George Alberts

THE

HOLY BIBLE

CONTAINING THE

OLD AND NEW TESTAMENTS

THE TEXT CAREFULLY PRINTED FROM THE
MOST CORRECT COPIES OF THE PRESENT
AUTHORIZED TRANSLATION, INCLUDING THE
MARGINAL READINGS AND PARALLEL TEXTS

WITH

A COMMENTARY AND CRITICAL NOTES

DESIGNED AS A HELP TO A BETTER UNDERSTANDING
OF THE SACRED WRITINGS

BY ADAM CLARKE, LL.D., F.S.A., &c.

A NEW EDITION, WITH THE
AUTHOR'S FINAL CORRECTIONS

For whatsoever things were written aforetime were written for our learning, that we through
patience and comfort of the Scriptures might have hope.—Rom. xv. 4.

THE OLD TESTAMENT

VOLUME II.—JOSHUA TO ESTHER

ABINGDON PRESS
NASHVILLE   ●   NEW YORK

ISBN 0-687-09124-1

PREFACE TO THE BOOK

OF

JOSHUA

JOSHUA, the son of Nun, of the tribe of Ephraim, was first called *Oshea* or *Hoshea*, הושע, Num. xiii. 16, which signifies *saved*, a *saviour*, or *salvation;* but afterwards Moses, guided no doubt by a prophetic spirit, changed his name into יהושע *Yehoshua* or *Joshua*, which signifies *he shall save*, or *the salvation of Jehovah;* referring, no doubt, to his being God's instrument in *saving the people* from the hands of their enemies, and leading them from victory to victory over the different Canaanitish nations, till he put them in possession of the promised land. On the change and meaning of the name, see the note on Num. xiii. 16. By the Septuagint he is called Ιησους Ναυη, *Jesus Naue*, or *Jesus son of Nave:* and in the New Testament he is expressly called Ιησους, JESUS; see Acts vii. 45; Heb. iv. 8. Joshua was denominated the *servant of Moses*, as he seems to have acted sometimes as his *secretary*, sometimes as his *aid-du-camp*, and sometimes as the *general* of the army. He was early appointed to be the *successor* of Moses, see Exod. xvii. 14; and under the instruction of this great master he was fully qualified for the important office. He was a great and pious man, and God honoured him in a most extraordinary manner, as the sequel of the history amply proves. From the preceding books it appears that he became attached to Moses shortly after the exodus from Egypt; that he was held by him in the highest esteem; had the command of the army confided to him in the war with the Amalekites; and accompanied his master to the Mount, when he went up to receive the Law from God. These were the highest honours he could possibly receive during the life-time of Moses.

Commentators and critics are divided in opinion whether the book that goes under his name was actually compiled by him.

It is argued by those who deny Joshua to be the author, that there are both *names* and *transactions* in it which did not exist till considerably after Joshua's time. The account we have, chap. iv. 9, of the twelve stones set up by Joshua in the midst of Jordan *remaining to the present day*, seems to prove that the book, at least this verse, was not written till after Joshua's time; the same may be said of the account of *Ai*, that Joshua made it *a heap for ever*, even *a desolation to the present day*, chap. viii. 28, which is a proof, however, that the book was not written after the time of the *kings*, as Ai subsisted after the return from the captivity; see Ezra ii. 28: *The men of Beth-el and Ai, two hundred twenty and three.* It is supposed also, that the relation of the *marriage of Achsah*, daughter of Caleb, with *Othniel* the son of Kenaz, necessarily belongs to the time of the Judges; Josh. xv. 16–19: as also the account of the capture of *Leshem* by the Danites; chap. xix. 47, compared with Judges xviii. 7, 29.

"What is related, chap. xv. 63, concerning the *Jebusites dwelling with the children of Judah at Jerusalem unto this day*, must certainly have been written *before the time of David;* for he took the strong hold of Zion, and expelled the Jebusites; see 2 Sam. v. 7–9. Also, what is said, chap. xvi. 10, *They drave not out the Canaanites that dwelt in Gezer, but they dwelt among the Ephraimites unto this day*, must have been written before the time of Solomon; for in his time Pharaoh, king of Egypt, had taken *Gezer*, burnt it with fire, slain the

Canaanites that dwelt in it, and given it a present to his daughter, the wife of Solomon, 1 Kings ix. 16. The country of *Cabul*, mentioned chap. xix. 27, had not this name till the time of Solomon, as appears from 1 Kings ix. 13; and the city called *Joktheel*, chap. xv. 38, had not this name till the reign of *Joash*, as appears from 2 Kings xiv. 7, it having been previously called *Selah*. The like may be said of *Tyre*, chap. xix. 29; and of *Galilee* cħap. xx. 7, and xxi. 32."

These are the principal objections which are made against the book as being the work of Joshua. Some of these difficulties might be so removed as to render it still probable that Joshua was the author of the whole book, as some think to be intimated chap. xxiv. 26; *And Joshua wrote these words in the book of the law of the Lord;* (but this probably refers to nothing more than the *words of the covenant* which was then made, and which is included in ver. 2–24;) but there are other difficulties that cannot be removed on the above supposition, and therefore it has been generally supposed that the book was written by some inspired person *after the time of Joshua;* and positively *before* many kings had reigned in Israel. The book has been attributed to *Samuel*, though some give this honour to *Ezra*.

After all, I cannot help considering the book in the main as the composition of *Joshua* himself. It is certain that Moses kept an accurate register of all the events that took place during *his* administration in the wilderness, at least from the giving of the law to the time of his death. And in that wilderness he wrote the book of *Genesis*, as well as the others that bear his name. Now, it is not likely that Joshua, the constant servant and companion of Moses, could see all this—be convinced, as he must be, of its utility—and not adopt the same practice; especially as at the death of Moses he came into the same office. I therefore take it for granted, that the Book of Joshua is as truly *his work*, as the Commentaries of Cæsar are *his;* and all the *real* difficulties mentioned above may be rationally and satisfactorily accounted for on the ground, that in transcribing this book in after ages, especially between the times of *Joshua* and the *Kings*, some few changes were made, and a very few slight additions, which referred chiefly to the insertion of names by which cities were *then* known instead of those by which they had been anciently denominated. This book therefore I conceive to be not the work of *Ezra*, nor of *Samuel*, nor of any other person of those times; nor can I allow that "it is called the Book of Joshua, because he is the chief subject of it, as the heroic poem of Virgil is called the *Æneis*, because of the prince whose travels and actions it relates;" but I conceive it to be called the Book of Joshua, 1. Because *Joshua wrote it.* 2. Because it is the relation of his own conduct in the conquest, division, and settlement of the promised land. 3. Because it contains a multitude of *particulars* that only *himself*, or a constant *eye-witness*, could possibly relate. 4. Because it was evidently designed to be a *continuation of the Book of Deuteronomy*, and is so *connected* with it, in narrative, as to prove that it must have been immediately *commenced* on the *termination* of the other. 5. I might add to this, that with the exception of a few individuals, the whole of the ancient Jewish and Christian Churches have uniformly acknowledged Joshua to be its author.

The Book of Joshua is one of the most important writings in the old covenant, and should never be separated from the Pentateuch, of which it is at once both the continuation and completion. Between *this Book* and the *five Books of Moses*, there is the same analogy as between the *four Gospels* and the *Acts of the Apostles*. The PENTATEUCH contains a history of the ACTS of the great Jewish *legislator*, and the LAWS on which the *Jewish Church* should be established. The *Book* of JOSHUA gives an account of the *establishment* of that Church in the Land of Canaan, according to the oft-repeated promises and declarations of God. The GOSPELS give an account of the *transactions* of JESUS CHRIST, the great Christian *legislator*, and of those LAWS on which *his* Church should be established, and by which it should be governed. The ACTS of the APOSTLES gives an account of the *actual establishment* of that Church, according to the predictions and promises of its great founder. Thus, then, the *Pentateuch* bears as pointed a relation to the *Gospels* as the Book of *Joshua* does to the *Acts of the Apostles*. And we might, with great appearance of probability, carry this analogy yet farther, and show that the writings of several of the *Prophets* bear as strict a relation to the *Apostolical Epistles*, as the Books of *Ezekiel* and *Daniel* do to the *Apocalypse*.

PREFACE TO JOSHUA

On this very ground of analogy Christ obviously founded the Christian Church; hence he had his *twelve disciples*, from whom the *Christian Church* was to spring, as the *Jewish Church* or *twelve tribes* sprang from the *twelve sons of Jacob*. He had his *seventy or seventy-two disciples*, in reference to the *seventy-two elders*, six chosen out of each of the twelve tribes, who were united with Moses and Aaron in the administration of justice, &c., among the people. CHRIST united in his person the characters both of Moses and Aaron, or legislator and high priest; hence he ever considers *himself*, and is considered by his *apostles* and *followers*, the *same* in the *Christian Church* that MOSES and AARON were in the Jewish. As a rite of *initiation* into his Church, he instituted *baptism* in the place of *circumcision*, both being types of the purification of the heart and holiness of life; and as a rite of *establishment* and *confirmation*, the holy *eucharist* in place of the *paschal lamb*, both being intended to commemorate the atonement made to God for the sins of the people. The analogies are so *abundant*, and indeed *universal*, that time would fail to enumerate them. On this very principle it would be a matter of high utility *to read these Old Testament and the New Testament books together*, as they reflect a strong and mutual light on each other, bear the most decided testimony to the words and truth of prophecy, and show the ample fulfilment of all the ancient and gracious designs of God. This appears particularly evident in the *five Books of Moses* and the *Book of Joshua* compared and collated with the *four Gospels* and the *Acts of the Apostles;* and the analogy will be the more complete as to the *number* of those books, though that is a matter of minor consideration, when we consider Joshua, as we ought, a *continuation* of the Book of Deuteronomy, though written by a different hand, which *two* books should be rated only as *one* history. Of *Judges* and *Ruth* it may be said they are a sort of supplement to the Book of Joshua.

Whoever goes immediately from the reading of the *Pentateuch* to the reading of the *Gospels*, and from the reading of *Joshua* to that of the *Acts*, will carry with him advantages which on no other plan he will be able to command. Even a commentator himself will derive advantages from this plan, which he will seek in vain from any other. To see the wisdom and goodness of God in the ritual of Moses, we must have an eye continually on the incarnation and death of Christ, to which it refers. And to have a proper view of the great atonement made by the sacrifice of our Lord, we must have a constant reference to the Mosaic law, where this is shadowed forth. *Without* this *reference* the law of Moses is a system of expensive and burdensome ceremonies, destitute of adequate meaning; and without this entering in of the law that the offence might abound, to show the exceeding sinfulness of sin, the frailty of man, and the holiness of God; the Gospel of Christ, including the account of his incarnation, preaching, miracles, passion, death, burial, ascension, and intercession, would not appear to have a sufficient *necessity* to explain and justify it. By the LAW is the *knowledge of sin*, and by the GOSPEL its *cure*. Either, taken separately, will not answer the purpose for which God gave these astonishing revelations of his *justice* and his *grace*.

TABLE OF CONTENTS TO THE BOOK OF JOSHUA

God commands Joshua to lead the people over the Jordan, and promises to put them in possession of the whole land. He encourages and commands him to be obedient, and promises him his continual presence and protection; chap. i.

Joshua sends two spies to examine the state of the inhabitants; they are received and concealed in the house of Rahab, with whom and her family they make a covenant. After three days they return to Joshua, and make a favourable report; chap. ii.

The whole Israelitish camp pass the Jordan, opposite to Jericho. The waters of the Jordan are miraculously cut off, and stand in a heap till the whole camp passed over; chap. iii.

By the command of God twelve stones are taken up from the bed of the river, and twelve other stones are set up *in* it as a memorial. The twelve stones brought out of the river are set up in *Gilgal* as a monument of the miraculous interposition of God; chap. iv.

At the command of God, Joshua circumcises the Israelites; they keep their first passover; and Joshua is encouraged by the appearance of an extraordinary person, who calls himself Captain of the Lord's host; chap. v.

The Israelites invest Jericho, and surround it seven days, the priests blowing with seven trumpets. On the seventh day, at the command of Joshua, the people shout, and the walls of Jericho fall down; the Israelites enter and put all to the sword, except Rahab and her family. The city is laid under a curse; chap. vi.

Three thousand men, being sent against *Ai*, are repulsed, and thirty-six of them slain; Joshua being distressed, and the people greatly discouraged, he inquires of the Lord why they fell before their enemies? And is answered that, contrary to the express command of God, some of the people had secreted part of the spoils of Jericho, which they had been ordered wholly to destroy. An inquiry is instituted, and *Achan*, the son of *Zerah*, is discovered to have taken a rich Babylonish garment, 200 shekels of silver, and a wedge of gold. He is sentenced to be stoned. He and all his property, his asses, sheep, oxen, and tent, are destroyed in the valley of *Achor*, and a heap of stones raised over the place; chap. vii.

Thirty thousand men attack Ai, and take it by stratagem; they put the inhabitants to the sword, to the amount of twelve thousand persons, and hang the king; they preserve the cattle and spoil to themselves. Joshua builds an altar to the Lord, and offers sacrifices, writes the law upon the stones of it and reads all the blessings and curses over against Mounts *Gerizim* and *Ebal*, as the Lord commanded Moses; chap. viii.

The Gibeonites send ambassadors to the Israelites, and, pretending to be of a very distant nation, get the princes of Israel to make a league with them; the deception is discovered, and they are condemned to a state of perpetual slavery; chap. ix.

The kings of Jerusalem, Hebron, Jarmuth, Lachish, and Eglon, attack the Gibeonites, because they had made a league with the Israelites. They send to Joshua for assistance. Joshua attacks those five kings, and during the battle, by an extraordinary fall of hail-stones, many are killed; and at the intercession of Joshua, the sun and moon stand still, and the day is prolonged till all the confederate Amorites are destroyed. The five kings are taken in a cave at Makkedah, brought out and hanged. The Israelites afterwards take and destroy Makkedah, Libnah, Lachish, Gezer, Eglon, Hebron, Debir, and all the country of the *hills*, *south*, *vale*, and *springs;* chap. x.

Many Canaanite, Amorite, Hittite, Perizzite, Jebusite, and Hivite kings join together against Israel; Joshua attacks and discomfits them at Merom. Afterwards he attacks the Anakim, and conquers the whole land; chap. xi.

A catalogue of all the kings and kingdoms that were conquered in this war; thirty-three in the whole, two on the east side of Jordan, and thirty-one on the west; chap. xii.

An account of the countries not yet subjugated to the Israelites. The manner in which the territories of Sihon and Og were divided among the Reubenites, Gadites, and the half tribe of Manasseh; chap. xiii.

Joshua, and Eleazar the priest, begin the distribution of the land by lot; Caleb's portion; chap. xiv.

The borders of the tribe of Judah described. Othniel smites Kirjath-sepher, and marries Achsah, the daughter of Caleb. The cities of the tribe of Judah are enumerated; chap. xv.

The boundaries of the children of Joseph. The Canaanites of Gezer are not expelled, but become tributary to the Ephraimites; chap. xvi.

The boundaries of the half tribe of Manasseh. The inheritance of the daughters of Zelophehad. The Canaanites are not expelled by the children of Manasseh, but serve under tribute. The children of Joseph complain that their portion is too small for them; and Joshua commands them to subdue and inhabit the mountain country of the Perizzites; chap. xvii.

The tabernacle of God is set up at Shiloh, and the remnant of the land is farther examined and divided by lot; Benjamin's portion is described; chap. xviii.

The lot of Simeon, Zebulun, Issachar, Asher, Naphtali, and Dan. The Danites take the city of Leshem; and the Israelites give Joshua the city of Timnath-serah, which he rebuilds and inhabits; chap. xix.

Six cities of refuge are appointed, at the commandment of God; chap. xx.

The Levites have forty-eight cities appointed to them out of the different tribes; they and their suburbs are described. The people enjoy rest, all the promises of God being accomplished; chap. xxi.

Joshua dismisses the two tribes of Reuben and Gad, and the half tribe of Manasseh. On their return, they build an altar of testimony on the east side of the Jordan, at which the other tribes are alarmed, fearing some idolatrous design; and preparing to go to war with them, they first send Phinehas and ten of the princes to require an explanation; they inquire into the business, and find that the altar was built to Jehovah, merely to prevent all idolatrous worship; and the people are satisfied; chap. xxii.

Joshua, in his old age, exhorts the people to be faithful to their God; chap. xxiii.

He assembles all the tribes at Shechem; recounts God's merciful dealings with them, and the deliverances he had wrought for them and their fathers; and causes them to make a solemn covenant, which he writes in the book of the law. Joshua dies aged 110 years, and shortly after Eleazar, the high priest, dies also; chap. xxiv.

N. B. In pursuance of the promise made in the General Preface, I have given in the Chronological note at the head of each transaction, in the following book, not only the Year of the World, the Year before Christ, and the Year of the Exodus from Egypt, but also the Year before the first OLYMPIAD. According to the Arundelian Marbles, and the most accurate computation, the *first* OLYMPIAD commenced in the 3938th year of the Julian Period; 3228 years from the Creation; 780 years from the foundation of the Athenian Empire; 408 years after the taking of Troy; 24 years before the building of Rome, and **776 before** the incarnation of our Lord.

THE BOOK

OF

JOSHUA

Year before the common Year of Christ, 1451.—Julian Period, 3263.—Cycle of the Sun, 10.—Dominical Letter, B.—Cycle of the Moon, 10.—Indiction, 15.—Creation from Tisri or September, 2553.

CHAPTER I

Moses being dead, God commissions Joshua to bring the people into the promised land, 1, 2. The extent of the land to be possessed, 3, 4. Joshua is assured of victory over all his enemies, and is exhorted to courage and activity, 5, 6; and to be careful to act, in all things, according to the law of Moses, in which he is to meditate day and night, 7, 8. He is again exhorted to courage, with the promise of continual support, 9. Joshua commands the officers to prepare the people for their passage over Jordan, 10, 11. The Reubenites, Gadites, and half tribe of Manasseh, are put in mind of their engagement to pass over with their brethren, 12–15. They promise the strictest obedience, and pray for the prosperity of their leader, 16–18.

A. M. 2553
B. C. 1451
An. Exod. Isr. 40
Anno ante
I. Olymp. 675

NOW after the death of Moses the servant of the LORD, it came to pass that the LORD spake unto Joshua the son of Nun, Moses' ᵃminister, saying,

2 ᵇMoses my servant is dead; now therefore arise, go over this Jordan, thou, and all this people, unto the land which I do give to them, *even* to the children of Israel.

3 ᶜEvery place that the sole of your foot shall tread upon, that have I given unto you, as I said unto Moses.

A. M. 2553
B. C. 1451
An. Exod. Isr. 40
Anno ante
I. Olymp. 675

ᵃExod. xxiv. 13; Deut. i. 38

ᵇDeut. xxxiv. 5——ᶜDeut. xi. 24; chap. xiv. 9

NOTES ON CHAP. I

Verse 1. *Now after the death of Moses*] ויהי *vayehi, and it was* or *happened* after the death of Moses. Even the first words in this book show it to be a *continuation* of the preceding, and intimately connected with the narrative in the last chapter in Deuteronomy, of which I suppose Joshua to have been the author, and that chapter to have originally made the *commencement* of this book. See the notes there. The *time* referred to here must have been at the conclusion of the *thirty* days in which they mourned for Moses.

Verse 2. *Moses my servant*] The word, servant, as applied both to Moses and Joshua, is to be understood in a very peculiar sense. It signifies God's *prime minister*, the person by whom he issued his orders, and by whom he accomplished all his purposes and designs. No person ever bore this title in the like sense but the Redeemer of mankind, of whom Moses and Joshua were types.

Go over this Jordan] The account given by Josephus of this river may not be unacceptable here. "*Panium* is thought to be the fountain of Jordan, but in reality it is carried thither in an occult manner from the place called *Phiala*.

This place lies on the road to Trachonitis, and is one hundred and twenty furlongs from Cæsarea, not far out of the road, on the right hand. It has its name *Phiala*, (a bowl or basin,) very justly, from the roundness of its circumference, being round like a wheel. It is always full, without ever sinking or running over. This origin of the Jordan was not known till the time of Philip, tetrarch of Trachonitis, who having ordered some *chaff* to be thrown in at *Phiala*, it was found at *Panium*. Jordan's *visible* stream arises from this cavern, (*Panium,*) and divides the marshes and fens of the lake *Semechon;* and when it has run another hundred and twenty furlongs, it first passes by the city *Julias*, and then passes through the middle of the lake *Gennesareth*, after which, running a long way over the desert, it empties itself into the lake *Asphaltites*."—WAR, book iii., chap. x., sect. 7. ᵈSee the note on Num. xxxiv. 12.

Verse 3. *The sole of your foot shall tread upon*] That is, the whole land occupied by the seven Canaanitish nations, and as far as the Euphrates on the *east;* for this was certainly the utmost of the grant now made to them; and all that was included in what is termed the *promised land*, the boundaries of which have already been defined. See Deut. xxxiv. 1-4, and

A. M. 2553
B. C. 1451
An. Exod. Isr.
40
Anno ante
I. Olymp. 675

4 ⁴From the wilderness and this Lebanon, even unto the great river, the river Euphrates, all the land of the Hittites, and unto the great sea, toward the going down of the sun, shall be your coast.

5 ᵉThere shall not any man be able to stand before thee all the days of thy life: ᶠas I was with Moses, *so* ᵍI will be with thee: ʰI will not fail thee, nor forsake thee.

6 ¹Be strong and of a good courage: for ᵏunto this people shalt thou divide for an inheritance the land, which I sware unto their fathers to give them.

7 Only be thou strong, and very courageous, that thou mayest observe to do according to all the law, ¹which Moses my servant commanded thee: ᵐturn not from it *to* the right

hand or *to* the left, that thou mayest ⁿprosper whithersoever thou goest.

A. M. 2553
B. C. 1451
An. Exod. Isr.
40
Anno ante
I. Olymp. 675

8 ᵒThis book of the law shall not depart out of thy mouth; but ᵖthou shalt meditate therein day and night, that thou mayest observe to do according to all that is written therein: for then thou shalt make thy way prosperous, and then thou shalt ᑫhave good success.

9 ʳHave not I commanded thee? Be strong and of a good courage; ˢbe not afraid, neither be thou dismayed: for the LORD thy God *is* with thee whithersoever thou goest.

10 Then Joshua commanded the officers of the people, saying,

11 Pass through the host, and command the people, saying, Prepare you victuals; for

---

ᵈGen. xv. 18; Exod. xxiii. 31; Num. xxxiv. 3–12
ᵉDeut. vii. 24——ᶠExod. iii. 12——ᵍDeut. xxxi. 8, 23;
ver. 9, 17; chap. iii. 7; vi. 27; Isa. xliii. 2, 5——ʰDeut.
xxxi. 6, 8; Heb. xiii. 5——ⁱDeut. xxxi. 7, 23——ᵏOr,
thou shalt cause this people to inherit the land, &c.

¹Num. xxvii. 23; Deut. xxxi. 7, chap. xi. 15——ᵐDeut.
v. 32; xxviii. 14——ⁿOr, *do wisely;* Deut. xxix. 9
ᵒDeut. xvii. 18, 19——ᵖPsa. i. 2——ᑫOr, *do wisely;*
ver. 7——ʳDeut. xxxi. 7, 8, 23——ˢPsa. xxvii. 1;
Jer. i. 8

---

see ver. 4 below. It has been supposed that the words, *Every place that the sole of your foot shall tread upon,* were intended to express the *ease* with which they were to conquer the whole land, an instance of which occurs in the taking of Jericho. It was only their unfaithfulness to God that rendered the conquest in any case difficult.

Verse 4. *From the wilderness and this Lebanon*] Joshua appears to be standing with his face towards the promised land, and pointing out the different places, or their situation, with his hand, THIS *Lebanon,* &c. The utmost of their limits should be from the desert of *Arabia Petræa* on the SOUTH to *Lebanon* on the NORTH; and from the *Euphrates* on the EAST to the *Mediterranean Sea* on the WEST. The Israelites did not possess the full extent of this grant till the days of David. See 2 Sam. viii. 3, &c., and 2 Chron. ix. 26.

Land of the Hittites] These are generally reputed to have been the most hardy and warlike of all the Canaanitish nations; and as they occupied the mountainous countries on the south of the land of Canaan, it is natural to suppose that they would be the most difficult to subdue, and on this account, it is supposed, God particularly specifies *these:* "Ye shall subdue and possess even all the land of the *Hittites;*" but it is probable that under this one term all the other nations are included, as it is certain they are in other places under the term *Amorites.*

Great sea: The *Mediterranean,* called *great* in respect of the *lakes* in the land of Judea, such as the sea of *Gennesareth,* or the sea of *Tiberias,* and the *Dead Sea,* which were comparatively *small lakes;* but the Hebrews gave the name of sea, ים *yam,* to every large collection of waters.

Verse 5. *Be able to stand before thee*] Because God shall be *with* thee, therefore thou shalt be irresistible. This **promise** was most punctually literally fulfilled.

Verse 7. *Only be thou strong, and very courageous*] Ισχυε ουν, και ανδριζου σφοδρα.—Sept. *Be strong therefore, and play the man to the uttermost.* Though God had promised him that no man should be able to stand before him, yet it was on condition that he should use all his military skill, and avail himself to the uttermost of all the *means,* natural and providential, which God should place within his reach. God will not have them who refuse to help themselves.

Verse 8. *This book of the law shall not depart out of thy mouth*] The law which had already been written by Moses, and from which he and the people were to take all those precepts by which their lives were to be governed. Though there was a copy of the law laid up in the sanctuary, yet this was not sufficient. Joshua must have a copy for himself, and he was to consult it incessantly, that his way might be made prosperous, and that he might have good success. If he kept God's word, God would keep him in body and soul; if he should observe to do according to that word, then God would cause all his way to be prosperous. Those who are obedient to God lack no manner of thing that is good.

Verse 10. *Commanded the officers*] שטרים *shoterim.* These were different from the שפטים *shophetim,* who were judges among the people, and whose business it was to determine in all civil cases. The *shoterim* have been supposed to be subordinate officers, whose business it was to see the decisions of the *shophetim* carried into effect. Calmet conjectures that the *shoterim* here may have been the *heralds* of the army like those so often met with in *Homer,* who were called the *messengers both of the gods and men;* who bore sceptres, and whose persons were ever held sacred. See on Deut. i. 13, 15.

Verse 11. *Prepare you victuals*] צדה *tsedah,* such *prey* or *provisions* as they had *taken* from the *conquered countries,* such as corn, oxen,

A. M. 2553
B. C. 1451
An. Exod. Isr. 40
Anno ante
I. Olymp. 675

¹within three days ye shall pass over this Jordan, to go in to possess the land, which the LORD your God giveth you to possess it.

12 And to the Reubenites, and to the Gadites, and to half the tribe of Manasseh, spake Joshua, saying,

13 Remember ᵘthe word which Moses the servant of the LORD commanded you, saying, The LORD your God hath given you rest, and hath given you this land.

14 Your wives, your little ones, and your cattle, shall remain in the land which Moses gave you on this side Jordan; but ye shall pass before your brethren ᵛarmed, all the mighty men of valour, and help them;

15 Until the LORD have given your brethren rest, as *he hath given* you, and they also have

possessed the land which the LORD your God giveth them: ᵂthen ye shall return unto the land of your possession, and enjoy it, which Moses the LORD's servant gave you on this side Jordan, toward the sun-rising.

A. M. 2553
B. C. 1451
An. Exod. Isr. 40
Anno ante
I. Olymp. 675

16 And they answered Joshua, saying, All that thou commandest us we will do, and whithersoever thou sendest us, we will go.

17 According as we hearkened unto Moses in all things, so will we hearken unto thee: only the LORD thy God ˣbe with thee, as he was with Moses.

18 Whosoever *he be* that doth rebel against thy commandment, and will not hearken unto thy words in all that thou commandest him, he shall be put to death: only be strong and of a good courage.

Chap. iii. 2; see Deut. ix. 1; xi. 31——ᵘNum. xxxii. 20–28; chap. xxii. 2, 3, 4

ᵛHeb. *marshalled by five;* as Exod. xiii. 18——ᵂChap. xxii. 4, &c.——ˣVer. 5; 1 Sam. xx. 13; 1 Kings i. 37

---

sheep, &c.; for the word signifies *prey,* or what is taken by *hunting,* &c. This was necessary, as they were about to undergo considerable fatigue in marching, and in making preparations for the passage of the Jordan; for although the manna had not ceased to fall, yet such other provisions as are mentioned above were necessary on this occasion.

For within three days ye shall pass] Calmet contends, with great appearance of truth, that these three days should be reckoned from the first day of their encamping at Jordan, three days after the return of the spies, i. e., on the eighth day of the first month, on the *tenth* of which they passed over Jordan. The text therefore is supposed to mean, *Prepare victuals for three days' march,* for "on the third day after your decampment from *Shittim* ye shall pass over this Jordan."

Verse 13. *Remember the word*] He puts the Reubenites, &c., in remembrance of the engagements they had made with Moses (See Num. xxxii. 20) when he granted them their portion on the east side of Jordan.

Verse 14. *Your wives, your little ones*] And with these it appears, from Num. xxxii. 17, were left behind 70,580 effective men to guard them and their property; only 40,000 having passed over Jordan to assist the *nine* tribes and half to conquer the land. See chap. iv. 13.

Armed] חמשים *chamushim, by fives;* in several lines, *five* in front, probably the usual method of marching; but it seems to signify *arrayed, equipped, accoutred, well-armed,* and ready for battle. See the note on Exod. xiii. 18.

Verse 15. *Toward the sun-rising.*] This is the EAST, as *toward the going down of the sun* signifies the WEST.

Verse 16. *All that thou commandest us we will do*] Here they acknowledge the Divine mission of Joshua, as they had done that of Moses, and consequently promise to follow his directions in all things.

Verse 17. *Only the Lord thy God be with thee*] Provided God be with *thee,* as he was

with Moses, we will implicitly obey thee. The words however may mean no more than an earnest prayer for Joshua's prosperity: May God be with *thee,* as he was with Moses!

Verse 18. *He shall be put to death*] This was *martial* law; he who disobeyed the command of his general should be put to death. To this the people agreed, and it was essentially necessary in order that proper discipline should be kept up in this great army. By insubordination their fathers had suffered much in the wilderness; they rejected the authority of Moses, mutinied and made themselves a leader to conduct them back to Egypt. (See Num. xiv. 4.) And Joshua himself, for attempting to encourage them against their fears, was near being stoned to death. It was necessary, therefore, that they should give him the most positive assurance that they would not act as their fathers had done.

1. NOTWITHSTANDING the great honour God put on his servants Moses, Aaron, Phinehas, and Joshua, yet we find him using every means to induce the people to trust in *himself* alone. Hence he is ever showing them that even those great men had nothing but what they had received, and that *they* were as fully dependent upon himself as the meanest of the people. What was even *Moses* without his GOD?

2. Is it not strange that at the death of Moses utter despair had not overwhelmed the whole camp, as he whom they expected to give them rest had died before any conquest was made in Canaan? We find, however, that they are not discouraged; he who gave them *Moses,* has now given them *Joshua* in his place; and they had now fully learned that if God be for them, none could be successfully against them.

3. From all this we may learn, that when God has a great work to accomplish, he will provide himself suitable instruments; and though one, which he has greatly honoured, appear to fail, we should know that he is not confined to work by that one alone. He has way every where,

and all things serve the purposes of his will. He will as surely support his Church on earth, as he will support the earth itself; and while the sun and moon endure, the Church shall flourish: this is for his own honour, and he certainly is more concerned for his own glory in the administration of justice, judgment, and salvation in the earth, than any of the children of men can possibly be.

4. Though God had so implicitly promised them his help, yet he strongly insists on their own *co-operation*. He requires the use of every power and talent he has given; even Joshua himself *must be strong and very courageous*, and the people must *obey him in all things*, in order that they may go over the Jordan to possess the good land; and without this they had never got into the promised rest. Shall we sup-

pose, then, that if *we* be not workers together with God we shall be saved? Vain expectation! He works in us to *will* and to *do*, i. e., he gives the *principle* of *volition* in things that are holy, and the principle of *power* to bring the *acts of will* into good practical effect; therefore, says the apostle, *work out your own salvation with fear and trembling*. Will, therefore, under the influence of the gracious principle of *volition;* act under the influence of the principle of *power*. Without the power you can neither *will* nor *do;* but having the power it is your duty to *will* and *do*. It is enough that God gives the power. It is our duty, when we receive these talents, to improve them. In a million of cases a man may be both able to *will* and to *do*, and yet do neither to the salvation of his soul.

CHAPTER II

Joshua sends out two spies to examine the state of the inhabitants of the land, particularly those of Jericho, who are entertained at the house of Rahab, 1. The king of Jericho is informed of their being in the town, and sends to Rahab, commanding her to deliver them up, 2, 3. She hides the spies, and tells the messengers that the men were departed and gone towards the mountain, 4, 5. When the officers of the king of Jericho were departed, she took the spies to the house-top, and covered them with flax, 6, 7. She relates to them that the fear of the Israelites had fallen on all the inhabitants of the country on hearing of their victories over the Amorites; that she knew none could resist the God of Israel, and therefore desired them to give her an oath that, when they took Jericho, they would preserve the lives of her and her family, 8–13. The spies swear to her, 14. She lets them down by a cord from the house-top, and gives them directions how to proceed, in order to avoid the pursuers, 15, 16. She is to tie a scarlet line to the window, through which she had let them down, which should be the sign to the Israelites to spare that house and its inhabitants, 17–19. Having bound her to secresy, they depart, 20, 21. After three days' stay in the mountain, they return to Joshua, and make a favourable report, 22–24.

A. M. 2553
B. C. 1451
An. Exod. Isr.
40
Anno ante
I. Olymp. 675

AND Joshua the son of Nun [a]sent [b]out of Shittim two men to spy secretly, saying, Go view the land, even Jericho. And they went, and [c]came into a harlot's house, named [d]Rahab, and [e]lodged there.

2 And [f]it was told the king of

A. M. 2553
B. C. 1451
An. Exod. Isr.
40
Anno ante
I. Olymp. 675

---

[a]Or, *had sent*——[b]Num. xxv. 1——[c]Heb. xi. 31; James ii. 25

[d]Matt. i. 5——[e]Heb. *lay*——[f]Psa. cxxvii. 1; Prov. xxi. 30

NOTES ON CHAP. II

Verse 1. *Joshua—sent—two men to spy secretly*] It is very likely that these spies had been sent out soon after the death of Moses, and therefore our marginal reading, *had sent*, is to be preferred. *Secretly*—It is very probable also that these were confidential persons, and that the transaction was between them and him alone. As they were to pass over the Jordan opposite to Jericho, it was necessary that they should have possession of this city, that in case of any reverses they might have no enemies in their rear. He sent the men, therefore, to see the state of the city, avenues of approach, fortifications, &c., that he might the better concert his mode of attack.

A harlot's house] Harlots and *inn-keepers* seem to have been called by the same name, as no doubt many who followed this mode of life, from their exposed situation, were not the most correct in their morals. Among the ancients *women* generally kept houses of entertainment, and among the Egyptians and Greeks this was common. I shall subjoin a few proofs. HE-

RODOTUS, speaking concerning the many differences between Egypt and other countries, and the peculiarity of their laws and customs, expressly says: Εν τοισι αἱ μεν γυναικες αγοραζουσι και καπηλευουσι· οἱ δε ανδρες, κατ᾽ οικους εοντες, ὑφαινουσι. "Among the Egyptians the women carry on all commercial concerns, and *keep taverns*, while the men continue at home and weave." Herod. in Euterp., c. xxxv. DIODORUS SICULUS, lib. i., s. 8, and c. xxvii., asserts that "the men were the slaves of the women in Egypt, and that it is stipulated in the marriage contract that the woman shall be the ruler of her husband, and that he shall obey her in all things." The same historian supposes that women had these high privileges among the Egyptians, to perpetuate the memory of the beneficent administration of *Isis*, who was afterwards deified among them.

NYMPHODORUS, quoted by the ancient scholiast on the *Œdipus Coloneus* of Sophocles, accounts for these customs: he says that "Sesostris, finding the population of Egypt rapidly increasing, fearing that he should not be able to govern the people or keep them united under one head,

A. M. 2553
B. C. 1451
An. Exod. Isr.
40
Anno ante
I. Olymp. 675

Jericho, saying, Behold, there came men in hither to-night of the children of Israel, ^gto search out the country.

3 And the king of Jericho sent unto Rahab, saying, Bring forth the men that are come to thee, which are entered into thine

A. M. 2553
B. C. 1451
An. Exod. Isr.
40
Anno ante
I. Olymp. 675

---

^gGen. lxii. 9–12, 31;   2 Sam. x. 3

---

obliged the *men* to assume the occupations of women, in order that they might be rendered effeminate."

Sophocles confirms the account given by Herodotus; speaking of Egypt he says:—

Εκει γαρ οι μεν αρσενες κατα στεγας
Θακουσιν ιστουργουντες· αι δε ξυννομοι
Τα 'ξω βιου τροφεια προσυνουσ' αει.
CEdip. Col. v. 352.

"There the men stay in their houses weaving cloth, while the women *transact all business out of doors*, provide food for the family," &c. It is on this passage that the scholiast cites *Nymphodorus* for the information given above, and which he says is found in the 13th chapter of his work "On the Customs of Barbarous Nations."

That the same custom prevailed among the *Greeks* we have the following proof from APULEIUS: *Ego vero quod primum ingressui stabulum conspicatus sum, accessi, et de* QUADAM ANU CAUPONA *illico percontor.*—Aletam. lib. i., p. 18, Edit. Bip. "Having entered into the first *inn* I met with, and there seeing a certain OLD WOMAN, the INN-KEEPER, I inquired of her."

It is very likely that women kept the places of public entertainment among the *Philistines;* and that it was with *such a one*, and not with a *harlot*, that Samson lodged; (see Judges xvi. 1, &c.;) for as this custom certainly did prevail among the *Egyptians*, of which we have the fullest proof above, we may naturally expect it to have prevailed also among the Canaanites and Philistines, as we find from *Apuleius* that it did afterwards among the Greeks. Besides, there is more than presumptive proof that this custom obtained among the Israelites themselves, even in the most polished period of their history; for it is much more reasonable to suppose that the *two women*, who came to Solomon for judgment, relative to the *dead child*, (1 Kings iii. 16, &c.,) were *inn-keepers*, than that they were *harlots*. It is well known that common prostitutes, from their abandoned course of life, scarcely ever have children; and the laws were so strict against such in Israel, (Deut. xxiii. 18,) that if these had been of that class it is not at all likely they would have dared to appear before Solomon. All these circumstances considered, I am fully satisfied that the term זונה *zonah* in the text, which we translate *harlot*, should be rendered *tavern* or *inn-keeper*, or *hostess*. The spies who were sent out on this occasion were undoubtedly the most confidential persons that Joshua had in his host; they went on an errand of the most weighty importance, and which involved the greatest consequences. The risk they ran of losing their lives in this enterprise was extreme. Is it therefore likely that persons who could not escape apprehension and death, without the miraculous interference of God, should in despite of that law which at this time must have been so well known unto them, go into a place where they might expect, not the blessing, but the

curse, of God? Is it not therefore more likely that they went rather to an *inn* to lodge than to a *brothel?* But what completes in my judgment the evidence on this point is, that this very Rahab, whom we call a *harlot*, was actually married to *Salmon*, a Jewish *prince*, see Matt. i. 5. And is it probable that a *prince of Judah* would have taken to wife such a person as our text represents Rahab to be?

It is granted that the Septuagint, who are followed by Heb. xi. 31, and James ii. 25, translate the Hebrew זונה *zonah* by πορνη, which generally signifies a *prostitute;* but it is not absolutely evident that the Septuagint used the word in this sense. Every scholar knows that the Greek word πορνη comes from περναω, to *sell*, as this does from περαω, to *pass from one to another; transire facio a me ad alterum:* DAMM. But may not this be spoken as well of the woman's *goods* as of her *person?* In this sense the Chaldee Targum understood the term, and has therefore translated it אתתא פונדקיתא *ittetha pundekitha*, a *woman*, a TAVERN-KEEPER. That this is the true sense many eminent men are of opinion; and the preceding arguments render it at least very probable. To all this may be added, that as our blessed Lord came through the line of this woman, it cannot be a matter of little consequence to know what moral character she sustained; as an *inn-keeper* she might be *respectable*, if not *honourable;* as a *public prostitute* she could be neither; and it is not very likely that the providence of God would have suffered a person of such a notoriously bad character to enter into the sacred line of his genealogy. It is true that the cases of Tamar and Bathsheba may be thought sufficient to destroy this argument; but whoever considers these two cases maturely will see that they differ totally from that of *Rahab*, if we allow the word *harlot* to be legitimate. As to the objection that her *husband* is nowhere mentioned in the account here given; it appears to me to have little weight. She might have been either a *single woman* or a *widow;* and in either of these cases there could have been no mention of a *husband;* or if she even had a husband it is not likely *he* would have been mentioned on this occasion, as the secret seems to have been kept religiously between *her* and the *spies*. If she were a *married* woman her husband might be included in the general terms, *all that she had*, and *all her kindred*, chap. vi. 23. But it is most likely that she was a *single woman* or a *widow*, who got her bread honestly by *keeping a house of entertainment for strangers*. See below.

Verse 3. *The king of Jericho sent unto Rahab*] This appears to be a proof of the preceding opinion: had she been a *prostitute* or a person of *ill fame* he could at once have sent officers to have seized the persons lodged with her as vagabonds; but if she kept a house of entertainment, the persons under her roof were *sacred*, according to the universal custom of the *Asiatics*, and could not be molested on any tri-

A. M. 2553
B. C. 1451
An. Exod. Isr.
40
Anno ante
I. Olymp. 675

house: for they be come to search out all the country.

4 [h]And the woman took the two men, and hid them, and said thus, There came men unto me, but I wist not whence they *were:*

5 And it came to pass *about the time* of shutting of the gate, when it was dark, that the men went out: whither the men went, I wot not: pursue after them quickly; for ye shall overtake them.

6 But [i]she had brought them up to the roof of the house, and hid them with the stalks of flax, which she had laid in order upon the roof.

7 And the men pursued after them, the way to Jordan, unto the fords: and as soon as they which pursued after them were gone out, they shut the gate.

8 And before they were laid down, she came up unto them upon the roof;

9 And she said unto the men, I know that the LORD hath given you the land, and that [k]your terror is fallen upon us, and that all the inhabitants of the land [l]faint because of you.

A. M. 2553
B. C. 1451
An. Exod. Isr.
40
Anno ante
I. Olymp. 675

10 For we have heard how the LORD [m]dried up the water of the Red Sea for you, when ye came out of Egypt; and [n]what ye did unto the two kings of the Amorites, that *were* on the other side Jordan, Sihon and Og, whom ye utterly destroyed.

11 And as soon as we had [o]heard *these things,* [p]our hearts did melt, neither [q]did there remain any more courage in any man, because of you: for [r]the LORD your God, he *is* God in heaven above, and in earth beneath.

12 Now therefore, I pray you, [s]swear unto me by the LORD, since I have showed you kindness, that ye will also show kindness unto 'my father's house, and [u]give me a true token:

---

[h]See 2 Sam. xvii. 19, 20——[i]See Exod. i. 17; 2 Sam. xvii. 19——[k]Gen. xxxv. 5; Exod. xxiii. 27; Deut. ii. 25; xi. 25——[l]Heb. *melt;* Exod. xv. 15——[m]Exod. xiv. 21; chap. iv. 23

[n]Num. xxi. 24, 34, 35——[o]Exod. xv. 14, 15 [p]Chap. v. 1; vii. 5; Isa. xiii. 7——[q]Heb. *rose up* [r]Deut. iv. 39——[s]See 1 Sam. xx. 14, 15, 17——[t]See 1 Tim. v. 8——[u]Ver. 18

---

fling grounds. A *guest* or a *friend* is sacred in whatever house he may be *received,* in every part of the *east* to the present day.

Verse 4. *And hid them*] Probably she secreted them for the time being in some private corner, till she had the opportunity of concealing them on the house-top in the manner mentioned ver. 6.

Verse 5. *When it was dark*] So it appears that it was after night that the king of Jericho sent to Rahab, ordering her to produce the persons who lodged with her. The *season* itself was friendly to the whole plot: had these transactions taken place in daylight, it is scarcely possible that the spies could have escaped. But this is no excuse for the woman's prevarication; for God could have saved his messengers independently of her *falsity.* God never says to any, Do evil that good may come of it. See at the end of the chapter.

Verse 6. *Hid them with the stalks of flax*] It is a matter of little consequence whether we translate פשתי העץ *pistey haets* stalks of flax, or stalks of hemp: the word עץ *ets,* which signifies *wood,* serves to show that whether it was *hemp* or *flax,* it was in its rough, unmanufactured state; and as this was about the season, viz., the end of March or the beginning of April, in which the flax is ripe in that country, consequently Rahab's *flax* might have been recently pulled, and was now drying on the roof of her house. The reader may find some useful remarks upon this subject in *Harmer's* Observations, vol. iv., p. 97, &c.

Upon the roof.] We have already seen that all the houses in the east were made *flat-roofed;* for which a law is given Deut. xxii. 8. On these flat roofs the Asiatics to this day walk, converse, and oftentimes even sleep and pass the

night. It is probable that this hiding was after that referred to in the *fourth* verse.

Verse 9. *I know that the Lord hath given you the land*] It is likely she had this only from *conjecture,* having heard of their successes against the Amorites, their prodigious numbers, and seeing the state of terror and dismay to which the inhabitants of her own land were reduced.

Verse 11. *He is God in heaven above, and in earth beneath.*] This confession of the true God is amazingly full, and argues considerable light and information. As if she had said, "I know your God to be omnipotent and omnipresent:" and in consequence of this faith she hid the spies, and risked her own life in doing it. But how had she this clear knowledge of the Divine nature? 1. Possibly the knowledge of the true God was general in the earth at this time, though *connected* with much superstition and idolatry; the people believing that there was a god for *every district,* and for *every people;* for the *mountains* and for the *valleys;* see 1 Kings xx. 23. 2. Or she received this instruction from the spies, with whom she appears to have had a good deal of conversation; or, 3. She had it from a supernatural influence of God upon her own soul. She probably made a better use of the light she had received than the rest of her countrymen, and God increased that light.

Verse 12. *Swear unto me by the Lord*] This is a farther proof that this woman had received considerable instruction in the Jewish faith; she acknowledged the *true God* by his essential character *Jehovah;* and knew that an *oath* in his name was the deepest and most solemn obligation under which a Jew could possibly come. Does not this also refer to the command of God,

A. M. 2553
B. C. 1451
An Exod. Isr.
40
Anno ante
I. Olymp. 675

13 And *that* ye will save alive my father, and my mother, and my brethren, and my sisters, and all that they have, and deliver our lives from death.

14 And the men answered her, Our life ᵛfor yours, if ye utter not this our business. And it shall be, when the Lᴏʀᴅ hath given us the land, that ʷwe will deal kindly and truly with thee.

15 Then she ˣlet them down by a cord through the window: for her house *was* upon the town wall, and she dwelt upon the wall.

16 And she said unto them, Get you to the mountain, lest the pursuers meet you; and hide yourselves there three days, until the pursuers be returned: and afterward may ye go your way.

17 And the men said unto her, We *will be* ʸblameless of this thine oath which thou hast made us swear;

18 ᶻBehold, *when* we come into the land, thou shalt bind this line of scarlet thread in the window which thou didst let us down by: ᵃand thou shalt ᵇbring thy father, and thy mother, and thy brethren, and all thy father's household, home unto thee.

19 And it shall be *that* whosoever shall go out of the doors of thy house into the street, his blood *shall be* upon his head, and we *will be* guiltless: and whosoever shall be with thee in the house, ᶜhis blood *shall be* on our head if *any* hand be upon him.

20 And if thou utter this our business, then we will be quit of thine oath which thou hast made us to swear.

21 And she said, According unto your words, so *be* it. And she sent them away, and they departed: and she bound the scarlet line in the window.

22 And they went, and came unto the mountain, and abode there three days, until the pursuers were returned: ᵈand the pursuers sought *them* throughout all the way, but found *them* not.

23 So the two men returned, and descended from the mountain, and passed over, and came to Joshua the son of Nun, and told him all *things* that befell them:

24 And they said unto Joshua, Truly ᵉthe Lᴏʀᴅ hath delivered into our hands all the land; for even all the inhabitants of the country do ᶠfaint because of us.

A. M. 2553
B. C. 1451
An. Exod. Isr.
40
Anno ante
I. Olymp. 675

ᵛHeb. *instead of you to die*——ʷJudg. i. 24; Matt. v. 7——ˣActs ix. 25——ʸExod. xx. 7——ᶻVer. 12 ᵃChap. vi. 23——ᵇHeb. *gather*

ᶜMatthew xxvii. 25——ᵈ2 Sam. xvii. 20; Psa. xxxii. 6——ᵉExodus xxiii. 31; chap. vi. 2; xxi. 44——ᶠHeb. *melt;* verse 9

Thou shalt fear the Lord, and shalt swear by his name? See the note on Deut. vi. 13.

Verse 13. *Deliver our lives from death.*] She had learned, either from the spies or otherwise, that all the inhabitants of the land were doomed to destruction, and therefore she obliges them to enter into a *covenant* with her for the preservation of herself and her household.

Verse 14. *Our life for yours*] "May our life be destroyed if we suffer yours to be injured!" This is what was anciently called in our country *pledging*—staking, a man's life for that of his neighbour or friend.

Verse 15. *Then she let them down by a cord, &c.*] The natural place of this verse is after the first clause of ver. 21; for it is certain that she did not let them down in the basket till all those circumstances marked from ver. 16 to 20 inclusive had taken place.

She dwelt upon the wall.] That is, either the wall of the city made a part of her house or her house was built close to the wall, so that the top or battlements of it were above the wall, with a window that looked out to the country. As the city gates were now shut there was no way for the spies to escape but through this window; and in order to this she let them down through the window in a basket suspended by

a cord, till they reached the ground on the outside of the wall.

Verse 16. *Hide yourselves there three days*] They were to travel by *night*, and hide themselves in the *day-time;* otherwise they might have been discovered by the pursuers who were in search of them.

Verse 18. *This line of scarlet thread*] תקות חוט השני *tikvath chut hashshani*. Probably this may mean, *this piece of scarlet cloth*, or, *this cloth* (made) *of scarlet thread*. When the Israelites took the city this piece of *red cloth* seems to have been hung out of the window by way of *flag;* and this was the sign on which she and the spies had agreed.

Verse 20. *If thou utter this our business*] It was prudent to make her *life* depend on her *secresy;* had it been otherwise she might have been tempted to give information, not only concerning the spies, but concerning the designs of the Israelites. But her life being at stake, added to every other motive, she kept the secret for the sake of her own personal safety and that of all her relatives.

Verse 23. *So the two men returned*] Having concealed themselves in the mountains that night, all the next day, and the night ensuing, on the third day they returned to Joshua.

Verse 24. *Truly the Lord hath delivered into*

our hands all the land] How different was this report from that brought by the spies on a former occasion! They found that all the inhabitants of the land were panic-struck. The people had heard of the great exploits of the Israelites on the other side of Jordan; and as they had destroyed the potent kings of the Amorites, they took it for granted that nothing could stand before them. This information was necessary to Joshua to guide him in forming the plan of his campaign.

1. It may be asked, Did not Rahab *lie* in the account she gave to the officers of the king of Jericho, (ver. 4, 5,) *There came men unto me,* &c.? I answer, She certainly did; and the inspired writer sets down the fact merely as it stood, without making the Spirit of God responsible for the dissimulation of the woman. But was she not rewarded, &c.? Yes; for her hospitality and faith, not for her *lie*. But could she have saved the spies without telling a lie? Yes, she certainly might; but what notion could a woman of her occupation, though nothing worse than an *inn-keeper*, have of the *nicer* distinctions between truth and falsehood, living among a most profligate and depraved people, where truth could scarcely be known?

2. There is a lax morality in the world that recommends a *lie* rather than the *truth*, when the purposes of *religion* and *humanity* can be served by it. But when can this be? The religion of Christ is one eternal system of truth, and can neither be served by a *lie* nor admit one. On this vile subject fine words have been spoken. *Tasso*, in his elegant episode of *Sophronia* and *Olindo*, in the *Gerusalemme Liberata*, b. ii., v. 22, represents the former as telling a lie to Saladdin, relative to the stealing of an image, for which, as he could not discover the culprit, he doomed all the Christians in his power to death. Sophronia, a pious Christian virgin, getting into the presence of the tyrant, in order to save her people, accuses herself, though perfectly innocent, of the theft. Her conduct on this occasion the poet embellishes in the following manner, for which the religion of that time, which dealt in *holy frauds*, would no doubt applaud him.

'Ed ella: il reo si trova al tuo cospetto;
Opra è il furto, Signor, di questa mano
Io l' immagine tolsi; Io son colei
Che tu ricerchi, e me punir ti dei.
  Cosi al pubblico fato il capo altero
Offerse, e 'l volle in se sol racorre.
Magnanima menzogna! or quando è il vero
Si bello, che si possa a te preporre?"

Then she: "Before thy sight the guilty stands;
The theft, O King, committed by these hands.
In me the thief who stole the image view!
To me the punishment decreed is due."
  Thus, filled with public zeal, the generous dame
A victim for her people's ransom came.
O *great deceit!* O *lie divinely fair!*
What *truth* with such a *falsehood* can compare!
                                              Hoole.

Thus a *lie* is ornamented with splendid decorations both by the *Italian* and *English* poet, and the whole formed into an anti-apostolic maxim, *Let us do* evil, *that* good *may come of it.*

A purer morality was taught by one of the most ancient *heathen* writers than is here preached by these *demi-christians:*—

Εχθρος γαρ μοι κεινος, ὁμως αϊδαο πυλῃσιν,
'Ος χ' ἑτερον μεν κευθει ενι φρεσιν, αλλο δε βαξει.
                                     Iliad. l. ix., v. 312.

My soul detests him as the gates of hell,
Who knows the *truth* and dares a *falsehood* tell,

The following is the advice of a genuine *Christian* poet, and one of the holiest men of his time:—

Lie *not;* but let thy *heart* be true to *God;*
Thy *tongue* to *it*, thy *actions* to them *both*.
Cowards tell lies, and those who *fear the rod;*
The stormy working soul spits *lies* and *froth*.
Dare to be true! *nothing* can need a *lie*.
The *fault* that *needs* it *most* grows two thereby.
                                              Herbert.

For other observations on this subject, see the notes on Gen. xii. at the end, and xx. 12.

3. Though the hand of God was evidently in every thing that concerned the Israelites, and they were taught to consider that by *his might alone* they were to be put in possession of the promised land; yet they were as fully convinced that if they did not use the counsel, prudence, and strength which they had received from him, they should not succeed. Hence, while they depended on the Divine direction and power, they exercised their own prudence, and put forth their own *strength;* and thus they were workers together with him, and did not receive the grace of God in vain. The application of this maxim is easy; and we cannot expect any success, either in things spiritual or temporal, unless *we* walk by the same rule and mind the same thing.

CHAPTER III

The Israelitish camp removes from Shittim to Jordan, 1. *The officers inform them how they are to pass the river, and the distance they are to keep from the ark,* 2–4. *Joshua directs the people,* 5, 6; *and the Lord gives directions to Joshua,* 7, 8. *He delivers the Lord's message to the people, and foretells the miraculous passage and division of Jordan,* 9–13. *The priests, bearing the ark, enter the river, and immediately the waters are cut off, and the priests stand on dry ground, in the bed of the river, till all the camp passes over,* 14–17.

A. M. 2553
B. C. 1451
An. Exod. Isr.
40
Anno ante
I. Olymp. 675

AND Joshua rose early in the morning; and they removed ᵃfrom Shittim, and came to Jordan, he and all the children of Israel, and lodged there before they passed over.

2 And it came to pass ᵇafter three days, that the officers went through the host;

3 And they commanded the people, saying, ᶜWhen ye see the ark of the covenant of the LORD your God, ᵈand the priests the Levites bearing it, then ye shall remove from your place, and go after it.

4 ᵉYet there shall be a space between you and it, about two thousand cubits by measure: come not near unto it, that ye may know the way by which ye must go: for ye have not passed *this* way ᶠheretofore.

5 And Joshua said unto the people, ᵍSanctify yourselves: for to-morrow the LORD will do wonders among you.

A. M. 2553
B. C. 1451
An. Exod. Isr.
40
Anno ante
I. Olymp. 675

6 And Joshua spake unto the priests, saying, ʰTake up the ark of the covenant, and pass over before the people. And they took up the ark of the covenant, and went before the people.

7 And the LORD said unto Joshua, This day will I begin to ⁱmagnify thee in the sight of all Israel, that they may know that, ᵏas I was with Moses, *so* I will be with thee.

8 And thou shalt command ˡthe priests that bear the ark of the covenant, saying, When ye are come to the brink of the water of Jordan, ᵐye shall stand still in Jordan.

9 And Joshua said unto the children of

ᵃChap. ii. 1——ᵇChap. i. 10, 11——ᶜSee Num. x. 33 ᵈDeut. xxxi. 9, 25——ᵉExod. xix. 12——ᶠHeb. *since yesterday, and the third day*——ᵍExod. xix. 10, 14, 15;

Lev. xx. 7; Num. xi. 18; chap. vii. 13; 1 Sam. xvi. 5; Joel ii. 16——ʰNum. iv. 15——ⁱCh. iv. 14; 1 Chron. xxix. 25; 2 Chron. i. 1——ᵏChap. i. 5——ˡVer. 3——ᵐVer. 17

NOTES ON CHAP. III

Verse 1. *Joshua rose early*] Archbishop Usher supposes that this was upon *Wednesday*, the 28th of April, A. M. 2553, the fortieth year after the exodus from Egypt. From Shittim, where they had lately been encamped, to Jordan, was about sixty stadia, according to Josephus; that is, about eight English miles.

Verse 2. *After three days*] These three days are probably to be thus understood: As soon as Joshua took the command of the army, he sent the spies to ascertain the state of Jericho; as we have seen chap. i. 12. They returned at the end of three days, or rather on the third day, and made their report. It was at this time, immediately on the return of the spies, that he made the proclamation mentioned here; in consequence of which the people immediately struck their tents, and marched forward to Jordan.

Verse 4. *About two thousand cubits*] This distance they were to keep, 1. For the greater *respect*, because the presence of the ark was the symbol and pledge of the Divine presence. 2. That the ark, which was to be their *pilot* over these waters, might be the more *conspicuous*, which it could not have been had the people crowded upon it.

Verse 5. *Sanctify yourselves*] What was implied in this command we are not informed; but it is likely that it was the same as that given by Moses, Exod. xix. 10-14. They were to wash themselves and their garments, and abstain from every thing that might indispose their minds from a profitable attention to the miracle about to be wrought in their behalf.

Verse 6. *Spake unto the priests, saying, Take up the ark*] It is remarkable that the *priests*, not the *Levites*, whose ordinary business it was, were employed to carry the ark on this occasion. Calmet conjectures that this was because it was probably carried *without being wrapped up in its curtains*, as it always was when the

Levites carried it. Though it was the business of the Levites, the sons of Kohath, to carry the ark; yet on certain occasions the priests alone performed this office. 1. In the present case. 2. When they encompassed Jericho, chap. vi. 6. 3. When it was carried to the war against the Philistines by the priests, the sons of Eli, 2 Sam. xv. 25. 4. When David sent it back to Jerusalem, at the time he was obliged to fly from it, through the rebellion of his son Absalom, 2 Sam. xv. 25; and, 5. At the time that it was taken out of the tabernacle, to be deposited in the temple; see 1 Kings viii. 6-11. These were the *most solemn* occasions, and on such alone, we may presume, the *priests* performed this office instead of the *Levites*.

In all their *former* marches the ark was carried in the *centre* of this immense camp; (see the scheme at the end of chap. ii. of the book of Numbers;) but *now* it was to proceed at the *head* of the army, and to go before them, and at such a distance, about three quarters of a mile, that the whole camp might see it as their *guide*.

Verse 7. *This day will I begin to magnify thee*] By making him the instrument in this miraculous passage, he did him honour and gave him high credit in the sight of the people: hence his authority was established, and obedience to him as their leader fully secured. What must have confirmed this authority was, his circumstantially foretelling how the waters should be cut off as soon as the feet of the priests had touched them, ver. 13. This *demonstrated* that the secret of the Lord was with *him*.

Verse 8. *Ye shall stand still in Jordan.*] The priests proceeded first with the ark, and entered into the bed of the river, the course of which was immediately arrested, the waters collecting *above* the place where the priests stood, while the stream fell off towards the Dead Sea; so that the whole channel below where the priests were standing became dry. The whole camp,

A. M. 2553
B. C. 1451
An. Exod. Isr.
40
Anno ante
I. Olymp. 675 Israel, Come hither, and hear the words of the LORD your God.

10 And Joshua said, Hereby ye shall know that ⁿthe living God *is* among you, and *that* he will without fail ᵒdrive out from before you the Canaanites, and the Hittites, and the Hivites, and the Perizzites, and the Girgashites, and the Amorites, and the Jebusites.

11 Behold, the ark of the covenant of ᵖthe LORD of all the earth passeth over before you into Jordan.

12 Now therefore �q take you twelve men out of the tribes of Israel, out of every tribe a man;

13 And it shall come to pass, ʳas soon as the soles of the feet of the priests that bear the ark of the LORD, ˢthe Lord of all the earth, shall rest in the waters of Jordan, *that* the waters of Jordan shall be cut off *from* the waters that come down from above; and they ᵗshall stand upon a heap.

A. M. 2553
B. C. 1451
An. Exod. Isr.
40
Anno ante
I. Olymp. 675

14 And it came to pass, when the people removed from their tents, to pass over Jordan, and the priests bearing the ᵘark of the covenant before the people;

15 And as they that bare the ark were come unto Jordan, and ᵛthe feet of the priests that bare the ark were dipped in the brim of the water, (for ᵂJordan overfloweth all his banks ˣall the time of harvest,)

16 That the waters which came down from above stood *and* rose up upon a heap, very far from the city Adam, that *is* beside ʸZaretan: and those that came down ᶻtoward the

---

ⁿDeut. v. 26; 1 Sam. xvii. 26; 2 Kings xix. 4; Hos. i. 10; Matt. xvi. 16; 1 Thess. i. 9——ᵒExod. xxxiii. 2; Deut. vii. 1; Psa. xliv. 2——ᵖVer. 13; Mic. iv. 13; Zech. iv. 14; vi. 5——q Chap. iv. 2——ʳVer. 15, 16——ˢVer. 11

ᵗPsa. lxxviii. 13; cxiv. 3——ᵘActs vii. 45——ᵛVer. 12 ᵂ1 Chron. xii. 15; Jer. xii. 5; xlix. 19; Ecclus. xxiv. 26 ˣChap. iv. 18; v. 10, 12——ʸ1 Kings iv. 12; vii. 46 ᶻDeut. iii. 17

---

therefore, passed over below where the priests were standing, keeping at the distance of two thousand cubits from the ark; this they would readily do, as the whole bed of the river was dry for many miles below the place where the priests entered.

Verse 10. *Hereby ye shall know that the living God is among you*] The Israelites were apt to be discouraged, and to faint at even the *appearance* of danger; it was necessary, therefore, that they should have the fullest assurance of the presence and assistance of God in the important enterprise on which they were now entering. They are to combat idolaters, who have nothing to trust in and help them but *gods* of *wood, stone,* and *metal:* whereas they are to have the *living God* in the midst of them—HE who is the author of *life* and of *being*—who can give, or take it away, at his pleasure; and who by this miracle proved that he had undertaken to guide and defend them: and Joshua makes *this* manifestation of God the proof that he will drive out the Hittites, Hivites, &c., before them.

With regard to the situation of each of these nations in the land of Canaan, Calmet remarks, that those called CANAANITES chiefly inhabited what is called *Phœnicia,* the environs of *Tyre* and *Sidon:* the HITTITES occupied the mountains, southward of the promised land: the HIVITES dwelt by *Ebal* and *Gerizim, Sichem* and *Gibeon,* towards the mountains of *Hermon:* the PERIZZITES were probably not a distinct nation or tribe, but rather *villagers,* scattered through the country in general: the GIRGASHITES possessed the country beyond the Jordan, towards the lake of Gennesareth: the JEBUSITES possessed Jerusalem: and the AMORITES occupied the mountainous country in the vicinity of the western part of the Dead Sea, and also that part of the land of Moab which the Israelites conquered from Sihon and Og.

Verse 12. *Take you twelve men*] See the note on chap. iv. 2.

Verse 15. *And the feet of the priests—were dipped in the brim of the water*] Thus we find that every thing occurred exactly in the way in which Joshua had foretold it. This must have greatly increased his credit among the people.

For Jordan overfloweth all his banks, &c.] It has often been remarked that there was no need of a miracle in crossing Jordan, as it is but an inconsiderable stream, easily fordable, being but about twenty yards in breadth. But the circumstance marked here by the sacred historian proves that there was a time in the year, viz., in the *harvest,* that this said river *overflowed its banks;* and this is confirmed by another place in Scripture, 1 Chron. xii. 15. As the miracle reported here took place about the beginning of April, a time in which rivers in general are less than in winter, it may be asked how there could be such an increase of waters at this time? The simple fact is, that the Jordan, as we have already seen, has its origin at the foot of Mount Lebanon, which mountain is always *covered with snow* during the winter months; in those months therefore the river is low: but when the summer's sun has melted these snows, there is consequently a prodigious increase of waters, so that the old channel is not capable of containing them; this accounts for the statement in the text that the Jordan *overfloweth his banks all the time of harvest;* and this was the time which God chose they should pass over it, that a miraculous interposition might be necessary, and that by the *miracle* they should be convinced of his omnipotence, who was not only their guide, but had promised to put them in possession of this good land.

Verse 16. *Rose up upon a heap*] That is, they continued to accumulate, filling up the whole of the channel toward the source, and the adjacent ground over which they were now spread, to a much greater depth, the power of God giving a contrary direction to the current. We need not suppose them to be gathered up *like a moun-*

A. M. 2553
B. C. 1451
An. Exod. Isr.
40
Anno ante
I. Olymp. 675

sea of the plain, *even* ᵃthe salt sea, failed, *and* were cut off: and the people passed over right against Jericho.

17 And the priests that bare the ark of the covenant of the LORD stood firm on dry ground in the midst of Jordan, ᵇand all the Israelites passed over on dry ground, until all the people were passed clean over Jordan.

A. M. 2553
B. C. 1451
An. Exod. Isr.
40
Anno ante
I. Olymp. 675

ᵃGen. xiv. 3; Num. xxxiv. 3

ᵇSee Exod. xiv. 29

---

tain, *instar montis*, as the *Vulgate* expresses it, but that they continued to flow back in the course of the channel; and ere they could have reached the lake of Gennesareth, where they might have been easily accumulated, the whole Israelitish army would have all got safely to the opposite side.

Very far from the city Adam—beside Zaretan] Where these places were it is difficult to say. The city *Adam* is wholly unknown. From 1 Kings iv. 12 we learn that *Zartanah* was below *Jezreel* near *Bethshean*, or *Scythopolis*, and not far from *Succoth*, 1 Kings vii. 46. And it appears from Gen. xxxiii. 17, Josh. xiii. 27, that *Succoth* lay on the east side of Jordan, not far from the lake of *Gennesareth;* and probably *Adam* was on the same side to the north of *Succoth.* It is probable that the Israelites crossed the Jordan near *Bethabara*, where John baptized, John i. 28, and which probably had its name, *the house of passage*, from this very circumstance. After all, it is extremely difficult to ascertain the exact situation of these places, as in the lapse of upwards of 3,000 years the face of the country must have been materially changed. Seas, rivers, and mountains, change not; and though we cannot ascertain the *spot*, it is sufficiently evident that we can come *near* to the *place.* It has been considered a lame objection against the truth of the *Iliad* that the situation of *Troy* cannot now be exactly ascertained. There are even many ancient cities and considerable towns in Europe, that, though they still bear their former names, do not occupy the same spot. There are not a few of those even in England; among such *Norwich, Salisbury,* &c., may be ranked, neither of which is in its primitive situation.

Right against Jericho.] It would be impossible for the *whole* camp to pass over in the space *opposite* to Jericho, as they must have taken up some *miles* in breadth, besides the 2,000 cubits which were left on the right between them and the ark; but the river was divided opposite to Jericho, and *there* the camp began to pass over.

Verse 17. *The priests—stood firm on dry ground*] They stood in the mid channel, and shifted not their position till the camp, consisting of nearly 600,000 effective men, besides women, children, &c., had passed over.

1. Is it not surprising that the Canaanites did not dispute this passage with the Israelites? It is likely they would, had they had any expectation that such a passage would have been attempted. They must have known that the Israelitish camp was on the other side of the Jordan, but could they have supposed that a passage for such a host was possible when the banks of the Jordan were quite overflowed? It was not merely because they were *panic struck* that they did not dispute this passage, but because they must have supposed it *impossible;* and when they found the attempt was made, the passage was effected before they could prepare to prevent it.

2. GOD now appears in such a way, and works in such a manner, as to leave no doubt concerning his *presence* or his *power*, or of his love to Israel. After this, was it possible for this people ever to doubt his being or his bounty? *This*, with the miraculous passage of the *Red Sea*, were well calculated to have established their faith for ever; and those who did not yield to the evidence afforded by these two miracles were incapable of rational conviction.

3. In some respects the *passage* of the *Jordan* was more strikingly miraculous than that even of the *Red Sea.* In the latter God was pleased to employ an *agent;* the *sea went back by a strong east wind all that night, and made the sea dry* land, Exod. xiv. 21. Nothing of this kind appeared in the passage of the Jordan; a very *rapid* river (for so all travellers allow it to be) went back to its source without any kind of agency but the invisible hand of the invisible God.

4. Through the whole period of the Jewish history these miracles, so circumstantially related, were never denied by any, but on the contrary conscientiously believed by all. Nor did any of them in their revolts from God, which were both foul and frequent, ever call these great facts in question, when even so full of enmity against God as to blaspheme his name, and give his glory to *dumb idols!* Is not this a manifest proof that these facts were incontestable? and that Jehovah had so done his marvellous works that they should be had in everlasting remembrance? Reader, the same God who is over all is rich in mercy to all that call upon him. HE *changes not*, neither is he weary: trust in the Lord for ever, for in the Lord Jehovah is everlasting strength; and HE ever saves his followers out of the hands of all their enemies, and, having guided them by his counsel, will receive them into his glory.

CHAPTER IV

When the people are passed over, Joshua commands twelve men, one taken out of each tribe, to take up a stone on his shoulder out of the midst of the river, and carry it to the other side, to be set up as a memorial of this miraculous passage, 1–7. They do so, and set up the stones in the place where they encamp the first night, 8, 9. The priests stand in the river, till all the people are passed over, 10, 11. Of the tribes of Reuben and

Gad, and the half tribe of Manasseh, 40,000 *fighting men pass over with the other tribes,* 12, 13. *Joshua is magnified in the sight of the people, and they fear him as they did Moses,* 14. *The priests are commanded to come up out of the river, which, on their leaving it, immediately returns, and overflows its banks as before,* 15–18. *This miraculous passage takes place the* tenth *day of the* first *month,* 19. *The stones are set up in Gilgal, and Joshua teaches the people what use they are to make of them,* 20–24.

A. M. 2553
B. C. 1451
An. Exod. Isr.
40
Anno ante
I. Olymp. 675

AND it came to pass, when all the people were clean passed ªover Jordan, that the LORD spake unto Joshua, saying,

2 ᵇTake you twelve men out of the people, out of every tribe a man,

3 And command ye them, saying, Take you hence out of the midst of Jordan, out of the place where ᶜthe priests' feet stood firm, twelve stones, and ye shall carry them over with you, and leave them in ᵈthe lodging place, where ye shall lodge this night.

4 Then Joshua called the twelve men, whom he had prepared of the children of Israel, out of every tribe a man:

5 And Joshua said unto them, Pass over before the ark of the LORD your God into the midst of Jordan, and take you up every man of you a stone upon his shoulder, according unto the number of the tribes of the children of Israel;

6 That this may be a sign among you, *that* ᵉwhen your children ask *their fathers* ᶠin time to come, saying, What *mean* ye by these stones?

A. M. 2553
B. C. 1451
An. Exod. Isr.
40
Anno ante
I. Olymp. 675

7 Then ye shall answer them, That ᵍthe waters of Jordan were cut off before the ark of the covenant of the LORD; when it passed over Jordan, the waters of Jordan were cut off: and these stones shall be for ʰa memorial unto the children of Israel for ever.

8 And the children of Israel did so, as Joshua commanded, and took up twelve stones out of the midst of Jordan, as the LORD spake unto Joshua, according to the number of the tribes of the children of Israel, and carried them over with them unto the place where they lodged, and laid them down there.

9 And Joshua set up twelve stones in the midst of Jordan, in the place where the feet of the priests which bare the ark of the cove-

---

ªDeuteronomy xxvii. 2; chapter iii. 17——ᵇChapter iii. 12——ᶜChapter iii. 13——ᵈVerse 19, 20 ᵉVerse 21; Exodus xii. 26; xiii. 14; Deuteronomy

vi. 20; Psa. xliv. 1; lxxviii. 3, 4, 5, 6——ᶠHeb. *to-morrow*——ᵍChap. iii. 13, 16——ʰExodus. xii. 14; Num. xvi. 40

NOTES ON CHAP. IV

Verse 2. *Take you twelve men*] From chap. iii. 12, it appears that the twelve men had been *before* appointed, one taken out of each of the twelve tribes; and now they are employed for that purpose for which they had been *before* selected.

Verse 3. *Where ye shall lodge this night.*] This was in the place that was afterwards called *Gilgal.* See ver. 19.

Verse 4. *Twelve men, whom he had prepared*] This must refer to their appointment, chap. iii. 12.

Verse 6. *This may be a sign*] Stand as a continual memorial of this miraculous passage, and consequently a proof of their lasting obligation to God.

Verse 9. *And Joshua set up twelve stones in the midst of Jordan*] It seems from this chapter that there were *two sets* of stones erected as a memorial of this great event; twelve at Gilgal, ver. 20, and twelve in the bed of Jordan, ver. 9. The twelve stones in the bed of Jordan might have been so placed on a base of strong stone-work so high as always to be visible, and serve to mark the very spot where the priests stood with the ark. The twelve stones set up at *Gilgal* would stand as a monument of the place of the *first encampment* after this miraculous passage. Though this appears to me to be the meaning of this place, yet Dr. Kennicott's

criticism here should not be passed by. "It is well known," says he, "that when Joshua led the Israelites over Jordan, he was commanded to take *twelve stones* out of the *midst of Jordan*, to be a memorial that the ground in the very *midst* of that river had been made dry. But *where* was this memorial to be set up? The ninth verse says: *Joshua set up these stones* IN *the midst of Jordan.* But is it likely that the stones should be placed or set down *where* they were *taken up;* and that the memorial should be erected there *where*, when the river was again united, it would be *concealed*, and of course could be no *memorial* at all? This however flatly contradicts the rest of the chapter, which says these stones were pitched in *Gilgal*, where Israel lodged in Canaan for the first time. The solution of this difficulty is, that בתוך *bethoch* IN *the midst*, should be here מתוך *mittoch*, FROM *the midst*, as in ver. 3, 8, 20, and as the word is here also in the *Syriac* version. The true rendering therefore is, *And Joshua set up the twelve stones* (taken) FROM *the midst of Jordan*," &c. I confess I see no need for this criticism, which is not supported by a single MS. either in his own or De Rossi's collection, though they amount to *four hundred and ninety-four* in number. Twelve stones might be *gathered* in different parts of the bed of the Jordan, and be set up as a pillar in another, and be a continual visible memorial of this grand event. And if twelve were set up in Gil-

A. M. 2553
B. C. 1451
An. Exod. Isr.
40
Anno ante
I. Olymp. 675

nant stood: and they are there unto this day.

10 For the priests which bare the ark stood in the midst of Jordan, until every thing was finished that the LORD commanded Joshua to speak unto the people, according to all that Moses commanded Joshua: and the people hasted and passed over.

11 And it came to pass, when all the people were clean passed over, that the ark of the LORD passed over, and the priests, in the presence of the people.

12 And ¹the children of Reuben, and the children of Gad, and half the tribe of Manasseh, passed over armed before the children of Israel, as Moses spake unto them:

13 About forty thousand ᵏprepared for war passed over before the LORD unto battle, to the plains of Jericho.

A. M. 2553
B. C. 1451
An. Exod. Isr.
40
Anno ante
I. Olymp. 675

14 On that day the LORD ¹magnified Joshua in the sight of all Israel; and they feared him, as they feared Moses, all the days of his life.

15 And the LORD spake unto Joshua, saying,

16 Command the priests that bear ᵐthe ark of the testimony, that they come up out of Jordan.

17 Joshua therefore commanded the priests, saying, Come ye up out of Jordan.

18 And it came to pass, when the priests that bare the ark of the covenant of the LORD were come up out of the midst of Jordan, *and* the soles of the priests' feet were ⁿlifted up unto the dry land, that the waters of Jordan returned unto their place, ᵒand ᵖflowed over all his banks, as *they did* before.

19 And the people came up out of Jordan on the tenth *day* of the first month, and encamped ᑫin Gilgal, in the east border of Jericho.

---

¹Num. xxxii. 20, 27, 28——ᵏOr, *ready armed*——ˡChap. iii. 7——ᵐExod. xxv. 16, 22

ⁿHebrew, *plucked up*——ᵒChapter iii. 15——ᵖHebrew, *went*——ᑫChap. v. 9

---

gal as a memorial of their first encampment in Canaan, it is still more likely that twelve would be set up in the bed of the river to show where it had been divided, and the place where the whole Israelitish host had passed over dry-shod. The reader may follow the opinion he judges most likely.

Verse 10. *And the people hasted and passed over.*] How very natural is this circumstance! The people seeing the waters divided, and Jordan running back, might be apprehensive that it would soon resume its wonted course; and this would naturally lead them to *hasten* to get over, with as much *speed* as possible. The circumstance itself thus marked is a proof that the relater was an eyewitness of this miraculous passage.

Verse 12. *The children of Reuben, and—Gad*] Concerning the numbers of these tribes that stayed behind to take care of the women, children, and cattle, and which amounted to 70,580 men, see the note on Num. xxxii. 17.

Passed over armed] See the note on chap. i. 14.

Verse 14. *The Lord magnified Joshua*] See the note on chap. iii. 7.

Verse 18. *The waters of Jordan returned unto their place*] It is particularly remarked by the sacred historian, that as soon as the soles of the priests' feet touched the water, the stream of the Jordan was cut off, chap. iii. 15, and the course of the river continued to be inverted all the time they continued in its channel; and that as soon as the soles of their feet had touched the dry land, on their return from the bed of the river, the waters immediately resumed their natural course. All this was done by the sovereign influence of that God whose *presence* was represented by the ark of the covenant.

Verse 19. *On the tenth day of the first month*] As the Israelites left Egypt on the *fifteenth* day of the first month, A. M. 2513, (see Exod. xiv.,)

and they entered into Canaan the *tenth* of the first month, A. M. 2553, it is evident that *forty* years, wanting *five* days, had elapsed from the time of their exodus from Egypt to their entrance into the promised inheritance.

Encamped in Gilgal] That is, in the place that was *afterwards* called Gilgal, see chap. v. 9; for here the name is given it by *anticipation*. In Hebrew, גַל *gal* signifies to *roll;* and the doubling of the root, גִלְגַּל *galgal* or *gilgal*, signifies *rolling round and round,* or *rolling off* or *away,* because, in circumcising the children that had been born in the wilderness, Joshua *rolled away, rolled off completely,* the reproach of the people. From this time Gilgal became a place of considerable eminence in the sacred history. 1. It was the place where the Israelitish camp rested the first night of their entering into that land which had been promised to their fathers from the days of Abraham. 2. It was the place in which Joshua circumcised all the people who had been born in the wilderness, during the forty years of their wandering, after they left Egypt. 3. It was the place in which Joshua had what we might term his fortified camp, and to which he and his army constantly returned after each of their expeditions against the inhabitants of the land. 4. It appears to have been the place where all the women, children, cattle, and goods, &c., were lodged, probably during the whole of the Canaanitish war. 5. It was the place where they celebrated the first passover they kept in the promised land. 6. It was the place where Saul, the first king of Israel, was proclaimed. 7. There the manna ceased to fall. And, 8. There the ark was fixed till, after the conquest of the country, it was removed to Shiloh.

Gilgal was about *ten* furlongs from Jericho, and *fifty* from Jordan: Jericho being on the

A. M. 2553
B. C. 1451
An. Exod. Isr.
40
Anno ante
I. Olymp. 675

20 And ʳthose twelve stones, which they took out of Jordan, did Joshua pitch in Gilgal.

21 And he spake unto the children of Israel, saying, ˢWhen your children shall ask their fathers, ᵗin time to come, saying, What *mean* these stones?

22 Then ye shall let your children know, saying, ᵘIsrael came over this Jordan on dry land.

23 For the LORD your God dried up the waters of Jordan from before you, until ye were passed over, as the LORD your God did to the Red Sea, ᵛwhich he dried up from before us, until we were gone over:

A. M. 2553
B. C. 1451
An. Exod. Isr.
40
Anno ante
I. Olymp. 675

24 ʷThat all the people of the earth might know the hand of the LORD, that it is ˣmighty: that ye might ʸfear the LORD your God ᶻfor ever.

ʳVer. 3——ˢVer. 6——ᵗHeb. *to-morrow*——ᵘChap. iii. 17——ᵛExod. xiv. 21——ʷ1 Kings viii. 42, 43; 2 Kings xix. 19; Psa. cvi. 8

ˣExod. xv. 16; 1 Chron. xxix. 12; Psa. lxxxix. 13 ʸExod. xiv. 31; Deut. vi. 2; Psa. lxxxix. 7; Jer. x. 7 ᶻHeb. *all days*

---

west, and Jordan on the east, Gilgal being between both. See *Josephus*, De Bello, &c., lib. v., c. 4, and *Calmet* on this place. Calmet supposes there was neither city nor town here before the arrival of the Israelites.

Verse 20. *Those twelve stones*] It is very likely that a base of mason-work was erected of some considerable height, and then the twelve stones placed on the top of it; and that this was the case both in Jordan and in Gilgal: for twelve such stones as a man could carry a considerable way on his shoulder, see ver. 5, could scarcely have made any observable altar, or pillar of memorial: but erected on a high base of mason-work they would be very conspicuous, and thus properly answer the end for which God ordered them to be set up.

Verse 22. *Then ye shall let your children know*] The necessity of an early religious education is inculcated through the whole oracles of God. The parents who neglect it have an awful account to give to the Judge of quick and dead.

Verse 24. *That all the people of the earth might know*] It is very likely that כל עמי הארץ *col ammey haarets* means simply, *all the people of this land*—all the Canaanitish nations, to whom, by the miracles wrought in behalf of his people, he intended to show his eternal power and Godhead, the excellence of his protection, and the unavailableness of human might against his omnipotence; and the miracles he wrought for this people, in the sight of the hea-

then, were well calculated to make these things *known*.

1. GOD intends that his religion should be maintained and propagated in the earth; therefore he has given a revelation of himself to men, that it may be taught in the world; and he particularly requires that parents should be diligent and fervent in teaching their children the knowledge of his name. 2. This is one great use of the *ordinances* of the Gospel, and the *rites* of religion. They are all significators of sacred things, and point out matters of infinite importance beyond themselves. 3. A spirit of inquiry is common to every child: the human heart is ever panting after knowledge; and if not rightly directed when young, will, like that of our first mother, go astray after forbidden science. 4. If we wish our children to be *happy*, we should show them where happiness is to be found. If we wish them to be *wise*, we should lead them unto God by means of his word and ordinances. It is natural for a child to inquire, "What do you mean by this baptism?—by this sacrament?—by praying?—by singing psalms and hymns?" &c. And what fine opportunities do such questions give pious and intelligent parents to instruct their children in every article of the Christian faith, and in every fact on which these articles are established! Oh why is this neglected, while the command of God is before our eyes, and the importance of the measure so strikingly obvious?

CHAPTER V

The effect produced on the minds of the Canaanites by the late miracle, 1. Joshua is commanded to circumcise the Israelites, 2. He obeys, 3. Who they were that were circumcised, and why it was now not done, 4-7. They abide in the camp till they are whole, 8. The place is called Gilgal, and why, 9. They keep the passover in the same place, 10. They eat unleavened cakes and parched corn, on the morrow after the passover, 11. The manna ceases, 12. The captain of the Lord's host appears to Joshua, 13-15.

A. M. 2553
B. C. 1451
An. Exod. Isr.
40
Anno ante
I. Olymp. 675

AND it came to pass, when all the kings of the Amorites, which *were* on the side of Jordan westward, and all the kings of the Canaanites, ᵃwhich *were* by the sea, ᵇheard that the LORD had dried up the waters of Jordan from before the chil-

A. M. 2553
B. C. 1451
An. Exod. Isr.
40
Anno ante
I. Olymp. 675

ᵃNum. xiii. 29——ᵇExod. xv. 14, 15; chap.

ii. 9, 10, 11; Psa. xlviii. 6; Ezek. xxi. 7

NOTES ON CHAP. V

Verse 1. *The Amorites which* were *on the side of Jordan westward*] It has already been

remarked that the term *Amorite* is applied sometimes to signify all the nations or tribes of Canaan. It appears from this verse that there were people thus denominated that dwelt

A. M. 2553
B. C. 1451
An. Exod. Isr.
40
Anno ante
I. Olymp. 675

dren of Israel, until we were passed over, that their heart melted, °neither was their spirit in them any more, because of the children of Israel.

2 At that time the LORD said unto Joshua, Make thee ᵈsharp ᵉknives, and circumcise

again the children of Israel the second time.

3 And Joshua made him sharp knives, and circumcised the children of Israel at ᶠthe hill of the foreskins.

4 And this *is* the cause why Joshua did circumcise: ᵍAll the people that came out of

A. M. 2553
B. C. 1451
An. Exod. Isr.
40
Anno ante
I. Olymp. 675

°1 Kings x. 5——ᵈOr, *knives of flints*——ᵉExodus iv. 25

ᶠOr, *Gibeath-haaraloth*——ᵍNum. xiv. 29; xxvi. 64, 65; Deut. ii. 16

---

on both sides of the Jordan. Those on the east side had already been destroyed in the war which the Israelites had with *Sihon* and *Og;* with those on the west side Joshua had not yet waged war. It is possible however that the *Amorites,* of whom we read in this verse, were the remains of those who dwelt on the east side of the Jordan, and who had taken refuge here on the defeat of Og and Sihon.

Verse 2. Make thee sharp knives] חרבות צרים *charboth tsurim, knives of rock, stone,* or *flint.* Before the use of iron was *common,* all the nations of the earth had their edge-tools made of *stones, flints,* &c. In the lately discovered islands this is found to be a common case. Our ancestors in these countries made their *arrow* and *spear-heads* of *flint:* these I have often seen turned up by the plough. But we cannot suppose that at the time here referred to the Israelites were destitute of *iron,* and were therefore obliged to use knives made of *stone* or *flint;* their different manufactures in the wilderness prove that they must have had both *iron* and *steel.* Why then use *knives* made of *stone?* Probably it was unlawful to use *metal* of any kind in this religious rite; and indeed this seems likely from the circumstance of Zipporah (Exod. iv. 25) taking a *sharp stone* and circumcising her son; and we find, from the most ancient and authentic accounts, that the Egyptians considered it unlawful or profane to use any kind of *metal* to make incisions in the human body, when preparing it for embalming; see the note on Gen. l. 2, and on Exod. iv. 25. That it was deemed improper to use any other kind of instrument in circumcision we have a proof in the tribe *Alnajab,* in Ethiopia, who follow the Mosaic institution, and perform the rite of circumcision, according to Ludolf, *cultris lapidibus,* with *knives made of stone.*—Hist. Æthiop., lib. iii., c. 1. And as God commanded the people to make him an altar of unhewn stones, on which no tool of iron had been lifted up, because this would *pollute* it, (see Exod. xx. 25, and Deut. xxvii. 5,) he might require that no instrument of iron should be used in a rite by which the body and soul of the person were in the most solemn and sacred manner dedicated to him to be his house and temple, the heart itself being the altar on which continual sacrifices to God must be offered. A physical reason has been given for preferring knives of *stone* in this operation, "the wound suffers less through inflammation, and is sooner healed." For this a reason may be given. It is almost impossible to get an edge made so even and firm as not to leave particles of the metal in the incisions made even in the most delicate flesh; these particles would soon become oxidized by the action of the air, and extra inflammation in the part would be the conse-

quence. The great aptitude of iron to be oxidized, i. e., to be converted to *rust,* is well known; but how far this reasoning, thus applied, may be supported by *fact,* I cannot pretend to determine: it is sufficiently evident that it was a common custom to use knives of stone in circumcision, and in all operations on those parts of the human body. I shall give a few examples. Pliny says, when they amputate certain parts they do it with a *sharp stone,* because nothing else could be employed without danger. *Samia testa virilitatem amputabant: nec aliter citra perniciem.*

Ovid, Fast. lib. iv., ver. 237, relates a circumstance where the *saxum acutum,* or *sharp stone,* was used about those parts:—

Ille etiam SAXO *corpus laniavit* ACUTO,
Longaque in immundo pulvere tracta coma est.
Voxque fuit, Merui; *meritas dem sanguine pœnas;*
Ah! *pereant partes, quæ nocuere mihi;*
Ah! *pereant; dicebat adhuc, onus inguinis aufert;*
Nullaque sunt subito signa relicta viri.

This quotation is produced in order to prove that a *knife* made of a *sharp stone* was used in making incisions and amputations of certain parts of the body, even when the use of iron was well known; but a translation of the verse is not necessary, and would be improper. The

Mollia qui RAPTA *secuit* GENITALIA TESTA

of *Juvenal* (Sat. vi., ver. 513) is a farther proof of this. Many other proofs might be produced; but those who wish for more may consult *Calmet* and *Scheuchzer.*

Circumcise again the children of Israel the second time.] This certainly does not mean that they should *repeat* circumcision on those who had already received it. This would have been as absurd as impracticable. But the command implies that they were to *renew* the observance of a rite which had been neglected in their travels in the desert: this is sufficiently evident from the following verses.

Verse 4. This is the cause why Joshua did circumcise] The text here explains itself. Before the Israelites left Egypt all the males were circumcised; and some learned men think that all those who were born during their encampment at *Sinai* were circumcised also, because there they celebrated the passover; but after that time, during the whole of their stay in the wilderness, there were none circumcised till they entered into the promised land. Owing to their unsettled state, God appears to have dispensed, for the time being, with this rite; but as they were about to celebrate another passover, it was necessary that all the males should

A. M. 2553
B. C. 1451
An. Exod. Isr. 40
Anno ante I. Olymp. 675

Egypt *that were* males, *even* all the men of war, died in the wilderness by the way, after they came out of Egypt.

5 Now all the people that came out were circumcised: but all the people *that were* born in the wilderness by the way as they came forth out of Egypt, *them* they had not circumcised.

6 For the children of Israel walked [h]forty years in the wilderness, till all the people *that were* men of war, which came out of Egypt, were consumed, because they obeyed not the voice of the LORD: unto whom the LORD sware that [i]he would not show them the land which the LORD sware unto their fathers that he would give us, [k]a land that floweth with milk and honey.

A. M. 2553
B. C. 1451
An. Exod. Isr. 40
Anno ante I. Olymp. 675

7 And [l]their children, *whom* he raised up in their stead, them Joshua circumcised: for they were uncircumcised, because they had not circumcised them by the way.

8 And it came to pass, [m]when they had done circumcising all the people, that they abode in their places in the camp [n]till they were whole.

9 And the LORD said unto Joshua, This day have I rolled away [o]the reproach of Egypt from off you. Wherefore the name of the place is called [p]Gilgal [q]unto this day.

10 And the children of Israel encamped in Gilgal, and kept the passover [r]on the four-

[h]Num. xiv. 33; Deut. i. 3; ii. 7, 14; Psa. xcv. 10 —— [i]Num. xiv. 23; Psa. xcv. 11; Heb. iii. 11 —— [k]Exod. iii. 8 —— [l]Num. xiv. 31; Deut. i. 39 —— [m]Heb. *when the people had made an end to be circumcised*

[n]See Gen. xxxiv. 25 —— [o]Gen. xxxiv. 14; 1 Sam. xiv. 6; see Lev. xviii. 3; chap. xxiv. 14; Ezek. xx. 7; xxiii. 3, 8; 1 Mac. iv. 58 —— [p]That is, *rolling* —— [q]Chap. iv. 19 —— [r]Exod. xii. 6; Num. ix. 5

be circumcised; for without this they could not be considered within the covenant, and could not keep the passover, which was the *seal* of that covenant. As baptism is generally understood to have succeeded to circumcision, and the holy eucharist to the passover; hence, in the Church of England, and probably in most others, no person is permitted to receive the sacrament of the *Lord's Supper* till he has been *baptized.*

Verse 8. *They abode—in the camp, till they were whole.*] This required several days; see the notes on Gen. xxxiv. Sir J. Chardin informs us that when adults were circumcised they were obliged to keep their beds for about three weeks, or at least during that time they are not able to walk about but with great difficulty. The account he had from several renegadoes, who had received circumcision among the Mohammedans. Is it not strange that during this time they were not attacked by the inhabitants of the land, and utterly destroyed, which might have been easily effected? See the case of the poor Shechemites, as related in Gen. xxxiv., with the notes there. Joshua, as an able general, would at once perceive that this very measure must expose his whole host to the danger of being totally annihilated; but he knew that GOD could not *err,* and that it was *his* duty to *obey;* therefore in the very teeth of his enemies he reduced the major part of his army to a state of total helplessness, simply trusting for protection in the arm of Jehovah! The sequel shows that his confidence was not misplaced; during the whole time God did not permit any of their enemies to disturb them. The path of duty is the path of safety; and it is impossible for any soul to be injured while walking in the path of obedience. But why did not God order them to be circumcised while they were on the east side of Jordan in a state of great security? Because he chose to bring them into straits and difficulties where no counsel or might but his own could infallibly direct and save them; and this he did that they might see that the excellence of the power was of God, and not of man. For the same reason he caused them to pass the Jordan at the time that it overflowed its banks, and not at the time when it was low and easily fordable, that he might have the better opportunity to show them that they were under his immediate care and protection; and convince them of his almighty power, that they might trust in him for ever, and not fear the force of any adversaries. In both cases how apparent are the wisdom, power, and goodness of God!

Verse 9. *The reproach of Egypt*] Their being *uncircumcised* made them like the uncircumcised Egyptians; and the Hebrews ever considered all those who were uncircumcised as being in a state of the grossest impurity. Being now *circumcised,* the reproach of uncircumcision was rolled away. This is another proof that the Israelites did not receive circumcision from the Egyptians; for they could not have considered those in a state of abomination, from whom they received that rite by which they conceived themselves to be made pure. The Israelites had this rite from Abraham; and Abraham had it from the express order of God himself. See Gen. xvii. 10, and the note there.

The place is called Gilgal] *A rolling away* or *rolling off.* See the note on chap. iv. 19, where the word is largely explained.

Verse 10. *Kept the passover on the fourteenth day of the month*] If the ceremony of circumcision was performed on the eleventh day of the month, as many think; and if the sore was at the worst on the thirteenth, and the passover was celebrated on the fourteenth, the people being then quite recovered; it must have been rather a *miraculous* than a *natural* healing. We have already seen from the account of Sir J. Chardin, that it required about three weeks to restore to soundness adults who had submitted to circumcision: if any thing like this took place in the case of the Israelites at Gilgal, they could not have celebrated the passover on the third or fourth day after their circumcision. The apparent impossibility of this led Mr. Harmer to suppose that they kept the pass-

A. M. 2553
B. C. 1451
An. Exod. Isr.
40
Anno ante
I. Olymp. 675

teenth day of the month at even, in the plains of Jericho.

11 And they did eat of the old corn of the land on the morrow after the passover, unleavened cakes, and parched *corn* in the self-same day.

12 And ˢthe manna ceased on the morrow after they had eaten of the old corn of the land; neither had the children of Israel manna any more; but they did eat of the fruit of the land of Canaan that year.

A. M. 2553
B. C. 1451
An. Exod. Isr.
40
Anno ante
I. Olymp. 675

13 And it came to pass, when Joshua was by Jericho, that he lifted up his eyes and looked, and, behold, there stood ᵗa man over against him, ᵘwith his sword drawn in his hand: and Joshua went unto him, and said unto him, *Art* thou for us, or for our adversaries?

14 And he said, Nay; but *as* ᵛcaptain of the host of the LORD am I now come. And Joshua ʷfell on his face to the earth, and did

---

ˢExod. xvi. 35——ᵗGen. xviii. 2; xxxii. 24; Exod. xxiii. 23; Zech. i. 8; Acts i. 10——ᵘNum. xxii. 23

ᵛOr, *prince;* see Exod. xxiii. 20; Dan. x. 13, 21; xii. 1; Rev. xii. 7; xix. 11, 14——ʷGen. xvii. 3

---

over on the fourteenth day of the *second* month, the preceding time having been employed in the business of the circumcision. See his *Observations,* vol. iv., p. 427, &c.

Verse 11. *They did eat of the old corn of the land*] The Hebrew word עבור *abur,* which we translate *old corn,* occurs only in this place in such a sense, if that sense be legitimate. The noun, though of doubtful signification, is evidently derived from עבר *abar,* to *pass over,* to *go beyond;* and here it may be translated simply *the produce,* that which *passes* from the *land* into the *hands* of the *cultivator;* or according to *Cocceius,* what passes from person to person in the way of *traffic;* hence *bought corn,* what they purchased from the inhabitants of the land.

On the morrow after the passover] That is, on the *fifteenth* day; for then the feast of unleavened bread began. But they could neither eat bread, nor parched corn, nor green ears, till the *first-fruits* of the harvest had been *waved* at the tabernacle; (see Lev. xxiii. 9, &c.;) and therefore in this case we may suppose that the Israelites had offered a sheaf of the *barley-harvest,* the only grain that was then ripe, before they ate of the unleavened cakes and parched corn.

Verse 12. *And the manna ceased—after they had eaten of the old corn*] This miraculous supply continued with them as long as they needed it. While they were in the wilderness they required such a provision; nor could such a multitude, in such a place, be supported without a miracle. Now they are got into the promised land, the anathematized inhabitants of which either fall or flee before them, they find an *old stock,* and they are brought in just at the commencement of the harvest; hence, as there is an ample provision made in the *ordinary* way of Providence, there is no longer any need of a *miraculous* supply; therefore the manna ceased which they had enjoyed for forty years. The circumstances in which it was first given, its continuance with them through all their peregrinations in the wilderness, its accompanying them over Jordan, and ceasing as soon as they got a supply in the ordinary way of Providence, all prove that it was a preternatural gift.

"On the fourteenth of Nisan they sacrificed the paschal lamb: on the fifteenth, i. e., according to our calculation, the same day after sunset, they disposed themselves for eating it, and actually did eat it. On the morrow, the six-

teenth, after having offered to God the *homer,* they began eating the corn of the country; and the seventeenth, the manna ceased to fall from heaven. What supports this calculation is, that the *homer* or *sheaf* was offered the sixteenth of Nisan, in broad daylight, though pretty late. Now the manna did not fall till night, or very early in the morning; so that it cannot be said to have ceased falling the same day that the Israelites began to eat of the produce of the country."—*Dodd.*

Verse 13. *When Joshua was by Jericho*] The sixth chapter should have commenced here, as this is an entirely new relation; or these two chapters should have made but one, as the present division has most unnaturally divided the communication which Joshua had from the angel of the Lord, and which is continued to ver. 5 of chap. vi. It is very likely that Joshua had gone out privately to reconnoitre the city of Jericho when he had this vision; and while contemplating the strength of the place, and probably reflecting on the extreme difficulty of reducing it, God, to encourage him, granted him this vision, and instructed him in the means by which the city should be taken.

There stood a man over against him] It has been a very general opinion, both among the ancients and moderns, that the person mentioned here was no other than the Lord Jesus in that form which, in the fulness of time, he was actually to assume for the redemption of man. That the appearance was supernatural is agreed on all hands; and as the name *Jehovah* is given him, (chap. vi. 2,) and he received from Joshua Divine adoration, we may presume that no *created angel* is intended.

And Joshua went unto him] This is a very natural relation, and carries with it all the appearances and characteristics of a simple relation of *fact.* The whole history of Joshua shows him to have been a man of the most *undaunted mind* and *intrepid courage*—a genuine HERO. An ordinary person, seeing this man armed, with a drawn sword in his hand, would have endeavoured to have regained the camp, and sought safety in flight; but Joshua, undismayed, though probably slightly armed, walks up to this terrible person and immediately questions him, *Art thou for us or for our adversaries?* probably at first supposing that he might be the Canaanitish general, coming to reconnoitre the Israelitish camp, as himself was come out to examine the city of Jericho.

Verse 14. *But as captain of the host of the*

A. M. 2553
B. C. 1451
An. Exod. Isr.
40
Anno ante
I. Olymp. 675

worship, and said unto him, What saith my lord unto his servant?

15 And the captain of the

Lord's host said unto Joshua, ˣLoose thy shoe from off thy foot; for the place whereon thou standest *is* holy. And Joshua did so.

A. M. 2553
B. C. 1451
An. Exod. Isr.
40
Anno ante
I. Olymp. 675

ˣExod. iii. 5;   Acts vii. 33

Lord am I now come.] By this saying Joshua was both encouraged and instructed. As if he had said, "Fear not; Jehovah hath sent from heaven to save thee and thy people from the reproach of them that would swallow thee up. Israel is the Lord's host; and the Lord of hosts is Israel's Captain. Thou thyself shalt only be captain under me, and I am now about to instruct thee relative to thy conduct in this war."

And Joshua—did worship] Nor was he reprehended for offering Divine worship to this person, which he would not have received had he been a *created angel.* See Rev. xxii. 8, 9.

Verse 15. *Loose thy shoe from off thy foot, &c.*] These were the same words which the angel, on Mount Sinai, spoke to Moses; (see Exod. iii. 5-8;) and from this it seems likely that it was the same person that appeared in both places: in the *first,* to encourage Moses to deliver the oppressed Israelites, and bring them to the promised land; in the *second,* to encourage Joshua in his arduous labour in expelling the ancient inhabitants, and establishing the people in the inheritance promised to their fathers.

There is scarcely a more unfortunate division of chapters in the whole Bible than that here. Through this very circumstance many persons

have been puzzled to know what was intended by this extraordinary appearance, because they supposed that the whole business ends with the chapter, whereas, it is continued in the succeeding one, the first verse of which is a mere parenthesis, simply relating the state of Jericho at the time that Joshua was favoured by this encouraging vision. We may draw two useful reflections from the subjects of this chapter:—

1. As the manna had now failed, the people, always greatly addicted to incredulity, might have been led to imagine that God had now given them up, and would be no longer in their armies, had he not given them this strong assurance, that the Angel of his presence should be with them as the guide and protector of the whole camp; for Joshua undoubtedly informed them of the encouragement he had received from the captain of the Lord's host.

2. By this vision he showed them that their help came from himself, and that it was not by human might or power, but by *the Lord of hosts,* they were to have the victory over all their adversaries; and he gave them the most convincing proof of this in the miraculous destruction of Jericho. By this means he continued to keep them dependent on his arm alone, without which dependence the spirit of religion could not have been preserved among them.

CHAPTER VI

The inhabitants of Jericho close their gates, 1. Continuation of the discourse between the captain of the Lord's host and Joshua. He commands the people to march round the city six days, the seven priests blowing with their trumpets; and to give a general shout, while marching round it on the seventh, *and promises that then the walls of the city shall fall down, 2–5. Joshua delivers these directions to the priests and to the people, 6, 7. The priests and people obey; the order of their procession, 8–16. He commands them to spare the house of Rahab, 17, and not to touch any part of the property of the city, the whole of which God had devoted to destruction, 18, 19. On the seventh day the walls fall down, and the Israelites take the city, 20, 21. The spies are ordered to take care of Rahab and her family—the city is burnt, but the silver, gold, brass, and iron, are put into the treasury of the house of the Lord, 22–24. Rahab dwells among the Israelites, 25; and the city is laid under a curse, 26.*

A. M. 2553
B. C. 1451
An. Exod. Isr.
40
Anno ante
I. Olymp. 675

NOW Jericho ᵃwas straitly shut up because of the children of Israel: none went out, and none came in.

2 And the Lord said unto Joshua, See, ᵇI have given into thine hand Jericho, and the ᶜking thereof, *and* the mighty men of valour.

A. M. 2553
B. C. 1451
An. Exod. Isr.
40
Anno ante
I. Olymp. 675

ᵃHeb. *did shut up, and was shut up*   ᵇChap. ii. 9, 24; viii. 1——ᶜDeut. vii. 24

NOTES ON CHAP. VI

Verse 1. *Now Jericho was straitly shut up*] The king of Jericho, finding that the spies had escaped, though the city was always kept shut by night, took the most proper precaution to prevent every thing of the kind in future, by keeping the city shut both day and night, having, no doubt, laid in a sufficiency of provisions to stand a siege, being determined to defend himself to the uttermost

Verse 2. *And the Lord said unto Joshua*] This is the same person who in the preceding chapter is called the *captain* or *prince of the Lord's host,* the discourse being here continued that was begun at the conclusion of the preceding chapter, from which the first verses of this are unnaturally divided.

I have given into thine hand Jericho, &c.] From ver. 11 of chap. xxiv. it seems as if there had been persons of all the seven Canaanitish nations then in Jericho, who might have come

A. M. 2553
B. C. 1451
An. Exod. Isr.
40
Anno ante
I. Olymp. 675

3 And ye shall compass the city, all *ye* men of war, *and* go round about the city once. Thus shalt thou do six days.

4 And seven priests shall bear before the ark seven ᵈtrumpets of rams' horns: and the seventh day ye shall compass the city seven times, and ᵉthe priests shall blow with the trumpets.

5 And it shall come to pass, that when they make a long *blast* with the ram's horn, *and* when ye hear the sound of the trumpet, all the people shall shout with a great shout; and the wall of the city shall fall down ᶠflat, and the people shall ascend up, every man straight before him.

6 And Joshua the son of Nun called the priests, and said unto them, Take up the ark of the covenant, and let seven priests bear seven trumpets of rams' horns before the ark of the LORD.

7 And he said unto the people, Pass on, and compass the city, and let him that is armed pass on before the ark of the LORD.

8 And it came to pass, when Joshua had spoken unto the people, that the seven priests

A. M. 2553
B. C. 1451
An. Exod. Isr.
40
Anno ante
I. Olymp. 675

bearing the seven trumpets of rams' horns passed on before the LORD, and blew with the trumpets: and the ark of the covenant of the LORD followed them.

9 And the armed men went before the priests that blew with the trumpets, ᵍand the ʰrereward came after the ark, *the priests* going on, and blowing with the trumpets.

10 And Joshua had commanded the people, saying, Ye shall not shout, nor ⁱmake any noise with your voice, neither shall *any* word proceed out of your mouth, until the day I bid you shout; then shall ye shout.

11 So the ark of the LORD compassed the city, going about *it* once: and they came into the camp, and lodged in the camp.

12 And Joshua rose early in the morning, ᵏand the priests took up the ark of the LORD.

13 And seven priests bearing seven trumpets of rams' horns before the ark of the LORD, went on continually, and blew with the trumpets: and the armed men went before them; but the rereward came after the ark of the LORD, *the priests* going on, and blowing with the trumpets.

ᵈSee Judg. vii. 16, 22——ᵉNum. x. 8——ᶠHeb. *under it*
ᵍNum. x. 25

ʰHeb. *gathering* host——ⁱHeb. *make your voice to be heard*——ᵏDeut. xxxi. 25

---

together at this time to help the king of Jericho against the invading Israelites. The Targum intimates that the place was very strong, having "*gates* of *iron* and *bars* of *brass;* and was shut up so closely that none came out, either to combat or make offers of peace."

Verse 3. *Ye shall compass the city*] In what order the people marched round the city does not exactly appear from the text. Some think they observed the same order as in their ordinary marches in the desert; (see the note on Num. x. 14, and see the *plans,* Num. ii;) others think that the soldiers marched first, then the priests who blew the trumpets, then those who carried the ark, and lastly the people.

Verse 4. *Seven trumpets of rams' horns*] The Hebrew word יובלים *yobelim* does not signify *rams' horns;* (see the note on Lev. xxv. 11;) nor do any of the ancient versions, the Chaldee excepted, give it this meaning. The instruments used on this occasion were evidently of the same kind with those used on the jubilee, and were probably made of horn or of silver; and the text in this place may be translated, *And seven priests shall bear before the ark the seven jubilee trumpets,* for they appear to have been the same kind as those used on the jubilee.

Seven times] The time was thus lengthened out that the besiegers and the besieged might be the more deeply impressed with that supernatural power by which *alone* the walls fell.

Verse 5. *The wall of the city shall fall down*

flat] Several commentators, both Jews and Christians, have supposed that the ground under the foundation of the walls opened, and the wall sunk into the chasm, so that there remained nothing but plain ground for the Israelites to walk over. Of this the text says nothing: ונפלה חומת העיר תחתיה *venaphelah chomath hair tachteyha,* literally translated, is, *The wall of the city shall fall down* UNDER ITSELF; which appears to mean no more than, *The wall shall fall down* FROM ITS VERY FOUNDATIONS. And this probably was the case in every part, though large breaches in different places might be amply sufficient to admit the armed men first, after whom the whole host might enter, in order to destroy the city.

Verse 9. *The rereward came after the ark*] The word מאסף *measseph,* from אסף *asaph,* to *collect* or *gather up,* may signify either the *rereward,* as our translation understands it, or the people who carried the baggage of the army; for on the seventh day this was necessary, as much fighting might be naturally expected in the assault, and they would need a supply of arms, darts, &c., as well as conveniences for those who *might* happen to be wounded: or the persons here intended might be such as carried the sacred articles belonging to the ark, or merely such people as might follow in the procession, without observing any particular *order.* The Jews think the division of Dan is meant, which always brought up the rear. See Num. x.

A. M. 2553
B. C. 1451
An. Exod. Isr.
40
Anno ante
I. Olymp. 675

14 And the second day they compassed the city once, and returned into the camp: so they did six days.

15 And it came to pass on the seventh day, that they rose early about the dawning of the day, and compassed the city after the same manner seven times: only on that day they compassed the city seven times.

16 And it came to pass at the seventh time, when the priests blew with the trumpets, Joshua said unto the people, Shout; for the LORD hath given you the city.

17 And the city shall be ¹accursed, *even* it, and all that *are* therein, to the LORD: only Rahab the harlot shall live, she and all that *are* with her in the house, because ᵐshe hid the messengers that we sent.

18 And ye, ⁿin any wise keep *yourselves* from the accursed thing, lest ye make *your-selves* accursed, when ye take of the accursed thing, and make the camp of Israel a curse, °and trouble it.

19 But all the silver, and gold, and vessels of brass and iron, *are* ᵖconsecrated unto the LORD: they shall come into the treasury of the LORD.

20 So the people shouted when *the priests* blew with the trumpets: and it came to pass, when the people heard the sound of the trumpet, and the people shouted with a great shout, that ᑫthe wall fell down ʳflat, so that the people went up into the city, every man straight before him, and they took the city.

21 And they ˢutterly destroyed all that *was*

A. M. 2553
B. C. 1451
An. Exod. Isr.
40
Anno ante
I. Olymp. 675

---

¹Or, *devoted;* Lev. xxvii. 28; Mic. iv. 13——ᵐChap. ii. 4 ⁿDeut. vii. 26; xiii. 17; chap. vii. 1, 11, 12——°Chap. vii.

25; 1 Kings xviii. 17, 18; Jonah i. 12——ᵖHeb. *holiness* ᑫVer. 5; Heb. xi. 30——ʳHeb. *under it*——ˢDeut. vii. 2

Verse 14. *So they did six days.*] It is not likely that the whole Israelitish host went each day round the city. This would have been utterly impossible: the fighting men alone amounted to nearly 600,000, independently of the people, who must have amounted at least to two or three millions; we may therefore safely assert that only a select number, such as was deemed necessary for the occasion, were employed. Jericho could not have been a large city; and to reduce it could not have required a hundredth part of the armed force under the command of Joshua.

Verse 15. *The seventh day—they rose early*] Because on this day they had to encompass the city seven times; a proof that the city could not have been very *extensive,* else this going round it seven times, and having time sufficient left to sack and destroy it, would have been impossible.

It is evident that in the course of these seven days there must have been a *Sabbath,* and that on this Sabbath the host must have encompassed the city as on the other days: the Jews themselves allow this, and *Rab. De Kimchi* says, "He who had ordained the observance of the Sabbath commanded it to be broken for the destruction of Jericho." But it does not appear that there could be any *breach* in the Sabbath by the people simply going round the city, the ark in company, and the priests sounding the sacred trumpets. This was a mere religious procession, performed at the command of God, in which no servile work was done. Therefore *Marcion's* objection, that the God of the Hebrews showed a changeableness of disposition in commanding the Sabbath to be kept sacred at one time, and then to be broken at another, is without foundation; for I must contend that no breach took place on this occasion, unless it could be made to appear that the day on which Jericho was taken was the Sabbath, which is very unlikely, and which none can prove. But if even this were to be conceded, it

is a sufficient answer to all such cavils, that the God who commanded the Sabbath to be set apart for rest and religious purposes, has always authority to suspend for a season the operation of merely ceremonial laws, or to abrogate them entirely, when the purpose of their institution is fulfilled. The Son of man is Lord even of the Sabbath.

Verse 17. *The city shall be accursed*] That is, it shall be devoted to destruction; ye shall take no spoils, and put *all that resist* to the sword. Though this may be the meaning of the word חרם *cherem* in some places, see the note on Lev. xxvii. 29, yet here it seems to imply the *total* destruction of all the inhabitants, see ver. 21; but it is likely that peace was offered to this city, and that the extermination of the inhabitants was in consequence of the rejection of this offer.

Verse 19. *But all the silver, and gold—shall come into the treasury*] The Brahmins will receive from any *caste,* however degraded, gold, silver, &c.: but to receive from *Shoodras* food, garments, &c., would be considered a great degradation.—*Ward.*

Verse 20. *The people shouted with a great shout, that the wall fell down*] There has been much learned labour spent to prove that the shouting of the people might be the natural cause that the wall fell down! To wait here, either to detail or refute any such arguments, would be lost time: enough of them may be seen in Scheuchzer. The whole relation evidently supposes it to have been a supernatural interference, as the blowing of the trumpets, and the shouting of the people, were too contemptible to be used even as instruments in this work, with the expectation of accomplishing it in a *natural* way.

Verse 21. *They utterly destroyed—both man, and woman, &c.*] As this act was ordered by God himself, who is the Maker and Judge of all men, it must be *right:* for the Judge of all the earth cannot do *wrong.* Nothing that

A. M. 2553
B. C. 1451
An. Exod. Isr.
40
Anno ante
I. Olymp. 675

in the city, both man and woman, young and old, and ox, and sheep, and ass, with the edge of the sword.

22 But Joshua had said unto the two men that had spied out the country, Go into the harlot's house, and bring out thence the woman, and all that she hath, [t]as ye sware unto her.

23 And the young men that were spies went in, and brought out Rahab, [u]and her father, and her mother, and her brethren, and all that she had; and they brought out all her [v]kindred, and left them without the camp of Israel.

24 And they burnt the city with fire, and all that *was* therein: [w]only the silver, and the gold, and the vessels of brass and of iron,

they put into the treasury of the house of the LORD.

A. M. 2553
B. C. 1451
An. Exod. Isr.
40
Anno ante
I. Olymp. 675

25 And Joshua saved Rahab the harlot alive, and her father's household, and all that she had; and [x]she dwelleth in Israel *even* unto this day; because she hid the messengers which Joshua sent to spy out Jericho.

26 And Joshua adjured *them* at that time, saying, [y]Cursed *be* the man before the LORD, that riseth up and buildeth this city Jericho: he shall lay the foundation thereof in his first-born, and in his youngest *son* shall he set up the gates of it.

27 [z]So the LORD was with Joshua; and [a]his fame was *noised* throughout all the country.

---

[t]Chap. ii. 14; Heb. xi. 31——[u]Chap. ii. 13——[v]Heb. *families*——[w]Ver. 19

[x]See Matt. i. 5——[y]1 Kings xvi. 34——[z]Chap. i. 5 [a]Chap. ix. 1, 3

---

breathed was permitted to live; hence the oxen, sheep, and asses, were destroyed, as well as the inhabitants.

Verse 23. *Brought out Rahab, and her father, &c.*] Rahab having been faithful to her vow of secrecy, the Israelites were bound by the oath of the spies, who acted as their representatives in this business, to preserve her and her family alive.

And left them without the camp] They were considered as persons *unclean*, and consequently left without the camp; (see Lev. xiii. 46; Num. xii. 14.) When they had abjured heathenism, were purified, and the males had received circumcision, they were doubtless admitted into the camp, and became incorporated with Israel.

Verse 24. *Only the silver, and the gold—they put into the treasury, &c.*] The people were to have no share of the spoils, because they had no hand in the conquest. God alone overthrew the city; and into his treasury only the spoils were brought. This is one proof that the agitation of the air, by the sound of the people's voice, was not the cause of the fall of the city walls.

Vessels of brass and of iron.—Instead of בלי *keley*, VESSELS, the Septuagint, in the Alexandrian copy, evidently have read בל *col*, ALL, with the omission of the י *yod;* for in ver. 19 they translate πας χαλκος και σιδηρος, ALL *the brass and iron:* but this reading does not appear in any of Kennicott's or De Rossi's MSS.

Verse 25. *And she dwelleth in Israel even unto this day*] This is one proof that the book was written *in the time* to which it is commonly referred; and certainly might have been done by the hand of Joshua himself, though doubtless many marginal notes may have since crept into the text, which, to superficial observers, give it the appearance of having been written after the days of Joshua. See the *preface* to this book.

Verse 26. *And Joshua adjured them at that time*] It appears that he had received intimations from God that this idolatrous city should continue a monument of the Divine displeasure: and having convened the princes and

elders of the people, he bound them by an oath that they should never rebuild it; and then, in their presence, pronounced a curse upon the person who should attempt it. The ruins of this city continuing would be a permanent proof, not only of God's displeasure against idolatry, but of the miracle which he had wrought in behalf of the Israelites; and for these reasons God willed that it should not be rebuilt: nevertheless, he left men to the operation of their own free will, and recorded the penalty which those must pay who should disobey him.

He shall lay the foundation thereof, &c.] This is a strange execration; but it may rather be considered in the light of a *prediction*. It seems to intimate that he who should attempt to rebuild this city, should lose all his children in the interim, from laying the foundation to the completion of the walls; which the author of 1 Kings xvi. 34 says was accomplished in Hiel the Beth-elite, who rebuilt Jericho under the reign of Ahab, and *laid the foundation of it in Abiram, his first-born, and set up its gates in his youngest son Segub:* this was 550 years after Joshua pronounced the curse. But we are not sure that this means that the children either died a natural or violent death on this occasion, for we may understand the history as relating to the slow progress of the work. Hiel having begun the work at the birth of his first-born, was not able to conclude before the birth of his last child, who was born many years after: and as their names are mentioned, it is very likely that the distance of time between the birth of each was well known when this history was written; and that the extraordinary length of time spent in the work, in which a multitude of vexatious delays had taken place, is that to which the prophetic execration relates. Yet the first opinion is the most probable. We must not suppose that Jericho had been wholly neglected from its overthrow by Joshua to the days of *Hiel;* if it be the same with the *city of palm trees,* mentioned Deut. xxxiv. 3. We find it mentioned as an inhabited place in the beginning of Judg. i. 16, a short time after the death of Joshua: *And the children of the Kenite,*

Moses' father-in-law, went up out of the city of palm trees, with the children of Judah, &c.; and this said city (if the same with the city of palm trees) was taken from the Israelites by Eglon king of Moab, Judg. iii. 13. The ambassadors of David, who were disgracefully treated by *Hanun* king of the Ammonites, were commanded to tarry at Jericho till their beards should grow, 2 Sam. x. 4, 5. It appears, therefore, that there was a city which went under this name long before the time of Hiel, unless we can suppose that the *city of palm trees* was a different place from Jericho, or that the name Jericho was given to some part of the circumjacent country after the city was destroyed, which is very probable.

After Hiel had rebuilt this city, it became of considerable consequence in the land of Judea: the courses of priests lodged there, who served in their turns at the temple; see Luke x. 30. There was a school of the prophets there, which was visited by Elijah and Elisha, 2 Kings ii. 4, 5, 18; and it was at this city that our Lord miraculously healed blind Bartimeus, Mark x. 46; Luke xviii. 35, &c. At present, Jericho is almost entirely deserted, having but thirty or forty miserable cabins in it, which serve for a place of refuge to some wretched Moors and Arabs, who live there like beasts. The plain of Jericho, formerly so celebrated for its fertility, is at present uncultivated, producing nothing but a few wild trees, and some very indifferent fruits. See *Calmet.*

Verse 27. *So the Lord was with Joshua*] Giving him miraculous assistance in all his enterprises; and this was what he was naturally led to expect from the communication made to him by the captain of the Lord's host, chap. v. 14, &c.

1. MANY attempts have been made either to deny the *miracle* in the fall of Jericho, or to account for it on natural causes. Reference has already been made to some of these in the note on ver. 20. But to those who believe the Divine authenticity of the New Testament, every objection of this kind is removed by the authority of the author of the Epistle to the Hebrews, chap. xi. 30: *By* FAITH *the walls of Jericho fell down, after they had been compassed about seven days.* Hence we find that it was a miraculous interference; and that Joshua's *faith* in the promise made to him by the captain of the Lord's host, was the instrument which God chose to employ in the accomplishment of this important purpose.

2. The same is said of Rahab: *By* FAITH *the harlot Rahab perished not with them that believed not, when she had received the spies with peace,* Heb. xi. 31. She believed that the true God was on the side of the Hebrews, and that all opposition to them must be in vain; and this faith led her to put herself under the Divine protection, and in virtue of it she escaped the destruction that fell on her countrymen. Thus God has ever chosen to put honour on *faith,* as the instrument by which he will perform his greatest miracles of *justice* and *mercy.* God, who cannot lie, has given the *promise;* he that believes shall have it accomplished; for with God nothing shall be impossible, and all things are possible to him that believes. These are Scriptural maxims, and God cannot deny himself.

3. On the curse pronounced by Joshua on those who should rebuild Jericho, it may be necessary to make a few remarks. In ancient history we have many instances of *execrations* against those who should rebuild those cities which had been destroyed in war, the revival of whose power and influence was dreaded; especially such cities as had been remarkable for oppression, insolence, or perfidy. *Strabo* observes, lib. xiii., p. 898, ed. 1707, that Agamemnon pronounced execrations on those who should rebuild *Troy,* as Crœsus did against those who should rebuild *Sidena,* in which the tyrant Glaucias had taken refuge; and this mode of execrating cities, according to Strabo, was an *ancient custom*—Ειτε και καταρασαμενου του Αγαμεμνονος κατα παλαιον εθος· καθαπερ και ὁ Κροισος εξελων την Σιδηνην, εις ἡν ὁ τυραννος κατεφυγε Γλαυκιας, αρας εθετο κατα των τειχιουντων παλιν τον τοπον.

The Romans made a decree full of execrations against those who should rebuild *Carthage,* which had been the rival of their empire; and which, from its advantageous situation, might again become formidable should it be rebuilt. See *Zonaras,* Anal.

The *Ionians,* according to *Isocrates,* pronounced the most awful execrations on those who should rebuild the *temples* destroyed by the *Persians,* that they might remain to posterity an endless monument of the impiety of those barbarians; and that none might put confidence in a people who were so wicked as to make war on the gods themselves. The other Greeks who had suffered by the Persians acted in the same way, leaving the desolated temples as a public monument of the enmity that should ever subsist between the two nations. See *Calmet,* and see the notes on Num. xxii. 6.

CHAPTER VII

The trespass of the Israelites, 1. Joshua sends men to view the state of Ai, 2. They return with a favourable report, 3. Three thousand men are sent against it, who are defeated, and thirty-six killed, 4, 5. Joshua is greatly distressed, prostrates himself, and inquires of the Lord the reason why he has abandoned Israel to their enemies, 6-9. The Lord raises him, and informs him that, contrary to the command, some of the people had secreted some of the spoils of Jericho, 10-12. He is directed how to discover the delinquent, 13-15. Joshua inquires in what TRIBE *the guilt is found, and finds it to be in the tribe of Judah; in what* FAMILY, *and finds it to be among the Zarhites; in what* HOUSEHOLD, *and finds it to be in that of Zabdi; in what* INDIVIDUAL, *and finds it to be Achan son of Carmi, son of Zabdi, 16-18. Joshua exhorts him to confess his sin, 19. He does so, and gives a circumstantial account, 20, 21. Joshua sends for the stolen articles, 22, 23. And Achan and all that belonged to him are brought to the valley of Achor, stoned and burnt, 24-26.*

A. M. 2553
B. C. 1451
An. Exod. Isr.
40
Anno ante
I. Olymp. 675

BUT the children of Israel committed a trespass in the accursed thing: for [a]Achan,[b] the son of Carmi, the son of [c]Zabdi, the son of Zerah, of the tribe of Judah, took of the accursed thing: and the anger of the LORD was kindled against the children of Israel.

2 And Joshua sent men from Jericho to Ai, which *is* beside Beth-aven, on the east side of Beth-el, and spake unto them, saying, Go up and view the country. And the men went up and viewed Ai.

3 And they returned to Joshua, and said unto him, Let not all the people go up; but let [d]about two or three thousand men go up

and smite Ai; *and* make not all the people to labour thither; for they *are but* few.

A. M. 2553
B. C. 1451
An. Exod. Isr.
40
Anno ante
I. Olymp. 675

4 So there went up thither of the people about three thousand men: [e]and they fled before the men of Ai.

5 And the men of Ai smote of them about thirty and six men: for they chased them *from* before the gate *even* unto Shebarim, and smote them [f]in the going down: wherefore [g]the hearts of the people melted, and became as water.

6 And Joshua [h]rent his clothes, and fell to the earth upon his face before the ark of the LORD, until the eventide, he and the elders of Israel, and [i]put dust upon their heads.

---

[a]Ch. xxii. 20——[b]1 Chron. ii. 7, *Achar*——[c]Or, *Zimri*, 1 Chron. ii. 6——[d]Heb. *about two thousand men, or about three thousand men*——[e]Lev. xxvi. 17; Deut. xxviii. 25

[f]Or, *in Morad*——[g]Chap. ii. 9, 11; Lev. xxvi. 36; Psa. xxii. 14——[h]Gen. xxxvii. 29, 34——[i]1 Sam. iv. 12; 2 Sam. i. 2; xiii. 19; Neh. ix. 1; Job ii. 12

NOTES ON CHAP. VII

Verse 1. *The children of Israel committed a trespass*] It is certain that *one* only was guilty; and yet the trespass is imputed here to the whole congregation; and the whole congregation soon suffered shame and disgrace on the account, as their armies were defeated, thirty-six persons slain, and general terror spread through the whole camp. Being one body, God attributes the crime of the individual to the whole till the trespass was discovered, and by a public act of justice inflicted on the culprit the congregation had purged itself of the iniquity. This was done to render every man extremely cautious, and to make the people watchful over each other, that sin might be no where tolerated or connived at, as one transgression might bring down the wrath of God upon the whole camp. See on ver. 12.

The accursed thing] A portion of the spoils of the city of Jericho, the whole of which God had commanded to be destroyed.

For Achan, the son of Carmi, &c.] Judah had two sons by Tamar: Pharez and Zarah. Zarah was father of Zabdi, and Zabdi of Carmi, the father of Achan. These five persons extend through a period of 265 years; and hence Calmet concludes that they could not have had children before they were fifty or fifty-five years of age. This *Achan, son of Zabdi*, is called, in 1 Chron. ii. 6, *Achar, son of Zimrie;* but this reading is corrected into *Achan* by some MSS. in the place above cited.

Verse 2. *Sent men from Jericho to Ai*] This is the place called *Hai*, Gen. xii. 8. It was in the east of Beth-el, north of Jericho, from which it was distant about ten or twelve miles. From verses 4 and 5 it appears to have been situated upon a *hill*, and belonged to the Amorites, as we learn from ver. 7. It is very likely that it was a *strong place*, as it chose to risk a siege, notwithstanding the extraordinary destruction of Jericho which it had lately witnessed.

Verse 4. *About three thousand men*] The spies sent to reconnoitre the place (ver. 3) reported that the town was meanly garrisoned, and that two or three thousand men would be

sufficient to take it. These were accordingly sent up, and were repulsed by the Amorites.

Verse 5. *They chased them* from *before the gate even unto Shebarim*] They seem to have presumed that the men of *Ai* would have immediately opened their gates to them, and therefore they marched up with confidence; but the enemy appearing, they were put to flight, their *ranks utterly broken*, and thirty-six of them killed. שברים *Shebarim* signifies *breaches* or *broken places*, and may here apply to the *ranks* of the Israelites, which were *broken* by the men of *Ai;* for the people were totally routed, though there were but few slain. They were panic-struck, and fled in the utmost confusion.

The hearts of the people melted] They were utterly discouraged; and by this gave an ample proof that without the supernatural assistance of God they could never have conquered the land.

Verse 6. *Joshua rent his clothes, &c.*] It was not in consequence of this slight discomfiture, simply considered in itself, that Joshua laid this business so much to heart; but 1. Because the *people melted, and became as water*, and there was little hope that they would make any stand against the enemy; and 2. Because this defeat evidently showed that God had turned his hand against them. Had it not been so, their enemies could not have prevailed.

Put dust upon their heads.] Rending the clothes, beating the breast, tearing the hair, putting dust upon the head, and falling down prostrate, were the usual marks of deep affliction and distress. Most nations have expressed their sorrow in a similar way. The example of the distressed family of King *Latinus*, so affectingly related by Virgil, may be adduced in illustration of many passages in the history of the patriarchs, prophets, apostles, &c.

*Regina ut tectis venientem prospicit hostem—
Purpureos moritura manu discindit amictus—
Filia prima manu* flavos *Lavinia* crines,
Et roseas laniata genas.—
. . . . . *It scissa veste Latinus—*
Caniticm immundo perfusam pulvere turpans.
Æn. lib. xii., ver. 594.

A. M. 2553
B. C. 1451
An. Exod. Isr.
40
Anno ante
I. Olymp. 675

7 And Joshua said, Alas, O Lord GOD, ^kwherefore hast thou at all brought this people over Jordan, to deliver us into the hand of the Amorites, to destroy us? would to God we had been content, and dwelt on the other side Jordan!

8 O LORD, what shall I say, when Israel turneth their ^lbacks before their enemies?

9 For the Canaanites and all the inhabitants of the land shall hear *of it,* and shall environ us round, and ^mcut off our name from the earth: and ⁿwhat wilt thou do unto thy great name?

10 And the LORD said unto Joshua, Get thee up; wherefore ^oliest thou thus upon thy face?

11 ^pIsrael hath sinned, and they have also transgressed my covenant which I commanded them; ^qfor they have even taken of the accursed thing, and have also stolen, and ^rdis-

sembled also, and they have put *it* even among their own stuff.

A. M. 2553
B. C. 1451
An. Exod. Isr.
40
Anno ante
I. Olymp. 675

12 ^sTherefore the children of Israel could not stand before their enemies, *but* turned *their* backs before their enemies, because ^tthey were accursed: neither will I be with you any more, except ye destroy the accursed from among you.

13 Up, ^usanctify the people, and say, ^vSanctify yourselves against to-morrow: for thus saith the LORD God of Israel, *There is* an accursed thing in the midst of thee, O Israel: thou canst not stand before thine enemies, until ye take away the accursed thing from among you.

14 In the morning therefore ye shall be brought according to your tribes: and it shall be, *that* the tribe which ^wthe LORD taketh shall come according to the families *thereof;* and the family which the LORD shall take shall

---

^kExod. v. 22; 2 Kings iii. 10——^lHeb. *necks*——^mPsa. lxxxiii. 4——ⁿSee Exod. xxxii. 12; Num. xiv. 13 ^oHeb. *fallest*——^pVer. 1——^qChap. vi. 17, 18

^rSee Acts v. 1, 2——^sSee Num. xiv. 45; Judg. ii. 14 ^tDeut. vii. 26; chap. vi. 18——^uExod. xix. 10 ^vChapter iii. 5——^wProv. xvi. 33

"The queen, who saw the foes invade the town,
And brands on tops of burning houses thrown,
She raves against the gods, she *beats her breast,*
And *tears,* with both her hands, her *purple vest.*
The sad Lavinia *rends* her yellow *hair,*
And *rosy cheeks;* the rest her sorrow share.
Latinus *tears his garments* as he goes,
Both for his public and his private woes;
With filth his venerable beard besmears,
And *sordid dust* deforms his *silver hairs.*"
DRYDEN.

Verse 7. *Alas, O Lord God*] Particles of exclamations and distress, or what are called *interjections,* are nearly the same in all languages; and the reason is because they are the simple voice of nature. The Hebrew word which we translate *alas* is אהה *ahah.* The complaint of Joshua in this and the following verses seems principally to have arisen from his deep concern for the glory of God, and the affecting interest he took in behalf of the people: he felt for the thousands of Israel, whom he considered as abandoned to destruction: and he felt for the glory of God, for he knew should Israel be destroyed God's name would be blasphemed among the heathen; and his expostulations with his Maker, which have been too hastily blamed by some, as savouring of too great freedom and impatience, are founded on God's own words, Deut. xxxii. 26, 27, and on the practice of Moses himself, who had used similar expressions on a similar occasion; see Exod. v. 22, 23; Num. xiv. 13-18.

Verse 10. *Wherefore liest thou thus upon thy face?*] It is plain there was nothing in Joshua's prayer or complaint that was offensive to God, for here there is no reprehension: *Why liest thou thus?* this is no time for complaint; something else is indispensably necessary to be done.

Verse 11. *Israel hath sinned*] It is impossible that God should turn *against* his people, if they had not turned *away from* him. *They have taken of the accursed thing,* notwithstanding my severe prohibition. *They have also stolen,* supposing, if not seen by their brethren, I should either not see or not regard it. *They have dissembled*—pretended to have kept strictly the command I gave them; *and have put it among their own stuff*—considered it now as a part of their own property.

Verse 12. *Because they were accursed*] From this verse it appears that the nature of the execration or anathema was such, that those who took of the thing doomed to destruction fell immediately under the same condemnation. The inhabitants of Jericho and all that they had were accursed; therefore they and all their substance were to be destroyed. The Israelites took of the *accursed thing,* and therefore became accursed with it. This was certainly understood when the curse was pronounced: Every man who touches this property shall be involved in the same execration. Achan therefore was sufficiently aware of the risk he ran in taking any part of the anathematized thing; and when viewed in this light, the punishment inflicted on him will appear to be perfectly just and proper.

Verse 13. *Up, sanctify the people*] Joshua, all the time that God spake, lay prostrate before the ark; he is now commanded to get up, and sanctify the people, i. e., cause them to wash themselves, and get into a proper disposition to hear the judgment of the Lord relative to the late transactions.

Verse 14. *Ye shall be brought according to your tribes*] It has been a subject of serious inquiry in what manner and by what means the culpable *tribe, family, household,* and *individual,* were discovered. The *Jews* have many conceits on the subject; the most rational is, that the tribes being, in their representa-

A. M. 2553
B. C. 1451
An. Exod. Isr.
40
Anno ante
I. Olymp. 675

come by households; and the household which the LORD shall take shall come man by man.

15 ˣAnd it shall be, *that* he that is taken with the accursed thing shall be burnt with fire, he and all that he hath: because he hath ʸtransgressed the covenant of the LORD, and because he ᶻhath wrought ᵃfolly in Israel.

16 So Joshua rose up early in the morning, and brought Israel by their tribes; and the tribe of Judah was taken:

17 And he brought the family of Judah; and he took the family of the Zarhites: and he brought the family of the Zarhites man by man; and Zabdi was taken:

18 And he brought his household man by man; and Achan, the son of Carmi, the son of Zabdi, the son of Zerah, of the tribe of Judah, ᵇwas taken.

A. M. 2553
B. C. 1451
An. Exod. Isr.
40
Anno ante
I. Olymp. 675

19 And Joshua said unto Achan, My son, ᶜgive, I pray thee, glory to the LORD God of Israel, ᵈand make confession unto him; and ᵉtell me now what thou hast done; hide *it* not from me.

20 And Achan answered Joshua, and said, Indeed I have sinned against the LORD God of Israel, and thus and thus have I done:

21 When I saw among the spoils a goodly Babylonish garment, and two hundred shekels of silver, and a ᶠwedge of gold of fifty shekels

---

ˣSee 1 Samuel xiv. 38, 39——ʸVerse 11——ᶻGenesis xxxiv. 7; Judges xx. 6——ᵃOr, *wickedness*——ᵇ1 Samuel xiv. 42——ᶜSee 1 Samuel vi. 5; Jeremiah xiii.

16; John ix. 24——ᵈNumbers v. 6, 7; 2 Chronicles xxx. 22; Psalm li. 3; Daniel ix. 4——ᵉ1 Samuel xiv. 43 ᶠHebrew, *tongue*

---

tives, brought before the high priest, the stone on the breastplate gave immediate intimation by suddenly losing its lustre. According to them, this is what is termed consulting God by *Urim* and *Thummim*. It is however most probable that the whole was determined by the *lot;* and that God chose this method to detect the guilty *tribe,* next the *family,* thirdly the *household,* and lastly the *individual.* This was nearly the plan pursued in the election of Saul by Samuel. "Now therefore," says he, "present yourselves before the Lord by your tribes, and by your thousands. And when Samuel had caused all the tribes of Israel to come near, the tribe of Benjamin was taken. When he had caused the tribe of Benjamin to come near by their families, the family of Matri was taken, and Saul the son of Kish was taken," 1 Sam. x. 19, 20. If the lot was used in the one case it was doubtless used in the other also, as the procedure in the main was entirely similar. The same mode was used to find out who it was that transgressed the king's command, when it was found that Jonathan had eaten a little honey, 1 Sam. xiv. 40-43. It is well known that the promised land was divided by lot among the Israelites; (see Num. xxvi. 55; xxxiii. 54; Deut. i. 38, &c.;) and that the courses of the priests were regulated by lot in the days of David, 1 Chron. xxiv. 5, &c. That this was a frequent mode of determining difficult questions, and appointed by God himself, is evident from Lev. xvi. 8; Psa. xxii. 18; Prov. xvi. 33; xviii. 18; Acts i. 26.

Verse 17. *And he brought the family of Judah*] Dr. Kennicott observes, "All Israel came near by TRIBES, and one *tribe* was fixed on; then that *tribe* came by its FAMILIES, and one *family* was fixed on; then came that *family* by its HOUSEHOLDS, and one *household* was fixed on; and then that *household,* coming MAN by MAN, one *man* was fixed on. Yet according to the present text, in the execution of this command, all *Israel* came, and the *tribe of Judah was* fixed on; secondly came the *families* of Judah, and *the family of the Zarhites* was fixed

on; thirdly came *the family of the Zarhites* MAN by MAN, and *Zabdi* was fixed on; and fourthly came *the household of Zabdi* MAN by MAN, and *Achan* was fixed on. So that in the third article the word for *by households* is most certainly left out; and the fourth article, *man by man,* is improperly expressed twice. Instead of לגברים *laggebarim,* MAN by MAN, in ver. 17, the true word לבתים *labbottim, by* HOUSEHOLDS, is preserved in six Hebrew copies, and the Syriac version. By this method was discovered *Achan,* as he is here five times called, though the valley in which he was stoned is called *Achor.* He is also called *Achar* in the text, and in all the versions, in 1 Chron. ii. 7. He is called *Achar* in the *five* places of *Joshua* in the Syriac version; also in all *five* in the Greek of the Vatican MS., and *twice* in the Alexandrian MS., and so in Josephus."—*Kennicott's* Observat.

Verse 19. *My son, give—glory to the Lord God*] The *person* being now detected, Joshua wishes him to acknowledge the omniscience of God, and confess his crime. And doubtless this was designed, not only for the edification of the people, and a vindication of the righteous judgment of God, but in reference to his own salvation; for as his *life* was now become forfeited to the law, there was the utmost necessity of humiliation before God that his *soul* might be saved. *Give glory to God* signifies the same as, Make a thorough confession as in the presence of God, and disguise no part of the truth. In this way and in these very words the Jews adjured the man who had been born blind that he would truly tell who had healed him; for they pretended to believe that Christ was such a sinner that God would not work a miracle by him. John ix. 24.

Verse 20. *I have sinned against the Lord God*] This seems a very honest and hearty confession, and there is hope that this poor culprit escaped perdition.

Verse 21. *A goodly Babylonish garment*] אדרת שנער *addereth shinar,* a *splendid* or *costly robe of Shinar;* but as Babylon or Babel was

A. M. 2553
B. C. 1451
An. Exod. Isr.
40
Anno ante
I. Olymp. 675

weight, then I coveted them, and took them; and, behold, they *are* hid in the earth in the midst of my tent, and the silver under it.

22 So Joshua sent messengers, and they ran unto the tent; and, behold, *it was* hid in his tent, and the silver under it.

23 And they took them out of the midst of the tent, and brought them unto Joshua, and unto all the children of Israel, and ᵍlaid them out before the LORD.

ᵍHeb. *poured*——ʰVer. 26; chap. xv. 7

---

built in the plain of *Shinar*, the word has in general been translated *Babylon* in this place. It is very probable that this was the robe of the king of Jericho, for the same word is used, Jonah iii. 6, to express the royal robe, of the king of Nineveh, which he laid aside in order to humble himself before God.

Bochart and *Calmet* have shown at large that Babylonish robes were very splendid, and in high reputation. "They are," says Calmet, "generally allowed to have been of *various colours*, though some suppose they were *woven* thus; others, that they were *embroidered* with the *needle;* and others, that they were *painted*. SILIUS ITALICUS appears to think they were *woven* thus:—

Vestis *spirantes referens subtemine vultus,*
Quos radio cælat BABYLON.
Punic. lib. xiv., ver. 657.

MARTIAL seems to say they were embroidered with the *needle:*—

Non ego prætulerim BABYLONICA PICTA *superbe Texta,* Semiramia *quæ variantur* ACU.
Lib. viii., E. 28, ver. 17.

PLINY (lib. viii., c. 48) and APULEIUS (Florid. lib. i.) speak of them as if *painted:* "Colores diversos picturæ intexere Babylon maxime celebravit, et nomen imposuit."

Thus far *Calmet:* but it may be observed that the clothes woven of divers colours at Babylon, which were so greatly celebrated, and hence called *Babylonish garments,* appear rather to have had the pictures *woven* or *embroidered* in them than *painted* on them, as Calmet supposes, though it is most likely the figures referred to were the work of the needle after the cloth came from the loom.

AQUILA translates the original, אדרת שנער *addereth shinar,* by στολην Βαβυλονικην, a *Babylonish robe;* SYMMACHUS, ενδυμα συναρ, a *robe of Synar;* the SEPTUAGINT, ψιλην ποικιλην, a *fine garment of different colours;* and the VULGATE, *pallium coccineum,* a *scarlet cloak.* There is no doubt it was both *beautiful* and *costly,* and on these grounds it was coveted by Achan.

Two hundred shekels of silver] At *three shillings* per shekel, amount to about 30*l.* sterling.

A wedge of gold] A tongue of gold, לשון זהב *leshon zahab* what we commonly call an *ingot of gold,* a corruption of the word *lingot,* signifying a *little tongue, of fifty shekels weight.*

VOL. II

24 And Joshua, and all Israel with him, took Achan the son of Zerah, and the silver, and the garment, and the wedge of gold, and his sons, and his daughters, and his oxen, and his asses, and his sheep, and his tent, and all that he had: and they brought them unto ʰthe valley of Achor.

A. M. 2553
B. C. 1451
An. Exod. Isr.
40
Anno ante
I. Olymp. 675

25 And Joshua said, ¹Why hast thou troubled us? the LORD shall trouble thee this day. ᵏAnd all Israel stoned him with stones, and

---

¹Chap. vi. 18; 1 Chron. ii. 7; Gal. v. 12——ᵏDeut. xvii. 5

These *fifty* shekels, in weight 29 oz. 15$\frac{15}{81}$ gr., at 2*l.* 5*s.* 2½ $\frac{42}{53}$*d.* per shekel, would be worth about 113*l.* 0*s.* 10$\frac{3}{4}$*d.*

This verse gives us a notable instance of the progress of sin. It 1, *enters* by the *eye;* 2. *sinks* into the *heart;* 3. *actuates* the *hand;* and, 4. leads to *secrecy* and *dissimulation. I saw, &c. I coveted, &c. I took* and *hid* them in the earth. Thus says St. James: "When lust (evil desire) is conceived it bringeth forth sin; and when sin is finished it bringeth forth death," chap. i. 15.

Verse 24. *Joshua—took Achan—and all that he had*] He and his cattle and substance were brought to the valley to be consumed; his sons and his daughters, probably, to witness the judgments of God inflicted on their disobedient parent. See ver. 25.

Verse 25. *Why hast thou troubled us?*] Here is a reference to the meaning of *Achan's* or *Achar's* name, מה עכרתנו *meh* ACHAR-*tanu;* and as עכר *achar* is used here, and not עכן *achan,* and the valley is called the *valley of Achor,* and not the *valley of Achan,* hence some have supposed that *Achar* was his proper name, as it is read 1 Chron. ii. 7, and in some MSS., and ancient versions. See the note on ver. 17.

And all Israel stoned him with stones, and burned them with fire, after they had stoned them with stones.] With great deference to the judgment of others, I ask, Can it be fairly proved from the text that the *sons* and *daughters* of Achan were stoned to death and burnt as well as their father? The text certainly leaves it *doubtful,* but seems rather to intimate that *Achan* alone was stoned, and that his *substance* was burnt with fire. The reading of the present HEBREW text is, *They stoned* HIM *with stones, and burnt* THEM *with fire, after they had stoned* THEM *with stones.* The *singular* number being used in the *first* clause of the verse, and the *plural* in the *last,* leaves the matter doubtful. The VULGATE is very clear: *Lapidavitque* EUM *omnis Israel; et cuncta quæ illius erant, igne consumpta sunt,* "All Israel stoned *him;* and all that he had was consumed with fire." The SEPTUAGINT add this and the first clause of the next verse together: Και ελιθοβολησαν αυτον λιθοις πας Ισραηλ, και επεστησαν αυτῳ σωρον λιθων μεγαν: *And all Israel stoned* HIM *with stones, and raised over* HIM *a great heap of stones.* The Syriac says simply, *They stoned* HIM *with stones, and burned what pertained to* HIM *with fire.* The TARGUM is the same as the *Hebrew.* The ANGLO-SAXON seems to refer the whole to *Achan* and his GOODS: **And hine**

A. M. 2553
B. C. 1451
An. Exod. Isr.
40
Anno ante
I. Olymp. 675

burned them with fire, after they had stoned them with stones.

26 And they [1] raised over him a great heap of stones unto this day. So

[m] the LORD turned from the fierceness of his anger. Wherefore the name of that place was called, [n] The valley of [o] Achor, unto this day.

A. M. 2553
B. C. 1451
An. Exod. Isr.
40
Anno ante
I. Olymp. 675

---

[1] Chap. viii. 29; 2 Sam. xviii. 17; Lam. iii. 53——[m] Deut. xiii. 17; 2 Sam. xxi. 14

[n] Verse 24; Isaiah lxv. 10; Hosea ii. 15——[o] That is, *trouble*

פֶּאןרְכֶּאנבּוֹן, anb hiר פּיןz רוֹנבֶּאןנבּוֹן, *And* HIM *they stoned there, and burnt his goods.* The ARABIC version alone says, *They stoned* HIM *and his* CHILDREN, *and his goods,* هو و بنيه و ماله In-stead of *burnt* THEM, אֹתָם *otham,* two of De Rossi's MSS. read אֹתוֹ *otho,* HIM; which reading, if genuine, would make the different members of the verse agree better. It is possible that *Achan,* his *oxen, asses, sheep, tent,* and all his *household goods,* were destroyed, but his *sons* and *daughters* left uninjured. But it may be asked, Why are *they* brought out into the valley with the rest? Why, that they might *see* and *fear,* and be for ever deterred by their father's punishment from imitating his example.

I have gone thus far into this important transaction, in which the *justice* and *mercy* of God are so much concerned, that I might be able to assign to each its due. That Achan's life was forfeited to justice by his transgression, no one doubts: *he* sinned against a known and positive law. His *children* could not suffer with him, because of the law, Deut. xxiv. 16, unless they had been accomplices in his guilt: of this there is no evidence; and the text in question, which speaks of Achan's punishment, is extremely *dubious,* as far as it relates to this point. One circumstance that strengthens the supposition that the children were not included, is the command of the Lord, ver. 15: "HE *that is taken with the accursed thing, shall be burnt with fire; he, and all that he hath.*" Now, *all that he hath* may certainly refer to his *goods,* and not to his *children;* and his punishment, and the destruction of his property would answer every purpose of public justice, both as a punishment and preventive of the crime; and both mercy and justice require that the innocent shall not suffer with the guilty, unless in very extraordinary cases, where God may permit the righteous or the innocent to be involved in those public calamities by which the ungodly are swept away from the face of the earth: but in the case before us, no necessity of this kind

urged it, and therefore I conclude that Achan *alone* suffered, and that his repentance and confession were genuine and sincere; and that, while JUSTICE required his *life,* MERCY was extended to the salvation of his *soul.*

Verse 26. *They raised over him a great heap of stones*] The burial-places, both of heroes and eminent culprits, were anciently thus distinguished; and transactions of this kind gave rise to those great piles of stones called *cairns,* that are so frequently to be met with, especially in northern countries.

FROM the whole of this account we may see the exceeding sinfulness of sin, and the great danger of not *withstanding* its first approaches. By *covetousness* many lives and many souls have been destroyed, and yet the living lay it not to heart! Who fears the *love of money,* provided he can get riches? Through the intensity of this desire, every part of the surface of the earth, and as far as possible its bowels, are ransacked in order to get wealth; and God alone can tell, who sees all things, to how many private crimes, *frauds,* and *dissimulations,* this gives birth; by which the wrath of God is brought down upon the community at large! Who is an enemy to his country? The sinner against his God. An *open foe* may be resisted and repelled, because he is *known;* but the *covetous* man, who, as far as his personal safety will admit, is outraging all the requisitions of justice, is an unseen pestilence, sowing the seeds of desolation and ruin in society. Achan's covetousness, which led him to break the law of God, had nearly proved the destruction of the Israelitish camp; nor would the Lord turn away from his displeasure till the evil was detected, and the criminal punished.

Reader, is the face of God turned against *thee,* because of some private transgression? Are not thy circumstances and family suffering in consequence of something in thy private life? O search and try thy ways, return to God, and humble thyself before him lest thy iniquity instantly *find thee out!*

CHAPTER VIII

The Lord encourages Joshua, and promises to deliver Ai into his hands, and instructs him how he is to proceed against it, 1, 2. *Joshua takes thirty thousand of his best troops, and gives them instructions concerning his intention of taking Ai by stratagem,* 3–8. *The men dispose themselves according to these directions,* 9–13. *The king of Ai attacks the Israelites, who, feigning to be beaten, fly before him, in consequence of which all the troops of Ai issue out, and pursue the Israelites,* 14–17. *Joshua, at the command of God, stretches out his spear towards Ai, and then five thousand men that he had placed in ambush in the valley rise up, enter the city, and set it on fire,* 18, 19. *Then Joshua and his men turned against the men of Ai, and, at the same time, those who had taken the city sallied forth and attacked them in the rear; thus the men of Ai were defeated, their king taken prisoner, the city sacked, and twelve thousand persons slain,* 20–26. *The Israelites take the spoils, and hang the king of Ai,* 27–29. *Joshua builds an altar to God on Mount Ebal, and writes* on it a copy of the law of Moses, 30–32. *The elders, officers, and judges, stand on each side of the ark, one half over against Mount Gerizim, and the other against Mount Ebal, and read all the blessings and curses of the law, according to the command of Moses, 33–35.*

A. M. 2553
B. C. 1451
An. Exod. Isr.
40
Anno ante
I. Olymp. 675

AND the LORD said unto Joshua, [a]Fear not, neither be thou dismayed: take all the people of war with thee, and arise, go up to Ai: see, [b]I have given into thy hand the king of Ai, and his people, and his city, and his land:

2 And thou shalt do to Ai and her king as thou didst unto [c]Jericho and her king: only [d]the spoil thereof, and the cattle thereof, shall ye take for a prey unto yourselves: lay thee an ambush for the city behind it.

3 So Joshua arose, and all the people of war, to go up against Ai: and Joshua chose out thirty thousand mighty men of valour, and sent them away by night.

A. M. 2553
B. C. 1451
An. Exod. Isr.
40
Anno ante
I. Olymp. 675

4 And he commanded them, saying, Behold, [e]ye shall lie in wait against the city, *even* behind the city: go not very far from the city, but be ye all ready:

5 And I, and all the people that *are* with me, will approach unto the city: and it shall

---

[a]Deut. i. 21; vii. 18; xxxi. 8; chap. i. 9——[b]Chap. vi. 2

[e]Chap. vi. 21——[d]Deut. xx. 14——[e]Judg. xx. 29

NOTES ON CHAP. VIII

Verse 1. *Fear not*] The iniquity being now purged away, because of which God had turned his hand against Israel, there was now no cause to dread any other disaster, and therefore Joshua is ordered to take courage.

Take all the people of war with thee] From the *letter* of this verse it appears that *all* that were capable of carrying arms were to march out of the camp on this occasion: *thirty thousand* chosen men formed an ambuscade in one place; *five thousand* he placed in another, who had all gained their positions in the night season: with the rest of the army he appeared the next morning before *Ai*, which the men of that city would naturally suppose were the whole of the Israelitish forces; and consequently be the more emboldened to come out and attack them. But some think that thirty thousand men were the whole that were employed on this occasion; five thousand of whom were placed as an ambuscade on the west side of the city between *Beth-el* and *Ai*, ver. 12, and with the rest he appeared before the city in the morning. The king of Ai seeing but about twenty-five thousand coming against him, and being determined to defend his city and crown to the last extremity, though he had but twelve thousand persons in the whole city, ver. 25, scarcely one half of whom we can suppose to be effective men, he was determined to risk a battle; and accordingly issued out, and was defeated by the stratagem mentioned in the preceding part of this chapter.

Several eminent commentators are of opinion that the whole Israelitish force was employed on this occasion, because of what is said in the first verse; but this is not at all likely. 1. It appears that but thirty thousand were chosen out of the whole camp for this expedition, the rest being drawn up in readiness should their co-operation be necessary. See verses 3 and 10. 2. That *all the people* were mustered in order to make this selection, ver. 1. 3. That these thirty thousand were sent off by night, ver. 3, Joshua himself continuing in the camp a part of that night, ver. 9, with the design of putting himself at the head of the army next morning. 4. That of the thirty thousand men *five thousand* were directed to lie in ambush between *Beth-el* and *Ai*, on the west side of the city, ver. 12;

the twenty-five thousand having taken a position on the north side of the city, ver. 11. 5. That the whole of the troops employed against Ai on this occasion were those on the north and west, ver. 13, which we know from the preceding verses were composed of thirty thousand chosen men. 6. That Joshua went in the course of the night, probably before daybreak, into the valley between *Beth-el* and *Ai*, where the ambuscade of five thousand men was placed, ver. 13, and gave them the proper directions how they were to proceed, and agreed on the sign he was to give them at the moment he wished them to act, see ver. 18: and that, after having done so, he put himself at the head of the twenty-five thousand men on the north side of the city: for we find him among them when the men of Ai issued out, ver. 15, though he was the night before in the valley on the west side, where the ambuscade lay, ver. 13. 7. That as Ai was but a small city, containing only twelve thousand inhabitants, it would have been absurd to have employed an army of several hundred thousand men against them. 8. This is confirmed by the opinion of the *spies*, chap. vii. 3, who, from the smallness of the place, the fewness of its inhabitants, and the panic-struck state in which they found them, judged that three thousand troops would be quite sufficient to reduce the place. 9. That it appears this judgment was correctly enough formed, as the whole population of the place amounted only to twelve thousand persons, as we have already seen, ver. 25. 10. That even a less force might have been sufficient for the reduction of this place, had they been supplied with battering-rams, and such like instruments, which it does not appear the Israelites possessed. 11. That this is the reason why Joshua employed the stratagems detailed in this chapter: having no proper instruments or machines by means of which he might hope to take the city by assault, (and to reduce it by famine, which was quite possible, would have consumed too much time,) he used the feigned flight, ver. 19, to draw the inhabitants from the city, that the ambush, ver. 12, 15, might then enter, and take possession of it. 12. That had he advanced with a greater force against the city the inhabitants would have had no confidence in risking a battle, and consequently would have kept within their walls, which would have defeated the design

A. M. 2553
B. C. 1451
An. Exod. Isr.
40
Anno ante
I. Olymp. 675

come to pass, when they come out against us, as at the first, that [f]we will flee before them,

6 (For they will come out after us,) till we have [g]drawn them from the city: for they will say, They flee before us, as at the first: therefore we will flee before them.

7 Then ye shall rise up from the ambush, and seize upon the city: for the LORD your God will deliver it into your hand.

8 And it shall be, when ye have taken the city, *that* ye shall set the city on fire: according to the commandment of the LORD shall ye do. [h]See, I have commanded you.

9 Joshua therefore sent them forth: and they went to lie in ambush, and abode between Beth-el and Ai, on the west side of Ai: but Joshua lodged that night among the people.

10 And Joshua rose up early in the morning, and numbered the people, and went up, he and the elders of Israel, before the people to Ai.

11 [i]And all the people, *even the people* of war that *were* with him, went up, and drew nigh, and came before the city, and pitched on the north side of Ai: now *there was* a valley between them and Ai.

12 And he took about five thousand men,

and set them to lie in ambush between Beth-el and Ai, on the west side [k]of the city.

A. M. 2553
B. C. 1451
An. Exod. Isr.
40
Anno ante
I. Olymp. 675

13 And when they had set the people, *even* all the hosts that *was* on the north of the city, and [l]their liers in wait on the west of the city, Joshua went that night into the midst of the valley.

14 And it came to pass, when the king of Ai saw *it,* that they hasted and rose up early, and the men of the city went out against Israel to battle, he and all his people, at a time appointed, before the plain; but he [m]wist not that *there were* liers in ambush against him behind the city.

15 And Joshua and all Israel [n]made as if they were beaten before them, and fled by the way of the wilderness.

16 And all the people that *were* in Ai were called together to pursue after them: and they pursued after Joshua, and were drawn away from the city.

17 And there was not a man left in Ai or Beth-el, that went not out after Israel: and they left the city open, and pursued after Israel.

18 And the LORD said unto Joshua, Stretch out the spear that *is* in thy hand toward Ai; for I will give it into thine hand. And Joshua

---

[f]Judg. xx. 32——[g]Heb. *pulled*——[h]2 Sam. xiii. 28
[i]Ver. 5——[k]Or, *of Ai*

[l]Heb. *their lying in wait,* ver. 4——[m]Judg. xx. 34; Eccles. ix. 12——[n]Judg. xx. 36, &c.

---

of the Israelites, which was to get them to issue from their city. 13. That, all these circumstances considered thirty thousand men, disposed as above, were amply sufficient for the reduction of the city, and were the whole of the Israelitish troops which were employed on the occasion.

Verse 8. *Ye shall set the city on fire*] Probably this means no more than that they should kindle a fire in the city, the smoke of which should be an indication that they had taken it. For as the spoils of the city were to be divided among the people, had they at this time set fire to the city itself, all the property must have been consumed, for the five thousand men did not wait to save any thing, as they immediately issued out to attack the men of Ai in the rear.

Verse 10. *Numbered the people*] ויפקד את העם *vaiyiphkod eth haam, he visited the people*—inspected their ranks to see whether every thing was in perfect readiness, that in case they should be needed they might be led on to the attack. There is no doubt that Joshua had left the rest of the army so disposed and ready, part of it having probably advanced towards Ai, that he might easily receive reinforcements in case of any disaster to the thirty thousand which had advanced against the city; and this consideration will serve to remove a part of the difficulty which arises from verses 1, 3, and 10,

collated with other parts of this chapter. Had he brought all his troops in sight, the people of Ai would not have attempted to risk a battle, and would consequently have kept within their walls, from which it was the object of Joshua to decoy them. See the preceding observations, particularly 10, 11, and 12.

Verse 17. *There was not a man left in Ai or Beth-el*] It is very likely that the principal strength of *Beth-el* had been previously brought into *Ai*, as the strongest place to make a stand in; Beth-el being but about three miles distant from Ai, and probably not greatly fortified. Therefore Ai contained on this occasion *all the men of Beth-el*—all the warriors of that city, as well as its own troops and inhabitants. Others think that the Beth-elites, seeing the Israelites fly, sallied out of their city as against a common enemy; but that, finding the men of Ai discomfited, and the city taken, they returned to Beth-el, which Joshua did not think proper to attack at this time. From Judges i. 24 we find that Beth-el was then a *walled city*, in the hands of the Canaanites, and was taken by the house of Joseph.

Verse 18. *Stretch out the spear*] It is very probable that Joshua had a *flag* or *ensign* at the end of his spear, which might be easily seen at a considerable distance; and that the *unfurling* or *waving* of this was the *sign* agreed on between him and the ambush, (see ver. 13, and

A. M. 2553
B. C. 1451
An. Exod. Isr.
40
Anno ante
I. Olymp. 675

stretched out the spear that *he* had in his hand toward the city.

19 And the ambush arose quickly out of their place, and they ran as soon as he had stretched out his hand: and they entered into the city, and took it, and hasted and set the city on fire.

20 And when the men of Ai looked behind them, they saw, and, behold, the smoke of the city ascended up to heaven, and they had no °power to flee this way or that way: and the people that fled to the wilderness turned back upon the pursuers.

21 And when Joshua and all Israel saw that the ambush had taken the city, and that the smoke of the city ascended, then they turned again, and slew the men of Ai.

22 And the other issued out of the city against them: so they were in the midst of Israel, some on this side, and some on that side: and they smote them, so that they ᴾlet none of them remain or escape.

23 And the king of Ai they took alive, and brought him to Joshua.

24 And it came to pass, when Israel had made an end of slaying all the inhabitants of Ai in the field, in the wilderness wherein they chased them, and when they were all fallen on the edge of the sword, until they were consumed, that all the Israelites returned unto Ai, and smote it with the edge of the sword.

A. M. 2553
B. C. 1451
An. Exod. Isr.
40
Anno ante
I. Olymp. 675

25 And *so* it was, *that* all that fell that day, both of men and women, *were* twelve thousand, *even* all the men of Ai.

26 For Joshua drew not his hand back, wherewith he stretched out the spear, until he had utterly destroyed all the inhabitants of Ai.

27 ۹Only the cattle and the spoil of that city Israel took for a prey unto themselves, according unto the word of the LORD which he ʳcommanded Joshua.

28 And Joshua burnt Ai, and made it ˢa heap for ever, *even* a desolation unto this day.

29 ᵗAnd the king of Ai he hanged on a tree until eventide: ᵘand as soon as the sun was down, Joshua commanded that they should

---

°Heb. *hand*——ᵖDeut. vii. 2——۹Num. xxxi. 22, 26
ʳVer. 2

ˢDeut. xiii. 16——ᵗChap. x. 26; Psalm cvii. 40; cx. 5
ᵘDeut. xxi. 23; chap. x. 27

---

the preceding observations on verse 1, observation 6;) and on seeing this *flag* or *ensign* unfurled, the men who lay in ambush arose and entered the city, making the fire previously agreed on. See ver. 8.

Verse 19. *Set the city on fire.*] See on ver. 8.

Verse 20. *They had no power to flee this way or that way*] They were in utter consternation; they saw that the city was taken, they found themselves in the midst of their foes; that their wives, children, and property, had fallen a prey to their enemies, in consequence of which they were so utterly panic-struck as to be incapable of making any resistance.

Verse 24. *Returned unto Ai, and smote it with the edge of the sword.*] This must refer to the women, children, and old persons, left behind; for it is likely that all the effective men had sallied out when they imagined the Israelites had fled. See ver. 16.

Verse 26. *Joshua drew not his hand back*] He was not only the *general*, but the *standard-bearer* or *ensign* of his own army, and continued in this employment during the whole of the battle. See on ver. 18. Some commentators understand this and ver. 18 *figuratively*, as if they implied that Joshua continued *in prayer to God* for the success of his troops; nor did he cease till the armies of Ai were annihilated, and the city taken and destroyed. The Hebrew word כידון *kidon*, which we render *spear*, is rendered by the Vulgate *clypeum*, *buckler;* and it must be owned that it seems to have this signification in several passages of Scripture: (see 1 Sam. xvii. 6, 45; Job xxxix.

23:) but it is clear enough also that it means a *spear*, or some kind of *offensive armour*, in other places: see Job xli. 29; Jer. vi. 23. I cannot therefore think that it has any *metaphorical* meaning, such as that attributed to the holding up of Moses's hands, Exod. xvii. 10-12, which is generally allowed to have a spiritual meaning, though it might be understood as the act of Joshua is here; and to this meaning an indirect glance is given in the note on the above place. But however the place in Exodus may be understood, that before us does not appear to have any metaphorical or equivocal meaning; Joshua continued to hold up or stretch out his spear, and did not slack from the pursuit till the forces of Ai were utterly discomfited.

Verse 27. *Only the cattle and the spoil*] In the case of Jericho these were all consigned to destruction, and therefore it was criminal to take any thing pertaining to the city, as we have already seen; but in the case before us the cattle and spoils were expressly given to the conquerors by the order of God. See ver. 2.

Verse 28. *Unto this day.*] This last clause was probably *added* by a later hand.

Verse 29. *The king of Ai he hanged on a tree*] He had gone out at the head of his men, and had been taken prisoner, ver. 23; and the battle being over, he was ordered to be hanged, probably after having been *strangled*, or in some way deprived of life, as in the case mentioned chap. x. 26, for in those times it was not customary to hang people *alive.*

As soon as the sun was down] It was not lawful to let the bodies remain all night upon

A. M. 2553
B. C. 1451
An. Exod. Isr.
40
Anno ante
I. Olymp. 675
take his carcass down from the tree, and cast it at the entering of the gate of the city, and ʳraise thereon a great heap of stones, *that remaineth* unto this day.

30 Then Joshua built an altar unto the Lᴏʀᴅ God of Israel ʷin Mount Ebal.

31 As Moses the servant of the Lᴏʀᴅ commanded the children of Israel, as it is written in the ˣbook of the law of Moses, an altar of whole stones, over which no man hath lift up *any* iron: and ʸthey offered thereon burnt-offerings unto the Lᴏʀᴅ, and sacrificed peace-offerings.

32 And ᶻhe wrote there upon the stones a copy of the law of Moses, which he wrote in the presence of the children of Israel.

33 And all Israel, and their elders, and offi-

cers, and their judges, stood on this side the ark, and on that side, before the priests the Levites, ᵃwhich bare the ark of the covenant of the Lᴏʀᴅ, as well ᵇthe stranger, as he that was born among them; half of them over against Mount Gerizim, and half of them over against Mount Ebal: ᶜas Moses the servant of the Lᴏʀᴅ had commanded before, that they should bless the people of Israel.

34 And afterward ᵈhe read all the words of the law, ᵉthe blessings and cursings, according to all that is written in the book of the law.

35 There was not a word of all that Moses commanded, which Joshua read not before all the congregation of Israel, ᶠwith the women, and the little ones, and ᵍthe strangers that ʰwere conversant among them.

A. M. 2553
B. C. 1451
An. Exod. Isr.
40
Anno ante
I. Olymp. 675

ᵛChap. vii. 26; x. 27——ʷDeut. xxvii. 4, 5——ˣExod. xx. 25; Deut. xxvii. 5, 6——ʸExod. xx. 24——ᶻDeut. xxvii. 2, 8——ᵃDeut. xxxi. 9, 25——ᵇDeut. xxxi. 12

ᶜDeut. xi. 29; xxvii. 12——ᵈDeut. xxxi. 11; Neh. viii. 3——ᵉDeut. xxviii. 2, 15, 45; xxix. 20, 21; xxx. 19 ᶠDeut. xxxi. 12——ᵍVer. 33——ʰHeb. *walked*

---

the tree. See the note on Deut. xxi. 23. The Septuagint say the king of *Ai* was hanged επι ξυλον διδυμον, upon a *double tree*, which probably means a *forked* tree, or something in the form of a *cross*. The tree on which criminals were hanged among the Romans was called *arbor infelix*, and *lignum infelix*, the *unfortunate, illfated*, or *accursed tree*.

Raise thereon a great heap of stones] This was a common custom through all antiquity in every country, as we have already seen in the case of *Achan*, chap. vii. 20.

Verse 30. *Then Joshua built an altar*] This was done in obedience to the express command of God, Deut. xxvii. 4-8. See the notes there.

Verse 32. *A copy of the law of Moses*] מִשְׁנֵה תּוֹרַת *mishneh torath*, the *repetition* of the *law;* that is, a *copy* of the *blessings* and *curses*, as commanded by Moses; not a copy of the *Decalogue*, as some imagine, nor of the book of Deuteronomy, as others think; much less of the whole Pentateuch; but merely of that part which contained the blessings and curses, and which was to be read on this solemn occasion. See the note on Deut. xxvii. 3.

Verse 33. *Half of them over against Mount Gerizim*] See the arrangement of the whole of this business in the note and observations on Deut. xxvii. 26. And see also the notes on chap. xxviii. of the same book.

Verse 35. *With the women and the little ones*] It was necessary that *all* should know that they were under the same obligations to obey; even the *women* are brought forward, not only because of their personal responsibility, but because to them was principally intrusted the education of the children. The *children* also witness this solemn transaction, that a salutary fear of offending God might be early, diligently, and deeply impressed upon their hearts. Thus every precaution is taken to ensure obedience to the Divine precepts, and con-

sequently to promote the happiness of the people; for this every ordinance of God is remarkable, as he ever causes the *interest* and *duty* of his followers to go hand in hand.

1. Iᴛ may be asked, Seeing God promised to deliver Ai into the hands of the Israelites, why needed they to employ so many men and so many stratagems in order to its reduction? To this it may be answered, that God will have man to put forth the wisdom and power with which he has endued him, in every important purpose of life; that he endued him with those powers for this very end; and that it would be inconsistent with his gracious design so to help man at any time as to render the powers he had given him useless.

2. It is only in the use of lawful means that we have any reason to expect God's blessing and help. One of the ancients has remarked, "Though God has made man without himself, he will not save him without himself;" and therefore man's own *concurrence* of *will*, and *co-operation* of *power* with God, are essentially necessary to his preservation and salvation. This co-operation is the grand condition, *sine qua non*, on which God will help or save. But is not this "endeavouring to *merit* salvation by our own works?" No: for this is impossible, unless we could prove that all the mental and corporeal powers which we possess came *from* and are *of ourselves*, and that we held them *independently* of the power and beneficence of our Creator; and that every act of these was of infinite value, to make it an equivalent for the heaven we wished to purchase. Putting forth the hand to receive the alms of a benevolent man, can never be considered a purchase-price for the bounty bestowed. For ever shall that word stand true in all its parts, *Christ is the* ᴀᴜᴛʜᴏʀ *of eternal salvation to all them that* ᴏʙᴇʏ *him*, Heb. v. 9.

CHAPTER IX

All the kings of the Hittites, Amorites, Canaanites, Perizzites, Hivites, and Jebusites, unite their forces against Joshua, 1, 2. The inhabitants of Gibeon, hearing what Joshua had done to Ai, sent ambassadors to him, feigning themselves to come from a very distant tribe, requesting a friendly alliance with him, 3–5. Their address to Joshua, and the means they used to deceive the Israelites, 6–13. The Israelitish elders are deceived, and make a league with them, which they confirm with an oath, 14, 15. After three days they are informed that the Gibeonites belong to the seven Canaanitish nations, yet they spare their cities, 16, 17. The congregation murmuring because of this, the elders excuse themselves because of their oath, 18, 19. They purpose to make the Gibeonites slaves to the congregation, 20, 21. Joshua calls them, and pronounces this sentence against them, 22, 23. They vindicate themselves, and submit to their lot, 24, 25. They are spared, and made hewers of wood and drawers of water to the congregation and to the altar, 26, 27.

A. M. 2553
B. C. 1451
An. Exod. Isr.
40
Anno ante
I. Olymp. 675

AND it came to pass, when all the kings which *were* on this side Jordan, in the hills, and in the valleys, and in all the coasts of ªthe great sea, over against Lebanon, ᵇthe Hittite, and the Amorite, the Canaanite, the Perizzite, the Hivite, and the Jebusite, heard *thereof;*

2 That they ᶜgathered themselves together, to fight with Joshua and with Israel, with one ᵈaccord.

3 And when the inhabitants of ᵉGibeon ᶠheard what Joshua had done unto Jericho and to Ai,

4 They did work wilily, and went and made as if they had been ambassadors, and took old sacks upon their asses, and wine bottles, old, and rent, and bound up;

5 And old shoes and clouted upon their feet, and old garments upon them; and all the bread of their provision was dry *and* mouldy.

A. M. 2553
B. C. 1451
An. Exod. Isr.
40
Anno ante
I. Olymp. 675

ªNumbers xxxiv. 6——ᵇExodus iii. 17; xxiii. 23
ᶜPsalm lxxxiii. 3, 5

ᵈHeb. *mouth*——ᵉChap. x. 2; 2 Sam. xxi. 1, 2
ᶠChapter vi. 27

NOTES ON CHAP. IX

Verse 1. *And it came to pass, when all the kings—heard* thereof] From this account it appears that the capture and destruction of *Jericho* and *Ai* had been heard of to the remotest parts of the land, that a general fear of the Israelitish arms prevailed, and that the different dynasties or petty governments into which the land was divided, felt all their interests at stake, and determined to make the defence of their country a common cause. This was the most prudent step they could take in their circumstances, and therefore they entered into a confederation in order to arrest the progress of the Israelites. The *Great Sea* mentioned here is the *Mediterranean Sea*, the coasts of which were inhabited by the *Phœnicians, Tyrians, Sidonians,* and *Philistines.* It is very likely that all these united with the Canaanites for their common safety.

Verse 3. *The inhabitants of Gibeon heard*] These alone did not join the confederation. Gibeon is supposed to have been the capital of the *Hivites.* In the division of the land it fell to the lot of Benjamin, chap. xviii. 25, and was afterwards given to the priests, chap. xxi. 17. See the note on chap. x. 2.

Verse 4. *They did work wilily*] Finesse of this kind is allowed by the conduct of all nations; and *stratagems* in war are all considered as legal. Nine tenths of the victories gained are attributable to *stratagem;* all sides practise them, and therefore none can condemn them. Much time and labour have been lost in the inquiry, "Did not the *Gibeonites* tell lies?" Certainly they did, and what is that to *us?* Does the word of God *commend* them for it? It does not. Are they held up to us as *examples?* Surely no. *They* did what any other nation would have done in their circumstances, and we have nothing to do with their example.

Had they come to the Israelites, and simply submitted themselves without opposition and without fraud, they had certainly fared much better. *Lying* and *hypocrisy* always defeat their own purpose, and at best can succeed only for a short season. *Truth* and *honesty* never wear out.

Old sacks—and wine bottles, old, &c.] They pretended to have come from a very distant country, and that their sacks and the *goat-skins* that served them for carrying their wine and water in, were worn out by the length of the journey.

Verse 5. *Old shoes and clouted*] Their sandals, they pretended had been worn out by long and difficult travelling, and they had been obliged to have them frequently *patched* during the way; their garments also were worn *thin;* and what remained of their bread was *mouldy*—spotted with age, or, as our old version has it, *bored*—pierced with many holes by the vermin which had bred in it, through the length of time it had been in their sacks; and this is the most literal meaning of the original נקדים *nik-kudim,* which means *spotted* or *pierced with many holes.*

The *old* and *clouted shoes* have been a subject of some controversy: the Hebrew word בלות *baloth* signifies *worn out,* from בלה *balah,* to *wear away;* and מטלאות *metullaoth,* from טלא *tala,* to *spot* or *patch,* i. e., *spotted* with *patches.* Our word *clouted,* in the Anglo-Saxon ᵹecluꞇoᵬ signifies *seamed up, patched;* from cluꞇ *clout, rag,* or *small piece of cloth,* used for piecing or patching. But some suppose the word here comes from *clouet,* the diminutive of *clou,* a small *nail,* with which the Gibeonites had fortified the soles of their shoes, to prevent them from wearing out in so long a journey; but this seems very unlikely; and our old English term

A. M. 2553
B. C. 1451
An. Exod. Isr.
40
Anno ante
I. Olymp. 675

6 And they went to Joshua [g]unto the camp at Gilgal, and said unto him, and to the men of Israel, We be come from a far country: now therefore make ye a league with us.

7 And the men of Israel said unto the [h]Hivites, Peradventure ye dwell among us; and [i]how shall we make a league with you?

8 And they said unto Joshua, [k]We *are* thy servants. And Joshua said unto them, Who *are* ye? and from whence come ye?

9 And they said unto him, [l]From a very far country thy servants are come, because of the name of the LORD thy God: for we have [m]heard the fame of him, and all that he did in Egypt.

10 [n]And all that he did to the two kings of the Amorites, that *were* beyond Jordan, to Sihon king of Heshbon, and to Og king of Bashan, which *was* at Ashtaroth.

11 Wherefore our elders and all the inhabitants of our country spake to us, saying, Take victuals [o]with you for the journey, and go to meet them, and say unto them, We *are* your servants: therefore now make ye a league with us.

A. M. 2553
B. C. 1451
An. Exod. Isr.
40
Anno ante
I. Olymp. 675

12 This our bread we took hot *for* our provision, out of our houses, on the day we came forth to go unto you; but now, behold, it is dry, and it is mouldy:

13 And these bottles of wine, which we filled, *were* new; and, behold, they be rent: and these our garments, and our shoes, are become old by reason of the very long journey.

14 And [p]the men took of their victuals, [q]and asked not *counsel* at the mouth of the LORD.

15 And Joshua [r]made peace with them, and made a league with them, to let them live: and the princes of the congregation sware unto them.

16 And it came to pass at the end of three

---

[g]Chap. v. 10——[h]Chap. xi. 19——[i]Exod. xxiii. 32; Deut. vii. 2; xx. 16; Judg. ii. 2——[k]Deut. xx. 11; 2 Kings x. 5——[l]Deut. xx. 15——[m]Exod. xv. 14; Josh. ii. 10——[n]Num. xxi. 24, 33——[o]Heb. *in your hand*

[p]Or, *they received the men by reason of their victuals* [q]Num. xxvii. 21; Isa. xxx. 1, 2; see Judg. i. 1; 1 Sam. xxii. 10; xxiii. 10, 11; xxx. 8; 2 Sam. ii. 1; v. 19 [r]Chap. xi. 19; 2 Sam. xxi. 2

---

clouted—seamed or *patched*—expresses the spirit of the Hebrew word.

Verse 6. Make ye a league with us.] כרתו לנו ברית *kirethu lanu berith, cut,* or *divide, the covenant sacrifice with us.* From this it appears that heathenism at this time had its sacrifices, and covenants were ratified by sacrificing to and invoking the objects of their adoration.

Verse 7. Peradventure ye dwell among us] It is strange they should have had such a suspicion, as the Gibeonites had acted so artfully; and it is as strange that, having such a suspicion, they acted with so little caution.

Verse 8. We are thy servants.] This appears to have been the only answer they gave to the question of the Israelitish elders, and this they gave to *Joshua,* not to *them,* as they saw that Joshua was commander-in-chief of the host.

Who are ye? and from whence come ye?] To these questions, from such an authority, they felt themselves obliged to give an explicit answer; and they do it very artfully by a mixture of *truth, falsehood,* and *hypocrisy.*

Verse 9. Because of the name of the Lord thy God] They pretend that they had undertaken this journey on a religious account; and seem to intimate that they had the highest respect for Jehovah, the object of the Israelites' worship; this was *hypocrisy.*

We have heard the fame of him] This was *true:* the wonders which God did in *Egypt,* and the discomfiture of *Sihon* and *Og,* had reached the whole land of Canaan; and it was on this account that the inhabitants of it were panic-struck. The Gibeonites, knowing that they could not stand where such mighty forces had fallen, wished to make the Israelites their

friends. This part of their relation was strictly *true.*

Verse 11. Wherefore our elders, &c.] All this, and what follows to the end of verse 13, was *false,* contrived merely for the purpose of deceiving the Israelites, and this they did to save their own lives; as they expected all the inhabitants of Canaan to be put to the sword.

Verse 14. The men took of their victuals] This was done in all probability in the way of *friendship;* for, from time immemorial to the present day, *eating together,* in the Asiatic countries, is considered a token of unalterable friendship; and those who eat even *salt* together, feel themselves bound thereby in a perpetual covenant. But the *marginal* reading of this clause should not be hastily rejected.

And asked not counsel *at the mouth of the Lord.*] They made the covenant with the Gibeonites without consulting God by *Urim* and *Thummim,* which was highly reprehensible in them, as it was a *state transaction* in which the interests and honour of God their king were intimately concerned.

Verse 15. Joshua made peace with them] Joshua agreed to receive them into a friendly connection with the Israelites, and to respect their lives and properties; and the elders of Israel bound themselves to the observance of it, and confirmed it with an *oath.* As the same words are used here as in verse 6, we may suppose that the covenant was made in the ordinary way, a sacrifice being offered on the occasion, and its blood poured out before the Lord. See on Gen. xv. 10, &c.

Verse 16. At the end of three days] Gibeon is reputed to be only about eight leagues distant from Gilgal, and on this account the fraud

A. M. 2553
B. C. 1451
An. Exod. Isr.
40
Anno ante
I. Olymp. 675

days after they had made a league with them, that they heard that they *were* their neighbours, and *that* they dwelt among them.

17 And the children of Israel journeyed, and came unto their cities on the third day. Now their cities *were* ⁸Gibeon, and Chephirah, and Beeroth, and Kirjath-jearim.

18 And the children of Israel smote them not, ᵗbecause the princes of the congregation had sworn unto them by the LORD God of Israel. And all the congregation murmured against the princes.

19 But all the princes said unto all the congregation, We have sworn unto them by the LORD God of Israel: now therefore we may not touch them.

20 This we will do to them; we will even let them live, lest ᵘwrath be upon us, because of the oath which we sware unto them.

A. M. 2553
B. C. 1451
An. Exod. Isr.
40
Anno ante
I. Olymp. 675

21 And the princes said unto them, Let them live; but let them be ᵛhewers of wood and drawers of water unto all the congregation; as the princes had ᵂpromised them.

22 And Joshua called for them, and he spake unto them, saying, Wherefore have ye beguiled us, saying, ˣWe *are* very far from you; when ʸye dwell among us?

23 Now therefore ye ᶻ*are* cursed, and there

---

⁸Chap. xviii. 25, 26, 28; Ezra ii. 25——ᵗEccles. v. 2; Psa. xv. 4——ᵘSee 2 Sam. xxi. 1, 2, 6; Ezek. xvii. 13, 15,

18, 19; Zech. v. 3, 4; Mal. iii. 5——ᵛDeut. xxix. 11 ᵂVer. 15——ˣVer. 6, 9——ʸVer. 16——ᶻGen. ix. 25

---

might be easily discovered in the time mentioned above.

Verse 17. *The children of Israel—came unto their cities*] Probably when the fraud was discovered, Joshua sent out a detachment to examine their country, and to see what use could be made of it in the prosecution of their war with the Canaanites. Some of the cities mentioned here were afterwards in great repute among the Israelites; and God chose to make one of them, *Kirjath-jearim*, the residence of the ark of the covenant for *twenty years*, in the reigns of *Saul* and *David*. There is no evidence that the *preservation* of the Gibeonites was displeasing to Jehovah.

Verse 18. *All the congregation murmured*] Merely because they were deprived of the *spoils* of the Gibeonites. They had now got under the full influence of a predatory spirit; God saw their proneness to this, and therefore, at particular times, totally interdicted the spoils of conquered cities, as in the case of Jericho.

Verse 19. *We have sworn unto them*] Although the Israelites were *deceived* in this business, and the covenant was made on a certain supposition which was afterwards proved to have had no foundation in truth, and consequently the whole engagement on the part of the *deceived* was hereby vitiated and rendered null and void; yet, because the elders had *eaten with them*, offered a *covenant sacrifice*, and *sworn by Jehovah*, they did not consider themselves at liberty to break the terms of the agreement, as far as the *lives* of the Gibeonites were concerned. That their conduct in this respect was highly pleasing to God is evident from this, that Joshua is nowhere reprehended for making this covenant, and sparing the Gibeonites; and that Saul, who four hundred years after this thought himself and the Israelites loosed from this obligation, and in consequence oppressed and destroyed the Gibeonites, was punished for the breach *of this treaty*, being considered as the violator of a most solemn oath and covenant engagement. See 2 Sam. xxi. 2-9, and Ezek. xvii. 18, 19.

All these circumstances laid together, prove that the command to destroy the Canaanites was not so *absolute* as is generally supposed:

and should be understood as rather referring to the destruction of the *political existence* of the Canaanitish *nations*, than to the destruction of their *lives*. See the notes on Deut. xx. 10, 17.

Verse 21. *Hewers of wood and drawers of water*] Perhaps this is a sort of proverbial expression, signifying the lowest state of servitude, though it may also be understood literally. See below.

Verse 23. *Now therefore ye are cursed*] Does not this refer to what was pronounced by Noah, Gen. ix. 25, against Ham and his posterity? Did not the curse of Ham imply *slavery*, and nothing else? *Cursed be Canaan, a servant of servants shall he be;* and does it not sufficiently appear that nothing else than perpetual *slavery* is implied in the curse of the Gibeonites? They were brought, no doubt, under tribute; performed the meanest offices for the Israelites, being in the same circumstances with the servile class of Hindoos called the *Chetrees;* had their national importance annihilated, and yet were never permitted to *incorporate* themselves with the Israelites. And we may reasonably suppose that this was the purpose of God relative to all the Canaanitish nations: those who would not renounce their idolatry, &c., were to be extirpated; those who *did* were to be preserved alive, on condition of becoming tributary, and serving as slaves. See the note on Deut. xx. 17.

Hewers of wood and drawers of water] The disgrace of this state lay not in the *laboriousness* of it, but in its being the common employment of the *females;* if the ancient customs among the same people were such as prevail now. The most intelligent travellers in those countries represent *collecting wood for fuel,* and *carrying water,* as the peculiar employment of the *females.* The Arab *women* of Barbary do so, according to Dr. *Shaw.* The *daughters* of the Turcomans in Palestine are employed, according to *D'Arvieux,* in fetching wood and water for the accommodation of their respective families. From these circumstances Mr. *Harmer* reasons thus: "The bitterness of the doom of the Gibeonites does not seem to have consisted in the laboriousness of the service enjoined them, for it was usual for *women* and

A. M. 2553
B. C. 1451
An. Exod. Isr.
40
Anno ante
I. Olymp. 675

shall ᵃnone of you be freed from being bondmen, and ᵇhewers of wood and drawers of water for the house of my God.

24 And they answered Joshua, and said, Because it was certainly told thy servants, how that the Lᴏʀᴅ thy God ᶜcommanded his servant Moses to give you all the land, and to destroy all the inhabitants of the land from before you, therefore ᵈwe were sore afraid of our lives because of you, and have done this thing.

25 And now, behold, we *are* ᵉin thine hand: as it seemeth good and right unto thee to do unto us, do.

26 And so did he unto them, and delivered them out of the hand of the children of Israel, that they slew them not.

27 And Joshua ᶠmade them that day ᵍhewers of wood and drawers of water for the congregation, and for the altar of the Lᴏʀᴅ, even unto this day, ʰin the place which he should choose.

A. M. 2553
B. C. 1451
An. Exod. Isr.
40
Anno ante
I. Olymp. 675

ᵃHeb. *not be cut off from you*——ᵇVer. 21, 27——ᶜExod. xxiii. 32; Deut. vii. 1, 2——ᵈExod. xv. 14

ᵉGen. xvi. 6——ᶠHeb. *gave, or, delivered to be;* 1 Chron. ix. 2; Ezra viii. 20——ᵍVer. 21, 23——ʰDeut. xii. 5

---

children to perform what was required of *them;* but its degrading them from the characteristic employment of *men,* that of *bearing arms;* and condemning them and their posterity for ever to the employment of *females.* The not receiving them as *allies* was bitter; the disarming them who had been warriors, and condemning them to the employment of *females,* was worse; but the extending this degradation to their *posterity,* was bitterest of all. It is no wonder that in these circumstances they are said to have been *cursed.*"—Obs., vol. iv., p. 297.

Verse 24. *We were sore afraid of our lives*] Self-preservation, which is the most powerful law of nature, dictated to them those measures which they adopted; and they plead this as the *motive* of their conduct.

Verse 25. *We are in thine hand*] Entirely in thy power.

As it seemeth good and right unto thee—do.] Whatever *justice* and *mercy* dictate to thee to do to us, that perform. They expect *justice,* because they *deceived* the Israelites; but they expect *mercy* also, because they were driven to use this expedient for fear of losing their lives. The appeal to Joshua is full of delicacy and cogent argument.

Verse 26. *And so did he unto them*] That is, he acted according to *justice* and *mercy:* he delivered them out of the hands of the people, so that they slew them not—here was *mercy;* and he made them hewers of wood and drawers of water for the congregation, and to the altar of God—here was *justice.* Thus Joshua did nothing but what was *good* and *right,* not only in his own eyes, but also in the eyes of the Lord.

How long the Gibeonites were preserved as a distinct people after this, we know not. That they existed in the time of David, is evident from the circumstance mentioned on ver. 19. They are not mentioned after the captivity; and it is probable that they were nearly annihilated by the persecution raised up against them by Saul. Some suppose that the Gibeonites existed under the appellation of *Nethinim;* but of this there is no decisive proof; the Nethinim were probably slaves of a different race.

Oɴ what we meet with in this chapter, we may make the following observations.

1. The Gibeonites told lies, in order to save their lives. No expediency can justify this, nor are *we* called to attempt it. The Gibeonites were *heathens,* and we can expect nothing better from them. See note at the end of chap. ii.

2. They did not profit by their falsity: had they come in fairly, sought peace, and renounced their idolatry, they would have had life on honourable terms. As it was, they barely escaped with their lives, and were utterly deprived of their political liberty. Even the *good* that is sought by *unlawful* means has God's curse on it.

3. We need not be solicitous for the character of the Gibeonites here; they are neither our models, nor believers in the true God, and therefore pure religion is not concerned in their prevarication and falsity.

4. We see here of what solemn importance an *oath* was considered among the people of God; they swore to their own hurt, and changed not. When once they had bound themselves to their Maker, they did not believe that any changing circumstances could justify a departure from so awful an obligation. Thus, reader, shouldst *thou* fear a lie, and tremble at an oath.

CHAPTER X

Adoni-zedec, *king of Jerusalem, hearing of the capture of Ai, and that the Gibeonites had made peace with Israel, calls to his assistance four other kings to fight against Gibeon, 1–4. They join forces, and encamp against Gibeon, 5. The Gibeonites send to Joshua for succour, 6, who immediately marches to their relief, receives encouragement from God, and falls suddenly on the confederate forces, 7–9, and defeats them; they fly, and multitudes of them are slain by a miraculous shower of hail-stones, 10, 11. Joshua, finding that the day began to fail, prayed that the sun and moon might stand still, that they might have time to pursue and utterly destroy these confederate forces, 12. The sun and moon stand still, and make that day as long as two, 13, 14. Joshua and the people return to their camp at Gilgal, 15. The five kings having taken shelter in a cave at Makkedah, Joshua commanded the people to roll great stones against the mouth of the cave, and set a watch to keep it, while Israel were pursuing their enemies, 16–19. The Israelites return to Makkedah, bring forth the five kings, then slay and hang them on five trees, 20–27. The Israelites take and destroy*

Makkedah, 28, *and* Libnah, 29, 30, *and* Lachish 31, 32, *and defeat* Horam *king of* Gezer, 33, *and take* Eglon, 34, 35, *and* Hebron, 36, 37, *and* Debir, 38, 39, *and all the country of the* hills, south, vale, *and* springs, *and the whole country from* Kadesh-Barnea *to Gibeon,* 40–42. *They return to Gilgal,* 43.

A. M. 2554
B. C. 1450
An. Exod. Isr. 41
Anno ante I. Olymp. 674

NOW it came to pass, when Adoni-zedec, king of Jerusalem, had heard how Joshua had taken Ai, and had utterly destroyed it; [a]as he had done to Jericho and her king, so he had done to [b]Ai and her king; and [c]how the inhabitants of Gibeon had made peace with Israel, and were among them;

2 That they [d]feared greatly, because Gibeon *was* a great city, as one of the [e]royal cities, and because it *was* greater than Ai, and all the men thereof *were* mighty.

3 Wherefore Adoni-zedec king of Jerusalem sent unto Hoham king of Hebron, and unto Piram king of Jarmuth, and unto Japhia king of Lachish, and unto Debir king of Eglon, saying,

4 Come up unto me, and help me, that we may smite Gibeon: [f]for it hath made peace with Joshua, and with the children of Israel.

5 Therefore the five kings of the Amorites,

the king of Jerusalem, the king of Hebron, the king of Jarmuth, the king of Lachish, the king of Eglon, [g]gathered themselves together, and went up, they and all their hosts, and encamped before Gibeon, and made war against it.

A. M. 2554
B. C. 1450
An. Exod. Isr. 41
Anno ante I. Olymp. 674

6 And the men of Gibeon sent unto Joshua [h]to the camp to Gilgal, saying, Slack not thy hand from thy servants; come up to us quickly, and save us, and help us: for all the kings of the Amorites that dwell in the mountains are gathered together against us.

7 So Joshua ascended from Gilgal, he, and [i]all the people of war with him, and all the mighty men of valour.

8 And the LORD said unto Joshua, [k]Fear them not: for I have delivered them into thine hand; [l]there shall not a man of them stand before thee.

9 Joshua therefore came unto them sud-

[a]Chap. vi. 21——[b]Chap. viii. 22, 26, 28——[c]Chap. ix. 15——[d]Exod. xv. 14, 15, 16; Deut. xi. 25——[e]Heb. *cities of the kingdom*

[f]Ver. 1; chap. ix. 15——[g]Chap. ix. 2——[h]Chap. v. 10, ix. 6——[i]Chap. viii. 1——[k]Chap. xi. 6; Judg. iv. 14——[l]Chap. i. 5

NOTES ON CHAP. X

Verse 1. *Adoni-zedec*] This name signifies the *Lord of justice* or *righteousness;* and it has been conjectured that the Canaanitish kings assumed this name in imitation of that of the ancient patriarchal king of this city, Melchizedek, whose name signifies *king of righteousness,* or *my righteous king:* a supposition that is not improbable, when the celebrity of Melchizedek is considered.

Jerusalem] ירושלם *Yerushalam*. This word has been variously explained; if it be compounded of שלם *shalam,* peace, perfection, &c., and ראה *raah,* he saw, it may signify *the vision of peace*—or, *he shall see peace* or *perfection.*

Verse 2. *As one of the royal cities*] Not a *regal* city, but great, well inhabited and well fortified, *as* those cities which served for the royal residence generally were. It does not appear that the Gibeonites had any king—they seem to have been a small but powerful *republic, all the men* thereof were *mighty,* merely governed by their *elders:* for in their address to Joshua, chap. ix. 11, they mention no *king,* but simply state that they were sent by their *elders and the inhabitants of their country;* nor do we any where read of their *king;* and therefore we may naturally suppose that they had none.

Verse 3. *Hoham king of Hebron*] This city was situated in the mountains, southward of Jerusalem, from which it was about thirty miles distant. It fell to the tribe of Judah.

Piram king of Jarmuth] There were two

cities of this name; one belonged to the tribe of *Issachar,* see chap. xxi. 29; that mentioned here fell to the tribe of *Judah,* see chap. xv. 35; it is supposed to have been about eighteen miles distant from Jerusalem.

Japhia king of Lachish] This city is celebrated in Scripture; in that city *Amaziah* was slain by conspirators, 2 Kings xiv. 19. It was besieged by *Sennacherib,* 2 Kings xviii. 14, 17; and without effect by the king of *Assyria,* as we learn from Isa. xxxvii. 8: it was also besieged by the army of *Nebuchadnezzar,* see Jer. xxxiv. 7; it also fell to the lot of *Judah,* chap. xv. 39.

Debir king of Eglon] Where this city was situated is very uncertain; but we learn from chap. xv. 39, that it fell to the lot of the tribe of *Judah.*

Verse 5. *The five kings of the Amorites*] This is a general name for the inhabitants of Canaan, otherwise called *Canaanites;* and it is very likely that they had this appellation because the Amorites were the most powerful tribe or nation in that country. The inhabitants of Jerusalem were *Jebusites,* chap. xv. 63; those of Hebron were *Hittites,* Gen. xxiii. 2, 3; xxv. 9, 10; and the Gibeonites were *Hivites,* Josh. ix. 7; and yet all these are called *Amorites* occasionally, probably for the reason already mentioned, viz., because that tribe was most numerous and powerful.

Verse 9. *Joshua—came unto them suddenly*] This he did by a forced march during the night, for he *went up from Gilgal all night;* from *Gilgal* to *Gibeon* was about eighteen or twenty miles; and, having fallen so unexpectedly on

A. M. 2554
B. C. 1450
An. Exod. Isr.
41
Anno ante
I. Olymp. 674
denly, *and* went up from Gilgal all night.

10 And the LORD [m]discomfited them before Israel, and slew them with a great slaughter at Gibeon, and chased them along the way that goeth up [n]to Beth-horon, and smote them to [o]Azekah, and unto Makkedah.

11 And it came to pass, as they fled from before Israel, *and* were in the going down to Beth-horon, [p]that the LORD cast down great

A. M. 2554
B. C. 1450
An. Exod. Isr.
41
Anno ante
I. Olymp. 674
stones from heaven upon them unto Azekah, and they died: *they were* more which died with hail-stones, than *they* whom the children of Israel slew with the sword.

12 Then spake Joshua to the LORD in the day when the LORD delivered up the Amorites before the children of Israel, and he said in the sight of Israel, [q]Sun, [r]stand thou still upon Gibeon; and thou Moon, in the valley of [s]Ajalon.

---

[m]Judg. iv. 15; 1 Sam. vii. 10, 12; Psa. xviii. 14; Isa. xxviii. 21——[n]Chap. xvi. 3, 5——[o]Chap. xv. 35

[p]Psa. xviii. 13, 14; lxxvii. 17; Isa. xxx. 30; Ecclus. xlvi. 6; Rev. xvi. 21——[q]Isa. xxviii. 21; Hab. iii. 11; Ecclus. xlvi. 4——[r]Heb. *be silent*——[s]Judg. xii. 12

---

these confederate kings, they were immediately thrown into confusion.

Verse 10. *Slew them with a great slaughter at Gibeon*] Multitudes of them fell in the *onset;* after which they fled, and the Israelites pursued them by the way of Beth-horon. There were two cities of this name, the *upper* and *lower*, both in the tribe of Ephraim, and built by *Sherah*, the daughter of Ephraim, 1 Chron. vii. 24. The situation of these two cities is not exactly known.

To Azekah, and unto Makkedah.] These two cities were in the tribe of Judah, chap. xv. 35-41.

Verse 11. *The Lord cast down great stones from heaven upon them*] Some have contended that stones, in the common acceptation of the word, are intended here; and that the term *hail-stones* is only used to point out the *celerity* of their fall, and their *quantity*. That stones have fallen from the *clouds*, if not from a greater height, is a most incontestable fact. That these have fallen in different parts of the world is also true; the East Indies, America, France, Germany, England, Ireland, &c., have all witnessed this phenomenon: of such stones I possess and have seen several fragments; some considerable pieces may be seen in the British Museum. That God might have cast down such stones as these on the Canaanites, there can be no doubt, because his power is unlimited; and the whole account proves that here there was a miraculous interference. But it is more likely that hail-stones, in the proper sense of the word, are *meant* as well as *expressed* in the text. That God on other occasions has made use of hail-stones to destroy both men and cattle, we have ample proof in the *plague of hail* that fell on the Egyptians. See the note on Exod. ix. 18. There is now before me a square of glass, taken out of a south window in the house of Mr. Ball of Crockerton, in the parish of Longbridge Deverell, county of Wilts., through which a hail-stone passed in a shower that fell there June 1, 1780, at two o'clock, P. M. The hole is an *obtuse ellipsis* or *oval*, and is cut as true as if it had been done with a diamond: it is three inches and a half in diameter; a proof that the stone that pierced it, which was about eleven inches in circumference, came with inconceivable velocity, else the glass must have been *shivered* to pieces. I have known a cannon ball go through a square of glass in the cabin window of a ship, and make precisely the same kind of hole, without either *shattering* or even

starring the glass. It is needless to add that this hail-shower did great damage, breaking even trees in pieces, and destroying the vegetation through the whole of its extent. But allowing that extraordinary showers of hail have fallen in *England* or *France*, is it likely that such showers ever fell in the promised land or its vicinity? They certainly have. *Albertus Aquensis*, one of the writers in the collection *Gesta Dei per Francos*, in describing the expedition of Baldwin I. in the Holy Land, observes that, when he and his army were in the *Arabian mountains*, in the vicinity of the *Dead Sea*, they suffered incredibly from *horrible hail, terrible frost*, and *indescribable rain* and *snow*, so that thirty of his men perished by them. His words are: *"Sexta vero die montanis permensis, in extremo illorum cacumine maxima pertulerunt pericula, in* GRANDINE *horribili, in* GLACIE *terribili, in* PLUVIA *et* NIVE *inaudita, quorum immanitate, et horrore ingruente ad triginta homines pedites præ frigore mortui sunt."*—Hist. Hieros., p. 307. I conclude, therefore, that a shower of *hail-stones* may be meant; and that this shower, though *natural* in itself, was *supernaturally* employed on this occasion, and *miraculously* directed to fall where it did, and do the execution described.

But I am ready to grant, notwithstanding, that as a most stupendous miracle was in this instance wrought, in causing the sun and moon to stand still; there can be no doubt that the shower of stones, which was also miraculous, might have been of *real stones* as well as *hail-stones*. Of late, this subject of the fall of real stones from the clouds has been very closely investigated, and not only the *possibility* of the fall of such stones from the *clouds*, or from much *higher* regions, but the *certainty* of the case has been fully demonstrated. These substances are now, in philosophical language denominated *aeroliths* or *air-stones;* and the following table constructed by M. *Izarn*, a foreign chemist, exhibits a variety of facts of this kind, and shows the *places* and *times* in which these substances fell, and the *testimony* by which these facts are supported. As it is as possible that God might have projected a shower of stones on these idolaters, even from the *moon*, as to arrest that planet in her course, I give the table, and leave the reader to decide, in the present case, for *aeroliths* or *hail-stones*, as may seem to him most congruous to the fact here related.

13 And the sun stood still, and the moon stayed, until the people had avenged themselves upon

†2 Sam. i. 18

their enemies. 'Is not this written in the book of ᵘJasher? So the sun stood still in the midst

ᵘOr, *the upright*

SUBSTANCES	PLACES WHERE THEY FELL	PERIOD OF THEIR FALL	TESTIMONY
Shower of stones	At Rome	Under Tullus Hostilius	Livy.
Shower of stones	At Rome	Consuls, C. Martius and M. Torquatus	J. Obsequens.
A very large stone	Near the river Negos, Thrace	Second year of the 78th Olympiad	Pliny.
Three large stones	In Thrace	Year before J. C., 452	Ch. of Count Marcellin.
Stone of 72 lbs	Near Larissa, Macedonia	January, 1706	Paul Lucas.
About 1,200 stones; one 120 lbs. Another of 60 lbs.	Near Padua in Italy	In 1510	Carden, Varcit.
Another of 59 lbs	On Mount Vasier, Provence	November 27, 1627	Gassendi.
Two large stones weighing 20 lbs.	Liponas, in Bresse	September, 1753	De La Lande.
A stony mass	Niort, Normandy	In 1750	De La Lande.
A stone of 7½ lbs	At Luce, in Le Maine	September 13, 1768	Bachelay.
A stone	At Aire, in Artois	In 1768	Gurson de Boyaval.
A stone	In Le Cotentin	In 1768	Morand.
Extensive shower of stones	Environs of Agen	July 24, 1790	St. Amand, Baudin, &c.
About 12 stones	Sienna, Tuscany	July, 1794	Earl of Bristol.
A large stone of 56 lbs	Wold Cottage, Yorkshire	December 13, 1795	Captain Topham.
A stone of 10 lbs	In Portugal	February 19, 1796	Southey.
A stone of about 120 lbs.	Salè, department of the Rhone	March 17, 1798	Le Lievre and De Drèe.
Shower of stones	Benares, East Indies	December 19, 1798	J. Lloyd Williams, Esq.
Shower of stones	At Plann, near Tabor, Bohemia	July 3, 1753	B. de Born.
Mass of iron, 70 cubic feet	America	April 5, 1800	Philosophical Magazine.
Mass of ditto, 14 quintals	Abakauk, Siberia	Very old	Pallas, Chladni, &c.
Shower of stones	Barboutan, near Roquefort	July, 1789	Darcet, jun., Lomet, &c.
Large stone, 260 lbs	Ensisheim, Upper Rhine	November 7, 1492	Butenschoen.
Two stones, 200 and 300 lbs.	Near Verona	In 1762	Acad. de Bourd.
A stone of 20 lbs	Sales, near Ville Franche	March 12, 1798	De Drèe.
Several ditto from 10 to 17 lbs.	Near L'Aigle, Normandy	April 26, 1803	Fourcroy.

These stones generally appear luminous in their descent, moving in oblique directions with very great velocities, and commonly with a hissing noise. They are frequently heard to explode or burst, and seem to fly in pieces, the larger parts falling first. They often strike the earth with such force as to sink several inches below the surface. They are always different from the surrounding bodies, but in every case are similar to one another, being semi-metallic, coated with a thin black incrustation. They bear strong marks of recent fusion. Chemists have found on examining these stones that they very nearly agree in their nature and composition, and in the proportions of their component parts. The stone which fell at Ensisheim in Alsace, in 1492, and those which fell at L'Aigle in France, in 1803, yielded, by the Analysis of Fourcroy and Vanquelin, as in this table:—

Ensisheim stone fell A. D. 1492	L'Aigle stone fell A. D. 1803	
56 0	54	of silica
30 0	36	—oxyd of iron
12 0	9	—magnesia
2 4	3	—oxyd of nickel
3 5	2	—sulphur
1 4	1	—lime
105 3	105	

Their specific gravities are generally about three of four times that of water, being heavier than common stones. From the above account it is reasonable to conclude that they have all the same origin. To account for this phenomenon, various hypotheses have appeared; we shall mention three: 1. That they are little planets, which, circulating in space, fall into the atmosphere, which, by its friction, diminishes the velocity, so that they fall by their weight. 2. That they are concretions formed in the atmosphere. 3. That they are projected from lunar volcanoes. These are the most probable conjectures we can meet with, and of these the two former possess a very small degree of probability, but there are very strong reasons in favour of the last. Among the reasons we may notice the following: 1. Volcanoes in the moon have been observed by means of the telescope. 2. The lunar volcanoes are very high, and the surface of that globe suffers frequent changes, as appears by the late observations of Schroeter. 3. If a body be projected from the moon to a distance greater than that of the point of equilibrium between the attraction of the earth and moon, it will, on the known principle of gravitation, fall to the earth. 4. That a body may be projected from the lunar volcanoes beyond the moon's influence, is not

A. M. 2554
B. C. 1450
An. Exod. Isr.
41
Anno ante
I. Olymp. 674

of heaven, and hasted not to go down about a whole day.

14 And there was ᵛno day like that before it or after it, that the

LORD hearkened unto the voice of a man: for ʷthe LORD fought for Israel.

15 ˣAnd Joshua returned, and

A. M. 2554
B. C. 1450
An. Exod. Isr.
41
Anno ante
I. Olymp. 674

ᵛSee Isa. xxxviii. 8

ʷDeut. i. 30; ver. 42; chap. xxiii. 3——ˣVer. 43

---

only possible but very probable; for on calculation it is found that four times the force usually given to a twelve pounder, will be quite sufficient for this purpose; it is to be observed that the point of equilibrium is much nearer the moon, and that a projectile from the moon will not be so much retarded as one from the earth, both on account of the moon's rarer atmosphere, and its less attractive force. On this subject, see Mr. Haward's valuable paper in the Philosophical Transactions for 1802, and Dr. Hutton's dissertation in the new abridgment, part xxi. It is highly probable that the *ancile,* or sacred shield, that fell from heaven in the reign of Numa Pompilius, was a stone of this sort. The description of its fall, as given by Ovid, *Fast.* lib. iii., bears a striking resemblance to recent accounts of stones falling from the atmosphere, particularly in the *luminous* appearance and *hissing* noise with which it was accompanied.

Dum loquitur, totum jam sol emerserat orbem,
  Et gravis æthereo venit ab axe *fragor.*
Ter tonuit sine nube *Deus,* tria *fulgura* misit:
  Credite dicenti; mira, sed *acta,* loquor.
A media cœlum regione *dehiscere* cœpit:
  Summisere oculos cum duce turba suos.
Ecce levi scutum versatum leniter aura
  Decidit, a pupulo clamor ad astra venit.
Tolit humo munus ————
Idque *ancile* vocat, quod ab omni parte recisum
  est.

It is very possible that the *Palladium* of *Troy,* and the *Image* of the *Ephesian Diana,* were stones which really fell from the atmosphere, bearing some rude resemblance to the human form. See the IMPERIAL ENCYCLOPÆDIA, article *Aerolith.*

I believe it is generally agreed among philosophers, 1. That all these aerial stones, chemically analyzed, show the same properties; 2. That no stone found on our earth possesses exactly the same properties, nor in the same proportions. This is an extraordinary circumstance, and deserves particular notice.

Verse 12. *Then spake Joshua to the Lord*] Though Joshua saw that the enemies of his people were put to flight, yet he well knew that all which escaped would rally again, and that he should be obliged to meet them once more in the field of battle if permitted now to escape; finding that the day was drawing towards a close, he feared that he should not have time sufficient to complete the destruction of the confederate armies; in this moment, being suddenly inspired with Divine confidence, he requested the Lord to perform the most stupendous miracle that had ever been wrought, which was no less than *to arrest the sun in his course,* and prolong the day till the destruction of his enemies had been completed!

Sun, stand thou still upon Gibeon; and thou, Moon, in the valley of Ajalon.] To account for this miracle, and to ascertain the *manner* in which it was wrought, has employed the pens

of the ablest *divines* and *astronomers,* especially of the last two centuries. By their learned labours many difficulties have been removed from the account in general; but the very different and contradictory methods pursued by several, in their endeavours to explain the whole, and make the relation accord with the present acknowledged system of the universe, and the phenomena of nature, tend greatly to puzzle the plain, unphilosophical reader. The subject cannot be well explained without a *dissertation;* and a dissertation is not consistent with the nature of short notes, or a commentary on Scripture. It is however necessary to attempt an explanation, and to bring that as much as possible within the apprehension of common readers; in order to this, I must beg leave to introduce a few preliminary observations, or what the reader may call *propositions* if he pleases.

1. I take it for granted that a *miracle* was wrought as nearly as circumstances could admit, in the *manner* in which it is here recorded. I shall not, therefore, seek for any *allegorical* or *metaphorical* interpretations; the miracle is recorded as a *fact,* and as a *fact* I take it up.

2. I consider the present accredited system of the universe, called sometimes the *Pythagorean, Copernican,* or *Newtonian* system, to be genuine; and also to be the system of the universe laid down in the Mosaic writings—that the SUN is in the *centre* of what is called the solar system; and that the *earth* and all the other *planets,* whether *primary* or *secondary,* move round him in certain periodical times, according to the quantity of their matter, and distance from him, their centre.

3. I consider the sun to have no revolution round any *orbit,* but to revolve round his own *axis,* and round the common centre of gravity in the planetary system, which centre of gravity is included within his own surface; and in all other respects I consider him to be at *rest* in the system.

4. I consider the earth, not only as *revolving round the sun* in 365 days, 5 hours, 48 minutes, and 48 seconds, but as *revolving round its own axis,* and making this revolution in 23 hours, 56 minutes, and 4 seconds; that in the course of 24 hours complete, every part of its surface is alternately turned to the sun; that this revolution constitutes our *day* and *night,* as the former does our *year;* and it is *day* to all those parts which have the sun *above* the horizon, and *night* to those which have the sun *below* it; and that this diurnal revolution of the earth, or revolving round its own axis, in a direction from west to east, occasions what is commonly called the *rising* and *setting of the sun,* which *appearance* is occasioned, not by any *motion* in the *sun* himself, but by this *motion of the earth;* which may be illustrated by a ball or globe suspended by a thread, and caused to turn round. If this be held opposite to a *candle,* it will appear half enlightened and half dark; but the dark parts will be seen to come *successively*

A. M. 2554
B. C. 1450
An. Exod. Isr.
41
Anno ante
I. Olymp. 674

all Israel with him, unto the camp to Gilgal.

16 But these five kings fled, and ^yhid themselves in a cave at Makkedah.

---

^yPsa. xlviii. 4, 5; Isa. ii. 10

---

into the *light*, and the enlightened parts into the *shade;* while the candle itself which gives the light is fixed, not changing its position.

5. I consider the solar influence to be the *cause* both of the *annual* and *diurnal* motion of the earth; and that, while that influence continues to act upon it according to the law which God originally impressed on both the earth and the sun, the *annual* and *diurnal* motions of the earth must continue; and that no power but the unlimited power of God can alter this influence, change, or suspend the operation of this law; but that he is such an infinitely FREE AGENT, that HE can, when his unerring wisdom sees good, alter, suspend, or even annihilate all secondary causes and their effects: for it would be degrading to the perfections of his nature to suppose that he had *so bound himself* by the laws which he has given for the preservation and direction of universal nature, that he could not change them, alter their effects, or suspend their operations when greater and better effects, in a certain *time* or *place*, might be produced by such temporary change or suspension.

6. I consider that the miracle wrought on this occasion served greatly to confirm the Israelites, not only in the belief of the being and perfections of God, but also in the doctrine of an especial providence, and in the nullity of the whole system of idolatry and superstition.

7. That no evil was done by this miraculous interference, nor any law or property of nature ultimately changed; on the contrary, a most important good was produced, which probably, to this people, could not have been brought about any other way; and that therefore the miracle wrought on this occasion was highly worthy of the wisdom and power of God.

8. I consider that the terms in the text employed to describe this miracle are not, when rightly understood, contrary to the well-established notions of the true system of the universe; and are not spoken, as some have contended, *ad captum vulgi*, to the prejudices of the common people, much less do they favour the *Ptolemaic* or any other *hypothesis* that places the *earth* in the centre of the solar system.

Having laid down these preliminaries, some short observations on the words of the text may be sufficient.

Joshua's address is in a *poetic* form in the original, and makes the two following hemistichs:—

שמש בגבעון דום
וירח בעמק אילן

Shemesh begibon dom:
Veyareach beemek Aiyalon.

Sun! upon Gibeon be dumb:
And the moon on the vale of Ajalon.

The effect of this command is related, ver. 13, in the following words:—

וידם השמש וירח עמד *vaiyiddom hashSHEMESH*

17 And it was told Joshua, saying, The five kings are found hid in a cave at Makkedah.

18 And Joshua said, ^zRoll great stones upon the mouth of the cave,

A. M. 2554
B. C. 1450
An. Exod. Isr.
41
Anno ante
I. Olymp. 674

---

^zVer. 22; Psa. xviii. 37-41

---

*ve*YAREACH *amad, And the sun was dumb* or *silent and the moon stood still.* And in the latter clause of this verse it is added: *And the sun stood still in the midst of heaven, and hasted not to go down about a whole day.*

It seems necessary here to answer the question, At what *time* of the day did this miracle take place? The expression בחצי השמים *bachatsi hashshamayim, in the midst of heaven*, seems to intimate that the sun was at that time on the *meridian* of Gibeon, and consequently had *one half* of its course to run; and this sense of the place has been strongly contended for as essential to the miracle, for the greater display of the glory of God: "Because," say its abettors, "had the miracle been wrought when the sun was near the going down, it might have been mistaken for some refraction of the rays of light, occasioned by a peculiarly moist state of the atmosphere in the horizon of that place, or by some such appearance as the *Aurora Borealis*." To me there seems no solidity in this reason. Had the sun been arrested in the *meridian*, the miracle could scarcely have been noticed, and especially in the hurry and confusion of that time; and we may be assured, that among the Canaanites there were neither *clocks* nor *time-keepers*, by which the preternatural length of such a day could have been accurately measured: but, on the contrary, had the sun been about the *setting*, when both the *pursuers* and the *pursued* must be apprehensive of its *speedy* disappearance, its continuance for several hours *above the horizon*, so near the point when it might be expected to go *down*, must have been very observable and striking. The *enemy* must see, feel, and deplore it; as their hope of escape must, in such circumstances, be founded on the speedy entering in of the night, through which alone they could expect to elude the pursuing Israelites. And the *Israelites* themselves must behold with astonishment and wonder that the *setting* sun *hasted not to go down about a whole day*, affording them supernatural time totally to destroy a routed foe, which otherwise might have had time to rally, confederate, choose a proper station, and attack in their turn with peculiar *advantages*, and a probability of *success*. It appears, therefore, much more reasonable that Joshua should require this miracle to be performed *when daylight was about to fail*, just as the sun was setting. If we were to consider the sun as being at the meridian of Gibeon, as some understand *the midst of heaven*, it may be well asked, How could Joshua know that he should not have time enough to complete the destruction of his enemies, who were now completely routed? Already multitudes of them had fallen by the hailstones and by the sword: and if he had yet half a day before him, it would have been natural enough for him to conclude that he had a sufficiency of time for the purpose, his men having been employed all night in a forced march, and half a day in close fighting; and indeed had he

A. M. 2554 B. C. 1450 An. Exod. Isr. 41 Anno ante I. Olymp. 674	and set men by it for to keep them: 19 And stay ye not, *but* pursue after your enemies, and ªsmite

the hindmost of them; suffer them not to enter into their cities: for the LORD your God hath delivered them into your hand.	A. M. 2554 B. C. 1450 An. Exod. Isr. 41 Anno ante I. Olymp. 674

ªHeb. *cut off*   the tail

---

not been under an especial inspiration, he could not have requested the miracle at all, knowing, as he must have done, that his men must be nearly exhausted by marching all night and fighting all day. But it may be asked, What is the meaning of בחצי השמים *bachatsi hashsha-mayim*, which we translate *in the midst of heaven?* If, with Mr. *Bate*, we translate חצה *chatsah, to part, divide asunder,* then it may refer to the *horizon,* which is the *apparent division* of the heavens into the *upper* and *lower hemisphere;* and thus the whole verse has been understood by some eminently learned men, who have translated the whole passage thus: *And the sun stood still in the* (upper) *hemisphere of heaven, and hasted not to go down when the day was complete;* that is, though the day was then complete, the sun being on the horizon— the line that to the eye constituted the *mid heaven*—yet it hasted not to go down; was miraculously sustained in its then almost *setting* position; and this seems still more evident from the moon's appearing at that time, which it is not reasonable to suppose could be visible in the glare of light occasioned by a *noon-day* sun.

But the main business relative to the standing still of the sun still remains to be considered.

I have already *assumed,* as a thoroughly demonstrated truth, that the sun is in the *centre* of the system, moving only round his own axis, and the common centre of the gravity of the planetary system, while all the planets revolve round *him,* Prop. 2 and 3; that his influence is the cause of the *diurnal* and *annual* revolutions of the earth; nor can I see what other purpose his revolution round his own axis can possibly answer, Prop. 5.

I consider that the word דום *dom,* in the text, refers to the *withholding* or *restraining* this influence, so that the cessation of the earth's motion might immediately take place. The desire of Joshua was, that the sun might not sink below the horizon; but as it appeared now to be over Gibeon, and the *moon* to be over the valley of Ajalon, he prayed that they might continue in these positions till the battle should be ended; or, in other words, that the day should be miraculously lengthened out.

Whether Joshua had a correct philosophical notion of the true system of the universe, is a subject that need not come into the present inquiry: but whether *he spoke* with strict propriety on this occasion is a matter of importance, because he must be considered as acting *under the Divine influence,* in requesting the performance of such a stupendous miracle; and we may safely assert that no man in his right mind would have thought of offering such a petition had he not felt himself under some Divine afflatus. Leaving, therefore, his philosophic knowledge out of the question, he certainly spoke as if he had known that the solar influence was the cause of the earth's *rotation,*

and therefore, with the strictest philosophic propriety, he requested that that influence might be for a time restrained, that the diurnal motion of the earth might be arrested, through which alone the sun could be kept above the horizon, and day be prolonged. His mode of expression evidently considers the sun as the great *ruler* or *master* in the system; and all the planets (or at least the earth) moving in their respective orbits at his *command.* He therefore desires him, in the name and by the authority of his Creator, to suspend his *mandate* with respect to the earth's motion, and that of its satellite, the moon. Had he said, *Earth, stand thou still,* the cessation of whose diurnal motion was the *effect* of his command, it could not have obeyed him; as it is not even the *secondary* cause either of its annual motion round the sun, or its diurnal motion round its own axis. Instead of doing so, he speaks to the sun, the *cause* (under God) of all these motions, as his great archetype did when, in the storm on the sea of Tiberias, he rebuked the *wind* first, and then said to the *waves,* Peace! be still! Σιωπα, πεφιμωσο· Be SILENT! be DUMB! Mark iv. 39; and the effect of this command was a cessation of the agitation in the *sea,* because the *wind* ceased to *command* it, that is, to exert its influence upon the waters.

The terms in this command are worthy of particular note: Joshua does not say to the sun, *Stand still,* as if he had conceived *him* to be *running his race round the earth;* but, *Be silent* or *inactive,* that is, as I understand it, *Restrain thy influence*—no longer act upon the earth, to cause it to revolve round its axis; a mode of speech which is certainly consistent with the strictest astronomical knowledge; and the writer of the account, whether Joshua himself or the author of the book of *Jasher,* in relating the consequence of this command is equally accurate, using a word widely different when he speaks of the *effect* the retention of the solar influence had on the moon: in the *first* case the sun was *silent* or *inactive,* דום *dom;* in the *latter,* the moon *stood still,* עמד *amad.* The *standing still* of the moon, or its continuance above the horizon, would be the natural effect of the cessation of the solar influence, which obliged the earth to discontinue her diurnal rotation, which of course would arrest the moon; and thus both it and the sun were kept above the horizon, probably for the space of a whole day. As to the address to the *moon,* it is not conceived in the same terms as that to the *sun,* and for the most obvious philosophical reasons; all that is said is simply, *and the moon on the vale of Ajalon,* which may be thus understood: "Let the sun restrain his influence or be inactive, as he appears now upon Gibeon, *that* the moon may continue as she appears now over the vale of Ajalon." It is worthy of remark that every word in this poetic address is apparently selected with the greatest caution and precision.

A. M. 2554
B. C. 1450
An. Exod. Isr.
41
Anno ante
I. Olymp. 674

20 And it came to pass, when Joshua and the children of Israel had made an end of slaying them with a very great slaughter,

till they were consumed, that the rest *which* remained of them entered into fenced cities.

21 And all the people returned

A. M. 2554
B. C. 1450
An. Exod. Isr.
41
Anno ante
I. Olymp. 674

Persons who are no friends to Divine revelation say "that the account given of this miracle supposes the *earth* to be in the *centre* of the system, and the sun moveable; and as this is demonstrably a false philosophy, consequently the history was never dictated by the Spirit of truth." Others, in answer, say "that the Holy Spirit condescends to accommodate himself to the apprehensions of the vulgar. The Israelites would naturally have imagined that Joshua was deranged had he bid the *earth stand still*, which they grant would have been the most accurate and philosophical mode of command on this occasion." But with due deference both to the *objectors* and *defenders* I must assert, that such a form of speech on such an occasion would have been utterly *unphilosophic;* and that the expressions found in the Hebrew text are such as Sir Isaac Newton himself might have denominated, every thing considered, elegant, correct, and sublime. Nor does it at all appear that the *prejudices of the vulgar* were consulted on this occasion; nor is there a word here, when properly understood, that is inconsistent with the purest axiom of the soundest philosophy, and certainly nothing that implies any *contradiction.* I grant that when the *people* have to do with *astronomical* and *philosophical* matters, then the terms of the science may be accommodated to their *apprehensions;* it is on this ground that Sir Isaac Newton himself speaks of the *rising* and of the *setting of the sun,* though all genuine philosophers know that these *appearances* are produced by the rotation of the *earth* on its own axis from west to east. But when matters of this kind are to be transacted between *God* and his *prophets,* as in the above case, then subjects relative to philosophy are conceived in their proper terms, and expressed according to their own nature. At the conclusion of the 13th verse a different expression is used when it is said, *So the sun stood still,* it is not דום *dom,* but עמד *amad;* ויעמד השמש *vaiyaamod hashshemesh,* which expression, thus varying from *that* in the command of Joshua, may be considered as implying that in order to *restrain his influence* which I have assumed to be the *cause* of the earth's motion, the sun himself became *inactive,* that is, ceased to revolve round his own axis, which revolution is probably one cause, not only of the revolution of the earth, but of all the other planetary bodies in our system, and might have affected all the planets at the time in question; but this neither could nor did produce any disorder in nature; and the delay of a few hours in the whole planetary motions dwindles away into an imperceptible point in the thousands of years of their revolutions. But the whole effect mentioned here might have been produced by the *cessation* of the *diurnal motion of the earth,* the *annual* being still continued; and I contend that this was possible to Omnipotence, and that such a cessation might have taken place without occasioning the slightest disturbance in the motions of any others of the planetary system. It is vain to cry out and say, "Such a cessation of motion in one planet

could not take place without disordering the motions of all the rest;" this I deny, and those who assert it neither know the *Scripture* nor the *power of God;* therefore they do greatly err. That the day was preternaturally lengthened, is a Scripture fact. That it was so by a *miracle,* is asserted; and whether that miracle was wrought *as above stated,* is a matter of little consequence; the thing is a Scripture fact, whether we know the *modus operandi* or not. I need scarcely add that the *command of Joshua to the sun* is to be understood as a *prayer to God* (from whom the sun derived his being and his continuance) that the effect might be what is expressed in the command: and therefore it is said, ver. 14, that the LORD HEARKENED UNTO THE VOICE OF A MAN, *for the Lord fought for Israel.*

I have thus gone through the different parts of this astonishing miracle, and have endeavoured to account for the whole in as plain and simple a manner as possible. It is not pretended that this account *should* satisfy every reader, and that every difficulty is solved; it would be impossible to do this in such a compass as that by which I am necessarily circumscribed; and I have been obliged, for the sake of brevity, to throw into the form of *propositions* or observations, several points which may appear to demand illustration and proof; for such I must refer the reader to Astronomical Treatises. Calmet, Scheuchzer, and Saurin, with several of our own countrymen, have spoken largely on this difficult subject, but in such a way as, I am obliged to confess, has given me little satisfaction, and which appears to me to leave the main difficulties unremoved. Conscious of the difficulties of this subject, I beg leave to address every candid reader in the often quoted words of an eminent author:—

Vive, Vale! si quid novisti rectius istis,
Candidus imperti; si non, his utere mecum.
　　　　HOR. Epist. l. i., E. vi., ver. 68.

Farewell! and if a better *system's* thine,
Impart it *frankly* or make use of *mine.*
　　　　　　　　FRANCIS.

Book of Jasher] The book of the upright. See the note on Num. xxi. 14. Probably this was a book which, in reference to Joshua and his transactions, was similar to the commentaries of Cæsar, on his wars with the Gauls. Critics and commentators are greatly divided in their sentiments relative to the nature of this book. The opinion above appears to me the most probable.

Verse 14. *And there was no day like that*] There was no period of time in which the sun was kept so long above the horizon as on that occasion. Some learned men have supposed that the *Fable of Phaeton* was founded on this historic fact. The fable may be seen with all the elegance of poetic embellishment in the commencement of the second book of Ovid's Metamorphoses; but I confess I can see nothing in the pretended copy that can justify the above opinion.

A. M. 2554
B. C. 1450
An. Exod. Isr.
41
Anno ante
I. Olymp. 674

to the camp to Joshua at Makkedah in peace: ᵇnone moved his tongue against any of the children of Israel.

22 Then said Joshua, Open the mouth of the cave, and bring out those five kings unto me out of the cave.

23 And they did so, and brought forth those five kings unto him out of the cave, the king of Jerusalem, the king of Hebron, the king of Jarmuth, the king of Lachish, *and* the king of Eglon.

24 And it came to pass, when they brought out those kings unto Joshua, that Joshua called for all the men of Israel, and said unto the captains of the men of war which went with him, Come near, ᶜput your feet upon the necks of these kings. And they came near, and put their feet upon the necks of them.

25 And Joshua said unto them, ᵈFear not,

nor be dismayed, be strong, and of good courage: for ᵉthus shall the LORD do to all your enemies against whom ye fight.

A. M. 2554
B. C. 1450
An. Exod. Isr.
41
Anno ante
I. Olymp. 674

26 And afterward Joshua smote them, and slew them, and hanged them on five trees: and they ᶠwere hanging upon the trees until the evening.

27 And it came to pass at the time of the going down of the sun, *that* Joshua commanded, and they ᵍtook them down off the trees, and cast them into the cave wherein they had been hid, and laid great stones in the cave's mouth, *which remain* until this very day.

28 And that day Joshua took Makkedah, and smote it with the edge of the sword, and the king thereof he utterly destroyed, them, and all the souls that *were* therein; he let none remain: and he did to the king of Makkedah ʰas he did unto the king of Jericho.

29 Then Joshua passed from Makkedah,

ᵇExod. xi. 7——ᶜPsa. cvii. 40; cx. 5; cxlix. 8, 9; Isa. xxvi. 5, 6; Mal. iv. 3——ᵈDeut. xxxi. 6, 8; chap. i. 9

ᵉDeut. iii. 21; vii. 19——ᶠChap. viii. 29——ᵍDeut. xxi. 23; chap. viii. 29——ʰChap. vi. 21

Verse 15. *And Joshua returned—unto the camp to Gilgal.*] That the Israelitish army did not return to the camp at Gilgal till *after* the hanging of the five kings and the destruction of their cities, is sufficiently evident from the subsequent parts of this chapter. When all this business was done, and not before, they returned unto the camp to Gilgal; see ver. 43. This verse is omitted by the *Septuagint* and by the *Anglo-Saxon;* and it does not appear to have existed in the ancient *hexaplar* versions; it stands in its proper place in ver. 43, and is not only useless where it is, but appears to be an encumbrance to the narrative. Should it be considered as genuine and in its proper place, I would propose that מקדה *makkedah* should be read instead of נלגלה *gilgalah*, for we find from ver. 21 that Joshua had a temporary camp there. *Then Joshua returned, and all Israel with him, unto the camp to* MAKKEDAH; after which we may suppose that Joshua having secured the cave, sent some detachments to scour the country and cut off all the remaining straggling Canaanites; when this was done *they* also returned to the camp at Makkedah, as is related ver. 21, and when the business was completed they struck the camp at Makkedah, and all returned to their fortified camp at Gilgal, ver. 43.

Verse 16. *Hid themselves in a cave*] It is very likely that this cave was a fortified place among some rocks; for there were many such places in different parts of Palestine.

Verse 21. *None moved his tongue*] The whole transaction of this important day had been carried on so evidently under the direction of God that there was not the least murmuring, nor cause for it, among them, for their enemies were all discomfited. There is an expression similar to this, Exod. xi. 7, on which the reader is requested to consult the note.

Verse 24. *Put your feet upon the necks of these kings.*] This act was done *symbolically*, as a token, not only of the present complete victory, but of their approaching triumph over all their adversaries, which is the interpretation given of it by Joshua in the succeeding verse.

Verse 26. *Smote—slew—and hanged them on five trees*] Hanging *alive* seems a barbarous custom: among the Hebrews, criminals were first deprived of life; this was the debt required by *justice:* then they were hanged up, perhaps generally by the *hands*, not by the *neck;* this was done by way of *example*, to deter others from committing the crimes for which those had suffered: but they were never permitted to hang thus exposed *all night*, as this could have answered no purpose, either of *justice* or *example*, as they could not be seen in the night-season. *One day* also was deemed enough for their exposure, it being thought sufficient to show the public that justice had been executed; and to have exhibited them *longer* would have appeared to be a barbarous cruelty which attempted to extend punishment beyond the possible requisitions of justice. See the note on Deut. xxi. 23.

Verse 28. *That day Joshua took Makkedah*] It is very possible that Makkedah was taken on the evening of the same day in which the miraculous *solstice* took place; but as to the other cities mentioned in this chapter, they certainly were subdued some days after, as it is not possible that an army, exhausted as this must have been with a whole night's march, and two days' hard fighting, could have proceeded farther than Makkedah that night; the other cities were successively taken in the following days.

Verse 29. *Fought against Libnah*] This city was near Makkedah, see chap. xv. 42, and fell to the tribe of Judah, ver. 20, 42, and was given to the priests, chap. xxi. 13. Sennacherib be-

A. M. 2554
B. C. 1450
An. Exod. Isr.
41
Anno ante
I. Olymp. 674

and all Israel with him, unto Libnah, and fought against Libnah: 30 And the LORD delivered it also, and the king thereof, into the hand of Israel: and he smote it with the edge of the sword, and all the souls that *were* therein; he let none remain in it; but did unto the king thereof as he did unto the king of Jericho.

31 And Joshua passed from [l]Libnah, and all Israel with him, unto Lachish, and encamped against it, and fought against it:

32 And the LORD delivered Lachish into the hand of Israel, which took it on the second day, and smote it with the edge of the sword, and all the souls that *were* therein, according to all that he had done to Libnah.

33 Then Horam king of Gezer came up to help Lachish; and Joshua smote him and his people, until he had left him none remaining.

34 And from Lachish Joshua passed unto Eglon, and all Israel with him: and they encamped against it, and fought against it:

35 And they took it on that day, and smote it with the edge of the sword, and all the souls that *were* therein he utterly destroyed that day, according to all that he had done to Lachish.

A. M. 2554
B. C. 1450
An. Exod. Isr.
41
Anno ante
I. Olymp. 674

36 And Joshua went up from Eglon, and all Israel with him, unto [k]Hebron; and they fought against it:

37 And they took it, and smote it with the edge of the sword, and the king thereof, and all the cities thereof, and all the souls that *were* therein: he left none remaining, according to all that he had done to Eglon; but destroyed it utterly, and all the souls that *were* therein.

38 And Joshua returned, and all Israel with him, to [l]Debir; and fought against it:

39 And he took it, and the king thereof, and all the cities thereof: and they smote them with the edge of the sword, and utterly destroyed all the souls that *were* therein; he left none remaining: as he had done to He-

---

[l]2 Kings viii. 22——[k]See chap. xiv. 13; xv. 13; Judg. i. 10

sieged it, after he had been obliged to raise the siege of Lachish. See 2 Kings xix. 8; Isa. xxxvii. 8.

Verse 32. *Lachish*] It appears that this was anciently a very strong place; notwithstanding the people were panic-struck, and the Israelites flushed with success, yet Joshua could not reduce it till the second day, and the king of Assyria afterwards was obliged to *raise the siege.* See above, and see the note on ver. 3.

Verse 33. *Horam king of Gezer*] It is likely that *Horam* was in a state of alliance with the king of *Lachish*, and therefore came to his assistance as soon as it appeared that he was likely to be attacked. Joshua probably sent a detachment against him, before he was able to form a junction with the forces of *Lachish;* and utterly destroyed him and his army.

Gezer is supposed to have been situated near Azotus. See 1 Mac. xvi. 34. It fell to the tribe of Ephraim, chap. xvi. 3, but was probably taken afterwards by some of the remnant of the Canaanitish nations; for we find it was given by Pharaoh to his son-in-law Solomon, 1 Kings ix. 16, which proves that it had got out of the possession of the Israelites previously to the days of Solomon.

Verse 34. *Eglon*] It is likely that this town was not any great distance from Lachish. See on ver. 3.

Verses 36 and 37. *Hebron—and the king thereof*] See the note on ver. 3. From ver. 23 we learn that the king of Hebron was one of those *five* whom Joshua slew and hanged on five trees at Makkedah. How then can it be said that he *slew the king of Hebron* when he took the city, which was some days after the

---

[l]See chap. xv. 15; Judg. i. 11

transactions at Makkedah? Either this slaying of the king of Hebron must refer to what had *already* been done, or the Hebronites, finding that their king fell in battle, had set up *another* in his place; which was the king Joshua slew, after he had taken the city and its dependencies, as is related ver. 37.

It appears that the city of *Hebron* had fallen back into the hands of the Canaanites, for it was again taken from them by the tribe of Judah, Judg. i. 10. *Debir* had also fallen into their hands, for it was reconquered by *Othniel*, the son-in-law of Caleb. ib. ver. 11-13. The manner in which Calmet accounts for this is very natural: Joshua, in his rapid conquests, contented himself with taking, demolishing, and burning those cities; but did not *garrison* any of them, for fear of weakening his army. In several instances no doubt the scattered Canaanites returned, repeopled, and put those cities in a state of defence. Hence the Israelites were obliged to conquer them a second time. This is a more rational way of accounting for these things, than that which supposes that the first chapter of Judges gives the more detailed account of the transactions recorded here; for there it is expressly said, that these transactions took place *after the death of Joshua*, (see Judg. i. 1,) and consequently cannot be the same that are mentioned here.

Verse 39. *Destroyed all the souls*] ויחרימו את נפש כל *vaiyacharimu eth col nephesh*, they brought every person under an *anathema;* they either slew them, or reduced them to a state of slavery. Is it reasonable to say those were slain who were *found in arms*, of the others they made *slaves?*

A. M. 2554
B. C. 1450
An. Exod. Isr.
41
Anno ante
I. Olymp. 674

bron so he did to Debir, and to the king thereof; as he had done also to Libnah, and to her king.

40 So Joshua smote all the country of the hills, and of the south, and of the vale, and of the springs, and all their kings: he left none remaining, but utterly destroyed all that breathed, as the LORD God of Israel ᵐcommanded.

41 And Joshua smote them from Kadesh-barnea, even unto ⁿGaza, °and all the country of Goshen, even unto Gibeon.

A. M. 2554
B. C. 1450
An. Exod. Isr.
41
Anno ante
I. Olymp. 674

42 And all these kings and their land did Joshua take at one time, ᴾbecause the LORD God of Israel fought for Israel.

43 And Joshua returned, and all Israel with him, unto the camp to Gilgal.

ᵐDeut. xx. 16, 17——ⁿGen. x. 19

°Chap. xi. 16——ᴾVer. 14

Verse 40. *All the country of the hills*] See the note on Deut. i. 7.

Destroyed all that breathed] Every person found in arms who continued to resist; these were all destroyed,—those who submitted were spared: but many no doubt made their escape, and afterwards reoccupied certain parts of the land. See ver. 36, 37.

Verse 41. *And all the country of Goshen*] Calmet contends that this was the very same country in which the Hebrews dwelt before their departure from Egypt; and according to this hypothesis he has constructed his *map,* causing it to extend from the Nile, which was called the river of Egypt, along the frontiers of the land of Cush or Arabia. It however appears plain that there was a city named *Goshen* in the tribe of Judah, see chap. xv. 51; and this probably gave name to the adjacent country, which may be that referred to above.

Verse 42. *Did Joshua take at one time*] That is, he defeated all those kings, and took all their cities, in ONE *campaign;* this appears to be the rational construction of the Hebrew. But these conquests were so rapid and stupendous, that they cannot be attributed either to the generalship of Joshua, or the valour of the Israelites; and hence the author himself, disclaiming the merit of them, modestly and piously adds, *because the Lord God of Israel fought for Israel.* It was by this aid that *Joshua took all these kings and their land at one time*—in a single campaign. And when all the circumstances related in this chapter are properly weighed, we shall find that GOD *alone* could have performed these works, and that both *reason* and *piety* require that to HIM *alone* they should be attributed.

1. THE principal subjects of this important chapter have been considered so much in detail in the preceding notes, that there is little room

to add any thing to what has already been said. The principal subject is the miracle of the sun's standing still; and to assert that all difficulties have been removed by the preceding notes and observations, would be to say what the writer does not believe, and what few readers would perhaps feel disposed to credit. Yet it is hoped that the chief difficulties have been removed, and the miracle itself shown to have nothing contradictory in it. If, as is generally believed, the sun and moon were objects of the Canaanitish adoration, the miracle was graciously calculated to check this superstition, and to show the Israelites, as well as the Canaanites, the vanity of such worship, and the folly of such dependence. Even their *gods* at the *command* of a *servant* of JEHOVAH, were *obliged to contribute to the destruction of their votaries.* This method of checking superstition and destroying idolatry God adopted in the plagues which he inflicted upon the Egyptians; and by it at once showed his *justice* and his *mercy.* See the concluding observations on Exod. xii.

2. The same God who appeared so signally in behalf of his people of old is still the governor of the heavens and the earth; and, if applied to, will do every thing essentially necessary for the extension of his truth and the maintenance of his religion among men. How is it that faith is so rarely exercised in his *power* and *goodness?* We have not, because we ask not. Our experience of his goodness is contracted, because we pray little and believe less. To holy men of old the object of faith was more obscurely revealed than to us, and *they* had fewer helps to their faith; yet they believed more, and witnessed greater displays of the power and mercy of their Maker. Reader, *have faith in God,* and know that to excite, exercise, and crown this, he has given thee his *word* and his *Spirit;* and learn to know that without him thou canst do nothing.

CHAPTER XI

The kings of Hazor, Madon, Shimron, and Achshaph, with those of the mountains, plains, &c., and various chiefs of the Canaanites and Amorites, confederate against Israel, 1–3. *They pitch their tents at the waters of Merom,* 4, 5. *The Lord encourages Joshua,* 6. *He attacks and discomfits them,* 7, 8. *Houghs all their horses, and burns all their chariots,* 9. *Takes and burns several of their cities,* 10–13. *The Israelites take the spoils,* 14, 15. *An account of the country taken by Joshua,* 16–18. *The Gibeonites only make peace with Israel,* 19. *All the rest resist and are overcome,* 20. *Joshua cuts off the Anakim,* 21, 22. *The conquered lands are given to Israel, and the war is concluded,* 23.

A. M. 2554
B. C. 1450
An. Exod. Isr.
41
Anno ante
I. Olymp. 674

AND it came to pass, when Jabin king of Hazor had heard *those things,* that he ᵃsent to Jobab king of Madon, and to the king ᵇof Shimron, and to the king of Achshaph,

2 And to the kings that *were* on the north of the mountains, and of the plains south of ᶜChinneroth, and in the valley, and in the borders ᵈof Dor on the west,

---

ᵃChap. x. 3——ᵇChap. xix. 15——ᶜNum. xxxiv. 11
ᵈChap. xvii. 11; Judg. i. 27; 1 Kings iv. 11

---

3 *And to* the Canaanite on the east and on the west, and *to* the Amorite, and the Hittite, and the Perizzite, and the Jebusite in the mountains, ᵉand *to* the Hivite under ᶠHermon ᵍin the land of Mizpeh.

A. M. 2554
B. C. 1450
An. Exod. Isr.
41
Anno ante
I. Olymp. 674

4 And they went out, they and all their hosts with them, much people, ʰeven as the sand that *is* upon the sea shore in multitude, with horses and chariots very many.

ᵉJudg. iii. 3——ᶠChap. xiii. 11——ᵍGen. xxxi. 49
ʰGen. xxii. 17; xxxii. 12; Judg. vii. 12; 1 Sam. xiii. 5

NOTES ON CHAP. XI

Verse 1. *Jabin king of Hazor*] It is probable that *Jabin* was the common name of all the kings of Hazor. That king, by whom the Israelites were kept in a state of slavery for twenty years, and who was defeated by Deborah and Barak, was called by this name; see Judg. iv. 2, 3, 23. The name signifies *wise* or *intelligent.* The *city* of *Hazor* was situated above the Lake *Semechon,* in Upper Galilee, according to Josephus, Antiq. lib. v., c. 6. It was given to the tribe of Naphtali, Josh. xix. 36, who it appears did not possess it long; for though it was burnt by Joshua, ver. 11, it is likely that the Canaanites rebuilt it, and restored the ancient government, as we find a powerful king there about one hundred and thirty years after the death of Joshua, Judg. iv. 1. It is the same that was taken by *Tiglath-pileser,* together with *Kadesh,* to which it is contiguous; see 2 Kings xv. 29. It is supposed to have given name to the *Valley* or *Plain* of *Hazor* or *Nasor,* situated between it and Kadesh, where Jonathan and Mattathias defeated the armies of *Demetrius,* and slew three thousand of their men, 1 Maccab. xi. 63-74. It was in ancient times the metropolitan city of all that district, and a number of petty kings or chieftains were subject to its king, see ver. 10; and it is likely that it was those tributary kings who were summoned to attend the king of Hazor on this occasion; for Joshua having conquered the southern part of the promised land, the northern parts seeing themselves exposed made now a common interest, and, joining with Jabin, endeavoured to put a stop to the progress of the Israelites. See *Calmet.*

Jobab king of Madon] This royal city is nowhere else mentioned in Scripture except in chap. xii. 19. The Vatican copy of the Septuagint reads Μαρων, *Maron,* which, if legitimate, Calmet thinks may mean *Maronia* or *Merath* in Phœnicia, to the north of Mount Libanus. The Hebrew text reads מרן *Meron,* chap. xii. 20, after *Shimron,* which is probably the same with מרן *Madon,* ver. 19, the word having casually dropped out of the preceding place into the latter, and the ר *resh* and ד *daleth* being interchanged, which might have easily happened from the great similarity of the letters. Hence Calmet conjectures that it may be the same place with מרן *Meroz,* Judg. v. 23, the ז *zain* and ן final *nun* being interchanged, which they might easily, as they are so very similar.

King of Shimron] This city is supposed to be the same with *Symira,* in Cœlosyria, joined

to *Maron* or *Marath,* by *Pliny* and *Pomponius Mela.* It cannot be *Samaria,* as that had its name long after by Omri king of Israel. See 1 Kings xvi. 24.

King of Achshaph] Calmet supposes this to have been the city of *Ecdippe,* mentioned by *Pliny, Ptolemy, Josephus,* and *Eusebius.* The latter places it within ten miles of *Ptolemais,* on the road to Tyre. It fell to the tribe of Asher. See chap. xix. 25.

Verse 2. *On the north of the mountains*] Or *the mountain,* probably *Hermon,* or some mountain not far from the lake of Gennesareth.

And of the plains] That is, the valleys of the above mountains, which had the sea of Chinneroth or Gennesareth on the south.

Chinneroth] This city is supposed by St. Jerome and several others since his time, to be the same as was afterwards called *Tiberias.* From this city or village the *sea of Chinneroth* or *Gennesareth* probably had its name.

And in the borders of Dor] Calmet supposes this to mean the champaign country of the higher and lower Galilee, on to the Mediterranean Sea, and to the village or city of *Dor,* which was the farthermost city of Phœnicia. *Dor* was in the lot of the half tribe of Manasseh, and was situated on the Mediterranean Sea, three leagues from Cæsarea, and seven from Ptolemais.

Verse 3. *The Canaanite on the east, &c.*] Those who dwelt on the borders of Jordan, south of the sea of Tiberias.

On the west] Those were the Phœnicians who dwelt on the coast of the Mediterranean Sea, from *Dor* northwards, on the way to Mount Libanus.—*Calmet.*

The Hivite under Hermon] Mount Hermon was to the east of Libanus and the fountains of Jordan; it is the same with *Syrion* and *Baal Hermon* in Scripture.

The land of Mizpeh.] There were several cities of this name: *one* in the tribe of *Judah,* (chap. xv. 38;) a *second* in the tribe of *Benjamin,* (chap. xviii. 26;) a *third* beyond Jordan, in the tribe of *Gad;* and a *fourth* beyond Jordan, in the tribe of *Manasseh,* which is that mentioned in the text. See *Wells's* Geography. Calmet supposes this Mizpeh to be the place where Laban and Jacob made their covenant, and from which circumstance it took its name. See Gen. xxxi. 48, 49.

Verse 4. *Much people, even as the sand*] This form of speech, by some called a *hyperbole,* conveys simply the idea of a vast or unusual number—a number of which no regular esti-

A. M. 2554
B. C. 1450
An. Exod. Isr.
41
Anno ante
I. Olymp. 674

5 And when all these kings were [l]met together, they came and pitched together at the waters of Merom, to fight against Israel.

6 And the LORD said unto Joshua, [k]Be not afraid because of them: for to-morrow about this time will I deliver them up all slain before Israel: thou shalt [l]hough their horses, and burn their chariots with fire.

7 So Joshua came, and all the people of war with him, against them by the waters of Merom suddenly; and they fell upon them.

8 And the LORD delivered them into the hand of Israel, who smote them, and chased them unto [m]great Zidon, and unto [n] [o]Misre-photh-maim, [p]and unto the valley of Mizpeh, eastward; and they smote them, until they left them none remaining.

9 And Joshua did unto them [q]as the LORD bade him: he houghed their horses, and burnt their chariots with fire.

10 And Joshua at that time turned back, and took Hazor, and smote the king thereof with the sword: for Hazor beforetime was the head of all those kingdoms.

11 And they smote all the souls that *were* therein with the edge of the sword, utterly destroying *them*: there was not [r]any left to breathe: and he burnt Hazor with fire.

A. M. 2554
B. C. 1450
An. Exod. Isr.
41
Anno ante
I. Olymp. 674

---

[l]Heb. *assembled by appointment*——[k]Chap. x. 8
[l]2 Sam. viii. 4——[m]Or, *Zidon-rabbah*

[n]Chap. xiii. 6——[o]Or, *salt pits*——[p]Heb. *burnings*
[q]Ver. 6——[r]Heb. *any breath*

---

mate could be easily formed. Josephus, who seldom finds difficulties in such cases, and makes no scruple of often speaking *without book*, tells us that the allied armies amounted to 300,000 *foot*, 10,000 *horse*, and 20,000 *chariots* of war.— Antiq. lib. v., c. 1.

That *chariots* were frequently used in war, all the records of antiquity prove; but it is generally supposed that among the Canaanites they were armed with iron scythes fastened to their *poles* and to the *naves* of their wheels. Terrible things are spoken of these, and the havoc made by them when furiously driven among the ranks of infantry. Of what sort the cavalry was, we know not; but from the account here given we may see what great advantages these allies possessed over the Israelites, whose armies consisted of *infantry* only.

Verse 5. *The waters of Merom*] Where these waters were, interpreters are not agreed. Whether they were the waters of the Lake *Semechon*, or the *waters of Megiddo*, mentioned Judg. v. 19, cannot be easily determined. The latter is the more probable opinion.

Verse 6. *Be not afraid—of them*] To meet such a formidable host so well equipped, in their own country, furnished with all that was necessary to supply a numerous army, required more than ordinary encouragement in Joshua's circumstances. This communication from God was highly necessary, in order to prevent the people from desponding on the eve of a conflict, in which their *all* was at stake.

Verse 7. *By the waters of Merom suddenly*] Joshua, being apprized of this grand confederation, lost no time, but marched to meet them; and before they could have supposed him at hand, fell suddenly upon them, and put them to the rout.

Verse 8. *Great Zidon*] If this were the same with the *Sidon* of the ancients, it was illustrious long before the Trojan war; and both it and its inhabitants are frequently mentioned by Homer as excelling in works of *skill* and *utility*, and abounding in *wealth*:—

Ενθ' εσαν οι πεπλοι παμποικιλοι, εογα γυναικων
Σιδονιων.   Iliad, lib. vi., ver. 289.

"There lay the vestures of no *vulgar* art,
SIDONIAN maids *embroidered* every part."
     POPE.

Αργυρεον κρητηρα τετυγμενον· εξ δ' αρα μετρα
Χανδανεν, αυταρ καλλει ενικα πασαν επ' αιαν
Πολλον, επι Σιδονες πολυδαιδαλοι ευ ησκησαν.
     Iliad, lib. xxiii., ver. 741.

"A *silver urn* that full six measures held,
By none in weight or *workmanship* excell'd;
SIDONIAN artists taught the *frame* to shine,
Elaborate with *artifice* divine."   POPE.

Εκ μεν Σιδωνος πολυχαλκου ευχομαι εναι.
     Odyss. xv. 424.

"I am of SIDON, famous for her *wealth*."

The art of making *glass* is attributed by Pliny to this city: SIDON *artifex vitri*, Hist. Nat. l. v., c. 19.

Misrephoth-maim] Or, Misrephoth of *the waters*. What this place was is unknown, but Calmet conjectures it to be the same with *Sarepta*, a city of Phœnicia, contiguous to Sidon. The word signifies the *burning of the waters*, or *inflammation;* probably it was a place noted for its *hot springs:* this idea seems to have struck Luther, as he translates it, die warme wasser, *the hot waters*.

Verse 9. *He houghed their horses*] The Hebrew word עקר *akar*, which we render to *hough* or *hamstring*, signifies to *wound, cut,* or *lop off*. It is very likely that it means here, not only an act by which they were rendered useless, but by which they were *destroyed;* as God had purposed that his people should not possess any cattle of this kind, that a warlike and enterprising spirit might not be cultivated among them; and that, when obliged to defend themselves and their country, they might be led to depend upon God for protection and victory. On the same ground, God had forbidden the kings of Israel *to multiply horses*, Deut. xvii. 16. See the note there containing the reasons on which this prohibition was founded.

Burnt their chariots] As these could have been of no use without the horses.

Verse 10. *Took Hazor*] See on ver. 1.

55

A. M. 2554–60
B. C. 1450–44
An. Exod. Isr. 41–47
Anno ante I.Olymp.674–68

12 And all the cities of those kings, and all the kings of them, did Joshua take, and smote them with the edge of the sword, *and* he utterly destroyed them, [s]as Moses the servant of the LORD commanded.

13 But *as for* the cities that stood still [t]in their strength, Israel burned none of them, save Hazor only; *that* did Joshua burn.

14 And all the spoil of these cities, and the cattle, the children of Israel took for a prey unto themselves; but every man they smote with the edge of the sword, until they had destroyed them, neither left they any to breathe.

15 [u]As the LORD commanded Moses his servant, so [v]did Moses command Joshua, and [w]so did Joshua; [x]he left nothing undone of all that the LORD commanded Moses.

A. M. 2554–60
B. C. 1450–44
An. Exod. Isr. 41–47
Anno ante I.Olymp.674–68

16 So Joshua took all that land, [y]the hills, and all the south country, [z]and all the land of Goshen, and the valley, and the plain, and the mountain of Israel, and the valley of the same;

17 [a]*Even* from [b]the mount Halak, that goeth up to Seir, even unto Baal-gad in the valley of Lebanon under Mount Hermon: and [c]all their kings he took, and smote them, and slew them.

18 [d]Joshua made war a long time with all those kings.

---

[s]Num. xxxiii. 52; Deut. vii. 2; xx. 16, 17——[t]Heb. *on their heap*——[u]Exod. xxxiv. 11, 12——[v]Deuteronomy vii. 2——[w]Chap. i. 7

[x]Heb. *he removed nothing*——[y]Chap. xii. 8——[z]Chap. x. 41——[a]Chap. xii. 7——[b]Or, *the smooth mountain*——[c]Deut. vii. 24; chap. xii. 7——[d]Till 1445; ver. 23

Verse 13. *The cities that stood still in their strength*] The word תִּלָּם *tillam,* which we translate *their strength,* and the margin, *their heap,* has been understood two ways. 1. As signifying those cities which had made peace with the Israelites, when conditions of peace were offered according to the command of the law; and consequently were not destroyed. Such as the cities of the *Hivites;* see ver. 19. 2. The cities which were situated upon *hills* and *mountains,* which, when taken, might be retained with little difficulty. In this sense the place is understood by the Vulgate, as pointing out the cities *quæ erant in collibus et tumulis sitæ,* "which were situated on hills and eminences." As the cities of the *plain* might be easily attacked and carried, Joshua destroyed them; but as those on *mountains, hills,* or other *eminences,* might be retained with little trouble, prudence would dictate their preservation, as places of refuge in any insurrection of the people, or invasion of their adversaries. The passage in Jeremiah, chap. xxx. 18, *Jerusalem shall be builded on her own heap,* תִּלָּהּ *tillah,* if understood as above, conveys an easy and clear sense: Jerusalem shall be re-established on her OWN HILL.

Verse 14. *All the spoil of these cities—Israel took*] With the exception of those things which had been employed for idolatrous purposes; see Deut. vii. 25.

Verse 16. *The mountain of Israel, and the valley of the same*] This place has given considerable trouble to commentators; and it is not easy to assign such a meaning to the place as may appear in all respects satisfactory. 1. If we consider this verse and the 21st to have been added after the times in which the kingdoms of Israel and Judah were divided, the difficulty is at once removed. 2. The difficulty will be removed if we consider that *mountain* and *valley* are put here for *mountains* and *valleys,* and that these include all mountains and valleys which were not in the lot that fell to the tribe of Judah. Or, 3. If by *mountain of Israel* we understand *Beth-el,* where God appeared to Jacob, afterwards called *Israel,* and promised

him the land of Canaan, a part of the difficulty will be removed. But the first opinion seems best founded; for there is incontestable evidence that several notes have been added to this book since the days of Joshua. See the preface.

Verse 17. *From the mount Halak*] All the mountainous country that extends from the south of the land of Canaan towards *Seir* unto *Baal-gad,* which lies at the foot of Mount Libanus or Hermon, called by some the mountains of *Separation,* which serve as a limit between the land of Canaan and that of Seir; see chap. xii. 7.

The valley of Lebanon] The whole extent of the plain which is on the south, and probably north, of Mount Libanus. Calmet conjectures that *Cœlesyria* is here meant.

Verse 18. *Joshua made war a long time*] The whole of these conquests were not effected in one campaign: they probably required *six* or *seven* years. There are some chronological notices in this book, and in Deuteronomy, by which the exact time may be nearly ascertained. Caleb was *forty* years old when he was sent from *Kadesh-barnea* by Moses to search out the land, about A. M. 2514; and at the end of this war he was *eighty-five* years old; (compare chap. xiv. 10 with Num. xiii. and Deut. i.;) consequently the war ended in 2559, which had begun, by the passage of Jordan, on the tenth day of the first month of the year 2554. From this date to the end of 2559 we find exactly six years; the *first* of which Joshua seems to have employed in the conquest of the *south* part of the land of Canaan, and the other *five* in the conquest of all the territories situated on the *north* of that country. See *Dodd.*

Calmet computes this differently, and allows the term of *seven* years for the conquest of the whole land. "Caleb was forty years old when sent from Kadesh-barnea to spy out the land. At the conclusion of the war he was eighty-five years old, as himself says, chap. xiv. 10. From this sum of eighty-five subtract forty, his age when he went from Kadesh-barnea, and the thirty-eight years which he spent in the wilderness after his return, and there will remain

A. M. 2554–60
B. C. 1450–44
An Exod. Isr.
41–47
Anno ante
I.Olymp.674-68

19 There was not a city that made peace with the children of Israel save ᵉthe Hivites, the inhabitants of Gibeon: all *other* they took in battle.

20 For ᶠit was of the LORD to harden their hearts, that they should come against Israel in battle, that he might destroy them utterly, *and* that they might have no favour, but that he might destroy them, ᵍas the LORD commanded Moses.

21 And at that time came Joshua, and cut off ʰthe Anakims from the mountains, from Hebron, from Debir, from Anab, and from all the mountains of Judah, and from all the mountains of Israel: Joshua destroyed *them* utterly with their cities.

A. M. 2554–60
B. C. 1450–44
An. Exod. Isr.
41–47
Anno ante
I.Olymp.674-68

22 There was none of the Anakims left in the land of the children of Israel: only in Gaza, in ⁱGath, ᵏand in Ashdod, there remained.

23 So Joshua took the whole land, ˡaccording to all that the LORD said unto Moses; and Joshua gave it for an inheritance unto Israel, ᵐaccording to their divisions by their tribes. ⁿAnd the land rested from war.

ᵉChapter ix. 3, 7——ᶠDeuteronomy ii. 30; Judges xiv. 4; 1 Samuel ii. 25; 1 Kings xii. 15; Romans ix. 18 ᵍDeuteronomy xx. 16, 17——ʰNumbers xiii. 22, 33; Deuteronomy i. 28; chap. xv. 13, 14

ⁱ1 Sam. xvii. 4——ᵏChap. xv. 46——ˡNum. xxxiv. 2, &c.——ᵐNum. xxvi. 53; chap. xiv., xv., xvi., xvii., xviii., and xix.——ⁿChap. xiv. 15; xxi. 44; xxii. 4; xxiii. 1; ver. 18

---

the sum of *seven* years, which was the time spent in the conquest of the land."

1. By protracting the war the Canaanites had time to repent, having sufficient opportunity to discern the hand of Jehovah. 2. Agriculture was carried on, and thus provision was made even for the support of the conquerors; for had the land been subdued and wasted at once, tillage must have stopped, and famine would have ensued. 3. Wild beasts would have multiplied upon them, and the land have been desolated by their means. 4. Had these conquests been more rapid the people of Israel would have been less affected, and less instructed by miracles that had passed in such quick succession before their eyes; and, as in this case they would have obtained the dominion with comparatively little exertion, they might have felt themselves less interested in the preservation of an inheritance, to obtain which they had been but at little trouble and little expense. What we *labour* under the Divine blessing to acquire we are careful to retain; but what *comes lightly* generally *goes lightly*. God obliged them to put forth their own strength in this work, and only blessed and prospered them while they were workers together with him. See the note on chap. xiii. 6.

Verse 20. *It was of the Lord to harden their hearts*] They had sinned against all the light they had received, and God left them justly to the hardness, obstinacy, and pride of their own hearts; for as they chose to retain their idolatry, God was determined that they should be cut off. For as no city made peace with the Israelites but Gibeon and some others of the Hivites, ver. 19, it became therefore necessary to destroy them; for their refusal to make peace was the proof that they wilfully persisted in their idolatry.

Verse 21. *Cut off the Anakims—from Hebron, from Debir*] This is evidently a recapitulation of the military operations detailed chap. x. 36-41.

Destroyed—their cities] That is, those of the Anakims; for from ver. 13 we learn that Joshua preserved certain other cities.

Verse 22. *In Gaza, in Gath, and in Ashdod*] The whole race of the Anakims was extirpated

in this war, except those who had taken refuge in the above cities, which belonged to the Philistines; and in which some of the descendants of Anak were found even in the days of David.

Verse 23. *So Joshua took the whole land*] All the country described here and in the preceding chapter. Besides the multitudes that perished in this war, many of the Canaanites took refuge in the confines of the land, and in the neighbouring nations. Some suppose that a party of these fugitive Canaanites made themselves masters of *Lower Egypt*, and founded a dynasty there known by the name of the *shepherd kings;* but it is more probable that the *shepherds* occupied Egypt long before the time that Jacob went thither to sojourn. It is said they founded *Tingris* or *Tangier*, where, according to Procopius, they erected two white pillars with an inscription in the Phœnician language, of which this is the translation: WE ARE THE PERSONS WHO HAVE FLED FROM THE FACE OF JOSHUA THE PLUNDERER, THE SON OF NAVE or *Nun*. See *Bochart*, Phaleg and Canaan, lib. i., c. xxiv., col. 476. Many, no doubt, settled in different parts of Africa, in Asia Minor, in Greece, and in the different islands of the Ægean and Mediterranean Sea: it is supposed also that colonies of this people were spread over different parts of Germany and Sclavonia, &c., but their descendants are now so confounded with the nations of the earth, as no longer to retain their original names, or to be discernible.

And Joshua gave it for an inheritance unto Israel] He claimed no peculiar jurisdiction over it; his own family had no peculiar share of it, and himself only the ruined city of *Timnath-serah*, in the tribe of Ephraim, which he was obliged to rebuild. See chap. xix. 49, 50, and see his character at the end of this book.

And the land rested from war.] The whole territory being now conquered, which God designed the Israelites should possess at *this time*.

ACCORDING to the apostle, Heb. iv. 8, &c., *Joshua* himself was a *type of Christ;* the *promised land.* of the *kingdom of heaven;* the *victories* which he gained, of the *victory* and triumph of Christ; and the *rest* he procured for Israel, of the *state of blessedness,* at the right hand of God. In this light we should view the whole history, in order to derive those advantages from it which, as a portion of the revelation of God, it was intended to convey. Those who finally reign with Christ are they who, through his grace, *conquer* the *world,* the *devil,* and the *flesh;* for it is only of those who thus *overcome* that he says, "They shall sit with me on my throne, as I have overcome, and am set down with the Father on the Father's throne;" Rev. iii. 21. Reader, art *thou* a conqueror?

CHAPTER XII

A list of the kings on the east of Jordan, which were conquered by MOSES, with their territories, 1–6. *A list of those on the west side of Jordan, conquered by JOSHUA, in number thirty-one,* 7–24.

A. M. 2554–60
B. C. 1450–44
An. Exod. Isr.
41–47
Anno ante
I.Olymp.674-68

NOW these *are* the kings of the land, which the children of Israel smote, and possessed their land on the other side Jordan toward the rising of the sun, [a]from the river Arnon [b]unto Mount Hermon, and all the plain on the east:

2 [c]Sihon king of the Amorites, who dwelt in Heshbon, *and* ruled from Aroer, which *is* upon the bank of the river Arnon, and from the middle of the river, and from half Gilead, even unto the river Jabbok, *which is* the border of the children of Ammon;

3 And [d]from the plain to the sea of Chinneroth on the east, and unto the sea of the plain, *even* the Salt Sea on the east, [e]the way

to Beth-jeshimoth; and from [f]the south, under [g]Ashdoth-pisgah:[h]

A. M. 2554–60
B. C. 1450–44
An. Exod. Isr.
41–47
Anno ante
I.Olymp.674-68

4 And [i]the coast of Og king of Bashan, *which was* of [k]the remnant of the giants, [l]that dwelt at Ashtaroth and at Edrei,

5 And reigned in [m]Mount Hermon, [n]and in Salcah, and in all Bashan, [o]unto the border of the Geshurites, and the Maachathites, and half Gilead, the border of Sihon king of Heshbon.

6 [p]Them did Moses the servant of the LORD and the children of Israel smite: and [q]Moses the servant of the LORD gave it *for* a possession unto the Reubenites, and the Gadites, and the half tribe of Manasseh.

---

[a]Num. xxi. 24——[b]Deut. iii. 8, 9——[c]Num. xxi. 24; Deut. ii. 33, 36; iii. 6, 16——[d]Deut. iii. 17——[e]Chap. xiii. 20——[f]Or, *Teman*——[g]Or, *the springs of Pisgah,* or *the hill*——[h]Deut. iii. 17; iv. 49

[i]Num. xxi. 35; Deut. iii. 4, 10——[k]Deut. iii. 11; chap. xiii. 12——[l]Deut. i. 4——[m]Deut. iii. 8——[n]Deut. iii. 10; chap. xiii. 11——[o]Deut. iii. 14——[p]Num. xxi. 24, 33——[q]Num. xxxii. 29, 33; Deut. iii. 11, 12; chap. xiii. 8

NOTES ON CHAP. XII

Verse 1. *From the river Arnon unto Mount Hermon*] Arnon was the boundary of all the *southern* coast of the land *occupied* by the Israelites beyond Jordan; and the mountains of Hermon were the boundaries on the *north.* Arnon takes its rise in the mountains of Gilead, and having run a long way from north to south falls into the Dead Sea, near the same place into which Jordan discharges itself.

And all the plain on the east] All the land from the plains of Moab to Mount Hermon.

Verse 2. *From Aroer*] Aroer was situated on the western side of the river Arnon, in the middle of the valley through which this river takes its course. The kingdom of Sihon extended from the river Arnon and the city of Aroer on the *south* to the river Jabbok on the *north.*

And from half Gilead] The mountains of Gilead extended from north to south from Mount Hermon towards the source of the river Arnon, which was about the *midst* of the extent of the kingdom of Sihon: thus Sihon is said to have possessed the *half of Gilead,* that is, the half of the mountains and of the country which bore the name of Gilead on the east of his territories.

River Jabbok] This river has its source in the *mountains of Gilead*; and, running from

east to west, falls into Jordan. It bounds the territories of Sihon on the north, and those of the Ammonites on the south.

Verse 3. *The sea of Chinneroth*] Or *Gennesareth,* the same as the lake or sea of *Tiberias.*

The Salt Sea on the east] מלח ים *yam hammelach,* which is here translated *the Salt Sea,* is understood by others to mean *the sea of the city Melach.* Where can we find any thing that can be called a *salt* sea on the east of the lake of Gennesareth? Some think that the lake Asphaltites, called also the *Dead Sea, Sea of the Desert, Sea of Sodom,* and *Salt Sea,* is here intended.

Beth-jeshimoth] A city near the Dead Sea in the plains of Moab.

Ashdoth-pisgah] Supposed to be a city at the foot of Mount Pisgah.

Verse 4. *Coast of Og king of Bashan*] Concerning this person see the notes on Deut. iii. 11, and on Num. xxi. 35, &c.

The remnant of the giants] Or, *Rephaim.* See the notes on Gen. vi. 4, xiv. 5, and Deut. ii. 7, 11.

Verse 5. *The border of the Geshurites*] The country of Bashan, in the days of Moses and Joshua, extended from the river Jabbok on the south to the frontiers of the Geshurites and Maachathites on the north, to the foot of the mountains of Hermon.

A. M. 2554–60
B. C. 1450–44
An. Exod. Isr.
41–47
Anno ante
I.Olymp.674–68

7 And these *are* the kings of the country ʳwhich Joshua and the children of Israel smote on this side Jordan on the west, from Baal-gad in the valley of Lebanon, even unto the mount Halak, that goeth up to ˢSeir; which Joshua ᵗgave unto the tribes of Israel, *for* a possession according to their divisions;

8 ᵘIn the mountains, and in the valleys, and in the plains, and in the springs, and in the wilderness, and in the south country; ᵛthe Hittites, the Amorites, and the Canaanites, the Perizzites, the Hivites, and the Jebusites:

9 ʷThe king of Jericho, one; ˣthe king of Ai, which *is* beside Beth-el, one;

10 ʸThe king of Jerusalem, one; the king of Hebron, one;

11 The king of Jarmuth, one; the king of Lachish, one;

12 The king of Eglon, one; ᶻthe king of Gezer, one;

13 ᵃThe king of Debir, one; the king of Geder, one;

14 The king of Hormah, one; the king of Arad, one;

15 ᵇThe king of Libnah, one; the king of Adullam, one;

16 ᶜThe king of Makkedah, one; ᵈthe king of Beth-el, one;

17 The king of Tappuah, one; ᵉthe king of Hepher, one;

18 The king of Aphek, one; the king of ᶠLasharon, one;

19 The king of Madon, one; ᵍthe king of Hazor, one;

20 The king of ʰShimron-meron, one; the king of Achshaph, one;

21 The king of Taanach, one; the king of Megiddo, one;

22 ⁱThe king of Kedesh, one; the king of Jokneam of Carmel, one;

23 The king of Dor in the ᵏcoast of Dor, one; the king of ˡthe nations of Gilgal, one;

24 The king of Tirzah, one: all the kings thirty and one.

A. M. 2554–60
B. C. 1450–44
An. Exod. Isr.
41–47
Anno ante
I.Olymp.674–68

ʳChap. xi. 17——ˢGen. xiv. 6; xxxii. 3; Deut. ii. 1, 4 ᵗChap. xi. 23——ᵘChap. x. 40; xi. 16——ᵛExod. iii. 8; xxiii. 23; chap. ix. 1——ʷChap. vi. 2——ˣChap. viii. 29 ʸChap. x. 23——ᶻChap. x. 33——ᵃChap. x. 38

ᵇCh. x. 29——ᶜCh. x. 28——ᵈChap. viii. 17; Judg. i. 22——ᵉ1 Kings iv. 10——ᶠOr, *Sharon;* Isa. xxxiii. 9——ᵍCh. xi. 10——ʰCh. xi. 1; xix. 15——ⁱChap. xix. 37——ᵏChap. xi. 2——ˡGen. xiv. 1, 2; Isa. ix. 1

Verse 7. *From Baal-gad*] A repetition of what is mentioned chap. xi. 17.

Verse 9. *The king of Jericho, &c.*] On this and the following verses see the notes on chap. x. 1-3.

Verse 13. *The king of Geder*] Probably the same with *Gedor*, chap. xv. 58; it was situated in the tribe of Judah.

Verse 14. *The king of Hormah*] Supposed to be the place where the Israelites were defeated by the Canaanites, see Num. xiv. 45; and which probably was called Hormah, חרמה *chormah*, or *destruction*, from this circumstance.

Verse 15. *Adullam*] A city belonging to the tribe of Judah, chap. xv. 35. In a cave at this place David often secreted himself during his persecution by Saul; 1 Sam. xxii. 1.

Verse 17. *Tappuah*] There were two places of this name: one in the tribe of Judah, chap. xv. 34, and another in the tribe of Ephraim on the borders of Manasseh; but which of the two is meant here cannot be ascertained. See the note on chap. xv. 53.

Hepher] The same, according to Calmet, as *Ophrah* in the tribe of Benjamin, chap. xviii. 23.

Verse 18. *Aphek*] There were several cities of this name: one in the tribe of Asher, chap. xix. 30; another in the tribe of Judah, 1 Sam. iv. 1, and xxix. 1; and a third in Syria, 1 Kings xx. 26, and 2 Kings xiii. 17. Which of the two former is here intended cannot be ascertained.

Lasharon] There is no city of this name known. Some consider the ל *lamed* in the word לשרן *lashsharon* to be the sign of the

genitive case; and in this sense it appears to have been understood by the *Vulgate*, which translates *rex Saron*, the king of Sharon. This was rather a district than a city, and is celebrated in the Scriptures for its fertility; Isa. xxxiii. 9; xxxv. 2. Some suppose it was the same with *Saron*, near *Lydda*, mentioned Acts ix. 35.

Verse 20. *Shimron-meron*] See on chap. xi. 1.

Verse 21. *Taanach*] A city in the half tribe of Manasseh, to the west of Jordan, not far from the frontiers of Zebulun, chap. xvii. 11. This city was assigned to the Levites, chap. xxi. 25.

Verse 22. *Kedesh*] There was a city of this name in the tribe of Naphtali, chap. xix. 37. It was given to the Levites, and was one of the cities of refuge, chap. xx. 7.

Jokneam of Carmel] This city is said to have been at the foot of Mount Carmel, near the river Belus, in the tribe of Zebulun, chap. xix. 11. It was given to the Levites, chap. xxi. 34.

Verse 23. *The king of Dor*] The city of this name fell to the lot of the children of Manasseh, chap. xvii. 11. Bochart observes that it was one of the oldest royal cities in Phœnicia. The Canaanites held it, Judg. i. 27. Antiochus Sydetes besieged it in aftertimes, but could not make himself master of it. See *Bochart*, Canaan, lib. i., c. 28, and *Dodd*.

The king of the nations of Gilgal] This is supposed to mean the higher Galilee, surnamed *Galilee of the Gentiles* or, *nations*, as the Hebrew word גוים *goyim* means. On this ground it should be read *king of Galilee of the nations*. Others suppose it is the same country with that of which *Tidal* was king; see Gen. xiv. 1. The place is very uncertain, and commentators have rendered it more so by their *conjectures*.

Verse 24. *King of Tirzah*] This city appears to have been for a long time the capital of the kingdom of Israel, and the residence of its kings. See 1 Kings xiv. 17; xv. 21, 33. Its situation cannot be exactly ascertained; but it is supposed to have been situated on a mountain about three leagues south of Samaria.

All the kings thirty and one.] The Septuagint say εικοσι εννεα, *twenty-nine,* and yet set down but *twenty-eight,* as they confound or omit the kings of *Beth-el, Lasharon,* and *Madon.* So many kings in so small a territory, shows that their kingdoms must have been very small indeed. The kings of *Beth-el* and *Ai* had but about 12,000 subjects in the whole; but in ancient times *all* kings had very small territories.

Every village or town had its chief; and this chief was independent of his neighbours, and exercised *regal* power in his own district. In reading all ancient histories, as well as the Bible, this circumstance must be kept constantly in view; for we ought to consider that in those times both *kings* and *kingdoms* were but a faint resemblance of those now.

Great Britain, in ancient times, was divided into many kingdoms: in the time of the *Saxons* it was divided into *seven,* hence called the *Saxon heptarchy.* But when Julius Cæsar first entered this island, he found *four* kings in Kent alone; *Cingetorix, Carnilius, Taximagulus,* and *Segonax.* Hence we need not wonder at the numbers we read of in the land of Canaan. Ancient Gaul was thus divided; and the great number of *sovereign princes, secular bishops, landgraves, dukes,* &c., &c., in Germany, are the modern remains of those ancient divisions.

CHAPTER XIII

Joshua being old, the Lord informs him of the land yet remaining to be possessed, 1. Of the unconquered land among the Philistines, 2, 3. Among the Canaanites, Sidonians, and Amorites, 4, 5. The inhabitants of the hill country and the Sidonians to be driven out, 6. The land on the east side of Jordan, that was to be divided among the tribes of Reuben and Gad, and the half tribe of Manasseh, 7–12. The Geshurites and the Maachathites not expelled, 13. The tribe of Levi receive no inheritance, 14. The possessions of REUBEN *described, 15–23. The possessions of* GAD, *24–28. The possessions of the half tribe of* Manasseh, *29–31. Recapitulation of the subjects contained in this chapter, 32, 33.*

A. M. 2560
B. C. 1444
An. Exod. Isr.
47
Anno ante
I. Olymp. 668

NOW Joshua ªwas old *and* stricken in years; and the LORD said unto him, Thou art old *and* stricken in years, and there remaineth yet very much land ᵇto be possessed.

2 ᶜThis *is* the land that yet remaineth: ᵈall the borders of the Philistines, and all ᵉGeshuri,

3 ᶠFrom Sihor, which *is* before Egypt, even unto the borders of Ekron northward, *which* is counted to the Canaanite: ᵍfive

A. M. 2560
B. C. 1444
An. Exod. Isr.
47
Anno ante
I. Olymp. 668

ªSee chap. xiv. 10; xxiii. 1——ᵇHeb. *to possess it;* Deut. xxxi. 3——ᶜJudg. iii. 1——ᵈJoel iii. 4

ᵉVer. 13; 2 Sam. iii. 3; xiii. 37, 38——ᶠJer. ii. 18
ᵍJudg. iii. 3; 1 Sam. vi. 4, 16; Zeph. ii. 5

NOTES ON CHAP. XIII

Verse 1. *Joshua was old*] He is generally reputed to have been at this time about a *hundred* years of age: he had spent about seven years in the conquest of the land, and is supposed to have employed about one year in dividing it; and he died about *ten* years after, aged one hundred and ten years. It is very likely that he intended to subdue the whole land before he made the division of it among the tribes; but God did not think proper to have this done. So unfaithful were the Israelites that he appears to have purposed that some of the ancient inhabitants should still remain to keep them in check, and that the respective tribes should have some labour to drive out from their allotted borders the remains of the Canaanitish nations.

There remaineth yet very much land to be possessed.] That is, very much when compared with that on the other side Jordan, which was all that could as yet be said to be in the hands of the Israelites.

Verse 2. *The borders of the Philistines, and all Geshuri*] The borders of the Philistines may mean the land which they possessed on

the sea-coast, southwest of the land of Canaan. There were several places named *Geshuri,* but that spoken of here was probably the region on the south of Canaan, towards Arabia, or towards Egypt.—*Calmet.* Cellarius supposes it to have been a country in the vicinity of the Amalekites.

Verse 3. *From Sihor, which is before Egypt*] Supposed by some to be the Pelusiac branch of the Nile, near to the Arabian Desert; called also the *river of Egypt,* Num. xxxiv. 5; Jer. ii. 18. On this subject an intelligent friend favours me with the following opinion:—

"The river *Sihor* is supposed by some to be the Nile, or a branch of it. Others think it the same as what is frequently called the *river of Egypt,* which lay *before* or towards the borders of *Egypt;* which arose out of the mountains of Paran, and ran westward, falling into that bay of the Mediterranean which lies south of the land of the Philistines. This river is often mentioned as the boundary of the Israelites to the southwest, as Euphrates, the *great river,* was on the northeast.

"There was a desert of considerable distance between what is called the *river of Egypt* and the isthmus of Suez. Solomon reigned to the

A. M. 2560
B. C. 1444
An. Exod. Isr.
47
Anno ante
I. Olymp. 668

lords of the Philistines; the Gazathites, and the Ashdothites, the Eshkalonites, the Gittites, and the Ekronites; also [h]the Avites:

4 From the south, all the land of the Canaanites, and [i]Mearah that *is* beside the Sidonians, [k]unto Aphek, to the borders of [l]the Amorites:

5 And the land of [m]the Giblites, and all

Lebanon, toward the sun-rising, [n]from Baal-gad under Mount Hermon unto the entering into Hamath.

A. M. 2560
B. C. 1444
An. Exod. Isr.
47
Anno ante
I. Olymp. 668

6 All the inhabitants of the hill country from Lebanon unto [o]Misrephoth-maim, *and* all the Sidonians, them [p]will I drive out from before the children of Israel: only [q]divide thou it by lot unto the Israelites for an inheritance, as I have commanded thee.

---

[h]Deut. ii. 23——[i]Or, *the cave*——[k]Chap. xix. 30
[l]See Judg. i. 34——[m]1 Kings v. 18; Psa. lxxxiii. 7:

Ezek. xxvii. 9——[n]Chap. xii. 7——[o]Chap. xi. 8
[p]See chap. xxiii. 13; Judg. ii. 21, 23——[q]Chap. xiv. 1, 2

---

borders of Egypt, i. e., to this desert; but not in Egypt, nor to the river Nile.

"Upon the whole, (though there are difficulties in the matter,) I incline to think that the river in question was not the Nile. *Sihor* (*black*) might, from some circumstances, be applied to another river as well as the Nile; though some places in Isaiah and Jeremiah seem to restrict it to the Nile."—*J. C.*

Ekron northward] Ekron was one of the five lordships of the Philistines, and the most *northern* of all the districts they possessed. *Baal-zebub*, its idol, is famous in Scripture; see 2 Kings i. 2, &c. The *five* lordships of the Philistines were *Gaza*, *Ashdod*, *Askalon*, *Gath*, and *Ekron*. There is no proof that ever the Israelites possessed *Ekron;* though, from chap. xv. 11, some think it was originally given to *Judah*, but the text does not say so; it only states that *the border* of the tribe of Judah *went out* UNTO THE SIDE of *Ekron*. From chap. xix. 43, we learn that it was a part of the lot of Dan, but it does not appear to have been possessed by any of those tribes.

Counted to the Canaanite] It is generally allowed that the original possessors of this country were the descendants of *Canaan*, the youngest son of Ham. The Philistines sprang from *Mizraim*, the second son of Ham, and, having dispossessed the *Avim* from the places they held in this land, dwelt in their stead. See Gen. x. 13, 14.

Five lords of the Philistines] These dynasties are famous in the Scriptures for their successful wars against the Israelites, of whom they were almost the perpetual scourge.

Also the Avites] These must not be confounded with the *Hivites*. The Avites seem to have been a very inconsiderable tribe, who dwelt in some of the skirts of Palestine. They had been originally deprived of their country by the *Caphtorim;* and though they lived as a distinct people, they had never afterwards arrived to any authority.

Verse 4. *The land of the Canaanites*] This lay on the south of the country of the Philistines, towards the sea-coast.

Mearah] Supposed to be the city *Maratha*, on the Mediterranean Sea.—*Calmet*. Or the river *Majora*, which falls into the Mediterranean Sea, between Sidon and Berytus. See PLINY, *Hist. Nat.* lib. v., c. 20.

Aphek] See on chap. xii. 18.

To the borders of the Amorites] Though the term *Amorite* is sometimes used to designate the inhabitants in general of the land of Canaan, yet it must be considered in a much more restricted sense in this place. As no Amorites are known to have dwelt in this quarter, Calmet supposes we should read *Aramites* or Syrians. Joshua, says he, proceeds from *Sidon* to *Aphek*, a city of Syria, between Heliopolis and Babylon, where was the temple of the Venus of Aphek; and which is spoken of in 1 Kings xx. 26; 2 Kings xiii. 17, as the capital of the kings of Syria. From this Joshua passes on to the frontiers of the Syrians, towards *Gebal* or Gabala, which, according to Ptolemy, was situated in Phœnicia. This conjecture of Calmet is not supported by any authority either from the ancient versions or MSS. *Houbigant*, however, approves of it: the emendation is simple, as it consists in the interchange of only two letters in the same word, הארמי *haarammi*, for האמרי *haemori*.

Verse 5. *The land of the Giblites*] This people dwelt beyond the precincts of the land of Canaan, on the east of Tyre and Sidon. See Ezek. xxvii. 9; Psa. lxxxiii. 7; their capital was named *Gebal*. See *Dodd*.

All Lebanon] See on chap. xi. 17.

Verse 6. *Misrephoth-maim*] See on chap. xi. 7.

Them will I drive out] That is, if the Israelites continued to be obedient; but they did not, and therefore they never fully possessed the *whole* of that land which, on this condition alone, God had promised them: the *Sidonians* were never expelled by the Israelites, and were only brought into a state of comparative subjection in the days of David and Solomon.

Some have taken upon them to deny the authenticity of Divine revelation relative to this business, "because," say they, "God is stated to have absolutely promised that Joshua should conquer the whole land, and put the Israelites in possession of it." This is a total mistake. 1. God never absolutely, i. e., *unconditionally*, promised to put them in possession of this land. The promise of their possessing the whole was suspended on their *fidelity* to God. They were not faithful, and therefore God was not bound by his promise to give them any part of the land, after their first act of national defection from his worship. 2. God never said that Joshua should conquer the whole land, and *give* it to them; the promise was simply this: "Thou shalt bring them into the land, and thou shalt divide it among them:" both of which he did, and procured them footing by his conquests, sufficient to have enabled them to establish themselves in it for ever. 3. It was never said, Thou shalt

A. M. 2560
B. C. 1444
An. Exod. Isr.
47
Anno ante
I. Olymp. 668

7 Now therefore divide this land for an inheritance unto the nine tribes, and the half tribe of Manasseh,

8 With whom the Reubenites and the Gadites have received their inheritance, [r]which Moses gave them, beyond Jordan eastward, *even* as Moses the servant of the LORD gave them;

9 From Aroer, that *is* upon the bank of the river Arnon, and the city that *is* in the midst of the river, [s]and all the plain of Medeba unto Dibon;

10 And [t]all the cities of Sihon king of the Amorites, which reigned in Heshbon, unto the border of the children of Ammon;

11 [u]And Gilead, and the border of the Geshurites and Maachathites, and all Mount Hermon, and all Bashan unto Salcah;

12 All the kingdom of Og in Bashan, which reigned in Ashtaroth and in Edrei, who remained of [v]the remnant of the giants: [w]for these did Moses smite, and cast them out.

13 Nevertheless the children of Israel expelled [x]not the Geshurites, nor the Maachathites: but the Geshurites and the Maachathites dwell among the Israelites until this day.

14 [y]Only unto the tribe of Levi he gave none inheritance; the sacrifices of the LORD

God of Israel made by fire *are* their inheritance, [z]as he said unto them.

15 And Moses gave unto the tribe of the children of Reuben *inheritance* according to their families.

16 And their coast was [a]from Aroer, that *is* on the bank of the river Arnon, [b]and the city that *is* in the midst of the river, [c]and all the plain by Medeba;

17 Heshbon, and all her cities that *are* in the plain; Dibon, and [d]Bamoth-baal, and Beth-baal-meon,

18 [e]And Jahaza, and Kedemoth, and Mephaath,

19 [f]And Kirjathaim, and [g]Sibmah, and Zareth-shahar in the mount of the valley,

20 And Beth-peor, and [h]Ashdoth-pisgah,[i] and Beth-jeshimoth;

21 [k]And all the cities of the plain, and all the kingdom of Sihon king of the Amorites, which reigned in Heshbon, [l]whom Moses smote [m]with the princes of Midian, Evi, and Rekem, and Zur, and Hur, and Reba, *which were* dukes of Sihon, dwelling in the country.

22 [n]Balaam also the son of Beor, the [o]soothsayer, did the children of Israel slay with the sword among them that were slain by them.

A. M. 2560
B. C. 1444
An. Exod. Isr.
47
Anno ante
I. Olymp. 668

---

[r]Num. xxxii. 33; Deut. iii. 12, 13; chap. xxii. 4
[s]Ver. 16; Num. xxi. 30——[t]Num. xxi. 24, 25——[u]Chap. xii. 5——[v]Deut. iii. 11; chap. xii. 4——[w]Num. xxi. 34, 35——[x]Ver. 11——[y]Num. xviii. 20, 23, 24; chap. xiv. 3, 4——[z]Ver. 33——[a]Chap. xii. 2——[b]Num. xxi. 28
[c]Num. xxi. 30; ver. 9

[d]Or, *the high places of Baal, and house of Baal-meon;* see Num. xxxii. 38——[e]Num. xxi. 23——[f]Num. xxxii. 37——[g]Num. xxxii. 38——[h]Deut. iii. 17; chap. xii. 3
[i]Or, *springs of Pisgah,* or *the hill*——[k]Deut. iii. 10
[l]Numbers xxi. 24——[m]Num. xxxi. 8——[n]Num. xxii. 5; xxxi. 8——[o]Or, *diviner*

---

conquer it all, and then *divide* it; no. Several of the tribes, *after* their quota was allotted them, were obliged to drive out the ancient inhabitants. See on chap. xi. 18.

Verse 7. *The nine tribes, and the half tribe of Manasseh*] The other half tribe of Manasseh, and the two tribes of Reuben and Gad, had got their inheritance on the other side of Jordan, in the land formerly belonging to Og king of Bashan, and Sihon king of the Amorites.

Verse 9. *From Aroer*] See on chap. xii. 2.

Verse 11. *Border of the Geshurites*] See on chap. xii. 5.

Verse 17. *Bamoth-baal*] The high places of Baal, probably so called from altars erected on hills for the impure worship of this Canaanitish Priapus.

Verse 18. *Jahaza*] A city near Medeba and Dibon. It was given to the Levites, 1 Chron. vi. 78.

Kedemoth] Mentioned Deut. ii. 26; supposed to have been situated beyond the river *Arnon.*

Mephaath] Situated on the frontiers of Moab,

on the eastern part of the desert. It was given to the Levites, chap. xxi. 37.

Verse 19. *Kirjathaim*] This city, according to Eusebius, was nine miles distant from Medeba, towards the east. It passed from the Emim to the Moabites, from the Moabites to the Amorites, and from the Amorites to the Israelites, Gen. xiv. 5; Deut. ii. 20. Calmet supposes the Reubenites possessed it till the time they were carried away by the Assyrians; and then the Moabites appear to have taken possession of it anew, as he collects from Jer. xlviii. and Ezek. xxv.

Sibmah] A place remarkable for its *vines.* See Isa. xvi. 8, 9; Jer. xlviii. 32.

Zareth-shahar, in the mount of the valley] This probably means a town situated on or near to a hill in some flat country.

Verse 20. *Beth-peor*] The *house* or *temple of Peor,* situated at the foot of the mountain of the same name. See Num. xxv. 3.

Verse 21. *The princes of Midian*] See the history of this war, Num. xxxi. 1, &c.; and

A. M. 2560
B. C. 1444
An. Exod. Isr.
47
Anno ante
I. Olymp. 668

23 And the border of the children of Reuben was Jordan, and the border *thereof*. This *was* the inheritance of the children of Reuben after their families, the cities and the villages thereof.

24 And Moses gave *inheritance* unto the tribe of Gad, *even* unto the children of Gad according to their families.

25 ᴾAnd their coast was Jazer, and all the cities of Gilead, ᑫand half the land of the children of Ammon, unto Aroer that *is* before ʳRabbah;

26 And from Heshbon unto Ramath-mizpeh, and Betonim; and from Mahanaim unto the border of Debir;

27 And in the valley, ˢBeth-aram, and Beth-nimrah, ᵗand Succoth, and Zaphon, the rest of the kingdom of Sihon king of Heshbon, Jordan and *his* border, *even* unto the edge ᵘof the sea of Chinneroth on the other side Jordan eastward.

28 This *is* the inheritance of the children of

Gad after their families, the cities, and their villages.

A. M. 2560
B. C. 1444
An. Exod. Isr.
47
Anno ante
I. Olymp. 668

29 And Moses gave *inheritance* unto the half tribe of Manasseh: and *this* was *the possession* of the half tribe of the children of Manasseh by their families.

30 And their coast was from Mahanaim, all Bashan, all the kingdom of Og king of Bashan, and ᵛall the towns of Jair, which *are* in Bashan, threescore cities:

31 And half Gilead, and ʷAshtaroth, and Edrei, cities of the kingdom of Og in Bashan, *were pertaining* unto the children of Machir the son of Manasseh, *even* to the one half of the ˣchildren of Machir by their families.

32 These *are the countries* which Moses did distribute for inheritance in the plains of Moab, on the other side Jordan, by Jericho, eastward.

33 ʸBut unto the tribe of Levi Moses gave not *any* inheritance: the LORD God of Israel *was* their inheritance, ᶻas he said unto them.

ᴾNum. xxxii. 35——ᑫCompare Num. xxi. 26, 28, 29, with Deut. ii. 19, and Judg. xi. 13, 15, &c.——ʳ2 Sam. xi. 1; xii. 26——ˢNum. xxxii. 36——ᵗGen. xxxiii. 17; 1 Kings vii. 46

ᵘNum. xxxiv. 11——ᵛNum. xxxii. 41; 1 Chron. ii. 23 ʷChap. xii. 4——ˣNum. xxxii. 39, 40——ʸVer. 14; chapter xviii. 7——ᶻNum. xviii. 20; Deut. x. 9; xviii. 1, 2

---

from that place this and the following verse seem to be borrowed, for the introduction of the death of Balaam here seems quite irrelevant.

Verse 23. *The cities and the villages*] By *villages*, חצרים *chatserim*, it is likely that *moveable villages* or *tents* are meant, such as are in use among the Bedouin Arabs; places where they were accustomed to feed and pen their cattle.

Verse 25. *Half the land of the children of Ammon*] This probably was land which had been taken from the Ammonites by Sihon, king of the Amorites, and which the Israelites possessed by right of conquest. For although the Israelites were forbidden to take the land of the Ammonites, Deut. ii. 37, yet this part, as having been united to the territories of Sihon, they might possess when they defeated that king and subdued his kingdom.

Verse 26. *Ramath-mizpeh*] The same as *Ramoth-gilead*. It was one of the cities of refuge, chap. xx. 8; Deut. iv. 47.

Mahanaim] Or the *two camps*. Situated on the northern side of the brook Jabbok, celebrated for the vision of the two camps of angels which Jacob had there; see Gen. xxxii. 2.

Verse 27. *Beth-aram*] This city was rebuilt by Herod, and called *Livias*, in honour of *Livia*, the wife of *Augustus*. Josephus calls it *Julias*, Julia being the name which the Greeks commonly give to *Livia.—Calmet*.

Succoth] A place between Jabbok and Jordan where Jacob pitched his *tents*, from which circumstance it obtained its name; see Genesis xxxiii. 17.

Verse 29. *The half tribe of Manasseh*] When the tribes of Reuben and Gad requested to have their settlement on the east side of Jordan, it does not appear that any part of the tribe of Manasseh requested to be settled in the same place. But as this tribe was numerous, and had much cattle, Moses thought proper to appoint one half of it to remain on the east of Jordan, and the other to go over and settle on the west side of that river.

Verse 30. *The towns of Jair*] These were sixty cities; they are mentioned afterwards, and in 1 Chron. ii. 21, &c. They are the same with the *Havoth-jair* mentioned Num. xxxii. 41. Jair was son of Segub, grandson of Esron or Hezron, and great-grandson of Machir by his grandmother's side, who married Hezron of the tribe of Judah. See his genealogy, 1 Chron. ii. 21-24.

Verse 32. *Which Moses did distribute*] Moses had settled every thing relative to these tribes before his death, having appointed them to possess the territories of Og king of Bashan, and Sihon king of the Amorites.

For particulars on this chapter, the reader, if he judge it of consequence, may consult *Calmet*.

CHAPTER XIV

Eleazar, Joshua, and the heads of the fathers, distribute the land by lot to the people, 1–3. The Levites receive no land, but cities to dwell in, and suburbs for their cattle, 4, 5. Caleb requests to have Mount Hebron for an inheritance, because of his former services, 6–12. Joshua grants his request, 13–15.

A. M. 2560
B. C. 1444
An. Exod. Isr.
47
Anno ante
I. Olymp. 668

AND these *are the countries* which the children of Israel inherited in the land of Canaan, ªwhich Eleazar the priest, and Joshua the son of Nun, and the heads of the fathers of the tribes of the children of Israel, distributed for inheritance to them.

2 ᵇBy lot *was* their inheritance, as the Lord commanded by the hand of Moses, for the nine tribes, and *for* the half tribe.

3 ᶜFor Moses had given the inheritance of two tribes and a half tribe on the other side Jordan: but unto the Levites he gave none inheritance among them.

4 For ᵈthe children of Joseph were two tribes, Manasseh and Ephraim: therefore they gave no part unto the Levites in the land, save cities to dwell *in,* with their suburbs for their cattle and for their substance.

A. M. 2560
B. C. 1444
An. Exod. Isr.
47
Anno ante
I. Olymp. 668

ªNum. xxxiv. 17, 18——ᵇNum. xxvi. 55; xxxiii. 54; xxxiv. 13

ᶜChap. xiii. 8, 32, 33——ᵈGen. xlviii. 5; 1 Chron. v. 1, 2

NOTES ON CHAP. XIV

Verse 1. *Eleazar the priest, &c.*] Eleazar, as being the minister of God in *sacred* things is mentioned *first.* Joshua, as having the supreme command in all things *civil,* is mentioned *next.* And the heads or princes of the twelve tribes, who in all things acted *under* Joshua, are mentioned *last.* These *heads* or *princes* were twelve, Joshua and Eleazar included; and the reader may find their names in Num. xxxiv. 19-28. It is worthy of remark that no prince was taken from the tribes of *Reuben* and *Gad,* because these had already received their inheritance on the other side of Jordan, and therefore could not be interested in this division.

Verse 2. *By lot* was *their inheritance*] Concerning the meaning and use of the lot, see the note on Num. xxxvi. 55; and concerning the manner of *casting lots* in the case of the *scapegoat,* see the note on Lev. xvi. 8, 9.

On this subject Dr. Dodd has selected some good observations from *Calmet* and *Masius,* which I here borrow: "Though God had sufficiently pointed out by the predictions of Jacob when dying, and those of Moses, what portions he designed for each tribe, we readily discern an admirable proof of his wisdom in the orders he gave to decide them by *lot.* By this means the false interpretations which might have been given to the words of Jacob and Moses were prevented; and by striking at the root of whatever might occasion *jealousies* and *disputes* among the tribes, he evidently secured the honesty of those who were to be appointed to distribute to them the conquered countries in the land of Canaan. Besides, the success of this method gave a fresh proof of the Divinity of the Jewish *religion,* and the truth of its *oracles.* Each tribe finding itself placed *by lot* exactly in the spot which Jacob and Moses had foretold, it was evident that Providence had equally directed both those *predictions* and that *lot.* The event justified the truth of the promises. The more singular it was, the more clearly we discern the finger of God in it. The portion, says *Masius,* fell to each tribe just as Jacob had declared two hundred and fifty years before

in the last moments of his life, and Moses, immediately before his death; for to the tribe of Judah fell a country abounding in *vineyards* and *pastures;* to Zebulun and Issachar, *seacoasts;* in that of Asher was plenty of *oil, wheat,* and *metals;* that of Benjamin, near to the *temple,* was, in a manner, *between the shoulders of the Deity;* Ephraim and Manasseh were distinguished with a territory blessed in a *peculiar* manner by Heaven; the land of Naphtali extended from the *west* to the *south* of the tribe of Judah. Since therefore the lot so well corresponded to these predictions, would it not be insolence and stupidity in the highest degree, not to acknowledge the *inspiration* of God in the *word* of Jacob and Moses, the *direction* of his *hand* in the *lot,* and his *providence* in the *event?*"

How the *lot* was cast in this case cannot be particularly determined. It is probable, 1. That the land was geographically divided into ten portions. 2. That each portion was called by a particular name. 3. That the name of each portion was written on a separate slip of parchment, wood, &c. 4. That the names of the claimants were also written on so many slips. 5. The names of the portions, and of the tribes, were put into separate vessels. 6. Joshua, for example, put his hand into the vessel containing the names of the tribes, and took out one slip; while Eleazar took out one from the other vessel, in which the names of the *portions* were put. 7. The *name* drawn, and the *portion* drawn, being read, it was immediately discerned what the *district* was which God had designed for such a *tribe.* This appears to be the most easy way to determine such a business.

Verse 4. *The children of Joseph were two tribes*] This was ascertained by the prophetic declaration of their grandfather Jacob, Gen. xlviii. 5, 6; and as *Levi* was taken out of the tribes for the service of the sanctuary, one of these sons of Joseph came in his place, and Joseph was treated as the first-born of Jacob, in the place of Reuben, who forfeited his right of primogeniture.

With their suburbs for their cattle] For the meaning of this passage the reader is referred to the note on Num. xxxv. 5.

A. M. 2560
B. C. 1444
An. Exod. Isr.
47
Anno ante
I. Olymp. 668

5 ^eAs the LORD commanded Moses, so the children of Israel did, and they divided the land.

6 Then the children of Judah came unto Joshua in Gilgal: and Caleb the son of Jephunneh the ^fKenezite said unto him, Thou knowest ^gthe thing that the LORD said unto Moses the man of God concerning me and thee ^hin Kadesh-barnea.

7 Forty years old *was* I when Moses the servant of the LORD ⁱsent me from Kadesh-barnea to espy out the land; and I brought him word again as *it was* in mine heart.

8 Nevertheless ^kmy brethren that went up with me made the heart of the people melt: but I wholly ^lfollowed the LORD my God.

9 And Moses sware on that day, saying, ^mSurely the land ⁿwhereon thy feet have trodden shall be thine inheritance, and thy children's for ever, because thou hast wholly followed the LORD my God.

10 And now, behold, the LORD hath kept me alive, ^oas he said, these forty and five years, even since the LORD spake this word unto Moses, while *the children of* Israel ^pwandered in the wilderness: and now, lo, I *am* this day fourscore and five years old.

A. M. 2560
B. C. 1444
An. Exod. Isr.
47
Anno ante
I. Olymp. 668

11 ^qAs yet I *am as* strong this day as *I was* in the day that Moses sent me; as my strength *was* then, even so *is* my strength now, for war, both ^rto go out, and to come in.

12 Now therefore give me this mountain, whereof the LORD spake in that day; for thou heardest in that day how ^sthe Anakims *were* there, and *that* the cities *were* great *and* fenced: ^tif so be the LORD *will be* with me, then ^uI shall be able to drive them out, as the LORD said.

13 And Joshua ^vblessed him, ^wand gave unto Caleb the son of Jephunneh Hebron for an inheritance.

^eNum. xxxv. 2; chap. xxi. 2——^fNum. xxxii. 12; chap. xv. 17——^gNum. xiv. 24, 30; Deut. i. 36, 38 ^hNum. xiii. 26——ⁱNum. xiii. 6; xiv. 6——^kNum. xiii. 31, 32; Deut. i. 28——^lNum. xiv. 24; Deut. i. 36 ^mNum. xiv. 23, 24; Deut. i. 36; chap. i. 3——ⁿSee Num. xiii. 22

^oNum. xiv. 30——^pHeb. *walked*——^qEcclus. xlvi. 9; see Deut. xxxiv. 7——^rDeut. xxxi. 2——^sNum. xiii. 28, 33——^tPsa. xviii. 32, 34; lx. 12; Rom. viii. 31——^uChap xv. 14; Judg. i. 20——^vChap. xxii. 6——^wChap. x. 37; xv. 13; Judg. i. 20; see chap. xxi. 11, 12; 1 Chron. vi. 55, 56

Verse 5. *They divided the land.*] This work was begun some time before at *Gilgal*, and was finished some time after at *Shiloh*. It must have required a very considerable time to make all the geographical arrangements that were necessary for this purpose.

Verse 6. *Caleb the son of Jephunneh the Kenezite*] In the note on the parallel place, Num. xxxii. 12, it is said Kenaz was probably the *father* of Jephunneh, and that Jephunneh, not Caleb, was the Kenezite; but still, allowing this to be perfectly correct, Caleb might also be called the *Kenezite*, as it appears to have been a *family* name, for *Othniel*, his nephew and son-in-law, is called the son of *Kenaz*, chap. xv. 17; Judg. i. 13, and 1 Chron. iv. 13; and a grandson of Caleb is also called the son of *Kenaz*, 1 Chron. iv. 15. In 1 Chron. ii. 18, Caleb is called the son of *Hezron*, but this is only to be understood of his having Hezron for one of his *ancestors;* and *son* here may be considered the same as *descendant;* for Hezron, of the tribe of Judah, having come into Egypt one hundred and seventy-six years before the birth of Caleb, it is not at all likely that he could be called his *father* in the proper sense of the term. Besides, the supposition above makes a very good sense, and is consistent with the use of the terms *father*, *son*, and *brother*, in different parts of the sacred writings.

Thou knowest the thing that the Lord said] In the place to which Caleb seems to refer, viz., Num. xiv. 24, there is not a word concerning a promise of *Hebron* to him and his posterity; nor in the place (Deut. i. 36) where Moses repeats what had been done at *Kadesh-barnea:* but it may be *included* in what is there spoken. God promises, *because he had another spirit*

within him, and had followed God fully, therefore he should enter into the land whereinto he came, and his seed should possess it. Probably this relates to *Hebron*, and was so understood by all parties at that time. This seems tolerably evident from the pointed reference made by Caleb to this transaction.

Verse 7. *As it was in mine heart.*] Neither *fear* nor *favour* influenced him on the occasion; he told what he believed to be the truth, the whole truth, and nothing but the truth.

Verse 9. *The land whereon thy feet have trodden*] This probably refers to *Hebron*, which was no doubt mentioned on this occasion.

Verse 10. *These forty and five years*] See the note on chap. xiii. 1.

Verse 11. *Even so is my strength now*] I do not ask this place because I wish to sit down now, and take my ease; on the contrary, I know I must fight, to drive out the Anakim, and I am as able and willing to do it as I was forty-five years ago, when Moses sent me to spy out the land.

Verse 12. *I shall be able to drive them out*] He cannot mean *Hebron* merely, for that had been taken before by Joshua; but in the request of Caleb doubtless all the *circumjacent country* was comprised, in many parts of which the Anakim were still in considerable force. It has been conjectured that Hebron itself had again fallen under the power of its former possessors, who, taking the advantage of the absence of the Israelitish army, who were employed in other parts of the country, re-entered the city, and restored their ancient domination. But the first opinion seems best founded.

Verse 13. *Joshua blessed him*] As the word *bless* often signifies to *speak good* or *well of* or

A. M. 2560
B. C. 1444
An. Exod. Isr.
47
Anno ante
I. Olymp. 668

14 ˣHebron therefore became the inheritance of Caleb the son of Jephunneh the Kenezite unto this day, because that he ʸwholly followed the LORD God of Israel.

15 And ᶻthe name of Hebron before *was* Kirjath-arba; *which Arba was* a great man among the Anakims. ᵃAnd the land had rest from war.

A. M. 2560
B. C. 1444
An. Exod. Isr.
47
Anno ante
I. Olymp. 668

ˣChap. xxi. 12; 1 Mac. ii. 56——ʸVer. 8, 9

ᶻGen. xxiii. 2; chap. xv. 13——ᵃChap. xi. 23

---

to any person, (see the note on Gen. ii. 3,) here it may mean the *praise* bestowed on Caleb's intrepidity and faithfulness by Joshua, as well as a *prayer* to God that he might have prosperity in all things; and especially that the Lord might be *with him*, as himself had expressed in the preceding verse.

Verse 14. *Hebron therefore became the inheritance of Caleb*] Joshua admitted his claim, recognized his right, and made a full conveyance of Hebron and its dependencies to Caleb and his posterity; and this being done in the sight of all the elders of Israel, the right was publicly acknowledged, and consequently this portion was excepted from the general determination by lot; God having long before made the cession of this place to him and to his descendants.

Verse 15. *And the name of Hebron before was Kirjath-arba*] That is, *the city of Arba*, or rather, *the city of the four*, for thus קרית ארבע *kiryath arba* may be literally translated. It is very likely that this city had its name from *four* Anakim, gigantic or powerful men, probably *brothers*, who built or conquered it. This conjecture receives considerable strength from chap. xv. 14, where it is said that Caleb drove from *Hebron* the *three sons of Anak, Sheshai, Ahiman*, and *Talmai:* now it is quite possible that Hebron had its former name, *Kirjath-arba*, the *city of the four*, from these *three sons* and their *father*, who, being men of uncommon stature or abilities, had rendered themselves famous by acts proportioned to their strength and influence in the country. It appears however from chap. xv. 13 that *Arba* was a proper name, as there he is called the *father of Anak*. The Septuagint call Hebron *the metropolis of the Enakim*, μητροπολις των Ενακιμ. It was probably the seat of government, being the *residence* of the above chiefs, from whose *conjoint* authority and power it might have been called חברון *chebron;* as the word חבר *chabar* literally signifies to *associate*, to *join in fellowship*, and appears to be used, Job xli. 6, for "*associated merchants*, or *merchants' companions*, who travelled

in the same caravan." Both these names are expressive, and serve to confirm the above conjecture. No notice need be taken of the tradition that this city was called *the city of the four* because it was the burial-place of *Adam, Abraham, Isaac*, and *Jacob*. Such traditions confute themselves.

The land had rest from war.] There were no more *general* wars; the inhabitants of Canaan collectively could make no longer any head, and when their confederacy was broken by the conquests of Joshua, he thought proper to divide the land, and let each tribe expel the ancient inhabitants that might still remain in its own territories. Hence the wars after this time were *particular* wars; there were no more general campaigns, as it was no longer necessary for the *whole* Israelitish body to act against an enemy now *disjointed* and *broken*. This appears to be the most rational meaning of the words, *The land had rest from war.*

THE Jewish economy furnishes, not only a history of God's revelations to man, but also a history of his providence, and an ample, most luminous, and glorious comment on that providence. Is it possible that any man can seriously and considerately sit down to the reading even of this book, without rising up a wiser and a better man? This is the true history which everywhere exhibits God as the *first mover* and *prime agent*, and men only as subordinate actors. What a miracle of God's power, wisdom, grace, justice, and providence are the people of Israel in every period of their history, and in every land of their dispersions! If their *fall* occasioned the *salvation* of the Gentile world, what shall their *restoration* produce! Their future *inheritance* is not left to what men would call the *fortuitous* decision of a *lot;* like Caleb's possession it is confirmed by the oath of the Lord; and when the end shall be, this people shall stand in their lot at the end of the days, and shall again be great to the ends of the earth.

CHAPTER XV

The lot of the tribe of Judah described, 1. *Their south border*, 2–4. *Their east border*, 5–11. *Their west border*, 12. *Caleb's conquest*, 13–15. *Promises his daughter to the person who should take Kirjath-sevher*, 16. *Othniel his kinsman renders himself master of it, and gets Achsah to wife*, 17. *Her request to her father to get a well-watered land, which is granted*, 18, 19. *The cities of the tribe of Judah are enumerated*, 20–63.

A. M. 2561
B. C. 1443
An. Exod. Isr.
48
Anno ante
I. Olymp. 667

*T*HIS then was the lot of the tribe of the children of Judah by their families; ᵃ*even* to the border of Edom the ᵇwilderness of Zin southward *was* the uttermost part of the south coast.

2 And their south border was from the shore of the Salt Sea, from the ᶜbay that looketh southward:

3 And it went out to the south side ᵈto ᵉMaaleh-acrabbim, and passed along to Zin, and ascended up on the south side unto Kadesh-barnea, and passed along to Hezron, and went up to Adar, and fetched a compass to Karkaa:

4 *From thence* it passed ᶠtoward Azmon, and went out unto the river of Egypt; and the goings out of that coast were at the sea: this shall be your south coast.

A. M. 2561
B. C. 1443
An. Exod. Isr.
48
Anno ante
I. Olymp. 667

ᵃNumbers xxxiv. 3——ᵇNumbers xxxiii. 36
ᶜHebrew, *tongue*

ᵈNum. xxxiv. 4——ᵉOr, *the going up to Acrabbim*
ᶠNum. xxxiv. 5

NOTES ON CHAP. XV

Verse 1. This *then was the lot of the tribe of—Judah*] The geography of the sacred writings presents many difficulties, occasioned by the changes which the civil state of the promised land has undergone, especially for the last two thousand years. Many of the ancient towns and villages have had their names so totally changed, that their former appellations are no longer discernible; several lie buried under their own ruins, and others have been so long destroyed that not one vestige of them remains. On these accounts it is very difficult to ascertain the situation of many of the places mentioned in this and the following chapters. But however this may embarrass the commentator, it cannot affect the *truth* of the narrative. Some of the principal cities in the universe, cities that were the seats of the most powerful empires, are not only reduced to *ruins*, but so completely blotted out of the map of the world that their situation cannot be ascertained. Where is *Babylon?* Where are *Nineveh, Carthage, Thebes, Tyre, Baalbec, Palmyra,* and the so far-famed and greatly celebrated TROY? Of the former and the latter, so renowned by *historians* and *poets,* scarcely a vestige, properly speaking, remains; nor can the learned agree on the *spot* once occupied by the buildings of those celebrated cities! Should this circumstance invalidate the whole history of the ancient world, in which they made so conspicuous a figure? And can the authenticity of our sacred historian be impaired, because several of the places *he* mentions no longer exist? Surely no: nor can it be called in question but by the *heedless* and *superficial,* or the *decidedly* profane. Although some of the cities of the holy land are destroyed, and it would be difficult to ascertain the geography of several, yet enough remain, either under their ancient names, or with such decisive characteristics, that through their new names their ancient appellatives are readily discernible.

It is natural to suppose that the *division* mentioned here was made after an accurate survey of the land, which might have been made by proper persons accompanying the conquering army of the Israelites. *Nine* tribes and a *half* were yet to be accommodated, and the land must be divided into *nine parts* and a *half.* This was no doubt done with the utmost judgment and discretion, the advantages and disadvantages of each division being carefully balanced. These were the portions which were divided by lot; and it appears that Judah drew the *first* lot; and, because of the importance and pre-eminence of this tribe, this lot is first described.

By their families] It is supposed that the *family divisions* were not determined by lot. These were left to the prudence and judgment of Joshua, Eleazar, and the ten princes, who appointed to each family a district in proportion to its number, &c., the general division being that alone which was determined by the *lot.*

To the border of Edom] The tribe of Judah occupied the most southerly part of the land of Canaan. Its limits extended from the extremity of the *Dead Sea* southward, along Idumea, possibly by the desert of *Sin,* and proceeding from east to west to the Mediterranean Sea, and the most eastern branch of the river Nile, or to what is called the river of Egypt. Calmet very properly remarks, that Joshua is particular in giving the limits of this tribe, as being the first, the most numerous, most important; that which was to furnish the *kings* of Judea; that in which *pure religion* was to be preserved, and that from which the *Messiah* was to spring.

Verse 2. *From the bay that looketh southward*] These were the southern limits of the tribe of Judah, which commenced at the extremity of the lake Asphaltites or Dead Sea, and terminated at *Sihor* or the river of Egypt, and Mediterranean Sea; though some think it extended to the *Nile.*

Verse 3. *Maaleh-acrabbim*] The ascent of the Mount of Scorpions, probably so called from the multitude of those animals found in that place.

Kadesh-barnea] This place was called *En-mishpat,* Gen. xiv. 7. It was on the edge of the wilderness of Paran, and about twenty-four miles from Hebron. Here Miriam, the sister of Moses and Aaron, died; and here Moses and Aaron rebelled against the Lord; hence the place was called *Meribah-Kadesh,* or *the contention of Kadesh.*

Karkaa] Supposed to be the *Coracea* of Ptolemy, in Arabia Petræa.—*Calmet.*

Verse 4. *Toward Azmon*] This was the last city they possessed toward Egypt.

The river of Egypt] The most eastern branch of the river Nile. See on chap. xiii. 3. But there is much reason to doubt whether any branch of the Nile be meant, and whether the promised land extended to that river. On this subject it is impossible to decide either way.

A. M. 2561
B. C. 1443
An. Exod. Isr.
48
Anno ante
I. Olymp. 667

5 And the east border *was* the Salt Sea, *even* unto the end of Jordan. And *their* border in the north quarter *was* from the bay of the sea at the uttermost part of Jordan:

6 And the border went up to ᵍBeth-hogla, and passed along by the north of Beth-arabah; and the border went up ʰto the stone of Bohan the son of Reuben:

7 And the border went up toward Debir from ⁱthe valley of Achor, and so northward, looking toward Gilgal, that *is* before the going

up to Adummim, which *is* on the south side of the river: and the border passed toward the waters of En-shemesh, and the goings out thereof were at ᵏEn-rogel:

8 And the border went up ˡby the valley of the son of Hinnom unto the south side of the ᵐJebusite; the same *is* Jerusalem: and the border went up to the top of the mountain that *lieth* before the valley of Hinnom westward, which *is* at the end ⁿof the valley of the giants northward:

9 And the border was drawn from the top of

A. M. 2561
B. C. 1443
An. Exod. Isr.
48
Anno ante
I. Olymp. 667

ᵍChap. xviii. 19——ʰChap. xviii. 17——ⁱChap. vii. 26
ᵏ2 Sam. xvii. 17; 1 Kings i. 9

ˡCh. xviii. 16; 2 Kings xxiii. 10; Jer. xix. 2, 6——ᵐCh. xviii. 28; Judg. i. 21; xix. 10——ⁿCh. xviii. 16

Verse 5. *The east border* was *the Salt Sea*] The Salt Sea is the same as the Dead Sea, lake Asphaltites, &c. And here it is intimated that the eastern border of the tribe of Judah extended along the Dead Sea, from its lowest extremity to the *end of Jordan*, i. e., to the place where Jordan falls into this sea.

Verse 6. *Beth-hogla*] A place between Jericho and the Dead Sea, belonging to the tribe of Benjamin, chap. xviii. 21, though here serving as a frontier to the tribe of Judah.

Stone of Bohan] This must have been some remarkable place, probably like the *stone of Jacob*, which afterwards became *Beth-el;* but where it was situated is uncertain.

Verse 7. *The valley of Achor*] Debir mentioned in this verse is unknown. The *valley of Achor* had its name from the punishment of *Achan.* See the account, chap. vii. 24, &c.

En-shemesh] The *fountain of the sun;* it was eastward of Jerusalem, on the confines of Judah and Benjamin.

Verse 8. *The valley of the son of Hinnom*] Who Hinnom was is not known, nor why this was called *his* valley. It was situated on the east of Jerusalem; and is often mentioned in Scripture. The image of the idol Molech appears to have been set up there; and there the idolatrous Israelites caused their sons and daughters to pass through the fire in honour of that demon, 2 Kings xxiii. 10. It was also called *Tophet*, see Jer. vii. 32. When King Josiah removed the image of this idol from this valley, it appears to have been held in such universal execration, that it became the general receptacle of all the filth and impurities which were carried out of Jerusalem; and it is supposed that *continual fires* were there kept up, to consume those impurities and prevent infection. From the Hebrew words גי בן הנם *gei ben Hinnom*, the *valley of the son of Hinnom*, and by contraction, גי הנם *gei Hinnom*, the *valley of Hinnom*, came the Γεεννα, *Gehenna* of the New Testament, called also Γεεννα του πυρος, the *Gehenna of fire*, which is the emblem of *hell*, or the place of the damned. See Matt. v. 22, 29, 30; x. 28; xviii. 9, &c.

In the *East* it is common to add the name of the *father* to that of the *son*, e. g., "This land belongs to *Goborka* the son of *Kake Prusada.*" But this addition is not made till after the father's death. This custom prevailed also in

the *west.* It is common among the aborigines of both *Ireland* and *Wales.*

The same is *Jerusalem*] This city was formerly called Jebus; a part of it was in the tribe of *Benjamin;* Zion, called its citadel, was in the tribe of *Judah.*

The valley of the giants] Of the *Rephaim.* See the notes on Gen. vi. 4; xiv. 5; Deut. ii. 7, 11.

On this subject, a very intelligent clergyman favours me with his opinion in the following terms:—

"The boundary between Judah and Benjamin went up from the valley of Hinnom on the east to the top of the hill southward, leaving Jebusi (or Jerusalem) to the northwest adjoining to Benjamin. This mount (Jebusi) lay between the two tribes, which the Jebusites possessed till the time of David. At the 63d verse here, it is said Judah could not drive out these people; and in Judg. i. 21, the same is said of the Benjamites. Each tribe might have attacked them at various times. There were various mounts or tops to these hills. Mount Zion and Moriah, where the temple stood, was in the tribe of Judah; Psa. lxxviii. 68, 69; lxxxvii. 2.

"In Deut. xxxiii. 12 it is said of Benjamin, *the Lord shall dwell by him*, i. e., near him, or beside his borders, *between his shoulders;* the line might be circular between the two hills or tops so as in part to encompass Mount Zion in the tribe of Judah, on which the temple stood. Benjamin's gate, (mentioned Jer. xxxvii. 12, 13, and xxxviii. 7,) was the gate leading out of the city, into the tribe of Benjamin. So the gate of Ephraim, (2 Kings xiv. 13,) was a gate which led towards the tribe of Ephraim. We give names to roads, &c., in the same way now.

"Mount Calvary, (which was on the outside of the gate,) seems to have been in the tribe of Benjamin. Query. Whether Calvary or Golgotha was so called from skulls being scattered about there, (as say some,) or rather from the figure of the rock being shaped like a man's skull, with one face of it nearly perpendicular? I incline to this latter opinion. I believe the Jews did not suffer human bones, even of malefactors, to lie about."—J. C.

Verse 9. *Baalah, which* is *Kirjath-jearim*] This place was rendered famous in Scripture, in consequence of its being the residence of the ark, for twenty years after it was sent back by the Philistines; see 1 Sam. v., vi., and vii. 1, 2.

A. M. 2561
B. C. 1443
An. Exod. Isr. 48
Anno ante I. Olymp. 667

the hill unto [o]the fountain of the water of Nephtoah, and went out to the cities of Mount Ephron; and the border was drawn [p]to Baalah, which *is* [q]Kirjath-jearim:

10 And the border compassed from Baalah westward unto Mount Seir, and passed along unto the side of Mount Jearim, which *is* Chesalon, on the north side, and went down to Beth-shemesh, and passed on to [r]Timnah:

11 And the border went out unto the side of [s]Ekron northward: and the border was drawn to Shicron, and passed along to Mount Baalah, and went out unto Jabneel; and the goings out of the border were at the sea.

12 And the west border *was* [t]to the great sea, and the coasts *thereof.* This *is* the coast of the children of Judah round about according to their families.

13 [u]And unto Caleb the son of Jephunneh he gave a part among the children of Judah, according to the commandment of the LORD to Joshua, *even* [v]the [w]city of Arba the father of Anak, which *city is* Hebron.

14 And Caleb drove thence [x]the three sons of Anak, [y]Sheshai, and Ahiman, and Talmai, the children of Anak.

15 And [z]he went up thence to the inhabitants of Debir: and the name of Debir before *was* Kirjath-sepher.

A. M. 2561
B. C. 1443
An. Exod. Isr. 48
Anno ante I. Olymp. 667

16 [a]And Caleb said, He that smiteth Kirjath-sepher, and taketh it, to him will I give Achsah my daughter to wife.

17 And [b]Othniel the [c]son of Kenaz, the brother of Caleb, took it: and he gave him Achsah his daughter to wife.

18 [d]And it came to pass, as she came *unto him,* that she moved him to ask of her father a field: and [e]she lighted off *her* ass; and Caleb said unto her, What wouldest thou?

19 Who answered, Give me a [f]blessing; for thou hast given me a south land; give me also springs of water. And he gave her the upper springs, and the nether springs.

20 This *is* the inheritance of the tribe of the children of Judah, according to their families.

21 And the uttermost cities of the tribe of the children of Judah, toward the coast of Edom southward, were Kabzeel, and Eder and Jagur,

22 And Kinah, and Dimonah, and Adadah,

23 And Kedesh, and Hazor, and Ithman,

---

[o]Chap. xviii. 15——[p]1 Chron. xiii. 6——[q]Judg. xviii. 12——[r]Gen. xxxviii. 13; Judg. xiv. 1——[s]Chap. xix. 43——[t]Verse 47; Num. xxxiv. 6, 7——[u]Chap. xiv. 13——[v]Chap. xiv. 15——[w]Or, *Kirjath-arba*

[x]Judg. i. 10, 20——[y]Num. xiii. 22——[z]Chap. x. 38; Judg. i. 11——[a]Judg. i. 12——[b]Judg. i. 13; iii. 9——[c]Num. xxxii. 12; chap. xiv. 6——[d]Judg. i. 14——[e]See Gen. xxiv. 64; 1 Sam. xxv. 23——[f]Gen. xxxiii. 11

Verse 10. *Beth-shemesh*] The *house* or *temple of the sun.* It is evident that the *sun* was an object of adoration among the Canaanites; and hence *fountains, hills,* &c., were dedicated to him. *Beth-shemesh* is remarkable for the slaughter of its inhabitants, in consequence of their prying *curiously,* if not *impiously,* into the ark of the Lord, when sent back by the Philistines. See 1 Sam. vii.

Verse 12. *The great sea*] The Mediterranean.

Verse 13. *And unto Caleb—he gave a part*] See the notes on chap. xiv. 14, &c.

Verse 14. *The three sons of Anak*] See on chap. xiv. 15.

Verse 15. *Kirjath-sepher.*] The *city of the book.* Why so named is uncertain. It was also called *Debir,* and *Kirpath-sannah.* See ver. 49.

Verse 16. *Will I give Achsah my daughter*] In ancient times fathers assumed an absolute right over their children, especially in disposing of them in marriage; and it was customary for a *king* or *great man* to promise his daughter in marriage to him who should take a city, kill an enemy, &c. So Saul promised his daughter in marriage to him who should kill Goliath, 1 Sam. xvii. 25; and Caleb offers his on this occasion to him who should take *Kirjath-sepher.* Profane writers furnish many similar examples.

Verse 18. *As she came*] As she was now departing from the house of her father to go to that of her husband.

She moved him] Othniel, to *ask of her father a field,* one on which she had set her heart, as contiguous to the patrimony already granted.

She lighted off her *ass*] ותצנח *vattitsnach,* she *nastily, suddenly* alighted, as if she had forgotten something, or was about to return to her father's house. Which being perceived by her father, he said, *What wouldest thou?* What is the matter? What dost thou want?

Verse 19. *Give me a blessing*] Do me an act of kindness. Grant me a particular request.

Thou hast given me a south land] Which was probably dry, or very ill, watered.

Give me also springs of water.] Let me have some fields in which there are *brooks* or *wells* already digged.

The upper springs, and the nether springs.] He gave her even more than she requested; he gave her a district among the *mountains* and another in the *plains* well situated and well watered. There are several difficulties in this account, with which I shall not trouble the reader. What is mentioned above appears to be the sense.

A. M. 2561
B. C. 1443
An. Exod. Isr.
48
Anno ante
I. Olymp. 667

24 Ziph, and Telem, and Bealoth,

25 And Hazor, Hadattah, and Kerioth, *and* Hezron, which *is* Hazor,

26 Amam, and Shema, and Moladah,

27 And Hazar-gaddah, and Heshmon, and Beth-palet,

28 And Hazar-shual, and Beer-sheba, and Bizjothjah,

29 Baalah, and Iim, and Azem,

30 And Eltolad, and Chesil, and Hormah,

31 And ᵍZiklag, and Madmannah, and Sansannah,

32 And Lebaoth, and Shilhim, and Ain, and Rimmon: all the cities *are* twenty and nine, with their villages:

33 *And* in the valley, ʰEshtaol, and Zoreah, and Ashnah,

34 And Zanoah, and En-gannim, Tappuah, and Enam,

35 Jarmuth, and Adullam, Socoh, and Azekah,

A. M. 2561
B. C. 1443
An. Exod. Isr.
48
Anno ante
I. Olymp. 667

36 And Sharaim, and Adithaim, and Gederah,ˡand Gederothaim; fourteen cities with their villages:

37 Zenan, and Hadashah, and Migdal-gad,

38 And Dilean, and Mizpeh, ᵏand Joktheel,

39 Lachish, and Bozkath, and Eglon,

40 And Cabbon, and Lahmam, and Kithlish,

41 And Gederoth, Beth-dagon, and Naamah, and Makkedah; sixteen cities with their villages:

42 Libnah, and Ether, and Ashan,

43 And Jiphtah, and Ashnah, and Nezib,

44 And Keilah, and Achzib, and Mareshah; nine cities with their villages:

45 Ekron, with her towns and her villages:

46 From Ekron even unto the sea, all that *lay* ˡnear Ashdod, with their villages:

47 Ashdod with her towns and her villages, Gaza with her towns and her villages, unto

---

ᵍ1 Sam. xxvii. 6——ʰNum. xiii. 23——ˡOr, *or*

ᵏ2 Kings xiv. 7——ˡHeb. *by the place of*

Verse 24. *Ziph*] There were two cities of this name in the tribe of Judah, that mentioned here, and another ver. 55. One of these two is noted for the refuge of David when persecuted by Saul; and the attempts made by its inhabitants to deliver him into the hands of his persecutor. See 1 Sam. xxiii. 14-24.

Verse 28. *Beer-sheba*] A city, famous in the book of Genesis as the residence of the patriarchs Abraham and Jacob, chap. xxii. 19; xxviii. 10; xlvi. 1. See the note on Gen. xxi. 31. It lay on the way between Canaan and Egypt, about forty miles from Jerusalem.

Verse 30. *Hormah*] A place rendered famous by the defeat of the Hebrews by the Canaanites. See Num. xiv. 45; Deut. i. 44.

Verse 31. *Ziklag*] The Philistines seem to have kept possession of this city till the time of David, who received it from Achish, king of Gath, 1 Sam. xxvii. 6; after which time it remained in the possession of the kings of Judah.

Verse 32. *All the cities* are *twenty and nine, with their villages*] But on a careful examination we shall find *thirty-eight;* but it is supposed that nine of these are excepted; viz., *Beersheba, Moladah, Hazarshual, Baalah, Azem, Hormah, Ziklag, Ain,* and *Rimmon,* which were afterwards given to the tribe of Simeon. This may appear satisfactory, but perhaps the truth will be found to be this: Several cities in the promised land are expressed by *compound* terms; not knowing the places, different translations combine what should be separated, and in many cases separate what should be combined. Through this we have *cities* formed out of *epithets.* On this ground we have *thirty-eight* cities as the sum here, instead of *twenty-nine.*

Verse 33. *Eshtaol, and Zoreah*] Here Samson was buried, it being the burial-place of his fathers; see Judges xvi. 31. These places, though first given to Judah, afterwards fell to the lot of Dan, chap. xix. 41.

Verse 35. *Jarmuth*] See the note on chap. x. 3.
Adullam] See the note on chap. xii. 15.
Socoh] It was near this place that David fought with and slew Goliath, the champion of the Philistines, 1 Sam. xvii. 1.

Verse 36. *Gederah*] See the note on chap. xii. 13.

Fourteen cities] Well reckoned, we shall find *fifteen* cities here; but probably Gederah and Gederothaim (ver. 36) are the same. See the note on ver. 32.

Verse 39. *Lachish—and Eglon*] See on chap. x. 3.

Verse 41. *Beth-dagon*] The *house* or *temple of Dagon.* This is a well known idol of the Philistines, and probably the place mentioned here was in some part of their territories; but the situation at present is unknown.

Verse 42. *Libnah*] See the note on chap. x. 29.
Ether] From chap. xix. 7 we learn that this city was afterwards given to the tribe of *Simeon.*

Verse 44. *Keilah*] This town was near Hebron, and is said to have been the burying-place of the prophet Habakkuk. David obliged the Philistines to raise the siege of it; (see 1 Sam. xxiii. 1-13;) but finding that its inhabitants had purposed to deliver him into the hands of Saul, who was coming in pursuit of him, he made his escape. See this remarkable case explained in the note on Deut. xxxii. 15.

Mareshah] Called also *Maresheth* and *Marasthi;* it was the birth-place of the prophet *Micah.* Near this place was the famous battle between Asa, king of Judah, and Zera, king of Cush or Ethiopia, who was at the head of one thousand thousand men, and three hundred chariots. Asa defeated this immense host and took much spoil; 2 Chron. xiv. 9-15.

Verse 46. *Ekron*] One of the five Philistine lordships; see the note on chap. xiii. 3.

Verse 47. *Ashdod*] Called also *Azotus,* Acts viii. 40.

A. M. 2561
B. C. 1443
An. Exod. Isr.
48
Anno ante
I. Olymp. 667

[m]the river of Egypt, and [n]the great sea, and the border *thereof:*

48 And in the mountains, Shamir, and Jattir, and Socoh,

49 And Dannah, and Kirjath-sannah, which *is* Debir,

50 And Anab, and Eshtemoh, and Anim,

51 [o]And Goshen, and Holon, and Giloh; eleven cities with their villages:

52 Arab, and Dumah, and Eshean,

53 And [p]Janum, and Beth-tappuah, and Aphekah,

54 And Humtah, and [q]Kirjath-arba, which *is* Hebron, and Zior; nine cities with their villages:

55 Maon, Carmel, and Ziph, and Juttah,

56 And Jezreel, and Jokdeam, and Zanoah,

57 Cain, Gibeah, and Timnah; ten cities with their villages:

58 Halhul, Beth-zur, and Gedor,

59 And Maarath, and Beth-anoth, and Eltekon; six cities with their villages:

60 [r]Kirjath-baal, which *is* Kirjath-jearim, and Rabbah; two cities with their villages:

61 In the wilderness, Beth-arabah, Middin, and Secacah,

62 And Nibshan, and the city of Salt, and En-gedi; six cities with their villages.

63 As for the Jebusites, the inhabitants of Jerusalem, [s]the children of Judah could not drive them out: [t]but the Jebusites dwell with the children of Judah at Jerusalem unto this day.

A. M. 2561
B. C. 1443
An. Exod. Isr.
48
Anno ante
I. Olymp. 667

---

[m]Verse 4——[n]Numbers xxxiv. 6——[o]Chap. x. 41; xi. 16
[p]Or, *Janus*

[q]Chap. xiv. 15; ver. 13——[r]Chap. xviii. 14——[s]See Judg. i. 8, 21; 2 Sam. v. 6——[t]Judg. i. 21

Unto the river of Egypt] The *Pelusiac* branch of the Nile, or *Sihor*. But see on ver. 4.

The great sea] The Mediterranean.

Verse 48. *Socoh*] See a town of this name, ver. 35.

Verse 49. *Kirjath-sannah*] See the note on ver. 15.

Verse 51. *Goshen*] See the note on chap. x. 41.

Giloh] The country of the traitor *Ahithophel*, 2 Sam. xv. 12.

Verse 53. *Beth-tappuah*] The *house of the apple* or *citron tree*. Probably a place where these grew in great abundance and perfection.

Aphekah] See the note on chap. xii. 18.

Verse 54. *Kirjath-arba*] See the note on chap. xiv. 15.

Verse 55. *Maon*] In a desert to which this town gave name, David took refuge for a considerable time from the persecution of Saul; and in this place Nabal the Carmelite had great possessions. See 1 Sam. xxiii. 24, 25; xxv. 2.

Carmel] Not the celebrated *mount* of that name, but a village, the residence of Nabal. See 1 Sam. xxv. 2. It was near *Maon*, mentioned above, and was about ten miles eastward of Hebron. It is the place where Saul erected a *trophy* to himself after the defeat of the Amalekites; see 1 Sam. xv. 12.

Ziph] See on ver. 24.

Verse 57. *Timnah*] A frontier town of the Philistines; it was in this place that Samson got his wife, see Judg. xiv. and xv.

Verse 58. *Gedor*] See the note on chap. xii. 13. In this place the Alexandrian MS. of the Septuagint and the Codex Vaticanus add the *eleven* following towns: *Theca, and Ephratha,* (that is, Bethlehem,) *and Phagor, and Etan, and Kulon, and Tatam, and Thebes, and Karam, and Galam, and Thether, and Manocho; eleven cities and their villages.* St. Jerome, on Mic. v. 1, mentions them, so that we find they were in the copies he used. Dr. Kennicott contends that they should be restored to the text, and accounts thus for their omission: "The same word וחצריהן *vechatsreyhen, and their villages,* occurring immediately *before* this passage and

at the *end* of it, the transcriber's eye passed from one to the other by mistake. A similar accident has caused the omission of two whole verses, the 35th and 36th of chap. xxi." See the note there.

Verse 60. *Kirjath-baal*] The same as *Baalah.* See on ver. 9.

Verse 62. *The city of Salt*] Or of *Melach.* This city was somewhere in the vicinity of the lake *Asphaltites*, the waters of which are the *saltest* perhaps in the world. The whole country abounds with *salt:* see the note on Gen. xix. 25. Some suppose that it is the same as Zoar, the place to which Lot escaped after the destruction of Sodom and Gomorrah.

En-gedi] The *well of the kid:* it was situated between Jericho and the lake of Sodom or Dead Sea.

Verse 63. *The Jebusites dwell—at Jerusalem unto this day.*] The whole history of Jerusalem, previously to the time of David, is encumbered with many difficulties. Sometimes it is attributed to *Judah*, sometimes to *Benjamin;* and it is probable that, being on the frontiers of both those tribes, each possessed a part of it. If the Jebusites were ever driven out before the time of David, it is certain they recovered it again, or at least a part of it— what is called the citadel or *strong hold of Zion,* (see 2 Sam. v. 7,) which he took from them; after which the city fell wholly into the hands of the Israelites. This verse is an additional proof that the book of Joshua was not written *after* the times of the Jewish kings, as some have endeavoured to prove; for when this verse was written, the Jebusites dwelt with the children of Judah, which they did not after the days of David; therefore the book was written before there were any *kings* in Judea.

It is very likely, not only that many cities have by the lapse of time changed their names or been totally destroyed, (see the note on ver. 1,) but that the names of those in the preceding catalogue have been changed also, several of them repeated that should have been mentioned but once, and not a few confounded with the terms by which they are described. But we must not suppose that every repetition of the name is through the carelessness of copyists; for there are often two places which bear the same name, which is frequently the case in England. But besides this, villages are mentioned as being apparently in the tribe of Judah, which afterwards appear to have been in another tribe. The reason appears to be this: many towns are mentioned which were frontier towns, and when the limits of a tribe are pointed out, such places must necessarily be mentioned, though allotted to a different tribe. This consideration will serve to remove several difficulties which occur in the reading of *this* and the following chapters.

CHAPTER XVI

Borders of the children of Joseph, 1–4. The borders of the Ephraimites, 5–9. The Canaanites dwell tributary among them, 10.

A. M. 2561
B. C. 1443
An. Exod. Isr.
48
Anno ante
I. Olymp. 667

AND the lot of the children of Joseph [a]fell from Jordan by Jericho, unto the water of Jericho on the east, to the wilderness that goeth up from Jericho throughout Mount Beth-el,

2 And goeth out from Beth-el to [b]Luz, and passeth along unto the borders of Archi to Ataroth,

3 And goeth down westward to the coast of Japhleti, [c]unto the coast of Beth-horon the nether, and to [d]Gezer: and the goings out thereof are at the sea.

4 [e]So the children of Joseph, Manasseh and Ephraim, took their inheritance.

5 And the border of the children of Ephraim according to their families was *thus:* even the border of their inheritance on the east side was [f]Ataroth-addar, [g]unto Beth-horon the upper;

6 And the border went out toward the sea

to [h]Michmethah on the north side; and the border went about eastward unto Taanath-shiloh, and passed by it on the east to Janohah;

A. M. 2561
B. C. 1443
An. Exod. Isr.
48
Anno ante
I. Olymp. 667

7 And it went down from Janohah to Ataroth, [i]and to Naarath, and came to Jericho, and went out at Jordan.

8 The border went out from Tappuah westward unto the [k]river Kanah; and the goings out thereof were at the sea. This *is* the inheritance of the tribe of the children of Ephraim by their families.

9 And [l]the separate cities for the children of Ephraim *were* among the inheritance of the children of Manasseh, all the cities with their villages.

10 [m]And they drave not out the Canaanites that dwelt in Gezer: but the Canaanites dwell among the Ephraimites unto this day, and serve under tribute.

---

[a]Heb. *went forth*——[b]Chap. xviii. 13; Judg. i. 26 [c]Chap. xviii. 13; 2 Chron. viii. 5——[d]1 Chron. vii. 28; 1 Kings ix. 15——[e]Chap. xvii. 14

[f]Chap. xviii. 13——[g]2 Chron. viii. 5——[h]Chap. xvii. 7——[i]1 Chron. vii. 28——[k]Chap. xvii. 9——[l]Chap. xvii. 9——[m]Judg. i. 29; see 1 Kings ix. 16

NOTES ON CHAP. XVI

Verse 1. *The children of Joseph*] Ephraim and Manasseh, and their descendants. The limits of the tribe of Ephraim extended along the borders of Benjamin and Dan, from *Jordan* on the *east* to the *Mediterranean* on the *west*.

Verse 2. *From Bethel to Luz*] From Gen. xxviii. 19 it appears that the place which Jacob called *Beth-el* was formerly called *Luz;* see the note there: but here they seem to be two distinct places. It is very likely that the place where Jacob had the vision was not in *Luz*, but in some place within a small distance of that city or village, (see the note on Gen. xxviii. 12,) and that sometimes the whole place was called *Beth-el*, at other times *Luz*, and sometimes, as in the case above, the two places were distinguished. As we find the term *London* comprises, not only *London*, but also the city of *Westminster* and the borough of *Southwark;* though at other times all three are distinctly mentioned.

Archi to Ataroth] Archi was the country of Hushai, the friend of David, 2 Sam. xv. 32, who

is called *Hushai the Archite*. Ataroth, called *Ataroth-addar*, Ataroth the illustrious, ver. 5, and simply *Ataroth*, ver. 7, is supposed to have been about fifteen miles from Jerusalem.

Verse 3. *Beth-horon the nether*] This city was about twelve miles from Jerusalem, on the side of *Nicopolis*, formerly *Emmaus.*—CALMET. See the note on chap. x. 10.

Verse 5. *Ataroth-addar*] See the note on ver. 2.

Beth-horon the upper] The situation of this town is little known. It was eastward of *Beth-horon the nether*, and consequently not far from it.

Verse 8. *Tappuah*] This was a city in the tribe of Manasseh, and gave name to a certain district called the *land of Tappuah*. See chap. xvii. 8.

The sea] The *Mediterranean*, as before.

Verse 9. *And the separate cities*] That is, the cities that were separated from the tribe of Manasseh to be given to Ephraim; see chap. xvii. 9.

Verse 10. *The Canaanites that dwelt in Gezer*] It appears that the Canaanites were not expelled from this city till the days of Solomon, when it was taken by the king of Egypt his father-in-law, who made it a present to his daughter, Solomon's queen. See 1 Kings ix. 16. And see the note on Josh. x. 33. The Ephraimites, however, had so far succeeded in subjecting these people as to oblige them to pay tribute, though they could not, or at least did not, totally expel them.

OF the *names* and *places* in this chapter, we may say the same as of others already mentioned. See the note on chap. xv. 1. Many of those towns were small, and, we may rationally conclude, slightly built, and consequently have

perished perhaps more than a thousand years ago. It would be therefore useless to look for such places *now*. Several of the towns in England, a land not exposed to such revolutions as that of Palestine has ever been, mentioned by Cæsar and other ancient writers, are no longer discernible. Several have changed their names, and not a few their situation. Tradition states that the city of Norwich anciently stood some miles from its present situation; and we have the fullest proof that this was the case with the city of Salisbury. Such changes do not affect the truth of the ancient geography of our own country; nor can they impeach that of the sacred historian before us.

CHAPTER XVII

The lot of the half tribe of Manasseh, 1, 2. Case of the daughters of Zelophehad, 3–6. The borders of Manasseh described, 7–11. The Canaanites dwell among them, but are laid under tribute, 12, 13. The children of Joseph complain of the scantiness of their lot, 14–16. Joshua authorizes them to possess the mountainous wood country of the Perizzites, and gives them encouragement to expel them, though they were strong and had chariots of iron, 17, 18.

A. M. 2561
B. C. 1443
An. Exod. Isr.
48
Anno ante
I. Olymp. 667

THERE was also a lot for the tribe of Manasseh; for he *was* the [a]first-born of Joseph; *to wit,* for [b]Machir, the first-born of Manasseh, the father of Gilead: because he was a man of war, therefore he had [c]Gilead and Bashan.

2 There was also *a lot* for [d]the rest of the children of Manasseh by their families; [e]for the children of [f]Abiezer, and for the children of Helek, [g]and for the children of Asriel, and for the children of Shechem, [h]and for the children of Hepher, and for the children of Shemida: these *were* the male children of Manasseh the son of Joseph by their families.

3 But [i]Zelophehad, the son of Hepher, the

son of Gilead, the son of Machir, the son of Manasseh, had no sons, but daughters: and these *are* the names of his daughters, Mahlah, and Noah, Hoglah, Milcah, and Tirzah.

A. M. 2561
B. C. 1443
An. Exod. Isr.
48
Anno ante
I. Olymp. 667

4 And they came near before [k]Eleazar the priest, and before Joshua the son of Nun, and before the princes, saying, [l]The LORD commanded Moses to give us an inheritance among our brethren. Therefore, according to the commandment of the LORD, he gave them an inheritance among the brethren of their father.

5 And there fell ten portions to Manasseh, beside the land of Gilead and Bashan, which *were* on the other side Jordan;

---

[a]Gen. xli. 51; xlvi. 20; xlviii. 18——[b]Gen. l. 23; Num. xxvi. 29; xxxii. 39, 40; 1 Chron. vii. 14——[c]Deut. iii. 15 [d]Num. xxvi. 29–32——[e]1 Chron. vii. 18

[f]Num. xxvi. 30; *Jezer*——[g]Num. xxvi. 31——[h]Num. xxvi. 32——[i]Num. xxvi. 33; xxvii. 1; xxxvi. 2 [k]Chap. xiv. 1——[l]Num. xxvii. 6, 7

NOTES ON CHAP. XVII

Verse 1. *There was also a lot for the tribe of Manasseh*] It was necessary to mark this because Jacob, in his blessing, (Gen. xlviii. 19, 20), did in a certain sense set Ephraim before Manasseh, though the latter was the first-born; but the place here shows that this preference did not affect the rights of primogeniture.

For Machir—because he was a man of war] It is not likely that Machir himself was now alive; if he were, he must have been nearly 200 years old: It is therefore probable that what is spoken here is spoken of his children, who now possessed the lot that was originally designed for their father, who it appears had signalized himself as a man of skill and valour in some of the former wars, though the circumstances are not marked. His descendants, being

of a warlike, intrepid spirit, were well qualified to defend a frontier country, which would be naturally exposed to invasion.

Verse 2. *The rest of the children of Manasseh*] That is, his *grandchildren;* for it is contended that Manasseh had no other son than *Machir;* and these were very probably the children of Gilead, the son of Machir.

Verse 3. *Zelophehad—had no sons, but daughters*] See this case considered at large in the notes on Num. xxvii. 1-7, and xxxvi. 1, &c.

Verse 5. *There fell ten portions to Manasseh*] The Hebrew word חבלי *chabley,* which we translate *portions,* signifies literally *cords* or *cables,* and intimates that by means of a *cord, cable,* or what we call a *chain,* the land was divided. We have but little account of the arts and sciences of the Hebrews, yet from the sketches

A. M. 2561
B. C. 1443
An. Exod. Isr.
48
Anno ante
I. Olymp. 667

6 Because the daughters of Manasseh had an inheritance among his sons: and the rest of Manasseh's sons had the land of Gilead.

7 And the coast of Manasseh was from Asher to ᵐMichmethah, that *lieth* before Shechem; and the border went along on the right hand unto the inhabitants of En-tappuah.

8 *Now* Manasseh had the land of Tappuah: but ⁿTappuah, on the border of Manasseh, *belonged* to the children of Ephraim:

9 And the coast descended ᵒunto the ᵖriver Kanah, southward of the river: �q these cities of Ephraim *are* among the cities of Manasseh: the coast of Manasseh also *was* on the north side of the river, and the outgoings of it were at the sea:

10 Southward *it was* Ephraim's, and northward *it was* Manasseh's, and the sea is his border; and they met together in Asher on the

A. M. 2561
B. C. 1443
An. Exod. Isr.
48
Anno ante
I. Olymp. 667

north, and in Issachar on the east.

11 ʳAnd Manasseh had in Issachar and in Asher ˢBethshean and her towns, and Ibleam and her towns, and the inhabitants of Dor and her towns, and the inhabitants of En-dor and her towns, and the inhabitants of Taanach and her towns, and the inhabitants of Megiddo and her towns, *even* three countries.

12 Yet ᵗthe children of Manasseh could not drive out *the inhabitants of* those cities; but the Canaanites would dwell in the land.

13 Yet it came to pass, when the children of Israel were waxen strong, that they put the Canaanites to ᵘtribute; but did not utterly drive them out.

14 ᵛAnd the children of Joseph spake unto Joshua, saying, Why hast thou given me *but* ᵂone lot and one portion to inherit, seeing I

ᵐChap. xvi. 6——ⁿChap. xvi. 8——ᵒChap. xvi. 8
ᵖOr, *brook of reeds*——q Chap. xvi. 9——ʳ1 Chron. vii. 29

ˢ1 Sam. xxxi. 10; 1 Kings iv. 12——ᵗJudg. i. 27, 28
ᵘChap. xvi. 10——ᵛChap. xvi. 4——ᵂGen. xlviii. 22

---

which we find in different parts of the Old Testament it appears that their minds were in many respects well cultivated; nor could the division, which is mentioned in this book, have been made without such a measure of geographical knowledge, as we find it difficult to grant them. Suppose even in this case, the land was not measured with a chain, which in some cases would have been impracticable, because the ancient inhabitants still occupied the places which were allotted to certain tribes or families; yet the allusion to this mode of measurement shows that it was well known among them.

As there were *six* sons and *five* daughters, among whom this division was to be made, there should be *eleven* portions; but Zelophehad, son of Hepher, having left five daughters in his place, neither he nor Hepher is reckoned. The lot of Manasseh therefore was divided into *ten* parts; five for the five sons of *Gilead*, who were Abiezer, Helek, Asriel, Shechem, and Shemida; and five for the five daughters of *Zelophehad*, viz., Mahlah, Noah, Hoglah, Milcah, and Tirzah.—CALMET.

Verse 9. *Unto the river Kanah*] Literally, the *river* or *valley of the reeds*, translated by the Vulgate, *vallis arundintei*. The tribe of Manasseh appears to have been bounded on the north by this *torrent* or *valley*, and on the south by the Mediterranean Sea.

Verse 10. *They met together in Asher on the north*] The tribe of Asher extended from the Mediterranean Sea to Mount Carmel, chap. xix. 26, and the tribe of Manasseh extended to *Dor* and her towns, (see the following verse,) which were in the vicinity of Carmel; and thus it appears that these two tribes formed a junction at the Mediterranean Sea. This may serve to

remove the difficulties in this verse; but still it does appear that in several cases the tribes were intermingled; for *Manasseh* had several towns, both in *Issachar* and in *Asher*, see ver. 11. In like manner, *Judah* had towns in *Dan* and *Simeon;* and *Simeon* had towns in *Judah;* and what is spoken of the *boundaries* of the tribes, may be sometimes understood of those *towns* which certain tribes had within the limits of others. For, in several cases, towns seem to be interchanged, or purchased, by mutual consent, so that in some instances the possessions were intermingled, without any confusion of the tribes or families.

Verse 11. *Beth-shean*] Called afterwards *Scythopolis;* the city of the *Scythians* or *Cuthites*, those who were sent into the different Samaritan cities by the kings of Assyria.

Dor] On the Mediterranean Sea, about eight miles from Cæsarea, on the road to Tyre.

En-dor] The *well* or *fountain of Dor*, the place where Saul went to consult the witch; 1 Sam. xxviii. 7, &c.

Verse 12. *Could not drive out, &c.*] They had neither *grace* nor *courage* to go against their enemies, and chose rather to share their territories with those whom the justice of God had proscribed, than exert themselves to expel them. But some commentators give a different turn to this expression, and translate the passage thus: *But the children of Manasseh could not* (resolve) *to destroy those cities, but the Canaanites consented to dwell in the land.* And as they were willing to pay tribute, and the others chose to tolerate them on those terms, they agreed to dwell together: but this paying of tribute seems not to have taken place till some time after, *when the children of Israel were waxen strong, &c.*

A. M. 2561
B. C. 1443
An. Exod. Isr.
48
Anno ante
I. Olymp. 667

am [x]a great people, forasmuch as the LORD hath blessed me hitherto?

15 And Joshua answered them, If thou *be* a great people, *then* get thee up to the wood *country,* and cut down for thyself there in the land of the Perizzites and of the [y]giants, if Mount Ephraim be too narrow for thee.

16 And the children of Joseph said, The hill is not enough for us: and all the Canaanites that dwell in the land of the valley have [z]chariots of iron, *both they* who *are* of Beth-

shean and her towns, and *they* who *are* [a]of the valley of Jezreel.

A. M. 2561
B. C. 1443
An. Exod. Isr
48
Anno ante
I. Olymp. 667

17 And Joshua spake unto the house of Joseph, *even* to Ephraim and to Manasseh, saying, Thou *art* a great people, and hast great power: thou shalt not have one lot *only:*

18 But the mountain shall be thine; for it *is* a wood, and thou shalt cut it down: and the outgoings of it shall be thine: for thou shalt drive out the Canaanites, [b]though they have iron chariots, *and* though they *be* strong.

---

[x]Gen. xlviii. 19; Num. xxvi. 34, 37——[y]Or, *Rephaims;* Gen. xiv. 5; xv. 20

[z]Judg. i. 19; iv. 3——[a]Chap. xix. 18; 1 Kings iv. 12 [b]Deut. xx. 1

Verse 15. If thou be *a great people*] Joshua takes them at their own word; they said, ver. 14, that they were a great people; then said he, *If thou be a great people* or *seeing thou art a great people, go to the wood country, and clear away for thyself.* Joshua would not reverse the decision of the lot; but as there was much woodland country, he gave them permission to clear away as much of it as they found necessary to extend themselves as far as they pleased.

Verse 16. The hill is not enough for us] The mountain of Gilboa being that which had fallen to them by lot.

Chariots of iron] We cannot possess the plain country, because that is occupied by the Canaanites; and we cannot conquer them, because they have *chariots of iron,* that is, very strong chariots, and *armed with scythes,* as is generally supposed.

Verse 18. The outgoings of it shall be thine] Clear away the wood, occupy the mountain, and you shall soon be able to command all the valleys; and, possessing all the defiles of the country, you shall drive out the Canaanites, though they have chariots of iron: your situation will be advantageous, your numbers very respectable, and the hand of God will be upon you for good.

1. FROM the whole history of the Israelites we find that it was difficult to please them; they

had a dissatisfied mind, and hence were rarely contented. From the above account we learn that the children of Joseph were much inclined to quarrel with Joshua, because they had not such a lot as they wished; though they could not be ignorant that their lot, as that of the others, had been determined by the especial providence of God.

2. Joshua treats them with great firmness; he would not attempt to alter the appointment of God, and he saw no reason to reverse or change the grant already made. They were both *numerous* and *strong,* and if they put forth their strength under the direction of even the ordinary providence of God, they had every reason to expect success.

3. *Slothfulness* is natural to man; it requires much training to induce him to labour for his daily bread; if God should miraculously send it he will *wonder* and *eat* it, and that is the whole. *Strive to enter in at the strait gate* is an ungracious word to many; they profess to trust in God's mercy, but *labour not* to enter into that rest: God will not reverse his *purpose* to meet their *slothfulness;* they alone who *overcome* shall sit with Jesus upon his throne. Reader, *take unto thee the whole armour of God, that thou mayest be able to stand in the evil day, and having done all—to* STAND. And remember, that he only who *endures to the end* shall be saved.

CHAPTER XVIII

The tabernacle is set up at Shiloh, 1. Seven of the tribes having not yet received their inheritance, 2, Joshua orders three men from each tribe to be chosen, and sent to examine the land and divide it into seven parts, which should be distributed among them by lot, 3–7. The men go and do as commanded, and return to Joshua, 8, 9. Joshua casts lots for them, 10. The lot of Benjamin, how situated, 11. Its northern boundaries, 12–14. Its southern boundaries, 15–19. Its eastern boundary, 20. Its cities, 21–28.

A. M. 2561
B. C. 1443
An. Exod. Isr.
48
Anno ante
I. Olymp. 667

A ND the whole congregation of the children of Israel assembled together [a]at Shiloh, and [b]set up the tabernacle of the

congregation there. And the land was subdued before them.

A. M. 2561
B. C. 1443
An. Exod. Isr.
48
Anno ante
I. Olymp. 667

2 And there remained among the children of Israel seven tribes,

---

[a]Chap. xix. 51; xxi. 2; xxii. 9; Jer. vii. 12

[b]Judg. xviii. 31; 1 Sam. i. 3, 24; iv. 3, 4

NOTES ON CHAP. XVIII
Verse 1. Israel assembled together at Shiloh]
This appears to have been a considerable town

about fifteen miles from Jerusalem, in the tribe of Ephraim, and nearly in the centre of the whole land. To this place both the camp of

A. M. 2561
B. C. 1443
An. Exod. Isr.
48
Anno ante
I. Olymp. 667 which had not yet received their inheritance.

3 And Joshua said unto the children of Israel, ^cHow long *are* ye slack to go to possess the land, which the LORD God of your fathers hath given you?

4 Give out from among you three men for *each* tribe: and I will send them, and they shall rise, and go through the land and describe it according to the inheritance of them; and they shall come *again* to me.

5 And they shall divide it into seven parts: ^dJudah shall abide in their coast on the south, and ^ethe house of Joseph shall abide in their coast on the north.

6 Ye shall therefore describe the land *into* seven parts, and bring *the description* hither to me, ^fthat I may cast lots for you here before the LORD our God.

7 ^gBut the Levites have no part among you; for the priesthood of the LORD *is* their in-

heritance: ^hand Gad, and Reuben, and half the tribe of Manasseh, have received their inheritance beyond Jordan on the east, which Moses the servant of the LORD gave them.

A. M. 2561
B. C. 1443
An. Exod. Isr.
48
Anno ante
I. Olymp. 667

8 And the men arose, and went away: and Joshua charged them that went to describe the land, saying, Go and walk through the land, and describe it, and come again to me, that I may here cast lots for you before the LORD in Shiloh.

9 And the men went and passed through the land, and described it by cities into seven parts in a book, and came *again* to Joshua to the host at Shiloh.

10 And Joshua cast lots for them in Shiloh before the LORD: and there Joshua divided the land unto the children of Israel according to their divisions.

11 And the lot of the tribe of the children of Benjamin came up according to their fami-

---

^cJudg. xviii. 9——^dChapter xv. 1——^eChapter xvi. 1, 4

^fChap. xiv. 2; ver. 10——^gChap. xiii. 33——^hChap. xiii. 8

Israel, and the ark of the Lord, were removed from Gilgal, after a residence there of *seven* years. Here the tabernacle remained one hundred and thirty years, as is generally supposed, being the most conveniently situated for access to the different tribes, and for safety, the Israelites having possession of the land on all sides; for it is here added, *the land was subdued before them*—the Canaanites were so completely subdued, that there was no longer any general resistance to the Israelitish arms.

Verse 3. *How long are ye slack to go to possess the land*] We find an unaccountable backwardness in this people to enter on the inheritance which God had given them! They had so long been supported by *miracle*, without any exertions of their own, that they found it difficult to shake themselves from their *inactivity*. When it was necessary that all the people should go out to battle, they went with a measure of confidence, expecting miraculous help from God, and confiding in their numbers, but when each tribe found it necessary to fight for itself, in order to its establishment and the extension of its borders, it was discouraged, and chose rather a life of inglorious ease than the possession of an inheritance which would cost it much labour to conquer.

Verse 4. *Three men for each tribe*] Probably meaning only *three* from each of the *seven* tribes who had not yet received their inheritance. It is likely that these twenty-one men were accompanied by a military guard, for without this they might have been easily cut off by straggling parties of the Canaanites.

They shall—describe it] It is likely they were persons well acquainted with geography and mensuration, without which it would have been impossible for them to have divided the land in the way necessary on this occasion.

Verse 5. *Judah shall abide—on the south,*

and the house of Joseph—on the north.] Joshua does not mean that the tribe of Judah occupied the *south*, and the tribe of Ephraim and Manasseh the *north* of the promised land; this was not the fact: but being now at Shiloh, a considerable way in the territory of Ephraim, and not far from that of Judah, he speaks of them in relation to *the place in which he then was*. Calmet considers him as thus addressing the deputies: "Go and examine the whole of the country which remains yet to be possessed; do not take into consideration the tribe of Judah, which is on the *south*, nor the tribe of Ephraim, which is on the *north* of where we now are, but carefully divide the remaining land which is not occupied by these tribes into seven equal parts." This makes a very good sense, and frees the place from embarrassment.

Verse 7. *The priesthood of the Lord is their inheritance*] We have already seen that the priests and Levites had the sacrifices, oblations, tithes, first-fruits, redemption-money of the first-born, &c., for their inheritance; they had no landed possessions in Israel; the LORD was their portion.

Verse 9. *And described it—in a book*] This, as far as I can recollect, is the first act of *surveying* on record. These men and their work differed widely from those who had searched the land in the time of Moses; *they* went only to discover the nature of the country, and the state of its inhabitants; but *these* went to take an actual *geographical survey* of it, in order to divide it among the tribes which had not yet received their portions. We may suppose that the country was exactly described *in a book*, that is, a *map*, pointing out the face of the country, accompanied with descriptions of each part.

Verse 11. *And the lot—of Benjamin came up*] On the manner of casting the lot, see on chap.

A. M. 2561
B. C. 1443
An. Exod. Isr.
48
Anno ante
I. Olymp. 667

lies: and the coast of their lot came forth between the children of Judah and the children of Joseph.

12 [i]And their border on the north side was from Jordan; and the border went up to the side of Jericho on the north side, and went up through the mountains westward; and the goings out thereof were at the wilderness of Beth-aven.

13 And the border went over from thence toward Luz, to the side of Luz, [k]which is Beth-el, southward; and the border descended to Ataroth-adar, near the hill that *lieth* on the south side [l]of the nether Beth-horon.

14 And the border was drawn *thence,* and compassed the corner of the sea southward, from the hill that *lieth* before Beth-horon southward; and the goings out thereof were at [m]Kirjath-baal, which is Kirjath-jearim, a city of the children of Judah: this *was* the west quarter.

15 And the south quarter *was* from the end of Kirjath-jearim, and the border went out on the west, and went out to [n]the well of waters of Nephtoah:

16 And the border came down to the end of the mountain that *lieth* before [o]the valley of the son of Hinnom, *and* which *is* in the valley of the giants on the north, and descended to the valley of Hinnom, to the side of Jebusi

on the south, and descended to [p]En-rogel,

A. M. 2561
B. C. 1443
An. Exod. Isr.
48
Anno ante
I. Olymp. 667

17 And was drawn from the north, and went forth to En-shemesh, and went forth toward Geliloth, which *is* over against the going up of Adummim, and descended to [q]the stone of Bohan the son of Reuben,

18 And passed along toward the side over against [r]Arabah [s]northward, and went down unto Arabah:

19 And the border passed along to the side of Beth-hoglah northward: and the outgoings of the border were at the north [t]bay of the Salt Sea at the south end of Jordan: this *was* the south coast.

20 And Jordan was the border of it on the east side. This *was* the inheritance of the children of Benjamin, by the coasts thereof round about, according to their families.

21 Now the cities of the tribe of the children of Benjamin according to their families were Jericho, and Beth-hoglah, and the valley of Keziz,

22 And Beth-arabah, and Zemaraim, and Beth-el,

23 And Avim, and Parah, and Ophrah,

24 And Chephar-haammonai, and Ophni, and Gaba; twelve cities with their villages:

25 Gibeon, and Ramah, and Beeroth,

26 And Mizpeh, and Chephirah, and Mozah,

---

[i]See Chap. xvi. 1——[k]Gen. xxviii. 19; Judg. i. 23
[l]Chap. xvi. 3——[m]See chap. xv. 9——[n]Chap. xv. 9

[o]Chap. xv. 8——[p]Chap. xv. 7——[q]Chap. xv. 6
[r]Chap. xv. 6——[s]Or, *the plain*——[t]Heb. *tongue*

---

xiv. 2, and Num. xxvi. 55. There were probably two *urns,* one of which contained the names of the seven tribes, and the other that of the seven portions. They therefore took out one name out of the first urn, and one portion out of the second, and thus the portion was adjudged to that tribe.

Verse 12. *The wilderness of Beth-aven.*] This was the same as *Beth-el;* but this name was not given to it till Jeroboam had fixed one of his golden calves there. Its first name signifies the *house of God;* its second, the *house of iniquity.*

Verse 16. *To the side of Jebusi*] The mountain of *Zion,* that was near *Jerusalem;* for *Jebusi,* or *Jebus,* was the ancient name of this city.

Verse 17. *En-shemesh*] The fountain of the sun; a proof of the idolatrous nature of the ancient inhabitants of this land.

Geliloth] As the word signifies *borders* or *limits,* it is probably not the proper name of a place: *And went forth towards the* BORDERS *which are over against the ascent to Adummim.*

Verse 19. *The north bay of the Salt Sea*] As the word לשׁון *leshon* signifies the *tongue,* it

may here refer to the *point* of the Dead or Salt Sea. Of these *tongues* or *points* it had *two,* one on the *north,* and the other on the *south.*

Verse 21. *Now the cities*] Some of these cities have been mentioned before, and described; of others we know nothing but the *name.*

Verse 24. *And Gaba*] Supposed to be the same as *Gibeah of Saul,* a place famous for having given ʰirth to the first king of Israel; and infamous for the shocking act towards the Levite's wife, mentioned Judg. xix., which was the cause of a war in which the tribe of Benjamin was nearly exterminated. Judg. xx.

Verse 25. *Gibeon*] See before, chap. x. This place is famous for the confederacy of the five kings against Israel, and their miraculous defeat. *Ramah,* a place about six or eight miles north of Jerusalem. *Beeroth,* i, e., *wells;* one of the four cities which belonged to the Gibeonites, who made peace with the Israelites by stratagem. See chap. ix.

Verse 26. *And Mizpeh*] This place is celebrated in the sacred writings. Here the people

A. M. 2561
B. C. 1443
An. Exod. Isr.
48
Anno ante
I. Olymp. 667

27 And Rekem, and Irpeel, and Taralah,

28 And Zelah, Eleph, and ᵘJebusi, which is Jerusalem, Gibeath,

and Kirjath; fourteen cities with their villages. This is the inheritance of the children of Benjamin according to their families.

A. M. 2561
B. C. 1443
An. Exod. Isr.
48
Anno ante
I. Olymp. 667

ᵘChap. xv. 8;   Num. xxvi. 54; xxxiii. 54

---

were accustomed to assemble often in the presence of the Lord, as in the deliberation concerning the punishment to be inflicted on the men of *Gibeah*, for the abuse of the Levite's wife. Judg. xx. 1-3. Samuel assembled the people here to exhort them to *renounce their idolatry*, 1 Sam. vii. 5, 6. In this same place *Saul* was chosen to be king, 1 Sam. x. 17. It was deemed a *sacred* place among the Israelites; for we find, from 1 Mac. iii. 46, that the Jews assembled here to seek God, when their enemies were in possession of the temple.

Verse 28. *And Zelah*] This was the burying-place of Saul, Jonathan, and the family of *Kish*. See 2 Sam. xxi. 14.

Jebusi, which is Jerusalem] We often meet with this name, and it is evident that it was the ancient name of Jerusalem, which was also

called *Salem*; and was probably the place in which Melchizedek reigned in the days of Abraham; though some think a different place is meant; for that there was another place of the same name, is evident from John iii. 23. This place, called Salim by the evangelist, is said to be near to Enon, and there John baptized, because there was much water in the place. This, however, must not be confounded with the *Salem* mentioned above; for that this was a name of Jerusalem, is evident from Psa. lxxvi. 1, 2: *In Judah is God known: his name is great in Israel. In* SALEM *also is his tabernacle, and his dwelling-place in Zion*. This must refer to *Jerusalem*, where the temple was situated. Whether *Jebus* or *Jebusi* had its name from the *Jebusites*, or the *Jebusites* from it, cannot be ascertained.

CHAPTER XIX

The lot of Simeon, 1–9. *Of* Zebulun, 10–16. *Of* Issachar, 17–23. *Of* Asher, 24–31. *Of* Naphtali, 32–39. *Of* Dan, 40–48. Joshua's *portion*, 49, 50. *The conclusion of the division of the land*, 51.

A. M. 2561
B. C. 1443
An. Exod. Isr.
48
Anno ante
I. Olymp. 667

AND the second lot came forth to Simeon, *even* for the tribe of the children of Simeon according to their families: ᵃand their inheritance was within the inheritance of the children of Judah.

2 And ᵇthey had in their inheritance Beer-sheba, Sheba, and Moladah,

3 And Hazar-shual, and Balah, and Azem,

4 And Eltolad, and Bethul, and Hormah,

5 And Hiklag, and Beth-marcaboth, and Hazar-susah,

6 And Beth-lebaoth, and Sharuhen; thirteen cities and their villages:

7 Ain, Remmon, and Ether, and Ashan; four cities and their villages:

8 And all the villages that *were* round about these cities to Baalath-beer, Ramath of the south. This *is* the inheritance of the tribe of the children of Simeon according to their families.

9 Out of the portion of the children of Judah *was* the inheritance of the children of Simeon: for the part of the children of Judah was too much for them: ᶜtherefore the children of Simeon had their inheritance within the inheritance of them.

10 And the third lot came up for the children of Zebulun according to their families: and the border of their inheritance was unto Sarid:

11 ᵈAnd their border went up toward the

A. M. 2561
B. C. 1443
An. Exod. Isr.
48
Anno ante
I. Olymp. 667

ᵃVer. 9——ᵇ1 Chron. iv. 28   ᶜVer. 1——ᵈGen. xlix. 13

NOTES ON CHAP. XIX

Verse 1. *The second lot came forth to Simeon*] In this appointment the providence of God may be especially remarked. For the iniquitous conduct of Simeon and Levi, in the massacre of the innocent Shechemites, Gen. xxxiv., Jacob, in the spirit of prophecy, foretold that they should be *divided in Jacob*, and *scattered in Israel*, Gen. xlix. 7. And this was most literally fulfilled in the manner in which God disposed of both these tribes afterwards. Levi was *scattered* through all Palestine, not having received any inheritance, only *cities to dwell in*, in different parts of the land; and *Simeon* was dis-

persed in Judah, with what could scarcely be said to be their *own*, or a *peculiar* lot. See the note on Gen. xlix. 7.

Verse 2. *Beer-sheba*] The *well of the oath*. See the note on Gen. xxi. 31.

Verse 3. *Hazar-shual*] For this and several of the following places, see the notes on chap. xv.

Verse 5. *Beth-marcaboth*] The *house* or *city of chariots*. Probably a place where their war-chariots and cavalry were laid up.

Verse 6. *Beth-lebaoth*] The *house* or *city of lionesses*. Probably so called from the numbers of those animals which bred there.

Verse 8. *Baalath-beer*] The *well of the mis-*

A. M. 2561
B. C. 1443
An. Exod. Isr.
48
Anno ante
I. Olymp. 667

sea, and Maralah, and reached to Dabbasheth, and reached to the river that *is* ebefore Jokneam;

12 And turned from Sarid eastward toward the sunrising unto the border of Chisloth-tabor, and then goeth out to Daberath, and goeth up to Japhia,

13 And from thence passeth on along on the east to Gittah-hepher, to Ittah-kazin, and goeth out to Remmon-fmethoar to Neah;

14 And the border compasseth it on the north side to Hannathon: and the outgoings thereof are in the valley of Jiphthah-el:

15 And Kattath, and Nahallal, and Shimron, and Idalah, and Beth-lehem; twelve cities with their villages.

16 This *is* the inheritance of the children of Zebulun according to their families, these cities with their villages.

17 *And* the fourth lot came out to Issachar, for the children of Issachar according to their families.

18 And their border was toward Jezreel, and Chesulloth, and Shunem,

19 And Haphraim, and Shihon, and Anaharath,

20 And Rabbith, and Kishion, and Abez,

21 And Remeth, and En-gannim, and En-haddah, and Beth-pazzez;

22 And the coast reacheth to Tabor, and Shahazimah, and Beth-shemesh; and the outgoings of their border were at Jordan: sixteen cities with their villages.

23 This *is* the inheritance of the tribe of the children of Issachar according to their families, the cities and their villages.

24 And the fifth lot came out for the tribe of the children of Asher according to their families.

25 And their border was Helkath, and Hali, and Beten, and Achshaph,

26 And Alammelech, and Amad, and Misheal; and reacheth to Carmel westward, and to Shihor-libnath;

27 And turneth toward the sunrising to Beth-dagon, and reacheth to Zebulun, and to the valley of Jiphthah-el toward the north

A. M. 2561
B. C. 1443
An. Exod. Isr.
48
Anno ante
I. Olymp. 667

---

eChap. xii. 22

fOr, *which is drawn*

---

tresses. Probably so called from some superstitious or impure worship set up there.

Verse 13. *Gittah-hepher*] The same as Gath-he-pher, the birth-place of the prophet Jonah.

Verse 15. *Shimron*] See on chap. xii.

Beth-lehem] The house of bread; a different place from that in which our Lord was born.

Verse 17. *The fourth lot came out to Issachar*] It is remarkable, that though Issachar was the eldest brother, yet the lot of Zebulun was drawn before his lot; and this is the order in which Jacob himself mentions them, Gen. xlix. 13, 14, though no reason appears, either here or in the place above, why this preference should be given to the younger; but that the apparently fortuitous lot should have distinguished them just as the prophetic Jacob did, is peculiarly remarkable. Known unto God are all his works from the beginning: he has reasons for his conduct, which in many cases are too great for any of his creatures to comprehend, but he works all things after the counsel of his own will, which is ever right and good; and in this case his *influence* may be as easily seen in the *decision* by the *lot*, as on the *mind* of the patriarch Jacob, when he *predicted* what should befall his children in the latter days, and his *providence* continued to ripen, and bring forward what his *judgment* had deemed right to be done.

Verse 18. *Jezreel*] This city, according to Calmet, was situated in an open country, having the town of *Legion* on the west, *Bethshan* on the east, on the south the mountains of *Gilboa*, and on the north those of *Hermon*.

Shunem] This city was rendered famous by

being the occasional abode of the prophet Elisha, and the place where he restored the son of a pious woman to life. 2 Kings iv. 8. It was the place where the Philistines were encamped on that ruinous day in which the Israelites were totally routed at *Gilboa*, and Saul and his sons Jonathan, Abinadab, and Malchi-shua, killed. 1 Sam. xxviii. 4; xxxi. 1, &c.

Verse 22. *Beth-shemesh*] The house or temple of the sun; there were several cities or towns of this name in Palestine; an ample proof that the worship of this celestial luminary had generally prevailed in that idolatrous country.

Verse 26. *Carmel*] The vineyard of God; a place greatly celebrated in Scripture, and especially for the miracles of Elijah; see 1 Kings xviii. The mountain of Carmel was so very fruitful as to pass into a proverb. There was another Carmel in the tribe of *Judah*, (see chap. xv. 55,) but this, in the tribe of *Asher*, was situated about one hundred and twenty furlongs south from Ptolemais, on the edge of the Mediterranean Sea. Calmet observes that there was, in the time of Vespasian, a temple on this mountain, dedicated to a god of the same name. There was a convent, and a religious order known by the name of *Carmelites*, established on this mountain in honour of *Elijah*: the time of the foundation of this order is greatly disputed. Some pretend that it was established by Elijah himself; while others, with more probability, fix it in A. D. 1180 or 1181, under the pontificate of Pope Alexander III.

Verse 27. *Cabul on the left hand*] That is, to the *north* of Cabul, for so the *left hand*, when

A. M. 2561
B. C. 1443
An. Exod. Isr.
48
Anno ante
I. Olymp. 667

side of Beth-emek, and Neiel, and goeth out to Cabul on the left hand,

28 And Hebron, and Rehob, and Hammon, and Kanah, ^g*even* unto great Zidon;

29 And *then* the coast turneth to Ramah, and to the strong city ^hTyre; and the coast turneth to Hosah; and the outgoings thereof are at the sea from the coast to ⁱAchzib:

30 Ummah also, and Aphek, and Rehob: twenty and two cities with their villages.

31 This *is* the inheritance of the tribe of

A. M. 2561
B. C. 1443
An. Exod. Isr.
48
Anno ante
I. Olymp. 667

the children of Asher according to their families, these cities with their villages.

32 The sixth lot came out to the children of Naphtali, *even* for the children of Naphtali according to their families.

33 And their coast was from Heleph, from Allon to Zaanannim, and Adami, Nekeb, and Jabneel, unto Lakum; and the outgoings thereof were at Jordan:

34 And *then* ^kthe coast turneth westward to Aznoth-tabor, and goeth out from thence to Hukkok, and reacheth to Zebulun on the

---

^gChap. xi. 8; Judg. i. 31——^hHeb. *Tzor;* 2 Sam. v. 11

ⁱGen. xxxviii. 5; Judg. i. 31; Mic. i. 14——^kDeut. xxxiii. 23

---

referring to *place*, is understood among the Hebrews.

We must not confound this *town* or *Cabul* with the twenty cities given by Solomon to Hiram, with which he was displeased, and which in contempt he called *the land of Cabul*, the *dirty* or *paltry land*, 1 Kings ix. 11-13: there was evidently a town of this name, widely different from the *land* so called, long before the time of Solomon, and therefore this cannot be adduced as an argument that the book of Joshua was written after the days of David. The town in question is supposed to be the same which Josephus in his Life calls Χωβουλω *Choboulo*, and which he says was situated by the sea-side, and nigh to Ptolemais. *De Bell. Jud.*, lib. iii., c. 4.

Verse 28. *Unto great Zidon*] The city of *Sidon* and the *Sidonians* are celebrated from the remotest antiquity. They are frequently mentioned by Homer. See the note on chap. xi. 8.

Verse 29. *The strong city Tyre*] I suspect this to be an improper translation. Perhaps the words of the original should be retained: *And the coast turneth to Ramah and to the city*, מבצר צר *mibtsar tsor*. Our translators have here left the *Hebrew*, and followed the *Septuagint* and *Vulgate*, a fault of which they are sometimes guilty. The former render the place έως πολεως οχυρωματος των Τυριων, *unto the fortified city of the Tyrians*. The Vulgate is nearly the same: *ad civitatem munitissimam Tyrum, to the well-fortified city Tyre;* but this must be incorrect, for the famous city of Tyre was not known till about A. M. 2760, about two hundred years after the days of Joshua. Homer, who frequently mentions *Sidon* and the *Sidonians*, never mentions *Tyre;* a proof that this afterwards very eminent city was not then known. Homer is allowed by some to have flourished in the time of Joshua, though others make him contemporary with the Israelitish judges.

The word צר *Tsor* or *Tsar*, which we translate or change into *Tyre*, signifies a *rock* or *strong place;* and as there were many *rocks* in the land of Judea, that with a little art were formed into strong places of defence, hence several places might have the name of *Tsar* or *Tyre*. The ancient and celebrated Tyre, so much spoken of both in *sacred* and *profane* history, was a *rock* or small island in the sea, about six or seven hundred paces from the main

land. In order to reduce this city, Alexander the Great was obliged to fill up the channel between it and the main land, and after all took it with much difficulty. It is generally supposed that a town on the main land, opposite to this fortified rock, went by the same name; one being called *old Tyre*, the other, *new Tyre:* it was out of the ruins of the old Tyre, or that which was situated on the main land, that Alexander is said to have filled up the channel between it and the new city. Of this city Isaiah, chap. xxiii., and Ezekiel, chap. xxvii. and xxviii., have given a very grand description, and also predicted its irreparable ruin, which prophecies have been most literally fulfilled. See more on the above places.

Achzib] Called afterwards *Ecdippe*, and now called *Zib;* it is about nine miles' distance from Ptolemais, towards *Tyre*.

Verse 30. *Twenty and two cities*] There are nearly thirty cities in the above enumeration instead of *twenty-two*, but probably several are mentioned that were but *frontier* towns, and that did not belong to this tribe, their border only passing *by* such cities; and on this account, though they are named, yet they do not enter into the *enumeration* in this place. Perhaps some of the *villages* are named as well as the *cities*.

Verse 34. *And to Judah upon Jordan*] It is certain that the tribe of Naphtali did not border on the east upon Judah, for there were several tribes betwixt them. Some think that as these two tribes were bounded by Jordan on the east, they might be considered as in some sort conjoined, because of the easy passage to each other by means of the river; but this might be said of several other tribes as well as of these. There is considerable difficulty in the text as it now stands; but if, with the *Septuagint*, we omit *Judah*, the difficulty vanishes, and the passage is plain: but this omission is supported by no MS. hitherto discovered. It is however very probable that some change has taken place in the words of the text, וביהודה הירדן *ubihudah haiyarden*, "and by Judah upon Jordan." Houbigant, who terms them *verba sine re ac sententia*, "words without sense or meaning," proposes, instead of them, to read ובגדות הירדן *ubigdoth haiyarden*, "and by the banks of Jordan;" a word which is used chap. iii. 15, and which here makes a very **good sense**.

A. M. 2561
B. C. 1443
An. Exod. Isr.
48
Anno ante
I. Olymp. 667

south side, and reacheth to Asher on the west side, and to Judah upon Jordan toward the sunrising.

35 And the fenced cities *are* Ziddim, Zer, and Hammath, Rakkath, and Chinnereth,

36 And Adamah, and Ramah, and Hazor,

37 And Kedesh, and Edrei, and En-hazor,

38 And Iron, and Migdal-el, Horem, and Beth-anath, and Beth-shemesh; nineteen cities with their villages.

39 This *is* the inheritance of the tribe of the children of Naphtali according to their families, the cities and their villages.

40 *And* the seventh lot came out for the tribe of the children of Dan according to their families.

41 And the coast of their inheritance was Zorah, and Eshtaol, and Ir-shemesh,

42 And [l]Shaalabbin, and Ajalon, and Jethlah,

43 And Elon, and Thimnathah, and Ekron,

44 And Eltekeh, and Gibbethon, and Baalath,

45 And Jehud, and Bene-berak, and Gath-rimmon,

46 And Me-jarkon, and Rakkon, with the border, [m]before [n]Japho.

47 And [o]the coast of the children of Dan went out *too little* for them: therefore the children of Dan went up to fight against Leshem, and took it, and smote it with the edge of the sword, and possessed it, and dwelt therein, and called Leshem, [p]Dan, after the name of Dan their father.

A. M. 2561
B. C. 1443
An. Exod. Isr.
48
Anno ante
I. Olymp. 667

48 This *is* the inheritance of the tribe of the children of Dan according to their families, these cities with their villages.

49 When they had made an end of dividing the land for inheritance by their coasts, the children of Israel gave an inheritance to Joshua the son of Nun among them:

50 According to the word of the LORD they gave him the city which he asked, *even* [q]Timnath-[r]serah in Mount Ephraim: and he built the city, and dwelt therein.

51 [s]These *are* the inheritances which Eleazar the priest, and Joshua the son of Nun, and the heads of the fathers of the tribes of the children of Israel, [t]divided for an inheritance by lot [u]in Shiloh before the LORD, at the door of the tabernacle of the congregation. So they made an end of dividing the country.

---

[l]Judg. i. 35——[m]Or, *over against*——[n]Or, *Joppa;* Acts ix. 36——[o]See Judg. xviii——[p]Judg. xviii. 29 [q]Chap. xxiv. 30

[r]1 Chron. vii. 24——[s]Num. xxxiv. 17; chap. xiv. 1 [t]Chap. xiv. 1; Num. xxiv. 17-29——[u]Chap. xviii. 1, 10

Verse 35. *Chinnereth*] See the note on chap. xi. 2.

Verse 36. *Hazor*] See the note on chap. xi. 1.

Verse 38. *Nineteen cities*] But if these cities be separately enumerated they amount to twenty-three; this is probably occasioned by reckoning *frontier* cities belonging to other tribes, which are only mentioned here as the *boundaries* of the tribe. See on ver. 30.

Verse 41. *Zorah, and Eshtaol*] See the note on chap. xv. 33.

Ir-shemesh] *The city of sun;* another proof of the idolatry of the Canaanites. Some think this was the same as *Beth-shemesh.*

Verse 42. *Shaalabbin*] *The foxes.* Of this city the Amorites kept constant possession. See Judg. i. 35.

Ajalon] There was a place of this name about two miles from Nicopolis or Emmaus, on the road to Jerusalem.—*Calmet.*

Verse 43. *Thimnathah*] Probably the same as Timnah. See on chap. xv. 57.

Ekron] A well-known city of the Philistines, and the metropolis of one of their *five* dynasties.

Verse 45. *Jehud, and Bene-berak*] Or Jehud of the children of Berak.

Verse 46. *Japho.*] The place since called Joppa, lying on the Mediterranean, and the chief sea-port, in the possession of the twelve tribes.

Verse 47. *Went out* too little *for them*] This is certainly the meaning of the passage; but our translators have been obliged to add the words

too little to make this sense apparent. Houbigant contends that an ancient copyist, meeting frequently with the words הגבול ויצא *vaiyetse haggebul,* in the preceding history, became so familiarized to them that he wrote them here instead of הגבול ויאץ *vaiyaats haggebul,* and the *border of the children of Dan was* STRAIT *for them.* It was on this account that they were obliged to go and fight against Leshem, and take and possess it, their former inheritance being too strait for their increasing population.

And called Leshem, Dan] This city was situated near the origin of Jordan, at the utmost northern extremity of the promised land, as *Beer-sheba* was at that of the south; and as after its capture by the Danites it was called *Dan,* hence arose the expression *from Dan even to Beer-sheba,* which always signified the whole extent of the promised land. Some suppose that *Leshem* was the same with *Cæsarea Philippi,* but others with reason reject this opinion. It must be granted that the whole account given in this verse refers indisputably to a fact which did not take place till after the death of Joshua. It is another of the marginal or explicative notes which were added by some *later* hand. The whole account of this expedition of the Danites against *Leshem* is circumstantially given in chap. xviii. of the book of Judges, and to that chapter the reader is referred.

Verse 50. *Timnath-serah*] Called *Timnath-heres* in Judg. ii. 9, where we find that the mountain on which it was built was called *Gaash*. It is generally allowed to have been a barren spot in a barren country.

Verse 51. *At the door of the tabernacle*] All the inheritances were determined by lot, and this was cast *before the Lord*—every thing was done in his immediate presence, as under his eye; hence there was no murmuring, each having received his inheritance as from the hand of God himself, though some of them thought they must have additional territory, because of the great increase of their families.

CHAPTER XX

Joshua is commanded to appoint cities of refuge, 1, 2. The purpose of their institution, 3–6. Three cities are appointed in the promised land, 7; and three on the east side of Jordan, 8, 9.

A. M. 2561
B. C. 1443
An. Exod. Isr. 48
Anno ante
I. Olymp. 667

THE LORD also spake unto Joshua, saying,

2 Speak to the children of Israel, saying, [a]Appoint out for you cities of refuge, whereof I spake unto you by the hand of Moses:

3 That the slayer that killeth *any* person unawares *and* unwittingly, may flee thither: and they shall be your refuge from the avenger of blood.

4 And when he that doth flee unto one of those cities, shall stand at the entering of [b]the gate of the city, and shall declare his cause in the ears of the elders of that city, they shall take him into the city unto them, and give him a place, that he may dwell among them.

5 [c]And if the avenger of blood pursue after him, then they shall not deliver the slayer up into his hand; because he smote his neighbour unwittingly, and hated him not beforetime.

A. M. 2561
B. C. 1443
An. Exod. Isr. 48
Anno ante
I. Olymp. 667

6 And he shall dwell in that city, [d]until he stand before the congregation for judgment, *and* until the death of the high priest that shall be in those days: then shall the slayer return, and come unto his own city, and unto his own house, unto the city from whence he fled.

7 And they [e]appointed [f]Kedesh in Galilee in Mount Naphtali, and [g]Shechem in Mount Ephraim, and [h]Kirjath-arba, which *is* Hebron, in the [i]mountain of Judah.

[a]Exodus xxi. 13; Num. xxxv. 6, 11, 14; Deut. xix. 2, 9——[b]Ruth iv. 1, 2——[c]Num. xxxv. 12——[d]Num. xxxv. 12, 25

[e]Heb. *sanctified*——[f]Chap. xxi. 32; 1 Chron. vi. 76 [g]Chap. xxi. 21; 2 Chron. x. 1——[h]Chap. xiv. 15; xxi. 11, 13——[i]Luke i. 39

NOTES ON CHAP. XX

Verse 2. *Cities of refuge*] An institution of this kind was essentially necessary wherever the patriarchal law relative to the right of redemption and the avenging of blood was in force; we have already seen that the *nearest of kin* to a deceased person had not only the right of redeeming an inheritance that had been forfeited or alienated, but had also authority to slay on the spot the person who had slain his relative. Now, as a man might *casually* kill another against whom he had no ill-will, and with whom he had no quarrel, and might have his life taken away by him who was called the *avenger of blood*, though he had not forfeited his life to the law; therefore these privileged cities were appointed, where the person might have protection till the cause had been fully heard by the magistrates, who certainly had authority to deliver him up to the avenger, if they found, on examination, that he was not entitled to this protection. On this subject see the notes on Num. xxxv. 11 to the end.

Verse 7. *They appointed Kedesh in Galilee*] The cities of refuge were distributed through the land at proper distances from each other, that they might be convenient to every part of the land; and it is said they were situated on *eminences*, that they might be easily seen at a distance, the *roads* leading to them being broad, even, and always kept in good repair. In the concluding note on Num. xxxv. it has been stated that these cities were a type of our blessed Lord, and that the apostle refers to them as such, Heb. vi. 17, 18. Hence their names have been considered as descriptive of some character or office of Christ. I shall give each and its signification, and leave the application to others.

1. קדש KEDESH, from *kadash*, to *separate* or *set apart*, because it implies the consecration of a person or thing to the worship or service of God alone; hence to *make* or *be holy*, and hence *Kedesh*, holiness, the *full consecration of a person to God*.

2. שכם SHECHEM, from *shacham*, to be *ready, forward*, and *diligent;* hence *Shechem*, the *shoulder*, because of its readiness to bear burdens, *prop up, sustain*, &c., and from this ideal meaning it has the metaphorical one of GOVERNMENT.

3. חברון *chebron*, HEBRON, from חבר *chabar*, to *associate, join, conjoin, unite as friends;* and hence *chebron, fellowship, friendly association*, or with the *diminutive* ן *nun*, the *little fellowship or association*.

4. בצר BEZER, from *batsar*, to *restrain, enclose, shut up*, or *encompass with a wall;* and hence the *goods* or *treasure* thus *secured*, and hence a *fortified* place, a *fortress*.

5. ראמות RAMOTH, from ראם *raam*, to be *raised, made high* or *exalted*, and hence *Ramoth, high places, eminences*.

6. גולן GOLAN, from גלה *galah*, to *remove*,

A. M. 2561
B. C. 1443
An. Exod. Isr.
48
Anno ante
I. Olymp. 667

8 And on the other side Jordan by Jericho eastward, they assigned [k]Bezer in the wilderness upon the plain out of the tribe of Reuben, and [l]Ramoth in Gilead out of the tribe of Gad, and [m]Golan in Bashan out of the tribe of Manasseh.

9 [n]These were the cities appointed for all the children of Israel, and for the stranger that sojourneth among them, that whosoever killeth *any* person at unawares might flee thither, and not die by the hand of the avenger of blood, [o]until he stood before the congregation.

A. M. 2561
B. C. 1443
An. Exod. Isr.
48
Anno ante
I. Olymp. 667

---

[k]Deut. iv. 43; chap. xxi. 36; 1 Chron. vi. 80——[l]Chap. xxi. 38

1 Kings xxii. 3——[m]Chap. xxi. 27——[n]Num. xxxv. 15
[o]Ver. 6

---

transmigrate, or *pass away;* hence *Golan,* a *transmigration* or *passage.* Some derive it from בָּל *gal,* to *rejoice,* hence GOLAN, *rejoicing* or *exultation.*

A person of the spirit and turn of *Origen* could preach the whole Gospel from these particulars.

Kedesh and *Hebron* were at the two extremities of the promised land; one was in Galilee, the other in the tribe of Judah, both in mountainous countries; and *Shechem* was in the tribe of Ephraim, nearly in the middle, between both.

Bezer was on the east side of Jordan, in the plain, opposite to Jericho.

Ramoth was about the midst of the country occupied by the two tribes and a half, about the middle of the mountains of Gilead.

Golan was the capital of a district called *Gaulonitis,* in the land of Bashan, towards the southern extremity of the lot of Manasseh.

Verse 9. *For all the children of Israel, and for the stranger*] As these typified the great provision which God was making for the salvation of both Jews and Gentiles, hence the

stranger as well as the Israelite had the same right to the benefits of these cities of refuge. Is HE the God of the *Jews* only? Is HE not also the God of the *Gentiles?*

Until he stood before the congregation.] The judges and elders of the people, in trying civil and criminal causes, always *sat;* the persons who came for judgment, or who were *tried,* always *stood;* hence the expressions so frequent in Scripture, STANDING *before the Lord,* the *judges,* the *elders,* &c.

It is worthy of remark that the cities of refuge were given to the *Levites;* see the following chapter. The *sacrificial* system alone afforded *refuge;* and while the suspected person was excluded from his family, &c., he had the advantage of being with those whose business it was to instruct the ignorant, and comfort the disconsolate. Thus he had the means constantly at hand, by a careful use of which he might grow wiser and better; secure the favour of his God, and a lot of blessedness in a better world. How wise, equal, and beneficent are all the institutions of God!

CHAPTER XXI

The Levites apply to Eleazar, Joshua, and the elders, for the cities to dwell in which Moses had promised, 1, 2. Their request is granted, 3. The priests receive thirteen cities out of the tribes of Judah, Simeon, and Benjamin, 4. The Levites receive ten cities out of the tribes of Ephraim, Dan, and the half tribe of Manasseh, 5; and thirteen out of the other half tribe of Manasseh, and the tribes of Issachar, Asher, and Naphtali, 6. The children of Merari had twelve cities out of the tribes of Reuben, Gad, and Zebulun, 7. The names of the cities given out of the tribes of Judah and Simeon, 8–16. Those granted out of the tribe of Benjamin, 17–19. Out of Ephraim, 20–22. Those out of Dan, 23, 24. Those out of both the halves of the tribe of Manasseh, 25–27. Those out of the tribe of Issachar, 28, 29. Those out of Asher, 30, 31. Those out of Naphtali, 32. These were the cities of the Gershonites, 33. The cities of the Merarites, 34–40. The sum of the cities given to the Levites, forty-eight, 41, 42. The exact fulfilment of all God's promises, 43–45.

A. M. 2561
B. C. 1443
An. Exod. Isr.
48
Anno ante
I. Olymp. 667

THEN came near the heads of the fathers of the Levites unto [a]Eleazar the priest, and unto Joshua the son of Nun, and

unto the heads of the fathers of the tribes of the children of Israel;

2 And they spake unto them at

A. M. 2561
B. C. 1443
An. Exod. Isr.
48
Anno ante
I. Olymp. 667

---

[a]Chap. xiv. 1:   xvii. 4

NOTES ON CHAP. XXI.

Verse I. *The heads of the fathers of the Levites*] The Levites were composed of *three* grand families, the *Gershonites, Koathites,* and *Merarites,* independently of the family of *Aaron,* who might be said to form a *fourth.* To none of these had God assigned any portion in the division of the land. But in this general division it must have been evidently intended that

the different tribes were to furnish them with *habitations;* and this was according to a positive command of God, Num. xxxv. 2, &c. Finding now that each tribe had its inheritance appointed to it, the heads of the Levites came before Eleazar, Joshua, and the chiefs of the tribes who had been employed in dividing the land, and requested that cities and suburbs should be granted them according to the Divine command.

A. M. 2561
B. C. 1443
An. Exod. Isr.
48
Anno ante
I. Olymp. 667

Shiloh, [b]in the land of Canaan, saying, [c]The LORD commanded, by the hand of Moses, to give us cities to dwell in, with the suburbs thereof for our cattle.

3 And the children of Israel gave unto the Levites out of their inheritance, at the commandment of the LORD, these cities and their suburbs.

4 And the lot came out for the families of the Kohathites: and [d]the children of Aaron the priest, *which were* of the Levites, [e]had by lot out of the tribe of Judah, and out of the tribe of Simeon, and out of the tribe of Benjamin thirteen cities.

5 And [f]the rest of the children of Kohath *had* by lot out of the families of the tribe of Ephraim, and out of the tribe of Dan, and out of the half tribe of Manasseh, ten cities.

6 And [g]the children of Gershon *had* by lot out of the families of the tribe of Issachar,

and out of the tribe of Asher, and out of the tribe of Naphtali, and out of the half tribe of Manasseh in Bashan, thirteen cities.

A. M. 2561
B. C. 1443
An. Exod. Isr.
48
Anno ante
I. Olymp. 667

7 [h]The children of Merari by their families *had* out of the tribe of Reuben, and out of the tribe of Gad, and out of the tribe of Zebulun, twelve cities.

8 [i]And the children of Israel gave by lot unto the Levites these cities with their suburbs, [k]as the LORD commanded by the hand of Moses.

9 And they gave out of the tribe of the children of Judah, and out of the tribe of the children of Simeon, these cities which are *here* [l]mentioned by name,

10 [m]Which the children of Aaron, *being* of the families of the Kohathites, *who were* of the children of Levi, had: for theirs was the first lot.

---

[b]Chap. xviii. 1——[c]Num. xxxv. 2——[d]Ver. 8, 19
[e]See chap. xxiv. 33——[f]Ver. 20, &c.

[g]Ver. 27, &c.——[h]Ver. 34, &c.——[i]Ver. 3——[k]Num.
xxxv. 2——[l]Heb. *called*——[m]Ver. 4

Verse 3. *And the children of Israel gave unto the Levites*] They cheerfully obeyed the Divine command, and cities for habitations were appointed to them out of the different tribes by *lot*, that it might as fully appear that God designed them their *habitations*, as he designed the others their *inheritances*.

Verse 4. *Out of the tribe of Judah—Simeon, and—Benjamin, thirteen cities.*] These tribes furnished more habitations to the Levites in proportion than any of the other tribes, because they possessed a more extensive inheritance; and Moses had commanded, Num. xxxv. 8, *From them that have many, ye shall give many; and from them that have few, ye shall give few: every one shall give of his cities unto the Levites, according to his inheritance.* It is worthy of remark, that the principal part of this tribe, whose business was to minister at the sanctuary, which sanctuary was afterwards to be established in Jerusalem, had their appointment nearest to that city; so that they were always within reach of the sacred work which God had appointed them.

Verse 5. *And the rest of the children of Kohath*] That is, the remaining part of that family that were not *priests*, for those who were priests had their lot in the preceding tribes. Those, therefore, of the family of Kohath, who were simply *Levites*, and not of the priests or Aaron's family, (see ver. 10,) had their habitations in *Ephraim, Dan*, and the half tribe of *Manasseh*.

It has been asked in what sense did the Levites possess those cities, seeing they had no inheritance? To which it may be answered, that it is not likely the Levites had the exclusive property of the cities in which they dwelt, for it is evident that the other Israelites dwelt among them. We know, says Calmet, by

history, that the cities of the Levites were almost entirely filled with Israelites of other tribes. For instance, Gibeah of Benjamin, which is here given to the Levites, ver. 17, was always peopled by the *Benjamites*, as appears from the history of the Levite, whose wife was so horribly abused by them; Judg. xix. Saul and all his family dwelt in the same city; and David and his court spent the first years of his reign at *Hebron*, which was also a city of the Levites, ver. 10. It appears, therefore, that they had no other property in those cities than merely the right to certain houses, which they might sell, but always with the right of perpetual redemption, for they could finally alienate nothing; and if the possessor of such a house, having sold it, did not redeem it at the year of jubilee, it reverted to the Levites. And as to their lands for their cattle, which extended two thousand cubits without the city, these they were not permitted to sell: they were considered as the Lord's property. See Lev. xxv. 32-34, and the notes there. It is therefore very likely that, in the first instance, the Levites had simply the right to choose, in all the cities assigned them, the houses in which they were to dwell, and that those of the tribe to which the city belonged occupied all the other dwellings. There is also reason to believe that in process of time, when the families of the Levites increased, they had more dwellings assigned to them, which were probably built at the public expense.

We may also observe that the Levites were not absolutely bound to live in these and no other cities: for when the tabernacle was at *Nob*, priests and Levites dwelt there, see 1 Sam. xxi. 1, &c.; and when the worship of God was established at Jerusalem, multitudes both of priests and Levites dwelt there, though it was no Levitical city: as did the *courses* of priests

A. M. 2561
B. C. 1443
An. Exod. Isr.
48
Anno ante
I. Olymp. 667

11 [n]And they gave them [o]the city of Arba the father of [p]Anak, which *city is* Hebron, [q]in the hill *country* of Judah, with the suburbs thereof round about it.

12 But [r]the fields of the city, and the villages thereof, gave they to Caleb the son of Jephunneh for his possession.

13 Thus [s]they gave to the children of Aaron the priest [t]Hebron with her suburbs, *to be* a city of refuge for the slayer; [u]and Libnah with her suburbs,

14 And [v]Jattir with her suburbs, [w]and Eshtemoa with her suburbs,

15 And [x]Holon with her suburbs, [y]and Debir with her suburbs,

16 And [z]Ain with her suburbs, [a]and Juttah with her suburbs, *and* [b]Beth-shemesh with her suburbs; nine cities out of those two tribes.

17 And out of the tribe of Benjamin, [c]Gibeon with her suburbs, [d]Geba with her suburbs,

18 Anathoth with her suburbs, and [e]Almon with her suburbs; four cities.

19 All the cities of the children of Aaron, the priests, *were* thirteen cities with their suburbs.

20 [f]And the families of the children of Kohath, the Levites which remained of the children of Kohath, even they had the cities of their lot out of the tribe of Ephraim.

21 For they gave them [g]Shechem with her suburbs in Mount Ephraim, *to be* a city of refuge for the slayer; and Gezer with her suburbs,

22 And Kibzaim with her suburbs, and

Beth-horon with her suburbs; four cities.

A. M. 2561
B. C. 1443
An. Exod. Isr.
48
Anno ante
I. Olymp. 667

23 And out of the tribe of Dan, Eltekeh with her suburbs, Gibbethon with her suburbs,

24 Aijalon with her suburbs, Gath-rimmon with her suburbs; four cities.

25 And out of the half tribe of Manasseh, Tanach with her suburbs, and Gath-rimmon with her suburbs; two cities.

26 All the cities *were* ten with their suburbs for the families of the children of Kohath that remained.

27 [h]And unto the children of Gershon, of the families of the Levites, out of the *other* half tribe of Manasseh, *they* gave [i]Golan in Bashan with her suburbs, *to be* a city of refuge for the slayer; and Beeshterah with her suburbs; two cities.

28 And out of the tribe of Issachar, Kishon with her suburbs, Dabareh with her suburbs,

29 Jarmuth with her suburbs, En-gannim with her suburbs; four cities.

30 And out of the tribe of Asher, Mishal with her suburbs, Abdon with her suburbs,

31 Helkath with her suburbs, and Rehob with her suburbs; four cities.

32 And out of the tribe of Naphtali, [k]Kedesh in Galilee with her suburbs, *to be* a city of refuge for the slayer; and Hammoth-dor with her suburbs, and Kartan with her suburbs; three cities.

33 All the cities of the Gershonites according to their families *were* thirteen cities with their suburbs.

34 [l]And unto the families of the children of Merari, the rest of the Levites, out of the

---

[n]1 Chron. vi. 55——[o]Or, *Kirjath-arba;* Genesis xxiii. 2
[p]Chap. xv. 13, 14——[q]Chap. xx. 7; Luke i. 39
[r]Chap. xiv. 14; 1 Chron. vi. 56——[s]1 Chron. vi. 57, &c.
[t]Chap. xv. 54; xx. 7——[u]Chap. xv. 42——[v]Chap. xv. 48
[w]Chap. xv. 50——[x]1 Chron. vi. 58, *Hilen;* chap. xv.
51——[y]Chap. xv. 49

[z]1 Chron. vi. 59, *Ashan;* chap. xv. 42——[a]Chap. xv.
55——[b]Chap. xv. 10——[c]Chap. xviii. 25——[d]Chap.
xviii. 24, *Gaba*——[e]1 Chron. vi. 60, *Alemeth*——[f]Verse
5; 1 Chron. vi. 66——[g]Chap. xx. 7——[h]Ver. 6; 1 Chron.
vi. 71——[i]Chap. xx. 8——[k]Chap. xx. 7——[l]Ver. 7; see
1 Chron. vi. 77

---

afterwards at Jericho. This was a circumstance which Moses had foreseen, and for which he had provided. See Deut. xviii. 6, &c.

Verse 11. *The city of Arba*] See the note on chap. xiv. 15.

Verse 12. *The fields of the city—gave they to Caleb*] This was an exclusive privilege to *him* and his *family*, with which the grant to the Levites did not interfere. See the notes on chap. xiv. 14.

Verse 18. *Anathoth.*] Celebrated as the birthplace of Jeremiah, about three miles northward of Jerusalem, according to St. Jerome.

Verse 19. *Thirteen cities with their suburbs.*] At the time mentioned here certainly thirteen cities were too large a proportion for the *priests*, as they and their families amounted to a very small number: but this ample provision was made in reference to their great increase in after times, when they formed twenty-four courses, as in the days of David.

Verse 22. *Beth-horon*] There were two cities of this name, the *upper* and the *nether;* but which is intended here, cannot be ascertained.

Verse 24. *Aijalon*] See on chap. x.

Verse 27. *Golan in Bashan*] On this and the

A. M. 2561
B. C. 1443
An. Exod. Isr. 48
Anno ante I. Olymp. 667

tribe of Zebulun, Jokneam with her suburbs, and Kartah with her suburbs,

35 Dimnah with her suburbs, Nahalal with her suburbs; four cities.

36 And out of the tribe of Reuben, [m]Bezer with her suburbs, and Jahazah with her suburbs,

37 Kedemoth with her suburbs, and Mephaath with her suburbs; four cities.

38 And out of the tribe of Gad, [n]Ramoth in Gilead with her suburbs, *to be* a city of refuge for the slayer; and Mahanaim with her suburbs,

39 Heshbon with her suburbs, Jazer with her suburbs; four cities in all.

40 So all the cities for the children of Merari by their families, which were remaining of the families of the Levites, were *by* their lot twelve cities.

41 [o]All the cities of the Levites within the possession of the children of Israel *were* forty and eight cities with their suburbs.

A. M. 2561
B. C. 1443
An. Exod. Isr. 48
Anno ante I. Olymp. 667

42 These cities were every one with their suburbs round about them: thus *were* all these cities.

43 And the LORD gave unto Israel [p]all the land which he sware to give unto their fathers; and they possessed it, and dwelt therein.

44 [q]And the LORD gave them rest round about, according to all that he sware unto their fathers: and [r]there stood not a man of all their enemies before them; the LORD delivered all their enemies into their hand.

45 [s]There failed not aught of any good thing which the LORD had spoken unto the house of Israel: all came to pass.

---

[m]Chap. xx. 8——[n]Chap. xx. 8——[o]Numbers xxxv. 7
[p]Gen. xiii. 15; xv. 18; xxvi. 3; xxviii. 4, 13

[q]Chap. xi. 23; xxii. 4——[r]Deut. vii. 24——[s]Chapter xxiii. 14

---

other cities of refuge mentioned here, see the note on chap. xx. ver. 7.

Verse 35. *Dimnah with her suburbs, &c.*] It is well known to every Hebrew scholar that the two following verses are wholly omitted by the Masora; and are left out in some of the most correct and authentic Hebrew Bibles. Between critics there is no small controversy relative to the authenticity of these verses; and those who wish to see the arguments at large on both sides, must consult the *Variæ Lectiones* of *De Rossi* on this place. Dr. Kennicott, who is a strenuous advocate for their authenticity, argues thus in their behalf: "Verses 41 and 42 of this chapter tell us that the Levitical cities were forty-eight, and that they had been *all* as such described; so that they must have been all specified in this chapter: whereas now in all the Hebrew copies printed in full obedience to the Masora, which excludes *two* verses containing *four* of these cities, the number amounts only to forty-four.

"The cities are first mentioned, in the general, as being *thirteen* and *ten*, with *thirteen* and *twelve*, which are certainly *forty-eight*. And yet when they are particularly named, verses 13 to 19 give *thirteen* cities; verses 20 to 26 give *ten* cities; verses 27 to 33 give *thirteen;* verses 34 and 35 give *four* cities; and then verses 35, 36, give *four* more, all which can make but *forty-four*. And what still increases the wonder is, that ver. 40 infers from the verses immediately preceding, that the cities allowed to the Merarites were *twelve,* though they here make *eight* only, unless we admit the *four* other cities expressed in those *two* verses, which have been rejected by that blind guide *the Masora.* In defiance of this authority these *two* verses, thus absolutely necessary, were inserted in the most early *editions* of the Hebrew text, and are found in Walton's Polyglot, as well as in our English Bible. But they have scarce ever been as yet printed completely, thus, *And out of the tribe of Reuben,* A CITY OF REFUGE FOR THE SLAYER, *Bezer,* IN THE WILDERNESS, *with her suburbs, and Jahazah with her suburbs, Kedemoth with her suburbs, and Mephaath with her suburbs; four cities.* See on this place my edition of the Hebrew Bible, where no less than *one hundred and forty-nine* copies are described, which happily preserve these verses, most clearly essential to the truth and consistency of this chapter. See also *General Discourse,* pp. 19, 26, 54."

Though this reasoning of Dr. Kennicott appears very conclusive, yet there are so many and important variations among the MSS. that retain, and those that reject these verses, as to render the question of their authenticity very difficult to be determined. To Dr. Kennicott's one hundred and forty-nine MSS. which have these two verses, may be added upwards of forty collated by De Rossi. Those who deny their authenticity say they have been inserted here from 1 Chron. vi. 78, 79, where they are found it is true, in general, but not exactly as they stand here, and in Dr. Kennicott's Hebrew Bible.

Verse 36. *Jahazah*] See on chap. xiii. 18.

Verse 41. *Forty and eight cities*] At the last census of the Hebrew people, related Num. xxvi., we find from ver. 62 that the tribe of Levi amounted only to 23,000; and it is supposed that *forty-eight cities* were too great a proportion for this tribe, the other tribes having so very few. But, 1. All the cities of the other tribes are not enumerated. 2. They had the circumjacent country as well as the cities. 3. The Levites had no other cities than those enumerated. 4. They had no country annexed to their cities, the 2,000 cubits for their cattle, &c., excepted. 5. Cities in those ancient times were very small, as most *villages* went under this appellation. 6. The Levites had now the appointment that was suited to their consequent increase. The other tribes might enlarge their borders and make conquests, but this was not suitable to the mere servants of God; besides, had they made conquests, they would have become proprietors of the conquered land; and God determined that they should have no inheritance in Israel, HE himself being their *portion*.

Verse 43. *And the Lord gave—all the land which he sware*] All was now divided by lot unto them, and their enemies were so completely discomfited that there was not a single army of the Canaanites remaining to make head against them; and those which were left in the land served under tribute, and the tribute that they paid was the amplest proof of their complete subjugation. Add to this, they had as much of the land in *actual* possession as they could occupy; and, as they increased, God enabled them to drive out the rest of the ancient inhabitants; but in consequence of the infidelity of the Israelites, God permitted their enemies often to straiten them, and sometimes to prevail against them. It should also be remembered, that God never promised to give them the land, or to maintain them in it, but on condition of *obedience;* and so punctually did he fulfil this intention, that there is not a single instance on record in which they were either straitened or subjugated, while obedient and faithful to their God.

The cavil is as foolish as it is unprincipled which states, "The Israelites never did possess the whole of the land which was promised to them, and therefore that promise could not come by Divine revelation." With as much reason might it be urged that Great Britain has not subdued the French West India Islands and Batavia, (Feb. 1812,) because the ancient inhabitants still remain in them; but is not their *serving under tribute* an absolute proof that they are *conquered*, and under the British dominion? So was the whole land of Canaan conquered, and its inhabitants subdued, though the whole of the ground was not occupied by the Israelites till the days of David and Solomon. In the most correct and literal sense it might be said, *There failed not aught of any good thing which the Lord had spoken unto the house of Israel: all came to pass.* Nor shall one word of his ever fail to any of his followers while the sun and moon endure.

CHAPTER XXII

Joshua assembles, commends, blesses, and then dismisses the two tribes of Reuben and Gad, and the half tribe of Manasseh, 1–8. They return and build an altar by the side of Jordan, 9, 10. The rest of the Israelites hearing of this, and suspecting that they had built the altar for idolatrous purposes, or to make a schism in the national worship, prepare to go to war with them, 11, 12; but first send a deputation to know the truth, 13, 14. They arrive and expostulate with their brethren, 15–20. The Reubenites, Gadites, and half tribe of Manasseh, make a noble defence, and show that their altar was built as a monument only to prevent idolatry, 21–29. The deputation are satisfied, and return to the ten tribes and make their report, 30–32. The people rejoice and praise God, 33; and the Reubenites and Gadites call the altar they had raised Ed, *that it might be considered a* witness *between them and their brethren on the other side Jordan, 34.*

A. M. 2561
B. C. 1443
An. Exod. Isr.
48
Anno ante
I. Olymp. 667

THEN Joshua called the Reubenites, and the Gadites, and the half tribe of Manasseh,

2 And said unto them, Ye have kept [a]all that Moses the servant of the LORD commanded you, [b]and have obeyed my voice in all that I commanded you:

3 Ye have not left your brethren these many days unto this day, but have kept the charge of the commandment of the LORD your God.

4 And now the LORD your God hath given rest unto your brethren, as he promised them: therefore now return ye, and get you unto your tents, *and* unto the land of your possession, [c]which Moses the servant of the LORD gave you on the other side Jordan.

A. M. 2561
B. C. 1443
An. Exod. Isr.
48
Anno ante
I. Olymp. 667

5 But [d]take diligent heed to do the commandment and the law, which Moses the servant of the LORD charged you, [e]to love the

---

[a]Numbers xxxii. 20; Deuteronomy iii. 18——[b]Chapter i. 16, 17

[c]Num. xxxii. 33; Deut. xxix. 8; chapter xiii. 8——[d]Deut. vi. 6, 17; xi. 22——[e]Deut. x. 12

NOTES ON CHAP. XXII

Verse 1. *Then Joshua called the Reubenites, &c.*] We have already seen that 40,000 men of the tribes of Reuben and Gad, and the half tribe of Manasseh, had passed over Jordan armed, with their brethren, according to their stipulation with Moses. The war being now concluded, Joshua assembles these warriors, and with commendations for their services and fidelity, he dismisses them, having first given them the most pious and suitable advices. They had now been about seven years absent from their respective families; and though there was only the river Jordan between the camp at Gilgal and their own inheritance, yet it does not appear that they had during that time ever revisited their own home, which they might have done any time in the year, the *harvest* excepted, as at all other times that river was easily fordable.

Verse 5. *But take diligent heed, &c.*] Let us examine the force of this excellent advice; they must ever *consider* that their prosperity and continued possession of the land depended on their fidelity and obedience to God; to this they must *take diligent heed.*

A. M. 2561
B. C. 1443
An. Exod. Isr.
48
Anno ante
I. Olymp. 667

LORD your God, and to walk in all his ways, and to keep his commandments, and to cleave unto him, and to serve him with all your heart and with all your soul.

6 So Joshua ᶠblessed them, and sent them away: and they went unto their tents.

7 Now to the *one* half of the tribe of Manasseh Moses had given *possession* in Bashanᵍ: but unto the *other* half thereof gave Joshua among their brethren on this side Jordan westward. And when Joshua sent them away also unto their tents, then he blessed them;

8 And he spake unto them, saying, Return with much riches unto your tents, and with very much cattle, with silver, and with gold, and with brass, and with iron, and with very much raiment: ʰdivide the spoil of your enemies with your brethren.

9 And the children of Reuben and the children of Gad and the half tribe of Manasseh returned, and departed from the children of Israel out of Shiloh, which *is* in the land

of Canaan, to go unto ⁱthe country of Gilead, to the land of their possession, whereof they were possessed, according to the word of the LORD by the hand of Moses.

A. M. 2561
B. C. 1443
An. Exod. Isr.
48
Anno ante
I. Olymp. 667

10 And when they came unto the borders of Jordan, that *are* in the land of Canaan, the children of Reuben and the children of Gad and the half tribe of Manasseh built there an altar by Jordan, a great altar to see to.

11 And the children of Israel ᵏheard say, Behold, the children of Reuben and the children of Gad and the half tribe of Manasseh have built an altar over against the land of Canaan, in the borders of Jordan, at the passage of the children of Israel.

12 And when the children of Israel heard *of it*, ˡthe whole congregation of the children of Israel gathered themselves together at Shiloh, to go up to war against them.

13 And the children of Israel ᵐsent unto the children of Reuben, and to the children of Gad, and to the half tribe of Manasseh, into

---

ᶠGen. xlvii. 7; Exod. xxxix. 43; chap. xiv. 13; 2 Sam. vi. 18; Luke xxiv. 50——ᵍChap. xvii. 5——ʰNum. xxxi. 27; 1 Sam. xxx. 14

ⁱNum. xxxii. 1, 26, 29——ᵏDeut. xiii. 12, &c.; Judg. xx. 12——ˡJudg. xx. 1——ᵐDeut. xiii. 14; Judg. xx. 12

Do the commandment] They must pay the strictest regard to every *moral* precept.

And the law] They must observe all the *rites* and *ceremonies* of their holy religion.

Love the Lord your God] Without an affectionate filial attachment to their Maker, duty would be irksome, grievous, and impossible.

Walk in all his ways] They must not only *believe* and *love*, but *obey:* walk not in *your own ways*, but walk in those which GOD has pointed out.

Keep his commandments] They must love him with all their heart, soul, mind, and strength, and their neighbour as themselves.

Cleave unto him] They must be *cemented* to him, in a union that should never be dissolved.

Serve him] They must consider him as their *Master*, having an absolute right to appoint them *when, where, how*, and in what *measure* they should do his work.

With all your heart] Having all their affections and passions sanctified and united to him.

And with all your soul.] Giving up their whole *life* to him, and employing their understanding, judgment, and will, in the contemplation and adoration of his perfections; that their love and obedience might increase in proportion to the cultivation and improvement of their *understanding*.

Verse 7. *Then he blessed them*] Spoke *respectfully* of their fidelity and exertions, *wished* them every *spiritual* and *temporal* good, *prayed to God* to protect and save them, and probably gave some *gifts* to those leaders among them that had most distinguished themselves in this seven years' war. In all the above senses the word *bless* is frequently taken in Scripture.

Verse 8. *Return with much riches*] It appears they had their full proportion of the spoils that were taken from the Canaanites, and that these spoils consisted in *cattle, silver, gold, brass, iron*, and *raiment*.

Divide the spoil—with your brethren.] It was right that those who stayed at home to defend the families of those who had been in the wars, and to cultivate the ground, should have a proper proportion of the spoils taken from the enemy; for had they not acted as they did, the others could not have safely left their families.

Verse 10. *The borders of Jordan, that* are *in —Canaan*] This verse can never mean that they built the altar on the west side of Jordan, for this was not in their territories; nor could it be a place for the purpose of public worship to their own people, if built on the opposite side of Jordan; besides, the next verse says it was built *over against the land of Canaan.* It appears that when they came to the river they formed the purpose of building the altar; and when they had crossed it they executed their purpose.

A great altar to see to.] A vast mass of earth, stones, &c., elevated to a great height, to serve as a memorial of the transactions that had already taken place. Probably it was intended also to serve as a kind of watchtower, being of a stupendous height, *altare infinitæ magnitudinis, an altar of an immense size*, as the Vulgate terms it.

Verse 12. *To go up to war against them.*] Supposing that they had built this altar in opposition to that which Moses, by the command of God, had erected, and were consequently become rebels against God and the Israelitish

A. M. 2561
B. C. 1443
An. Exod. Isr.
48
Anno ante
I. Olymp. 667

the land of Gilead, [n]Phinehas the son of Eleazar the priest,

14 And with him ten princes, of each [o]chief house a prince throughout all the tribes of Israel, and [p]each one *was* a head of the house of their fathers among the thousands of Israel.

15 And they came unto the children of Reuben, and to the children of Gad, and to the half tribe of Manasseh, unto the land of Gilead, and they spake with them, saying,

16 Thus saith the whole congregation of the LORD, What trespass *is* this that ye have committed against the God of Israel, to turn away this day from following the LORD, in that ye have builded you an altar, [q]that ye might rebel this day against the LORD?

17 *Is* the iniquity [r]of Peor too little for us, from which we are not cleansed until this day, although there was a plague in the congregation of the LORD,

18 But that ye must turn away this day from following the LORD? and it will be, *seeing* ye rebel to-day against the LORD, that to-morrow [s]he will be wroth with the whole congregation of Israel.

A. M. 2561
B. C. 1443
An. Exod. Isr.
48
Anno ante
I. Olymp. 667

19 Notwithstanding, if the land of your possession *be* unclean, *then* pass ye over unto the land of the possession of the LORD, [t]wherein the LORD's tabernacle dwelleth, and take possession among us: but rebel not against the LORD, nor rebel against us, in building you an altar beside the altar of the LORD our God.

20 [u]Did not Achan the son of Zerah commit a trespass in the accursed thing, and wrath fell on all the congregation of Israel? and that man perished not alone in his iniquity.

21 Then the children of Reuben and the children of Gad and the half tribe of Manasseh answered, and said unto the heads of the thousands of Israel,

22 The LORD [v]God of gods, the LORD God of gods, he [w]knoweth, and Israel he shall know; if *it be* in rebellion, or if in transgression against the LORD, (save us not this day,)

---

[n]Exod. vi. 25; Num. xxv. 7——[o]Heb. *house of the father*——[p]Num. i. 4——[q]See Lev. xvii. 8, 9; Deut. xii. 13, 14——[r]Num. xxv. 3, 4; Deut. iv. 3——[s]Num. xvi. 22

[t]Chap. xviii. 1——[u]Chap. vii. 1, 5——[v]Deut. x. 17
[w]1 Kings viii. 39; Job x. 7; xxiii. 10; Psa. xliv. 21; cxxxix. 1, 2; Jer. xii. 3; 2 Cor. xi. 11, 31

---

constitution, and should be treated as such. Their great concern for the glory of God led them to take this step, which at first view might appear precipitate; but, that they might do nothing rashly, they first sent Phinehas and ten princes, one out of each tribe, to require an explanation of their motives in erecting this altar.

Verse 17. *Is the iniquity of Peor too little*] See this history, Num. xxv. 3, &c., and the notes there. Phinehas takes it for granted that this altar was built in opposition to the altar of God erected by Moses, and that they intended to have a *separate* service, priesthood, &c., which would be rebellion against God, and bring down his curse on them and their posterity; and, in order to show that God is jealous of his glory, he refers to the business of Baal Peor, which took place in that very country they were now about to possess, the destructive consequences of which *he*, through his zeal for the glory of God, was the means of preventing.

Verse 19. *If the land of your possessions be unclean*] The generous mind of Phinehas led him to form this excuse for them. If ye suppose that this land is impure, as not having been originally included in the covenant, and ye think that ye cannot expect the blessing of God unless ye have an altar, sacrifices, &c., then *pass ye over unto the land of the possession of the Lord, wherein the Lord's tabernacle dwelleth*, the only legitimate place where sacrifices and offerings can be made. We will divide this land with you, and rather straiten ourselves than that you should conceive yourselves to be under any necessity of erecting a new altar *besides the altar of the Lord our God.*

Verse 20. *Did not Achan the son of Zerah*] Your sin will not be merely against yourselves; your transgressions will bring down the wrath of God upon all the people; this was the case in the transgression of Achan; he alone sinned, and yet God on that account turned his face against the whole congregation, so that they fell before their enemies. We cannot therefore be unconcerned spectators of your transgression, we may all be implicated in its criminality; let this and the dishonour which we apprehend is done to our God plead our excuse, and vindicate the necessity of the present warlike appearance which we make before you. See the history of Achan referred to here, (chap. vii.,) and the notes there.

Verse 21. *Then the children of Reuben—answered*] Though conscious of their own innocency they permitted Phinehas to finish his discourse, though composed of little else than accusations; there was a decency in this, and such a full proof of good breeding, as does them the highest credit. There are many public assemblies in the present day which lay claim to the highest refinement, who might take a very useful lesson from these Reubenites and their associates.

Verse 22. *The Lord God of gods*] The original words are exceedingly emphatic, and cannot be easily translated. אל אלהים יהוה *El Elohim Yehovah*, are the three principal names by which the supreme God was known among the Hebrews, and may be thus translated, *the strong God, Elohim, Jehovah*, which is nearly the version of *Luther*, der ſtarcte Gott der Herr,

A. M. 2561
B. C. 1443
An. Exod. Isr.
48
Anno ante
I. Olymp. 667

23 That we have built us an altar to turn from following the LORD, or if to offer thereon burnt-offering or meat-offering, or if to offer peace-offerings thereon, let the LORD himself ˣrequire *it;*

24 And if we have not *rather* done it for fear of *this* thing, saying, ʸIn time to come your children might speak unto our children, saying, What have ye to do with the LORD God of Israel?

25 For the LORD hath made Jordan a border between us and you, ye children of Reuben and children of Gad; ye have no part in the LORD: so shall your children make our children cease from fearing the LORD.

26 Therefore we said, Let us now prepare to build us an altar; not for burnt-offering, nor for sacrifice;

27 But *that* it *may be* ᶻa witness between us and you, and our generations after us, that we might ᵃdo the service of the LORD before him with our burnt-offerings, and with our sacrifices, and with our peace-offerings; that your children may not say to our children in time to come, Ye have no part in the LORD.

28 Therefore said we, that it shall be, when they should *so* say to us or to our generations in time to come, that we may say *again,* Be-

hold the pattern of the altar of the LORD, which our fathers made, not for burnt-offerings, nor for sacrifices; but it *is* a witness between us and you.

A. M. 2561
B. C. 1443
An. Exod. Isr.
48
Anno ante
I. Olymp. 667

29 God forbid that we should rebel against the LORD, and turn this day from following the LORD, ᵇto build an altar for burnt-offerings, for meat-offerings, or for sacrifices, beside the altar of the LORD our God that *is* before his tabernacle.

30 And when Phinehas the priest, and the princes of the congregation and heads of the thousands of Israel which *were* with him, heard the words that the children of Reuben and the children of Gad and the children of Manasseh spake, ᶜit pleased them.

31 And Phinehas the son of Eleazar the priest said unto the children of Reuben, and to the children of Gad, and to the children of Manasseh, This day we perceive that the LORD *is* ᵈamong us, because ye have not committed this trespass against the LORD: ᵉnow ye have delivered the children of Israel out of the hand of the LORD.

32 And Phinehas the son of Eleazar the priest, and the princes, returned from the children of Reuben, and from the children of Gad, out of the land of Gilead, unto the land of

---

ˣDeut. xviii. 19; 1 Sam. xx. 16——ʸHeb. *To-morrow*
ᶻGen. xxxi. 48; chap. xxiv. 27; ver. 34——ᵃDeut. xii. 5, 6, 11, 12, 17, 18, 26, 27

ᵇDeut. xii. 13, 14——ᶜHeb. *it was good in their eyes*——ᵈLev. xxvi. 11, 12; 2 Chron. xv. 2——ᵉHeb. *then*

"The strong God the LORD." And the Reubenites, by using these in their very solemn appeal, expressed at once their strong unshaken faith in the God of Israel; and by this they fully showed the deputation from the ten tribes, that their religious *creed* had not been changed; and, in the succeeding part of their defence they show that their *practice* corresponded with their *creed.* The *repetition* of these solemn names by the *Reubenites,* &c., shows their deep concern for the honour of God, and their anxiety to wipe off the reproach which they consider cast on them by the supposition that they had been capable of defection from the pure worship of God, or of disaffection to their brethren.

Save us not this day] This was putting the affair to the most solemn issue; and nothing but the utmost consciousness of their own integrity could have induced them to make such an appeal, and call for such a decision. "Let God the Judge cause us to perish this day, if in principle or practice we have knowingly departed from him."

Verse 24. *For fear of this thing*] The motive that actuated us was directly the reverse of that of which we have been suspected.

Verse 26. *An altar, not for burnt-offering, nor*

for sacrifice] Because this would have been in flat opposition to the law, Lev. xvii. 8, 9; Deut. xii. 4, 5, 6, 10, 11, 13, 14, which most positively forbade any sacrifice or offering to be made in any other place than that *one* which the Lord should choose. Therefore the altar built by the Reubenites, &c., was for no religious purpose, but merely to serve as a testimony that they were one people with those on the west of Jordan, having the same religious and civil constitution, and bound by the same interests to keep that constitution inviolate.

Verse 29. *God forbid that we should rebel*] These words not only express their strong abhorrence of this crime, but also show that without God they could do no good thing, and that they depended upon him for that strength by which alone they could abstain from evil.

Verse 31. *We perceive that the Lord is among us*] Or, according to the Targum of *Jonathan,* "This day we know that the majesty of Jehovah dwelleth among us, because ye have not committed this prevarication against the WORD of the Lord, and thus ye have delivered the children of Israel from the hand of the WORD of the Lord." They rejoice to find them innocent, and that there is no ground of quarrel between

A. M. 2561
B. C. 1443
An. Exod. Isr.
48
Anno ante
I. Olymp. 667

Canaan, to the children of Israel, and brought them word again.

33 And the thing pleased the children of Israel; and the children of Israel [f]blessed God, and did not intend to go up against them in battle, to destroy

the land wherein the children of Reuben and Gad dwelt.

34 and the children of Reuben and the children of Gad called the altar [g]*Ed:* for it *shall be* a witness between us that the LORD is God.

A. M. 2561
B. C. 1443
An. Exod. Isr.
48
Anno ante
I. Olymp. 667

---

[f]1 Chron. xxix. 20; Neh. viii. 6; Dan. ii. 19; Luke ii. 28

[g]That is, a witness; so chap. xxiv. 27

---

the children of the same family. And from this they draw a very favourable conclusion, that as God was among them as the sole object of their religious worship, so he would abide with them as their protector and their portion; and as they were *his* friends, they take it for granted that he will deliver them from the hands of their enemies.

Verse 33. *And did not intend to go up against them in battle*] That is, they now relinquished the intention of going against them in battle, as this explanation proved there was no cause for the measure.

Verse 34. *Called the altar* Ed] The word עֵד *ED*, which signifies *witness* or *testimony*, is not found in the common editions of the Hebrew Bible, and is supplied in Italics by our translators, at least in our modern copies; for in the *first edition* of this translation it stands in the text without any note of this kind; and it is found in several of *Kennicott's* and *De Rossi's* MSS., and also in the *Syriac* and *Arabic*. Several also of the early printed editions of the Hebrew Bible have the word עֵד, either in the text or in the margin, and it must be allowed to be necessary to complete the sense. It is very probable that an *inscription* was put on this altar, which pointed out the purposes for which it was erected.

FROM the contents of this chapter we learn that the Israelites were dreadfully alarmed at the prospect of a *schism* in their own body, both as it related to *ecclesiastical* and *civil* matters. A few observations on this subject may not be useless.

Schism in religion is a dangerous thing, and should be carefully avoided by all who fear God. But this word should be well understood. Σχισμα, in theology, is generally allowed to signify a *rent* in, or departure from, the *doctrine* and *practice* of the apostles, especially among those who had been previously *united* in that doctrine and practice. A departure from *human institutions* in religion is no *schism*, for this reason, that the WORD OF GOD alone is the sufficient rule

of the faith and practice of Christians; and as to *human* institutions, forms, modes, &c., those of one *party* may be as good as those of *another*.

When the majority of a nation agrees in some particular forms and modes in their religious service; no conscientious man will *lightly* depart from these; nor depart at all, unless he find that they are not only not authorized by the word of God, but *repugnant* to it. It is an object greatly to be desired, that a whole people, living under the same laws may, as much as possible, glorify God, not only with one *heart*, but also with one *mouth*.

But there may be a *dissent* from established forms without *schism;* for if that dissent make no *rent* in the *doctrines* or *practice* of Christianity, as laid down in the New Testament, it is an abuse of terms to call it a *schism;* besides, there may be a dissent among religious people relative to certain points both in *creed* and *practice*, which, not affecting the *essentials* of Christianity, nor having any direct tendency to alienate the affections of Christians from each other, cannot be called a *schism;* but when professing Christians separate from each other, to set up one *needless* or *non-essential* form, &c., in the place of others which they call needless or non-essential, they are highly culpable. This not only produces no good, but tends to much evil; for both parties, in order to make the points of their difference of sufficient consequence to justify their dissension, magnify these non-essential matters beyond all *reason*, and sometimes beyond *conscience* itself: and thus *mint* and *cummin* are tithed, while the weightier matters of the law—judgment and the love of God—are utterly neglected. If Christians either cannot or will not think alike on all points, surely they can agree to disagree, and let each go to heaven his own way. "But should we take this advice, would it not lead to a total *indifference* about religion?" Not at all; for in the things which concern the *essentials* of Christianity, both in *doctrine* and *practice*, we should ever feel zealously affected, and *earnestly contend for the faith once delivered to the saints.*

CHAPTER XXIII

Joshua, being old, calls for the rulers and different heads of the Israelites, 1, 2, to whom he relates how God had put them in possession of the promised land, 3, 4; from which all their remaining enemies should be expelled, 5. Exhorts them to be faithful to God, and to avoid all connections with the idolatrous nations, 6–8. Encourages them with the strongest promises, that no enemy should ever be able to prevail against them, if they continued to love the Lord their God, 9–11. Lays also before them the consequences of disobedience, 12, 13. Shows them that as all God's promises had been fulfilled to them while they were obedient, so his threatenings should be fulfilled on them if they revolted from his service; and that if they did so, they should be utterly destroyed from off the good land, 14–16.

A. M. 2561
B. C. 1443
An. Exod. Isr.
48
Anno ante
I. Olymp. 667

AND it came to pass a long time after that the LORD [a]had given rest unto Israel from all their enemies round about, that Joshua [b]waxed old *and* [c]stricken in age.

2 And Joshua [d]called for all Israel, *and* for their elders, and for their heads, and for their judges, and for their officers, and said unto them, I am old *and* stricken in age:

3 And ye have seen all that the LORD your God hath done unto all these nations because of you; for the [e]LORD your God *is* he that hath fought for you.

4 Behold, [f]I have divided unto you by lot these nations that remain, to be an inheritance for your tribes, from Jordan, with all the nations that I have cut off, even unto the great sea [g]westward.

5 And the LORD your God, [h]he shall expel them from before you, and drive them from out of your sight; and ye shall possess their land, [i]as the LORD your God hath promised unto you.

A. M. 2561
B. C. 1443
An. Exod. Isr.
48
Anno ante
I. Olymp. 667

6 [k]Be ye therefore very courageous to keep and to do all that is written in the book of the law of Moses, [l]that ye turn not aside therefrom *to* the right hand or *to* the left;

7 That ye [m]come not among these nations, these that remain among you; neither [n]make mention of the name of their gods, nor cause to swear *by them*, neither serve them, nor bow yourselves unto them:

8 [o]But [p]cleave unto the LORD your God, as ye have done unto this day.

9 [q]For [r]the LORD hath driven out from

---

[a]Chap. xxi. 44; xxii. 4——[b]Chap. xiii. 1——[c]Heb. *come into days*——[d]Deut. xxxi. 28; chap. xxiv. 1; 1 Chron. xxviii. 1——[e]Exod. xiv. 14; chap. x. 14, 42 [f]Chap. xiii. 2, 6; xviii. 10——[g]Heb. *at the sunset* [h]Exod. xxiii. 30; xxxiii. 2; xxxiv. 11; Deut. xi. 23; chap. xiii. 6——[i]Num. xxxiii. 53

[k]Chap. i. 7——[l]Deut. v. 22; xxviii. 14——[m]Exod. xxiii. 33; Deut. vii. 2, 3; Prov. iv. 14; Eph. v. 11 [n]Exod. xxiii. 13; Psa. xvi. 4; Jer. v. 7; Zeph. i. 5; see Num. xxxii. 38——[o]Or, *For if ye will cleave*, &c. [p]Deut. x. 20; xi. 22; xiii. 4; chap. xxii. 5——[q]Or, *Then the LORD will drive*——[r]Deut. xi. 23

NOTES ON CHAP. XXIII

Verse 1. *A long time after that the Lord had given rest*] This is supposed to have been in the last or one hundred and tenth year of the life of Joshua, about thirteen or fourteen years after the conquest of Canaan, and *seven* after the division of the land among the tribes.

Verse 2. *Joshua called for all Israel*] There are four degrees of civil distinction mentioned here: 1. זְקֵנִים *zekenim*, the *elders* or *senate*, the PRINCES of the *tribes*. 2. רָאשִׁים *rashim*, or *rashey aboth*, the CHIEFS or HEADS of *families*. 3. שֹׁפְטִים *shophetim*, the JUDGES who interpreted and decided according to the law. 4. שֹׁטְרִים *shoterim*, the OFFICERS, serjeants, &c., who executed the decisions of the judges. Whether this assembly was held at *Timnath-serah*, where Joshua lived, or at *Shiloh*, where the *ark* was, or at *Shechem*, as in chap. xxiv. 1, we cannot tell. Some think that the meaning here, and that mentioned in chap. xxiv., were the same, and if so, *Shechem* was the place of assembling; but it is more likely that the two chapters treat of two distinct assemblies, whether held at the same place or not.

Verse 3. *For the Lord your God is he that hath fought for you.*] There is much both of *piety* and *modesty* in this address. It was natural for the Israelites to look on their veteran, worn-out general, who had led them on from conquest to conquest, with profound respect; and to be ready to say, "Had we not had such a commander, we had never got possession of this good land." Joshua corrects this opinion, and shows them that all their enemies had been defeated, because the Lord their God had fought for them. That the battle was the Lord's, and not his; and that God *alone* should have the glory.

Verse 4. *I have divided—these nations that*

remain] The whole of the promised land had been portioned out, as well those parts which had not yet been conquered, as those from which the ancient inhabitants had been expelled. The Canaanitish armies had long ago been broken in pieces, so that they could make no head against the Israelites, but in many districts the old inhabitants remained, more through the supineness of the Israelites, than through their own bravery.

From Jordan—unto the great sea] All the land that lay between the river *Jordan*, from *Phiala*, where it rose, to the southern extremity of the *Dead Sea*, and to the *Mediterranean Sea*, through the whole extent of its coast, opposite to Jordan.

Verse 5. *And drive them—out—and ye shall possess*] The same Hebrew word יָרַשׁ *yarash* is used here to signify to *expel from an inheritance*, and to *succeed* those thus expelled. *Ye shall disinherit them from your sight, and ye shall inherit their land.*

Verse 6. *Be ye therefore very courageous to keep and to do, &c.*] It requires no small courage to keep a sound *creed* in the midst of *scoffers*, and not less to maintain a godly *practice* among the *profane and profligate*.

That is written in the book] By the word of God alone his followers are bound. Nothing is to be received as an article of *faith* which God has *not* spoken.

Verse 7. *Come not among these nations*] Have no civil or social contracts with them, (see ver. 12,) as these will infallibly lead to *spiritual* affinities, in consequence of which ye will make honourable *mention of the name of their gods, swear by them* as the judges of your motives and actions, *serve them* in their abominable rites, and *bow yourselves unto them* as your creators and preservers; thus giving the whole worship of God to idols: and all this

A. M. 2561
B. C. 1443
An. Exod. Isr.
48
Anno ante
I. Olymp. 667

before you great nations and strong: but *as for* you, ᵉno man hath been able to stand before you unto this day.

10 ᵗOne man of you shall chase a thousand: for the LORD your God, he *it is* that fighteth for you, ᵘas he hath promised you.

11 ᵛTake good heed therefore unto ʷyourselves, that ye love the LORD your God.

12 Else if ye do in any wise ˣgo back, and cleave unto the remnant of these nations, *even* these that remain among you, and shall ʸmake marriages with them, and go in unto them, and they to you:

13 Know for a certainty that ᶻthe LORD your God will no more drive out *any of* these nations from before you; ᵃbut they shall be snares and traps unto you, and scourges in your sides, and thorns in your eyes, until ye perish from off this good land which the LORD your God hath given you.

14 And, behold, this day ᵇI am going the way of all the earth: and ye know in all your hearts and in all your souls, that ᶜnot one thing hath failed of all the good things which the LORD your God spake concerning you; all are come to pass unto you, *and* not one thing hath failed thereof.

A. M. 2561
B. C. 1443
An. Exod. Isr.
48
Anno ante
I. Olymp. 667

15 ᵈTherefore it shall come to pass, *that* as all good things are come upon you, which the LORD your God promised you; so shall the LORD bring upon you ᵉall evil things, until he have destroyed you from off this good land which the LORD your God hath given you.

16 When ye have transgressed the covenant of the LORD your God, which he commanded you, and have gone and served other gods, and bowed yourselves to them; then shall the anger of the LORD be kindled against you, and ye shall perish quickly from off the good land which he hath given unto you.

ᵃChap. i. 5——ᵗLev. xxvi. 8; Deut. xxxii. 30; see Judg. iii. 31; xv. 15; 2 Sam. xxiii. 8——ᵘExod. xiv. 14; xxiii. 27; Deut. iii. 22——ᵛChap. xxii. 5——ʷHeb. *your souls*——ˣHeb. x. 38, 39; 2 Pet. ii. 20, 21——ʸDeut. vii. 3——ᶻJudg. ii. 3

ᵃExod. xxiii. 33; Num. xxxiii. 55; Deut. vii. 16; 1 Kings xi. 4——ᵇ1 Kings ii. 2; see Heb. ix. 27 ᶜChap. xxi. 45; Luke xxi. 33——ᵈDeut. xxviii. 63 ᵉLev. xxvi. 16; Deut. xxviii. 15, 16, &c.; Judg. iii. 8, 12; iv. 1, 2; vi. 1; x. 6, 7; xiii. 1; 2 Chron. xxxvi. 16, 17

---

will follow from simply *coming among them.* He who *walks* in the counsel of the ungodly will soon *stand* in the way of *sinners,* and shortly *sit* in the seat of the *scornful. Nemo repente fuit turpissimus.* "No man rises to the highest stages of iniquity but by *degrees.*" NERO himself, under the instructions of *Seneca,* was a promising *youth.*

Verse 10. *One man of you shall chase a thousand*] Do not remain inactive on the supposition that you must be much more numerous before you can drive out your enemies, for it is the Lord that shall drive out nations great and strong; and under his direction and influence *one of you shall chase a thousand.*

Verse 11. *Take good heed—unto yourselves that ye love the Lord*] לנפשתיכם *lenaphshotheychem, Take heed* TO YOUR SOULS, literally; but נפש *nephesh* and نفس *nefs,* both in *Hebrew* and *Arabic,* signify the *whole self,* as well as *soul* and *life;* both soul and body must be joined in this work, for it is written, *Thou shalt love the Lord thy God with all thy heart, soul, mind, and strength.*

Verse 12. *Else if ye do—go back*] The soldier who draws back when going to meet the enemy, forfeits his life. These were the Lord's soldiers, and if they drew back they drew back unto *perdition,* their lives being forfeited by their infidelity.

Verse 13. *They shall be snares*] לפח *lephach,* a *net* or *gin,* set by the artful fowler to catch heedless birds.

And traps] מוקש *mokesh,* any snare, toil, or trap, placed on the ground to catch the unwary traveller or wild beast by the foot.

Scourges in your sides, and thorns in your eyes] Nothing can be conceived more vexatious and distressing than a continual *goad* in the *side,* or *thorn* in the *eye.* They will *drive* you into obedience to their false gods, *and put out the eyes of your understandings* by their idolatries. And God will preserve them merely to distress and punish you.

Verse 14. *The way of all the earth*] I am about to die; I am going into the grave.

Not one thing hath failed, &c.] God had so remarkably and literally fulfilled his promises, that not one of his enemies could state that even the smallest of them had not had its most literal accomplishment: this all Israel could testify.

Verse 15. *So shall the Lord bring upon you all evil things*] His faithfulness in fulfilling his *promises* is a proof that he will as faithfully accomplish his *threatenings,* for the veracity of God is equally pledged for both.

Verse 16. *Ye shall perish quickly from off the good land*] The following note from Mr. John Trapp is very judicious: "This judgment Joshua inculcates ver. 13, 15, and here, because he knew it would be a very grievous thing to them to forego so goodly a land, so lately gotten, and so short a while enjoyed. In the beginning of a speech τα ηθη, the *milder affections,* suit best; but towards the end τα παθη, *passionate* and *piercing passages;* according to the orator. This rule Joshua observes, being *Ex utroque Cæsar;* no less an *orator* than a *warrior.*"

IN all this exhortation we see how closely Joshua copies the example of his great master

Moses. See Lev. xxvi. 7, 8, 14, &c.; Deut. xxviii. 7, xxxii. 30. He was tenderly concerned for the welfare of the people, and with a deeply affected heart he spoke to their hearts. No people ever were more fairly and fully warned, and no people profited less by it. The threatenings pronounced here were accomplished in the Babylonish captivity, but more fully in their general dispersion since the crucifixion of our Lord. And should not every *Christian* fear when he reads, *If God spared not the natural branches, take heed that he spare not thee?* Surely a worldly, carnal, and godless *Christian* has no more reason to expect indulgence from the justice of God than a profligate *Jew.* We have a goodly land, but the justice of God can decree a captivity from it, or a state of bondage in it. The privileges that are abused are thereby forfeited. And this is as applicable to the individual as to the whole system.

CHAPTER XXIV

Joshua gathers all the tribes together at Shechem, 1; *and gives them a history of God's gracious dealings with Abraham,* 2, 3; *Isaac, Jacob, and Esau,* 4; *Moses and Aaron, and their* fathers *in Egypt,* 5, 6. *His judgments on the Egyptians,* 7. *On the Amorites,* 8. *Their deliverance from Balak and Balaam,* 9, 10. *Their conquests in the promised land, and their establishment in the possession of it,* 11–13. *Exhorts them to abolish idolatry, and informs them of his and his family's resolution to serve Jehovah,* 14, 15. *The people solemnly promise to serve the Lord alone, and mention his merciful dealings towards them,* 16–18. *Joshua shows them the holiness of God, and the danger of apostasy,* 19, 20. *The people again promise obedience,* 21. *Joshua calls them to witness against themselves, that they had promised to worship God alone, and exhorts them to put away the strange gods,* 22, 23. *They promise obedience,* 24. *Joshua makes a covenant with the people, writes it in a book, sets up a stone as a memorial of it, and dismisses the people,* 25–28. *Joshua's death,* 29, *and burial,* 30. *The people continue faithful during that generation,* 31. *They bury the bones of Joseph in Shechem,* 32. *Eleazar the high priest dies also,* 33.

A. M. 2561
B. C. 1443
An. Exod. Isr.
48
Anno ante
I. Olymp. 667

AND Joshua gathered all the tribes of Israel to ᵃShechem, and ᵇcalled for the elders of Israel, and for their heads, and for their judges, and for their officers; and they ᶜpresented themselves before God.

2 And Joshua said unto all the people, Thus saith the Lᴏʀᴅ God of Israel, ᵈYour fathers dwelt on the other side of the flood in old time, *even* Terah, the father of Abraham, and the father of Nachor: and ᵉthey served other gods.

3 And ᶠI took your father Abraham from the other side of the flood, and led him throughout all the land of Canaan, and multiplied his seed, and ᵍgave him Isaac.

4 And I gave unto Isaac ʰJacob and Esau: and I gave unto ⁱEsau Mount Seir, to possess it; ᵏbut Jacob and his children went down into Egypt.

5 ˡI sent Moses also and Aaron, and ᵐI plagued Egypt, according to that which I did among them: and afterward I brought you out.

A. M. 2561
B. C. 1443
An. Exod. Isr.
48
Anno ante
I. Olymp. 667

ᵃGen. xxxv. 4——ᵇChap. xxiii. 2——ᶜ1 Sam. x. 19
ᵈGen. xi. 26, 31; Judith v. 6, 7——ᵉGen. xxxi. 53
ᶠGen. xii. 1; Acts vii. 2, 3

ᵍGen. xxi. 2, 3; Psa. cxxvii. 3——ʰGen. xxv. 24, 25, 26
ⁱGen. xxxvi. 8; Deut. ii. 5——ᵏGen. xlvi. 1, 6; Acts vii. 15——ˡExod. iii. 10——ᵐExod. vii., viii., ix., x., xii

NOTES ON CHAP. XXIV

Verse 1. *Joshua gathered all the tribes*] This must have been a different assembly from that mentioned in the preceding chapter, though probably held not long after the former.

To Shechem] As it is immediately added that *they presented themselves before God,* this must mean the *tabernacle;* but at this time the tabernacle was not at *Shechem* but at *Shiloh.* The Septuagint appear to have been struck with this difficulty, and therefore read Σηλω, *Shiloh,* both here and in ver. 25, though the *Aldine* and *Complutensian* editions have Συχεμ, *Shechem,* in both places. Many suppose that this is the original reading, and that *Shechem* has crept into the text instead of *Shiloh.* Perhaps there is more of imaginary than real difficulty in the text. As Joshua was now old and incapable of travelling, he certainly had a right to assemble the representatives of the tribes wherever he found most convenient, and to bring the ark of the covenant to the place of assembling: and this was probably done on this occasion. Shechem is a place famous in the patriarchal history. Here Abraham settled on his first coming into the land of Canaan, Gen. xii. 6, 7; and here the patriarchs were buried, Acts vii. 16. And as Shechem lay between Ebal and Gerizim, where Joshua had before made a covenant with the people, chap. viii. 30, &c., the very circumstance of the *place* would be undoubtedly friendly to the solemnity of the present occasion. *Shuckford* supposes that the covenant was made at *Shechem,* and that the people went to *Shiloh* to confirm it before the Lord. Mr. *Mede* thinks the Ephraimites had a *proseucha,* or temporary oratory or house of prayer, at Shechem, whither the people resorted for Divine worship when they could not get to the tabernacle; and that this is what is called *before the Lord;* but this conjecture seems not at all likely, God having forbidden this kind of worship.

Verse 2. *On the other side of the flood*] The river *Euphrates.*

They served other gods.] Probably Abraham as well as Terah his father was an idolater, till he received the call of God to leave that

A. M. 2561
B. C. 1443
An. Exod. Isr.
48
Anno ante
I. Olymp. 667

6 And I [n]brought your fathers out of Egypt: and [o]ye came unto the sea; [p]and the Egyptians pursued after your fathers with chariots and horsemen unto the Red Sea.

7 And when they [q]cried unto the LORD, [r]he put darkness between you and the Egyptians, [s]and brought the sea upon them, and covered them; and [t]your eyes have seen what I have done in Egypt: and ye dwelt in the wilderness [u]a long season.

8 And I brought you into the land of the Amorites, which dwelt on the other side Jordan; [v]and they fought with you: and I gave them into your hand, that ye might possess their land; and I destroyed them from before you.

9 Then [w]Balak the son of Zippor, king of Moab, arose and warred against Israel, and [x]sent and called Balaam the son of Beor to curse you:

10 [y]But I would not hearken unto Balaam; [z]therefore he blessed you still: so I delivered you out of his hand.

A. M. 2561
B. C. 1443
An. Exod. Isr.
48
Anno ante
I. Olymp. 667

11 And [a]ye went over Jordan, and came unto Jericho: and [b]the men of Jericho fought against you, the Amorites, and the Perizzites, and the Canaanites, and the Hittites, and the Girgashites, the Hivites, and the Jebusites; and I delivered them into your hand.

12 And [c]I sent the hornet before you, which drave them out from before you, *even* the two kings of the Amorites; *but* [d]not with thy sword, nor with thy bow.

13 And I have given you a land for which ye did not labour, and [e]cities which ye built not, and ye dwell in them; of the vineyards and oliveyards which ye planted not, do ye eat.

14 [f]Now therefore fear the LORD, and serve him in [g]sincerity and in truth: and [h]put away the gods which your fathers served on the other side of the flood, and [i]in Egypt; and serve ye the LORD.

15 And if it seem evil unto you to serve the LORD, [k]choose you this day whom ye will serve; whether [l]the gods which your fathers

---

[n]Exod. xii. 37, 51——[o]Exod. xiv. 2——[p]Exod. xiv. 9
[q]Exodus xiv. 10——[r]Exodus xiv. 20——[s]Exodus xiv.
27, 28——[t]Deut. iv. 34; xxix. 2——[u]Chap. v. 6
[v]Num. xxi. 21, 33; Deut. ii. 32; iii. 1——[w]See Judg. xi.
25——[x]Num. xxii. 5; Deut. xxiii. 4——[y]Deut. xxiii. 5
[z]Num. xxiii. 11, 20; xxiv. 10——[a]Chap. iii. 14, 17; iv. 10,
11, 12——[b]Chap. vi. 1; x. 1; xi. 1——[c]Exod. xxiii. 28;
Deut. vii. 20——[d]Psa. xliv. 3, 6——[e]Deut. vi. 10, 11;
chap. xi. 13——[f]Deut. x. 12; 1 Sam. xii. 24——[g]Gen.
xvii. 1; xx. 5; Deut. xviii. 13; Psa. cxix. 1; 2 Cor. i. 12;
Eph. vi. 24——[h]Ver. 2, 33; Lev. xvii. 7; Ezekiel
xx. 18——[i]Ezek. xx. 7, 8; xxiii. 3——[k]See Ruth i.
15; 1 Kings xviii. 21; Ezek. xx. 39; John vi. 67
[l]Ver. 14

---

land. See on Gen. xi. 31; xii. 1. And for the rest of the history referred to here, see the notes on the parallel passages in the margin.

Verse 9. *Then Balak—arose and warred against Israel*] This circumstance is not related in Num. xxii., nor does it appear in that history that the Moabites attacked the Israelites; and probably the *warring* here mentioned means no more than his attempts to destroy them by the curses of Balaam, and the wiles of the Midianitish women.

Verse 11. *The men of Jericho fought against you*] See the notes on chap. iii. and chap. vi. 1, &c. The people of Jericho are said to have fought against the Israelites, because they *opposed* them by *shutting their gates,* &c., though they did not attempt to meet them in the field.

Verse 12. *I sent the hornet before you*] See the note on Exod. xxiii. 28.

Verse 14. *Fear the Lord*] Reverence him as the sole object of your religious worship.

Serve him] Perform his will by obeying his commands.

In sincerity] Having your whole heart engaged in his worship.

And in truth] According to the directions he has given you in his infallible word.

Put away the gods, &c.] From this exhortation of Joshua we learn of what sort the gods were, to the worship of whom these Israelites were still attached. 1. Those which their

fathers worshipped on the other side of the flood: i. e., the gods of the CHALDEANS, *fire, light, the sun.* 2. Those of the EGYPTIANS, *Apis, Anubis,* the *ape, serpents, vegetables,* &c. 3. Those of the CANAANITES, MOABITES, &c., *Baalpeor* or *Priapus, Astarte* or *Venus,* &c., &c. All these he refers to in this and the following verse. See at the conclusion of verse 33.

How astonishing is this, that, after all God had done for them, and all the miracles they had seen, there should till be found among them both *idols* and *idolaters!* That it was so we have the fullest evidence, both here and in ver. 23; Amos v. 26; and in Acts vii. 41. But what excuse can be made for such stupid, not to say brutish, blindness? Probably they thought they could the better represent the Divine nature by using *symbols* and *images,* and perhaps they professed to worship *God* through the *medium* of these. At least this is what has been alleged in behalf of a gross class of Christians who are notorious for image worship. But on such conduct God will never look with any allowance, where he has given his word and testimony.

Verse 15. *Choose you this day whom ye will serve*] Joshua well knew that all service that was not *free* and *voluntary* could be only *deceit* and *hypocrisy,* and that God loveth a *cheerful giver.* He therefore calls upon the people to make their *choice,* for God himself would not *force* them—they must serve him *with all their*

A. M. 2561
B. C. 1443
An. Exod. Isr. 48
Anno ante I. Olymp. 667

served that *were* on the other side of the flood, or [m]the gods of the Amorites, in whose land ye dwell: [n]but as for me and my house, we will serve the LORD.

16 And the people answered and said, God forbid that we should forsake the LORD, to serve other gods;

17 For the LORD our God, he *it is* that brought us up and our fathers out of the land of Egypt, from the house of bondage, and which did those great signs in our sight, and preserved us in all the way wherein we went, and among all the people through whom we passed:

18 And the LORD drave out from before us all the people, even the Amorites which dwelt in the land: *therefore* will we also serve the LORD; for he *is* our God.

19 And Joshua said unto the people, [o]Ye cannot serve the LORD: for he *is* a [p]holy God; he *is* [q]a jealous God; [r]he will not forgive your transgressions nor your sins.

A. M. 2561
B. C. 1443
An. Exod. Isr. 48
Anno ante I. Olymp. 667

20 [s]If ye forsake the LORD, and serve strange gods, [t]then he will turn and do you hurt, and consume you after that he hath done you good.

21 And the people said unto Joshua, Nay; but we will serve the LORD.

22 And Joshua said unto the people, Ye *are* witnesses against yourselves that [u]ye have chosen you the LORD, to serve him. And they said, *We are* witnesses.

23 Now therefore [v]put away, *said he,* the strange gods which *are* among you, and incline your heart unto the LORD God of Israel.

24 And the people said unto Joshua, The LORD our God will we serve, and his voice will we obey.

25 So Joshua [w]made a covenant with the people that day, and set them a statute and an ordinance [x]in Shechem.

26 And Joshua [y]wrote these words in the

[m]Exod. xxiii. 24, 32, 33; xxxiv. 15; Deut. xiii. 7; xxix. 18; Judg. vi. 10——[n]Gen. xviii. 19——[o]Matt. vi. 24——[p]Lev. xix. 2; 1 Sam. vi. 20; Psa. xcix. 5, 9; Isa. v. 16——[q]Exod. xx. 5——[r]Exod. xxiii. 21——[s]1 Chron. xxviii. 9; 2 Chron. xv. 2; Ezra viii. 22; Isa. i. 28; lxv. 11, 12; Jer. xvii. 13——[t]Chap. xxiii. 15; Isa. lxiii. 10; Acts vii. 42——[u]Psa. cxix. 173——[v]Ver. 14; Gen. xxxv. 2; Judg. x. 16; 1 Sam. vii. 3——[w]See Exod. xv. 25; 2 Kings xi. 17——[x]Ver. 26——[y]Deut. xxxi. 24

heart if they served him at all. As for himself and family, he shows them that their choice was already fixed, for they had taken JEHOVAH for their portion.

Verse 16. *God forbid that we should forsake the Lord*] That they were now *sincere* cannot be reasonably doubted, for they served the Lord all the days of Joshua, and the elders that outlived him, ver. 31; but afterwards they turned aside, and did serve other gods. "It is ordinary," says Mr. Trapp, "for the many-headed multitude to turn with the stream—to be of the same religion with their superiors: thus at Rome, in DIOCLETIAN's time, they were *pagans;* in CONSTANTINE'S *Christians;* in CONSTANTIUS'S, *Arians;* in JULIAN's *apostates;* and in JOVINIAN'S, *Christians* again! And all this within less than the age of a man. It is, therefore, a good thing that the heart be established with grace."

Verse 19. *Ye cannot serve the Lord: for he is a holy God*] If we are to take this literally, we cannot blame the Israelites for their defection from the worship of the true God; for if it was impossible for them to serve God, they could not but come short of his kingdom: but surely this was not the case. Instead of לא תוכלו *lo thuchelu, ye* CANNOT *serve,* &c., some eminent critics read לא תכלו *lo thechallu, ye shall not* CEASE *to serve,* &c. This is a very ingenious emendation, but there is not one MS. in all the collections of *Kennicott* and *De Rossi* to support it. However, it appears very possible that the first ו *vau* in תוכלו did not make a part of the word originally. If the common reading be preferred, the meaning of the place must be, "Ye cannot serve the Lord, for he is holy and jealous, *unless* ye put away the gods which your fathers served beyond the flood. For he is a jealous God, and will not give to nor divide his glory with any other. He is a holy God, and will not have his people defiled with the impure worship of the Gentiles."

Verse 21. *And the people said—Nay; but we will serve, &c.*] So they understood the words of Joshua to imply no moral impossibility on their side: and had they earnestly sought the gracious assistance of God, they would have continued steady in his covenant.

Verse 22. *Ye are witnesses against yourselves*] Ye have been sufficiently apprised of the difficulties in your way—of GOD's holiness—your own weakness and inconstancy—the need you have of Divine help, and the awful consequences of apostasy; and now ye deliberately make your choice. Remember then, that ye are witnesses against yourselves, and your own conscience will be *witness, judge,* and *executioner;* or, as one terms it, *index, judex, vindex.*

Verse 23. *Now therefore put away*] As you have promised to reform, begin instantly the work of reformation. A man's promise to serve God soon loses its moral hold of his conscience, if he do not instantaneously begin to put it in practice. The grace that enables him to promise is that by the strength of which he is to begin the performance.

Verse 25. *Joshua made a covenant*] Literally, *Joshua cut the covenant,* alluding to the *sacrifice* offered on the occasion.

And set them a statute and an ordinance]

A. M. 2561
B. C. 1443
An. Exod. Isr.
48
Anno ante
I. Olymp. 667

book of the law of God, and took [z]a great stone, and [a]set it up there, [b]under an oak, that *was* by the sanctuary of the LORD.

27 And Joshua said unto all the people, Behold, this stone shall be [c]a witness unto us; for [d]it hath heard all the words of the LORD which he spake unto us: it shall be therefore a witness unto you, lest ye deny your God.

28 So [e]Joshua let the people depart, every man unto his inheritance.

29 [f]And it came to pass after these things, that Joshua the son of Nun, the servant of the LORD, died, *being* a hundred and ten years old.

30 And they buried him in the border of his inheritance in [g]Timnath-serah, which *is* in Mount Ephraim, on the north side of the hill of Gaash.

A. M. 2561
B. C. 1443
An. Exod. Isr.
48
Anno ante
I. Olymp. 667

31 And [h]Israel served the LORD all the days of Joshua, and all the days of the elders that [i]overlived Joshua, and which had [k]known all the works of the LORD, that he had done for Israel.

32 And [l]the bones of Joseph, which the children of Israel brought up out of Egypt, buried they in Shechem, in a parcel of ground [m]which Jacob bought of the sons of Hamor the father of Shechem for a hundred [n]pieces of silver: and it became the inheritance of the children of Joseph.

33 And Eleazar the son of Aaron died; and they buried him in a hill *that pertained* to [o]Phinehas his son, which was given him in Mount Ephraim.

---

[z]See Judg. ix. 6——[a]See Gen. xxviii. 18; chap. iv. 3 [b]Gen. xxxv. 4——[c]See Gen. xxxi. 48, 52; Deut. xxxi. 19, 21, 26; chap. xxii. 27, 28, 34——[d]Deut. xxxii. 1 [e]Judg. ii. 6——[f]Judg. ii. 8

[g]Chap. xix. 50; Judg. ii. 9——[h]Judg. ii. 7——[i]Heb. *prolonged* their *days after Joshua*——[k]See Deut. xi. 2, xxxi. 13——[l]Gen. l. 25; Exod. xiii. 19——[m]Gen. xxxiii. 19——[n]Or, *lambs*——[o]Exod. vi. 25; Judg. xx. 28

He made a solemn and public act of the whole, which was signed and witnessed by himself and the people, in the presence of Jehovah; and having done so, he wrote the words of the covenant in the book of the law of God, probably in some part of the skin constituting the great roll, on which the laws of God were written, and of which there were some blank columns to spare. Having done this, he took a great stone and set it up under an oak—that this might be עֵד *ed* or *witness* that, at such a time and place, this covenant was made, the terms of which might be found written in the book of the law, which was laid up *beside the ark.* See Deut. xxxi. 26.

Verse 27. *This stone—hath heard all the words*] That is, the stone itself, from its permanency, shall be in all succeeding ages as competent and as substantial a witness as one who had been present at the transaction, and heard all the words which on both sides were spoken on the occasion.

Verse 28. *So Joshua*] After this verse the Septuagint insert ver. 31.

Verse 29. *Joshua the son of Nun—died*] This event probably took place shortly after this public assembly; *for he was old and stricken in years* when he held the assembly mentioned chap. xxiii. 2; and as his work was now all done, and his soul ripened for a state of blessedness, God took him to himself, being one hundred and ten years of age; exactly the same age as that of the patriarch Joseph. See Gen. l. 26.

Verse 30. *And they buried him—in Timnath-serah*] This was his own inheritance, as we have seen chap. xix. 50. The Septuagint add here, "And they put with him there, in the tomb in which they buried him, the knives of stone with which he circumcised the children of Israel in Gilgal, according as the Lord commanded when he brought them out of Egypt; and there they are till this day." St. Augus-

tine quotes the same passage in his thirtieth question on the book of Joshua, which, in all probability, he took from some copy of the Septuagint. It is very strange that there is no account of any public mourning for the death of this eminent general; probably, as he was buried in his own inheritance, he had forbidden all funeral pomp, and it is likely he was privately interred.

Verse 31. *And Israel served the Lord, &c.*] Though there was private idolatry among them, for they had strange gods, yet there was no public idolatry all the days of Joshua and of the elders that overlived Joshua; most of whom must have been advanced in years at the death of this great man. Hence Calmet supposes that the whole of this time might amount to about fifteen years. It has already been noted that this verse is placed by the Septuagint after ver. 28.

Verse 32. *And the bones of Joseph*] See the note on Gen. l. 25, and on Exod. xiii. 19. This burying of the bones of Joseph probably took place when the conquest of the land was completed, and each tribe had received its inheritance; for it is not likely that this was deferred till after the death of Joshua.

Verse 33. *And Eleazar—died*] Probably about the same time as Joshua, or soon after; though some think he outlived him six years. Thus, nearly all the persons who had witnessed the miracles of God in the wilderness were gathered to their fathers; and their descendants left in possession of the great inheritance, with the Law of God in their hands, and the bright example of their illustrious ancestors before their eyes. It must be added that they possessed every advantage necessary to make them a great, a wise, and a holy people. How they used, or rather how they abused, these advantages, their subsequent history, given in the sacred books, amply testifies.

A hill that pertained to *Phinehas his son*]

This grant was probably made to Phinehas as a token of the respect of the whole nation, for his zeal, courage, and usefulness: for the priests had properly no inheritance. At the end of this verse the Septuagint add:—

"In that day the children of Israel, taking up the ark of the covenant of God, carried it about with them, and Phinehas succeeded to the high priest's office in the place of his father until his death; and he was buried in Gabaath, which belonged to himself.

"Then the children of Israel went every man to his own place, and to his own city.

"And the children of Israel worshipped Astarte and Ashtaroth, and the gods of the surrounding nations, and the Lord delivered them into the hands of Eglon king of Moab, and he tyrannized over them for eighteen years."

THE last six verses in this chapter were, doubtless, not written by Joshua; for no man can give an account of his own death and burial. Eleazar, Phinehas, or Samuel, might have added them, to bring down the narration so as to connect it with their own times; and thus preserve the thread of the history unbroken. This is a common case; many men write histories of their own lives, which, in the last circumstances, are finished by others, and who has ever thought of impeaching the authenticity of the preceding part, because the subsequent was the work of a different hand? *Hirtius's* supplement has never invalidated the authenticity of the *Commentaries* of *Cæsar;* nor the work of *Quintus Smyrnæus*, that of the *Iliad* and *Odyssey* of *Homer;* nor the 13th book of *Æneid*, by *Mapheus Viggius*, the authenticity of the preceding twelve, as the genuine work of *Virgil*. We should be thankful that an adequate and faithful hand has supplied those circumstances which the original author could not write, and without which the work would have been incomplete.

Mr. Saurin has an excellent dissertation on this grand federal act formed by Joshua and the people of Israel on this very solemn occasion, of the substance of which the reader will not be displeased to find the following very short outline, which may be easily filled up by any whose business it is to instruct the public; for such a circumstance may with great propriety be brought before a *Christian* congregation at any time:—

"SEVEN things are to be considered in this renewal of the covenant.

   I. The *dignity* of the *mediator*.
  II. The *freedom* of those who *contracted*.
 III. The *necessity* of the *choice*.
 IV. The *extent* of the *conditions*.
  V. The *peril* of the *engagement*.
 VI. The *solemnity* of the *acceptance*.
VII. The *nearness* of the *consequence*.

"I. The *dignity* of the *mediator*.—Take a view of his names, *Hosea* and *Jehoshua*. God will save: he will save. The first is like a *promise;* the second, the fulfilment of that *promise*. God will save some time or other:—this is the very person by whom he will accomplish his promise. Take a view of Joshua's life: his faith, courage, constancy, heroism, and success. A remarkable type of Christ. See Heb. iv. 8.

"II. The *freedom* of those who *contracted*.— Take away the gods which your fathers served beyond the flood; and in Egypt, &c., ver. 14, &c. Joshua exhibits to the Israelites all the religions

which were then known: 1. That of the *Chaldeans*, which consisted in the adoration of *fire*. 2. That of the *Egyptians*, which consisted in the worship of the ox *Apis*, *cats*, *dogs*, and *serpents;* which had been preceded by the worship even of *vegetables*, such as the *onion*, &c. 3. That of the people of *Canaan*, the principal objects of which were *Astarte*, (Venus), and *Baal Peor*, (Priapus.) Make remarks on the liberty of choice which every man has, and which God, in matters of religion, applies to, and calls into action.

"III. The *necessity* of the *choice*.—To be without *religion*, is to be without happiness here, and without any title to the kingdom of God. To have a *false* religion, is the broad road to perdition; and to have the true religion, and live agreeably to it, is the high road to heaven. Life is precarious—death is at the door—the Judge calls—much is to be done, and perhaps little time to do it in! Eternity depends on the present moment. Choose—choose speedily— determinately, &c.

"IV. The *extent* of the *conditions*.—*Fear the Lord, and serve him in truth and righteousness*. Fear the Lord. Consider his *being*, his *power*, *holiness*, *justice*, &c. This is the gate to religion. Religion itself consists of two parts. I. TRUTH. 1. In opposition to the detestable *idolatry* of the forementioned nations. 2. In reference to that *revelation* which God gave of himself. 3. In reference to that solid peace and comfort which false religions may promise, but cannot give; and which the true religion communicates to all who properly embrace it. II. UPRIGHTNESS or *integrity*, in opposition to those abominable vices by which themselves and the neighbouring nations had been defiled. 1. The major part of men have one religion for *youth*, another for old *age*. But he who serves God in *integrity*, serves him with all his heart in every part of life. 2. Most men have a religion of *times*, *places*, and *circumstances*. This is a *defective* religion. *Integrity* takes in every time, every place, and every circumstance; God's law being ever kept before the eyes, and his love in the heart, dictating purity and perfection to every thought, word, and work. 3. Many content themselves with abstaining from vice, and think themselves sure of the kingdom of God because they do not sin as others. But he who serves God in *integrity*, not only abstains from the *act* and the *appearance* of evil, but steadily performs every moral *good*. 4. Many think that if they practise some kind of virtues, to which they feel less of a natural repugnance, they bid fair for the kingdom; but this is opposite to *uprightness*. The religion of God equally forbids every species of vice, and recommends every kind of virtue.

"V. The *peril* of the *engagement*.—This covenant had in it the nature of an *oath;* for so much the phrase *before the Lord* implies: therefore those who entered into this covenant bound themselves by oath unto the Lord, to be steady and faithful in it. But it may be asked, 'As human nature is very corrupt, and exceedingly fickle, is there not the greatest danger of breaking such a covenant; and is it not better not to make it, than to run the risk of breaking it, and exposing one's self to superadded punishment on that account?' Answer: He who makes such a covenant in God's strength, will have that strength to enable him to prove faithful to it. Besides, if the soul do not feel itself under the most solemn obligation to live

A. M. 2553
B. C. 1451
An. Exod. Isr.
40
Anno ante
I. Olymp. 675

burned them with fire, after they had stoned them with stones.

26 And they [1]raised over him a great heap of stones unto this day. So

---

[1]Chap. viii. 29; 2 Sam. xviii. 17; Lam. iii. 53——[m]Deut. xiii. 17; 2 Sam. xxi. 14

פה רחמבון, אנב היר פינג יונבאמנבון, *And* HIM *they stoned there, and burnt his goods.* The ARABIC version alone says, *They stoned* HIM *and his* CHILDREN, *and his goods,* هو و بنیه و ماله In-stead of *burnt* THEM, אתם *otham,* two of De Rossi's MSS. read אתו *otho,* HIM; which reading, if genuine, would make the different members of the verse agree better. It is possible that *Achan,* his *oxen, asses, sheep, tent,* and all his *household goods,* were destroyed, but his *sons* and *daughters* left uninjured. But it may be asked, Why are *they* brought out into the valley with the rest? Why, that they might *see* and *fear,* and be for ever deterred by their father's punishment from imitating his example.

I have gone thus far into this important transaction, in which the *justice* and *mercy* of God are so much concerned, that I might be able to assign to each its due. That Achan's life was forfeited to justice by his transgression, no one doubts: *he* sinned against a known and positive law. His *children* could not suffer with him, because of the law, Deut. xxiv. 16, unless they had been accomplices in his guilt: of this there is no evidence; and the text in question, which speaks of Achan's punishment, is extremely *dubious,* as far as it relates to this point. One circumstance that strengthens the supposition that the children were not included, is the command of the Lord, ver. 15: "HE *that is taken with the accursed thing, shall be burnt with fire; he, and all that he hath.*" Now, *all that he hath* may certainly refer to his *goods,* and not to his *children;* and his punishment, and the destruction of his property would answer every purpose of public justice, both as a punishment and preventive of the crime; and both mercy and justice require that the innocent shall not suffer with the guilty, unless in very extraordinary cases, where God may permit the righteous or the innocent to be involved in those public calamities by which the ungodly are swept away from the face of the earth: but in the case before us, no necessity of this kind

[m]the LORD turned from the fierceness of his anger. Wherefore the name of that place was called, [n]The valley of [o]Achor, unto this day.

A. M. 2553
B. C. 1451
An. Exod. Isr.
40
Anno ante
I. Olymp. 675

---

[n]Verse 24; Isaiah lxv. 10; Hosea ii. 15——[o]That is, *trouble*

---

urged it, and therefore I conclude that Achan *alone* suffered, and that his repentance and confession were genuine and sincere; and that, while JUSTICE required his *life,* MERCY was extended to the salvation of his *soul.*

Verse 26. *They raised over him a great heap of stones*] The burial-places, both of heroes and eminent culprits, were anciently thus distinguished; and transactions of this kind gave rise to those great piles of stones called *cairns,* that are so frequently to be met with, especially in northern countries.

FROM the whole of this account we may see the exceeding sinfulness of sin, and the great danger of not *withstanding* its first approaches. By *covetousness* many lives and many souls have been destroyed, and yet the living lay it not to heart! Who fears the *love of money,* provided he can get riches? Through the intensity of this desire, every part of the surface of the earth, and as far as possible its bowels, are ransacked in order to get wealth; and God alone can tell, who sees all things, to how many private crimes, *frauds,* and *dissimulations,* this gives birth; by which the wrath of God is brought down upon the community at large! Who is an enemy to his country? The sinner against his God. An *open foe* may be resisted and repelled, because he is *known;* but the *covetous* man, who, as far as his personal safety will admit, is outraging all the requisitions of justice, is an unseen pestilence, sowing the seeds of desolation and ruin in society. Achan's covetousness, which led him to break the law of God, had nearly proved the destruction of the Israelitish camp; nor would the Lord turn away from his displeasure till the evil was detected, and the criminal punished.

Reader, is the face of God turned against *thee,* because of some private transgression? Are not thy circumstances and family suffering in consequence of something in thy private life? O search and try thy ways, return to God, and humble thyself before him lest thy iniquity instantly *find thee out!*

CHAPTER VIII

The Lord encourages Joshua, and promises to deliver Ai into his hands, and instructs him how he is to proceed against it, 1, 2. Joshua takes thirty thousand of his best troops, and gives them instructions concerning his intention of taking Ai by stratagem, 3–8. The men dispose themselves according to these directions, 9–13. The king of Ai attacks the Israelites, who, feigning to be beaten, fly before him, in consequence of which all the troops of Ai issue out, and pursue the Israelites, 14–17. Joshua, at the command of God, stretches out his spear towards Ai, and then five thousand men that he had placed in ambush in the valley rise up, enter the city, and set it on fire, 18, 19. Then Joshua and his men turned against the men of Ai, and, at the same time, those who had taken the city sallied forth and attacked them in the rear; thus the men of Ai were defeated, their king taken prisoner, the city sacked, and twelve thousand persons slain, 20–26. The Israelites take the spoils, and hang the king of Ai, 27–29. Joshua builds an altar to God on Mount Ebal, and writes on it a copy of the law of Moses, 30–32. *The elders, officers, and judges, stand on each side of the ark, one half over against Mount Gerizim, and the other against Mount Ebal, and read all the blessings and curses of the law, according to the command of Moses, 33–35.*

A. M. 2553
B. C. 1451
An. Exod. Isr.
40
Anno ante
I. Olymp. 675

AND the Lord said unto Joshua, ªFear not, neither be thou dismayed: take all the people of war with thee, and arise, go up to Ai: see, ᵇI have given into thy hand the king of Ai, and his people, and his city, and his land:

2 And thou shalt do to Ai and her king as thou didst unto ᶜJericho and her king: only ᵈthe spoil thereof, and the cattle thereof, shall ye take for a prey unto yourselves: lay thee an ambush for the city behind it.

3 So Joshua arose, and all the people of war, to go up against Ai: and Joshua chose out thirty thousand mighty men of valour, and sent them away by night.

A. M. 2553
B. C. 1451
An. Exod. Isr.
40
Anno ante
I. Olymp. 675

4 And he commanded them, saying, Behold, ᵉye shall lie in wait against the city, *even* behind the city: go not very far from the city, but be ye all ready:

5 And I, and all the people that *are* with me, will approach unto the city: and it shall

---

ªDeut. i. 21; vii. 18; xxxi. 8; chap. i. 9——ᵇChap. vi. 2

ᶜChap. vi. 21——ᵈDeut. xx. 14——ᵉJudg. xx. 29

NOTES ON CHAP. VIII

Verse 1. *Fear not*] The iniquity being now purged away, because of which God had turned his hand against Israel, there was now no cause to dread any other disaster, and therefore Joshua is ordered to take courage.

Take all the people of war with thee] From the *letter* of this verse it appears that *all* that were capable of carrying arms were to march out of the camp on this occasion: *thirty thousand* chosen men formed an ambuscade in one place; *five thousand* he placed in another, who had all gained their positions in the night season: with the rest of the army he appeared the next morning before *Ai*, which the men of that city would naturally suppose were the whole of the Israelitish forces; and consequently be the more emboldened to come out and attack them. But some think that thirty thousand men were the whole that were employed on this occasion; five thousand of whom were placed as an ambuscade on the west side of the city between *Beth-el* and *Ai*, ver. 12, and with the rest he appeared before the city in the morning. The king of Ai seeing but about twenty-five thousand coming against him, and being determined to defend his city and crown to the last extremity, though he had but twelve thousand persons in the whole city, ver. 25, scarcely one half of whom we can suppose to be effective men, he was determined to risk a battle; and accordingly issued out, and was defeated by the stratagem mentioned in the preceding part of this chapter.

Several eminent commentators are of opinion that the whole Israelitish force was employed on this occasion, because of what is said in the first verse; but this is not at all likely. 1. It appears that but thirty thousand were chosen out of the whole camp for this expedition, the rest being drawn up in readiness should their co-operation be necessary. See verses 3 and 10. 2. That *all the people* were mustered in order to make this selection, ver. 1. 3. That these thirty thousand were sent off by night, ver. 3, Joshua himself continuing in the camp a part of that night, ver. 9, with the design of putting himself at the head of the army next morning. 4. That of the thirty thousand men *five thousand* were directed to lie in ambush between *Beth-el* and *Ai*, on the west side of the city, ver. 12;

the twenty-five thousand having taken a position on the north side of the city, ver. 11. 5. That the whole of the troops employed against Ai on this occasion were those on the north and west, ver. 13, which we know from the preceding verses were composed of thirty thousand chosen men. 6. That Joshua went in the course of the night, probably before daybreak, into the valley between *Beth-el* and *Ai*, where the ambuscade of five thousand men was placed, ver. 13, and gave them the proper directions how they were to proceed, and agreed on the sign he was to give them at the moment he wished them to act, see ver. 18: and that, after having done so, he put himself at the head of the twenty-five thousand men on the north side of the city: for we find him among them when the men of Ai issued out, ver. 15, though he was the night before in the valley on the west side, where the ambuscade lay, ver. 13. 7. That as Ai was but a small city, containing only twelve thousand inhabitants, it would have been absurd to have employed an army of several hundred thousand men against them. 8. This is confirmed by the opinion of the *spies*, chap. vii. 3, who, from the smallness of the place, the fewness of its inhabitants, and the panic-struck state in which they found them, judged that three thousand troops would be quite sufficient to reduce the place. 9. That it appears this judgment was correctly enough formed, as the whole population of the place amounted only to twelve thousand persons, as we have already seen, ver. 25. 10. That even a less force might have been sufficient for the reduction of this place, had they been supplied with battering-rams, and such like instruments, which it does not appear the Israelites possessed. 11. That this is the reason why Joshua employed the stratagems detailed in this chapter: having no proper instruments or machines by means of which he might hope to take the city by assault, (and to reduce it by famine, which was quite possible, would have consumed too much time,) he used the feigned flight, ver. 19, to draw the inhabitants from the city, that the ambush, ver. 12, 15, might then enter, and take possession of it. 12. That had he advanced with a greater force against the city the inhabitants would have had no confidence in risking a battle, and consequently would have kept within their walls, which would have defeated the design

A. M. 2553
B. C. 1451
An. Exod. Isr.
40
Anno ante
I. Olymp. 675

come to pass, when they come out against us, as at the first, that ᶠwe will flee before them,

6 (For they will come out after us,) till we have ᵍdrawn them from the city: for they will say, They flee before us, as at the first: therefore we will flee before them.

7 Then ye shall rise up from the ambush, and seize upon the city: for the LORD your God will deliver it into your hand.

8 And it shall be, when ye have taken the city, *that* ye shall set the city on fire: according to the commandment of the LORD shall ye do. ʰSee, I have commanded you.

9 Joshua therefore sent them forth: and they went to lie in ambush, and abode between Beth-el and Ai, on the west side of Ai: but Joshua lodged that night among the people.

10 And Joshua rose up early in the morning, and numbered the people, and went up, he and the elders of Israel, before the people to Ai.

11 ⁱAnd all the people, *even the people* of war that *were* with him, went up, and drew nigh, and came before the city, and pitched on the north side of Ai: now *there was* a valley between them and Ai.

12 And he took about five thousand men,

and set them to lie in ambush between Beth-el and Ai, on the west side ᵏof the city.

A. M. 2553
B. C. 1451
An. Exod. Isr.
40
Anno ante
I. Olymp. 675

13 And when they had set the people, *even* all the hosts that *was* on the north of the city, and ˡtheir liers in wait on the west of the city, Joshua went that night into the midst of the valley.

14 And it came to pass, when the king of Ai saw *it,* that they hasted and rose up early, and the men of the city went out against Israel to battle, he and all his people, at a time appointed, before the plain; but he ᵐwist not that *there were* liers in ambush against him behind the city.

15 And Joshua and all Israel ⁿmade as if they were beaten before them, and fled by the way of the wilderness.

16 And all the people that *were* in Ai were called together to pursue after them: and they pursued after Joshua, and were drawn away from the city.

17 And there was not a man left in Ai or Beth-el, that went not out after Israel: and they left the city open, and pursued after Israel.

18 And the LORD said unto Joshua, Stretch out the spear that *is* in thy hand toward Ai; for I will give it into thine hand. And Joshua

---

ᶠJudg. xx. 32——ᵍHeb. *pulled*——ʰ2 Sam. xiii. 28
ⁱVer. 5——ᵏOr, *of Ai*

ˡHeb. *their lying in wait,* ver. 4——ᵐJudg. xx. 34;
Eccles. ix. 12——ⁿJudg. xx. 36, &c.

---

of the Israelites, which was to get them to issue from their city. 13. That, all these circumstances considered thirty thousand men, disposed as above, were amply sufficient for the reduction of the city, and were the whole of the Israelitish troops which were employed on the occasion.

Verse 8. *Ye shall set the city on fire*] Probably this means no more than that they should kindle a fire in the city, the smoke of which should be an indication that they had taken it. For as the spoils of the city were to be divided among the people, had they at this time set fire to the city itself, all the property must have been consumed, for the five thousand men did not wait to save any thing, as they immediately issued out to attack the men of Ai in the rear.

Verse 10. *Numbered the people*] ויפקד את העם *vaiyiphkod eth haam, he visited the people*—inspected their ranks to see whether every thing was in perfect readiness, that in case they should be needed they might be led on to the attack. There is no doubt that Joshua had left the rest of the army so disposed and ready, part of it having probably advanced towards Ai, that he might easily receive reinforcements in case of any disaster to the thirty thousand which had advanced against the city; and this consideration will serve to remove a part of the difficulty which arises from verses 1, 3, and 10,

collated with other parts of this chapter. Had he brought all his troops in sight, the people of Ai would not have attempted to risk a battle, and would consequently have kept within their walls, from which it was the object of Joshua to decoy them. See the preceding observations, particularly 10, 11, and 12.

Verse 17. *There was not a man left in Ai or Beth-el*] It is very likely that the principal strength of *Beth-el* had been previously brought into *Ai,* as the strongest place to make a stand in; Beth-el being but about three miles distant from Ai, and probably not greatly fortified. Therefore Ai contained on this occasion *all the men of Beth-el*—all the warriors of that city, as well as its own troops and inhabitants. Others think that the Beth-elites, seeing the Israelites fly, sallied out of their city as against a common enemy; but that, finding the men of Ai discomfited, and the city taken, they returned to Beth-el, which Joshua did not think proper to attack at this time. From Judges i. 24 we find that Beth-el was then a *walled city,* in the hands of the Canaanites, and was taken by the house of Joseph.

Verse 18. *Stretch out the spear*] It is very probable that Joshua had a *flag* or *ensign* at the end of his spear, which might be easily seen at a considerable distance; and that the *unfurling* or *waving* of this was the *sign* agreed on between him and the ambush, (see ver. 13, and

A. M. 2553
B. C. 1451
An. Exod. Isr.
40
Anno ante
I. Olymp. 675
stretched out the spear that *he had* in his hand toward the city.

19 And the ambush arose quickly out of their place, and they ran as soon as he had stretched out his hand: and they entered into the city, and took it, and hasted and set the city on fire.

20 And when the men of Ai looked behind them, they saw, and, behold, the smoke of the city ascended up to heaven, and they had no °power to flee this way or that way: and the people that fled to the wilderness turned back upon the pursuers.

21 And when Joshua and all Israel saw that the ambush had taken the city, and that the smoke of the city ascended, then they turned again, and slew the men of Ai.

22 And the other issued out of the city against them: so they were in the midst of Israel, some on this side, and some on that side: and they smote them, so that they ᴾlet none of them remain or escape.

23 And the king of Ai they took alive, and brought him to Joshua.

24 And it came to pass, when Israel had made an end of slaying all the inhabitants of Ai in the field, in the wilderness wherein they chased them, and when they were all fallen on the edge of the sword, until they were consumed, that all the Israelites returned unto Ai, and smote it with the edge of the sword.

A. M. 2553
B. C. 1451
An. Exod. Isr.
40
Anno ante
I. Olymp. 675

25 And *so* it was, *that* all that fell that day, both of men and women, *were* twelve thousand, *even* all the men of Ai.

26 For Joshua drew not his hand back, wherewith he stretched out the spear, until he had utterly destroyed all the inhabitants of Ai.

27 �q Only the cattle and the spoil of that city Israel took for a prey unto themselves, according unto the word of the LORD which he ʳcommanded Joshua.

28 And Joshua burnt Ai, and made it ˢa heap for ever, *even* a desolation unto this day.

29 ᵗ And the king of Ai he hanged on a tree until eventide: ᵘand as soon as the sun was down, Joshua commanded that they should

---

°Heb. *hand*——ᴾDeut. vii. 2——qNum. xxxi. 22, 26
ʳVer. 2

ˢDeut. xiii. 16——ᵗChap. x. 26; Psalm cvii. 40; cx. 5
ᵘDeut. xxi. 23; chap. x. 27

---

the preceding observations on verse 1, observation 6;) and on seeing this *flag* or *ensign* unfurled, the men who lay in ambush arose and entered the city, making the fire previously agreed on. See ver. 8.

Verse 19. *Set the city on fire.*] See on ver. 8.

Verse 20. *They had no power to flee this way or that way*] They were in utter consternation; they saw that the city was taken, they found themselves in the midst of their foes; that their wives, children, and property, had fallen a prey to their enemies, in consequence of which they were so utterly panic-struck as to be incapable of making any resistance.

Verse 24. *Returned unto Ai, and smote it with the edge of the sword.*] This must refer to the women, children, and old persons, left behind; for it is likely that all the effective men had sallied out when they imagined the Israelites had fled. See ver. 16.

Verse 26. *Joshua drew not his hand back*] He was not only the *general*, but the *standard-bearer* or *ensign* of his own army, and continued in this employment during the whole of the battle. See on ver. 18. Some commentators understand this and ver. 18 *figuratively*, as if they implied that Joshua continued *in prayer to God* for the success of his troops; nor did he cease till the armies of Ai were annihilated, and the city taken and destroyed. The Hebrew word כידון *kidon*, which we render *spear*, is rendered by the Vulgate *clypeum, buckler;* and it must be owned that it seems to have this signification in several passages of Scripture: (see 1 Sam. xvii. 6, 45; Job xxxix.

23:) but it is clear enough also that it means a *spear*, or some kind of *offensive armour*, in other places: see Job xli. 29; Jer. vi. 23. I cannot therefore think that it has any *metaphorical* meaning, such as that attributed to the holding up of Moses's hands, Exod. xvii. 10-12, which is generally allowed to have a spiritual meaning, though it might be understood as the act of Joshua is here; and to this meaning an indirect glance is given in the note on the above place. But however the place in Exodus may be understood, that before us does not appear to have any metaphorical or equivocal meaning; Joshua continued to hold up or stretch out his spear, and did not slack from the pursuit till the forces of Ai were utterly discomfited.

Verse 27. *Only the cattle and the spoil*] In the case of Jericho these were all consigned to destruction, and therefore it was criminal to take any thing pertaining to the city, as we have already seen; but in the case before us the cattle and spoils were expressly given to the conquerors by the order of God. See ver. 2.

Verse 28. *Unto this day.*] This last clause was probably *added* by a later hand.

Verse 29. *The king of Ai he hanged on a tree*] He had gone out at the head of his men, and had been taken prisoner, ver. 23; and the battle being over, he was ordered to be hanged, probably after having been *strangled*, or in some way deprived of life, as in the case mentioned chap. x. 26, for in those times it was not customary to hang people *alive*.

As soon as the sun was down] It was not lawful to let the bodies remain all night upon

A. M. 2553
B. C. 1451
An. Exod. Isr.
40
Anno ante
I. Olymp. 675

take his carcass down from the tree, and cast it at the entering of the gate of the city, and ᵛraise thereon a great heap of stones, *that remaineth* unto this day.

30 Then Joshua built an altar unto the LORD God of Israel ᵂin Mount Ebal.

31 As Moses the servant of the LORD commanded the children of Israel, as it is written in the ˣbook of the law of Moses, an altar of whole stones, over which no man hath lift up *any* iron: and ʸthey offered thereon burnt-offerings unto the LORD, and sacrificed peace-offerings.

32 And ᶻhe wrote there upon the stones a copy of the law of Moses, which he wrote in the presence of the children of Israel.

33 And all Israel, and their elders, and offi-

cers, and their judges, stood on this side the ark, and on that side, before the priests the Levites, ᵃwhich bare the ark of the covenant of the LORD, as well ᵇthe stranger, as he that was born among them; half of them over against Mount Gerizim, and half of them over against Mount Ebal: ᶜas Moses the servant of the LORD had commanded before, that they should bless the people of Israel.

34 And afterward ᵈhe read all the words of the law, ᵉthe blessings and cursings, according to all that is written in the book of the law.

35 There was not a word of all that Moses commanded, which Joshua read not before all the congregation of Israel, ᶠwith the women, and the little ones, and ᵍthe strangers that ʰwere conversant among them.

A. M. 2553
B. C. 1451
An. Exod. Isr.
40
Anno ante
I. Olymp. 675

ᵛChap. vii. 26; x. 27——ᵂDeut. xxvii. 4, 5——ˣExod. xx. 25; Deut. xxvii. 5, 6——ʸExod. xx. 24——ᶻDeut. xxvii. 2, 8——ᵃDeut. xxxi. 9, 25——ᵇDeut. xxxi. 12

ᶜDeut. xi. 29; xxvii. 12——ᵈDeut. xxxi. 11; Neh. viii. 3——ᵉDeut. xxviii. 2, 15, 45; xxix. 20, 21; xxx. 19 ᶠDeut. xxxi. 12——ᵍVer. 33——ʰHeb. *walked*

---

the tree. See the note on Deut. xxi. 23. The Septuagint say the king of *Ai* was hanged επι ξυλον διδυμον, upon a *double tree*, which probably means a *forked* tree, or something in the form of a *cross*. The tree on which criminals were hanged among the Romans was called *arbor infelix*, and *lignum infelix*, the *unfortunate, ill-fated,* or *accursed tree.*

Raise thereon a great heap of stones] This was a common custom through all antiquity in every country, as we have already seen in the case of *Achan*, chap. vii. 20.

Verse 30. *Then Joshua built an altar*] This was done in obedience to the express command of God, Deut. xxvii. 4-8. See the notes there.

Verse 32. *A copy of the law of Moses*] משנה תורת *mishneh torath*, the *repetition* of the *law;* that is, a *copy* of the *blessings* and *curses*, as commanded by Moses; not a copy of the *Decalogue*, as some imagine, nor of the book of Deuteronomy, as others think; much less of the whole Pentateuch; but merely of that part which contained the blessings and curses, and which was to be read on this solemn occasion. See the note on Deut. xxvii. 3.

Verse 33. *Half of them over against Mount Gerizim*] See the arrangement of the whole of this business in the note and observations on Deut. xxvii. 26. And see also the notes on chap. xxviii. of the same book.

Verse 35. *With the women and the little ones*] It was necessary that *all* should know that they were under the same obligations to obey; even the *women* are brought forward, not only because of their personal responsibility, but because to them was principally intrusted the education of the children. The *children* also witness this solemn transaction, that a salutary fear of offending God might be early, diligently, and deeply impressed upon their hearts. Thus every precaution is taken to ensure obedience to the Divine precepts, and con-

sequently to promote the happiness of the people; for this every ordinance of God is remarkable, as he ever causes the *interest* and *duty* of his followers to go hand in hand.

1. IT may be asked, Seeing God promised to deliver Ai into the hands of the Israelites, why needed they to employ so many men and so many stratagems in order to its reduction? To this it may be answered, that God will have man to put forth the wisdom and power with which he has endued him, in every important purpose of life; that he endued him with those powers for this very end; and that it would be inconsistent with his gracious design so to help man at any time as to render the powers he had given him useless.

2. It is only in the use of lawful means that we have any reason to expect God's blessing and help. One of the ancients has remarked, "Though God has made man without himself, he will not save him without himself;" and therefore man's own *concurrence* of *will*, and *co-operation* of *power* with God, are essentially necessary to his preservation and salvation. This co-operation is the grand condition, *sine qua non*, on which God will help or save. But is not this "endeavouring to *merit* salvation by our own works?" No: for this is impossible, unless we could prove that all the mental and corporeal powers which we possess came *from* and are *of ourselves*, and that we held them *independently* of the power and beneficence of our Creator; and that every act of these was of infinite value, to make it an equivalent for the heaven we wished to purchase. Putting forth the hand to receive the alms of a benevolent man, can never be considered a purchase-price for the bounty bestowed. For ever shall that word stand true in all its parts, *Christ is the* AUTHOR *of eternal salvation to all them that* OBEY *him*, Heb. v. 9.

CHAPTER IX

All the kings of the Hittites, Amorites, Canaanites, Perizzites, Hivites, *and* Jebusites, *unite their forces against Joshua,* 1, 2. *The inhabitants of* Gibeon, *hearing what Joshua had done to Ai, sent ambassadors to him, feigning themselves to come from a very distant tribe, requesting a friendly alliance with him,* 3–5. *Their address to Joshua, and the means they used to deceive the Israelites,* 6–13. *The Israelitish elders are deceived, and make a league with them, which they confirm with an oath,* 14, 15. *After three days they are informed that the* Gibeonites *belong to the seven Canaanitish nations, yet they spare their cities,* 16, 17. *The congregation murmuring because of this, the elders excuse themselves because of their oath,* 18, 19. *They purpose to make the Gibeonites slaves to the congregation,* 20, 21. *Joshua calls them, and pronounces this sentence against them,* 22, 23. *They vindicate themselves, and submit to their lot,* 24, 25. *They are spared, and made hewers of wood and drawers of water to the congregation and to the altar,* 26, 27.

A. M. 2553
B. C. 1451
An. Exod. Isr.
40
Anno ante
I. Olymp. 675

AND it came to pass, when all the kings which *were* on this side Jordan, in the hills, and in the valleys, and in all the coasts of ᵃthe great sea, over against Lebanon, ᵇthe Hittite, and the Amorite, the Canaanite, the Perizzite, the Hivite, and the Jebusite, heard *thereof ;*

2 That they ᶜgathered themselves together, to fight with Joshua and with Israel, with one ᵈaccord.

3 And when the inhabitants of ᵉGibeon ᶠheard what Joshua had done unto Jericho and to Ai,

4 They did work wilily, and went and made as if they had been ambassadors, and took old sacks upon their asses, and wine bottles, old, and rent, and bound up ;

5 And old shoes and clouted upon their feet, and old garments upon them ; and all the bread of their provision was dry *and* mouldy.

A. M. 2553
B. C. 1451
An. Exod. Isr.
40
Anno ante
I. Olymp. 675

ᵃNumbers xxxiv. 6——ᵇExodus iii. 17; xxiii. 23 ᶜPsalm lxxxiii. 3, 5

ᵈHeb. *mouth*——ᵉChap. x. 2; 2 Sam. xxi. 1, 2 ᶠChapter vi. 27

NOTES ON CHAP. IX

Verse 1. *And it came to pass, when all the kings—heard* thereof] From this account it appears that the capture and destruction of *Jericho* and *Ai* had been heard of to the remotest parts of the land, that a general fear of the Israelitish arms prevailed, and that the different dynasties or petty governments into which the land was divided, felt all their interests at stake, and determined to make the defence of their country a common cause. This was the most prudent step they could take in their circumstances, and therefore they entered into a confederation in order to arrest the progress of the Israelites. The *Great Sea* mentioned here is the *Mediterranean Sea,* the coasts of which were inhabited by the *Phœnicians, Tyrians, Sidonians,* and *Philistines.* It is very likely that all these united with the Canaanites for their common safety.

Verse 3. *The inhabitants of Gibeon heard*] These alone did not join the confederation. Gibeon is supposed to have been the capital of the *Hivites.* In the division of the land it fell to the lot of Benjamin, chap. xviii. 25, and was afterwards given to the priests, chap. xxi. 17. See the note on chap. x. 2.

Verse 4. *They did work wilily*] Finesse of this kind is allowed by the conduct of all nations; and *stratagems* in war are all considered as legal. Nine tenths of the victories gained are attributable to *stratagem;* all sides practise them, and therefore none can condemn them. Much time and labour have been lost in the inquiry, "Did not the *Gibeonites* tell lies?" Certainly they did, and what is that to *us?* Does the word of God *commend* them for it? It does not. Are they held up to us as *examples?* Surely no. *They* did what any other nation would have done in their circumstances, and we have nothing to do with their example.

Had they come to the Israelites, and simply submitted themselves without opposition and without fraud, they had certainly fared much better. *Lying* and *hypocrisy* always defeat their own purpose, and at best can succeed only for a short season. *Truth* and *honesty* never wear out.

Old sacks—and wine bottles, old, &c.] They pretended to have come from a very distant country, and that their sacks and the *goat-skins* that served them for carrying their wine and water in, were worn out by the length of the journey.

Verse 5. *Old shoes and clouted*] Their sandals, they pretended had been worn out by long and difficult travelling, and they had been obliged to have them frequently *patched* during the way; their garments also were worn *thin;* and what remained of their bread was *mouldy*—spotted with age, or, as our old version has it, *bored*—pierced with many holes by the vermin which had bred in it, through the length of time it had been in their sacks; and this is the most literal meaning of the original נקדים *nik-kudim,* which means *spotted* or *pierced with many holes.*

The *old* and *clouted shoes* have been a subject of some controversy: the Hebrew word בלות *baloth* signifies *worn out,* from בלה *balah,* to *wear away;* and מטלאות *metullaoth,* from טלא *tala,* to *spot* or *patch,* i. e., *spotted* with *patches.* Our word *clouted,* in the Anglo-Saxon ᵹecluꞇod signifies *seamed up, patched;* from cluꞇ *clout, rag,* or *small piece of cloth,* used for piecing or patching. But some suppose the word here comes from *clouet,* the diminutive of *clou,* a small *nail,* with which the Gibeonites had fortified the soles of their shoes, to prevent them from wearing out in so long a journey; but this seems very unlikely; and our old English term

A. M. 2553
B. C. 1451
An. Exod. Isr.
40
Anno ante
I. Olymp. 675

6 And they went to Joshua ᵍunto the camp at Gilgal, and said unto him, and to the men of Israel, We be come from a far country: now therefore make ye a league with us.

7 And the men of Israel said unto the ʰHivites, Peradventure ye dwell among us; and ⁱhow shall we make a league with you?

8 And they said unto Joshua, ᵏWe *are* thy servants. And Joshua said unto them, Who *are* ye? and from whence come ye?

9 And they said unto him, ˡFrom a very far country thy servants are come, because of the name of the LORD thy God: for we have ᵐheard the fame of him, and all that he did in Egypt.

10 ⁿAnd all that he did to the two kings of the Amorites, that *were* beyond Jordan, to Sihon king of Heshbon, and to Og king of Bashan, which *was* at Ashtaroth.

A. M. 2553
B. C. 1451
An. Exod. Isr.
40
Anno ante
I. Olymp. 675

11 Wherefore our elders and all the inhabitants of our country spake to us, saying, Take victuals °with you for the journey, and go to meet them, and say unto them, We *are* your servants: therefore now make ye a league with us.

12 This our bread we took hot *for* our provision, out of our houses, on the day we came forth to go unto you; but now, behold, it is dry, and it is mouldy:

13 And these bottles of wine, which we filled, *were* new; and, behold, they be rent: and these our garments, and our shoes, are become old by reason of the very long journey.

14 And ᵖthe men took of their victuals, �q and asked not *counsel* at the mouth of the LORD.

15 And Joshua ʳmade peace with them, and made a league with them, to let them live: and the princes of the congregation sware unto them.

16 And it came to pass at the end of three

ᵍChap. v. 10——ʰChap. xi. 19——ⁱExod. xxiii. 32; Deut. vii. 2; xx. 16; Judg. ii. 2——ᵏDeut. xx. 11; 2 Kings x. 5——ˡDeut. xx. 15——ᵐExod. xv. 14; Josh. ii. 10——ⁿNum. xxi. 24, 33——°Heb. *in your hand*

ᵖOr, *they received the men by reason of their victuals* �q Num. xxvii. 21; Isa. xxx. 1, 2; see Judg. i. 1; 1 Sam. xxii. 10; xxiii. 10, 11; xxx. 8; 2 Sam. ii. 1; v. 19 ʳChap. xi. 19; 2 Sam. xxi. 2

---

clouted—seamed or *patched*—expresses the spirit of the Hebrew word.

Verse 6. *Make ye a league with us.*] כרתו לנו ברית *kirethu lanu berith, cut,* or *divide, the covenant sacrifice with us.* From this it appears that heathenism at this time had its sacrifices, and covenants were ratified by sacrificing to and invoking the objects of their adoration.

Verse 7. *Peradventure ye dwell among us*] It is strange they should have had such a suspicion, as the Gibeonites had acted so artfully; and it is as strange that, having such a suspicion, they acted with so little caution.

Verse 8. *We are thy servants.*] This appears to have been the only answer they gave to the question of the Israelitish elders, and this they gave to *Joshua,* not to *them,* as they saw that Joshua was commander-in-chief of the host.

Who are ye? and from whence come ye?] To these questions, from such an authority, they felt themselves obliged to give an explicit answer; and they do it very artfully by a mixture of *truth, falsehood,* and *hypocrisy.*

Verse 9. *Because of the name of the Lord thy God*] They pretend that they had undertaken this journey on a religious account; and seem to intimate that they had the highest respect for Jehovah, the object of the Israelites' worship; this was *hypocrisy.*

We have heard the fame of him] This was *true:* the wonders which God did in *Egypt,* and the discomfiture of *Sihon* and *Og,* had reached the whole land of Canaan; and it was on this account that the inhabitants of it were panic-struck. The Gibeonites, knowing that they could not stand where such mighty forces had fallen, wished to make the Israelites their

friends. This part of their relation was strictly *true.*

Verse 11. *Wherefore our elders, &c.*] All this, and what follows to the end of verse 13, was *false,* contrived merely for the purpose of deceiving the Israelites, and this they did to save their own lives; as they expected all the inhabitants of Canaan to be put to the sword.

Verse 14. *The men took of their victuals*] This was done in all probability in the way of *friendship;* for, from time immemorial to the present day, *eating together,* in the Asiatic countries, is considered a token of unalterable friendship; and those who eat even *salt* together, feel themselves bound thereby in a perpetual covenant. But the *marginal* reading of this clause should not be hastily rejected.

And asked not counsel at the mouth of the Lord.] They made the covenant with the Gibeonites without consulting God by *Urim* and *Thummim,* which was highly reprehensible in them, as it was a *state transaction* in which the interests and honour of God their king were intimately concerned.

Verse 15. *Joshua made peace with them*] Joshua agreed to receive them into a friendly connection with the Israelites, and to respect their lives and properties; and the elders of Israel bound themselves to the observance of it, and confirmed it with an *oath.* As the same words are used here as in verse 6, we may suppose that the covenant was made in the ordinary way, a sacrifice being offered on the occasion, and its blood poured out before the Lord. See on Gen. xv. 10, &c.

Verse 16. *At the end of three days*] *Gibeon* is reputed to be only about eight leagues distant from Gilgal, and on this account the fraud

A. M. 2553
B. C. 1451
An. Exod. Isr.
40
Anno ante
I. Olymp. 675

days after they had made a league with them, that they heard that they *were* their neighbours, and *that* they dwelt among them.

17 And the children of Israel journeyed, and came unto their cities on the third day. Now their cities *were* ⁸Gibeon, and Chephirah, and Beeroth, and Kirjath-jearim.

18 And the children of Israel smote them not, ᵗbecause the princes of the congregation had sworn unto them by the LORD God of Israel. And all the congregation murmured against the princes.

19 But all the princes said unto all the congregation, We have sworn unto them by the LORD God of Israel: now therefore we may not touch them.

20 This we will do to them; we will even let them live, lest ᵘwrath be upon us, because of the oath which we sware unto them.

21 And the princes said unto them, Let them live; but let them be ᵛhewers of wood and drawers of water unto all the congregation; as the princes had ʷpromised them.

22 And Joshua called for them, and he spake unto them, saying, Wherefore have ye beguiled us, saying, ˣWe *are* very far from you; when ʸye dwell among us?

23 Now therefore ye ᶻ*are* cursed, and there

A. M. 2553
B. C. 1451
An. Exod. Isr.
40
Anno ante
I. Olymp. 675

---

⁸Chap. xviii. 25, 26, 28; Ezra ii. 25——ᵗEccles. v. 2; Psa. xv. 4——ᵘSee 2 Sam. xxi. 1, 2, 6; Ezek. xvii. 13, 15, 18, 19; Zech. v. 3, 4; Mal. iii. 5——ᵛDeut. xxix. 11 ——ʷVer. 15——ˣVer. 6, 9——ʸVer. 16——ᶻGen. ix. 25

---

might be easily discovered in the time mentioned above.

Verse 17. *The children of Israel—came unto their cities*] Probably when the fraud was discovered, Joshua sent out a detachment to examine their country, and to see what use could be made of it in the prosecution of their war with the Canaanites. Some of the cities mentioned here were afterwards in great repute among the Israelites: and God chose to make one of them, *Kirjath-jearim*, the residence of the ark of the covenant for *twenty years*, in the reigns of *Saul* and *David*. There is no evidence that the *preservation* of the Gibeonites was displeasing to Jehovah.

Verse 18. *All the congregation murmured*] Merely because they were deprived of the *spoils* of the Gibeonites. They had now got under the full influence of a predatory spirit; God saw their proneness to this, and therefore, at particular times, totally interdicted the spoils of conquered cities, as in the case of Jericho.

Verse 19. *We have sworn unto them*] Although the Israelites were *deceived* in this business, and the covenant was made on a certain supposition which was afterwards proved to have had no foundation in truth, and consequently the whole engagement on the part of the *deceived* was hereby vitiated and rendered null and void; yet, because the elders had *eaten with them*, offered a *covenant sacrifice*, and *sworn by Jehovah*, they did not consider themselves at liberty to break the terms of the agreement, as far as the *lives* of the Gibeonites were concerned. That their conduct in this respect was highly pleasing to God is evident from this, that Joshua is nowhere reprehended for making this covenant, and sparing the Gibeonites; and that Saul, who four hundred years after this thought himself and the Israelites loosed from this obligation, and in consequence oppressed and destroyed the Gibeonites, was punished for the breach *of this treaty*, being considered as the violator of a most solemn oath and covenant engagement. See 2 Sam. xxi. 2-9, and Ezek. xvii. 18, 19.

All these circumstances laid together, prove that the command to destroy the Canaanites was not so *absolute* as is generally supposed:

and should be understood as rather referring to the destruction of the *political existence* of the Canaanitish *nations*, than to the destruction of their *lives*. See the notes on Deut. xx. 10, 17.

Verse 21. *Hewers of wood and drawers of water*] Perhaps this is a sort of proverbial expression, signifying the lowest state of servitude, though it may also be understood literally. See below.

Verse 23. *Now therefore ye* are *cursed*] Does not this refer to what was pronounced by Noah, Gen. ix. 25, against Ham and his posterity? Did not the curse of Ham imply *slavery*, and nothing else? *Cursed be Canaan, a servant of servants shall he be;* and does it not sufficiently appear that nothing else than perpetual *slavery* is implied in the curse of the Gibeonites? They were brought, no doubt, under tribute; performed the meanest offices for the Israelites, being in the same circumstances with the servile class of Hindoos called the *Chetrees;* had their national importance annihilated, and yet were never permitted to *incorporate* themselves with the Israelites. And we may reasonably suppose that this was the purpose of God relative to all the Canaanitish nations: those who would not renounce their idolatry, &c., were to be extirpated; those who *did* were to be preserved alive, on condition of becoming tributary, and serving as slaves. See the note on Deut. xx. 17.

Hewers of wood and drawers of water] The disgrace of this state lay not in the *laboriousness* of it, but in its being the common employment of the *females;* if the ancient customs among the same people were such as prevail now. The most intelligent travellers in those countries represent *collecting wood for fuel*, and *carrying water*, as the peculiar employment of the *females.* The Arab *women* of Barbary do so, according to Dr. *Shaw.* The *daughters* of the Turcomans in Palestine are employed, according to *D'Arvieux,* in fetching wood and water for the accommodation of their respective families. From these circumstances Mr. *Harmer* reasons thus: "The bitterness of the doom of the Gibeonites does not seem to have consisted in the laboriousness of the service enjoined them, for it was usual for *women* and

A. M. 2553
B. C. 1451
An. Exod. Isr.
40
Anno ante
I. Olymp. 675

shall ªnone of you be freed from being bondmen, and ᵇhewers of wood and drawers of water for the house of my God.

24 And they answered Joshua, and said, Because it was certainly told thy servants, how that the LORD thy God ᶜcommanded his servant Moses to give you all the land, and to destroy all the inhabitants of the land from before you, therefore ᵈwe were sore afraid of our lives because of you, and have done this thing.

25 And now, behold, we *are* ᵉin thine hand: as it seemeth good and right unto thee to do unto us, do.

A. M. 2553
B. C. 1451
An. Exod. Isr.
40
Anno ante
I. Olymp. 675

26 And so did he unto them, and delivered them out of the hand of the children of Israel, that they slew them not.

27 And Joshua ᶠmade them that day ᵍhewers of wood and drawers of water for the congregation, and for the altar of the LORD, even unto this day, ʰin the place which he should choose.

ªHeb. *not be cut off from you*——ᵇVer. 21, 27——ᶜExod. xxiii. 32; Deut. vii. 1, 2——ᵈExod. xv. 14

ᵉGen. xvi. 6——ᶠHeb. *gave, or, delivered to be;* 1 Chron. ix. 2; Ezra viii. 20——ᵍVer. 21, 23——ʰDeut. xii. 5

---

children to perform what was required of *them;* but its degrading them from the characteristic employment of *men,* that of *bearing arms;* and condemning them and their posterity for ever to the employment of *females.* The not receiving them as *allies* was bitter; the disarming them who had been warriors, and condemning them to the employment of *females,* was worse; but the extending this degradation to their *posterity,* was bitterest of all. It is no wonder that in these circumstances they are said to have been *cursed.*"—Obs., vol. iv., p. 297.

Verse 24. *We were sore afraid of our lives*] Self-preservation, which is the most powerful law of nature, dictated to them those measures which they adopted; and they plead this as the *motive* of their conduct.

Verse 25. *We are in thine hand*] Entirely in thy power.

As it seemeth good and right unto thee—do.] Whatever *justice* and *mercy* dictate to thee to do to us, that perform. They expect *justice,* because they *deceived* the Israelites; but they expect *mercy* also, because they were driven to use this expedient for fear of losing their lives. The appeal to Joshua is full of delicacy and cogent argument.

Verse 26. *And so did he unto them*] That is, he acted according to *justice* and *mercy:* he delivered them out of the hands of the people, so that they slew them not—here was *mercy;* and he made them hewers of wood and drawers of water for the congregation, and to the altar of God—here was *justice.* Thus Joshua did nothing but what was *good* and *right,* not only in his own eyes, but also in the eyes of the Lord.

How long the Gibeonites were preserved as a distinct people after this, we know not. That they existed in the time of David, is evident from the circumstance mentioned on ver. 19. They are not mentioned after the captivity; and it is probable that they were nearly annihilated by the persecution raised up against them by Saul. Some suppose that the Gibeonites existed under the appellation of *Nethinim;* but of this there is no decisive proof; the Nethinim were probably slaves of a different race.

ON what we meet with in this chapter, we may make the following observations.

1. The Gibeonites told lies, in order to save their lives. No expediency can justify this, nor are *we* called to attempt it. The Gibeonites were *heathens,* and we can expect nothing better from them. See note at the end of chap. ii.

2. They did not profit by their falsity: had they come in fairly, sought peace, and renounced their idolatry, they would have had life on honourable terms. As it was, they barely escaped with their lives, and were utterly deprived of their political liberty. Even the *good* that is sought by *unlawful* means has God's curse on it.

3. We need not be solicitous for the character of the Gibeonites here; they are neither our models, nor believers in the true God, and therefore pure religion is not concerned in their prevarication and falsity.

4. We see here of what solemn importance an *oath* was considered among the people of God; they swore to their own hurt, and changed not. When once they had bound themselves to their Maker, they did not believe that any changing circumstances could justify a departure from so awful an obligation. Thus, reader, shouldst *thou* fear a lie, and tremble at an oath.

CHAPTER X

Adoni-zedec, *king of Jerusalem, hearing of the capture of* Ai, *and that the Gibeonites had made peace with* Israel, *calls to his assistance four other kings to fight against Gibeon,* 1–4. *They join forces, and encamp against Gibeon,* 5. *The Gibeonites send to Joshua for succour,* 6, *who immediately marches to their relief, receives encouragement from God, and falls suddenly on the confederate forces,* 7–9, *and defeats them; they fly, and multitudes of them are slain by a miraculous shower of hail-stones,* 10, 11. *Joshua, finding that the day began to fail, prayed that the sun and moon might stand still, that they might have time to pursue and utterly destroy these confederate forces,* 12. *The sun and moon stand still, and make that day as long as two,* 13, 14. *Joshua and the people return to their camp at* Gilgal, 15. *The five kings having taken shelter in a cave at* Makkedah, *Joshua commanded the people to roll great stones against the mouth of the cave, and set a watch to keep it, while* Israel *were pursuing their enemies,* 16–19. *The Israelites return to* Makkedah, *bring forth the five kings, then slay and hang them on five trees,* 20–27. *The Israelites take and destroy*

Makkedah, 28, *and* Libnah, 29, 30, *and* Lachish 31, 32, *and defeat* Horam *king of* Gezer, 33, *and take* Eglon, 34, 35, *and* Hebron, 36, 37, *and* Debir, 38, 39, *and all the country of the* hills, south, vale, *and* springs, *and the whole country from* Kadesh-Barnea *to Gibeon*, 40–42. *They return to Gilgal*, 43.

A. M. 2554
B. C. 1450
An. Exod. Isr.
41
Anno ante
I. Olymp. 674

NOW it came to pass, when Adoni-zedec, king of Jerusalem, had heard how Joshua had taken Ai, and had utterly destroyed it; [a]as he had done to Jericho and her king, so he had done to [b]Ai and her king; and [c]how the inhabitants of Gibeon had made peace with Israel, and were among them;

2 That they [d]feared greatly, because Gibeon *was* a great city, as one of the [e]royal cities, and because it *was* greater than Ai, and all the men thereof *were* mighty.

3 Wherefore Adoni-zedec king of Jerusalem sent unto Hoham king of Hebron, and unto Piram king of Jarmuth, and unto Japhia king of Lachish, and unto Debir king of Eglon, saying,

4 Come up unto me, and help me, that we may smite Gibeon: [f]for it hath made peace with Joshua, and with the children of Israel.

5 Therefore the five kings of the Amorites, the king of Jerusalem, the king of Hebron, the king of Jarmuth, the king of Lachish, the king of Eglon, [g]gathered themselves together, and went up, they and all their hosts, and encamped before Gibeon, and made war against it.

A. M. 2554
B. C. 1450
An. Exod. Isr.
41
Anno ante
I. Olymp. 674

6 And the men of Gibeon sent unto Joshua [h]to the camp to Gilgal, saying, Slack not thy hand from thy servants; come up to us quickly, and save us, and help us: for all the kings of the Amorites that dwell in the mountains are gathered together against us.

7 So Joshua ascended from Gilgal, he, and [i]all the people of war with him, and all the mighty men of valour.

8 And the LORD said unto Joshua, [k]Fear them not: for I have delivered them into thine hand; [l]there shall not a man of them stand before thee.

9 Joshua therefore came unto them sud-

---

[a]Chap. vi. 21——[b]Chap. viii. 22, 26, 28——[c]Chap. ix. 15——[d]Exod. xv. 14, 15, 16; Deut. xi. 25——[e]Heb. *cities of the kingdom*

[f]Ver. 1; chap. ix. 15——[g]Chap. ix. 2——[h]Chap. v. 10, ix. 6——[i]Chap. viii. 1——[k]Chap. xi. 6; Judg. iv. 14——[l]Chap. i. 5

NOTES ON CHAP. X

Verse 1. *Adoni-zedec*] This name signifies the *Lord of justice* or *righteousness;* and it has been conjectured that the Canaanitish kings assumed this name in imitation of that of the ancient patriarchal king of this city, Melchizedek, whose name signifies *king of righteousness,* or *my righteous king:* a supposition that is not improbable, when the celebrity of Melchizedek is considered.

Jerusalem] יְרוּשָׁלֵם *Yerushalam.* This word has been variously explained; if it be compounded of שָׁלַם *shalam,* peace, perfection, &c., and רָאָה *raah, he saw,* it may signify *the vision of peace*—or, *he shall see peace* or *perfection.*

Verse 2. *As one of the royal cities*] Not a *regal* city, but great, well inhabited and well fortified, *as* those cities which served for the royal residence generally were. It does not appear that the Gibeonites had any king—they seem to have been a small but powerful *republic, all the men* thereof were *mighty*, merely governed by their *elders:* for in their address to Joshua, chap. ix. 11, they mention no *king,* but simply state that they were sent by their *elders and the inhabitants of their country;* nor do we any where read of their *king;* and therefore we may naturally suppose that they had none.

Verse 3. *Hoham king of Hebron*] This city was situated in the mountains, southward of Jerusalem, from which it was about thirty miles distant. It fell to the tribe of Judah.

Piram king of Jarmuth] There were two

cities of this name; one belonged to the tribe of *Issachar,* see chap. xxi. 29; that mentioned here fell to the tribe of *Judah,* see chap. xv. 35; it is supposed to have been about eighteen miles distant from Jerusalem.

Japhia king of Lachish] This city is celebrated in Scripture; in that city *Amaziah* was slain by conspirators, 2 Kings xiv. 19. It was besieged by *Sennacherib,* 2 Kings xviii. 14, 17; and without effect by the king of *Assyria,* as we learn from Isa. xxxvii. 8: it was also besieged by the army of *Nebuchadnezzar,* see Jer. xxxiv. 7; it also fell to the lot of *Judah,* chap. xv. 39.

Debir king of Eglon] Where this city was situated is very uncertain; but we learn from chap. xv. 39, that it fell to the lot of the tribe of *Judah.*

Verse 5. *The five kings of the Amorites*] This is a general name for the inhabitants of Canaan, otherwise called *Canaanites;* and it is very likely that they had this appellation because the Amorites were the most powerful tribe or nation in that country. The inhabitants of Jerusalem were *Jebusites,* chap. xv. 63; those of Hebron were *Hittites,* Gen. xxiii. 2, 3; xxv. 9, 10; and the Gibeonites were *Hivites,* Josh. ix. 7; and yet all these are called *Amorites* occasionally, probably for the reason already mentioned, viz., because that tribe was most numerous and powerful.

Verse 9. *Joshua—came unto them suddenly*] This he did by a forced march during the night, for he *went up from Gilgal all night;* from Gilgal to Gibeon was about eighteen or twenty miles; and, having fallen so unexpectedly on

A. M. 2554
B. C. 1450
An. Exod. Isr.
41
Anno ante
I. Olymp. 674

denly, *and* went up from Gilgal all night.

10 And the LORD ^mdiscomfited them before Israel, and slew them with a great slaughter at Gibeon, and chased them along the way that goeth up ⁿto Beth-horon, and smote them to ^oAzekah, and unto Makkedah.

11 And it came to pass, as they fled from before Israel, *and* were in the going down to Beth-horon, ^pthat the LORD cast down great stones from heaven upon them unto Azekah, and they died: *they were* more which died with hail-stones, than *they* whom the children of Israel slew with the sword.

A. M. 2554
B. C. 1450
An. Exod. Isr.
41
Anno ante
I. Olymp. 674

12 Then spake Joshua to the LORD in the day when the LORD delivered up the Amorites before the children of Israel, and he said in the sight of Israel, ^qSun, ^rstand thou still upon Gibeon; and thou Moon, in the valley of ^sAjalon.

---

^mJudg. iv. 15; 1 Sam. vii. 10, 12; Psa. xviii. 14; Isa. xxviii. 21——ⁿChap. xvi. 3, 5——^oChap. xv. 35

^pPsa. xviii. 13, 14; lxxvii. 17; Isa. xxx. 30; Ecclus. xlvi. 6; Rev. xvi. 21——^qIsa. xxviii. 21; Hab. iii. 11; Ecclus. xlvi. 4——^rHeb. *be silent*——^sJudg. xii. 12

---

these confederate kings, they were immediately thrown into confusion.

Verse 10. *Slew them with a great slaughter at Gibeon*] Multitudes of them fell in the *onset;* after which they fled, and the Israelites pursued them by the way of Beth-horon. There were two cities of this name, the *upper* and *lower,* both in the tribe of Ephraim, and built by *Sherah,* the daughter of Ephraim, 1 Chron. vii. 24. The situation of these two cities is not exactly known.

To Azekah, and unto Makkedah.] These two cities were in the tribe of Judah, chap. xv. 35-41.

Verse 11. *The Lord cast down great stones from heaven upon them*] Some have contended that stones, in the common acceptation of the word, are intended here; and that the term *hail-stones* is only used to point out the *celerity* of their fall, and their *quantity.* That stones have fallen from the *clouds,* if not from a greater height, is a most incontestable fact. That these have fallen in different parts of the world is also true; the East Indies, America, France, Germany, England, Ireland, &c., have all witnessed this phenomenon: of such stones I possess and have seen several fragments; some considerable pieces may be seen in the British Museum. That God might have cast down such stones as these on the Canaanites, there can be no doubt, because his power is unlimited; and the whole account proves that here there was a miraculous interference. But it is more likely that hail-stones, in the proper sense of the word, are *meant* as well as *expressed* in the text. That God on other occasions has made use of hail-stones to destroy both men and cattle, we have ample proof in the *plague of hail* that fell on the Egyptians. See the note on Exod. ix. 18. There is now before me a square of glass, taken out of a south window in the house of Mr. Ball of Crockerton, in the parish of Longbridge Deverell, county of Wilts., through which a hail-stone passed in a shower that fell there June 1, 1780, at two o'clock, P. M. The hole is an *obtuse ellipsis* or oval, and is cut as true as if it had been done with a diamond: it is three inches and a half in diameter; a proof that the stone that pierced it, which was about eleven inches in circumference, came with inconceivable velocity, else the glass must have been *shivered* to pieces. I have known a cannon ball go through a square of glass in the cabin window of a ship, and make precisely the same kind of hole, without either *shattering* or ᵃven

starring the glass. It is needless to add that this hail-shower did great damage, breaking even trees in pieces, and destroying the vegetation through the whole of its extent. But allowing that extraordinary showers of hail have fallen in *England* or *France,* is it likely that such showers ever fell in the promised land or its vicinity? They certainly have. *Albertus Aquensis,* one of the writers in the collection *Gesta Dei per Francos,* in describing the expedition of Baldwin I. in the Holy Land, observes that, when he and his army were in the *Arabian mountains,* in the vicinity of the *Dead Sea,* they suffered incredibly from *horrible hail, terrible frost,* and *indescribable rain* and *snow,* so that thirty of his men perished by them. His words are: "*Sexta vero die montanis permensis, in extremo illorum cacumine maxima pertulerunt pericula, in* GRANDINE *horribili, in* GLACIE *terribili, in* PLUVIA *et* NIVE *inaudita, quorum immanitate, et horrore ingruente ad triginta homines pedites præ frigore mortui sunt.*"— Hist. Hieros., p. 307. I conclude, therefore, that a shower of *hail-stones* may be meant; and that this shower, though *natural* in itself, was *supernaturally* employed on this occasion, and *miraculously* directed to fall where it did, and do the execution described.

But I am ready to grant, notwithstanding, that as a most stupendous miracle was in this instance wrought, in causing the sun and moon to stand still; there can be no doubt that the shower of stones, which was also miraculous, might have been of *real stones* as well as *hail-stones.* Of late, this subject of the fall of real stones from the clouds has been very closely investigated, and not only the *possibility* of the fall of such stones from the *clouds,* or from much *higher regions,* but the *certainty* of the case have been fully demonstrated. These substances are now, in philosophical language denominated *aeroliths* or *air-stones;* and the following table constructed by M. *Izarn,* a foreign chemist, exhibits a variety of facts of this kind, and shows the *places* and *times* in which these substances fell, and the *testimony* by which these facts are supported. As it is as possible that God might have projected a shower of stones on these idolaters, even from the *moon,* as to arrest that planet in her course, I give the table, and leave the reader to decide, in the present case, for *aeroliths* or *hail-stones,* as may seem to him most congruous to the fact here related.

A. M. 2554
B. C. 1450
An. Exod. Isr.
41
Anno ante
I. Olymp. 674

13 And the sun stood still, and the moon stayed, until the people had avenged themselves upon

†2 Sam. i. 18

their enemies. †Is not this written in the book of ᵘJasher? So the sun stood still in the midst

A. M. 2554
B. C. 1459
An. Exod. Isr.
41
Anno ante
I. Olymp. 674

ᵘOr, *the upright*

SUBSTANCES	PLACES WHERE THEY FELL	PERIOD OF THEIR FALL	TESTIMONY
Shower of stones.........	At Rome.............	Under Tullus Hostilius...	Livy.
Shower of stones.........	At Rome.............	Consuls, C. Martius and M. Torquatus	J. Obsequens.
A very large stone......	Near the river Negos, Thrace.............	Second year of the 78th Olympiad....	Pliny.
Three large stones.......	In Thrace........	Year before J. C., 452....	Ch. of Count Marcellin.
Stone of 72 lbs..........	Near Larissa, Macedonia.	January, 1706..........	Paul Lucas.
About 1,200 stones; one 120 lbs...... Another of 60 lbs.......	Near Padua in Italy.....	In 1510................	Carden, Varcit.
Another of 59 lbs........	On Mount Vasier, Provence	November 27, 1627......	Gassendi.
Two large stones weighing 20 lbs.............	Liponas, in Bresse.......	September, 1753........	De La Lande.
A stony mass.............	Niort, Normandy.......	In 1750.............	De La Lande.
A stone of 7½ lbs........	At Luce, in Le Maine....	September 13, 1768......	Bachelay.
A stone...............	At Aire, in Artois......	In 1768...........	Gurson de Boyaval.
A stone................	In Le Cotentin..........	In 1768...........	Morand.
Extensive shower of stones.	Environs of Agen.......	July 24, 1790.........	St. Amand, Baudin, &c.
About 12 stones.........	Sienna, Tuscany.......	July, 1794............	Earl of Bristol.
A large stone of 56 lbs....	Wold Cottage, Yorkshire.	December 13, 1795....	Captain Topham.
A stone of 10 lbs	In Portugal............	February 19, 1796......	Southey.
A stone of about 120 lbs.	Salè, department of the Rhone.............	March 17, 1798........	Le Lievre and De Drèe.
Shower of stones.........	Benares, East Indies....	December 19, 1798.....	J. Lloyd Williams, Esq.
Shower of stones.........	At Plann, near Tabor, Bohemia.........	July 3, 1753............	B. de Born.
Mass of iron, 70 cubic feet..	America.............	April 5, 1800..........	Philosophical Magazine.
Mass of ditto, 14 quintals..	Abakauk, Siberia........	Very old..............	Pallas, Chladni, &c.
Shower of stones........	Barboutan, near Roquefort	July, 1789.............	Darcet, jun., Lomet, &c.
Large stone, 260 lbs......	Ensisheim, Upper Rhine.	November 7, 1492.......	Butenschoen.
Two stones, 200 and 300 lbs.	Near Verona............	In 1762.............	Acad. de Bourd.
A stone of 20 lbs.........	Sales, near Ville Franche..	March 12, 1798........	De Drèe.
Several ditto from 10 to 17 lbs..............	Near L'Aigle, Normandy	April 26, 1803.........	Fourcroy.

These stones generally appear luminous in their descent, moving in oblique directions with very great velocities, and commonly with a hissing noise. They are frequently heard to explode or burst, and seem to fly in pieces, the larger parts falling first. They often strike the earth with such force as to sink several inches below the surface. They are always different from the surrounding bodies, but in every case are similar to one another, being semi-metallic, coated with a thin black incrustation. They bear strong marks of recent fusion. Chemists have found on examining these stones that they very nearly agree in their nature and composition, and in the proportions of their component parts. The stone which fell at Ensisheim in Alsace, in 1492, and those which fell at L'Aigle in France, in 1803, yielded, by the Analysis of Fourcroy and Vanquelin, as in this table:—

Ensisheim stone fell A. D. 1492	L'Aigle stone fell A. D. 1803	
56 0	54	of silica
30 0	36	—oxyd of iron
12 0	9	—magnesia
2 4	3	—oxyd of nickel
3 5	2	—sulphur
1 4	1	—lime
105 3	105	

Their specific gravities are generally about three of four times that of water, being heavier than common stones. From the above account it is reasonable to conclude that they have all the same origin. To account for this phenomenon, various hypotheses have appeared; we shall mention three: 1. That they are little planets, which, circulating in space, fall into the atmosphere, which, by its friction, diminishes the velocity, so that they fall by their weight. 2. That they are concretions formed in the atmosphere. 3. That they are projected from lunar volcanoes. These are the most probable conjectures we can meet with, and of these the two former possess a very small degree of probability, but there are very strong reasons in favour of the last. Among the reasons we may notice the following: 1. Volcanoes in the moon have been observed by means of the telescope. 2. The lunar volcanoes are very high, and the surface of that globe suffers frequent changes, as appears by the late observations of Schroeter. 3. If a body be projected from the moon to a distance greater than that of the point of equilibrium between the attraction of the earth and moon, it will, on the known principle of gravitation, fall to the earth. 4. That a body may be projected from the lunar volcanoes beyond the moon's influence, is not

A. M. 2554
B. C. 1450
An. Exod. Isr. 41
Anno ante
I. Olymp. 674

of heaven, and hasted not to go down about a whole day.

14 And there was ᵛno day like that before it or after it, that the

LORD hearkened unto the voice of a man: for ᵂthe LORD fought for Israel.

15 ˣAnd Joshua returned, and

A. M. 2554
B. C. 1450
An. Exod. Isr. 41
Anno ante
I. Olymp. 674

ᵛSee Isa. xxxviii. 8

ᵂDeut. i. 30; ver. 42; chap. xxiii. 3——ˣVer. 43

---

only possible but very probable; for on calculation it is found that four times the force usually given to a twelve pounder, will be quite sufficient for this purpose; it is to be observed that the point of equilibrium is much nearer the moon, and that a projectile from the moon will not be so much retarded as one from the earth, both on account of the moon's rarer atmosphere, and its less attractive force. On this subject, see Mr. Haward's valuable paper in the Philosophical Transactions for 1802, and Dr. Hutton's dissertation in the new abridgment, part xxi. It is highly probable that the *ancile*, or sacred shield, that fell from heaven in the reign of Numa Pompilius, was a stone of this sort. The description of its fall, as given by Ovid, *Fast.* lib. iii., bears a striking resemblance to recent accounts of stones falling from the atmosphere, particularly in the *luminous* appearance and *hissing* noise with which it was accompanied.

Dum loquitur, totum jam sol emerserat orbem,
  Et gravis æthereo venit ab axe *fragor*.
Ter tonuit sine nube *Deus*, tria *fulgura* misit:
  Credite dicenti; mira, sed *acta*, loquor.
A media cœlum regione *dehiscere* cœpit:
  Summisere oculos cum duce turba suos.
Ecce levi scutum versatum leniter aura
  Decidit, a pupulo clamor ad astra venit.
Tolit humo munus ——————
Idque *ancile* vocat, quod ab omni parte recisum
  est.

It is very possible that the *Palladium* of *Troy*, and the *Image* of the *Ephesian Diana*, were stones which really fell from the atmosphere, bearing some rude resemblance to the human form. See the IMPERIAL ENCYCLOPÆDIA, article *Aerolith*.

I believe it is generally agreed among philosophers, 1. That all these aerial stones, chemically analyzed, show the same properties; 2. That no stone found on our earth possesses exactly the same properties, nor in the same proportions. This is an extraordinary circumstance, and deserves particular notice.

Verse 12. *Then spake Joshua to the Lord*] Though Joshua saw that the enemies of his people were put to flight, yet he well knew that all which escaped would rally again, and that he should be obliged to meet them once more in the field of battle if permitted now to escape; finding that the day was drawing towards a close, he feared that he should not have time sufficient to complete the destruction of the confederate armies; in this moment, being suddenly inspired with Divine confidence, he requested the Lord to perform the most stupendous miracle that had ever been wrought, which was no less than *to arrest the sun in his course*, and prolong the day till the destruction of his enemies had been completed!

Sun, stand thou still upon Gibeon; and thou, Moon, in the valley of Ajalon.] To account for this miracle, and to ascertain the *manner* in which it was wrought, has employed the pens

of the ablest *divines* and *astronomers*, especially of the last two centuries. By their learned labours many difficulties have been removed from the account in general; but the very different and contradictory methods pursued by several, in their endeavours to explain the whole, and make the relation accord with the present acknowledged system of the universe, and the phenomena of nature, tend greatly to puzzle the plain, unphilosophical reader. The subject cannot be well explained without a *dissertation;* and a dissertation is not consistent with the nature of short notes, or a commentary on Scripture. It is however necessary to attempt an explanation, and to bring that as much as possible within the apprehension of common readers; in order to this, I must beg leave to introduce a few preliminary observations, or what the reader may call *propositions* if he pleases.

1. I take it for granted that a *miracle* was wrought as nearly as circumstances could admit, in the *manner* in which it is here recorded. I shall not, therefore, seek for any *allegorical* or *metaphorical* interpretations; the miracle is recorded as a *fact*, and as a *fact* I take it up.

2. I consider the present accredited system of the universe, called sometimes the *Pythagorean*, *Copernican*, or *Newtonian* system, to be genuine; and also to be the system of the universe laid down in the Mosaic writings—that the SUN is in the *centre* of what is called the solar system; and that the *earth* and all the other *planets*, whether *primary* or *secondary*, move round him in certain periodical times, according to the quantity of their matter, and distance from him, their centre.

3. I consider the sun to have no revolution round any *orbit*, but to revolve round his own *axis*, and round the common centre of gravity in the planetary system, which centre of gravity is included within his own surface; and in all other respects I consider him to be at *rest* in the system.

4. I consider the earth, not only as *revolving round the sun* in 365 days, 5 hours, 48 minutes, and 48 seconds, but as *revolving round its own axis*, and making this revolution in 23 hours, 56 minutes, and 4 seconds; that in the course of 24 hours complete, every part of its surface is alternately turned to the sun; that this revolution constitutes our *day* and *night*, as the former does our *year;* and it is *day* to all those parts which have the sun *above* the horizon, and *night* to those which have the sun *below* it; and that this diurnal revolution of the earth, or revolving round its own axis, in a direction from west to east, occasions what is commonly called the *rising* and *setting* of *the sun*, which *appearance* is occasioned, not by any *motion* in the *sun* himself, but by this *motion of the earth;* which may be illustrated by a ball or globe suspended by a thread, and caused to turn round. If this be held opposite to a *candle*, it will appear half enlightened and half dark; but the dark parts will be seen to come *successively*

A. M. 2554
B. C. 1450
An. Exod. Isr.
41
Anno ante
I. Olymp. 674

all Israel with him, unto the camp to Gilgal.

16 But these five kings fled, and ʸhid themselves in a cave at Makkedah.

17 And it was told Joshua, saying, The five kings are found hid in a cave at Makkedah.

18 And Joshua said, ᶻRoll great stones upon the mouth of the cave,

A. M. 2554
B. C. 1450
An. Exod. Isr.
41
Anno ante
I. Olymp. 674

ʸPsa. xlviii. 4, 5; Isa. ii. 10

ᶻVer. 22; Psa. xviii. 37–41

---

into the *light*, and the enlightened parts into the *shade;* while the candle itself which gives the light is fixed, not changing its position.

5. I consider the solar influence to be the *cause* both of the *annual* and *diurnal* motion of the earth; and that, while that influence continues to act upon it according to the law which God originally impressed on both the earth and the sun, the *annual* and *diurnal* motions of the earth must continue; and that no power but the unlimited power of God can alter this influence, change, or suspend the operation of this law; but that he is such an infinitely FREE AGENT, that HE can, when his unerring wisdom sees good, alter, suspend, or even annihilate all secondary causes and their effects: for it would be degrading to the perfections of his nature to suppose that he had *so bound himself* by the laws which he has given for the preservation and direction of universal nature, that he could not change them, alter their effects, or suspend their operations when greater and better effects, in a certain *time* or *place*, might be produced by such temporary change or suspension.

6. I consider that the miracle wrought on this occasion served greatly to confirm the Israelites, not only in the belief of the being and perfections of God, but also in the doctrine of an especial providence, and in the nullity of the whole system of idolatry and superstition.

7. That no evil was done by this miraculous interference, nor any law or property of nature ultimately changed; on the contrary, a most important good was produced, which probably, to this people, could not have been brought about any other way; and that therefore the miracle wrought on this occasion was highly worthy of the wisdom and power of God.

8. I consider that the terms in the text employed to describe this miracle are not, when rightly understood, contrary to the well-established notions of the true system of the universe; and are not spoken, as some have contended, *ad captum vulgi*, to the prejudices of the common people, much less do they favour the *Ptolemaic* or any other *hypothesis* that places the *earth* in the centre of the solar system.

Having laid down these preliminaries, some short observations on the words of the text may be sufficient.

Joshua's address is in a *poetic* form in the original, and makes the two following hemistichs:—

שמש בגבעון דום
וירח בעמק אילון

Shemesh begibon dom:
Veyareach beemek Aiyalon.

Sun! upon Gibeon be dumb:
And the moon on the vale of Ajalon.

The effect of this command is related, ver. 13, in the following words:—

וידם השמש וירח עמד *vaiyiddom hash*SHEMESH

*ve*YAREACH *amad, And the sun was dumb* or *silent and the moon stood still.* And in the latter clause of this verse it is added: *And the sun stood still in the midst of heaven, and hasted not to go down about a whole day.*

It seems necessary here to answer the question, At what *time* of the day did this miracle take place? The expression בחצי השמם *bachatsi hashshamayim, in the midst of heaven,* seems to intimate that the sun was at that time on the *meridian* of Gibeon, and consequently had *one half* of its course to run; and this sense of the place has been strongly contended for as essential to the miracle, for the greater display of the glory of God: "Because," say its abettors, "had the miracle been wrought when the sun was near the going down, it might have been mistaken for some refraction of the rays of light, occasioned by a peculiarly moist state of the atmosphere in the horizon of that place, or by some such appearance as the *Aurora Borealis.*" To me there seems no solidity in this reason. Had the sun been arrested in the *meridian,* the miracle could scarcely have been noticed, and especially in the hurry and confusion of that time; and we may be assured, that among the Canaanites there were neither *clocks* nor *time-keepers,* by which the preternatural length of such a day could have been accurately measured: but, on the contrary, had the sun been about the *setting,* when both the *pursuers* and the *pursued* must be apprehensive of its *speedy* disappearance, its continuance for several hours *above the horizon,* so near the point when it might be expected to go *down,* must have been very observable and striking. The *enemy* must see, feel, and deplore it; as their hope of escape must, in such circumstances, be founded on the speedy entering in of the night, through which alone they could expect to elude the pursuing Israelites. And the *Israelites* themselves must behold with astonishment and wonder that the *setting* sun *hasted not to go down about a whole day,* affording them supernatural time totally to destroy a routed foe, which otherwise might have had time to rally, confederate, choose a proper station, and attack in their turn with peculiar *advantages,* and a probability of *success.* It appears, therefore, much more reasonable that Joshua should require this miracle to be performed *when daylight was about to fail,* just as the sun was *setting.* If we were to consider the sun as being at the meridian of Gibeon, as some understand *the midst of heaven,* it may be well asked, How could Joshua know that he should not have time enough to complete the destruction of his enemies, who were now completely routed? Already multitudes of them had fallen by the hailstones and by the sword: and if he had yet half a day before him, it would have been natural enough for him to conclude that he had a sufficiency of time for the purpose, his men having been employed all night in a forced march, and half a day in close fighting; and indeed had he

A. M. 2554
B. C. 1450
An. Exod. Isr.
41
Anno ante
I. Olymp. 674

and set men by it for to keep them:

19 And stay ye not, *but* pursue after your enemies, and ^asmite the hindmost of them; suffer them not to enter into their cities: for the LORD your God hath delivered them into your hand.

A. M. 2554
B. C. 1450
An. Exod. Isr.
41
Anno ante
I. Olymp. 674

---

^aHeb. *cut off*   *the tail*

---

not been under an especial inspiration, he could not have requested the miracle at all, knowing, as he must have done, that his men must be nearly exhausted by marching all night and fighting all day. But it may be asked, What is the meaning of בחצי השמים *bachatsi hashshamayim*, which we translate *in the midst of heaven?* If, with Mr. *Bate*, we translate חצה *chatsah*, *to part, divide asunder*, then it may refer to the *horizon*, which is the *apparent division* of the heavens into the *upper* and *lower hemisphere;* and thus the whole verse has been understood by some eminently learned men, who have translated the whole passage thus: *And the sun stood still in the* (upper) *hemisphere of heaven, and hasted not to go down when the day was complete;* that is, though the day was then complete, the sun being on the horizon—the line that to the eye constituted the *mid heaven*—yet it hasted not to go down; was miraculously sustained in its then almost *setting* position; and this seems still more evident from the moon's appearing at that time, which it is not reasonable to suppose could be visible in the glare of light occasioned by a *noon-day* sun.

But the main business relative to the standing still of the sun still remains to be considered.

I have already *assumed*, as a thoroughly demonstrated truth, that the sun is in the *centre* of the system, moving only round his own axis, and the common centre of the gravity of the planetary system, while all the planets revolve round *him*, Prop. 2 and 3; that his influence is the cause of the *diurnal* and *annual* revolutions of the earth; nor can I see what other purpose his revolution round his own axis can possibly answer, Prop. 5.

I consider that the word דום *dom*, in the text, refers to the *withholding* or *restraining* this influence, so that the cessation of the earth's motion might immediately take place. The desire of Joshua was, that the sun might not sink below the horizon; but as *it* appeared now to be over Gibeon, and the *moon* to be over the valley of Ajalon, he prayed that they might continue in these positions till the battle should be ended; or, in other words, that the day should be miraculously lengthened out.

Whether Joshua had a correct philosophical notion of the true system of the universe, is a subject that need not come into the present inquiry: but whether *he spoke* with strict propriety on this occasion is a matter of importance, because he must be considered as acting *under the Divine influence*, in requesting the performance of such a stupendous miracle; and we may safely assert that no man in his right mind would have thought of offering such a petition had he not felt himself under some Divine afflatus. Leaving, therefore, his philosophic knowledge out of the question, he certainly spoke as if he had known that the solar influence was the cause of the earth's *rotation*, and therefore, with the strictest philosophic propriety, he requested that that influence might be for a time restrained, that the diurnal motion of the earth might be arrested, through which alone the sun could be kept above the horizon, and day be prolonged. His mode of expression evidently considers the sun as the great *ruler* or *master* in the system; and all the planets (or at least the earth) moving in their respective orbits at his *command*. He therefore desires him, in the name and by the authority of his Creator, to suspend his *mandate* with respect to the earth's motion, and that of its satellite, the moon. Had he said, *Earth, stand thou still*, the cessation of whose diurnal motion was the *effect* of his command, it could not have obeyed him; as it is not even the *secondary* cause either of its annual motion round the sun, or its diurnal motion round its own axis. Instead of doing so, he speaks to the sun, the *cause* (under God) of all these motions, as his great archetype did when, in the storm on the sea of Tiberias, he rebuked the *wind* first, and then said to the *waves*, Peace! be still! Σιωπα, πεφιμωσο· *Be* SILENT! *be* DUMB! Mark iv. 39; and the effect of this command was a cessation of the agitation in the *sea*, because the *wind* ceased to *command* it, that is, to exert its influence upon the waters.

The terms in this command are worthy of particular note: Joshua does not say to the sun, *Stand still*, as if he had conceived *him* to be *running his race round the earth;* but, *Be silent* or *inactive*, that is, as I understand it, *Restrain thy influence*—no longer act upon the earth, to cause it to revolve round its axis; a mode of speech which is certainly consistent with the strictest astronomical knowledge; and the writer of the account, whether Joshua himself or the author of the book of *Jasher*, in relating the consequence of this command is equally accurate, using a word widely different when he speaks of the *effect* the retention of the solar influence had on the moon: in the *first* case the sun was *silent* or *inactive*, דום *dom;* in the *latter*, the moon *stood still*, עמד *amad*. The *standing still* of the moon, or its continuance above the horizon, would be the natural effect of the cessation of the solar influence, which obliged the earth to discontinue her diurnal rotation, which of course would arrest the moon; and thus both it and the sun were kept above the horizon, probably for the space of a whole day. As to the address to the *moon*, it is not conceived in the same terms as that to the *sun*, and for the most obvious philosophical reasons; all that is said is simply, *and the moon on the vale of Ajalon*, which may be thus understood: "Let the sun restrain his influence or be inactive, as he appears now upon Gibeon, *that* the moon may continue as she appears now over the vale of Ajalon." It is worthy of remark that every word in this poetic address is apparently selected with the greatest caution and precision.

A. M. 2554
B. C. 1450
An. Exod. Isr. 41
Anno ante
I. Olymp. 674

20 And it came to pass, when Joshua and the children of Israel had made an end of slaying them with a very great slaughter,

till they were consumed, that the rest *which* remained of them entered into fenced cities.

21 And all the people returned

A. M. 2554
B. C. 1450
An. Exod. Isr. 41
Anno ante
I. Olymp. 674

Persons who are no friends to Divine revelation say "that the account given of this miracle supposes the *earth* to be in the *centre* of the system, and the sun moveable; and as this is demonstrably a false philosophy, consequently the history was never dictated by the Spirit of truth." Others, in answer, say "that the Holy Spirit condescends to accommodate himself to the apprehensions of the vulgar. The Israelites would naturally have imagined that Joshua was deranged had he bid the *earth stand still*, which they grant would have been the most accurate and philosophical mode of command on this occasion." But with due deference both to the *objectors* and *defenders* I must assert, that such a form of speech on such an occasion would have been utterly *unphilosophic;* and that the expressions found in the Hebrew text are such as Sir Isaac Newton himself might have denominated, every thing considered, elegant, correct, and sublime. Nor does it at all appear that the *prejudices of the vulgar* were consulted on this occasion; nor is there a word here, when properly understood, that is inconsistent with the purest axiom of the soundest philosophy, and certainly nothing that implies any *contradiction.* I grant that when the *people* have to do with *astronomical* and *philosophical* matters, then the terms of the science may be accommodated to their *apprehensions;* it is on this ground that Sir Isaac Newton himself speaks of the *rising* and of the *setting of the sun*, though all genuine philosophers know that these *appearances* are produced by the rotation of the *earth* on its own axis from west to east. But when matters of this kind are to be transacted between *God* and his *prophets*, as in the above case, then subjects relative to philosophy are conceived in their proper terms, and expressed according to their own nature. At the conclusion of the 13th verse a different expression is used when it is said, *So the sun stood still*, it is not דום *dom*, but עמד *amad*; ויעמד השמש *vaiyaamod hashshemesh*, which expression, thus varying from *that* in the command of Joshua, may be considered as implying that in order to *restrain his influence* which I have assumed to be the *cause* of the earth's motion, the sun himself became *inactive*, that is, ceased to revolve round his own axis, which revolution is probably one cause, not only of the revolution of the earth, but of all the other planetary bodies in our system, and might have affected all the planets at the time in question; but this neither could nor did produce any disorder in nature; and the delay of a few hours in the whole planetary motions dwindles away into an imperceptible point in the thousands of years of their revolutions. But the whole effect mentioned here might have been produced by the *cessation* of the *diurnal motion of the earth*, the *annual* being still continued; and I contend that this was possible to Omnipotence, and that such a cessation might have taken place without occasioning the slightest disturbance in the motions of any others of the planetary system. It is vain to cry out and say, "Such a cessation of motion in one planet

could not take place without disordering the motions of all the rest;" this I deny, and those who assert it neither know the *Scripture* nor the *power of God;* therefore they do greatly err. That the day was preternaturally lengthened, is a Scripture fact. That it was so by a *miracle*, is asserted; and whether that miracle was wrought *as above stated*, is a matter of little consequence; the thing is a Scripture fact, whether we know the *modus operandi* or not. I need scarcely add that the *command of Joshua to the sun* is to be understood as a *prayer to God* (from whom the sun derived his being and his continuance) that the effect might be what is expressed in the command: and therefore it is said, ver. 14, that the LORD HEARKENED UNTO THE VOICE OF A MAN, *for the Lord fought for Israel.*

I have thus gone through the different parts of this astonishing miracle, and have endeavoured to account for the whole in as plain and simple a manner as possible. It is not pretended that this account *should* satisfy every reader, and that every difficulty is solved; it would be impossible to do this in such a compass as that by which I am necessarily circumscribed; and I have been obliged, for the sake of brevity, to throw into the form of *propositions* or observations, several points which may appear to demand illustration and proof; for such I must refer the reader to Astronomical Treatises. Calmet, Scheuchzer, and Saurin, with several of our own countrymen, have spoken largely on this difficult subject, but in such a way as, I am obliged to confess, has given me little satisfaction, and which appears to me to leave the main difficulties unremoved. Conscious of the difficulties of this subject, I beg leave to address every candid reader in the often quoted words of an eminent author:—

Vive, Vale! si quid novisti rectius istis,
Candidus imperti; si non, his utere mecum.

HOR. Epist. l. i., E. vi., ver. 68.

Farewell! and if a better *system's* thine,
Impart it *frankly* or make use of *mine.*

FRANCIS.

Book of Jasher] The book of the upright. See the note on Num. xxi. 14. Probably this was a book which, in reference to Joshua and his transactions, was similar to the commentaries of Cæsar, on his wars with the Gauls. Critics and commentators are greatly divided in their sentiments relative to the nature of this book. The opinion above appears to me the most probable.

Verse 14. *And there was no day like that*] There was no period of time in which the sun was kept so long above the horizon as on that occasion. Some learned men have supposed that the *Fable of Phaeton* was founded on this historic fact. The fable may be seen with all the elegance of poetic embellishment in the commencement of the second book of Ovid's Metamorphoses; but I confess I can see nothing in the pretended copy that can justify the above opinion.

A. M. 2554
B. C. 1450
An. Exod. Isr. 41
Anno ante
I. Olymp. 674

to the camp to Joshua at Makkedah in peace: [b]none moved his tongue against any of the children of Israel.

22 Then said Joshua, Open the mouth of the cave, and bring out those five kings unto me out of the cave.

23 And they did so, and brought forth those five kings unto him out of the cave, the king of Jerusalem, the king of Hebron, the king of Jarmuth, the king of Lachish, *and* the king of Eglon.

24 And it came to pass, when they brought out those kings unto Joshua, that Joshua called for all the men of Israel, and said unto the captains of the men of war which went with him, Come near, [c]put your feet upon the necks of these kings. And they came near, and put their feet upon the necks of them.

25 And Joshua said unto them, [d]Fear not,

nor be dismayed, be strong, and of good courage: for [e]thus shall the LORD do to all your enemies against whom ye fight.

A. M. 2554
B. C. 1450
An. Exod. Isr. 41
Anno ante
I. Olymp. 674

26 And afterward Joshua smote them, and slew them, and hanged them on five trees: and they [f]were hanging upon the trees until the evening.

27 And it came to pass at the time of the going down of the sun, *that* Joshua commanded, and they [g]took them down off the trees, and cast them into the cave wherein they had been hid, and laid great stones in the cave's mouth, *which remain* until this very day.

28 And that day Joshua took Makkedah, and smote it with the edge of the sword, and the king thereof he utterly destroyed, them, and all the souls that *were* therein; he let none remain: and he did to the king of Makkedah [h]as he did unto the king of Jericho.

29 Then Joshua passed from Makkedah,

---

[b]Exod. xi. 7——[c]Psa. cvii. 40; cx. 5; cxlix. 8, 9; Isa. xxvi. 5, 6; Mal. iv. 3——[d]Deut. xxxi. 6, 8; chap. i. 9

[e]Deut. iii. 21; vii. 19——[f]Chap. viii. 29——[g]Deut. xxi. 23; chap. viii. 29——[h]Chap. vi. 21

Verse 15. *And Joshua returned—unto the camp to Gilgal.*] That the Israelitish army did not return to the camp at Gilgal till *after* the hanging of the five kings and the destruction of their cities, is sufficiently evident from the subsequent parts of this chapter. When all this business was done, and not before, they returned unto the camp to Gilgal; see ver. 43. This verse is omitted by the *Septuagint* and by the *Anglo-Saxon;* and it does not appear to have existed in the ancient *hexaplar* versions; it stands in its proper place in ver. 43, and is not only useless where it is, but appears to be an encumbrance to the narrative. Should it be considered as genuine and in its proper place, I would propose that מקדה *makkedah* should be read instead of נלגלה *gilgalah*, for we find from ver. 21 that Joshua had a temporary camp there. *Then Joshua returned, and all Israel with him, unto the camp to* MAKKEDAH; after which we may suppose that Joshua having secured the cave, sent some detachments to scour the country and cut off all the remaining straggling Canaanites; when this was done *they* also returned to the camp at Makkedah, as is related ver. 21, and when the business was completed they struck the camp at Makkedah, and all returned to their fortified camp at Gilgal, ver. 43.

Verse 16. *Hid themselves in a cave*] It is very likely that this cave was a fortified place among some rocks; for there were many such places in different parts of Palestine.

Verse 21. *None moved his tongue*] The whole transaction of this important day had been carried on so evidently under the direction of God that there was not the least murmuring, nor cause for it, among them, for their enemies were all discomfited. There is an expression similar to this, Exod. xi. 7, on which the reader is requested to consult the note.

Verse 24. *Put your feet upon the necks of these kings.*] This act was done *symbolically*, as a token, not only of the present complete victory, but of their approaching triumph over all their adversaries, which is the interpretation given of it by Joshua in the succeeding verse.

Verse 26. *Smote—slew—and hanged them on five trees*] Hanging *alive* seems a barbarous custom: among the Hebrews, criminals were first deprived of life; this was the debt required by *justice:* then they were hanged up, perhaps generally by the *hands*, not by the *neck;* this was done by way of *example*, to deter others from committing the crimes for which those had suffered: but they were never permitted to hang thus exposed *all night*, as this could have answered no purpose, either of *justice* or *example*, as they could not be seen in the night-season. *One day* also was deemed enough for their exposure, it being thought sufficient to show the public that justice had been executed; and to have exhibited them *longer* would have appeared to be a barbarous cruelty which attempted to extend punishment beyond the possible requisitions of justice. See the note on Deut. xxi. 23.

Verse 28. *That day Joshua took Makkedah*] It is very possible that Makkedah was taken on the evening of the same day in which the miraculous *solstice* took place; but as to the other cities mentioned in this chapter, they certainly were subdued some days after, as it is not possible that an army, exhausted as this must have been with a whole night's march, and two days' hard fighting, could have proceeded farther than Makkedah that night; the other cities were successively taken in the following days.

Verse 29. *Fought against Libnah*] This city was near Makkedah, see chap. xv. 42, and fell to the tribe of Judah, ver. 20, 42, and was given to the priests, chap. xxi. 13. Sennacherib be-

A. M. 2554
B. C. 1450
An. Exod. Isr.
41
Anno ante
I. Olymp. 674

and all Israel with him, unto Libnah, and fought against Libnah:

30 And the LORD delivered it also, and the king thereof, into the hand of Israel: and he smote it with the edge of the sword, and all the souls that *were* therein; he let none remain in it; but did unto the king thereof as he did unto the king of Jericho.

31 And Joshua passed from ¹Libnah, and all Israel with him, unto Lachish, and encamped against it, and fought against it:

32 And the LORD delivered Lachish into the hand of Israel, which took it on the second day, and smote it with the edge of the sword, and all the souls that *were* therein, according to all that he had done to Libnah.

33 Then Horam king of Gezer came up to help Lachish; and Joshua smote him and his people, until he had left him none remaining.

34 And from Lachish Joshua passed unto Eglon, and all Israel with him: and they encamped against it, and fought against it:

35 And they took it on that day, and smote it with the edge of the sword, and all the souls that *were* therein he utterly destroyed that day, according to all that he had done to Lachish.

A. M. 2554
B. C. 1450
An. Exod. Isr.
41
Anno ante
I. Olymp. 674

36 And Joshua went up from Eglon, and all Israel with him, unto ᵏHebron; and they fought against it:

37 And they took it, and smote it with the edge of the sword, and the king thereof, and all the cities thereof, and all the souls that *were* therein: he left none remaining, according to all that he had done to Eglon; but destroyed it utterly, and all the souls that *were* therein.

38 And Joshua returned, and all Israel with him, to ¹Debir; and fought against it:

39 And he took it, and the king thereof, and all the cities thereof: and they smote them with the edge of the sword, and utterly destroyed all the souls that *were* therein; he left none remaining: as he had done to He-

---

ʲ2 Kings viii. 22——ᵏSee chap. xiv. 13; xv. 13; Judg. i. 10

ˡSee chap. xv. 15; Judg. i. 11

---

sieged it, after he had been obliged to raise the siege of Lachish. See 2 Kings xix. 8; Isa. xxxvii. 8.

Verse 32. *Lachish*] It appears that this was anciently a very strong place; notwithstanding the people were panic-struck, and the Israelites flushed with success, yet Joshua could not reduce it till the second day, and the king of Assyria afterwards was obliged to *raise the siege.* See above, and see the note on ver. 3.

Verse 33. *Horam king of Gezer*] It is likely that *Horam* was in a state of alliance with the king of *Lachish,* and therefore came to his assistance as soon as it appeared that he was likely to be attacked. Joshua probably sent a detachment against him, before he was able to form a junction with the forces of *Lachish;* and utterly destroyed him and his army.

Gezer is supposed to have been situated near Azotus. See 1 Mac. xvi. 34. It fell to the tribe of Ephraim, chap. xvi. 3, but was probably taken afterwards by some of the remnant of the Canaanitish nations; for we find it was given by Pharaoh to his son-in-law Solomon, 1 Kings ix. 16, which proves that it had got out of the possession of the Israelites previously to the days of Solomon.

Verse 34. *Eglon*] It is likely that this town was not any great distance from Lachish. See on ver. 3.

Verses 36 and 37. *Hebron—and the king thereof*] See the note on ver. 3. From ver. 23 we learn that the king of Hebron was one of those *five* whom Joshua slew and hanged on five trees at Makkedah. How then can it be said that he *slew the king of Hebron* when he took the city, which was some days after the

transactions at Makkedah? Either this slaying of the king of Hebron must refer to what had *already* been done, or the Hebronites, finding that their king fell in battle, had set up *another* in his place; which was the king Joshua slew, after he had taken the city and its dependencies, as is related ver. 37.

It appears that the city of *Hebron* had fallen back into the hands of the Canaanites, for it was again taken from them by the tribe of Judah, Judg. i. 10. *Debir* had also fallen into their hands, for it was reconquered by *Othniel,* the son-in-law of Caleb. ib. ver. 11-13. The manner in which Calmet accounts for this is very natural: Joshua, in his rapid conquests, contented himself with taking, demolishing, and burning those cities; but did not *garrison* any of them, for fear of weakening his army. In several instances no doubt the scattered Canaanites returned, repeopled, and put those cities in a state of defence. Hence the Israelites were obliged to conquer them a second time. This is a more rational way of accounting for these things, than that which supposes that the first chapter of Judges gives the more detailed account of the transactions recorded here; for there it is expressly said, that these transactions took place *after the death of Joshua,* (see Judg. i. 1,) and consequently cannot be the same that are mentioned here.

Verse 39. *Destroyed all the souls*] את ויחרימו כל נפש *vaiyacharimu eth col nephesh,* they brought every person under an *anathema;* they either slew them, or reduced them to a state of slavery. Is it reasonable to say those were slain who were *found in arms,* of the others they made *slaves?*

A. M. 2554
B. C. 1450
An. Exod. Isr. 41
Anno ante
I. Olymp. 674

bron so he did to Debir, and to the king thereof; as he had done also to Libnah, and to her king.

40 So Joshua smote all the country of the hills, and of the south, and of the vale, and of the springs, and all their kings: he left none remaining, but utterly destroyed all that breathed, as the LORD God of Israel ᵐcommanded.

41 And Joshua smote them from Kadesh-barnea, even unto ⁿGaza, ᵒand all the country of Goshen, even unto Gibeon.

A. M. 2554
B. C. 1450
An. Exod. Isr. 41
Anno ante
I. Olymp. 674

42 And all these kings and their land did Joshua take at one time, ᵖbecause the LORD God of Israel fought for Israel.

43 And Joshua returned, and all Israel with him, unto the camp to Gilgal.

ᵐDeut. xx. 16, 17——ⁿGen. x. 19

ᵒChap. xi. 16——ᵖVer. 14

Verse 40. *All the country of the hills*] See the note on Deut. i. 7.

Destroyed all that breathed] Every person found in arms who continued to resist; these were all destroyed,—those who submitted were spared: but many no doubt made their escape, and afterwards reoccupied certain parts of the land. See ver. 36, 37.

Verse 41. *And all the country of Goshen*] Calmet contends that this was the very same country in which the Hebrews dwelt before their departure from Egypt; and according to this hypothesis he has constructed his *map,* causing it to extend from the Nile, which was called the river of Egypt, along the frontiers of the land of Cush or Arabia. It however appears plain that there was a city named *Goshen* in the tribe of Judah, see chap. xv. 51; and this probably gave name to the adjacent country, which may be that referred to above.

Verse 42. *Did Joshua take at one time*] That is, he defeated all those kings, and took all their cities, in ONE *campaign;* this appears to be the rational construction of the Hebrew. But these conquests were so rapid and stupendous, that they cannot be attributed either to the generalship of Joshua, or the valour of the Israelites; and hence the author himself, disclaiming the merit of them, modestly and piously adds, *because the Lord God of Israel fought for Israel.* It was by this aid that *Joshua took all these kings and their land at one time*—in a single campaign. And when all the circumstances related in this chapter are properly weighed, we shall find that GOD *alone* could have performed these works, and that both *reason* and *piety* require that to HIM *alone* they should be attributed.

1. THE principal subjects of this important chapter have been considered so much in detail in the preceding notes, that there is little room to add any thing to what has already been said. The principal subject is the miracle of the sun's standing still; and to assert that all difficulties have been removed by the preceding notes and observations, would be to say what the writer does not believe, and what few readers would perhaps feel disposed to credit. Yet it is hoped that the chief difficulties have been removed, and the miracle itself shown to have nothing contradictory in it. If, as is generally believed, the sun and moon were objects of the Canaanitish adoration, the miracle was graciously calculated to check this superstition, and to show the Israelites, as well as the Canaanites, the vanity of such worship, and the folly of such dependence. Even their *gods* at the *command* of a *servant* of JEHOVAH, were *obliged to contribute to the destruction of their votaries.* This method of checking superstition and destroying idolatry God adopted in the plagues which he inflicted upon the Egyptians; and by it at once showed his *justice* and his mercy. See the concluding observations on Exod. xii.

2. The same God who appeared so signally in behalf of his people of old is still the governor of the heavens and the earth; and, if applied to, will do every thing essentially necessary for the extension of his truth and the maintenance of his religion among men. How is it that faith is so rarely exercised in his *power* and *goodness?* We have not, because we ask not. Our experience of his goodness is contracted, because we pray little and believe less. To holy men of old the object of faith was more obscurely revealed than to us, and *they* had fewer helps to their faith; yet they believed more, and witnessed greater displays of the power and mercy of their Maker. Reader, *have faith in God,* and know that to excite, exercise, and crown this, he has given thee his *word* and his *Spirit;* and learn to know that without him thou canst do nothing.

CHAPTER XI

The kings of Hazor, Madon, Shimron, and Achshaph, with those of the mountains, plains, &c., and various chiefs of the Canaanites and Amorites, confederate against Israel, 1–3. They pitch their tents at the waters of Merom, 4, 5. The Lord encourages Joshua, 6. He attacks and discomfits them, 7, 8. Houghs all their horses, and burns all their chariots, 9. Takes and burns several of their cities, 10–13. The Israelites take the spoils, 14, 15. An account of the country taken by Joshua, 16–18. The Gibeonites only make peace with Israel, 19. All the rest resist and are overcome, 20. Joshua cuts off the Anakim, 21, 22. The conquered lands are given to Israel, and the war is concluded, 23.

A. M. 2554
B. C. 1450
An. Exod. Isr.
41
Anno ante
I. Olymp. 674

AND it came to pass, when Jabin king of Hazor had heard *those things*, that he [a]sent to Jobab king of Madon, and to the king [b]of Shimron, and to the king of Achshaph,

2 And to the kings that *were* on the north of the mountains, and of the plains south of [c]Chinneroth, and in the valley, and in the borders [d]of Dor on the west,

3 *And to* the Canaanite on the east and on the west, and *to* the Amorite, and the Hittite, and the Perizzite, and the Jebusite in the mountains, [e]and *to* the Hivite under [f]Hermon [g]in the land of Mizpeh.

A. M. 2554
B. C. 1450
An. Exod. Isr.
41
Anno ante
I. Olymp. 674

4 And they went out, they and all their hosts with them, much people, [h]even as the sand that *is* upon the sea shore in multitude, with horses and chariots very many.

---

[a]Chap. x. 3——[b]Chap. xix. 15——[c]Num. xxxiv. 11
[d]Chap. xvii. 11; Judg. i. 27; 1 Kings iv. 11

[e]Judg. iii. 3——[f]Chap. xiii. 11——[g]Gen. xxxi. 49
[h]Gen. xxii. 17; xxxii. 12; Judg. vii. 12; 1 Sam. xiii. 5

NOTES ON CHAP. XI

Verse 1. *Jabin king of Hazor*] It is probable that *Jabin* was the common name of all the kings of Hazor. That king, by whom the Israelites were kept in a state of slavery for twenty years, and who was defeated by Deborah and Barak, was called by this name; see Judg. iv. 2, 3, 23. The name signifies *wise* or *intelligent*. The *city* of *Hazor* was situated above the Lake *Semechon*, in Upper Galilee, according to Josephus, Antiq. lib. v., c. 6. It was given to the tribe of Naphtali, Josh. xix. 36, who it appears did not possess it long; for though it was burnt by Joshua, ver. 11, it is likely that the Canaanites rebuilt it, and restored the ancient government, as we find a powerful king there about one hundred and thirty years after the death of Joshua, Judg. iv. 1. It is the same that was taken by *Tiglath-pileser*, together with *Kadesh*, to which it is contiguous; see 2 Kings xv. 29. It is supposed to have given name to the *Valley* or *Plain* of *Hazor* or *Nasor*, situated between it and Kadesh, where Jonathan and Mattathias defeated the armies of *Demetrius*, and slew three thousand of their men, 1 Maccab. xi. 63-74. It was in ancient times the metropolitan city of all that district, and a number of petty kings or chieftains were subject to its king, see ver. 10; and it is likely that it was those tributary kings who were summoned to attend the king of Hazor on this occasion; for Joshua having conquered the southern part of the promised land, the northern parts seeing themselves exposed made now a common interest, and, joining with Jabin, endeavoured to put a stop to the progress of the Israelites. See *Calmet*.

Jobab king of Madon] This royal city is nowhere else mentioned in Scripture except in chap. xii. 19. The Vatican copy of the Septuagint reads Μαρων, *Maron*, which, if legitimate, Calmet thinks may mean *Maronia* or *Merath* in Phœnicia, to the north of Mount Libanus. The Hebrew text reads מרון *Meron*, chap. xii. 20, after *Shimron*, which is probably the same with מדון *Madon*, ver. 19, the word having casually dropped out of the preceding place into the latter, and the ר *resh* and ד *daleth* being interchanged, which might have easily happened from the great similarity of the letters. Hence Calmet conjectures that it may be the same place with מרון *Meroz*, Judg. v. 23, the ז *zain* and נ final *nun* being interchanged, which they might easily, as they are so very similar.

King of Shimron] This city is supposed to be the same with *Symira*, in Cœlosyria, joined

to *Maron* or *Marath*, by *Pliny* and *Pomponius Mela*. It cannot be *Samaria*, as that had its name long after by Omri king of Israel. See 1 Kings xvi. 24.

King of Achshaph] Calmet supposes this to have been the city of *Ecdippe*, mentioned by *Pliny, Ptolemy, Josephus*, and *Eusebius*. The latter places it within ten miles of *Ptolemais*, on the road to Tyre. It fell to the tribe of Asher. See chap. xix. 25.

Verse 2. *On the north of the mountains*] Or *the mountain*, probably *Hermon*, or some mountain not far from the lake of Gennesareth.

And of the plains] That is, the valleys of the above mountains, which had the sea of Chinneroth or Gennesareth on the south.

Chinneroth] This city is supposed by St. Jerome and several others since his time, to be the same as was afterwards called *Tiberias*. From this city or village the *sea of Chinneroth* or *Gennesareth* probably had its name.

And in the borders of Dor] Calmet supposes this to mean the champaign country of the higher and lower Galilee, on to the Mediterranean Sea, and to the village or city of *Dor*, which was the farthermost city of Phœnicia. *Dor* was in the lot of the half tribe of Manasseh, and was situated on the Mediterranean Sea, three leagues from Cæsarea, and seven from Ptolemais.

Verse 3. *The Canaanite on the east, &c.*] Those who dwelt on the borders of Jordan, south of the sea of Tiberias.

On the west] Those were the Phœnicians who dwelt on the coast of the Mediterranean Sea, from *Dor* northwards, on the way to Mount Libanus.—*Calmet*.

The Hivite under Hermon] Mount Hermon was to the east of Libanus and the fountains of Jordan; it is the same with *Syrion* and *Baal Hermon* in Scripture.

The land of Mizpeh.] There were several cities of this name: *one* in the tribe of *Judah*, (chap. xv. 38;) a *second* in the tribe of *Benjamin*, (chap. xviii. 26;) a *third* beyond Jordan, in the tribe of *Gad;* and a *fourth* beyond Jordan, in the tribe of *Manasseh*, which is that mentioned in the text. See *Wells's* Geography. Calmet supposes this Mizpeh to be the place where Laban and Jacob made their covenant, and from which circumstance it took its name. See Gen. xxxi. 48, 49.

Verse 4. *Much people, even as the sand*] This form of speech, by some called a *hyperbole*, conveys simply the idea of a vast or unusual number—a number of which no regular esti-

A. M. 2554
B. C. 1450
An. Exod. Isr.
41
Anno ante
I. Olymp. 674

5 And when all these kings were ¹met together, they came and pitched together at the waters of Merom, to fight against Israel.

6 And the LORD said unto Joshua, ᵏBe not afraid because of them: for to-morrow about this time will I deliver them up all slain before Israel: thou shalt ˡhough their horses, and burn their chariots with fire.

7 So Joshua came, and all the people of war with him, against them by the waters of Merom suddenly; and they fell upon them.

8 And the LORD delivered them into the hand of Israel, who smote them, and chased them unto ᵐgreat Zidon, and unto ⁿ °Misre-

photh-maim, ᵖand unto the valley of Mizpeh, eastward; and they smote them, until they left them none remaining.

A. M. 2554
B. C. 1450
An. Exod. Isr.
41
Anno ante
I. Olymp. 674

9 And Joshua did unto them ᑫas the LORD bade him: he houghed their horses, and burnt their chariots with fire.

10 And Joshua at that time turned back, and took Hazor, and smote the king thereof with the sword: for Hazor beforetime was the head of all those kingdoms.

11 And they smote all the souls that *were* therein with the edge of the sword, utterly destroying *them:* there was not ʳany left to breathe: and he burnt Hazor with fire.

---

¹Heb. *assembled by appointment*——ᵏChap. x. 8
ˡ2 Sam. viii. 4——ᵐOr, *Zidon-rabbah*

ⁿChap. xiii. 6——°Or, *salt pits*——ᵖHeb. *burnings*
ᑫVer. 6——ʳHeb. *any breath*

---

mate could be easily formed. Josephus, who seldom finds difficulties in such cases, and makes no scruple of often speaking *without book*, tells us that the allied armies amounted to 300,000 *foot*, 10,000 *horse*, and 20,000 *chariots* of war.— Antiq. lib. v., c. 1.

That *chariots* were frequently used in war, all the records of antiquity prove; but it is generally supposed that among the Canaanites they were armed with iron scythes fastened to their *poles* and to the *naves* of their wheels. Terrible things are spoken of these, and the havoc made by them when furiously driven among the ranks of infantry. Of what sort the cavalry was, we know not; but from the account here given we may see what great advantages these allies possessed over the Israelites, whose armies consisted of *infantry* only.

Verse 5. *The waters of Merom*] Where these waters were, interpreters are not agreed. Whether they were the waters of the Lake *Semechon*, or the *waters of Megiddo*, mentioned Judg. v. 19, cannot be easily determined. The latter is the more probable opinion.

Verse 6. *Be not afraid—of them*] To meet such a formidable host so well equipped, in their own country, furnished with all that was necessary to supply a numerous army, required more than ordinary encouragement in Joshua's circumstances. This communication from God was highly necessary, in order to prevent the people from desponding on the eve of a conflict, in which their *all* was at stake.

Verse 7. *By the waters of Merom suddenly*] Joshua, being apprized of this grand confederation, lost no time, but marched to meet them; and before they could have supposed him at hand, fell suddenly upon them, and put them to the rout.

Verse 8. *Great Zidon*] If this were the same with the *Sidon* of the ancients, it was illustrious long before the Trojan war; and both it and its inhabitants are frequently mentioned by Homer as excelling in works of *skill* and *utility*, and abounding in *wealth:*—

Ενθ' εσαν οι πεπλοι παμποικιλοι, εσγα γυναικων
Σιδονιων.   Iliad, lib. vi., ver. 289.

"There lay the vestures of no *vulgar* art,
SIDONIAN maids *embroidered* every part."
          POPE.

Αργυρεον κρητηρα τετυγμενον· εξ δ' αρα μετρα
Χανδανεν, αυταρ καλλει ενικα πασαν επ' αιαν
Πολλον, επι Σιδονες πολυδαιδαλοι ευ ησκησαν.
          Iliad, lib. xxiii., ver. 741.

"A *silver urn* that full six measures held,
By none in weight or *workmanship* excell'd;
SIDONIAN *artists* taught the *frame* to shine,
Elaborate with *artifice* divine."   POPE.

Εκ μεν Σιδωνος πολυχαλκου ευχομαι ειναι.
          Odyss. xv. 424.

"I am of SIDON, famous for her *wealth*."

The art of making *glass* is attributed by Pliny to this city: SIDON *artifex vitri*, Hist. Nat. l. v., c. 19.

Misrephoth-maim] Or, Misrephoth of *the waters*. What this place was is unknown, but Calmet conjectures it to be the same with *Sarepta*, a city of Phœnicia, contiguous to Sidon. The word signifies the *burning of the waters*, or *inflammation;* probably it was a place noted for its *hot springs:* this idea seems to have struck Luther, as he translates it, die warme wasser, *the hot waters.*

Verse 9. *He houghed their horses*] The Hebrew word עקר *akar*, which we render to *hough* or *hamstring*, signifies to *wound, cut*, or *lop off.* It is very likely that it means here, not only an act by which they were rendered useless, but by which they were *destroyed;* as God had purposed that his people should not possess any cattle of this kind, that a warlike and enterprising spirit might not be cultivated among them; and that, when obliged to defend themselves and their country, they might be led to depend upon God for protection and victory. On the same ground, God had forbidden the kings of Israel *to multiply horses*, Deut. xvii. 16. See the note there containing the reasons on which this prohibition was founded.

Burnt their chariots] As these could have been of no use without the horses.

Verse 10. *Took Hazor*] See on ver. 1.

A. M. 2554–60
B. C. 1450–44
An. Exod. Isr.
41–47
Anno ante
I.Olymp.674–68

12 And all the cities of those kings, and all the kings of them, did Joshua take, and smote them with the edge of the sword, *and* he utterly destroyed them, ⁸as Moses the servant of the LORD commanded.

13 But *as for* the cities that stood still ᵗin their strength, Israel burned none of them, save Hazor only; *that* did Joshua burn.

14 And all the spoil of these cities, and the cattle, the children of Israel took for a prey unto themselves; but every man they smote with the edge of the sword, until they had destroyed them, neither left they any to breathe.

15 ᵘAs the LORD commanded Moses his servant, so ᵛdid Moses command Joshua, and ʷso did Joshua; ˣhe left nothing undone of all that the LORD commanded Moses.

A. M. 2554–60
B. C. 1450–44
An. Exod. Isr.
41–47
Anno ante
I.Olymp.674–68

16 So Joshua took all that land, ʸthe hills, and all the south country, ᶻand all the land of Goshen, and the valley, and the plain, and the mountain of Israel, and the valley of the same;

17 ᵃ*Even* from ᵇthe mount Halak, that goeth up to Seir, even unto Baal-gad in the valley of Lebanon under Mount Hermon: and ᶜall their kings he took, and smote them, and slew them.

18 ᵈJoshua made war a long time with all those kings.

ˢNum. xxxiii. 52; Deut. vii. 2; xx. 16, 17——ᵗHeb. *on their heap*——ᵘExod. xxxiv. 11, 12——ᵛDeuteronomy vii. 2——ʷChap. i. 7

ˣHeb. *he removed nothing*——ʸChap. xii. 8——ᶻChap. x. 41——ᵃChap. xii. 7——ᵇOr, *the smooth mountain* ᶜDeut. vii. 24; chap. xii. 7——ᵈTill 1445; ver. 23

Verse 13. *The cities that stood still in their strength*] The word תלם *tillam*, which we translate *their strength*, and the margin, *their heap*, has been understood two ways. 1. As signifying those cities which had made peace with the Israelites, when conditions of peace were offered according to the command of the law; and consequently were not destroyed. Such as the cities of the *Hivites;* see ver. 19. 2. The cities which were situated upon *hills* and *mountains*, which, when taken, might be retained with little difficulty. In this sense the place is understood by the Vulgate, as pointing out the cities *quæ erant in collibus et tumulis sitæ*, "which were situated on hills and eminences." As the cities of the *plain* might be easily attacked and carried, Joshua destroyed them; but as those on *mountains*, *hills*, or other *eminences*, might be retained with little trouble, prudence would dictate their preservation, as places of refuge in any insurrection of the people, or invasion of their adversaries. The passage in Jeremiah, chap. xxx. 18, *Jerusalem shall be builded on her own heap*, תלה *tillah*, if understood as above, conveys an easy and clear sense: Jerusalem shall be re-established on her OWN HILL.

Verse 14. *All the spoil of these cities—Israel took*] With the exception of those things which had been employed for idolatrous purposes; see Deut. vii. 25.

Verse 16. *The mountain of Israel, and the valley of the same*] This place has given considerable trouble to commentators; and it is not easy to assign such a meaning to the place as may appear in all respects satisfactory. 1. If we consider this verse and the 21st to have been added after the times in which the kingdoms of Israel and Judah were divided, the difficulty is at once removed. 2. The difficulty will be removed if we consider that *mountain* and *valley* are put here for *mountains* and *valleys*, and that these include all mountains and valleys which were not in the lot that fell to the tribe of Judah. Or, 3. If by *mountain of Israel* we understand *Beth-el*, where God appeared to Jacob, afterwards called *Israel*, and promised

him the land of Canaan, a part of the difficulty will be removed. But the first opinion seems best founded; for there is incontestable evidence that several notes have been added to this book since the days of Joshua. See the preface.

Verse 17. *From the mount Halak*] All the mountainous country that extends from the south of the land of Canaan towards *Seir* unto *Baal-gad*, which lies at the foot of Mount Libanus or Hermon, called by some the mountains of *Separation*, which serve as a limit between the land of Canaan and that of Seir; see chap. xii. 7.

The valley of Lebanon] The whole extent of the plain which is on the south, and probably north, of Mount Libanus. Calmet conjectures that *Cælesyria* is here meant.

Verse 18. *Joshua made war a long time*] The whole of these conquests were not effected in one campaign: they probably required *six* or *seven* years. There are some chronological notices in this book, and in Deuteronomy, by which the exact time may be nearly ascertained. Caleb was *forty* years old when he was sent from *Kadesh-barnea* by Moses to search out the land, about A. M. 2514; and at the end of this war he was *eighty-five* years old; (compare chap. xiv. 10 with Num. xiii. and Deut. i.;) consequently the war ended in 2559, which had begun, by the passage of Jordan, on the tenth day of the first month of the year 2554. From this date to the end of 2559 we find exactly six years; the *first* of which Joshua seems to have employed in the conquest of the *south* part of the land of Canaan, and the other *five* in the conquest of all the territories situated on the *north* of that country. See *Dodd.*

Calmet computes this differently, and allows the term of *seven* years for the conquest of the whole land. "Caleb was forty years old when sent from Kadesh-barnea to spy out the land. At the conclusion of the war he was eighty-five years old, as himself says, chap. xiv. 10. From this sum of eighty-five subtract forty, his age when he went from Kadesh-barnea, and the thirty-eight years which he spent in the wilderness after his return, and there will **remain**

A. M. 2554-60
B. C. 1450-44
An Exod. Isr.
41-47
Anno ante
I.Olymp.674-68

19 There was not a city that made peace with the children of Israel save ^ethe Hivites, the inhabitants of Gibeon: all *other* they took in battle.

20 For ^fit was of the LORD to harden their hearts, that they should come against Israel in battle, that he might destroy them utterly, *and* that they might have no favour, but that he might destroy them, ^gas the LORD commanded Moses.

21 And at that time came Joshua, and cut off ^hthe Anakims from the mountains, from Hebron, from Debir, from Anab, and from all the mountains of Judah, and from all the mountains of Israel: Joshua destroyed *them* utterly with their cities.

A. M. 2554-60
B. C. 1450-44
An. Exod. Isr.
41-47
Anno ante
I.Olymp.674-68

22 There was none of the Anakims left in the land of the children of Israel: only in Gaza, in ⁱGath, ^kand in Ashdod, there remained.

23 So Joshua took the whole land, ^laccording to all that the LORD said unto Moses; and Joshua gave it for an inheritance unto Israel, ^maccording to their divisions by their tribes. ⁿAnd the land rested from war.

---

^eChapter ix. 3, 7——^fDeuteronomy ii. 30; Judges xiv. 4; 1 Samuel ii. 25; 1 Kings xii. 15; Romans ix. 18 ^gDeuteronomy xx. 16, 17——^hNumbers xiii. 22, 33; Deuteronomy i. 28; chap. xv. 13, 14

ⁱ1 Sam. xvii. 4——^kChap. xv. 46——^lNum. xxxiv. 2, &c.——^mNum. xxvi. 53; chap. xiv., xv., xvi., xvii., xviii., and xix.——ⁿChap. xiv. 15; xxi. 44; xxii. 4; xxiii. 1; ver. 18

---

the sum of *seven* years, which was the time spent in the conquest of the land."

1. By protracting the war the Canaanites had time to repent, having sufficient opportunity to discern the hand of Jehovah. 2. Agriculture was carried on, and thus provision was made even for the support of the conquerors; for had the land been subdued and wasted at once, tillage must have stopped, and famine would have ensued. 3. Wild beasts would have multiplied upon them, and the land have been desolated by their means. 4. Had these conquests been more rapid the people of Israel would have been less affected, and less instructed by miracles that had passed in such quick succession before their eyes; and, as in this case they would have obtained the dominion with comparatively little exertion, they might have felt themselves less interested in the preservation of an inheritance, to obtain which they had been but at little trouble and little expense. What we *labour* under the Divine blessing to acquire we are careful to retain; but what *comes lightly* generally *goes lightly*. God obliged them to put forth their own strength in this work, and only blessed and prospered them while they were workers together with him. See the note on chap. xiii. 6.

Verse 20. *It was of the Lord to harden their hearts*] They had sinned against all the light they had received, and God left them justly to the hardness, obstinacy, and pride of their own hearts; for as they chose to retain their idolatry, God was determined that they should be cut off. For as no city made peace with the Israelites but Gibeon and some others of the Hivites, ver. 19, it became therefore necessary to destroy them; for their refusal to make peace was the proof that they wilfully persisted in their idolatry.

Verse 21. *Cut off the Anakims—from Hebron, from Debir*] This is evidently a recapitulation of the military operations detailed chap. x. 36-41.

Destroyed—their cities] That is, those of the Anakims; for from ver. 13 we learn that Joshua preserved certain other cities.

Verse 22. *In Gaza, in Gath, and in Ashdod*] The whole race of the Anakims was extirpated in this war, except those who had taken refuge in the above cities, which belonged to the Philistines; and in which some of the descendants of Anak were found even in the days of David.

Verse 23. *So Joshua took the whole land*] All the country described here and in the preceding chapter. Besides the multitudes that perished in this war, many of the Canaanites took refuge in the confines of the land, and in the neighbouring nations. Some suppose that a party of these fugitive Canaanites made themselves masters of *Lower Egypt*, and founded a dynasty there known by the name of the *shepherd kings;* but it is more probable that the *shepherds* occupied Egypt long before the time that Jacob went thither to sojourn. It is said they founded *Tingris* or *Tangier*, where, according to Procopius, they erected two white pillars with an inscription in the Phœnician language, of which this is the translation: WE ARE THE PERSONS WHO HAVE FLED FROM THE FACE OF JOSHUA THE PLUNDERER, THE SON OF NAVE or *Nun*. See *Bochart*, Phaleg and Canaan, lib. i., c. xxiv., col. 476. Many, no doubt, settled in different parts of Africa, in Asia Minor, in Greece, and in the different islands of the Ægean and Mediterranean Sea: it is supposed also that colonies of this people were spread over different parts of Germany and Sclavonia, &c., but their descendants are now so confounded with the nations of the earth, as no longer to retain their original names, or to be discernible.

And Joshua gave it for an inheritance unto Israel] He claimed no peculiar jurisdiction over it; his own family had no peculiar share of it, and himself only the ruined city of *Timnath-serah*, in the tribe of Ephraim, which he was obliged to rebuild. See chap. xix. 49, 50, and see his character at the end of the book.

And the land rested from war.] The whole territory being now conquered, which God designed the Israelites should possess at *this time*.

ACCORDING to the apostle, Heb. iv. 8, &c., *Joshua* himself was a *type of Christ;* the *promised land,* of the *kingdom of heaven;* the *victories* which he gained, of the *victory* and triumph of Christ; and the *rest* he procured for Israel, of the *state of blessedness*, at the right hand of God. In this light we should view the whole history, in order to derive those advantages from it which, as a portion of the revelation of God, it was intended to convey. Those who finally reign with Christ are they

who, through his grace, *conquer* the *world*, the *devil*, and the *flesh;* for it is only of those who thus *overcome* that he says, "They shall sit with me on my throne, as I have overcome, and am set down with the Father on the Father's throne;" Rev. iii. 21. Reader, art *thou* a conqueror?

CHAPTER XII

A list of the kings on the east of Jordan, which were conquered by MOSES, with their territories, 1–6. A list of those on the west side of Jordan, conquered by JOSHUA, in number thirty-one, 7–24.

A. M. 2554–60
B. C. 1450–44
An. Exod. Isr.
41–47
Anno ante
I.Olymp.674–68

NOW these *are* the kings of the land, which the children of Israel smote, and possessed their land on the other side Jordan toward the rising of the sun, [a]from the river Arnon [b]unto Mount Hermon, and all the plain on the east:

2 [c]Sihon king of the Amorites, who dwelt in Heshbon, *and* ruled from Aroer, which *is* upon the bank of the river Arnon, and from the middle of the river, and from half Gilead, even unto the river Jabbok, *which is* the border of the children of Ammon;

3 And [d]from the plain to the sea of Chinneroth on the east, and unto the sea of the plain, *even* the Salt Sea on the east, [e]the way to Beth-jeshimoth; and from [f]the south, under [g]Ashdoth-pisgah: [h]

4 And [i]the coast of Og king of Bashan, *which was* of [k]the remnant of the giants, [l]that dwelt at Ashtaroth and at Edrei,

5 And reigned in [m]Mount Hermon, [n]and in Salcah, and in all Bashan, [o]unto the border of the Geshurites, and the Maachathites, and half Gilead, the border of Sihon king of Heshbon.

6 [p]Them did Moses the servant of the LORD and the children of Israel smite: and [q]Moses the servant of the LORD gave it *for* a possession unto the Reubenites, and the Gadites, and the half tribe of Manasseh.

A. M. 2554–60
B. C. 1450–44
An. Exod. Isr.
41–47
Anno ante
I.Olymp.674–68

---

[a]Num. xxi. 24——[b]Deut. iii. 8, 9——[c]Num. xxi. 24; Deut. ii. 33, 36; iii. 6, 16——[d]Deut. iii. 17——[e]Chap. xiii. 20——[f]Or, *Teman*——[g]Or, *the springs of Pisgah, or the hill*——[h]Deut. iii. 17; iv. 49

[i]Num. xxi. 35; Deut. iii. 4, 10——[k]Deut. iii. 11; chap. xiii. 12——[l]Deut. i. 4——[m]Deut. iii. 8——[n]Deut. iii. 10; chap. xiii. 11——[o]Deut. iii. 14——[p]Num. xxi. 24, 33——[q]Num. xxxii. 29, 33; Deut. iii. 11, 12; chap. xiii. 8

NOTES ON CHAP. XII

Verse 1. *From the river Arnon unto Mount Hermon*] Arnon was the boundary of all the *southern* coast of the land *occupied* by the Israelites beyond Jordan; and the mountains of Hermon were the boundaries on the *north*. Arnon takes its rise in the mountains of Gilead, and having run a long way from north to south falls into the Dead Sea, near the same place into which Jordan discharges itself.

And all the plain on the east] All the land from the plains of Moab to Mount Hermon.

Verse 2. *From Aroer*] Aroer was situated on the western side of the river Arnon, in the middle of the valley through which this river takes its course. The kingdom of Sihon extended from the river Arnon and the city of Aroer on the *south* to the river Jabbok on the *north*.

And from half Gilead] The mountains of Gilead extended from north to south from Mount Hermon towards the source of the river Arnon, which was about the *midst* of the extent of the kingdom of Sihon: thus Sihon is said to have possessed the *half of Gilead*, that is, the half of the mountains and of the country which bore the name of Gilead on the east of his territories.

River Jabbok] This river has its source in the mountains of Gilead; and, running from

east to west, falls into Jordan. It bounds the territories of Sihon on the north, and those of the Ammonites on the south.

Verse 3. *The sea of Chinneroth*] Or *Gennesareth*, the same as the lake or sea of *Tiberias*.

The Salt Sea on the east] ים המלח *yam hammelach*, which is here translated *the Salt Sea*, is understood by others to mean *the sea of the city Melach*. Where can we find any thing that can be called a *salt* sea on the east of the lake of Gennesareth? Some think that the lake Asphaltites, called also the *Dead Sea, Sea of the Desert, Sea of Sodom*, and *Salt Sea*, is here intended.

Beth-jeshimoth] A city near the Dead Sea in the plains of Moab.

Ashdoth-pisgah] Supposed to be a city at the foot of Mount Pisgah.

Verse 4. *Coast of Og king of Bashan*] Concerning this person see the notes on Deut. iii. 11, and on Num. xxi. 35, &c.

The remnant of the giants] Or, *Rephaim*. See the notes on Gen. vi. 4, xiv. 5, and Deut. ii. 7, 11.

Verse 5. *The border of the Geshurites*] The country of Bashan, in the days of Moses and Joshua, extended from the river Jabbok on the south to the frontiers of the Geshurites and Maachathites on the north, to the foot of the mountains of Hermon.

A. M. 2554–60
B. C. 1450–44
An. Exod. Isr.
41–47
Anno ante
I.Olymp.674–68

7 And these *are* the kings of the country ʳwhich Joshua and the children of Israel smote on this side Jordan on the west, from Baal-gad in the valley of Lebanon, even unto the mount Halak, that goeth up to ˢSeir; which Joshua ᵗgave unto the tribes of Israel, *for* a possession according to their divisions;

8 ᵘIn the mountains, and in the valleys, and in the plains, and in the springs, and in the wilderness, and in the south country; ᵛthe Hittites, the Amorites, and the Canaanites, the Perizzites, the Hivites, and the Jebusites:

9 ʷThe king of Jericho, one; ˣthe king of Ai, which *is* beside Beth-el, one;

10 ʸThe king of Jerusalem, one; the king of Hebron, one;

11 The king of Jarmuth, one; the king of Lachish, one;

12 The king of Eglon, one; ᶻthe king of Gezer, one;

13 ᵃThe king of Debir, one; the king of Geder, one;

14 The king of Hormah, one;

A. M. 2554–60
B. C. 1450–44
An. Exod. Isr.
41–47
Anno ante
I.Olymp.674–68

the king of Arad, one;

15 ᵇThe king of Libnah, one; the king of Adullam, one;

16 ᶜThe king of Makkedah, one; ᵈthe king of Beth-el, one;

17 The king of Tappuah, one; ᵉthe king of Hepher, one;

18 The king of Aphek, one; the king of ᶠLasharon, one;

19 The king of Madon, one; ᵍthe king of Hazor, one;

20 The king of ʰShimron-meron, one; the king of Achshaph, one;

21 The king of Taanach, one; the king of Megiddo, one;

22 ⁱThe king of Kedesh, one; the king of Jokneam of Carmel, one;

23 The king of Dor in the ᵏcoast of Dor, one; the king of ˡthe nations of Gilgal, one;

24 The king of Tirzah, one: all the kings thirty and one.

ʳChap. xi. 17——ˢGen. xiv. 6; xxxii. 3; Deut. ii. 1, 4
ᵗChap. xi. 23——ᵘChap. x. 40; xi. 16——ᵛExod. iii. 8;
xxiii. 23; chap. ix. 1——ʷChap. vi. 2——ˣChap. viii. 29
ʸChap. x. 23——ᶻChap. x. 33——ᵃChap. x. 38

ᵇCh. x. 29——ᶜCh. x. 28——ᵈChap. viii. 17; Judg.
i. 22——ᵉ1 Kings iv. 10——ᶠOr, *Sharon;* Isa. xxxiii.
9——ᵍCh. xi. 10——ʰCh. xi. 1; xix. 15——ⁱChap.
xix. 37——ᵏChap. xi. 2——ˡGen. xiv. 1, 2; Isa. ix. 1

Verse 7. *From Baal-gad*] A repetition of what is mentioned chap. xi. 17.

Verse 9. *The king of Jericho, &c.*] On this and the following verses see the notes on chap. x. 1-3.

Verse 13. *The king of Geder*] Probably the same with *Gedor*, chap. xv. 58; it was situated in the tribe of Judah.

Verse 14. *The king of Hormah*] Supposed to be the place where the Israelites were defeated by the Canaanites, see Num. xiv. 45; and which probably was called Hormah, חרמה *chormah*, or *destruction*, from this circumstance.

Verse 15. *Adullam*] A city belonging to the tribe of Judah, chap. xv. 35. In a cave at this place David often secreted himself during his persecution by Saul; 1 Sam. xxii. 1.

Verse 17. *Tappuah*] There were two places of this name: one in the tribe of Judah, chap. xv. 34, and another in the tribe of Ephraim on the borders of Manasseh; but which of the two is meant here cannot be ascertained. See the note on chap. xv. 53.

Hepher] The same, according to Calmet, as *Ophrah* in the tribe of Benjamin, chap. xviii. 23.

Verse 18. *Aphek*] There were several cities of this name: one in the tribe of Asher, chap. xix. 30; another in the tribe of Judah, 1 Sam. iv. 1, and xxix. 1; and a third in Syria, 1 Kings xx. 26, and 2 Kings xiii. 17. Which of the two former is here intended cannot be ascertained.

Lasharon] There is no city of this name known. Some consider the ל *lamed* in the word לשרון *lashsharon* to be the sign of the

genitive case; and in this sense it appears to have been understood by the *Vulgate*, which translates *rex Saron*, the king of Sharon. This was rather a district than a city, and is celebrated in the Scriptures for its fertility; Isa. xxxiii. 9; xxxv. 2. Some suppose it was the same with *Saron*, near *Lydda*, mentioned Acts ix. 35.

Verse 20. *Shimron-meron*] See on chap. xi. 1.

Verse 21. *Taanach*] A city in the half tribe of Manasseh, to the west of Jordan, not far from the frontiers of Zebulun, chap. xvii. 11. This city was assigned to the Levites, chap. xxi. 25.

Verse 22. *Kedesh*] There was a city of this name in the tribe of Naphtali, chap. xix. 37. It was given to the Levites, and was one of the cities of refuge, chap. xx. 7.

Jokneam of Carmel] This city is said to have been at the foot of Mount Carmel, near the river Belus, in the tribe of Zebulun, chap. xix. 11. It was given to the Levites, chap. xxi. 34.

Verse 23. *The king of Dor*] The city of this name fell to the lot of the children of Manasseh, chap. xvii. 11. Bochart observes that it was one of the oldest royal cities in Phœnicia. The Canaanites held it, Judg. i. 27. Antiochus Sydetes besieged it in aftertimes, but could not make himself master of it. See *Bochart*, Canaan, lib. i., c. 28, and *Dodd*.

The king of the nations of Gilgal] This is supposed to mean the higher Galilee, surnamed *Galilee of the Gentiles* or, *nations*, as the Hebrew word נוים *goyim* means. On this ground it should be read king of Galilee of the nations. Others suppose it is the same country with that of which *Tidal* was king; see Gen. xiv. 1. The place is very uncertain, and commentators have rendered it more so by their *conjectures.*

Verse 24. *King of Tirzah*] This city appears to have been for a long time the capital of the kingdom of Israel, and the residence of its kings. See 1 Kings xiv. 17; xv. 21, 33. Its situation cannot be exactly ascertained; but it is supposed to have been situated on a mountain about three leagues south of Samaria.

All the kings thirty and one.] The Septuagint say εικοσι εννεα, *twenty-nine*, and yet set down but *twenty-eight*, as they confound or omit the kings of *Beth-el, Lasharon*, and *Madon.*

So many kings in so small a territory, shows that their kingdoms must have been very small indeed. The kings of *Beth-el* and *Ai* had but about 12,000 subjects in the whole; but in ancient times *all* kings had very small territories.

Every village or town had its chief; and this chief was independent of his neighbours, and exercised *regal* power in his own district. In reading all ancient histories, as well as the Bible, this circumstance must be kept constantly in view; for we ought to consider that in those times both *kings* and *kingdoms* were but a faint resemblance of those now.

Great Britain, in ancient times, was divided into many kingdoms: in the time of the *Saxons* it was divided into *seven*, hence called the *Saxon heptarchy.* But when Julius Cæsar first entered this island, he found *four* kings in Kent alone; *Cingetorix, Carnilius, Taximagulus*, and *Segonax.* Hence we need not wonder at the numbers we read of in the land of Canaan. Ancient Gaul was thus divided; and the great number of *sovereign princes, secular bishops, landgraves, dukes*, &c., &c., in Germany, are the modern remains of those ancient divisions.

CHAPTER XIII

Joshua being old, the Lord informs him of the land yet remaining to be possessed, 1. Of the unconquered land among the Philistines, 2, 3. Among the Canaanites, Sidonians, and Amorites, 4, 5. The inhabitants of the hill country and the Sidonians to be driven out, 6. The land on the east side of Jordan, that was to be divided among the tribes of Reuben and Gad, and the half tribe of Manasseh, 7–12. The Geshurites and the Maachathites not expelled, 13. The tribe of Levi receive no inheritance, 14. The possessions of REUBEN *described, 15–23. The possessions of* GAD, *24–28. The possessions of the half tribe of* Manasseh, *29–31. Recapitulation of the subjects contained in this chapter, 32, 33.*

A. M. 2560
B. C. 1444
An. Exod. Isr.
47
Anno ante
I. Olymp. 668

NOW Joshua [a]was old *and* stricken in years; and the LORD said unto him, Thou art old *and* stricken in years, and there remaineth yet very much land [b]to be possessed.

2 [c]This *is* the land that yet remaineth: [d]all the borders of the Philistines, and all [e]Geshuri,

3 [f]From Sihor, which *is* before Egypt, even unto the borders of Ekron northward, *which* is counted to the Canaanite: [g]five

A. M. 2560
B. C. 1444
An. Exod. Isr.
47
Anno ante
I. Olymp. 668

---

[a]See chap. xiv. 10; xxiii. 1——[b]Heb. *to possess it;* Deut. xxxi. 3——[c]Judg. iii. 1——[d]Joel iii. 4

[e]Ver. 13; 2 Sam. iii. 3; xiii. 37, 38——[f]Jer. ii. 18
[g]Judg. iii. 3; 1 Sam. vi. 4, 16; Zeph. ii. 5

NOTES ON CHAP. XIII

Verse 1. *Joshua was old*] He is generally reputed to have been at this time about a *hundred* years of age: he had spent about seven years in the conquest of the land, and is supposed to have employed about one year in dividing it; and he died about *ten* years after, aged one hundred and ten years. It is very likely that he intended to subdue the whole land before he made the division of it among the tribes; but God did not think proper to have this done. So unfaithful were the Israelites that he appears to have purposed that some of the ancient inhabitants should still remain to keep them in check, and that the respective tribes should have some labour to drive out from their allotted borders the remains of the Canaanitish nations.

There remaineth yet very much land to be possessed.] That is, very much when compared with that on the other side Jordan, which was all that could as yet be said to be in the hands of the Israelites.

Verse 2. *The borders of the Philistines, and all Geshuri*] The borders of the Philistines may mean the land which they possessed on

the sea-coast, southwest of the land of Canaan. There were several places named *Geshuri*, but that spoken of here was probably the region on the south of Canaan, towards Arabia, or towards Egypt.—*Calmet.* Cellarius supposes it to have been a country in the vicinity of the Amalekites.

Verse 3. *From Sihor, which* is *before Egypt*] Supposed by some to be the Pelusiac branch of the Nile, near to the Arabian Desert; called also the *river of Egypt*, Num. xxxiv. 5; Jer. ii. 18. On this subject an intelligent friend favours me with the following opinion:—

"The river *Sihor* is supposed by some to be the Nile, or a branch of it. Others think it the same as what is frequently called the *river of Egypt*, which lay *before* or towards the borders of *Egypt;* which arose out of the mountains of Paran, and ran westward, falling into that bay of the Mediterranean which lies south of the land of the Philistines. This river is often mentioned as the boundary of the Israelites towards southwest, as Euphrates, the *great river*, was on the northeast.

"There was a desert of considerable distance between what is called the *river of Egypt* and the isthmus of Suez. Solomon reigned to the

A. M. 2560
B. C. 1444
An. Exod. Isr.
47
Anno ante
I. Olymp. 668

lords of the Philistines; the Gazathites, and the Ashdothites, the Eshkalonites, the Gittites, and the Ekronites; also [h]the Avites:

4 From the south, all the land of the Canaanites, and [i]Mearah that *is* beside the Sidonians, [k]unto Aphek, to the borders of [l]the Amorites:

5 And the land of [m]the Giblites, and all

Lebanon, toward the sun-rising, [n]from Baal-gad under Mount Hermon unto the entering into Hamath.

A. M. 2560
B. C. 1444
An. Exod. Isr.
47
Anno ante
I. Olymp. 668

6 All the inhabitants of the hill country from Lebanon unto [o]Misrephoth-maim, *and* all the Sidonians, them [p]will I drive out from before the children of Israel: only [q]divide thou it by lot unto the Israelites for an inheritance, as I have commanded thee.

---

[h]Deut. ii. 23——[i]Or, *the cave*——[k]Chap. xix. 30
[l]See Judg. i. 34——[m]1 Kings v. 18; Psa. lxxxiii. 7:

Ezek. xxvii. 9——[n]Chap. xii. 7——[o]Chap. xi. 8
[p]See chap. xxiii. 13; Judg. ii. 21, 23——[q]Chap. xiv. 1, 2

---

borders of Egypt, i. e., to this desert; but not in Egypt, nor to the river Nile.

"Upon the whole, (though there are difficulties in the matter,) I incline to think that the river in question was not the Nile. *Sihor* (*black*) might, from some circumstances, be applied to another river as well as the Nile; though some places in Isaiah and Jeremiah seem to restrict it to the Nile."—*J. C.*

Ekron northward] Ekron was one of the five lordships of the Philistines, and the most *northern* of all the districts they possessed. *Baal-zebub,* its idol, is famous in Scripture; see 2 Kings i. 2, &c. The *five* lordships of the Philistines were *Gaza, Ashdod, Askalon, Gath,* and *Ekron.* There is no proof that ever the Israelites possessed *Ekron;* though, from chap. xv. 11, some think it was originally given to *Judah,* but the text does not say so; it only states that *the border* of the tribe of Judah *went out* UNTO THE SIDE *of Ekron.* From chap. xix. 43, we learn that it was a part of the lot of Dan, but it does not appear to have been possessed by any of those tribes.

Counted to the Canaanite] It is generally allowed that the original possessors of this country were the descendants of *Canaan,* the youngest son of Ham. The Philistines sprang from *Mizraim,* the second son of Ham, and, having dispossessed the *Avim* from the places they held in this land, dwelt in their stead. See Gen. x. 13, 14.

Five lords of the Philistines] These dynasties are famous in the Scriptures for their successful wars against the Israelites, of whom they were almost the perpetual scourge.

Also the Avites] These must not be confounded with the *Hivites.* The Avites seem to have been a very inconsiderable tribe, who dwelt in some of the skirts of Palestine. They had been originally deprived of their country by the *Caphtorim;* and though they lived as a distinct people, they had never afterwards arrived to any authority.

Verse 4. *The land of the Canaanites*] This lay on the south of the country of the Philistines, towards the sea-coast.

Mearah] Supposed to be the city *Maratha,* on the Mediterranean Sea.—*Calmet.* Or the river *Majora,* which falls into the Mediterranean Sea, between Sidon and Berytus. See PLINY, *Hist. Nat.* lib. v., c. 20.

Aphek] See on chap. xii. 18.

To the borders of the Amorites] Though the term *Amorite* is sometimes used to designate the inhabitants in general of the land of Ca-

naan, yet it must be considered in a much more restricted sense in this place. As no Amorites are known to have dwelt in this quarter, Calmet supposes we should read *Aramites* or Syrians. Joshua, says he, proceeds from *Sidon* to *Aphek,* a city of Syria, between Heliopolis and Babylon, where was the temple of the Venus of Aphek; and which is spoken of in 1 Kings xx. 26; 2 Kings xiii. 17, as the capital of the kings of Syria. From this Joshua passes on to the frontiers of the Syrians, towards *Gebal* or Gabala, which, according to Ptolemy, was situated in Phœnicia. This conjecture of Calmet is not supported by any authority either from the ancient versions or MSS. *Houbigant,* however, approves of it: the emendation is simple, as it consists in the interchange of only two letters in the same word, הארמי *haarammi,* for האמרי *haemori.*

Verse 5. *The land of the Giblites*] This people dwelt beyond the precincts of the land of Canaan, on the east of Tyre and Sidon. See Ezek. xxvii. 9; Psa. lxxxiii. 7; their capital was named *Gebal.* See *Dodd.*

All Lebanon] See on chap. xi. 17.

Verse 6. *Misrephoth-maim*] See on chap. xi. 7.

Them will I drive out] That is, if the Israelites continued to be obedient; but they did not, and therefore they never fully possessed the *whole* of that land which, on this condition alone, God had promised them: the *Sidonians* were never expelled by the Israelites, and were only brought into a state of comparative subjection in the days of David and Solomon.

Some have taken upon them to deny the authenticity of Divine revelation relative to this business, "because," say they, "God is stated to have absolutely promised that Joshua should conquer the whole land, and put the Israelites in possession of it." This is a total mistake. 1. God never absolutely, i. e., *unconditionally,* promised to put them in possession of this land. The promise of their possessing the whole was suspended on their *fidelity* to God. They were not faithful, and therefore God was not bound by his promise to give them any part of the land, after their first act of national defection from his worship. 2. God never said that Joshua should conquer the whole land, and *give* it to them; the promise was simply this: "Thou shalt bring them into the land, and thou shalt divide it among them:" both of which he did, and procured them footing by his conquests, sufficient to have enabled them to establish themselves in it for ever. 3. It was never said, Thou shalt

A. M. 2560
B. C. 1444
An. Exod. Isr. 47
Anno ante
I. Olymp. 668

7 Now therefore divide this land for an inheritance unto the nine tribes, and the half tribe of Manasseh,

8 With whom the Reubenites and the Gadites have received their inheritance, ʳwhich Moses gave them, beyond Jordan eastward, *even* as Moses the servant of the LORD gave them;

9 From Aroer, that *is* upon the bank of the river Arnon, and the city that *is* in the midst of the river, ˢand all the plain of Medeba unto Dibon;

10 And ᵗall the cities of Sihon king of the Amorites, which reigned in Heshbon, unto the border of the children of Ammon;

11 ᵘAnd Gilead, and the border of the Geshurites and Maachathites, and all Mount Hermon, and all Bashan unto Salcah;

12 All the kingdom of Og in Bashan, which reigned in Ashtaroth and in Edrei, who remained of ᵛthe remnant of the giants: ʷfor these did Moses smite, and cast them out.

13 Nevertheless the children of Israel expelled ˣnot the Geshurites, nor the Maachathites: but the Geshurites and the Maachathites dwell among the Israelites until this day.

14 ʸOnly unto the tribe of Levi he gave none inheritance; the sacrifices of the LORD God of Israel made by fire *are* their inheritance, ᶻas he said unto them.

A. M. 2560
B. C. 1444
An. Exod. Isr. 47
Anno ante
I. Olymp. 668

15 And Moses gave unto the tribe of the children of Reuben *inheritance* according to their families.

16 And their coast was ᵃfrom Aroer, that *is* on the bank of the river Arnon, ᵇand the city that *is* in the midst of the river, ᶜand all the plain by Medeba;

17 Heshbon, and all her cities that *are* in the plain; Dibon, and ᵈBamoth-baal, and Beth-baal-meon,

18 ᵉAnd Jahaza, and Kedemoth, and Mephaath,

19 ᶠAnd Kirjathaim, and ᵍSibmah, and Zareth-shahar in the mount of the valley,

20 And Beth-peor, and ʰAshdoth-pisgah,ⁱ and Beth-jeshimoth;

21 ᵏAnd all the cities of the plain, and all the kingdom of Sihon king of the Amorites, which reigned in Heshbon, ˡwhom Moses smote ᵐwith the princes of Midian, Evi, and Rekem, and Zur, and Hur, and Reba, *which were* dukes of Sihon, dwelling in the country.

22 ⁿBalaam also the son of Beor, the °soothsayer, did the children of Israel slay with the sword among them that were slain by them.

ʳNum. xxxii. 33; Deut. iii. 12, 13; chap. xxii. 4 ˢVer. 16; Num. xxi. 30——ᵗNum. xxi. 24, 25——ᵘChap. xii. 5——ᵛDeut. iii. 11; chap. xii. 4——ʷNum. xxi. 34, 35——ˣVer. 11——ʸNum. xviii. 20, 23, 24; chap. xiv. 3, 4——ᶻVer. 33——ᵃChap. xii. 2——ᵇNum. xxi. 28 ᶜNum. xxi. 30; ver. 9

ᵈOr, *the high places of Baal, and house of Baal-meon;* see Num. xxxii. 38——ᵉNum. xxi. 23——ᶠNum. xxxii. 37——ᵍNum. xxxii. 38——ʰDeut. iii. 17; chap. xii. 3 ⁱOr, *springs of Pisgah,* or *the hill*——ᵏDeut. iii. 10 ˡNumbers xxi. 24——ᵐNum. xxxi. 8——ⁿNum. xxii. 5; xxxi. 8——°Or, *diviner*

---

conquer it all, and then *divide* it; no. Several of the tribes, *after* their quota was allotted them, were obliged to drive out the ancient inhabitants. See on chap. xi. 18.

Verse 7. *The nine tribes, and the half tribe of Manasseh*] The other half tribe of Manasseh, and the two tribes of Reuben and Gad, had got their inheritance on the other side of Jordan, in the land formerly belonging to Og king of Bashan, and Sihon king of the Amorites.

Verse 9. *From Aroer*] See on chap. xii. 2.

Verse 11. *Border of the Geshurites*] See on chap. xii. 5.

Verse 17. *Bamoth-baal*] The high places of Baal, probably so called from altars erected on hills for the impure worship of this Canaanitish Priapus.

Verse 18. *Jahaza*] A city near Medeba and Dibon. It was given to the Levites, 1 Chron. vi. 78.

Kedemoth] Mentioned Deut. ii. 26; supposed to have been situated beyond the river *Arnon.*

Mephaath] Situated on the frontiers of Moab,

on the eastern part of the desert. It was given to the Levites, chap. xxi. 37.

Verse 19. *Kirjathaim*] This city, according to Eusebius, was nine miles distant from Medeba, towards the east. It passed from the Emim to the Moabites, from the Moabites to the Amorites, and from the Amorites to the Israelites, Gen. xiv. 5; Deut. ii. 20. Calmet supposes the Reubenites possessed it till the time they were carried away by the Assyrians; and then the Moabites appear to have taken possession of it anew, as he collects from Jer. xlviii. and Ezek. xxv.

Sibmah] A place remarkable for its *vines.* See Isa. xvi. 8, 9; Jer. xlviii. 32.

Zareth-shahar, in the mount of the valley] This probably means a town situated on or near to a hill in some flat country.

Verse 20. *Beth-peor*] The *house* or *temple of Peor,* situated at the foot of the mountain of the same name. See Num. xxv. 3.

Verse 21. *The princes of Midian*] See the history of this war, Num. xxxi. 1, &c.; and

A. M. 2560
B. C. 1444
An. Exod. Isr. 47
Anno ante I. Olymp. 668

23 And the border of the children of Reuben was Jordan, and the border *thereof*. This *was* the inheritance of the children of Reuben after their families, the cities and the villages thereof.

24 And Moses gave *inheritance* unto the tribe of Gad, *even* unto the children of Gad according to their families.

25 [p]And their coast was Jazer, and all the cities of Gilead, [q]and half the land of the children of Ammon, unto Aroer that *is* before [r]Rabbah;

26 And from Heshbon unto Ramath-mizpeh, and Betonim; and from Mahanaim unto the border of Debir;

27 And in the valley, [s]Beth-aram, and Beth-nimrah, [t]and Succoth, and Zaphon, the rest of the kingdom of Sihon king of Heshbon, Jordan and *his* border, *even* unto the edge [u]of the sea of Chinneroth on the other side Jordan eastward.

28 This *is* the inheritance of the children of Gad after their families, the cities, and their villages.

A. M. 2560
B. C. 1444
An. Exod. Isr. 47
Anno ante I. Olymp. 668

29 And Moses gave *inheritance* unto the half tribe of Manasseh: and *this* was *the possession* of the half tribe of the children of Manasseh by their families.

30 And their coast was from Mahanaim, all Bashan, all the kingdom of Og king of Bashan, and [v]all the towns of Jair, which *are* in Bashan, threescore cities:

31 And half Gilead, and [w]Ashtaroth, and Edrei, cities of the kingdom of Og in Bashan, *were pertaining* unto the children of Machir the son of Manasseh, *even* to the one half of the [x]children of Machir by their families.

32 These *are the countries* which Moses did distribute for inheritance in the plains of Moab, on the other side Jordan, by Jericho, eastward.

33 [y]But unto the tribe of Levi Moses gave not *any* inheritance: the LORD God of Israel *was* their inheritance, [z]as he said unto them.

---

[p]Num. xxxii. 35——[q]Compare Num. xxi. 26, 28, 29, with Deut. ii. 19, and Judg. xi. 13, 15, &c.——[r]2 Sam. xi. 1; xii. 26——[s]Num. xxxii. 36——[t]Gen. xxxiii. 17; 1 Kings vii. 46

[u]Num. xxxiv. 11——[v]Num. xxxii. 41; 1 Chron. ii. 23——[w]Chap. xii. 4——[x]Num. xxxii. 39, 40——[y]Ver. 14; chapter xviii. 7——[z]Num. xviii. 20; Deut. x. 9; xviii. 1, 2

---

from that place this and the following verse seem to be borrowed, for the introduction of the death of Balaam here seems quite irrelevant.

Verse 23. *The cities and the villages*] By *villages*, חצרים *chatserim*, it is likely that *moveable villages* or *tents* are meant, such as are in use among the Bedouin Arabs; places where they were accustomed to feed and pen their cattle.

Verse 25. *Half the land of the children of Ammon*] This probably was land which had been taken from the Ammonites by Sihon, king of the Amorites, and which the Israelites possessed by right of conquest. For although the Israelites were forbidden to take the land of the Ammonites, Deut. ii. 37, yet this part, as having been united to the territories of Sihon, they might possess when they defeated that king and subdued his kingdom.

Verse 26. *Ramath-mizpeh*] The same as *Ramoth-gilead*. It was one of the cities of refuge, chap. xx. 8; Deut. iv. 47.

Mahanaim] Or the *two camps*. Situated on the northern side of the brook Jabbok, celebrated for the vision of the two camps of angels which Jacob had there; see Gen. xxxii. 2.

Verse 27. *Beth-aram*] This city was rebuilt by Herod, and called *Livias*, in honour of *Livia*, the wife of *Augustus*. Josephus calls it *Julias*, Julia being the name which the Greeks commonly give to *Livia*.—*Calmet*.

Succoth] A place between Jabbok and Jordan where Jacob pitched his *tents*, from which circumstance it obtained its name; see Genesis xxxiii. 17.

Verse 29. *The half tribe of Manasseh*] When the tribes of Reuben and Gad requested to have their settlement on the east side of Jordan, it does not appear that any part of the tribe of Manasseh requested to be settled in the same place. But as this tribe was numerous, and had much cattle, Moses thought proper to appoint one half of it to remain on the east of Jordan, and the other to go over and settle on the west side of that river.

Verse 30. *The towns of Jair*] These were sixty cities; they are mentioned afterwards, and in 1 Chron. ii. 21, &c. They are the same with the *Havoth-jair* mentioned Num. xxxii. 41. Jair was son of Segub, grandson of Esron or Hezron, and great-grandson of Machir by his grandmother's side, who married Hezron of the tribe of Judah. See his genealogy, 1 Chron. ii. 21-24.

Verse 32. *Which Moses did distribute*] Moses had settled every thing relative to these tribes before his death, having appointed them to possess the territories of Og king of Bashan, and Sihon king of the Amorites.

For particulars on this chapter, the reader, if he judge it of consequence, may consult *Calmet*.

CHAPTER XIV

Eleazar, Joshua, and the heads of the fathers, distribute the land by lot to the people, 1–3. The Levites receive no land, but cities to dwell in, and suburbs for their cattle, 4, 5. Caleb requests to have Mount Hebron for an inheritance, because of his former services, 6–12. Joshua grants his request, 13–15.

A. M. 2560
B. C. 1444
An. Exod. Isr.
47
Anno ante
I. Olymp. 668

AND these *are the countries* which the children of Israel inherited in the land of Canaan, ªwhich Eleazar the priest, and Joshua the son of Nun, and the heads of the fathers of the tribes of the children of Israel, distributed for inheritance to them.

2 ᵇBy lot *was* their inheritance, as the LORD commanded by the hand of Moses, for the nine tribes, and *for* the half tribe.

3 ᶜFor Moses had given the inheritance of two tribes and a half tribe on the other side Jordan: but unto the Levites he gave none inheritance among them.

A. M. 2560
B. C. 1444
An. Exod. Isr.
47
Anno ante
I. Olymp. 668

4 For ᵈthe children of Joseph were two tribes, Manasseh and Ephraim: therefore they gave no part unto the Levites in the land, save cities to dwell *in,* with their suburbs for their cattle and for their substance.

ªNum. xxxiv. 17, 18——ᵇNum. xxvi. 55; xxxiii. 54; xxxiv. 13

ᶜChap. xiii. 8, 32, 33——ᵈGen. xlviii. 5; 1 Chron. v. 1, 2

NOTES ON CHAP. XIV

Verse 1. Eleazar the priest, &c.] ELEAZAR, as being the minister of GOD in *sacred* things is mentioned *first.* JOSHUA, as having the supreme command in all things *civil,* is mentioned *next.* And the HEADS or PRINCES of the twelve tribes, who in all things acted *under* Joshua, are mentioned *last.* These *heads* or *princes* were twelve, Joshua and Eleazar included; and the reader may find their names in Num. xxxiv. 19-28. It is worthy of remark that no prince was taken from the tribes of *Reuben* and *Gad,* because these had already received their inheritance on the other side of Jordan, and therefore could not be interested in this division.

Verse 2. By lot was *their inheritance*] Concerning the meaning and use of the lot, see the note on Num. xxxvi. 55; and concerning the manner of *casting lots* in the case of the *scapegoat,* see the note on Lev. xvi. 8, 9.

On this subject Dr. Dodd has selected some good observations from *Calmet* and *Masius,* which I here borrow: "Though God had sufficiently pointed out by the predictions of Jacob when dying, and those of Moses, what portions he designed for each tribe, we readily discern an admirable proof of his wisdom in the orders he gave to decide them by *lot.* By this means the false interpretations which might have been given to the words of Jacob and Moses were prevented; and by striking at the root of whatever might occasion *jealousies* and *disputes* among the tribes, he evidently secured the honesty of those who were to be appointed to distribute to them the conquered countries in the land of Canaan. Besides, the success of this method gave a fresh proof of the Divinity of the Jewish *religion,* and the truth of its *oracles.* Each tribe finding itself placed *by lot* exactly in the spot which Jacob and Moses had foretold, it was evident that Providence had equally directed both those *predictions* and that *lot.* The event justified the truth of the promises. The more singular it was, the more clearly we discern the finger of God in it. The portion, says *Masius,* fell to each tribe just as Jacob had declared two hundred and fifty years before

in the last moments of his life, and Moses, immediately before his death; for to the tribe of JUDAH fell a country abounding in *vineyards* and *pastures;* to ZEBULUN and ISSACHAR, *seacoasts;* in that of ASHER was plenty of *oil, wheat,* and *metals;* that of BENJAMIN, near to the *temple,* was, in a manner, *between the shoulders of the Deity;* EPHRAIM and MANASSEH were distinguished with a territory blessed in a *peculiar* manner by Heaven; the land of NAPHTALI extended from the *west* to the *south* of the tribe of Judah. Since therefore the lot so well corresponded to these predictions, would it not be insolence and stupidity in the highest degree, not to acknowledge the *inspiration* of God in the *word* of Jacob and Moses, the *direction* of his *hand* in the *lot,* and his *providence* in the *event?*"

How the *lot* was cast in this case cannot be particularly determined. It is probable, 1. That the land was geographically divided into ten portions. 2. That each portion was called by a particular name. 3. That the name of each portion was written on a separate slip of parchment, wood, &c. 4. That the names of the *claimants* were also written on so many slips. 5. The names of the portions, and of the tribes, were put into separate vessels. 6. Joshua, for example, put his hand into the vessel containing the names of the tribes, and took out one slip; while Eleazar took out one from the other vessel, in which the names of the *portions* were put. 7. The *name* drawn, and the *portion* drawn, being read, it was immediately discerned what the *district* was which God had designed for such a *tribe.* This appears to be the most easy way to determine such a business.

Verse 4. The children of Joseph were two tribes] This was ascertained by the prophetic declaration of their grandfather Jacob, Gen. xlviii. 5, 6; and as *Levi* was taken out of the tribes for the service of the sanctuary, one of these sons of Joseph came in his place, and Joseph was treated as the first-born of Jacob, in the place of Reuben, who forfeited his right of primogeniture.

With their suburbs for their cattle] For the meaning of this passage the reader is referred to the note on Num. xxxv. 5.

A. M. 2560
B. C. 1444
An. Exod. Isr.
47
Anno ante
I. Olymp. 668

5 [e]As the LORD commanded Moses, so the children of Israel did, and they divided the land.

6 Then the children of Judah came unto Joshua in Gilgal: and Caleb the son of Jephunneh the [f]Kenezite said unto him, Thou knowest [g]the thing that the LORD said unto Moses the man of God concerning me and thee [h]in Kadesh-barnea.

7 Forty years old *was* I when Moses the servant of the LORD [i]sent me from Kadesh-barnea to espy out the land; and I brought him word again as *it was* in mine heart.

8 Nevertheless [k]my brethren that went up with me made the heart of the people melt: but I wholly [l]followed the LORD my God.

9 And Moses sware on that day, saying, [m]Surely the land [n]whereon thy feet have trodden shall be thine inheritance, and thy children's for ever, because thou hast wholly followed the LORD my God.

A. M. 2560
B. C. 1444
An. Exod. Isr.
47
Anno ante
I. Olymp. 668

10 And now, behold, the LORD hath kept me alive, [o]as he said, these forty and five years, even since the LORD spake this word unto Moses, while *the children of* Israel [p]wandered in the wilderness: and now, lo, I *am* this day fourscore and five years old.

11 [q]As yet I *am as* strong this day as *I was* in the day that Moses sent me; as my strength *was* then, even so *is* my strength now, for war, both [r]to go out, and to come in.

12 Now therefore give me this mountain, whereof the LORD spake in that day; for thou heardest in that day how [s]the Anakims *were* there, and *that* the cities *were* great *and* fenced: [t]if so be the LORD *will be* with me, then [u]I shall be able to drive them out, as the LORD said.

13 And Joshua [v]blessed him, [w]and gave unto Caleb the son of Jephunneh Hebron for an inheritance.

---

[e]Num. xxxv. 2; chap. xxi. 2——[f]Num. xxxii. 12; chap. xv. 17——[g]Num. xiv. 24, 30; Deut. i. 36, 38 [h]Num. xiii. 26——[i]Num. xiii. 6; xiv. 6——[k]Num. xiii. 31, 32; Deut. i. 28——[l]Num. xiv. 24; Deut. i. 36 [m]Num. xiv. 23, 24; Deut. i. 36; chap. i. 3——[n]See Num. xiii. 22

[o]Num. xiv. 30——[p]Heb. *walked*——[q]Ecclus. xlvi. 9; see Deut. xxxiv. 7——[r]Deut. xxxi. 2——[s]Num. xiii. 28, 33——[t]Psa. xviii. 32, 34; lx. 12; Rom. viii. 31——[u]Chap xv. 14; Judg. i. 20——[v]Chap. xxii. 6——[w]Chap. x. 37; xv. 13; Judg. i. 20; see chap. xxi. 11, 12; 1 Chron. vi. 55, 56

Verse 5. *They divided the land.*] This work was begun some time before at *Gilgal*, and was finished some time after at *Shiloh*. It must have required a very considerable time to make all the geographical arrangements that were necessary for this purpose.

Verse 6. *Caleb the son of Jephunneh the Kenezite*] In the note on the parallel place, Num. xxxii. 12, it is said Kenaz was probably the *father* of Jephunneh, and that Jephunneh, not Caleb, was the Kenezite; but still, allowing this to be perfectly correct, Caleb might also be called the *Kenezite*, as it appears to have been a *family* name, for *Othniel*, his nephew and son-in-law, is called the son of *Kenaz*, chap. xv. 17; Judg. i. 13, and 1 Chron. iv. 13; and a grandson of Caleb is also called the son of *Kenaz*, 1 Chron. iv. 15. In 1 Chron. ii. 18, Caleb is called the son of *Hezron*, but this is only to be understood of his having Hezron for one of his *ancestors;* and *son* here may be considered the same as *descendant;* for Hezron, of the tribe of Judah, having come into Egypt one hundred and seventy-six years before the birth of Caleb, it is not at all likely that he could be called his *father* in the proper sense of the term. Besides, the supposition above makes a very good sense, and is consistent with the use of the terms *father, son,* and *brother,* in different parts of the sacred writings.

Thou knowest the thing that the Lord said] In the place to which Caleb seems to refer, viz., Num. xiv. 24, there is not a word concerning a promise of *Hebron* to him and his posterity; nor in the place (Deut. i. 36) where Moses repeats what had been done at *Kadesh-barnea:* but it may be *included* in what is there spoken. God promises, *because he had another spirit*

within him, and had *followed God fully*, therefore he should enter into the land whereinto he came, and his seed should possess it. Probably this relates to *Hebron*, and was so understood by all parties at that time. This seems tolerably evident from the pointed reference made by Caleb to this transaction.

Verse 7. *As it was in mine heart.*] Neither *fear* nor *favour* influenced him on the occasion; he told what he believed to be the truth, the whole truth, and nothing but the truth.

Verse 9. *The land whereon thy feet have trodden*] This probably refers to *Hebron*, which was no doubt mentioned on this occasion.

Verse 10. *These forty and five years*] See the note on chap. xiii. 1.

Verse 11. *Even so is my strength now*] I do not ask this place because I wish to sit down now, and take my ease; on the contrary, I know I must fight, to drive out the Anakim and I am as able and willing to do it as I was forty-five years ago, when Moses sent me to spy out the land.

Verse 12. *I shall be able to drive them out*] He cannot mean *Hebron* merely, for that had been taken before by Joshua; but in the request of Caleb doubtless all the *circumjacent country* was comprised, in many parts of which the Anakim were still in considerable force. It has been conjectured that Hebron itself had again fallen under the power of its former possessors, who, taking the advantage of the absence of the Israelitish army, who were employed in other parts of the country, re-entered the city, and restored their ancient domination. But the first opinion seems best founded.

Verse 13. *Joshua blessed him*] As the word *bless* often signifies to *speak good* or *well of* or

A. M. 2560
B. C. 1444
An. Exod. Isr.
47
Anno ante
I. Olymp. 668

14 ˣHebron therefore became the inheritance of Caleb the son of Jephunneh the Kenezite unto this day, because that he ʸwholly followed the LORD God of Israel.

15 And ᶻthe name of Hebron before *was* Kirjath-arba; *which Arba was* a great man among the Anakims. ᵃAnd the land had rest from war.

A. M. 2560
B. C. 1444
An. Exod. Isr.
47
Anno ante
I. Olymp. 668

ˣChap. xxi. 12; 1 Mac. ii. 56——ʸVer. 8, 9

ᶻGen. xxiii. 2; chap. xv. 13——ᵃChap. xi. 23

---

to any person, (see the note on Gen. ii. 3,) here it may mean the *praise* bestowed on Caleb's intrepidity and faithfulness by Joshua, as well as a *prayer* to God that he might have prosperity in all things; and especially that the Lord might be *with him*, as himself had expressed in the preceding verse.

Verse 14. *Hebron therefore became the inheritance of Caleb*] Joshua admitted his claim, recognized his right, and made a full conveyance of Hebron and its dependencies to Caleb and his posterity; and this being done in the sight of all the elders of Israel, the right was publicly acknowledged, and consequently this portion was excepted from the general determination by lot; God having long before made the cession of this place to him and to his descendants.

Verse 15. *And the name of Hebron before was Kirjath-arba*] That is, *the city of Arba*, or rather, *the city of the four*, for thus קרית ארבע *kiryath arba* may be literally translated. It is very likely that this city had its name from *four* Anakim, gigantic or powerful men, probably *brothers*, who built or conquered it. This conjecture receives considerable strength from chap. xv. 14, where it is said that Caleb drove from *Hebron* the *three sons of Anak, Sheshai, Ahiman*, and *Talmai:* now it is quite possible that Hebron had its former name, *Kirjath-arba*, the *city of the four*, from these *three sons* and their *father*, who, being men of uncommon stature or abilities, had rendered themselves famous by acts proportioned to their strength and influence in the country. It appears however from chap. xv. 13 that *Arba* was a proper name, as there he is called the *father of Anak*. The Septuagint call Hebron *the metropolis of the Enakim*, μητροπολις των Ενακιμ. It was probably the seat of government, being the *residence* of the above chiefs, from whose *conjoint* authority and power it might have been called חברון *chebron;* as the word חבר *chabar* literally signifies to *associate*, to *join in fellowship*, and appears to be used, Job xli. 6, for "*associated merchants*, or *merchants' companions*, who travelled

in the same caravan." Both these names are expressive, and serve to confirm the above conjecture. No notice need be taken of the tradition that this city was called *the city of the four* because it was the burial-place of *Adam, Abraham, Isaac*, and *Jacob*. Such traditions confute themselves.

The land had rest from war.] There were no more *general* wars; the inhabitants of Canaan collectively could make no longer any head, and when their confederacy was broken by the conquests of Joshua, he thought proper to divide the land, and let each tribe expel the ancient inhabitants that might still remain in its own territories. Hence the wars after this time were *particular* wars; there were no more general campaigns, as it was no longer necessary for the *whole* Israelitish body to act against an enemy now *disjointed* and *broken*. This appears to be the most rational meaning of the words, *The land had rest from war*.

THE Jewish economy furnishes, not only a history of God's revelations to man, but also a history of his providence, and an ample, most luminous, and glorious comment on that providence. Is it possible that any man can seriously and considerately sit down to the reading even of this book, without rising up a wiser and a better man? This is the true history which everywhere exhibits God as the *first mover* and *prime agent*, and men only as subordinate actors. What a miracle of God's power, wisdom, grace, justice, and providence are the people of Israel in every period of their history, and in every land of their dispersions! If their *fall* occasioned the *salvation* of the Gentile world, what shall their *restoration* produce! Their future *inheritance* is not left to what men would call the *fortuitous* decision of a *lot;* like Caleb's possession it is confirmed by the oath of the Lord; and when the end shall be, this people shall stand in their lot at the end of the days, and shall again be great to the ends of the earth.

CHAPTER XV

A. M. 2759
B. C. 1245
An. Exod. Isr.
246
Anno ante
I. Olymp. 469

and set *it* before thee. And he said, I will tarry until thou come again.

19 ᵉAnd Gideon went in, and made ready ᶠa kid, and unleavened cakes of an ephah of flour: the flesh he put in a basket, and he put the broth in a pot, and brought *it* out unto him under the oak, and presented *it*.

20 And the angel of God said unto him, Take the flesh and the unleavened cakes, and ᵍlay *them* upon this rock, and ʰpour out the broth. And he did so.

21 Then the angel of the LORD put forth the end of the staff that *was* in his hand, and touched the flesh and the unleavened cakes;

and ⁱthere rose up fire out of the rock, and consumed the flesh and the unleavened cakes. Then the angel of the LORD departed out of his sight.

A. M. 2759
B. C. 1245
An. Exod. Isr.
246
Anno ante
I. Olymp. 469

22 And when Gideon ᵏperceived that he *was* an angel of the LORD, Gideon said, Alas, O Lord GOD! ˡfor because I have seen an angel of the LORD face to face.

23 And the LORD said unto him, ᵐPeace *be* unto thee; fear not: thou shalt not die.

24 Then Gideon built an altar there unto the LORD, and called it ⁿJehovah-shalom: unto this day it *is* yet ᵒin Ophrah of the Abiezrites.

ᵉGenesis xviii. 6, 7, 8——ᶠHeb. *a kid of the goats* ᵍChap. xiii. 19——ʰSee 1 Kings xviii. 33, 34——ⁱLev. ix. 24; 1 Kings xviii. 38; 2 Chron. vii. 1——ᵏChap. xiii. 21

ˡGen. xvi. 13; xxxii. 30; Exod. xxxiii. 20; chap. xiii. 22——ᵐDan. x. 19——ⁿThat is, *the LORD send peace:* see Gen. xxii. 14; Exod. xvii. 15; Jer. xxxiii. 16; Ezek. xlviii. 35——ᵒChap. viii. 32

---

oil, flour, and such like. It seems from this that Gideon supposed the person to whom he spoke to be a Divine person. Nevertheless, what he prepared and brought out appears to be intended simply as an entertainment to refresh a respectable stranger.

Verse 19. *Made ready a kid—the flesh he put in a basket, and he put the broth in a pot*] The manner in which the Arabs entertain strangers will cast light on this verse. Dr. Shaw observes: "Besides a bowl of milk, and a basket of figs, raisins, or dates, which upon our arrival were presented to us to stay our appetite, the master of the tent fetched us from his flock according to the number of our company, a kid or a goat, a lamb or a sheep; half of which was immediately seethed by his wife, and served up with cucasoe; the rest was made *kab-ab*, i. e., cut to pieces and roasted, which we reserved for our breakfast or dinner next day." May we not suppose, says Mr. *Harmer*, that Gideon, presenting some slight refreshment to the supposed prophet, according to the present Arab mode, desired him to stay till he could provide something more substantial; that he immediately killed a kid, seethed part of it, and, when ready, brought out the stewed meat in a *pot*, with unleavened cakes of bread which he had baked; and the other part, the *kab-ab*, in a *basket*, for him to carry with him for some after-repast in his journey. See *Shaw's* and *Pococke's Travels*, and *Harmer's Observations*.

Brought it *out unto him under the oak*] Probably where he had a tent, which, with the shade of the oak, sheltered them from the heat of the sun, and yet afforded the privilege of the refreshing breeze. Under a shade in the open air the Arabs, to the present day, are accustomed to receive their guests.

Verse 20. *Take the flesh, &c.*] The angel intended to make the flesh and bread an *offering* to God, and the broth a *libation*.

Verse 21. *The angel—put forth the end of the staff*] He appeared like a traveller with a staff in his hand; this he put forth, and having touched the flesh, fire rose out of the rock and consumed it. Here was the most evident proof of supernatural agency.

Then the angel—departed out of his sight.] Though the angel vanished out of his sight, yet God continued to converse with him either by secret inspiration in his own heart, or by an audible voice.

Verse 22. *Alas, O Lord God! for because I have seen*] This is an elliptical sentence, a natural expression of the distressed state of Gideon's mind: as if he had said, Have mercy on me, O Lord God! else I shall die; because I have seen an angel of Jehovah face to face. We have frequently seen that it was a prevalent sentiment, as well *before* as *under* the *law*, that if any man saw God, or his representative angel, he must surely die. On this account Gideon is alarmed, and prays for his life. This notion prevailed among the heathens, and we find an instance of it in the fable of *Jupiter* and *Semele*. She wished to see his glory; she saw it, and was struck dead by the effulgence. See the notes on Exod. xxxiii. 20. We find that ⌐ similar opinion prevailed very anciently among the Greeks. In the hymn of Callimachus, Εις Λουτρα της Παλλαδος, ver. 100, are these words:—

Κρονιοι δ' ὡδε λεγοντι νομοι·
Ὁς κε τιν' αθανατων, ὀκα μη θεος αυτος ἐληται,
Ἀθρησῃ, μισθῳ τουτον ιδειν μεγαλῳ.

"The laws of Saturn enact, that if any man see any of the immortal gods, unless that god himself shall choose it, he shall pay dearly for that sight."

Verse 23. *Fear not: thou shalt not die.*] Here the discovery is made by God himself: Gideon is not curiously prying into forbidden mysteries, therefore he shall not die.

Verse 24. *Gideon built an altar—and called it Jehovah-shalom*] The words יהוה שלום *Yehovah shalom* signify *The Lord is my peace,* or *The peace of Jehovah;* and this name he gave the altar, in reference to what God had said, ver. 23, *Peace be unto thee,* שלום לך *shalom lecha,* "Peace to thee;" which implied, not only a *wish,* but a *prediction* of the prosperous issue of the enterprise in which he was about to engage. It is likely that this is the altar which

A. M. 2759
B. C. 1245
An. Exod. Isr. 246
Anno ante I. Olymp. 469

25 And it came to pass the same night, that the LORD said unto him, Take thy father's young bullock, [p]even the second bullock of seven years old, and throw down the altar of Baal that thy father hath, and [q]cut down the grove that *is* by it:

26 And build an altar unto the LORD thy God upon the top of this [r]rock, [s]in the ordered place, and take the second bullock, and offer a burnt-sacrifice with the wood of the grove which thou shalt cut down.

27 Then Gideon took ten men of his servants, and did as the LORD had said unto him: and *so* it was, because he feared his father's household, and the men of the city, that he could not do *it* by day, that he did *it* by night.

28 And when the men of the city arose early in the morning, behold, the altar of Baal was cast down, and the grove was cut down that *was* by it, and the second bullock was offered upon the altar *that was* built.

A. M. 2759
B. C. 1245
An. Exod. Isr. 246
Anno ante I. Olymp. 469

29 And they said one to another, Who hath done this thing? And when they inquired and asked, they said, Gideon the son of Joash hath done this thing.

30 Then the men of the city said unto Joash, Bring out thy son, that he may die: because he hath cast down the altar of Baal, and because he hath cut down the grove that *was* by it.

31 And Joash said unto all that stood against him, Will ye plead for Baal? will ye save him? he that will plead for him, let him be put to death whilst *it is yet* morning: if he *be* a god, let him plead for himself, because *one* hath cast down his altar.

[p]Or, *and*——[q]Exod. xxxiv. 13; Deut. vii. 5

[r]Heb. *strong place*——[s]Or, *in an orderly manner*

is mentioned in verse 26, and is spoken of here merely by anticipation.

Verse 25. *Take thy father's young bullock, even the second bullock*] There is some difficulty in this verse, for, according to the Hebrew text, *two* bullocks are mentioned here; but there is only one mentioned in verses 26 and 28. But what was this *second* bullock? Some think that it was a bullock that was fattened in order to be offered in sacrifice to Baal. This is very probable, as the *second bullock* is so particularly distinguished from *another* which belonged to Gideon's father. As the altar was built upon the ground of Joash, yet appears to have been public property, (see verses 29, 30,) so this *second ox* was probably reared and fattened at the expense of the men of that village, else why should they so particularly *resent* its being offered to Jehovah?

Verse 26. *With the wood of the grove*] It is probable that אשרה *Asherah* here signifies *Astarte;* and that there was a *wooden image* of this goddess on the altar of Baal. Baal-peor was the same as *Priapus,* Astarte as *Venus;* these two impure idols were proper enough for the same altar. In early times, and among rude people, the images of the gods were made of *wood.* This is the case still with the inhabitants of the South Sea Islands, with the Indians of America, and with the inhabitants of Ceylon: many of the images of Budhoo are of wood. The Scandinavians also had *wooden gods.*

Verse 27. *He feared his father's household*] So it appears that his father was an idolater: but as Gideon had *ten men* of his own servants whom he could trust in this matter, it is probable that he had preserved the true faith, and had not bowed his knee to the image of Baal.

Verse 28. *The second bullock was offered*] It appears that the second bullock was offered, because it was just *seven* years old, ver. 25, being calved about the time that the Midianitish oppression began; and it was now to be slain to indicate that their slavery should end with its life. The young bullock, ver. 25, is supposed to have been offered for a *peace-offering;* the bullock of seven years old, for a *burnt-offering.*

Verse 29. *Gideon the son of Joash hath done this thing.*] They fixed on him the more readily because they knew he had not joined with them in their idolatrous worship.

Verse 30. *The men of the city said*] They all felt an interest in the continuance of rites in which they had often many sensual gratifications. Baal and Ashtaroth would have more worshippers than the true God, because their *rites* were more adapted to the fallen nature of man.

Verse 31. *Will ye plead for Baal?*] The words are very emphatic: "Will ye plead in earnest תריבון for Baal? Will ye תושיעון really save *him?* If *he* be God, אלהים *Elohim,* let him contend for himself, seeing his altar is thrown down." The *paragogic* letters in the words *plead* and *save* greatly increase the sense. Joash could not slay his son; but he was satisfied he had insulted Baal: if Baal were the true God, he would avenge his own injured honour. This was a sentiment among the heathens. Thus *Tacitus,* lib. i., c. 73, A. U. C. 768, mentioning the letter of Tiberius to the consuls in behalf of *Cassius* and *Rubrius,* two Roman knights, one of whom was accused of having sold a statue of Augustus in the auction of his gardens; and the other, of having sworn falsely by the name of Augustus, who had been deified by the senate; among other things makes him say: Non ideo decretum patri suo cœlum, ut in perniciem civium is honor verteretur. Nec contra religiones fieri quod effigies ejus, utalia nu minum simulachra, venditionibus hortorum, et domuum accedant. Jusjurandum perinde æstimandum quam si Jovem fefellisset: *deorum injuriœ diis curœ*—"That Divine honours were

A. M. 2759
B. C. 1245
An. Exod. Isr.
246
Anno ante
I. Olymp. 469

32 Therefore on that day he called him [t]Jerubbaal, [u]saying, Let Baal plead against him, because he hath thrown down his altar.

33 Then all [v]the Midianites and the Amalekites and the children of the east were gathered together, and went over, and pitched in [w]the valley of Jezreel.

34 But [x]the Spirit of the LORD [y]came upon Gideon, and he [z]blew a trumpet; and Abi-ezer [a]was gathered after him.

35 And he sent messengers throughout all Manasseh; who also was gathered after him: and he sent messengers unto Asher, and unto Zebulun, and unto Naphtali; and they came up to meet them.

36 And Gideon said unto God, If thou wilt save Israel by mine hand, as thou hast said,

37 [b]Behold, I will put a fleece of wool in the floor; *and* if the dew be on the fleece only, and *it be* dry upon all the earth *beside,* then shall I know that thou wilt save Israel by mine hand, as thou hast said.

A. M. 2759
B. C. 1245
An. Exod. Isr.
246
Anno ante
I. Olymp. 469

38 And it was so: for he rose up early on the morrow, and thrust the fleece together, and wringed the dew out of the fleece, a bowl full of water.

39 And Gideon said unto God, [c]Let not thine anger be hot against me, and I will speak but this once: let me prove, I pray thee, but this once with the fleece; let it now be dry only upon the fleece, and upon all the ground let there be dew.

40 And God did so that night: for it was dry upon the fleece only, and there was dew on all the ground.

---

[t]That is, *Let Baal plead*——[u]1 Sam. xii. 11; 2 Sam. xi. 21; *Jerubbesheth;* that is, *Let the shameful thing plead;* see Jer. xi. 13; Hos. ix. 10——[v]Ver. 3 [w]Josh. xvii. 16

[x]Chap. iii. 10; 1 Chron. xii. 18; 2 Chron. xxiv. 20 [y]Heb. *clothed*——[z]Num. x. 3; chap. iii. 27——[a]Heb. *was called after him*——[b]See Exod. iv. 3, 4, 6, 7 [c]Gen. xviii. 32

---

not decreed to his father (Augustus) to lay snares for the citizens; and if his statue, in common with the images of the gods in general, was put up to sale with the houses and gardens, it could not be considered an injury to religion. That any oath must be considered as an attempt to deceive Jupiter himself; *but the gods themselves must take cognizance of the injuries done unto them.*" *Livy* has a similar sentiment, Hist. lib. x., c. 6, where, speaking of some attempts made to increase the number of the augurs out of the commons, with which the senators were displeased, he says: *Simulabant ad deos id magis, quam ad se pertinere; ipsos visuros, ne sacra sua polluantur.*—"They pretended that these things belonged *more to the gods than themselves; and that they would take care that their sacred rites were not polluted.*"

Verse 32. *He called him Jerubbaal*] That is, *Let Baal contend;* changed, 2 Sam. xi. 21, into *Jerubbesheth, he shall contend against confusion or shame;* thus changing *baal, lord,* into *bosheth, confusion* or *ignominy.* Some think that Jerubbaal was the same with *Jerombalus,* who, according to *Sanchoniatho* and *Porphyry,* was a priest of *Jevo.* But the history of Sanchoniatho is probably a forgery of Porphyry himself, and worthy of no credit.

Verse 33. *Then all the Midianites*] Hearing of what Gideon had done, and apprehending that this might be a forerunner of attempts to regain their liberty, they formed a general association against Israel.

Verse 34. *The Spirit of the Lord came upon Gideon*] He was endued with preternatural courage and wisdom.

Verse 36. *If thou wilt save Israel*] Gideon was very bold, and God was very condescending. But probably the request itself was suggested by the Divine Spirit.

ON the miracle of the *fleece, dew,* and *dry ground,* Origen, in his eighth homily on the book of Judges, has many curious and interesting thoughts. I shall insert the substance of the whole:—

The *fleece* is the *Jewish nation.* The *fleece covered with dew,* while *all around is dry,* the Jewish nation favoured with the *law* and the *prophets.* The *fleece dry,* the Jewish nation cast off for rejecting the *Gospel. All around watered,* the Gospel preached to the *Gentiles,* and they converted to God. The *fleece on the threshing-floor,* the *Jewish people* in the land of Judea, *winnowed, purged,* and *fanned* by the *Gospel.* The *dew wrung out into the bowl,* the doctrines of Christianity, extracted from the Jewish writings, shadowed forth by Christ's pouring water into a basin, and washing the disciples' feet. The pious father concludes that he has now wrung this water out of the fleece of the book of *Judges,* as he hopes by and by to do out of the fleece of the book of *Kings,* and out of the fleece of the book of *Isaiah* or *Jeremiah;* and he has received it into the basin of his heart, and there conceived its true sense; and is desirous to wash the feet of his brethren, that they may be able to walk in the way of the preparation of the Gospel of peace.—ORIGEN, *Op.* vol. ii., p. 475, edit. *Benedict.*

All this to some will doubtless appear trifling; but it is not too much to say that scarcely any pious mind can consider the homily of this excellent man without drinking into a measure of the same spirit, so much sincerity, deep piety, and unction, appear throughout the whole: yet as I do not follow such practices, I cannot recommend them. Of dealers in such *small wares,* we have many that imitate *Benjamin Keach,* but few that come nigh to *Origen.*

CHAPTER VII

The Lord commands Gideon to make a selection of a small number of his men to go against the Midianites. Three hundred only are selected; and into the hands of these God promises to deliver the whole Midianitish host, 1–8. Gideon is directed to go down unto the host in the night, that he may be encouraged on hearing what they say, 9–12. He obeys, and hears a Midianite tell a remarkable dream unto his fellow, which predicted the success of his attack, 13–15. He takes encouragement, divides his men into three companies, and gives each a trumpet with a lighted lamp concealed in a pitcher, with directions how to use them, 16–18. They come to the Midianitish camp at night, when all suddenly blowing their trumpets and exposing their lamps, the Midianites are thrown into confusion, fly, and are stopped by the Ephraimites at the passage of Jordan, and slain, 19–24. Oreb and Zeeb, two Midianitish princes, are slain, 25.

A. M. 2759
B. C. 1245
An. Exod. Isr.
246
Anno ante
I. Olymp. 469

THEN ᵃJerubbaal, who *is* Gideon, and all the people that *were* with him, rose up early, and pitched beside the well of Harod; so that the host of the Midianites were on the north side of them, by the hill of Moreh, in the valley.

2 And the LORD said unto Gideon, The people that *are* with thee *are* too many for me to give the Midianites into their hands, lest Israel ᵇvaunt themselves against me, saying, Mine own hand hath saved me.

3 Now therefore go to, proclaim in the ears of the people, saying, ᶜWhosoever *is* fearful and afraid, let him return and depart early from Mount Gilead. And there returned of

the people twenty and two thousand; and there remained ten thousand.

A. M. 2759
B. C. 1245
An. Exod. Isr.
246
Anno ante
I. Olymp. 469

4 And the LORD said unto Gideon, The people *are* yet *too* many; bring them down unto the water, and I will try them for thee there: and it shall be, *that* of whom I say unto thee, This shall go with thee, the same shall go with thee; and of whomsoever I say unto thee, This shall not go with thee, the same shall not go.

5 So he brought down the people unto the water: and the LORD said unto Gideon, Every one that lappeth of the water with his tongue as a dog lappeth, him shalt thou set by himself; likewise every one that boweth down upon his knees to drink.

ᵃChap. vi. 32——ᵇDeut. viii. 17; Isa. x. 13; 1 Cor. i. 29; 2 Cor. iv. 7——ᶜDeut. xx. 8; 1 Mac. iii. 56

NOTES ON CHAP. VII

Verse 1. *Then Jerubbaal, who is Gideon*] It appears that Jerubbaal was now a *surname* of Gideon, from the circumstance mentioned chap. vi. 32. See chap. viii. 35.

The well of Harod] If this was a *town* or *village*, it is nowhere else mentioned. Probably, as חרד *charad* signifies to *shake* or *tremble through fear*, the fountain in question may have had its name from the *terror* and *panic* with which the Midianitish host was seized at this place.

Verse 2. *The people that* are *with thee* are *too many*] Had he led up a numerous host against his enemies, the excellence of the power by which they were discomfited might have appeared to be of man and not of God. By the manner in which this whole transaction was conducted, both the Israelites and Midianites must see that the thing was of God. This would inspire the Israelites with confidence, and the Midianites with fear.

Verse 3. *Whosoever* is *fearful and afraid, let him return—from Mount Gilead*] Gideon was certainly not at Mount *Gilead* at this time, but rather near Mount *Gilboa*. Gilead was on the other side of Jordan. Calmet thinks there must either have been two Gileads, which does not from the Scripture appear to be the case, or that the Hebrew text is here corrupted, and that for *Gilead* we should read *Gilboa*. This read-

ing, though adopted by *Houbigant*, is not countenanced by any MS., nor by any of the *versions*.

Dr. Hales endeavours to reconcile the whole, by the supposition that there were in Gideon's army many of the eastern Manassites, who came from Mount Gilead; and that these probably were more afraid of their neighbours, the Midianites, than the western tribes were; and therefore proposes to read the text thus: *Whosoever from Mount Gilead is fearful and afraid, let him return* (home) *and depart early. So there returned* (home) *twenty-two thousand of the people.* Perhaps this is on the whole the best method of solving this difficulty.

There returned of the people twenty and two thousand] Gideon's army was at this time thirty-two thousand strong, and after the above address twenty-two thousand went away. How astonishing, that in thirty-two thousand men there should be found not less than twenty-two thousand poltroons, who would neither fight for God nor their oppressed country! A state of slavery debases the mind of man, and renders it incapable of being influenced by the pure principles of patriotism or religion. In behalf of the army of Gideon we may say, if the best appointed armies in Europe had the same address, *bona fide*, from their generals as the Israelites had, at least an equal proportion would return home.

Verse 5. *Every one that lappeth of the water —as a dog*] The original word ילק *yalok* is

A. M. 2759
B. C. 1245
An. Exod. Isr.
246
Anno ante
I. Olymp. 469

6 And the number of them that lapped, *putting* their hand to their mouth, were three hundred men: but all the rest of the people bowed down upon their knees to drink water.

7 And the LORD said unto Gideon, [d]By the three hundred men that lapped will I save you, and deliver the Midianites into thine hand: and let all the *other* people go every man unto his place.

8 So the people took victuals in their hand, and their trumpets: and he sent all *the rest of* Israel every man unto his tent, and retained those three hundred men: and the host of Midian was beneath him in the valley.

9 And it came to pass the same [e]night, that the LORD said unto him, Arise, get thee down unto the host; for I have delivered it into thine hand.

10 But if thou fear to go down, go thou with Phurah thy servant down to the host:

11 And thou shalt [f]hear what they say: and afterward shall thine hands be strengthened to go down unto the host. Then went he down with Phurah his servant unto the outside of the [g]armed men that *were* in the host.

12 And the Midianites and the Amalekites and [h]all the children of the east lay along in the valley like grasshoppers for multitude; and their camels *were* without number, as the sand by the sea-side for multitude.

13 And when Gideon was come, behold, *there was* a man that told his dream unto his fellow, and said, Behold, I dreamed a dream, and, lo, a cake of barley bread tumbled into the host of Midian, and came unto a tent, and smote it that it fell, and overturned it, that the tent lay along.

14 And his fellow answered and said, This *is* nothing else save the sword of Gideon the son of Joash, a man of Israel: *for* into his hand hath God delivered Midian, and all the host.

15 And it was *so,* when Gideon heard the telling of the dream, and [i]the interpretation thereof, that he worshipped, and returned into the host of Israel, and said, Arise; for the LORD hath delivered into your hand the host of Midian.

16 And he divided the three hundred men *into* three companies, and he put [k]a trumpet in every man's hand, with empty pitchers, and [l]lamps within the pitchers.

17 And he said unto them, Look on me, and do likewise: and, behold, when I come to the outside of the camp, it shall be *that,* as I do, so shall ye do.

18 When I blow with a trumpet, I and all that *are* with me, then blow ye the trumpets also on every side of all the camp, and say, *The sword* of the LORD, and of Gideon.

A. M. 2759
B. C. 1245
An. Exod. Isr.
246
Anno ante
I. Olymp. 469

---

[d]1 Sam. xiv. 6——[e]Gen. xlvi. 2, 3——[f]Ver. 13, 14, 15; see Gen. xxiv. 14; 1 Sam. xiv. 9, 10——[g]Or, *ranks by five;* Exod. xiii. 18

[h]Chapter vi. 5, 33; viii. 10——[i]Hebrew, *the breaking thereof*——[k]Heb. *trumpets in the hand of all of them* [l]Or, *firebrands,* or *torches*

---

precisely the sound which a dog makes when he is drinking.

Verse 6. *The number of them that lapped*] From this account it appears that some of the people went down on their knees, and putting their mouths to the water, sucked up what they needed; the others stooped down, and taking up water in the hollow of their hands, applied it to their mouth.

Verse 8. *So the people took victuals*] The three hundred men that he reserved took the victuals necessary for the day's expenditure, while the others were dismissed to their tents and their houses as they thought proper.

Verse 9. *I have delivered it into thine hand.*] I have determined to do it, and it is as sure as if it were done.

Verse 11. *Unto the outside of the armed men*] No doubt the vast multitudes of Midianites, &c., which came merely for plunder, were wholly unarmed; but they had a guard of armed men, as all the caravans have, and those guards were on the outside of the multitudes; it was to these that Gideon and his servant came.

Verse 13. *Told a dream*] Both the dream and the interpretation were inspired by God for the purpose of increasing the confidence of Gideon, and appalling his enemies.

Verse 14. *Into his hand hath God delivered Midian*] This is a full proof that God had inspired both the dream and its interpretation.

Verse 16. *He divided the three hundred men*] Though the victory was to be from the Lord, yet he knew that he ought to use prudential means; and those which he employed on this occasion were the best calculated to answer the end. If he had not used these means, it is not likely that God would have delivered the Midianites into his hands. Sometimes, even in working a miracle, God will have natural means used: *Go, dip thyself seven times in Jordan. Go, wash in the pool Siloam.*

Verse 18. The sword *of the Lord, and of*

A. M. 2759
B. C. 1245
An. Exod. Isr.
246
Anno ante
I. Olymp. 469

19 So Gideon, and the hundred men that *were* with him, came unto the outside of the camp in the beginning of the middle watch; and they had but newly set the watch: and ᵐthey blew the trumpets, and brake the pitchers that *were* in their hands.

20 And the three companies blew the trumpets, and brake the pitchers, and held the lamps in their left hands, and the trumpets in their right hands to blow *withal:* and ⁿthey

cried, The sword of the LORD, and of Gideon.

21 And they °stood every man in his place round about the camp: ᴾand all the host ran, and cried, and fled.

22 And the three hundred ᑫblew the trumpets, and ʳthe LORD set ˢevery man's sword against his fellow, even throughout all the host: and the host fled to Beth-shittah ᵗin Zererath, *and* to the ᵘborder of Abel-meholah, unto Tabbath.

A. M. 2759
B. C. 1245
An. Exod. Isr.
246
Anno ante
I. Olymp. 469

ᵐVerse 18, 22——ⁿVerse 18——°Exodus xiv. 13, 14; 2 Chronicles xx. 17——ᴾ2 Kings vii. 7, 15——ᑫJosh. vi. 4, 16, 20; see 2 Corinthians iv. 7

ʳPsalm lxxxiii. 9; Isaiah ix. 4——ˢ1 Samuel xiv. 20; 2 Chronicles xx. 23——ᵗOr, *toward* ᵘHebrew, *lip*

Gideon.] The word חרב *chereb,* "sword," is not found in this verse, though it is necessarily implied, and is found in ver. 20. But it is found in this place in the *Chaldee, Syriac,* and *Arabic,* and in eight of *Kennicott's* and *De Rossi's* MSS. The reading appears to be genuine.

Verse 20. *Blew the trumpets, and brake the pitchers*] How astonishing must the effect be, in a dark night, of the sudden glare of three hundred torches, darting their splendour, in the same instant, on the half-awakened eyes of the terrified Midianites, accompanied with the clangour of three hundred trumpets, alternately mingled with the thundering shout of

חרב ליהוה ולגדעון *chereb layhovah ulegidon,* "A sword for the Lord and for Gideon!"

Origen, in his ninth homily on this book, makes these three hundred men types of the *preachers of the Gospel;* their *trumpets* of the *preaching of Christ crucified;* and their *lights* or *torches,* of the *holy conduct* of righteous men. In some verses of an ancient author, attributed to *Tertullian,* and written against the heretic *Marcion,* Gideon's three hundred men are represented as horsemen; and in this number he finds the mystery of the cross; because the Greek letter T, *tau,* which is the numeral for 300, is itself the sign of the cross. The verses, which may be found in vol. v. of the *Pisaurian* Collection of the Latin heathen and Christian poets, *Advers, Marcion.,* lib. 3, ver. 18, as being very curious, and not often to be met with, I shall here subjoin:—

Ex quibus ut Gideon dux agminis, acer in hostem,
Non virtute sua tutelam acquirere genti,
Firmatusque fide signum petit excita menti,
Quo vel non posset, vel posset vincere bellum,
Vellus ut in noctem positum de rore maderet,
Et tellus omnis circum siccata jaceret,
Hoc inimicorum palmam coalescere mundo;
Atque iterum solo remanenti vellere sicco,
Hoc eadem tellus roraret nocte liquore,
Hoc etenim signo prædonum stravit acervos.
Congressus populo Christi, sine milite multo:
Tercenteno equite (numerus Tau littera Græca)
Armatis facibusque et cornibus ore canentum.
Vellus erat populus ovium de semine sancto.
Nam tellus variæ gentes fusæque per orbem,
Verbum quod nutrit, sed nox est mortis imago.
Tau signum crucis et cornu præconia vitæ,
Lucentesque faces in lychno spiritus ardens.

"Gideon, keen in arms, was captain of the host,
And acquired redemption for his people, but not by his own power.
Being strengthened in faith, his heart was influenced to ask a sign
By which he might know whether or not he should be successful in battle.
A *fleece* was so placed by night, that it might be wet with dew;
And all the surrounding earth remain dry.
By this he was to learn that he should gain the victory over his enemies.
The sign was reversed; the fleece remaining dry while all the ground was moist;
And by this sign he was to know that he should slaughter those troops of robbers.
The people of Christ conquer without any military force;
Three hundred horsemen, (for the Greek letter T, *tau,* is the emblem of the number,)
Armed with torches, and blowing with trumpets.
The *fleece* of the sheep are the people sprung from the Messiah,
And the *earth* are the various nations dispersed over the world.
It is the *word* which nourishes; but *might* is the image of *death.*
Tau is the sign of the *cross;* and the *trumpets,* the emblems of the *heralds of life;*
And the *burning torches* in the *pitchers,* the emblems of the *Holy Spirit.*"

We see here what abstruse meanings a strong imagination, assisted by a little piety, may extract from what was never intended to be understood as a mystery.

Verse 21. *They stood every man in his place*] Each of the three companies kept its station, and continued to sound their trumpets. The Midianites seeing this, and believing that they were the trumpets of a numerous army which had then penetrated their camp, were thrown instantly into confusion; and supposing that their enemies were in the midst of them, they turned their swords against every man they met, while at the same time they endeavoured to escape for their lives. No stratagem was ever better imagined, better executed, or more completely successful.

Verse 22. *Fled to Beth-shittah*] This is nowhere else mentioned in Scripture.

A. M. 2759
B. C. 1245
An. Exod. Isr.
246
Anno ante
I. Olymp. 469

23 And the men of Israel gathered themselves together out of Naphtali, and out of Asher, and out of all Manasseh, and pursued after the Midianites.

24 And Gideon sent messengers throughout all ᵛMount Ephraim, saying, Come down against the Midianites, and take before them the waters unto Beth-barah and Jordan. Then all the men of Ephraim gathered themselves together, and ᵂtook the waters unto ˣBeth-barah and Jordan.

A. M. 2759
B. C. 1245
An. Exod. Isr.
246
Anno ante
I. Olymp. 469

25 And they took ʸtwo princes of the Midianites, Oreb and Zeeb; and they slew Oreb upon ᶻthe rock Oreb, and Zeeb they slew at the winepress of Zeeb, and pursued Midian, and brought the heads of Oreb and Zeeb to Gideon, on the ᵃother side Jordan.

ᵛChapter iii. 27——ᵂChapter iii. 28——ˣJohn i. 28

ʸChap. viii. 3; Psa. lxxxiii. 11——ᶻIsa. x. 26——ᵃChap. viii. 4

Zererath] This and *Tabbath* are nowhere else to be found.

Abel-meholah] This was the birth-place of the prophet Elisha, 1 Kings xix. 16. It was beyond Jordan, in the tribe of Manasseh, 1 Kings iv. 12. The *Zartanah*, mentioned in this last quoted verse, was probably the same as *Zererath*. Its situation corresponds well with Abel-meholah.

Verse 23. *The men of Israel gathered*] It is very likely that these were some persons whom Gideon had sent home the day before, who now hearing that the Midianites were routed, went immediately in pursuit.

Verse 24. *Take before them the waters unto Beth-barah*] This is probably the same place as that mentioned John i. 28, where the Hebrews forded Jordan under the direction of Joshua. To this place the Midianites directed their flight that they might escape into their own country; and here, being met by the Ephraimites, they appear to have been totally overthrown, and their two generals taken.

Verse 25. *They slew Oreb upon the rock Oreb*] These two generals had taken shelter, one in the cavern of the rock, the other in the vat of a winepress; both of which places were, from this circumstance, afterwards called by their names.

Brought the heads of Oreb and Zeeb to Gideon] OREB signifies a *raven*, and ZEEB a *wolf*. In all ancient nations we find generals and princes taking their names from both birds and beasts; the Romans had their *Gracchi*, jackdaws; *Corvini*, crows; *Aquilini*, eagles, &c. We have the same in our *Crows*, *Wolfs*, *Lyons*, *Hawkes*. *Bulls*, *Kidds*, &c. Among barbarous nations the *head* of the conquered chief was often brought to the conqueror. Pompey's head was brought to Cæsar; Cicero's head, to Mark Antony; the heads of Ahab's children, to Jehu, &c. These barbarities are not often practised now, except among the Mohammedans or the savages of Africa and America; and for the credit of human nature it is a pity that such barbarous atrocities had ever been committed.

CHAPTER VIII

The Ephraimites are angry with Gideon because he did not call them particularly to his assistance; he pacifies them, 1–3. Gideon and his three hundred men pass over Jordan, pursuing the Midianites; and, being faint, ask victuals from the princes of Succoth, but are refused, 4–7. They make the like application to the people of Penuel, and are also refused, 8, 9. Gideon defeats Zebah and Zalmunna, the two kings of Midian, and takes them prisoners, 10–12. He chastises the men of Succoth and Penuel, 13–17. He slays Zebah and Zalmunna, who had killed his brethren, 18–21. The Israelites offer him the kingdom, which he refuses, 22, 23. He requires from them the gold rings which they had takem from the Ishmaelites, and makes an ephod, which he sets up at Ophrah; and it became an instrument of idolatry, 24–27. The land enjoys peace forty years; Gideon dies, having seventy-one sons, 28–32. The Israelites fall into idolatry, and forget their obligations to Gideon's family, 33–35.

A. M. 2759
B. C. 1245
An. Exod. Isr.
246
Anno ante
I. Olymp. 469

AND ᵃthe men of Ephraim said unto him, ᵇWhy hast thou served us thus, that thou calledst us not, when thou wentest to fight with the Midianites? And they did chide with him ᶜsharply.

A. M. 2759
B. C. 1245
An. Exod. Isr.
246
Anno ante
I. Olymp. 469

2 And he said unto them, What have I done now in comparison of you? *Is* not the gleaning of the grapes

---

ᵃSee chap. xii. 1; 2 Sam. xix. 41——ᵇHeb. *What*

thing is *this thou hast done unto us?*——ᶜHeb. *strongly*

NOTES ON CHAP. VIII

Verse 1. *The men of Ephraim said*] This account is no doubt displaced; for what is mentioned here could not have taken place till the return of Gideon from the pursuit of the Midianites; for he had not yet passed Jordan, ver. 4. And it was when he was beyond that river that the Ephraimites brought the heads of Oreb and Zeeb to him, chap. vii. 25.

Verse 2. *Is* not *the gleaning*, &c.] That is, The Ephraimites have performed more important services than Gideon and his men; and he supports the assertion by observing that it was they who took the two Midianitish generals, having discomfited their hosts at the passes of Jordan.

A. M. 2759
B. C. 1245
An. Exod. Isr.
246
Anno ante
I. Olymp. 469

of Ephraim better than the vintage of Abi-ezer?

3 ^dGod hath delivered into your hands the princes of Midian, Oreb and Zeeb: and what was I able to do in comparison of you? Then their ^eanger ^fwas abated toward him, when he had said that.

4 And Gideon came to Jordan, *and* passed over, he, and the three hundred men that *were* with him, faint, yet pursuing *them.*

5 And he said unto the men of ^gSuccoth, Give, I pray you, loaves of bread unto the people that follow me; for they *be* faint, and I am pursuing after Zebah and Zalmunna, kings of Midian.

6 And the princes of Succoth said, ^h*Are* the hands of Zebah and Zalmunna now in thine hand, that ⁱwe should give bread unto thine army?

7 And Gideon said, Therefore, when the LORD hath delivered Zebah and Zalmunna into mine hand, ^kthen I will ^ltear your flesh with the thorns of the wilderness and with briers.

8 And he went up thence ^mto Penuel, and spake unto them likewise: and the men of Penuel answered him as the men of Succoth had answered *him.*

9 And he spake also unto the men of Penuel, saying, When I ⁿcome again in peace, ^oI will break down this tower.

A. M. 2759
B. C. 1245
An. Exod. Isr.
246
Anno ante
I. Olymp. 469

10 Now Zebah and Zalmunna *were* in Karkor, and their hosts with them, about fifteen thousand *men,* all that were left of ^pall the hosts of the children of the east: for there fell ^qa hundred and twenty thousand men that drew sword.

11 And Gideon went up by the way of them that dwelt in tents on the east of ^rNobah and Jogbehah, and smote the host: for the host was ^ssecure.

12 And When Zebah and Zalmunna fled, he pursued after them, and ^ttook the two kings of Midian, Zebah and Zalmunna, and ^udiscomfited all the host.

13 And Gideon the son of Joash returned from battle before the sun *was up,*

14 And caught a young man of the men of Succoth, and inquired of him: and he ^vdescribed unto him the princes of Succoth, and the elders thereof, *even* threescore and seventeen men.

15 And he came unto the men of Succoth, and said, Behold Zebah and Zalmunna, with whom ye did ^wupbraid me, saying, *Are* the

---

^dChap. vii. 24, 25; Phil. ii. 3——^eHeb. *spirit*
^fProv. xv. 1——^gGen. xxxiii. 17; Psa. lx. 6——^hSee
1 Kings xx. 11——ⁱSee 1 Sam. xxv. 11——^kVer. 16
^lHeb. *thresh*——^mGen. xxxii. 30; 1 Kings xii. 25
ⁿ1 Kings xxii. 27——^oVer. 17

^pChap. vii. 12——^qOr, *a hundred and twenty thousand every one drawing a sword;* chap. xx. 2, 15, 17, 25;
2 Kings iii. 26——^rNumbers xxxii. 35, 42——^sChapter
xviii. 27; 1 Thess. v. 3——^tPsa. lxxxiii. 11——^uHeb. *terrified*——^vHeb. *writ*——^wVer. 6

Verse 3. *Then their anger was abated*] A soft answer turneth away wrath. He might have said that he could place but little dependence on his brethren when, through faintheartedness, 22,000 left him at one time; but he passed this by, and took a more excellent way.

Verse 4. *Faint, yet pursuing*] The Vulgate paraphrases this, *et præ lassitudine, fugientes persequi non poterant;* "and, through fatigue, unable to pursue the fugitives."

Verse 5. *Give, I pray you, loaves of bread*] As Gideon was engaged in the common cause of Israel, he had a right to expect succour from the people at large. His request to the men of Succoth and Penuel was both just and reasonable.

Verse 6. *Are the hands of Zebah and Zalmunna now in thine hand*] They feared to help Gideon, lest, if he should be overpowered, the Midianites would revenge it upon them; and they dared not trust God.

Verse 7. *I will tear your flesh*] What this punishment consisted in I cannot say; it must mean a severe punishment: as if he had said, I will thresh your flesh with briers and thorns, as corn is threshed out with threshing instruments; or, Ye shall be trodden down under the

feet of my victorious army, as the corn is trodden out with the feet of the ox.

Succoth was beyond Jordan, in the tribe of Gad. *Penuel* was also in the same tribe, and not far distant from Succoth.

Verse 9. *I will break down this tower.*] Probably they had not only denied him, but insultingly pointed to a tower in which their chief defence lay; and intimated to him that he might do his worst, for they could amply defend themselves.

Verse 10. *Zebah and Zalmunna were in Karkor*] If this were a *place,* it is nowhere else mentioned in Scripture. Some contend that קרקר *karkor* signifies *rest;* and thus the Vulgate understood it: Zebah and Zalmunna *requiescebant, rested,* with all their army. And this seems the most likely, for it is said, ver. 11, that Gideon smote the host, for the host was *secure.*

Verse 13. *Returned from battle before the sun was up*] This does not appear to be a proper translation of מלמעלה החרס *milmaaleh hechares.* It should be rendered *from the ascent of Chares:* this is the reading of the Septuagint, the *Syriac,* and the *Arabic.*

Verse 14. *He described unto him the princes of Succoth*] The young man probably gave

A. M. 2759
B. C. 1245
An. Exod. Isr.
246
Anno ante
I. Olymp. 469

hands of Zebah and Zalmunna now in thine hand, that we should give bread unto thy men *that are* weary?

16 [x]And he took the elders of the city, and thorns of the wilderness, and briers, and with them he [y]taught the men of Succoth.

17 [z]And he beat down the tower of [a]Penuel, and slew the men of the city.

18 Then said he unto Zebah and Zalmunna, What manner of men *were they* whom ye slew at [b]Tabor? And they answered, As thou *art,* so *were* they; each one [c]resembled the children of a king.

A. M. 2759
B. C. 1245
An. Exod. Isr.
246
Anno ante
I. Olymp. 469

19 And he said, They *were* my brethren, *even* the sons of my mother: as the LORD liveth, if ye had saved them alive, I would not slay you.

20 And he said unto Jether his first-born, Up, *and* slay them. But the youth drew not his sword: for he feared, because he *was* yet a youth.

21 Then Zebah and Zalmunna said, Rise thou, and fall upon us: for as the man *is, so is* his strength. And Gideon arose, and [d]slew Zebah and Zalmunna, and took away the [e]ornaments that *were* on their camels' necks.

[x]Ver. 7——[y]Heb. *made to know*——[z]Ver. 9——[a]1 Kings xii. 25——[b]Chap. iv. 6; Psa. lxxxix. 12

[c]Heb. *according to the form,* &c.——[d]Psa. lxxxiii. 11
[e]Or, *ornaments like the moon*

him the names of seventy persons, the chief men of Succoth, who were those who were most concerned in refusing him and his men the refreshment he requested.

Verse 16. *He taught the men of Succoth.*] Instead of וירע *he taught,* Houbigant reads וירש *he tore;* and this is not only agreeable to what Gideon had threatened, ver. 7, but is supported by the *Vulgate, Septuagint, Chaldee, Syriac,* and *Arabic.* The Hebrew text might have been easily corrupted in this place by the change of ש *shin* into ע *ain,* letters very similar to each other.

Verse 18. *What manner of men were they whom ye slew at Tabor?*] We have no antecedent to this question; and are obliged to conjecture one: it seems as if Zebah and Zalmunna had massacred the family of Gideon, while he was absent on this expedition. Gideon had heard some confused account of it, and now questions them concerning the fact. They boldly acknowledge it, and describe the persons whom they slew, by which he found they were *his own brethren.* This determines him to avenge their death by slaying the Midianitish kings, whom he otherwise was inclined to save. He might have heard that his brethren had been taken prisoners, and might have hoped to have exchanged them for the kings now in his hand; but when he found they had been all slain, he decrees the death of their murderers. There is something in this account similar to that in the 12th Æneis of Virgil:—When Turnus was overthrown, and supplicated for his life, and Æneas was inclined to spare him; he saw the belt of his friend Pallas, whom Turnus had slain, and which he now wore as a trophy: this immediately determined the Trojan to sacrifice the life of Turnus to the manes of his friend. The story is well told:—

Stetit acer in armis
Æneas, volvens oculos, dextramque repressit.
Et jam jamque magis cunctantem flectere sermo
Cœperat: infelix humero cum apparuit ingens
Balteus, et notis fulserunt cingula bullis
Pallantis pueri; victum quem vulnere Turnus
Straverat, atque humeris inimicum insigne
gerebat.
Ille oculis postquam sævi monumenta doloris
Exuviasque hausit: furiis accensus et ira

Terribilis: Tune hinc spoliis indute meorum
Eripiare mihi?—Pallas, te hoc vulnere Pallas
Immolat; et pœnam scelerato ex sanguine
sumit.
Hoc dicens furrum adverso sub pectore condit
Fervidus.   VIRG. *Æn.* lib. xii., ver. 938.

"In deep suspense the Trojan seem'd to stand,
And, just prepared to strike, repress'd his hand.
He roll'd his eyes, and every moment felt
His manly soul with more compassion melt.
When, casting down a casual glance, he spied
The golden belt that glitter'd on his side;
The fatal spoils which haughty Turnus tore
From dying Pallas, and in triumph wore.
Then roused anew to wrath, he loudly cries,
(Flames, while he spoke, came flashing from his eyes,)
Traitor! dost thou! dost *thou* to grace pretend,
Clad, as thou art, in trophies of my friend?—
To his sad soul a grateful offering go;
'Tis Pallas, Pallas gives this deadly blow.
He rais'd his arm aloft; and at the word,
Deep in his bosom drove the shining sword."
                                            DRYDEN.

The same principle impels Gideon to slay Zebah and Zalmunna which induced Æneas to kill Turnus: and perhaps the ornaments which he took from their camels' necks, ver. 21, were some of the spoils of his slaughtered brethren.

Verse 20. *He said unto Jether his first-born*] By the ancient laws of war, prisoners taken in war might be either slain, sold, or kept for slaves. To put a captive enemy to death no *executioner* was required. *Gideon* slays Zebah and Zalmunna with his own hand. So *Samuel* is said to have hewn Agag in pieces, 1 Sam. xv. 33. *Benaiah* slew Joab, 1 Kings ii. 25. *Saul* orders his guards to slay the priests who had contributed to the escape of David, 1 Sam. xxii. 17; and *David* caused one of his attendants to slay the Amalekite who pretended to have slain Saul, 2 Sam. i. 15.

Verse 21. *Then Zebah and Zalmunna said, Rise, thou, and fall upon us*] It was disgraceful to fall by the hands of a *child;* and the death occasioned by the blows of such a person must be much more lingering and tormenting. Some have even employed children to despatch

A. M. 2759
B. C. 1245
An. Exod. Isr.
246
Anno ante
I. Olymp. 469

22 Then the men of Israel said unto Gideon, Rule thou over us, both thou, and thy son, and thy son's son also: for thou hast delivered us from the hand of Midian.

23 And Gideon said unto them, I will not rule over you, neither shall my son rule over you: [f]the LORD shall rule over you.

24 And Gideon said unto them, I would desire a request of you, that ye would give me every man the ear-rings of his prey. (For they had golden ear-rings, [g]because they were Ishmaelites.)

25 And they answered, We will willingly give *them*. And they spread a garment, and did cast therein every man the ear-rings of his prey.

A. M. 2759
B. C. 1245
An. Exod. Isr.
246
Anno ante
I. Olymp. 469

26 And the weight of the golden ear-rings that he requested was a thousand and seven hundred *shekels* of gold; beside ornaments, and [h]collars, and purple raiment that *was* on the kings of Midian, and beside the chains that *were* about their camels' necks.

27 And Gideon [i]made an ephod thereof, and put it in his city, *even* [k]in Ophrah: and all

---

[f]1 Sam. viii. 7; x. 19; xii. 12——[g]Gen. xxv. 13; xxxvii. 25, 28

[h]Or, *sweet jewels*——[i]Chapter xvii. 5
[k]Chap. vi. 24

---

captives. *Civilis*, a Roman knight, headed a revolt of the Gauls against Rome, in the year of the city 824. Of him *Tacitus* says, *Hist.* lib. iv., c. 61: *Ferebatur parvulo filio quosdam captivorum sagittis jaculisque puerilibus figendos obtulisse:* "He is said to have given to his little son some prisoners, as butts to be shot at with little darts and arrows." This was for their greater torment and dishonour; and to inure his child to blood! Could any thing like this have been the design of Gideon?

The ornaments that were *on their camels' necks.*] The heads, necks, bodies, and legs of camels, horses, and elephants, are highly ornamented in the eastern countries; and indeed this was common, from the remotest antiquity, in all countries. *Virgil* refers to it as a thing long before his time, and thus describes the horses given by King Latinus to the ambassadors of Æneas.—*Æn.* lib. vii., ver. 274.

Hæc effatus equos numero pater eligit omni.
Stabant tercentum nitidi in præsepibus altis:
Omnibus extemplo Teucris jubet ordine duci
Instratos ostro alipedes *pictisque tapetis.*
Aurea pectoribus demissa *monilia* pendent:
Tecti auro fulvum mandunt sub dentibus aurum.

"He said, and order'd steeds to mount the band:
In lofty stalls three hundred coursers stand;
Their shining sides with *crimson* cover'd o'er;
The sprightly steeds *embroider'd trappings* wore,
With *golden chains*, refulgent to behold:
Gold were their *bridles*, and they *champ'd* on gold."   PITT.

Instead of *ornaments*, the *Septuagint* translate τους μηνισκους, *the crescents* or *half-moons;* and this is followed by the *Syriac* and *Arabic.* The worship of the *moon* was very ancient; and, with that of the *sun*, constituted the earliest idolatry of mankind. We learn from ver. 24 that the Ishmaelites, or Arabs, as they are termed by the *Targum, Syriac*, and *Arabic*, had *golden ear-rings*, and probably a *crescent* in each; for it is well known that the Ishmaelites, and the Arabs who descended from them, were addicted very early to the worship of the *moon;* and so attached were they to this superstition, that although *Mohammed* destroyed the idolatrous use of the *crescent*, yet it was universally borne in their ensigns, and on the

tops of their mosques, as well as in various ornaments.

Verse 22. *Rule thou over us, both thou, and thy son, and thy son's son*] That is, Become our king, and let the crown be hereditary in thy family. What a weak, foolish, and inconstant people were these! As yet their government was a *theocracy;* and now, dazzled with the success of a man who was only an instrument in the hands of God to deliver them from their enemies, they wish to throw off the Divine yoke, and shackle themselves with an *unlimited* hereditary monarchy! An *unlimited* monarchy is a *curse;* a *limited* monarchy may be a blessing: the latter may be an appointment of God; the former never can. Those who cast off their allegiance to their Maker, are guilty of folly and extravagance of every kind.

Verse 23. *The Lord shall rule over you*] Few with such power at their command would have acted as Gideon. His speech calls them back to their first principles, and should have excited in them both shame and contrition. How different is this speech from that of *Oliver Cromwell* when the commons offered him the crown of England!

Verse 24. *Give me every man the ear-rings of his prey.*] The *spoils* taken from their enemies in this warfare. This is a transaction very like to that of the Israelites and Aaron; when they brought him their *golden ear-rings*, out of which he made the *molten calf*, Exod. xxxii. 2, &c. Whether Gideon designed this ephod for an instrument of worship, or merely as a *trophy*, is not very clear. It is most likely that he had intended to establish a place of worship at Ophrah; and he took this occasion to provide the proper sacerdotal vestments.

Verse 26. *The weight of the golden ear-rings —was a thousand and seven hundred* shekels *of gold*] Taking the shekel at *half an ounce* weight, the sum of the gold collected in earrings was seventy pounds ten ounces; and worth, as gold now rates, about £3,100 sterling.

This computation of the weight of the golden *ear-rings*, taken from the slaughtered Ishmaelites, will bring to the reader's mind the slaughter of the Roman knights by the Carthaginians at the battle of *Cannæ*, from whose spoils Hannibal sent *three bushels* of gold rings to the city of Carthage!

Verse 27. *Gideon made an ephod thereof*]

A. M. 2759
B. C. 1245
An. Exod. Isr.
246
Anno ante
I. Olymp. 469

Israel [l]went thither a whoring after it: which thing became [m]a snare unto Gideon, and to his house.

28 Thus was Midian subdued before the children of Israel, so that they lifted up their heads no more. [n]And the country was in quietness forty years in the days of Gideon.

29 And Jerubbaal the son of Joash went and dwelt in his own house.

30 And Gideon had [o]threescore and ten sons [p]of his body begotten: for he had many wives.

31 [q]And his concubine that *was* in Shechem, she also bare him a son, whose name he [r]called Abimelech.

32 And Gideon the son of Joash died [s]in a good old age, and was buried in the sepulchre of Joash his father, [t]in Ophrah of the Abi-ezrites.

A. M. 2799
B. C. 1205
An. Exod. Isr.
286
Anno ante
I. Olymp. 429

33 And it came to pass, [u]as soon as Gideon was dead, that the children of Israel turned again, and [v]went a whoring after Baalim, [w]and made Baal-berith their god.

34 And the children of Israel [x]remembered not the LORD their God, who had delivered them out of the hands of all their enemies on every side:

35 [y]Neither showed they kindness to the house of Jerubbaal, *namely,* Gideon, according to all the goodness which he had showed unto Israel.

---

[l]Psa. cvi. 39——[m]Deut. vii. 16——[n]Chap. v. 31
[o]Chap. ix. 2, 5——[p]Hebrew, *going out of his thigh*
[q]Chapter ix. 1——[r]Heb. *set*——[s]Gen. xxv. 8; Job. v. 26

[t]Ver. 27; chap. vi. 24——[u]Chap. ii. 19——[v]Chap. ii.
17——[w]Chap. ix. 4, 46——[x]Psa. lxxviii. 11, 42; cvi. 13,
21——[y]Chap. ix. 16, 17, 18; Eccles. ix. 14, 15

That is, he made an ephod *out of this* mass of gold; but he could not employ it *all* in making this one garment, for it is not likely that any man could wear a coat of nearly one hundred pounds weight. It is likely that he made a whole tabernacle service in miniature out of this gold.

All Israel went thither a whoring after it] This form of speech often occurs, and has been often explained. The whole Jewish nation is represented as being *united to God* as a *wife is to her husband.* Any act of *idolatry* is considered as a *breach of their covenant* with God, as an act of *whoredom* is the breach of the *marriage agreement* between man and wife. God calls himself the *husband* of the Jewish nation; and their *idolatries* acts of *whoredom, adultery,* and *fornication.* All Israel paid idolatrous worship to the ephod or sacerdotal establishment made by Gideon at Ophrah, and this is called *going a whoring after it;* see on ver. 33. For a description of the *ephod,* see Exod. xxv. 7; and for the other garments of the priests, see Exod. xxviii. 4, &c.

Verse 28. Forty years in the days of Gideon.] The Midianites were so completely humbled that they could make head no more against Israel during the forty years in which the government of Gideon lasted.

Verse 31. His concubine] A *lawful* but *secondary wife,* whose children could not *inherit.*

Whose name he called Abimelech.] That is, *my father is king,* or *my father hath reigned.* This name was doubtless given by the *mother,* and so it should be understood here; she wished to raise her son to the supreme government, and therefore gave him a name which might serve to stimulate him to seek that which she hoped he should enjoy in his father's right. See the following chapter.

Verse 32. Gideon—died in a good old age] Supposed to have been A. M. 2799; B. C. 1205.

Verse 33. A whoring after Baalim] This term has probably a different meaning here from what it has ver. 7; for it is very likely

that in most parts of the pagan worship there were many *impure* rites, so that *going a whoring after Baalim* may be taken in a *literal* sense.

Baal-berith] Literally, *the lord of the covenant;* the same as *Jupiter fœderis,* or *Mercury,* among the Romans; the deity whose business it was to preside over *compacts, leagues, treaties, covenants,* &c. Some of the *versions* understand it as if the Israelites had made a *covenant* or agreement *to have Baal for their god;* so the VULGATE: *Percusseruntque cum Baal fœdus, ut esset eis in deum.*

Verse 34. Remembered not the Lord their God] They attributed their deliverance to some other cause, and did not give him the glory of their salvation.

Verse 35. Neither showed they kindness to the house of—Gideon] They were both *unthankful* and *unholy.* Though they had the clearest proofs of God's power and goodness before their eyes, yet they forgot him. And although they were under the greatest obligations to Gideon, and were once so sensible of them that they offered to settle the kingdom on him and his family, yet they forgot him also; for, becoming *foes* to GOD, they could not be friends to MAN.

Jerubbaal, namely, Gideon.—This is improper; it should be *Jerubbaal Gideon,* as we say *Simon Peter,* or call any man by his *Christian name* and *surname.*

THE ancients, particularly St. *Ambrose* and *Augustine,* have endeavoured to find out a *parallel* between our blessed Lord and Gideon. We have already seen what *Origen* has made of the whole account, who is followed in the main by the above Latin fathers. As I believe no such parallel was intended by the Spirit of God, I must be excused from going into their details. It is no credit either to Christ or Christianity to be compared to such persons and their transactions.

1. Of Gideon the most we can say is that

which the angel said, he was *a mighty man of valour.*

2. He was also a *true patriot;* he loved his country, and hazarded his life for it; and yet he would not stir till he had the most incontestable proofs that God would, by his supernatural assistance, make him victorious.

3. He was most evidently *disinterested,* and void of *ambition;* he refused the kingdom when it was offered to him and to his heirs after him. But, consistently with the belief he had in God, he could not accept it, as this would have been a complete alteration of the Jewish constitution, which acknowledged no ruler but God himself.

4. His motive in making the ephod is not well understood; probably it was done with no reprehensible *design.* But the *act* was totally wrong; he had no Divine authority to make such an innovation in the religious worship of his country. The ark was at Shechem; and *there* was the proper and only accredited priest. The *act* therefore can never be excused, whatever may be said of his *motive.*

5. His private character does not appear to have been very exemplary; he had *many wives,* and seventy sons by them, besides one by a concubine, which he kept at Shechem, where he was often obliged to go as *judge,* for the purpose of administering justice. In short, there is scarcely a trait in his character worthy to be compared with any thing in the conduct of the Redeemer of mankind.

6. Parallels to Christ, and the work of his Spirit in the salvation of men, have been diligently sought in the sacred writings, by both commentators and preachers; and we have had voluminous treaties on types and antitypes; and how little has sound doctrine or true piety derived from them! They have often served to unsettle the former, and have been rather inimical than favourable to the interests of the latter. When the Spirit of God says such things are *types* and such things are *allegories,* it is our duty to believe and examine; when men produce their types and metaphors, it may be our duty to doubt, be suspicious, and pass on.

CHAPTER IX

Abimelech is made king; and, to secure himself in the kingdom, slays his brethren; Jotham, the youngest only escapes, 1–6. Jotham reproves him and the Shechemites by a curious and instructive parable, 7–21. Abimelech having reigned three years, the Shechemites, headed by Gaal the son of Ebed, conspire against him, 22–29. Zebul, governor of the city, apprises Abimelech of the insurrection, who comes with his forces, and discomfits Gaal, 30–40. Abimelech assaults the city, takes, beats it down, and sows it with salt, 41–45. Several of the Shechemites take refuge in the temple of Baal-berith; Abimelech sets fire to it, and destroys in it about one thousand men and women, 46–50. He afterwards besieges and takes Thebez; but while he is assaulting the citadel, a woman threw a piece of millstone upon his head, and killed him. Thus God requited him and the men of Shechem for their wickedness, and their ingratitude to the family of Gideon, 51–57.

A. M. 2799
B. C. 1205
An. Exod. Isr.
286
Anno ante
I. Olymp. 429

AND Abimelech the son of Jerubbaal went to Shechem unto ªhis mother's brethren, and communed with them, and with all the family of the house of his mother's father, saying,

2 Speak, I pray you, in the ears of all the men of Shechem, ᵇWhether *is* better for you, either that all the sons of Jerubbaal, *which are* ᶜthreescore and ten persons, reign over you,

or that one reign over you? remember also that I *am* ᵈyour bone and your flesh.

A. M. 2799
B. C. 1205
An. Exod. Isr.
286
Anno ante
I. Olymp. 429

3 And his mother's brethren spake of him in the ears of all the men of Shechem all these words: and their hearts inclined ᵉto follow Abimelech; for they said, He *is* our ᶠbrother.

4 And they gave him threescore and ten *pieces* of silver out of the house of ᵍBaal-

---

ªChapter viii. 31——ᵇHebrew, *What is good? whether,* &c.——ᶜChap. viii. 30

ᵈGenesis xxix. 14——ᵉHebrew, *after*——ᶠGenesis xxix. 15——ᵍChap. viii. 33

NOTES ON CHAP. IX

Verse 1. *Abimelech—went to Shechem*] We have already seen that Abimelech was the son of Gideon, by his concubine at Shechem. His going thither immediately after his father's death was to induce his townsmen to proclaim him governor in the place of his father. Shechem was the residence of his mother, and of all her relatives.

Verse 2. *Whether is better for you, either that all the sons*] This was a powerful argument: Whether will you have seventy tyrants or only *one?* For, as he had no right to the government, and God alone was *king* at that

time in Israel; so he must support his usurped rule by whatever means were most likely to effect it: a usurped government is generally supported by oppression and the sword.

Verse 3. *He is our brother.*] We shall be raised to places of trust under him, and our city will be the capital of the kingdom.

Verse 4. *Threescore and ten pieces of silver*] Probably *shekels;* and this was the whole of his exchequer. As he was now usurping the government of God, he begins with a *contribution* from the idol temple. A work begun under the name and influence of the devil is not likely to end to the glory of God, or to the welfare of man.

A. M. 2799
B. C. 1205
An. Exod. Isr.
286
Anno ante
I. Olymp. 429

berith, wherewith Abimelech hired [h]vain and light persons, which followed him.

5 And he went unto his father's house [i]at Ophrah, and [k]slew his brethren the sons of Jerubbaal, *being* threescore and ten persons, upon one stone; notwithstanding, yet Jotham the youngest son of Jerubbaal was left; for he hid himself.

6 And all the men of Shechem gathered together, and all the house of Millo, and went and made Abimelech king, [l]by the plain of the pillar that *was* in Shechem.

7 And when they told *it* to Jotham, he went and stood in the top of [m]Mount Gerizim, and lifted up his voice, and cried, and said unto them, Hearken unto me, ye men of Shechem, that God may hearken unto you.

A. M. 2799
B. C. 1205
An. Exod. Isr.
286
Anno ante
I. Olymp. 429

8 [n]The trees went forth *on a time* to anoint a king over them; and they said unto the olive tree, [o]Reign thou over us.

9 But the olive tree said unto them, Should I leave my fatness, [p]wherewith by me they honour God and man, and [q]go to be promoted over the trees?

10 And the trees said to the fig tree, Come thou, *and* reign over us.

---

[h]Chap. xi. 3; 2 Chron. xiii. 7; Prov. xii. 11; Acts xvii. 5——[i]Chap. vi. 24——[k]2 Kings xi. 1, 2——[l]Heb. or, *by the oak of the pillar; see* Josh. xxiv. 26

[m]Deut. xi. 29; xxvii. 12; Joshua viii. 33; John iv. 20 [n]See 2 Kings xiv. 9——[o]Chap. viii. 22, 23——[p]Psa. civ. 15——[q]Heb. *go up and down for other trees*

Hired vain and light persons] אנשים ריקים ופחזים *anashim reykim uphochazim, worthless and dissolute men;* persons who were living on the public, and had nothing to lose. Such was the foundation of his *Babel* government. By a cunning management of such rascals most revolutions have been brought about.

Verse 5. *Slew his brethren*] His brothers by the father's side, chap. viii. 30. This was a usual way of securing an ill-gotten throne; the person who had no right destroying all those that had right, that he might have no competitors.

Yet Jotham—was left] That is, all the seventy were killed except Jotham, if there were not seventy *besides* Jotham. All the histories of all the nations of the earth are full of cruelties similar to those of Abimelech: cousins, uncles, brothers, husbands, and fathers have been murdered by their cousins, nephews, brothers, wives, and children, in order that they might have the undisturbed possession of an ill-gotten throne. Europe, Asia, and Africa, can witness all this. Even now, some of these horribly obtained governments exist.

Verse 6. *And all the house of Millo*] If *Millo* be the name of a *place*, it is nowhere else mentioned in the sacred writings. But it is probably the name of a *person* of note and influence in the city of Shechem—*the men of Shechem and the family of Millo.*

Verse 7. *Stood in the top of Mount Gerizim*] *Gerizim* and *Ebal* were mounts very near to each other; the former lying to the north, the latter to the south, and at the foot of them Shechem. But see some remarks on the extent of the human voice in some hilly countries in the following extract from a late traveller in the East:—

"The great extent to which the sound of the voice is conveyed may be mentioned. Some persons have thought this a proof of the extreme rarity of the atmosphere. A similar observation is made by Captain Parry in his Voyage of Discovery to the Polar Regions in 1819-20, where he states that in the depth of winter the sound of the men's voices was heard at a much greater distance than usual. This phenomenon is constantly observed on the *Neilgherries.* I have heard the natives, especially in the morning and evening, when the air was still, carry on conversation from one hill to another, and that apparently without any extraordinary effort. They do not *shout* in the manner that strangers think necessary in order to be heard at so great a distance, but utter every syllable as distinctly as if they were conversing face to face. When listening to them, I have often been reminded of those passages in holy writ where it is recorded that Jotham addressed the ungrateful men of Shechem from Mount Gerizim, that David cried 'from the top of a hill afar off' to Abner and to the people that lay about their master Saul, and that Abner addressed Joab from the top of a hill."—*Letters on the Climate, Inhabitants, Productions, &c., &c., of the Neilgherries, or Blue Mountains of Coimbatoor, South India, by James Hough, of Madras: 1829.*

That God may hearken unto you.] It appears that Jotham received this message from God, and that he spoke on this occasion by Divine inspiration.

Verse 8. *The trees went forth* on a time] This is the *oldest,* and without exception the *best fable* or *apologue* in the world. See the observations at the end of this chapter.

It is not to be supposed that a fable, if well formed, requires much illustration; every part of this, a few expressions excepted, illustrates itself, and tells its own meaning.

To anoint a king] Hence it appears that *anointing* was usual in the installation of kings, long before there was any king in Israel; for there is much evidence that the book of Judges was written before the days of Saul and David.

The olive tree] The *olive* was the most *useful* of all the trees in the field or forest, as the *bramble* was the meanest and the most worthless.

Verse 9. *Wherewith—they honour God and man*] I believe the word אלהים *elohim* here should be translated *gods,* for the parable seems to be accommodated to the idolatrous state of the Shechemites. Thus it was understood by the *Vulgate, Arabic,* and others. It is true that *olive oil* was often used in the service of God: the priests were *anointed* with it; the lamps

A. M. 2799
B. C. 1205
An. Exod. Isr.
286
Anno ante
I. Olymp. 429

11 But the fig tree said unto them, Should I forsake my sweetness, and my good fruit, and go to be promoted over the trees?

12 Then said the trees unto the vine, Come thou, *and* reign over us.

13 And the vine said unto them, Should I leave my wine, ^rwhich cheereth God and man, and go to be promoted over the trees?

14 Then said all the trees unto the ^sbramble, Come thou, *and* reign over us.

A. M. 2799
B. C. 1205
An. Exod. Isr.
286
Anno ante
I. Olymp. 429

---

^rPsa. civ. 15

^sOr, *thistle*

---

in the tabernacle *lighted* with it; almost all the offerings of fine flour, cakes prepared in the pan, &c., had *oil* mingled with them; therefore Jotham might say that *with it they honour God;* and as *priests, prophets,* and *kings* were *anointed,* and their office was the most honourable, he might with propriety say, *therewith they honour man.* But I am persuaded he used the term in the first sense. See on ver. 13.

Verse 11. *But the fig tree said—Should I forsake my sweetness*] The fruit of the fig tree is the *sweetest* or most *luscious* of all fruits. A full-ripe fig, in its own climate, has an indescribable sweetness; so much so that it is almost impossible to eat it, till a considerable time after it is gathered from the trees, and has gone through an artificial preparation. This I have often noticed.

Verse 13. *Which cheereth God and man*] I believe אלהים *elohim* here is to be taken in the same sense proposed on ver. 9. Vast libations of *wine,* as well as much *oil,* were used in heathenish sacrifices and offerings; and it was their opinion that the gods *actually partook* of, and were *delighted* with, both the *wine* and *oil.* The pagan mythology furnishes the most exquisite *wines* to its gods in heaven, and hence the *nectar* and *ambrosia* so much talked of and praised by the ancients. It is not reasonable to suppose that Jotham makes any reference here to the sacrifices, oblations, and perfumes offered to the true God. This language the idolatrous Shechemites could scarcely understand. What could the worshippers of *Baalberith* know of the worship of the God who gave his law to Moses? And it is not very likely that Jotham himself was well acquainted with the sacred rites of the Mosaic religion, as they had been little preached in his time.

Verse 14. *Then said all the trees unto the bramble*] The word אטד *atad,* which we translate *bramble,* is supposed to mean the *rhamnus,* which is the largest of thorns, producing dreadful spikes, similar to darts. See *Theodoret* on Psa. lviii. 10.

There is much of the *moral* of this fable contained in the different kinds of *trees* mentioned. 1. The *olive;* the most *profitable* tree to its owner, having few equals either for food or medicine. 2. The *fig tree;* one of the most *fruitful* of trees, and yielding one of the most delicious fruits, and superior to all others for *sweetness.* 3. The *vine,* which alone yields a liquor that, when properly prepared, and taken in strict moderation, is friendly both to the body and mind of man, having a most direct tendency to invigorate both. 4. The *bramble* or *thorn,* which, however useful as a hedge, is dangerous to come near; and is here the emblem of an impious, cruel, and oppressive king. As the *olive, fig,* and *vine,* are said in this fable to refuse the royalty, because in consequence,

they intimate, they should lose their *own privileges,* we learn that to be *invested with power* for the *public good* can be no *privilege* to the sovereign. If he discharge the office faithfully, it will plant his pillow with thorns, fill his soul with anxious cares, rob him of rest and quiet, and, in a word, will be to him a source of distress and misery. All this is represented here under the emblem of the trees losing their *fatness,* their *sweetness* and *good fruits,* and their *cheering influence.* In short, we see from this most sensible fable that the *beneficent, benevolent,* and highly *illuminated* mind, is ever averse from the love of power; and that those who *do seek it* are the *thoughtless,* the *vain,* the *ambitious,* and those who wish for power merely for the purpose of *self-gratification;* persons who have neither the *disposition* nor the *knowledge* to use power for the advantage of the *community;* and who, while they boast great things, and make great pretensions and promises, are the tyrants of the people, and often through their ambition, like the bramble in the fable, kindle a flame of foreign or domestic war, in which their subjects are consumed.

The sleepless nights and corroding cares of sovereignty, are most forcibly described by a poet of our own, whose equal in describing the inward workings of the human heart, in all varieties of character and circumstances, has never appeared either in ancient or modern times. Hear what he puts in the mouth of two of his care-worn kings:—

"How many thousand of my poorest subjects
Are at this hour asleep?—Sleep, gentle sleep,
Nature's soft nurse! how have I frighted thee,
That thou no more wilt weigh my eyelids down,
And steep my senses in forgetfulness?
Why rather, sleep, liest thou in smoky cribs,
Upon uneasy pallets stretching thee,
And hush'd with buzzing night-flies to thy slumber
Than in the perfumed chambers of the great,
Under the canopies of costly state,
And lull'd with sounds of sweetest melody?
O thou dull god! why liest thou with the vile
In loathsome beds; and leav'st the kingly couch
A watch-case, or a common 'larum bell?
Wilt thou upon the high and giddy mast
Seal up the ship-boy's eyes, and rock his brains
In cradle of the rude imperious surge;
And in the visitation of the winds,
Who take the ruffian billows by the top,
Curling their monstrous heads and hanging them,
With deafening clamours, in the slippery clouds,
That, with the hurly, death itself awakes?
Canst thou, O partial sleep! give thy repose
To the wet sea-boy, in an hour so rude;
And, in the calmest and most stillest night,

A. M. 2799
B. C. 1205
An. Exod. Isr.
286
Anno ante
I. Olymp. 429

15 And the bramble said unto the trees, If in truth ye anoint me king over you, *then* come *and* put your trust in my ᵗshadow: and if not, ᵘlet fire come out of the bramble, and devour the ᵛcedars of Lebanon.

16 Now therefore, if ye have done truly and sincerely, in that ye have made Abimelech king, and if ye have dealt well with Jerubbaal and his house, and have done unto him ʷaccording to the deserving of his hands;

17 (For my father fought for you, and ˣadventured his life far, and delivered you out of the hand of Midian:

18 ʸAnd ye are risen up against my father's house this day, and have slain his sons, threescore and ten persons, upon one stone, and have made Abimelech, the son of his maidservant, king over the men of Shechem, because he *is* your brother;)

19 If ye then have dealt truly and sincerely

with Jerubbaal and with his house this day, *then* ᶻrejoice ye in Abimelech, and let him also rejoice in you:

20 But if not, ᵃlet fire come out from Abimelech, and devour the men of Shechem, and the house of Millo; and let fire come out from the men of Shechem, and from the house of Millo, and devour Abimelech.

21 And Jotham ran away, and fled, and went to ᵇBeer, and dwelt there, for fear of Abimelech his brother.

A. M. 2799
B. C. 1205
An. Exod. Isr.
286
Anno ante
I. Olymp. 429

22 When Abimelech had reigned three years over Israel,

A. M. 2802
B. C. 1202
An. Exod. Isr.
289
Anno ante
I. Olymp. 426

23 Then ᶜGod sent an evil spirit between Abimelech and the men of Shechem; and the men of Shechem ᵈdealt treacherously with Abimelech:

24 ᵉThat the cruelty *done* to the threescore and ten sons of Jerubbaal might come, and their blood be laid upon Abimelech their bro-

---

ᵗIsa. xxx. 2; Dan. iv. 12; Hos. xiv. 7——ᵘVerse 20; Num. xxi. 28; Ezek. xix. 14——ᵛ2 Kings xiv. 9; Psa. civ. 16; Isa. ii. 13; xxxvii. 24; Ezek. xxxi. 3——ʷChap. viii. 35——ˣHeb. *cast his life*——ʸVer. 5, 6——ᶻIsa. viii. 6; Phil. iii. 3

ᵃVer. 15, 56, 57——ᵇ2 Sam. xx. 14——ᶜ1 Sam. xvi. 14; xviii. 9, 10; see 1 Kings xii. 15; xxii. 22; 2 Chron. x. 15; xviii. 19, &c.; Isa. xix. 2, 14——ᵈIsa. xxxiii. 1 ᵉ1 Kings ii. 32; Esth. ix. 25; Psa. vii. 16; Matt. xxiii. 35, 36

With all appliances and means to boot,
Deny it to a king? Then, happy low, lie down!
Uneasy lies the head that wears a crown."——
"O hard condition! twin-born with greatness,
Subjected to the breath of every fool,
Whose sense no more can feel but his own
　　wringing!
What infinite heart's ease must kings neglect,
That private men enjoy!
And what have kings, that privates have not
　　too,
Save ceremony, save general ceremony?"——
"'Tis not the balm, the sceptre, and the ball,
The sword, the mace, the crown imperial,
The intertissued robe of gold and pearl,
The farced title running 'fore the king,
The throne he sits on, nor the tide of pomp
That beats upon the high shore of this world,
No, not all these, thrice gorgeous ceremony,
Not all these, laid in bed majestical,
Can sleep so soundly as the wretched slave."
　　　　　　　　　　　SHAKSPEARE.

This is precisely the sentiment expressed in the denial of the olive, fig tree, and vine.

Verse 15. *Come* and *put your trust in my shadow*] The vain boast of the *would-be* sovereign; and of the man who is seeking to be put into power by the suffrages of the people. All *promise*, no *performance.*

Let fire come out of the bramble] A strong catachresis. The bramble was *too low* to give shelter to any tree; and so far from being able to *consume* others, that the smallest fire will reduce it to *ashes*, and that in the *shortest time.* Hence the very *transitory* mirth of fools is said to be *like the cracking of thorns under a pot.* Abimelech was the *bramble;* and the *cedars* of

Lebanon, all the *nobles* and *people* of Israel. Could they therefore suppose that such a lowborn, uneducated, cruel, and murderous man, could be a proper protector, or a humane governor? He who could imbrue his hands in the blood of his brethren in order to get into power, was not likely to stop at any means to retain that power when possessed. If, therefore, they took him for their king, they might rest assured that desolation and blood would mark the whole of his reign.

The condensed moral of the whole fable is this: Weak, worthless, and wicked men, will ever be foremost to thrust themselves into power; and, in the end, to bring ruin upon themselves, and on the unhappy people over whom they preside.

Verse 20. *Let fire come out from Abimelech*] As the thorn or bramble may be the means of kindling other wood, because it may be easily ignited; so shall Abimelech be the cause of kindling a *fire* of civil discord among you, that shall consume the rulers and great men of your country. A prophetic declaration of what would take place.

Verse 21. *Went to Beer*] Mr. Maundrell, in his journey from Aleppo to Jerusalem, p. 64, 5th edit., mentions a place of this name, which he thinks to be that to which Jotham fled, and supposed to be the same as Michmash, 1 Sam. xiv. It is situated, he says, towards the south, on an easy declivity; and has a *fountain* of excellent water at the bottom of the hill from which it has taken its name.

Verse 23. *God sent an evil spirit*] He permitted jealousies to take place which produced factions; and these factions produced insurrections, civil contentions, and slaughter.

A. M. 2802
B. C. 1202
An. Exod. Isr. 289
Anno ante
I. Olymp. 426

ther, which slew them; and
upon the men of Shechem,
which [f]aided him in the killing
of his brethren.
25 And the men of Shechem set liers in
wait for him in the top of the mountains, and
they robbed all that came along that way by
them: and it was told Abimelech.
26 And Gaal the son of Ebed came with
his brethren, and went over to Shechem: and
the men of Shechem put their confidence in
him.
27 And they went out into the fields, and
gathered their vineyards, and trode *the
grapes,* and made [g]merry, and went into [h]the
house of their god, and did eat and drink,
and cursed Abimelech.
28 And Gaal the son of Ebed said, [i]Who
is Abimelech, and who *is* Shechem, that we
should serve him? *is* not *he* the son of Jerubbaal? and Zebul his officer? serve the
men of [k]Hamor the father of Shechem: for
why should we serve him?
29 And [l]would to God this people were
under my hand! then would I remove Abimelech. And he said to Abimelech, Increase
thine army, and come out.
30 And when Zebul the ruler of the city
heard the words of Gaal the son of Ebed, his
anger was [m]kindled.
31 And he sent messengers unto Abimelech
[n]privily, saying, Behold, Gaal
the son of Ebed and his brethren
be come to Shechem; and, behold, they fortify the city against
thee.

A. M. 2802
B. C. 1202
An. Exod. Isr. 289
Anno ante
I. Olymp. 426

32 Now therefore up by night, thou and the
people that *is* with thee, and lie in wait in
the field:
33 And it shall be, *that* in the morning, as
soon as the sun is up, thou shalt rise early,
and set upon the city: and, behold, *when* he
and the people that *is* with him come out
against thee, then mayest thou do to them [o]as
thou shalt find occasion.
34 And Abimelech rose up, and all the people that *were* with him, by night, and they
laid wait against Shechem in four companies.
35 And Gaal the son of Ebed went out, and
stood in the entering of the gate of the city:
and Abimelech rose up, and the people that
were with him, from lying in wait.
36 And when Gaal saw the people, he said
to Zebul, Behold, there come people down
from the top of the mountains. And Zebul
said unto him, Thou seest the shadow of the
mountains as *if they were* men.
37 And Gaal spake again and said, See,
there come people down by the [p]middle of
the land, and another company come along
by the plain of [q]Meonenim.
38 Then said Zebul unto him, Where *is*

[f]Heb. *strengthened his hands to kill*——[g]Or, *songs;* see Isa. xvi. 9, 10; Jer. xxv. 30——[h]Verse 4——[i]1 Samuel xxv. 10; 1 Kings xii. 16——[k]Gen. xxxiv. 2, 6——[l]2 Sam. xv. 4

[m]Or, *hot*——[n]Heb. *craftily,* or, *to Tormah*——[o]Heb. *as thine hand shall find;* 1 Sam. x. 7; xxv. 8; Eccles. ix. 10——[p]Heb. *navel*——[q]Or, *the regarders of the times;* Deut. xviii. 14

Verse 25. *The men of Shechem set liers in wait*] It pleased God to punish this bad man by the very persons who had contributed to his iniquitous elevation. So God often makes the instruments of men's sins the means of their punishment. It is likely that although Abimelech had his chief residence at *Shechem,* yet he frequently went to *Ophrah,* the city of his father; his claim to which there was none to oppose, as he had slain all his brethren. It was probably in his passage between those two places that the Shechemites had posted cut-throats, in order to assassinate him; as such men had no moral principle, they robbed and plundered all who came that way.

Verse 26. *Gaal the son of Ebed*] Of this person we know no more than is here told. He was probably one of the descendants of the Canaanites, who hoped from the state of the public mind, and their disaffection to Abimelech, to cause a revolution, and thus to restore the ancient government as it was under *Hamor,* the father of *Shechem.*

Verse 28. *Zebul his officer*] פקידו *pekido, his overseer;* probably governor of Shechem in his absence.

Verse 29. *Would to God this people were under my hand*] The very words and conduct of a sly, hypocritical demagogue.

Increase thine army, and come out.] When he found his party strong, and the public feeling warped to his side, then he appears to have sent a challenge to Abimelech, to come out and fight him.

Verse 31. *They fortify the city against thee.*] Under pretence of repairing the walls and towers, they were actually putting the place in a state of defence, intending to seize on the government as soon as they should find Abimelech coming against them. *Fortifying the city* may mean seducing the inhabitants from their loyalty to Abimelech.

Verse 35. *Stood in the entering of the gate*] Having probably got some intimation of the designs of Zebul and Abimelech.

Verse 37. *By the plain of Meonenim.*] Some translate, *by the way of the oaks,* or oaken groves; others, *by the way of the magicians,* or

A. M. 2802
B. C. 1202
An. Exod. Isr.
289
Anno ante
I. Olymp. 426

now thy mouth, wherewith thou [r]saidst, Who *is* Abimelech, that we should serve him? *is* not this the people that thou hast despised? go out, I pray now, and fight with them.

39 And Gaal went out before the men of Shechem, and fought with Abimelech.

40 And Abimelech chased him, and he fled before him, and many were overthrown *and* wounded, *even* unto the entering of the gate.

41 And Abimelech dwelt at Arumah: and Zebul thrust out Gaal and his brethren, that they should not dwell in Shechem.

42 And it came to pass on the morrow that the people went out into the field; and they told Abimelech.

43 And he took the people, and divided them into three companies, and laid wait in the field, and looked, and, behold, the people *were* come forth out of the city: and he rose up against them, and smote them.

44 And Abimelech, and the company that *was* with him, rushed forward, and stood in the entering of the gate of the city: and the two *other* companies ran upon all *the people* that *were* in the fields, and slew them.

45 And Abimelech fought against the city all that day; and [s]he took the city, and slew the people that *was* therein, and [t]beat down the city, and sowed it with salt.

46 And when all the men of the tower of

Shechem heard *that,* they entered into a hold of the house [u]of the god Berith.

A. M. 2802
B. C. 1202
An. Exod. Isr.
289
Anno ante
I. Olymp. 426

47 And it was told Abimelech, that all the men of the tower of Shechem were gathered together.

48 And Abimelech gat him up to Mount [v]Zalmon, he and all the people that *were* with him; and Abimelech took an axe in his hand, and cut down a bough from the trees, and took it, and laid *it* on his shoulder, and said unto the people that *were* with him, What ye have seen [w]me do, make haste, *and* do as I *have done.*

49 And all the people likewise cut down every man his bough, and followed Abimelech, and put *them* to the hold, and set the hold on fire upon them; so that all the men of the tower of Shechem died also, about a thousand men and women.

50 Then went Abimelech to Thebez, and encamped against Thebez, and took it.

51 But there was a strong tower within the city, and thither fled all the men and women, and all they of the city, and shut *it* to them, and gat them up to the top of the tower.

52 And Abimelech came unto the tower, and fought against it, and went hard unto the door of the tower to burn it with fire.

53 And a certain woman [x]cast a piece of a millstone upon Abimelech's head, and all to break his skull.

54 Then [y]he called hastily unto the young

---

[r]Ver. 28, 29——[s]Ver. 20——[t]Deut. xxix. 23; 1 Kings xii. 25; 2 Kings iii. 25

[u]Chap. viii. 33——[v]Psalm lxviii. 14——[w]Heb. *I have done*——[x]2 Sam. xi. 21——[y]So 1 Sam. xxxi. 4

---

regarders of the times, as in our *margin.* Probably it was a place in which augurs and soothsayers dwelt.

Verse 45. *And sowed it with salt.*] Intending that the destruction of this city should be a *perpetual* memorial of his achievements. The *salt* was not designed to render it *barren,* as some have imagined; for who would think of cultivating a city? but as *salt* is an emblem of *incorruption* and *perpetuity,* it was no doubt designed to *perpetuate* the memorial of this transaction, and as a token that he wished this desolation to be *eternal.* This *sowing a place with salt* was a custom in different nations to express *permanent desolation* and *abhorrence.* *Sigonius* observes that when the city of *Milan* was taken, in A. D. 1162, the walls were razed, and *it was sown with salt.* And *Brantome* informs us that it was ancient custom in France to *sow the house* of a man *with salt,* who had been declared a *traitor* to his king. Charles IX., king of France, the most base and perfidious of human beings, caused the house of the *Admiral Coligni* (whom he and the Duke of *Guise* caused to be murdered, with thousands

more of Protestants, on the eve of St. Bartholomew, 1572) to *be sown with salt!* How many houses have been since *sown with salt* in France by the just judgments of God, in revenge for the massacre of the Protestants on the eve of St. Bartholomew! *Yet for all this God's wrath is not turned away, but his hand is stretched out still.*

Verse 46. *A hold of the house of the god Berith.*] This must mean the *precincts* of the temple, as we find there were a thousand men and women together in that place.

Verse 53. *A piece of a millstone*] פלח רכב *pelach recheb,* a piece of a *chariot wheel;* but the word is used in other places for *upper millstones,* and is so understood here by the *Vulgate, Septuagint, Syriac,* and *Arabic.*

And all to break his skull.] A most nonsensical version of ותריץ את גלגלתו *vattarits eth gulgolto,* which is literally, *And she brake,* or *fractured, his skull.* Plutarch, in his life of Pyrrhus, observes that this king was killed at the siege of Thebes, by a *piece of a tile,* which a *woman* threw upon his head.

Verse 54. *Draw thy sword, and slay me*] It

A. M. 2802
B. C. 1202
An. Exod. Isr.
289
Anno ante
I. Olymp. 426 man his armour-bearer, and said unto him, Draw thy sword, and slay me, that men say not of me, A woman slew him. And his young man thrust him through, and he died.

55 And when the men of Israel saw that Abimelech was dead, they departed every man unto his place.

ªVer. 24; Job xxxi. 3; Psa. xciv.

---

was a disgrace to be killed by a woman; on this account, Seneca the tragedian deplores the death of Hercules:—

O turpe fatum! femina Herculeæ necis
Autor feritur.   Herc. Oetæus, ver. 1177.

"O dishonourable fate! a woman is reported to have been author of the death of Hercules."

Abimelech was also afraid that if he fell thus mortally wounded into the hands of his enemies, they might treat him with cruelty and insult.

Verse 56. *Thus God rendered, &c.*] Both the fratricide Abimelech, and the unprincipled men of Shechem, had the iniquity visited upon them of which they had been guilty. Man's judgment may be avoided; but there is no escape from the judgments of God.

I HAVE said that the fable of Jotham is the *oldest*, and perhaps the *best*, in the world; and referred for other particulars to the end of the chapter.

On the general subject of fable, apologue, and parable, the reader will find a considerable dissertation at the end of Matt. xiii.; I shall add but a few things here, and they shall refer to the oldest *collection* of fables extant. These are of *Indian origin*, and are preserved in the *Sanscreet*, from which they have been translated into different languages, both Asiatic and European, under various titles. The *collection* is called *Hitopadesa*, and the author *Veshnoo Sarma;* but they are known in Europe by *The Tales and Fables of Bidpay, or Pilpay, an ancient Indian Philosopher*. Of this collection Sir William Jones takes the following notice:—
"The fables of Veshnoo Sarma, whom we ridiculously call *Pilpay*, are the most beautiful, if not the most ancient, collection of apologues in the world. They were first translated from the Sanscreet, in the sixth century, by *Buzerchumihr*, or *bright as the sun*, the chief physician, and afterwards the vizir of the great *Anushirwan;* and are extant under various names, in more than *twenty* languages. But their original title is *Hitopadesa*, or *amicable instruction;* and as the very existence of *Æsop*, whom the Arabs believe to have been an *Abyssinian*, appears rather doubtful, I am not disinclined to suppose that the first moral fables which appeared in Europe were of *Indian* or *Æthiopian origin*."

Mr. Frazer, in his collection of Oriental MSS. at the end of his History of *Nadir Shah*, gives us the following account of this curious and instructive work:—

"The ancient brahmins of India, after a good deal of time and labour, compiled a treatise, (which they called *Kurtuk Dumnik*,) in which

56 ᶻThus God rendered the wickedness of Abimelech, which he did unto his father, in slaying his seventy brethren:

57 And all the evil of the men of Shechem did God render upon their heads: and upon them came ªthe curse of Jotham the son of Jerubbaal.

23; Prov. v. 22——ªVer. 20

---

were inserted the choicest treasure of wisdom, and the most perfect rules for governing a people. This book they presented to their *rajahs*, who kept it with the greatest secrecy and care. About the time of *Mohammed's* birth or the latter end of the sixth century, *Noishervan* the Just, who then reigned in Persia, discovered a great inclination to see that book; for which purpose *Burzuvia*, a physician, who had a surprising talent in learning several languages, particularly *Sanskerritt*, was introduced to him as the most proper person to be employed to get a copy of it. He went to *India*, where, after some years' stay, and great trouble, he procured it. It was translated into the *Pehluvi* (the ancient Persian language) by him and *Buzrjumehr*, the vizir. *Noishervan*, ever after, and all his successors, the Persian kings, had this book in high esteem, and took the greatest care to keep it secret. At last *Abu Jaffer Munsour zu Nikky*, who was the second caliph of the Abassi reign, by great search got a copy of it in the *Pehluvi* language, and ordered *Imam Hassan Abdal Mokaffa*, who was the most learned of the age, to translate it into *Arabic*. This prince ever after made it his guide, not only in affairs relating to the government, but also in private life.
"In the year 380 of the *Hegira*, Sultan *Mahmud Ghazi* put into verse; and afterwards, in the year 515, by order of *Bheram Shah ben Massaud*, that which *Abdal Mokaffa* had translated was retranslated into *Persic* by *Abdul Mala Nasser Allah Mustofi;* and this is that *Kulila Dumna* which is now extant. As this latter had too many Arabic verses and obsolete phrases in it, *Molana Ali ben Hessein Vaes*, at the request of *Emir Soheli*, keeper of the seals to Sultan *Hossein Mirza*, put it into a more modern style, and gave it the title of *Anuar Soheli*.
"In the year 1002, the great moghul *Jalal o Din Mohommed Akbar* ordered his own secretary and vizir, the learned *Abul Fazl*, to illustrate the obscure passages, abridge the long digressions, and put it into such a style as would be most familiar to all capacities; which he accordingly did, and gave it the name of *Ayar Danish*, or the *Criterion* of *Wisdom*." This far Mr. *Frazer*, under the word *Ayar Danish*.
"In the year 1709," says Dr. *Wilkins*, "the *Kulila Dumna*, the Persian version of *Abul Mala Nasser Allah Mustofi*, made in the 515th year of the *Hegira*, was translated into *French*, with the title of *Les Conseils et les Maximes de Pilpay, Philosophe Indien, sur les divers Etats de la Vie*. This edition resembles the *Hitopadesa* more than any other then seen; and is evidently the immediate original of the

English *Instructive and entertaining Fables of Pilpay, an ancient Indian philosopher,* which, in 1775, had gone through *five* editions.

"The *Anuar Soheli,* above mentioned, about the year 1540, was rendered into the *Turkish* language; and the translator is said to have bestowed twenty years' labour upon it. In the year 1724, this edition M. *Galland* began to translate into French, and the first four chapters were then published; but, in the year 1778, M. *Cardonne* completed the work, in three volumes, giving it the name of *Contes et Fables Indiennes de Bidpai et de Lokman; traduites d' Ali Tcheleby ben Saleh, auteur Turk;* 'Indian Tales and Fables of Bidpay and Lockman, translated from Aly Tcheleby ben Saleh, a Turkish author.' "

The fables of *Lockman* were published in *Arabic* and *Latin,* with notes, by *Erpenius,* 4to. Amstel., 1636; and by the celebrated *Golius,* at the end of his edition of *Erpen's* Arabic Grammar, Lugd. Bat., 1656, with additional notes; and also in the edition of the same Grammar, by *Albert Schultens,* Lugd. Bat., 1748, 4to. They are only thirty-seven in number.

Of the *Hitopadesa,* or fables of *Veshnoo Sarma,* we have two very elegant *English* transla-tions from the original Sanscreet: one by Sir *William Jones,* printed in his works, 4to., vol. 6, Lond. 1799; the other by the father of Sanscreet literature in Europe, Dr. *Charles Wilkins,* of the India House, 8vo., Bath, 1787, with a collection of very important notes.

The *Bahar Danush,* or *Sea of Wisdom,* abounds with maxims, apothegms, &c., similar to those in the preceding works; this was most faithfully translated from the *Persian,* by Dr. *Jonathan Scott,* late Persian secretary to his excellency *Warren Hastings,* published in three vols. 12mo., with notes, Shrewsbury, 1799. This is the most correct version of any Persian work yet offered to the public. The original is by *Einaut Ullah.* Of these works it may be said, they contain the wisdom of the oriental world; and many of the numerous maxims interspersed through them yield in importance only to those in the sacred writings. The fables attributed to *Æsop* have been reapeatedly published in *Greek* and *Latin,* as well as in all the languages of Europe, and are well known. Those of *Phœdrus* are in general only a metrical version of the fables of *Æsop.* The compositions of *La Fontaine,* in French, and those of Mr. *Gay,* in English, are very valuable.

CHAPTER X

Tola judges Israel twenty-three years, 1, 2. Jair is judge twenty-two years, 3–5. After him the Israelites rebel against God, and are delivered into the hands of the Philistines and Ammonites eighteen years, 6–9. They humble themselves, and God reproves them, 10–14. They put away their strange gods, and gather together against the Ammonites, 15–17. The chiefs of Gilead inquire concerning a captain to head them against the Ammonites, 18.

A. M. 2802
B. C. 1202
An. Exod. Isr.
289
Anno ante
I. Olymp. 426

AND after Abimelech there [a]arose to [b]defend [c]Israel Tola the son of Puah, the son of Dodo, a man of Issachar; and he dwelt in Shamir in Mount Ephraim.

A. M. 2825
B. C. 1179
An. Exod. Isr.
312
Anno ante
I. Olymp. 403

2 And he judged Israel twenty and three years, and died, and was buried in Shamir.

3 And after him arose Jair, a Gileadite, and judged Israel twenty and two years.

4 And he had thirty sons that [d]rode on thirty ass colts, and they had thirty cities, [e]which are called [f]Havoth-jair unto this day, which *are* in the land of Gilead.

A. M. 2825
B. C. 1179
An. Exod. Isr.
312
Anno ante
I. Olymp. 403

5 And Jair died, and was buried in Camon.

6 And [g]the children of Israel did evil again in the sight of the LORD, and [h]served Baalim, and Ashtaroth, and [i]the gods of Syria, and the gods of [k]Zidon, and the gods

A. M. 2847
B. C. 1157
An. Exod. Isr.
334
Anno ante
I. Olymp. 381

---

[a]Ch. ii. 16—— [b]Or, *deliver*—— [c]Heb. *save*——[d]Ch. v. 10; xii. 14—— [e]Deut. iii. 14—— [f]Or, *the villages of Jair;*

Num. xxxii. 41—— [g]Ch. ii. 11; iii. 7; iv. 1; vi. 1; xiii. 1 [h]Ch. ii. 13—— [i]Ch. ii. 12—— [k]1 Kings xi. 33; Psa. cvi. 36

NOTES ON CHAP. X

Verse 1. Tola the son of Puah] As this Tola continued twenty-three years a judge of Israel after the troubles of Abimelech's reign, it is likely that the land had rest, and that the enemies of the Israelites had made no hostile incursions into the land during his presidency and that of Jair; which, together continued forty-five years.

Verse 4. He had thirty sons, &c.] It appears that there was both peace and prosperity during the time that Jair governed Israel; he had, it seems, provided for his family, and given a village to each of his thirty sons; which were, in consequence, called *Havoth Jair* or the *villages of Jair.* Their *riding on thirty ass colts* seems to intimate that they were persons of consideration, and kept up a certain dignity in their different departments.

Verse 6. And served Baalim] They became *universal idolaters,* adopting every god of the surrounding nations. *Baalim* and *Ashtaroth* may signify *gods* and *goddesses* in general. These are enumerated: 1. *The gods of Syria; Bel* and *Saturn,* or *Jupiter* and *Astarte.* 2. *Gods of Zidon; Ashtaroth, Astarte* or *Venus.* 3. *The gods of Moab; Chemosh.* 4. *Gods of the children of Ammon; Milcom.* 5. *Gods of the Philistines; Dagon.* See 1 Kings xi. 33, and 1 Sam. v. 2. These are called *gods* because their images and places of worship were multiplied throughout the land.

A. M. 2847
B. C. 1157
An. Exod. Isr. 334
Anno ante I. Olymp. 381

of Moab, and the gods of the children of Ammon, and the gods of the Philistines, and forsook the LORD, and served not him.

7 And the anger of the LORD was hot against Israel, and he ¹sold them into the hands of the Philistines, and into the hands of the children of Ammon.

8 And that year they vexed and ᵐoppressed the children of Israel eighteen years, all the children of Israel that *were* on the other side Jordan in the land of the Amorites, which *is* in Gilead.

9 Moreover the children of Ammon passed over Jordan to fight also against Judah, and against Benjamin, and against the house of Ephraim; so that Israel was sore distressed.

10 ⁿAnd the children of Israel cried unto the LORD, saying, We have sinned against thee, both because we have forsaken our God, and also served Baalim.

11 And the LORD said unto the children of Israel, *Did* not *I deliver you* ᵒfrom the Egyptians, and ᵖfrom the Amorites, �qfrom the children of Ammon, ʳand from the Philistines?

12 ˢThe Zidonians also, ᵗand the Amalek-ites, and the Maonites, ᵘdid oppress you; and ye cried to me, and I delivered you out of their hand.

A. M. 2847
B. C. 1157
An. Exod. Isr. 334
Anno ante I. Olymp. 381

13 ᵛYet ye have forsaken me, and served other gods: wherefore I will deliver you no more.

14 Go and ᵂcry unto the gods which ye have chosen; let them deliver you in the time of your tribulation.

15 And the children of Israel said unto the LORD, We have sinned: ˣdo thou unto us whatsoever ʸseemeth good unto thee; deliver us only, we pray thee, this day.

16 ᶻAnd they put away the ªstrange gods from among them, and served the LORD: and ᵇhis soul ᶜwas grieved for the misery of Israel.

17 Then the children of Ammon were ᵈgathered together, and encamped in Gilead. And the children of Israel assembled themselves together, and encamped in ᵉMizpeh.

18 And the people *and* princes of Gilead said one to another, What man *is he* that will begin to fight against the children of Ammon? he shall ᶠbe head over all the inhabitants of Gilead.

ˡChap. ii. 14; 1 Sam. xii. 9——ᵐHeb. *crushed*——ⁿ1 Sam. xii. 10——ᵒExod. xiv. 30——ᵖNum. xxi. 21, 24, 25 qChap. iii. 12, 13——ʳChap. iii. 31——ˢChap. v. 19 ᵗCh. vi. 3——ᵘPsa. cvi. 42, 43——ᵛDeut. xxxii. 15; Jer. ii. 13——ᵂDeut. xxxii. 37, 38; 2 Kings iii. 13; Jer. ii. 28

ˣ1 Sam. iii. 18; 2 Sam. xv. 26——ʸHeb. *is good in thine eyes*——ᶻ2 Chron. vii. 14; xv. 8; Jer. xviii. 7, 8 ªHeb. *gods of strangers*——ᵇPsa. cvi. 44, 55; Isa. lxiii. 9 ᶜHeb. *was shortened*——ᵈHeb. *cried together*——ᵉChap. xi. 11, 29; Gen. xxxi. 49——ᶠChap. xi. 8, 11

Verse 7. *The anger of the Lord was hot*] This Divine displeasure was manifested in delivering them into the hands of the Philistines and the Ammonites. The former dwelt on the *western* side of Jordan; the latter, on the *eastern:* and it appears that they joined their forces on this occasion to distress and ruin the Israelites, though the Ammonites were the most active.

Verse 11. *And the Lord said*] By what means these reproofs were conveyed to the Israelites, we know not: it must have been by an *angel*, a *prophet*, or some *holy man* inspired for the occasion.

Verse 15. *We have sinned*] The reprehension of this people was kind, pointed, and solemn; and their repentance deep. And they gave proofs that their repentance was genuine, by putting away all their idols: but they were ever *fickle* and *uncertain*.

Verse 16. *And his soul was grieved for the misery of Israel.*] What a proof of the *philanthropy* of God! Here his compassions moved on a *small scale;* but it was the same principle that led him to give his Son Jesus Christ to be a sacrifice for the sins of the WHOLE *world.* God *grieves* for the miseries to which his creatures are reduced by their own sins. Be astonished, ye heavens, at this; and shout for joy, all ye

inhabitants of the earth! for, through the love whence this compassion flowed, God has visited and redeemed a lost world!

Verse 17. *The children of Ammon were gathered together*] Literally, *they cried against Israel*—they sent out *criers* in different directions to stir up all the enemies of Israel; and when they had made a mighty collection, they encamped in Gilead.

Verse 18. *What man* is he *that will begin to fight*] It appears that, although the spirit of *patriotism* had excited the people at large to come forward against their enemies, yet they had no general, none to lead them forth to battle. God, however, who had accepted their sincere repentance, raised them up an able captain in the person of Jephthah; and in him the suffrages of the people were concentrated, as we shall see in the following chapter.

In those ancient times much depended on the onset; a war was generally terminated in one battle, the first impression was therefore of great consequence, and it required a person *skilful, valorous,* and *strong,* to head the attack. Jephthah was a person in whom all these qualifications appear to have met. When God purposes to deliver, he, in the course of his providence, will find out, employ, and direct the proper *means.*

CHAPTER XI

The history of Jephthah, and his covenant with the Gileadites, 1–10. He is elected by the people, 11. Sends an embassy to the king of the Ammonites, to inquire why they invaded Israel; and receives an answer, to which he sends back a spirited reply, 12–27. This is disregarded by the Ammonites, and Jephthah prepares for battle, 28, 29. His vow, 30, 31. He attacks and defeats them, 32, 33. On his return to Mizpeh he is met by his daughter, whom, according to his vow, he dedicates to the Lord, 34–40.

A. M. 2847
B. C. 1157
An. Exod. Isr.
334
Anno ante
I. Olymp. 381

NOW [a]Jephthah the Gileadite was [b]a mighty man of valour, and he *was* the son of [c]a harlot: and Gilead begat Jephthah.

2 And Gilead's wife bare him sons; and his wife's sons grew up, and they thrust out Jephthah, and said unto him, Thou shalt not inherit in our father's house; for thou *art* the son of a strange woman.

3 Then Jephthah fled [d]from his brethren, and dwelt in the land of Tob: and there were gathered [e]vain men to Jephthah, and went out with him.

A. M. 2865
B. C. 1139
An. Exod. Isr.
352
Anno ante
I. Olymp. 363

4 And it came to pass [f]in process of time, that the children of Ammon made war against Israel.

5 And it was so, that when the children of Ammon made war against Israel, the elders of Gilead went to fetch Jephthah out of the land of Tob:

6 And they said unto Jephthah, Come, and be our captain, that we may fight with the children of Ammon.

7 And Jephthah said unto the children of Gilead, [g]Did not ye hate me, and expel me out of my father's house? and why are ye come unto me now when ye are in distress?

A. M. 2865
B. C. 1139
An. Exod. Isr.
352
Anno ante
I. Olymp. 363

8 [h]And the elders of Gilead said unto Jephthah, Therefore we [i]turn again to thee now, that thou mayest go with us, and fight against the children of Ammon, and be [k]our head over all the inhabitants of Gilead.

9 And Jephthah said unto the elders of Gilead, If ye bring me home again to fight against the children of Ammon, and the LORD deliver them before me, shall I be your head?

10 And the elders of Gilead said unto Jephthah, [l]The LORD [m]be witness between us, if we do not so according to thy words.

11 Then Jephthah went with the elders of Gilead, and the people made him [n]head and captain over them: and Jephthah uttered all his words [o]before the LORD in Mizpeh.

---

[a]Heb. xi. 32, called, *Jephthae*——[b]Chap. vi. 12; 2 Kings v. 1——[c]Heb. *a woman a harlot*——[d]Heb. *from the face*——[e]Chap. ix. 4; 1 Sam. xxii. 2——[f]Heb. *after days*

[g]Gen. xxvi. 27——[h]Chap. x. 18——[i]Luke xvii. 4 [k]Chap. x. 18——[l]Jer. xlii. 5——[m]Heb. *be the hearer between us*——[n]Ver. 8——[o]Chap. x. 17; xx. 1; 1 Sam. x. 17; xi. 15

NOTES ON CHAP. XI

Verse 1. *Now Jephthah—was the son of a harlot*] I think the word זונה *zonah*, which we here render *harlot*, should be translated, as is contended for on Josh. ii. 1, viz. a *hostess, keeper of an inn* or *tavern* for the accommodation of travellers; and thus it is understood by the Targum of Jonathan on this place: והוא בר אתתא פונדקיתא *vehu bar ittetha pundekitha*, "and he was the son of a woman, a *tavern keeper*." See the note referred to above. She was very probably a Canaanite, as she is called, ver. 2, a *strange woman*, אשה אחרת *ishshah achereth*, a *woman of another race;* and on this account his brethren drove him from the family, as he could not have a full right to the inheritance, his mother not being an Israelite.

Verse 3. *There were gathered vain men to Jephthah*] אנשים ריקים *anashim reykim, empty men*—persons destitute of good sense, and profligate in their manners. The word may, however, mean in this place *poor persons*, without property, and without employment. The *versions* in general consider them as *plunderers*.

Verse 4. *The children of Ammon made war*] They had invaded the land of Israel, and were now encamped in Gilead. See chap. x. 17.

Verse 6. *Come, and be our captain*] The Israelites were assembled in Mizpeh, but were without a captain to lead them against the Ammonites. And we find, from the conclusion of the preceding chapter, that they offered the command to any that would accept it.

Verse 8. *Therefore we turn again to thee now*] We are convinced that we have dealt unjustly by thee, and we wish now to repair our fault, and give thee this sincere proof of our regret for having acted unjustly, and of our confidence in thee.

Verse 11. *Jephthah went with the elders*] The *elders* had chosen him for their head; but, to be valid, this choice must be confirmed by the *people;* therefore, it is said, *the people made him head.* But even this did not complete the business; God must be brought in as a party to this transaction; and therefore *Jephthah uttered all his words before the Lord*—the terms made with the elders and the people on which he had accepted the command of the

A. M. 2865
B. C. 1139
An. Exod. Isr.
352
Anno ante
I. Olymp. 363

12 And Jephthah sent messengers unto the king of the children of Ammon, saying, What hast thou to do with me, that thou art come against me to fight in my land?

13 And the king of the children of Ammon answered unto the messengers of Jephthah, ᵖBecause Israel took away my land, when they came up out of Egypt, from Arnon even unto ᑫJabbok, and unto Jordan: now therefore restore those *lands* again peaceably.

14 And Jephthah sent messengers again unto the king of the children of Ammon:

15 And said unto him, Thus saith Jephthah, ʳIsrael took not away the land of Moab, nor the land of the children of Ammon:

16 But when Israel came up from Egypt, and ˢwalked through the wilderness unto the Red Sea, and ᵗcame to Kadesh;

17 Then ᵘIsrael sent messengers unto the king of Edom, saying, Let me, I pray thee, pass through thy land: ᵛbut the king of Edom would not hearken *thereto*. And in like manner they sent unto the king of Moab: but he would not *consent:* and Israel ʷabode in Kadesh.

18 Then they went along through the wilderness, and ˣcompassed the land of Edom,

and the land of Moab, and ʸcame by the east side of the land of Moab, ᶻand pitched on the other side of Arnon, but came not within the border of Moab: for Arnon *was* the border of Moab.

A. M. 2865
B. C. 1139
An. Exod. Isr.
352
Anno ante
I. Olymp. 363

19 And ᵃIsrael sent messengers unto Sihon king of the Amorites, the king of Heshbon; and Israel said unto him, ᵇLet us pass, we pray thee, through thy land unto my place.

20 ᶜBut Sihon trusted not Israel to pass through his coast: but Sihon gathered all his people together, and pitched in Jahaz, and fought against Israel.

21 And the LORD God of Israel delivered Sihon and all his people into the hand of Israel, and they ᵈsmote them: so Israel possessed all the land of the Amorites, the inhabitants of that country.

22 And they possessed ᵉall the coasts of the Amorites, from Arnon even unto Jabbok, and from the wilderness even unto Jordan.

23 So now the LORD God of Israel hath dispossessed the Amorites from before his people Israel, and shouldest thou possess it?

24 Wilt not thou possess that which ᶠChemosh thy god giveth thee to possess? So whomsoever ᵍthe LORD our God shall drive

---

ᵖNum. xxi. 24, 25, 26——ᑫGen. xxxii. 22——ʳDeut. ii. 9, 19——ˢNum. xiv. 25; Deut. i. 40; Josh. v. 6 ᵗNum. xiii. 26; xx. 1; Deut. i. 46——ᵘNum. xx. 14 ᵛNum. xx. 18, 21——ʷNum. xx. 1——ˣNum. xxi. 4; Deut. ii. 1-8——ʸNum. xxi. 11

ᶻNum. xxi. 13; xxii. 36——ᵃNum. xxi. 21; Deut. ii. 26 ᵇNum. xxi. 22; Deut. ii. 27——ᶜNum. xxi. 23; Deut. ii. 32——ᵈNum. xxi. 24, 25; Deut. ii. 33, 34——ᵉDeut. ii. 36——ᶠNum. xxi. 29; 1 Kings xi. 7; Jer. xlviii. 7 ᵍDeut. ix. 4, 5; xviii. 12; Josh. iii. 10

---

army; and, being sure of the Divine approbation, he entered on the work with confidence.

Verse 12. *Jephthah sent messengers*] He wished the Ammonites to explain their own motives for undertaking a war against Israel; as then the justice of his cause would appear more forcibly to the people.

Verse 13. *From Arnon even unto Jabbok, and unto Jordan*] That is, all the land that had formerly belonged to the Amorites, and to the Moabites, who it seems were confederates on this occasion.

Verse 22. *From the wilderness even unto Jordan.*] From Arabia Deserta on the east to Jordan on the west.

Verse 23. *The Lord God of Israel hath dispossessed the Amorites*] Jephthah shows that the Israelites did not take the land of the Moabites or Ammonites, but that of the *Amorites,* which they had conquered from Sihon their king, who had, without cause or provocation, attacked them; and although the Amorites had taken the lands in question from the Ammonites, yet the title by which Israel held them was good, because they took them not from the Ammonites, but conquered them from the Amorites. *So now the Lord—hath dispossessed the*

Amorites.—The circumstances in which the Israelites were when they were attacked by the Amorites, plainly proved, that, unless Jehovah had helped them, they must have been overcome. God defeated the Amorites, and made a grant of their lands to the Israelites; and they had, in consequence, possessed them for *three hundred years,* ver. 26.

Verse 24. *Wilt not thou possess that which Chemosh thy god giveth thee*] As if he had said: "It is a maxim with you, as it is among all nations, that the lands which they conceive to be given them by their gods, they have an absolute right to, and should not relinquish them to any kind of claimant. You suppose that the land which you possess was given you by your god *Chemosh;* and therefore you will not relinquish what you believe you hold by a Divine right. Now, we know that Jehovah, our God, who is the Lord of heaven and earth, has given the Israelites the land of the Amorites; and therefore we will not give it up." The ground of Jephthah's remonstrance was sound and good.

1. The Ammonites had lost their lands in their contests with the Amorites.

2. The Israelites conquered these lands from

A. M. 2865
B. C. 1139
An. Exod. Isr.
352
Anno ante
I. Olymp. 363

out from before us, them will we possess.

25 And now *art* thou any thing better than [h]Balak the son of Zippor, king of Moab? did he ever strive against Israel, or did he ever fight against them,

26 While Israel dwelt in [i]Heshbon and her towns, and in [k]Aroer and her towns, and in all the cities that *be* along by the coasts of Arnon, three hundred years? why therefore did ye not recover *them* within that time?

27 Wherefore I have not sinned against thee, but thou doest me wrong to war against me: the LORD [l]the Judge [m]be judge this day between the children of Israel and the children of Ammon.

28 Howbeit the king of the children of

Ammon hearkened not unto the words of Jephthah which he sent him.

A. M. 2865
B. C. 1139
An. Exod. Isr.
352
Anno ante
I. Olymp. 363

29 Then [n]the Spirit of the LORD came upon [o]Jephthah, and he passed over Gilead, and Manasseh, and passed over Mizpeh of Gilead, and from Mizpeh of Gilead he passed over *unto* the children of Ammon.

30 And Jephthah [p]vowed a vow unto the LORD, and said, If thou shalt without fail deliver the children of Ammon into mine hands,

31 Then it shall be that [q]whatsoever cometh forth of the doors of my house to meet me, when I return in peace from the children of Ammon, [r]shall surely be the LORD's, [s]and [t]I will offer it up for a burnt-offering.

---

[h]Num. xxii. 2; see Josh. xxiv. 9——[i]Num. xxi. 25 [k]Deut. ii. 36——[l]Gen. xviii. 25——[m]Gen. xvi. 5; xxxi. 53; 1 Sam. xxiv. 12, 15——[n]Chap. iii. 10——[o]Jephthah seems to have been judge only of northeast *Israel*

[p]Gen. xxviii. 20; 1 Sam. i. 11——[q]Heb. *that which cometh forth, which shall come forth*——[r]See Lev. xxvii. 2, 3, &c.; 1 Sam. i. 11, 28; ii. 18——[s]Or, *or I will offer it*, &c.——[t]Psa. lxvi. 13; see Lev. xxvii. 11, 12

---

the Amorites, who had waged a most unprincipled war against them.

3. God, who is the Maker of heaven and earth, had given those very lands as a Divine grant to the Israelites.

4. In consequence of this they had possession of them for upwards of three hundred years.

5. These lands were never reclaimed by the Ammonites, though they had repeated opportunities of doing it, whilst the Israelites dwelt in Heshbon, in Aroer, and in the coasts of Arnon; but they did not reclaim them because they knew that the Israelites held them legally. The present pretensions of Ammon were unsupported and unjustifiable.

Verse 27. *The Lord the Judge be judge—between the children of Israel*] If *you* be right, and *we* be wrong, then Jehovah, who is the sovereign and incorruptible Judge, shall determine in your favour; and to Him I submit the righteousness of my cause.

Verse 29. *Then the Spirit of the Lord came upon Jephthah*] The Lord qualified him for the work he had called him to do, and thus gave him the most convincing testimony that his cause was good.

Verse 31. *Shall surely be the Lord's, and I will offer it up for a burnt-offering.*] The text is היה ליהוה והעליתיהו עולה *vehayah layhovah, vehaalithihu olah;* the translation of which, according to the most accurate Hebrew scholars, is this: *I will consecrate it to the Lord, or I will offer it for a burnt-offering;* that is, "If it be a thing fit for a *burnt-offering*, it shall be made one; if fit for the *service of God*, it shall be consecrated to him." That conditions of this kind must have been implied in the vow, is evident enough; to have been made without them, it must have been the vow of a *heathen*, or a *madman.* If a *dog* had met him, this could not have been made a *burnt-offering*; and if his neighbour or friend's *wife, son,* or *daughter*, &c., had been returning from a visit to his fami-

ly, his vow gave him no right over them. Besides, *human sacrifices* were ever an abomination to the Lord; and this was one of the grand reasons why God drove out the Canaanites, &c., because they offered their sons and daughters to Molech in the fire, i. e., made burnt-offerings of them, as is generally supposed. That Jephthah was a deeply pious man, appears in the whole of his conduct; and that he was well acquainted with the *law of Moses*, which prohibited all such sacrifices, and stated *what* was to be offered in sacrifice, is evident enough from his expostulation with the king and people of Ammon, ver. 14-27. Therefore it must be granted that he never made that rash vow which several suppose he did; nor was he capable, if he had, of executing it in that most shocking manner which some Christian writers ("tell it not in Gath") have contended for. He could not commit a crime which himself had just now been an executor of God's justice to punish in others.

It has been supposed that "the text itself might have been read differently in former times; if instead of the words והעליתיהו עולה, *I will offer IT a burnt-offering*, we read והעליתי הוא עולה, *I will offer HIM* (i. e., the Lord) *a burnt-offering:* this will make a widely different sense, more consistent with every thing that is sacred; and it is formed by the addition of only a *single letter*, (א *aleph*,) and the separation of the *pronoun* from the verb. Now the letter א *aleph* is so like the letter ע *ain*, which immediately follows it in the word עולה *olah*, that the one might easily have been lost in the other, and thus the *pronoun* be joined to the *verb* as at present, where it expresses the *thing* to be sacrificed instead of the *person* to *whom* the sacrifice was to be made. With this emendation the passage will read thus: *Whatsoever cometh forth of the doors of my house to meet me—shall be the Lord's; and I will offer HIM a*

A. M. 2865
B. C. 1139
An. Exod. Isr.
352
Anno ante
I. Olymp. 363

32 So Jephthah passed over unto the children of Ammon to fight against them; and the Lord delivered them into his hands.

33 And he smote them from Aroer, even till thou come to ᵘMinnith, *even* twenty cities, and unto ᵛthe plain of the vineyards, with a very great slaughter. Thus the children of Ammon were subdued before the children of Israel.

34 And Jephthah came to ʷMizpeh unto his house, and, behold, ˣhis daughter came out to meet him with timbrels and with

---

ᵘEzek. xxvii. 17——ᵛOr, *Abel*——ʷChap. x. 17; ver. 11 ˣExodus xv. 20; 1 Sam. xviii. 6; Psa. lxviii. 25; Jer. xxxi. 4——ʸOr, *he had not of his own either son or daughter*

---

dances: and she *was his* only child; ʸbesides ᶻher he had neither son nor daughter.

A. M. 2865
B. C. 1139
An. Exod. Isr.
352
Anno ante
I. Olymp. 363

35 And it came to pass, when he saw her, that he ᵃrent his clothes, and said, Alas, my daughter! thou hast brought me very low, and thou art one of them that trouble me: for I ᵇhave opened my mouth unto the Lord, and ᶜI cannot go back.

36 And she said unto him, My father, *if* thou hast opened thy mouth unto the Lord, ᵈdo to me according to that which hath proceeded out of thy mouth; forasmuch as ᵉthe

---

ᶻHeb. *of himself*——ᵃGen. xxxvii. 29, 34——ᵇEccles. v. 2——ᶜNum. xxx. 2; Psa. xv. 4; Eccles. v. 4, 5 ᵈNum. xxx. 2——ᵉ2 Sam. xviii. 19, 31

---

burnt-offering." For this criticism there is no absolute need, because the pronoun הוּ *hu,* in the above verse, may with as much propriety be translated *him* as *it.* The latter part of the verse is, literally, *And I will offer him a burnt-offering,* עוֹלה *olah,* not לְעוֹלה *leolah,* FOR *a burnt-offering,* which is the common Hebrew form when *for* is intended to be expressed. This is strong presumption that the text should be thus understood: and this avoids the very disputable construction which is put on the ו *vau,* in והעליתיהו *vehaalithihu,* OR *I will offer IT up,* instead of AND *I will offer* HIM *a burnt-offering.* "From ver. 39 it appears evident that Jephthah's daughter *was not* SACRIFICED *to God,* but *consecrated* to him in a state of *perpetual virginity;* for the text says, *She knew no man, for this was a statute in Israel.* ותהי חק בישראל *vattehi chok beyishrael;* viz., that persons thus *dedicated* or *consecrated to God,* should live in a state of unchangeable *celibacy.* Thus this celebrated place is, without violence to any part of the text, or to any proper rule of construction, cleared of all difficulty, and caused to speak a language consistent with itself, and with the nature of God."

Those who assert that Jephthah did sacrifice his daughter, attempt to justify the opinion from the barbarous usages of those times: but in answer to this it may be justly observed, that Jephthah was now under the influence of the Spirit of God, ver. 29; and that Spirit could not permit him to imbrue his hands in the blood of his own child; and especially under the pretence of offering a *pleasing* sacrifice to that God who is the Father of mankind, and the Fountain of love, mercy, and compassion.

The *versions* give us but little assistance in clearing the difficulties of the text. In the *Targum* of Jonathan there is a remarkable *gloss* which should be mentioned, and from which it will appear that the Targumist supposed that the daughter of Jephthah was actually sacrificed: "And he fulfilled the vow which he had vowed upon her; and she knew no man: and it was made a statute in Israel, [that no man should offer his son or his daughter for a burnt-offering, as did Jephthah the Gileadite, who did not consult Phinehas the priest; for if he had

consulted Phinehas the priest, he would have redeemed her with money."]

The Targumist refers here to the *law,* Lev. xxvii. 1-5, where the Lord prescribes the *price* at which either males or females, who had been *vowed to the Lord,* might be *redeemed.* "When a man shall make a singular vow, the persons shall be for the Lord at thy estimation: the male from twenty years old even unto sixty, shall be fifty shekels of silver; and if it be a female, then thy estimation shall be thirty shekels; and from five years old unto twenty years, the male twenty shekels, and for the female ten." This also is an argument that the daughter of Jephthah was not sacrificed; as the father had it in his power, at a very moderate price, to have redeemed her: and surely the blood of his daughter must have been of more value in his sight than *thirty* shekels of silver.

Dr. Hales has entered largely into the subject: his observations may be seen at the end of this chapter.

Verse 33. *Twenty cities*] That is, he either *took* or *destroyed* twenty cities of the Ammonites, and completely routed their whole army.

Verse 34. *With timbrels and with dances*] From this instance we find it was an ancient custom for women to go out to meet returning conquerors with musical instruments, songs, and dances; and that it was continued afterwards is evident from the instance given 1 Sam. xviii. 6, where David was met, on his return from the defeat of Goliath and the Philistines, by women from all the cities of Israel, with singing and dancing, and various instruments of music.

Verse 35. *Thou hast brought me very low*] He was greatly distressed to think that his daughter, who was his only child, should be, in consequence of his vow, prevented from continuing his family in Israel; for it is evident that he had not any other child, for *besides her,* says the text, *he had neither son nor daughter,* ver. 34. He might, therefore, well be grieved that thus his family was to become extinct in Israel.

Verse 36. *And she said unto him*] What a pattern of filial piety and obedience! She was at once obedient, pious, and patriotic. A woman to have no offspring was considered to

A. M. 2865
B. C. 1139
An. Exod. Isr. 352
Anno ante
I. Olymp. 363

LORD hath taken vengeance for thee of thine enemies, *even* of the children of Ammon.

37 And she said unto her father, Let this thing be done for me; let me alone two months, that I may [f]go up and down upon the mountains, and bewail my virginity, I and my fellows.

38 And he said, Go. And he sent her away *for* two months; and she went with her companions, and bewailed her virginity upon the mountains.

39 And it came to pass at the end of two months, that she returned unto her father, who [g]did with her *according* to his vow which he had vowed: and she knew no man. And it was a [h]custom in Israel,

40 *That* the daughters of Israel went [l]yearly [k]to lament the daughter of Jephthah the Gileadite four days in a year.

A. M. 2865
B. C. 1139
An. Exod. Isr. 352
Anno ante
I. Olymp. 363

---

[f]Heb. *go and go down*——[g]Verse 31; 1 Samuel i. 22, 24; ii. 18

[h]Or, *ordinance*——[i]Heb. *from year to year*——[k]Or, *to talk with*, chap. v. 11

---

be in a state of the utmost degradation among the Hebrews; but she is regardless of all this, seeing her father is in safety, and her country delivered.

Verse 37. *I and my fellows*] Whether she meant the young women of her own acquaintance, or those who had been consecrated to God in the same way, though on different accounts, is not quite clear; but it is likely she means her own *companions*: and her *going up and down upon the mountains* may signify no more than her paying each of them a visit at their own houses, previously to her being shut up at the tabernacle; and this visiting of each at their own home might require the space of *two months*. This I am inclined to think is the meaning of this difficult clause.

Verse 39. *And she knew no man*] She continued a *virgin* all the days of her life.

Verse 40. *To lament the daughter of Jephthah*] I am satsified that this is not a correct translation of the original לתנות לבת יפתח *lethannoth lebath yiphtach*. Houbigant translates the whole verse thus: *Sed iste mos apud Israel invaluit, ut virgines Israel, temporibus diversis, irent ad filiam Jepthe-ut eam quotannis dies quatuor consolarentur;* "But this custom prevailed in Israel, that the virgins of Israel went at different times, four days in the year, to the daughter of Jephthah, that they might comfort her." This verse also gives evidence that the daughter of Jephthah was not sacrificed: nor does it appear that the custom or statute referred to here lasted after the death of Jephthah's daughter.

THE following is Dr. *Hales'* exposition of Jephthah's vow:—

"When *Jephthah* went forth to battle against the *Ammonites*, he vowed a vow unto the Lord, and said, 'If thou wilt surely give the children of *Ammon* into my hand, then it shall be that *whatsoever cometh out of the doors of my house to meet me*, when I return in peace from the children of *Ammon, shall either be the Lord's, or I will offer it up (for) a burnt-offering,*' Judg. xi. 30, 31. According to this rendering of the two conjunctions, ו *vau*, in the last clause *'either,' 'or,'* (which is justified by the *Hebrew* idiom; thus, 'He that curseth his father *and* his mother,' Exod. xxi. 17, is necessarily rendered disjunctively, 'His father *or* his mother,' by the *Septuagint, Vulgate, Chaldee,* and *English,* confirmed by Matt. xv. 4, the paucity of connecting particles in that language making it necessary

that this conjunction should often be understood disjunctively,) the vow consisted of two parts: 1. That what *person* soever met him should *be the Lord's* or be dedicated to his service; and, 2. That what *beast* soever met him, if *clean,* should be offered up for a *burnt-offering* unto the Lord.

"This rendering and this interpretation is warranted by the *Levitical* law about vows.

"The נדר *neder,* or *vow,* in general, included either *persons, beasts,* or *things* dedicated to the Lord for pious uses; which, if it was a simple vow, was redeemable at certain prices, if the person repented of his vow, and wished to commute it for money, according to the age or sex of the person, Lev. xxvii. 1-8: this was a wise regulation to remedy rash vows. But if the vow was accompanied with חרם *cherem, devotement,* it was irredeemable, as in the following case, Lev. xxvii. 28.

"Notwithstanding, no devotement which a man shall devote unto the Lord, (either) of *man,* or *beast,* or of *land* of his own property, shall be sold or redeemed. Every thing devoted is most holy to the Lord.

"Here the three ו *vaus* in the original should necessarily be rendered disjunctively, or as the last actually is in our translation, because there are three distinct subjects of devotement there to be applied to distinct uses, the *man* to be dedicated to the service of the Lord, as *Samuel* by his mother *Hannah,* 1 Sam. i. 11; the *cattle,* if clean, such as *oxen, sheep, goats, turtle-doves,* or *pigeons,* to be sacrificed; and if unclean, as *camels, horses, asses,* to be employed for carrying burdens in the service of the tabernacle or temple; and the *lands,* to be sacred property.

"This law therefore expressly applied in its first branch to *Jephthah's* case, who had *devoted* his daughter to the Lord, or *opened his mouth to the Lord,* and therefore *could not go back,* as he declared in his grief at seeing his daughter and only child coming to meet him with timbrels and dances: she was, therefore necessarily devoted, but with her own consent, to perpetual *virginity* in the service of the tabernacle, chap. xi. 36, 37; and such service was customary, for in the division of the spoils taken in the first Midianitish war, of the whole number of captive virgins the Lord's *tribute was thirty-two persons,* Num. xxxi. 15-40. This instance appears to be decisive of the nature of her devotement.

"Her father's extreme grief on the occasion and her requisition of a respite for two months to *bewail her virginity*, are both perfectly natural. Having no other issue, he could only look forward to the extinction of his name or family; and a state of celibacy, which is reproachful among women everywhere, was peculiarly so among the *Israelites*, and was therefore no ordinary sacrifice on her part; who, though she generously gave up, could not but regret the loss of, becoming 'a *mother* in *Israel*.' And *he did with her according to his vow* which he had vowed, and *she knew no man*, or remained a virgin, all her life, ver. 34-39.

"There was also another case of *devotement* which was irredeemable, and follows the former, Lev. xxvii. 29. This case differs materially from the former.

"1. It is confined to PERSONS devoted, omiting *beasts* and *lands*. 2. It does not relate to *private property*, as in the foregoing. And, 3. The subject of it was to be *utterly destroyed*, instead of being *most holy unto the Lord*. This law, therefore, related to *aliens*, or *public enemies* devoted to destruction *either* by GOD, the *people*, or by the *magistrate*. Of all these we have instances in Scripture.

"1. The *Amalekites* and *Canaanites* were devoted by God himself. *Saul* was, therefore, guilty of a breach of the law for sparing *Agag* the king of the *Amalekites*, as Samuel reproached him, 1 Sam. xv. 33: 'And Samuel hewed Agag in pieces before the Lord;' not as a *sacrifice*, according to *Voltaire*, but as a *criminal*, whose sword had made many women childless. By this law the Midianitish women who had been spared in battle were slain, Num. xxxi. 14-17.

"2. In Mount *Hor*, when the Israelites were attacked by Arad, king of the southern Canaanites, who took some of them prisoners, they vowed a vow unto the Lord that they would utterly destroy the *Canaanites* and their cities, if the Lord should deliver them into their hand, which the Lord ratified; whence the place was called *Hormah*, because the vow was accompanied by *cherem*, or devotement to destruction, Num. xxi. 1-3; and the vow was accomplished, chap. i. 17.

"3. In the *Philistine* war *Saul* adjured the people, and cursed any one who should taste food till the evening. His own son *Jonathan* inadvertently ate a honey-comb, not knowing his father's oath, for which *Saul* sentenced him to die. But the people interposed, and rescued him for his public services; thus assuming the power of *dispensing*, in their collective capacity, with an unreasonable oath. This latter case, therefore, is utterly irrelative to *Jephthah's* vow, which did not regard a foreign enemy or a domestic transgressor devoted to destruction, but on the contrary was a vow of thanksgiving, and therefore properly came under the former case. And that *Jephthah* could not possibly have sacrificed his daughter, (according to the vulgar opinion,) may appear from the following considerations:—

"1. The sacrifice of children to *Molech* was an abomination to the Lord, of which in numberless passages he expresses his detestation, and it was prohibited by an express law, under pain of death, as a *defilement of God's sanctuary, and a profanation of his holy name*, Lev. xx. 2, 3. Such a sacrifice, therefore, unto the Lord himself, must be a still higher abomination, and there is no precedent of any such under the law in the OLD TESTAMENT.

"2. The case of *Isaac* before the law is irrel-

evant, for *Isaac* was not sacrificed, and it was only proposed for a trial of *Abraham's* faith.

"3. No father, merely by his own authority, could put an offending, much less an innocent, child to death upon any account, without the sentence of the magistrate, (Deut. xxi. 18-21,) and the consent of the people, as in *Jonathan's* case.

"4. The *Mischna*, or traditional law of the Jews is pointedly against it; ver. 212. 'If a Jew should devote his *son* or *daughter*, his *man* or *maid servant*, who are *Hebrews*, the devotement would be void, because no man can devote *what is not his own*, or *whose life he has not the absolute disposal of*.' These arguments appear to be decisive against the sacrifice; and that *Jephthah* could not have devoted his daughter to celibacy against her will is evident from the history, and from the high estimation in which she was always held by the daughters of Israel for her filial duty and her hapless fate, which they celebrated by a regular anniversary commemoration four days in the year; chap. xi. 40."—*New Analysis of Chronology*, vol. iii., p. 319.

The celebrated sacrifice of Iphigenia has been supposed by many learned men to be a fable founded on this account of Jephthah's daughter; and M. De Lavaur, *Conference de la Fable avec l' Histoire Sainte*, has thus traced the parallel:—

"The fable of *Iphigenia*, offered in sacrifice by *Agamemnon* her father, sung by so many poets, related after them by so many historians, and celebrated in the *Greek* and *French* theatres, has been acknowledged by all those who knew the sacred writings, and who have paid a particular attention to them, as a changed copy of the history of the daughter of *Jephthah*, offered in sacrifice by her father. Let us consider the several parts particularly, and begin with an exposition of the original, taken from the eleventh chapter of the book of Judges.

"The sacred historian informs us that *Jephthah*, the son of *Gilead*, was a great and valiant captain. The *Israelites*, against whom God was irritated, being forced to go to war with the *Ammonites*, (nearly about the time of the siege of Troy,) assembled themselves together to oblige *Jephthah* to come to their succour, and chose him for their captain against the *Ammonites*. He accepted the command on conditions that, if God should give him the victory, they would acknowledge him for their prince. This they promised by oath; and all the people elected him in the city of *Mizpeh*, in the tribe of *Judah*. He first sent ambassadors to the king of the *Ammonites* to know the reason why he had committed so many acts of injustice, and so many ravages on the coast of *Israel*. The other made a pretext of some ancient damages his people had suffered by the primitive *Israelites*, to countenance the ravages he committed, and would not accord with the reasonable propositions made by the *ambassadors* of *Jephthah*. Having now supplicated the Lord, and being filled with his Spirit, he marched against the *Ammonites*, and being zealously desirous to acquit himself nobly, and to ensure the success of so important a war, he made a vow to the Lord to offer in sacrifice or as a burnt-offering the first thing that should come out of the house to meet him at his return from victory.

"He then fought with and utterly discomfited

the *Ammonites;* and returning victorious to his house, God so permitted it that his only daughter was the first who met him. *Jephthah* was struck with terror at the sight of *her*, and tearing his garments, he exclaimed, *Alas! alas! my daughter, thou dost exceedingly trouble me; for I have opened my mouth against thee, unto the Lord, and I cannot go back.* His daughter, full of courage and piety, understanding the purport of his vow, exhorted him to accomplish what he had vowed to the Lord, which to her would be exceedingly agreeable, seeing the Lord had avenged him of his and his country's enemies; desiring liberty only to go on the mountains with her companions, and to bewail the dishonour with which sterility was accompanied in *Israel*, because each hoped to see the *Messiah* born of his or her family. *Jephthah* could not deny her this request. She accordingly went, and at the end of two months returned, and put herself into the hands of her father, who did with her according to his vow.

"Several of the *rabbins*, and many very learned Christian expositors, believe that *Jephthah's* daughter was not really sacrificed, but that her virginity was consecrated to God, and that she separated from all connection with the world; which indeed seems to be implied in the sacred historian's account: *And she knew no man.* This was a kind of mysterious death, because it caused her to lose all hope of the glory of a posterity from which the *Messiah* might descend. From this originated the custom, observed afterwards in *Israel*, that on a certain season in the year the virgins assembled themselves on the mountains to bewail the daughter of *Jephthah* for the space of four days. Let us now consider the leading characters of the fable of *Iphigenia.* According to good chronological reckonings, the time of the one and of the other very nearly agree. The opinion that the name of *Iphigenia* is taken from the daughter of Jephthah, appears well founded; yea, the conformity is palpable. By a very inconsiderable change *Iphigenia* makes *Iphthygenia*, which signifies literally, *the daughter of Jephthah. Agamemnon*, who is described as a valiant warrior and admirable captain, was chosen by the *Greeks* for their prince and *general* against the *Trojans*, by the united consent of all *Greece*, assembled together at *Aulis* in *Bœotia.*

"As soon as he had accepted the command, he sent ambassadors to *Priam*, king of *Troy*, to demand satisfaction for the rape of *Helen*, of which the *Greeks* complained. The *Trojans* refusing to grant this, *Agamemnon*, to gain over to his side the gods, who appeared irritated against the *Greeks* and opposed to the success of their enterprise, after having sacrificed to them went to consult their interpreter, *Chalchas*, who declared that the gods, and particularly Diana, would not be appeased but by the

sacrifice of *Iphigenia*, the daughter of *Agamemnon.*

"*Cicero*, in his *Offices*, says that Agamemnon. in order to engage the protection of the gods in his war against the *Trojans*, vowed to sacrifice to them the most beautiful of all that should be born in his kingdom; and as it was found that his daughter *Iphigenia* surpassed all the rest in beauty, he believed himself bound by his vow to sacrifice her. *Cicero* condemns this, rightly judging *that it would have been a less evil to have falsified his vow than to have committed parricide.* This account of *Cicero* renders the fable entirely comformable to the history.

"*Agamemnon* was at first struck with and troubled at this order, nevertheless consented to it: but he afterwards regretted the loss of his daughter. He is represented by the poets as deliberating, and being in doubt whether the gods could require such a *parricide;* but at last a sense of his duty and honour overcame his paternal affection, and his daughter, who had warmly exhorted him to fulfil his vow to the gods, was led to the altar amidst the lamentations of her companions; as *Ovid* and *Euripides* relate, see *Met.*, lib. 13.

"Some authors have thought she really was sacrificed; but others, more humane, say she was caught up in a cloud by the gods, who, contented with the intended sacrifice, substituted a *hind* in her place, with which the sacrifice was completed. *Dictys Cretensis* says that this animal was substituted to save *Iphigenia.*

"The chronology of times so remote cannot, in many respects, but be uncertain. Both the *Greeks* and *Romans* grant that there was nothing else than fables before the first *Olympiad*, the beginning of which was at least four hundred and fifty years after the destruction of *Troy*, and two hundred and forty years after *Solomon.* As to the time of *Solomon*, nothing can be more certain than what is related in the sixth chapter of the first book of Kings, that from the going out of *Egypt*, under *Moses*, till the time in which he began to build the temple, was four hundred and eighty years.

"According to the common opinion, the taking of *Troy* is placed one hundred and eighty years before the reign of *Solomon;* but his reign preceded *Homer three centuries*, according to some learned men, and always at least *one century* by those who related it lowest. Indeed, there is much uncertainty in fixing the express time in which *Homer* flourished.

"*Pausanias* found so much difference concerning this in authors, that he was at a loss how to judge of it. However, it is sufficient for us that it was granted that *Solomon* was at least a century before *Homer*, who wrote more than two centuries after the taking of *Troy*, and who is the most ancient historian of this famous siege."

CHAPTER XII

The Ephraimites are incensed against Jephthah, because he did not call them to war against the Ammonites; and threaten his destruction, 1. *He vindicates himself,* 2, 3; *and arms the Gileadites against the men of Ephraim; they fight against them, and kill* forty-two thousand *Ephraimites at the passages of Jordan,* 4-6. *Jephthah dies, having judged Israel* six years, 7. *Ibzan judge* seven years, 8. *His posterity and death,* 9, 10. *Elon judge* ten years, *and dies,* 11, 12. *Abdon judge* eight years, 13. *His posterity and death,* 14, 15.

A. M. 2865
B. C. 1139
An. Exod. Isr. 352
Anno ante
I. Olymp. 363

AND [a]the men of Ephraim [b]gathered themselves together, and went northward, and said unto Jephthah, Wherefore passedst thou over to fight against the children of Ammon, and didst not call us to go with thee? we will burn thine house upon thee with fire.

2 And Jephthah said unto them, I and my people were at great strife with the children of Ammon; and when I called you, ye delivered me not out of their hands.

3 And when I saw that ye delivered *me* not, I [c]put my life in my hands, and passed over against the children of Ammon, and the LORD delivered them into my hand: wherefore then

are ye come up unto me this day, to fight against me?

A. M. 2865
B. C. 1139
An. Exod. Isr. 352
Anno ante
I. Olymp. 363

4 Then Jephthah gathered together all the men of Gilead, and fought with Ephraim: and the men of Gilead smote Ephraim, because they said, Ye [d]Gileadites *are* fugitives of Ephraim among the Ephraimites, *and* among the Manassites.

5 And the Gileadites took [e]the passages of Jordan before the Ephraimites: and it was *so*, that when those Ephraimites which were escaped said, Let me go over; that the men of Gilead said unto him, *Art* thou an Ephraimite? If he said, Nay,

6 Then said they unto him, Say now [f]Shibboleth; and he said Sibboleth: for he could

---

[a]See chap. viii. 1——[b]Heb. *were* called——[c]1 Sam. xix. 5; xxviii. 21; Job xiii. 14; Psa. cxix. 109——[d]See 1 Sam. xxv. 10; Psa. lxxviii. 9

[e]Josh. xxii. 11; chap. iii. 28; vii. 24——[f]Which signifieth *a stream* or *flood;* Psa. lxix. 2, 15; Isa. xxvii. 12

NOTES ON CHAP. XII

Verse 1. *The men of Ephraim gathered themselves together*] ויצעק *vaiyitstsaek, they called each other to arms;* summoning all their tribe and friends to arm themselves to destroy Jephthah and the Gileadites, being jealous lest they should acquire too much power.

Verse 3. *I put my life in my hands*] I exposed myself to the greatest difficulties and dangers. But whence did this form of speech arise? Probably from a man's laying hold of his sword, spear, or bow. "This is the defender of my life; on this, and my proper use of it, my life depends." When a man draws his sword against his foe, his enemy will naturally aim at his life; and his sword in his hand is his sole defence. It is then, Fight and conquer, or die. Thus Jephthah took his life in his hand. This phrase occurs in some other places of Scripture; see 1 Sam. xix. 5; xxviii. 21. And the words of the Conqueror, Isa. lxiii. 5, seem to confirm the above view of the subject: *I looked, and* there was *none to help; and I wondered* there was *none to uphold; therefore mine own arm brought salvation unto me;* i. e., by mine own arm I saved my life, and brought destruction on mine enemies.

Verse 4. *And fought with Ephraim*] Some commentators suppose that there were *two* battles in which the Ephraimites were defeated: the first mentioned in the above clause; and the second occasioned by the taunting language mentioned in the conclusion of the verse, *Ye Gileadites are fugitives of Ephraim.* Where the *point* of this reproach lies, or what is the reason of it, cannot be easily ascertained.

Verse 6. *Say now Shibboleth; and he said Sibboleth*] The original differs only in the first letter ס *samech,* instead of ש *sheen;* אמר נא שבלת ויאמר סבלת *emar na Shibboleth, vaiyomer Sibboleth.* The difference between ש *seen,* without a point, which when pointed is pronounced *sheen,* and ס *samech,* is supposed by many to be imperceptible. But there can be

no doubt there was, to the ears of a Hebrew, a most sensible distinction. Most Europeans, and, indeed, most who have written grammars of the language, perceive scarcely any difference between the Arabic ﺱ *seen* and ﺹ *saad;* but as both those letters are *radical* not only in Arabic but in Hebrew, the difference of enunciation must be such as to be plainly perceivable by the ear; else it would be impossible to determine the root of a word into which either of these letters entered, except by guessing, unless by pronunciation the sounds were distinct. One to whom the Arabic is vernacular, hearing a native speak, discerns it in a moment; but the delicate enunciation of the characteristic difference between those letters ש *seen* and ס *samech,* and ﺱ *seen* and ﺹ *saad,* is seldom caught by a European. Had there been no distinction between the *seen* and *samech* but what the Masoretic point gives now, then ס *samech* would not have been used in the word סבלת *sibboleth,* but ש *seen,* thus שבלת: but there must have been a very remarkable difference in the pronunciation of the Ephraimites, when instead of שבלת *shibboleth,* an *ear of corn,* (see Job xxiv. 24,) they said סבלת *sibboleth,* which signifies *a burden,* Exod. vi. 6; and a heavy burden were they obliged to bear who could not pronounce this *test* letter. It is likely that the Ephraimites were, in reference to the pronunciation of *sh,* as different from the Gileadites as the people in some parts of the north of England are, in the pronunciation of the letter *r,* from all the other inhabitants of the land. The sound of *th* cannot be pronounced by the Persians in general; and yet it is a common sound among the Arabians. To this day multitudes of the German Jews cannot pronounce ת *th,* but put *ss* in the stead of it: thus for בית *beith* (a house) they say *bess.*

Mr. Richardson, in his "Dissertation on the Languages, Literature, and Manners of the Eastern Nations," prefixed to his Persian and Arabic Dictionary, p. ii., 4to. edition, makes

A. M. 2865
B. C. 1139
An. Exod. Isr. 352
Anno ante
I. Olymp. 363

not frame to pronounce *it right.* Then they took him, and slew him at the passages of Jordan: and there fell at that time of the Ephraimites forty and two thousand.

7 And Jephthah judged Israel six years. Then died Jephthah the Gileadite, and was buried in *one of* the cities of Gilead.

A. M. 2871
B. C. 1133
An. Exod. Isr. 358
Anno ante
I. Olymp. 357

8 And after him ᵍIbzan of Beth-lehem judged Israel.

9 And he had thirty sons, and thirty daughters, *whom* he sent abroad, and took in thirty daughters from abroad for his sons. And he judged Israel seven years.

10 Then died Ibzan, and was buried at Beth-lehem.

11 And after him ʰElon, a Zebulonite, judged Israel; and he judged Israel ten years.

A. M. 2878
B. C. 1126
An. Exod. Isr. 365
Anno ante
I. Olymp. 350

12 And Elon the Zebulonite died, and was buried in Aijalon in the country of Zebulun.

13 And after him ⁱAbdon the son of Hillel, a Pirathonite, judged Israel.

A. M. 2888
B. C. 1116
An. Exod. Isr. 375
Anno ante
I. Olymp. 340

14 And he had forty sons and thirty ᵏnephews, that ˡrode on threescore and ten ass colts: and he judged Israel eight years.

15 And Abdon the son of Hillel the Pirathonite died, and was buried in Pirathon in the land of Ephraim, in ᵐthe mount of the Amalekites.

ᵍHe seems to have been only a civil judge to do justice in northeast *Israel*——ʰA civil judge in northeast *Israel*

ⁱA civil judge in northeast *Israel*——ᵏHeb. *sons' sons* ˡChap. v. 10; x. 4——ᵐChap. iii. 13, 27; v. 14

---

some observations on the different dialects which prevailed in Arabia Felix, the chief of which were the *Hemyaret* and *Koreish;* and to illustrate the point in hand, he produces the following story from the Mohammedan writers: "An envoy from one of the feudatory states, having been sent to the *tobba,* (the sovereign,) that prince, when he was introduced, pronounced the word *T'heb,* which in the *Hemyaret* implied, *Be seated:* unhappily it signified, in the native dialect of the ambassador, *Precipitate thyself;* and he, with a singular deference for the orders of his sovereign, threw himself instantly from the castle wall and perished." Though the Ephraimites had not a different *dialect,* they had, it appears, a different pronunciation, which confounded, to others, letters of the same organ, and thus produced, not only a different sound, but even an opposite meaning. This was a sufficient test to find out an Ephraimite; and he who spake not as he was commanded, at the fords of Jordan, spoke against his own life.

For he could not frame to pronounce it right.] This is not a bad rendering of the original ולא יבין לדבר כן *velo yachin ledabber ken;* "and they did not *direct* to speak it thus." But instead of יבין *yachin,* to *direct,* thirteen of Kennicott's and De Rossi's MSS., with two ancient editions, read יבין *yabin;* "they did not *understand* to speak it thus."

The *versions* take great latitude in this verse. The *Vulgate* makes a paraphrase: *Dic ergo Shibboleth, quod interpretatur spica: qui respondebat Sibboleth; eadem litera spicam exprimere non valens.* "Say therefore, Shibboleth; which interpreted is an *ear of corn:* but he answered, Sibboleth; not being able to express an ear of corn by that letter." In my very ancient copy of the *Vulgate,* probably the *editio princeps,* there is *sebboleth* in the first instance as the test word, and *thebboleth* as the Ephraimite pronunciation. But *cebboleth* is the reading of the *Complutensian* Polyglot, and is supported

by one of my own MSS.; yet the former reading, *thebboleth,* is found in *two* of my MSS. The *Chaldee* has שובלתא *shubbaltha* for the Gileaditish pronunciation, and סבלתא *subbaltha* for that of Ephraim. The *Syriac* has ܫܒܠܐ *shelba* and ܣܒܠܐ *sebla.* The Arabic has the same word, with ش *sheen* and س *seen;* and adds, "He said *Sebla,* for the Ephraimites could not pronounce the letter *sheen.*" These notices, however trivial at first view, will not be thought unimportant by the Biblical critic.

Verse 8. *And after him Ibzan*] It appears that during the administration of *Jephthah,* six years—*Ibzan,* seven years—*Elon,* ten years—and *Abdon,* eight years, (in the whole thirty-one years,) the Israelites had peace in all their borders; and we shall find by the following chapter that in this time of rest they corrupted themselves, and were afterwards delivered into the power of the Philistines.

1. WE find that *Ibzan* had a numerous family, sixty children; and *Abdon* had forty sons and thirty grandsons; and that they lived splendidly, which is here expressed by their *riding on seventy young asses;* what we would express by *they all kept their carriages;* for the riding on fine asses in those days was not less dignified than riding in coaches in ours.

2. It does not appear that any thing particular took place in the civil state of the Israelites during the time of these latter judges; nothing is said concerning their administration, whether it was good or bad; nor is any thing mentioned of the state of religion. It is likely that they enjoyed peace without, and their judges were capable of preventing discord and sedition within. Yet, doubtless, God was at work among them, though there were none to record the operations either of his hand or his Spirit; but the people who feared him no doubt bore testimony to the word of his grace.

CHAPTER XIII

The Israelites corrupt themselves, and are delivered into the hands of the Philistines forty years, 1. An Angel appears to the wife of Manoah, foretells the birth of her son, and gives her directions how to treat both herself and her child, who was to be a deliverer of Israel, 2–5. She informs her husband of this transaction, 6, 7. Manoah prays that the Angel may reappear; he is heard, and the Angel appears to him and his wife, and repeats his former directions concerning the mother and the child, 8–14. Manoah presents an offering to the Lord, and the Angel ascends in the flame, 15–20. Manoah is alarmed, but is comforted by the judicious reflections of his wife, 21–23. Samson is born, and begins to feel the influence of the Divine Spirit, 24, 25.

A. M. 2847
B. C. 1157
An. Exod. Isr.
334
Anno ante
I. Olymp. 381

AND the children of Israel [a]did [b]evil again in the sight of the LORD; [c]and the LORD delivered them [d]into the hands of the Philistines forty years.

2 And there was a certain man of [e]Zorah, of the family of the Danites, whose name *was* Manoah; and his wife *was* barren, and bare not.

3 And the [f]angel of the LORD appeared unto the woman, and said unto her, Behold now, thou *art* barren, and bearest not: but thou shalt conceive, and bear a son.

4 Now therefore beware, I pray thee, and [g]drink not wine nor strong drink, and eat not any unclean *thing:*

5 For, lo, thou shalt conceive, and bear a son; and no [h]razor shall come on his head: for the child shall be [i]a Nazarite unto God

from the womb: and he shall [k]begin to deliver Israel out of the hand of the Philistines.

A. M. 2847
B. C. 1157
An. Exod. Isr.
334
Anno ante
I. Olymp. 381

6 Then the woman came and told her husband, saying, [1]A man of God came unto me, and his [m]countenance *was* like the countenance of an angel of God, very terrible: but I [n]asked him not whence he *was,* neither told he me his name:

7 But he said unto me, Behold, thou shalt conceive, and bear a son; and now drink no wine nor strong drink, neither eat any unclean *thing:* for the child shall be a Nazarite to God from the womb to the day of his death.

8 Then Manoah entreated the LORD, and said, O my LORD, let the man of God which thou didst send come again unto us, and teach us what we shall do unto the child that shall be born.

9 And God hearkened to the voice of Ma-

---

[a]Heb. *added to commit,* &c.——[b]Chap. ii. 11; iii. 7; iv. 1; vi. 1; x. 6——[c]This seems a partial captivity——[d]1 Sam. xii. 9——[e]Josh. xix. 41——[f]Chap. vi. 12; Luke i. 11, 13, 28, 31——[g]Ver. 14; Num. vi. 2, 3; Luke i. 15

[h]Num. vi. 5; 1 Sam. i. 11——[i]Num. vi. 2——[k]See 1 Sam. vii. 13; 2 Sam. viii. 1; 1 Chron. xviii. 1——[l]Deut. xxxiii. 1; 1 Sam. ii. 27; ix. 6; 1 Kings xvii 24 [m]Matt. xxviii. 3; Luke ix. 29; Acts vi. 15——[n]Ver. 17,18

NOTES ON CHAP. XIII

Verse 1. *Delivered them into the hand of the Philistines*] It does not appear that after Shamgar, to the present time, the Philistines were in a condition to oppress Israel, or God had not permitted them to do it; but now they have a commission, the Israelites having departed from the Lord. Nor is it evident that the Philistines had entirely subjected the Israelites, as there still appears to have been a sort of commerce between the two people. They had often vexed and made inroads upon them, but they had them not in entire subjection; see chap. xv. 11.

Verse 2. *A certain man of Zorah*] A town in the tribe of Judah, but afterwards given to Dan.

Verse 3. *The angel of the Lord*] Generally supposed to have been the same that appeared to Moses, Joshua, Gideon, &c., and no other than the second person of the ever-blessed Trinity.

Verse 4. *Beware—drink not wine*] As Samson was designed to be a *Nazarite from the womb,* it was necessary that, while his mother carried and nursed him, *she* should live the life of a Nazarite, neither drinking wine nor any inebriating liquor, nor eating any kind of forbidden meat. See the account of the Nazarite and his vow in the notes on Num. vi. 2, &c.

Verse 5. *He shall begin to deliver Israel*] Samson only *began* this deliverance, for it was not till the days of David that the Israelites were completely redeemed from the power of the Philistines.

Verse 6. *But I asked him not whence he* was, *neither told he me his name*] This clause is rendered very differently by the Vulgate, the negative NOT being omitted: *Quem cum interrogassem quis esset, et unde venisset, et quo nomine vocaretur, noluit mihi dicere; sed hoc respondit.* "Who, when I asked who he was and whence he came, and by what name he was called, would not tell me; but this he said," &c.

The *negative* is also wanting in the *Septuagint,* as it stands in the *Complutensian Polyglot:* Και ηρωτων αυτον ποθεν εστιν, και το ονομα αυτου ουκ απηγγειλε μοι; "And I asked him whence he was, and his name, *but* he did not tell me." This is also the reading of the *Codex Alexandrinus;* but the *Septuagint,* in the London Polyglot, together with the *Chaldee, Syriac,* and *Arabic,* read the *negative* particle with the Hebrew text, *I asked* NOT *his name,* &c.

Verse 9. *The angel of God came again*] This second appearance of the angel was probably essential to the peace of Manoah, who might have been jealous of his wife had he not had this proof that the thing was of the Lord.

A. M. 2847
B. C. 1157
An. Exod. Isr.
334
Anno ante
I. Olymp. 381

noah; and the angel of God came again unto the woman as she sat in the field: but Manoah her husband *was* not with her.

10 And the woman made haste, and ran, and showed her husband, and said unto him, Behold, the man hath appeared unto me, that came unto me the *other* day.

11 And Manoah arose, and went after his wife, and came to the man, and said unto him, *Art* thou the man that spakest unto the woman? And he said, I *am*.

12 And Manoah said, Now let thy words come to pass. °How shall we order the child, and P*how* ⁹shall we do unto him?

13 And the angel of the Lord said unto Manoah, Of all that I said unto the woman, let her beware.

14 She may not eat of any *thing* that cometh of the vine, ʳneither let her drink wine or strong drink, nor eat any unclean *thing:* all that I commanded her let her observe.

15 And Manoah said unto the angel of the Lord, I pray thee, ˢlet us detain thee, until we shall have made ready a kid ᵗfor thee.

16 And the angel of the Lord said unto Manoah, Though thou detain me, I will not eat of thy bread: and if thou wilt offer a burnt-offering, thou must offer it unto the

Lord. For Manoah knew not that he *was* an angel of the Lord.

A. M. 2847
B. C. 1157
An. Exod. Isr.
334
Anno ante
I. Olymp. 381

17 And Manoah said unto the angel of the Lord, What *is* thy name, that when thy sayings come to pass we may do thee honour?

18 And the angel of the Lord said unto him, ᵘWhy askest thou thus after my name, seeing it *is* ᵛsecret?

19 So Manoah took a kid with a meat-offering, ʷand offered *it* upon a rock unto the Lord: and *the angel* did wondrously; and Manoah and his wife looked on.

20 For it came to pass, when the flame went up toward heaven from off the altar, that the angel of the Lord ascended in the flame of the altar. And Manoah and his wife looked on *it*, and ˣfell on their faces to the ground.

21 And the angel of the Lord did no more appear to Manoah and to his wife. ʸThen Manoah knew that he *was* an angel of the Lord.

22 And Manoah said unto his wife, ᶻWe shall surely die, because we have seen God.

23 But his wife said unto him, If the Lord were pleased to kill us, he would not have received a burnt-offering and a meat-offering at our hands; neither would he have showed us all these *things,* nor would as at this time have told us *such things* as these.

°Heb. *What shall be the manner of the,* &c.——P Or, what *shall he do?*——⁹Heb. what shall be *his work?* ʳVer. 4——ˢGen. xviii. 5; chap. vi. 18——ᵗHeb. *before thee*——ᵘGen. xxxii. 29

ᵛOr, *wonderful;* Isa. ix. 6——ʷChap. vi. 19, 20 ˣLev. ix. 24; 1 Chron. xxi. 16; Ezek. i. 28; Matt. xvii. 6 ʸChap. vi. 22——ᶻGen. xxxii. 30; Exod. xxxiii. 20; Deut. v. 26; chap. vi. 22

Verse 15. *Until we shall have made ready a kid*] Not knowing his quality, Manoah wished to do this as an act of hospitality.

Verse 16. *I will not eat of thy bread*] As I am a spiritual being, I subsist not by earthly food.

And if thou wilt offer a burnt-offering] Neither shall I receive that homage which belongs to God; thou must therefore offer thy burnt-offering to Jehovah.

Verse 18. *Seeing it is secret?*] It was because it was *secret* that they wished to know it. The angel does not say that it was *secret*, but פלאי הוא *hu peli, it is* WONDERFUL; the very character that is given to Jesus Christ, Isa. ix.

6: *His name shall be called,* פלא *Wonderful;* and it is supposed by some that the angel gives this as his name, and consequently that he was our blessed Lord.

Verse 19. The angel *did wondrously*] He acted according to his name; he, being *wonderful*, performed wonderful things; probably causing fire to arise out of the rock and consume the sacrifice, and then ascending in the flame.

Verse 22. *We shall surely die, because we have seen God.*] See the note on chap. vi. 22.

Verse 23. *If the Lord were pleased to kill us, &c.*] This is excellent reasoning, and may be of great use to every truly religious mind, in cloudy and dark dispensations of Divine Providence. It is not likely that God, who has preserved thee so long, borne with thee so long, and fed and supported thee all thy life long, girding thee when thou knewest him not, is less willing to save and provide for thee and thine now than he was when, probably, thou trustedst less in him. He who freely gave his Son to redeem thee, can never be indifferent to thy welfare; and if he give thee power to pray to and trust in him, is it at all likely that he is now seeking an occasion against thee, in order to destroy thee? Add to this the very *light* that shows thee thy wretchedness, ingratitude, and disobedience, is in itself a proof that he is waiting to be gracious to thee; and the penitential pangs thou feelest, and thy bitter regret for thy unfaithfulness, argue that the *light* and *fire* are of God's own kindling, and are sent to direct and refine, not to drive thee out of the way and destroy thee. *Nor would he have told*

A. M. 2848
B. C. 1156
An. Exod. Isr.
335
Anno ante
I. Olymp. 380

24 And the woman bare a son, and called his name [a]Samson: and [b]the child grew, and the Lord blessed him.

25 [c]And the Spirit of the Lord began to move him at times in [d]the camp of Dan, [e]between Zorah and Eshtaol.

A. M. 2863
B. C. 1141
An. Exod. Isr.
350
Anno ante
I. Olymp. 365

---

[a]Heb. xi. 32——[b]1 Sam. iii. 19; Luke i. 80; ii. 52
[c]Chap. iii. 10; 1 Sam. xi. 6; Matt. iv. 1

[d]Heb. *Mahaneh-dan,* as chap. xviii. 12——[e]Josh. xv. 33;
chap. xviii. 11

---

thee such things of his love, mercy, and kindness, and unwillingness to destroy sinners, as he has told thee in his sacred word, if he had been determined not to extend his mercy to thee.

Verse 24. And called his name Samson] The original שמשון *shimshon,* which is from the root שמש *shamash, to serve,* (whence *shemesh, the sun,*) probably means either a *little sun,* or a *little servant;* and this latter is so likely a name to be imposed on an only son, by maternal fondness, that it leaves but little doubt of the propriety of the etymology.]

And the Lord blessed him.] Gave evident proofs that the child was under the peculiar protection of the Most High; causing him to increase daily in stature and extraordinary strength.

Verse 25. The Spirit of the Lord began to

move him] He felt the degrading bondage of his countrymen, and a strong desire to accomplish something for their deliverance. These feelings and motions he had from the Divine Spirit.

Camp of Dan] Probably the place where his parents dwelt; for they were Danites, and the place is supposed to have its name from its being the spot where the Danites stopped when they sent some men of their company to rob Micah of his teraphim, &c. See chap. xviii.

As he had these influences between Zorah and Eshtaol, it is evident that this was *while* he dwelt at home with his parents; for Zorah was the place where his father dwelt; see ver. 2. Thus God began, from his infancy, to qualify him for the work to which he had called him.

CHAPTER XIV

Samson marries a wife of the Philistines, 1–4. Slays a young lion at Timnath, in the carcass of which he afterwards finds a swarm of bees, 5–9. He makes a feast; they appoint him thirty companions, to whom he puts forth a riddle, which they cannot expound, 10–14. They entice his wife to get the interpretation from him; she succeeds, informs them, and they tell the explanation, 15–18. He is incensed, and slays thirty of the Philistines, 19, 20.

A. M. 2867
B. C. 1137
An. Exod. Isr.
354
Anno ante
I. Olymp. 361

AND Samson went down [a]to Timnath, and [b]saw a woman in Timnath of the daughters of the Philistines.

2 And he came up, and told his father and his mother, and said, I have seen a woman in Timnath of the daughters of the Philistines: now therefore [c]get her for me to wife.

3 Then his father and his mother said unto him, *Is there* never a woman among the daughters of [d]thy brethren, or among all my people, that thou goest to take a wife of the [e]uncircumcised Philistines? And Samson said unto his father, Get her for me; for [f]she pleaseth me well.

4 But his father and his mother knew not that it *was* [g]of the Lord, that he sought an occasion against the Philistines: for at that time [h]the Philistines had dominion over Israel.

A. M. 2867
B. C. 1137
An. Exod. Isr.
354
Anno ante
I. Olymp. 361

---

[a]Gen. xxxviii. 13; Josh. xv. 10——[b]Gen. xxxiv. 2
[c]Gen. xxi. 21; xxxiv. 4——[d]Gen. xxiv. 3, 4——[e]Gen.
xxxiv. 14; Exod. xxxiv. 16; Deut. vii. 3

[f]Heb. *she is right in mine eyes*——[g]Josh. xi. 20;
1 Kings xii. 15; 2 Kings vi. 33; 2 Chron. x. 15; xxii. 7;
xxv. 20——[h]Chap. xiii. 1; Deut. xxviii. 48

NOTES ON CHAP. XIV

Verse 1. Went down to Timnath] A frontier town of the Philistines, at the beginning of the lands belonging to the tribe of *Judah,* Josh. xv. 57; but afterwards given up to Dan, Josh. xix. 43. David took this place from the Philistines, but they again got possession of it in the reign of Ahaz, 2 Chron. xxviii. 18.

Verse 3. Is there never a woman] To marry with any that did not belong to the Israelitish stock, was contrary to the law, Exod. xxxiv. 16; Deut. vii. 3. But this marriage of Samson was said to be *of the Lord,* ver. 4; that is, God *permitted* it, (for in no other sense can we understand the phrase,) that it might be a means of bringing about the deliverance of Israel.

For she pleaseth me well.] כי היא ישרה בעיני *ki hi yisherah beeynai, for she is right in my eyes.* This is what is supposed to be a sufficient reason to justify either man or woman in their random choice of wife or husband; the maxim is the same with that of the poet:—

"Thou hast no fault, or I no fault can spy;
Thou art all beauty or all blindness I."

When the *will* has sufficient power, its determinations are its own rule of right. That *will* should be pure and well directed that says, *It shall be so, because I* WILL *it should be so.* A reason of this kind is similar to that which I have seen in a motto on the brass ordnance of Lewis XIV., ULTIMA RATIO REGUM, *the sum*

A. M. 2867
B. C. 1137
An. Exod. Isr.
354
Anno ante
I. Olymp. 361

5 Then went Samson down, and his father and his mother, to Timnath, and came to the vineyards of Timnath: and, behold, a young lion roared ¹against him.

6 And ᵏthe Spirit of the LORD came mightily upon him, and he rent him as he would have rent a kid, and *he had* nothing in his hand: but he told not his father or his mother what he had done.

7 And he went down, and talked with the woman; and she pleased Samson well.

8 And after a time he returned to take her, and he turned aside to see the carcass of the lion: and, behold, *there was* a swarm of bees and honey in the carcass of the lion.

A. M. 2868
B. C. 1136
An. Exod. Isr.
355
Anno ante
I. Olymp. 360

9 And he took thereof in his hands, and went on eating, and came to his father and mother, and he gave them, and they did eat: but he told not them that he had taken the honey out of the carcass of the lion.

10 So his father went down unto the woman: and Samson made there a feast; for so used the young men to do.

11 And it came to pass, when they saw him, that they brought thirty companions to be with him.

12 And Samson said unto them, I will now ¹put forth a riddle unto you: if ye can certainly declare it me ᵐwithin the seven days of the feast, and find *it* out, then I will give

---

ⁱHeb. *in meeting him*——ᵏChap. iii. 10; xiii. 25; 1 Sam. xi. 6

¹1 Kings x. 1; Ezek. xvii. 2; Luke xiv. 7——ᵐGen. xxix. 27

---

of regal logic; i. e., "My will, backed by these instruments of destruction, shall be the rule of right and wrong." The rules and principles of this *logic* are now suspected; and it is not likely to be generally received again without *violent demonstration.*

Verse 5. *A young lion roared against him.*] Came fiercely out upon him, ready to tear him to pieces.

Verse 6. *He rent him as he would have rent a kid*] Now it is not intimated that he did this by his own natural strength, but by the *Spirit of the Lord coming mightily upon him:* so that his strength does not appear to be his own, nor to be at his command; his might was, *by the will of God,* attached to his *hair* and to his *Nazarate.*

Verse 7. *And talked with the woman*] That is, concerning marriage; thus forming the espousals.

Verse 8. *After a time*] Probably about one year; as this was the time that generally elapsed between espousing and wedding.

A swarm of bees and honey in the carcass] By length of time the flesh had been entirely consumed off the bones, and a swarm of bees had formed their combs within the region of the thorax, nor was it an improper place; nor was the thing unfrequent, if we may credit ancient writers; the carcasses of slain beasts becoming a receptacle for wild bees. The beautiful espisode in the 4th Georgic of Virgil, beginning at ver. 317, proves that the ancients believed that bees might be engendered in the body of a dead ox:—

Pastor Aristæus fugiens Peneia Tempe——
Quatuor eximios præstanti corpore tauros
Ducit, et intacta totidem cervice juvencas.
Post, ubi nona suos Aurora induxerat ortus.
Inferias Orphei mittit, lucumque revisit.
Hic ver o subitum, ac dietu mirabile monstrum
Adspiciunt, liquefacta boum per viscera toto
Stridere apes utero, et ruptis effervere costis;
Immensasque trahi nubes, jamque arbore summa
Confluere, et lentis uvam demittere ramis.
VIRG. Geor. lib. iv., ver. 550.

"Sad Aristæus from fair Tempe fled,
His bees with famine or diseases dead——
Four altars raises, from his herd he culls
For slaughter four the fairest of his *bulls;*
Four *heifers* from his female store he took,
All fair, and all unknowing of the yoke.
Nine mornings thence, with sacrifice and prayers,
The powers atoned, he to the grove repairs.
Behold a prodigy! for, from within
The broken bowels, and the bloated skin,
A buzzing noise of *bees* his ears alarms,
Straight issuing through the sides assembling swarms!
Dark as a cloud, they make a wheeling flight,
Then on a neighbouring tree descending light,
Like a large cluster of black grapes they show,
And make a large dependance from the bough.
DRYDEN.

Verse 10. *Samson made there a feast*] The marriage feast, when he went to marry his espoused wife.

Verse 11. *They brought thirty companions*] These are called in Scripture *children of the bride-chamber,* and *friends of the bridegroom.* See the whole of this subject particularly illustrated in the observations at the end of John iii.

Verse 12. *I will now put forth a riddle*] Probably this was one part of the amusements at a marriage-feast; each in his turn proposing a riddle, to be solved by any of the rest on a particular forfeit; the proposer forfeiting, if solved, the same which the company must forfeit if they could not solve it.

Thirty sheets] I have no doubt that the Arab *hayk,* or *hyke,* is here meant; a dress in which the natives of the East wrap themselves, as a Scottish Highlander does in his *plaid.* In Asiatic countries the dress scarcely ever changes; being nearly the same now that it was 2000 years ago. Mr. Jackson, in his account of the Empire of Morocco, thus mentions the Moorish dress: "It resembles," says he, "that of the ancient patriarchs, as represented in paintings; (*but the paintings are taken from Asiatic models;*) that of the men consists of a *red cap* and turban, a ·(*kumja*) shirt, which

A. M. 2868
B. C. 1136
An. Exod. Isr. 355
Anno ante
i. Olymp. 360

you thirty [n]sheets and thirty [o]change of garments:

13 But if ye cannot declare it me, then shall ye give me thirty sheets and thirty change of garments. And they said unto him, Put forth thy riddle, that we may hear it.

14 And he said unto them, Out of the eater came forth meat, and out of the strong came forth sweetness. And they could not in three days expound the riddle.

[n]Or, *shirts*——[o]Gen. xlv. 22; 2 Kings v. 22——[p]Chapter xvi. 5

15 And it came to pass on the seventh day, that they said unto Samson's wife, [p]Entice thy husband, that he may declare unto us the riddle, [q]lest we burn thee and thy father's house with fire: have ye called us [r]to take that we have? *is it* not *so?*

16 And Samson's wife wept before him, and said, [s]Thou dost but hate me, and lovest me not: thou hast put forth a riddle unto the children of my people, and hast not told *it* me.

A. M. 2868
B. C. 1136
An. Exod. Isr. 355
Anno ante
I. Olymp. 360

[q]Chapter xv. 6——[r]Heb. *to possess,* or, *to impoverish us*
[s]Chap. xvi. 15

hangs outside of the drawers, and comes down below the knee; a (*caftan*) coat, which buttons close before, and down to the bottom, with large open sleeves; over which, when they go out of doors, they throw carelessly, and sometimes elegantly, a *hayk,* or garment of white cotton, silk, or wool, five or six yards long, and five feet wide. The Arabs often dispense with the caftan, and even with the shirt, wearing nothing but the hayk." When an Arab does not choose to wrap himself in the hayk, he throws it over his left shoulder, where it hangs till the weather, &c., obliges him to wrap it round him. The hayk is either *mean* or *elegant,* according to the quality of the cloth, and of the person who wears it. I have myself seen the natives of Fez, with hayks, or hykes, both elegant and costly. By the *changes of garments,* it is very likely that the *kumja* and *caftan* are meant, or at least the caftan; but most likely both: for the Hebrew has חליפות בגדים *chaliphoth begadim, changes* or *succession of garments.* Samson, therefore, engaged to *give* or *receive* thirty *hayks,* and thirty *kumjas* and *caftans,* on the issue of the interpretation or non-interpretation of his riddle: these were complete suits.

Verse 14. *And he said unto them*] Thus he states or proposes his riddle:—

Out of the eater came forth meat,
And out of the strong came forth sweetness.

Instead of *strong,* the *Syriac* and *Arabic* have *bitter.* I have no doubt that the riddle was in *poetry;* and perhaps the two hemistichs above preserve its order. This was scarcely a fair riddle; for unless the fact to which it refers were known, there is no rule of interpretation by which it could be found out. We learn from the Scholiast, on Aristophanes, *Vesp.* v. 20, that it was a custom among the ancient Greeks to propose at their festivals, what were called γρϕοι, *griphoi,* riddles, enigmas, or very obscure sayings, both curious and difficult; and to give a recompense to those who found them out, which generally consisted in either a festive crown, or a goblet full of wine. Those who failed to solve them were condemned to drink a large portion of fresh water, or of wine mingled with a sea-water, which they were compelled to take down at one draught, without drawing their breath, their hands being tied behind their backs. Sometimes they gave the crown to the deity in honour of whom the festival was made: and if none could solve the riddle, the reward was given to him who proposed it.

Of these enigmas proposed at entertainments, &c., we have numerous examples in ATHENÆUS, *Deipnosoph,* lib. x., c. 15, p. 142, edit. Argentorat., and some of them very like this of Samson; for example:—

Διδους τις ουκ εδωκεν, ουδ' εχων εχει;

"Who gives, and does not give?
Who has not, and yet has?"

This may be spoken of an enigma and its proposer: he gives *it,* but he does not give the sense; the other has it, but has not the meaning.

Εστι ϕυσις θηλεια βρεϕη σοζουσ' υπο κολποις
Αυτης· ταυτα δ' αϕωνα βοην ιστησι γεγωνον.
Και δια ποντιον οιδμα, και ηπειρου δια πασης,
Οις εθελει θνητων· τοις δ' ου παρεουσιν ακουειν
Εξεστι· κωϕην δ' ακοης αισθησιν εχουσιν.

"There is a feminine Nature, fostering her children in her bosom; who, although they are dumb, send forth a distinct voice over every nation of the earth, and every sea, to whomsoever they please. It is possible for those who are absent to hear, and for those who are deaf to hear also."

The relator brings in Sappho interpreting it thus:—

Θηλεια μεν ουν εστι ϕυσις, επιστολη.
Βρεϕη δ' εν αυτη περιϕερει τα γραμματα
Αϕωνα δ' οντα ταυτα τοις πορρω λαλει,
Οις βουλεθ'· ετερος δ' αν τυχη τις πλησιον
Εστως αναγινωσκοντος, ουκ ακουσεται.

"The Nature, which is feminine, signifies an epistle; and her children whom she bears are alphabetical characters: and these, being dumb, speak and give counsel to any, even at a distance; though he who stands nigh to him who is silently reading, hears no voice."

Here is another, attributed by the same author to *Theodectes:*—

Της ϕυσεως οσα γαια ϕερει τροϕος, ουδ' οσα ποντος,
Ουτε βροτοισιν εχει γυιων αυξησιν ομοιαν.
Αλλ' εν μεν γενεσει πρωτοσπορῳ εστι μεγιστη,
Εν δε μεσαις ακμαις μικρα, γηρα δε προς αυτῳ
Μορϕη και μεγεβει μειζων παλιν εστιν απαντωι.

"Neither does the nourishing earth so bear by nature, nor the sea, nor is there among mortals a like increase of parts; for at the period of its birth it is greatest, but in its middle age it is small, and in its old age it is again greater in form and size than all."

A. M. 2868
B. C. 1136
An. Exod. Isr. 355
Anno ante
I. Olymp. 360

And he said unto her, Behold, I have not told *it* my father nor my mother, and shall I tell *it* thee?

17 And she wept before him [t]the seven days, while their feast lasted: and it came to pass on the seventh day, that he told her, because she lay sore upon him: and she told the riddle to the children of her people.

18 And the men of the city said unto him on the seventh day before the sun went down, What *is* sweeter than honey? and what *is*

stronger than a lion? And he said unto them, If ye had not ploughed with my heifer, ye had not found out my riddle.

A. M. 2868
B. C. 1136
An. Exod. Isr. 355
Anno ante
I. Olymp. 360

19 And [u]the Spirit of the LORD came upon him, and he went down to Askelon, and slew thirty men of them, and took their [v]spoil, and gave change of garments unto them which expounded the riddle. And his anger was kindled, and he went up to his father's house.

20 But Samson's wife [w]was *given* to his companion, whom he had used as [x]his friend.

---

[t]Or, the rest of *the seven days*, &c.——[u]Chap. iii. 10; xiii. 25——[v]Or, *apparel*——[w]Chap. xv. 2——[x]John iii. 29

This is spoken of a *shadow*. At the rising of the sun in the east, the shadow of an object is projected illimitably across the earth towards the west; at noon, if the sun be vertical to that place, the shadow of the object is entirely lost; at sunsetting, the shadow is projected towards the east, as it was in the morning towards the west.

Here is another, from the same author:—

Εισι κασιγνηται διτται, ὠν ἡ μια τικτει
Την ἑτεραν, αυτη δε τεκουσ' ὑπο τησδε τεκνουται.

"There are two sisters, the one of whom begets the other, and she who is begotten produces her who begat her."

Day and *night* solve this enigma.

The following I have taken from *Theognis:*—

Ηδη γαρ με κεκληκε θαλαττιος οικαδε νεκρος,
Τεθνηκως, ζωῳ φθεγγομενος στοματι.
THEOGN. *Gnom.*, in fine.

"A dead seaman calls me to his house;
And, although he be dead, he speaks with a living mouth."

This dead seaman is a conch or large shell-fish, of which the poet was about to eat. The mouth by which it spoke signifies its being used as a *horn;* as it is well known to produce, when opened at the spiral end and blown, a very powerful sound.

Verse 17. *And she wept before him*] Not through any love to him, for it appears she had none, but to oblige her paramours; and of this he soon had ample proof.

Verse 18. *If ye had not ploughed with my heifer*] If my wife had not been unfaithful to my bed, she would not have been unfaithful to my secret; and, you being her paramours, your interest was more precious to her than that of her husband. She has betrayed me through her attachment to you.

Calmet has properly remarked, in quoting the *Septuagint*, that to *plough with one's heifer*, or to *plough in another man's ground*, are delicate turns of expression used both by the Greeks and Latins, as well as the Hebrews, to point out a wife's infidelities.

Thus Theognis, Gnom. v. 581:—

Εχθαιρω δε γυναικα περιδρομον, ανδρα τε μαργον,
Ὁς την αλλονριην βουλετ' αρουραν αρουν.

"I detest a woman who gads about, and also a libidinous man, who wishes to plough in another man's ground."

Fundum alienum arat, incultum familiarem deserit.   PLAUTUS.

"He ploughs another's farm, and leaves his own heritage uncultivated."

Milo domi non est, peregre at Milone profecto Arva vacant, uxor non minus inde parit.
MARTIAL.

"Milo is not at home, and Milo being from home, his field lies uncultivated; his wife, nevertheless, continues to breed, and brings forth children."

There is the same metaphor in the following lines of *Virgil:*—

*Hoc faciunt, nimo ne luxu obtusior usus,
Sit genitali arvo, sulcosque oblimet inertes.*
Geor. l. iii., v. 135.

In this sense Samson's words were understood by the *Septuagint*, by the *Syriac*, and by Rabbi *Levi*. See BOCHART, Hierozoic. p. 1., lib. ii., cap. 41., col. 406.

The metaphor was a common one, and we need seek for no other interpretation of the words of Samson.

Verse 19. *The Spirit of the Lord came upon him*] "The spirit of fortitude from before the Lord."—*Targum.* He was inspired with unusual courage, and he felt strength proportioned to his wishes.

He—slew thirty men—and took their spoils] He took their *hayks*, their *kumjas*, and *caftans*, and gave them to the thirty persons who, by unfair means, had solved his riddle; thus they had what our version calls *thirty sheets, and thirty changes of raiment*. See the note on ver. 12.

Verse 20. *But Samson's wife was* given *to his companion*] This was the same kind of person who is called the friend of the bridegroom, John iii. 29. And it is very likely that she loved this person better than she loved her husband, and went to him as soon as Samson had gone to his father's house at Zorah. She might, however, have thought herself abandoned by him, and therefore took another; this appears to have been the persuasion of her father, chap. xv. 2. But her betraying his secret and his interests to his enemies was a full proof he was not very dear to her; though, to persuade him to the contrary, she shed many crocodile tears; see ver. 16. He could not keep his own secret, and he was fool enough to suppose that another would be more faithful to him than he was to himself. Multitudes complain of the treachery of friends betraying their secrets, &c., never

considering that they themselves have been their first betrayers, in confiding to others what they pretend to wish should be a secret to the whole world! If a man never let his secret out of his own bosom, it is impossible that he should ever be betrayed.

CHAPTER XV

Samson, going to visit his wife, finds her bestowed on another, 1, 2. He is incensed, vows revenge, and burns the corn of the Philistines, 3–5. They burn Samson's wife and her father, 6. He is still incensed, makes a great slaughter among them, 7, 8. The Philistines gather together against Israel, and to appease them the men of Judah bind Samson, and deliver him into their hands, 9–13. The Spirit of the Lord comes upon him; he breaks his bonds, finds the jaw-bone of an ass, and therewith kills a thousand men, 14–16. He is sorely fatigued; and, being thirsty, God miraculously produces water from an opening of the ground in Lehi, and he is refreshed, 17–19. He judges Israel in the time of the Philistines twenty years, 20.

A. M. 2869
B. C. 1135
An. Exod. Isr.
356
Anno ante
I. Olymp. 359

BUT it came to pass within a while after, in the time of wheat harvest, that Samson visited his ^awife with a kid; and he said, I will go in to my wife into the chamber. But her father would not suffer him to go in.

2 And her father said, I ^bverily thought that thou hadst utterly hated her; therefore I gave her to thy ^ccompanion: *is* not her younger sister fairer than she? ^dtake her, I pray thee, instead of her.

3 And Samson said concerning them, ^eNow shall I be more blameless than the Philistines, though I do them a displeasure.

A. M. 2869
B. C. 1135
An. Exod. Isr.
356
Anno ante
I. Olymp. 359

4 And Samson went and caught three hundred foxes, and took ^ffirebrands, and turned tail to tail, and put a firebrand in the midst between two tails.

5 And when he had set the brands on fire, he let *them* go into the standing corn of the Philistines, and burnt up both the shocks, and also the standing corn, with the vineyards *and* olives.

---

^aChap. xiv. 2——^bChap. xiv. 16——^cChap. xiv. 20
^dHeb. *let her be thine*

^eOr, *Now shall I be blameless from the Philistines,
though, &c.*——^fOr, *torches*

NOTES ON CHAP. XV

Verse 1. *Visited his wife with a kid*] On her betraying him, he had, no doubt, left her in great disgust. After some time his affection appears to have returned; and, taking a kid, or perhaps a *fawn*, as a present, he goes to make reconciliation, and finds her given to his brideman; probably, the person to whom she betrayed his riddle.

Verse 2. *Thou hadst utterly hated her*] As he was conscious she had given him great cause so to do.

Her younger sister] The father appears to have been perfectly sincere in this offer.

Verse 4. *Went and caught three hundred foxes*] There has been much controversy concerning the meaning of the term שׁוּעָלִים *shua-lim*, some supposing it to mean *foxes* or *jackals*, and others *handfuls* or *sheaves of corn*. Much of the force of the objections against the common version will be diminished by the following considerations:—

1. Foxes, or jackals, are common and gregarious in that country.

2. It is not hinted that Samson collected them *alone*; he might have employed several hands in this work.

3. It is not said he collected them all in *one day*; he might have employed several days, as well as many persons, to furnish him with these means of vengeance.

4. In other countries, where ferocious beasts were less numerous, great multitudes have been

exhibited at once. *Sylla*, in a public show to the Roman citizens, exhibited *one hundred* lions; *Cæsar, four hundred*, and *Pompey*, nearly *six hundred*. The Emperor *Probus* let loose in the theatre, at one time, *one thousand* ostriches, *one thousand* stags, *one thousand* wild boars, *one thousand* does, and a countless multitude of other wild animals; at another time he exhibited *one hundred* leopards from Libya, *one hundred* from Syria, and *three hundred* bears. —See *Flavius Vopiscus* in the Life of *Probus*, cap. xix., beginning with *Dedit Romanis etiam voluptates*, &c.

That foxes, or the creature called *shual*, abounded in Judea, is evident from their frequent mention in Scripture, and from several places bearing their name. 1. It appears they were so numerous that even their cubs ruined the vineyards; see Cant. ii. 15: *Take us the foxes, the little foxes, that spoil our vines.* Jeremiah complains that the *foxes* had occupied the mountains of Judea, Lam. v. 18. They are mentioned as making incursions into *enclosures*, &c., Neh. iv. 3. Ezekiel compares the numerous false prophets to these animals, chap. xiii. 4. In Josh. xv. 28 we find a place called *Hazar Shual*, "the court of the *foxes*;" and in chap. xix. 42 a place called *Shaal-abbin*, "the foxes;" no doubt from the number of those animals in that district. And mention is made of the *land of Shual*, or of the *fox*, 1 Sam. xiii. 17.

The creature called *shual* is represented by travellers and naturalists who have been in

A. M. 2869
B. C. 1135
An. Exod. Isr.
356
Anno ante
I. Olymp. 359

6 Then the Philistines said, Who hath done this? And they answered, Samson the son-in-law of the Timnite, because he had taken his wife, and given her to his companion. ᵍAnd the Philistines came up and burnt her and her father with fire.

7 And Samson said unto them, Though ye have done this, yet will I be avenged of you, and after that I will cease.

8 And he smote them hip and thigh with a great slaughter: and he went down and dwelt in the top of the rock Etam.

9 Then the Philistines went up, and pitched

in Judah, and spread themselves ʰin Lehi.

A. M. 2869
B. C. 1135
An. Exod. Isr.
356
Anno ante
I. Olymp. 359

10 And the men of Judah said, Why are ye come up against us? And they answered, To bind Samson are we come up, to do to him as he hath done to us.

11 Then three thousand men of Judah ⁱwent to the top of the rock Etam, and said to Samson, Knowest thou not that the Philistines *are* ᵏrulers over us? what *is* this *that* thou hast done unto us? And he said unto them, As they did unto me, so have I done unto them.

12 And they said unto him, We are come down to bind thee, that we may deliver thee

---

ᵍChap. xiv. 15——ʰVer. 19

ⁱHeb. *went down*——ᵏChap. xiv. 4

Judea, as an animal between a wolf and a fox. *Hasselquist*, who was on the spot, and saw many of them, calls it the *little Eastern fox*. They are frequent in the East, and often destroy infirm persons and children.

Dr. *Kennicott*, however, objects to the common interpretation; and gives reasons, some of which are far from being destitute of weight. "The *three hundred foxes*," says he, "caught by Samson, have been so frequently the subject of banter and ridicule, that we should consider whether the words may not admit a more rational interpretation: for, besides the improbability arising here from the *number* of these *foxes*, the *use* made of them is also very strange. If these animals were tied *tail to tail*, they would probably pull contrary ways, and consequently stand still; whereas a firebrand tied to the tail of each fox singly would have been far more likely to answer the purpose here intended. To obviate these difficulties it has been well remarked, that the word שׁוּעָלִים *shualim*, here translated *foxes*, signifies also *handfuls*, Ezek. xiii. 19, *handfuls of barley;* if we leave out that one letter ו *vau*, which has been inserted or omitted elsewhere, almost at pleasure. No less than *seven* Hebrew MSS. want that letter here, and read שְׁעָלִים *shealim*. Admitting this version, we see that Samson took *three hundred handfuls* or *sheaves of corn*, and *one hundred and fifty firebrands;* that he turned the sheaves *end* to *end*, and put a firebrand between the two ends in the midst; and then, setting the brands on fire, sent the fire into the standing corn of the Philistines. The same word is now used twice in one chapter, (Ezek. xiii. 4 and 19;) in the former verse signifying *foxes*, in the latter *handfuls:* and in 1 Kings xx. 10, where we render it *handfuls*, it is ἀλωπεξ, *foxes*, in the Greek version."—*Remarks on Select Passages.*

The reasoning of Dr. Kennicott in the first part of this criticism has already been answered; other parts shall be considered below. Though there are seven MSS., which agree in the reading contended for by Dr. Kennicott, yet all the *versions* are on the other side. I see no improbability in the common version.

Turned tail to tail] Had he put a firebrand to each, which Dr. Kennicott thinks more reasonable, the creature, naturally terrified at fire,

would have instantly taken to *cover;* and thus the design of Samson would have been frustrated. But, tying *two* of them *together by their tails*, they would frequently thwart each other in running, pull hither and thither, and thus make the greater devastation. Had he tied them all together, the confusion would have been so great that no execution could have been done.

Verse 6. *Burnt her and her father*] This was probably done to *appease* Samson: as they saw he had been unjustly treated both by his wife and her father; therefore they destroyed them both, that they might cause his wrath to cease from them. And this indeed seems intimated in the following verse: *And Samson said —Though ye have done this, yet will I be avenged of you;* that is, I am not yet satisfied: ye have done me great wrongs, I must have proportionate redress; then I shall rest satisfied.

Verse 8. *He smote them hip and thigh*] This also is variously understood; but the general meaning seems plain; he appears to have had no kind of defensive weapon, therefore he was obliged to grapple with them; and, according to the custom of *wrestlers, trip up their feet*, and then bruise them to death. Some translate *heaps upon heaps;* others, *he smote horsemen and footmen;* others, *he wounded them from their legs to their thighs*, &c., &c. See the different *versions*. Some think in their running away from him he *kicked* them down, and then trod them to death: thus his *leg* or *thigh* was against their *hip;* hence the expression.

The top of the rock Etam.] It is very likely that this is the same place as that mentioned 1 Chron. iv. 32; it was in the tribe of Simeon, and on the borders of Dan, and probably a *fortified* place.

Verse 10. *To bind Samson are we come up*] It seems they did not wish to come to an open rupture with the Israelites, provided they would deliver up him who was the cause of their disasters.

Verse 11. *Three thousand men of Judah went*] It appears evidently from this that Samson was strongly posted, and they thought that no less than *three thousand* men were necessary to reduce him.

Verse 12. *That ye will not fall upon me your-*

A. M. 2869
B. C. 1135
An. Exod. Isr.
356
Anno ante
I. Olymp. 359
into the hand of the Philistines. And Samson said unto them, Swear unto me, that ye will not fall upon me yourselves.

13 And they spake unto him, saying, No; but we will bind thee fast, and deliver thee into their hand: but surely we will not kill thee. And they bound him with two new cords, and brought him up from the rock.

14 *And* when he came unto Lehi, the Philistines shouted against him: and [l]the Spirit of the LORD came mightily upon him, and the cords that *were* upon his arms became as flax that was burnt with fire, and his bands [m]loosed from off his hands.

15 And he found a [n]new jaw-bone of an ass, and put forth his hand, and took it, and [o]slew a thousand men therewith.

16 And Samson said, With the jaw bone of an ass, [p]heaps upon heaps, with the jaw of an ass have I slain a thousand men.

A. M. 2869
B. C. 1135
An. Exod. Isr.
356
Anno ante
I. Olymp. 359

17 And it came to pass, when he had made an end of speaking, that he cast away the jaw-bone out of his hand, and called that place [q]Ramath-lehi.

18 And he was sore athirst, and called on the LORD, and said, [r]Thou hast given this great deliverance into the hand of thy servant: and now shall I die for thirst, and fall into the hand of the uncircumcised?

19 But God clave a hollow place that *was* in [s]the jaw, and there came water thereout; and when he had drunk, [t]his spirit came again, and he revived: wherefore he called the name thereof [u]En-hakkore, which *is* in Lehi unto this day.

20 [v]And he judged Israel [w]in the days of the Philistines twenty years.

---

[l]Chap. iii. 10; xiv. 6——[m]Heb. *were melted*——[n]Heb. *moist*——[o]Chap. iii. 31; Lev. xvi. 8; Josh. xxiii. 10 [p]Heb. *a heap, two heaps*——[q]That is, *the lifting up of the jaw-bone*, or, *casting away of the jaw-bone*——[r]Psa. iii. 7

[s]Or, *Lehi*——[t]Gen. xlv. 27; Isa. xl. 29——[u]That is, *the well of him that called*, or *cried;* Psa. xxxiv. 6——[v]He seems to have judged southwest Israel during twenty years of their servitude of the Philistines——[w]Chap. xiii. 1

---

selves.] He could not bear the thought of contending with and slaying his own countrymen; for there is no doubt that he could have as easily rescued himself from their hands as from those of the Philistines.

Verse 13. *They bound him with two new cords*] Probably his *hands* with one and his *legs* with the other.

Verse 14. *When he came unto Lehi*] This was the name of the *place* to which they brought him, either to put him to death, or keep him in perpetual confinement.

Shouted against him] His capture was a matter of public rejoicing.

Verse 15. *He found a new jaw-bone of an ass*] I rather think that the word טריה *teriyah*, which we translate *new*, and the margin *moist*, should be understood as signifying the *tabia* or *putrid state* of the ass from which this jawbone was taken. He found there a dead ass in a state of putrefaction; on which account he could the more easily separate the jaw from its integuments; this was a circumstance proper to be recorded by the historian, and a mark of the providence of God. But were we to understand it of a *fresh jaw-bone*, very lately separated from the head of an ass, the circumstance does not seem worthy of being recorded.

With the jaw-bone of an ass, heaps upon heaps] I cannot see the propriety of this rendering of the Hebrew words בלחי החמור חמור חמרתים *bilchi hachamor, chamor chamorathayim;* I believe they should be translated thus:—

"With the jaw-bone of this ass, an ass (the foal) of two asses;
"With the jaw-bone of this ass I have slain a thousand men."

This appears to have been a triumphal song on the occasion; and the words are variously rendered both by the versions, and by expositors.

Verse 17. *Ramath-lehi.*] The *lifting up* or *casting away of the jaw-bone*. Lehi was the name of the place before, *Ramath* was now added to it here; he *lifted up* the jaw-bone against his enemies, and slew them.

Verse 18. *I die for thirst*] The natural consequence of the excessive fatigue he had gone through in this encounter.

Verse 19. *God clave a hollow place that was in the jaw*] אשר בלחי *asher ballechi, that was in Lehi;* that is, there was a *hollow* place in this Lehi, and God caused a fountain to spring up in it. Because the place was *hollow* it was capable of containing the water that rose up in it, and thus of becoming a *well*.

En-hakkore] The *well of the implorer;* this name he gave to the *spot* where the water rose, in order to perpetuate the bounty of God in affording him this miraculous supply.

Which is *in Lehi unto this day.*] Consequently not IN the *jaw-bone of the ass*, a most unfortunate rendering.

Verse 20. *He judged Israel—twenty years.*] In the margin it is said, *He seems to have judged southwest Israel during twenty years of their servitude of the Philistines*, chap. xiii. 1. Instead of עשרים שנה *esrim shanah, twenty years*, the Jerusalem Talmud has ארבעים שנה *arbaim shanah, forty years;* but this reading is not acknowledged by any MS. or version. According to Calmet, the twenty years of the judicature of Samson began the eighteenth year of the subjection of Israel to the Philistines; and these twenty years are included in the judicature of the high priest *Eli.*

THE burning of the Philistines' corn by the means of foxes and firebrands is a very remarkable circumstance; and there is a story told by Ovid, in the 4th book of his *Fasti*, that bears a striking similitude to this; and is supposed by some learned men to allude to *Samson* and his *foxes*. The poet is at a loss to account for this custom, but brings in an old man of Carseoli, with what must have appeared to himself a very unsatisfactory solution. The passage begins as follows:—

Tertia post Hyadas cum luxerit orta remotas,
   Carcere partitos Circus habebit equos
Cur igitur missæ vinctis ardentia tædis
   Terga ferant vulpes, causa docenda mihi?
      Vid. OVID, *Fastor.* lib. iv., ver. 679.

The substance of the whole account, which is too long to be transcribed, is this: It was a custom in Rome, celebrated in the month of April, to let loose a number of *foxes* in the circus, with lighted flambeaux on their backs; and the Roman people took pleasure in seeing these animals run about till roasted to death by the flames with which they were eneveloped. The poet wishes to know what the origin of this custom was, and is thus informed by an old man of the city of Carseoli: "A frolicksome young lad, about ten years of age, found, near a thicket, a fox that had stolen away many fowls from the neighbouring roosts. Having enveloped his body with hay and straw, he set it on fire, and let the fox loose. The animal, in order to avoid the flames, took to the standing corn which was then ready for the sickle; and the wind, driving the flames with double violence, the crops were everywhere consumed. Though this transaction is long since gone by, the com-

memoration of it still remains; for, by a law of this city, every fox that is taken is burnt to death. Thus the nation awards to the foxes the punishment of being burnt alive, for the destruction of the ripe corn formerly occasioned by one of these animals."

Both *Serrarius* and *Bochart* reject this origin of the custom given by Ovid; and insist that the custom took its rise from the burning of the Philistines' corn by Samson's foxes. The *origin* ascribed to the custom by the Carseolian they consider as too frivolous and unimportant to be commemorated by a national festival. The *time* of the observation does not accord with the time of *harvest* about Rome and in Italy, but it perfectly accords with the time of harvest in Palestine, which was at least as early as April. Nor does the circumstance of the fox wrapped in hay and let loose, the hay being set on fire, bear any proper resemblance to the foxes let loose in the circus with burning brands on their backs.

These learned men therefore conclude that it is much more natural to suppose that the Romans derived the custom from Judea, where probably the burning of the Philistines' corn might, for some time, have been annually commemorated.

The whole account is certainly very singular, and has not a very satisfactory solution in the old man's tale, as related by the Roman poet.

All public institutions have had their origin in *facts;* and if, through the lapse of time or loss of records, the original facts be lost, we may legitimately look for them in cases where there is so near a resemblance as in that above.

CHAPTER XVI

Samson comes to Gaza; they lay wait for him; he rises by night, and carries away the city gates, 1–3. Falls in love with Delilah, 4. The lords of the Philistines promise her money if she will obtain from Samson the secret in which his strength lay, 5. By various artifices she at last obtains this; and communicates it to the Philistines, who seize and bind him, put out his eyes, and cause him to grind in the prison-house, 6–21. At a public festival to Dagon he is brought out to make sport; when, being weary, he requests to be placed between the two pillars which supported the roof of the house, on which three thousand men and women were stationed to see him make sport, 22–27. He prays to God to strengthen him, and pulls down the pillars; by which (the house falling) both himself, the lords of the Philistines, and a vast multitude of the people, are slain, 28–30. His relatives come and take away his body, and bury it, 31.

A. M. 2884
B. C. 1120
An. Exod. Isr.
371
Anno ante
I. Olymp. 344

THEN went Samson to Gaza, and saw there a [a]harlot, and went in unto her.

2 *And it was told* the Gazites, saying, Samson is come hither. And they [b]compassed *him* in, and laid wait for him all night in the gate of the city, and were

A. M. 2884
B. C. 1120
An. Exod. Isr.
371
Anno ante
I. Olymp. 344

---

[a]Heb. *a woman a harlot*

[b]1 Sam. xxiii. 26; Psa. cxviii. 10, 11, 12; Acts ix. 24

NOTES ON CHAP. XVI

Verse 1. *Then went Samson to Gaza, and saw there a harlot*] The Chaldee, as in the former case, renders the clause thus: *Samson saw there a woman, an inn-keeper.* Perhaps the word זונה *zonah* is to be taken here in its *double* sense; one who keeps a house for the entertainment of travellers, and who also prostitutes her person.

Gaza was situated near the Mediterranean Sea, and was one of the most southern cities of Palestine. It has been supposed by some to have derived its name from the *treasures* de-

posited there by Cambyses, king of the Persians; because they say Gaza, in *Persian*, signifies *treasure;* so Pomponius Mela, and others. But it is more likely to be a Hebrew word, and that this city derived its name, עזה *azzah*, from עזז *azaz*, to be strong, it being a strong or well fortified place.

The Hebrew ע *ain* in this word is, by the *Septuagint*, the *Arabic*, and the *Vulgate*, rendered *G;* hence instead of *azzah*, with a strong guttural breathing, we have *Gaza*, a name by which this town could not be recognised by an ancient Hebrew.

Verse 2. *They compassed him in*] They shut

A. M. 2884
B. C. 1120
An. Exod. Isr.
371
Anno ante
I. Olymp. 344
^cquiet all the night, saying, In the morning, when it is day, we shall kill him.

3 And Samson lay till midnight, and arose at midnight, and took the doors of the gate of the city, and the two posts, and went away with them, ^dbar and all, and put *them* upon his shoulders, and carried them up to the top of a hill that *is* before Hebron.

4 And it came to pass afterward, that he loved a woman ^ein the valley of Sorek, whose name *was* Delilah.

5 And the lords of the Philistines came up unto her, and said unto her, ^fEntice him, and see wherein his great strength *lieth,* and by what *means* we may prevail against him, that we may bind him to ^gafflict him: and we will give thee every one of us eleven hundred *pieces* of silver.

6 And Delilah said to Samson, Tell me, I pray thee, wherein thy great strength *lieth,* and wherewith thou mightest be bound to afflict thee.

A. M. 2884
B. C. 1120
An. Exod. Isr.
371
Anno ante
I. Olymp. 344

7 And Samson said unto her, If they bind me with seven ^hgreen ⁱwiths that were never dried, then shall I be weak and be as ^kanother man.

8 Then the lords of the Philistines brought up to her seven green withs which had not been dried, and she bound him with them.

9 Now *there were* men lying in wait, abiding with her in the chamber. And she said unto him, The Philistines *be* upon thee, Samson. And he brake the withs, as a thread of tow is broken when it ^ltoucheth the fire. So his strength was not known.

10 And Delilah said unto Samson, Behold, thou hast mocked me, and told me lies: now tell me, I pray thee, wherewith thou mightest be bound.

---

^cHeb. *silent*——^dHeb. *with the bar*——^eOr, *by the brook*——^fCh. xiv. 15; see Prov. ii. 16–19; v. 3–11; vi.

24, 25, 26; vii. 21, 22, 23——^gOr, *humble*——^hOr, *new cords*——ⁱHeb. *moist*——^kHeb. *one*——^lHeb. *smelleth*

---

up all the avenues, secured the gates, and set persons in ambush near them, that they might attack him on his leaving the city early the next morning.

Verse 3. *Took the doors of the gate*] Though Samson was a very strong man, yet we do not find that he was a *giant;* consequently we may conjecture that the gates of the city were not very large, as he took at once the *doors,* the *two posts,* and the *bar,* with him. The *cities* of those days would appear to disadvantage among modern *villages.*

A hill—before Hebron.] Possibly there were *two* Hebrons; it could not be the city generally understood by the word Hebron, as that was about twenty miles distant from Gaza: unless we suppose that עַל פְּנֵי חֶבְרוֹן *al peney Chebron* is to be understood of the road *leading to Hebron:* he carried all to the top of that hill which was on the road leading to Hebron.

Verse 4. *He loved a woman in the valley of Sorek*] Some think Samson took this woman for his *wife;* others, that he had her as a *concubine.* It appears she was a Philistine; and however strong his love was for her, she seems to have had none for him. He always matched improperly, and he was cursed in all his matches. Where the *valley* or *brook* of *Sorek* was, is not easy to be ascertained. Eusebius and Jerome say it lay southward of *Eleutheropolis;* but where was Eleutheropolis? Ancient writers take all their measurements from this city; but as it is nowhere mentioned in the Scriptures, it is impossible to fix its situation, for we know not its ancient name.

Verse 5. *See wherein his great strength* lieth] They saw that his *stature* was not remarkable: and that, nevertheless, he had most extraordinary strength; therefore they supposed that it was the effect of some *charm* or *amulet.* The

lords of the Philistines were the five following: Gaza, Gath, Askelon, Ekron, and Ashdod. All these considered Samson as a public enemy; and they promised this bad woman a large sum of money if she would obtain from him the important secret wherein his strength lay, that, depriving him of this *supernatural power,* they might be able to reduce him to bondage.

Verse 7. *Seven green withs*] That is, any kind of *pliant, tough wood,* twisted in the form of a cord or rope. Such are used in many countries formed out of *osiers, hazel, &c.* And in Ireland, very long and strong ropes are made of the *fibres of bog-wood,* or the larger roots of the fir, which is often dug up in the *bogs* or *mosses* of that country. But the *Septuagint,* by translating the Hebrew יְתָרִים לַחִים *yetharim lachim* by νευραις υγραις, and the *Vulgate* by *nerviceis funibus,* understand these bonds to be *cords made of the nerves of cattle,* or perhaps rather out of *raw hides,* these also making an exceedingly strong cord. In some countries they take the skin of the horse, cut it lengthwise from the hide into thongs about two inches broad, and after having laid them in salt for some time, take them out for use. This practice is frequent in the country parts of Ireland; and both customs, the wooden cord, and that made of the raw or green hide, are among the most ancient perhaps in the world. Among the Irish peasantry this latter species of cord is called the *tug,* and is chiefly used for agricultural purposes, particularly for drawing the *plough* and the *harrow,* instead of the *iron chains* used in other countries.

Verse 9. *Men lying in wait*] They probably did not appear, as Samson immediately broke his bonds when this bad woman said, *The Philistines be upon thee.*

A. M. 2884
B. C. 1120
An. Exod. Isr.
371
Anno ante
I. Olymp. 344

11 And he said unto her, If they bind me fast with new ropes [m]that never were occupied, then shall I be weak, and be as another man.

12 Delilah therefore took new ropes, and bound him therewith, and said unto him, The Philistines *be* upon thee, Samson. And *there were* liers in wait abiding in the chamber. And he brake them from off his arms like a thread.

13 And Delilah said unto Samson, Hitherto thou hast mocked me, and told me lies: tell me wherewith thou mightest be bound. And he said unto her, If thou weavest the seven locks of my head with the web.

14 And she fastened *it* with the pin, and said unto him, The Philistines *be* upon thee, Samson. And he awaked out of his sleep, and went away with the pin of the beam, and with the web.

15 And she said unto him, [n]How canst

thou say, I love thee, when thine heart *is* not with me? thou hast mocked me these three times, and hast not told me wherein thy great strength *lieth*.

A. M. 2884
B. C. 1120
An. Exod. Isr.
371
Anno ante
I. Olymp. 344

16 And it came to pass, when she pressed him daily with her words, and urged him, *so* that his soul was [o]vexed unto death;

17 That he [p]told her all his heart, and said unto her, [q]There hath not come a razor upon mine head; for I *have been* a Nazarite unto God from my mother's womb; if I be shaven, then my strength will go from me, and I shall become weak, and be like any *other* man.

18 And when Delilah saw that he had told her all his heart, she sent and called for the lords of the Philistines, saying, Come up this once, for he hath showed me all his heart. Then the lords of the Philistines came up unto her, and brought money in their hand.

19 [r]And she made him sleep upon her knees; and she called for a man, and caused

---

[m]Heb. *wherewith work hath not been done*——[n]Chapter xiv. 16——[o]Heb. *shortened*

[p]Mic. vii. 5——[q]Num. vi. 5; chap. xiii. 5——[r]Proverbs vii. 26, 27

Verse 11. *If they bind me fast with new ropes*] Samson wishes to keep up the opinion which the Philistines held; viz., that his mighty strength was the effect of some *charm;* and therefore he says, *Seven green withs which had not been dried; new ropes that were never occupied; weave the seven locks of my hair with the web,* &c.; the *green* withs, the *new* ropes, and the number *seven*, are such matters as would naturally be expected in a charm or spell.

Verse 13. *The seven locks of my head*] Probably Samson had his long hair plaited into *seven divisions*, and as his vow of a Nazarite obliged him to *wear his hair*, so, *seven* being a number of perfection among the Hebrews, his hair being divided into *seven locks* might more particularly point out the *perfection* designed by his *Nazarite state.*

Every person must see that this verse ends abruptly, and does not contain a full sense. Houbigant has particularly noticed this, and corrected the text from the *Septuagint, the reading* of which I shall here subjoin: Εαν υφανης τας επτα σειρας της κεφαλης μου συν τω διασματι, και εγκρουσης τω πασσαλω εις τον τοιχον, και εσομαι ως εις των ανθρωπων ασθενης· Και εγενετο εν τω κοιμασθαι αυτον, και ελαβε Δαλιδα τας επτα σειρας της κεφαλης αυτου, και υφανεν εν τω διασματι, και επηξε τω πασσαλω εις τον τοιχον; "If thou shalt weave the seven locks of my head with the web, *and shalt fasten them with the pin in the wall, I shall become weak like other men: And so it was that, when he slept, Dalida took the seven locks of his head, and wove them with the web, and fastened it with the pin to the wall* and said unto him," &c. All the words printed here in *italic*, are wanting in the present Hebrew copies; but

are preserved in the *Septuagint*, and are most obviously necessary to complete the sense; else Delilah appears to do something that she is not ordered to do, and to omit what she was commanded.

Verse 16. *His soul was vexed unto death*] What a consummate *fool* was this *strong* man! Might he not have seen, from what already took place, that Delilah intended his ruin? After trifling with her, and lying thrice, he at last commits to her his fatal secret, and thus becomes a traitor to himself and to his God. Well may we adopt the sensible observation of Calmet on this passage: *La foiblesse du cœur de Samson, dans toute cette histoire, est encore plus etonnante que la force de son corps;* "The weakness of Samson's heart in the whole of this history, is yet more astonishing than the strength of his body."

Verse 17. *If I be shaven, then my strength will go from me*] The miraculous strength of Samson must not be supposed to reside either in his *hair* or in his *muscles*, but in that *relation* in which he stood to God as a Nazarite, such a person being bound by a solemn vow to walk in a strict conformity to the laws of his Maker. It was a part of the Nazarite's vow to permit no razor to pass on his head; and his long *hair* was the mark of his Nazirate, and of his vow to God. When Samson permitted his hair to be shorn off, he renounced and broke his Nazir vow; in consequence of which God abandoned him; and therefore we are told, in ver. 20, that *the Lord was departed from him.*

Verse 19. *She began to afflict him*] She had probably tied his hands slyly, while he was asleep, and after having cut off his hair, she began to insult him before she called the Philistines, to try whether he were really reduced to

A. M. 2884
B. C. 1120
An. Exod. Isr.
371
Anno ante
I. Olymp. 344

him to shave off the seven locks of his head; and she began to afflict him, and his strength went from him.

20 And she said, The Philistines *be* upon thee, Samson. And he awoke out of his sleep, and said, I will go out as at other times before, and shake myself. And he wist not that the LORD [s]was departed from him.

21 But the Philistines took him, and [t]put out his eyes, and brought him down to Gaza, and bound him with fetters of brass; and he did grind in the prison-house.

22 Howbeit the hair of his head began to grow again, [u]after he was shaven.

23 Then the lords of the Philistines gathered them together for to offer a great sacrifice unto Dagon their god, and to rejoice:

for they said, Our god hath delivered Samson our enemy into our hand.

A. M. 2884
B. C. 1120
An. Exod. Isr.
371
Anno ante
I. Olymp. 344

24 And when the people saw him, they [v]praised their god: for they said, Our god hath delivered into our hands our enemy, and the destroyer of our country [w]which slew many of us.

25 And it came to pass, when their hearts were [x]merry, that they said, Call for Samson, that he may make us sport. And they called for Samson out of the prison-house; and he [y]made them sport: and they set him between the pillars.

26 And Samson said unto the lad that held him by the hand, Suffer me that I may feel the pillars whereupon the house standeth, that I may lean upon them.

---

[s]Numbers xiv. 9, 42, 43; Josh. vii. 12; 1 Sam. xvi. 14; xviii. 12; xxviii. 15, 16; 2 Chron. xv. 2——[t]Heb. *bored out*

[u]Or, *as when he was shaven*——[v]Daniel v. 4——[w]Heb. *and who multiplied our slain*——[x]Chap. ix. 27——[y]Heb. *before them*

---

a state of weakness. Finding he could not disengage himself, she called the Philistines, and he, being alarmed, rose up, thinking he could exert himself as before, *and shake himself,* i. e., disengage himself from his bonds and his enemies: but *he wist not that the Lord was departed from him;* for as Delilah had cut off his locks while he was *asleep,* he had not yet perceived that they were gone.

Verse 21. *Put out his eyes*] Thus was the lust of the eye, in looking after and gazing on strange women, punished. As the Philistines did not know that his strength might not return, they put out his eyes, that he might never be able to plan any enterprise against them.

He did grind in the prison-house.] Before the invention of *wind* and *water-mills,* the grain was at first bruised between two stones, afterwards ground in *hand-mills.* This is practised in China and in different parts of the East still; and *women* and *slaves* are the persons who are obliged to turn these mills.

Such instruments were anciently used in this country, and called *querns,* from the Anglo-Saxon cpeopn and cpypn *cweorn* and *cwyrn,* which has the signification of a *mill;* hence cpeopn ſtan *cweorn stan,* a millstone: and as *quern* conveys the notion of *grinding,* hence opeopnteð, *cweornteth,* the *dentes molares* or *grinders* in the jaws of animals. This clause of the verse is thus translated in the Saxon Octateuch: Anð þa Philiſtei ƷeƷenƷon hine ſona—anð Ʒeleðdon hine apeƷ—to heoþa biþiƷ. Anð on cþeaþtenne belucon-hetton hine Ʒhinðan æt hiþa hanðcþyne. "And the Philistines laid their fangs, (seized) him soon, and led him away to their burgh, (city,) and shut him up in prison, and made him grind at their *hand-querne.*" So late as half a century ago I have seen these *querns* or hand-mills in *these* kingdoms.

Verse 22. *The hair of his head began to grow again*] And may we not suppose that, sensible of his sin and folly, he renewed his *Nazir vow*

to the Lord, in consequence of which his supernatural strength was again restored?

Verse 23. *Unto Dagon their god*] Diodorus Siculus describes their god thus: Το μεν προσωπον εχει γυναικος, το δ' αλλο σωμα παν ιχθυος; "It had the head of a woman, but all the rest of the body resembled a fish." Dagon was called *Dorceto* among the heathens.

Horace, in the following lines, especially in the *third* and *fourth,* seems to have in view the image of *Dagon:*—

Humano capiti cervicem pictor equinam
Pingere si velit; et varias inducere plumas,
Undique collatis membris; ut *turpiter atrum*
Desinat in piscem mulier formosa superne;
Spectatum admissi risum teneatis amici?
DE ART. POET., v. 1.

"Suppose a painter to a human head
Should join a horse's neck; and wildly spread
The various plumage of the feather'd kind
O'er limbs of different beasts, absurdly join'd;
Or if he gave to view a *beauteous maid,*
Above the waist with every charm array'd,
Should a *foul fish her lower parts* infold,
Would you not smile such pictures to behold?"
FRANCIS.

Verse 25. *Call for Samson, that he may make us sport*] What the sport was we cannot tell; probably it was an exhibition of his prodigious strength. This seems to be intimated by what is said, ver. 22, of the restoration of his *hair;* and the exertions he was obliged to make will account for the *weariness* which gave him the pretence to ask for leave to *lean against the pillars.* Some think he was brought out to be a *laughing-stock,* and that he was variously *insulted* by the Philistines; hence the version of the Septuagint: και ερραπιζον αυτον, *and they buffeted him.* Josephus, Antiq. Jud. lib. v., cap. 8, s. 12, says: *He was brought out,* οπως ενυβρισωσιν αυτον παρα τον ποτον, *that they might insult him in their cups.*

A. M. 2884
B. C. 1120
An. Exod. Isr. 371
Anno ante I. Olymp. 344

27 Now the house was full of men and women; and all the lords of the Philistines *were* there; and *there were* upon the ^zroof about three thousand men and women, that beheld while Samson made sport.

28 And Samson called unto the LORD, and said, O LORD God, ^aremember me, I pray thee, and strengthen me, I pray thee, only this once, O God, that I may be at once avenged of the Philistines for my two eyes.

29 And Samson took hold of the two middle pillars upon which the house stood, and ^bon which it was borne up, of the one with his right hand, and of the other with his left.

A. M. 2884
B. C. 1120
An. Exod. Isr. 371
Anno ante I. Olymp. 344

30 And Samson said, Let ^cme die with the Philistines. And he bowed himself with *all his* might; and the house fell upon the lords, and upon all the people that *were* therein. So the dead which he slew at his death were more than *they* which he slew in his life.

31 Then his brethren and all the house of his father came down, and took him, and brought *him* up, and ^dburied him between Zorah and Eshtaol in the burying-place of Manoah his father. And he judged Israel twenty years.

---

^zDeut. xxii. 8——^aJer. xv. 15——^bOr, *he leaned*   on them——^cHeb. *my soul*——^dChap. xiii. 25

Verse 27. *Now the house was full of men*] It was either the prison-house, house of assembly, or a *temple* of Dagon, raised on pillars, open on all sides, and flat-roofed, so that it could accommodate a multitude of people on the top.

Verse 28. *Samson called unto the Lord*] It was in consequence of his *faith* in God that he should be strengthened to overthrow his enemies and the enemies of his country, that he is mentioned, Heb. xi., among those who were remarkable for their *faith*.

Verse 29. *The two middle pillars upon which the house stood*] Much learned labour has been lost on the attempt to prove that a building like this might stand on two pillars. But what need of this? There might have been as many pillars here as were in the temple of Diana at Ephesus, and yet the two centre pillars be the *key of the building;* these being once pulled down, the whole house would necessarily fall.

Verse 30. *So the dead which he slew*] We are informed that the house was *full of men and women*, with about *three thousand* of both sexes on the top; now as the whole house was pulled down, consequently the principal part of all these were slain; and among them we find there were the *lords of the Philistines*. The death of *these*, with so many of the inferior chiefs of the people, was such a crush to the Philistine ascendancy, that they troubled Israel no more for several years, and did not even attempt to hinder Samson's relatives from taking away and burying his dead body.

Verse 31. *He judged Israel twenty years.*] It is difficult to ascertain the *time* of Samson's magistracy, and the *extent* of country over which he presided. His jurisdiction seems to have been very limited, and to have extended no farther than over those parts of the *tribe of Dan* contiguous to the land of the Philistines. This is what our *margin* intimates on ver. 20 of chap. xv. Many suppose that *he* and *Eli* were contemporaries, Samson being rather an *executor of the Divine justice* upon the enemies of his people, than an *administrator* of the *civil* and *religious* laws of the Hebrews. Allowing Eli and Samson to have been contemporaries, this latter part might have been entirely committed to the care of Eli.

1. SAMSON does not appear to have left any posterity. His amours with the different women mentioned in the history were unproductive as to issue. Had he married according to the laws of his country, he would have been both a more useful and a more happy man, and not have come to a violent death.

2. We seldom find much *mental energy* dwelling in a body that in *size* and *bulk* greatly surpasses the *ordinary pitch* of man; and wherever there are great *physical powers*, we seldom find proportionate *moral faculties*. Samson was a man of a *little mind*, a slave to his passions, and the wretched dupe of his mistresses. He was not a *great* though he was a *strong* man; and even his muscular force would have been lost, or spent in beating the air, had he not been frequently under the impulse of the *Divine Spirit*. He often got himself into broils and difficulties from which nothing but supernatural interposition could have saved him. His attacks upon the Philistines were never *well planned*, as he does not appear to have asked counsel from God; indeed, he seems to have consulted nothing but his own passions, particularly those of *inordinate* love and *revenge;* and the last effort of his extraordinary strength was, not to avenge his people for the oppressions which they had suffered under the Philistinian yoke, nor to avenge the quarrel of God's covenant against the enemies of his truth, but to be *avenged of the Philistines for the loss of his two eyes*.

3. Samson is a solemn proof how little corporeal *prowess* avails where *judgment* and *prudence* are wanting, and how dangerous all such gifts are in the hands of any man who has not his passions under proper discipline, and the fear of God continually before his eyes.

4. A *parallel* has been often drawn between Samson and our blessed Lord, of whom he has been supposed to be a *most illustrious type*. By a fruitful imagination, and the torture of words and facts, we may force resemblances everywhere; but that not one will *naturally* result from a cool comparison between Jesus Christ and Samson, is most demonstrable. A more exceptionable character is not to be found in the sacred oracles. It is no small dishonour to Christ to be thus compared. There is no

resemblance in the *qualities* of Samson's mind, there is none in his moral conduct, that can entitle him even to the most distant comparison with the chaste, holy, benevolent, and immaculate Jesus. That man dishonours the law of unchangeable righteousness, who endeavours to make Samson a type of any thing or person that can be called holy, just, and pure.

5. Those who compare him to *Hercules* have been more successful. Indeed, the heathen god of strength appears to have been borrowed from the Israelitish judge; but if we regard what is called the *choice of Hercules*, his preference of *virtue* to *pleasure*, we shall find that the heathen is, morally speaking, vastly superior to the Jew. M. *De Lavaur*, in his *Conference de la Fable avec l' Histoire Sainte*, vol. ii., p. 1, has traced the parallel between Hercules and Samson in the following manner:—

"Hercules was figured by the poets as supernatural both in his birth and actions, and was therefore received by the people as a god of the first order. They attributed to him the miracles wrought by several illustrious chiefs among the people of God, which they found described in the sacred oracles, more ancient than their most ancient accounts, or which they had learned by tradition, and their commerce with the Egyptians and Phœnicians, who were spread through various countries, but particularly in Greece. It is also to the time of these chiefs, and to the government of the Israelites by their judges, that the heroes and grand events of fable owe their origin; to which time, indeed, they are referred by the common consent of authors, sacred and profane.

"Every ancient nation, which had writers who left monuments of their country's glory, had a Hercules of its own, forged on the same plan. Varro reckons more than forty, and Cicero reckons six. (Book iii. *De Natura Deorum*.)

"Herodotus, (book ii., entitled *Euterpe*,) only speaks of the Egyptian and Greek Hercules. Although a Greek himself, this father of history, as Cicero calls him, who lived the nearest of any of these writers to the period he describes, informs us that Greece had borrowed its Hercules from Egypt, and that Amphitryon his father, and Alcmena his mother, were both Egyptians; so that, notwithstanding the desire the Greeks had to make Hercules a native of their country, they could not conceal his origin, which was either Egyptian or Hebrew; for the Greeks and Phœnicians looked upon the Israelites, who were settled in Canaan or Phœnicia, as Egyptians, whose ancestors, after residing in Egypt some centuries, had certainly come from that country.

"M. Jaquelot, in his '*Treatise on the Existence of God*,' believes that the Tyrian Hercules, who was the most ancient, was no other than Joshua. But St. Augustine (*City of God*, book xviii., chap. 19) has made it appear that it was after Samson (because of his prodigious and incomparable strength) that they forged their Hercules; first in Egypt, afterwards in Phœnicia, and lastly in Greece, each of whose writers has united in him all the miraculous actions of the others. In fact, it appears that Samson, judge of the Israelites from about A. M. 2867 to 2887, celebrated in the book of Judges, and mentioned by Josephus in his history, is the original and essential Hercules of fable: and although the poets have united these several particulars, drawn from Moses and Joshua, and have added their own inventions;

yet the most capital and considerable belong to Samson, and are distinguished by characteristics so peculiar to him, as to render *him* easily discerned throughout the whole.

"In Hebrew the name of Samson (שמשון) signifies the *sun*, and in Syriac (servitium vel ministerium ejus) *subjection to some one, servitude*. Macrobius says that the name of Hercules signifies only the *sun;* for, he adds, in Greek Hercules means, *it is glory of the air*, or *the light of the sun*. The Greeks and Egyptians have exactly followed the Syriac signification by imposing on their Hercules, during the whole of his life, a subjection to Eurystheus in all his exploits, and who appointed him his famous enterprises. This necessity they attribute to fate and the law of his birth. Having spoken of his name, we will now examine the circumstances of his birth, as mentioned in the sacred writings, Judg., chap. xiii., and in the History of the Jews, chap. x.

"Manoah, of the tribe of Dan, had married a woman who was barren, which led them to pray earnestly that the Lord would bless them with an offspring. One day, this woman being alone, an angel appeared to her, and told her he was sent by God to inform her she should have a son of the most extraordinary strength, who was to raise the glory of their nation, and to humble their enemies. Upon the arrival of her husband, she imparted to him the message and discourse of the angel. Some time after this heavenly messenger showed himself to them both as they were in the house together, and ascended up to heaven in their sight, after having confirmed the promises made before to the woman, who soon after became pregnant, and was in due time delivered of Samson.

"The singular birth of Hercules, in fable, is similar to the above account, with a trifling alteration taken from the ideas the poets entertained of their gods. Amphitryon, the most considerable person and the chief of the Thebans, had married Alcmena, whom he loved to distraction, but had not any children by her. Jupiter, desirous of making her the mother of Hercules, repaired to Alcmena one night, in the absence and under the figure of her husband. On Amphitryon's return, his wife said she had seen him before, on such a night, mentioning the visit she had received. Amphitryon, transported with jealousy, and enraged with his wife, whatever good opinion he might entertain of her virtue, would neither be appeased nor consoled till Jupiter appeared to vindicate her conduct; and, in order to convince Amphitryon of his being a god, visibly ascended up to heaven, after informing him that he alone had visited Alcmena, assuring him of her virtue, and promising him a son, who was to be distinguished for his strength; whose glory was to confer honour on his race and family; who was to humble their enemies; and who, finally, was to be immortal.

"The Spirit of God, with which Samson was from the very first endowed, caused him, even in his youth, to effect prodigies of strength. He once met with a furious young lion which attacked him; Samson, then unarmed, immediately rent the lion in pieces, as if it had been a lamb; and, resolving to revenge himself upon the Philistines, who had grievously afflicted the children of Israel, he slew vast numbers of them at different times, weakened them excessively, and thus began to deliver Israel out of the hands of their enemies as the angel had predicted.

"Fable, likewise, causes Hercules to perform exploits requiring prodigious strength; but, as its exaggerations are beyond all bounds, it attributes to him, while still an infant, the strangling enormous serpents which fell upon him in his cradle; and the first and most illustrious exploit of his youth was the defeat of a terrible lion in the Nemæan forest, which he slew without the help of any weapon of defence: the skin of this lion he afterwards wore as a garment. He likewise formed and executed the design of delivering his country from the tyrannic oppression of the Myrmidons. We ought not to be surprised that fable, which disfigures so many events by transforming them to its fancy, has altered the other adventures of Samson; that it has added to them others of its own invention; that it attributes to him the actions of other chiefs and heroes, and ascribes some of the performances of Samson to other persons than Hercules; for this reason we find the account of the foxes Samson caught and tied by the tail preserved indeed, but transferred to another country.

"Fable then borrows in favour of our hero, Hercules, the miracle which God wrought for Joshua, when he assisted the Gibeonites against the five kings of the Amorites, when the Lord cast down great stones upon them from heaven, so that more of those who fled from the Israelites perished by the hail than did by the sword. In imitation of this miracle, fable says (Pliny, book iii., chap. iv.; Pomponius Mela, De Situ Orbis, book ii., chap. v.) that when Hercules was engaged in a combat with the Ligurians, Jupiter assisted him by sending him a shower of stones. The quantity of stones which are still to be seen on the plains of Crau (called by the ancients Campi Lapidei) in Provence, has occasioned the poets to consider this place as the theatre of the above miracle.

"The jaw-bone of the ass, rendered so famous from Samson having slain one thousand Philistines with it, has been changed into the celebrated club of Hercules with which he defeated giants, and slew the many enemies that opposed him. The similarity of the Greek words κορρη and κορυνη may have given rise to this alteration; *corre* signifying *jaw*, and *corune*, a *mace* or *club*. The change of one of these words for the other is not difficult, especially as it seemed more suitable to arm Hercules with a club than with the jaw-bone of an ass. But fable has, however, more clearly preserved the miracle of the spring of water that God produced in this bone, to preserve Samson from perishing with thirst, after the defeat of the Philistines; for it relates that when Hercules had slain the dragon that guarded the golden apples in the garden of the Hesperides, and he was in danger of perishing with thirst in the scorching deserts of Libya, the gods caused a fountain to issue from a rock he struck with his foot; Apol. book xxxvi. of Argonauts, ver. 1446.

"The extraordinary strength of Samson was accompanied with a constant and surprising weakness, viz., his love for women. These two characteristics compose his history, and are equally conspicuous throughout the whole of his life: the latter however predominated; and after having frequently exposed him to great danger, at length completed his ruin. Fable has not omitted this characteristic weakness in

its Hercules; in him this passion was excited by every woman that presented herself to his view; it led him to the performance of many base actions, and, after precipitating him into several dangers, at length put an end to his miserable existence. Samson, who well knew that his strength depended upon the preservation of his hair, was so imprudent as to impart this secret to Delilah, his mistress. This woman, whose sole design in importuning him was to betray him, cut his hair off while asleep, and delivered him, thus deprived of all his strength, into the hands of the Philistines, who took from him both his liberty and eyesight, and treated him as the vilest and most wretched of slaves. Tradition, which spoils and disfigures the ancient histories and those of distant countries, has transferred this adventure to Nisus, king of Megara, and his daughter Scylla. Megara was also the name of one of Hercules' wives, the daughter of Creon, king of Thebes. The name of Scylla is taken from the crime and impiety of the daughter of Nisus, from the Greek verb συλαω, *sulao*, which signifies to *rob* or *strip with impiety*. The destiny or welfare of Nisus depended on the preservation of a lock of purple hair which grew on his head. Scylla, having conceived an affection for Minos, who was at that time besieging the capital of her father's kingdom, betrayed her parent, cut off this lock of purple hair while he was asleep, and delivered him into the hands of his enemy. Nisus lost both his senses and his life, and, according to fable, was changed into a bird. —*Ovid, Met.*, book viii.

"But the most remarkable and striking event in the history of Samson, is that by which he lost his life. The Philistines, when offering solemn sacrifices to their god, by way of thanksgiving for his having delivered into their hands their formidable enemy, caused Samson to be brought out of prison, in order to make a laughing-stock of him. Samson, as though wishing to rest himself, requested his conductors to let him lean against the pillars which supported the temple, which was at that time filled with a great multitude of persons, among whom were many princes of the Philistines. Samson then, invoking the Lord, and exerting all his strength, which was returning with the growth of his hair, laid hold of the pillars with both his hands, and shook them so violently as to pull the building down upon the whole multitude therein assembled. By this fatal catastrophe Samson killed a greater number of Philistines than he had done during his life.

"Fable and tradition could not efface this event in the copy of Samson, which is Hercules. Herodotus relates it as a fabulous tradition, invented by the Greeks, and rejects it as having no foundation either in the history itself, or in the manners and customs of the Egyptians; among whom the Greeks say this event had happened. They relate (says this historian, book ii., entitled *Euterpe*, p. 47) that Hercules, having fallen into the hands of the Egyptians, was condemned to be sacrificed to Jupiter. He was adorned like a victim, and led with much pomp to the foot of the altar: after permitting himself to be conducted thus far, and stopping a moment to collect his strength, he fell upon and massacred all those who were assembled to be either actors in, or spectators of, this pompous sacrifice, to the number of many thousands.

"The conformity between these adventures

of Samson and Hercules is self-evident, and proves beyond a doubt that the fable of the one was composed from the history of the other. The remark of Herodotus respecting the impossibility of this last adventure, according to the Greek tradition, and the folly of attributing it to the Egyptians, serves to confirm the truth of its having been borrowed, and of its being but a disfigured copy, whose original must be sought for elsewhere.

"In fact, it appears that Samson, judge of the Israelites, particularly mentioned in the book of Judges, and by Josephus, Ant. lib. v., c. 10,

is the original and essential Hercules of fable; and although the poets have united some particulars drawn from Moses and Joshua, and have added their own inventions, yet the most capital and considerable belong to Samson, and are distinguished by characteristics so peculiar to him, as render him easily discernible throughout the whole."

The above is the substance of what M. De Lavaur has written on the subject, and contains, as some think, a very clear case; and is an additional proof how much the *heathens* have been indebted to the *Bible.*

CHAPTER XVII

Micah, an Ephraimite, restores to his mother eleven hundred *shekels of silver, which he had taken from her,* 1, 2. *She dedicates this to God; and out of a part of it makes a graven image and a molten image, and gets them up in the house of Micah, 3, 4; who consecrates one of his sons to be his priest, 5. He afterwards finds a Levite, whom he consecrates for a priest, and gives him annually* ten *shekels of silver, with his food and clothing, 6–13.*

A. M. 2598
B. C. 1406
An. Exod. Isr.
85
Anno ante
I. Olymp. 630

AND there was a man of Mount Ephraim, whose name *was* Micah.

2 And he said unto his mother, The eleven hundred *shekels* of silver that were taken from thee, about which thou cursedst, and spakest of also in mine ears, behold, the silver *is* with me; I took it. And his mother said, [a]Blessed *be thou* of the LORD, my son.

3 And when he had restored the eleven hundred *shekels* of silver to his mother, his mother said, I had wholly dedicated the silver unto the LORD from my hand for my son, to [b]make

a graven image and a molten image: now therefore I will restore it unto thee.

4 Yet he restored the money unto his mother; and his mother [c]took two hundred *shekels* of silver, and gave them to the founder, who made thereof a graven image and a molten image: and they were in the house of Micah.

5 And the man Micah had a house of gods, and made an [d]ephod, and [e]teraphim, and [f]consecrated one of his sons, who became his priest.

A. M. 2598
B. C. 1406
An. Exod. Isr.
85
Anno ante
I. Olymp. 630

---

[a]Gen. xiv. 19; Ruth iii. 10——[b]See Exodus xx. 4, 23; Lev. xix. 4——[c]Isa. xlvi. 6——[d]Chap. viii. 27

[e]Gen. xxxi. 19, 30; Hos. iii. 4——[f]Heb. *filled the hand;* Exod. xxix. 9; 1 Kings xiii. 33

NOTES ON CHAP. XVII

Verse 1. *And there was a man of Mount Ephraim*] It is extremely difficult to fix the *chronology* of this and the following transactions. Some think them to be here in their natural order; others, that they happened in the time of *Joshua,* or immediately after the *ancients* who outlived Joshua. All that can be said with certainty is this, that they happened when there was no king in Israel; i. e., about the time of the *Judges,* or in some time of the anarchy, ver. 6.

Verse 2. *About which thou cursedst*] Houbigant and others understand this of *putting the young man to his oath.* It is likely that when the mother of Micah missed the money, she poured imprecations on the thief; and that Micah, who had secreted it, hearing this, was alarmed, and restored the money lest the curses should fall on him.

Verse 3. *I had wholly dedicated*] From this it appears that Micah's mother, though she made a superstitious use of the money, had no *idolatrous* design, for she expressly says she had dedicated it ליהוה *layhovah, to Jehovah;* and this appears to have been the reason why

she poured imprecations on him who had taken it.

Verse 4. *A graven image and a molten image*] What these images were, we cannot positively say; they were most probably some resemblance of matters belonging to the tabernacle. See below.

Verse 5. *The man Micah had a house of gods*] בית אלהים *beith Elohim* should, I think, be translated *house* or *temple of God;* for it is very likely that both the mother and the son intended no more than a private or domestic chapel, in which they proposed to set up the worship of the true God.

Made an ephod] Perhaps the whole of this case may be stated thus: Micah built a *house of God*—a chapel in imitation of the *sanctuary;* he made a *graven image* representing the *ark,* a *molten image* to represent the *mercy-seat,* *teraphim* to represent the *cherubim* above the *mercy-seat,* and an *ephod* in imitation of the *sacerdotal garments;* and he consecrated one of his sons to be priest. Thus gross idolatry was not the crime of Micah; he only set up in his own house an epitome of the Divine worship as performed at Shiloh. What the *teraphim* were, see the note on Gen. xxxi. 19; for the

A. M. 2598
B. C. 1406
An. Exod. Isr. 85
Anno ante
I. Olymp. 630

6 ᵍIn those days *there was* no king in Israel, ʰ*but* every man did *that which was* right in his own eyes.

7 And there was a young man out of ⁱBeth-lehem-judah of the family of Judah, who *was* a Levite, and he sojourned there.

8 And the man departed out of the city from Beth-lehem-judah to sojourn where he could find *a place:* and he came to Mount Ephraim to the house of Micah, ᵏas he journeyed.

9 And Micah said unto him, Whence comest thou? And he said unto him, I *am* a Levite of Beth-lehem-judah, and I go to sojourn where I may find *a place.*

A. M. 2598
B. C. 1406
An. Exod. Isr. 85
Anno ante
I. Olymp. 630

10 And Micah said unto him, Dwell with me, ˡand be unto me a ᵐfather and a priest, and I will give thee ten *shekels* of silver by the year, and ⁿa °suit of apparel, and thy victuals. So the Levite went in.

11 And the Levite was content to dwell with the man; and the young man was unto him as one of his sons.

12 And Micah ᵖconsecrated the Levite; and the young man �q became his priest, and was in the house of Micah.

13 Then said Micah, Now know I that the LORD will do me good, seeing I have a Levite to *my* priest.

ᵍChap. xviii. 1; xix. 1; xxi. 25; Deut. xxxiii. 5 ʰDeut. xii. 8——ⁱSee Josh. xix. 15; chap. xix. 1; Ruth i. 1, 2; Mic. v. 2; Matt. ii. 1, 5, 6

ᵏHeb. *in making his way*——ˡCh. xviii. 19——ᵐGen. xlv. 8; Job xxix. 16——ⁿOr, *a double suit,* &c.——°Heb. *an order of garments*——ᵖVer. 5——qChap. xviii. 30

---

ephod, see the note on Exod. xxv. 7; and for the *sacerdotal vestments* in general, see the note on Exod. xxviii. 4, &c.

Who became his priest.] כהן *cohen,* which the Targum translates *chumera.* The word כהן *cohen* is the common name in Hebrew for a *priest* of the true God; but sometimes it is applied to idolatrous priests. When it is to be understood in the former sense, the Targum renders it *cahen;* when in the latter, it uses the word כומרא *chumera,* by which it always understands an *idolatrous* priest. But that this was not a case of idolatry, and that the true God was worshipped here, is evident from the word *Jehovah* being used, ver. 4, and *oracular* answers being given at this house, as we see from chap. xviii.

Verse 6. There was *no king in Israel*] The word מלך *melech,* which generally means *king,* is sometimes taken for a supreme *governor, judge, magistrate,* or *ruler* of any kind; (see Gen. xxxvi. 31, and Deut. xxxiii. 5;) and it is likely it should be so understood here.

Every man did that which was *right in his own eyes.*] He was his own governor, and what he did he said was right; and, by his cunning and strength, defended his conduct. When a man's own will, passions, and caprice, are to be made the rule of law, society is in a most perilous and ruinous state. Civil government is of God; and without it the earth must soon be desolated. There was a time when there was no king in *England;* and that was, in general, a time of scandal to religion, and oppression to men.

Verse 7. *Of the family of Judah*] The word *family* may be taken here for *tribe;* or the young man might have been of the tribe of *Judah* by his *mother,* and of the tribe of *Levi* by his *father,* for he is called here a *Levite;* and it is probable that he might have officiated at Shiloh, in the Levitical office. A Levite might marry into any other tribe, providing the woman was not an *heiress.*

Verse 8. *To sojourn where he could find*] He went about the country seeking for some employment, for the Levites had no inheritance:

besides, no secure residence could be found where there was no civil government.

Verse 10. *Be unto me a father and a priest*] Thou shalt be *master* of my house, as if thou wert my father; and, as *priest,* thou shalt appear in the presence of God for me. The term *father* is often used to express *honour* and *reverence.*

Ten shekels *of silver*] About thirty shillings per annum, with board, lodging, and clothes. Very good wages in those early times.

Verse 11. *The Levite was content*] He thought the place a good one, and the wages respectable.

Verse 12. *Micah consecrated the Levite*] וימלא את יד *vayemalle eth yad, he filled his hands;* i. e., he gave him an *offering* to present before the Lord, that he might be accepted by him. He *appointed* him to be priest; God was to *accept* and *consecrate* him; and for this purpose he *filled his hand;* i. e., furnished him with the proper offering which he was to present on his inauguration.

Verse 13. *Now know I that the Lord will do me good*] As he had already provided an epitome of the *tabernacle,* a model of the *ark, mercy-seat,* and *cherubim;* and had got proper *sacerdotal vestments,* and a *Levite* to officiate; he took for granted that all was right, and that he should now have the benediction of God. Some think that he expected great gain from the concourse of the people to his temple; but of this there is no evidence in the text. Micah appears to have been perfectly sincere in all that he did.

I HAVE already remarked that there is no positive evidence that Micah or his mother intended to establish any idolatrous worship. Though they acted without any Divine command in what they did; yet they appear, not only to have been perfectly *sincere,* but also perfectly *disinterested.* They put themselves to considerable *expense* to *erect* this place of worship, and to *maintain,* at their own proper charges, a priest to officiate there; and without this the place, in all probability, would have been destitute of the worship and knowledge of the true God. His *sincerity, disinterestedness,* and *attachment* to the *worship* of the God of his fathers, are farther seen in the *joy* which he expressed on finding a *Levite* who might *legally* officiate in his house. It is true, he had not a Divine warrant for what he did; but the state of the land, the profligacy of his countrymen, his distance from Shiloh, &c., considered,

he appears to deserve more *praise* than *blame,* though of the latter he has received a most liberal share from every quarter. This proceeds from that often-noticed propensity in man to take every thing which concerns the character of another by the worst handle. It cannot be considered any particular crime, should these notes be found at any time leaning to the other side.

CHAPTER XVIII

Some Danites, seeking an inheritance, send five men to search the land, who arrive at the house of Micah, 1, 2. They employ the Levite, who served in his house as priest, to ask counsel for them of God, 3–5. He inquires, and promises them success, 6. They depart, and go to Laish, and find the inhabitants secure, 7. They return to their brethren, and encourage them to attempt the conquest of the place, 8–10. They send six hundred men, who, coming to the place where Micah dwelt, enter the house, and carry off the priest and his consecrated things, 11–21. Micah and his friends pursue them; but, being threatened, are obliged to return, 22–26. The Danites come to Laish, and smite it, and build a city there, which they call Dan, 27–29. They make the Levite their priest, and set up the images at this new city, 30, 31.

A. M. 2598
B. C. 1406
An. Exod. Isr.
85
Anno ante
I. Olymp. 630

IN ªthose days *there was* no king in Israel: and in those days ᵇthe tribe of the Danites sought them an inheritance to dwell in; for unto that day *all their* inheritance had not fallen unto them among the tribes of Israel.

2 And the children of Dan sent of their family five men from their coasts, ᶜmen of valour, from ᵈZorah, and from Eshtaol, ᵉto spy out the land, and to search it; and they said unto them, Go, search the land: who when they came to Mount Ephraim, to the ᶠhouse of Micah, they lodged there.

3 When they *were* by the house of Micah, they knew the voice of the young man the Levite: and they turned in thither, and said unto him, Who brought thee hither? and what makest thou in this *place?* and what hast thou here?

A. M. 2598
B. C. 1406
An. Exod. Isr.
85
Anno ante
I. Olymp. 630

4 And he said unto them, Thus and thus dealeth Micah with me, and hath ᵍhired me, and I am his priest.

5 And they said unto him, ʰAsk counsel, we pray thee, ⁱof God, that we may know whether our way which we go shall be prosperous.

ªChap. xvii. 6; xxi. 25——ᵇJosh. xix. 47——ᶜHeb. *sons* ᵈChap. xiii. 25——ᵉNum. xiii. 17; Josh. ii. 1

ᶠChap. xvii. 1——ᵍChap. xvii. 10——ʰ1 Kings xxii. 5; Isa. xxx. 1; Hos. iv. 12——ⁱSee chap. xvii. 5; ver. 14

NOTES ON CHAP. XVIII

Verse 1. *There was no king in Israel*] See chap. xvii. 6. The circumstances related here show that this must have happened about the time of the preceding transactions.

The tribe of the Danites] That is, a part of this tribe; some families of it.

All their inheritance] That is, they had not got an extent of country sufficient for them. Some families were still unprovided for, or had not sufficient territory; for we find from Josh. chap. xix. 40, &c., that, although the tribe of Dan did receive their inheritance with the rest of the tribes of Israel, yet *their coasts went out too little for them, and they went and fought against* LESHEM, (called here *Laish,*) *and took it,* &c. This circumstance is marked here more particularly than in the book of Joshua. See on Josh. xix. 47.

Verse 2. *Five men—men of valour*] The Hebrew word חיל *chayil* has been applied to *personal prowess,* to *mental energy,* and to *earthly possessions.* They sent those in whose courage, judgment, and prudence, they could safely confide.

Verse 3. *They knew the voice of the young man*] They knew, by his dialect or mode of *pronunciation,* that he was not an Ephraimite. We have already seen (chap. xii. 6) that the Ephraimites could not pronounce certain letters. See the note there.

Verse 5. *Ask counsel—of God*] As the Danites use the word אלהים *Elohim* here for *God,* we are necessarily led to believe that they meant the true God; especially as the Levite answers, ver. 6, *Before the* LORD (יהוה *Yehovah*) *is your way.* Though the former word may be sometimes applied to *idols,* whom their votaries clothed with the *attributes* of God; yet the latter is never applied but to the *true God* alone. As the Danites succeeded according to the oracle delivered by the Levite, it is a strong presumption that the *worship* established by Micah was not of an *idolatrous* kind. It is really begging the question to assert, as many commentators have done, that the answer was either a *trick of the Levite,* or *suggested by the devil;* and that the success of the Danites was merely *accidental.* This is taking the thing by the worst handle, to support an hypothesis, and

A. M. 2598
B. C. 1406
An. Exod. Isr.
85
Anno ante
I. Olymp. 630

6 And the priest said unto them, [k]Go in peace: before the LORD *is* your way wherein ye go.

7 Then the five men departed, and came to [l]Laish, and saw the people that *were* therein, [m]how they dwelt careless, after the manner of the Zidonians, quiet and secure: and *there was* no [n]magistrate in the land, that might put *them* to shame in *any* thing; and they *were* far from the Zidonians, and had no business with *any* man.

8 And they came unto their brethren to [o]Zorah and Eshtaol: and their brethren said unto them, What *say* ye?

9 And they said, [p]Arise, that we may go up against them: for we have seen the land, and behold, it *is* very good: and *are* ye [q]still? be not slothful to go, *and* to enter to possess the land.

10 When ye go, ye shall come unto a people [r]secure, and to a large land: for God hath given it into your hands; [s]a place where *there is* no want of any thing that *is* in the earth.

11 And there went from thence of the family of the Danites, out of Zorah and out of Eshtaol, six hundred men [t]appointed with weapons of war.

A. M. 2598
B. C. 1406
An. Exod. Isr.
85
Anno ante
I. Olymp. 630

12 And they went up, and pitched in [u]Kirjath-jearim, in Judah; wherefore they called that place [v]Mahaneh-dan unto this day: behold, *it is* behind Kirjath-jearim:

13 And they passed thence unto Mount Ephraim, and came unto [w]the house of Micah.

14 [x]Then answered the five men that went to spy out the country of Laish, and said unto their brethren, Do ye know that [y]there is in these houses an ephod, and teraphim, and a graven image, and a molten image? now therefore consider what ye have to do.

15 And they turned thitherward, and came to the house of the young man the Levite, *even* unto the house of Micah, and [z]saluted him.

16 And the [a]six hundred men appointed with their weapons of war, which *were* of the children of Dan, stood by the entering of the gate.

17 And [b]the five men that went to spy out the land, went up, *and* came in thither, *and* took [c]the graven image, and the ephod, and the teraphim, and the molten image: and the priest stood in the entering of the gate with the six hundred men *that were* appointed with weapons of war.

---

[k]1 Kings xxii. 6——[l]Josh. xix. 47, called *Leshem*
[m]Ver. 27, 28——[n]Heb. *possessor,* or *heir of restraint*
[o]Verse 2——[p]Num. xiii. 30; Josh. ii. 23, 24——[q]1 Kings xxii. 3——[r]Ver. 7, 27——[s]Deut. viii. 9

[t]Heb. *girded*——[u]Josh. xv. 60——[v]Chap. xiii. 25
[w]Ver. 2——[x]1 Sam. xiv. 28——[y]Chap. xvii. 5——[z]Heb. *asked him of peace;* Gen. xliii. 27; 1 Sam. xvii. 22
[a]Ver. 11——[b]Ver. 2, 14——[c]Chap. xvii. 4, 5

---

to serve a system. See the end of the preceding chapter.

Verse 7. After the manner of the Zidonians] Probably the people of *Laish* or *Leshem* were originally a colony of the *Sidonians,* who, it appears, were an opulent people; and, being in possession of a *strong city,* lived in a state of security, not being afraid of their neighbours. In this the Leshemites imitated them, though the sequel proves they had not the same reason for their confidence.

They were far from the Zidonians] Being, as above supposed, a *Sidonian colony,* they might naturally expect help from their countrymen; but, as they dwelt a considerable distance from Sidon, the Danites saw that they could strike the blow before the news of invasion could reach *Sidon;* and, consequently, before the people of Laish could receive any succours from that city.

And had no business with any man.] In the most correct copies of the Septuagint, this clause is thus translated: Και λογος ουκ ην αυτοις μετα Συριας; *and they had no transactions with* SYRIA. Now it is most evident that, instead of אדם *adam,* MAN, they read ארם *aram,* SYRIA; words which are so nearly similar that the difference which exists is only between the ר *resh*

and ד *daleth,* and this, both in MSS. and printed books, is often indiscernible. This reading is found in the *Codex Alexandrinus,* in the *Complutensian* Polyglot, in the *Spanish* Polyglot, and in the edition of the Septuagint published by *Aldus.* It may be proper to observe, that *Laish* was on the frontiers of Syria; but as they had no intercourse with the *Syrians,* from whom they might have received the promptest assistance, this was an additional reason why the Danites might expect success.

Verse 9. Arise, &c.] This is a very plain and nervous address; full of good sense, and well adapted to the purpose. It seems to have produced an instantaneous effect.

Verse 11. Six hundred men] These were not the whole, for we find they had children, &c., ver. 21; but these appear to have been six hundred *armed* men.

Verse 12. Mahaneh-dan] "The camp of Dan;" so called from the circumstance of this armament *encamping* there. See chap. xiii. 25, which affords some proof that this transaction was previous to the days of Samson.

Verse 14. Consider what ye have to do.] They probably had formed the design to carry off the priest and his sacred utensils.

A. M. 2598
B. C. 1406
An. Exod. Isr.
85
Anno ante
I. Olymp. 630

18 And these went into Mi-cah's house, and fetched the carved image, the ephod, and the teraphim, and the molten image. Then said the priest unto them, What do ye?

19 And they said unto him, Hold thy peace, ^dlay thine hand upon thy mouth, and go with us, ^eand be to us a father and a priest: *is it* better for thee to be a priest unto the house of one man, or that thou be a priest unto a tribe and a family in Israel?

20 And the priest's heart was glad, and he took the ephod, and the teraphim, and the graven image, and went in the midst of the people.

21 So they turned and departed, and put the little ones and the cattle and the carriage before them.

22 *And* when they were a good way from the house of Micah, the men that *were* in the houses near to Micah's house were gathered together, and overtook the children of Dan.

23 And they cried unto the children of Dan. And they turned their faces, and said unto Micah, What aileth thee, ^fthat thou comest with such a company?

24 And he said, Ye have taken away my gods which I made, and the priest, and ye are gone away: and what have I more? and what *is* this *that* ye say unto me, What aileth thee?

25 And the children of Dan said unto him,

Let not thy voice be heard among us, lest ^gangry fellows run upon thee, and thou lose thy life, with the lives of thy household.

A. M. 2598
B. C. 1406
An. Exod. Isr
85
Anno ante
I. Olymp. 630

26 And the children of Dan went their way: and when Micah saw that they *were* too strong for him, he turned and went back unto his house.

27 And they took *the things* which Micah had made, and the priest which he had, and ^hcame unto Laish, unto a people *that were* at quiet and secure: ⁱand they smote them with the edge of the sword, and burnt the city with fire.

28 And *there was* no deliverer, because it *was* ^kfar from Zidon, and they had no business with *any* man; and it was in the valley that *lieth* ^lby Beth-rehob. And they built a city, and dwelt therein.

29 And ^mthey called the name of the city ⁿDan, after the name of Dan their father, who was born unto Israel: howbeit the name of the city *was* Laish at the first.

30 And the children of Dan set up the graven image: and Jonathan the son of Gershom, the son of Manasseh, he and his sons were priests to the tribe of Dan ^ountil the day of the captivity of the land.

31 And they set them up Micah's graven image, which he made, ^pall the time that the house of God was in Shiloh.

---

^dJob xxi. 5; xxix. 9; xl. 4; Prov. xxx. 32; Mic. vii. 16 ^eChap. xvii. 10——^fHeb. *that thou art gathered together* ^gHeb. *bitter of soul;* 2 Sam. xvii. 8——^hVer. 7, 10 Deut. xxxiii. 22——ⁱJosh. xix. 47

^kVer. 7——^lNum. xiii. 21; 2 Sam. x. 6——^mJosh. xix. 47——ⁿGen. xiv. 14; chap. xx. 1; 1 Kings xii. 29, 30; xv. 20——^oChap. xiii. 1; 1 Sam. iv. 2, 3, 10, 11; Psa. lxxviii. 60, 61——^pJosh. xviii. 1; chap. xix. 18; xxi. 12

Verse 18. *These went into Micah's house*] The five men went in, while the six hundred armed men stood at the gate.

Verse 19. *Lay thine hand upon thy mouth*] This was the token of *silence*. The god of silence, *Harpocrates*, is represented on ancient statues with *his finger pressed on his lips*.

Verse 20. *Went in the midst of the people.*] He was glad to be employed by the Danites; and went into the *crowd*, that he might not be discovered by Micah or his family.

Verse 21. *The little ones and the cattle, &c.*] These men were so confident of success that they removed their whole families, household goods, cattle, and all.

And the carriage] כבודה *kebudah*, their *substance, precious things*, or *valuables; omne quod erat pretiosum*, VULGATE: or rather the *luggage* or *baggage;* what *Cæsar* calls in his commentaries *impedimenta;* and what the *Septuagint* here translate βαρος, *weight* or *baggage*. We are not to suppose that any *wheel carriage* is meant.

Verse 24. *Ye have taken away my gods*] As

Micah was a worshipper of the true God, as we have seen, he cannot mean any kind of *idols* by the word אלהי *elohai* here used. He undoubtedly means those *representations* of Divine things, and symbols of the Divine presence; such as the teraphim, ephod, &c.; for they are all evidently included under the word *elohai*, which we translate *my gods*.

Verse 25. *And thou lose thy life*] This was *argumentum ad hominem;* he must put up with the loss of his substance, or else lose his life! It was the mere language of a modern highwayman: *Your life or your money*.

Verse 27. *Unto a people—at quiet and secure*] They found the report given by the spies to be correct. The people were apprehensive of no danger, and were unprepared for resistance; hence they were all put to the sword, and their city burnt up.

Verse 28. *There was no deliverer*] They had no succour; because the Sidonians, from whom they might have expected it, were at too great a *distance*.

Verse 29. *Called the name of the city Dan*]

This city was afterwards very remarkable as one of the *extremities* of the promised land. The extent of the Jewish territories was generally expressed by the phrase, *From* DAN *to* BEER-SHEBA; that is, From the most *northern* to the *southern* extremity.

Verse 30. *The children of Dan set up the graven image*] They erected a chapel, or temple, among themselves, as Micah had done before; having the same implements and the same priest.

And Jonathan the son of Gershom] Either this was the name of the young *Levite;* or they had turned him off, and got this Jonathan in his place.

The son Manasseh] Who this Manasseh was, none can tell; nor does the reading appear to be genuine. He could not be Manasseh the son of *Joseph,* for he had no son called *Gershom;* nor could it be Manasseh king of *Israel,* for he lived *eight hundred* years afterwards.

Instead of מנשה *Manasseh,* the word should be read משה *Mosheh,* MOSES, as it is found in some MSS., in the *Vulgate,* and in the *concessions* of the most intelligent Jews. The Jews, as *R. D. Kimchi* acknowledges, have suspended the letter נ *nun,* over the word משה *Mosheh,*

נ
thus, משה—which, by the addition of the *points,* they have changed into MANASSEH, because they think it would be a great reproach to their legislator to have had a grandson who was an idolater. That *Gershom* the son of *Moses* is here intended, is very probable. See the arguments urged by *Dr. Kennicott,* Dissertation I., p. 55, &c.; and see the *Var. Lect.* of *De Rossi* on this place.

Until the day of the captivity of the land.] Calmet observes, "The posterity of this Jonathan executed the office of priest in the city of Dan, all the time that the idol of Micah (the teraphim, ephod, &c.) was there. But this was only while the house of the Lord was at Shiloh;

and, consequently, the sons of Jonathan were priests at Dan only till the time in which the ark was taken by the Philistines, which was the last year of Eli, the high priest; for after that the ark no more returned to Shiloh." This is evident; and on this very ground *Houbigant* contends that, instead of הארץ *haarets, the* LAND, we should read הארון *haaron, the* ARK; for nothing is easier than the ו *vau* and ן *final nun* to be mistaken for the ץ *final tsade,* which is the only difference between *the captivity of the* LAND and *the captivity of the* ARK. And this conjecture is the more likely, because the next verse tells us that Micah's graven image, &c., continued at Dan *all the time that the house of God was at Shiloh;* which was, till the ark was taken by the Philistines. Those who wish to see more on this subject may consult *Calmet,* and the writers in *Pool's Synopsis.* This chapter is an important supplement to the conclusion of the 19th chapter of Joshua, on which it casts considerable light.

THE Danites were properly the first *dissenters* from the public *established* worship of the Jews; but they seem to have departed *as little* as possible from the Jewish *forms,* their worship being conducted in the same *way,* but not in the same place. Surely it was better to have had this, allowing it to be unconstitutional worship, than to have been wholly destitute of the ordinances of God.

I think we have not sufficient ground from the text to call these persons *idolaters;* I believe they worshipped the true God according to their light and circumstances, from a conviction that they could not prosper without his approbation, and that they could not expect that approbation if they did not offer to him a religious worship. They endeavoured to please him, though the means they adopted were not the most proper.

CHAPTER XIX

A Levite and his concubine disagree; and she leaves him and goes to her father's house, 1, 2. He follows to bring her back, and is kindly entertained by her father five days, 3–8. He returns; and lodges the first night at Gibeah, in the tribe of Benjamin, 9–21. The men of Gibeah attack the house, and insist on abusing the body of the Levite; who, to save himself, delivers to them his concubine, whose life falls a victim to their brutality, 22–27. The Levite divides her dead body into twelve pieces, and sends one to each of the twelve tribes; they are struck with horror, and call a council on the subject, 28–30.

A. M. 2598
B. C. 1406
An. Exod. Isr. 85
Anno ante
I. Olymp. 630

AND it came to pass in those days, [a]when *there was* no king in Israel, that there was a certain Levite sojourning on the side of Mount Ephraim, who took to him [b]a concubine out of [c]Beth-lehem-judah.

2 And his concubine played

A. M. 2598
B. C. 1406
An. Exod. Isr. 85
Anno ante
I. Olymp. 630

---

[a]Chap. xvii. 5; xviii. 1; xxi. 25——[b]Heb. *a woman a*　　*concubine, or, a wife a concubine*——[c]Chap. xvii. 7

NOTES ON CHAP. XIX

Verse 1. There was *no king in Israel*] All sorts of *disorders* are attributed to the want of *civil government;* justice, right, truth, and humanity, had fallen in the streets.

Took to him a concubine] We have already seen that the *concubine* was a sort of *secondary wife;* and that such connections were not disreputable, being according to the general cus-

tom of those times. The word פילגש *pilegesh, concubine,* is supposed by Mr. Parkhurst to be compounded of פלג *palag,* "to divide, or share;" and נגש *nagash,* "to approach;" because the husband *shared* or *divided* his attention and affections between her and the real wife; from whom she differed in nothing material, except in her posterity not *inheriting.*

Verse 2. *Played the whore*] Neither the *Vul-*

A. M. 2598
B. C. 1406
An. Exod. Isr.
85
Anno ante
I. Olymp. 630

the whore against him, and went away from him unto her father's house to Beth-lehem-judah, and was there ᵈfour ᵉwhole months.

3 And her husband arose, and went after her, to speak ᶠfriendly unto her, *and* to bring her again, having his servant with him, and a couple of asses: and she brought him into her father's house: and when the father of the damsel saw him, he rejoiced to meet him.

4 And his father-in-law, the damsel's father, retained him; and he abode with him three days: so they did eat and drink, and lodged there.

5 And it came to pass on the fourth day, when they arose early in the morning, that he rose up to depart: and the damsel's father said unto his son-in-law, ᵍComfort ʰthine heart with a morsel of bread, and afterward go your way.

6 And they sat down, and did eat and drink both of them together: for the damsel's father had said unto the man, Be content, I pray thee, and tarry all night, and let thine heart be merry.

7 And when the man rose up to depart, his father-in-law urged him: therefore he lodged there again.

8 And he arose early in the morning on the fifth day to depart: and the damsel's father said, Comfort thine heart, I pray thee. And

they tarried ⁱuntil afternoon, and they did eat both of them.

A. M. 2598
B. C. 1406
An. Exod. Isr
85
Anno ante
I. Olymp. 630

9 And when the man rose up to depart, he and his concubine, and his servant, his father-in-law, the damsel's father, said unto him, Behold, now the day ᵏdraweth toward evening, I pray you tarry all night: behold, ˡthe day groweth to an end, lodge here, that thine heart may be merry; and to-morrow get you early on your way that thou mayest go ᵐhome.

10 But the man would not tarry that night, but he rose up and departed, and came ⁿover against ᵒJebus, which *is* Jerusalem; and *there were* with him two asses saddled, his concubine also *was* with him.

11 *And* when they wᵉre by Jebus, the day was far spent; and the servant said unto his master, Come, I pray thee, and let us turn in into this city ᵖof the Jebusites, and lodge in it.

12 And his master said unto him, We will not turn aside hither into the city of a stranger that *is* not of the children of Israel; we will pass over ᑫto Gibeah.

13 And he said unto his servant, Come, and let us draw near to one of these places to lodge all night, in Gibeah, or in ʳRamah.

14 And they passed on and went their way; and the sun went down upon them *when they were* by Gibeah, which *belongeth* to Benjamin.

15 And they turned aside thither, to go in

ᵈOr, *a year* and *four months*——ᵉHeb. *days four months*——ᶠHeb. *to her heart;* Gen. xxxiv. 3——ᵍHeb. *strengthen*——ʰGen. xviii. 5——ⁱHeb. *till the day declined*——ᵏHeb. *is weak*

ⁱHeb. it is *the pitching* time *of the day*——ᵐHeb. *to thy tent*——ⁿHeb. *to over against*——ᵒJosh. xviii. 28 ᵖJosh. xv. 8, 63; chap. i. 21; 2 Sam. v. 6——ᑫJosh. xviii. 28——ʳJosh. xviii. 25

---

gate, *Septuagint, Targum,* nor *Josephus,* understand this word as implying any act of conjugal infidelity on the woman's part. They merely state that the *parties disagreed,* and the woman returned to her father's house. Indeed all the circumstances of the case vindicate this view of the subject. If she had been a *whore,* or *adulteress,* it is not very likely that her husband would have gone after her tᵒ *speak friendly,* literally, *to speak to her heart,* and entreat her to return. The *Vulgate* simply states, *quæ reliquit eum,* that she *left him;* the *Septuagint,* ωργισθη αυτῳ, that she *was angry with* him; the *Targum* ובסרת עלוהי *ubserath alohi,* that she *despised him; Josephus,* αλλοτιως ειχε, that she *was alienated,* or *separated* herself, from him. *Houbigant* translates the clause: *quæ cum ab eo alienata esset, vel irata in eum esset, eum reliquit;* "who when she was *alienated* from him, or *angry with* him, left him;" and he defends this version in his note. I think the true meaning to be among the above interpretations. They had *contentions;* she ceased to love him,

her *affections were alienated* from him; and she *left his house,* and *went home* to her *father.*

Verse 3. *He rejoiced to meet him.*] He hoped to be able completely to reconcile his daughter and her husband.

Verse 8. *And they tarried until afternoon*] Merely that they might avoid the *heat of the day,* which would have been very inconvenient in travelling.

Verse 9. *The day groweth to an end*] חנות היום *chanoth haiyom,* "the day is about to pitch its tent;" that is, it was near the time in which travellers ordinarily pitched their tents, to take up their lodging for the night.

Verse 11. *When they* were *by Jebus*] This was *Jerusalem,* in which, though after the death of Joshua it appears to have been partly conquered by the tribe of Judah, yet the Jebusites kept the strong hold of Zion till the days of David, by whom they were finally expelled. See the note on chap. i. 8.

Verse 15. *No man—took them into his house to lodging.*] There was probably no *inn* or

A. M. 2598
B. C. 1406
An. Exod. Isr.
85
Anno ante
I. Olymp. 630

and to lodge in Gibeah: and when he went in, he sat him down in a street of the city: for *there was* no man that ˢtook them into his house to lodging.

16 And, behold, there came an old man from ᵗhis work out of the field at even, which *was* also of Mount Ephraim; and he sojourned in Gibeah: but the men of the place *were* Benjamites.

17 And when he had lifted up his eyes, he saw a wayfaring man in the street of the city: and the old man said, Whither goest thou? and whence comest thou?

18 And he said unto him, We *are* passing from Beth-lehem-judah toward the side of Mount Ephraim; from thence *am* I: and I went to Beth-lehem-judah, but I *am now* going to ᵘthe house of the LORD; and there *is* no man that ᵛreceiveth me to house.

19 Yet there is both straw and provender for our asses; and there is bread and wine also for me and for thy handmaid, and for the young man *which is* with thy servants: *there is* no want of any thing.

20 And the old man said, ʷPeace *be* with thee; howsoever, *let* all thy wants *lie* upon me; ˣonly lodge not in the street.

21 ʸSo he brought him into his house, and gave provender unto the asses: ᶻand they washed their feet, and did eat and drink.

22 *Now* as they were making their hearts merry, behold, ᵃthe men of the city, certain ᵇsons of Belial, beset the house round about, *and* beat at the door, and spake to the master of the house, the old man, saying, ᶜBring forth the man that came into thine house, that we may know him.

23 And ᵈthe man, the master of the house, went out unto them, and said unto them, Nay, my brethren, *nay,* I pray you, do not *so* wickedly; seeing that this man is come into mine house, ᵉdo not this folly.

24 ᶠBehold, *here is* my daughter, a maiden, and his concubine; them I will bring out now, and ᵍhumble ye them, and do with them what seemeth good unto you: but unto this man do not ʰso vile a thing.

25 But the men would not hearken to him: so the man took his concubine, and brought

A. M. 2598
B. C. 1406
An. Exod. Isr.
85
Anno ante
I. Olymp. 630

ᵃMatt. xxv. 43; Heb. xiii. 2——ᵗPsa. civ. 23 ᵘJosh. xviii. 1; chap. xviii. 31; xx. 18; 1 Sam. i. 3, 7 ᵛHeb. *gathereth;* ver. 15——ʷGen. xliii. 23; chap. vi. 23 ˣGen. xix. 2——ʸGen. xxiv. 32; xliii. 24——ᶻGen. xviii. 4; John xiii. 5

ᵃGen. xix. 4; chap. xx. 5; Hos. ix. 9; x. 9——ᵇDeut. xiii. 13——ᶜGen. xix. 5; Rom. i. 26, 27——ᵈGen. xix. 6, 7——ᵉ2 Sam. xiii. 12——ᶠGen. xix. 8——ᵍGen. xxxiv. 2; Deut. xxi. 14——ʰHeb. *the matter of this folly.*

---

house of *public entertainment* in this place, and therefore they could not have a lodging unless furnished by mere *hospitality.* To say that there were *no inns in those primitive times,* is not true; there were such places, though not very frequent. Joseph's brethren found their money in their sacks when they loosed them at an *inn,* Gen. xlii. 27. The house of Rahab was an *inn,* Josh. ii. 1. And the woman whose house Samson frequented at Gaza was a *hostess,* or one who kept a place of *public entertainment.*

Verse 19. *There is both straw and provender for our asses.*] In the countries principally devoted to *pasturage,* there was no *hay;* but as they raised some corn, they took great care of their *straw,* chopped it very small, and having mixed it with *barley, beans,* or the pounded kernels of *dates,* made it into *balls,* and fed their cattle with it. *Straw,* cut into what is called *chaff,* is not unfrequently used in England for the same purpose.

Verse 20. *All thy wants lie upon me*] Here was genuine hospitality: "Keep your bread and wine for yourselves, and your straw and provender for your asses; you may need them before you finish your journey; I will supply all your wants for this night, therefore do not lodge in the street."

Verse 22. *Sons of Belial*] Profligate fellows. See the notes on Deut. xiii. 13.

That we may know him.] See Gen. xix. These were genuine sodomites as to their practice; sons of Belial, rascals and miscreants of the deepest dye; worse than brutes, being a compound of beast and devil inseparably blended.

Verse 24. Here is *my daughter, a maiden*] Such a proposal was made by *Lot* to the men of Sodom, Gen. xix., but nothing can excuse either. That the rights of *hospitality* were sacred in the East, and most highly regarded, we know; and that a man would defend, at the expense of his life, the stranger whom he had admitted under his roof, is true; but how a *father* could make such a proposal relative to his *virgin daughter,* must remain among those things which are incomprehensible.

Verse 25. *So the man took his concubine*] The word יחזק *yachazek,* which we here translate simply *took,* signifies rather to *take* or *seize by violence.* The woman would not go out to them; but her graceless husband *forced* her to go, in order that he might save his own body. He could have but little love for her, and this was the cause of their separation before.

The *men of Gibeah* who wished to abuse the body of the Levite; the *Levite* who wished to save his body at the expense of the modesty, reputation, and life of his wife; and the *old man* who wished to save his guest at the expense of the violation of his daughter; are all

A. M. 2598
B. C. 1406
An. Exod. Isr. 85
Anno ante
I. Olymp. 630

her forth unto them; and they [i]knew her, and abused her all the night until the morning: and when the day began to spring, they let her go.

26 Then came the woman in the dawning of the day, and fell down at the door of the man's house where her lord *was*, till it was light.

27 And her lord rose up in the morning, and opened the doors of the house, and went out to go his way: and, behold, the woman his concubine was fallen down *at* the door of the house, and her hands *were* upon the threshold.

28 And he said unto her, Up, and let us be going. But [k]none answered. Then the man took her *up* upon an ass, and the man rose up, and gat him unto his place.

A. M. 2598
B. C. 1406
An. Exod. Isr. 85
Anno ante
I. Olymp. 630

29 And when he was come into his house, he took a knife, and laid hold on his concubine, and [l]divided her, *together* with her bones, into twelve pieces, and sent her into all the coasts of Israel.

30 And it was so, that all that saw it said, There was no such deed done nor seen from the day that the children of Israel came up out of the land of Egypt unto this day: consider of it, [m]take advice, and speak *your minds*.

---

[i]Gen. iv. 1——[k]Chap. xx. 5——[l]Chap. xx. 6;

see 1 Sam. xi. 7——[m]Chap. xx. 7; Prov. xiii. 10

---

characters that humanity and modesty wish to be buried in everlasting oblivion.

When the day began to spring] Their turpitude could not bear the full light of the day; and they dismissed the poor woman when the day began to break.

Verse 26. Fell down at the door] She had strength to reach the door, but not to knock for admittance: when she reached the door she fell down dead! The reason of this abominable and horrid catastrophe is strongly signified by the original words, ver. 25: וידעו אותה ויתעללו בה כל הלילה *vaiyedu othah, vaiyithallelu bah col hallailah,* which we modestly translate, *and they knew her, and they abused her all the night.* More literally, but still not fully: *Illi cum ea rem habuerunt, et alternatim in eam tota nocte ascenderunt.* The *hithpahel* used here in the verb עלל greatly increases the sense: *Conjugatio* hithpahel *frequentiam actus et immanem libidinem designat.* The Arabic is not too strong; the following is its meaning: *Exercuerunt in ea cupiditates suas, et mœchati sunt in ea ad matutinum usque.*

Verse 29. Divided her—into twelve pieces] There is no doubt that with the *pieces* he sent to each tribe a circumstantial account of the barbarity of the men of Gibeah; and it is very likely that they considered each of the pieces as expressing an *execration*, "If ye will not come and avenge my wrongs, may ye be hewn in pieces like this abused and murdered woman!"

It was a custom among the ancient Highlanders in Scotland, when one clan wished to call all the rest to avenge its wrongs, to take a *wooden cross, dip it in blood,* and send it by a special messenger through all the clans. This was called the *fire cross,* because at sight of it each clan *lighted a fire* or *beacon,* which gave notice to all the adjoining clans that a general rising was immediately to take place.

Verse 30. There was no such deed done nor seen] They were all struck with the enormity of the crime; and considered it a sovereign disgrace to all the tribes of Israel.

Consider of it] Literally, *Put it to yourselves; take counsel upon it; and speak.* This was the prelude to the council held, and the subsequent operations, which are mentioned in the following chapter.

I HAVE passed over the abominable transactions of this chapter as lightly as I could, and shall make no apology to the learned or unlearned reader for leaving some things untranslated.

What a blessing are wholesome laws, and a vigorous and attentive magistracy! These wretched people had no form of government, and every one did what was right in his own eyes: their own eye (corrupt inclination) was the measure and rule of their conduct; and how bad a rule, the abuse and murder of the Levite's wife testify. Reader, bless God for a civil government.

CHAPTER XX

The heads of the eleven tribes come before the Lord in Mizpeh, and examine the Levite relative to the murder of his wife, who gives a simple narrative of the whole affair, 1–7. They unanimously resolve to avenge the wrong, and make provision for a campaign against the Benjamites, 8–11. They desire the Benjamites to deliver up the murderers; they refuse, and prepare for battle, having assembled an army of twenty-six thousand seven hundred men, 12–16. The rest of the Israelites amount to four hundred thousand, who, taking counsel of God, agree to send the tribe of Judah against the Benjamites, 17, 18. They attack the Benjamites, and are routed with the loss of twenty-two thousand men, 19–21. They renew the battle next day, and are discomfited with the loss of eighteen thousand men, 22–25. They weep, fast, and pray, and offer sacrifices; and again inquire of the Lord, who promises to deliver Benjamin into their hands, 26–28. They concert plans, attack the Benjamites, and rout them, killing twenty-five thousand one hundred men, and destroy the city of Gibeah, 29–37. A recapitulation of the different actions in which they were killed, 38–46. Six hundred men escape to the rock Rimmon, 47. The Israelites destroy all the cities of the Benjamites, 48.

A. M. 2598
B. C. 1406
An. Exod. Isr.
85
Anno ante
I. Olymp. 630

THEN [a]all the children of Israel went out, and the congregation was gathered together as one man, from [b]Dan even to Beer-sheba, with the land of Gilead, unto the LORD [c]in Mizpeh.

2 And the chief of all the people, *even* of all the tribes of Israel, presented themselves in the assembly of the people of God, four hundred thousand footmen [d]that drew sword.

3 (Now the children of Benjamin heard that the children of Israel were gone up to Mizpeh.) Then said the children of Israel, Tell *us,* how was this wickedness?

4 And [e]the Levite, the husband of the woman that was slain, answered and said, [f]I came into Gibeah that *belongeth* to Benjamin, I and my concubine, to lodge.

5 [g]And the men of Gibeah rose against me, and beset the house round about upon me by night, *and* thought to have slain me: [h]and my concubine have they [i]forced, that she is dead.

6 And [k]I took my concubine, and cut her in pieces, and sent her throughout all the country of the inheritance of Israel: for they [l]have committed lewdness and folly in Israel.

7 Behold, ye *are* all children of Israel; [m]give here your advice and counsel.

8 And all the people arose as one man, saying, We will not any *of us* go to his tent, neither will we any *of us* turn into his house.

A. M. 2598
B. C. 1406
An. Exod. Isr.
85
Anno ante
I. Olymp. 630

9 But now this *shall be* the thing which we will do to Gibeah; *we will go up* by lot against it;

10 And we will take ten men of a hundred throughout all the tribes of Israel, and a hundred of a thousand, and a thousand out of ten thousand, to fetch victual for the people, that they may do, when they come to Gibeah of Benjamin, according to all the folly that they have wrought in Israel.

11 So all the men of Israel were gathered against the city, [n]knit together as one man.

12 [o]And the tribe of Israel sent men through all the tribe of Benjamin, saying, What wickedness *is* this that is done among you?

13 Now therefore deliver *us* the men, [p]the children of Belial, which *are* in Gibeah, that we may put them to death, and [q]put away evil from Israel. But the children of Benjamin would not hearken to the voice of their brethren the children of Israel:

14 But the children of Benjamin gathered themselves together out of the cities unto Gi-

---

[a]Deut. xiii. 12; Josh. xxii. 12; chap. xxi. 5; 1 Sam. xi. 7——[b]Chap. xviii. 29; 1 Sam. iii. 20; 2 Sam. iii. 10; xxiv. 2——[c]Chap. x. 17; xi. 11; 1 Sam. vii. 5; x. 17 [d]Chap. viii. 10——[e]Heb. *the man the Levite*——[f]Chap. xix. 15

[g]Chap. xix. 22——[h]Chap. xix. 25, 26——[i]Heb. *humbled*——[k]Chap. xix. 29——[l]Josh. vii. 15——[m]Chap. xix. 30——[n]Heb. *fellows*——[o]Deut. xiii. 14; Josh. xxii. 13, 16——[p]Deut. xiii. 13; chap. xix. 22——[q]Deut. xvii. 12

NOTES ON CHAP. XX

Verse 1. *Unto the Lord in Mizpeh.*] This city was situated on the confines of Judah and Benjamin, and is sometimes attributed to the one, sometimes to the other. It seems that there was a *place* here in which the Lord was consulted, as well as at Shiloh; in 1 Mac. iii. 46 we read, *In Maspha was the place where they prayed aforetime in Israel.* These two passages cast light on each other.

Some think that *Shiloh* is meant, because the ark was there; but the phrase *before the Lord* may signify no more than meeting in the *name of God* to consult him, and make prayer and supplication. Wherever God's people are, there is God himself; and it ever was true, that wherever two or three were assembled in his name, he was in the midst of them.

Verse 2. *The chief of all the people*] The *corners* פנות *pinnoth;* for as the *corner-stones* are the *strength* of the walls, so are the *chiefs* the strength of the people. Hence Christ is called the *chief corner-stone.*

In the assembly of the people of God] The Septuagint translate, *And all the tribes of Israel stood up before the face of the Lord,* εν εκκλησιᾳ του λαου του Θεου, *in the Church of the people*

of God. Here was a *Church,* though there was no *priest;* for, as *Tertullian* says, *Ubi tres, ecclesia est, licet laici;* "Wheresoever three are gathered together in the name of the Lord, there is a *Church,* although there be none but the *laity.*"

Verse 3. *Tell us, how was this wickedness?*] They had heard before, by the messengers he sent with the fragments of his wife's body; but they wish to hear it, in full council, from himself.

Verse 8. *We will not any of us go to his tent*] We will have satisfaction for this wickedness before we return home.

Verse 10. *Ten men of a hundred*] Expecting that they might have a long contest, they provide suttlers for the camp; and it is probable that they chose these tenths by lot.

Verse 13. *Deliver us the men*] Nothing could be fairer than this. They wish only to make the murderers answerable for their guilt.

Benjamin would not hearken] Thus making their whole tribe partakers of the guilt of the men of Gibeah. By not delivering up those bad men, they in effect said: "We will stand by them in what they have done, and would have acted the same part had we been present." This proves that the whole tribe was excessively depraved.

A. M. 2598
B. C. 1406
An. Exod. Isr.
85
Anno ante
I. Olymp. 630

beah, to go out to battle against the children of Israel.

15 And the children of Benjamin were numbered at that time out of the cities twenty and six thousand men that drew sword, beside the inhabitants of Gibeah, which were numbered seven hundred chosen men.

16 Among all this people *there were* seven hundred chosen men 'left-handed; every one could sling stones at a hair *breadth,* and not miss.

17 And the men of Israel, beside Benjamin, were numbered four hundred thousand men that drew sword: all these *were* men of war.

18 And the children of Israel arose, and 'went up to the house of God, and 'asked counsel of God, and said, Which of us shall go up first to the battle against the children

of Benjamin? And the LORD said, Judah *shall go up* first.

A. M. 2598
B. C. 1406
An. Exod. Isr.
85
Anno ante
I. Olymp. 630

19 And the children of Israel rose up in the morning, and encamped against Gibeah.

20 And the men of Israel went out to battle against Benjamin; and the men of Israel put themselves in array to fight against them at Gibeah.

21 And "the children of Benjamin came forth out of Gibeah, and destroyed down to the ground of the Israelites that day twenty and two thousand men.

22 And the people, the men of Israel, encouraged themselves, and set their battle again in array in the place where they put themselves in array the first day.

23 ('And the children of Israel went up and wept before the LORD until even, and asked

---

'Chap. iii. 15; 1 Chron. xii. 2——'Ver. 23, 26——'Num.   xxvii. 21; chap. i. 1——"Gen. xlix. 27——'Ver. 26, 27

Verse 15. *Twenty and six thousand*] Some copies of the *Septuagint* have twenty-three thousand, others twenty-five thousand. The *Vulgate* has this latter number; the *Complutensian* Polyglot and Josephus have the same.

Verse 16. *Left-handed*] They were *ambidexters*—could use the right hand and the left with equal ease and effect. See the note on chap. iii. 15.

Could sling stones at a hair—and not miss]

ולא יחטא *velo yachati, and not sin:* και ουκ εξαμαρτανοντες; *Sept.* Here we have the true import of the term *sin;* it signifies simply *to miss the mark,* and is well translated in the New Testament by αμαρτανω, from a, *negative,* and μαρπτω, *to hit the mark.* Men miss the mark of true *happiness* in aiming at sensual gratifications; which happiness is to be found only in the possession and enjoyment of the favour of God, *from* whom their *passions* continually lead them. He alone *hits the mark,* and ceases from *sin,* who attains to God through Christ Jesus.

It is worthy of remark that the Persian

كردن خطا *khuta kerden,* which literally signifies *to sin* or *mistake,* is used by the Mohammedans to express *to miss the mark.*

The *sling* was a very ancient warlike instrument, and, in the hands of those who were skilled in the use of it, it produced astonishing effects. The inhabitants of the isles called *Baleares,* now *Majorca* and *Minorca,* were the most celebrated slingers of antiquity. They did not permit their children to break their fast till they had struck down the bread they were to eat from the top of a pole, or some distant eminence. They had their name *Baleares* from the Greek word βαλλειν, *to dart, cast,* or *throw.*

Concerning the *velocity* of the ball out of the sling, there are strange and almost incredible things told by the ancients. The leaden ball, when thus projected, is said to have *melted* in its course. So OVID, Met. lib. ii., ver. 726:

Obstupuit forma Jove natus: et æthere pendens
Non secus *exarsit,* quam cum *balearica plumbum
Funda jacit;* volat illud, et *incandescit* eundo;
Et, quos non habuit, sub nubibus invenit *ignes.*

Hermes was fired as in the clouds he hung;
So the *cold bullet* that, with fury *slung*
From *Balearic engines,* mounts on high,
Glows in the whirl, and *burns* along the sky.
DRYDEN.

This is not a *poetic* fiction; SENECA, the philosopher, in lib. iii. *Quæst. Natural.,* c. 57, says the same thing: *Sic liquescit excussa glans funda, et adtritu aeris velut igne distillat;* "Thus the ball projected from the sling melts, and is liquefied by the friction of the air, as if it were exposed to the action of fire." I have often, by the *sudden* and *violent compression of the air,* produced *fire;* and by this *alone* inflamed tinder, and lighted a match.

Vegetius de Re Militari, lib. ii., cap. 23, tells us that slingers could in general hit the mark at six hundred feet distance. *Funditores scopas —pro signo ponebant; ita ut* SEXCENTOS PEDES *removerentur a signo—signum sæpius tangerent.* These things render credible what is spoken here of the Benjamite slingers.

Verse 18. *Went up to the house of God*] Some think that a deputation was sent from *Shiloh,* where Phinehas the high priest was, to inquire, not concerning the *expediency* of the war, nor of its *success,* but which of the tribes should begin the attack. Having so much right on their side, they had no doubt of the *justice* of their cause. Having such a *superiority* of numbers, they had no doubt of success. See the note on ver. 1.

And the Lord said, Judah] But he did not say that they should conquer.

Verse 21. *Destroyed down to the ground—twenty-two thousand men.*] That is, so many were left dead on the field of battle.

Verse 23. *Go up against him.*] It appears most evident that the Israelites did not seek

A. M. 2598
B. C. 1406
An. Exod. Isr.
85
Anno ante
I. Olymp. 630

counsel of the LORD, saying, Shall I go up again to battle against the children of Benjamin my brother? And the LORD said, Go up against him.)

24 And the children of Israel came near against the children of Benjamin the second day.

25 And ʷBenjamin went forth against them out of Gibeah the second day, and destroyed down to the ground of the children of Israel again eighteen thousand men; all these drew the sword.

26 Then all the children of Israel, and all the people, ˣwent up, and came unto the house of God, and wept, and sat there before the LORD, and fasted that day until even, and offered burnt-offerings and peace-offerings before the LORD.

27 And the children of Israel inquired of the LORD, (for ʸthe ark of the covenant of God *was* there in those days,

28 ᶻAnd Phinehas, the son of Eleazar, the son of Aaron, ᵃstood before it in those days,) saying, Shall I yet again go out to battle against the children of Benjamin my brother, or shall I cease? And the LORD said, Go up, for to-morrow I will deliver them into thine hand.

29 And Israel ᵇset liers in wait round about Gibeah.

30 And the children of Israel went up against the children of Benjamin on the third day, and put themselves in array against Gibeah, as at other times.

A. M. 2598
B. C. 1406
An. Exod. Isr.
85
Anno ante
I. Olymp. 630

31 And the children of Benjamin went out against the people, *and* were drawn away from the city; and they began ᶜto smite of the people, *and* kill, as at other times, in the highways, of which one goeth up to ᵈthe house of God, and the other to Gibeah in the field, about thirty men of Israel.

32 And the children of Benjamin said, They *are* smitten down before us as at the first. But the children of Israel said, Let us flee, and draw them from the city unto the highways.

33 And all the men of Israel rose up out of their place, and put themselves in array at Baal-tamar: and the liers in wait of Israel came forth out of their places, *even* out of the meadows of Gibeah.

34 And there came against Gibeah ten thousand chosen men out of all Israel, and the battle was sore: ᵉbut they knew not that evil *was* near them.

35 And the LORD smote Benjamin before Israel: and the children of Israel destroyed of the Benjamites that day twenty and five thousand and a hundred men: all these drew the sword.

ʷVerse 21——ˣVerse 18——ʸJosh. xviii. 1; 1 Sam. iv. 3, 4——ᶻJosh. xxiv. 33——ᵃDeut. x. 8; xviii. 5

ᵇSo Josh. viii. 4——ᶜHeb. *to smite of the people wounded as at*——ᵈOr, *Beth-el*——ᵉJosh. viii. 14; Isa. xlvii. 11

---

the protection of God. They trusted in the *goodness of their cause* and in the *multitude of their army.* God humbled them, and delivered them into the hands of their enemies, and showed them that the race was not to the swift, nor the battle to the strong.

Verse 26. *And wept*] Had they humbled themselves, fasted, and prayed, and offered sacrifices at first, they had not been discomfited.

And fasted that day until even] This is the first place where *fasting* is mentioned as a religious ceremony, or as a means of obtaining help from God. And in this case, and many since, it has been powerfully effectual. At present it is but little used; a strong proof that *self-denial* is wearing out of fashion.

Verse 28. *Phinehas, the son of Eleazar*] This was the same Phinehas who is mentioned Num. xxv., and consequently these transactions must have taken place shortly after the death of Joshua.

Verse 29. *Israel set liers in wait*] Though God had promised them success, they knew they could expect it only in the use of the

proper means. They used all prudent precaution, and employed all their military skill.

Verse 32. *Let us—draw them from the city*] They had two reasons for this: 1. They had placed an ambuscade behind Gibeah, which was to enter and burn the city as soon as the Benjamites had left it. 2. It would seem that the slingers, by being within the city and its fortifications, had great advantage against the Israelites by their slings, whom they could not annoy with their swords, unless they got them to the plain country.

Verse 33. *Put themselves in array at Baal-tamar*] The Israelites seem to have divided their army into three divisions; one was at Baal-tamar, a second behind the city in ambush, and the third skirmished with the Benjamites *before* Gibeah.

Verse 35. *Twenty and five thousand and a hundred*] As the Benjamites consisted only of twenty-six thousand and seven hundred slingers; or, as the Vulgate, Septuagint, and others read, twenty-five thousand, which is most probably the true reading; then the whole of the

A. M. 2598
B. C. 1406
An. Exod. Isr. 85
Anno ante I. Olymp. 630

36 So the children of Benjamin saw that they were smitten: [f]for the men of Israel gave place to the Benjamites, because they trusted unto the liers in wait which they had set beside Gibeah.

37 [g]And the liers in wait hasted, and rushed upon Gibeah: and the liers in wait [h]drew *themselves* along, and smote all the city with the edge of the sword.

38 Now there was an appointed [i]sign between the men of Israel [k]and the liers in wait, that they should make a great [l]flame with smoke to rise up out of the city.

39 And when the men of Israel retired in the battle, Benjamin began [m]to smite *and* kill of the men of Israel about thirty persons: for they said, Surely they are smitten down before us, as *in* the first battle.

40 But when the flame began to arise up out of the city with a pillar of smoke, the Benjamites [n]looked behind them, and, behold, [o]the flame of the city ascended up to heaven.

41 And when the men of Israel turned again, the men of Benjamin were amazed: for they saw that evil [p]was come upon them.

42 Therefore they turned *their backs* before the men of Israel unto the way of the wilderness; but the battle overtook them; and them which *came* out of the cities they destroyed in the midst of them.

A. M. 2598
B. C. 1406
An. Exod. Isr. 85
Anno ante I. Olymp. 630

43 *Thus* they enclosed the Benjamites round about, *and* chased them, *and* trode them down [q]with ease [r]over against Gibeah toward the sunrising.

44 And there fell of Benjamin eighteen thousand men; all these *were* men of valour.

45 And they turned and fled toward the wilderness unto the rock of [s]Rimmon: and they gleaned of them in the highways five thousand men, and pursued hard after them unto Gidom, and slew two thousand men of them.

46 So that all which fell that day of Benjamin were twenty and five thousand men that drew the sword; all these *were* men of valour.

47 [t]But six hundred men turned and fled to the wilderness unto the rock Rimmon, and abode in the rock Rimmon four months.

48 And the men of Israel turned again upon the children of Benjamin, and smote them with the edge of the sword, as well the men of *every* city, as the beast, and all that [u]came to hand: also they set on fire all the cities that [v]they came to.

---

[f]Josh. viii. 15——[g]Josh. viii. 19——[h]Or, *made a long sound with the trumpets;* Josh. vi. 5——[i]Or, *time* [k]Heb. *with*——[l]Heb. *elevation*——[m]Heb. *to smite the wounded*——[n]Josh. viii. 20

[o]Heb. *the whole consumption*——[p]Heb. *touched them* [q]Or, from *Menuchah, &c.*——[r]Heb. *unto over against* [s]Josh. xv. 32——[t]Chap. xxi. 13——[u]Heb. *was found* [v]Heb. *were found*

Benjamites were cut to pieces, except six hundred men, who we are informed fled to the rock Rimmon, where they fortified themselves.

Verse 38. *Now there was an appointed sign*] From this verse to the end of the chapter we have the *details* of the same operations which are mentioned, in a general way, in the preceding part of the chapter.

Verse 45. *Unto the rock of Rimmon*] This was some strong place, but where situated is not known. Here they maintained themselves four months, and it was by these alone that the tribe of Benjamin was preserved from utter extermination. See the following chapter.

It is scarcely possible to imagine any thing more horrid than the indiscriminate and relentless slaughter of both innocent and guilty mentioned in this chapter. The crime of the men of Gibeah was great, but there was no adequate cause for this relentless extermination of a whole tribe. There was neither justice nor judgment in this case; they were on all sides brutal, cruel, and ferocious: and no wonder; *there was no king in Israel*—no effective civil government, and *every man did what was right in his own eyes.* There was no proper leader; no man that had authority and influence to repress the disorderly workings of the pell-mell mob.

CHAPTER XXI

The Israelites mourn because of the desolation of Benjamin, and consult the Lord, 1–4. *They inquire who of Israel had not come to this war, as they had vowed that those who would not make this a common cause should be put to death,* 5, 6. *They consult how they shall procure wives for the six hundred men who had fled to the rock Rimmon,* 7. *Finding that the men of Jabesh-gilead had not come to the war, they send twelve thousand men against them, smite them, and bring off four hundred virgins, which they give for wives to those who had taken refuge in Rimmon,* 8–14. *To provide for the two hundred which remained, they propose to carry off two hundred virgins of the daughters of Shiloh, who might come to the annual feast of the Lord, held at that place,* 15–22. *They take this counsel, and each carries away a virgin from the feast,* 23–25.

A. M. 2598
B. C. 1406
An. Exod. Isr.
85
Anno ante
I. Olymp. 630

NOW [a]the men of Israel had sworn in Mizpeh, saying, There shall not any of us give his daughter unto Benjamin to wife.

2 And the people came [b]to the house of God, and abode there till even before God, and lifted up their voices, and wept sore;

3 And said, O LORD God of Israel, why is this come to pass in Israel, that there should be to-day one tribe lacking in Israel?

4 And it came to pass on the morrow, that the people rose early, and [c]built there an altar, and offered burnt-offerings and peace-offerings.

5 And the children of Israel said, Who is there among all the tribes of Israel that came not up with the congregation unto the LORD? [d]For they had made a great oath concerning him that came not up to the LORD to Mizpeh, saying, He shall surely be put to death.

6 And the children of Israel repented them for Benjamin their brother, and said, There is one tribe cut off from Israel this day.

7 How shall we do for wives for them that remain, seeing we have sworn by the LORD

A. M. 2598
B. C. 1406
An. Exod. Isr.
85
Anno ante
I. Olymp. 630

that we will not give them of our daughters to wives?

8 And they said, What one is there of the tribes of Israel that came not up to Mizpeh to the LORD? And, behold, there came none to the camp from [e]Jabesh-gilead to the assembly.

9 For the people were numbered, and, behold, there were none of the inhabitants of Jabesh-gilead there.

10 And the congregation sent thither twelve thousand men of the valiantest, and commanded them, saying, [f]Go and smite the inhabitants of Jabesh-gilead with the edge of the sword, with the women and the children.

11 And this is the thing that ye shall do, [g]Ye shall utterly destroy every male, and every woman that hath [h]lain by man.

12 And they found among the inhabitants of Jabesh-gilead four hundred [i]young virgins, that had known no man by lying with any male: and they brought them unto the camp to [k]Shiloh, which is in the land of Canaan.

13 And the whole congregation sent some [l]to speak to the children of Benjamin [m]that

---

[a]Chap. xx. 1——[b]Chap. xx. 18, 26——[c]2 Sam. xxiv. 25——[d]Judg. v. 23——[e]1 Sam. xi. 1; xxxi. 11——[f]Ver. 5; chap. v. 23; 1 Sam. xi. 7

[g]Num. xxxi. 17——[h]Heb. *knoweth the lying* with *man* [i]Heb. *young women virgins*——[k]Josh. xviii. 1——[l]Heb. *and spake and called*——[m]Chap. xx. 47

NOTES ON CHAP. XXI

Verse 1. *Now the men of Israel had sworn*] Of this oath we had not heard before; but it appears they had commenced this war with a determination to destroy the Benjamites utterly, and that if any of them escaped the sword, no man should be permitted to give him his daughter to wife. By these means the remnant of the tribe must soon have been annihilated.

Verse 2. *The people came to the house of God*] Literally, *the people came* בֵּית־אֵל *to Beth-el;* this is considered as the name of a *place* by the Chaldee, Syriac, Arabic, and Septuagint.

And wept sore] Their revenge was satisfied, and now reflection brings them to contrition for what they had done.

Verse 3. *Why is this come to pass*] This was a very impertinent question. They knew well enough *how* it came to pass. It was right that the men of Gibeah should be punished, and it was right that they who vindicated them should share in that punishment; but they carried their revenge too far, they endeavoured to exterminate both man and beast, chap. xx. 48.

Verse 4. *Built there an altar*] This affords some evidence that this was not a *regular* place of worship, else an altar would have been found in the place; and their act was not according to the law, as may be seen in several places of the Pentateuch. But there was neither king nor law among them, and they did whatever appeared right in their own eyes.

Verse 7. *How shall we do for wives for them*] From this it appears that they had destroyed all the Benjamitish *women* and children! They had set out with the purpose of exterminating the whole tribe, and therefore they massacred the *women*, that if any of the men escaped, they might neither find wife nor daughter; and they bound themselves under an oath not to give any of their females to any of the remnant of this tribe, that thus the whole tribe might utterly perish.

Verse 8. *There came none to the camp from Jabesh-gilead*] As they had sworn to destroy those who would not assist in this war, ver. 5, they determined to destroy the men of Jabesh, and to leave none alive except the *virgins*, and to give these to the six hundred Benjamites that had escaped to the rock Rimmon. So twelve thousand men went, smote the city, and killed all the males and all the *married* women. The whole account is dreadful; and none could have been guilty of all these enormities but those who were abandoned of God. The crime of the men of Gibeah was of the deepest die; the punishment, involving both the guilty and innocent, was extended to the most criminal excess; and their mode or redressing the evil which they had occasioned was equally abominable.

Verse 13. *And to call peaceably unto them.*] To *proclaim peace* to them; to assure them that the enmity was all over, and that they might with safety leave their strong hold.

A. M. 2598
B. C. 1406
An. Exod. Isr.
85
Anno ante
I. Olymp. 630

were in the rock Rimmon, and to ⁿcall peaceably unto them.

14 And Benjamin came again at that time; and they gave them wives which they had saved alive of the women of Jabesh-gilead: and yet so they sufficed them not.

15 And the people °repented them for Benjamin, because that the LORD had made a breach in the tribes of Israel.

16 Then the elders of the congregation said, How shall we do for wives for them that remain, seeing the women are destroyed out of Benjamin?

17 And they said, *There must be* an inheritance for them that be escaped of Benjamin, that a tribe be not destroyed out of Israel.

18 Howbeit we may not give them wives of our daughters: ᵖfor the children of Israel have sworn, saying, Cursed *be* he that giveth a wife to Benjamin.

19 Then they said, Behold, *there is* a feast of the LORD in Shiloh �q*yearly in a place* which *is* on the north side of Beth-el, ʳon the east side ˢof the highway that goeth up from Beth-el to Shechem, and on the south of Lebonah.

20 Therefore they commanded the children of Benjamin, saying, Go, and lie in wait in the vineyards;

21 And see, and, behold, if the daughters of Shiloh come out ᵗto dance in dances, then come ye out of the vineyards, and catch you every man his wife of the daughters of Shiloh, and go to the land of Benjamin.

22 And it shall be, when their fathers or their brethren come unto us to complain, that we will say unto them, ᵘBe favourable unto them for our sakes: because we reserved not to each man his wife in the war: for ye did not give unto them at this time, *that* ye should be guilty.

A. M. 2598
B. C. 1406
An. Exod. Isr.
85
Anno ante
I. Olymp. 630

ⁿOr, *proclaim peace;* Deut. xx. 10——°Ver. 6——ᵖVer. 1; Judg. xi. 35——qHeb. *from year to year*——ʳOr, *toward* *the sunrising*——ˢOr, *on*——ᵗSee Exod. xv. 20; ch. xi. 34; 1 Sam. xviii. 6; Jer. xxxi. 13——ᵘOr, *gratify us in time*

Verse 14. *Yet so they sufficed them not.*] There were six hundred men at Rimmon, and all the young women they saved from Jabesh were only four hundred; therefore, there were two hundred still wanting.

Verse 19. There is *a feast of the Lord*] What this feast was is not known: it might be either the passover, pentecost, or the feast of tabernacles, or indeed some other peculiar to this place. All the above feasts were celebrated at that time of the year when the vines were in full *leaf;* therefore the Benjamites might easily conceal themselves in the vineyards; and the circumstances will answer to any of those feasts.

On the east side of the highway, &c.] I can see no reason for this minute description, unless it intimates that this feast was to be held this year in rather a *different* place to that which was usual: and, as the Benjamites had been shut up in their strong hold in Rimmon, they might not have heard of this alteration; and it was necessary, in such a case, to give them the most circumstantial information, that they might succeed in their enterprise without being discovered.

Verse 21. *And catch you every man his wife*] That is, Let each man of the two hundred Benjamites seize and carry off a *woman*, whom he is, from that hour, to consider as his *wife*.

Verse 22. *Be favourable unto them*] They promise to use their influence with the men of Shiloh to induce them to consent to a connection thus fraudulently obtained, and which the necessity of the case appeared to them to justify.

We reserved not to each man his wife in the war] The reading of the *Vulgate* is very remarkable: Miseremini eorum, non enim rapuerunt eas jure bellantium atque victorum, sed rogantibus ut acciperent non dedistis, et a vestra parte peccatum est.—"Pardon them, for

they have not taken them as victors take captives in war; but when they requested you to give them you did not; therefore the fault is your own." Here it is intimated that application had been made to the people of Shiloh to furnish these *two hundred* Benjamites with wives, and that they had refused; and it was this refusal that induced the Benjamites to seize and carry them off. Does not St. Jerome, the translator, refer to the history of the rape of the *Sabine virgins?* See below. *Houbigant* translates the Hebrew thus: Veniam quæso illis date; non enim ad bellum duxerant suam quisque uxorem; et nisi eas illis nunc concedetis, delicti rei eritis.—"Pardon them, I beseech you, for they have not each taken his wife to the war; and unless you now give these to them, you will sin." This intimates that, as the Benjamites had not taken their wives with them to the war, where some, if not all, of them might have escaped; and the Israelites found them in the cities, and put them all to the sword; therefore the people of Shiloh should give up those *two hundred* young women to them for wives; and if they did not, it would be a sin, the circumstances of the case being considered.

Our translation seems to give as a reason to the men of Shiloh why they should pardon this rape, that as they had not permitted the women to live in their war with Benjamin, therefore these men are now destitute; and the concession which they wish them to make may be considered as more of an obligation to the Israelites than to the Benjamites. It is an obscure sentence; and the reader, if not pleased with what is laid down, may endeavour to satisfy himself with others which he may find in different *versions* and *commentators.* The *Vulgate* gives a good sense to the passage; but probably Houbigant comes nearest to the meaning.

A. M. 2598
B. C. 1406
An. Exod. Isr.
85
Anno ante
I. Olymp. 630

23 And the children of Benjamin did so, and took *them* wives, according to their number, of them that danced, whom they caught: and they went and returned unto their inheritance, and [v]repaired the cities, and dwelt in them.

24 And the children of Israel departed thence at that time, every man to his tribe and to his family, and they went out from thence every man to his inheritance.

A. M. 2598
B. C. 1406
An. Exod. Isr.
85
Anno ante
I. Olymp. 630

25 [w]In those days *there was* no king in Israel: [x]every man did *that which was* right in his own eyes.

---

[v]See chap. xx. 48——[w]Chap. xvii. 6; xviii. 1: xix. 1

[x]Deut. xii. 8; chap. xvii. 6

Verse 23. *They went and returned unto their inheritance*] It appears that the Benjamites acted in the most honourable way by the women whom they had thus violently carried off; and we may rest assured they took them to an inheritance at least equal to their own, for it does not appear that any part of the lands of the Benjamites was alienated from them, and the *six hundred* men in question shared, for the present, the inheritance of many thousands.

Verse 24. *Every man to his tribe*] Though this must have been *four months* after the war with Benjamin, chap. xx. 47; yet it appears the armies did not disband till they had got the remnant of Benjamin settled, as is here related.

Verse 25. *In those days* there was *no king in Israel*] Let no one suppose that the sacred writer, by relating the atrocities in this and the preceding chapters, justifies the actions themselves; by no means. Indeed, they cannot be justified; and the writer by relating them gives the strongest proof of the authenticity of the whole, by such an impartial relation of facts that were highly to be discredit of his country.

I HAVE already referred to the rape of the Sabine virgins. The story is told by *Livy*, Hist. lib. i., cap. 9, the substance of which is as follows: Romulus having opened an *asylum* at his new-built city of Rome for all kinds of persons, the number of men who flocked to his standard was soon very considerable; but as they had few *women*, or, as Livy says, *penuria mulierum*, a dearth of women, he sent to all the neighbouring states to invite them to make intermarriages with his people. Not one of the tribes around him received the proposal; and some of them insulted his ambassador, and said, *Ecquod feminis quoque asylum aperuissent? Id enim demum compar connubium fore?* "Why have you not also opened an asylum for WOMEN, which would have afforded you suitable matches?" This exasperated Romulus, but he

concealed his resentment; and, having published that he intended a great *feast* to *Neptune Equester*, invited all the neighbouring tribes to come to it: they did so, and were received by the Romans with the greatest cordiality and friendship. The *Sabines*, with their wives and children, came in great numbers, and each Roman citizen entertained a stranger. When the games began, and each was intent on the spectacle before them, at a signal given the young Romans rushed in among the Sabine women, and each carried off one, whom however they used in the kindest manner, marrying them according to their own rites with due solemnity, and admitting them to all the rights and privileges of the new commonwealth. The number carried off on this occasion amounted to near *seven hundred;* but this act of violence produced disastrous wars between the Romans and the Sabines, which were at last happily terminated by the *mediation* of the very women whose rape had been the cause of their commencement. The story may be seen at large in *Livy, Plutarch,* and others.

Thus ends the book of *Judges;* a work which, while it *introduces* the history of *Samuel* and that of the *kings* of Judah and Israel, forms in some sort a *supplement* to the book of *Joshua,* and furnishes the only account we have of those times of anarchy and confusion, which extended nearly from the times of the elders who survived Joshua, to the establishment of the Jewish *monarchy* under Saul, David, and their successors. For other *uses* of this book, see the *preface.*

MASORETIC NOTES ON THE BOOK OF JUDGES

The number of *verses* in this book is *six hundred and eighteen.*

Its Masoretic *chapters* are *fourteen.*

And its middle verse is ver. 8, of chap. x.: *And that year they vexed and oppressed the children of Israel,* &c.

Corrected for a new edition, December 1, 1827.—A. C.

PREFACE TO THE BOOK

OF

RUTH

WHEN and by *whom* the *book of Ruth* was written, are points not agreed on among critics and commentators.

As to the transactions recorded in it, they are variously placed. In the book itself there is no other notation of *time* than merely this, that the things *came to pass in the days when the judges ruled;* therefore some have placed these transactions under *Ehud;* others, under *Gideon;* others, under *Barak;* others, under *Abimelech;* and others, under *Shamgar.* This last is the opinion of Archbishop Usher; and most chronologers adopt it. The book is evidently an *Appendix* to the book of Judges, and contains a perfect history in itself; and therefore should not be inserted in any part of that book. It also seems to be an *Introduction* to the books of Samuel, in which the history of David is contained, as it gives the genealogy of this prince. It is also not without its use in matters which respect the *Gospels,* as it ascertains the line by which Jesus Christ came.

As to the *author,* he is as uncertain as the *time.* It has been attributed to *Hezekiah,* to *Ezra,* and to *Samuel;* and it is most likely that the author of the two books of Samuel was also the writer of this little book, as it seems necessary to complete his plan of the history of David. See the *preface* to the first book of Samuel.

The sum of the history contained in this book is the following: A man of Bethlehem, named Elimelech, with his wife Naomi, and his two sons Mahlon and Chilion, left his own country in the time of a famine, and went to sojourn in the land of Moab. There he died; and Naomi married her two sons to two Moabitish women: Mahlon married Ruth, who is the chief subject of this book; and Chilion married one named Orpah. In about ten years both these brethren died; and Naomi, accompanied by her two daughters-in-law, set out to return to the land of Judah, she having heard that plenty was again restored to her country. On the way she besought her daughters to return to their own country and kindred. Orpah took her advice, and, after an affectionate parting, returned; but Ruth insisted on accompanying her mother-in-law. They arrived in Bethlehem about the time of *harvest;* and Ruth went into the fields to glean for their support. The ground on which she was accidentally employed belonged to Boaz, one of the relatives of Elimelech, her father-in-law; who, finding who she was, ordered her to be kindly treated, and appointed her both meat and drink with his own servants. Finding that she was by marriage his *kinswoman,* he purposed to take her to wife, if a nearer kinsman who was then living should refuse. He was accordingly applied to, refused to take Ruth, and surrendered his right to her, according to the custom of those times, at the gate of Bethlehem, before the elders of the city. Boaz then took her to wife, by whom she had Obed, who was father to Jesse, the father of David.

To the questions, Who was *Boaz?* and, Who was *Ruth?* no satisfactory answer can be given: all we know for certain is, that *Boaz* was an *Ephraimite* of Bethlehem; and *Ruth* a *Moabitess,* and consequently educated a heathen. But what we want in certainty, several have attempted to supply by conjecture; with them Boaz was the same as *Ibzan*, Judg. xii. 8–10; and Ruth was the daughter of *Eglon*, king of Moab. This is the opinion maintained by the Chaldee *Targum* on this book; to which I shall, in the course of the notes, have farther occasion to refer. The rabbins say that Elimelech was brother to Salmon, who married Rahab; and that Naomi was his niece.

The genealogy of David, as stated in this book, is as follows:—

A. M. 2236. Judah,	Nahshon,
Pharez,	Salmon, who married Rahab,
Ezron, called also *Hezron*,	Boaz, who married Ruth,
Aram, called also *Ram*,	Obed, who begat Jesse,
Amminadab,	A. M. 2919. David born.

This chronology is according to Archbishop Usher; and includes, from Judah to David *six hundred and seventy years*.

THE

BOOK OF RUTH

Year before the common year of Christ, 1186.—Year from the Flood, 1162.—Year before the first Olympiad, 410.—Creation from Tisri, or September, 2818.—This chronology is upon the supposition that Obed was forty years of age at the birth of Jesse; and Jesse, fifty at the birth of David.

CHAPTER I

Elimelech, his wife Naomi, and their two sons, Mahlon and Chilion, flee from a famine in the land of Israel, and go to sojourn in Moab, 1, 2. Here his two sons marry; and, in the space of ten years, both their father and they die, 3–6. Naomi sets out on her return to her own country, accompanied by her daughters-in-law Orpah and Ruth; whom she endeavours to persuade to return to their own people, 7–13. Orpah returns, but Ruth accompanies her mother-in-law, 14–18. They arrive at Beth-lehem in the time of the barley harvest, 19–22.

A. M. 2818
B. C. 1186
An. Exod. Isr. 305
Anno ante
I. Olymp. 410

NOW it came to pass in the days when [a]the judges [b]ruled, that there was [c]a famine in the land. And a certain man of [d]Beth-lehem-judah went to sojourn in the country of Moab, he, and his wife, and his two sons.

2 And the name of the man *was* Elimelech, and the name of his wife Naomi, and the name of his two sons Mahlon and Chilion, [e]Ephrathites of Beth-lehem-judah. And they came [f]into the country of Moab, and [g]continued there.

3 And Elimelech Naomi's husband died, and she was left, and her two sons.

A. M. 2818
B. C. 1186
An. Exod. Isr. 305
Anno ante
I. Olymp. 410

4 And they took them wives of the women of Moab; the name of the one *was* Orpah, and the name of the other Ruth: and they dwelled there about ten years.

5 And Mahlon and Chilion died also both of them; and the woman was left of her two sons and her husband.

6 Then she arose with her daughters-in-

[a]Judg. ii. 16——[b]Heb. *judged*——[c]See Gen. xii. 10; xxvi. 1; 2 Kings viii. 1

[d]Judg. xvii. 8——[e]See Gen. xxxv. 19——[f]Judg. v. 30 [g]Heb. *were*

NOTES ON CHAP. I

Verse 1. *When the judges ruled*] We know not under what judge this happened; some say under *Ehud*, others under *Shamgar*. See the *preface*.

There was a famine] Probably occasioned by the depredations of the Philistines, Ammonites, &c., carrying off the corn as soon as it was ripe, or destroying it on the field.

The *Targum* says: "God has decreed ten grievous famines to take place in the world, to punish the inhabitants of the earth, before the coming of Messiah the king. The *first* in the days of Adam; the *second* in the days of Lamech; the *third* in the days of Abraham; the *fourth* in the days of Isaac; the *fifth* in the days of Jacob; the *sixth* in the days of Boaz, who is called Abstan, (Ibzan,) the just, of Beth-lehem-judah; the *seventh* in the days of David, king of Israel; the *eighth* in the days of Elijah the prophet; the *ninth* in the days of Elisha, in Samaria; the *tenth* is yet to come, and it is not a famine of *bread* or of *water*, but

of hearing the word of prophecy from the mouth of the Lord; and even now this famine is grievous in the land of Israel."

Verse 2. *Elimelech*] That is, *God is my king.*

Naomi] *Beautiful* or *amiable.*

Mahlon] *Infirmity.*

Chilion] *Finished, completed.*

Verse 3. *Elimelech—died*] Probably a short time after his arrival in Moab.

Verse 4. *And they took them wives*] The Targum very properly observes, that *they transgressed the decree of the word of the Lord, and took to themselves strange women.*

Verse 5. *And Mahlon and Chilion died*] The Targum adds, *And because they transgressed the decree of the word of the Lord, and joined affinity with strange people, therefore their days were cut off.* It is very likely that there is more here than conjecture.

Verse 6. *She had heard*] *By the mouth of an angel*, says the *Targum.*

The Lord had visited his people] "Because of the righteousness of Ibzan the judge, and

A. M. 2828
B. C. 1176
An. Exod. Isr.
315
Anno ante
I. Olymp. 400

law, that she might return from the country of Moab: for she had heard in the country of Moab how that the LORD had [h]visited his people in [i]giving them bread.

7 Wherefore she went forth out of the place where she was, and her two daughters-in-law with her; and they went on the way to return unto the land of Judah.

8 And Naomi said unto her two daughters-in-law, [k]Go, return each to her mother's house: [l]the LORD deal kindly with you, as ye have dealt with [m]the dead, and with me.

9 The LORD grant you that ye may find [n]rest, each *of you* in the house of her husband. Then she kissed them; and they lifted up their voice, and wept.

10 And they said unto her, Surely we will return with thee unto thy people.

11 And Naomi said, Turn again, my daughters: why will ye go with me? *are* there yet any more sons in my womb, [o]that they may be your husbands?

A. M. 2828
B. C. 1176
An. Exod. Isr.
315
Anno ante
I. Olymp. 400

12 Turn again, my daughters, go *your way;* for I am too old to have a husband. If I should say, I have hope, [p]*if* I should have a husband also to-night, and should also bear sons;

13 Would ye [q]tarry for them till they were grown? would ye stay for them from having husbands? nay, my daughters; for [r]it grieveth me much for your sakes, that [s]the hand of the LORD is gone out against me.

14 And they lifted up their voice, and wept again: and Orpah [t]kissed her mother-in-law; but Ruth [u]clave unto her.

15 And she said, Behold, thy sister-in-law is gone back unto her people, and unto [v]her gods: [w]return thou after thy sister-in-law.

16 And Ruth said, [x]Entreat [y]me not to leave thee, *or* to return from following after

---

[h]Exod. iv. 31; Luke i. 68——[i]Psa. cxxxii. 15; Matt. vi. 11——[k]See Josh. xxiv. 15——[l]2 Tim. i. 16, 17, 18
[m]Verse 5; chap. ii. 20——[n]Chap. iii. 1——[o]Gen. xxxviii. 11; Deut. xxv. 5——[p]Or, *if I were with a husband*
[q]Heb. *hope*——[r]Heb. *I have much bitterness*

[s]Judg. ii. 15; Job xix. 21; Psa. xxxii. 4; xxxviii. 2; xxxix. 9, 10——[t]Ecclus. xii. 9——[u]Proverbs xvii. 17; xviii. 24——[v]Judges xi. 24——[w]See Joshua xxiv. 15, 19; 2 Kings ii. 2; Luke xxiv. 28——[x]Or, *be not against me*
[y]2 Kings ii. 2, 4, 6

---

because of the supplications of pious Boaz."—*Targum.*

It is imagined, and not without probability, that Mahlon and Chilion are the same with *Joash* and *Saraph*, mentioned 1 Chron. iv. 22, where the Hebrew should be thus translated, *and Joash and Saraph, who married in Moab, and dwelt in Lehem.* See the *Hebrew.*

Verse 11. Are *there yet* any more *sons*] This was spoken in allusion to the *custom*, that when a married brother died without leaving posterity, his brother should take his widow; and the children of such a marriage were accounted the children of the deceased brother. There is something very persuasive and affecting in the address of Naomi to her daughters-in-law. Let us observe the particulars:—

1. She intimates that she had no other sons to give them.

2. That she was not with child; so there could be no expectation.

3. That she was too old to have a husband.

4. That though she should marry that night, and have children, yet they could not wait till such sons were marriageable; she therefore begs them to return to their own country, where they might be comfortably settled among their own kindred.

Verse 14. *And Orpah kissed her mother-in-law*] The Septuagint add, Και επεστρεψεν εις τον λαον αυτης, *And returned to her own people.* The *Vulgate, Syriac,* and *Arabic,* are to the same purpose.

Verse 15. *Gone back—unto her gods*] They were probably both idolaters; their having been *proselytes* is an unfounded conjecture. Chemosh was the grand idol of the Moabites.

The conversion of Ruth probably commenced at this time.

Verse 16. *And Ruth said*] A more perfect surrender was never made of friendly feelings to a friend: *I will not leave thee*—I will follow thee: *I will lodge where thou lodgest*—take the same fare with which thou meetest; *thy people shall be my people*—I most cheerfully abandon my own country, and determine to end my days in thine. *I will also henceforth have no god but thy God,* and be joined with thee in worship, as I am in affection and consanguinity. I will cleave unto thee *even unto death; die where thou diest; and be buried,* if possible, in the same grave. This was a most extraordinary attachment, and evidently without any secular motive.

The Targum adds several things to this conversation between Naomi and Ruth. I shall subjoin them: "And Ruth said, Entreat me not to leave thee," *for I desire to become a proselyte. And Naomi said, We are commanded to keep the Sabbath and other holy days; and on it not to travel more than* two thousand cubits. *And Ruth said,* "Whither thou goest, I will go." *And Naomi said, We are commanded not to lodge with the Gentiles. Ruth answered,* "Where thou lodgest, I will lodge." *And Naomi said, We are commanded to observe the* one hundred and thirteen *precepts. Ruth answered, What thy people observe, that will I observe;* as if they had been my people of old. *And Naomi said, We are commanded not to worship with any strange worship. Ruth answered,* "Thy God shall be my God." *Naomi said, We have four kinds of capital punishment for criminals; stoning, burning, beheading, and*

A. M. 2828
B. C. 1176
An. Exod. Isr. 315
Anno ante
I. Olymp. 400

thee: for whither thou goest, I will go; and where thou lodgest, I will lodge; ᶻthy people *shall be* my people, and thy God my God:

17 Where thou diest, will I die, and there will I be buried: ᵃthe LORD do so to me, and more also, *if aught* but death part thee and me.

18 ᵇWhen she saw that she ᶜwas steadfastly minded to go with her, then she left speaking unto her.

19 So they two went until they came to Beth-lehem. And it came to pass, when they were come to Beth-lehem, that ᵈall the city

was moved about them, and they said, ᵉ*Is* this Naomi?

A. M. 2828
B. C. 1176
An. Exod. Isr. 315
Anno ante
I. Olymp. 400

20 And she said unto them, Call me not ᶠNaomi, call me ᵍMara: for the Almighty hath dealt very bitterly with me.

21 I went out full, ʰand the LORD hath brought me home again empty: why *then* call ye me Naomi, seeing the LORD hath testified against me, and the Almighty hath afflicted me?

22 So Naomi returned, and Ruth the Moabitess, her daughter-in-law, with her, which returned out of the country of Moab: and they came to Beth-lehem ⁱin the beginning of barley harvest.

ᶻChap. ii. 11, 12——ᵃ1 Sam. iii. 17; xxv. 22; 2 Sam. xix. 13; 2 Kings vi. 31——ᵇActs xxi. 14——ᶜHeb. *strengthened herself*——ᵈMatt. xxi. 10

ᵉSee Isa. xxiii. 7; Lam. ii. 15——ᶠThat is, *pleasant* ᵍThat is, *bitter*——ʰJob i. 21——ⁱExod. ix. 31, 32; chap. ii. 23; 2 Sam. xxi. 9

---

hanging. *Ruth answered,* "In whatsoever manner thou diest, I will die." *Naomi said, We have a house of burial. Ruth answered,* "And there will I be buried."

It is very likely that some such conversation as this took place between the *elders* and those who were becoming *proselytes.* This verse is famous among those who strive to *divine* by the Bible. I should relate the particulars, but am afraid they might lead to a continuance of the practice. In my youth I have seen it done, and was then terrified.

Verse 17. The Lord do so to me, and more] May he inflict any of those punishments on me, and any worse punishment, if I part from thee till death. And it appears that she was true to her engagement; for Naomi was nourished in the house of Boaz in her old age, and became the fosterer and nurse of their son Obed, chap. iv. 15, 16.

Verse 19. All the city was moved about them] It appears that Naomi was not only well known, but highly respected also at Bethlehem; a proof that Elimelech was of high consideration in that place.

Verse 20. Call me not Naomi] That is, *beautiful* or *pleasant.*

Call me Mara; That is, *bitter;* one whose life is grievous to her.

The Almighty] שׁדי *Shaddai,* He who is *self-sufficient,* has taken away the props and supports of my life.

Verse 21. I went out full] Having a *husband* and *two sons.*

The Lord hath brought me home again empty] Having lost all *three* by death. It is also likely that Elimelech took considerable property with him into the land of Moab; for as he fled from the face of the famine, he would naturally take his property with him; and on this Naomi subsisted till her return to Bethlehem, which she might not have thought of till all was spent.

Verse 22. In the beginning of barley harvest.] This was in the beginning of *spring,* for the barley harvest began immediately after the passover, and that feast was held on the 15th of the month *Nisan,* which corresponds nearly with our *March.*

The *Targum* says, "They came to Beth-lehem on that day in which the children of Israel began to mow the sheaf of barley which was to be waved before the Lord." This circumstance is the more distinctly marked, because of Ruth's *gleaning,* mentioned in the succeeding chapter.

1. THE native, the amiable *simplicity,* in which the story of the preceding chapter is told, is a proof of its *genuineness.* There are several sympathetic circumstances recorded here which no *forger* could have invented. There is too much of *nature* to admit any thing of *art.*

2. On the marriage of Orpah and Ruth, and the wish of Naomi that they might find *rest* in the house of their husbands, there are some pious and sensible observations in Mr. NESS's *History and Mystery of the Book of Ruth,* from which I shall lay the following extract before my readers:—

"A married estate is a state of *rest;* so it is called here, and in chap. iii. 1. Hence marriage is called *portus juventutis,* the *port* or *haven* of *young people;* whose affections, while unmarried, are continually *floating* or *tossed* to and *fro,* like a *ship* upon the *waters,* till they come into this *happy harbour.* There is a natural propension in most persons towards nuptial communion, as all created beings have a natural tendency towards their proper centre, (*leve sursum, et grave deorsum,*) and are restless out of it; so the rabbins say, *Requiret vir costam suam, et requiret femina sedem suam,* 'The man is restless while he misses his rib that was taken out of his side; and the woman is restless till she get under the man's arm, from whence she was taken.' O! look up to God then, ye unmarried ones, and cry with good *Naomi, The Lord grant me rest* for my roving affections in the house of some good consort, that I may live in peace and plenty, with content and comfort all my days. Know that your marriage is, of all your civil affairs, of the greatest importance, having an influence upon your whole life. It is either your making or marring in this world; 'tis like a stratagem in war, wherein a miscarriage cannot be recalled when we will, for we marry for life. I am thine, and thou art mine, *brevis quidem cantiuncula est*, 'is a short song,' *sed longum habet epiphonema*, 'but it hath a long under-

song.' So an error here is irrecoverable; you have need of Argus's hundred eyes to look withal before you leap." This is good advice; but who among the persons concerned will have grace enough to take it?

CHAPTER II

Ruth goes to glean in the field of Boaz, 1–3. Boaz finds her, and inquires who she is, 4–7. He speaks kindly to her, gives her permission to follow his reapers, and orders them to use her well, 8–16. She returns in the evening to Naomi, and tells her of her fare; from whom she receives encouragement and advice, 17–23.

A. M. 2828
B. C. 1176
An. Exod. Isr.
315
Anno ante
I. Olymp. 400

AND Naomi had a [a]kinsman of her husband's, a mighty man of wealth, of the family of Elimelech; and his name *was* [b]Boaz.[c]

2 And Ruth the Moabitess said unto Naomi, Let me now go to the field, and [d]glean ears of corn after *him* in whose sight I shall find grace. And she said unto her, Go, my daughter.

3 And she went, and came, and gleaned in the field after the reapers: and her [e]hap was to light on a part of the field *belonging* unto Boaz, who *was* of the kindred of Elimelech.

A. M. 2828
B. C. 1176
An. Exod. Isr.
315
Anno ante
I. Olymp. 400

4 And, behold, Boaz came from Beth-lehem, and said unto the reapers, [f]The LORD *be* with you. And they answered him, The LORD bless thee.

5 Then said Boaz unto his servant that was set over the reapers, Whose damsel *is* this?

---

[a]Chap. iii. 2, 12——[b]Chap. iv. 21——[c]Called *Booz;* Matt. i. 5——[d]Lev. xix. 9; Deut. xxiv. 19

[e]Heb. *hap happened*——[f]Psa. cxxix. 7, 8; Luke i. 28; 2 Thess. iii. 16

NOTES ON CHAP. II

Verse 1. *A mighty man of wealth*] We have already seen that some suppose Boaz to have been one of the judges of Israel; he was no doubt a man of considerable property.

Verse 2. *Glean ears of corn*] The word *glean* comes from the French *glaner*, to gather ears or grains of corn. This was formerly a general custom in England and Ireland; the poor went into the fields and collected the straggling ears of corn after the reapers; and it was long supposed that this was their *right*, and that the *law* recognised it. But although it has been an old *custom*, I find that it is now settled, by a solemn judgment in the court of common pleas, that a right to glean in the harvest field cannot be claimed by any person at common law; see *Law Dictionary,* article *gleaning.* Any person may *permit* or *prevent* it in his own grounds. By the Irish acts, 25 Hen. VIII., c. 1, and 28 Hen. VIII., c. 24, *gleaning* and *leasing* are so restricted as to be in fact prohibited in that part of the United Kingdom. See the note on Lev. xix. 10.

After him *in whose sight I shall find grace.*] She did not mean Boaz; but she purposed to go out where they were now reaping, and glean after *any person* who might permit her, or use her in a friendly manner. The words seem to intimate that, notwithstanding the law of Moses, the gleaners might be prevented by the owner of the field.

Verse 3. *And her hap was*] So she was *accidentally* or *providentially* led to that part of the cultivated country which belonged to Boaz.

Verse 4. *Boaz came from Beth-lehem*] This salutation between Boaz and his reapers is

worthy of particular regard; he said, יהוה עמכם *Yehovah immachem*, "Jehovah be with you!" They said, יברכך יהוה *yebarechecha Yehovah*, "May Jehovah bless thee!" Can a pious mind read these godly salutations without wishing for a return of those simple primitive times? The words may be thus paraphrased: "May God be with you, to preserve you from accidents, and strengthen you to accomplish your work!" "May God bless THEE with the increase of the field, and grace to use his bounty to the glory of the Giver!"

Verse 5. *His servant that was set over the reapers*] This was a kind of steward or hind who had the under management of the estate. Some think that an *officer* of this kind is intended in the description given by Homer of the labours of a harvest field, as represented by Vulcan on one compartment of the shield which he made for Achilles:—

Εν δ' ετιθει τεμενος βαθυληϊον· ενθα δ' εριθοι
Ἡμων, οξειας δρεπανας εν χερσιν εχοντες·
Δραγματα δ' αλλα μετ' ογμον επητριμα πιπτον εραξε,
Αλλα δ' αμαλλοδετηρες εν ελλεδανοισι δεοντο.
Τρεις δ' αρ' αμαλλοδετηρες εφεστασαν· αυταρ οπισθε
Παιδες δραγμευοντες, εν αγκαλιδεσσι φεροντες,
Ασπερχες παρεχον· βασιλευς δ' εν τοισι σιωπη
Σκηπτρον εχων ἑστηκει επ' ογμου γηθοσυνος κηρ.
Κηρυκες δ' απανευθεν ὑπο δρυϊ δαιτα πενοντο·
Βουν δ' ἱερευσαντες μεγαν, αμφεπον· αἱ δε γυναικες
Δειπνον εριθοισιν, λευκ' αλφιτα πολλα παλυνον.

Iliad xviii., v. 550.

There too he form'd the likeness of a field
Crowded with corn, in which the reapers toil'd,
Each with a sharp-tooth'd sickle in his hand.

A. M. 2828
B. C. 1176
An. Exod. Isr.
315
Anno ante
I. Olymp. 400

6 And the servant that was set over the reapers answered and said, It *is* the Moabitish damsel [g]that came back with Naomi out of the country of Moab:

7 And she said, I pray you, let me glean and gather after the reapers among the sheaves: so she came, and hath continued even from the morning until now, that she tarried a little in the house.

8 Then said Boaz unto Ruth, Hearest thou not, my daughter? Go not to glean in another field, neither go from hence, but abide here fast by my maidens:

9 *Let* thine eyes *be* on the field that they do reap, and go thou after them: have I not charged the young men that they shall not touch thee? and when thou art athirst, go unto the vessels, and drink of *that* which the young men have drawn.

10 Then she [h]fell on her face, and bowed herself to the ground, and said unto him, Why have I found grace in thine eyes, that thou shouldest take knowledge of me, seeing I *am* a stranger?

A. M. 2828
B. C. 1176
An. Exod. Isr.
315
Anno ante
I. Olymp. 400

11 And Boaz answered and said unto her, It hath fully been showed me, [i]all that thou hast done unto thy mother-in-law since the death of thine husband: and *how* thou hast left thy father and thy mother, and the land of thy nativity, and art come unto a people which thou knewest not heretofore.

12 [k]The LORD recompense thy work, and a full reward be given thee of the LORD God of Israel, [l]under whose wings thou art come to trust.

13 Then she said, [m]Let [n]me find favour in thy sight, my lord; for that thou hast comforted me, and for that thou hast spoken [o]friendly unto thine handmaid, [p]though I be not like unto one of thine handmaidens.

---

[g]Chap. i. 22——[h]1 Sam. xxv. 23——[i]Chap. i. 14, 16, 17——[k]1 Sam. xxiv. 19——[l]Chap. i. 16; Psa. xvii. 8; xxxvi. 7; lvii. 1; lxiii. 7

[m]Or, *I find favour*——[n]Gen. xxxiii. 15; 1 Sam. i. 18 [o]Heb. *to the heart;* Gen. xxxiv. 3; Judg. xix. 3——[p]1 Sam. xxv. 41

Along the furrow *here,* the harvest fell
In frequent handfuls; *there,* they bound the sheaves.
Three binders of the sheaves their sultry task
All plied industrious, and behind them boys
Attended, filling with the corn their arms,
And offering still their bundles to be bound.
Amid them, staff in hand, the master stood,
Enjoying, mute, the order of the field:
While, shaded by an oak, apart his train
Prepared the banquet—a well thriven ox
New slain, and the attendant maidens mix'd
Large supper for the hinds, of whitest flour.
                                    COWPER.

This scene is well described; and the person who acts as *overseer* is here called βασιλευς, *king,* and his *staff* is called σκηπτρον, a *sceptre;* and he *stands* in *mute dignity,* merely to see that the work is well done, and that each person performs his task; and there appear to me to be *gleaners* in the description, viz., the *boys who gather the handfuls after the three binders.* See the *Greek.*

Verse 7. *That she tarried a little in the house.*] It seems as if the reapers were now resting in their *tent,* and that Ruth had just gone in with them to take her rest also.

Verse 8. *Abide here fast by my maidens*] These were probably employed in making *bands,* and laying on them enough to form a *sheaf,* which the binders would tie and form into *shocks* or *thraves.* When the maidens had gathered up the scattered handfuls thrown down by the reapers, Ruth picked up any straggling heads or ears which they had left.

Verse 9. *The young men that they shall not touch thee*] This was peculiarly necessary, as she was a stranger and unprotected.

Verse 10. *Then she fell on her face*] Prostrated herself, as was the custom in the East when inferiors approached those of superior rank. The *Targum* adds to the conversation between Ruth and Boaz: "How, says she, have I obtained grace in thy sight, that thou shouldest acknowledge me who am a stranger and one of the daughters of Moab, of whom it is said, The unclean shall not enter into the congregation of the Lord? And Boaz, answered, It has been certainly told me by the word of the wise, that what the Lord hath decreed, he hath not decreed concerning the *women* but the *men.* And it hath been surely said to me by prophecy, that kings and prophets shall proceed from thee because of the good which thou hast done," &c.

Verse 12. *The Lord recompense thy work*] The dutiful respect which thou hast paid to thy husband, and thy tender and affectionate attachment to thy aged mother-in-law.

And a full reward be given thee] This is spoken with great modesty and piety: The kindness I show thee is little in comparison of thy desert; God alone can give thee a *full reward* for thy kindness to thy husband and mother-in-law; and he will do it, because *thou art come to trust under his wings*—to become a *proselyte* to his religion. The metaphor is taken from the young of fowls, who, seeing a bird of prey, run to their mother to be covered by her wings from danger, and also to take shelter from storms, tempests, cold, &c. It is evident from this that Ruth had already attached herself to the Jewish religion.

Verse 13. *Not like unto one of thine handmaidens.*] I am as unworthy of thy regards as any of thine own maid-servants, and yet thou showest me distinguished kindness.

A. M. 2828
B. C. 1176
An. Exod. Isr.
315
Anno ante
I. Olymp. 400

14 And Boaz said unto her, At mealtime come thou hither, and eat of the bread, and dip thy morsel in the vinegar. And she sat beside the reapers: and he reached her parched *corn,* and she did eat, and ꝗwas sufficed, and left.

15 And when she was risen up to glean, Boaz commanded his young men, saying, Let her glean even among the sheaves, and ʳreproach her not:

16 And let fall also *some* of the handfuls of purpose for her, and leave *them,* that she may glean *them,* and rebuke her not:

17 So she gleaned in the field until even, and beat out that she had gleaned: and it was about an ephah of barley.

18 And she took *it* up, and went into the city: and her mother-in-law saw what she had gleaned: and she brought forth, and gave to her ˢthat she had reserved after she was sufficed.

19 And her mother-in-law said unto her, Where hast thou gleaned to-day? and where

wroughtest thou? blessed be he that did ᵗtake knowledge of thee. And she showed her mother-in-law with whom she had wrought, and said, The man's name with whom I wrought to-day *is* Boaz.

A. M. 2828
B. C. 1176
An. Exod. Isr.
315
Anno ante
I. Olymp. 400

20 And Naomi said unto her daughter-in-law, ᵘBlessed *be* he of the LORD, who ᵛhath not left off his kindness to the living and to the dead. And Naomi said unto her, The man *is* near of kin unto us, ʷoneˣ of our next kinsmen.

21 And Ruth the Moabitess said, He said unto me also, Thou shalt keep fast by my young men, until they have ended all my harvest.

22 And Naomi said unto Ruth her daughter-in-law, *It is* good, my daughter, that thou go out with his maidens, that they ʸmeet thee not in any other field.

23 So she kept fast by the maidens of Boaz to glean unto the end of barley harvest and of wheat harvest: and dwelt with her mother-in-law.

ꝗVer. 18——ʳHeb. *shame her not*——ˢVer. 14——ᵗVer. 10; Psa. xli. 1——ᵘCh. iii. 10; 2 Sam. ii. 5; Job xxix. 13

ᵛProv. xvii. 17——ʷCh. iii. 9; iv. 6——ˣOr, *one that hath right to redeem;* see Lev. xxv. 25——ʸOr, *fall upon thee*

Verse 14. *Dip thy morsel in the vinegar.*] The חמץ *chomets,* which we here translate *vinegar,* seems to have been some refreshing kind of *acid sauce* used by the reapers to dip their bread in, which both cooled and refreshed them. *Vinegar, rob of fruits,* &c., are used for this purpose in the East to the present day; and the custom of the Arabs, according to Dr. Shaw, is to *dip the bread* and hand together into these cooling and refreshing articles.

Parched corn] This was a frequent repast among the ancients in almost all countries; see the notes on Lev. ii. 1-14.

Verse 15. *Let her glean even among the sheaves*] This was a privilege; for no person should glean till the sheaves were all bound, and the shocks set up.

Verse 17. *An ephah of barley.*] Not less than *seven gallons and a half;* a good day's work. On Hebrew measures of capacity, see the note on Exod. xvi. 16.

Verse 18. *And gave to her that she had reserved*] As Ruth had received a distinct portion at dinner-time, of which she had more than she could eat, ver. 14; it appears she brought the rest home to her mother-in-law, as is here related.

Verse 20. *To the living and to the dead.*] Naomi and Ruth were the *living;* and they were also the representatives of *Elimelech* and *Mahlon,* who were dead. Naomi was of the *family;* and Ruth, though not of the family, was a *representative* of one of its deceased branches, being the *widow* of Mahlon.

One of our next kinsmen.] מגאלינו *miggoaleynu,*

VOL. II

of our *redeemers;* one who has the right to redeem the forfeited inheritance of the family. The word גאל *goel* signifies a *near kinsman*—one who by the Mosaic law had a right to *redeem* an inheritance, and also was permitted to *vindicate* or *revenge* the death of his relation by killing the slayer, if he found him out of the cities of refuge.

In order to prevent families from running to decay, if a brother died childless, the next unmarried brother took his widow; and the children from that marriage were reputed the children of the deceased brother. The office of the next akin was *threefold:* 1. It belonged to him to buy back the forfeited inheritance, or the liberty of him who had been obliged to sell himself for a servant. 2. It was his right to avenge the blood of any of the family who had been killed, by killing the murderer. 3. It belonged to him to take the widow of a deceased brother or relative, if he died childless. If the nearest akin in any case refused, he was treated with indignity, lost his right to the inheritance, and the next akin to him might come forward and take the widow, &c., as in the case of Boaz. See chap. iv.

Verse 21. *Keep fast by my young men*] The word הנערים *hannearim* should be translated *servants,* both the *male* and *female* being included in it; the latter especially, as we see in ver. 22, 23.

Verse 23. *And of wheat harvest*] That is, she was to continue gleaning in the farm of Boaz to the end of the *barley* harvest; and then, when the *wheat* harvest began, to continue to its conclusion in the same way. In the interim, as well as each night, she lodged with her mother-inlaw.

1. RUTH seems to have been a woman of a very amiable mind: she was *modest*, and she was *industrious*, and most probably a *comely* woman; and all these things served to attract the *attention* of Boaz, and to engage his *affection*. Her *attachment* also to her mother-in-in-law could not fail to secure his *esteem*. All these things worked together in the course of Providence, to bring about a matrimonial connection, which in its issue was intimately connected with the salvation of a lost world; for, from this very *line*, Jesus Christ, according to the flesh, sprang; and Ruth showed herself as worthy to be one of His progenitors as the

Virgin Mary was to be His mother. See the notes on Matt. i.

2. We should carefully attend to the *leadings* and to the *workings* of God's providence; it is our *duty* and our *interest* to do both, for the path of duty is ever the way of *safety*. Had not Ruth acted thus, how dreary and uncomfortable must her life have been! but she followed God fully, and in a path apparently *dangerous*, and yet, not only sustained no injury, but succeeded well in all things: from this, as well as from innumerable other circumstances, we see the truth of that word, *Acknowledge him in all thy ways, and he will direct thy steps;* and with this we may ever connect, *Trust in the Lord with thy whole heart, and lean not to thy own understanding.* Whosoever follows God in simplicity of heart, will most assuredly be guided into all truth.

CHAPTER III

Naomi's advice to Ruth, how to procure herself a marriage with Boaz, 1–5. She acts according to her mother-in-law's direction, and is kindly received by Boaz, who promises to marry her, should her nearer kinsman refuse, 6–13. He gives her six measures of barley, and sends her away privately to her mother-in-law, who augurs favourably of the issue of the plan she had laid, 14–18.

A. M. 2828
B. C. 1176
An. Exod. Isr.
315
Anno ante
I. Olymp. 400

THEN Naomi her mother-in-law said unto her, My daughter, [a]shall I not seek [b]rest for thee, that it may be well with thee?

2 And now *is* not Boaz of our kindred, [c]with whose maidens thou wast? Behold, he winnoweth barley to-night in the threshing-floor.

3 Wash thyself, therefore, [d]and anoint thee, and put thy raiment upon thee, and get thee down to the floor: *but* make not thyself known unto the man, until he shall have done eating and drinking.

4 And it shall be, when he lieth down, that thou shalt mark the place where he shall lie, and thou shalt go in, and [e]uncover his feet, and lay thee down; and he will tell thee what thou shalt do.

A. M. 2828
B. C. 1176
An. Exod. Isr.
315
Anno ante
I. Olymp. 400

5 And she said unto her, All that thou sayest unto me I will do.

6 And she went down unto the floor, and did according to all that her mother-in-law bade her.

7 And when Boaz had eaten and drunk, and [f]his heart was merry, he went to lie down at the end of the heap of corn; and she came softly, and uncovered his feet, and laid her down.

[a]1 Cor. vii. 36; 1 Tim. v. 8——[b]Chap. i. 9——[c]Chap. ii. 8——[d]2 Sam. xiv. 2

[e]Or, *lift up the clothes that are on his feet*——[f]Judg. xix. 6, 9, 22; 2 Sam. xiii. 28; Esth. i. 10

NOTES ON CHAP. III

Verse 1. *Shall I not seek rest for thee*] That is, Shall I not endeavour to procure thee a *proper husband?* See chap. i. 9, and the observations at the end of that chapter.

Verse 2. *He winnoweth barley to-night*] It is very likely that the winnowing of grain was effected by taking up, in a broad thin vessel or sieve, a portion of the corn, and letting it down slowly in the wind; thus the *grain* would, by its own weight, fall in one place, while the *chaff*, &c., would be carried to a distance by the wind. It is said here that this was done *at night;* probably what was threshed out in the day was winnowed in the evening, when the *sea breeze* set in, which was common in Palestine; and as this took place in the *evening* only, that was the time in which they would naturally winnow their corn.

Verse 3. *Wash thyself, therefore*] She made Ruth put on her best dress, that Boaz might,

in the course of the day, be the more attracted by her person, and be the better disposed to receive her as Naomi wished.

Verse 4. *Uncover his feet, and lay thee down*] It is said that women in the East, when going to the bed of their lawful husbands, through modesty, and in token of *subjection*, go to the bed's foot, and gently raising the clothes, creep under them up to their place. See *Calmet*.

On the whole, we must say, had not Boaz been a person of extraordinary piety, prudence, and continence, this experiment might have been fatal to Ruth. We cannot easily account for this transaction; probably Naomi knew more than she revealed to her daughter-in-law. The experiment however was dangerous, and should in no sense be imitated.

He will tell thee what thou shalt do] The *Targum* reads the clause thus: *Thou shalt ask counsel from him*, "and he shall tell thee what thou shouldest do."

Verse 7. *When Boaz had eaten and drunk*]

A. M. 2828
B. C. 1176
An. Exod. Isr. 315
Anno ante
I. Olymp. 400

8 And it came to pass at midnight, that the man was afraid, and 8turned himself: and, behold, a woman lay at his feet.

9 And he said, Who *art* thou? And she answered, I *am* Ruth thine handmaid: hspread therefore thy skirt over thine handmaid; for thou *art* ia knear kinsman.

10 And he said, lBlessed *be* thou of the LORD, my daughter: *for* thou hast showed more kindness in the latter end than mat the beginning, inasmuch as thou followedst not young men, whether poor or rich.

11 And now, my daughter, fear not; I will do to thee all that thou requirest: for all the ncity of my people doth know that thou *art* oa virtuous woman.

A. M. 2828
B. C. 1176
An. Exod. Isr. 315
Anno ante
I. Olymp. 400

12 And now it is true that I am *thy* pnear kinsman: howbeit qthere is a kinsman nearer than I.

13 Tarry this night, and it shall be in the morning, *that* if he will rperform unto thee the part of a kinsman, well; let him do the kinsman's part: but if he will not do the part of a kinsman to thee, then will I do the part of a kinsman to thee, sas the LORD liveth: lie down until the morning.

14 And she lay at his feet until the morning: and she rose up before one could know another. And he said, tLet it not be known that a woman came into the floor.

15 Also he said, Bring the uveil that *thou hast* upon thee, and hold it. And when she

---

gOr, *took hold on*——hEzek. xvi. 8——iOr, *one that hath right to redeem*——kChap. ii. 20; ver. 12——lChapter ii. 20——mChap. i. 8——nHeb. *gate*——oProv. xii. 4 pVer. 9

qChap. iv. 1——rDeut. xxv. 5; chap. iv. 5; Matt. xxii. 24——sJudg. viii. 19; Jer. iv. 2——tRom. xii. 17; xiv. 16; 1 Cor. x. 32; 2 Cor. viii. 21; 1 Thess. v. 22 uOr, *sheet*, or *apron*

The *Targum* adds, "He blessed the name of the Lord, who had heard his prayer, and removed famine from the land of Israel."

Went to lie down] As the threshing-floors of the Eastern nations are in general in the *open* air, it is very likely that the *owner* or some confidential person continued in the fields till the grain was secured, having a *tent* in the place where the corn was threshed and winnowed. Boaz seems to have acted thus.

Verse 8. *The man was afraid, and turned himself*] The verb ילפת *yillapheth*, which we render *turned himself*, has puzzled even the Targumist, who translates the clause thus: "The man trembled, and his flesh became like a (boiled) turnip through fear." It is fully evident Boaz had no intimation of the present proceedings. To this verse the Targumist adds much; he says, "Boaz subdued his concupiscence, and acted towards her as Joseph did to the Egyptian wife of his master, and as Pelatiel, the son of Laish the pious, did to Michal, the daughter of Saul, the wife of David, who put a sword between Michal and himself, because he would not approach to her."

Verse 9. *Spread therefore thy skirt over thine handmaid*] Hebrew, *Spread thy wing*. The *wing* is the emblem of *protection*, and is a metaphor taken from the young of fowls, which run under the wings of their mothers, that they may be saved from birds of prey. The meaning here is, *Take me to thee for wife;* and so the Targum has translated it, *Let thy name be called on thy handmaid to take me for wife, because thou art the redeemer;* i. e., thou art the נאל *goel*, the *kinsman*, to whom the right of *redemption* belongs. See on chap. ii. 20. Even to the present day, when a Jew marries a woman, *he throws the skirt or end of his talith over her*, to signify that he has taken her under his protection.

Verse 10. *In the latter end than at the beginning*] It is not easy to find out what Boaz means. Perhaps חסד *chesed*, which we translate

kindness, means *piety;* as if he had said: Thou hast given great proof of thy *piety* in this latter instance, when thou hast avoided the young, and those of thy own age, to associate thyself with an elderly man, merely for the purpose of having the Divine injunction fulfilled, viz., that the brother, or next akin, might take the wife of the deceased, and raise a family to him who had died childless, that his name might not become extinct in Israel: this latter act is a greater proof of thy piety and sincerity than any thing that could be inferred from thy becoming a proselyte.

Whether poor or rich.] So it appears from this that it was not to mend her condition in life that Ruth endeavoured to get Boaz for her husband, for she might have had a *rich young man*, but she preferred the building up the house of her deceased husband. See above.

Verse 12. *There is a kinsman nearer than I.*] It is very likely that Naomi was not acquainted with this circumstance. Some have supposed that there was a *brother* of Elimelech remaining, who was nearer than Boaz, who is supposed to have been only a *nephew;* the former, therefore, must have a prior right.

Verse 13. *As the Lord liveth*] Thus he bound himself by an *oath* to take her to wife if the other should refuse.

Verse 15. *Bring the veil*] המטפחת *hammit-pachath;* this seems to have been a cloak, plaid, or what the Arabs call *hayk*, which has been largely explained elsewhere. See Judg. xiv. 12.

Six measures *of barley*] We supply the word *measures*, for the Hebrew mentions no *quantity*. The Targum renders *six seahs*, שית סאין *shith sein;* which, as a seah was about *two gallons and a half*, must have been a very heavy load for a woman; and so the Targumist thought, for he adds, *And she received strength from the Lord to carry it.* If the *omer* be meant, which is about *six pints*, the load would not be so great, as this would amount to but about *four gallons and a half;* a very goodly

A. M. 2828
B. C. 1176
An. Exod. Isr.
315
Anno ante
I. Olymp. 400
held it, he measured six *mea-sures* of barley, and laid *it* on her: and she went into the city. 16 And when she came to her mother-in-law, she said, Who *art* thou, my daughter? And she told her all that the man had done to her.

17 And she said, These six *measures* of

barley gave he me; for he said to me, Go not empty unto thy mother-in-law.

18 Then said she, ᵛSit still, my daughter, until thou know how the matter will fall: for the man will not be in rest, ʷuntil he have finished the thing this day.

A. M. 2828
B. C. 1176
An. Exod. Isr.
315
Anno ante
I. Olymp. 400

ᵛPsa. xxxvii. 3, 5

ʷIsa. xxviii. 16

---

present. The Targum says, that on receiving these six measures "it was said, in the spirit of prophecy, that from her should proceed the six righteous persons of the world, viz., David, Daniel, Shadrach, Meshach, Abednego, and the King Messiah; each of whom should be blessed with six benedictions." It is, however, remarkable, that the Targum makes the *Messiah* to spring from her through the line of David, and goes down to Daniel and his companions;

which Daniel prophesied so clearly, not only of the advent of *Messiah the prince*, but also of the very *time* in which he was to come, and the *sacrificial* death he was to die.

Verse 18. *Until thou know how the matter will fall*] That is, whether he who is nearer of kin than Boaz will take thee to wife; do not return again till this thing is determined. Boaz lost no time to bring this to an issue, as we shall see in the following chapter.

CHAPTER IV

Boaz gathers a council of the elders at the city gates, states the case, and proposes to the nearest kinsman to redeem the inheritance of Elimelech, and take Ruth to wife, 1–5. The kinsman refuses, and relinquishes his right to Boaz, 6. The manner of redemption in such cases, 7, 8. Boaz redeems the inheritance in the presence of the elders, and of the people, who witness the contract, and pray for God's blessing upon the marriage, 9–12. Boaz takes Ruth for wife, and she bears a son, 13. The people's observations on the birth of the child, 14, 15. It is given to Naomi to nurse, 16. The neighbouring women name the child, and the book concludes with the genealogy of David, 17–22.

A. M. 2828
B. C. 1176
An. Exod. Isr.
315
Anno ante
I. Olymp. 400
THEN went Boaz up to the gate, and sat him down there: and, behold, ᵃthe kinsman of whom Boaz spake came by; unto whom he said, Ho, such a one! turn aside,

sit down here. And he turned aside, and sat down.

2 And he took ten men of ᵇthe elders of the city, and said, Sit ye down here. And they sat down.

A. M. 2828
B. C. 1176
An. Exod. Isr.
315
Anno ante
I. Olymp. 400

ᵃChap. iii. 12

ᵇ1 Kings xxi. 8; Prov. xxxi. 23

NOTES ON CHAP. IV

Verse 1. *Then went Boaz up to the gate*] We have often had occasion to remark that the *gate* or *entrance* to any city or town was the place where the court of justice was ordinarily kept. For an account of the officers in such places, see the note on Deut. xvi. 18.

Ho, such a one!—sit down here.] This familiar mode of compellation is first used here. The original is שבה פה פלני אלמני *shebah poh, peloni almoni!* "Hark ye, Mr. Such-a-one of such a place! come and sit down here." This is used when the *person* of the individual is known, and his *name* and *residence* unknown. אלמני *almoni* comes from אלם *alam, to be silent* or *hidden*, hence the Septuagint render it by κρυφε, *thou unknown person:* פלני *peloni* comes from פלה *palah, to sever* or *distinguish;* you of such a *particular* place. Modes of compellation of this kind are common in all languages.

Verse 2. *He took ten men*] Probably it required this number to constitute a court. How simple and how rational was this proceeding!

1. The man who had a suit went to the city gates. 2. Here he stopped till the person with whom he had the suit came to the gate on his way to his work. 3. He called him by name, and he stopped and sat down. 4. Then ten elders were called, and they came and sat down. 5. When all this was done, the appellant preferred his suit. 6. Then the appellee returned his answer. 7. When the elders heard the case, and the response of the appellee, they pronounced judgment, which judgment was always according to the *custom* of the place. 8. When this was done, the people who happened to be present witnessed the issue. And thus the business was settled without lawyers or legal casuistry. A question of this kind, in one of our courts of justice, in these enlightened times, would require many days' previous preparation of the attorney, and several hours' arguing between counsellor *Botherum* and counsellor *Borum*, till even an enlightened and conscientious judge would find it extremely difficult to decide whether *Naomi might sell* her *own land*, and whether *Boaz* or *Peloni* might *buy* it! O, glorious uncertainty of modern law!

A. M. 2828
B. C. 1176
An. Exod. Isr.
315
Anno ante
I. Olymp. 400

3 And he said unto the kinsman, Naomi, that is come again out of the country of Moab, selleth a parcel of land, which *was* our brother Elimelech's:

4 And °I thought to advertise thee, saying, ᵈBuy *it* ᵉbefore the inhabitants, and before the elders of my people. If thou wilt redeem *it*, redeem *it:* but if thou wilt not redeem *it, then,* tell me, that I may know: ᶠfor *there is* none to redeem *it* beside thee; and I *am* after thee. And he said, I will redeem *it.*

5 Then said Boaz, What day thou buyest the field of the hand of Naomi, thou must buy *it* also of Ruth the Moabitess, the wife of the dead, ᵍto raise up the name of the dead upon his inheritance.

6 ʰAnd the kinsman said, I cannot redeem *it* for myself, lest I mar mine own inheritance: redeem thou my right to thyself; for I cannot redeem *it.*

7 ¹Now this *was the manner* in former time in Israel concerning redeeming and concerning changing, for to confirm all things; a man plucked off his shoe, and gave *it* to his neighbour: and this *was* a testimony in Israel.

8 Therefore the kinsman said unto Boaz, Buy *it* for thee. So he drew off his shoe.

9 And Boaz said unto the elders, and *unto* all the people, Ye *are* witnesses this day, that I have bought all that *was* Elimelech's, and all that *was* Chilion's and Mahlon's, of the hand of Naomi.

10 Moreover Ruth the Moabitess, the wife of Mahlon, have I purchased to be my wife, to raise up the name of the dead upon his inheritance, ᵏthat the name of the dead be not cut off from among his brethren, and from the gate of his place: ye *are* witnesses this day.

11 And all the people that *were* in the gate, and the elders, said, *We are* witnesses. ¹The

A. M. 2828
B. C. 1176
An. Exod. Isr.
315
Anno ante
I. Olymp. 400

°Heb. *I said I will reveal* in *thine ear*——ᵈJeremiah xxxii. 7, 8——ᵉGenesis xxiii. 18——ᶠLeviticus xxv. 25

ᵍGen. xxxviii. 8; Deut. xxv. 5, 6; chap. iii. 13; Matt. xxii. 24——ʰChap. iii. 12, 13——¹Deut. xxv. 7, 9——ᵏDeut. xxv. 6——¹Psa. cxxvii. 3; cxxviii. 3

Verse 3. *Naomi—selleth a parcel of land*] She was reduced to want; the immediate inheritors were extinct; and it was now open for the next heir to purchase the land, and thus preserve the inheritance in the family according to the custom of Israel.

Verse 4. *I thought to advertise thee*] Both Dr. *Kennicott* and Father *Houbigant* have noticed several corruptions in the *pronouns* of this and the following verses; and their criticisms have been confirmed by a great number of MSS. since collated. The text corrected reads thus: "And I said I will reveal this to thy ear, saying, Buy it before the inhabitants, and before the elders of my people. If thou wilt redeem it, redeem it; but if thou wilt not redeem it, tell me, that I may know; for there is none to redeem it but thou, and I who am next to thee. And he said, I will redeem it. And Boaz said, In the day that thou redeemest the land from the hand of Naomi, thou wilt also acquire Ruth, the wife of the dead, that thou mayest raise up the name of the dead upon his inheritance;" ver. 4, 5.—See *Kennicott's Dissertations*, vol. i., p. 449; *Houbigant in loco;* and the *Variæ Lectiones* of *Kennicott* and *De Rossi.* This is Boaz's statement of the case before the kinsman, and before the people and the elders.

I will redeem it.] I will pay down the money which it is worth. He knew not of the following condition.

Verse 5. *Thou must buy* it *also of Ruth*] More properly, *Thou wilt also acquire Ruth.* Thou canst not get the land without taking the wife of the deceased; and then the children which thou mayest have shall be reputed the children of Mahlon, thy deceased kinsman.

Verse 6. *I cannot redeem* it *for myself*] The

Targum gives the proper sense of this passage: "And the kinsman said, On this ground I cannot redeem it, because I have a wife already; and I have no desire to take another, lest there should be contention in my house, and I should become a corrupter of my inheritance. Do thou redeem it, for thou hast no wife; for I cannot redeem it." This needs no comment. But still the gloss of the *Targum* has no foundation in the *law* of Moses. See the law, Deut. xxv. 5-9.

Verse 7. *A man plucked off his shoe*] The law of such a case is given at large in Deut. xxv. 5-9. It was simply this: If a brother, who had married a wife, died without children, the eldest brother was to take the widow, and raise up a family to the brother deceased; and he had a right to redeem the inheritance, if it had been alienated. But if the person who had the right of redemption would not take the woman, she was to pull off his shoe and spit in his face; and he was ever after considered as a disgraced man. In the present case the *shoe* only is taken off, probably because the circumstances of the man were such as to render it *improper* for him to redeem the ground and take Ruth to his wife; and because of this reasonable excuse, the *contemptuous* part of the ceremony is omitted. See the note on Deut. xxv. 9.

Verse 11. We are *witnesses.*] It is not very likely that any writing was drawn up. There was an appeal made to the people then present, whether they had seen and understood the transaction; who answered, We have witnessed it. If any minutes of court were kept, then the transaction was entered probably in some such words as these: "On —— day of ——, Boaz bought the land of Elimelech from Naomi his

A. M. 2828
B. C. 1176
An. Exod. Isr. 315
Anno ante
I. Olymp. 400
LORD make the woman that is come into thine house like Rachel and like Leah, which two did [m]build the house of Israel: and [n]do thou worthily in [o]Ephratah, and [p]be famous in Beth-lehem:

12 And let thy house be like the house of Pharez, [q]whom Tamar bare unto Judah, of [r]the seed which the LORD shall give thee of this young woman.

A. M. 2829
B. C. 1175
An. Exod. Isr. 316
Anno ante
I. Olymp. 399
13 So Boaz [s]took Ruth, and she was his wife: and when he went in unto her, [t]the LORD gave her conception, and she bare a son.

14 And [u]the women said unto Naomi, Blessed be the LORD, which hath not [v]left thee this day without a [w]kinsman, that his name may be famous in Israel.

A. M. 2829
B. C. 1175
An. Exod. Isr. 316
Anno ante
I. Olymp. 399

15 And he shall be unto thee a restorer of thy life, and a [x]nourisher [y]of thine old age; for thy daughter-in-law, which loveth thee, which is [z]better to thee than seven sons, hath borne him.

16 And Naomi took the child, and laid it in her bosom, and became nurse unto it.

17 [a]And the women her neighbours gave it a name, saying, There is a son born to Naomi; and they called his name Obed: he is the father of Jesse, the father of David.

18 Now these are the generations of Pharez; [b]Pharez begat Hezron,

A.M.2289-2919
B.C.1715-1085
Ante I. Olymp. 939-309

---

[m]Deut. xxv. 9——[n]Or, get the riches, or, power
[o]Genesis xxxv. 16, 19——[p]Heb. proclaim thy name
[q]Gen. xxxviii. 29; 1 Chron. ii. 4; Matt. i. 3——[r]1 Sam. ii. 20——[s]Chap. iii. 11——[t]Gen. xxix. 31; xxxiii. 5

[u]Luke i. 58; Rom. xii. 15——[v]Heb. caused to cease unto thee——[w]Or, redeemer——[x]Heb. to nourish; Gen. xlv. 11; Psa. lv. 22——[y]Heb. thy gray hairs——[z]1 Sam. i. 8——[a]Luke i. 58, 59——[b]1 Chron. ii. 4, &c.; Matt. i. 3

---

widow, and took Ruth, her daughter-in-law, to wife; ——, who had the nearest right, refusing to buy the land on the conditions then proposed."

The Lord make this woman—like Rachel and like Leah] May thy family be increased by her means, as the tribes were formed by means of Rachel and Leah, wives of the patriarch Jacob!

Which two did build the house of Israel] We have already seen that בֵן ben, a son, comes from the root בנה banah, he built; and hence אבן eben, a stone, because as a house is built of stones, so is a family of children. There is a similar figure in PLAUTUS, Mostell. Act i., sec. 2, ver. 37.

————— Nunc etiam volo
Dicere, ut homines ædium esse similes arbitremini.
Primum dum parentes fabri liberum sunt,
Et fundamentum liberorum substruunt.

"I would also observe, that ye men are similar to houses; ye parents are the fabricators of the children, and they are the foundation of the building."

Verse 12. Like the house of Pharez] This was very appropriate; for from Pharez, the son of Judah, by Tamar, came the family of the Beth-lehemites and that of Elimelech.

Verse 13. So Boaz took Ruth] The law of Moses had prohibited the Moabites, even to the tenth generation, from entering into the congregation of the Lord: but this law, the Jews think, did not extend to women; and even if it had, Ruth's might be considered an exempt case, as she had been already incorporated into the family by marriage; and left her own country, people, and gods, to become a proselyte to the true God in the land of Israel.

Verse 15. Better to thee than seven sons] If Naomi had had even a numerous family of sons, it is most likely that they would have been scattered to different quarters from her, and settled in life; whereas Ruth cleaved to her,

and it was by her affectionate services that Naomi was preserved alive.

Verse 16. Naomi took the child] This might do for Naomi, but it was bad for the child. A child, unless remarkably healthy and robust, will suffer considerably by being nursed by an old woman, especially if the child sleep with her. The aged gain refreshment and energy by sleeping with the young; and from the same means the young derive premature decrepitude. The vigour which is absorbed by the former is lost by the latter. It is a foolish and destructive custom to permit young children, which is a common case, to sleep with aged aunts and old grandmothers. Bacon's grand secret of the cure of old age, couched in so many obscure and enigmatical terms, is simply this: Let young persons sleep constantly with those who are aged and infirm. And it was on this principle that the physicians of David recommended a young healthy girl to sleep with David in his old age. They well knew that the aged infirm body of the king would absorb a considerable portion of healthy energy from the young woman.

Verse 17. The neighbours gave it a name] That is, they recommended a name suitable to the circumstances of the case; and the parents and grandmother adopted it.

They called his name Obed] עוֹבֵד obed, serving, from עבד abad, he served. Why was this name given? Because he was to be the nourisher of her old age, ver. 15. And so he must be by lying in her bosom, even if services in future life were wholly left out of the question. These neighbours of Naomi were skilful people. See on ver. 16. Other meanings, of which I am not ignorant, have been derived from these words; those who prefer them have my consent.

He is the father of Jesse, the father of David.] And for the sake of this conclusion, to ascertain the line of David, and in the counsel of God to fix and ascertain the line of the Messiah, was this instructive little book written.

Verse 18. Now these are the generations]

A.M.2289-2919
B.C. 1715-1085
Ante I.Olymp.
939–309
19 And Hezron begat Ram, and Ram begat Amminadab, 20 And Amminadab ^cbegat Nahshon, and Nahshon begat ^dSalmon,^e

21 And Salmon begat Boaz, and Boaz begat Obed, 22 And Obed begat Jesse, and Jesse begat ^fDavid.

A.M.2289-2919
B.C. 1715-1085
Ante I. Olymp.
939–309

---

^cNum. i. 7——^dMatt. i. 4, &c.

^eOr, *Salmah*——^f1 Chron. ii. 15; Matt. i. 6

The Targum gives a copious paraphrase on this and the following verses; I shall insert the principal parts in their proper places.

Verse 19. *Hezron begat Ram*] He is called *Aram* here by the *Septuagint*, and also by St. Matthew, chap. i. 3.

Verse 20. *Amminadab begat Nahshon*] The Targum adds, "And Nahshon was chief of the house of his father in the tribe of Judah."

Nahshon begat Salmon] In the Hebrew it is שלמה *Salmah*, which *Houbigant* thinks was an error of an ancient scribe, before any final letters were acknowledged in the Hebrew alphabet: for then the word would be written שלמן *Salmon*, which a scribe, after final letters were admitted, might mistake for שלמה *Salmah*, and so write it, instead of שלמן *Salmon*, the ו *vau* and ן *final nun* in conjunction (ון) bearing some resemblance to ה.

The *Targum* calls him "Salmah the Just; he was the Salmah of Beth-lehem and Netopha, whose sons abolished the watches which Jeroboam set over the highways; and their works and the works of their father were good in Netopha."

Verse 21. *And Salmon begat Boaz*] The *Targum* goes on, "And Salmon begat *Absan* the judge; he is *Boaz* the Just, on account of whose righteousness the people of the house of Israel were redeemed from the hands of their enemies; and at whose supplication the famine departed from the land of Israel."

And Boaz begat Obed] "Who served the Lord in this world with a perfect heart."

Verse 22. *And Obed begat Jesse*] "Who," says the *Targum*, "also is called Nachash, נחש because neither iniquity nor corruption was found in him, that he should be delivered into the hands of the angel of death, that he might take away his soul from him. And he lived many days until the counsel was remembered before the Lord, that the serpent gave to Eve the wife of Adam, that she should eat of the tree; by eating of the fruit of which they became wise, to distinguish between good and evil: and by that counsel all the inhabitants of the earth became guilty of death; and by this iniquity Jesse the Just died." Here is no mean or indistinct reference to the doctrine of *original sin:* and it shows us, at least, what the very ancient rabbins thought on the subject. I should observe that these *additions* are taken from the *London Polyglot;* they are not found in that of *Antwerp;* but they are the same that appear in the Targum of the great Bible printed by *Bomberg*, at Venice, in 1547-49.

And Jesse begat David] To this no comment is added by the Targumist, as the history of this king is found in the following book.

The *ten* persons whose genealogy is recorded in the five last verses, may be found, with a trifling change of name, in the genealogical list in Matt. i. 3-6, as forming important links in the *line* of the Messiah. To introduce this appears to have been the principal object of the writer, as introductory to the following books, where the history of David, the regal progenitor and type of the Messiah, is so particularly detailed.

FOR the account of the birth of Pharez and his brother Zarah, the reader is requested to refer to Gen. xxxviii. 12-30, and to the notes there; and for several particulars in the genealogy itself, to the notes on Matt. i. and Luke iii., where the wisdom, goodness, and providence of God, in the preservation of this line, are particularly noticed.

MASORETIC NOTES ON RUTH

Number of verses in Ruth is 85.
Middle verse is the 21st of chap. ii.
We have already seen that Archbishop Usher places the event mentioned here in A. M. 2686, about one hundred years after the conquest of Canaan.

PREFACE

TO THE

FIRST BOOK OF SAMUEL,

OTHERWISE CALLED

THE FIRST BOOK OF THE KINGS

THIS and the three following books were formerly termed the *first, second, third,* and *fourth books of Kings,* and the two books of *Samuel* made in ancient times but one; the separation which has taken place seems to have been done without reason or necessity. These books are, properly speaking, a continuation of the book of *Judges,* as they give us an account of the remaining judges of Israel, down to the election of Saul; and of all the kings of Israel and Judah to the Babylonish captivity.

Of this book, called the first book of Samuel, the following are the contents: The birth and education of Samuel; the high priesthood of Eli; the Philistines attack the Israelites, overthrow them with a terrible slaughter, take the ark of the Lord, and set it up in the temple of their god Dagon; they are visited with Divine judgments, and are obliged to send back the ark with offerings and presents; Samuel, long acknowledged as a prophet of the Lord, takes the government of the people. Under his wise and pious administration, the affairs of Israel become re-established, and the Philistines are subdued. The sons of Samuel, who principally administered the secular concerns of the kingdom, acting unworthily, the people desire to have a *king,* who should be supreme, both in civil and military affairs. Samuel, after expostulations, yields to their entreaties; and, under the direction of God, Saul the son of Kish, whilst seeking the lost asses of his father, is met by the prophet, and anointed king over Israel. This man, not conducting himself in the government according to the direction of God, is rejected, and David the son of Jesse anointed king in his place, though Saul continues still in the government. This person soon becomes advantageously known to Israel by his single combat with a gigantic Philistine chief, called *Goliath,* whom he slays; on which the Israelites attack the Philistines, and give them a total overthrow. Saul, envious of David's popularity, seeks his destruction; he is in consequence obliged to escape for his life, and take refuge sometimes among the Moabites, sometimes among the Philistines, and sometimes in the caves of the mountains of Judah, everywhere pursued by Saul, and everywhere visibly protected by the Lord. At last Saul, being pressed by the Philistines, and finding that the Lord had forsaken him, had recourse to a witch that dwelt at Endor, whom he consulted relative to the issue of the present war with the Philistines; he loses the battle, and being sorely wounded, and his three sons slain, he falls on his own sword, and expires on Mount Gilboa. The Philistines find his body, and the bodies of his three sons, among the slain; they cut off Saul's head, and affix the bodies to the walls of Beth-shan. The men of Jabesh-gilead, hearing this, go by night, and take the bodies from the walls of Beth-shan, bring them to Jabesh, burn them there, bury the bones, and mourn over their fallen king, fasting seven days. Thus concludes the first book of Samuel.

Concerning the *author* of these books there have been various conjectures. Because, in most of the Hebrew copies, they bear the name of *Samuel,* as a running title, it has been generally supposed that *he* was the author. But his name does not appear to have been anciently prefixed to these books, at least in those copies used by the Greek interpreters, commonly called the *Septuagint,* as they simply term each βασιλεῶν, The *History* or *Book of*

Kingdoms. The *Chaldee* has no inscription. The *Syriac* and *Arabic* call each The *Book of Samuel the Prophet;* and the *Vulgate,* The *Book of Samuel,* simply. The Jews, in *general,* believe that *Samuel* is the author of the first twenty-seven chapters of this book, which contain the history of his own life and government, and what respects Saul and David during that time. The remaining four chapters they suppose were added by the prophets Gad and Nathan. This opinion is founded on what is said 1 Chron. xxix. 29: *Now the acts of David the king, first and last, behold they are written in the book of Samuel the seer, and in the book of Nathan the prophet, and in the book of Gad the seer.* Others suppose the books to be more recent than the persons already named, but that they were compiled out of their *memoirs.*

But who was the compiler? Some of the most learned among the Jews suppose it to have been *Jeremiah* the prophet, and that the style bears a near resemblance to his prophecies. That they were the work of a more recent author than Samuel, &c., *Grotius* thinks evident from this circumstance, that the names of the *months* are comparatively *modern,* and were not known among the ancient Jews. Others have attributed them to David; others, to Hezekiah; and others, to Ezra the scribe, on his return from the Babylonish captivity.

Calmet's opinion is as probable as any, viz., "That these books were written by the same hand, though composed out of the memoirs left by persons of that time; and that the compiler has generally used the same terms he found in those memoirs, adding here and there something of his own by way of illustration." The equality of the *style,* the frequent eulogiums on the character of Samuel, the connection of the materials, particular quotations, and remarks on certain events, are, he thinks, proofs sufficiently clear of what he assumes. These books contain remarks or expressions which could only proceed from a *contemporary* author, and others which are evidences of a much *later* age.

1. For instance, we read, chap. iii. 1, *The word of the Lord was precious in those days; there was no open vision;* i. e., in the days of Eli, the high priest: hence it is evident that the author lived in times in which prophecy was *more common;* which, in fact, it was after Samuel, under David, and the succeeding kings of Israel and Judah.

2. Again, in the time of the author of this book, *Beth-el* was called *Beth-aven,* chap. xiii. 5, which name was given to it in derision *after* Jeroboam had placed there his golden calves.

3. Again, it is said, chap. vi. 18, that the ark of the Lord was set down in the field of *Joshua the Beth-shemite, where it remained to the time of this author;* and yet, in chap. vii. 15, he speaks of Samuel as being already dead: *And Samuel judged Israel all the days of his life.*

4. It is not natural to suppose that Samuel would have spoken of himself as is done chap. ii. 26: *And the child Samuel grew, and was in favour both with the Lord and with men;* but if he were *dead* when this book was written, any author might have added this with the strictest propriety.

5. In chap. xxvii. 6, it is said that Achish gave Ziklag to David, *Wherefore Ziklag pertaineth to the kings of Judah unto this day.* This is a proof that when this book was written the kingdoms of Judah and Israel were *separated;* and that, although the tribe of Simeon belonged to the kings of *Israel,* yet *Ziklag,* which was in that tribe, remained in the hands of the kings of *Judah.*

Here, therefore, are proofs that this book contains matters which must have been written by a *contemporary* author; and others which could not have been inserted but in times *much posterior.* These seeming contradictions are reconciled by the hypothesis that the books were compiled, by a comparatively recent author, out of materials of a much earlier date, the author not changing many of the expressions which he found in those ancient documents.

Several other proofs might be here adduced to support this opinion; but as the reader will find them noticed in the places where they occur, it is not necessary to repeat them here. Those who wish to see the subject farther discussed, may consult *Calmet.* We may rest satisfied with these *three* things: 1. That the books of Samuel were constructed out of original and authentic documents. 2. That the compiler was not contemporary with the facts he narrates. And, 3. That both the author and time in which he compiled his history, though comparatively more recent than the facts themselves, are nevertheless both *uncertain.*

THE
FIRST BOOK OF SAMUEL

Year from the Creation, 2833.—Year before the Incarnation, 1171.—Year before the first Olympiad, 395.—Year before the building of Rome, 418.—Year of the Julian Period, 3543.—Year of the Dionysian Period, 351.—Cycle of the Sun, 15.—Cycle of the Moon, 9.

CHAPTER I

Some account of Elkanah and his two wives, Peninnah and Hannah, 1, 2. His annual worship at Shiloh and the portions he gave at such times to his wives, 3–5. Hannah, being barren, is reproached by Peninnah, especially in their going up to Shiloh; at which she is sorely grieved, 6, 7. Elkanah comforts her, 8. Her prayer and vow in the temple, that if God would give her a son, she would consecrate him to His service, 9–11. Eli, the high priest, indistinctly hearing her pray, charges her with being drunk, 12–14. Her defence of her conduct, 15, 16. Eli, undeceived, blesses her; on which she takes courage, 17, 18. Hannah and Elkanah return home; she conceives, bears a son, and calls him Samuel, 19, 20. Elkanah and his family go again to Shiloh to worship; but Hannah stays at home to nurse her child, purposing, as soon as he is weaned, to go and offer him to the Lord, according to her vow, 21–23. When weaned, she takes him to Shiloh, presents her child to Eli to be consecrated to the Lord, and offers three bullocks, an ephah of flour, and a bottle of wine, for his consecration, 24–28.

A. M. 2833
B. C. 1171
An. Exod. Isr.
320
Anno ante
I. Olymp. 395

NOW there was a certain man of Ramathaim-zophim, of Mount Ephraim, and his name was [a]Elkanah, the son of Jeroham, the son of Elihu, the son of Tohu, the son of Zuph, [b]an Ephrathite:

2 And he had two wives; the name of the one was Hannah, and the name of the other Peninnah: and Peninnah had children, but Hannah had no children.

3 And this man went up out of his city [c]yearly[d] [e]to worship and to sacrifice unto the LORD of hosts in [f]Shiloh. And the two sons of Eli, Hophni and Phinehas, the priests of the LORD, were there.

4 And when the time was that Elkanah [g]offered, he gave to Peninnah his wife, and to all her sons and her daughters, portions:

[a]1 Chron. vi. 27, 34——[b]Ruth i. 2——[c]Exod. xxiii. 14; Deut. xvi. 16; Luke ii. 41

[d]Heb. *from year to year*——[e]Deut. xii. 5, 6, 7——[f]Josh. xviii. 1——[g]Deut. xii. 17, 18; xvi. 11

NOTES ON CHAP. I

Verse 1. *Ramathaim-zophim*] Literally, *the two high places of the watchman;* these were, no doubt, two contiguous hills, on which watchtowers were built, and in which watchmen kept continual guard for the safety of the country, and which afterwards gave name to the place.

Verse 2. *He had two wives*] The custom of those times permitted polygamy; but wherever there was more than *one wife*, we find the peace of the family greatly disturbed by it.

The name of the one was Hannah] חנה *Channah,* which signifies *fixed* or *settled;* and *the other* פננה *Peninnah,* which signifies a *jewel* or *pearl.*

Verse 3. *Went up out of his city yearly to worship*] As the ark was at Shiloh, *there* was the temple of God, and thither all the males were bound by the law to go once a year, on each of the great national festivals: viz., the *passover, pentecost,* and *feast of tabernacles.*

The Lord of hosts] יהוה צבאות *Yehovah tsebaoth, Jehovah of armies.* As all the heavenly bodies were called the *hosts of heaven,* צבא

השמים *tseba hashshamayim,* Jehovah being called Lord of this host showed that he was their Maker and Governor; and consequently *He,* not *they,* was the proper object of religious worship. The *sun, moon, planets,* and *stars,* were the highest objects of religious worship to the heathens in general. The Jewish religion, teaching the knowledge of a Being who was the Lord of all these, showed at once its superiority to all that heathenism could boast. This is the *first place* where *Lord of hosts* is mentioned in the Bible; and this is so much in the style of the prophets *Isaiah, Jeremiah,* &c., that it gives some weight to the supposition that this book was written by a person who lived *in* or *after* the times of these prophets. See the *preface.*

Verse 4. *He gave—portions*] The sacrifices which were made were probably *peace-offerings,* of which the *blood* was poured out at the foot of the altar; the *fat* was burnt on the fire; the *breast* and *right shoulder* were the portion of the priest; and the *rest* belonged to him who made the offering; on it he and his family feasted, each receiving his *portion;* and to these feasts God commands them to invite the *Levite,*

VOL. II
206

A. M. 2833
B. C. 1171
An. Exod. Isr.
320
Anno ante
I. Olymp. 395

5 But unto Hannah he gave [h]a worthy portion; for he loved Hannah: [i]but the LORD had shut up her womb.

6 And her adversary also [k]provoked [l]her sore, for to make her fret, because the LORD had shut up her womb.

7 And *as* he did so year by year, [m]when [n]she went up to the house of the LORD, so she provoked her; therefore she wept, and did not eat.

8 Then said Elkanah her husband to her, Hannah, why weepest thou? and why eatest thou not? and why is thy heart grieved? *am* not I [o]better to thee than ten sons?

9 So Hannah rose up after they had eaten in Shiloh, and after they had drunk. Now Eli the priest sat upon a seat by a post of [p]the temple of the LORD.

10 [q]And she *was* [r]in bitterness of soul, and

prayed unto the LORD, and wept sore.

A. M. 2833
B. C. 1171
An. Exod. Isr.
320
Anno ante
I. Olymp. 395

11 And she [s]vowed a vow, and said, O LORD of hosts, if thou wilt indeed [t]look on the affliction of thine handmaid, and [u]remember me, and not forget thine handmaid, but wilt give unto thine handmaid [v]a man-child, then I will give him unto the LORD all the days of his life, and [w]there shall no razor come upon his head.

12 And it came to pass, as she [x]continued praying before the LORD, that Eli marked her mouth.

13 Now Hannah, she spake in her heart; only her lips moved, but her voice was not heard: therefore Eli thought she had been drunken.

14 And Eli said unto her, How long wilt thou be drunken? put away thy wine from thee.

15 And Hannah answered and said, No, my

---

[h]Or, *a double portion*——[i]Gen. xxx. 2——[k]Heb. *angered her*——[l]Job xxiv. 21——[m]Or, *from the time that she,* &c.——[n]Heb. *from her going up*——[o]Ruth iv. 15 [p]Chap. iii. 3——[q]Job vii. 11; x. 1——[r]Heb. *bitter of soul;* 2 Sam. xvii. 8

[s]Genesis xxviii. 20; Numbers xxx. 6; Judges xi. 30 [t]Genesis xxix. 32; Exodus iv. 31; 2 Samuel xvi. 12; Psalm xxv. 18——[u]Genesis viii. 1; xxx. 22——[v]Heb. *seed of men*——[w]Numbers vi. 5; Judges xiii. 5——[x]Heb. *multiplied to pray*

---

the *poor,* the *widow,* and the *orphan,* Deut. xvi. 11.

Verse 5. *Unto Hannah he gave a worthy portion*] The Hebrew here is very obscure, יתן מנה אחת אפים *yitten manah achath appayim; he gave her one portion of two faces;* which the *Syriac* renders, *he gave her one* DOUBLE PART; and the *Chaldee, he gave her one* CHOSEN *part;* the *Arabic* is nearly the same; the *Vulgate* Annæ autem dedit unam partem tristis, *but to Anna he being sorrowful gave one part.* As the *shew-bread* that was presented to the Lord was called לחם פנים *lechem panim,* the *bread of faces,* because it was placed before the *face* or *appearances* of the Lord; probably this was called מנה אפים *manah appayim,* because it was the portion that belonged to, or was placed *before,* the person who had offered the sacrifice. On this ground it might be said that Elkanah gave Hannah *his own portion,* or a part of that which was placed *before himself.* Whatever it was, it was intended as a proof of his especial love to her; *for,* it is added, *he loved Hannah.*

Verse 6. *And her adversary*] That is, Peninnah.

Provoked her sore] Was constantly striving to irritate and vex her, *to make her fret*—to make her discontented with her lot, because the Lord had denied her children.

Verse 7. *And as he did so year by year*] As the whole family went up to Shiloh to the annual festivals, Peninnah had both *sons* and *daughters* to accompany her, ver. 4, but Hannah had none; and Peninnah took this opportunity particularly to twit Hannah with her barrenness, by making an ostentatious exhibition of her children.

Therefore she wept] She was greatly distressed, because it was a great reproach to a

woman among the Jews to be barren; because, say some, every one hoped that the *Messiah* should spring from her line.

Verse 8. *Am not I better to thee than ten sons?*] TEN, a certain for an uncertain number. Is not my especial affection to thee better than all the comfort thou couldst gain, even from a numerous family

Verse 9. *Eli—sat upon a seat*] על הכסא *al hakkisse,* upon the throne, i. e., of judgment; for he was then *judge* of Israel.

By a post of the temple of the Lord.] I think this is the first place where היכל יהוה *heychal Yehovah,* "temple of Jehovah," is mentioned. This gives room for a strong suspicion that the books of Samuel were not compiled *till the first temple was built,* or *after the days of Solomon.* After this the word *temple* is frequent in the books of Kings, Chronicles, and in the prophets. Perhaps those *Psalms* in which this word occurs were, like many others in the Psalms, not of David's composition; some of them were evidently made long after his time.

Verse 11. *I will give him unto the Lord*] Samuel, as a descendant of the house of *Levi,* was the Lord's property from *twenty-five* years of age till *fifty;* but the vow here implies that he should be consecrated to the Lord from his infancy to his death, and that he should not only act as a *Levite,* but as a *Nazarite,* on whose head no razor should pass.

Verse 13. *Spake in her heart; only her lips moved*] She prayed; her whole heart was engaged: and though she spake not with an audible voice, yet her lips formed themselves according to the pronunciation of the words which her *heart* uttered.

Verse 15. *I have drunk neither wine nor strong drink*] Neither wine nor inebriating drink has

A. M. 2833
B. C. 1171
An. Exod. Isr.
320
Anno ante
I. Olymp. 395

lord, I *am* a woman [y]of a sorrowful spirit: I have drunk neither wine nor strong drink, but have [z]poured out my soul before the LORD.

16 Count not thine handmaid for a daughter of [a]Belial: for out of the abundance of my [b]complaint and grief have I spoken hitherto.

17 Then Eli answered and said, [c]Go in peace: and [d]the God of Israel grant *thee* thy petition that thou hast asked of him.

18 And she said, [e]Let thine handmaid find grace in thy sight. So the woman [f]went her way, and did eat, and her countenance was no more *sad*.

19 And they rose up in the morning early, and worshipped before the LORD, and returned, and came to their house to Ramah: and Elkanah [g]knew Hannah his wife; and [h]the LORD remembered her.

20 Wherefore it came to pass, [i]when the time was come about after Hannah had conceived, that she bare a son, and called his name [k]Samuel, *saying,* Because I have asked him of the LORD.

A. M. 2833
B. C. 1171
An. Exod. Isr.
320
Anno ante
I. Olymp. 395

A. M. 2834
B. C. 1170
An. Exod. Isr.
321
Anno ante
I. Olymp. 394

21 And the man Elkanah, and all his house, [l]went up to offer unto the LORD the yearly sacrifice, and his vow.

22 But Hannah went not up; for she said unto her husband, *I will not go up* until the child be weaned, and *then* I will [m]bring him, that he may appear before the LORD, and there [n]abide [o]for ever.

23 And [p]Elkanah her husband said unto her, Do what seemeth thee good: tarry until thou have weaned him; [q]only the LORD establish his word. So the woman abode, and gave her son suck until she weaned him.

24 And when she had weaned him, she [r]took him up with her, with three bullocks, and one ephah of flour, and a bottle of wine,

[y]Heb. *hard of spirit*——[z]Psa. lxii. 8; cxlii. 2
[a]Deut. xiii. 13——[b]Or, *meditation*——[c]Judg. xviii. 6; Mark v. 34; Luke vii. 50; viii. 48——[d]Psa. xx. 4, 5
[e]Gen. xxxiii. 15; Ruth ii. 13——[f]Eccles. ix. 7——[g]Gen. iv. 1

[h]Gen. xxx. 22——[i]Heb. *in revolution of days*
[k]That is, *asked of God*——[l]Ver. 3——[m]Luke ii. 22
[n]Ver. 11. 28; chap. ii. 11, 18; iii. 1——[o]Exod. xxi. 6
[p]Num. xxx. 7——[q]2 Sam. vii. 25——[r]Deut. xii. 5, 6, 11

been *poured out unto me;* but I have *poured out my soul unto the Lord.* There is a great deal of delicacy and point in this vindication.

Verse 16. *Count not thine handmaid for a daughter of Belial*] אל תתן את אמתך לפני בת בליעל *al titten eth amathecha liphney bath Beliyaal;* "Put not thy handmaiden before the faces of a daughter of Belial." "If I am a drunkard, and strive by the most execrable hypocrisy (praying in the house of God) to cover my iniquity, then I am the chief of the daughters of Belial." Or, "Give not thy handmaid (to reproach) before the faces of the daughters of Belial." Several of *these* probably attended there for the purposes of prostitution and gain; for it is said, chap. ii. 22, that Eli's sons lay with the women at the door of the tabernacle, though this may refer to the women who kept the door.

Verse 17. *Grant* thee *thy petition*] He was satisfied he had formed a wrong judgment, and by it had added to the distress of one already sufficiently distressed.

The fact that Eli supposed her to be *drunken,* and the other of the conduct of Eli's sons already mentioned, prove that religion was at this time at a very low ebb in Shiloh; for it seems *drunken women* did come to the place, and *lewd women* were to be found there.

Verse 18. *Let thine handmaid find grace*] Continue to think favourably of me, and to pray for me.

Verse 20. *Called his name Samuel*] As she gave this name to her son because she had *asked him of the Lord,* the word שמואל *Shemuel* must be here considerably contracted; if it express this sentiment, the component parts of it are the following: שאול מאל *shaul meEl,* "asked of God." This name would put both the mother and the son in continual remembrance of the Divine interposition at his birth. See on ver. 28.

Verse 21. *The man Elkanah and all his house*] He and the whole of his family, Hannah and her child excepted, who purposed not to go up to Shiloh till her son was old enough to be employed in the Divine service.

And his vow] Probably *he* had also made some vow to the Lord on the occasion of his wife's prayer and vow; in which, from his love to her, he could not be less interested than herself.

Verse 23. *Until thou have weaned him*] On the nature of this *weaning,* and the time in which it was usually done, the reader will be pleased to refer to the note on Gen. xxi. 8.

The Lord establish his word.] Or, *may the Lord establish his word*—preserve the child, cause him to grow up, and make him a blessing to Israel.

Verse 24. *With three bullocks*] The *Septuagint,* the *Syriac,* and the *Arabic,* read, *a bullock of three years old;* and this is probably correct, because we read, ver. 25, that they slew את הפר *eth happar,* THE *bullock.* We hear of no more, and we know that a *bullock* or *heifer* of *three years old* was ordinarily used; see Gen. xv. 9.

One ephah of flour] Seven *gallons and a half.*

A bottle of wine] נבל יין *nebel yayin,* a *skin full of wine.* Their bottles for wine and fluids in general were made out of skins of goats, stripped off without being cut up; the places whence the legs were extracted sewed up, as also the lower part; and the top tied. See the notes on Gen. xxi. 14, and Matt. ix. 17. These

A. M. 2834
B. C. 1170
An. Exod. Isr.
321
Anno ante
I. Olymp. 394

and brought him unto [s]the house of the LORD in Shiloh: and the child *was* young.

25 And they slew a bullock, and [t]brought the child to Eli.

26 And she said, O my lord, [u]*as* thy soul liveth, my lord, I *am* the woman that stood by thee here, praying unto the LORD.

27 [v]For this child I prayed; and the LORD hath given me my petition which I asked of him.

A. M. 2834
B. C. 1170
An. Exod. Isr.
321
Anno ante
I. Olymp. 394

28 [w]Therefore also I have [x]lent him to the LORD; as long as he liveth [y]he shall be lent to the LORD. And he [z]worshipped the LORD there.

---

[s]Joshua xviii. 1——[t]Luke ii. 22——[u]Genesis xlii. 15; 2 Kings ii. 2, 4, 6——[v]Matthew vii. 7——[w]Verse 11, 22——[x]Or, *returned him, whom I have obtained*

by petition, to the LORD——[y]Or, *he whom I have obtained by petition shall be returned*——[z]Genesis xxiv. 26, 52

---

three things, the *ox*, the *flour*, and the *wine*, probably constituted the *consecration-offering*.

Verse 26. *As thy soul liveth*] As sure as thou art a living soul, so surely am I the person who stood by thee here praying.

Verse 28. *Therefore also I have lent him to the Lord*] There is here a continual reference to her *vow*, and to the *words* which she used in making that vow.

The word *Samuel*, as we have already seen, is a contraction of the words שאול מאל *Shaul meEl*, that is, *asked* or *lent of God;* for his mother said, ver. 27, *The Lord hath given me my petition, which* שאלתי SHAALTI, *I* ASKED *of him.* In ver. 28 she says: הוא שאול ליהוה *hu* SHAUL *layhovah, he shall be* LENT *unto the Lord:* here we find the verb is the same; and it is remarked by grammarians that שאל *shaal, he asked,* making in the participle *pahul* שאול *shaul,* ASKED, in the conjugation *hiphil* signifies to *lend;* therefore, says his mother, ver. 28,

השאלתיהו ליהוה HISHILTIHU *layhovah, I have* LENT *him to the Lord.* This twofold meaning of the Hebrew root is not only followed by our translators, but also by the *Vulgate, Septuagint,* and *Syriac.*

And he worshipped the Lord there.] Instead of וישתחו *vaiyishtachu,* HE *worshipped,* וישתחוו *vaiyishtachavu, and* THEY *worshipped,* is the reading of six of *Kennicott's* and *De Rossi's* MSS., of some copies of the *Septuagint,* and of the *Vulgate, Syriac,* and *Arabic.*

This and the following chapter are *connected* in most copies of the *Septuagint* and *Vulgate* thus: *And Anna worshipped, and said, My soul is strengthened in the Lord,* &c. It is very likely that the whole passage, from the beginning of ver. 26 to the end of ver. 10 of the ensuing chapter, contains the words of Hannah *alone;* and *that* even the clause, *He worshipped the Lord there,* should be, *And she worshipped the Lord there,* and prayed, and said, &c. Indeed this latter clause is wanting in the *Polyglot Septuagint,* as I have stated above.

CHAPTER II

Hannah's prophetic hymn, 1–10. Samuel ministers to the Lord, 11. The abominable conduct of Eli's sons, 12–17. Farther account of Samuel, and of the Divine blessing on Elkanah and Hannah, 18–21. Eli's reprehensible remissness towards his sons in not restraining them in their great profligacy, 22–26. The message of God to Eli, and the prophecy of the downfall of his family, and slaughter of his wicked sons Hophni and Phinehas, 27–36.

A. M. 2839
B. C. 1165
An. Exod. Isr.
326
Anno ante
I. Olymp. 389

AND Hannah [a]prayed, and said, [b]My heart rejoiceth in the LORD, [c]mine horn is exalted in the LORD; my mouth is enlarged over mine enemies; because I [d]rejoice in thy salvation.

2 [e]*There is* none holy as the

A. M. 2839
B. C. 1165
An. Exod. Isr.
326
Anno ante
I. Olymp. 389

---

[a]Phil. iv. 6——[b]See Luke i. 46, &c.——[c]Psa. xcii. 10; cxii. 9——[d]Psa. ix. 14; xiii. 5; xx. 5; xxxv. 9

[e]Exodus xv. 11; Deut. iii. 24; xxxii. 4; Psalm lxxxvi. 8, lxxxix. 6, 8

NOTES ON CHAP. II

Verse 1. *And Hannah prayed, and said*] The *Chaldee* very properly says, *And Hannah prayed in the spirit of prophecy;* for indeed the whole of this prayer, or as it may be properly called *oracular declaration,* is a piece of regular prophecy, every part of it having respect to the future, and perhaps not a little of it declaratory of the Messiah's kingdom.

Dr. *Hales* has some very good observations on this prophetic song.

"This admirable hymn excels in simplicity of composition, closeness of connection, and

uniformity of sentiment; breathing the pious effusions of a devout mind, deeply impressed with a conviction of God's mercies to herself in particular, and of his providential government of the world in general; exalting the poor in spirit or the humble-minded, and abasing the rich and the arrogant; rewarding the righteous, and punishing the wicked. *Hannah* was also a prophetess of the first class; besides predicting her own fruitfulness, ver. 5, (for she bore six children in all, chap. ii. 21,) she foretold not only the more immediate judgments of God upon the *Philistines* during her son's administration, chap. ii. 10, but his remoter judgments

A. M. 2839
B. C. 1165
An. Exod. Isr.
326
Anno ante
I. Olymp. 389
LORD: for *there is* ᶠnone beside thee: neither *is there* any rock like our God.

3 Talk no more so exceeding

proudly; ᵍlet *not* ʰarrogancy come out of your mouth: for the LORD *is* a God of knowledge, and by him actions are weighed.
A. M. 2839
B. C. 1165
An. Exod. Isr.
326
Anno ante
I. Olymp. 389

ᶠDeut. iv. 35; 2 Sam. xxii. 32

ᵍPsa. xciv. 4; Mal. iii. 13; Jude 15——ʰHeb. *hard*

'upon the ends of the earth,' ver. 10, in the true spirit of the prophecies of *Jacob, Balaam,* and *Moses.* Like them, she describes the promised Saviour of the world as a KING, before there was any king in Israel; and she first applied to him the remarkable epithet MESSIAH in Hebrew, CHRIST in Greek, and ANOINTED in English, which was adopted by *David, Nathan, Ethan, Isaiah, Daniel,* and the succeeding prophets of the Old Testament; and by the apostles and inspired writers of the New. And the allusion thereto by Zacharias, the father of the Baptist, in his hymn, Luke i. 69, where he calls Christ a *'horn of salvation,'* and the beautiful imitation of it by the blessed *Virgin* throughout in her hymn, Luke i. 46-55, furnishing the finest commentary thereon, clearly prove that *Hannah* in her rejoicing had respect to something higher than *Peninnah* her rival, or to the triumphs of *Samuel,* or even of *David* himself; the expressions are too magnificent and sublime to be confined to such objects. Indeed the learned rabbi, *David Kimchi,* was so struck with them that he ingenuously confessed that 'the *King* of whom *Hannah* speaks is the MESSIAH,' of whom she spake either by *prophecy* or *tradition;* for, continues he, 'there was a tradition among the *Israelites,* that *a great King should arise in Israel;* and she seals up her song with celebrating this King *who was to deliver them from all their enemies.'* The tradition, as we have seen, was founded principally on Balaam's second and third prophecies, Num. xxiv. 7-17; and we cannot but admire that *gracious* dispensation of spiritual gifts to *Hannah* (whose name signifies *grace*) in ranking her among the prophets who should first unfold a leading title of the *blessed Seed of the woman.*"

In the best MSS. the whole of this hymn is written in hemistich or poetic lines. I shall here produce it in this order, following the plan as exhibited in *Kennicott's* Bible, with some trifling alterations of our present version:—

Ver. 1. My heart exulteth in Jehovah;
    My horn is exalted in Jehovah.
    My mouth is incited over mine enemies,
    For I have rejoiced in thy salvation.
Ver. 2. There is none holy like Jehovah,
    For there is none besides thee;
    There is no rock like our God.
Ver. 3. Do not magnify yourselves, speak not
    proudly, proudly.
    Let not prevarication come out of your mouth;
    For the God of knowledge is Jehovah,
    And by him actions are directed.
Ver. 4. The bows of the heroes are broken,
    And the tottering are girded with strength.
Ver. 5. The full have hired out themselves for bread,
    And the famished cease for ever.
    The barren hath borne seven,
    And she who had many children is greatly enfeebled.

Ver. 6. Jehovah killeth, and maketh alive;
    He bringeth down to the grave, and bringeth up.
Ver. 7. Jehovah maketh poor, and maketh rich;
    He bringeth down, and he even exalteth.
Ver. 8. He lifteth up the poor from the dust;
    From the dunghill he exalteth the beggar,
    To make him sit with the nobles,
    And inherit the throne of glory.
    For to Jehovah belong the pillars of the earth,
    And upon them he hath placed the globe.
Ver. 9. The foot of his saints he shall keep,
    And the wicked shall be silent in darkness;
    For by strength shall no man prevail.
Ver. 10. Jehovah shall bruise them who contend with him;
    Upon them shall be thunder in the heavens.
    Jehovah shall judge the ends of the earth;
    And he shall give strength to his King,
    And shall exalt the horn of his Messiah.

It is not particularly stated here when Hannah composed or delivered this hymn; it appears from the connection to have been at the very time in which she dedicated her son to God at the tabernacle, though some think that she composed it immediately on the birth of Samuel. The former sentiment is probably the most correct.

Mine horn is exalted in the Lord] We have often seen that *horn* signifies power, might, and dominion. It is thus constantly used in the Bible, and was so used among the heathens. The following words of Horace to his jar are well known, and speak a sentiment very similar to that above:—

Tu spem reducis mentibus anxiis,
Viresque et addis CORNUA *pauperi.*
    Hor. Odar. lib. iii., Od. 21, v. 18.

Thou bringest back hope to desponding minds;
And thou addest strength and *horns* to the poor man.

Paraphrastically expressed by Mr. Francis:—

    "Hope, by thee, fair fugitive,
    Bids the wretched strive to live.
    To the beggar you dispense
    Heart and brow of confidence."

In which scarcely any thing of the *meaning* is preserved.

My mouth is enlarged] My faculty of speech is *incited, stirred up,* to express God's disapprobation against my adversaries.

Verse 2. *None holy*] HOLINESS is peculiar to the God of Israel; no false god ever pretended to *holiness;* it was no attribute of heathenism, nor of any religion ever professed in the world before or since the true revelation of the true God.

There is none beside thee] There can be but

A. M. 2839
B. C. 1165
An. Exod. Isr.
326
Anno ante
I. Olymp. 389

4 [l]The bows of the mighty men *are* broken, and they that stumbled are girded with strength.

5 [k]*They that were* full have hired out themselves for bread; and *they that were* hungry ceased: so that [l]the barren hath borne seven; and [m]she that hath many children is waxed feeble.

6 [n]The LORD killeth, and maketh alive: he bringeth down to the grave, and bringeth up.

7 The LORD [o]maketh poor, and maketh rich: [p]he bringeth low, and lifteth up.

---

[l]Psa. xxxvii. 15, 17; lxxvi. 3——[k]Psa. xxxiv. 10; Luke i. 53——[l]Psa. cxiii. 9——[m]Isa. liv. 1; Jer. xv. 9 [n]Deut. xxxii. 39; Job v. 18; Hos. vi. 1; Tob. xiii. 2; Wisd. xvi. 13——[o]Job i. 21——[p]Psa. lxxv. 7

---

one unoriginated, infinite, and eternal Being; that Being is Jehovah.

Any rock like our God.] Rabbi *Maimon* has observed that the word צור *tsur*, which we translate *rock*, signifies, when applied to Jehovah, *fountain, source, spring.* There is no *source* whence continual help and salvation can arise but our God.

Verse 3. *A God of knowledge*] He is the most wise, *teaching* all good, and *knowing* all things.

Actions are weighed] נתכנו *nithkenu*, they are *directed;* it is by his counsel alone that we can successfully *begin, continue,* or *end,* any work.

Verse 3. *The bows of the mighty*] The *Targum* considers the *first* verse as including a prophecy against the *Philistines;* the *second* verse, against *Sennacherib* and his army; the *third,* against *Nebuchadnezzar* and the *Chaldeans;* the *fourth,* against the *Greeks;* the *fifth,* against *Haman* and his posterity; and the *tenth,* against *Magog,* and the enemies of the Messiah.

Verse 5. They that were *full*] All the things mentioned in these verses frequently happen in the course of the Divine providence; and indeed it is the particular providence of God that Hannah seems more especially to celebrate through the whole of this simple yet sublime ode.

Verse 6. *The Lord killeth*] God is the arbiter of life and death; he only can give life, and he only has a right to take it away.

He bringeth down to the grave] The Hebrew word שאול *sheol,* which we translate *grave,* seems to have the same meaning in the Old Testament with ἄδης, *hades* in the New, which is the word generally used by the *Septuagint* for the other. It means the *grave,* the *state* of the *dead,* and the *invisible place,* or place of *separate spirits.* Sometimes we translate it *hell,* which now means the *state of perdition,* or place of *eternal torments;* but as this comes from the Saxon **helan,** to *cover* or *conceal,* it means only the *covered place.* In some parts of England the word *helling* is used for the *covers* of a book, the *slating* of a house, &c. The *Targum* seems to understand it of death and the resurrection. "He kills and commands

8 [q]He raiseth up the poor out of the dust, *and* lifteth up the beggar from the dunghill, [r]to set *them* among princes, and to make them inherit the throne of glory; for [s]the pillars of the earth *are* the LORD'S, and he hath set the world upon them.

9 [t]He will keep the feet of his saints, and the wicked shall be silent in darkness; for by strength shall no man prevail.

10 The adversaries of the LORD shall be [u]broken to pieces; [v]out of heaven shall he thunder upon them: [w]the LORD shall judge

A. M. 2839
B. C. 1165
An. Exod. Isr.
326
Anno ante
I. Olymp. 389

---

[q]Psa. cxiii. 7, 8; Dan. iv. 17; Luke i. 52——[r]Job xxxvi. 7——[s]Job xxxviii. 4, 5, 6; Psa. xxiv. 2; cii. 25; civ. 5; Heb. i. 3——[t]Psa. xci. 11; cxxi. 3——[u]Psa. ii. 9 [v]Chap. vii. 10; Psa. xviii. 13——[w]Psa. xcvi. 13; xcviii. 9

---

to give life; he causes to descend into Sheol, that in the time to come he may bring them into the lives of eternity," i. e., the *life* of shame and everlasting contempt, and the *life* of glory.

Verse 7. *The Lord maketh poor*] For many cannot bear affluence, and if God should continue to trust them with riches, they would be their ruin.

Maketh rich] Some he can trust, and therefore makes them stewards of his secular bounty.

Verse 8. *To set* them *among princes*] There have been many cases where, in the course of God's providence, a person has been raised from the lowest and most abject estate to the highest; from the *plough* to the *imperial dignity;* from the *dungeon* to the *throne;* from the *dunghill* to *nobility.* The story of *Cincinnatus* is well known; so is that of the patriarch *Joseph;* but there is one not less in point, that of *Roushen Akhter,* who was brought out of a dungeon, and exalted to the throne of Hindustan. On this circumstance the following elegant couplet was made:—

روشن اختر بوده اکنون ماه شد
یوسف از زندان بر آمد شاه شد

"He was a *bright star,* but now is become a *moon,*
Joseph is taken from prison, and is become a *king.*"

There is a play here on *Roushen Akhter,* which signifies a *bright star;* and there is an allusion to the history of the patriarch *Joseph,* because of the similarity of fortune between him and the Mohammedan prince.

For the pillars of the earth are *the Lord's*] He is almighty, and upholds all things by the word of his power.

Verse 9. *He will keep the feet of his saints*] He will order and direct all their goings, and keep them from every evil way.

The wicked shall be silent in darkness] The *Targum* understands this of their being sent to the *darkness of hell;* they shall be slain.

By strength shall no man prevail.] Because God is *omnipotent,* and no power can be successfully exerted against him.

Verse 10. *The adversaries of the Lord shall*

A. M. 2839
B. C. 1165
An. Exod. Isr.
326
Anno ante
I. Olymp. 389

the ends of the earth; and he shall give strength unto his King, and exalt ˣthe horn of his anointed.

11 And Elkanah went to Ramah to his house. ʸAnd the child did minister unto the LORD before Eli the priest.

12 Now the sons of Eli *were* ᶻsons of Belial; ᵃthey knew not the LORD.

13 And the priest's custom with the people *was, that,* when any man offered sacrifice, the priest's servant came, while the flesh was in seething, with a flesh-hook of three teeth in his hand;

14 And he struck *it* into ᵇthe pan, or kettle, or caldron, or pot; all that the flesh-hook brought up the priest took for himself. So

they did in Shiloh unto all the Israelites that came thither.

A. M. 2839
B. C. 1165
An. Exod. Isr.
326
Anno ante
I. Olymp. 389

15 Also before they ᶜburnt the fat, the priest's servant came, and said to the man that sacrificed, Give flesh to roast for the priest; for he will not have sodden flesh of thee, but raw.

16 And *if* any man said unto him, Let them not fail to burn the fat ᵈpresently, and *then* take *as much* as thy soul desireth; then he would answer him, *Nay;* but thou shalt give *it me* now: and if not, I will take *it* by force.

17 Wherefore the sin of the young men was very great ᵉbefore the LORD: for men ᶠabhorred the offering of the LORD.

18 ᵍBut Samuel ministered before the LORD, *being* a child, ʰgirded with a linen ephod.

ˣPsa. lxxxix. 24——ʸVer. 18; chap. iii. 1——ᶻDeut. xiii. 3——ᵃJudg. ii. 10; Jer. xxii. 16; Rom. i. 28 ᵇSee 1 Esd. i. 12

ᶜLev. iii. 3, 4, 5, 16——ᵈHeb. *as on the day*——ᵉGen. vi. 11——ᶠMal. ii. 8——ᵍVer. 11——ʰExod. xxviii. 4; 2 Sam. vi. 14

---

be broken] Those who *contend with him,* מריביו, *meribaiv,* by sinning against his laws, opposing the progress of his word, or persecuting his people.

Shall judge the ends of the earth] His empire shall be extended over all mankind by the preaching of the everlasting Gospel, for to this the afterpart of the verse seems to apply: *He shall give strength unto his King, and shall exalt the horn of his Christ,* or, as the *Targum* says, ורבי מלכות משיחיה *viribbey malcuth Meshicheyh,* "he shall multiply the kingdom of the Messiah." Here the horn means spiritual as well as secular dominion.

After the clause, *The adversaries of the Lord shall be broken to pieces,* the Septuagint add the following words: Μη καυχασθω ὁ φρονιμος εν τη φρονησει αυτου, κ. τ. λ. *Let not the wise man glory in his wisdom; and let not the rich man glory in his riches; but let him who glorieth rather glory in this, that he understandeth and knoweth the Lord; and that he executeth judgment and righteousness in the midst of the earth.* This is a very long addition, and appears to be taken from Jer. ix. 23, but on collating the two places the reader will find the *words* to be materially different. This clause is wanting in the *Complutensian* Polyglot, but it is in the edition of *Aldus,* in that of Cardinal *Caraffa,* and in the *Codex Alexandrinus.*

Verse 11. *And Elkanah went to Ramah*] Immediately after the 10th verse, the Septuagint add, Και κατελιπεν αυτον εκει ενωπιον Κυριου· και απηλθεν εις Αραμαθαια, *And she left him there before the Lord, and went unto Arimathea.* Thus the Septuagint suppose that the song of Hannah was composed when she brought Samuel to present him to the Lord; and as soon as she had completed this fine ode, she delivered him into the hands of Eli the high priest, and the child entered immediately on his ministration, under the direction and instructions of Eli.

Verse 12. *The sons of Eli were sons of Belial*] They were perverse, wicked, profligate men; devil's children. *They knew not the Lord.*

"THEY *know!* nor would an angel show Him; They *would* not know, nor *choose* to know Him."

These men were the principal cause of all the ungodliness of Israel. Their most execrable conduct, described from ver. 13 to 17, caused the people to abhor the Lord's offering. An impious priesthood is the grand cause of the transgressions and ruin of any nation; witness France, Germany, Spain, &c., from 1792 to 1814.

Verse 13. *When any man offered sacrifice*] That is, when a *peace-offering* was brought, the right shoulder and the breast belonged to the priest, the fat was burnt upon the altar, and the blood was poured at the bottom of the altar; the rest of the flesh belonged to the offerer. Under pretence of taking only their own part, they took the *best* of all they chose, and *as much* as they chose.

Verse 14. *Kettle—caldron,* or *pot*] We know not what these were, nor of what capacity; nor is it of any consequence.

Verse 15. *Before they burnt the fat*] They would serve *themselves* before GOD was served! This was iniquity and arrogance of the first magnitude.

He will not have sodden flesh] He chooses *roast* meat, not *boiled;* and if they had it in the pot before the servant came, he took it out that it might be roasted.

Verse 17. *Wherefore the sin of the young men was very great*] That is, Hophni and Phinehas, the sons of Eli.

Men abhorred the offering] As the people saw that the priests had no piety, and that they acted as if there was no God; they despised God's service, and became infidels.

A national priesthood, when the foundation is right, may be a great blessing; but if the priesthood becomes corrupt, though the foundation itself stand sure, the corruption of the national manners will be the unavoidable consequence.

Verse 18. *Girded with a linen ephod*] This the Targum translates אסיר כרדוט דבוץ *asir car-*

A. M. 2839
B. C. 1165
An. Exod. Isr.
326
Anno ante
I. Olymp. 389

19 Moreover his mother made him a little coat, and brought *it* to him from year to year, when she [i]came up with her husband to offer the yearly sacrifice.

20 And Eli [k]blessed Elkanah and his wife, and said, The LORD give thee seed of this woman for the [l]loan which is [m]lent to the LORD. And they went unto their own home.

21 And the LORD [n]visited Hannah, so that she conceived, and bare three sons and two daughters. And the child Samuel [o]grew before the LORD.

22 Now Eli was very old, and heard all that his sons did unto all Israel; and how they lay with [p]the women that [q]assembled *at* the door of the tabernacle of the congregation.

23 And he said unto them, Why do ye such things? for [r]I hear of your evil dealings by all this people.

A. M. 2839
B. C. 1165
An. Exod. Isr.
326
Anno ante
I. Olymp. 389

24 Nay, my sons; for *it is* no good report that I hear: ye make the LORD's people [s]to transgress.

25 If one man sin against another, the judge shall judge him: but if a man [t]sin against the LORD, who shall entreat for him? Notwithstanding, they hearkened not unto the voice of their father, [u]because the LORD would slay them.

26 And the child Samuel [v]grew on, and was [w]in favour both with the LORD, and also with men.

27 [x]And there came a man of God unto Eli, and said unto him, Thus saith the LORD, [y]Did I plainly appear unto the house of thy father, when they were in Egypt in Pharaoh's house?

---

[i]Chap. i. 3——[k]Gen. xiv. 19——[l]Or, *petition which she asked,* &c.——[m]Chap. i. 28——[n]Gen. xxi. 1 [o]Ver. 26; chap. iii. 19; Judg. xiii. 24; Luke i. 80; ii. 40 [p]See Exod. xxxviii. 8——[q]Heb. *assembled by troops*

[r]Or, *I hear evil words of you*——[s]Or, *to cry out* [t]Num. xv. 30——[u]Josh. xi. 20; Prov. xv. 10——[v]Ver. 21——[w]Prov. iii. 4; Luke ii. 52; Acts ii. 47; Rom. xiv. 18 [x]1 Kings xiii. 1——[y]Exod. iv. 14, 27

---

dut debuts, "Girded with a cardit of byssus, or *fine linen*." The word *cardut* they seem to have borrowed from the Greek χειριδωτος, a *tunic,* having χειριδας, i. e., *sleeves* that came down to, or covered, the *hands.* This was esteemed an effeminate garment among the Romans. See Buxtorf's *Talmudic Lexicon.*

Verse 19. *Made him a little coat*] מעיל קטן *meil katon, a little cloak,* or *surtout;* an *upper garment:* probably intended to keep him from the cold, and to save his other clothes from being abused in his meaner services. It is probable that she furnished him with a *new one* each year, when she came up to one of the annual sacrifices.

Verse 20. *Eli blessed Elkanah*] The natural place of this verse seems to be before the 11th; after which the 21st should come in; after the 21st, perhaps the 26th should come in. The subjects in this chapter seem very much entangled and confused by the wrong position of the verses.

Verse 22. *They lay with the women that assembled*] It is probable that these were persons who had some *employment* about the tabernacle. See the note on Exod. xxxviii. 8, where the Hebrew text is similar to that in this place.

Verse 23. *Why do ye such things?*] Eli appears to have been a fondly affectionate, easy father, who wished his sons to do well, but did not bring them under proper *discipline,* and did not use his *authority* to restrain them. As *judge,* he had power to cast them immediately out of the vineyard, as wicked and unprofitable servants; this he did not, and his and their ruin was the consequence.

Verse 25. *If one man sin against another*] All differences between man and man may be settled by the proper judge; but if a man sin against the Supreme Judge, God himself, who

shall reconcile him to his Maker? Your sin is immediately against God himself, and is the highest insult that can be offered, because it is in the matter of his own worship; therefore ye may expect his heaviest judgments.

But if a man sin against the Lord, who shall entreat for him?] This was a question of the most solemn importance under the old covenant, especially after the death of Moses, the mediator. The law had determined *what* sins should be punished with *death;* and it was supposed that there was not any appeal from the decision there pronounced. 1 John ii. 1 is an answer to this question; but it is an answer which the *Gospel* alone can give: *My little children, these things write I unto you, that ye sin not; but if any man sin, we have an Advocate with the Father, Jesus Christ the righteous.*

Because the Lord would slay them.] The particle כי *ki,* which we translate *because,* and thus make their continuance in sin the *effect* of God's determination to destroy them, should be translated *therefore,* as it means in many parts of the sacred writings. See *Noldius's* Particles, where the very text in question is introduced: *Sed non auscultarunt, &c.;* IDEO *voluit Jehova eos interficere;* "But they would not hearken, &c.; THEREFORE God purposed to destroy them." It was their not hearkening that induced the Lord to will their destruction.

Verse 27. *There came a man of God*] Who this was we know not, but the Chaldee terms him נביא דיי *nebiya daya, a prophet of Jehovah.*

Unto the house of thy father] That is, to *Aaron;* he was the first high priest; the priesthood descended from him to his eldest son Eleazar, then to *Phinehas.* It became afterwards established in the younger branch of the family of Aaron; for Eli was a descendant of *Ithamar,* Aaron's youngest son. From Eli it

A. M. 2839
B. C. 1165
An. Exod. Isr.
326
Anno ante
I. Olymp. 389

28 And did I [z]choose him out of all the tribes of Israel *to be* my priest, to offer upon mine altar, to burn incense, to wear an ephod before me? and [a]did I give unto the house of thy father all the offerings made by fire of the children of Israel?

29 Wherefore [b]kick ye at my sacrifice and at mine offering, which I have commanded *in my* [c]habitation; and honourest thy sons above me, to make yourselves fat with the chiefest of all the offerings of Israel my people?

30 Wherefore the LORD God of Israel saith, [d]I said indeed *that* thy house, and the house of thy father, should walk before me for ever: but now the LORD saith, [e]Be it far from me; for them that honour me [f]I will honour, and [g]they that despise me shall be lightly esteemed.

31 Behold, [h]the days come, that I will cut off thine arm, and the arm of thy father's house, and there shall not be an old man in thine house.

A. M. 2839
B. C. 1165
An. Exod. Isr.
326
Anno ante
I. Olymp. 389

32 And thou shalt see [i]an enemy *in my* habitation, in all *the wealth* which *God* shall give Israel: and there shall not be [k]an old man in thine house for ever.

33 And the man of thine, *whom* I shall not cut off from mine altar, *shall be* to consume thine eyes, and to grieve thine heart: and all the increase of thine house shall die [l]in the flower of their age.

34 And this *shall be* [m]a sign unto thee, that shall come upon thy two sons, on Hophni and Phinehas; [n]in one day they shall die both of them.

---

[z]Exod. xxviii. 1, 4; Num. xvi. 5; xviii. 1, 7——[a]Lev. ii. 3, 10; vi. 16; vii. 7, 8, 34, 35; x. 14, 15; Num. v. 9, 10; xviii. 8-19——[b]Deut. xxxii. 15——[c]Deut. xii. 5, 6 [d]Exodus xxix. 9——[e]Jer. xviii. 9, 10——[f]Psa. xviii. 20; xci. 14——[g]Mal. ii. 9

[h]1 Kings ii. 27; Ezek. xliv. 10; see chapter iv. 11, 18, 20; xiv. 3; xxii. 18, &c.——[i]Or, *the affliction of the tabernacle, for all the wealth which God would have given Israel* [k]See Zech. viii. 4——[l]Heb. *men*——[m]1 Kings xiii. 3 [n]Chap. iv. 11

---

was transferred back again to the family of *Eleazar*, because of the profligacy of Eli's sons.

Verse 28. *And did I choose him*] The high priesthood was a place of the greatest *honour* that could be conferred on man, and a place of considerable *emolument;* for from their part of the sacrifices they derived a most comfortable livelihood.

Verse 29. *Wherefore kick ye at my sacrifice*] They disdained to take the *part* allowed by law; and would take for themselves *what* part they pleased, and *as much* as they pleased, ver. 13-16: thus they kicked at the sacrifices.

Honourest thy sons above me] Permitting them to deal, as above, with the offerings and sacrifices, and take their part *before* the fat, &c., was burnt unto the Lord: thus they were *first* served. At this Eli *connived*, and thus honoured his sons *above* God.

Verse 30. *Should walk before me for ever*] See Exod. xxix. 9; xl. 15; Num. xxv. 10-13, where it is positively promised that the priesthood should be continued in the *family of Aaron* FOR EVER. But although this promise appears to be *absolute*, yet we plainly see that, like all other apparently absolute promises of God, it is *conditional*, i. e., a condition is *implied* though not *expressed*.

But now—be it far from me] You have walked unworthily; I shall annul my promise, and reverse my ordinance. See Jer. xviii. 9, 10.

For them that honour me] This is a plan from which God will never depart; this can have no *alteration;* every promise is made in reference to it; "they who honour God shall be honoured; they who despise him shall be lightly esteemed."

Verse 31. *I will cut off thine arm*] I will destroy the strength, power, and influence of thy family.

Verse 32. *Thou shalt see an enemy* in my

habitation] Every version and almost every commentator understands this clause differently. The word צר *tsar*, which we translate an *enemy*, and the Vulgate *æmulum*, a *rival*, signifies *calamity;* and this is the best sense to understand it in here. The calamity which he saw was the defeat of the Israelites, the capture of the ark, the death of his wicked sons, and the triumph of the Philistines. All this he *saw*, that is, knew to have taken place, before he met with his own tragical death.

In all the wealth which God shall give Israel] This also is dark. The meaning may be this: God has spoken good concerning Israel; he will, in the end, make the triumph of the Philistines their own confusion; and the capture of the ark shall be the desolation of their gods; but the Israelites shall first be sorely pressed with *calamity*. See the *margin*.

There shall not be an old man] This is repeated from the *preceding* verse; all the family shall die in the flower of their years, as is said in the following verse.

Verse 33. *And the man of thine*] Of this passage Calmet observes: "The posterity of Eli possessed the high priesthood to the time of Solomon; and even when that dynasty was transferred to another family, God preserved that of Eli, not to render it more happy, but to punish it by seeing the prosperity of its enemies, to the end that it might see itself destitute and despised. This shows the depth of the judgments of God and the grandeur of his justice, which extends even to distant generations, and manifests itself to sinners both in life and death; both in their own disgrace, and in the prosperity of their enemies."

Verse 34. *They shall die both of them.*] Hophni and Phinehas were both killed very shortly after in the great battle with the Philistines in which the Israelites were completely routed, and the ark taken. See chap. iv.

A. M. 2839
B. C. 1165
An. Exod. Isr.
326
Anno ante
I. Olymp. 389

35 And °I will raise me up a faithful priest, *that* shall do according to *that* which *is* in mine heart and in my mind: and ᴾI will build him a sure house; and he shall walk before ᑫmine Anointed for ever.

A. M. 2839
B. C. 1165
An. Exod. Isr.
326
Anno ante
I. Olymp. 389

36 ʳAnd it shall come to pass, *that* every one that is left in thine house shall come *and* crouch to him for a piece of silver and a morsel of bread, and shall say, ˢPut me, I pray thee, into ᵗone of the priests' offices, that I may eat a piece of bread.

°1 Kings ii. 35; 1 Chron. xxix. 22; Ezek. xliv. 15
ᴾ2 Sam. vii. 11, 27; 1 Kings xi. 38

ᑫPsalm ii. 2; xviii. 50——ʳ1 Kings ii. 27——ˢHeb. *join*
ᵗOr, *somewhat about the priesthood*

Verse 35. *A faithful priest*] This seems to have been spoken of Zadok, who was anointed high priest in the room of Abiathar, the last descendant of the house of Eli; see 1 Kings ii. 26, 27. Abiathar was removed because he had joined with Adonijah, who had got himself proclaimed king; see 1 Kings i. 7.

I will build him a sure house] I will continue the priesthood in his family.

He shall walk before mine Anointed] He shall minister before Solomon, and the *kings* which shall reign in the land. The *Targum* says, "He shall walk קדם משיחי *kodam Meshichi, before my* MESSIAH," and the *Septuagint* expresses it, ενωπιον Χριστου μου, *"before my* CHRIST;"* for, in their proper and more extended sense, these things are supposed to belong to our great High Priest and the Christian system: but the word may refer to the *Israelitish people.* See the note on Heb. ix. 26.

Verse 36. *Shall come* and *crouch to him*] Shall *prostrate* himself before him in the most abject manner, begging to be employed even in the meanest offices about the tabernacle, in order to get even the most scanty means of support.

A piece of silver] אגורת כסף *agorath keseph,* translated by the *Septuagint,* οβολου αργυριον, an *obolus of silver.* The *Targum* translates it מעא *mea,* which is the same as the Hebrew *gerah,* and weighed about sixteen grains of barley.

A morsel of bread] A mouthful; what might be sufficient to keep body and soul together. See the *sin* and its *punishment.* They formerly *pampered* themselves, and *fed to the full* on the Lord's sacrifices; and now they are reduced to a *morsel of bread.* They fed themselves *without fear;* and now they have *cleanness of teeth* in all their dwellings. They *wasted* the Lord's heritage, and now they *beg their bread!*

IN religious establishments, vile persons, who have no higher motive, may and do get into the priest's office, that they may clothe themselves with the wool, and feed themselves with the fat, while they starve the flock. But where there is no law to back the claims of the worthless and the wicked, men of piety and solid merit only can find support; for they must live on the *free-will offerings* of the people. Where religion is established by law, the strictest ecclesiastical discipline should be kept up, and all *hireling priests* and ecclesiastical *drones* should be expelled from the Lord's vineyard. An established religion, where the *foundation* is good, as is ours, I consider a great blessing; but it is liable to this continual abuse, which nothing but careful and rigid ecclesiastical discipline can either cure or prevent. If *our* high priests, our archbishops and bishops, do not their duty, the whole body of the clergy may become corrupt or inefficient. If *they* be faithful, the establishment will be an honour to the kingdom, and a praise in the earth.

The words *pillars of the earth,* מצקי ארץ *metsukey erets,* Mr. Parkhurst translates and defends thus: "The *compressors of the earth;* i. e., the columns of the celestial fluid which compress or keep its parts together." This is all *imaginary;* we do not know this compressing *celestial fluid;* but there is one that answers the same end, which we do know, i. e., the AIR, the *columns* of which *press* upon the earth *in all directions; above, below, around,* with a weight of *fifteen pounds* to every *square inch;* so that a *column of air* of the height of the atmosphere, which on the surface of the globe measures one square inch, is known by the most accurate and indubitable experiments to weigh *fifteen pounds.* Now as a *square foot* contains one hundred and forty-four square inches, each foot must be compressed with a weight of incumbent atmospheric *air* equal to two thousand one hundred and sixty pounds. And as the earth is known to contain a surface of *five thousand five hundred and seventy-five billions* of square feet; hence, allowing *two thousand one hundred and sixty pounds* to each square foot, the whole surface of the globe must sustain a pressure of atmospheric air equal to *twelve trillions and forty-one thousand billions of pounds;* or *six thousand and twenty-one billions of tons.* This pressure, independently of what is called *gravity,* is sufficient to keep all the parts of the earth *together,* and perhaps to counteract all the influence of *centrifugal* force. But adding to this all the influence of *gravity* or *attraction,* by which every particle of matter tends to the *centre,* these *compressors of the earth* are sufficient to poise, balance, and preserve the whole terraqueous globe. These *pillars* or *compressors* are an astonishing provision made by the wisdom of God for the necessities of the globe. Without this, water could not rise in fountains, nor the sap in vegetables. Without this, there could be no respiration for man or beast, and no circulation of the blood in any animal. In short, both vegetable and animal life depend, under God, on these *pillars* or *compressors of the earth;* and were it not for this *compressing* power, the air contained in the vessels of all plants and animals would by its elasticity expand and instantly rupture all those vessels, and cause the destruction of all animal and vegetable life: but God in his wisdom has so balanced these two forces, that, while they appear to counteract and balance each other, they serve, by mutual dilations and compressions, to promote the circulation of the sap in vegetables, and the blood in animals.

CHAPTER III

Samuel ministers to the Lord before Eli, 1. He is thrice called by the Lord; who informs him of the evils which shall be brought on the house of Eli, 2–15. Eli inquires of Samuel what the Lord had said, 16, 17. He gives a faithful relation of the whole, which Eli receives with great submission, 18. Samuel prospers; is established as a prophet in Israel; and the Lord reveals himself to him in Shiloh, 19–21.

A. M. 2839
B. C. 1165
An. Exod. Isr. 326
Anno ante I. Olymp. 389

AND ᵃthe child Samuel ministered unto the LORD before Eli. And ᵇthe word of the LORD was precious in those days; *there was* no open vision.

A. M. 2862
B. C. 1142
An. Exod. Isr. 349
Anno ante I. Olymp. 366

2 And it came to pass at that time, when Eli *was* laid down in his place, ᶜand his eyes began to wax dim, *that* he could not see;

3 And ere ᵈthe lamp of God went out ᵉin the temple of the LORD, where the ark of God *was,* and Samuel was laid down *to sleep;*

4 That the LORD called Samuel: and he answered, Here *am* I.

5 And he ran unto Eli, and said, Here *am* I; for thou calledst me. And he said, I called not; lie down again. And he went and lay down.

6 And the LORD called yet again, Samuel. And Samuel arose and went to Eli, and said, Here *am* I; for thou didst call me. And he

answered, I called not, my son; lie down again.

A. M. 2862
B. C. 1142
An. Exod. Isr. 349
Anno ante I. Olymp. 366

7 ᶠNow Samuel ᵍdid not yet know the LORD, neither was the word of the LORD yet revealed unto him.

8 And the LORD called Samuel again the third time. And he arose and went to Eli, and said, Here *am* I; for thou didst call me. And Eli perceived that the LORD had called the child.

9 Therefore Eli said unto Samuel, Go, lie down: and it shall be, if he call thee, that thou shalt say, Speak, LORD; for thy servant heareth. So Samuel went and lay down in his place.

10 And the LORD came, and stood, and called as at the other times, Samuel, Samuel. Then Samuel answered, Speak; for thy servant heareth.

11 And the LORD said to Samuel, Behold, I will do a thing in Israel, ʰat which both the

---

ᵃChap. ii. 11——ᵇPsa. lxxiv. 9; Amos viii. 11; see ver. 21——ᶜGen. xxvii. 1; xlviii. 10; chap. ii. 22; iv. 15 ᵈExod. xxvii. 21; Lev. xxiv. 3; 2 Chron. xiii. 11 ᵉChap. i. 9

ᶠOr, *Thus did Samuel before he knew the LORD, and before the word of the LORD was revealed unto him* ᵍSee Acts xix. 2——ʰ2 Kings xxi. 12; Jeremiah xix. 3

NOTES ON CHAP. III

Verse 1. *Samuel ministered unto the Lord*] He performed minor services in the tabernacle, under the direction of Eli, such as *opening the doors,* &c. See ver. 15.

The word of the Lord was precious] There were but few revelations from God; and because the word was *scarce,* therefore it was *valuable.* The author of this book probably lived at a time when prophecy was frequent. See the *preface.*

There was *no open vision.*] There was no public accredited prophet; one with whom the secret of the Lord was known to dwell, and to whom all might have recourse in cases of doubt or public emergency.

Verse 2. *Eli was laid down in his place*] It is very likely that as the ark was a long time at Shiloh, they had built near to it certain apartments for the high priest and others more immediately employed about the tabernacle. In one of these, near to that of Eli, perhaps under the same roof, Samuel lay when he was called by the Lord.

Verse 3. *Ere the lamp of God went out*] Before sunrise; for it is likely that the lamps were extinguished before the rising of the sun. See Exod. xxvii. 21; Lev. xxiv. 3.

Verse 4. *The Lord called Samuel*] The voice

probably came from the holy place, near to which Eli and Samuel were both lying.

Verse 7. *Samuel did not yet know the Lord*] He had not been accustomed to receive any revelation from him. He *knew* and *worshipped* the God of Israel; but he did not know him as communicating especial revelation of His will.

Verse 9. *Speak, Lord; for thy servant heareʰ*] This was the usual way in which the prophets spoke, when they had intimations that the Lord was about to make some especial revelation.

Verse 10. *The Lord came, and stood*] He heard the voice as if it was approaching nearer and nearer; till at last, from the sameness of the tone, he could imagine that it ceased to approach: and this is what appears to be represented under the notion of God *standing* and calling.

Verse 11. *The Lord said to Samuel*] He probably saw nothing, and only heard the *voice;* for it was not likely that any extraordinary *representation* could have been made to the *eyes* of a person so young. He heard a voice, but saw no *similitude.*

The ears—shall tingle.] It shall be a *piercing* word to all Israel; it shall astound them all; and, after having heard it, it will still continue to *resound* in their ears.

A. M. 2862
B. C. 1142
An. Exod. Isr.
349
Anno ante
I. Olymp. 366

ears of every one that heareth it shall tingle.

12 In that day I will perform against Eli [i]all *things* which I have spoken concerning his house: [k]when I begin, I will also make an end.

13 [l]For [m]I have told him that I will [n]judge his house for ever for the iniquity which he knoweth; because [o]his sons made themselves [p]vile, and he [q]restrained [r]them not.

14 And therefore I have sworn unto the house of Eli, that the iniquity of Eli's house [s]shall not be purged with sacrifice nor offering for ever.

15 And Samuel lay until the morning, and opened the doors of the house of the LORD. And Samuel feared to show Eli the vision.

16 Then Eli called Samuel, and said, Samuel, my son. And he answered, Here *am* I.

A. M. 2862
B. C. 1142
An. Exod. Isr.
349
Anno ante
I. Olymp. 366

17 And he said, What *is* the thing that *the LORD* hath said unto thee? I pray thee hide *it* not from me: [t]God do so to thee, and [u]more also, if thou hide *any* [v]thing from me of all the things that he said unto thee.

18 And Samuel told him [w]every whit, and hid nothing from him. And he said, [x]It *is* the LORD: let him do what seemeth him good.

19 And Samuel [y]grew, and [z]the LORD was with him, [a]and did let none of his words fall to the ground.

20 And all Israel [b]from Dan even to Beersheba knew that Samuel *was* [c]established *to be* a prophet of the LORD.

21 And the LORD appeared again in Shiloh: for the LORD revealed himself to Samuel in Shiloh by [d]the word of the LORD.

---

[i]Chap. ii. 30–36——[k]Heb. *beginning and ending*
[l]Or, *And I will tell him,* &c.——[m]Chap. ii. 29, 30, 31, &c.
[n]Ezek. vii. 3; xviii. 30——[o]Chap. ii. 12, 17, 22——[p]Or,
accursed——[q]Heb. *frowned not upon them*——[r]Chap. ii.
23, 25——[s]Num. xv. 30, 31; Isa. xxii. 14

[t]Ruth i. 17——[u]Heb. *so add*——[v]Or, *word*——[w]Heb.
all the things, or *words*——[x]Job i. 21; ii. 10; Psa. xxxix.
9; Isa. xxxix. 8——[y]Chap. ii. 21——[z]Gen. xxxix. 2, 21,
23——[a]Chap. ix. 6——[b]Judg. xx. 1——[c]Or, *faithful*
[d]Ver. 1, 4

Verse 12. *I will perform—all* things *which I have spoken*] That is, what He had declared by the prophet, whose message is related chap. ii. 27, &c.

When I begin, I will also make an end.] I will not delay the execution of my purpose: when I begin, nothing shall deter me from bringing all my judgments to a conclusion.

Verse 13. *I will judge his house for ever*] I will continue to execute judgments upon it till it is destroyed.

His sons made themselves vile] See chap. ii. 12-17, 22-25.

He restrained them not.] He did not use his parental and juridical authority to curb them, and prevent the disorders which they committed. See at the conclusion of the chapter.

Verse 14. *Shall not be purged with sacrifice nor offering*] That is, God was determined that they should be removed by a violent death. They had committed the *sin unto death;* and no *offering* or *sacrifice* could prevent this. What is spoken here relates to their *temporal death* only.

Verse 15. *Samuel feared to show Eli*] He reverenced him as a father, and he feared to distress him by showing what the Lord had purposed to do. It does not appear that God had commanded Samuel to deliver this message: he, therefore, did not attempt it till adjured by Eli, ver. 17.

Verse 17. *God do so to thee, and more also*] This was a very solemn adjuration: he suspected that God had threatened severe judgments, for he knew that his house was very criminal; and he wished to know what God had spoken. The words imply thus much: If thou do not tell me fully what God has threatened, may the same and greater curses fall on thyself.

Verse 18. *Samuel told him every whit*] Our word *whit,* or *wid,* comes from the Anglo-Saxon ᵖᶦᵇᵗ, which signifies *person, thing,* &c.; *every whit* is *every thing.* The Hebrew את כל הדברים *et col haddebarim,* "all these words."

It is the Lord] He is *Sovereign,* and will do what he *pleases;* he is *righteous,* and will do nothing but what is *just.*

Let him do what seemeth him good.] There is much of a godly submission, as well as a deep sense of his own unworthiness, found in these words. He also had sinned, so as to be punished with *temporal death;* but surely there is no evidence that the displeasure of the Lord against him was extended to a future state.

Verse 19. *Samuel grew*] Increased to manhood.

The Lord was with him] Teaching him, and filling him with grace and holiness.

None of his words fall] Whatever prediction he uttered, God fulfilled it; and his counsels were received as coming from the Lord.

Verse 20. *All Israel from Dan even to Beersheba*] Through the whole extent of Palestine; Dan being at the *northern,* Beer-sheba at the *southern* extremity.

Was established to be *a prophet*] The word נאמן *neeman,* which we translate *established,* signifies *faithful: The faithful Samuel was a prophet of the Lord.*

Verse 21. *The Lord appeared again*] ויסף יהוה להראה *vaiyoseph Yehovah leheraoh,* "And Jehovah *added* to appear;" that is, he continued to reveal himself to Samuel at Shiloh.

By the word of the Lord.] By the *spirit* and *word* of *prophecy.*

IN this chapter we read again of the fearful consequences of a neglected religious education.

Eli's sons were wicked: their father knew the Lord; but he neither taught his children, nor restrained them by his parental authority. I have already had occasion to remark, that were a proper line of conduct pursued in the education of children, how few *profligate* sons *and daughters*, and how few *broken-hearted* parents should we find! The neglect of early *religious education*, connected with a *wholesome* and *affectionate* restraint, is the ruin of millions. Many parents, to excuse their indolence and most criminal neglect, say, "We cannot give our children grace." What do they *mean* by this? That God, not *themselves*, is the author of the irregularities and viciousness of their children. They may shudder at this imputation: but when they reflect that they have not given them right precepts, have not brought them under firm and affectionate restraint; have not showed them, by their own spirit, temper, and conduct, how they should be regulated in theirs; when either the worship of God has not been established in their houses, or they have permitted their children, on the most trifling pretences, to absent themselves from it; when all these things are considered, they will find that, speaking after the manner of men, it would have been a very extraordinary miracle indeed if the children had been found preferring a path in which they did not see their parents conscientiously tread. Let those parents who continue to excuse themselves by saying, "*We cannot give grace to our children*," lay their hand on their conscience, and say whether they ever knew an instance where God withheld *his* grace, while they were, in humble subserviency to him, performing *their* duty. The real state of the case is this: parents cannot do God's work, and God will not do *theirs;* but if they use the means, and *train up the child in the way he should go*, God will not withhold his blessing.

It is not parental *fondness*, nor parental *authority*, taken *separately*, that can produce this beneficial effect. A father may be as *fond* of his offspring as *Eli*, and his children be sons of Belial; he may be as *authoritative* as the

grand Turk, and his children despise and plot rebellion against him. But let parental *authority* be tempered with *fatherly affection;* and let the rein of discipline be steadily held by this powerful but affectionate hand; and there shall the pleasure of God prosper; there will he give his blessing, even life for evermore. Many fine families have been *spoiled*, and many *ruined*, by the *separate* exercise of these two principles. Parental *affection*, when *alone*, infallibly degenerates into *foolish fondness;* and parental authority frequently degenerates into *brutal tyranny* when standing by *itself*. The first sort of parents will be *loved* without being respected; the second sort will be *dreaded*, without either *respect* or *esteem*. In the first case obedience is not *exacted*, and is therefore felt to be unnecessary, as offences of great magnitude pass without punishment or reprehension: in the second case, rigid exaction renders obedience almost impossible; and the smallest delinquency is often punished with the extreme of torture, which, hardening the mind, renders duty a matter of perfect indifference.

Parents, lay these things to heart: remember Eli and his sons; remember the dismal end of both! Teach your children to fear God—use wholesome discipline—be determined—begin in time—mingle *severity* and *mercy* together in all your conduct—and earnestly pray to God to second your godly discipline with the power and grace of his Spirit.

Education is generally defined that series of means by which the human understanding is gradually enlightened, and the dispositions of the heart are corrected, formed, and brought forth, between early infancy and the period when a young person is considered as qualified to take a part in active life. Whole *nations* have been corrupted, enfeebled, and destroyed, through the want of proper education: through this multitudes of *families* have degenerated; and a countless number of *individuals* have come to an untimely end. Parents who neglect this, neglect the present and eternal interests of their offspring.

CHAPTER IV

A battle between Israel and the Philistines, in which the former are defeated, with the loss of four thousand men, 1, 2. They resolve to give the Philistines battle once more, and bring the ark of the Lord, with Hophni and Phinehas the priests, into the camp, 3, 4. They do so, and become vainly confident, 5. At this the Philistines are dismayed, 6–9. The battle commences; the Israelites are again defeated, with the loss of thirty thousand men; Hophni and Phinehas are among the slain; and the ark of the Lord is taken, 10, 11. A Benjamite runs with the news to Eli; who, hearing of the capture of the ark, falls from his seat, and breaks his neck, 12–18. The wife of Phinehas, hearing of the death of her husband, and father-in-law, and of the capture of the ark, is taken in untimely travail, brings forth a son, calls him I-chabod, and expires, 19–22.

A. M. 2863
B. C. 1141
An. Ex. Isr. 350
Anno ante
I. Olymp. 365

AND the word of Samuel [a]came [b]to all Israel. Now Israel went out against the Philistines to battle, and pitched beside [c]Eben-ezer: and the Philistines pitched in Aphek.

A. M. 2863
B. C. 1141
An. Ex. Isr. 350
Anno ante
I. Olymp. 365

---

[a]Or, *came to pass*——[b]Heb. *was*

[c]Chap. v. 1; vii. 12

NOTES ON CHAP. IV

Verse 1. *The word of Samuel came to all Israel*] This clause certainly belongs to the preceding chapter, and is so placed by the *Vulgate, Septuagint, Syriac*, and *Arabic*.

Pitched beside Eben-ezer] This name was

not given to this place till more than *twenty* years *after* this battle, see chap. vii. 12; for the monument called אבן העזר *haeben haezer*, the "Stone of Help," was erected by Samuel in the place which was afterwards from this circumstance, called *Eben-ezer*, when the Lord had given the Israelites a signal victory over the

A. M. 2863
B. C. 1141
An. Exod. Isr. 350
Anno ante
I. Olymp. 365

2 And the Philistines put themselves in array against Israel: and when ^dthey joined battle, Israel was smitten before the Philistines: and they slew of ^ethe army in the field about four thousand men.

3 And when the people were come into the camp, the elders of Israel said, Wherefore hath the LORD smitten us to-day before the Philistines? Let us ^ffetch the ark of the covenant of the LORD out of Shiloh unto us, that, when it cometh among us, it may save us out of the hand of our enemies.

4 So the people sent to Shiloh, that they might bring from thence the ark of the covenant of the LORD of hosts, ^gwhich dwelleth *between* ^hthe cherubims: and the two sons of Eli, Hophni and Phinehas, *were* there with the ark of the covenant of God.

5 And when the ark of the covenant of the LORD came into the camp, all Israel shouted with a great shout, so that the earth rang again.

6 And when the Philistines heard the noise of the shout, they said, What *meaneth* the noise of this great shout in the camp of the Hebrews? And they understood that the ark of the LORD was come into the camp.

A. M. 2863
B. C. 1141
An. Exod. Isr. 350
Anno ante
I. Olymp. 365

7 And the Philistines were afraid, for they said, God is come into the camp. And they said, Wo unto us! for there hath not been such a thing ⁱheretofore.

8 Wo unto us! who shall deliver us out of the hand of these mighty Gods? these *are* the Gods that smote the Egyptians with all the plagues in the wilderness.

9 ^kBe strong, and quit yourselves like men, O ye Philistines, that ye be not servants unto the Hebrews, ^las they have been to you: ^mquit yourselves like men, and fight.

10 And the Philistines fought, and ⁿIsrael was smitten, and they fled every man into his tent: and there was a very great slaughter; for there fell of Israel thirty thousand footmen.

---

^dHeb. *the battle was spread*——^eHeb. *the array* ^fHeb. *take unto us*——^g2 Sam. vi. 2; Psa. lxxx. 1; xcix. 1 ^hExod. xxv. 18, 22; Num. vii. 89

ⁱHeb. *yesterday*, or *the third day*——^k1 Cor. xvi. 13 ^lJudg. xiii. 1——^mHeb. *be men*——ⁿVer. 2; Lev. xxvi. 17; Deut. xxviii. 25; Psa. lxxviii. 9, 62

Philistines. It was situated in the tribe of Judah, between *Mizpeh* and *Shen*, and not far from the *Aphek* here mentioned. This is another proof that this book was compiled *after* the times and transcactions which it records, and probably from *memoranda* which had been made by a contemporary writer.

Verse 2. *Put themselves in array*] There is no doubt that both the Philistines and Israelites had what might be called *the art of war*, according to which they marshalled their troops in the field, constructed their camps, and conducted their retreats, sieges, &c.; but we know not the principles on which they acted.

They slew of the army in the field about four thousand men.] This must have been a severe conflict, as *four thousand* were left dead on the field of battle. The contest also must have lasted some considerable time, as these were all slain hand to hand; swords and spears being in all probability the only weapons then used.

Verse 3. *Let us fetch the ark*] They vainly supposed that the ark could save them, when the God of it had departed from them because of their wickedness. They knew that in former times their fathers had been *beaten* by their enemies, when they took not the ark with them to battle; as in the case of their wars with the Caanaanites, Num. xiv. 44, 45; and that they had *conquered* when they took this with them, as in the case of the destruction of Jericho, Josh. vi. 4. From the latter clause they took confidence; but the *cause* of their miscarriage in the former they laid not to heart. It was customary with all the nations

of the earth to take their *gods* and *sacred ensigns* with them to war. The *Persians*, *Indians*, *Greeks*, *Romans*, *Germans*, *Philistines*, &c., did so. *Consecrated crosses, blessing* and *hallowing of colours* and *standards*, are the *modern* remains of those ancient *superstitions*.

Verse 4. *The Lord of hosts*] See on chap. i. 3.

Dwelleth between the cherubims] Of what shape the cherubim were, we know not; but there was one of these representative figures placed at each end of the ark of the covenant; and between them, on the *lid* or *cover* of that ark, which was called the *propitiatory* or *mercy-seat*, the *shechinah*, or symbol of the Divine presence, was said to dwell. They thought, therefore, if they had the ark, they must necessarily have the *presence* and *influence* of *Jehovah*.

Verse 5. *All Israel shouted*] Had they *humbled* themselves, and *prayed* devoutly and fervently for success, they would have been heard and saved. Their shouting proved both their vanity and irreligion.

Verse 7. *God is come into the camp.*] They took for granted, as did the Israelites, that his presence was inseparable from his ark or shrine.

Verse 8. *These mighty Gods*] מיד האלהים האדירים *miyad haelohim haaddirim, from the hand of these illustrious Gods.* Probably this should be translated in the *singular*, and not in the *plural: Who shall deliver us from the hand of this illustrious God?*

Verse 9. *Be strong, &c.*] This was the address to the whole army, and very forcible it

---

A. M. 2863
B. C. 1141
An. Exod. Isr.
350
Anno ante
I. Olymp. 365

11 And °the ark of God was taken; and Pthe two sons of Eli, Hophni and Phinehas, ⁹were slain.

12 And there ran a man of Benjamin out of the army, and ʳcame to Shiloh the same day with his clothes rent, and ˢwith earth upon his head.

13 And when he came, lo, Eli sat upon a ᵗseat by the wayside watching: for his heart

trembled for the ark of God. And when the man came into the city, and told *it,* all the city cried out.

A. M. 2863
B. C. 1141
An. Exod. Isr.
350
Anno ante
I. Olymp. 365

14 And when Eli heard the noise of the crying, he said, What *meaneth* the noise of the tumult? And the man came in hastily, and told Eli.

15 Now Eli was ninety and eight years old; and ᵘhis eyes ᵛwere dim, that he could not see.

°Chap. ii. 32; Psa. lxxviii. 61——PChap. ii. 34; Psa. lxxviii. 64——⁹Heb. *died*——ʳ2 Sam. i. 2

ˢJosh. vii. 6; 2 Sam. xiii. 19; xv. 32; Neh. ix. 1; Job ii. 12
ᵗChap. i. 9——ᵘChap. iii. 2——ᵛHeb. *stood*

---

was. "If ye do not fight, and acquit yourselves like men, ye will be servants to the Hebrews, as they have been to you; and you may expect that they will avenge themselves of you for all the cruelty you have exercised towards *them.*"

Verse 11. *Hophni and Phinehas were slain.*] They probably attempted to defend the ark, and lost their lives in the attempt.

Verse 12. *Came to Shiloh the same day*] The field of battle could not have been at any great distance, for this young man reached Shiloh the same evening after the defeat.

With his clothes rent, and with earth upon his head.] These were signs of *sorrow* and *distress* among all nations. The *clothes rent,* signified the *rending, dividing,* and *scattering,* of the *people;* the *earth,* or *ashes on the head,* signified their *humiliation:* "We are brought down to the *dust* of the earth; we are near to our *graves.*" When the Trojan fleet was burnt, Æneas is represented as *tearing his robe from his shoulder,* and invoking the aid of his gods:—

Tum pius Æneas *humeris abscindere vestem,*
Auxilioque vocare Deos, et tendere palmas.
           VIRG. Æn. lib. v., ver. 685.

"The prince then *tore his robes* in deep despair,
Raised high his hands, and thus address'd his prayer."   PITT.

We have a remarkable example in the same poet, where he represents the queen of King Latinus resolving on her own death, when she found that the Trojans had taken the city by storm:—

Purpueros moritura manu *discindit amictus.*
           Æn. lib. xii., ver. 603.

She *tears* with both her hands her *purple vest.*

But the image is complete in King Latinus himself, when he heard of the death of his queen, and saw his city in flames:—

————It *scissa veste* Latinus,
Conjugis attonitus fatis, urbisque ruina,
Canitiem immundo *perfusam pulvere* turpans.
           Ib., ver. 609.

Latinus *tears his garments* as he goes.
Both for his public and his private woes:
With *filth* his venerable beard besmears,
And *sordid dust* deforms his *silver hairs.*
           DRYDEN.

We find the same custom expressed in one line by *Catullus:*—

Canitiem terra, *atque* infuso pulvere fœdans.
      EPITH. *Pelei et Thetidos,* ver. 224.

Dishonouring her *hoary locks* with *earth* and *sprinkled dust.*

The ancient Greeks in their mourning often *shaved off their hair:*—

Τουτο νυ και γερας οιον οἴζυροισι βροτοισι,
Κειρασθαι τε κομην, βαλεειν τ' απο δακρυ παρειων.
      HOM. *Odyss.* lib. iv., ver. 197.

"Let each deplore his dead: the *rites* of wo
Are all, alas! the living can bestow
O'er the congenial dust, enjoin'd to *shear*
The *graceful curl,* and drop the tender tear."
           POPE.

And again:—

Κατθεμεν εν λεχεεσσι καθηραντες χροα καλον
'Υδατι τε λιαρῳ και αλειφατι· πολλα δε σ' αμφις
Δακρυα θερμα χεον Δαναοι, κειροντο τε χαιτας.
      Ib., lib. xxiv., ver. 44.

"Then unguents sweet, and tepid streams, we shed;
Tears flow'd from every eye; and o'er the dead
Each *clipp'd* the *curling honours* of his *head.*"
           POPE.

The whole is strongly expressed in the case of Achilles, when he heard of the death of his friend Patroclus:—

'Ως φατο· τον δ' αχεος νεφελη εκαλυψε μελαινα
Αμφοτερῃσι δε χερσιν ἑλων κονιν αιθαλοεσσαν,
Χευατο κακ κεφαλης, χαριεν δ' ῃσχυνε προσωπον·
Νεκταρεῳ δε χιτωνι μελαιν' αμφιξανε τεφρη.
      Iliad, lib. xviii., ver. 22.

"A sudden horror shot through all the chief,
And wrapp'd his senses in the cloud of grief.
Cast *on the ground,* with furious hands he spread
The *scorching ashes* o'er his *graceful head:*
His *purple garments,* and his *golden hairs.*
Those he deforms with *dust,* and *these* with tears."   POPE.

It is not unusual, even in *Europe,* and in the most *civilized* parts of it, to see grief expressed by *tearing the hair, beating the breasts,* and *rending* the garments; all these are *natural* signs, or expression of deep and excessive grief, and are common to all the nations of the world.

Verse 13. *His heart trembled for the ark of God*] He was a most mild and affectionate father, and yet the safety of the *ark* lay nearer

A. M. 2863
B. C. 1141
An. Exod. Isr. 350
Anno ante
I. Olymp. 365

16 And the man said unto Eli, I *am* he that came out of the army, and I fled to-day out of the army. And he said, ^wWhat ^xis there done, my son?

17 And the messenger answered and said, Is-

rael is fled before the Philistines, and there hath been also a great slaughter among the people, and thy two sons also, Hophni and Phinehas, are dead, and the ark of God is taken.

18 And it came to pass, when he made

A. M. 2863
B. C. 1141
An. Exod. Isr. 350
Anno ante
I. Olymp. 365

^w2 Sam. i. 4

^xHeb. *is the thing*

to his heart than the safety of his *two sons.* Who can help feeling for this aged, venerable man?

Verse 17. *And the messenger answered*] Never was a more afflictive message, containing such a variety of woes, each rising above the preceding, delivered in so few words.

1. *Israel is fled before the Philistines.*

This was a sore evil: that *Israel* should *turn their backs upon their enemies,* was *bad;* and that they should turn their backs on such enemies as the *Philistines,* was yet worse; for now they might expect the chains of their slavery to be strengthened and riveted more closely.

2. *There hath also been a great slaughter among the people.*

A *rout* might have taken place without any *great previous slaughter;* but in this case the field was warmly contested, *thirty thousand* were laid dead on the spot. This was a deeper cause of distress than the preceding; as if he had said, "The flower of our armies is destroyed; scarcely a veteran now to take the field."

3. *Thy two sons also, Hophni and Phinehas, are dead.*

This was still more afflictive to him as a father, to lose *both* his sons, the only hope of the family; and to have them taken away by a *violent death* when there was so little prospect of their having died *in the peace of God,* was more grievous than all.

4. *The ark of God is taken.*

This was the most dreadful of the whole; now Israel is dishonoured in the sight of the heathen, and the name of the Lord will be blasphemed by them. Besides, the capture of the ark shows that God is departed from Israel; and now there is no farther hope of restoration for the people, but every prospect of the destruction of the nation, and the final ruin of all religion! How high does each wo rise on the back of the preceding! And with what apparent *art* is this very laconic message constructed! And yet, probably, no art at all was used, and the messenger delivered the tidings just as the facts rose up in his own mind.

How vapid, diffused, and alliterated, is the report of the messenger in the Persæ of Æschylus, who comes to the queen with the tremendous account of the destruction of the whole naval power of the Persians, at the battle of Salamis? I shall give his first speech, and leave the reader to compare the two accounts.

Ω γης απασης Ασιδος πολισματα,
Ω Περσις αια, και πολυς πλουτου λιμην,
'Ως εν μια πληγη κατεφθαρται πολυς
Ολβος, το Περσων δ' ανθος οιχεται πεσον.
Ωμοι, κακον μεν πρωτον αγγελλειν κακα·
'Ομως δ' αναγχη παν αναπτυξαι παθος
Περσαις, στρατος γαρ πας ολωλε βαρβαρων.

Of which I subjoin the following translation by Mr. Potter:—

Wo to the towns through Asia's peopled realms!
Wo to the land of Persia, once the port
Of boundless wealth! how is thy glorious state
Vanish'd at once, and all thy spreading honours
Fallen, lost! Ah me! unhappy is his task
That bears unhappy tidings; but constraint
Compels me to relate this tale of wo:
Persians! the whole barbaric host is fallen.

This is the sum of his account, which he afterwards details in about a dozen of speeches.

Heroes and conquerors, ancient and modern, have been celebrated for comprising a vast deal of information in a few words. I will give *three* examples, and have no doubt that the Benjamite in the text will be found to have greatly the advantage.

1. *Julius Cæsar* having totally defeated *Pharnaces,* king of *Pontus,* wrote a letter to the Roman senate, which contained only these three words:—

VENI, VIDI, VICI;
I came, I saw, I conquered.

This war was begun and ended in *one day.*

2. *Admiral* HAWKE having totally defeated the French fleet, in 1759, off the coast of Brittany, wrote as follows to King George II.:—

"SIRE, *I have taken, burnt, and destroyed all the French fleet, as per margin.*—HAWKE."

3. NAPOLEON BUONAPARTE, then general-in-chief of the French armies in Italy, wrote to *Josephine,* his wife, the evening before he attacked Field Marshal *Alvinzi,* the imperial general:—

"*Demain j'attaquerai l'enemie; je le battrai; et j'en finirai.*" "*To-morrow I shall attack the enemy; I shall defeat them, and terminate the business.*" He did so: the imperialists were totally defeated, *Mantua* surrendered, and the campaign for that year (1796) was concluded.

In the above examples, excellent as they are in their kind, we find little more than *one idea,* whereas the report of the Benjamite includes *several;* for, in the most forcible manner, he points out the *general* and *particular disasters* of the *day,* the *rout of the army,* the *great slaughter,* the *death of the priests,* who were in effect the whole generals of the army, and the *capture of the ark;* all that, on such an occasion, could affect and distress the heart of an Israelite. And all this he does in *four simple assertions.*

Verse 18. *When he made mention of the ark of God*] Eli bore all the relation till the messenger came to this solemn word; he had *trembled* before *for the ark,* and now, hearing that it was *captured,* he was transfixed with grief, fell down from his seat, and dislocated his neck! Behold the judgments of God! But

A. M. 2863
B. C. 1141
An. Exod. Isr.
350
Anno ante
I. Olymp. 365

mention of the ark of God, that he fell from off the seat backward by the side of the gate, and his neck brake, and he died: for he was an old man, and heavy. ʸAnd he had judged Israel forty years.

19 And his daughter-in-law, Phinehas's wife, was with child, *near* ᶻto be delivered: and when she heard the tidings that the ark of God was taken, and that her father-in-law and her husband were dead, she bowed herself and travailed; for her pains ᵃcame upon her.

20 And about the time of her death, ᵇthe women that stood by her said unto her, Fear not; for thou hast borne a son. But she answered not, ᶜneither did she regard *it*.

A. M. 2863
B. C. 1141
An. Exod. Isr.
350
Anno ante
I. Olymp. 365

21 And she named the child ᵈI-chabod,ᵉ saying, ᶠThe glory is departed from Israel: because the ark of God was taken, and because of her father-in-law and her husband.

22 And she said, The glory is departed from Israel: for the ark of God is taken.

ʸHe seems to have been a judge to do justice only, and that in southwest *Israel*——ᶻOr, *to cry out* ᵃHeb. *were turned*——ᵇGen. xxxv. 17

ᶜHeb. *set not her heart*——ᵈThat is, *where* is *the glory?* or, there is *no glory*——ᵉChapter xiv. 3——ᶠPsalm xxvi. 8; lxxviii. 61

---

shall we say that this man, however remiss in the education of his children, and criminal in his indulgence towards his profligate sons, which arose more from the *easiness* of his disposition than from a desire to encourage vice, is gone to perdition? God forbid! No man ever died with such benevolent and religious feelings, and yet perished.

He had judged Israel forty years] Instead of *forty* years, the Septuagint has here εικοσι ετη, *twenty years*. All the other versions, as well as the Hebrew text, have *forty* years.

Verse 19. *And his daughter-in-law*] This is another very affecting story; the defeat of Israel, the capture of the ark, the death of her father-in-law, and the slaughter of her husband, were more than a woman in her circumstances, near the time of her delivery, could bear. She bowed, travailed, was delivered of a son, gave the child a name indicative of the ruined state of Israel, and expired!

Verse 20. *But she answered not*] She paid no attention to what the women had said concerning her having borne a son; that information she *regarded not*.

Verse 21. *She named the child I-chabod*] The versions are various on the original words

אי כבוד *I-chabod; the Septuagint,* ουαιβαρχαβωθ *ouaibrachaboth;* the Syriac, ܐܝܟܒܘܪ *yochobor;* the Arabic, يوخابله *yochabad.* But none of these give us much light on the subject. It is pretty evident they did not know well what signification to give the name; and we are left to collect its meaning from what she says afterwards, *The glory is departed from Israel;* the words literally mean, *Where is the glory?* And indeed where was it, when the armies of Israel were defeated by the Philistines, the priests slain, the supreme magistrate dead, and the ark of the Lord taken?

THIS is a very eventful, interesting, and affecting chapter, and prepares the reader for those signal manifestations of God's power and providence by which the ark was restored, the priesthood re-established, an immaculate judge given to Israel, the Philistine yoke broken, and the people of the Most High caused once more to triumph. God humbled them that he might exalt them; he suffered his glory for a time to become eclipsed, that he might afterwards cause it to break out with the greater effulgence.

CHAPTER V

The Philistines set up the ark in the temple of Dagon at Ashdod; whose image is found next morning prostrate before it, broken in pieces, 1–5. The Philistines are also smitten with a sore disease, 6. The people of Ashdod refuse to let the ark stay with them; and the lords of the Philistines, with whom they consulted, order it to be carried to Gath, 7, 8. They do so; and God smites the inhabitants of that city, young and old, with the same disease, 9. They send the ark to Ekron, and a heavy destruction falls upon that city, and they resolve to send it back to Shiloh, 10–12.

A. M. 2863
B. C. 1141
An. Exod. Isr.
350
Anno ante
I. Olymp. 365

AND the Philistines took the ark of God, and brought it ᵃfrom Eben-ezer unto Ashdod.

2 When the Philistines took the ark of God, they brought it into the house of ᵇDagon, and set it by Dagon.

A. M. 2863
B. C. 1141
An. Exod. Isr.
350
Anno ante
I. Olymp. 365

3 And when they of Ashdod

ᵃChap. iv. 1; vii. 12

ᵇJudg. xvi. 23

NOTES ON CHAP. V

Verse 1. *Brought it from Eben-ezer unto Ashdod.*] Ashdod or Azotus was one of the five *satrapies* or *lordships* of the Philistines.

Verse 2. *The house of Dagon*] On this idol, which was supposed to be partly in a *human* form, and partly in that of a *fish*, see the note on Judg. xvi. 23. Some think that this idol was the same with *Dirceto, Attergatis,* the

A. M. 2863
B. C. 1141
An. Exod. Isr.
350
Anno ante
I. Olymp. 365

arose early on the morrow, behold, Dagon *was* ᶜfallen upon his face to the earth before the ark of the LORD. And they took Dagon, and ᵈset him in his place again.

4 And when they arose early on the morrow morning, behold, Dagon *was* fallen upon his face to the ground before the ark of the LORD; and ᵉthe head of Dagon, and both the palms of his hands *were* cut off upon the threshold; only ᶠ*the stump of* Dagon was left to him.

5 Therefore neither the priests of Dagon, nor any that come into Dagon's house, ᵍtread on the threshold of Dagon in Ashdod unto this day.

A. M. 2863
B. C. 1141
An. Exod. Isr.
350
Anno ante
I. Olymp. 365

6 But ʰthe hand of the LORD was heavy upon them of Ashdod, and he ⁱdestroyed them, and smote them with ᵏemerods, *even* Ashdod and the coasts thereof.

7 And when the men of Ashdod saw that *it was* so, they said, The ark of the God of Israel

---

ᶜIsa. xix. 1; xlvi. 1, 2——ᵈIsa. xlvi. 7——ᵉJer. l. 2; Ezek. vi. 4, 6; Mic. i. 7——ᶠOr, *the fishy part*——ᵍSee Zeph. i. 9

ʰVer. 7, 11; Exod. ix. 3; Psa. xxxii. 4; Acts xiii. 11 ⁱChap. vi. 5——ᵏDeuteronomy xxviii. 27; Psalm lxxviii. 66

Venus of Askelon, and the *Moon*.—See Calmet's *Dissertation on the gods of the Philistines*.

The *motive* which induced the Philistines to set up the ark in the temple of Dagon, may be easily ascertained. It was customary, in all nations, to dedicate the spoils taken from an enemy to their gods: 1. As a *gratitude-offering* for the help which they supposed them to have furnished; and, 2. As a *proof* that their gods, i. e., the gods of the conquerors, were *more powerful* than those of the conquered. It was, no doubt, to insult the God of Israel, and to insult and terrify his people, that they placed his ark in the temple of Dagon. When the Philistines had conquered Saul, they hung up his armour in the temple of Ashtaroth, chap. xxxi. 10. And when David slew Goliath, he laid up his sword in the tabernacle of the Lord, chap. xxi. 8, 9. We have the remains of this custom in the depositing of colours, standards, &c., taken from an enemy, in our *churches;* but whether this may be called superstition or a religious act, is hard to say. If the *battle* were the *Lord's*, which few battles are, the dedication might be right.

Verse 3. *They of Ashdod arose early on the morrow*] Probably to perform some act of their superstition in the temple of their idol.

Dagon was fallen upon his face] This was one proof, which they little expected, of the *superiority* of the God of Israel.

Set him in his place again.] Supposing his fall might have been merely *accidental*.

Verse 4. *Only the stump of Dagon was left*] Literally, Only רגן *dagon* (i. e., the *little fish*) was left. It has already been remarked that Dagon had the head, arms, and hands of a man or woman, and that the rest of the idol was in the form of a *fish*, to which Horace is supposed to make allusion in the following words:—

Desinat in piscem mulier formosa superne

"The upper part resembling a *beautiful woman;* the lower, a *fish*."

All that was *human* in his form was broken off from what resembled a *fish*. Here was a proof that the affair was not accidental; and these proofs of God's *power* and *authority* prepared the way for his *judgments*.

Verse 5. *Tread on the threshold*] Because the arms, &c., of Dagon were broken off by his fall on the threshold, the threshold became sacred, and neither his priests nor worshippers ever tread on the threshold. Thus it was ordered, in the Divine providence, that, by a re-

ligious custom of their own, they should perpetuate their disgrace, the insufficiency of their worship, and the superiority of the God of Israel.

It is supposed that the idolatrous Isrelites, in the time of *Zephaniah*, had adopted the worship of Dagon: and that in this sense chap. i. 9 is to be understood: *In the same day will I punish all those who leap upon the threshold.* In order to go into such temples, and not tread on the threshold, the people must *step* or *leap over* them; and in this way the above passage may be understood. Indeed, the *thresholds* of the temples in various places were deemed so sacred that the people were accustomed to fall down and *kiss* them. When Christianity became corrupted, this *adoration* of the thresholds of the churches took place.

Verse 6. *Smote them with emerods*] The word עפלים *apholim*, from עפל *aphal*, to be *elevated*, probably means the disease called the *bleeding piles*, which appears to have been accompanied with dysentery, bloody flux, and ulcerated anus.

The Vulgate says, *Et percussit in secretiori parte natium;* "And he smote them in the more secret parts of their posteriors." To this the psalmist is supposed to refer, Psa. lxxviii. 66, *He smote all his enemies in the* HINDER PARTS; *he put them to a perpetual reproach.* Some copies of the *Septuagint* have εξεξεσεν αυτοις εις τας ναυς, "he inflamed them in their ships:" other copies have εις τας εδρας, "in their posteriors." The *Syriac* is the same. The *Arabic* enlarges: "He smote them in their posteriors, so that they were affected with a dysenteria." I suppose them to have been affected with enlargements of the *hæmorrhoidal* veins, from which there came frequent discharges of blood.

The *Septuagint* and *Vulgate* make a very material *addition* to this verse: Και μεσον της χωρας αυτης ανεφυεσιν μυες· και εγενετο συγχυσις θανατου μεγαλη εν τη πολει; *Et ebullierunt villæ et agri in medio regionis illius; et nati sunt mures, et facta est confusio mortis magnæ in civitate:* "And the cities and fields of all that region burst up, and mice were produced, and there was the confusion of a great death in the city." This addition *Houbigant* contends was originally in the Hebrew text; and this gives us the reason why golden *mice* were sent, as well as the images of the emerods, (chap. vi. 4,) when the ark was restored.

Verse 7. *His hand is sore upon us, and upon Dagon our god.*] Here the *end* was completely

A. M. 2863 B. C. 1141 An. Exod. Isr. 350 Anno ante I. Olymp. 365

shall not abide with us: for his
hand is sore upon us, and upon
Dagon our god.
8 They sent therefore and ga-
thered all the lords of the Philistines unto
them, and said, What shall we do with the ark
of the God of Israel? And they answered,
Let the ark of the God of Israel be carried
about unto Gath. And they carried the ark
of the God of Israel about *thither*.
9 And it was *so*, that, after they had carried
it about, [l]the hand of the LORD was against
the city [m]with a very great destruction: and
[n]he smote the men of the city, both small and
great, and they had emerods in their secret
parts.
10 Therefore they sent the ark of God to
Ekron. And it came to pass, as
the ark of God came to Ekron,
that the Ekronites cried out, saying, They have brought about
the ark of the God of Israel to [o]us, to slay us
and our people.
11 So they sent and gathered together
all the lords of the Philistines, and said,
Send away the ark of the God of Israel,
and let it go again to his own place, that
it slay [p]us not, and our people: for there
was a deadly destruction throughout all
the city; [q]the hand of God was very heavy
there.
12 And the men that died not were smitten
with the emerods: and the cry of the city
went up to heaven.

A. M. 2863 B. C. 1141 An. Exod. Isr. 350 Anno ante I. Olymp. 365

---

[l]Deut. ii. 15; chap. vii. 13; xii. 15——[m]Ver. 11——[n]Ver. 6; Psa. lxxviii. 66

[o]Heb. *me, to slay me and my*——[p]Heb. *me not, and my*——[q]Ver. 6, 9

---

answered: they now saw that they had not prevailed against Israel, on account of their god being more *powerful* than *Jehovah;* and they now feel how easily this God can confound and destroy their whole nation.

Verse 8. *The lords of the Philistines*] The word סרני *sarney*, which we translate *lords*, is rendered by the *Chaldee* טורני *tureney*, *tyrants*. The *Syriac* is the same. By the *Vulgate* and *Septuagint*, *satrapæ*, satraps. Palestine was divided into five *satrapies:* Ashdod, Ekron, Askelon, Gath, and Gaza. See Josh. xiii. 8. But these were all federates, and acted under one general government, for which they assembled in council.

Let the ark—be carried about] They probably thought that their affliction rose from some *natural* cause; and therefore they wished the ark to be carried about from place to place, to see what the effects might be. If they found the same evil produced wherever it came, then they must conclude that it was a judgment from the God of Israel.

Verse 9. *The hand of the Lord was against the city*] As it was at *Ashdod*, so it was at *Gath*. The *Vulgate* says, *Et computrescebant prominenter extales eorum;* which conveys the idea of a bloody flux, dysentery, and ulcerated anus; and it adds, what is not to be found in the Hebrew text, nor many of the versions, except some traces in the Septuagint, *Et fecerunt sibi sedes pelliceas*, "And they made unto themselves *seats of skins;*" for the purpose of sitting more easy, on account of the malady already mentioned.

Verse 11. *Send away the ark*] It appears that it had been received at Ekron, for *there was a deadly destruction through the whole city*. They therefore concluded that the ark should be sent back to Shiloh.

Verse 12. *The men that died not*] Some it seems were smitten with *instant death;* others, with the *hæmorrhoids;* and there was a universal consternation; and *the cry of the city went up to heaven*—it was an exceeding great cry.

IT does not appear that the Philistines had any correct knowledge of the nature of Jehovah, though they seemed to acknowledge his *supremacy*. They imagined that every country, district, mountain, and valley, had its peculiar deity; who, in its *place*, was supreme over all others. They thought therefore to appease Jehovah by sending him back his ark or shrine; and, in order to be redeemed from their plagues, they send golden mice and emerods as *telesms*, probably made under some particular configurations of the planets. See at the end of chap. vi.

CHAPTER VI

After the ark had been seven months in the land of the Philistines, they consult their priests and diviners about sending it to Shiloh, 1, 2. *They advise that it be sent back with a trespass-offering of five golden emerods, and five golden mice*, 3–6. *They advise also that it be sent back on a new cart, drawn by two milch kine, from whom their calves shall be tied up; and then conclude that if these cows shall take the way of Beth-shemesh, as going to the Israelitish border, then the* LORD *had afflicted them; if not, then their evils were* accidental, 7–9. *They do as directed; and the kine take the way of Beth-shemesh*, 10–13. *They stop in the field of Joshua; and the men of Beth-shemesh take them, and offer them to the Lord for a burnt-offering, and cleave the wood of the cart to burn them, and make sundry other offerings*, 14, 15. *The offerings of the five lords of the Philistines*, 16–18. *For too curiously looking into the ark, the men of Beth-shemesh are smitten of the Lord*, 19, 20. *They send to the inhabitants of Kirjath-jearim, that they may take away the ark*, 21.

A. M. 2864
B. C. 1140
An. Exod. Isr. 351
Anno ante I. Olymp. 364

AND the ark of the LORD was in the country of the Philistines seven months.

2 And the Philistines [a]called for the priests and the diviners, saying, What shall we do to the ark of the LORD? tell us wherewith we shall send it to his place.

3 And they said, If ye send away the ark of the God of Israel, send it not [b]empty; but in any wise return him [c]a trespass-offering: then ye shall be healed, and it shall [d]be known to you why his hand is not removed from you.

4 Then said they, What *shall be* the trespass-offering which we shall return to him? They answered, Five golden emerods, and five golden mice, [e]*according to* the number of the lords of the Philistines: for one plague *was* on [f]you all, and on your lords.

5 Wherefore ye shall make images of your emerods, and images of your mice that [g]mar the land; and ye shall [h]give glory unto the God of Israel: peradventure he will [i]lighten his hand from off you, and from off [k]your gods, and from off your land.

A. M. 2864
B. C. 1140
An. Exod. Isr. 351
Anno ante I. Olymp. 364

6 Wherefore then do ye harden your hearts, [l]as the Egyptians and Pharaoh hardened their hearts? when he had wrought [m]wonderfully among them, [n]did they not let [o]the people go and they departed?

7 Now therefore make [p]a new cart, and take two milch kine, [q]on which there hath come no yoke, and tie the kine to the cart, and bring their calves home from them:

8 And take the ark of the LORD and lay it upon the cart; and put [r]the jewels of gold, which ye return him *for* a trespass-offering, in a coffer by the side thereof: and send it away, that it may go.

9 And see, if it goeth up by the way of his own coast to [s]Beth-shemesh, *then* [t]he hath

[a]Gen. xli. 8; Exod. vii. 11; Dan. ii. 2; v. 7; Matt. ii. 4 —— [b]Exod. xxiii. 15; Deut. xvi. 16 —— [c]Lev. v. 15, 16 —— [d]Ver. 9 —— [e]See ver. 17, 18; Josh. xiii. 3; Judg. iii. 3 —— [f]Heb. *them* —— [g]Chap. v. 6 —— [h]Josh. vii. 19; Isa. xlii. 12; Mal. ii. 2; John ix. 24

[i]See chap. v. 6, 11; Psa. xxxix. 10 —— [k]Chap. v. 3, 4, 7 —— [l]Exod. vii. 13; viii. 15; xiv. 17 —— [m]Or, *reproachfully* —— [n]Exod. xii. 31 —— [o]Heb. *them* —— [p]2 Sam. vi. 3 —— [q]Num. xix. 2 —— [r]Ver. 4, 5 —— [s]Josh. xv. 10 —— [t]Or, *it*

NOTES ON CHAP. VI

Verse 2. *The diviners*] קסמים *kosemim*, from קסם *kasam*, to *presage* or *prognosticate*. See Deut. xviii. 10. In what their pretended art consisted, we know not.

Verse 3. *Send it not empty*] As it appears ye have *trespassed* against him, send him an offering for this trespass.

Why his hand is not removed] The sense is, If you send him a trespass-offering, and ye be cured, then ye shall know why his judgments have not been taken away from you previously to this offering.

It is a common opinion, says *Calmet*, among all people, that although the Supreme Being needs nothing of his creatures, yet he requires that they should consecrate to him all that they have; for the same argument that proves his independence, infinitude, and self-sufficiency, proves our dependence, and the obligation we are under to acknowledge him by offering him due marks of our gratitude and submission. Such sentiments were common among all people; and God himself commands his people not to appear before him without an offering, Exod. xxiii. 15: *None shall appear before me empty.*

Verse 4. *Five golden emerods, and five golden mice*] *One* for each satrapy. The *emerods* had afflicted their bodies; the *mice* had marred their land. Both, they considered, as sent by God; and, making an image of each, and sending them as a trespass-offering, they acknowledged this. See at the end.

Verse 5. *He will lighten his hand from off you*] The whole land was afflicted; the ground was marred by the *mice* the common people and the lords afflicted by the *hæmorrhoids*, and their gods broken in pieces.

Verse 6. *Wherefore then do ye harden your hearts*] They had heard how God punished the Egyptians, and they are afraid of similar plagues. It appears that they had kept the ark long enough.

Did they not let the people go] And has he not *wrought wonderfully among us?* And should we not send back his ark?

Verse 7. *Make a new cart*] It was indecent and improper to employ in any part of the worship of God any thing that had before served for a *common* purpose. Every thing in the worship of God is said to be *sanctified:* now the general meaning of that word is, *to separate a thing from all earthly and common uses*, and *devote it solely to the service of God.*

When David removed the ark from the house of Abinadab, he put it on a *new* cart, 2 Sam. vi. 3.

Bring their calves home from them] So it appears that their calves had been with them in the fields. This was a complete trial: unless they were supernaturally *influenced*, they would not leave their calves; unless supernaturally *directed*, they would not leave their home, and take a way unguided, which they had never gone before.

Verse 8. *The jewels of gold*] The word כלי *keley*, which our translators so often render *jewels*, signifies *vessels*, *implements*, *ornaments*, &c. A *jewel of gold* has an odd sound to those who always attach the idea of a *precious stone* to the term.

Verse 9. *A chance that happened to us*] The word מקרה *mikreh*, from קרה *karah*, to *meet* or *coalesce*, signifies an event that naturally arises

A. M. 2864
B. C. 1140
An. Exod. Isr. 351
Anno ante
I. Olymp. 364

done us this great evil: but if not, then [u]we shall know that *it is* not his hand *that* smote us; it *was* a chance *that* happened to us.

10 And the men did so; and took two milch kine, and tied them to the cart, and shut up their calves at home:

11 And they laid the ark of the LORD upon the cart, and the coffer with the mice of gold and the images of their emerods.

12 And the kine took the straight way to the way of Beth-shemesh, *and* went along the highway, lowing as they went, and turned not aside *to* the right hand or *to* the left; and the lords of the Philistines went after them unto the border of Beth-shemesh.

13 And *they of* Beth-shemesh *were* reaping their wheat harvest in the valley; and they lifted up their eyes, and saw the ark, and rejoiced to see *it.*

14 And the cart came into the field of Joshua, a Beth-shemite, and stood there, where *there was* a great stone: and they clave the wood of the cart, and offered the kine a burnt-offering unto the LORD.

A. M. 2864
B. C. 1140
An. Exod. Isr. 351
Anno ante
I. Olymp. 364

15 And the Levites took down the ark of the LORD, and the coffer that *was* with it, wherein the jewels of gold *were,* and put *them* on the great stone; and the men of Beth-shemesh offered burnt-offerings and sacrificed sacrifices the same day unto the LORD.

16 And when [v]the five lords of the Philistines had seen *it,* they returned to Ekron the same day.

17 [w]And these *are* the golden emerods which the Philistines returned *for* a trespass-offering unto the LORD; for Ashdod one, for Gaza one, for Askelon one, for Gath one, for Ekron one;

18 And the golden mice, *according to* the number of all the cities of the Philistines *belonging* to the five lords, *both* of fenced cities, and of country villages, even unto the [x]great *stone of* Abel, whereon they set down the ark of the LORD: *which stone remaineth* unto this day in the field of Joshua, the Beth-shemite.

19 And [y]he smote the men of Beth-shemesh

---

[u]Ver. 3——[v]Josh. xiii. 3——[w]Ver. 4——[x]Or, *great stone*

[y]See Exod. xix. 21; Num. iv. 5, 15, 20; 2 Sam. vi. 7

---

from such concurring causes as, in the order and nature of things, must produce it.

Thus a bad state of the atmosphere, putrid exhalations, bad diet, occasioned by any general scarcity, might have produced the disease in question; and to something of this kind they would attribute it, if the other evidences did not concur. This gives us the proper notion of *chance;* and shows us that it is a matter as dependent upon the *Divine* providence, as any thing can be: in short, that these *occurrences* are parts of the *Divine government.*

The word *chance,* though often improperly used to signify such an occurrence as is not under the Divine government, is of itself, not only *simple,* but expressive; and has nearly the meaning of the Hebrew word: it comes from the French *cheoir,* or *escheoir, to fall out, to occur, to fall to.* Hence our law-term *escheat,* any lands that fall to the lord of the manor by forfeiture, or for want of heirs: i. e., these are the *occurrences* which *naturally* throw the lands into the hands of the lord.

Verse 12. *Lowing as they went*] Calling for their calves.

To *the right hand or to the left*] Some think they were placed where two roads met; one going to *Ekron,* the other to *Beth-shemesh.* It is possible that they were put in such circumstances as these for the greater certainty of the affair: to have turned from their own homes, from their calves and known pasture, and to have taken the road to a strange country, must argue supernatural influence.

The lords of the Philistines went after] They were so jealous in this business that they would

trust no eyes but their own. All this was wisely ordered, that there might be the fullest conviction of the *being* and *interposition* of God.

Verse 14. *They clave the wood of the cart*] Both the *cart* and the *cattle* having been thus employed, could no longer be devoted to any secular services; therefore the *cattle* were *sacrificed,* and the *cart* was *broken up* for fuel to consume the sacrifice.

Verse 15. *The Levites took down*] It appears there were some of the tribe of Levi among the people of Beth-shemesh: to them appertained the service of the tabernacle.

Verse 17. *These* are *the golden emerods*] Each of these cities, in what may be called its *corporate capacity,* sent a golden emerod.

Verse 18. *And the golden mice*] The desolation that had been made through the land by these animals had excited a general concern; and it appears from the text, that *all* the cities of the Philistines, as well *fenced* as without *walls,* sent a golden mouse as a trespass-offering.

Remaineth unto this day] Some think the *ark* is intended, which continued on the stone of Abel for some considerable time after it was placed there; and that the memoranda from which this book was afterwards compiled, were made before it was removed: but it is not likely that it remained any time exposed in the open field. Therefore it is most natural to suppose that it is the *stone of Abel* which is here intended; and so our translators have understood the place, and have used supplementary words to express this sentiment: "Which *stone remaineth* unto this day."

Verse 19. *He smote of the people fifty thou*

A. M. 2864
B. C. 1140
An. Exod. Isr. 351
Anno ante
I. Olymp. 364

because they had looked into the ark of the LORD, even he smote of the people fifty thousand and threescore and ten men: and the people lamented because the LORD had smitten *many* of the people with a great slaughter.

20 And the men of Beth-shemesh said, [z]Who is able to stand before this holy LORD God? and to whom shall he go up from us?

A. M. 2864
B. C. 1140
An. Exod. Isr 351
Anno ante
I. Olymp. 364

21 And they sent messengers to the inhabitants of [a]Kirjath-jearim, saying, The Philistines have brought again the ark of the LORD; come ye down, *and* fetch it up to you.

---

[z]2 Sam. vi. 9; Mal. iii. 2

[a]Josh. xviii. 14; Judg. xviii. 12; 1 Chron. xiii. 5, 6

---

sand and threescore and ten men] The present Hebrew text of this most extraordinary reading stands thus: ויך באנשי בית־שמש—ויך בעם שבעים איש חמשים אלף איש *vaiyach beanshey Beith-shemesh—vaiyach baam shibim ish, chamish-shim eleph ish;* "And he smote among the men of Beth-shemesh, (because they looked into the ark of Jehovah,) and he smote among the people SEVENTY men, FIFTY THOUSAND *men*."

From the manner in which the text stands, and from the great improbability of the thing, it is most likely that there is a corruption in this text, or that some explanatory word is lost, or that the number *fifty thousand* has been added by ignorance or design; it being very improbable that such a small village as Beth-shemesh should *contain* or be *capable* of *employing fifty thousand* and *seventy* men in the fields at wheat harvest, much less that they could all peep into the ark on the stone of Abel, in the corn-field of Joshua.

That the words are not naturally connected in the Hebrew text, is evident; and they do not stand better in the *versions.*

1. The VULGATE renders it thus:—*Et percussit de populo* SEPTUAGINTA *viros; et* QUINQUAGINTA MILLIA *plebis;* "And he smote of the (chief) people SEVENTY men, and FIFTY THOUSAND of the (common) people." This distinction, I suppose, St. Jerome intended between *plebis* and *populus;* which he might think was warranted by the אנשים *anashim,* and איש *ish,* of the Hebrew text.

2. The TARGUM of *Jonathan* is something similar to the *Vulgate:*—"And he smote בסבי besabey amma, of the *elders* of the people SEVENTY men; ובקהלא *ubekahala,* and of the *congregation* FIFTY THOUSAND men."

3. The SEPTUAGINT follow the Hebrew text: Καὶ ἐπάταξεν ἐν αὐτοῖς ἑβδομήκοντα ἄνδρας, καὶ πεντήκοντα χιλιάδας ἀνδρῶν; "And he smote of them SEVENTY men; and FIFTY THOUSAND men." Ἐκ τοῦ λαοῦ, *of the people,* is added by some copies.

4. The SYRIAC has *forty-five thousand* less!

It is as follows: ܘܡܚܐ ܡܪܝܐ ܒܥܡܐ ܚܡܫܐ ܐܠܦܝܢ ܘܫܒܥܝܢ ܓܒܪܝܢ *wamacho Morio beamo chamesho alapin weshabein gabrin;* "And the Lord smote among the people FIVE *thousand* and SEVENTY men."

5. The ARABIC is nearly similar: "*And the* LORD *smote among the people; and there died of* them خمسة الف وسبعون FIVE *thousand* and SEVENTY men."

We have no other *versions* from which we can receive any farther light.

6. JOSEPHUS is different from all the rest, and has *fifty thousand* less, for he renders the place thus, *Antiq. Jud.* libe. vi., cap. i., sect. 4: Ὀργὴ δὲ καὶ χόλος τοῦ Θεοῦ μέτεισιν, ὥστε ἑβδομήκοντα τῶν ἐκ τῆς Βηθσαμῆς κωμῆς—βαλὼν ἀπέκτεινεν; "But the displeasure and wrath of God pursued them so, that SEVENTY *men* of the village of Beth-shemesh, approaching the ark, which they were not worthy to touch, (not being priests,) were struck with lightning." Here we find the whole *fifty thousand* is omitted.

7. *Rabbi Solomon Jarchi,* giving the opinion of other rabbins as well as his own, says, "Our rabbins say SEVENTY *men,* and each of them was worth *fifty thousand* men; or *fifty thousand,* every one of whom was worth the seventy of the Sanhedrin." This only shows embarrassment, but gives very little light.

All these discordances, together with the utter improbability of the thing, lead us to suppose there must be a corruption in this place, either by *adding* or *omitting.*

Dr. *Kennicott* has found *three* very reputable MSS. in which the words חמשים אלף איש *chamishshim eleph ish, fifty thousand men,* are wanting. The 1st, No. 84, a MS. from *Holland;* the 2d, No. 210, one of the *Parisian MSS.;* the 3d, No. 418, a MS. belonging to *Milan;* all three written about the beginning of the *twelfth* century, and numbered as above in Dr. K's Bible.

Perhaps the omission in these MSS. was occasioned by a mistake of the transcriber, which might have easily happened, because of the word איש *ish,* which occurs both after שבעים *shibim* and after אלף *eleph;* for, having written the *first,* and taking his eye off, when he recommenced he might have supposed he had written the latter, and so proceed, leaving the words in question *out* of his copy. Two, *three,* or *more* persons might have been thus deceived, and so produce the above MSS.; or the mistake once made, all the MSS. copied from that would show the same omission. The common reading may be defended, if we only suppose the *omission* of a single letter, the particle of *comparison* כ *ke,* like, as, or equal to, before the word חמשים *chamishshim:* thus בחמשים *kechamishshim;* the passage would then read: "And he smote of the people SEVENTY men, *equal to* FIFTY THOUSAND men;" that is, they were the *elders* or *governors* of the people.

Some solve the difficulty by translating, "He slew SEVENTY men OUT OF *fifty thousand* men." There are various *other* methods invented by learned men to remove this difficulty, which I shall not stop to examine; all, however, issue in this point, that only SEVENTY MEN were slain; and this is, without doubt the most probable. The FIFTY THOUSAND, therefore, must be an *in-*

terpolation, or be understood in some such way as that mentioned above. But the omission of the particle of *similitude* solves every difficulty; and this would account for the reading in *Josephus*, who in his recital would naturally leave out such an explanation of the *worth* of the *seventy* men, as his Roman readers could not easily comprehend such *comparisons*.

With a great slaughter.] *Seventy* men slain, out of an inconsiderable village in a harvest day, was certainly a *great slaughter*.

Verse 20. *Who is able to stand*] Why this exclamation? They knew that God had forbidden any to touch his ark but the priests and Levites; but they endeavoured to throw that blame on God, as a Being *hard to be pleased*, which belonged solely to themselves.

Verse 21. *To the inhabitants of Kirjath-jearim*] They wished the ark away out of their village, but *why* they sent to this city instead of sending to *Shiloh*, does not appear: probably Shiloh had been destroyed by the Philistines, after the late defeat of Israel. This is most likely, as the ark was never more taken back to that place.

It was a very ancient usage, when a plague or other calamity infested a country, city, &c., for the magicians to form an *image* of the *destroyer*, or of the *things* on which the plague particularly rested, in gold, silver, ivory, wax, clay, &c., under certain configurations of the heavens; and to set this up in some proper place, that the evils thus represented might be driven away. These consecrated images were the same that are called *talismans*, or rather *telesms*, among the Asiatics. Mr. Locke calls the diviners *talismans*, but this is a mistake; the *image*, not the *fabricator*, was called by this name.

I have seen several of these *talismans*, of different countries; and such images were probably the origin of all the forms of gods which, in after times, were the objects of religious worship. It is well known that Ireland is not infested with any venomous creature; no serpent of any kind is found in it:—

"No poison there infects, no scaly snake
Lurks in the grass, nor toads annoy the lake."

This has been attributed to a *telesm*, formed with certain rites under the sign *Scorpio*. Such opinions have been drawn from very ancient pagan sources: e. g.: A stone engraved with the figure of a *scorpion*, while the *moon* is in the sign *Scorpio*, is said to cure those who are stung by this animal. *Apollonius Tyaneus* is said to have prevented *flies* from infesting Antioch, and *storks* from appearing in Byzantium, by figures of those animals formed under certain constellations. A *brazen scorpion*, placed on a pillar in the city of *Antioch*, is said to have expelled all such animals from that country. And a *crocodile* of lead is also said to have preserved *Cairo* from the depredations of those monsters. See *Calmet*.

Virgil refers to this custom, Eclogue viii., ver. 80, where he represents a person making two images or *telesms*, one of *wax*, another of *clay*, which were to represent an absent person, who was to be alternately *softened* or *hardened*, as the *wax* or *clay* image was exposed to the fire:—

Limus ut hic durescit, et hæc ut cera liquescit
Uno et eodem igni: sic nostro Daphnis amore.

"As this clay hardens, and this wax softens, by one and the same fire, so may Daphnis by my love."

This thought is borrowed from *Theocritus*, Idyl. ii., ver. 28.

A beautiful marble figure of *Osiris*, about four inches and a quarter high, now stands before me, entirely covered with *hieroglyphics*; he is *standing*, and holds in each hand a *scorpion* and a *snake* by the tails, and with each foot he stands on the neck of a *crocodile*. This I have no doubt was a *telesm*, formed under some peculiar *configuration* of the heavens, intended to drive away both scorpions and crocodiles. This image is of the highest antiquity, and was formed probably long before the Christian era.

Tavernier observes that something like what is mentioned in the text is practised among the Indians; for when a pilgrim goes to one of the idol temples for a cure, he brings the *figure* of the *member* affected, made either of *gold, silver,* or *copper*, according to his circumstances, which he offers to his god. This custom was common among the heathens, and they consecrated to their gods the *monuments* of their deliverance. From heathenism it was adopted by *corrupt Christianity*; and *Theodoret* informs us that in his time there might be seen about the tombs of the martyrs figures of *eyes, hands, feet,* and other parts of the body, which represented those of the offerers which they supposed had been healed by the intercession of those holy persons! This degrading superstition is continued among the papists to the present day: I have seen at *St. Winifred's well*, in *Holywell*, Flintshire, several *staves, crutches,* and *handbarrows*, hung up in different places, which were reported to be the votive offerings of the maimed, the halt, the withered, &c., who had received their cure by the virtue of the saint! It is true the crutches are such as no man or woman could ever walk with; and the *barrows* are such as most evidently never carried any human being. But they serve the purpose of superstition, and keep up an idolatrous reverence for the well and the legendary virgin.

After all, I need not say that the system of judicial astrology is vain, unfounded, absurd, and wicked. It in effect presumes to take the government of the world out of the hand of an all-wise God, and to abandon it to the most fortuitous and unconnected occurrences of life; for the stars have their influences according to this pretended science, conformably to the occurrences here below: e. g., if a child be born but one hour sooner or later than a particular configuration of the heavens, his destiny will be widely different from what it otherwise would have been; and as an almost infinite number of casualties may accelerate or retard a birth, consequently the whole destiny of man is influenced and ruled by these casualties: to say nothing of the absurdity, that those omnipotent stars ever can affect the infant while invested with a thin covering of flesh in the womb of its parent. But the whole science is a tissue of absurdities.

CHAPTER VII

The men of Kirjath-jearim bring the ark from Beth-shemesh, and consecrate Eleazar, the son of Abinadab, to keep it; and there it continued twenty years, 1, 2. Samuel reproves and exhorts the people, and gathers them together at Mizpeh, where they fast and pray, and confess their sins, 3–6. The Philistines go up against them; the Israelites cry unto the Lord for help; Samuel offers sacrifices; and the Lord confounds the Philistines with thunder; Israel discomfits and pursues them to Beth-car, 7–11. Samuel erects a stone for a memorial, and calls it Eben-ezer, 12. The Philistines are totally subdued, and Israel recovers all its lost cities, 13, 14. Samuel acts as an itinerant judge in Israel, 15–17.

A. M. 2864
B. C. 1140
An. Exod. Isr.
351
Anno ante
I. Olymp. 364

AND the men of ^aKirjath-jearim came, and fetched up the ark of the Lord, and brought it into the house of ^bAbinadab in the hill, and sanctified Eleazar his son to keep the ark of the Lord.

2 And it came to pass, while the ark abode in Kirjath-jearim, that the time was long; for it was twenty years: and all the house of Israel lamented after the Lord.

A. M. 2884
B. C. 1120
An. Exod. Isr.
371
Anno ante
I. Olymp. 344

3 And Samuel spake unto all the house of Israel, saying, If ye do ^creturn unto the Lord with all your hearts, *then* ^dput away the strange gods and ^eAshtaroth from among you, and ^fprepare your hearts unto the Lord, and ^gserve him only; and he will deliver you out of the hand of the Philistines.

A. M. 2884
B. C. 1120
An. Exod. Isr.
371
Anno ante
I. Olymp. 344

4 Then the children of Israel did put away ^hBaalim and Ashtaroth, and served the Lord only.

5 And Samuel said, ⁱGather all Israel to Mizpeh, and I will pray for you unto the Lord.

6 And they gathered together to Mizpeh, ^kand drew water, and poured *it* out before the Lord, and ^lfasted on that day, and said

---

^aChap. vi. 21; Psa. cxxxii. 6——^b2 Sam. vi. 4
^cDeut. xxx. 2–10; 1 Kings viii. 48; Isa. lv. 7; Hos. vi. 1;
Joel ii. 12——^dGen. xxxv. 2; Josh. xxiv. 14, 23
^eJudg. ii. 13——^f2 Chron. xxx. 19; Job. xi. 13, 14

^gDeut. vi. 13; x. 20; xiii. 4; Matthew iv. 10; Luke
iv. 8——^hJudg. ii. 11——ⁱJudg. xx. 1; 2 Kings xxv. 23
^k2 Samuel xiv. 14——^lNeh. ix. 1, 2; Dan. ix. 3, 4, 5;
Joel ii. 12

NOTES ON CHAP. VII

Verse 1. *Fetched up the ark*] When these people received the message of the Beth-shemites, they probably consulted Samuel, with whom was the counsel of the Lord, and he had encouraged them to go and bring it up, else they might have expected such destruction as happened to the Beth-shemites.

Sanctified Eleazar] Perhaps this sanctifying signifies no more than *setting* this man *apart*, simply to take care of the ark.

Verse 2. *It was twenty years*] This chapter contains the transactions of at least *twenty* years, but we know not the date of each event.

Verse 3. *And Samuel spake*] We have heard nothing of this judge since he served in the tabernacle. He was now grown up, and established for a prophet in the land of Israel.

If ye do return] From your backsliding and idolatry.

With all your hearts] For outward services and professions will avail nothing.

Put away the strange gods] Destroy their *images, altars,* and *groves:* they are *strange;* you do not know them as *helpers, saviours,* or *defenders.*

Prepare your hearts] Let your hearts be *straight* and *steady.*

And serve him only] Have no other religious service but his, and *obey* his laws.

He will deliver you] Vain are your own exertions; he will deliver you in such a way as to show that the excellence of the power is of himself alone.

Verse 4. *Put away Baalim and Ashtaroth*] These were not two *particular deities,* but two *genera* of idols; the one *masculine,* Baalim; the other *feminine,* Ashtaroth; both the words are in the *plural* number, and signify all their *gods* and *goddesses.*

Verse 5. *Gather all Israel to Mizpeh*] This appears to have been an *armed* assembly, though probably collected principally for religious and political purposes; but Samuel knew that an *unarmed* multitude could not safely be convened in the vicinity of the Philistines.

Verse 6. *Drew water, and poured it out*] It is not easy to know what is meant by this; it is true that *pouring out water,* in the way of *libation,* was a religious ordinance among the *Hebrews,* (Isa. xii. 3,) and among most other nations, particularly the *Greeks* and *Romans,* who used, not only *water,* but *wine, milk, honey,* and *blood,* as we find by Homer, Virgil, Euripides, Sophocles, Porphyry, and Lucian. Our Lord seems to allude to this ceremony, John vii. 37, 38, where see the note.

The *Chaldee Paraphrast* understands the place differently, for he translates: "And they *poured out their hearts* in *penitence, as* waters, before the Lord." That deep penitential sorrow was represented under the notion of *pouring out water,* we have a direct proof in the case of David, who says, Psa. xxii. 14, *I am* poured out like water, *my heart is like* wax; *it is* melted *in the midst of my bowels.* And to repentance, under this very similitude, the prophet exhorts fallen Jerusalem: *Arise, cry out in the night; in the beginning of the watches* pour out *thine* heart like water *before the face of the Lord;* Lam. ii. 19. David uses the same image, Psa. lxii. 8: *Trust in him at all times, ye people;* pour out *your hearts before him.* The same

A. M. 2884
B. C. 1120
An. Exod. Isr. 371
Anno ante
I. Olymp. 344

there, [m]We have sinned against the LORD. And Samuel [n]judged the children of Israel in Mizpeh.

7 And when the Philistines heard that the children of Israel were gathered together to Mizpeh, the lords of the Philistines went up against Israel. And when the children of Israel heard *it,* they were afraid of the Philistines.

8 And the children of Israel said to Samuel, [o]Cease [p]not to cry unto the LORD our God for us, that he will save us out of the hand of the Philistines.

9 [q]And Samuel took a sucking lamb, and offered *it for* a burnt-offering wholly unto the LORD: and [r]Samuel cried unto the LORD for Israel; and the LORD [s]heard him.

10 And as Samuel was offering up the burnt-offering, the Philistines drew near to battle against Israel: [t]but the LORD thundered with a great thunder on that day upon the Philis-

tines, and discomfited them; and they were smitten before Israel.

A. M. 2884
B. C. 1120
An. Exod. Isr. 371
Anno ante
I. Olymp. 344

11 And the men of Israel went out of Mizpeh, and pursued the Philistines, and smote them, until *they came* under Beth-car.

12 Then Samuel [u]took a stone, and set *it* between Mizpeh and Shen, and called the name of it [v]Eben-ezer, saying, Hitherto hath the LORD helped us.

13 [w]So the Philistines were subdued, and they [x]came no more into the coast of Israel: and the hand of the LORD was against the Philistines all the days of Samuel.

14 And the cities which the Philistines had taken from Israel were restored to Israel, from Ekron even unto Gath; and the coasts thereof did Israel deliver out of the hands of the Philistines. And there was peace between Israel and the Amorites.

15 And Samuel [y]judged Israel all the days of his life.

---

[m]Judges x. 10; 1 Kings viii. 47; Psalm cvi. 6 [n]Ecclus. xlvi. 14——[o]Hebrew, *Be not silent from us from crying*——[p]Isa. xxxvii. 4——[q]Ecclus. xlvi. 16——[r]Psalm xcix. 6; Jer. xv. 1——[s]Or, *answered*

[t]See Josh. x. 10; Judg. iv. 15; v. 20; chap. ii. 10; 2 Sam. xxii. 14, 15; Ecclus. xlvi. 17——[u]Gen. xxviii. 18; xxxi. 45; xxxv. 14; Josh. iv. 9; xxiv. 26——[v]That is, *The stone of help;* chap. iv. 1——[w]Judg. xiii. 1——[x]Chap. xiii. 5——[y]Ver. 6; chap. xii. 11; Judg. ii. 16

---

figure is used by *Hannah* in chap. i. 15 of this book; *I am a woman of a sorrowful spirit; I have* POURED OUT *my soul before the Lord.* Perhaps the *drawing* and *pouring out* of *water* mentioned in the text was done *emblematically,* to represent the *contrition* of their hearts.

And Samuel judged] He gave them ordinances, heard and redressed grievances, and taught them how to get reconciled to God. The assembly, therefore, was held for religio-politico-military purposes.

Verse 7. *The Philistines went up against Israel*] They went to give them battle before that, by continual accessions of numbers, they should become too powerful.

Verse 8. *Cease not to cry unto the Lord*] They had strong confidence in the intercession of Samuel, because they knew he was a holy man of God.

Verse 9. *Samuel took a sucking lamb*] This sucking lamb must have been *eight days under its mother* before it could be offered, as the law says, Lev. xxii. 27.

Though Samuel was not a *priest,* yet he offered this sacrifice; or he might have ordered *Eleazar* to offer it, and still be said to have done it himself: *Qui facit per alterum, facit per se;* "He who *procures* a thing to be done, may be said to *do* it *himself."*

His not sacrificing at the *tabernacle* was justified by the necessity of the case; neither tabernacle nor ark was at hand.

Verse 10. *The Lord thundered with a great thunder*] Literally, *The Lord thundered with*

a great voice—he confounded them with a mighty tempest of thunder and lightning, and no doubt slew many by the lightning.

Verse 11. *Under Beth-car.*] We know not where this place was; the *Septuagint* have *Beth-chor;* the *Targum, Beth-saron;* and the *Syriac* and *Arabic, Beth-jasan.*

Verse 12. *Called the name of it Eben-ezer*] אבן העזר *Eben haezer,* "The Stone of Help;" perhaps a *pillar* is meant by the word *stone.*

Verse 13. *They came no more into the coast of Israel*] Perhaps a more signal victory was never gained by Israel; the Lord had brought them low, almost to extermination; and now, by his miraculous interference, he lifts them completely up, and humbles to the dust their proud oppressors. God often suffers nations and individuals to be brought to the lowest extremity, that he may show his mercy and goodness by suddenly rescuing them from destruction, when all *human* help has most evidently failed.

Verse 14. *The cities which the Philistines had taken*] We are not informed of the particulars of these reprisals, but we may rest assured all this was not done in one day: perhaps the *retaking* of the cities was by slow degrees, through the space of several years.

There was peace between Israel and the Amorites.] That is, all the remaining Canaanites kept quiet, and did not attempt to molest the Israelites, when they found the Philistines, the most powerful of the ancient inhabitants of the land, broken and subdued before them.

Verse 15. *Samuel judged Israel all the days*

A.M.2873-2947
B.C. 1131-1057
Anno ante
I. Olymp.
355-281

16 And he went from year to year in ᶻcircuit to Beth-el, and Gilgal, and Mizpeh, and judged Israel in all those places.

17 And ᵃhis return *was* to Ramah; for there *was* his house; and there he judged Israel; and there he ᵇbuilt an altar unto the LORD.

A.M.2873-2947
B.C. 1131-1057
Anno ante
I. Olymp.
355-281

ᶻHeb. *and he circuited*

ᵃChap. viii. 4——ᵇJudg. xxi. 4

---

of his life.] Samuel is supposed to have lived *one hundred* years; he did not begin to judge Israel till he was about *forty* years of age; and if he was *one hundred* years of age when he died, he must have been a judge *sixty* years, and consequently filled that office during the whole of Saul's reign. But that he had been dead before Saul's last battle, is evident from the transactions of that king with the witch of Endor, and probably not long before. Samuel was the *prophet* of that time; declared the will of the Lord, and frequently directed both the *civil* and *military* transactions of the kingdom. Samuel seems, in many respects, to have been considered the *governor of the people,* while Saul was only looked on as the *general of the armies.*

Verse 16. *He went from year to year in circuit*] When he was at BETH-EL, the tribe of Ephraim, and all the northern parts of the country, could attend him; when at GILGAL, the tribe of Benjamin, and those beyond Jordan, might have easy access to him; and when at MIZPEH, he was within reach of Judah, Simeon, and Gad; but *Ramah* was the place of his ordinary abode; and there he held his court, for *there* he *judged Israel;* and, as it is probable that *Shiloh* was destroyed, it is said, ver. 17, that *there* (viz., at Ramah) *he built an altar unto the Lord.* This altar, being duly consecrated, the worship performed at it was strictly legal.

Ramah, which is said to be about six miles from Jerusalem, was the *seat of prophecy* during the life of Samuel; and there it is probable all Israel came to consult him on matters of a spiritual nature, as *there* was the only *altar* of God in the land of Israel.

CHAPTER VIII

Samuel, grown old, makes his sons judges in Beer-sheba, 1, 2. They pervert judgment; and the people complain, and desire a king, 3–5. Samuel is displeased, and inquires of the Lord, 6. The Lord is also displeased; but directs Samuel to appoint them a king, and to show them solemnly the consequences of their choice, 7–9. Samuel does so; and shows them what they may expect from an absolute monarch, and how afflicted they should be under his administration, 10–18. The people refuse to recede from their demand; and Samuel lays the matter before the Lord, and dismisses them, 19–22.

A. M. 2892
B. C. 1112
An. Exod. Isr.
379
Anno ante
I. Olymp. 336

AND it came to pass, when Samuel was old, that he ᵃmade his sons ᵇjudges over Israel.

2 Now the name of his first-born was ᶜJoel; and the name of his second, Abiah: *they were* judges in Beer-sheba.

3 And his sons ᵈwalked not in his ways, but turned aside ᵉafter lucre, and ᶠtook bribes, and perverted judgment.

4 Then all the elders of Israel gathered themselves together, and came to Samuel unto Ramah,

A. M. 2982
B. C. 1112
An. Exod. Isr.
379
Anno ante
I. Olymp. 336

ᵃDeut. xvi. 18; 2 Chron. xix. 5——ᵇSee Judg. x. 4; xii. 14, compared with Judg. v. 10——ᶜ*Vashni,* 1

Chron. vi. 28——ᵈJer. xxii. 15, 16, 17——ᵉExod. xviii. 21; 1 Tim. iii. 3; vi. 10——ᶠDeut. xvi. 19; Psa. xv. 5

NOTES ON CHAP. VIII

Verse 1. *When Samuel was old*] Supposed to be about *sixty.*

He made his sons judges] He appointed them as his lieutenants to superintend certain affairs in Beer-sheba, which he could not conveniently attend to himself. But they were never *judges* in the proper sense of the word; Samuel was the last judge in Israel, and he judged it to the day of his death. See chap. vii. 15.

Verse 3. *His sons walked not in his ways*] Their iniquity is pointed out in *three* words: 1. *They turned aside after lucre;* the original (בצע *batsa*) signifies to *cut, clip, break off;* and therefore Mr. Parkhurst thinks that it means nearly the same with our *clipping of coin.* It however expresses here the idea of *avarice,* of *getting money by hook or by crook.* The Tar-

gum says, "They looked after ממון דשקר *mamon dishkar, the mammon of unrighteousness;*" of which they did not make unto themselves *friends* but *enemies;* see the note on Matt. vi. 24. 2. *They took bribes;* שחד *shochad, gifts* or *presents,* to blind their eyes. 3. *They perverted judgment*—they *turned judgment aside;* they put it out of its *regular path;* they *sold* it to the highest bidder: thus the wicked rich man had his cause, and the poor man was oppressed and deprived of his right. This was the custom in our own country before MAGNA CHARTA was obtained; he that would speed in the *king's court* must *bribe* all the *officers,* and fee both the *king* and *queen!* I have found in our ancient records the most barefaced and shameful examples of this kind; but it was totally abolished, *invito rege,* by that provision in the above charter which states, *Nulli vendemus,*

A. M. 2909 B. C. 1095 An. Exod. Isr. 396 Anno ante I. Olymp. 319

5 And said unto him, Behold, thou art old, and thy sons walk not in thy ways: now [g]make us a king to judge us like all the nations.

6 But the thing [h]displeased Samuel, when they said, Give us a king to judge us. And Samuel prayed unto the LORD.

7 And the LORD said unto Samuel, Hearken unto the voice of the people in all that they say unto thee: for [i]they have not rejected thee, but [k]they have rejected me, that I should not reign over them.

8 According to all the works which they have done since the day that I brought them up out of Egypt, even unto this day, wherewith they have forsaken me, and served other gods, so do they also unto thee.

9 Now therefore [l]hearken unto their voice: [m]howbeit yet protest solemnly unto them, and [n]show them the manner of the king that shall reign over them.

10 And Samuel told all the words of the Lord unto the people that asked of him a king.

11 And he said, [o]This will be the manner of the king that shall reign over you: [p]He will take your sons, and appoint *them* for himself, for his chariots, and *to be* his horsemen; and *some* shall run before his chariots.

A. M. 2909 B. C. 1095 An. Exod. Isr. 396 Anno ante I. Olymp. 319

12 And he will appoint him captains over thousands, and captains over fifties; and *will set them* to ear his ground, and to reap his harvest, and to make his instruments of war, and instruments of his chariots.

13 And he will take your daughters *to be* confectionaries, and *to be* cooks, and *to be* bakers.

14 And [q]he will take your fields and your vineyards, and your oliveyards, *even* the best *of them,* and give *them* to his servants.

15 And he will take the tenth of your seed, and of your vineyards, and give to his [r]officers, and to his servants.

16 And he will take your men-servants, and your maid-servants, and your goodliest young men, and your asses, and put *them* to his work.

17 He will take the tenth of your sheep: and ye shall be his servants.

18 And ye shall cry out in that day because of your king which ye shall have chosen you;

---

[g]Ver. 19, 20; Deut. xvii. 14; Hos. xiii. 10; Acts xiii. 21——[h]Heb. *was evil in the eyes of Samuel*——[i]See Exodus xvi. 8——[k]Chap. x. 19; xii. 17, 19; Hos. xiii. 10, 11——[l]Or, *obey*——[m]Or, *notwithstanding when thou hast solemnly protested against them, then thou shalt show,* &c.——[n]Ver. 11——[o]See Deut. xvii. 16, &c.; chap. x. 25——[p]Chap. xiv. 52——[q]1 Kings xxi. 7; see Ezek. xlvi. 18——[r]Heb. *eunuchs;* Gen. xxxvii. 36

---

nulli negabimus aut differemus rectum aut judicium; "To no man will we sell, to no man will we deny or defer, justice and right." It was customary in those inauspicious times, for judgment to be *delayed in banco regis*, in the king's court, as long as there was any hope that *more money* would be paid in order to bring it to *issue.* And there were cases, where the king did not like the party, in which he *denied justice* and *judgment* entirely! *Magna Charta* brought them to book, and brought the subject to his right.

Of those times it might well be said, as Homer did, Iliad xvi., ver. 387.

Οἱ βιῃ ειν αγορῃ σκολιας κρινωσι θεμιστας,
Εκ δε δικην ελασωσι, θεων οπιν ουκ αλεγοντες.

"When guilty mortals break the eternal laws,
Or judges, bribed, betray the righteous cause."

"When the laws are perverted by force; when justice is expelled from her seat; when judges are swayed from the right, regardless of the vengeance of Heaven." Or, in other words, these were times in which the streams of justice were poisoned in their source, and judges neither feared God nor regarded man.

Verse 5. *Make us a king*] Hitherto, from the time in which they were a people, the Israelites were under a *theocracy*, they had no other king but GOD. Now they desire to have a king like the other nations around them, who may be their general in battle; for this is the point at which they principally aim.

Verse 6. *The thing displeased Samuel*] Because he saw that this amounted to a formal renunciation of the Divine government.

Samuel prayed unto the Lord] He begged to know his mind in this important business.

Verse 7. *They have rejected me*] They wish to put that government in the hands of a *mortal*, which was always in the hands of their GOD. But *hearken unto their voice*—grant them what they request. So we find God grants that in his *displeasure* which he withholds in his *mercy.*

Verse 9. *Show them the manner of the king*] The word משפט *mishpat*, which we here render *manner*, signifies simply what the king would and might require, according to the *manner* in which kings in general ruled; all of whom, in those times, were *absolute* and *despotic.*

The whole of this *manner of the king* is well illustrated by Puffendorf. "Hitherto," says he, "the people of Israel had lived under governors raised up of God, who had exacted no tribute of them, nor put them to any charge; but, little content with this form of government, they de-

A. M. 2909
B. C. 1095
An. Exod. Isr. 396
Anno ante
I. Olymp. 319

and the LORD ᵍwill not hear you in that day.

19 Nevertheless the people ᵗrefused to obey the voice of Samuel; and they said, Nay; but we will have a king over us;

20 That we also may be ᵘlike all the nations; and that our king may judge us, and go out before us, and fight our battles.

ᵍProv. i. 25, 26, 27, 28; Isa. i. 15; Mic. iii. 4

21 And Samuel heard all the words of the people, and he rehearsed them in the ears of the LORD.

A. M. 2909
B. C. 1095
An. Exod. Isr. 396
Anno ante
I. Olymp. 319

22 And the LORD said to Samuel, ᵛHearken unto their voice, and make them a king. And Samuel said unto the men of Israel, Go ye every man unto his city.

ᵗJer. xliv. 16——ᵘVer. 5——ᵛVer. 7; Hos. xiii. 11

sire to have *a king like other nations*, who should live in magnificence and pomp, keep *armies*, and be able to resist any invasion. Samuel informs them what it was they desired; that when they understood it, they might consider whether they would persist in their choice. If they would have a king splendidly attended, he tells them that he *would take their sons for his chariots*, &c.; if they would have him keep up constant *forces*, then he would appoint them for *colonels* and *captains*, and employ those in his *wars* who were accustomed to follow their family business; and since, after the *manner* of other kings, he must keep a *stately court*, they must be content that their *daughters* should serve in several offices, which the king would think below the dignity of his wives and daughters, ver. 13. Many ministers also, in several departments, both of war and peace, must have *salaries* to support them, which must be paid out of their *fields* and *vineyards*, ver. 14. In one word, that to sustain his dignity their king would exact the *tenth* of all they possessed, and be maintained in a royal manner out of their estates."

It is perfectly vain in *Grotius*, or any one else, to state that this shows what a king, as king, *may* any where in virtue of his *office*, claim and *exact;* and that he can take the *property* and *persons* of his subjects, and dispose of them as *he may judge necessary* for the exigence of the state. This was the *manner* of *Saul*, but Saul was not a king of *God's choosing:* "He gave him in his wrath, and took him away in his displeasure;" and the *manner* of such a king should not be arrogated by any potentate who affects to rule *jure divino*, by Divine right. The *manner* of the king of God's choice is distinctly detailed, Deut. xvii. 15-20, to which the reader will do well to refer, that he may have an impartial statement of the subject.

Verse 19. *The people refused to obey*] They *would* have the *king*, his *manner* and all, notwithstanding the solemn warning which they here receive.

Verse 20. *May judge us*] This appears to be a rejection of Samuel.

Go out before us] Be in every respect our head and governor.

And fight our battles.] Be the general of our armies.

Verse 21. *Rehearsed them in the ears of the Lord.*] He went to the altar, and in his secret devotion laid the whole business before God.

Verse 22. *Hearken unto their voice*] Let them have what they desire, and let them abide the consequences.

Go ye every man unto his city.] It seems the elders of the people had tarried all this time with Samuel, and when he had received his ultimate answer from God, he told them of it and dismissed them.

ON this account we may observe: 1. That GOD did not change the government of Israel; it was the *people* themselves who changed it. 2. That though God permitted them to have a king, yet he did not *approve* of him. 3. That, notwithstanding he did not suffer them to choose the *man*, he ordered his servant Samuel to choose him by lot, he disposing of that lot. 4. That God never gave up the supreme government; he was still KING *in Israel*, and the king, so called, was only the *vicegerent* or *deputy* of the Lord. 5. That no king of Judah attempted to be supreme, therefore they never *made new laws*, nor *altered the old;* which was a positive confession that God was the supreme Legislator. 6. That an *absolute monarchy* is always an evil, and is contrary to all the rights, civil and religious, of mankind; a mode of government that all people should avoid, as pregnant with evils to mankind. 7. That although it was a sin in the Israelites to *desire a king*, that is, *to change a constitution* of which God was the author, yet *kingly government*, properly understood, is a good of the first magnitude to the civil happiness of mankind. 8. That by kingly government, *properly understood*, I mean such a monarchical government as that of *Great Britain*, where the *king*, the *nobles*, and the *people*, are duly *mixed*, each having his proper part in the government, and each preventing the other from running to excess, and all limited by law. 9. That the *three* grand forms of government which have obtained among mankind, viz., *monarchy*, *aristocracy*, and *democracy*, have each certain *advantages* without which no state can be well preserved; but they have *evils* by which any state may be injured. 10. That, from a proper *mixture* of these, the advantages of the whole may be reaped without any of their attendant evils, and that this is the *British constitution;* which, not merely the *wisdom of our ancestors*, but the *providence of God* has given unto us, and of which no other state has had common sense enough to avail themselves, though they see that *because of this* the British empire is the most *powerful* and the most *happy* in the universe, and likely at last *to give laws to the whole world.* The *manner of our* king is *constitutional*, widely different from that of Saul, and from that of any other potentate in the four quarters of the globe. He is the *father* of his people, and the people *feel* and *love* him as *such.* He has all the *power* necessary to do good; they have all the *liberty* necessary to their political happiness, had they only a diminution of taxes, which at present are too heavy for any nation to bear.

CHAPTER IX

Saul's lineage and description; he is sent by his father to seek some lost asses, 1–5. Not finding them, he purposes to go and consult Samuel concerning the proper method of proceeding, 6–14. The Lord informs Samuel that he should anoint Saul king, 15, 16. Samuel invites Saul to dine with him, and informs him that the asses are found; and gives him an intimation that he is to be king, 17–21. Saul dines with Samuel, and afterwards he is taken to the house-top, where both commune together, 22–27.

A. M. 2909
B. C. 1095
An. Exod. Isr.
396
Anno ante
I. Olymp. 319

NOW there was a man of Benjamin, whose name *was* ᵃKish, the son of Abiel, the son of Zeror, the son of Bechorath, the son of Aphiah, ᵇa Benjamite, a mighty man of ᶜpower.

2 And he had a son, whose name *was* Saul, a choice young man, and a goodly: and *there was* not among the children of Israel a goodlier person than he: ᵈfrom his shoulders and upward *he was* higher than any of the people.

3 And the asses of Kish, Saul's father, were lost. And Kish said to Saul his son, Take now one of the servants with thee, and arise, go seek the asses.

4 And he passed through Mount Ephraim, and passed through the land of ᵉShalisha, but they found *them* not: then they passed through the land of Shalim, and *there they were* not:

and he passed through the land of the Benjamites, but they found *them* not.

A. M. 2909
B. C. 1095
An. Exod. Isr.
396
Anno ante
I. Olymp. 319

5 *And* when they were come to the land of Zuph, Saul said to his servant that *was* with him, Come, and let us return; lest my father leave *caring* for the asses, and take thought for us.

6 And he said unto him, Behold now, *there is* in this city ᶠa man of God, and *he is* an honourable man: ᵍall that he saith cometh surely to pass: now let us go thither; peradventure he can show us our way that we should go.

7 Then said Saul to his servant, But, behold, *if* we go, ʰwhat shall we bring the man? for the bread ⁱis spent in our vessels, and *there is* not a present to bring to the man of God: what ᵏhave we?

ᵃChap. xiv. 51; 1 Chron. viii. 33; ix. 39——ᵇOr, *the son of a man of Jemini*——ᶜOr, *substance*——ᵈChap. x. 23——ᵉ2 Kings iv. 42——ᶠDeut. xxxiii. 1; 1 Kings xiii. 1

ᵍChap. iii. 19——ʰSee Judg. vi. 18; xiii. 17; 1 Kings xiv. 3; 2 Kings iv. 42; viii. 8——ⁱHeb. *is gone out of*, &c. ᵏHeb. *is with us*

NOTES ON CHAP. IX

Verse 1. *A mighty man of power.*] Literally, a *strong man;* this appears to be the only *power* he possessed; and the physical strength of the father may account for the extraordinary size of the son. See ver. 2.

Verse 2. *From his shoulders and upwards*] It was probably from this very circumstance that he was chosen for king; for, where kings were *elective*, in all ancient times great respect was paid to *personal appearance*.

Verse 3. *The asses of Kish—were lost*] What a wonderful train of occurrences were connected in order to bring Saul to the throne of Israel! Every thing seems to go on according to the *common course of events*, and yet all conspired to favour the election of a man to the kingdom who certainly did not come there by the *approbation* of God.

Asses grow to great perfection in the East; and at this time, as there were no *horses* in Judea, they were very useful; and on them kings and princes rode.

Verse 5. *Were come to the land of Zuph*] Calmet supposes that Saul and his servant went from Gibeah to Shalisha, in the tribe of Dan; from thence to Shalim, near to Jerusalem; and thence, traversing the tribe of Benjamin, they purposed to return to Gibeah; but passing through the land of Zuph, in which Ramatha,

the country of Samuel, was situated, they determined to call on this prophet to gain some directions from him; the whole of this circuit he supposes to have amounted to no more than about *twenty-five* leagues, or three days' journey. We do not know where the places were situated which are here mentioned: the Targum translates thus: "And he passed through the mount of the house of *Ephraim*, and went into the *southern* land, but did not meet with them. And he passed through the land of *Mathbera*, but they were not there; and he passed through the land of the tribe of *Benjamin*, but did not find them; then they came into the land where the *prophet of the Lord* dwelt. And Saul said to his servant," &c.

Verse 7. There is *not a present to bring to the man of God*] We are not to suppose from this that the prophets took money to predict future events: Saul only refers to an invariable custom, that no man approached a *superior* without a *present* of some kind or other. We have often seen this before; even God, who needs nothing, would not that his people should approach him with *empty hands*. "It is very common in Bengal for a person, who is desirous of asking a favour from a superior, to take a present of *fruits* or *sweetmeats* in his hand. If not accepted, the feelings of the offerer are greatly wounded. The making of presents to appease a superior is also very common in Bengal."—WARD's *Customs*.

A. M. 2909
B. C. 1095
An. Exod. Isr.
396
Anno ante
I. Olymp. 319

8 And the servant answered Saul again, and said, Behold, [1]I have here at hand the fourth part of a shekel of silver: *that* will I give to the man of God, to tell us our way.

9 (Beforetime in Israel, when a man [m]went to inquire of God, thus he spake, Come, and let us go to the seer: for *he that is* now *called* a prophet was beforetime called [n]a seer.)

10 Then said Saul to his servant, [o]Well said; come, let us go. So they went unto the city where the man of God *was*.

11 *And* as they went up [p]the hill to the city, [q]they found young maidens going out to draw water, and said unto them, Is the seer here?

12 And they answered them, and said, He is; behold, *he is* before you: make haste now, for he came to-day to the city; for [r]*there is* a [s]sacrifice of the people to-day[t]in the high place:

13 As soon as ye be come into the city, ye shall straightway find him, before he go up to the high place to eat: for the people will not eat until he come, because he doth bless the sacrifice: *and* afterwards they eat that be bidden. Now therefore get you up; for about [u]this time ye shall find him.

14 And they went up into the city: *and* when they were come into the city, behold, Samuel came out against them, for to go up to the high place.

15 [v]Now the LORD had [w]told Samuel in his ear a day before Saul came, saying,

16 To-morrow about this time I will send thee a man out of the land of Benjamin, [x]and thou shalt anoint him *to be* captain over my people Israel, that he may save my people out of the hand of the Philistines: for I have

A. M. 2909
B. C. 1095
An. Exod. Isr.
396
Anno ante
I. Olymp. 319

---

[1]Heb. *there is found in my hand*——[m]Gen. xxv. 22
[n]2 Sam. xxiv. 11; 2 Kings xvii. 13; 1 Chron. xxvi. 28;
xxix. 29; 2 Chron. xvi. 7, 10; Isa. xxx. 10; Amos vii. 12
[o]Heb. *Thy word is good*

[p]Heb. *in the ascent of the city*——[q]Gen. xxiv. 11
[r]Gen. xxxi. 54; chap. xvi. 2——[s]Or, *feast*——[t]1 Kings
iii. 2——[u]Heb. *to-day*——[v]Chap. xv. 1; Acts xiii. 21
[w]Heb. *revealed the ear of Samuel;* ch. xx. 2——[x]Ch. x. 1

Verse 8. *The fourth part of a shekel of silver*] We find from the preceding verse, that the *bread* or *provisions* which they had brought with them for their journey was expended, else a *part of that* would have been thought a suitable present; and here the *fourth part of a shekel of silver*, about *ninepence* of our money, was deemed sufficient: therefore the present was intended more as a *token of respect* than as an *emolument.*

Verse 9. *Beforetime in Israel*] This passage could not have been a part of this book originally: but we have already conjectured that Samuel, or some contemporary author, wrote the memoranda, out of which a later author *compiled* this book. This hypothesis, sufficiently reasonable in itself, solves all difficulties of this kind.

Was beforetime called a seer.] The word *seer,* ראה *roeh,* occurs for the first time in this place; it literally signifies a *person who* SEES; particularly *preternatural* sights. A *seer* and a *prophet* were the same in most cases; only with this difference, the seer was always a *prophet,* but the prophet was not always a *seer.* A seer seems to imply one who *frequently* met with, and *saw,* some symbolical representation of God. The term *prophet* was used a long time before this; Abraham is called a *prophet,* Gen. xx. 7, and the term frequently occurs in the law. Besides, the word *seer* does not occur before this time; but often occurs *afterwards* down through the prophets, for more than *three hundred* years. See Amos vii. 12; Mic. iii. 7.

All prophets, false and true, profess to see God; see the case of *Balaam,* Num. xxiv. 4, 16, and Jer. xiv. 14. All *diviners,* in their enthusiastic flights, boasted that they had those things *exhibited* to their *sight* which should come to pass. There is a remarkable account in *Virgil* which may serve as a specimen of the whole; the *Sibyl* professes to be a seer:—

——————*Bella, horrida bella,*
Et Tyberim multo spumantem sanguine CERNO.
ÆN. lib. vi., ver. 86.

Wars, horrid wars, I VIEW; a field of blood;
And Tyber rolling with a purple flood.

I think the 9th verse comes more naturally in after the 11th.

Verse 11. *Young maidens going out to draw water*] So far is it from being true, that young women were always kept closely shut up at home, that we find them often in the field, drawing and carrying water, as here.

Verse 12. *He came to-day to the city*] Though Samuel lived chiefly in *Ramah,* yet he had a dwelling in the country, at a place called Naioth, where it is probable there was a school of the prophets. See chap. xix. 18-24.

A sacrifice of the people] A great *feast.* The animals used were first sacrificed to the Lord; that is, their blood was poured out before him; and then all the people fed on the flesh. By *high place* probably Samuel's *altar* is alone meant; which no doubt was raised on an eminence.

Verse 13. *He doth bless the sacrifice*] He alone can perform the religious rites which are used on this occasion.

Afterwards they eat that be bidden.] Among the Arabs, often a large feast is made of sacrificed *camels,* &c., and then the people of the vicinity are invited to come and partake of the sacrifice. This is the custom to which allusion is made here.

Verse 14. *Come out against them*] Met them.

Verse 15. *Now the Lord had told Samuel*] How this communication was made, we cannot tell.

Verse 16. *Thou shalt anoint him* to be *cap-*

A. M. 2909
B. C. 1095
An. Exod. Isr.
396
Anno ante
I. Olymp. 319

ylooked upon my people, because their cry is come unto me.

17 And when Samuel saw Saul, the LORD said unto him, zBehold the man whom I spake to thee of! this same shall areign over my people.

18 Then Saul drew near to Samuel in the gate, and said, Tell me, I pray thee, where the seer's house *is*.

19 And Samuel answered Saul, and said, I *am* the seer: go up before me unto the high place; for ye shall eat with me to-day, and to-morrow I will let thee go, and will tell thee all that *is* in thine heart.

20 And as for bthine asses that were lost cthree days ago, set not thy mind on them; for they are found. And on whom d*is* all the desire of Israel? *Is it* not on thee, and on all thy father's house?

21 And Saul answered and said, e*Am* not I a Benjamite, of the fsmallest of the tribes of Israel? and gmy family the least of all the families of the tribe of Benjamin? wherefore then speakest thou hso to me?

22 And Samuel took Saul and his servant, and brought them into the parlour, and made them sit in the chiefest place among them

that were bidden, which *were* about thirty persons.

A. M. 2909
B. C. 1095
An. Exod. Isr.
396
Anno ante
I. Olymp. 319

23 And Samuel said unto the cook, Bring the portion which I gave thee, of which I said unto thee, Set it by thee.

24 And the cook took up ithe shoulder, and *that* which *was* upon it, and set *it* before Saul. And *Samuel* said, Behold that which is kleft! set *it* before thee, *and* eat: for unto this time hath it been kept for thee since I said, I have invited the people. So Saul did eat with Samuel that day.

25 And when they were come down from the high place into the city, *Samuel* communed with Saul upon lthe top of the house.

26 And they arose early: and it came to pass about the spring of the day, that Samuel called Saul to the top of the house, saying, Up, that I may send thee away. And Saul arose, and they went out both of them, he and Samuel, abroad.

27 *And* as they were going down to the end of the city, Samuel said to Saul, Bid the servant pass on before us, (and he passed on,) but stand thou still ma while, that I may show thee the word of God.

---

yExod. ii. 25; iii. 7, 9——zChap. xvi. 12; Hos. xiii. 11
aHeb. *restrain in*——bVer. 3——cHeb. *to-day three days*
dChap. viii. 5, 19; xii. 13——eChap. xv. 17——fJudg.
xx. 46, 47, 48; Psa. lxviii. 27

gSee Judges vi. 15——hHebrew, *according to this word*——iLeviticus vii. 32, 33; Ezekiel xxiv. 4——kOr, *reserved*——lDeuteronomy xxii. 8; 2 Samuel xi. 2; Acts x. 9——mHebrew, *to-day*

---

tain] Not to be *king*, but to be נָגִיד *nagid* or captain of the Lord's host. But in ancient times no king was esteemed who was not an able warrior. *Plutarch* informs us that Alexander the Great esteemed the following verse the most correct, as to its sentiment, of any in the whole Iliad of Homer:—

Ουτος γ' Ατρειδης ευρυκρειων Αγαμεμνων,
Αμφοτερον βασιλευς τ' αγαθος, κρατερος
τ' αιχμητης.

"The king of kings, Atrides, you survey;
Great in the war, and *great in acts of sway*."
POPE.

Verse 17. *Behold the man whom I spake to thee of*] What an intimate communion must Samuel have held with his God! A constant familiarity seems to have existed between them.

Verse 19. *I am the seer*] This declaration would prepare Saul for the communications afterwards made.

Verse 20. *As for thine asses*] Thus he shows him that he knew what was in his heart, God having previously revealed these things to Samuel.

And on whom is all the desire of Israel?] Saul understood this as implying that he was chosen to be king.

Verse 21. Am *not I a Benjamite*] This

speech of Saul is exceedingly *modest;* he was now becomingly humble; but who can bear *elevation* and *prosperity?* The tribe of Benjamin had not yet recovered its strength, after the ruinous war it had with the other tribes, Judg. xx.

Verse 22. *Brought them into the parlour*] It might as well be called *kitchen;* it was the place where they sat down to feast.

Verse 23. *Said unto the cook*] טבּח *tabbach*, here rendered *cook;* the singular of טבּחות *tabbachoth, female cooks*, chap. viii. 13, from the root *tabach*, to *slay* or *butcher*. Probably the *butcher* is here meant.

Verse 24. *The shoulder, and* that *which was upon it*] Probably the shoulder was covered with a part of the caul, that it might be the better roasted. The Targum has it, *the shoulder and its thigh;* not only the *shoulder* merely, but the *fore-leg bone* to the knee; perhaps the whole *fore-quarter*. Why was the *shoulder* set before Saul? Not because it was the *best part*, but because it was an emblem of the *government* to which he was now called. See Isa. ix. 6: *And the government shall be upon his* SHOULDER.

Verse 25. *Upon the top of the house.*] All the houses in the East were flat-roofed; on these people walked, talked, and frequently *slept*, for the sake of fresh and cooling air.

Verse 26. *Called Saul to the top of the*

house] Saul had no doubt slept there all night; and now, it being the *break of day*, "Samuel called to Saul on the top of the house, saying, Up, that I may send thee away." There was no calling him *to* the house-top a *second* time; he was sleeping there, and Samuel called him up.

Verse 27. *As they were going down*] So it appears that Saul arose immediately, and Samuel accompanied him out of the town, and sent the servant on that he might show Saul the *word*—the *counsel* or *design*, of the Lord. What this was we shall see in the following chapter.

CHAPTER X

Samuel anoints Saul captain of the Lord's inheritance, 1. *Instructs him concerning his return home, whom he should meet, and what he should do,* 2–8. *Saul meets a company of prophets, the Spirit of the Lord comes on him, and he prophesies among them,* 9–13. *He meets his uncle, and converses with him,* 14–16. *Samuel calls the people together to Mizpeh, and upbraids them for having rejected the Lord as their king,* 17–19. *Lots are cast to find out the person proper to be appointed king; Saul is chosen,* 20–24. *Samuel shows the manner of the king, and writes it in a book,* 25. *Saul goes to Gibeah; and certain persons refuse to acknowledge him as king,* 26, 27.

A. M. 2909
B. C. 1095
An. Exod. Isr.
396
Anno ante
I. Olymp. 319

THEN ªSamuel took a vial of oil, and poured *it* upon his head, ᵇand kissed him, and said, *Is it* not because ᶜthe LORD hath anointed thee *to be* captain over ᵈhis inheritance?

2 When thou art departed from me to-day, then thou shalt find two men by ᵉRachel's sepulchre in the border of Benjamin ᶠat Zelzah; and they will say unto thee, The asses which thou wentest to seek are found: and lo, thy father hath left ᵍthe care of the asses, and sorroweth for you, saying, What shall I do for my son?

3 Then shalt thou go on forward from thence, and thou shalt come to the plain of Tabor, and there shall meet thee three men going up ʰto God to Beth-el, one carrying three kids, and another carrying three loaves of bread, and another carrying a bottle of wine:

4 And they will ⁱsalute thee, and give thee two *loaves* of bread; which thou shalt receive of their hands.

5 After that thou shalt come to ᵏthe hill of God, ˡwhere *is* the garrison of the Philistines: and it shall come to pass, when thou art come thither to the city, that thou shalt meet a com-

A. M. 2909
B. C. 1095
An. Exod. Isr.
396
Anno ante
I. Olymp. 319

ªChapter ix. 16; xvi. 13; 2 Kings ix. 3, 6——ᵇPsalm ii. 12——ᶜActs xiii. 21——ᵈDeut. xxxii. 9; Psa. lxxviii. 71——ᵉGen. xxxv. 19, 20

ⁱJosh. xviii. 28——ᵍHeb. *the business*——ʰGen. xxviii. 29; xxxv. 1, 3, 7——ⁱHeb. *ask thee of peace:* as Judg. xviii. 15——ᵏVer. 10——ˡChap. xiii. 3

NOTES ON CHAP. X

Verse 1. *Took a vial of oil*] The reasons of this rite the reader will find largely stated in the note on Exod. xxix. 7. The anointing mentioned here took place in the *open field.* See th preceding chapter, ver. 26, 27. How simple was the ancient ceremony of consecrating a king! A *prophet* or *priest* poured oil *upon his head*, and *kissed him;* and said, *Thus the Lord hath anointed thee to be captain over his inheritance.* This was the whole of the ceremony. Even in this anointing, Saul is not acknowledged as *king*, but simply נגיד *nagid, a captain* —one who *goes before* and *leads* the people.

Verse 2. *Rachel's sepulchre*] This was nigh to Bethlehem. See Gen. xxxv. 19.

At Zelzah] If this be the name of a *place*, nothing is known of it.

The Hebrew בצלצח *betseltsach* is translated by the *Septuagint* ἀλλομενους μεγαλα, *dancing greatly:* now this may refer to the *joy* they felt and expressed on finding the asses, or it may refer to those *religious exultations*, or *playing on instruments of music*, mentioned in the succeeding verses.

Verse 3. *Three men going up to God to Bethel*] Jacob's altar was probably there still, Gen. xxviii. 19. However this might be, it was still considered, as its name implies, *the house*

of God; and to it they were now going, to offer *sacrifice.*

The *three kids* were for *sacrifice;* the *three loaves of bread* to be offered probably as a *thank-offering;* and *the bottle* or skin full of *wine*, for a *libation.* When the blood was poured out before the Lord, then they feasted on the *flesh* and on the *bread;* and probably had a sufficiency of the *wine* left for their own drinking.

Verse 4. *And they will salute thee*] ושאלו לך לשלום *veshaalu lecha leshalom*, "And they will inquire of thee concerning peace," i. e., *welfare.* In the East, if this salutation be given, then the person or persons giving it may be reckoned friends; if the others return it, then there is friendship on both sides. *Salaam alicum*, Peace to you! is the mode of compellaticn: *Alicum essalaam*, To you be peace! is the return. If you give the former and receive not the latter, you may expect hostility. The meaning of the prophet is, When you come to the plain of Tabor, ye shall meet three men; you need not be afraid of them, for they are *friends;* and they will show this friendship, not only by bidding you good speed, but by giving you two loaves of bread, a provision which you will need for the remaining part of your journey.

Verse 5. *The hill of God*] The Targum says,

A. M. 2909
B. C. 1095
An. Exod. Isr.
396
Anno ante
I. Olymp. 319

pany of prophets coming down ᵐfrom the high place with a psaltery, and a tabret, and a pipe, and a harp, before them; ⁿand they shall prophesy:

6 And the °spirit of the LORD will come upon thee, and ᵖthou shalt prophesy with them, and shalt be turned into another man.

A. M. 2909
B. C. 1095
An. Exod. Isr.
396
Anno ante
I. Olymp. 319

ᵐChap. ix. 12——ⁿExod. xv. 20, 21; 2 Kings iii. 15;
1 Cor. xiv. 1

°Numbers xi. 25; chap. xvi. 13——ᵖVerse 10; chapter
xix. 23, 24

"The hill on which *the ark of the Lord was.* Calmet supposes it to be a height near Gibeah.

The garrison of the Philistines] Probably they kept a watch on the top of this hill, with a company of soldiers to keep the country in check.

A company of prophets] A company of scribes, says the Targum. Probably the scholars of the prophets; for the prophets seem to have been the only accredited teachers, at particular times, in Israel; and at this time there does not appear to have been any other prophet besides Samuel in this quarter. Probably the teacher of this school was not an inspired man, but one acting under the direction of Samuel. Mr. Harmer thinks that the following custom among the Mohammedans greatly illustrates this obscure place: "When the children have gone through the Koran, their relations borrow a fine horse and furniture, and *carry them about the town in procession*, with the book in their hand, the rest of their *companions* following, and all sorts of music of the country going before. Dr. Shaw, in p. 195, mentions the same custom; adding the *acclamations* of their *school-fellows*, but taking no notice of the music. We have no reason, however, to doubt the fact on account of the doctor's silence; especially as it relates to another part of Barbary, and is given us by those who resided some years in that country. The doctor makes no use of this circumstance relating to the education of youth in Barbary; but the account of the procession above given seems to be a lively comment on that ancient Jewish custom mentioned in these verses. That the word *prophet* often signifies *sons* or *scholars* of the prophets, and that *prophesying* often implies *singing*, has been already remarked; but no author that I know of Las given any account of the nature of this procession, or its design. We are sometimes told that *high places* were used for sacrifices; and in one case *music*, it is certain, played before them when they went up to worship, Isa. xxx. 29. But did they not also return from sacrifice with it? We are told that music was used by the prophets to calm and compose them, and to invite the Divine influences; which is indeed very true. But is it to the purpose? Did they go forth in this manner *from their college* into the *noise* and *interruptions* of the world, to call down the prophetic impulse? But if we consider them as a company of the *sons of the prophets*, going in procession with *songs* of *praise* and *music* playing before them, and recollect that it is usual in this day for young scholars to go in procession with acclamations and music, the whole mystery seems to be unravelled. To which may be added, that Saul was to *meet them,* and find himself *turned into another man;* into a man, perhaps, who is instantaneously made as knowing in the law of God as the youth to whom they were doing the above honours, or any of his convoy; which acquain-

tance with the law of God was very necessary for one who was to judge among his brethren as their king. For this reason the Jewish kings were to write out a copy of the law of God, and read it continually, that they might be perfect masters of it, Deut. xvii. 18, 20, which accomplishment some youth had gained whom Saul met with, and who was honoured with the solemnity the sacred historian speaks of, if the customs of South Barbary may be supposed to be explanatory of those of Judea."

On the word *prophet,* and the general account given here, I shall introduce the following illustrations from another work:—

"The word *prophet* generally conveys the idea of a person so far acquainted with *futurity* as to discern some purpose of the Divine Being relative to his government of the natural and moral world, but which is not sufficiently matured by the economy of Providence to make, as yet, its public appearance among men, and to *prophesy* is usually understood to imply the *foretelling* such an event, the *time* of its appearance, and the *place* of its operation, with some preceding and subsequent circumstances. But that this was the *original* and *only meaning* of the word prophet or prophesy, is very far from being clear. The first place the word occurs in is Gen. xx. 7, where the Lord says of Abraham to Abimelech, He is a *prophet,* (נביא הוא *nabi hu,*) *and will pray* (ויתפלל *veyith-pallel,* will make earnest intercession) *for thee.* In the common acceptation of the word it is certain Abraham was *no prophet;* but here it seems to signify a man well acquainted with the Supreme Being, capable of teaching others in Divine things, and especially a *man of prayer*— one who had great influence with the God he worshipped, and whose intercessions were available in the behalf of others. And in this sense the original word נביא *nabi* is used in several places in the Old Testament.

"It was through inattention to this meaning of the word, which appears to me to be the true, original, and ideal one, that all the commentators and critics that I have met with have been so sadly puzzled with that part of the history of Saul which is related chap. x. 9-13, and xix. 20-24. In these passages the sacred historian represents Saul, who was neither a prophet nor the son of one, associating with the prophets, and *prophesying among them,* to which he was led by *the Spirit of the Lord which came upon him.*

"That this can mean no more here than prayer and *supplication* to God, accompanied probably with edifying *hymns* of *praise* and *thanksgiving,* (for they had instruments of music, chap. x. 5,) needs, in my opinion, little proof. If Saul had prophesied in the common acceptation of the word, it is not likely that we should have been kept absolutely in the dark concerning the subject and design of his predictions, of which, by the way, not one syllable is spoken in the oracles of God. The

A. M. 2909
B. C. 1095
An. Exod. Isr. 396
Anno ante
I. Olymp. 319

7 And �q let it be, when these ʳsigns are come unto thee, ˢ*that* thou do as occasion serve thee; for ᵗGod *is* with thee.

8 And thou shalt go down before me ᵘto Gilgal; and, behold, I will come down unto thee, to offer burnt-offerings, *and* to sacrifice sacrifices of peace-offerings: ᵛseven days shalt thou tarry, till I come to thee, and show thee what thou shalt do.

9 And it was *so,* that when he had turned his ʷback to go from Samuel, God ˣgave him another heart: and all those signs came to pass that day.

A. M. 2909
B. C. 1095
An. Exod. Isr. 396
Anno ante
I. Olymp. 319

10 And ʸwhen they came thither to the hill, behold, ᶻa company of prophets met him; and ᵃthe Spirit of God came upon him; and he prophesied among them.

11 And it came to pass, when all that knew

�q Heb. *it shall come to pass, that when these signs,* &c.
ʳ Exod. iv. 8; Luke ii. 12——ˢ Heb. *do for thee as thine hand shall find;* Judg. ix. 33

ᵗ Judg. vi. 12——ᵘ Chap. xi. 14, 15; xiii. 4——ᵛ Chap. xiii. 8——ʷ Heb. *shoulder*——ˣ Heb. *turned*——ʸ Ver. 5
ᶻ Chap. xix. 20——ᵃ Ver. 6

---

simple fact seems to have been this: God, who had chosen this man to govern Israel, designed to teach *him* that the Most High alone is the fountain of power, and that by him only kings could reign so as to execute justice properly, and be his ministers for good to the people. To accomplish this gracious purpose, *he gave him another heart* (ver. 9)—a disposition totally different from what he had ever before possessed, and taught him *to pray.*

"Coming among the sons of the prophets, on whom the Spirit of the Lord rested, and who were under the instruction of Samuel, (chap. xix. 20,) while they worshipped God with music and supplication, Saul also was made a partaker of the same Divine influence, and *prophesied,* i. e., made prayer and supplication among them. To see one who did not belong to the prophetic school *thus incorporated* with the prophets, pouring out his soul in prayer and supplication, was an unusual sight, which could not pass unnoticed, especially by those of Saul's acquaintance who probably knew him in times past to have been as careless and ungodly as themselves, (for it was only *now* he got that other good Spirit from God, a sufficient proof that he had it not *before.*) These companions of his, being unacquainted with that grace which can in a moment influence and change the heart, would, according to an invariable custom, express their astonishment with a sneer: *Is* Saul *also among the prophets?* That is, in modern language, 'Can this man *pray* or *preach?* He whose education has been the same as our own, employed in the same secular offices, and formerly companion with us in what he now affects to call folly and sin? Can such a person be among the prophets?' Yes, for God may have *given him* a *new heart;* and the *Spirit of God,* whose inspiration *alone* can give sound understanding in sacred things, may have *come upon him* for this very purpose, that he might announce unto *you* the righteousness of the Lord, and speak unto your ruined souls *to edification, and to exhortation, and to comfort.*

"The history of Elijah and the priests of Baal, mentioned in 1 Kings xviii., throws farther light on this subject. In ver. 26 it is said, 'They (the priests of Baal) took a bullock and dressed it, and called on the name of Baal, from morning to noon, saying, O Baal, hear us! And they leaped upon the altar, and cried aloud, and cut themselves with knives, till the blood gushed out; and they *prophesied* (ויתנבאו

vaiyithnabbeu, and they made supplication) until the time of the evening sacrifice.' From the whole context it is plain that *earnest, importunate prayer,* is alone what is meant by *prophesying* in this text. See also 1 Cor. xiv. 3.

"And as all the prophets of God, whose principal business it was to instruct the people in the way of righteousness, were *men of prayer,* who were continually interceding with God in behalf of those to whom they ministered, the term נביא *nabi* became their proper appellative; and thus a part of their office, *intercessors for the people,* might have given rise to that name by which the Spirit of God thought proper in after times to distinguish those whom he sent, not only to *pray for* and *instruct the people,* but also to *predict* those future events which concerned the punishment of the incorrigible and the comfort and exaltation of his own servants." See a sermon which I have printed on 1 Cor. xiv. 3, entitled, "The Christian Prophet and his Work;" and see the note on Gen. xx. 7.

A psaltery] נבל *nebel.* As the word signifies in other places a *bottle* or *flagon,* it was probably something like the *utricularia tibia* or BAG-PIPE. It often occurs both with the Greeks and Romans, and was evidently borrowed from the *Hebrews.*

A tabret] תף *toph;* a sort of *drum* or *cymbal.*

A pipe] חליל *chalil,* from חל *chal, to make a hole* or *opening;* a sort of *pipe, flute, hautboy, clarionet,* or the like.

A harp] כנור *kinnor;* a stringed instrument similar to our harp, or that on the model of which a harp was formed. On these different instruments I shall have occasion to speak more at large when I come to the *Psalms.*

Verse 7. *Thou do as occasion serve thee*] After God has shown thee all these signs that thou art under his especial guidance, fear not to undertake any thing that belongs to thy office, for God is with thee.

What a number of circumstances thus precisely foretold! Does not this prove that Samuel was under the continual inspiration of the Almighty?

Verse 8. *Seven days shalt thou tarry*] I will come to thee within seven days, offer sacrifices, receive directions from the Lord, and deliver them to thee. It is likely that these seven *days referred* to the time in which Samuel came to Saul to Gilgal, offered sacrifices, and confirmed the kingdom to him, after he had defeated the Ammonites. See chap. xi. 14, 15.

A. M. 2909
B. C. 1095
An. Exod. Isr.
396
Anno ante
I. Olymp. 319

him beforetime saw that, behold, he prophesied among the prophets, then the people said [b]one to another, What *is* this *that* is come unto the son of Kish? [c]*Is* Saul also among the prophets?

12 And one [d]of the same place answered and said, But [e]who *is* their father? Therefore it became a proverb, *Is* Saul also among the prophets?

13 And when he had made an end of prophesying, he came to the high place.

14 And Saul's uncle said unto him and to his servant, Whither went ye? And he said, To seek the asses: and when we saw that *they were* nowhere, we came to Samuel.

15 And Saul's uncle said, Tell me, I pray thee, what Samuel said unto you.

16 And Saul said unto his uncle, He told us plainly that the asses were found. But of the matter of the kingdom, whereof Samuel spake, he told him not.

17 And Samuel called the people together [f]unto the LORD [g]to Mizpeh;

18 And said unto the children of Israel, [h]Thus saith the LORD God of Israel, I brought up Israel out of Egypt, and delivered you out of the hand of the Egyptians, and out of the hand of all kingdoms, *and* of them that oppressed you:

19 [i]And ye have this day rejected your God, who himself saved you out of all your adversities and your tribulations; and ye have said unto him, *Nay,* but set a king over us. Now therefore present yourselves before the LORD by your tribes, and by your thousands.

20 And when Samuel had [k]caused all the tribes of Israel to come near, the tribe of Benjamin was taken.

21 When he had caused the tribe of Benjamin to come near by their families, the family of Matri was taken, and Saul the son of Kish was taken: and when they sought him, he could not be found.

22 Therefore they [l]inquired of the LORD farther, if the man should yet come thither. And the LORD answered, Behold, he hath hid himself among the stuff.

23 And they ran and fetched him thence: and when he stood among the people, [m]he was higher than any of the people from his shoulders and upward.

24 And Samuel said to all the people, See ye him [n]whom the LORD hath chosen, that *there is* none like him among all the people? And all the people shouted, and said, [o]God [p]save the king.

25 Then Samuel told the people [q]the manner of the kingdom, and wrote *it* in a

A. M. 2909
B. C. 1095
An. Exod. Isr.
396
Anno ante
I. Olymp. 319

---

[b]Heb. *a man to his neighbour*——[c]Ch. xix. 24; Matt. xiii. 54, 55; John vii. 15; Acts iv. 13——[d]Heb. *from thence*——[e]Isa. liv. 13; John vi. 45; vii. 16——[f]Judg. xi. 11; xx. 1; ch. xi. 15——[g]Ch. vii. 5, 6——[h]Judg. vi. 8, 9

[i]Ch. viii. 7, 19; xii. 12——[k]Josh. vii. 14, 16, 17; Acts i. 24, 26——[l]Ch. xxiii. 2, 4, 10, 11——[m]Ch. ix. 2——[n]2 Sam. xxi. 6——[o]1 Kings i. 25, 39; 2 Kings xi. 12 [p]Heb. *Let the king live*——[q]See Deut. xvii. 14, &c.; chap. viii. 11

Verse 10. *Behold, a company of prophets*] See on ver. 5, &c.

Verse 12. *But who is their father?*] The Septuagint, in its principal editions, adds ουκ Κεις; *is it not Kish?* This makes the sense more complete.

Verse 13. *He came to the high place.*] I suppose this to mean the place where Saul's father lived; as it is evident the next verse shows him to be at *home.*

Verse 14. *Saul's uncle*] The word דוד *dod* signifies a *beloved one, love,* a *lover, friend,* &c.; and is the same as *David.* It is supposed to mean *uncle* here; but I think it means some *familiar friend.*

Verse 18. *I brought up Israel out of Egypt*] These are similar to the upbraidings in chap. viii. 7, &c.

Verse 19. *Present yourselves—by your tribes*] It appears that, in order to find out the proper person who should be made their king, they must determine by lot: 1. The *tribe.* 2. The *thousands* or *grand divisions* by families. 3. The *smaller divisions* by families. And, 4. The *individual.* When the lot was cast for

the *tribe, Benjamin* was taken; when for the *thousand,* the division of *Matri* was taken; when for the *family,* the family of *Kish* was taken; when for the *individual, Saul,* the son of Kish, was taken.

Verse 21. *When they sought him, he could not be found.*] Through modesty or fear he had secreted himself.

Verse 22. *The Lord answered*] What a continual access to God! and what condescension in his attention to all their requests!

The *stuff* among which he had secreted himself may mean the *carts, baggage,* &c., brought by the people to Mizpeh.

Verse 24. *God save the king.*] There is no such word here; no, nor in the whole Bible; nor is it countenanced by any of the *versions.* The words which we thus translate here and elsewhere are simply יחי המלך *yechi hammelech,* "May the king live;" and so all the *versions,* the *Targum* excepted, which says, *May the king prosper!* The French *Vive le roi!* is a proper version of the Hebrew.

Verse 25. *The manner of the kingdom*] It is the same word as in chap. viii. 9; and doubt-

A. M. 2909
B. C. 1095
An. Exod. Isr.
396
Anno ante
I Olymp. 319

book, and laid *it* up before the LORD. And Samuel sent all the people away, every man to his house.

26 And Saul also went home ʳto Gibeah; and there went with him a band

of men, whose hearts God had touched.

27 ˢBut the ᵗchildren of Belial said, How shall this man save us? And they despised him, ᵘand brought him no presents. But ᵛhe held his peace.

A. M. 2909
B. C. 1095
An. Exod. Isr.
396
Anno ante
I. Olymp. 319

ʳJudg. xx. 14; chap. xi. 4——ˢChap. xi. 12——ᵗDeut. xiii. 13——ᵘ2 Sam. viii. 2; 1 Kings iv. 21; x. 25; 2 Chron.

xvii. 5; Psa. lxxii. 10; Matt. ii. 11——ᵛOr, *he was as though he had been deaf*

---

less the same thing is implied as is there related. But possibly there was some kind of *compact* or *covenant* between *them* and *Saul;* and this was the thing that was *written in a book*, and *laid up before the Lord*, probably near the *ark*.

Verse 26. *A band of men*] Not a *military band*, as I imagine, but some *secret friends*, or *companions*, who were personally attached to him. Others think that all the men fit to bear arms are intended; but this seems inconsistent with the life that Saul led for some time afterwards; for he appears to have gone into his agricultural concerns, and waited for a call from the Divine providence. See the next chap. ver. 5.

Verse 27. *Brought him no presents*] They gave him no proofs that they acknowledged either the Divine appointment or his authority. The Arab chiefs are, to this day, when on a march or excursion of any kind, supplied with

every necessary by the *free-will offerings* or *presents* of the people in the villages or places where they encamp. Saul was now a public character, and had a right to support from the public. These sons of Belial refused to bear their part; they *brought him no presents*. He marked it, but at present held his peace; *he was as if he were deaf:* so says the text. He was prudent, and did not immediately assume all the consequence to which his office entitled him. It is probable, however, that *tribute* is meant by the word *present*. The people in general finding they had now a king, took it for granted that they must pay tribute or taxes to him. This was a part of the *manner of the king* which Samuel had shown them; the great majority had done so, but certain refractory people refused to pay any thing, on the pretence that such a person as Saul could not be a deliverer of Israel. *How*, say they, *shall this man save us?*

CHAPTER XI

Nahash, king of the Ammonites, besieges Jabesh-gilead; and proposes to its inhabitants the most degrading conditions of peace, 1, 2. They apply to their brethren for help, 3, 4. Saul hears of their distress; takes a yoke of oxen, hews them in pieces, and sends them throughout the coasts of Israel, with the threat that all who did not come to his standard should have his cattle served in like manner; in consequence of which he is soon at the head of an army of three hundred and thirty thousand men, 5–8. He sends to Jabesh-gilead, and promises help, 9, 10. Saul attacks the Ammonites next morning, and gives them a total overthrow, 11. The people are greatly encouraged, and propose to put to death those who are opposed to Saul's government: but this he prevents, 12, 13. Samuel leads the people to Gilgal: they offer sacrifices, and renew the kingdom to Saul, 14, 15.

A. M. 2909
B. C. 1095
An. Exod. Isr.
396
Anno ante
I. Olymp. 319

THEN ᵃNahash the Ammonite came up, and encamped against ᵇJabesh-gilead: and all the men of Jabesh said unto

Nahash, ᶜMake a covenant with us, and we will serve thee.

2 And Nahash the Ammonite answered them, On this *condition*

A. M. 2909
B. C. 1095
An. Exod. Isr.
396
Anno ante
I. Olymp. 319

ᵃChap. xii. 12——ᵇJudg. xxi. 8——ᶜGen. xxvi. 28;

Exod. xxiii. 32; 1 Kings xx. 34; Job xli. 4; Ezek. xvii. 13

NOTES ON CHAP. XI

Verse 1. *Nahash the Ammonite*] In the *Vulgate* this chapter begins thus: *Et factum est quasi post mensem,* "And it came to pass about a month after." This addition appears also in the principal copies of the *Septuagint;* though it is wanting in the Complutensian edition, both in the *Greek* and *Latin*, and is not acknowledged by any of the *Oriental versions*. But it is in *Josephus*, and probably was inserted from him into some copies of the *Septuagint*, and thence into the *Vulgate*. It appears to be of very little authority.

We know little about *Nahash;* there was a king of this name among the Ammonites in the time of David, 2 Sam. x. 2, but prob-

ably not the same person. *Nahash* might have been a common name of the Ammonitish kings.

Make a covenant with us] They found they were in no condition to risk a war; and they wish to have peace, and desire to know his conditions.

Verse 2. *I may thrust out all your right eyes*] This cruel condition would serve at once as a badge of their *slavery*, and a means of incapacitating them from being effective warriors. *Theodoret* observes, "He who opposes his shield to the enemy with his left hand, thereby hides his left eye, and looks at his enemy with his right eye; he therefore who plucks out that right eye makes men useless in war." *Josephus* gives the same reason.

A. M. 2909
B. C. 1095
An. Exod. Isr.
396
Anno ante
I. Olymp. 319

will I make *a covenant* with you, that I may thrust out all your right eyes, and lay it *for* ^da reproach upon all Israel.

3 And the elders of Jabesh said unto him, ^eGive us seven days' respite, that we may send messengers unto all the coasts of Israel: and then, if *there be* no man to save us, we will come out to thee.

4 Then came the messengers ^fto Gibeah of Saul, and told the tidings in the ears of the people: and ^gall the people lifted up their voices, and wept.

5 And, behold, Saul came after the herd out of the field; and Saul said, What *aileth* the people that they weep? And they told him the tidings of the men of Jabesh.

6 ^hAnd the Spirit of God came upon Saul when he heard those tidings, and his anger was kindled greatly.

7 And he took a yoke of oxen, and ⁱhewed them in pieces, and sent *them* throughout all

the coasts of Israel by the hands of messengers, saying, ^kWhosoever cometh not forth after Saul and after Samuel, so shall it be done unto his oxen. And the fear of the LORD fell on the people, and they came out ^lwith one consent.

8 And when he numbered them in ^mBezek, the children ⁿof Israel were three hundred thousand, and the men of Judah thirty thousand.

9 And they said unto the messengers that came, Thus shall ye say unto the men of Jabesh-gilead, To-morrow, by *that time* the sun be hot, ye shall have ^ohelp. And the messengers came and showed *it* to the men of Jabesh: and they were glad.

10 Therefore the men of Jabesh said, To-morrow ^pwe will come out unto you, and ye shall do with us all that seemeth good unto you.

11 And it was *so* on the morrow, that ^qSaul put the people ^rin three companies; and they

A. M. 2909
B. C. 1095
An. Exod. Isr.
396
Anno ante
I. Olymp. 319

---

^dGen. xxxiv. 14; chap. xvii. 26——^eHeb. *Forbear us*
^fChap. x. 26; xv. 34; 2 Sam. xxi. 6——^gJudg. ii. 4; xxi. 2
^hJudg. iii. 10; vi. 34; xi. 29; xiii. 25; xiv. 6; chap. x. 10;
xvi. 13

ⁱJudg. xix. 29——^kJudg. xxi. 5, 8, 10——^lHeb. *as
one man;* Judg. xx. 1——^mJudg. i. 5——ⁿ2 Sam. xxiv. 9
^oOr, *deliverance*——^pVer. 3——^qSee chap. xxxi. 11
^rJudg. vii. 16

Verse 3. *Give us seven days' respite*] Such promises are frequently made by besieged places: "We will surrender if not relieved in so many days;" and such conditions are generally received by the besiegers.

Verse 4. *Then came the messengers to Gibeah*] It does not appear that the people of Jabesh-gilead knew any thing of Saul's appointment to the kingdom, for the message is not directed to him but to the *people*.

The people lifted up their voices and wept.] They saw no hope of deliverance, and they expected that their reproach would be laid on all Israel.

Verse 5. *Saul came after the herd*] He had been bred up to an *agricultural* life, and after his consecration he returned to it, waiting for a call of Divine providence, which he considered he had now received in the message from Jabesh-gilead.

It has often been remarked, that mighty kings and accomplished generals have been chosen from among those who were engaged in agricultural concerns. In these observations one fact is lost sight of, viz., that in ancient times *agriculture* was the *only* employment. *Trade* and *commerce* were scarcely known; therefore all descriptions of official dignities must be chosen out of this class, there being no other to choose them from. We need not wonder at these words of the poet:—

Jura dabat populis posito modo consul aratro;
Pascebatque suas ipse senator oves.

"The consul, having now laid aside his plough,
    gives laws to the people;
And the senator himself feeds his own sheep."
      OVID, *Fast.* lib. i., v. 204-207.

Verse 6. *The Spirit of God came upon Saul*] He felt himself *strongly excited* to attempt the relief of his brethren.

And his anger was kindled greatly.] I believe this means no more than that *his courage was greatly excited*—he felt himself strong for fight, and confident of success.

Verse 7. *He took a yoke of oxen*] The sending the *pieces* of the oxen was an act similar to that of the Levite, Judg. xix. 29, where see the note. And both customs are similar to the sending about of the *bloody cross*, to call the clans to battle, practised by the ancient Highlanders of Scotland. See at the end of this chapter.

Verse 8. *The children of Israel were three hundred thousand, and the men of Judah thirty thousand.*] This was a vast army, but the *Septuagint* make it even more: "All the men of Israel were ἑξακοσίας χιλιάδας, SIX HUNDRED *thousand;* and the men of Judah ἑβδομήκοντα χιλιάδας, SEVENTY *thousand.*" *Josephus* goes yet higher with the number of the Israelites: "He found the number of those whom he had gathered together to be ἑβδομήκοντα μυριάδας, SEVEN HUNDRED *thousand.*" Those of the tribe of Judah he makes *seventy* thousand, with the Septuagint. These numbers are not all right; and I suspect even the Hebrew text to be exaggerated, by the mistake or design of some ancient scribe.

Verse 10. *To-morrow we will come out unto you*] They concealed the information they had received of Saul's promised assistance. They did *come* out unto them; but it was in a different manner to what the Ammonites expected.

Verse 11. *Put the people in three companies*] Intending to attack the Ammonites in three different points, and to give his own men more *room* to act.

A. M. 2909
B. C. 1095
An. Exod. Isr.
396
Anno ante
I. Olymp. 319

came into the midst of the host in the morning watch, and slew the Ammonites until the heat of the day: and it came to pass, that they which remained were scattered, so that two of them were not left together.

12 And the people said unto Samuel, *Who is he that said, Shall Saul reign over us? bring the men, that we may put them to death.

13 And Saul said, "There shall not a man

be put to death this day: for to-day ᵛthe LORD hath wrought salvation in Israel.

A. M. 2909
B. C. 1095
An. Exod. Isr.
396
Anno ante
I. Olymp. 319

14 Then said Samuel to the people, Come, and let us go ʷto Gilgal, and renew the kingdom there.

15 And all the people went to Gilgal; and there they made Saul king ˣbefore the LORD in Gilgal; and ʸthere they sacrificed sacrifices of peace-offerings before the LORD; and there Saul and all the men of Israel rejoiced greatly.

ˢChapter x. 27——ᵗSee Luke xix. 27——ᵘ2 Samuel xix. 22

ᵛExod. xiv. 13, 30; chap. xix. 5——ʷChap. x. 8
ˣChap. x. 17——ʸChap. x. 8

In the morning watch] He probably began his march in the evening, passed Jordan in the night, and reached the camp of the Ammonites by daybreak.

That two of them were not left together.] This proves that the rout was complete.

Verse 12. *Who is he that said, Shall Saul reign*] Now, flushed with victory and proud of their leader, they wished to give him a proof of their attachment by slaying, even in cool blood, the persons who were at first averse from his being intrusted with the supreme power! The common soldier is scarcely ever inspired by his victory to acts of *magnanimity;* he has shed blood—he wishes to shed more!

Verse 13. *There shall not a man be put to death*] This was as much to Saul's credit as the lately proposed measure was to the discredit of his soldiers.

Verse 14. *Renew the kingdom*] The unction of Saul, in the first instance, was a very private act; and his being appointed to be king was not known to the people in general. He had now shown himself worthy to command the people; and Samuel takes advantage of this circumstance to gain the general consent in his favour. Josephus says that Saul was anointed a *second time* at this convocation.

Verse 15. *There they made Saul king*] It is likely, from these words, that Saul was anointed a second time; he was now publicly acknowledged, and there was no gainsayer. Thus far Saul acted well, and the kingdom seemed to be confirmed in his hand; but soon through *imprudence* he lost it.

ON the custom referred to in ver. 7 I am favoured with the following observations by a learned correspondent:—

"It is considered that the authenticity of records respecting a peculiar people cannot be better illustrated, or the fidelity of the historian more clearly ascertained, than by proving that the manners and customs recorded are in unison with, or bear a resemblance to, the manners and customs of other nations of the same antiquity; or, what may be more correct, in a similar state of improvement; and the records of such rites and customs may possibly acquire

an additional mark of authenticity, when the similarity is not so exact as to admit a presumption that the customs of one nation were merely copied from the other.

"Sir Walter Scott, in the third canto of the *Lady of the Lake,* describes the rites, incantations, and imprecations, used prior to the fiery cross being circulated, to summon the rough warriors of ancient times to the service of their chief; and in the first note of this canto he alludes to this ancient custom which, in comparatively modern times, has been used in Scotland, and proves that a similar punishment of death or destruction of the houses for disobeying the summons was inflicted by the ancient Scandinavians, as recorded by Olaus Magnus, in his history of the Goths. A custom still more in point than the one cited may be found to have existed in a more ancient nation, whose history is supposed the most, if not the only, authentic narrative of deeds of ancient times; and which also records the sanguinary manners of uncultivated nations; see the preceding chapter, first eight verses. The similarity of the custom is to be found in the seventh verse; with the Highlanders a goat was slain; with the Israelites, an ox. The exhibition of a cross stained with the blood of the sacrificed animal was the summons of the former, while part of the animal was the mandate of the latter. Disobedience in the one nation was punished with the death of the parties, and burning of their dwellings; in the other, the punishment was more simple, and more allusive to the sacrificed emblem, the forfeiture or destruction of their oxen. It is not difficult to judge whether the comparison be correct.

"The first verses record the sanguinary practices of ancient times, which to many appear merely as the gratification of revenge, or as proofs of victory; yet when it is considered that the right eye must chiefly aid the warrior in aiming at his adversary, whether the weapon be of ancient or modern warfare, here arises a military reason, corroborative of the truth of history, for the deprivation, and in some degree lessening the cruelty of the mutilation, which would be increased if it were caused by revenge or wantonness; though Nahash declares it to be a reproach upon all Israel."

CHAPTER XII

Samuel, grown old, testifies his integrity before the people, which they confirm, 1–5. He reproves them for their ingratitude and disobedience; and gives a summary of the history of their fathers, 6–12. He exhorts them to future obedience, and calls for a sign from heaven to confirm his authority, and to show them their disobedience: God sends an extraordinary thunder and rain, 13–19. He warns them against idolatry, and exhorts to obedience, and promises to intercede for them, 20–23. Sums up their duty, and concludes with a solemn warning, 24, 25.

A. M. 2909
B. C. 1095
An. Exod. Isr.
396
Anno ante
I. Olymp. 319

AND Samuel said unto all Israel, Behold, I have hearkened unto [a]your voice in all that ye said unto me, and [b]have made a king over you.

2 And now, behold, the king [c]walketh before you: [d]and I am old and gray-headed; and, behold, my sons *are* with you: and I have walked before you from my childhood unto this day.

3 Behold, [e]here I *am:* witness against me before the LORD, and before [f]his anointed: [g]whose ox have I taken? or whose ass have I taken? or whom have I defrauded? whom have I oppressed? or of whose hand have I received *any* [h]bribe [i]to [k]blind mine eyes therewith? and I will restore it you.

4 And they said, Thou hast not defrauded us, nor oppressed us, neither hast thou taken aught of any man's hand.

5 And he said unto them, The LORD *is* witness against you, and his anointed *is* witness this day, [l]that ye have not found aught [m]in my hand. And they answered, *He is* witness.

A. M. 2909
B. C. 1095
An. Exod. Isr.
396
Anno ante
I. Olymp. 319

6 And Samuel said unto the people, [n]*It is* the LORD that [o]advanced Moses and Aaron, and that brought your fathers up out of the land of Egypt.

7 Now therefore stand still, that I may [p]reason with you before the LORD of all the [q]righteous acts of the LORD, which he did [r]to you and to your fathers.

8 [s]When Jacob was come into Egypt, and your fathers [t]cried unto the LORD, then the LORD [u]sent Moses and Aaron, which brought forth your fathers out of Egypt, and made them dwell in this place.

9 And when they [v]forgat the LORD their God, [w]he sold them into the hand of Sisera, captain of the host of Hazor, and into the hand of

---

[a]Chap. viii. 5, 19, 20——[b]Chap. x. 24; xi. 14, 15
[c]Num. xxvii. 17; chap. viii. 20——[d]Chap. viii. 1, 5
[e]Ecclus. xlvi. 19——[f]Ver. 5; chap. x. 1; xxiv. 6; 2 Sam.
i. 14, 16——[g]Num. xvi. 15; Acts xx. 33; 1 Thess. ii. 5
[h]Heb. *ransom*——[i]Or, *that I should hide mine eyes at him*——[k]Deut. xvi. 19

[l]John xviii. 38; Acts xxiii. 9; xxiv. 16, 20——[m]Exodus
xxii. 4——[n]Mic. vi. 4——[o]Or, *made*——[p]Isa. i. 18; v.
3, 4; Mic. vi. 2, 3——[q]Heb. *righteousnesses,* or, *benefits;*
Judg. v. 11; [r]Heb. *with*——[s]Gen. xlvi. 5, 6——[t]Exod.
ii. 23——[u]Exodus iii. 10; iv. 26——[v]Judg. iii. 7
[w]Judg. iv. 2

NOTES ON CHAP. XII

Verse 1. *And Samuel said*] It is very likely that it was at this public meeting Samuel delivered the following address; no other time seems to be given for it, and this is the most proper that could be chosen.

Verse 2. *My sons* are *with you*] It is generally agreed that these words intimate that Samuel had deprived them of their public employ, and reduced them to a level with the common people.

Have walked before you from my childhood] He had been a long, steady, and immaculate servant of the public.

Verse 3. *Witness against me*] Did ever a minister of state, in any part of the world, resign his office with so much self-consciousness of integrity, backed with the universal approbation of the public? No man was oppressed under his government, no man defrauded! He had accumulated no riches for himself; he had procured none for his friends; nor had one needy dependant been provided for out of the *public purse.* He might have pardoned his own sons, who had acted improperly, before he quitted the government; but though he was the

most tender of parents, he would not, but abandoned them to national justice, with only a tacit solicitation of mercy: *Behold, my sons are with you!* They have acted improperly; I deprived them of their authority; they are amenable to *you* for their past conduct; I have walked uprightly and disinterestedly among you; they have not followed my steps: but can you forgive them for their father's sake? As a *minister of justice,* he abandons them to their fate; as a *tender father,* he indirectly and modestly pleads for them on the ground of his own services. Had he not acted thus in both these relations, he would have been unworthy of that character which he so deservedly bears.

Verse 4. *They said, Thou hast not defrauded*] Of what minister or governor can any nation under heaven say such things?

Verse 7. *Now therefore stand still*] I have arraigned *myself* before God and you; I now arraign *you* before God.

Verse 8. *The Lord sent Moses and Aaron*] He shows them that through all their history God had ever raised them up deliverers, when their necessities required such interference.

Verse 9. *The hand of Sisera*] See these transactions in the book of Judges, as **marked**

A. M. 2909
B. C. 1095
An. Exod. Isr. 396
Anno ante
I. Olymp. 319

[x]the Philistines, and into the hand of the king [y]of Moab, and they fought against them.

10 And they cried unto the LORD, and said, [z]We have sinned, because we have forsaken the LORD, [a]and have served Baalim and Ashtaroth: but now [b]deliver us out of the hand of our enemies, and we will serve thee.

11 And the LORD sent [c]Jerubbaal, and Bedan, and [d]Jephthah, and [e]Samuel, and delivered you out of the hand of your enemies on every side, and ye dwelled safe.

12 And when ye saw that [f]Nahash the king of the children of Ammon came against you, [g]ye said unto me, Nay; but a king shall reign over us: when [h]the LORD your God *was* your king.

13 Now therefore [i]behold the king [k]whom ye have chosen, *and* whom ye have desired! and, behold, [l]the LORD hath set a king over you.

14 If ye will [m]fear the LORD, and serve him, and obey his voice, and not rebel against the

[n]commandment of the LORD, then shall both ye and also the king that reigneth over you [o]continue following the LORD your God:

A. M. 2909
B. C. 1096
An. Exod. Isr. 396
Anno ante
I. Olymp. 319

15 But if ye will [p]not obey the voice of the LORD, but rebel against the commandment of the LORD, then shall the hand of the LORD be against you, [q]as *it was* against your fathers.

16 Now therefore [r]stand and see this great thing, which the LORD will do before your eyes.

17 *Is it* not [s]wheat harvest to-day? [t]I will call unto the LORD, and he shall send thunder and rain; that ye may perceive and see that [u]your wickedness *is* great, which ye have done in the sight of the LORD, in asking you a king.

18 So Samuel called unto the LORD; and the LORD sent thunder and rain that day: and [v]all the people greatly feared the LORD and Samuel.

19 And all the people said unto Samuel, [w]Pray for thy servants unto the LORD thy God, that we die not: for we have added unto

---

[x]Judges x. 7; xiii. 1——[y]Judges iii. 12——[z]Judges x. 10——[a]Judges ii. 13——[b]Judg. x. 15, 16——[c]Judg. vi. 14, 32——[d]Judg. xi. 1——[e]Chap. vii. 13——[f]Chap. xi. 1——[g]Chap. viii. 3, 19——[h]Judg. viii. 23; chap. viii. 7; x. 19——[i]Chap. x. 24——[k]Chap. viii. 5; ix. 20——[l]Hos. xiii. 11——[m]Josh. xxiv. 14; Psa. lxxxi. 13, 14

[n]Heb. *mouth*——[o]Heb. *be after*——[p]Lev. xxvi. 14, 15, &c.; Deut. xxviii. 15, &c.; Josh. xxiv. 20——[q]Ver. 9 [r]Exodus xiv. 13, 31——[s]Prov. xxvi. 1——[t]Josh. x. 12; chap. vii. 9, 10; James v. 16, 17, 18——[u]Chap. viii. 7 [v]Exod. xiv. 31; see Ezra x. 9——[w]Exod. ix. 28; x. 17; James v. 15; 1 John v. 16

---

in the margin; and see the notes on those passages.

Verse 11. *Jerubbaal*] That is, Gideon. *And Bedan:* instead of *Bedan,* whose name occurs nowhere else as a judge or deliverer of Israel, the *Septuagint* have *Barak;* the same reading is found in the *Syriac* and *Arabic.* The *Targum* has *Samson.* Many commentators are of this opinion; but *Calmet* thinks that *Jair* is intended, who judged Israel *twenty-two* years, Judg. x. 3.

Instead of *Samuel,* the *Syriac* and *Arabic* have *Samson;* and it is most natural to suppose that Samuel does not mention *himself* in this place. St. Paul's authority confirms these alterations: *The time would fail me,* says he, *to tell of Gideon,* of *Barak,* of *Samson,* of *Jephthah,* of *David,* &c.

Verse 12. *When ye saw that Nahash*] This was not the first time they had demanded a *king;* see before, chap. viii. 5. But at the crisis mentioned here they became more importunate; and it was in consequence of this that the kingdom was a second time confirmed to Saul. Saul was *elected* at *Mizpeh,* he was *confirmed* at *Gilgal.*

Verse 14. *If ye will fear the Lord, &c.*] On condition that ye rebel no more, God will take you and your king under his merciful protection, and he and his kingdom shall be confirmed and *continued.*

Verse 16. *This great thing*] This unusual occurrence.

Verse 17. Is it *not wheat harvest to-day?*] That is, This is the *time of wheat harvest.* According to St. Jerome, who spent several years in the promised land, this harvest commenced about the end of *June* or beginning of *July,* in which he says he never saw rain in Judea: Nunquam enim in fine mensis Junii, sive in mense Julio, in his provinciis, maximeque in Judea, pluvias vidimus.—HIER. in Amos iv. 7; where he refers to this very history. What occurred now hardly ever occurs there but in the winter months.

Verse 18. *The Lord sent thunder and rain that day*] This was totally unusual; and, as it came at the *call of Samuel,* was a most evident *miracle.*

Greatly feared the Lord] They dreaded His terrible majesty; and *they feared Samuel,* perceiving that he had so much power with God.

Verse 19. *Pray for thy servants—that we die not*] As they knew they had rebelled against God, they saw that they had every thing to fear from his justice and power.

We have added unto all our sins this evil] It is no sin to have a king; a good king is one of the greatest blessings of God's providence; but it is a sin to put a *man* in the place of *God.* Is it not strange that they did not now attempt to repair their fault? They might have done it, but they did not; they acknowledged their sin, but did not put it away. This is the general way of mankind. "God help us, we are all sinners!" is the general language of all people;

A. M. 2909
B. C. 1095
An. Exod. Isr.
396
Anno ante
I. Olymp. 319

all our sins *this* evil, to ask us a king.

20 And Samuel said unto the people, Fear not: ye have done all this wickedness: yet turn not aside from following the LORD, but serve the LORD with all your heart;

21 And *x*turn ye not aside: *y*for *then should ye go* after vain *things,* which cannot profit nor deliver; for they *are* vain.

22 For *z*the LORD will not forsake his people *a*for his great name's sake: because *b*it

hath pleased the LORD to make you his people.

A. M. 2909
B. C. 1095
An. Exod. Isr.
396
Anno ante
I. Olymp. 319

23 Moreover, as for me, God forbid that I should sin against the LORD *c*in *d*ceasing to pray for you: but *e*I will teach you the *f*good and the right way:

24 *g*Only fear the LORD, and serve him in truth with all your heart: for *h*consider *i*how *k*great *things* he hath done for you.

25 But if ye shall still do wickedly, *l*ye shall be consumed, *m*both ye and your king.

---

*x*Deut. xi. 16——*y*Jer. xvi. 19; Hab. ii. 18; 1 Cor. viii. 4——*z*1 Kings vi. 13; Psa. xciv. 14——*a*Josh. vii. 9; Psa. cvi. 8; Jer. xiv. 21; Ezek. xx. 9, 14——*b*Deut. vii. 7, 8; xiv. 2; Mal. i. 2——*c*Heb. *from ceasing*——*d*Acts xii. 5; Rom. i. 9; Col. i. 9; 2 Tim. i. 3

*e*Psa. xxxiv. 11; Prov. iv. 11——*f*1 Kings viii. 36: 2 Chron. vi. 27; Jer. vi. 16——*g*Eccles. xii. 13——*h*Isa. v. 12——*i*Or, *what a great* thing, &c.——*k*Deut. x. 21; Psalm cxxvi. 2, 3——*l*Josh. xxiv. 20——*m*Deut. xxviii. 36

---

but though to be a *sinner* is to be in the most *solemn* and *awful* circumstances, yet they are contented to bear the character, heedless of the consequences!

Verse 20. *Ye have done all this wickedness*] That is, *although* ye have done all this wickedness: what was past God would pass by, provided they would be obedient in future.

Verse 21. *After vain* things] That is, *idols;* which he calls here התהו *hattohu*, the same expression found Gen. i. 2. *The earth was* תהו *tohu;* it was *waste, empty,* and *formless:* so idols; they are *confusion,* and things of *naught,* for *an idol is nothing in the world*—it is not the representative of any intelligent being.

Verse 22. *The Lord will not forsake his people*] He will not as yet cast you off, though you have deserved it. His purpose in preserving them in their land and religion was not yet accomplished. It was not however *for their sake* that he would not cast them off, but *for his own great name's sake.* He drew his reasons from himself.

Verse 23. *God forbid that I should sin*] They had earnestly begged him, ver. 19, to pray to God for them, that they might not die; and he tells them that he should consider himself a sinner, should he cease to be their intercessor.

But I will teach you the good and the right way] I will show you, as long as I am with you, what *true religion* is; it is the *way* to

happiness and *heaven.* It is *right*—there is no *crookedness* in it; it is *good*—there is no *evil* in it.

Verse 24. *Only fear the Lord*] Know, respect, and *reverence* him.

Serve him] Consider him your *Lord* and *Master;* consider yourselves his *servants.*

In truth] Be ever *honest,* ever *sincere; with all your heart*—have every *affection* engaged in the work of obedience; act not merely from a principle of *duty,* but also from a *pious, affectionate sense* of obligation. Act towards your God as an affectionate *child* should act towards a tender and loving *parent.*

Consider how great things] Review the history of your *fathers,* review your own life; see what interpositions of power, mercy, goodness, and truth, God has displayed in your behalf! Has he not daily loaded you with his benefits?

Verse 25. *Ye shall be consumed*] If ye do wickedly *you* shall be destroyed, your *kingdom* destroyed, and your *king* destroyed. Here they had set before them life and good, death and evil. Never was a people more fully warned, and never did a people profit less by the warning; and they continue to this day monuments of God's justice and forbearance. Reader, What art thou? Perhaps a similar monument. Consider therefore what great things God has done for *thee.*

CHAPTER XIII

Saul chooses a body of troops, 1, 2. Jonathan smites a garrison of the Philistines, 3, 4. The Philistines gather together an immense host against Israel, 5. The Israelites are afraid; and some hide themselves in caves, and others flee over Jordan, 6, 7. Samuel delaying his coming, Saul offers sacrifice, 8, 9. Samuel comes and reproves him, and Saul excuses himself, 10–12. Samuel shows him that God has rejected him from being captain over his people, 13, 14. Samuel departs; and Saul and Jonathan, with six hundred *men abide in Gibeah, 15, 16. The Philistines send out foraging companies, and waste the land, 17, 18. Desolate state of the Israelitish army, having no weapons of defence against their enemies, 19–23.*

A. M. 2909
B. C. 1095
An. Exod. Isr. 396
Anno ante
I. Olymp. 319

SAUL [a]reigned one year; and when he had reigned two years over Israel,

A. M. 2911
B. C. 1093
An. Exod. Isr. 398
Anno ante
I. Olymp. 317

2 Saul chose him three thousand *men* of Israel; *whereof* two thousand were with Saul in Michmash and in Mount Beth-el, and a thousand were with Jonathan in [b]Gibeah of Benjamin: and the rest of the people he sent every man to his tent.

3 And Jonathan smote the [c]garrison of the Philistines that *was* in [d]Geba, and the Philistines heard *of it*. And Saul blew the trumpet throughout all the land, saying, Let the Hebrews hear.

4 And all Israel heard say *that* Saul had smitten a garrison of the Philistines, and *that* Israel also [e]was had in abomination with the Philistines. And the people were called together after Saul to Gilgal.

5 And the Philistines gathered themselves together to fight with Israel, thirty thousand chariots, and six thousand horsemen, and people as the sand which *is* on the sea-shore in multitude: and they came up, and pitched in Michmash, eastward from Beth-aven.

A. M. 2911
B. C. 1093
An. Exod. Isr. 398
Anno ante
I. Olymp. 317

6 When the men of Israel saw that they were in a strait, (for the people were distressed,) then the people [f]did hide themselves in caves, and in thickets, and in rocks, and in high places, and in pits.

7 And *some of* the Hebrews went over Jordan to the land of Gad and Gilead. As for Saul, he *was* yet in Gilgal, and all the people [g]followed him trembling.

8 [h]And he tarried seven days, according to the set time that Samuel *had appointed:* but Samuel came not to Gilgal; and the people were scattered from him.

---

[a]Heb. *the son of one year in his reigning*——[b]Chapter x. 26——[c]Chap. x. 5——[d]Or, *the hill*

[e]Heb. *did stink;* Gen. xxxiv. 30; Exod. v. 21——[f]Judg. vi. 2——[g]Heb. *trembled after him*——[h]Chap. x. 8

NOTES ON CHAP. XIII

Verse 1. *Saul reigned one year*] A great deal of learned labour has been employed and lost on this verse, to reconcile it with propriety and common sense. I shall not recount the meanings put on it. I think this clause belongs to the preceding chapter, either as a part of the whole, or a chronological note added afterwards; as if the writer had said, *These things* (related in chap. xii.) *took place in the first year of Saul's reign:* and then he proceeds in the next place to tell us what took place in the *second year,* the *two* most remarkable years of Saul's reign. In the first he is appointed, anointed, and twice confirmed, viz., at *Mizpeh* and at *Gilgal;* in the *second,* Israel is brought into the lowest state of degradation by the Philistines, Saul acts unconstitutionally, and is rejected from being king. These things were worthy of an especial *chronological* note.

And when he had reigned] This should begin the chapter, and be read thus: "And when Saul had reigned two years over Israel, he chose him three thousand," &c. The *Septuagint* has left the clause out of the text entirely, and begins the chapter thus: "And Saul chose to himself three thousand men out of the men of Israel."

Verse 2. *Two thousand were with Saul*] Saul, no doubt, meditated the redemption of his country from the Philistines; and having chosen three thousand men, he thought best to divide them into companies, and send one against the Philistine garrison at *Michmash,* another against that at *Beth-el,* and the third against that at *Gibeah:* he perhaps hoped, by *surprising* these garrisons, to get *swords* and *spears* for his men, of which we find, (ver. 22,) they were entirely destitute.

Verse 3. *Jonathan smote*] He appears to have taken this garrison by surprise, for his men had no arms for a regular battle, or taking the place by storm. This is the first place in which this brave and excellent man appears; a man who bears one of the most amiable characters in the Bible.

Let the Hebrews hear.] Probably this means the people who *dwelt beyond Jordan,* who might very naturally be termed here העברים *haibrim,* from עבר *abar, he passed over;* those who are beyond the river Jordan: as Abraham was called עברי *Ibri* because he dwelt beyond the river Euphrates.

Verse 4. *The people were called together*] The smiting of this garrison was the commencement of a war, and in effect the shaking off of the Philistine yoke; and now the people found that they must stand together, and fight for their lives.

Verse 5. *Thirty thousand chariots, and six thousand horsemen*] There is no proportion here between the *chariots* and the *cavalry.* The largest armies ever brought into the field, even by mighty emperors, never were furnished with *thirty thousand* chariots.

I think שלשים *sheloshim,* THIRTY, is a false reading for שלש *shalosh,* THREE. The *Syriac* has ܬܠܬܐ ܐܠܦܝܢ *telotho alpin,* and the *Arabic* ثلاثة الف *thalathato alf,* both signifying THREE *thousand;* and this was a fair proportion to the *horsemen.* This is most likely to be the true reading.

Verse 6. *The people did hide themselves*] They, being few in number, and totally unarmed as to *swords* and *spears,* were terrified at the very numerous and well-appointed army of the Philistines. Judea was full of *rocks, caves, thickets,* &c., where people might shelter themselves from their enemies. While some hid themselves, others fled beyond Jordan:

VOL. II

A. M. 2911
B. C. 1093
An. Exod. Isr.
398
Anno ante
I. Olymp. 317

9 And Saul said, Bring hither a burnt-offering to me, and peace-offerings. And he offered the burnt-offering.

10 And it came to pass, that as soon as he had made an end of offering the burnt-offering, behold, Samuel came; and Saul went out to meet him, that he might ¹salute him.

11 And Samuel said, What hast thou done? And Saul said, Because I saw that the people were scattered from me, and *that* thou camest not within the days appointed, and *that* the Philistines gathered themselves together at Michmash:

12 Therefore said I, The Philistines will come down now upon me to Gilgal, and I have not ᵏmade supplication unto the Lord: I forced myself therefore, and offered a burnt-offering.

13 And Samuel said to Saul, ¹Thou hast done foolishly: ᵐthou hast not kept the commandment of the Lord thy God, which he commanded thee: for now would the Lord have established thy kingdom upon Israel for ever.

A. M. 2911
B. C. 1093
An. Exod. Isr.
398
Anno ante
I. Olymp. 317

14 ⁿBut now thy kingdom shall not continue: ᵒthe Lord hath sought him a man after his own heart, and the Lord hath commanded him *to be* captain over his people, because thou hast not kept *that* which the Lord commanded thee.

15 And Samuel arose, and gat him up from Gilgal unto Gibeah of Benjamin. And Saul numbered the people *that were* ᵖpresent with him, ᑫabout six hundred men.

16 And Saul, and Jonathan his son, and the people *that were* present with them, abode in ʳGibeah of Benjamin: but the Philistines encamped in Michmash.

ⁱHeb. *bless him*——ᵏHeb. *entreated the face*——¹2 Chron. xvi. 9——ᵐChap. xv. 11——ⁿChap. xv. 28

ᵒPsalm lxxxix. 20; Acts xiii. 22——ᵖHebrew, *found* ᑫChap. xiv. 2——ʳHeb. *Geba;* ver. 3

---

and those who did cleave to Saul *followed him trembling.*

Verse 8. *He tarried seven days according to the set time*] Samuel in the beginning had told Saul to wait *seven days*, and he would come to him, and *show him what to do,* chap. x. 8. What is here said cannot be understood of that appointment, but of a different one. Samuel had at this time promised to come to him within seven days, and he kept his word, for we find him there before the day was ended; but as Saul found he did not come at the beginning of the *seventh day,* he became impatient, took the whole business into his own hand, and acted the parts of prophet, priest, and king; and thus he attempted a most essential change in the Israelitish constitution. In it the king, the prophet, and the priest, are in their nature perfectly distinct. What such a rash person might have done, if he had not been deprived of his authority, who can tell? But his conduct on this occasion sufficiently justifies that deprivation. That he was a rash and headstrong man is also proved by his senseless *adjuration* of the people about *food,* chap. xiv. 24, and his unfeeling resolution to put the brave Jonathan, his own son, to death, because he had unwittingly acted contrary to this adjuration, ver. 44. Saul appears to have been a brave and honest man, but he had few of those qualities which are proper for a king, or the governor of a people.

Verse 9. *And he offered the burnt-offering.*] This was most perfectly unconstitutional; he had no authority to offer, or cause to be offered, any of the Lord's sacrifices.

Verse 10. *Behold, Samuel came*] Samuel was punctual to his appointment; one hour longer of delay would have prevented every evil, and by it no good would have been lost. How often are the effects of *precipitation* fatal!

Verse 11. *And Saul said*] Here he offers three excuses for his conduct: 1. The people were fast leaving his standard. 2. Samuel did not come *at the time,* למועד *lemoed;* at the very *commencement* of the time he did not come, but *within* that time he did come. 3. The Philistines were coming fast upon him. Saul should have waited *out* the time; and at all events he should not have gone contrary to the counsel of the Lord.

Verse 12. *I forced myself*] It was with great reluctance that I did what I did. In all this Saul was sincere, but he was rash, and regardless of the *precept of the Lord,* which precept or command he most evidently had received, ver. 13. And one part of this precept was, that the *Lord should tell him what he should do.* Without this information, in an affair under the immediate cognizance of God, he should have taken no step.

Verse 14. *The Lord hath sought him a man after his own heart*] That this man was *David* is sufficiently clear from the sequel. But in what sense was he *a man after God's own heart?* Answer: 1. In his strict attention to the law and worship of God. 2. In his admitting, in the whole of his conduct, that God was King in Israel, and that he himself was but his vicegerent. 3. In never attempting to alter any of those laws, or in the least change the Israelitish constitution. 4. In all his *public official conduct* he acted according to the Divine mind, and fulfilled the will of his Maker: thus was he *a man after God's own heart.* In reference to his *private* or *personal moral* conduct, the word is never used. This is the sense alone in which the word is used here and elsewhere; and it is unfair and wicked to put another meaning on it in order to ridicule the revelation of God, as certain infidels have done.

Verse 15. *And Samuel arose*] Though David, in the Divine purpose, is appointed to

A. M. 2911
B. C. 1093
An. Exod. Isr.
398
Anno ante
I. Olymp. 317

17 And the spoilers came out of the camp of the Philistines in three companies: one company turned unto the way *that leadeth to* ᵍOphrah, unto the land of Shual:

18 And another company turned the way *to* ᵗBeth-horon: and another company turned *to* the way of the border that looketh to the valley of ᵘZeboim toward the wilderness.

19 Now ᵛthere was no smith found throughout all the land of Israel: for the Philistines said, Lest the Hebrews make *them* swords or spears:

20 But all the Israelites went down to the Philistines, to sharpen every man his share, and his coulter, and his axe, and his mattock.

A. M. 2911
B. C. 1093
An. Exod. Isr.
398
Anno ante
I. Olymp. 317

21 Yet they had ʷa file for the mattocks, and for the coulters, and for the forks, and for the axes, and ˣto sharpen the goads.

22 So it came to pass in the day of battle, that ʸthere was neither sword nor spear found in the hand of any of the people that *were* with Saul and Jonathan: but with Saul and with Jonathan his son was there found.

23 ᶻAnd the ᵃgarrison of the Philistines went out to the passage of Michmash.

ˢJosh. xviii. 23——ᵗJosh. xvi. 3; xviii. 13, 14——ᵘNeh. xi. 34——ᵛSee 2 Kings xxiv. 14; Jer. xxiv. 1

ʷHeb. *a file with mouths*——ˣHeb. *to set*——ʸSo Judg. v. 8——ᶻChap. xiv. 1, 4——ᵃOr, *standing camp*

---

be *captain over the people*, yet Saul is not to be removed from the government during his life; Samuel therefore accompanies him to Gibeah, to give him the requisite help in this conjuncture.

About six hundred men.] The whole of the Israelitish army at this time, and not one sword or spear among them!

Verse 17. *The spoilers came out*] The Philistines, finding that the Israelites durst not hazard a battle, divided their army into three bands, and sent them in three different directions to pillage and destroy the country. Jonathan profited by this circumstance, and attacked the remains of the army at Michmash, as we shall see in the succeeding chapter.

Verse 19. *Now there was no smith found*] It is very likely that in the former wars the Philistines carried away all the smiths from Israel, as Porsenna did in the peace which he granted to the Romans, not permitting any iron to be forged except for the purposes of agriculture: "Ne ferro, nisi in agricultura, uterentur." The Chaldeans did the same to the Jews in the time of Nebuchadnezzar; they carried away all the artificers, 2 Kings xxiv. 14; Jer. xxiv. 1; xxix. 2. And in the same manner did Cyrus treat the Lydians, *Herod.* lib. i., c. 145. See several examples in *Calmet.*

Verse 20. *But all the Israelites went down to the Philistines*] We find from this that they did not grant them as much as Porsenna did to the Romans; he permitted the people to manufacture the implements of *husbandry.*

Verse 21. *Yet they had a file*] The Hebrew פְּצִירָה *petsirah,* from פָּצַר *patsar,* to *rub hard,* is translated very differently by the versions and by critics. Our translation may be as likely as any: they permitted them the use of *files,* (I believe the word means *grindstone,*) to restore the blunted edges of their *tridents, axes,* and *goads.*

Verse 22. *In the day of battle—there was*

neither sword nor spear] But if the Israelites enjoyed such profound peace and undisturbed dominion under Samuel, how is it that they were totally destitute of *arms,* a state which argues the lowest circumstances of oppression and vassalage? In answer to this we may observe, that the *bow* and the *sling* were the principal arms of the Israelites; for these they needed no *smith:* the most barbarous nations, who have never seen *iron,* have nevertheless *bows* and *arrows;* the arrow *heads* generally made of *flint.* Arrows of this kind are found among the inhabitants of the South Sea islands; and even axes, and different implements of war, all made of stone, cut and polished by stone, are frequent among them. The arms of the aboriginal Irish have been of this kind. I have frequently seen heads of *axes* and *arrows* of *stone,* which have been dug up out of the ground, formed with considerable taste and elegance. The former the common people term *thunderbolts;* the latter, *elf-stones.* Several of these from *Ireland,* from *Zetland,* and from the *South Sea islands,* are now before me.

Now it is possible that the Israelites had still *bows* and *arrows:* these they could have without the *smith;* and it is as likely that they had *slings,* and for these they needed none. But then these were *missiles;* if they came into *close* fight, they would avail them nothing: for attacks of this kind they would require *swords* and *spears;* of these none were found but with Saul and Jonathan.

WE see, in this chapter, Israel brought to as low a state as they were under Eli; when they were totally discomfited, their priests slain, their ark taken, and the judge dead. After that, they rose by the strong hand of God; and in this way they are now to rise, principally by means of David, whose history will soon commence.

CHAPTER XIV

Jonathan and his armour-bearer purpose to attack a garrison of the Philistines, 1. Saul and his army, with Ahiah the priest, tarry in Gibeah, 2, 3. Jonathan plans his attack of the Philistine garrison, 4–10. He and his armour-bearer climb over a rock: attack and rout the garrison, 11–15. Saul and his company,

A. M. 2917
B. C. 1087
An. Exod. Isr. 404
Anno ante
I. Olymp. 311

NOW [a]it came to pass upon a day, that Jonathan the son of Saul said unto the young man that bare his armour, Come and let us go over to the Philistines' garrison, that *is* on the other side. But he told not his father.

2 And Saul tarried in the uttermost parts of Gibeah under a pomegranate tree which *is* in Migron: and the people that *were* with him *were* [b]about six hundred men;

3 And [c]Ahiah, the son of Ahitub, [d]I-chabod's brother, the son of Phinehas, the son of Eli, the LORD's priest in Shiloh, [e]wearing an ephod. And the people knew not that Jonathan was gone.

4 And between the passages, by which Jonathan sought to go over [f]unto the Philistines' garrison, *there was* a sharp rock on the one side, and a sharp rock on the other side: and the name of the one *was* Bozez, and the name of the other Seneh.

5 The [g]fore-front of the one *was* situate

northward over against Mich-mash, and the other southward over against Gibeah.

A. M. 2917
B. C. 1087
An. Exod. Isr. 404
Anno ante
I. Olymp. 311

6 And Jonathan said to the young man that bare his armour, Come, and let us go over unto the garrison of these uncircumcised: it may be that the LORD will work for us: for *there is* no restraint to the LORD [h]to save by many or by few.

7 And his armour-bearer said unto him, Do all that *is* in thine heart: turn thee; behold, I *am* with thee according to thy heart.

8 Then said Jonathan, Behold, we will pass over unto *these* men, and we will discover ourselves unto them.

9 If they say thus unto us, [i]Tarry until we come to you; then we will stand still in our place, and will not go up unto them.

10 But if they say thus, Come up unto us; then we will go up; for [k]the LORD hath delivered them into our hand: and [l]this *shall be* a sign unto us.

11 And both of them discovered themselves

---

[a]Or, *there was a day*——[b]Chap. xiii. 15——[c]Chap. xxii. 9, 11, 20, called *Ahimelech*——[d]Chap. iv. 21 [e]Chapter ii. 28——[f]Chap. xiii. 23

[g]Heb. *tooth*——[h]Judg. vii. 4, 7; 2 Chron. xiv. 11; 1 Mac. iii. 18——[i]Heb. *be still*——[k]1 Mac. iv. 30 [l]See Gen. xxiv. 14; Judg. vii. 11

NOTES ON CHAP. XIV

Verse 1. *Come, and let us go over*] This action of Jonathan was totally contrary to the laws of war; no military operation should be undertaken without the knowledge and command of the general. But it is likely that he was led to this by a Divine influence.

The *armour-bearer* is the origin of what we call *esquire*, from *escu*, old French, a *shield;* *armiger* is the Latin, from *arma, weapons*, and *gero, I bear.* In the times of chivalry, the *armiger*, or *esquire*, was the *servant* of the knight who went after him, and carried his lance, shield, &c. It is now (strange to tell!) a title of *honour.*

Verse 2. *Under a pomegranate tree*] Under *Rimmon*, which not only signifies a *pomegranate tree*, but also a strong rock, in which *six hundred* Benjamites took shelter, Judg. xx. 45. Probably it was in this very rock that Saul and his six hundred men now lay hidden.

Verse 3. *Ahiah, the son of Ahitub*] Phinehas, son of Eli the high priest, had two sons, Ahitub

and I-chabod; the latter was born when the ark was taken, and his mother died immediately after. Ahiah is also called Ahimelech, chap. xxii. 9.

Wearing an ephod.] That is, performing the functions of the high priest. This man does not appear to have been with Saul when he offered the sacrifices, chap. xiii. 9, &c.

Verse 4. *The name of the one was Bozez*] *Slippery;* and the name of the other Seneh, *treading down.*—Targum.

Verse 6. *Let us go over*] Moved, doubtless, by a Divine impulse.

There is *no restraint to the Lord*] This is a fine sentiment; and where there is a promise of defence and support, the weakest, in the face of the strongest enemy, may rely on it with the utmost confidence.

Verse 7. *Behold, I* am *with thee*] I shall accompany thee whithersoever thou goest, and share all thy dangers.

Verse 9. *If they say thus unto us*] Jonathan had no doubt asked this as a sign from God;

A. M. 2917
B. C. 1087
An. Exod. Isr. 404
Anno ante I. Olymp. 311

unto the garrison of the Philistines: and the Philistines said, Behold, the Hebrews come forth out of the holes where they had hid themselves.

12 And the men of the garrison answered Jonathan and his armour-bearer, and said, Come up to us, and we will show you a thing. And Jonathan said unto his armour-bearer, Come up after me; for the LORD hath delivered them into the hands of Israel.

13 And Jonathan climbed up upon his hands and upon his feet, and his armour-bearer after him: and they fell before Jonathan; and his armour-bearer slew after him.

14 And that first slaughter, which Jonathan and his armour-bearer made, was about twenty men, within as it were ^ma half acre of land, *which* a yoke *of oxen might plough.*

15 And ⁿthere was trembling in the host, in the field, and among all the people: the garrison, and ^othe spoilers, they also trembled, and the earth quaked: so it was ^pa ^qvery great trembling.

16 And the watchmen of Saul in Gibeah of Benjamin looked; and, behold, the multitude melted away, and they ^rwent on beating down *one another.*

A. M. 2917
B. C. 1087
An. Exod. Isr. 404
Anno ante I. Olymp. 311

17 Then said Saul unto the people that *were* with him, Number now, and see who is gone from us. And when they had numbered, behold, Jonathan and his armour-bearer *were* not *there.*

18 And Saul said unto Ahiah, Bring hither the ark of God. For the ark of God was at that time with the children of Israel.

19 And it came to pass, while Saul ^stalked unto the priest, that the ^tnoise that *was* in the host of the Philistines went on and increased: and Saul said unto the priest, Withdraw thine hand.

20 And Saul and all the people that *were* with him ^uassembled themselves, and they came to the battle: and, behold, ^vevery man's sword was against his fellow, *and there was a* very great discomfiture.

21 Moreover the Hebrews *that* were with

---

^mOr, *half a furrow of an acre of land;* Judges vii. 21
ⁿ2 Kings vii. 7; Job xviii. 11——^oChap. xiii. 17
^pHeb. *a trembling of God*

^qGen. xxxv. 5——^rVer. 20——^sNum. xxvii. 21
^tOr, *tumult*——^uHeb. *were cried together*——^vJudg. vii. 22; 2 Chron. xx. 23

---

exactly as Eliezer the servant of Abraham did, Gen. xxiv. 12.

Verse 12. *Come up to us, and we will show you a thing.*] This was the favourable sign which Jonathan had requested. The Philistines seem to have meant, Come, and we will show you how well fortified we are, and how able to quell all the attacks of your countrymen.

Verse 13. *Jonathan climbed up*] It seems he had a part of the rock still to get over. When he got over he began to slay the guards, which were about twenty in number; these were of a sort of outpost or advanced guard to the garrison.

Slew after him] Jonathan knocked them down, and the armour-bearer despatched them. This seems to be the meaning.

Verse 14. *A half acre of land*] The ancients measured land by the quantum which a yoke of oxen could plough in a day. The original is obscure, and is variously understood. It is probably a proverbial expression for a *very small space.*

Verse 15. *There was trembling in the host*] They were terrified and panic-struck; the people in general round about, those in the garrison, the spoilers, and the whole country, were struck with terror; the commotion was universal and most extraordinary. The trembling of the earth is probably not to be taken literally, but as a metaphor for a great commotion in the country, though God might have interposed in an extraordinary manner, and produced a real earthquake; but their being panic-struck was sufficient to produce all the requisite confusion and dismay.

Verse 16. *The watchmen of Saul*] Those who were sent out as scouts to observe the motions of the army.

Melted away] There was no order in the Philistine camp, and the people were dispersing in all directions. The Vulgate has, *Et ecce multitudo prostrata,* "And behold the multitude were prostrate;" many lay dead upon the field, partly by the sword of Jonathan and his armour-bearer, and partly by the swords of each other, ver. 20.

Verse 17. *Number now*] Saul perceived that the Philistines were routed, but could not tell by what means; supposing that it must be by some of his own troops, he called a muster to see who and how many were absent.

Verse 18. *Bring hither the ark of God*] He wished to inquire what use he should make of the present favourable circumstances, and to proceed in the business as God should direct.

Verse 19. *While Saul talked unto the priest*] Before he had made an end of consulting him, the increasing noise of the panic-struck Philistines called his attention; and finding there was no time to lose, he immediately collected his men and fell on them.

Verse 21. *The Hebrews that were with the Philistines*] We may understand such as they held in bondage, or who were their servants. Instead of *Hebrews* the *Septuagint* read, οἱ δουλοι, *the slaves;* from which it is evident that, instead of עברים *Ibrim, Hebrews,* they found in their text עבדים *abadim, servants.* But this reading is not countenanced by any other version, nor by any MS. yet discovered.

A. M. 2917
B. C. 1087
An. Exod. Isr.
404
Anno ante
I. Olymp. 311

the Philistines before that time, which went up with them into the camp *from the country* round about, even they also *turned* to be with the Israelites that *were* with Saul and Jonathan.

22 Likewise all the men of Israel which ^whad hid themselves in Mount Ephraim, *when* they heard that the Philistines fled, even they also followed hard after them in the battle.

23 ^xSo the LORD saved Israel that day: and the battle passed over ^yunto Beth-aven.

24 And the men of Israel were distressed that day: for Saul had ^zadjured the people, saying, Cursed *be* the man that eateth *any* food until evening, that I may be avenged on mine enemies. So none of the people tasted *any* food.

25 ^aAnd all *they of* the land came to a wood; and there was ^bhoney upon the ground.

26 And when the people were come into the wood, behold, the honey dropped; but no man put his hand to his mouth: for the people feared the oath.

27 But Jonathan heard not when his father charged the people with the oath: wherefore he put forth the end of the rod that *was* in his hand, and dipped it in a honey-comb, and put his hand to his mouth; and his eyes were enlightened.

28 Then answered one of the people, and said, Thy father straitly charged the people

with an oath, saying, Cursed *be* the man that eateth *any* food this day. And the people were ^cfaint.

A. M. 2917
B. C. 1087
An. Exod. Isr.
404
Anno ante
I. Olymp. 311

29 Then said Jonathan, My father hath troubled the land: see, I pray you, how mine eyes have been enlightened, because I tasted a little of this honey.

30 How much more, if haply the people had eaten freely to-day of the spoil of their enemies which they found? for had there not been now a much greater slaughter among the Philistines?

31 And they smote the Philistines that day from Michmash to Aijalon: and the people were very faint.

32 And the people flew upon the spoil, and took sheep, and oxen, and calves, and slew *them* on the ground: and the people did eat *them* ^dwith the blood.

33 Then they told Saul, saying, Behold, the people sin against the LORD, in that they eat with the blood. And he said, Ye have ^etransgressed: roll a great stone unto me this day.

34 And Saul said, Disperse yourselves among the people, and say unto them, Bring me hither every man his ox, and every man his sheep, and slay *them* here, and eat; and sin not against the LORD in eating with the blood. And all the people brought every man his ox ^fwith him that night, and slew *them* there.

35 And Saul ^gbuilt an altar unto the LORD:

---

^wChap. xiii. 6——^xExod. xiv. 30; Psa. xliv. 6, 7; Hos. i. 7——^yChap. xiii. 5——^zJosh. vi. 26——^aDeut. ix. 28; Matt. iii. 5——^bExod. iii. 8; Num. xiii. 27; Matt. iii. 4

^cOr, *weary*——^dLev. iii. 17; vii. 26; xvii. 10; xix. 26; Deut. xii. 16, 23, 24——^eOr, *dealt treacherously* ^fHeb. *in his hand*——^gChap. vii. 17

Verse 22. *The men—which had hid themselves*] See chap. xiii. 6.

The *Vulgate* and the *Septuagint* add here, *And there were with Saul about ten thousand men;* but this is supported by no other authority.

Verse 24. *Saul had adjured the people*] He was afraid, if they waited to refresh themselves, the Philistines would escape out of their hands, and therefore he made the taking any food till sunset a capital crime. This was the very means of defeating his own intention; for as the people were exhausted for want of food, they could not continue the pursuit of their enemies: had it not been for this foolish adjuration, there had been a greater slaughter of the Philistines, ver. 30.

Verse 25. *There was honey upon the ground*] There were many wild bees in that country, and Judea is expressly said to be a land flowing with milk and *honey*.

Verse 26. *The honey dropped*] It seems to have dropped from the *trees* on the ground. Honey

dews, as they are called, are not uncommon in most countries; and this appears to have been something of this kind. I have seen *honey* in considerable quantity on the *trees* and long *grass* in the fields, and have often eaten of it.

Verse 27. *His eyes were enlightened.*] Hunger and fatigue affect and dim the sight; on taking food, this affection is immediately removed. This most people know to be a fact.

Verse 31. *They smote the Philistines—from Michmash to Aijalon*] The distance Calmet states to be three or four leagues.

Verse 32. *The people did eat* them *with the blood.*] They were faint through hunger, and did not take time to bleed the cattle on which they fed. This was another bad effect of Saul's rash adjuration.

Verse 33. *Roll a great stone unto me*] Probably this means that they should set up an altar to the Lord, on which the animals might be properly slain, and the blood poured out upon the earth; and a *large stone* was erected for an *altar*.

Verse 35. *Saul built an altar*] And this we

A. M. 2917
B. C. 1087
An. Exod. Isr.
404
Anno ante
I. Olymp. 311

[h]the same was the first altar that he built unto the LORD.

36 And Saul said, Let us go down after the Philistines by night, and spoil them until the morning light, and let us not leave a man of them. And they said, Do whatsoever seemeth good unto thee. Then said the priest, Let us draw near hither unto God.

37 And Saul asked counsel of God, Shall I go down after the Philistines? wilt thou deliver them into the hand of Israel? But [i]he answered him not that day.

38 And Saul said, [k]Draw ye near hither, all the [l]chief of the people: and know and see wherein this sin hath been this day.

39 For, [m]*as* the LORD liveth, which saveth Israel, though it be in Jonathan my son, he shall surely die. But *there was* not a man among all the people *that* answered him.

40 Then said he unto all Israel, Be ye on one side, and I and Jonathan my son will be on the other side. And the people said unto

Saul, Do what seemeth good unto thee.

41 Therefore Saul said unto the LORD God of Israel, [n]Give [o]a perfect *lot.* [p]And Saul and Jonathan were taken: but the people [q]escaped.

42 And Saul said, Cast *lots* between me and Jonathan my son. And Jonathan was taken.

43 Then said Saul to Jonathan, [r]Tell me what thou hast done. And Jonathan told him, and said, [s]I did but taste a little honey with the end of the rod that *was* in mine hand, *and,* lo, I must die.

44 And Saul answered, [t]God do so and more also: [u]for thou shalt surely die, Jonathan.

45 And the people said unto Saul, Shall Jonathan die, who hath wrought this great salvation in Israel? God forbid: [v]*as* the LORD liveth, there shall not one hair of his head fall to the ground; for he hath wrought with God this day. So the people rescued Jonathan, that he died not.

A. M. 2917
B. C. 1087
An. Exod. Isr.
404
Anno ante
I. Olymp. 311

---

[h]Heb. *that altar he began to build unto the LORD* [i]Chap. xxviii. 6——[k]Josh. vii. 14; chap. x. 19——[l]Heb. *corners;* Judg. xx. 2——[m]2 Sam. xii. 5——[n]Or, *Show the innocent*

[o]Prov. xvi. 33; Acts i. 24——[p]Josh. vii. 16; chap. x. 20, 21——[q]Heb. *went forth*——[r]Josh. vii. 19——[s]Ver. 27——[t]Ruth. i. 17——[u]Ver. 39——[v]2 Sam. xiv. 11; 1 Kings i. 52; Luke xxi. 18

---

are informed was *the first* he had built; Samuel, as prophet had hitherto erected the altars, and Saul thought he had sufficient authority to erect one himself without the prophet, as he once offered sacrifice without him.

Verse 36. *Then said the priest*] It is evident that Ahiah doubted the propriety of pursuing the Philistines that night; and as a reverse of fortune might be ruinous after such a victory, he wished to have specific directions from the Lord.

Verse 37. *He answered him not that day.*] Why was this answer delayed? Surely Jonathan's eating the honey was no *sin.* This could not have excited God's displeasure. And yet the *lot* found out Jonathan! But did this argue that he had incurred guilt in the sight of God? I answer: It did not; for Jonathan was delivered, by the authority of the people, from his father's rash curse; no propitiation is offered for his supposed transgression to induce God to pardon it; nor do we find any displeasure of God manifested on the occasion. See below.

Verse 41. *Lord God of Israel, Give a perfect lot.*] Both the *Vulgate* and *Septuagint* add much to this verse: *And Saul said to the Lord God of Israel, Lord God of Israel, give judgment. Why is it that thou hast not answered thy servant to-day? If the iniquity be in me, or Jonathan my son, make it manifest. Or if this iniquity be in thy people, give sanctification.*

Verse 42. *And Jonathan was taken.*] The object of the inquiry most evidently was, "Who has gone contrary to the king's *adjuration* to-day?" The answer to that *must* be JONATHAN. But was this a proof of the Divine displeasure

against the man? By no means: the holy oracle told the truth, but neither that oracle nor the God who gave it fixed any blame upon Jonathan, and his own conscience acquits him. He seeks not pardon from God, because he is conscious he had not transgressed. But why did not God answer the priest that day? Because he did not think it proper to send the people by night in pursuit of the vanquished Philistines. Saul's motive was perfectly vindictive: *Let us go down after the Philistines by night, and spoil them unto the morning light, and let us not leave a man of them;* that is, Let us burn, waste, destroy, and slay all before us! Was it right to indulge a disposition of this kind, which would have led to the destruction of many innocent country people, and of many Israelites who resided among the Philistines? Besides, was there not a most manifest reason in the *people* why God could not be among them? Multitudes of them were defiled in a very solemn manner; they had eaten the *flesh with the blood;* and however sacrifices might be offered to atone for this transgression of the law, they must continue unclean till the evening. Here were reasons enough why God would not go on with the people for that night.

Verse 44. *And Saul answered—thou shalt surely die, Jonathan.*] To save thy rash oath! So must John Baptist's head be taken off at the desire of an impure woman, because a Herod had sworn to give her whatever she might request! Unfeeling brute! However, the king was JUDGE. But what said the *people,* who were the JURY?

Verse 45. *And the people said*] "Shall Jona-

A. M. 2917
B. C. 1087
An. Exod. Isr.
404
Anno ante
I. Olymp. 311

46 Then Saul went up from following the Philistines: and the Philistines went to their own place.

47 So Saul took the kingdom over Israel, and fought against all his enemies on every side, against Moab, and against the children of ᵂAmmon, and against Edom, and against the kings of ˣZobah, and against the Philistines: and whithersoever he turned himself, he vexed *them*.

48 And he ʸgathered a host, and ᶻsmote the Amalekites, and delivered Israel out of the hands of them that spoiled them.

49 Now ᵃthe sons of Saul were Jonathan, and Ishui, and Melchi-shua: and the names of his two daughters *were these;* the name of the firstborn Merab, and the name of the younger Michal:

A. M. 2917
B. C. 1087
An. Exod. Isr.
404
Anno ante
I. Olymp. 311

50 And the name of Saul's wife *was* Ahinoam, the daughter of Ahimaaz: and the name of the captain of his host *was* ᵇAbner, the son of Ner, Saul's uncle.

51 ᶜAnd Kish *was* the father of Saul; and Ner the father of Abner *was* the son of Abiel.

52 And there was sore war against the Philistines all the days of Saul: and when Saul saw any strong man, or any valiant man, ᵈhe took him unto him.

ᵂChap. xi. 11——ˣ2 Sam. x. 6——ʸOr, *wrought mightily*
ᶻChap. xv. 3, 7

ᵃChap. xxxi. 2; 1 Chron. viii. 33——ᵇHeb. *Abiner*
ᶜChap. ix. 1——ᵈChap. viii. 11

---

than die, who hath wrought this great salvation in Israel? God forbid! As the Lord liveth, there shall not one hair of his head fall to the ground." Here was a righteous and impartial *jury,* who brought in a *verdict* according to the *evidence:* No man should *die* but for a *breach of the law of God;* but Jonathan hath *not broken any law of God;* therefore Jonathan *should not die.* And because he *should* not, therefore he *shall* not.

He hath wrought with God this day.] God has been commander-in-chief; Jonathan has acted under his directions.

So the people rescued Jonathan] And God testified no displeasure; and perhaps he permitted all this that he might correct Saul's propensity to rashness and precipitancy.

Verse 47. *So Saul took the kingdom*] The Targum appears to give the meaning of this expression: "Saul prospered in his government over Israel." And the proofs of his prosperity are immediately subjoined.

Fought against all his enemies] Of the wars which are mentioned here we have no particulars; they must have endured a long time, and have been, at least in general, successful.

Verse 48. *Smote the Amalekites.*] This war is mentioned in the following chapter.

Verse 49. *Now the sons of Saul*] We do not find Ishbosheth here. *Calmet* says it was "because he was too young, and did not go with him to the war, for he mentions only those who were with him." Why then mention his *daughters* and his *wife?* Did *they* go with him to the war?

Verse 52. *When Saul saw any strong man*] This was very politic. He thus continued to recruit his army with strong and effective men.

CHAPTER XV

Samuel sends Saul to destroy the Amalekites, and all their substance, 1–3. Saul collects an immense army and comes against their city, 4, 5. He desires the Kenites to remove from among the Amalekites, 6. He smites the Amalekites, and takes their king, Agag, prisoner, and saves the best of the spoil, 7–9. The Lord is displeased, and sends Samuel to reprove him, 10, 11. The conversation between Samuel and Saul, in which the latter endeavours to justify his conduct, 12–23. He is convinced that he has done wrong, and asks pardon, 24–31. Samuel causes Agag to be slain; for which he assigns the reasons, 32–35.

A. M. 2925
B. C. 1079
An. Exod. Isr.
412
Anno ante
I. Olymp. 303

SAMUEL also said unto Saul, ᵃThe LORD sent me to anoint thee *to be* king over his people, over Israel: now therefore hearken thou unto the voice of the words of the LORD.

2 Thus saith the LORD of hosts, I remember *that* which Amalek did to Israel, ᵇhow he laid *wait* for him in the way, when he came up from Egypt.

A. M. 2925
B. C. 1079
An. Exod. Isr.
412
Anno ante
I. Olymp. 303

ᵃChap. ix. 16——ᵇExod. xvii. 8, 14;

Num. xxiv. 20; Deut. xxv. 17, 18, 19

NOTES ON CHAP. XV

Verse 1. *The Lord sent me to anoint thee*] This gave him a right to say what immediately follows.

Verse 2. *I remember* that *which Amalek did*] The Amalekites were a people of Arabia Petræa,

who had occupied a tract of country on the frontiers of Egypt and Palestine. They had acted with great cruelty towards the Israelites on their coming out of Egypt. (See Exod. xvii. 8, and the notes there.) They came upon them *when they were faint and weary, and smote the hindermost of the people*—those who were too

A. M. 2925
B. C. 1079
An. Exod. Isr. 412
Anno ante I. Olymp. 303

3 Now go and smite Amalek, and [c]utterly destroy all that they have, and spare them not; but slay both man and woman, infant and suckling, ox and sheep, camel and ass.

4 And Saul gathered the people together, and numbered them in Telaim, two hundred thousand footmen, and ten thousand men of Judah.

5 And Saul came to a city of Amalek, and [d]laid wait in the valley.

6 And Saul said unto [e]the Kenites, [f]Go, depart, get you down from among the Amalekites, lest I destroy you with them: for [g]ye showed kindness to all the children of Israel, when they came up out of Egypt. So the Kenites departed from among the Amalekites.

7 [h]And Saul smote the Amalekites from [i]Havilah *until* thou comest to [k]Shur, that *is* over against Egypt.

8 And [l]he took Agag the king of the Amalekites alive, and [m]utterly destroyed all the people with the edge of the sword.

9 But Saul and the people [n]spared Agag, and the best of the sheep, and of the oxen, and [o]of the fatlings, and the lambs, and all *that was* good, and would not utterly destroy them: but every thing *that was* vile and refuse, that they destroyed utterly.

A. M. 2925
B. C. 1079
An. Exod. Isr. 412
Anno ante I. Olymp. 303

10 Then came the word of the LORD unto Samuel, saying,

11 [p]It repenteth me that I have set up Saul *to be* king: for he is [q]turned back from following me, [r]and hath not performed my commandments. And it [s]grieved Samuel; and he cried unto the LORD all night.

12 And when Samuel rose early to meet Saul in the morning, it was told Samuel, saying, Saul came to [t]Carmel, and, behold, he set him up a place, and is gone about and passed on, and gone down to Gilgal.

13 And Samuel came to Saul: and Saul said unto him, [u]Blessed *be* thou of the LORD: I have performed the commandment of the LORD.

14 And Samuel said, What *meaneth* then this bleating of the sheep in mine ears, and the lowing of the oxen which I hear?

15 And Saul said, They have brought them from the Amalekites: [v]for the people spared

[c]Lev. xxvii. 28, 29; Josh. vi. 17, 21——[d]Or, *fought*——[e]Num. xxiv. 21; Judg. i. 16; iv. 11——[f]Gen. xviii. 25; xix. 12, 14; Rev. xviii. 4——[g]Exod. xviii. 10, 19; Num. x. 29, 32——[h]Chap. xiv. 48——[i]Gen. ii. 11; xxv. 18——[k]Gen. xvi. 7——[l]See 1 Kings xx. 34, 35, &c.——[m]See chap. xxx. 1

[n]Ver. 3, 15——[o]Or, *of the second sort*——[p]Ver. 35; Gen. vi. 6, 7; 2 Sam. xxiv. 16——[q]Josh. xxii. 16; 1 Kings ix. 6——[r]Chap. xiii. 13; ver. 3, 9——[s]Ver. 35; chap. xvi. 1——[t]Josh. xv. 55——[u]Gen. xiv. 19; Judg. xvii. 2; Ruth iii. 10——[v]Ver. 9, 21; Gen. iii. 12; Prov. xxviii. 13

weak to keep up with the rest. (See Deut. xxv. 18.) And God then purposed that Amalek, as a nation, should be blotted out from under heaven; which purpose was now fulfilled by Saul upwards of *four hundred* years afterwards!

Verse 3. *Slay both man and woman*] Nothing could justify such an exterminating decree but the absolute authority of God. This was given: all the reasons of it we do not know; but this we know well, *The Judge of all the earth doth right*. This war was not for *plunder*, for God commanded that all the *property* as well as all the *people* should be destroyed.

Verse 4. *Two hundred thousand—and ten thousand*] The *Septuagint*, in the *London Polyglot*, have FOUR HUNDRED *thousand companies of Israel*, and THIRTY *thousand companies of Judah*. The *Codex Alexandrinus* has TEN *thousand* of each. The *Camplutensian Polyglot* has TWO HUNDRED *thousand companies of Israel*, and TEN *thousand of Judah*. And *Josephus* has FOUR HUNDRED *thousand of Israel*, and THIRTY *thousand of Judah*. All the other *versions* are the same with the *Hebrew* text; and there is no difference in the MSS.

Verse 5. *Saul came to a city of Amalek*] I believe the original should be translated, *and Saul came to the city Amalek;* their capital being called by the *name* of their *tribe*.

Verse 6. *Said unto the Kenites*] The Kenites were an ancient people. Jethro, the father-in-law of Moses, was a Kenite. Hobab his son (if the same person be not meant) was guide to the Hebrews through the wilderness. They had a portion of the promised land, near to the city Arad. See Judg. i. 16; and for more particulars concerning them and the Amalekites, see the notes on Num. xxvi. 20, 21.

Verse 7. *From Havilah—to Shur*] From Pelusium in Egypt, unto the Red Sea.—*Josephus*. But Havilah lay eastward from the Red Sea; the Amalekites lay between this and the way to Egypt towards Shur.

Verse 11. *It repenteth me that I have set up Saul*] That is, I placed him on the throne; I intended, if he had been obedient, to have established his kingdom. He has been disobedient; I change my purpose, and the kingdom shall not be *established in his family*. This is what is meant by God's *repenting—changing a purpose* according to conditions already laid down or mentally determined.

Verse 12. *He set him up a place*] Literally, a *hand*, יד *yad*. Some say it was a *monument;* others, a *triumphal arch:* probably it was no more than a *hand*, pointing out the place where Saul had gained the victory. *Absalom's pillar* is called *the hand of Absalom*, 2 Sam. xviii. 18.

Verse 15. *The people spared the best of the*

A. M. 2925
B. C. 1079
An. Exod. Isr.
412
Anno ante
I. Olymp. 303
the best of the sheep and of the oxen, to sacrifice unto the Lord thy God; and the rest we have utterly destroyed.

16 Then Samuel said unto Saul, Stay, and I will tell thee what the Lord hath said to me this night. And he said unto him, Say on.

17 And Samuel said, ʷWhen thou *wast* little in thine own sight, *wast* thou not *made* the head of the tribes of Israel, and the Lord anointed thee king over Israel?

18 And the Lord sent thee on a journey, and said, Go and utterly destroy the sinners the Amalekites, and fight against them until ˣthey be consumed.

19 Wherefore then didst thou not obey the voice of the Lord, but didst fly upon the spoil, and didst evil in the sight of the Lord?

20 And Saul said unto Samuel, Yea, ʸI have obeyed the voice of the Lord, and have gone the way which the Lord sent me, and have brought Agag the king of Amalek, and have utterly destroyed the Amalekites.

21 ᶻBut the people took of the spoil, sheep and oxen, the chief of the things which should have been utterly destroyed, to sacrifice unto the Lord thy God in Gilgal.

22 And Samuel said, ᵃHath the Lord as great delight in burnt-offerings and sacrifices, as in obeying the voice of the Lord? Behold, ᵇto obey *is* better than sacrifice, *and* to hearken than the fat of rams.

A. M. 2925
B. C. 1079
An. Exod. Isr.
412
Anno ante
I. Olymp. 303

23 For rebellion *is as* the sin of ᶜwitchcraft, and stubbornness *is as* iniquity and idolatry. Because thou hast rejected the word of the Lord, ᵈhe hath also rejected thee from *being* king.

24 ᵉAnd Saul said unto Samuel, I have sinned: for I have transgressed the commandment of the Lord, and thy words: because I ᶠfeared the people, and obeyed their voice.

25 Now, therefore, I pray thee, pardon my sin, and turn again with me, that I may worship the Lord.

26 And Samuel said unto Saul, I will not return with thee: ᵍfor thou hast rejected the word of the Lord, and the Lord hath rejected thee from being king over Israel.

27 And as Samuel turned about to go away, ʰhe laid hold upon the skirt of his mantle, and it rent.

28 And Samuel said unto him, ⁱThe Lord hath rent the kingdom of Israel from thee this day, and hath given it to a neighbour of thine, *that is* better than thou.

ʷChap. ix 21——ˣHeb. *they consume*——ʸVer. 13
ᶻVer. 15——ᵃPsa. l. 8, 9; Prov. xxi. 3; Isa. i. 11, 12, 13, 16, 17; Jer. vii. 22, 23; Mic. vi. 6, 7, 8; Heb. x. 6, 7, 8, 9——ᵇEccles. v. 1; Hos. vi. 6; Matt. v. 24; ix. 13; xii. 7; Mark xii. 33

ᶜHebrew, *divination;* Deut. xviii. 10——ᵈChapter xiii. 14——ᵉSee 2 Sam. xii. 13——ᶠExod. xxiii. 2; Prov. xxix. 25; Isa. li. 12, 13——ᵍSee chap. ii. 30 ʰSee 1 Kings xi. 30——ⁱChapter xxviii. 17, 18; 1 Kings xi. 31

---

sheep] It is very likely that the people did spare the best of the prey; and it is as likely that Saul might have *restrained* them if he would. That they might not *love war*, God had interdicted *spoil* and *plunder;* so the war was undertaken merely from a sense of *duty*, without any hope of enriching themselves by it.

Verse 17. *Little in thine own sight*] Who can bear *prosperity?* Is it not of the Lord's great goodness that the majority of the inhabitants of the earth are in comparative *poverty?*

Verse 21. *To sacrifice unto the Lord*] Thus he endeavours to *excuse* the people. They did not take the spoil in order to *enrich themselves* by it, but to *sacrifice unto the Lord;* and did not this motive justify their conduct?

Verse 22. *Hath the Lord as great delight, &c.*] This was a very proper answer to, and refutation of Saul's excuse. Is not obedience to the will of God the end of all religion, of its rites, ceremonies, and sacrifices?

Verse 23. *For rebellion* is as *the sin of witchcraft, and stubbornness* is as *iniquity and idolatry.*] This is no translation of those difficult words, כי חטאת קסם מרי ואון ותרפים הפצר *ki chattath kesem meri veaven utheraphim haphtsar.* It appears to me that the three nouns which occur first in the text refer each to the three last in order. Thus, חטאת *chattath*, TRANSGRESSION, refers to און *aven*, INIQUITY, which is the principle whence *transgression* springs. קסם *kesem*, DIVINATION, refers to תרפים *teraphim*, consecrated images or *telesms*, vulgarly *talismans*, used in incantations. And מרי *meri*, REBELLION, refers evidently to הפצר *haphstar*, STUBBORNNESS, whence *rebellion* springs. The meaning therefore of this difficult place may be the following: As transgression comes from iniquity, divination from teraphim, and rebellion from stubbornness, so, because thou hast rejected the word of the Lord, he hath also rejected thee from being king. All the *versions* are different.

Verse 24. *I have sinned—because I feared the people*] This was the best excuse he could make for himself; but had he *feared* God *more*, he need have *feared the* PEOPLE *less.*

Verse 25. *Pardon my sin*] Literally, *bear my sin;* take it away; forgive what I have done against thee, and be my intercessor with God, that he may forgive my offence against him; *turn again with me, that I may worship the Lord.*

Verse 26. *I will not return with thee*] I

A. M. 2925
B. C. 1079
An. Exod. Isr.
412
Anno ante
I. Olymp. 303

29 And also the [k]Strength of Israel [l]will not lie nor repent; for he *is* not a man, that he should repent.

30 Then he said, I have sinned: *yet* [m]honour me now, I pray thee, before the elders of my people, and before Israel, and turn again with me, that I may worship the LORD thy God.

31 So Samuel turned again after Saul; and Saul worshipped the LORD.

32 Then said Samuel, Bring ye hither to me Agag the king of the Amalekites. And Agag came unto him delicately. And Agag

said, Surely the bitterness of death is past.

33 And Samuel said, [n]As thy sword hath made women childless, so shall thy mother be childless among women. And Samuel hewed Agag in pieces before the LORD in Gilgal.

34 Then Samuel went to Ramah; and Saul went up to his house to [o]Gibeah of Saul.

35 And [p]Samuel came no more to see Saul until the day of his death: nevertheless Samuel [q]mourned for Saul: and the LORD [r]repented that he had made Saul king over Israel.

A. M. 2925
B. C. 1079
An. Exod. Isr.
412
Anno ante
I. Olymp. 303

---

[k]Or, *eternity,* or *victory*——[l]Num. xxiii. 19; Ezek. xxiv. 14; 2 Tim. ii. 13; Tit. i. 2——[m]John v. 44; xii. 43

[n]Exod. xvii. 11; Num. xiv. 45; see Judg. i. 7——[o]Ch. xi. 4——[p]See ch. xix. 24——[q]Ver. 11; ch. xvi. 1——[r]Ver.11

---

cannot acknowledge thee as king, seeing the Lord hath rejected thee.

Verse 29. *The Strength of Israel will not lie*] What God has purposed he will bring to pass, for he has all power in the heavens and in the earth; and he will not *repent*—change his purpose—concerning thee.

We may say it was some extenuation of Saul's fault that the people *insisted* on preserving the best of the prey; for who could resist the demands of a victorious mob? But his crime was in *consenting;* had he not, the crime would have been *theirs alone.*

Verse 32. *Agag came unto him delicately.*] The Septuagint have τρεμων, *trembling;* the original, מעדנת *maadannoth, delicacies;* probably איש *ish,* man, understood; *a man of delights,* a pleasure-taker: the Vulgate, *pinguissimus et tremens,* "very fat and trembling."

Surely the bitterness of death is past.] Almost all the versions render this differently from ours. *Surely death is bitter,* is their general sense; and this seems to be the true meaning.

Verse 33. *As thy sword hath made women childless*] It appears that Agag had forfeited his life by his own personal transgressions, and that his death now was the retribution of his *cruelties.*

And Samuel hewed Agag in pieces] 1. What Samuel did here he did in his magisterial capacity; and, 2. It is not likely he did it by his *own sword,* but by that of an *executioner.* What kings, magistrates, and generals do, in an official way, by their subjects, servants, or soldiers, they are said to do themselves; *qui facit per alterum, facit per se.*

Verse 35. *And Samuel came no more to see Saul*] But we read, chap. xix. 22-24, that *Saul* went to *see Samuel* at Naioth, but this does not affect what is said here. From this time Samuel had no *connection* with Saul; he never more acknowledged him as king; he mourned and prayed for him, and continued to perform his prophetic functions at Ramah, and at Naioth, superintending the school of the prophets in that place.

CHAPTER XVI

Samuel is sent from Ramah to Beth-lehem, to anoint David, 1–13. The Spirit of the Lord departs from Saul, and an evil spirit comes upon him, 14. His servants exhort him to get a skilful harper to play before him, 15, 16. He is pleased with the counsel, and desires them to find such a person, 17. They recommend David, 18. He is sent for, comes, plays before Saul, and finds favour in his sight, 19–23.

A. M. 2941
B. C. 1063
An. Exod. Isr.
428
Anno ante
I. Olymp. 287

AND the LORD said unto Samuel, [a]How long wilt thou mourn for Saul, seeing [b]I have rejected him from reigning over Israel? [c]fill thine horn with oil, and go, I will

send thee to Jesse the Beth-lehemite: for [d]I have provided me a king among his sons.

2 And Samuel said, How can I go? if Saul hear *it,* he will kill me. And

A. M. 2941
B. C. 1063
An. Exod. Isr.
428
Anno ante
I. Olymp. 287

---

[a]Ch. xv. 35——[b]Ch. xv. 23——[c]Ch. ix. 16; 2 Kings

ix. 1——[d]Psa. lxxviii. 70; lxxxix. 19, 20; Acts xiii. 22

NOTES ON CHAP. XVI

Verse 1. *Fill thine horn with oil*] Horns appear to have been the *ancient* drinking vessels of all nations; and we may suppose that most persons who had to travel much, always carried one with them, for the purpose of taking up water from the fountains to quench

their thirst. Such a *horn* had Samuel; and on this occasion he was commanded to fill it with oil, for the purpose of consecrating a king over Israel from among the sons of Jesse.

Verse 2. *Take a heifer with thee, and say, I am come to sacrifice*] This was strictly *true;* Samuel *did offer a sacrifice;* and it does not appear that he could have done the work which

A. M. 2941
B. C. 1063
An. Exod. Isr.
428
Anno ante
I. Olymp. 287

the LORD said, Take a heifer
[e]with thee, and say, [f]I am come
to sacrifice to the LORD.

3 And call Jesse to the sacrifice, and [g]I will show thee what thou shalt do: and [h]thou shalt anoint unto me *him* whom I name unto thee.

4 And Samuel did that which the LORD spake, and came to Beth-lehem. And the elders of the town [i]trembled at his [k]coming, and said, [l]Comest thou peaceably?

5 And he said, Peaceably: I am come to sacrifice unto the LORD: [m]sanctify yourselves, and come with me to the sacrifice. And he sanctified Jesse and his sons, and called them to the sacrifice.

6 And it came to pass, when they were come, that he looked on [n]Eliab, and [o]said, Surely the LORD's anointed *is* before him.

7 But the LORD said unto Samuel, Look not on [p]his countenance, or on the height of his stature; because I have refused him: [q]for *the LORD seeth* not as man seeth; for man [r]looketh on the [s]outward appearance, but the LORD looketh on the [t]heart.

8 Then Jesse called [u]Abinadab, and made him pass before Samuel. And he said, Neither hath the LORD chosen this.

A. M. 2941
B. C. 1063
An. Exod. Isr.
428
Anno ante
I. Olymp. 287

9 Then Jesse made [v]Shammah [w]to pass by. And he said, Neither hath the LORD chosen this.

10 Again, Jesse made seven of his sons to pass before Samuel. And Samuel said unto Jesse, The LORD hath not chosen these.

11 And Samuel said unto Jesse, Are here all *thy* children? And he said, [x]There remaineth yet the youngest, and, behold, he keepeth the sheep. And Samuel said unto Jesse, [y]Send and fetch him: for we will not sit [z]down till he come hither.

12 And he sent, and brought him in. Now he *was* [a]ruddy, *and* withal [b]of a beautiful countenance, and goodly to look to. [c]And the LORD said, Arise, anoint him: for this *is* he.

13 Then Samuel took the horn of oil, and [d]anointed him in the midst of his brethren: and [e]the Spirit of the LORD came upon David from that day forward. So Samuel rose up, and went to Ramah.

14 [f]But the Spirit of the LORD departed

---

[e]Heb. *in thine hand*——[f]Chap. ix. 12; xx. 29
[g]Exod. iv. 15——[h]Ch. ix. 16——[i]Ch. xxi. 1——[k]Heb. *meeting*——[l]1 Kings ii. 13; 2 Kings ix. 22——[m]Exod. xix. 10, 14——[n]Ch. xvii. 13; called *Elihu,* 1 Chron. xxvii. 18
[o]1 Kings xii. 26——[p]Psa. cxlvii. 10, 11——[q]Isa. lv. 8
[r]2 Cor. x. 7——[s]Heb. *eyes*——[t]1 Kings viii. 39;
1 Chron. xxviii. 9; Psa. vii. 9; Jer. xi. 20; xvii. 10;
xx. 12; Acts i. 24

[u]Chap. xvii. 13——[v]Chap. xvii. 13——[w]*Shimeah,*
2 Sam. xiii. 3; *Shimma,* 1 Chron. ii. 13——[x]Chap. xvii.
12——[y]2 Sam. vii. 8; Psa. lxxviii. 70——[z]Heb. *round*
[a]Chap. xvii. 42; Cant. v. 10——[b]Heb. *fair of eyes*
[c]So chap. ix. 17——[d]Ch. x. 1; Psa. lxxxix. 20——[e]See
Num. xxvii. 18; Judg. xi. 29; xiii. 25; xiv. 6; chap. x. 6
10——[f]Chap. xi. 6; xviii. 12; xxviii. 15; Judg. xvi. 20;
Psa. li. 11

God designed, unless he had offered this sacrifice, and called the elders of the people together, and thus collected Jesse's sons. But he did not tell the principal design of his coming; had he done so, it would have produced *evil* and *no good:* and though no man, in any circumstances, should ever *tell a lie,* yet in all circumstances he is not obliged to tell the *whole* truth, though in every circumstance he must tell *nothing but the truth,* and in every case so tell the truth that the hearer shall not believe a lie by it.

Verse 3. *Call Jesse to the sacrifice*] The common custom was, after the blood of the victim had been poured out to God, and the fat burnt, to feast on the flesh of the sacrifice. This appears to have been the case in all, except in the *whole burnt-offering;* this was entirely consumed.

Verse 4. *The elders of the town trembled at his coming*] They knew he was a prophet of the Lord, and they were afraid that he was now come to denounce some judgments of the Most High against their city.

Verse 5. *Sanctify yourselves*] Change your clothes, and wash your bodies in pure water, and prepare your minds by meditation, reflection, and prayer; that, being in the spirit of sacrifice, ye may offer acceptably to the Lord.

Verse 7. *Man looketh on the outward appearance*] And it is well he *should,* and confine his looks to *that;* for when he pretends to sound the *heart,* he usurps the prerogative of God.

In what way were these communications made from God to Samuel? It must have been by direct inspirations into his heart. But what a state of holy familiarity does this argue between God and the prophet! I believe Moses himself was not more highly favoured than Samuel.

Verse 10. *Seven of his sons*] This certainly was not done *publicly;* Samuel, Jesse, and his children, must have been in a *private* apartment, previously to the public feast on the sacrifice; for Samuel says, ver. 11, We will not *sit down till he* (David) *come.*

Verse 12. *He* was *ruddy*] I believe the word here means *red-haired,* he had *golden locks.* Hair of this kind is ever associated with a delicate skin and florid complexion.

Verse 13. *The Spirit of the Lord came upon David*] God qualified him to be governor of his people, by infusing such graces as wisdom, prudence, counsel, courage, liberality, and magnanimity.

Verse 14. *The Spirit of the Lord departed from Saul*] He was thrown into such a state of mind by the judgments of God, as to be de-

A. M. 2941
B. C. 1063
An. Exod. Isr.
428
Anno ante
I. Olymp. 287

from Saul, and [g]an evil spirit from the LORD [h]troubled him.

15 And Saul's servants said unto him, Behold now, an evil spirit from God troubleth thee.

16 Let our lord now command thy servants, *which are* [i]before thee, to seek out a man, *who is* a cunning player on a harp: and it shall come to pass, when the evil spirit from God is upon thee, that he shall [k]play with his hand, and thou shalt be well.

17 And Saul said unto his servants, Provide me now a man that can play well, and bring *him* to me.

18 Then answered one of the servants, and

said, Behold, I have seen a son of Jesse the Beth-lehemite *that is* cunning in playing, and [l]a mighty valiant man, and a man of war, and prudent in [m]matters, and a comely person, and [n]the LORD *is* with him.

A. M. 2941
B. C. 1063
An. Exod. Isr.
428
Anno ante
I. Olymp. 287

19 Wherefore Saul sent messengers unto Jesse, and said, Send me David thy son, [o]which *is* with the sheep.

20 And Jesse [p]took an ass *laden* with bread, and a bottle of wine, and a kid, and sent *them* by David his son unto Saul.

21 And David came to Saul, and [q]stood before him: and he loved him greatly; and he became his armour-bearer.

---

[g]Judg. ix. 23; ch. xviii. 10; xix. 9——[h]Or, *terrified* [i]Gen. xli. 46; ver. 21, 22; 1 Kings x. 8——[k]Ver. 23; 2 Kings iii. 15——[l]Ch. xvii. 32, 34, 35, 36——[m]Or, *speech*

[n]Chap. iii. 19; xviii. 12, 14——[o]Ver. 11; chap. xvii. 15, 34——[p]See chap. x. 27; xvii. 18; Gen. xliii. 11: Prov. xviii. 16——[q]Gen. xli. 46; 1 Kings x. 8; Prov. xxii. 29

---

prived of any regal qualities which he before possessed. God seems to have taken what gifts he had, and given them to David; and then the evil spirit came upon Saul; for what God fills not, the devil will.

And evil spirit from the Lord] The evil spirit was either immediately sent from the Lord, or permitted to come. Whether this was a diabolic possession, or a mere mental malady, the learned are not agreed; it seems to have partaken of both. That Saul had fallen into a deep melancholy, there is little doubt; that the devil might work more effectually on such a state of mind, there can be but little question. There is an old proverb, Satan delights to fish in troubled waters; and Saul's situation of mind gave him many advantages.

The theory of Dr. Scheuchzer, in his *Physica Sacra*, on the malady of Saul, is allowed to be very ingenious. It is in substance as follows: Health consists in a moderate tension of the *fibres*, which permits all the *fluids* to have an entire freedom of circulation, and to the *spirits*, that of diffusing themselves through all the limbs; on the contrary, *disease* consists in tensions of the fibres morbidly weak or morbidly strong. This latter seems to have been the case of Saul; and as the undulations of the air which convey *sound* communicate themselves to and through the most solid bodies, it is easy to suppose that by the modulations of music all the fibres of his body, which were under the influence of the morbidly increased tension, might be so relaxed as to be brought back into their natural state, and thus permit the re-establishment of a free and gentle circulation of the fluids, and consequently of the animal spirits, and thus induce calmness and tranquillity of mind. I believe this theory to be correct, and I should find no difficulty to amplify and to illustrate the subject. Even a skilful playing upon the harp was one means to bring a disordered state of the nervous and fibrous system into a capacity of affording such uninterrupted tranquillity to the mind as to render it capable of receiving the prophetic influence; see the case of Elisha, 2 Kings iii. 14, 15. It has been said—

"Music hath charms to sooth the savage breast."

This has been literally proved: a musician was brought to play on his instrument while they were feeding a *savage lion* in the tower of London; the beast immediately left his food, came towards the grating of his den, and began to *move* in such a way as to show himself affected by the music. The musician ceased, and the lion returned to his food; he recommenced, and the lion left off his prey, and was so affected as to seem by his motions to dance with delight. This was repeatedly tried, and the effects were still the same.

Verse 18. *I have seen a son of Jesse*] Dr. Warburton supposes the story is anticipated from ver. 14 to 23, and that the true chronology of this part of David's life is the following:— 1. David is anointed by Samuel; 2. Carries provisions to his brethren in the army; 3. Fights with and kills Goliath; 4. Is received into the king's court; 5. Contracts a friendship with Jonathan; 6. Incurs Saul's jealousy; 7. Retires to his father's house; 8. Is after some time sent for by Saul to sooth his melancholy with his harp; 9. Again excites Saul's jealousy, who endeavours to smite him with his javelin. This anticipation between the 14th and 23d verse comes in, in the order of time, between verses 9 and 10 of chap. xviii., where the breach is apparent.

Verse 20. *Took an ass laden with bread*] He must send a present to Saul to introduce his son, and this was probably the best he had. Dr. Warburton pleads still farther on the propriety of his rectification of the chronology in this place. David had at this time vanquished the Philistine, was become a favourite with the people, had excited Saul's jealousy, and retired to shun its effects. In the interim Saul was seized with the disorder in question, and is recommended by his servants to try the effects of music. They were acquainted with David's skill on the harp, and likewise with Saul's bad disposition towards him; the point was delicate, it required to be managed with address, and therefore they recommend David in this artful manner: "As you must have one constantly in

A. M. 2941
B. C. 1063
An. Exod. Isr.
428
Anno ante
I. Olymp. 287

22 And Saul sent to Jesse, saying, Let David, I pray thee, stand before me; for he hath found favour in my sight.

23 And it came to pass, when ʳthe *evil*

ʳ1 Samuel,

spirit from God was upon Saul, that David took a harp, and played with his hand: so Saul was refreshed, and was well, and the evil spirit departed from him.

A. M. 2941
B. C. 1063
An. Exod. Isr.
428
Anno ante
I. Olymp. 287

chap. xvi. 14, 16

attendance, both in court and on your military expeditions, to be always at hand on occasion, the son of Jesse will become both stations well; he will strengthen your camp and adorn your court, for he is a tried soldier and of a graceful presence. You have nothing to fear from his ambition, for you saw with what prudence he went into voluntary banishment when his popularity had incurred your displeasure." Accordingly Saul is prevailed on, David is sent for, and succeeds with his music; this dissipates all former umbrage, and, as one who is ever to be in attendance, he is *made Saul's armour-bearer.* This sunshine still continued till his great successes awakened Saul's jealousy afresh, and then the lifted *javelin* was to strike off all obligations. Thus we see what light is thrown upon the whole history by the supposition of an *anticipation* in the latter part of this chapter; an anticipation the most natural, proper, and necessary, for the purpose of the historian. Thus reasons Bishop *Warburton,* and with very considerable plausibility, though the intelligent reader may still have his doubts.

Verse 23. *The* evil *spirit from God*] The word *evil* is not in the common Hebrew text, but it is in the *Vulgate, Septuagint, Targum,*

Syriac, and *Arabic,* and in *eight* of *Kennicott's* and *De Rossi's* MSS., which present the text thus: רוח אלהים רעה *ruach Elohim raah, spiritus Domini malus, the evil spirit of God.* The *Septuagint* leave out Θεου, *of God,* and have πνευμα πονηρον, *the evil spirit.* The *Targum* says, *The evil spirit from before the Lord;* and the *Arabic* has it. *The evil spirit by the permission of God;* this is at least the sense.

And the evil spirit departed from him.] The *Targum* says, *And the evil spirit descended up from off him.* This considers the malady of Saul to be more than a *natural* disease.

THERE are several difficulties in this chapter; those of the *chronology* are pretty well cleared, in the opinion of some, by the observations of Bishop Warburton; but there is still something more to be done to make this point entirely satisfactory. Saul's *evil spirit,* and the influence of *music* upon it, are not easily accounted for. I have considered his malady to be of a *mixed* kind, *natural* and *diabolical;* there is too much of apparent *nature* in it to permit us to believe it was all *spiritual,* and there is too much of apparent *supernatural* influence to suffer us to believe that it was all *natural.*

CHAPTER XVII

The Philistines gather together against Israel at Ephes-dammim, and Saul and his men pitch their camp near the valley of Elah, 1–3. Goliath of Gath, a gigantic man, whose height was six cubits and a span, defies the armies of Israel, and proposes to end all contests by single combat; his armour is described, 4–11. Saul and his host are greatly dismayed, 12. David, having been sent by his father with provisions to his brethren in the army, hears the challenge, inquires into the circumstances, thinks it a reproach to Israel that no man can be found to accept the challenge, is brought before Saul, and proposes to undertake the combat, 13–32. Saul objects to his youth and inexperience, 33. David shows the grounds on which he undertakes it, 34–37. Saul arms him with his own armour: but David, finding them an encumbrance, puts them off, and takes his staff, his sling, and five stones out of the brook, and goes to meet Goliath, 38–40. The Philistine draws near, despises, defies, and curses him, 41–44. David retorts his defiance, 45–47. They draw near to each other, and David slings a stone, hits Goliath in the forehead, slays him, and cuts off his head with his own sword, 48–51. The Philistines flee, and are pursued by the Israelites, 52, 53. David brings the head of the Philistine to Jerusalem, 54. Conversation between Saul and Abner concerning David, who is in consequence brought before Saul, 55–58.

A. M. 2941
B. C. 1063
An. Exod. Isr.
428
Anno ante
I. Olymp. 287

NOW the Philistines ᵃgathered together their armies to battle, and were gathered together at ᵇShochoh, which be-

longeth to Judah, and pitched between Shochoh and Azekah, in ᶜEphes-dammim.

2 And Saul and the men of

A. M. 2941
B. C. 1063
An. Exod. Isr.
428
Anno ante
I. Olymp. 287

ᵃChap. xiii. 5——ᵇJosh. xv. 35; 2 Chron.
xxviii. 18

ᶜOr, *the coast of Dammim;* called *Pas-dammim,*
1 Chron. xi. 13

NOTES ON CHAP. XVII

Verse 1. *Now the Philistines gathered together*] Calmet thinks that this war happened *eight* years after the anointing of David, and *ten* or *twelve* years after the war with the Amalekites. We have already seen that there was war between Saul and the Philistines all his days. See chap. xiv. 52.

Shochoh and Azekah] Places which lay to the south of Jerusalem and to the west of Bethlehem; about five leagues from the former. Ephes-dammim was somewhere in the vicinity, but it is not known *where.* See *Calmet.*

Verse 2. *The valley of Elah*] Some translate this the *turpentine valley,* or *the valley of the terebinth trees;* and others, *the valley of oaks.* The situation of this valley is well known.

A. M. 2941
B. C. 1063
An. Exod. Isr.
428
Anno ante
I. Olymp. 287
Israel were gathered together, and pitched by the valley of Elah, and ^dset the battle in array against the Philistines.

3 And the Philistines stood on a mountain on the one side, and Israel stood on a mountain on the other side: and *there was* a valley between them.

4 And there went out a champion out of the

camp of the Philistines, named ^eGoliath, of ^fGath, whose height *was* six cubits and a span.

A. M. 2941
B. C. 1063
An. Exod. Isr.
428
Anno ante
I. Olymp. 287

5 And *he had* a helmet of brass upon his head, and he *was* ^garmed with a coat of mail; and the weight of the coat *was* five thousand shekels of brass.

6 And *he had* greaves of brass upon his legs, and a ^htarget of brass between his shoulders.

---

^dHeb. *ranged the battle*——^e2 Sam. xxi. 19

^fJosh. xi. 22——^gHeb. *clothed*——^hOr, *gorget*

Verse 3. *The Philistines stood on a mountain*] These were two eminences or hills, from which they could see and talk with each other.

Verse 4. *There went out a champion*] Our word *champion* comes from *campus*, the field; Campio *est enim ille qui pugnat in* campo, *hoc est, in castris*, "Champion is he, properly, who fights in the *field;* i. e., in *camps.*" A man well skilled in arms, strong, brave, and patriotic.

But is this the meaning of the original איש הבנים *ish habbenayim*, a *middle man*, the *man between two;* that is, as here, the *man* who undertakes to settle the disputes *between two armies* or nations. So our ancient *champions* settled disputes between *contending parties* by what was termed *camp fight;* hence the *campio* or *champion.* The *versions* know not well what to make of this man. The *Vulgate* calls him *vir spurius*, "a bastard;" the *Septuagint*, ανηρ δυνατος, "a strong or powerful man;" the *Targum*, נברא מביניהון *gabra mibbeyneyhon*, "a man from between them;" the *Arabic*, رجل جبار *rujil jibar*, "a great or gigantic man;" the *Syriac* is the same; and Josephus terms him ανηρ παμμεγεθιστατος, "an immensely great man." The *Vulgate* has given him the notation of *spurius* or *bastard*, because it considered the original as expressing *a son of two*, i. e., a man whose parents are unknown. Among all these I consider our word *champion*, as explained above, the best and most appropriate to the original terms.

Whose height was *six cubits and a span.*] The word cubit signifies the length from *cubitus*, the elbow, to the top of the middle finger, which is generally rated at *one foot six inches.* The *span* is the distance from the top of the middle finger to the end of the thumb, when extended as far as they can stretch on a *plain;* this is ordinarily *nine inches.* Were we sure that these were the measures, and their extent, which are intended in the original words, we could easily ascertain the height of this Philistine; it would then be *nine feet nine inches*, which is a tremendous height for a man. But the *versions* are not all agreed in his height. The *Septuagint* read τεσσαρων πηχεων και σπιθαμης, *four cubits and a span;* and *Josephus* reads the same. It is necessary however to observe that the *Septuagint*, in the *Codex Alexandrinus*, read with the Hebrew text. But what was the *length* of the ancient cubit? This has been variously computed; *eighteen inches, twenty inches and a half*, and *twenty-one inches.* If we take the first measurement, he was *nine feet nine;* if the second, and read *palm* instead of *span*, with the Vulgate and others, he was *ten feet seven inches and a half;* if we take the last, which is the estimate of Grævius, with

the *span*, he was *eleven feet three inches;* or if we go to the exactest measurement, as laid down in Bishop Cumberland's tables, where he computes the cubit at 21.888 inches, the span at 10.944 inches, and the palm at 3.684 inches, then the six cubits and the span will make exactly 11 feet 10.272 inches. If we take the *palm* instead of the *span*, then the height will be 11 feet 3.012 inches. But I still think that the *nine feet nine inches* is the most reasonable.

Verse 5. *He* was *armed with a coat of mail*] The words in the original, שריון קשקשים *shiryon kaskassim*, mean *a coat of mail* formed of *plates of brass overlapping each other, like the scales of a fish*, or *tiles of a house.* This is the true notion of the original terms.

With thin *plates* of *brass* or *iron, overlapping* each other, were the ancient coats of mail formed in different countries; many formed in this way may be now seen in the tower of London.

The weight—five thousand shekels] Following Bishop Cumberland's tables, and rating the *shekel* at *two hundred and nineteen grains*, and the *Roman* ounce at *four hundred and thirty-eight grains*, we find that Goliath's coat of mail, weighing *five thousand shekels*, was exactly *one hundred and fifty-six pounds four ounces* avoirdupois. A vast weight for a coat of mail, but not all out of proportion to the man.

Verse 6. *Greaves of brass upon his legs*] This species of armour may be seen on many ancient monuments. It was a *plate of brass* (though perhaps sometimes formed of *laminæ* or *plates*, like the *mail*) which covered the *shin* or fore part of the leg, from the knee down to the instep, and was buckled with straps behind the leg. From ancient monuments we find that it was commonly worn only on one leg. VEGETIUS, *de Re Militari*, says, *Pedites Scutati etiam ferreas ocreas in dextris cruribus cogebantur accipere.* "The foot soldiers, called Scutati, from their particular species of shield, were obliged to use iron *greaves* on their *right legs.*" One of these may be seen in the monument of the gladiator *Buto*, in *Montfaucon;* and another in the Mosaic pavement at *Bognor*, in Surrey.

A target of brass between his shoulders.] When not actually engaged, soldiers threw their shields behind their back, so that they appeared to rest or hang between the shoulders.

There are different opinions concerning this piece of armour, called here כידון *kidon.* Some think it was a *covering* for the *shoulders;* others, that it was a *javelin* or *dart;* others, that it was a *lance;* some, a *club;* and others, a *sword.* It is certainly distinguished from the shield, ver. 41, and is translated a *spear*, Josh. viii. 18.

A. M. 2941
B. C. 1063
An. Exod. Isr. 428
Anno ante
I. Olymp. 287

7 And the [i]staff of his spear *was* like a weaver's beam; and his spear's head *weighed* six hundred shekels of iron: and one bearing a shield went before him.

8 And he stood and cried unto the armies of Israel, and said unto them, Why are ye come out to set *your* battle in array? *am* not I a Philistine, and ye [k]servants to Saul? choose you a man for you, and let him come down to me.

9 If he be able to fight with me, and to kill me, then will we be your servants: but if I prevail against him, and kill him, then shall ye be our servants, and [l]serve us.

10 And the Philistine said, I [m]defy the armies of Israel this day; give me a man, that we may fight together.

A. M. 2941
B. C. 1063
An. Exod. Isr. 428
Anno ante
I. Olymp. 287

11 When Saul and all Israel heard those words of the Philistine, they were dismayed, and greatly afraid.

12 Now David *was* [n]the son of that [o]Ephrathite of Beth-lehem-judah, whose name *was* Jesse; and he had [p]eight sons: and the man went among men *for* an old man in the days of Saul.

13 And the three eldest sons of Jesse went *and* followed Saul to the battle: and the [q]names of his three sons that went to the battle *were* Eliab the first-born, and next unto him Abinadab, and the third Shammah.

---

[i]2 Sam. xxi. 19——[k]Chap. viii. 17——[l]Chap. xi. 1——[m]Ver. 26; 2 Sam. xxi. 21——[n]Ver. 58; Ruth iv. 22; chap. xvi. 1, 18——[o]Gen. xxxv. 19——[p]Chap. xvi. 10, 11; see 1 Chron. ii. 13, 14, 15——[q]Chapter xvi. 6, 8, 9; 1 Chronicles ii. 13

Verse 7. *The staff of his spear* was *like a weaver's beam*] Either like that on which the *warp* is *rolled*, or that on which the *cloth* is *rolled*. We know not how *thick* this was, because there were several sorts of *looms*, and the sizes of the beams very dissimilar. Our *woollen*, *linen*, *cotton*, and *silk* looms are all different in the *size* of their *beams;* and I have seen several that I should not suppose *too thick*, though they might be *too short*, for Goliath's spear.

His spear's head weighed *six hundred shekels of iron*] That is, his spear's head was of *iron*, and it weighed *six hundred shekels;* this, according to the former computation, would amount to *eighteen pounds twelve ounces*.

And one bearing a shield] הצנה *hatstsinnah*, from צן *tsan, pointed* or *penetrating*, if it do not mean some kind of a *lance*, must mean a *shield*, with what is called the *umbo*, a sharp protuberance, in the middle, with which they could as effectually annoy their enemies as defend themselves. Many of the old Highland targets were made with a projecting *dagger* in the centre. Taking the proportions of things *unknown* to those *known*, the armour of Goliath is supposed to have weighed not less than *two hundred and seventy-two pounds thirteen ounces!* Plutarch informs us that the ordinary weight of a soldier's *panoply*, or complete armour, was one *talent*, or *sixty pounds;* and that one Alcimus, in the army of Demetrius, was considered as a prodigy, because his panoply weighed *two talents*, or *one hundred and twenty pounds*.

Verse 8. *I a Philistine*] The *Targum* adds much to this speech. This is the substance: "I am Goliath the Philistine of Gath, who killed the two sons of Eli, Hophni and Phinehas the priests; and led into captivity the ark of the covenant of Jehovah, and placed it in the temple of Dagon my god; and it remained in the cities of the Philistines seven months. Also, in all our battles I have gone at the head of the army, and we conquered and cut down men, and laid them as low as the dust of the earth; and to this day the Philistines have not granted me the honour of being chief of a thousand men. And ye, men of Israel, what noble exploit has Saul, the son of Kish, of Gibeah, done, that ye should have made him king over you? If he be a hero, let him come down himself and fight with me; but if he be a weak or cowardly man, then choose you out a man that he may come down to me."

Verse 9. *Then will we be your servants*] Of this stipulation we hear nothing farther.

Verse 10. *I defy*] אני חרפתי *ani cheraphti*, "I *strip* and *make bare*," the armies of Israel; for none dared to fight him. From the *Dhunoor Veda Shastra* it appears that, among the Hindoos, it was common, before the commencement of an engagement, to challenge the enemy by throwing out some terms of abuse, similar to those used by Goliath. We find this also in Homer: his heroes scold each other heartily before they begin to fight. See on ver. 43.

Verse 11. *Saul and all Israel—were dismayed*] They saw no man able to accept the challenge.

Verse 12. The 12th verse, to the 31st inclusive, are wanting in the *Septuagint;* as also the 41st verse; and from the 54th to the end; with the first *five* verses of chap. xviii., and the 9th, 10th, 11th, 17th, 18th, and 19th of the same.

All these parts are found in the *Codex Alexandrinus;* but it appears that the MS. from which the Codex Alexandrinus was copied, had them not. See observations at the end of this chapter. Dr. *Kennicott* has rendered it very probable that these portions are not a genuine part of the text.

Notwithstanding what Bishop Warburton and others have done to clear the chronology of the present printed Hebrew, it is impossible to make a clear consistent sense of the history unless these verses are omitted. Let any one read the *eleventh* verse in connection with the *thirty-second*, leave out the *forty-first*, and connect the *fifty-fourth* with the *sixth* of chap. *xviii.*, and he will be perfectly convinced that there is nothing wanting to make the sense complete; to say nothing of the other omissions noted above. If the above be taken in as genuine, the ingenuity of man has hitherto failed to free the whole from apparent contradiction and

A. M. 2941
B. C. 1063
An. Exod. Isr.
428
Anno ante
I. Olymp. 287

14 And David *was* the youngest: and the three eldest followed Saul.

15 But David went and returned from Saul [r]to feed his father's sheep at Beth-lehem.

16 And the Philistine drew near morning and evening, and presented himself forty days.

17 And Jesse said unto David his son, Take now for thy brethren an ephah of this parched *corn,* and these ten loaves, and run to the camp to thy brethren;

18 And carry these ten [s]cheeses unto the [t]captain of *their* thousand, and [u]look how thy brethren fare, and take their pledge.

19 Now Saul, and they, and all the men of Israel, *were* in the valley of Elah, fighting with the Philistines.

20 And David rose up early in the morning, and left the sheep with a keeper, and took, and went, as Jesse had commanded him; and he came to the [v]trench, as the host was going forth to the [w]fight, and shouted for the battle.

21 For Israel and the Philistines had put the battle in array, army against army.

22 And David left [x]his carriage in the hand of the keeper of the carriage, and ran into the army, and came and [y]saluted his brethren.

23 And as he talked with them, behold, there came up the champion, the Philistine of Gath, Goliath by name, out of the armies of the Philistines, and spake [z]according to the same words: and David heard *them.*

24 And all the men of Israel, when they saw the man, fled [a]from him, and were sore afraid.

25 And the men of Israel said, Have ye seen this man that is come up? surely to defy Israel is he come up: and it shall be, *that* the man who killeth him, the king will enrich him with great riches, and [b]will give him his daughter, and make his father's house free in Israel.

A. M. 2941
B. C. 1063
An. Exod. Isr.
428
Anno ante
I. Olymp. 287

26 And David spake to the men that stood by him, saying, What shall be done to the man that killeth this Philistine, and taketh away [c]the reproach from Israel? for who *is* this [d]uncircumcised Philistine, that he should [e]defy the armies of [f]the living God?

27 And the people answered him after this manner, saying, [g]So shall it be done to the man that killeth him.

28 And Eliab his eldest brother heard when he spake unto the men; and Eliab's [h]anger was kindled against David, and he said, Why camest thou down hither? and with whom hast thou left those few sheep in the wilderness? I know thy pride and the naughtiness of thine heart; for thou art come down that thou mightest see the battle.

29 And David said, What have I now done? [i]*Is there* not a cause?

30 And he turned from him toward another and [k]spake after the same [l]manner: and the people answered him again after the former manner.

31 And when the words were heard which David spake, they rehearsed them before Saul: and he [m]sent for him.

32 And David said to Saul, [n]Let no man's heart fail because of him; [o]thy servant will go and fight with this Philistine.

33 And Saul said to David, [p]Thou art not

---

[r]Chap. xvi. 19——[s]Heb. *cheeses of milk*——[t]Heb. *captain of a thousand*——[u]Gen. xxxvii. 14——[v]Or, *place of the carriage;* chap. xxvi. 5——[w]Or, *battle array,* or, *place of fight*——[x]Heb. *the vessels from upon him*——[y]Heb. *asked his brethren of peace,* as Judg. xviii. 15——[z]Ver. 8

[a]Heb. *from his face*——[b]Josh. xv. 16——[c]Chap. xi. 2 [d]Chap. xiv. 6——[e]Verse 10——[f]Deut. v. 26——[g]Verse 25——[h]Gen. xxxvii. 4, 8, 11; Matt. x. 36——[i]Ver. 17 [k]Ver. 26, 27——[l]Heb. *word*——[m]Heb. *took him* [n]Deut. xx. 1, 3——[o]Chap. xvi. 18——[p]See Num. xiii. 31; Deut. ix. 2

---

absurdity. I must confess that where every one else has failed, I have no hope of succeeding: I must, therefore, leave all farther attempts to justify the chronology; and refer to those who have written *for* and *against* the genuineness of this part of the common Hebrew text. At the end of the chapter I shall introduce some extracts from *Kennicott* and *Pilkington:* and leave the whole with the unprejudiced and discerning reader.

Verse 18. *Carry these ten cheeses*] *Cheeses of milk,* says the *margin.* In the East they do not make what we call *cheese:* they press the milk

but slightly, and carry it in rush baskets. It is highly salted, and little different from *curds.*

Verse 19. *Fighting with the Philistines.*] See at the end of the chapter.

Verse 29. Is there *not a cause?*] הלא דבר הוא *halo dabar hu.* I believe the meaning is what several of the versions express: *I have spoken but a word.* And should a man be made an offender for a word?

Verse 32. *And David said*] This properly connects with the eleventh verse.

Verse 33. *Thou art but a youth*] Supposed

A. M. 2941
B. C. 1063
An. Exod. Isr.
428
Anno ante
I. Olymp. 287

able to go against this Philistine to fight with him; for thou *art but* a youth, and he a man of war from his youth.

34 And David said unto Saul, Thy servant kept his father's sheep, and there came a lion, and a bear, and took a ⁹lamb out of the flock:

35 And I went out after him, and smote him, and delivered *it* out of his mouth: and when he arose against me, I caught *him* by his beard, and smote him, and slew him.

36 Thy servant slew both the lion and the bear: and this uncircumcised Philistine shall be as one of them, seeing he has defied the armies of the living God.

37 David said moreover, ʳThe LORD that delivered me out of the paw of the lion, and

out of the paw of the bear, he will deliver me out of the hand of this Philistine. And Saul said unto David, Go, and ˢthe LORD be with thee.

A. M. 2941
B. C. 1063
An. Exod. Isr
428
Anno ante
I. Olymp. 287

38 And Saul ᵗarmed David with his armour, and he put a helmet of brass upon his head; also he armed him with a coat of mail.

39 And David girded his sword upon his armour, and he assayed to go; for he had not proved *it*. And David said unto Saul, I cannot go with these; for I have not proved *them*. And David put them off him.

40 And he took his staff in his hand, and chose him five smooth stones out of the ᵘbrook, and put them in a shepherd's ᵛbag which he had, even in a scrip; and his sling *was* in his

---

⁹Or, *kid*——ʳPsa. xviii. 16, 17; lxiii. 7; lxxvii. 11; 2 Cor. i. 10; 2 Tim. iv. 17, 18

ˢChap. xx. 13; 1 Chron. xxii. 11, 16——ᵗHeb. *clothed David with his clothes*——ᵘOr, *valley*——ᵛHeb. *vessel*

---

to be about *twenty-two* or *twenty-three* years of age.

Verse 34. *Thy servant kept his father's sheep*] He found it necessary to give Saul the *reasons* why he undertook this combat; and why he expected to be victorious. 1. I have *courage* to undertake it, and *strength* to perform it. 2. Both have been tried in a very signal manner: (1.) A *lion* came upon my flock, and seized a lamb; I ran after him, he attacked me, I seized hold of him by his shaggy locks, smote and slew him, and delivered the lamb. (2.) A *bear* came in the same way, and I attacked and slew him. 3. This, with whom I am to fight, is a *Philistine*, an *uncircumcised* man; one who is an enemy to God: God therefore will not be on *his* side. On that ground I have nothing to fear. 4. He has defied the armies of the Lord; and has in effect defied Jehovah himself: therefore the battle is the Lord's, and he will stand by *me*. 5. I have perfect confidence in his protection and defence; for they that trust in him shall never be confounded. 6. I conclude, therefore, that the Lord, who delivered me out of the paw of the lion, and out of the paw of the bear, will deliver me out of the hand of the Philistine.

Verse 35. The slaying of the lion and the bear mentioned here, must have taken place at *two* different times; perhaps the verse should be read thus: *I went out after him,* (the lion,) *and smote him,* &c. *And when he* (the bear) *rose up against me, I caught him by the beard and slew him.*

Verse 37. *Go, and the Lord be with thee.*] Saul saw that these were reasonable grounds of confidence, and therefore wished him success.

Verse 38. *Saul armed David*] He knew that although the battle was the Lord's, yet prudent means should be used to secure success.

Verse 39. *I cannot go with these*] In ancient times it required considerable *exercise* and *training* to make a man expert in the use of such heavy armour; armour which in the present day scarcely a man is to be found who is able to carry; and so it must have been *then*, until that *practice* which arises from frequent use had made the proprietor perfect. *I have not*

proved them says David: I am wholly unaccustomed to such armour and it would be an encumbrance to me.

Verse 40. *He took his staff*] What we would call his *crook*.

Five smooth stones] 1. Had they been *rough* or *angular*, they would not have passed easily through the air, and their asperities would, in the course of their passage, have given them a *false direction*. 2. Had they not been *smooth*, they could not have been readily despatched from the *sling*.

A shepherd's bag] That in which he generally carried his provisions while keeping his sheep in the open country.

And his sling] The sling, both among the Greeks and Hebrews, has been a powerful offensive weapon. See what has been said in Judg. xx. 16. It is composed of *two strings* and a *leathern strap;* the strap is in the *middle,* and is the place where the *stone* or *bullet* lies. The string on the right end of the strap is firmly fastened to the hand; that on the *left* is held between the thumb and middle joint of the fore finger. It is then whirled two or three times round the head; and when discharged, the finger and thumb let go their hold of the left end string. The velocity and force of the sling are in proportion to the distance of the strap, where the bullet lies, from the shoulder joint. Hence the ancient *Baleares,* or inhabitants of *Majorca* and *Minorca,* are said to have had *three* slings of different lengths, the *longest* they used when the enemy was at the greatest distance; the *middle* one, on their nearer approach; and the *shortest,* when they came into the ordinary fighting distance in the field. The shortest is the most *certain,* though not the most *powerful.* The *Balearians* are said to have had *one* of their slings constantly bound about their *head,* to have used the *second* as a *girdle,* and to have carried the *third* always in their *hand.* See DIOD. Sic. lib. v., c. 18, p. 286 edit. *Bipont.*

In the use of the sling it requires much *practice* to hit the mark; but when once this dexterity is acquired, the sling is nearly as fatal as

A. M. 2941
B. C. 1063
An. Exod. Isr.
428
Anno ante
I. Olymp. 287

hand: and he drew near to the Philistine.

41 And the Philistine came on and drew near unto David; and the man that bare the shield *went* before him.

42 And when the Philistine looked about, and saw David, he ʷdisdained him: for he was *but* a youth, and ˣruddy, and of a fair countenance.

43 And the Philistine said unto David, ʸ*Am I a dog*, that thou comest to me with staves? And the Philistine cursed David by his gods.

44 And the Philistine ᶻsaid to David, Come to me, and I will give thy flesh unto the fowls of the air, and to the beasts of the field.

45 Then said David to the Philistine, Thou comest to me with a sword, and with a spear, and with a shield: ᵃbut I come to thee in the name of the LORD of hosts, the God of the armies of Israel, whom thou hast ᵇdefied.

46 This day will the LORD ᶜdeliver thee

into mine hand; and I will smite thee, and take thine head from thee; and I will give ᵈthe carcasses of the host of the Philistines this day unto the fowls of the air, and to the wild beasts of the earth; ᵉthat all the earth may know that there is a God in Israel.

47 And all this assembly shall know that the LORD ᶠsaveth not with sword and spear: for ᵍthe battle *is* the LORD's, and he will give you into our hands.

48 And it came to pass, when the Philistine arose, and came and drew nigh to meet David, that David hasted, and ran toward the army to meet the Philistine.

49 And David put his hand in his bag, and took thence a stone, and slang *it*, and smote the Philistine in his forehead, that the stone sunk into his forehead; and he fell upon his face to the earth.

A. M. 2941
B. C. 1063
An. Exod. Isr.
428
Anno ante
I. Olymp. 287

ʷPsa. cxxiii. 4, 5; 1 Cor. i. 27, 28——ˣChap. xvi. 12 ʸChap. xxiv. 14; 2 Sam. iii. 8; ix. 8; xvi. 9; 2 Kings viii. 13——ᶻ1 Kings xx. 10, 11——ᵃ2 Sam. xxii. 33, 35; Psa. cxxiv. 8; cxxv. 1; 2 Cor. x. 4; Heb. xi. 33, 34

ᵇVerse 10——ᶜHebrew, *shut thee up*——ᵈDeut. xxviii. 26——ᵉJosh. iv. 24; 1 Kings viii. 43; xviii. 36; 2 Kings xix. 19; Isa. lii. 10——ᶠPsa. xliv. 6, 7; Hos. i. 7; Zech. iv. 6——ᵍ2 Chron. xx. 15

---

the musket or bow; see on ver. 49. David was evidently an expert marksman; and his sling gave him greatly the *advantage* over Goliath; an advantage of which the giant does not seem to have been aware. He could hit him within any speaking distance; if he missed once, he had as many *chances* as he had *stones;* and after all, being unencumbered with armour, young, and athletic, he could have saved his life by flight. Against him the Philistine could do but little, except in close fight; it is true he appears to have had a *javelin* or *missile spear*, (see on ver. 6,) but David took care to prevent the use of all such weapons, by giving him the first blow.

Verse 41. *The man that bare the shield*] See on ver. 7.

Verse 42. *He disdained him*] He held him in contempt; he saw that he was young, and from his *ruddy complexion* supposed him to be *effeminate*.

Verse 43. *Am I a dog, that thou comest to me with staves?*] It is very likely that Goliath did not perceive the *sling*, which David might have kept coiled up within his hand.

Cursed David by his gods.] Prayed his gods to curse him. This long parley between David and Goliath is quite in the style of those times. A Hindoo sometimes in a fit of anger says to his enemy, *The goddess Kalee shall devour thee! May Doorga destroy thee!* Homer's heroes have generally an altercation before they engage; and sometimes enter into geographical and genealogical discussions, and vaunt and scold most contemptibly.

Verse 44. *Come to me, and I will give thy flesh*] He intended, as soon as he could lay hold on him, to pull him to pieces.

Verse 45. *Thou comest to me with a sword*] *I come to thee with the name* (בשם *beshem*) *of Jehovah of hosts; the God of the armies of Israel*. What Goliath expected from his *arms*, David expected from the ineffable *name*.

Verse 46. *This day will the Lord deliver thee into mine hand*] This was a direct and circumstantial prophecy of what did take place.

Verse 47. *For the battle* is *the Lord's*] It is the Lord's war: you are fighting *against* him and his religion, as the champion of your party; I am fighting *for* God, as the champion of his cause.

Verse 48. *The Philistine arose*] This was an end of the parley; the Philistine came forward to meet David, and David on his part ran forward to meet the Philistine.

Verse 49. *Smote the Philistine in his forehead*] Except his *face*, Goliath was everywhere covered over with strong armour. Either he had no *beaver* to his helmet, or it was lifted up so as to expose his forehead; but it does not appear that the ancient helmets had any covering for the face. The *Septuagint* however supposes that the stone passed through the helmet, and sank into his forehead: Και διεδυ ὁ λιθος δια της περικεφαλαιας εις το μετωπον αυτου, "and the stone passed through his helmet, and sank into his skull." To some this has appeared perfectly improbable; but we are assured by ancient writers that scarcely any thing could resist the force of the *sling*.

Diodorus Siculus, lib. v., c. 18, p. 287, edit. *Bipont*, says, "The Baleares, in time of war, sling greater stones than any other people, and with *such force*, that they seem as if projected from a *catapult*. Διο και κατα τας τειχομαχιας εν ταις προσβολαις τυπτοντες τους προ των επαλξεων

A. M. 2941
B. C. 1063
An. Exod. Isr.
428
Anno ante
I. Olymp. 287
50 So [h]David prevailed over the Philistine with a sling and with a stone, and smote the Philistine, and slew him; but *there was* no sword in the hand of David.

51 Therefore David ran, and stood upon the Philistine, and took his sword, and drew it out of the sheath thereof, and slew him, and cut off his head therewith. And when the Philistines saw their champion was dead, [i]they fled.

52 And the men of Israel and of Judah arose, and shouted, and pursued the Philistines, until thou come to the valley, and to the gates of Ekron. And the wounded of the Philistines fell down by the way to [k]Shaaraim, even unto Gath, and unto Ekron.

53 And the children of Israel returned from chasing after the Philistines, and they spoiled their tents.

54 And David took the head of the Philistine, and brought it to Jerusalem; but he put his armour in his tent.

A. M. 2941
B. C. 1063
An. Exod. Isr.
428
Anno ante
I. Olymp. 287

55 And when Saul saw David go forth against the Philistine, he said unto Abner, the captain of the host, Abner, [l]whose son *is* this youth? And Abner said, *As* thy soul liveth, O king, I cannot tell.

56 And the king said, Inquire thou whose son the stripling *is*.

57 And as David returned from the slaughter of the Philistine, Abner took him, and brought him before Saul [m]with the head of the Philistine in his hand.

58 And Saul said to him, Whose son *art* thou, *thou* young man? And David answered, [n]*I am* the son of thy servant Jesse the Bethlehemite.

---

[h]Chap. xxi. 9; Ecclus. xlvii. 4; 1 Mic. iv. 30; see Judg. iii. 31; xv. 15; chap. xxiii. 21

[i]Heb. xi. 34——[k]Josh. xv. 36——[l]See chap. xvi. 21, 22
[m]Ver. 54——[n]Ver. 12

εφεστωτας κατατραυματιζουσιν· εν δε ταις παραταξεσι τους τε θυρεους, και τα κρανη, και παν σκεπαστηριον οπλον συντριβουσι. Κατα δε την ευστοχιαν ουτως ακριβεις εισιν, ωστε κατα το πλειστον μη αμαρτανειν του προκειμενου σκοπου. Therefore, in assaults made on fortified towns, they grievously wound the besieged; and in battle they *break in pieces* the *shields, helmets,* and every *species* of *armour* by which the body is defended. And they are such exact marksmen that they scarcely *ever miss* that at which they *aim.*"

The historian accounts for their great *accuracy* and *power* in the use of the *sling,* from this circumstance: Αιτιαι δε τουτων, κ. τ. λ. "They attain to this perfection by frequent exercise from their childhood; for while they are young and under their mother's care, they are obliged to learn to sling; for they fasten bread for a mark at the top of the pole; and till the child hit the bread he must remain fasting; and when he has hit it, the mother gives it to him to eat."—*Ibid.*

I have given these passages at large, because they contain several curious facts, and sufficiently account for the *force* and *accuracy* with which David slung his stone at Goliath. We find also in the μη αμαρτανειν, *not miss the mark,* of the historian, the true notion of αμαρτανειν, *to sin,* which I have contended for elsewhere. He who *sins,* though he *aims* thereby at his *gratification* and *profit, misses the mark* of present and eternal felicity.

Verse 51. *When the Philistines saw their champion was dead, they fled.*] They were panic-struck; and not being willing to fulfil the condition which was stipulated by Goliath, they precipitately left the field. The Israelites took a proper advantage of these circumstances, and totally routed their enemies.

Verse 54. *David took the head of the Philistine*] It has been already remarked that this,

with the following verses, and the five first verses of the eighteenth chapter, are omitted by the Septuagint. See the observations at the end.

Verse 58. *Whose son* art *thou,* thou *young man?*] That Saul should not know David with whom he had treated a little before, and even armed him for the combat, and that he should not know who his father was, though he had sent to his father for permission to David to reside constantly with him, (chap. xvi. 22,) is exceedingly strange! I fear all Bishop Warburton's attempts to rectify the chronology by assumed *anticipations,* will not account for this. I must honestly confess they do not satisfy me; and I must refer the reader to what immediately follows on the authenticity of the verses which concern this subject.

ON the subject of that large omission in the Septuagint of which I have spoken on ver. 12, I here subjoin the reasons of Mr. *Pilkington* and Dr. *Kennicott* for supposing it to be an interpolation of some rabbinical writer, added at a very early period to the Hebrew text.

"Had every version of the Hebrew text," says Mr. Pilkington, "agreed to give a translation of this passage, as we now find, the attempts of clearing it from its embarrassments would have been attended with very great difficulties; but as in several other cases before mentioned, so here, the providence of God seems to have so far secured the credit of those who were appointed to be the penmen of the oracles of truth, that the defence of their original records may be undertaken upon good grounds, and supported by sufficient evidence. For we are now happily in possession of an ancient version of these two chapters, which appears to have been made from a *Hebrew* copy, which had none of the thirty-nine verses which are here supposed to have been interpolated, nor was similar to what we have at present in those places which are here supposed to have been altered. This version is found in the *Vatican* copy of the *Seventy*, which whoever reads and considers, will find the accounts there given regular, consistent, and probable. It will be proper, therefore, to examine the several parts where such alterations are supposed to have been made in the *Hebrew* text, in order to produce such other external or internal evidence, as shall be necessary to support the charge of interpolation, which ought not to be laid merely upon the authority of any single version.

"The first passage, which is not translated in the *Vatican* copy of the *Greek* version, is from the 11th to the 32d verse of the xviith chapter, wherein we have an account: 1. Of *David's* being sent to the camp to visit his brethren. 2. Of his conversation with the men of *Israel*, relating to *Goliath's* challenge; and their informing him of the premium *Saul* had offered to any one that should accept it, and come off victorious. 3. Of *Eliab's* remarkable behaviour to his brother *David*, upon his making this inquiry. And, 4. Of *Saul's* being made acquainted with what *David* had said upon this occasion.

"It is obvious to remark upon this passage:—

"1. That, after *David* had been of so much service to the king, in causing the evil spirit to depart from him; after its being recorded how greatly *Saul* loved him, and that he had made him his armour-bearer; after the king had sent to *Jesse* to signify his intention of keeping his son with him; all of which are particularly mentioned in the latter part of the preceding chapter; the account of his keeping his father's sheep afterwards, and being sent to his brethren upon this occasion, must appear to be somewhat improbable. 2. That what is here said of the premium that *Saul* had offered to him who should conquer the *Philistine*, is not well consistent with the accounts afterwards given, of which we shall have occasion to take particular notice. 3. That *Eliab's* behaviour, as here represented, is not only remarkable but unaccountable and absurd. And, 4. That the inquiries of a young man, who is not said to have declared any intentions of accepting the challenge of the *Philistine*, would scarcely have been related to the king. But now, if this passage be supposed to have been interpolated, we must see how the connection stands upon its being omitted.

"Verse 11. 'When *Saul* and all *Israel* heard these words of the *Philistine*, they were dismayed, and greatly afraid.'

"Verse 32. 'Then *David* said unto *Saul*, Let no man's heart fail because of him; thy servant will go and fight with this *Philistine*.'

"No connection can be more proper, and in this view *David* is represented as being at that time an attendant upon the king; and when we had been told just before, (chap. xvi. 21,) that *Saul* had made him his armour-bearer, we might justly expect to find him with him when the battle was set in array; chap. xvii. 2. In this connection *David* is also represented as fully answering the character before given of him: 'A mighty valiant man, and a man of war,' chap. xvi. 18, and ready to fight with the *giant* upon the first proposal, (for the account of the *Philistine* presenting himself forty days is in this passage here supposed to have been interpolated, chap. xvii. 16.) I shall leave it to the critical *Hebrew* reader to make what particular remarks he may think proper in respect to the style and manner of expression in these twenty

verses; and let *Jesse go for an old man amongst men in the days of Saul*, &c."—PILKINGTON'S Remarks upon several Passages of Scripture, p. 62.

"The authorities," says Dr. *Kennicott*, "here brought to prove this great interpolation are the internal evidence arising from the *context*, and the external arising from the *Vatican* copy of the Greek version. But how then reads the *Alexandrian* MS.? The remarks acknowledge that this MS. agrees here with the corrupted *Hebrew;* and therefore was probably translated, in this part, from some late Hebrew copy which had thus been interpolated; see pages 72, 75. Now that these two MSS. do contain different readings in some places, I observed in pages 398-404, and 414. And in this xviith chapter of *Samuel*, ver. 4, the *Alexandrian* MS. says, agreeably to the present *Hebrew*, that the height of Goliath was *six cubits and a span*, i. e., above *eleven feet;* but the *Vatican* MS., agreeably to *Josephus*, that it was *four cubits and a span*, i. e., near *eight feet*. And in ver. 43, what the *Vatican* renders *he cursed David by his gods*, the *Alexandrian* renders *by his idols*. But though the *Hebrew* text might be consulted, and a few words differently rendered by the transcriber of one of these MSS., or by the transcribers of the MSS. from which these MSS. were taken; yet, as these MSS. do contain, in this chapter, such Greek as is almost universally the same, (in verb, noun, and particle,) I presume that they contain here the same translation with the designed alteration of a few words, and with the difference of the interpolated verses found in the *Alexandrian* MS.

"But, after all, what if the *Alexandrian* MS., which now has these verses, should *itself* prove them interpolated? What if the *very words of this very MS.* demonstrate that these verses were not in some former *Greek* MS.? Certainly if the *Alexandrian* MS. should be thus found, at last, not to contradict, but to confirm the *Vatican* in its omission of these twenty verses, the concurrence of these authorities will render the argument much more forcible and convincing.

"Let us then state the present question; which is, Whether the twenty verses between ver. 11 and 32, which are now in the *Hebrew* text, are interpolated? The *Vatican* MS. goes on immediately from the end of the 11th verse (και εφοβηθησαν σφοδρα) to ver. 32, which begins και ειπε Δαυιδ: whereas the 12th verse in the Hebrew begins, *not with a speech*, but with David's birth and parentage. If then the *Alexandrian* MS. begins its present 12th verse as the 32d verse begins, and as the 12th verse could not begin properly, I appeal to any man of judgment *whether the transcriber was not certainly copying from a MS. in which the 32d verse succeeded the 11th verse;* and if so, then *from a MS. which had not these intermediate verses?* Now that this is the fact, the case will at once appear upon examining the *Alexandrian* copy, where the 12th verse begins with ΚΑΙ ΕΙΠΕ ΔΑΤΙΔ; exactly as the 32d verse begins, and as the 12th verse could not begin properly.

"The case seems clearly to be, that the transcriber, having wrote what is now in the 11th verse, was beginning what is now the 32d verse; when, after writing και ειπε Δαυιδ, he perceived that either the *Hebrew*, or some other *Greek* copy, or the margin of his own copy, had several intermediate verses: upon which, without blotting out the significant word ΕΙΠΕ, he goes on to write the addition: thus fortunately leaving a decisive proof of his own great interpolation. If this addition was in the margin of that MS. from which the *Alexandrian* was transcribed, it might be inserted by that transcriber; but if it was inserted either from the *Hebrew*, or from any other *Greek* copy, the transcriber of this MS. seems to have had too little learning for such a proceeding. If it was done by the writer of that *former* MS., then the interpolation may be *a hundred* or *a hundred and fifty* years older than the *Alexandrian* MS. Perhaps the earliest Christian writer who enlarges upon the strong circumstance of David's coming from the sheep to the army, is Chrysostom, in his homily upon David and Saul; so that it had then been long in some copies of the *Greek* version. The truth seems to be, that the addition of these twenty verses took its first rise from what *Josephus* had inserted in his variation and embellishment of this history; but that many circumstances were afterwards added to his additions.

"For (and it is extremely remarkable) though *Josephus* has some, he has not half the improbabilities which are found *at present* in the sacred history: as for instance: Nothing of *the armies being fighting in the valley*, or *fighting at all*, when David was sent by his father, as in ver. 19. Nothing of *the host going forth, and shouting for the battle*, at the time of David's arrival, as in ver. 20. Nothing of *all the men of Israel fleeing from Goliath*, as in ver. 24; on the contrary, *the two armies*, (it should seem,) continued upon their two mountains. Nothing of *David's long conversation with the soldiers*, ver. 25-27, in seasons so very improper, as, whilst they were *shouting for the battle*, or whilst they were *fleeing from Goliath;* and *fleeing* from a man after they had seen him and heard him *twice* in every day *for forty days together*, ver. 16, the two armies, all this long while, leaning upon their arms, and looking very peaceably at one another. Nothing of Goliath's repeating his challenge *every morning and every evening*, as in ver. 16. David, (it is said, ver. 23,) happened to hear one of these challenges; but if he heard the *evening* challenge, it would have been then too late for the several transactions before, and the long pursuit after, Goliath's death; and David could not well hear the *morning* challenge, because he could scarce have arrived so early, after travelling from *Beth-lehem* to the army, (about *fifteen* miles,) and bringing with him *an ephah of parched corn, and ten loaves, and ten cheeses*, as in ver. 17, 18. Nothing of encouraging any man to fight Goliath, by *an offer of the king's daughter*, ver. 25; which, as it seems from the subsequent history, had never been thought of; and which, had it been offered, would probably have been accepted by some man or other out of the whole army. Nothing of Eliab's reprimanding David for *coming to see the battle*, as in ver. 28; but for a very different reason; and, indeed, it is highly improbable that Eliab should treat him at all with contempt and scurrility, after having seen Samuel anoint him for the future king of Israel, see chap. xvi. 1-13. Nothing of a *second conversation* between David and the soldiers, as in ver. 30, 31. Nothing of *Saul and Abner's not knowing who was David's father*, at the time of his going forth against the Philistine, as in ver. 55. Nothing of *David's being introduced to the king by Abner*, in form, after killing the Philistine, ver. 57, at a time when the king and the captain of the host had

no leisure for complimental ceremony; but were set out, ver. 57, in *immediate and full pursuit of the Philistines*. Nor, lastly, is any notice taken *here* by *Josephus* of what now begins the xviiith chapter, *Jonathan's friendship for David*, which is related elsewhere, and in a different manner; on the contrary, as soon as *Josephus* has mentioned Goliath's death, and told us that Saul and all Israel shouted, and fell at once upon the Philistines, and that, when the pursuit was ended, the head of Goliath was carried *by David into his own tent*, (and he could have then *no tent of his own* if he had not been then an officer in the army:) I say, as soon as *Josephus* has recorded these circumstances, he goes on to *Saul's envy and hatred of David, arising from the women's songs of congratulation;* exactly as these capital parts of the history are connected in the VATICAN MS. And with this circumstance I shall conclude these remarks; earnestly recommending the whole to the learned reader's attentive examination.

"It must not however be forgot, that the learned F. Houbigant has, in his Bible, placed these twenty verses (from the 11th to the 32d) between *hooks*, as containing a passage which comes in very improperly.

"If it be inquired as to this interpolation in *Samuel, when* it could possibly be introduced into the text? It may be observed that, *about the time of Josephus*, the Jews seem to have been fond of enlarging and, as they vainly thought, embellishing the sacred history, by inventing speeches, and prayers, and hymns, and also new articles of history, and these of considerable length; witness the several additions to the book of Esther; witness the long story concerning *wine, women, and truth*, inserted amidst parts of the genuine history of *Ezra* and *Nehemiah*, and worked up into what is now called the *First Book of Esdras;* witness the hymn of the three children in the fiery furnace, added to *Daniel;* and witness also the many additions in *Josephus*. Certainly, then, some few remarks might be noted by the Jews, and some few of their historical additions might be inserted in the margin of their Hebrew copies; which might afterwards be taken into the text itself by injudicious transcribers.

"The history of David's conquest of the mighty and insulting Philistine is certainly very engaging; and it gives a most amiable description of a brave young man, relying with firm confidence upon the aid of the GOD *of battle* against the blaspheming enemy. It is not therefore very strange that some fanciful rabbin should be particularly struck with the strange circumstances of the Philistines daring to challenge all Israel; and David's cutting off the giant's head with the giant's own sword. And then, finding that Josephus had said that *David came from the sheep to the camp, and happened to hear the challenge*, the rabbin might think it very natural that David should be indignant against the giant, and talk valorously to the soldiers, and that the soldiers should mightily encourage David; and then, to be sure, this was the most lucky season to introduce the celebrated friendship of Jonathan for David; particularly when, according to these additions, Jonathan had seen *Abner leading David in triumph to the king's presence;* every one admiring the young hero, as he proudly advanced with the grim *head of the Philistine in his hand*. So that this multiform addition and fanciful embellishment of the rabbin reminds one of the motley absurdity described by the poet in the famous lines:—

Humano capiti cervicem pictor equinam
Jungere si velit, et varias inducere plumas, &c.

"The passage supposed to be interpolated here, was in the Hebrew text before the time of Aquila; because there are preserved a few of the differences in those translations of it which were made by Aquila, Theodotion, and Symmachus. These verses, being thus acknowledged at that time, would doubtless be found in such copies as the Jews then declared to be *genuine*, and which they delivered afterwards to Origen as such. And that Origen did refer to the Jews for such copies as *they held genuine*, he allows in his epistle to Africanus; for there he speaks of *soothing* the Jews, in order to get *pure* copies from them."—KENNICOTT's *Second Dissertation on the Hebrew Text*, p. 419.

In the *general dissertation* which Dr. Kennicott has prefixed to his edition of the Hebrew Bible, he gives additional evidence that the verses in question were not found originally in the *Septuagint*, and consequently not in the *Hebrew copy* used for that version. Several MSS. in the royal library at Paris either omit these verses, or have them with *asterisks* or notes of *dubiousness*. And the collation by Dr. *Holmes* and his continuators has brought farther proof of the fact. From the whole, there is considerable evidence that these verses were not in the Septuagint in the time of *Origen;* and if they were not in the MSS. used by Origen, it is very probable they were not in that version *at first;* and if they were not in the Septuagint at first, it is very probable that they were not in the *Hebrew text* one hundred and fifty years before Christ; and if not *then* in the Hebrew text, it is very probable they were not in that text *originally*. See *Dissertation on Gen.*, p. 9; and *Remarks on Select Passages*, p. 104.

I have only to remark here, that the *historical books* of the Old Testament have suffered more by the carelessness or infidelity of transcribers than any other parts of the sacred volume; and of this the two books of *Samuel*, the two books of *Kings*, and the two books of *Chronicles*, give the most decided and unequivocal proofs. Of this also the reader has already had considerable evidence; and he will find this greatly increased as he proceeds.

It seems to me that the Jewish copyists had not the same opinion of the *Divine inspiration* of those books as they had of those of the *law* and the *prophets;* and have therefore made no scruple to insert some of their own *traditions*, or the glosses of their doctors, in different

parts; for as the whole must evidently appear to them as a *compilation* from their *public records*, they thought it no harm to make *different alterations* and *additions* from *popular statements* of the same facts, which they found in general circulation. This is notoriously the case in *Josephus;* this will account, and it does to me very satisfactorily, for many of the *various readings* now found in the Hebrew text of the *historical books*. They were held in less *reverence*, and they were copied with less *care*, and emended with less *critical skill*, than the *pentateuch* and the *prophets;* and on them the hands of careless, ignorant, and temerarious scribes, have too frequently been laid. To deny this, only betrays a portion of the same ignorance which was the parent of those disorders; and attempts to blink the question, though they may with some be an argument of *zeal*, yet with all the sincere and truly enlightened friends of Divine revelation, will be considered to be as dangerous as they are absurd.

Where the rash or ignorant hand of man has fixed a *blot* on the Divine records, let them who in the providence of God are qualified for the task wipe it off; and while they have the thanks of all honest men, God will have the glory.

There have been many who have affected to deny the existence of *giants*. There is no doubt that the accounts given of several are either fabulous or greatly exaggerated. But men of an extraordinary size are not uncommon even in our own day: I knew two brothers of the name of *Knight*, who were born in the same township with myself, who were *seven feet six inches high;* and another, in the same place, *Charles Burns*, who was *eight feet six!* These men were well and proportionately made. I have known others of this height, whose limbs were out of all proportion; their knees bent in, and joints rickety.

Ireland, properly speaking, is the only nation on the earth that produces GIANTS; and let me tell the *poor*, that this is the only nation in the world that may be said to live on *potatoes;* with little *bread*, and less *flesh-meat*.

I have seen and entertained in my house the famous Polish dwarf, the *Count Boruwlaski*, who was about *thirty-six inches* high, every part of whose person was formed with the most perfect and delicate symmetry. The prodigious height and bulk of *Charles Burns*, and the astonishing diminutiveness of *Count Boruwlaski*, could not be properly estimated but by comparing both together. Each was a perfect man; and yet, in quantum, how disproportionate! *Man* is the only creature in whom the extremes of minuteness and magnitude are so apparent, and yet the proportion of the parts in each strictly correlative.

CHAPTER XVIII

Jonathan and David commence a lasting friendship; and David acts prudently with respect to Saul, 1–5 Saul becomes jealous of David, on account of the esteem in which he is held in Israel; and, in his fury, endeavours to destroy him, 6–12. David is made captain over a thousand; and the people love and respect him, 13–16. Saul, in order to ensnare him, offers him his daughter in marriage, 17–24; and requires a hundred foreskins of the Philistines for dowry; hoping that, in endeavouring to procure them, David might fall by the hands of the Philistines, 25. David agrees to the conditions, fulfils them, and has Michal to wife, 26–30.

A. M. 2941
B. C. 1063
An. Exod. Isr.
428
Anno ante
I. Olymp. 287

AND it came to pass, when he had made an end of speaking unto Saul, that [a]the soul of Jonathan was knit with the soul of David, [b]and Jonathan loved him as his own soul.

2 And Saul took him that day, [c]and would let him go no more home to his father's house.

3 Then Jonathan and David made a covenant, because he loved him as his own soul.

4 And Jonathan stripped himself of the robe that *was* upon him, and gave it to David, and his garments, even to his sword, and to his bow, and to his girdle.

5 And David went out whithersoever Saul sent him, *and* [d]behaved himself wisely: and Saul set him over the men of war, and he was accepted in the sight of all the people, and also in the sight of Saul's servants.

6 And it came to pass as they came, when David was returned from the slaughter of the [e]Philistine, that [f]the women came out of all the cities of Israel, singing and dancing, to meet King Saul, with tabrets, with joy, and with [g]instruments of music.

A. M. 2941
B. C. 1063
An. Exod. Isr.
428
Anno ante
I. Olymp. 287

7 And the women [h]answered *one another* as they played, and said, [i]Saul hath slain his thousands, and David his ten thousands.

8 And Saul was very wroth, and the saying [k]displeased [l]him; and he said, They have ascribed unto David ten thousands, and to me they have ascribed *but* thousands: and *what* can he have more but [m]the kingdom?

9 And Saul eyed David from that day and forward.

10 And it came to pass on the morrow, that [n]the evil spirit from God came upon Saul,

---

[a]Gen. xliv. 30——[b]Chap. xix. 2; xx. 17; 2 Sam. i. 26; Deut. xiii. 6——[c]Chap. xvii. 15——[d]Or, *prospered;* ver. 14, 15, 30——[e]Or, *Philistines*——[f]Exod. xv. 20; Judg. xi. 34

[g]Heb. *three-stringed instruments*——[h]Exod. xv. 21 [i]Chap. xxi. 11; xxix. 5; Ecclus. xlvii. 6——[k]Heb. *was evil in his eyes*——[l]Eccles. iv. 4——[m]Chap. xv. 28 [n]Chap. xvi. 14

NOTES ON CHAP. XVIII

Verse 1. When he had made an end of speaking] These *first five verses* are omitted by the *Septuagint.* See the notes on the preceding chapter.

Jonathan loved him as his own soul] The most intimate friendship subsisted between them; and they loved each other with pure hearts fervently. No love was lost between them; each was worthy of the other. They had a friendship which could not be affected with changes or chances, and which exemplified all that the ancients have said on the subject; Τὴν φιλιαν ισοτητα ειναι, και μιαν ψυχην, τον φιλον ἑτερον αυτον; "Friendship produces an entire sameness; it is one soul in two bodies: a friend is another self."

Verse 4. Jonathan stripped himself] Presents of *clothes* or *rich robes,* in token of respect and friendship, are frequent in the East. And how frequently *arms* and *clothing* were presented by warriors to each other in token of friendship, may be seen in Homer and other ancient writers.

Verse 5. Set him over the men of war] Made him *generalissimo;* or what we would call *field marshal.*

Verse 6. When David was returned] This verse connects well with the 54th verse of the preceding chapter; and carries on the narration without any break or interruption. See the notes there.

The women came out] It was the principal business of certain women to celebrate *victories,* sing at *funerals,* &c.

With instruments of music.] The original word (שלשים *shalishim*) signifies instruments with *three strings;* and is, I think, properly translated by the Vulgate, *cum sistris,* "with *sistrums.*" This instrument is well known as being used among the ancient Egyptians: it was made of brass, and had *three,* sometimes more, brass rods across; which, being loose in their holes, made a jingling noise when the instrument was shaken.

Verse 7. Saul hath slain his thousands] As it cannot literally be true that Saul had slain thousands, and David ten thousands; it would be well to translate the passage thus: *Saul hath smitten* or *fought against thousands; David against tens of thousands.* "Though Saul has been victorious in all *his* battles; yet he has not had such *great odds* against him as David has had; Saul, indeed, has been *opposed by thousands;* David, by *ten thousands.*" We may here remark that the Philistines had drawn out their whole forces at this time: and when Goliath was slain, they were totally discomfited by the Israelites, led on chiefly by David.

Verse 10. The evil spirit from God] See on chap. xvi. 14, &c.

He prophesied in the midst of the house] He was *beside himself;* made *prayers, supplications,* and incoherent *imprecations:* "God preserve my life," "Destroy my enemies," or such like prayers, might frequently escape from him in his agitated state. The Arabic intimates that he was actually possessed by an evil spirit, and that through it he uttered a sort of demoniacal predictions.

But let us examine the original more closely: it is said that Saul prophesied in the midst of his house, that is, he *prayed* in his family, while David was playing on the harp; and then suddenly threw his javelin, intending to have killed David. Let it be observed that the word ויתנבא *vaiyithnabbe* is the third person singular of the future *hithpael;* the sign of which is not only to do an action on or for one's self, but also to *feign* or *pretend* to do it. The meaning seems to be, Saul *pretended* to be *praying*

A. M. 2941
B. C. 1063
An. Exod. Isr.
428
Anno ante
I. Olymp. 287

°and he prophesied in the midst of the house: and David played with his hand, as at other times: ᵖand *there was* a javelin in Saul's hand.

11 And Saul qcast the javelin; for he said, I will smite David even to the wall *with it.* And David avoided out of his presence twice.

12 And Saul was ʳafraid of David, because ˢthe LORD was with him, and was ᵗdeparted from Saul.

13 Therefore Saul removed him from him, and made him his captain over a thousand; and ᵘhe went out and came in before the people.

14 And David ᵛbehaved himself wisely in all his ways; and ʷthe LORD *was* with him.

15 Wherefore when Saul saw that he behaved himself very wisely, he was afraid of him.

16 But ˣall Israel and Judah loved David, because he went out and came in before them.

17 And Saul said to David, Behold my elder daughter Merab, ʸher will I give thee to wife: only be thou ᶻvaliant for me, and fight ᵃthe LORD's battles. For Saul said, ᵇLet not mine hand be upon him, but let the hand of the Philistines be upon him.

18 And David said unto Saul, ᶜWho *am* I?

and what *is* my life, *or* my father's family in Israel, that I should be son-in-law to the king?

19 But it came to pass at the time when Merab Saul's daughter should have been given to David, that she was given unto ᵈAdriel the ᵉMeholathite to wife.

20 ᶠAnd Michal Saul's daughter loved David: and they told Saul, and the thing ᵍpleased him.

21 And Saul said, I will give him her, that she may be ʰa snare to him, and that ⁱthe hand of the Philistines may be against him. Wherefore Saul said to David, Thou shalt ᵏthis day be my son-in-law in *the one of* the twain.

22 And Saul commanded his servants, *saying,* Commune with David secretly, and say, Behold, the king hath delight in thee, and all his servants love thee: now therefore be the king's son-in-law.

23 And Saul's servants spake those words in the ears of David. And David said, Seemeth it to you *a* light *thing* to be a king's son-in-law, seeing that I *am* a poor man, and lightly esteemed?

24 And the servants of Saul told him, saying, ˡOn this manner spake David.

25 And Saul said, Thus shall ye say to

A. M. 2941
B. C. 1063
An. Exod. Isr.
428
Anno ante
I. Olymp. 287

°Chap. xix. 24; 1 Kings xviii. 29; Acts xvi. 16
ᵖChap. xix. 9——qChap. xix. 10; xx. 33; Prov. xxvii. 4
ʳVer. 15, 29——ˢChap. xvi. 13, 18——ᵗChap. xvi. 14;
xxviii. 15——ᵘVer. 16; Num. xxvii. 17; 2 Sam. v. 2
ᵛOr, *prospered;* ver. 5——ʷGen. xxxix. 2, 3, 23; Josh.
vi. 27——ˣVer. 5——ʸChap. xvii. 25

ᶻHeb. *a son of valour*——ᵃNum. xxxii. 20, 27, 29;
chapter xxv. 28——ᵇVer. 21, 25; 2 Sam. xii. 9——ᶜSee
ver. 23; chap. ix. 21; 2 Sam. vii. 18——ᵈ2 Sam. xxi. 8
ᵉJudg. vii. 22——ᶠVer. 28——ᵍHeb. *was right in his
eyes*——ʰExod. x. 7——ⁱVer. 17——ᵏSee ver. 26
ˡHeb. *According to these words*

---

in his family, the better to conceal his murderous intentions, and render David unsuspicious; who was, probably, at this time performing the musical part of the family worship. This view of the subject makes the whole case natural and plain.

Verse 11. *Saul cast the javelin*] The *javelin* or *spear* was the emblem of regal authority; kings always had it at hand, and in ancient monuments they are always represented with it.

In ancient times, says *Justin,* kings used a *spear* instead of a diadem: *Per ea tempora reges* hastas *pro* diademate *habebant, Hist.* lib. xliii. And as *spears* were the emblems of supreme power, hence they were reputed as attributes of the Divinity, and were worshipped as representatives of the gods. *Ab origine rerum, pro* DIIS *immortalibus veteres* HASTAS *coluerunt, ob cujus religionis memoriam, adhuc deorum simulachris* HASTÆ *adduntur.—*Ibid.

Verse 13. *Made him his captain*] This was under pretence of doing him honour, when it was in effect only to rid himself of the object of his envy.

Verse 15. *He was afraid of him.*] He saw

that, by his prudent conduct, he was every day gaining increasing influence.

Verse 17. *Fight the Lord's battles.*] Mr. Calmet properly remarks that the wars of the Hebrews, while conducted by the express orders of God, were truly *the wars of the Lord;* but when the spirit of worldly ambition and domination became mingled with them, they were no longer the wars of the Lord, but wars of lust and profanity.

Verse 21. *That she may be a snare to him*] Saul had already determined the condition on which he would give his daughter to David; viz., that he *should slay one hundred Philistines:* this he supposed he would undertake for the love of Michal, and that he must necessarily perish in the attempt; and *thus* Michal would become a *snare to him.*

Verse 25. *But a hundred foreskins*] That is, Thou shalt slay one hundred Philistines, and thou shalt produce their *foreskins,* as a proof, not only that thou hast killed one hundred men, but that these are of the *uncircumcised.* A custom similar to this still prevails among the Abyssinians, according to Bruce. See his Travels.

A. M. 2941
B. C. 1063
An. Exod. Isr.
428
Anno ante
I. Olymp. 287

David, The king desireth not any [m]dowry, but a hundred foreskins of the Philistines, to be [n]avenged of the king's enemies. But Saul [o]thought to make David fall by the hand of the Philistines.

26 And when his servants told David these words, it pleased David well to be the king's son-in-law: and [p]the days were not [q]expired.

27 Wherefore David arose and went, he and [r]his men, and slew of the Philistines two hundred men; and [s]David brought their foreskins, and they gave them in full tale to the king,

that he might be the king's son-in-law. And Saul gave him Michal his daughter to wife.

A. M. 2941
B. C. 1063
An. Exod. Isr.
428
Anno ante
I. Olymp. 287

28 And Saul saw and knew that the LORD *was* with David, and *that* Michal Saul's daughter loved him.

29 And Saul was yet the more afraid of David; and Saul became David's enemy continually.

30 Then the princes of the Philistines [t]went forth: and it came to pass, after they went forth, *that* David [u]behaved himself more wisely than all the servants of Saul; so that his name was much [v]set by.

---

[m]Gen. xxxiv. 12; Exod. xxii. 17——[n]Chap. xiv. 24 [o]Ver. 17——[p]See ver. 21——[q]Heb. *fulfilled*——[r]Ver. 13

[s]2 Sam. iii. 14——[t]2 Sam. xi. 1——[u]Ver. 5——[v]Heb. *precious;* chap. xxvi. 21; 2 Kings i. 13; Psa. cxvi. 15

Verse 27. *Slew—two hundred men.*] The Septuagint has only *one hundred men.* Saul covenanted with David for a *hundred;* and David himself says, 2 Sam. iii. 14, that he espoused Michal for a *hundred:* hence it is likely that *one hundred* is the true reading.

Verse 30. *Then the princes of the Philistines went forth*] Probably to avenge themselves

on David and the Israelites: but of this war we know no more than that David was more skilful and successful in it than any of the other officers of Saul. His military skill was greater, and his success was proportionate to his skill and courage; hence it is said, he behaved himself more wisely than all the servants of Saul.

CHAPTER XIX

Jonathan pleads for David before Saul, who is for the present reconciled, 1–7. David defeats the Philistines; and Saul becomes again envious, and endeavours to slay him, but he escapes, 8–10. Saul sends men to David's house, to lie in wait for him; but Michal saves him by a stratagem, 11–17. David flees to Samuel, at Ramah, 18. Saul, hearing of it, sends messengers three several times to take him; but the Spirit of God coming upon them, they prophesy, 19–21. Saul, hearing of this, goes after David himself, and falls under the same influence, 22–24.

A. M. 2941
B. C. 1063
An. Exod. Isr.
428
Anno ante
I. Olymp. 287

AND Saul spake to Jonathan his son, and to all his servants, that they should kill David.

2 But Jonathan Saul's son [a]delighted much in David: and Jonathan told David, saying, Saul my father [b]seeketh to kill thee: now therefore, I pray thee, take heed to thyself until the morning, and abide in a secret *place,* and hide thyself:

3 And I will go out and stand beside my father in the field where thou *art,* and I will

commune with my father of thee; and what I see, that I will tell thee.

A. M. 2941
B. C. 1063
An. Exod. Isr.
428
Anno ante
I. Olymp. 287

4 And Jonathan [c]spake good of David unto Saul his father, and said unto him, Let not the king [d]sin against his servant, against David; because he hath not sinned against thee, and because his works *have been* to thee-ward very good:

5 For he did put his [e]life in his hand, and [f]slew the Philistine, and [g]the LORD wrought

---

[a]Chap. xviii. 1——[b]Ver. 8——[c]Prov. xxxi. 8, 9 [d]Gen. xlii. 22; Psa. xxxv. 12; cix. 5; Prov. xvii. 13; Jer. xviii. 20

[e]Judg. ix. 17; xii. 3; chap. xxviii. 21; Psalm cxix. 109 [f]Chapter xvii. 49, 50——[g]1 Samuel xi. 13; 1 Chron. xi. 14

NOTES ON CHAP. XIX

Verse 1. *That they should kill David.*] Nothing less than the especial interposition of God could have saved David's life, when every officer about the king's person, and every soldier, had got positive orders to despatch him.

Verse 2. *Take heed to thyself until the morn-*

ing] Perhaps the order was given to slay him the *next day;* and therefore Jonathan charges him to be particularly on his guard at that time, and to hide himself.

Verse 4. *Jonathan spake good of David*] It is evident that Jonathan was satisfied that David was an innocent man; and that his father was most *unjustly* incensed against him.

A. M. 2941
B. C. 1063
An. Exod. Isr.
428
Anno ante
I. Olymp. 287

a great salvation for all Israel: thou sawest *it,* and didst rejoice: [h]wherefore then wilt thou [i]sin against innocent blood, to slay David without a cause?

6 And Saul hearkened unto the voice of Jonathan: and Saul sware, *As* the LORD liveth, he shall not be slain.

7 And Jonathan called David, and Jonathan showed him all those things. And Jonathan brought David to Saul, and he was in his presence, [k]as [l]in times past.

A. M. 2942
B. C. 1062
An. Exod. Isr.
429
Anno ante
I. Olymp. 286

8 And there was war again: and David went out, and fought with the Philistines, and slew them with a great slaughter; and they fled from [m]him.

9 And [n]the evil spirit from the LORD was upon Saul, as he sat in his house with his javelin in his hand: and David played with *his* hand.

10 And Saul sought to smite David even to the wall with the javelin; but he slipped away out of Saul's presence, and he smote the javelin into the wall: and David fled, and escaped that night.

11 [o]Saul also sent messengers unto David's house, to watch him, and to slay him in the morning: and Michal David's wife told him, saying, If thou save not thy life to-night, to-morrow thou shalt be slain.

A. M. 2942
B. C. 1062
An. Exod. Isr.
429
Anno ante
I. Olymp. 286

12 So Michal [p]let David down through a window: and he went, and fled, and escaped.

13 And Michal took an [q]image, and laid *it* in the bed, and put a pillow of goats' *hair* for his bolster, and covered *it* with a cloth.

14 And when Saul sent messengers to take David, she said, He *is* sick.

15 And Saul sent the messengers *again* to see David, saying, Bring him up to me in the bed, that I may slay him.

16 And when the messengers were come in, behold, *there was* an image in the bed, with a pillow of goats' *hair* for his bolster.

17 And Saul said unto Michal, Why hast thou deceived me so, and sent away mine enemy, that he is escaped? And Michal answered Saul, He said unto me, Let me go; [r]why should I kill thee?

---

[h]Chap. xx. 32——[i]Matt. xxvii. 4——[k]Chap. xvi. 21; xviii. 2, 13——[l]Heb. *yesterday third day*——[m]Heb. *his face*——[n]Chap. xvi. 14; xviii. 10, 11

[o]Psalm lix. title——[p]So Josh. ii. 15; Acts ix. 24, 25 [q]Heb. *teraphim;* Gen. xxxi. 19; Judg. xvii. 5——[r]2 Samuel ii. 22

Verse 5. *For he did put his life in his hand*] The pleadings in this verse, though short, are exceedingly cogent; and the argument is such as could not be resisted.

Verse 6. *He shall not be slain.*] In consequence of this *oath,* we may suppose he issued orders contrary to those which he had given the preceding day.

Verse 7. *He was in his presence, as in times past.*] By Jonathan's advice he had secreted himself on that day on which he was to have been assassinated: the king having sworn that he should not be slain, David resumes his place in the palace of Saul.

Verse 9. *And the evil spirit from the Lord*] His envy and jealousy again returned, producing distraction of mind, which was exacerbated by diabolic influence. See on chap. xvi. 14.

Verse 10. *But he slipped away*] He found he could not trust Saul; and therefore was continually on his watch. His agility of body was the means of his preservation at this time.

Verse 11. *To slay him in the morning*] When they might be able to *distinguish* between him and Michal his wife; for, had they attempted his life in the night season, there would have been some danger to Michal's life. Besides, Saul wished to represent him as a *traitor;* and consequently an attack upon him was justifiable at any time, even in the fullest daylight.

Verse 12. *Let David down through a win-*

dow] As Saul's messengers were sent to David's house to *watch him,* they would naturally guard the gate, or lie in wait in that place by which David would come out. Michal, seeing this, let him down to the ground through a window, probably at the *back part* of the house; and there being neither entrance nor issue that way, the liers in wait were easily eluded.

Verse 13. *Michal took an image*] את התרפים *eth hatteraphim, the teraphim.* The Hebrew word appears to mean any kind of *image,* in any kind of *form,* as a representative of some *reality.* Here it must have been something in the *human form;* because it was intended to represent a man lying in bed indisposed.

A pillow of goats' hair] Perhaps she formed the appearance of a sick man's *head* muffled up by this pillow or bag of goats' hair. So I think the original might be understood. The *goats' hair* was merely accidental; unless we could suppose that it was designed to represent the *hair of David's head,* which is not improbable.

Verse 17. *Let me go; why should I kill thee?*] That is, If thou do not let me go, I will kill thee. This she said to excuse herself to her father: as a *wife* she could do not less than favour the escape of her husband, being perfectly satisfied that there was no guilt in him. It is supposed that it was on this occasion that David wrote the fifty-ninth Psalm, *Deliver me from mine enemies, &c.*

A. M. 2942
B. C. 1062
An. Exod. Isr.
429
Anno ante
I. Olymp. 286

18 So David fled, and escaped, and came to Samuel to Ramah, and told him all that Saul had done to him. And he and Samuel went and dwelt in Naioth.

19 And it was told Saul, saying, Behold, David *is* at Naioth in Ramah.

20 And ˢSaul sent messengers to take David: ᵗand when they saw the company of the prophets prophesying, and Samuel standing *as* appointed over them, the Spirit of God was upon the messengers of Saul, and they also ᵘprophesied.

21 And when it was told Saul, he sent other messengers, and they prophesied likewise. And Saul sent messengers again the third time, and they prophesied also.

22 Then went he also to Ramah, and came to a great well that *is* in Sechu: and he asked and said, Where *are* Samuel and David? And *one* said, Behold, *they be* at Naioth in Ramah.

23 And he went thither to Naioth in Ramah: and ᵛthe Spirit of God was upon him also, and he went on, and prophesied, until he came to Naioth in Ramah.

24 ʷAnd he stripped off his clothes also, and prophesied before Samuel in like manner, and ˣlay down ʸnaked all that day and all that night. Wherefore they say, ᶻ*Is* Saul also among the prophets?

A. M. 2942
B. C. 1062
An. Exod. Isr.
429
Anno ante
I. Olymp. 286

ˢSee John vii. 32, 45, &c.——ᵗ1 Cor. xiv. 3, 24, 25; chap. x. 5, 6——ᵘNum. xi. 25; Joel ii. 28

ᵛChap. x. 10——ʷIsa. xx. 2——ˣHeb. *fell;* Num. xxiv. 4 ʸMic. i. 8; see 2 Sam. vi. 14, 20——ᶻChap. x. 11

Verse 18. *David fled, and escaped—to Samuel*] He, no doubt, came to this holy man to ask advice; and Samuel thought it best to retain him for the present, with himself at Naioth, where it is supposed he had a school of prophets.

Verse 20. *The company of the prophets prophesying*] Employed in religious exercises. *Samuel—appointed over them*] Being *head* or *president* of the school at this place.

The Spirit of God was upon the messengers] They partook of the same influence, and joined in the same exercise; and thus were prevented from seizing David.

Verse 23. *He went on, and prophesied*] The Divine Spirit seemed to have seized him at the well of Sechu; and he went on from that *prophesying*—praying, singing praises, &c.— till he came to Naioth.

Verse 24. *He stripped off his clothes*] Threw off his royal robes or military dress, retaining only his *tunic;* and continued so all that day and all that night, uniting with the sons of the prophets in *prayers, singing praises,* and other *religious exercises,* which were unusual to kings and warriors; and this gave rise to the saying, *Is Saul also among the prophets?* By bringing both him and his men thus under a Divine influence, God prevented them from injuring the person of David. See the notes on chap. x. 6, &c.; and see my sermon on *The Christian Prophet and his Work.*

CHAPTER XX

David complains to Jonathan of Saul's enmity against him; Jonathan comforts him, 1–10. They walk out into the field, and renew their covenant, 11–17. David asks Jonathan's leave to absent himself from Saul's court; and Jonathan informs him how he shall ascertain the disposition of his father towards him, 18–23. David hides himself; is missed by Saul; Jonathan is questioned concerning his absence; makes an excuse for David; Saul is enraged, and endeavours to kill Jonathan, 24–33. Jonathan goes out to the field; gives David the sign which they had agreed on, and by which he was to know that the king had determined to take away his life, 34–39. He sends his servant back into the city; and then he and David meet, renew their covenant, and have a very affectionate parting, 40–42.

A. M. 2942
B. C. 1062
An. Exod. Isr.
429
Anno ante
I. Olymp. 286

AND David fled from Naioth in Ramah, and came and said before Jonathan, What have I done? what *is* mine iniquity? and what *is* my sin before thy father, that he seeketh my life?

2 And he said unto him, God forbid; thou shalt not die: behold, my father will do nothing either great or small, but that he will ᵃshow it me: and why should my father hide this thing from me? it *is* not *so.*

A. M. 2942
B. C. 1062
An. Exod. Isr.
429
Anno ante
I. Olymp. 286

ᵃHeb. *uncover mine ear;*

ver. 12; chap. ix. 15

NOTES ON CHAP. XX

Verse 1. *David fled from Naioth*] On hearing that Saul had come to that place, knowing that he was no longer in safety, he fled for his life.

Verse 2. *My father will do nothing*] Jonathan thought that his father could have no evil design against David, because of the oath which he had sworn to himself, chap. xix. 6; and at any rate, that he would do nothing against David without informing him.

A. M. 2942
B. C. 1062
An. Exod. Isr.
429
Anno ante
I. Olymp. 286

3 And David sware moreover, and said, Thy father certainly knoweth that I have found grace in thine eyes; and he saith, Let not Jonathan know this, lest he be grieved: but truly *as* the LORD liveth, and *as* thy soul liveth, *there is* but a step between me and death.

4 Then said Jonathan unto David, ^bWhatsoever thy soul ^cdesireth, I will even do *it* for thee.

5 And David said unto Jonathan, Behold, to-morrow *is* the ^dnew moon, and I should not fail to sit with the king at meat: but let me go, that I may ^ehide myself in the field unto the third *day* at even.

6 If thy father at all miss me, then say, David earnestly asked *leave* of me that he might run ^fto Beth-lehem his city: for *there is* a yearly ^gsacrifice there for all the family.

7 ^hIf he say thus, *It is* well; thy servant shall have peace: but if he be very wroth, *then* be sure that ⁱevil is determined by him.

8 Therefore thou shalt ^kdeal kindly with thy servant; for ^lthou hast brought thy servant into a covenant of the LORD with thee:

notwithstanding, ^mif there be in me iniquity, slay me thyself; for why shouldest thou bring me to thy father?

A. M. 2942
B. C. 1062
An. Exod. Isr.
429
Anno ante
I. Olymp. 286

9 And Jonathan said, Far be it from thee: for if I knew certainly that evil were determined by my father to come upon thee, then would not I tell it thee?

10 Then said David to Jonathan, Who shall tell me? or what *if* thy father answer thee roughly?

11 And Jonathan said unto David, Come, and let us go out into the field. And they went out both of them into the field.

12 And Jonathan said unto David, O LORD God of Israel, when I have ⁿsounded my father about to-morrow any time, *or* the third *day,* and behold, *if there be* good toward David, and I then send not unto thee, and ^oshow it thee;

13 ^pThe LORD do so and much more to Jonathan: but if it please my father *to do* thee evil, then I will show it thee, and send thee away, that thou mayest go in peace: and ^qthe LORD be with thee, as he hath been with my father.

---

^bOr, *Say what* is *thy mind, and I will do,* &c.——^cHeb. *speaketh,* or, *thinketh*——^dNum. x. 10; xxviii. 11 ^eCh. xix. 2——^fCh. xvi. 4——^gOr, *feast;* ch. ix. 12 ^hSee Deut. i. 23; 2 Sam. xvii. 4——ⁱCh. xxv. 17; Esth.

vii. 7——^kJosh. ii. 14——^lVer. 16; chap. xviii. 3; xxiii. 18——^m2 Sam. xiv. 32——ⁿHeb. *searched*——^oHeb. *uncover thine ear;* ver. 2——^pRuth i. 17——^qJosh. i. 5; chap. xvii. 37; 1 Chron. xxii. 11, 16

Verse 3. There is *but a step between me and death.*] My life is in the most imminent danger. Your father has, most assuredly, determined to destroy me.

The same figure used here, *there is but a step between me and death,* may be found in *Juvenal,* who, satirizing those who risk their lives for the sake of gain in perilous voyages, speaks thus:—

I nunc et ventis animam committe, dolato Confisus ligno, digitis a morte remotus Quatuor aut septem, *si sit latissima teda.*
SAT. xii., ver. 57.

"Go now, and commit thy life to the winds, trusting to a hewn plank, *four* or *seven* fingers thick, if the beam out of which it has been cut have been large enough."

Verse 5. *To-morrow* is *the new moon*] The months of the Hebrews were *lunar* months, and they reckoned from new moon to new moon. And as their other feasts, particularly the passover, were reckoned according to this, they were very scrupulous in observing the first appearance of each new moon. On these new moons they offered sacrifices, and had a feast; as we learn from Num. x. 10; xxviii. 11. And we may suppose that the families, on such occasions, sacrificed and feasted together. To this David seems to refer; but the gathering together all the families of a whole tribe seems

to have taken place only once in the year. *There is a yearly sacrifice there for all the family,* ver. 6.

Verse 8. *If there be in me iniquity*] If thou seest that I am plotting either against the state, or the life of thy father, then slay me thyself.

Verse 10. *Who shall tell me?*] Who shall give me the necessary information? What means wilt thou use to convey this intelligence to me?

Verse 11. *Come, and let us go out into the field*] In answer to David's question, he now shows him how he shall convey this intelligence to him.

Verse 12. *Jonathan said—O Lord God of Israel*] There is, most evidently, something wanting in this verse. The *Septuagint* has, *The Lord God of Israel doth* KNOW. The *Syriac* and *Arabic, The Lord God of Israel* is WITNESS. Either of these makes a good sense. But two of Dr. Kennicott's MSS. supply the word חי *chai,* "liveth;" and the text reads thus, *As the Lord God of Israel* LIVETH, *when I have sounded my father—if there be good, and I then send not unto thee, and show it thee, the Lord do so and much more to Jonathan.* This makes a still better sense.

Verse 13. *The Lord be with thee, as he hath been with my father.*] From this, and other passages here it is evident that Jonathan knew that the Lord had appointed David to the kingdom.

A. M. 2942
B. C. 1062
An. Exod. Isr.
429
Anno ante
I. Olymp. 286

14 And thou shalt not only, while yet I live, show me the kindness of the LORD, that I die not:

15 But *also* ʳthou shalt not cut off thy kindness from my house for ever: no, not when the LORD hath cut off the enemies of David every one from the face of the earth.

16 So Jonathan ˢmade *a covenant* with the house of David, *saying,* ᵗLet the LORD even require *it* at the hand of David's enemies.

17 And Jonathan caused David to swear again, ᵘbecause he loved him: ᵛfor he loved him as he loved his own soul.

18 Then Jonathan said to David, ʷTo-morrow *is* the new moon: and thou shalt be missed, because thy seat will be ˣempty.

19 And *when* thou hast stayed three days, *then* thou shalt go down ʸquickly, ᶻand come to ᵃthe place where thou didst hide thyself, ᵇwhen the business was *in hand,* and shalt remain by the stone ᶜEzel.

20 And I will shoot three arrows on the side *thereof,* as though I shot at a mark.

21 And, behold, I will send a lad, *saying,* Go, find out the arrows. If I expressly say unto the lad, Behold, the arrows *are* on this side of thee, take them; then come thou: for *there is* peace to thee, and ᵈno hurt; ᵉas the LORD liveth.

22 But if I say thus unto the young man, Behold, the arrows *are* beyond thee; go thy way: for the LORD hath sent thee away.

23 And *as touching* ᶠthe matter which thou and I have spoken of, behold, the LORD *be* between thee and me for ever.

A. M. 2942
B. C. 1062
An. Exod. Isr.
429
Anno ante
I. Olymp. 286

24 So David hid himself in the field: and when the new moon was come, the king sat him down to eat meat.

25 And the king sat upon his seat, as at other times, *even* upon a seat by the wall: and Jonathan arose, and Abner sat by Saul's side, and David's place was empty.

26 Nevertheless Saul spake not any thing that day: for he thought, Something hath befallen him, he *is* ᵍnot clean; surely he *is* not clean.

27 And it came to pass on the morrow, *which was* the second *day* of the month, that David's place was empty: and Saul said unto Jonathan his son, Wherefore cometh not the son of Jesse to meat, neither yesterday nor to-day?

28 And Jonathan ʰanswered Saul, David earnestly asked *leave* of me *to go* to Beth-lehem:

29 And he said, Let me go, I pray thee; for our family hath a sacrifice in the city; and my brother, he hath commanded me *to be there:* and now, if I have found favour in thine eyes, let me get away, I pray thee, and see my brethren. Therefore he cometh not unto the king's table.

30 Then Saul's anger was kindled against Jonathan, and he said unto him, ⁱThou ᵏson of the perverse rebellious *woman,* do not I

ʳ2 Sam. ix. 1, 3, 7; xxi. 7——ˢHeb. *cut*——ᵗCh. xxv. 22; see ch. xxxi. 2; 2 Sam. iv. 7; xxi. 8——ᵘOr, *by his love toward him*——ᵛChap. xviii. 1——ʷVer. 5——ˣHeb. *missed* ʸOr, *diligently*——ᶻHeb. *greatly*——ᵃChap. xix. 2

ᵇHeb. *in the day of the business*——ᶜOr, *that showeth the way*——ᵈHeb. *not* any *thing*——ᵉJer. iv. 2——ᶠVer. 14, 15; see ver. 42——ᵍLev. vii. 21; xv. 5, &c.——ʰVer. 6 ⁱOr, *Thou perverse rebel*——ᵏHeb. *son of perverse rebellion*

Verse 14. *Show me the kindness of the Lord*] When thou comest to the kingdom, if I am alive, thou shalt show kindness to me, and thou shalt continue that kindness to my family after me.

Verse 20. *I will shoot three arrows*] Jonathan intended that David should stay at the stone Ezel, where probably there was some kind of *cave,* or *hiding place;* that, to prevent all suspicion, he would not go to him himself, but take his servant into the fields, and pretend to be exercising himself in archery; that he would shoot three arrows, the better to cover his design; and that, if he should say to his servant, who went to bring back the arrows, "The arrows are on this side of thee," this should be a sign to David that he might safely return to court, no evil being designed; but if he should say, "The arrows are beyond thee," then David should escape for his life, Saul having determined his destruction.

Verse 25. *The king sat upon his seat*] It

seems that there was one table for Saul, Jonathan, David, and Abner; Saul having the chief seat, that *next to the wall.* As only *four* sat at this table, the absence of any one would soon be noticed.

Verse 29. *Our family hath a sacrifice*] Such sacrifices were undoubtedly *festal* ones; the beasts slain for the occasion were first *offered to God,* and *their blood poured out before him;* afterwards all that were bidden to the feast ate of the flesh. This was a family entertainment, at the commencement of which God was peculiarly honoured.

Verse 30. *Thou son of the perverse rebellious* woman] This clause is variously translated and understood. The *Hebrew* might be translated, *Son of an unjust rebellion;* that is, "Thou art a rebel against thy own father." The Vulgate, *Fili mulieris virum ultro rapientis;* "Son of the woman who, of her own accord, forces the man." The Septuagint is equally curious,

A. M. 2942
B. C. 1062
An. Exod. Isr.
429
Anno ante
I. Olymp. 286

know that thou hast chosen the son of Jesse to thine own confusion, and unto the confusion of thy mother's nakedness?

31 For as long as the son of Jesse liveth upon the ground, thou shalt not be established, nor thy kingdom. Wherefore now send and fetch him unto me, for he ¹shall surely die.

32 And Jonathan answered Saul his father, and said unto him, ᵐWherefore shall he be slain? What hath he done?

33 And Saul ⁿcast a javelin at him to smite him: ᵒwhereby Jonathan knew that it was determined of his father to slay David.

34 So Jonathan arose from the table in fierce anger, and did eat no meat the second day of the month: for he was grieved for David, because his father had done him shame.

35 And it came to pass in the morning, that Jonathan went out into the field at the time appointed with David, and a little lad with him.

36 And he said unto his lad, Run, find out now the arrows which I shoot. *And* as the lad ran, he shot an arrow ᵖbeyond him.

37 And when the lad was come to the place of the arrow which Jonathan had shot, Jonathan cried after the lad, and said, *Is* not the arrow beyond thee?

A. M. 2942
B. C. 1062
An. Exod. Isr.
429
Anno ante
I. Olymp. 286

38 And Jonathan cried after the lad, Make speed, haste, stay not. And Jonathan's lad gathered up the arrows, and came to his master.

39 But the lad knew not any thing: only Jonathan and David knew the matter.

40 And Jonathan gave his ۹artillery unto ʳhis lad, and said unto him, Go, carry *them* to the city.

41 *And* as soon as the lad was gone, David arose out of *a place* toward the south, and fell on his face to the ground, and bowed himself three times; and they kissed one another, and wept one with another, until David exceeded.

42 And Jonathan said to David, ˢGo in peace, ᵗforasmuch as we have sworn both of us in the name of the LORD, saying, The LORD be between me and thee, and between my seed and thy seed for ever. And he arose and departed: and Jonathan went into the city.

---

¹Heb. is *the son of death*——ᵐChap. xix. 5; Matt. xxvii. 23; Luke xxiii. 22——ⁿChap. xviii. 11——ᵒVer. 7 ᵖHeb. *to pass over him*

۹Heb. *instruments*——ʳHeb. *that* was *his*——ˢChap. i. 17——ᵗOr, the LORD be witness of that *which*, &c.; see ver. 23

Τίε κορασιων αυτομολουντων; "Son of the damsels who came of their own accord." Were these the meaning of the *Hebrew*, then the bitter reflection must refer to some *secret* transaction between Saul and Jonathan's mother; which certainly reflects more dishonour on himself than on his brave son. Most sarcasms bear as hard upon the speaker, as they do on him against whom they are spoken. Abusive language always argues a mean, weak, and malevolent heart.

Verse 34. *Jonathan arose—in fierce anger*] We should probably understand this rather of Jonathan's *grief* than of his *anger*, the latter clause explaining the former: *for he was grieved for David.* He was grieved for his *father*—he was grieved for his *friend.*

Verse 38. *Make speed, haste, stay not.*] Though these words appear to be addressed to the lad, yet they were spoken to David, indicating that his life was at stake, and only a prompt flight could save him.

Verse 40. *Jonathan gave his artillery*] I believe this to be the only place in our language where the word *artillery* is not applied to *cannon* or *ordance.* The original (כלי *keley*) signifies simply *instruments*, and here means the bow, quiver, and arrows.

Verse 41. *Until David exceeded.*] David's dis-

tress must, in the nature of things, be the *greatest.* Besides his friend Jonathan, whom he was now about to lose for ever, he lost his wife, relatives, country; and, what was most afflictive, the altars of his God, and the ordinances of religion.

Saul saw David's growing popularity, and was convinced of his own maladministration. He did not humble himself before God, and therefore became a prey to envy, pride, jealousy, cruelty, and every other malevolent temper. From him David had every thing to fear, and therefore he thought it was safer to yield to the storm, than attempt to brave it; though he could have even raised a very powerful party in Israel, had he used the means which were so much in his power. But as he neither sought not affected the kingdom, he left it to the providence of God to bring him in by such means, at such a way, and in such a time, as was most suited to his godly wisdom. He that believeth shall not make haste: God's *way* and *time* are ever the best; and he who, even in God's way, runs before he is sent, runs at random; runs without light, and without Divine strength. Feeble, therefore, must be his own might, his own counsel, and his own wisdom: though he encompass himself with his own sparks, yet this hath he at the Lord's hand—he shall lie down in sorrow.

CHAPTER XXI

David comes to Ahimelech at Nob, receives provisions from him, and the sword of Goliath; and is noticed by Doeg, one of the servants of Saul, 1–9. He leaves Nob, and goes to Achish, king of Gath, 10. But on being recognised as the vanquisher of Goliath by the servants of Achish, he feigns himself deranged, and Achish sends him away, 11-15.

A. M. 2942
B. C. 1062
An. Exod. Isr.
429
Anno ante
I. Olymp. 286

THEN came David to Nob to ᵃAhimelech the priest: and Ahimelech was ᵇafraid at the meeting of David, and said unto him, Why *art* thou alone, and no man with thee?

2 And David said unto Ahimelech the priest, The king hath commanded me a business, and hath said unto me, Let no man know any thing of the business whereabout I send thee, and what I have commanded thee: and I have appointed *my* servants to such and such a place.

3 Now therefore what is under thine hand? give *me* five *loaves of* bread in mine hand, or what there is ᶜpresent.

4 And the priest answered David, and said, *There is* no common bread under mine hand, but there is ᵈhallowed bread; ᵉif the young men have kept themselves at least from women.

5 And David answered the priest, and said unto him, Of a truth women *have been* kept from us about these three days, since I came out, and the ᶠvessels of the young men are holy, and *the bread is* in a manner common, ᵍyea, though it were sanctified this day ʰin the vessel.

6 So the priest ⁱgave him hallowed *bread*:

for there was no bread there but the shew-bread, ᵏthat was taken from before the LORD, to put hot bread in the day when it was taken away.

A. M. 2942
B. C. 1062
An. Exod. Isr.
429
Anno ante
I. Olymp. 286

7 Now a certain man of the servants of Saul *was* there that day, detained before the LORD; and his name *was* ¹Doeg, an Edomite, the chiefest of the herdmen that *belonged* to Saul.

8 And David said unto Ahimelech, And is there not here under thine hand spear or sword? for I have neither brought my sword nor my weapons with me, because the king's business required haste.

9 And the priest said, The sword of Goliath the Philistine, whom thou slewest in ᵐthe valley of Elah, ⁿbehold, it *is here* wrapped in a cloth behind the ephod: if thou wilt take that, take *it:* for *there is* no other save that here. And David said, *There is* none like that; give it me.

10 And David arose, and fled that day for fear of Saul, and went to ᵒAchish the king of Gath.

11 And ᵖthe servants of Achish said unto him, *Is* not this David the king of the land? Did they not sing one to another of him in

---

ᵃChap. xiv. 3, called *Ahiah;* called also *Abiathar,* Mark ii. 26——ᵇChap. xvi. 4——ᶜHeb. *found* ᵈExod. xxv. 30; Lev. xxiv. 5; Matt. xii. 4——ᵉExod. xix. 15; Zech. vii. 3——ᶠ1 Thess. iv. 4——ᵍOr, *especially when this day there is* other *sanctified in the vessel*

ʰLev. viii. 26——ⁱMatt. xii. 3, 4; Mark ii. 25, 26; Luke vi. 3, 4——ᵏLev. xxiv. 8, 9——ˡChap. xxii. 9; Psa. lii. title——ᵐChap. xvii. 2, 50——ⁿSee chap. xxxi. 10——ᵒOr, *Abimelech,* Psa. xxxiv. title——ᵖPsa. lvi. title

---

NOTES ON CHAP. XXI

Verse 1. *Then came David to Nob*] There were two places of this name, one on this side, the second on the other side of Jordan; but it is generally supposed that Nob, near Gibeah of Benjamin, is the place here intended; it was about twelve miles from Jerusalem.

Why art *thou alone*] Ahimelech probably knew nothing of the difference between Saul and David; and as he knew him to be the king's son-in-law, he wondered to see him come without any attendants.

Verse 2. *The king hath commanded me a business*] All said here is an untruth, and could not be dictated by the Spirit of the Lord; but there is no reason to believe that David was under the influence of Divine inspiration at this time. It is well known that from all antiquity it was held no crime to tell a lie, in order to save life. Thus *Diphilus:*—

Ὑπολαμβανω το ψευδος επι σωτηρια
Λεγομενον, ουδεν περιποιεισθαι δυσχερες.

"I hold it right to tell a lie, in order to procure my personal safety; nothing should be avoided in order to save life."

A *heathen* may *say* or *sing* thus; but no *Chris-*

tian can act thus, and *save his soul,* though he by doing so may *save his life.*

Verse 6. *So the priest gave him hallowed bread*] To this history our Lord alludes, Mark ii. 25, in order to show that in cases of *absolute necessity* a breach of the *ritual* law was no sin. It was lawful for the priests only to eat the shew-bread; but David and his companions were starving, no other bread could be had at the time, and therefore he and his companions ate of it without sin.

Verse 7. *Detained before the Lord*] Probably fulfilling some vow to the Lord, and therefore for a time resident at the tabernacle.

And his name was *Doeg*] From chap. xxii. 9 we learn that this man betrayed David's secret to Saul, which caused him to destroy the city, and slay eighty-five priests. We learn from its title that the fifty-second Psalm was made on this occasion; but titles are not to be implicitly trusted.

Verse 9. *The sword of Goliath*] It has already been conjectured (see chap. xvii.) that the sword of Goliath was laid up as a trophy in the tabernacle.

Verse 10. *Went to Achish the king of Gath.*] This was the worst place to which he could have gone: it was the very city of Goliath, whom he had slain, and whose sword he now

A. M. 2942
B. C. 1062
An. Exod. Isr.
429
Anno ante
I. Olymp. 286

dances, saying, ᵠSaul hath slain his thousands, and David his ten thousands?

12 And David ʳlaid up these words in his heart, and was sore afraid of Achish the king of Gath.

13 And ˢhe changed his behaviour before them, and feigned himself mad in their hands, and ᵗscrabbled on the doors of the gate, and

let his spittle fall down upon his beard.

14 Then said Achish unto his servants, Lo, ye see the man ᵘis mad: wherefore *then* have ye brought him to me?

15 Have I need of madmen, that ye have brought this *fellow* to play the madman in my presence? shall this *fellow* come into my house?

A. M. 2942
B. C. 1062
An. Exod. Isr.
429
Anno ante
I. Olymp. 286

ᵠChapter xviii. 7; xxix. 5; Ecclus. xlvii. 6
ʳLuke ii. 19

ˢPsa. xxxiv. title——ᵗOr, *made marks*——ᵘOr, *playeth*
the madman

---

wore; and he soon found, from the conversation of the servants of Achish, that his life was in the most imminent danger in this place.

Verse 13. *And he changed his behaviour*] Some imagine David was so *terrified* at the danger to which he was now exposed, that he was thrown into a kind of *frenzy*, accompanied with *epileptic fits*. This opinion is countenanced by the *Septuagint*, who render the passage thus: Ιδου ιδετε ανδρα επιληπτον; "Behold, ye see an epileptic man. Why have ye introduced him to me?" Μη ελαττουμαι επιληπτων εγω; "Have I any need of epileptics, that ye have brought him to have his fits before me, (επιληπτευεσθαι προς με?") It is worthy of remark, that the *spittle falling upon the beard*, i. e., *slavering* or *frothing at the mouth*, is a genuine concomitant of an epileptic fit.

If this translation be allowed, it will set the conduct of David in a clearer point of view than the present translation does. But others think the whole was a feigned conduct, and that he acted the part of a lunatic or madman in order to get out of the hands of Achish and his

courtiers. Many vindicate this conduct of David; but if *mocking be catching*, according to the proverb, he who *feigns* himself to be *mad* may, through the just judgment of God, *become* so. I dare not be the apologist of *insincerity* or *lying*. Those who wish to look farther into this subject may consult Dr. *Chandler*, Mr. *Saurin*, and *Ortlob*, in the first volume of *Dissertations*, at the end of ᵗhe Dutch edition of the *Critici Sacri*.

Verse 15. *Shall this* fellow *come into my house?*] I will not take into my service a man who is liable to so grievous a disease. *Chandler*, who vindicates David's *feigning himself, mad*, concludes thus: "To deceive the deceiver is in many instances meritorious, in none criminal. And what so likely to deceive as the very reverse of that character which they had so misconstrued? He was undone as a *wise man*, he had a chance to escape as a *madman;* he tried, and the experiment succeeded." I confess I can neither feel the *force* nor the *morality* of this. Deceit and hypocrisy can never be pleasing in the sight of God.

CHAPTER XXII

David flees to the cave of Adullam, where he is joined by four hundred men of various descriptions, 1, 2. *He goes afterwards to Moab; and by the advice of the prophet Gad, to the forest of Hareth,* 3–5. *Saul, suspecting his servants of infidelity, upbraids them,* 6–8. *Doeg informs him of David's coming to Nob; of his being entertained by Ahimelech; on which Saul slays Ahimelech and all the priests, to the number of* eighty-five, *and destroys the city of Nob,* 9–19. *Abiathar, the son of Ahimelech, only escapes; he joins with David, by whom he is assured of protection,* 20–23.

A. M. 2942
B. C. 1062
An. Exod. Isr.
429
Anno ante
I. Olymp. 286

DAVID therefore departed thence, and ᵃescaped ᵇto the cave Adullam: and when his brethren and all his father's house heard *it*, they went down thither to him.

2 ᶜAnd every one *that was* in distress, and

every one that ᵈ*was* in debt, and every one *that was* ᵉdiscontented, gathered themselves unto him; and he became a captain over them: and there were with him about four hundred men.

A. M. 2942
B. C. 1062
An. Exod. Isr.
429
Anno ante
I. Olymp. 286

ᵃPsa. lvii. title, and cxlii. title——ᵇ2 Sam.
xxiii. 13

ᶜJudg. xi. 3——ᵈHebrew, *had a creditor*——ᵉHeb.
bitter of soul

NOTES ON CHAP. XXII

Verse 1. *The cave Adullam*] This was in the tribe of Judah, and, according to Eusebius and Jerome, ten miles eastward of what they call *Eleutheropolis*.

Verse 2. *And every one that was in distress --debt--discontented*] It is very possible that these several disaffected and exceptionable characters might at first have supposed that David, unjustly persecuted, would be glad to

avail himself of their assistance that he might revenge himself upon Saul, and so they in the mean time might profit by plunder, &c. But if this were their design they were greatly disappointed, for David never made any improper use of them. They are never found plundering or murdering; on the contrary, they always appear under good discipline, and are only employed in services of a beneficent nature, and in defence of their country. Whatever they were before they came to David, we find that he suc-

A. M. 2942
B. C. 1062
An. Exod. Isr.
429
Anno ante
I. Olymp. 286

3 And David went thence to Mizpeh of Moab: and he said unto the king of Moab, Let my father and my mother, I pray thee, come forth, *and be* with you, till I know what God will do for me.

4 And he brought them before the king of Moab, and they dwelt with him all the while that David was in the hold.

5 And the prophet ᶠGad said unto David, Abide not in the hold; depart, and get thee into the land of Judah. Then David departed, and came into the forest of Hareth.

6 When Saul heard that David was discovered, and the men that *were* with him, (now Saul abode in Gibeah under a ᵍtree in Ramah, having his spear in his hand, and all his servants *were* standing about him;)

7 Then Saul said unto his servants that stood about him, Hear now, ye Benjamites; will the son of Jesse ʰgive every one of you fields and vineyards, *and* make you all captains of thousands, and captains of hundreds;

8 That all of you have conspired against me, and *there is* none that ⁱshoweth me that ᵏmy son hath made a league with the son of Jesse, and *there is* none of you that is sorry for me, or showeth unto me that my son hath

stirred up my servant against me, to lie in wait, as at this day?

9 Then answered ¹Doeg the Edomite, which was set over the servants of Saul, and said, I saw the son of Jesse coming to Nob, to ᵐAhimelech the son of ⁿAhitub.

10 ᵒAnd he inquired of the Lord for him, ᵖand gave him victuals, and gave him the sword of Goliath the Philistine.

11 Then the king sent to call Ahimelech the priest, the son of Ahitub, and all his father's house, the priests that *were* in Nob: and they came all of them to the king.

12 And Saul said, Hear now, thou son of Ahitub. And he answered, �q Here I *am*, my lord.

13 And Saul said unto him, Why have ye conspired against me, thou and the son of Jesse, in that thou hast given him bread, and a sword, and hast inquired of God for him that he should rise against me, to lie in wait as at this day?

14 Then Ahimelech answered the king, and said, And who *is so* faithful among all thy servants as David, which is the king's son-in-law, and goeth at thy bidding, and is honourable in thine house?

15 Did I then begin to inquire of God for

A. M. 2942
B. C. 1062
An. Exod. Isr.
429
Anno ante
I. Olymp. 286

ᶠ2 Sam. xxiv. 11; 1 Chron. xxi. 9; 2 Chron. xxix. 25 ᵍOr, *grove in a high place*——ʰChap. viii. 14——ⁱHeb. *uncovereth mine ear; chap. xx. 2*

ᵏChap. xviii. 3; xx. 30——¹Chap. xxi. 7; Psa. lii. title, and ver. 1, 2, 3——ᵐChapter xxi. 1——ⁿChap. xiv. 3 ᵒNum. xxvi. 21——ᵖCh. xxi. 6, 9——q Heb. *Behold me*

---

ceeded in civilizing them, and making profitable to the state those who were before unprofitable. It is not necessary to strain the words of the original in order to prove that these were *oppressed* people, and not exceptionable characters, as some have done.

Verse 3. *He said unto the king of Moab*] David could not trust his parents within the reach of Saul, and he found it very inconvenient to them to be obliged to go through all the fatigues of a military life, and therefore begs the king of Moab to give them shelter. The king of Moab, being one of Saul's enemies, would be the more ready to oblige a person from whom he might at least expect *friendship,* if not considerable *services.*

Verse 5. *Get thee into the land of Judah*] Gad saw that in this place alone he could find safety.

Verse 6. *Saul abode in Gibeah*] Saul and his men were in pursuit of David, and had here, as is the general custom in the East, encamped on a *height,* for so *Ramah* should be translated, as in the margin. His *spear,* the ensign of power, (see on chap. xviii. 11,) was at hand, that is, stuck in the ground where he rested, which was the *mark* to the soldiers that *there* was their general's tent.

And all his servants were *standing about*

him] That is, they were encamped around him, or perhaps here there is a reference to a sort of council of war called by Saul for the purpose of delivering the speech recorded in the following verses.

Verse 8. There is *none that showeth me*] He conjectured that Jonathan had made a league with David to dethrone him, and he accuses them of disloyalty for not making the discovery of this unnatural treason. Now it was impossible for any of them to show what did not exist, no such league having ever been made between David and Jonathan.

Verse 9. *Doeg the Edomite, which was set over the servants of Saul*] In chap. xxi. 7 he is said to be *the chiefest of the herdmen that belonged to Saul,* and the *Septuagint* intimate that he was *over the mules of Saul.* Probably he was what we call the king's *equery* or *groom.*

Verse 10. *And he inquired of the Lord for him*] This circumstance is not related in history; but it is probably true, as David would most naturally wish to know where to direct his steps in this very important crisis.

Verse 14. *And who is so faithful*] The word נאמ *neeman,* which we here translate *faithful,* is probably the name of an *officer.* See the note on Num. xii. 7.

Verse 15. *Did I then begin to inquire of God*]

A. M. 2942
B. C. 1062
An. Exod. Isr.
429
Anno ante
I. Olymp. 286 him? be it far from me: let not the king impute *any* thing unto his servant, *nor* to all the house of my father: for thy servant knew nothing of all this, [r]less or more.

16 And the king said, Thou shalt surely die, Ahimelech, thou, and all thy father's house.

17 And the king said unto the [s]footmen [t]that stood about him, Turn, and slay the priests of the LORD; because their hand also *is* with David, and because they knew when he fled, and did not show it to me. But the servants of the king [u]would not put forth their hand to fall upon the priests of the LORD.

18 And the king said to Doeg, Turn thou, and fall upon the priests. And Doeg the Edomite turned, and he fell upon the priests, and [v]slew on that day fourscore and five persons that did wear a linen ephod.

19 [w]And Nob, the city of the priests, smote he with the edge of the sword, both men and women, children and sucklings, and oxen, and asses, and sheep, with the edge of the sword.

20 [x]And one of the sons of Ahimelech the son of Ahitub, named Abiathar, [y]escaped, and fled after David.

21 And Abiathar showed David that Saul had slain the LORD's priests.

22 And David said unto Abiathar, I knew *it* that day, when Doeg the Edomite *was* there, that he would surely tell Saul: I have occasioned *the death* of all the persons of thy father's house.

23 Abide thou with me, fear not: [z]for he that seeketh my life seeketh thy life: but with me thou *shalt be* in safeguard.

A. M. 2942
B. C. 1062
An. Exod. Isr.
429
Anno ante
I. Olymp. 286

---

[r]Heb. *little or great*——[s]Or, *guard*——[t]Heb. *runners*
[u]See Exod. i. 17

[v]See chap. ii. 31——[w]Ver. 9, 11——[x]Chap. xxiii. 6
[y]Chap. ii. 33——[z]1 Kings ii. 26

He probably means that his inquiring *now* for David was no *new thing*, having often done so before, and without ever being informed it was either wrong in itself, or displeasing to the king. Nor is it likely that Ahimelech knew of any disagreement between Saul and David. He knew him to be the king's son-in-law, and he treated him as such.

Verse 17. *But the servants of the king would not*] They dared to disobey the commands of the king in a case of such injustice, inhumanity, and irreligion.

Verse 18. *And Doeg—fell upon the priests*] A ruthless Edomite, capable of any species of iniquity.

Fourscore and five persons] The Septuagint read τριακοσιους και πεντε ανδρας, *three hundred and five men;* and Josephus has *three hundred and eighty-five men.* Probably the eighty-five were priests; the three hundred, the families of the priests; three hundred and eighty-five being the whole population of Nob.

That did wear a linen ephod.] That is, persons who did actually administer, or had a right to administer, in sacred things. The *linen ephod* was the ordinary clothing of the priests.

Verse 19. *And Nob—smote he with the edge of the sword*] This is one of the worst acts in the life of Saul; his malice was implacable, and his wrath was cruel, and there is no motive of justice or policy by which such a barbarous act can be justified.

Verse 20. *Abiathar, escaped*] This man carried with him his *sacerdotal garments*, as we find from chap. xxiii. 6, 9.

Verse 22. *I knew it that day*] When I saw Doeg there, I suspected he would make the matter known to Saul.

I have occasioned the death *of all the persons*] I have been the innocent cause of their destruction.

Verse 23. *He that seeketh my life seeketh thy life*] The enmity of Saul is directed against thee as well as against me, and thou canst have no safety but in being closely attached to me; and I will defend thee even at the risk of my own life. This he was bound in duty and conscience to do.

CHAPTER XXIII

David succours Keilah, besieged by the Philistines; defeats them, and delivers the city, 1–6. Saul, hearing that David was at Keilah, determines to come and seize him, 7, 8. David inquires of the Lord concerning the fidelity of the men of Keilah towards him; is informed that if he stays in the city, the men of Keilah will betray him to Saul, 9–12. David and his men escape from the city, and come to the wilderness of Ziph, 13–15. Jonathan meets David in the wood of Ziph, strengthens his hand in God, and they renew their covenant, 16–18. The Ziphites endeavour to betray David to Saul, but he and his men escape to Maon, 19–22. Saul comes to Maon; and having surrounded the mountain on which David and his men were, they must inevitably have fallen into his hands, had not a messenger come to call Saul to the succour of Judah, then invaded by the Philistines, 25–27. Saul leaves the pursuit of David, and goes to succour the land; and David escapes to En-gedi, 28, 29.

A. M. 2942
B. C. 1062
An. Exod. Isr.
429
Anno ante
I. Olymp. 286

THEN they told David, saying, Behold, the Philistines fight against ^aKeilah, and they rob the threshing-floors.

2 Therefore David ^binquired of the LORD, saying, Shall I go and smite these Philistines? And the LORD said unto David, Go and smite the Philistines, and save Keilah.

3 And David's men said unto him, Behold, we be afraid here in Judah: how much more then if we come to Keilah against the armies of the Philistines?

4 Then David inquired of the LORD yet again. And the LORD answered him, and said, Arise, go down to Keilah; for I will deliver the Philistines into thine hand.

5 So David and his men went to Keilah, and fought with the Philistines, and brought away their cattle, and smote them with a great slaughter. So David saved the inhabitants of Keilah.

6 And it came to pass, when Abiathar the son of Ahimelech ^cfled to David to Keilah, *that* he came down *with* an ephod in his hand.

7 And it was told Saul that David was come to Keilah. And Saul said, God hath delivered him into mine hand; for he is shut in, by entering into a town that hath gates and bars.

A. M. 2943
B. C. 1061
An. Exod. Isr.
430
Anno ante
I. Olymp. 285

8 And Saul called all the people together to war, to go down to Keilah, to besiege David and his men.

9 And David knew that Saul secretly practised mischief against him; and ^dhe said to Abiathar the priest, Bring hither the ephod.

10 Then said David, O LORD God of Israel, thy servant hath certainly heard that Saul seeketh to come to Keilah, ^eto destroy the city for my sake.

11 Will the men of Keilah deliver me up into his hand? will Saul come down, as thy servant hath heard? O LORD God of Israel, I beseech thee, tell thy servant. And the LORD said, He will come down.

12 Then said David, Will the men of Keilah ^fdeliver me and my men into the hand of Saul? And the LORD said, They will deliver thee up.

---

^aJosh. xv. 44——^bVer. 4, 6, 9; chap. xxx. 8; 2 Sam. v. 19, 23——^cChap. xxii. 20

^dNum. xxvii. 21; chap. xxx. 7——^eChapter xxii. 19
^fHeb. *shut up*

NOTES ON CHAP. XXIII

Verse 1. *The Philistines fight against Keilah*] Keilah was a fortified town in the tribe of Judah near to Eleutheropolis, on the road to Hebron.

Rob the threshing-floors.] This was an ancient custom of the Philistines, Midianites, and others. See Judg. vi. 4. When the corn was ripe and fit to be threshed, and they had collected it at the threshing-floors, which were always in the open field, then their enemies came upon them and spoiled them of the fruits of their harvest.

Verse 2. *Therefore David inquired of the Lord*] In what way David made this inquiry we are not told, but it was probably by means of Abiathar; and therefore I think, with Houbigant, that the sixth verse should be read immediately after the first. The adventure mentioned here was truly noble. Had not David loved his country, and been above all motives of private and personal revenge, he would have rejoiced in this invasion of Judah as producing a strong diversion in his favour, and embroiling his inveterate enemy. In most cases a man with David's wrongs would have joined with the enemies of his country, and avenged himself on the author of his adversities; but he thinks of nothing but succouring Keilah, and using his power and influence in behalf of his brethren! This is a rare instance of disinterested heroism.

The Lord said—Go and smite] He might now go with confidence, being assured of success. When God promises success, who need be afraid of the face of any enemy?

Verse 4. *David inquired of the Lord yet again*] This was to satisfy his men, who made the strong objections mentioned in the preceding verse.

Verse 5. *Brought away their cattle*] The forage and spoil which the Philistines had taken, driving the country before them round about Keilah.

Verse 6. *Came down with an ephod.*] I think this verse should come immediately after ver. 1. See the note there.

Verse 8. *Saul called all the people together*] That is, all the people of that region or district, that they might scour the country, and hunt out David from all his haunts.

Verse 9. *Bring hither the ephod.*] It seems as if David himself, clothed with the ephod, had consulted the Lord; and the 10th, 11th, and 12th verses contain the words of the consultation, and the Lord's answer. But see on ver. 2.

Verses 11, 12. In these verses we find the following questions and answers:—David said, *Will Saul come down to Keilah?* And the Lord said, *He will come down.* *Will the men of Keilah deliver me and my men into the hand of Saul?* And the Lord said, *They will deliver thee up.* In this short history we find an ample proof that there is such a thing as *contingency* in human affairs; that is, God has poised many things between a possibility of being and not being, leaving it to the will of the creature to turn the scale. In the above answers of the Lord the following *conditions* were evidently implied:—IF thou *continue* in Keilah, Saul will certainly come down; and IF *Saul come down,* the men of Keilah will deliver thee into his

A. M. 2943
B. C. 1061
An. Exod. Isr. 430
Anno ante I. Olymp. 285

13 Then David and his men, [g]*which were* about six hundred, arose and departed out of Keilah, and went whithersoever they could go. And it was told Saul that David was escaped from Keilah; and he forbare to go forth.

14 And David abode in the wilderness in strong holds, and remained in [h]a mountain in the wilderness of [i]Ziph. And Saul [k]sought him every day, but God delivered him not into his hand.

15 And David saw that Saul was come out to seek his life; and David *was* in the wilderness of Ziph in a wood.

16 And Jonathan Saul's son arose, and went to David into the wood, and strengthened his hand in God.

17 And he said unto him, Fear not: for the hand of Saul my father shall not find thee; and thou shalt be king over Israel, and I shall be next unto thee; and [l]that also Saul my father knoweth.

18 And they two [m]made a covenant before the LORD: and David abode in the wood, and Jonathan went to his house.

19 Then [n]came up the Ziphites to Saul to Gibeah, saying, Doth not David hide himself with us in strong holds in the wood, in the hill of Hachilah, which *is* [o]on the south of [p]Jeshimon?

A. M. 2943
B. C. 1061
An. Exod. Isr. 430
Anno ante I. Olymp. 285

20 Now therefore, O king, come down according to all the desire of thy soul to come down; and [q]our part *shall be* to deliver him into the king's hand.

21 And Saul said, Blessed *be* ye of the LORD; for ye have compassion on me.

22 Go, I pray you, prepare yet, and know and see his place where his [r]haunt is, *and* who hath seen him there: for it is told me *that* he dealeth very subtilly.

23 See therefore, and take knowledge of all the lurking places where he hideth himself, and come ye again to me with the certainty, and I will go with you: and it shall come to pass, if he be in the land, that I will search him out throughout all the thousands of Judah.

24 And they arose, and went to Ziph before Saul: but David and his men *were* in the wilderness [s]of Maon, in the plain on the south of Jeshimon.

25 Saul also and his men went to seek *him*. And they told David: wherefore he came down [t]into a rock, and abode in the wilderness of Maon. And when Saul heard *that*, he pursued after David in the wilderness of Maon.

26 And Saul went on this side of the mountain, and David and his men on that side of the mountain: [u]and David made haste to get away for fear of Saul; for Saul and his men

---

[g]Ch. xxii. 2; xxv. 13——[h]Psa. xi. 1——[i]Josh. xv. 55——[k]Psa. liv. 3, 4——[l]Ch. xxiv. 20——[m]Ch. xviii. 3; xx. 16, 42; 2 Sam. xxi. 7——[n]See chap. xxvi. 1; Psa. liv. title

[o]Heb. *on the right hand*——[p]Or, *the wilderness*——[q]Psa. liv. 3——[r]Heb. *foot shall be*——[s]Josh. xv. 55; chap. xxv. 2——[t]Or, *from the rock*——[u]Psa. xxxi. 22

---

hands. Now though the text positively asserts that Saul would come to Keilah, yet he did not come; and that the men of Keilah would deliver David into his hand, yet David was not thus delivered to him. And why? Because David left Keilah; but had he stayed, Saul would have come down, and the men of Keilah would have betrayed David. We may observe from this that, however positive a declaration of God may appear that refers to any thing in which man is to be employed, the prediction is not intended to *suspend* or *destroy free agency*, but always comprehends in it some particular condition.

Verse 14. *Wilderness of Ziph*] Ziph was a city in the southern part of Judea, not far from Carmel.

Verse 16. *And Jonathan—strengthened his hand in God.*] It is probable that there was always a secret intercourse between David and Jonathan, and that by this most trusty friend he was apprized of the various designs of Saul to take away his life. As Jonathan well knew that God had appointed David to the kingdom, he came now to encourage him to trust in the Most High, and to assure him that the hand of Saul should not prevail against him; and at this interview they renewed their covenant of friendship. Now all this Jonathan could do, consistently with his *duty* to his *father* and his *king*. He knew that David had delivered the kingdom; he saw that his father was ruling unconstitutionally; and he knew that God had appointed David to succeed Saul. This he knew would come about in the order of Providence; and neither he nor David took one step to hasten the time. Jonathan, by his several interferences, prevented his father from imbruing his hands in innocent blood: a more filial and a more loyal part he could not have acted; and therefore, in his attachment to David, he is wholly free of blame.

Verse 25. *The wilderness of Maon.*] Maon was a mountainous district in the most southern parts of Judah. Calmet supposes it to be the city of *Menois*, which Eusebius places in the vicinity of Gaza; and the *Mænœmi Castrum*, which the Theodosian code places near to Beersheba.

Verse 26. *Saul went on this side of the moun-*

A. M. 2943
B. C. 1061
An. Exod. Isr.
430
Anno ante
I. Olymp. 285

ᵛcompassed David and his men round about to take them.

27 ʷBut there came a messenger unto Saul, saying, Haste thee, and come; for the Philistines have ˣinvaded the land.

28 Wherefore Saul returned from pursuing after David, and went against the Philistines: therefore they called that place ʸSela-hammah-lekoth.

29 And David went up from thence, and dwelt in strong holds at ᶻEn-gedi.

A. M. 2943
B. C. 1061
An. Exod. Isr.
430
Anno ante
I. Olymp. 285

ᵛPsa. xvii. 6——ʷSee 2 Kings xix. 9——ˣHeb. *spread themselves upon*, &c.

ʸThat is, *the rock of divisions*——ᶻ2 Chronicles xx. 2

---

tain] Evidently not knowing that David and his men were on the other side.

Verse 27. *There came a messenger*] See the providence of God exerted for the salvation of David's life! David and his men are almost surrounded by Saul and his army, and on the point of being taken, when a messenger arrives, and informs Saul that the Philistines had invaded the land! But behold the workings of Providence! God had already prepared the invasion of the land by the Philistines, and kept Saul ignorant how much David was in his power; but as his advanced guards and scouts must have discovered him in a very short time, the messenger arrives just at the point of time to prevent it. Here David was delivered by God, and in such a manner too as rendered the Divine interposition visible.

Verse 28. *They called that place Sela-hammah-lekoth.*] That is, *the rock of divisions;* because, says the *Targum, the heart of the king was divided to go hither and thither.* Here Saul was obliged to *separate* himself from David, in order to go and oppose the invading Philistines.

Verse 29. *Strong holds at En-gedi.*] En-gedi was situated near to the western coast of the *Dead Sea*, not far from Jeshimon: it literally signifies the *kid's well*, and was celebrated for its *vineyards*, Cant. i. 14. It was also celebrated for its *balm.* It is reported to be a mountainous territory, filled with caverns; and consequently proper for David in his present circumstances.

How *threshing-floors* were made among the ancients, we learn from CATO, *De Re Rustica*, chap. xci. and cxxix. And as I believe it would be an excellent method to make the most durable and efficient *barn-floors*, I will set it down:—

Aream sic facito. Locum ubi facies confodito; postea amurca conspergito bene, sinito-

que combibat. Postea comminuito glebas bene. Deinde coæquato, et paviculis verberato. Postea denuo amurca conspergito, sinitoque arescat. Si ita feceris neque formicæ nocebunt, neque herbæ nascentur: et cum pluerit, lutum non erit. "Make a threshing-floor thus: dig the place thoroughly; afterwards sprinkle it well with the lees of oil, and give it time to soak in. Then beat the clods very fine, make it level, and beat it well down with a paver's rammer. When this is done, sprinkle it afresh with the oil lees, and let it dry. This being done, the mice cannot burrow in it, no grass can grow through it, nor will the rain dissolve the surface to raise mud."

The directions of COLUMELLA are nearly the same; but as there as some differences of importance, I will subjoin his account:—

Area quoque si terrena erit, ut sit ad trituram satis habilis, primum radatur, deinde confodiatur, permixtis paleis cum amurca, quæ salem non accepit, extergatur; nam ea res a populatione murium formicarumque frumenta defendit. Tum æquata paviculis, vel molari lapide condensetur, et rursus subjectis paleis inculcetur, atque ita solibus siccanda relinquatur.— *De Re Rustica*, lib. ii., c. 20. "If you would have a threshing-floor made on the open ground, that it may be proper for the purpose, first pare off the surface, then let it be well digged, and mixed with lees of oil, unsalted, with which chaff has been mingled, for this prevents the mice and ants from burrowing and injuring the corn. Then level it with a paver's rammer, or press it down with a millstone. Afterwards scatter chaff over it, tread it down, and leave it to be dried by the sun."

This may be profitably used within doors, as well as in the field; and a durable and solid floor is a matter of very great consequence to the husbandman, as it prevents the flour from being injured by sand or dust.

CHAPTER XXIV

Saul is informed that David is at En-gedi, and goes to seek him with three thousand men, 1, 2. He goes into a cave to repose, where David and his men lay hid; who, observing this, exhort David to take away his life: David refuses, and contents himself with privily cutting off Saul's skirt, 3–7. When Saul departed, not knowing what was done, David called after him; showed him that his life had been in his power; expostulates strongly with him; and appeals to God, the Judge of his innocence, 8–15. Saul confesses David's uprightness; acknowledges his obligation to him for sparing his life; and causes him to swear that, when he should come to the kingdom, he would not destroy his seed, 17–21. Saul returns home, and David and his men stay in the hold, 22.

A. M. 2943
B. C. 1061
An. Exod. Isr.
430
Anno ante
I. Olymp. 285

A ND it came to pass, [a]when Saul was returned from [b]following the Philistines, that it was told him, saying, Behold, David *is* in the wilderness of En-gedi.

2 Then Saul took three thousand chosen men out of all Israel, and [c]went to seek David and his men upon the rocks of the wild goats.

3 And he came to the sheep-cotes by the way, where *was* a cave; and [d]Saul went in to [e]cover his feet; and [f]David and his men remained in the sides of the cave.

4 [g]And the men of David said unto him, Behold the day of which the LORD said unto thee, Behold, I will deliver thine enemy into thine hand, that thou mayest do to him as it shall seem good unto thee. Then David arose, and cut off the skirt of [h]Saul's robe privily.

5 And it came to pass afterward, that [i]David's heart smote him, because he had cut off Saul's skirt.

6 And he said unto his men, [k]The LORD

A. M. 2943
B. C. 1061
An. Exod. Isr.
430
Anno ante
I. Olymp. 285

---

[a]Chap. xxiii. 28——[b]Heb. *after*——[c]Psa. xxxviii. 12 [d]Psa. cxli. 6——[e]Judg. iii. 24——[f]Psa. lvii. title; and

cxlii. title——[g]Chap. xxvi. 8——[h]Heb. *the robe which was Saul's*——[i]2 Sam. xxiv. 10——[k]Chap. xxvi. 11

NOTES ON CHAP. XXIV

Verse 1. *Saul was returned*] It is very probable that it was only a small marauding party that had made an excursion in the Israelitish borders, and this invasion was soon suppressed.

Verse 2. *Rocks of the wild goats.*] The original (צורי היעלים *tsurey haiyeelim*) is variously understood. The VULGATE makes a *paraphrase: Super abruptissimas petras quæ solis ibicibus perviæ sunt;* "On the most precipitous rocks over which the ibexes alone can travel." The TARGUM: *the caverns of the rocks.* The SEPTUAGINT make the original a proper name; for out of צרוי היעלים *tsurey haiyeelim,* they make Σαδδαιεμ *Saddaiem,* and in some copies Αειαμειν *Aeiamein,* which are evidently corruptions of the Hebrew.

Verse 3. *The sheep-cotes*] Caves in the rocks, in which it is common, even to the present time, for shepherds and their flocks to lodge. According to *Strabo* there are caverns in Syria, one of which is capable of containing *four thousand men:* Ὧν ἐν και τετρακισχιλιους ανθρωπους δεξασθαι δυναμενον; lib. xvi. p. 1096. Edit. 1707.

Saul went in to cover his feet] Perhaps this phrase signifies exactly what the *Vulgate* has rendered it, *ut purgaret ventrem.* The *Septuagint,* the *Targum,* and the *Arabic* understand it in the same way. It is likely that, when he had performed this *act of necessity,* he lay down to repose himself, and it was while he was asleep that David cut off the skirt of his robe. It is strange that Saul was not aware that there might be men lying in wait in such a place; and the rabbins have invented a most curious conceit to account for Saul's security: "God, foreseeing that Saul would come to this cave, *caused a spider to weave her web over the mouth of it,* which, when Saul perceived, he took for granted that no person had lately been there, and consequently he entered it without suspicion." This may be *literally* true; and we know that even a *spider* in the hand of God may be the instrument of a great salvation. This is a Jewish tradition, and one of the most elegant and instructive in their whole collection.

David and his men remained in the sides of the cave.] This is no hyperbole; we have not only the authority of *Strabo* as above mentioned, but we have the authority of the most accurate travellers, to attest the fact of the vast capacity of caves in the East.

Dr. *Pococke* observes: "Beyond the valley (of Tekoa) there is a very large grotto, which the Arabs call *El Maamah,* a hiding place; the high rocks on each side of the valley are almost perpendicular, and the way to the grotto is by a terrace formed in the rock, which is very narrow. There are two entrances into it; we went by the farthest, which leads by a narrow passage into a large grotto, the rock being supported by great natural pillars; the top of it rises in several parts like domes; the grotto is perfectly dry. There is a tradition that the people of the country, to the number of *thirty thousand,* retired into this grotto to avoid a bad air. This place is so strong that one would imagine it to be one of the strong holds of *En-gedi,* to which David and his men fled from Saul; and possibly it may be that very cave in which he cut off Saul's skirt, for David and his men might with great ease lie hid there and not be seen by him."—*Pococke's Travels,* vol. ii., part 1, p. 41.

Verse 4. *And the men of David said*] We know not to what promise of God the men of David refer; they perhaps meant no more than to say, "Behold, the Lord hath delivered thine enemy into thy land, now do to him as he wishes to do to thee."

Then David arose] Though I have a high opinion of the character of David, yet the circumstances of the case seem to indicate that he arose to take away the life of Saul, and that it was in reference to this that his heart smote him. It appears that he rose up immediately at the desire of his men to slay his inveterate enemy, and one whom he knew the Lord had rejected; but when about to do it he was prevented by the remonstrance of God in his conscience, and instead of cutting off his head, as he might have done, an act which the laws and usages of war would have justified, he contented himself with cutting off the skirt of his robe; and he did this only to show Saul how much he had been in his power.

Verse 6. *The Lord's anointed*] However unworthily Saul was now acting, he had been appointed to his high office by God himself, and he could only be removed by the authority which placed him on the throne. Even David, who knew he was appointed to reign in his stead, and whose life Saul had often sought to destroy, did not conceive that he had any right to take away his life; and he grounds the reasons of his forbearance on this—He is my *mas-*

A. M. 2943
B. C. 1061
An. Exod. Isr.
430
Anno ante
I. Olymp. 285

forbid that I should do this thing unto my master, the LORD's anointed, to stretch forth mine hand against him, seeing he *is* the anointed of the LORD.

7 So David 1stayed mhis servants with these words, and suffered them not to rise against Saul. But Saul rose up out of the cave, and went on *his* way.

8 David also arose afterward, and went out of the cave, and cried after Saul, saying, My lord the king. And when Saul looked behind him, David stooped with his face to the earth, and bowed himself.

9 And David said to Saul, nWherefore hearest thou men's words, saying, Behold, David seeketh thy hurt?

10 Behold, this day thine eyes have seen how that the LORD hath delivered thee to-day into mine hand in the cave: and *some* bade *me* kill thee: but *mine eye* spared thee; and I said, I will not put forth mine hand against my lord; for he *is* the LORD's anointed.

11 Moreover, my father, see, yea, see the skirt of thy robe in my hand: for in that I cut off the skirt of thy robe, and killed thee not, know thou and see that *there is* oneither evil nor transgression in mine hand, and I

have not sinned against thee; yet thou phuntest my soul to take it.

A. M. 2943
B. C. 1061
An. Exod. Isr.
430
Anno ante
I. Olymp. 285

12 qThe LORD judge between me and thee, and the LORD avenge me of thee: but mine hand shall not be upon thee.

13 As saith the proverb of the ancients, Wickedness proceedeth from the wicked: but mine hand shall not be upon thee.

14 After whom is the king of Israel come out? after whom dost thou pursue? rAfter a dead dog, after sa flea?

15 tThe LORD therefore be judge, and judge between me and thee; and usee, and vplead my cause, and wdeliver me out of thine hand.

16 And it came to pass when David had made an end of speaking these words unto Saul, that Saul said, xIs this thy voice, my son David? And Saul lifted up his voice and wept.

17 yAnd he said to David, Thou *art* zmore righteous than I: for athou hast rewarded me good, whereas I have rewarded thee evil.

18 And thou hast showed this day how that thou hast dealt well with me: forasmuch as when bthe LORD had cdelivered me into thine hand, thou killedst me not.

1Heb. *cut off*——mPsa. vii. 4; Matt. v. 44; Rom. xii. 17, 19——nPsa. cxli. 6; Prov. xvi. 28; xvii. 9——oPsa. vii. 3; xxxv. 7——pChap. xxvi. 20——qGen. xvi. 5; Judg. xi. 27; chap. xxvi. 10; Job v. 8——rChap. xvii. 43; 2 Sam. ix. 8——sChap. xxvi. 20

tVer. 12——u2 Chron. xxiv. 22——vPsa. xxxv. 1; xliii. 1; cxix. 154; Mic. vii. 9——wHeb. *judge*——xChap. xxvi. 17——yChap. xxvi. 21——zGen. xxxviii. 26 aMatthew v. 44——bChap. xxvi. 23——cHeb. *shut up*; chap. xxiii. 12; xxvi. 8

---

ter, I am his *subject*. He is the *Lord's anointed*, and therefore *sacred* as to his *person* in the Lord's sight. It is an awful thing to kill a king, even the most untoward, when he has once been constitutionally appointed to the throne. No experiment of this kind has ever succeeded; the Lord abhors *king killing*. Had David taken away the life of Saul at this time, he would, in the sight of God, have been a *murderer*.

Verse 7. *Suffered them not to rise against Saul.*] As he could restrain them, it was his duty to do so; had he *connived* at *their* killing him, David would have been the *murderer*. In praying for the king we call God *the only Ruler of princes*, for this simple reason, that their authority is the *highest* among men, and next to that of God himself; hence he alone is above them. We find this sentiment well expressed by an elegant poet:—

Regum timendorum in proprios greges,
Reges in ipsos imperium est Jovis.
HORACE, *Odar.* lib. iii., Od. i., ver. 5.

Kings are supreme over their own subjects;
Jove is supreme over kings themselves.

Verse 12. *The Lord judge between me and*

thee] Appeals of this kind to God are the common refuge of the poor and oppressed people. So also among the *Hindoos: God will judge between us. Mother Kalee will judge.* Sometimes this springs from a consciousness of innocence, and sometimes from a desire of revenge.

Verse 13. *Wickedness proceedeth from the wicked*] This proverb may be thus understood: He that does a wicked act, gives proof thereby that he is a wicked man. From him who is wicked, wickedness will proceed; he who is wicked will add one iniquity to another. Had I conspired to dethrone thee, I should have taken thy life when it was in my power, and thus added *wickedness* to *wickedness*.

Verse 14. *After a dead dog*] A term used among the Hebrews to signify the most sovereign contempt; see 2 Sam. xvi. 9. One utterly incapable of making the least resistance against Saul, and the troops of Israel. The same idea is expressed in the term *flea*. The *Targum* properly expresses both thus: *one who is weak, one who is contemptible.*

Verse 15. *The Lord therefore be judge*] Let God determine who is guilty.

Verse 16. *My son David?*] David had called

A. M. 2943
B. C. 1061
An. Exod. Isr.
430
Anno ante
I. Olymp. 285

19 For if a man find his enemy, will he let him go well away? wherefore the Lord reward thee good for that thou hast done unto me this day.

20 And now, behold, ^dI know well that thou shalt surely be king, and that the kingdom of Israel shall be established in thine hand.

21 ^eSwear now therefore unto me by the Lord, ^fthat thou wilt not cut off my seed after me, and that thou wilt not destroy my name out of my father's house.

22 And David sware unto Saul. And Saul went home; but David and his men gat them up unto ^gthe hold.

A. M. 2943
B. C. 1061
An. Exod. Isr.
430
Anno ante
I. Olymp. 285

---

^dChap. xxiii. 17——^eGen. xxi. 23——^f2 Sam. xxi.

6, 8——^gChap. xxiii. 29; Ecclus. xii. 10, 11

Saul his *master, lord,* and *king.* Saul accosts him here as his *son,* to show that he felt perfectly reconciled to him, and wished to receive him as formerly into his family.

Verse 19. *If a man find his enemy, will he let him go well away?*] Or rather, *Will he send him in a good way?* But *Houbigant* translates the whole clause thus: *Si quis, inimicum suum reperiens, dimittit eum in viam bonam,* redditur ei adomino sua merces; "If a man, finding his enemy, send him by a good way, *the Lord will give him his reward.*" The words which are here put in italic, are not in the *Hebrew text,* but they are found, at least in the sense, in the *Septuagint, Syriac,* and *Arabic,* and seem necessary to complete the sense; *therefore,* adds Saul, *the Lord will reward thee good for what thou hast done unto me.*

Verse 20. *I know well that thou shalt surely be king*] Hebrew, *Reigning, thou shalt reign.* He knew this before; and yet he continued to pursue him with the most deadly hatred.

Verse 21. *Swear now*] Saul knew that an oath would bind *David,* though it was insufficient to bind *himself;* see chap. xix. 6. He had sworn to his son Jonathan that David should not be slain; and yet sought by all means in his power to destroy him!

Verse 22. *Saul went home*] Confounded at a sense of his own baseness, and overwhelmed with a sense of David's generosity.

David and his men gat them up unto the hold.] *Went up to Mizpeh,* according to the *Syriac* and *Arabic.* David could not trust Saul with his life; the utmost he could expect from him was that he should cease from persecuting him; but even this was too much to expect from a man of such a character as Saul. He was no longer under the Divine guidance; an evil spirit had full dominion over his soul. What God fills not, the devil will occupy.

CHAPTER XXV

The death of Samuel, 1. The history of Nabal, and his churlishness towards David and his men, 2–12. David, determining to punish him, is appeased by Abigail, Nabal's wife, 13–35. Abigail returns, and tells Nabal of the danger that he has escaped: who on hearing it is thunderstruck, and dies in ten days, 36–38. David, hearing of this, sends and takes Abigail to wife, 39–42. He marries also Ahinoam of Jezreel, Saul having given Michal, David's wife, to Phalti, the son of Laish, 43, 44.

A. M. 2944
B. C. 1060
An. Exod. Isr.
431
Anno ante
I. Olymp. 284

AND ^aSamuel died: and all the Israelites were gathered together, and ^blamented him, and buried him in his house at Ramah. And David arose, and went down ^cto the wilderness of Paran.

2 And *there was* a man ^din Maon, whose

^epossessions *were* in ^fCarmel; and the man *was* very great, and he had three thousand sheep, and a thousand goats: and he was shearing his sheep in Carmel.

3 Now the name of this man *was* Nabal; and the name of his wife Abigail: and *she was*

A. M. 2944
B. C. 1060
An. Exod. Isr.
431
Anno ante
I. Olymp. 284

---

^aChapter xxviii. 3——^bNumbers xx. 29; Deuteronomy xxxiv. 8

^cGen. xxi. 21; Psa. cxx. 5——^dChap. xxiii. 24——^eOr, business——^fJosh. xv. 55

NOTES ON CHAP. XXV

Verse 1. *And Samuel died*] Samuel lived, as is supposed, about *ninety-eight years;* was in the government of Israel before Saul from *sixteen* to *twenty* years; and ceased to live, according to the Jews, about *four months* before the death of Saul; but according to *Calmet* and others, *two years.* But all this is very uncertain; how long he died before Saul, cannot be ascertained. For some account of his character, see the end of the chapter.

Buried him in his house] Probably this means, not his *dwelling-house,* but the *house* or *tomb* he had made for his sepulture; and thus

the *Syriac* and *Arabic* seem to have understood it.

David—went down to the wilderness of Paran.] This was either on the confines of Judea, or in Arabia Petræa, between the mountains of Judah and Mount Sinai; it is evident from the history that it was not far from *Carmel,* on the south confines of Judah.

Verse 3. *The name of the man was Nabal*] The word נבל *nabal* signifies to be *foolish, base,* or *villanous;* and hence the Latin word *nebulo, knave,* is supposed to be derived.

The name of his wife Abigail] The *joy* or *exultation of my father.* A woman of sense

A. M. 2944
B. C. 1060
An. Exod. Isr.
431
Anno ante
I. Olymp. 284

a woman of good understanding, and of a beautiful countenance: but the man *was* churlish and evil in his doings; and he *was* of the house of Caleb.

4 And David heard in the wilderness that Nabal did ᵍshear his sheep.

5 And David sent out ten young men, and David said unto the young men, Get you up to Carmel, and go to Nabal, and ʰgreet him in my name:

6 And thus shall ye say to him that liveth *in prosperity,* ⁱPeace *be* both to thee, and peace *be* to thine house, and peace *be* unto all that thou hast.

7 And now I have heard that thou hast shearers: now thy shepherds which were with us, we ᵏhurt them not, ˡneither was there aught missing unto them, all the while they were in Carmel.

8 Ask thy young men, and they will show thee. Wherefore let the young men find favour in thine eyes; for we come in ᵐa good day: give, I pray thee, whatsoever cometh to thine hand unto thy servants, and to thy son David.

9 And when David's young men came, they spake to Nabal according to all those words in the name of David, and ⁿceased.

10 And Nabal answered David's servants, and said, ᵒWho *is* David? and who *is* the son of Jesse? there be many servants now-a-days that break away every man from his master.

A. M. 2944
B. C. 1060
An. Exod. Isr.
431
Anno ante
I. Olymp. 284

11 ᵖShall I then take my bread, and my water, and my �q flesh that I have killed for my shearers, and give *it* unto men, whom I know not whence they *be?*

12 So David's young men turned their way, and went again, and came and told him all those sayings.

13 And David said unto his men, Gird ye on every man his sword. And they girded on every man his sword; and David also girded on his sword: and there went up after David about four hundred men; and two hundred ʳabode by the stuff.

14 But one of the young men told Abigail, Nabal's wife, saying, Behold, David sent messengers out of the wilderness to salute our master; and he ˢrailed on them.

15 But the men *were* very good unto us, and ᵗwe were not ᵘhurt, neither missed we any thing, as long as we were conversant with them, when we were in the fields:

16 They were ᵛa wall unto us both by night and day, all the while we were with them keeping the sheep.

ᵍGen. xxxviii. 13; 2 Sam. xiii. 23——ʰHeb. *ask him in my name of peace;* chap. xvii. 22——ⁱ1 Chron. xii. 18; Psa. cxxii. 7; Luke x. 5——ᵏHeb. *shamed*——ˡVer. 15, 21——ᵐNeh. viii. 10; Esth. ix. 19

ⁿHeb. *rested*——ᵒJudg. ix. 28; Psa. lxxiii. 7, 8; cxxiii. 3, 4——ᵖJudg. viii. 6——�q Heb. *slaughter*——ʳChap. xxx. 24——ˢHeb. *flew upon them*——ᵗVer. 7——ᵘHeb. *shamed*——ᵛExod. xiv. 22; Job i. 10

---

and beauty, married to the boor mentioned above, probably because he was *rich.* Many women have been thus sacrificed.

Of the house of Caleb] כלבי וְהוּא *vehu Chalibbi,* "he was a Calebite." But as the word *caleb* signifies *a dog,* the *Septuagint* have understood it as implying a man of a *canine disposition,* and translate it thus, και ὁ ανθρωπος κυνικος, *he was a doggish man.* It is understood in the same way by the *Syriac* and *Arabic.*

Verse 6. *Peace be both to thee*] This is the ancient form of sending greetings to a friend: *Peace to* THEE, *peace to thy* HOUSEHOLD, *and peace to all that* THOU HAST. That is, May both *thyself,* thy *family,* and all that *pertain* unto thee, be in continual *prosperity!*

Perhaps David, by this salutation, wished Nabal to understand that he had acted so towards him and his property that nothing had been destroyed, and that all had been protected; see ver. 15-17.

Verse 7. *Thy shepherds which were with us, we hurt them not*] It is most evident that David had a *claim* upon Nabal, for very essential services performed to his herdmen at Carmel. He not only did them *no hurt,* and took

none of their *flocks* for the supply of his necessities, but he protected them from the rapacity of others; *they were a* WALL *unto us,* said Nabal's servants, *both by night and day.* In those times, and to the present day, wandering hordes of Arabs, under their several *chiefs,* think they have a right to exact contributions of provisions, &c., wherever they come; David had done nothing of this kind, but protected them against those who would.

Verse 8. *Whatsoever cometh to thine hand*] As thou art making a great feast for thy servants, and I and my men, as having essentially served thee, would naturally come in for a share were we present; send a portion by my ten young men, for me and my men, that we also may rejoice with you. Certainly this was a very reasonable and a very modest request. This mode of address is not unfrequent among the Hindoos: "O father, fill the belly of thy son; he is in distress."

Verse 10. *Who is David?*] Nabal's answer shows the *surliness* of his disposition. It was unjust to refuse so reasonable a request; and the *manner* of the refusal was highly insulting. It is true what his own servants said of him,

VOL. II

A. M. 2944
B. C. 1060
An. Exod. Isr. 431
Anno ante
I. Olymp. 284

17 Now therefore know and consider what thou wilt do; for ^wevil is determined against our master, and against all his household: for he *is such* a son of ^xBelial, that *a man* cannot speak to him.

18 Then Abigail made haste, and ^ytook two hundred loaves, and two bottles of wine, and five sheep ready dressed, and five measures of parched *corn,* and a hundred ^zclusters of raisins, and two hundred cakes of figs, and laid *them* on asses.

19 And she said unto her servants, ^aGo on before me; behold, I come after you. But she told not her husband Nabal.

20 And it was *so, as* she rode on the ass, that she came down by the covert of the hill, and, behold, David and his men came down against her; and she met them.

21 Now David had said, ^bSurely in vain have I kept all that this *fellow* hath in the wilderness, so that nothing was missed of all that *pertained* unto him: and he hath ^crequited me evil for good.

22 ^dSo and more also do God unto the enemies of David, if I ^eleave of all that *pertain* to him by the morning light ^fany that pisseth against the wall.

A. M. 2944
B. C. 1060
An. Exod. Isr. 431
Anno ante
I. Olymp. 284

23 And when Abigail saw David, she hasted, ^gand lighted off the ass, and fell before David on her face, and bowed herself to the ground,

24 And fell at his feet, and said, Upon me, my lord, *upon* me *let this* iniquity *be:* and let thine handmaid, I pray thee, speak in thine ^haudience, and hear the words of thine handmaid.

25 Let not my lord, I pray thee, ⁱregard this man of Belial, *even* Nabal: for as his name *is,* so *is* he; ^kNabal *is* his name, and folly *is* with him: but I thine handmaid saw not the young men of my lord, whom thou didst send.

26 Now therefore, my lord, ^l*as* the LORD liveth, and *as* thy soul liveth, seeing the LORD hath ^mwithholden thee from coming to *shed* blood, and from ⁿavenging ^othyself with thine own hand, now ^plet thine enemies, and they that seek evil to my lord, be as Nabal.

27 And now ^qthis ^rblessing which thine handmaid hath brought unto my lord, let it even be given unto the young men that ^sfollow my lord.

28 I pray thee, forgive the trespass of thine handmaid: for ^tthe LORD will certainly make my lord a sure house; because my lord ^ufighteth the battles of the LORD, and ^vevil hath not

---

^wChap. xx. 7——^xDeut. xiii. 13; Judg. xix. 22 ^yGen. xxxii. 13; Prov. xviii. 16; xxi. 14——^zOr, *lumps* ^aGen. xxii. 16, 20——^bEcclus. xii. 1——^cPsa. cix. 5; Prov. xvii. 13——^dRuth i. 17; chap. iii. 17; xx. 13, 16 ^eVer. 34——^f1 Kings xiv. 10; xxi. 21; 2 Kings ix. 8 ^gJosh. xv. 18; Judg. i. 14——^hHeb. *ears*——ⁱHeb. *lay it to his heart*

^kThat is, *fool*——^l2 Kings ii. 2——^mGen. xx. 6; ver. 33——ⁿHeb. *saving thyself*——^oRom. xii. 19——^p2 Sam. xviii. 32——^qGen. xxxiii. 11; chap. xxx. 26; 2 Kings v. 15——^rOr, *present*——^sHeb. *walk at the feet of, &c.;* ver. 42; Judg. iv. 10——^t2 Sam. vii. 11, 27; 1 Kings ix. 5; 1 Chron. xvii. 10, 25——^uChap. xviii. 17 ^vChap. xxiv. 11

He is such a son of Belial that one cannot speak to him, ver. 17.

Verse 18. *Took two hundred loaves*] The Eastern bread is ordinarily both *thin* and *small;* and answers to our *cakes.*

Two bottles of wine] That is, two goat-skins full. The hide is pulled off the animal without *ripping up;* the places where the legs, &c., were are sewed up, and then the skin appears one *large bag.* This is properly the Scripture and Eastern *bottle.* There is one such before me.

Five sheep] Not one sheep to one hundred men.

Clusters of raisins] Raisins dried in the sun.

Cakes of figs] Figs cured, and then pressed together. We receive the former in jars, and the latter in small *barrels;* and both articles answer the description here given.

Now all this provision was a matter of little worth, and, had it been granted in the first instance, it would have perfectly satisfied David, and secured the good offices of him and his men. Abigail showed both her wisdom and prudence in making this provision. Out of *three thousand sheep* Nabal could not have missed *five;*

and as this claim was made only in the time of sheep-shearing, it could not have been made more than once in the year: and it certainly was a small price for such important services.

Verse 20. *She came down—and David—came down*] David was coming down Mount Paran; Abigail was coming down from Carmel.—*Calmet.*

Verse 22. *So and more also do God*] Nothing can justify this part of David's conduct. Whatever his provocation might have been, he had suffered, properly speaking, no wrongs; and his resolution to cut off a whole innocent family, because Nabal had acted ungenerously towards him, was abominable and cruel, not to say diabolic. He who attempts to vindicate this conduct of David is, at least constructively, a foe to God and truth. David himself condemns this most rash and unwarrantable conduct, and thanks God for having prevented him from doing this evil, ver. 32, &c.

Any that pisseth against the wall.] This expression certainly means either *men* or *dogs,* and should be thus translated, *if I leave—any male;* and this will answer both to *men* and *dogs,* and the offensive mode of expression be

A. M. 2944
B. C. 1060
An. Exod. Isr.
431
Anno ante
I. Olymp. 284

been found in thee *all* thy days.

29 Yet a man is risen to pursue thee, and to seek thy soul: but the soul of my lord shall be bound in the bundle of life with the LORD thy God; and the souls of thine enemies, them shall he ʷsling out, ˣ*as out* of the middle of a sling.

30 And it shall come to pass, when the LORD shall have done to my lord according to all the good that he hath spoken concerning thee, and shall have appointed thee ruler over Israel;

31 That this shall be ʸno grief unto thee, nor offence of heart unto my lord, either that thou hast shed blood causeless, or that my lord hath avenged himself: but when the LORD shall have dealt well with my lord, then remember thine handmaid.

32 And David said to Abigail, ᶻBlessed *be* the LORD God of Israel, which sent thee this day to meet me:

33 And blessed *be* thy advice, and blessed *be* thou, which hast ᵃkept me this day from coming to *shed* blood, and from avenging myself with mine own hand.

34 For in very deed, *as* the LORD God of Israel liveth, which hath ᵇkept me back from hurting thee, except thou hadst hasted and come to meet me, surely there had ᶜnot been left unto Nabal by the morning light any that pisseth against the wall.

35 So David received of her hand *that* which she had brought him, and said unto her, ᵈGo up in peace to thine house; see, I have hearkened to thy voice, and have ᵉaccepted thy person.

36 And Abigail came to Nabal; and, behold,

ᶠhe held a feast in his house, like the feast of a king; and Nabal's heart *was* merry within him, for he *was* very drunken: wherefore she told him nothing, less or more, until the morning light.

A. M. 2944
B. C. 1060
An. Exod. Isr.
431
Anno ante
I. Olymp. 284

37 But it came to pass in the morning, when the wine was gone out of Nabal, and his wife had told him these things, that his heart died within him, and he became *as* a stone.

38 And it came to pass about ten days *after,* that the LORD smote Nabal, that he died.

39 And when David heard that Nabal was dead, he said, ᵍBlessed *be* the LORD, that hath ʰpleaded the cause of my reproach from the hand of Nabal, and hath ⁱkept his servant from evil: for the LORD hath ᵏreturned the wickedness of Nabal upon his own head. And David sent and communed with Abigail, to take her to him to wife.

40 And when the servants of David were come to Abigail to Carmel, they spake unto her, saying, David sent us unto thee, to take thee to him to wife.

41 And she arose, and bowed herself on *her* face to the earth, and said, Behold, *let* ˡthine handmaid *be* a servant to wash the feet of the servants of my lord.

42 And Abigail hasted, and arose, and rode upon an ass, with five damsels of hers that went ᵐafter her; and she went after the messengers of David, and became his wife.

43 David also took Ahinoam ⁿof Jezreel; ᵒand they were also both of them his wives.

44 But Saul had given ᵖMichal his daughter, David's wife, to ᵠPhalti the son of Laish, which *was* of ʳGallim.

ʷJer. x. 18——ˣHeb. *in the midst of the bow of a sling* ʸHeb. *no staggering,* or, *stumbling*——ᶻGen. xxiv. 27; Exod. xviii. 10; Psa. xli. 13; lxxii. 18; Luke i. 68 ᵃVerse 26——ᵇVer. 26——ᶜVer. 22——ᵈChap. xx. 42; 2 Sam. xv. 9; 2 Kings v. 19; Luke vii. 50; viii. 48

ᵉGen. xix. 21——ᶠ2 Sam. xiii. 23——ᵍVer. 32——ʰProv. xxii. 23——ⁱVer. 26, 34——ᵏ1 Kings ii. 44; Psa. vii. 16 ˡRuth ii. 10, 13; Prov. xv. 33——ᵐHeb. *at her feet;* ver. 27——ⁿJosh. xv. 56——ᵒCh. xxvii. 3; xxx. 5——ᵖ2 Sam. iii. 14——ᵠ*Phaltiel;* 2 Sam. iii. 15——ʳIsa. x. 30

---

avoided. I will not enter farther into the subject: *Bochart* and *Calmet* have done enough, and more than enough; and in the *plainest language* too.

Verse 28. *And evil hath not been found in thee*] Thou hast not committed any act of this kind hitherto.

Verse 29. *Shall be bound in the bundle of life*] Thy life shall be precious in the sight of the Lord: it shall be found in the bundle of life; it shall be supported by Him who is the *Spring and Fountain of life,* and ever be found *united* to those who are most favoured by the Almighty.

Them shall he sling out] Far from being

bound and *kept together* in union with the Fountain of life, he will cast them off from himself as a stone is cast out from a sling. This betokens both *force* and *violence.*

Verse 37. *His heart died within him, and he became as a stone.*] He was thunderstruck, and was so terrified at the apprehension of what he had escaped, that the fear overcame his mind, he became insensible to all things around him, probably refused all kinds of nourishment, and died in ten days.

Verse 39. *To take her to him to wife.*] It is likely that he had heard before this that Saul, to cut off all his pretensions to the throne, had married Michal to Phalti; and this justified

David in taking Abigail or any other woman; and, according to the then custom, it was not unlawful for David to take several wives. By his marriage with Abigail, it is probable he became possessed of all Nabal's property in Carmel and Maon.

Verse 43. David also took Ahinoam] Many think that this was his wife before he took Abigail; she is always mentioned first in the list of his wives, and she was the mother of his eldest son Ammon.

Of Jezreel] There were two places of this name; one in the tribe of Issachar, the other in the tribe of Judah.

Verse 44. Phalti] Called also *Phaltiel*, 2 Sam. iii. 15.

Of Gallim.] Probably a city or town in the tribe of Benjamin; see Isa. x. 30. It is likely therefore that Saul chose this man because he was of his own tribe.

In this chapter we have the account of the death of Samuel, who from his infancy had been devoted to God and the service of his people. He was born at a time in which religion was at a very low ebb in Israel, as there were but very few prophets, and *no open vision*—scarcely any revelation from God. Those who might be called *prophets* had no regular ministry of God's word; they were extraordinary messengers sent for a particular purpose, and not continued in the work any longer than the time necessary to deliver their extraordinary message.

Samuel is supposed to have been the first who established *academies* or *schools for prophets*, at least we do not hear of them before his time; and it is granted that they continued till the Babylonish captivity. This was a wise institution, and no doubt contributed much to the maintenance of pure religion, and the prevention of idolatry among that people.

Samuel reformed many abuses in the Jewish state, and raised it to a pitch of political consequence to which it had been long a stranger. He was very zealous for the honour of God, and supported the rights of pure religion, of the king, and of the people, against all encroachments. He was *chief magistrate* in Israel before the appointment of a *king*, and afterwards he acted as *prime minister* to Saul, though without being chosen or formally appointed to that station. Indeed, he seems on the whole to have been the *civil* and *ecclesiastical governor*, Saul being little more than *general of the Israelitish forces*.

In his office of *minister* in the state, he gave the brightest example of zeal, diligence, inflexible integrity, and uncorruptedness. He reproved both the people and the king for their transgressions, with a boldness which nothing but his sense of the Divine *authority* could inspire, and yet he tempered it with a sweetness which showed the interest he felt in their welfare, and the deep and distressing concern he felt for their back-slidings and infidelities.

He was incorrupt; he received no man's *bribe;* he had no *pension* from the *state;* he *enriched* none of his *relatives* from the *public purse;* left no *private debts* to be discharged by his country. He was among the Hebrews what *Aristides* is said to have been among the Greeks, so poor at his death, though a minister of state, that he did not leave property enough to bury him. *Justice* was by him duly and impartially administered, and oppression and wrong had no existence.

If there ever was a *heaven-born minister,* it was Samuel; in whose public and private conduct there was no blemish, and whose parallel cannot be found in the ancient or modern history of any country in the universe.

Let ministers of state who have sought for nothing but their own glory, and have increased the public burdens by their improvident expenditure; who have endeavoured, by their wordy representations, to dazzle and elude the people, and impose *false grandeur* in the place of *true greatness* and *solid prosperity;* who have *oppressed* the *many,* and *enriched* the *worthless few;* fall down at the feet of THIS *heaven-born man,* and learn, from this immaculate judge of Israel, what a faithful servant to his king, and an incorruptible *minister of state,* means; and in retiring from their high station, or in going to appear before the judgment-seat of God, see whether, in the presence of their king, and in the face of the thousands of their people, they can boldly say, "Behold, here am I! Witness against me before the Lord and before his anointed. Whose ox have I taken? Whose ass have I seized? Whom have I defrauded? Whom have I oppressed, by the imposition of heavy taxes for the support of *needless expenses,* and the payment of *venal men?* Or of whose hand have I taken any bribe to blind my eyes? Scrutinize my conduct, examine the state of my family, compare their present circumstances with what they were previously to my administration, and see if you can find aught in my hands." See chap. xii. 1, &c.

O, how seldom in the annals of the world, from the assembled heads of the great body politic, can the departing prime minister hear, "Thou hast not defrauded us; thou hast not oppressed us; neither hast thou taken aught of any man's hand!" This voice can be heard from Gilgal; but of what other minister can this be spoken but of *Samuel the seer,* who was the gift of God's mercy to the people of Israel; whose memory was too precious to be intrusted to public monuments, but stands, and alas; almost *unique,* in the BOOK OF GOD? Of *Daniel,* and his administration, I shall have occasion to speak elsewhere.

A prime minister, deeply devoted to God, and faithful to his king and to his country, is so rare a character in the world, that when he does occur, he should be held up to public admiration. But I have no *parallel* for Samuel. See the notes on chap. xii. and on chap. xxiv. 6.

CHAPTER XXVI

A. M. 2944
B. C. 1060
An. Exod. Isr.
431
Anno ante
I. Olymp. 284

AND the Ziphites came unto Saul to Gibeah, saying, [a]Doth not David hide himself in the hill of Hachilah, *which is* before Jeshimon?

2 Then Saul arose, and went down to the wilderness of Ziph, having three thousand chosen men of Israel with him, to seek David in the wilderness of Ziph.

3 And Saul pitched in the hill of Hachilah, which *is* before Jeshimon, by the way. But David abode in the wilderness, and he saw that Saul came after him into the wilderness.

4 David therefore sent out spies, and understood that Saul was come in very deed.

5 And David arose, and came to the place where Saul had pitched: and David beheld the place where Saul lay, and [b]Abner the son of Ner, the captain of his host: and Saul lay in the [c]trench, and the people pitched round about him.

6 Then answered David and said to Ahimelech the Hittite, and to Abishai [d]the son of Zeruiah, brother to Joab, saying, Who will [e]go down with me to Saul to the camp? And

Abishai said, I will go down with thee.

7 So David and Abishai came to the people by night: and, behold, Saul lay sleeping within the trench, and his spear stuck in the ground at his bolster: but Abner and the people lay round about him.

8 Then said Abishai to David, God hath [f]delivered thine enemy into thine hand this day: now therefore let me smite him, I pray thee, with the spear even to the earth at once, and I will not *smite* him the second time.

9 And David said to Abishai, Destroy him not: [g]for who can stretch forth his hand against the LORD'S anointed, and be guiltless?

10 David said furthermore, *As* the LORD liveth, [h]the LORD shall smite him; or [i]his day shall come to die; or he shall [k]descend into battle, and perish.

11 [l]The LORD forbid that I should stretch forth mine hand against the LORD'S anointed: but, I pray thee, take thou now the spear that *is* at his bolster, and the cruse of water, and let us go.

12 So David took the spear, and the cruse

A. M. 2944
B. C. 1060
An. Exod. Isr.
431
Anno ante
I. Olymp. 284

---

[a]Chap. xxiii. 19; Psa. liv. title——[b]Chap. xiv. 50; xvii. 55——[c]Or, *midst of his carriages;* chap. xvii. 20 [d]1 Chron. ii. 16——[e]Judg. vii. 10, 11——[f]Heb. *shut up;* chap. xxiv. 18——[g]Chap. xxiv. 6, 7; 2 Sam. i. 16

[h]Chapter xxv. 38; Psa. xciv. 1, 2, 23; Luke xviii. 7; Rom. xii. 19——[i]See Gen. xlvii. 29; Deut. xxxi. 14; Job vii. 1; xiv. 5; Psa. xxxvii. 13——[k]Chap. xxxi. 6 [l]Chapter xxiv. 6, 12

NOTES ON CHAP. XXVI

Verse 1. *The Ziphites came*] This is the second time that these enemies of David endeavoured to throw him into the hands of Saul. See chap. xxiii. 19.

Verse 2. *Three thousand chosen men*] Though they knew that David was but six hundred strong, yet Saul thought it was not safe to pursue such an able general with a less force than that mentioned in the text; and, that he might the better depend on them, they were all *elect* or *picked men* out of the whole of his army.

Verse 5. *David arose*] As David and his men knew the country, they had many advantages over Saul and his men; and no doubt could often watch them without being discovered.

Saul lay in the trench] The word במעגל *bammaegal,* which we translate *in the trench,* and in the margin *in the midst of his carriages,* is rendered by some *in a ring of carriages,* and by others *in the circle,* i. e., which was formed by his troops. Luther himself translates it **wagenburg,** a *fortress* formed of *wagons* or *carriages.*

As עגל *agal* signifies any thing *round,* it may here refer to a *round pavilion* or *tent* made for Saul, or else to the *form* of his *camp.* The Arabs, to the present day, always form a *circle* in their encampments, and put their principal officers in the centre.

Verse 6. *Abishai the son of Zeruiah*] She was David's sister; and therefore Abishai and Joab were nephews to David.

Verse 8. *God hath delivered thine enemy into thine hand*] Here Abishai uses the same language as did David's men, when Saul came into the cave at En-gedi, (see chap. xxiv. 4, &c.,) and David uses the same language in reply.

Verse 10. *The Lord shall smite him*] He shall die by a stroke of the Divine judgment; *or his day shall come to die*—he shall die a natural death; which in the course of things must be before mine, and thus I shall get rid of mine enemy; *or he shall descend into the battle, and perish*—he shall fall by the enemies of his country. These are the *three* ordinary ways by which man accomplishes, as a hireling, his day. *Murder* David could not consider to be lawful; this would have been taking the matter out of God's hand, and this David would not do.

Verse 12. *David took the spear and the cruse*] The *spear,* we have already seen, was the emblem of *power* and *regal dignity.* But it is usual, in Arab camps, for every man to have his lance stuck in the ground beside him, that he may be ready for action in a moment. The cruse of water resembled, in some measure, the *canteens* of our soldiers. In such a climate, where water was always scarce, it was neces-

A. M. 2944
B. C. 1060
An. Exod. Isr. 431
Anno ante I. Olymp. 284

of water from Saul's bolster; and they gat them away, and no man saw *it,* nor knew *it,* neither awaked: for they *were* all asleep; because [m]a deep sleep from the LORD was fallen upon them.

13 Then David went over to the other side, and stood on the top of a hill afar off; a great space *being* between them:

14 And David cried to the people, and to Abner the son of Ner, saying, Answerest thou not, Abner? Then Abner answered and said, Who *art* thou *that* criest to the king?

15 And David said to Abner, *Art* not thou a *valiant* man? and who *is* like to thee in Israel? wherefore then hast thou not kept thy lord the king? for there came one of the people in to destroy the king thy lord.

16 This thing *is* not good that thou hast done. *As* the LORD liveth, ye *are* [n]worthy to die, because ye have not kept your master, the LORD's anointed. And now see where the king's spear *is,* and the cruse of water that *was* at his bolster.

17 And Saul knew David's voice, and said, [o]*Is* this thy voice, my son David? And David said, *It is* my voice, my lord, O king.

18 And he said, [p]Wherefore doth my lord thus pursue after his servant? for what have I done? or what evil *is* in mine hand?

19 Now therefore, I pray thee, let my lord the king hear the words of his servant. If the LORD have [q]stirred thee up against me, let him [r]accept an offering: but if *they be* the children of men, cursed *be* they before the LORD; [s]for they have driven me out this day from [t]abiding in the [u]inheritance of the LORD, saying, Go, serve other gods.

A. M. 2944
B. C. 1060
An. Exod. Isr. 431
Anno ante I. Olymp. 284

20 Now therefore, let not my blood fall to the earth before the face of the LORD: for the king of Israel is come out to seek [v]a flea, as when one doth hunt a partridge in the mountains.

21 Then said Saul, [w]I have sinned: return, my son David: for I will no more do thee harm, because my soul was [x]precious in thine eyes this day: behold, I have played the fool, and have erred exceedingly.

22 And David answered and said, Behold the king's spear! and let one of the young men come over and fetch it.

23 [y]The LORD render to every man his righteousness and his faithfulness: for the LORD delivered thee into *my* hand to-day, but I would not stretch forth mine hand against the LORD's [z]anointed.

24 And, behold, as thy life was much set by this day in mine eyes, so let my life be much set by in the eyes of the LORD, and let

[m]Gen. ii. 21; xv. 12——[n]Heb. *the sons of death;* 2 Samuel xii. 5——[o]Chap. xxiv. 16——[p]Chap. xxiv. 9, 11——[q]2 Sam. xvi. 11; xxiv. 1——[r]Heb. *smell;* Gen. viii. 21; Lev. xxvi. 31

[s]Deut. iv. 28; Psa. cxx. 5——[t]Heb. *cleaving*——[u]2 Sam. xiv. 16; xx. 19——[v]Chap. xxiv. 14——[w]Chap. xv. 24; xxiv. 17——[x]Chap. xviii. 30——[y]Psa. vii. 8; xviii. 20——[z]Chap. xxiv. 6

sary for each man to carry a little with him, to refresh him on his march.

A deep sleep from the Lord] It is the same word which is used, Gen. ii. 21, to describe the *sleep* which God caused to fall upon Adam, when he formed Eve out of his side.

Verse 15. Art *not thou a* valiant *man?*] This is a strong irony. *Ye are worthy to die; ye are sons of death*—ye deserve death for this neglect of your king. And had not Saul been so deeply affected with David's generosity in preserving his life, he had doubtless put Abner and his chief officers to death; though they were not to blame, as their apparent neglect was the effect of a supernatural sleep.

Verse 19. *Let him accept an offering*] If God have stirred thee up against me, why, then, let him deliver my life into thy hand, and accept it as a sacrifice. But as the word is מנחה *minchah,* a gratitude-offering, perhaps the sense may be this: Let God accept a gratitude-offering from thee, for having purged the land of a worker of iniquity; for, were I not such, God would never stir thee up against me.

But if they be *the children of men*] If men have, by false representations, lies, and slanders, stirred thee up against an innocent man, then *let them be cursed before the Lord.* If I am guilty, I deserve to die; if not, those who seek my life should be destroyed.

Saying, Go, serve other gods.] His being *obliged* to leave the tabernacle, and the place where the true worship of God was performed, and take refuge among *idolaters,* said in effect, *Go, serve other gods.*

Verse 20. *As when one doth hunt a partridge*] It is worthy of remark that the Arabs, observing that partridges, being put up several times, soon become so weary as not to be able to fly; they in this manner hunt them upon the mountains, till at last they can knock them down with their clubs.

It was in this manner that Saul hunted David, coming hastily upon him, and putting him up from time to time, in hopes that he should at length, by frequent repetitions of it, be able to destroy him. See *Harmer.*

Verse 21. *I have sinned*] Perhaps the word חטאתי *chatathi,* "I have sinned," should be read, *I have erred,* or, *have been mistaken.* I have

A. M. 2944
B. C. 1060
An. Exod. Isr.
431
Anno ante
I. Olymp. 284

him deliver me out of all tribulation.

25 Then Saul said to David, Blessed *be* thou, my son David:

thou shalt both do great *things,* and also shalt still ªprevail. So David went on his way, and Saul returned to his place.

A. M. 2944
B. C. 1060
An. Exod. Isr.
431
Anno ante
I. Olymp. 284

ªGenesis,

chap. xxxii. 28

---

taken thee to be a very different man from what I find thee to be. Taken literally, it was strictly true. He often purposed the spilling of David's blood; and thus, again and again, *sinned* against his life.

Verse 25. *Thou shalt both do great* things, *and also shalt still prevail.*] The Hebrew is גם עשה תעשה וגם יכל תוכל *gam asoh thaaseh, vegam yachol tuchal;* "Also in doing thou shalt do, and being able thou shalt be able; which the Targum translates, *also in reigning thou shalt reign, and in prospering thou shalt prosper;* which in all probability is the meaning.

There is a vast deal of dignity in this speech of David, arising from a consciousness of his own innocence. He neither begs his life from Saul, nor offers one argument to prevail upon

him to desist from his felonious attempts, but refers the whole matter to God, as the judge and vindicator of oppressed innocence. Saul himself is speechless, except in the simple acknowledgment of his sin; and in the behalf of their king not one of his officers has one word to say! It is strange that none of them offered now to injure the person of David; but they saw that he was most evidently under the guardian care of God, and that their master was apparently abandoned by him. Saul invites David to *return,* but David knew the uncertainty of Saul's character too well to trust himself in the power of this infatuated king. How foolish are the counsels of men against God! When he undertakes to save, who can destroy? And who can deliver out of his hands?

CHAPTER XXVII

David flies to Achish, king of Gath, who receives him kindly, and gives him Ziklag to dwell in, where he continues a year and four months, 1–7. David invades the Geshurites and Amalekites, and leaves neither man nor woman alive, 8, 9. He returns to Achish, and pretends that he had been making inroads on the Israelites, and Achish believes it, 10–12.

A. M. 2946
B. C. 1058
An. Exod. Isr.
433
Anno ante
I. Olymp. 282

AND David said in his heart, I shall now ªperish one day by the hand of Saul: *there is* nothing better for me than that I should speedily escape into the land of the Philistines; and Saul shall despair of me, to seek me any more in any coast of Israel: so shall I escape out of his hand.

2 And David arose, ᵇand he passed over with the six hundred men that *were* with him ᶜunto Achish, the son of Maoch, king of Gath.

3 And David dwelt with Achish at Gath, he and his men, every man with his household, *even* David ᵈwith his two wives, Ahinoam the Jezreelitess, and Abigail the Carmelitess, Nabal's wife.

4 And it was told Saul that David was fled to Gath: and he sought no more again for him.

5 And David said unto Achish, If I have now found grace in thine eyes, let them give

A. M. 2946
B. C. 1058
An. Exod. Isr.
433
Anno ante
I. Olymp. 282

ªHeb. *be consumed*——ᵇChap. xxv. 13

ᶜChap. xxi. 10——ᵈChap. xxv. 43

NOTES ON CHAP. XXVII

Verse 1. *I shall now perish one day by the hand of Saul*] This was a very hasty conclusion: God had so often interposed in behalf of his life, that he was authorized to believe the reverse. God had hitherto confounded all Saul's stratagems, and it was not at all likely that he would now abandon him: there was now no *additional* reason why he should withdraw from David his helping hand.

Verse 2. *David arose, and he passed over—unto Achish*] There is not one circumstance in this transaction that is not blameable. David joins the enemies of his God and of his country, acts a most inhuman part against the Geshurites and Amalekites, without even the pretence of a Divine authority; tells a most deliberate falsehood to Achish, his protector, relative to the people against whom he had per-

petrated this cruel act; giving him to understand that he had been destroying the Israelites, his enemies. I undertake no defence of this conduct of David; it is all bad, all defenceless; God vindicates him not. The inspired penman tells what he did, but passes no *eulogium* upon his conduct; and it is false to say that, because these things are *recorded,* therefore they are *approved.* In all these transactions David was in no sense a man after God's own heart. Chandler attempts to vindicate all this conduct: those who can receive his saying, let them receive it.

Verse 3. *Every man with his household*] So it appears that the men who consorted with David had wives and families. David and his company resembled a tribe of the wandering Arabs.

Verse 5. *Why should thy servant dwell in the royal city*] He seemed to intimate that

A. M. 2946
B. C. 1058
An. Exod. Isr.
433
Anno ante
I. Olymp. 282

me a place in some town in the country, that I may dwell there: for why should thy servant dwell in the royal city with thee?

6 Then Achish gave him Ziklag that day: wherefore eZiklag pertaineth unto the kings of Judah unto this day.

7 And fthe time that David dwelt in the country of the Philistines was ga full year and four months.

8 And David and his men went up, and invaded hthe Geshurites, iand the kGezrites, and the lAmalekites: for those *nations were* of old the inhabitants of the land, mas thou goest to Shur, even unto the land of Egypt.

9 And David smote the land, and left neither man nor woman alive, and took away the

sheep, and the oxen, and the asses, and the camels, and the apparel, and returned, and came to Achish.

A. M. 2946
B. C. 1058
An. Exod. Isr.
433
Anno ante
I. Olymp. 282

10 And Achish said, nWhither have ye made a road to-day? And David said, Against the south of Judah, and against the south of othe Jerahmeelites, and against the south of pthe Kenites.

11 And David saved neither man nor woman alive, to bring *tidings* to Gath, saying, Lest they should tell on us, saying, So did David, and so *will be* his manner all the while he dwelleth in the country of the Philistines.

12 And Achish believed David, saying, He hath made his people Israel qutterly to abhor him; therefore he shall be my servant for ever.

---

eSee Josh. xv. 31; xix. 5——fHeb. *the number of days*
gHeb. a year *of days; see* chap. xxix. 3, till 1056——hJosh.
xiii. 2——iJosh. xvi. 10; Judg. i. 29——kOr, *Gerzites*

lExod. xvii. 16; see chap. xv. 7, 8——mGen. xxv. 18
nOr, *Did you not make a road, &c.*——oSee 1 Chron. ii.
9, 25——pJudg. i. 16——qHeb. *to stink*

---

two princely establishments in the same city were too many. Achish appears to have felt the propriety of his proposal, and therefore appoints him Ziklag.

Verse 6. *Achish gave him Ziklag*] Ziklag was at first given to the tribe of *Judah*, but afterwards it was ceded to that of *Simeon*, Josh. xv. 31; xix. 5. The Philistines had, however, made themselves masters of it, and held it to the time here mentioned; it then fell into the tribe of Judah again, and continued to be the property of the kings of Judah. This verse is a proof that this book was written long after the days of Samuel, and that it was formed by a later hand, out of materials which had been collected by a contemporary author. See the *preface.*

Verse 9. *David smote the land*] Here was a complete extirpation of all these people, not one being left alive, lest he should carry tidings of the disasters of his country! The *spoil*

which David took consisted of *sheep, oxen, asses, camels,* and *apparel.*

Verse 10. *Whither have ye made a road to-day?*] He had probably been in the habit of making predatory excursions. This seems to be implied in the question of Achish.

Verse 12. *He hath made his people—utterly to abhor him*] This deception, which Dr. Delaney says "*did harm to nobody, and to the account of which he is at an utter loss what degree of guilt to charge,*" imposed upon Achish, had the most direct tendency to make him imagine himself secure, while in the utmost danger; and to have a faithful friend and able ally in David, while he was the veriest enemy he could possibly have. Shame on him who becomes the apologist of such conduct! As to Dr. Chandler, he should know that no *lie* is of the *truth,* and that all *falsity* is an abomination to the Lord.

CHAPTER XXVIII

The Philistines prepare to attack the Israelites, and Achish informs David that he shall accompany him to battle, 1, 2. Saul, unable to obtain any answer from God, applies to a witch at En-dor to bring up Samuel, that he may converse with him on the issue of the war, 3–11. Samuel appears, 12–14. He reproaches Saul with his misconduct, and informs him of his approaching ruin, 15–19. His is greatly distressed; but at the solicitations of the woman and his own servants, he takes some food, and departs the same night, 20–25.

A. M. 2948
B. C. 1056
An. Exod. Isr.
435
Anno ante
I. Olymp. 280

AND ait came to pass in those days, that the Philistines gathered their armies together for warfare, to fight with Israel.

And Achish said unto David, Know thou assuredly, that thou shalt go out with me to battle, thou and thy men.

A. M. 2948
B. C. 1056
An. Exod. Isr.
435
Anno ante
I. Olymp. 280

---

a1 Samuel,   chap. xxix. 1

NOTES ON CHAP. XXVIII

Verse 1. *The Philistines gathered their armies together*] Sir Isaac Newton conjectures that the Philistines had got a great increase to their armies by vast numbers of men which

Amasis had driven out of Egypt. This, with Samuel's death, and David's disgrace, were no inconsiderable motives to a new war, from which the Philistines had now every thing to hope.

Thou shalt go out with me to battle] This he

A. M. 2948
B. C. 1056
An. Exod. Isr. 435
Anno ante
I. Olymp. 280

2 And David said to Achish, Surely thou shalt know what thy servant can do. And Achish said to David, Therefore will I make thee keeper of mine head for ever.

3 Now ᵇSamuel was dead, and all Israel had lamented him, and buried him in Ramah, even in his own city. And Saul had put away ᶜthose that had familiar spirits, and the wizards, out of the land.

4 And the Philistines gathered themselves together, and came and pitched in ᵈShunem: and Saul gathered all Israel together, and they pitched in ᵉGilboa.

5 And when Saul saw the host of the Philistines, he was ᶠafraid, and his heart greatly trembled.

6 And when Saul inquired of the LORD, ᵍthe LORD answered him not, neither by ʰdreams, nor ⁱby Urim, nor by prophets.

7 Then said Saul unto his servants, Seek me a woman that hath a familiar spirit, that I may go to her, and inquire of her. And his servants said to him, Behold, *there is* a woman that hath a familiar spirit at En-dor.

A. M. 2948
B. C. 1056
An. Exod. Isr. 435
Anno ante
I. Olymp. 280

8 And Saul disguised himself, and put on other raiment, and he went, and two men with him, and they came to the woman by night: and ᵏhe said, I pray thee, divine unto me by the familiar spirit, and bring me *him* up, whom I shall name unto thee.

9 And the woman said unto him, Behold, thou knowest what Saul hath done, how he ˡhath cut off those that have familiar spirits, and the wizards, out of the land: wherefore then layest thou a snare for my life, to cause me to die?

10 And Saul sware to her by the LORD, saying, *As* the LORD liveth, there shall no punishment happen to thee for this thing.

11 Then said the woman, Whom shall I bring up unto thee? And he said, Bring me up Samuel.

ᵇChap. xxv. 1——ᶜVer. 9; Exod. xxii. 18; Lev. xix. 31; xx. 27; Deut. xviii. 10, 11——ᵈJosh. xix. 18; 2 Kings iv. 8——ᵉChap. xxxi. 1——ᶠJob xviii. 11

ᵍChap. xiv. 37; Prov. i. 28; Lam. ii. 9——ʰNum. xii. 6——ⁱExod. xxviii. 30; Num. xxvii. 21; Deut. xxxiii. 8 ᵏDeut. xviii. 11; 1 Chron. x. 13; Isa. viii. 19——ˡVer. 3

---

said, being deceived by what David had told him.

Verse 2. *Surely thou shalt know what thy servant can do*] This was another equivocal answer; and could only be understood by his succeeding conduct. It might imply what he *could do* in *favour* of the *Philistines* against Israel; or in favour of *Israel* against the Philistines. Achish understood it in the former sense; and therefore he said to David, *I will make thee keeper of my head for ever;* i. e., Thou shalt be captain of my *life-guards*.

Verse 3. *Samuel was dead*] And there was no longer a public accredited prophet to consult.

Those that had familiar spirits, and the wizards] See the note on Lev. xix. 31, and Exod. xxii. 18.

Verse 5. *When Saul saw*] He saw from the superiority of his enemies, from the state of his army, and especially from his own state towards God, that he had every thing to fear.

Verse 6. *The Lord answered him not*] He used the *three methods* by which supernatural intelligence was ordinarily given:—

1. *Dreams.*—The person prayed for instruction; and begged that God would answer by a significant dream.

2. *Urim.*—This was a kind of oracular answer given to the high priest when clothed with the ephod, on which were the *Urim* and *Thummim.* How these communicated the answer, is not well known.

3. *Prophets.*—Who were requested by the party concerned to consult the Lord on the subject in question, and to report his answer. The *prophets* at that time could only be those in the *schools of the prophets*, which Samuel had established at *Naioth* and *Gibeah.* These

were the only successors of Samuel that we know of.

Verse 7. *Seek me a woman that hath a familiar spirit*] Literally, Seek me a woman, בעלת אוב *baalath ob, the mistress of the Ob or Pythonic spirit*—one who had a familiar spirit, whom she could invoke when she pleased, and receive answers from him relative to futurity.

Strange that a man, who had banished all such from the land, as dangerous to the state, as impostors and deceivers, should now have recourse to them as the only persons in whom he could safely put his confidence in the time in which *Jehovah* had refused to help him!

At En-dor.] This was a city in the valley of Jezreel, at the foot of Mount Gilboa, where the army of Saul had now encamped.

Verse 8. *Saul disguised himself*] That he might not be known by the woman, lest she, being terrified, should refuse to use her art.

Verse 11. *Whom shall I bring up*] The woman certainly meant no more than making her *familiar* personify whomsoever the querist should wish. In the evocation of spirits this is all that, according to the professed rules of their art, such persons pretend to; for over human souls in *paradise* or in the *infernal regions* they have no power. If we allow that there is such an art founded on true principles, all it can pretend to is, to bring up the *familiar;* cause him when necessary to assume the *form* and *character* of some particular person, and to give such notices relative to *futurity* as he is able to collect. And this even in the cases to which authenticity is generally allowed, is often scanty, vague, and uncertain, for fallen spirits do not abound in *knowledge:* this is an attribute of God, and rays of this perfection are

A. M. 2948
B. C. 1056
An. Exod. Isr. 435
Anno ante I. Olymp. 280

12 And when the woman saw Samuel, she cried with a loud voice: and the woman spake to Saul, saying, Why hast thou deceived me? for thou *art* Saul.

13 And the king said unto her, Be not afraid: for what sawest thou? And the woman said unto Saul, I saw [m]gods ascending out of the earth.

14 And he said unto her, [n]What form *is* he of? And she said, An old man cometh up; and he *is* covered with [o]a mantle. And Saul perceived that it *was* [p]Samuel, and he stooped with *his* face to the ground, and bowed himself.

15 And Samuel said to Saul, Why hast thou disquieted me, to bring me up? And Saul answered, [q]I am sore distressed; for the Philistines make war against me, and [r]God is departed from me, and [s]answereth me no more, neither [t]by prophets, nor by dreams: therefore I have called thee, that thou mayest make known unto me what I shall do.

A. M. 2948
B. C. 1056
An. Exod. Isr. 435
Anno ante I. Olymp. 280

16 [u]Then said Samuel, Wherefore then dost thou ask of me, seeing the LORD is departed from thee, and is become thine enemy?

17 And the LORD hath done [v]to him [w]as he spake by [x]me: for the LORD hath rent the kingdom out of thine hand, and given it to thy neighbour, *even* to David:

18 [y]Because thou obeyedst not the voice of the LORD, nor executedst his fierce wrath upon Amalek, therefore hath the LORD done this thing unto thee this day.

19 Moreover the LORD will also deliver Israel with thee into the hand of the Philis-

[m]Exod. xxii. 28——[n]Hebrew, *What* is *his form?* [o]Chap. xv. 27; 2 Kings ii. 8, 13——[p]Ecclus. xlvi. 20 [q]Proverbs v. 11, 12, 13; xiv. 14——[r]Chap. xviii. 12 [s]Ver. 6

[t]Heb. *by the hand of prophets*——[u]Ecclus. xlvi. 20 [v]Or, *for himself;* Prov. xvi. 4——[w]Chapter xv. 28 [x]Heb. *mine hand*——[y]Chap. xv. 9; 1 Kings xx. 42; 1 Chron. x. 13; Jer. xlviii. 10

imparted to pure and holy intelligences; and even *Satan* himself, as may be seen from most of his temptations, is far from *excelling in knowledge*. He may be *cunning* and *insidious*, but he certainly is not *wise* and *prudent;* we in general give this fallen spirit credit for much more wisdom than he possesses.

Verse 12. *When the woman saw Samuel*] That *Samuel did* appear on this occasion, is most evident from the text; nor can this be denied from any legitimate mode of interpretation: and it is as evident that he was neither raised by the power of the devil nor the incantations of the witch, for the appearances which took place at this time were such as she was wholly unacquainted with. Her *familiar* did not appear; and from the confused description she gives, it is fully evident that she was both surprised and alarmed at what she saw, being so widely different from what she expected to see.

Verse 13. *I saw gods ascending out of the earth.*] The word אלהים *elohim,* which we translate *gods*, is the word which is used for the Supreme Being throughout the Bible; but all the *versions*, the *Chaldee* excepted, translate it in the *plural* number, as we do. The *Chaldee* has, *I see* מלאכא דיי *malacha dayeya, an angel of the Lord, ascending from the earth.* This sight alarmed the woman; it was what she did not expect; in this she could not recognise her familiar, and she was terrified at the appearance.

Verse 14. *An old man cometh up; and he is covered with a mantle.*] This seems to have been a *second* apparition; she cannot mean that she had seen *gods* ascending out of the earth, and these *gods* were like an *old man with a mantle.* The angelic appearance first mentioned prepared the way for Samuel; and the whole was done so as to show to the woman that her art had not prevailed in the present instance, and that what was now taking place was wholly independent of *her incantations.*

Saul perceived that it was *Samuel*] The description was suitable to his person and clothing.

Verse 15. *Why hast thou disquieted me*] The complaint is not directed against the *woman* but against *Saul.* Indeed, her incantations had no influence in the business, and it does not appear that she had commenced her operations before the *angels* had prepared the way of the prophet, and before the *prophet* himself had made his appearance.

That thou mayest make known unto me what I shall do.] In his former difficulties, and when pressed by his enemies, he was in the habit of consulting Samuel; and now he applies to him as his former preceptor. God, he knew, might answer by such a man as Samuel, when he would answer by no other means.

Verse 16. *Wherefore then dost thou ask of me*] Was ever I wont to give answers that were not dictated by the Lord? It is his counsel alone that I communicate.

Verse 17. *The Lord hath done to him*] I believe these words are spoken *of* Saul; and as they are spoken *to* him, it seems evident that *him* should be *thee.* The Vulgate has *tibi*, the Septuagint *σοι, to* THEE: and this is the reading of *five* of *Kennicott's* and *De Rossi's* MSS., as well as of both the Bibles printed at Venice in 1518, where we read לך *lecha, to* THEE, instead of לו *lo, to* HIM.

As he spake by me] Here was no illusion; none but *Samuel* could say this.

Verse 18. *Nor executedst his fierce wrath upon Amalek*] See chap. xv. and the notes there.

Verse 19. *To-morrow* shalt *thou and thy sons* be *with me*] What an awful message! In the course of the ensuing day thou shalt be slain,

A. M. 2948
B. C. 1056
An. Exod. Isr. 435
Anno ante
I. Olymp. 280

tines: and to-morrow *shalt* thou and thy sons *be* with me: the LORD also shall deliver the host of Israel into the hand of the Philistines.

20 Then Saul ᶻfell straightway all along on the earth, and was sore afraid, because of the words of Samuel: and there was no strength in him; for he had eaten no bread all the day, nor all the night.

21 And the woman came unto Saul, and saw that he was sore troubled, and said unto him, Behold, thine handmaid hath obeyed thy voice, and I have ᵃput my life in my hand, and have hearkened unto thy words which thou spakest unto me.

22 Now therefore, I pray thee, hearken thou

also unto the voice of thine handmaid, and let me set a morsel of bread before thee; and eat, that thou mayest have strength when thou goest on thy way.

A. M. 2948
B. C. 1056
An. Exod. Isr. 435
Anno ante
I. Olymp. 280

23 But he refused, and said, I will not eat. But his servants, together with the woman, compelled him; and he hearkened unto their voice. So he arose from the earth, and sat upon the bed.

24 And the woman had a ᵇfat calf in the house; and she hasted, and killed it, and took flour, and kneaded *it,* and did bake ᶜunleavened bread thereof:

25 And she brought *it* before Saul, and before his servants; and they did eat. Then they rose up, and went away that night.

ᵃHebrew, *made haste, and fell with the fulness of his stature*

ᵃJudg. xii. 3; chap. xix. 5; Job xiii. 14――ᵇGen. xviii. 6, 7, 8――ᶜGen. xix. 3

---

thy three sons shall be slain, and the armies of Israel shall be delivered into the hands of the Philistines! Can any person read this, properly considering the situation of this unfortunate monarch, the triumph of the enemies of God, and the speedy ruin in which the godlike Jonathan is about to be involved, without feeling the keenest anguish of heart?

But Samuel says, "He and his sons should be *with him.*" Does not this mean that they were to go to *paradise?* I suppose it means no more than that they should all *die.* Yet the paraphrase of the Rev. C. Wesley is beautiful:—

"What do these solemn words portend?
A ray of hope when life shall end.
Thou and thy sons, *though slain,* shall be
To-morrow in *repose* with me.
Not in a state of hellish pain,
If Saul with Samuel do remain:
Not in a state of damn'd *despair,*
If loving Jonathan be *there.*"

Saul had committed *the sin unto death*—the sin to be visited with a violent death, while the mercy of God was extended to the soul. Thus say my *faith,* my *hope,* and my *charity;* and doth not the *mercy* of God say the same?

Verse 20. *Then Saul fell straightway all along on the earth.*] Literally, *he fell with his own length,* or *with the fulness of his stature.* He was so overwhelmed with this most dreadful message, that he swooned away, and thus *fell at his own length upon the ground.* The woman, being terrified, had probably withdrawn to some distance at the first appearance of the prophet; and Saul was left alone with Samuel. After some short time, *the woman came* again unto Saul, found him *sore troubled,* and offered him those succours which humanity dictated.

Verse 23. *I will not eat.*] It is no wonder that not only his *strength,* but also his *appetite,* had departed from him.

And sat upon the bed] Beds or *couches* were the common places on which the ancients sat to take their repasts.

Verse 24. *The woman had a fat calf*] The ancients used great despatch in their cookery.

In hot countries they could not keep flesh meat by them any length of time; hence they generally kept young animals, such as *calves, lambs,* and *kids,* ready for slaughter; and when there was occasion, one of them was killed, and dressed immediately.

Unleavened bread] There was not time to bake *leavened bread;* that would have taken considerable time, in order that the leaven might leaven the whole lump.

Verse 25. *They rose up, and went away that night.*] The transactions of this chapter occupy one night only. 1. Saul came by night to *En-dor,* ver. 8. 2. He consulted the woman, and had his conference with Samuel the same night; for no time whatever appears to have been lost after his arrival at *En-dor.* 3. He was overcome by the heavy tidings which he heard; and which for a time appear to have deprived him of all power. 4. The woman kills a calf; dresses a part; makes and bakes bread; and Saul and his servants eat. And, 5. They rose and went away *that night,* ver. 25. The *next day,* in all probability, the battle happened in which Israel was defeated, and Saul and his sons lost their lives.

THERE is a considerable diversity of opinion, both among learned and pious men, relative to the subject mentioned in this chapter, that of *raising Samuel from the dead.* Some deny the *possibility* of the thing, and say that it was the *devil* that personified *Samuel;* and others, that the whole was the *imposition* of this cunning woman, and that there was no *supernatural* agency in the business. This is not a proper place to argue the point. I have given my opinion in the notes. I may sum up in a few particulars.

1. I believe there is a *supernatural* and *spiritual* world, in which HUMAN spirits, both good and bad, live in a state of consciousness.

2. I believe there is an *invisible world,* in which various orders of spirits, not *human,* live and act.

3. I believe that any of these spirits may, according to the order of God, in the laws of

their place of residence, have intercourse with this world, and become visible to mortals.

4. I believe there is a possibility, by arts not strictly good, to evoke and have intercourse with spirits, *not* HUMAN; and to employ, in a certain limited way, their power and influence.

5. I believe that the woman of En-dor had no power over *Samuel;* and that *no incantation* can avail over any *departed saint of God*, nor indeed over any *human* disembodied spirit.

6. I believe *Samuel did actually appear to Saul;* and that he was sent by the especial *mercy of God* to warn this infatuated king of his approaching death, that he might have an opportunity to make his peace with his Maker.

7. I believe that the woman found, from the *appearances*, that her *real* or *pretended charms* had no effect; and that what now took place came from a totally different disposition of things from those with which she was conversant.

8. I believe that direct, circumstantial, and unequivocal oracles were now delivered concerning things which neither human nor diabolical wisdom could foresee or penetrate; that the defeat of the Israelites, and the death of Saul and his three sons on the following day, were matters which, from their nature, could only be known to God himself; and that no demon or bad spirit could be employed in such a transaction.

CHAPTER XXIX

The Philistines gather their armies together against Israel, and encamp at Aphek; while the Israelites encamp at Jezreel, 1. The lords of the Philistines refuse to let David go to battle with them, lest he should betray them, 2-5. Achish expresses his confidence in David; but begs him to return, 6-10. David and his men return, 11.

A. M. 2948
B. C. 1056
An. Exod. Isr. 435
Anno ante I. Olymp. 280

NOW [a]the Philistines gathered together all their armies [b]to Aphek: and the Israelites pitched by a fountain which *is* in Jezreel.

2 And the lords of the Philistines passed on by hundreds, and by thousands: but David and his men passed on in the rere-ward [c]with Achish.

3 Then said the princes of the Philistines, What *do* these Hebrews *here?* And Achish said unto the princes of the Philistines, *Is* not this David, the servant of Saul the king of Israel, which hath been with me [d]these days, or these years, and I have [e]found no fault in him since he fell *unto me* unto this day?

4 And the princes of the Philistines were wroth with him; and the princes of the Philistines said unto him, [f]Make this fellow return,

that he may go again to his place which thou hast appointed him, and let him not go down with us to battle, lest [g]in the battle he be an adversary to us: for wherewith should he reconcile himself unto his master? *should* it not *be* with the heads of these men?

5 *Is* not this David, of whom they sang one to another in dances, saying, [h]Saul slew his thousands, and David his ten thousands?

6 Then Achish called David, and said unto him, Surely, *as* the LORD liveth, thou hast been upright, and [i]thy going out and thy coming in with me in the host *is* good in my sight: for [k]I have not found evil in thee since the day of thy coming unto me unto this day: nevertheless [l]the lords favour thee not.

7 Wherefore now return, and go in peace, that

A. M. 2948
B. C. 1056
An. Exod. Isr. 435
Anno ante I. Olymp. 280

---

[a]Chap. xxviii. 1——[b]Chap. iv. 1——[c]Chapter xxviii. 1, 2——[d]See chap. xxvii. 7——[e]Dan. vi. 5——[f]1 Chron. xii. 19——[g]As chap. xiv. 21

[h]Chap. xviii. 7; xxi. 11——[i]2 Sam. iii. 25; 2 Kings xix. 27——[k]Ver. 3——[l]Heb. *thou art not good in the eyes of the lords*

NOTES ON CHAP. XXIX

Verse 1. *To Aphek*] This was a place in the valley of Jezreel, between Mounts Tabor and Gilboa.

Pitched by a fountain] To be near a *fountain*, or *copious spring of water*, was a point of great importance to an army in countries such as these, where water was so very scarce. It is supposed, as William of Tyre says, that it was at this *same fountain* that Saladin pitched his camp, while Baldwin, king of Jerusalem, pitched his by another fountain between Nazareth and Sephoris; each being anxious to secure that without which it was impossible for their armies to subsist.

Verse 2. *By hundreds, and by thousands*] They were probably divided, as the Jewish armies, by *fifties, hundreds,* and *thousands;* each having its proper officer or captain.

Verse 3. *These days, or these years*] I suppose these words to mark no *definite time*, and may be understood thus: "Is not this David, who has been with me for a considerable time?"

Verse 4. *The princes of the Philistines were wroth*] It is strange that they had not yet heard of David's destruction of a village of the Geshurites, Gezrites, and Amalekites, chap. xxvii. Had they heard of this, they would have seen much more cause for suspicion.

Verse 6. *Thou hast been upright*] So he

A. M. 2948
B. C. 1056
An. Exod. Isr.
435
Anno ante
I. Olymp. 280

thou ᵐdisplease not the lords of the Philistines.

8 And David said unto Achish, But what have I done? and what hast thou found in thy servant so long as I have been ⁿwith thee unto this day, that I may not go fight against the enemies of my lord the king?

9 And Achish answered and said to David, I know that thou *art* good in my sight, °as an angel of God: notwithstanding, ᵖthe princes of

the Philistines have said, He shall not go up with us to the battle.

10 Wherefore now rise up early in the morning with thy master's servants that are come with thee: �q and as soon as ye be up early in the morning, and have light, depart.

11 So David and his men rose up early to depart in the morning, to return into the land of the Philistines. ʳAnd the Philistines went up to Jezreel.

A. M. 2948
B. C. 1056
An. Exod. Isr.
435
Anno ante
I. Olymp. 280

ᵐHeb. *do not evil in the eyes of the lords*——ⁿHebrew, *before thee*

°2 Sam. xiv. 17, 20; xix. 27——ᵖVer. 4——qGen. xliv. 3
ʳ2 Sam. iv. 4

---

thought; for as yet he had not heard of the above transaction; David having given him to understand that he had been fighting against Israel.

Verse 8. David said—what have I done?] Dr. Chandler and others may say what they will to make David act a *consistent* part in this business; but it is most evident, whatever his *intentions* might be as to the part he was to take in the approaching battle, he did intend to persuade Achish that he would fight *against Israel;* and affects to feel his reputation injured by not being permitted on this occasion to show his fidelity to the king of Gath.

It was in the order of God's gracious providence that the Philistine lords refused to let David go with them to this battle. Had he gone, he had his choice of two sins—*First,* If he had fought *for the Philistines,* he would have fought *against God* and his *country. Secondly,* If he had in the battle *gone over to the Israelites,* he would have *deceived* and become a *traitor* to the hospitable Achish. God, therefore, so ordered it in his mercy that he was not permitted to go to a battle in which he was sure to be disgraced, whatever side he

took, or with what success soever he might be crowned.

Verse 9. As an angel of God] There is some reason to think that Achish had actually embraced or was favourably disposed towards the Jewish religion. He speaks here of *the angels of God,* as a Jew might be expected to speak; and in ver. 6 he appeals to, and swears by, *Jehovah;* which, perhaps, no Philistine ever did. It is possible that he might have learned many important truths from David, during the time he sojourned with him.

Verse 10. With thy master's servants] Who were these? has been very properly asked; and to this question there can be but two answers:—

1. The *six hundred Israelites* which were with him; and who might still be considered the *subjects of* Saul, though now residing in a foreign land.

2. The servants of Achish; i. e., David's men thus considered; because on his coming to Gath, he had in effect given up himself and his men to Achish. But Saul may be the master to whom Achish refers, and the words convey a delicate information to David that he is no vassal, but still at liberty.

CHAPTER XXX

While David is absent with the army of Achish, the Amalekites invade Ziklag, and burn it with fire, and carry away captive David's wives, and those of his men, 1, 2. David and his men return; and, finding the desolate state of their city, are greatly affected, 3–5. The men mutiny, and threaten to stone David, who encourages himself in the Lord, 6. David inquires of the Lord, and is directed to pursue the Amalekites, with the promise that he shall recover all, 7, 8. He and his men begin the pursuit, but two hundred, through fatigue, are obliged to stay behind at the brook Besor, 9, 10. They find a sick Egyptian, who directs them in their pursuit, 11–15. David finds the Amalekites secure, feasting on the spoils they had taken; he attacks and destroys the whole host, except four hundred, who escape on camels, 16, 17. The Israelites recover their wives, their families, and all their goods, 18–20. They come to the two hundred who were so faint as not to be able to pursue the enemy, with whom they divide the spoil; and this becomes a statute in Israel, 21–25. David sends part of the spoil which he had taken to different Jewish cities, which had suffered by the incursion of the Amalekites; and where David and his men had been accustomed to resort, 26–31.

A. M. 2948
B. C. 1056
An. Exod. Isr. 435
Anno ante
I. Olymp. 280

AND it came to pass, when David and his men were come to Ziklag on the third day, that the [a]Amalekites had invaded the south, and Ziklag, and smitten Ziklag, and burned it with fire;

2 And had taken the [b]women captives, that *were* therein: they slew not any, either great or small, but carried *them* away, and went on their way.

3 So David and his men came to the city, and, behold, *it was* burned with fire; and their wives, and their sons, and their daughters, were taken captives.

4 Then David and the people that *were* with him lifted up their voice and wept, until they had no more power to weep.

5 And David's [c]two wives were taken captives, Ahinoam the Jezreelitess, and Abigail the wife of Nabal the Carmelite.

6 And David was greatly distressed; [d]for the people spake of stoning him, because the soul of all the people was [e]grieved, every man for his sons and for his daughters: [f]but David encouraged himself in the LORD his God.

7 [g]And David said to Abiathar the priest, Ahimelech's son, I pray thee, bring me hither the ephod. And Abiathar brought thither the ephod to David.

8 [h]And David inquired at the LORD, saying, Shall I pursue after this troop? shall I overtake them? And he answered him, Pursue: for thou shalt surely overtake *them* and without fail recover *all*.

A. M. 2948
B. C. 1056
An. Exod. Isr. 435
Anno ante
I. Olymp. 280

9 So David went, he and the six hundred men that *were* with him, and came to the brook Besor, where those that were left behind stayed.

10 But David pursued, he and four hundred men: [i]for two hundred abode behind, which were so faint that they could not go over the brook Besor.

11 And they found an Egyptian in the field, and brought him to David, and gave him bread, and he did eat; and they made him drink water;

12 And they gave him a piece of a cake of figs, and two clusters of raisins: and [k]when he had eaten, his spirit came again to him: for he had eaten no bread, nor drunk *any* water, three days and three nights.

13 And David said unto him, To whom *belongest* thou? and whence *art* thou? And he said, I *am* a young man of Egypt, servant to an Amalekite; and my master left me, because three days agone I fell sick.

---

[a]See ch. xv. 7; xxvii. 8——[b]Ver. 5, 6——[c]Ch. xxv. 42, 43; 2 Sam. ii. 2——[d]Exod. xvii. 4——[e]Heb. *bitter;* Judg. xviii. 25; chap. i. 10; 2 Sam. xvii. 8; 2 Kings iv. 27

[f]Psa. xlii. 5; lvi. 3, 4, 11; Hab. iii. 17, 18——[g]Chap. xxiii. 6, 9——[h]Chap. xxiii. 2, 4——[i]Ver. 21——[k]So Judg. xv. 19; chap. xiv. 27

NOTES ON CHAP. XXX

Verse 1. *On the third day*] This was the third day after he had left the Philistine army at Aphek. *Calmet* supposes that Aphek was distant from Ziklag more than *thirty* leagues.

The Amalekites had invaded] These were, doubtless, a travelling predatory *horde,* who, availing themselves of the war between the Philistines and the Israelites, plundered several unprotected towns, and among them Ziklag. It is likely they had not heard of what David did to some of their tribes, else they would have avenged themselves by slaying all they found in Ziklag.

Verse 4. *Wept, until they had no more power to weep.*] This marks great distress; they wept, as says the Vulgate, till their tears failed them.

Verse 6. *The people spake of stoning him*] David had done much to civilize those men; but we find by this of what an unruly and ferocious spirit they were; and yet they strongly felt the ties of natural affection, they "grieved every man for his sons and for his daughters."

David encouraged himself in the Lord] He found he could place very little confidence in his men; and, as he was conscious that this evil had not happened either through his neg-

lect or folly, he saw he might the more confidently expect succour from his Maker.

Verse 7. *Bring me hither the ephod.*] It seems as if David had put on the ephod, and inquired of the Lord for himself; but it is more likely that he caused Abiathar to do it.

Verse 9. *The brook Besor*] This had its source in the mountain of Idumea, and fell into the Mediterranean Sea beyond Gaza. Some suppose it to have been the same with the river of the wilderness, or the river of Egypt. The sense of this and the following verse is, that when they came to the brook Besor, there were found *two hundred* out of his *six hundred* men so spent with fatigue that they could proceed no farther. The baggage or *stuff* was left there, ver. 24, and they were appointed to guard it.

Verse 12. *A cake of figs*] See on chap. xxv. 18.

Verse 13. *My master left me, because three days agone I fell sick.*] This was very inhuman: though they had booty enough, and no doubt asses sufficient to carry the invalids, yet they left this poor man to perish; and God visited it upon them, as he made this very person the means of their destruction, by the information which he was enabled to give to David and his men.

A. M. 2948
B. C. 1056
An. Exod. Isr.
435
Anno ante
I. Olymp. 280

14 We made an invasion *upon* the south of [1]the Cherethites, and upon *the coast* which *belongeth* to Judah, and upon the south of [m]Caleb; and we burned Ziklag with fire.

15 And David said to him, Canst thou bring me down to this company? And he said, Swear unto me by God, that thou wilt neither kill me, nor deliver me into the hands of my master, and I will bring thee down to this company.

16 And when he had brought him down, behold, *they were* spread abroad upon all the earth, [n]eating and drinking, and dancing, because of all the great spoil that they had taken out of the land of the Philistines, and out of the land of Judah.

17 And David smote them from the twilight even unto the evening of [o]the next day: and there escaped not a man of them, save four hundred young men, which rode upon camels, and fled.

18 And David recovered all that the Amalekites had carried away: and David rescued his two wives.

19 And there was nothing lacking to them, neither small nor great, neither sons nor daughters, neither spoil, nor any *thing* that they had taken to them: [p]David recovered all.

20 And David took all the flocks and the herds, *which* they drave before those *other* cattle, and said, This *is* David's spoil.

A. M. 2948
B. C. 1056
An. Exod. Isr.
435
Anno ante
I. Olymp. 280

21 And David came to the [q]two hundred men, which were so faint that they could not follow David, whom they had made also to abide at the brook Besor: and they went forth to meet David, and to meet the people that *were* with him: and when David came near to the people, he [r]saluted them.

22 Then answered all the wicked men, and *men* [s]of Belial, of [t]those that went with David, and said, Because they went not with us, we will not give them *aught* of the spoil that we have recovered, save to every man his wife and his children, that they **may** lead *them* away, and depart.

23 Then said David, Ye shall not do so, my brethren, with that which the LORD hath given us, who hath preserved us, and delivered the company that came against us into our hand.

24 For who will hearken unto you in this matter? but [u]as his part *is* that goeth down to the battle, so *shall* his part *be* that tarrieth by the stuff: they shall part alike.

25 And it was *so* from that day [v]forward, that he made it a statute and an ordinance for Israel unto this day.

---

[1]Ver. 16; 2 Sam. viii. 18; 1 Kings i. 38, 44; Ezek. xxv. 16; Zeph. ii. 5——[m]Josh. xiv. 13; xv. 13——[n]1 Thess. v. 3——[o]Heb. *their morrow*——[p]Verse 8——[q]Verse 10

[r]Or, *asked them how they did;* Judg. xviii. 15——[s]Deut xiii. 13; Judg. xix. 22——[t]Heb. *men*——[u]See Num. xxxi. 27; Josh. xxii. 8; 2 Mac. viii. 28——[v]Heb. *and forward*

Verse 14. Upon *the south of the Cherethites*] Calmet and others maintain, that the כרתי *kerethi*, which, without the points, might be read *Creti*, were not only at this time *Philistines*, but that they were aborigines of *Crete*, from which they had their name *Cherethites* or *Cretans*, and are those of whom Zephaniah speaks, chap. ii. 5: *Wo to the inhabitants of the sea-coasts, the nation of the Cherethites.* And by Ezekiel, chap. xxv. 16: *Behold, I will stretch out mine hand upon the Philistines, and will cut off the Cherethim.* In 2 Sam. xv. 18 we find that the *Cherethites* formed a part of David's guards.

South of Caleb] Somewhere about *Kirjath-arba*, or Hebron, and *Kirjath-sepher;* these being in the possession of Caleb and his descendants.

Verse 15. *Swear unto me*] At the conclusion of this verse, the *Vulgate, Syriac,* and *Arabic* add, that *David swore to him.* This is not expressed in the *Hebrew,* but is necessarily implied.

Verse 16. *Out of the land of the Philistines*] That *these* Amalekites were enemies to the Philistines is evident, but it certainly does not follow from this that *those* whom David destroyed were enemies also. This, I think, has been too hastily assumed by Dr. Chandler and

others, in order the better to vindicate the character of David.

Verse 17. *There escaped not a man of them*] It is well known to every careful reader of the Bible, that the *Amalekites* were a proscribed people, even by God himself, and that in extirpating them it has been supposed David fulfilled the express will of God. But all this depends on whether *he* had an express commission to do so, received from God himself, as Saul had.

Verse 20. *And David took all the flocks*] He and his men not only recovered all their own property, but they recovered all the spoil which these Amalekites had taken from the south of Judah, the Cherethites, and the south of Caleb. When this was separated from the rest, it was given to David, and called *David's spoil.*

Verse 22. Men *of Belial*] This is a common expression to denote the *sour,* the *rugged,* the *severe,* the *idle,* and the *profane.*

Verse 23. *That which the Lord hath given us*] He very properly attributes this victory to God; the numbers of the Amalekites being so much greater than his own. Indeed, as many fled away on camels as were in the whole host of David.

Verse 25. *He made it a statute and an ordi-*

A. M. 2948
B. C. 1056
An. Exod. Isr. 435
Anno ante
I. Olymp. 280

26 And when David came to Ziklag, he sent of the spoil unto the elders of Judah, *even* to his friends, saying, Behold a ^wpresent for you of the spoil of the enemies of the LORD;

27 To *them* which *were* in Beth-el, and to *them* which *were* in ^xsouth Ramoth, and to *them* which *were* in ^yJattir,

28 And to *them* which *were* in ^zAroer, and to *them* which *were* in Siphmoth, and to *them* which *were* in ^aEshtemoa,

29 And to *them* which *were* in Rachal, and to *them* which *were* in the cities of ^bthe Jerahmeelites, and to *them* which *were* in the cities of the ^cKenites,

30 And to *them* which *were* in ^dHormah, and to *them* which *were* in Chor-ashan, and to *them* which *were* in Athach,

31 And to *them* which *were* in ^eHebron, and to all the places where David himself and his men were wont to haunt.

A. M. 2948
B. C. 1056
An. Exod. Isr. 435
Anno ante
I. Olymp. 280

---

^wHeb. *blessing;* Gen. xxxiii. 11; chap. xxv. 27——^xJosh. xix. 8——^yJosh. xv. 48——^zJosh. xiii. 16

^aJosh. xv. 50——^bChap. xxvii. 10——^cJudg. i. 16 ^dJudg. i. 17——^eJosh. xiv. 13; 2 Sam. ii. 1

---

nance for Israel] Nothing could be more just and proper than this law: he who stays at home to defend house and property, has an equal right to the booty taken by those who go out to the war. There was a *practice* of this kind among the Israelites long before this time; see Num. xxxi. 27; Josh. xxii. 8; and the note on this latter verse.

Unto this day.] This is another indication that this book was composed long after the facts it commemorates. See the hypothesis in the preface.

Verse 26. *Unto the elders of Judah*] These were the persons among whom he sojourned during his exile, and who had given him shelter and protection. Gratitude required these presents.

Verse 27. *To* them *which* were *in Beth-el*] This was in the tribe of Ephraim.

South Ramoth] So called to distinguish it from *Ramoth Gilead,* beyond Jordan. This *Ramoth* belonged to the tribe of *Simeon,* Josh. xix. 8.

In Jattir] Supposed by Calmet to be the same as *Ether,* Josh. xv. 42, but more probably *Jattir,* ver. 48. It was situated in the mountains, and belonged to *Judah.*

Verse 28. *In Aroer*] Situated beyond Jordan, on the banks of the river Arnon, in the tribe of *Gad.*

Siphmoth] Supposed to be the same with *Shepham,* Num. xxxiv. 10, on the eastern border of the promised land.

Eshtemoa] Another city in the tribe of *Judah.* See Josh. xv. 50.

Verse 29. Them *which* were *in Rachal*] We know not where this place was; it is mentioned nowhere else in the Bible. Calmet conjectures that *Hachilah,* chap. xxiii. 19, may be the same place; here we know David did conceal himself

for some time, till the Ziphites endeavoured to betray him to Saul.

The cities of the Jerahmeelites] See before, chap. xxvii. 10.

And—the cities of the Kenites] A very small tract on the southern coast of the *Dead Sea.*

Verse 30. *Hormah*] The general name of those cities which belonged to *Arad,* king of Canaan; and were devoted to destruction by the Hebrews, and thence called *Hormah.* See Num. xxi. 1-3.

In Chor-ashan] Probably the same as *Ashan* in the tribe of *Judah:* see Josh. xv. 42. It was afterwards ceded to *Simeon,* Josh. xix. 7.

To them *which* were *in Athach*] Probably the same as *Ether,* Josh. xix. 7.

Verse 31. *To* them *which* were *in Hebron*] This was a place strongly attached to David, and David to it, and the place where he was proclaimed king, and where he reigned more than seven years previously to the death of Ish-bosheth, Saul's son, who was, for that time, his competitor in the kingdom.

David's having sent presents to all these places, not only shows his sense of *gratitude,* but that the *booty* which he took from the Amalekites must have been exceedingly great. And we learn from this also that David sojourned in many places which are not mentioned in the preceding history; for *these* are all said to be places *where David and his men were wont to haunt.*

WE are not to suppose that the transactions mentioned here and in the preceding chapter took place after Saul's interview with the woman of *En-dor;* they were considerably antecedent to this, but how long we do not know. What is recorded in the following chapter must have taken place the next day after Saul left En-dor.

CHAPTER XXXI

A battle in Mount Gilboa between Israel and the Philistines; in which the former are defeated, and Saul's three sons slain, 1, 2. Saul, being mortally wounded, and afraid to fall alive into the hands of the Philistines, desires his armour-bearer to despatch him; which he refusing, Saul falls on his sword, and his armour-bearer does the same, 3–6. The Israelites on the other side of the valley forsake their cities, and the Philistines come and dwell in them, 7. The Philistines, finding Saul and his three sons among the slain, strip them of their armour, which they put in the house of Ashtaroth, cut off their heads, send the news to all the houses of their idols, and fasten the bodies of Saul and his three sons to the walls of Beth-shan, 8–10. Valiant men of Jabesh-gilead go by night, and take away the bodies; burn them at Jabesh; bury their bones under a tree; and fast seven days, 11–13.

A. M. 2948
B. C. 1056
An. Exod. Isr.
435
Anno ante
I. Olymp. 280

NOW [a]the Philistines fought against Israel: and the men of Israel fled from before the Philistines, and fell down [b]slain in Mount [c]Gilboa.

2 And the Philistines followed hard upon Saul and upon his sons; and the Philistines slew [d]Jonathan, and Abinadab, and Melchishua, Saul's sons.

3 And [e]the battle went sore against Saul, and the [f]archers [g]hit him; and he was sore wounded of the archers.

4 [h]Then said Saul unto his armour-bearer, Draw thy sword, and thrust me through therewith; lest [i]these uncircumcised come and thrust me through, and [k]abuse me. But his armour-bearer would not; [l]for he was sore afraid. Therefore Saul took a sword, and [m]fell upon it.

5 And when his armour-bearer saw that Saul was dead, he fell likewise upon his sword, and died with him.

6 So Saul died, and his three sons, and his armour-bearer, and all his men, that same day together.

7 And when the men of Israel that *were* on the other side of the valley, and *they* that *were* on the other side Jordan, saw that the men of Israel fled, and that Saul and his sons were dead, they forsook the cities, and fled; and the Philistines came and dwelt in them.

8 And it came to pass on the morrow, when the Philistines came to strip the slain, that they found Saul and his three sons fallen in Mount Gilboa.

9 And they cut off his head, and stripped off his armour, and sent into the land of the Philistines round about, to [n]publish *it in* the house of their idols, and among the people.

A. M. 2948
B. C. 1056
An. Exod. Isr.
435
Anno ante
I. Olymp. 280

---

[a]1 Chron. x. 1–12——[b]Or, *wounded*——[c]Chap. xxviii. 4——[d]Chap. xiv. 49; 1 Chron. viii. 33——[e]See 2 Sam. i. 6, &c.——[f]Heb. *shooters, men with bows*

[g]Heb. *found him*——[h]So Judg. ix. 54——[i]Chap. xiv. 6; xvii. 26——[k]Or, *mock me*——[l]2 Sam. i. 14 [m]2 Sam. i. 10——[n]2 Sam. i. 20

NOTES ON CHAP. XXXI

Verse 1. *Now the Philistines fought*] This is the continuation of the account given in chap. xxix.

The men of Israel fled] It seems as if they were thrown into confusion at the first onset, and turned their backs upon their enemies.

Verse 2. *Followed hard upon Saul and upon his sons*] They, seeing the discomfiture of their troops, were determined to sell their lives as dear as possible, and therefore maintained the battle till the three brothers were slain.

Verse 3. *He was sore wounded of the archers.*] It is likely that Saul's sons were slain by the archers, and that Saul was now mortally wounded by the same. Houbigant translates, *The archers rushed upon him, from whom he received a grievous wound.* He farther remarks that had not Saul been grievously wounded, and beyond hope of recovery, he would not have wished his armour-bearer to despatch him; as he might have continued still to fight, or have made his escape from this most disastrous battle. Some of the versions render it, *He* FEARED *the archers greatly;* but this is by no means likely.

Verse 4. *Draw thy sword, and thrust me through*] Dr. Delaney has some good observations on this part of the subject: "Saul and his armour-bearer died by the same sword. That his armour-bearer died by his own sword is out of all doubt; the text expressly tells us so; and that Saul perished by the same sword is sufficiently evident. *Draw* THY *sword*, says he to him, *and thrust me through;* which, when he refused, *Saul*, says the text, *took* THE *sword*, (את החרב *eth hachereb, the very sword,*) *and fell upon it.* What sword? Not his *own*, for then the text would have said so; but, in the plain natural grammatical construction, the

sword before mentioned must be the sword now referred to, that is, his armour-bearer's, 1 Chron. x. 4, 5. Now it is the established tradition of all the Jewish nation that this armour-bearer was *Doeg*, and I see no reason why it should be discredited; and if so, then Saul and his executioner both fell by that weapon with which they had before massacred the priests of God. So *Brutus* and *Cassius* killed themselves with the same swords with which they stabbed *Cæsar;* and *Catippus* was stabbed with the same sword with which he stabbed *Dio*."

Verse 6. *And all his men*] Probably meaning those of his troops which were his *life* or *body guards:* as to the bulk of the army, it fled at the commencement of the battle, ver. 1.

Verse 7. *The men of Israel that* were *on the other side of the valley*] They appear to have been panic-struck, and therefore fled as far as they could out of the reach of the Philistines. As the Philistines possessed *Beth-shan*, situated near to *Jordan*, the people on *the other side* of that river, fearing for their safety, fled also.

Verse 8. *On the morrow*] It is very likely that the battle and pursuit continued till the night, so that there was no time till the next day to strip and plunder the slain.

Verse 9. *And they cut off his head*] It is possible that they cut off the heads of his three sons likewise; for although only *his head* is said to be cut off, and *his body* only to be fastened to the walls of Beth-shan, yet we find that the men of Jabesh-gilead found both *his body* and the *bodies* of *his three sons*, fastened to the walls, ver. 12.

Perhaps they only took off Saul's head, which they sent about to their temples as a trophy of their victory, when they sent the news of the defeat of the Israelites through all their coasts, and at last placed it in the temple of Dagon, 1 Chron. x. 10.

A. M. 2948
B. C. 1056
An. Exod. Isr.
435
Anno ante
I. Olymp. 280

10 °And they put his armour in the house of ᵖAshtaroth: and �q they fastened his body to the wall of ʳBeth-shan.

11 ˢAnd when the inhabitants of Jabesh-gilead heard ᵗof that which the Philistines had done to Saul,

12 ᵘAll the valiant men arose, and went all

night, and took the body of Saul, and the bodies of his sons, from the wall of Beth-shan, and came to Jabesh, and ᵛburnt them there.

A. M. 2948
B. C. 1056
An. Exod. Isr.
435
Anno ante
I. Olymp. 280

13 And they took their bones, and ʷburied *them* under a tree at Jabesh, and ˣfasted seven days.

°Chap. xxi. 9——ᵖJudg. ii. 13——�q2 Sam. xxi. 12
ʳJosh. xvii. 11; Judg. i. 27——ˢChap. xi. 3, 9, 11
ᵗOr, *concerning him*

ᵘSee chap. xi. 1–11; 2 Sam. ii. 4–7——ᵛ2 Chron. xvi. 14; Jer. xxxiv. 5; Amos vi. 10——ʷ2 Sam. ii. 4, 5; xxi. 12, 13, 14——ˣGen. l. 10

Verse 10. *They put his armour in the house of Ashtaroth*] As David had done in placing the sword of Goliath in the tabernacle. We have already seen that it was common for the conquerors to consecrate armour and spoils taken in war, to those who were the objects of religious worship.

They fastened his body to the wall] Probably by means of iron hooks; but it is said, 2 Sam. xxi. 12, that these bodies *were fastened in the* STREET *of Beth-shan*. This may mean that the place where they were fastened to the wall was the main *street* or *entrance* into the city.

Verse 11. *When the inhabitants of Jabesh-gilead heard*] This act of the men of Jabesh-gilead was an act of gratitude due to Saul, who, at the very commencement of his reign, rescued them from Nahash, king of the Ammonites, (see chap. xi. 1, &c.,) and by his timely succours saved them from the deepest degradation and the most oppressive tyranny. This heroic act, with the seven days' *fast*, showed that they retained a due sense of their obligation to this unfortunate monarch.

Verse 12. *And burnt them there.*] It has been denied that the Hebrews *burnt* the bodies of the dead, but that they *buried* them in the earth, or *embalmed* them, and often burnt spices *around them*, &c. These no doubt were the common forms of sepulture, but neither of these could be conveniently practised in the present case. They could not have *buried* them about Beth-shan without being discovered; and as to *embalming*, that was most likely out of all question, as doubtless the bodies were now too *putrid* to bear it. They therefore *burnt* them, because there was no other way of disposing of them at that time so as to do them honour; and the *bones* and *ashes* they collected, and *buried under a tree* or in a *grove at Jabesh*.

Verse 13. *And fasted seven days.*] To testify their sincere regret for his unfortunate death, and the public calamity that had fallen upon the land.

THUS ends the troublesome, and I had almost said the useless, reign of Saul. A king was chosen in opposition to the will of the Most High; and the government of God in effect rejected, to make way for this king.

Saul was at first a very humble young man, and conducted himself with great propriety; but his elevation made him proud, and he soon became tyrannical in his private conduct and in his political measures. His natural temper was not good; he was peevish, fretful, and often outrageous; and these bad dispositions, unchecked by proper application to the grace of

God, became every day more headstrong and dangerous. Through their violence he seems at times to have been wholly carried away and deranged; and this derangement appears to have been occasionally greatly exacerbated by diabolical influences. This led him to take his friends for his foes; so that in his paroxysms he strove to imbrue his hands in their blood, and more than once attempted to assassinate his own son; and most causelessly and inhumanly ordered the innocent priests of the Lord at Nob to be murdered. This was the worst act in his whole life.

Saul was but ill qualified for a proper discharge of the *regal* functions. The reader will remember that he was chosen rather as a *general* of the *armies* than as *civil governor*. The administration of the affairs of the *state* was left chiefly to Samuel, and Saul led forth the armies to battle.

As a *general* he gave proof of considerable capacity; he was courageous, prompt, decisive, and persevering; and, except in the last unfortunate battle in which he lost his life, generally led his troops to *victory*.

Saul was a weak man, and very capricious; this is amply proved by his unreasonable jealousy against David, and his continual suspicion that all were leagued against him. It is also evident, in his foolish adjuration relative to the matter of the honey (see chap. xiv.) in which, to save his rash and nonsensical oath, he would have sacrificed Jonathan his son!

The question, "Was Saul a good king?" has already in effect been answered. He was on the whole a good *man*, as far as we know, in private life; but he was a *bad king;* for he endeavoured to reign independently of the Jewish constitution; he in effect assumed the sacerdotal office and functions, and thus even changed what was essential to that constitution. He not only offered sacrifices which belonged to the priests alone; but in the most positive manner went opposite to the orders of that God whose *vicegerent* he was.

Of his conduct in visiting the woman at *En-dor* I have already given my opinion, and to this I must refer. His desperate circumstances imposed on the weakness of his mind; and he did in that instance an act which, in his jurisprudential capacity, he had disapproved by the edict which banished all witches, &c., from Israel. Yet in this act he only wished to avail himself of the counsel and advice of his *friend* Samuel.

To the question, "Was not Saul a *self-murderer?*" I scruple not to answer, "No." He was to all appearance mortally wounded, when he begged his armour-bearer to extinguish the remaining spark of life; and he was afraid that the Philistines might *abuse* his body, if they found him alive; and we can scarcely say how much of *indignity* is implied in this *word;* and his falling on his sword was a fit of desperation, which doubtless was the issue of a mind greatly agitated, and full of distraction. A few minutes longer, and his life would in all probability have ebbed out; but though this wound accelerated his death, yet it could not be properly

the cause of it, as he was mortally wounded before, and did it on the conviction that he could not survive.

Taking Saul's state and circumstances together, I believe there is not a *coroner's inquest* in this nation that would not have brought in a verdict of *derangement;* while the pious and the humane would everywhere have consoled themslves with the hope that God had extended mercy to his soul.

MILLBROOK, June 11, 1818.

Ended this examination August 13, 1827.—A. C.

INTRODUCTION

TO THE

SECOND BOOK OF SAMUEL,

OTHERWISE CALLED

THE SECOND BOOK OF THE KINGS

AS this is a continuation of the preceding history, without any interruption, it can scarcely be called *another* book. Originally this and the preceding made but one book, and they have been separated without reason or necessity. For a general account of both, see the *preface* to the *first* book of Samuel.

It is generally allowed that this book comprehends a period of forty years, from about A. M. 2949 to 2989. See the prefixed chronological account.

It has been divided into *three* parts: in the *first* we have an account of the happy commencement of David's reign, chap. i.–x. In the *second*, David's unhappy fall, and its miserable consequences, chap. xi.–xviii. In the *third*, his restoration to the Divine favour, the re-establishment of his kingdom, and the events which signalized the latter part of his reign, chap. xix.–xxiv.

THE
SECOND BOOK OF SAMUEL

Year from the Creation, 2949.—Year before the Incarnation, 1055.—Year before the first Olympiad, 279.—Year before the building of Rome, 302.—Year of the Julian Period, 3659.—Year of the Dionysian Period, 467.—Cycle of the Sun, 19.—Cycle of the Moon, 11.

CHAPTER I

An Amalekite comes to David, and informs him that the Philistines had routed the Israelites; and that Saul and his sons were slain, 1–4. And pretends that he himself had despatched Saul, finding him ready to fall alive into the hands of the Philistines, and had brought his crown and bracelets to David, 5–10. David and his men mourn for Saul and his sons, 11, 12. He orders the Amalekite, who professed that he had killed Saul, to be slain, 13–16. David's funeral song for Saul and Jonathan, 17–27.

A. M. 2949
B. C. 1055
An. Exod. Isr.
436
Anno ante
I. Olymp. 279

NOW it came to pass after the death of Saul, when David was returned from ᵃthe slaughter of the Amalekites, and David had abode two days in Ziklag;

2 It came even to pass on the third day, that, behold, ᵇa man came out of the camp from Saul ᶜwith his clothes rent, and earth upon his head: and *so* it was, when he came to David, that he fell to the earth, and did obeisance.

3 And David said unto him, From whence comest thou? And he said unto him, Out of the camp of Israel am I escaped.

4 And David said unto him, ᵈHow went the matter? I pray thee, tell me. And he answered, That the people are fled from the battle, and many of the people also are fallen and dead; and Saul and Jonathan his son are dead also.

5 And David said unto the young man that told him, How knowest thou that Saul and Jonathan his son be dead?

6 And the young man that told him, said,

As I happened by chance upon ᵉMount Gilboa, behold, ᶠSaul leaned upon his spear; and, lo, the chariots and horsemen followed hard after him.

A. M. 2949
B. C. 1055
An. Exod. Isr.
436
Anno ante
I. Olymp. 279

7 And when he looked behind him, he saw me, and called unto me. And I answered, ᵍHere *am* I.

8 And he said unto me, Who *art* thou? And I answered him, I *am* an Amalekite.

9 He said unto me again, Stand, I pray thee, upon me, and slay me: for ʰanguish is come upon me, because my life *is* yet whole in me.

10 So I stood upon him, and ⁱslew him, because I was sure that he could not live after that he was fallen: and I took the crown that *was* upon his head, and the bracelet that *was* on his arm, and have brought them hither unto my lord.

11 Then David took hold on his clothes, and ᵏrent them; and likewise all the men that *were* with him:

12 And they mourned, and wept, and fasted until even, for Saul, and for Jonathan his son,

---

ᵃ1 Sam. xxx. 17, 26——ᵇChap. iv. 10——ᶜ1 Sam. iv. 12——ᵈHeb. *what was,* &c.; 1 Sam. iv. 16——ᵉ1 Sam. xxxi. 1——ᶠSee 1 Sam. xxxi. 2, 3, 4

ᵍHeb. *Behold me*——ʰOr, *my coat of mail,* or, *my embroidered coat hindereth me, that my,* &c.——ⁱJudg. ix. 54 ᵏChap. iii. 31; xiii. 31

NOTES ON CHAP. I

Verse 2. *A man came out of the camp*] The whole account which this young man gives is a fabrication: in many of the particulars it is grossly *self-contradictory.* There is no *fact* in the case but the bringing of the *crown,* or *diadem,* and *bracelets* of Saul; which, as he appears to have been a plunderer of the slain, he

found on the field of battle; and he brought them to David, and told the lie of having despatched Saul, merely to ingratiate himself with David.

Verse 8. *I am an Amalekite.*] Dr. Delaney remarks that an Amalekite took that crown from off the head of Saul, which he had forfeited by his disobedience in the case of Amalek.

Verse 10. *The crown—and the bracelet*] The

A. M. 2949
B. C. 1055
An. Exod. Isr. 436
Anno ante I. Olymp. 279

and for the people of the LORD, and for the house of Israel; because they were fallen by the sword.

13 And David said unto the young man that told him, Whence *art* thou? And he answered, I *am* the son of a stranger, an Amalekite.

14 And David said unto him, [l]How wast thou not [m]afraid to [n]stretch forth thine hand to destroy the LORD's anointed?

15 And [o]David called one of the young men, and said, Go near, *and* fall upon him. And he smote him that he died.

16 And David said unto him, [p]Thy blood *be* upon thy head; for [q]thy mouth hath testified against thee, saying, I have slain the LORD's anointed.

17 And David lamented with this lamentation over Saul and over Jonathan his son:

18 ([r]Also he bade them teach the children of Judah *the use of* the bow: behold, *it is* written [s]in the book [t]of Jasher.)

19 The beauty of Israel is slain upon thy high places: [u]how are the mighty fallen!

20 [v]Tell *it* not in Gath, publish *it* not in the streets of Askelon; lest [w]the daughters of the [x]Philistines rejoice, lest the daughters of the uncircumcised triumph.

A. M. 2949
B. C. 1055
An. Exod. Isr. 436
Anno ante I. Olymp. 279

21 Ye [y]mountains of Gilboa, [z]*let there be* no dew, neither *let there be* rain upon you, nor fields of offerings: for there the shield of the mighty is vilely cast away, the shield of Saul, *as though he had* not *been* [a]anointed with oil.

22 From the blood of the slain, from the fat of the mighty, [b]the bow of Jonathan turned not back, and the sword of Saul returned not empty.

23 Saul and Jonathan *were* lovely and [c]pleasant in their lives, and in their death they were not divided: they were swifter than eagles, they were [d]stronger than lions.

24 Ye daughters of Israel, weep over Saul, who clothed you in scarlet, with *other* delights, who put on ornaments of gold upon your apparel.

25 How are the mighty fallen in the midst of the battle! O Jonathan, *thou wast* slain in thine high places.

26 I am distressed for thee, my brother Jonathan: very pleasant hast thou been unto me: [e]thy love to me was wonderful, passing the love of women.

27 [f]How are the mighty fallen, and the weapons of war perished!

---

[l]Num. xii. 8——[m]1 Sam. xxxi. 4——[n]1 Sam. xxiv. 6; xxvi. 9; Psa. cv. 15——[o]Chap. iv. 10, 12——[p]1 Sam. xxvi. 9; 1 Kings ii. 32, 33, 37——[q]Ver. 10; Luke xix. 22 [r]1 Sam. xxxi. 3——[s]Josh. x. 33——[t]Or, *of the upright* [u]Ver. 27; 1 Mac. ix. 21——[v]1 Sam. xxxi. 9; Mic. i. 10; see Judg. xvi. 23

[w]See Exod. xv. 20; Judg. xi. 34; 1 Sam. xviii. 6——[x]1 Sam. xxxi. 4——[y]1 Sam. xxxi. 1——[z]So Judg. v. 23; Job iii. 3, 4; Jer. xx. 14——[a]1 Sam. x. 1——[b]1 Sam. xviii. 4——[c]Or, *sweet*——[d]Judg. xiv. 18——[e]1 Sam. xviii. 1, 3; xix. 2; xx. 17, 41; xxiii. 16——[f]Verse 19

---

crown was probably no more than a royal *fillet* or *diadem*, both being the ensigns of royalty. It is sometimes customary in the *East* for a sovereign prince to give a *crown* and *bracelets*, when investing others with dominion or authority over certain provinces. Had Saul these in token of his being God's *vicegerent*, and that he held the kingdom from him alone?

Verse 16. *Thy blood* be *upon thy head*] If he killed Saul, as he said he did, then he deserved death; at that time it was not known to the contrary, and this man was executed on his own confession.

Verse 17. *David lamented*] See this lamentation, and the notes on it at the end of this chapter.

Verse 18. The use of *the bow*] *The use of* is not in the Hebrew; it is simply *the bow*, that is, a song thus entitled. See the observations at the end.

Verse 21. As though he had *not* been] Instead of בלי *beli*, NOT, I read כלי *keley*, INSTRUMENTS.

Anointed with oil.] See the observations at the end.

Chap. i. ver. 18, &c.: *He bade them teach the children of Judah* the use of *the bow*, קשת *kasheth*.

The word *kasheth* is to be understood of the title of the song which immediately follows, and not of the use of the bow, as our translation intimates.

Many of David's Psalms have titles prefixed to them; some are termed *Shosannim*, some *Maschil, Nehiloth, Neginoth*, &c., and this one here, *Kadesh* or *The Bow*, because it was occasioned by the Philistine archers. 1 Sam. xxxi. 3: "And the archers hit him."

But especially respecting the *bow* of Jonathan, "which returned not back from the blood of the slain," as the song itself expresses. And David could not but remember the *bow* of Jonathan, out of which "the arrow was shot beyond the lad," 1 Sam. xx. 36. It was the time when that covenant was made, and that affection expressed between them "which was greater than the love of women."

On these accounts the song was entitled *Kasheth*, or *The song of the Bow;* and David commanded the chief musicians, Ethan, Heman, and Jeduthun, to teach the children of Judah to sing it.

"It is written in the book of Jasher." *Sept.*, επι βιβλιου του ευθους, "in the book of the upright."

ספרא דאוריתא *siphra deoraitha*, "The book of the Law."—*Jonathan.*

The *Arabic* says, "Behold it is written in the book of Ashee; this is the book of Samuel;" the interpretation of which is, "book of songs or canticles."

This lamentation is justly admired as a picture of distress the most tender and the most striking; unequally divided by grief into longer and shorter breaks, as nature could pour them forth from a mind interrupted by the alternate recurrence of the most lively images of *love* and *greatness.*

His reverence for Saul and his love for Jonathan have their strongest colourings; but their *greatness* and *bravery* come full upon him, and are expressed with peculiar energy.

Being himself *a warrior*, it is in that character he sees their greatest excellence; and though his imagination hurries from one point of recollection to another, yet we hear him—at first, at last, everywhere—lamenting, *How are the mighty fallen!*

It is almost impossible to read the noble original without finding every word *swollen* with a *sigh* or *broken* with a *sob*. A heart pregnant with distress, and striving to utter expressions descriptive of its feelings, which are repeatedly interrupted by an excess of grief, is most sensibly painted throughout the whole. Even an *English* reader may be convinced of this, from the following specimen in European characters:—

19. Hatstsebi Yishrael al bamotheycha chalal;
     Eych naphelu gibborim;

20. Al taggidu begath,
     Al tebasseru bechutsoth Ashkelon;
     Pen tismachnah benoth Pelishtim,
     Pen taalozenah benoth haarelim.

21. Harey baggilboa al tal,
     Veal matar aleychem usedey terumoth;
     Ki sham nigal magen Gibborim.
     Magen Shaul keley Mashiach bashshamen!

22. Middam chalalim, mecheleb gibborim,
     Kesheth Yehonathan lo nashog achor;
     Vechereb Shaul lo thashub reykam.

23. Shaul Vihonathan,
     Hanneehabim vehanneimim bechaiyeyhem,
     Ubemotham lo niphradu.
     Minnesharim kallu, mearayoth gaberu!

24. Benoth Yishrael el Shaul becheynah;
     Hammalbishchem shani im adanim,
     Hammaaleh adi zahab al lebushechen.

25. Eych naphelu gibborim bethoch hammilchamah!
     Yehonathan al bamotheycha chalal!

26. Tsar li aleycha achi
     Yehonathan, naamta li meod,
     Niphleathah ahabathecha li meahabath nashim!

27. Eych naphelu gibborim,
     Vaiyobedu keley milchamah!

The three last verses in this sublime lamentation have *sense* and *sound* so connected as to strike every reader.

Dr. *Kennicott*, from whom I have taken several of the preceding remarks, gives a fine Latin version of this song, which I here subjoin:—

O decus Israelis, super excelsa tua MILES!
  Quomodo ceciderunt FORTES!
  Nolite indicare in Gatho,
Nolite indicare in plateis Ascalonis:
Ne lætentur filiæ Philistæorum,
Ne exultent filiæ incircumcisorum.
  Montes Gilboani super vos
Nec ros, nec pluvia, neque agri primitiarum;
Ibi enim abjectus fuit clypeus fortium.
Clypeus Saulis, arma inuncti olec!
  Sine sanguine MILITUM,
  Sine adipe FORTIUM.
Arcus Jonathanis non retrocesserat;
Gladiusque Saulis non redierat incassum.
  Saul et Jonathan
Amabiles erant et jucundi in vitis suis,
Et in morte sua non separati.
  Præ aquilis veloces!
  Præ leonibus fortes!
Filiæ Israelis deflete Saulem;
Qui coccino cum deliciis vos vestivit,
Qui vestibus vestris ornamenta imposuit aurea!
Quomodo ceciderunt FORTES, in medio belli!
  O Jonathan, super excelsa tua MILES!
  Versor in angustiis, tui causa,
    Frater mi, Jonathan!
Mihi fuisti admodum jucundus!
Mihi tuus amor admodum mirabilis,
  Mulierum exuperans amorem!
Quomodo ceciderunt fortes,
  Et perierunt arma belli!

DISSERTATION I., p. 122.

In verse 21 I have inserted כלי *keley* for בלי *beli*. Dr. *Delaney* rightly observes that the particle בלי *beli* is not used in any part of the Bible in the sense of *quasi non, as though not*, in which sense it must be used here if it be retained as a genuine reading: The shield of Saul *as though it had not been* anointed with oil.

In a MS. written about the year 1200, numbered 30 in *Kennicott's Bible*, כלי *keley* is found; and also in the *first edition of the whole Hebrew Bible*, printed *Soncini* 1488. Neither the *Syriac* nor *Arabic* versions, nor the *Chaldee* paraphrase, acknowledge the negative particle בלי *beli*, which they would have done had it been in the copies from which they translated. It was easy to make the mistake, as there is such a similarity between ב *beth* and כ *caph*; the line therefore should be read thus: The shield of Saul, *weapons* anointed with oil.

In verse 22 נשוג *nashog*, to *obtain, attain*, seems to have been written for נסוג *nasog*, to *recede, return*. The former destroys the sense; the latter, which our translation has followed, and which is supported by the authority of 30 MSS., makes it not only intelligible but beautiful.

In verses 19, 22, and 25, חלל *chalal* and חללים *chalalim* occur, which we translate the SLAIN, but which Dr. *Kennicott*, I think from good authority, renders *soldier* and *soldiers;* and thus the version is made more consistent and beautiful.

חלל *chalal* signifies to *bore* or *pierce through;* and this epithet might be well given to a soldier, q. d., the PIERCER, because his business is to *transfix* or *pierce* his enemies with sword, spear, and arrows.

If it be translated *soldiers* in the several places of the Old Testament, where we translate it SLAIN or WOUNDED, the sense will be much mended; see Judg. xx. 31, 39; Psa. lxxxix. 11;

Prov. vii. 26; Jer. li. 4, 47, 49; Ezek. xi. 6, 7; xxi. 14. In several others it retains its radical signification of *piercing, wounding,* &c.

AFTER these general observations I leave the particular beauties of this inimitable song to be sought out by the intelligent reader. Much has been written upon this, which cannot, consistently with the plan of these notes, be admitted here. See *Delaney, Kennicott, Lowth,* &c.; and, above all, let the reader examine the *Hebrew* text.

CHAPTER II

David, by the direction of God, goes up to Hebron, and is there anointed king over the house of Judah, 1–4. He congratulates the inhabitants of Jabesh-gilead on their kindness in rescuing the bodies of Saul and his sons from the Philistines, 5–7. Abner anoints Ish-bosheth, Saul's son, king over Gilead, the Ashurites, Jezreel, Ephraim, Benjamin, and all Israel; over whom he reigned two years, 8–10. David reigns over Judah, in Hebron, seven years and six months, 11. Account of a battle between Abner, captain of the Israelites, and Joab, captain of the men of Judah; in which the former are routed with the loss of three hundred and sixty men: but Asahel, the brother of Joab, is killed by Abner, 12–32.

A. M. 2949
B. C. 1055
An. Exod. Isr. 436
Anno ante
I. Olymp. 279

AND it came to pass after this, that David [a]inquired of the LORD, saying, Shall I go up into any of the cities of Judah? And the LORD said unto him, Go up. And David said, Whither shall I go up? And he said, Unto [b]Hebron.

2 So David went up thither, and his [c]two wives also, Ahinoam the Jezreelitess, and Abigail, Nabal's wife, the Carmelite.

3 And [d]his men that *were* with him did David bring up, every man with his household: and they dwelt in the cities of Hebron.

4 [e]And the men of Judah came; and there they anointed David king over the house of Judah. And they told David, saying, *That*

[f]the men of Jabesh-gilead *were they* that buried Saul.

5 And David sent messengers unto the men of Jabesh-gilead, and said unto them, [g]Blessed *be* ye of the LORD, that ye have showed this kindness unto your lord, *even* unto Saul, and have buried him.

6 And now [h]the LORD show kindness and truth unto you: and I also will requite you this kindness, because ye have done this thing.

7 Therefore now let your hands be strengthened, and [i]be ye valiant: for your master Saul is dead, and also the house of Judah have anointed me king over them.

8 But [k]Abner the son of Ner, captain of

A. M. 2949
B. C. 1055
An. Exod. Isr. 436
Anno ante
I. Olymp. 279

---

[a]Judg. i. 1; 1 Sam. xxiii. 2, 4, 9; xxx. 7, 8——[b]1 Sam. xxx. 31; ver. 11; chap. v. 1, 3; 1 Kings ii. 11——[c]1 Sam. xxx. 5——[d]1 Sam. xxvii. 2, 3; xxx. 1; 1 Chron. xii. 1

[e]Ver. 11; chap. v. 5; 1 Mac. ii. 57——[f]1 Sam. xxxi. 11, 13——[g]Ruth ii. 20; iii. 10; Psa. cxv. 15——[h]2 Tim. i. 16, 18——[i]Heb. *be ye the sons of valour*——[k]1 Sam. xiv. 50

NOTES ON CHAP. II

Verse 1. David inquired of the Lord] By means of Abiathar the priest; for he did not know whether the different tribes were willing to receive him, though he was fully persuaded that God had appointed him king over Israel.

Unto Hebron.] The metropolis of the tribe of Judah, one of the richest regions in Judea. The mountains of Hebron were famed for fruits, herbage, and honey; and many parts were well adapted for vines, olives, and different kinds of grain, abounding in springs of excellent water, as the most accurate travellers have asserted.

Verse 4. Anointed David king] He was anointed before by Samuel, by which he acquired *jus ad regnum, a right* TO *the kingdom;* by the present anointing he had *jus in regno, authority* OVER *the kingdom.* The other parts of the kingdom were, as yet, attached to the family of Saul.

Verse 5. David sent messengers unto—Jabesh-gilead] This was a generous and noble act, highly indicative of the grandeur of David's mind. He respected Saul as his once legitimate sovereign; he loved Jonathan as his most inti-

mate friend. The former had greatly injured him, and sought his destruction; but even this did not cancel his respect for him, as the anointed of God, and as the king of Israel. This brings to my remembrance that fine speech of Saurin, when speaking of the banishment of the Protestants from France by the revocation of the edict of Nantes. He thus at the Hague apostrophizes Louis XIV., their persecutor: *Et toi, prince redoubtable, que j'honorai jadis comme mon roi, et que je respecte encore comme le fleau du Seigneur.* "And thou, O formidable prince, whom I once honoured as my king, and whom I still reverence as the scourge of the Lord!"

Verse 7. Now let your hands be strengthened] David certainly wished to attach the men of Jabesh to his interest; he saw that they were generous and valiant, and must be of great service to him whose part they espoused; and he was no doubt afraid that they would attach themselves to the house of Saul, in consideration of the eminent services Saul had rendered them in rescuing them from Nahash, king of the Ammonites.

Verse 8. Abner the son of Ner] This **man**

A. M. 2949
B. C. 1055
An. Exod. Isr.
436
Anno ante
I. Olymp. 279

[1]Saul's host, took [m]Ish-bosheth the son of Saul, and brought him over to Mahanaim;

9 And made him king over Gilead, and over the Ashurites, and over Jezreel, and over Ephraim, and over Benjamin, and over all Israel.

10 Ish-bosheth Saul's son *was* forty years old when he began to reign over Israel, and reigned two years. But the house of Judah followed David.

11 And [n]the [o]time that David was king in Hebron over the house of Judah was seven years and six months.

A. M. 2951
B. C. 1053
An. Exod. Isr.
438
Anno ante
I. Olymp. 277

12 And Abner the son of Ner, and the servants of Ish-bosheth the son of Saul, went out from Mahanaim to [p]Gibeon.

13 And Joab the son of Zeruiah, and the servants of David, went out, and met [q]together by the [r]pool of Gibeon: and they sat down, the one on the one side of the pool, and the other on the other side of the pool.

A. M. 2951
B. C. 1053
An. Exod. Isr
438
Anno ante
I. Olymp. 277

14 And Abner said to Joab, Let the young men now arise, and play before us. And Joab said, Let them arise.

15 Then there arose and went over by number twelve of Benjamin, which *pertained* to Ish-bosheth the son of Saul, and twelve of the servants of David.

16 And they caught every one his fellow by the head, and *thrust* his sword in his fellow's side; so they fell down together: wherefore that place was called [s]Helkath-hazzurim, which *is* in Gibeon.

17 And there was a very sore battle that day; and Abner was beaten, and the men of Israel, before the servants of David.

18 And there were [t]three sons of Zeruiah there, Joab, and Abishai, and Asahel: and Asahel *was* [u]*as* light [v]of foot [w]as [x]a wild roe.

---

[l]Heb. *the host which* was *Saul's*——[m]Or, *Esh-baal;* 1 Chron. viii. 33; ix. 39——[n]Chap. v. 5; 1 Kings ii. 11 [o]Heb. *number of days*——[p]Josh. xviii. 25——[q]Heb. *them together*——[r]Jer. xli. 12

[s]That is, *The field of strong men*——[t]1 Chron. ii. 16 [u]1 Chron. xii. 8——[v]Heb. *of his feet*——[w]Heb. *as one of the roes that* is *in the field*——[x]Psa. xviii. 33; Cant. ii. 17; viii. 14

---

had long been one of the chief captains of Saul's army, and commander-in-chief on several occasions; he was probably envious of David's power, by whom he had often been out-generalled in the field.

Verse 9. *Made him king over Gilead*] These were places beyond Jordan; for as the Philistines had lately routed the Israelites, they were no doubt in possession of some of the principal towns, and were now enjoying the fruits of their victory. Abner was therefore afraid to bring the new king to any place where he was likely to meet with much resistance, till he had got his army well recruited.

Who the *Ashurites* were is not generally agreed; probably men of the tribe of Ashur.

Verse 10. *Ish-bosheth—reigned two years.*] It is well observed that Ish-bosheth reigned *all the time that David reigned in Hebron*, which was *seven years and six months.* Perhaps the meaning of the writer is this: Ish-bosheth reigned two years before any but the tribe of Judah had attached themselves to the interest of David. Some think that Abner in effect reigned the last five years of Ish-bosheth, who had only the name of king after the first two years. Or the text may be understood thus: *When Ish-bosheth had reigned two years over Israel, he was forty years of age.*

Houbigant, dissatisfied with all the common modes of solution, proposes to read שֵׁשִׁית שָׁנָה *shishshith shanah, six years,* for the שָׁתַיִם שָׁנִים *shetayim shanim, two years,* of the text, which he contends is a *solecism;* for in pure Hebrew the words would be שָׁתֵי שָׁנָה as they are everywhere read in the first book; and שָׁנָה is the reading of eleven of Kennicott's MSS., and nine of De Rossi's; but the number *two* is acknowledged by all the ancient versions, and by all the MSS. yet collated. The critical reader may examine Houbigant on the place. After all, probably the expedition mentioned in the succeeding verses is that to which the writer refers, and from which he *dates.* Ish-bosheth had reigned two years without any rupture with David or his men, till under the direction of Abner, captain of his host, the Israelites passed over Jordan, from Mahanaim to Gibeon; and being opposed by Joab, captain of David's host, that battle took place which is described in the following verses.

Verse 14. *Let the young men—play before us.*] This was diabolical play, where each man thrust his sword into the body of the other, so that the twenty-four (twelve on each side) fell down dead together! But this was the signal for that sanguinary skirmish which immediately took place.

Verse 16. *Caught every one his fellow by the head*] Probably by the beard, if these persons were not too young to have one, or by the hair of the head. Alexander ordered all the Macedonians to shave their beards; and being asked by Parmenio why they should do so, answered, "Dost thou not know that in battle there is no better hold than the beard?"

Helkath-hazzurim] "The portion of the mighty;" or, "The inheritance of those who were slain," according to the *Targum.*

Verse 18. *Asahel was as light of foot as a wild roe*] To be *swift of foot* was deemed a great accomplishment in the heroes of antiquity; ποδας ωκυς Αχιλλευς, *the swift-footed Achilles,* is an epithet which Homer gives to that hero no less than thirty times in the course of the Ilias. It was a qualification also among the Roman soldiers; they were taught both to *run swiftly,* and to *swim well.*

A. M. 2951
B. C. 1053
An. Exod. Isr.
438
Anno ante
I. Olymp. 277

19 And Asahel pursued after Abner; and in going he turned not to the right hand nor to the left ʸfrom following Abner.

20 Then Abner looked behind him, and said, *Art* thou Asahel? And he answered, I *am.*

21 And Abner said to him, Turn thee aside to thy right hand or to thy left, and lay thee hold on one of the young men, and take thee his ᶻarmour. But Asahel would not turn aside from following him.

22 And Abner said again to Asahel, Turn thee aside from following me: wherefore should I smite thee to the ground? how then should I hold up my face to Joab thy brother?

23 Howbeit he refused to turn aside: wherefore Abner with the hinder end of the spear smote him ᵃunder the fifth *rib,* that the spear came out behind him; and he fell down there, and died in the same place: and it came to pass, *that* as many as came to the place where Asahel fell down and died stood still.

24 Joab also and Abishai pursued after Abner: and the sun went down when they were come to the hill of Ammah, that *lieth* before Giah by the way of the wilderness of Gibeon.

25 And the children of Benjamin gathered themselves together after Abner, and became one troop, and stood on the top of a hill.

A. M. 2951
B. C. 1053
An. Exod. Isr.
438
Anno ante
I. Olymp. 277

26 Then Abner called to Joab, and said, Shall the sword devour for ever? knowest thou not that it will be bitterness in the latter end? how long shall it be then, ere thou bid the people return from following their brethren?

27 And Joab said, *As* God liveth, unless ᵇthou hadst spoken, surely then ᶜin the morning the people had ᵈgone up every one from following his brother.

28 So Joab blew a trumpet, and all the people stood still, and pursued after Israel no more, neither fought they any more.

29 And Abner and his men walked all that night through the plain, and passed over Jordan, and went through all Bithron, and they came to Mahanaim.

30 And Joab returned from following Abner: and when he had gathered all the people together, there lacked of David's servants nineteen men and Asahel.

31 But the servants of David had smitten of Benjamin, and of Abner's men, *so that* three hundred and threescore men died.

32 And they took up Asahel, and buried him in the sepulchre of his father, which *was in* Beth-lehem. And Joab and his men went all night, and they came to Hebron at break of day.

ʸHeb. *from after Abner*——ᶻOr, *spoil; Judg. xiv. 19 ᵃChap. iii. 27; iv. 6; xx. 10

ᵇVer. 14; Prov. xvii. 14——ᶜHeb. *from the morning* ᵈOr, *gone away*

Verse 21. *Take thee his armour.*] It seems Asahel wished to get the armour of Abner as a trophy; this also was greatly coveted by ancient heroes. Abner wished to spare him, for fear of exciting Joab's enmity; but as Asahel was obstinate in the pursuit, and was swifter of foot than Abner, the latter saw that he must either kill or be killed, and therefore he *turned his spear* and ran it through the body of Asahel. This *turning about* that he might pierce him is what we translate "the hinder end of his spear." This slaying of Asahel cost Abner his life, as we shall find in the next chapter.

Verse 27. *And Joab said*] The meaning of this verse appears to be this: If Abner had not provoked the battle, (see ver. 14,) Joab would not have attacked the Israelites that day; as his orders were probably to act on the defensive. Therefore the blame fell upon Israel.

Verse 29. *They came to Mahanaim.*] So they returned to the place whence they set out. See ver. 12. This was the commencement of the civil wars between Israel and Judah, and properly the commencement of the division of the two kingdoms, through which both nations were deluged with blood.

CHAPTER III

A. M. 2951
B. C. 1053
An. Exod. Isr.
438
Anno ante
I. Olymp. 277

NOW there was long war between the house of Saul and the house of David: but David waxed stronger and stronger, and the house of Saul waxed weaker and weaker.

2 And ªunto David were sons born ᵇin Hebron: and his first-born was Amnon, ᶜof Ahinoam the Jezreelitess;

3 And his second, ᵈChileab, of Abigail the wife of Nabal the Carmelite; and the third, Absalom the son of Maacah, the daughter of Talmai king of ᵉGeshur;

4 And the fourth, ᶠAdonijah the son of Haggith; and the fifth, Shephatiah, the son of Abital;

5 And the sixth, Ithream, by Eglah, David's wife. These were born to David in Hebron.

6 And it came to pass, while there was war between the house of Saul and the house of David, that Abner made himself strong for the house of Saul.

7 And Saul had a concubine, whose name *was* ᵍRizpah, the daughter of Aiah: and *Ish-bosheth* said to Abner, Wherefore hast thou ʰgone in unto my father's concubine?

8 Then was Abner very wroth for the words of Ish-bosheth, and said, *Am* I ¹a dog's head, which against Judah do show kindness this day unto the house of Saul thy father, to his brethren, and to his friends, and have not

delivered thee into the hand of David, that thou chargest me to-day with a fault concerning this woman?

A. M. 2951
B. C. 1053
An. Exod. Isr.
438
Anno ante
I. Olymp. 277

9 ᵏSo do God to Abner, and more also, except ¹as the Lᴏʀᴅ hath sworn to David, even so I do to him;

10 To translate the kingdom from the house of Saul, and to set up the throne of David over Israel and over Judah, ᵐfrom Dan even to Beer-sheba.

11 And he could not answer Abner a word again, because he feared him.

12 And Abner sent messengers to David on his behalf, saying, Whose *is* the land? saying *also,* Make thy league with me, and, behold, my hand *shall be* with thee, to bring about all Israel unto thee.

A. M. 2956
B. C. 1048
An. Exod. Isr.
443
Anno ante
I. Olymp. 272

13 And he said, Well; I will make a league with thee: but one thing I require of thee, ⁿthat is, ᵒThou shalt not see my face, except thou first bring ᵖMichal, Saul's daughter, when thou comest to see my face.

14 And David sent messengers to Ish-bosheth Saul's son, saying, Deliver *me* my wife Michal, which I espoused to me �q for a hundred foreskins of the Philistines.

15 And Ish-bosheth sent, and took her from *her* husband, *even* from ʳPhaltiel the son of Laish.

ª1 Chron. iii. 1–4——ᵇ1 Chron. xxix. 27——ᶜ1 Sam. xxv. 43——ᵈOr, *Daniel;* 1 Chron. iii. 1——ᵉ1 Sam. xxvii. 8; chap. xiii. 37——ᶠ1 Kings i. 5——ᵍChap. xxi. 8, 10——ʰChap. xvi. 21——ⁱDeut. xxiii. 18; 1 Sam. xxiv. 15; chap. ix. 8; xvi. 9

ᵏRuth i. 17; 1 Kings xix. 2——¹1 Sam. xv. 28; xvi. 1, 12; xxviii. 17; 1 Chron. xii. 23——ᵐJudg. xx. 1; chap. xvii. 11; 1 Kings iv. 25——ⁿHeb. *saying*——ᵒSo Gen. xliii. 3——ᵖ1 Sam. xviii. 20——q1 Sam. xviii. 25, 27 ʳ1 Sam. xxv. 44, *Phalti*

NOTES ON CHAP. III

Verse 1. *There was long war*] Frequent battles and skirmishes took place between the followers of David and the followers of Ish-bosheth, after the two years mentioned above, to the end of the fifth year, in which Ish-bosheth was slain by Rechab and Baanah.

Verse 6. *Abner made himself strong*] This strengthening of himself, and going in to the late king's concubine, were most evident proofs that he wished to seize upon the government. See 1 Kings ii. 21, 22; xii. 8; xvi. 21.

Verse 8. Am *I a dog's head*] Dost thou treat a man with indignity who has been the only prop of thy tottering kingdom, and the only person who could make head against the house of David?

Verse 9. *Except, as the Lord hath sworn to David*] And why did he not do this before, when he knew that God had given the kingdom to David? Was he not now, according to his own concession, fighting against God?

Verse 11. *He could not answer Abner a word*]

Miserable is the lot of a king who is governed by the general of his army, who may strip him of his power and dignity whenever he pleases! Witness the fate of poor Charles I. of England, and Louis XVI. of France. Military men, above all others, should never be intrusted with any *civil* power, and should be great only in the *field.*

Verse 13. *Except thou first bring Michal*] David had already *six wives* at Hebron; and none of them could have such pretensions to *legitimacy* as Michal, who had been taken away from him and married to Phaltiel. However distressing it was to take her from a husband who loved her most tenderly, (see ver. 16,) yet prudence and policy required that he should strengthen his own interest in the kingdom as much as possible; and that he should not leave a princess in the possession of a man who might, in her right, have made pretensions to the throne. Besides, she was his own lawful wife, and he had a right to demand her when he pleased.

Verse 14. *Deliver* me *my wife*] It is supposed that he meant to screen Abner; and to prevent

A. M. 2956
B. C. 1048
An. Exod. Isr.
443
Anno ante
I. Olymp. 272

16 And her husband went with her ⁵along weeping behind her to ᵗBahurim. Then said Abner unto him, Go, return. And he returned.

17 And Abner had communication with the elders of Israel, saying, Ye sought for David ᵘin times past *to be* king over you:

18 Now then do *it:* ᵛfor the LORD hath spoken of David, saying, By the hand of my servant David I will save my people Israel out of the hand of the Philistines, and out of the hand of all their enemies.

19 And Abner also spake in the ears of ʷBenjamin: and Abner went also to speak in the ears of David in Hebron all that seemed good to Israel, and that seemed good to the whole house of Benjamin.

20 So Abner came to David to Hebron, and twenty men with him. And David made Abner and the men that *were* with him a feast.

21 And Abner said unto David, I will arise and go, and ˣwill gather all Israel unto my lord the king, that they may make a league with thee, and that thou mayest ʸreign over all that thine heart desireth. And David sent Abner away; and he went in peace.

22 And, behold, the servants of David and Joab came from *pursuing* a troop, and brought in a great spoil with them: but Abner *was* not with David in Hebron; for he had sent him away, and he was gone in peace.

23 When Joab and all the host that *was* with him were come, they told Joab, saying,

Abner the son of Ner came to the king, and he hath sent him away, and he is gone in peace.

A. M. 2956
B. C. 1048
An. Exod. Isr.
443
Anno ante
I. Olymp. 272

24 Then Joab came to the king, and said, What hast thou done? behold, Abner came unto thee; why *is it that* thou hast sent him away, and he is quite gone?

25 Thou knowest Abner the son of Ner, that he came to deceive thee, and to know ᶻthy going out and thy coming in, and to know all that thou doest.

26 And when Joab was come out from David, he sent messengers after Abner, which brought him again from the well of Sirah: but David knew *it* not.

27 And when Abner was returned to Hebron, Joab ᵃtook him aside in the gate to speak with him ᵇquietly, and smote him there ᶜunder the fifth *rib,* that he died, for the blood of ᵈAsahel his brother.

28 And afterward when David heard *it,* he said, I and my kingdom *are* guiltless before the LORD for ever from the blood of ᵉAbner the son of Ner:

29 ᶠLet it rest on the head of Joab, and on all his father's house; and let there not ᵍfail from the house of Joab one ʰthat hath an issue, or that is a leper, or that leaneth on a staff, or that falleth on the sword, or that lacketh bread.

30 So Joab and Abishai his brother slew Abner, because he had slain his brother ⁱAsahel at Gibeon in the battle.

31 And David said to Joab, and to all the

ˢHeb. *going and weeping*——ᵗCh. xix. 16——ᵘHeb. *both yesterday and the third day*——ᵛVer. 9——ʷ1 Chron. xii. 29——ˣVer. 10, 12——ʸ1 Kings xi. 37 ᶻ1 Sam. xxix. 6; Isa. xxxvii. 28——ᵃ1 Kings ii. 5; so

chapter xx. 9, 10——ᵇOr, *peaceably*——ᶜChapter iv. 6——ᵈCh. ii. 23——ᵉHeb. *bloods*——ᶠ1 Kings ii. 32, 33——ᵍHeb. *be cut off*——ʰLev. xv. 2——ⁱChap. ii. 23

---

that *violence* which he might have used in carrying off Michal.

Verse 16. *Weeping behind her*] If genuine affection did not still subsist between David and Michal, it was a pity to have taken her from Phaltiel, who had her to wife from the conjoint authority of her *father* and her *king.* Nevertheless David had a legal right to her, as she had never been divorced, for she was taken from him by the hand of violence.

Verse 18. *The Lord hath spoken of David*] *Where* is this spoken? Such a promise is not extant. Perhaps it means no more than, "Thus, it may be presumed, God hath determined."

Verse 21. *He went in peace.*] David dismissed him in good faith, having no sinister design in reference to him.

Verse 27. *And smote him there*] Joab feared that, after having rendered such essential serv-

ices to David, Abner would be made captain of the host: he therefore determined to prevent it by murdering the man, under pretence of avenging the death of his brother Asahel.

The murder, however, was one of the most unprovoked and wicked: and such was the power and influence of this nefarious general, that the king dared not to bring him to justice for his crime. In the same way he murdered *Amasa,* a little time afterwards. See chap. xx. 10. Joab was a cool-blooded, finished murderer. "Treason and murder ever keep together, like two yoke-devils."

Verse 29. *Let it rest on the head*] All these verbs may be rendered in the *future* tense: it *will* rest on the head of Joab, &c. This was a prophetic declaration, which sufficiently showed the displeasure of God against this execrable man.

Verse 31. *David said to Joab*] He com-

A. M. 2956
B. C. 1048
An. Exod. Isr.
443
Anno ante
I. Olymp. 272

people that *were* with him, ᵏRend your clothes, and ˡgird you with sackcloth, and mourn before Abner. And king David *himself* followed the ᵐbier.

32 And they buried Abner in Hebron: and the king lifted up his voice, and wept at the grave of Abner; and all the people wept.

33 And the king lamented over Abner, and said, Died Abner as a ⁿfool dieth?

34 Thy hands *were* not bound, nor thy feet put into fetters: as a man falleth before ᵒwicked men, *so* fellest thou. And all the people wept again over him.

35 And when all the people came ᵖto cause David to eat meat while it was yet day,

David sware, saying, �qSo do God to me, and more also, if I taste bread, or aught else, ʳtill the sun be down.

A. M. 2956
B. C. 1048
An. Exod. Isr.
443
Anno ante
I. Olymp. 272

36 And all the people took notice *of it,* and it ˢpleased them: as whatsoever the king did pleased all the people.

37 For all the people and all Israel understood that day that it was not of the king to slay Abner the son of Ner.

38 And the king said unto his servants, Know ye not that there is a prince and a great man fallen this day in Israel?

39 And I *am* this day ᵗweak, though anointed king; and these men the sons of Zeruiah ᵘ*be* too hard for me: ᵛthe LORD shall reward the doer of evil according to his wickedness.

ᵏJosh. vii. 6; chap. i. 2, 11——ˡGen. xxxvii. 34 ᵐHeb. *bed*——ⁿChap. xiii. 12, 13——ᵒHeb. *children of iniquity*——ᵖChap. xii. 17; Jer. xvi. 7——qRuth i. 17

ʳChap. i. 12——ˢHeb. *was good in their eyes*——ᵗHeb. *tender*——ᵘChap. xix. 7——ᵛSee chap. xix. 13; 1 Kings ii. 5, 6, 33, 34; Psa. xxviii. 4; lxii. 12; 2 Tim. iv. 14

---

manded him to take on him the part of a principal mourner.

Verse 33. *The king lamented over Abner*] This lamentation, though short, is very pathetic. It is a high strain of poetry; but the *measure* cannot be easily ascertained. Our own translation may be measured thus:—

> Died Abner as a fool dieth?
> Thy hands were not bound,
> Nor thy feet put into fetters.
> As a man falleth before the wicked.
> *So* hast thou fallen!

Or thus:—

> Shall Abner die
> A death like to a villain's?
> Thy hands not bound,
> Nor were the fetters to thy feet applied.
> Like as one falls before the sons of guilt,
> So hast *thou* fallen!

He was not taken away by the hand of *justice*, nor in *battle*, nor by *accident:* he died the death of a culprit by falling into the hands of a villain.

This song was a heavy reproof to Joab; and must have galled him extremely, being sung by all the people.

Verse 36. *The people took notice*] They saw that the king's grief was sincere, and that he had no part nor device in the murder of Abner: see ver. 37.

Verse 39. *I am this day weak*] Had Abner

lived, all the tribes of Israel would have been brought under my government.

Though anointed king] I have little else than the title: *first*, having only one tribe under my government; and *secondly*, the sons of Zeruiah, Joab and his brethren, having usurped all the power, and reduced me to the shadow of royalty.

The Lord shall reward the doer of evil] That is, Joab, whom he appears afraid to name.

WE talk much of ancient manners, their *simplicity* and *ingenuousness;* and say that *the former days were better than these.* But who says this who is a judge of the times? In those days of celebrated *simplicity*, &c., there were not so *many* crimes as at present I grant: but what they wanted in *number* they made up in *degree:* deceit, cruelty, rapine, murder, and *wrong* of almost every kind, then flourished. We are *refined* in our vices; they were *gross* and *barbarous* in theirs: they had neither so many *ways* nor so many *means* of sinning; but the *sum* of their moral turpitude was greater than ours. We have a sort of *decency* and *good breeding*, which lay a certain restraint on our passions; they were boorish and beastly, and their bad passions were ever in full play. Civilization prevents barbarity and atrocity; mental cultivation induces decency of manners: those primitive times were generally without these. Who that knows them would wish such ages to return?

CHAPTER IV

Some account of Rechab and Baanah, two of Ish-bosheth's captains, and of Mephibosheth, the son of Jonathan, 1–4. *Rechab and Baanah murder Ish-bosheth, and escape; and bring his head to David,* 5–8. *David is greatly irritated, and commands them to be slain,* 9–12.

A. M. 2956
B. C. 1048
An. Exod. Isr. 443
Anno ante
I. Olymp. 272

AND when Saul's son heard that Abner was dead in Hebron, [a]his hands were feeble, and all the Israelites were [b]troubled.

2 And Saul's son had two men *that were* captains of bands: the name of the one *was* Baanah, and the name of the [c]other Rechab, the sons of Rimmon a Beerothite, of the children of Benjamin: (for [d]Beeroth also was reckoned to Benjamin:

3 And the Beerothites fled to [e]Gittaim, and were sojourners there until this day.)

4 And [f]Jonathan, Saul's son, had a son *that was* lame of *his* feet. He was five years old when the tidings came of Saul and Jonathan [g]out of Jezreel, and his nurse took him up, and fled: and it came to pass, as she made haste to flee, that he fell, and became lame. And his name *was* [h]Mephibosheth.

5 And the sons of Rimmon the Beerothite, Rechab and Baanah, went, and came about the heat of the day to the house of Ish-bosheth, who lay on a bed at noon.

6 And they came thither into the midst of the house, *as though* they would have fetched

wheat; and they smote him [i]under the fifth *rib:* and Rechab and Baanah his brother escaped.

7 For when they came into the house, he lay on his bed in his bed-chamber, and they smote him, and slew him, and beheaded him, and took his head, and gat them away through the plain all night.

8 And they brought the head of Ish-bosheth unto David to Hebron, and said to the king, Behold the head of Ish-bosheth the son of Saul thine enemy, [k]which sought thy life; and the LORD hath avenged my lord the king this day of Saul, and of his seed.

9 And David answered Rechab and Baanah his brother, the sons of Rimmon the Beerothite, and said unto them, *As* the LORD liveth, [l]who hath redeemed my soul out of all adversity,

10 When [m]one told me, saying, Behold, Saul is dead, [n]thinking to have brought good tidings, I took hold of him, and slew him in Ziklag, [o]who *thought* that I would have given him a reward for his tidings:

11 How much more when wicked men have

A. M. 2956
B. C. 1048
An. Exod. Isr. 443
Anno ante
I. Olymp. 272

---

[a]Ezra iv. 4; Isa. xiii. 7——[b]Matt. ii. 3——[c]Heb. *second*——[d]Josh. xviii. 25——[e]Neh. xi. 33——[f]Chap. ix. 3——[g]1 Sam. xxix. 1, 11——[h]Or, *Merib-baal;* 1 Chron. viii. 34; ix. 40——[i]Chap. ii. 23

[k]1 Sam. xix. 2, 10, 11; xxiii. 15; xxv. 29——[l]Gen. xlviii. 16; 1 Kings i. 29; Psa. xxxi. 7——[m]Ch. i. 2, 4, 15 [n]Heb. *he was in his own eyes as a bringer,* &c.——[o]Or, *which* was *the reward I gave him for his tidings*

NOTES ON CHAP. IV

Verse 1. *All the Israelites were troubled*] Abner was their great support; and on him they depended; for it appears that Ish-bosheth was a feeble prince, and had few of those qualities requisite for a sovereign.

Verse 2. *Captains of bands*] *Principes latronum,* captains of banditti, says the *Vulgate;* the *Syriac* is the same. Whether Ish-bosheth kept bands of *marauders,* whose business it was to make sudden incursions into the country places, and carry off grain, provisions, cattle, &c., we know not; but such persons would be well qualified for the bloody work in which these two men were afterwards employed.

Verse 3. *The Beerothites fled to Gittaim*] Probably the same as *Gath;* as *Ramathaim* is the same as *Ramah.*

Verse 4. *He fell, and became lame*] Dislocated his *ankle, knee,* or *thigh;* which was never after reduced; and thus he became lame. Lovely Jonathan! unfortunate in thy life, and in thy progeny.

Verse 5. *Lay on a bed at noon.*] It is a custom in all hot countries to travel or work very *early* and very *late,* and rest at *noonday,* in which the *heat* chiefly prevails.

Verse 6. As though *they would have fetched wheat*] The king's stores were probably near his own dwelling; and these men were accustomed to go thither for provisions for them-

selves, their cattle, and their men. This supposition, which is natural, renders unnecessary all the emendations of *Houbigant* and others.

As these men were accustomed to bring wheat from these stores, from which it appears there was an easy passage to the king's chamber, (especially if we consider this a *summer-house,* as it most probably was,) no man would suspect their present errand, as they were in the habit of going frequently to that place.

Verse 8. *They brought the head—unto David*] They thought, as did the poor lying Amalekite, to ingratiate themselves with David by this abominable act.

Verse 9. *Who hath redeemed my soul out of all adversity*] This was, in David's case, a very proper view of the goodness and watchful providence of God towards him. His *life* was frequently in danger; murderers had often laid wait for it: but God, the *living* God, had always *redeemed that life* from *all adversity;* and called on him now to punish such evil-minded and blood-thirsty men.

Verse 10. *A reward for his tidings*] Ὦ ἔδει με δοῦναι εὐαγγέλια, Septuagint. Here is a proof that εὐαγγελιον, *evangelium* or *gospel,* signifies the *reward* which the bringer of good tidings is entitled to receive. See my *preface* to St. Matthew's Gospel.

Verse 11. *How much more*] Here are sev-

A. M. 2956
B. C. 1048
An. Exod. Isr.
443
Anno ante
I. Olymp. 272 slain a righteous person in his own house upon his bed? shall I not therefore now ᵖrequire his blood of your hand, and take you away from the earth?

12 And David �q commanded his young men, and they slew them, and cut off their hands and their feet, and hanged *them* up over the pool in Hebron. But they took the head of Ish-bosheth, and buried *it* in the ʳsepulchre of Abner in Hebron. A. M. 2956
B. C. 1048
An. Exod. Isr.
443
Anno ante
I. Olymp. 272

ᵖGen. ix. 5, 6——�q Chap. i. 15

ʳChap. iii. 32

---

eral things which aggravated the guilt of those wicked men. 1. Ish-bosheth was an *innocent man*, and therefore none could have any ground of quarrel against him. 2. He was in *his own house*, which was his sanctuary, and none but the worst of men would disturb him there. 3. He was *upon his bed*, resting in the heat of the day, and so free from suspicion that he was not even attended by his guards, nor had he his doors secured. To take away the life of such a man, in such circumstances, whom also they professed to hold as their sovereign, was the most abandoned treachery.

Verse 12. *And they slew them*] None ever more richly deserved death; and by this act of justice, David showed to all Israel that he was a decided enemy to the destruction of Saul's family; and that none could lift up their hands against any of them without meeting with condign punishment. In all these cases I know not that it was possible for David to show more sincerity, or a stricter regard for justice.

CHAPTER V

The elders of all the tribes of Israel come and anoint David king over all Israel, 1–5. He goes against the Jebusites, and takes the strong hold of Zion, and afterwards the city itself; which is called the city of David, 6–9. David's prosperity, and friendship with Hiram, king of Tyre, 10–12. He takes more concubines, and begets several sons and daughters, 13–16. The Philistines gather together against him in the valley of Rephaim; he defeats them; they abandon their idols, and David and his men burn them, 17–21. They assemble once more in the valley of Rephaim, and David smites them from Geba to Gazer, 22–25.

A. M. 2956
B. C. 1048
An. Exod. Isr.
443
Anno ante
I. Olymp. 272 THEN ᵃcame all the tribes of Israel to David unto Hebron, and spake, saying, Behold, ᵇwe *are* thy bone and thy flesh.

2 Also in time past, when Saul was king over us, ᶜthou wast he that leddest out and broughtest in Israel: and the LORD said to thee, ᵈThou shalt feed my people Israel, and thou shalt be a captain over Israel.

3 ᵉSo all the elders of Israel came to the king to Hebron; ᶠand king David made a league with them in Hebron ᵍbefore the LORD: and they anointed David king over Israel.

4 David *was* thirty years old when he began to reign, ʰ*and* he reigned forty years. A. M. 2956
B. C. 1048
An. Exod. Isr.
443
Anno ante
I. Olymp. 272

5 In Hebron he reigned over Judah ⁱseven years and six months: and in Jerusalem he reigned thirty and three years over all Israel and Judah.

6 And the king and his men went ᵏto Jerusalem unto ˡthe Jebusites, the inhabitants of the land; which spake unto David, saying, Except thou take away the blind and the lame, thou shalt not come in hither: ᵐthinking, David cannot come in hither.

ᵃ1 Chron. xi. 1; xii. 23——ᵇGen. xxix. 14——ᶜ1 Sam. xviii. 13——ᵈ1 Sam. xvi. 1, 12; Psa. lxxviii. 71; see ch. vii. 7——ᵉ1 Chron. xi. 3——ᶠ2 Kings xi. 17——ᵍJudg. xi. 11; 1 Sam. xxiii. 18

ʰ1 Chronicles xxvi. 31; xxix. 27——ⁱChapter ii. 11; 1 Chronicles iii. 4——ᵏJudges i. 21——ˡJoshua xv. 63; Judges i. 8; xix. 11, 12——ᵐOr, *saying, David shall not*, &c.

NOTES ON CHAP. V

Verse 1. *Then came all the tribes of Israel*] Ish-bosheth the king, and Abner the general, being dead, they had no hope of maintaining a separate kingdom, and therefore thought it better to submit to David's authority. And they founded their resolution on *three* good arguments: 1. David was their own countryman; *We are thy bone and thy flesh.* 2. Even in Saul's time David had been their general, and had always led them to victory; *Thou wast he that leddest out and broughtest in Israel.* 3. God had appointed him to the kingdom, to govern and protect the people; *The Lord said to thee, Thou shalt feed my people and be a captain over Israel.*

Verse 3. *They anointed David king*] This was the third time that David was anointed, having now taken possession of the *whole* kingdom.

Verse 6. *The king and his men went to Jerusalem*] This city was now in the hands of the Jebusites; but how they got possession of it is not known; probably they took it during the wars between Ish-bosheth and David. After Joshua's death, what is called the *lower city* was taken by the Israelites; and it is evident that the whole city was in their possession in the time of Saul, for David brought the head of Goliath thither, 1 Sam. xvii. 54. It appears to have been a very strong fortress, and, from what follows, deemed impregnable by the Jebusites. It was right that the Israelites should

A. M. 2956
B. C. 1048
An. Exod. Isr. 443
Anno ante I. Olymp. 272

7 Nevertheless David took the
strong hold of Zion: [n]the same
is the city of David.
8 And David said on that day,
Whosoever getteth up to the gutter, and smiteth the Jebusites, and the lame and the blind
that are hated of David's soul, [o]*he shall be
chief and captain.* [p]Wherefore they said, The
blind and the lame shall not come into the
house.
9 So David dwelt in the fort, and called it
[q]The city of David. And David built round
about from Millo and inward.
10 And David [r]went on, and grew great,
and the LORD God of hosts *was* with him.

A. M. 2961
B. C. 1043
An. Exod. Isr. 448
Anno ante I. Olymp. 267

11 And [s]Hiram king of Tyre
sent messengers to David, and
cedar trees, and carpenters, and
[t]masons: and they built David
a house.

A. M. 2957
B. C. 1047
An. Exod. Isr. 444
Anno ante I. Olymp. 271

12 And David perceived that
the LORD had established him
king over Israel, and that he had
exalted his kingdom for his people Israel's sake.
13 And [u]David took *him* more concubines
and wives out of Jerusalem, after he was come
from Hebron: and there were yet sons and
daughters born to David.
14 And [v]these *be* the names of those that
were born unto him in Jerusalem; [w]Sham-
muah, and Shobab, and Nathan, and Solomon,
15 Ibhar also, and [x]Elishua, and Nepheg,
and Japhia,
16 And Elishama, and [y]Eliada, and Eliphalet.

A. M. 2957
B. C. 1047
An. Exod. Isr. 444
Anno ante I. Olymp. 271

17 [z]But when the Philistines
heard that they had anointed
David king over Israel, all the
Philistines came up to seek

[n]Ver. 9; 1 Kings ii. 10; viii. 1——[o]1 Chron. xi. 6–9——[p]Or, *because they had said, even the blind, and the lame, he shall not come into the house*——[q]Ver. 7——[r]Heb. *went going and growing*——[s]1 Kings v. 2; 1 Chron. xiv. 1

[t]Heb. *hewers of the stone of the wall*——[u]Deut. xvii. 17; 1 Chron. iii. 9; xiv. 3——[v]1 Chron. iii. 5; xiv. 4——[w]Or, *Shimea*, 1 Chron. iii. 5——[x]Or, *Elishama*, 1 Chron. iii. 6——[y]Or, *Beeliada*, 1 Chron. xiv. 7——[z]1 Chron. xi. 16; xiv. 8

repossess it; and David very properly began his reign over the whole country by the siege of this city.

Except thou take away the blind and the lame] Scarcely a passage in the sacred oracles has puzzled commentators more than this. For my own part, I do not think that it is worth the labour spent upon it, nor shall I encumber these pages with the discordant opinions of learned men. From the general face of the text it appears that the Jebusites, vainly confiding in the strength of their fortress, placed *lame* and *blind men* upon the walls, and thus endeavoured to turn into ridicule David's attempt to take the place: *Thou shalt not come in hither, except thou take away the blind and the lame;* nothing could be more cutting to a warrior.

Dr. *Kennicott* has taken great pains to correct this passage, as may be seen in his *First Dissertation on the Hebrew Text*, pages 27 to 47. I shall insert our present version with his amended text line for line, his translation being distinguished by *italics;* and for farther information refer to Dr. K.'s work.

Verse 6. And the king and his men went to
K. *And the king and his men went to Jeru-*
Jerusalem unto the Jebusites, the inhabitants
K. *salem unto the Jebusites, the inhabitants of*
of the land: who spake unto David, saying,
K. *the land; who spake unto David, saying;*
Except thou take away the blind and the
K. *Thou shalt not come in hither; for the blind*
lame, thou shalt not come in hither: think-
K. *and the lame shall drive thee away by say-*
ing, David cannot come in hither.
K. *ing, "David shall not come in hither."*

Verse 8. And David said—Whosoever getteth
K. *And David said—Whosoever smiteth the*
up to the gutter, and smiteth the Jebusites,
K. *Jebusites, and through the subterranean pas-*
and the lame and the blind, that are hated
K. *sage reacheth the lame and the blind who*
of David's soul—Wherefore they said, The
K. *hate the life of David (because the blind and*
blind and the lame shall not come into the
K. *the lame said, "He shall not come into the*
house. * * * * * * * * * * *
K. *house,") shall be chief and captain. So*
* * * * * * * * * * * * * *
K. *Joab the son of Zeruiah went up first, and*
* * * * * * * * * * * * * *
K. *was chief.*

Verse 11. *Hiram king of Tyre*] He was a very friendly man, and no doubt a believer in the true God. He was not only a friend to David, but also of his son Solomon, to whom, in building the temple, he afforded the most important assistance.

Verse 13. *David took* him *more concubines*] He had, in all conscience, enough before; he had, in the whole, *eight wives* and *ten concubines.* That dispensation permitted *polygamy,* but from the beginning it was not so; and as upon an average there are about *fourteen* males born to *thirteen* females, polygamy is unnatural, and could never have entered into the original design of God.

Verse 14. *These* be *the names*] *Eleven* children are here enumerated in the Hebrew text; but the *Septuagint* has no less than *twenty-four.* I shall insert their names, and the reader if he please may collate them with the text: *Sammus, Sobab, Nathan, Solomon, Ebear, Elisue, Naphek, Jephies, Elisama, Elidae, Eliphalath, Samae, Jessibath, Nathan, Galimaan, Jebaar, Theesus, Eliphalat, Naged, Naphek, Jonathan, Leasamus, Baalimath,* and *Eliphaath.* There is no doubt some corruption in these names; there are two of the name of *Nathan,* two of *Eliphalath,* and two of *Naphek;* and probably *Sammus* and *Samae* are the same.

Verse 17. *The Philistines came up to seek*

A. M. 2957
B. C. 1047
An. Exod. Isr.
444
Anno ante
I. Olymp. 271

David; and David heard *of it,* *a*and went down to the hold.

18 The Philistines also came and spread themselves in *b*the valley of Rephaim.

19 And David *c*inquired of the LORD, saying, Shall I go up to the Philistines? wilt thou deliver them into mine hand? And the LORD said unto David, Go up: for I will doubtless deliver the Philistines into thine hand.

20 And David came to *d*Baal-perazim, and David smote them there, and said, The LORD hath broken forth upon mine enemies before me, as the breach of waters. Therefore he called the name of that place *e*Baal-perazim.

21 And there they left their images, and

David and his men *f*burned *g*them.

22 *h*And the Philistines came up yet again, and spread themselves in the valley of Rephaim.

23 And when *i*David inquired of the LORD, he said, Thou shalt not go up; *but* fetch a compass behind them, and come upon them over against the mulberry trees.

24 And let it be, when thou *k*hearest the sound of a going in the tops of the mulberry trees, that then thou shalt bestir thyself: for then *l*shall the LORD go out before thee, to smite the host of the Philistines.

25 And David did so, as the LORD had commanded him; and smote the Philistines from *m*Geba until thou come to *n*Gazer.

A. M. 2957
B. C. 1047
An. Exod. Isr.
444
Anno ante
I. Olymp. 271

---

*a*Ch. xxiii. 14——*b*Josh. xv. 8; Isa. xvii. 5——*c*Ch. ii. 1; 1 Sam. xxiii. 2, 4; xxx. 8——*d*Isa. xxviii. 21——*e*That is, *the plain of breaches*——*f*Deut. vii. 5, 25; 1 Chron. xiv. 12

*g*Or, *took them away*——*h*1 Chron. xiv. 13——*i*Verse 19——*k*So 2 Kings vii. 6——*l*Judg. iv. 14——*m*1 Chron. xiv. 16, *Gibeon*——*n*Josh. xvi. 10

David] Ever since the defeat of the Israelites and the fall of Saul and his sons, the Philistines seem to have been in undisturbed possession of the principal places in the land of Israel; now, finding that David was chosen king by the *whole nation,* they thought best to attack him before his army got too numerous, and the affairs of the kingdom were properly settled.

Verse 19. *David inquired of the Lord*] He considered himself only the captain of the Lord's host, and therefore would not strike a stroke without the command of his Superior.

Verse 20. *The Lord hath broken forth*] He very properly attributes the victory of Jehovah, without whose strength and counsel he could have done nothing.

Baal-perazim.] The *plain* or *chief of breaches,* because of the *breach* which God made in the Philistine army; and thus he commemorated the interference of the Lord.

Verse 21. *They left their images*] It was the custom of most nations to carry their gods with them to battle: in imitation of this custom the Israelites once took the ark and lost it in the field; see 1 Sam. iv.

Verse 23. *Fetch a compass behind them*] When they may be had, God will not work without using *human means.* By this he taught David caution, prudence, and dependence on the Divine strength.

Verse 24. *When thou hearest the sound of a going*] If there had not been an evident *supernatural interference,* David might have thought that the *sleight* or *ruse de guerre* which he had used was the cause of his victory. By the *going in the tops of the mulberry trees* probably only a *rustling among the leaves* is intended. The Targum says, *a noise;* the Arabic has it, *the noise of horses' hoofs.*

Verse 25. *And David did so*] He punctually obeyed the directions of the Lord, and then every thing succeeded to his wish.

How is it that such supernatural directions and assistances are not communicated now?

Because they are not asked for; and they are not asked for because they are not expected; and they are not expected because men have not faith; and they have not faith because they are under a refined spirit of atheism, and have no spiritual intercourse with their Maker. Who believes that God sees all things and is everywhere? Who supposes that he concerns himself with the affairs of his creatures? Who acknowledges him in all his ways? Who puts not his own wisdom, prudence, and strength, in the place of God Almighty? Reader, hast *thou* faith in God? Then exercise it, cultivate it, and thou mayest remove mountains.

It is worthy of remark that David was, by the appointment of God, *to feed the people.* As he had formerly the care of a flock of sheep, which he was to watch over, defend, lead in and out, and for which he was to find pasture; now he is to watch over, defend, lead in and out, feed, and protect, the Israelites. He is to be *the shepherd of the people,* not the tyrant or oppressor.

In ancient times, among the Greeks, kings were denominated ποιμενες λαου, *shepherds of the people;* and all good kings were really such: but, in process of time, this pleasing title was changed for βασιλευς and τυραννος, *sovereign* and *tyrant;* in neither of which names does any thing of the original title exist. And such are the different political constitutions of the kingdoms of the earth, that it is impossible that in any of them, the British excepted, the king can be the *shepherd* and *father of his people.* All the other regal constitutions under the sun permit the sovereign to be *despotic,* and consequently *oppressive* and *tyrannical* if he please. The British alone gives no power of this kind to the prince; by the constitution he is a *patriotic king,* and by the influence of those maxims of state which are continually presented to his view, and according to which all acts of government are formed, he becomes *habitually* the *father of his people,* and in this light alone do the British people behold the British king.

David, by his own authority, *without any form of law,* could slay the Amalekite who said he had killed Saul; and could cut off the heads of Rechab and Baanah, who murdered Ish-bosheth; but, in the government of Britain, the culprit is to be heard in his vindication, witnesses are to be examined, the facts viewed by an upright judge in the light of the law; and then the alleged criminality is left to the decision of twelve honest men, the equals of the accused, who are bound by a solemn oath to decide *according to the evidence* brought before them. The Israelitish constitution was radically good, but the British constitution is much better. In the former, while the king ruled ac-cording to the *spirit* of the constitution, he could do no wrong, because he was only the *vicegerent* of the Almighty; in the latter, the king can do no wrong, because he is bound both by the *spirit* and *letter* of the law, to do noth-ing but what is according to the rules of eternal justice and equity laid down in that law: noth-ing is left to mere regal power or authority, and nothing trusted to human fickleness or caprice. In all his acts he is directed by his nobles and commons; who, being the representatives of all classes of the people, are always sup-posed to speak their mind. Well may it be said, Blessed are the people who are in such a case!

CHAPTER VI

David goes with thirty thousand *men to bring the ark from Kirjath-jearim to Jerusalem,* 1–5. *The oxen stum-bling, Uzzah, who drove the cart on which the ark was placed, put forth his hand to save it from falling: the Lord was displeased, and smote him so that he died,* 6, 7. *David, being alarmed, carries the ark to the house of Obed-edom,* 8–10. *Here it remained three months; and God prospered Obed-edom, in whose house it was deposited,* 11. *David, hearing of this, brings the ark, with sacrifices and solemn rejoicings, to Jerusalem,* 12–15. *Michal, seeing David dance before the ark, despises him,* 16. *He offers burnt-offerings and peace-offerings, and deals among all the people, men and women, a cake of bread, a good piece of flesh, and a flagon of wine each,* 17–19. *Michal coming to meet him, and seeing him dance extravagantly before the ark, reproaches him for his conduct: he vindicates himself, reproves her, and she dies childless,* 20–23.

A. M. 2962
B. C. 1042
An. Exod. Isr.
449
Anno ante
I. Olymp. 266

AGAIN, David gathered to-gether all *the* chosen *men* of Israel, thirty thousand.

2 And ªDavid arose, and went with all the people that *were* with him from ᵇBaale of Judah, to bring up from thence the ark of God, ᶜwhose name is called by the name of the LORD of hosts ᵈthat dwelleth *between* the cherubims.

3 And they ᵉset the ark of God ᶠupon a new cart, and brought it out of the house of Abinadab that *was* in ᵍGibeah:

and Uzzah and Ahio, the sons of Abinadab, drave the new cart.

A. M. 2962
B. C. 1042
An. Exod. Isr.
449
Anno ante
I. Olymp. 266

4 And they brought it out of ʰthe house of Abinadab which *was* at Gibeah, ⁱaccompanying the ark of God: and Ahio went before the ark.

5 And David and all the house of Israel played before the LORD on all manner of *in-struments made of* fir wood, even on harps, and on psalteries, and on timbrels, and on cor-nets, and on cymbals.

ª1 Chron. xiii. 5, 6——ᵇOr, *Baalah, that is, Kirjath-jearim,* Josh. xv. 9, 60——ᶜOr, *at which the name, even the name of the LORD of hosts, was called upon*

ᵈ1 Sam. iv. 4; Psa. lxxx. 1——ᵉHeb. *made to ride* ᶠSee Num. vii. 9; 1 Sam. vi. 7——ᵍOr, *the hill*——ʰ1 Sam. vii. 1——ⁱHeb. *with*

NOTES ON CHAP. VI

Verse 1. *Thirty thousand.*] This is supposed to have been a new levy; and thus he augment-ed his army by 30,000 fresh troops. The *Sep-tuagint* has 70,000.

Verse 2. *From Baale of Judah*] This is sup-posed to be the same city which, in Josh. xv. 60, is called *Kirjath-baal* or *Kirjath-jearim;* (see 1 Chron. xiii. 6;) or *Baalah,* Josh. xv. 9.

Whose name is called by the name of the Lord] That is, The ark is called *the ark of the Lord of hosts.* But this is not a *literal* version; the word שׁם *shem,* NAME, occurs twice together; probably one of them should be read שׁם *sham,* THERE. *There* the name of the Lord of hosts was invoked, &c.

Verse 3. *A new cart*] Every thing used in the worship of God was hallowed or *set apart*

for that purpose: a new cart was used through respect, as that had never been applied to any profane or common purpose. But this was not sufficient, for the ark should have been carried on the shoulders of the priests; and the neglect of this ceremony was the cause of the death of Uzzah.

Verse 5. *On all manner of* instruments made of *fir wood*] This place should be corrected from the parallel place, 1 Chron. xiii. 8: "All Israel played before God, with all their might, and with singing, and with harps, and with psalteries," &c. Instead of עֲצֵי בְּכֹל *bechol atsey,* "with all woods" or "trees;" the parallel place is עֹז בְּכֹל *bechol oz,* "with all their strength:" this makes a good sense, the first makes none. The *Septuagint,* in this place, has the same reading: εν ισχυϊ, *with might,*

A. M. 2962
B. C. 1042
An. Exod. Isr.
449
Anno ante
I. Olymp. 266

6 And when they came to [k]Nachon's threshing-floor, Uzzah [l]put forth *his hand* to the ark of God, and took hold of it; for the oxen [m]shook it.

7 And the anger of the LORD was kindled against Uzzah; and [n]God smote him there for *his* [o]error; and there he died by the ark of God.

8 And David was displeased because the LORD had [p]made a breach upon Uzzah: and he called the name of the place [q]Perez-uzzah to this day.

9 And [r]David was afraid of the LORD that day, and said, How shall the ark of the LORD come to me?

10 So David would not remove the ark of the LORD unto him into the city of David: but David carried it aside into the house of Obed-edom [s]the Gittite.

11 [t]And the ark of the LORD continued in the house of Obed-edom the Gittite three months: and the LORD [u]blessed Obed-edom, and all his household.

12 And it was told King David, saying, The LORD hath blessed the house of Obed-edom, and all the *pertaineth* unto him, because of the ark of God. [v]So David went and brought up the ark of God from the house of Obed-edom into the city of David with gladness.

A. M. 2962
B. C. 1042
An. Exod. Isr.
449
Anno ante
I. Olymp. 266

13 And it was so, that when [w]they that bare the ark of the LORD had gone six paces, he sacrificed [x]oxen and fatlings.

14 And David [y]danced before the LORD with all *his* might; and David *was* girded [z]with a linen ephod.

15 [a]So David and all the house of Israel brought up the ark of the LORD with shouting, and with the sound of the trumpet.

16 And [b]as the ark of the LORD came into the city of David, Michal Saul's daughter looked through a window, and saw King David leaping and dancing before the LORD; and she despised him in her heart.

17 [c]And they brought in the ark of the LORD, and set it in [d]his place, in the midst of the tabernacle that David had [e]pitched for it: and David [f]offered burnt-offerings and peace-offerings before the LORD.

18 And as soon as David had made an end of offering burnt-offerings and peace-offerings, [g]he blessed the people in the name of the LORD of hosts.

---

[k]1 Chron. xiii. 9, he is called, *Chidon*——[l]See Num. iv. 15——[m]Or, *stumbled*——[n]1 Sam. vi. 19——[o]Or, *rashness*——[p]Heb. *broken*——[q]That is, *the breach of Uzzah*——[r]Psa. cxix. 120; see Luke v. 8, 9——[s]1 Chron. xiii. 13——[t]1 Chronicles xiii. 14——[u]Genesis xxx. 27; xxix. 5——[v]1 Chronicles xv. 25

[w]Num. iv. 15; Josh. iii. 3; 1 Chron. xv. 2, 15——[x]See 1 Kings viii. 5; 1 Chron. xv. 26——[y]See Exod. xv. 20; Psa. xxx. 11——[z]1 Sam. ii. 18; 1 Chron. xv. 27——[a]1 Chron. xv. 28——[b]1 Chron. xv. 19——[c]1 Chron. xvi. 1 [d]1 Chron. xv. 1; Psa. cxxxii. 8——[e]Heb. *stretched*——[f]1 Kings viii. 5, 62, 63——[g]1 Kings viii. 55; 1 Chron. xvi. 2

Verse 6. *Uzzah put forth* his hand] In Num. iv. 15-20, the Levites are forbidden to touch the ark *on pain of death;* this penalty was inflicted upon Uzzah, and he was the first that suffered for a breach of this law.

Verse 7. *Smote him there for* his *error*] Uzzah sinned through ignorance and precipitancy; he had not time to *reflect;* the oxen suddenly stumbled; and, fearing lest the ark should fall, he suddenly stretched out his hand to prevent it. Had he touched the ark with impunity, the populace might have lost their respect for it and its sacred service; the example of Uzzah must have filled them with fear and sacred reverence; and, as to Uzzah, no man can doubt of his eternal safety. He committed a sin unto death, but doubtless the mercy of God was extended to his soul.

Verse 10. *But David carried it aside*] The house of Obed-edom appears to have been very near the city, which they were about to enter, but were prevented by this accident, and lodged the ark with the nearest friend.

Verse 11. *The Lord blessed Obed-edom*] And why? Because he had the ark of the Lord in his house. Whoever entertains God's messengers, or consecrates his house to the service of God, will infallibly receive God's blessing.

Verse 12. *So David—brought up the ark*] The *Vulgate* adds to this verse: *And David had seven choirs, and a calf for a sacrifice.* The *Septuagint* make a greater addition: "And he had seven choirs carrying the ark, a sacrifice, a calf, and lambs. And David played on harmonious organs before the Lord; and David was clothed with a costly tunic; and David, and all the house of Israel, brought the ark of the Lord with rejoicing, and the sound of a trumpet." Nothing of this is found in any MS., nor in the *Chaldee*, the *Syriac*, nor the *Arabic*, nor in the parallel place, 1 Chron. xv. 25.

Verse 14. *And David danced before the Lord*] Dancing is a religious ceremony among the Hindoos, and they consider it an act of devotion to their idols. It is evident that David considered it in the same light. What connection dancing can have with devotion I cannot tell. This I know, that unpremeditated and involuntary *skipping* may be the effect of sudden mental elation.

Verse 16. *She despised him in her heart.*] She did not blame him outwardly; she thought he had disgraced himself, but she kept her mind to herself.

Verse 18. *He blessed the people in the name of the Lord*] David acted here as priest, for it

A. M. 2962
B. C. 1042
An. Exod. Isr.
449
Anno ante
I. Olymp. 266

19 [h]And he dealt among all the people, *even* among the whole multitude of Israel, as well to the women as men, to every one a cake of bread, and a good piece *of flesh,* and a flagon *of wine.* So all the people departed every one to his house.

20 [i]Then David returned to bless his household. And Michal the daughter of Saul came out to meet David, and said, How glorious was the king of Israel to-day, who [k]uncovered himself to-day in the eyes of the handmaids of his servants, as one of the [l]vain fellows [m]shamelessly uncovereth himself!

---

[h]1 Chron. xvi. 3——[i]Psa. xxx. title——[k]Ver. 14, 16; 1 Sam. xix. 24——[l]Judg. ix. 4——[m]Or, *openly*

---

was the general prerogative of the priests to bless the people; but it appears, by both David and Solomon, that it was the prerogative of the kings also.

Verse 19. *A cake of bread*] Such as those which are baked without leaven, and are made very thin.

A good piece of flesh, *and a flagon* of wine.] The words *of flesh* and *of wine* we add; they are not in the Hebrew. The *Chaldee* translates *one part* and *one portion;* but all the other versions understand the Hebrew as we do.

Verse 20. *To bless his household.*] This was according to the custom of the *patriarchs,* who were priests in their own families. It is worthy of remark, that David is called *patriarch* by Stephen, Acts ii. 29, though living upwards of *four hundred* years after the termination of the patriarchal age.

How glorious was the king of Israel] This is a strong irony. From what Michal says, it is probable that David used some *violent* gesticulations, by means of which some parts of his body became uncovered. But it is very probable that we cannot guess all that was implied in this reproach.

Verse 21. It was *before the Lord, which chose*

A. M. 2962
B. C. 1042
An. Exod. Isr.
449
Anno ante
I. Olymp. 266

21 And David said unto Michal, *It was* before the LORD, [n]which chose me before thy father, and before all his house, to appoint me ruler over the people of the LORD, over Israel: therefore will I play before the LORD.

22 And I will yet be more vile than thus, and will be base in mine own sight: and [o]of the maid-servants which thou hast spoken of, of them shall I be had in honour.

23 Therefore Michal the daughter of Saul had no child [p]unto the day of her death.

---

[n]1 Sam. xiii. 14; xv. 28——[o]Or, *of the handmaids* of my servants——[p]See 1 Sam. xv. 35; Isa. xxii. 14; Matt. i. 25

---

me] David felt the reproach, and was strongly irritated, and seems to have spoken to Michal with sufficient asperity.

Verse 22. *I will yet be more vile*] The plain meaning of these words appears to be this: "I am not ashamed of *humbling* myself before that God who rejected thy father because of his *obstinacy* and *pride,* and chose me in his stead to rule his people; and even those maid-servants, when they come to know the motive of my conduct, shall acknowledge its propriety, and treat me with additional respect; and as for thee, thou shalt find that thy conduct is as little pleasing to God as it is to me." Then it is said, *Michal had no child till the day of her death:* probably David never more took her to his bed; or God, in his providence, might have subjected her to *barrenness,* which in Palestine was considered both a misfortune and a *reproach.* Michal formed her judgment without reason, and meddled with that which she did not understand. We should be careful how we attribute actions, the reasons of which we cannot comprehend, to motives which may appear to us unjustifiable or absurd. Rash judgments are *doubly* pernicious; they hurt those who form them, and those of whom they are formed.

CHAPTER VII

David consults the prophet Nathan about building a temple for the Lord, and is encouraged by him to do it, 1-3. That night Nathan receives a revelation from God, stating that Solomon, not David, should build the temple, 4-16. Nathan delivers the Divine message, and David magnifies God for his mercies, and makes prayer and supplication, 17-29.

A. M. 2962
B. C. 1042
An. Exod. Isr.
449
Anno ante
I. Olymp. 266

AND it came to pass, [a]when the king sat in his house, and the LORD had given him rest round about from all his enemies;

A. M. 2962
B. C. 1042
An. Exod. Isr.
449
Anno ante
I. Olymp. 266

2 That the king said unto Nathan the prophet, See now, I dwell in [b]a house of cedar, [c]but the ark of God dwelleth within [d]curtains.

---

[a]1 Chron. xvii. 1, &c.——[b]Chap. v. 11

[c]See Acts vii. 46——[d]Exod. xxvi. 1; xl. 21

NOTES ON CHAP. VII

Verse 1. *When the king sat in his house*] That is, when he became resident in the palace which Hiram, king of Tyre, had built for him.

And the Lord had given him rest] This was after he had defeated the Philistines, and cast them out of all the strong places in Israel which they had possessed after the overthrow of Saul; but before he had carried his arms beyond the

A. M. 2962
B. C. 1042
An. Exod. Isr. 449
Anno ante I. Olymp. 266

3 And Nathan said to the king, Go, do all that *is* [e]in thine heart; for the LORD *is* with thee.

4 And it came to pass that night, that the word of the LORD came unto Nathan, saying,

5 Go and tell [f]my servant David, Thus saith the LORD, [g]Shalt thou build me a house for me to dwell in?

6 Whereas I have not dwelt in *any* house [h]since the time that I brought up the children of Israel out of Egypt, even to this day; but have walked in [i]a tent and in a tabernacle.

7 In all *the places* wherein I have [k]walked with all the children of Israel spake I a word with [l]any of the tribes of Israel, whom I commanded [m]to feed my people Israel, saying, Why build ye not me a house of cedar?

8 Now therefore so shalt thou say unto my servant David, Thus saith the LORD of hosts, [n]I took thee from the sheep-cote, [o]from following the sheep, to be ruler over my people, over Israel:

9 And [p]I was with thee whithersoever thou wentest, [q]and have cut off all thine enemies [r]out of thy sight, and have made thee [s]a great name, like unto the name of the great *men* that *are* in the earth.

A. M. 2962
B. C. 1042
An. Exod. Isr. 449
Anno ante I. Olymp. 266

10 Moreover I will appoint a place for my people Israel, and will [t]plant them, that they may dwell in a place of their own, and move no more; [u]neither shall the children of wickedness afflict them any more, as before time,

11 And as [v]since the time that I commanded judges *to be* over my people Israel, and have [w]caused thee to rest from all thine enemies. Also the LORD telleth thee [x]that he will make thee a house.

12 And [y]when thy days be fulfilled, and thou [z]shalt sleep with thy fathers, [a]I will set up thy seed after thee, which shall proceed out of thy bowels, and I will establish his kingdom.

13 [b]He shall build a house for my name, and I will [c]establish the throne of his kingdom for ever.

---

[e]1 Kings viii. 17, 18; 1 Chron. xxii. 7; xxviii. 2 —— [f]Heb. *to my servant, to David* —— [g]See 1 Kings v. 3; viii. 19; 1 Chron. xxii. 8; xxviii. 3 —— [h]1 Kings viii. 16 —— [i]Exod. xl. 18, 19, 34 —— [k]Lev. xxvi. 11, 12; Deut. xxiii. 14 —— [l]1 Chron. xvii. 6, *any of the judges* —— [m]Chap. v. 2; Psa. lxxviii. 71, 72; Matt. ii. 6; Acts xx. 28 —— [n]1 Sam. xvi. 11, 12; Psa. lxxviii. 70 —— [o]Heb. *from after* —— [p]1 Sam. xviii. 14; chap. v. 10; viii. 6, 14

[q]1 Sam. xxxi. 6; Psa. lxxxix. 23 —— [r]Heb. *from thy face* —— [s]Gen. xii. 2 —— [t]Psa. xliv. 2; lxxx. 8; Jer. xxiv. 6; Amos ix. 15 —— [u]Psa. lxxxix. 22 —— [v]Judg. ii. 14, 15, 16; 1 Sam. xii. 9, 11; Psa. cvi. 42 —— [w]Ver. 1 —— [x]Exod. i. 21; ver. 27; 1 Kings xi. 38 —— [y]1 Kings ii. 1 —— [z]Deut. xxxi. 16; 1 Kings i. 21; Acts xiii. 36 —— [a]1 Kings viii. 20; Psa. cxxxii. 11 —— [b]1 Kings v. 5; vi. 12; viii. 19; 1 Chron. xxii. 10; xxviii. 6 —— [c]Ver. 16; Psa. lxxxix. 4, 29, 36, 37

---

land of Israel, against the Moabites, Syrians, and Idumeans. See chap. viii.

Verse 2. *I dwell in a house of cedar*] That is, a house whose principal beams, ceiling, and wainscot, were cedar.

Dwelleth within curtains.] Having no other residence but the tabernacle, which was a place covered with the *skins* of beasts, Exod. xxvi.

Verse 3. *Nathan said to the king*] In this case he gave his judgment as a pious and prudent man, not as a prophet; for the prophets were not always under a Divine afflatus; it was only at select times they were thus honoured.

For the Lord is *with thee.*] Thou hast his blessing in all that thou doest, and this pious design of thine will most certainly meet with his approbation.

Verse 5. *Shalt thou build me a house*] That is, Thou shalt not: this is the force of the interrogative in such a case.

Verse 7. *With any of the tribes*] "Spake I a word to any of the JUDGES" is the reading in the parallel place, 1 Chron. xvii. 6; and this is probably the true reading. Indeed, there is but *one letter* of difference between them, and letters which might be easily mistaken for each other: שבטי *shibtey, tribes*, is almost the same in *appearance* with שפטי *shophetey, judges;* the ב *beth* and the פ *pe* being the same letter, the apex under the upper stroke of the פ *pe* excepted. If this were but a little effaced in a MS., it would be mistaken for the other, and then we should have *tribes* instead of *judges.* This reading seems confirmed by ver. 11.

Verse 10. *I will appoint a place*] I *have* appointed a place, and *have* planted them. See the observations at the end.

Verse 11. *The Lord—will make thee a house.*] Thou hast in thy heart to make *me* a house; I have it in my heart to make *thee* a house: thy family shall be built up, and shall prosper in the throne of Israel; and thy spiritual posterity shall remain for ever. God is the author of all our holy purposes, as well as of our good works; he first excites them; and if we be workers together with him, he will crown and reward them as though they were our own, though he is their sole author.

Verse 13. *He shall build*] That is, Solomon shall build my temple, not thou, because *thou hast shed blood abundantly, and hast made great wars.* See 1 Chron. xxii. 8; and see also the observations at the end.

The throne of his kingdom for ever.] This is a reference to the government of the *spiritual kingdom*, the kingdom of the *Messiah*, agreeably to the predictions of the prophet long after, and by which this passage is illustrated: "Of the increase of *his* government and peace *there shall be* no end, upon the throne of David, and upon his kingdom, to order it, and to estab-

A. M. 2962
B. C. 1042
An. Exod. Isr.
449
Anno ante
I. Olymp. 266

14 [d]I will be his father, and he shall be my son. [e]If he commit iniquity, I will chasten him with the rod of men, and with the stripes of the children of men:

15 But my mercy shall not depart away from him, [f]as I took *it* from Saul, whom I put away before thee.

16 And [g]thine house and thy kingdom shall be established for ever before thee: thy throne shall be established for ever.

17 According to all these words, and according to all this vision, so did Nathan speak unto David.

18 Then went King David in, and sat before the LORD, and he said, [h]Who *am* I, O LORD God? and what *is* my house, that thou hast brought me hitherto?

19 And this was yet a small thing in thy sight, O LORD God; [i]but thou hast spoken also of thy servant's house for a great while to come. [k]And *is* this the [l]manner of man, O LORD God?

20 And what can David say more unto thee? for thou, LORD God, [m]knowest thy servant.

21 For thy word's sake, and according to thine own heart, hast thou done all these great things, to make thy servant know *them.*

22 Wherefore [n]thou art great, O LORD God: for [o]*there is* none like thee, neither *is there* any God beside thee, according to all that we have heard with our ears.

A. M. 2962
B. C. 1042
An. Exod. Isr.
449
Anno ante
I. Olymp. 266

23 And [p]what one nation in the earth *is* like thy people, *even* like Israel, whom God went to redeem for a people to himself, and to make him a name, and to do for you great things and terrible, for thy land, before [q]thy people, which thou redeemedst to thee from Egypt, *from* the nations and their gods?

24 For [r]thou hast confirmed to thyself thy people Israel *to be* a people unto thee for ever: [s]and thou, LORD, art become their God.

25 And now, O LORD God, the word that thou hast spoken concerning thy servant, and concerning his house, establish *it* for ever, and do as thou hast said.

26 And let thy name be magnified for ever, saying, The LORD of hosts is the God over Israel: and let the house of thy servant David be established before thee.

27 For thou, O LORD of hosts, God of Israel, hast [t]revealed to thy servant, saying, I will build thee a house: therefore hath thy servant found in his heart to pray this prayer unto thee.

28 And now, O LORD God, thou *art* that God, and [u]thy words be true, and thou hast promised this goodness unto thy servant:

29 Therefore now [v]let it please thee to bless the house of thy servant, that it may continue for ever before thee: for thou, O LORD God, hast spoken *it:* and with thy blessing let the house of thy servant be blessed [w]for ever.

---

[d]Psa. lxxxix. 26, 27; Heb. i. 5——[e]Psa. lxxxix. 30, 31, 32, 33——[f]1 Sam. xv. 23, 28; xvi. 14; 1 Kings xi. 13, 34 [g]Ver. 13; Psa. lxxxix. 36, 37; John xii. 34——[h]Gen. xxxii. 10——[i]Ver. 12, 13——[k]Isa. lv. 8——[l]Heb. *law* [m]Gen. xviii. 19; Psa. cxxxix. 1——[n]1 Chron. xvi. 25; 2 Chron. ii. 5; Psa. xlviii. 1; lxxxvi. 10; xcvi. 4; cxxxv. 5; cxlv. 3; Jer. x. 6

[o]Deut. iii. 24; iv. 35; xxxii. 39; 1 Sam. ii. 2; Psa. lxxxvi. 8; lxxxix. 6, 8; Isa. xlv. 5, 18, 22——[p]Deut. iv. 7, 32, 34; xxxiii. 29; Psa. cxlvii. 20——[q]Deut. ix. 26; Neh. i. 10——[r]Deut. xxvi. 18——[s]Psa. xlviii. 14 [t]Heb. *opened the ear;* Ruth iv. 4; 1 Sam. ix. 15——[u]John xvii. 17——[v]Heb. *be thou pleased, and bless*——[w]Chap. xxii. 51

---

lish it, with judgment and with justice, from henceforth even for EVER." Isa. ix. 7.

Verse 14. *If he commit iniquity*] Depart from the holy commandment delivered to him; *I will chasten him with the rod of men*—he shall have affliction, but his government shall not be utterly subverted. But this has a higher meaning. See the observations at the end.

Verse 15. *But my mercy shall not depart away from him, as I took* it *from Saul*] His house shall be a lasting house, and he shall die in the throne of Israel, his children succeeding him; and the spiritual seed, Christ, possessing and ruling in that throne to the end of time.

The family of Saul became *totally extinct;* the family of David remained till the incarnation. Joseph and Mary were both of that family; Jesus was the *only heir* to the kingdom of Israel; he did not choose to sit on the *secular* throne, he ascended the *spiritual* throne, and now he is exalted to the right hand of God, a

PRINCE and a Saviour, to give repentance and remission of sins. See the observations at the end of the chapter.

Many have applied these verses and their *parallels* to support the doctrine of *unconditional final perseverance;* but with it the text has nothing to do; and were we to press it, because of the antitype, Solomon, the doctrine would most evidently be ruined, for there is neither *proof* nor *evidence* of Solomon's salvation.

Verse 18. *Sat before the Lord*] Sometimes, when a Hindoo seeks a favour from a superior, he sits down in his presence in silence; or if he solicits some favour of a *god,* as *riches, children,* &c., he places himself before the idol, and remains in a *waiting posture,* or repeats the name of the god, counting the beads in his necklace.—WARD.

Verse 19. *And is this the manner of man*] Literally: *And this, O Lord God, is the law of*

Adam. Does he refer to the promise made to Adam, *The seed of the woman shall bruise the head of the serpent?* From my line shall the Messiah spring, and be the spiritual and triumphant King, for ever and ever. See the additions at the end.

Verse 20. *What can David say more*] How can I express my endless obligation to thee?

Verse 25. *And do as thou hast said.*] David well knew that all the promises made to himself and family were *conditional;* and therefore he prays that they may be fulfilled. His posterity did not walk with God, and therefore they were driven from the throne. It was taken from *them* by the neighbouring nations, and it is now in the hands of the Mohammedans; all the promises have failed to David and his *natural posterity,* and to Christ and his spiritual seed alone are they fulfilled. Had David's posterity been faithful, they would, according to the promises of God, have been sitting on the Israelitish throne at this day.

It is worthy of remark how seldom God employs a soldier in any spiritual work, just for the same reason as that given to David; and yet there have been several eminently pious men in the army, who have laboured for the conversion of sinners. I knew a remarkable instance of this; I was acquainted with Mr. *John Haime,* a well known preacher among the people called *Methodists.* He was a soldier in the queen's eighth regiment of dragoons, in Flanders, in the years 1739-46. He had his horse shot under him at the battle of *Fontenoy,* May 11, 1745; and was in the hottest fire of the enemy for above seven hours; he preached among his fellow soldiers frequently, and under the immediate patronage of his royal highness the *Duke of Cumberland,* commander-in-chief; and was the means of reforming and converting many hundreds of the soldiers. He was a man of amazing courage and resolution, and of inflexible loyalty. One having expressed a wonder "how he could reconcile *killing men* with *preaching the Gospel of the grace and peace of Christ,*" he answered, "I never killed a man." "How can you tell that? were you not in several battles?" "Yes, but I am confident I never killed nor wounded a man." "How was this? did you not do your *duty?*" "Yes, with all my might; but when in battle, either my horse jumped aside or was wounded, or was killed, or my carbine missed fire, and I could never draw the blood of the enemy." "And would you have done it if you could?" "Yes, I would have slain the whole French army, had it been in my power; I fought in a good cause, for a good king, and for my country; and though I struck in order to cut, and hack, and hew, on every side, I could kill no man." This is the substance of his answers to the above questions, and we see from it a remarkable interfering Providence; God had appointed this man to *build a spiritual house* in the British army, in Flanders, and would not permit him to shed the blood of his fellow creatures.

"This chapter is one of the most important in the Old Testament, and yet some of its most interesting verses are very improperly rendered in our translation; it therefore demands our most careful consideration. And as in the course of these *remarks* I propose to consider, and hope to explain, some of the prophecies descriptive of THE MESSIAH, which were fulfilled in JESUS CHRIST, among which prophecies *that*

contained in this chapter is worthy of particular attention, I shall introduce it with a general state of this great argument.

"It having pleased God that, between the time of *a Messiah* being promised and the time of his coming, there should be delivered by the prophets a variety of *marks* by which *the Messiah* was to be known, and distinguished from every other man; it was impossible for any one to prove himself *the Messiah,* whose *character* did not answer to these *marks;* and of course it was necessary that *all these criteria,* thus Divinely *foretold,* should be *fulfilled* in the character of *Jesus Christ.* That these prophetic descriptions of the Messiah were *numerous,* appears from Christ and his apostles, (Luke xxiv. 27, 44; Acts xvii. 2, 3; xxviii. 23, &c.,) who referred the Jews to the Old Testament as containing abundant evidence of *his* being THE MESSIAH, because *he fulfilled all the prophecies* descriptive of that *singular* character. The chief of these prophecies related to his being *miraculously born of a virgin;* the *time* and *place* of his birth; the *tribe* and *family* from which he was to descend; the miracles he was to perform; the *manner* of his preaching; his *humility* and *mean* appearance; the perfect *innocence* of his life; the greatness of his *sufferings;* the *treachery* of his betrayer; the circumstances of his *trial;* the nature of his *death* and *burial;* and his *miraculous resurrection.* Now amongst all the circumstances which form this chain of prophecy, the first reference made in the New Testament relates to his *descent;* for the New Testament begins with asserting that JESUS CHRIST *was the son of David, the son of Abraham.* As to the descent of Christ from ABRAHAM, every one knows that Christ was born a *Jew,* and consequently descended from Jacob, the grandson of Abraham. And we all know that the promise given to Abraham concerning the Messiah is *recorded* in the *history* of Abraham's life, in Gen. xxii. 18. Christ being also to descend from DAVID, there can be no doubt that this promise, as made to David, was recorded likewise in the *history* of David. It is remarkable that David's life is given more at large than that of any other person in the Old Testament; and can it be supposed that the historian omitted to record *that promise* which was more honourable to David than any other circumstance? The *record* of this promise, if written at all, must have been written in this chapter; in the message *from God by Nathan to David,* which is here inserted. Here, I am fully persuaded, the promise was, and still is, recorded; and the chief reason why our divines have so frequently missed it, or been so much perplexed about it, is owing to our very improper translation of the 10th and 14th verses.

"This wrong translation in a part of Scripture so very interesting, has been artfully laid hold of, and expatiated upon splendidly, by the deistical author of *The Ground and Reasons of the Christian Religion;* who pretends to demonstrate that the promise of a Messiah could not be here recorded. His reasons, hitherto I believe unanswered, are three: 1. Because, in ver. 10, the prophet speaks of *the future* prosperity of the Jews, as to be afterwards *fixed,* and *no more afflicted;* which circumstances are totally repugnant to the fate of the Jews, as connected with the birth and death of Christ. 2. Because the son here promised was (ver. 13) to *build a house;* which house, it is pretended, must mean the temple *of Solomon;* and of course *Solomon* must be the son here promised. And, 3. Because ver. 14 supposes that this son *might commit iniquity,* which could not be supposed of *the Messiah.* The first of these objections is founded on our wrong translation of ver. 10, where the words should be expressed as relating to the time *past* or *present.* For the prophet is there declaring what great things God *had already done* for David and his people; that he *had* raised David from the sheepfold to the throne; and that he *had* planted the Israelites in a place of safety, at rest from all those enemies who had so often before afflicted them. That the verbs ושמתי *vesamti,* and ונטעתי *unetati,* may be rendered in the time *past* or *present,* is allowed by our own translators; who here (ver. 11) render והניחתי *vahanichothi, and have caused thee to rest,* and also render והגיד *vehiggid, and telleth;* which construction, made necessary here by the context, might be confirmed by other proofs almost innumerable. The translation, therefore, should run thus: *I took thee from the sheepcote; and have made thee a great name; and I* HAVE APPOINTED *a place for my people Israel; and* HAVE PLANTED *them, that they may dwell in a place of their own, and move no more. Neither* DO *the children of wickedness afflict them any more; as before-time, and as since the time that I commanded judges to be over Israel: and I* HAVE CAUSED *thee to rest from all thine enemies.*

"Objection the second is founded on a mistake in the sense. David indeed had proposed to build a house for God, which God did not permit. Yet, approving the piety of David's intention, God was pleased to reward it by promising that he *would make a house for* DAVID; which house, to be thus erected by God, was certainly *not material,* or made of stones, but *a spiritual house,* or *family,* to be raised up for the honour of God, and the salvation of mankind. And this house, which God would make, was to be built by *David's* SEED; and this seed was to be raised up AFTER *David slept with his fathers;* which words clearly exclude *Solomon,* who was set up and placed upon the throne BEFORE *David was dead.* This building promised by God, was to be erected by one of David's descendants, who was also to be *an everlasting king;* and indeed the *house* and the *kingdom* were both of them to be *established for ever.* Now that this *house* or spiritual building was to be set up, together with a *kingdom,* by the Messiah, is clear from *Zechariah;* who very emphatically says, (ch. vi. 12, 13,) *Behold the man whose name is The Branch;* HE SHALL BUILD THE TEMPLE *of the Lord. Even* HE SHALL BUILD THE TEMPLE *of the Lord; and he shall bear the glory, and shall sit and rule upon his* THRONE, &c. Observe also the language of the *New* Testament. In 1 Cor. iii. 9-17, St. Paul says, *Ye are God's* BUILDING—*Know ye not that* YE *are the temple of God—the temple of God is holy, which temple* YE *are.* And the author of the Epistle to the Hebrews seems to have his eye upon this very promise in *Samuel* concerning a *son* to David, and of the *house* which he should build; when he says, (iii. 6,) CHRIST, AS A SON OVER HIS OWN HOUSE, WHOSE HOUSE ARE WE.

"As to the third and greatest difficulty, *that* also may be removed by a more just translation of ver. 14; for the Hebrew words do not properly signify what they are now made to speak. It is certain that the principal word, בהעותו

behaavotho, is not the active infinitive of *kal,* which would be בעותו, but העות from עוה is in *niphal,* as הגלות from גלה. It is also certain that a verb, which in the active voice signifies to *commit iniquity,* may, in the passive signify to *suffer for iniquity;* and hence it is that nouns from such verbs sometimes signify *iniquity,* sometimes *punishment.* See Lowth's Isaiah, p. 187, with many other authorities which shall be produced hereafter. The way being thus made clear, we are now prepared for abolishing our translation, *if he commit iniquity;* and also for adopting the true one, *even in his suffering for iniquity.* The Messiah, who is thus the person possibly here spoken of, will be made still more manifest from the whole verse thus translated: *I will be his father, and he shall be my son:* EVEN IN HIS SUFFERING FOR INIQUITY, *I shall chasten him with the rod of men,* (with the rod *due to men,) and with the stripes* (due to) *the children of* ADAM. And this construction is well supported by Isa. liii. 4, 5: *He hath carried* OUR SORROWS, (i. e., the sorrows *due to* us, and which we must otherwise have suffered,) *he was wounded for our transgressions, he was bruised for our iniquities: the chastisement of our peace was upon him; and with his stripes we are healed.* See note, p. 479, in Hallet, on Heb. xi. 26. Thus, then, God declares himself the Father of the Son here meant; (see also Heb. i. 5;) and promises that, even amidst the *sufferings* of this Son, (as they would be for the sins of others, not for his own,) his mercy should still attend him: nor should his favour be ever removed from *this king,* as it had been from *Saul.* And thus (as it follows) *thine house* (O David) *and thy kingdom shall,* in Messiah, *be established for ever before* ME: (before GOD:) *thy throne shall be established for ever.* Thus the angel, delivering his message to the virgin mother, Luke i. 32, 33, speaks as if he was quoting from this very prophecy: *The Lord God shall give unto him the throne of his father David, and he shall reign over the house of Jacob* FOR EVER: *and of his kingdom there shall be no end.* In ver. 16, לפניך *lephaneycha,* is rendered as לפני *lephanai,* on the authority of *three* Hebrew MSS., with the Greek and Syriac versions; and, indeed, nothing could be established *for ever* in the presence of *David,* but in the presence of God only.

"Having thus shown that the words fairly admit here the promise made to David, that *from his seed* should arise *Messiah, the everlasting King;* it may be necessary to add that, if the *Messiah* be the person here meant, as suffering innocently for the sins of others, *Solomon* cannot be; nor can this be a prophecy admitting such double sense, or be applied properly to two such opposite characters. *Of whom speaketh the prophet this? of* HIMSELF, *or of* SOME OTHER *man?* This was a question properly put by the Ethiopian treasurer, (Acts viii. 34,) who never dreamed that such a description as he was reading could relate to different persons; and Philip shows him that the person was *Jesus* only. So here it may be asked, *Of whom speaketh the prophet this? of Solomon, or of Christ?* It must be answered, *Of Christ:* one reason is, because the description does *not agree* to *Solomon;* and therefore *Solomon* being necessarily excluded in a single sense, must also be excluded in a double. Lastly, if it would be universally held absurd to consider the promise of Messiah made to Abraham as relating to *any other* person *besides* MESSIAH; why is there not an equal absurdity in giving a *double* sense to the promise of Messiah thus made to DAVID?

"Next to our present very improper translation, the cause of the common confusion here has been—not distinguishing the promise here made as to *Messiah* alone, from another made as to *Solomon* alone: the *first* brought by *Nathan*, the *second* by *Gad;* the *first* near the *beginning* of David's reign, the *second* near the *end* of it; the *first* relating to Messiah's *spiritual* kingdom, *everlasting without conditions,* the *second* relating *to the fate* of the *temporal* kingdom of Solomon, and his heirs, depending entirely on their *obedience* or *rebellion,* 1 Chron. xxii. 8-13, xxviii. 7. Let the first message be compared with this second in 1 Chron. xxii. 8-13, which the Syriac version (at ver. 8) tells us was delivered by *a prophet,* and the Arabian says by *the prophet* GAD. This *second* message was after David's *many wars,* when he *had shed much blood;* and it was this *second* message that, out of all David's sons, appointed *Solomon* to be his successor. At the time of the *first message* Solomon was *not born;* it being delivered soon after David became king at Jerusalem: but Solomon *was born* at the time of this *second message.* For though our translation very wrongly says, (1 Chron. xxii. 9,) *a son* SHALL BE *born to thee—and his name shall be Solomon;* yet the Hebrew text expressly speaks of him as *then born—Behold a son,* (נולד, *natus est,*) IS BORN *to thee:* and therefore the words following must be rendered, *Solomon* IS *his name, and I will give peace in his days: he shall build a house for my name,* &c.

"From David's address to God, after receiving the message by Nathan, it is plain that David understood the *Son promised* to be THE MESSIAH: in whom *his house* was to be *established for ever.* But the words which seem most expressive of this are in this verse now rendered very unintelligibly: *And is this the manner of man?* Whereas the words וזאת תורת האדם *vezoth torath haadam* literally signify, *and this is* (or *must be*) *the law of the man,* or *of the Adam;* i. e., this promise must relate to *the law* or ordinance made by God to *Adam,* concerning *the seed of the woman; the man,* or *the second*

ADAM; as the Messiah is expressly called by St. Paul, 1 Cor. xv. 45, 47. This meaning will be yet more evident from the parallel place, 1 Chron. xvii. 17, where the words of David are now miserably rendered thus: *And thou hast regarded me according to the estate of a man of high degree;* whereas the words וראיתני כתור ‎האדם המעלה *ureithani kethor haadam hammaalah* literally signify, *and thou hast regarded me according to the order of the* ADAM THAT IS FUTURE, or THE MAN THAT IS FROM ABOVE: (for the word המעלה *hammaalah* very remarkably signifies *hereafter* as to time, and *from above* as to place:) and thus St. Paul, including both senses—THE SECOND MAN *is* THE LORD FROM HEAVEN—and *Adam is the figure of him that was to come,* or *the future,* Rom. v. 14.—See the *Preface* of the late learned Mr. *Peters* on *Job,* referred to and confirmed as to this interesting point in a note subjoined to my Sermon on A VIRGIN SHALL CONCEIVE, &c., p. 46-52, 8vo. 1765. A part of that note here follows: 'The speech of David (2 Sam. vii. 18-29) is such as one might naturally expect from a person overwhelmed with the greatness of the promised blessing: for it is abrupt, full of wonder, and fraught with repetitions. *And now what can David say unto thee?* What, indeed! *For thou,* LORD GOD *knowest thy servant*—thou knowest the hearts of all men, and seest how full my own heart is. *For thy word's sake*—for the sake of former prophecies, *and according to thine own heart*—from the mere motive of thy wisdom and goodness, *hast thou done all these great things, to make thy servant know them.* I now perceive the reason of those miraculous providences which have attended me from my youth up; *taken from following the sheep,* and conducted through all difficulties *to be ruler of thy people;* and shall I distrust the promise now made me? *Thy words be true.* If the preceding remarks on this whole passage be just and well grounded, then may we see clearly the chief foundation of what St. Peter tells us (Acts ii. 30) concerning DAVID: that *being a prophet, and* KNOWING *that God had sworn with an oath to him, that of the fruit of his loins, according to the flesh, he would raise up* CHRIST *to sit on his throne; he, seeing this before, spake of the resurrection of Christ,* &c.' "

CHAPTER VIII

A. M. 2964
B. C. 1040
An. Exod. Isr. 451
Anno ante
I. Olymp. 264

AND [a]after this it came to pass, that David smote the Philistines, and subdued them: and David took [b]Metheg-ammah out of the hand of the Philistines.

2 And [c]he smote Moab, and measured them with a line, cast-

A. M. 2964
B. C. 1040
An. Exod. Isr. 451
Anno ante
I. Olymp. 264

---

[a]1 Chron. xviii. 1, &c.

[b]Or, *the bridle of Ammah*——[c]Num. xxiv. 17

NOTES ON CHAP. VIII

Verse 1. *David took Metheg-ammah*] This is variously translated. The Vulgate has, *Tulit David frœnum tributi, David removed the bond-*

age of the tribute, which the Israelites paid to the Philistines. Some think it means a *fortress,* city, or strong town; but no such place as *Metheg-ammah* is known. Probably the Vulgate is nearest the truth. The versions are all

A. M. 2964
B. C. 1040
An. Exod. Isr. 451
Anno ante
I. Olymp. 264 ing them down to the ground; even with two lines measured he to put to death, and with one full line to keep alive. And *so* the Moabites ᵈbecame David's servants, *and* ᵉbrought gifts.

3 David smote also ᶠHadadezer, the son of Rehob, king of ᵍZobah, as he went to recover ʰhis border at the river Euphrates.

4 And David took ⁱfrom him a thousand ᵏ*chariots,* and seven hundred horsemen, and twenty thousand footmen: and David ˡhoughed

all the chariot *horses,* but reserved of them *for* a hundred chariots. A. M. 2964
B. C. 1040
An. Exod. Isr. 451
Anno ante
I. Olymp. 264

5 ᵐAnd when the Syrians of Damascus came to succour Hadadezer king of Zobah, David slew of the Syrians two and twenty thousand men.

6 Then David put garrisons in Syria of Damascus: and the Syrians ⁿbecame servants to David, *and* brought gifts. ᵒAnd the LORD preserved David whithersoever he went.

7 And David took ᵖthe shields of gold that

ᵈVer. 6, 14——ᵉPsa. lxxii. 10; see 1 Sam. x. 27 ᶠOr, *Hadarezer,* 1 Chron. xviii. 3——ᵍChap. x. 6; Psa. lx. title——ʰGen. xv. 18

ⁱOr, *of his*——ᵏAs 1 Chron. xviii. 4——ˡJosh. xi. 6, 9 ᵐ1 Kings xi. 23, 24, 25——ⁿVer. 2——ᵒVer. 14; chap. vii. 9——ᵖSee 1 Kings x. 16

---

different. See the following comparison of the principal passages here collated with the parallel place in 1 Chron.

S. 8, 1—David took Metheg-ammah 3. David
C. 18, 1—*David took Gath and her towns.* 3. *David*
S. smote Hadadezer 4. And David took from him
C. *smote Hadarezer* 4. *And David took from him*
S. 1000 and 700 horsemen, and 20,000 foot.
C. 1000 *chariots, and 7000 horsemen, and 20,000 foot.*
S. 6. Then David put garrisons in Syria 8. And
C. 6. *Then David put* *in Syria* 8. *And*
S. from Betah and Berothai cities of Hadadezer. 9.
C. *from Tibhath and Chun cities of Hadarezer.* 9.
S. When Toi heard that David had smitten
C. *When Tou heard that David had smitten*
S. Hadadezer 10. Then Toi sent Joram his son
C. *Hadarezer* 10. *He sent Hadoram his son*
S. 12—Syria and Moab 13—Syrians, in the valley
C. 11—*Edom and Moab* 12—*Edomites, in the valley*
S. of salt, 18,000 17—Ahimelech—and Seraiah
C. *of salt,* 18,000 16—*Abimelech—and Shavsha*
S. was the scribe. 10, 16. Shobach the captain
C. *was scribe.* 19, 16. *Shophach the captain*

S. 17. David passed over Jordan, and came חלאמה
C. 17. *David passed over Jordan and came* אלהם
S. to Helam. 18. David slew 700
C. *upon them* 18. *David slew of the Syrians* 7000
S. chariots of the Syrians, and 40,000 horsemen,
C. *chariots,* *and 40,000 footmen;*
S. and smote Shobach, &c.
C. *and killed Shophach, &c.*

Verse 2. *And measured them with a line— even with two lines*] It has been generally conjectured that David, after he had conquered Moab, consigned *two-thirds* of the inhabitants *to the sword;* but I think the text will bear a meaning much more reputable to that king. The first clause of the verse seems to determine the sense; *he measured them with a line, casting them down to the ground*—to put to death, and with one line to keep alive. *Death* seems here to be referred to the cities by way of metaphor; and, from this view of the subject we may conclude that two-thirds of the cities, that is, the *strong places* of Moab, were erased; and not having strong places to trust to, the text adds, *So the Moabites became David's servants, and brought gifts,* i. e., were obliged to pay tribute. The word *line* may mean the same here as our *rod,* i. e., the instrument by which land is measured. There are various opinions on this verse, with which I shall not trouble

the reader. Much may be seen in *Calmet* and *Dodd.*

Verse 3. *David smote—Hadadezer*] He is supposed to have been king of all Syria, except Phœnicia; and, wishing to extend his dominions to the Euphrates, invaded a part of David's dominions which lay contiguous to it; but being attacked by David, he was totally routed.

Verse 4. *A thousand* chariots] It is strange that there were a *thousand* chariots, and only *seven hundred horsemen* taken, and twenty thousand foot. But as the discomfiture appears complete, we may suppose that the *chariots,* being less manageable, might be more easily taken, while the *horsemen* might, in general, make their escape. The *infantry* also seem to have been surrounded, when twenty thousand of them were taken prisoners.

David houghed all the chariot horses] If he did so, it was both unreasonable and inhuman; for, as he had so complete a victory, there was no danger of these horses falling into the enemy's hands; and if he did not choose to keep them, which indeed the law would not permit, he should have killed them outright; and then the poor innocent creatures would have been put out of pain. But does the text speak of houghing *horses* at all? It does not. Let us

hear; ויעקר דוד את כל הרכב *vayeakker David eth col harecheb, And David disjointed all the chariots,* except a hundred chariots which he reserved for himself. Now, this destruction of the *chariots,* was a matter of sound *policy,* and strict *piety.* God had censured those who trusted in chariots; *piety* therefore forbade David the use of them: and lest they should fall into the enemy's hands, and be again used against him, *policy* induced him to destroy them. The Septuagint render the words nearly as I have done, και παρελυσε Δαυιδ παντα τα αρματα.

He kept however one hundred; probably as a sort of baggage or forage wagons.

Verse 6. *Brought gifts*] Paid tribute.

Verse 7. *David took the shields of gold*] We know not what these were. Some translate *arms,* others *quivers,* others *bracelets,* others *collars,* and others *shields.* They were probably costly ornaments by which the Syrian soldiers were decked and distinguished. And those who are called *servants* here, were probably the *choice troops* or *body-guard* of Hada-

A. M. 2964
B. C. 1040
An. Exod. Isr.
451
Anno ante
I. Olymp. 264

were on the servants of Hadadezer, and brought them to Jerusalem.

8 And from qBetah, and from rBerothai, cities of Hadadezer, King David took exceeding much brass.

9 When sToi king of Hamath heard that David had smitten all the host of Hadadezer,

10 Then Toi sent tJoram his son unto King David, to usalute him, and to bless him, because he had fought against Hadadezer, and smitten him: for Hadadezer vhad wars with Toi. And *Joram* wbrought with him vessels of silver, and vessels of gold, and vessels of brass:

11 Which also king David xdid dedicate unto the LORD, with the silver and gold that he had dedicated of all nations which he subdued;

12 Of Syria, and of Moab, and of the children of Ammon, and of the Philistines, and of Amalek, and of the spoil of Hadad-

ezer, son of Rehob, king of Zobah.

A. M. 2964
B. C. 1040
An. Exod. Isr.
451
Anno ante
I. Olymp. 264

13 And David gat *him* a name when he returned from ysmiting of the Syrians in zthe valley of salt, abeing beighteen thousand *men.*

14 And he put garrisons in Edom; throughout all Edom put he garrisons, and call they of Edom became David's servants. dAnd the LORD preserved David whithersoever he went.

15 And David reigned over all Israel; and David executed judgment and justice unto all his people.

16 eAnd Joab the son of Zeruiah *was* over the host; and fJehoshaphat the son of Ahilud *was* grecorder;

17 And hZadok the son of Ahitub, and Ahimelech the son of Abiathar, *were* the priests; and Seraiah *was* the iscribe;

18 kAnd Benaiah the son of Jehoiada *was over* both the lCherethites and the Pelethites; and David's sons were mchief rulers.

---

qOr, *Tibhath*——rOr, *Chun,* 1 Chron. xviii. 8
sTou, 1 Chron. xviii. 9——t1 Chron. xviii. 10, *Hadoram*
uHeb. *ask him of peace*——vHeb. *was a man of wars with*
wHeb. *in his hand were*——x1 Kings vii. 51; 1 Chron.
xviii. 11; xxvi. 26——yHeb. *his smiting*——z2 Kings
xiv. 7——aSee 1 Chron. xviii. 12; Psa. lx. title——bOr,

slaying——cGen. xxvii. 29, 37, 40; Num. xxiv. 18
dVer. 6——eChap. xix. 13; xx. 23; 1 Chron. xi. 6; xviii. 15
f1 Kings iv. 3——gOr, *remembrancer, or, writer of chronicles*——h1 Chron. xxiv. 3——iOr, *secretary*
k1 Chron. xviii. 17——l1 Sam. xxx. 14——mOr, *princes;*
chap. xx. 26

---

dezer, as *the argyraspides* were of Alexander the Great. See Quintus Curtius.

Verse 9. *Toi king of Hamath*] Hamath is supposed to be the famous city of *Emesa,* situated on the *Orontes,* in Syria. This was contiguous to Hadadezer; and led him to wage war with Toi, that he might get possession of his territories. For a comparison of the 10th verse, see 1 Chron. xviii. 9.

Verse 13. *David gat him a name*] Became a very celebrated and eminent man. The Targum has it, *David collected troops;* namely, to *recruit* his army when he returned from smiting the Syrians. His many battles had no doubt greatly thinned his army.

The valley of salt] Supposed to be a large plain abounding in this mineral, about a league from the city of *Palmyra* or Tadmor in the wilderness.

Verse 4. *He put garrisons in Edom*] He repaired the strong cities which he had taken, and put garrisons in them to keep the country in awe.

Verse 16. *Joab—was over the host*] General and commander-in-chief over all the army.

Ahilud—recorder] מזכיר *mazkir, remembrancer;* one who kept a strict journal of all

the proceedings of the king and operations of his army; a chronicler. See the margin.

Verse 17. *Seraiah—the scribe*] Most likely the king's private secretary. See the margin.

Verse 18. *Benaiah*] The chief of the second class of David's worthies. We shall meet with him again.

The Cherethites and the Pelethites] The former supposed to be those who accompanied David when he fled from Saul; the latter, those who came to him at Ziklag. But the Targum translates these two names thus, *the archers and the slingers;* and this is by far the most likely. It is not at all probable that David was without a company both of *archers* and *slingers.* The *bow* is celebrated in the funeral lamentation over Saul and Jonathan; and the *sling* was renowned as the weapon of the Israelites, and how expert David was in the use of it we learn from the death of Goliath. I take for granted that the Chaldee paraphrast is correct. No weapons then known were equally powerful with these; the spears, swords, and javelins, of other nations, were as stubble before them. The bow was the grand weapon of our English ancestors; and even after the invention of firearms, they were with difficulty persuaded to prefer them and leave their archery.

CHAPTER IX

David inquires after the family of Jonathan, and is informed of Mephibosheth his son, 1–4. He sends for him and gives him all the land of Saul, 5–8; and appoints Ziba the servant of Saul, and his family, to till the ground for Mephibosheth, 9–13.

A. M. 2964
B. C. 1040
An. Exod. Isr.
451
Anno ante
I. Olymp. 264

AND David said, Is there yet any that is left of the house of Saul, that I may ^ashow him kindness for Jonathan's sake?

2 And *there was* of the house of Saul a servant whose name *was* ^bZiba. And when they had called him unto David, the king said unto him, *Art* thou Ziba? And he said, Thy servant *is* he.

3 And the king said, *Is* there not yet any of the house of Saul, that I may show ^cthe kindness of God unto him? And Ziba said unto the king, Jonathan hath yet a son, *which is* ^dlame on *his* feet.

4 And the king said unto him, Where *is* he? and Ziba said unto the king, Behold, he *is* in the house of ^eMachir, the son of Ammiel, in Lo-debar.

5 Then King David sent, and fetched him out of the house of Machir, the son of Ammiel, from Lo-debar.

6 Now when ^fMephibosheth, the son of Jonathan, the son of Saul, was come unto David, he fell on his face, and did reverence.

And David said, Mephibosheth. And he answered, Behold thy servant!

A. M. 2964
B. C. 1040
An. Exod. Isr.
451
Anno ante
I. Olymp. 264

7 And David said unto him, Fear not: ^gfor I will surely show thee kindness for Jonathan thy father's sake, and will restore thee all the land of Saul thy father; and thou shalt eat bread at my table continually.

8 And he bowed himself, and said, What *is* thy servant, that thou shouldest look upon such ^ha dead dog as I *am?*

9 Then the king called to Ziba, Saul's servant, and said unto him, ⁱI have given unto thy master's son all that pertained to Saul and to all his house.

10 Thou therefore, and thy sons, and thy servants, shall till the land for him, and thou shalt bring in *the fruits,* that thy master's son may have food to eat: but Mephibosheth thy master's son ^kshall eat bread alway at my table. Now Ziba had ^lfifteen sons and twenty servants.

11 Then said Ziba unto the king, According to all that my lord the king hath commanded

---

^a1 Sam. xviii. 3; xx. 14, 15, 16, 17, 42; Prov. xxvii. 10
^bChap. xvi. 1; xix. 17, 29——^c1 Sam. xx. 14——^dChap. iv. 4——^eChap. xvii. 27

^fCalled *Merib-baal,* 1 Chron. viii. 34——^gVer. 1, 3
^h1 Sam. xxiv. 14; chap. xvi. 9——ⁱSee chap. xvi. 4;
xix. 29——^kVer. 7, 11, 13; chap. xix. 28——^lCh. xix. 17

NOTES ON CHAP. IX

Verse 1. *Is there yet any that is left*]
David recollecting the covenant made with his friend Jonathan, now inquires after his family. It is supposed that *political* considerations prevented him from doing this *sooner.* *Reasons of state* often destroy all the charities of life.

Verse 3. *That I may show the kindness of God unto him?*] That is, the *utmost,* the *highest degrees of kindness;* as the *hail of God,* is very great hail, the *mountains of God,* exceeding high mountains: besides, this kindness was according to the *covenant of God* made between him and the family of Jonathan.

Verse 4. *Lo-debar.*] Supposed to have been situated beyond Jordan; but there is nothing certain known concerning it.

Verse 7. *Will restore thee all the land*] I believe this means the *mere family estate* of the house of Kish, which David as *king* might have retained, but which most certainly belonged, according to the Israelitish law, to the descendants of the family.

And thou shalt eat bread at my table] This was kindness, (the giving up the land was *justice,*) and it was the highest honour that any subject could enjoy, as we may see from the

reference made to it by our Lord, Luke xxii. 30: *That ye may eat and drink at my table in my kingdom.* For such a person David could do no more. His lameness rendered him unfit for any public employment.

Verse 9. *I have given unto thy master's son*] Unless Ziba had been servant of Jonathan, this seems to refer to Micha, son of Mephibosheth, and so some understand it; but it is more likely that Mephibosheth is meant, who is called *son of Saul* instead of *grandson.* Yet it is evident enough that the produce of the land went to the support of Micha, (see ver. 10,) for the father was provided for at the table of David; but all the patrimony belonged to Mephibosheth.

Verse 10. *Thou therefore, and thy sons—shall till the land*] It seems that Ziba and his family had the care of the whole estate, and cultivated it at their own expense, yielding the half of the produce to the family of Mephibosheth. Ziba was properly the *hind,* whose duty and interest it was to take proper care of the ground, for the better it was cultivated the more it produced; and his *half* would consequently be the greater.

Verse 11. *So shall thy servant do.*] The promises of Ziba were fair and specious, but he was a traitor in his heart, as we shall see in

A. M. 2964
B. C. 1040
An. Exod. Isr.
451
Anno ante
I. Olymp. 264

his servant, so shall thy servant do. As for Mephibosheth, *said the king,* he shall eat at my table, as one of the king's sons.

12 And Mephibosheth had a young son, [m]whose name *was* Micha. And all that dwelt

in the house of Ziba *were* servants unto Mephibosheth.

13 So Mephibosheth dwelt in Jerusalem: [n]for he did eat continually at the king's table; and [o]was lame on both his feet.

A. M. 2964
B. C. 1040
An. Exod. Isr.
451
Anno ante
I. Olymp. 264

---

[m]1 Chron. viii. 34

[n]Ver. 7, 10——[o]Ver. 3

---

the rebellion of Absalom, and David's indulgence to this man is a blot in his character; at this time however he suspected no evil; circumstances alone can develope the human character. The *internal* villain can be known only when circumstances occur which can call

his propensities into action; till then he may be reputed an honest man.

Verse 13. *Did eat continually at the king's table*] He was fit for no public office, but was treated by the king with the utmost respect and affection.

CHAPTER X

The king of Ammon being dead, David sends ambassadors to comfort his son Hanun, 1, 2. Hanun, misled by his courtiers, treats the messengers of David with great indignity, 3–5. The Ammonites, justly dreading David's resentment, send, and hire the Syrians to make war upon him, 6. Joab and Abishai meet them at the city of Medeba, and defeat them, 7–14. The Syrians collect another army, but are defeated by David with great slaughter, and make with him a separate peace, 15–19.

A. M. 2967
B. C. 1037
An. Exod. Isr.
454
Anno ante
I. Olymp. 261

AND it came to pass after this, that the [a]king of the children of Ammon died, and Hanun his son reigned in his stead.

2 Then said David, I will show kindness unto Hanun the son of Nahash, as his father showed kindness unto me. And David sent to comfort him by the hand of his servants for his father. And David's servants came into the land of the children of Ammon.

3 And the princes of the children of Ammon said unto Hanun their lord, [b]Thinkest thou that David doth honour thy father, that he hath sent comforters unto thee? hath not

David *rather* sent his servants unto thee, to search the city, and to spy it out, and to overthrow it?

4 Wherefore Hanun took David's servants, and shaved off the one half of their beards, and cut off their garments in the middle, [c]*even* to their buttocks, and sent them away.

5 When they told *it* unto David, he sent to meet them, because the men were greatly ashamed: and the king said, Tarry at Jericho until your beards be grown, and *then* return.

6 And when the children of Ammon saw

A. M. 2967
B. C. 1037
An. Exod. Isr.
454
Anno ante
I. Olymp. 261

---

[a]1 Chron. xix. 1, &c.——[b]Heb. *In thine*

eyes doth David?——[c]Isa. xx. 4; xlvii. 2

NOTES ON CHAP. X

Verse 2. *I will show kindness unto Hanun the son of Nahash*] We do not know exactly the nature or extent of the obligation which David was under to the king of the Ammonites; but it is likely that the Nahash here mentioned was the same who had attacked Jabesh-gilead, and whom Saul defeated: as David had taken refuge with the Moabites, (1 Sam. xxii. 3,) and this was contiguous to the king of the Ammonites, his hatred to Saul might induce him to show particular kindness to David.

Verse 3. *Thinkest thou that David doth honour thy father*] It has been a matter of just complaint through all the history of mankind, that there is little sincerity in courts. Courtiers, especially, are suspicious of each other, and often mislead their sovereigns. They feel themselves to be insincere, and suspect others to be so too.

Verse 4. *Shaved off the one half of their*

beards] The *beard* is held in high respect in the East: the possessor considers it his greatest ornament; often swears by it; and, in matters of great importance, *pledges* it. Nothing can be more secure than a pledge of this kind; its owner will redeem it at the hazard of his life. The beard was never cut off but in *mourning,* or as a sign of *slavery.* Cutting off half of the beard and the clothes rendered the men ridiculous, and made them look like slaves: what was done to these men was an accumulation of insult.

Verse 5. *Tarry at Jericho*] This city had not been rebuilt since the time of Joshua; but there were, no doubt, many cottages still remaining, and larger dwellings also, but the *walls* had not been repaired. As it must have been comparatively a *private* place, it was proper for these men to tarry in, as they would not be exposed to public notice.

Verse 6. *The children of Ammon saw that they stank*] That is, that their conduct ren-

A. M. 2967
B. C. 1037
An. Exod. Isr.
454
Anno ante
I. Olymp. 261

that they ᵈstank before David, the children of Ammon sent and hired ᵉthe Syrians of Beth-rehob, and the Syrians of Zoba, twenty thousand footmen, and of King Maacah a thousand men, and of ᶠIsh-tob twelve thousand men.

7 And when David heard of *it,* he sent Joab, and all the host of ᵍthe mighty men.

8 And the children of Ammon came out, and put the battle in array at the entering in of the gate: and ʰthe Syrians of Zoba, and of Rehob, and Ish-tob, and Maacah, *were* by themselves in the field.

9 When Joab saw that the front of the battle was against him before and behind, he chose of all the choice *men* of Israel, and put *them* in array against the Syrians:

10 And the rest of the people he delivered into the hand of Abishai his brother, that he might put *them* in array against the children of Ammon.

11 And he said, If the Syrians be too strong for me, then thou shalt help me: but if the children of Ammon be too strong for thee, then I will come and help thee.

12 ⁱBe of good courage, and let us ᵏplay the men for our people, and for the cities of our God: and ˡthe Lord do that which seemeth him good.

13 And Joab drew nigh, and the people that *were* with him, unto the battle against the Syrians: and they fled before him.

14 And when the children of Ammon saw that the Syrians were fled, then fled they also before Abishai, and entered into the city. So Joab returned from the children of Ammon, and came to Jerusalem.

A. M. 2967
B. C. 1037
An. Exod. Isr.
454
Anno ante
I. Olymp. 261

15 And when the Syrians saw that they were smitten before Israel, they gathered themselves together.

A. M. 2968
B. C. 1036
An. Exod. Isr.
455
Anno ante
I. Olymp. 260

16 And Hadarezer sent, and brought out the Syrians that *were* beyond ᵐthe river: and they came to Helam; and ⁿShobach the captain of the host of Hadarezer *went* before them.

17 And when it was told David, he gathered all Israel together, and passed over Jordan, and came to Helam. And the Syrians set themselves in array against David, and fought with him.

18 And the Syrians fled before Israel; and David slew *the men of* seven hundred chariots of the Syrians, and forty thousand ᵒhorsemen, and smote Shobach the captain of their host, who died there.

19 And when all the kings *that were* servants of Hadarezer saw that they were smitten before Israel, they made peace with Israel, and ᵖserved them. So the Syrians feared to help the children of Ammon any more.

ᵈGen. xxxiv. 30; Exod. v. 21; 1 Sam. xiii. 4——ᵉChap. viii. 3, 5——ᶠOr, *the men of Tob:* see Judg. xi. 3, 5 ᵍChap. xxiii. 8——ʰVer. 6——ⁱDeut. xxxi. 6

ᵏ1 Sam. iv. 9; 1 Cor. xvi. 13——ˡ1 Sam. iii. 18 ᵐThat is, *Euphrates*——ⁿOr, *Shophach,* 1 Chron. xix. 16 ᵒ1 Chron. xix. 18, *footmen*——ᵖChap. viii. 6

---

dered them abominable. This is the Hebrew mode of expressing such a feeling. See Gen. xxxiv. 30.

The Syrians of Beth-rehob] This place was situated at the extremity of the valley between Libanus and Anti-libanus. The Syrians of Zoba were subject to Hadadezer. *Maacah* was in the vicinity of Mount Hermon, beyond Jordan, in the Trachonitis.

Ish-tob] This was probably the same with *Tob,* to which Jephthah fled from the cruelty of his brethren. It was situated in the land of Gilead.

Verse 7. *All the host of the mighty*] All his *worthies,* and the flower of his army.

Verse 8. *At the entering in of the gate*] This was the city of *Medeba,* as we learn from 1 Chron. xix. 7.

Verse 9. *Before and behind*] It is probable that one of the armies was in the *field,* and the other in the *city,* when Joab arrived. When he fronted this army, the other appears to have issued from the city, and to have taken him in the rear; he was therefore obliged to divide his army as here mentioned; one part to face the Syrians commanded by himself, and the other to face the Ammonites commanded by his brother Abishai.

Verse 12. *Be of good courage*] This is a very fine military address, and is equal to any thing in ancient or modern times. Ye fight *pro aris et focis;* for every good, sacred and civil; for God, for your families, and for your country.

Verse 14. *The Syrians were fled*] They betook themselves to their own confines, while the Ammonites escaped into their own city.

Verse 16. *The Syrians that* were *beyond the river*] That is, the *Euphrates.*

Hadarezer] This is the same that was overthrown by David, chap. viii., and there called *Hadadezer;* which is the reading here of about *thirty* of Kennicott's and De Rossi's MSS. But the ר *resh* and ד *daleth* are easily interchanged.

Verse 17. *David—gathered all Israel together*] He thought that such a war required his own presence.

Verse 18. Seven hundred *chariots—and forty thousand* horsemen] In the parallel place, 1

Chron. xix. 18, it is said, *David slew of the Syrians* SEVEN THOUSAND *men*, which fought in *chariots*. It is difficult to ascertain the right number in this and similar places. It is very probable that, in former times, the Jews expressed, as they often do *now*, their numbers, not by *words at full length*, but by *numeral letters;* and, as many of the letters bear a great similarity to each other, mistakes might easily creep in when the numeral letters came to be expressed by *words at full length*. This alone will account for the many mistakes which we find in the numbers in these books, and renders a mistake here very probable. The letter ז *zain*, with a dot above, stands for *seven thousand*, ן *nun* for *seven hundred:* the great similarity of these letters might easily cause the one to be mistaken for the other, and so produce an error in this place.

Verse 19. *Made peace with Israel*] They made this peace separately, and were obliged to pay tribute to the Israelites. Some copies of the Vulgate add here after the word *Israel*, *Expaverunt et fugerunt quinquaginta et octo millia coram Israel;* "and they were panic-struck, and fled *fifty-eight thousand* of them before Israel." This reading is nowhere else to be found. "Thus," observes Dr. *Delaney*, "the arms of David were blessed; and God accom-

plished the promises which he had made to Abraham, Gen. xv. 18, and renewed to Joshua, i. 2, 4." And thus, in the space of *nineteen* or *twenty* years, David had the good fortune to finish gloriously *eight* wars, all righteously undertaken, and all honourably terminated; viz., 1. The civil war with *Ish-bosheth*. 2. The war against the *Jebusites*. 3. The war against the *Philistines* and their *allies*. 4. The war against the *Philistines* alone. 5. The war against the *Moabites*. 6. The war against *Hadadezer*. 7. The war against the *Idumeans*. 8. The war against the *Ammonites* and *Syrians*. This last victory was soon followed by the complete conquest of the kingdom of the Ammonites, abandoned by their allies. What glory to the monarch of Israel, had not the splendour of this illustrious epoch been obscured by a complication of crimes, of which one could never have even suspected him capable!

WE have now done with the first part of this book, in which we find David great, glorious, and pious: we come to the *second* part, in which we shall have the pain to observe him fallen from God, and his horn defiled in the dust by crimes of the most flagitious nature. Let him that most assuredly standeth take heed lest he fall.

CHAPTER XI

David sends Joab against the Ammonites, who besieges the city of Rabbah, 1. He sees Bath-sheba, the wife of Uriah, bathing; is enamoured of her; sends for and takes her to his bed, 2–4. She conceives, and informs David, 5. David sends to Joab, and orders him to send to him Uriah, 6. He arrives; and David having inquired the state of the army, dismisses him, desiring him to go to his own house, 7, 8. Uriah sleeps at the door of the king's house, 9. The next day the king urges him to go to his house; but he refuses to go, and gives the most pious and loyal reasons for his refusal, 10–11. David after two days sends him back to the army, with a letter to Joab, desiring him to place Uriah in the front of the battle, that he may be slain, 12–15. He does so; and Uriah falls, 16, 17. Joab communicates this news in an artful message to David, 18–25. David sends for Bath-sheba and takes her to wife, and she bears him a son, 26, 27.

A. M. 2969
B. C. 1035
An. Exod. Isr.
456
Anno ante
I. Olymp. 259

AND it came to pass ª after the year was expired, at the time when kings go forth *to battle,* that ᵇDavid sent Joab, and his servants with him, and all Israel; and they destroyed the children of Ammon, and besieged Rabbah. But David tarried still at Jerusalem.

2 And it came to pass in an evening-tide, that David arose from off his bed, ᶜand walked upon the roof of the king's house: and from the roof he ᵈsaw a woman washing herself; and the woman *was* very beautiful to look upon.

3 And David sent and inquired after the

A. M. 2969
B. C. 1035
An. Exod. Isr.
456
Anno ante
I. Olymp. 259

ªHeb. *at the return of the year*, 1 Kings xx. 22, 26; 2 Chron. xxxvi. 10

ᵇ1 Chron. xx. 1——ᶜDeut. xxii. 8——ᵈGen. xxxiv. 2; Job xxxi. 1; Matt. v. 28

NOTES ON CHAP. XI

Verse 1. *When kings go forth*] This was about a year after the war with the Syrians spoken of before, and about the *spring* of the year, as the most proper season for military operations. Calmet thinks they made *two campaigns*, one in *autumn* and the other in *spring;* the *winter* being in many respects inconvenient, and the *summer* too hot.

Verse 2. *In an evening-tide—David arose*] He had been reposing on the roof of his house, to enjoy the breeze, as the noonday was too hot for the performance of business. This is still a constant custom on the flat-roofed houses in the East.

He saw a woman washing herself] How could any woman of delicacy expose herself where she could be so fully and openly viewed? Did she not know that she was at least in view of the king's terrace? Was there no *design* in all this? *Et fugit ad salices, et se cupit ante videri.* In a Bengal town pools of water are to be seen everywhere, and women *may be seen* morning and evening *bathing* in them, and carrying water home. Thus David might have seen Bath-sheba, and no blame attach to her.

Verse 4 shows us that this washing was at the termination of a particular period.

Verse 3. *The daughter of Eliam*] Called, 1 Chron. iii. 5, Ammiel; a word of the same meaning, *The people of my God, The God of my*

A. M. 2969
B. C. 1035
An. Exod. Isr.
456
Anno ante
I. Olymp. 259

woman. And *one* said, *Is* not this ᵉBath-sheba, the daughter of ᶠEliam, the wife ᵍof Uriah the Hittite?

4 And David sent messengers, and took her; and she came in unto him, and ʰhe lay with her; ⁱfor she was ᵏpurified from her uncleanness: and she returned unto her house.

5 And the woman conceived, and sent and told David, and said, I *am* with child.

6 And David sent to Joab, *saying,* Send me Uriah the Hittite. And Joab sent Uriah to David.

7 And when Uriah was come unto him, David demanded of him ˡhow Joab did, and how the people did, and how the war prospered.

8 And David said to Uriah, Go down to thy house, and ᵐwash thy feet. And Uriah departed out of the king's house, and there ⁿfollowed him a mess *of meat* from the king.

9 But Uriah slept at the door of the king's house with all the servants of his lord, and went not down to his house.

10 And when they had told David, saying,

A. M. 2969
B. C. 1035
An. Exod. Isr.
456
Anno ante
I. Olymp. 259

Uriah went not down unto his house, David said unto Uriah, Camest thou not from *thy* journey? why *then* didst thou not go down unto thine house?

11 And Uriah said unto David, ᵒThe ark, and Israel, and Judah, abide in tents; and ᵖmy lord Joab, and the servants of my lord, are encamped in the open fields; shall I then go into mine house, to eat and to drink, and to lie with my wife? *as* thou livest, and *as* thy soul liveth, I will not do this thing.

12 And David said to Uriah, Tarry here to-day also, and to-morrow I will let thee depart. So Uriah abode in Jerusalem that day, and the morrow.

13 And when David had called him, he did eat and drink before him; and he made him �q drunk; and at even he went out to lie on his bed ʳwith the servants of his lord, but went not down to his house.

14 And it came to pass in the morning, that David ˢwrote a letter to Joab, and sent *it* by the hand of Uriah.

ᵉOr, *Bath-shuah*, 1 Chron. iii. 5——ᶠOr, *Ammiel* ᵍChap. xxiii. 39——ʰPsa. li. title; James i. 14——ⁱOr, *and when she had purified herself, &c., she returned* ᵏLev. xv. 19, 28; xviii. 19

ˡHeb. *of the peace of*, &c.——ᵐGen. xviii. 4; xix. 2 ⁿHeb. *went out after him*——ᵒChap. vii. 2, 6——ᵖChap. xx. 6——q Gen. xix. 33, 35——ʳVer. 9——ˢSee 1 Kings xxi. 8, 9

---

people. This name expressed the covenant—*I will be your God; We will be thy people.*

Verse 4. *And she came in unto him*] We hear nothing of her reluctance, and there is no evidence that she was taken by force.

Verse 5. *And the woman conceived*] A proof of the observation on ver. 4; as that is the time in which women are most apt to conceive.

Verse 8. *Go down to thy house, and wash thy feet.*] Uriah had come off a journey, and needed this refreshment; but David's design was that he should go and lie with his wife, that the child now conceived should pass for his, the honour of Bath-sheba be screened, and his own crime concealed. At this time he had no design of the murder of Uriah, nor of taking Bath-sheba to wife.

A mess of meat *from the king.*] All this was artfully contrived.

Verse 9. *Slept at the door*] That is, in one of the apartments or niches in the court of the king's house. But in Bengal servants and others generally sleep on the verandahs or porches in face of their master's house.

Verse 10. *Camest thou not from thy journey?*] It is not *thy* duty to keep watch or guard; thou art come from a journey, and needest rest and refreshment.

Verse 11. *The ark, and Israel—abide in tents*] It appears therefore that they had taken the ark with them to battle.

This was the answer of a brave, generous, and disinterested man. I will not indulge myself while all my fellow soldiers are exposed to

hardships, and even the ark of the Lord in danger. Had Uriah no suspicion of what had been done in his absence?

Verse 13. *He made him drunk*] Supposing that in this state he would have been off his guard, and hastened down to his house.

Verse 14. *David wrote a letter*] This was the sum of treachery and villany. He made this most noble man the carrier of letters which prescribed the mode in which he was to be murdered. This case some have likened to that of Bellerophon, son of Glaucus, king of Ephyra, who being in the court of Prœtus, king of the Argives, his queen Antia, or as others Sthenobœa, fell violently in love with him; but he, refusing to gratify her criminal passions, was in revenge accused by her to Prœtus her husband, as having attempted to corrupt her. Prœtus not willing to violate the laws of hospitality by slaying him in his own house, wrote letters to Jobates, king of Lycia, the father of Sthenobœa, and sent them by the hand of Bellerophon, stating his crime, and desiring Jobates to put him to death. To meet the wishes of his son-in-law, and keep his own hands innocent of blood, he sent him with a small force against a very warlike people called the *Solymi;* but, contrary to all expectation, he not only escaped with his life, but gained a complete victory over them. He was afterwards sent upon several equally dangerous and hopeless expeditions, but still came off with success; and to reward him Jobates gave him one of his daughters to wife, and a part of his

A. M. 2969
B. C. 1035
An. Exod. Isr.
456
Anno ante
I. Olymp. 259

15 And he wrote in the letter, saying, Set ye Uriah in the forefront of the [t]hottest battle, and retire ye [u]from him, that he may [v]be smitten, and die.

16 And it came to pass, when Joab observed the city, that he assigned Uriah unto a place where he knew that valiant men *were*.

17 And the men of the city went out, and fought with Joab: and there fell *some* of the people of the servants of David; and Uriah the Hittite died also.

18 Then Joab sent and told David all the things concerning the war;

19 And charged the messenger, saying, When thou hast made an end of telling the matters of the war unto the king,

20 And if so be that the king's wrath arise, and he say unto thee, Wherefore approached ye so nigh unto the city when ye did fight? knew ye not that they would shoot from the wall?

21 Who smote [w]Abimelech the son of [x]Jerubbesheth? did not a woman cast a piece of a millstone upon him from the wall, that he died in Thebez? why went ye nigh the wall?

then say thou, Thy servant Uriah the Hittite is dead also.

A. M. 2969
B. C. 1035
An. Exod. Isr.
456
Anno ante
I. Olymp. 25&

22 So the messenger went, and came and showed David all that Joab had sent him for.

23 And the messenger said unto David, Surely the men prevailed against us, and came out unto us into the field, and we were upon them even unto the entering of the gate.

24 And the shooters shot from off the wall upon thy servants; and *some* of the king's servants be dead, and thy servant Uriah the Hittite is dead also.

25 Then David said unto the messenger, Thus shalt thou say unto Joab, Let not this thing [y]displease thee, for the sword devoureth [z]one as well as another: make thy battle more strong against the city, and overthrow it: and encourage thou him.

26 And when the wife of Uriah heard that Uriah her husband was dead, she mourned for her husband.

27 And when the mourning was past, David sent and fetched her to his house, and she [a]became his wife, and bare him a son. But the thing that David had done [b]displeased the LORD.

---

[t]Heb. *strong*——[u]Heb. *from after him*——[v]Chap. xii. 9
[w]Judg. ix. 53——[x]Judg. vi. 32, *Jerubbaal*

[y]Heb. *be evil in thine eyes*——[z]Heb. *so and such*
[a]Chap. xii. 9——[b]Heb. *was evil in the eyes of*

---

kingdom. Sthenobœa, hearing this, through rage and despair killed herself.

I have given this history at large, because many have thought it not only to be parallel to that of Uriah, but to be a fabulous formation from the Scripture fact: for my own part, I scarcely see in them any correspondence, but in the simple circumstance that both carried those letters which contained their own condemnation. From the fable of Bellerophon came the proverb, *Bellerophontis literas portare*, "to carry one's own condemnation."

Verse 17. *Uriah the Hittite died also.*] He was led to the attack of a place defended by valiant men; and in the heat of the assault, Joab and his men retired from this brave soldier, who cheerfully gave up his life for his king and his country.

Verse 20. *If—the king's wrath arise*] It is likely that Joab had by some indiscretion suffered loss about this time; and he contrived to get rid of the odium by connecting the transaction with the death of Uriah, which he knew would be so pleasing to the king.

Verse 25. *The sword devoureth one as well as another*] What abominable hypocrisy was here! He well knew that Uriah's death was no *chance-medley;* he was by his own order thrust on the edge of the sword.

Verse 26. *She mourned for her husband.*] The whole of her conduct indicates that she

observed the *form* without feeling the *power* of *sorrow.* She lost a *captain* and got a *king* for her spouse; this must have been deep affliction indeed: and therefore

—— Lachrymas non sponte cadentes
Effudit; gemitusque expressit pectore læto.

"She shed reluctant tears, and forced out groans from a joyful heart."

Verse 27. *When the mourning was past*] Probably it lasted only *seven days.*

She became his wife] This hurried marriage was no doubt intended on both sides to cover the pregnancy.

But the thing that David had done displeased the Lord.] It was necessary to add this, lest the splendour of David's former virtues should induce any to suppose his crimes were passed over, or looked on with an indulgent eye, by the God of purity and justice. Sorely he sinned, and sorely did he suffer for it; he sowed one *grain* of sweet, and reaped a long *harvest* of calamity and wo.

ON a review of the whole, I hesitate not to say that the preceding chapter is an illustrious proof of the truth of the sacred writings. Who that intended to deceive, by trumping up a religion which he designed to father on the purity of God, would have inserted such an account of one of its most zealous advocates, and once its brightest ornament? God alone, whose character is impartiality, has done it, to show that his religion, *librata ponderibus suis,* will ever stand independently of the conduct of its professors.

Drs. Delaney, Chandler, and others, have taken great pains to excuse and varnish this conduct of David; and while I admire their ingenuity, I abhor the tendency of their doctrine, being fully convinced that he who writes on this subject should write like the inspired penman, who tells the TRUTH, the WHOLE TRUTH, and NOTHING BUT THE TRUTH.

David may be *pitied* because he had fallen from great eminence; but who can help *deploring* the fate of the brave, the faithful, the incorruptible *Uriah? Bath-sheba* was probably *first* in the transgression, by a too public display of her charms; by which, accidentally, the heart of David was affected, wounded, and blinded. He committed one crime which he employed many shifts to conceal; these all failing, he is led from step to step to the highest degree of guilt. Not only does he feel that his and her *honour,* but even their *lives,* are at stake; for death, by the law of Moses, was the punishment of adultery. He thought therefore that either Uriah must die, or he and Bath-sheba perish for their iniquity; for that law had made no provision to save the life of even a *king* who transgressed its precepts. He must not imbrue his own hands in the blood of this brave man; but he employs him on a service from which his bravery would not permit him to shrink; and in which, from the nature of his circumstances, he must inevitably perish! The awful trial is made, and it succeeds! The criminal king and his criminal paramour are for a moment concealed; and one of the bravest of men falls an affectionate victim for the safety and support of him by whom his spotless blood is shed! But what shall we say of *Joab,* the wicked executor of the base commands of his fallen master? He was a *ruffian,* not a *soldier;* base and barbarous beyond example, in his calling; a pander to the vices of his monarch, while he was aware that he was outraging every law of religion, piety, honour, and arms! It is difficult to state the characters, and sum up and apportion the quantity of vice chargeable on each.

Let *David,* once a pious, noble, generous, and benevolent hero, who, when almost perishing with thirst, would not taste the water which his brave men had acquired at the hazard of their lives; let this David, I say, be considered an awful example of *apostacy* from religion, justice, and virtue; *Bath-sheba,* of lightness and conjugal infidelity; *Joab,* of base, unmanly, and cold-blooded cruelty; *Uriah,* of untarnished heroism, inflexible fidelity, and unspotted virtue; and then justice will be done to each character. For my own part, I must say, I *pity* David; I *venerate* Uriah; I *detest* Joab, and *think meanly* of Bath-sheba. Similar crimes have been repeatedly committed in similar circumstances. I shall take my leave of the whole with

Id commune malum; semel insanivimus omnes; Aut sumus, aut fuimus, aut possumus, omne quod hic est.

God of purity and mercy! save the reader from the ευπεριστατος αμαρτια, *well circumstanced sin;* and let him learn,

"Where many mightier have been slain, By thee unsaved, he falls."

See the notes on the succeeding chapter.

CHAPTER XII

The Lord sends Nathan the prophet to reprove David; which he does by means of a curious parable, 1–4. David is led, unknowingly, to pronounce his own condemnation, 5, 6. Nathan charges the guilt home on his conscience; and predicts a long train of calamities which should fall on him and his family, 7–12. David confesses his sin; and Nathan gives him hope of God's mercy, and foretells the death of the child born in adultery, 13, 14. The child is taken ill; David fasts and prays for its restoration, 15–17. On the seventh day the child dies, and David is comforted, 18–24. Solomon is born of Bath-sheba, 25, 26. Joab besieges Rabbah of the Ammonites, takes the city of waters, and sends for David to take Rabbah, 27, 28. He comes, takes it, gets much spoil, and puts the inhabitants to hard labour, 29–31.

A. M. 2970
B. C. 1034
An. Exod. Isr. 457
Anno ante
I. Olymp. 258

AND the LORD sent Nathan unto David. And [a]he came unto him, and [b]said unto him, There were two men in one city; the one rich, and the other poor.

2 The rich *man* had exceeding many flocks and herds:

3 But the poor *man* had nothing, save one little ewe lamb, which he had bought and nourished up: and

A. M. 2970
B. C. 1034
An. Exod. Isr. 457
Anno ante
I. Olymp. 258

---

[a]Psa. li. title——[b]See chap. xiv. 5, &c.; 1 Kings xx. 35–41; Isa. v. 3

NOTES ON CHAP. XII

Verse 1. *There were two men in one city]* See a *discourse* on *fables* at the end of Judg. ix.; and a *discourse* on *parabolic writing* at the end of the thirteenth chapter of Matthew. There is nothing in this parable that requires illustration; its bent is evident; and it was constructed to make David, unwittingly, pass sentence on himself. It was in David's hand, what his own letters were in the hands of the brave but unfortunate Uriah.

Verse 3. *And lay in his bosom]* This can only mean that this lamb was what we call a *pet* or *favourite* in the family, else the circumstance would be very *unnatural,* and most likely would have prevented David from making the application which he did, as otherwise it would have

A. M. 2970
B. C. 1034
An. Exod. Isr.
457
Anno ante
I. Olymp. 258

it grew up together with him, and with his children; it did eat of his own ᶜmeat, and drank of his own cup, and lay in his bosom, and was unto him as a daughter.

4 And there came a traveller unto the rich man, and he spared to take of his own flock and of his own herd, to dress for the wayfaring man that was come unto him; but took the poor man's lamb, and dressed it for the man that was come to him.

5 And David's anger was greatly kindled against the man; and he said to Nathan, *As* the LORD liveth, the man that hath done this *thing* shall surely ᵈdie:

6 And he shall restore the lamb ᵉfourfold, because he did this thing, and because he had no pity.

7 And Nathan said to David, Thou *art* the man. Thus saith the LORD God of Israel, I ᶠanointed thee king over Israel, and I delivered thee out of the hand of Saul;

8 And I gave thee thy master's house, and thy master's wives into thy bosom, and gave thee the house of Israel and of Judah: and if *that had been* too little, I would moreover have given unto thee such and such things.

A. M. 2970
B. C. 1044
An. Exod. Isr.
457
Anno ante
I. Olymp. 258

9 ᵍWherefore hast thou ʰdespised the commandment of the LORD, to do evil in his sight? ⁱthou hast killed Uriah the Hittite with the sword, and hast taken his wife *to be* thy wife, and hast slain him with the sword of the children of Ammon.

10 Now therefore ᵏthe sword shall never depart from thine house; because thou hast despised me, and hast taken the wife of Uriah the Hittite to be thy wife.

11 Thus saith the LORD, Behold, I will raise up evil against thee out of thine own house, and I will ˡtake thy wives before thine eyes, and give *them* unto thy neighbour, and he shall lie with thy wives in the sight of this sun.

12 For thou didst *it* secretly: ᵐbut I will do this thing before all Israel, and before the sun.

13 ⁿAnd David said unto Nathan, ᵒI have

ᶜHeb. *morsel*——ᵈOr, is *worthy to die*, or, is *a son of death;* 1 Sam. xxvi. 16——ᵉExod. xxii. 1; Luke xix. 8——ᶠ1 Sam. xvi. 13——ᵍ1 Sam. xv. 19——ʰNum. xv. 31

ⁱChap. xi. 15, 16, 17, 27——ᵏAmos vii. 9——ˡDeut. xxviii. 30; chap. xvi. 22——ᵐChap. xvi. 22——ⁿSee 1 Sam. xv. 24——ᵒChap. xxiv. 10; Job vii. 20; Psa. xxxii. 5; li. 4; Prov. xxviii. 13

---

appeared absurd. It is the only part of this parable which is at variance with *nature* and *fact.*

Verse 5. *The man—shall surely die*] Literally מות בן *ben maveth*, "he is a son of death," a very *bad man*, and one who *deserves to die.* But the law did not sentence a sheep-stealer to death; let us hear it: *If a man steal an ox or a sheep, he shall restore* FIVE OXEN *for an ox, and* FOUR SHEEP *for a sheep*, Exod. xxii. 1; and hence David immediately says, *He shall restore the lamb* FOURFOLD.

Verse 7. *Thou* art *the man.*] What a terrible word! And by it David appears to have been transfixed, and brought into the dust before the messenger of God.

THOU ART *this son of death*, and thou shalt restore this lamb FOURFOLD. It is indulging fancy too much to say David was called, in the course of a just Providence to pay this fourfold debt? to lose *four sons* by untimely deaths, viz., this son of Bath-sheba, on whom David had set his heart, was slain by the Lord; *Amnon*, murdered by his brother Absalom; *Absalom*, slain in the oak by Joab; and *Adonijah*, slain by the order of his brother Solomon, even at the altar of the Lord! The sword and calamity did not depart from his house, from the murder of wretched *Amnon* by his brother to the slaughter of the sons of *Zedekiah*, before their father's eyes, by the king of Babylon. His *daughter* was dishonoured by her own brother, and his *wives* contaminated publicly by his own son! How dreadfully, then, was David punished for his sin! Who would repeat his transgression to share in its penalty? Can

his conduct ever be an inducement to, or an encouragement in, sin? Surely, No. It must ever fill the reader and the hearer with horror. Behold the goodness and severity of God! Reader, lay all these solemn things to heart.

Verse 8. *Thy master's wives into thy bosom*] Perhaps this means no more than that he had given him *absolute power* over every thing possessed by Saul; and as it was the custom for the new king to succeed even to the *wives* and *concubines*, the *whole harem* of the deceased king, so it was in this case; and the possession of the wives was a sure proof that he had got all regal rights. But could David, as the *son-in-law* of Saul, take the *wives* of his *father-in-law?* However, we find delicacy was seldom consulted in these cases; and Absalom lay with his own father's wives in the most public manner, to show that he had seized on the kingdom, because the wives of the preceding belonged to the succeeding king, and to none other.

Verse 9. *Thou hast killed Uriah*] THOU art the MURDERER, as having planned his death; the sword of the Ammonites was THY instrument only.

Verse 11. *I will take thy wives*] That is, In the course of my providence I will *permit* all this to be done. Had David been faithful, God, by his providence, would have turned all this aside; but now, by his sin, he has made that providence his enemy which before was his friend.

Verse 13. *The Lord—hath put away thy sin*] Many have supposed that David's sin was *now actually pardoned*, but this is perfectly erroneous; David, as an adulterer, was *condemned*

A. M. 2970
B. C. 1034
An. Exod. Isr.
457
Anno ante
I. Olymp. 258 sinned against the LORD. And Nathan said unto David, ᵖThe LORD also hath ᑫput away thy sin: thou shalt not die.

14 Howbeit, because by this deed thou hast given great occasion to the enemies of the LORD ʳto blaspheme, the child also *that is* born unto thee shall surely die.

15 And Nathan departed unto his house. And the LORD struck the child that Uriah's wife bare unto David, and it was very sick.

16 David therefore besought God for the child; and David ˢfasted, and went in, and ᵗlay all night upon the earth.

17 And the elders of his house arose, *and went* to him, to raise him up from the earth: but he would not, neither did he eat bread with them.

18 And it came to pass on the seventh day, that the child died. And the servants of David feared to tell him that the child was dead: for they said, Behold, while the child was yet alive, we spake unto him, and he would not hearken unto our voice: how will he then ᵘvex himself, if we tell him that the child is dead?

19 But when David saw that his servants whispered, David perceived that the child was dead: therefore David said unto his servants, Is the child dead? And they said, He is dead.

A. M. 2970
B. C. 1034
An. Exod. Isr
457
Anno ante
I. Olymp. 258

20 Then David arose from the earth, and washed, and ᵛanointed *himself,* and changed his apparel, and came into the house of the LORD, and ʷworshipped: then he came to his own house; and when he required, they set bread before him, and he did eat.

21 Then said his servants unto him, What thing *is* this that thou hast done? thou didst fast and weep for the child *while it was* alive; but when the child was dead, thou didst rise and eat bread.

22 And he said, While the child was yet alive, I fasted and wept: ˣfor I said, Who can tell *whether* God will be gracious to me, that the child may live?

23 But now he is dead, wherefore should I fast? can I bring him back again? I shall go to him, but ʸhe shall not return to me.

ᵖEcclus. xlvii. 11——ᑫChap. xxiv. 10; Psa. xxxii. 1; Job vii. 21; Mic. vii. 18; Zech. iii. 4——ʳIsa. lii. 5; Ezek. xxxvi. 20, 23; Rom. ii. 24

ˢHeb. *fasted a fast*——ᵗChap. xiii. 31——ᵘHeb. *do hurt*——ᵛRuth iii. 3——ʷJob i. 20——ˣSee Isa. xxxviii. 1, 5; Jonah iii. 9——ʸJob vii. 8, 9, 10

---

to death by the law of God; and he had according to that law passed sentence of death upon himself. God alone, whose law that was could revoke that sentence, or dispense with its execution; therefore Nathan, who had charged the guilt home upon his conscience, is authorized to give him the assurance that he should not die a *temporal death* for it: *The Lord hath put away thy sin; thou shalt not die.* This is all that is contained in the assurance given by Nathan: Thou shalt not die that temporal death; thou shalt be preserved alive, that thou mayest have time to repent, turn to God, and find mercy. If the fifty-first Psalm, as is generally supposed, was written on this occasion, then it is evident (as the Psalm must have been written *after* this interview) that David had not received pardon for his sin from God at the time he composed it; for in it he confesses the crime in order to find mercy.

There is something very remarkable in the words of Nathan: *The Lord also hath* PUT AWAY *thy sin; thou shalt not die;* גם יהוה העביר חטאתך לא תמות אלא *gam Yehovah heebir chattathecha, lo thamuth, Also Jehovah* HATH CAUSED *thy sin* TO PASS OVER, *or transferred thy sin;* THOU *shalt not die.* God has *transferred* the legal punishment of this sin to the *child;* HE shall die, THOU shalt not die; and this is the very point on which the prophet gives him the most direct information: *The child that is born unto thee shall* SURELY *die;* מות ימות *moth yamuth, dying he shall die*—he shall be in a *dying* state seven days, and then he shall *die.* So God immediately *struck the child, and it was very sick.*

Verse 16. *David—besought God for the child*] How could he do so, after the solemn assurance that he had from God that the child should die? The justice of God absolutely required that the penalty of the law should be exacted; either the *father* or the *son* shall die. This could not be reversed.

Verse 20. *David arose from the earth, and washed*] Bathing, anointing the body, and changing the apparel, are the first outward signs among the Hindoos of coming out of a state of *mourning* or sickness.

Verse 22. *Who can tell*] David, and indeed all others under the Mosaic dispensation, were so satisfied that all God's *threatenings* and *promises* were *conditional*, that even in the most positive assertions relative to judgments, &c., they sought for a change of purpose. And notwithstanding the positive declaration of Nathan, relative to the death of the child, David sought for its life, not knowing but *that* might depend on some unexpressed *condition*, such as earnest *prayer*, *fasting*, *humiliation*, &c., and in these he continued while there was hope. When the child *died*, he ceased to grieve, as he now saw that this must be fruitless. This appears to be the sole reason of David's importunity.

Verse 23. *I shall go to him, but he shall not return to me.*] It is not clear whether David by this expressed his faith in the *immortality*

A. M. 2971
B. C. 1033
An. Exod. Isr. 458
Anno ante
I. Olymp. 257

24 And David comforted Bath-sheba his wife, and went in unto her, and lay with her: and ᶻshe bare a son, and ᵃhe called his name Solomon: and the LORD loved him.

25 And he sent by the hand of Nathan the prophet; and he called his name ᵇJedidiah, because of the LORD.

26 And ᶜJoab fought against ᵈRabbah of the children of Ammon, and took the royal city.

27 And Joab sent messengers to David, and

said, I have fought against Rabbah, and have taken the city of waters.

A. M. 2971
B. C. 1033
An. Exod. Isr. 458
Anno ante
I. Olymp. 257

28 Now therefore gather the rest of the people together, and encamp against the city, and take it: lest I take the city, and ᵉit be called after my name.

29 And David gathered all the people together, and went to Rabbah, and fought against it, and took it.

30 ᶠAnd he took their king's crown from off his head, the weight whereof *was* a talent

---

ᶻMatt. i. 6——ᵃ1 Chron. xxii. 9——ᵇThat is, *Beloved of the Lord*

ᶜ1 Chron. xx. 1——ᵈDeut. iii. 11——ᵉHeb. *my name be called upon it*——ᶠ1 Chron. xx. 2

---

of the soul; going to him may only mean, *I also shall die, and be gathered to my fathers, as he is.* But whether David expressed this or not, we know that the thing is true; and it is one of the most solid grounds of consolation to surviving friends that they shall by and by be joined to them in a state of conscious existence. This doctrine has a very powerful tendency to *alleviate* the miseries of human life, and reconcile us to the death of most beloved friends. And were we to admit the contrary, grief, in many cases, would wear out its subject before it wore out itself. Even the heathens derived consolation from the reflection that they should meet their friends in a state of conscious existence. And a saying in Cicero *De Senectute*, which he puts in the mouth of Cato of Utica, has been often quoted, and is universally admired:—

O præclarum diem, cum ad illud divinum animorum concilium cœtumque proficiscar, cumque ex hac turba et colluvione discedam! Proficiscar enim non ad eos solum viros de quibus ante dixi; sed etiam ad Catonem meum quo nemo vir melior natus est, nemo pietate præstantior: cujus a me corpus crematum est; quod contra decuit ab illo meum. Animus vero non me deserens, sed respectans, in ea profecto loca discessit, quo mihi ipsi cernebat esse veniendum: quem ego meum catum fortiter ferre visus sum: non quod æquo animo ferrem: sed me ipse consolabar, existimans, non longinquum inter nos digressum et discessum fore.

CATO MAJOR, *De Senectute*, in fin.

"O happy day, (says he,) when I shall quit this impure and corrupt multitude, and join myself to that divine company and council of souls who have quitted the earth before me! There I shall find, not only those illustrious personages to whom I have spoken, but also my Cato, who I can say was one of the best men ever born, and whom none ever excelled in virtue and piety. I have placed his body on that funeral pile whereon he ought to have laid mine. But his soul has not left me; and, without losing sight of me, he has only gone before into a country where he saw I should soon rejoin him. This my lot I seem to bear courageously; not indeed that I do bear it with resignation, but I shall comfort myself with the persuasion that the interval between his departure and mine will not be long."

And we well know who has taught us *not to sorrow as those without hope* for departed friends.

Verse 24. *David comforted Bath-sheba*] His extraordinary attachment to this beautiful woman was the cause of all his misfortunes.

He called his name Solomon] This name seems to have been given prophetically, for שלמה *sholomah* signifies *peaceable*, and there was almost uninterrupted *peace* during his reign.

Verse 25. *Called—Jedidiah*] ידידיה, literally, *the beloved of the Lord.* This is the first instance I remember of a minister of God being employed to give a name to the child of one of his servants. But it is strange that the name given by the father was that alone which prevailed.

Verse 26. *And took the royal city.*] How can this be, when Joab sent to David to come to take the city, in consequence of which David did come and take that city? The explanation seems to be this: Rabbah was composed of a *city* and *citadel;* the former, in which was the king's residence, Joab had taken, and supposed he could soon render himself master of the latter, and therefore sends to David to come and take it, lest, he taking the whole, the city should be called after his name.

Verse 27. *And have taken the city of waters.*] The city where the *tank* or *reservoir* was that supplied the city and suburbs with water. Some think that the original, לכדתי את עיר המים *lachadti eth ir hammayim*, should be translated, *I have intercepted, or cut off, the waters of the city:* and Houbigant translates the place, *et aquas ab urbe jam derivavi;* "And I have already drawn off the waters from the city." This perfectly agrees with the account in *Josephus*, who says τῶν τε ὑδάτων αὐτοὺς ἀποτεμνόμενος, *having cut off their waters*, Antiq., lib. vii., cap. 7. This was the reason why David should come speedily, as the citadel, *deprived of water*, could not long hold out.

Verse 30. *The weight whereof* was *a talent of gold*] If this talent was only *seven pounds*, as Whiston says, David might have carried it on his head with little difficulty; but this weight, according to common computation, would amount to more than *one hundred pounds!*

If, however, משקלה *mishkalah* be taken for the *value*, not the *weight*, then all is plain, as the worth of the crown will be about £5075 15s. 7d. sterling. Now this seems to be the true sense, because of the added words *with the precious stones;* i. e., the *gold* of the crown, and

A. M. 2971
B. C. 1033
An. Exod. Isr.
458
Anno ante
I. Olymp. 257

of gold with the precious stones: and it was *set* on David's head. And he brought forth the spoil of the city ^gin great abundance.

31 And he brought forth the people that *were* therein, and put *them* under saws, and under

harrows of iron, and under axes of iron, and made them pass through the brick-kiln: and thus did he unto all the cities of the children of Ammon. So David and all the people returned unto Jerusalem.

A. M. 2971
B. C. 1033
An. Exod. Isr.
458
Anno ante
I. Olymp. 257

---

^gHebrew,   *very great*

---

the *jewels* with which it was adorned, were equal in *value* to a talent of gold.

Verse 31. *He brought forth the people*] And put them *under saws*. From this representation a great cry has been raised against "David's unparalleled, if not diabolic, cruelty." I believe this interpretation was chiefly taken from the parallel place, 1 Chron. xx. 3, where it is said, *he cut* them *with saws, and with axes*, &c. Instead of וַיָּשַׂר *vaiyasar, he sawed*, we have here (in Samuel) וַיָּשֶׂם *vaiyasem, he put them;* and these two words differ from each other only in a *part of a single letter*, ר *resh* for ם *mem*. And it is worthy of remark, that instead of וַיָּשַׂר *vaiyasar, he sawed*, in 1 Chron. xx. 3, six or seven MSS. collated by Dr. Kennicott have וַיָּשֶׂם *vaiyasem, he put them;* nor is there found any various reading in all the MSS. yet collated for the text in this chapter, that favours the common reading in Chronicles. The meaning therefore is, He made the people *slaves*, and employed them in *sawing, making iron harrows*, or *mining*, (for the word means both,) and in *hewing of wood*, and *making of brick.*

Sawing asunder, hacking, chopping, and hewing human beings, have no place in this text, no more than they had in David's conduct towards the Ammonites.

It is surprising, and a thing to be deplored, that in this and similar cases our translators had not been more careful to sift the sense of the original words by which they would have avoided a profusion of exceptionable meanings with which they have clothed many passages of the sacred writings. Though I believe our translation to be by far the best in any language, ancient or modern, yet I am satisfied it stands much in need of revision. Most of the advantages which our unbelievers have appeared to have over certain passages of Scripture, have arisen from an inaccurate or false translation of the terms in the original; and an appeal to this has generally silenced the gainsayers. But in the time in which our translation was made, Biblical criticism was in its infancy, if indeed it did exist; and we may rather wonder that we find things so well, than be surprised that they are no better.

CHAPTER XIII

Amnon falls in love with his half-sister Tamar, and feigns himself sick, and requests her to attend him, 1–6. David sends her to him, and he violates her, 7–14. He then hates her, and expels her from his house, 15–17. She rends her garments, puts ashes on her head, and goes forth weeping, 18, 19. She is met by Absalom her brother, who, understanding her case, determines the death of Amnon, 20–22. Two years after, he invites all his brothers to a sheep-shearing, when he orders his servants to murder Amnon, 23–29. Tidings come to David that Absalom has slain all the king's sons, which fill him with the bitterest distress, 30, 31. The rest soon arrive, and he finds that Amnon only is killed, 32–36. Absalom flees to Talmai, king of Geshur, where he remains three years, 37, 38. David longs after Absalom, having become reconciled to the death of Amnon, 39.

A. M. 2972
B. C. 1032
An. Exod. Isr.
459
Anno ante
I. Olymp. 256

AND it came to pass after this, ^athat Absalom the son of David had a fair sister, whose name was ^bTamar; and Amnon the son of David loved her.

2 And Amnon was so vexed that he fell sick

for his sister Tamar; for she *was* a virgin; and ^cAmnon thought it hard for him to do any thing to her.

3 But Amnon had a friend, whose name *was* Jonadab, ^dthe son of Shimeah, David's

A. M. 2972
B. C. 1032
An. Exod. Isr.
459
Anno ante
I. Olymp. 256

---

^aCh. iii. 2, 3——^b1 Chron. iii. 9——^cHeb. *it was marvel-*   *lous* or *hidden in the eyes of Amnon*——^dSee 1 Sam. xvi. 9

NOTES ON CHAP. XIII

Verse 1. *Whose name was Tamar*] Tamar was the daughter of David and Maacah, daughter of the king of Geshur, and the uterine sister of Absalom. Amnon was David's eldest son by Ahinoam. She was therefore sister to Amnon only by the father's side, i. e., *half-sister;* but *whole sister* to Absalom.

Verse 2. *Amnon was so vexed—for she* was *a virgin*] It has been well remarked that "the passion of love is nowhere so wasting and vexatious, as where it is unlawful. A quick sense of guilt, especially where it is enormous,

as in the present instance, strikes the soul with horror; and the impossibility of an innocent gratification loads that horror with desperation: a conflict too cruel and too dreadful for human bearing."—*Delaney.*

Verse 3. *Jonadab* was *a very subtle man.*] And most diabolic advice did he give to his cousin. We talk of the simplicity and excellence of primitive times! "Say not thou what is *the cause* that the former days were better than these." Take them altogether, we may thank God that they are past, and pray him that they may never return.

A. M. 2972
B. C. 1032
An. Exod. Isr.
459
Anno ante
I. Olymp. 256

brother: and Jonadab *was* a very subtle man.

4 And he said unto him, Why art thou, *being* the king's son, [e]lean [f]from day to day? wilt thou not tell me? And Amnon said unto him, I love Tamar, my brother Absalom's sister.

5 And Jonadab said unto him, Lay thee down on thy bed, and make thyself sick; and when thy father cometh to see thee, say unto him, I pray thee, let my sister Tamar come, and give me meat, and dress the meat in my sight, that I may see *it,* and eat *it* at her hand.

6 So Amnon lay down, and made himself sick: and when the king was come to see him, Amnon said unto the king, I pray thee, let Tamar my sister come, and [g]make me a couple of cakes in my sight, that I may eat at her hand.

7 Then David sent home to Tamar, saying, Go now to thy brother Amnon's house, and dress him meat.

8 So Tamar went to her brother Amnon's house; and he was laid down. And she took [h]flour, and kneaded *it,* and made cakes in his sight, and did bake the cakes.

9 And she took a pan, and poured *them* out before him; but he refused to eat. And Amnon said, [i]Have out all men from me. And they went out every man from him.

10 And Amnon said unto Tamar, Bring the meat into the chamber, that I may eat of thine hand. And Tamar took the cakes which she had made, and brought *them* into the chamber to Amnon her brother.

11 And when she had brought *them* unto him to eat, he [k]took hold of her, and said unto her, Come lie with me, my sister.

12 And she answered him, Nay, my brother,

do not [l]force me; for [m]no [n]such thing ought to be done in Israel: do not thou this [o]folly.

A. M. 2972
B. C. 1032
An. Exod. Isr.
459
Anno ante
I. Olymp. 256

13 And I, whither shall I cause my shame to go? and as for thee, thou shalt be as one of the fools in Israel. Now therefore, I pray thee, speak unto the king; [p]for he will not withhold me from thee.

14 Howbeit he would not hearken unto her voice: but, being stronger than she, [q]forced her, and lay with her.

15 Then Amnon hated her [r]exceedingly; so that the hatred wherewith he hated her *was* greater than the love wherewith he had loved her. And Amnon said unto her, Arise, be gone.

16 And she said unto him, *There is* no cause: this evil in sending me away *is* greater than the other that thou didst unto me. But he would not hearken unto her.

17 Then he called his servant that ministered unto him, and said, Put now this *woman* out from me, and bolt the door after her.

18 And *she had* [s]a garment of divers colours upon her: for with such robes were the king's daughters *that were* virgins apparelled. Then his servant brought her out, and bolted the door after her.

19 And Tamar put [t]ashes on her head, and rent her garment of divers colours that *was* on her, and [u]laid her hand on her head, and went on crying.

20 And Absalom her brother said unto her, Hath [v]Amnon thy brother been with thee? but hold now thy peace, my sister: he *is* thy brother; [w]regard not this thing. So Tamar remained [x]desolate in her brother Absalom's house.

21 But when King David heard of all these things, he was very wroth.

---

[e]Heb. *thin*——[f]Heb. *morning by morning*——[g]Gen. xviii. 6——[h]Or, *paste*——[i]Gen. xlv. 1——[k]Gen. xxxix. 12——[l]Heb. *humble me;* Gen. xxxiv. 2——[m]Lev. xviii. 9, 11; xx. 17——[n]Heb. *it ought not so to be done*——[o]Gen. xxxiv. 7; Judges xix. 23; xx. 6

[p]See Lev. xviii. 9, 11——[q]Deut. xxii. 25; see chap. xii. 11——[r]Heb. *with great hatred greatly*——[s]Gen. xxxvii. 3; Judg. v. 30; Psa. xlv. 14——[t]Josh. vii. 6; chap. i. 2; Job ii. 12——[u]Jer. ii. 37——[v]Heb. *Aminon*——[w]Heb. *set not thine heart*——[x]Heb. *and desolate*

Verse 12. *Nay, my brother*] There is something exceedingly tender and persuasive in this speech of Tamar; but Amnon was a mere brute, and it was all lost on him.

Verse 13. *Speak unto the king*] So it appears that she thought that the king, her father, would give her to him as wife. This is another strong mark of indelicacy in those simple but barbarous times. There might have been some excuse for such connections under the patriarchal age, but there was none now. But perhaps she said this only to divert him from his

iniquitous purpose, that she might get out of his hands.

Verse 15. *Hated her exceedingly*] Amnon's conduct to his sister was not only brutal but inexplicable. It would be easy to form *conjectures* concerning the *cause,* but we can arrive at no certainty.

Verse 18. *A garment of divers colours*] See the note on Gen. xxxvii. 3, where the same words occur.

Verse 21. *But when King David heard*] To this verse the *Septuagint* add the following

A. M. 2974
B. C. 1030
An. Exod. Isr.
461
Anno ante
I. Olymp. 254

22 And Absalom spake unto his brother Amnon [y]neither good nor bad: for Absalom [z]hated Amnon, because he had forced his sister Tamar.

23 And it came to pass after two full years, that Absalom [a]had sheep-shearers in Baal-hazor, which *is* beside Ephraim: and Absalom invited all the king's sons.

24 And Absalom came to the king, and said, Behold now, thy servant hath sheep-shearers; let the king, I beseech thee, and his servants go with thy servant.

25 And the king said to Absalom, Nay, my son, let us not all now go, lest we be chargeable unto thee. And he pressed him: howbeit he would not go, but blessed him.

26 Then said Absalom, If not, I pray thee, let my brother Amnon go with us. And the king said unto him, Why should he go with thee?

27 But Absalom pressed him, that he let Amnon and all the king's sons go with him.

28 Now Absalom had commanded his servants, saying, Mark ye now when Amnon's [b]heart is merry with wine, and when I say unto you, Smite Amnon; then kill him, fear not: [c]have not I commanded you? be courageous, and be [d]valiant.

29 And the servants of Absalom did unto Amnon as Absalom had commanded. Then all the king's sons arose, and every man [e]gat him up upon his mule, and fled.

30 And it came to pass, while they were in the way, that tidings came to David, saying, Absalom hath slain all the king's sons, and there is not one of them left.

A. M. 2974
B. C. 1030
An. Exod. Isr.
461
Anno ante
I. Olymp. 254

31 Then the king arose, and [f]tare his garments, and [g]lay on the earth; and all his servants stood by with their clothes rent.

32 And [h]Jonadab the son of Shimeah, David's brother, answered and said, Let not my lord suppose *that* they have slain all the young men the king's sons; for Amnon only is dead: for by the [i]appointment of Absalom this hath been [k]determined from the day that he forced his sister Tamar.

33 Now therefore [l]let not my lord the king take the thing to his heart, to think that all the king's sons are dead: for Amnon only is dead.

34 [m]But Absalom fled. And the young man that kept the watch lifted up his eyes, and looked, and, behold, there came much people by the way of the hill-side behind him.

35 And Jonadab said unto the king, Behold, the king's sons come: [n]as thy servant said, so it is.

36 And it came to pass, as soon as he had made an end of speaking, that, behold, the king's sons came, and lifted up their voice and wept: and the king also and all his servants wept [o]very sore.

37 But Absalom fled, and went to [p]Talmai, the son of [q]Ammihud, king of Geshur. And *David* mourned for his son every day.

---

[y]Gen. xxiv. 50; xxxi. 24——[z]Lev. xix. 17, 18——[a]See Gen. xxxviii. 12, 13; 1 Sam. xxv. 4, 36——[b]Judg. xix. 6, 9, 22; Ruth iii. 7; 1 Sam. xxv. 36; Esth. i. 10; Psa. civ. 15 [c]Or, *will you not, since I have commanded you?* Josh. i. 9 [d]Heb. *sons of valour*

[e]Heb. *rode*——[f]Chap. i. 11——[g]Chap. xii. 16 [h]Ver. 3——[i]Heb. *mouth*——[k]Or, *settled*——[l]Chap. xix. 19——[m]Ver. 38——[n]Heb. *according to the word of thy servant*——[o]Heb. *with a great weeping greatly*——[p]Chap. iii. 3——[q]Or, *Ammihur*

---

words: Και ουκ ελυπησε το πνευμα Αμνων του υιου αυτου, ότι ηγαπα αυτον, ότι πρωτοτοκος αυτου ην; "But he would not grieve the soul of Amnon his son, for he loved him, because he was his first-born." The same addition is found in the *Vulgate* and in *Josephus*, and it is possible that this once made a part of the Hebrew text.

Verse 23. *Absalom had sheep-shearers*] These were times in which feasts were made, to which the neighbours and relatives of the family were invited.

Verse 26. *Let my brother Amnon go*] He urged this with the more plausibility, because Amnon was the first-born, and presumptive heir to the kingdom; and he had disguised his resentment so well before, that he was not suspected.

Verse 30. *Absalom hath slain all the king's sons*] *Fame* never *lessens* but always *magnifies*

a fact. *Report*, contrary to the nature of all other things, *gains strength by going.*

Virgil has given, in his best manner, a fine personification of *Fame* or *Evil Report.*—ÆN. iv., 173.

Extemplo Libyæ magnas it *Fama* per urbes; *Fama*, malum qua non aliud velocius ullum, Mobilitate viget, viresque adquirit eundo, &c.

"Now *Fame*, tremendous fiend! without delay, Through Libyan cities took her rapid way; *Fame*, the swift plague, that *every moment grows*, And *gains new strength* and *vigour as she goes*," &c.

Verse 32. *And Jonadab—said—Amnon only is dead*] This was a very bad man, and here speaks coolly of a most bloody tragedy, which himself had contrived.

Verse 37. *Absalom fled*] As he had com-

A. M. 2974–77
B. C. 1030–27
An. Exod. Isr.
461–464

38 So Absalom fled, and went to ʳGeshur, and was there three years.

39 And *the soul of* King David ˢlonged

ʳChap. xiv. 23, 32; xv. 8——ˢOr, *was*

mitted wilful murder, he could not avail himself of a city of refuge, and was therefore obliged to leave the land of Israel, and take refuge with Talmai, king of Geshur, his grandfather by his mother's side. See chap. iii. 3.

Verse 39. *David longed to go forth unto Absalom*] We find that he had a very strong paternal affection for this young man, who appears to have had little to commend him but the beauty of his person. David wished either to go to him, or to bring him back; for

to go forth unto Absalom: for he was ᵗcomforted concerning Amnon, seeing he was dead.

A. M. 2974–77
B. C. 1030–27
An. Exod. Isr.
461–464

consumed; Psa. lxxxiv. 2——ᵗGen. xxxviii. 12

the hand of time had now wiped off his tears for the death of his son Amnon. Joab had marked this disposition, and took care to work on it, in order to procure the return of Absalom. It would have been well for all parties had Absalom ended his days at Geshur. His return brought increasing wretchedness to his unfortunate father. And it may be generally observed that those undue, unreasonable paternal attachments are thus rewarded.

CHAPTER XIV

A woman of Tekoah, by the advice of Joab, comes to the king; and by a fictitious story persuades him to recall Absalom, 1–20. Joab is permitted to go to Geshur, and bring Absalom from thence, 21–23. Absalom comes to Jerusalem to his own house, but is forbidden to see the king's face, 24. An account of Absalom's beauty, and the extraordinary weight of his hair, 25, 26. His children, 27. He strives to regain the king's favour, and employs Joab as an intercessor, 28–32. David is reconciled to him, 33.

A. M. 2977
B. C. 1027
An. Exod. Isr.
464
Anno ante
I. Olymp. 251

NOW Joab the son of Zeruiah perceived that the king's heart *was* ᵃtoward Absalom.

2 And Joab sent to ᵇTekoah, and fetched thence a wise woman, and said unto her, I pray thee, feign thyself to be a mourner, ᶜand put on now mourning apparel, and anoint not thyself with oil, but be as a woman that had a long time mourned for the dead:

3 And come to the king, and speak on this manner unto him. So Joab ᵈput the words in her mouth.

4 And when the woman of Tekoah spake to

the king, she ᵉfell on her face to the ground, and did obeisance, and said, ᶠHelp, ᵍO king.

A. M. 2977
B. C. 1027
An. Exod. Isr.
464
Anno ante
I. Olymp. 251

5 And the king said unto her, What aileth thee? And she answered, ʰI *am* indeed a widow woman, and mine husband is dead.

6 And thy handmaid had two sons, and they two strove together in the field, and *there was* ⁱnone to part them, but the one smote the other, and slew him.

7 And, behold, ᵏthe whole family is risen against thine handmaid, and they said, De-

ᵃCh. xiii. 39——ᵇ2 Chron. xi. 6——ᶜSee Ruth iii. 3
ᵈVer. 19; Exod. iv. 15——ᵉ1 Sam. xx. 41; chap. i. 2
ᶠHeb. *save*

ᵍSee 2 Kings vi. 26, 28——ʰSee chap. xii. 1——ⁱHeb. *no deliverer between them*——ᵏNum. xxxv. 19; Deut. xix. 12

NOTES ON CHAP. XIV

Verse 2. *Joab sent to Tekoah*] Tekoah, according to St. *Jerome*, was a little city in the tribe of Judah, about twelve miles from Jerusalem.

There are several circumstances relative to this woman and her case which deserve to be noticed:—

1. She was a *widow*, and therefore her condition of life was the better calculated to excite compassion.

2. She lived at some *distance* from Jerusalem, which rendered the case difficult to be readily inquired into; and consequently there was the less danger of detection.

3. She was *advanced in years*, as Josephus says, that her application might have the more weight.

4. She put on *mourning*, to heighten the idea of distress.

5. She framed *a case similar to that in which*

David stood, in order to convince him of the reasonableness of sparing Absalom.

6. She did not make the similitude *too plain* and *visible*, lest the king should see her intention before she had obtained a grant of pardon. Thus her circumstances, her mournful tale, her widow's weeds, her aged person, and her impressive manner, all combined to make one united impression on the king's heart. We need not wonder at her success. See Bishop *Patrick*.

Verse 5. *I am indeed a widow woman*] It is very possible that the principal facts mentioned here were real, and that Joab found out a person whose circumstances bore a near resemblance to that which he wished to represent.

Verse 7. *The whole family is risen*] They took on them the part of the *avenger of blood;* the nearest akin to the murdered person having a right to slay the murderer.

They shall quench my coal which is left] A man and his descendants or successors are often termed in Scripture *a lamp* or *light*. So,

A. M. 2977
B. C. 1027
An. Exod. Isr.
464
Anno ante
I. Olymp. 251

liver him that smote his brother, that we may kill him, for the life of his brother whom he slew; and we will destroy the heir also: and so they shall quench my coal which is left, and shall not leave to my husband *neither* name nor remainder [1]upon the earth.

8 And the king said unto the woman, Go to thine house, and I will give charge concerning thee.

9 And the woman of Tekoah said unto the king, My lord, O king, [m]the iniquity *be* on me, and on my father's house: [n]and the king and his throne *be* guiltless.

10 And the king said, Whosoever saith *aught* unto thee, bring him to me, and he shall not touch thee any more.

11 Then said she, I pray thee, let the king remember the LORD thy God, [o]that thou wouldest not suffer [p]the revengers of blood to destroy any more, lest they destroy my son. And he said, [q]*As* the LORD liveth, there shall not one hair of thy son fall to the earth.

12 Then the woman said, Let thine handmaid, I pray thee, speak *one* word unto my lord the king. And he said, Say on.

A. M. 2977
B. C. 1027
An. Exod. Isr.
464
Anno ante
I. Olymp. 251

13 And the woman said, Wherefore then hast thou thought such a thing against [r]the people of God? for the king doth speak this thing as one which is faulty, in that the king doth not fetch home again [s]his banished.

14 For we [t]must needs die, and *are* as water spilt on the ground, which cannot be gathered up again; [u]neither doth God respect *any* person: yet doth he [v]devise means that his banished be not expelled from him.

15 Now therefore that I am come to speak of this thing unto my lord the king, *it is* because the people have made me afraid: and thy handmaid said, I will now speak unto the king; it may be that the king will perform the request of his handmaid.

16 For the king will hear, to deliver his handmaid out of the hand of the man *that would* destroy me and my son together out of the inheritance of God.

---

[1]Heb. *upon the face of the earth*——[m]Gen. xxvii. 13; 1 Sam. xxv. 24; Matt. xxvii. 25——[n]Chap. iii. 28, 29; 1 Kings ii. 33——[o]Heb. *that the revenger of blood do not multiply to destroy*——[p]Num. xxxv. 19

[q]1 Sam. xiv. 45; Acts xxvii. 34——[r]Judg. xx. 2 [s]Chap. xiii. 37, 38——[t]Job xxxiv. 15, Heb. ix. 27 [u]Or, *because God hath not taken away* his *life, he hath also devised means*, &c.——[v]Num. xxxv. 15, 25, 28

---

chap. xxi. 17, the men of David said, when they sware that he should no more go out with them to battle, *That thou* QUENCH *not the* LIGHT *of Israel.* See also Psa. cxxxii. 17. And to *raise up a lamp* to a person signifies his having a posterity to continue his name and family upon the earth: thus, *quench my coal that is left* means destroying all hope of posterity, and extinguishing the family from among the people. The heathens made use of the same similitude. The few persons who survived the deluge of Deucalion are termed ζώπυρα *living coals*, because by them the *vital flame* of the human race was to be *rekindled* on the earth.

Verse 8. *I will give charge concerning thee.*] This would not do; it was too distant; and she could not by it bring her business to a conclusion: so she proceeds—

Verse 9. *The iniquity be on me*] She intimates that, if the king should suppose that the not bringing the offender to the assigned punishment might reflect on the administration of justice in the land, she was willing that all blame should attach to her and her family, and the king and his throne be guiltless.

Verse 10. *Whosoever saith* aught *unto thee*] Neither did this bring the matter to such a bearing that she could come to her conclusion, which was, to get the king pledged by a *solemn promise* that all proceedings relative to the case should be stopped.

Verse 11. *Let the king remember the Lord thy God*] Consider that when God is earnestly requested to show mercy, he does it in the promptest manner; he does not wait till the

case is hopeless: the danger to which my son is exposed is imminent; if the king do not decide the business instantly, it may be too late.

And he said, As the Lord liveth] Thus he binds himself by a most solemn promise and oath; and this is what the woman wanted to extort.

Verse 13. *Wherefore then hast thou thought such a thing*] The woman, having now got the king's promise confirmed by an oath, that her son should not suffer for the murder of his brother, comes immediately to her conclusion: Is not the king to blame? Does he now act a consistent part? He is willing to pardon the meanest of his subjects the murder of a brother at the instance of a poor widow, and he is not willing to pardon his son Absalom, whose restoration to favour is the desire of the whole nation. Is that clemency to be refused to the king's son, the hope of the *nation* and heir to the throne, which is shown to a private individual, whose death or life can only be of consequence to one family? Why, therefore, dost thou not bring back thy banished child?

Verse 14. *For we must needs die*] Whatever is done must be done quickly; all must die; God has not exempted any person from this common lot. Though Amnon be dead, yet the death of Absalom cannot bring him to life, nor repair this loss. Besides, for his crime, he justly deserved to die; and thou, in this case, didst not administer justice. Horrible as this fratricide is, it is a pardonable case: the crime of Amnon was the most flagitious; and the offence to Absalom, the ruin of his beloved

A. M. 2977
B. C. 1027
An. Exod. Isr.
464
Anno ante
I. Olymp. 251

17 Then thine handmaid said, The word of my lord the king shall now be ^wcomfortable: for ^xas an angel of God, so *is* my lord the king ^yto discern good and bad: therefore the LORD thy God will be with thee.

18 Then the king answered and said unto the woman, Hide not from me, I pray thee, the thing that I shall ask thee. And the woman said, Let my lord the king now speak.

19 And the king said, *Is not* the hand of Joab with thee in all this? And the woman answered and said, *As* thy soul liveth, my lord the king, none can turn to the right hand or to the left from aught that my lord the king hath spoken: for thy servant Joab, he bade me, and ^zhe put all these words in the mouth of thine handmaid:

20 To fetch about this form of speech hath thy servant Joab done this thing: and my lord *is* wise, ^aaccording to the wisdom of an angel of God, to know all *things* that *are* in the earth.

21 And the king said unto Joab, Behold now, I have done this thing: go therefore, bring the young man Absalom again.

22 And Joab fell to the ground on his face, and bowed himself, and ^bthanked the king: and Joab said, To-day thy servant knoweth that I have found grace in thy sight, my lord, O king, in that the king hath fulfilled the request of ^chis servant.

A. M. 2977
B. C. 1027
An. Exod. Isr.
464
Anno ante
I. Olymp. 251

23 So Joab arose ^dand went to Geshur, and brought Absalom to Jerusalem.

24 And the king said, Let him turn to his own house, and let him ^enot see my face. So Absalom returned to his own house, and saw not the king's face.

25 ^fBut in all Israel there was none to be so much praised as Absalom for his beauty: ^gfrom the sole of his foot even to the crown of his head there was no blemish in him.

26 And when he polled his head, (for it was at every year's end that he polled *it:* because *the hair* was heavy on him, therefore he polled it:) he weighed the hair of his head at two hundred shekels after the king's weight.

27 And ^hunto Absalom there were born three sons, and one daughter, whose name *was* Tamar: she was a woman of a fair countenance.

---

^wHeb. *for rest*——^xVer. 20; chap. xix. 27——^yHeb. *to hear*——^zVer. 3——^aVer. 17; chap. xix. 27——^bHeb. *blessed*——^cOr, *thy*——^dChap. xiii. 37

^eGen. xliii. 3; chap. iii. 13——^fHeb. *And as Absalom there was not a beautiful man in all Israel to praise greatly*——^gIsa. i. 6——^hSee chap. xviii. 18

---

sister, indescribably great. Seeing, then, that the thing is so, and that Amnon can be no more recalled to life than water spilt upon the ground can be gathered up again; and that God, whose vicegerent thou art, and whose example of clemency as well as justice thou art called to imitate, devises means that those who were banished from him by sin and transgression, may not be finally expelled from his mercy and his kingdom; restore thy son to favour, and pardon his crime, as thou hast promised to restore my son, and the Lord thy God will be with thee. This is the sum and sense of the woman's argument.

The argument contained in this 14th verse is very elegant, and powerfully persuasive; but one clause of it has been variously understood, *Neither doth God respect* any *person;* the Hebrew is, ולא ישא אלהים נפש *velo yissa Elohim nephesh,* "And God doth not take away the soul." The Septuagint has it, Και ληψεται ὁ Θεος την ψυχην; *And God will receive the soul.* This intimates that, after human life is ended, the soul has a state of separate existence with God. This was certainly the opinion of these translators, and was the opinion of the ancient Jews, at least *three hundred years* before the incarnation; about which time this translation was made. The Vulgate has, *Nec vult Deus perire animam,* "Nor does God will the destruction of the soul." God is not the author of death; neither hath he pleasure in the destruction of the living; imitate him; pardon and recall thy son.

Verse 20. *According to the wisdom of an angel of God*] This is quite in the style of Asiatic flattery. A European is often addressed, "*Saheb can do every thing;* we can do nothing; none can prevent the execution of Saheb's commands; Saheb is God." See WARD.

Verse 21. *And the king said unto Joab*] It appears that Joab was present at the time when the woman was in conference with the king, and no doubt others of David's courtiers or officers were there also.

Verse 24. *Let him not see my face.*] He would not at once restore him to favour, though he had now remitted his crime; so that he should not die for it. It was highly proper to show this detestation of the crime, and respect for justice.

Verse 25. *None to be so much praised as Absalom*] It was probably his *personal* beauty that caused the people to interest themselves so much in his behalf; for the great mass of the public is ever caught and led by *outward appearances.*

There was no blemish in him.] He was perfect and regular in all his features, and in all his proportions.

Verse 26. *When he polled his head*] Not at any particular period, but when the hair became too heavy for him. On this account of the extraordinary weight of Absalom's hair, see the observations at the end of this chapter.

Verse 27. *Unto Absalom there were born*]

A. M. 2977–79
B. C. 1027–25
An. Exod. Isr.
464–66
28 So Absalom dwelt two full years in Jerusalem, ¹and saw not the king's face.

29 Therefore Absalom sent for Joab, to have sent him to the king; but he would not come to him: and when he sent again the second time, he would not come.

30 Therefore he said unto his servants, See, Joab's field is ᵏnear mine, and he hath barley there; go and set it on fire. And Absalom's servants set the field on fire.

31 Then Joab arose, and came to Absalom unto *his* house, and said unto him, Wherefore have thy servants set my field on fire.

32 And Absalom answered Joab, Behold, I sent unto thee, saying, Come hither, that I may send thee to the king, to say, Wherefore am I come from Geshur? *it had been* good for me *to have been* there still: now therefore let me see the king's face; and if there be *any* iniquity in me, let him kill me.

A. M. 2977–79
B. C. 1027–25
An. Exod. Isr.
464–66

33 So Joab came to the king, and told him: and when he had called for Absalom, he came to the king, and bowed himself on his face to the ground before the king: and the king ¹kissed Absalom.

A. M. 2979
B. C. 1025
An. Exod. Isr.
466
Anno ante
I. Olymp. 249

---

¹Ver. 24——ᵏHeb. *near my place*

---

¹Gen. xxxiii. 4; xlv. 15; Luke xv. 20

These children did not survive him; see chap. xviii. 18.

Tamar] The Septuagint adds, *And she became the wife of Roboam, the son of Solomon, and bare to him Abia;* see Matt. i. 7. Josephus says the same. This addition is not found in the other versions.

Verse 30. *Go and set it on fire*] This was strange conduct, but it had the desired effect. He had not used his influence to get Absalom to court; now he uses it, and succeeds.

ADDITIONAL observations on ver. 26:—
"And at every year's end, he (Absalom) polled his head; and he weighed the hair at *two hundred* shekels."

The very learned *Bochart* has written a dissertation on this subject (vide *Bocharti Opera*, vol. iii., col. 883, edit. Lugd. 1692) in a letter to his friend M. *Faukell*. I shall give the substance in what follows.

There is nothing more likely than that corruptions in the Scripture numerals have taken place. *Budæus de Asse* (lib. ii., p. 49 and 51, also lib. iii., p. 67, &c.) complains loudly of this.

This might easily have happened, as in former times the numbers in the sacred writings appear to have been expressed by single letters. The letter ר *resh* stands for *two hundred*, and might in this place be easily mistaken for ד *daleth*, which signifies *four;* but this may be thought to be too little, as it would not amount to more than a quarter of a pound; yet, if the *two hundred* shekels be taken in, the amount will be utterly incredible; for *Josephus* says, (Antiq. lib. vii., cap. 8,) Σικλους διακοσιους, ουτοι δε εισι πεντε μναι, i. e., "Two hundred shekels make five minæ," and in lib. xiv., cap. 12. he says, Ἡ δε μνα παρ᾽ ἡμιν ισχει λιτρας β᾽ και ημισυ; "And a mina with us (i. e., the Jews) weighs two pounds and a half." This calculation makes Absalom's hair weigh *twelve pounds and a half! Credat Judæus Apella!*

Indeed, the same person tells us that the hair of *Absalom* was so thick, &c., ὡς μολις αυτην ἡμεραις αποκειρειν οκτω, "that eight days were scarcely sufficient to cut it off in!" This is rabbinism, with a witness.

Epiphanius, in his treatise *De Ponderibus et Mensuris*, casts much more light on this place, where he says, Σικλος ὁ λεγεται και κοδραντης τε-

ταρτον μεν εστι της ουγκιας, ἡμισυ δε του στατηρος, δυο δραχμας εχων; "A shekel, (i. e., a *common* or *king's* shekel, equal to half a shekel *of the sanctuary*,) which is called also a *quarter*, is the fourth part of an ounce, or half a stater; which is about two drachms." This computation seems very just, as the half-shekel, (i. e., of the sanctuary,) Exod. xxx. 13, which the Lord commanded the children of Israel to give as an offering for their souls, is expressly called in Matt. xvii. 24, το διδραχμον, "two drachms:" and our Lord wrought a miracle to pay this, which the Romans then exacted by way of tribute: and Peter took out of the fish's mouth a *stater*, which contained exactly four drachms or one shekel, (of the sanctuary), the tribute money for our Lord and himself.

The king's shekel was about the fourth part of an ounce, according to what *Epiphanius* says above; and *Hesychius* says the same: Δυναται δε ὁ σικλος δυο δραχμας Αττικας; "A shekel is equal to, or worth, two Attic drachms." The whole amount, therefore, of the *two hundred* shekels is about *fifty ounces*, which make *four pounds two ounces*, Troy weight, or *three pounds two ounces*, Avoirdupois. This need not, says my learned author, be accounted incredible, especially as abundance of *oil* and *ointments* were used by the ancients in dressing their heads; as is evident, not only from many places in the Greek and Roman writers, but also from several places in the sacred writings. See Psa. xxiii. 5; Eccles. ix. 8; Matt. vi. 17.

Josephus also informs us that the Jews not only used *ointments*, but that they put *gold dust* in their hair, that it might flame in the sun; and this they might do in considerable quantities, as gold was so plentiful among them. I must own I have known an instance that makes much for Bochart's argument: an *officer*, who had upwards of *two pounds* of powder and ointments put on his head daily, whose hair did not weigh a fourth part of that weight. And *Absalom*, being exceedingly vain, might be supposed to make a very extensive use of these things. There are some, however, who endeavour to solve the difficulty by understanding שקל *shakal* to mean rather the *value* than the *weight*.

Bochart concludes this elaborate dissertation, in which he appears to have ransacked all the

Hebrew, Greek, and Roman authors for proofs of his opinion, by exhorting his friend in these words of *Horace:*—

—*Si quid novisti rectius istis,*
Candidus imperti; si non, his utere mecum.

To me the above is quite unsatisfactory; and, with due deference to so great a character, I think I have found out *something better.*

I believe the text is not here in its original form; and that a mistake has crept into the numeral letters. I imagine that **ל** *lamed,* THIRTY, was first written; which, in process of time, became changed for **ר** *resh,* TWO HUNDRED, which might easily have happened from the similarity of the letters. But if this be supposed to be *too little,* (which I think it is not,) being only *seven ounces and a half* in the course of a year; let it be observed that the sacred text does not limit it to that quantity of time, for **מקץ ימים לימים** *mikkets yamim laiyamim* signifies literally, "From the end of days to days;" which *Jonathan* properly renders, **מזמן עדן לעדן** *mizzeman iddan leiddan,* "at proper or convenient times," viz., when it

grew too long or weighty, which it might be several times in the year. Besides, this was not all his hair; for his head was not *shaved* but *polled,* i. e., the redundancy cut off.

But how was it probable that these two numerals should be interchanged? Thus; if the upper stroke of the **ל** *lamed* were but a little impaired, as it frequently is both in MSS. and printed books, it might be very easily taken for **ר** *resh,* and the remains of the upper part of the *lamed* might be mistaken for the stroke over the **ר**, which makes it the character of *two hundred.*

But how could **מאתים** *mathayim, two hundred,* in the text, be put in the place of **שלשים** *sheloshim, thirty?* Very easily, when the numbers became expressed by words *at length* instead of *numeral letters.*

The common reading of the text appears to me irreconcilable with truth; and I humbly hope that what I have offered above solves every difficulty, and fully accounts for all that the sacred historian speaks of this vain-comely lad.

Verse 27. "Absalom had a daughter, whose name was *Tamar.*"

CHAPTER XV

Absalom conspires against his father, and uses various methods to seduce the people from their allegiance to their king, 1–6. Under pretence of paying a vow at Hebron, he obtains leave from David to go thither; and, by emissaries sent through the land, prepares the people for revolt, 7–11. He gains over Ahithophel, David's counsellor, 12. David is informed of the general defection of the people; on which he, and his life-guards and friends, leave the city, and go towards the wilderness, 13–18. The steadfast friendship of Ittai, the Gittite, 19–22. David's affecting departure from the city, 23. He sends Zadok and Abiathar with the ark back to Jerusalem, 24–29. He goes up Mount Olivet; prays that the counsel of Ahithophel may be turned into foolishness, 30–31. He desires Hushai to return to Jerusalem, and to send him word of all that occurs, 32–37.

A. M. 2980
B. C. 1024
An. Exod. Isr.
467
Anno ante
I. Olymp. 248

A ND [a]it came to pass after this, that Absalom [b]prepared him chariots and horses, and fifty men to run before him.

2 And Absalom rose up early, and stood beside the way of the gate: and it was *so,* that when any man that had a controversy [c]came to the king for judgment, then Absalom called unto him, and said, Of what city *art* thou? And he said, Thy servant *is* of one of the tribes of Israel.

3 And Absalom said unto him, See, thy matters *are* good and right; but [d]*there is* no man deputed of the king to hear thee.

A. M. 2980
B. C. 1024
An. Exod. Isr.
467
Anno ante
I. Olymp. 248

4 Absalom said moreover, [e]O that I were made judge in the land, that every man which hath any suit or cause might come unto me, and I would do him justice!

5 And it was *so,* that when any man came nigh *to him* to do him obeisance, he put forth his hand, and took him, and kissed him.

---

[a]Chap. xii. 11——[b]1 Kings i. 5——[c]Heb. *to come*

[d]Or, *none will hear thee from the king* downward
[e]Judg. ix. 29

NOTES ON CHAP. XV

Verse 1. *Absalom prepared him chariots and horses*] After all that has been said to prove that *horses* here mean *horsemen,* I think it most likely that the writer would have us to understand *chariots* drawn by *horses;* not by *mules* or such like cattle.

Fifty men to run before him.] Affecting in every respect the regal state by this establishment. Of this man *Calmet* collects the following character: "He was a bold, violent, revengeful, haughty, enterprising, magnificent, eloquent, and popular prince; he was also rich,

ambitious, and vain of his personal accomplishments: after the death of Amnon, and his reconciliation to his father, he saw no hindrance in his way to the throne. He despised Solomon because of the meanness of his birth, and his tender years. He was himself of the blood royal, not only by his father David, but also by his mother Maacah, daughter to Talmai, king of Geshur: and, doubtless, in his own apprehension, of sufficient age, authority, and wisdom, to sustain the weight of government. There was properly now no competitor in his way: Amnon, David's *first-born,* was dead. Of Chileab, his *second* son by Abigail, we hear nothing; and

A. M. 2980
B. C. 1024
An. Exod. Isr.
467
Anno ante
I. Olymp. 248

6 And on this manner did Absalom to all Israel that came to the king for judgment: [f]so Absalom stole the hearts of the men of Israel.

A. M. 2981
B. C. 1023
An. Exod. Isr.
468
Anno ante
I. Olymp. 247

7 And it came to pass [g]after forty years, that Absalom said unto the king, I pray thee, let me go and pay my vow, which I have vowed unto the LORD, in Hebron.

8 [h]For thy servant [i]vowed a vow [k]while I abode at Geshur in Syria, saying, If the LORD shall bring me again indeed to Jerusalem, then I will serve the LORD.

9 And the king said unto him, Go in peace. So he arose, and went to Hebron.

10 But Absalom sent spies throughout all the tribes of Israel, saying, As soon as ye hear the sound of the trumpet, then ye shall say, Absalom reigneth in Hebron.

A. M. 2981
B. C. 1023
An. Exod. Isr.
468
Anno ante
I. Olymp. 247

11 And with Absalom went two hundred men out of Jerusalem, *that were* [l]called; and they went [m]in their simplicity, and they knew not any thing.

12 And Absalom sent for Ahithophel the Gilonite, [n]David's counsellor, from his city, *even* from [o]Giloh, while he offered sacrifices. And the conspiracy was strong; for the people [p]increased continually with Absalom.

13 And there came a messenger to David,

---

[f]Rom. xvi. 18——[g]1 Sam. xvi. 1——[h]1 Sam. xvi. 2
[i]Gen. xxviii. 20, 21——[k]Chap. xiii. 38

[l]1 Sam. ix. 13; xvi. 3, 5——[m]Gen. xx. 5——[n]Psa. xli. 9;
lv. 12, 13, 14——[o]Josh. xv. 51——[p]Psa. iii. 1

Absalom was the *third:* see chap. iii. 2-5. He, therefore, seemed to stand *nearest to the throne;* but his sin was, that he sought it during his father's life, and endeavoured to dethrone him in order to sit in his stead."

Verse 6. *So Absalom stole the hearts*] His manner of doing this is circumstantially related above. He was thoroughly versed in the arts of the *demagogue;* and the common people, the vile mass, heard him gladly. He used the *patriot's* arguments, and was every thing of the kind, as far as *promise* could go. He found fault with men in power; and he only wanted their place, like all other pretended patriots, that he might act as they did, or worse.

Verse 7. *After forty years*] There is no doubt that this reading is corrupt, though supported by the commonly printed *Vulgate,* the *Septuagint,* and the *Chaldee.* But the *Syriac* has

ܐܪܒܥ ܫܢܝܢ *arba shanin,* FOUR *years;* the *Arabic* the same أربعة سنين *arba shinin,* FOUR *years;* and *Josephus* has the same; so also the *Sixtine edition* of the *Vulgate,* and several MSS. of the same version. *Theodoret* also reads *four,* not *forty;* and most learned men are of opinion that ארבעים *arbaim,* FORTY, is an error for ארבע *arba,* FOUR; yet this reading is not supported by any Hebrew MS. yet discovered. But *two* of those collated by Dr. *Kennicott* have יום *yom* instead of שנה *shanah,* i. e., *forty* DAYS, instead of *forty* YEARS; and this is a reading more likely to be true than that in the commonly received text. We know that Absalom did stay THREE *years* with his grandfather at Geshur, chap. xiii. 38; and this probably was *a year after his return:* the era, therefore, may be the time of his slaying his brother Amnon; and the *four* years include the time from his flight till the conspiracy mentioned here.

Verse 8. *While I abode at Geshur in Syria*] Geshur, the country of Talmai, was certainly not in *Syria,* but lay on the south of *Canaan,* in or near *Edom,* as is evident from Judg. i. 10; 1 Sam. xxvii. 8; chap. xiii. 37. Hence it is probable that ארם *Aram, Syria,* is a mistake for אדם *Edom;* ד *daleth* and ר *resh* being easily inter-

changeable. *Edom* is the reading both of the *Syriac* and *Arabic.*

I will serve the Lord.] Here he pretended to be a strict follower of Jehovah, even while he was in a *heathen* country; and now he desires liberty to go and perform a vow at Hebron, which he pretends to have made while he was resident at Geshur. And all this was the more perfectly to organize his system of rebellion against his venerable father.

Verse 10. *Absalom sent spies*] These persons were to go into every tribe; and the trumpet was to be blown as a signal for all to arise, and proclaim Absalom in every place. The trumpet was probably used as a kind of *telegraph* by the spies: trumpet exciting trumpet from place to place; so that, in a few minutes all Israel would hear the proclamation.

Verse 11. *Went two hundred men*] These were probably soldiers, whom he supposed would be of considerable consequence to him. They had been seduced by his specious conduct, but knew nothing of his present *design.*

Verse 12. *Sent for Ahithophel*] When Absalom got *him,* he in effect got the *prime minister* of the kingdom to join him.

Verse 13. *The hearts of the men of Israel are after Absalom.*] It is very difficult to account for this general defection of the people. Several reasons are given: 1. David was old or afflicted, and could not well attend to the administration of justice in the land. 2. It does appear that the king did not attend to the affairs of state, and that there were no properly appointed judges in the land; see ver. 3. 3. Joab's power was overgrown; he was wicked and insolent, oppressive to the people, and David was afraid to execute the laws against him. 4. There were still some partisans of the house of Saul, who thought the crown not fairly obtained by David. 5. David was under the displeasure of the Almighty, for his adultery with Bath-sheba, and his murder of Uriah; and God let his enemies loose against him. 6. There are always troublesome and disaffected men in every state, and under every government; who can never rest, and are ever hoping for something from a

A. M. 2981
B. C. 1023
An. Exod. Isr.
468
Anno ante
I. Olymp. 247 saying, qThe hearts of the men of Israel are after Absalom.

14 And David said unto all his servants that *were* with him at Jerusalem, Arise, and let us ʳflee; for we shall not *else* escape from Absalom: make speed to depart, lest he overtake us suddenly, and ˢbring evil upon us, and smite the city with the edge of the sword.

15 And the king's servants said unto the king, Behold, thy servants *are ready to do* whatsoever my lord the king shall ᵗappoint.

16 And ᵘthe king went forth, and all his household ᵛafter him. And the king left ʷten women, *which were* concubines, to keep the house.

17 And the king went forth, and all the people after him, and tarried in a place that was far off.

18 And all his servants passed on beside him; ˣand all the Cherethites, and all the Pelethites, and all the Gittites, six hundred men which came after him from Gath, passed on before the king.

19 Then said the king to ʸIttai the Gittite, Wherefore goest thou also with us? return to thy place, and abide with the king: for thou *art* a stranger, and also an exile.

20 Whereas thou camest *but* yesterday, should I this day ᶻmake thee go up and down with us? seeing I go ᵃwhither I may, return thou, and take back thy brethren: mercy and truth *be* with thee.

A. M. 2981
B. C. 1023
An. Exod. Isr.
468
Anno ante
I. Olymp. 247

21 And Ittai answered the king, and said, ᵇ*As* the LORD liveth, and *as* my lord the king liveth, surely in what place my lord the king shall be, whether in death or life, even there also will thy servant be.

22 And David said to Ittai, Go and pass over. And Ittai the Gittite passed over, and all his men, and all the little ones that *were* with him.

23 And all the country wept with a loud voice, and all the people passed over: the king also himself passed over the brook ᶜKidron, and all the people passed over toward the way of the ᵈwilderness.

24 And lo, Zadok also, and all the Levites *were* with him, ᵉbearing the ark of the covenant of God: and they set down the ark of God; and Abiathar went up, until all the people had done passing out of the city.

25 And the king said unto Zadok, Carry back the ark of God into the city: if I shall find favour in the eyes of the LORD, he ᶠwill bring me again, and show me *both* it and his habitation:

---

qVer. 6; Judg. ix. 3——ʳCh. xix. 9; Psa. iii. title
ˢHeb. *thrust*——ᵗHeb. *choose*——ᵘPsa. iii. title——ᵛHeb. *at his feet*——ʷChap. xvi. 21, 22——ˣChap. viii. 18
ʸChap. xviii. 2

ᶻHeb. *make thee wander in going*——ᵃ1 Sam. xxiii. 13
ᵇRuth i. 16, 17; Prov. xvii. 17; xviii. 24——ᶜCalled, John xviii. 1, *Cedron*——ᵈChap. xvi. 2——ᵉNum. iv. 15——ᶠPsa. xliii. 3

---

change. 7. Absalom appeared to be the *real* and was the *undisputed* heir to the throne; David could not, in the course of nature, live very long; and most people are more disposed to hail the beams of the *rising*, than exult in those of the *setting*, sun. No doubt some of these causes operated, and perhaps most of them exerted less or more influence in this most scandalous business.

Verse 14. *David said—Arise—let us flee*] This, I believe, was the first time that David turned his back to his enemies. And why did he *now* flee? Jerusalem, far from not being in a state to sustain a siege, was so strong that even the blind and the lame were supposed to be a sufficient defence for the walls, see chap. v. 6. And he had still with him his faithful *Cherethites* and *Pelethites;* besides six hundred faithful Gittites, who were perfectly willing to follow his fortunes. There does not appear any reason why such a person, in such circumstances, should not act on the *defensive;* at least till he should be fully satisfied of the real complexion of affairs. But he appears to take all as *coming from the hand of God;* therefore he humbles himself, weeps, goes barefoot, and covers his head! He does not even *hasten* his

departure, for the habit of mourners is not the habit of those who are *flying* before the face of their enemies. He sees the storm, and he yields to what he conceives to be the tempest of the Almighty.

Verse 17. *And tarried in a place*] He probably waited till he saw all his friends safely out of the city.

Verse 19. *Thou* art *a stranger, and also an exile.*] Some suppose that Ittai was the son of Achish, king of Gath, who was very much attached to David, and banished from his father's court on that account. He and his *six hundred* men are generally supposed to have been proselytes to the Jewish religion.

Verse 20. *Mercy and truth be with thee.*] May God ever show thee mercy, as thou showest it to me, and his truth ever preserve thee from error and delusion!

Verse 23. *The brook Kidron*] This was an inconsiderable brook, and only furnished with water in *winter*, and in the *rains*. See John xviii. 1.

Verse 24. *Bearing the ark*] The priests knew that God had given the kingdom to David; they had no evidence that he had deposed him: they therefore chose to accompany him, and

A. M. 2981
B. C. 1023
An. Exod. Isr.
468
Anno ante
I. Olymp. 247

26 But if he thus say, I have no ^gdelight in thee; behold, *here am* I, ^hlet him do to me as seemeth good unto him.

27 The king said also unto Zadok the priest, *Art not* thou a ⁱseer? return into the city in peace, and ^kyour two sons with you, Ahimaaz thy son, and Jonathan the son of Abiathar.

28 See, ^lI will tarry in the plain of the wilderness, until there come word from you to certify me.

29 Zadok therefore and Abiathar carried the ark of God again to Jerusalem: and they tarried there.

30 And David went up by the ascent of *Mount* Olivet, ^mand wept as he went up, and ⁿhad his head covered, and he went ^obarefoot: and all the people that *was* with him ^pcovered every man his head, and they went up, ^qweeping as they went up.

31 And *one* told David, saying, ^rAhithophel *is* among the conspirators with Absalom. And David said, O LORD, I pray thee, ^sturn the counsel of Ahithophel into foolishness.

32 And it came to pass, that *when* David was come to the top *of the mount,* where he worshipped God, behold, Hushai the ^tArchite came to meet him ^uwith his coat rent, and earth upon his head:

A. M. 2981
B. C. 1023
An. Exod. Isr.
468
Anno ante
I. Olymp. 247

33 Unto whom David said, If thou passest on with me, then thou shalt be ^va burden unto me:

34 But if thou return to the city, and say unto Absalom, ^wI will be thy servant, O king; *as* I *have been* thy father's servant hitherto, so *will* I now also *be* thy servant: then mayest thou for me defeat the counsel of Ahithophel.

35 And *hast thou* not there with thee Zadok and Abiathar the priests? therefore it shall be, *that* what thing soever thou shalt hear out of the king's house, ^xthou shalt tell *it* to Zadok and Abiathar the priests.

36 Behold, *they have* there ^ywith them their two sons, Ahimaaz Zadok's *son,* and Jonathan Abiathar's *son;* and by them ye shall send unto me every thing that ye can hear.

37 So Hushai ^zDavid's friend came into the city, ^aand Absalom came into Jerusalem.

---

^gNum. xiv. 8; chap. xxii. 20; 1 Kings x. 9; 2 Chron. ix. 8; Isa. lxii. 4——^h1 Sam. iii. 18——ⁱ1 Sam. ix. 9 ^kSee chap. xvii. 17——^lChap. xvii. 16——^mHeb. *going up, and weeping*——ⁿChap. xix. 4; Esth. vi. 12——^oIsa. xx. 2, 4

^pJer. xiv. 3, 4——^qPsa. cxxvi. 6——^rPsa. iii. 1, 2; lv. 12, &c.——^sChap. xvi. 23; xvii. 14, 23——^tJosh. xvi. 2——^uChap. i. 2——^vChap. xix. 35——^wChap. xvi. 19——^xChap. xvii. 15, 16——^yVer. 27——^zChap. xvi. 16; 1 Chron. xxvii. 33——^aChap. xvi. 15

---

take the ark, the object of their charge, with them.

Verse 25. *Carry back the ark*] David shows here great confidence in God, and great humility. The ark was too precious to be exposed to the dangers of his migrations; he knew that God would restore him if he delighted in him, and he was not willing to carry off from the city of God that without which the *public worship* could not be carried on. He felt, therefore, more for this public worship and the honour of God, than he did for his own personal safety.

Verse 27. *Art not thou a seer? return into the city in peace*] That is, As thou art the only organ of the public worship, that worship cannot be carried on without thee; and as thou art the *priest of God,* thou hast no cause to fear for thy personal safety: the nation has not abandoned their God, though they have abandoned their king. It appears also, that he wished these priests, by means of their sons, Ahimaaz the son of Zadok, and Jonathan the son of Abiathar, to send him frequent intelligence of the motions and operations of the enemy.

Verse 30. *Had his head covered*] This was not only the attitude of a *mourner,* but even of a *culprit;* they usually had their heads covered when condemned. See the case of Haman. When the king had pronounced his condemnation, they immediately covered his face, and led him out to punishment; Esth. vii. 8. See also Quintus Curtius, De Philota, cap. vi.: *I, Lictor; caput obnubito.*

Verse 31. *Turn the counsel of Ahithophel*

into foolishness.] Ahithophel was a wise man, and well versed in state affairs; and God alone could confound *his* devices.

Verse 32. *Where he worshipped God*] Though in danger of his life, he stops on the top of Mount Olivet for prayer! How true is the adage, *Prayer and provender never hinder any man's journey!* Reader, dost thou do likewise?

Hushai the Archite] He was the particular friend of David, and was now greatly affected by his calamity.

Verse 33. *Then thou shalt be a burden unto me.*] It appears that Hushai was not a warrior, but was a wise, prudent, and discreet man, who could well serve David by gaining him intelligence of Absalom's conspiracy; and he directs him to form a strict confederacy with the priests Zadok and Abiathar, and to make use of their sons as couriers between Jerusalem and David's place of retreat.

Verse 37. *Absalom came into Jerusalem.*] It is very probable that he and his partisans were not far from the city when David left it, and this was one reason which caused him to hurry his departure.

READER, behold in the case of David a sad vicissitude of human affairs, and a fearful proof of their instability. Behold a king, the greatest that ever lived, a profound politician, an able general, a brave soldier, a poet of the most sublime genius and character, a prophet of the Most High God, and the deliverer of his country, driven from his dominions by his own son, abandoned by his fickle people, and for a time even by his God! See in his desolate state that there is none so exalted that God cannot abase, and none so abased that God cannot exalt. He was forsaken for a time, and his enemies triumphed; God returned, and his enemies were confounded. His crime, it is true, was great; and God had declared by Nathan what had now come to pass. God is just, and in numberless instances sees right to show his displeasure even at those sins which his mercy has forgiven. In all cases it is a fearful and bitter thing to sin against the Lord.

CHAPTER XVI

Ziba, servant of Mephibosheth, meets David with provisions, and by false insinuations obtains the grant of his master's property, 1–4. Shimei abuses and curses David, who restrains Abishai from slaying him, 5–14. Hushai makes a feigned tender of his services to Absalom, 15–19. Absalom calls a council and Ahithophel advises him to go in to his father's concubines, 20–22. Character of Ahithophel as a counsellor, 23.

A. M. 2981
B. C. 1023
An. Exod. Isr. 468
Anno ante
I. Olymp. 247

AND [a]when David was a little past the top *of the hill*, behold, [b]Ziba the servant of Mephibosheth met him, with a couple of asses saddled, and upon them two hundred *loaves* of bread, and a hundred bunches of raisins, and a hundred of summer fruits, and a bottle of wine.

2 And the king said unto Ziba, What meanest thou by these? And Ziba said, The asses *be* for the king's household to ride on; and the bread and summer fruit for the young men to eat; and the wine, [c]that such as be faint in the wilderness may drink.

3 And the king said, And where *is* thy master's son? [d]And Ziba said unto the king, Behold, he abideth at Jerusalem: for he said, To-day shall the house of Israel restore me the kingdom of my father.

4 [e]Then said the king to Ziba, Behold, thine *are* all that *pertained* unto Mephibosheth.

And Ziba said, [f]I humbly beseech thee *that* I may find grace in thy sight, my lord, O king.

A. M. 2981
B. C. 1023
An. Exod. Isr. 468
Anno ante
I. Olymp. 247

5 And when King David came to Bahurim, behold thence came out a man of the family of the house of Saul, whose name *was* [g]Shimei, the son of Gera: [h]he came forth, and cursed still as he came.

6 And he cast stones at David, and at all the servants of King David: and all the people and all the mighty men *were* on his right hand and on his left.

7 And thus said Shimei when he cursed, Come out, come out, thou [i]bloody man, and thou [k]man of Belial:

8 The LORD hath [l]returned upon thee all [m]the blood of the house of Saul, in whose stead thou hast reigned; and the LORD hath delivered the kingdom into the hand of Absalom thy son: and, [n]behold, thou *art taken* in thy mischief, because thou *art* a bloody man.

---

[a]Ch. xv. 30, 32——[b]Ch. ix. 2——[c]Ch. xv. 23; xvii. 29
[d]Ch. xix. 27——[e]Prov. xviii. 13——[f]Heb. *I do obeisance*
[g]Ch. xix. 16; 1 Kings ii. 8, 44——[h]Or, *he still came forth*

and cursed——[i]Heb. *man of blood*——[k]Deut. xiii. 13
[l]Judg. ix. 24, 56, 57; 1 Kings ii. 32, 33——[m]See chap. i. 16; iii. 28, 29; iv. 11, 12——[n]Heb. *behold thee in thy evil*

NOTES ON CHAP. XVI

Verse 1. *Two hundred* loaves *of bread*] The word *loaf* gives us a false idea of the ancient Jewish bread; it was *thin cakes*, not *yeasted* and *raised* like ours.

Bunches of raisins] See on 1 Sam. xxv. 18.

Summer fruits] These were probably *pumpions, cucumbers*, or *water-melons*. The two latter are extensively used in those countries to refresh travellers in the burning heat of the summer. Mr. Harmer supposes they are called *summer fruits* on this very account.

A bottle of wine.] A *goat's skin full of wine;* this I have already shown was the general *bottle* in the Eastern countries; see on 1 Sam. xxv. 18.

Verse 2. *The asses* be *for the king's household*] This is the Eastern method of speaking when any thing is presented to a great man: "This and this is for the slaves of the servants of your majesty," when at the same time the presents are intended for the sovereign himself, and are so understood. It is a high Eastern compliment: These presents are not worthy of *your* acceptance; they are only fit for the slaves of your slaves.

Verse 3. *To-day shall the house of Israel*] What a base wretch was Ziba! and how unfounded was this accusation against the peaceable, loyal, and innocent Mephibosheth!

Verse 4. *Thine* are *all*] This conduct of David was very rash; he spoiled an honourable man to reward a villain, not giving himself time to look into the circumstances of the case. But David was in heavy afflictions, and these sometimes make even a *wise man* mad. Nothing should be done rashly; he who is in the habit of obeying the first impulse of his passions or feelings, will seldom do a right action, and never keep a clear conscience.

Verse 5. *David came to Bahurim*] This place lay northward of Jerusalem, in the tribe of Benjamin. It is called *Almon*, Josh. xxi. 18; and

A. M. 2981
B. C. 1023
An. Exod. Isr.
468
Anno ante
I. Olymp. 247

9 Then said Abishai the son of Zeruiah unto the king, Why should this °dead dog ᴾcurse my lord the king? let me go over, I pray thee, and take off his head.

10 And the king said, �ۥWhat have I to do with you, ye sons of Zeruiah? so let him curse, because ʳthe Lᴏʀᴅ hath said unto him, Curse David. ˢWho shall then say, Wherefore hast thou done so?

11 And David said to Abishai, and to all his servants, Behold, ᵗmy son, which ᵘcame forth of my bowels, seeketh my life: how much more now *may this* Benjamite *do it?* let him alone, and let him curse; for the Lᴏʀᴅ hath bidden him.

12 It may be that the Lᴏʀᴅ will look on mine ᵛaffliction, ʷand that the Lᴏʀᴅ will ˣrequite me good for his cursing this day.

13 And as David and his men went by the way, Shimei went along on the hill's side over against him, and cursed as he went, and threw stones at him, and ʸcast dust.

14 And the king, and all the people that *were* with him, came weary, and refreshed themselves there.

15 And ᶻAbsalom, and all the people the

men of Israel, came to Jerusalem, and Ahithophel with him.

A. M. 2981
B. C. 1023
An. Exod. Isr.
468
Anno ante
I. Olymp. 247

16 And it came to pass, when Hushai the Archite, ᵃDavid's friend, was come unto Absalom, that Hushai said unto Absalom, ᵇGod save the king, God save the king.

17 And Absalom said to Hushai, *Is* this thy kindness to thy friend? ᶜwhy wentest thou not with thy friend?

18 And Hushai said unto Absalom, Nay; but whom the Lᴏʀᴅ, and this people, and all the men of Israel, choose, his will I be, and with him will I abide.

19 And again, ᵈwhom should I serve? *should I* not *serve* in the presence of his son? as I have served in thy father's presence, so will I be in thy presence.

20 Then said Absalom to Ahithophel, Give counsel among you what we shall do.

21 And Ahithophel said unto Absalom, Go in unto thy father's ᵉconcubines, which he hath left to keep the house; and all Israel shall hear that thou ᶠart abhorred of thy father: then shall ᵍthe hands of all that *are* with thee be strong.

22 So they spread Absalom a tent upon the

°1 Sam. xxiv. 14; chap. ix. 8——ᴾExod. xxii. 28 �q Chap. xix. 22; 1 Pet. ii. 23——ʳSee 2 Kings xviii. 25; Lam. iii. 38——ˢRom. ix. 20——ᵗChapter xii. 11 ᵘGen. xv. 4——ᵛOr, *tears*——ʷHeb. *eye;* Gen. xxix. 32; 1 Sam. i. 11; Psa. xxv. 18——ˣRom. viii. 28——ʸHeb.

dusted him *with dust*——ᶻChap. xv. 37——ᵃChap. xv. 37——ᵇHeb. *Let the king live*——ᶜChap. xix. 25; Prov. xvii. 17——ᵈChap. xv. 34——ᵉChap. xv. 16; xx. 3 ᶠGen. xxxiv. 30; 1 Sam. xiii. 4——ᵍChap. ii. 7; Zech. viii. 13

Alemeth, 1 Chron. vi. 60. Bahurim signifies *youths,* and Almuth *youth;* so the names are of the same import.

Cursed still as he came.] Used imprecations and execrations.

Verse 10. *Because the Lord hath said*] The particle וכי *vechi* should be translated *for if,* not *because.* Fᴏʀ ɪꜰ *the Lord hath said unto him, Curse David, who shall then say, Wherefore hast thou done so?*

Verse 11. *Let him curse; for the Lord hath bidden him.*] No soul of man can suppose that ever God bade one man to curse another, much less that he commanded such a wretch as Shimei to curse such a man as David; but this is a peculiarity of the Hebrew language, which does not always distinguish between *permission* and *commandment.* Often the Scripture attributes to God what he only *permits* to be done; or what in the course of his providence he does not *hinder.* David, however, considers all this as being permitted of God for his chastisement and humiliation. I cannot withhold from my readers a very elegant poetic paraphrase of this passage, from the pen of the Rev. *Charles Wesley,* one of the first of Christian poets:—

"Pure from the blood of *Saul* in vain,
    He dares not to the charge reply:

Uriah's doth the charge maintain,
    Uriah's doth against him cry!
Let Shimei curse: the rod he bears
    For sins which mercy had forgiven:
And in the wrongs of man reveres
    The awful righteousness of heaven.
Lord, I adore thy righteous will,
    Through every instrument of ill
    My Father's goodness see;
Accept the complicated wrong
Of *Shimei's* hand and *Shimei's* tongue
    As kind rebukes from ᴛʜᴇᴇ."

Verse 15. *The men of Israel*] These words are wanting in the *Chaldee, Septuagint, Syriac, Vulgate,* and *Arabic,* and in two of *Kennicott's* and *De Rossi's* MSS.

Verse 18. *Whom the Lord and this people—choose*] Here is an *equivocation;* Hushai meant *in his heart* that God and all the people of Israel had chosen *David;* but he spake so as to make Absalom believe that he spoke of *him:* for whatever of insincerity may appear in this, Hushai is alone answerable. What he says afterwards may be understood in the same way.

Verse 21. *Go in unto thy father's concubines*] It may be remembered that David left *ten* of them behind to take care of the house, see chap. xv. 16. Ahithophel advised this infernal meas-

A. M. 2981
B. C. 1023
An. Exod. Isr.
468
Anno ante
I. Olymp. 247

top of the house; and Absalom went in unto his father's concubines [h]in the sight of all Israel.

23 And the counsel of Ahithophel, which he

counselled in those days, *was* as if a man had inquired at the [i]oracle of God: so *was* all the counsel of Ahithophel [k]both with David and with Absalom.

A. M. 2981
B. C. 1023
An. Exod. Isr.
468
Anno ante
I. Olymp. 247

---

[h]Chap. xii. 11, 12

[i]Heb. *word*——[k]Chap. xv. 12

---

ure, in order to prevent the possibility of a *reconciliation* between David and his son; thus was the prophecy to Nathan fulfilled, chap. xii. 11. And this was probably transacted in the very same place where David's eye took the adulterous view of Bath-sheba; see chap. xi. 2.

The wives of the conquered king were always the property of the conqueror; and in possessing these, he appeared to possess the right to the kingdom. *Herodotus* informs us that Smerdis, having seized on the Persian throne after the death of Cambyses, espoused all the wives of his predecessor, lib. iii., c. 68. But for a son to take his father's wives was the sum of abomi-

nation, and was *death* by the law of God, Lev. xx. 11. This was a sin rarely found, even among the *Gentiles*.

Every part of the conduct of Absalom shows him to have been a most profligate young man; he was proud, vindictive, adulterous, incestuous, a parricide, and, in fine, reprobate to every good word and work. We still however recollect that David had grievously sinned, and we should also recollect that he suffered grievously for it; and that his humiliation, repentance, and amendment, were most decisive and exemplary. Reader, God is as *just* as he is *merciful*.

CHAPTER XVII

Ahithophel counsels Absalom to pursue his father with twelve thousand men, 1–4. Hushai gives a different counsel, and is followed, 5–14. Hushai informs Zadok and Abiathar; and they send word to David, 15–21. David and his men go beyond Jordan, 22. Ahithophel, finding his counsel slighted, goes home, sets his house in order, and hangs himself, 23. David moves to Mahanaim; and Absalom follows him over Jordan, 24–26. Several friends meet David at Mahanaim with refreshments and provisions, 27–29.

A. M. 2981
B. C. 1023
An. Exod. Isr.
468
Anno ante
I. Olymp. 247

MOREOVER, Ahithophel said unto Absalom, Let me now choose out twelve thousand men, and I will arise and pursue after David this night:

2 And I will come upon him while he *is* [a]weary and weak-handed, and will make him afraid: and all the people that *are* with him shall flee; and I will [b]smite the king only:

3 And I will bring back all the people unto thee: the man whom thou seekest *is* as if all returned: *so* all the people shall be in peace.

4 And the saying [c]pleased Absalom well, and all the elders of Israel.

5 Then said Absalom, Call now Hushai the Archite also, and let us hear likewise [d]what he saith.

6 And when Hushai was come to Absalom, Absalom spake unto him, saying, Ahithophel hath spoken after this manner, shall we do *after* his [e]saying? if not, speak thou.

7 And Hushai said unto Absalom, The counsel that Ahithophel hath [f]given *is* not good at this time.

8 For, said Hushai, thou knowest thy father and his men, that they *be* mighty men, and they *be* [g]chafed in their minds, as [h]a bear robbed of her whelps in the field: and thy father *is* a man of war, and will not lodge with the people.

9 Behold, he is hid now in some pit, or in some *other* place: and it will come to pass, when some of them be [i]overthrown at the

A. M. 2981
B. C. 1023
An. Exod. Isr.
468
Anno ante
I. Olymp. 247

---

[a]See Deut. xxv. 18; ch. xvi. 14——[b]Zech. xiii. 7
[c]Heb. *was right in the eyes of*, &c.; 1 Sam. xviii. 20
[d]Heb. *what is in his mouth*

[e]Hebrew, *word*——[f]Heb. *counselled*——[g]Hebrew, *bitter of soul*; Judg. xviii. 25——[h]Hosea xiii. 8——[i]Hebrew, *fallen*

NOTES ON CHAP. XVII

Verse 1. *Let me now choose out twelve thousand men*] Had this counsel been followed, David and his little troop would soon have been destroyed; nothing but the miraculous interposition of God could have saved them. *Twelve thousand* chosen troops coming against him, in

his totally unprepared state, would have soon settled the business of the kingdom. Ahithophel well saw that, this advice neglected, all was lost.

Verse 3. *The man whom thou seekest* is *as if all returned*] Only secure David, and all Israel will be on thy side. He is the soul of the whole; destroy him, and all the rest will submit.

Verse 8. *As a bear robbed of her whelps*]

A. M. 2981
B. C. 1023
An. Exod. Isr.
468
Anno ante
I. Olymp. 247
first, that whosoever heareth it will say, There is a slaughter among the people that follow Absalom.

10 And he also *that is* valiant, whose heart *is* as the heart of a lion, shall utterly ᵏmelt: for all Israel knoweth that thy father *is* a mighty man, and *they* which *be* with him *are* valiant men.

11 Therefore I counsel that all Israel be generally gathered unto thee, ˡfrom Dan even to Beer-sheba, ᵐas the sand that *is* by the sea for multitude; and ⁿthat thou go to battle in thine own person.

12 So shall we come upon him in some place where he shall be found, and we will light upon him as the dew falleth on the ground: and of him and of all the men that *are* with him there shall not be left so much as one.

13 Moreover, if he be gotten into a city, then shall all Israel bring ropes to that city, and we will draw it into the river, until there be not one small stone found there.

14 And Absalom and all the men of Israel said, The counsel of Hushai the Archite *is* better than the counsel of Ahithophel. For ᵒthe Lᴏʀᴅ had ᵖappointed to defeat the good counsel of Ahithophel, to the intent that the Lᴏʀᴅ might bring evil upon Absalom.

15 ᑫThen said Hushai unto Zadok and to Abiathar the priests, Thus and thus did Ahi-

thophel counsel Absalom and the elders of Israel; and thus and thus have I counselled.

A. M. 2981
B. C. 1023
An. Exod. Isr.
468
Anno ante
I. Olymp. 247

16 Now therefore send quickly, and tell David, saying, Lodge not this night ʳin the plains of the wilderness, but speedily pass over; lest the king be swallowed up, and all the people that *are* with him.

17 ˢNow Jonathan and Ahimaaz ᵗstayed by ᵘEn-rogel; for they might not be seen to come into the city: and a wench went and told them; and they went and told King David.

18 Nevertheless a lad saw them, and told Absalom: but they went both of them away quickly, and came to a man's house ᵛin Bahurim, which had a well in his court; whither they went down.

19 And ʷthe woman took and spread a covering over the well's mouth, and spread ground corn thereon; and the thing was not known.

20 And when Absalom's servants came to the woman to the house, they said, Where *is* Ahimaaz and Jonathan? And ˣthe woman said unto them, They be gone over the brook of water. And when they had sought and could not find *them,* they returned to Jerusalem.

21 And it came to pass, after they were departed, that they came up out of the well, and went and told King David, and said unto

---

ᵏJosh. ii. 11——ˡJudg. xx. 1——ᵐGen. xxii. 17
ⁿHeb. *that thy face* or *presence go,* &c.——ᵒChap. xv.
31, 34——ᵖHeb. *commanded*——ᑫChap. xv. 35

ʳChap. xv. 28——ˢChap. xv. 27, 36——ᵗJosh. ii. 4,
&c.——ᵘJosh. xv. 7; xviii. 16——ᵛChap. xvi. 5——ʷSee
Josh. ii. 6——ˣSee Exod. i. 19; Josh. ii. 4, 5

All wild beasts are very furious when robbed of their young; but we have some remarkable instances of the maternal affection of the bear in such circumstances; see one at the end of the chapter.

Verse 13. *Shall all Israel bring ropes to that city*] The original word חבלים *chabalim,* which signifies *ropes,* and from which we have our word *cable,* may have some peculiarity of meaning here; for it is not likely that any city could be pulled down with ropes. The *Chaldee,* which should be best judge in this case, translates the original word by משרין *mashreyan, towers:* this gives an easy sense.

Verse 17. *En-rogel*] The *fullers' well;* the place where they were accustomed to *tread* the clothes with their *feet;* hence the name עין *ein,* a *well,* and רגל *regel,* the *foot,* because of the *treading* above mentioned.

And a wench went and told them] The word *wench* occurs nowhere else in the Holy Scriptures: and, indeed, has no business here; as the

Hebrew word שפחה *shiphchah,* should have been translated *girl, maid, maid-servant.* The word either comes from the Anglo-Saxon **pencle.** a *maid,* or the Belgic *wunch, desire, a thing wished for:* multum enim ut plurimum *Puellæ* a Juvenibus *desiderantur,* seu *appetuntur.* So *Minsheu. Junius* seems more willing to derive it from *wince,* to frisk, to be skittish, &c.; for reasons sufficiently obvious, and which he gives at length. After all, it may as likely come from the Gothic *wens* or *weins,* a word frequently used in the gospels of the Codex Argenteus for *wife. Coverdale's* Bible, 1535, has *damsell. Becke's* Bible, 1549, has *wenche.* The same in *Cardmarden's* Bible, 1566; but it is *maid* in *Barker's* Bible, 1615. *Wench* is more of a Scotticism than *maid* or *damsel;* and King James probably restored it, as he is said to have done *lad* in Gen. xxi. 12, and elsewhere. In every other place where the word occurs, our translators render it *handmaid, bondmaid, maiden, womanservant, maidservant,* and *servant.* Such is the latitude with which they translate the

A. M. 2981
B. C. 1023
An. Exod. Isr.
468
Anno ante
I. Olymp. 247

David, [y]Arise, and pass quickly over the water: for thus hath Ahithophel counselled against you.

22 Then David arose, and all the people that *were* with him, and they passed over Jordan: by the morning light there lacked not one of them that was not gone over Jordan.

23 And when Ahithophel saw that his counsel was not [z]followed, he saddled *his* ass, and arose, and gat him home to his house, to [a]his city, and [b]put his household in order, and [c]changed himself, and died, and was buried in the sepulchre of his father.

24 Then David came to [d]Mahanaim. And Absalom passed over Jordan, he and all the men of Israel with him.

25 And Absalom made Amasa captain of the host instead of Joab: which Amasa *was* a man's son whose name *was* [e]Ithra, an Israelite,

that went in to [f]Abigail [g]the daughter of [h]Nahash, sister to Zeruiah, Joab's mother.

A. M. 2981
B. C. 1023
An. Exod. Isr.
468
Anno ante
I. Olymp. 247

26 So Israel and Absalom pitched in the land of Gilead.

27 And it came to pass, when David was come to Mahanaim, that [i]Shobi the son of Nahash of Rabbah of the children of Ammon, and [k]Machir the son of Ammiel of Lo-debar, and [l]Barzillai the Gileadite of Rogelim,

28 Brought beds, and [m]basons, and earthen vessels, and wheat, and barley, and flour, and parched *corn,* and beans, and lentiles and parched *pulse,*

29 And honey, and butter, and sheep, and cheese of kine, for David, and for the people that *were* with him, to eat: for they said, The people *is* hungry, and weary, and thirsty [n]in the wilderness.

---

[y]Ver. 15, 16——[z]Heb. *done*——[a]Chap. xv. 12 [b]Heb. *gave charge concerning his house;* 2 Kings xx. 1 [c]Matt. xxvii. 5——[d]Gen. xxxii. 2; Josh. xiii. 26; chap. ii. 8——[e]Or, *Jether an Ishmaelite*

[f]1 Chron. ii. 16, 17——[g]Heb. *Abigal*——[h]Or, *Jesse;* see 1 Chron. ii. 13, 16——[i]See chap. x. 1; xii. 30 [k]Chap. ix. 4——[l]Chap. xix. 31, 32; 1 Kings ii. 7 [m]Or, *cups*——[n]Chap. xvi. 2

---

same Hebrew term in almost innumerable instances.

Verse 23. *Put his household in order*] This self-murder could not be called *lunacy,* as every step to it was deliberate. He foresaw Absalom's ruin; and he did not choose to witness it, and share in the disgrace: and he could expect no mercy at the hands of David. He was a very bad man, and died an unprepared and accursed death.

Verse 25. *Amasa captain of the host*] From the account in this verse, it appears that Joab and Amasa were sisters' children, and both nephews to David.

Verse 28. *Brought beds*] These no doubt consisted in *skins* of beasts, *mats, carpets,* and such like things.

Basons] ספות *sappoth.* Probably *wooden bowls,* such as the Arabs still use to eat out of, and to knead their bread in.

Earthen vessels] כלי יוצר *keley yotser.* Probably clay vessels, baked in the sun. These were perhaps used for lifting water, and boiling those articles which required to be cooked.

Wheat, and barley, &c.] There is no direct mention of *flesh-meat* here; little was eaten in that country, and it would not keep. Whether the *sheep* mentioned were brought for their *flesh* or their *milk,* I cannot tell.

According to Mr. Jones, "the Moors of west Barbary use the flour of parched barley, which is the chief provision they make for their *journeys,* and often use it at *home;* and this they carry in a leathern satchel." These are ordinarily made of *goat-skins.* One of them now lies before me: it has been drawn off the animal before it was cut up; the places where the fore legs, the tail, and the anus were, are elegantly closed, and have leathern thongs attached to

them, by which it can be slung over the back of man, ass, or camel. The place of the neck is left open, with a running string to draw it up, purse-like, when necessary. The skin itself is tanned; and the upper side is curiously embroidered with red, black, blue, yellow, and flesh-coloured leather, in very curious and elegant forms and devices. Bags of this kind are used for carrying wine, water, milk, butter, grain, flour, clothes, and different articles of merchandise. This is, as I have before stated, the Scripture *bottle.* Mr. Jones farther says: "Travellers use *zumeet, tumeet,* and *limereece. Zumeet* is flour mixed with honey, butter, and spice; *tumeet* is flour done up with organ oil; and *limereece* is flour mixed with water for drink. This quenches the thirst much better than water alone; satisfies a hungry appetite; cools and refreshes tired and weary spirits; overcoming those ill effects which a hot sun and fatiguing journey might well occasion."

This flour might be made of grain or pulse of any kind: and probably may be that which we here term *parched corn* and *parched pulse;* and in the forms above mentioned was well calculated, according to Mr. Jones's account, for *the people hungry, weary, and thirsty, in the wilderness.* This was a timely supply for David and his men, and no doubt contributed much to the victory mentioned in the following chapter.

A REMARKABLE account of maternal affection in a she-bear: "In the year 1772, the *Seahorse* frigate and *Carcass* bomb, under the command of the Hon. Captain C. J. Phipps, afterwards Lord Mulgrave, were sent on a voyage of discovery to the north seas. In this expedition the late celebrated admiral Lord Nelson served as midshipman. While the *Carcass* lay locked in the ice, early one morning, the man at the masthead gave notice that three bears were making their way very fast over the frozen sea, and were directing their course towards the ship. They had no doubt been invited by the scent of some blubber of a seahorse that the crew had killed a few days before, which had been set on fire, and was burning on the ice at the time of their approach. They proved to be a she-bear and her two cubs, but the cubs were nearly as large as the dam. They ran eagerly to the fire, and drew out from the flames part of the flesh of the seahorse that remained unconsumed, and ate voraciously. The crew from the ship threw great lumps of flesh of the seahorse, which they had still left upon the ice, which the old bear fetched away singly, laid every lump before her cubs as she brought it, and dividing it, gave each a share, reserving but a small portion to herself. As she was fetching away the last piece, they levelled their muskets at the cubs, and shot them both dead; and in her retreat they wounded the dam, but not mortally. It would have drawn tears of pity from any but unfeeling minds, to have marked the affectionate concern expressed by this poor beast in the dying moments of her expiring young. Though she was sorely wounded, and could but just

crawl to the place where they lay, she carried the lump of flesh she had fetched away, as she had done the others before, tore it in pieces, and laid it down before them; and when she saw that they refused to eat, she laid her paws first upon one, and then upon the other, and endeavoured to raise them up; all this while it was piteous to hear her moan. When she found she could not move them, she went off; and being at some distance, looked back and moaned. This not availing to entice them away, she returned, and smelling around them, began to lick their wounds. She went off a second time, as before; and having crawled a few paces, looked again behind her, and for some time stood moaning. But still her cubs not rising to follow her, she returned to them again, and with signs of inexpressible fondness went round one, and round the other, pawing them and moaning. Finding at last that they were cold and lifeless, she raised her head towards the ship, and growled a curse upon the murderers, which they returned with a volley of musket balls. She fell between her cubs, and died licking their wounds."

Had this animal got among the destroyers of her young, she would have soon shown what was implied in the *chafed mind of a bear robbed of her whelps.*

CHAPTER XVIII

David reviews and arranges the people, and gives the command to Joab, Abishai, and Ittai, 1, 2. On his expressing a desire to accompany them to the battle, they will not permit him, 3. He reviews them as they go out of the city, and gives commandment to the captains to save Absalom, 4, 5. They join battle with Absalom and his army, who are discomfited with the loss of twenty thousand men, 6–8. Absalom, fleeing away, is caught by his head in an oak; Joab finds him, and transfixes him with three darts, 9–15. The servants of David are recalled, and Absalom buried, 16–18. Ahimaaz and Cushi bring the tidings to David, who is greatly distressed at hearing of the death of Absalom, and makes bitter lamentation for him, 19–33.

A. M. 2981
B. C. 1023
An. Exod. Isr.
468
Anno ante
I. Olymp. 247

AND David [a]numbered the people that *were* with him, and set captains of thousands and captains of hundreds over them.

2 And David sent forth a third part of the people under the hand of Joab, [b]and a third part under the hand of Abishai the son of Zeruiah, Joab's brother, [c]and a third part under the hand of Ittai the Gittite. And the king said unto the people, I will surely go forth with you myself also.

3 [d]But the people answered, Thou shalt not go forth: for if we flee away, they will not [e]care for us; neither if half of us die, will

they care for us: but now *thou art* [f]worth ten thousand of us: therefore now *it is* better that thou [g]succour us out of the city.

A. M. 2981
B. C. 1023
An. Exod. Isr
468
Anno ante
I. Olymp. 247

4 And the king said unto them, What seemeth you best I will do. And the king stood by the gate side, and all the people came out by hundreds and by thousands.

5 And the king commanded Joab and Abishai and Ittai, saying, *Deal* gently for my sake with the young man, *even* with Absalom. [h]And all the people heard when the king gave all the captains charge concerning Absalom.

6 So the people went out into the field

---

[a]Psa. iii. 1——[b]1 Sam. xxvi. 6——[c]Chap. xv. 19
[d]Chap. xxi. 17——[e]Heb. *set their heart on us*

[f]Hebrew, *as ten thousand of us*——[g]Hebrew, *be to succour*
[h]Ver. 12

NOTES ON CHAP. XVIII

Verse 1. *And set captains of thousands*] By this time David's small company was greatly recruited; but what its number was we cannot tell. Josephus says it amounted to *four thousand* men. Others have supposed that they amounted to *ten thousand*; for thus they understand a clause in ver. 3, which they think should be read, *We are now ten thousand* strong.

Verse 3. *But now* thou art *worth ten thou-*

sand of us] The particle עַתָּה *attah, now,* is doubtless a mistake for the pronoun אַתָּה *attah, thou;* and so it appears to have been read by the *Septuagint,* the *Vulgate,* and the *Chaldee,* and by *two* of *Kennicott's* and *De Rossi's* MSS.

Verse 5. Deal *gently—with the young man*] David was the *father* of this worthless young man; and is it to be wondered at that he feels *as a father?* Who in his circumstances, that had such feelings as every *man* should have, would have felt, or acted otherwise?

A. M. 2981
B. C. 1023
An. Exod. Isr.
468
Anno ante
I. Olymp. 247

against Israel: and the battle was in the [i]wood of Ephraim;

7 Where the people of Israel were slain before the servants of David, and there was there a great slaughter that day of twenty thousand *men.*

8 For the battle was there scattered over the face of all the country: and the wood [k]devoured more people that day than the sword devoured.

9 And Absalom met the servants of David. And Absalom rode upon a mule, and the mule went under the thick boughs of a great oak, and his head caught hold of the oak, and he was taken up between the heaven and the earth; and the mule that *was* under him went away.

10 And a certain man saw *it,* and told Joab, and said, Behold, I saw Absalom hanged in an oak.

11 And Joab said unto the man that told him, And, behold, thou sawest *him,* and why didst thou not smite him there to the ground?

and I would have given thee ten *shekels* of silver, and a girdle.

A. M. 2981
B. C. 1023
An. Exod. Isr.
468
Anno ante
I. Olymp. 247

12 And the man said unto Joab, Though I should [l]receive a thousand *shekels* of silver in mine hand *yet* would I not put forth mine hand against the king's son: [m]for in our hearing the king charged thee and Abishai and Ittai, saying, [n]Beware that none *touch* the young man Absalom.

13 Otherwise I should have wrought falsehood against mine own life: for there is no matter hid from the king, and thou thyself wouldest have set thyself against *me.*

14 Then said Joab, I may not tarry thus [o]with thee. And he took three darts in his hand, and thrust them through the heart of Absalom, while he *was* yet alive in the [p]midst of the oak.

15 And ten young men that bare Joab's armour compassed about and smote Absalom, and slew him.

16 And Joab blew the trumpet, and the people returned from pursuing after Israel:

---

[i]Josh. xvii. 15, 18——[k]Heb. *multiplied to devour*
[l]Hebrew, *weigh upon mine hand*

[m]Ver. 5——[n]Heb. *Beware whosoever ye be of,* &c.
[o]Heb. *before thee*——[p]Heb. *heart*

Verse 7. *Twenty thousand* men.] Whether these were slain on the field of battle, or whether they were reckoned with those slain in the *wood* of Ephraim, we know not.

Verse 8. *The wood devoured more people*] It is generally supposed that, when the army was broken, they betook themselves to the wood, fell into pits, swamps, &c., and, being entangled, were hewn down by David's men; but the *Chaldee, Syriac,* and *Arabic,* state that they were *devoured* by *wild beasts* in the wood.

Verse 9. *And his head caught hold of the oak*] It has been supposed that Absalom was caught by the *hair,* but no such thing is intimated in the text. Probably his neck was caught in the fork of a strong bough, and he was nearly dead when Joab found him; for it is said, ver. 14, *he was yet alive,* an expression which intimates he was *nearly dead.*

Verse 10. *I saw Absalom hanged in an oak.*] He must have hung there a considerable time. This man saw him hanging; how long he had been hanging *before* he saw him, we cannot tell. He came and informed Joab; this must have taken up a considerable time. Joab *went* and pierced him through with three darts; this must have taken up still more time. It is therefore natural to conclude that his life must have been nearly gone after having been so long suspended, and probably was past recovery, even if Joab had taken him down.

Verse 11. *And a girdle.*] The military belt was the chief ornament of a soldier, and was highly prized in all ancient nations; it was also a rich present from one chieftain to another. *Jonathan* gave his to *David,* as the highest pledge of his esteem and perpetual friendship,

1 Sam. xviii. 4. And *Ajax* gave his to *Hector,* as a token of the highest respect.—*Hom.* Il. vii., ver. 305.

Verse 13. *Thou thyself wouldest have set thyself against* me.] This is a strong appeal to Joab's loyalty, and respect for the orders of David; but he was proof against every fine feeling, and against every generous sentiment.

Verse 14. *I may not tarry thus with thee*] He had nothing to say in vindication of the purpose he had formed.

Thrust them through the heart of Absalom] He was determined to make sure work, and therefore he pierced his *heart.*

Joab should have obeyed the king's commandment: and yet the safety of the state required the sacrifice of Absalom. But independently of this, his life was quadruply forfeited to the law:— 1. In having murdered his brother Amnon. 2. In having excited an insurrection in the state. 3. In having taken up arms against his own father, Deut. xxi. 18, 21. 4. In having lain with his father's concubines, Lev. xviii. 29. Long ago he should have died by the hand of justice; and now all his crimes are visited on him in his last act of rebellion. Yet, in the present circumstances, Joab's act was base and disloyal, and a cowardly murder.

Verse 15. *Ten young men—smote Absalom and slew him.*] That is, they all pierced the body; but there could be no life in it after three darts had been thrust through the heart: but they added as much as would have killed him had he been alive.

Verse 16. *Joab blew the trumpet*] He knew that the rebellion was now extinguished by the

A. M. 2981
B. C. 1023
An. Exod. Isr.
468
Anno ante
I. Olymp. 247

for Joab held back the peo-ple.

17 And they took Absalom, and cast him into a great pit in the wood, and qlaid a very great heap of stones upon him: and all Israel fled every one to his tent.

18 Now Absalom in his lifetime had taken and reared up for himself a pillar, which *is* in rthe king's dale: for he said, sI have no son to keep my name in remembrance: and he called the pillar after his own name: and it is called unto this day, Absalom's place.

19 Then said Ahimaaz the son of Zadok, Let me now run, and bear the king tidings, how that the LORD hath tavenged him of his enemies.

20 And Joab said unto him, Thou shalt not ubear tidings this day, but thou shalt bear tidings another day: but this day thou shalt bear no tidings, because the king's son is dead.

21 Then said Joab to Cushi, Go tell the king what thou hast seen. And Cushi bowed himself unto Joab, and ran.

22 Then said Ahimaaz the son of Zadok yet again to Joab, But vhowsoever, let me, I pray thee, also run after Cushi. And Joab said, Wherefore wilt thou run, my son, seeing that thou hast no tidings wready?

23 But howsoever, *said he,* let me run. And he said unto him, Run. Then Ahimaaz

ran by the way of the plain, and overran Cushi.

A. M. 2981
B. C. 1023
An. Exod. Isr.
468
Anno ante
I. Olymp. 247

24 And David sat between the two gates: and xthe watchman went up to the roof over the gate unto the wall, and lifted up his eyes, and looked, and behold a man running alone.

25 And the watchman cried, and told the king. And the king said, If he *be* alone, *there is* tidings in his mouth. And he came apace, and drew near.

26 And the watchman saw another man run-ning: and the watchman called unto the porter, and said, Behold *another* man running alone. And the king said, He also bringeth tidings.

27 And the watchman said, yMethinketh the running of the foremost is like the run-ning of Ahimaaz the son of Zadok. And the king said, He *is* a good man, and cometh with good tidings.

28 And Ahimaaz called and said unto the zking, aAll is well. And he fell down to the earth upon his face before the king, and said, Blessed *be* the LORD thy God, which hath bdelivered up the men that lifted up their hand against my lord the king.

29 And the king said, cIs the young man Absalom safe? And Ahimaaz answered, When Joab sent the king's servant, and *me* thy serv-ant, I saw a great tumult, but I knew not what it *was.*

---

qJosh. vii. 26——rGen. xiv. 17——sSee ch. xiv. 27
tHeb. *judged him from the hand,* &c.——uHeb. *be a man of tidings*——vHeb. *be what may*

wOr, *convenient*——x2 Kings ix. 17——yHeb. *I see the running*——zOr, *Peace* be to thee——aHeb. *Peace*
bHeb. *shut up*——cHeb. Is there *peace?*

---

death of Absalom; and was not willing that any farther slaughter should be made of the deluded people.

Verse 17. *And laid a very great heap of stones*] This was the method of burying heroes, and even traitors, the heap of stones being de-signed to perpetuate the memory of the event, whether good or bad. The ancient *cairns* or heaps of stones, in different parts of the world, are of this kind. The various *tumuli* or *bar-rows* in England are the same as the *cairns* in different parts of Ireland and Scotland. In the former, *stones* were not plenty; hence they heaped up great *mounds of earth.*

Verse 18. *Reared up for himself a pillar*] There was a marble pillar in the time of Jose-phus called *Absalom's pillar:* and there is one shown to the present day under this name; but it is comparatively a modern structure.

Absalom's place.] Literally Absalom's HAND. See the note on 1 Sam. xv. 12.

Verse 21. *Tell the king what thou hast seen*] At this time the death of Absalom was not pub-

licly known; but Joab had given Cushi private information of it. This Ahimaaz had not, for he could not tell the king whether Absalom were dead. To this Joab seems to refer, ver. 22: "Thou hast no tidings ready."

Verse 24. *David sat between the two gates*] He was probably in the seat of justice. Before the gate of the city it is supposed there was an enclosure, which had its gate also; David sat in the space between these two doors. Over the larger gate there appears to have been a turret, on which a sentinel or watchman stood con-tinually, and gave information of what he saw in the country.

Verse 25. *If he be alone, there is tidings*] That is, *good tidings.* For if the battle had been lost men would have been running in dif-ferent directions through the country.

Verse 29. *I saw a great tumult*] It was very probable that Ahimaaz did not know of the death of Absalom; he had seen the rout of his army, but did not know of his death. Others think he knew all, and told this untruth that

A. M. 2981
B. C. 1023
An. Exod. Isr.
468
Anno ante
I. Olymp. 247

30 And the king said *unto him,* Turn aside, *and* stand here. And he turned aside, and stood still.

31 And, behold, Cushi came; and Cushi said, [d]Tidings, my lord the king: for the LORD hath avenged thee this day of all them that rose up against thee.

32 And the king said unto Cushi, *Is* the young man Absalom safe? And Cushi an-

swered, The enemies of my lord the king, and all that rise against thee to do *thee* hurt, be as *that* young man *is.*

33 And the king was much moved, and went up to the chamber over the gate, and wept: and as he went, thus he said, [e]O my son Absalom, my son, my son Absalom! would God I had died for thee, O Absalom, my son, my son!

A. M. 2981
B. C. 1023
An. Exod. Isr.
468
Anno ante
I. Olymp. 247

---

[d]Heb. *tidings is brought*

---

he might not be the messenger of bad news to David.

Verse 30. *Stand here.*] He intended to confront two messengers, and compare their accounts.

Verse 32. Is *the young man Absalom safe?*] This was the utmost of his solicitude, and it well merited the reproof which Joab gave him, chapter xix. 5.

Verse 33. *O my son Absalom*] It is allowed by the most able critics that this lamentation is exceedingly pathetic. In what order the words were pronounced, for much depends on this, we cannot say. Perhaps it was the following:—

בני אבשלום בני
Beni Abshalom, beni!
My son Absalom! O my son!

בני אבשלום
Beni Abshalom!
O my son Absalom!

---

[e]Chap. xix. 4

מי יתן מותי אני תחתיך
Mi yitten muthi ani thachteicha.
O that I had died in thy stead!

אבשלום בני בני
Abshalom, beni! beni!
O Absalom, my son, my son!

Is there no hope for the soul of this profligate young man? He died in his iniquity: but is it not possible that he implored the mercy of his Maker while he hung in the tree? And is it not possible that the mercy of God was extended to him? And was not that suspension a respite, to the end that he might have time to deprecate the wrath of Divine justice?

This is at least a charitable conjecture, and humanity will delight in such a case to lay hold even on *possibilities.* If there be any room for *hope* in such a death, who that knows the worth of an immortal soul, would not wish to indulge in it?

CHAPTER XIX

David continues his lamentation for his son, and the people are greatly discouraged, 1–4. Joab reproves and threatens him with the general defection of the people, 5–7. David lays aside his mourning, and shows himself to the people, who are thereby encouraged, 8. The tribes take counsel to bring the king back to Jerusalem, 9–12. He makes Amasa captain of the host in place of Joab, 13. The king, returning, is met by Judah at Gilgal, 14, 15. Shimei comes to meet David, and entreats for his life, which David grants, 16–23. Mephibosheth also meets him, and shows how he had been slandered by Ziba, 24–30. David is met by Barzillai, and between them there is an affecting interview, 31–40. Contention between the men of Judah and the men of Israel, about bringing back the king, 41–43.

A. M. 2981
B. C. 1023
An. Exod. Isr.
468
Anno ante
I. Olymp. 247

AND it was told Joab, Behold, the king weepeth and mourneth for Absalom.

2 And the [a]victory that day was *turned* into mourning unto all the people: for the people heard say that day how the king was grieved for his son.

3 And the people gat them by stealth that day [b]into the city, as people being ashamed steal away when they flee in battle.

4 But the king [c]covered his face, and the king cried with a loud voice, [d]O my son Absalom, O Absalom, my son, my son!

A. M. 2981
B. C. 1023
An. Exod. Isr.
468
Anno ante
I. Olymp. 247

---

[a]Heb. *salvation* or *deliverance*——[b]Ver. 32

NOTES ON CHAP. XIX

Verse 2. *The victory—was* turned *into mourning*] Instead of rejoicing that a most unnatural and ruinous rebellion had been quashed, the people mourned over their own success, because they saw their king so immoderately afflicted for the loss of his worthless son.

Verse 4. *The king covered his face*] This was the custom of mourners.

O my son Absalom] Calmet has properly remarked that the frequent repetition of the name

---

[c]Chap. xv. 30——[d]Chap. xviii. 33

---

of the defunct, is common in the language of lamentation. Thus VIRGIL, *Ecl.* v., ver. 51:—

——Daphnin *que tuum tollemus ad astra;*
Daphnin *ad astra feremus: amavit nos quoque*
Daphnis.

"With yours, my song I cheerfully shall join,
To raise your *Daphnis* to the powers Divine.
Daphnis I'll raise unto the powers above,
For dear to me was *Daphnis'* well tried love,"

See the notes on the preceding chapter.

A. M. 2981
B. C. 1023
An. Exod. Isr. 468
Anno ante
I. Olymp. 247

5 And Joab came into the house to the king, and said, Thou hast shamed this day the faces of all thy servants, which this day have saved thy life, and the lives of thy sons and of thy daughters, and the lives of thy wives, and the lives of thy concubines;

6 eIn that thou lovest thine enemies, and hatest thy friends. For thou hast declared this day, fthat thou regardest neither princes nor servants: for this day I perceive that if Absalom had lived, and all we had died this day, then it had pleased thee well.

7 Now therefore arise, go forth, and speak gcomfortably unto thy servants: for I swear by the LORD, if thou go not forth, there will not tarry one with thee this night: and that will be worse unto thee than all the evil that befell thee from thy youth until now.

8 Then the king arose, and sat in the gate. And they told unto all the people, saying, Behold, the king doth sit in the gate. And all the people came before the king: for Israel had fled every man to his tent.

9 And all the people were at strife throughout all the tribes of Israel, saying, The king saved us out of the hand of our enemies, and he delivered us out of the hands of the Philistines; and now he is hfled out of the land for Absalom.

10 And Absalom, whom we anointed over us, is dead in battle. Now therefore why ispeak ye not a word of bringing the king back?

11 And King David sent to Zadok and to Abiathar the priests, saying, Speak unto the elders of Judah, saying, Why are ye the last to bring the king back to his house? seeing the speech of all Israel is come to the king, *even* to his house.

A. M. 2981
B. C. 1023
An. Exod. Isr. 468
Anno ante
I. Olymp. 247

12 Ye *are* my brethren, ye *are* kmy bones and my flesh: wherefore then are ye the last to bring back the king?

13 lAnd say ye to Amasa, *Art* thou not of my bone, and of my flesh? mGod do so to me, and more also, if thou be not captain of the host before me continually in the room of Joab.

14 And he bowed the heart of all the men of Judah neven as *the heart of* one man; so that they sent *this word* unto the king, Return thou, and all thy servants.

15 So the king returned, and came to Jordan. And Judah came to oGilgal, to go to meet the king, to conduct the king over Jordan.

16 And pShimei the son of Gera, a Benjamite, which *was* of Bahurim, hasted and came down with the men of Judah to meet King David.

17 And *there were* a thousand men of Benjamin with him, and qZiba the servant of the house of Saul, and his fifteen sons and his twenty servants with him: and they went over Jordan before the king.

18 And there went over a ferry-boat to carry over the king's household, and to do rwhat he thought good. And Shimei the son of Gera

---

eHeb. *by loving*, &c.——fHeb. *that princes or servants are not to thee*——gHeb. *to the heart of thy servants;* Gen. xxxiv. 3——hChap. xv. 14——iHeb. *are ye silent?*

kCh. v. 1——lCh. xvii. 25——mRuth i. 17——nJudg. xx. 1——oJosh. v. 9——pChap. xvi. 5; 1 Kings ii. 8 qCh. ix. 2, 10; xvi. 1, 2——rHeb. *the good in his eyes*

Verse 5. *Thou hast shamed this day*] Joab's speech to David on his immoderate grief for the death of his rebellious son is not only remarkable for the *insolence of office*, but also for good sense and firmness. Every man who candidly considers the state of the case, must allow that David acted imprudently at least; and that Joab's firm reproof was necessary to arouse him to a sense of his duty to his people. But still, in his *manner*, Joab had far exceeded the bonds of that reverence which a servant owes to his master, or a subject to his prince. Joab was a good soldier, but in every respect a bad man, and a dangerous subject.

Verse 8. *The king—sat in the gate.*] The place where justice was administered to the people.

Verse 11. *Speak unto the elders of Judah*] David was afraid to fall out with this tribe: they were in possession of Jerusalem, and this was a city of great importance to him. They had joined Absalom in his rebellion; and doubtless were now ashamed of their conduct. David

appears to take no notice of their infidelity, but rather to place confidence in them, that their confidence in him might be naturally excited: and, to oblige them yet farther, purposes to make Amasa captain of the host in the place of Joab.

Verse 14. *And he bowed the heart of all the men of Judah*] The measures that he pursued were the best calculated that could be to accomplish this salutary end. Appear to distrust those whom you have some reason to suspect, and you increase their caution and distrust. Put as much confidence in them as you safely can, and this will not fail to excite their confidence towards you.

Verse 16. *Shimei the son of Gera*] It appears that Shimei was a powerful chieftain in the land; for he had here, in his retinue, no less than a thousand men.

Verse 18. *There went over a ferry-boat*] This is the first mention of any thing of the kind. Some think a bridge or raft is what is here intended.

A. M. 2981
B. C. 1023
An. Exod. Isr.
468
Anno ante
I. Olymp. 247

fell down before the king, as he was come over Jordan;

19 And said unto the king, [s]Let not my lord impute iniquity unto me, neither do thou remember [t]that which thy servant did perversely the day that my lord the king went out of Jerusalem, that the king should [u]take it to his heart.

20 For thy servant doth know that I have sinned: therefore, behold, I am come the first this day of all [v]the house of Joseph to go down to meet my lord the king.

21 But Abishai the son of Zeruiah answered and said, Shall not Shimei be put to death for this, because he [w]cursed the LORD's anointed?

22 And David said, [x]What have I to do with you, ye sons of Zeruiah, that ye should this day be adversaries unto me? [y]shall there any man be put to death this day in Israel? for do not I know that I *am* this day king over Israel?

23 Therefore [z]the king said unto Shimei, Thou shalt not die. And the king sware unto him.

24 And [a]Mephibosheth the son of Saul came down to meet the king, and had neither dressed his feet, nor trimmed his beard, nor washed his clothes, from the day the king departed until the day he came *again* in peace.

25 And it came to pass, when he was come to Jerusalem to meet the king, that the king said unto him, [b]Wherefore wentest not thou with me, Mephibosheth?

26 And he answered, My lord, O king, my servant deceived me: for thy servant said, I will saddle me an ass, that I may ride thereon, and go to the king; because thy servant *is* lame.

27 [c]And he hath slandered thy servant unto my lord the king; [d]but my lord the king *is* as an angel of God: do therefore *what is* good in thine eyes.

28 For all *of* my father's house were but [e]dead men before my lord the king: [f]yet didst thou set thy servant among them that did eat at thine own table. What right therefore have I yet to cry any more unto the king?

29 And the king said unto him, Why speakest thou any more of thy matters? I have said, Thou and Ziba divide the land.

30 And Mephibosheth said unto the king, Yea, let him take all, forasmuch as my lord the king is come again in peace unto his own house.

31 And [g]Barzillai the Gileadite came down from Rogelim, and went over Jordan with the king, to conduct him over Jordan.

32 Now Barzillai was a very aged man, *even* fourscore years old: and [h]he had provided the king of sustenance while he lay at Mahanaim; for he *was* a very great man.

A. M. 2981
B. C. 1023
An. Exod. Isr.
468
Anno ante
I. Olymp. 247

---

[s]1 Sam. xxii. 15——[t]Chap. xvi. 5, 6, &c.——[u]Chap. xiii. 33——[v]See ch. xvi. 5——[w]Exod. xxii. 28——[x]Ch. xvi. 10——[y]1 Sam. xi. 13——[z]1 Kings ii. 8, 9, 37, 46

[a]Ch. ix. 6——[b]Ch. xvi. 17——[c]Ch. xvi. 3——[d]Chap. xiv. 17, 20——[e]Heb. *men of death;* 1 Sam. xxvi. 16 [f]Ch. ix. 7, 10, 13——[g]1 Kings ii. 7——[h]Ch. xvii. 27

Verse 20. *For thy servant doth know that I have sinned*] This was all he could do; his subsequent conduct alone could prove his sincerity. On such an avowal as this David could not but grant him his life.

Verse 24. *Neither dressed his feet*] He had given the fullest proof of his sincere attachment to David and his cause; and by what he had done, amply refuted the calumnies of his servant Ziba.

Verse 27. *The king is as an angel of God*] As if he had said, I state my case plainly and without guile; thou art too wise not to penetrate the motives from which both myself and servant have acted. I shall make no appeal; with whatsoever thou determinest I shall rest contented.

Verse 29. *I have said, Thou and Ziba divide the land.*] At first, David gave the land of Saul to Mephibosheth; and Ziba, his sons, and his servants, were to work that land; and to Mephibosheth, as the lord, he was to give the *half of the produce.* Ziba met David in his distress with provisions, and calumniated Mephibosheth: David, too slightly trusting to his misrepresentation, and supposing that Mephibosheth was

actually such a traitor as Ziba represented him, made him on the spot a grant of his master's land. Now he finds that he has acted too rashly, and therefore confirms the *former grant;* i. e., that Ziba should cultivate the ground, and still continue to give to Mephibosheth, as the lord, the half of the produce. This was merely placing things *in statu quo,* and utterly annulling the gift that he had made to Ziba. But why did he leave this treacherous man any thing? Answer, 1. He was one of the domestics of Saul, and David wished to show kindness to that house. 2. He had supplied him with the necessaries of life when he was in the greatest distress; and he thinks proper to continue him in his old office, by way of remuneration. But it was certainly too great a compensation for his services, however then important, when all the circumstances are considered.

Verse 32. *Barzillai was a very aged man*] This venerable person had given full proof of his attachment to David by the supplies he had given him when he lay at Mahanaim, where his case was all but desperate; the sincerity of his congratulations now none can suspect. David's offer to him was at once noble and liberal: he

A. M. 2981
B. C. 1023
An. Exod. Isr.
468
Anno ante
I. Olymp. 247

33 And the king said unto Barzillai, Come thou over with me, and I will feed thee with me in Jerusalem.

34 And Barzillai said unto the king, [1]How long have I to live, that I should go up with the king unto Jerusalem?

35 I *am* this day [k]fourscore years old: *and* can I discern between good and evil? can thy servant taste what I eat or what I drink? can I hear any more the voice of singing men and singing women? Wherefore then should thy servant be yet a burden unto my lord the king?

36 Thy servant will go a little way over Jordan with the king: and why should the king recompense it me with such a reward?

37 Let thy servant, I pray thee, turn back again, that I may die in mine own city, *and be buried* by the grave of my father and of my mother. But behold thy servant [l]Chimham; let him go over with my lord the king; and do to him what shall seem good unto thee.

38 And the king answered, Chimham shall go over with me, and I will do to him that which shall seem good unto thee: and whatsoever thou shalt [m]require of me, *that* will I do for thee.

39 And all the people went over Jordan. And when the king was come over, the king [n]kissed Barzillai, and blessed him; and he returned unto his own place.

A. M. 2981
B. C. 1023
An. Exod. Isr.
468
Anno ante
I. Olymp. 247

40 Then the king went on to Gilgal, and [o]Chimham went on with him: and all the people of Judah conducted the king, and also half the people of Israel.

41 And, behold, all the men of Israel came to the king, and said unto the king, Why have our brethren the men of Judah stolen thee away, and [p]have brought the king, and his household, and all David's men with him, over Jordan?

42 And all the men of Judah answered the men of Israel, Because the king *is* [q]near of kin to us: wherefore then be ye angry for this matter? have we eaten at all of the king's cost? or hath he given us any gift?

43 And the men of Israel answered the men of Judah, and said, We have ten parts in the king, and we have also more *right* in David than ye: why then did ye [r]despise us, that our advice should not be first had in bringing back our king? And the words of the men of Judah were fiercer than [s]the words of the men of Israel.

---

[i]Heb. *how many days* are *the years of my life?*——[k]Psa. xc. 10——[l]1 Kings ii. 7; Jer. xli. 17——[m]Hebrew, *choose*

[n]Gen. xxxi. 55——[o]Heb. *Chimhan*——[p]Ver. 15——[q]Ver. 12——[r]Heb. *set us at light*——[s]See Judg. viii. 1; xii. 1

---

wished to compensate *such a man*, and he wished to have at hand *such a friend*.

Verse 35. *Can thy servant taste what I eat*] Here is at once an affecting description of the infirmities of old age; and a correct account of the mode of living at an Eastern court in ancient times.

Barzillai was fourscore years old; his *ear* was become dull of hearing, and his *relish* for his food was gone: he therefore appears to have been not only an old man, but an *infirm* old man. Besides *delicate meats* and *drinks*, we find that *vocal music* constituted a principal part of court entertainments: male and female singers made a necessary appendage to these banquets, as they do in most Eastern courts to the present day. As David was a most sublime poet, and emphatically styled the *sweet singer of Israel*, he no doubt had his court well supplied with vocal as well as *instrumental* performers; and, probably, with *poets* and *poetesses;* for it is not likely that *he* was the only poet of his time, though he undoubtedly was the most excellent.

Verse 37. *Thy servant Chimham*] It is generally understood that this was Barzillai's son; and this is probable from 1 Kings ii. 7, where, when David was dying, he said, *Show kindness to the sons of Barzillai:* and it is very probable that this Chimham was one of them. In Jer. xli. 17 mention is made of the *habitation of*

Chimham, which was near to Bethlehem; and it is reasonably conjectured that David had left that portion, which was probably a part of his paternal estate, to this son of Barzillai.

Verse 39. *The king kissed Barzillai, and blessed him*] The *kiss* was the token of *friendship* and *farewell;* the *blessing* was a *prayer to God* for his prosperity, probably a prophetical benediction.

Verse 42. *Wherefore then be ye angry for this matter?*] We have not done this for our own advantage; we have gained nothing by it; we did it through loyal attachment to our king.

Verse 43. *We have ten parts in the king, and —more right*] We are ten tribes to one, or we are ten times so many as you; and consequently should have been consulted in this business.

The words of the men of Judah were fiercer than the words of the men of Israel.] They had more weight, for they had more reason on their side.

IT is pleasant when every province, canton, district, and county, vie with each other in personal attachment to the prince, and loyal attachment to his government. From such contentions as these civil wars are never likely to arise. And how blessed it must be for the country where the king merits all this! where the prince is the pastor and father of his people, and in all things the minister of God to them for good!

It is criminal in the prince not to endeavour to deserve the confidence and love of his people; and it is highly criminal in the people not to repay such endeavours with the most loyal and affectionate attachment.

Where the government is not *despotic,* the king acts by the counsels of his ministers; and while he does so he is not chargeable with miscarriages and misfortunes; they either came through bad counsels, or directly thwarting providences. On this ground is that political maxim in our laws formed, *the king can do no wrong.* Sometimes God will have things other-

wise than the best counsels have determined, because he sees that the results will, on the whole, be better for the peace and prosperity of that state. "God is the only Ruler of princes." And as the peace of the world depends much on civil government, hence kings and civil governors are peculiar objects of the Almighty's care. Wo to him who labours to bring about a general disaffection; as such things almost invariably end in general disappointment and calamity. It is much easier to unsettle than to settle; to pull down than to build up.

CHAPTER XX

Sheba raises an insurrection, and gains a party in Israel, 1, 2. David shuts up the ten concubines who were defiled by Absalom, 3. Amasa is sent to assemble the men of Judah, 4, 5. And in the mean time Abishai is sent to pursue Sheba, 6, 7. Joab treacherously murders Amasa, 8–12. Joab and the army continue the pursuit of Sheba, 13, 14. He is besieged in Abel; and, by the counsels of a wise woman, the people of Abel cut off his head, and throw it over the wall to Joab; who blows the trumpet of peace, and he and his men return to Jerusalem, 15–22. Account of David's civil and military officers, 23–26.

A. M. 2982
B. C. 1022
An. Exod. Isr.
469
Anno ante
I. Olymp. 246

AND there happened to be there a man of Belial, whose name *was* Sheba, the son of Bichri, a Benjamite: and he blew a trumpet, and said, ªWe have no part in David, neither have we inheritance in the son of Jesse: ᵇevery man to his tents, O Israel.

2 So every man of Israel went up from after David, *and* followed Sheba the son of Bichri: but the men of Judah clave unto their king, from Jordan even to Jerusalem.

3 And David came to his house at Jerusalem; and the king took the ten women *his* ᶜconcubines, whom he had left to keep the house, and put them in ᵈward, and fed them, but went not in unto them. So they were ᵉshut up unto the day of their death, ᶠliving in widowhood.

4 Then said the king to Amasa, ᵍAssemble ʰme the men of Judah within three days, and be thou here present.

A. M. 2982
B. C. 1022
An. Exod. Isr.
469
Anno ante
I. Olymp. 246

5 So Amasa went to assemble *the men of* Judah: but he tarried longer than the set time which he had appointed him.

6 And David said to Abishai, Now shall Sheba the son of Bichri do us more harm than *did* Absalom: take thou ⁱthy lord's servants, and pursue after him, lest he get him fenced cities, and ᵏescape us.

7 And there went out after him Joab's men, and the ˡCherethites, and the Pelethites, and all the mighty men: and they went out of Jerusalem, to pursue after Sheba the son of Bichri.

8 When they *were* at the great stone which

ªCh. xix. 43——ᵇ1 Kings xii. 16; 2 Chron. x. 16
ᶜChap. xv. 16; xvi. 21, 22——ᵈHeb. *a house of ward*
ᵉHeb. *bound*——ᶠHeb. *in widowhood of life*

ᵍChap. xix. 13——ʰHeb. *call*——ⁱChap. xi. 11;
1 Kings i. 33——ᵏHeb. *deliver himself from our eyes*
ˡChap. viii. 18; 1 Kings i. 38

NOTES ON CHAP. XX

Verse 1. *Sheba, the son of Bichri*] As this man was a *Benjamite,* he probably belonged to the family of Saul; and he seems to have had considerable influence in Israel to raise such an insurrection: but we know nothing farther of him than what is related in this place.

We have no part in David] We of Israel, we of the ten tribes, are under no obligation to the house of David. Leave him, and let every man fall into the ranks under his own leader.

Verse 3. *The ten women*] He could not well divorce them; he could not punish them, as they were not in the transgression; he could no more be familiar with them, because they had been defiled by his son; and to have married them to other men might have been dangerous to the state: therefore he shut them up and *fed them*

—made them quite comfortable, and they continued as widows to their death.

Verse 4. *Then said the king to Amasa*] Thus he invests him with the command of the army, and sends him to collect the men of Judah, and to come back to receive his orders in relation to Sheba, in three days. It appears that Amasa found more difficulty in collecting his countrymen than was at first supposed; and this detaining him beyond the three days, David, fearing that Sheba's rebellion would get head, sent Abishai, who it appears was accompanied by Joab, to pursue after Sheba.

Amasa, it seems, got up with them at Gibeon, ver. 8, where he was treacherously murdered by the execrable Joab.

Verse 8. *Joab's garment*] It appears that this was not a military garment; and that Joab had no arms but a short sword, which he had

A. M. 2982
B. C. 1022
An. Exod. Isr.
469
Anno ante
I. Olymp. 246

is in Gibeon, Amasa went before them. And Joab's garment that he had put on was girded unto him, and upon it a girdle *with* a sword fastened upon his loins in the sheath thereof; and as he went forth it fell out.

9 And Joab said to Amasa, *Art* thou in health, my brother? [m]And Joab took Amasa by the beard with the right hand to kiss him.

10 But Amasa took no heed to the sword that *was* in Joab's hand: so [n]he smote him therewith [o]in the fifth *rib,* and shed out his bowels to the ground, and [p]struck him not again; and he died. So Joab and Abishai his brother pursued after Sheba the son of Bichri.

11 And one of Joab's men stood by him, and said, He that favoureth Joab, and he that *is* for David, *let him go* after Joab.

12 And Amasa wallowed in blood in the midst of the highway. And when the man saw that all the people stood still, he removed Amasa out of the highway into the field, and cast a cloth upon him, when he saw that every one that came by him stood still.

13 When he was removed out of the high-

way, all the people went on after Joab, to pursue after Sheba the son of Bichri.

A. M. 2982
B. C. 1022
An. Exod. Isr.
469
Anno ante
I. Olymp. 246

14 And he went through all the tribes of Israel unto [q]Abel, and to Beth-maachah, and all the Berites: and they were gathered together, and went also after him.

15 And they came and besieged him in Abel of Beth-maachah, and they [r]cast up a bank against the city, and [s]it stood in the trench: and all the people that *were* with Joab [t]battered the wall, to throw it down.

16 Then cried a wise woman out of the city, Hear, hear; say, I pray you, unto Joab, Come near hither, that I may speak with thee.

17 And when he was come near unto her, the woman said, *Art* thou Joab? And he answered, I *am he.* Then she said unto him, Hear the words of thine handmaid. And he answered, I do hear.

18 Then she spake, saying, [u]They were wont to speak in old time, saying, They shall surely ask *counsel* at Abel: and so they ended *the matter.*

---

[m]Matthew xxvi. 49; Luke xxii. 47——[n]1 Kings ii. 5——[o]Chapter ii. 23——[p]Hebrew, *doubled not his stroke*——[q]2 Kings xv. 29; 2 Chronicles xvi. 4——[r]2 Kings xix. 32

[s]Or, *it stood against the outmost wall*——[t]Heb. *marred to throw down*——[u]Or, *they plainly spoke in the beginning, saying, Surely they will ask of Abel, and so make an end;* see Deut. xx. 11

---

concealed in his girdle; and this *sword,* or *knife,* was so loose in its sheath that it could be easily drawn out. It is thought farther, that Joab, in passing to Amasa, stumbled, (for so some of the versions, and able critics, understand the words *it fell out,*) and that the sword fell down when he stumbled; that he took it up with his left hand as if he had no bad intention; and then, taking Amasa by the beard with his right hand, pretending to kiss him, he, with his sword in his left hand, ripped up his bowels. This seems to be the meaning of this very obscure verse. It is worthy of remark that in the Eastern country it is the *beard,* not the *man,* which is usually kissed.

Verse 10. *In the fifth* rib] I believe חמש *chomesh,* which we render here and elsewhere the *fifth rib,* means any part of the abdominal region. The *Septuagint* translate it την ψοαν, *the groin;* the *Targum, the right side of the thigh,* i. e., (the phrase of the Targumist being interpreted,) *the privy parts.* That it means some part of the abdominal region, is evident from what follows, *And shed out his bowels to the ground.* It appears from this that, in plain English, he ripped up his belly.

Verse 11. *He that favoureth Joab*] As if he had said, There is now no other commander besides Joab; and Joab is steadily attached to David: let those therefore who are loyal follow Joab.

Verse 12. *Amasa wallowed in blood*] It is very likely that Amasa did not immediately die; I have known instances of persons living several hours after their bowels had been shed out.

Verse 14. *Unto Abel*] This is supposed to have been the capital of the district called Abilene in St. Luke's Gospel, chap. iii. 1.

Beth-maachah] Is supposed to have been in the northern part of the Holy Land, on the confines of Syria, and probably in the tribe of Naphtali.

Verse 15. *They cast up a bank against the city*] The word סללה *solelah,* which we render *bank,* means, most probably, a *battering engine* of some kind, or a *tower* overlooking the walls, on which archers and slingers could stand and annoy the inhabitants, while others of the besiegers could proceed to sap the walls. That it cannot be a *bank that stood in the trench,* is evident from the circumstance thus expressed.

Verse 16. *A wise woman*] She was probably governess.

Verse 18. *They shall surely ask* counsel *at Abel*] This is a proverb, but from what it originated we know not; nor can we exactly say what it means: much must be supplied to bring it to speak sense. Abel was probably famed for the wisdom of its inhabitants; and parties who had disputes appealed to their judgment, which appears to have been in such high reputation as

A. M. 2982
B. C. 1022
An. Exod. Isr.
469
Anno ante
I. Olymp. 246

19 I *am one of them that are* peaceable *and* faithful in Israel: thou seekest to destroy a city and a mother in Israel: why wilt thou swallow up ᵛthe inheritance of the LORD?

20 And Joab answered and said, Far be it, far be it from me, that I should swallow up or destroy.

21 The matter *is* not so: but a man of Mount Ephraim, Sheba the son of Bichri ᵂby name, hath lifted up his hand against the king, *even* against David: deliver him only, and I will depart from the city. And the woman said unto Joab, Behold, his head shall be thrown to thee over the wall.

22 Then the woman went unto all the people

ˣin her wisdom. And they cut off the head of Sheba the son of Bichri, and cast *it* out to Joab. And he blew a trumpet, and they ʸretired from the city, every man to his tent. And Joab returned to Jerusalem unto the king.

A. M. 2982
B. C. 1022
An. Exod. Isr.
469
Anno ante
I. Olymp. 246

23 Now ᶻJoab *was* over all the host of Israel: and Benaiah the son of Jehoiada *was* over the Cherethites and over the Pelethites:

24 And Adoram *was* ᵃover the tribute: and ᵇJehoshaphat the son of Ahilud *was* ᶜrecorder:

25 And Sheva *was* scribe: and ᵈZadok and Abiathar *were* the priests:

26 ᵉAnd Ira also the Jairite was ᶠa chief ruler about David.

ᵛ1 Sam. xxvi. 19; chap. xxi. 3——ᵂHeb. *by his name* ˣEccles. ix. 14, 15——ʸHeb. *were scattered*——ᶻChap. viii. 16, 18——ᵃ1 Kings iv. 6

ᵇChap. viii. 16; 1 Kings iv. 3——ᶜOr, *remembrance* ᵈCh. viii. 17; 1 Kings iv. 4——ᵉChap. xxiii. 38——ᶠOr, *a prince;* Gen. xli. 45; Exod. ii. 16; chap. viii. 18

---

to be final by consent of all parties. To this the wise woman refers, and intimates to Joab that he should have proceeded in this way before he began to storm the city, and destroy the peaceable inhabitants.

Verse 19. *I—peaceable* and *faithful in Israel*] I am for peace, not contention of any kind; I am *faithful*—I adhere to David, and neither seek nor shall sanction any rebellion or anarchy in the land. Why then dost thou proceed in such a violent manner? Perhaps the woman speaks here in the *name* and on *behalf* of the *city:* "I am a peaceable city, and am faithful to the king."

A mother in Israel] That is, a chief city of a district; for it is very likely that the woman speaks of the city, not of herself.

Verse 21. *His head shall be thrown to thee*] Thus it appears she had great sway in the counsels of the city; and that the punishment of a state rebel was then, what it is now in this kingdom, *beheading.*

Verse 23. *Joab* was *over all the host*] He had murdered Amasa, and seized on the supreme command: and such was his power at present, and the service which he had rendered to the state by quelling the rebellion of Sheba,

that David was obliged to continue him; and dared not to call him to account for his murders without endangering the safety of the state by a civil war.

Benaiah—over the Cherethites] Benaiah was over the *archers* and *slingers.* See the notes on chap. viii. 18.

Verse 24. *Adoram* was *over the tribute*] Probably the chief receiver of the taxes; or *Chancellor of the Exchequer,* as we term it.

Jehoshaphat—recorder] The registrar of public events.

Verse 25. *Shevah* was *scribe*] The king's secretary.

Verse 26. *Ira—was a chief ruler about David.*] The Hebrew is כהן לדויד *cohen ledavid, a priest to David;* and so the *Vulgate, Septuagint, Syriac,* and *Arabic.* The *Chaldee* has רב *rab, a prince,* or *chief.* He was probably a sort of *domestic chaplain* to the king. We know that the kings of Judah had their *seers,* which is nearly the same: Gad was David's seer, chap. xxiv. 11; and Jeduthun was the seer of King Josiah, 2 Chron. xxxv. 15.

The conclusion of this chapter is very similar to the conclusion of chap. viii., where see the notes.

CHAPTER XXI

A famine taking place three successive years in Israel, David inquired of the Lord the cause; and was informed that it was on account of Saul and his bloody house, who had slain the Gibeonites, 1. David inquires of the Gibeonites what atonement they require, and they answer, seven sons of Saul, that they may hang them up in Gibeah, 2–6. Names of the seven sons thus given up, 7–9. Affecting account of Rizpah, who watched the bodies through the whole of the time of harvest, to prevent them from being devoured by birds and beasts of prey, 10. David is informed of Rizpah's conduct, and collects the bones of Saul, Jonathan, and the seven men that were hanged at Gibeah, and buries them; and God is entreated for the land, 11–14. War between the Israelites and Philistines, in which David is in danger of being slain by Ishbi-benob, but is succoured by Abishai, 15–17. He, and several gigantic Philistines, are slain by David and his servants, 18–22.

A. M. 2983
B. C. 1021
An. Exod. Isr.
470
Anno ante
I. Olymp. 245

THEN there was a famine in the days of David three years, year after year; and David [a]inquired of the LORD. And the LORD answered, *It is* for Saul and for *his* bloody house, because he slew the Gibeonites.

2 And the king called the Gibeonites, and said unto them; (now the Gibeonites *were* not of the children of Israel, but [b]of the remnant of the Amorites; and the children of Israel had sworn unto them: and Saul sought to slay them in his zeal to the children of Israel and Judah;)

3 Wherefore David said unto the Gibeonites, What shall I do for you? and wherewith shall I make the atonement, that ye may bless [c]the inheritance of the LORD?

4 And the Gibeonites said unto him, [d]We will have no silver nor gold of Saul, nor of his house; neither for us shalt thou kill any man in Israel. And he said, What ye shall say, *that* will I do for you.

5 And they answered the king, The man that consumed us, and that [e]devised against us *that* we should be destroyed from remaining in any of the coasts of Israel,

6 Let seven men of his sons be delivered unto us, and we will hang them up unto the LORD [f]in Gibeah of Saul, [g]whom [h]the LORD did choose. And the king said, I will give *them*.

A. M. 2983
B. C. 1021
An. Exod. Isr.
470
Anno ante
I. Olymp. 245

7 But the king spared Mephibosheth, the son of Jonathan the son of Saul, because of [i]the LORD'S oath that *was* between them, between David and Jonathan the son of Saul.

8 But the king took the two sons of [k]Rizpah the daughter of Aiah, whom she bare unto Saul, Armoni and Mephibosheth; and the five sons of [l]Michal the daughter of Saul, whom she [m]brought up for Adriel the son of Barzillai the Meholathite:

9 And he delivered them into the hands of the Gibeonites, and they hanged them in the hill [n]before the LORD: and they fell all seven together, and were put to death in the days of harvest, in the first *days,* in the beginning of barley harvest.

A. M. 2985
B. C. 1019
An. Exod. Isr.
472
Anno ante
I. Olymp. 243

10 And [o]Rizpah the daughter of Aiah took sackcloth, and spread it for her upon the rock, [p]from the beginning of harvest until water dropped upon them out of heaven, and suffered neither the birds of the air to rest on them by day, nor the beasts of the field by night.

---

[a]Heb. *sought the face,* &c.; see Numbers xxvii. 21 [b]Josh. ix. 3, 15, 16, 17——[c]Chap. xx. 19——[d]Or, It is *not silver nor gold that we have to do with Saul or his house, neither* pertains it *to us to kill,* &c.——[e]Or, *cut us off*——[f]1 Sam. x. 26; xi. 4

[g]1 Sam. x. 24——[h]Or, *chosen of the LORD*——[i]1 Sam. xviii. 3; xx. 8, 15, 42; xxiii. 18——[k]Ch. iii. 7——[l]Or, *Michal's sister*——[m]Heb. *bare to Adriel;* 1 Sam. xviii. 19 [n]Chap. vi. 17——[o]Ver. 8; chap. iii. 7——[p]See Deut. xxi. 23

NOTES ON CHAP. XXI

Verse 1. *Then there was a famine*] Of this famine we know nothing; it is not mentioned in any part of the history of David.

Because he slew the Gibeonites.] No such fact is mentioned in the life and transactions of Saul; nor is there any reference to it in any other part of Scripture.

Verse 2. *The remnant of the Amorites*] The Gibeonites were *Hivites,* not Amorites, as appears from Josh. xi. 19: but *Amorites* is a name often given to the Canaanites in general, Gen. xv. 16; Amos ii. 9, and elsewhere.

Verse 3. *Wherewith shall I make the atonement*] It is very strange that a choice of this kind should be left to such a people. Why not ask this of God himself?

Verse 6. *Seven men of his sons*] Meaning sons, grandsons, or other near branches of his family. It is supposed that the persons chosen were principal in assisting Saul to exterminate the Gibeonites. But where is the proof of this?

Verse 8. *Five sons of Michal—whom she brought up*] Michal, Saul's daughter, was never married to *Adriel,* but to David, and afterwards to Phaltiel; though it is here said *she bore* יָלְדָה

yaledah, not *brought up,* as we falsely translate it: but we learn from 1 Sam. xviii. 19, that *Merab,* one of Saul's daughters, was married to Adriel.

Two of Dr. *Kennicott's* MSS. have *Merab,* not Michal; the *Syriac* and *Arabic* have *Nadab;* the *Chaldee* has properly *Merab;* but it renders the passage thus:—*And the five sons of Merab which Michal the daughter of Saul brought up, which she brought forth to Adriel the son of Barzillai.* This *cuts* the knot.

Verse 9. *In the beginning of barley harvest.*] This happened in Judea about the vernal equinox, or the 21st of *March.*

Verse 10. *Rizpah—took sackcloth*] Who can read the account of Rizpah's maternal affection for her sons that were now hanged, without feeling his mind deeply impressed with sorrow?

Did God require this sacrifice of Saul's sons, probably all innocent of the alleged crime of their father? Was there no other method of averting the Divine displeasure? Was the requisition of the Gibeonites to have Saul's sons sacrificed to God, to be considered as an oracle of God? Certainly not; God will not have man's blood for sacrifice, no more than he will have swine's blood. The famine might have been re-

A. M. 2985
B. C. 1019
An. Exod. Isr. 472
Anno ante I. Olymp. 243

11 And it was told David what Rizpah the daughter of Aiah, the concubine of Saul, had done.

12 And David went and took the bones of Saul and the bones of Jonathan his son from the men of [q]Jabesh-gilead, which had stolen them from the street of Beth-shan, where the [r]Philistines had hanged them, when the Philistines had slain Saul in Gilboa:

A. M. 2986
B. C. 1018
An. Exod. Isr. 473
Anno ante I. Olymp. 242

13 And he brought up from thence the bones of Saul and the bones of Jonathan his son; and they gathered the bones of them that were hanged.

14 And the bones of Saul and Jonathan his son buried they in the country of Benjamin in [s]Zelah, in the sepulchre of Kish his father: and they performed all that the king commanded. And after that [t]God was entreated for the land.

15 Moreover the Philistines had yet war again with Israel; and David went down, and his servants with him; and fought against the Philistines; and David waxed faint.

A. M. 2986
B. C. 1018
An. Exod. Isr. 473
Anno ante I. Olymp. 242

16 And Ishbi-benob, which *was* of the sons of [u]the giant, the weight of whose [v]spear *weighed* three hundred *shekels* of brass in weight, he being girded with a new *sword,* thought to have slain David.

17 But Abishai the son of Zeruiah succoured him, and smote the Philistine, and killed him. Then the men of David sware unto him, saying, [w]Thou shalt go no more out with us to battle, that thou quench not the [x]light [y]of Israel.

18 [z]And it came to pass after this, that there was again a battle with the Philistines at Gob: then [a]Sibbechai the Hushathite slew [b]Saph, which *was* of the sons of [c]the giant.

19 And there was again a battle in Gob with the Philistines, where Elhanan the son of [d]Jaare-oregim, a Beth-lehemite, slew [e]*the brother of* Goliath the Gittite, the staff of whose spear *was* like a weaver's beam.

---

[q]1 Samuel xxxi. 11, 12, 13——[r]1 Samuel xxxi. 10 [s]Joshua xviii. 28——[t]So Joshua vii. 26; chap. xxiv. 25 [u]Or, *Rapha*——[v]Heb. *the staff*, or, *the head*——[w]Chap. xviii. 3

[x]1 Kings xi. 36; xv. 4; Psa. cxxxii. 17——[y]Heb. *candle*, or, *lamp*——[z]1 Chron. xx. 4——[a]1 Chron. xi. 29 [b]Or, *Sippai*——[c]Or, *Rapha*——[d]Or, *Jair*——[e]See 1 Chron. xx. 5

---

moved, and the land properly purged, by offering the sacrifices prescribed by the law, and by a general humiliation of the people.

Until water dropped upon them] Until the time of the *autumnal* rains, which in that country commence about October. Is it possible that this poor broken-hearted woman could have endured the fatigue, (and probably in the open air,) of watching these bodies for more than five months? Some think that the *rain dropping on them out of heaven* means the removal of the famine which was occasioned by *drought,* by now sending *rain,* which might have been shortly after these men were hanged; but this by no means agrees with the manner in which the account is introduced: "They were put to death in the days of harvest, in the first *days,* in the beginning of barley harvest. And Rizpah—took sackcloth, and spread it for her on the rock, from the beginning of harvest, until water dropped upon them out of heaven." No casual or immediately providential rain can be here intended; the reference must be to the *periodical* rains above mentioned.

Verse 12. *Took the bones of Saul*] The reader will recollect that the men of Jabesh-gilead burned the bodies of Saul and his sons, and buried the remaining bones under a tree at Jabesh. See 1 Sam. xxxi. 12, 13. These David might have digged up again, in order to bury them in the family sepulchre.

Verse 15. *Moreover the Philistines had yet war*] There is no mention of this war in the parallel place, 1 Chron. xx. 4, &c.

David waxed faint.] This circumstance is nowhere else mentioned.

Verse 16. *Being girded with a new* sword] As the word *sword* is not in the original, we may apply the term *new* to his *armour* in general; he had got new arms, a new coat of mail, or something that defended him well, and rendered him very formidable: or it may mean a strong or sharp sword.

Verse 17. *That thou quench not the light of Israel.*] David is here considered as the *lamp* by which all Israel was guided, and without whom all the nation must be involved in darkness. The lamp is the emblem of *direction* and *support.* Light is used in this sense by Homer:—

> Ουδε τι Πατροκλῳ γενομην φαος, αυδ' ἑταροισι
> Τοις αλλοις, οἱ δη πολεες δαμεν Ἑκτορι διῳ.
>
> *Iliad*, lib. xviii. ver. 102.

"I have neither been a LIGHT to Patroclus, nor to his companions, who have been slain by the noble Hector."

Verse 18. *A battle—at Gob*] Instead of *Gob*, several editions, and about *forty* of *Kennicott's* and *De Rossi's* MSS., have *nob*; but *Gezer* is the name in the parallel place, 1 Chron. xx. 4.

Verse 19. *Elhanan the son of Jaare-oregim—slew—Goliath the Gittite*] Here is a most manifest corruption of the text, or gross mistake of the transcriber; *David*, not *Elhanan*, slew *Goliath*. In 1 Chron. xx. 5, the parallel place, it stands thus: "Elhanan, the son of Jair, slew Lahmi, the brother of Goliath the Gittite, whose spear-staff *was* like a weaver's beam." This is plain; and our translators have *borrowed* some words from Chronicles to make

A. M. 2986
B. C. 1018
An. Exod. Isr.
473
Anno ante
I. Olymp. 242

20 And ᶠthere was yet a battle in Gath, where was a man of *great* stature, that had on every hand six fingers, and on every foot six toes, four and twenty in number; and he also was born to ᵍthe giant.

21 And when he ʰdefied Israel, Jonathan the son of ᶦShimeah the brother of David slew him.

A. M. 2986
B. C. 1018
An. Exod. Isr.
473
Anno ante
I. Olymp. 242

22 ᵏThese four were born to the giant in Gath, and fell by the hand of David, and by the hand of his servants.

ᶠ1 Chron. xx. 6——ᵍOr, *Rapha*——ʰOr, *reproached;* 1 Sam. xvii. 10, 25, 26

ᶦ1 Samuel xvi. 9, *Shammah*——ᵏ1 Chronicles xx. 8

---

both texts agree. The corruption may be easily accounted for by considering that ארגים *oregim,* which signifies *weavers,* has slipped out of one line into the other; and that בית הלחמי *beith hallachmi,* the *Beth-lehemite,* is corrupted from את לחמי *eth Lachmi;* then the reading will be the same as in Chronicles. Dr. *Kennicott* has made this appear very plain in his *First Dissertation on the Hebrew Text,* p. 78, &c.

Verse 20. *On every hand six fingers*] This is not a solitary instance: *Tavernier* informs us that the eldest son of the emperor of Java, who reigned in 1648, had *six fingers* on each hand, and *six toes* on each foot. And *Maupertuis,* in his seventeenth letter, says that he met with two families near Berlin, where *sedigitism* was equally transmitted on both sides of father and mother. I saw once a young girl, in the county of Londonderry, in Ireland, who had six fingers on each hand, and six toes on each foot, but her stature had nothing gigantic in it. The daughters of *Caius Horatius,* of patrician dignity, were called *sedigitæ,* because they had *six fingers* on each hand. *Volcatius,* a poet, was called *sedigitus* for the same reason. See *Pliny's* Hist. Nat., lib. xi., cap. 43.

THERE are evidently many places in this chapter in which the text has suffered much from the ignorance or carelessness of transcribers; and indeed I suspect the whole has suffered so materially as to distort, if not misrepresent the principal facts. It seems as if a Gibeonite has had something to do with the copies that are come down to us, or that the first fourteen verses have been inserted from a less authentic document than the rest of the book. I shall notice some of the most unaccountable, and apparently exceptionable particulars:—

1. The *famine,* ver. 1, is not spoken of anywhere else, nor at all referred to in the books of *Kings* or *Chronicles;* and, being of three years' duration, it was too remarkable to be omitted in the history of David.

2. The circumstance of Saul's *attempt to exterminate the Gibeonites* is nowhere else mentioned; and, had it taken place, it is not likely it would have been passed over in the history of Saul's transgressions. Indeed, it would have been such a breach of the good faith by which the whole nation was bound to this people, that an attempt of the kind could scarcely have failed to raise an insurrection through all Israel.

3. The wish of David that the Gibeonites, little better than a heathenish people, *should bless the inheritance of the Lord,* is unconstitutional and unlikely.

4. That God should leave the choice of the atonement to such a people, or indeed to any people, seems contrary to his established laws and particular providence.

5. That he should require seven innocent men to be hung up in place of their offending father,

in whose iniquity they most likely never had a share, seems inconsistent with justice and mercy.

6. In ver. 8, there is mention made of *five sons of Michal,* which she bore (ילדה *yaledah*) unto Adriel. Now, 1. Michal was never the wife of Adriel, but of David and Phaltiel. 2. She never appears to have had any children, see chap. vi. 23; this I have been obliged to correct in the preceding notes by putting *Merab* in the place of *Michal.*

7. The seven sons of Saul, mentioned here, are represented as a *sacrifice* required by God, to make an *atonement* for the sin of Saul. Does God in any case require *human blood* for sacrifice? And is it not *such a sacrifice* that is represented here? Dr. Delaney and others imagine that these seven sons were *principal agents* in the execution of their father's purpose; but of this there is *no proof.* Mephibosheth, the son of Jonathan, certainly had no hand in this projected massacre; he was ever *lame,* and could not be so employed; and yet he would have been one of the seven had it not been for the covenant made before with his father: *But the king spared Mephibosheth the son of Jonathan—because of the Lord's oath that was between them,* ver. 7.

8. The circumstance of Rizpah's watching the bodies of those victims, upon a rock, and probably in the open air, both day and night, from March to October, or even *for a much less period,* is, as it is here related, very extraordinary and improbable.

9. The hanging the bodies *so long* was against an express law of God, which ordained that those who were hanged on a tree should be taken down before sunset, and *buried the same day, lest the land should be defiled,* (Deut. xxi. 22, 23.) Therefore, 1. God did not command a breach of his own law. 2. David was too exact an observer of that law to require it. 3. The people could not have endured it; for, in that sultry season, the land would indeed have been *defiled* by the *putrefaction* of the dead bodies; and this would, in all likelihood, have added *pestilence* to *famine.*

10. The story of collecting and *burying the bones* of Saul and Jonathan is not very likely, considering that the men of Jabesh-gilead had burned their bodies, and buried the remaining bones under a tree at Jabesh, 1 Sam. xxxi. 12, 13; yet still it is possible.

11. Josephus takes as much of this story as he thinks proper, but says not one word about Rizpah, and her long watching over her slaughtered sons.

12. Even the *facts* in this chapter, which are mentioned in other places, (see 1 Chron. xx. 4, &c.,) are greatly distorted and corrupted; for we have already seen that *Elhanan* is made here to *kill Goliath the Gittite,* whom it is well known David slew; and it is only by means of

the parallel place above that we can restore this to historical truth.

That there have been attempts to remove some of these objections, I know; and I know also that these attempts have been in general without success.

Till I get farther light on the subject, I am led to conclude that the whole chapter is not *now* what it would be coming from the pen of an inspired writer; and that this part of the Jewish records has suffered much from rabbinical glosses, alterations, and additions. The *law*,

the *prophets*, and the *hagiographa*, including *Psalms*, *Proverbs*, *Ecclesiastes*, &c., have been ever considered as possessing the *highest title to Divine inspiration;* and therefore have been most carefully preserved and transcribed; but the *historical books*, especially *Samuel*, *Kings*, and *Chronicles*, have not ranked so high, have been less carefully preserved, and have been the subjects of frequent alteration and corruption. Yet still the great foundation of God standeth sure and is sufficiently attested by his own broad seal of consistency, truth, and holiness.

CHAPTER XXII

David's psalm of thanksgiving for God's powerful deliverance and manifold blessings, including prophetic declarations relative to the humiliation and exaltation of the Messiah, 1–51.

A. M. 2986
B. C. 1018
An. Exod. Isr.
473
Anno ante
I. Olymp. 242

AND David ᵃspake unto the LORD the words of this song in the day *that* the LORD had ᵇdelivered him out of the hand of all his enemies, and out of the hand of Saul.

2 And he said, ᶜThe LORD *is* my rock, and my fortress, and my deliverer:

3 The God of my rock; ᵈin him will I trust: *he is* my ᵉshield, and the ᶠhorn of my salvation, my high ᵍtower, and my ʰrefuge, my saviour; thou savest me from violence.

4 I will call on the LORD, *who is* worthy to be praised: so shall I be saved from mine enemies.

5 When the ¹waves of death compassed me, the floods of ᵏungodly men made me afraid;

6 The ¹sorrows ᵐof hell compassed me about; the snares of death prevented me;

A. M. 2986
B. C. 1018
An. Exod. Isr.
473
Anno ante
I. Olymp. 242

7 In my distress ⁿI called upon the LORD, and cried to my God: and he did ᵒhear my voice out of his temple, and my cry *did enter* into his ears.

8 Then ᵖthe earth shook and trembled; �q the foundations of heaven moved and shook, because he was wroth.

9 There went up a smoke ʳout of his nostrils, and ˢfire out of his mouth devoured: coals were kindled by it.

10 He ᵗbowed the heavens also, and came down; and ᵘdarkness *was* under his feet.

11 And he rode upon a cherub, and did fly; and he was seen ᵛupon the wings of the wind.

ᵃExod. xv. 1; Judg. v. 1——ᵇPsa. xviii. title; xxxiv. 19 ᶜDeut. xxxii. 4; Psa. xviii. 2, &c.; xxxi. 3; lxxi. 3; xci. 2; cxliv. 2——ᵈHeb. ii. 13——ᵉGen. xv. 1——ᶠLuke i. 69 ᵍProv. xviii. 10——ʰPsa. ix. 9; xiv. 6; lix. 16; lxxi. 7; Jer. xvi. 19——ⁱOr, *pangs*——ᵏHeb. *Belial*——¹Or, *cords*

ᵐPsa. cxvi. 3——ⁿPsa. cxvi. 4; cxx. 1; Jonah ii. 2 ᵒExod. iii. 7; Psa. xxxiv. 6, 15, 17——ᵖJudg. v. 4; Psa. lxxvii. 18; xcvii. 4——qJob xxvi. 11——ʳHeb. *by* ˢPsa. xcvii. 3; Hab. iii. 5; Heb. xii. 29——ᵗPsa. cxliv. 5; Isa. lxiv. 1——ᵘExod. xx. 21; 1 Kings viii. 12; Psa. xcvii. 2——ᵛPsa. civ. 3

NOTES ON CHAP. XXII

Verse 1. *David spake unto the Lord the words of this song*] This is the same in *substance*, and almost in *words*, with Psa. xviii.; and therefore the exposition of it must be reserved till it occurs in its course in that book, with the exception of a very few observations, and Dr. *Kennicott's* general view of the subject.

Verse 5. *When the waves of death compassed me*] Though in a primary sense many of these things belong to David, yet generally and fully they belong to the Messiah alone.

Verse 11. *He rode upon a cherub, and did fly —he was seen upon the wings of the wind.*] In the *original* of this sublime passage, *sense* and *sound* are astonishingly well connected. I shall insert the *Hebrew*, represent it in *English letters* for the sake of the unlearned reader, and have only to observe, he must read from the right to the left.

רוח כנפי על וירא ויעף כרוב על וירכב

ruach canphey al vaiyera : vaiyaoph kerub al vayirkab

wind the of wings the upon seen was he and ; fly did and cherub a upon rode he

The *clap* of the *wing*, the *agitation* and *rush* through the air are expressed here in a very extraordinary manner.

Other beauties of this kind will be noted in the exposition of the Psalm alluded to above.

I NOW subjoin Dr. *Kennicott's* remarks on this chapter:—

"The very sublime poetry contained in this chapter is universally admired, and yet it cannot be perfectly understood, till it is known WHO is the *speaker*, who the person thus triumphant over mighty enemies, *whose* sufferings occasioned such a dreadful convulsion of nature, and, *who*, upon his deliverance, inflicted such vengeance on his own people, and also became thus a king over the heathen. Should we be told that this person was *David*, it will be very difficult to show how this description can possibly agree with that character: but if it did in fact agree, yet would it contradict St. Paul, who quotes part of it as predicting *the conversion of the Gentiles under Christ the Messiah*, Rom. xv. 9; Heb. ii. 13; and see *Peirce's* Commentary, p. 50. Now if the person represented

A. M. 2986
B. C. 1018
An. Exod. Isr. 473
Anno ante
I. Olymp. 242

12 And he made [w]darkness pavilions round about him, [x]dark waters, *and* thick clouds of the skies.

13 Through the brightness before him were [y]coals of fire kindled.

14 The LORD [z]thundered from heaven, and the Most High uttered his voice.

15 And he sent out [a]arrows, and scattered them; lightning, and discomfited them.

16 And the channels of the sea appeared, the foundations of the world were discovered, at the [b]rebuking of the LORD, at the blast of the breath of his [c]nostrils.

17 [d]He sent from above, he took me; he drew me out of [e]many waters;

18 [f]He delivered me from my strong enemy, *and* from them that hated me: for they were too strong for me.

19 They prevented me in the day of my calamity: but the LORD was my stay.

20 [g]He brought me forth also into a large place: he delivered me, because he [h]delighted in me.

21 [i]The LORD rewarded me according to my righteousness: according to the [k]cleanness of my hands hath he recompensed me.

22 For I have [l]kept the ways of the LORD, and have not wickedly departed from my God.

23 For all his [m]judgments *were* before me: and *as for* his statutes, I did not depart from them.

A. M. 2986
B. C. 1018
An. Exod. Isr. 473
Anno ante
I. Olymp. 242

24 I was also [n]upright [o]before him, and have kept myself from mine iniquity.

25 Therefore [p]the LORD hath recompensed me according to my righteousness; according to my cleanness [q]in his eyesight.

26 With [r]the merciful thou wilt show thyself merciful, *and* with the upright man thou wilt show thyself upright.

27 With the pure thou wilt show thyself pure; and [s]with the froward thou wilt [t]show thyself unsavoury.

28 And the [u]afflicted people thou wilt save: but thine eyes *are* upon [v]the haughty, *that* thou mayest bring *them* down.

29 For thou *art* my [w]lamp, O LORD: and the LORD will lighten my darkness.

30 For by thee I have [x]run through a troop: by my God have I leaped over a wall.

31 *As for* God, [y]his way *is* perfect; [z]the word of the [a]LORD *is* tried: he *is* a buckler to all them that trust in him.

32 For [b]who *is* God, save the LORD? and who *is* a rock, save our God?

33 God *is* my [c]strength *and* power: and he [d]maketh [e]my way [f]perfect.

34 He [g]maketh my feet [h]like hinds' *feet:* and [i]setteth me upon my high places.

---

[w]Verse 10; Psalm xcvii. 2——[x]Heb. *binding of waters* [y]Ver. 9——[z]Judg. v. 20; 1 Sam. ii. 10; vii. 10; Psa. xxix. 3; Isa. xxx. 30——[a]Deut. xxxii. 23; Psa. vii. 13; lxxvii. 17; cxliv. 6; Hab. iii. 11——[b]Exod. xv. 8; Psa. cvi. 9; Nah. i. 4; Matt. viii. 26——[c]Or, *anger;* Psa. lxxiv. 1 [d]Psa. cxliv. 7——[e]Or, *great*——[f]Ver. 1——[g]Psa. xxxi 8; cxviii. 5——[h]Ch. xv. 26; Psa. xxii. 8——[i]Ver. 25; 1 Sam. xxvi. 23; 1 Kings viii. 32; Psa. vii. 8——[k]Psa. xxiv. 4——[l]Gen. xviii. 19; Psa. cxix. 3; cxxviii. 1; Prov. viii. 32——[m]Deut. vii. 12; Psa. cxix. 30, 102——[n]Genesis vi. 9; xvii. 1; Job i. 1——[o]Heb. *to him*——[p]Ver. 21

[q]Heb. *before his eyes*——[r]Matt. v. 7——[s]Lev. xxvi. 23, 24, 27, 28——[t]Or, *wrestle;* Psa. xviii. 26——[u]Exod. iii. 7, 8; Psa. lxxii. 12, 13——[v]Job xl. 11, 12; Isa. ii. 11, 12, 17; v. 15; Dan. iv. 37——[w]Or, *candle;* Job xxix. 3; Psa. xxvii. 1——[x]Or, *broken a troop*——[y]Deut. xxxii. 4; Dan. iv. 37; Rev. xv. 3——[z]Psa. xii. 6; cxix. 140; Prov. xxx. 5——[a]Or, *refined*——[b]1 Sam. ii. 2; Isa. xlv. 5, 6 [c]Exod. xv. 2; Psalm xxvii. 1; xxviii. 7, 8; xxxi. 4; Isa. xii. 2——[d]Heb. *riddeth,* or, *looseth*——[e]Heb. xiii. 21 [f]Deut. xviii. 13; Job xxii. 3; Psa. ci. 2, 6; cxix. 1 [g]Heb. *equalleth*——[h]Chap. ii. 18; Hab. iii. 19——[i]Deut. xxxii. 13; Isa. xxxiii. 16; lviii. 14

---

as speaking through this Divine ode be *David only*, the Messiah is excluded. In consequence of the difficulties resulting from each of these suppositions, the general idea has been that it relates *both to David and to the Messiah* as *a prophecy of a double sense;* first, as spoken by David of *himself*, and yet to be understood in a secondary sense, of the *Messiah.* But it must be remarked here, that if spoken only of David, it is not *a prediction* of any thing future, but a *thanksgiving* for favours past, and therefore is no *prophecy* at all. And farther, it could not be a prophecy descriptive of David unless the particulars agreed to David, which they evidently do not. If then David be here necessarily excluded from the *single* sense, he must be excluded also from the *double* sense, because nothing can be intended by any sacred writer, to relate to *two* persons, unless it be TRUE of *both;* but it not being the case here as to David, we must conclude that this song relates only to the *Messiah;* and on this subject an excellent Dissertation, by the late Mr. *Peirce*, is subjoined to his comment on the *Epistle to the Hebrews.* It may be necessary to add here two remarks: the twenty-fourth verse now ends with, *I have kept myself from mine iniquity*, which words, it is objected, are not proper, if applied to the Messiah. But this difficulty is removed, in part, by the context, which represents the speaker as *perfectly innocent and righteous;* and this exactly agrees with the proof arising from the *Syriac* and *Arabic* versions, and also the Chaldee paraphrase, that this word was anciently מעונים *ab iniquitatibus;* consequently, this is one of the many instances where the ם *final mem*

A. M. 2986
B. C. 1018
An. Exod. Isr.
473
Anno ante
I. Olymp. 242

35 [k]He teacheth my hands [l]to war; so that a bow of steel is broken by mine arms.

36 Thou hast also given me the shield of thy salvation: and thy gentleness hath [m]made me great.

37 Thou hast [n]enlarged my steps under me; so that my [o]feet did not slip.

38 I have pursued mine enemies, and destroyed them; and turned not again until I had consumed them.

39 And I have consumed them, and wounded them, that they could not arise: yea, they are fallen [p]under my feet.

40 For thou hast [q]girded me with strength to battle: [r]them that rose up against me hast thou [s]subdued under me.

41 Thou hast also given me the [t]necks of mine enemies, that I might destroy them that hate me.

42 They looked, but *there was* none to save; *even* [u]unto the LORD, but he answered them not.

43 Then did I beat them as small [v]as the dust of the earth, I did stamp them [w]as the mire of the street, *and* did spread them abroad.

44 [x]Thou also hast delivered me from the strivings of my people, thou hast kept me *to be* [y]head of the heathen: [z]a people *which* I knew not shall serve me.

A. M. 2986
B. C. 1018
An. Exod. Isr.
473
Anno ante
I. Olymp. 242

45 [a]Strangers shall [b]submit [c]themselves unto me: as soon as they hear, they shall be obedient unto me.

46 Strangers shall fade away, and they shall be afraid [d]out of their close places.

47 The LORD liveth; and blessed *be* my rock; and exalted be the God of the [e]rock of my salvation.

48 It *is* God that [f]avengeth me, and that [g]bringeth down the people under me,

49 And that bringeth me forth from mine enemies: thou also hast lifted me up on high above them that rose up against me: thou hast delivered me from the [h]violent man.

50 Therefore I will give thanks unto thee, O LORD, among [i]the heathen, and I will sing praises unto thy name.

51 [k]*He is* the tower of salvation for his king: and showeth mercy to his [l]anointed, unto David, and [m]to his seed for evermore.

---

[k]Psa. cxliv. 1——[l]Heb. *for the war*——[m]Heb. *multiplied me*——[n]Prov. iv. 12——[o]Heb. *ankles*——[p]Mal. iv. 3——[q]Psa. xviii. 32, 39——[r]Psa. xliv. 5——[s]Heb. *caused to bow*——[t]Gen. xlix. 8; Exod. xxiii. 27; Josh. x. 24——[u]Job xxvii. 9; Prov. i. 28; Isa. i. 15; Mic. iii. 4 [v]2 Kings xiii. 7; Psa. xxxv. 5; Dan. ii. 35——[w]Isa. x. 6; Mic. vii. 10; Zech. x. 5——[x]Chap. iii. 1; v. 1; xix. 9, 14; xx. 1, 2, 22

[y]Deut. xxviii. 13; chap. viii. 1–14; Psa. ii. 8——[z]Isa. lv. 5——[a]Hebrew, *sons of the stranger*——[b]Or, *yield feigned obedience*——[c]Heb. *lie;* see Deut. xxxiii. 29; Psa. lxvi. 3; lxxxi. 15——[d]Mic. vii. 17——[e]Psa. lxxxix. 26 [f]Heb. *giveth avengement for me;* 1 Sam. xxv. 39; chap. xviii. 19, 31——[g]Psa. cxliv. 2——[h]Psa. cxl. 1——[i]Rom. xv. 9——[k]Psa. cxliv. 10——[l]Psa. lxxxix. 20——[m]Chap. vii. 12, 13; Psa. lxxxix. 29

---

is improperly omitted by the Jewish transcribers. See my *General Dissertation*, p. 12. Lastly, the difficulty arising from the *title*, which ascribes the Psalm to *David*, and which seems to make *him* the speaker in it, may be removed, either by supposing that the title here, like those now prefixed to several Psalms, is of no sufficient authority; or *rather*, by considering this title as only meant to describe *the time* when David composed this prophetic hymn, that *when delivered from all his other enemies as well as from the hand of Saul*, he *then* consecrated his leisure by composing this sublime prophecy concerning MESSIAH, his son, *whom* he represents here as *speaking*, (just as in Psa. xxii., xl., and other places,) and as describing, 1. His triumph over death and hell; 2. The manifestations of Omnipotence in his favour, earth and heaven, trembling at God's awful presence; 3. The speaker's innocence thus divinely attested; 4. The vengeance he was to take on *his own people* the Jews, in the destruc-

tion of Jerusalem; and, 5. The adoption of the *heathen*, over whom he was to be the head and ruler.

"Another instance of *a title* denoting only *the time* of a prophecy, occurs in the very next chapter; where a prophecy concerning the Messiah is entitled, *The* LAST *words of David;* i. e., a hymn which he composed a little before his death, *after all his other prophecies*. And perhaps this ode in chap. xxii., which immediately precedes that in chap. xxiii., was composed but a little while before; namely, *when all his wars were over*. Let it be added, that *Josephus*, immediately before he speaks of David's mighty men, which follow in this same chapter of Samuel, considers the two hymns in chap. xxii. and xxiii. as both written after his wars were over —*Jam Davides, bellis et periculis perfunctus, pacemque deinceps profundam agitans, odas in Deum hymnosque composuit.* Tom. i., page 401."

CHAPTER XXIII

The last words of David, 1–7. *The names and exploits of his* thirty-seven *worthies,* 8–39.

A. M. 2986
B. C. 1018
An. Exod. Isr.
473
Anno ante
I. Olymp. 242

NOW these *be* the last words of David. David the son of Jesse said, [a]and the man *who was* raised up on high, [b]the anointed of the God of Jacob, and the sweet psalmist of Israel, said,

2 [c]The Spirit of the LORD spake by me, and his word *was* in my tongue.

3 The God of Israel said, [d]the Rock of Israel spake to me, [e]He that ruleth over men *must be* just, ruling [f]in the fear of God.

4 And [g]*he shall be* as the light of the morning, *when* the sun riseth, *even* a morning without clouds; *as* the tender grass *springing*

out of the earth by clear shining after rain.

5 Although my house *be* not so with God; [h]yet he hath made with me an everlasting covenant, ordered in all *things,* and sure: for *this is* all my salvation, and all *my* desire, although he make *it* not to grow.

6 But *the sons* of Belial *shall be* all of them as thorns thrust away, because they cannot be taken with hands:

7 But the man *that* shall touch them must be [i]fenced with iron and the staff of a spear: and they shall be utterly burned with fire in the *same* place.

A. M. 2986
B. C. 1018
An. Exod. Isr.
473
Anno ante
I. Olymp. 242

---

[a]Ch. vii. 8, 9; Psa. lxxviii. 70, 71; lxxxix. 27——[b]1 Sam. xvi. 12, 13; Psa. lxxxix. 20——[c]2 Pet. i. 21 [d]Deut. xxxii. 4, 31; chap. xxii. 2, 32——[e]Or, *be thou ruler, &c.*; Psa. cx. 2

[f]Exod. xviii. 21; 2 Chron. xix. 7, 9——[g]Judg. v. 31; Psalm lxxxix. 36; Prov. iv. 18; Hos. vi. 5; see Psa. cx. 3 [h]Chap. vii. 15, 16; Psa. lxxxix. 29; Isa. lv. 3——[i]Heb. *filled*

NOTES ON CHAP. XXIII

Verse 1. These be the last words of David.] I suppose the *last poetical composition* is here intended. He might have spoken many words after these in *prose,* but none in *verse.* Other meanings are given; this I prefer.

The words of this song contain a glorious prediction of the Messiah's kingdom and conquests, in highly poetic language.

The sweet psalmist of Israel] This character not only belonged to him as the finest poet in *Israel,* but as the finest and most Divine poet of the whole *Christian* world. The *sweet psalmist of Israel* has been the sweet psalmist of every part of the habitable world, where religion and piety have been held in reverence.

Verse 2. The Spirit of the Lord spake by me] Hence the matter of his writing came by direct and immediate inspiration.

His word was *in my tongue.*] Hence the *words* of this writing were as directly inspired as the *matter.*

Verse 3. The Rock of Israel] The *Fountain* whence Israel was derived.

He that ruleth over men must be *just*] More literally, מושל באדם צדיק *moshel baadam tsaddik, He that ruleth in man is the just one;* or, *The just one is the ruler among men.*

Ruling in the fear of God.] It is by God's fear that Jesus Christ rules the hearts of all his followers; and he who has not the fear of God before his eyes, can never be a Christian.

Verse 4. He shall be *as the light of the morning*] This verse is very obscure, for it does not appear from it *who* the person is of whom the prophet speaks. As the Messiah seems to be the whole subject of these last words of David, he is probably the person intended. One of Dr. *Kennicott's* MSS. supplies the word יהוה *Ye-*

hovah; and he therefore translates, *As the light of the morning ariseth Jehovah* (see below)— He shall be the Sun of righteousness, bringing salvation in his rays, and *shining*—illuminating the children of men, with increasing splendour, as long as the sun and moon endure.

As the tender grass] The effects of this *shining,* and of the rays of his grace, shall be like the shining of the sun upon the young grass or corn, after a plentiful shower of rain.

Verse 5. Although my house be *not so with God*] Instead of בן *ken, so,* read כן *kun, established;* and let the whole verse be considered as an *interrogation,* including a positive *assertion;* and the sense will be at once clear and consistent: "for is not my house (family) *established* with God; because he hath made with me an everlasting covenant, ordered in all, and preserved? For this (He) is all my salvation, and all my desire, although he make it (or him) not to spring up." All is sure relative to my spiritual successor, though he do not *as yet* appear; the covenant is firm, and it will spring forth in due time. See the observations at the end of the chapter.

Verse 6. But the sons *of Belial* shall be *all of them as thorns*] There is no word in the text for *sons;* it is simply *Belial,* the *good-for-nothing man,* and may here refer—first to Saul, and secondly to the enemies of our Lord.

As thorns thrust away] A metaphor taken from *hedging;* the workman thrusts the thorns aside either with his *bill* or hand, protected by his impenetrable *mitten* or glove, till, getting a fair blow at the roots, he cuts them all down. The man is *fenced with iron,* and the handle of his bill is *like the staff of a spear.* This is a good representation of the *dubbing-bill,* with which they *slash the thorn hedge* on each side before they level the tops by the *pruning-shears.* The handle is five or six feet long. This is a perfectly natural and intelligible image.

A. M. 2949–89
B. C. 1055–15
An. Exod. Isr.
436–76
8 These *be* the names of the mighty men whom David had: [k]The Tachmonite that sat in the seat, chief among the captains: the same *was* Adino the Eznite: [l]he *lift up his spear* against eight hundred, [m]whom he slew at one time.

9 And after him *was* [n]Eleazar the son of Dodo the Ahohite, *one* of the three mighty men with David, when they defied the Philistines *that* were there gathered together to battle, and the men of Israel were gone away:

10 He arose, and smote the Philistines until his hand was weary, and his hand clave unto the sword: and the Lord wrought a great victory that day; and the people returned after him only to spoil.

11 And after him *was* [o]Shammah the son of Agee the Hararite. [p]And the Philistines were gathered together [q]into a troop, where was a piece of ground full of lentiles: and the people fled from the Philistines.

12 But he stood in the midst of the ground, and defended it, and slew the Philistines; and the Lord wrought a great victory.

A. M. 2949–89
B. C. 1055–15
An. Exod. Isr.
436–76

13 And [r]three [s]of the thirty chief went down, and came to David in the harvest time unto [t]the cave of Adullam: and the troop of the Philistines pitched in [u]the valley of Rephaim.

14 And David *was* then in [v]a hold, and the garrison of the Philistines *was* then *in* Beth-lehem.

15 And David longed, and said, O that one would give me drink of the water of the well of Beth-lehem, which *is* by the gate!

16 And the three mighty men brake through the host of the Philistines, and drew water out of the well of Beth-lehem, that *was* by the gate, and took *it,* and brought *it* to David: nevertheless he would not drink thereof, but poured it out unto the Lord.

---

[k]Or, *Josheb-bassebet the Tachmonite, head of the three* [l]See 1 Chron. xi. 11; xxvii. 2——[m]Heb. *slain*——[n]1 Chron. xi. 12; xxvii. 4——[o]1 Chron. xi. 27

[p]See 1 Chron. xi. 13, 14——[q]Or, *for foraging*——[r]1 Chron. xi. 15——[s]Or, *the three captains over the thirty* [t]1 Sam. xxii. 1——[u]Chap. v. 18——[v]1 Sam. xxii. 4, 5

Verse 8. *These* be *the names of the mighty* men] This chapter should be collated with the parallel place, 1 Chron. xi.; and see *Kennicott's* First Dissertation on the printed Hebrew text, pages 64-471.

The Tachmonite that sat in the seat] Literally and properly, *Jashobeam the Hachmonite.* See 1 Chron. xi. 11.

The same was *Adino the Eznite*] This is a corruption for *he lift up his spear.* See 1 Chron. xi. 11.

Eight hundred, whom he slew at one time.] THREE *hundred* is the reading in Chronicles, and seems to be the true one. The word חלל *chalal,* which we translate *slain,* should probably be translated *soldiers,* as in the *Septuagint,* στρατιωτας; he withstood *three hundred* SOLDIERS at one time. See the note on David's lamentation over Saul and Jonathan, chap. i., and *Kennicott's* First Dissertation, p. 101. Dr. Kennicott observes: "This one verse contains *three* great corruptions in the Hebrew text: 1. The proper name of the hero *Jashobeam* is turned into two common words, rendered, *that sat in the seat.* 2. The words, *he lift up his spear,* הוא עורר את חניתו *hu orer eth chanitho,* are turned into two proper names wholly inadmissible here: הוא עדינו העצני *hu Adino haetsni, he was Adino the Eznite;* it being nearly as absurd to say that Jashobeam the Hachmonite was the same with Adino the Eznite, as that David the Beth-lehemite was the same with Elijah the Tishbite. 3. The number *eight hundred* was probably at first *three hundred,* as in 1 Chron. xi. 11." See *Kennicott,* ubi supr.

Verse 9. *When they defied the Philistines that* were *there gathered*] This is supposed to refer to the war in which David slew Goliath.

Verse 11. *A piece of ground full of lentiles*] In 1 Chron. xi. 13 it is *a parcel of ground full of*

barley. There is probably a mistake of עדשים *adashim, lentiles,* for שעורים *seorim, barley,* or *vice versa.* Some think there were both *lentiles* and *barley* in the field, and that a marauding party of the Philistines came to destroy or carry them off, and these worthies defeated the whole, and saved the produce of the field. This is not unlikely.

Verse 13. *And three of the thirty*] The word שלשים *shalishim,* which we translate *thirty,* probably signifies an *office* or *particular description* of men. Of these *shalishim* we have here *thirty-seven,* and it can scarcely be said with propriety that we have *thirty-seven* out of *thirty;* and besides, in the parallel place, 1 Chron. xi., there are *sixteen* added. The *captains* over Pharaoh's chariots are termed שלשים *shalishim,* Exod. xiv. 7.

The Philistines pitched in the valley of Rephaim.] This is the same war which is spoken of chap. v. 17, &c.

Verse 15. *The water of the well of Beth-lehem*] This was David's city, and he knew the excellence of the water which was there; and being near the place, and parched with thirst, it was natural for him to wish for a draught of water out of that well. These three heroes having heard it, though they received no command from David, broke through a company of the Philistines, and brought away some of the water. When brought to David he refused to drink it: for as the men got it at the hazard of their lives, he considered it as their blood, and gave thereby a noble instance of self-denial. There is no evidence that David had requested them to bring it; they had gone for it of their own accord, and without the knowledge of David.

Verse 16. *Poured it out unto the Lord.*] To make *libations,* both of *water* and *wine,* was a

A. M. 2949–89
B. C. 1055–15
An. Exod. Isr.
436–76

17 And he said, Be it far from me, O LORD, that I should do this: *is not this* [w]the blood of the men that went in jeopardy of their lives? therefore he would not drink it. These things did these three mighty men.

18 And [x]Abishai, the brother of Joab, the son of Zeruiah, was chief among three. And he lifted up his spear against three hundred, [y]*and* slew *them,* and had the name among three.

19 Was he not most honourable of three? therefore he was their captain: howbeit he attained not unto the *first* three.

20 And Benaiah the son of Jehoiada, the son of a valiant man, of [z]Kabzeel, [a]who had done many acts, [b]he slew two [c]lion-like men of Moab: he went down also and slew a lion in

A. M. 2949–89
B. C. 1055–15
An. Exod. Isr.
436–76

the midst of a pit in time of snow:

21 And he slew an Egyptian, [d]a goodly man: and the Egyptian had a spear in his hand; but he went down to him with a staff, and plucked the spear out of the Egyptian's hand, and slew him with his own spear.

22 These *things* did Benaiah the son of Jehoiada, and had the name among three mighty men.

23 He was [e]more honourable than the thirty, but he attained not to the *first* three. And David set him [f]over his [g]guard.[h]

24 [i]Asahel the brother of Joab *was* one of the thirty; Elhanan the son of Dodo of Bethlehem,

---

[w]Lev. xvii. 10——[x]1 Chron. xi. 20——[y]Heb. *slain*
[z]Josh. xv. 21——[a]Heb. *great of acts*——[b]Exod. xv. 15;
1 Chron. xi. 22——[c]Hebrew, *lions of God*——[d]Hebrew,
a man of countenance, or, *sight;* called, 1 Chron. xi. 23,

a man of great *stature*——[e]Or, *honourable among the thirty*——[f]Chapter viii. 18; xx. 23——[g]Or, *council*
[h]Hebrew, *at his command;* 1 Sam. xxii. 14——[i]Chap.
ii. 18

---

frequent custom among the heathens. We have an almost similar account in *Arrian's* Life of Alexander: "When his army was greatly oppressed with heat and thirst, a soldier brought him a cup of water; he ordered it to be carried back, saying, I cannot bear to drink alone while so many are in want, and this cup is too small to be divided among the whole." Tunc poculo pleno sicut oblatum est reddito: Non solus, inquit, bibere sustineo, nec tam exiguum dividere omnibus possum.—ARRIAN, lib. vi.

The example was noble in both cases, but David added *piety* to *bravery;* he poured it out unto the Lord.

Verse 20. *Two lion-like men of Moab*] Some think that two *real lions* are meant; some that they were two savage *gigantic* men; others, that two *fortresses* are meant. The words שני אראל מואב *sheney ariel Moab* may signify, as the Targum has rendered it, ית תרין רברבי מואב *yath terein rabrebey Moab,* "The two princes of Moab."

Verse 21. *He slew an Egyptian*] This man in 1 Chron. xi. 23 is stated to have been *five cubits* high, about *seven feet six inches.*

He went down to him with a staff] I have known men who, with a *staff* only for their defence, could render the sword of the best practised soldier of no use to him. I have seen even a parallel instance of a man with his staff being attacked by a soldier with his hanger; he soon beat the weapon out of the soldier's hand, and could easily have slain him with his own sword.

We have a good elucidation of this in a duel between *Dioxippus* the Athenian and *Horratas* a Macedonian, before Alexander: "The Macedonian, proud of his military skill, treated the naked Athenian with contempt, and then challenged him to fight with him the ensuing day. The Macedonian came armed *cap-a-pie* to the place; on his left arm he had a brazen shield, and in the same hand a spear called *sarissa;* he had a javelin in his right hand, and a sword

girded on his side; in short, he appeared armed as though he were going to contend with a host. Dioxippus came into the field with a chaplet on his head, a purple sash on his left arm, his body naked, smeared over with oil, and in his right hand a strong knotty club, (*dextra validum nodosumque stipitem præferebat.*) Horratas, supposing he could easily kill his antagonist while at a distance, threw his javelin, which Dioxippus, suddenly stooping, dexterously avoided, and, before Horratas could transfer the spear from his left to his right hand, sprang forward, and with one blow of his club, broke it in two. The Macedonian being deprived of both his spears, began to draw his sword; but before he could draw it out Dioxippus seized him, tripped up his heels, and threw him with great violence on the ground, (*pedibus repente subductis arietavit in terram.*) He then put his foot on his neck, drew out his sword, and lifting up his club, was about to dash out the brains of the overthrown champion, had he not been prevented by the king."—*Q. Curt.* lib. ix., cap. 7.

How similar are the two cases! *He went down to him with a staff, and plucked the spear out of the Egyptian's hands, and slew him with his own spear.* Benaiah appears to have been just such another *clubsman* as Dioxippus.

Verse 23. *David set him over his guard.*] The *Vulgate* renders this, *Fecitque eum sibi David auricularium a secreto,* "David made him his privy counsellor;" or, according to the Hebrew, *He put him to his ears,* i. e. confided his secrets to him. Some think he made him a *spy* over the rest. It is supposed that the meaning of the fable which attributes to *Midas very long ears,* is, that this king carried the system of *espionage* to a great length; that he had a multitude of spies in different places.

Verse 24. *Asahel—was one of the thirty*] Asahel was one of those officers, or troops, called the *shalishim.* This Asahel, brother of Joab, was the same that was killed by Abner, chap. ii. 23.

A. M. 2949–89
B. C. 1055–15
An. Exod. Isr.
436–76

25 [k]Shammah the Harodite, Elika the Harodite,

26 Helez the Paltite, Ira the son of Ikkesh the Tekoite,

27 Abiezer the Anethothite, Mebunnai the Hushathite,

28 Zalmon the Ahohite, Maharai the Netophathite,

29 Heleb the son of Baanah, a Netophathite, Ittai the son of Ribai out of Gibeah of the children of Benjamin,

30 Benaiah the Pirathonite, Hiddai of the [l]brooks of [m]Gaash,

31 Abi-albon the Arbathite, Azmaveth the Barhumite,

32 Eliahba the Shaalbonite, of the sons of Jashen, Jonathan,

A. M. 2946–89
B. C. 1055–15
An. Exod. Isr.
436–76

33 Shammah the Hararite, Ahiam the son of Sharar the Hararite,

34 Eliphelet the son of Ahasbai, the son of the Maachathite, Eliam the son of Ahithophel the Gilonite,

35 Hezrai the Carmelite, Paarai the Arbite,

36 Igal the son of Nathan of Zobah, Bani the Gadite,

37 Zelek the Ammonite, Naharai the Beerothite, armour-bearer to Joab the son of Zeruiah.

38 [n]Ira an Ithrite, Gareb an Ithrite,

39 [o]Uriah the Hittite: thirty and seven in all.

---

[k]See 1 Chron. xi. 27——[l]Or, *valleys*, Deut. i. 24

[m]Judg. ii. 9——[n]Chap. xx. 26——[o]Chap. xi. 3, 6

Verse 25. *Shammah the Harodite*] There are several varieties in the names of the following *shalishim;* which may be seen by comparing these verses with 1 Chron. xi. 27.

Verse 39. *Uriah the Hittite: thirty and seven in all.*] To these the author of 1 Chron. xi. 41 adds *Zabad* son of *Ahlai.*

Verse 42.—*Adina* the son of *Shiza* the Reubenite, a captain of the Reubenites, and thirty with him.

Verse 43.—*Hanan* the son of *Maachah*, and *Joshaphat* the Mithnite,

Verse 44.—*Uzzia* the Ashterathite, *Shama* and *Jehiel* the sons of *Hothan* the Aroerite,

Verse 45.—*Jediael* the son of *Shimri*, and *Joha* his brother, the Tizite,

Verse 46.—*Eliel* the Mahavite, and *Jeribai*, and *Joshaviah*, the sons of *Elnaam*, and *Ithmah* the Moabite,

Verse 47.—*Eliel*, and *Obed*, and *Jasiel* the Mesobaite.

THE 4th and 5th verses are very obscure; *L. De Dieu* gives them a good meaning, if not the true one:—

"The *perpetuity* of his kingdom David amplifies by a comparison to three natural things, which are very grateful to men, but not *constant* and *stable.* For the *sun* arises and goes down again; the *morning* may be clear, but clouds afterwards arise; and the *tender grass* springs up, but afterwards withers. Not so,

said he, is my kingdom before God; it is flourishing like all these, but *perpetual*, for he has made an everlasting covenant with me, though some afflictions have befallen me; and he has not made all my *salvation* and *desire* to grow."

De Dieu repeats כ *ke*, the note of similitude, *thrice;* and the following is his version:—

"The God of Israel said, the Rock of Israel spake unto me, (or concerning me:) The just man ruleth among men; he ruleth in the fear of God. And, as the sun ariseth with a shining light; as the morning is without clouds by reason of its splendour; as, from rain, the tender grass springeth out of the earth; truly so is not my house with God: because he hath made an *everlasting* covenant with me; disposed in all things, and well *kept* and *preserved* in that order. Although he doth not make all my deliverance and desire to grow, i. e., though some adversities happen to me and my family; yet, *that* always remains, which, in the covenant of God made with me, is in all things orderly, disposed, and preserved."

See Bishop *Patrick* on the place.

Once more I must beg the reader to refer to the *First Dissertation* of Dr. *Kennicott*, on the *present state of the printed Hebrew text;* in which there is not only great light cast on this subject, several corruptions in the Hebrew text being demonstrated, but also many valuable criticisms on different texts in the sacred writings. There are two *Dissertations*, 2 vols. 8vo.; and both very valuable.

CHAPTER XXIV

David is tempted by Satan to number Israel and Judah, 1. *Joab remonstrates against it, but the king determines that it shall be done; and Joab and the captains accomplish the work, and bring the sum total to the king:* viz.: *eight hundred thousand warriors in Israel, and five hundred thousand in Judah,* 2–9. *David is convinced that he has done wrong; and the prophet Gad is sent to him, to give him his choice of three judgments, one of which God is determined to inflict upon the nation,* 10–13. *David humbles himself before God; and a pestilence is sent, which destroys* seventy thousand *men,* 14, 15. *The angel of the Lord being about to destroy Jerusalem, David makes intercession, and the plague is stayed,* 16, 17. *Gad directs him to build an altar to the Lord on the threshing-floor of Araunah, where the plague was stayed,* 18. *He purchases this place for the purpose, and offers burnt-offerings and peace-offerings.* 19–25.

A. M. 2987
B. C. 1017
An. Exod. Isr.
474
Anno ante
I. Olymp. 241

AND ªagain the anger of the LORD was kindled against Israel, and ᵇhe moved David against them to say, ᶜGo, number Israel and Judah.

2 For the king said to Joab the captain of the host, which *was* with him, ᵈGo now through all the tribes of Israel, ᵉfrom Dan even to Beer-sheba, and number ye the people, that ᶠI may know the number of the people.

3 And Joab said unto the king, Now the LORD thy God add unto the people, how many soever they be, a hundred-fold, and that the eyes of my lord the king may see *it:* but why doth my lord the king delight in this thing?

4 Notwithstanding the king's word prevailed against Joab, and against the captains

of the host. And Joab and the captains of the host went out from the presence of the king, to number the people of Israel.

A. M. 2987
B. C. 1017
An. Exod. Isr.
474
Anno ante
I. Olymp. 241

5 And they passed over Jordan, and pitched in ᵍAroer, on the right side of the city that *lieth* in the midst of the ʰriver of Gad, and toward ⁱJazer:

6 Then they came to Gilead, and to the ᵏland of Tahtim-hodshi; and they came to ˡDan-jaan, and about to ᵐZidon;

7 And came to the ⌁trong hold of Tyre, and to all the cities of the Hivites, and of the Canaanites: and they went out to the south of Judah, *even* to Beer-sheba.

8 So when they had gone through all the land, they came to Jerusalem at the end of nine months and twenty days.

ªCh. xxi. 1——ᵇ*Satan,* see 1 Chron. xxi. 1; James i. 13, 14——ᶜ1 Chron. xxvii. 23, 24——ᵈOr, *compass*——ᵉJudg. xx. 1——ᶠJer. xvii. 5——ᵍDeut. ii. 36; Josh. xiii. 9, 16

ʰOr, *valley*——ⁱNum. xxxii. 1, 3——ᵏOr, *nether land newly inhabited*——ˡJosh. xix. 47; Judg. xviii. 29 ᵐJosh. xix. 28; Judg. xviii. 28

NOTES ON CHAP. XXIV

Verse 1. *He moved David against them*] God could not be angry with David for numbering the people if *he moved him to do it;* but in the parallel place (1 Chron. xxi. 1) it is expressly said, *Satan stood up against Israel, and provoked David to number Israel.* David, in all probability, slackening in his piety and confidence toward God, and meditating some extension of his dominions without the Divine counsel or command, was naturally curious to know whether the number of fighting men in his empire was sufficient for the work which he had projected. See more on ver. 10. He therefore orders Joab and the captains to take an exact account of all the effective men in Israel and Judah. God is justly displeased with this conduct, and determines that the *props* of his vain ambition shall be taken away, either by *famine, war,* or *pestilence.*

Verse 3. *Joab said unto the king*] This very bad man saw that the measure now recommended by the king was a wrong one, and might be ruinous to the people, and therefore he remonstrates against it in a very sensible speech; but the king was infatuated, and would hear no reason.

Verse 5. *And pitched in Aroer*] This was beyond Jordan, on the river Arnon, in the tribe of Gad: hence it appears, says *Calmet,* that they began their census with the most *eastern* parts of the country beyond Jordan.

Verse 6. *Tahtim-hodshi*] Where this place was is not exactly known: some think that the words refer to a newly conquered country, as our margin, *the nether land newly inhabited;* and if so, this was probably the country *eastward* of Gilead, which the Israelites, in the time of Saul, had conquered from the Hagarites, and dwelt in themselves. See 1 Chron. v. 10, where this transaction is recorded.

To Dan-jaan] Or, to *Dan of the woods.* This is the place so frequently mentioned, situated

at the foot of Mount Libanus, near to the source of the Jordan, the most *northern* city of all the possessions of the Israelites in what was called the promised land, as Beer-sheba was the most *southern:* hence the common form of speech, *From Dan to Beer-sheba,* i. e., from *north* to *south.*

Verse 7. *The strong hold of Tyre*] This must have been the old city of Tyre, which was built on the main land: the new city was built on a rock in the sea.

Verse 8. *Nine months and twenty days.*] This was a considerable time; but they had much work to do, nor did they complete the work, as appears from 1 Chron. xxi. 6; xxvii. 24. *William the Conqueror* made a survey of all England, particularizing "how many hides or carucates the land is taxed at; whose it was in the time of his predecessor Edward; who the present owners and sub-tenants; what and how much arable land, meadow, pasture, and wood there is; how much in demesne, i. e., held and cultivated by the landowners; how much in tenancy, and what number of ploughs it will keep; what mills and fisheries; how many sockmen, freemen, co-liberti, cotarii, bordarii, radmanni, radchenisters, villains, maid-servants, and bondmen, there are; how many hogs the woods would support; how many churches, priests, or parsons; what customary rents, prestations, and services, are to be paid and rendered out of the lands; what has been added to the manor; what has been withheld from it, and by whom; what land is waste, and what the whole was let for in the time of King Edward; and what the nett rent, and whether it was too dear rented, and whether it might be improved." This survey was begun in the year 1080, and was finished in the year 1086, *six years* having been employed in the work. This most important document is still preserved; it is in the *Chapter House, Westminster,* in two volumes, one in *folio,* on *three hundred and eighty-two* leaves of vellum, the other in *quarto,* on *four*

A. M. 2987
B. C. 1017
An. Exod. Isr.
474
Anno ante
I. Olymp. 241
9 And Joab gave up the sum of the number of the people unto the king: [n]and there were in Israel eight hundred thousand valiant men that drew the sword; and the men of Judah *were* five hundred thousand men.

10 And [o]David's heart smote him after that he had numbered the people. And David said unto the Lord, [p]I have sinned greatly in that I have done: and now, I beseech thee, O Lord, take away the iniquity of thy servant; for I have [q]done very foolishly.

11 For when David was up in the morning, the word of the Lord came unto the prophet [r]Gad, David's [s]seer, saying,

12 Go and say unto David, Thus saith the Lord, I offer thee three *things;* choose thee one of them, that I may *do it* unto thee.

13 So Gad came to David, and told him, and said unto him, Shall [t]seven years of famine come unto thee in thy land? or wilt thou flee three months before thine enemies, while they pursue thee? or that there be three days' pestilence in thy land? now advise, and see what answer I shall return to him that sent me.

A. M. 2987
B. C. 1017
An. Exod. Isr.
474
Anno ante
I. Olymp. 241

14 And David said unto Gad, I am in a great strait: let us fall now into the hand of the Lord; [u]for his mercies *are* [v]great: and [w]let me not fall into the hand of man.

15 So [x]the Lord sent a pestilence upon Israel from the morning even to the time appointed: and there died of the people from Dan even to Beer-sheba seventy thousand men.

16 [y]And when the angel stretched out his hand upon Jerusalem to destroy it, [z]the Lord

---

[n]See 1 Chron. xxi. 5——[o]1 Sam. xxiv. 5——[p]Chap. xii. 13——[q]1 Sam. xiii. 13——[r]1 Sam. xxii. 5——[s]1 Sam. ix. 9; 1 Chron. xxix. 29——[t]See 1 Chron. xxi. 12 [u]Psa. ciii. 3, 13, 14; cxix. 156

[v]Or, *many*——[w]See Isa. xlvii. 6; Zech. i. 15 [x]1 Chron. xxi. 14; xxvii. 24——[y]Exod. xii. 23; 1 Chron. xxi. 15——[z]Genesis vi. 6; 1 Sam. xv. 11: Joel ii. 13, 14

---

hundred and fifty leaves; and is in as good preservation as it was *seven hundred* years ago. This work was much more difficult than that which was performed by Joab and his fellows. The work itself is known by the name *Domesday Book.*

Verse 9. *In Israel eight hundred thousand— the men of Judah* were *five hundred thousand*] In the parallel place, 1 Chron. xxi. 5, the sums are widely different: in Israel *one million one hundred thousand*, in Judah *four hundred and seventy thousand*. Neither of these sums is too great, but they cannot be both correct; and which is the true number is difficult to say. The former seems the most likely; but more corruptions have taken place in the *numbers* of the historical books of the Old Testament, than in any other part of the sacred records. To attempt to reconcile them in every part is lost labour; better at once acknowledge what cannot be successfully denied, that although the original writers of the Old Testament wrote under the influence of the Divine Spirit, yet we are not told that the same influence descended on all *copiers* of their words, so as absolutely to prevent them from making mistakes. They might mistake, and they did mistake; but a careful collation of the different historical books serves to correct all essential errors of the scribes. See the *Dissertations* of Dr. *Kennicott* mentioned at the conclusion of the preceding chapter.

Verse 10. *David said—I have sinned greatly*] We know not exactly in what this sin consisted. I have already hinted, ver. 1, that probably David now began to covet an extension of empire, and purposed to unite some of the neighbouring states with his own; and having, through the suggestions of Satan or some other *adversary,* (for so the word implies,) given way to this covetous disposition, he could not well look to God for help, and therefore wished to know whether the thousands of Israel and Judah might be deemed equal to the conquests which he meditated. When God is offended and refuses assistance, vain is the help of man.

Verse 11. *For when David was up*] It is supposed that David's contrition arose from the reproof given by Gad, and that in the order of time the reproof came before the confession stated in the 10th verse.

David's seer] A holy man of God, under the Divine influence, whom David had as a domestic chaplain.

Verse 13. *Shall seven years of famine*] In 1 Chron. xxi. 12, the number is *three*, not *seven;* and here the *Septuagint* has *three*, the same as in Chronicles: this is no doubt the true reading, the letter ז *zain*, SEVEN, being mistaken for ג *gimel*, THREE. A mistake of this kind might be easily made from the similarity of the letters.

Verse 14. *I am in a great strait: let us fall now into the hand of the Lord*] David acted nobly in this business. Had he chosen *war*, his own *personal safety* was in no danger, because there was already an ordinance preventing him from going to battle. Had he chosen *famine*, his own wealth would have secured his and his own family's support. But he showed the greatness of his mind in choosing the *pestilence*, to the ravages of which himself and household were exposed equally with the meanest of his subjects.

Verse 15. *From the morning—to the time appointed*] That is, from the morning of the day after David had made his election till the *third day*, according to the condition which God had proposed, and he had accepted: but it seems that the plague was terminated before the conclusion of the third day, for Jerusalem might have been destroyed, but it was not. Throughout the land, independently of the city, *seventy thousand* persons were slain! This was a terrible mortality in the space of less than three days.

Verse 16. *The angel stretched out his hand*

A. M. 2987
B. C. 1017
An. Exod. Isr.
474
Anno ante
I. Olymp. 241

repented him of the evil, and said to the angel that destroyed the people, It is enough: stay now thine hand. And the angel of the LORD was by the threshing-place of [a]Araunah the Jebusite.

17 And David spake unto the LORD when he saw the angel that smote the people, and said, Lo, [b]I have sinned, and I have done wickedly: but these sheep, what have they done? let thine hand, I pray thee, be against me, and against my father's house.

18 And Gad came that day to David, and said unto him, [c]Go up, rear an altar unto the LORD in the threshing-floor of [d]Araunah the Jebusite.

19 And David, according to the saying of Gad, went up as the LORD commanded.

20 And Araunah looked, and saw the king and his servants coming on toward him: and Araunah went out, and bowed himself before the king on his face upon the ground.

21 And Araunah said, Wherefore is my lord

the king come to his servant? [e]And David said, To buy the threshing-floor of thee, to build an altar unto the LORD, that [f]the plague may be stayed from the people.

A. M. 2987
B. C. 1017
An. Exod. Isr.
474
Anno ante
I. Olymp. 241

22 And Araunah said unto David, Let my lord the king take and offer up what *seemeth* good unto him: [g]behold, *here be* oxen for burnt-sacrifice, and threshing instruments and *other* instruments of the oxen for wood.

23 All these *things* did Araunah, *as* a king, give unto the king. And Araunah said unto the king, The LORD thy God [h]accept thee.

24 And the king said unto Araunah, Nay; but I will surely buy *it* of thee at a price; neither will I offer burnt-offerings unto the LORD my God of that which doth cost me nothing. So [i]David bought the threshing-floor and the oxen for fifty shekels of silver.

25 And David built there an altar unto the LORD, and offered burnt-offerings and peace offerings. [k]So the LORD was entreated for the land, and [l]the plague was stayed from Israel.

---

[a]1 Chron. xxi. 15, *Ornan;* see verse 18; 2 Chron. iii. 1 [b]1 Chron. xxi. 17——[c]1 Chron. xxi. 18, &c.——[d]Hebrew, *Araniah*

[e]See Gen. xxiii. 8–16——[f]Num. xvi. 48, 50——[g]1 Kings xix 21——[h]Ezek. xx. 40, 41——[i]See 1 Chron. xxi. 24, 25——[k]Chap. xxi. 14——[l]Ver. 21

---

upon Jerusalem] By what means this destruction took place, we know not: it appears that an angel was employed in it, and that this minister of Divine justice actually appeared as an object of sight; for it is said, ver. 17, *When David saw the angel that smote the people, he said,* &c.; and both Ornan and his four sons saw him and were affrighted, 1 Chron. xxi. 20.

The threshing-place of Araunah] These *threshing-places*, we have already seen, were made in the open air. In the parallel place, 1 Chron. xxi. 15, 20, &c., this person is called *Ornan*. The word that we render *Araunah* is written in this very chapter אורנה *Avarnah*, ver. 16, ארניה *Araniah*, ver. 18, ארונה *Araunah* or *Aravnah*, ver. 20, and the following: but in every place in 1 Chron. xxi. where it occurs it is written ארנן *Ornan*. It is likely he had both names, *Araunah* and *Ornan:* but the *varieties* of spelling in 2 Sam. must arise from the blunders of transcribers.

Verse 17. *But these sheep, what have they done?*] It seems that in the order of Providence there is no way of punishing kings in their *regal* capacity, but by afflictions on their land, in which the people must necessarily suffer. If the king, therefore, by his own personal offences, in which the people can have no part, bring down God's judgments upon his people, (though they suffer innocently,) grievous will be the account that he must give to God. The people generally suffer for the miscarriages of their governors: this has been observed in every age.

Quicquid delirant reges, plectuntur Achivi.

VOL. II

"When doting monarchs urge
Unsound resolves, their subjects feel the scourge." HOR. Ep. lib. i., ep. 2, ver. 14.

Against my father's house.] That is, against his own family; even to cut it off from the face of the earth.

Verse 18. *Go up, rear an altar unto the Lord*] This place is supposed to be Mount Moriah: on which, according to the rabbins, Cain and Abel offered their sacrifices; where Abraham attempted to sacrifice Isaac, and where the temple of Solomon was afterwards built.

Verse 22. Here be *oxen for burnt-sacrifice*] He felt for the *king;* and showed his loyalty to him by this offer. He felt for the *people;* and was willing to make any sacrifice to get the plague stayed. He felt for *his own personal safety;* and therefore was willing to give up all to save his life. He felt for the *honour of God;* and therefore was glad that he had a sacrifice to offer, so that God might magnify both his justice and mercy.

Verse 23. *As a king, give unto the king.*] Literally, *All these did King Araunah give unto the king.* That there could not be a king of the Jebusites on Mount Moriah, is sufficiently evident; and that there was no other king than David in the land, is equally so: the word המלך *hammelech,* "the king," given here to Araunah, is wanting in the *Septuagint, Syriac,* and *Arabic;* in *three* of Kennicott's and De Rossi's MSS., and in the parallel place in Chronicles: and, it is very probable, never made a part of the text. Perhaps it should be read, *All these did Araunah give unto the king.*

There is, however, a difficulty here. David had taken the fortress of the Jebusites many years before; yet it is evident that Araunah was proprietor of the soil at this time. It is not clear that he was a subject of David; but he paid him respect as a neighbour and a king. This is merely *possible*.

Verse 24. *Neither will I offer burnt-offerings*] It is a maxim from heaven, "Honour the Lord with thy substance." He who has a religion that *costs him nothing*, has a religion that is *worth nothing:* nor will any man esteem the ordinances of God, if those ordinances cost him nothing. Had Araunah's noble offer been accepted, it would have been *Araunah's sacrifice*, not *David's;* nor would it have answered the end of turning away the displeasure of the Most High. It was David that sinned, not Araunah: therefore David must offer sacrifice, and at his own expense too.

Verse 25. *David—offered burnt-offerings*] And that these sacrifices were pleasing to the Lord, is evident from a circumstance marked in the parallel place, 1 Chron. xxi. 26: *David called upon the Lord, and he answered him*

from heaven by fire upon the altar of burnt-offering.

The plague was stayed] Jerusalem did not share in the common calamity, seventy thousand being the whole that were slain throughout the land.

THIS book is unfinished, and requires 1 Chron. xxii., xxiii., xxiv., xxv., xxvi., xxvii., xxviii., and xxix., to complete it. A few things relative to this history may be found in the beginning of the following book; but the information in 1 Chron. is much more extensive and satisfactory.

MASORETIC NOTES ON THE TWO BOOKS OF SAMUEL

In the time of the Masoretes the two books of Samuel were considered but as one, and thus divided:—

Number of *verses* in these two books, 1506.
Number of *Masoretic sections*, 34.

The *middle verse* is 1 Sam. xxviii. 24: *And the woman had a fat calf in the house, and she hasted and killed it, and took flour and kneaded it, and did bake unleavened bread thereof.*

PREFACE

TO THE

FIRST BOOK OF THE KINGS,

OTHERWISE CALLED

THE THIRD BOOK OF THE KINGS

IN the most correct and ancient editions of the Hebrew Bible, the two books of Kings make but *one*, with sometimes a little break, the first book beginning with 1 Sam. xxii. 40. Some of the ancient fathers seem to have begun the First Book of Kings at the death of David, chap. ii. 12. The more modern copies of the Hebrew Bible have the same division as ours; but in the time of the Masoretes they certainly made but one book; as both, like the books of Samuel, are included under one enumeration of sections, verses, &c., in the Masora.

The *titles* to these books have been various, though it appears from Origen that they had their name from their first words, והמלך דוד *vehammelech David*, "and King David;" as *Genesis* had its name from בראשית *bereshith*, "in the beginning." The *Septuagint* simply term it βασιλειων, *of reigns*, or kingdoms; of which it calls Samuel the *first* and *second*, and these two the *third* and *fourth*. The *Vulgate* has *Liber Regum tertius; secundum Hebræos, Liber Malachim:* "The Third Book of Kings; but, according to the Hebrews, the First Book of Malachim." The *Syriac* has, "Here follows the Book of the Kings who flourished among this ancient people; and in this is also exhibited the history of the prophets who flourished in their times." The *Arabic* has the following title: "In the name of the most merciful and compassionate God; the Book of Solomon, the son of David the prophet, whose benedictions be upon us.—Amen."

The author of these books is unknown: that they are a *compilation* out of public and private records, as the books of Samuel are, there is little doubt; but by whom this compilation was made nowhere appears. Some have attributed it to Isaiah and to Jeremiah, because there are several chapters in both these prophets which are similar to some found in the first and second books of Kings; compare 2 Kings xviii., xix., and xx., with Isa. xxxvi., xxxvii., xxxviii., and xxxix.; and 2 Kings xxiv. 18, and xxv. 1, &c., with Jer. lii. 1, &c. But rather than allow those prophets to be the authors or compilers of these books, some very learned men have judged that the chapters in question have been taken from the books of Kings in after times, and inserted in those prophets. It is worthy of remark that the fifty-second chapter found in Jeremiah is marked so as to intimate that *it is not the composition of that prophet;* for at the end of chap. li. we find these words, *Thus far* are *the words of Jeremiah;* intimating that the following chapter *is* not *his.*

But the most common opinion is, that *Ezra* was the author, or rather the compiler of the history found in these books. Allowing only the existence of ancient documents from which it was compiled, it appears,

1. That it is the work of one person; as is sufficiently evident from the uniformity of the style, and the connection of events.

2. That this person had ancient documents from which he compiled, and which he often only abridged, is evident from his own words, *The rest of the acts* of such and such a prince, *are they not written in the Chronicles of the Kings of Judah*, or *of Israel*, which occur frequently.

3. These books were written during or after the Babylonish captivity, as at the end of the second book that event is particularly described. The author states also, 2 Kings xvii. 23, that Israel was, in his time, in captivity in Assyria, according to the declaration of God by his prophets.

4. That the writer was not *contemporary* with the facts which he relates, is evident from the reflections he makes on the facts that he found in the memoirs which he consulted. See 2 Kings xvii. from ver. 6 to ver. 24.

5. There is every reason to believe that the author was a *priest* or a *prophet;* he studies less to describe acts of heroism, successful battles, conquests, political address, &c., than what regards the temple, religion, religious ceremonies, festivals, the worship of God, the piety of princes, the fidelity of the prophets, the punishment of crimes, the manifestation of God's anger against the wicked, and his kindness to the righteous. He appears everywhere strongly attached to the house of David; he treats of the kings of Israel only accidentally; his principal object seems to be the kingdom of Judah, and the matters which concern it.

Now, all this agrees well with the supposition that *Ezra* was the compiler of these books. He was not only a *priest*, a zealous servant of God, and a reformer of the corruptions which had crept into the Divine worship, but is universally allowed by the Jews to have been the collector and compiler of the whole sacred code, and author of the arrangement of the different books which constitute the Old Testament. If some things be found in these books of Kings which do not agree to his time, they may be easily accounted for on his often taking the facts as he found them in the documents which he consults, without any kind of alteration; and this is so far a proof of his great sincerity and scrupulous exactness.

The First Book of Kings contains the history of *one hundred and nineteen* years, from A. M. 2989 to A. M. 3108. It contains a great variety of interesting particulars, the chief of which are the following: The death of David; the reign of Solomon; the building and dedication of the temple; the building of Solomon's palace; an account of his great wisdom; his magnificence, and his fall; the division of Israel and Judah under Rehoboam; the idolatry of the ten tribes over whom Jeroboam became king. It states how Judah, Benjamin, and Levi attached themselves to the house of David; how Rehoboam was attacked by Shishak, king of Egypt, who pillaged the temple; how Baasha destroyed the house of Jeroboam, and seized on the government of Israel; how Jehu predicted the ruin of Baasha; how Ahab married the impious Jezebel, and persecuted the prophets of the Lord. It relates the acts of Elijah; the destruction of the prophets of Baal; the cruel death of Naboth; the death of Ahab; the good reign of Jehoshaphat, king of Judah; and the wicked reign of Ahaziah, king of Israel, &c. See *Calmet's* preface to the first and second books of Kings.

THE
FIRST BOOK OF THE KINGS

Year from the Creation, according to the English Bible, 2989.—Year before the Incarnation, 1015.—Year from the destruction of Troy, according to Dionysius of Halicarnassus, 170.—Year before the first Olympiad, 239.—Year before the building of Rome, 262.—Year of the Julian Period, 3699.—Year of the Dionysian Period, 507.—Cycle of the Sun, 3.—Cycle of the Moon, 13.—Year of Acastus, the second perpetual archon of the Athenians, 31.—Pyritiades was king over the Assyrians about this time, according to Scaliger, Langius, and Strauchius. He was the *thirty-seventh* monarch, (including Belus,) according to Africanus, and the *thirty-third* according to Eusebius.—Year of Alba Silvius, the sixth king of the Latins, 15.—Year of David, king of the Hebrews, 40.

CHAPTER I

David, grown old, is, by the advice of his physicians, cherished by Abishag the Shunammite, 1–4. Adonijah conspires with Joab and Abiathar to seize on the government, 5–10. Nathan and Bath-sheba communicate these tidings to the aged king, 11–27. David immediately pronounces Solomon his successor, and causes Zadok and Nathan to proclaim and anoint him king, 28–40. Adonijah and his friends hear of it, are afraid, and flee away, Adonijah laying hold on the horns of the altar, from which he refuses to go till Solomon shall promise him his life; this he does, and banishes him to his own house, 41–53.

A. M. 2989
B. C. 1015
An. Exod. Isr.
476
Anno ante
I. Olymp. 239

NOW King David was old *and* ᵃstricken in years; and they covered him with clothes, but he gat no heat.

2 Wherefore his servants said unto him, ᵇLet there be sought for my lord the king ᶜa young virgin: and let her stand before the king, and let her ᵈcherish him, and let her lie in thy bosom, that my lord the king may get heat.

3 So they sought for a fair damsel through-

out all the coasts of Israel, and found Abishag a ᵉShunammite, and brought her to the king.

4 And the damsel *was* very fair and cherished the king, and ministered to him: but the king knew her not.

5 Then ᶠAdonijah the son of Haggith exalted himself, saying, I will ᵍbe king: ʰand he prepared him chariots and horsemen, and fifty men to run before him.

6 And his father had not displeased him ⁱat

A. M. 2989
B. C. 1015
An. Exod. Isr.
476
Anno ante
I. Olymp. 239

ᵃHeb. *entered into days*——ᵇHeb. *let them seek*——ᶜHeb. *a damsel, a virgin*——ᵈHeb. *be a cherisher unto him*

ᵉJosh. xix. 18——ᶠ2 Sam. iii. 4——ᵍHeb. *reign*——ʰ2 Sam. xv. 1——ⁱHeb. *from his days*

NOTES ON CHAP. I

Verse 1. *Now King David was old*] He was probably now about *sixty-nine* years of age. He was *thirty* years old when he began to reign, reigned *forty*, and died in the *seventieth* year of his age, 2 Sam. v. 4, and chap. ii. 11; and the transactions mentioned here are supposed to have taken place about a year before his death.

But he gat no heat.] Sixty-nine was not an advanced age; but David had been exhausted with various fatigues, and especially by family afflictions, so that he was much older in constitution than he was in years. Besides he seems to have laboured under some wasting maladies, to which there is frequent reference in the Psalms.

Verse 2. *Let there be sought—a young virgin*] This was the best remedy which in his state could be prescribed. His nearly exhausted frame would infallibly absorb from her young and healthy body an additional portion of ani-

mal heat, and consequently trim and revive the flame of animal life. This is properly, as I have elsewhere expressed it, Friar Bacon's secret for the cure of old age.

Verse 4. *The king knew her not.*] The maxim of Bacon in his enigmatical cure is, "Take all you can from the medicine, but give nothing to it; if you give any thing, it increases the disease and hastens death." I have seen this abundantly verified; but it is a subject on which it would be improper to dilate except in a medical work. An extract from Friar Bacon's *Cure of Old Age* may be found at the end of the chapter.

Verse 5. *Adonijah the son of Haggith*] Who this woman was we know not; Adonijah was evidently David's eldest son now living, and one of whom his father was particularly fond; see ver. 6.

Prepared him chariots and horsemen] He copied the conduct of his brother Absalom in every respect. See 2 Sam. xv. 1.

A. M. 2989
B. C. 1015
An. Exod. Isr.
476
Anno ante
I. Olymp. 239

any time in saying, Why hast thou done so? and he also *was* a very goodly *man;* [k]and *his mother* bare him after Absalom.

7 And [l]he conferred with Joab the son of Zeruiah, and with [m]Abiathar the priest: and [n]they [o]following Adonijah helped *him.*

8 But Zadok the priest, and Benaiah the son of Jehoiada, and Nathan the prophet, and [r]Shimei, and Rei, and [q]the mighty men which *belonged* to David, were not with Adonijah.

9 And Adonijah slew sheep and oxen and fat cattle by the stone of Zoheleth, which *is* by [r]En-rogel, and called all his brethren the king's sons, and all the men of Judah the king's servants:

10 But Nathan the prophet, and Benaiah, and the mighty men, and Solomon his brother, he called not.

11 Wherefore Nathan spake unto Bath-sheba the mother of Solomon, saying, Hast thou not heard that Adonijah the son of [s]Haggith doth reign, and David our lord knoweth *it* not?

12 Now therefore come, let me, I pray thee, give thee counsel, that thou mayest save thine own life, and the life of thy son Solomon.

13 Go and get thee in unto King David, and say unto him, Didst not thou, my lord, O king, swear unto thine handmaid, saying, [t]Assuredly Solomon thy son shall reign after me, and he

shall sit upon my throne? why then doth Adonijah reign?

14 Behold, while thou yet talkest there with the king, I also will come in after thee, and [u]confirm thy words.

15 And Bath-sheba went in unto the king into the chamber: and the king was very old, and Abishag the Shunammite ministered unto the king.

16 And Bath-sheba bowed, and did obeisance unto the king. And the king said, [v]What wouldest thou?

17 And she said unto him, My lord, [w]thou swarest by the LORD thy God unto thine handmaid, *saying,* Assuredly Solomon thy son shall reign after me, and he shall sit upon my throne.

18 And now, behold, Adonijah reigneth; and now, my lord the king, thou knowest *it* not:

19 [x]And he hath slain oxen and fat cattle and sheep in abundance, and hath called all the sons of the king, and Abiathar the priest, and Joab the captain of the host: but Solomon thy servant hath he not called.

20 And thou, my lord, O king, the eyes of all Israel *are* upon thee, that thou shouldest tell them who shall sit on the throne of my lord the king after him.

A. M. 2989
B. C. 1015
An. Exod. Isr.
476
Anno ante
I. Olymp. 239

---

[k]2 Sam. iii. 3, 4; 1 Chron. iii. 2——[l]Heb. *his words were with Joab*——[m]2 Sam. xx. 25——[n]Chap. ii. 22, 28 [o]Heb. *helped after Adonijah*——[p]Chap. iv. 18——[q]2

Sam. xxiii. 8——[r]Or, *the well Rogel;* 2 Sam. xvii. 17 [s]2 Sam. iii. 4——[t]1 Chron. xxii. 9——[u]Heb. *fill up* [v]Heb. *what to thee?*——[w]Ver. 13, 30——[x]Ver. 7, 8, 9, 25

Verse 7. *And he conferred with Joab*] Joab well knew, if *he made the new king,* he would necessarily be continued in the command of the army, and so govern him.

Verse 8. *And Nathan*] Some suppose that he was the preceptor of Solomon.

Verse 9. *Slew sheep and oxen*] Making a royal feast, in reference to his inauguration. As he had Abiathar the *priest* with him, no doubt these animals were offered *sacrificially,* and then the guests fed on the flesh of the victims. He had not only a splendid feast, but a great sacrifice; and he gave by this a popular colour to his pretensions, by affecting to receive his authority from *God.*

Verse 11. *Hast thou not heard that Adonijah the son of Haggith doth reign*] He was now considered as being legally appointed to the regal office, and no doubt was about to begin to perform its functions.

Verse 12. *Save thine own life, and the life of thy son*] Nathan took for granted that Adonijah would put both Bath-sheba and Solomon to death as state criminals, if he got established on the throne. O cursed lust of rule! a father will destroy his son, a son depose his

father, and a brother murder a brother, in order to obtain a crown! At this time the monarchy of Israel was *unsettled;* no man knew who was to succeed to the crown, and the minds of the people were as unsettled as the succession. I have examined both systems, and find that, with all its alleged disadvantages, *hereditary monarchy* has a high balance of evidence in its favour beyond that which is *elective,* and is every way more safe for the state and more secure for the subject.

Verse 13. *Go and get thee in unto King David*] He knew that this woman had a sovereign influence over the king. If Bath-sheba was a source of pleasure to David, must she not also have been a source of pain to him? For could he ever forget the guilty manner in which he acquired her?

Didst not thou—swear] It is very likely that David made such an oath, and that was known only to Bath-sheba and Nathan. It is nowhere else mentioned.

Verse 20. *That thou shouldest tell—who shall sit on the throne*] This was a monarchy neither *hereditary* nor *elective;* the king simply *named his successor.* This obtained less or more, anciently, in most countries.

A. M. 2989
B. C. 1015
An. Exod. Isr.
476
Anno ante
I. Olymp. 239

21 Otherwise it shall come to pass, when my lord the king shall ʸsleep with his fathers, that I and my son Solomon shall be counted ᶻoffenders.

22 And, lo, while she yet talked with the king, Nathan the prophet also came in.

23 And they told the king, saying, Behold Nathan the prophet. And when he was come in before the king, he bowed himself before the king with his face to the ground.

24 And Nathan said, My lord, O king, hast thou said, Adonijah shall reign after me, and he shall sit upon my throne?

25 ᵃFor he is gone down this day, and hath slain oxen and fat cattle and sheep in abundance, and hath called all the king's sons, and the captains of the host, and Abiathar the priest; and, behold, they eat and drink before him, and say, ᵇGod ᶜsave King Adonijah.

26 But me, *even* me thy servant, and Zadok the priest, and Benaiah the son of Jehoiada, and thy servant Solomon, hath he not called.

27 Is this thing done by my lord the king, and thou hast not showed *it* unto thy servant, who should sit on the throne of my lord the king after him?

28 Then King David answered and said, Call me Bath-sheba. And she came ᵈinto the king's presence, and stood before the king.

29 And the king sware, and said, ᵉ*As the* LORD liveth, that hath redeemed my soul out of all distress,

30 ᶠEven as I sware unto thee by the LORD God of Israel, saying, Assuredly Solomon thy son shall reign after me, and he shall sit upon my throne in my stead; even so will I certainly do this day.

31 Then Bath-sheba bowed with *her* face to the earth, and did reverence to the king, and said, ᵍLet my lord King David live for ever.

32 And King David said, Call me Zadok the priest, and Nathan the prophet, and Benaiah the son of Jehoiada. And they came before the king.

33 The king also said unto them, ʰTake with you the servants of your lord, and cause Solomon my son to ride upon ⁱmine own mule, and bring him down to ᵏGihon:

34 And let Zadok the priest and Nathan the prophet ˡanoint him there king over Israel: and ᵐblow ye with the trumpet, and say, God save King Solomon.

35 Then ye shall come up after him, that he may come and sit upon my throne; for he shall be king in my stead: and I have appointed him to be ruler over Israel and over Judah.

36 And Benaiah the son of Jehoiada answered the king, and said, Amen: the LORD God of my lord the king say so *too*.

37 ⁿAs the LORD hath been with my lord

A. M. 2989
B. C. 1015
An. Exod. Isr.
476
Anno ante
I. Olymp. 239

ʸDeut. xxxi. 16; chapter ii. 10——ᶻHeb. *sinners*
ᵃVer. 19——ᵇ1 Sam. x. 24——ᶜHeb. *let King Adonijah live*——ᵈHeb. *before the king*——ᵉ2 Sam. iv. 9——ᶠVer. 17——ᵍNeh. ii. 3; Dan. ii. 4——ʰ2 Sam. xx. 6

ⁱHeb. *which* belongeth *to me;* see Esth. vi. 8——ᵏ2 Chron xxxii. 30——ˡ1 Sam. x. 1; xvi. 3, 12; 2 Sam. ii. 4; v. 3; ch. xix. 16; 2 Kings ix. 3; xi. 12——ᵐ2 Sam. xv. 10; 2 Kings ix. 13; xi. 14——ⁿJosh. i. 5, 17; 1 Sam. xx. 13

Verse 21. *Shall be counted offenders.*] When Adonijah and his party shall find that I and my son have had this promise from thee by oath, he will slay us both.

Verse 28. *Call me Bath-sheba.*] She had gone out when Nathan came in, and he retired when she was re-admitted. Each had a separate audience, but to Nathan the king did not express any will.

Verse 33. *Take with you the servants of your lord*] By these we may understand the *king's guards,* the *guards* of the *city,* the *Cherethites* and *Pelethites,* who were under the command of Benaiah; and in short, all the disposable force that was at hand.

Solomon—to ride upon mine own mule] No subject could use any thing that belonged to the prince, without forfeiting his life. As David offered Solomon to ride on his own mule, this was full evidence that he had appointed him his successor.

Verse 34. *Blow ye with the trumpet*] After he has been anointed, make proclamation that he is king.

Verse 35. *Sit upon my throne*] The matter of conducting a business of this kind seems to have been this: 1. The king elect was *placed on the mule of his predecessor,* and caused *to ride abroad* to one of the public wells, or to a river where there was the greatest concourse of people, that they might see who he was that was appointed. Solomon was here taken to the river *Gihon,* in order to be anointed; the continual stream or constantly running fountain, denoting the perpetuity of the kingdom. 2. The *priest* and the *prophet anointed* him in the name of the Lord; and thereby signified that he should be endued with all the kingly virtues; that he should reign *by, under,* and *for* the Lord. 3. The *trumpet* was then to be *blown,* and solemn proclamation made, that he was anointed king. 4. He was then brought and solemnly *placed on the throne,* to signify that he had now assumed the reins of government, and was about to administer justice and judgment to the people.

Verse 37. *Make his throne greater than the throne of—David.*] A wish of this kind a *king*

A. M. 2989 B. C. 1015 An. Exod. Isr. 476 Anno ante I. Olymp. 239

the king, even so be he with Solomon, and [o]make his throne greater than the throne of my lord king David.

38 So Zadok the priest, and Nathan the prophet, [p]and Benaiah the son of Jehoiada, and the Cherethites, and the Pelethites, went down, and caused Solomon to ride upon King David's mule, and brought him to Gihon.

39 And Zadok the priest took a horn of [q]oil out of the tabernacle, and [r]anointed Solomon. And they blew the trumpet; [s]and all the people said, God save King Solomon.

40 And all the people came up after him, and the people piped with [t]pipes, and rejoiced with great joy, so that the earth rent with the sound of them.

41 And Adonijah and all the guests that *were* with him heard *it* as they had made an end of eating. And when Joab heard the sound of the trumpet, he said, Wherefore *is this* noise of the city being in an uproar?

42 And while he yet spake, behold, Jonathan the son of Abiathar the priest came: and Adonijah said unto him, Come in; for [u]thou *art* a valiant man, and bringest good tidings.

43 And Jonathan answered and said to Adonijah, Verily, our lord King David hath made Solomon king.

A. M. 2989 B. C. 1015 An. Exod. Isr. 476 Anno ante I. Olymp. 239

44 And the king hath sent with him Zadok the priest, and Nathan the prophet, and Benaiah the son of Jehoiada, and the Cherethites, and the Pelethites, and they have caused him to ride upon the king's mule:

45 And Zadok the priest and Nathan the prophet have anointed him king in Gihon: and they are come up from thence rejoicing, so that the city rang again. This *is* the noise that ye have heard.

46 And also Solomon [v]sitteth on the throne of the kingdom.

47 And moreover the king's servants came to bless our lord King David, saying, [w]God make the name of Solomon better than thy name, and make his throne greater than thy throne. [x]And the king bowed himself upon his bed.

48 And also thus said the king, Blessed *be* the LORD God of Israel, which hath [y]given *one* to sit on my throne this day, mine eyes even seeing *it*.

49 And all the guests that *were* with Adonijah were afraid, and rose up, and went every man his way.

[o]Ver. 47.——[p]2 Sam. viii. 18; xxiii. 20-23——[q]Exod. xxx. 23, 25, 32; Psa. lxxxix. 20——[r]1 Chron. xxix. 22——[s]1 Sam. x. 24

[t]Or, *flutes*——[u]2 Samuel xviii. 27——[v]1 Chron. xxix. 23——[w]Verse 37——[x]Gen. xlvii. 31——[y]Chap. iii. 6; Psa. cxxxii. 11, 12

will suffer in behalf of his *son*, but it is never in ordinary cases considered a *compliment* to say, "I hope this child will make a better man than his father," because it seems to insinuate some reflections on his father's conduct or character. Many foolish people deal in such compliments, and they may rest assured, for the reasons given above, that they are far from being either welcome or agreeable.

Claudian, in his panegyric *De Quarto Consulatu Honorii Augusti*, ver. 428, has words something similar to those of Benaiah, when he describes a father, worn out with toils and difficulties, committing the reins of government to the hands of his son:—

Adspice, completur votum: jam natus adæquat
Te meritis; et, quod magis est optabile, vincit.

"Behold, thy desire is accomplished. Even now thy son equals thee in worth; and what is still more desirable, surpasses thee."

Verse 39. *Zadok—took a horn of oil*] *Pottery* and *glass* were little in use in those times; and *horns* were frequently used to hold *oil* and *wine*. The old used here was the *holy anointing oil*, which was laid up in the tabernacle, and which was used for the anointing of both *priests* and *kings*.

Verse 40. *The people piped with pipes*] They danced, sang, and played on what instruments of music they possessed.

The earth rent] We use a similar expression in precisely the same sense: They *rent the air* with their cries.

Verse 43. *Jonathan answered*] He was properly a *messenger* about the court; we have met with him and Ahimaaz before, 2 Sam. xv. 36. He had now been an *observer*, if not a *spy*, on all that was doing, and relates the transactions to Adonijah, in the very order in which they took place.

1. David has nominated Solomon his successor.

2. Zadok, Nathan, and Benaiah, have been appointed to set him on the king's mule.

3. They have taken him to Gihon, and anointed him there.

4. They have brought him up to Jerusalem and placed him on the throne of the kingdom.

Verse 47. *Moreover, the king's servants came*] The king himself was at this time confined to his own house, and probably to his bed, and could not possibly see these ceremonies; therefore his confidential servants came and told him. We know not how Jonathan, in so short a time, possessed himself of so much information.

A. M. 2989
B. C. 1015
An. Exod. Isr.
476
Anno ante
I. Olymp. 239

50 And Adonijah feared because of Solomon, and arose, and went, and ᶻcaught hold on the horns of the altar.

51 And it was told Solomon, saying, Behold, Adonijah feareth king Solomon: for, lo, he hath caught hold on the horns of the altar, saying, Let King Solomon swear unto me to-day that he will not slay his servant with the sword.

52 And Solomon said, If he will show himself a worthy man, ᵃthere shall not a hair of him fall to the earth: but if wickedness shall be found in him, he shall die.

A. M. 2989
B. C. 1015
An. Exod. Isr.
476
Anno ante
I. Olymp. 239

53 So King Solomon sent, and they brought him down from the altar. And he came and bowed himself to King Solomon: and Solomon said unto him, Go to thine house.

ᶻChap. ii. 28——ᵃ1 Sam. xiv. 45; 2 Sam. xiv. 11; Acts xxvii. 34

Verse 50. *Adonijah feared*] He knew he had usurped the kingdom, and had not his father's consent; and, as he finds now that Solomon is appointed by David, he knows well that the people will immediately respect that appointment, and that his case is hopeless; he therefore took sanctuary, and, fleeing to the tabernacle, laid hold on one of the horns of the altar, as if appealing to the protection of God against the violence of men. The altar was a privileged place, and it was deemed sacrilege to molest a man who had taken refuge there. See chap. ii. 28.

Verse 52. *If he will show himself a worthy man*] If, from henceforth, he behave well, show himself to be contented, and not endeavour to make partisans, or stir up insurrections among the people, he shall be safe; *but if wickedness be found in him*—if he act at all contrary to this—*he shall die;* his blood shall be upon him.

Verse 53. *Go to thine house.*] Intimating that he should have no place about the king's person, nor under the government. Adonijah must have seen that he stood continually on his good behaviour.

Friar Bacon's method of restoring and strengthening the Natural Heat

"I have read many volumes of the wise: I find few things in physic which restore the *natural heat*, weakened by dissolution of the innate moisture, or increase of a foreign one.

"But certain wise men have *tacitly* made mention of some medicine, which is likened to that which *goes out of the mine of the noble animal.* They affirm that in it there is a *force* and *virtue* which restores and increases the *natural heat.* As to its disposition, they say it is like *youth* itself, and contains an equal and temperate complexion.

"And the signs of a temperate complexion in men are, when their colour is made up of *white* and *red,* when the hair is *yellow,* inclined to redness and curling.

"This *medicine* indeed is like *to such a complexion,* for it is of a temperate heat: its flame is temperate and sweet, and grateful to the smell. When it departs from this temperature, it departs so far from its virtue and goodness.

"This medicine therefore *temperately heats,* because it is temperately hot; it therefore *heals* because it is *whole.* When it is *sick,* it makes a man *sick;* when it is distempered, it breeds distempers, and changes the body to its own disposition, because of the similitude it has with the body.

"For the infirmity of a *brute* animal rarely passes into a *man,* but into another animal of the *same kind;* but the infirmity of *man* passes into *man;* and so does *health,* because of *like, ness.*

"This thing is seldom found; and although sometimes it be found, yet *it cannot commodiously be had of all men.*

"Now, when this thing is *like to youth,* that is, of temperate complexion, it has good operations; if its temperature be better, it produces better effects: sometimes it is even in the *highest degree of its perfection,* and then it operates best; and then there is that property whereof we have spoken before.

"This differs from other medicines and nutriments, which heat and moisten after a certain temperate manner, and are good for old men. For other medicines principally heat and moisten the body; and, secondarily, they strengthen the *native heat,* and after that refresh the body, by moistening and heating it. For it brings back this heat in old men, who have it but weakly and deficient, to a certain stronger and more vehement power.

"If a *plaster* be made hereof, and applied to the *stomach,* it will help very much, for it will refresh the stomach itself, and excite an appetite; it will very much *recreate an old man,* and change *him to a kind of youth;* and will make complexions, by what means soever depraved or corrupted, better. But it is to be observed, that *Venus* doth weaken and diminish the power and virtue of this thing!

"And it is very likely that the son of the prince, in his second canon of the *Operations of Simple Medicines* spoke of this thing, where he saith, that there is a certain medicine, concealed by wise men, lest the *incontinent* should offend their Creator. There is such a *heat* in this thing, as is in young men of sound complexion; and if I durst declare the properties of this heat, this most hidden secret should presently be revealed. For this heat doth help the palsical, it restores and preserves the wasted strength of the native heat, and causeth it to flourish in all the members, and gently revives the aged.

"But the simple medicine which restores the *native heat,* when wasted and weakened, is that which is likened to the complexion of a healthy young man."

All this covered and enigmatical description is intended simply to point out that very medicine recommended by the Jewish physicians to restore and invigorate the dying king. I could show the bearing of every sentence, but I must leave something to the good sense of my readers. By attending to the words in *italics,* the sense will be more easily discovered. See my note on Ruth iv. 16.

CHAPTER II

David leaves his dying charge with Solomon, relative to his own personal conduct, 1–4; to Joab, 5, 6; to Barzillai, 7; to Shimei, 8, 9. He dies, and Solomon is established in the kingdom, 10–12. Adonijah requests to have Abishag to wife, and is put to death by Solomon, 13–25. Abiathar the priest is banished to his estate at Anathoth, 26, 27. Joab, fearing for his life, flees to the horns of the altar, and is slain there by Benaiah, 28–34. Benaiah is made captain of the host in his stead, 35. Shimei is ordered to confine himself to Jerusalem, and never leave it on pain of death, 36–38. After three years he follows some of his runaway servants to Gath, and thereby forfeits his life, 39, 40. Solomon sends for him, upbraids him, and commands him to be slain by Benaiah, 41–46.

A. M. 2989
B. C. 1015
An. Exod. Isr. 476
Anno ante
I. Olymp. 239

NOW [a]the days of David drew nigh that he should die; and he charged Solomon his son, saying,

2 [b]I go the way of all the earth: [c]be thou strong therefore, and show thyself a man;

3 And keep the charge of the LORD thy God, to walk in his ways, to keep his statutes, and his commandments, and his judgments, and his testimonies, as it is written in the law of Moses, that thou mayest [d]prosper [e]in all that thou doest, and whithersoever thou turnest thyself.

A. M. 2989
B. C. 1015
An. Exod. Isr. 476
Anno ante
I. Olymp. 239

---

[a]Gen. xlvii. 29; Deut. xxxi. 14——[b]Josh. xxiii. 14
[c]Deut. xvii. 19, 20

[d]Deut. xxix. 9; Josh. i. 7; 1 Chron. xxii. 12, 13——[e]Or,
do wisely; 1 Sam. xviii. 5, 14, 40

NOTES ON CHAP. II

Verse 2. *I go the way of all the earth*] I am dying. All the inhabitants of the earth must come to the dust. In *life*, some follow one occupation, some another; but all must, sooner or later, come to the *grave*. Death is no respecter of persons; he visits the palace of the king as well as the cottage of the peasant.

Pallida mors æquo pulsat pede pauperum
   tabernas,
Regumque turres.
     —HOR. *Odar.* lib. i., *od.* iv., ver. 13.

"With equal pace, impartial fate
Knocks at the *palace* as the *cottage* gate."
     FRANCIS.

———— Sed omnes una manet nox,
Et calcanda semel via lethi.
     —*Ib. od.* xxviii., ver. 15.

"One dreary night for all mankind remains,
And once we all must tread the shadowy plains."
     Ibid.

There is no respect to *age* or *youth* more than to *station* or external *circumstance:*—

Mixta senum ac juvenum densantur funera:
   nullum
Sæva caput Proserpina fugit.
     —*Ib. od.* xxviii., ver. 19.

Thus *age* and *youth* promiscuous crowd the
   tomb;
No mortal head can shun the impending doom."
     Ibid.

And it is not merely *man* that is subjected to this necessity; all that have in them the *breath of life* must lose it; *it is the way of all the earth*, both of *men* and inferior *animals.*

———— Terrestria quando
Mortales animas vivunt sortita, neque ulla
   est
Aut parvo aut magno lethi fuga.—
Vive memor quam sis ævi brevis.
     HOR. *Sat.* l. ii., *s.* vi., ver. 93.

"All that tread the earth are subject to mortality; neither *great* nor *small* can avoid death. Live therefore conscious that your time is short."

It is painful to the pride of the great and

mighty that, however decorated their tombs may be, they must undergo the same *dissolution* and *corruption* with the vulgar dead; for the grave is the house appointed for all living: man is born to die.

Omnium idem exitus est, sed et idem domicilium.

"For all have the *same end*, and are huddled together in the same narrow house."

Here emperors, kings, statesmen, *warriors, heroes,* and *butchers* of all kinds, with peasants and beggars, meet; however various their routes, they terminate in the same point. This and all other kindred sentiments on the subject are well expressed in that excellent little poem of Mr. Blair, entitled THE GRAVE, which opens with the following lines:—

While some affect the sun, and some the shade;
Some flee the city, some the hermitage;
Their aims as various as the roads they take
In journeying through life; the task be mine
To paint the gloomy horrors of the tomb,
The *appointed place of rendezvous*, where all
These *travellers meet.*

Show thyself a man] Act like a *rational being*, and not like a *brute;* and remember, that he acts most like a *man* who is most devoted to his GOD.

Verse 3. *Keep the charge of the Lord*] Keep what God has given thee to keep.

1. *Walk in his ways.* Not in thine own, nor in the ways of a wicked, perishing world.

2. *Keep his statutes.* Consider all his appointments to be holy, just, and good; receive them as such; and conscientiously observe them.

3. *Keep his commandments.* Whatever he has bidden thee to do, perform; what he has forbidden thee to do, omit.

4. *Keep his judgments.* What he has *determined* to be right, is essentially and inherently right; what he has determined to be wrong or evil, is inherently and essentially so. A thing is not good because God has commanded it; a thing is not evil because he has forbidden it. He has commanded the *good*, because it is in its own nature *good* and *useful;* he has forbidden the *evil*, because it is in its own nature *bad* and *hurtful.* Keep therefore his judgments.

A. M. 2989
B. C. 1015
An. Exod. Isr.
476
Anno ante
I. Olymp. 239

4 That the Lord may [f]continue his word which he spake concerning me, saying, [g]If thy children take heed to their way, to [h]walk before me in truth with all their heart and with all their soul, [i]there shall not [k]fail thee (said he) a man on the throne of Israel.

5 Moreover thou knowest also what Joab the son of Zeruiah [l]did to me, *and* what he did to the two captains of the hosts of Israel, unto [m]Abner the son of Ner, and unto [n]Amasa the son of Jether, whom he slew, and [o]shed the blood of war in peace, and put the blood of war upon his girdle that *was* about his loins, and in his shoes that *were* on his feet.

6 Do therefore [p]according to thy wisdom, and let not his hoar head go down to the grave in peace.

7 But show kindness unto the sons of [q]Barzillai the Gileadite, and let them be of those that [r]eat at thy table: for so [s]they came to me when I fled because of Absalom thy brother.

8 And, behold, *thou hast* with thee [t]Shimei the son of Gera, a Benjamite of Bahurim, which cursed me with a [u]grievous curse in the day when I went to Mahanaim: but [v]he came down to meet me at Jordan, and [w]I sware to him by the Lord, saying, I will not put thee to death with the sword.

9 Now therefore [x]hold him not guiltless: for thou *art* a wise man, and knowest what thou oughtest to do unto him; but his hoar head [y]bring thou down to the grave with blood.

10 So [z]David slept with his fathers, and was buried in [a]the city of David.

A. M. 2990
B. C. 1014
An. Exod. Isr.
477
Anno ante
I. Olymp. 238

11 And the days that David

---

[f]2 Sam. vii. 25——[g]Psa. cxxxii. 12——[h]2 Kings xx. 3
[i]2 Sam. vii. 12, 13; chap. viii. 25——[k]Heb. *be cut off from thee from the throne*——[l]2 Sam. iii. 39; xviii. 5, 12, 14; xix. 5, 6, 7——[m]2 Sam. iii. 27——[n]2 Sam. xx. 10
[o]Heb. *put*——[p]Ver. 9; Prov. xx. 26

[q]2 Sam. xix. 31, 38——[r]2 Sam. ix. 7, 10; xix. 28——[s]2 Sam. xvii. 27——[t]2 Sam. xvi. 5——[u]Heb. *strong*——[v]2 Samuel xix. 18——[w]2 Sam. xix. 23——[x]Exod. xx. 7; Job ix. 28——[y]Gen. xlii. 38; xliv. 31——[z]Chap. i. 21; Acts ii. 29; xiii. 36——[a]2 Sam. v. 7

---

5. *Keep his testimonies.* Bear witness to all to which he has borne witness. His testimonies are true; there is no deceit or falsity in them. His testimonies refer also to future good things and good times; they are the significators of coming blessedness: as such, respect them.

That thou mayest prosper] If thou hast God's approbation, thou wilt have God's blessing. If thy ways please him, he will not withhold from thee any manner of thing that is good.

Verse 4. *That the Lord may continue his word*] The prosperity which God has promised to grant to my family will depend on their faithfulness to the good they receive; if they live to God, they shall sit for ever on the throne of Israel. But alas! they did not; and God's justice cut off the entail made by his mercy.

Verse 5. *Thou knowest—what Joab—did to me*] He did every thing bad and dishonourable in itself, in the murder of Abner and Amasa, and indeed in the death of the profligate Absalom.

Shed the blood of war—upon his girdle—and in his shoes] He stabbed them while he pretended to *embrace* them, so that their blood gushed out on his girdle, and fell into his shoes! This was a most abominable aggravation of his crimes.

Verse 6. *Let not his hoar head go down to the grave in peace.*] It would have been an insult to justice not to have taken the life of Joab. David was culpable in delaying it so long; but probably the circumstances of his government would not admit of his doing it sooner. According to the law of God, Joab, having murdered Abner and Amasa, should die. And had not David commanded Solomon to perform this act of justice, he could not have died in the approbation of his Maker.

Verse 7. *But show kindness unto the sons of Barzillai*] See the notes on 2 Sam. xix. 31, &c.

Verse 8. Thou hast *with thee Shimei*] See on 2 Sam. xvi. 5, &c., and the notes on 2 Sam. xix. 18-23.

Verse 9. *Hold him not guiltless*] Do not consider him as an innocent man, though I have sworn to him that I would not put him to death by the sword; yet as thou art a wise man, and knowest how to treat such persons, treat him as he deserves; only as I have sworn to him, and he is an aged man, let him not die a violent death; bring *not* down his hoary head to the grave with blood. So Solomon understood David, and so I think David should be understood; for the negative particle לא *lo*, in the former clause, *hold him* NOT *guiltless*, should be repeated in this latter clause, though not expressed, *his hoary head bring thou* NOT *down;* instances of which frequently occur in the Hebrew Bible. See Dr. *Kennicott's* note at the end of this chapter.

Verse 10. *David slept with his fathers*] His life was a life of remarkable providences, of much piety, and of great public usefulness. In general he lived well, and it is most evident that he died well; and as a king, a general, a poet, a father, and a friend, he has had few *equals*, and no *superior*, from his own time to the present day. But I shall reserve a more particular consideration of his character till I come to the book of Psalms, in which that character, with all its lights and shades, is exhibited by his own masterly hand. And it is from this composition alone that we can know David, and the maxims by which he was governed in public and private life.

Was buried in the city of David.] And Solomon, says Josephus, deposited immense treasures

A. M. 2990
B. C. 1014
An. Exod. Isr.
477
Anno ante
I. Olymp. 238

[b]reigned over Israel *were* forty years: seven years reigned he in Hebron, and thirty and three years reigned he in Jerusalem.

12 [c]Then sat Solomon upon the throne of David his father; and his kingdom was established greatly.

13 And Adonijah the son of Haggith came to Bath-sheba the mother of Solomon. And she said, [d]Comest thou peaceably? And he said, Peaceably.

14 He said moreover, I have somewhat to say unto thee. And she said, Say on.

15 And he said, Thou knowest that the kingdom was [e]mine, and *that* all Israel set their faces on me, that I should reign: howbeit the kingdom is turned about, and is become my brother's: for [f]it was his from the LORD.

16 And now I ask one petition of thee, [g]deny me not. And she said unto him, Say on.

17 And he said, Speak, I pray thee, unto Solomon the king, (for he will not say thee nay,) that he give me [h]Abishag the Shunammite to wife.

18 And Bath-sheba said, Well; I will speak for thee unto the king.

19 Bath-sheba therefore went unto King So-

lomon, to speak unto him for Adonijah. And the king rose up to meet her, and [i]bowed himself unto her, and sat down on his throne, and caused a seat to be set for the king's mother; [k]and she sat on his right hand.

A. M. 2990
B. C. 1014
An. Exod. Isr.
477
Anno ante
I. Olymp. 238

20 Then she said, I desire one small petition of thee; *I pray thee,* say me not nay. And the king said unto her, Ask on, my mother: for I will not say thee nay.

21 And she said, Let Abishag the Shunammite be given to Adonijah thy brother to wife.

22 And King Solomon answered and said unto his mother, And why dost thou ask Abishag the Shunammite for Adonijah? ask for him the kingdom also; for he *is* mine elder brother; even for him, and for [l]Abiathar the priest, and for Joab the son of Zeruiah.

23 Then King Solomon sware by the LORD saying, [m]God do so to me, and more also, if Adonijah have not spoken this word against his own life.

24 Now therefore, *as* the LORD liveth, which hath established me, and set me on the throne of David my father, and who hath made me a house, as he [n]promised, Adonijah shall be put to death this day.

---

[b]2 Sam. v. 4; 1 Chron. xxix. 26, 27——[c]1 Chron. xxix. 23; 2 Chron. i. 1——[d]1 Sam. xvi. 4, 5——[e]Ch. i. 5——[f]1 Chron. xxii. 9, 10; xxviii. 5, 6, 7; Prov. xxi. 30; Dan. ii. 21

[g]Heb. *turn not away my face;* Psa. cxxxii. 10——[h]Ch. i. 3, 4——[i]Exod. xx. 12——[h]See Psa. xlv. 9——[l]Ch. i. 7 [m]Ruth i. 17——[n]2 Sam. vii. 11, 13; 1 Chron. xxii. 10

---

with him, in the grave, where they continued unmolested for *thirteen hundred* years, till Hyrcanus, the high priest, being besieged by Antiochus, opened the sepulchre, and took thence *three thousand* talents, part of which he gave to Antiochus, to raise the siege. It is added that, many years afterwards, Herod the Great ransacked this tomb and got considerable riches. Little credit is due to this account, though we know that was customary in ancient times to deposit with the more illustrious dead, gold, silver, and precious stones. That the tomb of David existed in the days of the *apostles*, we learn from Acts ii. 29, where St. Peter, addressing the Jews, says, *Men and brethren, let me speak freely to you of the patriarch David; that he is both dead and buried, and his sepulchre is with us unto this day.* St. Jerome speaks of it as existing in his time, and modern travellers pretend that it is still in existence. But both monks and Mohammedans have long united to impose on Christian pilgrims; and there is scarcely any dependence to be placed on any of their relations; absurdity and self-contradiction are their principal characteristics.

Verse 15. *Thou knowest that the kingdom was mine*] It certainly was *his* by the right of *primogeniture*, and it was his by the *voice of the people*, and the consent of the *high priest*.

But there was a right paramount to all these, the *right of God;* it was his kingdom; the kings were his *lieutenants*, and he had a right to give the crown to whomsoever he pleased, and he was pleased to give it to Solomon.

Verse 17. *That he give me Abishag—to wife.*] He cheerfully gives up all right to the kingdom, and only desires to have this young woman, who, though she had been his father's wife or concubine, was still in a state of virginity. Some think that Joab and Abiathar had advised Adonijah to make this application, not doubting, if he got Abishag, that the popular tide would again turn in his favour, and that Solomon, whom they did not like, might soon be deposed; and that it was on this account that Solomon was so severe. But there is little evidence to support these conjectures. It does not appear that Adonijah by desiring to have Abishag had any thought of the kingdom, or of maintaining any right to it, though Solomon appears to have understood him in this sense. But without farther evidence, this was a flimsy pretext to imbrue his hands in a brother's blood. The fable of the *wolf and lamb* is here very applicable, and the old English proverb not less so: *It is an easy thing to find a staff to beat a dog with.* We readily find an excuse for whatever we are determined to do. He who attempts to varnish

A. M. 2990
B. C. 1014
An. Exod. Isr.
477
Anno ante
I. Olymp. 238

25 And King Solomon sent by the hand of Benaiah the son of Jehoiada; and he fell upon him that he died.

26 And unto Abiathar the priest said the king, Get thee to °Anathoth, unto thine own fields; for thou *art* ᵖworthy of death: but I will not at this time put thee to death, ᑫbecause thou barest the ark of the Lord GOD before David my father, and because ʳthou hast been afflicted in all wherein my father was afflicted.

27 So Solomon thrust out Abiathar from being priest unto the LORD; that he might ˢfulfil the word of the LORD, which he spake concerning the house of Eli in Shiloh.

28 Then tidings came to Joab: for Joab ᵗhad turned after Adonijah, though he turned not after Absalom. And Joab fled unto the tabernacle of the LORD, and ᵘcaught hold on the horns of the altar.

29 And it was told King Solomon that Joab was fled unto the tabernacle of the LORD; and, behold, *he is* by the altar. Then Solomon sent Benaiah the son of Jehoiada, saying, Go, fall upon him.

A. M. 2990
B. C. 1014
An. Exod. Isr.
477
Anno ante
I. Olymp. 238

30 And Benaiah came to the tabernacle of the LORD, and said unto him, Thus saith the king, Come forth. And he said, Nay; but I will die here. And Benaiah brought the king word again, saying, Thus saith Joab, and thus he answered me.

31 And the king said unto him, ᵛDo as he hath said, and fall upon him, and bury him; ʷthat thou mayest take away the innocent blood, which Joab shed, from me, and from the house of my father.

32 And the LORD ˣshall return his blood upon his own head, who fell upon two men more righteous ʸand better than he, and slew them with the sword, my father David not knowing *thereof, to wit,* ᶻAbner the son of Ner, captain of the host of Israel, and ᵃAmasa

---

°Josh. xxi. 18——ᵖHeb. *a man of death*——ᑫ1 Sam. xxiii. 6; 2 Sam. xv. 24, 29——ʳ1 Sam. xxii. 20, 23; 2 Sam. xv. 24——ˢ1 Sam. ii. 31–35——ᵗChap. i. 7

ᵘChap. i. 50——ᵛExod. xxi. 14——ʷNum. xxxv. 33; Deut. xix. 13; xxi. 8, 9——ˣJudg. ix. 24, 57; Psa. vii. 16 ʸ2 Chron. xxi. 13——ᶻ2 Sam. iii. 27——ᵃ2 Sam. xx. 10

---

over this conduct of Solomon by either *state necessity* or a *Divine command,* is an enemy, in my mind, to the cause of God and truth. See on ver. 25.

Verse 25. *Solomon sent—Benaiah—and he fell upon him that he died.*] Benaiah seems to have been the public state executioner, and yet he was generalissimo of all the forces. See him employed in a similar work, ver. 34, 46. I suppose him to have been such another general as *Suwarrow,* butcher-general of the Turks and Poles to the late Empress Catharine of Russia: like mistress, like man. But they have long since been called to an impartial tribunal.

That this was an act of cruelty towards Adonijah, needs no proof. He is suspected, condemned, and slain, without a hearing. *Calmet* vindicates all this by various assumptions, and lays down a doctrine that is calculated for the meridian of *Fez* or *Morocco;* hear him: Un prince, dans ses jugemens, ne peut pas toujours suivre les regles de la plus parfaite morale; la politique, et le bien de l'état, obligent souvent à des choses opposées aux conseils de l'evangile; "A prince in his judgments cannot always follow the rules of the most perfect morality; policy and the good of the state often require things to be done which are contrary to the counsels of the Gospel." What a diabolic maxim is this! And is this indeed the way that *French kings* ruled and ministers decreed judgment? Then we need not wonder at a revolution in that state, nor of the scourge that desolated the land. O England! magnify God for your *constitution,* your *constitutional king,* and the *laws* according to which he reigns.

Verse 27. *So Solomon thrust out Abiathar*] This was for having taken part before with

Adonijah, but by it a remarkable prophecy was fulfilled; see 1 Sam. ii. 13-35, and the notes there. God had told Eli that the priesthood should depart from his house; Abiathar was the last of the descendants of *Ithamar,* of which family was Eli the high priest. Zadok, who was made priest in the stead of Abiathar, was of the family of *Eliezer;* and by this change the priesthood reverted to its ancient channel. Abiathar deserved this degradation; he supported Adonijah in his unnatural assumption of the royal dignity, even during the life of his father. This was the head and front of his offending.

Verse 28. *Tidings came to Joab*] He heard that Adonijah had been slain and Abiathar banished, and probably he had heard of David's dying charge to Solomon. Fearing therefore for his personal safety, he takes refuge at the tabernacle, as claiming Divine protection, and desiring to have his case decided by God alone; or perhaps a spark of remorse is now kindled; and, knowing that he must die, he wishes to die in the house of God, as it were under the shadow, that he might receive the mercy of the Almighty.

Verse 30. *Nay; but I will die here.*] The altars were so sacred among all the people, that, in general, even the vilest wretch found safety, if he once reached the altar. This led to many abuses, and the perversion of public justice; and at last it became a maxim that the guilty should be punished, should they even have taken refuge at the altars. God decreed that the presumptuous murderer who had taken refuge at the altar should be dragged thence, and put to death; see Exod. xxi. 14. The heathens had the same kind of ordinance; hence *Euripides:*—

A. M. 2990
B. C. 1014
An. Exod. Isr.
477
Anno ante
I. Olymp. 238
the son of Jether, captain of the host of Judah.

33 Their blood shall therefore return upon the head of Joab, and [b]upon the head of his seed for ever: [c]but upon David, and upon his seed, and upon his house, and upon his throne, shall there be peace for ever from the LORD.

34 So Benaiah the son of Jehoiada went up, and fell upon him, and slew him: and he was buried in his own house in the wilderness.

35 And the king put Benaiah the son of Jehoiada in his room over the host: and [d]Zadok the priest did the king put in the room of [e]Abiathar.

36 And the king sent and called for [f]Shimei, and said unto him, Build thee a house in Jerusalem, and dwell there, and go not forth thence any whither.

37 For it shall be, *that* on the day thou goest out, and passest over [g]the brook Kidron, thou shalt know for certain that thou shalt surely die: [h]thy blood shall be upon thine own head.

38 And Shimei said unto the king, The saying *is* good: as my lord the king hath said, so will thy servant do. And Shimei dwelt in Jerusalem many days.

A. M. 2993
B. C. 1011
An. Exod. Isr.
480
Anno ante
I. Olymp. 235
39 And it came to pass at the end of three years, that two of the servants of Shimei ran away unto [l]Achish son of Maachah

king of Gath. And they told Shimei, saying, Behold, thy servants *be* in Gath.

A. M. 2993
B. C. 1011
An. Exod. Isr.
480
Anno ante
I. Olymp. 235

40 And Shimei arose, and saddled his ass, and went to Gath to Achish to seek his servants: and Shimei went, and brought his servants from Gath.

41 And it was told Solomon that Shimei had gone from Jerusalem to Gath, and was come again.

42 And the king sent and called for Shimei, and said unto him, Did I not make thee to swear by the LORD, and protested unto thee, saying, Know for a certain, on the day thou goest out, and walkest abroad any whither, that thou shalt surely die? and thou saidst unto me, The word *that* I have heard *is* good.

43 Why then hast thou not kept the oath of the Lord, and the commandment that I have charged thee with?

44 The king said moreover to Shimei, Thou knowest [k]all the wickedness which thine heart is privy to, that thou didst to David my father: therefore the LORD shall [l]return thy wickedness upon thine own head;

45 And King Solomon *shall be* blessed, and [m]the throne of David shall be established before the LORD for ever.

46 So the king commanded Benaiah the son of Jehoiada; which went out, and fell upon him, that he died. And the [n]kingdom was established in the hand of Solomon.

---

[b]2 Sam. iii. 29——[c]Prov. xxv. 5——[d]Num. xxv. 11, 12, 13; 1 Samuel ii. 35; see 1 Chron. vi. 53; xxiv. 3 [e]Ver. 27——[f]2 Sam. xvi. 5; ver. 8——[g]2 Sam. xv. 23

[h]Lev. xx. 9; Josh. ii. 29; 2 Sam. i. 16——[i]1 Sam. xxvii. 2——[k]2 Sam. xvi. 5——[l]Psa. vii. 16; Ezek. xvii. 19 [m]Prov. xxv. 5——[n]Ver. 12; 2 Chron. i. 1

Εγω γαρ οστις μη δικαιος ων ανηρ
Βωμον προσιζει, τον νομον χαιρειν εων,
Προς την δικην αγοιμ' αν, αυ τρεσας θεους·
Κακον γαρ ανδρα χρη κακως πασχειν αει.
EURIPID. *Frag.* 42. Edit. *Musg.*

"If an unrighteous man, availing himself of the law, should claim the protection of the altar, I would drag him to justice, nor fear the wrath of the gods; for it is necessary that every wicked man should suffer for his crimes."

Verse 34. *So Benaiah—went up—and slew him*] It appears he slew him at the very altar. Joab must have been both old and infirm at this time, and now he bleeds for *Abner*, he bleeds for *Amasa*, and he bleeds for *Uriah*. The two former he murdered; of the blood of the latter he was not innocent; yet he had done the state much service, and they knew it. But he was a murderer, and vengeance would not suffer such to live.

Verse 36. *Build thee a house*] Thus he gave him the whole city for a prison, and this certainly could have reduced him to no hardships.

Verse 37. *Thy blood shall be upon thine own head.*] Thou knowest what to expect; if thou disobey my orders thou shalt certainly be slain, and then thou shalt be considered as a *self-murderer;* thou alone shalt be answerable for thy own death. Solomon knew that Shimei was a seditious man, and he chose to keep him under his own eye; for such a man at large, in favourable circumstances, might do much evil. His bitter revilings of David were a sufficient proof.

Verse 40. *And Shimei—went to Gath*] It is astonishing that with his eyes wide open he would thus run into the jaws of death.

Verse 45. *King Solomon shall be blessed*] He seems to think that, while such bad men remained unpunished, the nation could not prosper; that it was an act of justice which God required him to perform, in order to the establishment and perpetuity of his throne.

Verse 46. *And the kingdom was established*]

He had neither foes within nor without. He was either dreaded or loved universally. His own subjects were affectionately bound to him, and the surrounding nations did not think proper to make him their enemy.

As there are serious doubts relative to the dying charge of David as it relates to *Shimei*, most believing that, in opposition to his own oath, David desired that Solomon should put him to death; I shall here insert Dr. *Kennicott's* criticism on this part of the text:—

"*David* is here represented in our *English* version as finishing his life with giving a command to Solomon to kill Shimei, and to kill him on account of that very crime for which, as David here says, he had sworn to him by the Lord he would not put him to death. The behaviour thus imputed to the king and prophet, and which would be justly censurable if true, should be examined very carefully as to the ground it stands upon; and when the passage is duly considered, I presume it will appear highly probable that an injury has been here done to this illustrious character. The point to which I now beg the reader's attention is this: That it is not uncommon in the Hebrew language to omit the negative in a second part of the sentence, and to consider it as repeated, when it has been once expressed, and is followed by the connecting particle. And thus on Isa. xiii. 22 the late learned annotator says: 'The *negative* is repeated or referred to by the conjunction *vau*, as in many other places.' So also Isa. xxiii. 4. The necessity of so very considerable an alteration as inserting the particle NOT, may be here confirmed by some other instances. Psa. i. 5: *The ungodly shall not stand in the judgment*, NOR (the Hebrew is AND, signifying *and not*) *sinners in the congregation of the righteous*. Psa. ix. 18: *The needy shall not alway be forgotten*, (and then the negative, under-stood as repeated by the conjunction, now dropped,) *the expectation of the poor shall* (NOT) *perish for ever*. Psa. xxxviii. 1: *O Lord, rebuke me not in thy wrath; neither* (AND, for *and not*) *chasten me in thy hot displeasure*. Psa. lxxv. 5: *Lift not up your horn on high*, (and then the negative, understood as repeated by the conjunction, now dropped,) *speak* (NOT) *with a stiff neck*. Prov. xxiv. 12, (our version is this:) *Doth not he, that pondereth the heart, consider it? and he that keepeth the soul, doth* (NOT) *he know it? and shall* (NOT) *he render to every man according to his works?* And Prov. xxx. 3: *I neither learned wisdom*, NOR (AND, for *and not*) *have the knowledge of the holy*. If then there are in fact many such instances, the question is, Whether the *negative* here, expressed in the former part of David's command, may not be understood as to be repeated in the latter part; and if this *may* be, a strong reason will be added why it *should* be, so interpreted. The passage will run thus: 'Behold, thou hast with thee Shimei, who cursed me—but I swore to him by the Lord, saying, I will not put thee to death by the sword. Now, therefore, hold him NOT guiltless, (for thou art a wise man, and knowest what thou oughtest to do unto him,) but bring NOT down his hoar head to the grave with blood.' Now if the language itself will admit of this construction, the sense thus given to the sentence derives a very strong support from the context. For how did Solomon understand this charge? Did he kill Shimei in consequence of it? Certainly he did not; for after he had immediately commanded Joab to be slain, in obedience to his father, he sends for Shimei, and knowing that Shimei ought to be well watched, confines him to a particular spot in Jerusalem for the remainder of his life; chap. ii. 36-42. See also Job xxiii. 17; xxx. 20; xxxi. 20." This is the best mode of interpreting this text.

CHAPTER III

Solomon marries Pharaoh's daughter, 1, 2. He serves God, and offers a thousand burnt-offerings upon one altar, at Gibeon, 3, 4. God appears to him in a dream at Gibeon; and asks what he shall give him, 5. He asks wisdom; with which God is well pleased, and promises to give him not only that, but also riches and honour; and, if obedient, long life, 6-14. He comes back to Jerusalem; and offers burnt-offerings and peace-offerings, and makes a feast for his servants, 15. His judgment between the two harlots, 16-27. He rises in the esteem of the people, 28.

A. M. 2990
B. C. 1014
An. Exod. Isr.
477
Anno ante
I. Olymp. 238

AND [a]Solomon made affinity with Pharaoh king of Egypt, and took Pharaoh's daughter, and brought her into the [b]city of David, until he had made an end of building his [c]own house, and [d]the house of the Lord, and [e]the wall of Jerusalem round about.

A. M. 2990
B. C. 1014
An. Exod. Isr.
477
Anno ante
I. Olymp. 238

---

[a]Chap. vii. 8; ix. 24——[b]2 Sam. v. 7——[c]Chap. vii. 1——[d]Chap. vi——[e]Chap. ix. 15, 19

NOTES ON CHAP. III

Verse 1. *Solomon made affinity with Pharaoh*] This was no doubt a *political* measure in order to strengthen his kingdom, and on the same ground he continued his alliance with the king of Tyre; and these were among the most powerful of his neighbours. But should political considerations prevail over express laws of God? God had strictly forbidden his people to form alliances with heathenish women, lest they should lead their hearts away from him into idolatry. Let us hear the law: *Neither shalt thou make marriages with them; thy daughter thou shalt not give unto his son, nor his daughter shalt thou take unto thy son; for they will turn away thy son from following me*, &c. Exod. xxxiv. 16; Deut. vii. 3, 4. Now Solomon acted in direct *opposition* to these laws; and perhaps in this alliance were sown those seeds of apostasy from God and goodness in which he so long lived, and in which he so awfully died.

Those who are, at all hazards, his determinate

A. M. 2990
B. C. 1014
An. Exod. Isr.
477
Anno ante
I. Olymp. 238

2 [f]Only the people sacrificed in high places, because there was no house built unto the name of the LORD, until those days.

3 And Solomon [g]loved the LORD, [h]walking in the statutes of David his father: only he sacrificed and burnt incense in high places.

4 And [i]the king went to Gibeon to sacrifice there; [k]for that *was* the great high place: a thousand burnt-offerings did Solomon offer upon that altar.

5 [l]In Gibeon the LORD appeared to Solomon [m]in a dream by night: and God said, Ask what I shall give thee.

A. M. 2990
B. C. 1014
An. Exod. Isr.
477
Anno ante
I. Olymp. 238

---

[f]Lev. xvii. 3, 4, 5; Deut. xii. 2, 4, 5; chap. xxii. 43
[g]Deut. vi. 5; xxx. 16, 20; Psa. xxxi. 23; Rom. viii. 28; 1 Cor. viii. 3

[h]Ver. 6, 14——[i]2 Chron. i. 3——[k]1 Chron. xvi. 39; 2 Chron. i. 3——[l]Chap. ix. 2; 2 Chron. i. 7——[m]Num. xii. 6; Matt. i. 20; ii. 13, 19

---

apologists, assume, 1. That Pharaoh's daughter must have been a *proselyte to the Jewish religion*, else Solomon would not have married her. 2. That God was not displeased with this match. 3. That the book of *Canticles*, which is supposed to have been his *epithalamium*, would not have found a place in the sacred canon had the spouse, whom it all along celebrates, been at that time an idolatress. 4. That it is certain we nowhere in Scripture find Solomon blamed for this match. See *Dodd*.

Now to all this I answer, 1. We have no evidence that the daughter of Pharaoh was a proselyte, no more than that her father was a true believer. It is no more likely that he sought a proselyte here than that he sought them among the Moabites, Hittites, &c., from whom he took many wives. 2. If God's law be positively against such matches, he could not possibly be *pleased* with this breach of it in Solomon; but his law is positively against them, therefore he was not pleased. 3. That the book of Canticles being found in the sacred canon, is, according to some critics, neither a proof that the marriage pleased God, nor that the book was written by Divine inspiration; much less that it celebrates the love between Christ and his Church, or is at all profitable for doctrine, for reproof, or for edification in righteousness. 4. That Solomon is most expressly reproved in Scripture for this very match, is to me very evident from the following passages: DID NOT SOLOMON, *king of Israel, SIN by these things? Yet among many nations was there no king like him, who was beloved of his God, and God made him king over all Israel; nevertheless even him did outlandish women cause to sin;* Neh. xiii. 26. Now it is certain that Pharaoh's daughter was an *outlandish woman;* and although it be not expressly said that Pharaoh's daughter is *here* intended, yet there is all reasonable evidence that she is included; and, indeed, the words seem to intimate that *she* is *especially referred to.* In ver. 3 it is said, *Solomon* LOVED THE LORD, *walking in the statutes of David;* and Nehemiah says, *Did not Solomon, king of Israel, SIN BY THESE THINGS, who WAS BELOVED of HIS GOD;* referring, most probably, to this early part of Solomon's history. But supposing that this is not sufficient evidence that this match is *spoken against in Scripture*, let us turn to chap. xi. 1, 2, of this book, where the cause of Solomon's apostacy is assigned; and there we read, *But King Solomon loved many STRANGE WOMEN, TOGETHER WITH THE DAUGHTER OF PHARAOH, women of the Moabites, Ammonites, Edomites, Zidonians, and Hittites: of the nations concerning which the Lord said unto the children of Israel,*

Ye shall not go in unto them; neither shall they come in unto you; for surely they will turn away your heart after their gods: SOLOMON CLAVE UNTO THESE IN LOVE. Here the marriage with Pharaoh's daughter is classed most positively with the most exceptionable of his matrimonial and concubinal alliances: as it no doubt had its predisposing share in an apostacy the most unprecedented and disgraceful.

Should I even be singular, I cannot help thinking that the reign of Solomon *began rather inauspiciously:* even a brother's blood must be shed to cause him to sit securely on his throne, and a most reprehensible alliance, the forerunner of many others of a similar nature, was formed for the same purpose. But we must ever be careful to distinguish between what God has commanded to be done, and what was done through the vile passions and foolish jealousies of men. Solomon had many advantages, and no man ever made a worse use of them.

Verse 2. *The people sacrificed in high places*] Could there be any sin in this, or was it unlawful till after the temple was built? for prophets, judges, the kings which preceded Solomon, and Solomon himself, sacrificed on high places, such as Gibeon, Gilgal, Shiloh, Hebron, Kirjath-jearim, &c. But after the temple was erected, it was sinful to offer sacrifices in any other place; yet here it is introduced as being morally wrong, and it is introduced, ver. 3, as being an exceptionable trait in the character of Solomon. The explanation appears to be this: as the *ark* and *tabernacle* were still in being, it was not right to offer sacrifices but where they were; and wherever they were, whether on a high place or a plain, there sacrifices might be lawfully offered, previously to the building of the temple. And the tabernacle was now at Gibeon, 2 Chron. i. 3. Possibly the *high places* may be like those among the Hindoos, large *raised-up terraces*, on which they place their gods when they bathe, anoint, and worship them. Juggernaut and Krishnu have large terraces or *high places*, on which they are annually exhibited. But there was no idol in the above case.

Verse 5. *The Lord appeared to Solomon in a dream*] This was the night after he had offered the sacrifices, (see 2 Chron. i. 7,) and probably after he had earnestly prayed for wisdom; see *Wisdom*, chap. vii. 7: *Wherefore I prayed, and understanding was given me: I called* upon God, *and the spirit of wisdom came to me.* If this were the case, the dream might have been the consequence of his earnest prayer for wisdom: the images of those things which occupy the mind during the day are most likely to recur during the night; and this, indeed, is the origin

A. M. 2990
B. C. 1014
An. Exod. Isr.
477
Anno ante
I. Olymp. 238

6 ⁿAnd Solomon said, Thou hast showed unto thy servant David my father great °mercy, according as he ^pwalked before thee in truth, and in righteousness, and in uprightness of heart with thee; and thou hast kept for him this great kindness, that thou ^qhast given him a son to sit on his throne, as *it is* this day.

7 And now, O LORD my God, thou hast made thy servant king instead of David my father: ^rand I *am but* a little child: I know not *how* ^sto go out or come in.

8 And thy servant *is* in the midst of thy people which thou ^thast chosen, a great people, ^uthat cannot be numbered nor counted for multitude.

9 ^vGive therefore thy servant an ^wunderstanding heart ^xto judge thy people, that I may ^ydiscern between good and bad: for who is able to judge this thy so great a people?

A. M. 2990
B. C. 1014
An. Exod. Isr.
477
Anno ante
I. Olymp. 238

10 And the speech pleased the LORD, that Solomon had asked this thing.

11 And God said unto him, Because thou hast asked this thing, and hast ^znot asked for thyself ^along life; neither hast asked riches for thyself, nor hast asked the life of thine enemies; but hast asked for thyself understanding, ^bto discern judgment:

12 ^cBehold, I have done according to thy words: ^dlo, I have given thee a wise and an understanding heart; so that there was none

---

ⁿ2 Chron. i. 8, &c.——°Or, *bounty*——^pChap. ii. 4; ix. 4; 2 Kings xx. 3; Psa. xv. 2——^qChap. i. 48——^r1 Chron. xxix. 1——^sNum. xxvii. 17——^tDeut. vii. 6 ^uGen. xiii. 16; xv. 5

^v2 Chron. i. 10; Prov. ii. 3-9; James i. 5——^wHeb. *hearing*——^xPsa. lxxii. 1, 2——^yHeb. v. 14——^zJames iv. 3——^aHeb. *many days*——^bHeb. *to hear*——^c1 John v. 14, 15——^dCh. iv. 29, 30, 31; v. 12; x. 24; Eccles. i. 16

---

of the greater part of our dreams. But this appears to have been *supernatural*.

Gregory Nyssen, speaking of different kinds of dreams, observes that our organs and brain are not unlike a musical instrument; while the strings of such instruments have their proper degree of tension, they give, when touched, a harmonious sound, but as soon as they are relaxed or screwed down, they give no sound at all. During our waking hours, our senses, touched by our reason, produce the most harmonious concert; but as soon as we are asleep, the instrument is no longer capable of emitting any sound, unless it happen that the remembrance of what passed during the day returns and presents itself to the mind while we are asleep, and so forms a dream; just as the strings of an instrument continue to emit feeble sounds for some time after the musician has ceased to strike them.—See GREG. NYSS. *De opificio hominis*, cap. xii., p. 77. *Oper.* vol. i., edit. *Morell.*, Par. 1638.

This may account, in some measure, for common dreams: but even suppose we should not allow that Solomon had been the day before earnestly requesting the gift of wisdom from God, yet we might grant that such a dream as this might be produced by the immediate influence of God upon the soul. And if Solomon received his wisdom by immediate inspiration from heaven, this was the kind of dream that he had; a dream by which that wisdom was actually communicated. But probably we need not carry this matter so much into miracle: God might be the author of his extraordinary *wisdom*, as he was the author of his extraordinary *riches*. Some say, "He lay down as ignorant as other men, and yet arose in the morning wiser than all the children of men." I think this is as credible as that he lay down with a scanty revenue, and in the morning, when he arose, found his treasury full. In short, God's especial blessing brought him riches through the medium of his own care and industry; as the inspiration of the Almighty gave him understanding, while

he gave his heart to seek and search out by his *wisdom, concerning all things under the sun,* Eccles. i. 13. God gave him the seeds of an extraordinary understanding, and, by much study and research, they grew up under the Divine blessing, and produced a plentiful harvest; but, alas! they did not continue to grow.

Verse 7. *I know not* how *to go out or come in.*] I am just like an infant learning to walk alone, and can neither go out nor come in without help.

Verse 9. *Give—an understanding heart to judge thy people*] He did not ask wisdom in general, but the true science of government. This wisdom he sought, and this wisdom he obtained.

Verse 12. *I have given thee a wise and an understanding heart*] I have given thee a capacious mind, one capable of knowing much: make a proper use of thy powers, under the direction of my Spirit, and thou shalt excel in wisdom all that have gone before thee; neither after thee shall any arise like unto thee. But, *query,* Was not all this *conditional? If he should walk in his ways, and keep his statutes and commandments,* ver. 14. Was it not to depend upon his proper use of initiatory inspirations? Did he ever receive *all* this wisdom? Did not his unfaithfulness prevent the fulfilment of the Divine purpose? Instead of being the *wisest* of men, did he not become more *brutish* than any man? Did he not even lose the *knowledge of his Creator,* and worship the abominations of the Moabites, Zidonians, &c., &c.! And was not such idolatry a proof of the *grossest stupidity?* How few proofs does his life give that the gracious purpose of God was fulfilled in him! He received *much;* but he would have received *much more,* had he been faithful to the grace given. No character in the sacred writings disappoints us more than the character of Solomon.

None like thee before thee] That is, no king, either in Israel or among the nations, as the following verse explains.

A. M. 2990
B. C. 1014
An. Exod. Isr.
477
Anno ante
I. Olymp. 238
like thee before thee, neither after thee shall any arise like unto thee.

13 And I have also [e]given thee that which thou hast not asked, both [f]riches and honour: so that there [g]shall not be any among the kings like unto thee all thy days.

14 And if thou wilt walk in my ways, to keep my statutes and my commandments, [h]as thy father David did walk, then I will [i]lengthen thy days.

15 And Solomon [k]awoke; and, behold, *it was* a dream. And he came to Jerusalem, and stood before the ark of the covenant of the LORD, and offered up burnt-offerings, and offered peace-offerings, and [l]made a feast to all his servants.

16 Then came there two women, *that were* harlots, unto the king, and [m]stood before him.

17 And the one woman said, O my lord, I and this woman dwell in one house; and I was delivered of a child with her in the house.

18 And it came to pass the third day after that I was delivered, that this woman was delivered also: and we *were* together; *there was* no stranger with us in the house, save we two in the house.

19 And this woman's child died in the night; because she overlaid it.

20 And she arose at midnight, and took my son from beside me, while thine handmaid slept, and laid it in her bosom, and laid her dead child in my bosom. A. M. 2990
B. C. 1014
An. Exod. Isr.
477
Anno ante
I. Olymp. 238

21 And when I rose in the morning to give my child suck, behold, it was dead: but when I had considered it in the morning, behold, it was not my son, which I did bear.

22 And the other woman said, Nay; but the living *is* my son, and the dead *is* thy son. And this said, No: but the dead *is* thy son, and the living *is* my son. Thus they spake before the king.

23 Then said the king, The one saith, This *is* my son that liveth, and thy son *is* the dead: and the other saith, Nay; but thy son *is* the dead, and my son *is* the living.

24 And the king said, Bring me a sword. And they brought a sword before the king.

25 And the king said, Divide the living child in two, and gave half to the one, and half to the other.

26 Then spake the woman whose the living child *was* unto the king, for [n]her bowels[o] yearned upon her son, and she said, O my lord, give her the living child, and in nowise slay it. But the other said, Let it be neither mine nor thine, *but* divide *it*.

---

[e]Wisd. vii. 11; Matt. vi. 33; Eph. iii. 20——[f]Ch. iv. 21, 24; x. 23, 25, &c.; Prov. iii. 16——[g]Or, *hath not been* [h]Chap. xv. 5——[i]Psa. xci. 16; Prov. iii. 2——[k]So Gen. xli. 7

[l]So Gen. xl. 20; chap. viii. 65; Esth. i. 3; Dan. v. 1; Mark vi. 21——[m]Num. xxvii. 2——[n]Gen. xliii. 30; Isa. xlix. 15; Jer. xxxi. 20; Hos. xi. 8——[o]Heb. *were hot*

Verse 16. *Then came there two women— harlots*] The word זנות *zonoth*, which we here, and in some other places, improperly translate *harlots*, is by the Chaldee (the best judge in this case) rendered פונדקין *pundekayan, tavern- keepers*. (See on Josh. ii. 1.) If these had been *harlots*, it is not likely they would have dared to appear before Solomon; and if they had been common women, it is not likely they would have had children; nor is it likely that such persons would have been permitted under the reign of David. Though there is no mention of their *husbands*, it is probable they might have been at this time in other parts, following their necessary occupations; and the settling the present business could not have been delayed till their return; the appeal to justice must be made immediately.

Verse 25. *Divide the living child in two*] This was apparently a very strange decision, and such as nothing could vindicate had it been carried into execution; but Solomon saw that the only way to find out the real mother was by the *affection* and *tenderness* which she would

necessarily show to her offspring. He plainly saw that the real mother would rather relinquish her claim to her child than see it hewn in pieces before her eyes, while it was probable the pretender would see this with indifference. He therefore orders such a mode of trial as would put the maternal affection of the real mother to the utmost proof; the plan was tried, and it succeeded. This was a proof of his sound judgment, penetration, and acquaintance with human nature; but surely it is not produced as a proof of extraordinary and supernatural wisdom. We have several similar decisions even among heathens.

Suetonius, in his life of the Emperor Claudius, cap. xv., whom he celebrates for his wonderful sagacity and penetration on some particular occasions, tells us, that this emperor discovered a woman to be the mother of a certain young man, whom she refused to acknowledge as her son, by commanding her to marry him, the proofs being doubtful on both sides; for, rather than commit this incest, she confessed the truth. His words are: Feminam, non agnoscentem

A. M. 2990
B. C. 1014
An. Exod. Isr. 477
Anno ante
I. Olymp. 238

27 Then the king answered and said, Give her the living child, and in no wise slay it: she *is* the mother thereof.

28 And all Israel heard of the judgment

pVer. 9, 11, 12

filium suum, dubia utrinque argumentorum fide, ad confessionem compulit, indicto matrimonio juvenis.

Ariopharnes, king of Thrace, being appointed to decide between three young men, who each professed to be the son of the deceased king of the Cimmerians, and claimed the crown in consequence, found out the real son by commanding each to shoot an arrow into the body of the dead king: two of them did this without hesitation; the third refused, and was therefore judged by Ariopharnes to be the real son of the deceased. *Grotius,* on this place, quotes this relation from *Diodorus Siculus;* I quote this on his authority, but have not been able to find

which the king had judged; and they feared the king: for they saw that the pwisdom of God *was* qin him, to do judgment.

A. M. 2990
B. C. 1014
An. Exod. Isr. 477
Anno ante
I. Olymp. 238

qHeb. *in the midst of him*

the place in Diodorus. This is a parallel case to that in the text; a covert appeal was made to the principle of *affection;* and the truth was discovered, as in the case of the mother of the living child.

Verse 28. They feared the king] This decision proved that they could not impose upon him; and they were afraid to do those things which might bring them before his judgment-seat.

They saw that the wisdom of God was *in him*] They perceived that he was taught of God, judged impartially, and could not be deceived. What was done to the other woman we are not told; justice certainly required that she should be punished for her lies and fraud.

CHAPTER IV

An account of Solomon's chief officers, 1–6. Names of the twelve officers that were over twelve districts, to provide victuals for the king's household monthly, 7–19. Judah and Israel are very populous; and Solomon reigns over many provinces, 20, 21. The daily provision for his family, 22, 23. The extent and peace of his dominions, 24, 25. His horses, chariots, and dromedaries; with the provision made for them, 26–28. His wisdom and understanding, 29–31. The number of his proverbs and songs; and his knowledge in natural history, 32, 33. People from all nations come to hear his wisdom, 34.

A.M.2989-3029
B.C.1015-975
Anno ante I.
Olymp.239-199

SO King Solomon was king over all Israel.

2 And these *were* the princes which he had; Azariah the son of Zadok the apriest.

3 Elihoreph and Ahiah, the sons of Shisha, bscribes; cJehoshaphat the son of Ahilud, the drecorder.

4 And eBenaiah the son of Jehoiada *was* over the host: and Zadok and fAbiathar *were* the priests.

5 And Azariah the son of Nathan *was* over gthe officers: and Zabud the son of Nathan *was* hprincipal officer, *and* ithe king's friend:

6 And Ahishar *was* over the household: and kAdoniram the son of Abda *was* over the ltribute.

A.M.2989-3029
B.C.1015-975
Anno ante I.
Olymp.239-199

7 And Solomon had twelve officers over all Israel, which provided victuals for the king and his household: each man his month in a year made provision.

8 And these *are* their names: mThe son of Hur, in Mount Ephraim:

9 nThe son of Dekar, in Makaz, and in Shaalbim, and Beth-shemesh, and Elon-beth-hanan:

10 oThe son of Hesed, in Aruboth; to him

aOr, *the chief officer*——bOr, *secretaries*——c2 Sam. viii. 16; xx. 24——dOr, *remembrancer*——eChap. ii. 35 fSee chap. ii. 27——gVer. 7

h2 Sam. viii. 18; xx. 26——i2 Sam. xv. 37; xvi. 16; 1 Chron. xxvii. 33——kChap. v. 14——lOr, *levy* mOr, *Ben-hur*——nOr, *Ben-dekar*——oOr, *Ben-hesed*

NOTES ON CHAP. IV

Verse 2. These were *the princes which he had; Azariah the son of Zadok the priest.*] These were his *great, chief,* or *principal* men. None of them were *princes* in the common acceptation of the word.

Verse 3. Elihoreph and Ahiah—scribes] *Secretaries* to the king.

Jehoshaphat—recorder] *Historiographer* to to the king, who chronicled the affairs of the kingdom. He was in this office under David, see 2 Sam. xx. 24.

Verse 5. Azariah—was over the officers] He had the *superintendence* of the twelve officers mentioned below; see ver. 7.

Zabud—was principal officer] Perhaps what we call *premier,* or *prime minister.*

The king's friend] His chief *favourite*—his *confidant.*

Verse 6. Ahishar was over the household] the king's *chamberlain.*

Adoniram—was over the tribute.] What we call *chancellor* of the *exchequer.* He received and brought into the treasury all the proceeds of *taxes* and *tributes.* He was in this office under David; see 2 Sam. xx. 24.

Verse 7. Twelve officers] The business of these twelve officers was to provide daily, each for a month, those provisions which were consumed in the king's household; see verses 22

A.M.2989-3029
B.C.1015-975
Anno ante I.
Olymp.239-199

pertained Sochoh, and all the land of Hepher:

11 pThe son of Abinadab, in all the region of Dor; which had Taphath the daughter of Solomon to wife;

12 Baana the son of Ahilud; *to him pertained* Taanach and Megiddo, and all Beth-shean, which *is* by Zartanah beneath Jezreel, from Beth-shean to Abel-meholah, *even* unto *the place that is* beyond Jokneam:

13 qThe son of Geber, in Ramoth-gilead; to him *pertained* rthe towns of Jair the son of Manasseh, which *are* in Gilead; to him *also pertained* sthe region of Argob, which *is* in Bashan, threescore great cities with walls and brazen bars:

14 Ahinadab the son of Iddo *had* tMahanaim:

15 Ahimaaz *was* in Naphtali; he also took Basmath the daughter of Solomon to wife:

16 Baanah the son of Hushai *was* in Asher and in Aloth:

17 Jehoshaphat the son of Paruah, in Issachar:

A.M.2989-3029
B.C. 1015-975
Anno ante I.
Olymp. 239-199

18 Shimei the son of Elah, in Benjamin:

19 Geber the son of Uri *was* in the country of Gilead, *in* uthe country of Sihon king of the Amorites, and of Og king of Bashan; and *he was* the only officer which *was* in the land.

20 Judah and Israel *were* many, vas the sand which *is* by the sea in multitude, weating and drinking, and making merry.

21 And xSolomon reigned over all kingdoms from ythe river unto the land of the Philistines, and unto the border of Egypt: zthey brought presents, and served Solomon all the days of his life.

22 And Solomon's aprovision for one day was thirty bmeasures of fine flour, and threescore measures of meal,

23 Ten fat oxen, and twenty oxen out of the pastures, and a hundred sheep, beside harts, and roebucks, and fallow deer, and fatted fowl.

---

pOr, *Ben-abinadab*——qOr, *Ben-geber*——rNumbers xxxii. 41——sDeut. iii. 4——tOr, *to Mahanaim* uDeut. iii. 8——vGen. xxii. 17; chap. iii. 8; Prov. xiv. 28

wPsa. lxxii. 3, 7; Mic. iv. 4——x2 Chron. ix. 26; Psa. lxxii. 8; Ecclus. xlvii. 13——yGen. xv. 18; Josh. i. 4 zPsa. lxviii. 29; lxxii. 10, 11——aHeb. *bread*——bHeb. *cors*

and 23. And the task for such a daily provision was not an easy one.

Verse 13. Threescore great cities with walls and brazen bars] These were fortified cities: their gates and bars covered with plates of brass. Such were the gates in Priam's palace:—

Ipse inter primos correpta dura bipenni Limina perrumpit, POSTES *que a cardine vellit* ÆRATOS.   VIRG. Æn., lib. ii. ver. 479.

Fierce Pyrrhus in the front, with forceful sway, Plied the huge axe, and hew'd the beams away; The solid timbers from the portal tore, And rent from every hinge the BRAZEN *door*.
         PITT.

Verse 20. Eating and drinking, and making merry.] They were very comfortable, very rich, very merry, and very corrupt. And this full feeding and dissipation led to a total corruption of manners.

Verse 21. Solomon reigned over all kingdoms] The meaning of this verse appears to be, that Solomon reigned over all the provinces from the river Euphrates to the land of the Philistines, even to the frontiers of Egypt. The Euphrates was on the *east* of Solomon's dominions; the Philistines were *westward* on the Mediterranean sea; and Egypt was on the *south*. Solomon had, therefore, as tributaries, the kingdoms of *Syria, Damascus, Moab,* and *Ammon,* which lay between the Euphrates and the Mediterranean. See *Calmet.* Thus he appears to have possessed all the land that God covenanted with Abraham to give to his posterity.

Verse 22. Solomon's provision for one day:—
Of fine flour - - 30 measures, or cors.
Of meal - - - 60 ditto.

Stall-fed oxen - - - 10
Ditto from the pasture 20
Sheep - - - - - - 100; with harts, roebucks, fallow deer, and fat fowls.

The כר *cor* was the same as the *homer,* and contained nearly *seventy-six gallons,* wine measure, according to Bishop Cumberland.

Sheep] צאן *tson,* comprehending both sheep and goats.

Harts] מאיל *meaiyal,* the deer.

Roebucks] צבי *tsebi,* the gazal, antelope, or wild goat.

Fallow deer] יחמור *yachmur,* the buffalo. See the notes on Deut. xii. 15, and xiv. 5.

Fatted fowl.] ברברים אבוסים *barburim abusim,* I suppose, means all the *wild fowls* in *season* during each month. Michaelis derives ברברים *barburim* from ברא *bara,* which in Chaldee, Syriac, and Arabic, signifies a *field,* a *desert;* all that is *without* the cities and habitations of men: hence ברא חיות *cheyvath bara,* wild beasts, Dan. ii. 38, תור בר *tor bar,* wild bull; and therefore *barburim* may signify creatures living in the *fields, woods,* and *deserts,* which are taken by *hunting,* and opposed to those which are *domesticated;* and, consequently, may include *beasts* as well as *fowls.* Many have translated the word *capons;* but, query, was any such thing known among the ancient Jews? Solomon's table, therefore, was spread with all the *necessaries* and *delicacies* which the *house* or the *field* could afford.

But how immense must the number of men have been who were fed daily at the palace of the Israelitish king! *Vilalpandus* computes the number to be not less than *forty-eight thousand, six hundred;* and Calvisius makes, by estimation from the consumption of food, *fifty-*

A.M.2989-3029
B.C.1015-975
Anno ante I.
Olymp.239-199

24 For he had dominion over all *the region* on this side the river, from Tiphsah even to Azzah, over ᶜall the kings on this side the river: and ᵈhe had peace on all sides round about him.

25 And Judah and Israel ᵉdwelt ᶠsafely, ᵍevery man under his vine and under his fig tree, ʰfrom Dan even to Beer-sheba, all the days of Solomon.

26 And ⁱSolomon had forty thousand stalls of ᵏhorses for his chariots, and twelve thousand horsemen.

27 And ˡthose officers provided victual for King Solomon, and for all that came unto King Solomon's table, every man in his month: they lacked nothing.

28 Barley also and straw for the horses and ᵐdromedaries brought they unto the place where *the officers* were, every man according to his charge.

A.M.2989-3029
B.C.1015-975
Anno ante I.
Olymp.239-199

29 And ⁿGod gave Solomon wisdom and understanding exceeding much, and largeness of heart, even as the sand that *is* on the sea-shore.

30 And Solomon's wisdom excelled the wisdom of all the children ᵒof the east country, and all the ᵖwisdom of Egypt.

31 For he was ᑫwiser than all men: ʳthan Ethan the Ezrahite, and Heman, ˢand Chalcol, and Darda, the sons of Mahol; and his fame was in all nations round about.

32 And ᵗhe spake three thousand proverbs;

ᶜPsa. lxxii. 11——ᵈ1 Chron. xxii. 9——ᵉSee Jer. xxiii. 6——ᶠHeb. *confidently*——ᵍMic. iv. 4; Zech. iii. 10 ʰJudg. xx. 1——ⁱChap. x. 26; 2 Chron. i. 14; ix. 25 ᵏSee Deut. xvii. 16——ˡVer. 7——ᵐOr, *mules or swift beasts;* Esth. viii. 14; Mic. i. 13

ⁿChap. iii. 12; Ecclus. xlvii. 14, 15, 16, 17——ᵒGen. xxv. 6——ᵖSee Acts vii. 22——ᑫChap. iii. 12——ʳ1 Chron. xv. 19; Psa. lxxxix. title——ˢSee 1 Chron. ii. 6; vi. 33; xv. 19; Psa. lxxxviii. title——ᵗProv. i. 1; Eccles. xii. 9

---

four thousand! These must have included all his guards, each of whom received a *ration* from the king's store.

Verse 25. *Every man under his vine*] They were no longer obliged to dwell in *fortified* cities for fear of their enemies; they spread themselves over all the country, which they everywhere cultivated; and had always the privilege of eating the fruits of their own labours. This is the meaning of the phrase.

Verse 26. *Solomon had forty thousand stalls of horses—and twelve thousand horsemen.*] In 2 Chron. ix. 25, instead of *forty thousand stalls*, we read *four thousand;* and even this number might be quite sufficient to hold horses for *twelve thousand* horsemen; for *stalls* and *stables* may be here synonymous. In chap. x. 26 it is said he had *one thousand four hundred chariots, and twelve thousand horsemen;* and this is the reading in 2 Chron. i. 14. In 2 Chron. ix. 25, already quoted, instead of *forty thousand stalls for horses*, the *Septuagint* has τεσσαρες χιλιαδες θηλειαι ιπποι, *four thousand mares;* and in this place the whole verse is omitted both by the *Syriac* and *Arabic*. In the *Targum* of Rabbi Joseph on this book we have ארבע מאה *arba meah, four hundred*, instead of the *four thousand* in Chronicles, and the *forty thousand* in the text. From this collation of parallel places we may rest satisfied that there is a *corruption* in the *numbers* somewhere; and as a sort of *medium*, we may take for the whole *four thousand stalls*, one thousand four hundred chariots, and twelve thousand horsemen.

Verse 28. *And dromedaries*] The word רכש *rechesh*, which we translate thus, is rendered *beasts*, or *beasts of burden*, by the *Vulgate; mares* by the *Syriac* and *Arabic; chariots* by the *Septuagint;* and *race-horses* by the *Chaldee*. The original word seems to signify a very *swift* kind of *horse*, and *race-horse* or *post-horse* is probably its true meaning. To communicate with so many distant provinces,

Solomon had need of many animals of this kind.

Verse 29. *God gave Solomon wisdom, &c.*] He gave him a capacious mind, and furnished him with extraordinary assistance to cultivate it.

Even as the sand that is on the sea-shore.] Lord *Bacon* observes on this: "As the sand on the sea-shore encloses a great body of waters, so Solomon's mind contained an ocean of knowledge." This is a happy and correct illustration.

Verse 30. *The children of the east country*] That is the Chaldeans, Persians, and Arabians, who, with the Egyptians, were famed for wisdom and knowledge through all the world.

Verse 31. *He was wiser than all men*] He was wiser than any of those who were most celebrated in his time, among whom were the *four* after mentioned, viz., *Ethan, Heman, Chalcol,* and *Darda*. Ethan was probably the same as is mentioned in some of the Psalms, particularly Psa. lxxxix., title; and among the *singers* in 1 Chron. vi. 42. There is a *Heman* mentioned in the title to Psa. lxxxviii. In 1 Chron. ii. 6 we have all the four names, but they are probably not the same persons, for they are there said to be the sons of *Zerah*, and he flourished long before Solomon's time.

Some suppose that בני מחול *beney machol* should be rendered *masters of dancing* or *music*, as מחול *machol* signifies not only a *dance* or *choir*, but also an instrument of *music* of the *pipe* kind. Perhaps a reference is here made to Solomon's skill in *music* and *poetry*, as he is compared to persons who appear to have been eminent *poets* and *musicians*.

Verse 32. *He spake three thousand proverbs*] The book of Proverbs, attributed to Solomon, contains only about *nine hundred* or *nine hundred and twenty-three* distinct proverbs; and if we grant with some that the first *nine chapters* are not the work of Solomon, then all

A.M.2989-3029
B. C. 1015-975
Anno ante I.
Olymp.239-199
and his ᵘsongs were a thousand and five.

33 And he spake of trees, from the cedar tree that *is* in Lebanon even unto the hyssop that springeth out of the wall; he spake also of beasts, and of

fowl, and of creeping things, and of fishes.

A.M.2989-3029
B. C. 1015-975
Anno ante I.
Olymp.239-199

34 And ᵛthere came of all people to hear the wisdom of Solomon, from all kings of the earth, which had heard of his wisdom.

ᵘCant. i. 1

ᵛChap. x. 1; 2 Chron. ix. 1, 23

---

that can be attributed to him is only about *six hundred* and *fifty.*

Of all his *one thousand* and *five songs* or *poems* we have only *one*, the book of Canticles, remaining, unless we include Psa. cxxvii., *Except the Lord build the house*, &c., which in the title is said to be *by* or *for* him, though it appears more properly to be a psalm of *direction*, left him by his father David, relative to the building of the temple.

Verse 33. *He spake of trees—beasts—fowl—creeping things, and of fishes.*] This is a complete system of natural history, as far as relates to the animal and vegetable kingdoms, and the first intimation we have of any thing of the kind: Solomon was probably the first *natural historian* in the world.

O, how must the heart of Tournefort, Ray, Linné, Buffon, Cuvier, Swammerdam, Blosch, and other naturalists, be wrung, to know that these works of Solomon are all and for ever lost! What light should we have thrown on the animal and vegetable kingdoms, had these works been preserved! But the providence of God has not thought fit to preserve them, and succeeding naturalists are left to invent the system which he probably left perfect. If there

be any remains of his wisdom, they must be sought among the orientals, among whom his character is well known, and rates as high as it does with either Jews or Christians. I shall give some extracts from their works relative to Solomon when I come to consider his character at the end of chap. xi.

Verse 34. *There came of all people to hear the wisdom of Solomon*] We learn from chap. x. that the *queen of Sheba* was one of those visitants, and perhaps the most remarkable, as we have the particulars of her visit, but not of the others.

It is astonishing that of a person so renowned for wisdom, so little should be left to prove the truth of a fact of which all the civilized nations of the world have heard, and of which scarcely any man has ever doubted. The people that came from all kings of the earth were probably ambassadors, who came to form and maintain friendship between their sovereigns and the Israelitish king. We cannot understand the place as speaking of people who, either through an idle or laudable curiosity, came to see and converse with Solomon; to give free access to such people would ill comport with the maintenance of his dignity.

CHAPTER V

Hiram, king of Tyre, sends to congratulate Solomon on his accession to the kingdom, 1. Solomon consults him on building a temple for the Lord, and requests his assistance, 2–6. Hiram is pleased, and specifies the assistance which he will afford, 7–9. He sends cedars and fir trees, 10. The return made by Solomon, 11. They form a league, 12. Solomon makes a levy of men in Israel to prepare wood and stones, 13–18.

A. M. 2990
B. C. 1014
An. Exod. Isr.
477
Anno ante
I. Olymp. 238
Aᴺᴰ ᵃHiram king of Tyre sent his servants unto Solomon; for he had heard that they had anointed him king in the room of his father: ᵇfor Hiram was ever a lover of David.

2 And ᶜSolomon sent to Hiram, saying,

3 Thou knowest how that David my father could not build a house unto the name of the Lᴏʀᴅ his God ᵈfor the wars which were about him on every side, until the Lᴏʀᴅ put them under the soles of his feet.

A. M. 2990
B. C. 1014
An. Exod. Isr.
477
Anno ante
I. Olymp. 238

4 But now the Lᴏʀᴅ my God hath given me

ᵃVer. 10, 18; 2 Chron. ii. 3, *Huram*——ᵇ2 Sam. v. 11; 1 Chron. xiv. 1; Amos i. 9

ᶜ2 Chronicles ii. 3——ᵈ1 Chronicles xxii. 8; xxviii. 3

NOTES ON CHAP. V

Verse 1. *Hiram king of Tyre*] It must have been at the beginning of Solomon's reign that these ambassadors were sent; and some suppose that the Hiram mentioned here is different from him who was the friend of David; but there seems no very solid reason for this supposition. As Hiram had intimate alliance with David, and built his palace, 2 Sam. v. 11, he wished to maintain the same good understanding with his son, of whose wisdom he had no doubt heard the most advantageous ac-

counts; and he loved the son because he always loved the father, *for Hiram was ever a lover of David.*

Verse 2. *Solomon sent to Hiram*] Made an interchange of ambassadors and friendly greetings. Josephus tells us that the correspondence between Hiram and Solomon was preserved in the archives of the Tyrians even in his time. But this, like many other assertions of the same author, is worthy of little cerdit.

Verse 4. There is *neither adversary*] אין שטן *eyn satan*, there is no *satan*—no opposer, nor any kind of evil; all is peace and quiet, both

A. M. 2990
B. C. 1014
An. Exod. Isr.
477
Anno ante
I. Olymp. 238

erest on every side, *so that there is* neither adversary nor evil occurrent.

5 fAnd, behold, I gpurpose to build a house unto the name of the LORD my God, has the LORD spake unto David my father, saying, Thy son, whom I will set upon thy throne in thy room, he shall build a house unto my name.

6 Now therefore command thou that they hew me icedar trees out of Lebanon; and my servants shall be with thy servants: and unto thee will I give hire for thy servants according to all that thou shalt kappoint: for thou knowest that *there is* not among us any that can skill to hew timber like unto the Sidonians.

7 And it came to pass, when Hiram heard the words of Solomon, that he rejoiced greatly, and said, Blessed *be* the LORD this day, which hath given unto David a wise son over this great people.

8 And Hiram sent to Solomon, saying, I have lconsidered the things which thou sentest to me for: *and* I will do all thy desire concerning timber of cedar, and concerning timber of fir.

9 My servants shall bring *them* down from Lebanon unto the sea: mand I will convey them by sea in floats unto the place that thou shalt nappoint me, and will cause them to be discharged there, and thou shalt receive *them*: and thou shalt accomplish my desire, oin giving food for my household.

A. M. 2990
B. C. 1014
An. Exod. Isr.
477
Anno ante
I. Olymp. 238

10 So Hiram gave Solomon cedar trees and fir trees *according to* all his desire.

11 pAnd Solomon gave Hiram twenty thousand qmeasures of wheat *for* food to his household, and twenty measures of pure oil: thus gave Solomon to Hiram year by year.

12 And the LORD gave Solomon wisdom ras he promised him: and there was peace between Hiram and Solomon; and they two made a league together.

---

eChap. iv. 24; 2 Chron. xxii. 9——f2 Chron. ii. 4
gHeb. *say*——h2 Sam. vii. 13; 1 Chron. xvii. 12; xxii. 10
i2 Chron. ii. 8, 10——kHeb. *say*

lHeb. *heard*——m2 Chron. ii. 16——nHeb. *send*
oSee Ezra iii. 7; Ezek. xxvii. 17; Acts xii. 20——pSee
2 Chron. ii. 10——qHeb. *cors*——rChap. iii. 12

---

without and within. God has given me this quiet that I may build his temple. *Deus nobis hœc otia fecit.*

Verse 5. *A house unto the name of the Lord*] The name of God is God himself. I purpose to build a house to that infinite and eternal Being called *Jehovah.*

Verse 6. *Any that can skill to hew timber*] An obsolete and barbarous expression for *any that know how to cut timber.* They had neither *sawyers, carpenters, joiners,* nor *builders* among them, equal to the Sidonians. Sidon was a part of the territories of Hiram, and its inhabitants appear to have been the most expert workmen. It requires more skill to *fell* and prepare timber than is generally supposed. *Vitruvius* gives some rules relative to this, lib. ii., cap. 9, the sum of which is this: 1. Trees should be felled in autumn, or in the winter, and in the wane of the moon; for in this season the trees recover their vigour and solidity, which was dispersed among their leaves, and exhausted by their fruit, in spring and summer; they will then be free from a certain moisture, very apt to engender worms and rot them, which in autumn and winter is consumed and dried up. 2. Trees should not be cut down *at once;* they should be cut carefully round towards the pith, that the sap may drop down and distil away, and thus left till thoroughly dry, and then cut down entirely. 3. When fully dried, a tree should not be exposed to the south sun, high winds, and rain; and should be smeared over with cow-dung to prevent its splitting. 4. It should never be drawn through the dew, but be removed in the afternoon. 5. It is not fit for floors, doors, or windows, till it has been felled three years. Perhaps these directions,

attended to, would prevent the dry rot. And we see from them that there is considerable skill required to *hew timber,* and in this the Sidonians excelled. We do every thing in a hurry, and our building is good for nothing.

Verse 7. *Blessed* be *the Lord this day*] From this, and indeed from every part of Hiram's conduct, it is evident that he was a worshipper of the true God; unless, as was the case with many of the heathens, he supposed that every country had its own god, and every god his own country, and he thanked the God of Israel that he had given so wise a prince to govern those whom he considered his friends and allies: but the first opinion seems to be the most correct.

Verse 9. *Shall bring* them *down from Lebanon unto the sea*] As the river *Adonis* was in the vicinity of the forest of Lebanon, and emptied itself into the Mediterranean sea, near *Biblos,* Hiram could transport the timber all squared, and not only cut to scantling, but cut so as to occupy the place it was intended for in the building, without any farther need of axe or saw. It might be readily sent down the coast on rafts and landed at *Joppa,* or Jamnia, just opposite to Jerusalem, **at the** distance of about *twenty-five* miles. See 2 Chron. ii. 16. The carriage could not be great, as the timber was all fitted for the building where it was hewn down. The materials had only to be put together when they arrived at Jerusalem. See chap. vi. 7.

Verse 11. *And Solomon gave Hiram, &c.*] The information in this verse of the annual stipend paid to Hiram, is *deficient,* and must be supplied out of 2 Chron. ii. 10. Here *twenty thousand* measures of wheat, and *twenty meas-*

A. M. 2990
B. C. 1014
An. Exod. Isr.
477
Anno ante
I. Olymp. 238

13 And King Solomon raised a [s]levy out of all Israel; and the levy was thirty thousand men. 14 And he sent them to Lebanon, ten thousand a month by courses: a month they were in Lebanon, *and* two months at home: and [t]Adoniram *was* over the levy.

15 [u]And Solomon had threescore and ten thousand that bare burdens, and fourscore thousand hewers in the mountains;

16 Besides the chief of Solomon's officers which *were* over the work, three thousand and three hundred, which ruled over the people that wrought in the work.

A. M. 2990
B. C. 1014
An. Exod. Isr.
477
Anno ante
I. Olymp. 238

17 And the king commanded, and they brought great stones, costly stones, *and* [v]hewed stones, to lay the foundation of the house.

18 And Solomon's builders and Hiram's builders did hew *them,* and the [w]stone-squarers: so they prepared timber and stones to build the house.

---

[s]Heb. *tribute* of men——[t]Chap. iv. 6——[u]Chap. ix. 21; 2 Chron. ii. 17, 18

[v]1 Chronicles xxii. 2——[w]Or, *Giblites,* as Ezekiel xxvii. 9

---

ures of pure oil, is all that is promised: there, *twenty thousand* measures of beaten wheat, *twenty thousand* measures of barley, *twenty thousand* baths of wine, and *twenty thousand* baths of oil, is the stipulation; unless we suppose the first to be for Hiram's own family, the latter for his workmen. Instead of *twenty* measures of oil, the Syriac, Arabic, and Septuagint, have *twenty thousand* measures, as in Chronicles. In 2 Chron., instead of *cors* of oil, it is *baths.* The *bath* was a measure much less than the *cor.*

Verse 13. *The levy was thirty thousand men.*] We find from the following verse that only *ten* thousand were employed at once, and those only for one month at a time; and having rested two months, they again resumed their labour. These were the persons over whom Adoniram was superintendent, and were all Israelites.

Verse 15. *Threescore and ten thousand that bare burdens*] These were all *strangers,* or *proselytes,* dwelling among the Israelites; as we learn from the parallel place, 2 Chron. ii. 17, 18.

Verse 16. *Besides—three thousand and three hundred which ruled over the people*] In the

parallel place, 2 Chron. ii. 18, it is *three thousand six hundred.* The Septuagint has here the same number.

Verse 17. *Great stones*] Stones of very large dimensions.

Costly stones] Stones that cost much labour and time to cut them out of the rock.

Hewed stones] Everywhere squared and polished.

Verse 18. *And the stone-squarers*] Instead of *stone-squarers* the *margin* very properly reads *Giblites,* הגבלים *haggiblim;* and refers to Ezek. xxvii. 9, where we find the inhabitants of *Gebal* celebrated for their knowledge in *ship-building.* Some suppose that these *Giblites* were the inhabitants of *Biblos,* at the foot of Mount Libanus, northward of Sidon, on the coast of the Mediterranean Sea; famous for its wines; and now called *Gaeta.* Both *Ptolemy* and *Stephanus Byzantinus* speak of a town called *Gebala,* to the east of Tyre: but this was different from *Gebal,* or *Biblos.* It seems more natural to understand this of a *people* than of *stone-squarers,* though most of the versions have adopted this idea which we follow in the text.

CHAPTER VI

In the four hundred and eightieth year from the exodus, in the fourth year of Solomon's reign, and in the second month, he laid the foundations of the temple; the length sixty cubits, the breadth twenty, and the height thirty cubits; besides the porch, which was twenty cubits in length, and ten cubits in height, 1-3. A description of its different external parts, 4-10. God's promise to Solomon, 11-13. Description of its interna' parts and contents, 14-36. Temple finished in the eighth month of the eleventh year of Solomon's reign, being seven years in building, 37, 38.

A. M. 2993
B. C. 1011
An. Exod. Isr.
480
Anno ante
I. Olymp. 235

AND [a]it came to pass in the four hundred and eightieth year after the children of Israel were come out of the land of Egypt, in the fourth year of Solomon's reign over Israel, in the month Zif, which *is* the second month, that [b]he [c]began

A. M. 2993
B. C. 1011
An. Exod. Isr.
480
Anno ante
I. Olymp. 235

---

[a]2 Chron. iii. 1, 2

[b]Acts vii. 47——[c]Heb. *built*

NOTES ON CHAP. VI

Verse 1. *In the four hundred and eightieth year*] The *Septuagint* has the *four hundred and fortieth* year. It need scarcely be noticed, that among chronologists there is a great difference of opinion concerning this epocha. *Glycas* has 330 years; *Melchior Canus,* 590 years; *Josephus,* 592 years; *Sulpicius Severus,* 588; *Clemens Alexandrinus,* 570; *Cedrenus,* 672;

Codomanus, 598; *Vossius* and *Capellus,* 580; *Serarius,* 680; *Nicholas Abraham,* 527; *Mæstlinus,* 592; *Petavius* and *Valtherus,* 520. Here are more than a dozen different opinions; and after all, that in the common Hebrew text is as likely to be the true one as any of the others.

The month Zif] This answers to a part of our April and May; and was the second month of the *sacred year,* but the eighth month of the civil year. Before the time of Solomon, the

A. M. 2993
B. C. 1011
An. Exod. Isr.
480
Anno ante
I. Olymp. 235
to build the house of the LORD.

2 And ᵈthe house which King Solomon built for the LORD, the length thereof *was* threescore cubits, and the breadth thereof twenty *cubits,* and the height thereof thirty cubits.

3 And the porch before the temple of the house, twenty cubits *was* the length thereof, according to the breadth of the house; *and* ten cubits *was* the breadth thereof before the house.

4 And for the house he made ᵉwindows ᶠof narrow lights.

5 And ᵍagainst the wall of the house he built ʰchambers ⁱround about, *against* the walls of the house round about, *both* of the temple ᵏand of the oracle: and he made ˡchambers round about:

6 The nethermost chamber *was* five cubits broad, and the middle *was* six cubits broad, and the third *was* seven cubits broad: for without *in the wall* of the house he made ᵐnarrowed rests round about, that *the beams* should not be fastened in the walls of the house.

7 And ⁿthe house, when it was in building, was built of stone made ready before it was brought thither: so that there was neither hammer nor axe *nor* any tool of iron heard in the house, while it was in building.

8 The door for the middle chamber *was* in the right ᵒside of the house: and they went up with winding stairs into the middle *chamber,* and out of the middle into the third.

A. M. 2993
B. C. 1011
An. Exod. Isr.
480
Anno ante
I. Olymp. 235

ᵈSee Ezek. xli. 1, &c.——ᵉSee Ezek. xl. 16; xli. 16
ᶠOr, *windows broad* within, and *narrow* without; or *skewed* and *closed*——ᵍOr, *upon* or *joining to*

ʰSee Ezek. xli. 6——ⁱHeb. *floors*——ᵏVer. 16, 19, 20, 21, 31——ˡHeb. *ribs*——ᵐHeb. *narrowings* or *rebatements*
ⁿSee Deut. xxvii. 5, 6; chap. v. 18——ᵒHeb. *shoulder*

Jews do not appear to have had any *names* for their months, but mentioned them in the order of their consecutive occurrence, *first* month, *second* month, *third* month, &c. In this chapter we find *Zif* and *Bul;* and in ch. viii. ver. 2, we find another, *Ethanim;* and these are supposed to be borrowed from the Chaldeans; and consequently this book was written after the Babylonish captivity. Before this time we find only the word *Abib* mentioned as the name of a month, Exod. xiii. 4. Whether there were any others at that time, or whether *Abib* were really intended as the *name* of a month, we cannot absolutely say. The present names of the Hebrew months are:—*Tisri,* answering to a part of *September* and *October, Marchesvan, Cisleu, Tebeth, Shebat, Adar, Nisan, Ijar, Sivan, Tamuz, Ab,* and *Elul.*

Verse 2. *The length thereof* was *threescore cubits*] A cubit, according to Bishop Cumberland, is 21 inches, and 888 decimals, or 1 foot, 9 inches, and 888 decimals.

	Yds.	Ft.	Inch.
According to this, the length, 60 cubits, was	36	1	5.28
The breadth, 20 cubits, was	12	0	5.76
The height, 30 cubits, was	18	0	8.64

This constituted what was called the *temple* or *house,* the *house of God,* &c. But, besides this, there were *courts* and *colonnades,* where the people might assemble to perform their devotions and assist at the sacrifices, without being exposed to the open air. The court surrounded the temple, or holy place, into which the priests alone entered. Sometimes the whole of the building is called the *temple;* at other times that, the measurement of which is given above. But as no proper account can be given of such a building in *notes;* and as there is a great variety of opinion concerning the temple, its structure, ornaments, &c., as mentioned in the books of *Kings* and *Chronicles,* in *Ezekiel,* and by *Josephus;* and as modern writers, such as *Vilalpandus,* Dr. *Lightfoot,* and Dr. *Prideaux,*

professing to be guided by the same principles, have produced very different buildings; I think it best to hazard nothing on the subject, but give that description at the end of the chapter which Calmet with great pains and industry has collected: at the same time, pledging myself to no particular *form* or *appearance,* as I find I cannot give any thing as the *likeness of Solomon's temple* which I could say, either in honour or conscience, bears any affinity to it. For other particulars I must refer the reader to the three large volumes of *Vilalpandus,* Dr. *Lightfoot's* Works, and to the *Connections of Dr. Prideaux.*

Verse 4. *Windows of narrow lights.*] The *Vulgate* says, *fenestras obliquas,* oblique windows; but what sort of windows could such be?

The Hebrew is חלוני שקפים אטמים *challoney shekuphim atumim, windows to look through, which shut.* Probably latticed windows: windows through which a person within could see well; but a person without, nothing. *Windows,* says the Targum, *which were open within and shut without.* Does he mean *windows* with *shutters;* or, are we to understand, with the Arabic, windows opening wide within, and narrow on the outside; such as we still see in ancient castles? This sense our *margin* expresses. We hear nothing of *glass* or any other *diaphanous* substance. Windows, perhaps originally *windore,* a *door* to let the *wind* in, in order to *ventilate* the building, and through which external objects might be discerned.

Verse 7. *The house—was built of stone*] It appears that every *stone* was hewn and squared, and its place in the building ascertained, before it came to Jerusalem: the *timbers* were fitted in like manner. This greatly lessened the trouble and expense of carriage. On this account, that all was prepared at Mount Lebanon, *there was neither hammer, axe, nor any tool of iron heard in the building;* nothing except mallets to drive the tenons into the mortices, and drive in the pins to fasten them, was neces-

A. M. 3000
B. C. 1004
Ante I. Ol. 228
An. Archippi, Arch. Athen. perpet. 9

9 [p]So he built the house, and finished it; and covered the house [q]with beams and boards of cedar.

10 And *then* he built chambers against all the house, five cubits high: and they rested on the house with timber of cedar.

11 And the word of the LORD came to Solomon, saying,

12 *Concerning* this house which thou art in building, [r]if thou wilt walk in my statutes, and execute my judgments, and keep all my commandments to walk in them; then will I perform my word with thee, [s]which I spake unto David thy father.

13 And [t]I will dwell among the children of Israel, and will not [u]forsake my people Israel.

A.M.2993-3000
B.C.1011-1004
Anno ante I. Olymp.235-228

14 [v]So Solomon built the house, and finished it.

15 And he built the walls of the house within with boards of cedar, [w]both the floor of the house, and the walls of the ceiling: *and* he covered *them* on the inside with wood, and covered the floor of the house with planks of fir.

16 And he built twenty cubits on the sides of the house, both the floor and the walls with boards of cedar: he even built *them* for it within, *even* for the oracle, *even* for the [x]most holy *place*.

17 And the house, that *is*, the temple before it, was forty cubits *long*.

A.M.2993-3000
B.C.1011-1004
Anno ante I. Olymp.235-228

18 And the cedar of the house within *was* carved with [y]knops and [z]open flowers: all *was* cedar; there was no stone seen.

19 And the oracle he prepared in the house within, to set there the ark of the covenant of the LORD.

20 And the oracle in the forepart *was* twenty cubits in length, and twenty cubits in breadth, and twenty cubits in the height thereof: and he overlaid it with [a]pure gold; and *so* covered the altar *which was of* cedar.

21 So Solomon overlaid the house within with pure gold: and he made a partition by the chains of gold before the oracle; and he overlaid it with gold.

22 And the whole house he overlaid with gold, until he had finished all the house; also [b]the whole altar that *was* by the oracle he overlaid with gold.

23 And within the oracle [c]he made two cherubims *of* [d]olive tree, [e]*each* ten cubits high.

24 And five cubits *was* the one wing of the cherub, and five cubits the other wing of the cherub: from the uttermost part of the one wing unto the uttermost part of the other *were* ten cubits.

25 And the other cherub *was* ten cubits; both the cherubims *were* of one measure and one size.

26 The height of the one cherub *was* ten cubits, and so *was it* of the other cherub.

---

[p]Ver. 14, 38——[q]Or, *the vault beams and the ceilings with cedar*——[r]Chap. ii. 4; ix. 4——[s]2 Sam. vii. 13; 1 Chron. xxii. 10——[t]Exod. xxv. 8; Lev. xxvi. 11; 2 Cor. vi. 16; Rev. xxi. 3——[u]Deut. xxxi. 6——[v]Ver. 38 [w]Or, *from the floor of the house unto the walls*, &c., and so ver. 16

[x]Exod. xxvi. 33; Lev. xvi. 2; chapter viii. 6; 2 Chron. iii. 8; Ezek. xlv. 3; Hebrews ix. 3——[y]Or, *gourds* [z]Hebrew, *openings of flowers*——[a]Hebrew, *shut up* [b]Exodus xxx. 1, 3, 6——[c]Exodus xxxvii. 7, 8, 9; 2 Chronicles iii. 10, 11, 12——[d]Or, *oily*——[e]Hebrew, *trees of oil*

---

sary: therefore there was no noise. But *why* is this so particularly marked? Is it not because the temple was a type of the kingdom of God; and the souls of men are to be prepared *here* for *that* place of blessedness? *There*, there is no preaching, exhortations, repentance, ears, cries, nor prayers; the stones must be all squared and fitted here for their place in the New Jerusalem; and, being *living stones*, must be built up a holy temple for a habitation of God through the Spirit.

Verse 9. *Covered the house with beams and boards of cedar.*] The Eastern custom is very different from ours: we *ceil* with *plaster*, and make our *floors* of *wood;* they make their *floors* of *plaster* or *painted tiles*, and make their *ceilings* of *wood.* But it may not be improper to observe that, in ancient times, our buildings were somewhat similar. Westminster Hall is a proof of this.

Verse 11. *The word of the Lord came to Solomon*] Some think that this is the same revelation as that mentioned chap. ix. 2, &c., which took place *after* the dedication of the temple: but to me it appears different; it was a word to encourage him *while* building; to warn him against apostacy, and to assure him of God's continued protection of him and his family, if they continued faithful to the grace which God had given.

Verse 15. *The walls of the ceiling*] See the note on ver. 9.

Verse 19. *The oracle he prepared*] See the description of the temple at the end of this chapter.

Verse 22. *The whole house he overlaid with gold*] It is impossible to calculate this expense, or the quantity of gold employed in this sacred building.

Verse 26. *The height of the one cherub* was *ten cubits*] Concerning the cherubs, their form, &c., see my note on Exod. xxv. 18. The

A.M.2993-3000
B.C.1011-1004
Anno ante I.
Olymp.235-228
27 And he set the cherubims within the inner house: and [f]they [g]stretched forth the wings of the cherubims, so that the wing of the one touched the *one* wall, and the wing of the other cherub touched the other wall; and their wings touched one another in the midst of the house.

28 And he overlaid the cherubims with gold.

29 And he carved all the walls of the house round about with carved figures of cherubims and palm trees and [h]open flowers, within and without.

30 And the floor of the house he overlaid with gold, within and without.

31 And for the entering of the oracle he made doors *of* olive tree: the lintel *and* side posts *were* [i]a fifth part *of the wall.*

32 The [k]two doors also *were of* olive tree; and he carved upon them carvings of cherubims and palm trees and [l]open flowers, and

overlaid *them* with gold, and spread gold upon the cherubims, and upon the palm trees.

A.M.2993-3000
B.C.1011-1044
Anno ante I.
Olymp.235-228

33 So also made he for the door of the temple posts *of* olive tree, [m]a fourth part *of the wall.*

34 And the two doors *were of* fir tree: the [n]two leaves of the one door *were* folding, and the two leaves of the other door *were* folding.

35 And he carved *thereon* cherubims and palm trees and open flowers: and covered *them* with gold fitted upon the carved work.

36 And he built the inner court with three rows of hewed stones, and a row of cedar beams.

37 [o]In the fourth year was the foundation of the house of the LORD laid, in the month Zif:

38 And in the eleventh year, in the month Bul, which *is* the eighth month, was the house finished [p]throughout all the parts thereof, and according to all the fashion of it. So was he [q]seven years in building it.

---

[f]Exodus xxv. 20; xxxvii. 9; 2 Chronicles v. 8——[g]Or, *the cherubims stretched forth their wings*——[h]Heb. *openings of flowers*——[i]Or, *five square*——[k]Or, *leaves of the door*

[l]Hebrew, *openings of flowers*——[m]Or, *four square*——[n]Ezek. xli. 23, 24, 25——[o]Ver. 1-——[p]Or, *with all the appurtenances thereof, and with all the ordinances thereof*——[q]Comp. ver. 1

---

height of each cherub was about *eighteen feet and three inches.*

Verse 36. *Three rows of hewed stone, and a row of cedar beams.*] Does not this intimate that there were three courses of stone, and then one course of timber all through this wall? Three strata of stone and one stratum of timber, and so on. If so, could such a building be very durable? This is also referred to in the succeeding chapter, ver. 11; and as both the temple and Solomon's house were built in the same manner, we may suppose that this was the ordinary way in which the better sort of buildings were constructed. Calmet thinks that to this mode of building the prophet alludes, Hab. ii. 11: *The stone shall cry out of the wall, and the beam out of the timber shall answer it.* But it should be observed that this was in the *inner* court, and therefore the timber was not exposed to the weather. The *outer* court does not appear to have been built stratum super stratum of stone and wood.

Verse 38. *In the eleventh year—was the house finished*] It is rather strange that this house required *seven* years and about six months to put all the stones and the timbers in their places, for we have already seen that they were all prepared before they came to Jerusalem; but the ornamenting, gilding, or overlaying with gold, making the carved work, cherubim, trees, flowers, &c., must have consumed a considerable time. The month *Bul* answers to a part of our *October* and *November*, as *Zif*, in which it was begun, answers to a part of *April* and *May*.

The *dedication* did not take place till the following year, the twelfth of Solomon, because then, according to Archbishop Usher, the jubilee happened.

So was he seven years in building it.] Prop-

erly seven years and six months; but the Scripture generally expresses things in *round numbers.*

DIANA's temple at Ephesus was one of the seven wonders of the world. It is said that almost all Asia was employed in the building of it for about *two hundred* years; but it was certainly more extensive than the temple at Jerusalem, for it may be justly questioned, notwithstanding the profusion of gold, silver, precious stones, &c., employed in the temple of Solomon, whether it cost any thing like the money expended on the temple of Diana.

Pliny informs us, *Hist. Nat.*, lib. xxxvi., cap. 12, that, in order to build one of the pyramids in Egypt, no less than *three hundred and sixty thousand* men were employed for the space of *twenty years.* But neither was the temple any such work as this. We may also observe that the temple was never intended to hold a vast concourse of people; it was only for the service of the Lord, and the priests were those alone who were employed in it. The courts, chambers, and other apartments, were far more extensive than the temple itself; it was never designed to be a place to worship *in*, but a place to worship *at.* There God was known to have a peculiar residence, and before him the tribes came, and the priests were a sort of mediators between him and the people. In short, the *temple* was to the *Jews* in the *promised land* what the *tabernacle* was to the *Hebrews* in the *wilderness;* the place where God's honour dwelt, and whither the people flocked to pay their adoration.

"Solomon laid the foundation of the temple in the year of the world 2992, before *Christ* 1008, before the vulgar era, 1012; and it was finished in the year of the world 3000, and dedicated in 3001, before Christ 999, before the vulgar era 1003; 1 Kings viii.; 2 Chron. v., vii., viii. The place that was pitched on for erecting this magnificent structure was on the side of Mount *Sion* called Moriah. Its entrance or frontispiece stood towards the east, and the most holy or most retired part was towards the west. The author of the first book of Kings, and of the second of Chronicles has chiefly made it his business to describe the *temple* properly so called, that is the sanctuary, the sanctum, and the apartments belonging to them, as also the vessels, the implements, and the ornaments of the temple, without giving any description scarcely of the courts and open areas, which, however, made a principal part of the grandeur of this august edifice.

"But *Ezekiel* has supplied this defect by the exact plan he has delineated of these necessary parts. Indeed it must be owned that the temple as described by *Ezekiel* was never restored after the captivity of *Babylon*, according to the model and the mensuration that this prophet has given of it. But as the measures he sets down for the sanctum and the sanctuary are, within a small matter, the same as those of the temple of Solomon; and as this prophet, who was himself a priest, had seen the first temple; it is to be supposed that the description he gives us of the temple of *Jerusalem* is the same as that of the temple of Solomon.

"The ground-plot upon which the temple was built was a square of six hundred cubits, or twenty-five thousand royal feet; Ezek. xlv. This space was encompassed with a wall of the height of six cubits, and of the same breadth. Beyond this wall was the court of the *Gentiles*, being fifty cubits wide. After this was seen a great wall, which encompassed the whole court of the children of *Israel*. This wall was a square of five hundred cubits. The court of *Israel* was a hundred cubits square, and was encompassed all round with magnificent galleries supported by two or three rows of pillars. It had four gates or entrances; one to the east, another to the west, a third to the north, and the fourth to the south. They were all of the same form and largeness, and each had an ascent of seven steps. The court was paved with marble of divers colours, and had no covering; but the people in case of need could retire under the galleries that were all round about. These apartments were to lodge the priests in, and to lay up such things as were necessary for the use of the temple. There were but three ways to come in, to the east, to the north, and to the south, and they went to it by an ascent of eight steps. Before, and over against the gate of the court of the priests, in the court of Israel, was erected a throne for the king, being a magnificent alcove, where the king seated himself when he came into the temple. Within the court of the priests, and over against the same eastern gate, was the altar of burnt-offerings, of twelve cubits square, according to Ezek. xliii. 16, or of ten cubits high and twenty broad, according to 2 Chron. iv. 1. They went up to it by stairs on the eastern side.

"Beyond this, and to the west of the altar of burnt-offerings was the temple, properly so called, that is to say, the *sanctuary*, the *sanctum*, and the *porch of entrance*. The porch was twenty cubits wide and six cubits deep. Its gate was fourteen cubits wide. The sanctum was forty cubits wide and twenty deep.

There stood the golden candlestick, the table of shew-bread, and the golden altar, upon which the incense was offered. The sanctuary was a square of twenty cubits. There was nothing in the sanctuary but the ark of the covenant, which included the tables of the law. The high priest entered here but once a year, and none but himself was allowed to enter. *Solomon* had embellished the inside of this holy place with palm trees in relief, and cherubim of wood covered with plates of gold, and in general the whole sanctuary was adorned, and as it were overlaid, with plates of gold.

"Round the sanctum and sanctuary were three stories of chambers, to the number of thirty-three. *Ezekiel* makes them but four cubits wide; but the first book of Kings, vi. 6, allows five cubits to the first story, six to the second, and seven to the third.

"Since the consecration or dedication of the temple by Solomon in the year of the world 3001, this edifice has suffered many revolutions, which it is proper to take notice of here.

"In the year of the world 3033, before Christ 967, before the vulgar era 971, *Shishak*, king of Egypt, having declared war with Rehoboam, king of Judah, took Jerusalem, and carried away the treasures of the temple; 1 Kings xiv.; 2 Chron. xii.

"In 3146, *Jehoash*, king of *Judah*, got silver together to go upon the repairs of the temple; they began to work upon it in earnest in 3148, before Christ 852, before the vulgar era 856; 2 Kings xii. 4, 5, and 2 Chron. xxiv. 7, 8, 9, &c.

"*Ahaz* king of Judah, having called to his assistance *Tiglath-pileser*, king of Assyria, against the kings of Israel and *Damascus*, who were at war with him, robbed the temple of the Lord of its riches to give away to this strange king, 2 Chron. xxviii. 21, 22, &c., in the year of the world 3264, before Christ 736, before the vulgar era 740; and not contented with this, he profaned this holy place by setting up there an altar like one he had seen at Damascus, and taking away the brazen altar that Solomon had made; 2 Kings xvi. 10, 11, 12, &c. He also took away the brazen sea from off the brazen oxen that supported it, and the brazen basons from their pedestals, and the king's throne or oratory, which was of brass. These he took away to prevent their being carried away by the king of *Assyria*. Nor did he stop here, but carried his wickedness so far as to sacrifice to strange gods, and to erect profane altars in all the corners of the streets of Jerusalem; 2 Chron. xxviii. 24, 25. He pillaged the temple of the Lord, broke the sacred vessels, and, lastly, shut up the house of God. This happened in the year of the world 3264, before Christ 736, before the vulgar era 740, to his death, which happened in 3278, before Christ 722, before the vulgar era 726.

"*Hezekiah*, the son and successor of Ahaz, opened again and repaired the gates of the temple which his father had shut up and robbed of their ornaments; 2 Chron. xxix. 3, 4, &c., in the year of the world 3278, before Christ 722, before the vulgar era 726. He restored the worship of the Lord and the sacrifices, and made new sacred vessels in the place of those that Ahaz had destroyed. But in the fourteenth year of his reign, 2 Kings xviii. 15, 16, in the year of the world 3291, before Christ 709, before the vulgar era 713, *Sennacherib*, king of *Assyria*, coming with an army into the land of *Judah*, *Hezekiah* was forced to take all the riches of the temple, and even the plates of gold that he himself had put upon the gates of the temple, and give them to the king of *Assyria*. But when Sennacherib was gone back into his own country, there is no doubt that Hezekiah restored all these things to their first condition.

"*Manasseh*, son and successor of *Hezekiah*, profaned the temple of the Lord, by setting up altars to all the host of heaven, even in the courts of the house of the Lord; 2 Kings xxi. 4, 5, 6, 7; 2 Chron. xxxiii. 5, 6, 7; in the year of the world 3306, and the following years. He set up *idols* there, and worshipped them. God delivered him into the hands of the king of *Babylon*, who loaded him with chains, and carried him away beyond the Euphrates; 2 Chron. xxxiii. 11, 12, &c.; in the year of the world 3328, before Christ 672, before the vulgar era 676. There he acknowledged and repented of his sins; and being sent back to his own dominions, he redressed the profanations he had made of the temple of the Lord, by taking away the idols, destroying the profane altars, and restoring the altar of burnt-offering, upon which he offered his sacrifices.

"*Josiah*, king of Judah, laboured with all his might in repairing the edifices of the temple, (2 Kings xxii. 4, 5, 6, &c.; 2 Chron. xxxiv. 8-10; in the year of the world 3380, before Christ 620, before the vulgar era 624,) which had been either neglected or demolished by the kings of *Judah*, his predecessors. He also commanded the priests and Levites to replace the ark of the Lord in the sanctuary, in its appointed place; and ordered that it should not any more be removed from place to place as it had been during the reigns of the wicked kings, his predecessors, 2 Chron. xxxv. 3.

"*Nebuchadnezzar* took away a part of the sacred vessels of the temple of the Lord, and placed them in the temple of his god at *Babylon*, under the reign of Jehoiakim, king of Judah; 2 Chron. xxxvi. 6, 7, in the year of the world 3398, before Christ 602, before the vulgar era 606. He also carried away others under the reign of Jehoiachin, 2 Chron. xxxvi. 10; in the year of the world 3405, before Christ 595, before the vulgar era 599. Lastly, he took the city of Jerusalem, and entirely destroyed the temple, in the eleventh year of Zedekiah, in the year of the world 3416, before Christ 584, before the vulgar era 588; 2 Kings xxv. 1, 2, 3, &c.; 2 Chron. xxxvi. 18, 19.

"The temple continued buried in its ruins for the space of fifty-two years, till the first year of *Cyrus* at Babylon, in the year of the world 3468, before Christ 532, before the vulgar era 536. Then Cyrus gave permission to the Jews to return to Jerusalem, and there to rebuild the temple of the Lord, Ezra i. 1, 2, 3, &c. The following year they laid the foundation of the second temple; but they had hardly been at work upon it one year, when either Cyrus or his officers, being gained over by the enemies of the Jews, forbade them to go on with their work; Ezra iv. 5; in the year of the world 3470, before Christ 530, before the vulgar era 534. After the death of *Cyrus* and *Cambyses*, they were again forbidden by the magian, who reigned after Cambyses, and whom the Scripture calls by the name of Artaxerxes; Ezra iv. 7, 17, 18, &c.; in the year of the world 3483, before Christ 517, before the vulgar era 521. Lastly, these prohibitions being superseded, under the reign of Darius, son

of *Hystaspes*, (Ezra v. 1; vi. 14; Hag. i. 1, &c.; in the year of the world 3485, before Christ 515, before the vulgar era 519,) the temple was finished and dedicated four years after, in the year of the world 3489, before Christ 511, before the vulgar era 515, twenty years after the return from the captivity.

"This temple was profaned by order of *Antiochus Epiphanes* in the year of the world 3837. The ordinary sacrifices were discontinued therein, and the idol of *Jupiter Olympus* was set up upon the altar. It continued in this condition for three years; then *Judas Maccabeus* purified it, and restored the sacrifice and the worship of the Lord, 1 Mac. iv. 36; in the year of the world 3840, before Christ 160, before the vulgar era 164.

"*Herod* the Great undertook to rebuild the whole temple of Jerusalem anew, in the eighteenth year of his reign, and in the year of the world 3986; *Joseph.*, Antiq., lib. xv., cap. 14. He began to lay the foundation of it in the year of the world 3987, forty-six years before the first passover of *Jesus Christ*, as the Jews observe to him by saying, *Forty and six years was this temple in building, and wilt thou rear it up in three days?* John ii. 20. This is not saying that *Herod* had employed six and forty years in building it; for *Josephus* assures us that he finished it in nine years and a half; *Joseph.*, Antiq., lib. xv., cap. 14. But, after the time of this prince, they all continued to make some new addition to it; and the same *Josephus* tells us that they went on working upon it, even to the beginning of the Jewish war; *Joseph.*, Antiq., lib. xx., cap. 8.

"This temple, built by *Herod*, did not subsist more than seventy-seven years, being destroyed in the year of the world 4073, of Christ 73, of the vulgar era 69. It was begun by *Herod* in 3987, finished in 3996, burnt and destroyed by the Romans in 4073.

"This temple of *Herod* was very different from that of *Solomon*, and from that which was rebult by *Zerubbabel* after the captivity. This is the description that *Josephus* has left us of it, who himself had seen it:—

"The temple, properly so called, was built sixty cubits high, and as many broad; but there were two sides of front, like two arms or shoulderings, which advanced twenty cubits on each side, which gave in the whole front a hundred cubits wide, as well as in height. The stones made use of in this building were white and hard, twenty-five cubits long, eight in height, and twelve in width; *Joseph.*, de Bell., lib. vi., p. 917.

"The front of this magnificent building resembled that of a royal palace. The two extremes of each face were lower than the middle, which middle was so exalted that those who were over against the temple, or that approached towards it at a distance, might see it, though they were many furlongs from it. The gates were almost of the same height as the temple; and on the top of the gates were veils or tapestry of several colours, embellished with purple flowers. On the two sides of the doors were two pillars, the cornices of which were adorned with the branches of a golden vine, which hung down with their grapes and clusters, and were so well imitated, that art did not at all yield to nature. *Herod* made very large and very high galleries about the temple, which were suitable to the magnificence of the rest of the building, and exceeded in beauty and sumptuousness all of the kind that had been seen before.

"The temple was built upon a very irregular mountain, and at first there was hardly place enough on the top of it for the site of the temple and altar. The rest of it was steep and sloping: *Joseph.*, de Bell, lib. vi., p. 915, εκφιδ.; Antiq., lib. xv., c. 14. But when King *Solomon* built it, he raised a wall towards the east, to support the earth on that side; and after this side was filled up, he then built one of the porticoes or galleries. At that time this face only was cased with stone, but in succeeding times, the people endeavouring to enlarge this space, and the top of the mountain being much extended, they broke down the wall which was on the north side, and enclosed another space as large as that which the whole

circumference of the temple contained at first. So that at last, against all hope and expectation, this work was carried so far that the whole mountain was surrounded by a treble wall. But, for the completing of this great work whole ages were no more than sufficient; and all the sacred treasures were applied to this use, that the devotion of the people had brought to the temple from all the provinces of the world. In some places these walls were above three hundred cubits high, and the stones used in these walls were some forty cubits long. They were fastened together by iron cramps and lead, to be able to resist the injuries of time. The platform on which the temple was built was a furlong square, or one hundred and twenty-five paces." Thus far *Calmet* and *Josephus.*

CHAPTER VII

Solomon builds his own house, and completes it in thirteen *years, 1. He builds another called the house of the forest of Lebanon; and a house for Pharaoh's daughter, 2–12. He brings Hiram, a coppersmith, out of Tyre, who makes much curious work for the temple, 13–20. He makes the two pillars Jachin and Boaz, 21, 22. The molten sea, and the twelve oxen that bare it, 23–26. And ten brazen bases, and the ten lavers, with pots, shovels, and basons, all of which he cast in the plain of Jordan, 27–46. The quantity of brass too great to be weighed; and the vessels of the temple were all of pure gold, 47–50. Solomon brings into the house the silver and gold which his father had dedicated, 51.*

A. M. 3000-3013
B. C. 1004-991
Anno ante I.
Olymp. 228-215

BUT Solomon was building his own house [a]thirteen years, and he finished all his house.

2 He built also the house of the forest of Lebanon; the length thereof *was* a hundred cubits, and the breadth thereof fifty cubits, and the height thereof thirty cubits, upon four rows of cedar pillars, with cedar beams upon the pillars.

3 And *it was* covered with cedar above upon the [b]beams, that *lay* on forty-five pillars, fifteen *in* a row.

4 And *there were* windows *in* three rows, and [c]light *was* against light *in* three ranks.

5 And all the [d]doors and posts *were* square, with the windows: and light *was* against light *in* three ranks.

6 And he made a porch of pillars; the length thereof *was* fifty cubits, and the breadth thereof thirty cubits: and the porch *was* [e]before them: and the *other* pillars and the thick beam *were* [f]before them.

A. M. 3000-3013
B. C. 1004-991
Anno ante I.
Olymp. 228-215

7 Then he made a porch for the throne where he might judge, *even* the porch of judgment: and *it was* covered with cedar [g]from one side of the floor to the other.

8 And his house where he dwelt *had* another court within the porch, *which* was of the like work. Solomon made also a house for Pharaoh's daughter, [h]whom he had taken *to* wife, like unto this porch.

9 All these *were of* costly stones, according to the measures of hewed stones, sawed with

---

[a]Ch. ix. 10; 2 Chron. viii. 1——[b]Heb. *ribs*——[c]Heb. *sight against sight*——[d]Or, *spaces and pillars* were *square in prospect*

[e]Or, *according to them*——[f]Or, *according to them* [g]Heb. *from floor to floor*——[h]Chap. iii. 1; 2 Chron. viii. 11

NOTES ON CHAP. VII

Verse 1. *Building his own house*] This house is said to have been situated in Jerusalem, and probably was, what some call it, his *winter's* residence. It is called the *king's house*, chap. ix. 10.

Verse 2. *The house of the forest of Lebanon*] It was not built in Lebanon, but is thought to have been on Mount Sion. And why it was called *the house of the forest of Lebanon* does not appear; probably it was because it was built *almost entirely* of materials brought from that place. See the following verses.

Verse 7. *A porch for the throne*] One porch appears to have been devoted to the purposes of administering judgment, which Solomon did in person.

Verse 8. *A house for Pharaoh's daughter*] This appears to have been a *third house;* probably the whole *three* made but *one building*, and were in the same place, but distinguished from each other; the first as Solomon's palace, the second as a house of judgment, a court-house; the third, the *harem*, or apartments for the women.

Verse 13. *Solomon sent and fetched Hiram out of Tyre.*] This was not the Tyrian

A.M.3000-3013
B.C. 1004-991
Anno ante I.
Olymp.228-215 saws within and without, even from the foundation unto the co-ping, and *so* on the outside toward the great court.

10 And the foundation *was of* costly stones, even great stones, stones of ten cubits, and stones of eight cubits.

11 And above *were* costly stones, after the measures of hewed stones, and cedars.

12 And the great court round about *was* with three rows of hewed stones, and a row of cedar beams, both for the inner court of the house of the LORD, ¹and for the porch of the house.

13 And King Solomon sent and fetched ᵏHiram out of Tyre.

14 ¹He *was* ᵐa widow's son of the tribe of Naphtali, and ⁿhis father *was* a man of Tyre, a worker in brass: and ᵒhe was filled with wisdom, and understanding, and cunning to work all works in brass. And he came to King Solomon, and wrought all his work.

15 For he ᵖcast ᑫtwo pillars of brass, of eighteen cubits high apiece: and a line of twelve cubits did compass either of them about.

16 And he made two chapiters *of* molten brass, to set upon the tops of the pillars: the height of the one chapiter *was* five cubits, and the height of the other chapiter *was* five cubits:

17 *And* nets of checker-work, and wreaths of chain-work, for the chapiters which *were* upon the top of the pillars; seven for the one chapiter, and seven for the other chapiter.

18 And he made the pillars, and two rows round about upon the one net-work, to cover the chapiters that *were* upon the top, with pomegranates: and so did he for the other chapiter.

19 And the chapiters that *were* upon the top of the pillars *were* of lily-work in the porch, four cubits.

20 And the chapiters upon the two pillars *had pomegranates* also above, over against the belly which *was* by the net-work: and the pomegranates *were* ʳtwo hundred in rows round about upon the other chapiter.

21 ˢAnd he set up the pillars in ᵗthe porch of the temple: and he set up the right pillar, and called the name thereof ᵘJachin: and he set up the left pillar, and called the name thereof ᵛBoaz.

22 And upon the top of the pillars *was* lily-work: so was the work of the pillars finished.

23 And he made ʷa molten sea, ten cubits ˣfrom the one brim to the other: *it was* round all about, and his height *was* five cubits: and a line of thirty cubits did compass it round about.

24 And under the brim of it round about *there were* knops compassing it, ten in a cubit, ʸcompassing the sea round about: the knops *were* cast in two rows, when it was cast.

25 It stood upon ᶻtwelve oxen, three looking toward the north, and three looking toward the west, and three looking toward the south, and three looking toward the east: and the sea *was set* above upon them, and all their hinder parts *were* inward.

26 And it *was* a hand-breadth thick, and the brim thereof was wrought like the brim of a cup, with flowers of lilies: it contained ᵃtwo thousand baths.

27 And he made ten bases of brass; four

A.M.3000-3013
B.C. 1004-991
Anno ante I.
Olymp.228-215

---

iJohn x. 23; Acts iii. 11——k2 Chron. iv. 11, *Huram;* see ver. 40——l2 Chron. ii. 14——mHeb. *the son of a widow woman*——n2 Chron. iv. 16——oExod. xxxi. 3; xxxvi. 1——pHebrew, *fashioned*——q2 Kings xxv. 17; 2 Chron. iii. 15; iv. 12; Jer. lii. 21——rSee 2 Chron. iii.

16; iv. 13; Jer. lii. 23——s2 Chron. iii. 17——tCh. vi. 3 uThat is, *He shall establish*—— vThat is, *In it is strength* w2 Kings xxv. 13; 2 Chron. iv. 2; Jer. lii. 17——xHeb. *from his brim to his brim*——y2 Chron. iv. 3——z2 Chron. iv. 4, 5; Jer. lii. 20——aSee 2 Chron. iv. 5

---

king, mentioned before, but a very intelligent coppersmith, of Jewish extraction by his mother's side, who was probably married to a Tyrian. In 2 Chron. ii. 14, this woman is said to be *of the daughters of Dan*, but here *of the tribe of Naphtali*. The king of Tyre, who gives the account as we have it in Chronicles, might have made the mistake, and confounded the two tribes; or she might have been of *Naphtali* by her *father*, and of *Dan* by her *mother*, and so be indifferently called *of the tribe of Naphtali* or *of the daughters of Dan*. This appears to be the best solution of the difficulty. The versions and MSS. give no help here.

VOL. II

Verse 15. *He cast two pillars—eighteen cubits high*] That is, about thirty feet in English measure.

A line of twelve cubits] In circumference. It would be difficult even now to procure a founder who could cast such massive pillars, whether solid or hollow.

Verse 21. *The right pillar—Jachin*] That is, *He shall establish*. *The left pillar—Boaz*, that is, *in strength*. These were no doubt emblematical; for notwithstanding their *names*, they seem to have supported no part of the building.

Verse 27. *He made ten bases*] That is, *pedestals*, for the *ten lavers* to rest on.

A.M.3000-3013
B.C.1004-991
Anno ante I.
Olymp.228-215
cubits *was* the length of one base, and four cubits the breadth thereof, and three cubits the height of it.

28 And the work of the bases *was* on this *manner:* they had borders, and the borders *were* between the ledges:

29 And on the borders that *were* between the ledges *were* lions, oxen, and cherubims: and upon the ledges *there was* a base above: and beneath the lions and oxen *were* certain additions made of thin work.

30 And every base had four brazen wheels, and plates of brass: and the four corners thereof had undersetters: under the laver *were* undersetters molten, at the side of every addition.

31 And the mouth of it within the chapiter and above *was* a cubit: but the mouth thereof *was* round *after* the work of the base, a cubit and a half: and also upon the mouth of it *were* gravings with their borders, four-square, not round.

32 And under the borders *were* four wheels; and the axletrees of the wheels *were* [b]*joined* to the base: and the height of a wheel *was* a cubit and a half cubit.

33 And the work of the wheels *was* like the work of a chariot-wheel; their axletrees, and their naves, and their felloes, and their spokes, *were* all molten.

34 And *there were* four undersetters to the four corners of one base: *and* the undersetters *were* of the very base itself.

35 And in the top of the base *was there* a round compass of half a cubit high: and on the top of the base the ledges thereof and the borders thereof *were* of the same.

36 For on the plates of the ledges thereof, and on the borders thereof, he graved cherubims, lions, and palm trees, according to the [c]proportion of every one, and additions round about.

37 After this *manner* he made
A.M.3000-3013
B.C.1004-991
Anno ante I.
Olymp. 228-215
the ten bases: all of them had one casting, one measure, *and* one size.

38 Then [d]made he ten lavers of brass: one laver contained forty baths: *and* every laver was four cubits: *and* upon every one of the ten bases one laver.

39 And he put five bases on the right [e]side of the house, and five on the left side of the house: and he set the sea on the right side of the house eastward over against the south.

40 And [f]Hiram made the lavers, and the shovels, and the basons. So Hiram made an end of doing all the work that he made King Solomon for the house of the LORD:

41 The two pillars, and the *two* bowls of the chapiters that *were* on the top of the two pillars; and the two [g]net-works, to cover the two bowls of the chapiters which *were* upon the top of the pillars;

42 And four hundred pomegranates for the two net-works, *even* two rows of pomegranates for one net-work, to cover the two bowls of the chapiters, that *were* [h]upon the pillars;

43 And the ten bases, and ten lavers on the bases;

44 And one sea, and twelve oxen under the sea;

45 [i]And the pots, and the shovels, and the basons: and all these vessels, which Hiram made to King Solomon for the house of the LORD, *were of* [k]bright brass.

46 [l]In the plain of Jordan did the king cast them, [m]in the clay ground between [n]Succoth and [o]Zarthan.

47 And Solomon left all the vessels *unweighed,* [p]because they were exceeding many: neither was the weight of the brass [q]found out.

48 And Solomon made all the vessels that *pertained* unto the house of the LORD: [r]the

---

[b]Heb. *in the base*——[c]Heb. *nakedness*——[d]2 Chron. iv. 6——[e]Heb. *shoulder*——[f]Heb. *Hirom; see ver* 13 [g]Ver. 17, 18——[h]Heb. *upon the face of the pillars* [i]Exod. xxvii. 3; 2 Chron. iv. 16——[k]Hebrew, *made bright*

or *scoured*——[l]2 Chron iv. 17——[m]Heb. *in the thickness of the ground*——[n]Gen. xxxiii. 17——[o]Josh. iii. 16 [p]Heb. *for the exceeding multitude*——[q]Heb. *searched;* 1 Chron. xxii. 14——[r]Exod. xxxvii. 25, &c.

Verse 38. *Then made he ten lavers*] These were set on the ten *bases* or *pedestals,* and were to hold water for the use of the priests in their sacred office, particularly to wash the victims that were to be offered as a burnt-offering, as we learn from 2 Chron. iv. 6; but the *brazen*

sea was for the priests to wash in. The whole was a building of vast art, labour, and expense.

Verse 40. *So Hiram made an end*] It is truly surprising, that in so short a time *one* artist could design and execute works of such magnitude, taste, and variety, however numerous his

A.M.3000-3013
B.C. 1004-991
Anno ante I.
Olymp.228-215

altar of gold, and [r]the table of gold, whereupon [t]the shew-bread *was,*

49 And the candlesticks of pure gold, five on the right *side,* and five on the left, before the oracle, with the flowers, and the lamps, and the tongs *of* gold,

50 And the bowls, and the snuffers, and the basons, and the spoons, and the [u]censers *of* pure gold; and the hinges *of* gold, *both* for the

doors of the inner house, the most holy *place, and* for the doors of the house, *to wit,* of the temple.

A.M.3000-3013
B.C. 1004-991
Anno ante I.
Olymp.228-215

51 So was ended all the work that King Solomon made for the house of the Lord. And Solomon brought in the [v]things [w]which David his father had dedicated; *even* the silver, and the gold, and the vessels, did he put among the treasures of the house of the Lord.

---

[s]Exodus xxxvii. 10, &c.——[t]Exodus xxv. 30; Lev. xxiv. 5–8

[u]Heb. *ash-pans*——[v]Heb. *holy things of David*——[w]2 Sam. viii. 11; 2 Chron. v. 1

---

assistants might be. The mere building of the house was a matter of little difficulty in comparison of these internal works.

Verse 46. *Cast them, in the clay ground*] In this place he found that particular kind of *clay* that was proper for his purpose. Some suppose that the place where Hiram had his foundry was on the *other* side, some on *this* side, of Jordan. Calmet supposes that it was near *Beth-shan.*

Verse 51. *Solomon brought in the things*] It has been a question whether Solomon, in the structure of the temple, used any of the gold and silver which David had provided? And here it seems answered in the negative; for after the house was finished, with all its utensils and ornaments, with its immense profusion of

gold, it is here said that *Solomon brought in the silver, and the gold, and the vessels, which David his father had dedicated.* It appears therefore that Solomon had employed four years to make preparation for the work before it was begun. During the whole time of the building, he was no doubt still appropriating a part of the public revenue for this purpose; and the provision made by his father he placed *among the treasures of the house;* but the temple was truly Solomon's, as he had provided all its materials, and borne every expense.

As the temple was built in some measure on the model of the tabernacle, and dedicated to the same use, I wish to refer the reader to the description of the former, in Exod. xxv.—xxvii., and xxxv.—xxxix., and the notes there.

CHAPTER VIII

Solomon assembles the elders of Israel, and brings up the ark, and the holy vessels, and the tabernacle, out of the city of David, and places them in the temple; on which account a vast number of sheep and oxen are sacrificed, 1–8. There was nothing in the ark save the two tables of stone, which Moses put there at Horeb, 9. The cloud of God's glory fills the house, 10, 11. Solomon blesses the people, 12–21. His dedicatory prayer, 22–53. Afterwards he blesses and exhorts the people, 54–61. They offer a sacrifice of twenty-two thousand oxen, and one hundred and twenty thousand sheep, 62, 63. He hallows the middle of the court for offerings; as the brazen altar which was before the Lord was too little, 64. He holds the feast of the dedication for seven days; and for other seven days, the feast of tabernacles; and on the eighth day blesses the people, and sends them away joyful, 65, 66.

A. M. 3000
B. C. 1004
Ante I. Ol. 228
An. Archippi,
Arch. Athen.
perpet. 9

THEN [a]Solomon assembled the elders of Israel, and all the heads of the tribes, the [b]chief of the fathers of the children of Israel, unto King Solo-

mon in Jerusalem, [c]that they might bring up the ark of the covenant of the Lord [d]out of the city of David, which *is* Zion.

A. M. 3000
B. C. 1004
Ante I. Ol. 228
An. Archippi,
Arch. Athen.
perpet. 9

---

[a]2 Chron. v. 2, &c.——[b]Heb. *princes*

[c]2 Sam. vi. 17——[d]2 Sam. v. 7, 9; vi. 12, 16

NOTES ON CHAP. VIII

Verse 1. *Then Solomon assembled*] It has already been observed that Solomon deferred the dedication of the temple to the following year after it was finished, because that year, according to Archbishop Usher, was a *jubilee.* "This," he observes, "was the *ninth* jubilee, opening the fourth *millenary* of the world, or A. M. 3001, wherein Solomon with great magnificence celebrated the dedication of the temple seven days, and the feast of tabernacles other seven days; and the celebration of the eighth day of tabernacles being finished, upon the twenty-third day of the seventh month the people were dismissed

every man to his home. The eighth day of the seventh month, viz., the thirtieth of our October, being *Friday,* was the first of the seven days of dedication; on the *tenth* day, Saturday, November 1, was the fast of expiation or atonement held; whereon, according to the Levitical law, the jubilee was proclaimed by sound of trumpet. The fifteenth day, *Friday,* November 6, was the feast of tabernacles; the twenty-second, November 13, being also *Friday,* was the feast of tabernacles, which was always very solemnly kept, 2 Chron. vii. 9; Lev. xxiii. 36; John vii. 37; and the day following, November 14, being our *Saturday,* when the Sabbath was ended, the people returned home.

A. M. 3000
B. C. 1004
Ante I. Ol. 228
An. Archippi,
Arch. Athen.
perpet. 9

2 And all the men of Israel assembled themselves unto King Solomon at the ^efeast in the month Ethanim, which *is* the seventh month.

3 And all the elders of Israel came, ^fand the priests took up the ark.

4 And they brought up the ark of the LORD, ^gand the tabernacle of the congregation, and all the holy vessels that *were* in the tabernacle, even those did the priests and the Levites bring up.

5 And King Solomon, and all the congregation of Israel, that were assembled unto him, *were* with him before the ark, ^hsacrificing sheep and oxen, that could not be told nor numbered for multitude.

6 And the priests ⁱbrought in the ark of the covenant of the LORD unto ^khis place, into the oracle of the house, to the most holy *place,* even ^lunder the wings of the cherubims.

7 For the cherubims spread forth *their* two wings over the place of the ark, and the cherubims covered the ark and the staves thereof above.

8 And they ^mdrew out the staves, that the ⁿends of the staves were seen out in the

^oholy *place* before the oracle, and they were not seen without: and there they are unto this day.

A. M. 3000
B. C. 1004
Ante I. Ol. 228
An. Archippi,
Arch. Athen.
perpet. 9

9 ^p*There was* nothing in the ark ^qsave the two tables of stone, which Moses ^rput there at Horeb, ^swhen ^tthe LORD made *a covenant* with the children of Israel, when they came out of the land of Egypt.

10 And it came to pass, when the priests were come out of the holy *place,* that the cloud ^ufilled the house of the LORD,

11 So that the priests could not stand to minister because of the cloud: for the glory of the LORD had filled the house of the LORD.

12 ^vThen spake Solomon, The LORD said that he would dwell ^win the thick darkness.

13 ^xI have surely built thee a house to dwell in, ^ya settled place for thee to abide in for ever.

14 And the king turned his face about, and ^zblessed all the congregation of Israel: (and all the congregation of Israel stood:)

15 And he said, ^aBlessed *be* the LORD God of Israel, which ^bspake with his mouth unto David my father, and hath with his hand fulfilled *it,* saying,

---

^eLev. xxiii. 34; 2 Chron. vii. 8——^fNum. iv. 15; Deut. xxxi. 9; Josh. iii. 3, 6; 1 Chron. xv. 14, 15——^gChap. iii. 4; 2 Chron. i. 3——^h2 Sam. vi. 13——ⁱ2 Sam. vi. 17 ^kExod. xxvi. 33, 34; chap. vi. 19——^lChap. vi. 27 ^mExod. xxv. 14, 15——ⁿHeb. *heads*——^oOr, *ark;* as 2 Chron. v. 9——^pExod. xxv. 21; Deut. x. 2

^qDeut. x. 5; Heb. ix. 4——^rExod. xl. 20——^sOr, *where*——^tExod. xxxiv. 27, 28; Deut. iv. 13; ver. 21 ^uExod. xl. 34, 35; 2 Chron. v. 13, 14; vii. 2——^v2 Chron. vi. 1, &c.——^wLev. xvi. 2; Psa. xviii. 11; xcvii. 2 ^x2 Sam. vii. 13——^yPsa. cxxxii. 14——^z2 Sam. vi. 18 ^aLuke i. 68——^b2 Sam. vii. 5, 25

"In the *thirteenth* year after the temple was built, Solomon made an end also of building his own house, having spent full twenty years upon both of them; seven and a half upon the temple, and thirteen or twelve and a half upon his own."—*Usher's Annals,* sub. A. M. 3001.

Verse 2. *At the feast in the month Ethanim*] The feast of tabernacles, which was celebrated in the *seventh* month of what is called the *ecclesiastical year.*

Verse 4. *They brought up—the tabernacle*] It is generally agreed that there were now *two* tabernacles at Gibeon, and the other in the city of David, which one David had constructed as a temporary residence for the ark, in the event of a temple being built. Which of these tabernacles was brought into the temple at this time, is not well known; some think *both* were brought in, in order to prevent the danger of idolatry. I should rather suppose that the tabernacle from Gibeon was brought in, and that the temporary one erected by David was demolished.

Verse 8. *And there they are unto this day.*] This proves that the book was written before the destruction of the first temple, but how long before we cannot tell.

Verse 9. *Save the two tables of stone*] See my notes on Heb. ix. 4.

Verse 10. *When the priests were come out*] That is, after having carried the ark into the holy of holies, before any sacred service had yet commenced.

Verse 11. *The glory of the Lord had filled the house*] The cloud, the symbol of the Divine glory and presence, appears to have filled not only the holy of holies, but the whole temple, court and all, and to have become evident to the people; and by this Solomon knew that God had honoured the place with his presence, and taken it for his habitation in reference to the people of Israel.

Verse 12. *The Lord said—he would dwell*] It was under the appearance of a cloud that God showed himself present with Israel in the wilderness; see Exod. xiv. 19, 20. And at the dedication of the tabernacle in the wilderness, God manifested himself in the same way that he did here at the dedication of the temple; see Exod. xl. 34, 35.

Verse 13. *I have surely built thee a house*] He was now fully convinced that the thing pleased God, and that he had taken this place for his settled habitation.

Verse 14. *Blessed all the congregation*] Though this blessing is not particularly stated, yet we may suppose that it was such as the

A. M. 3000
B. C. 1004
Ante I. Ol. 228
An. Archippi,
Arch. Athen.
perpet. 9

16 ^cSince the day that I brought forth my people Israel out of Egypt, I chose no city out of all the tribes of Israel to build a house, that ^dmy name might be therein; but I chose ^eDavid to be over my people Israel.

17 And ^fit was in the heart of David my father to build a house for the name of the LORD God of Israel.

18 ^gAnd the LORD said unto David my father, Whereas it was in thine heart to build a house unto my name, thou didst well that it was in thine heart.

19 Nevertheless ^hthou shalt not build the house; but thy son that shall come forth out of thy loins, he shall build the house unto my name.

20 And the LORD hath performed his word that he spake, and I am risen up in the room of David my father, and sit on the throne of Israel, ⁱas the LORD promised, and have built a house for the name of the LORD God of Israel.

A. M. 3000
B. C. 1004
Ante I. Ol. 228
An. Archippi,
Arch. Athen.
perpet. 9

21 And I have set there a place for the ark, wherein *is* ^kthe covenant of the LORD, which he made with our fathers, when he brought them out of the land of Egypt.

22 And Solomon stood before ^lthe altar of the LORD in the presence of all the congregation of Israel, and ^mspread forth his hands toward heaven:

23 And he said, ⁿLORD God of Israel, ^o*there is* no God like thee, in heaven above,

---

^c2 Sam. vii. 6; 2 Chron. vi. 5, &c.——^dVer. 29; Deut. xii. 11——^e1 Sam. xvi. 1; 2 Sam. vii. 8; 1 Chron. xxviii. 4——^f2 Samuel vii. 2; 1 Chron. xvii. 1——^g2 Chron. vi. 8, 9

^h2 Sam. vii. 5, 12, 13; ch. v. 3, 5——ⁱ1 Chron. xxviii. 5, 6——^kVer. 9; Deut. xxxi. 26——^l2 Chron. vi. 12, &c.——^mExod. ix. 33; Ezra ix. 5; Isa. i. 15——ⁿ2 Mac. ii. 8——^oExod. xv. 11; 2 Sam. vii. 22

---

high priest pronounced upon the people: "The Lord bless thee, and keep thee! The Lord make his face shine upon thee, and be gracious unto thee! The Lord lift up his countenance upon thee, and give thee peace!" (see Num. vi. 24-26,) for Solomon seems now to be acting the part of the high priest. But he may have in view more particularly the conduct of *Moses*, who, when he had seen that the people had done all the work of the tabernacle, as the Lord had commanded them, he blessed them, Exod. xxxix. 43; and the conduct of his father David, who, when the ark had been brought into the city of David, and the burnt-offerings and peace-offerings completed, blessed the people in the name of the Lord; 2 Sam. vi. 18.

Verse 16. *Since the day, &c.*] Mention is here made, says Dr. Kennicott, of some one *place* and some one *person* preferred before all others; and the preference is that of *Jerusalem* to other *places*, and of *David* to other *men*. In consequence of this remark, we shall see the necessity of correcting this passage by its parallel in 2 Chron. vi. 5, 6, where the thirteen Hebrew words now lost in Kings are happily preserved. Let us compare the passages:—

K. *Since the day that I brought forth my people*
C. Since the day that I brought forth my people
K. *Israel out of*   *Egypt, I chose no* CITY
C.   out of the land of Egypt, I chose no CITY
K. *out of all the tribes of Israel to build a house,*
C. among all the tribes of Israel to build a house in,
K. *that my name might be therein;* * * *
C. that my name might be there; neither chose I
K. * * * * * * *
C. any MAN to be a ruler over my people Israel:
K. * * * * * * *
C. but I have chosen JERUSALEM, that my name
K. * * * *but I*   *chose David to be*
C. might be there; and have chosen DAVID to be
K. *over my people Israel.*
C. over my people Israel.

I would just observe here, that I do not think these *thirteen words* ever made a part of Kings, and, consequently, are not *lost* from it; nor do they exist here in any of the versions; but their being found in Chronicles helps to complete the sense.

Verse 21. *Wherein is the covenant of the Lord*] As it is said, ver. 9, that *there was nothing in the ark but the two tables of stone*, consequently these are called *the Covenant*, i. e., a *sign* of the covenant; as our Lord calls the *cup* the *new covenant in his blood*, that is, the *sign* of the new covenant: for *This is my body* implies, This is the *sign* or *emblem* of my body.

Verse 22. *Stood*] He ascended the *brazen scaffold*, five cubits long, and five cubits broad, and three cubits high, and then *kneeled down upon his knees*, with his hands spread up to heaven, and offered up the following prayer: see ver. 54, and 2 Chron. v. 12, 13.

And spread forth his hands toward heaven] This was a usual custom in all nations: in prayer the *hands were stretched out to heaven*, as if to invite and receive assistance from thence; while, humbly *kneeling* on their knees, they seemed acknowledge at once their *dependence* and *unworthiness*. On this subject I have spoken elsewhere. In the Scriptures we meet with several examples of the kind: *Hear my voice—when I* LIFT UP MY HANDS *toward thy holy oracle;* Psa. xxviii. 2. LIFT UP YOUR HANDS *in the sanctuary, and bless the Lord;* Psa. cxxxiv. 2. *Let my prayer be set forth—and the* LIFTING UP OF MY HANDS *as the evening sacrifice;* Psa. cxli. 2. And see 1 Tim. ii. 8, &c.

In heathen writers examples are not less frequent:

SUSTULIT exutas vinclis ad sidera PALMAS.
Vos æterni ignes, et non violabile vestrum
Testor numen, ait.
            VIRG. Æn. lib. ii., ver. 153.

Ye lamps of heaven, he said, and LIFTED HIGH
HIS HANDS, now free; thou venerable sky,
Inviolable powers!

And that they *kneeled* down when supplicating I have also proved. Of this too the Scriptures afford abundant evidence, as do also the *heathen* writers. I need add but one word:—

A. M. 3000
B. C. 1004
Ante I. Ol. 228
An. Archippi,
Arch. Athen.
perpet. 9

or on earth beneath, Pwho keepest covenant and mercy with thy
servants that qwalk before thee
with all their heart:

24 Who hast kept with thy servant David
my father that thou promisedst him: thou
spakest also with thy mouth, and hast fulfilled *it* with thine hand, as *it is* this day.

25 Therefore now, LORD God of Israel,
keep with thy servant David my father that
thou promisedst him, saying, rThere sshall
not fail thee a man in my sight to sit on the
throne of Israel; tso that thy children take
heed to their way, that they walk before me
as thou hast walked before me.

26 uAnd now, O God of Israel, let thy
word, I pray thee, be verified, which thou
spakest unto thy servant David my father.

27 But vwill God indeed dwell on the earth?
behold, the heaven and wheaven of heavens

cannot contain thee; how much
less this house that I have
builded?

A. M. 3000
B. C. 1004
Ante I. Ol. 228
An. Archippi,
Arch. Athen.
perpet. 9

28 Yet have thou respect unto
the prayer of thy servant, and to his supplication, O LORD my God, to hearken unto the
cry and to the prayer which thy servant
prayeth before thee to-day:

29 That thine eyes may be open toward this
house night and day, *even* toward the place
of which thou hast said, xMy name shall be
there: that thou mayest hearken unto the
prayer which thy servant shall make ytoward
zthis place.

30 aAnd hearken thou to the supplication of
thy servant, and of thy people Israel, when
they shall pray btoward this place: and hear
thou in heaven thy dwelling-place: and when
thou hearest, forgive.

31 If any man trespass against his neigh-

---

pDeut. vii. 9; Neh. i. 5; Dan. ix. 4——qGen. xvii. 1;
chap. iii. 6; 2 Kings xx. 3——rChap. ii. 4; 2 Sam. vii.
12, 16——sHeb. *there shall not be cut off unto thee a man
from my sight*——tHeb. *only if*

u2 Sam. vii. 25——v2 Chron. ii. 6; Isa. lxvi. 1;
Jer. xxiii. 24; Acts vii. 49; xvii. 24——w2 Cor. xii. 2
xDeut. xii. 11——yDan. vi. 10——zOr, *in this place*
a2 Chron. xx. 9; Neh. i. 6——bOr, *in this place*

Et GENIBUS PRONIS supplex, similisque roganti,
Circumfert tacitos, tanquam sua brachia, vultus.
OVID, Met. lib. iii., f. 3, ver. 240.

Indeed, so universal were these forms in praying, that one of the heathens has said, "All men,
in praying, lift up their hands to heaven."
Verse 24. *Who has kept with thy servant
David*] This is in reference to 2 Sam. vii. 13,
where God promises to David that Solomon
shall build a house for the name of the Lord.
The temple being now completed, this promise
was literally fulfilled.
Verse 27. *But will God indeed dwell on the
earth?*] This expression is full of astonishment, veneration, and delight. He is struck
with the immensity, dignity, and grandeur of
the Divine Being, but especially at his *condescension* to dwell with men: and though he sees,
by his filling the place, that he has come now
to make his abode with them, yet he cannot help
asking the question, How can such a God dwell
in such a place, and with such creatures?
Behold, the heaven] The words are all in the
plural number in the Hebrew: השמים ושמי השמים
hashshamayim, ushemey hashshamayim; "the
heavens, and the heavens of heavens." What
do these words imply? That there are *systems*,
and *systems of systems*, each possessing its *sun*,
its *primary* and *secondary* planets, all extending beyond each other in unlimited space, in the
same regular and graduated order which we
find to prevail in what we call our *solar system;*
which probably, in its thousands of millions of
miles in diameter, is, to some others, no more
than the area of the lunar orbit to that of the
Georgium Sidus. When God, his manifold wisdom, his creative energy, and that *space* which
is unlimited, are considered, it is no hyperbole
to say that, although the earth has been created
nearly *six thousand* years ago, suns, the centres

of systems, may have been created at so immense a distance that their light has not yet
reached our earth, though travelling at the rate
of *one hundred and ninety thousand* miles every
second, or upwards of a *million* times swifter
than the motion of a cannon ball! This may
be said to be inconceivable; but what is even
all this to the vast immensity of space! Had
God created a system like ours in every six
days since the foundation of the world, and
kept every seventh as a Sabbath; and though
there might have been by this time [A. M. 5823
ineunte, A. D. 1819, *ineunte*] three hundred and
three thousand five hundred and seventy-five
mundane systems; they would occupy but a
speck in the inconceivable immensity of *space*.
Reader, all this and millions more is demonstrably possible; and if so, what must God
be—*illud inexprimibile*—who i-n-h-a-b-i-t-e-t-h
E-t-e-r-n-i-t-y!
Verse 29. *My name shall be there*] I will
there show forth my power and my glory by
enlightening, quickening, pardoning, sanctifying, and saving all my sincere worshippers.
Verse 30. *Toward this place*] Both tabernacle and temple were types of our Lord Jesus,
or of *God manifested in the flesh;* and he was
and is the Mediator between God and man. All
prayer, to be acceptable, and to be entitled to
a hearing, must go to God *through Him.* The
human nature of Christ is the temple in which
dwelt all the fulness of the Godhead bodily;
therefore with propriety all prayer must be
offered to God through Him. "If they pray toward this place, hear thou in heaven thy dwelling-place; and when thou hearest, forgive."
This appears to me to be the true sense and
doctrine of this verse.
Verse 31. *If any man trespass against his
neighbour*] Solomon puts here *seven cases*, in
all of which the mercy and intervention of God

A. M. 3000
B. C. 1004
Ante I. Ol. 228
An. Archippi,
Arch. Athen.
perpet. 9

bour, ^cand ^dan oath be laid upon him to cause him to swear, and the oath come before thine altar in this house:

32 Then hear thou in heaven, and do, and judge thy servants, ^econdemning the wicked, to bring his way upon his head; and justifying the righteous, to give him according to his righteousness.

33 ^fWhen thy people Israel be smitten down before the enemy, because they have sinned against thee, and ^gshall turn again to thee, and confess thy name, and pray, and make supplication unto thee ^hin this house:

34 Then hear thou in heaven, and forgive the sin of thy people Israel, and bring them again unto the land which thou gavest unto their fathers.

35 ⁱWhen heaven is shut up, and there is no rain, because they have sinned against thee; if they pray toward this place, and confess thy name, and turn from their sin, when thou afflictest them:

36 Then hear thou in heaven, and forgive

the sin of thy servants, and of thy people Israel, that thou ^kteach them ^lthe good way wherein they should walk, and give rain upon thy land, which thou hast given to thy people for an inheritance.

A. M. 3000
B. C. 1004
Ante I. Ol. 228
An. Archippi,
Arch. Athen.
perpet. 9

37 ^mIf there be in the land famine, if there be pestilence, blasting, mildew, locust, *or* if there be caterpillar; if their enemy besiege them in the land of their ⁿcities; whatsoever plague, whatsoever sickness *there be;*

38 What prayer and supplication soever be *made* by any man, *or* by all thy people Israel, which shall know every man the plague of his own heart, and spread forth his hands toward this house:

39 Then hear thou in heaven thy dwelling-place, and forgive, and do, and give to every man according to his ways, whose heart thou knowest; (for thou, *even* thou only, ^oknowest the hearts of all the children of men;)

40 ^pThat they may fear thee all the days that they live in the land which thou gavest unto our fathers.

---

^cHeb. *and he require an oath of him;* Lev. v. 1——^dExod. xxii. 11——^eDeut. xxv. 1——^fLev. xxvi. 17; Deut. xxviii. 25——^gLev. xxvi. 39, 40; Neh. i. 9——^hOr, *toward*——ⁱLev. xxvi. 19; Deut. xxviii. 23——^kPsa. xxv. 4; xxvii. 11; xciv.

12; cxliii. 8——^l1 Sam. xii. 23——^mLev. xxvi. 16, 25, 26; Deut. xxviii. 21, 22, 27, 38, 42, 52; 2 Chron. xx. 9——ⁿOr, *jurisdiction*——^o1 Sam. xvi. 7; 1 Chron. xxviii. 9; Psa. xi. 4; Jer. xvii. 10; Acts i. 24——^pPsa. cxxx. 4

---

would be indispensably requisite; and he earnestly bespeaks that mercy and intervention on condition that the people pray towards that holy place, and with a feeling heart make earnest supplication.

The FIRST case is one of *doubtfulness;* where a man has sustained an injury, and charges it on a suspected person, though not able to bring direct evidence of the fact, the accused is permitted to come before the altar of God, and purge himself by his personal oath. Solomon prays that God may not permit a false oath to be taken, but that he will discover the truth, so that the wicked shall be condemned, and the righteous justified.

Verse 33. *When thy people Israel be smitten down, &c.*] The SECOND case. When their enemies make inroads upon them, and defeat them in battle, and lead them into captivity, because God, being displeased with their transgressions, has delivered them up; then if they shall turn again; confess the name of God, which they had in effect denied, by either neglecting his worship, or becoming *idolatrous;* and pray and make supplication; *then,* says Solomon, *hear thou in heaven—and bring them again unto the land which thou gavest unto their fathers.*

Verse 35. *When the heaven is shut up, and there is no rain*] The THIRD case. When, because of their sin, and their ceasing to *walk in the good way* in which they should have walked, God refuses to send the *early* and *latter rain,* so that the appointed weeks of harvest come in vain, as there is no crop: then, if they

pray and confess their sin, hear thou in heaven, &c.

Verse 37. *If there be in the land famine—pestilence*] The FOURTH case includes several kinds of evils: 1. *Famine;* a scarcity or total want of bread, necessarily springing from the preceding cause, *drought.* 2. *Pestilence;* any general and contagious disease. 3. *Blasting;* any thing by which the crops are injured, so that the ear is never matured; but instead of wholesome grain, there is a *black offensive dust.* 4. *Mildew;* any thing that vitiates or corrodes the texture of the *stalk,* destroys the flowers and blossoms, or causes the young shaped fruits to fall off their stems. 5. *Locust,* a well known curse in the East; a species of *grasshopper* that multiplies by *millions,* and covers the face of the earth for many miles square, destroying every green thing; leaving neither herb nor grass upon the earth, nor leaf nor bark upon the trees. 6. *Caterpillar;* the locust in its young or *nympha* state. The *former* refers to *locusts* brought by winds *from other countries* and settling *on* the land; the latter, to the young *locusts* bred in the land. 7. An *enemy,* having *attacked* their *defenced cities,* the keys and barriers of the land. 8. Any other kind of *plague;* that which affects the *surface* of the body; blotch, blain, leprosy, ophthalmia, &c. 9. *Sickness;* whatever impaired the strength, or affected the intestines, disturbing or destroying their natural functions. All such cases were to be brought before the Lord, the persons *having a deep sense* of the wickedness which in-

A. M. 3000
B. C. 1004
Ante I. Ol. 228
An. Archippi,
Arch. Athen.
perpet. 9

41 Moreover, concerning a stranger that *is* not of thy people Israel, but cometh out of a far country for thy name's sake;

42 (For they shall hear of thy great name, and of thy qstrong hand, and of thy stretched-out arm;) when he shall come and pray toward this house;

43 Hear thou in heaven thy dwelling-place, and do according to all that the stranger calleth to thee for: rthat all people of the earth may know thy name, to sfear thee, as *do* thy people Israel; and that they may know that tthis house, which I have builded, is called by thy name.

44 If thy people go out to battle against their enemy, whithersoever thou shalt send them, and shall pray unto the LORD utoward the city which thou hast chosen, and *toward* the house that I have built for thy name:

45 Then hear thou in heaven their prayer and their supplication, and maintain their vcause.

A. M. 3000
B. C. 1004
Ante I. Ol. 228
An. Archippi,
Arch. Athen.
perpet. 9

46 If they sin against thee, (wfor *there is* no man that sinneth not,) and thou be angry with them, and deliver them to the enemy, so that they carry them away captives xunto the land of the enemy far or near;

47 yYet if they shall zbethink themselves in the land whither they were carried captives, and repent, and make supplication unto thee in the land of them that carried them captives, asaying, We have sinned, and have done perversely, we have committed wickedness;

48 And *so* breturn unto thee with all their heart, and with all their soul, in the land of their enemies, which led them away captive, and cpray unto thee toward their land, which thou gavest unto their fathers, the city which thou hast chosen, and the house which I have built for thy name:

---

qDeut. iii. 24——r1 Sam. xvii. 46; 2 Kings xix. 19; Psa. lxvii. 2——sPsa. cii. 15——tHeb. *thy name is called upon this house*——uHeb. *the way of the city*——vOr, *right*——w2 Chron. vi. 36; Prov. xx. 9; Eccles. vii. 20; James iii. 2; 1 John i. 8, 10——xLev. xxvi. 34, 44; Deut. xxviii. 36, 64——yLev. xxvi. 40——zHebrew, *bring back to their heart*——aNeh. i. 6; Psa. cvi. 6; Dan. ix. 5 bJer. xxix. 12, 13, 14——cDaniel vi. 10

---

duced God thus to afflict, or permit them to be afflicted: for only those who knew the *plague of their own hearts*, (ver. 38,) the deep-rooted moral corruption of their nature, and the destructive nature and sinfulness of sin, were likely to pray in such a manner as to induce God to hear and forgive.

Verse 41. *Moreover, concerning a stranger*] The FIFTH case relates to *heathens* coming from other countries with the design to become proselytes to the true religion; that they might be received, blessed, and protected as the true Israelites, that the name of Jehovah might be known over the face of the earth.

Verse 44. *If thy people go out to battle*] The SIXTH case refers to wars undertaken by Divine appointment: *whithersoever thou shalt send them;* for in no other wars could they expect the blessing and concurrence of the Lord; in none other could the God of truth and justice *maintain their cause.* There were such wars under the Mosaic dispensation, there are none such under the Christian dispensation: nor can there be any; for the Son of man is come, not to destroy men's lives, but to save them. Except mere *defensive* war, all others are diabolic; and, *query,* if there were no *provocations,* would there be any *attacks,* and consequently any need of *defensive* wars?

Verse 46. *If they sin against thee*] This SEVENTH case must refer to some general defection from truth, to some species of false worship, idolatry, or corruption of the truth and ordinances of the Most High; as for it they are here stated to be *delivered into the hands of their enemies* and *carried away captive,* which was the general punishment for idolatry, and what is called, verse 47, *acting perversely* and *committing wickedness.*

In ver. 46 we read, *If they sin against thee,*

for there is *no man that sinneth not.* On this verse we may observe that the second clause, as it is here translated, renders the *supposition* in the first clause entirely nugatory; for if there be *no man that sinneth not,* it is useless to say, IF *they sin;* but this contradiction is taken away by reference to the original, כי יחטאו לך *ki yechetu lach,* which should be translated IF *they shall sin against thee,* or *should they sin against thee;* כי אין אדם אשר לא יחטא *ki ein Adam asher lo yecheta, for there is no man that* MAY *not sin;* i. e., there is no man *impeccable,* none *infallible,* none that is not *liable* to transgress. This is the true meaning of the phrase in various parts of the Bible, and so our translators have understood the original: for even in the thirty-first verse of this chapter they have translated יחטא *yecheta,* IF *a man* TRESPASS; which certainly implies he *might* or *might not* do it; and in this way they have translated the same word, IF *a soul* SIN, in Lev. v. 1; vi. 2; 1 Sam. ii. 25; 2 Chron. vi. 22, and in several other places. The truth is, the Hebrew has no mood to express words in the *permissive* or *optative* way, but to express this sense it uses the *future* tense of the conjugation *kal.*

This text has been a wonderful strong hold for all who believe that there is no redemption from sin in this life, that no man can live without committing sin, and that we cannot be entirely freed from it till we die. 1. The text speaks no such doctrine: it only speaks of the possibility of every man sinning, and this must be true of a state of *probation.* 2. There is not another text in the Divine records that is more to the purpose than this. 3. The doctrine is flatly in opposition to the design of the Gospel; for Jesus came to save his people from their sins, and to destroy the works of the devil. 4.

A. M. 3000
B. C. 1004
Ante I. Ol. 228
An. Archippi, Arch. Athen. perpet. 9

49 Then hear thou their prayer and their supplication in heaven thy dwelling-place, and maintain their [d]cause,

50 And forgive thy people that have sinned against thee, and all their transgressions wherein they have transgressed against thee, and [e]give them compassion before them who carried them captive, that they may have compassion on them:

51 For [f]they *be* thy people, and thine inheritance, which thou broughtest forth out of Egypt, [g]from the midst of the furnace of iron:

52 That thine eyes may be open unto the supplication of thy servant, and unto the supplication of thy people Israel, to hearken unto them in all that they call for unto thee.

53 For thou didst separate them from among all the people of the earth, *to be* thine inheritance, [h]as thou spakest by the hand of Moses thy servant, when thou broughtest our fathers out of Egypt, O Lord GOD.

54 And it was *so,* that when Solomon had made an end of praying all this prayer and supplication unto the LORD, he arose from before the altar of the LORD, from kneeling on his knees with his hands spread up to heaven.

55 And he stood, [i]and blessed all the congregation of Israel with a loud voice, saying,

56 Blessed *be* the LORD, that hath given rest unto his people Israel, according to all that he promised: [k]there hath not [l]failed one word of all his good promise, which he promised by the hand of Moses his servant.

A. M. 3000
B. C. 1004
Ante I. Ol. 228
An. Archippi, Arch. Athen. perpet. 9

57 The LORD our God be with us, as he was with our fathers: [m]let him not leave us, nor forsake us:

58 That he may [n]incline our hearts unto him, to walk in all his ways, and to keep his commandments, and his statutes, and his judgments, which he commanded our fathers.

59 And let these my words, wherewith I have made supplication before the LORD, be nigh unto the LORD our God day and night, that he maintain the cause of his servant, and the cause of his people Israel [o]at all times, as the matter shall require:

60 [p]That all the people of the earth may know that [q]the LORD *is* God, *and that there is* none else.

61 Let your [r]heart therefore be perfect with the LORD our God, to walk in his statutes, and to keep his commandments, as at this day.

62 And [s]the king, and all Israel with him, offered sacrifice before the LORD.

63 And Solomon offered a sacrifice of peace-offerings, which he offered unto the LORD, two and twenty thousand oxen, and a hundred and twenty thousand sheep. So the king and all the children of Israel dedicated the house of the LORD.

64 [t]The same day did the king hallow the middle of the court that *was* before the house of the LORD: for there he offered burnt-offerings, and meat-offerings, and the fat of the peace-offerings: because [u]the brazen altar that

[d]Or, *right*——[e]Ezra vii. 6; Psa. cvi. 46——[f]Deut. ix. 29; Neh. i. 10——[g]Deut. iv. 20; Jer. xi. 4——[h]Exod. xix. 5; Deut. ix. 26, 29; xiv. 2——[i]2 Samuel vi. 18 [k]Deut. xii. 10; Josh. xxi. 45; xxiii. 14——[l]Heb. *fallen* [m]Deut. xxxi. 6; Josh. i. 5

[n]Psa. cxix. 36——[o]Heb. *the thing of a day in his day* [p]Josh. iv. 24; 1 Sam. xvii. 46; 2 Kings xix. 19——[q]Deut. iv. 35, 39——[r]Chapter xi. 4; xv. 3, 14; 2 Kings xx. 3 [s]2 Chronicles vii. 4, &c.——[t]2 Chronicles vii. 7——[u]2 Chron. iv. 1

It is a dangerous and destructive doctrine, and should be blotted out of every Christian's creed. There are too many who are seeking to excuse their crimes by all means in their power; and we need not embody their excuses in a creed, to complete their deception, by stating that their sins are *unavoidable.*

Verse 50. *And give them compassion before them who carried them captive*] He does not pray that they may be delivered out of that captivity, but that their enemies may use them well; and that they may, as formerly, be kept a separate and distinct people.

Verse 55. *He stood, and blessed all the congregation*] This blessing is contained in verses 57 and 58.

Verse 59. *And let these my words*] This and the following verse is a sort of supplement to the prayer which ended ver. 53; but there is an important addition to this prayer in the parallel place, 2 Chron. vi. 41, 42: "Now therefore arise, O LORD God, into thy resting place, thou and the ark of thy strength: let thy priests, O LORD God, be clothed with salvation, and let thy saints rejoice in goodness. O LORD God, turn not away the face of thine anointed: remember the mercies of David thy servant."

Verse 61. *Let your heart therefore be perfect*] Be sincere in your faith, be irreproachable in your conduct.

Verse 63. *Two and twenty thousand oxen*] This was the whole amount of the victims that had been offered during the *fourteen days;* i. e., the *seven* days of the *dedication,* and the *seven* days of the *feast of tabernacles.* In what way could they dispose of the *blood* of so many victims?

Verse 64. *Did the king hallow the middle of*

A. M. 3000
B. C. 1004
Ante I. Ol. 228
An. Archippi,
Arch. Athen.
perpet. 9

was before the Lord, *was* too little to receive the burnt-offerings, and meat-offerings, and the fat of the peace-offerings.

65 And at that time Solomon held ᵛa feast, and all Israel with him, a great congregation, from ʷthe entering in of Hamath unto ˣthe river of Egypt, before the Lord our

God, ʸseven days and seven days, *even* fourteen days.

66 ᶻOn the eighth day he sent the people away: and they ᵃblessed the king, and went unto their tents joyful and glad of heart for all the goodness that the Lord had done for David his servant, and for Israel his people.

A. M. 3000
B. C. 1004
Ante I. Ol. 228
An. Archippi,
Arch. Athen.
perpet. 9

ᵛVer. 2; Lev. xxiii. 34——ʷNum. xxxiv. 8; Josh. xiii. 5; Judg. iii. 3; 2 Kings xiv. 25

ˣGen. xv. 18; Num. xxxiv. 5——ʸ2 Chronicles vii. 8 ᶻ2 Chron. vii. 9, 10——ᵃOr, *thanked*

---

the court] The great altar of burnt-offerings was not sufficient for the number of sacrifices which were then made; therefore the middle of the court was *set apart*, and an altar erected there for the same purpose.

Verse 65. *From—Hamath*] Supposed to be *Antioch* of Syria; *unto the river of Egypt*—to the *Rhinocorura;* the former being on the *north*, the latter on the *south:* i. e., from one extremity of the land to the other.

Verse 66. *They blessed the king*] Wished him all spiritual and temporal happiness. They were contented with their king, at peace among themselves, and happy in their God; so that they returned to their houses magnifying their God for all his bounty to them, their country, and their king. How happy must these people have been, and how prosperous, had their king continued to walk uprightly before God! But alas! the king fell, and the nation followed his example.

CHAPTER IX

The Lord appears a second time to Solomon, and assures him that he had heard his prayer; and that he would establish his worship for ever in that temple, and him and his successors on the throne of Israel, provided he and they would keep his statutes and judgments, 1–5; but if they should transgress and forsake the Lord, then they should be cast off, the temple itself abandoned, and their enemies permitted to prevail over them, 6–9. Solomon having finished the temple and the king's house, about which he was employed twenty years, and having received assistance from Hiram king of Tyre, he gave him in return twenty cities in Galilee, with which he was not pleased, 10–14. Solomon's levies, buildings, and the persons employed 15–23. Pharaoh's daughter comes to the city of David, 24. He sacrifices thrice a year at the temple, 25. Solomon's navy, and the gold they brought from Ophir, 26–28.

A. M. 3013
B. C. 991
Ante I. Ol. 215
An. Thersippi,
Arch. Athen.
perpet. 3

AND ᵃit came to pass, when Solomon had finished the building of the house of the Lord, ᵇand the king's house, and ᶜall Solomon's desire which he was pleased to do,

2 That the Lord appeared to Solomon the second time, ᵈas he had appeared unto him at Gibeon.

3 And the Lord said unto him, ᵉI have heard thy prayer and thy supplication, that thou hast made before me: I have hallowed this house, which thou hast built, ᶠto put my name there for ever; ᵍand mine eyes and mine heart shall be there perpetually.

4 And if thou wilt ʰwalk before me, ⁱas

David thy father walked, in integrity of heart, and in uprightness, to do according to all that I have commanded thee, *and* wilt keep my statutes and my judgments:

5 Then I will establish the throne of thy kingdom upon Israel for ever, ᵏas I promised to David thy father, saying, There shall not fail thee a man upon the throne of Israel.

6 ˡ*But* if ye shall at all turn from following me, ye or your children, and will not keep my commandments *and* my statutes which I have set before you, but go and serve other gods, and worship them:

7 ᵐThen will I cut off Israel out of the land

A. M. 3013
B. C. 991
Ante I. Ol. 215
An. Thersippi,
Arch. Athen.
perpet. 3

ᵃ2 Chron. vii. 11——ᵇChap. vii. 1——ᶜ2 Chron. viii. 6 ᵈChap. iii. 5——ᵉ2 Kings xx. 5; Psa. x. 17——ᶠChap. viii. 29——ᵍDeut. xi. 12——ʰGen. xvii. 1——ⁱChap. xi. 4, 6, 38; xiv. 8; xv. 5

ᵏ2 Sam. vii. 12, 16; chap. ii. 4; vi. 12; 1 Chron. xxii. 10; Psa. cxxxii. 12——ˡ2 Sam. vii. 14; 2 Chron. vii. 19, 20; Psa. lxxxix. 30, &c——ᵐDeut. iv. 26; 2 Kings xvii. 23; xxv. 21

NOTES ON CHAP. IX

Verse 2. *The Lord appeared to Solomon*] The design of this appearance, which was in a dream, as that was at Gibeon, was to assure Solomon that God had accepted his service, and had taken that house for his dwelling-

place, and would continue it, and establish him and his descendants upon the throne of Israel for ever, provided they served him with an upright heart; but, on the contrary, if they forsook him, he would abandon both them and his temple.

Verse 7. *A proverb and a by-word among*

A. M. 3013
B. C. 991
Ante I. Ol. 215
An. Thersippi,
Arch. Athen.
perpet. 3

which I have given them; and this house which I have hallowed [n]for my name, will I cast out of my sight; [o]and Israel shall be a proverb and a by-word among all people:

8 And [p]at this house, *which* is high, every one that passeth by it shall be astonished, and shall hiss; and they shall say, [q]Why hath the LORD done thus unto this land, and to this house?

9 And they shall answer, Because they forsook the LORD their God, who brought forth their fathers out of the land of Egypt, and have taken hold upon other gods, and have worshipped them, and served them: therefore hath the LORD brought upon them all this evil.

10 [r]And it came to pass at the end of twenty years, when Solomon had built the two houses, the house of the LORD, and the king's house,

11 ([s]*Now* Hiram the king of Tyre had furnished Solomon with cedar trees and fir trees, and with gold, according to all his desire,)

A. M. 3013
B. C. 991
Ante I. Ol. 215
An. Thersippi,
Arch. Athen.
perpet. 3

that then King Solomon gave Hiram twenty cities in the land of Galilee.

12 And Hiram came out from Tyre to see the cities which Solomon had given him; and they [t]pleased him not.

13 And he said, What cities *are* these which thou hast given me, my brother? [u]And he called them the land of [v]Cabul unto this day.

14 And Hiram sent to the king sixscore talents of gold.

A.M. 2989-3029
B. C. 1015-975
Anno ante I.
Olymp. 239-199

15 And this *is* the reason of [w]the levy which King Solomon raised; for to build the house of the LORD, and his own house, and [x]Millo, and the wall of Jerusalem, and [y]Hazor, and [z]Megiddo, and [a]Gezer.

16 *For* Pharaoh king of Egypt had gone up, and taken Gezer, and burnt it with fire, [b]and slain the Canaanites that dwelt in the city, and

---

[n]Jeremiah vii. 14——[o]Deut. xxviii. 37; Psa. xliv. 14
[p]2 Chron. vii. 21——[q]Deut. xxix. 24, 25, 26; Jer. xxii. 8, 9——[r]Chap. vi. 37, 38; vii. 1; 2 Chron. viii. 1
[s]2 Chron. viii. 2

[t]Heb. *were not right in his eyes*——[u]Josh. xix. 27
[v]That is, *displeasing* or *dirty*——[w]Ch. v. 13——[x]Ver. 24; 2 Sam. v. 9——[y]Josh. xix. 36——[z]Josh. xvii. 11
[a]Josh. xvi. 10; Judg. i. 29——[b]Josh. xvi. 10

---

all people] And so they are to the present; the *unbelieving Jews*, the *stubborn, stiff-necked Jews*, are words still in common use. They forsook the Lord, rejected his Christ, and are cast off, their temple destroyed, and they scattered over the face of the earth.

Verse 9. *Have taken hold upon other gods*] When an indigent person claims the protection of a superior, he casts himself down before him, and *lays hold of his feet;* and this expression is frequently used when there is no prostration: *I have taken hold of thy feet.* When a person is called into the presence of the *Burman* monarch, he is said to go to the *golden foot.*—WARD'S *Customs.*

Verse 10. *At the end of twenty years*] He employed seven years and a half in building the temple, and twelve years and a half in building the king's house; see chap. vii. 1; 2 Chron. viii. 1.

Verse 11. *Solomon gave Hiram twenty cities*] It is very likely that Solomon did not give those cities to Hiram so that they should be annexed to his Tyrian dominions, but rather gave him the produce of them till the money was paid which he had advanced to Solomon for his buildings. It appears however that either Hiram did not accept them, or that, having received the produce till he was paid, he then restored them to Solomon; for in the parallel place, 2 Chron. viii. 2, it is said, *The cities which Hiram had restored to Solomon, Solomon built them, and caused the children of Israel to dwell there.* Some think that they were *heathen cities* which Solomon had conquered, and therefore had a right to give them if he pleased, as they were not any part of the land given by promise to the Israelites.

Verse 13. *Called them the land of Cabul*]

Whether this epithet was given to this land by Hiram as a mark of disapprobation, or what is its proper meaning, the learned are not agreed. That there was a country of this name in the promised land in the time of Joshua, is evident enough from Josh. xix. 27, as it was one part of the boundary of the tribe of Asher; hence some interpret the word *border* or *boundary*, and so the *Septuagint* understood it, for they have translated the Hebrew word ὅριον, which signifies the same. The margin gives another meaning.

Verse 14. *Sixscore talents of gold.*] This was the sum which Hiram had lent, and in order to pay this Solomon had laid a tax upon his people, as we afterward learn. The whole is very darkly expressed.

Verse 15. *This is the reason of the levy*] That is, in order to pay Hiram the sixscore talents of gold which he had borrowed from him (Hiram not being willing to take the Galilean cities mentioned above; or, having taken them, soon restored them again) he was obliged to lay a tax upon the people; and that this was a grievous and oppressive tax we learn from chap. xii. 1-4, where the elders of Israel came to Rehoboam, complaining of their heavy state of taxation, and entreating that their yoke might be made lighter.

And Millo] This is supposed to have been a deep valley between Mount Sion and what was called the city of Jebus, which Solomon filled up, and it was built on, and became a sort of fortified place, and a place for public assemblies.—See *Calmet.*

Verse 16. *Pharaoh—had gone up, and taken Gezer*] This city Joshua had taken from the Canaanites, Josh. x. 33, and xii. 12, and it was divided by lot to the tribe of Ephraim, and was

A.M.2989-3029
B.C.1015-975
Anno ante I.
Olymp.239-199

given it *for* a present unto his daughter, Solomon's wife.

17 And Solomon built Gezer, and ᶜBeth-horon the nether,

18 And ᵈBaalath, and Tadmor in the wilderness, in the land,

19 And all the cities of store that Solomon had, and cities for ᵉhis chariots and cities for his horsemen, and ᶠthat which Solomon ᵍdesired to build in Jerusalem, and in Lebanon, and in all the land of his dominion.

20 ʰ*And* all the people *that were* left of the Amorites, Hittites, Perizzites, Hivites, and Jebusites, which *were* not of the children of Israel,

21 Their children ⁱthat were left after them in the land, ᵏwhom the children of Israel also were not able utterly to destroy, ˡupon those did Solomon levy a tribute of ᵐbond-service unto this day.

22 But of the children of Israel did Solomon ⁿmake no bondmen: but they *were* men of war, and his servants, and his princes, and his captains, and rulers of his chariots, and his horsemen.

A.M.2989-3029
B.C.1015-975
Anno ante I.
Olymp.239-199

23 These *were* the chief of the officers that *were* over Solomon's work, ᵒfive hundred and fifty, which bare rule over the people that wrought in the work.

24 But ᵖPharaoh's daughter came up out of the city of David unto ᑫher house which *Solomon* had built for her: ʳthen did he build Millo.

25 ˢAnd three times in a year did Solomon offer burnt-offerings and peace-offerings upon the altar which he built unto the LORD, and he burnt incense ᵗupon the altar that *was* before the LORD. So he finished the house.

26 And ᵘKing Solomon made a navy of ships in ᵛEzion-geber, which *is* beside Eloth, on the ʷshore of the Red Sea, in the land of Edom.

27 ˣAnd Hiram sent in the navy his servants, shipmen that had knowledge of the sea, with the servants of Solomon.

28 And they came to ʸOphir, and fetched from thence gold, four hundred and twenty talents, and brought *it* to King Solomon.

ᶜJosh. xvi 3; xxi. 22; 2 Chron. viii. 5——ᵈJosh. xix. 44: 2 Chron. viii. 4, 6, &c.——ᵉChap. iv. 26——ᶠHeb. *the desire of Solomon which he desired*——ᵍVer. 1——ʰ2 Chron viii. 7, &c.——ⁱJudg. i. 21, 27, 29; iii. 1——ᵏJosh. xv. 63; xvii. 12——ˡJudg. i. 28——ᵐSee GEN. ix. 25, 26; Ezra ii. 55, 58; Neh. vii. 57; xi. 3

ⁿLev. xxv. 39——ᵒSee 2 Chron. viii. 10——ᵖChap. iii. 1; 2 Chron. viii. 11——ᑫChap. vii. 8——ʳ2 Sam. v. 9; chap. xi. 27, 2 Chron. xxxii. 5——ˢ2 Chron. viii. 12, 13, 16——ᵗHeb. *upon it*——ᵘ2 Chron. viii. 17, 18 ᵛNum. xxxiii. 35; Deut. ii. 8; chap. xxii. 48——ʷHeb. *lip*——ˣChap. x. 11——ʸJob xxii. 24

---

intended to be one of the Levitical cities; but it appears that the Canaanites had retaken it, and kept possession till the days of Solomon, when his father-in-law, Pharaoh king of Egypt, retook it, and gave it to Solomon in dowry with his daughter.

Verse 18. *And Tadmor in the wilderness*] This is almost universally allowed to be the same with the celebrated *Palmyra* the ruins of which remain to the present day, and give us the highest idea of Solomon's splendour and magnificence. *Palmyra* stood upon a fertile plain surrounded by a barren desert, having the river Euphrates on the east. The ruins are well described by Messrs. *Dawkes* and *Wood*, of which they give fine representations. They are also well described in the ancient part of the *Universal History*, vol. i. p. 367-70. The description concludes thus: "The world never saw a more glorious city; the pride, it is likely, of ancient times, and the reproach of our own; a city not more remarkable for the state of her buildings and unwontedness of her situation than for the extraordinary *personages* who once flourished there, among whom the renowned *Zenobia* and the incomparable *Longinus* must for ever be remembered with admiration and regret."

Verse 19. *And all the cities of store*] Though, by the multitude and splendour of his buildings, Solomon must have added greatly to the magnificence of his reign; yet, however plenteous silver and gold were in his times, his subjects must have been greatly oppressed with the taxation necessary to defray such a vast public expenditure.

Verse 21. *A tribute of bond-service*] He made them do the most laborious part of the public works, the *Israelites* being generally exempt. When *Sesostris*, king of Egypt, returned from his wars, he caused temples to be built in all the cities of Egypt, but did not employ one *Egyptian* in the work, having built the whole by the hands of the *captives* which he had taken in his wars. Hence he caused this inscription to be placed upon each temple:—

Ουδεις εγχωριος εις αυτα μεμοχθηκε.

No native has laboured in these.
Diodor. Sic. Bibl., lib. i., c. 56.

It appears that Solomon might with propriety have placed a similar inscription on most of his works.

Verse 25. *Three times in a year did Solomon offer*] These three times were: 1. The *passover*. 2. The feast of *pentecost*. 3. The feast of *tabernacles*.

Verse 26. *A navy of ships*] Literally, אֳנִי *oni, a ship:* in the parallel place, 2 Chron. viii. 17, it is said that Hiram sent him אֳנִיּוֹת *oniyoth, ships;* but it does not appear that Solomon in this case built more than one ship, and this was manned principally by the Tyrians.

Verse 28. *And they came to Ophir*] No man knows certainly, to this day, where this *Ophir* was situated. There were two places of this name; one somewhere in India, beyond the

Ganges, and another in Arabia, near the country of the Sabæans, mentioned by Job, chap. xxii. 24: *Then shalt thou lay up gold as dust; and the* gold *of Ophir as the stones of the brooks.* And chap. xxviii. 16: *It cannot be valued with the gold of Ophir, with the precious onyx, or the sapphire.* Calmet places this country at the sources of the Euphrates and Tigris.

But there are several reasons to prove that this was not the Ophir of the Bible, which it seems was so situated as to require a voyage of *three years* long to go out, load, and return. Mr. *Bruce* has discussed this subject at great length; see his *Travels*, vol. ii., chap. iv., p. 354, &c. He endeavours to prove that *Ezion-geber* is situated on the Elanitic branch of the Arabian Gulf or Red Sea. 2. That *Tharshish* is Moka, near to Melinda, in the Indian Ocean, in about *three* degrees south latitude. 3. That *Ophir* lies somewhere in the land of *Sofala*,

or in the vicinity of the *Zambeze* river, opposite the island of Madagascar, where there have been gold and silver mines in great abundance from the remotest antiquity. And he proves, 4. That no vessel could perform this voyage *in less than* THREE *years*, because of the *monsoons;* that more time *need not* be employed, and that this is the precise time mentioned in chap. x. 22. 5. That this is the country of the queen of *Sheba*, or *Sabia*, or *Azeba*, who on her visit to Solomon, brought him *one hundred and twenty* talents of gold, and of spices and precious stones great store, ver 10. And that gold, ivory, silver, &c., are the natural productions of this country. To illustrate and prove his positions he has given a map on a large scale, "showing the track of Solomon's fleet in their three years' voyage from the Elanitic Gulf to Ophir and Tharshish;" to which, and his description, I must refer the reader.

CHAPTER X

The queen of Sheba visits Solomon, and brings rich presents; and tries him by hard questions, which he readily solves, 1–3. She expresses great surprise at his wisdom, his buildings, his court, &c.; and praises God for placing him on the Jewish throne, 4–9. She gives him rich presents, 10. What the navy of Hiram brought from Ophir, 11, 12. The queen of Sheba returns, 13. Solomon's annual revenue, 14, 15. He makes two hundred targets and three hundred shields of gold, 16, 17. His magnificent ivory throne, 18–20. His drinking vessels all of gold, 21. What the navy of Tharshish brought every three years to Solomon, 22. His great riches, numerous chariots, and horsemen, 23–27. He brings chariots and horses out of Egypt, 28, 29.

A. M. 3014
B. C. 990
Ante I. Ol. 214
An. Thersippi,
Arch. Athen.
perpet. 4

A ND when the [a]queen of Sheba heard of the fame of Solomon, concerning the name of the LORD, she came [b]to prove him with hard questions.

2 And she came to Jerusalem with a very great train, with camels that bare spices, and very much gold, and precious stones: and when she was come to Solomon, she communed with him of all that was in her heart.

A. M. 3014
B. C. 990
Ante I. Ol. 214
An. Thersippi,
Arch. Athen.
perpet. 4

---

[a]2 Chron. ix. 1, &c.; Matt. vii. 42; Luke xi. 31   [b]See Judg. xiv. 12; Prov. i. 6

NOTES ON CHAP. X

Verse 1. *When the queen of Sheba heard*] As our Lord calls her *queen of the south*, (Matt. xii. 42), it is likely the name should be written *Saba, Azab*, or *Azaba*, all of which signify the *south*. She is called *Balkis* by the Arabians, but by the Abyssinians *Maqueda*. See the account at the end of this chapter.

With hard questions.] בחידות *bechidoth; Septuagint, εν αινγμασι, riddles. With parables and riddles*, says the Arabic.

Verse 2. *She came to Jerusalem with— spices, &c.*] Those who contend that she was queen of the Sabæans, a people of Arabia Felix, towards the southern extremity of the Red Sea, find several proofs of their opinion: 1. That the Sabæans abounded in riches and spices.

India mittit ebur, molles sua thura Sabæi

"India furnishes ivory, and the effeminate *Sabæans* their *frankincense*."
        VIRG. *Geor.* i., ver. 57.

And again:—

Divisæ arboribus patriæ: sola India nigrum Fert ebenum; solis est thurea virga Sabæis.
        Geor. ii., ver. 116.

All sorts of trees their several countries know: Black ebon only will in India grow;

And *odorous frankincense* on the *Sabæan* bough.
        DRYDEN.

————*Ubi templum illi centumque* Sabæo *Thure calent aræ.*

Where to her fame a hundred altars rise, And pour *Sabæan* odours to the skies.

PLINY (*Hist. Nat.* lib. xii., c. 17) observes, *Non alia ligni genera in usu sunt quam odorata; cibosque* Sabæi *coquunt thuris ligno; alii myrrhæ*. "The *Sabæans* use *odorous wood* only, and even use the *incense tree* and *myrrh* to cook their victuals."

2. All ancient authors speak, not only of their *odoriferous woods*, but of their rich *gold and silver mines*, and of their *precious stones*. See *Pliny, Hist. Nat.* lib. xxxvii., c. 6, &c.

3. It is also well known that the Sabæans had queens for their sovereigns, and not *kings*. So *Claudian*, in Eutrop. lib. i.

————*Medis levibusque* Sabæis *Imperat hic sexus*, reginarumque *sub armis* Barbariæ *pars magna jacet.*

By this is meant, says Mr. Bruce, the country between the tropic and mountains of Abyssinia, the country of shepherds, from *berber*, a shepherd. And he contends that these *Sabæans* were a distinct *people* from the *Ethiopians* and the *Arabs*, and that SABA was a distinct *state*.

A. M. 3014
B. C. 990
Ante I. Ol. 214
An. Thersippi,
Arch. Athen.
perpet. 4

3 And Solomon told her all her ᶜquestions: there was not any thing hid from the king, which he told her not.

4 And when the queen of Sheba had seen all Solomon's wisdom, and the house that he had built,

5 And the meat of his table, and the sitting of his servants, and the ᵈattendance of his ministers, and their apparel, and his ᵉcup-bearers, ᶠand his ascent by which he went up unto the house of the LORD; there was no more spirit in her.

6 And she said to the king, It was a true ᵍreport that I heard in mine own land of thy ʰacts and of thy wisdom.

7 Howbeit I believed not the words, until I came, and mine eyes had seen *it:* and, behold,

the half was not told me: ⁱthy wisdom and prosperity exceedeth the fame which I heard.

A. M. 3014
B. C. 990
Ante I. Ol. 214
An. Thersippi,
Arch. Athen.
perpet. 4

8 ᵏHappy *are* thy men, happy *are* these thy servants, which stand continually before thee, *and* that hear thy wisdom.

9 ˡBlessed be the LORD thy God, which delighted in thee, to set thee on the throne of Israel: because the LORD loved Israel for ever, therefore made he thee king, ᵐto do judgment and justice.

10 And she ⁿgave the king a hundred and twenty talents of gold, and of spices very great store, and precious stones: there came no more such abundance of spices as these which the queen of Sheba gave to King Solomon.

11 ᵒAnd the navy also of Hiram, that

ᶜHebrew, *words*——ᵈHeb. *standing*——ᵉOr, *butlers* ᶠ1 Chron. xxvi. 16——ᵍHeb. *word*——ʰOr, *sayings* ⁱHeb. *thou hast added wisdom and goodness to the fame*

ᵏProverbs viii. 34——ˡChapter v. 7——ᵐ2 Sam. viii. 15; Psa. lxxii. 2; Prov. viii. 15——ⁿPsa. lxxii. 10, 15——ᵒChap. ix. 27

Verse 3. *Solomon told her all her questions*] Riddles, problems, fables, apologues, &c., formed the principal part of the wisdom of the East; indeed they use and delight in them to the present day. See the case of Samson and his friends, Judg. xiv. 12, 14, and the notes there.

Verse 4. *Had seen all Solomon's wisdom*] By the answers which he gave to her subtle questions.

And the house that he had built] Most probably his own house.

Verse 5. *The meat of his table*] The immense supply of all kinds of food daily necessary for the many thousands which were fed at and from his table. See chap. iv. 22, 23, and the notes there.

And the sitting of his servants] The various orders and distinctions of his officers.

The attendance of his ministers] See the account of these and their attendance, chap. iv. 1, &c.

And their apparel] The peculiarity of their robes, and their splendour and costliness.

And his cup-bearers] The original משקיו *mashkaiv* may as well be applied to his *beverage*, or to his *drinking utensils*, as to his *cup-bearers*.

And his ascent by which he went up] It seems very strange that the *steps* to the temple should be such a separate matter of astonishment. The original is ועלתו אשר יעלה בית יהוה which all the versions have translated, *And the holocausts which he offered in the house of the Lord.* The *Vulgate, Septuagint, Chaldee, Syriac,* and *Arabic,* all express this sense: so does the *German* translation of *Luther,* from which, in this place, we have most pitifully departed: Unb seine Brandopfer, die er in dem Hause des Herrn opferte; "And his burnt-offering which he offered in the house of the Lord."

There was no more spirit in her.] She was overpowered with astonishment; she fainted. I have seen precisely the same effect produced; a lady who was herself an artist, viewing some

exquisitely finished oriental paintings, was so struck with astonishment that she twice nearly fainted, and was obliged to leave the room. What happened to the queen of Sheba is a natural and not an uncommon effect which will be produced in a delicate sensible mind at the sight of rare and extraordinary productions of art.

Of the profusion of Solomon's sacrifices we have already had proof, chap. viii. 63, and ix. 25.

Verse 8. *Happy are thy men*] All these are very natural expressions from a person in her state of mind.

Verse 10. *A hundred and twenty talents of gold*] The worth of these one hundred and twenty talents of gold, according to Mr. Reynolds, is equal to £843,905. 10s. 4¾d. of our British sterling. But the *spices* and *precious stones* might have been yet of more value. After this verse the 13th should be read, which is here most evidently misplaced; and then the account of the queen of Sheba will be concluded, and that of Solomon's revenue will stand without interruption.

Verse 13. *All her desire whatsoever she asked*] Some imagine she desired progeny from the wise king of Israel; and all the traditions concerning her state that she had a son by Solomon called *Menilek,* who was brought up at the Israelitish court, succeeded his mother in the kingdom of Saba, and introduced among his subjects the Jewish religion. See at the end of the chapter.

Verse 11. *Great plenty of almug trees*] In the parallel place, 2 Chron. ix. 10, 11, these are called *algum trees,* the ם *mem* and the ג *gimel* being transposed; probably the latter is the more correct orthography. What the *algum trees* were we do not exactly know. The *Vulgate* calls it *ligna thyina,* the *thya* or *lignum vitæ* wood; and Mr. Parkhurst thinks that the original אלגומים *algumim,* comes from אל *al, not,* and גם *gem, to fill;* because the lignum

A. M. 3014
B. C. 990
Ante I. Ol. 214
An. Thersippi,
Arch. Athen.
perpet. 4

brought gold from Ophir, brought in from Ophir great plenty of ᴾalmug trees, and precious stones.

12 �q And the king made of the almug trees ʳpillars ˢfor the house of the LORD, and for the king's house, harps also and psalteries for singers: there came no such ᵗalmug trees, nor were seen unto this day.

13 And King Solomon gave unto the queen of Sheba all her desire, whatsoever she asked, beside *that* which Solomon gave her ᵘof his royal bounty. So she turned and went to her own country, she and her servants.

A.M.2989-3029
B.C.1015-975
Anno ante I.
Olymp.239-199

14 Now the weight of gold that came to Solomon in one year was six hundred threescore and six talents of gold.

15 Beside *that he had* of the merchantmen, and of the traffic of the spice merchants, and ᵛof all the kings of Arabia, and of the ʷgovernors of the country.

16 And King Solomon made two hundred targets *of* beaten gold: six hundred *shekels* of gold went to one target.

17 And *he made* ˣthree hundred shields *of* beaten gold; three pounds of gold went to one shield: and the king put them in the ʸhouse of the forest of Lebanon.

18 ᶻMoreover the king made a great throne of ivory, and overlaid it with the best gold.

19 The throne had six steps, and the top of the throne *was* round ᵃbehind: and *there were* ᵇstays on either side on the place of the seat, and two lions stood beside the stays.

20 And twelve lions stood there on the one side and on the other upon the six steps: there was not ᶜthe like made in any kingdom.

21 ᵈAnd all King Solomon's drinking vessels *were of* gold, and all the vessels of the house of the forest of Lebanon *were of* pure gold; ᵉnone *were of* silver: it was nothing accounted of in the days of Solomon.

22 For the king had at sea a navy of ᶠTharshish with the navy of Hiram: once in three years came the navy of Tharshish, bringing gold, and silver, ᵍivory, and apes, and peacocks.

23 So ʰKing Solomon exceeded all the kings

A.M.2989-3029
B. C. 1015-975
Anno ante I.
Olymp.239-199

ᵖ2 Chron. ii. 8; ix. 10, 11, *algum trees*——q2 Chron. ix. 11——ʳOr, *rails*——ˢHeb. *a prop*——ᵗ2 Chron. ix. 10——ᵘHeb. *according to the hand of King Solomon* ᵛ2 Chron. ix. 24; Psa. lxxii. 10——ʷOr, *captains* ˣChap. xiv. 26——ʸChap. vii. 2

ᶻ2 Chron. ix. 17, &c.——ᵃHeb. *on the hinder part thereof*——ᵇHeb. *bands*——ᶜHeb. *so*——ᵈ2 Chron. ix. 20, &c.——ᵉOr, there was *no silver* in them——ᶠGen. x. 4; 2 Chron. xx. 36——ᵍOr, *elephants' teeth*——ʰChap. iii. 12, 13; iv. 30

---

vitæ is of so close a texture that it can imbibe no water, and cannot be affected by wet weather. The *Septuagint* translate it ξύλα πυκινα, *pine timber;* the *Syriac* ܟܐܝܣܐ ܕܩܝܣܘ *kaise dakisotho*, probably *cypress wood*, or what the translators render *ligna brasilica;* the *Arabic* translates *coloured wood*, and subjoins a paraphrase, *for that wood was by nature painted with various colours*. Perhaps the Arabic comes nearest the truth; *wood shaded* of different colours, such as the *rose wood* and such like, which are brought to us from various parts of the East Indies. The whole passage as it stands in the Arabic is this: "And the ships of Hiram brought gold from the land of Hind, (India,) and they carried also much *coloured wood*, (but this wood is *naturally painted of various colours*,) and very precious jewels. And Solomon put some of that same *painted wood* which was brought to him in the house of the Lord, and in his own house; and with it he adorned them." And for inlaying and veneering nothing can be finer than this wood.

Verse 14. *The weight of gold—was six hundred threescore and six talents*] This would amount in our money to £4,683,675 12s. 8½d. sterling. This seems to be what he got annually of *bullion;* but independently of this, he had *tribute* of all the kings of Arabia, duties from merchantmen, and the traffic of spice merchants; see ver. 25.

Verse 16. *Solomon made two hundred targets*

of beaten gold] I have already conjectured that the צנה *tsinnah* might resemble the Highland targe or target, with a dagger projecting from the UMBO or centre.

Verse 17. He made *three hundred shields*] The מגן *magen* was a large shield by which the whole body was protected.

Mr. Reynolds computes that the *two hundred targets*, on each of which were employed *three hundred shekels* of gold, were worth £28,131 16s. 9½d.

And the *three hundred shields*, in forming each of which *three pounds of gold* were employed, were worth £210,976 7s. 7d.

Verse 19. *The throne was round behind: and there were stays on either side*] This description seems to indicate that the throne was in the form of one of our ancient *round-topped, two-armed* chairs. This throne or chair of state was raised on a platform, the ascent to which consisted of six steps. What we call *stays* is in the Hebrew ידת *yadoth, hands*, which serves to confirm the conjecture above.

Verse 22. *A navy of Tharshish*] For probable conjectures concerning this place, and the *three years' voyage*, see at the end of this and the preceding chapter.

Apes] קפים *kophim;* probably a species of *monkey* rather than *ape*.

Verse 23. *Solomon exceeded all the kings of the earth for riches*] Mr. Reynolds, stating the yearly tribute of Solomon, 666 talents of

A.M.2989-3029
B. C. 1015-975
Anno ante I.
Olymp.239-199

of the earth for riches and for wisdom.

24 And all the earth [i]sought to Solomon, to hear his wisdom, which God had put in his heart.

25 And they brought every man his present, vessels of silver, and vessels of gold, and garments, and armour, and spices, horses, and mules, a rate year by year.

26 [k]And Solomon [l]gathered together chariots and horsemen: and he had a thousand and four hundred chariots, and twelve thousand horsemen, whom he bestowed in the cities for chariots, and with the king at Jerusalem.

27 [m]And the king [n]made silver *to be* in Jerusalem as stones, and cedars made he *to be* as the sycamore trees that *are* in the vale, for abundance.

A.M.2989-3029
B. C. 1015-975
Anno ante I.
Olymp.239-199

28 [o]And [p]Solomon had horses brought out of Egypt, and [q]linen yarn: the king's merchants received the linen yarn at a price.

29 And a chariot came up and went out of Egypt for six hundred *shekels* of silver, and a horse for a hundred and fifty: [r]and so for all the kings of the Hittites, and for the kings of Syria, did they bring *them* out [s]by their means.

---

[i]Heb. *sought the face of*——[k]Chap. iv. 26; 2 Chron. i. 14; ix. 25——[l]Deut. xvii. 16——[m]2 Chron. i. 15–17 [n]Heb. *gave*——[o]Deut. xvii. 16; 2 Chron. i. 16; ix. 28

[p]Heb. *And the going forth of the horses which* was *Solomon's*——[q]Ezek. xxvii. 7——[r]Josh. i. 4; 2 Kings vii. 6——[s]Heb. *by their hand*

---

gold, at about four times as much as his father left him, hence reckons that he had £4,909,371 8s. 8d. each year, £94,410 19s. 9¼d. per week, £13,487 5s. 8d. per day, taking each *day*, *week*, and *year*, one with another.

Verse 25. *They brought every man his present*] This means *tribute; and* it shows us of what sort that tribute was, viz., *vessels* of *gold* and *silver*, probably *ingots; garments* of very rich stuffs; *armour*, for little of this kind was ever made in Judea; *spices*, which doubtless sold well in that country; *horses*, which were very rare; and *mules*, the most *necessary* animal for all the purposes of life.

Verse 26. *He had a thousand and four hundred chariots*] See the note on chap. iv. 26.

Verse 27. *Made silver—as stones*] He destroyed its value by making it so exceedingly plenty.

As the sycamore trees] He planted many cedars, and doubtless had much cedar wood imported; so that it became as common as the *sycamore trees*, which appear to have grown there in great abundance. This is considered to be a tree that partakes of the nature of the *fig tree*, and of the *mulberry*. Of the former it has the *fruit*, and of the latter the *leaves; that* is, the fruit had a considerable resemblance to the fig, and the *leaf* to that of the *mulberry tree:* hence its name *sycamore*, from the Greek συκον, a fig, and μορεα, a *mulberry tree*.

Verse 28. *Horses brought out of Egypt*] It is thought that the first people who used horses in *war* were the Egyptians; and it is well known that the nations who knew the use of this creature in battle had greatly the advantage of those who did not. God had absolutely prohibited horses to be imported or used; but in many things Solomon paid little attention to the Divine command.

And linen yarn] The original word, מקוה *mikveh*, is hard to be understood, if it be not indeed a *corruption*.

The versions are all puzzled with it: the *Vulgate* and *Septuagint* make it a proper name: "And Solomon had horses brought out of Egypt, and from *Coa*, or *Tekoa*." Some think it signifies a *tribute*, thus *Bochart:* "They brought horses to Solomon out of Egypt; and

as to the tribute, the farmers of this prince received it at a price." They farmed the tribute, gave so much annually for it, taking the different kinds to themselves, and giving a round sum for the whole.

Some suppose that MIKVEH signifies the *string* or *cord* by which one horse's head is tied to the tail of another; and that the meaning is, Solomon brought *droves* of horses, thus tied, out of Egypt.

Rabbi Solomon Jarchi, in his comment on the parallel place, 2 Chron. i. 14, says that מקוה *mikveh* signifies a collection or drove of horses, or what the Germans call ſtutte, a *stud*. He observes on that place, "That he has heard that there was a company of merchants in Egypt, who bought horses from the Egyptians at a certain price, on condition that no person should be permitted to bring a horse out of Egypt but through them."

Houbigant supposes the place to be *corrupt*, and that for מקוה *mikveh* we should read מרכבה *mercabah*, *chariots:* "And Solomon had horses brought out of Egypt, and chariots; and the king's merchants received the chariots at a price: and a chariot came up and went out of Egypt for *six hundred* shekels of silver," &c. This makes a very good and consistent sense; but none of the versions acknowledged it, nor is there any various reading here in any of the MSS. yet collated.

If we understand it of *thread*, it may refer to the *byssus* or *fine flax* for which Egypt was famous; but I do not see on what authority we translate it *linen thread*. *Bochart's* opinion appears to me the most probable, as the text now stands; but the *charge* contended for by Houbigant makes the text far more simple and intelligible.

Verse 29. *A chariot came up—for six hundred* shekels] This was the ordinary price of a *chariot*, as *a hundred and fifty shekels* were for a *horse*.

Kings of the Hittites] These must have been the remains of the original inhabitants of Canaan, who had gone to some other country, probably Syria, and formed themselves into a principality there. It seems that neither horses nor chariots came out of Egypt but by means of Solomon's servants.

"WE are not to wonder, if the prodigious hurry and flow of business, and the immensely valuable transactions they had with each other, had greatly familiarized the Tyrians and Jews with their correspondents, the Cushites and shepherds, on the coast of Africa. This had gone so far as, very naturally, to create a desire in the queen of Azab, the sovereign of that country, to go herself and see the application of the immense treasures that had been exported from her country for a series of years, and the prince who so magnificently employed them. There can be no doubt of this expedition; as Pagan, Arab, Moor, Abyssinian, and all the countries around, vouch for it nearly in the terms of Scripture.

"Her name, the Arabs say, was Belkis; the Abyssinians, Maqueda. Our Saviour calls her queen of the south, without mentioning any other name, but gives his sanction to the truth of the voyage. 'The queen of the south (or Saba, or Azab) shall rise up in judgment with this generation, and shall condemn it, for she came from the uttermost parts of the earth to hear the wisdom of Solomon; and behold a greater than Solomon is here.' No other particulars, however, are mentioned about her in Scripture; and it is not probable that our Saviour would have said she came from the uttermost parts of the earth, if she had been an Arab, and had near *fifty degrees* of the continent behind her. But when we consider that the boundaries of the known land, to the southward, were at that time Raptum or Prassum, as we have just seen, these, being the uttermost parts of the known earth, were, with great propriety, so styled by our Saviour; and of these she was undoubtedly sovereign. The gold, the myrrh, cassia, and frankincense were all the produce of her own country.

"Whether she was a Jewess or a pagan is uncertain. Sabaism was the religion of all the East; it was the constant attendant and stumbling block of the Jews: but considering the multitude of that people then trading from Jerusalem, and the long time it continued, it is not improbable she was a Jewess. 'And when the queen of Sheba heard of the fame of Solomon, concerning the name of the Lord, she came to prove him with hard questions,' 1 Kings x. 1; 2 Chron. ix. 1. Our Saviour moreover speaks of her with praise, pointing her out as an example to the Jews. And in her thanksgiving before Solomon, she alludes to God's blessing on the seed of Israel for ever, which is by no means the language of a pagan, but of a person skilled in the ancient history of this nation.

"She likewise appears to have been a person of learning, and of that sort of learning which was then almost peculiar to Palestine, not to Ethiopia; for we know that one of the reasons of her coming was to examine whether Solomon was really the learned man he was said to be. She came to try him in allegories or parables, in which Nathan had instructed him.

"The annals of the Abyssinians, being very full upon this point, have taken a middle opinion, and by no means an improbable one. They say she was a pagan when she left Azab, but, being full of admiration at Solomon's works, she was converted to Judaism in Jerusalem, and bore him a son whom he called Menilek, and who was their first king.

"The Abyssinians, both Jews and Christians, believe the forty-fifth Psalm to be a prophecy of the queen's voyage to Jerusalem; that she was attended by a daughter of Hiram's from Tyre to Jerusalem; and that the last part of it contains a declaration of her having a son by Solomon, who was to be a king over a nation of the Gentiles.

"To Saba or Azab, then, she returned with her son Menilek; whom, after keeping him some years, she sent back to his father to be instructed. Solomon did not neglect his charge; and he was anointed and crowned king of Ethiopia in the temple of Jerusalem, and at his inauguration took the name of David. After this he returned to Azab, and brought with him a colony of Jews, among whom were many doctors of the law of Moses, particularly one of each tribe, to make judges of in his kingdom; from whom the present *umbares*, or supreme judges (three of whom always attended the king) are said and believed to be descended. With these came also Azarias, the son of Zadok the priest, and brought with him a Hebrew transcript of the law, which was delivered into his custody, as he bore the title of *nebret*, or high priest; and this charge, though the book itself was burnt with the church of Axum, in the Moorish war of Adel, is still continued, as it is said, in the lineage of Azarias, who are *nebrets*, or keepers of the church of Axum, at this day. All Abyssinia was thereupon converted, and the government of the church and state modelled according to what was then in use at Jerusalem.

"By the last act of the queen of Saba's reign, she settled the mode of succession in her country for the future. *First*, she enacted, that the crown should be hereditary in the family of Solomon for ever. *Secondly*, that, after her, no woman should be capable of wearing that crown, or being queen; but that it should descend to the heir male, however distant, in exclusion of all heirs female, however near; and that these two articles should be considered as the fundamental laws of the kingdom, never to be altered or abolished. And, lastly, that the heirs male of the royal house should always be sent prisoners to a high mountain, where they were to continue till their death, or till the succession should open to them.

"The queen of Saba having made these laws irrevocable by all her posterity, died after a long reign of forty years, in 986 before Christ, placing her son Menilek upon the throne, whose posterity, the annals of Abyssinia would teach us to believe, have ever since reigned. So far, indeed, we must bear witness to them that this is no new doctrine, but has been steadfastly and uniformly maintained from their earliest account of time; first, when Jews, then in later days, after they had embraced Christianity. We may farther add, that the testimony of all the neighbouring nations is with them on this subject, whether friends or enemies. They only differ in the name of the queen, or in giving her two names.

"I shall therefore now give a list of their kings of the race of Solomon, descended from the queen of Saba, whose device is a lion passant, proper, upon a field gules; and their motto, *Mo Anbasa am Nizilet Solomon am Negade Juda;* which signifies 'The lion of the race of Solomon and tribe of Judah hath overcome.'

List of the kings of Abyssinia, from Maqueda, Queen of Saba, to the Nativity

Reigned yrs.		Reigned yrs.	
Menilek, or David I	4	Katzina	9
Hendedya, or Zagdur	1	Wazeha	1
Awida	11	Hazer	2
Ausyi	3	Kalas	6
Sawe	31	Solaya	16
Gesaya	15	Falaya	26
Katar	15	Aglebu	3
Mouta	20	Asisena	1
Bahas	9	Brus	29
Kawida	2	Mohesa	1
Kanaza	10	Bazen	16

Bruce's Travels, vol. ii., p. 395.

Mr. Bruce justly finds fault with this table as being *defective;* several kings must necessarily have been lost out of this list. It is probably a late invention, the genealogical tables having been lost or destroyed; and no wonder when we consider the numerous predatory wars in which the people of Abyssinia have been frequently engaged.

I need scarcely add that the very learned *Samuel Bochart* has endeavoured to prove by arguments not to be despised, that the Scripture *Ophir* is the island *Taprobanes* or *Serendib,* now called *Ceylon.* With any other opinions on this subject I think it unnecessary to trouble the reader. That the voyage which Mr. Bruce describes would take up three years, I think he has satisfactorily proved; but on other points and resemblances many readers will doubtless hesitate, while some may suppose his theory is the most plausible of any yet offered to the public on this very obscure subject.

CHAPTER XI

Solomon's attachment to strange women, and consequent idolatry, 1, 2. Number of his wives and concubines, 3. In his old age they turn away his heart from God, 4. He builds temples to idols, burns incense and sacrifices to them, 5–8. The Lord is angry with him, and threatens to deprive him of the kingdom, but will leave one tribe for David's sake, 9–13. The Lord stirs up Hadad, the Edomite, to be his enemy; the history of this man, 14–22. He stirs another adversary against him, Rezon the son of Eliadah. He and Hadad plague Israel, 23–25. Jeroboam also becomes his enemy, and the reason why, 26–28. Ahijah the prophet meets Jeroboam, and promises, in the name of the Lord, that God will rend Israel from the family of Solomon, and give him ten tribes, 29–39. Solomon, hearing of this, seeks to put Jeroboam to death, who escapes to Egypt, where he continues till the death of Solomon, 40. Solomon dies, after having reigned over Israel forty years; and his son Rehoboam reigns in his stead, 41–43.

A.M.3020-3029
B.C. 984-975
Anno ante I.
Olymp.208-199

BUT [a]King Solomon loved [b]many strange women, [c]together with the daughter of Pharaoh, women of the Moabites, Ammonites, Edomites, Zidonians, *and* Hittites;

2 Of the nations *concerning* which the LORD said unto the children of Israel, [d]Ye shall not go in to them, neither shall they come in unto you: *for* surely they will turn away your heart after their gods: Solomon clave unto these in love.

A.M.3020-3029
B.C. 984-975
Anno ante I.
Olymp.208-199

3 And he had seven hundred wives, princesses, and three hundred concubines: and his wives turned away his heart.

4 For it came to pass, when Solomon was old, [e]that his wives turned away his heart after other gods: and his [f]heart was not per-

---

[a]Neh. xiii. 26——[b]Deut. xvii. 17; Ecclus. xlvii. 19
[c]Or, *beside*

[d]Exod. xxxiv. 16; Deut. vii. 3, 4——[e]Deut. xvii. 17; Neh. xiii. 26——[f]Chap. viii. 61

NOTES ON CHAP. XI

Verse 1. *Many strange women*] That is, idolaters; *together with the daughter of Pharaoh:* she was also one of those strange women and an idolater. But many think she became a proselyte to the Jewish religion; of this there is no evidence.

Verse 3. *He had seven hundred wives, princesses*] How he could get so many of the blood royal from the different surrounding nations, is astonishing; but probably the daughters of *noblemen, generals,* &c., may be included.

And three hundred concubines] These were *wives of the second rank,* who were taken according to the usages of those times; but their offspring could not inherit. Sarah was to Abraham what these *seven hundred* princesses were to Solomon; and the *three hundred* concubines stood in the same relation to the Israelitish king as *Hagar* and *Keturah* did to the patriarch.

Here then are *one thousand wives* to form this great bad man's *harem!* Was it possible that such a person could have any piety to God, who was absorbed by such a number of women? We scarcely allow a man to have the fear of God who has a *second wife* or *mistress;* in what state then must the man be who has *one thousand* of them? We may endeavour to excuse all this by saying, "It was a custom in the East to have a multitude of women, and that there were many of those whom Solomon probably never saw," &c., &c. But was there any of them whom he *might not have seen?* Was it for reasons of state, or merely court splendour, that he had so many? How then is it said that *he loved many strange women?*—that *he clave to them in love?* And did he not give them the utmost proofs of his *attachment* when he not only *tolerated* their iniquitous worship in the land, but *built temples* to their idols, and more, *burnt incense* to them *himself?* As we should not condemn what God justifies, so we should

A.M.3020-3029
B. C. 984-975
Anno ante I.
Olymp.208-199

fect with the LORD his God, ^gas *was* the heart of David his father.

5 For Solomon went after ^hAshtoreth the goddess of the Zidonians, and after ⁱMilcom the abomination of the Ammonites.

6 And Solomon did evil in the sight of the LORD, and ^kwent not fully after the LORD, as *did* David his father.

7 ^lThen did Solomon build a high place for ^mChemosh, the abomination of Moab, in ⁿthe hill that *is* before Jerusalem, and for Molech, the abomination of the children of Ammon.

8 And likewise did he for all his strange wives, which burnt incense and sacrificed unto their gods.

9 And the LORD was angry with Solomon, because ^ohis heart was turned from the LORD God of Israel, ^pwhich had appeared unto him twice,

10 And ^qhad commanded him

A.M.3020-3029
B. C. 984-975
Anno ante I.
Olymp.208-199

concerning this thing, that he should not go after other gods: but he kept not that which the LORD commanded.

11 Wherefore the LORD said unto Solomon, Forasmuch as this ^ris done of thee, and thou hast not kept my covenant and my statutes, which I have commanded thee, ^sI will surely rend the kingdom from thee, and will give it to thy servant.

12 Notwithstanding in thy days I will not do it for David thy father's sake: *but* I will rend it out of the hand of thy son.

13 ^tHowbeit I will not rend away all the kingdom; *but* will give ^uone tribe to thy son for David my servant's sake, and for Jerusalem's sake, ^vwhich I have chosen.

14 And the LORD stirred ^wup an adversary unto Solomon, Hadad the Edomite: he *was* of the king's seed in Edom.

---

^gChap. ix. 4——^hVer. 33; Judg. ii. 13; 2 Kings xxiii. 13——ⁱCalled *Molech*, ver. 7——^kHeb. *fulfilled not after;* Num. xiv. 24——^lNum. xxxiii. 52——^mNum. xxi. 29; Judg. xi. 24——ⁿ2 Kings xxiii. 13

^oVer. 2, 3——^pChap. iii. 5; ix. 2——^qChap. vi. 12; ix. 6——^rHeb. *is with thee*——^sVer. 31; chap. xii. 15, 16 ^t2 Sam. vii. 15; Psa. lxxxix. 33——^uChap. xii. 20 ^vDeut. xii. 11——^w1 Chron. v. 26

---

not justify what God condemns. He went after *Ashtaroth,* the impure *Venus* of the *Sidonians;* after *Milcom,* the *abomination of the Ammonites;* after *Chemosh,* the *abomination of the Moabites;* and after the murderous *Molech,* the *abomination of the children of Ammon.* He seems to have gone as far in iniquity as it was possible.

Verse 7. *The hill that* is *before Jerusalem*] This was the *Mount of Olives.*

Verse 9. *The Lord was angry with Solomon*] Had not this man's delinquency been strongly marked by the Divine disapprobation, it would have had a fatal effect on the morals of mankind. Vice is *vice,* no matter who commits it. And God is as much displeased with sin in Solomon as he can be with it in the most profligate, *uneducated* wretch. And although God sees the same sin in precisely the *same degree* of *moral turpitude* as to the *act itself,* yet there may be *circumstances* which greatly aggravate the offence, and subject the offender to greater punishment. Solomon was wise; he knew better; his understanding showed him the vanity as well as the wickedness of idolatry. God had *appeared unto him twice,* and thus given him the most direct proof of his being and of his providence. The *promises* of God had been *fulfilled to him* in the most remarkable manner, and in such a way as to prove that they came by a Divine counsel, and not by any kind of *casualty.* All these were *aggravations* of Solomon's crimes, as to their demerit; for the same crime has, in every case, the same degree of moral turpitude in the sight of God; but circumstances may so aggravate, as to require the *offender* to be more grievously *punished;* so the punishment may be legally *increased* where

the crime is the same. Solomon deserved more punishment for his worship of Ashtaroth than any of the Sidonians did, though they performed precisely the same acts. The Sidonians had never known the true God; Solomon had been fully acquainted with him.

Verse 11. *Forasmuch as this is done of thee*] Was not this another warning from the Lord? And might not Solomon have yet recovered himself? Was there not mercy in this message which he might have sought and found?

Verse 13. *Will give one tribe—for David my servant's sake*] The line of the *Messiah* must be preserved. The *prevailing lion* must come out of the tribe of Judah: not only the tribe must be preserved, but the *regal line* and the *regal right.* All this must be done for the *true David's* sake: and this was undoubtedly what God had in view by thus miraculously preserving the tribe of Judah, and the royal line, in the midst of so general a defection.

And for Jerusalem's sake] As *David* was a type of the *Messiah,* so was *Jerusalem* a type of the *true Church:* therefore the OLD *Jerusalem* must be preserved in the hands of the tribe of Judah, till the *true David* should establish the NEW *Jerusalem* in the same land, and in the same city. And what a series of providences did it require to do all these things!

Verse 14. *The Lord stirred up an adversary*] A *satan,* שטן. When he sent to Hiram to assist him in building the temple of the Lord, he could say, *There was no satan,* see chap. v. 4; and all his kingdom was in peace and security;—*every man dwelt under his vine, and under his fig tree,* chap. iv. 25: but now that he had turned away from God, three *satans* rise up against him at once, *Hadad, Rezon,* and *Jeroboam.*

A.M.3020-3029
B. C. 984-975
Anno ante I.
Olymp.208-199

15 [x]For it came to pass when David was in Edom, and Joab the captain of the host was gone up to bury the slain, [y]after he had smitten every male in Edom;

16 (For six months did Joab remain there with all Israel, until he had cut off every male in Edom:)

17 That Hadad fled, he and certain Edomites of his father's servants with him, to go into Egypt; Hadad *being* yet a little child.

18 And they arose out of Midian, and came to Paran: and they took men with them out of Paran, and they came to Egypt, unto Pharaoh king of Egypt; which gave him a house, and appointed him victuals, and gave him land.

19 And Hadad found great favour in the sight of Pharaoh, so that he gave him to wife the sister of his own wife, the sister of Tahpenes the queen.

20 And the sister of Tahpenes bare him Genubath his son, whom Tahpenes weaned in Pharaoh's house: and Genubath was in Pharaoh's household among the sons of Pharaoh.

21 [z]And when Hadad heard in Egypt that David slept with his fathers, and that Joab the captain of the host was dead, Hadad said to

Pharaoh, [a]Let me depart, that I may go to mine own country.

A.M.3020-3029
B. C. 984-975
Anno ante I.
Olymp.208-199

22 Then Pharaoh said unto him, But what hast thou lacked with me, that, behold, thou seekest to go to thine own country? and he answered, [b]Nothing: howbeit let me go in any wise.

23 And God stirred him up *another* adversary, Rezon the son of Eliadah, which fled from his lord [c]Hadadezer king of Zobah:

24 And he gathered men unto him, and became captain over a band, [d]when David slew them *of Zobah:* and they went to Damascus, and dwelt therein, and reigned in Damascus.

25 And he was an adversary to Israel all the days of Solomon, beside the mischief that Hadad *did:* and he abhorred Israel, and reigned over Syria.

26 And [e]Jeroboam the son of Nebat, an Ephrathite of Zereda, Solomon's servant, whose mother's name *was* Zeruah, a widow woman, even he [f]lifted up *his* hand against the king.

A. M. 3024
B. C. 980
Ante I. Ol. 204
An. Thersippi,
Arch. Athen.
perpet. 14

27 And this was the cause that he lifted up *his* hand against the king: [g]Solomon built Millo, *and* [h]repaired the breaches of the city of David his father.

---

[x]2 Sam. viii. 14; 1 Chron. xviii. 12, 13——[y]Num. xxiv. 19; Deut. xx. 13——[z]1 Kings ii. 10, 34——[a]Heb. *send me away*——[b]Heb. *not*

[c]2 Sam. viii. 3——[d]2 Sam. viii. 3; x. 8, 18——[e]Chap. xii. 2; 2 Chron. xiii. 6——[f]2 Sam. xx. 21——[g]Chap. ix. 24——[h]Heb. *closed*

Verse 15. *Was gone up to bury the slain*] The slain Edomites; for Joab had in the course of six months exterminated all the males, except Hadad and his servants, who escaped to Egypt. Instead of *bury the slain*, the Targum has *to take the spoils of the slain.*

Verse 17. *Hadad being yet a little child.*] נער קטן *naar katan, a little boy;* one who was apprehensive of his danger, and could, with his father's servants, make his escape: not an infant.

Verse 18. *They arose out of Midian*] They at first retired to Midian, which lay to the southwest of the Dead Sea. Not supposing themselves in safety there, they went afterwards to *Paran* in the south of Idumea, and getting a number of persons to join them in Paran, they went straight to Egypt, where we find Hadad became a favourite with Pharaoh, who gave him his sister-in-law to wife; and incorporated him and his family with his own.

Verse 22. *Let me go in any wise.*] It does not appear that he avowed his real intention to Pharaoh; for at this time there must have been peace between Israel and Egypt, Solomon having married the daughter of Pharaoh.

Verse 23. *Rezon the son of Eliadah*] Thus God fulfilled his threatening by the prophet Nathan: *If he commit iniquity, I will chasten*

him with the rod of men, and with the stripes of the children of men; 2 Sam. vii. 14.

Verse 24. *And reigned in Damascus.*] Rezon was one of the captains of Hadadezer, whom David defeated. It seems that at this time Rezon escaped with his men; and having lived, as is supposed, some time by plunder, he seized on Damascus, and reigned there till David took Damascus, when he subdued Syria, and drove out Rezon. But after Solomon's defection from God, Rezon, finding that God had departed from Israel, recovered Damascus; and joining with Hadad, harassed Solomon during the remaining part of his reign. But some think that Hadad and Rezon were the same person.

Verse 26. *Jeroboam the son of Nebat*] From the context we learn that Jeroboam while a young man was employed by Solomon to superintend the improvements and buildings at *Millo*, and had so distinguished himself there by his industry and good conduct as to attract general notice, and to induce Solomon to set him over all the labourers employed in that work, belonging to the tribes of *Ephraim and Manasseh*, called here the *house* of *Joseph.* At first it appears that Solomon employed none of the *Israelites* in any *drudgery;* but it is likely that, as he grew profane, he grew tyrannical and oppressive; and at the works of *Millo* he

A. M. 3024
B. C. 980
Ante I. Ol. 204
An. Thersippi,
Arch. Athen.
perpet. 14

28 And the man Jeroboam *was* a mighty man of valour: and Solomon seeing the young man that he [1]was industrious, he made him ruler over all the [k]charge of the house of Joseph.

29 And it came to pass at that time when Jeroboam went out of Jerusalem, that the prophet, [l]Ahijah the Shilonite found him in the way; and he had clad himself with a new garment; and they two *were* alone in the field:

30 And Ahijah caught the new garment that *was* on him, and [m]rent it *in* twelve pieces:

31 And he said to Jeroboam, Take thee ten pieces: for [n]thus saith the LORD, the God of Israel, Behold, I will rend the kingdom out of the hand of Solomon, and will give ten tribes to thee:

32 (But he shall have one tribe for my servant David's sake, and for Jerusalem's sake, the city which I have chosen out of all the tribes of Israel:)

33 [o]Because that they have forsaken me, and have worshipped Ashtoreth the goddess of the Zidonians, Chemosh the god of the Moabites, and Milcom the god of the children of Ammon, and have not walked in my ways to do *that which is* right in mine eyes, and *to keep* my statutes and my judgments, as *did* David his father.

A. M. 3024
B. C. 980
Ante I. Ol. 204
An. Thersippi,
Arch. Athen.
perpet. 14

34 Howbeit I will not take the whole kingdom out of his hand: but I will make him prince all the days of his life for David my servant's sake, whom I chose, because he kept my commandments, and my statutes:

35 But [p]I will take the kingdom out of his son's hand, and will give it unto thee, *even* ten tribes.

36 And unto his son will I give one tribe, that [q]David my servant may have a [r]light alway before me in Jerusalem, the city which I have chosen me to put my name there.

37 And I will take thee, and thou shalt reign according to all that thy soul desireth, and shall be king over Israel.

38 And it shall be, if thou wilt hearken unto all that I command thee, and wilt walk in my ways, and do *that is* right in my sight, to keep my statutes and my commandments, as David my servant did; that [s]I will be with thee, and [t]build thee a sure house, as I built for David, and will give Israel unto thee.

39 And I will for this afflict the seed of David, but not for ever.

40 Solomon sought therefore to kill Jeroboam. And Jeroboam arose, and fled into Egypt, unto Shishak king of Egypt, and was in Egypt until the death of Solomon.

---

[i]Hebrew, *did work*——[k]Hebrew, *burden*——[l]Chapter xiv. 2——[m]See 1 Samuel xv. 27; xxiv. 5——[n]Verse 11, 13——[o]Verse 5, 6, 7——[p]Chapter xii. 16, 17——[q]1 Kings xv. 4; 2 Kings viii. 19; Psalm cxxxii. 17——[r]Heb. *lamp,* or *candle*——[s]Joshua i. 5——[t]2 Samuel vii. 11, 27

---

changed his conduct; and there, in all probability, were the seeds of disaffection sown. And Jeroboam, being a clever and enterprising man, knew well how to avail himself of the general discontent.

Verse 29. *When Jeroboam went out of Jerusalem*] On what errand he was going out of Jerusalem, we know not.

Ahijah the Shilonite] He was one of those who wrote the history of the reign of Solomon, as we find from 2 Chron. ix. 29, and it is supposed that it was by him God spake twice to Solomon; and particularly delivered the message which we find in this chapter, ver. 11-13.

Verse 31. *Take thee ten pieces*] The *garment* was the symbol of the *kingdom of Israel;* the *twelve pieces* the symbol of the *twelve tribes;* the *ten pieces* given to Jeroboam, of the *ten tribes* which should be given to him, and afterwards form the *kingdom* of Israel, ruling in Samaria, to distinguish it from the *kingdom* of Judah, ruling in Jerusalem.

Verse 36. *That David my servant may have a light alway*] That his posterity may never fail, and the regal line never become extinct. This, as we have already seen, was in reference to the Messiah. He was not only *David's light,* but he was a *light to enlighten the Gentiles.*

Verse 37. *According to all that thy soul desireth*] It appears from this that Jeroboam had affected the kingdom, and was seeking for an opportunity to seize on the government. God now tells him, by his prophet, *what he shall have,* and *what he shall not have,* in order to prevent him from attempting to seize on the whole kingdom, to the prejudice of the spiritual seed of David.

Verse 38. *And build thee a sure house*] He would have continued his posterity on the throne of Israel, had he not by his wickedness forfeited the promises of God, and thrown himself out of the protection of the Most High.

Verse 39. *But not for ever.*] They shall be in affliction and distress till the Messiah come, who shall sit on the throne of David to order it and establish it in judgment and justice for ever. Jarchi says, on this verse, "When the Messiah comes, the kingdom shall be restored to the house of David."

Verse 40. *Sought—to kill Jeroboam.*] He thought by this means to prevent the punishment due to his crimes.

A. M. 3024
B. C. 980
Ante I. Ol. 204
An. Thersippi,
Arch. Athen.
perpet. 14

41 And ^uthe rest of the ^vacts of Solomon, and all that he did, and his wisdom, *are* they not written in the book of the acts of Solomon?

42 ^wAnd the ^xtime that Solomon reigned in

Jerusalem over all Israel *was* forty years.

A. M. 3029
B. C. 975
Ante I. Ol. 199
An. Thersippi
Arch. Athen.
perpet. 19

43 ^yAnd Solomon slept with his fathers, and was buried in the city of David his father: and ^zRehoboam his son reigned in his stead.

---

^u2 Chron. ix. 29——^vOr, *words,* or, *things*——^w2 Chron. ix. 30

^xHeb. *days*——^y2 Chron. ix. 31——^zMatt. i. 7, called *Roboam*

Unto Shishak king of Egypt] This is the first time we meet with the *proper name* of an Egyptian king, *Pharaoh* being the common name for all the sovereigns of that country. Some suppose that this *Shishak* was the *Sesostris* so renowned for his wars and his conquests. But it is likely that this king lived long before Solomon's time.

Verse 41. *The book of the acts of Solomon?*] These acts were written by Nathan the prophet, Ahijah the Shilonite, and Iddo the seer; as we learn from 2 Chron. ix. 29. Probably from these were the Books of Kings and Chronicles composed; but the original documents are long since lost.

Verse 42. *Solomon reigned—forty years.*] Josephus says *fourscore years,* which is sufficiently absurd. Calmet supposes him to have been *eighteen* years old when he came to the throne, and that he died A. M. 3029, aged *fifty-eight* years; and, when we consider the excess in which he lived, and the criminal passions which he must have indulged among his thousand wives, and their idolatrous and impure worship, this life was as long as could be reasonably expected.

Verse 43. *Solomon slept with his fathers*] He died in almost the flower of his age, and, it appears unregretted. His government was no blessing to Israel; and laid, by its exactions and oppressions, the foundation of that schism which was so fatal to the unhappy people of Israel and Judah, and was the most powerful procuring cause of the miseries which have fallen upon the Jewish people from that time until now.

I. IT may now be necessary to give a more distinct outline of the character of this king.

1. In his infancy and youth he had the high honour of being peculiarly *loved by the Lord;* and he had a *name* given him by the express authority of God himself, which to himself and others must ever call to remembrance this peculiar favour of the Most High.

There is little doubt that he was a most amiable youth, and his whole conduct appeared to justify the high expectations that were formed of him.

2. He ascended the Israelitish throne at a time the most favourable for the cultivation of those arts so necessary to the comfort and improvement of life. Among all the surrounding nations Israel had not one open enemy; *there was neither adversary, nor evil occurrent,* chap. v. 4. He had *rest on every side,* and from the universal and profound peace which he enjoyed, the very important name *Jedidiah,* "beloved of the Lord," which was given him by Divine authority, was changed to that of Solomon, *the Peaceable,* 2 Sam. xii. 24, 25, which at once indicated the state of the country, and the character of his own mild, pacific mind.

3. To the dying charge of his pious father relative to the building a temple for the Lord, he paid the most punctual attention. He was fond of *architecture,* as we may learn from the account that is given of his numerous buildings and improvements; and yet it does not appear that he at all excelled in architectural knowledge. Hiram, the amiable king of Tyre, and his excellent workmen, were the grand directors and executors of the whole. By his public buildings he doubtless rendered Jerusalem highly respectable; but his *passion* for such works was not on the whole an advantage to his subjects, as it obliged him to have recourse to a burdensome system of taxation, which at first oppressed and exasperated his people, and ultimately led to the fatal separation of Israel and Judah.

4. That he improved the *trade* and *commerce* of his country is sufficiently evident: by his public buildings vast multitudes were employed; and knowledge in the most beneficial arts must have been greatly increased, and the spirit of *industry* highly cultivated.

Commerce does not appear to have been much regarded, if even known, in Israel, previously to the days of Solomon. The most celebrated maritime power then in the world was that of the Tyrians. With great address and prudence he availed himself of their experience and commercial knowledge, sent his ships in company with theirs to make long and dangerous but lucrative voyages, and, by getting their sailors aboard of his own vessels, gained possession of their nautical skill, and also a knowledge of those safe ports in which they harboured, and of the rich countries with which they traded. His friendly alliance with the king of Tyre was a source of advantage to Israel, and might have been much more so had it been prudently managed. But after the time of Solomon we find it scarcely mentioned, and therefore it does not appear that the Jews continued to follow a track which had been so successfully opened to them; their endless contentions, and the ruinous wars of the two kingdoms, paralyzed all their commercial exertions: till at length all the maritime skill which they had acquired from the expert and industrious Tyrians, dwindled down to the puny art of managing a few boats on the internal lakes of their own country. Had it not been for the destructive feuds that reigned between the two kingdoms of Israel and Judah, that country might have become one of the best and richest maritime powers of either Asia or Europe. Their situation was grand and commanding, but their execrable jealousies deprived them of its advantages, exposed them to the aggressions of their enemies, and finally brought them to ruin.

5. I have intimated that Solomon was truly *pious* in his youth; of this there can be no doubt; it was on this account that the *Lord loved*

him, and his zeal in the cause of true religion, and high respect for the honour of God, are strong indications of such a frame of mind. Had we no other proof of this than his *prayer for wisdom*, and his *prayer* at the *dedication* of the *temple*, it would put the matter for ever beyond dispute, independently of the direct testimonies we have from God himself on the subject. He loved the *worship* and *ordinances* of *God*, and was a pattern to his subjects of the strictest attention to religious duties. He even exceeded the requisitions of the *law* in the multitude of his sacrifices, and was a careful observer of those annual festivals so necessary to preserve the memory of the principal facts of the Israelitish history, and those miraculous interventions of God in the behalf of that people.

6. There can be no doubt that Solomon possessed the *knowledge* of *governing well;* of the importance of this knowledge he was duly aware, and this was the *wisdom* that he so particularly sought from God. "I am," said he, "but a little child; I know not how to go out or come in; and thy servant is in the midst of a great people that cannot be counted for multitude. Give therefore thy servant an *understanding heart to judge thy people*, and that I may *discern between good and bad;* for who is able to judge this thy so great a people? And the speech pleased the Lord that Solomon had asked this thing;" chap. iii. 8-10. This *wisdom* he did receive from God; and he is here a pattern to all kings, who, as they are the vicegerents of the Lord, should earnestly seek that wisdom which is from above, that they may be able to know how to govern the people intrusted to their care; because, in every civil government, there are a multitude of things on which a king may be called to decide, concerning which neither the laws, nor the commonly received political maxims by which, in particular cases, the conduct of a governor is to be regulated, can give any specific direction.

7. But the wisdom of Solomon was not confined to the art of government; he appears to have possessed a *universal knowledge*. The sages of the East were particularly distinguished by their accurate *knowledge of human nature*, from which they derived innumerable maxims for the regulation of man in every part of his moral conduct, and in all the relations in which he could possibly be placed. Hence their vast profusion of *maxims, proverbs, instructive fables, apologues, enigmas*, &c.; great collections of which still remain locked up in the languages of Asia, particularly the *Sanscrit, Arabic*, and *Persian;* besides those which, by the industry of learned men, have been translated and published in the languages of Europe. Much of this kind appears in the books of *Wisdom* and *Ecclesiasticus* in the *Apocrypha*, and in the very excellent collections of *D'Herbelot, Visdelou*, and *Galand*, in the *Bibliothèque Orientale*. That Solomon possessed this wisdom in a very high degree, the book of *Proverbs* bears ample testimony, leaving *Ecclesiastes* for the present out of the consideration.

8. As a *poet*, Solomon stands deservedly high, though of his *one thousand and five poems* not one, except the book of *Canticles*, remains. This ode alone, taken in a *literary* point of view, is sufficient to raise any man to a high degree of poetic fame. It is a most interesting drama, where what *Racine* terms the *genie createur*, the creative genius, every where appears; in which the imagery, which is always borrowed from nature, is impressive and sublime; the characters accurately distinguished and defined, the strongest passion, in its purest and most vigorous workings, elegantly portrayed; and in which allusions the most delicate, to transactions of the tenderest complexion, while sufficiently described to make them intelligible, are nevertheless hidden from the eye of the gross vulgar by a tissue as light as a gossamer covering. Such is the nature of this inimitable ode, which, had it not been perverted by weak but well designing men to purposes to which it can never legitimately apply, would have ranked with the highest productions of the *Epithalamian* kind that ever came from the pen of man. But alas! for this exquisite poem, its true sense has been perverted; it has been *forced* to speak a language that was never intended, a language far from being honourable to the *cause* which it was brought to support, and subversive of the unity and simplicity of the ode itself. By a forced mode of interpretation it has been hackneyed to death, and allegorized to destruction. It is now little read, owing to the injudicious manner in which it has been interpreted.

It was scarcely to be expected that the son of such a father should not, independently of inspiration, have caught a portion of the pure *poetic fire*. Though the spirit of poetry, strictly speaking, is not transmissible by ordinary generation, yet most celebrated poets have had poetical parents; but in many cases the talent has degenerated into that of *music*, and the *spirit of poetry* in the *sire* has become a mere musical instrument in the hands of the *son*. This however was not the case with the son of David, for though vastly inferior to his father in this gift, he had nevertheless the spirit and powers of a first-rate *poet*.

9. His knowledge in *natural history* must have been very extensive; it is said, "He spake of *trees*, from the cedar that is in Lebanon even unto the hyssop that springeth out of the wall. He spake also of *beasts*, of *fowls*, of *reptiles*, and of *fishes;*" chap. iv. 33. All this knowledge has perished; his countrymen, the prophets excepted, were without *taste*, and took no pains to preserve what they did not relish. A man of such mental power and comprehension under the direction of Divine light must have spoken of things as they are. His doctrine therefore of *generation* and *corruption*, of *nutrition, vegetation, production, aliments, tribes, classes, families*, and *habits*, relative to the different subjects in *botany, zoology, ornithology, entomology*, and *ichthyology*, which are all evidently referred to here, must have been at once correct, instructive, and delightful. I have already lamented the labour it has cost our *Rays, Tourneforts, Linnés, Buffons, Willoughbys, Swammerdams*, and *Bloschs*, to regain those sciences which possibly were possessed in their highest degree by the Israelitish king, and which, alas! are all lost, except a few traces in the book of Ecclesiastes, if that work can be traced to so remote an age as that of Solomon.

10. As a *moral philosopher* the author of the book of *Ecclesiastes* occupies no mean rank. At present we may consider this work as a production of Solomon, though this is disputed, and the question shall be considered in its proper place. This book contains such a fund of wisdom, applied to the *regulation of life*, and all referred to the proper end, that it most deserv-

edly occupies a high place in Biblical *ethics*, and deserves the closest attention of every reader.

11. The proofs of Solomon's vast wisdom, as brought into *practical* effect, lie in a very small compass, because his history in the Bible is short, his own writings in general lost, and the annals of his reign, as compiled by Nathan the prophet, Ahijah the Shilonite, and Iddo the seer, long since perished. The decision between the two harlots is almost the only instance.

Of his interesting interview with the *queen of Sheba*, and the discussions into which they entered, we have only the *fact* stated, without the least detail of particulars. Those who have read the *Concessus of Harari*, or the *Heetopadesa*, of *Veeshnoo Sarma*, will regret that the conversations of the wisest of men, with probably the most intelligent of women, should have been lost to the world, which may be reasonably concluded to have been as far superior to the excellent works above referred to, as they are beyond the *maxims* of *Rochefoucault*, and the *sayings* of *Madame Maintenon*.

12. The wisdom of the East has ever been celebrated; and if we may believe their own best writers, much of what they possess has been derived from Solomon. Encomiums of his wisdom are everywhere to be met with in the Asiatic writers; and his name is famous in every part of the East. Most of the oriental historians, poets, and philosophers, mention *Soliman ben Daoud*, "Solomon the son of David." They relate that he ascended the throne of Israel at the death of his father, when he was only *twelve* years of age, and that God subjected to his government, not only *men*, but good and evil *spirits*, the *fowls* of the air, and the *winds* of heaven. They agree with the sacred writers in stating that he employed *seven years* in building the temple at Jerusalem.

Solomon's *seal*, and Solomon's *ring*, are highly celebrated by them, and to these they attribute a great variety of magical effects. They state that without his ring he had not the science of government; and having once lost it, he did not remount his throne for forty days, as being destitute of that wisdom without which he could not decide according to truth and equity. But these things are probably spoken *allegorically* by their oldest writers. Of the *throne* of this prince they speak in terms of the most profound admiration. I have met with the most minute description of its magnificence, its ivory, gold, and jewels, and an estimate of its cost in lacs of rupees! According to those writers it had 12,000 seats of gold on the right hand for patriarchs and prophets, and as many on the left for the doctors of the law, who assisted him in the distribution of justice.

In various parts of the *Koran* Solomon is spoken of in terms of the highest respect, and is represented as a true believer; though, through the envy of demons, magic and sorcery were attributed to him. Mohammed speaks of this in the second surat of his Koran. The story, in sum, is this: The devils, by God's permission, having tempted Solomon without success, made use of the following stratagem to blast his reputation: they wrote several books of magic, and hid them under his throne; and, after his death, told the chief men that if they wished to know by what means Solomon had obtained absolute dominion over *men, genii*, and the *winds*, they should dig under his throne. This they did, and found the aforesaid books

full of impious superstitions. The better sort would not learn these incantations; but the common people did, and published them as the genuine works of Solomon. From this imputation the Koran justifies him, by saying, *Solomon was not an unbeliever*, surat 2. From the wonder-working *signet* and *ring* of the Asiatics came the *Clavicle* of Solomon, so celebrated among the Jewish rabbins, and the Christian occult philosophers; for such things found in Cornelius Agrippa, and such like writers, are not late inventions, but have descended from a very remote antiquity, as the Koran and the various commentators on it sufficiently prove.—See *Calmet* and *Sale*.

The oriental traditions concerning this prince have been embodied in the *Soliman Nameh* of *Ferdusi*, in Persian, and in the *Soliman Nameh* of *Uscobi*, in Turkish. D'Herbelot mentions one of these histories in Persian verse, containing 1571 couplets.

Indeed, the traditions concerning the wonderful knowledge of Solomon, which abound so much in the East, are at least an indirect proof that many things relative to this prince have been preserved among them which are not mentioned in our sacred books, but which they have blended so miserably with fables that it is impossible now to distinguish the precious from the vile.

Works attributed to Solomon have existed in different ages, from his time till the present. *Eusebius* states that Hezekiah, finding the Jews putting too much confidence in the books of Solomon, relative to *cures* and *different occult arts*, ordered them to be suppressed. *Josephus* positively says that Solomon did compose *books* of *charms* to cure *diseases*, and *conjurations* to *expel demons*, Antiq., lib. viii., cap. 2. He states farther, that a Jew named Eliezar cured several demoniacs in the presence of Vespasian, by reciting the *charms* which had been invented by Solomon. *R. D. Kimchi* speaks of a book of Solomon entitled *The Cure of Diseases*, which *Genebrard* supposes to be the same work of which Josephus speaks. And *Origen* speaks of conjurations which were used by the Jews in his time, and which they professed to derive from the books of Solomon.

There are still extant books of this kind attributed to Solomon, such as *The Enchantments, The Clavicle, The Ring, The Hygromantia, The New Moons*, and *The Shadows of Ideas;* but these, as they now stand, are the inventions of quacks and impostors, and entitled to no regard. If there were any books containing the wisdom of Solomon, they are either irrecoverably lost, or exist in mutilated fragments among the Asiatic sages; and are disfigured by being connected with improbable tales, and pretended *mantras* or *charms*.

II. Hitherto we have looked only at the bright side of Solomon's character: we must now take a much less satisfactory view of this singular man; one in whom every thing great, glorious, wise, and holy, and every thing little, mean, foolish, and impious, predominated by turns. He forsook the God of his mercies in a great variety of ways.

1. Whatever may be thought of the step in a political point of view, he most assuredly went out of the way of God's providence, and acted contrary to his law, in making *affinity with Pharaoh's daughter*. The sacred writers frequently refer to this; and it is never mentioned

with *approbation:* it is rather associated with circumstances that place it in a reprehensible point of view. She was doubtless an *idolater;* and the question of her becoming a *proselyte* is far from being satisfactorily settled. I believe she was the first means of drawing off his heart from the true God.

2. His expensive buildings obliging him to have recourse to a system of oppressive taxation, was another flaw in his character. Though with great zeal and honourable industry, and at great expense, he built a temple for the Lord, which he completed in seven years, yet the expense here was little in comparison of what was incurred by *his own house,* called the *house of the forest of Lebanon,* in which he spent incredible sums, and consumed nearly *thirteen* years; almost twice the time employed in building the temple at Jerusalem. This would have had no evil operation provided he had not been obliged to impose heavy taxes on his subjects, which produced an almost universal disaffection. Add to this, he had a most expensive household; *one thousand* women, part wives, part mistresses, would require immense riches to support their pomp and gratify their ambition. The people therefore justly complained of an establishment which, notwithstanding the riches brought into the country, must be both odious and oppressive.

3. He began his reign by an inauspicious act, the death of his brother Adonijah. This was a sin against God and nature: and no art of man can ever wash out its guilt. If *state policy* required it, which is very questionable, what had that to do with the *feelings* of *humanity,* and the *love of God?* On no pretence whatever is Solomon justified in this act.

4. His inordinate love of women. He had no doubt formed matrimonial alliances with all kingdoms and neighbouring states, by taking their *sisters* and *daughters* to be his wives, to the fearful amount of no less than *seven hundred!* Politicians may endeavour to justify these acts by asserting, that in the Asiatic countries they were matters of a sound policy, rather than an argument of the prevalence of an irregular and unbridled passion. Let this stand for its value; but what can such apologists say for the *additional three hundred concubines,* for the taking of whom no such necessity can be pleaded? But even allowing that state policy might require such extensive alliances, what are we to say to the flagrant breaches of a most positive law of God? Most solemnly and most authoritatively had he said that his people should not give their daughters to the heathen, nor take the daughters of the heathen to be their wives; lest they should turn their hearts away from serving the Lord. In the face of this most positive declaration, Solomon took wives of the most idolatrous of the surrounding nations; who succeeded, according to what was foretold, in turning his heart away from God.

5. He became an idolater. He worshipped "Ashtaroth, the Venus of the Sidonians; Milcom, the abomination of the Ammonites; Chemosh, the abomination of the Moabites; and Molech, the abomination of the children of Ammon." He did more: he built a temple to each of these; "and to all the gods of all his strange wives, which burned incense, and sacrificed unto their gods," chap. xi. 5-8.

6. By this time we may suppose that the light of God had entirely departed from his mind. He who knew so well the true God, now served him not; or, if he did, it was in conjunction with those idols, thus bringing the Supreme Being on a level with demons, or the figments of impure hearts and disordered fancies. We need not wonder at the tale of the mighty Samson betraying his life's secret in the lap of Delilah; or of the unconquerable Hercules handling the distaff among the maids of Omphale, queen of Lydia; when we see the son of David, the once well-beloved of the Lord, the wisest of human beings, for the love of his *millenary* of wives and concubines, erecting temples to devils, and burning incense to them that were no gods; not considering that an idol is nothing in the world. To what an indescribable state of blindness and fatuity must this man have been brought, before he could have been capable of such acts as these! O Lucifer, son of the morning, how art thou fallen!

7. I have already hinted that Solomon's oppressive taxation laid the foundation of that discontent which shortly after his death produced the separation of Israel and Judah; also the long and ruinous wars which drenched these states in blood: and this was doubtless the cause that ten-twelfths of the Jewish people became idolaters; which crime was punished, by the just judgments of God, by the Babylonish captivity, which lasted seventy years; and by the carrying away of the ten Israelitish tribes by the Assyrians, who are lost from the map of the universe, and no longer numbered among the children of men!

8. What greatly aggravates the whole of this most dismal tale is, that this strange defection from God, truth, reason, and common sense, was persisted in to his old age; or that in his old age, meaning undoubtedly his latter days, his wives turned away his heart from God. But his idolatry must have been of *many years'* standing; he meddled with it in his connection with the princes of Egypt; each of his idolatrous wives in succession increased the propensity: to chastise him for this very idolatry the Lord stirred up an adversary unto him. *Hadad,* the Edomite, and *Rezon,* the son of Eliadah, who was an adversary to Israel all the days of Solomon, 1 Kings xi. 14-25, which surely intimates that this idolatry was not the sin merely of his *old age;* as to chastise him for it Rezon was an adversary to Israel all his days. And as Solomon reigned forty years, we may fairly presume that a principal part of that time was spent in idolatrous practices.

9. This dismal account has a more dismal close still; for, in the same place in which we are informed of his *apostasy,* we are informed of his *death,* without the slightest intimation that he ever repented and turned to God. It is true that what is wanting in *fact* is supplied by *conjecture;* for it is firmly believed that "he did repent, and wrote the *book of Ecclesiastes* after his conversion, which is a decided proof of his repentance." I am sorry I cannot strengthen this opinion; of which I find not the shadow of a proof. 1. The book of Ecclesiastes, though it speaks much of the vanity of the creatures, yet speaks little or nothing of the *vanity* or *sin* of *idolatry.* 2. It is not the *language* of a man who was recovering from a state of the most awful backsliding. Is there any direct *confession of sin* in it? Is there any thing in it like the *penitential confessions* of his father, or like

the *lamentations* of Jeremiah? Is there any where to be heard in it the *sighing of a broken heart*, or strong crying and tears to deprecate the justice and implore the mercy of a deeply offended God? Does it any where exhibit the language of a *penitent*, or expressions suitable to the state and circumstances of this supposed penitent king of Israel? Excellent as it is in its kind, is it any thing more than a valuable collection of experimental ethics, relative to the *emptiness of the creature*, and the folly of earthly pursuits and worldly anxieties? 3. Nor is it even past doubt that Solomon wrote this book: it certainly does in several places bear evidences of times posterior to those of Solomon. Eminent scholars have discerned a deterioration in the *style* from the pure classical Hebrew, with an admixture of exotic terms that did not exist in the Hebrew language previously to the Babylonish captivity. But supposing that they are mistaken here, I still contend that it is not the language of a penitent soul. 4. It has been supposed, that, as Solomon was a *type* of Christ, it is not likely that he has finally perished. To this I answer, (1.) I know not that Solomon was a type of Christ. The reference to Cant. iii. 7; viii. 11, 12, is to me no proof whatever of the point. (2.) Were it even otherwise, this would be no proof of his repentance, when the Scriptures are silent on the subject. The *brazen serpent* was a type of Christ, John iii. 14, and was held in great veneration for a considerable time among the Jews; but when it became an *incitement* to *idolatry*, it was called *nehushtan*, a *brazen trifle*, taken down, and destroyed; 2 Kings xviii. 4. Typical persons and typical things may perish as well as others; the antitype alone will infallibly remain. 5. Finally, there seems every evidence that he died in his sins. His crimes were greatly aggravated: he forsook the Lord, who had appeared to him twice; his wives turned away his heart in his old age: there is not a single testimony in the Old or New Testament that intimates he died in a safe state. That awful denunciation of Divine justice stands point blank in the way of all contrary suppositions: "If thou forsake the Lord, he will cast thee off for ever," 1 Chron. xxviii. 9. He did forsake the Lord; and he forsook him in his very last days; and there is no evidence that he ever again clave to him. *Ergo,*

Reader, let him that standeth take heed lest he fall; not only foully but finally. Certainly, unconditional final perseverance will find little support in the case of Solomon. He was once most incontrovertibly in grace. He lost that grace and sinned most grievously against God. He was found in this state in his old age. He died, as far as the Scripture informs us, without repentance. Even the doubtfulness in which the bare letter of the Scripture leaves the eternal state of this man, is a blast of lightning to the syren song of "Once in grace, and still in grace;" "Once a child, and a child for ever."

I shall close these observations with the account given by Abul Farage, an Arabic writer of the thirteenth century, in his work entitled *The History of the Dynasties*, p. 55. "But in this Solomon transgressed, because towards the end of his life he took other women of foreign nations besides the daughter of Pharaoh; nations with whom God had forbidden the children of Israel to form matrimonial alliances; but leaning towards their gods, he worshipped their idols. In the *thirty-fourth* year of his reign he built a house for idols in the mount which is opposite to Jerusalem; and the length of it was one hundred cubits, its breadth fifty, and its height thirty. He made also for himself golden shields, and a brazen sea, supported on the horns of brazen oxen. God reproved him for his infidelity, and gave him for punishment in this world that he took away from his son the greater part of the kingdom. Moreover, the duration of his reign was *forty* years; ومات عومير توبه *and he died without repentance*, and was buried in the sepulchre of his father David."

For other particulars relative to the different transactions of this reign, the reader is referred to the *notes* in the order of their occurrence; and to those treatises which have been written on the probability that Solomon *did* or *did not* repent of his idolatry: and also to the notes on *Ecclesiastes*, where the subject will be again reviewed.

CHAPTER XII

A. M. 3029
B. C. 975
Ante I Ol. 199
An. Thersippi,
Arch. Athen.
perpet. 19

AND [a]Rehoboam went to Shechem: for all Israel were come to Shechem to make him king.

2 And it came to pass, when [b]Jeroboam the son of Nebat, who was yet in [c]Egypt, heard *of it,* (for he was fled from the presence of King Solomon, and Jeroboam dwelt in Egypt;)

3 That they sent and called him. And Jeroboam and all the congregation of Israel came, and spake unto Rehoboam, saying,

4 Thy father made our [d]yoke grievous: now therefore make thou the grievous service of thy father, and his heavy yoke which he put upon us, lighter, and we will serve thee.

5 And he said unto them, Depart yet *for* three days, then come again to me. And the people departed.

6 And King Rehoboam consulted with the old men, that stood before Solomon his father

A. M. 3029
B. C. 975
Ante I. Ol. 199
An. Thersippi,
Arch. Athen.
perpet. 19

while he yet lived, and said, How do ye advise that I may answer this people?

7 And they spake unto him, saying, [e]If thou wilt be a servant unto this people this day, and wilt serve them, and answer them, and speak good words to them, then they will be thy servants for ever.

8 But he forsook the counsel of the old men, which they had given him, and consulted with the young men that were grown up with him, *and* which stood before him.

9 And he said unto them, What counsel give ye that we may answer this people, who have spoken to me, saying, Make the yoke which thy father did put upon us lighter?

10 And the young men that were grown up with him spake unto him, saying, Thus shalt thou speak unto this people that spake unto thee, saying, Thy father made our yoke heavy, but make thou *it* lighter unto us; thus shalt

---

[a]2 Chronicles x. 1, &c.——[b]Chap. xi. 26——[c]Chap. xi. 40

[d]1 Sam. viii. 11–18; chap. iv. 7——[e]2 Chron. x. 7; Prov. xv. 1

NOTES ON CHAP. XII

Verse 1. *Rehoboam went to Shechem*] Rehoboam was probably the only son of Solomon; for although he had a *thousand* wives, he had not the blessing of a numerous offspring; and although he was the wisest of men himself, his son was a poor, unprincipled fool. Had Solomon kept himself within reasonable bounds in matrimonial affairs, he would probably have had more children; and such as would have had common sense enough to discern the delicacy of their situation, and rule according to reason and religion.

Verse 4. *The grievous service—and—heavy yoke*] They seem here to complain of two things—excessively laborious service, and a heavy taxation. At first it is supposed Solomon employed no Israelite in drudgery: afterwards, when he forsook the God of compassion, he seems to have used them as *slaves,* and to have revived the Egyptian bondage.

Verse 7. *If thou wilt be a servant unto this people*] This is a constitutional idea of a king: he is the *servant,* but not the *slave* of his people; every regal act of a just king is an act of *service* to the state. The king is not only the *fountain of law* and *justice;* but as he has the appointment of all *officers* and *judges,* consequently he is the *executor of the laws;* and all justice is administered in his name. Properly speaking, a good and constitutional king is the servant of his people; and in being such he is their father and their king.

They will be thy servants for ever.] The way to insure the obedience of the people is to hold the reins of empire with a steady and impartial hand; let the people see that the king *lives for them,* and not for *himself;* and they will obey, love, and defend him. The state is maintained on the part of the ruler and the ruled by mutual acts of service and benevolence. A good king has no self-interest; and such a king will ever have obedient and loving subjects. The haughty, proud tyrant will have a *suspicious* and *jealous* people, hourly ripening for *revolt.* The king is made for the people, not the people for the king. Let every *potentate* wisely consider this; and let every *subject* know that the heaviest cares rest on the heart, and the heaviest responsibility rests on the head, of the king. Let them therefore, under his government, fashion themselves as obedient children; acknowledge him their head; and duly consider *whose authority he has;* that they may love, honour and obey him. Happy are the people who have such a king; safe is the king who has such a people.

Verse 10. *And the young men that were grown up with him*] It was a custom in different countries to educate with the heir to the throne young noblemen of nearly the same age. This, as Calmet observes, answered two great and important ends:—1. It excited the prince to emulation; that he might, as far as possible, surpass in all manly exercises, and in all acts of prudence and virtue, those whom one day he was to surpass in the elevation and dignity of his station. 2. That he might acquire a correct knowledge of the disposition and views of those who were likely to be, under him, the highest officers of the state; and consequently, know the better how to trust and employ them. The old counsellors Rehoboam did not know; with the young nobility he had been familiar.

My little finger *shall be thicker*] A proverbial mode of expression: "My little *finger* is thicker than my father's *thigh.*" As much as the *thigh* surpasses the *little finger* in thickness, so much does my power exceed that of my father; and the use that I shall make of it, to employ and tax you, shall be in proportion.

A. M. 3029
B. C. 975
Ante I. Ol. 199
An. Thersippi,
Arch. Athen.
perpet. 19

thou say unto them, My little *finger* shall be thicker than my father's loins.

11 And now, whereas my father did lade you with a heavy yoke, I will add to your yoke: my father hath chastised you with whips, but I will chastise you with scorpions.

12 So Jeroboam and all the people came to Rehoboam the third day, as the king had appointed, saying, Come to me again the third day.

13 And the king answered the people ʳroughly, and forsook the old men's counsel that they gave him;

14 And spake to them after the counsel of the young men, saying, My father made your yoke heavy, and I will add to your yoke: my father *also* chastised you with whips, but I will chastise you with scorpions.

15 Wherefore the king hearkened not unto the people; ᵍfor the cause was from the LORD, that he might perform his saying, which the LORD ʰspake by Ahijah the Shilonite unto Jeroboam the son of Nebat.

16 So when all Israel saw that the king hearkened not unto them; the people answered the king, saying, ⁱWhat portion have we in David? neither *have we* inheritance in the son of Jesse: to your tents, O Israel: now see to thine own house, David. So Israel departed unto their tents.

A. M. 3029
B. C. 975
Ante I. Ol. 199
An. Thersippi,
Arch. Athen.
perpet. 19

17 But ᵏ*as for* the children of Israel which dwelt in the cities of Judah, Rehoboam reigned over them.

18 Then King Rehoboam ˡsent Adoram, who *was* over the tribute; and all Israel stoned him with stones, that he died. Therefore King Rehoboam ᵐmade speed to get him up to his chariot, to flee to Jerusalem.

19 So ⁿIsrael ᵒrebelled against the house of David unto this day.

20 And it came to pass, when all Israel heard that Jeroboam was come again, that they sent and called him unto the congregation, and made him king over all Israel: there was none that followed the house of David, but the tribe of Judah ᵖonly.

21 And when ᑫRehoboam was come to Jerusalem, he assembled all the house of Judah, with the tribe of Benjamin, a hundred and fourscore thousand chosen men, which were warriors, to fight against the house of Israel, to bring the kingdom again to Rehoboam the son of Solomon.

22 But ʳthe word of God came unto Shemaiah the man of God, saying,

---

ᶠHeb. *hardly*——ᵍVer. 24; Judg. xiv. 4; 2 Chron. x. 15; xxii. 7; xxv. 20——ʰChap. xi. 11, 31——ⁱ2 Sam. xx. 1——ᵏChap. xi. 13, 36

ˡChap. iv. 6; v. 14——ᵐHeb. *strengthened himself* ⁿ2 Kings xvii. 21——ᵒOr, *fell away*——ᵖChap. xi. 13, 32 ᑫ2 Chron. xii. 1——ʳ2 Chron. xi. 2

Verse 11. *Chastise you with scorpions*] Should you rebel, or become disaffected, my father's *whip* shall be a *scorpion* in my hand. His was *chastisement*, mine shall be *punishment*. St. Isidore, and after him Calmet and others, assert that the scorpion was a sort of severe whip, the lashes of which were armed with iron points, that sunk into and tore the flesh. We know that the *scorpion* was a military engine among the Romans for *shooting arrows*, which, being poisoned, were likened to the scorpion's sting, and the wound it inflicted.

Verse 15. *The cause was from the Lord*] God left him to himself, and did not incline his heart to follow the counsel of the wise men. This is making the best of our present version; but if we come to inquire into the meaning of the CAUSE of all this confusion and anarchy, we shall find it was Rehoboam's *folly, cruelty*, and *despotic tyranny:* and was *this* from the Lord? But does the text speak this bad doctrine? No: it says סבה *sibbah, the* REVOLUTION, *was from the Lord.* This is consistent with all the declarations which went before. God stirred up the people to revolt from a man who had neither skill nor humanity to govern them. We had such a סבה *revolution* in these nations in 1688;

and, thank God, we have never since needed another. None of our ancient translations understood the word as our present version does: they have it either *the* TURNING AWAY *was from the Lord*, or *it was the Lord's* ORDINANCE; viz., that they should turn away from this foolish king.

Verse 16. *So Israel departed unto their tents*] That is, the ten tribes withdrew their allegiance from Rehoboam; only Judah and Benjamin, frequently reckoned one tribe, remaining with him.

Verse 18. *King Rehoboam sent Adoram*] As this was the person who was superintendent over the *tribute*, he was probably sent to collect the ordinary taxes; but the people, indignant at the *master* who had given them such a brutish answer, stoned the *servant* to death. The sending of Adoram to collect the taxes, when the public mind was in such a state of fermentation, was another proof of Rehoboam's folly and incapacity to govern.

Verse 20. *Made him king over all Israel*] What is called Israel here, was ten-twelfths of the whole nation; and had they a right to call another person to the throne? They had not, —they had neither *legal* nor *constitutional right.* Jeroboam was not of the blood royal;

A. M. 3029
B. C. 975
Ante I. Ol. 199
An. Thersippi,
Arch. Athen.
perpet. 19

23 Speak unto Rehoboam the son of Solomon, king of Judah, and unto all the house of Judah and Benjamin, and to the remnant of the people, saying,

24 Thus saith the LORD, Ye shall not go up, nor fight against your brethren the children of Israel: return every man to his house; ^sfor this thing is from me. They hearkened therefore to the word of the LORD, and returned to depart, according to the word of the LORD.

25 Then Jeroboam ^tbuilt Shechem in Mount Ephraim, and dwelt therein; and went out from thence, and built ^uPenuel.

26 And Jeroboam said in his heart, Now shall the kingdom return to the house of David:

27 If this people ^vgo up to do sacrifice in the house of the LORD at Jerusalem, then shall the heart of this people turn again unto their lord, *even* unto Rehoboam king of Judah, and they shall kill me and go again to Rehoboam king of Judah.

28 Whereupon the king took counsel, and ^wmade two calves *of* gold, and said unto them,

It is too much for you to go up to Jerusalem: ^xbehold thy gods, O Israel, which brought thee up out of the land of Egypt.

A. M. 3029
B. C. 975
Ante I. Ol. 199
An. Thersippi,
Arch. Athen.
perpet. 19

29 And he set the one in ^yBeth-el, and the other put he in ^zDan.

30 And this thing became ^aa sin: for the people went *to worship* before the one, *even* unto Dan.

31 And he made a ^bhouse of high places, ^cand made priests of the lowest of the people, which were not of the sons of Levi.

32 And Jeroboam ordained a feast in the eighth month, on the fifteenth day of the month, like unto ^dthe feast that *is* in Judah, and he ^eoffered upon the altar. So did he in Beth-el, ^fsacrificing unto the calves that he had made; and ^ghe placed in Beth-el the priests of the high places which he had made.

33 So he ^hoffered upon the altar which he had made in Beth-el the fifteenth day of the eighth month, *even* in the month which he had ⁱdevised of his own heart; and ordained a feast unto the children of Israel: and he offered upon the altar, ^kand burnt ^lincense.

---

^sVerse 15——^tSee Judges ix. 45——^uJudges viii. 17 ^vDeut. xii. 5, 6——^w2 Kings x. 29; xvii. 16——^xExodus xxxii. 4, 8——^yGen. xxviii. 19; Hosea iv. 15——^zJudges xviii. 29——^aChap. xiii. 34; 2 Kings xvii. 21——^bChap. xiii. 32

^cNum. iii. 10; ch. xiii. 33; 2 Kings xvii. 32; 2 Chron. xi. 14, 15; Ezek. xliv. 7, 8——^dLev. xxiii. 33, 34; Num. xxix. 12; ch. viii. 2, 5——^eOr, *went up to the altar*, &c.—— ^fOr, *to sacrifice*——^gAmos vii. 13——^hOr, *went up to the altar*, &c. ⁱNum. xv. 39——^kHeb. *to burn incense*——^lCh. xiii. 1

---

he had no affinity to the kingdom. Nothing could justify this act, but the just judgment of God. God thus punished a disobedient and gainsaying people; and especially Solomon's family, whose sins against the Lord were of no ordinary magnitude.

Verse 24. *For this thing is from me.*] That is, the *separation* of the ten tribes from the house of David.

They—returned to depart] This was great deference, both in Rehoboam and his officers, to relinquish, at the demand of the prophet, a war which they thought they had good grounds to undertake. *The remnant of the people* heard the Divine command gratefully, for the mass of mankind are averse from war. No nations would ever rise up against each other, were they not instigated to it or compelled by the rulers.

Verse 27. *And they shall kill me*] He found he had little cause to trust this fickle people; though they had declared for him it was more from *caprice, desire of change,* and *novelty,* than from any regular and praiseworthy *principle.*

Verse 28. *Made two calves* of *gold*] He invented a political religion, instituted feasts in his own times different from those appointed by the Lord, gave the people certain objects of devotion, and pretended to think it would be both inconvenient and oppressive to them to have to go up to Jerusalem to worship. This was not the last time that religion was made a state engine to serve political purposes. It is strange

that in pointing out his calves to the people, he should use the same words that Aaron used when he made the golden calf in the wilderness, when they must have heard what terrible judgments fell upon their forefathers for this idolatry.

Verse 29. *One in Beth-el, and the other—in Dan.*] One at the *southern* and the other at the *northern* extremity of the land. Solomon's idolatry had prepared the people for Jeroboam's abominations!

Verse 31. *A house of high places*] A temple of temples; he had many *high places* in the land, and to imitate the temple at Jerusalem, he made one chief over all the rest, where he established a priesthood of his own ordination. Probably a place of *separate appointment,* where *different idols* were set up and worshipped; so it was a sort of *pantheon.*

Made priests of the lowest of the people] He took the people indifferently as they came, and made them priests, till he had enough, without troubling himself whether they were of the family of Aaron or the house of Levi, or not. Any priests would do well enough for such gods. But those whom he took seem to have been worthless, good-for-nothing fellows, who had neither piety nor good sense. Probably the *sons of Levi* had grace enough to refuse to sanction this new priesthood and idolatrous worship.

Verse 32. *Ordained a feast*] The Jews held their *feast of tabernacles* on the fifteenth day

---

of the *seventh* month; Jeroboam, who would meet the prejudices of the people as far as he could, appointed a similar feast on the fifteenth of the *eighth* month; thus appearing to hold the thing while he subverted the ordinance.

Verse 33. *He offered upon the altar*] Jeroboam probably performed the functions of high priest himself, that he might in his own person condense the civil and ecclesiastical power.

CHAPTER XIII

A man of God prophesies against Jeroboam's altar, and foretells the destruction of that altar, and of its idolatrous priests by Josiah; and gives Jeroboam a sign that the prophecy should be accomplished, 1–3. Jeroboam is enraged, and orders the man of God to be seized; and stretching out his hand for this purpose, his arm dries up, 4. The altar is rent, and the ashes poured out, according to the sign given by the man of God; and at his intercession Jeroboam's arm is restored, 5, 6. Jeroboam wishes to engage him in his service, but he refuses, and tells him that he was ordered by God not even to eat or drink in that place; and he accordingly departs, 7–10. An old prophet that dwelt at Beth-el, hearing of this, rides after the man of God; deceives him; brings him back to his house, and persuades him to eat and drink, 11–19. While he is eating, the word of the Lord comes to the old prophet, and he foretells the death of the man of God; who departing is met by a lion, and slain, 20–25. On hearing this, the old prophet goes to the place, finds the carcass, brings it home, buries it, and mourns over it, charging his sons to bury him, when dead, in the same grave, 26–32. Notwithstanding these warnings, Jeroboam continues in his idolatry, 33, 34.

A. M. 3030
B. C. 974
Ante I. Ol. 198
An. Thersippi,
Arch. Athen.
perpet. 20

AND, behold, there came ᵃa man of God out of Judah by the word of the Lord unto Beth-el: ᵇand Jeroboam stood by the altar ᶜto burn incense.

2 And he cried against the altar in the word of the Lord, and said, O altar, altar, thus saith the Lord; Behold, a child shall be born unto the house of David, ᵈJosiah by name; and upon thee shall he offer the priests of the high

places that burn incense upon thee, and men's bones shall be burnt upon thee.

A. M. 3030
B. C. 974
Ante I. Ol. 198
An. Thersippi,
Arch. Athen.
perpet. 20

3 And he gave ᵉa sign the same day, saying, This *is* the sign which the Lord hath spoken; Behold, the altar shall be rent, and the ashes that *are* upon it shall be poured out.

4 And it came to pass, when King Jeroboam heard the saying of the man of God, which

---

ᵃ2 Kings xxiii. 17——ᵇChap. xii. 32, 33——ᶜOr, *to offer*

ᵈ2 Kings xxiii. 15, 16——ᵉIsa. vii. 14; John ii. 18; 1 Cor. i. 22

NOTES ON CHAP. XIII

Verse 1. *There came a man of God*] Who this was we know not. The *Chaldee, Syriac,* and *Arabic* call him a *prophet.* The *Vulgate* and *Septuagint* follow the *Hebrew.* איש אלהים *ish elohim* means a Divine person, one wholly devoted to God's service. Some have thought it was Shemaiah, others Joel, and others Iddo. It could not have been the latter, for he wrote the acts of Jeroboam, 2 Chron. ix. 29, and the prophet was killed before he returned home; but conjecture is idle on such a subject.

Jeroboam stood by the altar] Like gods, like priest; he made himself high priest, and he took of the lowest of the people, and made them priests of the high places; they proved themselves to be *fools* by worshipping *calves.*

Verse 2. *He cried against the altar*] He denounced the destruction of this idolatrous system.

A child shall be born—Josiah by name] This is one of the most remarkable and most singular prophecies in the Old Testament. It here most circumstantially foretells a fact which took place *three hundred and forty* years after the prediction; a fact which was attested by the two nations. The *Jews,* in whose behalf this prophecy was delivered, would guard it most sacredly; and it was the interest of the *Israel-*

ites, against whom it was levelled, to impugn its authenticity and expose its falsehood, had this been possible. This prediction not only showed the *knowledge* of God, but his *power.* He gave, as it were, this warning to idolatry, that it might be on its guard, and defend itself against this Josiah whenever a person of that name should be found sitting on the throne of David; and no doubt it was on the alert, and took all prudent measures for its own defence; but all in vain, for Josiah, in the *eighteenth* year of his reign, literally accomplished this prophecy, as we may read, 2 Kings, chap. xxiii. 15-20. And from this latter place we find that the prophecy had *three* permanent testimonials of its truth. 1. The house of Israel; 2. The house of Judah; and, 3. The tomb of the prophet who delivered this prophecy, who, being slain by a lion, was brought back and buried at Beth-el, the *superscription* on whose tomb remained till the day on which Josiah destroyed that altar, and burnt dead men's bones upon it. See above, verses 16, 17, and 18.

Verse 3. *And he gave a sign*] A miracle to prove that the prophecy should be fulfilled in its season.

Verse 4. *Lay hold on him.*] No doubt, stretching out his own hand at the same time, through rage, pride, and haste, to execute his own orders.

And his hand—dried up] The whole arm became suddenly rigid; the nerves no longer com-

A. M. 3030
B. C. 974
Ante I. Ol. 198
An. Thersippi,
Arch. Athen.
perpet. 20

had cried against the altar in Beth-el, that he put forth his hand from the altar, saying, Lay hold on him. And his hand, which he put forth against him, dried up, so that he could not pull it in again to him.

5 The altar also was rent, and the ashes poured out from the altar, according to the sign which the man of God had given by the word of the LORD.

6 And the king answered and said unto the man of God, [f]Entreat now the face of the LORD thy God, and pray for me, that my hand may be restored me again. And the man of God besought [g]the LORD, and the king's hand was restored to him again, and became as *it was* before.

7 And the king said unto the man of God, Come home with me, and refresh thyself, and [h]I will give thee a reward.

8 And the man of God said unto the king, [i]If thou wilt give me half thine house, I will not go in with thee, neither will I eat bread nor drink water in this place:

9 For so was it charged me by the word of the LORD, saying, [k]Eat no bread, nor drink water, nor turn again by the same way that thou camest.

10 So he went another way, and returned not by the way that he came to Beth-el.

A. M. 3030
B. C. 974
Ante I. Ol. 198
An. Thersippi,
Arch. Athen.
perpet. 20

11 Now there dwelt an old prophet in Beth-el; and his [l]sons came and told him all the works that the man of God had done that day in Beth-el: the words which he had spoken unto the king, them they told also to their father.

12 And their father said unto them, What way went he? For his sons had seen what way the man of God went, which came from Judah.

13 And he said unto his sons, Saddle me the ass. So they saddled him the ass: and he rode thereon,

14 And went after the man of God, and found him sitting under an oak: and he said unto him, *Art* thou the man of God that camest from Judah? And he said, I *am*.

15 Then he said unto him, Come home with me, and eat bread.

16 And he said, [m]I may not return with thee, nor go in with thee: neither will I eat bread nor drink water with thee in this place:

17 For [n]it was said to me [o]by the word of the LORD, Thou shalt eat no bread nor drink water there, nor turn again to go by the way that thou camest.

18 He said unto him, I *am* a prophet also as

---

[f]Exod. viii. 8; ix. 28; x. 17; Num. xxi. 7; Acts viii. 24; James v. 16——[g]Heb. *the face of the LORD*——[h]1 Sam. ix. 7; 2 Kings v. 15

[i]So Num. xxii. 18; xxiv. 13——[k]1 Cor. v. 11——[l]Heb. *son*——[m]Ver. 8, 9——[n]Heb. *a word* was——[o]Chap. xx. 35; 1 Thess. iv. 15

---

municated their influence, and the muscles ceased to obey the dictates of the will.

Verse 5. *The altar was also rent*] It split or clave of its own accord; and, as the split parts would decline at the top from the line of their perpendicular, so the ashes and coals would fall off, or be poured out.

Verse 6. *Entreat—the face of the Lord thy God*] The *face* of God is his *favour*, as we see in many parts of the sacred writings. He says, *thy God;* for Jeroboam knew that he was not *his God*, for he was now in the very act of acknowledging other gods, and had no portion in the God of Jacob.

And the king's hand was restored] Both miracles were wrought to show the truth of the Jewish religion, and to convince this bold innovator of his wickedness, and to reclaim him from the folly and ruinous tendency of his idolatry.

Verse 7. *Come home with me—and I will give thee a reward.*] Come and be one of my priests, and I will give thee a proper salary.

Verse 9. *For so it was charged me—Eat no bread, &c.*] That is, Have no kind of communication with those idolaters. He was charged also not to return by the way that he came; probably lest the account of what was done should have reached the ears of any of the peo-

ple through whom he *had passed*, and he suffer inconveniences on the account, either by persecution from the idolaters, or from curious people delaying him, in order to cause him to give an account of the transactions which took place at Beth-el. This is *a* reason why he should not return by the same way; but what *the* reason of this part of the charge was, if not the above, is not easy to see.

Verse 11. *An old prophet*] Probably once a prophet of the Lord, who had fallen from his steadfastness, and yet not so deeply as to lose the knowledge of the true God, and join with Jeroboam in his idolatries. We find he was not at the king's sacrifice, though his sons were there; and perhaps even they were there, not as idolaters, but as spectators of what was done.

Verse 14. *And went after the man of God*] I can hardly think that this was with any evil design. His sons had given him such an account of the prediction, the power, and influence of this prophet, that he wished to have a particular acquaintance with him, in order that he might get farther information relative to the solemn import of the prophecy which he had denounced against the idolatry at Beth-el. This good man could not have been an object of the old prophet's malevolence.

Verse 18. *An angel spake unto me*] That *he*

A. M. 3030
B. C. 974
Ante I. Ol. 198
An. Thersippi,
Arch. Athen.
perpet. 20

thou *art;* and an angel spake unto me by the word of the LORD, saying, Bring him back with thee into thine house, that he may eat bread and drink water. *But* he lied unto him.

19 So he went back with him, and did eat bread in his house, and drank water.

20 And it came to pass, as they sat at the table, that the word of the LORD came unto the prophet that brought him back:

21 And he cried unto the man of God that came from Judah, saying, Thus saith the LORD, Forasmuch as thou hast disobeyed the

mouth of the LORD, and hast not kept the commandment which the LORD thy God commanded thee,

A. M. 3030
B. C. 974
Ante I. Ol. 198
An. Thersippi,
Arch. Athen.
perpet. 20

22 But camest back, and hast eaten bread and drunk water in the place, Pof the which *the LORD* did say to thee, Eat no bread, and drink no water; thy carcass shall not come unto the sepulchre of thy fathers.

23 And it came to pass, after he had eaten bread, and after he had drunk, that he saddled for him the ass, *to wit,* for the prophet whom he had brought back.

24 And when he was gone, qa lion met him

PVerse 9

qChap. xx. 36

---

lied unto him is here expressly asserted, and is amply proved by the event. But why should he deceive him? The simple principle of curiosity to know all about this prediction, and the strange facts which had taken place, of which he had heard at second hand by means of his sons, was sufficient to induce such a person to get the intelligence he wished by any means. We may add to this, that, as he found the man of God sitting under an oak, probably *faint* with *fatigue* and *fasting,* for he had had no refreshment, his *humanity* might have led him to practise this deception, in order to persuade him to take some refreshment. Having fallen from God, as I have supposed, ver. 11, his own tenderness of conscience was gone; and he would not scruple to do a *moral evil,* if even a *temporal good* could come of it. Again, is it not possible that the old prophet was himself *deceived?* for, though he *lied unto him,* it is possible that he was not conscious of his lie, for Satan, as *an angel of light,* might have deceived him in order to lead him to deceive the other. He does not say, as the man of God did, *It was said to me by the word of the Lord;* no: but, *An angel spake unto me by the word of the Lord.* And I think it very likely that an angel did appear to him on the occasion; an *angel of darkness* and *idolatry,* in the garb of *an angel of light,* who wished to use him as an instrument to bring discredit on the awful transactions which had lately taken place, and to destroy him who had foretold the destruction of his power and influence.

Verse 19. *So he went back with him]* He permitted himself to be imposed on; he might have thought, as he had accomplished every purpose for which God sent him, and had actually begun to return by another way, God, who had given him the charge, had authority to say, "As thy purpose was to obey every injunction, even to the letter, I now permit thee to go with this old prophet, and take some refreshment." Now God might as well have dispensed with this part of the injunction, as he did in the case of Abraham: *Take thy son Isaac, thy only son, whom thou lovest—and offer him for a burnt-offering;* but, when he saw his perfect readiness, he dispensed with the *actual offering,* and accepted a ram in his stead. Thus much may be said in vindication of the man of God: but if this be so, why should he be punished with *death,* for

doing what he had *reason* and *precedent* to believe might be the will of God? I answer: He should not have taken a step back, till he had remission of the clause from the same authority which gave him the general message. He should have had it from the *word of the Lord to himself,* in both cases, as Abraham had; and not taken an apparent contradiction of what was before delivered unto him, from the mouth of a *stranger,* who only professed to have it from *an angel,* who pretended to speak unto him *by the word of the Lord.* In this, and in this alone, lay the *sinfulness* of the act of the man of God, who came out of Judah.

Verse 20. *The word of the Lord came unto the prophet that brought him back]* "A great clamour," says Dr. *Kennicott,* "has been raised against this part of the history, on account of God's denouncing sentence on the *true* prophet by the mouth of the *false* prophet: but if we examine with attention the original words here, they will be found to signify either *he who brought him back;* or, *whom he had brought back;* for the very same words, אשר השיבו *asher heshibo,* occur again in ver. 23, where they are now translated, *whom he had brought back;* and where they cannot be translated otherwise. This being the case, we are at liberty to consider the word of the Lord as delivered to the *true* prophet thus brought back; and then the sentence is pronounced by GOD himself, calling to him out of heaven, as in Gen. xxii. 11. And that this doom was thus pronounced by *God,* not by the false prophet, we are assured in ver. 26: 'The Lord hath delivered him unto the lion, according to the word of the *Lord* which HE spake unto him.' *Josephus* expressly asserts that the sentence was declared by God to the *true* prophet." The *Arabic* asserts the same.

Verse 21. *And he]* That is, according to the above interpretation, *the voice of God* from heaven addressing the man of God, the old prophet having nothing to do in this business.

Verse 22. *Thy carcass shall not come]* This intimated to him that he was to *die an untimely death,* but probably did not *specify* by what means.

Verse 24. *A lion met him—and slew him]* By permitting himself to be seduced by the old prophet, when he should have acted only on the expressly declared counsel of God, he committed *the sin unto death;* that is, such a sin as God

A. M. 3030
B. C. 974
Ante I. Ol. 198
An. Thersippi,
Arch. Athen.
perpet. 20

by the way, and slew him: and his carcass was cast in the way, and the ass stood by it, the lion also stood by the carcass.

25 And, behold, men passed by, and saw the carcass cast in the way, and the lion standing by the carcass: and they came and told *it* in the city where the old prophet dwelt.

26 And when the prophet that brought him back from the way heard *thereof,* he said, It *is* the man of God, who was disobedient unto the word of the LORD: therefore the LORD hath delivered him unto the lion, which hath ʳtorn him, and slain him, according to the word of the LORD, which he spake unto him.

27 And he spake to his sons, saying, Saddle me the ass. And they saddled *him.*

28 And he went and found his carcass cast in the way, and the ass and the lion standing by the carcass: the lion had not eaten the carcass, nor ˢtorn the ass.

A. M. 3030
B. C. 974
Ante I. Ol. 198
An. Thersippi,
Arch. Athen.
perpet. 20

29 And the prophet took up the carcass of the man of God, and laid it upon the ass, and brought it back: and the old prophet came to the city, to mourn and to bury him.

30 And he laid his carcass in his own grave; and they mourned over him, *saying,* ᵗAlas, my brother!

31 And it came to pass, after he had buried him, that he spake to his sons, saying, When I am dead, then bury me in the sepulchre wherein the man of God *is* buried; ᵘlay my bones beside his bones:

32 ᵛFor the saying which he cried by the word of the LORD against the altar in Beth-el, and against all the houses of the high places which *are* in the cities of ʷSamaria, shall surely come to pass.

33 ˣAfter this thing Jeroboam returned not from his evil way, but ʸmade again of the

---

ʳHeb. *broken*——ˢHeb. *broken*——ᵗJer. xxii. 18——ᵘ2 Kings xxiii. 17, 18——ᵛVer. 2; 2 Kings xxiii. 16, 19

ʷSee chap. xvi. 24——ˣChap. xii. 31, 32; 2 Chron. xi. 15; xiii. 9——ʸHeb. *returned and made*

---

will punish with the death of the body, while he extends mercy to the soul. See my notes on 1 John v. 16, 17.

From the instance here related, we see, as in various other cases, that often *judgment begins at the house of God.* The true prophet, for receiving that as a revelation from God which was opposed to the revelation which himself had received, and which was confirmed by so many miracles, is slain by a lion, and his body deprived of the burial of his fathers; while the wicked king, and the old fallen prophet, are both permitted to live! If this was *severity* to the man of God, it was *mercy* to the others, neither of whom was prepared to meet his judge. Here we may well say, "If the righteous scarcely be saved, where shall the ungodly and the sinner appear?"

Verse 28. *The lion had not eaten the carcass, nor torn the ass.*] All here was preternatural. The lion, though he had killed the man, does not devour him; the ass stands quietly by, not fearing the lion; and the lion does not attempt to tear the ass: both stand as guardians of the fallen prophet. How evident is the hand of God in all!

Verse 30. *Alas, my brother!*] This lamentation is very simple, very short, and very pathetic. Perhaps the old prophet said it as much in reference to *himself,* who had been the cause of his untimely death, as in reference to the man of God, whose corpse he now committed to the tomb. But the words may be no more than the *burden* of each line of the lamentation which was used on this occasion. See instances of this among the Asiatics in the note on Jer. xxii. 18.

Verse 31. *Lay my bones beside his bones*] This argues a strong conviction in the mind of the old prophet, that the deceased was a good and holy man of God; and he is willing to have place with him in the general resurrection.

Verse 32. *In the cities of Samaria*] It is most certain that Samaria, or as it is called in Hebrew *Shomeron,* was not built at this time. We are expressly told that Omri, king of Israel, founded this city on the hill which he bought for two talents of silver, from a person of the name of *Shemer,* after whom he called the city Samaria or *Shomeron;* (see chap. xvi. 24;) and this was fifty years after the death of Jeroboam. How then could the old prophet speak of *Samaria,* not then in existence, unless he did it by the spirit of prophecy, calling things that are not as though they were; as the man of God called Josiah by name *three hundred* years before he was born? Some suppose that the historian adds these words because Samaria existed in *his* time, and he well knew that it did not exist in the time of the old prophet; for himself, in the sixteenth chapter, gives us the account of its foundation by Omri. After all, it is possible that God might have given this revelation to the old prophet; and thus by anticipation which is the language of prophecy, spoke of Samaria as then existing. This is the solution of *Houbigant,* and is thought sound by many good critics.

Verse 33. *Jeroboam returned not from his evil way*] There is something exceedingly obstinate and perverse, as well as blinding and infatuating, in idolatry. The prediction lately delivered at Beth-el, and the miracles wrought in confirmation of it, were surely sufficient to have affected and alarmed any heart, not wholly and incorrigibly hardened; and yet they had no effect on Jeroboam!

Made—the lowest of the people priests] So hardy was this bad man in his idolatry that he did not even attempt to form any thing according to the model of God's true worship: he would have nothing like God and truth. In his *calves,* or rather *oxen,* he copied the manner of

A.M.3030-3050
B. C. 974–954
Anno ante I.
Olymp.198-178

lowest of the people priests of the high places: whosoever would, he ᶻconsecrated him, and he became *one* of the priests of the high places.

ᵃHeb. *filled his hand; Judg.* xvii. 12

Egypt; and in the formation of his priesthood, he seems to have gone aside from all models. Amongst the worst of heathens, the priesthood was filled with respectable men; but Jeroboam took of the lowest of the people, and put them in that office.

Whosoever would, he consecrated him] He made no discrimination: any vagabond that offered was accepted even of those who had no character, who were too idle to work, and too stupid to learn.

Verse 34. And this thing became sin] These abominations were too glaring, and too insulting to the Divine Majesty, to be permitted to last; therefore his house was cut off, and destroyed from the face of the earth.

A HOLY priesthood, a righteous ministry, is a blessing to any state, because it has a most powerful effect on the *morals* of the community; inducing order, sobriety, and habits of industry, among the people: on the contrary, the profligacy of the clergy, and false principles of religion, are the most likely to unsettle a kingdom, and to bring about destructive revolutions in the state. This is the principle on which all

34 ᵃAnd this thing became sin unto the house of Jeroboam, even ᵇto cut *it* off, and to destroy *it* from off the face of the earth.

A.M.3030-3050
B. C. 974–954
Anno ante I.
Olymp.198-178

ᵃChap. xii. 30——ᵇChap. xiv. 10

---

national establishments of religion were originally formed. The state thought proper to secure a permanency of religion, that religion might secure the safety of the state; because it was supposed from the general aversion of men from good, that, if left to themselves, they would have no religion at all. Where the religion of the country is pure, founded solely on the oracles of God, it deserves the utmost sanction of the state, as well as the attention of every individual. A Christian state has surely authority to enact, *The Christian religion is and shall be the religion of this land;* and, prejudice apart, should not the laws provide for the permanence of this system? Is the form of Christianity likely to be preserved in times of general profligacy, if the laws do not secure its permanence? What would our nation have been if we had not had a version of the sacred writings established by the authority of the laws: and a form of sound words for general devotion established by the same authority? Whatever the reader may do the writer thanks God for the religious establishment of his country. For *abuses* in *church* or *state*, he is the last to contend.

CHAPTER XIV

Abijah, son of Jeroboam, falls sick, 1. Jeroboam sends his wife disguised to Ahijah the prophet, and with her a present, to inquire concerning his son, 2–4. Ahijah discovers her by a Divine intimation and delivers to her a heavy message concerning the destruction of Jeroboam's house, and the death of her son, 5–16. The child dies, according to the prediction of Ahijah, 17. Jeroboam's reign and death, 18–20. Rehoboam's bad reign, and the apostasy of Judah, 21–24. Shishak, king of Egypt, invades Judea, spoils the temple, and takes away the golden shields made by Solomon; instead of which Rehoboam makes others of brass, 25–28. Rehoboam's reign and death, 29–31.

A. M. 3048
B. C. 956
Ante I. Ol. 180
An. Thersippi,
Arch. Athen.
perpet. 38

AT that time Abijah the son of Jeroboam fell sick.

2 And Jeroboam said to his wife, Arise, I pray thee, and disguise thyself, that thou be not known to be the wife of Jeroboam; and get thee to Shiloh: behold, there *is* Ahijah the prophet, which told me that ᵃI *should be* king over this people.

3 ᵇAnd take ᶜwith thee ten loaves, and

ᵈcracknels, and a ᵉcruse of honey, and go to him: he shall tell thee what shall become of the child.

A. M. 3048
B. C. 956
Ante I. Ol. 180
An. Thersippi,
Arch. Athen.
perpet. 38

4 And Jeroboam's wife did so, and arose, ᶠand went to Shiloh, and came to the house of Ahijah. But Ahijah could not see; for his eyes ᵍwere set by reason of his age.

5 And the LORD said unto Ahijah, Behold,

ᵃChap. xi. 31——ᵇSee 1 Sam. ix. 7, 8——ᶜHeb. *in thine hand*——ᵈOr, *cakes*

ᵉOr, *bottle*——ᶠChapter xi. 29——ᵍHebrew, *stood for his hoariness*

NOTES ON CHAP. XIV

Verse 1. Abijah—fell sick] This was but a prelude to the miseries which fell on the house of Jeroboam; but it was another merciful warning, intended to turn him from his idolatry and wickedness.

Verse 3. Ten loaves] Probably common or household bread.

Cracknels] נקדים *nikkuddim, spotted,* or per-

forated bread; thin cakes, pierced through with many holes, the same as is called *Jews' bread* to the present day, and used by them at the passover. It was customary to give presents to all great personages; and no person consulted a prophet without bringing something in his hand.

Verse 5. Feign herself to be *another* woman.] It would have been discreditable to Jero-

A. M. 3048 B. C. 956 Ante I. Ol. 180 An. Thersippi, Arch. Athen. perpet. 38

the wife of Jeroboam cometh to ask a thing of thee for her son; for he *is* sick: thus and thus shalt thou say unto her: for it shall be, when she cometh in, that she shall feign herself *to be* another *woman.*

6 And it was *so,* when Ahijah heard the sound of her feet, as she came in at the door, that he said, Come in, thou wife of Jeroboam; why feignest thou thyself *to be* another? for I *am* sent to thee *with* [h]heavy *tidings.*

7 Go, tell Jeroboam, Thus saith the LORD God of Israel, [i]Forasmuch as I exalted thee from among the people, and made thee prince over my people Israel,

8 And [k]rent the kingdom away from the house of David, and gave it thee: and *yet* thou hast not been as my servant David, [l]who kept my commandments, and who followed me with all his heart, to do *that* only *which was* right in mine eyes:

9 But hast done evil above all that were before thee: [m]for thou hast gone and made thee other gods, and molten images, to provoke me to anger, and [n]hast cast me behind thy back:

10 Therefore, behold, [o]I will bring evil upon the house of Jeroboam, and [p]will cut off from Jeroboam him that pisseth against the wall, [q]*and* him that is shut up and left in Israel, and will take away the remnant of the house of Jeroboam, as a man taketh away dung, till it be all gone.

11 [r]Him that dieth of Jeroboam in the city shall the dogs eat; and him that dieth in the field shall the fowls of the air eat: for the LORD hath spoken *it.*

12 Arise thou, therefore, get thee to thine own house: *and* [s]when thy feet enter into the city, the child shall die.

A. M. 3048 B. C. 956 Ante I. Ol. 180 An. Thersippi, Arch. Athen. perpet. 38

13 And all Israel shall mourn for him, and bury him: for he only of Jeroboam shall come to the grave, because in him [t]there is found *some* good thing toward the LORD God of Israel in the house of Jeroboam.

14 [u]Moreover the LORD shall raise him up a king over Israel, who shall cut off the house of Jeroboam that day: but what? even now.

15 For the LORD shall smite Israel, as a reed is shaken in the water, and he shall [v]root up Israel out of this [w]good land, which he gave to their fathers, and shall scatter them [x]beyond the river, [y]because they have made their groves, provoking the LORD to anger.

16 And he shall give Israel up because of the sins of Jeroboam, [z]who did sin, and who made Israel to sin.

17 And Jeroboam's wife arose, and departed, and came to [a]Tirzah: *and* [b]when she came to the threshold of the door, the child died;

18 And they buried him; and all Israel mourned for him, [c]according to the word of the LORD, which he spake by the hand of his servant Ahijah the prophet.

A.M.3029-3050 B. C. 975-954 Anno ante I. Olymp.199-178

19 And the rest of the acts of Jeroboam, how he [d]warred, and how he reigned, behold, they *are* written in the book of the chronicles of the kings of Israel.

20 And the days which Jeroboam reigned *were* two and twenty years: and he [e]slept with his fathers, and Nadab his son reigned in his stead.

---

[h]Heb. *hard*——[i]See 2 Sam. xii. 7, 8; chap. xvi. 2——[k]Chap. xi. 31——[l]Chap. xi. 33, 38; xv. 5——[m]Chap. xii. 28; 2 Chron. xi. 15——[n]Neh. ix. 26; Psa. l. 17; Ezek. xxiii. 35——[o]Chap. xv. 29——[p]Chap. xxi. 21; 2 Kings ix. 8——[q]Deut. xxxii. 36; 2 Kings xiv. 26——[r]Chap. xvi. 4; xxi. 24——[s]Ver. 17

[t]2 Chron. xii. 12; xix. 3——[u]Ch. xv. 27, 28, 29——[v]2 Kings xvii. 6; Psa. lii. 5——[w]Josh. xxiii. 15, 16——[x]2 Kings xv. 29——[y]Exod. xxxiv. 13; Deut. xii. 3, 4——[z]Chap. xii. 30; xiii. 34; xv. 30, 34; xvi. 2——[a]Chap. xvi. 6, 8, 15, 23; Cant. vi. 4——[b]Ver. 12——[c]Ver. 13——[d]2 Chron. xiii. 2, &c.——[e]Heb. *lay down*

---

boam's calves, if it had been known that he had consulted a prophet of Jehovah.

Verse 8. *And rent the kingdom away from the house of David*] That is, *permitted* it to be rent, because of the folly and insolence of Rehoboam.

Verse 10. *Him that pisseth against the wall*] Every *male.* The phrase should be thus rendered wherever it occurs.

Verse 11. *Shall the dogs eat*] They shall not have an honourable burial: and shall not come into the sepulchres of their fathers.

Verse 13. *In him there is found* some *good thing*] Far be it from God to destroy the righteous with the wicked; God respects even a *little good,* because it is a seed from himself. The kingdom of heaven is like a grain of mustard seed.

Verse 15. *For the Lord shall smite Israel*] See this prophecy fulfilled, chap. xv. 28-30, when Baasha destroyed all the house and posterity of Jeroboam.

Verse 19. *The rest of the acts of Jeroboam—are written in the—chronicles*] For some im-

A.M.3029-3046
B. C. 975-958
Anno ante I.
Olymp.199-182 21 And Rehoboam the son of Solomon reigned in Judah. ᶠRehoboam *was* forty and one years old when he began to reign, and he reigned seventeen years in Jerusalem, the city ᵍwhich the LORD did choose out of all the tribes of Israel, to put his name there. ʰAnd his mother's name *was* Naamah an Ammonitess.

22 ⁱAnd Judah did evil in the sight of the LORD, and they ᵏprovoked him to jealousy with their sins which they had committed, above all that their fathers had done.

23 For they also built them ˡhigh places, and ᵐimages, ⁿand groves, on every high hill, and ᵒunder every green tree.

24 ᵖAnd there were also sodomites in the land: *and* they did according to all the abominations of the nations which the LORD cast out before the children of Israel.

A. M. 3034
B. C. 970
Ante I. Ol. 194
An. Thersippi,
Arch. Athen.
perpet. 24 25 ᑫAnd it came to pass in the fifth year of King Rehoboam, *that* Shishak king of Egypt came up against Jerusalem:

26 ʳAnd he took away the treasures of the house of the LORD, and the treasures of the king's house; he even took away all: and he took away all the shields of gold ˢwhich Solomon had made.

A. M. 3034
B. C. 970
Ante I. Ol. 194
An. Thersippi,
Arch. Athen.
perpet. 24

27 And King Rehoboam made in their stead brazen shields, and committed *them* unto the hands of the chief of the ᵗguard, which kept the door of the king's house.

28 And it was *so,* when the king went into the house of the LORD, that the guard bare them, and brought them back into the guard chamber.

29 ᵘNow the rest of the acts of Rehoboam, and all that he did, *are* they not written in the book of the chronicles of the kings of Judah?

A.M.3029-3046
B. C. 975-958
Anno ante I.
Olymp.199-182

30 And there was ᵛwar between Rehoboam and Jeroboam all *their* days.

31 ʷAnd Rehoboam slept with his fathers, and was buried with his fathers in the city of David. ˣAnd his mother's name *was* Naamah an Ammonitess. And ʸAbijam his son reigned in his stead.

A. M. 3046
B. C. 958
Ante I. Ol. 182
An. Thersippi,
Arch. Athen.
perpet. 36

ᶠ2 Chron. xii. 13——ᵍCh. xi. 36——ʰVer. 31——ⁱ2 Chron. xii. 1——ᵏDeut. xxxii. 21; Psa. lxxviii. 58; 1 Cor. x. 22——ˡDeut. xii. 2; Ezek. xvi. 24, 25——ᵐOr, *standing images* or *statues*——ⁿ2 Kings xvii. 9, 10——ᵒIsa. lvii. 5——ᵖDeut. xxiii. 17; ch. xv. 12; xxii. 46; 2 Kings xxiii. 7

ᑫChap. xi. 40; 2 Chronicles xii. 2——ʳ2 Chronicles xii. 9, 10, 11——ˢChapter x. 17——ᵗHebrew, *runners* ᵘ2 Chronicles xii. 15——ᵛChapter xii. 24; xv. 6; 2 Chronicles xii. 15——ʷ2 Chronicles xii. 16——ˣVerse 21——ʸ2 Chronicles xii. 16, *Abijah;* Matthew i. 7, *Abia*

---

portant particulars relative to this reign, see 2 Chron. xiii. 1-20.

Verse 24. *There were also sodomites in the land*] קדשים *kedeshim, consecrated persons;* persons who had devoted themselves, in practices of the greatest impurity, to the service of the most impure idols.

Verse 26. *He took away the treasures*] All the treasures which Solomon had amassed, both in the temple and in his own houses; a booty the most immense ever acquired in one place.

All the shields of gold which Solomon had made.] These were *three hundred* in number, and were all made of beaten gold. See a computation of their value in the note on chap. x. 17.

Verse 28. *The guard bare them*] The guard probably were just *three hundred,* answering to the number of the shields.

Verse 31. *Naamah an Ammonitess.*] He was born of a heathen mother, and begotten of an apostate father. From such an impure fountain could sweet water possibly spring?

Abijam his son reigned in his stead.] Though righteousness cannot be propagated, because it is *supernatural,* yet unrighteousness may, for that is a genuine offspring of nature. Abijam was the wicked son of an apostate father and heathenish mother. Grace may be grafted on a crab stock; but let none do evil that good may come of it. A bad stock will produce bad fruit.

Dr. *Kennicott* observes that the name of this king of Judah is now expressed *three* ways: here and in four other places it is *Abijam* or *Abim;* in *two* others it is *Abihu;* but in *eleven* other places it is *Abiah,* as it is expressed by St. Matt. i. 7, Ῥοβοαμ εγεννησε τον ABIA; and this is the reading of *thirteen* of *Kennicott's* and *De Rossi's* MSS., and of *thirteen* respectable editions of the Hebrew Bible. The *Syriac* is the same. The *Septuagint* in the London Polyglot has Αβιον, *Abihu;* but in the *Complutensian* and *Antwerp* Polyglots, it is Αβια, *Abiah.* Though the common printed *Vulgate* has *Abiam,* yet the *Editio Princeps* of the *Vulgate,* some MSS., and the text in the *Complutensian* and *Antwerp* Polyglots, have *Abia;* which without doubt is the reading that should in all cases be followed.

The rabbins say, and particularly *Rab. Sol. Jarchi,* that the Shishak mentioned in this chapter is Pharaoh Necho, and that he invaded Israel in order to get the ivory throne of his son-in-law Solomon, which he had always coveted; and this throne he carried away. It appears however that he spoiled the temple, the king's palace, &c., and in short took every thing away without resistance which he chose to carry off. It is very likely that this had a good effect on Rehoboam; it probably caused him to frequent the temple, ver. 28, which it is likely he had before neglected. This history is more particularly told in 2 Chron. xii., to which the reader will do well to refer; and as to Rehoboam, though so much positive iniquity is not laid to his charge as to his father, yet little can be said

for his piety; the idolatry introduced by Solomon does not appear to have been lessened in the days of Rehoboam.

CHAPTER XV

Abijam's wicked reign, and death, 1–8. Asa succeeds him in the kingdom of Judah, and rules well, 9–15. He makes a league with the king of Syria against Baasha king of Israel, who is obliged to desist in his attempts against Judah, 16–22. He is diseased in his feet and dies, and is succeeded by his son Jehoshaphat, 23–25. Nadab, son of Jeroboam, reigns over Israel; but is slain by Baasha, who reigns in his stead, 26–28. Baasha destroys all the house of Jeroboam, according to the prediction of Ahijah, 29, 30. Baasha continues the idolatry of Jeroboam, 31–34.

A.M.3046-3049
B. C. 958–955
Anno ante I.
Olymp.182-179

NOW [a]in the eighteenth year of King Jeroboam the son of Nebat reigned Abijam over Judah.

2 Three years reigned he in Jerusalem. [b]And his mother's name *was* [c]Maachah, the daughter of [d]Abishalom.

3 And he walked in all the sins of his father, which he had done before him: and [e]his heart was not perfect with the LORD his God, as the heart of David his father.

4 Nevertheless [f]for David's sake did the LORD his God give him a [g]lamp in Jerusalem, to set up his son after him, and to establish Jerusalem:

5 Because David [h]did *that which was* right in the eyes of the LORD, and turned not aside from any *thing* that he commanded him all

the days of his life, [i]save only in the matter of Uriah the Hittite.

A.M.3046-3049
B. C. 958–955
Anno ante I.
Olymp.182-179

6 [k]And there was war between Rehoboam and Jeroboam all the days of his life.

7 [l]Now the rest of the acts of Abijam, and all that he did, *are* they not written in the book of the chronicles of the kings of Judah? And there was war between Abijam and Jeroboam.

8 [m]And Abijam slept with his fathers; and they buried him in the city of David: and Asa his son reigned in his stead.

A. M. 3049
B. C. 955
Ante I. Ol. 179
An. Thersippi,
Arch. Athen.
perpet. 39

9 And in the twentieth year of Jeroboam king of Israel reigned Asa over Judah.

10 And forty and one years reigned he in Jerusalem. And his [n]mother's name *was* Maachah, the daughter of Abishalom.

A.M.3049-3090
B. C. 955-914
Anno ante I.
Olymp.179-138

---

[a]2 Chron. xiii. 1, 2——[b]2 Chron. xi. 20, 21, 22——[c]2 Chron. xiii. 2, *Michaia, the daughter of Uriel*——[d]2 Chron. xi. 21, *Absalom*——[e]Chap. xi. 4; Psa. cxix. 80 [f]Chap. xi. 32, 36: 2 Chron. xxi. 7

[g]Or, *candle;* chapter xi. 36——[h]Chapter xiv. 8——[i]2 Sam. xi. 4, 15; xii. 9——[k]Chapter xiv. 30——[l]2 Chron. xiii. 2, 3, 22——[m]2 Chron. xiv. 1——[n]That is, *grandmother's;* ver. 2

NOTES ON CHAP. XV

Verse 1. *Reigned Abijam over Judah.*] Of this son of Rehoboam, of his brethren, and of Rehoboam's family in general, see 2 Chron. xii., where many particulars are added.

Verse 3. *His heart was not perfect*] He was an idolater, or did not support the worship of the true God. This appears to be the general meaning of *the heart not being perfect with God.*

Verse 4. *The Lord—give him a lamp*] That is, a son to succeed him; see chap. xi. 36.

Verse 5. *Save only in the matter of Uriah*] Properly speaking, this is the only flagrant fault or crime in the life of David. It was a horrible offence, or rather a *whole system of offences.* See the notes on 2 Sam. xi. and xii.

Verse 6. *There was war between Rehoboam and Jeroboam*] This was mentioned in the preceding chapter, ver. 30, and it can mean no more than this: there was a *continual spirit of hostility* kept up between the two kingdoms, and no doubt frequent *skirmishing* between bordering parties; but it never broke out into *open war*, for this was particularly forbidden. See chap. xii. 24. Hostility did exist, and no

doubt frequent skirmishes; but *open war* and *pitched* battles there were none.

But why is this circumstance *repeated*, and the history of Abijam interrupted by the repetition? There is some reason to believe that *Rehoboam* is not the true reading, and that it should be *Abijam:* "Now there was war between *Abijam* and Jeroboam all the days of his life." And this is the reading of *fourteen* of *Kennicott's* and *De Rossi's* MSS. The *Syriac* has *Abia the son of Rehoboam;* the *Arabic* has *Abijam.* In the *Septuagint* the whole verse is omitted in the London Polyglot, but it is extant in those of *Complutum* and *Antwerp.* Some copies of the *Targum* have *Abijam* also, and the *Editio Princeps* of the *Vulgate* has *Abia.* This is doubtless the true reading, as we know there was a very memorable war between Abia and Jeroboam; see it particularly described 2 Chron. xiii. 3, &c.

Verse 10. *His mother's name*] Our translators thought that *grandmother* was likely to be *the meaning,* and therefore have put it in the *margin.*

The daughter of Abishalom.] She is called, says *Calmet,* the *daughter of Absalom,* according to the custom of the Scriptures, which give

A.M.3049-3090 B. C. 955-914 Anno ante I. Olymp.179-138

11 [o]And Asa did *that which* *was* right in the eyes of the LORD, as *did* David his father.

12 [p]And he took away the sodomites out of the land, and removed all the idols that his fathers had made.

13 And also [q]Maachah his mother, even her he removed from *being* queen, because she had made an idol in a grove; and Asa [r]destroyed her idol, and [s]burnt *it* by the brook Kidron.

14 [t]But the high places were not removed: nevertheless Asa's [u]heart was perfect with the LORD all his days.

15 And he brought in the [v]things which his father had dedicated, and the things which himself had dedicated, into the house of the LORD, silver, and gold, and vessels.

A.M.3051-3074 B. C. 953-930 Anno ante I. Olymp.177-154

16 And there was war between Asa and Baasha king of Israel all their days.

A. M. 3074 B. C. 930 Ante I. Ol. 154 An. Phorbæ, Arch. Athen. perpet. 23

17 And [w]Baasha king of Israel went up against Judah, and built [x]Ramah, [y]that he might not suffer any to go out or come in to Asa king of Judah.

18 Then Asa took all the silver and the gold

[o]2 Chronicles xiv. 2——[p]Chapter xiv. 24; xxii. 46——[q]2 Chronicles xv. 16——[r]Hebrew, *cut off*——[s]So Exodus xxxii. 20——[t]Chapter xxii. 43; 2 Chronicles xv. 17, 18——[u]See verse 3——[v]Hebrew, *holy*——[w]2 Chron. xvi. 1, &c.——[x]Josh. xviii. 25——[y]See chap. xii. 27

the name of *daughter* indifferently to the *niece*, the *grand-daughter*, and *great grand-daughter*.

Verse 12. *The sodomites*] הקדשים *hakkedeshim;* literally, *the holy* or *consecrated ones*. See on chap. xiv. 24.

Verse 13. *She had made an idol in a grove*] The original word, מפלצת *miphletseth*, is variously understood. I shall give its different views in the *versions:*—

"Besides, he removed his mother Maacha from being chief in the sacred rites of Priapus, and in his grove which she had consecrated."—VULGATE.

"And Ana, [other copies Maacha,] he removed from being governess, because she had made an assembly in her grove."—SEPTUAGINT.

"Moreover, he deprived Maacha, his mother, of her own magnificence, because she had celebrated a solemnity to her own worship."—SYRIAC.

"And even Maacha, his mother, he removed from the kingdom, because she had made an idol in a grove."—CHALDEE.

"Besides, he removed Maacha, his mother, from her kingdom, because she had made a high tree into an idol."—ARABIC.

"Also he removed Maacha, his mother, from the kingdom, because she had made a horrible statue; and our rabbins say that it was called מפלצת *miphletseth*, because מפליא ליצנותא *maphli leytsanutha*, it *produced wonderful ridicule;* for she made it *ad instar membri virilis*, and she used it daily."—RABBI SOLOMON JARCHI.

From the whole, it is pretty evident that the image was a mere *Priapus*, or something of the same nature, and that Maachah had an assembly in the grove where this image was set up, and doubtless worshipped it with the most impure rites. What the Roman *Priapus* was I need not tell the learned reader; and as to the unlearned, it would not profit him to know. *Maachah* was most likely another *Messalina;* and Asa probably did for his *mother* what Claudius did for his *wife*.

Verse 14. *The high places were not removed*] He was not able to make a thorough *reformation;* this was reserved for his son Jehoshaphat.

Asa's heart was perfect] He worshipped the true God, and zealously promoted his service; see on ver. 3. And even the *high places* which he did not remove were probably those where the true God alone was worshipped; for that there were such high places the preceding history amply proves, and Jarchi intimates that these were places which individuals had erected for the worship of Jehovah.

Verse 15. *Which his father had dedicated*] On what account he and his father dedicated the things mentioned below, we know not; but it appears that Asa thought himself bound by the vow of his father.

Verse 16. *There was war*] That is, there was continual enmity; see on ver. 6. But there was no open war till the *thirty-sixth* year of Asa, when Baasha, king of Israel, began to build Ramah, that he might prevent all communication between Israel and Judah; see 2 Chron. xv. 19, and xvi. 1. But this does not agree with what is said here, chap. xvi. 8, 9, that Elah, the son and successor of Baasha, was killed by Zimri, in the *twenty-sixth* year of the reign of Asa. Chronologers endeavour to reconcile this by saying that the years should be reckoned, not from the beginning of the reign of Asa, but from the separation of the kingdoms of Israel and Judah. It is most certain that Baasha could not make war upon Asa in the *thirty-sixth* year of his reign, when it is evident from this chapter that he was dead in the *twenty-sixth* year of that king. We must either adopt the mode of solution given by chronologists, or grant that there is a mistake in some of the numbers; most likely in the parallel places in Chronicles, but which we have no direct means of correcting. But the reader may compare 2 Chron. xiv. 1, with xv. 10, 19, and xvi. 1.

Verse 17. *And Baasha—built Ramah*] As the word signifies a *high place*, what is here termed *Ramah* was probably a *hill*, (commanding a *defile* through which lay the principal road to Jerusalem,) which Baasha fortified in order to prevent all intercourse with the kingdom of Judah, lest his subjects should cleave to the

A. M. 3074
B. C. 930
Ante I. Ol. 154
An. Phorbæ,
Arch. Athen.
perpet. 23
that were left in the treasures of the house of the LORD, and the treasures of the king's house, and delivered them into the hand of his servants: and King Asa sent them to ᶻBen-hadad, the son of Tabrimon, the son of Hezion, king of Syria, that dwelt at ᵃDamascus, saying,

19 *There is* a league between me and thee, *and* between my father and thy father: behold, I have sent unto thee a present of silver and gold; come and break thy league with Baasha king of Israel, that he may ᵇdepart from me.

20 So Ben-hadad hearkened unto King Asa, and sent the captains of the hosts which he had against the cities of Israel, and smote ᶜIjon, and ᵈDan, and ᵉAbel-beth-maachah, and all Cinneroth, with all the land of Naphtali.

21 And it came to pass, when Baasha heard *thereof,* that he left off building of Ramah, and dwelt in Tirzah.

22 ᶠThen King Asa made a proclamation throughout all Judah, none *was* ᵍexempted: and they took away the stones of Ramah, and the timber thereof, wherewith Baasha had builded; and King Asa built with them ʰGeba of Benjamin, and ⁱMizpah.

23 The rest of all the acts of Asa, and all

his might, and all that he did, and the cities which he built, *are* they not written in the book of the chronicles of the kings of Judah? Nevertheless ᵏin the time of his old age he was diseased in his feet.

A. M. 3074
B. C. 930
Ante I. Ol. 154
An. Phorbæ,
Arch. Athen.
perpet. 23

24 And Asa slept with his fathers, and was buried with his fathers in the city of David his father: ˡand ᵐJehoshaphat his son reigned in his stead.

A. M. 3090
B. C. 914
Ante I. Ol. 138
An. Megaclis,
Arch. Athen.
perpet. 8

25 And Nadab the son of Jeroboam ⁿbegan to reign over Israel in the second year of Asa king of Judah, and reigned over Israel two years.

A.M.3050-3051
B. C. 954–953
Anno ante I.
Olymp.178-177

26 And he did evil in the sight of the LORD, and walked in the way of his father, and in ᵒhis sin wherewith he made Israel to sin.

27 ᵖAnd Baasha the son of Ahijah, of the house of Issachar, conspired against him; and Baasha smote him at �qGibbethon, which *belonged* to the Philistines; for Nadab and all Israel laid siege to Gibbethon.

A. M. 3051
B. C. 953
Ante I. Ol. 177
An. Thersippi,
Arch. Athen.
perpet. 41

28 Even in the third year of Asa king of Judah did Baasha slay him, and reigned in his stead.

ᶻ2 Chron. xvi. 2——ᵃChap. xi. 23, 24——ᵇHebrew, *go up*——ᶜ2 Kings xv. 29——ᵈJudg. xviii. 29——ᵉ2 Sam. xx. 14——ᶠ2 Chron. xvi. 6——ᵍHebrew, *free* ʰJosh. xxi. 17——ⁱJosh. xviii. 26——ᵏ2 Chronicles

xvi. 12——ˡ2 Chronicles xvii. 1——ᵐMatt. i. 8, called *Josaphat*——ⁿHeb. *reigned*——ᵒChap. xii. 30; xiv. 16 ᵖChapter xiv. 14——�q Joshua xix. 44; xxi. 23; chapter xvi. 15

---

house of David. Ramah was about *two* leagues northward of Jerusalem.

Verse 18. *Asa took all the silver*] Shishak, king of Egypt, had not taken the whole; or there had been some treasures brought in since that time.

Ben-hadad] This was the grandson of Rezon, called here Hezion, who founded the kingdom of Damascus. See chap. xi. 23, 24; and *Calmet.*

Verse 19. There is *a league between me and thee*] Or, Let there be a league between me and thee; as there was between my father and thy father. There was no reason why Asa should have emptied his treasures at this time to procure the aid of the Syrian king; as it does not appear that there was any danger which himself could not have turned aside. He probably wished to destroy the kingdom of Israel; and to effect this purpose, even robbed the house of the Lord.

Verse 20. *Ijon, and Dan, &c.*] He appears to have attacked and taken those towns which constituted the principal strength of the kingdom of Israel.

Verse 21. *Dwelt in Tirzah.*] This seems to have been the *royal city;* see ver. 33, and chap. xiv. 17; and in this Baasha was probably obliged to shut himself up.

Verse 22. *None* was *exempted*] Every man was obliged to go and help to dismantle the fortress at Ramah which Baasha had built. This was a general *levee en masse* of the people: every one was obliged to lend a helping hand, as the state was then supposed to be in danger, and all exemptions necessarily ceased. This is a maxim of civil policy, *Ubi adversus hostem muniendi sunt limites, omnis immunitas cessat:* "Where the boundaries are to be fortified against an enemy, then all exemptions cease."

Verse 23. *And the cities which he built*] Such as *Geba* and *Mizpah,* which he built out of the spoils of Ramah.

He was diseased in his feet.] Probably he had a strong rheumatic affection, or the *gout.* This took place in the *thirty-ninth* year of his reign, *three years* before his death; and it is said that he sought to physicians rather than to the Lord, 2 Chron. xvi. 12, 13.

Verse 24. *Asa slept with his fathers*] Of his splendid and costly funeral we read 1 Chron. xvi. 14.

Verse 25. *Nadab—began to reign over Israel*] He began his reign in the *second* year of the reign of Asa, and reigned *two* years.

Verse 27. *Smote him at Gibbethon*] This

A. M. 3051
B. C. 953
Ante I. Ol. 177
An. Thersippi,
Arch. Athen.
perpet. 41

29 And it came to pass, when he reigned, *that* he smote all the house of Jeroboam; he left not to Jeroboam any that breathed, until he had destroyed him, according unto ʳthe saying of the LORD, which he spake by his servant Ahijah the Shilonite:

30 ˢBecause of the sins of Jeroboam which he sinned, and which he made Israel sin, by his provocation wherewith he provoked the LORD God of Israel to anger.

31 Now the rest of the acts of Nadab, and all that he did, *are* they not written

in the book of the chronicles of the kings of Israel?

32 ᵗAnd there was war between Asa and Baasha king of Israel all their days.

33 In the third year of Asa king of Judah began Baasha the son of Ahijah to reign over all Israel in Tirzah, twenty and four years.

34 And he did evil in the sight of the LORD, and walked in ᵘthe way of Jeroboam, and in his sin wherewith he made Israel to sin.

A.M.3050-3051
B. C. 954-953
Anno ante I.
Olymp.178-177

A.M.3051-3074
B. C. 953-930
Anno ante I.
Olymp.177-154

ʳChap. xiv. 10, 14——ˢChap. xiv. 9, 16

ᵗVer. 16——ᵘChap. xii. 28, 29; xiii. 33; xiv. 16

---

was a city in the tribe of Dan, and generally in the possession of the Philistines.

Verse 29. *He smote all the house of Jeroboam*] This was according to Ahijah's prophetic declaration; see chap. xiv. 10, 14. Thus God made use of one wicked man to destroy another.

Verse 32. *There was war*] See on ver. 16.

Verse 34. *Walked in the way of Jeroboam*] The *entail* of iniquity cannot be cut off but by a thorough *conversion* of the soul to God; and of this, these bad kings seem to have had no adequate notion. The wicked followed the steps of the wicked, and became still more wicked; sin gathers strength by *exercise* and *age*.

CHAPTER XVI

Jehu the prophet denounces the destruction of Baasha, 1–7. Zimri conspires against him, and slays him and his family, and reigns seven days, 8–15. The people make Omri king, and besiege Zimri in Tirzah; who, finding no way to escape, sets fire to his palace, and consumes himself in it, 16–20. The people are divided, half following Tibni, and half Omri; the latter faction overcomes the former, Tibni is slain, and Omri reigns alone, 21–23. He founds Samaria, 24. His bad character and death, 25–28. Ahab reigns in his stead; marries Jezebel, restores idolatry, and exceeds his predecessors in wickedness, 29–33. Hiel the Beth-elite rebuilds Jericho, 34.

A. M. 3073
B. C. 931
Ante I. Ol. 155
An. Phorbæ,
Arch. Athen.
perpet. 22

THEN the word of the LORD came to ᵃJehu the son of Hanani against Baasha, saying,

2 ᵇForasmuch as I exalted thee out of the dust, and made thee prince over my people Israel; and ᶜthou hast walked in the way of Jeroboam, and hast made my people Israel to sin, to provoke me to anger with their sins;

3 Behold, I will ᵈtake away the posterity of Baasha, and the posterity of his house; and will make thy house like ᵉthe house of Jeroboam the son of Nebat.

4 ᶠHim that dieth of Baasha in the city shall the dogs eat; and him that dieth of his in the fields shall the fowls of the air eat.

5 Now the rest of the acts of Baasha, and what he did, and his might, ᵍ*are* they not written in the book of the chronicles of the kings of Israel?

6 So Baasha slept with his fathers, and was buried in ʰTirzah: and Elah his son reigned in his stead.

7 And also by the hand of the prophet

A. M. 3073
B. C. 931
Ante I. Ol. 155
An. Phorbæ,
Arch. Athen.
perpet. 22

A.M.3051-3074
B. C. 953-930
Anno ante I.
Olymp.177-154

A. M. 3074
B. C. 930
Ante I. Ol. 154
An. Phorbæ,
Arch. Athen.
perpet. 23

ᵃVer. 7; 2 Chron. xix. 2; xx. 34——ᵇChapter xiv. 7
ᶜChap. xv. 34——ᵈVer. 11

ᵉChap. xiv. 10; xv. 29——ᶠChap. xiv. 11——ᵍ2 Chron. xvi. 1——ʰChap. xiv. 17; xv. 21

NOTES ON CHAP. XVI

Verse 1. *Then the word of the Lord came to Jehu*] Of this prophet we know nothing but from this circumstance. It appears from 2 Chron. xvi. 7-10, that his father *Hanani* was also a prophet, and suffered imprisonment in consequence of the faithful discharge of his ministry to Asa.

Verse 2. *Made thee prince over my people*] That is, in the course of my providence, I

suffered thee to become king; for it is impossible that God should make a rebel, a traitor, and a murderer, king over *his* people, or over any people. God is ever represented in Scripture as *doing* those things which, in the course of his providence, he *permits* to be done.

Verse 7. *And because he killed him.*] This the Vulgate understands of *Jehu the prophet*, put to death by Baasha; *Ob hanc causam*

A. M. 3074
B. C. 930
Ante I. Ol. 154
An. Phorbæ,
Arch. Athen.
perpet. 23

[i]Jehu the son of Hanani came the word of the LORD against Baasha, and against his house, even for all the evil that he did in the sight of the LORD, in provoking him to anger with the work of his hands, in being like the house of Jeroboam; and because [k]he killed him.

A.M.3074-3075
B. C. 930–929
Anno ante I.
Olymp.154-153

8 In the twenty and sixth year of Asa king of Judah began Elah the son of Baasha to reign over Israel in Tirzah, two years.

A. M. 3075
B. C. 929
Ante I. Ol. 153
An. Phorbæ,
Arch. Athen.
perpet 24

9 [l]And his servant Zimri, captain of half *his* chariots, conspired against him as he was in Tirzah, drinking himself drunk in the house of Arza, [m]steward of *his* house in Tirzah.

10 And Zimri went in and smote him, and killed him, in the twenty and seventh year of Asa king of Judah, and reigned in his stead.

11 And it came to pass, when he began to reign, as soon as he sat on his throne, *that* he slew all the house of Baasha: he left him [n]not one that pisseth against a wall, [o]neither of his kinsfolks, nor of his friends.

12 Thus did Zimri destroy all the house of Baasha, [p]according to the word of the LORD, which he spake against Baasha [q]by [r]Jehu the prophet,

13 For all the sins of Baasha, and the sins of Elah his son, by which they sinned, and by which they made Israel to sin, in provoking the LORD God of Israel to anger [s]with their vanities.

14 Now the rest of the acts of Elah, and all that he did, *are* they not written in the book of the chronicles of the kings of Israel?

A.M.3074-3075
B. C. 930–929
Anno ante I.
Olymp.154-153

15 In the twenty and seventh year of Asa king of Judah did Zimri reign seven days in Tirzah. And the people *were* encamped [t]against Gibbethon, which *belonged* to the Philistines.

A. M. 3075
B. C. 929
Ante I. Ol. 153
An. Phorbæ,
Arch. Athen.
perpet. 24

16 And the people *that were* encamped heard say, Zimri hath conspired, and hath also slain the king: wherefore all Israel made Omri, the captain of the host, king over Israel that day in the camp.

17 And Omri went up from Gibbethon, and all Israel with him, and they besieged Tirzah.

18 And it came to pass, when Zimri saw that the city was taken, that he went into the palace of the king's house, and burnt the king's house over him with fire, and died,

19 For his sins which he sinned in doing evil in the sight of the LORD, [u]in walking in the way of Jeroboam, and in his sin which he did, to make Israel to sin.

20 Now the rest of the acts of Zimri, and his treason that he wrought, *are* they not written in the book of the chronicles of the kings of Israel?

21 Then were the people of Israel divided into two parts: half of the people followed Tibni the son of Ginath, to make him king; and half followed Omri.

22 But the people that followed Omri pre-

---

[i]Ver. 1——[k]Chap. xv. 27, 29; see Hos. i. 4——[l]2 Kings ix. 31——[m]Heb. *which* was *over*——[n]1 Sam. xxv. 22——[o]Or, *both his kinsmen and his friends*——[p]Ver. 3

[q]Heb. *by the hand of*——[r]Ver. 1——[s]Deut. xxxii. 21; 1 Sam. xii. 21; Isa. xli. 29; Jon. ii. 8; 1 Cor. viii. 4; x. 19 [t]Chap. xv. 27——[u]Chap. xii. 28; xv. 26, 34

---

occidit eum, hoc est, Jehu filium Hanani prophetam; "On this account he killed him, that is, Jehu the prophet, the son of Hanani." Some think *Baasha* is intended, others *Jeroboam*, and others *Nadab* the son of Jeroboam. This last is the sentiment of *Rab. Sol. Jarchi*, and of some good critics. The order is here confused; and the *seventh* verse should probably be placed between the 4th and 5th.

Verse 9. *Captain of half his chariots*] It is probable that Zimri, and some other who is not here named, were commanders of the cavalry.

Verse 11. *He slew all the house of Baasha*] He endeavoured to exterminate his race, and blot out his memory; and the Jews say, when such a matter is determined, they not only destroy the house of the person himself, *but the five neighbouring houses*, that the memory of such a person may perish from the earth.

Verse 13. *For all the sins of Baasha*] We see why it was that God permitted such judgments to fall on this family. Baasha was a grievous offender, and so also was his son Elah; and they caused the people to sin; and they provoked God to anger by their idolatries.

Verse 15. *The people* were *encamped against Gibbethon*] It appears that, at this time, the Israelites had war with the Philistines, and were now besieging Gibbethon, one of their cities. This army, hearing that Zimri had rebelled and killed Elah, made Omri, their general, king, who immediately raised the siege of Gibbethon, and went to attack Zimri in the royal city of Tirzah; who, finding his affairs desperate, chose rather to consume himself in his palace than to fall into the hands of his enemies.

Verse 21. *Divided into two parts*] Why this

A. M. 3075
B. C. 929
Ante I. Ol. 153
An. Phorbæ,
Arch. Athen.
perpet. 24

vailed against the people that followed Tibni the son of Ginath: so Tibni died, and Omri reigned.

A.M.3079-3086
B. C. 925-918
Anno ante I.
Olymp.149-142

23 In the thirty and first year of Asa king of Judah began Omri to reign over Israel, twelve years: six years reigned he in Tirzah.

24 And he bought the hill Samaria of Shemer for two talents of silver, and built on the hill, and called the name of the city which he built, after the name of Shemer, owner of the hill, ᵛSamaria.ʷ

25 But ˣOmri wrought evil in the eyes of the LORD, and did worse than all that *were* before him.

26 For he ʸwalked in all the way of Jeroboam the son of Nebat, and in his sin wherewith he made Israel to sin, to provoke the

LORD God of Israel to anger with their ᶻvanities.

A.M.3079-3086
B. C. 925-918
Anno ante I.
Olymp.149-142

27 Now the rest of the acts of Omri which he did, and his might that he showed, *are* they not written in the book of the chronicles of the kings of Israel?

28 So Omri slept with his fathers, and was buried in Samaria: and Ahab his son reigned in his stead.

A. M. 3086
B. C. 918
Ante I. Ol. 142
An. Megaclis,
Arch. Athen.
perpet. 4

29 And in the thirty and eighth year of Asa king of Judah began Ahab the son of Omri to reign over Israel: and Ahab the son of Omri reigned over Israel in Samaria twenty and two years.

A.M.3086-3107
B. C. 918-897
Anno ante I.
Olymp.142-121

30 And Ahab the son of Omri did evil in the sight of the LORD above all that *were* before him.

31 And it came to pass, ᵃas if it had been

ᵛHeb. *Shomeron*——ʷSee chap. xiii. 32; 2 Kings xvii. 24; John iv. 4

ˣMic. vi. 16——ʸVer. 19——ᶻVer. 13——ᵃHeb. *was it a light thing*, &c.

---

division took place we cannot tell; the *people* appear to have been for Tibni, the *army* for Omri; and the latter prevailed.

Verse 23. *In the thirty and first year of Asa*] There must be a mistake here in the number *thirty-one;* for, in ver. 10 and 15, it is said that Zimri slew his master, and began to reign *in the twenty-seventh year of Asa;* and as Zimri reigned only *seven days,* and Omri *immediately* succeeded him, this could not be in the *thirty-first,* but in the *twenty-seventh year of Asa,* as related above. *Rab. Sol. Jarchi* reconciles the two places thus: "The division of the kingdom between Tibni and Omri began in the *twenty-seventh* year of Asa; this division lasted *five years,* during which Omri had but a *share* of the kingdom. Tibni dying, Omri came into the possession of the *whole* kingdom, which he held *seven years;* this was in the *thirty-first* year of Asa. *Seven years* he reigned *alone; five years* he reigned over *part* of Israel; *twelve years* in the whole. The two dates, the *twenty-seventh* and *thirty-first* of Asa, answering, the first to the beginning of the division, the second to the sole reign of Omri." *Jarchi* quotes *Sedar Olam* for this solution.

Verse 24. *He bought the hill Samaria of Shemer*] This should be read, "He bought the hill of Shomeron from Shomer, and called it Shomeron, (*i. e.,* Little Shomer,) after the name of Shomer, owner of the hill." At first the kings of Israel dwelt at Shechem, and then at Tirzah; but this place having suffered much in the civil broils, and the place having been burnt down by Zimri, Omri purposed to found a new city, to which he might transfer the seat of government. He fixed on a hill that belonged to a person of the name of *Shomer;* and bought it from him for *two talents of silver,* about £707 3s. 9d. Though this was a large sum in those days, yet we cannot suppose that the hill was very large which was purchased for so little; and probably no other building

VOL. II

upon it than Shomer's house, if indeed he had one there. *Shomeron,* or, as it is corruptly written, *Samaria,* is situated in the midst of the tribe of Ephraim, not very far from the coast of the Mediterranean Sea, and about midway between Dan and Beer-sheba: thus Samaria became the capital of the ten tribes, the metropolis of the kingdom of Israel, and the residence of its kings. The kings of Israel adorned and fortified it; Ahab built a *house of ivory* in it, chap. xxii. 39; the kings of Syria had *magazines* or *storehouses* in it, for the purpose of commerce; see chap. xx. 34. And it appears to have been a place of considerable importance and great strength.

Samaria endured several sieges; Ben-hadad, king of Syria, besieged it twice, chap. xx. 1, &c.; and it cost Shalmaneser a siege of three years to reduce it, 2 Kings xvii. 6, &c. After the death of Alexander the Great, it became the property of the kings of Egypt; but Antiochus the Great took it from the Egyptians; and it continued in the possession of the kings of Syria till the Asmoneans took and razed it to the very foundation. *Gabinius,* pro-consul of Syria, partially rebuilt it, and called it *Gabiniana.* Herod the Great restored it to its ancient splendour, and placed in it a colony of *six thousand* men, and gave it the name of *Sebaste,* in honour of *Augustus.* It is now a place of little consequence.

Verse 25. *Did worse than all—before him*] Omri was, 1. An idolater in principle; 2. An idolater in practice; 3. He led the people to idolatry by *precept* and *example;* and, which was that in which he *did worse* than all before him, 4. He made *statutes* in favour of idolatry, and obliged the people by law to commit it. See Mic. vi. 16, where this seems to be intended: *For the statutes of Omri are kept, and all the works of the house of Ahab.*

Verse 31. *He took to wife Jezebel*] This was the head and chief of his offending; he

A.M.3086-3107
B. C. 918–897
Anno ante I.
Olymp.142-121 a light thing for him to walk in the sins of Jeroboam the son of Nebat, [b]that he took to wife Jezebel the daughter of Ethbaal king of the [c]Zidonians, [d]and went and served Baal, and worshipped him.

32 And he reared up an altar for Baal in [e]the house of Baal, which he had built in Samaria.

33 [f]And Ahab made a grove; and Ahab

[g]did more to provoke the LORD God of Israel to anger than all the kings of Israel that were before him.

A.M.3086-3107
B. C. 918–897
Anno ante I.
Olymp.142-121

34 In his days did Hiel the Beth-elite build Jericho: he laid the foundation thereof in Abiram his first-born, and set up the gates thereof in his youngest *son* Segub, [h]according to the word of the LORD, which he spake by Joshua the son of Nun.

---

[b]Deut. vii. 3——[c]Judg. xviii. 7——[d]Chap. xxi. 25, 26; 2 Kings x. 18; xvii. 16——[e]2 Kings x. 21, 26, 27

[f]2 Kings xiii. 6; xvii. 10; xxi. 3; Jer. xvii. 2——[g]Verse 30; chap. xxi. 25——[h]Josh. vi. 26

---

took to wife, not only a *heathen*, but one whose hostility to the true religion was well known, and carried to the utmost extent. 1. She was the idolatrous daughter of an idolatrous king; 2. She practised it openly; 3. She not only countenanced it in others, but protected it, and gave its partisans honours and rewards; 4. She used every means to persecute the true religion; 5. She was hideously cruel, and put to death the prophets and priests of God; 6. And all this she did with the most zealous perseverance and relentless cruelty.

Notwithstanding Ahab had built a temple, and made an altar for Baal, and set up the worship of *Asherah*, the Sidonian *Venus*, which we, ver. 33, have transformed into a *grove;* yet so well known was the hostility of Jezebel to all good, that his marrying her was esteemed the highest pitch of vice, and an act the most provoking to God, and destructive to the prosperity of the kingdom.

Verse 33. *Ahab made a grove*] אשרה *Asherah, Astarte,* or *Venus;* what the *Syriac* calls an *idol,* and the *Arabic,* a *tall tree;* probably meaning, by the last, an image of *Priapus*, the obscene keeper of groves, orchards, and gardens.

Verse 34. *Did Hiel the Beth-elite build Jericho*] I wish the reader to refer to my note on Josh. vi. 26, for a general view of this subject. I shall add a few observations. Joshua's curse is well known: "Cursed be the man before the Lord that riseth up and buildeth this city Jericho; he shall lay the foundation thereof in his first-born; and in his youngest son shall he set up the gates of it," Josh. vi. 26. This is the curse, but the meaning of its terms is not very obvious. Let us see how this is to be understood from the manner in which it was accomplished.

"In his days did Hiel the Beth-elite build Jericho; he laid the foundation thereof in Abiram his first-born, and set up the gates thereof in his youngest son Segub; according to the word of the Lord, which he spake by Joshua the son of Nun." This prediction was delivered upwards of *five hundred* years before the event; and though it was most circumstantially fulfilled, yet we know not the precise meaning of some of the terms used in the original execration, and in this place, where its fulfilment is mentioned. There are *three* opinions on the words, *lay the foundation in his first-born, and set up the gates in his youngest son.*

1. It is thought that when he laid the foundation of the city, his eldest son, the hope of

his family, died by the hand and judgment of God, and that all his children died in succession; so that when the doors were ready to be hung, his youngest and last child died, and thus, instead of securing himself a name, his whole family became extinct.

2. These expressions signify only *great delay* in the building; that he who should undertake it should *spend nearly his whole life* in it; all the time in which he was capable of procreating children; in a word, that if a man laid the foundation when his first-born came into the world, his youngest and last son should be born before the walls should be in readiness to admit the gates to be set up in them; and that the expression is of the proverbial kind, intimating *greatly protracted labour,* occasioned by *multitudinous hinderances and delays.*

3. That he who rebuilt this city should, in laying the foundation, *slay* or *sacrifice* his first-born, in order to consecrate it, and secure the assistance of the objects of his idolatrous worship; and should slay his youngest at the completion of the work, as a gratitude-offering for the assistance received. This latter opinion seems to be countenanced by the *Chaldee,* which represents Hiel as *slaying* his first-born Abiram, and his youngest son *Segub.*

But who was *Hiel the Beth-elite?* The *Chaldee* calls him *Hiel* of *Beth-mome,* or the *Beth-momite;* the *Vulgate,* Hiel of *Beth-el;* the *Septuagint,* Hiel the *Baithelite;* the *Syriac* represents *Ahab* as the builder: "Also in his days did Ahab build Jericho, the place of execration;" the *Arabic,* "Also in his days did Hiel build the house of idols—to wit, Jericho." The MSS. give us no help. None of these versions, the Chaldee excepted, intimates that the children were either *slain* or *died;* which circumstance seems to strengthen the opinion, that the passage is to be understood of *delays* and *hinderances.* Add to this, Why should the innocent children of Hiel suffer for their father's presumption? And is it likely that, if Hiel lost his first-born when he laid the foundation, he would have proceeded under this evidence of the Divine displeasure, and at the risk of losing his whole family? Which of these opinions is the right one, or whether any of them be correct, is more than I can pretend to state. A curse seems to rest still upon Jericho: it is not yet blotted out of the map of Palestine; but it is reduced to a miserable village, consisting of about *thirty* wretched cottages, and the governor's *dilapidated castle;* nor is there any *ruin* there to indicate its former splendour.

CHAPTER XVII

Elijah's message to Ahab concerning the three years' drought, 1. He is commanded to go to the brook Cherith; where he is fed by ravens, 2–7. He afterwards goes to a widow's house at Zarephath, and miraculously multiplies her meal and oil, 8–16. Her son dies, and Elijah restores him to life, 17–24.

A. M. 3094
B. C. 910
Ante I. Ol. 134
An. Megaclis,
Arch. Athen.
perpet. 12

AND ªElijah the Tishbite, *who was* of the inhabitants of Gilead, said unto Ahab, ᵇ*As* the LORD God of Israel liveth, ᶜbefore whom I stand, ᵈthere shall not be dew nor rain ᵉthese years, but according to my word.

2 And the word of the LORD came unto him, saying,

3 Get thee hence, and turn thee eastward, and hide thyself by the brook Cherith, that *is* before Jordan.

4 And it shall be, *that* thou shalt drink of the brook; and I have commanded the ravens to feed thee there.

A. M. 3094
B. C. 910
Ante I. Ol. 134
An. Megaclis,
Arch. Athen.
perpet. 12

5 So he went and did according unto the word of the LORD: for he went and dwelt by the brook Cherith, that *is* before Jordan.

6 And the ravens brought him bread and flesh in the morning, and bread and flesh in the evening; and he drank of the brook.

ªHebrew, *Elijahu;* Luke i. 17; iv. 25, he is called *Elias*
ᵇ2 Kings iii. 14

ᶜDeut. x. 8——ᵈEcclus. xlviii. 3; James v. 17——ᵉLuke iv. 25

NOTES ON CHAP. XVII

Verse 1. *Elijah the Tishbite*] The history of this great man is introduced very abruptly; his origin is enveloped in perfect obscurity. He is here said to be a *Tishbite.* Tishbeh, says Calmet, is a city beyond Jordan, in the tribe of Gad, and in the land of Gilead. Who was his father, or from what tribe he sprang, is not intimated; he seems to have been the prophet of *Israel* peculiarly, as we never find him prophesying in *Judah.* A number of apocryphal writers have trifled at large about his parentage, miraculous birth, of his continual celibacy, his academy of the prophets, &c., &c., all equally worthy of credit. One opinion, which at first view appears strange, bears more resemblance to truth than any of the above, viz., that he had no earthly parentage known to any man; that he was an angel of God, united for a time to a human body, in order to call men back to perfect purity, both in doctrine and manners, from which they had totally swerved. His Hebrew name, which we have corrupted into *Elijah* and *Elias*, is אליהו *Alihu,* or, according to the vowel points, *Eliyahu;* and signifies *he is my God.* Does this give countenance to the supposition that this great personage was a manifestation in the flesh of the Supreme Being? He could not be the Messiah; for we find him with Moses on the mount of transfiguration with Christ. The conjecture that he was an *angel* seems countenanced by the manner of his departure from this world; yet, in James v. 17, he is said to be a man ὁμοιοπαθης, *of like passions,* or rather *with real human propensities:* this, however, is irreconcilable with the conjecture.

There shall not be dew nor rain these years] In order to remove the abruptness of this address, R. S. Jarchi dreams thus:—"Elijah and Ahab went to comfort Hiel in his grief, concerning his sons. And Ahab said to Elijah, Is it possible that the curse of Joshua, the son of Nun, who was only the servant of Moses, should be fulfilled; and the curse of Moses, our teacher, not be fulfilled; who said, Deut. xi.

16, 17: *If ye turn aside, and serve other gods, and worship them, then the Lord's wrath shall be kindled against you; and he will shut up the heaven that there be no rain?* Now all the Israelites serve other gods, and yet the rain is not withheld. Then Elijah said unto Ahab, *As the Lord God of Israel liveth, before whom I stand, there shall not be dew nor rain these years, but according to my word.*" This same mode of connecting this and the preceding chapter, is followed by the Jerusalem and Babylonish Talmuds, Sedar Olam, Abarbanel, &c.

Verse 3. *Hide thyself by the brook Cherith*] This brook, and the valley through which it ran, are supposed to have been on the western side of Jordan, and not far from Samaria. Others suppose it to have been on the eastern side, because the prophet is commanded to go *eastward,* ver. 3. It was necessary, after such a declaration to this wicked and idolatrous king, that he should immediately hide himself; as, on the first drought, Ahab would undoubtedly seek his life. But what a proof was this of the power of God, and the vanity of idols! As God's prophet prayed, so there was rain or drought; and all the gods of Israel could not reverse it! Was not this sufficient to have converted all Israel?

Verse 4. *I have commanded the ravens to feed thee*] Thou shalt not lack the necessaries of life; thou shalt be supplied by an especial providence. See more on this subject at the end of the chapter.

Verse 6. *And the ravens brought him bread and flesh*] The *Septuagint,* in the Codex Vaticanus, and some ancient *fathers,* read the passage thus:—Και οἱ κορακες εφερον αυτῳ αρτους το πρωϊ, και κρεα το δειλης, *And the crows brought him bread in the morning, and flesh in the evening:* but all the other versions agree with the Hebrew text. This is the first account we have of flesh-meat breakfasts and flesh-meat suppers; and as this was the food appointed by the Lord for the sustenance of the prophet, we may naturally conjecture that it was the food of the people at large.

A. M. 3095
B. C. 909
Ante I. Ol. 133
An. Megaclis,
Arch. Athen.
perpet. 13

7 And it came to pass ᶠafter a while, that the brook dried up, because there had been no rain in the land.

8 And the word of the LORD came unto him, saying,

9 Arise, get thee to ᵍZarephath, which *belongeth* to Zidon, and dwell there: behold, I have commanded a widow woman there to sustain thee.

10 So he arose and went to Zarephath. And when he came to the gate of the city, behold, the widow woman *was* there gathering of sticks: and he called to her, and said, Fetch me, I pray thee, a little water in a vessel, that I may drink.

11 And as she was going to fetch *it,* he called to her, and said, Bring me, I pray thee, a morsel of bread in thine hand.

12 And she said, *As* the LORD thy God liveth, I have not a cake, but a handful of meal in a barrel, and a little oil in a cruse: and, behold, I *am* gathering two sticks, that I may go in and dress it for me and my son, that we may eat it, and die.

13 And Elijah said unto her, Fear not; go *and* do as thou hast said: but make me thereof a little cake first, and bring *it* unto me, and after make for thee and for thy son.

14 For thus saith the LORD God of Israel, The barrel of meal shall not waste, neither shall the cruse of oil fail, until the day *that* the LORD ʰsendeth rain upon the earth.

A. M. 3095
B. C. 909
Ante I. Ol. 133
An. Megaclis,
Arch. Athen.
perpet. 13

15 And she went and did according to the saying of Elijah, and she, and he, and her house did eat ⁱ*many* days.

16 *And* the barrel of meal wasted not, neither did the cruse of oil fail, according to the word of the LORD, which he spake ᵏby Elijah.

A.M.3095-3098
B. C. 909-906
Anno ante I.
Olymp.133-130

17 And it came to pass after these things, *that* the son of the woman, the mistress of the house, fell sick; and his sickness was so sore, that there was no breath left in him.

A. M. 3096
B. C. 908
Ante I. Ol. 132
An. Megaclis,
Arch. Athen.
perpet. 14

18 And she said unto Elijah, ˡWhat have I to do with thee, O thou man of God? art thou come unto me to call my sin to remembrance, and to slay my son?

19 And he said unto her, Give me thy son. And he took him out of her bosom, and carried him up into a loft, where he abode, and laid him upon his own bed.

20 And he cried unto the LORD, and said, O LORD my God, hast thou also brought evil

---

ᶠHeb. *at the end of days*——ᵍObad. 20; Luke iv. 26, called *Sarepta*

ʰHeb. *giveth*——ⁱOr, *a full year*——ᵏHeb. *by the hand of* ˡSee Luke v. 8

Verse 7. *The brook dried up*] Because there had been no rain in the land for some time, God having sent this drought as a testimony against the idolatry of the people: see Deut. xi. 16, 17.

Verse 9. *Get thee to Zarephath*] This was a town between Tyre and Sidon, but nearer to the latter, and is therefore called in the text *Zarephath* which belongeth *to Sidon;* or, as the *Vulgate* and other versions express it, *Sarepta of the Sidonians.* Sarepta is the name by which it goes in the New Testament; but its present name is *Sarphan.* Mr. Maundrell, who visited it, describes it as consisting of a few houses only on the tops of the mountains; but supposes that it anciently stood in the plain below, where there are still ruins of a considerable extent.

Verse 12. *A handful of meal in a barrel*] The word כד *cad* is to be understood as implying an *earthen jar;* not a *wooden vessel,* or *barrel* of any kind. In the East they preserve their corn and meal in such vessels; without which precaution the insects would destroy them. Travellers in Asiatic countries abound with observations of this kind.

The word *cruse,* צפחת *tsappachath,* says Jarchi, signifies what in our tongue is ex-

pressed by *bouteille,* a bottle. Jarchi was a French rabbin.

Verse 13. *But make me thereof a little cake first*] This was certainly putting the widow's faith to an extraordinary trial: to take and give to a stranger, of whom she knew nothing, the small pittance requisite to keep her child from perishing, was too much to be expected.

Verse 16. *The barrel of meal wasted not*] She continued to take out of her *jar* and out of her *bottle* the quantity of *meal* and *oil* requisite for the consumption of her household; and without carefully estimating what was left, she went with confidence each time for a supply, and was never disappointed. This miracle was very like that wrought by Jesus at the marriage at Cana in Galilee: as the servants drew the water out of the pots, they found it turned into wine; and thus they continued to draw *wine* from the *water-pots* till the guests had been sufficiently supplied.

Verse 17. *There was no breath left in him*] He ceased to breathe and died.

Verse 18. *To call my sin to remembrance*] She seems to be now conscious of some secret sin, which she had either forgotten, or too carelessly passed over; and to punish this she supposes the life of her son was taken away.

A. M. 3096
B. C. 908
Ante I. Ol. 132
An. Megaclis,
Arch. Athen.
perpet. 14

upon the widow with whom I sojourn, by slaying her son?

21 ᵐAnd he ⁿstretched himself upon the child three times, and cried unto the LORD, and said, O LORD my God, I pray thee, let this child's soul come °into him again.

22 And the LORD heard the voice of Elijah; and the soul of the child came into him again, and he ᴾrevived.

23 And Elijah took the child,
A. M. 3096
B. C. 908
Ante I. Ol. 132
An. Megaclis,
Arch. Athen.
perpet. 14

and brought him down out of the chamber into the house, and delivered him unto his mother: and Elijah said, See, thy son liveth.

24 And the woman said to Elijah, Now by this ۹I know that thou *art* a man of God, *and* that the word of the LORD in thy mouth *is* truth.

ᵐ2 Kings iv. 34, 35——ⁿHeb. *measured*——°Heb. *into*

his inward parts——ᴾHeb. xi. 35——۹John iii. 2; xvi. 30

It is mostly in times of adversity that we duly consider our moral state; outward afflictions often bring deep searchings of heart.

Verse 21. *Stretched himself upon the child three times*] It is supposed that he did this in order to communicate some *natural warmth* to the body of the child, in order to dispose it to receive the departed spirit. *Elisha*, his disciple, did the same in order to restore the dead child of the Shunammite, 2 Kings iv. 34. And St. Paul appears to have stretched himself on Eutychus in order to restore him to life, Acts xx. 10.

Let this child's soul come into him again] Surely this means no more than the *breath.* Though the word נפש *nephesh* may sometimes signify the *life,* yet does not this imply that the spirit must take possession of the body in order to produce and maintain the flame of animal life? The expressions here are singular:

Let his soul, נפש *nephesh, come into him,* על קרבו *al kirbo, into the midst of him.*

Verse 22. *And the soul*] נפש *nephesh, of the child came into him again,* על קרבו *al kirbo,* into the midst of him; and he revived, ויחי *vaiyechi, and he became alive.* Did he not become alive from the circumstance of the immaterial principle coming again into him?

Although רוח *ruach* is sometimes put for the *breath,* yet נפש generally means the immortal spirit, and where it seems to refer to *animal life* alone, it is only such a life as is the immediate and necessary effect of the presence of the immortal spirit.

The words and mode of expression here appear to me a strong proof, not only of the existence of an immortal and immaterial spirit in man, but also that that spirit can and does exist in a separate state from the body. It is here represented as being *in the midst* of the child, like a *spring* in the centre of a machine, which gives motion to every part, and without which the whole would stand still.

Verse 24. *The word of the Lord in thy mouth* is *truth.*] *Three* grand effects were produced by this temporary affliction: 1. The woman was led to examine her heart, and try her ways; 2. The power of God became highly manifest in the resurrection of the child; 3. She was convinced that the word of the Lord was truth, and that not one syllable of it could fall to the ground. Through a little suffering all this good was obtained.

THE subject in the fourth verse of this chapter deserves a more particular consideration. *I have commanded the ravens to feed thee.*—

It is contended that if we consider ערבים *orebim* to signify *ravens,* we shall find any interpretation on this ground to be clogged with difficulties. I need mention but a few. The *raven* is an unclean bird, *And these ye shall have in abomination among the fowls—every raven after his kind;* Lev. xi. 13-15; that is, every *species* of this *genus* shall be considered by you *unclean* and *abominable.* Is it therefore likely that God would employ this most unclean bird to feed his prophet? Besides, where could the ravens get any *flesh* that was not *unclean? Carrion* is their food; and would God send any thing of this kind to his prophet? Again: If the flesh was *clean* which God sent, *where* could ravens get it? Here must be at least three miracles: *one* to bring from some *table* the flesh to the ravens; *another,* to induce the ravenous bird to give it up; and the *third,* to conquer its timidity towards man, so that it could come to the prophet without fear. Now, although God might employ a fowl that would naturally strive to prey on the flesh, and oblige it, contrary to its nature, to give it up; yet it is by no means likely that he would employ a bird that his *own law* had pronounced *abominable.* Again, he could not have employed this means without working a *variety* of *miracles* at the same time, in order to accomplish *one simple end;* and this is never God's method: his plan is ever to accomplish the greatest purposes by the simplest means.

The original word *orebim* has been considered by some as meaning *merchants,* persons occasionally trading through that country, whom God directed, by inspiration, to supply the prophet with food. To get a constant supply from such hands in an extraordinary way was *miracle enough;* it showed the superintendence of God, and that the hearts of all men are in his hands.

But in answer to this it is said, that the "original word never signifies merchants; and that the learned *Bochart* has proved this." I have carefully read over cap. 13, part. ii., lib. 2, of the *Hierozoicon* of this author, where he discusses this subject; and think that he has never succeeded less than in his attempt to prove that *ravens* are meant in this passage. He allows that the Tyrian merchants are described by this periphrasis, ערבי מערבך, *the occupiers of thy merchandise,* Ezek. xxvii. 27; and asserts that ערבים *orebim, per se, mercatores nusquam significat,* "by itself, never signifies *merchants.*" Now, with perfect deference to so great an authority, I assert that ערבי *oreby,* the contracted form of ערבים *orebim,* does signify *merchants,* both in Ezek. xxvii.

9 and xxvii. 27, and that מערב *maarab* signifies *a place for merchandise*, the *market-place* or *bazaar*, in Ezek. xxvii. 9, 13, 17, 19; as also the *goods* sold in such places, Ezek. xxvii. 33; and therefore that ערבים may, for aught proved to the contrary, signify *merchants* in the text.

As to Bochart's objection, that, the prophet being ordered to go to the brook Cherith, that he might lie hid, and the place of his retreat not be known, if any traders or merchants supplied his wants, they would most likely discover where he was, &c., I think there is no weight in it; for the men might be as well bound by the secret inspiration of God not to discover the place of his retreat, as they were to supply his wants; besides, they might have been of the number of *those* seven thousand *men who had not bowed their knees to the image of Baal*, and consequently would not inform Ahab and Jezebel of their prophet's hiding place.

Some have supposed that the original means *Arabians;* but Bochart contends that there were no Arabians in that district: this is certainly more than he or any other man can prove. Colonies of Arabs, and hordes and families of the same people, have been widely scattered over different places for the purpose of temporal sojournment and trade; for they were a wandering people, and often to be found in different districts remote enough from the place of their birth. But, letting this pass merely for what it is worth, and feeling as I do the weight of the objections that may be brought against the supposition of *ravens* being the agents employed to feed the prophet, I would observe that there was a town or city of the name of *Orbo*, that was not far from the place where Elijah was commanded to hide himself. In *Bereshith Rabba*, a rabbinical comment on Genesis, we have these words עיר היא בתחום ביתשאן ושמה ערבו *ir hi bithchom Beithshean, veshemo Orbo;* "There is a town in the vicinity of Beth-shan, (Scythopolis,) and its name is Orbo." We may add to this from St. Jerome,

Orbim, accolæ villæ in finibus Arabum, Eliæ dederunt alimenta; "The Orbim, inhabitants of a town in the confines of the Arabs, gave nourishment to Elijah." Now, I consider Jerome's testimony to be of great worth, because he spent several years in the holy land, that he might acquire the most correct notion possible of the language and geography of the country, as well as of the customs and habits of the people, in order to his translating the sacred writings, and explaining them. Had there not been such a place in his time, he could not have written as above: and although in this place the common printed editions of the *Vulgate* have *corvi,* "crows or ravens;" yet in 2 Chron. xxi. 16, St. Jerome translates the same word ערבים, "the Arabians;" and the same in Neh. iv. 7; it is therefore most likely that the inhabitants of *Oreb* or *Orbo*, as mentioned above, furnished the aliment by which the prophet was sustained; and that they did this being specially moved thereto by the Spirit of the Lord. Add to all these testimonies that of the Arabic version, which considers the words as meaning a people, عوربيم *Orabim*, and not ravens or fowls of any kind. In such a case this version is high authority.

It is contended that those who think the *miracle* is lost if the *ravens* be not admitted, are bound to show, 1. With what propriety the raven, an unclean animal, could be employed? 2. Why the *dove*, or some such clean creature, was not preferred? 3. How the ravens could get properly *dressed* flesh to bring to the prophet? 4. From whose table it was taken; and by what means? 5. Whether it be consistent with the wisdom of God, and his general conduct, to work a *tissue* of miracles where *one* was sufficient? 6. And whether it be not best, in all cases of this kind, to adopt that mode of interpretation which is most simple; the wisdom, goodness, and providence of God being as equally apparent as in those cases where a multitude of miracles are resorted to in order to solve difficulties?

CHAPTER XVIII

Elijah is commanded by the Lord to show himself to Ahab, 1, 2. Ahab, and Obadiah his steward, search the land to find provender for the cattle, 3–6. Obadiah meets Elijah, who commands him to inform Ahab that he is ready to present himself before him, 7–15. Elijah and Ahab meet, 16–18. Elijah proposes that the four hundred and fifty priests of Baal should be gathered together at Mount Carmel; that they should offer a sacrifice to their god, and he to Jehovah; and the God who should send down fire to consume the sacrifice should be acknowledged as the true God, 19–24. The proposal is accepted, and the priests of Baal call in vain upon their god through the whole day, 25–29. Elijah offers his sacrifice, prays to God, and fire comes down from heaven and consumes it; whereupon the people acknowledge Jehovah to be the true God, and slay all the prophets of Baal, 30–40. Elijah promises Ahab that there shall be immediate rain; it comes accordingly, and Ahab and Elijah come to Jezreel, 41–46.

A. M. 3098
B. C. 906
Ante I. Ol. 130
An. Megaclis,
Arch. Athen.
perpet. 16

AND it came to pass *after* [a]many days, that the word of the LORD came to Elijah in the third year, saying, Go, show thyself unto Ahab; and [b]I will send rain upon the earth.

2 And Elijah went to show himself unto Ahab. And

A. M. 3098
B. C. 906
Ante I. Ol. 130
An. Megaclis,
Arch. Athen.
perpet. 16

---

[a]Luke iv. 25; James v. 17   [b]Deut. xxvii. 12

NOTES ON CHAP. XVIII

Verse 1. *After many days—in the third year*] We learn from our Lord, Luke iv. 25, that the drought which brought on the famine in Israel

lasted *three years and six months*. St. James, v. 17, gives it the same duration. Probably Elijah spent six months at the brook Cherith, and three years with the widow at *Sarepta*.

I will send rain upon the earth.] The word

A. M. 3098
B. C. 906
Ante I. Ol. 130
An. Megaclis,
Arch. Athen.
perpet. 16

there was a sore famine in Samaria.

3 And Ahab called ᶜObadiah, which *was* ᵈthe governor of *his* house. (Now Obadiah feared the LORD greatly:

4 For it was *so,* when ᵉJezebel cut off the prophets of the LORD, that Obadiah took a hundred prophets, and hid them by fifty in a cave, and fed them with bread and water.)

5 And Ahab said unto Obadiah, Go into the land, unto all fountains of water, and unto all brooks: peradventure we may find grass to save the horses and mules alive, ᶠthat we lose not all the beasts.

6 So they divided the land between them to pass throughout it: Ahab went one way by himself, and Obadiah went another way by himself.

7 And as Obadiah was in the way, behold, Elijah met him: and he knew him, and fell on his face, and said, *Art* thou that my lord Elijah?

8 And he answered him, I *am:* go, tell thy lord, Behold, Elijah *is here.*

9 And he said, What have I sinned, that thou wouldst deliver thy servant into the hand of Ahab, to slay me?

10 *As* the LORD thy God liveth, there is no nation or kingdom, whither my lord hath not sent to seek thee: and when they said, *He is* not *there;* he took an oath of the kingdom and nation, that they found thee not.

A. M. 3098
B. C. 906
Ante I. Ol. 130
An. Megaclis,
Arch. Athen.
perpet. 16

11 And now thou sayest, Go, tell thy lord, Behold, Elijah *is here.*

12 And it shall come to pass, *as soon as* I am gone from thee, that ᵍthe Spirit of the LORD shall carry thee whither I know not; and *so* when I come and tell Ahab, and he cannot find thee, he shall slay me: but I thy servant fear the LORD from my youth.

13 Was it not told my lord what I did when Jezebel slew the prophets of the LORD, how I hid a hundred men of the LORD's prophets by fifty in a cave, and fed them with bread and water?

14 And now thou sayest, Go, tell thy lord, Behold, Elijah *is here:* and he shall slay me.

15 And Elijah said, *As* the LORD of hosts liveth, before whom I stand, I will surely show myself unto him to-day.

16 So Obadiah went to meet Ahab, and told him: and Ahab went to meet Elijah.

17 And it came to pass, when Ahab saw Elijah, that Ahab said unto him, ʰ*Art* thou he that ⁱtroubleth Israel?

18 And he answered, I have not troubled Israel; but thou, and thy father's house, ᵏin that ye have forsaken the commandments of the LORD, and thou hast followed Baalim.

ᶜHebrew, *Obadiahu*——ᵈHebrew, *over* his *house* ᵉHebrew, *Izabel*——ᶠHebrew, *that we cut not off* ourselves *from the beasts*——ᵍ2 Kings ii. 16; Ezekiel iii.

12, 14; Matthew iv. 1; Acts viii. 39——ʰChapter xxi. 20——ⁱJoshua vii. 25; Acts xvi. 20——ᵏ2 Chronicles xv. 2

אדמה *haadamah* should be translated *the ground* or *the land,* as it is probable that this drought did not extend beyond the land of Judea.

Verse 3. *Obadiah feared the Lord greatly*] He was a sincere and zealous worshipper of the true God, and his conduct towards the persecuted prophets was the full proof both of his *piety* and *humanity.*

Verse 4. *Fed them with bread and water.*] By these are signified the necessaries of life, of whatsoever kind.

Verse 5. *Unto all fountains of water*] All marshy or well-watered districts, where grass was most likely to be preserved.

Verse 10. *There is no nation or kingdom*] He had sent through all his own states and to the neighbouring governments to find out the prophet, as he knew, from his own declaration, that both rain and drought were to be the effect of his prayers. Had he found him, he no doubt intended to oblige him to procure rain, or punish him for having brought on this drought.

He took an oath] Ahab must have had considerable power and authority among the neighbouring nations to require and exact this, and Elijah must have kept himself very secret to have shunned such an extensive and minute search.

Verse 12. *The Spirit of the Lord shall carry thee*] Obadiah supposed that the Spirit of the Lord had carried him to some strange country during the three years and a half of the drought; and as he had reason to think that Ahab would slay Elijah if he found him, and that the God of the prophet would not suffer his servant to fall into such murderous hands, he took for granted that as soon as he should come into danger, so soon would the Spirit of the Lord carry him away, or direct him to some hiding place.

Verse 13. *When Jezebel slew the prophets*] This persecution was probably during the dearth, for as this bad woman would attribute the public calamity to Elijah, not being able to find him, she would naturally wreak her vengeance on the prophets of Jehovah who were within her reach.

Verse 18. *I have not troubled Israel*] Here the *cause* of the dearth is placed on its true ground: the king and the people had forsaken the true God, and God *shut up the heavens that there was no rain.* Elijah was only the minister whom God used to dispense this judgment.

A. M. 3098
B. C. 906
Ante I. Ol. 130
An. Megaclis,
Arch. Athen.
perpet. 16

19 Now therefore send, *and*
gather to me all Israel unto
Mount [l]Carmel, and the prophets of Baal four hundred and
fifty, [m]and the prophets of the groves four
hundred, which eat at Jezebel's table.
20 So Ahab sent unto all the children of
Israel, and [n]gathered the prophets together
unto Mount Carmel.
21 And Elijah came unto all the people, and
said, [o]How long halt ye between two [p]opin-
ions? if the LORD *be* God, follow him: but if
[q]Baal, *then* follow him. And the people answered him not a word.
22 Then said Elijah unto the people, [r]I *even*
I only, remain a prophet of the LORD; [s]but
Baal's prophets *are* four hundred and fifty
men.
23 Let them therefore give us two bullocks;
and let them choose one bullock for themselves,
and cut it in pieces, and lay *it* on
wood, and put no fire *under:* and
I will dress the other bullock, and
lay *it* on wood, and put no fire
under.
24 And call ye on the name of your gods,
and I will call on the name of the LORD: and
the God that [t]answereth by fire, let him be
God. And all the people answered and said,
[u]It is well spoken.
25 And Elijah said unto the prophets of
Baal, Choose you one bullock for yourselves,
and dress *it* first; for ye *are* many; and call on
the name of your gods, but put no fire *under.*
26 And they took the bullock which was
given them, and they dressed *it,* and called on
the name of Baal from morning even until
noon, saying, O Baal, [v]hear us. But *there*
was [w]no voice, nor any that [x]answered. And
they [y]leaped upon the altar which was made.

A. M. 3098
B. C. 906
Ante I. Ol. 130
An. Megaclis,
Arch. Athen.
perpet. 16

[l]Josh. xix. 26——[m]Chap. xvi. 33——[n]Chap. xxii. 6——[o]2 Kings xvii. 41; Matt. vi. 24——[p]Or, *thoughts*——[q]See Josh. xxiv. 15——[r]Chap. xix. 10, 14——[s]Ver. 19

[t]Ver. 38; 1 Chron. xxi. 26——[u]Heb. *the word is good*——[v]Or, *answer*——[w]Psa. cxv. 5; Jer. x. 5; 1 Cor. viii. 4; xii. 2——[x]Or, *heard*——[y]Or, *leaped up and down at the altar*

Verse 19. *Gather to me all Israel*] The heads of tribes and families; the rulers of the people.

The prophets of Baal four hundred and fifty—the prophets of the groves four hundred] The king and queen had different religious establishments; the king and his servants worshipped Baal, the supreme lord and master of the world, the sun. For this establishment *four hundred and fifty* priests were maintained. The queen and her women worshipped אשרה *Asherah, Astarte,* or *Venus;* and for this establishment *four hundred* priests were maintained. These latter were in high honour; they ate at Jezebel's table; they made a part of her household. It appears that those *eight hundred and fifty* priests were the domestic chaplains of the king and queen, and probably not all the priests that belonged to the rites of Baal and Asherah in the land; and yet from the following verse we learn that Ahab had sent to all the children of Israel to collect these prophets; but Jezebel had certainly *four hundred* of them in her own house who were not at the assembly mentioned here. Those of Baal might have a more extensive jurisdiction than those of Asherah, the latter being constantly resident in Samaria.

Verse 21. *How long halt ye between two opinions?*] Literally, "How long hop ye about upon two boughs?" This is a metaphor taken from birds hopping about from bough to bough, not knowing on which to settle. Perhaps the idea of *limping* through *lameness* should not be overlooked. They were *halt,* they could not walk uprightly; they dreaded Jehovah, and therefore could not totally abandon him; they feared the king and queen, and therefore thought they *must* embrace the religion of the state. Their conscience forbade them to do the former; their fear of man persuaded them to do the latter; but in neither were they heartily engaged; and at this juncture their minds seemed in equipoise, and they were waiting for a favourable opportunity to make their decision. Such an opportunity now, through the mercy of God, presented itself.

Verse 22. *I only, remain a prophet of the Lord*] That is, I am the only prophet of God *present,* and can have but the influence of *an individual;* while the prophets of Baal are *four hundred and fifty* men! It appears that the queen's prophets, amounting to *four hundred,* were not at this great assembly; and these are they whom we meet with chap. xxii. 6, and whom the king consulted relative to the battle at Ramoth-gilead.

Verse 24. *The God that answereth by fire*] Elijah gave them every advantage when he granted that the God who answered by *fire* should be acknowledged as the true God; for as the Baal who was worshipped here was incontestably *Apollo,* or the sun, he was therefore the *god of fire,* and had only to work in *his own element.*

Verse 25. *For ye are many*] And therefore shall have the preference, and the advantage of being first in your application to the deity.

Verse 26. *From morning even until noon*] It seems that the priests of Baal employed the whole day in their desperate rites. The time is divided into two periods: 1. *From morning until noon;* this was employed in preparing and offering the sacrifice, and in earnest supplication for the celestial fire. Still there was no answer, and at *noon* Elijah began to mock and ridicule them, and this excited them to commence anew. And, 2. They continued *from noon till the time of offering the evening sacrifice,* dancing up and down, cutting themselves with knives, mingling their own blood with their sacrifice, praying, supplicating, and acting in the most frantic manner.

A. M. 3098
B. C. 906
Ante I. Ol. 130
An. Megaclis,
Arch. Athen.
perpet. 16

27 And it came to pass at noon, that Elijah mocked them, and said, Cry [z]aloud: for he *is* a god; either [a]he is talking, or he [b]is pursuing, or he is in a journey, *or* peradventure he sleepeth, and must be awaked.

28 And they cried aloud, and [c]cut themselves after their manner with knives and lan-

cets, till [d]the blood gushed out upon them.

29 And it came to pass, when midday was past, [e]and they prophesied until the *time* of the [f]offering of the *evening* sacrifice, that *there was* [g]neither voice, nor any to answer, nor any [h]that regarded.

30 And Elijah said unto all the people, Come

A. M. 3098
B. C. 906
Ante I. Ol. 130
An. Megaclis,
Arch. Athen.
perpet. 16

---

[a]Heb. *with a great voice*——[a]Or, *he meditateth*——[b]Heb. *hath a pursuit*——[c]Lev. xix. 28; Deut. xiv. 1

[d]Heb. *poured out blood upon them*——[e]1 Cor. xi. 4, 5
[f]Heb. *ascending*——[g]Ver. 26——[h]Heb. *attention*

And they leaped upon the altar] Perhaps it will be more correct to read with the margin, *they leaped up and down at the altar;* they danced round it with strange and hideous cries and gesticulations, tossing their heads to and fro, with a great variety of bodily contortions.

A heathen priest, a high priest of Budhoo, has been just showing me the manner in which they dance and jump up and down, and from side to side, twisting their bodies in all manner of ways, when making their offerings to their demon gods; a person all the while beating furiously on a tom-tom, or drum, to excite and sustain those frantic attitudes; at the same time imploring the succour of their god, frequently in some such language as this: "O loving brother devil, hear me, and receive my offering!" To perform these sacrificial attitudes they have persons who are taught to practise them from their earliest years, according to directions laid down in religious books; and to make the joints and body pliant, much anointing of the parts and mechanical management are used; and they have masters, whose business it is to teach these attitudes and contortions according to the rules laid down in those books. It seems therefore that this was a very general practice of idolatry, as indeed are the others mentioned in this chapter.

Verse 27. *At noon—Elijah mocked them*] Had not Elijah been conscious of the Divine protection, he certainly would not have used such freedom of speech while encompassed by his enemies.

Cry aloud] Make a great noise; oblige him by your *vociferations* to attend to your suit.

For he is a god] הוא אלהים כי *ki Elohim hu, he is the supreme God,* you worship him as such, he must needs be such, and no doubt jealous of his own honour and the credit of his votaries! A strong irony.

He is talking] He may be giving audience to some others; let him know that he has other worshippers, and must not give too much of his attention to one. Perhaps the word שיח *siach* should be interpreted as in the margin, *he meditateth;* he is in a profound revery; he is making some god-like projects; he is considering how he may best keep up his credit in the nation. Shout! let him know that all is now at stake.

He is pursuing] He may be taking his pleasure in hunting, and may continue to pursue the game in heaven, till he have lost all his credit and reverence on earth.

The original words, לו שיג *sig lo,* are variously translated; *He is in a hotel, in diversorio,* VULGATE. *Perhaps he is delivering oracles,* μη ποτε

χρηματιζει αυτος, SEPTUAGINT. Or, he is on some special business. Therefore, cry aloud!

He is in a journey] He has left his audience chamber, and is making some excursions; call aloud to bring him back, as his all is at stake.

Peradventure he sleepeth] Rab. S. Jarchi gives this the most degrading meaning; I will give it in Latin, because it is too coarse to be put in English; *Fortassis ad locum secretum abiit, ut ventrem ibi exomeret;* "Perhaps he is gone to the ————." This certainly reduces Baal to the lowest degree of contempt, and with it the ridicule and sarcasm are complete.

Among Asiatic idolaters their gods have different functions to fulfil, and require *sleep* and *rest.* *Vishnoo* sleeps four months in the year. *Budhoo* is represented in his temple as sleep, though his eyes are open. *Vayoo* manages the winds; *Varoona,* the waters; *Indra,* the clouds, &c.; and according to many fables in the *Pooranas,* the gods are often *out on journeys,* expeditions, &c.

Verse 28. *They cried aloud*] The poor fools acted as they were bidden.

And cut themselves after their manner] This was done according to the *rites* of that barbarous religion; if the blood of the bullock would not move him they thought their *own blood* might; and with it they smeared themselves and their sacrifice. This was not only the custom of the idolatrous Israelites, but of the Syrians, Persians, Greeks, Indians, and in short of all the heathen world.

Verse 29. *They prophesied*] They made incessant *prayer* and *supplication;* a farther proof that *to pray* or *supplicate* is the proper ideal meaning of the word נבא *naba,* which we constantly translate *to prophesy,* when even all the circumstances of the time and place are against such a meaning. See what is said on the case of *Saul among the prophets,* in the note on 1 Sam. x. 5.

Verse 30. *He repaired the altar of the Lord*] There had been an altar of Jehovah in that place, called, even among the heathens, *the altar of Carmel,* probably built in the time of the judges, or, as the rabbins imagine, by *Saul.* *Tacitus* and *Suetonius* mention an altar on Mount Carmel, which Vespasian went to consult; there was no temple nor statue, but simply an altar that was respectable for its antiquity. "Est Judæam inter Syriamque *Carmelus; ita* vocant montem Deumque: nec simulachrum Deo, aut templum situm tradidere majores: *aram* tantum, et reverentiam."—TACIT. *Hist.* lib. ii., c. 78. A priest named *Basilides* officiated at that altar, and assured Vespasian that all his projects would be crowned with success.

Suetonius speaks to this purpose: "Apud Judæam Carmeli Dei oraculum consulentem ita

A. M. 3098 B. C. 906 Ante I. Ol. 130 An. Megaclis, Arch. Athen. perpet. 16

near unto me. And all the people came near unto him. [i]And he repaired the altar of the LORD *that was* broken down.

31 And Elijah took twelve stones, according to the number of the tribes of the sons of Jacob, unto whom the word of the LORD came, saying, [k]Israel shall be thy name:

32 And with the stones he built an altar [l]in the name of the LORD: and he made a trench about the altar, as great as would contain two measures of seed.

33 And he [m]put the wood in order, and cut the bullock in pieces, and laid *him* on the wood, and said, Fill four barrels with water, and [n]pour *it* on the burnt-sacrifice, and on the wood.

34 And he said, Do *it* the second time. And they did *it* the second time. And he said, Do *it* the third time. And they did *it* the third time.

A. M. 3098 B. C. 906 Ante I. Ol. 130 An. Megaclis, Arch. Athen. perpet. 16

35 And the water [o]ran round about the altar; and he filled [p]the trench also with water.

36 And it came to pass at *the time of* the offering of the *evening* sacrifice, that Elijah the prophet came near, and said, LORD [q]God of Abraham, Isaac, and of Israel, [r]let it be known this day that thou *art* God in Israel, and *that* I *am* thy servant, and *that* [s]I have done all these things at thy word.

37 Hear me, O LORD, hear me, that this people may know that thou *art* the LORD God, and *that* thou hast turned their heart back again.

38 Then [t]the fire of the LORD fell, and

---

[i]Chap. xix. 10——[k]Gen. xxxii. 28; xxxv. 10; 2 Kings xvii. 34——[l]Col. iii. 17——[m]Lev. i. 6, 7, 8——[n]See Judg. vi. 20——[o]Heb. *went*

[p]Ver. 32, 38——[q]Exod. iii. 6——[r]Ch. viii. 43; 2 Kings xix. 19; Psa. lxxxiii. 18——[s]Num. xvi. 28 [t]Lev. ix. 24; Judg. vi. 21; 1 Chron. xxi. 26; 2 Chron. vii. 1

---

confirmavere sortes, ut quicquid cogitaret volveretque animo quamlibet magnum, id esse proventurum pollicerentur." SUET. in *Vespas.* cap. 5. The mount, the absence of a temple, no image, but a simple altar, very ancient, and which was held in reverence on account of the true answers which had been given there, prove that this was originally the altar of Jehovah; though in the time of Vespasian it seems to have been occupied by a heathen priest, and devoted to lying vanities.

Verse 31. *Took twelve stones*] He did this to show that all the twelve tribes of Israel should be joined in the worship of Jehovah.

Verse 32. *He made a trench*] This was to detain the water that might fall down from the altar when the barrels should be poured upon it, ver. 35.

Verse 33. *Fill four barrels*] This was done to prevent any kind of suspicion that there was *fire concealed under the altar.* An ancient writer under the name of *Chrysostom,* quoted by Calmet, says that he had seen under the altars of the heathens holes dug in the earth with funnels proceeding from them, and communicating with openings on the tops of the altars. In the former the priests concealed fire, which, communicating through the funnels with the holes, set fire to the wood and consumed the sacrifice; and thus the simple people were led to believe that the sacrifice was consumed by a miraculous fire. Elijah showed that no such knavery could be practised in the present case. Had there been a *concealed fire* under the altar, as in the case mentioned above, the water that was thrown *on* the altar must have extinguished it most effectually. This very precaution has for ever put this miracle beyond the reach of suspicion.

Verse 36. *Lord God of Abraham*] He thus addressed the Supreme Being, that they might know when the answer was given, that it was the *same God,* whom the patriarchs and their fathers worshipped, and thus have *their hearts turned back again* to the true religion of their ancestors.

Verse 38. *Then the fire of the Lord fell*] It did not *burst out* from the altar; this might still, notwithstanding the water, have afforded some ground for suspicion that fire had been concealed, after the manner of the heathens, under the altar.

Pindar's account of the Rhodians' settling in the isle of Rhodes, and their first sacrifice there, bears a near affinity to the account here given: *the shower of gold* descending on the sacrifice *offered up without fire,* to show the approbation of their god, is little more than a *poetic* account of the above transactions.

Καιτοι γαρ αιθουσας εχοντες
Σπερμ' ανεβαν φλογος ου
Τευξαν δ' απυροις ἱεροις
Αλσος εν ακροπολει· κεινοι-
σι μεν ξαν-
θαν αγαγων νεφελαι·
Πολυν ὑσε χρυσον

Pind. Olymp. Od. 7, ver. 86.

The Rhodians, mindful of their sire's behest,
Straight *in the citadel an altar reared;*
But with imperfect rites the Power addressed,
And without fire their sacrifice prepared;
Yet Jove, approving, o'er the assembly spread
A yellow cloud, that dropped with golden dews.
WEST.

Consumed the burnt-sacrifice] The process of this consumption is very remarkable, and all calculated to remove the possibility of a suspicion that there was any concealed fire. 1. The fire *came down* from heaven. 2. The *pieces of the sacrifice* were *first* consumed. 3. The *wood next,* to show that it was not even by *means of the wood* that the flesh was burned. 4. The *twelve stones* were also consumed, to show that it was no *common fire,* but one whose agency nothing could resist. 5. The *dust,* the *earth* of

A. M. 3098
B. C. 906
Ante I. Ol. 130
An. Megaclis,
Arch. Athen.
perpet. 16 consumed the burnt-sacrifice, and the wood, and the stones, and the dust, and licked up the water that *was* in the trench.

39 And when all the people saw *it,* they fell on their faces: and they said, ^uThe LORD, he *is* the God; the LORD, he *is* the God.

40 And Elijah said unto them, ^vTake ^wthe prophets of Baal; let not one of them escape. And they took them: and Elijah brought them down to the brook Kishon, and ^xslew them there.

41 And Elijah said unto Ahab, Get thee up, eat and drink; for *there is* ^ya sound of abundance of rain.

42 So Ahab went up to eat and to drink. And Elijah went up to the top of Carmel; ^zand he cast himself down upon the earth, and put his face between his knees,

43 And said to his servant, Go up now, look toward the sea. And he went up, and looked, and said, There is nothing. And he said, Go again seven times. A. M. 3098
B. C. 906
Ante I. Ol. 130
An. Megaclis,
Arch. Athen.
perpet. 16

44 And it came to pass at the seventh time, that he said, Behold, there ariseth a little cloud out of the sea, like a man's hand. And he said, Go up, say unto Ahab, ^aPrepare *thy chariot,* and get thee down, that the rain stop thee not.

45 And it came to pass in the mean while, that the heaven was black with clouds and wind, and there was a great rain. And Ahab rode, and went to Jezreel.

46 And the hand of the LORD was on Elijah; and he ^bgirded up his loins, and ran before Ahab ^cto the entrance of Jezreel.

---

^uVerse 24——^vOr, *apprehend*——^w2 Kings x. 25
^xDeut. xiii. 5; xviii. 20——^yOr, *a sound of a noise of rain*

^zJames v. 17, 18——^aHeb. *tie* or *bind*——^b2 Kings iv.
29; ix. 1——^cHeb. *till thou come to Jezreel*

---

which the altar was constructed, was burned up. 6. The *water* that was in the trench was, by the action of this fire, entirely evaporated. 7. The action of this fire was in every case *downward,* contrary to the nature of all earthly and material fire. Nothing can be more simple and artless than this description, yet how amazingly full and satisfactory is the whole account!

Verse 39. *Fell on their faces*] Struck with awe and reverence at the sight of this incontestable miracle.

And they said] We should translate the words thus: JEHOVAH, *He is the God!* JEHOVAH, *He is the God!* Baal is not the God; Jehovah alone is the God of Israel.

As our term *Lord* is very equivocal, we should every where insert the original word יהוה, which we should write *Yeve* or *Yeheveh,* or *Yahvah* or *Yehueh,* or, according to the points, *Yehovah.*

Verse 40. *Let not one of them escape.*] They had committed the highest crime against the state and the people by introducing idolatry, and bringing down God's judgments upon the land; therefore their lives were forfeited to that law which had ordered every idolater to be slain. It seems also that Ahab, who was present, consented to this act of impartial justice.

Verse 41. *Get thee up, eat and drink*] It appears most evidently that Ahab and the prophet were now on good terms, and this is a farther evidence that the slaying of the false prophets was by the king's consent.

Verse 42. *Put his face between his knees*] He kneeled down, and then bowed his head to the earth, so that, while his face was between his knees, his forehead touched the ground.

Verse 43. *Look toward the sea.*] From the top of Mount Carmel the Mediterranean Sea was full in view.

Verse 44. *There ariseth a little cloud out of the sea, like a man's hand.*] כְּכַף אִישׁ *kechaph ish, like the hollow of a man's hand.* In the form of the hand bent, the concave side down-

most. I have witnessed a resemblance of this kind at sea previously to a violent storm, a little cloud the size of a man's hand first appearing, and this increasing in size and density every moment, till at last it covered the whole heavens, and then burst forth with incredible fury.

Mr. Bruce mentions a similar appearance in Abyssinia:—"Every morning, in Abyssinia, is clear, and the sun shines. About nine a *small cloud, not above four hundred feet broad,* appears in the east, whirling violently round, as if upon an axis; but arrived near the zenith, it first abates its motion, then loses its form, and extends itself greatly, and seems to call up vapours from all opposite quarters. These clouds, having attained nearly the same height, rush against each other with great violence, and put me always in mind of Elijah foretelling rain on Mount Carmel."—*Travels,* vol. v., page 336, edit. 1805.

Verse 46. *Ran before Ahab*] Many think that Elijah ran before the king in order *to do him honour;* and much learned labour has been spent on this passage in order to show that Elijah had put himself at the head of a company of chanters who ran before the king reciting his praises, or the praises of God; a custom which still exists in Arabian countries! I believe all these entirely mistake the writer's meaning: Ahab yoked his chariot, and made all speed to Jezreel. The hand of the Lord, or, as the *Targum* says, the *spirit of strength,* came upon Elijah, and he girded up his loins, that is, tucked up his long garments in his girdle, and ran; and notwithstanding the advantage the king had by means of his chariot, the prophet reached Jezreel before him. There is no intimation here that he ran before the horses' heads. All this was intended to show that he was under the peculiar influence and inspiration of the Almighty, that the king might respect and fear him, and not do or permit to be done to him any kind of outrage.

CHAPTER XIX

Ahab tells Jezebel what Elijah had done; she is enraged, and threatens to take away his life, 1, 2. He leaves Jezreel, and comes to Beer-sheba, and thence to the wilderness, where he is fed and encouraged by an angel, 3–9. His complaint, and the vision by which God instructs him, 10–14. He is sent to Damascus, in order to anoint Hazael king over Syria, and Jehu king over Israel, 15–18. He meets with Elisha, who becomes his servant, 19–21.

A. M. 3098
B. C. 906
Ante I. Ol. 130
An. Megaclis,
Arch. Athen.
perpet. 16

AND Ahab told Jezebel all that Elijah had done, and withal how he had ªslain all the prophets with the sword.

2 Then Jezebel sent a messenger unto Elijah, saying, ᵇSo let the gods do *to me,* and more also, if I make not thy life as the life of one of them by to-morrow about this time.

3 And when he saw *that,* he arose, and went for his life, and came to Beer-sheba, which *belongeth* to Judah, and left his servant there.

4 But he himself went a day's journey into the wilderness, and came and sat down under a juniper tree: and he ᶜrequested ᵈfor himself that he might die; and said, It is enough; now, O Lᴏʀᴅ, take away my life; for I *am* not better than my fathers.

5 And as he lay and slept under a juniper tree, behold, then an angel touched him, and said unto him, Arise *and* eat.

6 And he looked, and, behold, *there was* a cake baken on the coals, and a cruse of water at his ᵉhead. And he did eat and drink, and laid him down again.

A. M. 3098
B. C. 906
Ante I. Ol. 130
An. Megaclis,
Arch. Athen.
perpet. 16

7 And the angel of the Lᴏʀᴅ came again the second time, and touched him, and said, Arise *and* eat; because the journey *is* too great for thee.

8 And he arose, and did eat and drink, and went in the strength of that meat ᶠforty days and forty nights unto ᵍHoreb the mount of God.

9 And he came thither unto a cave, and lodged there; and, behold, the word of the Lᴏʀᴅ *came* to him, and he said unto him, What doest thou here, Elijah?

10 And he said, ʰI have been very ¹jealous for the Lᴏʀᴅ God of hosts: for the children of Israel have forsaken thy covenant, thrown

---

ªChap. xvii. 40——ᵇRuth i. 17; chap. xx. 10; 2 Kings vi. 31——ᶜNum. xi. 15; Jonah iv. 3, 8——ᵈHeb. *for his life*——ᵉHeb. *bolster*

ᶠSo Exodus xxxiv. 28; Deuteronomy ix. 9, 18; Matt. iv. 2——ᵍExodus iii. 1——ʰRom. xi. 3——¹Numbers xxv. 11, 13; Psa. lxix. 9

NOTES ON CHAP. XIX

Verse 1. *Ahab told Jezebel*] Probably with no evil design against Elijah.

Verse 2. *So let the gods do*] If I do not slay thee, let the gods slay me with the most ignominious death.

Verse 3. *He arose, and went for his life*] He saw it was best to give place to this storm, and go to a place of safety. He probably thought that the miracle at Carmel would have been the means of effecting the conversion of the whole court and of the country, but, finding himself mistaken, he is greatly discouraged.

To Beer-sheba] This being at the most southern extremity of the promised land, and under the jurisdiction of the king of Judah, he might suppose himself in a place of safety.

Left his servant there.] Being alone, he would be the more unlikely to be discovered; besides, he did not wish to risk the life of his servant.

Verse 4. *A day's journey into the wilderness*] Probably in his way to Mount Horeb. See ver. 8.

Juniper tree] A tree that afforded him a shade from the scorching sun.

It is enough] I have lived long enough! I can do no more good among this people; let me now end my days.

Verse 5. *As he lay and slept*] Excessive anguish of mind frequently induces sleep, as well as great fatigue of body.

An angel touched him] He needed refreshment, and God sent an angel to bring him what was necessary.

Verse 6. *A cake baken on the coals*] All this seems to have been *supernaturally* provided.

Verse 7. *The journey* is *too great for thee.*] From Beer-sheba to Horeb was about *one hundred and fifty* miles.

Verse 8. *Forty days and forty nights*] So he fasted just the same time as Moses did at Horeb, and as Christ did in the wilderness.

Verse 9. *He came thither unto a cave*] Conjectured by some to be the same cave in which God put Moses that he might give him a glimpse of his glory. See Exod. xxxiii. 22.

What doest thou here, Elijah?] Is this a reproach for having fled from the face of Jezebel, through what some call *unbelieving fears,* that God would abandon him to her rage?

Verse 10. *I have been very jealous for the Lord*] The picture which he draws here of apostate Israel is very affecting:—

1. *They have forsaken thy covenant*] They have now cleaved to and worshipped other gods.

2. *Thrown down thine altars*] Endeavoured, as much as they possibly could, to abolish thy worship, and destroy its remembrance from the land.

3. *And slain thy prophets*] That there might be none to reprove their iniquity, or teach the truth; so that the restoration of the true worship might be impossible.

A. M. 3098
B. C. 906
Ante I. Ol. 130
An. Megaclis,
Arch. Athen.
perpet. 16

down thine altars, and [k]slain thy prophets with the sword; and [l]I, *even* I only, am left; and they seek my life, to take it away.

11 And he said, Go forth, and stand upon [m]the mount before the LORD. And, behold, the LORD passed by, and [n]a great and strong wind rent the mountains, and brake in pieces the rocks before the LORD; *but* the LORD *was* not in the wind: and after the wind an earthquake; *but* the LORD *was* not in the earthquake:

12 And after the earthquake a fire; *but* the LORD *was* not in the fire: and after the fire a still small voice.

13 And it was *so,* when Elijah heard *it,*

that [o]he wrapped his face in his mantle, and went out, and stood in the entering in of the cave. [p]And, behold, *there came* a voice unto him, and said, What doest thou here, Elijah?

A. M. 3098
B. C. 906
Ante I. Ol. 130
An. Megaclis,
Arch. Athen.
perpet. 16

14 [q]And he said, I have been very jealous for the LORD God of hosts: because the children of Israel have forsaken thy covenant, thrown down thine altars, and slain thy prophets with the sword; and I, *even* I only, am left; and they seek my life, to take it away.

15 And the LORD said unto him, Go, return on thy way to the wilderness of Damascus: [r]and when thou comest, anoint Hazael *to be* king over Syria:

16 And [s]Jehu the son of Nimshi shalt thou

[F] [k]Ch. xviii. 4——[l]Ch. xviii. 22; Rom. xi. 3——[m]Exod. xxiv. 12——[n]Ezek. i. 4; xxxvii. 7——[o]So Exod. iii. 6;

Isa. vi. 2——[p]Verse 9——[q]Ver. 10——[r]2 Kings viii. 12, 13——[s]2 Kings ix. 1–3; Ecclus. xlviii. 8

---

4. *I only, am left*] They have succeeded in destroying all the rest of the prophets, and they are determined not to rest till they slay me.

Verse 11. *Stand upon the mount before the Lord.*] God was now treating Elijah nearly in the same way that he treated Moses; and it is not unlikely that Elijah was now standing on the same place where Moses stood, when God revealed himself to him in the giving of the law. See Exod. xix. 9, 16.

The Lord passed by] It appears that the *passing by* of the Lord occasioned the *strong wind,* the *earthquake,* and the *fire;* but in none of these was God to make a discovery of himself unto the prophet; yet these, in some sort, prepared his way, and prepared Elijah to hear the *still small voice.* The apparatus, indicating the presence of the Divine Majesty, is nearly the same as that employed to minister the law to Moses; and many have supposed that God intended these things to be understood thus: that God intended to display himself to mankind not in *judgment,* but in *mercy;* and that as the *wind,* the *earthquake,* and the *fire,* were only the forerunners of the *still small voice,* which proclaimed the benignity of the Father of spirits; so the *law,* and all its *terrors,* were only intended to introduce that mild spirit of the Gospel of Jesus, proclaiming glory to God in the highest, and on earth peace, and good will unto men. Others think that all this was merely *natural;* and that a real earthquake, and its accompaniments, are described. 1. Previously to earthquakes the atmosphere becomes greatly disturbed, mighty winds and tempests taking place. 2. This is followed by the actual agitation of the earth. 3. In this agitation *fire* frequently escapes, or a burning *lava* is poured out, often accompanied with *thunder* and *lightning.* 4. After these the air becomes serene, the thunder ceases to roll, the forked lightnings no longer play, and nothing remains but a *gentle breeze.* However correct all this may be, it seems most probably evident that what took place at this time was out of the ordinary course of nature; and although the things, as mentioned here, may often be the accompaniments of an earthquake that has nothing super-

natural in it; yet here, though every thing is produced in its *natural order,* yet the exciting cause of the whole is *supernatural.* Thus the Chaldee understands the whole passage: "And behold the Lord was revealed; and before him was a host of the angels of the wind, tearing the mountains, and breaking the rocks before the Lord, but the Majesty (*Shechinah*) of the Lord was not in the host of the angels of the wind. And after the host of the angels of the wind, there was a host of the angels of commotion; but the Majesty of the Lord was not in the host of the angels of commotion. And after the host of the angels of commotion, a fire; but the Majesty of the Lord was not in the host of the angels of fire. And after the host of the angels of fire, a voice singing in silence," &c.; that is, a sound with which no other sound was mingled. Perhaps the whole of this is intended to give an emblematical representation of the various displays of Divine providence and grace.

Verse 13. *Wrapped his face in his mantle*] This he did to signify his *respect;* so Moses hid his face, for he dared not to look upon God, Exod. iii. 6. *Covering the face* was a token of respect among the Asiatics, as *uncovering the head* is among the Europeans.

Verse 15. *To the wilderness of Damascus*] He does not desire him to take a road by which he might be likely to meet Jezebel, or any other of his enemies.

Anoint Hazael] For what reason the Lord was about to make all these *revolutions,* we are told in ver. 17. God was about to bring his judgments upon the land, and especially on the house of Ahab. This he exterminated by means of Jehu; and Jehu himself was a scourge of the Lord to the people. Hazael also grievously afflicted Israel; see the accomplishment of these purposes, 2 Kings viii. and ix.

Verse 16. *Elisha—shalt thou anoint to be prophet in thy room.*] Jarchi gives a strange turn to these words: "Thy prophecy (or execution of the prophetic office) does not please me, because thou art the constant accuser of my children." With all their abominations, this rabbin would have us to believe that those vile idolaters and murderers were still the *beloved*

A. M. 3098
B. C. 906
Ante I. Ol. 130
An. Megaclis,
Arch. Athen.
perpet. 16

anoint *to be* king over Israel: and ᵗElisha the son of Shaphat of Abel-meholah shalt thou anoint *to be* prophet in thy room.

17 And ᵘit shall come to pass, *that* him that escapeth the sword of Hazael shall Jehu slay: and him that escapeth from the sword of Jehu ᵛshall Elisha slay.

18 ʷYet ˣI have left *me* seven thousand in Israel, all the knees which have not bowed unto Baal, ʸand every mouth which hath not kissed him.

19 So he departed thence, and found Elisha the son of Shaphat, who *was* ploughing *with* twelve yoke *of oxen* before him, and he with

the twelfth: and Elijah passed by him, and cast his mantle upon him.

A. M. 3098
B. C. 906
Ante I. Ol. 13C
An. Megaclis,
Arch. Athen.
perpet. 16

20 And he left the oxen, and ran after Elijah, and said, ᶻLet me, I pray thee, kiss my father and my mother, and *then* I will follow thee. And he said unto him, ᵃGo back again: for what have I done to thee?

21 And he returned back from him, and took a yoke of oxen, and slew them, and ᵇboiled their flesh with the instruments of the oxen, and gave unto the people, and they did eat. Then he arose, and went after Elijah, and ministered unto him.

ᵗLuke iv. 27, called *Eliseus*——ᵘ2 Kings viii. 12; ix. 14, &c.; x. 6, &c.; xiii. 3——ᵛSee Hos. vi. 5 ʷRomans xi. 4

ˣOr, *I will leave*——ʸSee Hosea xiii. 2——ᶻMatthew viii. 21, 22; Luke ix. 61, 62——ᵃHebrew, *go return* ᵇ2 Samuel xxiv. 22

---

children of God! And why? Because God had made a *covenant* with their fathers; therefore said the ancient as well as the modern *siren song:* "Once in the covenant, always in the covenant; once a son, and a son for ever." And yet we have here the testimony of God's own prophet, and the testimony of their history, that they had *forsaken the covenant,* and consequently renounced all their interest in it.

Verse 17. *Shall Elisha slay.*] We do not find that Elisha either used the sword, or commissioned it to be used, though he delivered solemn prophecies against this disobedient people: and this is probably the sense in which this should be understood, as Elisha was prophet before Hazael was king, and Hazael was king before Jehu; and the heavy famine which he brought on the land took place before the reign either of Jehu or Hazael. The meaning of the prophecy may be this: Hazael, Jehu, and Elisha, shall be the ministers of my vengeance against this disobedient and rebellious people. The *order of time,* here, is not to be regarded.

Verse 18. *Seven thousand in Israel*] That is, *many* thousands; for *seven* is a number of perfection, as we have often seen: so, *The barren has borne seven*—has had a *numerous* offspring; *Gold seven times purified*—purified till *all the dross is perfectly separated* from it. The court and multitudes of the people had gone after Baal; but perhaps the majority of the common people still worshipped in secret the God of their fathers.

Every mouth which hath not kissed him.] Idolaters often *kissed their hand* in honour of their idols; and hence the origin of *adoration*— *bringing the hand to the mouth* after touching the idol, if it were within reach; and if not, kissing the right hand in token of respect and subjection. The word is compounded of *ad, to,* and *os, oris, the mouth. Dextera manu deum contingentes, ori admovebant:* "Touching the god with their right hand, they applied it to their mouth." So *kissing the hand,* and *adoration,* mean the same thing—thus Pliny, *Inter adorandum, dexteram ad osculum referimus, totum corpus circumagimus:* Nat. Hist. lib. xxviii., cap. 2.—"In the act of adoration we kiss

the right hand, and turn about the whole body." *Cicero* mentions a statue of Hercules, the chin and lips of which were considerably *worn* by the frequent kissing of his worshippers: *Ut rictus ejus, et mentum paulo sit attritius, quod in precibus et gratulationibus, non solum id venerari, sed etiam osculari solent.—Orat.* in VERREM.

I have seen several instances of this, especially in the paintings of old saints: the lips and mouth of beautiful paintings literally worn away by the unmerciful *osculations* of devotees.

Verse 19. *Twelve yoke* of oxen] Elisha must have had a considerable estate, when he kept *twelve* yoke of oxen to till the ground. If, therefore, he obeyed the prophetic call, he did it to considerable secular loss.

He with the twelfth] Every owner of an inheritance among the Hebrews, and indeed among the *ancients* in general, was a principal *agent* in its cultivation.

Cast his mantle upon him] Either this was a *ceremony* used in a call to the prophetic office, or it indicated that he was called to be the *servant* of the prophet. The *mantle,* or *pallium,* was the peculiar garb of the prophet, as we may learn from Zech. xiii. 4; and this was probably made of *skin dressed with the hair on.* See also 2 Kings i. 8. It is likely, therefore, that Elijah threw his mantle on Elisha to signify to him that he was called to the prophetic office. See more on this subject below.

Verse 20. *Let me—kiss my father and my mother*] Elisha fully understood that he was called by this ceremony to the prophetic office: and it is evident that he conferred not with flesh and blood, but resolved, immediately resolved, to obey; only he wished to bid farewell to his relatives. See below.

What have I done to thee?] Thy call is not from *me,* but from *God:* to *him,* not to *me,* art thou accountable for thy use or abuse of it.

Verse 21. *He returned back*] He went home to his house; probably he yet lived with his parents, for it appears he was a single man: and *he slew a yoke of the oxen*—he made a feast for his household, having boiled the flesh of the oxen with his agricultural implements, probably in token that he had *abandoned* secular life: then, having bidden them an affectionate farewell, he arose, went after Elijah, who probably still awaited his coming in the field or its vicinity, and ministered unto him.

ON the call of Elisha, I may make a few remarks.

1. Elijah is commanded, ver. 16, to *anoint* Elisha prophet in his room. Though it is generally believed that *kings, priests,* and *prophets,* were inaugurated into their respective offices by the right of *unction,* and this I have elsewhere supposed; yet this is the only instance on record where a prophet is commanded to be *anointed;* and even this case is problematical, for it does not appear that Elijah did *anoint* Elisha. Nothing is mentioned in his call to the prophetic office, but the casting the mantle of Elijah upon him; wherefore it is probable that the word *anoint,* here signifies no more than the *call to the office,* accompanied by the *simple rite* of having the prophet's *mantle thrown over his shoulders.*

2. A call to the ministerial office, though it completely sever from all secular occupations, yet never supersedes the duties of filial affection. Though Elisha must leave his oxen, and become a prophet to Israel: yet he may first go home, eat and drink with his parents and relatives, and bid them an affectionate farewell.

3. We do not find any attempt on the part of his parents to hinder him from obeying the Divine call: they had too much respect for the authority of God, and they left their son to the dictates of his conscience. Wo to those parents who strive, for filthy lucre's sake, to prevent their sons from embracing a call to preach Jesus to their perishing countrymen, or to the heathen, because they see that the life of a true evangelist is a life of comparative poverty, and they had rather he should *gain money* than *save souls.*

4. The *cloak,* we have already observed, was the prophet's peculiar habit; it was probably in imitation of this that the Greek philosophers wore a sort of *mantle,* that distinguished them from the common people; and by which they were at once as easily known as certain academical characters are by their *gowns* and *square caps.* The *pallium* was as common among the *Greeks* as the *toga* was among the *Romans.* Each of these was so peculiar to those nations, that *Palliatus* is used to signify a *Greek,* as *Togatus* is to signify a *Roman.*

5. Was it from this act of Elijah, conveying the prophetic office and its authority to Elisha by throwing his mantle upon him, that the popes of Rome borrowed the ceremony of collating an archbishop to the spiritualities and temporalities of his *see,* and investing him with plenary sacerdotal authority, by sending him what is well known in ecclesiastical history by the name *pallium, pall,* or cloak? I think this is likely; for as we learn from Zech. xiii. 4, and 2 Kings i. 8, that this *mantle* was a *rough* or *hairy garment,* so we learn from *Durandus* that the *pallium* or *pall* was made of *white wool,* after the following manner:—

The nuns of St. *Agnes,* annually on the festival of their patroness, offer two *white lambs* on the altar of their church, during the time they sing *Agnus Dei,* in a solemn mass; which lambs are afterwards taken by two of the canons of the Lateran church, and by them given to the pope's sub-deacons, who send them to pasture till shearing time; and then they are shorn, and the *pall* is made of their wool, mixed with other white wool. The pall is then carried to the Lateran church, and there placed on the high altar by the deacons, on the bodies of St. *Peter* and St. *Paul;* and, after a usual watching or vigil, it is carried away in the night, and delivered to the sub-deacons, who lay it up safely. Now, because it was taken from the body of St. Peter, it signifies the plenitude of ecclesiastical power: and, therefore, the popes assume it as their prerogative, being the professed successors of this apostle, to invest other prelates with it. This was at first confined to *Rome,* but afterwards it was sent to popish prelates in different parts of the world.

6. It seems, from the place in Zechariah, quoted above, that this *rough cloak* or *garment* became the covering of *hypocrites* and *deceivers;* and that persons assumed the *prophetic dress* without the *prophetic call,* and God threatens to *unmask* them. We know that this became general in the popish Church in the beginning of the 16th century; and God stripped those false prophets of their false and wicked pretensions, and exposed them to the people. Many of them profited by this exposure, and became reformed; and the whole community became at least more *cautious.* The Romish Church should be thankful to the Reformation for the moral purity which is now found in it; for, had not its vices, and usurpations, and super-scandalous sales of indulgences, been thus checked, the whole fabric had by this time been probably dissolved. Should it carry its reformation still farther, it would have a more legitimate pretension to the title of *apostolic.* Let them compare their *ritual* with the Bible and common sense, and they will find cause to lop many cumbrous and rotten branches from a good tree.

CHAPTER XX

hadad and his courtiers, being closely besieged in Aphek, and unable to escape, surrender themselves with sackcloth on their loins, and halters on their heads; the king of Israel receives them in a friendly manner, and makes a covenant with Ben-hadad, 31–34. A prophet, by a symbolical action, shows him the impolicy of his conduct in permitting Ben-hadad to escape, and predicts his death and the slaughter of Israel, 35–43.

A. M. 3103
B. C. 901
Ante I. Ol. 125
An. Megaclis,
Arch. Athen.
perpet. 21

AND Ben-hadad the king of Syria gathered all his host together: and *there were* thirty and two kings with him, and horses, and chariots: and he went up and besieged Samaria, and warred against it.

2 And he sent messengers to Ahab king of Israel into the city, and said unto him, Thus saith Ben-hadad,

3 Thy silver 'and thy gold *is* mine: thy wives also and thy children, *even* the goodliest, *are* mine.

4 And the king of Israel answered and said, My lord, O king, according to thy saying, I *am* thine, and all that I have.

5 And the messengers came again, and said, Thus speaketh Ben-hadad, saying, Although I have sent unto thee, saying, Thou shalt deliver me thy silver, and thy gold, and thy wives, and thy children;

6 Yet I will send my servants unto thee to-morrow about this time, and they shall search thine house, and the houses of thy servants; and it shall be, *that* whatsoever is [a]pleasant in thine eyes, they shall put *it* in their hand, and take *it* away.

7 Then the king of Israel called all the elders of the land, and said, Mark, I pray you, and see how this *man* seeketh [b]mischief: for he sent unto me for my wives, and for my children, and for my silver, and for my gold; and [c]I denied him not.

A. M. 3103
B. C. 901
Ante I. Ol. 125
An. Megaclis,
Arch. Athen.
perpet. 21

8 And all the elders and all the people said unto him, Hearken not *unto him,* nor consent.

9 Wherefore he said unto the messengers of Ben-hadad, Tell my lord the king, All that thou didst send for to thy servant at the first I will do: but this thing I may not do. And the messengers departed, and brought him word again.

10 And Ben-hadad sent unto him, and said, [d]The gods do so unto me, and more also, if the dust of Samaria shall suffice for handfuls for all the people that [e]follow me.

11 And the king of Israel answered and said, Tell *him,* Let not him that girdeth on *his harness* boast himself as he that putteth it off.

12 And it came to pass, when *Ben-hadad* heard this [f]message, as he *was* [g]drinking, he and the kings in the [h]pavilions, that he said unto his servants, [i]Set *yourselves in array.*

---

[a] Heb. *desirable*——[b] 2 Kings v. 7——[c] Heb. *I kept not back from him*——[d] Ch. xix. 2——[e] Heb. are *at my feet;* so Exod. xi. 8; Judg. iv. 10——[f] Heb. *word*——[g] Ver. 16——[h] Or, *tents*——[i] Or, *place* the engines; *and they placed* engines

---

NOTES ON CHAP. XX

Verse 1. *Ben-hadad*] Several MSS., and some early printed editions, have *Ben-hadar,* or *the son of Hadar,* as the Septuagint. He is supposed to be the same whom Asa stirred up against the king of Israel, xv. 18; or, as others, his *son* or *grandson.*

Thirty and two kings] Tributary chieftains of Syria and the adjacent countries. In former times every town and city had its independent chieftain. Both the *Septuagint* and *Josephus* place this war after the history of *Naboth.*

Verse 4. *I am thine, and all that I have.*] He probably hoped by this humiliation to soften this barbarous king, and perhaps to get better conditions.

Verse 6. *Whatsoever is pleasant in thine eyes*] It is not easy to discern in what this *second* requisition differed from the *first;* for surely his *silver, gold, wives,* and *children,* were among his *most pleasant* or *desirable things.* *Jarchi* supposes that it was the *book of the law of the Lord* which Ben-hadad meant, and of which he intended to deprive Israel. It is however evident that Ben-hadad meant to *sack the whole city,* and after having taken the royal treasures, and the *wives* and *children* of the king, to deliver up the whole to be *pillaged* by his soldiers.

Verse 8. *Hearken not unto him*] The elders had every thing at stake, and they chose rather to make a desperate defence than tamely to yield to such degrading and ruinous conditions.

Verse 10. *If the dust of Samaria shall suffice*] This is variously understood. Jonathan translates thus: "If the dust of Shomeron shall be sufficient for the soles of the feet of the people that shall accompany me;" i. e., I shall bring such an army that there will scarcely be room for them to stand in Samaria and its vicinity.

Verse 11. *Let not him that girdeth on*] This was no doubt a proverbial mode of expression. *Jonathan* translates, "Tell him, Let not him who girds himself and goes down to the battle, boast as he who has conquered and returned from it."

Verse 12. *In the pavilions*] This word comes from *papilio,* a *butterfly,* because tents, when pitched or spread out, resembled such animals; partly because of the mode of their *expansion,* and partly because of the manner in which they were *painted.*

Set yourselves in array.] The **original** word.

A. M. 3103
B. C. 901
Ante I. Ol. 125
An. Megaclis,
Arch. Athen.
perpet. 21 And they set *themselves in array* against the city.

13 And, behold, there [k]came a prophet unto Ahab king of Israel, saying, Thus saith the LORD, Hast thou seen all this great multitude? behold, [l]I will deliver it into thine hand this day; and thou shalt know that I *am* the LORD.

14 And Ahab said, By whom? And he said, Thus saith the LORD, *Even* by the [m]young men of the princes of the provinces. Then he said, Who shall [n]order the battle? And he answered, Thou.

15 Then he numbered the young men of the princes of the provinces, and they were two hundred and thirty-two: and after them he numbered all the people, *even* all the children of Israel, *being* seven thousand.

16 And they went out at noon. But Ben-hadad *was* [o]drinking himself drunk in the pavilions, he and the kings, the thirty and two kings that helped him.

17 And the young men of the princes of the provinces went out first; and Ben-hadad sent out, and they told him, saying, There are men come out of Samaria.

18 And he said, Whether they be come out for peace, take them alive; or whether they be come out for war, take them alive.

19 So these young men of the princes of the provinces came out of the city, and the army which followed them.

A. M. 3103
B. C. 901
Ante I. Ol. 125
An. Megaclis,
Arch. Athen.
perpet. 21

20 And they slew every one his man: and the Syrians fled; and Israel pursued them: and Ben-hadad the king of Syria escaped on a horse with the horsemen.

21 And the king of Israel went out, and smote the horses and chariots, and slew the Syrians with a great slaughter.

22 And the prophet came to the king of Israel, and said unto him, Go, strengthen thyself, and mark, and see what thou doest: [p]for at the return of the year the king of Syria will come up against thee.

23 And the servants of the king of Syria said unto him, Their gods *are* gods of the hills; therefore they were stronger than we; but let us fight against them in the plain, and surely we shall be stronger than they.

24 And do this thing, Take the kings away, every man out of his place, and put captains in their rooms:

25 And number thee an army, like the army [q]that thou hast lost, horse for horse, and chariot for chariot: and we will fight against them in the plain, *and* surely we shall be stronger than they. And he hearkened unto their voice, and did so.

שׂימוּ *simu*, which we translate by this long periphrasis, is probably a military term for *Begin the attack, Invest the city, Every man to his post*, or some such like expression.

Verse 13. *There came a prophet*] Who this was we cannot tell; *Jarchi* says it was *Micaiah, son of Imlah*. It is strange that on such an occasion we hear nothing of Elijah or Elisha. Is it not possible that this was one of them disguised?

Verse 14. *By the young men of the princes of the provinces*.] These were probably some chosen persons out of the militia of different districts, raised by the *princes of the provinces;* the same as we would call *lord-lieutenants* of counties.

Verse 15. *Two hundred and thirty-two*] These were probably the king's *life* or *body guards;* not all the militia, but *two hundred and thirty* of them who constituted the royal guard in Samaria. They were therefore the king's own regiment, and he is commanded by the prophet to put himself at their head.

Seven thousand.] How low must the state of Israel have been at this time! These *Jarchi* thinks were the seven thousand who had not bowed the knee to Baal.

Verse 18. *Take them alive.*] He was confident of victory. Do not slay them; bring them to me, they may give us some useful information.

Verse 20. *The Syrians fled*] They were doubtless panic-struck.

Verse 23. *Their gods* are *gods of the hills*] It is very likely that the small Israelitish army availed itself of the *heights* and *uneven* ground, that they might fight with greater advantage against the Syrian *cavalry*, for Ben-hadad came up against Samaria *with horses and chariots,* ver. 1. These therefore must be soon thrown into confusion when charging in such circumstances; indeed, the *chariots* must be nearly useless.

Let us fight against them in the plain] There our horses and chariots will all be able to bear on the enemy, and there their gods, whose influence is confined to the hills, will not be able to help them. It was a general belief in the heathen world that each *district* had its tutelary and protecting deity, who could do nothing out of his own sphere.

Verse 24. *Take the kings away*] These were not acquainted with military affairs, or they had **not** competent skill. Put experienced *cap-*

A. M. 3104
B. C. 900
Ante I. Ol. 124
An. Megaclis,
Arch. Athen.
perpet. 22

26 And it came to pass at the return of the year, that Ben-hadad numbered the Syrians, and went up to ʳAphek, ˢto fight against Israel.

27 And the children of Israel were numbered, and ᵗwere all present, and went against them: and the children of Israel pitched before them like two little flocks of kids; but the Syrians filled the country.

28 And there came a man of God, and spake unto the king of Israel, and said, Thus saith the Lord, Because the Syrians have said, The Lord *is* God of the hills, but he *is* not God of the valleys, therefore ᵘwill I deliver all this great multitude into thine hand, and ye shall know that I *am* the Lord.

29 And they pitched one over against the other seven days. And *so* it was, that in the seventh day the battle was joined: and the children of Israel slew of the Syrians a hundred thousand footmen in one day.

30 But the rest fled to Aphek, into the city; and *there* a wall fell upon twenty and seven

thousand of the men *that were* left. And Ben-hadad fled and came into the city, ᵛinto ʷan inner chamber.

A. M. 3104
B. C. 900
Ante I. Ol. 124
An. Megaclis,
Arch. Athen.
perpet. 22

31 And his servants said unto him, Behold now, we have heard that the kings of the house of Israel *are* merciful kings: let us, I pray thee, ˣput sackcloth on our loins, and ropes upon our heads, and go out to the king of Israel: peradventure he will save thy life.

32 So they girded sackcloth on their loins, and *put* ropes on their heads, and came to the king of Israel, and said, Thy servant Ben-hadad saith, I pray thee, let me live. And he said, *Is* he yet alive? he *is* my brother.

33 Now the men did diligently observe whether *any thing would come* from him, and did hastily catch *it;* and they said, Thy brother Ben-hadad. Then he said, Go ye, bring him. Then Ben-hadad came forth to him; and he caused him to come up into the chariot.

34 And *Ben-hadad* said unto him, ʸThe cities, which my father took from thy father, I will restore; and thou shalt make streets for thee

---

ʳJosh. xiii. 4——ˢHeb. *to the war with Israel*——ᵗOr, *were victualled*——ᵘVer. 13——ᵛOr, *from chamber to*

chamber——ʷHeb. *into a chamber within a chamber;* chap. xxii. 25——ˣGen. xxxvii. 34——ʸChap. xv. 20

---

tains in their place, and fight not but on the plains, and you will be sure of victory.

Verse 26. *Ben-hadad numbered the Syrians, and went up to Aphek*] There were several towns of this name; see the notes on Josh. xii. 18. It is supposed that the town mentioned here was situated in *Libanus,* upon the river *Adonis,* between *Heliopolis* and *Biblos.*

Verse 28. *Because the Syrians have said*] God resents their blasphemy, and is determined to punish it. They shall now be discomfited in such a way as to show that God's power is every where, and that the multitude of a host is nothing against him.

Verse 29. *Slew—a hundred thousand footmen in one day.*] This number is enormous; but the MSS. and versions give no various reading.

Verse 30. *A wall fell upon twenty and seven thousand*] From the first view of this text it would appear that when the Syrians fled to Aphek, and shut themselves within the walls, the Israelites immediately brought all hands, and sapped the walls, in consequence of which a large portion fell, and buried *twenty-seven thousand* men. But perhaps the hand of God was more immediately in this disaster; probably a *burning wind* is meant. See at the end of the chapter.

Came into the city, into an inner chamber.] However the passage above may be understood, the city was now, in effect, taken; and Ben-hadad either betook himself with his few followers to the citadel or to some secret hiding-place, where he held the council with his servants immediately mentioned.

Verse 31. *Put sackcloth on our loins, and ropes upon our heads*] Let us show ourselves humbled in the deepest manner, and let us put ropes about our necks, and go submitting to his mercy, and deprecating his wrath. The citizens of Calais are reported to have acted nearly in the same way when they surrendered their city to Edward III., king of England, in 1346. See at the end.

Verse 32. *Thy servant Ben-hadad*] See the vicissitude of human affairs! A little before he was the haughtiest of all tyrants, and Ahab calls him his *lord;* now, so much is he humbled, that he will be glad to be reputed Ahab's *slave!*

Verse 33. *Did hastily catch* it] They were watching to see if any kind word should be spoken by him, from which they might draw a favourable omen; and when they heard him use the word *brother,* it gave them much encouragement.

Verse 34. *Thou shalt make streets for thee in Damascus*] It appears that it was customary for foreigners to have a place assigned to them, particularly in maritime towns, where they might deposit and vend their merchandise. This was the very origin of European settlements in Asiatic countries: "The people gave an *inch* to those strangers; and in consequence they took an *ell.*" Under the pretence of strengthening the place where they kept their wares, to prevent depredations, they built forts, and soon gave laws to their entertainers. In vain did the natives wish them away; they had got power, and would retain it; and at last subjected these countries to their own dominion.

A. M. 3104
B. C. 900
Ante I. Ol. 124
An. Megaclis,
Arch. Athen.
perpet. 22

in Damascus, as my father made in Samaria. Then *said Ahab,* I will send thee away with this covenant. So he made a covenant with him, and sent him away.

35 And a certain man of ᶻthe sons of the prophets said unto his neighbour ᵃin the word of the LORD, Smite me, I pray thee. And the man refused to smite him.

36 Then said he unto him, Because thou hast not obeyed the voice of the LORD, behold, as soon as thou art departed from me, a lion shall slay thee. And as soon as he was departed from him, ᵇa lion found him, and slew him.

37 Then he found another man, and said, Smite me, I pray thee. And the man smote him, ᶜso that in smiting he wounded *him.*

38 So the prophet departed, and waited for the king by the way, and disguised himself with ashes upon his face.

39 And ᵈas the king passed by, he cried unto the king: and he said, Thy servant went out into the midst of the battle; and, behold, a man turned aside, and brought a man unto me, and said, Keep this man: if by any means he be missing, then ᵉshall thy life be for his life, or else thou shalt ᶠpay a talent of silver.

A. M. 3104
B. C. 900
Ante I. Ol. 124
An. Megaclis,
Arch. Athen.
perpet. 22

40 And as thy servant was busy here and there, ᵍhe was gone. And the king of Israel said unto him, So *shall* thy judgment *be;* thyself hast decided *it.*

41 And he hasted, and took the ashes away from his face; and the king of Israel discerned him that he *was* of the prophets.

42 And he said unto him, Thus saith the LORD, ʰBecause thou hast let go out of *thy* hand a man whom I appointed to utter destruction, therefore thy life shall go for his life, and thy people for his people.

43 And the king of Israel ⁱwent to his house heavy and displeased, and came to Samaria.

ᶻ2 Kings ii. 3, 5, 15——ᵃCh. xiii. 17, 18——ᵇCh. xiii. 24.——ᶜHeb. *smiting and wounding*——ᵈSee 2 Sam. xii. 1, &c.——ᵉ2 Kings x. 24——ᶠHeb. *weigh*——ᵍHeb. *he was not*——ʰChap. xxii. 31–37——ⁱChap. xxi. 4

It was customary also, in the time of the crusades, to give those nations which were engaged in them *streets, churches,* and *post dues,* in those places which they assisted to conquer. The Genoese and Venetians had each a street in *Accon,* or St. Jean d'Acre, in which they had their own jurisdiction; with oven, mill, bagnio, weights, and measures.—See *William of Tyre,* and *Harmer's Observations.*

He made a covenant with him] According to the words recited above, putting him under no kind of disabilities whatsoever.

Verse 35. *In the word of the Lord*] By the word or command of the Lord; that is, God has commanded thee to smite me. Refusing to do it, this man forfeited his life, as we are informed in the next verse.

By this emblematical action he intended to inform Ahab that, as the man forfeited his life who refused to smite him when he had the Lord's command to do it; so he (Ahab) had forfeited his life, because he did not smite Benhadad when he had him in his power.

Verse 36. *A lion found him, and slew him.*] This seems a hard measure, but there was ample reason for it. This person was also one of the sons of the prophets, and he knew that God frequently delivered his counsels in this way, and should have immediately obeyed; for the smiting could have had no evil in it when God commanded it, and it could be no outrage or injury to his fellow when he himself required him to do it.

Verse 38. *Disguised himself with ashes upon his face.*] It does not immediately appear how putting *ashes* upon his face could disguise him. Instead of אֵפֶר *apher, dust, Houbigant* conjectures that it should be אֲפַד *aphad,* a *fillet* or *bandage.* It is only the *corner* of the last letter which makes the difference; for the ר *daleth* and ר *resh* are nearly the same, only the *shoulder* of the former is *square,* the latter *round.* That *bandage,* not *dust,* was the original reading, seems pretty evident from its remains in two of the oldest versions, the *Septuagint* and the *Chaldee;* the former has Καὶ κατεδήσατο ἐν τελαμῶνι τοὺς ὀφθαλμοὺς αὐτοῦ, "And he bound his eyes with a fillet." The latter has וכריך במעפריא עינוהי *ukerich bemaaphira einohi;* "And he covered his eyes with a cloth." The MSS. of *Kennicott* and *De Rossi* contain no various reading here; but *bandage* is undoubtedly the true one. However, in the way of *mortification,* both the *Jews* and *Hindoos* put ashes upon their *heads* and *faces,* and make themselves sufficiently disgusting.

Verse 39. *Keep this man*] The drift of this is at once seen; but Ahab, not knowing it, was led to pass sentence on himself.

Verse 41. *Took the ashes away*] He took the bandage from off his eyes: see on ver. 38. It was no doubt of thin cloth, through which he could see, while it served for a sufficient disguise.

Verse 42. *Thy life shall go for his life*] This was fulfilled at the battle of Ramoth-gilead, where he was slain by the Syrians; see chap. xxii. 34, 35.

Verse 43. *Heavy and displeased*] Heavy or afflicted, because of these dreadful tidings; and displeased with the prophet for having announced them. Had he been displeased with himself, and humbled his soul before God, even those judgments, so circumstantially foretold, might have been averted.

1. WE have already seen, in ver. 30, that according to our text, *twenty-seven thousand* men

were slain by the falling of a wall. Serious doubts are entertained concerning the legitimacy of this rendering. I have, in the note, given the conjecture concerning sapping the foundation of the wall, and thus overthrowing them that were upon it. If instead of חומה *chomah*, a *wall*, we read הומה *confusion* or *disorder*, then the destruction of the *twenty-seven thousand* men may appear to have been occasioned by the *disorganized* state into which they fell; of which their enemies taking advantage, they might destroy the whole with ease.

But חומה *chomah*, a *wall*, becomes, as Dr. *Kennicott* has observed, a very different word when written without the ו *vau*, חמה which signifies *heat*; sometimes the *sun*, *vehement heat*, or the *heat of the noon-day sun;* and also the name of a *wind*, from its suffocating, *parching* quality.

The same noun, from יחם *yacham*, Dr. Castel explains by *excandescentia, furor, venenum; burning, rage, poison*. These renderings, says Dr. *Kennicott*, all concur to establish the sense of a *burning wind*, eminently blasting and destructive. I shall give a few instances from the Scripture:—

We read in Job xxvii. 21: *The east wind carrieth him away;* where the word קדים *kadim* is καυσων, *burning*, in the *Septuagint;* and in the *Vulgate, ventus urens, a burning wind*. In Ezek. xix. 12: *She was plucked up* בחמה *she was cast down to the ground, and the east wind dried up her fruit; her strong rods were withered, and the fire consumed them*. Hosea (xiii. 15) mentions the desolation brought by *an east wind, the wind of the Lord*. What in Amos iv. 9 is, *I have smitten you with blasting*, in the Vulgate is, *in vento vehemente*, "with a vehement wind;" and in the Syriac, *with a hot wind*.

Let us apply these to the history: when Benhadad, king of Syria, was besieging Samaria the second time, the Israelites slew of the Syrians *one hundred thousand* footmen in one day; and it follows, that when the rest of the army fled to Aphek, *twenty-seven thousand* of the men that were left were suddenly destroyed by החומה *hachomah*, or החמה *hachamah*, a *burning wind*. That such is the true interpretation, will appear more clearly if we compare the destruction of Ben-hadad's army with that of Sennacherib, whose sentence is that God would send upon him a BLAST, רוח *ruach*, a *wind;* doubtless such a wind as would be suddenly destructive. The event was said to that in the night *one hundred and eighty-five thousand* Assyrians were smitten by the angel of the Lord, 2 Kings xix. 7, 35. The connection of this sentence with the execution of it is given by the psalmist, who says, civ. 4: *God maketh his angels* רחות *ruchoth, winds;* or, *maketh the winds his angels*, i. e., *messengers for the performance of his will*. In a note on Psa. xi. 6, Professor Michaelis has these words: *Ventus Zilgaphoth, pestilens eurus est, orientalibus notissimus, qui obvia quævis necat;* "The wind Zilgaphoth is a *pestilent east wind*, well known to the Asiatics, which suddenly kills those who are exposed to it." *Thevenot* mentions such a wind in 1658, that in one night suffocated *twenty thousand* men. And the *Samiel* he mentions as having, in 1665, suffocated *four thousand* persons. "Upon the whole, I conclude," says the doctor, "that as *Thevenot* has mentioned *two* great multitudes destroyed by this *burning wind*, so has holy Scripture recorded

the destruction of *two* much greater multitudes by a similar cause; and therefore we should translate the words thus: *But the rest fled to Aphek, into the city; and* THE BURNING WIND *fell upon the twenty and seven thousand of the men that were left*."

2. On the case of Ben-hadad and his servants coming out to Ahab with *sackcloth on their loins* and *ropes about their necks*, ver. 31, I have referred to that of the six citizens of Calais, in the time of Edward III. I shall give this affecting account from Sir *John Froissart*, who lived in that time, and relates the story circumstantially, and with that simplicity and detail that give it every appearance of truth. He is the only writer, of all his contemporaries, who gives the relation; and as it is not only illustrative of the text in question, but also very curious and affecting, I will give it in his own words; only observing that, King Edward having closely invested the city in 1346, and the king of France having made many useless attempts to raise the siege, at last withdrew his army, and left it to its fate. "Then," says *Froissart*, chap. cxliv., "after the departure of the king of France with his army, the Calesians saw clearly that all hopes of succour were at an end; which occasioned them so much sorrow and distress that the hardiest could scarcely support it. They entreated therefore, most earnestly, the lord *John de Vienne*, their governor, to mount upon the battlements, and make a sign that he wished to hold a parley.

"The king of England, upon hearing this, sent to him Sir *Walter Manny* and Lord *Basset*. When they were come near, the lord de Vienne said to them: 'Dear gentlemen, you, who are very valiant knights, know that the king of France, whose subjects we are, has sent us hither to defend this town and castle from all harm and damage. This we have done to the best of our abilities; all hopes of help have now left us, so that we are most exceedingly straitened; and if the gallant king, your lord, have not pity upon us, we must perish with hunger. I therefore entreat that you would beg of him to have compassion upon us, and to have the goodness to allow us to depart in the state we are in; and that he will be satisfied with having possession of the town and castle, with all that is within them, as he will find therein riches enough to content him.' To this Sir Walter Manny replied: 'John, we are not ignorant of what the king our lord's intentions are, for he has told them to us; know then, that it is not his pleasure that you should get off so, for he is resolved that you surrender yourselves wholly to his will, to allow those whom he pleases their ransom, or to be put to death; for the Calesians have done him so much mischief, and have, by their obstinate defence, cost him so many lives, and so much money, that he is mightily enraged.'

"The lord de Vienne answered: 'These conditions are too hard for us; we are but a small number of knights and squires, who have loyally served our lord and master, as you would have done, and have suffered much ill and disquiet: but we will endure more than any men ever did in a similar situation, before we consent that the smallest boy in the town should fare worse than the best. I therefore once more entreat you, out of compassion, to return to the king of England, and beg of him to have pity on us; he will, I trust, grant you this favour; for I have such an opinion of his gallantry as to hope that, through God's mercy, he will alter his mind.'

"The two lords returned to the king and related what had passed. The king said: 'He had no intention of complying with the request, but should insist that they surrendered themselves unconditionally to his will.' Sir Walter replied: 'My lord, ye may be to blame in this, as you will set us a very bad example; for if you order us to go to any of your castles, we shall not obey you so cheerfully if you put these people to death, for they will retaliate upon us in a similar case.'

"Many barons who were present supported this opinion; upon which the king replied: 'Gentlemen, I am not so obstinate as to hold my opinion alone against you all. Sir Walter, you will inform the governor of Calais, that the only grace he is to expect from me is, that six of the principal citizens of Calais march out of the town with bare heads and feet, *with ropes round their necks*, and the keys of the town and castle in their hands. These six persons shall be at my absolute disposal, and the remainder of the inhabitants pardoned.'

"Sir Walter returned to the lord de Vienne, who was waiting for him on the battlements, and told him all that he had been able to gain from the king. 'I beg of you,' replied the governor, 'that you would be so good as to remain here a little, whilst I go and relate all that has passed to the townsmen; for, as they have desired me to undertake this, it is but proper that they should know the result of it.'

"He went to the market place, and caused the bell to be rung; upon which all the inhabitants, men and women, assembled in the town-hall. He then related to them what he had said, and the answers he had received, and that he could not obtain any conditions more favourable; to which they must give a short and immediate answer.

"This information caused the greatest lamentations and despair, so that the hardest heart would have had compassion on them; even the lord de Vienne wept bitterly.

"After a short time the most wealthy citizen of the town, by name *Eustace de St. Pierre*, rose up and said: 'Gentlemen, both high and low, it would be a very great pity to suffer so many people to die through famine, if any means could be found to prevent it; and it would be highly meritorious in the eyes of our Saviour, if such misery could be averted. I have such faith and trust in finding grace before God, if I die to save my townsmen, that I name myself as first of the six.'

"When Eustace had done speaking, they all rose up and almost worshipped him: many cast themselves at his feet with tears and groans. Another citizen, very rich and respected, rose up and said, 'He would be the *second* to his companion *Eustace;*' his name was *John Daire*. After him *James Wisant*, who was very rich in merchandise and lands, offered himself as companion to his two cousins, as did *Peter Wisant*, his brother. Two others then named themselves, which completed the number demanded by the king of England. The lord John de Vienne then mounted a small hackney, for it was with difficulty he could walk, (he had been wounded in the siege,) and conducted them to the gate. There was the greatest sorrow and lamentation over all the town; and in such manner were they attended to the gate, which the governor ordered to be opened and then shut

upon him and the six citizens, whom he led to the barriers, and said to Sir Walter Manny, who was there waiting for him, 'I deliver up to you, as governor of Calais, with the consent of the inhabitants, these six citizens; and I swear to you that they were, and are at this day, the most wealthy and respectable inhabitants of Calais. I beg of you, gentle sir, that you would have the goodness to beseech the king that they may not be put to death.' 'I cannot answer for what the king will do with them,' replied Sir Walter; 'but you may depend that I will do all in my power to save them.'

"The barriers were opened, when these six citizens advanced towards the pavilion of the king, and the lord de Vienne re-entered the town.

"When Sir Walter Manny had presented these six citizens to the king, they fell upon their knees, and with uplifted hands said: 'Most gallant king, see before you six citizens of Calais, who have been capital merchants, and who bring you the keys of the castle and of the town. We surrender ourselves to your absolute will and pleasure, in order to save the remainder of the inhabitants of Calais, who have suffered much distress and misery. Condescend, therefore, out of your nobleness of mind, to have mercy and compassion upon us.' All the barons, knights, and squires, that were assembled there in great numbers, wept at this sight.

"The king eyed them with angry looks, (for he hated much the people of Calais, for the great losses he had formerly suffered from them at sea,) and ordered their heads to be stricken off. All present entreated the king that he would be more merciful to them, but he would not listen to them. Then Sir Walter Manny said: 'Ah, gentle king, let me beseech you to restrain your anger; you have the reputation of great nobleness of soul, do not therefore tarnish it by such an act as this, nor allow any one to speak in a disgraceful manner of you. In this instance all the world will say you have acted cruelly, if you put to death six such respectable persons, who of their own free will have surrendered themselves to your mercy, in order to save their fellow citizens.' Upon this the king gave a wink, saying, *Be it so*, and ordered the headsman to be sent for; for that the Calesians had done him so much damage, it was proper they should suffer for it.

"The queen of England, who was at that time very big with child, fell on her knees, and with tears said: 'Ah, gentle sir, since I have crossed the sea with great danger to see you, I have never asked you one favour; now I most humbly ask as a gift, for the sake of the Son of the blessed Mary, and for your love to me, that you will be merciful to these six men.' The king looked at her for some time in silence, and then said: 'Ah, lady, I wish you had been any where else than here; you have entreated in such a manner that I cannot refuse you; I therefore give them to you, to do as you please with them.'

"The queen conducted the six citizens to her apartments, and had the halters taken from round their necks, new clothed, and served them with a plentiful dinner; she then presented each with nobles, and had them escorted out of the camp in safety."

This is the whole of this affecting account, which is mentioned by no other writer, and has been thought a proper subject for the pen of the poet, the pencil of the painter, and the burin of the engraver; and which has seldom been fairly represented in the accounts we have of it from our historians. The translation I have borrowed from the accurate edition of Froissart, by Mr. Johns, of Hafod; and to his work, vol. i., p. 367, I must refer for objections to the authenticity of some of the facts stated by the French historian. We see in *Eustace de*

St. Pierre and his five companions the portrait of genuine patriotism.—a principle, almost as rare in the world as the Egyptian phœnix, which leads its possessors to devote their property and consecrate their lives to the public weal; widely different from that spurious birth which is deep in the cry of *My country!* while it has nothing in view but its places, pensions, and profits. Away with it!

CHAPTER XXI

Ahab covets the vineyard of Naboth, and wishes to have it either by purchase or exchange, 1, 2. Naboth refuses to alienate it on any account, because it was his inheritance from his fathers, 3. Ahab becomes disconsolate, takes to his bed, and refuses to eat, 4. Jezebel, finding out the cause, promises to give him the vineyard, 5-7. She writes to the nobles of Jezreel to proclaim a fast, to accuse Naboth of blasphemy, carry him out, and stone him to death; which is accordingly done, 8-14. She then tells Ahab to go and take possession of the vineyard; he goes, and is met by Elijah, who denounces on him the heaviest judgments, 15-24. Ahab's abominable character, 25, 26. He humbles himself; and God promises not to bring the threatened public calamities in his days, but in the days of his son, 27-29.

A. M. 3105
B. C. 899
Ante I. Ol. 123
An. Megaclis,
Arch. Athen.
perpet. 23

AND it came to pass after these things, *that* Naboth the Jezreelite had a vineyard, which *was* in Jezreel, hard by the palace of Ahab king of Samaria.

2 And Ahab spake unto Naboth, saying, Give me thy ªvineyard, that I may have it for a garden of herbs, because it *is* near unto my house: and I will give thee for it a better vineyard than it; *or,* if it ᵇseem good to thee, I will give thee the worth of it in money.

3 And Naboth said to Ahab, The LORD forbid it me, ᶜthat I should give the inheritance of my fathers unto thee.

A. M. 3105
B. C. 899
Ante I. Ol. 123
An. Megaclis,
Arch. Athen.
perpet. 23

4 And Ahab came into his house heavy and displeased, because of the word which Naboth the Jezreelite had spoken to him: for he had said, I will not give thee the inheritance of my fathers. And he laid him down upon his bed, and turned away his face, and would eat no bread.

ª1 Sam. viii. 14——ᵇHeb. be *good in thine eyes*

ᶜLev. xxv. 23; Num. xxxvi. 7; Ezek. xlvi. 18

NOTES ON CHAP. XXI

Verse 1. *After these things*] This and the twentieth chapter are transposed in the *Septuagint;* this preceding the account of the Syrian war with Ben-hadad. *Josephus* gives the history in the same order.

Verse 2. *Give me thy vineyard*] The request of Ahab seems at first view fair and honourable. Naboth's vineyard was nigh to the palace of Ahab, and he wished to add it to his own for a *kitchen garden,* or perhaps a *grass-plat,* גן ירק *gan yarak;* and he offers to give him either a better vineyard for it, or to give him its worth in money. Naboth rejects the proposal with horror: *The Lord forbid it me, that I should give the inheritance of my fathers to thee.* No man could *finally* alienate any part of the parental inheritance; it might be sold or mortgaged till the *jubilee,* but at that time it must revert to its original owner, if not redeemed before; for this God had particularly enjoined, Lev. xxv. 14-17, 25-28: therefore Naboth properly said, ver. 3, *The Lord forbid it me, to give the inheritance of my fathers.* Ahab most evidently wished him to *alienate* it *finally,* and this is what God's law had expressly forbidden; therefore he could not, consistently with his duty to God, indulge Ahab; and it was high

iniquity in Ahab to tempt him to do it; and to covet it showed the depravity of Ahab's soul. But we see farther that, despotic as those kings were, they dared not seize on the inheritance of any man. This would have been a flagrant breach of the *law* and *constitution* of the country; and this indeed would have been inconsistent with the character which they sustained, viz., the *Lord's vicegerents.* The Jewish kings had no authority either to *alter* the old laws, or to *make new ones.* "The Hindoos," says Mr. *Ward,* "are as strongly attached to their *homesteads* as the Jews were. Though the heads of the family be employed in a distant part of the country, and though the *homesteads* may be almost in ruins, they cling still to the *family inheritance* with a fondness bordering on superstition."

Verse 4. *He laid him down upon his bed*] Poor soul! he was lord over ten-twelfths of the land, and became miserable because he could not get a poor man's vineyard added to all that he possessed! It is a true saying, "That soul in which God dwells not, has no happiness: and he who has God has a satisfying portion." Every privation and cross makes an unholy soul unhappy; and privations and crosses it must ever meet with, therefore—

"Where'er it goes is hell; itself is hell!"

A. M. 3105
B. C. 899
Ante I. Ol. 123
An. Megaclis,
Arch. Athen.
perpet. 23

5 But Jezebel his wife came to him, and said unto him, Why is thy spirit so sad, that thou eatest no bread?

6 And he said unto her, Because I spake unto Naboth the Jezreelite, and said unto him, Give me thy vineyard for money; or else, if it please thee, I will give thee *another* vineyard for it: and he answered, I will not give thee my vineyard.

7 And Jezebel his wife said unto him, Dost thou now govern the kingdom of Israel? arise, *and* eat bread, and let thine heart be merry: I will give thee the vineyard of Naboth the Jezreelite.

8 So she wrote letters in Ahab's name, and sealed *them* with his seal, and sent the letters unto the elders and to the nobles that *were* in his city, dwelling with Naboth.

9 And she wrote in the letters, saying, Proclaim a fast, and set Naboth ᵈon high among the people:

10 And set two men, sons of Belial, before him, to bear witness against him, saying, Thou didst ᵉblaspheme God and the king. And *then* carry him out, and ᶠstone him, that he may die.

11 And the men of his city, *even* the elders and the nobles who were the inhabitants in his city, did as Jezebel had sent unto them, *and* as it *was* written in the letters which she had sent unto them.

A. M. 3105
B. C. 899
Ante I. Ol. 123
An. Megaclis,
Arch. Athen.
perpet. 23

12 ᵍThey proclaimed a fast, and set Naboth on high among the people.

13 And there came in two men, children of Belial, and sat before him: and the men of Belial witnessed against him, *even* against Naboth, in the presence of the people, saying, Naboth did blaspheme God and the king. ʰThen they carried him forth out of the city, and stoned him with stones, that he died.

14 Then they sent to Jezebel, saying, Naboth is stoned, and is dead.

15 And it came to pass, when Jezebel heard that Naboth was stoned, and was dead, that Jezebel said to Ahab, Arise, take possession of the vineyard of Naboth the Jezreelite, which he refused to give thee for money: for Naboth is not alive, but dead.

16 And it came to pass, when Ahab heard that Naboth was dead, that Ahab rose up to go

---

ᵈHeb. *in the top of the people*——ᵉExod. xxii. 28; Lev. xxiv. 15, 16; Acts vi. 11

ᶠLeviticus xxiv. 14——ᵍIsaiah lviii. 4——ʰSee 2 Kings ix. 26

Verse 7. *Dost thou now govern the kingdom of Israel?*] Naboth, not Ahab, is king. If *he* have authority to *refuse*, and *thou* have no power to *take*, he is the greater man of the two. This is the vital language of *despotism* and *tyranny*.

Verse 8. *She wrote letters in Ahab's name*] She counterfeited his authority by his own consent; and he lent his signet to stamp that authority.

Verse 9. *Proclaim a fast*] Intimate that there is some great calamity coming upon the nation, because of some evil tolerated in it.

Set Naboth on high] Bring him to a public trial.

Verse 10. *Set two men*] For life could not be attainted but on the evidence of two witnesses at least.

Sons of Belial] Men who will not scruple to tell lies and take a false oath.

Thou didst blaspheme God and the king.] Thou art an *atheist* and a *rebel*. Thou hast spoken words injurious to the perfections and nature of God; and thou hast spoken words against the crown and dignity of the king. The words literally are, Naboth hath BLESSED *God and the king;* or, as Parkhurst contends, "Thou hast blessed the false gods and Molech," ברכת אלהים ומלך. And though Jezebel was herself an abominable idolatress; yet, as the law of Moses

still continued in force, she seems to have been wicked enough to have destroyed Naboth, upon the false accusation of *blessing the heathen Aleim and Molech*, which subjected him to death by Deut. xii. 6; xvii. 2-7. The first meaning appears the most simple.

Many think that the word ברך *barach* signifies both to *bless* and *curse;* and so it is interpreted in most Lexicons: it is passing strange that out of the same word proceedeth *blessing* and *cursing;* and to give such opposite and self-destructive meanings to any word is very dangerous. Parkhurst denies that it ever has the meaning of *cursing*, and examines all the texts where it is said to occur with this meaning; and shows that *blessing*, not *cursing*, is to be understood in all those places: see him under ברך, sec. vi.

Verse 13. *And stoned him with stones*] As they pretended to find him guilty of treason against God and the king, it is likely they destroyed the whole of his *family;* and then the king seized on his grounds as confiscated, or as *escheated* to the king, without any heir at law. That his *family* was destroyed appears strongly intimated, 2 Kings ix. 26; *Surely I have seen yesterday the blood of Naboth*, AND THE BLOOD OF HIS SONS, *saith the Lord.*

Verse 15. *Arise, take possession*] By what *rites* or in what *forms* this was done, we do not know.

A. M. 3105
B. C. 899
Ante I. Ol. 123
An. Megaclis,
Arch. Athen.
perpet. 23

down to the vineyard of Naboth the Jezreelite, to take possession of it.

17 [1]And the word of the LORD came to Elijah the Tishbite, saying,

18 Arise, go down to meet Ahab king of Israel, [k]which *is* in Samaria: behold, *he is* in the vineyard of Naboth, whither he is gone down to possess it.

19 And thou shalt speak unto him, saying, Thus saith the LORD, Hast thou killed, and also taken possession? And thou shalt speak unto him, saying, Thus saith the LORD, [l]In the place where dogs licked the blood of Naboth shall dogs lick thy blood, even thine.

20 And Ahab said to Elijah, [m]Hast thou found me, O mine enemy? And he answered, I have found *thee:* because [n]thou hast sold thyself to work evil in the sight of the LORD.

21 Behold, [o]I will bring evil upon thee, and will take away thy posterity, and will cut off from Ahab [p]him that pisseth against the wall, and [q]him that is shut up and left in Israel,

22 And will make thine house like the house of [r]Jeroboam the son of Nebat, and like the house of [s]Baasha the son of Ahijah, for the provocation wherewith thou hast provoked *me* to anger, and made Israel to sin.

23 And [t]of Jezebel also spake the LORD, saying, The dogs shall eat Jezebel by the [u]wall of Jezreel.

A. M. 3105
B. C. 899
Ante I. Ol. 123
An. Megaclis,
Arch. Athen.
perpet. 23

24 [v]Him that dieth of Ahab in the city the dogs shall eat; and him that dieth in the field shall the fowls of the air eat.

25 But [w]there was none like unto Ahab, which did sell himself to work wickedness in the sight of the LORD, [x]whom Jezebel his wife [y]stirred up.

A.M.3086-3107
B. C. 918-897
Anno ante I.
Olymp.142-121

26 And he did very abominably in following idols, according to all *things* [z]as did the Amorites, whom the LORD cast out before the children of Israel.

27 And it came to pass, when Ahab heard those words, that he rent his clothes, and [a]put sackcloth upon his flesh, and fasted, and lay in sackcloth, and went softly.

A. M. 3105
B. C. 899
Ante I. Ol. 123
An. Megaclis,
Arch. Athen.
perpet. 23

28 And the word of the LORD came to Elijah the Tishbite, saying,

29 Seest thou how Ahab humbleth himself before me? because he humbleth himself before me, I will not bring the evil in his days: *but* [b]in his son's days will I bring the evil upon his house.

---

[i]Psa. ix. 12——[k]Chap. xiii. 32; 2 Chron. xxii. 9
[l]Ch. xxii. 38——[m]Ch. xviii. 17——[n]2 Kings xvii. 17;
Rom. vii. 14——[o]Ch. xiv. 10; 2 Kings ix. 8——[p]1 Sam.
xxv. 22——[q]Chap. xiv. 10——[r]Chap. xv. 29

[s]Chap. xvi. 3, 11——[t]2 Kings ix. 36——[u]Or, *ditch*
[v]Ch. xiv. 11; xvi. 4——[w]Chap. xvi. 30, &c.——[x]Chap.
xvi. 31——[y]Or, *incited*——[z]Gen. xv. 16; 2 Kings xxi. 11
[a]Gen. xxxvii. 34——[b]2 Kings ix. 25

Verse 18. *Go down to meet Ahab*] This was the next day after the murder, as we learn from the above quotation, 2 Kings ix. 26.

Verse 19. *In the place where dogs licked, &c.*] It is in vain to look for a *literal fulfilment* of this prediction. Thus it would have have been fulfilled, but the humiliation of Ahab induced the merciful God to say, *I will not bring the evil in his days, but in the days of his son,* ver. 29. Now dogs did lick the blood of Ahab; but it was at the pool of Samaria, where his chariot and his armour were washed, after he had received his death wound at Ramoth-gilead; but some think this was the place where Naboth was stoned: see chap. xxii. 38. And how literally the prediction concerning *his son* was fulfilled, see 2 Kings ix. 25, where we find that the body of Jehoram his son, just then slain by an arrow that had passed through his heart, was thrown *into the portion of the field of Naboth the Jezreelite;* and there, doubtless, the dogs licked his blood, if they did not even devour his body. There is a similar idea of the propriety of punishment overtaking the culprit in the place where he had committed the crime, expressed by *Orestes* to *Ægisthus*, SOPH. *Elect.* 1495.

———Χωρει δ' ενθαπερ κατεκτανες
Πατερα τον α''ον, ώς άν εν ταυτῳ θανῃς.

———Go where thou slew'st my father,
That in the self-same place thou too may'st die.

Verse 20. *Thou hast sold thyself to work evil*] See a similar form of speech, Rom. vii. 14. Thou hast totally abandoned thyself to the service of sin. Satan is become thy *absolute master*, and thou his *undivided slave*.

Verse 23. *The dogs shall eat Jezebel*] This was most literally fulfilled; see 2 Kings ix. 36. The carcasses of poor *Hindoos*, and of persons who have received public punishment, are thrown into the *rivers*, and floating to the side, are devoured by *dogs, vultures,* and *crows*.

Verse 25. *Did sell himself to work wickedness*] He hired himself to the devil for this very purpose, that he might *work* wickedness. This was to be his *employment*, and at this he *laboured*.

In the sight of the Lord, whom Jezebel his wife stirred up.] A good wife is from the Lord; a bad wife is from the devil: Jezebel was of this kind; and she has had many successors.

Verse 27. *He rent his clothes*] He was penetrated with sorrow, and that evidently unfeigned.

Put sackcloth upon his flesh] He humbled himself before God and man.

And fasted] He afflicted his body for his soul's benefit.

Lay in sackcloth] Gave the fullest proof that his repentance was real.

And went softly.] *Walked barefooted;* so the *Chaldee, Syriac,* and *Arabic.* The *Vulgate* has *demisso capite,* "with his head hanging down." *Houbigant* translates *went groaning. Jarchi* says that the word כֹּן *at,* used here, signifies *to be unshod.* This is its most likely sense. All these things prove that Ahab's repentance was genuine; and God's approbation of it puts it out of doubt. The *slow* and *measured pace* which always accompanies deep and reflective sorrow is also alluded to by Æschylus, where the *Chorus* are thus shortly addressed on the defeat of Xerxes.—ÆSCH. *Pers.* 1073.

Γ'οασθ' ἀβροβαται

"With light and noiseless step lament."

Verse 29. *Seest thou how Ahab humbleth himself*] He did abase himself; he did *truly repent him of his sins,* and it was such a repentance as was genuine in the *sight of God: He humbleth himself* BEFORE ME.

The *penitent* heart ever meets the *merciful* eye of God; repentance is highly esteemed by the Father of compassion, even where it is comparatively shallow and short-lived. Any measure of godly sorrow has a proportionate measure of God's regard; where it is deep and lasting, the heart of God is set upon it. He that mourns shall be comforted; thus hath God spoken, and though repentance for our past sins can *purchase* no favour, yet without it God will not grant us his salvation.

CHAPTER XXII

Jehoshaphat king of Judah, and Ahab king of Israel, unite against the Syrians, in order to recover Ramoth-gilead, 1-4. They inquire of false prophets, who promise them success. Micaiah, a true prophet, foretells the disasters of the war, 5-17. A lying spirit in the mouths of Ahab's prophets persuades Ahab to go up against Ramoth, 18-29. The confederate armies are routed, and the king of Israel slain, 30-36. Death and burial of Ahab, 37-40. Character of Jehoshaphat, 41-47. He makes a fleet in order to go to Ophir for gold, which is wrecked at Ezion-geber, 48. His death, 49. He is succeeded by his son Jehoram, 50. Ahaziah succeeds his father Ahab, and reigns wickedly, 51, 52.

A.M.3104-3107
B. C. 900-897
Anno ante I.
Olymp.124-121

AND they continued three years without war between Syria and Israel.

A. M. 3107
B. C. 897
Ante I. Ol. 121
An. Megaclis,
Arch. Athen.
perpet. 25

2 And it came to pass in the third year, that [a]Jehoshaphat the king of Judah came down to the king of Israel.

3 And the king of Israel said unto his servants, Know ye that [b]Ramoth in Gilead *is* ours, and we *be* [c]still, *and* take it not out of the hand of the king of Syria?

4 And he said unto Jehoshaphat, Wilt thou go with me to battle to Ramoth-gilead? And Jehoshaphat said to the king of Israel, [d]I *am* as thou *art,* my people as thy people, my horses as thy horses.

5 And Jehoshaphat said unto the king of Israel, Inquire, I pray thee, at the word of the LORD to-day.

A. M. 3107
B. C. 897
Ante I. Ol. 121
An. Megaclis,
Arch. Athen.
perpet. 25

6 Then the king of Israel [e]gathered the prophets together, about four hundred men, and said unto them, Shall I go against Ramoth-gilead to battle, or shall I forbear? And they said, Go up; for the LORD shall deliver *it* into the hand of the king.

7 And [f]Jehoshaphat said, *Is there* not here a prophet of the LORD besides, that we might inquire of him?

8 And the king of Israel said unto Jehoshaphat, *There is* yet one man, Micaiah the son of Imlah, by whom we may inquire of the LORD: but I hate him; for he doth not prophesy good concerning me, but evil. And

---

[a]2 Chron. xviii. 2, &c.—[b]Deut. iv. 43——[c]Heb. *silent from taking it*

[d]2 Kings iii. 7——[e]Chapter xviii. 19——[f]2 Kings iii. 11

NOTES ON CHAP. XXII

Verse 1. *Three years without war*] That is, from the time that Ahab made the covenant with Ben-hadad, mentioned chap. xx. 34. And probably in that treaty it was stipulated that Ramoth-gilead should be restored to Israel; which not being done, Ahab formed a confederacy with Judah, and determined to take it by force.

Verse 4. *Wilt thou go with me*] We find that there was a good understanding between Jehoshaphat and Ahab, which no doubt was the consequence of a matrimonial alliance between the son of the former, Jehoram, and the

daughter of the latter, Athaliah; see 2 Chron. xviii. 1; 2 Kings viii. 18. This coalition did not please God, and Jehoshaphat is severely reproved for it by Jehu the seer, 2 Chron. xix. 1-3.

Verse 6. *About four hundred men*] These were probably the *prophets of Asherah* or *Venus,* maintained by Jezebel, who were not present at the contention on Mount Carmel. See chap. xviii. 19, &c.

Verse 8. *Micaiah the son of Imlah*] The Jews suppose that it was this prophet who reproved Ahab for dismissing Ben-hadad, chap. xx. 35, &c. And that it was because of the judgments with which he had threatened him,

A. M. 3107
B. C. 897
Ante I. Ol. 121
An. Megaclis,
Arch. Athen.
perpet. 25

Jehoshaphat said, Let not the king say so.

9 Then the king of Israel called an ᵍofficer, and said, Hasten *hither* Micaiah the son of Imlah.

10 And the king of Israel and Jehoshaphat the king of Judah sat each on his throne, having put on their robes, in a ʰvoid place in the entrance of the gate of Samaria; and all the prophets prophesied before them.

11 And Zedekiah the son of Chenaanah made him horns of iron: and he said, Thus saith the LORD, With these shalt thou push the Syrians, until thou have consumed them.

12 And all the prophets prophesied so, saying, Go up to Ramoth-gilead, and prosper: for the LORD shall deliver *it* into the king's hand.

13 And the messenger that was gone to call

Micaiah spake unto him, saying, Behold now, the words of the prophets *declare* good unto the king with one mouth: let thy word, I pray thee, be like the word of one of them, and speak *that which is* good.

A. M. 3107
B. C. 897
Ante I. Ol. 121
An. Megaclis,
Arch. Athen.
perpet. 25

14 And Micaiah said, *As* the LORD liveth, ⁱwhat the LORD saith unto me, that will I speak.

15 So he came to the king. And the king said unto him, Micaiah, shall we go against Ramoth-gilead to battle, or shall we forbear? And he answered him, Go, and prosper: for the LORD shall deliver *it* into the hand of the king.

16 And the king said unto him, How many times shall I adjure thee that thou tell me nothing but *that which is* true in the name of the LORD?

ᵍOr, *eunuch*——ʰHeb. *floor*   ⁱNum. xxii. 38

---

that Ahab hated him: *I hate him, for he doth not prophesy good concerning me, but evil.*

Verse 9. *The king of Israel called an officer*] סריס *saris*, literally *a eunuch;* probably a foreigner, for it was not lawful to disgrace an Israelite by reducing him to such a state.

Verse 11. *Zedekiah—made him horns of iron*] This was in imitation of that sort of prophecy which instructed by significative actions. This was frequent among the prophets of the Lord.

Verse 13. *The words of the prophets declare good*] What notion could these men have of *prophecy*, when they supposed it was in the power of the prophet to model the prediction as he pleased, and have the result accordingly?

Verse 15. *Go, and prosper*] This was a strong *irony;* as if he had said, All your prophets have predicted success; you wish me to speak as they speak: *Go, and prosper; for the Lord will deliver it into the hand of the king.* These were the precise words of the false prophets, (see ver. 6 and 12,) and were spoken by Micaiah in such a tone and manner as at once showed to Ahab that he did not believe them; hence the king *adjures* him, ver. 16, that he *would speak to him nothing but truth;* and on this the prophet immediately relates to him the prophetic vision which pointed out the disasters which ensued.

It is worthy of remark that this prophecy of the king's prophets is couched in the same *ambiguous terms* by which the false prophets in the heathen world endeavoured to maintain their credit, while they deluded their votaries. The reader will observe that the word *it* is not in the original: *The Lord will deliver* IT *into the hand of the king;* and the words are so artfully constructed that they may be interpreted *for* or *against;* so that, be the event whatever it might, the *juggling prophet* could save his credit by saying he meant what had happened. Thus then the prophecy might have been understood: *The Lord will deliver* (Ramoth-gilead) *into the king's* (Ahab's)

hand; or, *The Lord will deliver* (Israel) *into the king's hand;* i. e., into the hand of the *king of Syria.* And Micaiah repeats these words of uncertainty in order to *ridicule* them and expose their fallacy.

The following oracles among the heathens were of this same *dubious* nature, in order that the priests' credit might be saved, let the event turn out as it might. Thus the Delphic oracle spoke to Crœsus words which are capable of a double meaning, and which he understood to his own destruction:—

Crœsus, Halym penetrans, magnam subvertet
     opum vim,

Which says, in effect—

"If you march against Cyrus, he will either overthrow *you*, or you will overthrow *him.*"

He trusted in the *latter*, the *former* took place. He was deluded, and yet the oracle maintained its credit. So in the following:—

Aio te, Æacida, Romanos vincere posse
Ibis redibis nunquam in bello peribis.

Pyrrhus, king of Epirus, understood by this that he should conquer the Romans, against whom he was then making war; but the oracle could be thus translated: "The Romans shall overcome thee." He trusted in the former, made unsuccessful war, and was overcome; and yet the juggling priest saved his credit. The latter line is capable of two *opposite* meanings:—

"Thou shalt go, thou shalt return, thou shalt *never perish* in war."

Or,

"Thou shalt go, thou shalt *never* return, thou shalt *perish* in war."

When prophecies and oracles were not delivered in this dubious way, they were generally couched in such intricate and dark terms

A. M. 3107
B. C. 897
Ante I. Ol. 121
An. Megaclis,
Arch. Athen.
perpet. 25

17 And he said, I saw all Israel *k*scattered upon the hills, as sheep that have not a shepherd: and the LORD said, These have no master: let them return every man to his house in peace.

18 And the king of Israel said unto Jehoshaphat, Did I not tell thee that he would prophesy no good concerning me, but evil?

19 And he said, Hear thou therefore the word of the LORD: *l*I saw the LORD sitting on his throne, *m*and all the host of heaven standing by him on his right hand and on his left:

20 And the LORD said, Who shall *n*persuade Ahab, that he may go up and fall at Ramothgilead? And one said on this manner, and another said on that manner.

21 And there came forth a spirit, and stood before the LORD, and said, I will persuade him.

22 And the LORD, said unto him, Wherewith? And he said, I will go forth, and I will be a lying spirit in the mouth of all his prophets. And he said, *o*Thou shalt persuade *him,* and prevail also: go forth, and do so.

A. M. 3107
B. C. 897
Ante I. Ol. 121
An. Megaclis,
Arch. Athen.
perpet. 25

23 *p*Now therefore, behold, the LORD hath put a lying spirit in the mouth of all these thy prophets, and the LORD hath spoken evil concerning thee.

24 But Zedekiah the son of Chenaanah went near, and smote Micaiah on the cheek, and said, *q*Which way went the Spirit of the LORD from me to speak unto thee?

25 And Micaiah said, Behold, thou shalt see in that day, when thou shalt go *r*into *s*an inner chamber to hide thyself.

26 And the king of Israel said, Take Micaiah, and carry him back unto Amon the governor of the city, and to Joash the king's son;

27 And say, Thus saith the king, Put this *fellow* in the prison, and feed him with bread of affliction, and with water of affliction, until I come in peace.

---

*k*Matthew ix. 36——*l*Isa. vi. 1; Daniel vii. 9——*m*Job i. 6; ii. 1; Psalm ciii. 20, 21; Daniel vii. 10; Zech. i. 10; Matthew xviii. 10; Hebrews i. 7, 14——*n*Or, *deceive*

*o*Judg. ix. 23; Job xii. 16; Ezek. xiv. 9; 2 Thess. ii. 11 *p*Ezek. xiv. 9——*q*2 Chron. xviii. 23——*r*Or, *from chamber to chamber*——*s*Heb. *a chamber in a chamber;* ch. xx. 30

---

that the assistance of the oracle was necessary to explain the oracle, and then it was *ignotum per ignotius,* a dark saying paraphrased by one yet more obscure.

Verse 17. *These have no master*] Here the prophet foretells the defeat of Israel, and the death of the king; they were as *sheep* that had not a *shepherd,* people that had no *master,* the political *shepherd* and *master* (Ahab) shall fall in battle.

Verse 19. *I saw the Lord sitting on his throne*] This is a mere *parable,* and only tells, in figurative language, what was in the womb of providence, the events which were shortly to take place, the agents employed in them, and the permission on the part of God for these agents to act. Micaiah did not choose to say before this angry and impious king, "Thy prophets are all liars; and the devil, the father of lies, dwells in them;" but he represents the whole by this parable, and says the same truths in language as forcible, but less offensive.

Verse 22. *Go forth, and do so.*] This is no more than, "God has *permitted* the spirit of lying to influence the whole of thy prophets; and he now, by my mouth, apprizes thee of this, that thou mayest not go and fall at Ramoth-gilead." Never was a man more circumstantially and fairly warned; he had counsels from the *God of truth,* and counsels from the *spirit of falsity;* he obstinately forsook the *former* and followed the *latter.* He was shown by this parable how every thing was going on, and that all was under the control and direction of God, and that still it was possible for him to make that God his friend whom by his continual transgressions he had made his enemy; but he would not: his blood was therefore upon his *own* head.

Verse 23. *The Lord hath put a lying spirit*] He hath *permitted* or *suffered* a lying spirit to influence thy prophets. Is it requisite again to remind the reader that the Scriptures repeatedly represent God as *doing* what, in the course of his providence, he only *permits* or *suffers* to be done? Nothing can be done in heaven, in earth, or hell, but either by his immediate *energy* or *permission.* This is the reason why the Scripture speaks as above.

Verse 24. *Which way went the Spirit of the Lord from me*] This is an expression of as great insolence as the act was of brutal aggression. "Did the Spirit of the Lord, who rests solely upon me, condescend to inspire thee? Was it at this ear [where he smote him] that it entered, in order to hold communion with thee?" Josephus tells an idle rabbinical tale about this business, which is as unworthy of repetition as it is of credit. See his *Antiq. of the Jews,* book viii., c. 10.

Verse 25. *When thou shalt go into an inner chamber*] It is probable that this refers to some Divine judgment which fell upon this deceiver. Hearing of the tragical result of the battle, he no doubt went into a secret place to hide himself from the resentment of Jezebel, and the Israelitish courtiers; and *there* it is probable he perished; but *how, when,* or *where,* is not mentioned.

Verse 27. *Feed him with bread of affliction.*] Deprive him of all the *conveniences* and *com-*

A. M. 3107
B. C. 897
Ante I. Ol. 121
An. Megaclis,
Arch. Athen.
perpet. 25

28 And Micaiah said, If thou return at all in peace, ᵗthe LORD hath not spoken by me. And he said, Hearken, O people, every one of you.

29 So the king of Israel and Jehoshaphat the king of Judah went up to Ramoth-gilead.

30 And the king of Israel said unto Jehoshaphat, ᵘI will disguise myself, and enter into the battle; but put thou on thy robes. And the king of Israel ᵛdisguised himself, and went into the battle.

31 But the king of Syria commanded his thirty and two captains that had rule over his chariots, saying, Fight neither with small nor great, save only with the king of Israel.

32 And it came to pass, when the captains of the chariots saw Jehoshaphat, that they said, Surely it *is* the king of Israel. And they turned aside to fight against him: and Jehoshaphat ʷcried out.

A. M. 3107
B. C. 897
Ante I. Ol. 121
An. Megaclis,
Arch. Athen.
perpet. 25

33 And it came to pass, when the captains of the chariots perceived that it *was* not the king of Israel, that they turned back from pursuing him.

34 And a *certain* man drew a bow ˣat a venture, and smote the king of Israel between the ʸjoints of the harness: wherefore he said unto the driver of his chariot, Turn thine hand, and carry me out of the host; for I am ᶻwounded.

35 And the battle ᵃincreased that day; and the king was stayed up in his chariot against the Syrians, and died at even: and the blood ran out of the wound into the ᵇmidst of the chariot.

36 And there went a proclamation throughout the host about the going down of the sun,

---

ᵗNum. xvi. 29; Deut. xviii. 20, 21, 22——ᵘOr, *when he was to disguise himself and enter into the battle*——ᵛ2 Chron. xxxv. 22——ʷ2 Chron. xviii. 31; Prov. xiii. 20

ˣHeb. *in his simplicity;* 2 Sam. xv. 11——ʸHeb. *joints and the breast-plate*——ᶻHeb. *made sick*——ᵃHeb. *ascended*——ᵇHeb. *bosom*

---

forts of life; treat him *severely;* just keep him alive, that he may see my triumph.

Verse 30. *I will disguise myself*] Probably he had heard of the orders given by Ben-hadad to his thirty-two captains, *to fight with the king of Israel only;* that is, to make their most powerful attack where he commanded, in order to take him prisoner, that he might lead him captive whose captive he formerly was; and therefore he *disguised* himself that he might not be known.

But put thou on thy robes.] What is meant by this? He could not mean, "Appear as the king of Judah, for they will not molest thee, as the matter of contention lies between them and me;" this is *Jarchi's* turn. For if Jehoshaphat aided Ahab, is it to be supposed that the Syrians would spare him in battle? A general in the civil wars of England, when he had brought his army in sight of their foes, thus addressed them: "Yonder are your enemies; if you do not kill *them,* they will kill *you.*" So it might be said in the case of Jehoshaphat and the Syrians.

The *Septuagint* gives the clause a different and more intelligible turn: "I will cover (conceal) myself, and enter into the battle; καὶ σὺ ἐνδύσαι τον ἱματισμον μου, *but put thou on* MY *robes.*" And does it not appear that he did put on Ahab's robes? And was it not this that caused the Syrians to mistake him for the king of Israel? ver. 32.

Verse 34. *Drew a bow at a venture*] It is supposed that he shot, as the archers in general did, not aiming at any person in particular.

The word לתמו *lethummo,* which we translate *in his simplicity,* has been variously understood; *in his integrity, his uprightness; in his perfection;* i. e., to the utmost of his *skill* and *strength.* This is most probably the meaning; and may imply both *aim* and *power,* having his *butt full in view.* In cases where the archers wished to do the greatest execution, they bent their bows, and pulled till the subtending string drew back the arrow *up to its head.* This they could not do *always,* because it required their whole strength; and they could not put forth their utmost effort each time, and continue to discharge many shots. Our old national ballad of the *Chevy-chace* mentions the slaying of Sir Hugh Montgomery, who had slain Earl Percy, in nearly the same way that Ahab appears to have been shot:—

> "And thus did both these nobles die,
>   Whose courage none could stain:
> An English archer then perceived
>   His noble lord was slain,
> Who had a bow bent in his hand
>   Made of a trusty tree;
> An *arrow, of a cloth-yard long,*
>   *Up to the head drew* he;
> *Against* Sir Hugh Montgomery then
>   So *right his shaft he set,*
> The gray goose wing that was thereon
>   In his heart's blood was wet."

Between the joints of the harness] "Between the *cuirass* and the lower part of the *helmet;*" and then the arrow must pass *through the neck,* just above the *breast:* or "between the *cuirass* and the *cuissarts;*" and then the arrow must pass through the *abdomen,* or just where the armour of the *thighs* joins to that which covers the *breast* and *belly.*

The *Vulgate* has *Inter pulmonem et stomachum;* "Between the lungs and the stomach;" consequently, in the region of the heart.

Verse 35. *The king was stayed up*] He did not wish his misfortune should be known, lest his troops should be discouraged.

Verse 36. *Every man to his city*] It appears that the Israelites and Jews maintained the fight the whole of the day; but when at eve-

A. M. 3107
B. C. 897
Ante I. Ol. 121
An. Megaclis,
Arch. Athen.
perpet. 25

saying, Every man to his city, and every man to his own country.

37 So the king died, and ᶜwas brought to Samaria; and they buried the king in Samaria.

38 And *one* washed the chariot in the pool of Samaria; and the dogs licked up his blood; and they washed his armour; according ᵈunto the word of the LORD which he spake.

A.M.3086-3107
B. C. 918-897
Anno ante I.
Olymp.142-121

39 Now the rest of the acts of Ahab, and all that he did, and ᵉthe ivory house which he made, and all the cities that he built, *are* they not written in the book of the chronicles of the kings of Israel?

A. M. 3107
B. C. 897
Ante I. Ol. 121
An. Megaclis,
Arch. Athen.
perpet. 25

40 So Ahab slept with his fathers; and Ahaziah his son reigned in his stead.

A. M. 3090
B. C. 914
Ante I. Ol. 130
An. Megaclis,
Arch. Athen.
perpet. 8

41 And ᶠJehoshaphat the son of Asa began to reign over Judah in the fourth year of Ahab king of Israel.

42 Jehoshaphat *was* thirty and

five years old when he began to reign: and he reigned twenty and five years in Jerusalem. And his mother's name *was* Azubah the daughter of Shilhi.

A.M.3090-3115
B. C. 914-889
Anno ante I.
Olymp.138-113

43 And ᵍhe walked in all the ways of Asa his father; he turned not aside from it, doing *that which was* right in the eyes of the LORD: nevertheless ʰthe high places were not taken away; *for* the people offered and burnt incense yet in the high places.

44 And ¹Jehoshaphat made peace with the king of Israel.

45 Now the rest of the acts of Jehoshaphat, and his might that he showed, and how he warred, *are* they not written in the book of the chronicles of the kings of Judah?

46 ᵏAnd the remnants of the sodomites, which remained in the days of his father Asa, he took out of the land.

47 ¹*There was* then no king in Edom: a deputy *was* king.

48 ᵐJehoshaphat ⁿmade ᵒships of Tharshish to go to Ophir for gold: ᵖbut they went

---

ᶜHeb. *came*——ᵈCh. xxi. 19——ᵉAmos iii. 15——ᶠ2 Chron. xx. 31——ᵍ2 Chron. xvii. 3——ʰCh. xiv. 23; xv. 14; 2 Kings xii. 3——¹2 Chron. xix. 2; 2 Cor. vi. 14

ᵏCh. xiv. 24; xv. 12——¹Gen. xxv. 23; 2 Sam. viii. 14; 2 Kings iii. 9; viii. 20——ᵐ2 Chron. xx. 35, &c.——ⁿOr, had *ten ships*——ᵒChap. x. 22——ᵖ2 Chron. xx. 37

---

ning the king died, and this was known, there was a proclamation made, probably with the consent of both Syrians and Israelites, that the war was over. Ahab being dead, his subjects did not choose to contend for Ramoth-gilead; so the Israelites went to their own *cities*, and the Syrians to their own *country*.

Verse 38. *The dogs licked up his blood*] Some of the rabbins think that this was in the *very place* where Naboth was stoned; see on chap. xxi. 19. The *Septuagint* translates this verse strangely: "And the swine and the dogs licked his blood, and the whores bathed themselves in his blood, according to the word of the Lord." It is certain that the Hebrew words, הזנות רחצו *hazzonoth rachatsu,* "washed his armour," might be translated as the *Septuagint* have done; "*and the whores* (or public women) *washed,*" &c. And so the rabbins seem to have understood the words; but then they suppose that Jezebel had made him *two images of prostitutes,* which he had with him in the chariot. It is not worth inquiring into the *use* for which they say these images were made. See *Kimchi* and *Jarchi.*

Verse 39. *Ivory house*] A royal palace which he built in Samaria, decorated with *ivory,* and hence called the *ivory house. Amos* the prophet speaks against this luxury, chap. iii. 15.

Verse 43. *The high places were not taken away*] In 2 Chron. xvii. 6, it is expressly said, that he *did take away the high places.* Allowing that the text is right in 2 Chron., the two places may be easily reconciled. There

were *two kinds* of *high places* in the land: 1. Those used for *idolatrous* purposes. 2. Those that were *consecrated to God,* and were used before the temple was built. The former he did take away; the latter he did not. But some think the parallel place in 2 Chron. xvii. 6 is corrupted, and that, instead of ועוד הסיר *veod hesir,* "and moreover he took away," we should read, ולא הסיר *velo hesir,* "and he did NOT take away."

Verse 46. *The remnant of the sodomites*] הקדש *of the consecrated persons;* or it may rather apply here to the *system* of pollution, effeminacy, and debauch. He destroyed the thing itself; the abominations of Priapus, and the rites of Venus, Baal, and Ashtaroth. No more of that impure worship was to be found in Judea.

Verse 47. *There was no king in Edom*] It is plain that the compiler of this book lived after the days of Jehoshaphat, in whose time the Edomites revolted; see 2 Kings viii. 22. David had conquered the Edomites, and they continued to be governed by *deputies,* appointed by the kings of Judah, till they recovered their liberty, as above. This note is introduced by the writer to account for Jehoshaphat's building ships at *Ezion-geber,* which was in the *territory* of the *Edomites,* and which showed them to be at that time under the Jewish yoke.

Verse 48. *Ships of Tharshish to go to Ophir for gold*] In the parallel place (2 Chron. xx. 36) it is said that Jehoshaphat joined himself to Ahaziah, *to make ships to go to Tharshish; and they made the ships in Ezion-geber.* Con-

A.M.3090-3115
B. C. 914–889
Anno ante I.
Olymp.138-113

not; for the ships were broken at ᑫEzion-geber.

49 Then said Ahaziah the son of Ahab unto Jehoshaphat, Let my servants go with thy servants in the ships. But Jehoshaphat would not.

A. M. 3115
B. C. 889
Ante I. Ol. 113
An. Diogeneti,
Arch. Athen.
perpet. 3

50 And ʳJehoshaphat slept with his fathers, and was buried with his fathers in the city of David his father: and Jehoram his son reigned in his stead.

51 ˢAhaziah the son of Ahab began to reign over Israel in Samaria the seventeenth year of Jehoshaphat king of Judah, and reigned two years over Israel.

A.M.3107-3108
B. C. 897–896
Anno ante I.
Olymp.121-120

52 And he did evil in the sight of the LORD, and ᵗwalked in the way of his father, and in the way of his mother, and in the way of Jeroboam the son of Nebat, who made Israel to sin:

53 For ᵘhe served Baal, and worshipped him, and provoked to anger the LORD God of Israel, according to all that his father had done.

ᑫChap. ix. 26——ʳ2 Chron. xxi. 1——ˢVer. 40

ᵗChap. xv. 26——ᵘJudg. ii. 11; chap. xvi. 31

---

cerning these places, and the voyage thither, see the notes on chap. ix. 26-28, and x. 11, 22. Some translate, instead of ships of *Tharshish*, ships of *burden*. See *Houbigant*, who expresses himself doubtful as to the meaning of the word.

Verse 49. *But Jehoshaphat would not.*] It appears from the above cited place in Chronicles that Jehoshaphat did join in making and sending ships to Tharshish, and it is possible that what is here said is spoken of a *second* expedition, in which Jehoshaphat *would not* join Ahaziah. But instead of ולא אבה *velo abah*, "he would not," perhaps we should read ולו אבה *velo abah*, "he consented to him;" two words pronounced exactly in the same way, and differing but in *one letter*, viz., an א *aleph* for a ו *vau*. This reading, however, is not supported by any MS. or version; but the emendation seems just; for there are several places in these historical books in which there are mistakes of transcribers which nothing but violent criticism can restore, and to this it is dangerous to re-

sort, but in cases of the last necessity. Critics have recommended the 48th and 49th verses to be read thus: "Jehoshaphat had built ships of burden at Ezion-geber, to go to Ophir for gold. 49. And Ahaziah, the son of Ahab, had said to Jehoshaphat, Let my servants, I pray thee, go with thy servants in the ships: to which Jehoshaphat consented. But the ships went not thither; for the ships were broken at Ezion-geber." This is *Houbigant's* translation, who contends that "the words of the 48th verse, *but they went not*, should be placed at the end of the 49th verse, for who can believe that the sacred writer should first relate that *the ships were broken*, and then that Ahaziah requested of Jehoshaphat that his servants might embark with the servants of Jehoshaphat?" This bold critic, who understood the Hebrew language better than any man in Europe, has, by happy conjectures, since verified by the testimony of MSS., removed the blots of many careless transcribers from the sacred volume.

THE
SECOND BOOK OF THE KINGS,

OTHERWISE CALLED

THE FOURTH BOOK OF THE KINGS

Year from the Creation, according to the English Bible, 3108.—Year before the birth of Christ, 892.—Year before the vulgar era of Christ's nativity, 896.—Year since the Deluge, according to Archbishop Usher and the English Bible, 1452.—Year of the Cali Yuga, or Indian era of the Deluge, 2206. Chronologers vary very considerably in their calculations of the time which elapsed between the flood and the birth of Abraham, the difference of the two extremes amounting to *nine hundred* years! Archbishop Usher's computation is from the common Hebrew text, with the single exception of fixing the birth of Abraham in the *one hundred and thirtieth* year of the life of his father, instead of the *seventieth*, in order to reconcile *Gen.* xi. 26, 32, with *Acts* vii. 4. But these passages are better reconciled, in the opinion of Dr. *Kennicott*, by stating (with the Samaritan Pentateuch) the whole life of Terah to have been *one hundred and forty-five* years, instead of *two hundred and five*, as in our common Bibles.—Year from the destruction of Troy, according to Dionysius of Halicarnassus, 289.—Year from the foundation of Solomon's temple, 115.—Year since the division of Solomon's monarchy into the kingdoms of Israel and Judah, 79.—Year before the era of Iphitus, who re-established the Olympic Games, *three hundred and thirty-eight* years after their institution by Hercules, or about *eight hundred and eighty-four* years before the commencement of the Christian era, 12.—Year before the conquest of Corœbus at Elis, usually styled the first Olympiad, (being the 28th Olympiad after their re-establishment by Iphitus,) 120.—Year before the Varronian or generally received era of the building of Rome, 143.—Year before the building of Rome, according to Cato and the Fasti Consulares, 144.—Year before the building of Rome, according to Polybius the historian, 145.—Year before the building of Rome, according to Fabius Pictor, who lived about *two hundred and twenty-five* years before the Christian era, 149.—Year before the commencement of the Nabonassarean era, 149. The years of this epoch contained uniformly 365 days, so that 1461 Nabonassarean were equal to 1460 Julian years. This era commenced on the fourth of the calends of March, (Feb. 26,) B. C. 747; which was the year in which Romulus laid the foundation of Rome, according to Fabius Pictor.—Year of the Julian Period, 3818.—Year of the Dionysian Period, 94.—Cycle of the Sun, 10.—Cycle of the Moon, 18.—Year of Megacles, the sixth perpetual archon of the Athenians, 26.—Ocrazeres, the immediate predecessor of Sardanapalus, was king over the Assyrians about this time, according to Strauchius: but when this king reigned is very uncertain, Scaliger fixing the fall of Sardanapalus, which ended the Assyrian empire, in the year of the Julian Period, 3841; Langius, in 3852 of the same epocha; and Eusebius, in the year before Christ, 820.—Year of Agrippa Silvius, the eleventh king of the Latins, 20.—Year of Jehoshaphat, king of Judah, 18.—Year of Ahaziah, king of Israel, 2.—Last year of the Prophet Elijah.—Tenth year of Elisha.

CHAPTER I

Ahaziah, being hurt by a fall, sends messengers to Baal-zebub to inquire whether he shall recover, 1, 2. They are met by Elijah, who sends them back with the information that he shall surely die, 3–8. The king sends a captain and fifty men, to bring Elijah to Samaria, on which fire comes down from heaven, and destroys both him and his men, 9, 10. Another captain and fifty men are sent, who are likewise destroyed, 11, 12. A third is sent, who behaves himself humbly, and Elijah is commanded to accompany him; he obeys, comes to the king, reproves his idolatry, and announces his death, 13–16. Ahaziah dies and Jehoram reigns in his stead, 17, 18.

A. M. 3108
B. C. 896
Ante I. Ol. 120
An. Megaclis,
Arch. Athen.
perpet. 26

THEN Moab [a]rebelled against Israel [b]after the death of Ahab.

2 And Ahaziah fell down through a lattice in his upper chamber that *was* in Samaria, and was sick: and he sent messengers, and said unto them, Go,

A. M. 3108
B. C. 896
Ante I. Ol. 120
An. Megaclis,
Arch. Athen.
perpet. 26

---

[a] 2 Sam. viii. 2

[b] Chap. iii. 5

In the *preface* to the First Book of Kings, I have spoken at large concerning both these books, the author, time of writing, &c., &c., to which I must refer my readers, as that preface is *common* to both.

The Second Book of Kings contains the his-

A. M. 3108
B. C. 896
Ante I. Ol. 120
An. Megaclis,
Arch. Athen.
perpet. 26

inquire of Baal-zebub the god of °Ekron whether I shall recover of this disease.

3 But the angel of the LORD said to Elijah the Tishbite, Arise, go up to meet the messengers of the king of Samaria, and say unto them, *Is it* not because *there is* not a God in Israel, *that* ye go to inquire of Baal-zebub the god of Ekron?

4 Now therefore thus saith the LORD, ᵈThou shalt not come down from that bed on which thou art gone up, but shalt surely die. And Elijah departed.

5 And when the messengers turned back unto him, he said unto them, Why are ye now turned back?

6 And they said unto him, There came a

man up to meet us, and said unto us, Go, turn again unto the king that sent you, and say unto him, Thus saith the LORD, *Is it* not because *there is* not a God in Israel, *that* thou sendest to inquire of Baal-zebub the god of Ekron? therefore thou shalt not come down from that bed on which thou art gone up, but shalt surely die.

A. M. 3108
B. C. 896
Ante I. Ol. 120
An. Megaclis,
Arch. Athen.
perpet. 26

7 And he said unto them, °What manner of man *was he* which came up to meet you, and told you these words?

8 And they answered him, *He was* ᶠa hairy man, and girt with a girdle of leather about his loins. And he said, It *is* Elijah the Tishbite.

9 Then the king sent unto him a captain of

°1 Sam. v. 10——ᵈHeb. *The bed whither thou art gone up, thou shalt not come down from it*

°Heb. *What was the manner of the man?*——ᶠSee Zech. xiii. 4; Matt. iii. 4

---

tory of *three hundred and eight* years, from the rebellion of Moab, A. M. 3108, to the ruin of the kingdom of Judah, A. M. 3416.

The history, on the whole, exhibits little less than a series of crimes, disasters, Divine benefits, and Divine judgments. In the *kingdom of Judah* we meet with a few kings who feared God, and promoted the interests of pure religion in the land; but the major part were idolaters and profligates of the highest order.

The *kingdom of Israel* was still more corrupt: all its kings were determined idolaters; profligate, vicious, and cruel tyrants. *Elijah* and *Elisha* stood up in the behalf of God and truth in this fallen, idolatrous kingdom, and bore a strong testimony against the corruptions of the princes, and the profligacy of the people: their powerful ministry was confined to the *ten tribes;* Judah had its own prophets, and those in considerable number.

At length the avenging hand of God fell first upon *Israel*, and afterwards upon *Judah*. Israel, after many convulsions, torn by domestic and foreign wars, was at length wholly subjugated by the king of Assyria, the people led away into captivity, and the land repeopled by strangers, A. M. 3287.

The kingdom of Judah continued some time longer, but was at last overthrown by Nebuchadnezzar; Zedekiah, its last king, was taken prisoner; his eyes put out; and the principal part of the people were carried into captivity, which lasted about *seventy* years. The captivity began under Jehoiakim, A. M. 3402, and ended under Belshazzar, A. M. 2470 or 3472. There was after this a partial restoration of the Jews, but they never more rose to any consequence among the nations; and at last their civil polity was finally dissolved by the Romans, and their temple burnt, A. D. 70; and from that time until now they became fugitives and vagabonds over the face of the earth, universally detested by mankind. But should they not be loved for their fathers' *sake?* Are they not men and brothers? Will persecution and contempt

convert them to *Christianity*, or to any thing that is good?

NOTES ON CHAP. I

Verse 1. *Moab rebelled*] The Moabites had been subdued by David, and laid under tribute, chap. iii. 4, and 2 Sam. viii. 2. After the division of the two kingdoms, the Moabites fell *partly* under the dominion of Israel, and partly under that of Judah, until the death of Ahab, when they arose and shook off this yoke. Jehoram confederated with the king of Judah and the king of Edom, in order to reduce them. See this war, chap. iii. 5.

Verse 2. *Fell down through a lattice*] Perhaps either through the flat roof of his house, or over or through the balustrades with which the roof was surrounded.

Go, inquire of Baal-zebub] Literally, the *fly-god*, or *master of flies*. The *Septuagint* has βααλ μυιαν, Baal the fly. He was the tutelary god of Ekron, and probably was used at first as a kind of *telesm*, to *drive away flies*. He became afterwards a very respectable devil, and was supposed to have great power and influence. In the New Testament Beelzebub is a common name for Satan himself, or the prince of devils. See my notes on Matt. x. 25.

Verse 4. *But shalt surely die.*] The true God tells you this; he in whose hands are both life and death, who can kill and make alive. Baalzebub can do nothing; God has determined that your master shall die.

Verse 8. He was *a hairy man*] That is, he wore a *rough garment*, either made of camels' hair, as his successor John Baptist's was; or he wore a skin *dressed with the hair on*. Some think that the meaning is, he had very *long hair* and a *long beard*. The ancient prophets all wore rough garments, or upper coats made of the *skins of beasts: They wandered about in sheep-skins and goat-skins*, says the apostle, Heb. xi. 37.

Verse 9. *A captain of fifty with his fifty.*] It is impossible that such a man as Ahaziah, in

A. M. 3108
B. C. 896
Ante I. Ol. 120
An. Megaclis,
Arch. Athen.
perpet. 26

fifty with his fifty. And he went up to him: and, behold, he sat on the top of a hill. And he spake unto him, Thou man of God, the king hath said, Come down.

10 And Elijah answered and said to the captain of fifty, If I *be* a man of God, then ᵍlet fire come down from heaven, and consume thee and thy fifty. And there came down fire from heaven, and consumed him and his fifty.

11 Again also he sent unto him another captain of fifty with his fifty. And he answered and said unto him, O man of God, thus hath the king said, Come down quickly.

12 And Elijah answered and said unto them, If I *be* a man of God, let fire come down from heaven, and consume thee and thy fifty. And the fire of God came down from heaven, and consumed him and his fifty.

13 And he sent again a captain of the third fifty with his fifty. And the third captain of fifty went up, and came and ʰfell on his knees before Elijah, and besought him, and said unto him, O man of God, I pray thee, let my life, and the life of these fifty thy servants, ⁱbe precious in thy sight.

14 Behold, there came fire down from heaven, and burnt up the two captains of the former fifties with their fifties:

A. M. 3108
B. C. 896
Ante I. Ol. 120
An. Megaclis,
Arch. Athen.
perpet. 26

therefore let my life now be precious in thy sight.

15 And the angel of the LORD said unto Elijah, Go down with him: be not afraid of him. And he arose, and went down with him unto the king.

16 And he said unto him, Thus saith the LORD, Forasmuch as thou hast sent messengers to inquire of Baal-zebub the god of Ekron, *is it* not because *there is* no God in Israel to inquire of his word? therefore thou shalt not come down off that bed on which thou art gone up, but shalt surely die.

17 So he died according to the word of the LORD which Elijah had spoken. And ᵏJehoram reigned in his stead, in the second year of Jehoram the son of Jehoshaphat king of Judah; because he had no son.

18 Now the rest of the acts of Ahaziah which he did, *are* they not written in the book of the chronicles of the kings of Israel?

A.M.3107-3108
B. C. 897-896
Anno ante I.
Olymp.121-120

ᵍLuke ix. 54──ʰHebrew, *bowed*──ⁱ1 Sam. xxvi. 21; Psa. lxxii. 14

ᵏThe second year that *Jehoram* was *Prorex*, and the eighteenth of *Jehoshaphat;* chap. iii. 1

---

such circumstances, could have had any *friendly* designs in sending a *captain and fifty soldiers* for the prophet; and the *manner* in which they are treated shows plainly that they went with a *hostile* intent.

And he spake unto him, Thou man of God] Thou prophet of the Most High.

Verse 10. *And there came down fire*] Some have blamed the prophet for destroying these men, by bringing down fire from heaven upon them. But they do not consider that it was no more possible for *Elijah* to bring down fire from heaven, than for *them* to do it. God alone could send the fire; and as he is *just* and *good,* he would not have destroyed these men had there not been a *sufficient cause* to justify the act. It was not to *please Elijah,* or to *gratify any vindictive humour* in him, that God thus acted; but to show his own *power* and *justice.* No entreaty of Elijah could have induced God to have performed an act that was *wrong* in itself. Elijah, personally, had no concern in the business. God led him simply to *announce* on these occasions what he himself had determined *to do. If I be a man of God,* i. e., as surely as I am a man of God, *fire* SHALL *come down from heaven,* and SHALL *consume thee and thy fifty.* This is the literal meaning of the original; and by it we see that Elijah's words were only *declarative,* and not *imprecatory.*

Verse 15. *And the angel of the Lord said— Go down with him*] This is an additional proof

that Elijah was then acting under *particular inspirations:* he had neither *will* nor *design* of his own. He waited to know the counsel, declare the will, and obey the command, of his God.

And he arose, and went down] He did not even regard his personal safety or his life; he goes without the least hesitation to the king, though he had reason to suppose he would be doubly irritated by his prediction, and the death of *one hundred* of his men. But with all these consequences *he* had nothing to do; he was the ambassador of the King eternal, and his honour and life were in the hands of his Master.

Verse 17. *And Jehoram reigned in his stead*] The *Vulgate, Septuagint,* and *Syriac* say, *Jehoram* HIS BROTHER *reigned in his stead, in the second year of Jehoram.* There were two *Jehorams* who were contemporary: the first, the son of *Ahab,* brother to Ahaziah, and his successor in the kingdom of Israel; the second, the *son of Jehoshaphat,* king of Judah, who succeeded his father in Judah. But there is a difficulty here: "How is it that Jehoram the brother of Ahaziah *began to reign in the second year of Jehoram son of Jehoshaphat,* seeing that, according to chap. iii. 1, he *began his reign in the eighteenth year of the reign of Jehoshaphat;* and, according to chap. viii. 16, *Jehoram son of Jehoshaphat began to reign in the fifth year of Jehoram king of Israel?*" *Calmet* and others answer thus: "Jehoram king of Israel began to reign in the eighteenth year of Jehoshaphat king of Judah, which was the second year after this same Jehoshaphat had given the *viceroyalty* to his son Jehoram; and afterwards Jehoshaphat communicated the royalty to Jehoram his successor, *two years before his death*, and *the fifth year of Jehoram*, king of Israel." Dr. *Lightfoot* takes another method:—"Observe," says he, "these texts, 1 Kings xxii. 51: *Ahaziah the son of Ahab began to reign over Israel in Samaria the seventeenth year of Jehoshaphat king of Judah, and reigned two years;* and 2 Kings i. 17: *And Ahaziah died according to the word of the Lord which Elijah had spoken, and Jehoram reigned in his stead, in the second year of Jehoram son of Jehoshaphat king of Judah;* and 2 Kings iii. 1: *Now Jehoram the son of Ahab began to reign over Israel in Samaria the eighteenth year of Jehoshaphat king of Judah.* By these scriptures it is most plain, that both Jehoram the son of Jehoshaphat, and Ahaziah the son of Ahab, began to reign in the seventeenth of Jehoshaphat; for who sees not in these texts that

Jehoshaphat's eighteenth, when Jehoram the son of Ahab began to reign, is called *the second year of Jehoram the son of Jehoshaphat?* Now Jehoshaphat's reign was not yet expired by *eight* or *nine years*, for this was in his *seventeenth year*, and he reigned *twenty-five years*, 1 Kings xxii. 42; nor was Ahab's reign expired by *two* or *three years*, for this was in his *twentieth year*, and he reigned *twenty-two years*, 1 Kings xvi. 29. But the reason why both their sons came thus into their thrones in their lifetime, and both in the *same year*, was because their fathers, Jehoshaphat and Ahab, were both engaged in the war against the *Syrians* about Ramoth-gilead: and while they were providing for it, and carrying it on, they made their sons viceroys, and set them to reign in their stead, while they were absent or employed upon that expedition." This is very probable, and seems well supported by the above texts, and would solve all the difficulties with which many have been puzzled and not a few stumbled, had we sufficient evidence for the viceroyalty here mentioned.

CHAPTER II

Elijah, about to be taken up to heaven, goes in company with Elisha from Gilgal to Beth-el, 1, 2. *Thence to Jericho,* 3–5. *And thence to Jordan,* 6, 7. *Elijah smites the waters with his mantle; they divide, and he and Elisha pass over on dry ground,* 8. *Elijah desires Elisha to ask what he should do for him; who requests a double portion of his spirit, which is promised on a certain condition,* 9, 10. *A chariot and horses of fire descend; and Elijah mounts, and ascends by a whirlwind to heaven,* 11. *Elisha gets his mantle, comes back to Jordan, smites the waters with it, and they divide, and he goes over,* 12–14. *The sons of the prophets see that the spirit of Elijah rests on Elisha,* 15. *They propose to send* fifty *men to seek Elijah, supposing the Spirit of the Lord might have cast him on some mountain or valley; after three days' search, they return, not having found him,* 16–18. *The people of Jericho apply to Elisha to heal their unwholesome water,* 19. *He casts salt into the spring in the name of Jehovah, and the water becomes wholesome,* 20–22. *Forty-two young persons of Beth-el, mocking him, are slain by two she-bears,* 23, 24. *He goes to Carmel, and returns to Samaria,* 25.

A. M. 3108
B. C. 896
Ante I. Ol. 120
An. Megaclis,
Arch. Athen.
perpet. 26

AND it came to pass, when the LORD would [a]take up Elijah into heaven by a whirlwind, that Elijah went with [b]Elisha from Gilgal.

2 And Elijah said unto Elisha, [c]Tarry here, I pray thee; for the LORD hath sent me to Beth-el. And Elisha said *unto him, As* the LORD liveth, and [d]*as* thy soul liveth, I will not leave thee. So they went down to Beth-el.

3 And [e]the sons of the prophets that *were* at Beth-el came forth to Elisha, and said unto him, Knowest thou that the LORD will take away thy master from thy head to-day? And

he said, Yea, I know *it;* hold ye your peace.

A. M. 3108
B. C. 896
Ante I. Ol. 120
An. Megaclis,
Arch. Athen.
perpet. 26

4 And Elijah said unto him, Elisha, tarry here, I pray thee; for the LORD hath sent me to Jericho. And he said, *As* the LORD liveth, and *as* thy soul liveth, I will not leave thee. So they came to Jericho.

5 And the sons of the prophets that *were* at Jericho came to Elisha, and said unto him, Knowest thou that the LORD will take away thy master from thy head to-day? And he answered, Yea, I know *it;* hold ye your peace.

6 And Elijah said unto him, Tarry, I pray

---

[a]Gen. v. 24——[b]1 Kings xix. 21——[c]See Ruth ii. 15, 16
[d]1 Sam. i. 26; ver. 4, 6; chap. iv. 30

[e]1 Kings xx. 35; verse 5, 7, 15; chapter iv. 1, 38; ix. 1

NOTES ON CHAP. II

Verse 1. *When the Lord would take up Elijah*] It appears that God had revealed this intended translation, not only to Elijah himself, but also to Elisha, and to the schools of the prophets, both at Beth-el and Jericho, so that they were all expecting this solemn event.

Verse 2. *Tarry here, I pray thee*] He either made these requests through *humility*, not wishing any person to be witness of the honour conferred on him by God, or with the desire to prove the fidelity of Elisha, whether he would continue to follow and serve him.

Verse 3. *Knowest thou that the Lord*] Thus we see that it was a matter well known to all

A. M. 3108
B. C. 896
Ante I. Ol. 120
An. Megaclis,
Arch. Athen.
perpet. 26

thee, here; for the LORD hath sent me to Jordan. And he said, *As* the LORD liveth, and *as* thy soul liveth, I will not leave thee. And they two went on.

7 And fifty men of the sons of the prophets went, and stood *[f]*to view afar off: and they two stood by Jordan.

8 And Elijah took his mantle, and wrapped *it* together, and smote the waters, and *[g]*they were divided hither and thither, so that they two went over on dry ground.

9 And it came to pass, when they were gone over, that Elijah said unto Elisha, Ask what

I shall do for thee, before I be taken away from thee. And Elisha said, I pray thee, let a double portion of thy spirit be upon me.

A. M. 3108
B. C. 896
Ante I. Ol. 120
An. Megaclis,
Arch. Athen.
perpet. 26

10 And he said, *[h]*Thou hast asked a hard thing: *nevertheless,* if thou see me *when I am* taken from thee, it shall be so unto thee; but if not, it shall not be *so.*

11 And it came to pass, as they still went on, and talked, that, behold, *there appeared* *[i]*a chariot of fire, and horses of fire, and parted them both asunder; and *[k]*Elijah went up by a whirlwind into heaven.

*[f]*Heb. *in sight* or *over against*——*[g]*So Exod. xiv. 21; Josh. iii. 16; ver. 14

*[h]*Heb. *thou hast done hard in asking*——*[i]*Chap. vi. 7, Psa. civ. 4——*[k]*Ecclus. xlviii. 9; 1 Mac. ii. 58

the sons of the prophets. This day the Lord will take thy master and instructer from thee.

Verse 7. *Fifty men of the sons of the prophets*] They fully expected this extraordinary event, and they could have known it only from Elijah himself, or by a direct revelation from God.

Verse 8. *Took his mantle*] Την μηλωτην αυτου, *his sheep-skin,* says the *Septuagint.* The skins of beasts, dressed with the hair on, were formerly worn by *prophets* and *priests* as the simple insignia of their office. As the *civil authority* was often lodged in the hands of such persons, particularly among the Jews, *mantles* of this kind were used by *kings* and *high civil officers* when they bore no sacred character. The custom continues to the present day; a *lamb's skin hood* or *cloak* is the badge which certain graduates in our universities wear; and the royal robes of kings and great officers of state are adorned with the *skins* of the animal called the *ermine.*

They were divided hither and thither] This was a most astonishing miracle, and could be performed only by the almighty power of God.

Verse 9. *A double portion of thy spirit be upon me.*] This in reference to the law, Deut. xxi. 17: *He shall acknowledge the first-born, by giving him a* DOUBLE PORTION *of all that he hath* —*the right of the first-born is his.* Elisha considered himself the only child or first-born of Elijah, as the disciples of eminent teachers were called their children; so here he claims a double portion of his spiritual influence, any other disciples coming in for a *single share* only. *Sons of the prophets* means no more than the *disciples* or *scholars* of the prophets. The original words פי שנים *pi shenayim,* mean rather *two parts,* than *double the quantity.*

Verse 10. *A hard thing*] This is what is not in *my* power, God alone can give this; yet *if thou see me taken away from thee, it shall be so.* Perhaps this means no more than, "If thou continue with me till I am translated, God will grant this to thee;" for on the mere *seeing* or *not seeing* him in the moment in which he was taken away, this Divine gift could not depend.

Verse 11. *A chariot of fire, and horses of fire*] That is a chariot and horses of the most *resplendent glory,* which, manifesting itself in *coruscations* or *shooting rays,* seemed to be like

blazing *fire,* or like the sun in his strength. Some think that this circumstance, known in the heathen world, gave rise to the fable of *Apollo,* or the *sun,* being seated in a *blazing chariot,* drawn by *horses which breathed and snorted fire.* These horses were *four,* and called Pyroeis, Eous, Æthon, and Phlegon; all which words signify *fire* or *resplendent light.* So OVID:—

Nec tibi quadrupedes animosos *ignibus* illis
Quos *in pectore* habent, quos *ore* et *naribus*
    efflant,
In promptu regere est: vix me patiuntur, ut acres
Incaluere animi; cervixque repugnat habenis.
                    OVID, Met. lib. ii., 84.

Interea volucres *Pyroeis, Eous,* et *Æthon,*
Solis equi, quartusque *Phlegon,* hinnitibus auras
Flammiferis implent, pedibusque repagula pul-
    sant   *Ib.* 153.

Meanwhile the restless horses neighed aloud,
Breathing out fire and pawing where they stood.
Nor would you find it easy to compose
The mettled steeds, when from their *nostrils*
    flows
The *scorching fire,* that in their *entrails glows.*
Even I their headstrong fury scarce restrain,
When they grow warm, and restiff to the rein.
                                     DRYDEN.

Perhaps the whole of this fable, which represents Phaethon son of Apollo *requesting to drive the chariot of his father (the horses and chariot of fire)* for one day, was borrowed from the *request of Elisha* to his spiritual father Elijah, whom he afterwards saw borne away *by a whirlwind,* in a *chariot of fire* drawn by *fiery steeds.*

Verse 11. *Elijah went up—into heaven*] He was truly *translated;* and the words here leave us no room to indulge the conjecture of Dr. Priestley, who supposes that as "*Enoch,* (probably *Moses,*) *Elijah,* and *Christ,* had no relation to any other world or planet, they are no doubt in this;" for we are told that Elijah *went up into heaven;* and we know, from the sure testimony of the Scripture, that our blessed Lord is at the right hand of the Majesty on high, ever living to make intercession for us.

A. M. 3108
B. C. 896
Ante I. Ol. 120
An. Megaclis,
Arch. Athen.
perpet. 26

12 And Elisha saw *it,* and he cried, [1]My father, my father, the chariot of Israel and the horsemen thereof. And he saw him no more: and he took hold of his own clothes, and rent them in two pieces.

13 He took up also the mantle of Elijah that fell from him, and went back, and stood by the [m]bank of Jordan:

14 And he took the mantle of Elijah that fell from him, and smote the waters, and said, Where *is* the LORD God of Elijah? And when he also had smitten the waters, [n]they parted hither and thither: and Elisha went over.

15 And when the sons of the prophets which *were* [o]to view at Jericho saw him, they said, The spirit of Elijah doth rest on Elisha. And they came to meet him, and bowed themselves to the ground before him.

16 And they said unto him, Behold now,

there be with thy servants fifty [p]strong men; let them go, we pray thee, and seek thy master: [q]lest peradventure the Spirit of the LORD hath taken him up, and cast him upon [r]some mountain, or into some valley. And he said, Ye shall not send.

A. M. 3108
B. C. 896
Ante I. Ol. 120
An. Megaclis,
Arch. Athen.
perpet. 26

17 And when they urged him till he was ashamed, he said, Send. They sent therefore fifty men; and they sought three days, but found him not.

18 And when they came again to him, (for he tarried at Jericho,) he said unto them, Did I not say unto you, Go not?

19 And the men of the city said unto Elisha, Behold, I pray thee, the situation of this city *is* pleasant, as my lord seeth: but the water *is* naught, and the ground [s]barren.

20 And he said, Bring me a new cruse, and put salt therein. And they brought *it* to him.

21 And he went forth unto the spring of the

---

[1]Chap. xiii. 14——[m]Heb. *lip*——[n]Ver. 8——[o]Ver. 7
[p]Heb. *sons of strength*——[q]See 1 Kings xviii. 12; Ezek.

viii. 3; Bel and Dragon 36; Acts viii. 39——[r]Heb. *one of the mountains*——[s]Heb. *causing to miscarry*

Verse 12. *The chariot of Israel and the horsemen thereof.*] The Chaldee translates these words thus: 'My master, my master! who, by thy intercession, wast of more use to Israel than horses and chariots." This is probably the *sense.*

In the Book of *Ecclesiasticus,* chap. xlviii. 1, &c., the *fiery horses* and *chariot* are considered as an *emblem* of that *burning zeal* which Elijah manifested in the whole of his ministry: "Then stood up Elijah the prophet *as fire,* and his word *burned as a lamp,*" &c.

And rent them in two pieces.] As a sign of *sorrow* for having lost so good and glorious a master.

Verse 13. *He took—the mantle*] The same with which he had been called by Elijah to the prophetic office, and the same by which Elijah divided Jordan. His having the *mantle* was a proof that he was *invested* with the authority and influence of his master.

Verse 14. *Where is the Lord God of Elijah?*] The Vulgate gives a strange turn to this verse: *Et percussit aquas,* et non sunt divisæ; *et dixu, Ubi est Deus Eliæ etiam nunc? Percussitque aquas, et divisæ sunt huc et illuc.* "And he smote the waters, *but they did not divide;* and he said, Where is the God of Elijah even now? And he struck the waters and they were divided hither and thither." The act of striking the waters seems to be twice repeated in the verse, though *we* get rid of the *second striking* by rendering the second clause, *when he also had smitten the* waters: which has the same Hebrew words as the first, and which we translate, *he smote the waters.* The Vulgate supposes he smote *once in vain,* perhaps confiding too much in his own strength; and then, having invoked the God of Elijah, he *succeeded.* This distinction is not followed by any of the other versions; nor is the clause, *et non sunt divisæ,*

"and they divided not," expressed by the *Hebrew* text.

Verse 15. *The spirit of Elijah doth rest on Elisha.*] This was a natural conclusion, from seeing him with the *mantle,* and working the same miracle. This disposed them to yield the same obedience to him they had done to his master: and in token of this, *they went out to meet him, and bowed themselves to the ground before him.*

Verse 16. *Fifty strong men*] Probably the *same fifty* who are mentioned ver. 7, and who saw Elijah taken up in the whirlwind.

Cast him upon some mountain] Though they saw him *taken up towards heaven,* yet they thought it possible that the Spirit of the Lord might have *descended* with him, and left him on some remote mountain or valley.

Ye shall not send.] He knew that he was translated to heaven, and that therefore it would be useless.

Verse 17. *Till he was ashamed*] He saw they would not be satisfied unless they made the proposed search; he felt therefore that he could not, with any good grace, resist their importunity any longer.

Verse 19. *The water* is *naught, and the ground barren.*] The barrenness of the ground was the effect of the badness of the water.

Verse 21. *And cast the salt in there*] He cast in the salt at the place where the waters sprang out of the earth. *Jarchi* well observes here, "Salt is a thing which corrupts water; therefore, it is evident that this was a true miracle." What Elisha did on this occasion, getting the new cruse and throwing in the salt, was only to make the miracle more conspicuous. If the salt could have had any *natural* tendency to render the water salubrious, it could have acted only for a *short time,* and only on that

A. M. 3108
B. C. 896
Ante I. Ol. 120
An. Megaclis,
Arch. Athen.
perpet. 26
waters, and ᵗcast the salt in there, and said, Thus saith the LORD, I have healed these waters; there shall not be from thence any more death or barren *land.*

22 So the waters were healed unto this day, according to the saying of Elisha which he spake.

23 And he went up from thence unto Bethel: and as he was going up by the way, there came forth little children out of the city, ᵘand

mocked him, and said unto him, Go up, thou bald head; go up, thou bald head.

A. M. 3108
B. C. 896
Ante I. Ol. 120
An. Megaclis,
Arch. Athen.
perpet. 26

24 And he turned back, and looked on them, and cursed them in the name of the LORD. And there came forth ᵛtwo she-bears out of the wood, and tare forty and two children of them.

25 And he went from thence to Mount Carmel, and from thence he returned to Samaria.

ᵗSee Exod. xv. 25; ch. iv. 41; vi. 6; John ix. 6——ᵘProv.

xx. 11; xxii. 6, 15——ᵛProv. xvii. 12; Lam. iii. 10

---

portion of the *stream* which now arose from the spring; and in a few moments its effects must have disappeared. But the miracle here was *permanent:* the death of men and cattle, which had been occasioned by the insalubrity of the waters, ceased; the land was no longer barren; and the waters became permanently fit for all agricultural and domestic uses.

Verse 23. *There came forth little children out of the city*] These were probably the school of some celebrated teacher; but under his instruction they had learned neither piety nor good manners.

Go up, thou bald head; go up, thou bald head.] עלה קרח עלה קרח *aleh kereach, aleh kereach.* Does not this imply the grossest insult? *Ascend, thou empty skull, to heaven,* as it is pretended thy master did! This was blasphemy against God; and their punishment (for they were Beth-elite idolaters) was only proportioned to their guilt. Elisha *cursed them,* i. e., pronounced a curse upon them, *in the name of the Lord,* בשם יהוה *beshem Yehovah, by the name* or *authority of Jehovah.* The spirit of their offence lies in their *ridiculing a miracle* of the Lord: the offence was against *Him,* and *He* punished it. It was no petulant humour of the prophet that caused him to pronounce this curse; it was God alone: had it proceeded from a wrong disposition of the prophet, no miracle would have been wrought in order to gratify it.

"But was it not a cruel thing to destroy *forty-two little children,* who, in mere childishness, had simply called the prophet *bare skull,* or *bald head?*" I answer, *Elisha* did not destroy them; he had no power by which he could bring two she-bears out of the wood to destroy them. It was evidently either accidental, or a Divine judgment; and if a judgment, God must be the sole author of it. Elisha's *curse* must be only *declaratory* of what God was about to do. See on chap. i. 10. "But then, as they were *little children,* they could scarcely be accountable for their conduct; and consequently, it was cruelty to destroy them." If it was a judgment of God, it could neither be *cruel* nor *unjust;* and I contend, that the prophet had no power by which

he could bring these she-bears to fall upon them. But were they *little children?* for *here* the strength of the objection lies. Now I suppose the objection means *children* from *four* to *seven* or *eight* years old; for so we use the word: but the original, נערים קטנים *nearim ketannim,* may mean *young men,* for קטן *katon* signifies to be *young,* in opposition to *old,* and is so translated in various places in our Bible; and נער *naar* signifies, not only a *child,* but a *young man,* a *servant,* or even a *soldier,* or one fit to go out to battle; and is so translated in a multitude of places in our common English version. I shall mention but a few, because they are sufficiently decisive: Isaac was called נער *naar* when *twenty-eight* years old, Gen. xxi. 5-12; and Joseph was so called when he was *thirty-nine,* Gen. xli. 12. Add to these 1 Kings xx. 14: "And Ahab said, By whom [shall the Assyrians be delivered into my hand?] And he said, Thus saith the Lord, by the YOUNG MEN, בנערי *benaarey, of the princes of the provinces.*" That these were *soldiers,* probably *militia,* or a selection from the militia, which served as a *bodyguard* to Ahab, the event sufficiently declares; and the persons that mocked Elisha were perfectly accountable for their conduct.

But is it not possible that these *forty-two* were a set of unlucky young men, who had been employed in the *wood,* destroying the *whelps* of these same *she-bears,* who now pursued them, and tore them to pieces, for the injury they had done? We have already heard of the ferocity of *a bear robbed of her whelps;* see at the end of 2 Sam. chap. xvii. The mention of SHE-*bears* gives some colour to the above conjecture; and, probably, at the time when these young fellows insulted the prophet, the bears might be tracing the footsteps of the murderers of their young, and thus came upon them in the midst of their insults, God's providence ordering these occurrences so as to make this natural effect appear as a Divine cause. If the conjecture be correct, the bears were prepared by their loss to execute the curse of the prophet, and God's justice guided them to the spot to punish the iniquity that had been just committed.

CHAPTER III

The reign and idolatry of Jehoram, king of Israel, 1–3. Mesha, king of Moab, rebels against Israel, 4, 5. Jehoram, Jehoshaphat, and the king of Edom join against the Moabites, and are brought into great distress for want of water, 6–10. The three kings go to Elisha to inquire of the Lord; who promises them water, and a complete victory, 11–19. Water comes the next morning, and fills the trenches which these kings had made in the valley, 20. The Moabites arm against them; and suppose, when they see the sun shining upon the waters, which look like blood, that the confederate kings have fallen out, and slain each other; and that they have nothing to do but take the spoil, 21–23. The Israelites attack and completely rout them, beat down their cities, and mar their land, 24, 25. The king of Moab, having made an unsuccessful attack on the king of Edom, takes his eldest son, and offers him for a burnt-offering upon the wall; and there is great indignation against Israel, 26, 27.

A. M. 3108
B. C. 896
Ante I. Ol. 120
An. Megaclis,
Arch. Athen.
perpet. 26

NOW ᵃJehoram the son of Ahab began to reign over Israel in Samaria the eighteenth year of Jehoshaphat king of Judah, and reigned twelve years.

2 And he wrought evil in the sight of the LORD; but not like his father, and like his mother: for he put away the ᵇimage of Baal ᶜthat his father had made.

3 Nevertheless he cleaved unto ᵈthe sins of Jeroboam the son of Nebat, which made Israel to sin; he departed not therefrom.

4 And Mesha king of Moab was a sheepmaster, and rendered unto the king of Israel a hundred thousand ᵉlambs, and a hundred thousand rams, with the wool.

5 But it came to pass, when ᶠAhab was dead, that the king of Moab rebelled against the king of Israel.

A. M. 3109
B. C. 895
Ante I. Ol. 119
An. Megaclis,
Arch. Athen.
perpet. 27

6 And King Jehoram went out of Samaria the same time, and numbered all Israel.

7 And he went and sent to Jehoshaphat the king of Judah,

A. M. 3109
B. C. 895
Ante I. Ol. 119
An. Megaclis,
Arch. Athen.
perpet. 27

saying, The king of Moab hath rebelled against me: wilt thou go with me against Moab to battle? And he said, I will go up: ᵍI *am* as thou *art,* my people as thy people, *and* my horses as thy horses.

8 And he said, Which way shall we go up? And he answered, The way through the wilderness of Edom.

9 So the king of Israel went, and the king of Judah, and the king of Edom: and they fetched a compass of seven days' journey; and there was no water for the host, and for the cattle ʰthat followed them.

10 And the king of Israel said, Alas! that the LORD hath called these three kings together, to deliver them into the hand of Moab!

11 But ⁱJehoshaphat said, *Is there* not here a prophet of the LORD, that we may inquire of the LORD by him? And one of the king of Israel's servants answered and said, Here

---

ᵃCh. i. 17——ᵇHeb. *statue*——ᶜ1 Kings xvi. 31, 32
ᵈ1 Kings xii. 28, 31, 32——ᵉSee Isa. xvi. 1

ᶠChap. i. 1——ᵍ1 Kings xxii. 4——ʰHeb. *at their feet;*
see Exod. xi. 8——ⁱ1 Kings xxii. 7

NOTES ON CHAP. III

Verse 2. *He put away the image of Baal*] He abolished his worship; but he continued that of the *calves* at Dan and Beth-el.

Verse 4. *Was a sheepmaster*] The original Is נקד *naked,* of which the Septuagint could make nothing, and therefore retained the Hebrew word νωκηδ: but the Chaldee has מרי גיתי *marey githey,* "a sheepmaster;" *Aquila* has ποιμνιοτροφος; and *Symmachus,* τρεφων βοσκηματα; all to the same sense. The original signifies one who *marks* or *brands,* probably from the *marking* of sheep. He fed many sheep, &c., and had them *all marked* in a particular way, in order to ascertain his property.

A hundred thousand lambs] The *Chaldee* and *Arabic* have a *hundred thousand fat oxen.*

Verse 7. *My people as thy people*] We find that Jehoshaphat maintained the same friendly intercourse with the *son,* as he did with the *father.* See 1 Kings xxii. 4.

Verse 8. *Through the wilderness of Edom.*] Because he expected the king of Edom to join them, as we find he did; for, being tributary to Judah, he was obliged to do it.

Verse 9. *A compass of seven days' journey*] By taking a circuitous route, to go round the southern part of the Dead Sea, they probably intended to surprise the Moabites; but it appears their journey was ill planned, as they at last got into a country in which it was impossible to obtain *water,* and they were brought in consequence to the utmost extremity.

Verse 10. *The Lord hath called these three kings together*] That is, This is a Divine judgment; God has judicially blinded us, and permitted us to take this journey to our destruction.

Verse 11. *Is there not here a prophet of the Lord*] The kings of Judah still acknowledged the true God, and him only.

Poured water on the hands of Elijah] That is, was his constant and confidential *servant.*

A. M. 3109
B. C. 895
Ante I. Ol. 119
An. Megaclis,
Arch. Athen.
perpet. 27

is Elisha the son of Shaphat, which poured water on the hands of Elijah.

12 And Jehoshaphat said, The word of the LORD is with him. So the king of Israel and Jehoshaphat and the king of Edom ᵏwent down to him.

13 And Elisha said unto the king of Israel, ˡWhat have I to do with thee? ᵐget thee to ⁿthe prophets of thy father, and to the prophets of thy mother. And the king of Israel said unto him, Nay: for the LORD hath called these three kings together, to deliver them into the hand of Moab.

14 And Elisha said, ᵒ*As* the LORD of hosts liveth, before whom I stand, surely, were it not that I regard the presence of Jehoshaphat the king of Judah, I would not look toward thee, nor see thee.

15 But now bring me a ᵖminstrel. And it came to pass, when the minstrel played, that ᑫthe hand of the LORD came upon him.

A. M. 3109
B. C. 895
Ante I. Ol. 119
An. Megaclis,
Arch. Athen.
perpet. 27

16 And he said, Thus saith the LORD, ʳMake this valley full of ditches.

17 For thus saith the LORD, Ye shall not see wind, neither shall ye see rain; yet that valley shall be filled with water, that ye may drink, both ye, and your cattle, and your beasts.

18 And this is *but* a light thing in the sight of the LORD: he will deliver the Moabites also into your hand.

19 And ye shall smite every fenced city, and every choice city, and shall fell every good tree, and stop all wells of water, and ˢmar every good piece of land with stones.

ᵏCh. ii. 25——ˡEzek. xiv. 3——ᵐSo Judg. x. 14; Ruth i. 15——ⁿ1 Kings xviii. 19

ᵒ1 Kings xvii. 1; ch. v. 16——ᵖSee 1 Sam. x. 5——ᑫEzek i. 3; iii. 14, 22; viii. 1——ʳCh. iv. 3——ˢHeb. *grieve*

Verse 12. *The word of the Lord is with him.*] He has the gift of prophecy.

Verse 13. *Get thee to the prophets of thy father*] This was a just but cutting reproof.

Nay] The Chaldee adds here, *I beseech thee, do not call the sins of this impiety to remembrance, but ask mercy for us;* because the Lord hath called, &c. The Arabic has, *I beseech thee, do not mention of our transgressions, but use kindness towards us.* It is very likely that some such words were spoken on the occasion; but these are the only *versions* which make this addition.

Verse 14. *Were it not that I regard the presence of Jehoshaphat*] He worshipped the true God; Jehoram was an idolater.

Verse 15. *Bring me a minstrel.*] A person who played on the *harp.* The rabbins, and many Christians, suppose that Elisha's mind was considerably irritated and grieved by the bad behaviour of the young men at Beth-el, and their tragical end, and by the presence of the idolatrous king of Israel; and therefore called for Divine psalmody, that it might calm his spirits, and render him more susceptible of the prophetic influence. To be able to discern the voice of God, and the operation of his hand, it is necessary that the *mind be calm,* and the *passions all in harmony,* under the direction of *reason;* that reason may be under the influence of the Divine Spirit.

The hand of the Lord came upon him.] The playing of the harper had the desired effect; his mind was calmed, and the power of God descended upon him. This effect of music was generally acknowledged in every civilized nation. *Cicero,* in his Tusculan Questions, lib. iv., says, that "the Pythagoreans were accustomed to calm their minds, and soothe their passions, by singing and playing upon the harp." *Pythagoræi mentes suas a cogitationum intentione cantu fidibusque ad tranquillitatem traduce-*

bant. I have spoken elsewhere of the heathen priests who endeavoured to imitate the true prophets, and were as *actually filled with the devil* as the others were *with the true God.* The former were thrown into *violent agitations* and *contortions* by the influence of the demons which possessed them, while the *latter* were in a state of the utmost serenity and composure.

Verse 16. *Make this valley full of ditches.*] The word נחל *nachal* may be translated *brook,* as it is by the *Vulgate* and *Septuagint.* There probably was a *river* here, but it was now *dry;* and the prophet desires that they would enlarge the channel, and cut out various canals from it, and reservoirs, where water might be collected for the refreshment of the army and of the cattle; and these were to be made so wide, that the reflection of the sun's rays from this water might be the means of confounding and destroying the Moabites.

Verse 17. *Ye shall not see wind*] There shall be no *wind* to collect vapours, and there shall be no *showers,* and yet the *whole* bed of this river, and all the *new made canals,* shall be filled with water.

Verse 19. *Shall fell every good tree*] Every tree by which your enemies may serve themselves for fortifications, &c. But surely *fruit trees* are not intended here; for this was positively against the law of God, Deut. xx. 19, 20: "When thou shalt besiege a city—thou shalt not destroy the trees thereof—for the tree of the field is man's life—only the trees which thou knowest that they be not trees for meat, thou shalt destroy and cut them down."

Stop all wells of water] In those hot countries this would lead sooner than any thing else to reduce an enemy.

Mar every good piece of land with stones.] Such a multitude of men, each throwing a stone on a good field as they passed, would completely destroy it.

A. M. 3109
B. C. 895
Ante I. Ol. 119
An. Megaclis,
Arch. Athen.
perpet. 27

20 And it came to pass in the morning, when 'the meat-offering was offered, that, behold, there came water by the way of Edom, and the country was filled with water.

21 And when all the Moabites heard that the kings were come up to fight against them, they ᵘgathered all that were able to ᵛput on armour, and upward, and stood in the border.

22 And they rose up early in the morning, and the sun shone upon the water, and the Moabites saw the water on the other side *as* red as blood:

23 And they said, This *is* blood: the kings are surely ʷslain, and they have smitten one another: now, therefore, Moab, to the spoil.

24 And when they came to the camp of Israel, the Israelites rose up and smote the Moabites, so that they fled before them: but

ˣthey went forward smiting the Moabites, even in *their* country.

A. M. 3109
B. C. 895
Ante I. Ol. 119
An. Megaclis,
Arch. Athen.
perpet. 27

25 And they beat down the cities, and on every good piece of land cast every man his stone, and filled it; and they stopped all the wells of water, and felled all the good trees: ʸonly in ᶻKirharaseth left they the stones thereof; howbeit the slingers went about *it,* and smote it.

26 And when the king of Moab saw that the battle was too sore for him, he took with him seven hundred men that drew swords, to break through *even* unto the king of Edom: but they could not.

27 Then ᵃhe took his eldest son that should have reigned in his stead, and offered him *for* a burnt-offering upon the wall. And there was great indignation against Israel: ᵇand they departed from him, and returned to *their own* land.

ᵗExodus xxix. 39, 40——ᵘHebrew, *were cried together* ᵛHebrew, *gird himself with a girdle*——ʷHebrew, *destroyed*

ˣOr, *they smote in it even smiting*——ʸHeb. *until he left the stones thereof in Kir-haraseth*——ᶻIsa. xvi. 7, 11 ᵃAmos ii. 1——ᵇChap. viii. 20

Verse 20. *When the meat-offering was offered*] This was the first of all offerings, and was generally made at sun-rising.

There came water] This supply was altogether miraculous, for there was neither *wind* nor *rain,* nor any other natural means by which it could be supplied.

Verse 22. *Saw the water on the other side as red as blood*] This might have been an optical deception; I have seen the like sight when there was no reason to suspect supernatural agency. The Moabites had never seen that valley full of water, and therefore did not suspect that their eyes deceived them, but took it for the blood of the confederate hosts, who they thought might have fallen into confusion in the darkness of night and destroyed each other, as the Midianites had formerly done, Judges vii. 22; and the Philistines lately, 1 Sam. xiv. 20.

Verse 23. *Therefore, Moab, to the spoil.*] Thus they came on in a disorderly manner, and fell an easy prey to their enemies.

Verse 25. *On every good piece of land*] On all cultivated ground, and especially fields that were sown.

Only in Kir-haraseth] This was the royal city of the Moabites, and, as we learn from Scripture, exceedingly strong; (see Isa. xvi. 7, 11;) so that it is probable the confederate armies could not easily reduce it. The *slingers,* we are informed, *went about the wall,* and smote all the men that appeared on it, while no doubt the besieging army was employed in sapping the foundations.

Verse 26. *Seven hundred men*] These were no doubt the choice of all his troops, and being afraid of being hemmed up and perhaps taken by his enemies, whom he found on the eve of gaining possession of the city, he made a desperate sortie in order to regain the open coun-

try; and supposing that the quarter of the Edomites was weakest, or less carefully guarded, he endeavoured to make his impression there; but they were so warmly received by the king of Edom that they failed in the attempt, and were driven back into the city. Hence he was led to that desperate act mentioned in the following verse.

Verse 27. *Took his eldest son*] The rabbins account for this horrible sacrifice in the following way:—

When the king of Moab found himself so harassed, and the royal city on the point of being taken, he called a council of his servants, and asked them how it was these Israelites could perform such prodigies, and that such miracles were wrought for them? His servants answered, that it was owing to their progenitor Abraham, who, having an only son, was commanded by Jehovah to offer him in sacrifice. Abraham instantly obeyed, and offered his only son for a burnt-offering; and the Israelites being his descendants, through his merits the holy blessed God wrought such miracles in their behalf. The king of Moab answered, I also have an only son, and I will go and offer him to my God. Then he offered him for a burnt-offering upon the wall.

Upon the wall] עַל הַחֹמָה *al hachamah.* Rab. Sol. Jarchi says that the letter ו *vau* is wanting in this word, as it should be written חומה *chomah,* to signify a *wall; but* חמה *chammah* signifies the *sun,* and this was the god of the king of Moab: "And he offered his first-born son for a burnt-offering unto the *sun.*" This is not very solid.

There was great indignation] The Lord was displeased with them for driving things to such an extremity: or the surrounding nations held them in abomination on the account; and they were so terrified themselves at this most horrid sacrifice, that they immediately raised the siege and departed. In cases of great extremity it was customary in various heathen nations to offer *human sacrifices*, or to *devote* to the infernal gods the most precious or excellent thing or person they possessed. This was frequent among the *Phœnicians*, *Romans*, and *Greeks;*

and it was the natural fruit of a religious system which had for the objects of its worship cruel and merciless divinities. How different the Christian system! "Wilt thou that we shall bring down fire from heaven and destroy them? Ye know not what manner of spirits ye are of; the Son of man is not come to destroy men's lives, but to save them."

CHAPTER IV

A widow of one of the prophets, oppressed by a merciless creditor, applies to Elisha, who multiplies her oil; by a part of which she pays her debt, and subsists on the rest, 1–7. His entertainment at the house of a respectable woman in Shunem, 8–10. He foretells to his hostess the birth of a son, 11–17. After some years the child dies, and the mother goes to Elisha at Carmel; he comes to Shunem, and raises the child to life, 18–37. He comes to Gilgal, and prevents the sons of the prophets from being poisoned by wild gourds, 38–41. He multiplies a scanty provision, so as to make it sufficient to feed one hundred men, 42–44.

A. M. 3109
B. C. 895
Ante I. Ol. 119
An. Megaclis,
Arch. Athen.
perpet. 27

NOW there cried a certain woman of the wives of [a]the sons of the prophets unto Elisha, saying, Thy servant my husband is dead; and thou knowest that thy servant did fear the LORD: and the creditor is come [b]to take unto him my two sons to be bondmen.

A. M. 3109
B. C. 895
Ante I. Ol. 119
An. Megaclis,
Arch. Athen.
perpet. 27

---

[a]1 Kings xx. 35

[b]See Lev. xxv. 39; Matt. xviii. 25

NOTES ON CHAP. IV

Verse 1. *Now there cried a certain woman*] This woman, according to the Chaldee, Jarchi, and the rabbins, was the wife of Obadiah.

Sons of the prophets] תלמידי נבייא *talmidey nebiyaiya*, "disciples of the prophets:" so the *Targum* here, and in all other places where the words occur, and properly too.

The creditor is come] This, says *Jarchi*, was *Jehoram* son of Ahab, who lent money on usury to Obadiah, because he had in the days of Ahab fed the Lord's prophets. The *Targum* says he borrowed money to feed these prophets, because he would not support them out of the property of Ahab.

To take unto him my two sons to be bondmen.] Children, according to the laws of the *Hebrews*, were considered the property of their parents, who had a right to dispose of them for the payment of their debts. And in cases of poverty, the law permitted them, expressly, to sell both themselves and their children; Exod. xxi. 7, and Lev. xxv. 39. It was by an extension of this law, and by virtue of another, which authorized them to sell the *thief* who could not make restitution, Exod. xxii. 3, that creditors were permitted to take the children of their debtors in payment. Although the law has not determined any thing precisely on this point, we see by this passage, and by several others, that this custom was common among the Hebrews. *Isaiah* refers to it very evidently, where he says, *Which of my creditors is it to whom I have sold you? Behold, for your iniquities have ye sold yourselves;* chap. l. 1. And our Lord alludes to it, Matt. xviii. 25, where he mentions the case of an insolvent debtor, *Forasmuch as he had not to pay, his lord commanded* HIM *to be* SOLD, *and his* WIFE *and* CHILDREN, *and all that he had;* which shows that the custom continued among the Jews to the very end of their republic. The *Romans, Athenians,* and

Asiatics in general had the same authority over their children as the Hebrews had: they sold them in time of poverty; and their creditors seized them as they would a sheep or an ox, or any *household goods. Romulus* gave the Romans an *absolute power* over their children which extended through the whole course of their lives, let them be in whatever situation they might. They could *cast them into prison, beat, employ them as slaves in agriculture, sell them for slaves,* or even *take away their lives!* —*Dionys. Halicarn.* lib. ii., pp. 96, 97.

Numa Pompilius first moderated this law, by enacting, that if a son married with the consent of his father, he should no longer have power to sell him for debt.

The emperors *Diocletian* and *Maximilian* forbade *freemen* to be sold on account of debt: Ob æs alienum servire liberos creditoribus, jura non patiuntur.—Vid. Lib. ob. æs C. de obligat. The ancient *Athenians* had the same right over their children as the *Romans;* but *Solon* reformed this barbarous custom.—Vid. *Plutarch in Solone.*

The people of Asia had the same custom, which *Lucullus* endeavoured to check, by moderating the laws respecting usury.

The *Georgians* may alienate their children; and their creditors have a right to sell the wives and children of their debtors, and thus exact the uttermost farthing of their debt.— *Tavernier,* lib. iii., c. 9. And we have reason to believe that this custom long prevailed among the inhabitants of the British isles. See *Calmet* here.

In short, it appears to have been the custom of all the inhabitants of the earth. We have some remains of it yet in this country, in the senseless and pernicious custom of throwing a man into prison for debt, though his own industry and labour be absolutely necessary to discharge it, and these cannot be exercised within the loathsome and contagious walls of a prison.

A. M. 3109
B. C. 895
Ante I. Ol. 119
An. Megaclis,
Arch. Athen.
perpet. 27

2 And Elisha said unto her, What shall I do for thee? tell me, what hast thou in the house? And she said, Thine handmaid hath not any thing in the house, save a pot of oil.

3 Then he said, Go, borrow thee vessels abroad of all thy neighbours, *even* empty vessels; ^cborrow ^dnot a few.

4 And when thou art come in, thou shalt shut the door upon thee and upon thy sons, and shalt pour out into all those vessels, and thou shalt set aside that which is full.

5 So she went from him, and shut the door upon her and upon her sons, who brought *the vessels* to her; and she poured out.

6 And it came to pass, when the vessels were full, that she said unto her son, Bring me yet a vessel. And he said unto her, *There is* not a vessel more. And the oil stayed.

7 Then she came and told the man of God. And he said, Go, sell the oil, and pay thy ^edebt, and live thou and thy children of the rest.

8 And ^fit fell on a day, that Elisha passed

to ^gShunem, where *was* a great woman; and she ^hconstrained him to eat bread. And *so* it was, *that* as oft as he passed by, he turned in thither to eat bread.

A. M. 3109
B. C. 895
Ante I. Ol. 119
An. Megaclis,
Arch. Athen.
perpet. 27

9 And she said unto her husband, Behold, Now, I perceive that this *is* a holy man of God, which passeth by us continually.

10 Let us make a little chamber, I pray thee, on the wall; and let us set for him there a bed, and a table, and a stool, and a candlestick: and it shall be, when he cometh to us, that he shall turn in thither.

11 And it fell on a day, that he came thither, and he turned into the chamber, and lay there.

12 And he said to Gehazi his servant, Call this Shunammite. And when he had called her, she stood before him.

13 And he said unto him, Say now unto her, Behold, thou hast been careful for us with all this care; what *is* to be done for thee? wouldest thou be spoken for to the king, or to the captain of the host? And she answered, I dwell among mine own people.

---

^cSee chap. iii. 16——^dOr, *scant not*——^eOr, *creditor*

^fHeb. *there was a day*——^gJosh. xix, 18——^hHeb. *laid hold on him*

Verse 2. *Save a pot of oil.*] Oil was used as *aliment*, for anointing the *body* after bathing, and to anoint the *dead*. Some think that this pot of oil was what this widow had kept for her burial: see Matt. xxvi. 12.

Verse 6. *And the oil stayed.*] While there was a vessel to fill, there was oil sufficient; and it only ceased to flow when there was no vessel to receive it. This is a good emblem of the grace of God. While there is an empty, longing heart, there is a continual overflowing fountain of salvation. If we find in any place or at any time that the oil ceases to flow, it is because there are no empty vessels there, no souls hungering and thirsting for righteousness. We find fault with the dispensations of God's mercy, and ask, Why were the former days better than these? Were we as much in earnest for our salvation as our *forefathers* were for theirs, we should have equal supplies, and as much reason to sing aloud of Divine mercy.

Verse 7. *Go, sell the oil, and pay thy debt*] He does not inveigh against the cruelty of this creditor, because the law and custom of the country gave him the authority on which he acted; and rather than permit a poor honest widow to have her children sold, or that even a Philistine should suffer loss who had given credit to a genuine Israelite, he would work a miracle to pay a debt which, in the course of providence, it was out of her power to discharge.

Verse 8. *Elisha passed to Shunem*] This city was in the tribe of Issachar, to the south

of the brook Kishon, and at the foot of Mount Tabor.

Where was *a great woman*] In *Pirkey Rab. Eliezer*, this woman is said to have been the sister of Abishag, the Shunammite, well known in the history of David.

Instead of *great woman*, the Chaldee has, *a woman fearing sin;* the Arabic, *a woman eminent for piety before God.* This made her truly *great.*

Verse 9. *This is a holy man of God*] That is, *a prophet*, as the *Chaldee* interprets it.

Which passeth by us continually.] It probably lay in his way to some school of the prophets that he usually attended.

Verse 10. *Let us make a little chamber*] See the note upon Judges iii. 20. As the woman was convinced that Elisha was a prophet, she knew that he must have need of more privacy than the general state of her house could afford; and therefore she proposes what she knew would be a great acquisition to him, as he could live in this little chamber in as much privacy as if he were in his own house. The *bed*, the *table*, the *stool*, and the *candlestick*, were really every thing he could need, by way of accommodation, in such circumstances.

Verse 12. *Gehazi his servant*] This is the first time we hear of this very indifferent character.

Verse 13. *Wouldest thou be spoken for to the king*] Elisha must have had considerable influence with the king, from the part he took in the late war with the Moabites. Jehoram had reason to believe that the prophet, under God,

A. M. 3109
B. C. 895
Ante I. Ol. 119
An. Megaclis,
Arch. Athen.
perpet. 27

14 And he said, What then *is* to be done for her? And Gehazi answered, Verily, she hath no child, and her husband is old.

15 And he said, Call her. And when he had called her, she stood in the door.

16 And he said, ¹About this ᵏseason, according to the time of life, thou shalt embrace a son. And she said, Nay, my lord, *thou* man of God, ¹do not lie unto thine handmaid.

17 And the woman conceived, and bare a son at that season that Elisha had said unto her, according to the time of life.

18 And when the child was grown, it fell on a day, that he went out to his father to the reapers.

19 And he said unto his father, My head, my head. And he said to a lad, Carry him to his mother.

20 And when he had taken him, and brought him to his mother, he sat on her knees till noon, and *then* died.

A. M. 3113
B. C. 891
Ante I. Ol. 115
An. Diogeneti,
Arch. Athen.
perpet. 1

21 And she went up, and laid him on the bed of the man of God, and shut *the door* upon him, and went out.

22 And she called unto her husband, and said, Send me, I pray thee, one of the young men, and one of the asses, that I may run to the man of God, and come again.

23 And he said, wherefore wilt thou go to him to-day? *it is* neither new moon nor Sabbath. And she said, It shall be ᵐwell.

24 Then she saddled an ass, and said to her servant, Drive, and go forward; ⁿslack not *thy* riding for me, except I bid thee.

25 So she went and came unto the man of God ᵒto Mount Carmel. And it came to pass, when the man of God saw her afar off, that he said to Gehazi his servant, Behold, *yonder is* that Shunammite:

26 Run now, I pray thee, to meet her, and say unto her, *Is it* well with thee? *is it* well

---

¹Gen. xviii. 10, 14——ᵏHeb. *set time*——¹Ver. 28 ᵐHeb. *peace*

ⁿHebrew, *restrain not for me to ride*——ᵒChapter ii. 25

---

was the sole cause of his success; and therefore he could have no doubt that the king would grant him any reasonable request.

Or to the captain of the host?] As if he had said, Wilt thou that I should procure thee and thy husband a place at court, or get any of thy *friends* a post in the *army?*

I dwell among mine own people.] I am perfectly satisfied and contented with my lot in life; I live on the best terms with my neighbours, and am here encompassed with my kindred, and feel no disposition to change my connections or place of abode.

How few are there like this woman on the earth! Who would not wish to be recommended to the king's notice, or get a post for a relative in the army, &c.? Who would not like to change the country for the town, and the rough manners of the inhabitants of the villages for the polished conversation and amusements of the court? Who is so contented with what he has as not to desire more? Who trembles at the prospect of riches; or believes there are any snares in an elevated state, or in the company and conversation of the great and honourable? How few are there that will not sacrifice every thing—peace, domestic comfort, their friends, their conscience, and their God—for *money, honours, grandeur,* and *parade?*

Verse 14. *What then is to be done for her?*] It seems that the woman retired as soon as she had delivered the answer mentioned in the preceding verse.

Verse 16. *Thou shalt embrace a son.*] This *promise,* and the *circumstances* of the parties, are not very dissimilar to that relative to the birth of Isaac, and those of Abraham and Sarah.

Do not lie] That is, Let thy words become true; or, as the rabbins understand it, Do not

mock me by giving me a son that shall soon be removed by death; but let me have one that shall survive me.

Verse 18. *When the child was grown*] We know not of what age he was, very likely *four* or *six,* if not more years; for he could go out to the reapers in the harvest field, converse, &c.

Verse 19. *My head, my head.*] Probably affected by the *coup de soleil,* or *sun stroke,* which might, in so young a subject, soon occasion death, especially in that hot country.

Verse 21. *Laid him on the bed of the man of God*] She had no doubt heard that Elijah had raised the widow's son of Zarephath to life; and she believed that he who had obtained this gift from God for her, could obtain his restoration to life.

Verse 23. *Wherefore wilt thou go*] She was a very prudent woman; she would not harass the feelings of her husband by informing him of the death of his son till she had tried the power of the prophet. Though the religion of the true God was not the religion of the state, yet there were no doubt multitudes of the people who continued to worship the true God alone, and were in the habit of going, as is here intimated, on *new moons* and *Sabbaths,* to consult the prophet.

Verse 24. *Drive, and go forward*] It is customary in the East for a servant to walk *along side* or *drive* the ass his master rides. Sometimes he walks *behind,* and goads on the beast; and when it is to turn, he directs its head with the long pole of the goad. It is probably to this custom that the wise man alludes when he says, "I have seen servants on horses, and *princes walking as servants* on the earth," on the *ground.*

Verse 26. It is *well.*] How strong was her faith in God and submission to his authority!

A. M. 3113
B. C. 891
Ante I. Ol. 115
An. Diogeneti,
Arch. Athen.
perpet. 1

with thy husband? *is it* well with the child? And she answered, *It is* well.

27 And when she came to the man of God to the hill, she caught [p]him by the feet: but Gehazi came near to thrust her away. And the man of God said, Let her alone; for her soul *is* [q]vexed within her: and the LORD hath hid *it* from me, and hath not told me.

28 Then she said, Did I desire a son of my lord? [r]did I not say, Do not deceive me?

29 Then he said to Gehazi, [s]Gird up thy loins, and take my staff in thine hand, and go thy way: if thou meet any man, [t]salute him not; and if any salute thee, answer him not again: and [u]lay my staff upon the face of the child.

30 And the mother of the child said, [v]As the LORD liveth, and *as* thy soul liveth, I will not leave thee. And he arose, and followed her.

A. M. 3113
B. C. 891
Ante I. Ol. 115
An. Diogeneti,
Arch. Athen.
perpet. 1

31 And Gehazi passed on before them, and laid the staff upon the face of the child; but *there was* neither voice nor [w]hearing. Wherefore he went again to meet him, and told him, saying, The child is [x]not awaked.

32 And when Elisha was come into the house, behold, the child was dead, *and* laid upon his bed.

33 He [y]went in therefore, and shut the door upon them twain, [z]and prayed unto the LORD.

34 And he went up, and lay upon the child, and put his mouth upon his mouth, and his eyes upon his eyes, and his hands upon his hands: and [a]he stretched himself upon the child; and the flesh of the child waxed warm.

35 Then he returned, and walked in the house [b]to and fro; and went up [c]and stretched

---

Though the heaviest family affliction that could befall her and her husband had now taken place; yet, believing that it was a dispensation of Providence which was in itself neither *unwise* nor *unkind,* she said, It is *well* with me, with my *husband,* and with my *child.* We may farther remark that, in her days, the doctrine of *reprobate infants* had not disgraced the pure religion of the God of endless compassion. She had no doubts concerning the welfare of her child, even with respect to another world; and who but a pagan or a stoic can entertain a contrary doctrine?

Verse 27. *The Lord hath hid it from me, and hath not told me.*] In reference to this point he had not now the *discernment of spirits.* This, and the *gift of prophecy,* were influences which God gave and suspended as his infinite wisdom saw good.

Verse 28. *Did I desire a son of my lord?*] I expressed no such wish to thee; I was contented and happy; and when thou didst promise me a son, *did I not say, Do not deceive me?* Do not mock me with a child which shall grow up to be attractive and engaging, but of whom I shall soon be deprived by death.

Verse 29. *Salute him not*] Make all the haste thou possibly canst, and lay my staff on the face of the child; he probably thought that it might be a case of mere *suspended animation* or a *swoon,* and that laying the staff on the face of the child might act as a *stimulus* to excite the animal motions.

Verse 30. *I will not leave thee.*] The prophet it seems had no design to accompany her; he intended to wait for Gehazi's return; but as the woman was well assured the child was *dead,* she was determined not to return till she brought the prophet with her.

Verse 32. *Behold, the child was dead*] The prophet then saw that the body and spirit of the child were separated.

Verse 33. *Prayed unto the Lord.*] He had no power of his own by which he could restore the child.

Verse 34. *Lay upon the child*] Endeavoured to convey a portion of his own natural warmth to the body of the child; and probably endeavoured, by blowing into the child's mouth, to inflate the lungs, and restore respiration. He uses every natural means in his power to restore life, while praying to the Author of it to exert a miraculous influence. Natural means are in our power; those that are supernatural belong to God. We should always do our own work, and beg of God to do his.

Verse 35. *Walked in the house to and fro*] In order, no doubt, that he might recover that natural warmth which was absorbed by the cold body of the child, that he might, by again taking it in his arms, communicate more warmth. *Caloric* or natural heat, when accumulated in any particular part, will diffuse itself to all bodies with which it comes in contact, till their temperature be equal; so a heated body will give out its caloric to the surrounding air, or to contiguous bodies, till the temperature of all be perfectly equalized. The body of the prophet gave out its natural heat, or caloric, to the cold body of the child; the prophet no doubt continued in contact with the child till he could bear it no longer; then covered up the child, rose up, and *walked smartly* on the floor, till, by increasing the circulation of the blood by activity and strong and quick respiration, he could again afford to communicate another portion of his natural heat. This appears to be the reason of what is mentioned in the text.

Verse 35. *The child sneezed seven times*] That is, it sneezed *abundantly.* When the nerv-

A. M. 3113
B. C. 891
Ante I. Ol. 115
An. Diogeneti,
Arch. Athen.
perpet. 1

himself upon him: and ᵈthe child sneezed seven times, and the child opened his eyes.

36 And he called Gehazi, and said, Call this Shunammite. So he called her. And when she was come in unto him, he said, Take up thy son.

37 Then she went in, and fell at his feet, and bowed herself to the ground, and ᵉtook up her son, and went out.

A. M. 3114
B. C. 890
Ante I. Ol. 114
An. Diogeneti,
Arch. Athen.
perpet. 2

38 And Elisha came again to ᶠGilgal: and *there was* a ᵍdearth in the land; and the sons of the prophets *were* ʰsitting before him: and he said unto his servant, Set on the great pot, and seethe pottage for the sons of the prophets.

39 And one went out into the field to gather herbs, and found a wild vine, and gathered thereof wild gourds his lap full, and came and shred *them* into the pot of pottage: for they knew *them* not.

40 So they poured out for the men to eat.

And it came to pass, as they were eating of the pottage, that they cried out, and said, O *thou* man of God, *there is* ⁱdeath in the pot. And they could not eat *thereof*.

A. M. 3114
B. C. 890
Ante I. Ol. 114
An. Diogeneti,
Arch. Athen.
perpet. 2

41 But he said, Then bring meal. And ᵏhe cast *it* into the pot; and he said, Pour out for the people, that they may eat. And there was no ˡharm in the pot.

42 And there came a man from ᵐBaal-sha-lisha, ⁿand brought the man of God bread oᵗ the first-fruits, twenty loaves of barley, and full ears of corn °in the husk thereof. And he said, Give unto the people, that they may eat.

43 And his servitor said, ᵖWhat, should I set this before a hundred men? He said again, Give the people, that they may eat: for thus saith the LORD, �q̣They shall eat, and shall leave *thereof*.

44 So he set *it* before them, and they did eat, ʳand left *thereof*, according to the word of the LORD.

ᵈChap. viii. 1, 5——ᵉ1 Kings xvii. 23; Heb. xi. 35
ᶠChap. ii. 1——ᵍChap. viii. 1——ʰChap. ii. 3; Luke x.
39; Acts xxii. 3——ⁱExod. x. 17——ᵏSee Exod. xv. 25;
chap. ii. 21; v. 10; John ix. 6

ˡHeb. *evil thing*——ᵐ1 Sam. ix. 4——ⁿ1 Sam. ix. 7;
1 Cor. ix. 11; Gal. vi. 6——°Or, *in his script* or *garment*
ᵖLuke ix. 13; John vi. 9——q̣Luke ix. 17; John vi. 11
ʳMatt. xiv. 20; xv. 37; John vi. 13

---

ous influence began to act on the muscular system, before the circulation could be in every part restored, particular muscles, if not the whole body, would be thrown into strong contractions and shiverings, and *sternutation* or sneezing would be a natural consequence; particularly as obstructions must have taken place in the *head* and its *vessels*, because of the disorder of which the child died. Most people, as well as philosophers and physicians, have remarked how beneficial sneezings are to the removal of obstructions in the head. *Sternutamenta*, says Pliny, *Hist. Nat.*, lib. xxviii., cap. 6, *gravedinem capitis emendant;* "Sneezing relieves disorders of the head."

Verse 37. *She went in and fell at his feet*] Few can enter into the feelings of this noble woman. What suspense must she have felt during the time that the prophet was employed in the slow process referred to above! for *slow* in its own nature it must have been, and exceedingly exhausting to the prophet himself.

Verse 38. *Came again to Gilgal*] He had been there before with his master, a short time prior to his translation.

Set on the great pot and seethe pottage for the sons of the prophets.] It was in a time of *dearth*, and all might now stand in need of refreshment; and it appears that the prophet was led to put forth the power he had from God to make a plentiful provision for those who were present. The father of the celebrated Dr. Young, author of the *Night Thoughts*, preaching a charity sermon for the benefit of the *sons of the clergy*, took the above words for his ᵗext; nor could they be said to be inappropriate.

Verse 39. *Wild gourds*] This is generally thought to be the *coloquintida*, the fruit of a plant of the same name, about the size of a large orange. It is brought hither from the Levant, and is often known by the name of the *bitter apple;* both the seeds and pulp are intensely bitter, and violently purgative. It ranks among vegetable poisons, as all intense bitters do; but, judiciously employed, it is of considerable use in medicine.

Verse 40. There is *death in the pot.*] As if they had said, "We have here a deadly mixture; if we eat of it, we shall all die."

Verse 41. *Bring meal.*] Though this might, in some measure, correct the strong acrid and purgative quality; yet it was only a miracle which could make a lapful of this fruit shred into pottage salutary.

Verse 42. *Bread of the first-fruits*] This was an offering to the prophet, as the first-fruits themselves were an offering to God.

Corn in the husk] Probably parched corn or corn to be parched, a very frequent food in the East; full ears, before they are ripe, parched on the fire.

Verse 43. *Thus saith the Lord, They shall eat, and shall leave* thereof.] It was God, not the prophet, who fed *one hundred* men with these *twenty* loaves, &c. This is something like our Lord's feeding the multitude miraculously. Indeed, there are many things in this chapter similar to facts in our Lord's history: and this prophet might be more aptly considered a type of our Lord, than most of the other persons in the Scriptures who have been thus honoured.

CHAPTER V

The history of Naaman, captain of the host of the king of Syria, a leper; who was informed by a little Israel-itish captive maid that a prophet of the Lord, in Samaria, could cure him, 1–4. The king of Syria sends him, with a letter and rich presents, to the king of Israel, that he should recover him of his leprosy, 5, 6. On receiving the letter, the king of Israel is greatly distressed, supposing that the Syrian king designed to seek a quarrel with him; in desiring him to cleanse a leper, when it was well known that none could cure that disorder but God, 7. Elisha, hearing this, orders Naaman to be sent to him, 8. He comes to Elisha's house in great state, 9. And the prophet sends a messenger to him, ordering him to wash in Jordan seven times, and he should be made clean, 10. Naaman is displeased that he is received with so little ceremony, and departs in a rage, 11, 12. His servants reason with him; he is persuaded, goes to Jordan, washes, and is made clean, 13, 14. He returns to Elisha; acknowledges the true God; and offers him a present, which the prophet refuses, 15, 16. He asks directions, promises never to sacrifice to any other god, and is dismissed, 17–19. Gehazi runs after him, pretends he is sent by his master for a talent of silver and two changes of raiment; which he receives, brings home, and hides, 20–24. Elisha questions him; convicts him of his wickedness; pronounces a curse of leprosy upon him, with which he is immediately afflicted; and departs from his master a leper, as white as snow, 25–27.

A. M. 3110
B. C. 894
Ante I. Ol. 118
An. Megaclis,
Arch. Athen.
perpet. 28

NOW ᵃNaaman, captain of the host of the king of Syria, was ᵇa great man ᶜwith his master, and ᵈhonourable, ᵉbecause by him the LORD had given ᶠdeliverance unto Syria: he was also a mighty man in valour, *but he was* a leper.

2 And the Syrians had gone out by companies, and had brought away captive out of the land of Israel a little maid; and she ᵍwaited on Naaman's wife.

A. M. 3110
B. C. 894
Ante I. Ol. 118
An. Megaclis,
Arch. Athen.
perpet. 28

3 And she said unto her mistress, Would God my lord *were* ʰwith the prophet that *is* in Samaria! for he would ⁱrecover him of his leprosy.

ᵃLuke iv. 27——ᵇExod. xi. 3——ᶜHeb. *before*——ᵈOr, *gracious*——ᵉHeb. *lifted up* or *accepted in countenance*

ᶠOr, *victory*——ᵍHebrew, *was before*——ʰHeb. *before*
ⁱHeb. *gather in*

NOTES ON CHAP. V

Verse 1. *Naaman, captain of the host*] Of Naaman we know nothing more than is related here. *Jarchi* and some others say that he was the man who *drew the bow at a venture*, as we term it, and slew Ahab: see 1 Kings xxii. 34, and the notes there. He is not mentioned by *Josephus*, nor has he any reference to this history; which is very strange, as it exists in the *Chaldee, Septuagint,* and *Syriac.*

King of Syria] The Hebrew is מלך ארם *melech Aram, king of Aram;* which is followed by the *Chaldee* and *Arabic.* The *Syriac* has ܐܕܘܡ *Adom;* but as the Syriac ܛ *dolath* is the same element as the Syriac ܪ *rish,* differing only in the position of the *diacritic point,* it may have been originally *Aram.* The *Septuagint* and *Vulgate* have *Syria;* and this is a common meaning of the term in Scripture. If the king of *Syria* be meant, it must be *Ben-hadad;* and the contemporary king of Israel was *Jehoram.*

A great man] He was held in the highest esteem.

And honourable] Had the peculiar favour and confidence of his master; and was promoted to the highest trusts.

Had given deliverance unto Syria] That is, as the rabbins state, by his slaying Ahab, king of Israel; in consequence of which the Syrians got the victory.

A mighty man in valour] *He was a giant, and very strong,* according to the *Arabic.* He had, in a word, all the qualifications of an able general.

But he was *a leper.*] Here was a heavy tax upon his grandeur; he was afflicted with a disorder the most loathsome and the most humiliating that could possibly disgrace a human being. God often, in the course of his providence, permits great defects to be associated with great eminence, that he may hide pride from man; and cause him to think soberly of himself and his acquirements.

Verse 2. *The Syrians had gone out by companies*] גדודים *gedudim, troops.* When *one hundred* or *two hundred* men go out by themselves to make prey of whatever they can get, that is called, says *Jarchi,* גדוד *gedud, a troop.* They had gone out in marauding parties; and on such occasions they bring away *grain, cattle,* and such of the inhabitants as are proper to make *slaves.*

A little maid] Who, it appears, had pious parents, who brought her up in the knowledge of the true God. Behold the goodness and the *severity* of the Divine providence! affectionate parents are deprived of their promising daughter by a set of lawless freebooters, without the smallest prospect that she should have any lot in life but that of misery, infamy, and wo.

Waited on Naaman's wife.] Her decent, orderly behaviour, the consequence of her sober and pious education, entitled her to this place of distinction; in which her servitude was at least easy, and her person safe.

If God permitted the parents to be deprived of their pious child by the hands of ruffians, he did not permit the child to be without a *guardian.* In such a case, were even the father and mother to forsake her, God would take her up.

Verse 3. *Would God my lord*] אחלי *achaley, I wish;* or, as the Chaldee, Syriac, and Arabic have, "*Happy would it be* for my master if he were with the prophet," &c.

A. M. 3110
B. C. 894
Ante I. Ol. 118
An. Megaclis,
Arch. Athen.
perpet. 28

4 And *one* went in, and told his lord, saying, Thus and thus said the maid that *is* of the land of Israel.

5 And the king of Syria said, Go to, go, and I will send a letter unto the king of Israel. And he departed, and ᵏtook ˡwith him ten talents of silver, and six thousand *pieces* of gold, and ten changes of raiment.

6 And he brought the letter to the king of Israel, saying, Now when this letter is come unto thee, behold, I have *therewith* sent Naaman my servant to thee, that thou mayest recover him of his leprosy.

7 And it came to pass, when the king of Israel had read the letter, that he rent his clothes, and said, *Am* I ᵐGod, to kill and to make alive, that this man doth send unto me to recover a man of his leprosy? wherefore

consider, I pray you, and see how he seeketh a quarrel against me.

A. M. 3110
B. C. 894
Ante I. Ol. 118
An. Megaclis,
Arch. Athen.
perpet. 28

8 And it was *so*, when Elisha the man of God had heard that the king of Israel had rent his clothes, that he sent to the king, saying, Wherefore hast thou rent thy clothes? let him come now to me, and he shall know that there is a prophet in Israel.

9 So Naaman came with his horses and with his chariot, and stood at the door of the house of Elisha.

10 And Elisha sent a messenger unto him, saying, Go and ⁿwash in Jordan seven times, and thy flesh shall come again to thee, and thou shalt be clean.

11 But Naaman was wroth, and went away, and said, Behold, ᵒI ᵖthought, He will surely come out to me, and stand, and call on the

---

ᵏ1 Sam. ix. 8; chap. viii. 8, 9——ˡHeb. *in his hand*
ᵐGen. xxx. 2; Deut. xxxii. 39; 1 Sam. ii. 6

ⁿSee chap. iv. 41; John ix. 7——ᵒHeb. *I said*——ᵖOr,
I said with myself, He will surely come out, &c.

Here the mystery of the Divine providence begins to develop itself. By the captivity of this little maid, one Syrian family at least, and that one of the most considerable in the Syrian empire, is brought to the knowledge of the true God.

Verse 4. *Thus and thus said the maid*] So well had this little pious maid conducted herself, that her words are credited; and credited so fully, that an embassy from the king of Syria to the king of Israel is founded upon them!

Verse 5. *The king of Syria said*] He judged it the best mode of proceeding to send immediately to the *king*, under whose control he supposed the prophet must be, that he would order the prophet to cure his general.

Ten talents of silver] This, at £353 11s. 10½d. the talent, would amount to £3,535 18s. 9d.

Six thousand pieces of gold] If *shekels* are here meant, as the *Arabic* has it, then the *six thousand* shekels, at £1 16s. 5d. will amount to £10,925; and the whole, to £14,460 18s. 9d. sterling: besides the value of the ten *caftans*, or *changes of raiment*. This was a princely present, and shows us at once how high Naaman stood in the esteem of his master.

Verse 7. *Am I God, to kill and to make alive*] He spoke thus under the conviction that God alone could cure the leprosy; which, indeed, was universally acknowledged: and must have been as much a maxim among the Syrians as among the Israelites, for the disorder was equally prevalent in both countries; and in both equally incurable. See the notes on Lev. xiii. and xiv. And it was this that led the king of Israel to infer that the Syrian king sought a quarrel with him, in desiring him to do a work which God only could do; and then declaring war upon him because he did not do it.

Verse 8. *Let him come now to me*] Do not be afflicted; the matter belongs to me, as the

prophet of the Most High; send him to me, and he shall know that I am such.

Verse 9. *Came with his horses and with his chariot*] In very great pomp and state. Closely inspected, this was preposterous enough; a *leper* sitting in state, and affecting it!

Verse 10. *Sent a messenger*] Did not come out to speak with him: he had got his orders from God, and he transmitted them to Naaman by his servant.

Wash in Jordan seven times] The waters of Jordan had no tendency to remove this disorder, but God chose to make them the means by which he *would* convey his healing power. He who is the author of life, health, and salvation, has a right to dispense, convey, and maintain them, by whatsoever means he pleases.

Verse 11. *Naaman was wroth*] And why? Because the prophet treated him without ceremony; and because he appointed him an expenseless and simple mode of cure.

Behold, I thought] God's ways are not as our ways; he appoints that mode of cure which he knows to be best. Naaman expected to be treated with great ceremony; and instead of humbling himself before the Lord's prophet, he expected the prophet of the Lord to humble himself before *him! Behold, I thought;*—and what did he think? Hear his words, for they are all very emphatic:—1. "*I thought, He will surely come* OUT *to* ME. He will never make his servant the medium of communication between ME and himself. 2. *And stand*—present himself before me, and stand as a servant to hear the orders of his God. 3. *And call on the name of Jehovah* HIS *God;* so that both his God and himself shall appear to do me service and honour. 4. *And strike his hand over the place;* for can it be supposed that any healing virtue can be conveyed without contact? Had he done these things, then the leper might have been recovered."

A. M. 3110
B. C. 894
Ante I. Ol. 118
An. Megaclis,
Arch. Athen.
perpet. 28

name of the LORD his God, and ᵠstrike his hand over the place and recover the leper.

12 *Are* not ʳAbana and Pharpar, rivers of Damascus, better than all the waters of Israel? may I not wash in them, and be clean? So he turned and went away in a rage.

13 And his servants came near, and spake unto him, and said, My father, *if* the prophet had bid thee *do some* great thing, wouldest thou not have done *it?* how much rather then, when he said to thee, Wash, and be clean?

14 Then he went down, and dipped himself seven times in Jordan, according to the saying

of the man of God: and ˢhis flesh came again like unto the flesh of a little child, and ᵗhe was clean.

A. M. 3110
B. C. 894
Ante I. Ol. 118
An. Megaclis,
Arch. Athen.
perpet. 28

15 And he returned to the man of God, he and all his company, and came, and stood before him: and he said, Behold, now I know that *there is* ᵘno God in all the earth, but in Israel: now therefore, I pray thee, take ᵛa blessing of thy servant.

16 But he said, ᵂAs the LORD liveth, before whom I stand, ˣI will receive none. And he urged him to take *it;* but he refused.

17 And Naaman said, Shall there not then, I pray thee, be given to thy servant two mules'

ᵠHeb. *move up and down*——ʳOr, *Amana*——ˢJob xxxiii. 25——ᵗLuke iv. 27.——ᵘDan. ii. 47; iii. 29; vi. 26, 27——ᵛGen. xxxiii. 11——ᵂChap. iii. 14——ˣGen. xiv. 23; see Matt. x. 8; Acts viii. 18, 20

Verse 12. *Are not Abana and Pharpar*] At present these rivers do not exist by these names; and where they are we know not; nor whether they were the *Orontes* and *Chrysorroes.* Mr. Maundrell, who travelled over all this ground, could find no vestige of the names *Abana* and *Pharpar.* The river *Barrady* he accurately describes: it has its source in Antilibanus; and, after having plentifully watered the city of Damascus and the gardens, dividing into three branches, (one of which goes through the city, and the two others are distributed among the gardens,) it is lost in the marshy country about five or six leagues from Damascus. Two of these branches were doubtless called in the time of Elisha *Abana*, or *Amana*, as many copies have it; and *Pharpar.* And in the time in which the *Arabic* version was made, one of these branches were called برد|وتوري *Barda* and *Toura*, for these are the names by which this version translates those of the text.

May I not wash in them, and be clean?] No, for God has directed thee to Jordan! and by *its* waters, or none, shalt thou be cleansed. *Abana* and *Pharpar* may be as good as Jordan; and in respect to thy cleansing, the simple difference is, God will convey his influence by the *latter*, and not by the *former.*

There is often contention among the people of Bengal and other places, concerning the superior efficacy of rivers; though the Ganges bears the bell in Bengal, as the Thames does in England, and the Nile in Egypt.

Verse 13. *My father*] A title of the highest respect and affection.

Had bid thee do some *great thing*] If the prophet had appointed thee to do something very *difficult* in itself, and very *expensive* to thee, wouldst thou not have done it? With much greater reason shouldst thou do what will occupy *little time*, be no *expense*, and is *easy* to be performed.

Verse 14. *Then went he down*] He felt the force of this reasoning, and made a trial, probably expecting little success.

Like unto the flesh of a little child] The loathsome scurf was now entirely removed; his flesh assumed the appearance and health of youth; and the whole mass of his blood, and

other juices, became purified, refined, and exalted! How mighty is God! What great things can he do by the simplest and feeblest of means!

Verse 15. *He returned to the man of God*] He saw that the hand of the Lord was upon him; he felt gratitude for his cleansing; and came back to acknowledge, in the most public way, his obligation to God and his servant.

Stood before him] He was now truly humbled, and left all his state behind him. It is often the case that those who have least to value themselves on are proud and haughty; whereas the most excellent of the earth are the most humble, knowing that they have nothing but what they have received. Naaman, the *leper*, was more proud and dictatorial than was when *cleansed* of his leprosy.

There is *no God in all the earth*] Those termed gods are no gods; the God of Israel is sole God in all the earth. See my sermon on this subject.

Take a blessing] Accept a present. *Take an expiatory gift.—Arabic.* He desired to offer something *for his cleansing.* He thought it right thus to acknowledge the hand from which he had received his healing, and thus honour the Lord by giving something to his servant.

Verse 16. *I will receive none.*] It was very common to give presents to all great and official men; and among these, *prophets* were always included: but as it might have appeared to the Syrians that he had taken the offered presents as a remuneration for the cure performed, he refused; for as God alone did the work, he alone should have all the glory.

Verse 17. *Shall there not then, I pray thee*] This verse is understood two different ways. I will give them both in a paraphrase:—

1. *Shall there not then be given unto thy servant* [viz., Naaman] *two mules' burden* of this Israelitish *earth*, that I may build an altar with it, on which I may offer sacrifices to the God of Israel? *For thy servant, &c.*

2. *Shall there not be given to thy* [Elisha's] *servant* [Gehazi] *two mules' burden of* this *earth?* i. e., the gold and silver which he brought with him; and which he esteemed as *earth*, or *dust*, in comparison of the cure he

A. M. 3110
B. C. 894
Ante I. Ol. 118
An. Megaclis,
Arch. Athen.
perpet. 28

burden of earth? for thy servant will henceforth offer neither burnt-offering nor sacrifice unto other gods, but unto the LORD.

18 In this thing the LORD pardon thy servant, *that* when my master goeth into the house of Rimmon to worship there, and ʸhe leaneth on my hand, and I bow myself in the house of Rimmon: when I bow down myself in the house of Rimmon, the LORD pardon thy servant in this thing.

19 And he said unto him, Go in peace. So he departed from him ᶻa little way.

A. M. 3110
B. C. 894
Ante I. Ol. 118
An. Megaclis,
Arch. Athen.
perpet. 28

20 But Gehazi, the servant of Elisha the man of God, said, Behold, my master hath spared Naaman this Syrian, in not receiving at his hands that which he brought: but, *as* the LORD liveth, I will run after him, and take somewhat of him.

21 So Gehazi followed after Naaman. And when Naaman saw *him* running after him, he

---

ʸChap. vii. 2, 17

ᶻHeb. *a little piece of ground,* as Gen. xxxv. 16

---

received. *For thy servant* [Naaman] *will henceforth, &c.*

Each of these interpretations has its difficulties. Why Naaman should *ask* for *two mules' burden of earth,* which he might have taken up any where on the confines of the land, without any such liberty, is not easy to see. As to the *prophet's permission,* though the boon was ever so small, it was not *his* to give; only the king of Israel could give such a permission: and what sort of an altar could he build with two mules' burden of earth, carried from Samaria to Damascus? If this be really the meaning of the place, the request was exceedingly foolish, and never could have come from a person enjoying the right use of his reason. The second opinion, not without its difficulties, seems less embarrassed than the former. It was natural for Naaman to wish to give something to the prophet's servant, as the master had refused his present. Again, impressed with the vast importance of the cure he had received, to take away all feeling of obligation, he might call *two* or *ten talents of silver* by the name of *earth,* as well as Habakkuk, chap. ii. 6, calls silver and gold *thick clay;* and by terms of this kind it has been frequently denominated, both by *prophets* and heathen writers: "Tyrus heaped up *silver* as the *dust,* and *fine gold* as the *mire of the streets;*" Zech. ix. 3. *And the king made silver and gold* at Jerusalem *as stones;* 2 Chron. i. 15. Which is agreeable to the sentiments of the heathen: Χρυσος τις κονις εστι, και αργυρος, Gold and *silver* are only a *certain kind of earth.*—ARIST. *Eth. Nicomach.*

Should it be said, The gold and silver could not be *two mules' burden;* I answer, Let the quantity that Naaman brought with him be only considered, and it will be found to be as much, when put into two bags, as could be well lifted upon the backs of two mules, or as those beasts could conveniently carry. The silver itself would weigh 233lbs. 9oz. 15½dwts., and the gold 1,140lbs. 7oz. 10dwts.; in the whole 1,374lbs. 5oz. 5½dwts. Troy weight. Should it be objected that, taken in this sense, there is no visible connection between the former and latter clauses of the verse, I answer that there is as much connection between the words taken in this sense as in the other, for something must be brought in to supply both; besides, this makes a more complete sense than the other: "Shall there not, I pray thee, be given to thy servant two mules' burden of this silver and gold, [to apply it as he may think proper; I regard it not,] for thy servant will henceforth offer

neither burnt-offering nor sacrifice unto other gods, [for the cure he has now received; or by way of worship at any time;] but unto Jehovah." The reader may choose which of these interpretations he pleases.

Verse 18. *In this thing the Lord pardon thy servant*] It is useless to enter into the controversy concerning this verse. By no rule of right reasoning, nor by any legitimate mode of interpretation, can it be stated that Naaman is asking pardon for offences which he *may commit,* or that he could ask or the prophet grant *indulgence* to bow himself in the temple of Rimmon, thus performing a decided act of *homage,* the very essence of that worshp which immediately before he solemnly assured the prophet he would never practise. The original may legitimately be read, and *ought* to be read, in the *past,* and not in the *future* tense. "For this thing the Lord pardon thy servant, for that when my master HATH GONE into the house of Rimmon to worship there, and he HATH LEANED upon mine hand, that I also HAVE BOWED myself in the house of Rimmon; for my worshipping in the house of Rimmon, the Lord pardon thy servant in this thing." This is the translation of Dr. *Lightfoot,* the most able Hebraist of his time in Christendom.

To admit the common interpretation is to admit, in effect, the doctrine of *indulgences;* and that we may do *evil* that *good* may come of it; that the *end* sanctifies the *means;* and that for political purposes we may do unlawful acts.

Verse 19. *And he said unto him*] There is a most singular and important reading in one of De Rossi's MSS., which he numbers 191. It has in the margin 'ק אל that is, "read אל *lo, not,* instead of לו *lo, to him.*" Now this reading supposes that Naaman *did* ask permission from the prophet to worship in Rimmon's temple; to which the prophet answers, *No; go in peace:* that is, maintain thy holy resolutions, be a consistent worshipper of the true God, and avoid all idolatrous practices. Another MS., No. 383, appears first to have written לו *to him,* but to have corrected it immediately by inserting an א *aleph* after the ו *vau;* and thus, instead of making it אל *no,* it has made it לוא *lu,* which is no word.

Verse 20. *My master hath spared—this Syrian*] He has neither taken any thing from him for himself, nor permitted him to give any thing to me.

Verse 21. *He lighted down from the chariot*]

A. M. 3110
B. C. 894
Ante I. Ol. 118
An. Megaclis,
Arch. Athen.
perpet. 28

lighted down from the chariot to meet him, and said, [a]*Is all well?*

22 And he said, All *is* well. My master hath sent me, saying, Behold, even now there be come to me from Mount Ephraim two young men of the sons of the prophets: give them, I pray thee, a talent of silver, and two changes of garments.

23 And Naaman said, Be content, take two talents. And he urged him, and bound two talents of silver in two bags, with two changes of garments, and laid *them* upon two of his servants; and they bare *them* before him.

24 And when he came to the [b]tower, he took *them* from their hand, and bestowed *them* in the house: and he let the men go, and they departed.

A. M. 3110
B. C. 894
Ante I. Ol. 118
An. Megaclis,
Arch. Athen.
perpet. 28

25 But he went in, and stood before his master. And Elisha said unto him, Whence *comest thou,* Gehazi? And he said, Thy servant went [c]no whither.

26 And he said unto him, Went not mine heart *with thee,* when the man turned again from his chariot to meet thee? *Is it* a time to receive money, and to receive garments, and oliveyards, and vineyards, and sheep, and oxen, and men-servants, and maid-servants?

27 The leprosy therefore of Naaman [d]shall cleave unto thee, and unto thy seed for ever. And he went out from his presence [e]a leper *as white* as snow.

---

[a]Is there *peace?*——[b]Or, *secret place*——[c]Heb. *not hither or thither*

[d]1 Tim. vi. 10——[e]Exod. iv. 6; Num. xii. 10; chap. xv. 5

He treats even the prophet's servant with the profoundest respect, alights from his chariot, and goes to meet him.

Is all well?] השלום *hashalom; Is it peace, or prosperity?*

Verse 22. And he said] שלום *shalom. It is peace; all is right.* This was a common mode of address and answer.

There be come to me from Mount Ephraim] There was probably a school of the prophets at this mount.

Verse 23. He—bound two talents of silver] It required two servants to carry these two talents, for, according to the computation above, each talent was about 120lbs. weight.

Verse 24. When he came to the tower] The Chaldee, Septuagint, Syriac, and Arabic understand the word עפל *ophel*, which we translate *tower*, as signifying a *secret, dark.* or *hiding place.* He was doing a deed of darkness, and he sought darkness to conceal it. He no doubt put them in a place little frequented, or one to which few had access besides himself. But the prophet's discerning spirit found him out.

Verse 26. Went not mine heart with thee] The *Chaldee* gives this a good turn: *By the prophetic spirit it was shown unto me, when the man returned from his chariot to meet thee.*

Is it a time to receive money] He gave him farther proof of this all-discerning prophetic spirit in telling him what he designed to do with the money; he intended to set up a splendid establishment, to have men-servants and maid-servants, to have oliveyards and vineyards, and sheep and oxen. This, as the Chaldee says, *he had thought in his heart to do.*

Verse 27. The leprosy of Naaman—shall cleave unto thee] Thou hast got much money, and thou shalt have much to do with it. Thou hast got Naaman's silver, and thou shalt have Naaman's leprosy. Gehazi is not the last who has got money in an unlawful way, and has got God's curse with it.

A leper as white *as snow.*] The moment the curse was pronounced, that moment the *signs* of the leprosy began to appear. The *white shining* spot was the sign that the infection had taken place. See on Lev. xiii. 2, and the notes at the end of that chapter.

1. Some have thought, because of the prophet's curse, *The leprosy of Naaman shall cleave unto thee and thy seed for ever,* that there are persons still alive who are this man's real descendants, and afflicted with this horrible disease. Mr. Maundrell when he was in Judea made diligent inquiry concerning this, but could not ascertain the truth of the supposition. To me it appears absurd; the denunciation took place in the posterity of Gehazi till it should become extinct, and under the influence of this disorder this must *soon* have taken place. The *for ever* implies as long as any of his posterity should remain. This is the import of the word לעולם *leolam.* It takes in the whole extent or duration of the thing to which it is applied. The *for ever* of Gehazi was till his posterity became extinct.

2. The god *Rimmon,* mentioned ver. 18, we meet with nowhere else in the Scriptures, unless it be the same which Stephen calls *Remphan.* See Acts vii. 43, and the note there. *Selden* thinks that *Rimmon* is the same with *Elion,* a god of the Phœnicians, borrowed undoubtedly from the עליון *Elion, the Most High,* of the Hebrews, one of the names of the supreme God, which *attribute* became a god of the Phœnicians. *Hesychius* has the word 'Ραμας Ramas, which he translates ὁ ὑψιστος Θεος, *the Most High God,* which agrees very well with the Hebrew רמון *Rimmon,* from רמה *ramah, to make high* or *exalt.* And all these agree with the sun, as being the *highest* or most *exalted* in what is called the solar system. Some think *Saturn* is intended, and others *Venus.* Much may be seen on this subject in Selden De Diis Syris.

3. Let us not suppose that the *offence* of Gehazi was too severely punished. 1. Look at the principle, *covetousness.* 2. *Pride* and *vanity;* he wished to become a great man. 3. His *lying,* in order to impose on Naaman: *Behold, even now there be come to me, &c.* 4. He in effect *sells* the cure of Naaman for so

much money; for if Naaman had not been cured, could he have pretended to ask the silver and raiment? 5. It was an act of *theft;* he applied that to his own use which Naaman gave him for his master. 6. He *dishonoured* his master by getting the money and raiment in his name, who had before so solemnly refused it. 7. He closed the whole by *lying to his master,* denying that he had gone after Naaman, or that he had received any thing from him. But was it not severe to *extend the punishment of his crime to his innocent posterity?* I answer, it does not appear that any of Gehazi's children, if he had any *prior* to this, were smitten with the leprosy; and as to those whom he might beget *after* this time, their leprosy must be the necessary consequence of their being engendered by a leprous father.

Reader, see the end of *avarice* and *ambition;* and see the truth of those words, "He that will be rich, shall fall into temptation, and a snare, and into divers hurtful lusts which drown men in destruction and perdition."—St. *Paul.*

4. We have already remarked the *apparently severe* and *manifestly kind providence* of God in this business. 1. A marauding party was permitted to spoil the confines of the land of Israel. 2. They brought away, to reduce to captivity, a little maid, probably the hope of her father's house. 3. She became Naaman's property, and waited on his wife. 4. She announced God and his prophet. 5. Naaman, on the faith of her account, took a journey to Samaria. 6. Gets healed of his leprosy. 7. Is converted to the Lord; and, doubtless, brought at least his whole family to believe to the saving of their souls. What was *severe* to the *parents* of the little maid was most kind to *Naaman* and his *family;* and the parents lost their child only a little time, that they might again receive her with honour and glory for ever. How true are the words of the poet!—

"Behind a *frowning* providence he hides a *smiling* face."

And see the benefits of a religious education! Had not this little maid been brought up in the knowledge of the true God, she had not been the instrument of so great a salvation. See my sermon on this subject 2 Kings v. 12.

CHAPTER VI

The sons of the prophets wish to enlarge their dwelling-place, and go to the banks of Jordan to cut down wood, when one of them drops his axe into the water, which Elisha causes to swim, 1–7. Elisha, understanding all the secret designs of the king of Syria against Israel, informs the king of Israel of them, 8–10. The king of Syria, finding that Elisha had thus penetrated his secrets and frustrated his attempts, sends a great host to Dothan, to take the prophet; the Lord strikes them with blindness; and Elisha leads the whole host to Samaria, and delivers them up to the king of Israel, 11–19. The Lord opens their eyes, and they see their danger, 20. But the king of Israel is prevented from destroying them; and, at the order of the prophet, gives them meat and drink, and dismisses them to their master, 21–23. Ben-hadad besieges Samaria, and reduces the city to great distress, of which several instances are given, 24–30. The king of Israel vows the destruction of Elisha, and sends to have him beheaded, 31–33.

A. M. 3111
B. C. 893
Ante I. Ol. 117
An. Megaclis,
Arch. Athen.
perpet. 29

AND [a]the sons of the prophets said unto Elisha, Behold now, the place where we dwell with thee is too strait for us.

2 Let us go, we pray thee, unto Jordan, and take thence every man a beam, and let us make us a place there, where we may dwell. And he answered, Go ye.

3 And one said, Be content, I pray thee, and go with thy servants. And he answered, I will go.

4 So he went with them. And when they came to Jordan they cut down wood.

A. M. 3111
B. C. 893
Ante I. Ol. 117
An. Megaclis,
Arch. Athen.
perpet. 29

5 But as one was felling a beam, the [b]axe head fell into the water: and he cried, and said, Alas, master! for it was borrowed.

6 And the man of God said, Where fell it? And he showed him the place. And [c]he cut down a stick, and cast *it* in thither; and the iron did swim.

---

[a]Chap. iv. 38——[b]Heb. *iron*　　　[c]Chap. ii. 21

NOTES ON CHAP. VI

Verse 1. *The place—is too strait for us.*] Notwithstanding the general profligacy of Israel, the schools of the prophets increased. This was no doubt owing to the influence of Elisha.

Verse 2. *Every man a beam*] They made a sort of *log-houses* with their own hands.

Verse 5. *Alas, master! for it was borrowed.*]

אהה אדני והוא שאול *ahah adonia, vehu shaul!*

Ah! ah, my master; and it has been sought. It has fallen in, and I have sought it in vain. Or, *it was borrowed,* and therefore I am the more afflicted for its loss; and *Jarchi* adds, I have nothing wherewith to repay it.

Verse 6. *He cut down a stick*] This had no natural tendency to raise the iron; it was only a sign or ceremony which the prophet chose to use on the occasion.

The iron did swim.] This was a real miracle; for the gravity of the metal must have for ever kept it at the bottom of the water.

A. M. 3111
B. C. 893
Ante I. Ol. 117
An. Megaclis,
Arch. Athen.
perpet. 29

7 Therefore said he, Take *it* up to thee. And he put out his hand, and took it.

8 Then the king of Syria warred against Israel, and took counsel with his servants, saying, In such and such a place *shall be* my ᵈcamp.

9 And the man of God sent unto the king of Israel, saying, Beware that thou pass not such a place; for thither the Syrians are come down.

10 And the king of Israel sent to the place which the man of God told him and warned him of, and saved himself there, not once nor twice.

11 Therefore the heart of the king of Syria was sore troubled for this thing; and he called his servants, and said unto them, Will ye not show me which of us *is* for the king of Israel?

12 And one of his servants said, ᵉNone, my lord, O king: but Elisha, the prophet that *is* in Israel, telleth the king of Israel the words that thou speakest in thy bed-chamber.

13 And he said, Go and spy where he *is,* that I may send and fetch him. And it was told him, saying, Behold, he *is* in ᶠDothan.

14 Therefore sent he thither horses, and chariots, and a ᵍgreat host: and they came by night, and compassed the city about.

15 And when the ʰservant of the man of God was risen early, and gone forth, behold, a host compassed the city both with horses and chariots. And his servant said unto him, Alas, my master! how shall we do?

16 And he answered, Fear not: for ⁱthey that *be* with us *are* more than they that *be* with them.

17 And Elisha prayed, and said, LORD, I pray thee, open his eyes, that he may see. And the LORD opened the eyes of the young man; and he saw: and, behold, the mountain *was* full of ᵏhorses and chariots of fire round about Elisha.

18 And when they came down to him, Elisha prayed unto the LORD, and said, Smite this people, I pray thee, with blindness. And ˡhe smote them with blindness, according to the word of Elisha.

19 And Elisha said unto them, This *is* not the way, neither *is* this the city: ᵐfollow me, and I will bring you to the man whom ye seek. But he led them to Samaria.

20 And it came to pass, when they were come into Samaria, that Elisha said, LORD,

A. M. 3111
B. C. 893
Ante I. Ol. 117
An. Megaclis,
Arch. Athen.
perpet. 29

ᵈOr, *encamping*——ᵉHeb. *No*——ᶠGen. xxxvii. 17
ᵍHeb. *heavy*——ʰOr, *minister*——ⁱ2 Chron. xxxii. 7; Psalm lv. 18; Romans viii. 31

ᵏChapter ii. 11; Psalm xxxiv. 7; lxviii. 17; Zechariah i. 8; vi. 1-7——ˡGenesis xix. 11——ᵐHebrew, *come ye after me*

Verse 8. *The king of Syria warred against Israel*] This was probably the same Ben-hadad who is mentioned ver. 24. What was the *real* or *pretended* cause of this war we cannot tell; but we may say, in numberless war cases, as Calmet says in this: "An ambitious and restless prince always finds a sufficiency of reasons to colour his enterprises."

In such and such a place] The Syrian king had observed, from the disposition of the Israelitish army, in what direction it was about to make its movements; and therefore laid ambuscades where he might surprise it to the greatest advantage.

Verse 9. *Beware that thou pass not such a place*] Elisha must have had this information by immediate revelation from heaven.

Verse 10. *Sent to the place*] To see if it were so. But the *Vulgate* gives it quite a different turn: *Misit rex Israel ad locum, et præoccupavit eum.* The king of Israel sent previously to the place, and took possession of it; and thus the Syrians were disappointed. This is very likely, though it is not expressed in the Hebrew text. The prophet knew the Syrians marked such a place; he told the king of Israel, and he hastened and sent a party of troops to pre-occupy it; and thus the Syrians found that their designs had been detected.

Verse 13. *Behold, he is in Dothan.*] This is supposed to be the same place as that mentioned in Gen. xxxvii. 17. It lay about twelve miles from Samaria.

Verse 14. *He sent thither horses*] It is strange he did not think that he who could penetrate his secrets with respect to the Israelitish army, could inform himself of all his machinations against his own life.

Verse 16. *For they that* be *with us* are *more, &c.*] What astonishing intercourse had this man with heaven! It seems the whole heavenly host had it in commission to help him.

Verse 17. *Lord—open his eyes*] Where is heaven? Is it not above, beneath, around us? And were our eyes open as were those of the prophet's servant, we should see the heavenly host in all directions. The horses and chariots of fire were there, before the eyes of Elisha's servant were opened.

Verse 18. *Smite this people—with blindness*] Confound their sight so that they may not know what they see, and so mistake one place for another.

Verse 19. *I will bring you to the man whom ye seek.*] And he did so; he was their guide to Samaria, and showed himself to them fully in that city.

Verse 20. *Open the eyes of these* men] Take

A. M. 3111
B. C. 893
Ante I. Ol. 117
An. Megaclis,
Arch. Athen.
perpet. 26

open the eyes of these *men,* that they may see. And the LORD opened their eyes, and they saw; and, behold, *they were* in the midst of Samaria.

21 And the king of Israel said unto Elisha, when he saw them, My father, shall I smite *them?* shall I smite *them?*

22 And he answered, Thou shalt not smite *them:* wouldest thou smite those whom thou hast taken captive with thy sword and with thy bow? ⁿset bread and water before them, that they may eat and drink, and go to their master.

23 And he prepared great provision for them: and when they had eaten and drunk, he sent them away, and they went to their master. So °the bands of Syria came no more into the land of Israel.

24 And it came to pass after this, that Ben-hadad king of Syria gathered all his host, and went up, and besieged Samaria.

A. M. 3112
B. C. 892
Ante I. Ol. 116
An. Megaclis,
Arch. Athen.
perpet. 30

25 And there was a great famine in Samaria: and, behold, they besieged it, until an ass's head was *sold* for fourscore *pieces* of silver, and the fourth part of a cab of dove's dung for five *pieces* of silver.

26 And as the king of Israel was passing by upon the wall, there cried a woman unto him, saying, Help, my lord, O king.

27 And he said, ᵖIf the LORD do not help thee, whence shall I help thee? out of the barn-floor, or out of the wine-press?

28 And the king said unto her, What aileth thee? And she answered, This woman said unto me, Give thy son, that we may eat him to-day, and we will eat my son to-morrow.

29 So ᑫwe boiled my son, and did eat him:

ⁿRom. xii. 20——°Ch. v. 2; ver. 8, 9——ᵖOr, *Let not the*
Lord save thee——ᑫLev. xxvi. 29; Deut. xxviii. 53, 57

---

away their confusion of vision, that they may discern things as they *are,* and distinguish *where* they are.

Verse 21. *My father, shall I smite*] This was dastardly; the utmost he could have done with these men, when thus brought into his hand, was to make them prisoners of war.

Verse 22. *Whom thou hast taken captive*] Those who in open *battle* either lay down their arms, or are surrounded, and have their retreat cut off, are entitled to their lives, much more those who are thus providentially put into thy hand, without having been in actual hostility against thee. Give them meat and drink, and send them home to their master, and let them thus know that thou fearest him not, and art incapable of doing an ungenerous or unmanly action.

Verse 23. *He prepared great provision for them*] These, on the return to their master, could tell him strange things about the power of the God of Israel, and the magnanimity of its king.

So the bands of Syria came no more] Marauding parties were no more permitted by the Syrian king to make inroads upon Israel. And it is very likely that for some considerable time after this, there was no war between these two nations. What is mentioned in the next verse was more than a year afterwards.

Verse 25. *And, behold, they besieged it*] They had closed it in on every side, and reduced it to the greatest necessity.

An ass's head was sold for fourscore pieces of silver] I suppose we are to take the *ass's head* literally; and if the *head* sold for so much, what must other parts sell for which were much to be preferred? The famine must be great that could oblige them to eat any part of an animal that was proscribed by the law; and it must be still greater that could oblige them to purchase so *mean a part* of this *unclean* animal at so *high a price.* The *piece of silver* was probably the *drachm,* with about

seven pence three farthings of our money; the whole amounting to about *two pounds nine shillings.*

And the fourth part of a cab of dove's dung] The *cab* was about a *quart* or *three pints.* Dove's dung, חריונים *chiriyonim.* Whether this means *pigeon's dung* literally, or a kind of *pulse,* has been variously disputed by learned men. After having written much upon the subject, illustrated with quotations from east, west, north, and south, I choose to spare my reader the trouble of wading through them, and shall content myself with asserting that it is probable a *sort of pease* are meant, which the Arabs to this day call by this name. "The *garvancos, cicer,* or *chick pea,*" says Dr. Shaw, "has been taken for the pigeon's dung, mentioned in the siege of Samaria; and as the *cicer* is *pointed* at one end, and acquires an *ash colour* in parching, the first of which circumstances answers to the *figure,* the second to the usual *colour* of *dove's* dung, the supposition is by no means to be disregarded."

I should not omit saying that *dove's dung* is of great value in the East, for its power in producing *cucumbers, melons,* &c., which has induced many learned men to take the words *literally.* Bochart has exhausted this subject, and concludes that a kind of *pulse* is meant. Most learned men are of his opinion.

Verse 27. *If the Lord do not help thee*] Some read this as an *imprecation, May God save thee not! how can I save thee?*

Verse 29. *So we boiled my son*] This is horrible; but for the sake of humanity we must allow that the children *died* through hunger, and then became food for their starved, desperate parents.

She hath hid her son.] He was already dead, says *Jarchi;* and she hid him, that she might eat him alone.

This very evil Moses had foretold should come upon them if they forsook God; see Deut. xxviii. 53, 57. The same evil came upon

A. M. 3112
B. C. 892
Ante I. Ol. 116
An. Megaclis,
Arch. Athen.
perpet. 30

and I said unto her on the 'next day, Give thy son, that we may eat him: and she hath hid her son.

30 And it came to pass, when the king heard the words of the woman, that he 'rent his clothes; and he passed by upon the wall, and the people looked, and, behold, *he had* sackcloth within upon his flesh.

31 Then he said, 'God do so and more also to me, if the head of Elisha the son of Shaphat shall stand on him this day.

32 But Elisha sat in his house, and "the

elders sat with him; and *the king* sent a man from before him: but ere the messenger came to him, he said to the elders, 'See ye how this son of "a murderer hath sent to take away mine head? look, when the messenger cometh, shut the door, and hold him fast at the door: *is* not the sound of his master's feet behind him?

33 And while he yet talked with them, behold, the messenger came down unto him: and he said, Behold, this evil *is* of the LORD; *What should I wait for the LORD any longer?

A. M. 3112
B. C. 892
Ante I. Ol. 116]
An. Megaclis,
Arch. Athen.
perpet. 30

'Hebrew, *other*——'1 Kings xxi. 27——'Ruth i. 17; 1 Kings xix. 2

"Ezek. viii. 1; xx. 1——'Luke xiii. 32——"1 Kings xviii. 4——'Job ii. 9

---

this wretched people when besieged by Nebuchadnezzar; see Ezek. v. 10. And also when Titus besieged Jerusalem; see *Josephus*, De Bell. Judaic. lib. vi., cap. 3, and my notes on Matt. xxiv. 19.

Verse 30. He had *sackcloth within upon his flesh.*] The king was in deep mourning for the distresses of the people.

Verse 31. *If the head of Elisha—shall stand on him*] Either he attributed these calamities to the prophet, or else he thought he could remove them, and yet would not. The miserable king was driven to desperation.

Verse 32. *This son of a murderer*] Jehoram, the son of Ahab and Jezebel. But Ahab is called a *murderer* because of the murder of Naboth.

Shut the door] He was obliged to make use of this method for his personal safety, as the king was highly incensed.

The sound of his master's feet behind him?] That is, King Jehoram is following his messenger, that he may see him take off my head.

Verse 33. *Behold, this evil is of the Lord*] It is difficult to know whether it be the *prophet*, the *messenger*, or the *king*, that says these words. It might be the answer of the *prophet*

from within to the messenger who was without, and who sought for admission, and gave his reason; to whom Elisha might have replied: "I am not the cause of these calamities; they are from the Lord; I have been praying for their removal; but why should I pray to the Lord any longer, for the time of your deliverance is at hand?" And *then Elisha said,*—see the following chapter, where the removal of the calamity is foretold in the most explicit manner; and indeed the chapter is unhappily divided from this. The seventh chapter should have begun with ver. 24 of this chapter, as, by the present division, the story is unnaturally interrupted.

How natural is it for men to lay the cause of their suffering on any thing or person but themselves! Ahab's iniquity was sufficient to have brought down God's displeasure on a whole nation; and yet he takes no blame to himself, but lays all on the prophet, who was the only *salt* that preserved the whole nation from corruption. How few take their sins to *themselves!* and till they do this, they cannot be true penitents; nor can they expect God's wrath to be averted till they feel themselves the chief of sinners.

CHAPTER VII

Elisha foretells abundant relief to the besieged inhabitants of Samaria, 1. One of the lords questions the possibility of it; and is assured that he shall see it on the morrow, but not taste of it, 2. Four lepers, perishing with hunger, go to the camp of the Syrians to seek relief, and find it totally deserted, 3-5. How the Syrians were alarmed, and fled, 6, 7. The lepers begin to take the spoil, but at last resolve to carry the good news to the city, 8-11. The king, suspecting some treachery, sends some horsemen to scour the country, and see whether the Syrians are not somewhere concealed; they return, and confirm the report that the Syrians are totally fled, 12-15. The people go out and spoil the camp, in consequence of which provisions become as plentiful as Elisha had foretold, 16. The unbelieving lord, having the charge of the gate committed to him, is trodden to death by the crowd, 17-20.

A. M. 3112
B. C. 892
Ante I. Ol. 116
An. Megaclis,
Arch. Athen.
perpet. 30

THEN Elisha said, Hear ye the word of the LORD; Thus saith the LORD, *To-morrow about this time *shall* a measure

of fine flour *be sold* for a shekel, and two measures of barley for a shekel, in the gate of Samaria.

A. M. 3112
B. C. 892
Ante I. Ol. 116
An. Megaclis,
Arch. Athen.
perpet. 30

---

*2 Kings

chap. vii. 18, 19

NOTES ON CHAP. VII

Verse 1. *To-morrow about this time*] This was in reply to the desponding language of the

king, and to vindicate himself from the charge of being author of this calamity. See the end of the preceding chapter.

A measure of fine flour—for a shekel] A seah

A. M. 3112
B. C. 892
Ante I. Ol. 116
An. Megaclis,
Arch. Athen.
perpet. 30

2 [b]Then [c]a lord on whose hand the king leaned answered the man of God, and said, Behold, [d]if the LORD would make windows in heaven, might this thing be? And he said, Behold, thou shalt see *it* with thine eyes, but shalt not eat thereof.

3 And there were four leprous men [e]at the entering in of the gate: and they said one to another, Why sit we here until we die?

4 If we say, We will enter into the city, then the famine *is* in the city, and we shall die there: and if we sit still here, we die also. Now therefore come, and let us fall unto the host of the Syrians: if they save us alive, we shall live; and if they kill us, we shall but die.

5 And they rose up in the twilight, to go unto the camp of the Syrians: and when they were come to the uttermost part of the camp of Syria, behold, *there was* no man there.

6 For the LORD had made the host of the Syrians [f]to hear a noise of chariots, and a noise of horses, *even* the noise of a great host: and they said one to another, Lo, the king of Israel hath hired against us [g]the kings of the Hittites, and the kings of the Egyptians, to come upon us.

7 Wherefore they [h]arose and fled in the twilight, and left their tents, and their horses, and their asses, even the camp as it *was,* and fled for their life.

8 And when these lepers came to the uttermost part of the camp, they went into one tent, and did eat and drink, and carried thence silver, and gold, and raiment, and went and hid *it;* and came again, and entered into another tent, and carried thence *also,* and went and hid *it.*

A. M. 3112
B. C. 892
Ante I. Ol. 116
An. Megaclis,
Arch. Athen.
perpet. 30

9 Then they said one to another, We do not well: this day *is* a day of good tidings, and we hold our peace: if we tarry till the morning light, [i]some mischief will come upon us: now therefore come, that we may go and tell the king's household.

10 So they came and called unto the porter of the city: and they told them, saying, We came to the camp of the Syrians, and, behold, *there was* no man there, neither voice of man, but horses tied, and asses tied, and the tents as they *were.*

11 And he called the porters; and they told *it* to the king's house within.

12 And the king arose in the night, and said unto his servants, I will now show you what the Syrians have done to us. They know that we *be* hungry; therefore are they gone out of the camp to hide themselves in the field, saying, When they come out of the city, we shall catch them alive, and get into the city.

13 And one of his servants answered and said, Let *some* take, I pray thee, five of the

---

[b]Ver. 17, 19, 20——[c]Heb. *a lord which* belonged *to the king leaning upon his hand,* chap. v. 18——[d]Mal. iii. 10——[e]Lev. xiii. 46

[f]2 Sam. v. 24; chap. xix. 7; Job xv. 21——[g]1 Kings x. 29——[h]Psa. xlviii. 4, 5, 6; Prov. xxviii. 1——[i]Heb. *we shall find punishment*

---

of fine flour: the *seah* was about *two gallons* and *a half;* the *shekel, two shillings* and *four-pence* at the lowest computation. A wide difference between this and the price of the ass's head mentioned above.

Verse 2. *Then a lord*] שָׁלִישׁ *shalish.* This word, as a name of *office,* occurs often, and seems to point out one of the highest offices in the state. So unlikely was this prediction to be fulfilled, that he thought God must pour out wheat and barley from heaven before it could have a literal accomplishment.

But shalt not eat thereof.] This was a mere prediction of his *death,* but not as a judgment for his unbelief; any person in his circumstances might have spoken as he did. He stated in effect that nothing but a miracle could procure the plenty predicted, and by a miracle alone was it done; and any person in his place might have been trodden to death by the crowd in the gate of Samaria.

Verse 3. *There were four leprous men*] The *Gemara* in *Sota, R. Sol. Jarchi,* and others, say that these four lepers were *Gehazi and his three sons.*

At the entering in of the gate] They were not permitted to mingle in civil society.

Verse 5. *The uttermost part of the camp*] Where the Syrian advanced guards should have been.

Verse 6. *The Lord had made the—Syrians to hear a noise*] This threw them into confusion; they imagined that they were about to be attacked by powerful auxiliaries, which the king of Israel had hired against them.

Verse 12. *The king arose in the night*] This king had made a noble defence; he seems to have shared in all the sufferings of the besieged, and to have been ever at his post. Even in vile Ahab there were some good things!

They know that we be *hungry*] This was a very natural conclusion; the Syrians by the closest blockade could not induce them to give up the city, but knowing that they were in a starving condition, they might make use of such a stratagem as that imagined by the king, in order to get possession of the city.

Verse 13. *And one of his servants answered*] This is a very difficult verse, and the great variety of explanations given of it cast but

A. M. 3112
B. C. 892
Ante I. Ol. 116
An. Megaclis,
Arch. Athen.
perpet. 30

horses that remain, which are left [k]in the city, (behold, they *are* as all the multitude of Israel that are left in it: behold, *I say,* they *are* even as all the multitude of the Israelites that are consumed:) and let us send and see.

14 They took therefore two chariot horses; and the king sent after the host of the Syrians, saying, Go and see.

15 And they went after them unto Jordan: and, lo, all the way *was* full of garments and vessels, which the Syrians had cast away in their haste. And the messengers returned, and told the king.

16 And the people went out, and spoiled the tents of the Syrians. So a measure of fine flour was *sold* for a shekel, and two measures of barley for a shekel, [l]according to the word of the LORD.

A. M. 3112
B. C. 892
Ante I. Ol. 116
An. Megaclis,
Arch. Athen.
perpet. 30

17 And the king appointed the lord on whose hand he leaned to have the charge of the gate: and the people trode upon him in the gate, and he died, [m]as the man of God had said, who spake when the king came down to him.

18 And it came to pass, as the man of God had spoken to the king, saying, [n]Two measures of barley for a shekel, and a measure of fine flour for a shekel, shall be to-morrow about this time in the gate of Samaria:

19 And that lord answered the man of God, and said, Now, behold, *if* the LORD should make windows in heaven, might such a thing be? And he said, Behold, thou shalt see it with thine eyes, but shalt not eat thereof.

20 And so it fell out unto him: for the people trode upon him in the gate, and he died.

---

[k]Heb. *in it*——[l]Ver. 1

[m]Chap. vi. 32; ver. 2——[n]Ver. 1

---

little light on the subject. I am inclined to believe, with Dr. *Kennicott,* that there is an *interpolation* here which puzzles, if not destroys, the sense. "Several instances," says he, "have been given of words improperly *repeated* by Jewish transcribers, who have been *careless* enough to make such *mistakes,* and yet *cautious* not to *alter* or *erase,* for fear of discovery. This verse furnishes another instance in a careless *repetition* of *seven Hebrew words,* thus:—

הנשארים אשר נשארו בה הנם בכל ההמון ישראל אשר

נשארו בה הנם בכל המון ישראל אשר תמי

The exact English of this verse is this: *And the servant said, Let them take now five of the remaining horses, which remain in it; behold they are as all the multitude of Israel, which* [remain in it; behold they are as all the multitude of Israel which] *are consumed; and let us send and see.*

"Whoever considers that the *second set* of these *seven words* is neither in the *Septuagint* nor *Syriac* versions, and that those translators who suppose these words to be genuine alter them to make them look like sense, will probably allow them to have been at first an improper *repetition;* consequently to be now an *interpolation* strangely continued in the Hebrew text." They are wanting in more than *forty* of *Kennicott's* and *De Rossi's* MSS. In some others they are left *without points;* in others they have been *written in,* and afterwards *blotted out;* and in others *four,* in others *five,* of the *seven words* are omitted. *De Rossi* concludes thus: *Nec verba hæc legunt* LXX., *Vulg., Syrus simplex, Syrus Heptaplaris Parisiensis, Targum.* They stand on little authority, and the text should be read, omitting the words enclosed by *brackets,* as above.

They are consumed] The words אשר תמו *asher tamu* should be translated, *which are perfect;* i. e., fit for service. The rest of the horses were either *dead* of the famine, *killed* for the subsistence of the besieged, or so *weak* as not to be able to perfom such a journey.

Verse 14. *They took—two chariot horses*] They had at first intended to send *five;* probably they found on examination that only two were effective. But if they sent two chariots, each would have two horses, and probably a single horse for crossing the country.

Verse 15. *All the way* was *full of garments and vessels*] A manifest proof of the hurry and precipitancy with which they fled.

Verse 17. *And the people trode upon him*] This officer being appointed by the king to have the command of the *gate,* the people rushing *out* to get spoil, and *in* to carry it to their houses, he was borne down by the multitude, and trodden to death. This also was foreseen by the spirit of prophecy. The literal and exact fulfilment of such predictions must have acquired the prophet a great deal of credit in Israel.

DR. *Lightfoot* remarks that, between the *first* and *last year* of Jehoram son of Jehoshaphat, there are very many occurrences mentioned which are not referred nor fixed to their *proper year;* and, therefore, they must be calculated in a *gross sum,* as coming to pass *in one of these years.* These are the stories contained in chapters iv., v., vi., and vii., of this book; and in 2 Chron, xxi. 6-19. They may be calculated thus: In the *first* year of Jehoram, Elisha, returning out of Moab into the land of Israel, multiplies the widow's oil; he is lodged in **Shunem,** and assures his hostess of a child. The *seven years'* famine was then begun, and he gives the Shunammite warning of its continuance.

The *second* year she bears her child in the land of the Philistines, chap. viii. 2. And Elisha resides among the disciples of the prophets at Gilgal, heals the poisoned pottage, and feeds *one hundred* men with *twenty* barley loaves and some ears of corn. That summer he cures Naaman of his leprosy, the only cure of this kind done till Christ came.

The *third* year he makes iron to swim, prevents the Syrians' ambushments, strikes those with blindness who were sent to seize him, and sends them back to their master.

The *fourth* year Jehoshaphat dies, and Edom rebels and shakes off the yoke laid upon them by David: Libnah also rebels.

The *fifth* year Samaria is besieged by Ben-hadad, the city is most grievously afflicted; and, after being nearly destroyed by famine, it is suddenly relieved by a miraculous interference of God, which had been distinctly foretold by Elisha.

The *sixth* year the Philistines and Arabians oppress Jehoram, king of Judah, and take captive his wives and children, leaving only one son behind.

The *seventh* year Jehoram falls into a grievous sickness, so that his bowels fall out, 2 Chron. xxi. 19. And in the same year the *seven years' famine ends* about the time of harvest; and at that harvest, the Shunammite's son dies, and is restored to life by Elisha,

though the story of his birth and death is related together; and yet some years must have passed between them. Not long after this the Shunammite goes to the king to petition to be restored to her own land, which she had left in the time of the famine, and had sojourned in the land of the Philistines.

This year Elisha is at Damascus; Ben-hadad falls sick; Hazael stifles him with a wet cloth, and reigns in his stead. All these things Dr. Lightfoot supposes happened between A. M. 3110 and 3117.—See *Lightfoot's* Works, vol. i., p. 88. In examining the facts recorded in these books, we shall always find it difficult, and sometimes impossible, to ascertain the exact chronology. The difficulty is increased by a custom common among these annalists, the giving the whole of a story *at once*, though several incidents took place at the *distance of some years from the commencement of the story:* as they seem unwilling to have to recur to the same history in the chronological order of its facts.

CHAPTER VIII

Account of the sojourning of the Shunammite in the land of the Philistines, during the seven years famine, 1, 2. She returns, and solicits the king to let her have back her land; which, with its fruits, he orders to be restored to her, 3–6. Elisha comes to Damascus, and finds Ben-hadad sick; who sends his servant Hazael to the prophet to inquire whether he shall recover, 7–9. Elisha predicts his death, tells Hazael that he shall be king, and shows him the atrocities he will commit, 10–14. Hazael returns, stifles his master with a wet cloth, and reigns in his stead, 15. Jehoram, son of Jehoshaphat, becomes king over Judah; his bad reign, 16–19. Edom and Libnah revolt, 20–22. Jehoram dies, and his son Ahaziah reigns in his stead, 23, 24. His bad reign, 25–27. He joins with Joram, son of Ahab, against Hazael; Joram is wounded by the Syrians, and goes to Jezreel to be healed, 28, 29.

A. M. 3113
B. C. 891
Ante I. Ol. 115
An. Diogeneti,
Arch. Athen.
perpet. 1

THEN spake Elisha unto the woman, [a]whose son he had restored to life, saying, Arise, and go thou and thine household, and sojourn wheresoever thou canst sojourn: for the LORD [b]hath called for a famine; and it shall also come upon the land seven years.

2 And the woman arose, and did after the saying of the man of God: and she went with her household, and sojourned in the land of the Philistines seven years.

A. M. 3119
B. C. 885
Ante I. Ol. 109
An. Diogeneti,
Arch. Athen.
perpet. 7

3 And it came to pass at the seven years' end, that the woman returned out of the land of the Philistines: and she went forth to cry unto the king for her house and for her land.

4 And the king talked with [c]Gehazi the servant of the man of God, saying, Tell me, I pray thee, all the great things that Elisha hath done.

5 And it came to pass, as he was telling the

---

[a]Chap. iv. 35——[b]Psa. cv. 16; Hag. i. 11

[c]Chap. v. 27

NOTES ON CHAP. VIII

Verse 1. *Then spake Elisha*] As this is the relation of an event far past, the words should be translated, "But Elisha *had spoken* unto the woman whose son he *had restored* unto life; and the woman *had arisen*, and acted according to the saying of the man of God, and *had gone* with her family, and *had sojourned* in the land of the Philistines seven years." What is mentioned in these two verses happened several years before the time specified in the *third* verse. See the observations at the end of the preceding chapter.

Verse 4. *The king talked with Gehazi*] This is supposed to have happened *before* the cleansing of Naaman, for is it likely that the king

would hold conversation with a leprous man; or that, knowing Gehazi had been dismissed with the highest disgrace from the prophet's service, he could hold any conversation with him concerning his late master, relative to whom he could not expect him to give either a true or impartial account?

Some think that this conversation might have taken place after Gehazi became leprous; the king having an insatiable curiosity to know the private history of a man who had done such astonishing things: and from whom could he get this information, except from the prophet's own confidential servant? It agrees better with the chronology to consider what is here related as having taken place *after* the cure of Naaman. As to the circumstance of

A. M. 3119
B. C. 885
Ante I. Ol. 109
An. Diogeneti,
Arch. Athen.
perpet. 7

king how he had ^drestored a dead body to life, that, behold, the woman, whose son he had restored to life, cried to the king for her house and for her land. And Gehazi said, My lord, O king, this *is* the woman, and this *is* her son, whom Elisha restored to life.

6 And when the king asked the woman, she told him. So the king appointed unto her a certain ^eofficer, saying, Restore all that *was* hers, and all the fruits of the field since the day that she left the land, even until now.

7 And Elisha came to Damascus; and Ben-hadad the king of Syria was sick; and it was told him, saying, The man of God is come hither.

8 And the king said unto ^fHazael, ^gTake a present in thine hand, and go, meet the man of God, and ^hinquire of the LORD by him, saying, Shall I recover of this disease?

9 So Hazael went to meet him, and took a present ⁱwith him, even of every good thing of Damascus, forty camels' burden, and came and stood before him, and said, Thy son Ben-hadad king of Syria hath sent me to thee, saying, Shall I recover of this disease?

A. M. 3119
B. C. 885
Ante I. Ol. 109
An. Diogeneti,
Arch. Athen.
perpet. 7

10 And Elisha said unto him, Go say unto him, Thou mayest certainly recover; howbeit the LORD hath showed me that ^khe shall surely die.

11 And he settled his countenance ^lsteadfastly, until he was ashamed: and the man of God ^mwept.

12 And Hazael said, Why weepeth my lord? And he answered, Because I know ⁿthe evil that thou wilt do unto the children of Israel: their strong holds wilt thou set on fire, and their young men wilt thou slay with the sword, and ^owilt dash their children, and rip up their women with child.

13 And Hazael said, But what, ^p*is* thy serv-

---

d Chap. iv. 35———e Or, *eunuch*———f 1 Kings xix. 15
g 1 Sam. ix. 7; 1 Kings xiv. 3; chap. v. 5———h Chap. i. 2
i Heb. *in his hand*———k Ver. 15

l Heb. *and set it*———m Luke xix. 41———n Chap. x. 32;
xii. 17; xiii. 3, 7; Amos i. 3———o Chap. xv. 16; Hos. xiii.
16; Amos i. 13———p 1 Sam. xvii. 43

Gehazi's disease, he might overlook that, and converse with him, keeping at a reasonable distance, as nothing but actual contact could defile.

Verse 5. *This is the woman, and this is her son, whom Elisha restored to life.*] This was a very providential occurrence in behalf of the Shunammite. The relation given by Gehazi was now corroborated by the woman herself; the king was duly affected, and gave immediate orders for the restoration of her land.

Verse 7. *Elisha came to Damascus*] That he might lead Gehazi to repentance; according to *Jarchi* and some others.

Verse 8. *Take a present in thine hand*] But what an immense present was this—*forty camels' burden of every good thing of Damascus!* The prophet would need to have a very large establishment at Damascus to dispose of so much property.

Verse 10. *Thou mayest certainly recover: howbeit the Lord hath showed me that he shall surely die.*] That is, God has not *determined* thy death, nor will it be a *necessary consequence* of the *disease* by which thou art now afflicted; but this wicked man will abuse the power and trust thou hast reposed in him, and take away thy life. Even when God has not *designed* nor *appointed* the death of a person, he may nevertheless die, though not without the *permission* of God. This is a farther proof of the doctrine of *contingent events:* he might live for all his sickness, but thou wilt put an end to his life.

Verse 11. *He settled his countenance steadfastly*] Of whom does the author speak? Of

Hazael, or of Elisha? Several apply this action to the prophet: he had a murderer before him, and he saw the bloody acts he was about to commit, and was greatly distressed; but he endeavoured to conceal his feelings: at last his face reddened with anguish, his feelings overcame him, and he burst out and wept.

The *Septuagint*, as it stands in the *Complutensian* and *Antwerp* Polyglots, makes the text very plain: Καὶ ἔστη Ἀζαὴλ κατα πρωσοπον αυτου, και παρεθηκεν ενωπιον αυτου δωρα, ἑως ᾑσχυνετο· και εκλαυσεν ὁ ανθρωπος του Θεου, *And Hazael stood before his face, and he presented before him gifts till he was ashamed; and the man of God wept.*

The Codex *Vaticanus*, and the Codex *Alexandrinus*, are nearly as the Hebrew. The *Aldine* edition agrees in some respects with the *Complutensian;* but all the *versions* follow the *Hebrew.*

Verse 12. *I know the evil that thou wilt do*] We may see something of the accomplishment of this prediction, chap. x. 32, 33, and xiii. 3, 7.

Verse 13. *But what, is thy servant a dog, that he should do this great thing?*] I believe this verse to be wrongly interpreted by the general run of commentators. It is generally understood that Hazael was struck with horror at the prediction; that these cruelties were most alien from his mind; that he then felt distressed and offended at the imputation of such evils to him; and yet, so little did he know his own heart, that when he got power, and had opportunity, he did the whole with a willing heart and a ready hand. On the contrary, I think he was *delighted* at the prospect; and his question rather implies a *doubt* whether a person so

A. M. 3119
B. C. 885
Ante I. Ol. 109
An. Diogeneti,
Arch. Athen.
perpet. 7

ant a dog, that he should do this great thing? And Elisha answered, ᵍThe LORD hath showed me that thou *shalt be* king over Syria.

14 So he departed from Elisha, and came to his master; who said to him, What said Elisha to thee? And he answered, He told me *that* thou shouldest surely recover.

15 And it came to pass on the morrow, that he took a thick cloth, and dipped *it* in water, and spread *it* on his face, so that he died: and Hazael reigned in his stead.

16 And in the fifth year of Joram the son of Ahab king of Israel, Jehoshaphat *being* then king of Judah, ʳJehoram the son of Jehoshaphat king of Judah ˢbegan to reign.

17 ᵗThirty and two years old was he when he began to reign, and he reigned eight years in Jerusalem.

A.M.3112-3119
B. C. 892-885
Anno ante I.
Olymp.116-109

18 And he walked in the way of the kings of Israel, as did the house of Ahab: for ᵘthe daughter of Ahab was his wife: and he did evil in the sight of the LORD.

19 Yet the LORD would not destroy Judah for David his servant's sake, ᵛas he promised him to give him alway a ʷlight, *and* to his children.

20 In his days ˣEdom revolted from under the hand of Judah, ʸand made a king over themselves.

21 So Joram went over to Zair, and all the

ᵠ1 Kings xix. 15——ʳ2 Chron. xxi. 3, 4——ˢHeb. *reigned.* Began to reign in consort with his father ᵗ2 Chron. xxi. 5, &c.——ᵘVer. 26

ᵛ2 Sam. vii. 13; 1 Kings xi. 36; xv. 4; 2 Chron. xxi. 7 ʷHeb. *candle* or *lamp*——ˣGen. xxvii. 40; chap. iii. 27; 2 Chron. xxi. 8, 9, 10——ʸ1 Kings xxii. 47

---

inconsiderable as he is shall ever have it in his power to do such *great*, not such *evil* things; for, in his sight, they had no turpitude. The Hebrew text stands thus: כי מה עבדך הכלב כי

יעשה הדבר הגדול הזה *ki mah abdecha hakkeleb, ki yaaseh haddabar haggadol hazzeh?* "But, what! thy servant, this dog! that *he* should do this great work!" Or, "Can such a poor, worthless fellow, such *a dead dog,* [ὁ κυων ὁ τεθνηκως, *Sept.*,] perform such mighty actions? thou fillest me with surprise." And that this is the true sense, his immediate murder of his master on his return fully proves. "Our common version of these words of Hazael," as Mr. *Patten* observes, "has stood in the front of many a fine declamation utterly wide of his real sentiment. His exclamation was not the result of *horror;* his expression has no tincture of it; but of the unexpected glimpse of a crown! The prophet's answer is plainly calculated to satisfy the astonishment he had excited. A *dog* bears not, in Scripture, the character of a *cruel*, but of a *despicable* animal; nor does he who is shocked with its barbarity call it a GREAT deed."—*David Vindicated.*

Verse 15. *A thick cloth*] The versions, in general, understand this of a *hairy* or *woollen* cloth.

So that he died] He was smothered, or suffocated.

Verse 16. *In the fifth year of Joram*] This verse, as it stands in the present Hebrew text, may be thus read: "And in the fifth year of Joram son of Ahab king of Israel, [and of Jehoshaphat, king of Judah,] reigned Jehoram son of Jehoshaphat king of Judah." The three

Hebrew words, ויהושפט מלך יהודה, *and of Jehoshaphat king of Judah,* greatly disturb the chronology in this place. It is certain that Jehoshaphat reigned *twenty-five* years, and that Jehoram his son reigned but *eight;* 1 Kings xxii. 42; 2 Kings viii. 17; 2 Chron. xx. 31, and xxi. 5. So that he could not have reigned during his father's life without being king *twenty* years, and *eight* years! These words are want-

ing in *three* of *Kennicott's* and *De Rossi's* MSS., in the *Complutensian* and *Aldine* editions of the *Septuagint*, in the *Peshito Syriac*, in the Parisian *Heptapler Syriac*, the *Arabic*, and in many copies of the *Vulgate*, collated by Dr. *Kennicott* and *De Rossi*, both *printed* and *manuscript;* to which may be added *two* MSS. in my own library, one of the fourteenth, the other of the eleventh century, and in what I judge to be the *Editio Princeps* of the Vulgate. And it is worthy of remark that in this latter work, after the fifteenth verse, ending with *Quo mortuo regnavit Azahel pro eo,* the following words are in a smaller character, *Anno quinto Joram filii Achab regis Israhel, regnavit Joram filius Josaphat rex Juda.* Triginta, &c. We have already seen that it is supposed that Jehoshaphat associated his son with him in the kingdom; and that the *fifth year* in this place only regards *Joram* king of Israel, and not *Jehoshaphat* king of Judah. See the notes on chap. i. 17.

Verse 17. *He reigned eight years in Jerusalem.*] Beginning with the fifth year of Joram, king of Israel. He reigned *three years* with *Jehoshaphat* his father, and *five years* alone; i. e., from A. M. 3112 to 3119, according to Archbishop Usher.

Verse 18. *The daughter of Ahab was his wife*] This was the infamous *Athaliah;* and through this marriage Jehoshaphat and Ahab were confederates; and this friendship was continued after Ahab's death.

Verse 19. *To give him alway a light*] To give him a *successor* in his own family.

Verse 21. *Joram went over to Zair*] This is the same as *Seir*, a chief city of Idumea. So Isa. xxi., 11: *The burden of Dumah* (Idumea.) *He calleth to me out of Seir.*

Smote the Edomites] It appears that the Israelites were *surrounded* by the Idumeans; and that in the night Joram and his men cut their way through them, and so got every man to his tent, for they were not able to make any farther head against these enemies; and therefore it is said, *that Edom revolted from under the hand of Judah unto this day.*

A.M.3112-3119
B. C. 892-885
Anno ante I.
Olymp.116-109

chariots with him: and he rose by night, and smote the Edomites which compassed him about, and the captains of the chariots: and the people fled into their tents.

22 [z]Yet Edom revolted from under the hand of Judah unto this day. [a]Then Libnah revolted at the same time.

23 And the rest of the acts of Joram, and all that he did, *are* they not written in the book of the chronicles of the kings of Judah?

A.M.3119-3120
B. C. 885-884
Anno ante I.
Olymp.109-108

24 And Joram slept with his fathers, and was buried with his fathers in the city of David: and [b]Ahaziah [c]his son reigned in his stead.

25 In the twelfth year of Joram the son of Ahab king of Israel did Ahaziah the son of Jehoram king of Judah begin to reign.

26 [d]Two and twenty years old *was* Ahaziah when he began to reign; and he reigned one year in Jerusalem. And his mother's name *was* Athaliah, the [e]daughter of Omri king of Israel.

A.M.3119-3120
B. C. 885-884
Anno ante I.
Olymp.109-108

27 [f]And he walked in the way of the house of Ahab, and did evil in the sight of the LORD, as *did* the house of Ahab: for he *was* the son-in-law of the house of Ahab.

28 And he went [g]with Joram the son of Ahab to the war against Hazael king of Syria in Ramoth-gilead; and the Syrians wounded Joram.

A. M. 3120
B. C. 884
Ante I. Ol. 108
An. Diogeneti,
Arch. Athen.
perpet. 8

29 And [h]King Joram went back to be healed in Jezreel of the wounds [i]which the Syrians had given him at [k]Ramah, when he fought against Hazael king of Syria. [l]And Ahaziah the son of Jehoram king of Judah went down to see Joram the son of Ahab in Jezreel, because he was [m]sick.

---

[z]And so fulfilled; Gen. xxvii. 40——[a]2 Chron. xxi. 10
[b]2 Chron. xxii. 1——[c]Called *Azariah*, 2 Chron. xxii. 6,
and *Jehoahaz*, 2 Chron. xxi. 17; xxv. 23——[d]See
2 Chron. xxii. 2——[e]Or, *grand-daughter; see ver. 18*

[f]2 Chron. xxii. 3, 4——[g]2 Chron. xxii. 5——[h]Chap.
ix. 15——[i]Heb. *wherewith the Syrians had wounded*
[k]Called *Ramoth*, ver. 28——[l]Chap. ix. 16; 2 Chron.
xxii. 6, 7——[m]Heb. *wounded*

Verse 23. *Are they not written in the book of the chronicles*] Several remarkable particulars relative to Joram may be found in 2 Chron. xxi.

Verse 26. *Two and twenty years old* was *Ahaziah when he began to reign*] In 2 Chron. xxii. 2, it is said, *forty and two years old was Ahaziah when he began to reign;* this is a heavy difficulty, to remove which several expedients have been used. It is most evident that, if we follow the reading in *Chronicles*, it makes the *son two years older* than his *own father!* for his father began to reign when he was *thirty-two* years old, and reigned *eight* years, and so died, being *forty* years old; see ver. 17. Dr. *Lightfoot* says, "The *original* meaneth thus: *Ahaziah was the son of two and forty years;* namely, of the house of *Omri*, of whose seed he was by the mother's side; and he walked in the ways of that house, and came to ruin at the same time with it. This the text directs us to look after, when it calleth his mother the *daughter of Omri*, who was indeed the *daughter of Ahab*. Now, these *forty-two* years are easily reckoned by any that will *count back* in the Chronicle to the *second of Omri*. Such another reckoning there is about *Jechoniah*, or Jehoiachin, 2 Kings xxiv. 8: *Jehoiachin was eighteen years old when he began to reign.* But, 2 Chron. xxxvi. 9, *Jehoiachin was the son of the eight* years; that is, the beginning of his reign fell in the *eighth* year of Nebuchadnezzar, and of Judah's first captivity."—Works, vol. i., p. 87.

After all, here is a most *manifest contradiction*, that cannot be removed but by having recourse to *violent modes* of solution. I am satisfied the reading in 2 Chron. xxii. 2, is a *mistake;* and that we should read there, as here, *twenty-two* instead of *forty-two* years; see the note there. And may we not say with *Calmet*, Which is most dangerous, to acknowledge that *transcribers* have made some mistakes in copying the sacred books, or to acknowledge that there are *contradictions* in them, and then to have recourse to solutions that can yield no satisfaction to any unprejudiced mind? I add, that no mode of solution yet found out has succeeded in removing the difficulty; and of all the MSS. which have been collated, and they amount to *several hundred, not one* confirms the reading of *twenty-two* years. And to it all the *ancient* versions are equally unfriendly.

Verse 28. *The Syrians wounded Joram*] Ahaziah went with Joram to endeavour to wrest Ramoth-gilead out of the hands of the Syrians, which belonged to Israel and Judah. Ahab had endeavoured to do this before, and was slain there; see 1 Kings xxii. 3, &c., and the notes there.

Verse 29. *Went back to be healed in Jezreel*] And there he continued till Jehu conspired against and slew him there. And thus the blood of the innocents, which had been shed by Ahab and his wife Jezebel, was visited on them in the total extinction of their family. See the following chapters, where the bloody tale of Jehu's conspiracy is told at large.

I HAVE already had to remark on the chronological difficulties which occur in the historical books; difficulties for which copyists alone are responsible. To remove them by the plan of *reconciliation*, is in many cases impracticable; to conjectural criticism we must have recourse. And is there a single ancient author of any kind, but particularly those who have written on matters of *history* and *chronology*, whose works have been transmitted to us free of similar errors, owing to the negligence of transcribers?

CHAPTER IX

Elisha sends one of the disciples of the prophets to Ramoth-gilead, to anoint Jehu king of Israel, 1–3. He acts according to his orders, and informs Jehu that he is to cut off the whole house of Ahab, 4–10. Jehu's captains proclaim him king, 11–14. He goes against Jezreel; where he finds Joram and Ahaziah king of Judah, who had come to visit him; he slays them both: the former is thrown into the portion of Naboth; the latter, having received a mortal wound, flees to Megiddo, and dies there, and is carried to Jerusalem, and buried in the city of David, 15–29. He commands Jezebel to be thrown out of her window; and he treads her under the feet of his horses; and the dogs eat her, according to the word of the Lord, 30–37.

A. M. 3120
B. C. 884
Ante I. Ol. 108
An. Diogeneti,
Arch. Athen.
perpet. 8

AND Elisha the prophet called one of [a]the children of the prophets, and said unto him, [b]Gird up thy loins, and take this box of oil in thine hand, [c]and go to Ramoth-gilead.

2 And when thou comest thither, look out there Jehu the son of Jehoshaphat the son of Nimshi, and go in, and make him arise up from among [d]his brethren, and carry him to an [e]inner chamber;

3 Then [f]take the box of oil, and pour *it* on his head, and say, Thus saith the Lord, I have anointed thee king over Israel. Then open the door, and flee, and tarry not.

4 So the young man, *even* the young man the prophet, went to Ramoth-gilead.

5 And when he came, behold, the captains of the host *were* sitting; and he said, I have an errand to thee, O captain. And Jehu said, Unto which of all us? And he said, To thee, O captain.

6 And he arose, and went into the house; and he poured the oil on his head, and said

unto him, [g]Thus saith the Lord God of Israel, I have anointed thee king over the people of the Lord, *even* over Israel.

A. M. 3120
B. C. 884
Ante I. Ol. 108
An. Diogeneti,
Arch. Athen.
perpet. 8

7 And thou shalt smite the house of Ahab thy master, that I may avenge the blood of my servants the prophets, and the blood of all the servants of the Lord, [h]at the hand of Jezebel.

8 For the whole house of Ahab shall perish: and [i]I will cut off from Ahab [k]him that pisseth against the wall, and [l]him that is shut up and left in Israel:

9 And I will make the house of Ahab like the house of [m]Jeroboam the son of Nebat, and like the house of [n]Baasha the son of Ahijah:

10 [o]And the dogs shall eat Jezebel in the portion of Jezreel, and *there shall be* none to bury *her*. And he opened the door, and fled.

11 Then Jehu came forth to the servants of his lord: and *one* said unto him, *Is* all well? wherefore came [p]this mad *fellow* to thee? And he said unto them, Ye know the man, and his communication.

---

[a]1 Kings xx. 35——[b]Ch. iv. 29; Jer. i. 17——[c]Chap. viii. 28, 29——[d]Ver. 5, 11——[e]Heb. *chamber in a chamber*——[f]1 Kings xix. 16——[g]1 Kings xix. 16; 2 Chron. xxii. 7——[h]1 Kings xviii. 4; xxi. 15——[i]1 Kings xiv. 10; xxi. 21

[k]1 Samuel xxv. 22——[l]Deuteronomy xxxii. 36 [m]1 Kings xiv. 10; xv. 29; xxi. 22——[n]1 Kings xvi. 3, 11——[o]1 Kings xxi. 23; verse 35, 36——[p]Jeremiah xxix. 26; John x. 20; Acts xxvi. 24; 1 Corinthians iv. 10

NOTES ON CHAP. IX

Verse 1. *One of the children of the prophets*] The Jews say that this was *Jonah* the prophet, the son of Amittai.

Gird up thy loins] What thou hast to do requires the utmost despatch.

Verse 4. *The young man the prophet*] This should be translated, *The servant of the prophet;* that is, the servant which Elisha now had in place of Gehazi.

Verse 6. *King over the people of the Lord*] This pointed out to Jehu that he was to rule that people according to God's law; and consequently, that he was to restore the pure worship of the Most High in Israel.

Verse 7. *Thou shalt smite the house of Ahab*] For their most cruel murders they have forfeited their own lives, according to that immutable law, "He that sheddeth man's blood, by man shall *his* blood be shed." This and the

two following verses contain the *commission* which Jehu received from the Lord against the bloody house of Ahab.

Verse 10. *The dogs shall eat Jezebel*] How most minutely was this prophecy fulfilled! See ver. 33, &c.

Verse 11. *Wherefore came this mad fellow to thee?*] Was it because he was a *holy man* of God that he was reputed by a club of irreligious officers to be a madman? In vain do such pretend that they fight for religion, and are the guardians of the public welfare and morals, if they persecute religion and scoff at holy men. But this has been an old custom with all the *seed*—the sons, *of the serpent*. As to religious soldiers, *they are far to seek, and ill to find,* according to the old proverb.

Ye know the man, and his communication.] Ye know that he is a *madman*, and that his message must be a message of folly. Jehu did not appear willing to tell them what had been

A. M. 3120
B. C. 884
Ante I. Ol. 108
An. Diogeneti,
Arch. Athen.
perpet. 8

12 And they said, *It is* false; tell us now. And he said, Thus and thus spake he to me, saying, Thus saith the LORD, I have anointed thee king over Israel.

13 Then they hasted, and �q took every man his garment, and put *it* under him on the top of the stairs, and blew with trumpets, saying, Jehu ʳis king.

14 So Jehu the son of Jehoshaphat the son of Nimshi conspired against Joram. (Now Joram had kept Ramoth-gilead, he and all Israel, because of Hazael king of Syria.

15 But ˢKing ᵗJoram was returned to be healed in Jezreel of the wounds which the Syrians ᵘhad given him, when he fought with Hazael king of Syria.) And Jehu said, If it be your minds, *then* ᵛlet none go forth *nor* escape out of the city to go to tell *it* in Jezreel.

16 So Jehu rode in a chariot, and went to Jezreel; for Joram lay there. ʷAnd Ahaziah king of Judah was come down to see Joram.

17 And there stood a watchman on the tower in Jezreel, and he spied the company of Jehu as he came, and said, I see a company. And Joram said, Take a horseman, and send to meet them, and let him say, *Is it* peace?

A. M. 3120
B. C. 884
Ante I. Ol. 108
An. Diogeneti,
Arch. Athen.
perpet. 8

18 So there went one on horseback to meet him, and said, Thus saith the king, *Is it* peace? And Jehu said, What hast thou to do with peace? turn thee behind me. And the watchman told, saying, The messenger came to them, but he cometh not again.

19 Then he sent out a second on horseback, which came to them, and said, Thus saith the king, *Is it* peace? And Jehu answered, What hast thou to do with peace? turn thee behind me.

20 And the watchman told, saying, He came even unto them, and cometh not again: and the ˣdriving *is* like the driving of Jehu the son of Nimshi; for he driveth ʸfuriously.

ᑫMatt. xxi. 7——ʳHeb. *reigneth*——ˢChap. viii. 29
ᵗHeb. *Jehoram*——ᵘHeb. *smote*

ᵛHeb. *let no escaper go,* &c.——ʷChap. viii. 29——ˣOr,
marching——ʸHeb. *in madness*

---

done, lest it should promote jealousy and envy.

Verse 12. *They said,* It is *false*] Or, as the Chaldee has it, *Thou liest.* Or, perhaps, it might be thus understood, "We know he has said nothing but folly and lies; nevertheless, let us hear what he has said."

Verse 13. *Took every man his garment*] This was a ceremony by which they acknowledged him as *king;* and it was by such a ceremony that the multitudes acknowledged Jesus Christ for the *Messiah and King of Israel,* a little before his passion: see Matt. xxi. 7, and the note there. The ceremony was expressive: "As we put our garments under his feet, so we place every thing under his authority, and acknowledge ourselves his servants."

On the top of the stairs] The *Chaldee,* the *rabbins,* and several interpreters, understand this of the *public sun-dial;* which, in those ancient times, was formed of *steps* like *stairs,* each *step* serving to indicate, by its *shadow,* one *hour,* or such division of time as was commonly used in that country. This *dial* was, no doubt, in the most *public place;* and upon the top of it, or on the *platform* on the top, would be a very proper place to set Jehu, while they blew their trumpets, and proclaimed him *king.*

The Hebrew מעלות *maaloth* is the same word which is used chap. xx. 9, 10, 11, to signify the *dial* of Ahaz; and this was probably the very same dial on which that miracle was afterwards wrought: and this dial, מעלות *maaloth,* from עלה *alah,* to go up, ascend, was most evidently made of *steps;* the *shadows* projected on which, by a gnomon, at the different elevations of the sun, would serve to show the popular divisions of time. See the notes on chap. xx. 9, &c., and the *diagram* at the end of that chapter.

Verse 14. *Joram had kept Ramoth-gilead*] The confederate armies appear to have taken this city; but they were obliged to watch their conquests, as they perceived that Hazael was determined to retake it if possible.

Verse 16. *Jehu—went to Jezreel; for Joram lay there.*] From the preceding verse we learn, that Joram had been wounded in his attack on Ramoth-gilead, and had gone to Jezreel to be cured; and neither he nor Ahaziah knew any thing of the conspiracy in Ramoth-gilead, because Jehu and his captains took care to prevent any person from leaving the city; so that the two kings at Jezreel knew nothing of what had taken place.

Verse 17. *A watchman on the tower*] These watchmen, fixed on elevated places, and generally within hearing of each other, served as a kind of *telegraphs,* to communicate intelligence through the whole country. But, in some cases, it appears that the intelligence was conveyed by a *horseman* to the next stage, as in the case before us. At this time, when the armies were at Ramoth-gilead, they were, no doubt, doubly watchful to observe the state of the country, and to notice every movement. See on 2 Sam. xiii. 34.

Verse 18. *What hast thou to do with peace?*] "What is it to thee whether there be peace or war? Join my company, and fall into the rear."

Verse 20. *He driveth furiously*] Jehu was a bold, daring, prompt, and precipitate general. In his various military operations he had established his character; and now it was almost proverbial.

A. M. 3120
B. C. 884
Ante I. Ol. 108
An. Diogeneti,
Arch. Athen.
perpet. 8
21 And Joram said, ²Make ready. And his chariot was made ready. And ªJoram king of Israel and Ahaziah king of Judah went out, each in his chariot, and they went out against Jehu, and ᵇmet him in the portion of Naboth the Jezreelite.

22 And it came to pass, when Joram saw Jehu, that he said, *Is it* peace, Jehu? And he answered, What peace, so long as the whoredoms of thy mother Jezebel and her witchcrafts *are so* many?

23 And Joram turned his hands, and fled, and said to Ahaziah, *There is* treachery, O Ahaziah.

24 And Jehu ᶜdrew a bow with his full strength, and smote Jehoram between his arms, and the arrow went out at his heart, and he ᵈsunk down in his chariot.

25 Then said *Jehu* to Bidkar his captain, Take up, *and* cast him in the portion of the field of Naboth the Jezreelite: A. M. 3120
B. C. 884
Ante I. Ol. 108
An. Diogeneti,
Arch. Athen.
perpet. 8 for remember how that, when I and thou rode together after Ahab his father, ᵉthe Lord laid this burden upon him;

26 Surely I have seen yesterday the ᶠblood of Naboth, and the blood of his sons, saith the Lord; and ᵍI will requite thee in this ʰplat, saith the Lord. Now therefore take *and* cast him into the plat *of ground,* according to the word of the Lord.

27 But when Ahaziah the king of Judah saw *this,* he fled by the way of the garden house. And Jehu followed after him, and said, Smite him also in the chariot. *And they did so* at the going up to Gur, which *is* by Ibleam. And he fled to ¹Megiddo, and died there.

28 And his servants carried him in a chariot to Jerusalem, and buried him in his sepulchre with his fathers in the city of David.

29 And in the eleventh year of Joram the

---

²Hebrew, *Bind*——ª2 Chron. xxii. 7——ᵇHeb. *found*
ᶜHeb. *filled his hand with a bow*——ᵈHeb. *bowed*
ᵉ1 Kings xxi. 29——ᶠHebrew, *bloods*——ᵍ1 Kings xxi.
19——ʰOr, *portion*

¹In the kingdom of *Samaria,* 2 Chron. xxii. 9. Then he began to reign as viceroy to his father in his sickness, 2 Chron. xxi. 18, 19. But in Joram's 12th year he began to reign alone, chap. viii. 25

Verse 21. *Joram—and Ahaziah—went out*] They had no suspicion of what was done at Ramoth-gilead; else they would not have ventured their persons as they now did.

Verse 22. *What peace, so long as the whoredoms*] Though the words *whoredom, adultery,* and *fornication,* are frequently used to express *idolatry,* and *false religion,* in general; yet here they may be safely taken in their *common* and most *obvious* sense, as there is much reason to believe that Jezebel was the patroness and supporter of a very impure system of religion; and to this Jehu might refer, rather than to the *calf-worship,* to which himself was most favourably disposed.

Verse 23. There is *treachery, O Ahaziah.*] This was the first intimation he had of it: he feels for the safety of his friend Ahaziah, and now they fly for their lives.

Verse 24. *Drew a bow with his full strength*] The marginal reading is correct: *He filled his hand with a bow.* That is, "He immediately took up his bow, set his arrow, and let fly." This is the only meaning of the passage.

Between his arms] That is, between his *shoulders;* for he was now *turned,* and was flying *from* Jehu.

Verse 25. *Cast him in the portion of the field*] This was predicted, 1 Kings xxi.; and what now happened to the son of Ahab is foretold in ver. 29 of that chapter.

Verse 26. *The blood of Naboth, and the blood of his sons*] We are not informed in 1 Kings xxi. that any of Naboth's *family* was slain but himself: but as the object both of Ahab and Jezebel was to have Naboth's vineyard entirely, and *for ever,* it is not likely that they would leave any of his posterity, who might at a future time reclaim it as their inheritance. Again, to secure this point, Jezebel had Naboth convicted of *treason* and *atheism;* in order that his whole family might be involved in his ruin.

Verse 27. *Fled by the way of the garden*] The account of the death of Ahaziah, as given in 2 Chron. xxii. 8, 9, is very different from that given *here: When Jehu was executing judgment upon the house of Ahab—he sought Ahaziah; and they caught him, (for he was hid in Samaria,) and brought him to Jehu; and when they had slain him, they buried him.* "The current of the story at large is this," says Dr. Lightfoot: "Jehu slayeth Joram in the *field of Jezreel,* as Ahaziah and Joram were together; Ahaziah, seeing this, flees, and gets into Samaria, and hides himself there. Jehu marcheth to Jezreel, and makes Jezebel dogs' meat: from thence he sends to Samaria for the heads of Ahab's children and posterity: which are brought him by night, and showed to the people in the morning. Then he marcheth to Samaria, and by the way slayeth *forty-two* of Ahab's kinsmen; and findeth Jehonadab, the father of the Rechabites. Coming into Samaria, he maketh search for Ahaziah: they find him hid, bring him to Jehu, and he commands to carry him up towards *Gur,* by *Ibleam,* and there to slay him. It may be, his father Joram had slain *his brethren there,* as Ahab had done *Naboth,* in *Jezreel.* They do so; smite him there in his chariot; and his charioteer driveth away to *Megiddo* before he dies. The story in the book of Kings is short: but the book of Chronicles shows the order." *Lightfoot's* Works, vol. i., p. 88.

Verse 29. *In the eleventh year of Joram*] The note in our *margin* contains as good an

A. M. 3118
B. C. 886
Ante I. Ol. 110
An. Diogeneti,
Arch. Athen.
perpet. 6

A. M. 3120
B. C. 884
Ante I. Ol. 108
An. Diogeneti,
Arch. Athen.
perpet. 8

son of Ahab began Ahaziah to reign over Judah.

30 And when Jehu was come to Jezreel, Jezebel heard *of it;* [k]and she [l]painted her face, and tired her head, and looked out at a window.

31 And as Jehu entered in at the gate, she said, [m]*Had* Zimri peace, who slew his master?

32 And he lifted up his face to the window, and said, Who *is* on my side? who? And there looked out to him two *or* three [n]eunuchs.

33 And he said, Throw her down. So they threw her down: and *some* of her blood was sprinkled on the wall, and on the horses: and he trode her under foot.

A. M. 3120
B. C. 884
Ante I. Ol. 108
An. Diogeneti,
Arch. Athen.
perpet. 8

34 And when he was come in, he did eat and drink, and said, Go, see now this cursed *woman,* and bury her; for [o]she *is* a king's daughter.

35 And they went to bury her: but they found no more of her than the skull, and the feet, and the palms of *her* hands.

36 Wherefore they came again, and told him. And he said, This *is* the word of the LORD, which he spake [p]by his servant Elijah the Tishbite, saying, [q]In the portion of Jezreel shall dogs eat the flesh of Jezebel:

37 And the carcass of Jezebel shall be [r]as dung upon the face of the field in the portion of Jezreel; *so* that they shall not say, This *is* Jezebel.

---

[k]Ezek. xxiii. 40——[l]Heb. *put her eyes in painting*
  [m]1 Kings xvi. 9-20——[n]Or, *chamberlains*

[o]1 Kings xvi. 31——[p]Heb. *by the hand of*——[q]1 Kings
    xxi. 23——[r]Psa. lxxxiii. 10

---

account of this chronological difficulty as can be reasonably required: *Then he began to reign as viceroy to his father in his sickness;* 2 Chron. xxi. 18, 19. *But in Joram's twelfth year he began to reign alone;* chap. viii. 26.

Verse 30. *She painted her face, and tired her head*] She endeavoured to improve the *appearance* of her *complexion* by paint, and the general effect of her countenance by a *tiara* or turban head-dress. *Jonathan,* the *Chaldee Targumist,* so often quoted, translates this וכחלת בצדידא עינהא *vechachalath bitsdida eynaha:* "She stained her eyes with *stibium* or *antimony.*" This is a custom in *Asiatic* countries to the present day. From a late traveller in Persia, I borrow the following account:—

"The Persians differ as much from us in their notions of *beauty* as they do in those of taste. *A large, soft, and languishing black eye,* with them, constitutes the perfection of beauty. It is chiefly on this account that the women *use the powder of antimony,* which, although it *adds to the vivacity of the eye, throws a kind of voluptuous languor over it,* which makes it appear, (if I may use the expression,) *dissolving in bliss.* The Persian women have a curious custom of making *their eye-brows meet;* and if this charm be denied them, *they paint the forehad* with a kind of preparation made for that purpose." *E. S. Waring's* Tour to Sheeraz, 4to., 1807, page 62.

This casts light enough on Jezebel's painting, &c.; and shows sufficiently with what design she did it, to conquer and disarm Jehu, and *induce him to take her for wife,* as *Jarchi* supposes. This staining of the eye with stibium and painting was a universal custom, not only in Asiatic countries, but also in all those that bordered on them, or had connections with them. The Prophet Ezekiel mentions the painting of the eyes, chap. xxiii. 40.

That the *Romans painted their eyes* we have the most positive evidence. Pliny says, *Tanta est decoris affectatio, ut tinguantur oculi quoque.* Hist. Nat. lib. xi., cap. 37. "Such is

their affection of ornament, that they paint their eyes also." That this *painting* was with *stibium* or *antimony,* is plain from these words of *St. Cyprian, De Opere et Eleemosynis, Inunge aculos tuos non stibio diaboli, sed collyrio Christi,* "Anoint your eyes, not with the devil's antimony, but with the eye-salve of Christ." Juvenal is plain on the same subject. Men as well as women in Rome practised it:—

*Ille supercilium madida fuligine tactum
Obliqua producit acu pingitque trementes
Attollens oculos.*   SAT. ii., ver. 93.

"With *sooty moisture* one his eye-brows dyes,
  And with a *bodkin* paints his *trembling eyes.*"

The *manner* in which the women in Barbary do it Dr. Russel particularly describes:—"Upon the principle of *strengthening* the sight, as well as an *ornament,* it is become a general practice among the women to *black the middle of their eye-lids* by applying a powder called *ismed.* Their method of doing it is by a cylindrical piece of *silver, steel,* or *ivory,* about two inches long, made very smooth, and about the size of a *common probe.* This they wet with water, in order that the powder may stick to it, *and applying the middle part horizontally to the eye, they shut the eye-lids upon it, and so drawing it through between them, it blacks the inside, leaving a narrow black rim all round the edge.* This is sometimes practised by the men, but is then regarded as foppish." RUSSEL'S *Nat. Hist.* of Aleppo, page 102. See *Parkhurst, sub voc.* פך.

Verse 31. *Had Zimri peace, who slew his master?*] Jarchi paraphrases this place thus: "If thou hast slain thy master, it is no new thing; for Zimri also slew Elah, the son of Baasha;" which words were rather intended to *conciliate* than to *provoke.* But the words are understood by most of the versions thus: Health to Zimri, the slayer of his master!

Verse 33. *So they threw her down*] What a terrible death! She was already, by the fall, almost dashed to pieces; and the brutal Jehu trampled her already mangled body under his horse's feet!

Verse 34. *She is a king's daughter.*] Jezebel was certainly a woman of a very *high lineage*. **She** was *daughter* of the king of Tyre; *wife* of Ahab, king of Israel; *mother* of Joram, king of Israel; *mother-in-law* of Joram, king of Judah; and *grandmother* of Ahaziah, king of Judah.

Verse 35. *The skull—the feet, and the palms of her hands.*] The dogs did not eat those parts, say *Jarchi* and *Kimchi*, because in her festal dances she danced like a dog, on her hands and feet, wantonly moving her head. What other meaning these rabbins had, I do not inquire. She was, no doubt, guilty of the foulest actions, and was almost too bad to be *belied.*

How literally was the prediction delivered in the preceding book, (1 Kings xxi. 23, *The*

dogs shall eat Jezebel, by the wall of Jezreel,) fulfilled! And how dearly did she and her husband Ahab pay for the murder of innocent Naboth!

Verse 37. *And the carcass of Jezebel shall be as dung*] As it was not *buried* under the earth, but was *eaten by the dogs*, this saying was also literally fulfilled.

They shall not say, This is Jezebel.] As she could not be buried, she could have no *funeral monument.* Though so great a woman by her birth, connections, and alliances, she had not the honour of a tomb! There was not even a *solitary stone* to say, *Here lies Jezebel!* not even a *mound of earth* to designate the place of her sepulture! Judgment is God's strange work; but when he contends, how terrible are his judgments! and when he ariseth to execute judgment, who shall stay his hand? How deep are his counsels, and how terrible are his workings!

CHAPTER X

Jehu sends an ironical letter to the elders of Samaria, telling them to choose one of the best of their master's sons, and put him on the throne; to which they return a submissive answer, 1–6. He writes a second letter, and orders them to send him the heads of Ahab's seventy sons; they do so, and they are laid in two heaps at the gate of Jezreel, 7, 8. Jehu shows them to the people, and excuses himself, and states that all is done according to the word of the Lord, 9, 10. He destroys all the kindred of Ahab that remained in Jezreel, 11. He also destroys forty-two men, the brethren of Ahaziah, king of Judah, 12–14. He meets with Jehonadab, and takes him with him in his chariot, 15, 16. He comes to Samaria, and destroys all that were of the kindred of Ahab there, 17. He pretends a great zeal for the worship of Baal, and gathers all his priests together, under the pretence of a grand sacrifice, and slays them all, 18–25. He burns Baal's images, and makes his temple a draught house, 26–28. But he does not depart from the sins of Jeroboam, and does not prosper, 29–31. Hazael vexes Israel, 32, 33. Jehu dies, having reigned over Israel, in Samaria, twenty-eight years, 34–36.

A. M. 3120
B. C. 884
Ante I. Ol. 108
An. Diogeneti,
Arch. Athen.
perpet. 8

AND Ahab had seventy sons in Samaria. And Jehu wrote letters, and sent to Samaria, unto the rulers of Jezreel, to the elders, and to [a]them that brought up Ahab's *children,* saying,

2 Now as soon as this letter cometh to you, seeing your master's sons *are* with you, and *there are* with you chariots and horses,

a fenced city also, and armour;

A. M. 3120
B. C. 884
Ante I. Ol. 108
An. Diogeneti,
Arch. Athen.
perpet. 8

3 Look even out of the best and meetest of your master's sons, and set *him* on his father's throne, and fight for your master's house.

4 But they were exceedingly afraid, and said, Behold, two kings stood not before him: how then shall we stand?

---

[a]Hebrew, *nourishers*

NOTES ON CHAP. X

Verse 1. *Ahab had seventy sons*] As he had several wives, he might have many children. The Israelites, from the earliest part of their history, were remarkably fruitful. How amazingly did they multiply in Egypt, even under the hand of the severest oppression! And as to the individuals of whose families we have an account, they are quite remarkable: *Rehoboam* had *thirty-eight* sons; *Abdon* had *forty; Tola* had *thirty; Ahab, seventy; and Gideon, seventy-one.*

Unto the rulers of Jezreel] It certainly should be, *unto the rulers of Samaria; for to them* and to that *city* the whole context shows us the letters were sent. See ver. 6.

To them that brought up Ahab's children]

It appears that the royal children of Israel and Judah were intrusted to the care of the nobles, and were brought up by them, (see ver. 6;) and to these, therefore, Jehu's letters are directed. It is supposed Isaiah (xlix. 23) alludes to this custom: *Kings shall be thy nursing fathers, and queens thy nursing mothers.*

Verse 2. *A fenced city also*] All here seems to refer to Samaria alone; in it were the magazines and implements of war, &c. No reader need be told that these letters were all *ironical.* It was the same as if he had said, "Ye have no means of defence; Israel is with *me:* if you yield not up yourselves and the city, I will put you all to the sword."

Verse 4. *Two kings stood not before him*] That is Joram and Ahaziah.

A. M. 3120
B. C. 884
Ante I. Ol. 108
An. Diogeneti,
Arch. Athen.
perpet. 8

5 And he that *was* over the house, and he that *was* over the city, the elders also, and the bringers up *of the children,* sent to Jehu, saying, We *are* thy servants, and will do all that thou shalt bid us; we will not make any king: do thou *that which is* good in thine eyes.

6 Then he wrote a letter the second time to them, saying, If ye *be* ᵇmine, and *if* ye will hearken unto my voice, take ye the heads of the men your master's sons, and come to me to Jezreel by to-morrow this time. Now the king's sons, *being* seventy persons, *were* with the great men of the city, which brought them up.

7 And it came to pass, when the letter came to them, that they took the king's sons, and ᶜslew seventy persons, and put their heads in baskets, and sent him *them* to Jezreel.

8 And there came a messenger, and told him, saying, They have brought the heads of the king's sons. And he said, Lay ye them in two heaps at the entering in of the gate until the morning.

9 And it came to pass in the morning, that he went out, and stood, and said to all the people, Ye be righteous: behold, ᵈI conspired against my master, and slew him: but who slew all these?

A. M. 3120
B. C. 884
Ante I. Ol. 108
An. Diogeneti,
Arch. Athen.
perpet. 8

10 Know now that there shall ᵉfall unto the earth nothing of the word of the LORD, which the LORD spake concerning the house of Ahab: for the LORD hath done *that* which he spake ᶠby ᵍhis servant Elijah.

11 So Jehu slew all that remained of the house of Ahab in Jezreel, and all his great men, and his ʰkinsfolks, and his priests, until he left him none remaining.

12 And he arose, and departed, and came to Samaria. *And* as he *was* at the ⁱshearing house in the way,

13 ᵏJehu ˡmet with the brethren of Ahaziah king of Judah, and said, Who *are* ye? And they answered, We *are* the brethren of Ahaziah; and we go down ᵐto salute the children of the king and the children of the queen.

14 And he said, Take them alive. And they took them alive, and slew them at the pit of the shearing house, *even* two and forty men; neither left he any of them.

15 And when he was departed thence, he

ᵇHeb. *for me*——ᶜ1 Kings xxi. 21——ᵈChap. ix. 14, 24——ᵉ1 Sam. iii. 19——ᶠ1 Kings xxi. 19, 21, 29 ᵍHebrew, *by the hand of*

ʰOr, *acquaintance*——ⁱHeb. *house of shepherds binding sheep*——ᵏCh. viii. 29; 2 Chron. xxii. 8——ˡHeb. *found* ᵐHeb. *to the peace of,* &c.

Verse 5. *He that* was *over the house, &c.*] Thus all the constituted authorities agreed to submit.

Will do all that thou shalt bid us] They made no conditions, and stood pledged to commit the horrid murders which this most execrable man afterwards commanded.

Verse 6. *Come to me to Jezreel*] Therefore the letters were not written to Jezreel, but from Jezreel to Samaria.

Verse 7. *Put their heads in baskets*] What cold-blooded wretches were the whole of these people!

Verse 8. *Lay ye them in two heaps*] It appears that the heads of these princes had arrived at Jezreel in the *night time:* Jehu ordered them to be left at the gate of the city, a place of public resort, that all the people might see them, and be struck with terror, and conclude that all resistance to such authority and power would be vain.

Verse 9. *Ye be righteous*] Another irony, intended partly to excuse himself, and to involve them in the odium of this massacre, and at the same time to justify the conduct of both, by showing that all was done according to the commandment of the Lord.

Verse 11. *Jehu slew all*] So it appears that the *great men* who had so obsequiously taken off the heads of Ahab's *seventy* sons, fell also

a sacrifice to the ambition of this incomparably bad man.

Verse 12. *The shearing house*] Probably the place where the shepherds met for the annual sheep shearing.

Verse 13. *The brethren of Ahaziah*] The relatives of his family; for it does not appear that he had any *brethren,* properly so called: but we know that the term brethren among the Jews signified the relatives of the same family, and especially *brothers'* and *sisters'* children; and that these were such, see 2 Chron. xxii. 8.

We go down to salute, &c.] So promptly had Jehu executed all his measures, that even the nearest relatives of the murdered kings had not heard of their death, and consequently had no time to escape. They were all taken as in a net.

Verse 14. *The pit of the shearing house*] Probably the place where they washed the *sheep* previously to shearing, or the *fleeces* after they were shorn off.

Verse 15. *Jehonadab the son of Rechab*] For particulars concerning this man, his *ancestry,* and *posterity,* see the notes on Jer. xxxv.

Is thine heart right] With me, in the prosecution of a reform in Israel; *as my heart is with thy heart* in the true religion of Jehovah, and the destruction of Baal?

It is.] I wish a reform in the religion of the

A. M. 3120
B. C. 884
Ante I. Ol. 108
An. Diogeneti,
Arch. Athen.
perpet. 8

[n]lighted on [o]Jehonadab the son of [p]Rechab, *coming* to meet him: and he [q]saluted him, and said to him, Is thine heart right, as my heart *is* with thy heart? and Jehonadab answered, It is. If it be, [r]give *me* thine hand. And he gave *him* his hand; and he took him up to him into the chariot.

16 And he said, Come with me, and see my [s]zeal for the LORD. So they made him ride in his chariot.

17 And when he came to Samaria, [t]he slew all that remained unto Ahab in Samaria, till he had destroyed him, according to the saying of the LORD, [u]which he spake to Elijah.

18 And Jehu gathered all the people together, and said unto them, [v]Ahab served Baal a little; *but* Jehu shall serve him much.

19 Now therefore call unto me all the [w]prophets of Baal, all his servants, and all his priests; let none be wanting: for I have a great sacrifice *to do* to Baal; whosoever shall be wanting, he shall not live. But Jehu did *it* in subtilty, to the intent that he might destroy the worshippers of Baal.

20 And Jehu said, [x]Proclaim a solemn assembly for Baal. And they proclaimed *it.*

A. M. 3120
B. C. 884
Ante I. Ol. 108
An. Diogeneti,
Arch. Athen.
perpet. 8

21 And Jehu sent through all Israel: and all the worshippers of Baal came, so that there was not a man left that came not. And they came into the [y]house of Baal; and the house of Baal was [z]full from one end to another.

22 And he said unto him that *was* over the vestry, Bring forth vestments for all the worshippers of Baal. And he brought them forth vestments.

23 And Jehu went, and Jehonadab the son of Rechab, into the house of Baal, and said unto the worshippers of Baal, Search, and look that there be here with you none of the servants of the LORD, but the worshippers of Baal only.

24 And when they went in to offer sacrifices and burnt-offerings, Jehu appointed fourscore men without, and said, *If* any of the men whom I have brought into your hands escape, *he that letteth him go,* [a]his life *shall be* for the life of him.

25 And it came to pass, as soon as he had made an end of offering the burnt-offering, that Jehu said to the guard and to the captains, Go in, *and* slay them; let none come forth.

---

[n]Heb. *found*——[o]Jer. xxxv. 6, &c.——[p]1 Chron. ii. 55
[q]Heb. *blessed*——[r]Ezra x. 19——[s]1 Kings xix. 10
[t]Chap. ix. 8; 2 Chron. xxii. 8——[u]1 Kings xxi. 21

[v]1 Kings xvi. 31, 32——[w]1 Kings xxii. 6——[x]Heb.
Sanctify——[y]1 Kings xvi. 32——[z]Or, *so full that they
stood mouth to mouth*——[a]1 Kings xx. 39

---

country; I am his friend who shall endeavour to promote it.

Give me *thine hand.*] This has been generally considered as exacting a *promise* from Jehonadab; but does it mean any more than his taking him by the hand, to help him to step into his chariot, in which Jehu was then sitting? Jehonadab was doubtless a very honourable man in Israel; and by carrying him about with him in his chariot, Jehu endeavoured to acquire the public esteem. "Jehu must be acting right, for Jehonadab is with him, and approves his conduct."

Verse 16. *Come with me, and see my zeal for the Lord.*] O thou ostentatious and murderous hypocrite! Thou have zeal for Jehovah and his pure religion! Witness thy calves at Dan and Bethel, and the general profligacy of thy conduct. He who can call another to witness his zeal for religion, or his works of charity, has as much of both as serves his *own* turn.

Verse 18. *Ahab served Baal a little*] Jehu had determined to have no worship in Israel but that of the golden calves at Dan and Bethel; therefore he purposes to destroy all the worshippers of Baal: and that he may do it without *suspicion*, he proclaims a great sacrifice; and that he may do it the more *easily*, he gathers them all together into one place.

Verse 19. *Whosoever shall be wanting, he shall not live.*] Because, as he will thereby show himself without zeal for the service of

his God, he will justly forfeit his life. All this was done in the very spirit of deceit.

Verse 22. *He said unto him that* was *over the vestry*] The word *vestry* comes from *vestiarium*, and that from *vestes, garments,* from *vestio,* I *clothe;* and signifies properly the *place* where the *sacerdotal robes* and *pontifical ornaments* are kept. The priests of Baal had their robes as well as the priests of the Lord; but the garments were such that one could be easily distinguished from the other.

Verse 23. *None of the servants of the Lord*] Though he was not attached to that service, yet he would tolerate it; and as he was led to suppose that he was fulfilling the will of Jehovah in what he was doing, he would of course treat his worship and worshippers with the more respect.

He might have ordered the search to be made on pretence of expelling any of those whom they would consider *the profane,* especially as this was "a solemn assembly for Baal," as was the custom with the heathen when any extraordinary exhibition of or for their god was expected; thus Callimachus, (Hymn to Apollo,) after imagining the temple and its suburbs to be shaken by the approach of Apollo, cries out, Εκας, εκας, οστις, αλιτρος. To prevent any suspicion of his real design, such might have been Jehu's plea, else alarm must have been excited, and perhaps some would have escaped.

Verse 25. *As soon as he had made an end*

A. M. 3120
B. C. 884
Ante I. Ol. 108
An. Diogeneti,
Arch. Athen.
perpet. 8
And they smote them with the ᵇedge of the sword; and the guard and the captains cast *them* out, and went to the city of the house of Baal.

26 And they brought forth the ᶜimages ᵈout of the house of Baal, and burned them.

27 And they brake down the image of Baal, and brake down the house of Baal, ᵉand made it a draught house unto this day.

A.M.3120-3148
B. C. 884-856
Anno ante I.
Olymp.108-80
28 Thus Jehu destroyed Baal out of Israel.

29 Howbeit *from* the sins of Jeroboam the son of Nebat, who made Israel to sin, Jehu departed not from after them, *to wit,* ᶠthe golden calves that *were* in Beth-el, and that *were* in Dan.

A. M. 3120
B. C. 884
Ante I. Ol. 108
An. Diogeneti,
Arch. Athen.
perpet. 8.
30 And the LORD said unto Jehu, Because thou hast done well in executing *that which is* right in mine eyes, *and* hast done unto the house of Ahab according to all that *was* in mine heart, ᵍthy children of the fourth *generation* shall sit on the throne of Israel.

31 But Jehu ʰtook no heed to walk in the law of the LORD God of Israel with all his heart: for he departed not from ⁱthe sins of Jeroboam, which made Israel to sin.

A.M.3120-3148
B. C. 884-856
Anno ante I.
Olymp. 108-80

32 In those days the LORD began ᵏto cut Israel short: and ˡHazael smote them in all the coasts of Israel;

33 From Jordan ᵐeastward, all the land of Gilead, the Gadites, and the Reubenites, and the Manassites, from Aroer, which *is* by the river Arnon, ⁿeven ᵒGilead and Bashan.

34 Now the rest of the acts of Jehu, and all that he did, and all his might, *are* they not written in the book of the chronicles of the kings of Israel?

A. M. 3148
B. C. 856
Ante I. Ol. 180
An. Pherecli,
Arch. Athen.
perpet. 8

35 And Jehu slept with his fathers: and they buried him in Samaria. And Jehoahaz his son reigned in his stead.

36 And ᵖthe time that Jehu reigned over Israel in Samaria *was* twenty and eight years.

A.M.3120-3148
B. C. 884-856
Anno ante I.
Olymp. 108-80

ᵇHebrew, *the mouth*——ᶜHebrew, *statues*——ᵈ1 Kings xiv. 23——ᵉEzra vi. 11; Daniel ii. 5; iii. 29 ᶠ1 Kings xii. 28, 29——ᵍSee verse 35; chapter xiii. 1, 10; xiv. 23; xv. 8, 12——ʰHebrew, *observed not*

ⁱ1 Kings xiv. 16——ᵏHebrew, *to cut off the ends*——ˡCh. viii. 12——ᵐHebrew, *toward the rising of the sun* ⁿOr, *even to Gilead and Bashan*——ᵒAmos i. 3——ᵖHeb. *the days* were

---

of offering] Had Jehu been a man of any conscientious principle in religion, he would have finished the tragedy before he offered the *burnt-offering;* but to a man of no religion, the worship of Jehovah and of Baal are alike. If he prefers either, it is merely as a *statesman,* for political purposes.

To the guard and to the captains] לרצים

ולשלשים *leratsim uleshalashim; to the couriers* or *runners, and the shalashim,* the men of the *third rank;* those officers who were next to the nobles, the king and these being only their superiors. The *runners* were probably a sort of *light infantry.*

The city of the house of Baal.] Does not this mean a sort of holy of holies, where the most sacred images of Baal were kept? A place separated from the temple of Baal, as the *holy of holies* in the temple of Jehovah was separated from what was called *the holy place.*

Verse 27. *Made it a draught house*] A place for human excrement; so all the *versions* understand it. Nothing could be more degrading than this; he made it a *public necessary.*

Verse 30. *Thy children of the fourth* generation] These four descendants of Jehu were *Jehoahaz, Jehoash, Jeroboam* the second, and *Zechariah;* see chap. xiv. and xv. This was all the compensation Jehu had in either world, as a recompense of *his zeal for the Lord.*

Verse 31. *Jehu took no heed*] He never made it his study; indeed, he never intended to walk in this way; it neither suited his *disposition* nor his *politics.*

Verse 32. *The Lord began to cut Israel short*] The *marginal* reading is best: *The Lord cut off the ends;* and this he did by permitting Hazael to seize on the *coasts,* to conquer and occupy the *frontier towns.* This was the commencement of those miserable ravages which Elisha predicted; see chap. viii. 12. And we find from the next verse that he seized on *all the land of Gilead,* and that of *Reuben* and *Gad,* and the *half tribe of Manasseh;* in a word, whatever Israel possessed on the east side of Jordan.

Verse 34. *Are they not written in the book of the chronicles*] We have no chronicles in which there is any thing farther spoken of this bad man. His reign was long, *twenty-eight* years; and yet we know nothing of it but the commencement.

FOR *barbarity* and *hypocrisy* Jehu has few parallels; and the cowardliness and baseness of the *nobles of Samaria* have seldom been equalled. Ahab's bloody house must be cut off; but did God ever design that it should be done by these means? The men were, no doubt, profligate and wicked, and God permitted their iniquity to manifest itself in this way; and thus the purpose of God, that Ahab's house should no more reign, was completely accomplished: see 1 Kings xxi. 19, 21, 29. And by this conduct Jehu is said to have executed what was right in God's eyes, ver. 30. The cutting off of Ahab's family was decreed by the Divine justice; the *means* by which it was done, or at least the *manner* of doing, were not entirely of his appointing: yet the commission given him by the young prophet, chap. ix. 7, was very

extensive. Yet still many things seem to be attributed to God, as the *agent*, which he does not execute, but only permits to be done.

CHAPTER XI

Athaliah destroys all that remain of the seed royal of Judah, 1. Jehosheba hides Joash the son of Ahaziah, and he remains hidden in the house of the Lord six years; and Athaliah reigns over the land, 2, 3. Jehoiada, the high priest, calls the nobles privately together into the temple, shows them the king's son, takes an oath of them, arms them, places guards around the temple, and around the young king's person; they anoint and proclaim him, 4–12. Athaliah is alarmed, comes into the temple, is seized, carried forth, and slain, 13–16. Jehoiada causes the people to enter into a covenant with the Lord; they destroy Baal's house, priest, and images, 17, 18. Joash is brought to the king's house, reigns, and all the land rejoices, 19–21.

A. M. 3120
B. C. 884
Ante I. Ol. 108
An. Diogeneti,
Arch. Athen.
perpet. 8

AND when ᵃAthaliah ᵇthe mother of Ahaziah saw that her son was dead, she arose and destroyed all the ᶜseed royal.

2 But ᵈJehosheba, the daughter of King Joram, sister of Ahaziah, took ᵉJoash the son of Ahaziah, and stole him from among the king's sons *which were* slain; and they hid him, *even* him and his nurse, in the bed-chamber from Athaliah, so that he was not slain.

A.M.3120-3126
B. C. 884-878
Anno ante I.
Olymp.108-102

3 And he was with her hid in the house of the LORD six years. And Athaliah did reign over the land.

A. M. 3126
B. C. 878
Ante I. Ol. 102
An. Diogeneti,
Arch. Athen.
perpet. 14

4 And ᶠthe seventh year Jehoiada sent and fetched the rulers over hundreds, with the captains and the guard, and brought them to him into the house of the LORD, and made a covenant with them, and took an oath of

them in the house of the LORD, and showed them the king's son.

A. M. 3126
B. C. 878
Ante I. Ol. 102
An. Diogeneti,
Arch. Athen.
perpet. 14

5 And he commanded them, saying, This *is* the thing that ye shall do; A third part of you that enter in ᵍon the Sabbath shall even be keepers of the watch of the king's house;

6 And a third part *shall be* at the gate of Sur; and a third part at the gate behind the guard: so shall ye keep the watch of the house, ʰthat it be not broken down.

7 And two ⁱparts ᵏof all you that go forth on the Sabbath, even they shall keep the watch of the house of the LORD about the king.

8 And ye shall compass the king round about, every man with his weapons in his hand: and he that cometh within the ranges, let him be slain: and be ye with the king as he goeth out and as he cometh in.

9 ˡAnd the captains over the hundreds did according to all *things* that Jehoiada the priest

---

ᵃ2 Chron. xxii. 10——ᵇChap. viii. 26——ᶜHeb. *seed of the kingdom*——ᵈ2 Chron. xxii. 11, *Jehoshabeath*
ᵉOr, *Jehoash*

ᶠ2 Chron. xxiii. 1, &c.——ᵍ1 Chron. ix. 25——ʰOr, *from breaking up*——ⁱOr, *companies*——ᵏHeb. *hands*
ˡ2 Chron. xxiii. 8

NOTES ON CHAP. XI

Verse 1. *Athaliah*] This woman was the daughter of Ahab, and grand-daughter of Omri, and wife of Joram king of Judah, and mother of Ahaziah.

Destroyed all the seed royal.] All that she could lay her hands on whom Jehu had left; in order that she might get undisturbed possession of the kingdom.

How dreadful is the lust of reigning! it destroys all the charities of life; and turns fathers, mothers, brothers, and children, into the most ferocious savages! Who, that has it in his power, makes any conscience

"To swim to sovereign rule through seas of blood?"

In what a dreadful state is that land that is exposed to political *revolutions*, and where the *succession* to the throne is not most positively settled by the clearest and most decisive law! Reader, beware of *revolutions;* there have been some useful ones, but they are in general the heaviest curse of God.

Verse 2. *Daughter of—Joram, sister of*

Ahaziah] It is not likely that Jehosheba was the daughter of *Athaliah;* she was sister, we find, to Ahaziah the son of Athaliah, but probably by a different mother. The mother of Jehoash was Zibiah of Beer-sheba; see chap. xii. 1.

Verse 3. *He was—hid in the house of the Lord*] This might be readily done, because none had access to the temple but the priests; and the high priest himself was the chief manager of this business.

Verse 4. *And the seventh year Jehoiada sent*] He had certainly sounded them all, and brought them into the interests of the young king, before this time; the plot having been laid, and now ripe for execution, he brings the chief officers of the army and those of the body guard into the temple, and there binds them by an oath of secrecy, and shows them the king's son, in whose behalf they are to rise.

Verse 5. *That enter in on the Sabbath*] It appears that Jehoiada chose the *Sabbath day* to proclaim the young king, because as that was a day of public concourse, the gathering together of the people who were in this secret would not be noticed; and it is likely that they

A. M. 3126
B. C. 878
Ante I. Ol. 102
An. Diogeneti,
Arch. Athen.
perpet. 14

commanded: and they took every man his men that were to come in on the Sabbath, with them that should go out on the Sabbath, and came to Jehoiada the priest.

10 And to the captains over hundreds did the priest give King David's spears and shields, that *were* in the temple of the LORD.

11 And the guard stood, every man with his weapons in his hand, round about the king, from the right ^mcorner of the temple to the left corner of the temple, *along* by the altar and the temple.

12 And he brought forth the king's son, and put the crown upon him, and *gave him* the testimony; and they made him king, and anointed him; and they clapped their hands, and said, ⁿGod ^osave the king.

13 ^pAnd when Athaliah heard the noise of the guard *and* of the people, she came to the people into the temple of the LORD.

14 And when she looked, behold, the king

stood by ^qa pillar, as the manner *was,* and the princes and the trumpeters by the king, and all the people of the land rejoiced, and blew with trumpets: and Athaliah rent her clothes, and cried, Treason, Treason.

A. M. 3126
B. C. 878
Ante I. Ol. 102
An. Diogeneti,
Arch. Athen.
perpet. 14

15 But Jehoiada the priest commanded the captains of the hundreds, the officers of the host, and said unto them, Have her forth without the ranges: and him that followeth her kill with the sword. For the priest had said, Let her not be slain in the house of the LORD.

16 And they laid hands on her; and she went by the way by the which the horses came into the king's house: and there was she slain.

17 ^rAnd Jehoiada made a covenant between the LORD and the king and the people, that they should be the LORD's people; ^sbetween the king also and the people.

18 And all the people of the land went into

---

^mHeb. *shoulder*——ⁿHeb. *Let the king live*——^o1 Sam. x. 24——^p2 Chron. xxiii. 12, &c.

^qChapter xxiii. 3; 2 Chron. xxxiv. 31——^r2 Chron. xxiii. 16——^s2 Sam. v. 3

---

all came *unarmed,* and were supplied by Jehoiada with the *spears* and *shields* which David had laid up in the temple, ver. 10.

The priests and Levites were divided into *twenty-four* classes by David, and each served a week by turns in the temple, and it was on the *Sabbath* that they began the weekly service; all this favoured Jehoiada's design.

Verse 10. *King David's spears and shields*] Josephus expressly says that David had provided an arsenal for the temple, out of which Jehoiada took those arms. His words are: Ανοιξας δε Ιωαδος την εν τῳ ιερῳ ὁπλοθηκην, ἡν Δαβιδης κατεσκευασε, διεμερισε τοις ἑκατονταρχαις ἁμα και ιεροισι και Λευιταις ἀπανθ᾽ ὁσα εὑρεν εν αυτῃ δορατα τε και φαρετρας, και ει τι ἑτερον ειδος ὁπλου κατελαβε. "And Jehoiada having opened the arsenal in the temple, which David had prepared, he divided among the centurions, priests, and Levites, the spears, (arrows,) and quivers, and all other kinds of weapons which he found there."—*Ant.* lib. ix., c. 7, s. 8.

Verse 12. *Put the crown upon him*] This was a *diadem,* or *golden band* that went round the head.

And—the testimony] Probably the *book of the law,* written on a roll of vellum. This was his *sceptre.* Some think that it was placed *upon his head,* as well as the diadem. The *diadem,* the *testimony,* and the *anointing oil,* were essential to his consecration.

They clapped their hands] This I believe is the first instance on record of *clapping the hands* as a testimony of joy.

God save the king] יחי המלך *yechi hammelech;*. *May the king live!* So the words should be translated wherever they occur.

Verse 14. *The king stood by a pillar*] Stood

on *a pillar* or *tribunal;* the place or throne on which they were accustomed to put the kings when they proclaimed them.

Treason, Treason.] קשר קשר *kesher, kashar; A conspiracy, A conspiracy!* from *kashar,* to *bind, unite together.*

Verse 15. *Have her forth*] She had pressed in among the guards into the temple.

And him that followeth] The person who takes her part, let him instantly be slain.

Verse 16. *By the way—which the horses came*] They probably brought her out near the king's stables. It has been supposed, from Ezek. xlvi. 1, 2, that the *east gate* of the inner court was that by which the king entered on the *Sabbath day,* whereas on all other days he entered by the *south gate.* And there was another gate, called the *horse gate,* in the wall of the city, (Jer. xxxi. 40,) for the king's horses to go out at from the stables at Millo, which is therefore called, 2 Chron. xxiii. 15, *the horse gate toward the king's house.*

Verse 17. *Jehoiada made a covenant*] A *general* covenant was *first* made between the Lord, the Supreme King, the *king* his viceroy, and the *people,* that they should all be *the Lord's people;* each being equally bound to live according to the Divine law.

Then, *secondly,* a *particular* covenant was made between the *king* and the *people,* by which the *king* was bound to rule according to the laws and constitution of the kingdom, and to watch and live for the safety of the public. And the *people* were bound on their part, to love, honour, succour, and obey the king. Where these mutual and just agreements are made and maintained, there can be nothing else than prosperity in the Church and the state.

Verse 18. *His altars and images brake they*

A. M. 3126
B. C. 878
Ante I. Ol. 102
An. Diogeneti,
Arch. Athen.
perpet. 14

the [t]house of Baal, and brake it down; his altars and his images [u]brake they in pieces thoroughly, and slew Mattan the priest of Baal before the altars. And [v]the priest appointed [w]officers over the house of the LORD.

19 And he took the rulers over hundreds, and the captains, and the guard, and all the people of the land; and they brought down

A. M. 3126
B. C. 878
Ante I. Ol. 102
An. Diogeneti,
Arch. Athen.
perpet. 14

the king from the house of the LORD, and came by the way of the gate of the guard to the king's house. And he sat on the throne of the kings.

20 And all the people of the land rejoiced, and the city was in quiet: and they slew Athaliah with the sword *beside* the king's house.

21 [x]Seven years old *was* Jehoash when he began to reign.

[t]Chapter x. 26——[u]Deuteronomy xii. 3; 2 Chronicles xii. 17

[v]2 Chron. xxiii. 18, &c.——[w]Heb. *officers*——[x]2 Chron. xxiv. 1

in pieces] It is probable that Athaliah had set up the worship of Baal in Judah, as Jezebel had done in Israel; or probably it had never been removed since the days of Solomon. It was no wonder that Jehoiada began his reform with this act, when we learn from 2 Chron. xxiv. 7, that *the sons of Athaliah, that wicked woman, had broken up the house of God; and also all the dedicated things of the house of the Lord did they bestow upon Baalim.*

Verse 20. *The people—rejoiced*] They were glad to get rid of the tyranny of Athaliah.

And the city was in quiet] She had no *partisans* to rise up and disturb the king's reign.

Verse 21. *Seven years old* was *Jehoash*] The first instance on record of making a child seven years old the king of any nation, and especially of such a nation as the Jews, who were at all times very difficult to be governed.

CHAPTER XII

Jehoash reigns well under the instructions of Jehoiada the priest, 1–3. *He directs the repairing of the temple; the account of what was done,* 4–16. *Hazael takes Gath; and, proceeding to besiege Jerusalem, is prevented by Jehoash, who gives him all the treasures and hallowed things of the house of the Lord,* 17, 18. *The servants of Jehoash conspire against and slay him,* 19–21.

A.M.3126-3165
B. C. 878-839
Anno ante I.
Olymp. 102-63

[I]N the seventh year of Jehu [a]Jehoash began to reign; and forty years reigned he in Jerusalem. And his mother's name *was* Zibiah of Beer-sheba.

A.M.3126-3162
B. C. 878-842
Anno ante I.
Olymp. 102-66

2 And Jehoash did *that which was* right in the sight of the LORD all his days wherein Jehoiada the priest instructed him.

3 But [b]the high places were not taken away: the people still sacrificed and burnt incense in the high places.

4 And Jehoash said to the priests, [c]All the money of the [d]dedicated [e]things that is brought into the house of the LORD, *even* [f]the money of every one that passeth *the account,* [g]the money that every man is set at, *and* all the money that [h]cometh[i] into any man's heart to bring into the house of the LORD,

A. M. 3148
B. C. 856
Ante I. Ol. 80
An. Pherecli,
Arch. Athen.
perpet. 8

5 Let the priests take *it* to them, every man of his acquaintance: and let them repair the breaches of the house, wheresoever any breach shall be found.

[a]2 Chron. xxiv. 1——[b]1 Kings xv. 14; xxii. 43; chap. xiv. 4——[c]Chap. xxii. 4——[d]Or, *holy things*——[e]Heb. *holiness*——[f]Exod. xxx. 13

[g]Heb. *the money of the souls of his estimation,* Lev. xxvii. 2——[h]Heb. *ascendeth upon the heart of a man* [i]Exod. xxxv. 5; 1 Chron. xxix. 9

NOTES ON CHAP. XII

Verse 2. *Jehoash did—right in the sight of the Lord*] While Jehoiada the priest, who was a pious, holy man, lived, Jehoash walked uprightly; but it appears from 2 Chron. xxiv. 17, 18, that he departed from the worship of the true God after the death of this eminent high priest, lapsed into idolatry, and seems to have had a share in the murder of Zechariah, who testified against his transgressions, and those of the princes of Judah. See above, ver. 20-22.

O how *few* of the *few* who begin to live to God *continue unto the end!*

Verse 3. *The high places were not taken away*] Without the total destruction of these there could be no *radical* reform. The toleration of any species of idolatry in the land, whatever else was done in behalf of true religion, left, and in effect fostered, a seed which, springing up, regenerated in time the whole infernal system. Jehoiada did not use his influence as he might have done; for as he had the king's heart and hand with him, he might have done what he pleased.

Verse 4. *All the money of the dedicated*

A. M. 3148 B. C. 856 Ante I. Ol. 80 An. Pherecli, Arch. Athen. perpet. 8

6 But it was *so, that* [k]in the
three and twentieth year of King
Jehoash [l]the priests had not repaired the breaches of the house.
7 [m]Then King Jehoash called for Jehoiada
the priest, and the *other* priests, and said unto
them, Why repair ye not the breaches of the
house? now therefore receive no *more* money
of your acquaintance, but deliver it for the
breaches of the house.
8 And the priests consented to receive no
more money of the people, neither to repair
the breaches of the house.
9 But Jehoiada the priest took [n]a chest, and
bored a hole in the lid of it, and set it beside
the altar, on the right side as one cometh into
the house of the LORD: and the priests that
kept the [o]door put therein all the money *that
was* brought into the house of the LORD.
10 And it was *so,* when they saw that *there
was* much money in the chest, that the king's
[p]scribe and the high priest came up, and they
[q]put up in bags, and told the money *that was*
found in the house of the LORD.
11 And they gave the money, being told,
into the hands of them that did
the work, that had the oversight
of the house of the LORD: and
they [r]laid it out to the carpenters and builders, that wrought upon the
house of the LORD,
12 And to masons and hewers of stone,
and to buy timber and hewed stone to repair
the breaches of the house of the LORD, and
for all that [s]was laid out for the house to
repair *it.*
13 Howbeit [t]there were not made for the
house of the LORD bowls of silver, snuffers,
basons, trumpets, any vessels of gold, or vessels of silver, of the money *that was* brought
into the house of the LORD.
14 But they gave that to the workmen, and
repaired therewith the house of the LORD.
15 Moreover [u]they reckoned not with the
men, into whose hand they delivered the
money to be bestowed on workmen: for they
dealt faithfully.
16 [v]The trespass money and sin money
was not brought into the house of the LORD:
[w]it was the priests'.

A. M. 3148 B. C. 856 Ante I. Ol. 80 An. Pherecli, Arch. Athen. perpet. 8

---

[k]Heb. *in the twentieth year and third year*——[l]2 Chron. xxiv. 5——[m]2 Chron. xxiv. 6——[n]2 Chron. xxiv. 8, &c.——[o]Heb. *threshold*——[p]Or, *secretary*

[q]Heb. *bound up*——[r]Heb. *brought it forth*——[s]Heb. *went forth*——[t]See 2 Chron. xxiv. 14——[u]Chap. xxii. 7 [v]Lev. v. 15, 18——[w]Lev. vii. 7; Num. xviii. 9

---

things] From all this account we find that the temple was in a very ruinous state; the walls were falling down, some had perhaps actually fallen, and there was no person so zealous for the pure worship of God, as to exert himself to shore up the falling temple!

The king himself seems to have been the first who noticed these dilapidations, and took measures for the necessary repairs. The repairs were made from the following sources: 1. The *things* which pious persons *had dedicated* to the service of God. 2. The *free-will offerings* of strangers who had visited Jerusalem: *the money of every one that passeth.* 3. The *half-shekel* which the males were obliged to pay from the age of *twenty* years (Exod. xxx. 12) for the redemption of their *souls,* that is their *lives,* which is here called *the money that every man is set at.* All these sources had ever been in some measure open, but instead of repairing the dilapidations in the Lord's house, the priests and Levites had converted the income to their own use.

Verse 6. *In the three and twentieth year*] In what year Jehoash gave the orders for these repairs, we cannot tell; but the account here plainly intimates that they had been long given, and that nothing was done, merely through the inactivity and *negligence of the priests;* see 2 Chron. xxiv. 5.

It seems that the people had brought money in abundance, and the pious Jehoiada was over the priests, and yet nothing was done! Though Jehoiada was a good man, he does not appear to have had much of the spirit of an active *zeal;* and simple *piety,* without zeal and activity, is of little use when a reformation in religion and manners is necessary to be brought about. *Philip Melancthon* was orthodox, pious, and learned, but he was a man of comparative *inactivity.* In many respects *Martin Luther* was by far his inferior, but in zeal and activity he was a flaming and consuming fire; and by him, under God, was the mighty Reformation, from the corruptions of popery, effected. Ten thousand *Jehoiadas* and *Melancthons* might have *wished* it in vain; Luther *worked,* and God worked *by* him, *in* him, and *for* him.

Verse 9. *Jehoiada—took a chest*] This chest was at first set *beside the altar,* as is here mentioned; but afterwards, for the convenience of the people, it was set *without the gate;* see 2 Chron. xxiv. 8.

Verse 10. *The king's scribe and the high priest*] It was necessary to associate with the high priest some *civil authority* and activity, in order to get the neglected work performed.

Verse 13. *Howbeit there were not made—bowls, &c.*] That is, there were no vessels made for the service of the temple till all the outward repairs were completed; but after this was done, *they brought the rest of the money before the king and Jehoiada, whereof were made vessels of gold and silver;* 2 Chron. xxiv. 14.

Verse 15. *They reckoned not with the men*]

A. M. 3164
B. C. 840
Ante I. Ol. 64
An. Ariphronis,
Arch. Athen.
perpet. 5

17 Then ˣHazael king of Syria went up, and fought against Gath, and took it: and ʸHazael set his face to go up to Jerusalem.

18 And Jehoash king of Judah ᶻtook all the hallowed things that Jehoshaphat, and Jehoram, and Ahaziah, his fathers, kings of Judah, had dedicated, and his own hallowed things, and all the gold *that was* found in the treasures of the house of the Lord, and in the king's house, and sent *it* to Hazael king of Syria: and he ᵃwent away from Jerusalem.

A. M. 3164
B. C. 840
Ante I. Ol. 64
An. Ariphronis,
Arch. Athen.
perpet. 5

19 And the rest of the acts of Joash, and all that he did, *are* they not written in the book of the chronicles of the kings of Judah?

20 And ᵇhis servants arose, and made a conspiracy, and slew Joash in ᶜthe house of Millo, which goeth down to Silla.

21 For ᵈJozachar the son of Shimeath, and Jehozabad the son of ᵉShomer, his servants, smote him, and he died; and they buried him with his fathers in the city of David: and ᶠAmaziah his son reigned in his stead.

ˣCh. viii. 12——ʸSee 2 Chron. xxiv. 23——ᶻ1 Kings xv. 18; ch. xviii. 15, 16——ᵃHeb. *went up*——ᵇCh. xiv. 5;

2 Chron. xxiv. 25——ᶜOr, *Beth-millo*——ᵈ2 Chron. xxiv. 26, *Zabad*——ᵉOr, *Shimrith*——ᶠ2 Chron. xxiv. 27

They placed great confidence in them, and were not disappointed, *for they dealt faithfully.*

Verse 17. *Hazael—fought against Gath, and took it*] This city, with its satrapy or *lordship*, had been taken from the Philistines by David, (see 2 Sam. viii. 1, and 1 Chron. xviii. 1;) and it had continued in the possession of the kings of Judah till this time. On what pretence Hazael seized it, we cannot tell; he had the *ultima ratio regum, power* to do it, and he *wanted more territory.*

Verse 18. *Took all the hallowed things*] He dearly bought a peace which was of *short duration*, for the next year Hazael returned, and Jehoash, having no more treasures, was obliged to hazard a battle, which he lost, with the principal part of his nobility, so that Judah was totally ruined, and Jehoash shortly after slain in his bed by his own servants; 2 Chron. xxiv. 23.

Verse 19. *The rest of the acts of Joash*] We have already seen that this man, so promising in the beginning of his reign, apostatized, became an idolater, encouraged idolatry among his subjects, and put the high priest Zechariah, the son of Jehoiada his benefactor, to death; and now God visited that blood upon him by the hands of the tyrannous king of Syria, and by his own servants.

Verse 20. *The house of Millo*] Was a royal

palace, built by David; (see 2 Sam. v. 9;) and *Silla* is supposed to be the name of the *road* or *causeway* that led to it. *Millo* was situated between the old city of Jerusalem, and the city of David.

Verse 21. *For Jozachar*] This person is called *Zabad* in 2 Chron. xxiv. 26; and *Shimeath* his mother is said to be an *Ammonitess*, as *Jehozabad* is said to be the son, not of *Shomer*, but of *Shimrith*, a Moabitess.

They buried him with his fathers in the city of David] But they did not bury him in the *sepulchres of the kings;* this is supposed to express the popular disapprobation of his conduct. Thus ended a reign full of promise and hope in the beginning, but profligate, cruel, and ruinous in the end. Never was the hand of God's justice more signally stretched out against an apostate king and faithless people, than at this time. Now Hazael had a plenary commission; the king, the nobles, and the people, were food for his sword, and by a handful of Syrians the mighty armies of Israel were overthrown: *For the army of the Syrians came with a small company of men, and the Lord delivered a very great host into their hand, because they had forsaken the Lord God,* 2 Chron. xxiv. 24. Thus as righteousness exalteth a nation, so sin is the disgrace and confusion of any people. Sin destroys both counsel and strength; and the wicked flee when none pursue.

CHAPTER XIII

Jehoahaz reigns in Israel seventeen years; his various acts, and wars with the Syrians, 1–8. He dies, and Joash reigns in his stead, and does evil in the sight of the Lord, 9–13. Elisha's last sickness; he foretells a three fold defeat of the Syrians, and dies, 14–20. A dead man raised to life by touching the bones of Elisha, 21 Hazael dies, having long oppressed Israel; but Jehoash recovers many cities out of the hands of Ben-hadad his successor, and defeats him three times, 22–25.

A. M. 3148
B. C. 856
Ante I. Ol. 80
An. Pherecli,
Arch. Athen.
perpet. 8

IN [a]the three and twentieth year of Joash, the son of Ahaziah king of Judah, Jehoahaz the son of Jehu began to reign over Israel in Samaria, *and reigned* seventeen years.

A.M.3148-3165
B. C. 856-839
Anno ante I.
Olymp. 80-63

2 And he did *that which was* evil in the sight of the LORD, and [b]followed the sins of Jeroboam the son of Nebat, which made Israel to sin; he departed not therefrom.

3 And [c]the anger of the LORD was kindled against Israel, and he delivered them into the hand of [d]Hazael king of Syria, and into the hand of Ben-hadad the son of Hazael, all *their* days.

4 And Jehoahaz [e]besought the LORD, and the LORD hearkened unto him: for [f]he saw the oppression of Israel, because the king of Syria oppressed them.

5 ([g]And the LORD gave Israel a saviour, so that they went out from under the hand of the Syrians: and the children of Israel dwelt in their tents, [h]as beforetime.

6 Nevertheless they departed not from the sins of the house of Jeroboam, who made Israel sin, *but* [i]walked therein: [k]and there [l]remained the grove also in Samaria.)

7 Neither did he leave of the people to Jehoahaz but fifty horsemen, and ten chariots, and ten thousand footmen; for the king of Syria had destroyed them, [m]and had made them like the dust by threshing.

8 Now the rest of the acts of Jehoahaz, and all that he did, and his might, *are* they not written in the book of the chronicles of the kings of Israel?

A.M.3148-3165
B. C. 856-839
Anno ante I.
Olymp. 80-63

9 And Jehoahaz slept with his fathers; and they buried him in Samaria: and [n]Joash his son reigned in his [o]stead.

A. M. 3165
B. C. 839
Ante I. Ol. 63
An. Ariphronis,
Arch. Athen.
perpet. 6

10 In the thirty and seventh year of Joash king of Judah began [p]Jehoash the son of Jehoahaz to reign over Israel in Samaria, *and reigned* sixteen years.

A.M.3163-3179
B. C. 841-825
Anno ante I.
Olymp. 65-49

11 And he did *that which was* evil in the sight of the LORD; he departed not from all the sins of Jeroboam the son of Nebat, who made Israel sin: *but* he walked therein.

12 [q]And the rest of the acts of Joash, and [r]all that he did, and [s]his might wherewith he fought against Amaziah king of Judah, *are* they not written in the book of the chronicles of the kings of Israel?

13 And Joash slept with his fathers; and Jeroboam sat upon his throne: and Joash was buried in Samaria with the kings of Israel.

A. M. 3179
B. C. 825
Ante I. Ol. 49
An. Ariphronis,
Arch. Athen.
perpet. 20

14 Now Elisha was fallen sick of his sickness whereof he died. And Joash the king of Israel came down unto him, and wept over his face, and said, O my father, my father, [t]the chariot of Israel, and the horsemen thereof.

A. M. 3166
B. C. 838
Ante I. Ol. 62
An. Ariphronis,
Arch. Athen.
perpet 7

---

[a]Hebrew, *the twentieth year and third year*——[b]Hebrew, *walked after*——[c]Judges ii. 14——[d]Chapter viii. 12 [e]Psalm lxxviii. 34——[f]Exodus iii. 7; chap. xiv. 26 [g]See ver. 25; chap. xiv. 25, 27——[h]Heb. *as yesterday and third day*

[i]Hebrew, *he walked*——[k]1 Kings xvi. 33——[l]Heb. *stood*——[m]Amos i. 3——[n]Ver. 10, *Jehoash*——[o]Alone [p]In consort with his father, chap. xiv. 1——[q]Chap. xiv. 15——[r]See ver. 14, 25——[s]Chap. xiv. 9, &c.; 2 Chron. xxv. 17, &c.——[t]Chap. ii. 12

NOTES ON CHAP. XIII

Verse 1. *In the three and twentieth year of Joash*] The chronology here is thus accounted for; Jehoahaz began his reign at the commencement of the *twenty-third* year of Joash, and reigned *seventeen* years, *fourteen* alone, and *three* years with his son Joash; the *fourteenth* year was but just begun.

Verse 5. *And the Lord gave Israel a saviour*] This was undoubtedly *Joash*, whose successful wars against the Syrians are mentioned at the conclusion of the chapter. *Houbigant* recommends to read the *seventh* verse after the *fourth*, then the *fifth* and *sixth*, and next the *eighth*, &c.

Verse 6. *The grove also in Samaria*] Asherah, or *Astarte*, remained in Samaria, and there was she worshipped, with all her abominable rites.

Verse 10. *In the thirty and seventh year*] Joash, the son of Jehoahaz, was associated with his father in the government two years before his death. It is this association that is spoken of here. He succeeded him two years after, a little before the death of Elisha. Joash reigned *sixteen years*, which include the years he governed *conjointly* with his father.—*Calmet*.

Verse 12. *Wherewith he fought against Amaziah*] This war with Amaziah may be seen in ample detail 2 Chron. xxv.; it ended in the total defeat of Amaziah, who was taken prisoner by Joash, and afterwards slain in a conspiracy at Lachish. Joash took Jerusalem, broke down *four hundred* cubits of the wall, and took all the royal treasures, and the treasures of the house of God. See 2 Chron. xxv. 20-27.

Verse 14. *Now Elisha was fallen sick*] This

A. M. 3166
B. C. 838
Ante I. Ol. 62
An. Ariphronis,
Arch. Athen.
perpet. 7

15 And Elisha said unto him, Take bow and arrows. And he took unto him bow and arrows. 16 And he said to the king of Israel, ᵘPut thine hand upon the bow. And he put his hand *upon it:* and Elisha put his hands upon the king's hands.

17 And he said, Open the window eastward. And he opened *it.* Then Elisha said, Shoot. And he shot. ᵛAnd he said, The arrow of the LORD's deliverance, and the arrow of deliverance from Syria: for thou shalt smite the Syrians in ʷAphek, till thou have consumed *them.*

18 And he said, Take the arrows. And he took *them.* And he said unto the king of Israel, Smite upon the ground. And he smote thrice, and stayed.

A. M. 3166
B. C. 838
Ante I. Ol. 62
An. Ariphronis,
Arch. Athen.
perpet. 7

19 And the man of God was wroth with him, and said, Thou shouldest have smitten five or six times; then hadst thou smitten Syria till thou hadst consumed *it:* ˣwhereas now thou shalt smite Syria *but* thrice.

20 And Elisha died, and they buried him. And the bands of the Moabites invaded the land at the coming in of the year.

A. M. 3167
B. C. 837
Ante I. Ol. 61
An. Ariphronis,
Arch. Athen.
perpet. 7

ᵘHeb. *Make thine hand to ride*——ᵛEcclus. xlviii. 13——ʷ1 Kings xx. 26——ˣVer. 25

---

is supposed to have taken place in the *tenth* year of Joash; and if so, Elisha must have prophesied about *sixty-five* years.

O my father, my father] "What shall I do now thou art dying? thou art the only defence of Israel." He accosts him with the same words which himself spoke to Elijah when he was translated; see chap. ii. 12, and the note there.

Verse 15. *Take bow and arrows.*] The *bow,* the *arrows,* and the *smiting on the ground,* were all emblematical things, indicative of the *deliverance of Israel* from Syria.

Verse 17. *Open the window eastward*] This was towards the country beyond Jordan, which Hazael had taken from the Israelites.

The arrow of—deliverance from Syria] That is, As surely as that arrow is shot towards the lands conquered from Israel by the Syrians, so surely shall those lands be reconquered and restored to Israel.

It was an ancient custom to *shoot an arrow* or *cast a spear* into the country which an army intended to invade. *Justin* says that, as soon as Alexander the Great had arrived on the coasts of Iona, he threw a dart into the country of the Persians. "Cum delati in continentem essent, primus Alexander jaculum velut in hostilem terram jacit."—Just. lib. ii.

The *dart, spear,* or *arrow* thrown, was an emblem of the commencement of hostilities. *Virgil* (Æn. lib. ix., ver. 51) represents *Turnus* as giving the signal of attack by *throwing a spear:*—

Ecquis erit mecum, O Juvenes, qui primus in
            hostem?
En, ait: et *jaculum* intorquens emittit in auras,
Principium pugnæ; et campo sese arduus infert.
"Who, first," he cried, "with me the foe will
            dare?"
Then hurled a *dart,* the *signal of the war.*
                                            PITT.

Servius, in his note upon this place, shows that it was a custom to proclaim war in this way: the *pater patratus,* or *chief* of the *Feciales,* a sort of *heralds,* went to the confines of the enemy's country, and, after some solemnities, said with a loud voice, *I wage war with you, for such and such reasons;* and then *threw in a spear.* It was then the business of the parties thus *defied* or *warned* to take the subject into

consideration; and if they did not, within *thirty* days, come to some accommodation, the war was begun.

Thou shalt smite the Syrians in Aphek] This was a city of Syria, and probably the place of the *first* battle; and there, it appears, they had a total overthrow. They were, in the language of the text, *consumed* or *exterminated.*

Verse 18. *Smite upon the ground*] As he was ordered to take his *arrows,* the smiting on the ground must mean *shooting arrows into it.*

He smote thrice, and stayed.] The prophet knew that this shooting was *emblematical:* probably the king was not aware of what depended on the *frequency* of the action; and perhaps it was of the Lord that he smote only *thrice,* as he had determined to give Israel those three victories *only* over the Syrians. Elisha's being *wroth* because there were only *three* instead of *five* or *six* shots does not prove that God was wroth, or that he had intended to give the Syrians *five* or *six* overthrows.

Verse 20. *And Elisha died*] The two prophets, *Elijah* and *Elisha,* were both most extraordinary men. Of the former, it is difficult to say whether he was a *man,* or an *angel in a human body.* The arguments *for* this latter opinion are strong, the objections against it very feeble. His being *fed by an angel* is no proof that he was not an *angel incarnate,* for *God manifest in the flesh* was fed by the same ministry. Of him the following from Ecclesiasticus (chap. xlviii. 1-11) is a nervous character:—

1. Then stood up Elias the prophet as fire, and his word burned like a lamp.

2. He brought a sore famine upon them, and by his zeal he diminished their number.

3. By the word of the Lord he shut up the heaven, and also three times brought down fire.

4. O Elias, how wast thou honoured in thy wondrous deeds! and who may glory like unto thee!

5. Who didst raise up a dead man from death, and his soul from the place of the dead, by the word of the Most High:

6. Who broughtest kings to destruction, and honourable men from their bed:

7. Who heardest the rebuke of the Lord in Sinai, and in Horeb the judgment of vengeance:

8. Who anointedst kings to take revenge, and prophets to succeed after him:

A. M. 3167
B. C. 837
Ante I. Ol. 61
An. Ariphronis,
Arch. Athen.
perpet. 8

21 And it came to pass, as they were burying a man, that, behold, they spied a band *of men;* and they cast the man into the sepulchre of Elisha: and when the man ʸwas let down, and touched the bones of Elisha, ᶻhe revived, and stood up on his feet.

A. M. 3148–3165
B. C. 856–839
Anno ante I.
Olymp. 80–63

22 But ªHazael king of Syria oppressed Israel all the days of Jehoahaz.

23 ᵇAnd the Lᴏʀᴅ was gracious unto them, and had compassion on them, and ᶜhad respect unto them, ᵈbecause of his covenant with Abraham, Isaac, and Jacob, and would not

destroy them, neither cast he them from his ᵉpresence as yet.

A. M. 3148–3165
B. C. 856–839
Anno ante I.
Olymp. 80–63

24 So Hazael king of Syria died; and Ben-hadad his son reigned in his stead.

A. M. 3165
B. C. 839
Ante I. Ol. 63
An. Ariphronis,
Arch. Athen.
perpet. 6

25 And Jehoash the son of Jehoahaz ᶠtook again out of the hand of Ben-hadad the son of Hazael the cities which he had taken out of the hand of Jehoahaz his father by war. ᵍThree times did Joash beat him, and recovered the cities of Israel.

A. M. 3168
B. C. 836
Ante I. Ol. 60
An. Ariphronis,
Arch. Athen.
perpet. 9

ʸHeb. *went* down——ᶻEcclus. xlviii. 14——ªChap. viii. 12——ᵇChap. xiv. 27——ᶜExod. ii. 24, 25

ᵈExod. xxxii. 13——ᵉHeb. *face*——ᶠHeb. *returned and took*——ᵍVer. 18, 19

---

9. Who wast taken up in a whirlwind of fire, and in a chariot of fiery horses:

10. Who wast ordained for reproofs in their times to pacify the wrath of the Lord's judgment, before it brake forth into fury; and to turn the heart of the father unto the son, and to restore the tribes of Jacob.

11. Blessed are they that saw thee, and slept in love; for we shall surely live.

Elisha was not less eminent than Elijah; the history of his ministry is more detailed than that of his master, and his miracles are various and stupendous. In many things there is a striking likeness between him and our blessed Lord, and especially in the very beneficent miracles which he wrought. Of him the same author gives this character, ib. ver. 12-14: *Elisha was filled with his spirit: whilst he lived, he was not moved with the presence of any prince; neither could any bring him into subjection. Nothing could overcome him; and after his death his body prophesied,* i. e., raised a dead man to life, as we learn from the following verse. *He did wonders in his life, and at his death were his works marvellous;* perhaps referring to his last acts with Joash.

The bands of the Moabites] *Marauding parties;* such as those mentioned chap. v. 2.

Verse 21. *They spied a band*] They saw one of these *marauding parties;* and through fear could not wait to bury their dead, but threw the body into the grave of Elisha, which chanced then to be open; and as soon as it touched the bones of the prophet, the man was restored to life. This shows that the prophet did not perform his miracles by any powers of his *own,* but by the power of God; and he chose to honour his servant, by making even his *bones* the instrument of another miracle after his death. This is the *first,* and I believe the *last,* account of a *true miracle* performed by the bones of a dead man; and yet on it and such like the whole system of miraculous working *relics* has been founded by the popish Church.

Verse 23. *And the Lord was gracious unto them*] ויחן *vaiyachon,* he had tender affection

for them, as a husband has for his wife, or a father for his own children.

And had compassion on them] וירחמם *vairachamem,* his *bowels yearned over them;* he *felt* for them, he *sympathized* with them in all their distress: *Therefore are my bowels troubled; I will surely have mercy upon him, saith the Lord,* Jer. xxxi. 20.

And had respect unto them] ויפן *vaiyiphen,* he turned face towards them, he received them again into *favour;* and this because of his *covenant* with their fathers: they must not be totally destroyed; the Messiah must come from them, and through them must come *that light which is to enlighten the Gentiles,* and therefore he would not make an entire end of them.

Neither cast he them from his presence as yet.] But *now* they are cast out from his presence; they have sinned against the only remedy for their souls. They sit in darkness and the shadow of death; the veil is upon their face; but if they yet turn to the Lord, the veil shall be taken away.

Verse 25. *Three times did Joash beat him*] The particulars of these battles we have not; but these three victories were according to the prediction of Elisha, ver. 19. That these victories were very *decisive* we learn from their fruits, for Joash took from the Syrians the cities which Hazael had taken from Israel: viz., Gilead, the possessions of Reuben, Gad, and the half-tribe of Manasseh, and the country of Bashan; see chap. x. 33.

Thus God accomplished his word of *judgment,* and his word of *mercy.* The Syrians found themselves to be but men, and the Israelites found they could do nothing without God. In the dispensations of his justice and mercy, God has ever in view, not only the comfort, support, and salvation of his followers, but also the conviction and salvation of his enemies; and by his judgments many of these have been awakened out of their sleep, turned to God, learned righteousness, and finally become as eminent for their *obedience,* as they were before for their *rebellion.*

CHAPTER XIV

Amaziah begins to reign well; his victory over the Edomites, 1–7. He challenges Jehoash, king of Israel, 8. Jehoash's parable of the thistle and the cedar, 9, 10. The two armies meet at Beth-shemesh; and the men of Judah are defeated, 11, 12. Jehoash takes Jerusalem, breaks down four hundred cubits of the wall; takes the treasures of the king's house, and of the temple; and takes hostages, and returns to Samaria, 13, 14. The death and burial of both these kings, 15–20. Azariah, the son of Amaziah, made king; he builds Elath, 21, 22. Jeroboam the second is made king over Israel: his wicked reign and death, 23–29.

A. M. 3165
B. C. 839
Ante I. Ol. 63
An. Ariphronis,
Arch. Athen.
perpet. 6

IN [a]the second year of Joash son of Jehoahaz king of Israel reigned [b]Amaziah the son of Joash king of Judah.

A. M. 3165–3194
B. C. 839–810
Anno ante I.
Olymp. 63–34

2 He was twenty and five years old when he began to reign, and reigned twenty and nine years in Jerusalem. And his mother's name *was* Jehoaddan of Jerusalem.

3 And he did *that which was* right in the sight of the LORD, yet not like David his father: he did according to all things as Joash his father did.

4 [c]Howbeit the high places were not taken away: as yet the people did sacrifice and burnt incense on the high places.

A. M. 3166
B. C. 838
Ante I. Ol. 62
An. Ariphronis,
Arch. Athen.
perpet. 7

5 And it came to pass, as soon as the kingdom was confirmed in his hand, that he slew his servants [d]which had slain the king his father.

6 But the children of the murderers he slew not: according unto that which is written in the book of the law of Moses, wherein the LORD commanded, saying, [e]The fathers shall not be put to death for the children, nor the children be put to death for the fathers; but every man shall be put to death for his own sin.

A. M. 3166
B. C. 838
Ante I. Ol. 62
An. Ariphronis,
Arch. Athen.
perpet. 7

7 [f]He slew of Edom in [g]the valley of salt ten thousand, and took [h]Selah by war, [i]and called the name of it Joktheel unto this day.

A. M. 3177
B. C. 827
Ante I. Ol. 51
An. Ariphronis,
Arch. Athen.
perpet. 18

8 [k]Then Amaziah sent messengers to Jehoash, the son of Jehoahaz son of Jehu, king of Israel, saying, [l]Come, let us look one another in the face.

A. M. 3178
B. C. 826
Ante I. Ol. 50
An. Ariphronis,
Arch. Athen.
perpet. 19

9 And Jehoash the king of Israel sent to Amaziah king of Judah, saying, [m]The thistle

---

[a]Chap. xiii. 10——[b]2 Chron. xxv. 1——[c]Chapter xii. 3——[d]Chap. xii. 20——[e]Deuteronomy xxiv. 16; Ezek. xviii. 4, 20——[f]2 Chron. xxv. 11

[g]2 Sam. viii. 13; Psa. lx. title——[h]Or, *the rock* [i]Josh. xv. 38——[k]2 Chron. xxv. 17, 18, &c.——[l]*Joseph.* Ant. IX——[m]See Judg. ix. 8

NOTES ON CHAP. XIV

Verse 1. *In the second year of Joash*] This second year should be understood as referring to the time when his father Jehoahaz associated him with himself in the kingdom: for he reigned *two* years with his father; so this *second* year of Joash is the *first* of his absolute and independent government.—See *Calmet.*

Verse 5. *As soon as the kingdom was confirmed in his hand*] No doubt those wicked men, *Jozachar* and *Jehozabad*, who murdered his father, had considerable power and influence; and therefore he found it dangerous to bring them to justice, till he was assured of the loyalty of his other officers: when this was clear, he called them to account, and put them to death.

Verse 6. *But the children of the murderers he slew not*] Here he showed his conscientious regard for the law of Moses; for God had positively said, *The fathers shall not be put to death for the children, neither shall the children be put to death for the fathers: every man shall be put to death for his own sin,* Deut. xxiv. 16.

Verse 7. *He slew of Edom in the valley of salt*] This war is more circumstantially related in 2 Chron. xxv. 5, &c. The Idumeans had

arisen in the reign of Joram king of Judah, and shaken off the yoke of the house of David. Amaziah determined to reduce them to obedience; he therefore levied an army of *three hundred thousand* men in his own kingdom, and hired *a hundred thousand* Israelites, at the price of *one hundred* talents. When he was about to depart at the head of this numerous army, a prophet came to him and ordered him to dismiss the Israelitish army, for God was not with *them:* and on the king of Judah expressing regret for the loss of his *hundred talents,* he was answered, that *the Lord could give him much more than that.* He obeyed, sent back the Israelites, and at the head of his own men attacked the Edomites in the valley of salt, slew *ten thousand* on the spot, and took *ten thousand* prisoners, all of whom he precipitated from the *rock,* or *Selah,* which was afterwards called *Joktheel,* a place or city supposed to be the same with *Petra,* which gave name to *Arabia Petræa,* where there must have been a great precipice, from which the place took its name of *Selah* or *Petra.*

Verse 8. *Come, let us look one another in the face.*] This was a real declaration of war; and the ground of it is most evident from this circumstance: that the *one hundred thousand* men of Israel that had been dismissed, though

A. M. 3178 B. C. 826 Ante I. Ol. 50 An. Ariphronis, Arch. Athen. perpet. 19	that *was* in Lebanon sent to the ⁿcedar that *was* in Lebanon, saying, Give thy daughter to my son to wife: and there passed by

a wild beast that *was* in Lebanon, and trode down the thistle.

10 Thou hast indeed smitten Edom, and ^othine heart hath lifted thee up: glory *of this,* and tarry ^pat home: for why shouldest thou meddle to *thy* hurt, that thou shouldest fall, *even* thou, and Judah with thee?

11 But Amaziah would not hear. Therefore Jehoash king of Israel went up: and he and Amaziah king of Judah looked one another in the face at ^qBeth-shemesh, which *belongeth* to Judah.

12 And Judah ^rwas put to the worse before Israel; and they fled every man to their tents.

13 And Jehoash king of Israel took Amaziah king of Judah, the son of Jehoash the son of Ahaziah, at Beth-shemesh, and came to Jerusalem, and brake down the wall of Jerusalem, from ^sthe gate of Ephraim unto ^tthe corner gate, four hundred cubits.

14 And he took all ^uthe gold and silver, and all the vessels that *were found* in the house of the LORD, and in the treasures of the king's house, and hostages, and returned to Samaria.

A. M. 3178 B. C. 826 Ante I. Ol. 50 An. Ariphronis, Arch. Athen. perpet. 19	

15 ^vNow the rest of the acts of Jehoash which he did, and his might, and how he fought with Amaziah king of Judah, *are* they not written in the book of the chronicles of the kings of Israel?

A. M. 3163–3179
B. C. 841–825
Anno ante I.
Olymp. 65–49

16 And Jehoash slept with his fathers, and was buried in Samaria, with the kings of Israel; and Jeroboam his son reigned in his stead.

A. M. 3179
B. C. 825
Ante I. Ol. 49
An. Ariphronis,
Arch. Athen.
perpet. 20

17 ^wAnd Amaziah the son of Joash king of Judah lived after the death of Jehoash son of Jehoahaz king of Israel fifteen years.

A. M. 3179–3194
B. C. 825–810
Anno ante I.
Olymp. 49–34

18 And the rest of the acts of Amaziah, *are* they not written in the book of the chronicles of the kings of Judah?

A. M. 3165–3194
B. C. 839–810
Anno ante I.
Olymp. 63–34

ⁿ1 Kings iv. 33——^oDeut. viii. 14; 2 Chron. xxxii. 25; Ezekiel xxviii. 2, 5, 17; Hab. ii. 4——^pHebrew, *at thy house*——^qJosh. xix. 38; xxi. 16

^rHeb. *was smitten*——^sNeh. viii. 16; xii. 39——^tJer. xxxi. 38; Zech. xiv. 10——^u1 Kings vii. 51——^vChapter xiii. 12——^w2 Chron. xxv. 25, &c.

---

they had the *stipulated money,* taking the advantage of Amaziah's absence, fell upon the *cities of Judah, from Samaria to Beth-horon, and smote three thousand men, and took much spoil,* 2 Chron. xxv. 10-13. Amaziah no doubt remonstrated with Jehoash, but to no purpose; and therefore he declared war against him.

Verse 9. *Jehoash—sent to Amaziah—saying*] The meaning of this parable is plain. *The thistle that* was *in Lebanon*—Amaziah, king of Judah, *sent to the cedar that* was *in Lebanon*—Jehoash, king of Israel, *saying, Give thy daughter*—a part of thy kingdom, *to my son to wife*—to be united to, and possessed by the kings of Judah. *And there passed by a wild beast*—Jehoash and his enraged army, *and trode down the thistle*--utterly discomfited Amaziah and his troops, pillaged the temple, and broke down the walls of Jerusalem: see verses 12-14. Probably Amaziah had required certain cities of Israel to be given up to Judah; if so, this accounts for that part of the parable, *Give thy daughter to my son to wife.*

Verse 10. *Glory of this, and tarry at home*] There is a vast deal of insolent dignity in this remonstrance of Jehoash: but it has nothing conciliatory; no proposal of making amends for the injury his army had done to the unoffending inhabitants of Judah. The ravages committed by the army of Jehoash were totally unprovoked, and they were base and cowardly; they fell upon women, old men, and children, and

butchered them in cold blood, for all the *effective* men were gone off with their king against the Edomites. The quarrel of Amaziah was certainly *just,* yet he was put to the rout; he did *meddle to his hurt; he fell,* and *Judah fell with him,* as Jehoash had said: but why was this? Why *it came of God;* for he had *brought the gods of Seir, and set them up to be his gods, and bowed down himself before them,* and *burnt incense to them;* therefore God *delivered them into the hands* of their enemies, *because they sought after the gods of Edom,* 2 Chron. xxv. 14, 20. This was the reason why the Israelites triumphed.

Verse 13. *Took Amaziah king of Judah*] It is plain that Amaziah afterwards had his liberty; but how or on what terms he got it, is not known. See on the following verse.

Verse 14. *And he took—hostages*] התערבות *hattaaruboth, pledges;* from ערב *arab,* to *pledge,* give *security,* &c., for the performance of some *promise.* See the meaning of this word interpreted in the note on Gen. xxxviii. 17. It is likely that Amaziah gave some of the *nobles* or some of his own family as *hostages,* that he might regain his liberty; and they were to get their liberty when he had fulfilled his engagements; but of what kind these were we cannot tell, nor, indeed, how he got his liberty.

Verse 15. *How he fought with Amaziah*] The only fighting between them was the battle already mentioned; and this is minutely related in 2 Chron. xxv.

A. M. 3194
B. C. 810
Ante I. Ol. 34
An. Thespiei,
Arch. Athen.
perpet. 15

19 Now ˣthey made a conspiracy against him in Jerusalem: and he fled to ʸLachish; but they sent after him to Lachish, and slew him there.

20 And they brought him on horses: and he was buried at Jerusalem with his fathers, in the city of David.

21 And all the people of Judah took ᶻAzariah, which *was* sixteen years old, and made him king instead of his father Amaziah.

22 He built ªElath, and restored it to Judah, after that the king slept with his fathers.

A. M. 3179–3220
B. C. 825–784
Anno ante I.
Olymp. 49-8

23 In the fifteenth year of Amaziah the son of Joash king of Judah, Jeroboam the son of Joash king of Israel began to reign in Samaria, *and reigned* forty and one years.

24 And he did *that which was* evil in the sight of the LORD: he departed not from all the sins of Jeroboam the son of Nebat, who made Israel to sin.

25 He restored the coast of Israel ᵇfrom the entering of Hamath unto ᶜthe sea of the plain, according to the word of the LORD God of Israel, which he spake by the hand of his servant ᵈJonah, the son of Amittai, the prophet, which *was* of ᵉGath-hepher.

A. M. 3179–3220
B. C. 825–784
Anno ante I.
Olymp. 49-8

26 For the LORD ᶠsaw the affliction of Israel, *that it was* very bitter: for ᵍ*there was* not any shut up, nor any left, nor any helper for Israel.

27 ʰAnd the LORD said not that he would blot out the name of Israel from under heaven: but he saved them by the hand of Jeroboam the son of Joash.

28 Now the rest of the acts of Jeroboam, and all that he did, and his might, how he warred, and how he recovered Damascus, and Hamath, ⁱ*which belonged* to Judah, for Israel, *are* they not written in the book of the chronicles of the kings of Israel?

29 And Jeroboam slept with his fathers, *even* with the kings of Israel; and ᵏZachariah his son reigned in his stead.

A. M. 3220
B. C. 784
Ante I. Ol. 8
An. Agamestoris,
Arch. Athen.
perpet. 14

ˣ2 Chron. xxv. 27——ʸJoshua x. 31——ᶻChapter xv. 13; 2 Chron. xxvi. 1, he is called *Uzziah*——ªChap. xvi. 6; 2 Chron. xxvi. 2; Now he begins to reign alone ᵇNum. xiii. 21; xxxiv. 8——ᶜDeut. iii. 17

ᵈJonah i. 1; Matt. xii. 39, 40, called *Jonas*——ᵉJosh. xix. 13——ᶠChap. xiii. 4——ᵍDeut. xxxii. 36——ʰCh. xiii. 5——ⁱ2 Sam. viii. 6; 1 Kings xi. 24; 2 Chron. viii. 3 ᵏAfter an interregnum of 11 years, chap. xv. 8

Verse 19. *They made a conspiracy against him*] His defeat by Jehoash, and the consequent pillaging of the temple, and emptying of the royal exchequer, and the dismantling of Jerusalem, had made him exceedingly unpopular; so that probably the whole of the last *fifteen* years of his life were a series of troubles and distresses.

Verse 21. *Took Azariah*] He is also called *Uzziah*, 2 Chron. xxvi. 1. The former signifies, *The help of the Lord;* the latter, *The strength of the Lord.*

Verse 22. *He built Elath*] This city belonged to the *Edomites;* and was situated on the *eastern branch of the Red Sea,* thence called the *Elanitic Gulf.* It had probably suffered much in the late war; and was now rebuilt by Uzziah, and brought entirely under the dominion of Judah.

Verse 25. *He restored the coast of Israel*] From the description that is here given, it appears that Jeroboam reconquered all the territory that had been taken from the kings of Israel; so that *Jeroboam the second* left the kingdom as ample as it was when the ten tribes separated under *Jeroboam the first.*

Verse 26. *The Lord saw the affliction of Israel*] It appears that about this time Israel had been greatly reduced; and great calamities had fallen upon all indiscriminately; even the *diseased* and *captives* in the dungeon had the hand of God heavy upon them, and there was *no helper;* and then God sent *Jonah* to en-

courage them, and to assure them of better days. He was the first of the prophets, after *Samuel*, whose writings are preserved; yet the prophecy delivered on this occasion is not extant; for what is now in the prophecies of Jonah, relates wholly to *Nineveh.*

Verse 28. *How he warred, and—recovered Damascus*] We learn from 1 Chron. xviii. 3-11, that David had conquered *all Syria*, and put garrisons in Damascus and other places, and laid all the Syrians under *tribute;* but this yoke they had not only shaken off, but they had conquered a considerable portion of the Israelitish territory, and added it to Syria. These latter Jeroboam now recovered; and thus the places which anciently *belonged to Judah* by David's conquests, and were repossessed by Syria, he now conquered, and added *to Israel.*

Verse 29. *Jeroboam slept with his fathers*] He died a natural death; and was regularly succeeded by his son *Zachariah*, who, reigning badly, was, after *six months*, slain by *Shallum*, who succeeded him, and reigned but *one month*, being slain by *Menahem*, who succeeded him, and reigned *ten years* over Israel. *Amos* the prophet lived in the reign of Jeroboam; and was accused by *Amaziah*, one of the idolatrous priests of Beth-el, of having predicted the death of Jeroboam by the sword, but this was a slander: what he did predict, and which came afterwards to pass, may be seen Amos vii. 10-17. The *interregnum* referred to in the *margin* cannot be accounted for in a satisfactory manner.

CHAPTER XV

Azariah begins to reign over Judah, and acts well, but does not remove the high places, 1–4. He becomes leprous, and dies, after having reigned fifty-two years; and Jotham, his son, reigns in his stead, 5–7. Zachariah reigns over Israel, and acts wickedly; and Shallum conspires against him and slays him, after he had reigned six months, 8–12. Shallum reigns one month, and is slain by Menahem, 13–15. Menahem's wicked and oppressive reign; he subsidizes the king of Assyria, and dies, after having reigned ten years, 16–22. Pekahiah, his son, reigns in his stead; does wickedly; Pekah, one of his captains, conspires against and kills him, after he had reigned two years, 23–26. Pekah reigns in his stead, and acts wickedly, 27–28. Tiglath-pileser, king of Assyria, carries into captivity the inhabitants of many cities, 29. Hoshea conspires against and slays Pekah, after he had reigned twenty years; and reigns in his stead, 30, 31. Jotham begins to reign over Judah; he reigns well; dies after a reign of sixteen years, and is succeeded by his son Ahaz, 32–38.

A. M. 3194
B. C. 810
Ante I. Ol. 34
An. Thespiei,
Arch. Athen.
perpet. 15

A. M. 3194–3246
B. C. 810–758
Ante Urbem
Conditam, 57–5

IN [a]the twenty and seventh year of Jeroboam king of Israel [b]began [c]Azariah son of Amaziah king of Judah to reign. 2 Sixteen years old was he when he began to reign, and he reigned two and fifty years in Jerusalem. And his mother's name *was* Jecholiah of Jerusalem.

3 And he did *that which was* right in the sight of the LORD, according to all that his father Amaziah had done;

A. M. 3194–3246
B. C. 810–758
Ante Urbem
Conditam, 57–5

4 [d]Save that the high places were not removed: the people sacrificed and burnt incense still on the high places.

5 And the LORD [e]smote the king, so that he was a leper unto the day of his death, and

---

[a]This is the 27th year of Jeroboam's partnership in the kingdom with his father, who made him consort at his going to the Syrian wars. It is the 16th year of Jeroboam's monarchy

[b]Chap. xiv. 21; 2 Chron. xxvi. 1, 3, 4——[c]Called *Uzziah,* verses 13, 30, &c.; and 2 Chronicles xxvi. 1 [d]Verse 35; chapter xii. 3; xiv. 4——[e]2 Chronicles xxvi. 19–21

NOTES ON CHAP. XV

Verse 1. *In the twenty and seventh year of Jeroboam*] Dr. *Kennicott* complains loudly here, because of "the corruption in the name of this king of Judah, who is expressed by *four* different names in this chapter: *Ozriah, Oziah, Ozrihu,* and *Ozihu.* Our oldest Hebrew MS. relieves us here by reading truly, in verses 1, 6, 7, עזיהו *Uzziah,* where the printed text is differently corrupted. This reading is called *true,* 1. *Because* it is supported by the *Syriac* and *Arabic* versions in these three verses. 2. *Because* the printed text itself has it so in ver. 32 and 34 of this very chapter. 3. *Because* it is so expressed in the parallel place in Chronicles; and, 4. *Because* it is not Ἀζαρίας, *Azariah,* but Ὀζίας, *Oziah,* (*Uzziah,*) in St. Matthew's genealogy." There are insuperable difficulties in the chronology of this place. The marginal note says, "This is the *twenty-seventh* year of Jeroboam's partnership in the kingdom with his father, who made him consort at his going to the Syrian wars. It is the *sixteenth* year of Jeroboam's monarchy." Dr. *Lightfoot* endeavours to reconcile this place with chap. xiv. 16, 17, thus: "At the death of Amaziah, his son and heir Uzziah was but *four* years old, for he was about *sixteen* in Jeroboam's *twenty-seventh* year; therefore, the throne must have been empty *eleven* years, and the government administered by protectors while Uzziah was in his minority." Learned men are not agreed concerning the mode of reconciling these differences; there is probably some mistake in the *numbers.* I must say to all the contending chronologers:—

Non nostrum inter vos tantas componere lites.

When *such men* disagree, *I* can't decide.

Verse 3. *He did that which was right*] It is said, 2 Chron. xxvi. 5, that he sought the Lord in the days of Zechariah the prophet, and God made him to prosper; that he fought against the *Philistines;* broke down the walls of *Gath, Jabneh,* and *Ashdod;* prevailed over the *Arabians* and *Mehunims;* and that the *Ammonites* paid him tribute; and his dominion extended abroad, even to the *entering in of Egypt;* that he built *towers* in Jerusalem, at the *corner gate, valley gate,* and *turning of the wall;* and built *towers* also in the *desert,* and digged many *wells;* that he had a very strong and well-regulated *military force,* which he provided with a well-stocked *arsenal;* and constructed many military *engines* to shoot *arrows* and project *great stones;* and that his fame was universally spread abroad.

Verse 5. *The Lord smote the king, so that he was a leper*] The reason of this plague is well told in the above quoted chapter, ver. 16. That his heart being elated, he went into the temple to burn incense upon the altar, assuming to himself the functions of the high priest; that Azariah the priest, with *fourscore* others, went in after him, to prevent him; and that while they were remonstrating against his conduct, the Lord struck him with the *leprosy,* which immediately appeared on his *forehead;* that they thrust him out as an unclean person; and that he himself *hurried to get out,* feeling that the Lord had smitten him; that he was obliged to dwell in a *house by himself,* being leprous, to the day of his death; and that during this time the affairs of the kingdom were administered by his son *Jotham.* A poet, ridiculing the conduct of those who, without an episcopal ordination, think they have authority from God to dispense all the ordinances of the Church, expresses himself thus:—

A. M. 3239–3246 [f]dwelt in a several house. And
B. C. 765–758
Ante Urbem Jotham the king's son *was* over
Conditam, 12–5 the house, judging the people
of the land.

A. M. 3194–3246 6 And the rest of the acts of
B. C. 810–758
Ante Urbem Azariah, and all that he did, *are*
Conditam, 57–5 they not written in the book of
the chronicles of the kings of Judah??

A. M. 3246 7 So Azariah slept with his
B. C. 758
Olymp. V. 3 fathers; and [g]they buried him
An. Æschyli,
Arch. Athen. with his fathers in the city of
perpet. 20 David: and Jotham his son
reigned in his stead.

A. M. 3231 8 [h]In the thirty and eighth
B. C. 773
Olymp. I. 4 year of Azariah king of Judah
An. Æschyli,
Arch. Athen. did Zachariah the son of Jero-
perpet. 5 boam reign over Israel in Sa-
maria six months.

9 And he did *that which was* evil in the
sight of the LORD, as his fathers had done:
he departed not from the sins of Jeroboam
the son of Nebat, who made Israel to sin.

A. M. 3232 10 And Shallum the son of
B. C. 772
Olymp. II. 1 Jabesh conspired against him,
An. Æschyli,
Arch. Athen. and [i]smote him before the peo-
perpet. 6 ple, and slew him, and reigned
in his stead.

11 And the rest of the acts of Zachariah,
behold, they *are* written in the book of the
chronicles of the kings of Israel.

12 This *was* [k]the word of the A. M. 3120
B. C. 884
LORD which he spake unto Ante I. Ol. 108
Jehu, saying, Thy sons shall sit An. Diogeneti,
Arch. Athen.
on the throne of Israel unto the perpet. 8
fourth *generation.* And so it came to pass.

13 Shallum the son of Jabesh A. M. 3232
B. C. 772
began to reign in the nine and Olymp. II. 1
thirtieth year of [l]Uzziah king of An. Æschyli,
Arch. Athen.
Judah; and he reigned [m]a full perpet. 6
month in Samaria.

14 For Menahem the son of Gadi went up
from [n]Tirzah, and came to Samaria, and
smote Shallum the son of Jabesh in Samaria,
and slew him, and reigned in his stead.

15 And the rest of the acts of Shallum, and
his conspiracy which he made, behold, they
are written in the book of the chronicles of
the kings of Israel.

16 Then Menahem smote [o]Tiphsah, and all
that *were* therein, and the coasts thereof from
Tirzah: because they opened not *to him,*
therefore he smote *it; and* all [p]the women
therein that were with child he ripped up.

17 In the nine and thirtieth A. M. 3232–3243
B. C. 772–761
year of Azariah king of Judah Ante Urbem
began Menahem the son of Gadi Conditam, 19–8
to reign over Israel, *and reigned* ten years in
Samaria.

18 And he did *that which was* evil in the
sight of the LORD: he departed not all his

---

[f]Lev. xiii. 46——[g]2 Chron. xxvi. 23——[h]There having been an interregnum for 11 years——[i]As prophesied, Amos vii. 9——[k]Chap. x. 30

[l]Matt. i. 8, 9, called *Ozias,* and ver. 11, *Azariah*
[m]Heb. *a month of days*——[n]1 Kings xiv. 17——[o]1
Kings iv. 24——[p]Chap. viii. 12

But now the warm enthusiast cries,
  The office to myself I take;
Offering the Christian sacrifice,
  Myself a lawful priest I make:
To me this honour appertains,
No need of *man* when GOD ordains.

[Some go into the contrary extreme, and in
effect say, *no need of* GOD *when* MAN *ordains.*]

Though *kings* may not so far presume,
  'Tis no presumption in a *clown,*
And, lo, without a call from Rome,
  My *flail* or *hammer* I lay down;
And if my *order's* name ye seek,
Come, see a new *Melchisedek!*
Ye upstart (men-made) priests, your sen-
    tence know,
  The marks you can no longer hide;
Your daring deeds too plainly show
  The loathsome leprosy of *pride;*
And if ye still your crime deny,
Who *lepers live* shall *lepers die.*

CHARLES WESLEY.

This is very severe, but applies to every man

who, through pride, presumption, or the desire
of gain, enters into the priest's office, though he
have the utmost authority that the highest
ecclesiastical officer can confer.

Verse 10. *Smote him before the people*] In
some public assembly: he probably became very
unpopular.

Verse 12. *This was the word of the Lord—
unto Jehu*] God had promised to Jehu that his
sons should sit on the throne of Israel *to the
fourth generation;* and so it came to pass, for
Jehoahaz, Joash, Jeroboam, and *Zachariah,* succeeded Jehu, to whom this promise was made.
But because he executed the Divine purpose
with an uncommanded *cruelty,* therefore God
cut his family short, according to his word by
Hosea, *I will avenge the blood of Jezreel upon
the house of Jehu; and I will cause to cease the
kingdom of the house of Israel,* i. 4.

Verse 13. *He reigned a full month*] Menahem is supposed to have been one of Zachariah's
generals. Hearing of the death of his master,
when he was with the troops at *Tirzah,* he
hastened to Samaria, and slew the murderer,
and had himself proclaimed in his stead. But,
as the people of *Tiphsah* did not open their

A. M. 3232–3243
B. C. 772–761
Ante Urbem
Conditam, 19–8

days from the sins of Jeroboam
the son of Nebat, who made
Israel to sin.

A. M. 3233
B. C. 771
Olymp. II. 2
An. Æschyli,
Arch. Athen.
perpet. 7

19 *And* [q]Pul the king of Assyria came against the land:
and Menahem gave Pul a thousand talents of silver, that his
hand might be with him to [r]confirm the kingdom in his hand.
20 And Menahem [s]exacted the money of
Israel, *even* of all the mighty men of wealth,
of each man fifty shekels of silver, to give to
the king of Assyria. So the king of Assyria
turned back, and stayed not there in the land.

A. M. 3232–3243
B. C. 772–761
Ante Urbem
Conditam, 19–8

21 And the rest of the acts of
Menahem, and all that he did,
are they not written in the book
of the chronicles of the kings of Israel?

A. M. 3243
B. C. 761
Olymp. IV. 4
An. Æschyli,
Arch. Athen.
perpet. 17

22 And Menahem slept with
his fathers; and Pekahiah his
son reigned in his stead.
23 In the fiftieth year of Aza-
riah king of Judah Pekahiah the son of Menahem began to reign over Israel in Samaria,
and reigned two years.

A. M. 3243–3245
B. C. 761–759
Ante Urbem
Conditam, 8–6

24 And he did *that which was*
evil in the sight of the LORD:
he departed not from the sins of
Jeroboam the son of Nebat, who made Israel
to sin.

A. M. 3245
B. C. 759
Olymp. V. 2
An. Æschyli,
Arch. Athen.
perpet. 19

25 But Pekah the son of Remaliah, a captain of his, conspired against him, and smote
him in Samaria, in the palace
of the king's house, with Argob and Arieh,
and with him fifty men of the Gileadites: and
he killed him, and reigned in his room.

A. M. 3243–3245
B. C. 761–759
Ante Urbem
Conditam, 8–6

26 And the rest of the acts of
Pekahiah, and all that he did,
behold, they *are* written in the
book of the chronicles of the kings of Israel.

A. M. 3245–3265
B. C. 759–739
Olymp. V. 2
—X. 2

27 In the two and fiftieth year
of Azariah king of Judah,
[t]Pekah the son of Remaliah
began to reign over Israel in Samaria, *and
reigned* twenty years.
28 And he did *that which was* evil in the
sight of the LORD: he departed not from the
sins of Jeroboam the son of Nebat, who made
Israel to sin.

A. M. 3264
B. C. 740
Olymp. X. 2
An. Æsimedis,
Arch. Athen.
decen. 3

29 In the days of Pekah king
of Israel [u]came Tiglath-pileser
king of Assyria, and took [v]Ijon,
and Abel-beth-maachah, and Ja-
noah, and Kedesh, and Hazor, and Gilead,
and Galilee, all the land of Naphtali, and carried them captive to Assyria.

A. M. 3265
B. C. 739
Olymp. X. 2
An. Æsimedis,
Arch. Athen.
decen. 4

30 And Hoshea the son of
Elah made a conspiracy against
Pekah the son of Remaliah, and

[q]1 Chron. v. 26; Isa. ix. 1; Hos. viii. 9——[r]Chap. xiv. 5
[s]Heb. *caused to come forth*

[t]Isaiah vii. 1——[u]1 Chron. v. 26; Isaiah ix. 1——[v]1 Kings xv. 20

gates to him, he took the place by assault; and as the text tells us, practised the most cruel barbarities, even *ripping up the women that were with child!*

Verse 19. *Pul, the king of Assyria*] This is the first time we hear of *Assyria* since the days of Nimrod, its founder, Gen. x. 11.

Dean *Prideaux* supposes that this *Pul* was father of the famous *Sardanapalus*, the son himself being called *Sardan;* to which, as was frequent in those times, the father's name, *Pul,* was added, making *Sardanpul* of which the Greeks and Latins made *Sardanapalus;* and this *Pul* is supposed to be the same that reigned in *Nineveh* when *Jonah* preached the terrors of the Lord to that city.

That his hand] That is, his *power* and *influence, might be with him:* in this sense is the word *hand* frequently used in Scripture.

Verse 20. *Each man fifty shekels of silver*] Upwards of *five pounds* sterling a man.

Verse 21. Are *they not written in—the chronicles*] There are no chronicles extant, in which there is any thing farther relative to this king.

Verse 25. *Smote him in Samaria, in the palace of the king's house, with Argob and Arieh*] Who Argob and Arieh were we know not; some make them *men,* some make them *statues.* Pekah had *fifty* Gileadites in the conspiracy with him.

Verse 29. *Came Tiglath-pileser*] He is supposed to have been the successor of Sardanapalus: Dean Prideaux makes him the same with *Arbaces,* called by Ælian *Thilgamus,* and by Usher *Ninus junior;* who, together with *Belesis,* headed the conspiracy against *Sardanapalus,* and fixed his seat at Nineveh, the ancient residence of the Assyrian kings; as did *Belesis,* who is called, in Isa. xxxix. 1, *Baladan,* fix his at Babylon.

Took Ijon] These places belonged to Israel; and were taken by Ben-hadad, king of Syria, when he was in league with Asa, king of Judah. See 1 Kings xv. 20. They were regained by *Jeroboam the second;* and now they are taken from Israel once more by *Tiglath-pileser.* From 1 Chron. v. 26, we learn that *Pul* and *Tiglath-pileser,* kings of Assyria, carried away into captivity the two tribes of *Reuben,* and *Gad,* and the half tribe of *Manasseh;* all that belonged to Israel, on the other side of Jordan. These were never restored to Israel.

Verse 30. *Hoshea the son of Elah—in the*

A. M. 3265
B. C. 739
Olymp. X. 2
An. Æsimedis,
Arch. Athen.
decen. 4

smote him, and slew him, and ʷreigned in his stead, ˣin the twentieth year of Jotham the son of Uzziah.

A. M. 3245–3265
B. C. 759–739
Olymp. V. 2
—X. 2

31 And the rest of the acts of Pekah, and all that he did, behold, they *are* written in the book of the chronicles of the kings of Israel.

A. M. 3246
B. C. 758
Olymp. V. 3
An. Æschyli,
Arch. Athen.
perpet. 20

32 In the second year of Pekah the son of Remaliah king of Israel began ʸJotham the son of Uzziah king of Judah to reign.

A. M. 3246–3262
B. C. 758–742
Olymp. V. 3
—IX. 3

33 Five and twenty years old was he when he began to reign, and he reigned sixteen years in Jerusalem. And his mother's name *was* Jerusha, the daughter of Zadok.

34 And he did *that which was* right in the sight of the LORD: he did ᶻaccording to all that his father Uzziah had done.

A. M. 3246–3262
B. C. 758–742
Olymp. V. 3
—IX. 3

35 ᵃHowbeit the high places were not removed: the people sacrificed and burned incense still in the high places. ᵇHe built the higher gate of the house of the LORD.

36 Now the rest of the acts of Jotham, and all that he did, *are* they not written in the book of the chronicles of the kings of Judah?

37 In ᶜthose days the LORD began to send against Judah ᵈRezin the king of Syria, and ᵉPekah the son of Remaliah.

A. M. 3262
B. C. 742
Olymp. IX. 3
An. Æsimedis,
Arch. Athen.
decen. 1

38 And Jotham slept with his fathers, and was buried with his fathers in the city of David his father: and Ahaz his son reigned in his stead.

ʷAfter an anarchy for some years, chap. xvii. 1; Hos. x. 3, 7, 15——ˣIn the fourth year of Ahaz, in the twentieth year after Jotham had begun to reign; *Ush*

ʸ2 Chron. xxvii. 1——ᶻVer. 3——ᵃVer. 4——ᵇ2 Chron. xxvii. 3, &c.——ᶜAt the end of Jotham's reign ᵈChap. xvi. 5; Isa. vii. 1——ᵉVer. 27

---

twentieth year of Jotham] There are many difficulties in the chronology of this place. To reconcile the whole, *Calmet* says: "Hoshea conspired against Pekah, the *twentieth* year of the reign of this prince, which was the *eighteenth* after the beginning of the reign of Jotham, king of Judah. Two years after this, that is, the *fourth* year of Ahaz, and the *twentieth* of Jotham, Hoshea made himself master of a *part* of the kingdom, according to ver. 30. Finally, the *twelfth* year of Ahaz, Hoshea had peaceable possession of the *whole* kingdom, according to chap. xvii. ver. 1."

Verse 36. *Now the rest of the acts of Jotham*] These acts are distinctly stated in 2 Chron. chap. xxvii. He built the high gate of the house of the Lord; and he built much on the wall of *Ophel.* He built cities in the mountains of Judah; and in the forests he built castles and towers. He overthrew the Ammonites; and obliged them to give him *one hundred* talents of silver, *ten thousand* measures of wheat, and *ten thousand* of barley, for *three* consecutive years. He was *twenty-five* years old when he began to reign, and he reigned *sixteen* years. These are the particulars which

we learn from the place in Chronicles quoted above; few of which are mentioned in this place. As to the *higher gate* of the house of the Lord, commentators are not well agreed: some think it was a gate which he then made, and which did not exist before, and is the same that is called the *new gate*, Jer. xxvi. 10; which is very likely.

Verse 37. *In those days the Lord began to send*] It was about this time that the Assyrian wars, so ruinous to the Jews, began; but it was in the following reigns that they arrived at their highest pitch of disaster to those unfaithful and unfortunate people. However much we may blame the Jews for their disobedience and obstinacy, yet we cannot help feeling for them under their severe afflictions. Grievously they have sinned, and grievously have they suffered for it. And if they be still objects of God's judgments, there is revelation to believe that they will yet be objects of God's goodness. Many think the signs of the times are favourable to this ingathering; but there is no evidence among the people themselves that the day of their redemption is at hand. They do not humble themselves; they do not seek the Lord.

CHAPTER XVI

Ahaz begins to reign, acts wickedly, and restores idolatry in Judea, 1–4. Rezin, king of Syria, besieges Jerusalem, but cannot take it; he takes Elath, and drives the Jews thence, 5, 6. Ahaz hires Tiglath-pileser against the king of Syria and the king of Israel, and gives him the silver and gold that were found in the treasures of the house of the Lord, 7, 8. Tiglath-pileser takes Damascus and slays Rezin, 9. Ahaz goes to meet him at Damascus: sees an altar there, a pattern of which he sends to Urijah, the priest; and orders him to make one like it, which he does, 10–15. He makes several alterations in the temple; dies; and Hezekiah his son reigns in his stead, 16–20.

A. M. 3262
B. C. 742
Olymp. IX. 3
An. Æsimedis,
Arch. Athen.
decen. 1

IN the seventeenth year of Pekah the [a]son of Remaliah, [b]Ahaz the son of Jotham king of Judah began to reign.

A. M. 3262-3278
B. C. 742-726
Olymp. IX. 3
—XIII. 3

2 Twenty years old *was* Ahaz when he began to reign, and reigned sixteen years in Jerusalem, and did not *that which was* right in the sight of the LORD his God, like David his father.

3 But he walked in the way of the kings of Israel, yea, [c]and made his son to pass through the fire, according to the [d]abomination of the heathen, whom the LORD cast out from before the children of Israel.

4 And he sacrificed and burnt incense in the high places, and [e]on the hills, and under every green tree.

A. M. 3262
B. C. 742
Olymp. IX. 3
An. Æsimedis,
Arch. Athen.
decen. 1

5 [f]Then Rezin king of Syria, and Pekah son of Remaliah king of Israel, came up to Jerusalem to war: and they besieged Ahaz, but could not overcome *him.*

A. M. 3262
B. C. 742
Olymp. IX. 3
An. Æsimedis,
Arch. Athen.
decen. 1

6 At that time Rezin king of Syria [g]recovered Elath to Syria, and drave the Jews from [h]Elath; and the Syrians came to Elath, and dwelt there unto this day.

7 So Ahaz sent messengers [i]to [k]Tiglath-pileser king of Assyria, saying, I *am* thy servant and thy son: come up, and save me out of the hand of the king of Syria, and out of the hand of the king of Israel, which rise up against me.

A. M. 3264
B. C. 740
Olymp. X. 1
An. Æsimedis,
Arch. Athen.
decen. 3

8 And Ahaz [l]took the silver and gold that was found in the house of the LORD, and in the treasures of the king's house, and sent *it for* a present to the king of Assyria.

9 And the king of Assyria hearkened unto him: for the king of Assyria went up against [m]Damascus, and [n]took it, and carried *the people of* it captive to Kir, and slew Rezin.

10 And King Ahaz went to Damascus to

---

[a]Isa. viii. 6——[b]2 Chron. xxviii. 1, &c.——[c]Lev. xviii. 21; 2 Chron. xxviii. 3; Psa. cvi. 37, 38——[d]Deut. xii. 31——[e]Deut. xii. 2; 1 Kings xiv. 23——[f]Isa. vii. 1, 4, &c.——[g]Chap. xiv. 22

[h]Heb. *Eloth*——[i]Ch. xv. 29——[k]Heb. *Tilgath-pileser,* 1 Chron. v. 26, and 2 Chron. xxviii. 20, *Tilgath-pilneser* [l]Chap. xii. 18; see 2 Chron. xxviii. 21——[m]Heb. *Dammesek*——[n]Foretold, Amos i. 5

NOTES ON CHAP. XVI

Verse 2. *Twenty years old was Ahaz*] Here is another considerable difficulty in the chronology. Ahaz was but *twenty years* old when he began to reign, and he died after he had reigned *sixteen* years; consequently his whole age amounted only to *thirty-six years.* But Hezekiah his son was *twenty-five* years old when he began to reign; and if this were so, then Ahaz must have been the father of Hezekiah when he was but *eleven* years of age! Some think that the *twenty years* mentioned here respect the beginning of the reign of Jotham, father of Ahaz; so that the passage should be thus translated: *Ahaz was twenty years of age when his father began to reign;* and consequently he was *fifty-two years* old when he died, seeing Jotham reigned *sixteen* years: and therefore Hezekiah was born when his father was *twenty-seven* years of age. This however is a violent solution, and worthy of little credit. It is better to return to the *text* as it stands, and allow that Ahaz might be only *eleven* or *twelve* years old when he had Hezekiah: this is not at all impossible; as we know that the youth of both sexes in the eastern countries are marriageable at *ten* or *twelve* years of age, and are frequently betrothed when they are but *nine.* I know a woman, an East Indian, who had the *second* of her *two* first children when she was only *fourteen* years of age, and must have had the *first* when between *eleven* and *twelve.* I hold it therefore quite a possible case that Ahaz might have had a son born to him when he was but *eleven* or *twelve* years old.

Verse 3. *Made his son to pass through the fire*] On this passage I beg leave to refer the reader to my notes on Lev. xviii. 21, xx. 2, 14, where the subject is considered at large.

Verse 5. *But could not overcome* him.] It is likely that this was the time when Isaiah was sent to console Ahaz; (see Isa. vii. 1;) and predicted the death both of Rezin and Pekah, his enemies.

Verse 6. *Recovered Elath to Syria*] See the note on chap. xiv. 22.

Verse 7. *I am thy servant and thy son*] I will *obey* thee in all, and become *tributary* to thee; only help me against Syria and Israel.

Verse 9. *The king of Assyria hearkened unto him*] It is said, 2 Chron. xxviii. 20, that *Tilgath-pileser distressed him, but strengthened him not.* Though he came against the Syrians, and took Damascus, and slew Rezin, yet he did *not help* Ahaz against the Philistines, nor did he lend him any forces to assist against Israel; and he distressed him by taking the royal treasures, and the treasures of the temple, and did him little service for so great a sacrifice. He helped him a little, but distressed him on the whole.

It appears that, about this time, Pekah king of Israel nearly ruined Judea: it is said, 2 Chron. xxviii. 6, *that he slew one hundred thousand valiant men in one day;* and that he *carried away captive to Samaria two hundred thousand women and children, and much spoil;* but, at the instance of the prophet Oded, these were all sent back, fed and clothed, ib. 8-15.

Verse 10. *Ahaz went to Damascus*] He had received so much help on the defeat of Rezin,

A. M. 3264
B. C. 740
Olymp. X. 1
An. Æsimedis,
Arch. Athen.
decen. 3 meet Tiglath-pileser king of Assyria, and saw an altar that *was* at Damascus: and King Ahaz sent to Urijah the priest the fashion of the altar, and the pattern of it, according to all the workmanship thereof.

11 And Urijah the priest built an altar according to all that King Ahaz had sent from Damascus: so Urijah the priest made *it* against King Ahaz came from Damascus.

12 And when the king was come from Damascus, the king saw the altar: and °the king approached to the altar, and offered thereon.

13 And he burnt his burnt-offering and his meat-offering, and poured his drink-offering, and sprinkled the blood of his ᵖpeace-offerings upon the altar.

14 And he brought also �q the brazen altar, which *was* before the LORD, from the forefront of the house, from between the altar and the house of the LORD, and put it on the north side of the altar.

15 And King Ahaz commanded Urijah the priest, saying, Upon the great altar burn ʳthe morning burnt-offering, and the evening meat-offering, and the king's burnt-sacrifice, and his meat-offering, with the burnt-offering of all

the people of the land, and their meat-offering, and their drink-offerings; and sprinkle upon it all the blood of the burnt-offering, and all the blood of the sacrifice: and the brazen altar shall be for me to inquire *by*. A. M. 3264
B. C. 740
Olymp. X. 1
An. Æsimedis,
Arch. Athen.
decen. 3

16 Thus did Urijah the priest, according to all that King Ahaz commanded.

17 ˢAnd King Ahaz cut off ᵗthe borders of the bases, and removed the laver from off them; and took down ᵘthe sea from off the brazen oxen that *were* under it, A. M. 3265
B. C. 739
Olymp. X. 2
An. Æsimedis,
Arch. Athen.
decen. 4 and put it upon a pavement of stones.

18 And the covert for the Sabbath that they had built in the house, and the king's entry without, turned he from the house of the LORD for the king of Assyria.

19 Now the rest of the acts of Ahaz which he did, *are* they not written in the book of the chronicles of the kings of Judah? A. M. 3262–3278
B. C. 742–726
Olymp. IX. 3
—XIII. 3

20 And Ahaz slept with his fathers, and ᵛwas buried with his fathers in the city of David: and Hezekiah his son reigned in his stead. A. M. 3278
B. C. 726
Olymp. XIII. 3
An. Clidici,
Arch. Athen.
decen. 7

°2 Chron. xxvi. 16, 19——ᵖHeb. *which* were *his*——q2 Chron. iv. 1——ʳExod. xxix. 39, 40, 41

ˢ2 Chron. xxviii. 25——ᵗ1 Kings vii. 27, 28——ᵘ1 Kings vii. 23, 24——ᵛ2 Chron. xxviii. 27

---

that he went to Damascus to meet the king of Assyria, and render him thanks.

Ahaz sent to Urijah the priest the fashion of the altar] This was some idolatrous altar, the *shape* and *workmanship* of which pleased Ahaz so well that he determined to have one like it at Jerusalem. For this he had no Divine authority, and the compliance of Urijah was both mean and sinful. That Ahaz did this for an idolatrous purpose, is evident from 2 Chron. xxviii. 21-25: "For he sacrificed to the gods of Damascus;—and he said, Because the gods of the kings of Syria help them, I will sacrifice to them, that they may help me. And he made high places to burn incense to other gods in every city of Judah."

Verse 14. *Put it on the north side*] He seems to have intended to *conform* every thing in the Lord's house as much as possible to the idolatrous temples which he saw at Damascus, and to model the Divine worship in the same way: in a word to honour and worship the gods of Syria, and not the God of heaven. All the alterations specified here were in contempt of the true God. Thus *he provoked to anger the Lord God of his fathers*, 2 Chron. xxviii. 25.

Verse 18. *And the covert for the Sabbath*] There are a great number of conjectures concerning this *covert*, or, as it is in the Hebrew, the מוסך *musach, of the Sabbath*. As the word, and others derived from the same root, signify

covering or booths, it is very likely that this means either a sort of *canopy* which was erected on the Sabbath days for the accommodation of the people who came to worship, and which Ahaz took away to discourage them from that worship; or a canopy under which the king and his family reposed themselves, and which he transported to some other place to accommodate the king of Assyria when he visited him. *Jarchi* supposes that it was a sort of *covert way* that the kings of Judah had to the temple, and Ahaz had it removed lest the king of Assyria, going by that way, and seeing the sacred vessels, should covet them. If that way had been open, he might have gone by it into the temple, and have seen the sacred vessels, and so have asked them from a man who was in no condition to refuse them, however unwilling he might be to give them up. The removing of this, whatever it was, whether *throne* or *canopy*, or *covered way*, cut off the communication between the king's house and the temple; and the king of Assyria would not attempt to go into that sacred place by that other passage to which the priests alone had access.

Verse 20. *Was buried with his fathers in the city of David*] But it is expressly declared, 2 Chron. xxviii. 27, that *he was not buried in the sepulchres of the kings of Israel;* and this was undoubtedly intended as a mark of *degradation*.

His reign was *disastrous* and *impious;* and it was *disastrous* because it was *impious.* He had been a *scourge,* not a *blessing,* to his people. He had not only made illegal *alterations* in the temple, and in the mode of worship prescribed by the true God, but he had *polluted* all the cities of Judah with *idolatry,* and brought ruin upon the nation. On the whole, a worse king than himself had not as yet sat on the Jewish throne; and yet he had many advantages: he had for *counsellor* one of the greatest men ever

produced in the Jewish nation, ISAIAH *the prophet;* and God condescended to interpose especially for him when grievously straitened by the kings of *Israel* and *Syria,* both of whom were cut off according to the prediction of this prophet. But he would not lay it to heart, and therefore the wrath of God fell heavily upon him, and upon the stiff-necked and rebellious people whom he governed. He had sufficient warning and was without excuse. He *would* sin, and therefore he *must* suffer.

CHAPTER XVII

Hoshea's wicked reign, 1, 2. Shalmaneser comes up against him, makes him tributary, and then casts him into prison, 3, 4. He besieges Samaria three years; and at last takes it, and carries Israel captive into Assyria, and places them in different cities of the Assyrians and Medes, 5, 6. The reason why Israel was thus afflicted; their idolatry, obstinacy, divination, &c., 7–18. Judah copies the misconduct of Israel, 19. The Lord rejects all the seed of Israel, 20–23. The king of Assyria brings different nations and places them in Samaria, and the cities from which the Israelites had been led away into captivity, 24. Many of these strange people are destroyed by lions, 25. The king of Assyria sends back some of the Israelitish priests to teach these nations the worship of Jehovah; which worship they incorporate with their own idolatry, 26–33. The state of the Israelites, and strange nations in the land of Israel, 34–41.

A. M. 3274
B. C. 730
Olymp. XII. 3
An. Clidici,
Arch. Athen.
decen. 3

IN the twelfth year of Ahaz king of Judah began [a]Hoshea the son of Elah to reign in Samaria over Israel nine years.

A. M. 3274–3283
B. C. 730–721
Olymp. XII. 3
—XIV. 4

2 And he did *that which was* evil in the sight of the LORD, but not as the kings of Israel that were before him.

3 Against him came up [b]Shalmaneser king of Assyria; and Hoshea became his servant, and [c]gave him [d]presents.

A. M. 3279
B. C. 725
Olymp. XIII. 4
An. Clidici,
Arch. Athen.
decen. 8

4 And the king of Assyria found conspiracy in Hoshea: for he had sent messengers to So, king of Egypt, and brought no present to the king of Assyria, as *he had done* year by year: therefore the king of Assyria shut him up, and bound him in prison.

5 Then [e]the king of Assyria came up throughout all the land, and went up to Samaria, and besieged it three years.

A. M. 3281–3283
B. C. 723–721
Olymp. XIV
2–4

6 [f]In the ninth year of Hoshea the king of Assyria took Samaria, and [g]carried Israel away into Assyria, and [h]placed them in Halah and in Habor *by* the river of Gozan, and in the cities of the Medes.

A. M. 3283
B. C. 721
Ol. XIV. 4
An. Hippomenis,
Arch. Athen.
decen. 2

7 For *so* it was, that the children of Israel had sinned against the LORD their God, which had brought them up out of the land of Egypt, from under the hand of Pharaoh king of Egypt, and had feared other gods,

8 And [i]walked in the statutes of the heathen, whom the LORD cast out from before the children of Israel, and of the kings

---

[a]After an interregnum, chapter xv. 30——[b]Chap. xviii. 9——[c]Heb. *rendered;* 2 Sam. viii. 2——[d]Or, *tribute* [e]Ch. xviii. 9——[f]Ch. xviii. 10, 11; Hos. xiii. 16, foretold

[g]Lev. xxvi. 32, 33; Deut. xxviii. 36, 64; xxix. 27, 28——[h]1 Chron. v. 26——[i]Lev. xviii. 3; Deut. xviii. 9; chapter xvi. 3

NOTES ON CHAP. XVII

Verse 3. *Shalmaneser*] This was the son and successor of *Tiglath-pileser.* He is called *Shalman* by Hosea, x. 14, and *Enemessar,* in the book of Tobit, i. 2.

Gave him presents.] Became tributary to him.

Verse 4. *Found conspiracy in Hoshea*] He had endeavoured to shake off the Assyrian yoke, by entering into a treaty with So, King of Egypt; and having done so, he ceased to send the annual tribute to Assyria.

Verse 5. *Besieged it three years.*] It must have been well fortified, well provisioned, and well defended, to have held out so long.

Verse 6. *Took Samaria*] According to the

prophets Hosea xiii. 16, and Micah i. 6. He exercised great cruelties on this miserable city, ripping up the women with child, dashing young children against the stones, &c., &c.

Carried Israel away into Assyria] What were the places to which the unfortunate Israelites were carried, or where their successors are now situated, have given rise to innumerable conjectures, dissertations, discourses, &c. Some maintain that they are found on the coast of *Guinea;* others, in *America;* the Indian tribes being the descendants of those carried away by the Assyrians. In vol. i. of the *Supplement* to Sir Wm. Jones's works, we find a translation of the *History of the Afghans,* by Mr. H. *Vansittart;* from which it appears that they derive their own descent from the Jews. On this

A. M. 3283
B. C. 721
Ol. XIV. 4
An. Hippome-
nis, Arch. Ath.
decen. 2

of Israel, which they had made.

9 And the children of Israel did secretly *those* things that *were* not right against the LORD their God, and they built them high places in all their cities, [k]from the tower of the watchmen to the fenced city.

10 [l]And they set them up [m]images and [n]groves [o]in every high hill, and under every green tree:

11 And there they burnt incense in all the high places, as *did* the heathen whom the LORD carried away before them; and wrought wicked things to provoke the LORD to anger:

12 For they served idols, [p]whereof the LORD had said unto them, [q]Ye shall not do this thing.

13 Yet the LORD testified against Israel and against Judah, [r]by all the prophets, *and by* all [s]the seers, saying, [t]Turn ye from your evil ways, and keep my commandments *and* my statutes, according to all the law which I commanded your fathers, and which I sent to you by my servants the prophets.

14 Notwithstanding they would not hear, but [u]hardened their necks, like to the neck of their fathers, that did not believe in the LORD their God.

A. M. 3283
B. C. 721
Ol. XIV. 4
An. Hippome-
nis, Arch. Ath.
decen. 2

15 And they rejected his statutes, [v]and his covenant that he made with their fathers, and his testimonies which he testified against them, and they followed [w]vanity, and [x]became vain, and went after the heathen that *were* round about them, *concerning* whom the LORD had charged them, that they should [y]not do like them.

16 And they left all the commandments of the LORD their God, and [z]made them molten images, *even* two calves, [a]and made a grove, and worshipped all the host of heaven, [b]and served Baal.

17 [c]And they caused their sons and their daughters to pass through the fire, and [d]used divination and enchantments, and [e]sold themselves to do evil in the sight of the LORD, to provoke him to anger.

18 Therefore the LORD was very angry with Israel, and removed them out of his sight:

---

[k]Ch. xviii. 8——[l]1 Kings xiv. 23; Isa. lvii. 5——[m]Heb *statutes*——[n]Exod. xxxiv. 13; Deut. xvi. 21; Mic. v. 14 [o]Deut. xii. 2; ch. xvi. 4——[p]Exod. xx. 3, 4; Lev. xxvi. 1; Deut. v. 7, 8——[q]Deut. iv. 19——[r]Heb. *by the hand of all*——[s]1 Sam. ix. 9——[t]Jer. xviii. 11; xxv. 5; xxxv. 15 [u]Deut. xxxi. 27; Prov. xxix. 1——[v]Deut. xxix. 25

[w]Deut. xxxii. 21; 1 Kings xvi. 13; 1 Cor. viii. 4 [x]Psalm cxv. 8; Romans i. 21——[y]Deut. xii. 30, 31 [z]Exod. xxxii. 8; 1 Kings xii. 28——[a]1 Kings xiv. 15, 23; xv. 13; xvi. 33——[b]1 Kings xvi. 31; xxii. 53; chap. xi. 18 [c]Lev. xviii. 21; chap. xvi. 3; Ezekiel xxiii. 37——[d]Deut. xviii. 10——[e]1 Kings xxi. 20

---

history Sir Wm. Jones writes the following note:—

"This account of the *Afghans* may lead to a very interesting discovery. We learn from *Esdras*, that the ten tribes, after a wandering journey, came to a country called *Arsaret*, where we may suppose they settled. Now the *Afghans* are said by the best Persian historians to be descended from the *Jews;* they have traditions among themselves of such a descent, and it is even asserted that their families are distinguished by the names of *Jewish tribes;* although, since their conversion to the *Islam*, they studiously conceal their origin. The *Pushtoo*, of which I have seen a dictionary, has a manifest resemblance to the *Chaldaic;* and a considerable district under their dominion is called *Hazarek* or *Hazaret*, which might easily have been changed into the word used by *Esdras*. I strongly recommend an inquiry into the literature and history of the Afghans." Every thing considered, I think it by far the most probable that the Afghans are the descendants of the Jews, who were led away captives by the Assyrian kings.

Thus ended the kingdom of Israel, after it had lasted *two hundred* and *fifty-four* years, from the death of Solomon and the schism of Jeroboam, till the taking of Samaria by Shalmaneser, in the *ninth* year of *Hoshea;* after which the remains of the ten tribes were carried away beyond the river Euphrates.

The rest of this chapter is spent in vindicating the Divine providence and justice; showing the reason why God permitted such a desolation to fall on a people who had been so long his peculiar children.

Verse 9. *Did secretly those things*] There was much *hidden iniquity* and *private idolatry* among them, as well as public and notorious crimes.

From the tower of the watchmen to the fenced city.] That is, the idolatry was *universal;* every place was made a place for some idolatrous rite or act of worship; from the largest city to the smallest village, and from the public watchtower to the shepherd's cot.

Verse 10. *Images and groves*] Images of different idols, and places for the abominable rites of *Ashtaroth* or *Venus*.

Verse 13. *Yet the Lord testified against Israel*] What rendered their conduct the more inexcusable was, that the Lord had preserved among them a succession of prophets, who testified against their conduct, and preached repentance to them, and the readiness of God to forgive, provided they would return unto him, and give up their idolatries.

Verse 17. *Sold themselves to do evil*] Abandoned themselves to the will of the devil, to work all iniquity with greediness.

Verse 18. *Removed them out of his sight*] Banished them from the promised land, from the temple, and from every ordinance of righteousness, as wholly unworthy of any kind of good.

A. M. 3283
B. C. 721
Ol. XIV. 4
An. Hippome-
nis, Arch. Ath.
decen. 2

there was none left ᶠbut the tribe of Judah only.

19 Also ᵍJudah kept not the commandments of the LORD their God, but walked in the statutes of Israel which they made.

20 And the LORD rejected all the seed of Israel, and afflicted them, and ʰdelivered them into the hand of spoilers, until he had cast them out of his sight.

21 For ⁱhe rent Israel from the house of David; and ᵏthey made Jeroboam the son of Nebat king: and Jeroboam drave Israel from following the LORD, and made them sin a great sin.

22 For the children of Israel walked in all the sins of Jeroboam which he did; they departed not from them;

23 Until the LORD removed Israel out of his sight, ˡas he had said by all his servants the prophets. ᵐSo was Israel carried away out of their own land to Assyria unto this day.

A. M. 3326
B. C. 678
Ol. XXV. 3
An. Numæ,
Regis Romano-
rum, 38

24 ⁿAnd the king of Assyria brought *men* ᵒfrom Babylon, and from Cuthah, and from ᵖAva, and from Hamath, and from Sepharvaim, and placed *them* in the cities of Samaria instead of the children of Israel: and they possessed Samaria, and dwelt in the cities thereof.

25 And *so* it was at the beginning of their dwelling there, *that* they feared not the LORD: therefore the LORD sent lions among them, which slew *some* of them.

26 Wherefore they spake to the king of Assyria, saying, The nations which thou hast removed, and placed in the cities of Samaria, know not the manner of the God of the land: therefore he hath sent lions among them, and, behold, they slay them, because they know not the manner of the God of the land.

27 Then the king of Assyria commanded, saying, Carry thither one of the priests whom ye brought from thence; and let them go and

---

ᶠ1 Kings xi. 13, 32——ᵍJer. iii. 8——ʰChap. xiii. 3; xv. 29——ⁱ1 Kings xi. 11, 31——ᵏ1 Kings xii. 20, 28

ˡ1 Kings xiv. 16——ᵐVer. 6——ⁿEzra iv. 2, 10——ᵒSee ver. 30——ᵖChap. xviii. 34, *Ivah*

None left but the tribe of Judah only.] Under this name all those of *Benjamin* and *Levi*, and the *Israelites*, who abandoned their idolatries and joined with Judah, are comprised. It was the *ten tribes* that were carried away by the Assyrians.

Verse 24. *The king of Assyria brought* men *from Babylon*] He removed one people entirely, and substituted others in their place; and this he did to cut off all occasion for mutiny or insurrection; for the people being removed from their *own land*, had no *object* worthy of attention to contend for, and no *patrimony* in the land of their captivity to induce them to hazard any opposition to their oppressors.

By men *from Babylon*, we may understand some cities of *Babylonia* then under the Assyrian empire; for at this time Babylon had a king of its own; but some parts of what was called Babylonia might have been still under the Assyrian government.

From Cuthah] This is supposed to be the same as *Cush*, the Chaldeans and Syrians changing שׁ *shin* into ת *tau;* thus they make כּוּשׁ *Cush* into כּוּת *Cuth;* and אַשּׁוּר *Ashshur, Assyria,* into אַתּוּר *Attur.* From these came the *Scythæ;* and from these the Samaritans were called *Cuthæans,* and their language *Cuthite.* The original language of this people, or at least the language they spake after their *settlement* in Israel, is contained in the *Samaritan version* of the Pentateuch, printed under the *Hebræo-Samaritan* in vol. i. of the London Polyglot. This *Cuthah* was probably the country in the land of *Shinar,* first inhabited by *Cush.*

From Ava] The *Avim* were an ancient people, expelled by the Caphtorim from *Hazerim,* Deut. ii. 23.

From Hamath] This was *Hemath* or *Emath*

of Syria, frequently mentioned in the sacred writings.

From Sepharvaim] There was a city called *Syphera,* near the Euphrates; others think the *Saspires,* a people situated between the *Colchians* and the *Medes,* are meant. There is much uncertainty relative to these places: all that we know is, that the Assyrians carried away the Israelites into Assyria, and placed them in cities and districts called *Halah* and *Habor by the river of Gozan,* and *in the cities of the Medes,* ver. 6; and it is very likely that they brought some of the inhabitants of those places into the cities of Israel.

Verse 25. *The Lord sent lions among them*] The land being deprived of its inhabitants, wild beasts would necessarily increase, even without any supernatural intervention; and this the superstitious new comers supposed to be a plague sent upon them, because they did not know how to worship him who was the God of the land; for they thought, like other heathens, that every district had its own *tutelary deity.* Yet it is likely that God did send lions as a scourge on this bad people.

Verse 26. *The manner of the God of the land.*] מִשְׁפָּט *mishpat,* the *judgment;* the way in which the God of the land is to be worshipped.

Verse 27. *Carry thither one of the priests*] Imperfect as this teaching was, it, in the end, overthrew the idolatry of these people, so that soon after the Babylonish captivity they were found to be as free from idolatry as the Jews themselves, and continue so to the present day. But they are now nearly annihilated: the small remains of them is found at *Naplouse* and *Jaffa;* they are about *thirty families;* and men, women, and children, amount to about *two*

A. M. 3326
B. C. 678
Ol. XXV. 3
An. Numæ,
Regis Romanorum, 38

dwell there, and let him teach them the manner of the God of the land.

28 Then one of the priests whom they had carried away from Samaria came and dwelt in Beth-el, and taught them how they should fear the LORD.

29 Howbeit every nation made gods of their own, and put *them* in the houses of the high places which the Samaritans had made, every nation in their cities wherein they dwelt.

30 And the men of [q]Babylon made Succoth-benoth, and the men of Cuth made Nergal, and the men of Hamath made Ashima,

31 [r]And the Avites made Nibhaz and Tartak, and the Sepharvites [s]burnt their children in fire to Adrammelech and Anammelech, the gods of Sepharvaim.

32 So they feared the LORD, [t]and made unto themselves of the lowest of them priests of the high places, which sacrificed for them in the houses of the high places.

33 [u]They feared the LORD, and served their own gods, after the manner of the nations [v]whom they carried away from thence.

A. M. 3326
B. C. 678
Ol. XXV. 3
An. Numæ,
Regis Romanorum, 38

34 Unto this day they do after the former manners: they fear not the LORD, neither do they after their statutes, or after their ordinances, or after the law and commandment which the LORD commanded the children of Jacob, [w]whom he named Israel;

35 With whom the LORD had made a covenant, and charged them, saying, [x]Ye shall not fear other gods, nor [y]bow yourselves to them, nor serve them, nor sacrifice to them:

36 But the LORD, who brought you up out of the land of Egypt with great power and [z]a stretched-out arm, [a]him shall ye fear, and him shall ye worship, and to him shall ye do sacrifice.

37 And the statutes, and the ordinances, and the law, and the commandment, which he wrote for you, [b]ye shall observe to do for evermore; and ye shall not fear other gods.

38 And the covenant that I have made with

[q]Ver. 24——[r]Ezra iv. 9——[s]Lev. xviii. 21; Deut. xii. 31——[t]1 Kings xii. 31——[u]Zeph. i. 5——[v]Or, *who carried them away from thence*

[w]Gen. xxxii. 28; xxxv. 10; 1 Kings xi. 31——[x]Judg. vi. 10——[y]Exod. xx. 5——[z]Exod. vi. 6——[a]Deut. x. 20 [b]Deut. v. 32

hundred persons! They have a synagogue, which they regularly attend every Sabbath; and they go thither clothed in white robes. The reader may find much curious information relative to this people, in a *Memoire sur L'Etat actuel des Samaritains*, by Baron *Sylvestre de Sacy*, 8vo., Paris, 1812.

Verse 29. *Every nation made gods of their own*] That is, they made gods after the fashion of those which they had worshipped in their own country.

Verse 30. *The men of Babylon made Succoth-benoth*] This, literally, signifies *the tabernacles of the daughters* or *young women*, and most evidently refers to those public prostitutions of young virgins at the temple of *Melitta* or *Venus* among the Babylonians. See at the end of the chapter. From *benoth* it is probable that the word *Venus* came, the *B* being changed into *V*, as is frequently the case, and the *th* into *s*, *benoth*, *Venos*. The rabbins say that her emblem was a *hen with her chickens;* see *Jarchi* on the place.

The men of Cuth made Nergal] This is supposed to have been the *solar orb* or *light*. According to the rabbins, his emblem was a *cock*. See at the end of the chapter.

The men of Hamath made Ashima] Perhaps *the fire;* from אשם *asham, to make atonement* or *to purify*. Jarchi says this was in the form of a *goat*. See below.

Verse 31. *The Avites made Nibhaz*] This was supposed to be the same as the *Anubis* of the Egyptians; and was in form partly of a *dog*, and partly of a *man*. A very ancient image of this kind now lies before me: it is cut out of stone, about *seven* inches high; has the *body*, *legs*, and *arms*, of a *man;* the *head* and *feet* of a *dog;* the *thighs* and *legs* covered with *scales;* the *head* crowned with a *tiara;* the *arms* crossed upon the breasts, with the fingers clenched. The figure stands upright, and the belly is very protuberant. See below.

And Tartak] This is supposed by some to be another name of the same idol; *Jarchi* says it was in the shape of an *ass*. Some think these were the representations of the *sun* in his *chariot; Nibhaz* representing the solar orb, and *Tartak* the chariot. See below.

Adrammelech] From אדר *adar, glorious*, and מלך *melech, king*. Probably the *sun*.

Anammelech] From *anah, to return*, and מלך *melech, king*. Probably, the *Moloch* of the Ammonites. *Jarchi* says, the first was in the form of a *mule*, the second in the form of a *horse;* this was probably the *moon*.

Verse 32. *Of the lowest of them priests*] One priest was not enough for this motley population; and, as the priesthood was probably neither *respectable* nor *lucrative*, it was only the lowest of the people who would enter into the employment.

Verse 33. *They feared the Lord, and served their own gods*] They did not relinquish their own *idolatry* but *incorporated* the worship of the true God with that of their idols. They were *afraid* of Jehovah, who had sent lions among them; and therefore they offered him a sort of worship that he might not thus afflict them: but they *served* other gods, devoted themselves *affectionately* to them, because their worship was such as gratified their *grossest passions*, and most sinful propensities.

Verse 36. *But the Lord*] JEHOVAH, the su-

A. M. 3326
B. C. 678
Ol. XXV. 3
An. Numæ,
Regis Romano-
rum, 38

you, [c]ye shall not forget; neither shall ye fear other gods.

39 But the LORD your God ye shall fear; and he shall deliver you out of the hand of all your enemies.

40 Howbeit they did not hearken, but

they did after their former manner.

41 [d]So these nations feared the LORD, and served their graven images, both their children and their children's children: as did their fathers, so do they unto this day.

A. M. 3326
B. C. 678
Ol. XXV. 3
An. Numæ,
Regis Romano-
rum, 38

---

[c]Deut. iv. 23

[d]Ver. 32, 33

---

preme, self-existent, and eternal Being; author of all *being* and *life*. This was to be the sole *object* of their adoration.

Who brought you up] This was a *strong reason* why they should adore *Him* only: he had saved them from the hands of their enemies, and he did it in such a *way* as to show his *power* to be irresistible; in such a Being they might safely confide.

Him shall ye fear] Here is the *manner* in which he is to be worshipped. Him ye shall *reverence* as your *Lawgiver* and *Judge;* ye shall *respect* and keep all his commandments; doing what he has enjoined, and avoiding what he has forbidden.

Him shall ye worship] Before Him ye shall *bow the knee;* living in the spirit of *obedience,* and performing every religious act in the *deepest humility.*

And to him shall ye do sacrifice.] Ye shall consider that, as ye have *sinned,* so ye deserve *death;* ye shall therefore bring your *living victims* to the altar of the Lord, and let their *life's* blood be poured out there, as an *atonement* for your souls. We see in this verse *three* important points: 1. The *object* of their worship. 2. The *reasons* of that worship; and, 3. The *spirit* and *manner* in which it was to be performed: viz., 1. In fear. 2. Humility; and, 3. By sacrifice.

Verse 41. *So do they unto this day.*] This must have been written before the Babylonish captivity; because, after that time, none of the Israelites ever lapsed into idolatry. But this may chiefly refer to the *heathenish* people who were sent to dwell among the remains of the ten tribes.

ON these *nations* and the *objects of their worship,* I present my readers with the following extracts from *Dodd* and *Parkhurst.*

Verse 30. *The men of Babylon made Succoth-benoth.* We have here an account of the idols which were consecrated by the different nations, transplanted by the king of Assyria to Samaria. It is difficult, however, and has afforded a large field for conjecture, to give any satisfactory account concerning them. The reader will find in Selden, Vossius, and Jurieu, much upon the subject. Succoth-benoth may be literally translated, *The Tabernacles of the Daughters,* or *Young Women;* or if *Benoth* be taken as the name of a female idol, from בנה *to build up, procreate children,* then the words will express the tabernacles sacred to the productive powers feminine. And, agreeably to this latter exposition, the rabbins say that the emblem was a hen and chickens. But however this may be, there is no room to doubt that these *succoth* were *tabernacles* wherein young women exposed themselves to prostitution in honour of the Babylonish goddess *Melitta.*

Herodotus, (lib. i., c. 199,) gives us a particular account of this detestable service. "Every young woman," says he, "of the country of Babylon must once in her life sit at the temple of Venus, [whom he afterwards tells us the Assyrians called *Melitta,*] and prostitute herself to some stranger. Those who are rich, and so disdain to mingle with the crowd, present themselves before the temple in covered chariots, attended by a great retinue. But the generality of the women sit near the temple, having crowns upon their heads, and holding a cord, some continually coming, others going. [See *Baruch* vi. 43.] The cords are held by them in such a manner as to afford a free passage among the women, that the strangers may choose whom they like. A woman who has once seated herself in this place must not return home till some stranger has cast money into her lap, and led her from the temple, and defiled her. The stranger who throws the money must say, 'I invoke the goddess Melitta for thee.' The money, however small a sum it may be, must not be refused, because it is appointed to sacred uses. [See *Deut.* xxiii. 18.] The woman must follow the first man that offers, and not reject him; and after prostitution, having now duly honoured the goddess, she is dismissed to her own house. In Cyprus," adds the historian, "they have the same custom." This abomination, implied by *Succoth-benoth,* the men of Babylon brought with them into the country of Samaria; and both the name of the idol *Melitta,* and the execrable service performed to her honour, show that by *Melitta* was originally intended the procreative or productive power of nature, the *Venus* of the Greeks and Romans. See the beginning of Lucretius's first book De Rerum Natura. Mr. Selden imagines that some traces of the Succoth-benoth may be found in Sicca Veneria, the name of a city of Numidia, not far from the borders of Africa Propria. The name itself bears a near allusion to the obscene custom above taken notice of, and seems to have been transported from Phœnicia: nor can this well be disputed, when we consider that here was a temple where women were obliged to purchase their marriage-money by the prostitution of their bodies. See *Univ. Hist.,* vol. xvii., p. 295, and Parkhurst's Lexicon on the word ‎סם‎.

The men of Cuth made Nergal.—*Cuth* was a province of Assyria, which, according to some, lies upon the Araxis: but others rather think it to be the same with *Cush,* which is said by Moses to be encompassed with the river Gihon; and must, therefore, be the same with the country which the Greeks call *Susiana,* and which to this day is called by the inhabitants *Chusesta.* Their idol, *Nergal,* seems to have been the *sun,* as the causer of the diurnal and annual revolutions of the planets; for it is naturally derived from נר *ner, light*, and גל *gal, to revolve.* The rabbins say that the idol was represented in the shape of a cock; and probably they tell us the truth, for this seems a very proper emblem. Among the latter heathens we find the cock was sacred to Apollo or the sun, (see *Pierii* Hieroglyph., p. 223,) "because," says Heliodorus, speaking of the time when cocks crow, "by a natural sensation of the sun's revolution to us, they are incited to salute the god." *Æthiop.* lib. i. And perhaps under this name, *Nergal*, they meant to worship the sun, not only for the diurnal return of its light upon the earth, but also for its annual return or revolution. We may observe that the emblem, a *cock*, is affected by the latter as well as by the former, and is frequently crowing both day and night, when the days begin to lengthen. See *Calmet's* Dictionary under the word, and *Parkhurst's* Lexicon.

The men of Hamath made Ashima.—There are several cities and countries which go under the name of *Hamath;* but what we take to be here meant is that province of Syria which lies upon the Orontes, wherein there was a city of the same name; which when Shalmaneser had taken, he removed the inhabitants from thence into Samaria. Their idol *Ashima* signifies the *atoner* or *expiator*, from אשם *asham.* The word is in a Chaldee form, and seems to be the same as אשמת שמרון *ashmath Shomeron, the sin of Samaria*, mentioned Amos viii. 14, where *ashmath* is rendered by the LXX. *propitiation.* It is known to every one who has the least acquaintance with the mythology of the heathen, how strongly and universally they retained the tradition of an *atonement* or *expiation for sin*, although they expected it from a false object and wrong means. We find it expressed in very clear terms among the Romans even so late as the time of Horace, lib. i., ode 2:—

> *Cui dabit partes scelus expiandi*
> *Jupiter?*

And whom, to expiate the horrid guilt,
Will Jove appoint?

The answer is, "Apollo," the god of light. Some think that, as *Asuman* or *Suman*, اسمان *asman*, in the Persian language, signifies *heaven*, the Syrians might from hence derive the name of this god; who, they suppose, was represented by a large stone pillar terminating in a conic or pyramidical figure, whereby they denoted *fire*. See *Parkhurst* on the word אשם *asham, Calmet's* Dictionary, and *Tennison* on Idolatry.

Verse 31. *The Avites made Nibhaz and Tartak.*—It is uncertain who these Avites were. The most probable opinion seems to be that which Grotius has suggested by observing that there are a people in Bactriana, mentioned by Ptolemy, under the name of *Avidia*, who possibly might be those transported at this time into Palestine by Shalmaneser. *Nibhaz*, according to the rabbins, had the shape of a dog, much like the *Anubis* of the Egyptians. In *Pierius's* Hieroglyphics, p. 53, is the figure of a *cunocephalus*, a kind of ape, with a head like a dog, standing upon his hinder feet, and *looking earnestly* at the moon. Pierius there teaches us that the *cunocephalus* was an animal emi-

nently sacred amongst the Egyptians, hieroglyphical of the moon, and kept in their temples to inform them of the moon's conjunction with the sun, at which time this animal is strangely affected, being deprived of sight, refusing food, and lying sick on the ground; but on the moon's appearance seeming to return thanks, and congratulate the return of light both to himself and her. See *Johnston's* Nat. Hist. de Quadruped., p. 100. This being observed, the נבחז *nibchaz*, (which may well be derived from נבח *nabach, to bark*, and חזה *chazah, to see*,) gives us reason to conclude that this idol was in the shape of a cunocephalus, or a dog looking, barking, or howling at the moon. It is obvious to common observation that dogs in general have this property; and an idol of the form just mentioned seems to have been originally designed to represent the power or influence of the moon on all sublunary bodies, with which the cunocephaluses and dogs are so eminently affected. So, as we have observed upon *Nergal*, the influence of the returning solar light was represented by a *cock;* and the generative power of the heavens by *Dagon*, a *fishy* idol. See *Parkhurst* on נבחז, who is of opinion that *Tartak* תרתק is compounded of תר *tar, to turn, go round*, and רתק *rathak, to chain, tether;* and plainly denotes the heavens, considered as confining the planets in their respective orbits, as if they were tethered. The Jews have a tradition that the emblem of this idol was an *ass;* which, considering the propriety of that animal when tethered to represent this idol, is not improbable; and from this idolatrous worship of the Samaritans, joined perhaps with some confused account of the cherubim, seems to have sprung that stupid story by the heathens, that the Jews had an ass's head in their holy of holies, to which they paid religious worship. See *Bochart*, vol. ii., p. 221. Jurieu is of opinion that as the word *Nibhaz*, both in the Hebrew and Chaldee, with a small variation, denotes *quick, swift, rapid;* and *tartak*, in the same languages, signifies a *chariot*, these two idols may both together denominate the *sun* mounted on his *car*, as the fictions of the poets and the notions of the mythologists were wont to represent that luminary.

The Sepharvites burned their children—to Adrammelech and Anammelech.—As these Sepharvites probably came from the cities of the Medes, whither the Israelites were carried captive, and as Herodotus tells us that between Colchis and Media are found a people called *Saspires*, in all likelihood they were the same with those here named *Sepharvites*. *Moloch, Milcom*, and *Melech*, in the language of different nations, all signify a *king*, and imply the *sun*, which was called the *king of heaven;* and consequently the addition of אדר *adar*, which signifies *powerful, illustrious*, to the one, and of ענה *anah*, which implies to *return*, to *answer*, to the other, means no more than the *mighty* or the *oracular Moloch.* And as the children were offered to him, it appears that he was the same with the Moloch of the Ammonites. See *Univ. Hist.* and *Calmet.* Mr. Locke is also of opinion that these two names were expressive of one and the same deity. What they were, or in what form, and how worshipped, we have not light from antiquity to determine.

CHAPTER XVIII

Hezekiah begins to reign; he removes the high places, breaks to pieces the brazen serpent, and walks uprightly before God, 1–6. He endeavours to shake off the Assyrian yoke, and defeats the Philistines, 7, 8. Shalmaneser comes up against Samaria, takes it, and carries the people away into captivity, 9–12. And then comes against Judah, and takes all the fenced cities, 13. Hezekiah sends a message to him at Lachish to desist, with the promise that he will pay him any tribute he chooses to impose; in consequence of which Shalmaneser exacts three hundred talents of silver, and thirty talents of gold; to pay which Hezekiah is obliged to take all his own treasures, and those belonging to the temple, 14–16. The king of Assyria sends, notwithstanding, a great host against Jerusalem; and his general, Rab-shakeh, delivers an insulting and blasphemous message to Hezekiah, 17–35. Hezekiah and his people are greatly afflicted at the words of Rab-shakeh, 36, 37.

A. M. 3278
B. C. 726
Ol. XIII. 3
An. Clidici,
Arch. Athen.
decen. 7

NOW it came to pass in the third year of Hoshea son of Elah king of Israel, *that* ᵃHezekiah the son of Ahaz king of Judah began to reign.

A. M. 3278–3306
B. C. 726–698
Ol. XIII. 3
—XX. 3

2 Twenty and five years old was he when he began to reign; and he reigned twenty and nine years in Jerusalem. His mother's name also *was* ᵇAbi, the daughter of Zachariah.

3 And he did *that which was* right in the sight of the LORD, according to all that David his father did.

A. M. 3278–3306
B. C. 726–698
Ol. XIII. 3
—XX. 3

4 ᶜHe removed the high places, and brake the ᵈimages, and cut down the groves, and brake in pieces the ᵉbrazen serpent that Moses had made: for unto those days the children of Israel did burn incense to it: and he called it ᶠNehushtan.

ᵃ2 Chron. xxviii. 27; xxix. 1; He is called *Ezekias*, Matt. i. 9——ᵇ2 Chron. xxix. 1, *Abijah*

ᶜ2 Chron. xxxi. 1——ᵈHeb. *statues*——ᵉNum. xxi. 9
ᶠThat is, *a piece of brass*

NOTES ON CHAP. XVIII

Verse 1. *Now—in the third year of Hoshea*]
See the note on chap. xvi. 1, where this chronology is considered.

Verse 3. *He did that which was right in the sight of the Lord*] In chap. xxix. of the second book of Chronicles, we have an account of what this pious king did to restore the worship of God. He caused the priests and Levites to cleanse the holy house, which had been shut up by his father Ahaz, and had been polluted with filth of various kinds; and this cleansing required no less than *sixteen* days to accomplish it. As the passover, according to the law, must be celebrated the *fourteenth* of the *first* month, and the Levites could not get the temple cleansed before the *sixteenth* day, he published the passover for the *fourteenth* of the *second* month, and sent through all Judah and Israel to collect all the men that feared God, that the passover might be celebrated in a proper manner. The concourse was great, and the feast was celebrated with great magnificence. When the people returned to their respective cities and villages, they began to throw down the idol altars, statues, images, and groves, and even to abolish the high places; the consequence was that a spirit of piety began to revive in the land, and a general reformation took place.

Verse 4. *Brake in pieces the brazen serpent.*]
The history of this may be seen in Num. xxi. 8, 9; see the notes there.

We find that this brazen serpent had become an object of idolatry, and no doubt was supposed to possess, as a *telesm* or *amulet,* extraordinary virtues, and that incense was burnt before it which should have been burnt before the true God.

And he called it Nehushtan.] נחשׁתּן. Not one of the *versions* has attempted to *translate* this word. *Jarchi* says, "He called it Nechustan, through contempt, which is as much as to say, *a brazen serpent.*" Some have supposed that the word is compounded of נחשׁ *nachash,* to divine, and תן *tan,* a *serpent,* so it signifies *the divining serpent;* and the *Targum* states that it was the *people,* not Hezekiah, that gave it this name. נחשׁ *nachash* signifies to *view, eye attentively, observe,* to *search, inquire accurately,* &c.; and hence is used to express *divination, augury.* As a *noun* it signifies *brass* or *copper, filth, verdigris,* and some *sea animal,* Amos ix. 3; see also Job xxvi. 13, and Isa. xxvi. 1. It is also frequently used for a *serpent;* and most probably for an animal of the genus *Simia,* in Gen. ii., where see the notes. This has been contested by some, ridiculed by a few, and believed by many. The objectors, because it signifies a *serpent* sometimes, suppose it must have the same signification *always!* And one to express his contempt and show his *sense,* has said, "Did Moses hang up an *ape* on a pole?" I answer, No; no more than he hanged up *you,* who ask the contemptible question. But this is of a piece with the conduct of the people of *Milan,* who show you to this day the brazen serpent which Moses hung up in the wilderness, and which Hezekiah broke in pieces *two thousand five hundred* years ago!

Of serpents there is a great variety. Allowing that נחשׁ *nachash* signifies a *serpent,* I may ask in my turn, What kind of a serpent was it that tempted Eve? Of what species was that which Moses hung up on the pole, and which Hezekiah broke to pieces? Who of the *wise men* can answer these questions? Till this is done I *assert,* that the word, Gen. iii. 1, &c., does *not* signify a serpent of *any kind;* and that with a creature of the genus *Simia* the whole account best agrees.

A. M. 3278–3306
B. C. 726–698
Ol. XIII. 3
—XX. 3

5 He ^gtrusted in the LORD God of Israel; ^hso that after him was none like him among all the kings of Judah, nor *any* that were before him.

6 For he ⁱclave to the LORD, *and* departed not ^kfrom following him, but kept his commandments, which the LORD commanded Moses.

7 And the LORD ^lwas with him; *and* he ^mprospered whithersoever he went forth: and he ⁿrebelled against the king of Assyria, and served him not.

8 ^oHe smote the Philistines, *even* unto ^pGaza, and the borders thereof, ^qfrom the tower of the watchmen to the fenced city.

A. M. 3281
B. C. 723
Ol. XIV. 2
An. Clidici,
Arch. Athen.
decen. 10

9 And ^rit came to pass in the fourth year of King Hezekiah, which *was* the seventh year of Hoshea, son of Elah king of Israel, *that* Shalmaneser king of Assyria came up against Samaria, and besieged it.

A. M. 3283
B. C. 721
Ol. XIV. 4
An. Hippome-
nis, Arch. Ath.
decen. 2

10 And at the end of three years they took it: *even* in the sixth year of Hezekiah, that *is* ^sthe ninth year of Hoshea king of Israel, Samaria was taken.

11 ^tAnd the king of Assyria did carry away Israel unto Assyria, and put them in ^uHalah and in Habor *by* the river of Gozan, and in the cities of the Medes:

12 ^vBecause they obeyed not the voice of the LORD their God, but transgressed his covenant, *and* all that Moses the servant of the LORD commanded, and would not hear *them* nor do *them*.

A. M. 3283
B. C. 721
Ol. XIV. 4
An. Hippome-
nis, Arch. Ath.
decen. 2

13 Now ^win the fourteenth year of King Hezekiah did ^xSennacherib king of Assyria come up against all the fenced cities of Judah, and took them.

A. M. 3291
B. C. 713
Ol. XVI. 4
An. Hippome-
nis, Arch. Ath.
decen. 10

14 And Hezekiah king of Judah sent to the king of Assyria to Lachish, saying, I have offended; return from me: that which thou puttest on me will I bear. And the king of Assyria appointed unto Hezekiah king of Judah three hundred talents of silver and thirty talents of gold.

15 And Hezekiah ^ygave *him* all the silver that was found in the house of the LORD, and in the treasures of the king's house.

16 At that time did Hezekiah cut off *the gold from* the doors of the temple of the LORD, and *from* the pillars which Hezekiah king of Judah had overlaid, and gave ^zit to the king of Assyria.

17 And the king of Assyria sent Tartan and Rabsaris and Rab-shakeh from Lachish to King Hezekiah with a ^agreat host against Jerusalem. And they went up and

A. M. 3294
B. C. 710
Ol. XVII. 3
An. Leocratis,
Arch. Athen.
decen. 3

---

^gChap. xix. 10; Job xiii. 15; Psa. xiii. 5——^hChap. xxiii. 25——ⁱDeut. x. 20; Josh. xxiii. 8——^kHeb. *from after him*——^l2 Chron. xv. 2——^m1 Sam. xviii. 5, 14; Psa. lx. 12——ⁿChap. xvi. 7——^o1 Chron. iv. 41; Isa. xiv. 29——^pHeb. *Azzah*

^qChap. xvii. 9——^rChap. xvii. 3——^sChap. xvii. 6 ^tChap. xvii. 6——^u1 Chron. v. 26——^vChap. xvii. 7; Dan. ix. 6, 10——^w2 Chron. xxxii. 1, &c.; Isa. xxxvi. 1, &c.; Ecclus. xlviii. 18——^xHeb. *Sanherib*——^yChap. xvi. 8——^zHeb. *them*——^aHeb. *heavy*

Verse 5. *He trusted in the Lord*] See the character of this good king: 1. *He trusted in the Lord God of Israel;* 2. He *clave to the Lord;* 3. He was steady in his religion; he *departed not from following the Lord;* 4. He *kept God's commandments.* And what were the consequences? 1. The *Lord was with him;* 2. He *prospered whithersoever he went.*

Verse 8. *From the tower of the watchmen*] See the same words, chap. xvii. 9. It seems a proverbial mode of expression: he reduced every kind of fortification; nothing was able to stand before him.

Verse 9. *In the fourth year*] This history has been already given, chap. xvii. 3, &c.

Verse 17. *The king of Assyria sent Tartan, &c.*] Calmet has very justly remarked that these are not the names of *persons*, but of *offices*. Tartan, תרתן *tartan* or *tantan*, as in the parallel place in Isaiah, in the Greek version, signifies he who *presides* over the *gifts* or *tribute;* chancellor of the exchequer.

Rabsaris] רב סרים, the *chief of the eunuchs*.

Rab-shakeh, רב שקה *master* or *chief* over the *wine cellar;* or he who had the care of the *king's drink.*

From Lachish] It seems as if the Assyrian troops had been *worsted* before Lachish, and were obliged to raise the siege, from which they went and sat down before *Libnah.* While Sennacherib was there with the Assyrian army, he heard that *Tirhakah,* king of Ethiopia, had invaded the Assyrian territories. Being obliged therefore to hasten, in order to succour his own dominions, he sent a considerable force under the aforementioned officers against Jerusalem, with a most *fearful* and *bloody manifesto,* commanding Hezekiah to pay him tribute, to deliver up his kingdom to him, and to submit, he and his people, to be carried away captives into Assyria! This manifesto was accompanied with the vilest *insults,* and the highest *blasphemies.* God interposed and the evils threatened against others fell upon himself.

Manifestoes of this kind have seldom been honourable to the senders. The conduct of Rab-

A. M. 3294
B. C. 710
Ol. XVII. 3
An. Leocratis,
Arch. Athen.
decen. 3

came to Jerusalem. And when they were come up, they came and stood by the conduit of the upper pool, [b]which *is* in the highway of the fuller's field.

18 And when they had called to the king, there came out to them Eliakim the son of Hilkiah, which *was* over the household, and Shebna the [c]scribe, and Joah the son of Asaph the recorder.

19 And Rab-shakeh said unto them, Speak ye now to Hezekiah, Thus saith the great king, the king of Assyria, [d]What confidence *is* this wherein thou trustest?

20 Thou [e]sayest, (but *they are but* [f]vain words,) [g]*I have* counsel and strength for the war. Now on whom dost thou trust, that thou rebellest against me?

21 [h]Now, behold, thou [i]trustest upon the staff of this bruised reed, *even* upon Egypt, on which if a man lean, it will go into his hand, and pierce it: so *is* Pharaoh king of Egypt unto all that trust on him.

22 But if ye say unto me, We trust in the LORD our God: *is* not that he, [k]whose high places and whose altars Hezekiah hath taken away, and hath said to Judah and Jerusalem, Ye shall worship before this altar in Jerusalem?

23 Now therefore, I pray thee, give [l]pledges to my lord the king of Assyria, and I will deliver thee two thousand horses, if thou be able on thy part to set riders upon them.

24 How then wilt thou turn away the face of one captain of the least of my master's servants, and put thy trust on Egypt for chariots and for horsemen?

25 Am I now come up without the LORD against this place to destroy it? The LORD said to me, Go up against this land, and destroy it.

26 Then said Eliakim the son of Hilkiah, and Shebna, and Joah, unto Rab-shakeh, Speak, I pray thee, to thy servants in the Syrian language; for we understand *it*: and

A. M. 3294
B. C. 710
Ol. XVII. 3
An. Leocratis,
Arch. Athen.
decen. 3

---

[b]Isaiah vii. 3——[c]Or, *secretary*——[d]2 Chronicles xxxii. 10, &c.——[e]Or, *talkest*——[f]Hebrew, *word of the lips*——[g]Or, *but counsel and strength are for the war*——[h]Ezekiel xxix. 6, 7——[i]Hebrew, *trustest thee*——[k]Verse 4; 2 Chronicles xxxi. 1; xxxii. 12——[l]Or, *hostages*

---

shakeh was unfortunately copied by the Duke of Brunswick, commander-in-chief of the allied army of the centre, in the French revolution, who was then in the plains of Champagne, August 27, 1792, at the head of *ninety thousand* men, *Prussians, Austrians,* and *emigrants,* on his way to Paris, which in his manifesto he threatened to reduce to ashes! This was the cause of the dreadful massacres which immediately took place. And shortly after this time the blast of God fell upon him, for in Sept. 20 of the same year, (three weeks after issuing the manifesto,) almost all his army was destroyed by a fatal disease, and himself obliged to retreat from the French territories with shame and confusion. This, and some other injudicious steps taken by the allies, were the cause of the ruin of the royal family of France, and of enormities and calamities the most extensive, disgraceful, and ruinous, that ever stained the page of history. From all such revolutions God in mercy save mankind!

Conduit of the upper pool] The aqueduct that brought the water from the *upper* or *eastern reservoir,* near to the valley of *Kidron,* into the city. Probably they had seized on this in order to distress the city.

The fuller's field.] The place where the washermen stretched out their clothes to dry.

Verse 18. *Called to the king*] They wished him to come out that they might get possession of his person.

Eliakim—over the household] What we would call lord chamberlain.

Shebna the scribe] The king's *secretary.*

Joah—the recorder.] The writer of the public *annals.*

Verse 19. *What confidence is this*] מה הבטחון הזה *ma habbittachon hazzeh.* The words are excessively insulting: *What little, foolish, or unavailing cause of confidence is it, in which thou trustest?* I translate thus, because I consider the word בטחון *bittachon* as a *diminutive,* intended to express the utmost contempt for Hezekiah's God.

Verse 21. *The staff of this bruised reed*] Egypt had already been greatly *bruised* and *broken,* through the wars carried on against it by the Assyrians.

Verse 22. *Whose high places and whose altars Hezekiah hath taken away*] This was artfully malicious. Many of the people sacrificed to Jehovah on the *high places;* Hezekiah had removed them, (ver. 4,) because they were incentives to idolatry: Rab-shakeh insinuates that by so doing he had offended Jehovah, deprived the people of their religious rights, and he could neither expect the blessing of God nor the cooperation of the people.

Verse 23. *I will deliver thee two thousand horses*] Another insult: Were I to give thee *two thousand* Assyrian horses, thou couldst not find riders for them. How then canst thou think that thou shalt be able to stand against even the *smallest division of my troops?*

Verse 25. *Am I now come up without the Lord*] As Rab-shakeh saw that the Jews placed the utmost confidence in God, he wished to persuade them that by Hezekiah's conduct Jehovah had departed from them, and was become ally to the king of Assyria, and therefore they could not expect any help from that quarter.

Verse 26. *Talk not with us in the Jews' language*] The object of this blasphemous caitiff

A. M. 3294
B. C. 710
Ol. XVII. 3
An. Leocratis,
Arch. Athen.
decen. 3
talk not with us in the Jews' language in the ears of the people that *are* on the wall.

27 But Rab-shakeh said unto them, Hath my master sent me to thy master, and to thee, to speak these words? *hath he not sent me* to the men which sit on the wall, that they may eat their own dung, and drink ᵐtheir own piss with you?

28 Then Rab-shakeh stood and cried with a loud voice in the Jews' language, and spake, saying, Hear the word of the great king, the king of Assyria:

29 Thus saith the king, ⁿLet not Hezekiah deceive you: for he shall not be able to deliver you out of his hand:

30 Neither let Hezekiah make you trust in the LORD, saying, The LORD will surely deliver us, and this city shall not be delivered into the hand of the king of Assyria.

31 Hearken not to Hezekiah: for thus saith the king of Assyria, °Make ᵖ*an agreement* with me by a present, and come out to me, and *then* eat ye every man of his own vine, and every one of his fig tree, and drink ye every one of the waters of his ᑫcistern:

32 Until I come and take you away to a land like your own land, ʳa land of corn and wine, a land of bread and vineyards, a land of oil olive and of honey, that ye may live, and not die: and hearken not unto Hezekiah, when he ˢpersuadeth you, saying, The LORD will deliver us.

33 ᵗHath any of the gods of the nations delivered at all his land out of the hand of the king of Assyria?

34 ᵘWhere *are* the gods of Hamath, and of Arpad? where *are* the gods of Sepharvaim, Hena, and ᵛIvah? have they delivered Samaria out of mine hand?

35 Who *are* they among all the gods of the countries, that have delivered their country out of mine hand, ʷthat the LORD should deliver Jerusalem out of mine hand?

36 But the people held their peace, and answered him not a word: for the king's commandment was, saying, Answer him not.

37 Then came Eliakim the son of Hilkiah, which *was* over the household, and Shebna the scribe, and Joah the son of Asaph the recorder, to Hezekiah ˣwith *their* clothes rent, and told him the words of Rab-shakeh.

A. M. 3294
B. C. 710
Ol. XVII. 3
An. Leocratis,
Arch. Athen.
decen. 3

ᵐHeb. *the water of their feet*——ⁿ2 Chron. xxxii. 15 °Or, *Seek my favour*——ᵖHeb. *Make with me a blessing;* Gen. xxxii. 20; xxxiii. 11; Prov. xviii. 16——ᑫOr, *pit*

ʳDeut. viii. 7, 8——ˢOr, *deceiveth*——ᵗCh. xix. 12; 2 Chron. xxxii. 14; Isa. x. 10, 11——ᵘCh. xix. 13 ᵛCh. xvii. 24, *Ava*——ʷDan. iii. 15——ˣIsa. xxxiii. 7

---

was to stir up the people to *sedition*, that the city and the king might be delivered into his hand.

Verse 27. *That they may eat their own dung*] That they may be duly apprized, if they hold on Hezekiah's side, Jerusalem shall be most straitly besieged, and they be reduced to such a state of *famine* as to be obliged to eat their own excrements.

Verse 28. *Hear the word of the great king— of Assyria*] This was all intended to cause the people to revolt from their allegiance to their king.

Verse 32. *Until I come and take you away*] This was well calculated to stir up a seditious spirit. Ye cannot be delivered; your destruction, if ye resist, is inevitable; Sennacherib will do with you, as he does with all the nations he conquers, lead you captive into another land: but if you will surrender without farther trouble, he will transport you into a land as good as your own.

Verse 34. *Where are the gods of Hamath*] Sennacherib is greater than any of the gods of the nations. The Assyrians have already overthrown the gods of Hamath, Arpad, Hena, and

Ivah; therefore, Jehovah shall be like one of them, and shall not be able to deliver Jerusalem out of the hand of my master.

The impudent blasphemy of this speech is without parallel. Hezekiah treated it as he ought: it was not properly against *him*, but against the LORD; therefore he refers the matter to Jehovah himself, who punishes this blasphemy in the most signal manner.

Verse 36. *Answer him not.*] The blasphemy is too barefaced; *Jehovah* is insulted, not *you;* let him avenge his own quarrel. See the succeeding chapter.

Verse 37. *Then came Eliakim—and Shebna— and Joah—to Hezekiah with their clothes rent*] It was the custom of the Hebrews, when they heard any blasphemy, to rend their clothes, because this was the greatest of crimes, as it immediately affected the majesty of God; and it was right that a religious people should have in the utmost abhorrence every insult offered to the object of their religious worship. These three ambassadors lay the matter before the *king*, as God's *representative;* he lays it before the *prophet*, as God's *minister;* and the prophet lays it before *God*, as the people's *mediator.*

CHAPTER XIX

Hezekiah is greatly distressed, and sends to Isaiah to pray for him, 1–4. Isaiah returns a comfortable answer, and predicts the destruction of the king of Assyria and his army, 5–8. Sennacherib, hearing that his kingdom was invaded by the Ethiopians, sends a terrible letter to Hezekiah, to induce him to surrender, 9-13. Hezekiah goes to the temple, spreads the letter before the Lord, and makes a most affecting prayer, 14–19. Isaiah is sent to him to assure him that his prayer is heard; that Jerusalem shall be delivered; and that the Assyrians shall be destroyed, 20–34. That very night a messenger of God slays one hundred and eighty-five thousand Assyrians, 35. Sennacherib returns to Nineveh, and is slain by his own sons, 36, 37.

A. M. 3294
B. C. 710
Ol. XVII. 3
An. Leocratis,
Arch. Athen.
decen. 3

A ND [a]it came to pass, when King Hezekiah heard *it*, that he rent his clothes, and covered himself with sackcloth, and went into the house of the LORD.

2 And he sent Eliakim, which *was* over the household, and Shebna the scribe, and the elders of the priests, covered with sackcloth, to [b]Isaiah the prophet the son of Amoz.

3 And they said unto him, Thus saith Hezekiah, This day *is* a day of trouble, and of rebuke, and of [c]blasphemy: for the children have come to the birth, and *there is* not strength to bring forth.

4 [d]It may be the LORD thy God will hear all the words of Rab-shakeh, [e]whom the king of Assyria his master hath sent to reproach the living God; and will [f]reprove the words

which the LORD thy God hath heard: wherefore lift up *thy* prayer for the remnant that are [g]left.

A. M. 3294
B. C. 710
Ol. XVII. 3
An. Leocratis,
Arch. Athen.
decen. 3

5 So the servants of King Hezekiah came to Isaiah.

6 [h]And Isaiah said unto them, Thus shall ye say to your master, Thus saith the LORD, Be not afraid of the words which thou hast heard, with which the [i]servants of the king of Assyria have blasphemed me.

7 Behold, I will send [k]a blast upon him, and he shall hear a rumour, and shall return to his own land; and I will cause him to fall by the sword in his own land.

8 So Rab-shakeh returned, and found the king of Assyria warring against Libnah: for he had heard that he was departed [l]from Lachish.

---

[a]Isaiah xxxvii. 1, &c.——[b]Luke iii. 4, called *Esaias* [c]Or, *provocation*——[d]2 Samuel xvi. 12——[e]Chapter xviii. 35——[f]Psalm l. 21

[g]Heb. *found*——[h]Isa. xxxvii. 6, &c.——[i]Chapter xviii. 17——[k]Verse 35, 36, 37; Jeremiah li. 1 [l]Chapter xviii. 14

NOTES ON CHAP. XIX

Verse 2. *To Isaiah the prophet*] His fame and influence were at this time great in Israel; and it was well known that the word of the Lord was with him. Here both the Church and the state unite in fervent application to, and strong dependence upon, God; and behold how they succeed!

Verse 3. *The children are come to the birth*] The Jewish state is here represented under the emblem of *a woman in travail*, who has been so long in the pangs of parturition, that her strength is now entirely exhausted, and her deliverance is hopeless, without a miracle. The image is very fine and highly appropriate.

A similar image is employed by Homer, when he represents the agonies which Agamemnon suffers from his wound:—

Οφρα οι αιμ' ετι θερμον ανηνοθεν εξ ωτειλης·
Αυταρ επει το μεν ελκος ετερσετο, παυσατο δ' αιμα,
Οξειαι οδυναι δυνον μενος Ατρειδαο·
Ωs δ' οταν ωδινουσαν εχη βελος οξυ γυναικα,
Δριμυ, το τε προϊεισι μογοστοκοι Ειλειθυιαι
'Ηρης θυγατερες, πικρας ωδινας εχουσαι·
'Ωs οξει' οδυναι δυνον μενος Ατρειδαο. *Il.* xi., ver. 266.

This, while yet warm, distill'd the purple flood;
But when the wound grew stiff with clotted blood,
Then *grinding tortures* his strong bosom rend.
Less keen *those darts* the fierce *Ilythiæ* send,

The powers that cause the *teeming matron's* throes,
Sad mothers of *unutterable woes*.　　POPE.

Better translated by *Macpherson;* but in neither *well:* "So long as from the gaping wound gushed forth, in its warmth, the blood; but when the wound became dry, when ceased the blood to flow amain, sharp pains pervade the strength of Atrides. Racking pangs glide through his frame; as when the Ilythiæ, who preside over *births*, the daughters of white armed Juno, fierce dealers of *bitter pains*, throw all their *darts* on hapless women, that travail with child. Such pains pervade the strength of Atrides."

Verse 4. *The remnant that are left*] That is, the *Jews;* the ten tribes having been already carried away captive by the kings of Assyria.

Verse 7. *Behold, I will send a blast—and he shall hear a rumour*] The *rumour* was, that Tirhakah had invaded Assyria. The *blast* was that which slew *one hundred and eighty-five thousand* of them in one night, see ver. 35.

Cause him to fall by the sword] Alluding to his death by the hands of his two sons, at Nineveh. See ver. 35-37.

Verse 8. *Libnah—Lachish.*] These two places were not very distant from each other; they were in the mountains of Judah, southward of Jerusalem.

A. M. 3294
B. C. 710
Ol. XVII. 3
An. Leocratis,
Arch. Athen.
decen. 3

9 And ^mwhen he heard say of Tirhakah king of Ethiopia, Behold, he is come out to fight against thee: he sent messengers again unto Hezekiah, saying,

10 Thus shall ye speak to Hezekiah king of Judah, saying, Let not thy God ⁿin whom thou trustest deceive thee, saying, Jerusalem shall not be delivered into the hand of the king of Assyria.

11 Behold, thou hast heard what the kings of Assyria have done to all lands by destroying them utterly: and shalt thou be delivered?

12 ^oHave the gods of the nations delivered them which my fathers have destroyed; *as* Gozan, and Haram, and Rezeph, and the children of ^pEden which *were* in Thelasar?

13 ^qWhere *is* the king of Hamath, and the king of Arpad, and the king of the city of Sepharvaim, of Hena, and Ivah?

14 ^rAnd Hezekiah received the letter of the hand of the messengers, and read it: and Hezekiah went up into the house of the LORD, and spread it before the LORD.

15 And Hezekiah prayed before the LORD, and said, O LORD God of Israel, ^swhich dwellest *between* the cherubims, ^tthou art the God, *even* thou alone, of all the kingdoms of the earth; thou hast made heaven and earth.

16 LORD, ^ubow down thine ear, and hear: ^vopen, LORD, thine eyes, and see: and hear the words of Sennacherib, ^wwhich hath sent

him to reproach the living God.

A. M. 3294
B. C. 710
Ol. XVII. 3
An. Leocratis,
Arch. Athen.
decen. 3

17 Of a truth, LORD, the kings of Assyria have destroyed the nations and their lands,

18 And have ^xcast their gods into the fire: for they *were* no gods, but ^ythe work of men's hands, wood and stone: therefore they have destroyed them.

19 Now therefore, O LORD our God, I beseech thee, save thou us out of his hand, ^zthat all the kingdoms of the earth may know that thou *art* the LORD God, *even* thou only.

20 Then Isaiah the son of Amoz sent to Hezekiah, saying, Thus saith the LORD God of Israel, ^a*That* which thou hast prayed to me against Sennacherib king of Assyria ^bI have heard.

21 This *is* the word that the LORD hath spoken concerning him; The virgin ^cthe daughter of Zion hath despised thee, *and* laughed thee to scorn; the daughter of Jerusalem ^dhath shaken her head at thee.

22 Whom hast thou reproached and blasphemed? and against whom hast thou exalted *thy* voice, and lifted up thine eyes on high! *even* against the ^eHoly *One* of Israel.

23 ^fBy ^gthy messengers thou hast reproached the LORD, and hast said, ^hWith the multitude of my chariots I am come up to the height of the mountains, to the sides of Lebanon, and will cut down ⁱthe tall cedar trees thereof, *and*

---

^mSee 1 Sam. xxiii. 27——ⁿChap. xviii. 5——^oChap. xviii. 33——^pEzek. xxvii. 23——^qChap. xviii. 34 ^rIsa. xxxvii. 14, &c.——^s1 Sam. iv. 4; Psa. lxxx. 1 ^t1 Kings xviii. 39; Isa. xliv. 6; Jer. x. 10, 11, 12 ^uPsa. xxxi. 2——^v2 Chron. vi. 40——^wVer. 4

^xHeb. *given*——^yPsa. cxv. 4; Jer. x. 3——^zPsa. lxxxiii. 18——^aIsa. xxxvii. 21, &c.——^bPsa. lxv. 2 ^cLam. ii. 13——^dJob xvi. 4; Psa. xxii. 7, 8; Lam. ii. 15 ^ePsa. lxxi. 22; Isa. v. 24; Jer. li. 5——^fHeb. *By the hand of* ^gChap. xviii. 17——^hPsa. xx. 7——ⁱHeb. *the tallness*, &c.

Verse 10. *Let not thy God in whom thou trustest*] This letter is nearly the same with the speech delivered by Rab-shakeh. See chap. xviii. 29.

Verse 14. *Spread it before the Lord*] The temple was considered to be *God's dwelling-place;* and that whatever was there was peculiarly under his eye. Hezekiah spread the letter before the Lord, as he wished him to read the blasphemies spoken against himself.

Verse 15. *Thou art the God, &c.*] Thou art not only God of Israel, but God also of Assyria, and of all the nations of the world.

Verse 21. *The virgin the daughter of Zion hath despised thee,* and *laughed thee to scorn; the daughter of Jerusalem hath shaken her head at thee.*] "So truly contemptible is thy power, and empty thy boasts, that even the *young women* of Jerusalem, under the guidance of Jehovah, shall be amply sufficient to discomfit all thy forces, and cause thee to return with

shame to thy own country, where the most disgraceful death awaits thee."

When Bishop *Warburton* had published his Doctrine of Grace, and chose to fall foul on some of the most religious people of the land, a *young woman* of the city of Gloucester exposed his *graceless* system in a pamphlet, to which she affixed the above words as a motto!

Verse 23. *The tall cedar trees—the choice fir trees*] Probably meaning the *princes* and *nobles* of the country.

The forest of his Carmel.] Better in the margin: *the forest* and *his fruitful field.*

Verse 24. *I have digged and drunk strange waters*] I have conquered *strange countries,* in which I have digged wells for my army; or, I have gained the *wealth* of strange countries.

With the sole of my feet] My *infantry* have been so numerous that they alone have been sufficient to drink up the rivers of the places I have besieged.

A. M. 3294
B. C. 710
Ol. XVII. 3
An. Leocratis,
Arch. Athen.
decen. 3

the choice fir trees thereof: and I will enter into the lodgings of his borders, *and into* [k]the forest of his Carmel.

24 I have digged and drunk strange waters, and with the sole of my feet have I dried up all the rivers of [l]besieged places.

25 [m]Hast thou not heard long ago *how* [n]I have done it, *and* of ancient times that I have formed it? now have I brought it to pass, that [o]thou shouldest be to lay waste fenced cities *into* ruinous heaps.

26 Therefore their inhabitants were [p]of small power, they were dismayed and confounded; they were *as* the grass of the field, and *as* the green herb, *as* [q]the grass on the house-tops, and *as corn* blasted before it be grown up.

27 But [r]I know thy [s]abode, and thy going out, and thy coming in, and thy rage against me.

28 Because thy rage against me and thy tumult is come up into mine ears, therefore [t]I will put my hook in thy nose, and my bridle in thy lips, and I will turn thee back [u]by the way by which thou camest.

A. M. 3294
B. C. 710
Ol. XVII. 3
An. Leocratis,
Arch. Athen.
decen. 3

29 And this *shall be* [v]a sign unto thee, Ye shall eat this year such things as grow of themselves, and in the second year that which springeth of the same; and in the third year sow ye, and reap, and plant vineyards, and eat the fruits thereof.

30 [w]And [x]the remnant that is escaped of the house of Judah shall yet again take root downward, and bear fruit upward.

31 For out of Jerusalem shall go forth a remnant, and [y]they that escape out of Mount Zion: [z]the zeal of the LORD *of hosts* shall do this.

32 Therefore thus saith the LORD concerning the king of Assyria, He shall not come into this city, nor shoot an arrow there, nor come before it with shield, nor cast a bank against it.

33 By the way that he came, by the same shall he return, and shall not come into this city, saith the LORD.

34 For [a]I will defend this city, to save it for mine own sake, and [b]for my servant David's sake.

[k]Or, *the forest* and *his fruitful field;* Isa. x. 18——[l]Or, *fenced*——[m]Or, *Hast thou not heard* how *I have made it long ago, and formed it of ancient times? should I now bring it to be laid waste,* and *fenced cities* to be *ruinous heaps?*——[n]Isa. xlv. 7——[o]Isa. x. 5——[p]Heb. *short of hand*——[q]Psa. cxxix. 6——[r]Psa. cxxxix. 1, &c.

[s]Or, *sitting*——[t]Job xli. 2; Ezek. xxix. 4; xxxviii. 4; Amos iv. 2——[u]Ver. 33, 36, 37——[v]1 Sam. ii. 34; chap. xx. 8, 9; Isa. vii. 11, 14; Luke ii. 12——[w]2 Chron. xxxii. 22, 23——[x]Heb. *the escaping of the house of Judah that remaineth*——[y]Heb. *the escaping*——[z]Isa. ix. 7——[a]Ch. xx. 6——[b]1 Kings xi. 12, 13

Verse 25. *Hast thou not heard*] Here *Jehovah* speaks, and shows this boasting king that what he had done was done by the *Divine appointment*, and that of his own counsel and might he could have done nothing. It was because God had appointed them to this civil destruction that he had overcome them; and it was not through *his* might; for God had made *their inhabitants of small power*, so that he only got the victory over men whom God had *confounded, dismayed*, and *enervated*, ver. 26.

Verse 28. *I will put my hook in thy nose*] This seems to be an allusion to the method of *guiding a buffalo;* he has a sort of ring put into his nose, to which a cord or bridle is attached, by which he can be *turned* to the *right*, or to the *left*, or *round about*, according to the pleasure of his driver.

Verse 29. *This* shall *be a sign unto thee*] To Hezekiah; for to him this part of the address is made.

Ye shall eat this year] Sennacherib had ravaged the country, and *seed-time* was now over, yet God shows them that he would so bless the land, that what should *grow of itself that year*, would be quite sufficient to supply the inhabitants and prevent all *famine;* and though the *second year* was the *sabbatical rest* or *jubilee for the land*, in which it was unlawful to plough or sow; yet even then the land, by an especial blessing of God, should bring forth a sufficiency for its inhabitants; and in the *third year* they should sow and plant, &c., and have abundance, &c. Now this was to be a *sign* to Hezekiah, that his deliverance had not been effected by *natural* or *casual* means; for as without a *miracle* the ravaged and uncultivated land could not yield food for its inhabitants, so not without *miraculous* interference could the Assyrian army be cut off and Israel saved.

Verse 30. *The remnant—shall yet again take root*] As your *corn* shall take root in the soil, and bring forth and abundantly *multiply* itself, so shall the Jewish people; the population shall be greatly increased, and the desolations occasioned by the sword soon be forgotten.

Verse 31. *Out of Jerusalem shall go forth a remnant*] The Jews shall be so multiplied as not only to fill *Jerusalem*, but all the adjacent country.

And they that escape out of Mount Zion] Some think that this refers to the going forth of the *apostles* to the Gentile world, and converting the nations by the preaching of the Gospel.

Verse 32. *He shall not, &c.*] Here follow the fullest proofs that Jerusalem shall not be taken by the Assyrians. 1. *He shall not come into this city;* 2. He shall not be able to get so near as to *shoot an arrow into it;* 3. He shall not be able to *bring an army* before it; 4. Nor shall he be able to raise any *redoubt* or *mound* against it; 5. No; not even an Assyrian *shield* shall be seen in the country; not even a foraging party shall come near the city.

Verse 33. *By the way that he came*] Though

A. M. 3294
B. C. 710
Ol. XVII. 3
An. Leocratis,
Arch. Athen.
decen. 3

35 And [c]it came to pass that night, that the angel of the LORD went out, and smote in the camp of the Assyrians a hundred fourscore and five thousand: and when they arose early in the morning, behold, they *were* all dead corpses.

36 So Sennacherib king of Assyria departed, and went and returned, and dwelt at [d]Nineveh.

37 And it came to pass, as he was worshipping in the house of Nisroch his god, that [e]Adrammelech and Sharezer [f]his sons [g]smote him with the sword: and they escaped into the land of [h]Armenia. And [i]Esarhaddon his son reigned in his stead.

A. M. 3294
B. C. 710
Ol. XVII. 3
An. Leocratis,
Arch. Athen.
decen. 3

---

[c]2 Chron. xxxii. 21; Isa. xxxvii. 36; Ecclus. xlviii. 21; 1 Mac. vii. 41; 2 Mac. viii. 19——[d]Gen. x. 11

[e]2 Chron. xxxii. 21——[f]Tob i. 21——[g]Ver. 7——[h]Heb. *Ararat*——[i]Ezra iv. 2

---

his army shall not return, yet *he* shall return to Assyria; for because of his blasphemy he is reserved for a more ignominious death.

Verse 35. *That night*] The very night after the blasphemous message had been sent, and this comfortable prophecy delivered.

The angel of the Lord went out] I believe this *angel* or *messenger of the Lord* was simply a *suffocating* or *pestilential* WIND; by which the Assyrian army was destroyed, as in a moment, without *noise, confusion,* or any *warning.* See the note 1 Kings chap. xx. ver. 30. Thus was the threatening, ver. 7, fulfilled, *I will send a* BLAST *upon him;* for he had heard the *rumour* that his territories were invaded; and on his way to save his empire, in one night the whole of his army was destroyed, without any one even seeing who had hurt them. This is called an *angel* or *messenger of the Lord:* that is, *something immediately sent* by him to execute his judgments.

When they arose early] That is, *Sennach-*

erib, and probably a *few associates,* who were preserved as *witnesses* and *relaters* of this most dire *disaster.* Rab-shakeh, no doubt, perished with the rest of the army.

Verse 36. *Dwelt at Nineveh.*] This was the capital of the Assyrian empire.

Verse 37. *Nisroch his god*] We know nothing of this deity; he is nowhere else mentioned.

Smote him with the sword] The rabbins say that his sons had learned that he intended to sacrifice them to this god, and that they could only prevent this by slaying *him.*

The same writers add, that he consulted his wise men how it was that such miracles should be wrought for the Israelites; who told him that it was because of the merit of Abraham, who had offered his only son to God: he then said, I will offer to him my two sons; which when *they* heard, they rose up and slew him. When a rabbin cannot untie a knot, he feels neither scruple nor difficulty to cut it.

CHAPTER XX

Hezekiah's sickness, and the message of the prophet to him, to prepare for death, 1. *His distress and prayer to God,* 2, 3. *The Lord hears, and promises to add* fifteen *years to his life, and Isaiah prescribes a means of cure,* 4–7. *Hezekiah seeks a sign; and to assure him of the truth of God's promise, the shadow on the dial of Ahaz goes back* ten *degrees,* 8–11. *The king of Babylon sends a friendly message to Hezekiah, to congratulate him on his recovery; and to these messengers he ostentatiously shows all his treasures,* 12, 13. *Isaiah reproves him, and foretells that the Babylonians will come and take away all those treasures, and take the people into captivity; and degrade the royal family of Judah,* 14–18. *Hezekiah bows to the Divine judgment,* 19. *His acts and death,* 20, 21.

A. M. 3291
B. C. 713
Ol. XVI. 4
An. Hippome-
nis, Arch. Ath.
decen. 10

IN [a]those days was Hezekiah sick unto death. And the prophet Isaiah the son of Amoz came to him, and said unto him, Thus saith the LORD, [b]Set thine house in order; for thou shalt die, and not live.

2 Then he turned his face to the wall, and prayed unto the LORD, saying,

A. M. 3291
B. C. 713
Ol. XVI. 4
An. Hippome-
nis, Arch. Ath.
decen. 10

---

[a]2 Chron. xxxii. 24, &c.; Isa. xxxviii. 1, &c.

[b]Heb. *Give charge concerning thine house;* 2 Sam. xvii. 23

NOTES ON CHAP. XX

Verse 1. *Set thine house in order*] It appears from the text that he was smitten with such a disorder as must *terminate in death,* without the miraculous interposition of God: and he is now commanded to *set his house in order,* or *to give charge concerning his house;* to dispose of his affairs, or in other words, to *make his will;* because his death was at hand. "This sickness," says *Jarchi,* "took place

three days before the defeat of Sennacherib." That it must have been *before* this defeat, is evident. Hezekiah reigned only *twenty-nine* years, chap. xviii. 2. He had reigned *fourteen* years when the war with Sennacherib began, chap. xviii. 13, and he reigned *fifteen* years after this sickness, chap. xx. 6; therefore 14+15=29, the term of his reign. Nothing can be clearer than this; that Hezekiah had reigned *fourteen* years before this time; and that he did live the *fifteen* years here promised. That

A. M. 3291
B. C. 713
Ol. XVI. 4
An. Hippome-
nis, Arch. Ath.
decen. 10

3 I beseech thee, O LORD, ^cremember now how I have ^dwalked before thee in truth and with a perfect heart, and have done *that which is* good in thy sight. And Hezekiah wept ^esore.

4 And it came to pass, afore Isaiah was gone out into the middle ^fcourt, that the word of the LORD came to him, saying,

5 Turn again, and tell Hezekiah ^gthe captain of my people, Thus saith the LORD, the God of David thy father, ^hI have heard thy prayer, I have seen ⁱthy tears: behold, I will heal thee: on the third day thou shalt go up unto the house of the LORD.

6 And I will add unto thy days fifteen years: and I will deliver thee and this city out of the hand of the king of Assyria; and ^kI will de-

fend this city for mine own sake, and for my servant David's sake.

A. M. 3291
B. C. 713
Ol. XVI. 4
An. Hippome-
nis, Arch. Ath.
decen. 10

7 And ^lIsaiah said, Take a lump of figs. And they took and laid *it* on the boil, and he recovered.

8 And Hezekiah said unto Isaiah, ^mWhat *shall be* the sign that the LORD will heal me, and that I shall go up into the house of the LORD the third day?

9 And Isaiah said, ⁿThis sign shalt thou have of the LORD, that the LORD will do the thing that he hath spoken: shall the shadow go forward ten degrees, or go back ten degrees?

10 And Hezekiah answered, It is a light thing for the shadow to go down ten degrees: nay, but let the shadow return backward ten degrees.

11 And Isaiah the prophet cried unto the

---

^cNeh. xiii. 22——^dGenesis xvii. 1; 1 Kings iii. 6
^eHeb. *with a great weeping*——^fOr, *city*——^g1 Sam. ix.
16; x. 1——^hChap. xix. 20; Psa. lxv. 2

ⁱPsa. xxxix. 12; lvi. 8——^kCh. xix. 34——^lIsa.
xxxviii. 21——^mSee Judg. vi. 17, 37, 39; Isa. vii. 11,
14; xxxviii. 22——ⁿSee Isa. xxxviii. 7, 8

Hezekiah's sickness happened before the destruction of Sennacherib's army, is asserted by the text itself: see ver. 6.

Verse 3. *I beseech thee, O Lord*] Hezekiah knew that, although the words of Isaiah were delivered to him in an *absolute* form, yet they were to be *conditionally* understood; else he could not have prayed to God to reverse a purpose which he knew to be irrevocable. Even this passage is a key to many prophecies and Divine declarations: see chap. xviii. of Jeremiah.

Hezekiah pleads his uprightness and holy conduct in his own behalf. Was it *impious* to do so? No; but it certainly did not savour much either of *humility* or of a *due sense of his own weakness*. If he had a *perfect heart*, who made it such?—God. If he did good in God's sight, who enabled him to do so?—God. Could he therefore plead in his behalf dispositions and actions which he could neither have felt nor practised but by the *power of the grace of God?* I trow not. But the times of this ignorance God winked at. The Gospel teaches us a different lesson.

Wept sore.] How clouded must his prospects of another world have been! But it is said that, as he saw the nation in danger from the Assyrian army, which was then invading it, and threatened to destroy the religion of the true God, he was greatly affected at the news of his death, as he wished to live to see the enemies of God overthrown. And therefore God promises that he *will deliver the city out of the hands of the king of Assyria*, at the same time that he promises him a respite of *fifteen* years, ver. 6. His lamentation on this occasion may be seen in Isaiah, chap. xxxviii.

Verse 4. *Into the middle court*] הצר *hatstser, the court*. This is the reading of the Masoretic *Keri:* העיר *haair*, "of the city," is the reading of the text, and of most MSS.; but the *versions* follow the *Keri*.

Verse 6. *I will add unto thy days fifteen years*]

This is the *first* and *only* man who was ever informed of the *term of his life*. And was this a *privilege?* Surely no. If Hezekiah was attached to life, as he appears to have been, how must his mind be affected to mark the *sinking years!* He knew he was to *die* at the end of *fifteen* years; and how must he feel at the end of every year, when he saw that so much was cut off from life? He must necessarily feel a thousand deaths in fearing one. I believe there would be nothing wanting to complete the misery of men, except the place of torment, were they informed of the precise time in which their lives *must* terminate. God, in his abundant mercy, has hidden this from their eyes.

Verse 7. *Take a lump of figs—and laid* it *on the boil*] We cannot exactly say in what Hezekiah's malady consisted. שחין *shechin* signifies any *inflammatory tumour, boil, abscess,* &c. The *versions* translate it *sore, wound*, and such like. Some think it was a *pleurisy;* others, that it was the *plague;* others, the *elephantiasis;* and others, that it was a *quinsey*. A poultice of figs might be very proper to maturate a boil, or to discuss any obstinate inflammatory swelling. This Pliny remarks, *Omnibus quæ maturanda aut discutienda sunt imponuntur*. But we cannot pronounce on the propriety of the *application*, unless we were certain of the nature of the *malady*. This, however, was the *natural* means which God chose to bless to the recovery of Hezekiah's health; and without this interposition he must have died.

Verse 8. *What* shall be *the sign*] He wished to be fully convinced that his cure was to be entirely supernatural; and, in order to this, he seeks one miracle to prove the truth of the other, that nothing might remain *equivocal*.

Verse 11. *He brought the shadow ten degrees backward*] We cannot suppose that these *ten degrees* meant *ten hours;* there were *ten divisions of time* on this dial: and perhaps it would

A. M. 3291
B. C. 713
Ol. XVI. 4
An. Hippomenis, Arch. Ath. decen. 10

LORD: and [o]he brought the shadow ten degrees backward, by which it had gone down in the [p]dial of Ahaz.

A. M. 3292
B. C. 712
Ol. XVII. 4
An. Leocratis, Arch. Athen. decen. 1

12 [q]At that time [r]Berodach-baladan, the son of Baladan, king of Babylon, sent letters and a present unto Hezekiah: for he had heard that Hezekiah had been sick.

13 And [s]Hezekiah hearkened unto them, and showed them all the house of his [t]precious things, the silver, and the gold, and the spices, and the precious ointment, and *all* the house of his [u]armour, [v]and all that was found in his treasures: there was nothing in his house, nor in all his dominion, that Hezekiah showed them not.

14 Then came Isaiah the prophet unto King Hezekiah, and said unto him, What said these men? and from whence came they unto thee? And Hezekiah said, They are come from a far country, *even* from Babylon.

A. M. 3292
B. C. 712
Ol. XVII. 1
An. Leocratis, Arch. Athen. decen. 1

15 And he said, What have they seen in thine house? And Hezekiah answered, [w]All *the things* that *are* in mine house have they seen: there is nothing among my treasures that I have not showed them.

16 And Isaiah said unto Hezekiah, Hear the word of the LORD.

17 Behold, the days come, that all that *is* in thine house, and that which thy fathers have laid up in store unto this day, [x]shall be carried into Babylon: nothing shall be left, saith the LORD.

18 And of thy sons that shall issue from thee, which thou shalt beget, [y]shall they take away; [z]and they shall be eunuchs in the palace of the king of Babylon.

19 Then said Hezekiah unto Isaiah, [a]Good *is* the word of the LORD which thou hast spoken. And he said, [b]*Is it* not *good,* if peace and truth be in my days?

---

[o]See Josh. x. 12, 14; Isa. xxxviii. 8; Ecclus. xlviii. 23 —— [p]Heb. *degrees* —— [q]Isa. xxxix. 1, &c. —— [r]Or, *Merodach-baladan* —— [s]2 Chron. xxxii. 27, 31 —— [t]Or, *spicery* —— [u]Or, *jewels* —— [v]Heb. *vessels* —— [w]Ver. 13

[x]Ch. xxiv. 13; xxv. 13; Jer. xxvii. 21, 22; lii. 17 —— [y]Ch. xxiv. 12; 2 Chron. xxxiii. 11 —— [z]Fulfilled, Dan. i. 3 —— [a]1 Sam. iii. 18; Job i. 21; Psa. xxxix. 9 —— [b]Or, *Shall there not be peace and truth, &c.*

---

not be right to suppose that the *sun* went ten degrees back in the heavens, or that the *earth* turned back upon its axis from *east* to *west,* in a contrary direction to its natural course. But the miracle might be effected by means of *refraction,* for a ray of light we know can be *varied* or *refracted* from a *right line* by passing through a dense medium; and we know also, by means of the refracting power of the atmosphere, the sun, when near rising and setting, seems to be higher above the horizon than he really is, and, by horizontal refraction, we find that the sun appears above the horizon when he is actually below it, and literally out of sight: therefore, by using dense clouds or vapours, the rays of light in that place might be *refracted* from their direct course *ten,* or any other number of degrees; so that the miracle might have been wrought by occasioning this extraordinary *refraction,* rather than by disturbing the course of the *earth,* or any other of the celestial bodies.

The dial of Ahaz.] See the note on chap. ix. 13, and the observations and *diagram* at the end of this chapter.

Verse 12. *At that time Berodach-baladan*] He is called *Merodach-Baladan,* Isa. xxxix. 1, and by the *Septuagint, Syriac,* and *Arabic* versions; and by several of *Kennicott's* and *De Rossi's* MSS.; and also by the *Babylonian* and *Jerusalem Talmuds.* The true reading seems to be *Merodach;* the מ *mem* and ב *beth* might be easily interchanged, and so produce the mistake.

Sent letters and a present] It appears that there was friendship between the king of Babylon and Hezekiah, when the latter and the Assyrians were engaged in a destructive war. The king of Babylon had not only heard of his *sickness,* but he had heard of the *miracle;* as we learn from 2 Chron. xxxii. 31.

Verse 13. *Hezekiah hearkened unto them*] Instead of וישמע *vaiyishma, he hearkened,* וישמח *vaiyismach, he rejoiced* or *was glad,* is the reading of *twelve* of *Kennicott's* and *De Rossi's* MSS., the *parallel* place, Isa. xxxix. 2, the *Septuagint, Syriac, Vulgate, Arabic,* some copies of the *Targum,* and the Babylonian *Talmud.*

All the house of his precious things] Interpreters are not well agreed about the meaning of the original נכתה *nechothoh,* which we here translate *precious things,* and in the margin *spicery* or *jewels.* I suppose the last to be meant.

There was nothing in his house] He showed them through a spirit of folly and exultation, all his treasures, and no doubt those in the house of the Lord. And it is said, 2 Chron. xxxii. 31, that in this business *God left him to try him, that he might know all* that was *in his heart;* and this trial proved that in his heart there was little else than *pride* and *folly.*

Verse 17. *Behold, the days come*] This was fulfilled in the days of the latter Jewish kings, when the Babylonians had led the people away into captivity, and stripped the land, the temple, &c., of all their riches. See Dan. i. 1-3.

Verse 18. *They shall be eunuchs*] Perhaps this means no more than that they should become *household servants* to the kings of Babylon. See the fulfillment, chap. xxiv. 13-15, and Dan. i. 1-3.

Verse 19. *Good* is *the word of the Lord*] He

A. M. 3278-3306
B. C. 726–698
Ol. XIII. 3
—XX. 3

20 ^cAnd the rest of the acts of Hezekiah, and all his might, and how he ^dmade a pool, and a conduit, and ^ebrought water into the city, *are* they not written in the book of the

chronicles of the kings of Judah?

21 And ^fHezekiah slept with his fathers: and Manasseh his son reigned in his stead.

A. M. 3306
B. C. 698
Ol. XX. 3
An. Apsandri,
Arch. Athen.
decen. 5

---

^c2 Chron. xxxii. 32——^dNeh. iii. 16

^e2 Chron. xxxii. 30——^f2 Chron. xxxii. 33

---

has spoken *right,* I have done *foolishly.* I submit to his judgments.

Is it not good if peace and truth be in my days?] I believe Hezekiah inquires whether there shall be peace and truth in his days. And the question seems to be rather of an interested nature. He does not appear to deplore the calamities that were coming on the land, provided peace and truth might prevail in his days.

Verse 20. *The rest of the acts of Hezekiah*] See the parallel places in Isaiah and in 2 Chronicles. In this latter book, chap. xxxii., we find several particulars that are not inserted here; especially concerning his pride, the increase of his riches, his storehouses of corn, wine, and oil; his stalls for all manner of beasts; his cities, flocks, and herds, in abundance; and the bringing the upper water course of Gihon to the west side of the city of David, by which he brought a plentiful supply of water into that city, &c., &c., &c.

ON the subject of the *Babylonian embassy* I may say a few words. However we may endeavour to excuse Hezekiah, it is certain that he made an exhibition of his riches and power in a spirit of great vanity; and that this did displease the Lord. It was also ruinous to Judea: when those foreigners had seen such a profusion of wealth, such princely establishments, and such a fruitful land, it was natural for them to conceive the *wish* that they had such treasures, and from that to covet the very treasures they saw. They made their report to their king and countrymen, and the *desire* to possess the Jewish wealth became general; and in consequence of this there is little doubt that the conquest of Jerusalem was *projected.* History is not barren in such instances: the same kind of cause has produced similar effects. Take two or three notable instances.

When the barbarous *Goth* and *Vandal* nations saw the pleasant and fruitful plains and hills of *Italy,* and the vast treasures of the Roman people, the abundance of the necessaries, conveniences, comforts, and luxuries of life, which met their eyes in every direction; they were never at rest till their swords put them in possession of the whole, and brought the mistress of the world to irretrievable ruin.

Vortigern, a British king, unhappily invited the *Saxons,* in 445, to assist him against his rebellious subjects: they came, saw the land that it was good, and in the end took possession of it, having driven out, or into the mountains of Wales, all the original Britons.

The *Danes,* in the *ninth century,* made some inroads into England, found the land better than their own, and never rested till they established themselves in this country, and, after having ruled it for a considerable time, were at last, with the utmost difficulty, driven out.

These nations had only to *see* a better land in order to *covet* it, and their *exertions* were not wanting in order to *possess* it.

How far other nations, since those times, have imitated the most foolish and impolitic conduct of the Jewish king, and how far their conduct may have been or may yet be marked with the same *consequences,* the pages of impartial history have shown and will show: God's ways are all equal, and the judge of all the earth will do right. But we need not wonder, after this, that the Jews fell into the hands of the Babylonians, for this was the political consequence of their own conduct: nor could it be otherwise, the circumstances of both nations considered, unless God, by a miraculous interposition, had saved them; and this it was inconsistent with his justice to do, because they had, in their pride and vanity, offended against him. To be lifted up with pride and vain glory in the possession of any blessings, is the most direct way to lose them; as it induces God, who dispensed them for our benefit, to resume them, because that which was designed for our good, through our own perversity becomes our bane.

1. I have intimated, in the note on ver. 11, that the shadow was brought back on the dial of Ahaz by means of *refraction.* On this subject some farther observations may not be improper.

2. Any person may easily convince himself of the effect of *refraction* by this simple experiment: Place a vessel on the floor, and put a piece of coin on the bottom, close to that part of the vessel which is *farthest off* from yourself; then move back till you find that the edge of the vessel next to yourself fairly covers the coin, and that it is now entirely out of sight. Stand exactly in that position, and let a person pour water gently into the vessel, and you will soon find the coin to reappear, and to be entirely in sight when the vessel is full, though neither it nor you have changed your positions in the least.

By the refracting power of the atmosphere we have *several minutes* more of the solar light each day than we should otherwise have. "The atmosphere refracts the sun's rays so as to bring him in sight every clear day, before he rises in the horizon, and to keep him in view for *some minutes* after he is really set below it. For at some times of the year we see the sun *ten minutes* longer above the horizon than he would be if there were no *refractions,* and above *six minutes* every day at a mean rate." —*Ferguson.*

And it is entirely owing to refraction that we have any morning or evening *twilight;* without this power in the atmosphere, the heavens would be as *black* as *ebony* in the absence of the sun; and at his *rising* we should pass in a moment from the *deepest darkness* into the *brightest light;* and at his *setting,* from the *most intense light* to the *most profound darkness,* which in a few days would be sufficient to destroy the visual organs of all the animals in *air, earth,* or *sea.*

That the rays of light can be *supernaturally refracted,* and the sun appear to be where he actually is not, we have a most remarkable instance in *Kepler*. Some Hollanders, who wintered in *Nova Zembla* in the year 1596, were surprised to find that after a continual night of three months, the sun began to rise *seventeen days* sooner than (according to computation deduced from the altitude of the pole, observed to be *seventy-six degrees*) he should have done; which can only be accounted for by a miracle, or by an *extraordinary refraction* of the sun's rays passing through the cold dense air in that climate. At that time the sun, as *Kepler* computes, was almost *five degrees* below the horizon when he appeared; and consequently the refraction of his rays was about *nine times* stronger than it is with us.

3. Now this might be all purely *natural*, though it was *extraordinary*, and it proves the *possibility* of what I have conjectured, even on *natural principles;* but the *foretelling* of this, and leaving the *going back* or *forward* to the choice of the king, and the thing occurring in the *place* and *time* when and where it was predicted, shows that it was *supernatural* and *miraculous*, though the means were purely *natural*. Yet in that climate, (LAT. *thirty-one degrees fifty minutes north*, and LONG. *thirty-five degrees twenty-five minutes east*,) where *vapours* to produce an extraordinary refraction of the solar rays could not be expected, the *collecting* or *producing* them *heightens* and *ascertains* the miracle. "But why contend that the thing was done by *refraction?* Could not God as easily have caused the *sun*, or rather the *earth*, to turn back, as to have produced this extraordinary and miraculous *refraction?*" I answer, Yes. But it is much more consistent with the wisdom and perfections of God to perform a work or accomplish an end by *simple* means, than by those that are *complex;* and had it been done in the other way, it would have required a miracle to *invert* and a miracle to *restore;* and a strong convulsion on the earth's surface to bring it ten degrees suddenly *back*, and to take it the same suddenly *forward*. The miracle, according to my supposition, was performed on the *atmosphere*, and without in the least disturbing even *that;* whereas, on the other supposition, it could not have been done without *suspending* or *interrupting* the *laws of the solar system*, and this without gaining a hair's breadth in credulity or conviction more by such stupendous interpositions than might be effected by the agency of *clouds* and *vapours*. The point to be gained was the *bringing back the shadow* on *the dial ten degrees:* this might have been gained by the means I have here described, as well as by the other; and these means being much more *simple*, were more worthy the Divine choice than those which are more *complex*, and could not have been used without producing the necessity of working at least double or treble miracles.

4. Before I proceed to the immediate object of inquiry, I shall beg leave to make some observations on the invention and construction of DIALS in general.

SUNDIALS must have been of great antiquity, though the earliest we hear of is that of *Ahaz;* but this certainly was not the *first* of its kind, though it is the first on record. Ahaz began his reign about *four hundred* years before Alexander, and about *twelve* years after the foundation of Rome.

Anaximenes, the Milesian, who flourished about *four hundred* years before Christ, is said

by *Pliny* to have been the first who made a *sundial*, the use of which he taught to the Spartans; but others give this honour to *Thales*, his countryman, who flourished *two hundred* years before him.

Aristarchus of Samos, who lived before *Archimedes*, invented a plain horizontal disc, with a *gnomon*, to distinguish the hours, and had its rim raised all around, to prevent the shadow from extending too far.

Probably all these were *rude* and *evanescent* attempts, for it does not appear that the *Romans*, who borrowed all their knowledge from the Greeks, knew any thing of a *sundial* before that set up by *Papirius Cursor*, about *four hundred* and *sixty* years after the foundation of Rome; before which time, says Pliny, there was no mention of any account of *time* but by the *rising* and *setting* of the sun. This dial was erected near the temple of *Quirinus*, but is allowed to have been very inaccurate. About *thirty* years after, the consul *Marcus Valerius Messala* brought a dial out of Sicily, which he placed on a pillar near the *rostrum;* but as it was not made for the latitude of Rome, it did not show the time exactly; however it was the only one they had for a *hundred* years, when *Martius Philippus* set up one more exact.

Since those times the science of *dialling* has been cultivated in most civilized nations, but we have no professed treatise on the subject before the time of the jesuit *Clavius*, who, in the latter part of the *sixteenth* century, demonstrated both the theory and practice of dialling; but he did this after the most rigid mathematical principles, so as to render that which was *simple* in itself exceedingly obscure. Though we have useful and correct works of this kind from *Rivard, De Parcieux, Dom. Bedos de Celles, Joseph Blaise Garnier, Gravesande, Emerson, Martin*, and *Leadbetter;* yet something more specific, more simple, and more general, is a desideratum in the science of *sciaterics* or *dialling*.

Observations on the nature and structure of the sundial of Ahaz, with a diagram of its supposed form.

5. When writing on the appointment of Jehu to be king of Israel, chap. ix., I was struck with the manner in which the subject of the thirteenth verse was understood by the *Chaldee:* "Then they hastened and took every man his garment, and put it under him, *on the* TOP *of the* STAIRS;" according to the Hebrew, אל גרם *el gerem hammaaloth*, which might be translated, *on the bare (naked* or *uncovered)* steps. This the Targumist has translated by לדרג שעיא *lidrag sheaiya, "at the* HOUR-STEPS." The other *versions*, knowing nothing of what was intended, have endeavoured to *guess* severally at a meaning. On turning to chap. xx. 11, where the same word מעלות *maaloth* is used, and most evidently there implies some kind of *sundial*, I found the *Chaldee* still more pointed, both in this and in the parallel place, Isa. xxxviii. 8, rendering the Hebrew words בצורת אבן שעיא *betsurath eben sheaiya, "by the shadow of the stone of hours,"* from which I was led to conclude that some kind of *gnomonic* figure, or *sundial*, was intended; and that the hours or divisions of time were shown by a *shadow*, projected on stone steps, *gradually ascending to a certain height*. This thought I communicated

to the Rev. *Philip Garrett*, one of the preachers among the people called Methodists, of whose rare knowledge in the science of *gnomonics*, and ingenuity in constructing every possible variety of dials, I had already indubitable proofs, and requested him, from the principle I had laid down, to try whether such an instrument could be constructed that might serve at once as a *public tribunal*, and as a *dial*, to ascertain all the *inequalities* of the Jewish *division of time?*

A more difficult problem in the science he was never called to solve. Though several had attempted to construct dials to show the mode by which different nations measured time, and among the rest the *Jews;* yet nothing properly satisfactory has been produced, although one nearly in the same form of outline with the present may be found in *Hutton's Mathematical Recreations*, vol. iii., p. 337, projected on a *plane superficies*, which could not possibly show the *ascending* and *descending* of the shadow like that now before the reader, which the ingenuity of the above gentleman has brought to almost as great a degree of perfection as can reasonably be expected. And that the dial of Ahaz was constructed on a similar principle, there can be but little doubt, as the words of the original seem to express this and no other form; and so the *Chaldee* appears to have understood it; nor is it easy to conceive that one on any other principle could ascertain in all seasons the varying admeasurement of the Jewish time.

6. Having said thus much relative to the circumstances which gave birth to this dial, it may be deemed necessary to give a general view of the natural and artificial divisions of time, and then a description of the dial itself.

The most obvious *division of time* is into *day* and *night;* these are marked out by the *rising* and *setting* of the sun. Modern writers call the time from sunrise to sunset the *natural day;* the *night* is the time from sunset to *sunrise;* these days and nights are subject to great inequalities in every part of the earth, except under the equator. The most ancient division of the equatorial day was into the morning and evening; the night was divided into watches.

Hours are either equal or unequal; an *unequal* hour is the *twelfth* part of a natural day, or the *twelfth* part of the night. In *summer*, when the days are the longest, the diurnal hours are the longest, and the nocturnal hours shortest; in *winter*, on the contrary, when the days are shortest, the hours of the day are the *shortest*, and the hours of the night *longest*. The difference between the hours of the day and those of the night is greatest at the *solstices*, because then there is the greatest inequality between the length of the day and that of the night. At the *equinoxes*, when the days and nights are of an equal length, all hours, both of days and nights, are equal.

The ancient *Jews* made use of *unequal* hours; with them *sunrise* was the beginning of the *first* hour of the day, *noon* was the end of the *sixth* hour, and the *twelfth* hour ended at *sunset*.

Doctor *Long* observes, "These *times* might be measured by an astronomer; but how *unequal* hours can be marked for common use, is not easy to say." He farther observes that "the ancients had *sundials;* but I think unequal hours could not be marked thereon exactly." And in a note on this observation he remarks, "The *sundials of the ancients*, to show unequal hours, were not made in the method used at

present, with a gnomon *parallel* to the axis of the earth, but had a *pin* set upright upon a plane, rounded at the upper end, the shadow whereof marked their *unequal* hours in the following manner: by means of an *analemma*, or projection of the sphere, *six curves* were drawn upon the plane, to show where the shadow of the *pin* at the several hours terminated every month in the year; one *curve* served for two months, because the shadows are of the same length in January as in December, in February as in November, in March as in October, &c.; each *curve* was drawn long enough to take in all the hours of the longest day in the respective months, and was divided into twelve equal parts. It is easy to see that a dial made by this method, in order to show the unequal hours exactly, *ought* to have *half* as many curves, or parallel lines, as there are days in the year; but this would require so many *lines* as would make it all confusion; it is possible they had only one line for a month, and that for the middle of the month."

The doctor is perfectly correct in observing, that "the sundials of the ancients, to show unequal hours, were not made in the method used at present, with a gnomon parallel to the axis of the earth;" because such a dial could not be of any use to those nations whose divisions of the solar hours were unequal, or more or less than *sixty* minutes to an hour. But the doctor is mistaken in supposing the difficulty, or rather impossibility, of constructing a sundial to show these *unequal* hours; for *eleven* lines are all that is necessary to show the hours for *every* day in the year; and *forty-four* lines would show all the *quarters:* whereas, on his plan, it would require near *eleven hundred* calculations of the *altitude of the sun*, and the same number to show where the shadow of the *gnomon* at the several hours terminated. His dial would therefore require above *one hundred and eighty* parallel lines, and nearly *eleven hundred* marks for the *hours* only; but if the quarters are inserted, *four thousand four hundred* marks would be necessary. This would require the labour of *six* or *eight months*, whereas the plan here adopted would not require in its calculations and construction as many hours.

7. *A description of the dial*. This dial consists of *eleven steps* placed parallel to the horizon, with a *perpendicular gnomon* fixed in the upper or middle step, which step is placed exactly *north* and *south*, and forms the *meridian* or sixth-hour line.

All the operations of this dial are determined by the *point* of the shadow projected from the gnomon on the steps of the dial.

Every day for *six months* the shadow from the point of the gnomon makes a *different angle* with the gnomon, which makes the hours of one day to differ in length from the hours of the preceding and following days. The same observations apply to the other six months in the year.

The shadow crosses each step of the dial every day in the year.

Each day in the year consists of *twelve* hours from the time of sunrise to sunset, which makes a difference of *twenty* minutes between an hour in the longest day and an hour in the shortest. The longest day, consisting of *twelve hours* of *seventy* minutes to an hour; and the shortest of *twelve* hours of *fifty* minutes to an hour; but when the sun enters *Aries* or *Libra*, each hour consists of *sixty* minutes.

To be able to understand this dial, one example will be sufficient: On the 21st of March, or the 23d of September, the shadow from the point of the gnomon will enter or *ascend* the *first* step of the dial, at the first hour of the day, at the *west* side of the dial on the equinoctial line; *eleven* minutes afterwards the shadow comes in contact with the circle marked *fifteen* degrees, which is the altitude of the sun at that time; *twenty-four* minutes afterwards the shadow touches the circle of *twenty* degrees; and in *twenty-five* minutes it ascends the *second* step, at the *second* hour of the day, when the altitude of the sun is *twenty-five* degrees *eight* minutes.

In *twenty-four* minutes the shadow comes to the circle of *thirty* degrees; and *twenty-five* minutes after it arrives at the circle of *thirty-five* degrees; and in *eleven* minutes it ascends the *third* step at the *third* hour of the day, when the altitude is *thirty-six* degrees *fifty-seven* minutes. In *sixteen* minutes the point of the shadow intersects the circle of *forty* degrees; and in *forty-four* minutes it ascends the *fourth* step at the *fourth* hour of the day, when the altitude of the sun is *forty-seven* degrees *twenty-two* minutes; and in *eighteen* minutes of time it comes in contact with the circle of *fifty* degrees, &c., &c., until it arrives at the *meridian step* or line at the *sixth* hour of the day, when the altitude is *fifty-eight* degrees *ten* minutes; then the shadow *descends* the *sixth* step, and moves on to the *seventh*, &c., *descending step after step*, tracing the equinoctial line on the *east* side of the dial; intersecting the *steps* or *hour lines*, and the *circles* of *altitude*, until it leaves the dial at the *eleventh* hour of the day.

A dial of this construction is the most simple, useful, and durable that can be made; and as exclusively and completely adapted to ascertain the ancient Jewish divisions of the solar hours.

The *steps* of this dial render the construction a little more difficult than it otherwise would be if the *lines* were drawn on a plane superficies, which would give exactly the same divisions of the hours.

N. B. A *vertical south dial*, in lat. *thirty-one* degrees *fifty* minutes, (the latitude of Jerusalem,) could be of little or no use to ascertain these divisions for several months in the year. The same remark may be made respecting a *south vertical concave* dial. The sun cannot shine upon a south vertical plane, in lat. *thirty-one* degrees *fifty* minutes in the longest day before *fifty-three* minutes past *eight*, or nearly *nine*, in the morning.

With respect to the dimensions of this dial, if we suppose the height of the stile from the bottom of the *lowest* step to be *four feet*, this would allow *six* inches for the thickness of each step, and *twelve* inches for the height of the *stile* above the upper step. According to this scale the *south* end of the dial would be *ten yards;* the *north* end *sixteen yards;* and the *east* and *west* sides *eight yards two feet*. The ground-work might be *eighteen* yards by *twelve*, making an oblong square facing the four cardinal points of the heavens.

N. B. All the lines upon a dial-plane are *inverted*, with respect to the *cardinal* points of the heavens.

The lines which show the hours from *sunrise* to the meridian, are on the *west* side of the dial-plane; and the lines which show the hours from the meridian to *sunset* are on the *east* side of the dial-plane; the *southern* tropic, Capricorn, is on the *north* end of the dial-plane; and the *northern* tropic, Cancer, is on the *south* end of the plane.

The *narrow* end of the dial looks towards the *south*, and is marked *north;* the *wide* end looks *north*, and is marked *south*. The side which looks *west* is marked *sunrise;* and the side which looks *east* is marked *sunset*.

8. In the annexed *diagram* a transverse section of the dial is represented where the *steps* are seen at one view *ascending* and *descending* to and *from* the gnomon or stile on the upper or sixth step. These steps are all equal in their height, but unequal on their upper surface, as the diagram shows, and for the reasons alleged above. Each of these steps might have been divided into parts or degrees, to mark the smaller divisions of time; and to this sort of division there appears to be a reference in the text, where it is said, *the shadow went back ten degrees*. It seems the miracle was wrought in the *afternoon*, for it is said, *The shadow was brought ten degrees* BACKWARD, *by which it had* GONE DOWN; so it appears that the shadow had reascended *ten* degrees on the afternoon steps; and when this was done, so that all were fully convinced of the miracle, the shadow again descended to its *true place* on the steps; and this would be the immediate consequence of dissipating the vapours which I have supposed to be the agent which God employed to produce, by *refraction*, this most extraordinary phenomenon.

A dial constructed in this way, in the *centre of a town*, or some *public place*, would serve, not only to give the *divisions of time*, but also as a place from which *proclamations* might be made; and especially from the *upper step*, where the speaker might stand by the *gnomon*, and be sufficiently elevated above the crowd below.

On such a place I have supposed Jehu to have been proclaimed king; and to do him honour his captains *spread their garments on the steps;* the *first, second, third, fourth*, and *fifth*, by which he ascended, to the *sixth step*, on which the *gnomon* was placed, and where he was proclaimed and acknowledged the king of Israel; for it is said, *The captains hasted, and took every man his* GARMENT, *and put* it *under him on the* TOP *of the* STAIRS, *and blew with trumpets, saying,* JEHU *is* KING! 2 Kings ix. 13; where see the note.

Pietro Nonius or *Nunnex*, a celebrated Portuguese mathematician about the middle of the *sixteenth* century, proved that the shadow on a stile in a sundial *might go backward without a miracle;* which was founded on the following theorem:—

"In all countries, the zenith of which is situated between the equator and the tropic, as long as the sun passes beyond the zenith, towards the apparent or elevated pole, he arrives *twice* before noon at the same azimuth; and the same thing takes place in the afternoon."

This gave rise to the demonstration that a dial might be constructed for any latitude on which the shadow shall *retrograde* or go *backward*. And it is effected in the following manner:—

Incline a plane turned directly *south* in such a manner that its zenith may fall between the tropic and equator; and nearly about the middle of the distance between these two circles.

In the latitude of London, for example, which is *fifty-one* degrees *thirty-one* minutes, the plane must make an angle of about *thirty-eight* degrees. In the middle of the plane fix an upright stile of such a length that its shadow shall go beyond the plane; and if several angular lines be then drawn from the bottom of the stile towards the *south*, about the time of the *solstice*, the shadow will retrograde twice in the course of the day, as mentioned above. This is evident, since the plane is parallel to the horizontal plane, having its zenith under the same meridian, at the distance of *twelve* degrees from the equator towards the *north;* the shadows of the two stiles must consequently move in the same manner in both.

Of these principles some have endeavoured to make an unholy use, contending that what the Holy Scriptures consider to be a *miracle*, in the case of the retrogradation of the shadow on the dial of Ahaz, was the effect of a mere *natural cause*, without any thing miraculous in it. On this subject Dr. *Hutton* very properly remarks: "It is very improbable, if the retrogradation which took place on the dial of that prince had been a natural effect, that it should not have been observed till the prophet announced it to him as the sign of his cure; for

in that case it must have always occurred when the sun was between the tropic and the zenith." *Hutton's* Mathematical Recreations, vol. iii. p. 323.

To this we may add, that if the dial of Ahaz had been thus constructed, the effect must have been generally known; and Hezekiah would never have taken that for a miracle which he and all his courtiers must have observed as an occurrence which at particular seasons, took place twice every day. And that the matter was known publicly to have been a *miracle* we learn from this circumstance: that Merodach-baladan, king of Babylon, sent his ambassadors to Jerusalem *to inquire after the wonder that was done in the land*, as well as after Hezekiah's health: see 2 Chron. xxxii. 31. But the miraculous interposition is so obvious, that infidelity must be driven to pitiful shifts when it is obliged to have recourse to the insinuation of imposture, in a case where the miraculous interference of God is so strikingly evident. Besides, such a dial could not be constructed for the latitude of Jerusalem without having the *north* end elevated *twenty* degrees *seven* minutes; which could not be used for the purpose which is indicated in the text. See No. 3 of the preceding observations.

SUPPOSED FORM OF THE SUNDIAL OF AHAZ

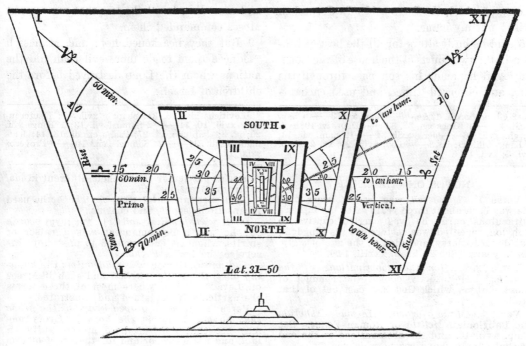

CHAPTER XXI

Manasseh succeeds his father Hezekiah, reigns fifty-five years, and fills Jerusalem and the whole land with abominable idolatry and murder, 1–9. God denounces the heaviest judgments against him and the land, 10–15. Manasseh's acts and death, 16–18. Amon his son succeeds him, and reigns two years; is equally profligate with his father; is slain by his servants, and buried in the garden of Uzza; and Josiah his son reigns in his stead, 19–26.

A. M. 3306–3361
B. C. 698–643
Olymp. XX. 3
—XXXIV. 2

MANASSEH [a]*was* twelve years old when he began to reign, and reigned fifty and five years in Jerusalem. And his mother's name *was* Hephzi-bah.

2 And he did *that which was* evil in the sight of the LORD, [b]after the abominations of the heathen, whom the LORD cast out before the children of Israel.

3 For he built up again the high places [c]which Hezekiah his father had destroyed; and he reared up altars for Baal, and made a grove, [d]as did Ahab king of Israel; and [e]worshipped all the host of heaven, and served them.

4 And [f]he built altars in the house of the LORD, of which the LORD said, [g]In Jerusalem will I put my name.

5 And he built altars for all the host of heaven in the two courts of the house of the LORD.

6 [h]And he made his son pass through the fire, and observed [i]times, and used enchant-

ments, and dealt with familiar spirits and wizards: he wrought much wickedness in the sight of the LORD, to provoke *him* to anger.

A. M. 3321
B. C. 683
Ol. XXIV. 2
Creonteu,
Arch. Athen.
annuo primo

7 And he set a graven image of the grove that he had made in the house, of which the LORD said to David, and to Solomon his son, [k]In this house and in Jerusalem, which I have chosen out of all tribes of Israel, will I put my name for ever:

A. M. 3306–3327
B. C. 698–677
Olymp. XX. 3
XXV. 4

8 [l]Neither will I make the feet of Israel move any more out of the land which I gave their fathers; only if they will observe to do according to all that I have commanded them, and according to all the law that my servant Moses commanded them.

9 But they hearkened not: and Manasseh [m]seduced them to do more evil than did the nations whom the LORD destroyed before the children of Israel.

---

[a]2 Chron. xxxiii. 1, &c.——[b]Chap. xvi. 3——[c]Chap. xviii. 4——[d]1 Kings xvi. 32, 33——[e]Deut. iv. 19; xvii. 3; ch. xvii. 16——[f]Jer. xxxii. 34——[g]2 Sam. vii. 13; 1 Kings viii. 29; ix. 3——[h]Lev. xviii. 21; xx. 2; chap. xvi. 3; xvii. 17

[i]Leviticus xix. 26, 31; chapter xvii. 17; Deuteronomy xviii. 10, 11——[k]2 Samuel vii. 13; 1 Kings viii. 29; ix. 3; chapter xxiii. 27; Psalm cxxxii. 13, 14; Jeremiah xxxii. 34——[l]2 Samuel vii. 10——[m]Proverbs xxix. 12

NOTES ON CHAP. XXI

Verse 1. *Manasseh was twelve years old*] He was born about three years after his father's miraculous cure; he was carried captive to Babylon, repented, was restored to his kingdom, put down idolatry, and died at the age of *sixty-seven* years. See 2 Chron. xxxiii. 1-20.

Verse 2. *After the abominations of the heathen*] He exactly copied the conduct of those nations which God had cast out of that land.

Verse 3. *Made a grove*] He made Asherah, the Babylonian *Melitta* or Roman *Venus*. See chap. xvii. 10, and the observations at the end of that chapter; and see here on ver. 7.

Worshipped all the host of heaven] All the *stars* and *planets*, but particularly the *sun* and the *moon*.

Verse 4. *Built altars*] He placed idolatrous altars even in the *temple*.

Verse 6. *Made his son pass through the fire*] Consecrated him to Moloch.

Observed times] וְעוֹנֵן *veonen;* he practised *divination* by the *clouds;* by observing their

course at particular times, their different kinds, contrary directions, &c., &c.

Used enchantments] וְנִחֵשׁ *venichesh;* he used incantations, spells, and charms.

Dealt with familiar spirits] וְעָשָׂה אוֹב *veasah ob;* he was a necromancer; was a raiser of spirits, whom he endeavoured to press into his service; he had a *Python.*

And wizards] וְיִדְּעֹנִים *veyiddeonim;* the knowing ones, the *white witches*, and such like; see on Lev. xix. 26-31, where most of these terms are particularly explained and illustrated.

Verse 7. *He set a graven image of the grove that he had made in the house*] Every one may see that *Asherah* here must signify an *idol*, and not a *grove;* and for the proof of this see the observations at the end of the chapter.

Verse 8. *Neither will I make the feet of Israel*] Had they been faithful to God's testimonies they never had gone into captivity, and should even at this day have been in possession of the promised land.

Verse 9. *Seduced them to do more evil*] He did all he could to pervert the national character, and totally destroy the worship of the true God; and he succeeded.

A. M. 3306–3327
B. C. 698–677
Olymp. XX. 3
XXV. 4

10 And the LORD spake by his
servants the prophets, saying,
11 [n]Because Manasseh king
of Judah hath done these abominations, [o]*and*
hath done wickedly above all that the Amorites did, which *were* before him, and [p]hath
made Judah also to sin with his idols:
12 Therefore thus saith the LORD God of
Israel, Behold, I *am* bringing *such* evil upon
Jerusalem and Judah, that whosoever heareth
of it, both [q]his ears shall tingle.
13 And I will stretch over Jerusalem [r]the
line of Samaria, and the plummet of the house
of Ahab: and I will wipe Jerusalem as *a man*
wipeth a dish, [s]wiping *it*, and turning *it* upside down.
14 And I will forsake the remnant of mine
inheritance, and deliver them into the hand of
their enemies; and they shall
become a prey and a spoil to all
their enemies;

A. M. 3306–3327
B. C. 698–677
Olymp. XX. 3
XXV. 4

15 Because they have done *that which*
was evil in my sight, and have provoked
me to anger, since the day their fathers
came forth out of Egypt, even unto this
day.
16 [t]Moreover Manasseh shed innocent blood
very much, till he had filled Jerusalem [u]from
one end to another; beside his sin wherewith
he made Judah to sin, in doing *that which*
was evil in the sight of the LORD.
17 Now [v]the rest of the acts
of Manasseh, and all that he
did, and his sin that he sinned,
are they not written in the book of the chronicles of the kings of Judah?

A. M. 3306–3361
B. C. 698–643
Olymp. XX. 3
—XXXIV. 2

---

[n]Chap. xxiii. 26, 27; xxiv. 3, 4; Jer. xv. 4——[o]1 Kings xxi, 26——[p]Ver. 9——[q]1 Sam. iii. 11; Jer. xix. 3
[r]See Isa. xxxiv. 11; Lam. ii. 8; Amos vii. 7, 8

[s]Heb. *he wipeth and turneth* it *upon the face thereof*
[t]Chap. xxiv. 4——[u]Heb. *from mouth to mouth*——[v]2 Chron. xxxiii. 11–19

Verse 10. *The Lord spake by—the prophets*] The prophets were Hosea, Joel, Nahum, Habakkuk, and Isaiah. These five following verses contain the sum of what these prophets spoke. It is said that Isaiah not only prophesied in those days, but also that he was put to death by Manasseh, being *sawn asunder by a wooden saw.*

Verse 12. *Both his ears shall tingle.*] תצלנה *titstsalnah;* something expressive of the *sound* in what we call, from the same sensation, the *tingling* of the ears. This is the consequence of having the ears suddenly pierced with a *loud* and *shrill noise;* the ears seem to *ring* for some time after. The prophets spoke to them vehemently, so that the sound seemed to be continued even when they had left off speaking. This was a faithful and solemn testimony.

Verse 13. *The line of Samaria*] I will treat Jerusalem as I have treated Samaria. Samaria was taken, pillaged, ruined, and its inhabitants led into captivity; Jerusalem shall have the same *measure.*

And the plummet of the house of Ahab] The house of Ahab was totally destroyed, and not a man of his race left to sit upon the throne of Israel: so shall it be done to the house or royal family of Judah; they shall be all finally destroyed, and not a man of their race shall any more sit on the throne of Judah; nor shall Judah have a throne to sit on. Thus Jerusalem shall have the same *weight* as well as the same *measure* as Samaria, because it has copied all the abominations which brought that kingdom to total destruction.

I will wipe Jerusalem as a man *wipeth a dish*] The Vulgate translates this clause as follows: *Delebo Jerusalem, sicut deleri solent tabulæ;* "I will blot out Jerusalem as tablets are wont to be blotted out." This is a metaphor taken from the ancient method of writing: they traced their letters with a stile on boards thinly spread over with *wax;* for this purpose one end of the stile was *sharp,* the other end blunt and smooth, with which they could rub out what they had written, and so smooth the place and spread back the wax, as to render it capable of receiving any other word. Thus the Lord had written down Jerusalem, never intending that its name or its memorial should be blotted out. It was written down *The Holy City, The City of the Great King;* but now God turns the stile and blots this out; and the Holy Jerusalem, the City of the Great King, is no longer to be found! This double use of the stile is pointed out in this ancient *enigma:*—

De summo planus; sed non ego planus in imo:
Versor utrinque manu, diverso et munere fungor:
Altera pars revocat, quicquid pars altera fecit.

"I am flat at the top, but sharp at the bottom;
I turn either end, and perform a double function:
One end destroys what the other end has made."

But the idea of *emptying out* and *wiping a dish* expresses the same meaning equally well. Jerusalem shall be emptied of all its wealth, and of all its inhabitants, as truly as a dish turned up is emptied of all its contents; and *it shall be turned upside down,* never to be filled again. This is true from that time to the present hour. Jerusalem is the *dish turned upside down,* the *tablet blotted out* to the present day! How great are God's mercies! and how terrible his judgments!

Verse 14. *I will forsake the remnant of mine inheritance*] One part (the *ten tribes*) was already forsaken, and carried into captivity; the *remnant* (the *tribe of Judah*) was now about to be forsaken.

Verse 16. *Shed innocent blood very much*] Like the deities he worshipped, he was *fierce* and *cruel;* an unprincipled, merciless tyrant: he slew innocent people and God's prophets.

Verse 17. *Now the rest of the acts*] In 2

A. M. 3361
B. C. 643
Ol. XXXIV. 2
An. Tulli Hostilii, Regis Romanorum, 30

18 ʷAnd Manasseh slept with his fathers, and was buried in the garden of his own house, in the garden of Uzza: and Amon his son reigned in his stead.

A. M. 3361–3363
B. C. 643–641
Ol. XXXIV. 2–4

19 ˣAmon *was* twenty and two years old when he began to reign, and he reigned two years in Jerusalem. And his mother's name *was* Meshullemeth, the daughter of Haruz of Jotbah.

20 And he did *that which was* evil in the sight of the LORD, ʸas his father Manasseh did.

21 And he walked in all the way that his father walked in, and served the idols that his father served, and worshipped them:

22 And he ᶻforsook the LORD God of his

fathers, and walked not in the way of the LORD.

A. M. 3363
B. C. 641
Ol. XXXIV. 4
An. Tulli Hostilii, Regis Romanorum, 32

23 ᵃAnd the servants of Amon conspired against him, and slew the king in his own house.

24 And the people of the land slew all them that had conspired against King Amon; and the people of the land made Josiah his son king in his stead.

25 Now the rest of the acts of Amon which he did, *are* they not written in the book of the chronicles of the kings of Judah?

A. M. 3361–3363
B. C. 643–641
Ol. XXXIV. 2–4

A. M. 3363
B. C. 641
Ol. XXXIV. 4
An. Tulli Hostilii, Regis Romanorum, 30

26 And he was buried in his sepulchre in the garden of Uzza: and ᵇJosiah his son reigned in his stead.

ʷ2 Chron. xxxiii. 20——ˣ2 Chron. xxxiii. 21–23
ʸVerse 2, &c.

ᵃ1 Kings xi. 33——ᵃ2 Chron. xxxiii. 24, 25——ᵇMatt.
i. 10, called *Josias*

Chron. xxxiii. 11, &c., we read that the Assyrians took Manasseh, bound him with fetters, and took him to Babylon; that there he repented, sought God, and was, we are not told how, restored to his kingdom; that he fortified the city of David, destroyed idolatry, restored the worship of the true God, and died in peace.

In 2 Chron. xxxiii. 18, 19, *His prayer unto God* is particularly mentioned. What is called his prayer, is found in the *Apocrypha*, just before the first book of the *Maccabees*. There are some good sentiments in it; but whether it be that which was made by Manasseh is more than can be proved. Even the Romish Church have not received it among the canonical books.

Are *they not written*] There are several particulars referred to here, and in 2 Chron. chap. xxxiii., which are not found in any chronicles or books which now remain, and what the *books of the seers* were, mentioned in Chronicles, we cannot tell.

Verse 18. *In the garden of his own house*] It was probably a burying-place made for his own family, for Amon his son is said to be buried in the same place, ver. 26.

Verse 19. *He reigned two years in Jerusalem.*] The remark of the rabbins is not wholly without foundation, that the sons of those kings who were idolaters, and who succeeded their fathers, seldom reigned more than *two years.* So *Nadab,* the son of Jeroboam, 1 Kings xv. 25; *Elah,* the son of Baasha, 1 Kings xvi. 8; *Ahaziah,* the son of Ahab, 1 Kings xxii. 51; and *Amon,* the son of Manasseh, as mentioned here, ver. 19.

Verse 23. *The servants of Amon conspired*] What their reason was for slaying their king we cannot tell. It does not seem to have been a popular act, for the people of the land rose up and slew the *regicides.* We hear enough of this man when we hear that he was as bad as his father was in the beginning of his reign, but did not copy his father's repentance.

Verse 26. *The garden of Uzza*] The family sepulchre or burying-place.

IT is said ver. 3 and 7, that "Manasseh made a grove; and he set a graven image of the grove," &c. וישם את פסל האשרה אשר עשה *vaiyasem eth pesel haasherah, asher asah:* "And he put the graven image of *Asherah,* which he had made," into the house.

Asherah, which we translate *grove,* is undoubtedly the name of an idol; and probably of one which was carved out of wood.

R. S. Jarchi, on Gen. xii. 3, says, "that אשרה *asherah* means a *tree* which was worshipped by the Gentiles;" like as the oak was worshipped by the ancient Druids in Britain.

Castel, in Lex. Hept. sub voce אשר, defines אשרה *asherah* thus, *Simulacrum ligneum* Astartæ *dicatum;* "A wooden image dedicated to *Astrate* or *Venus.*"

The *Septuagint* render the words by αλσος; and *Flamminius Nobilis,* on 2 Kings xxiii. 4, says *Rursus notat Theodoretus* το αλσος *esse Astartem et Venerem, et ab aliis interpretibus dictum Ashatroth;* i. e. "Again *Theodoret* observes, αλσος is *Astarte* and *Venus;* and by other interpreters called *Ashtaroth.*"

The *Targum* of *Ben Uzziel,* on Deut. vii. 5, ואשירהם תגדעון *vaasheyrehem tegaddeun;* i. e., "Their groves shall ye cut down"—translates the place thus, ואילני סינדיהון תקצצון *veilaney sigedeyhon tekatsetsun;* "And the oaks of their adoration shall ye cut down."

From the above it is pretty evident that *idols,* not *groves,* are generally intended where אשרה *asherah* and its derivatives are used.

Here follow proofs:—

In chap. xxiii. 6, it is said that "Josiah brought out the grove from the house of the Lord." This translation seems very absurd; for what *grove* could there be in the temple? There was none planted there, nor was there room for any. The plain meaning of ויצא את האשרה מבית יהוה *vaiyotse eth haasherah mibbeyth Yehovah,* is, "And he brought out the (goddess) *Asherah* from the house of the Lord, and burnt it," &c.

That this is the true meaning of the place appears farther from ver. 7, where it is said, "He broke down the houses of the sodomites," (הקדשים *hakkedeshim*, of the *whoremongers*,) "where the women wove hangings for the grove" (בתים לאשרה *bottim laasherah*, "houses or shrines for *Asherah*.") Similar perhaps to those which the silversmiths made for *Diana*, Acts xix. 24. It is rather absurd to suppose that the women were employed in making curtains to encompass a *grove*.

The *Syriac* and *Arabic* versions countenance the interpretation I have given above. In ver. 6, the former says, "He cast out the idol, ܕܚܠܬܐ *dechlotho*, from the house of the Lord;" and in

ver. 7: "He threw down the houses, ܕܙܘܢܐ *dazoine*, of the prostitutes; and the women who wove garments, ܠܕܚܠܬܐ *ledechlotho*, for the idols which were there." The *Arabic* is exactly the same.

From the whole it is evident that Asherah was no other than *Venus;* the nature of whose worship is plain enough from the mention of *whoremongers* and *prostitutes*.

I deny not that there were groves consecrated to idolatrous worship among the Gentiles, but I am sure that such are not intended in the above-cited passages; and the text, in most places, reads better when understood in this way.

CHAPTER XXII

Josiah succeeds Amon his father, and reigns thirty-one *years,* 1, 2. *He repairs the breaches of the temple,* 3–7. *Hilkiah finds the book of the law in the temple,* 8. *It is read by Shaphan the scribe, before the king and his servants,* 9, 10. *The king, greatly affected, sends to inquire of Huldah the prophetess,* 11–13. *She delivers an afflictive prophecy concerning the evils that were coming upon the land,* 14–17. *But promises Josiah that these evils shall not come in his time,* 18–20.

A. M. 3363–3394
B. C. 641–610
Ol. XXXIV. 4
—XLII. 3

JOSIAH [a]*was* eight years old when he began to reign, and he reigned thirty and one years in Jerusalem. And his mother's name *was* Jedidah, the daughter of Adaiah of [b]Boscath.

2 And he did *that which was* right in the sight of the Lord, and walked in all the way of David his father, and [c]turned not aside to the right hand or to the left.

A. M. 3380
B. C. 624
Ol. XXXIX. 1
An. Anci Martii,
Regis Romano-
rum, 17

3 [d]And it came to pass in the eighteenth year of King Josiah, *that* the king sent Shaphan the son of Azaliah, the son of Meshullam, the scribe, to the house of the Lord, saying,

4 Go up to Hilkiah the high priest, that he may sum the silver which is [e]brought into the

house of the Lord, which [f]the keepers of the [g]door have gathered of the people:

A. M. 3380
B. C. 624
Ol. XXXIX. 1
An. Anci Martii,
Regis Romano-
rum, 17

5 And let them [h]deliver it into the hand of the doers of the work, that have the oversight of the house of the Lord: and let them give it to the doers of the work which *is* in the house of the Lord, to repair the breaches of the house,

6 Unto carpenters, and builders, and masons, and to buy timber and hewn stone to repair the house.

7 Howbeit [i]there was no reckoning made with them of the money that was delivered into their hand, because they dealt faithfully.

8 And Hilkiah the high priest said unto Shaphan the scribe, [k]I have found the book

---

[a]2 Chronicles xxxiv. 1——[b]Joshua xv. 39——[c]Deuteronomy v. 32——[d]2 Chronicles xxxiv. 8, &c. [e]Chapter xii. 4——[f]Chapter xii. 9; Psalm lxxxiv.

10——[g]Hebrew, *threshold*——[h]Chapter xii. 11, 12, 14——[i]Chapter xii. 15——[k]Deuteronomy xxxi. 24, &c.; 2 Chron. xxxiv. 14, &c.

NOTES ON CHAP. XXII

Verse 1. *Josiah* was *eight years old*] He was one of the best, if not the best, of all the Jewish kings since the time of David. He began well, continued well, and ended well.

Verse 4. *That he may sum the silver*] As Josiah began to seek the Lord as soon as he began to reign, we may naturally conclude that the worship of God that was neglected and suppressed by his father, was immediately restored; and the people began their accustomed offerings to the temple. Ten years therefore had elapsed since these offerings began; no one had, as yet, taken account of them; nor were they applied to the use for which they were given, viz., the repairing the breaches of the temple.

Verse 8. *I have found the book of the law*] Was this the *autograph* of Moses? It is very

probable that it was, for in the parallel place, 2 Chron. xxxiv. 14, it is said to be the book of *the law of the Lord by Moses*. It is supposed to be that part of Deuteronomy, (xxviii., xxix., xxx., and xxxi.,) which contains the renewing of the covenant in the plains of Moab, and which contains the most terrible invectives against the corrupters of God's word and worship.

The rabbins say that Ahaz, Manasseh, and Amon endeavoured to destroy all the copies of the law, and this only was saved by having been buried under a paving-stone. It is scarcely reasonable to suppose that this was the *only copy* of the law that was found in Judea; for even if we grant that Ahaz, Manasseh, and Amon had endeavoured to destroy all the books of the law, yet they could not have succeeded so as to destroy the whole. Besides, Manasseh endeavoured after his conversion to *restore*

A. M. 3380
B. C. 624
Ol. XXXIX. 1
An. Anci Martii,
Regis Romano-
rum, 17 of the law in the house of the
Lord. And Hilkiah gave the
book to Shaphan, and he
read it.

9 And Shaphan the scribe came to the king,
and brought the king word again, and said,
Thy servants have ¹gathered the money that
was found in the house, and have delivered it
into the hand of them that do the work, that
have the oversight of the house of the Lord.

10 And Shaphan the scribe showed the king,
saying, Hilkiah the priest hath delivered me a
book. And Shaphan read it before the king.

11 And it came to pass, when the king had
heard the words of the book of the law, that
he rent his clothes.

12 And the king commanded Hilkiah the
priest, and Ahikam the son of Shaphan, and
ᵐAchbor the son of ⁿMichaiah, and Shaphan
the scribe, and Asahiah a servant of the king,
saying,

13 Go ye, inquire of the Lord for me, and
for the people, and for all Judah, concerning

the words of this book that is A. M. 3380
B. C. 624
Ol. XXXIX.
An. Anci Martii,
Regis Romano-
rum, 17
found: for great *is* °the wrath
of the Lord that is kindled
against us, because our fathers
have not hearkened unto the words of this
book, to do according unto all that which is
written concerning us.

14 So Hilkiah the priest, and Ahikam, and
Achbor, and Shaphan, and Asahiah, went unto
Huldah the prophetess, the wife of Shallum
the son of ᵖTikvah, the son of ۹Harhas, keeper
of the ʳwardrobe; (now she dwelt in Jerusalem ˢin the college;) and they communed
with her.

15 And she said unto them, Thus saith the
Lord God of Israel, Tell the man that sent
you to me,

16 Thus saith the Lord, Behold, ᵗI will
bring evil upon this place, and upon the inhabitants thereof, *even* all the words of the book
which the king of Judah hath read:

17 ᵘBecause they have forsaken me, and
have burned incense unto other gods, that they

---

¹Heb. *melted*——ᵐAbdon, 2 Chron. xxxiv. 20——ⁿOr,
Micah——°Deut. xxix. 27——ᵖ*Tikvath*, 2 Chron. xxxiv.
22——۹Or, *Hasrah*

ʳHebrew, *garments*——ˢOr, *in the second part*
ᵗDeut. xxix. 27; Daniel ix. 11, 12, 13, 14——ᵘDeut.
xxix. 25, 26, 27

---

every part of the Divine worship, and in this
he could have done nothing without the Pentateuch; and the succeeding reign of Amon was
too short to give him opportunity to undo
every thing that his penitent father had reformed. Add to all these considerations, that
in the time of Jehoshaphat teaching from the
law was *universal* in the land, for he set on
foot an *itinerant ministry*, in order to instruct
the people fully: for "he sent to his princes to
teach in the cities of Judah; and with them he
sent Levites and priests; and they went about
through all the cities of Judah, and taught the
people, having the book of the Lord with
them;" see 2 Chron. xvii. 7-9. And if there be
any thing wanting to show the improbability
of the thing, it must be this, that the transactions mentioned here took place in the *eighteenth* year of the reign of Josiah, who had,
from the time he came to the throne, employed
himself in the restoration of the pure worship
of God; and it is not likely that during these
eighteen years he was without a copy of the
Pentateuch. The simple fact seems to be this,
that this was the original of the covenant renewed by Moses with the people in the plains
of Moab, and which he ordered to be laid up
beside the ark; (Deut. xxxi. 26;) and now
being unexpectedly found, its *antiquity*, the
occasion of its being made, the present *circumstances* of the people, the *imperfect state* in
which the reformation was as yet, after all that
had been done, would all concur to produce the
effect here mentioned on the mind of the pious
Josiah.

Verse 14. *Went unto Huldah the prophetess*]

This is a most singular circumstance: At this
time *Jeremiah* was certainly a prophet in Israel, but it is likely he now dwelt at *Anathoth*,
and could not be readily consulted; *Zephaniah*
also prophesied under this reign, but probably
he had not yet *begun; Hilkiah* was *high priest*,
and the priest's lips should retain knowledge.
Shaphan was *scribe*, and must have been conversant in sacred affairs to have been at all
fit for his office; and yet *Huldah*, a prophetess,
of whom we know nothing but by this circumstance, is consulted on the meaning of the book
of the law; for the secret of the Lord was
neither with *Hilkiah* the high priest, *Shaphan*
the scribe, nor any other of the *servants* of the
king, or *ministers* of the *temple!* We find from
this, and we have many facts in all ages to
corroborate it, that a pontiff, a pope, a bishop,
or a priest, may, in some cases, not possess the
true knowledge of God; and that a simple
woman, possessing the life of God in her soul,
may have more knowledge of the Divine testimonies than many of those whose office it is to
explain and enforce them.

On this subject Dr. Priestley in his note
makes the following very judicious remark:
—"It pleased God to distinguish several women
with the spirit of prophecy, as well as other
great attainments, to show that in his sight,
and especially in things of a *spiritual nature*,
there is no essential pre-eminence in the male
sex, though in some things the female be subject to the male."

Verse 17. *My wrath shall be kindled*] The
decree is gone forth; Jerusalem shall be delivered into the hands of its enemies; the peo-

A. M. 3380
B. C. 624
Ol. XXXIX. 1
An. Anci Martii,
Regis Romano-
rum, 17

might provoke me to anger with all the works of their hands; therefore my wrath shall be kindled against this place, and shall not be quenched.

18 But to ᵛthe king of Judah which sent you to inquire of the LORD, thus shall ye say to him, Thus saith the LORD God of Israel, *As touching* the words which thou hast heard;

19 Because thine ʷheart was tender, and thou hast ˣhumbled thyself before the LORD,

when thou heardest what I spake against this place, and against the inhabitants thereof, that they should become ʸa desolation and ᶻa curse, and hast rent thy clothes, and wept before me; I also have heard *thee*, saith the LORD.

20 Behold, therefore, I will gather thee unto thy fathers, and thou ᵃshalt be gathered into thy grave in peace; and thine eyes shall not see all the evil which I will bring upon this place. And they brought the king word again.

A. M. 3380
B. C. 624
Ol. XXXIX. 1
An. Anci Martii,
Regis Romano-
rum, 17

ᵛ2 Chron. xxxiv. 26, &c.——ʷPsa. li. 17; Isa. lvii. 15
ˣ1 Kings xxi. 29

ʸLev. xxvi. 31, 32——ᶻJer. xxvi. 6; xliv. 22——ᵃPsa. xxxvii. 37; Isa. lvii. 1, 2

---

ple will revolt more and more; towards them longsuffering is useless; the *wrath of God is kindled, and shall not be quenched.* This was a dreadful message.

Verse 19. *Because thine heart was tender*] Because thou hast feared the Lord, and trembled at his word, and hast wept before me, I have heard thee, so far that these evils shall not come upon the land in thy lifetime.

Verse 20. *Thou shalt be gathered into thy grave in peace*] During thy life *none of these calamities* shall fall upon the people, and no *adversary* shall be permitted to disturb the peace of Judea, and thou shalt die in peace with God. But was Josiah *gathered to the grave in peace?* Is it not said, chap. xxiii. 29, that Pharaoh-nechoh slew him at Megiddo? On this we may remark, that the Assyrians and the Jews were at peace; that Josiah might feel it his duty to oppose the Egyptian king going against his friend and ally, and endeavour to prevent him from passing through his territories; and that in his endeavours to oppose him he was mortally wounded at Megiddo: but certainly was not killed *there;* for his servants put him in his second chariot and brought him to *Jerusalem,* where he died in peace. See *2 Chron.* xxxv. 24. So that, however we take the place here, we shall find that the words of Huldah were true: he *did die in peace,* and *was gathered to his fathers in peace.*

FROM the account in the above chapter, where we have this business detailed, we find that

Josiah should not have meddled in the quarrel between the Egyptian and the Assyrian kings, for God had given a commission to the former against the latter; but he did it in error, and suffered for it. But this unfortunate end of this pious man does not at all impeach the credit of Huldah; he died in peace in his own kingdom. He died in peace with God, and there was neither war nor desolation in his land: nor did the king of Egypt proceed any farther against the Jews during his life; for he said, "What have I to do with thee, thou king of Judah? I come not against thee, but the house wherewith I have war; for God commanded me to make haste: forbear then from meddling with God, who is with me, that he destroy thee not. Nevertheless, Josiah would not turn his face from him, and hearkened not to the words of Nechoh, from the mouth of God. And the archers shot at King Josiah: and the king said, Bear me away, for I am sore wounded. And his servants took him out of that chariot, and put him in the second chariot, and they brought him to Jerusalem, and he died and was buried in the sepulchre of his fathers;" 2 Chron. xxxv. 21-24.

It seems as if the Egyptian king had brought his troops by sea to Cæsarea, and wished to cross the Jordan about the southern point of the sea of Tiberias, that he might get as speedily as possible into the Assyrian dependencies; and that he took this road, for *God,* as he said, *had commanded him to make haste.*

CHAPTER XXIII

Josiah reads in the temple to the elders of Judah, the priests, the prophets, and the people, the book of the covenant which had been found, 1, 2. *He makes a covenant, and the people stand to it,* 3. *He destroys the vessels of Baal and Asherah, and puts down the idolatrous priests; breaks down the houses of the sodomites, and the high places; defiles Topheth; takes away the horses of the sun; destroys the altars of Ahaz; breaks in pieces the images; and breaks down and burns Jeroboam's altar at Beth-el,* 4-15. *Fulfils the word of the prophet, who cried against the altar at Beth-el,* 16-18. *Destroys the high places in Samaria, slays the idolatrous priests, and celebrates a great passover,* 19-23; *and puts away all the dealers with familiar spirits, &c.,* 24. *His eminent character; he is mortally wounded at Megiddo, and buried at Jerusalem,* 25-30. *Jehoahaz reigns in his stead, and does evil in the sight of the Lord,* 31, 32. *Is dethroned by Pharaoh-nechoh; and Eliakim, his brother, called also Jehoiakim, made king in his stead; the land is laid under tribute by the king of Egypt, and Jehoiakim reigns wickedly,* 33-37.

A. M. 3380
B. C. 624
Ol. XXXIX. 1
An. Anci Martii,
Regis Romano-
rum, 17

AND [a]the king sent, and they gathered unto him all the elders of Judah and of Jerusalem.

2 And the king went up into the house of the LORD, and all the men of Judah and all the inhabitants of Jerusalem with him, and the priests, and the prophets, and all the people, [b]both small and great: and he read in their ears all the words of the book of the covenant [c]which was found in the house of the LORD.

3 And the king [d]stood by a pillar, and made a covenant before the LORD, to walk after the LORD, and to keep his commandments and his testimonies and his statutes with all *their* heart and all *their* soul, to perform the words of this covenant that were written in this book. And all the people stood to the covenant.

4 And the king commanded Hilkiah the high priest, and the priests of the second order, and the keepers of the door, to bring

forth out of the temple of the LORD all the vessels that were made for Baal, and for [e]the grove, and for all the host of heaven: and he burned them without Jerusalem, in the fields of Kidron, and carried the ashes of them unto Beth-el.

A. M. 3380
B. C. 624
Ol. XXXIX. 1
An. Anci Martii,
Regis Romano-
rum, 17

5 And he [f]put down [g]the idolatrous priests, whom the kings of Judah had ordained to burn incense in the high places in the cities of Judah, and in the places round about Jerusalem; them also that burned incense unto Baal, to the sun, and to the moon, and to the [h]planets, and to [i]all the host of heaven.

6 And he brought out the [k]grove from the house of the LORD, without Jerusalem, unto the brook Kidron, and burned it at the brook Kidron, and stamped *it* small to powder, and cast the powder thereof upon [l]the graves of the children of the people.

---

[a]2 Chron. xxxiv. 29, 30, &c.——[b]Heb. *from small even unto great*——[c]Chap. xxii. 8——[d]Chap. xi. 14, 17 [e]Chap. xxi. 3, 7——[f]Heb. *caused to cease*

[g]Heb. *chemarim;* Hosea x. 5; foretold, Zeph. i. 4 [h]Or, *twelve signs* or *constellations*——[i]Chap. xxi. 3 [k]Chap. xxi. 7——[l]2 Chron. xxxiv. 4

NOTES ON CHAP. XXIII

Verse 2. *The king went up into the house of the Lord*] Here is another very singular circumstance. The high priest, scribes, priest, and prophets, are gathered together, with all the elders of the people, and the king *himself* reads the book of the covenant which had been lately found! It is strange that either the high priest, Jeremiah, Zephaniah, or some other of the prophets, who were certainly there present, did not read the sacred book! It is likely that the king considered himself a *mediator* between God and them, and therefore read and made the covenant.

Verse 3. *Stood by a pillar*] He stood, עַל הָעַמּוּד *al haammud*, "upon the *stairs* or *pulpit*." This is what is called the *brazen scaffold* or *pulpit* which Solomon made, and on which the kings were accustomed to stand when they addressed the people. See 2 Chron. vi. 13, and the parallel places.

Made a covenant] This was expressed, 1. In *general*. To walk after Jehovah; to have no gods besides him. 2. To take his law for the regulation of their *conduct*. 3. In *particular*. To bend their whole heart and soul to the observance of it, so that they might not only have *religion* without, but *piety* within. To this *all the people stood up*, thus giving their consent, and binding themselves to obedience.

Verse 4. *The priests of the second order*] These were probably such as supplied the place of the high priest when he was prevented from fulfilling the functions of his office. So the Chaldee understood the place—*the sagan of the high priests*. But the words may refer to those of the *second course* or *order* established by David: though it does not appear that those orders were now in use, yet the *distinction* was

continued even to the time of our Lord. We find the *course of Abia*, which was the *eighth*, mentioned Luke i. 5; where see the note.

All the vessels] These *had* been used for idolatrous purposes; the king is now to destroy them; for although no longer used in this way, they might, if permitted to remain, be an incentive to idolatry at a future time.

Verse 5. *The idolatrous priests*] הכמרים *hakkemarim*. Who these were is not well known. The *Chaldee*, *Syriac*, and *Arabic*, call them the *priests* simply, *which the kings of Judah had ordained*. Probably they were an *order* made by the idolatrous kings of Judah, and called *kemarim*, from כמר *camar*, which signifies to be *scorched*, *shrivelled together*, *made dark*, or *black*, because their business was constantly to attend *sacrificial fires*, and probably they were *black garments;* hence the Jews in derision call Christian ministers *kemarim*, because of their *black clothes* and *garments*. Why we should *imitate*, in our *sacerdotal dress*, those priests of Baal, is strange to think and hard to tell.

Unto Baal, to the sun] Though *Baal* was certainly the *sun*, yet here they are distinguished; Baal being worshipped under different forms and attributes, *Baal-peor, Baal-zephon, Baal-zebub*, &c.

The planets] מזלות *mazzaloth*. The *Vulgate* translates this *the twelve signs*, i. e., the *zodiac*. This is as likely as any of the other conjectures which have been published relative to this word. See a similar word Job xxxvii. 9, and xxxviii. 32.

Verse 6. *He brought out the grove*] He brought out the idol Asherah. See at the end of chap. xxi.

Upon the graves of the children of the people.] I believe this means the burial-place of the common people.

A. M. 3380
B. C. 624
Ol. XXXIX. 1
An. Anci Martii,
Regis Romano-
rum, 17

7 And he brake down the houses ^mof the sodomites, that *were* by the house of the LORD, ⁿwhere the women wove ^ohangings for the grove.

8 And he brought all the priests out of the cities of Judah, and defiled the high places where the priests had burned incense, from ^pGeba to Beer-sheba, and brake down the high places of the gates that *were* in the entering in of the gate of Joshua the governor of the city, which *were* on a man's left hand at the gate of the city.

9 ^qNevertheless the priests of the high places came not up to the altar of the LORD in Jerusalem, ^rbut they did eat of the unleavened bread among their brethren.

10 And he defiled ^sTopheth, which *is* in ^tthe valley of the children of Hinnom, ^uthat no man might make his son or his daughter to pass through the fire to Molech.

A. M. 3380
B. C. 624
Ol. XXXIX. 1
An. Anci Martii,
Regis Romano-
rum, 17

11 And he took away the horses that the kings of Judah had given to the sun, at the entering in of the house of the LORD, by the chamber of Nathan-melech the ^vchamberlain, which *was* in the suburbs, and burned the chariots of the sun with fire.

12 And the altars that *were* ^won the top of the upper chamber of Ahaz, which the kings of Judah had made, and the altars which ^xManasseh had made in the two courts of the house of the LORD, did the king beat down, and ^ybrake *them* down from thence, and cast the dust of them into the brook Kidron.

13 And the high places that *were* before Jerusalem, which *were* on the right hand of ^zthe mount of corruption, which ^aSolomon the king of Israel had builded for Ashtoreth the abomination of the Zidonians, and for Chemosh the abomination of the Moabites, and for Milcom the abomination of the chil-

---

^m1 Kings xiv. 24; xv. 12——ⁿEzek. xvi. 16——^oHeb. *houses*——^p1 Kings xv. 22——^qSee Ezek. xliv. 10–14 ^r1 Sam. ii. 36——^sIsa. xxx. 33; Jer. vii. 31; xix. 6, 11, 12, 13——^tJosh. xv. 8

^uLev. xviii. 21; Deut. xviii. 10; Ezek. xxiii. 37, 39 ^vOr, *eunuch* or *officer*——^wSee Jer. xix. 13; Zeph. i. 5 ^xChap. xxi. 5——^yOr, *ran from thence*——^zThat is, the mount of Olives——^a1 Kings xi. 7

Verse 7. *The houses of the sodomites*] We have already often met with these קדשים *kedeshim* or *consecrated persons.* The word implies all kinds of *prostitutes*, as well as *abusers of themselves with mankind.*

Wove hangings for the grove.] For *Asherah;* curtains or tent coverings for the places where the rites of the impure goddess were performed. See at the end of chap. xxi.

Verse 8. *The gate of Joshua*] The place where he, as governor of the city, heard and decided causes. Near this we find there were public altars, where sometimes the true God, at other times false gods, were honoured.

Verse 9. *The priests of the high places came not up*] As these priests had offered sacrifices on the *high places*, though it was to the *true God*, yet they were not thought proper to be employed *immediately* about the *temple;* but as they were acknowledged to belong to the *priest-hood*, they had a right to their support; therefore a portion of the tithes, offerings, and unleavened bread, shew-bread, &c., was appointed to them for their support. Thus they were treated as *priests* who had some infirmity which rendered it improper for them to minister at the altar. See Lev. xxi. 17, &c., and particularly verses 22 and 23.

Verse 10. *He defiled Topheth*] St. Jerome says that Topheth was a fine and pleasant place, well watered with fountains, and adorned with gardens. The valley of the son of Hinnom, or *Gehenna*, was in one part; here it appears the sacred rites of Molech were performed, and to this all the filth of the city was carried, and perpetual fires were kept up in order to consume it. Hence it has been considered a *type* of *hell;* and in this sense it is used in the New Testament.

It is here said that Josiah *defiled* this place

that no man might make his son or his daughter to pass through the fire. He destroyed the *image* of Molech, and so polluted the place where he stood, or his temple, that it was rendered in every way abominable. The rabbins say that Topheth had its name from תף *toph*, a *drum*, because instruments of this kind were used to drown the cries of the children that were put into the burning arms of Molech, to be scorched to death. This may be as true as the following definition: "Topheth, or the valley of the son of Hinnom, was a place near Jerusalem, where the filth and offal of the city were thrown, and where a constant fire was kept up to consume the wretched remains of executed criminals. It was a human shambles, a public chopping-block, where the arms and legs of men and women were quartered off by thousands." *Query*, On what *authority* do such descriptions rest?

Verse 11. *The horses that the kings of Judah had given to the sun.*] *Jarchi* says that those who adored the *sun* had *horses* which they mounted every morning to go out to meet the sun at his rising. Throughout the East the *horse*, because of his *swiftness* and *utility*, was dedicated to the *sun;* and the Greeks and Romans feigned that the *chariot of the sun* was drawn by *four horses*—Pyroeis, Eous, Æthon, and Phlegon. See the note on chap. ii.

Whether these were *living* or *sculptured* horses, we cannot tell; the latter is the more *reasonable* supposition.

Verse 12. *On the top of the upper chamber*] Altars built on the *flat roof* of the house. Such altars were erected to the *sun, moon, stars*, &c.

Verse 13. *Mount of corruption*] This, says *Jarchi*, following the *Chaldee*, was the mount of *Olives*, for this is the mount המשחה *ham-*

A. M. 3380
B. C. 624
Ol. XXXIX. 1
An.Anci Martii,
Regis Romano-
rum, 17
dren of Ammon, did the king defile.

14 And he [b]brake in pieces the [c]images, and cut down the groves, and filled their places with the bones of men.

15 Moreover the altar that *was* at Beth-el, *and* the high place [d]which Jeroboam the son of Nebat, who made Israel to sin, had made, both that altar and the high place he brake down, and burned the high place, *and* stamped *it* small to powder, and burned the grove.

16 And as Josiah turned himself, he spied the sepulchres that *were* there in the mount, and sent, and took the bones out of the sepulchres, and burned *them* upon the altar, and polluted it, according to the [e]word of the LORD which the man of God proclaimed, who proclaimed these words.

17 Then he said, What title *is* that that I see? And the men of the city told him, It is [f]the sepulchre of the man of God, which came from Judah and proclaimed these things that thou hast done against the altar of Beth-el.

18 And he said, Let him alone; let no man move his bones. So they let his bones [g]alone, with the bones of [h]the prophet that came out of Samaria.

19 And all the houses also of the high places

that *were* [i]in the cities of Sama- A. M. 3380
B. C. 624
Ol. XXXIX. 1
An. Anci Martii,
Regis Romano-
rum, 17
ria, which the kings of Israel had made to provoke *the LORD* to anger, Josiah took away, and did to them according to all the acts that he had done in Beth-el.

20 And [k]he[l] [m]slew all the priests of the high places that *were* there upon the altars, and [n]burned men's bones upon them, and returned to Jerusalem.

21 And the king commanded all the people, saying, [o]Keep the passover unto the LORD your God, [p]as *it is* written in the book of this covenant.

22 Surely [q]there was not holden such a passover from the days of the judges that judged Israel, nor in all the days of the kings of Israel, nor of the kings of Judah;

23 But in the eighteenth year of King Josiah, *wherein* this passover was holden to the LORD in Jerusalem.

24 Moreover [r]the *workers with* familiar spirits, and the wizards, and the [s]images, and the idols, and all the abominations that were spied in the land of Judah and in Jerusalem, did Josiah put away, that he might perform the words of [t]the law which were written in the book that Hilkiah the priest found in the house of the LORD.

---

[b]Exod. xxiii. 24; Deut. vii. 5, 25——[c]Heb. *statues*
[d]1 Kings xii. 28, 33——[e]1 Kings xiii. 2——[f]1 Kings xiii.
1, 30——[g]Heb. *to escape*——[h]1 Kings xiii. 31——[i]See
2 Chron. xxxiv. 6, 7——[k]1 Kings xiii. 2——[l]Or, *sacrificed*——[m]Exod. xxii. 20; 1 Kings xviii. 40; chap. xi. 18

[n]2 Chron. xxxiv. 5——[o]2 Chron. xxxv. 1; 1 Esd. i. 1
[p]Exod. xii. 3; Lev. xxiii. 5; Num. ix. 2; Deut. xvi. 2
[q]2 Chron. xxxv. 18, 19; His eighteenth year ending
[r]Chap. xxi. 6——[s]Or, *teraphim*, Gen. xxxi. 19——[t]Lev.
xix. 31; xx. 27; Deut. xviii. 11

---

mishchah, of *unction;* but because of the idolatrous purposes for which it was used, the Scripture changed the appellation to the *mount* המשחית *hammashchith, of corruption.*

Ashtoreth the abomination, &c.] See on 1 Kings xi. 7.

Verse 14. *Filled their places with the bones of men.*] This was allowed to be the utmost defilement to which any thing could be exposed.

Verse 16. *And as Josiah turned himself*] This verse is much more *complete* in the *Septuagint,* and in the *Hexaplar Syriac* version at Paris. I shall give the whole, making a distinction where, in those versions, any thing is added: "And as Josiah turned himself, he spied the sepulchres that were there in the mount, and sent and took the bones out of the sepulchres, and burnt them upon the altar, and polluted it: according to the word of the Lord which the man of God proclaimed [when Jeroboam stood by the altar at the feast. And turning about, *he* cast his eyes on the sepulchre of the man of God] who proclaimed these words." See 1 Kings xiii. 2, where these things were predicted, and see the notes there.

Verse 17. *What title is that*] There was either a *stone,* an *image,* or an *inscription* here:

the old prophet no doubt took care to have the place made sufficiently remarkable.

Verse 18. *The prophet that came out of Samaria*] See the note on 1 Kings xiii. 32.

Verse 19. *That were in the cities of Samaria*] Israel had now no king; and Josiah, of the blood royal of Judah, had certainly a direct right to the kingdom; he had, at this time, an especial commission from God, to reform every abuse through the whole land—all that ground that was given by the Lord as an inheritance to the *twelve sons* of Jacob. Therefore he had every right to carry his plans of reformation into the Samaritan states.

Verse 20. *Slew all the priests*] The lives of these, as corrupters of the people, were forfeited to the law.

Verse 22. *Surely there was not holden such a passover*] Not one on *purer* principles, more *heartily* joined in by the *people* present, more *literally consecrated,* or more *religiously* observed. The words do not apply to the number present, but to the manner and spirit. See the *particulars* and *mode* of celebrating this passover in 2 Chron. xxxv. 1-18.

Verse 24. *The* workers with *familiar spirits*] See on chap. xxi. 5.

A. M. 3363–3394
B. C. 641–610
Ol. XXXIV. 4
—XLII. 3

25 [u]And like unto him was there no king before him, that turned to the LORD with all his heart, and with all his soul, and with all his might, according to all the law of Moses; neither after him arose there *any* like him.

26 Notwithstanding the LORD turned not from the fierceness of his great wrath, wherewith his anger was kindled against Judah, [v]because of all the [w]provocations that Manasseh had provoked him withal.

27 And the LORD said, I will remove Judah also out of my sight, as [x]I have removed Israel, and will cast off this city Jerusalem which I have chosen, and the house of which I said, [y]My name shall be there.

28 Now the rest of the acts of Josiah, and all that he did, *are* they not written in the book of the chronicles of the kings of Judah?

A. M. 3394
B. C. 610
Ol. XLII 3
An. Tarquinii
Prisci, Reg.
Rom. 7

29 [z]In his days Pharaoh-nechoh king of Egypt went up against the king of Assyria to the river Euphrates: and King Josiah went against him; and he slew him at [a]Megiddo, when he [b]had seen him.

A. M. 3394
B. C. 610
Ol. XLII. 3
An. Tarquinii
Prisci, Reg.
Rom. 7

30 [c]And his servants carried him in a chariot dead from Megiddo, and brought him to Jerusalem, and buried him in his own sepulchre. And [d]the people of the land took Jehoahaz the son of Josiah, and anointed him, and made him king in his father's stead.

31 [e]Jehoahaz *was* twenty and three years old when he began to reign; and he reigned three months in Jerusalem. And his mother's name *was* [f]Hamutal, the daughter of Jeremiah of Libnah.

32 And he did *that which was* evil in the sight of the LORD, according to all that his fathers had done.

33 And Pharaoh-nechoh put him in bands [g]at Riblah in the land of Hamath, [h]that he might not reign in Jerusalem; and [i]put the land to a tribute of a hundred talents of silver, and a talent of gold.

34 And [k]Pharaoh-nechoh made Eliakim the

---

[u]Ch. xviii. 5——[v]Ch. xxi. 11, 12; xxiv. 3, 4; Jer. xv. 4——[w]Heb. *angers*——[x]Ch. xvii. 18, 20; xviii. 11; xxi. 13
[y]1 Kings viii. 29; ix. 3; ch. xxi. 4, 7——[z]2 Chron. xxxv.
20——[a]Zech. xii. 11——[b]Chap. xiv. 8——[c]2 Chron.
xxxv. 24

[d]2 Chron. xxxvi. 1——[e]Called *Shallum*, 1 Chron.
iii. 15; Jer. xxii. 11——[f]Chap. xxiv. 18——[g]Chap.
xxv. 6; Jer. lii. 27——[h]Or, *because he reigned*——[i]Heb.
set a mulct upon the land; 2 Chron. xxxvi. 3——[k]2
Chron. xxxvi. 4

And the images] The *teraphim.* See the note on Gen. xxxi. 19.

Verse 25. *Like unto him was there no king*] Perhaps not one from the time of David; and, morally considered, including David himself, none ever sat on the Jewish throne, so truly exemplary in his own conduct, and so thoroughly zealous in the work of God. David was a *greater* but not a *better* man than Josiah.

Verse 26. *The Lord turned not*] It was of no use to try this fickle and radically depraved people any longer. They were respited merely during the life of Josiah.

Verse 29. *In his days Pharaoh-nechoh*] See the note on the death of Josiah, chap. xxii. 20.

Nechoh is supposed to have been the son of *Psammitichus*, king of Egypt; and the Assyrian king, whom he was now going to attack, was the famous *Nabopolassar.* What the cause of this quarrel was, is not known. Some say it was on account of *Carchemish*, a city on the Euphrates, belonging to the Egyptians, which Nabopolassar had seized. See Isa. x. 9.

Verse 30. *Dead from Megiddo*] The word מת *meth* should here be considered as a participle, *dying*, for it is certain he was not *dead:* he was *mortally wounded* at Megiddo, was carried in a *dying state* to Jerusalem, and *there* he *died* and was buried. See 2 Chron. xxxv. 24.

Herodotus, lib. i., c. 17, 18, 25, and lib. ii. 159, appears to refer to the same war which is here mentioned. He says that Nechoh, in the *sixth* year of his reign, went to attack the king of Assyria at *Magdolum*, gained a complete victory, and took *Cadytis.* Usher and others believe that *Magdolum* and *Megiddo* were the same place. The exact place of the battle seems to have been *Hadadrimmon*, in the valley of Megiddo, for there Zechariah tells us, chap. xii. 11, was the great mourning for Josiah. Compare this with 2 Chron. xxxv. 24, 25.

Verse 31. *Jehoahaz was twenty and three years old*] This was not the *eldest* son of Josiah, which is evident from this, that he was *twenty-three* years old when he began to reign; that he reigned but *three months;* that, being dethroned, his brother *Eliakim* was put in his place, who was then *twenty-five years* of age. Eliakim, therefore, was the eldest brother; but Jehoahaz was probably raised to the throne by the people, as being of a more active and martial spirit.

Verse 33. *Nechoh put him in bands*] But what was the cause of his putting him in bands? It is conjectured, and not without reason, that Jehoahaz, otherwise called *Shallum*, raised an army, met Nechoh in his return from *Carchemish*, fought, was beaten, taken prisoner, put in chains, and taken into Egypt, where he died; ver. 34, and Jer. xxii. 11, 12. *Riblah* or *Diblath*, the place of this battle, was probably a town in *Syria*, in the land or district of *Hamath.*

Verse 34. *Turned his name to Jehoiakim*] These names are precisely the same in signification: ELIAKIM is *God shall arise;* JEHOIAKIM,

A. M. 3394
B. C. 610
Ol. XLII. 3
An. Tarquinii
Prisci, Reg.
Rom. 7 son of Josiah king in the room of Josiah his father, and ¹turned his name to ᵐJehoiakim, and took Jehoahaz away: ⁿand he came to Egypt, and died there.

35 And Jehoiakim gave °the silver and the gold to Pharaoh; but he taxed the land to give the money according to the commandment of Pharaoh; he exacted the silver and the gold of the people of the land, of every one

according to his taxation, to give *it* unto Pharaoh-nechoh. A. M. 3394–3405
B. C. 610–599
Ol. XLII. 3
XLV. 2

36 ᵖJehoiakim *was* twenty and five years old when he began to reign: and he reigned eleven years in Jerusalem. And his mother's name *was* Zebudah, the daughter of Pedaiah of Rumah.

37 And he did *that which was* evil in the sight of the LORD, according to all that his fathers had done.

---

¹See chap. xxiv. 17; Dan. i. 7——ᵐMatthew i. 11, called *Jakim*

ⁿJer. xxii. 11, 12; Ezek. xix. 3, 4——°Ver. 33——ᵖ2 Chron. xxxvi. 5

Jehovah shall arise; or, the *resurrection of God;* the *resurrection of Jehovah.* That is, God's rising again to show his power, justice, &c. The *change* of the name was to show Nechoh's *supremacy,* and that Jehoiakim was only his *vassal* or *viceroy.* Proofs of this mode of changing the name, when a person of greater power put another in office under himself, may be seen in the case of *Mattaniah,* changed into *Zedekiah; Daniel, Mishael, Hananiah,* and *Azariah,* into *Belteshazzar, Shadrach, Meshach,* and *Abed-nego;* and *Joseph* into *Zaphnath-paaneah.* See Dan. i. 6, 7; Gen. xli. 45.

Verse 35. *Jehoiakim gave the silver and the*

gold] Nechoh had placed him there as viceroy, simply to *raise* and *collect his taxes.*

Every one according to his taxation] That is, each was assessed in proportion to his property: that was the principle avowed: but there is reason to fear that this bad king was not governed by it.

Verse 37. *He did* that which was *evil in the sight of the Lord*] He was a most unprincipled and oppressive tyrant. *Jeremiah* gives us his character at large, chap. xxii. 13-19, to which the reader will do well to refer. Jeremiah was at that time in the land, and was an eyewitness of the abominations of this cruel king.

CHAPTER XXIV

Nebuchadnezzar brings Jehoiakim under subjection; who, after three years, rebels, 1. Bands of Chaldeans, Syrians, Moabites, and Ammonites, invade the land, 2-4. Jehoiakim dies, and Jehoiachin his son reigns in his stead, 5, 6. The Babylonians overcome the Egyptians, 7. Nebuchadnezzar takes Jehoiachin and his family, and all his treasures, and those of the temple, and all the chief people and artificers, and carries them to Babylon, 8-16; and makes Mattaniah, brother of Jehoiakim, king, who reigns wickedly, and rebels against the king of Babylon, 17-20.

A.M. 3394–3405
B. C. 610–599
Ol. XLII. 3
—XLV. 2 IN ᵃhis days Nebuchadnezzar king of Babylon came up, and Jehoiakim became his servant three years: then he turned and rebelled against him.

2 ᵇAnd the LORD sent against him bands of the Chaldees, and bands of the Syrians, and bands of the Moabites, and bands of the children of Ammon, and sent them against Judah to destroy it, ᶜaccording to the word of the

LORD, which he spake ᵈby his servants the prophets. A.M. 3394–3405
B. C. 610–599
Ol. XLII. 3
—XLV. 2

3 Surely at the commandment of the LORD came *this* upon Judah, to remove *them* out of his sight, ᵉfor the sins of Manasseh, according to all that he did;

4 ᶠAnd also for the innocent blood that he shed: for he filled Jerusalem with innocent blood; which the LORD would not pardon.

5 Now the rest of the acts of Jehoiakim,

ᵃ2 Chron. xxxvi. 6; Jer. xxv. 1, 9; Dan. i. 1——ᵇEzek. xix. 8; Jer. xxv. 9; xxxii. 28

ᶜChap. xx. 17; xxi. 12, 13, 14; xxiii. 27——ᵈHeb. *by the hand of*——ᵉChap. xxi. 2, 11; xxiii. 26——ᶠCh. xxi. 16

NOTES ON CHAP. XXIV

Verse 1. *Nebuchadnezzar*] This man, so famous in the writings of the prophets, was son of *Nabopolassar.* He was sent by his father against the rulers of several provinces that had revolted; and he took Carchemish, and all that belonged to the Egyptians, from the Euphrates to the Nile. Jehoiakim, who was tributary to Nechoh king of Egypt, he attacked and re-

duced; and obliged to become tributary to Babylon. At the end of *three* years he revolted; and then a mixed army, of Chaldeans, Syrians, Moabites, and Ammonites, was sent against him, who ravaged the country, and took *three thousand and twenty-three* prisoners, whom they brought to Babylon, Jer. lii. 28.

Verse 2. *According to the word of the Lord*] See what *Huldah* predicted, chap. xxii. 16, and see chap. xiv., xv. and xvi. of Jeremiah.

A. M. 3394–3405
B. C. 610–599
Ol. XLII. 3
—XLV. 2

A. M. 3405
B. C. 599
Ol. XLV. 2
An. Tarquinii
Prisci, Reg.
Rom. 18

and all that he did, *are* they not written in the book of the chronicles of the kings of Judah?

6 ᵍSo Jehoiakim slept with his fathers: and Jehoiachin his son reigned in his stead.

7 And ʰthe king of Egypt came not again any more out of his land: for ⁱthe king of Babylon had taken from the river of Egypt unto the river Euphrates all that pertained to the king of Egypt.

8 ᵏJehoiachin ˡ*was* eighteen years old when he began to reign, and he reigned in Jerusalem three months. And his mother's name *was* Nehushta, the daughter of Elnathan of Jerusalem.

9 And he did *that which was* evil in the sight of the LORD, according to all that his father had done.

10 ᵐAt that time the servants of Nebuchadnezzar king of Babylon came up against Jerusalem, and the city ⁿwas besieged.

11 And Nebuchadnezzar king of Babylon came against the city, and his servants did besiege it.

12 ᵒAnd Jehoiachin the king of Judah went

A. M. 3405
B. C. 599
Ol. XLV. 2
An. Tarquinii
Prisci, Reg.
Rom. 18

out to the king of Babylon, he, and his mother, and his servants, and his princes, and his ᵖofficers: ᑫand the king of Babylonʳtook himˢin the eighthyear of his reign.

13 ᵗAnd he carried out thence all the treasures of the house of the LORD, and the treasures of the king's house, and ᵘcut in pieces all the vessels of gold which Solomon king of Israel had made in the temple of the LORD, ᵛas the LORD had said.

14 And ʷhe carried away all Jerusalem, and all the princes, and all the mighty men of valour, ˣ*even* ten thousand captives, and ʸall the craftsmen and smiths: none remained, save ᶻthe poorest sort of the people of the land.

15 And ᵃhe carried away Jehoiachin to Babylon, and the king's mother, and the king's wives, and his ᵇofficers, and the mighty of the land, *those* carried he into captivity from Jerusalem to Babylon.

16 And ᶜall the men of might, *even* seven thousand, and craftsmen and smiths a thousand, all *that were* strong *and* apt for war, even them the king of Babylon brought captive to Babylon.

ᵍSee 2 Chron. xxxvi. 6, 8; Jer. xxii. 18, 19; xxxvi. 30 ʰSee Jer. xxxvii. 5, 7——ⁱJer. xlvi. 2——ᵏCalled *Jeconiah*, 1 Chron. iii. 16; Jer. xxiv. 1; and *Coniah*, Jer. xxii. 24, 28——ˡ2 Chron. xxxvi. 9——ᵐDan. i. 1 ⁿHeb. *came into siege*——ᵒJer. xxiv. 1; xxix. 1, 2; Ezekiel xvii. 12——ᵖOr, *eunuchs*

ᑫ*Nebuchadnezzar's* eighth year; Jer. xxv. 1——ʳSee ch. xxv. 27——ˢSee Jer. lii. 28——ᵗCh. xx. 17; Isa. xxxix. 6——ᵘSee Dan. v. 2, 3——ᵛJer. xx. 5——ʷJer. xxiv. 1——ˣSee Jer. lii. 28——ʸSo 1 Sam. xiii. 19, 22 ᵃCh. xxv. 12; Jer. xl. 7——ᵃ2 Chron. xxxvi. 10; Esth. ii. 6; Jer. xxii. 24, &c.——ᵇOr, *eunuchs*——ᶜSee Jer. lii. 28

Verse 6. *Jehoiachin his son*] As this man reigned only *three months*, and was a mere *vassal* to the Babylonians, his reign is scarcely to be reckoned; and therefore Jeremiah says of Jehoiakim, *He shall have none to sit upon the throne of David,* chap. xxxvi. 30, for at that time it belonged to the king of Babylon, and Jehoiachin was a mere viceroy or governor. Jehoiachin is called *Jechonias* in Matt. i. 11.

Verse 7. *The king of Egypt came not again*] He was so crushed by the Babylonians that he was obliged to confine himself within the limits of his own states, and could no more attempt any conquests. The text tells us how much he had lost by the Babylonians. See on ver. 1.

Verse 8. *Jehoiachin was eighteen years old*] He is called *Jeconiah*, 1 Chron. iii. 16, and *Coniah*, Jer. xxii. 24. In 2 Chron. xxxvi. 9, he is said to be only *eight* years of age, but this must be a mistake; for we find that, having reigned only *three* months, he was carried captive to Babylon, and there he had *wives;* and it is very improbable that a child between *eight* and *nine* years of age could have *wives;* and of such a tender age, it can scarcely be said that, as a *king,* he *did that which was evil in the sight of the Lord.* The place in Chronicles must be corrupted.

That he was a grievous offender against God, we learn from Jer. xxii. 24, which the reader may consult; and in the man's punishment, see his crimes.

Verse 12. *Jehoiachin—went out*] He saw that it was useless to attempt to defend himself any longer; and he therefore surrendered himself, hoping to obtain better terms.

Verse 13. *He carried out thence all the treasures*] It has been remarked that Nebuchadnezzar spoiled the temple *three times:*—1. He took away the greater part of those treasures when he took Jerusalem under Jehoiakim: and the vessels that he took then he placed in the temple of his god, Dan. i. 2. And these were the vessels which Belshazzar *profaned,* Dan. v. 2; and which *Cyrus* restored to *Ezra,* when he went up to Jerusalem, Ezra i. 2. It was at this time that he took Daniel and his companions. 2. He took the remaining part of those vessels, and broke them or cut them in pieces, when he came the second time against Jerusalem under Jeconiah; as is mentioned here, ver. 13. 3. He pillaged the temple, took away all the brass, the brazen pillars, brazen vessels, and vessels of gold and silver, which he found there when he besieged Jerusalem under Zedekiah, chap. xxv. 13-17.

Verse 14. *He carried away all Jerusalem*] That is, all the chief men, the nobles, and arti-

A. M. 3405
B. C. 599
Ol. XLV. 2
An. Tarquinii
Prisci, Reg.
Rom. 18

17 And ᵈthe king of Babylon made Mattaniah ᵉhis father's brother king in his stead, and ᶠchanged his name to Zedekiah.

A. M. 3405–3416
B. C. 599–588
Ol. XLV. 2
—XLVIII. 1

18 ᵍZedekiah *was* twenty and one years old when he began to reign, and he reigned eleven years in Jerusalem. And his mother's name *was* ʰHamutal, the daughter of Jeremiah of Libnah.

19 ⁱAnd he did *that which was* evil in the sight of the LORD, according to all that Jehoiakim had done.

A. M. 3405–3416
B. C. 599–588
Olymp. XLV. 2
—XLVIII. 1

20 For through the anger of the LORD it came to pass in Jerusalem and Judah, until he had cast them out from his presence, ᵏthat Zedekiah rebelled against the king of Babylon.

ᵈJer. xxxvii. 1——ᵉ1 Chron. iii. 15; 2 Chron. xxxvii. 10——ᶠSo ch. xxiii. 34; 2 Chron. xxxvi. 4——ᵍ2 Chron.

xxxvi. 11; Jer. xxxvii. 1; lii. 1——ʰCh. xxiii. 31——ⁱ2 Chron. xxxvi. 12——ᵏ2 Chron. xxxvi. 13; Ezek. xvii. 15

---

ficers. Among these there were of mighty men *seven thousand;* of craftsmen and smiths, *one thousand.*

Verse 17. *Made Mattaniah his father's brother king in his stead*] He was the son of Josiah, and brother to Jehoiakim.

Changed his name to Zedekiah.] See the note on chap. xxiii. 34.

Verse 19. *He did—evil*] How astonishing is this! not one of them takes warning by the

judgments of God, which fell on their sinful predecessors.

Verse 20. *Zedekiah rebelled*] This was in the eighth year of his reign: and he is strongly reproved for having violated the oath he took to the king of Babylon: see 2 Chron. xxxvi. 13. This was the filling up of the measure of iniquity; and now the wrath of God descends upon this devoted king, city, and people, to the uttermost. See the catastrophe in the next chapter.

CHAPTER XXV

Nebuchadnezzar besieges Jerusalem; it is taken, after having been sorely reduced by famine, &c.; and Zedekiah, endeavouring to make his escape, is made prisoner, his sons slain before his eyes; then, his eyes being put out, he is put in chains and carried to Babylon, 1–7. Nebuzar-adan burns the temple, breaks down the walls of Jerusalem, and carries away the people captives, leaving only a few to till the ground, 8–12. He takes away all the brass, and all the vessels of the temple, 13–17. Several of the chief men and nobles found in the city, he brings to Nebuchadnezzar at Riblah, who puts them all to death, 18–21. Nebuchadnezzar makes Gedaliah governor over the poor people that were left, against whom Ishmael rises, and slays him, and others with him; on which the people in general, fearing the resentment of the Chaldeans, flee to Egypt, 22–26. Evil-merodach, king of Babylon, releases Jehoiachin out of prison, treats him kindly, and makes him his friend, 27–30.

A. M. 3414
B. C. 590
Ol. XLVII. 3
An. Tarquinii
Prisci, Reg.
Rom. 27

AND it came to pass, ᵃin the ninth year of his reign, in the tenth month, in the tenth *day* of the month, *that* Nebuchadnezzar king of Babylon came, he, and all

his host, against Jerusalem, and pitched against it; and they built forts against it round about.

A. M. 3414
B. C. 590
Ol. XLVII. 3
An. Tarquinii
Prisci, Reg.
Rom. 27

2 And the city was besieged unto the eleventh year of King Zedekiah.

ᵃ2 Chron. xxxvi. 17; Jer. xxxiv. 2;

xxxix. 1; lii. 4, 5; Ezek. xxiv. 1

NOTES ON CHAP. XXV

Verse 1. *In the ninth year of his reign*] Zedekiah, having revolted against the Chaldeans, Nebuchadnezzar, wearied with his treachery, and the bad faith of the Jews, determined the total subversion of the Jewish state. Having assembled a numerous army, he entered Judea on the *tenth day* of the *tenth month* of the *ninth year* of the reign of Zedekiah; this, according to the computation of Archbishop Usher, was on *Thursday, January* 30, A. M. 3414, which was a *sabbatical year:* whereon the men of Jerusalem, hearing that the Chaldean army was approaching, proclaimed liberty to their servants; see Jer. xxxiv. 8, 9, 10, according to the law, Exod. xxi. 2; Deut. xv. 1, 2, 12: for Nebuchadnezzar, marching with

his army against Zedekiah, having wasted all the country, and taken their strong holds, except Lachish, Azekah, and Jerusalem, came against the latter with all his forces. See Jer. xxxiv. 1-7. On the very day, as the same author computes, the siege and utter destruction of Jerusalem were revealed to Ezekiel the prophet, then in Chaldea, under the type of a *seething pot;* and his wife died in the evening, and he was charged not to mourn for her, because of the extraordinary calamity that had fallen upon the land. See Ezek. xxiv. 1, 2, &c.

Jeremiah, having predicted the same calamities, Jer. xxxiv. 1-7, was by the command of Zedekiah shut up in prison, xxxii. 1-16.

Pharaoh Hophra, or *Vaphris,* hearing how Zedekiah was pressed, and fearing for the safety of his own dominions should the Chal-

A. M. 3416
B. C. 588
Ol. XLVIII. 1
An. Tarquinii
Prisci, Reg.
Rom. 29

3 And on the ninth *day* of the *b fourth* month the famine prevailed in the city, and there was no bread for the people of the land.

4 And *c* the city was broken up, and all the men of *war* fled by night by the way of the gate between two walls, which *is* by the king's garden: (now the Chaldees *were* against the city round about:) and *d the king* went the way toward the plain.

5 And the army of the Chaldees pursued after the king, and overtook him in the plains of Jericho: and all his army were scattered from him.

6 So they took the king, and brought him up to the king of Babylon *e* to Riblah: and they *f* gave judgment upon him.

7 And they slew the sons of Zedekiah before his eyes, and *g* put *h* out the eyes of Zedekiah, and bound him with fetters of brass, and carried him to Babylon.

8 And in the fifth month, *l* on the seventh *day* of the month, which *is* *k* the nineteenth year of King Nebuchadnezzar king of Babylon, *l* came Nebuzar-adan, *m* captain of the guard, a servant of the king of Babylon, unto Jerusalem:

9 *n* And he burnt the house of the Lord,

o and the king's house, and all the houses of Jerusalem, and every great *man's* house burnt he with fire.

10 And all the army of the Chaldees, that *were with* the captain of the guard, *p* brake down the walls of Jerusalem round about.

11 *q* Now the rest of the people *that were* left in the city, and the *r* fugitives that fell away to the king of Babylon, with the remnant of the multitude, did Nebuzar-adan the captain of the guard carry away.

12 But the captain of the guard *s* left of the poor of the land *to be* vine-dressers and husbandmen.

13 And *t* the *u* pillars of brass that *were* in the house of the Lord, and *v* the bases, and *w* the brazen sea that *was* in the house of the Lord, did the Chaldees break in pieces, and carried the brass of them to Babylon.

14 And *x* the pots, and the shovels, and the snuffers, and the spoons, and all the vessels of brass wherewith they ministered, took they away.

15 And the fire-pans, and the bowls, *and* such things as *were* of gold, *in* gold, and of silver, *in* silver, the captain of the guard took away.

A. M. 3416
B. C. 588
Ol. XLVIII. 1
An. Tarquinii
Prisci, Reg.
Rom. 29

---

b Jer. xxxix. 2; lii. 6——*c* Jer. xxxix. 2; lii. 7, &c. *d* Jer. xxxix. 4–7; lii. 7; Ezek. xii. 12——*e* Chap. xxiii. 33; Jer. lii. 9——*f* Heb. *spake judgment with him*——*g* Heb. *made blind*——*h* Jer. xxxix. 7; Ezek. xii. 13——*i* See Jer. lii. 12–14——*k* See chap. xxiv. 12; ver. 27——*l* Jer. xxxix. 9——*m* Or, *chief marshal*

n 2 Chron. xxxvi. 19; Psa. lxxix. 1——*o* Jer. xxxix. 8; Amos ii. 5——*p* Neh. i. 3; Jer. lii. 14——*q* Jer. xxxix. 9; lii. 15——*r* Heb. *fallen away*——*s* Ch. xxiv. 14; Jer. xxxix. 10; xl. 7; lii. 16——*t* Ch. xx. 17; Jer. xxvii. 19, 22; lii. 17, &c.——*u* 1 Kings vii. 15——*v* 1 Kings vii. 27 *w* 1 Kings vii. 23——*x* Exod. xxvii. 3; 1 Kings vii. 45, 50

---

deans succeed against Jerusalem, determined to succour Zedekiah. Finding this, the Chaldeans raised the siege of Jerusalem, and went to meet the Egyptian army, which they defeated and put to flight. *Joseph. Antiq.,* lib. 10, cap. 10. In the interim the Jews, thinking their danger was passed, reclaimed their servants, and put them again under the yoke; Jer. xxxiv. 8, &c.

Verses 2-4. *And the city was besieged, &c.*] Nebuchadnezzar, having routed the Egyptian army, returned to Jerusalem, and besieged it so closely that, being reduced by famine, and a breach made in the wall, the Chaldeans entered it on the *ninth day of the fourth month,* (*Wednesday, July* 27,) Zedekiah and many others endeavouring to make their escape by night.

Verse 5. *The army of the Chaldeans pursued*] Zedekiah was taken, and brought captive to Riblah in Syria, where Nebuchadnezzar then lay, who ordered his sons to be slain before his face, and then put out his eyes; and having loaded him with chains, sent him to Babylon, (see Jer. xxxix. 4, 7, lii. 7, 11,) thus fulfilling the prophetic declarations, that *his*

eyes should see the eyes of the king of Babylon, Jer. xxxii. 4, and xxxiv. 3; but *Babylon he should not see,* though he was to die there; Ezek. xii. 13.

Verse 8. *In the fifth month*] On the *seventh day of the fifth month,* (answering to Wednesday, *Aug.* 24,) Nebuzar-adan made his entry into the city; and having spent two days in making provision, on the *tenth day* of the same month, (*Saturday, Aug.* 27,) he set fire to the temple and the king's palace, and the houses of the nobility, and burnt them to the ground; Jer. lii. 13, compared with xxxix. 8. Thus the temple was destroyed in the *eleventh* year of Zedekiah, the *nineteenth* of Nebuchadnezzar, the *first* of the XLVIIIth Olympiad, in the *one hundred and sixtieth* current year of the era of Nabonassar, *four hundred and twenty-four* years *three* months and *eight* days from the time in which Solomon laid its foundation stone.

Verse 10. *Brake down the walls*] In the same *fifth month,* Jer. i. 3, the walls of Jerusalem being razed to the ground, all that were left in the city, and all that had fled over for-

A. M. 3416
B. C. 588
Ol. XLVIII. 1
An. Tarquinii
Prisci, Reg.
Rom. 29

16 The two pillars, ʸone sea, and the bases which Solomon had made for the house of the LORD; ᶻthe brass of all these vessels was without weight.

17 ᵃThe height of the one pillar *was* eighteen cubits, and the chapiter upon it *was* brass: and the height of the chapiter three cubits; and the wreathen work, and pomegranates upon the chapiter round about, all of brass: and like unto these had the second pillar with wreathen work:

18 ᵇAnd the captain of the guard took ᶜSeraiah the chief priest, and ᵈZephaniah the second priest, and the three keepers of the ᵉdoor:

19 And out of the city he took an ᶠofficer, that was set over the men of war, and ᵍfive men of them that ʰwere in the king's presence, which were found in the city, and the ⁱprincipal scribe of the host, which mustered the people of the land, and threescore men of the people of the land *that were* found in the city:

20 And Nebuzar-adan captain of the guard took these, and brought them to the king of Babylon to Riblah:

21 And the king of Babylon smote them, and slew them at Riblah in the land of Ra-

math. ᵏSo Judah was carried away out of their land.

22 ¹And *as for* the people that remained in the land of Judah, whom Nebuchadnezzar king of Babylon had left, even over them he made Gedaliah the son of Ahikam, the son of Shaphan, ruler.

A. M. 3416
B. C. 588
Ol. XLVIII. 1
An. Tarquinii
Prisci, Reg.
Rom. 29

23 And when all the ᵐcaptains of the armies, they and their men, heard that the king of Babylon had made Gedaliah governor, there came to Gedaliah to Mizpah, even Ishmael the son of Nethaniah, and Johanan the son of Careah, and Seraiah the son of Tanhumeth the Netophathite, and Jaazaniah the son of a Maachathite, they and their men.

24 And Gedaliah sware to them, and to their men, and said unto them, Fear not to be the servants of the Chaldees: dwell in the land, and serve the king of Babylon; and it shall be well with you.

25 But ⁿit came to pass in the seventh month, that Ishmael the son of Nethaniah, the son of Elishama, of the seed ᵒroyal, came, and ten men with him, and smote Gedaliah, that he died, and the Jews and the Chaldees that were with him at Mizpah.

26 And all the people, both small and great, and the captains of the armies, arose, ᵖand came to Egypt: for they were afraid of the Chaldees.

ʸHeb. *the one sea*——ᶻ1 Kings vii. 47——ᵃ1 Kings vii. 15; Jer. lii. 21——ᵇJer. lii. 24, &c.——ᶜ1 Chron. vi. 14; Ezra vii. 1——ᵈJer. xxi. 1; xxix. 25——ᵉHeb. *threshold* ᶠOr, *eunuch*——ᵍSee Jer. lii. 25——ʰHeb. *saw the king's face;* Esth. i. 14

ⁱOr, *scribe of the captain of the host*——ᵏLev. xxvi. 33; Deut. xxviii. 36, 64; chapter xxiii. 27——¹Jeremiah xl. 5——ᵐJeremiah xl. 7, 8, 9——ⁿJeremiah xli, 1, 2——ᵒHebrew, *of the kingdom*——ᵖJeremiah xliii. 4, 7

---

merly to Nebuchadnezzar, and all the common people of the city, with all the king's treasures, those of the nobles, and the whole furniture of the temple, did Nebuzar-adan carry off to Babylon. See Jer. xxxix. 8, 9, lii. 14, 23. And thus was Judah carried away out of her own land, *four hundred and sixty-eight* years after David began to reign over it; from the division of the ten tribes *three hundred and eighty-eight* years; and from the destruction of the kingdom of Israel, *one hundred and thirty-four* years; A. M. 3416, and before Christ *five hundred and ninety.* And thus ends what is called the *fifth age of the world.* See USHER'S *Annals.*

Verse 18. *Seraiah the chief priest—Zephaniah*] The person who is here called the *second priest* was what the Jews call *sagan,* a sort of *deputy,* who performed the functions of the high priest when he was prevented by any infirmity from attending the temple service. See on chap. xxiii. 4.

Verse 19. *And five men of them that were in the king's presence*] These were principal counsellors, and confidential officers.

In Jer. lii. 25, it is said he took *seven* men who were near the king's person, and the same

number is found in the *Arabic* in this place; and the *Chaldee* has no less than *fifty men;* but in Jeremiah this, as well as all the rest of the *versions,* reads *seven.* Probably they were no more than *five* at first, or, perhaps Jeremiah reckoned with the five the *officer* that was set *over the men of war,* and the *principal scribe* of the host mentioned here, as *two* with the five; and thus made *seven* in the whole.

Verse 21. *The king of Babylon smote them*] He had, no doubt, found that these had counselled Zedekiah to revolt.

Verse 22. *Made Gedaliah—ruler.*] This was no *regal* dignity; he was only a sort of *hind* or *overseer,* appointed to regulate the *husbandmen.*

Verse 23. *To Mizpah*] This is said to have been situated on the *east* side of the river Jordan, and most contiguous to Babylon, and therefore the most proper for the residence of Gedaliah, because nearest to the place from which he was to receive his instructions. But there were several places of this name, and we do not exactly know where *this* was situated.

Verse 24. *Gedaliah sware to them*] He pledged himself in the most solemn manner to encourage and protect them.

A. M. 3442
B. C. 562
Ol. LIV. 3
An. Servii Tul-
lii, Regis Ro-
manorum, 17

27 �q And it came to pass in the seven and thirtieth year of the captivity of Jehoiachin king of Judah, in the twelfth month, on the seven and twentieth *day* of the month, *that* Evil-merodach king of Babylon in the year that he began to reign ʳdid lift up the head of Jehoiachin king of Judah out of prison;

28 And he spake ˢkindly to him, and set his throne above the throne of the kings that *were* with him in Babylon;

A. M. 3442
B. C. 562
Ol. LIV. 3
An. Servii Tul-
lii, Regis Ro-
manorum, 17

29 And changed his prison garments: and he did ᵗeat bread continually before him all the days of his life.

30 And his allowance *was* a continual allowance given him of the king, a daily rate for every day, all the days of his life.

�q Jer. lii. 31, &c.——ʳSee Gen. xl. 13, 20

ˢHeb. *good things with him*——ᵗ2 Sam. ix. 7

Verse 25. *Smote Gedaliah*] This was at an entertainment which Gedaliah had made for them; see Jer. xli. 1, &c. He was not content with this murder, but slew fourscore more, who were coming with offerings to the temple, and took several as prisoners, among whom were some of the *king's daughters;* and set off to go to the Ammonites: but Johanan, the son of Careah, hearing of these outrages, raised a number of men, and pursued Ishmael; upon which Ishmael's prisoners immediately turned and joined Johanan; so that *he,* and *eight* of his accomplices, with difficulty escaped to the Ammonites. See Jer. xli. 1, &c. *Baalis,* king of the *Ammonites,* had sent Ishmael to murder Gedaliah; and of this he was informed by Johanan, who offered to prevent it, by taking away the life of this murderer. But Gedaliah could not believe that he harboured such foul designs, and therefore took no precaution to save his life. See Jer. xl. 13-16.

Verse 27. *And it came to pass*] Nebuchadnezzar was just now dead; and Evil-merodach, his son, succeeded to the kingdom in the *thirty-seventh year of the captivity of Jehoiachin:* and on the *seven and twentieth* day [Jeremiah says *five and twentieth*] of the *twelfth month* of that year, (*Tuesday, April* 15, A. M. 3442,) he brought the long captivated Jewish king out of prison; treated him kindly; and ever after, during his life, reckoned him among the king's friends. This is particularly related in the four last verses of the book of *Jeremiah.*

Verse 30. *A continual allowance given him of the king*] He lived in a *regal style,* and had his *court* even in the city of Babylon, being supplied with every requisite by the munificence and friendship of the king. In about *two years* after this, Evil-merodach was slain in a conspiracy; and it is supposed that Jehoiachin, then about fifty-eight years of age, fell with his friend and protector. Thus terminates the catastrophe of the Jewish kings, people, and state; the consequence of unheard-of rebellions and provocations against the Majesty of heaven.

MASORETIC NOTES ON THE FIRST AND SECOND BOOKS OF KINGS

WE have already seen that the Hebrews consider these two books as one:—

The NUMBER of verses in both is *one thousand five hundred and thirty-four.*

MASORETIC SECTIONS, *thirty-five.*

MIDDLE VERSE, 1 Kings xxi. 6. *And he said unto her, Because I spake unto Naboth the Jezreelite, and said unto him, Give me, &c.*

TWO BOOKS OF CHRONICLES

<hr/>

ANCIENTLY these *two* books were considered but as *one:* for this we have not only the testimony of St. *Jerome,* but also that of the *Masoretes,* who gave the *sum* of all the sections, chapters, and verses, under one *notation* at the end of the second book, without mentioning any division; and although the modern Jews divide them, yet they give the *Masoretic* enumeration of sections, &c., as it was given of old; and all editors of the Masoretic Bibles, whether Jewish or Christian, follow the same plan.

These books have had several *names.* In Hebrew they are denominated דברי הימים *dibrey haiyamim;* literally, *The Words of the Days,* i. e., *The Journals,* particularly of the kings of Israel and kings of Judah. But this name does not appear to have been given by the inspired writer.

The *Syriac* has, *The Book of the Transactions in the days of the Kings of Judah: which is called, Dibrey Yamim;* referring to the Hebrew title.

The *Arabic* has, *The Book of the Annals, which is called in Hebrew, Dibrey Haiyamim.*

The *Septuagint* has, παραλειπομενων, *of the things that were left* or *omitted;* supposing that these books were a *supplement* either to *Samuel* and to the *books of Kings,* or to the *whole Bible.* To this the Greek translators might have been led by finding that these books in their time closed the Sacred Canon, as they still do in the most correct editions of the Hebrew Bible.

The *Vulgate* uses the same term as the *Septuagint,* referring, like the *Syriac* and *Arabic,* to the *Hebrew name.*

In our *English Bibles* these books are termed *Chronicles,* from the Greek χρονικα, from χρονος, *time,* i. e., *A History of Times;* or, as the matter of the work shows, "A History of Times, Kingdoms, States, Religion, &c., with an Account of the most memorable *Persons* and *Transactions* of those Times and Nations."

Concerning the *author* of these books, nothing certain is known. Some think they are the works of *different* authors; but the uniformity of the style, the connection of the facts, together with the recapitulations and reflections which are often made, prove that they are the work of *one* and the *same person.*

The Jews, and Christian interpreters in general, believe they were the work of EZRA, assisted by the prophets *Haggai, Zechariah,* and *Malachi.* That EZRA was the author is, on the whole, the most probable opinion. That he lived at the conclusion of the Babylonish captivity is well known; and the second book of Chronicles terminates at that period, barely reciting the *decree of Cyrus* to permit the return of the captivated Israelites to their own land; which subject is immediately taken up in *the book of Ezra,* in which the operation of that decree is distinctly marked.

There are words and terms, both in Chronicles and Ezra, which are similar, and prove that each was written *after* the captivity, and probably by the same person, as those terms were not in use previously to that time, and some of them are peculiar to *Ezra* himself: e. g., we have כפורי זהב *kipporey zahab,* "golden cups;" Ezra i. 10; viii. 27; and in

1 Chron. xxviii. 17; and דרכמן *darkemon* or *drakmon*, "a drachma" or *drachm;* 1 Chron. xxix. 7; Ezra ii. 69; Neh. vii. 70; and רפסדות *raphsodoth*, "rafts" or *floats*, 2 Chron. ii. 16, widely differing from דברות *doberoth*, 1 Kings v. 9, which we there translate in the same way. *Calmet* considers these words as strong evidence that these books were the work of *Ezra*, and penned after the captivity.

We are not to suppose that these books are the *Chronicles of the Kings of Judah and Israel* so often referred to in the historical books of the Old Testament; these have been long lost, and the books before us can only be abridgments, either of such chronicles, or of works of a similar kind.

That the ancient Jews took great care to *register* their civil, military, and ecclesiastical transactions, is sufficiently evident from frequent reference to such works in the sacred writings; and that these *registers* were carefully and correctly formed, we learn from the *character* of the *persons* by whom they were compiled: they were in general prophets, and seem to have been employed by the kings under whom they lived to compile the annals of their reigns; or most likely this was considered a part of the prophet's regular office.

Samuel, Nathan, and *Gad,* wrote under the reign of DAVID; 1 Chron. xxix. 29.

The acts of the reign of SOLOMON were written by *Nathan, Ahijah,* and *Iddo;* 2 Chron. ix. 29.

Shemaiah and *Iddo* wrote those of REHOBOAM; 2 Chron. xii. 15.

Iddo wrote also those of ABIJAH; 2 Chron. xiii. 22.

It is likely that *Hanani* the seer wrote those of Asa; 2 Chron. xvi. 7.

Jehu the prophet, the son of Hanani, 1 Kings xvi. 1, 7, wrote the acts of JEHOSHAPHAT; 2 Chron. xx. 34. Under this same reign we find *Jahaziel* the prophet, 2 Chron. xx. 14; and *Eliezer* the prophet, *ib.* v. 37.

Isaiah recorded the transactions of UZZIAH, 2 Chron. xxvi. 22; and those of HEZEKIAH, 2 Chron. xxxii. 32; and of AHAZ, of whose reign we find the principal facts in the fifth, sixth, and ninth chapters of his prophecies. Under this reign we find *Oded* the prophet, 2 Chron. xxviii. 9.

Hosea wrote the history of the reign of MANASSEH. See 2 Chron. xxxiii. 19, in the *margin.*

And *Jeremiah* wrote the history of JOSIAH and his descendants, the last kings of Judah.

This was such a succession of *historians* as no nation of the world could ever boast. Men, all of whom wrote under the *inspiration* of God's Holy Spirit; some of whom had minds the most highly cultivated, and of the most extraordinary powers. Whether the prophets who flourished in the reigns of the *kings of Israel* wrote the annals of *those* kings, we know not, because it is not positively declared. We know that *Ahijah* the Shilonite lived under JEROBOAM, the son of Nebat; 1 Kings xi. 29, and xiv. 2; and *Jehu,* son of Hanani, under BAASHA; 1 Kings xvi. 7.

Elijah and many others flourished under the reign of AHAB. *Elisha, Jonah,* and many more, succeeded him in the prophetic office.

Besides these prophets and prophetic men, we find other persons, whose office it was to *record* the transactions of the kings under whom they lived. These were called *secretaries* or *recorders;* so, under DAVID and SOLOMON, *Jehoshaphat* the son of Ahilud was *recorder,* מזכיר *mazkir,* "remembrancer;" 2 Sam. viii. 16, and 1 Chron. xviii. 15. And under HEZE-KIAH we find *Joah,* the son of *Asaph;* 2 Kings xviii. 18. And under JOSIAH, *Joah* the son of *Joahaz,* who filled the office; 2 Chron. xxxiv. 8.

The real object of the author of these books is not very easy to be ascertained. But it is evident that he never could have intended them as a *supplement* to the preceding books, as he relates many of the same circumstances which occur in them, and often in *greater detail;* and, except by way of *amplification, adds* very little that can be called *new,* and *omits* many things of importance, not only in the ancient history of the Israelites, but even of those mentioned in the preceding books of Samuel and Kings. *Nine chapters* of his work are occupied with extensive *genealogical tables*, but even these are far from being *perfect*. His history, properly speaking, does not begin till the *tenth chapter*, and then it commences abruptly with the last unsuccessful battle of Saul and his death, but not a word of his history.

Though the writer gives many curious and important particulars in the life of David, yet he passes by his *adultery* with Bath-sheba, and all its consequences. He says nothing of the *incest* of Amnon with his sister *Tamar*, nor a word of the *rebellion* and *abominations* of Absalom. He says very little of the kings of Israel, and takes no notice of what concerned that state, from the capture of Amaziah king of Judah by Joash king of Israel; 2 Chron. xxv. 17, &c. And of the last wars of these kings, which terminated in the captivity of the ten tribes, he says not one word!

The principal design of the writer appears to have been this: to point out, from the public registers, which were still preserved, what had been the state of the different families previously to the captivity, that at their return they might enter on and repossess their respective inheritances. He enters particularly into the functions, genealogies, families, and orders of the *priests* and *Levites;* and this was peculiarly necessary after the return from the captivity, to the end that the worship of God might be conducted in the same way as before, and by the proper legitimate persons.

He is also very particular relative to what concerns religion, the worship of God, the temple and its utensils, the kings who *authorized* or *tolerated* idolatry, and those who maintained the worship of the true God. In his distribution of praise and blame, these are the qualities which principally occupy his attention, and influence his pen.

It may be necessary to say something here concerning the *utility* of these books. That they are in this respect in low estimation, we may learn from the manner in which they are treated by commentators: they say very little concerning them, and suppose the subject has been anticipated in the books of *Samuel* and *Kings*. That the persons who treat them thus have never studied them, is most evident, else their judgment would be widely different. Whatever history these books possess, *in common* with the books of Samuel and Kings, may, in a commentary, be fairly introduced in the examination of the latter; and this I have endeavoured to do, as the reader may have already seen. But there are various *details*, and *curious facts* and *observations*, which must be considered in these books alone: nor will a *slight* mention of such circumstances do them justice.

St. Jerome had the most exalted opinion of the books of Chronicles. According to him, "they are an epitome of the Old Testament." He asserts, that "they are of such high moment and importance, that he who supposes himself to be acquainted with the sacred writings, and does not know *them*, only deceives himself; and that innumerable questions relative to the Gospel are here explained." *Paralipomenon liber, id est, Instrumenti Veteris* επιτομη, *tantus ac talis est, ut absque illo, si quis scientiam Scripturarum sibi voluerit arrogare, seipsum irrideat. Per singula quippe nomina, juncturasque verborum, et prætermissæ in* REGUM *libris tanguntur historiæ, et innumerabiles explicantur Evangelii Quæstiones.*—Epis. Secund. ad Paulinum Presbyterum., OPER. Edit. Benedict. vol. iv., col. 574. And in another place he asserts, that "all Scripture knowledge is contained in these books;" *Omnis eruditio Scripturarum in hoc libro continetur.*—Præfat. in lib. Paral. justa Septuaginta Interpret. OPER. Edit. Bened., vol. i., col. 1418. This may be going too far; but St. Jerome believed that there was a mystery and meaning in every proper name, whether of *man, woman, city,* or *country*, in the book. And yet he complains greatly of the corruption of those names, some having been *divided*, so as to make *two* or *three* names out of one, and sometimes names condensed, so as of *three* names to make but *one*. To cure this evil he laboured hard, and did much; but still the confusion is great, and in many cases past remedy. To assist the reader in this respect I wish to refer him to the *marginal readings* and *parallel texts*, which are here carefully represented in the inner margin; these should be constantly consulted, as they serve to remove many difficulties and reconcile several seeming contradictions. In addition to these helps I have carefully examined the different *ancient versions*, and the *various readings* in the MSS. of *Kennicott* and *De Rossi*, which often help to remove such difficulties.

There is one mode of exposition which I have applied to these books, which has not, as far as I know, been as yet used: I mean the *Targum, or Chaldee Paraphrase*, of Rabbi JOSEPH. It is well known to all oriental scholars, that a *Chaldee* Targum, or Paraphrase, has been found and published in the Polyglots, on every book of the Old Testament, *purely Hebrew*, the books of *Chronicles* excepted. Neither in the Complutensian, Antwerp, Parisian, nor London Polyglot, is such a *Targum* to be found; none having been discovered when these works were published. But shortly after the London Polyglot was finished, a MS. was found in the University of Cambridge, containing the *Targum* on these books: this, with several other pieces, *Arabic, Persian, Syriac*, &c., Dr. *Samuel Clarke* collected, and intended to publish, as a *supplementary volume* to the Polyglot, but was prevented by premature death. The MS. was afterwards copied by Mr. *David Wilkins*, and printed, with a Latin translation, at Amsterdam, quarto, 1715. Of this work the reader will find I have made a liberal use, as I have of the *Targum* of *Jonathan ben Uzziel*, on the preceding books. *Rabbi Joseph*, the author, lived about *three hundred years* after the destruction of the second temple, or about A. D. 400. The MS. in question formerly belonged to the celebrated *Erpen*, and was purchased by the duke of Buckingham, then Chancellor of the University of Cambridge, and by him presented to the public library of that University.

It is worthy of remark, that the term מימרא *meymera*, "word," and מימרא דיי *meymera dayeya*, "the word of Jehovah," is used *personally* in this Targum; never as a *word spoken*, but as a PERSON *acting:* see the notes on John i. 1.

The *first book of Chronicles* contains a sort of genealogical history from the creation of the world to the death of David, A. M. 2989.

THE FIRST BOOK

OF

THE CHRONICLES

Chronological Notes relative to this Book

Year of the World, 1.—Year before Christ, according to Archbishop Usher, 4004.—Year before the Flood, according to the common Hebrew Bible, 1656.—Year of the Julian period, 710.

CHAPTER I

The genealogy of Adam to Noah, 1–3. Of Noah to Abraham, 4–27. The sons of Abraham, Ishmael, and Isaac, 28. The sons of Ishmael, 29, 33. The sons of Esau, 34–42. A list of the kings of Edom, 43–50. A list of the dukes of Edom, 51–54.

A. M. 1, &c.
B. C. 4004, &c.
Ante Diluvium,
1656, &c.

ADAM, ^aSheth, Enosh,
2 Kenan, Mahalaleel, Jered,
3 Henoch, Methuselah, Lamech,

4 Noah, Shem, Ham, and Japheth.

5 ^bThe sons of Japheth; Gomer, and Magog, and Madai, and Javan, and Tubal, and Meshech, and Tiras.

6 And the sons of Gomer; Ashchenaz, and ^cRiphath, and Togarmah.

7 And the sons of Javan; Elishah, and Tarshish, Kittim, and ^dDodanim.

8 ^eThe sons of Ham; Cush, and Mizraim, Put, and Canaan.

A. M. 1, &c.
B. C. 4004, &c.
Ante Diluvium,
1656, &c.

9 And the sons of Cush; Seba, and Havilah, and Sabta, and Raamah, and Sabtecha. And the sons of Raamah; Sheba, and Dedan.

10 And Cush ^fbegat Nimrod: he began to be mighty upon the earth.

11 And Mizraim begat Ludim, and Anamim, and Lehabim, and Naphtuhim,

---

^aGen. iv. 25, 26; v. 3, 9——^bGen. x. 2, &c.——^cOr, *Diphath*, as it is in some copies

^dOr, *Rodanim*, according to some copies——^eGen. x. 6, &c.——^fGen. x. 8, 13, &c.

NOTES ON CHAP. I

Verse 1. *Adam, Sheth, Enosh*] That is, Adam was the father of Sheth or Seth, Seth was the father of Enosh, Enosh the father of Kenan, and so on. No notice is taken of *Cain* and *Abel*, or of any of the other sons of Adam. One line of patriarchs, from Adam to Noah, is what the historian intended to give; and to have mentioned the posterity of *Cain* or *Abel* would have been useless, as Noah was not the immediate descendant of either. Besides, all their posterity had perished in the deluge, none remaining of the Adamic family but Noah and his children; and from these all the nations of the earth sprang.

How learned must those men be who can take for a text "*The first verse of the first chapter of the first book* of CHRONICLES," and find a *mystery* in each *name;* which, in the aggregate, amounts to a full view of the *original perfection, subsequent fall, consequent misery,* and *final restoration,* of MAN! O ye profound illustrators of the names of *men* and *cities!* why do ye not give us the *key* of your wisdom, write comments, and enlighten the world?

Verse 5. After *Tiras,* the Targum adds, "And the names of their countries were Africa, and Germany, and Media, and Macedonia, Bithynia, and Mœsia, and Thrace." *And in another copy,* "Germany, Getia, and Media, and Ephesus, Bithynia, and Mœsia, and Thrace."

Verse 6. To this verse the Targum adds, "And the names of their countries were Asia, and Persia, and Barbary."

Verse 7. *The sons of Javan*] "But the sons of Macedon, Alsu, and Tarsus, Ilation, and Dardania; or, according to others, Elisha, Alam, Titsas, Achzavia, and Dardania, Ridom, and Chamen, and Antioch." So says this Targum, which I shall henceforth designate by the letter *T.*

Verse 8. *The sons of Ham; Cush, and Mizraim*] "Arabia and Egypt."—*T.*

Verse 9. *Seba, and Havilah*] "Sindi and Hindi, and Semadæi, and Libyes and the Zingitæ; but the sons of the Mauritanians, Demargad and Mesag."—*T.*

Verse 10. *He began to be mighty upon the earth.*] "He began to be bold in sin, a murderer of the innocent, and a rebel before the Lord."—*T.*

Verse 11. *Ludim, &c.*] "The Nivitæi, the Mariotæi, the Libakæi, and the Pentaskenæi."—*T.*

A. M. 1, &c.
B. C. 4004, &c.
Ante Diluvium,
1656, &c.

12 And Pathrusim, and Caslu-him, (of whom came the Philistines,) and ᵍCaphthorim.

13 And ʰCanaan begat Zidon his first-born, and Heth.

14 The Jebusite also, and the Amorite, and the Girgashite,

15 And the Hivite, and the Arkite, and the Sinite,

16 And the Arvadite, and the Zemarite, and the Hamathite.

17 The sons of ¹Shem; Elam, and Asshur, and Arphaxad, and Lud, and Aram, and Uz, and Hul, and Gether, and ᵏMeshech.

18 And Arphaxad begat Shelah, and Shelah begat Eber.

19 And unto Eber were born two sons: the name of the one *was* ¹Peleg; because in his days the earth was divided: and his brother's name *was* Joktan.

20 And ᵐJoktan begat Almodad, and Sheleph, and Hazarmaveth, and Jerah,

21 Hadoram also, and Uzal, and Diklah,

22 And Ebal, and Abimael, and Sheba,

23 And Ophir, and Havilah, and Jobab. All these *were* the sons of Joktan.

24 ⁿShem, Arphaxad, Shelah,

25 ºEber, Peleg, Reu,

26 Serug, Nahor, Terah,

27 ᵖAbram; the same *is* Abraham.

28 The sons of Abraham; ۹Isaac, and ʳIshmael.

29 These *are* their generations: The ˢfirst-born of Ishmael, Nebaioth; then Kedar, and Adbeel, and Mibsam,

30 Mishma, and Dumah, Massah, ᵗHadad, and Tema,

31 Jetur, Naphish, and Kedemah. These are the sons of Ishmael.

32 Now ᵘthe sons of Keturah, Abraham's concubine: she bare Zimran, and Jokshan, and Medan, and Midian, and Ishbak, and Shuah. And the sons of Jokshan; Sheba, and Dedan.

33 And the sons of Midian; Ephah, and Epher, and Henoch, and Abida, and Eldaah. All these *are* the sons of Keturah.

34 And ᵛAbraham begat Isaac. ʷThe sons of Isaac; Esau and Israel.

35 The sons of ˣEsau; Eliphaz, Reuel, and Jeush, and Jaalam, and Korah.

36 The sons of Eliphaz; Teman, and Omar, ʸZephi, and Gatam, Kenaz, and Timna, and Amalek.

37 The sons of Reuel; Nahath, Zerah, Shammah, and Mizzah.

38 ᶻAnd the sons of Seir; Lotan, and Shobal, and Zibeon, and Anah, and Dishon, and Ezar, and Dishan.

39 And the sons of Lotan; Hori, and ᵃHomam: and Timna *was* Lotan's sister.

40 The sons of Shobal; ᵇAlian, and Manahath, and Ebal, ᶜShephi, and Onam. And the sons of Zibeon; Aiah, and Anah.

41 The sons of Anah; ᵈDishon. And the sons of Dishon; ᵉAmram, and Eshban, and Ithran, and Cheran.

42 The sons of Ezer; Bilhan, and Zavan, *and* ᶠJakan. The sons of Dishan; Uz, and Aran.

A. M. 1, &c.
B. C. 4004, &c.
Ante Diluvium,
1656, &c.

ᵍDeut. ii. 23——ʰGen. x. 15, &c.——¹Gen. x. 22; xi. 10——ᵏOr, *Mash*, Gen. x. 23——¹That is, *Division*, Gen. x. 25——ᵐGen. x. 26——ⁿGen. xi. 10, &c.; Luke iii. 34, &c.——ºGen. xi. 15——ᵖGen. xvii. 5 ۹Gen. xxi. 2, 3——ʳGen. xvi. 11, 15——ˢGen. xxv. 13–16——ᵗOr, *Hadar*, Gen. xxv. 15——ᵘGen. xxv. 1, 2

ᵛGen. xxi. 2, 3——ʷGen. xxv. 25, 26——ˣGen. xxxvi. 9, 10——ʸOr, *Zepho*, Gen. xxxvi. 11——ᶻGen. xxxvi. 20——ᵃOr, *Heman*, Gen. xxxvi. 22——ᵇOr, *Alvan*, Gen. xxxvi. 23——ᶜOr, *Shepho*, Gen. xxxvi. 23——ᵈGen. xxxvi. 25——ᵉOr, *Hemdan*, Gen. xxxvi. 26——ᶠOr, *Akan*, Gen. xxxvi. 27

Verse 12. *Caphthorim.*] "The Cappadocians." —T.

Verse 13. *Canaan begat Zidon*] "Canaan begat Bothniam, his first-born, who built Sidon."—T.

Verse 19. *The name of the one* was *Peleg*] "Because in his days the inhabitants of the earth were *divided* according to their languages. And the name of his brother was *Joktan*, because in his days the years of men began to be shortened, on account of their iniquities."—T.

Verse 20. *Joktan begat Almodad*] "He divided and measured the earth by lines. *Sheleph;* he assigned rivers to be boundaries. *Hazarmaveth;* he prepared a place of snares to kill by the highways. *Jerah;* he built inns, and when any person came to eat and drink, he gave

him deadly poison, and so took his property." —T.

According to these traditions, the two first were *geographers;* the third, a public *robber;* and the fourth, an unprincipled *innkeeper*, who gave poison to his rich guests, that he might get their property. Such things have been done even in *modern* times.

Verse 23. *And Ophir*] "Whence gold is brought." *And Havilah;* "whence pearls are brought."—T.

Verse 24. *Shem*] "The great priest."—T.

Verse 32. *Keturah, Abraham's concubine*] Abraham's *pilegesh*, or *wife* of the second rank; she was neither *whore, harlot,* nor *concubine*, in our sense of these words.

A. M. 1, &c.
B. C. 4004, &c.
Ante Diluvium,
1656, &c.
43 Now these *are* the ᵍkings that reigned in the land of Edom before *any* king reigned over the children of Israel; Bela the son of Beor: and the name of his city *was* Dinhabah.

44 And when Belah was dead, Jobab, the son of Zerah of Bozrah, reigned in his stead.

45 And when Jobab was dead, Husham of the land of the Temanites reigned in his stead.

46 And when Husham was dead, Hadad the son of Bedad, which smote Midian in the field of Moab, reigned in his stead: and the name of his city *was* Avith.

47 And when Hadad was dead, Samlah of Masrekah reigned in his stead.

48 ʰAnd when Samlah was dead, Shaul of Rehoboth by the river reigned in his stead.

49 And when Shaul was dead, Baal-hanan the son of Achbor reigned in his stead.

50 And when Baal-hanan was dead, ¹Hadad reigned in his stead: and the name of his city *was* ᵏPai; and his wife's name *was* Mehetabel, the daughter of Matred, the daughter of Mezahab.

51 Hadad died also. And the ¹dukes of Edom were; duke Timnah, duke ᵐAliah, duke Jetheth,

52 Duke Aholibamah, duke Elah, duke Pinon,

53 Duke Kenaz, duke Teman, duke Mibzar,

54 Duke Magdiel, duke Iram. These *are* the dukes of Edom.

A. M. 1, &c.
B. C. 4004, &c.
Ante Diluvium,
1656, &c.

ᵍGen. xxxvi. 31, &c.——ʰGen. xxxvi. 37——ⁱOr, *Hadar*, Gen. xxxvi. 39

ᵏOr, *Pau*, Genesis xxxvi. 39——¹Genesis xxxvi. 40 ᵐOr, *Alvah*

Verse 43. *Before* any *king reigned over—Israel*] See Gen. xxxvi. 31, &c., where the same verses occur, as I have supposed borrowed from this place; and see the notes there.

Bela the son of Beor] "Balaam the impious son of Beor, the same as Laban the Syrian, who formed a confederacy with the sons of Esau, to destroy Jacob and his children; and he studied to destroy them utterly. Afterwards he reigned in Edom; and the name of his royal city was Dinhabah, because it was undeservedly given to him."—*T.*

Verse 44. *Bela was dead*] "Being killed by Phineas, in the wilderness."—*T.*

Jobab the son of Zerah] Supposed by some to be the same as *Job*, whose book forms a part of the canon of Scripture. But in their names there is no similarity; Job being written אִיוֹב *aiyob;* Jobab, יוֹבָב *yobab.* See the notes on Job, and the parallel place in Genesis.

Verse 46. *Smote Midian*] Nothing is known of this war.

Verse 48. *By the river*] "Shaul of Plathiutha, a great city, built on the banks of the Euphrates."—*T.*

Verse 50. *Daughter of Mezahab.*] This word מֵי זָהָב *mey zahab*, is literally *the golden waters;* or *What is gold?* The Targumist paraphrases thus: "Mehetabel, the daughter of Matred, was so earnest and diligent in business that she became immensely rich; but when she was converted, she said, *What is this silver,* and *What is this gold?* That is, They are of no real worth."

Verse 51. *Hadad died*] "And his kingdom ended; for his land was subdued by the children of Esau, and the dukes of Edom ruled in the land of Gebala."—*T.*

For various particulars in this chapter, see Gen. x. and xxxvi., and the parallel places.

CHAPTER II

The twelve sons of Jacob, 1, 2. The posterity of Judah down to David, 3–15. The posterity of the children of Jesse and Caleb, 16–55.

A. M. 2252, &c.
B. C. 1752, &c.
Post Diluvium,
596, &c.
THESE *are* the sons of ᵃIsrael; ᵇReuben, Simeon, Levi, and Judah, Issachar, and Zebulun,

2 Dan, Joseph, and Benjamin, Naphtali, Gad, and Asher.

3 The sons of ᶜJudah; Er, and Onan, and Shelah: *which* three were born unto him of the daughter of ᵈShua the Canaanitess. And ᵉEr, the first-born of Judah, was evil in the sight of the LORD; and he slew him.

4 And ᶠTamar his daughter-in-law bare him Pharez and Zerah. All the sons of Judah *were* five.

5 The sons of ᵍPharez; Hezron, and Hamul.

A. M. 2252, &c.
B. C. 1752, &c.
Post Diluvium,
596, &c.

ᵃOr, *Jacob*——ᵇGen. xxix. 32; xxx. 5; xxxv. 18, 22; xlvi. 8, &c.——ᶜGen. xxxviii. 3; xlvi. 12; Num. xxvi. 19

ᵈGen. xxxviii. 2——ᵉGen. xxxviii. 7——ᶠGen. xxxviii. 29, 30; Matt. i. 3——ᵍGen. xlvi. 12; Ruth iv. 18

NOTES ON CHAP. II

Verse 1. *These are the sons of Israel*] For this genealogy see the parallel places pointed out in the margin.

A. M. 2252, &c.
B. C. 1752, &c.
Post Diluvium, 596, &c.

6 And the sons of Zerah; [h]Zimri, [i]and Ethan, and Heman, and Calcol, and [k]Dara: five of them in all.

7 And the sons of [l]Carmi; [m]Achar, the troubler of Israel, who transgressed in the thing [n]accursed.

8 And the sons of Ethan; Azariah.

9 The sons also of Hezron, that were born unto him; Jerahmeel, and [o]Ram, and [p]Chelubai.

10 And Ram [q]begat Amminadab; and Amminadab begat Nahshon, [r]prince of the children of Judah;

11 And Nahshon begat [s]Salma, and Salma begat Boaz,

12 And Boaz begat Obed, and Obed begat Jesse,

13 [t]And Jesse begat his first-born Eliab, and Abinadab the second, and [u]Shimma the third,

14 Nethaneel the fourth, Raddai the fifth,

15 Ozem the sixth, David the seventh:

16 Whose sisters *were* Zeruiah, and Abigail. [v]And the sons of Zeruiah; Abishai, and Joab, and Asahel, three.

17 And [w]Abigail bare Amasa: and the father of Amasa *was* [x]Jether the Ishmeelite.

18 And Caleb the son of Hezron begat *children* of Azubah *his* wife, and of Jerioth: her sons *are* these; Jesher, and Shobab, and Ardon.

19 And when Azubah was dead, Caleb took unto him [y]Ephrath, which bare him Hur.

20 And Hur begat Uri, and Uri begat [z]Bezaleel.

21 And afterward Hezron went in to the daughter of [a]Machir the father of Gilead, whom he [b]married when he *was* threescore years old; and she bare him Segub.

22 And Segub begat Jair, who had three and twenty cities in the land of Gilead.

23 [c]And he took Geshur, and Aram, with the towns of Jair, from them, with Kenath, and the towns thereof, *even* threescore cities. All these *belonged to* the sons of Machir the father of Gilead.

A. M. 2252, &c.
B. C. 1752, &c.
Post Diluvium, 596, &c.

24 And after that Hezron was dead in Caleb-ephratah, then Abiah, Hezron's wife, bare him [d]Ashur the father of Tekoa.

25 And the sons of Jerahmeel the first-born of Hezron were, Ram the first-born, and Bunah, and Oren, and Ozem, *and* Ahijah.

26 Jerahmeel had also another wife, whose name *was* Atarah; she *was* the mother of Onam.

27 And the sons of Ram the first-born of Jerahmeel were, Maaz, and Jamin, and Eker.

28 And the sons of Onam were, Shammai, and Jada. And the sons of Shammai; Nadab, and Abishur.

29 And the name of the wife of Abishur *was* Abihail, and she bare him Ahban, and Molid.

30 And the sons of Nadab; Seled, and Appaim: but Seled died without children.

31 And the sons of Appaim; Ishi. And the sons of Ishi; Sheshan. And [e]the children of Sheshan; Ahlai.

32 And the sons of Jada the brother of Shammai; Jether, and Jonathan: and Jether died without children.

33 And the sons of Jonathan; Peleth, and Zaza. These were the sons of Jerahmeel.

34 Now Sheshan had no sons, but daughters. And Sheshan had a servant, an Egyptian, whose name *was* Jarha.

35 And Sheshan gave his daughter to Jarha his servant to wife; and she bare him Attai.

36 And Attai begat Nathan, and Nathan begat [f]Zabad,

37 And Zabad begat Ephlal, and Ephlal begat Obed,

38 And Obed begat Jehu, and Jehu begat Azariah,

---

[h]Or, *Zabdi*, Josh. vii. 1——[i]1 Kings iv. 31——[k]Or, *Darda* [l]See ch. iv. 1——[m]Or, *Achan*——[n]Josh. vi. 18; vii. 1 [o]Or, *Aram*, Matt. i. 3, 4——[p]Or, *Caleb*, ver. 18, 42 [q]Ruth iv. 19, 20; Matt. i. 4——[r]Num. i. 7; ii. 3——[s]Or, *Salmon*, Ruth iv. 21; Matt. i. 4——[t]2 Sam. xvi. 6

[u]Or, *Shammah*, 1 Sam. xvi. 9——[v]2 Sam. ii. 18——[w]2 Sam. xvii. 25——[x]2 Sam. xvii. 25, *Ithra an Israelite* [y]Ver. 50——[z]Exod. xxxi. 2——[a]Num. xxxvii. 1——[b]Heb. *took*——[c]Num. xxxii. 41; Deut. iii. 14; Josh. xiii. 30 [d]Chap. iv. 5——[e]See ver. 34, 35——[f]Chap. xi. 41

Verse 6. *Five of them in all.*] "These were all chief men; and on them the spirit of prophecy rested."—*T.*

Verse 17. *Jether the Ishmeelite.*] "They called him Jether, because he girded himself with his sword, that he might assist David with the Arabians, when Abner was endeavouring to destroy David and the whole race of Jesse, as being unfit to enter into the congregation of the Lord, on account of Ruth the Moabitess."—*T.*

Verse 18. *Azubah*] "And why was she called Azubah? Because she was barren and despised. But her injury was manifested before the Lord; and she was comforted, and adorned with wisdom; and she span, skilfully, goats' hair for the court of the tabernacle."—*T.*

Verse 20. *Uri begat Bezaleel*] This was

A. M. 2252, &c.
B. C. 1752, &c.
Post Diluvium,
596, &c.

39 And Azariah begat Helez, and Helez begat Eleasah,

40 And Eleasah begat Sisamai, and Sisamai begat Shallum,

41 And Shallum begat Jekamiah, and Jekamiah begat Elishama.

42 Now the sons of Caleb the brother of Jerahmeel *were,* Mesha his first-born, which *was* the father of Ziph; and the sons of Mareshah the father of Hebron.

43 And the sons of Hebron; Korah, and Tappuah, and Rekem, and Shema.

44 And Shema begat Raham, the father of Jorkoam; and Rekem begat Shammai.

45 And the son of Shammai *was* Maon: and Maon *was* the father of Beth-zur.

46 And Ephah, Caleb's concubine, bare Haran, and Moza, and Gazez: and Haran begat Gazez.

47 And the sons of Jahdai; Regem, and Jotham, and Gesham, and Pelet, and Ephah, and Shaaph.

48 Maachah, Caleb's concubine, bare Sheber and Tirhanah.

A. M. 2252, &c.
B. C. 1752, &c.
Post Diluvium,
596, &c.

49 She bare also Shaaph the father of Madmannah, Sheva the father of Machbenah, and the father of Gibea: and the daughter of Caleb *was* [g]Achsah.

50 These were the sons of Caleb the son of Hur, the first-born of [h]Ephratah; Shobal the father of Kirjath-jearim,

51 Salma the father of Beth-lehem, Hareph the father of Beth-gader.

52 And Shobal the father of Kirjath-jearim had sons; [i]Haroeh, *and* [k]half of the Manahethites.

53 And the families of Kirjath-jearim; the Ithrites, and the Puhites, and the Shumathites, and the Mishraites; of them came the Zareathites, and the Eshtaulites.

54 The sons of Salma; Beth-lehem, and the Netophathites, [l]Ataroth, the house of Joab, and half of the Manahethites, the Zorites.

55 And the families of the scribes which dwelt at Jabez; the Tirathites, the Shimeathites, *and* Suchathites. These *are* the [m]Kenites that came of Hemath, the father of the house of [n]Rechab.

---

[g]Josh. xv. 17——[h]Or, *Ephrath,* ver. 19——[i]Or, *Reaiah,* chap. iv. 2——[k]Or, *half of the Menuchites* or

probably the famous artist mentioned Exod. xxxi. 2, &c., where see the notes.

Verse 34. *Whose name was Jarha.*] "And he gave him his liberty, and gave him Sheshan his daughter to wife."—*T.*

Verse 42. *Now the sons of Caleb*] This was not Caleb the son of Jephunneh, but Caleb the son of Hezron, ver. 18, 50. But some think that Caleb the son of Hezron was the *grandson* of Caleb, son of Jephunneh; but this is probably fanciful.

The father of Ziph] "The prince of the Ziphites."—*T.*

Verse 52. *Shobal—had sons*] "Disciples and priests, to whom belonged the half of the oblations."—*T.*

Verse 53. *The families of Kirjath-jearim*] "These were the children of Moses, which Zipporah bare to him, viz., the Jethrites, the Shumathites, and the Mishraites; of these came the disciples of the prophets Zarah and *Eshtaol.*"—*T.*

Verse 54. *The sons of Salma*] "The righteous Bethlehemites, who had a good name, as the Netophathites, who removed the guards which Jeroboam had placed in the way lest the people should carry the first-fruits to Jerusalem: for the sons of Salma carried baskets full of first-fruits privately to Jerusalem; and having cloven wood, they made ladders, and

Hatsi-hammenuchoth——[l]Or, *Asarites* or *crowns of the house of Joab*——[m]Judg i. 16——[n]Jer. xxxv. 2

brought them to Jerusalem to be laid up in Beth-mokad for oblations. These came from the lineage of Joab the son of Zeruiah; and some of them were priests; and they divided the residue of the sacrifices with the sons of the prophets who were in Zorah."—*T.*

Verse 55. *The families*] "The families of the Rechabites, the sons of Eliezer the son of Misco, the disciple of Jabez; he was Othniel, the son of Kenaz. And he was called *Jabez,* because in his *council* he instituted a school of disciples; they were called *Tirathim,* because in their hymns their voice was like *trumpets;* and *Shimathim,* because in *hearing* they lifted up their faces, i. e., in prayer; and *Suchathim,* because they were *overshadowed* by the Spirit of prophecy. These Salmæi were the children of Zipporah, who were numbered among the Levites who came from the stock of Moses, the master of Israel, whose righteousness profited them more than chariots and horses."—*T.* See on chap. iv. 9, 10.

In the above explanation of *Tirathites, Shimeathites,* and *Suchathites,* the Targumist refers to the import of the Hebrew roots, whence these names are derived. See chap. iv. 10. In this chapter many names of *cities* are given as the names of *men.*

CHAPTER III

*The children of David which were born to him in Hebron, 1–4. Those born to him in Jerusalem, 5–9.
The regal line from Solomon, 10–24.*

A. M. 2951, &c.
B. C. 1053, &c.
Post Diluvium,
1295, &c.

NOW these were the sons of David, which were born unto him in Hebron; the first-born [a]Amnon, of Ahinoam the [b]Jezreelitess; the second, [c]Daniel, of Abigail the Carmelitess:

2 The third, Absalom the son of Maachah the daughter of Talmai king of Geshur: the fourth, Adonijah the son of Haggith:

3 The fifth, Shephatiah of Abital: the sixth, Ithream by [d]Eglah his wife.

4 *These* six were born unto him in Hebron; and [e]there he reigned seven years and six months: and [f]in Jerusalem he reigned thirty and three years.

5 [g]And these were born unto him in Jerusalem; [h]Shimea, and Shobab, and Nathan, and [i]Solomon, four, of [k]Bath-shua the daughter of [l]Ammiel:

6 Ibhar also, and [m]Elishama, and Eliphelet,

7 And Nogah, and Nepheg, and Japhia,

8 And Elishama, and [n]Eliada, and Eliphelet, [o]nine.

9 *These were* all the sons of David, besides the sons of the concubines, and [p]Tamar their sister.

A. M. 2951, &c.
B. C. 1053, &c.
Post Diluvium,
1295, &c.

10 And Solomon's son *was* [q]Rehoboam, [r]Abia his son, Asa his son, Jehoshaphat his son,

11 Joram his son, [s]Ahaziah his son, Joash his son,

12 Amaziah his son, [t]Azariah his son, Jotham his son,

13 Ahaz his son, Hezekiah his son, Manasseh his son,

14 Amon his son, Josiah his son.

15 And the sons of Josiah *were,* the first-born, [u]Johanan, the second, [v]Jehoiakim, the third, [w]Zedekiah, the fourth, Shallum.

16 And the sons of [x]Jehoiakim; [y]Jeconiah his son, Zedekiah [z]his son.

17 And the sons of Jeconiah; Assir, [a]Salathiel [b]his son,

---

[a]2 Sam. iii. 2——[b]Josh. xv. 56——[c]Or, *Chileab,* 2 Sam. iii. 3——[d]2 Sam. iii. 5——[e]2 Sam. ii. 11——[f]2 Sam. v. 5 [g]2 Sam. v. 14; chap. xiv. 4——[h]Or, *Shammua,* 3 Sam. v. 14——[i]2 Sam. xii. 24——[k]Or, *Bath-sheba,* 2 Sam. xi. 3——[l]Or, *Eliam,* 2 Sam. xi. 3——[m]*Elishua,* 2 Sam. v. 15 [n]Or, *Beeliada,* chap. xiv. 7——[o]See 2 Sam. v. 14, 15, 16——[p]2 Samuel xiii. 1——[q]1 Kings xi. 43; xv. 6

[r]Or, *Abijam,* 1 Kings xv. 1——[s]Or, *Azariah,* 2 Chron. xxii. 6; or *Jehoahaz,* 2 Chron. xxi. 17——[t]Or, *Uzziah,* 2 Kings xv. 30——[u]Or, *Jehoahaz,* 2 Kings xxiii. 30——[v]Or, *Eliakim,* 2 Kings xxiii. 34——[w]Or, *Mattaniah,* 2 Kings xxiv. 17——[x]Matt. i. 11——[y]Or, *Jehoiachin,* 2 Kings xxiv. 6; or *Coniah,* Jer. xxii. 24——[z]2 Kings xxiv. 17, being his uncle——[a]Heb. *Shealtiel*——[b]Matt. i. 12

NOTES ON CHAP. III

Verse 1. *The second, Daniel*] In 2 Sam. iii. 3, this person is called *Chileab;* he probably had two names. The Targum says, "The second, Daniel, who was also called Chileab, because he was in every respect like to his father." The Targumist refers here to the import of the word כלאב *ke-le-ab, like to the father.* Jarchi says the two names were given to this person because David, having taken Abigail immediately after the death of Nabal, it could not be ascertained whether this child were the son of *David* or of *Nabal,* therefore David called him דניאל *Daniel, God is my Judge,* and כלאב *Chileab,* he who is *like to the father;* probably from the striking resemblance he bore to David, his reputed father. "God is my Judge, I have not fathered another man's child; this is entirely like unto myself."

Verse 3. *By Eglah his wife.*] The Targum, Jarchi, and others, maintain that this was *Michal,* the daughter of Saul; but this does not well agree with 2 Sam. vi. 23: *Michal had no child to the day of her death.* Yet she might have had a child *before* the time that is mentioned above.

Verse 5. *Shimea, and Shobab*] Solomon is mentioned *last,* though he was the *eldest* of these four sons, because the genealogy was to be continued from him. *Bath-shua* בת שוע, is the same as *Bath-sheba,* בת שבע the ו *vau* being put by mistake in the former for ב *beth* in the latter.

Verse 6. *Elishama, and Eliphelet*] In this and the eighth verse these two names occur twice; some think this is a mistake, but others suppose that two persons of these names died young, and that the next born received the name of the deceased.—See *Jarchi.*

Verse 8. *Nine.*] There are *thirteen* if we count the *four* sons of Bath-sheba, and *nine* without them; and in the second book of Samuel there are *eleven,* reckoning the above *four,* and without them only *seven.* In the book of *Samuel* probably only those who were *alive* were reckoned, while the author of the *Chronicles* comprises those also who were *dead* in this enumeration. Jarchi supposes that the duplicate *Elishama* and *Eliphelet* are those which increase the regular number *seven* to *nine;* and that the dead without posterity, as well as the living, are mentioned to increase the number of David's descendants; for, says he, the whole book is written for the honour of David and his seed.

Verse 9. *And Tamar their sister.*] This is the only *daughter* of David whose name is on record; and yet he is said to have had both SONS and DAUGHTERS, 2 Sam. v. 13.

Verse 15. *Jehoiakim*] For the difference of several names in these lists, see the *marginal readings* and *references.*

Shallum.] "So called because the kingdom departed from the house of David in his days."—*T.*

Verse 16. *Zedekiah his son.*] If this be the same who was the last king of Judah, before the captivity, the word *son* must be taken here to signify *successor;* for it is certain that Zede-

A. M. 2951, &c.
B. C. 1053, &c.
Post Diluvium,
1295, &c.

18 Malchiram also, and Pedaiah, and Shenazar, Jecamiah, Hoshama, and Nedabiah.

19 And the sons of Pedaiah *were,* Zerubbabel, and Shimei: and the sons of Zerubbabel, Meshullam, and Hananiah, and Shelomith their sister:

20 And Hashubah, and Ohel, and Berechiah, and Hasadiah, Jushab-hesed, five.

21 And the sons of Hananiah; Pelatiah, and Jesaiah: the sons of Rephaiah, the sons

of Arnan, the sons of Obadiah, the sons of Shechaniah.

A. M. 2951, &c.
B. C. 1053, &c.
Post Diluvium,
1295, &c.

22 And the sons of Shechaniah; Shemaiah: and the sons of Shemaiah; cHattush, and Igeal, and Bariah, and Neariah, and Shaphat, six.

23 And the sons of Neariah; Elioenai, and dHezekiah, and Azrikam, three.

24 And the sons of Elioenai *were,* Hodaiah, and Eliashib, and Pelaiah, and Akkub, and Johanan, and Dalaiah, and Anani, seven.

---

cEzra viii. 2

dHeb. *Hiskijahu*

---

kiah was the successor of Jeconiah, and that Zedekiah was the son of Josiah, and not of Jehoiakim.

Verse 17. *The sons of Jeconiah*] Jeremiah has said (chap. xxii. 30) that Jeconiah, or, as he calls him, *Coniah,* should be *childless;* but this must refer to his *posterity* being deprived of the throne, and indeed thus the prophet interprets it himself: *For no man of his seed shall prosper, sitting upon the throne of David, and ruling any more in Judah.*

Assir] Salathiel was not the son of *Assir,* but of Jeconiah, Matt. i. 12. Who then was *Assir?* Possibly *nobody;* for as the Hebrew אסר *assir* signifies a *prisoner,* it may be considered as an epithet of Jeconiah, who we know was a very long time *prisoner* in Babylon. See 2 Kings xxiv. 15, and *Calmet.*

Verse 18. *Malchiram also*] Calmet supposes we should read here, *And the sons of Salathiel were Malchiram and Pedaiah,* &c.

Verse 19. *The sons of Pedaiah*] Houbigant

thinks these words should be omitted. *Pedaiah* is wanting in the *Arabic* and *Syriac.* If this be omitted, Zerubbabel will appear to be the son of *Salathiel,* according to Matt. i. 12, and not the son of *Pedaiah,* as here stated.

Verse 22. *The sons of Shemaiah—six.*] Five only are found in the text, and the *versions* give us no assistance; neither do the MSS. correct the place. If the *father* be not here included with his *sons,* some *name* must be lost out of the text.

Verse 24. *And Anani*] "This is the King Messiah who is to be revealed."—*T. Jarchi* says the same, and refers to Dan. vii. 13: *Behold, one like the Son of man came with the clouds (עננ* *ananey) of heaven.* For this application of the word he gives a fanciful reason, not worthy to be repeated. The *Syriac* and *Arabic* omit several names in this table, and make only *twenty-three* verses in the chapter: but such differences are frequent in the books of Chronicles.

CHAPTER IV

A second genealogy of Judah, 1–23. *The account of Jabez,* 9, 10. *The genealogy of Simeon,* 24–27. *Their cities,* 28–31. *Their villages, and where situated,* 32, 33. *The heads of families,* 34–38. *Where they settled; and what was their occupation,* 39–43.

A. M. 2704, &c.
B. C. 1300, &c.
Post Diluvium,
1048, &c.

THE sons of Judah; aPharez, Hezron, and bCarmi, and Hur, and Shobal.

2 And cReaiah the son of Shobal begat Jahath; and Jahath begat Ahumai and Lahad. These *are* the families of the Zorathites.

3 And these *were of* the father of Etam; Jezreel, and Ishma, and Idbash: and the name of their sister *was* Hazelelponi:

4 And Penuel the father of Gedor, and Ezer the father of Hushah. These *are* the sons of dHur, the first-born of Ephratah, the father of Beth-lehem.

A. M. 2704, &c.
B. C. 1300, &c.
Post Diluvium,
1048, &c.

5 And eAshur the father of Tekoa had two wives, Helah and Naarah.

6 And Naarah bare him Ahuvam, and Hepher, and Temeni, and Haahashtari. These *were* the sons of Naarah.

---

aGen. xxxviii. 29; xlvi. 12——bOr, *Chelubai,* chap. ii. 9, or *Caleb,* chap. ii. 18

cOr, *Haroah,* chapter ii. 52——dChap. ii. 50——eChap. ii. 24

NOTES ON CHAP. IV

Verse 1. *The sons of Judah*] A genealogy of this tribe has already been given in the *second* chapter. It is here introduced again, with some variations. Probably there were different copies in the public registers; and the

writer of this book, finding that this *second* one contained some remarkable particulars, thought proper to insert it in this place: and no reader will regret the insertion, when he carefully considers the matter.

Verse 3. *These* were of *the father of Etam*] "And these are the rabbins (*doctors*) living at Etam, Jezreel, Ishma, and Idbash."—*T.*

A. M. 2704, &c.
B. C. 1300, &c.
Post Diluvium, 1048, &c.

7 And the sons of Helah were, Zereth, and Jezoar, and Ethnan.

8 And Coz begat Anub, and Zobebah, and the families of Aharhel the son of Harum.

9 And Jabez was [f]more honourable than his brethren: and his mother called his name [g]Jabez, saying, Because I bare him with sorrow.

10 And Jabez called on the God of Israel, saying, [h]O that thou wouldest bless me indeed, and enlarge my coast, and that thine hand might be with me, and that thou wouldest [i]keep me from evil, that it may not grieve me! And God granted him that which he requested.

11 And Chelub the brother of Shuah begat Mehir, which was the father of Eshton.

A. M. 2704, &c.
B. C. 1300, &c.
Post Diluvium, 1048, &c.

12 And Eshton begat Beth-rapha, and Paseah, and Tehinnah the father of [k]Ir-nahash. These are the men of Rechah.

13 And the sons of Kenaz; [l]Othniel and Seraiah: and the sons of Othniel; [m]Hathath.

14 And Meonothai begat Ophrah: and Seraiah begat Joab, the father of [n]the [o]valley of [p]Charashim; for they were craftsmen.

15 And the sons of Caleb the son of Jephunneh; Iru, Elah, and Naam: and the sons of Elah, [q]even Kenaz.

16 And the sons of Jehaleleel; Ziph, and Ziphah, Tiria, and Asareel.

17 And the sons of Ezra were, Jether, and Mered, and Epher, and Jalon; and she bare

---

[f]Gen. xxxiv. 19——[g]That is, sorrowful——[h]Heb. If thou wilt, &c.——[i]Heb. do me——[k]Or, the city of Nahash [l]Josh. xv. 17

[m]Or, Hathath, and Meonothai, who begat, &c. [n]Neh. xi. 35——[o]Or, inhabitants of the valley——[p]That is, craftsmen——[q]Or, Uknaz

---

Verse 7. And Ethnan.] After this word we should, with the Targum, read Coz, whose posterity is mentioned in the next verse. Coz was probably the same as Kenaz.

Verse 8. The son of Harum.] Jabez should be mentioned at the end of this verse, else he is as a consequent without an antecedent.

Verse 9. And Jabez was more honourable] This whole account is variously understood by some of the principal versions. I shall subjoin a translation of each.

SEPTUAGINT.—"And Igabes was more glorious than his brethren; and his mother called his name Igabes, saying, I have brought thee forth as Gabes. And Igabes invoked the God of Israel, saying, If in blessing thou wilt bless me, and enlarge my borders, and thy hand be with me, and wilt give me understanding not to depress me: and God brought about all that he requested."

SYRIAC.—"And one of these was dear to his father and to his mother; and he called his name ܥܝܢܝ ainai, MY EYE. And he said to him, In blessing may the Lord bless thee, and enlarge thy boundary; and may his hand be with thee; and may he preserve thee from evil, that it may not rule over thee; and may he give to thee whatsoever thou shalt request of him!"

ARABIC.—"And this one (Hastahar or Harum) was beloved of his father and his mother: and they called his name عينى aina, MY EYE; and they said unto him, May the Lord bless thee, and multiply thy people, and may his hand be present with thee, because thou wast born in Beth-lehem!"

These two latter versions seem to have copied each other, and the Vulgate is nearly, like ours, a literal rendering of the Hebrew; but the Chaldee is widely different from all the rest:—

CHALDEE.—"And Jabets also, he is Othniel, honourable and skilled in the law beyond his brethren, whose mother called his name Jabets, because she had borne him with sorrow. And Jabets prayed to the God of Israel, saying, O

that in blessing thou wouldest bless me with children, and enlarge my borders with disciples; and that thy hand may be with me in business, that thou mayest make me like to my companions, that evil concupiscence may the less grieve me! And the Lord granted that which he prayed for."

Of this honourable person we know nothing but what is here mentioned, nor does the name occur in any other part of Scripture except in chap. ii. 55, where it appears to be the name of a place, but is understood by the Chaldee to be the name of a person, as here. Though I have noticed this particularly in the note on that place, yet I think it right to add the Chaldee here, that all that concerns this worthy person may be seen at one view:—

Chap. ii. 55: "The families of the Rechabites, the son of Eliezer, the son of Moses, the disciples of Jabets; he was Othniel, the son of Kenaz. And he was called Jabets, יעבץ Yabets, because in his counsel [בעיצתיה beytsatih, from יעץ yaats, he counselled, advised, &c.] he instituted a school for disciples. They were called Tirathim, תרעתים, because in their hymns their voices were like trumpets, [from רע ra, to sound like a trumpet; see Num. x. 9; 2 Chron. xiii. 12,] and Shimathim, שמעתים, because, in hearing, they lifted up their faces, i. e., in prayer, [from שמע shama, he heard, hearkened,] and Suchathim, שוכתים, because they were overshadowed with the spirit of prophecy, [from סך sach, a tabernacle, or extended covering.]" For farther particulars, see at the end of this chapter.

Verse 12. These are the men of Rechah.] "These are the men of the great Sanhedrin."—T.

Verse 15. Caleb the son of Jephunneh] We have already met with this eminent person in Num. xiii. 6, 30, xiv. 24, and elsewhere; and seen his courageous piety and inflexible integrity. The Targum says here, "They called him Caleb, the son of Jephunneh, because he had purged his soul from the counsel of the spies."

A. M. 2704, &c.
B. C. 1300, &c.
Post Diluvium,
1048, &c.

Miriam, and Shammai, and Ishbah the father of Eshtemoa.

18 And his wife ʳJehudijah bare Jered the father of Gedor, and Heber the father of Socho, and Jekuthiel the father of Zanoah. And these *are* the sons of Bithiah the daughter of Pharaoh, which Mered took.

19 And the sons of *his* wife ˢHodiah the sister of Naham, the father of Keilah the Garmite, and Eshtemoa the Maachathite.

20 And the sons of Shimon *were,* Amnon, and Rinnah, Ben-hanan, and Tilon. And the sons of Ishi *were,* Zoheth, and Ben-zoheth.

21 The sons of Shelah ᵗthe son of Judah *were,* Er the father of Lecah, and Laadah the father of Mareshah, and the families of the house of them that wrought fine linen, of the house of Ashbea,

22 And Jokim, and the men of Chozeba, and Joash, and Saraph, who had the dominion in Moab, and Jashubi-lehem. And *these are* ancient things.

23 These *were* the potters, and those that dwelt among plants and hedges: there they dwelt with the king for his work.

A. M. 2704, &c.
B. C. 1300, &c.
Post Diluvium,
1048, &c.

24 The sons of Simeon *were,* ᵘNemuel, and Jamin, ᵛJarib, Zerah, *and* Shaul:

25 Shallum his son, Mibsam his son, Mishma his son.

26 And the sons of Mishma; Hamuel his son, Zacchur his son, Shimei his son.

27 And Shimei had sixteen sons and six daughters; but his brethren had not many children, neither did all their family multiply, ʷlike to the children of Judah.

28 And they dwelt at ˣBeer-sheba, and Moladah, and Hazar-shual,

29 And at ʸBilhah, and at Ezem, and at ᶻTolad,

30 And at Bethuel, and at Hormah, and at Ziklag,

31 And at Beth-marcaboth, and ᵃHazarsusim, and at Beth-birei, and at Shaaraim.

ʳOr, *the Jewess*——ˢOr, *Jehudijah,* mentioned before ᵗGen. xxxviii. 1, 5; xlvi. 12——ᵘOr, *Jemuel,* Gen. xlvi. 10; Exod. vi. 15; Num. xxvi. 12

ᵛOr, *Jachin, Zohar*——ʷHeb. *unto*——ˣJosh. xix. 2 ʸOr, *Balah,* Josh. xix. 3——ᶻOr, *Eltolad,* Josh. xix. 4 ᵃOr, *Hazar-susah,* Josh. xix. 5

Verse 18. *And his wife Jehudijah*] The Targum considers the names in this verse as *epithets* of Moses: "And his wife Jehuditha educated Moses after she had drawn him out of the water: and she called his name *Jered,* because he caused the manna to *descend* upon Israel; and Prince *Gedor,* because he *restored* the desolations of Israel; *Heber* also, because he *joined* Israel to their heavenly Father; and Prince *Socho,* because he *overshadowed* Israel with his righteousness; and *Jekuthiel,* because the Israelites *waited* on the God of heaven in his time, forty years in the desert; and prince *Zanoah,* because God, on his account, had *passed* by the sins of Israel. These names *Bithiah,* the daughter of Pharaoh, called him by the spirit of prophecy, for she became a proselyte; and Mered took her to himself to wife: he is Caleb, and was so called because he *opposed* the counsel of the spies."—*T.* A similar explanation is given by *Jarchi.*

Verse 21. *That wrought fine linen*] "Of the family of those who worked in fine flax to make garments for kings and priests."—*T.*

Verse 22. *And Joash, and Saraph*] "And the prophets and scribes which sprang from the seed of Joshua, and the Gibeonites, whose office it was to serve in the house of the sanctuary, because they had lied to the princes of Israel; also *Joash,* who is the same as *Mahlon;* and *Saraph,* who is the same as *Chilion,* who took wives of the daughters of Moab and Boaz, the chief of the wise men of the college of Bethlehem, and of those who existed in former days."—*T.*

Verse 23. *These* were *the potters*] "These are the disciples of the law, for whose sake the world was created; who preside in judgment,

and establish the world; and they build and perfect the fallen down house of Israel: they dwelt there with the Shechinah of the King of the world, in the study of the law and the intercalation or months, and determining the commencement of years and festivals: and they computed the times from heaven in the days of Ruth, the mother of kingdoms, to the days of Solomon the king."—*T.* I am afraid this paraphrase gives us as little light as the text itself, which speaks *of potters, and those who dwelt among plants and hedges.* They were probably *brickmakers;* perhaps *potters* also, who had their dwelling in low grounds, and fabricated the clay into pots and bricks that was digged up in forming fences in the king's domains.

Verse 24. *The sons of Simeon*] This genealogy is very different from that given in Gen. xlvi. 10, and Num. xxvi. 12. This may be occasioned by the same person having several names, one *list* taking one name, another list some other, and so on: to reconcile is impossible; to attempt it, useless.

Verse 27. *Neither did all their family multiply*] In Num. i. 23 the number of all the families of Simeon was *fifty-nine thousand three hundred;* and that of Judah was, ver. 27, not less than *seventy-four thousand six hundred.* When the next census was made, Num. xxvi., the tribe of Judah amounted to *seventy-six thousand five hundred,* an increase of *one thousand nine hundred;* while the tribe of Simeon amounted only to *twenty-two thousand two hundred,* a decrease of *thirty-seven thousand one hundred.* It was at that time the smallest tribe in Israel.

Verse 31. *These* were *their cities unto the*

A. M. 2704, &c.
B. C. 1300, &c.
Post Diluvium,
1048, &c.

These *were* their cities unto the reign of David.

32 And their villages *were* ᵇEtam, and Ain, Rimmon, and Tochen, and Ashan, five cities:

33 And all their villages that *were* round about the same cities, unto ᶜBaal. These *were* their habitations, and ᵈtheir genealogy.

34 And Meshobab, and Jamlech, and Joshah the son of Amaziah,

35 And Joel, and Jehu the son of Josibiah, the son of Seraiah, the son of Asiel,

36 And Elioenai, and Jaakobah, and Jeshohaiah, and Asaiah, and Adiel, and Jesimiel, and Benaiah,

37 And Ziza the son of Shiphi, the son of Allon, the son of Jedaiah, the son of Shimri, the son of Shemaiah;

38 These ᵉmentioned by *their* names *were* princes in their families: and the house of their fathers increased greatly.

39 And they went to the entrance of Gedor, *even* unto the east side of the valley, to seek pasture for their flocks.

A. M. 3289
B. C. 715
Olymp. XVI. 2
An. Hezekiæ,
regis Judæorum,
12

40 And they found fat pasture and good, and the land *was* wide, and quiet, and peaceable: for *they* of Ham had dwelt there of old.

41 And these written by name came in the days of Hezekiah king of Judah, and ᶠsmote their tents, and the habitations that were found there, and destroyed them utterly unto this day, and dwelt in their rooms: because *there was* pasture there for their flocks.

42 And *some* of them, *even* of the sons of Simeon, five hundred men, went to Mount Seir, having for their captains Pelatiah, and Neariah, and Rephaiah, and Uzziel, the sons of Ishi,

43 And they smote ᵍthe rest of the Amalekites that were escaped, and dwelt there unto this day.

ᵇOr, *Ether,* Josh. xix. 7——ᶜOr, *Baalath-beer,* Josh. xix. 8
ᵈOr, *as they divided themselves by nations among them*

ᵉHebrew, *coming*——ᶠ2 Kings xviii. 8——ᵍSee 1 Sam. xv. 8; xxx. 17; 2 Sam. viii. 12

---

reign of David.] It appears that David took some of the cities of the Simeonites, and added them to Judah; *Ziklag* for instance, 1 Sam. xxvii. 6.

As the tribe of Simeon had withdrawn their allegiance from the house of David, the kings of Judah extended their domination as far as possible into the territories of that tribe, so that they were obliged to seek pasture for their flocks at *Gedor,* and in the mountains of *Seir,* as we find ver. 39-42.

Verse 40. They *of Ham had dwelt there of old.*] These were probably either *Philistines* or *Egyptians,* who dwelt at Gedor, which was situated in the environs of *Joppa* and *Samnia.* Those whom the *five hundred* Simeonites expelled from Seir were *Amalekites,* ver. 43.

Verse 43. *They smote the rest of the Amalekites*] Those who had escaped in the war which Saul made against them, (see 1 Sam. xiv. 48,) and from David, who had attacked them afterwards, 2 Sam. viii. 12.

THE expedition of the Simeonites mentioned here, against *Gedor* and *Seir,* was in the days of Hezekiah; and, as Calmet conjectures, near about the time of the captivity of the ten tribes, when the remnant of Simeon would feel themselves obliged to retire more *southward,* into Arabia Petræa, for fear of the Jews. These may be probable conjectures.—See *Calmet.*

There are several things in the account of Jabez that are very instructive:—

1. He appears to have been a child brought into the world with great *difficulty,* at the *risk* of his *own life* and that of his *mother.* So much seems to be implied in, *she bare him with sorrow,* i. e., with peculiar sorrow and danger.

2. To perpetuate the merciful interposition of God in her own and her son's behalf, she gave him a *name* that must have recalled to her and his *remembrance* the *danger* to which both their lives were exposed, and from which they could not have been extricated but by the especial help of God. *She called his name Jabez,* &c.

3. He was brought up in the fear of God; he was no *idolater;* he worshipped the *God of Israel,* and he showed the sincerity of his faith by frequent and earnest *prayer.*

4. His *prayer* was at once both *enlightened* and *pious.* He had *piety* towards God, and therefore he *trusted* in him: he *knew* that he was the fountain of all good, and therefore he sought all necessaries both for body and soul from him. *He prayed to the God of Israel.*

5. Both the *matter* and *manner* of his prayer were excellent. His heart was deeply impressed with its wants, and therefore he was *earnest* and *fervent; O that thou wouldest bless me indeed;* אם ברך תברכני *im barech tebarecheni;* "O that in blessing thou wouldest bless me!" Let me live under thy benediction! Do thou *diligently* and *frequently bless* me!

6. He prays for the things necessary for the *body* as well as for the *soul: And enlarge my coasts*—grant me as much territory as may support my family. Let the means of *living* be adequate to the demands of life; let me have the *necessaries, conveniences,* and, as far as they may be safely intrusted with me, the *comforts* of life! *O that thou wouldest enlarge my coasts!*

7. He is conscious that without the continual support of God he must fail; and therefore he prays to be upheld by his power: *That thy hand might be with me!* May I ever walk with thee, and ever feel the *hand* of thy *power* to *support* and *cover* me in all the trials, dangers, and difficulties of life; and the *hand* of thy

providence to *supply* all my wants in reference to both worlds!

8. He dreads both *sin* and *suffering*, and therefore prays against both: *O that thou wouldest keep me from evil, that it may not grieve me! Sin* and *misery* are in every step of the journey of life; keep me from *sin*, that I *grieve thee* not; and keep me from sin, that I render not *myself miserable!* We can never *offend God* without *injuring ourselves;* he that *sins* must *suffer. Thorns* and *scorpions* are everywhere in the way to perdition; and he that walks in it must be *torn* and *stung.* He alone is *happy* who walks in the ways of God. *Keep me from evil, that it may not grieve me.* 9. Prayers that have a *right aim* will have a *right answer;* Jabez did not pray in vain, *for God granted him that which he requested.* He was continually blessed; his family was increased; the hand of God was upon him for good. He was saved from sin, and saved from the pangs and sufferings of a guilty conscience.

10. If we take up the character and conduct of Jabez in the view given by the *Chaldee*, we shall not only see him as a *pious* and *careful* man, deeply interested in behalf of *himself* and his *family*, but we shall see him as a *benevolent* man, labouring for the welfare of others, and especially for the religious instruction of *youth*. He founded *schools*, in which the young and rising generation were taught useful knowledge, and especially the knowledge of God. He had

disciples, which were divided into *three classes*, who distinguished themselves by their *fervour* in the *worship of God*, by their *docility* in obediently hearing and treasuring up the advices and instructions of their teachers, and by their deep piety to God in bringing forth the fruits of the Spirit. The *spirit of prophecy*, that is, of *prayer* and *supplication*, rested *upon them*.

11. He did not do these things merely as a *duty* he owed to God and his fellows, but from the *abundance* of a *generous* and *loving heart: In his counsel he erected a school of disciples.* God had blessed him with temporal things, and he secures their continuance by devoting them to his service; he honours God with his substance, and God honours him with his especial blessing and approbation.

12. On these accounts he was *more honourable than his brethren.* He was of the same stock and the same lineage; he had neither nobility of birth, nor was distinguished by earthly titles; in all these respects he was on a level with his brethren: but God tells us that he was *more honourable than them all;* and why? because he *prayed*, because he *served his Maker*, and because he *lived to do good among men;* therefore he received the honour that cometh from God. Reader, imitate the conduct of this worthy Israelite, that thou mayest be a partaker of his blessings.

The things added by the Targumist might have been derived from authentic tradition.

CHAPTER V

The genealogies of Reuben, 1–10. Of Gad, 11–17. The exploits of Reuben, Gad, and the half tribe of Manasseh, 18–22. The genealogy of the half tribe of Manasseh, 23, 24. The idolatry of these tribes and their captivity by the Assyrians, 25, 26.

A. M. 2704, &c.
B. C. 1300, &c.
Post Diluvium,
1048, &c.

NOW the sons of Reuben the first-born of Israel, (for [a]he *was* the first-born; but, forasmuch as he [b]defiled his father's bed, [c]his birthright was given unto the sons of Joseph the son of Israel: and the genealogy is not to be reckoned after the birthright.

2 For [d]Judah prevailed above his brethren, and of him *came* the [e]chief [f]ruler;

but the birthright *was* Joseph's:)

A. M. 2704, &c.
B. C. 1300, &c.
Post Diluvium,
1048, &c.

3 The sons, I *say*, of [g]Reuben the first-born of Israel *were,* Hanoch, and Pallu, Hezron, and Carmi.

4 The sons of Joel; Shemaiah his son, Gog his son, Shimei his son,

5 Micah his son, Reaia his son, Baal his son,

6 Beerah his son, whom [h]Tilgath-pilneser

---

[a]Genesis xxix. 32; xlix. 3——[b]Genesis xxxv. 22; xlix. 4——[c]Genesis xlviii. 15, 22——[d]Genesis xlix. 8, 10; Psalm lx. 7; cviii. 8——[e]Micah v. 2; Matthew ii. 6——[f]Or, *prince*——[g]Genesis xlvi. 9; Exodus vi. 14; Numbers xxvi. 5——[h]Or, *Tiglath-pileser*, 2 Kings xv. 29; xvi. 7

NOTES ON CHAP. V

Verse 1. *The sons of Reuben the first-born*] As Reuben was the *eldest* son of Jacob, why was not his genealogy reviewed first? This verse answers the question; he lost the birthright because of the transgression mentioned Gen. xxxv. 22, and xlix. 4, and the *precedency* was given to Judah; from him therefore came the chief ruler. This appears to be the meaning of the place.

Verse 2. *And of him* came *the chief ruler*] This is, by both the Syriac and Arabic, understood of *Christ:* "From Judah the King Messiah shall proceed." The *Chaldee* paraphrases the verse thus: "Seeing Judah prevailed over his

brethren, so the kingdom was taken from Reuben and given to Judah; and because he was strong, so was his kingdom. Levi also was godly, and did not transgress in the matter of the golden calf; therefore the high priesthood was taken away from the children of Reuben, and on their account from all the first-born, and given to Aaron and his sons. The custody of the sanctuary belonged to the Levites, but the birthright to Joseph."—*T.*

Verse 6. *Beerah his son*] After their separation from the house of David the ten tribes continued to have princes of the tribes; and this continued till the time that Tiglath-pileser carried them captives into Assyria. At that time *Beerah* was their *prince* or *chief;* and with

A. M. 2704, &c.
B. C. 1300, &c.
Post Diluvium,
1048, &c.
king of Assyria carried away *captive:* he *was* prince of the Reubenites.

7 And his brethren by their families, [i]when the genealogy of their generations was reckoned, *were* the chief, Jeiel, and Zechariah,

8 And Bela the son of Azaz, the son of [k]Shema, the son of Joel, who dwelt in [l]Aroer, even unto Nebo and Baal-meon:

9 And eastward he inhabited unto the entering in of the wilderness from the river Euphrates: because their cattle were multiplied [m]in the land of Gilead.

10 And in the days of Saul they made war [n]with the Hagarites, who fell by their hand: and they dwelt in their tents [o]throughout all the east *land* of Gilead.

11 And the children of Gad dwelt over against them in the land of [p]Bashan, unto Salcah:

12 Joel the chief, and Shapham the next, and Jaanai, and Shaphat in Bashan.

13 And their brethren of the house of their fathers *were* Michael, and Meshullam, and Sheba, and Jorai, and Jachan, and Zia, and Heber, seven.

14 These *are* the children of Abihail the son of Huri, the son of Jaroah, the son of Gilead, the son of Michael, the son of Jeshishai, the son of Jahdo, the son of Buz;

15 Ahi the son of Abdiel, the son of Guni, chief of the house of their fathers.

A. M. 2704, &c.
B. C. 1300, &c.
Post Diluvium,
1048, &c.

16 And they dwelt in Gilead in Bashan, and in her towns, and in all the suburbs of [q]Sharon, upon [r]their borders.

17 All these were reckoned by genealogies in the days of [s]Jotham king of Judah, and in the days of [t]Jeroboam king of Israel.

18 The sons of Reuben, and the Gadites, and half the tribe of Manasseh, [u]of valiant men, men able to bear buckler and sword, and to shoot with bow, and skilful in war, *were* four and forty thousand seven hundred and threescore, that went out to the war.

19 And they made war with the Hagarites, with [v]Jetur, and Nephish, and Nodab.

20 And [w]they were helped against them, and the Hagarites were delivered into their hand, and all that *were* with them: for they cried to God in the battle, and he was entreated of them; because they [x]put their trust in him.

21 And they [y]took away their cattle; of their camels fifty thousand, and of sheep two hundred and fifty thousand, and of asses two thousand, and of [z]men a hundred thousand.

22 For there fell down many slain, because the war *was* of God. And they dwelt in their steads until [a]the captivity.

---

[i]See ver. 17——[k]Or, *Shemaiah,* ver. 4——[l]Josh. xiii. 15, 16——[m]Josh. xxii. 9——[n]Gen. xxv. 12——[o]Heb. *upon all the faces of the east*——[p]Josh. xiii. 11, 24 [q]Chap. xxvii. 29——[r]Heb. *their goings forth*

[s]2 Kings xv. 5, 32——[t]2 Kings xiv. 16, 20——[u]Heb. *sons of valour*——[v]Gen. xxv. 15; ch. i. 31——[w]See ver. 22——[x]Psa. xxii. 4, 5——[y]Heb. *led captive*——[z]Heb. *souls of men;* as Num. xxxi. 35——[a]2 Kings xv. 29; xvii. 6

---

him this species of dominion or precedency terminated. According to the Targum, *Beerah* was the same as Baruch the prophet.

Verse 8. *Who dwelt in Aroer*] This town was situated on the river *Arnon;* and *Nebo* was both a city and a mountain in the same country. They both lay on the other side of Jordan.

Verse 10. *And they dwelt in their tents*] The *Hagarites* were tribes of *Nomade,* or *Scenite,* Arabs; people who lived in *tents,* without any fixed dwellings, and whose property consisted in *cattle.* The descendants of Reuben extirpated these Hagarites, seized on their property and their tents, and dwelt in their place.

Verse 12. *Joel the chief*] "Joel, prince of the Sanhedrin; and Shapham, master of the college; and Jaanai and Shaphat, judges in Mathnan."—*T.*

Verse 13. *And their brethren*] This verse is wanting both in the *Syriac* and in the *Arabic.*

Verse 16. *The suburbs of Sharon*] There were *three* places of this name: that mentioned here was a district in the country of Bashan beyond Jordan, (see Josh. xii. 18;) there was

another that lay between Cæsarea of Palestine and Joppa; and there was a third between Mount Tabor and the Sea of Tiberias. See *Calmet.*

Verse 19. *They made war with the Hagarites*] This is probably the same war that is mentioned ver. 10. Those called *Hagarites* in the text are everywhere denominated by the Targum הונגראיי *Hongaraai,* Hongarites.

Verse 20. *They put their trust in him.*] Or, as the Targum says, "Because they trusted במימריה *bemeymriah, in his* WORD."

Verse 21. *They took away their cattle*] This was a war of extermination as to the political state of the people, which nothing could justify but an especial direction of God; and this he could never give against any, unless the cup of their iniquity had been full. The Hagarites were full of idolatry: see ver. 25.

Verse 22. *For there fell down many slain*] The *hundred thousand men* mentioned above were probably made *slaves,* and were not slain. The Targum says, *one hundred thousand souls of men.*

The war was of God.] The Targum says, the

A. M. 2704, &c.
B. C. 1300, &c.
Post Diluvium,
1048, &c.

23 And the children of the half tribe of Manasseh dwelt in the land: they increased from Bashan unto Baal-hermon and Senir, and unto Mount Hermon.

24 And these *were* the heads of the house of their fathers, even Epher, and Ishi, and Eliel, and Azriel, and Jeremiah, and Hodaviah, and Jahdiel, mighty men of valour, [b]famous men, *and* heads of the house of their fathers.

25 And they transgressed against the God of their fathers, and went a [c]whoring after the gods of the people of the land, whom God destroyed before them.

A. M. 2704, &c.
B. C. 1300, &c.
Post Diluvium,
1048, &c.

26 And the God of Israel stirred up the spirit of [d]Pul king of Assyria, and the spirit of [e]Tilgath-pilneser king of Assyria, and he carried them away, even the Reubenites, and the Gadites, and the half tribe of Manasseh, and brought them unto [f]Halah, and Habor, and Hara, and to the river Gozan, unto this day.

---

[b]Heb. *men of names*——[c]2 Kings xvii. 7——[d]2 Kings xv. 19——[e]2 Kings xv. 29——[f]2 Kings xvii. 6; xviii. 11

---

war was מן מימרא דיי *min meymera dayai,* "from the WORD of the Lord."

Verse 25. *The gods of the people of the land*] We see the reason why God delivered the Hagarites into the hands of these tribes; they were abominable *idolaters,* and therefore God destroyed them.

Verse 26. *Tilgath-pilneser*] Many MSS. have תגלת *Tiglath* instead of תלגת *Tilgath.* The

Syriac, the *Septuagint,* and the *Chaldee,* have the same reading as in 2 Kings xv. 29, &c.

Brought them unto Halah] See the *notes* on the parallel places marked in the margin, for many particulars of these wars, and consequent captivity. It is a pity that some method were not found out to *harmonize* the books of Kings with the books of Chronicles, that the *variations* might be seen at one view.

CHAPTER VI

The genealogy of Levi and Aaron, 1–30. *The offices of the priests and Levites,* 31–53. *The cities assigned them,* 54–81.

A. M. 2704, &c.
B. C. 1300, &c.
Post Diluvium,
1048, &c.

THE sons of Levi; [a]Gershon, [b]Kohath, and Merari.

2 And the sons of Kohath; Amram, [c]Izhar, and Hebron, and Uzziel.

3 And the children of Amram; Aaron, and Moses, and Miriam. The sons also of Aaron; [d]Nadab, and Abihu, Eleazar, and Ithamar.

4 Eleazar begat Phinehas, Phinehas begat Abishua,

5 And Abishua begat Bukki, and Bukki begat Uzzi,

6 And Uzzi begat Zerahiah, and Zerahiah begat Meraioth,

A. M. 2704, &c.
B. C. 1300, &c.
Post Diluvium,
1048, &c.

7 Meraioth begat Amariah, and Amariah begat Ahitub,

8 And [e]Ahitub begat Zadok, and [f]Zadok begat Ahimaaz,

9 And Ahimaaz begat Azariah, and Azariah begat Johanan,

10 And Johanan begat Azariah, (he *it is* [g]that executed the priest's office [h]in the [i]temple that Solomon built in Jerusalem:)

---

[a]Gen. xlvi. 11; Exodus vi. 16; Num. xxvi. 57; chapter xxiii. 6——[b]Or, *Gershom,* verse 16——[c]See verse 22
[d]Lev. x. 1

[e]2 Samuel viii. 17——[f]2 Samuel xv. 27——[g]See 2 Chron. xxvi. 17, 18——[h]Heb. *in the house*——[i]1 Kings vi; 2 Chron. iii

---

NOTES ON CHAP. VI

Verse 1. *The sons of Levi*] It has been well remarked that the genealogy of *Levi* is given here more ample and correct than that of any of the others. And this is perhaps an additional proof that the author was a *priest,* felt much for the priesthood, and took care to give the genealogy of the Levitical and sacerdotal families, from the most correct tables; for with such tables we may presume he was intimately acquainted.

Verse 4. *Eleazar begat Phinehas*] As the high priesthood continued in this family for a

long time, the sacred historian confines himself to this chiefly, omitting *Nadab* and *Abihu,* and even the family of *Ithamar.*

Verse 8. *Ahitub begat Zadok*] Through this person the high priesthood came again into the family of Eleazar.

Verse 10. *Johanan*] Supposed to be the same as *Jehoiada.*

Executed the priest's office] Probably this refers to the dignified manner in which Azariah opposed King Uzziah, who wished to invade the priest's office, and offer incense in the temple. See 2 Chron. xxvi. 17, 18.

A. M. 2704, &c.
B. C. 1300, &c.
Post Diluvium, 1048, &c.

11 And ᵏAzariah begat Amariah, and Amariah begat Ahitub,

12 And Ahitub begat Zadok, and Zadok begat ˡShallum,

13 And Shallum begat Hilkiah, and Hilkiah begat Azariah,

14 And Azariah begat ᵐSeraiah, and Seraiah begat Jehozadak,

15 And Jehozadak went *into captivity,* ⁿwhen the LORD carried away Judah and Jerusalem by the hand of Nebuchadnezzar.

16 The sons of Levi; ᵒGershom, ᵖKohath, and Merari.

17 And these *be* the names of the sons of Gershom; Libni, and Shimei.

18 And the sons of Kohath *were,* Amram, and Izhar, and Hebron, and Uzziel.

19 The sons of Merari; Mahli, and Mushi. And these *are* the families of the Levites according to their fathers.

20 Of Gershom; Libni his son, Jahath his son, �q Zimmah his son,

21 ʳJoah his son, ˢIddo his son, Zerah his son, ᵗJeaterai his son.

22 The sons of Kohath; ᵘAmminadab his son, Korah his son, Assir his son,

23 Elkanah his son, and Ebiasaph his son, and Assir his son,

24 Tahath his son, ᵛUriel his son, Uzziah his son, and Shaul his son.

25 And the sons of Elkanah; ʷAmasai and Ahimoth.

26 *As for* Elkanah: the sons of Elkanah; ˣZophai his son, and ʸNahath his son,

27 ᶻEliab his son, Jeroham his son, Elkanah his son.

A. M. 2704, &c.
B. C. 1300, &c.
Post Diluvium, 1048, &c.

28 And the sons of Samuel; the first-born ªVashni, and Abiah.

29 The sons of Merari; Mahli, Libni his son, Shimei his son, Uzza his son,

30 Shimea his son, Haggiah his son, Asaiah his son.

31 And these *are they* whom David set over the service of song in the house of the LORD, after that the ᵇark had rest.

32 And they ministered before the dwelling-place of the tabernacle of the congregation with singing, until Solomon had built the house of the LORD in Jerusalem: and *then* they waited on their office according to their order.

33 And these *are* they that ᶜwaited with their children. Of the sons of the Kohathites: Heman, a singer, the son of Joel, the son of Shemuel,

34 The son of Elkanah, the son of Jeroham, the son of Eliel, the son of ᵈToah,

35 The son of ᵉZuph, the son of Elkanah, the son of Mahath, the son of Amasai,

36 The son of Elkanah, the son of ᶠJoel, the son of Azariah, the son of Zephaniah,

37 The son of Tahath, the son of Assir, the son of ᵍEbiasaph, the son of Korah,

38 The son of Izhar, the son of Kohath, the son of Levi, the son of Israel.

39 And his brother Asaph, who stood on his right hand, *even* Asaph the son of Berachiah, the son of Shimea.

ᵏSee Ezra vii. 3——ˡOr, *Meshullam,* chap. ix. 11
ᵐNeh. xi. 11——ⁿ2 Kings xxv. 18——ᵒExod. vi. 16
ᵖOr, *Gershon,* ver. 1——q Ver. 42——ʳOr, *Ethan,* ver. 42
ˢOr, *Adaiah,* ver. 41——ᵗOr, *Ethni,* ver. 41——ᵘOr, *Izhar,* ver. 2, 18——ᵛOr, *Zephaniah, Azariah, Joel,* ver. 36

ʷSee ver. 35, 36——ˣOr, *Zuph,* ver. 35; 1 Samuel i. 1
ʸVer. 34, *Toah*——ᶻVer. 34, *Eliel*——ªCalled also *Joel,* ver. 33; 1 Sam. viii. 2——ᵇChap. xvi. 1——ᶜHeb. *stood*
ᵈVer. 26, *Nahath*——ᵉOr, *Zophia*——ᶠVer. 24, *Shaul, Uzziah, Uriel*——ᵍExod. vi. 24

Verse 14. *Seraiah*] He was put to death by Nebuchadnezzar, 2 Kings xxv. 18, 21.

Verse 22. *Korah*] See the history of this man, and his rebellion, Num. xvi.

Verse 28. *The first-born Vashni, and Abiah.*] There is a great mistake in this verse: in 1 Sam. viii. 2 we read, *Now the name of his* (Samuel's) *first-born was Joel; and the name of his second Abiah.* The word יוֹאֵל *Joel* is lost out of the text in this place, and ישְׁנִי *vesheni,* which signifies *the second,* and which refers to *Abiah,* is made here into a proper name. The *Septuagint, Vulgate,* and *Chaldee,* copy this blunder; but the *Syriac* and *Arabic* read as in 1 Sam. viii. The MSS. have all copied the corrupted Hebrew in this place. *Jarchi* labours to restore the true reading, and yet preserve the integrity of the text, by paraphrasing thus: "*And the second,* (ישְׁנִי *vesheni,*) in respect of

the first, he was *Abiah; and the second,* in respect of Abiah, he was *Joel.*"

These, *Joel* and *Abiah,* were the two sons of Samuel, who administered justice so badly that the people, being oppressed, began to murmur, and demanded a king. See 1 Sam. viii. 1, &c.

Verse 31. *After that the ark had rest.*] The Targum says, "These are they whom David set over the service of the singing, in the house of the sanctuary, or tabernacle of the Lord, at the time in which the ark was brought into it;" that is, when it was brought from the house of Obed-edom.

Verse 32. *According to their order.*] This order is specified below.

Verse 39. *Asaph*] This person, with *Heman,* the sons of *Kora, Ethan, Jeduthun,* &c., are celebrated in these books, and in the Psalms,

A. M. 2704, &c.
B. C. 1300, &c.
Post Diluvium, 1048, &c.

40 The son of Michael, the son of Baaseiah, the son of Malchiah,

41 The son of [h]Ethni, the son of Zerah, the son of Adaiah,

42 The son of Ethan, the son of Zimmah, the son of Shimei,

43 The son of Jahath, the son of Gershom, the son of Levi.

44 And their brethren the sons of Merari *stood* on the left hand: [i]Ethan the son of [k]Kishi, the son of Abdi, the son of Malluch,

45 The son of Hashabiah, the son of Amaziah, the son of Hilkiah,

46 The son of Amzi, the son of Bani, the son of Shamer,

47 The son of Mahli, the son of Mushi, the son of Merari, the son of Levi.

48 Their brethren also the Levites *were* appointed unto all manner of service of the tabernacle of the house of God.

49 But Aaron and his sons offered [l]upon the altar of the burnt-offering, and [m]on the altar of incense, *and were appointed* for all the work of the *place* most holy, and to make an atonement for Israel, according to all that Moses the servant of God had commanded.

50 And these *are* the sons of Aaron; Eleazar his son, Phinehas his son, Abishua his son,

51 Bukki his son, Uzzi his son, Zerahiah his son,

52 Meraioth his son, Amariah his son, Ahitub his son,

53 Zadok his son, Ahimaaz his son.

54 [n]Now these *are* their dwelling-places throughout their castles in their coasts, of the sons of Aaron, of the families of the Kohathites: for theirs was the lot.

A. M. 2704, &c.
B. C. 1300, &c.
Post Diluvium, 1048, &c.

55 [o]And they gave them Hebron in the land of Judah, and the suburbs thereof round about it.

56 [p]But the fields of the city, and the villages thereof, they gave to Caleb the son of Jephunneh.

57 And [q]to the sons of Aaron they gave the cities of Judah, *namely,* Hebron, *the city* of refuge, and Libnah with her suburbs, and Jattir, and Eshtemoa, with their suburbs,

58 And [r]Hilen with her suburbs, Debir with her suburbs,

59 And [s]Ashan with her suburbs, and Bethshemesh with her suburbs:

60 And out of the tribe of Benjamin; Geba with her suburbs, and [t]Alemeth with her suburbs, and Anathoth with her suburbs. All their cities throughout their families *were* thirteen cities.

61 And unto the sons of Kohath, [u]*which were* left of the family of that tribe, *were cities given* out of the half tribe, *namely, out of* the half *tribe* of Manasseh, [v]by lot, ten cities.

62 And to the sons of Gershom throughout their families out of the tribe of Issachar, and out of the tribe of Asher, and out of the tribe of Naphtali, and out of the tribe of Manasseh in Bashan, thirteen cities.

---

[h]See ver. 21——[i]Called *Jeduthun,* chap. ix. 16; xxv. 1, 3, 6——[k]Or, *Kushaiah,* chap. xv. 17——[l]Lev. i. 9 [m]Exod. xxx. 7——[n]Josh. xxi——[o]Josh. xxi. 11, 12

[p]Josh. xiv. 13; xv. 13——[q]Josh. xxi. 13——[r]Or, *Holon,* Josh. xxi. 15——[s]Or, *Ain,* Josh. xxi. 16——[t]Or, *Almon,* Josh. xxi. 18——[u]Ver. 66——[v]Josh. xxi. 5

---

for their skill in singing, and the part they performed in the public worship of God.

It is very likely that their singing was only a kind of recitative or chanting, such as we still find in the synagogues. It does not appear that God had especially appointed these singers, much less any musical instruments, (the silver trumpets excepted,) to be employed in his service. Musical instruments in the house of God are, at least under the Gospel, repugnant to the *spirit* of Christianity, and tend not a little to corrupt the worship of God. Those who are fond of music in the theatre are fond of it in the house of God when they go thither; and some, professing Christianity, set up such a spurious worship in order to draw people to hear the Gospel! This is doing evil that good may come of it; and by this means, light and trifling people are introduced into the Church of Christ, and when in, are generally very troublesome, hard to be pleased, and difficult to be saved.

Verse 50. *These* are *the sons of Aaron*] We have already had a list of these, (see ver. 3-16;) this is a second, but less extensive, and is a proof that the writer of this book had several lists before him, from which he borrowed as he judged proper.

Verse 54. *Theirs was the lot.*] All the tribes and families obtained their respective inheritances by lot, but to the sons of Aaron was the *first lot;* and so the *Syriac* and *Arabic* have understood this place. The first lot, says *Jarchi,* fell to Judah, that they might give to the priests and the Levites the cities marked below. See an account of the possessions of the priests and Levites, Josh. xx., xxi.

Verse 60. *All their cities—were thirteen*] But there are only *eleven* reckoned here, *Gibeon* and *Juttah* being omitted, and the names of some of the others changed. None of the versions give the full number of names, although they all give the whole sum *thirteen.*

A. M. 2704, &c.
B. C. 1300, &c.
Post Diluvium,
1048, &c.

63 Unto the sons of Merari *were given* by lot, throughout their families, out of the tribe of Reuben, and out of the tribe of Gad, and out of the tribe of Zebulun, ʷtwelve cities.

64 And the children of Israel gave to the Levites *these* cities with their suburbs.

65 And they gave by lot out of the tribe of the children of Judah, and out of the tribe of the children of Simeon, and out of the tribe of the children of Benjamin, these cities, which are called by *their* names.

66 And ˣ*the residue* of the families of the sons of Kohath had cities of their coasts out of the tribe of Ephraim.

67 ʸAnd they gave unto them, *of* the cities of refuge, Shechem in Mount Ephraim with her suburbs; *they gave* also Gezer with her suburbs,

68 And ᶻJokmeam with her suburbs, and Beth-horon with her suburbs,

69 And Aijalon with her suburbs, and Gath-rimmon with her suburbs:

70 And out of the half tribe of Manasseh; Aner with her suburbs, and Bileam with her suburbs, for the family of the remnant of the sons of Kohath.

71 Unto the sons of Gershom *were given* out of the family of the half tribe of Manasseh,

Golan in Bashan with her suburbs, and Ashtaroth with her suburbs:

A. M. 2704, &c.
B. C. 1300, &c.
Post Diluvium,
1048, &c.

72 And out of the tribe of Issachar; Kedesh with her suburbs, Daberath with her suburbs,

73 And Ramoth with her suburbs, and Anem with her suburbs:

74 And out of the tribe of Asher; Mashal with her suburbs, and Abdon with her suburbs,

75 And Hukok with her suburbs, and Rehob with her suburbs:

76 And out of the tribe of Naphtali; Kedesh in Galilee with her suburbs, and Hammon with her suburbs, and Kirjathaim with her suburbs.

77 Unto the rest of the children of Merari *were given* out of the tribe of Zebulun, Rimmon with her suburbs, Tabor with her suburbs:

78 And on the other side Jordan by Jericho, on the east side of Jordan, *were given them* out of the tribe of Reuben, Bezer in the wilderness with her suburbs, and Jahzah with her suburbs,

79 ᵃKedemoth also with her suburbs, and Mephaath with her suburbs:

80 And out of the tribe of ᵇGad; Ramoth in Gilead with her suburbs, and Mahanaim with her suburbs,

81 And Heshbon with her suburbs, and Jazer with her suburbs.

ʷJoshua xxi. 7, 34——ˣVerse 61——ʸJoshua xxi. 21

ᶻSee Josh. xxi. 22–35, where many of these cities have other names——ᵃJosh. xxi. 37——ᵇJosh. xxi. 38, 39

Verse 65. *Which are called by* their *names.*] Probably each family gave its own name to the city that fell to its lot.

Verse 69. *Aijalon with her suburbs*] There are the *two* cities wanting here, *Eltekeh* and *Gibethon.* See Josh. xxi. 23.

Verses 71-77. We shall see from Josh. xxi. 28, &c., that several of these cities have different names.

How barren to us is this register, both of incident and interest! and yet, as barren rocks and sandy deserts make integral and necessary parts of the globe; so do these genealogical tables make necessary parts of the history of providence and grace in the maintenance of truth, and the establishment of the Church of Christ. Therefore, no one that fears God will either despise or lightly esteem them.

CHAPTER VII

The genealogy of Issachar, 1–5. Of Benjamin, 6–12. Of Naphtali, 13. Of Manasseh, 14–19. Of Ephraim, 20–29. And of Asher, 30–40.

A. M. 2704, &c.
B. C. 1300, &c.
Post Diluvium,
1048, &c.

NOW the sons of Issachar *were,* ᵃTola, and ᵇPuah, Jashub, and Shimrom, four.

2 And the sons of Tola; Uzzi, and Rephaiah, and Jeriel, and Jahmai, and Jibsam, and She-

A. M. 2704, &c.
B. C. 1300, &c.
Post Diluvium,
1048, &c.

ᵃGen. xlvi. 13; Num. xxvi. 23

ᵇOr, *Phuvah, Job*

NOTES ON CHAP. VII

Verse 2. *Whose number* was *in the days of David*] Whether this was the number returned

by Joab and his assistants, when they made that census of the people with which God was so much displeased, we know not. It is worthy of remark that we read here the sum of three

A. M. 2704, &c.
B. C. 1300, &c.
Post Diluvium,
1048, &c.

muel, heads of their father's house, *to wit,* of Tola: *they were* valiant men of might in their generations; [c]whose number *was* in the days of David two and twenty thousand and six hundred.

3 And the sons of Uzzi; Izrahiah: and the sons of Izrahiah; Michael, and Obadiah, and Joel, Ishiah, five: all of them chief men.

4 And with them, by their generations, after the house of their fathers, *were* bands of soldiers for war, six and thirty thousand *men:* for they had many wives and sons.

5 And their brethren among all the families of Issachar *were* valiant men of might, reckoned in all by their genealogies fourscore and seven thousand.

6 *The sons* of [d]Benjamin; Bela, and Becher, and Jediael, three.

7 And the sons of Bela; Ezbon, and Uzzi, and Uzziel, and Jerimoth, and Iri, five; heads of the house of *their* fathers, mighty men of valour; and were reckoned by their genealogies twenty and two thousand and thirty and four.

8 And the sons of Becher; Zemira, and Joash, and Eliezer, and Elioenai, and Omri, and Jerimoth, and Abiah, and Anathoth, and Alameth. All these *are* the sons of Becher.

9 And the number of them, after their genealogy by their generations, heads of the house of their fathers, mighty men of valour, *was* twenty thousand and two hundred.

10 The sons also of Jediael; Bilhan: and

the sons of Bilhan; Jeush, and Benjamin, and Ehud, and Chenaanah, and Zethan, and Tharshish, and Ahishahar.

A. M. 2704, &c.
B. C. 1300, &c.
Post Diluvium,
1048, &c.

11 All these the sons of Jediael, by the heads of their fathers, mighty men of valour, *were* seventeen thousand and two hundred *soldiers,* fit to go out for war *and* battle.

12 [c]Shuppim also, and Huppim, the children of [f]Ir, *and* Hushim, the sons of [g]Aher.

13 The sons of Naphtali; Jahziel, and Guni, and Jezer, and [h]Shallum, the sons of Bilhah.

14 The sons of Manasseh; Ashriel, whom she bare: (*but* his concubine the Aramitess bare Machir the father of Gilead:

15 And Machir took to wife *the sister* of Huppim and Shuppim, whose sister's name *was* Maachah;) and the name of the second *was* Zelophehad: and Zelopehad had daughters.

16 And Maachah the wife of Machir bare a son, and she called his name Peresh; and the name of his brother *was* Sheresh: and his sons *were* Ulam and Rakem.

17 And the sons of Ulam; [i]Bedan. These *were* the sons of Gilead, the son of Machir, the son of Manasseh.

18 And his sister Hammoleketh bare Ishod, and [k]Abiezer, and Mahalah.

19 And the sons of Shemidah were Ahian, and Shechem, and Likhi, and Aniam.

20 And [l]the sons of Ephraim; Shuthelah, and Bered his son, and Tahath his son, and Eladah his son, and Tahath his son,

21 And Zabad his son, and Shuthelah his son,

---

[c]2 Sam. xxiv. 1, 2; chap. xxvii. 1——[d]Gen. xlvi. 21; Num. xxvi. 38; chap. viii. 1, &c.——[e]Num. xxvi. 39, *Shupham* and *Hupham*

[f]Or, *Iri,* ver. 7——[g]Or, *Ahiram,* Num. xxvi. 38 [h]Gen. xlvi. 24, *Shillem*——[i]1 Sam. xii. 11——[k]Num. xxvi. 30, *Jezer*——[l]Num. xxvi. 35

---

tribes, Benjamin, Issachar, and Asher, under the reign of David, which is mentioned nowhere else; and yet we have no account here of the other tribes, probably because the author found no public registers in which such enumeration was recorded.

Verse 3. *The sons of Izrahiah—five*] There are, however, only *four* names in the text. Instead of *five,* the *Syriac* and *Arabic* read *four.* If *five* be the true reading, then *Izrahiah* must be reckoned with his *four sons.*

Verse 6. *The sons of Benjamin; Bela, and Becher, and Jediael*] In Gen. xlvi. 21, *ten* sons of Benjamin are reckoned; viz., *Bela, Becher, Ashbel, Gera, Naaman, Eri, Rosh, Muppim, Huppim,* and *Ard.* In Num. xxvi. 38, &c., *five* sons only of Benjamin are mentioned, *Bela, Ashbel, Ahiram, Shupham,* and *Hupham:* and Ard and Naaman are there said to be the sons of Bela;

consequently grandsons of Benjamin. In the beginning of the following chapter, *five* sons of Benjamin are mentioned, viz., *Bela, Ashbel, Aharah, Nohah,* and *Rapha;* where also *Addar, Gera, Abihud, Abishua, Naaman, Ahoah,* a second *Gera, Shephuphan,* and *Huram,* are all represented as *grandsons,* not *sons,* of Benjamin: hence we see that in many cases *grandsons* are called *sons,* and both are often confounded in the genealogical tables. To attempt to reconcile such discrepancies would be a task as endless as it would be useless. The rabbins say that Ezra, who wrote this book, did not know whether some of these were *sons* or *grandsons;* and they intimate also that the tables from which he copied were often defective, and here we must leave all such matters.

Verse 21. *Whom the men of Gath—slew*] We know nothing of this circumstance but what

A. M. 2704, &c.
B. C. 1300, &c.
Post Diluvium,
1048, &c.

and Ezer, and Elead, whom the men of Gath *that were* born in *that* land slew, because they came down to take away their cattle.

22 And Ephraim their father mourned many days, and his brethren came to comfort him.

23 And when he went in to his wife, she conceived, and bare a son, and he called his name Beriah, because it went evil with his house.

24 (And his daughter *was* Sherah, who built Beth-horon the nether, and the upper, and Uzzensherah.)

25 And Rephah *was* his son, also Resheph, and Telah his son, and Tahan his son,

26 Laadan his son, Ammihud his son, Elishama his son,

27 ᵐNon his son, Jehoshuah his son.

28 And their possessions and habitations *were,* Beth-el and the towns thereof, and eastward ⁿNaaran, and westward Gezer, with the °towns thereof; Shechem also and the towns thereof, unto ᵖGaza and the towns thereof:

29 And by the borders of the children of ۹Manasseh, Beth-shean and her towns, Taanach and her towns, ʳMegiddo and her towns, Dor and her towns. In these dwelt the children of Joseph the son of Israel.

30 ˢThe sons of Asher; Imnah, and Isuah, and Ishuai, and Beriah, and Serah their sister.

A. M. 2704, &c.
B. C. 1300, &c.
Post Diluvium,
1048, &c.

31 And the sons of Beriah; Heber, and Malchiel, who *is* the father of Birzavith.

32 And Heber begat Japhlet; and ᵗShomer, and Hotham, and Shua their sister.

33 And the sons of Japhlet; Pasach, and Bimhal, and Ashvath. These *are* the children of Japhlet.

34 And the sons of ᵘShamer; Ahi, and Rohgah, Jehubbah, and Aram.

35 And the sons of his brother Helem; Zophah, and Imna, and Shelesh, and Amal.

36 The sons of Zophah; Suah, and Harnepher, and Shual, and Beri, and Imrah,

37 Bezer, and Hod, and Shamma, and Shilshah, and Ithran, and Beera.

38 And the sons of Jether; Jephunneh, and Pispah, and Ara.

39 And the sons of Ulla; Arah, and Haniel, and Rezia.

40 All these *were* the children of Asher, heads of *their* father's house, choice *and* mighty men of valour, chief of the princes. And the number throughout the genealogy of them that were apt to the war *and* to battle *was* twenty and six thousand men.

ᵐOr, *Nun,* Num. xiii. 8, 16——ⁿJosh. xvi. 7, *Naarath*
°Heb. *daughters*——ᵖOr, *Adasa,* 1 Mac. vii. 45

۹Josh. xvii. 7——ʳJosh. xvii. 11——ˢGen. xlvi. 17; Num. xxvi. 44——ᵗVer. 34, *Shamer*——ᵘVer. 32, *Shomer*

---

is related here. The Targum paraphrases the whole thus: "These were the leaders of the house of Ephraim; and they computed their period [or boundary, קיצא *kitsa*] from the time in which the Word of the Lord of the universe spake with Abraham between the divisions, [i. e., the separated parts of the covenant sacrifice; see Gen. xv.,] but they erred, for they should have counted from the time in which Isaac was born; they went out of Egypt therefore thirty years before the period: for, thirty years before the birth of Isaac the Word of the Lord of the universe spake with Abraham between the divisions. And when they went out of Egypt, there were with them *two hundred thousand* warriors of the tribe of Ephraim, whom the men of Gath, the natives of the land of the Philistines, slew, because they came down that they might carry away their cattle. 22.— And Ephraim their father mourned for them

many days, and all his brethren came to comfort him. 23.—And he went in to his wife, and she conceived and bare a son, and called his name Beriah, (בריעה *in evil,*) because *he was born in the time in which this evil happened to his house.*"

Verse 24. *His daughter* was *Sherah*] That is, *remnant;* "called so," says the Targum, "because she was the *remnant that escaped from the slaughter* mentioned above."

Verse 32. *And Shua their sister.*] It is very rarely that *women* are found in the Jewish genealogies, and they are never inserted but for especial reasons.

Verse 40. *The children of Asher*] The rabbins say that the daughters of Asher were very beautiful, and were all matched with *kings* or *priests.* Several things relative to the subjects in this chapter may be found explained in the parallel places marked in the margin.

CHAPTER VIII

A. M. 2704, &c.
B. C. 1300, &c.
Post Diluvium,
1048, &c.

NOW Benjamin begat [a]Bela his first-born, Ashbel the second, and Aharah the third,

2 Nohah the fourth, and Rapha the fifth.

3 And the sons of Bela were, [b]Addar, and Gera, and Abihud,

4 And Abishua, and Naaman, and Ahoah,

5 And Gera, and [c]Shephuphan, and Huram.

6 And these *are* the sons of Ehud: these are the heads of the fathers of the inhabitants of Geba, and they removed them to [d]Manahath:

7 And Naaman, and Ahiah, and Gera, he removed them, and begat Uzza, and Ahihud.

8 And Shaharaim begat *children* in the country of Moab, after he had sent them away; Hushim and Baara *were* his wives.

9 And he begat of Hodesh his wife, Jobab, and Zibia, and Mesha, and Malcham,

10 And Jeuz, and Shachia, and Mirma. These *were* his sons, heads of the fathers.

11 And of Hushim he begat Abitub, and Elpaal.

12 The sons of Elpaal; Eber, and Misham, and Shamed, who built Ono, and Lod, with the towns thereof:

13 Beriah also, and [e]Shema, who *were* heads of the fathers of the inhabitants of Aijalon, who drove away the inhabitants of Gath:

14 And Ahio, Shashak, and Jeremoth,

15 And Zebadiah, and Arad, and Ader,

16 And Michael, and Ispah, and Joha, the sons of Beriah;

17 And Zebadiah, and Meshullam, and Hezeki, and Heber,

18 Ishmerai also, and Jezliah and Jobab, the sons of Elpaal;

19 And Jakim, and Zichri, and Zabdi,

20 And Elienai, and Zilthai, and Eliel,

21 And Adaiah, and Beraiah, and Shimrath, the sons of [f]Shimhi;

22 And Ishpan, and Heber, and Eliel,

23 And Abdon, and Zichri, and Hanan,

24 And Hananiah, and Elam, and Antothijah,

25 And Iphedeiah, and Penuel, the sons of Shashak;

26 And Shamsherai, and Shehariah, and Athaliah,

27 And Jaresiah, and Eliah, and Zicri, the sons of Jeroham.

28 These *were* heads of the fathers, by their generations, chief *men*. These dwelt in Jerusalem.

29 And at Gibeon dwelt the [g]father of Gibeon; whose [h]wife's name *was* Maachah:

30 And his first-born son Abdon, and Zur, and Kish, and Baal, and Nadab,

31 And Gedor, and Ahio, and [i]Zacher.

32 And Mikloth begat [k]Shimeah. And these also dwelt with their brethren in Jerusalem, over against them.

33 And [l]Ner begat Kish, and Kish begat Saul, and Saul begat Jonathan, and Malchishua, and [m]Abinadab, and [n]Esh-baal.

34 And the son of Jonathan *was* [o]Meribbaal; and Merib-baal begat [p]Micah.

A. M. 2704, &c.
B. C. 1300, &c.
Post Diluvium,
1048, &c.

---

[a]Gen. xlvi. 21; Num. xxvi. 38; ch. vii. 6——[b]Or, *Ard*, Gen. xlvi. 21——[c]Or, *Shuphan*, Num. xxvi. 39; see ch. vii. 12——[d]Ch. ii. 52——[e]Ver. 21——[f]Or, *Shema*, ver. 13——[g]Called *Jehiel*, ch. ix. 35——[h]Chap. ix. 35

[i]Or, *Zechariah*, ch. ix. 37——[k]Or, *Shimeam*, ch. ix. 38 [l]1 Sam. xiv. 51——[m]1 Sam. xiv. 49, *Ishui*——[n]Or, *Ishbosheth*, 2 Sam. ii. 8——[o]Or, *Mephibosheth*, 2 Sam. iv. 4; ix. 6, 10——[p]2 Sam. ix. 12

NOTES ON CHAP. VIII

Verse 1. *Now Benjamin begat, &c.*] See what has been said on the preceding chapter, ver. 6.

Verse 9. *He begat of Hodesh his wife*] In the preceding verse it is said that *Hushim and Baara* were *his wives;* and here it is said *he begat of Hodesh his wife, &c.* And then his children by *Hushim* are mentioned, but not a word of *Baara!* It is likely therefore that *Hodesh* was another name for *Baara,* and this is asserted by the Targum: *And he begot of Baara, that is Chodesh, his wife;* so called *because he espoused her anew.* It is supposed that he had put her away before, and now remarried her.

Verse 12. *Who built Ono, and Lod*] The Targum adds, "Which the children of Israel

ravaged and burnt with fire, when they made war on the tribe of Benjamin in Gibeah."

Verse 28. *These* were *heads of the fathers*] On the following verses Dr. Kennicott has laboured hard to restore the true reading. See his detailed *comparison* of these and their parallel passages in his Hebrew Bible, vol. ii., p. 657.

Verse 29. *And at Gibeon*] This passage to the end of the 38th verse is found, with a little variety in the names, chap. ix. 35-44.

The rabbins say that Ezra, having found *two books* that had these passages with a variety in the names, as they agreed in general, he thought best to insert them both, not being able to discern which was the best.

His general plan was to collate all the copies he had, and to follow the *greater number* when he found them to agree; those which disagreed from the majority were thrown aside as spuri-

A. M. 2704, &c.
B. C. 1300, &c.
Post Diluvium,
1048, &c.

35 And the sons of Micah *were,* Pithon, and Melech, and ᵠTarea, and Ahaz.

36 And Ahaz begat ʳJehoadah; and Jehoadah begat Alemeth, and Azmaveth, and Zimri; and Zimri begat Moza,

37 And Moza begat Binea: ˢRapha *was* his son, Eleasah his son, Azel his son:

38 And Azel had six sons, whose names *are* these, Azrikam, Bocheru, and Ishmael, and

Sheariah, and Obadiah, and Hanan. All these *were* the sons of Azel.

A. M. 2704, &c.
B. C. 1300, &c.
Post Diluvium,
1048, &c.

39 And the sons of Eshek his brother *were,* Ulam his first-born, Jehush the second, and Eliphelet the third.

40 And the sons of Ulam were mighty men of ᵗvalour, archers, and had many sons, and sons' sons, a hundred and fifty. All these *are* of the sons of Benjamin.

ᵠOr, *Tahrea,* ch. ix. 41——ʳ*Jarah,* ch. ix. 42——ˢCh. ix. 43, *Rephaiah*

ᵗJudg. vi. 12; 1 Kings xi. 28; 2 Kings v. 1; chap. xii. 28; 2 Chron. xvii. 17

---

ous; and yet, in many cases, probably the rejected copies contained the true text.

If Ezra proceeded as R. Sol. Jarchi says, he had a very imperfect notion of the rules of true criticism; and it is no wonder that he has left so many faults in his text.

Verse 34. *Merib-baal*] The same as *Mephibosheth;* for, as the Israelites detested *Baal,* which signifies *lord,* they changed it into *bosheth,* which signifies *shame* or *reproach.*

Verse 40. *The sons of Ulam were mighty men of valour*] The Targum speaks honourably of them: "The sons of Ulam were mighty and strong men, subduing by wisdom their evil

concupiscence, as men bend a bow; therefore they had many sons and grandsons."

Of the six sons of Azel, mentioned ver. 38, R. S. Jarchi says that their allegorical expositions were sufficient to load *thirteen thousand* camels! No doubt these were reputed to be *deeply learned* men. There was a time when the *allegorizers* and *metaphor-men* ranked very high among *theologians,* even in our own enlightened and critical country. At present they are almost totally out of fashion. May they never recover their footing! But what a shameful hyperbole is that of Jarchi! The writings of six men a load for *thirteen thousand camels!*

CHAPTER IX

All Israel reckoned by genealogies, 1. *The first inhabitants of Jerusalem, after their return from their captivity, who were chiefs of the fathers,* 2–9. *Of the priests,* 10–13; *Levites,* 14–16; *porters, their work, lodgings, &c.,* 17–29; *other officers,* 30–32; *the singers,* 33, 34. *A repetition of the genealogy of Saul and his sons,* 35–44.

A. M. 2804, &c.
B. C. 1200, &c.
Post Diluvium,
1148, &c.

SO ᵃall Israel were reckoned by genealogies; and, behold, they *were* written in the book of the kings of Israel and Judah, *who* were carried away to Babylon for their transgression.

2 ᵇNow the first inhabitants that *dwelt* in their possessions in their cities *were,* the

Israelites, the priests, Levites, and ᶜthe Nethinims.

A. M. 2804, &c.
B. C. 1200, &c.
Post Diluvium,
1148, &c.

3 And in ᵈJerusalem dwelt of the children of Judah, and of the children of Benjamin, and of the children of Ephraim, and Manasseh;

4 Uthai the son of Ammihud, the son of

ᵃEzra ii. 59——ᵇEzra ii. 70; Neh. vii. 73

ᶜJosh. ix. 27; Ezra ii. 43; viii. 20——ᵈNeh. xi. 1

NOTES ON CHAP. IX

Verse 1. *Were reckoned by genealogies*] Jarchi considers these as the words of Ezra, the compiler of the book; as if he had said: I have given the genealogies of the Israelites as I have found them in a book which was carried into Babylon, when the people were carried thither for their transgressions; and this book which I found is that which I have transcribed in the preceding chapters.

Verse 2. *Now the first inhabitants*] This is spoken of those who returned from the Babylonish captivity, and of the time in which they returned; for it is insinuated here that *other persons afterwards* settled at Jerusalem, though these mentioned here were the *first* on the return from the captivity. Properly speaking, the divisions mentioned in this verse constituted the *whole* of the Israelitish people, who were, ever since the days of Joshua, divided into

the *four* following classes: 1. The *priests.* 2. The *Levites.* 3. The *common people,* or *simple Israelites.* 4. The *Nethinim,* or *slaves of the temple,* the remains of the Gibeonites, who, having deceived Joshua, were condemned to this service, Josh. ix. 21, &c. In David's time it is probable that other conquered people were added, as the successors of the Gibeonites were not sufficient to perform all the drudgery of the temple service.

Verse 3. *And in Jerusalem dwelt*] Several of the tribes of Judah, Benjamin, Ephraim, and Manasseh, took advantage of the proclamation of Cyrus to return to Jerusalem, and so mingled with the Israelites, and those to whom Jerusalem had previously appertained; and this was necessary in order to provide a sufficient population for so large a city.

Verse 4. *Uthai the son of Ammihud*] The list here is nearly the same with those found in *Ezra* and *Nehemiah,* and contains those who

A. M. 2804, &c.
B. C. 1200, &c.
Post Diluvium,
1148, &c.
Omri, the son of Imri, the son of Bani, of the children of Pharez the son of Judah.

5 And of the Shilonites; Asaiah the first-born, and his sons.

6 And of the sons of Zerah; Jeuel, and their brethren, six hundred and ninety.

7 And of the sons of Benjamin; Sallu the son of Meshullam, the son of Hodaviah, the son of Hasenuah,

8 And Ibneiah the son of Jeroham, and Elah the son of Uzzi, the son of Michri, and Meshullam the son of Shephatiah, the son of Reuel, the son of Ibnijah;

9 And their brethren, according to their generations, nine hundred and fifty and six. All these men *were* chief of the fathers in the house of their fathers.

10 [e]And of the priests; Jedaiah, and Jehoiarib, and Jachin,

11 And [f]Azariah the son of Hilkiah, the son of Meshullam, the son of Zadok, the son of Meraioth, the son of Ahitub, the ruler of the house of God;

12 And Adaiah the son of Jeroham, the son of Pashur, the son of Malchijah, and Maasiai the son of Adiel, the son of Jahzerah, the son of Meshullam, the son of Meshillemith, the son of Immer;

13 And their brethren, heads of the house of their fathers, a thousand and seven hundred and threescore; [g]very able men for the work of the service of the house of God.

14 And of the Levites; Shemaiah the son of Hasshub, the son of Azrikam, the son of Hashabiah, of the sons of Merari;

15 And Bakbakkar, Heresh, and Galal, and

Mattaniah the son of Micah, the A. M. 2804, &c.
B. C. 1200, &c.
Post Diluvium,
1148, &c. son of Zichri, the son of Asaph;

16 And Obadiah the son of Shemaiah, the son of Galal, the son of Jeduthun, and Berechiah the son of Asa, the son of Elkanah, that dwelt in the villages of the Netophathites.

17 And the porters *were,* Shallum, and Akkub, and Talmon, and Ahiman, and their brethren: Shallum *was* the chief;

18 Who hitherto *waited* in the king's gate eastward: they *were* porters in the companies of the children of Levi.

19 And Shallum the son of Kore, the son of Ebiasaph, the son of Korah, and his brethren, of the house of his father, the Korahites, *were* over the work of the service, keepers of the [h]gates of the tabernacle: and their fathers, *being* over the host of the LORD, *were* keepers of the entry.

20 And [i]Phinehas the son of Eleazar was the ruler over them in time past, *and* the LORD *was* with him.

21 *And* Zechariah the son of Meshelemiah *was* porter of the door of the tabernacle of the congregation.

22 All these *which were* chosen to be porters in the gates *were* two hundred and twelve. These were reckoned by their genealogy in their villages, whom [k]David and Samuel [l]the seer [m]did ordain in their [n]set office.

23 So they and their children *had* the oversight of the gates of the house of the LORD, *namely,* the house of the tabernacle, by wards.

24 In four quarters were the porters, toward the east, west, north, and south.

25 And their brethren, *which were* in their

---

[e]Neh. xi. 10, &c.——[f]Neh. xi. 11, *Seraiah*——[g]Heb. *mighty men of valour*——[h]Heb. *thresholds*

[i]Num. xxxi. 6——[k]Chap. xxvi. 1, 2——[l]1 Sam. ix. 9
[m]Heb. *founded*——[n]Or, *trust*

---

returned to Jerusalem with Zerubbabel; but the list in Nehemiah is more ample, probably because it contains those who came *afterwards.* The object of the sacred writer here was to give the list of those who came *first. Now the first inhabitants, &c.*

Verse 11. *The ruler of the house of God.*] The high priest at this time was *Jeshua* the son of *Jozadak,* (Ezra iii. 8,) and *Seraiah,* (Neh. xi. 11,) called here *Azariah,* was the *ruler of the house;* the person next in authority to the high priest, and who probably had the guard of the temple and command of the priests, Levites, &c. It is likely that the person here was the same as is called the *second priest,* 2 Kings xxv. 18, who was the *sagan* or high priest's deputy. See the note there.

Verse 13. *And their brethren*] What a prodigious number of ecclesiastics to perform the Divine service of one temple! no less than *one thousand seven hundred* and *eighty* able-bodied men! and this number is reckoned independently of the *two hundred* and *twelve* porters who served at the gates of the house of the Lord, ver. 22.

Verse 18. *The king's gate*] That by which the kings of Judah went to the temple; see on 2 Kings xvi. 18.

Verse 19. *Keepers of the entry.*] Whose business it was to suffer no person to come to the tabernacle but the priests, during the performance of the sacred service; see *Jarchi.*

Verse 20. *And Phinehas*] The Targum says,

A. M. 2804, &c. B. C. 1200, &c. Post Diluvium, 1148, &c.

villages, *were* to come [o]after seven days from time to time with them.

26 For these Levites, the four chief porters, were in *their* [p]set office, and were over the [q]chambers and treasuries of the house of God.

27 And they lodged round about the house of God, because the charge *was* upon them, and the opening thereof every morning *pertained* to them.

28 And *certain* of them had the charge of the ministering vessels, that they should [r]bring them in and out by tale.

29 *Some* of them also *were* appointed to oversee the vessels, and all the [s]instruments of the sanctuary, and the fine flour, and the wine, and the oil, and the frankincense, and the spices.

30 And *some* of the sons of the priests made [t]the anointment of the spices.

31 And Mattithiah, *one* of the Levites, who *was* the first-born of Shallum the Korahite, had the [u]set office [v]over the things that were made [w]in the pans.

32 And *other* of their brethren, of the sons of the Kohathites, [x]*were* over the [y]shew-bread, to prepare *it* every Sabbath.

33 And these *are* [z]the singers, chief of the fathers of the Levites, *who remaining* in the chambers *were* free: for [a]they were employed in *that* work day and night.

A. M. 2804, &c. B. C. 1200, &c. Post Diluvium, 1148, &c.

34 These chief fathers of the Levites *were* chief throughout their generations; these dwelt at Jerusalem.

35 And in Gibeon dwelt the father of Gibeon, Jehiel, whose wife's name *was* [b]Maachah:

36 And his first-born son Abdon, then Zur, and Kish, and Baal, and Ner, and Nadab,

37 And Gedor, and Ahio, and Zechariah, and Mikloth.

38 And Mikloth begat Shimeam. And they also dwelt with their brethren at Jerusalem, over against their brethren.

39 [c]And Ner begat Kish; and Kish begat Saul; and Saul begat Jonathan, and Malchi-shua, and Abinadab, and Esh-baal.

40 And the son of Jonathan *was* Merib-baal: and Merib-baal begat Micah.

41 And the sons of Micah *were*, Pithon, and Melech, and Tahrea, [d]*and Ahaz.*

42 And Ahaz begat Jarah; and Jarah begat Alemeth, and Azmaveth, and Zimri; and Zimri begat Moza;

43 And Moza begat Binea; and Rephaiah his son, Eleasah his son, Azel his son.

44 And Azel had six sons, whose names *are* these, Azrikam, Bocheru, and Ishmael, and Sheariah, and Obadiah, and Hanan: these *were* the sons of Azel.

[o]2 Kings xi. 5——[p]Or, *trust*——[q]Or, *storehouses*——[r]Heb. *bring them in by tale, and carry them out by tale*——[s]Or, *vessels*——[t]Exod. xxx. 23——[u]Or, *trust*——[v]Lev. ii. 5; vi. 21

[w]Or, *on flat plates* or *slices*——[x]Lev. xxiv. 8——[y]Heb. *bread of ordering*——[z]Chap. vi. 31; xxv. 1——[a]Heb. *upon them*——[b]Chap. viii. 29——[c]Chap. viii. 33——[d]Ch. viii. 35

"And Phinehas, the son of Eleazar, was ruler over them from ancient times, from the day in which the tabernacle was set up in the wilderness; and the WORD of the Lord was his assistant."

Verse 30. *The sons of the priests made the ointment*] Only the priests were permitted to make this ointment; all others were forbidden to do it on pain of death; see Exod. xxx. 34-38, and the notes there.

Verse 35. *Whose wife's name was Maachah*] Here our translators have departed from the original, for the word is אחתו *achotho*, his SISTER; but the *Vulgate*, *Septuagint*, *Syriac*, *Arabic*, and *Chaldee*, have WIFE; to which may be added chap. viii. 29, the parallel place. Almost all the early editions, as well as the MS. editions, have the same reading. Of all the *Polyglots* the *Complutensian* alone has אשתו *ishto*, his WIFE. *His wife* is the reading also of Vatablus's Polyglot, but in the margin he observes that other copies have *his sister*. There is most certainly a *fault* somewhere, for *Maachah* could not be both the *sister* and *wife* of *Jehiel*. Whether, therefore, chap. viii. 29 has been altered from *this*, or this altered from *that*, who can tell? A *single letter* makes the whole difference: if the word be written with ח *cheth*, it is SISTER; if with ש *shin*, it is WIFE. The latter is most probably the true reading. It is so in three very ancient MSS. in my own possession.

Verse 41. And Ahaz.] This is added by our translators from chap. viii. 35, but such liberties should only be taken in a note; for although the words are now sufficiently distinguished from the text by being printed in *Italics*, yet it is too much to expect that every editor of a Bible will attend to such distinctions, and in process of time the words will be found incorporated with the text.

Verse 35, and the following verses, are a repetition of what we find in chap. viii. 29-38, where see the notes.

CHAPTER X

A fatal battle between the Israelites and Philistines in Gilboa, in which Saul is mortally wounded, and his three sons slain, 1–6. The Israelites being totally routed, the Philistines, coming to strip the dead, find Saul and his three sons among the slain; they cut off Saul's head, and send it and his armour about the country to the idol temples; and then fix them up in the house of Dagon, 7–10. The men of Jabesh-gilead come by night, and take away the bodies of Saul and his three sons, and bury them in Jabesh, 11, 12. The reason of Saul's tragical death; the kingdom is transferred to David, 13, 14.

A. M. 2949
B. C. 1055
An. Exod. Isr.
436
Anno ante I.
Olymp. 279

NOW [a]the Philistines fought against Israel; and the men of Israel fled from before the Philistines, and fell down [b]slain in Mount Gilboa.

2 And the Philistines followed hard after Saul, and after his sons; and the Philistines slew Jonathan, and [c]Abinadab, and Malchishua, the sons of Saul.

3 And the battle went sore against Saul, and the [d]archers [e]hit him, and he was wounded of the archers.

4 Then said Saul to his armour-bearer, Draw thy sword, and thrust me through therewith; lest these uncircumcised come and [f]abuse me. But his armour-bearer would not; for he was sore afraid. So Saul took a sword, and fell upon it.

5 And when his armour-bearer saw that Saul was dead, he fell likewise on the sword, and died.

6 So Saul died, and his three sons, and all his house died together.

7 And when all the men of Israel that *were* in the valley saw that they fled, and that Saul and his sons were dead, then they forsook their cities, and fled: and the Philistines came and dwelt in them.

8 And it came to pass on the morrow, when the Philistines came to strip the slain, that they found Saul and his sons fallen in Mount Gilboa.

A. M. 2949
B. C. 1055
An. Exod. Isr.
436
Anno ante I.
Olymp. 279

9 And when they had stripped him, they took his head, and his armour, and sent into the land of the Philistines round about, to carry tidings unto their idols, and to the people.

10 [g]And they put his armour in the house of their gods, and fastened his head in the temple of Dagon.

11 And when all Jabesh-gilead heard all that the Philistines had done to Saul,

12 They arose, all the valiant men, and took away the body of Saul, and the bodies of his sons, and brought them to Jabesh, and buried their bones under the oak in Jabesh, and fasted seven days.

13 So Saul died for his transgression which he [h]committed against the LORD, [i]*even* against the word of the LORD, which he kept not, and also for asking *counsel* of *one that had* a familiar spirit, [k]to inquire *of it;*

14 And inquired not of the LORD: therefore he slew him, and [l]turned the kingdom unto David, the son of [m]Jesse.

---

[a]1 Sam. xxxi. 1, 2——[b]Or, *wounded*——[c]Or, *Ishui,* 1 Sam. xiv. 49——[d]Heb. *shooters with bows*——[e]Heb. *found him*——[f]Or, *mock me*

[g]1 Sam. xxxi. 10——[h]Heb. *transgressed*——[i]1 Sam. xiii. 13; xv. 23——[k]1 Sam. xxviii. 7——[l]1 Sam. xv. 28; 2 Sam. iii. 9, 10; v. 3——[m]Heb. *Isai*

NOTES ON CHAP. X

Verse 1. *Now the Philistines fought against Israel*] The reader will find the same history in almost the same words, in 1 Sam. xxxi. 1-13, to the notes on which he is referred for every thing important in this.

Verse 6. *So Saul died—and all his house*] Every branch of his family that had followed him to the war was cut off; his *three sons* are mentioned as being the chief. No doubt all his officers were slain.

Verse 11. *When all Jabesh-gilead heard*] For a general account of the principles of *heroism* and *gratitude* from which this action of the men of Jabesh-gilead proceeded, see the note on 1 Sam. xxxi. 11, 12.

By the kindness of a literary friend, I am enabled to lay a farther illustration of this noble act before the reader, which he will find at the conclusion of the chapter.

Verse 13. *Saul died for his transgression*] See the concluding observations on the first book of Samuel.

Verse 14. *Inquired not of the Lord*] On these two last verses the Targum speaks thus: "And Saul died for the transgression by which he transgressed against the WORD of the Lord, and because he did not keep the commandment of the Lord when he warred against the house of Amalek; and because he consulted Pythons, and sought oracular answers from them. Neither did he ask counsel from before the Lord by Urim and Thummim, for he had slain the priests that were in Nob; therefore the Lord slew him, and transferred the kingdom to David the son of Jesse."

A LITERARY friend furnishes the following remarks:—

"The sacred writer, in the first book of Samuel, chap. xxxi. 11-13, and 1 Chron. x. 11, 12, after relating the defeat and death of Saul, and the ignominious treatment of his remains, thus concludes:—

"'And when the inhabitants of Jabesh-gilead heard of that which the Philistines had done to Saul, all the valiant men arose, and went all night, and took the body of Saul, and the bodies of his sons, from the wall of Beth-shan, and came to Jabesh, and burnt them there; and they took the bones, and buried them under a tree at Jabesh, and fasted seven days.'

"Often has this account been read with admiration of the bravery and devotedness of the men of Jabesh-gilead, but without considering that these men had any greater cause than others for honouring the remains of their sovereign; but, on reflection, it will be perceived that the strong impulse of gratitude prompted them to this honourable exertion. They remembered their preservation from destruction, and, which to brave men is more galling, from bearing marks of having been defeated, and being deprived of the honourable hope of wiping off disgrace, or defending their country at future seasons.

"Reading these verses in conjunction with the attack of Nahash, we perceive the natural feelings of humanity, of honourable respect, prompting the men of Jabesh to act as they did in rescuing the bones of Saul and his family.

"The father of Grecian poetry relates in how great a degree the warriors of ancient days honoured the remains of their leaders; how severe were the contests for the body of the fallen chief, more determined oftentimes than the struggle for victory: this point of military honour was possibly excited or heightened by the religious idea so prevalent in his age, and after times, respecting the fate of the spirits of those who were unburied.

"Homer wrote of events passing at no distant period from those recorded in the first volume of Samuel; and these accounts mutually corroborate each other, being in unison, not only with the feelings of humanity, but with the customs of ancient nations. These may be farther illustrated by comparing the conduct of the Philistines with regard to Saul and his sons, with that of the hero of the Iliad towards Hector, the most finished character of the poem. Saul had been a severe scourge to the Philistines throughout a long series of years; the illustrious chief of Troy had long warded off the ruin of his country, and destroyed the flower of her foes, independently of his last victory over Patroclus, which drew on his remains that dishonour which, however, fell only on his destroyer.

"Should the siege of Troy be considered a fable, it may then be concluded that Homer introduced into his poems the customs and manners known to those for whose perusal he wrote, if these customs were not prevalent among his readers; but anxiety for the body of the illustrious dead, or regret for his death, has often caused success when all exertions prior to this powerful stimulus have not availed; and this even in our days.

"The Philistines had long been confined to the southwest angle of the promised land, and in the earlier part of Saul's reign had suffered many and severe losses; yet it appears by this chapter that, alone or in conjunction with allies, they had been able to penetrate nearly to the banks of the Jordan, to fight the battle on Mount Gilboa. This could only have been effected by a march through great part of the kingdom of Israel.

"Doubtless the attention of Saul in its defence might have been greatly distracted by his pursuit and fear of David, which appeared to have absorbed his whole mind; and it may account for the defenceless or weakened state of his forces.

"These circumstances appear to corroborate the authenticity of these books, independently of the many private transactions therein recorded; particularly the interesting and singular friendship of Jonathan and David, a transaction not likely to occur to a forger of a narrative. **J. W.**"

CHAPTER XI

David is anointed king in Hebron, 1-3. He wars against the Jebusites, and takes their city, 4-9. An account of David's three mightiest heroes; and particularly of their hazardous exploit in bringing water from the well of Beth-lehem, 10-19. A list of the rest, and an account of their acts, 20-47.

A. M. 2956
B. C. 1048
An. Exod. Isr.
443
Anno ante I.
Olymp. 272

THEN [a]all Israel gathered themselves to David unto Hebron, saying, Behold, we *are* thy bone and thy flesh.

2 And moreover [b]in time past, even when Saul was king, thou *wast* he that leddest out and broughtest in Israel: and the LORD thy God said unto thee, Thou shalt [c]feed [d]my people Israel, and thou shalt be ruler over my people Israel.

A. M. 2956
B. C. 1048
An. Exod. Isr.
443
Anno ante I.
Olymp. 272

3 Therefore came all the elders of Israel to the king to Hebron; and David made a covenant with them in Hebron before the LORD; and [e]they anointed David king over Israel, according to the word of the LORD [f]by [g]Samuel.

---

[a]2 Sam. v. 1——[b]Heb. *both yesterday and the third day* [c]Or, *rule*

[d]Psa. lxxviii. 71——[e]2 Sam. v. 3——[f]Heb. *by the hand of*——[g]1 Sam. xvi. 1, 12, 13

NOTES ON CHAP. XI

Verse 1. *Then all Israel gathered themselves*

to David] See 2 Sam. v. 1-10, for the history contained in the first nine verses of this chapter, and the notes there.

A. M. 2956
B. C. 1048
An. Exod. Isr.
443
Anno ante I.
Olymp. 272

4 And David and all Israel [h]went to Jerusalem, which *is* Jebus; [i]where the Jebusites *were,* the inhabitants of the land.

5 And the inhabitants of Jebus said to David, Thou shalt not come hither. Nevertheless David took the castle of Zion, which *is* the city of David.

6 And David said, Whosoever smiteth the Jebusites first shall be [k]chief and captain. So Joab the son of Zeruiah went first up, and was chief.

7 And David dwelt in the castle; therefore they called it [l]the city of David.

8 And he built the city round about, even from Millo round about: and Joab [m]repaired the rest of the city.

9 So David [n]waxed greater and greater: for the LORD of hosts *was* with him.

10 [o]These also *are* the chief of the mighty men whom David had, who [p]strengthened themselves with him in his kingdom, *and* with

all Israel, to make him king, according to [q]the word of the LORD concerning Israel.

A. M. 2956
B. C. 1048
An. Exod. Isr.
443
Anno ante I.
Olymp. 272

11 And this *is* the number of the mighty men whom David had; Jashobeam, [r]a Hachmonite, the chief of the captains: he lifted up his spear against three hundred slain *by him* at one time.

12 And after him *was* Eleazar the son of Dodo, the Ahohite, who *was one* of the three mighties.

13 He was with David at [s]Pas-dammim, and there the Philistines were gathered together to battle, where was a parcel of ground full of barley; and the people fled from before the Philistines.

A. M. 2957
B. C. 1047
An. Exod. Isr.
444
Anno ante I.
Olymp. 271

14 And they [t]set themselves in the midst of *that* parcel, and delivered it, and slew the Philistines; and the LORD saved *them* by a great [u]deliverance.

15 Now [v]three of the thirty captains [w]went

---

[b]2 Samuel v. 6——[i]Judg. i. 21; xix. 10——[k]Heb. *head*
[l]That is, *Zion,* 2 Sam. v. 7——[m]Heb. *revived*——[n]Heb. *went in going and increasing*——[o]2 Sam. xxiii. 8——[p]Or, *held strongly with him*

[q]1 Sam. xvi. 1, 12——[r]Or, *son of Hachmoni*——[s]Or, *Ephes-dammim,* 1 Samuel xvii. 1——[t]Or, *stood*——[u]Or, *salvation*——[v]Or, *three captains over the thirty*——[w]2 Samuel xxiii. 13

Verse 11. *The number of the mighty men*] See 2 Sam. xxiii. 8, &c., and the notes there. The Targum has a remarkable addition here.

"These are the numbers of the strong men who were with David; he was the potent chief of the army; he sat upon the throne of judgment, anointed with the holy oil, all the prophets and wise men standing about him. When he went to battle, he was assisted from on high; and when he sat down to teach the law, the true meaning arose up in his mind. He was elect and pleasant, of a beautiful mien and lovely countenance, exercised in wisdom, prudent in counsel, and strong in virtue; the prince of the assembly, of a melodious voice, master in hymns, and chief among the mighty. He was instructed in the use of martial weapons; he carried a spear, to which was appended the ensign of the host of Judah; he went forth according to the voice of the Holy Spirit, was victorious in battle, and overthrew with his spear *three hundred* men at one time."—*T.*

On this and some of the following verses there is a judicious note of Dr. *Kennicott,* which I shall take the liberty to introduce, referring to his *first Dissertation on the Hebrew text* for farther illustration and proof, p. 128-144.

"Among the parallel places, a comparison of which may be of very considerable service, scarce any passages will appear more effectually to correct each other than the catalogue of David's mighty men of valour, as it now stands in 2 Sam. xxiii. 8-40, and in this chapter. About *thirty-four Hebrew words* have been lost out of this part of the passage in *Chronicles,* which are happily preserved in *Samuel.*

"The chief point of proof is this, that the

catalogue divides these *thirty-seven* warriors into the *captain-general,* a *first three,* a *second three,* and the remaining *thirty;* and yet that the *third* captain of the first ternary is now here omitted. The following juxtaposition will show the whole deficiency, and properly supply it. But let it be observed that *Jashobeam,* the *first* captain of the first ternary, had been already mentioned, and that the history is here speaking of the *second* captain, namely, *Eleazar.*

2 Sam. xxiii. 9: And after him was Eleazar the son
1 Chron. xi. 12: *And after him was Eleazar the son*
S. of Dodo, the Ahohite,   one of the three mighty
C. *of Dodo, the Ahohite, who was one of the three mighties.*
S. men   with David when they defied
C. 13. *He was with David at Pas-dammim, and there*
S. the Philistines that were there gathered together to
C. *the Philistines*   *were*   *gathered together to*
S. battle, and the men of Israel were gone away.
C. *battle,*   *   *   *   *   *   *
S. 10. He arose and smote the Philistines until his
C.   *   *   *   *   *   *
S. hand was weary, and his hand clave unto the
C.   *   *   *   *   *   *
S. sword; and the Lord wrought a great victory
C.   *   *   *   *   *   *
S. that day: and the people returned after him only
C.   *   *   *   *   *   *
S. to spoil. 11. And after him was SHAMMAH, the
C.   *   *   *   *   *   *
S. son of Agee, the Hararite: and the Philistines
C.   *   *   *   *   *   *
S. were gathered together into a troop, where was
C.   *   *   *   *   *where was*
S. a piece of ground full of lentiles: and the people
C. *a parcel of ground full of barley, and the people*

A. M. 2957
B. C. 1047
An. Exod. Isr.
444
Anno ante
I. Olymp. 271

down to the rock to David, unto the cave of Adullam; and the host of the Philistines encamped ˣin the valley of Rephaim.

16 And David *was* then in the hold, and the Philistines' garrison *was* then at Beth-lehem.

17 And David longed, and said, O that one would give me drink of the water of the well of Beth-lehem, that *is* at the gate!

18 And the three brake through the host of the Philistines, and drew water out of the well of Beth-lehem, that *was* by the gate, and took *it,* and brought *it* to David: but David would not drink *of* it, but poured it out to the LORD,

19 And said, My God forbid it me, that I should do this thing: shall I drink the blood of these men ʸthat have put their lives in jeopardy? for with *the jeopardy of* their lives they brought it. Therefore he would not drink it. These things did these three mightiest.

20 ᶻAnd Abishai the brother of Joab, he was chief of the three: for lifting up his spear against three hundred, he slew *them,* and had a name among the three.

21 ᵃOf the three, he was more honourable than the two; for he was their captain: howbeit he attained not to the *first* three.

22 Benaiah the son of Jehoiada, the son of a valiant man of Kabzeel, ᵇwho had done many acts; ᶜhe slew two lion-like men of Moab: also he went down and slew a lion in a pit in a snowy day.

23 And he slew an Egyptian, ᵈa man of *great* stature, five cubits high; and in the Egyptian's hand *was* a spear like a weaver's beam; and he went down to him with a staff,

and plucked the spear out of the Egyptian's hand, and slew him with his own spear.

24 These *things* did Benaiah the son of Jehoiada, and had a name among the three mighties.

25 Behold, he was honourable among the thirty, but attained not to the *first* three: and David set him over his guard.

26 Also the valiant men of the armies *were,* ᵉAsahel the brother of Joab, Elhanan the son of Dodo of Beth-lehem,

27 ᶠShammoth the ᵍHarorite, Helez the ʰPelonite,

28 Ira the son of Ikkesh the Tekoite, Abiezer the Antothite,

29 ˡSibbecai the Hushathite, ᵏIlai the Ahohite,

30 Maharai the Netophathite, ˡHeled the son of Baanah the Netophathite,

31 Ithai the son of Ribai of Gibeah, *that pertained* to the children of Benjamin, Benaiah the Pirathonite,

32 ᵐHurai of the brooks of Gaash, ⁿAbiel the Arbathite,

33 Azmaveth the Baharumite, Eliahba the Shaalbonite,

34 The sons of ᵒHashem the Gizonite, Jonathan the son of Shage the Hararite,

35 Ahiam the son of ᵖSacar the Hararite, �q Eliphal the son of ʳUr,

36 Hepher the Mecherathite, Ahijah the Pelonite,

37 ˢHezro the Carmelite, ᵗNaarai the son of Ezbai,

38 Joel the brother of Nathan, Mibhar ᵘthe son of Haggeri,

39 Zelek the Ammonite, Naharai the Bero-

A. M. 2957
B. C. 1047
An. Exod. Isr.
444
Anno ante
I. Olymp. 271

ˣChap. xiv. 9——ʸHeb. *with their lives*——ᶻ2 Sam. xxiii. 18, &c.——ᵃ2 Sam. xxiii. 19, &c.——ᵇHeb. *great of deeds*——ᶜ2 Sam. xxiii. 20——ᵈHeb. *a man of measure* ᵉ2 Sam. xxiii. 24——ᶠOr, *Shammah*——ᵍOr, *Harodite,* 2 Sam. xxiii. 25——ʰOr, *Paltite,* 2 Sam. xxiii. 26

ⁱOr, *Mebunnai*——ᵏOr, *Zalmon*——ˡOr, *Heleb* ᵐOr, *Hiddai*——ⁿOr, *Abialbon*——ᵒOr, *Jashen;* see 2 Sam. xxiii. 32, 33——ᵖOr, *Sharar*——�q Or, *Eliphelet* ʳOr, *Ahasbai*——ˢOr, *Hezrai*——ᵗOr, *Paaria the Arbite* ᵘOr, *the Haggerite*

S. fled from   the Philistines.   12. But he
C. *fled from before the Philistines.*   14. *And they set*
S. stood   in the midst of the ground and defended
C. *themselves, in the midst of that parcel, and delivered*
S. it, and slew the Philistines: and the Lord
C. *it, and slew the Philistines: and the Lord*
S. wrought   a great victory.
C. *saved them by a great deliverance.*

Verse 17. *David longed*] See the notes on 2 Sam. xxiii. 15-17.

Verse 22. *Benaiah—slew two lion-like men of Moab*] The *Targum* says, "Benaiah was a valiant man, fearing sin, and of a righteous con-

duct in Kabzeel; he slew two of the nobles of Moab, who were like two strong lions. He was a great and righteous man as any in the second sanctuary. On a certain day, having struck his foot against a dead tortoise, he went down to Shiloh, and having broken pieces of ice, he washed himself with them, and afterward went up, and read the book of the law of the priests, in which much is contained, in a short winter's day, viz., the tenth of the month Tebeth."

Verse 23. *Plucked the spear out of the Egyptian's hand, and slew him with his own spear.*] See the note on 2 Sam. xxiii. 21.

A. M. 2957
B. C. 1047
An. Exod. Isr.
444
Anno ante I.
Olymp. 271

thite, the armour-bearer of Joab the son of Zeruiah,

40 Ira the Ithrite, Gareb the Ithrite,

41 Uriah the Hittite, Zabad the son of Ahlai,

42 Adina the son of Shiza the Reubenite, a captain of the Reubenites, and thirty with him,

43 Hanan the son of Maachah, and Joshaphat the Mithnite,

44 Uzzia the Ashterathite, Shama and Jehiel the sons of Hothan the Aroerite,

45 Jediael the ᵛson of Shimri, and Joha his brother, the Tizite,

46 Eliel the Mahavite, and Jeribai, and Joshaviah, the sons of Elnaam, and Ithmah the Moabite,

47 Eliel, and Obed, and Jasiel the Mesobaite.

A. M. 2957
B. C. 1047
An. Exod. Isr.
444
Anno ante I.
Olymp. 271

ᵛOr, *Shimrite*

Verse 25. *David set him over his guard*] "Made him chief ruler over his disciples." —*T.*

FOR other particulars, see the notes on the parallel places, where the subject is farther considered.

CHAPTER XII

The different persons, captains, &c., who joined themselves to David at Ziklag, 1–22. Those who joined him at Hebron, out of the different tribes; Judah, Simeon, Levi, the house of Aaron, Benjamin, Ephraim, Manasseh, Issachar, Zebulun, Naphtali, Dan, Asher, Reuben, &c., to the amount of a hundred and twenty thousand, 23–37. Their unanimity, and the provisions they brought for his support, 38–40.

A. M. 2946
B. C. 1058
An. Exod. Isr.
433
Anno ante I.
Olymp. 282

NOW ᵃthese *are* they that came to David to ᵇZiklag, ᶜwhile he yet kept himself close because of Saul the son of Kish: and they *were* among the mighty men, helpers of the war.

2 *They were* armed with bows, and could use both the right hand and ᵈthe left in *hurling* stones, and *shooting* arrows out of a bow, *even* of Saul's brethren of Benjamin.

3 The chief *was* Ahiezer, then Joash, the sons of ᵉShemaah the Gibeathite; and Jeziel, and Pelet, the sons of Azmaveth; and Berachah, and Jehu the Antothite,

4 And Ismaiah the Gibeonite, a mighty man among the thirty, and over the thirty; and Jeremiah, and Jahaziel, and Johanan, and Josabad the Gederathite,

5 Eluzai, and Jerimoth, and Bealiah, and Shemariah, and Shephatiah the Haruphite,

6 Elkanah, and Jesiah, and Azareel, and Joezer, and Jashobeam, the Korhites,

7 And Joelah, and Zebadiah, the sons of Jeroham of Gedor.

8 And of the Gadites there separated themselves unto David into the hold to the wilderness men of might, *and* men ᶠof war fit for the battle, that could handle shield and buckler, whose faces *were like* the faces of lions, and *were* ᵍas ʰswift as the roes upon the mountains;

9 Ezer the first, Obadiah the second, Eliab the third,

10 Mishmannah the fourth, Jeremiah the fifth,

11 Attai the sixth, Eliel the seventh,

12 Johanan the eighth, Elzabad the ninth,

13 Jeremiah the tenth, Machbanai the eleventh.

14 These *were* of the sons of Gad, captains of the host: ⁱone of the least *was* over a hundred, and the greatest over a thousand.

A. M. 2946
B. C. 1058
An. Exod. Isr.
433
Anno ante I.
Olymp. 282

ᵃ1 Sam. xxvii. 2——ᵇ1 Sam. xxvii. 6——ᶜHeb. *being yet shut up*——ᵈJudg. xx. 16——ᵉOr, *Hasmaah* ᶠHeb. *of the host*

ᵍ2 Sam. ii. 18——ʰHeb. *as the roes upon the mountains to make haste*——ⁱOr, *one that was least could resist a hundred, and the greatest a thousand*

NOTES ON CHAP. XII

Verse 1. *Came to David to Ziklag*] Achish, king of Gath, had given Ziklag to David, as a safe retreat from the wrath of Saul.

Verse 8. *And were as swift as the roes*] That *swiftness* was considered to be a grand accomplishment in a warrior, appears from all ancient writings which treat of military affairs.

A. M. 2946
B. C. 1058
An. Exod. Isr.
433
Anno ante I.
Olymp. 282
15 These *are* they that went over Jordan in the first month, when it had ᵏoverflown all his ˡbanks; and they put to flight all *them* of the valleys, *both* toward the east, and toward the west.

16 And there came of the children of Benjamin and Judah to the hold unto David.

17 And David went out ᵐto meet them, and answered and said unto them, If ye be come peaceably unto me to help me, mine heart shall ⁿbe knit unto you: but if *ye be come* to betray me to mine enemies, seeing *there is* no ᵒwrong in mine hands, the God of our fathers look *thereon,* and rebuke *it.*

18 Then ᵖthe spirit came upon �q Amasai, *who was* chief of the captains, *and he said,* Thine *are* we, David, and on thy side, thou son of Jesse: peace, peace *be* unto thee, and peace *be* to thine helpers; for thy God helpeth thee. Then David received them, and made them captains of the band.

19 And there fell *some* of Manasseh to David, ʳwhen he came with the Philistines against Saul to battle: but they helped them not: for the lords of the Philistines upon advisement sent him away, saying, ˢHe will fall to his master Saul, ᵗto *the jeopardy of* our heads.

20 As he went to Ziklag, there fell to him of Manasseh, Adnah, and Jozabad, and Jediael, and Michael, and Jozabad, and Elihu, and Zilthai, captains of the thousands that *were* of Manasseh.

21 And they helped David ᵘagainst ᵛthe band *of the rovers:* for they *were* all mighty men of valour, and were captains in the host.

22 For at *that* time day by day there came to David to help him, until *it was* a great host, like the host of God.
A. M. 2946
B. C. 1058
An. Exod. Isr.
433
Anno ante I.
Olymp. 282

23 And these *are* the numbers of the ʷbands ˣ*that were* ready armed to the war, *and* ʸcame to David to Hebron, to ᶻturn the kingdom of Saul to him, ᵃaccording to the word of the LORD.
A. M. 2956
B. C. 1048
An. Exod. Isr.
443
Anno ante I.
Olymp. 272

24 The children of Judah that bare shield and spear *were* six thousand and eight hundred, ready ᵇarmed to the war.

25 Of the children of Simeon, mighty men of valour for the war, seven thousand and one hundred.

26 Of the children of Levi four thousand and six hundred.

27 And Jehoiada *was* the leader of the Aaronites, and with him *were* three thousand and seven hundred;

28 And ᶜZadok, a young man mighty of valour, and of his father's house twenty and two captains.

29 And of the children of Benjamin, the ᵈkindred of Saul, three thousand: for hitherto ᵉthe ᶠgreatest part of them had kept the ward of the house of Saul.

30 And of the children of Ephraim twenty thousand and eight hundred, mighty men of valour, ᵍfamous throughout the house of their fathers.

31 And of the half tribe of Manasseh eighteen thousand, which were expressed by name, to come and make David king.

32 And of the children of Issachar, ʰ*which*

ᵏHeb. *filled over*——ˡJosh. iii. 15——ᵐHeb. *before them*——ⁿHeb. *be one*——ᵒOr, *violence*——ᵖHeb. *the spirit clothed Amasai; so* Judg. vi. 34——q2 Sam. xvii. 25 ʳ1 Sam. xxix. 2——ˢ1 Sam. xxix. 4——ᵗHeb. *on our heads*——ᵘOr, *with a band*——ᵛ1 Sam. xxx. 1, 9, 10 ʷOr, *captains; or, men*

ˣHeb. *heads*——ʸ2 Samuel ii. 3, 4; v. 1; chapter xi. 1——ᶻChapter x. 14——ᵃ1 Samuel xvi. 1, 3——ᵇOr, *prepared*——ᶜ2 Samuel viii. 17——ᵈHebrew, *brethren,* Genesis xxxi. 23——ᵉHebrew, *a multitude of them* ᶠ2 Sam. ii. 8, 9——ᵍHebrew, *men of names*——ʰEsth. i. 13

Verse 15. *In the first month*] Perhaps this was the month Nisan, which answers to a part of our *March* and *April*. This was probably before the snows on the mountains were melted, just as Jordan began to overflow its banks; or if we allow that it had already overflowed its banks, it made their attempt more hazardous, and afforded additional proof of their heroism.

Verse 18. *The spirit came upon Amasai*] "The spirit of fortitude clothed Amasai, the chief of the mighty men; and he answered, For thy sake, O David, are we come, that we may be with thee, thou son of Jesse. Prosperity be to thee by night and by day; and prosperity be

to thy helpers; for the Word of the Lord is thy assistant."—*T.*

Verse 22. *Like the host of God.*] "That is, a very numerous army; like the army of the angel of God."—*T.*

Verse 23. And *came to David to Hebron*] That is, after the death of Ish-bosheth, Saul's son. See 2 Sam. iv. 5.

Verse 27. *Jehoiada was the leader of the Aaronites*] Abiathar was then high priest, and Jehoiada captain over the warriors of the house of Aaron.

Verse 32. *Children of Issachar*] According to the Targum they were all astronomers and

A. M. 2956
B. C. 1048
An. Exod. Isr.
443
Anno ante I.
Olymp. 272

were men that had understanding of the times, to know what Israel ought to do; the heads of them *were* two hundred; and all their brethren *were* at their command.

33 Of Zebulun, such as went forth to battle, ʲexpert in war, with all instruments of war, fifty thousand, which could ᵏkeep rank: *they were* ˡnot of double heart.

34 And of Naphtali a thousand captains, and with them with shield and spear thirty and seven thousand.

35 And of the Danites expert in war twenty and eight thousand and six hundred.

36 And of Asher, such as went forth to battle, ᵐexpert in war, forty thousand.

37 And on the other side of Jordan, of the Reubenites, and the Gadites, and of the half

A. M. 2956
B. C. 1048
An. Exod. Isr.
443
Anno ante I.
Olymp. 272

tribe of Manasseh, with all manner of instruments of war for the battle, a hundred and twenty thousand.

38 All these men of war, that could keep rank, came with a perfect heart to Hebron, to make David king over all Israel: and all the rest also of Israel *were* of one heart to make David king.

39 And there they were with David three days, eating and drinking: for their brethren had prepared for them.

40 Moreover they that were nigh them, *even* unto Issachar and Zebulun and Naphtali, brought bread on asses, and on camels, and on mules, and on oxen, *and* ⁿmeat, meal, cakes of figs, and bunches of raisins, and wine, and oil, and oxen, and sheep abundantly: for *there was* joy in Israel.

ʲOr, *rangers of battle*, or *ranged in battle*——ᵏOr, *set the battle in array*

ˡHeb. *without a heart and a heart*, Psa. xii. 2——ᵐOr, *keeping their rank*——ⁿOr, *victual of meal*

---

astrologers: "and the sons of Issachar, who had understanding to know the times, and were skilled in fixing the beginnings of years, the commencement of months, and the intercalation of months and years; skilful in the changes of the moon, and in fixing the lunar solemnities to their proper times; skilful also in the doctrine of the solar periods; astrologers in signs and stars, that they might show Israel what to do; and their teachers were *two hundred* chiefs of the Sanhedrin: and all their brethren excelled in the words of the law, and were endued with wisdom, and were obedient to their command."—*T.* It appears that in their wisdom, experience, and skill, their brethren had the fullest confidence; and nothing was done but by their direction and advice.

Verse 39. *They were with David three days*] These were the *deputies* of the different people

mentioned here: it is not possible that all the thousands mentioned above could have feasted with David for three days; and yet it appears there was even of these a great number, for the men of Issachar, Zebulun, and Naphtali, who were nearest to this place of rendezvous, had brought all the necessaries for such a feast. From the whole it appears most evident that the great majority of the tribes of Israel wished to see the kingdom confirmed in the hands of David; nor was there ever in any country a man more worthy of the public choice. As a statesman, warrior, hero, poet, and divine, he stands unrivalled in the annals of the world: by him alone were the Israelites raised to a pitch of the highest splendour; and their name became a terror to their enemies, and a praise in the earth. But, alas, how are the mighty now fallen!

CHAPTER XIII

David consults with his officers, and resolves to bring back the ark from the house of Abinadab, 1–4. They place it on a new cart, and Uzza and Ahio drive the cart; the oxen stumbling, Uzza puts forth his hand to save the ark from falling, and he is smitten by the Lord, 5–10. David is displeased, and orders the ark to be carried to the house of Obed-edom the Gittite, 11–13. The ark abides there three months, and the Lord blesses Obed-edom, 14.

A. M. 2959
B. C. 1045
An. Exod. Isr.
446
Anno ante I.
Olymp. 269

AND David consulted with the captains of thousands and hundreds, *and* with every leader.

2 And David said unto all the

A. M. 2959
B. C. 1045
An. Exod. Isr.
446
Anno ante I.
Olymp. 269

congregation of Israel, If *it seem* good unto you, and *that it be* of the LORD our God, ᵃlet us send abroad unto our brethren every

---

ᵃHeb. *let us break*

forth and *send*

NOTES ON CHAP. XIII

Verse 1. *David consulted*] Having taken the

strong hold of Zion from the Jebusites, organized his army, got assurances of the friendly disposition of the Israelites towards him, he

A. M. 2959
B. C. 1045
An. Exod. Isr.
446
Anno ante I.
Olymp. 269

where, *that are* [b]left in all the land of Israel, and with them *also* to the priests and Levites *which are* [c]in their cities *and* suburbs, that they may gather themselves unto us:

3 And let us [d]bring again the ark of our God to us: [e]for we inquired not at it in the days of Saul.

4 And all the congregation said that they would do so; for the thing was right in the eyes of all the people.

5 So [f]David gathered all Israel together, from [g]Shihor of Egypt even unto the entering of Hemath, to bring the ark of God [h]from Kirjath-jearim.

6 And David went up, and all Israel, to [i]Baalah, *that is,* to Kirjath-jearim, which *belonged* to Judah, to bring up thence the ark of God the LORD, [k]that dwelleth *between* the cherubims, whose name is called *on it.*

7 And they [l]carried the ark of God [m]in a new cart [n]out of the house of Abinadab: and Uzza and Ahio drave the cart.

8 [o]And David and all Israel played before God with all *their* might, and with [p]singing,

and with harps, and with psalteries, and with timbrels, and with cymbals, and with trumpets.

A. M. 2959
B. C. 1045
An. Exod. Isr.
446
Anno ante I.
Olymp. 269

9 And when they came unto the threshing-floor of [q]Chidon, Uzza put forth his hand to hold the ark; for the oxen [r]stumbled.

10 And the anger of the LORD was kindled against Uzza, and he smote him, [s]because he put his hand to the ark: and there he [t]died before God.

11 And David was displeased, because the LORD had made a breach upon Uzza: wherefore that place is called [u]Perez-uzza to this day.

12 And David was afraid of God that day, saying, How shall I bring the ark of God *home* to me?

13 So David [v]brought not the ark *home* to himself to the city of David, but carried it aside into the house of Obed-edom the Gittite.

14 [w]And the ark of God remained with the family of Obed-edom in his house three months. And the LORD blessed [x]the house of Obed-edom, and all that he had.

---

[b]1 Sam. xxxi. 1; Isa. xxxvii. 4——[c]Heb. *in the cities of their suburbs*——[d]Heb. *bring about*——[e]1 Sam. vii. 1, 2 [f]1 Sam. vii. 1; 2 Sam. vi. 1——[g]Josh. xiii. 3——[h]1 Sam. vi. 21; vii. 1——[i]Josh. xv. 9, 60——[k]1 Sam. iv. 4; 2 Sam. vi. 2——[l]Heb. *made the ark to ride*——[m]See

Num. iv. 15; ch. xv. 2, 13——[n]1 Sam. vii. 1——[o]2 Sam. vi.5 [p]Heb. *songs*——[q]Called *Nachon,* 2 Sam. vi. 6——[r]Heb. *shook it*——[s]Num. iv. 15; ch. xv. 13, 15——[t]Lev. x. 2 [u]That is, *The breach of Uzza*——[v]Heb. *removed*——[w]2 Sam. vi. 11——[x]As Gen. xxx. 27; chap. xxvi. 5

---

judged it right to do what he could for the establishment of religion in the land; and as a first step, consulted on the propriety of bringing the ark from an obscure village, where it had remained during the reign of Saul, to the royal city or seat of government.

Verse 5. *From Shihor of Egypt even unto the entering of Hemath*] "Therefore David gathered all Israel, from the *Nile,* נילום *Nilos,* of Egypt, even to the entrance of Antioch."—*T.*

Verse 6. *Whose name is called* on it.] "Where his name is invoked."—*T.* And so the Hebrew, אשר נקרא שם *asher nikra shem,* should be understood, his name was not *called on it,* but *invoked at it.*

Verse 7. *In a new cart*] Lest it should be profaned by being placed on any carriage that had been employed about common uses.

Uzza and Ahio] All the *versions* understand אחיו *achyo* as signifying *brother* or *brothers;* so

does *Jarchi,* who observes, from 2 Sam. vi. 3, that these were the sons of Abinadab.

Verse 9. *Uzza put forth his hand*] See this transaction explained 2 Sam. vi. 6, &c.

Verse 14. *The Lord blessed the house of Obed-edom*] That this man was only a sojourner at Gath, whence he was termed Gittite, and that he was originally a *Levite,* is evident from chap. xv. 17, 18.

The *Targum* ends this chapter thus: "And the Word of the Lord blessed Obed-edom, and his children, and his grand-children; and his wife conceived, and his eight daughters-in-law: and each brought forth eight at one birth, insomuch that in one day there were found, of fathers and children, *fourscore* and *one;* and He blessed and increased greatly all that belonged to him." This exposition will not be generally received; but all rabbins must be allowed to deal in the marvellous.

For other remarks see on 2 Sam. vi. 1, &c.

CHAPTER XIV

Hiram sends artificers and materials to David, to build him a house, 1, 2. David's wives and children, 3–7. He defeats the Philistines in two battles: one in the valley of Rephaim, 8–12; and the other at Gibeon and Gazer, 13–16. His fame goes out into all the surrounding nations, 17.

A. M. 2961
B. C. 1043
An. Exod. Isr. 448
Anno ante I. Olymp. 267

NOW ^aHiram king of Tyre sent messengers to David, and timber of cedars, with masons and carpenters, to build him a house.

2 And David perceived that the LORD had confirmed him king over Israel, for his kingdom was lifted up on high, because of his people Israel.

3 And David took ^bmore wives at Jerusalem: and David begat more sons and daughters.

4 Now ^cthese *are* the names of *his* children which he had in Jerusalem; Shammua, and Shobab, Nathan, and Solomon,

5 And Ibhar, and Elishua, and Elpalet,

6 And Nogah, and Nepheg, and Japhia,

7 And Elishama, and ^dBeeliada, and Eliphalet.

8 And when the Philistines heard that ^eDavid was anointed king over all Israel, all the Philistines went up to seek David. And David heard *of it,* and went out against them.

A. M. 2957
B. C. 1047
An. Exod. Isr. 444
Anno ante I. Olymp. 271

9 And the Philistines came and spread themselves ^fin the valley of Rephaim.

10 And David inquired of God, saying, Shall I go up against the Philistines? and wilt thou deliver them into mine hand?

And the LORD said unto him, Go up; for I will deliver them into thine hand.

A. M. 2957
B. C. 1047
An. Exod. Isr. 444
Anno ante I. Olymp. 271

11 So they came up to Baal-perazim; and David smote them there. Then David said, God hath broken in upon mine enemies by mine hand like the breaking forth of waters: therefore they called the name of that place ^gBaal-perazim.

12 And when they had left their gods there, David gave a commandment, and they were burned with fire.

13 ^hAnd the Philistines yet again spread themselves abroad in the valley.

14 Therefore David inquired again of God; and God said unto him, Go not up after them; turn away from them, ⁱand come upon them over against the mulberry trees.

15 And it shall be, when thou shalt hear a sound of going in the tops of the mulberry trees, *that* then thou shalt go out to battle: for God is gone forth before thee to smite the host of the Philistines.

16 David therefore did as God commanded him: and they smote the host of the Philistines from ^kGibeon even to Gazer.

17 And ^lthe fame of David went out into all lands; and the LORD ^mbrought the fear of him upon all nations.

---

^a2 Sam. v. 11, &c.——^bHeb. *yet*——^cChap. iii. 5 ^dOr, *Eliada,* 2 Sam. v. 16——^e2 Sam. v. 17——^fChap. xi. 15—— ^gThat is, *a place of breaches*

^h2 Samuel v. 22——ⁱ2 Samuel v. 23——^k2 Sam. v. 25, *Geba*——^lJosh. vi. 27; 2 Chron. xxvi. 8——^mDeut. ii. 25; xi. 25

NOTES ON CHAP. XIV

Verse 1. *Now Hiram king of Tyre*] See the transactions of this chapter related 2 Sam. v. 11-25.

Verse 4. *These* are *the names of* his *children*] In 2 Sam. v. 14-16, *eleven* persons only are mentioned in the *Hebrew* text, but the *Septuagint* has *twenty-four;* here there are *thirteen,* and all the *versions* have the same number, with certain varieties in the names.—See the notes there.

Verse 8. *The Philistines went up to seek David*] See on 2 Sam. v. 17.

Verse 10. *David inquired of God*] "David consulted the WORD of the Lord."—*T.*

Verse 11. *Like the breaking forth of waters*] "And David said, The Lord hath broken the enemies of David like to the breaking of a potter's vessel full of water."—*T.*

Verse 15. *A sound of going*] "When thou shalt hear the sound of the angels coming to thy assistance, then go out to battle; for an angel is sent from the presence of God, that he may render thy way prosperous."—*T.*

Verse 17. *Into all lands*] That is, all the surrounding or neighbouring lands and nations, for no others can possibly be intended.

CHAPTER XV

David prepares to bring home the ark, and musters the Levites, 1–11. They sanctify themselves, and bear the ark upon their shoulders, 12–15. The solemnities observed on the occasion, 16–26. David dances before the ark, and is despised by his wife Michal, 27–29.

A. M. 2962
B. C. 1042
An. Exod. Isr.
449
Anno ante I.
Olymp. 266

AND *David* made him houses in the city of David, and prepared a place for the ark of God, [a]and pitched for it a tent.

2 Then David said, [b]None ought to carry the [c]ark of God but the Levites: for them hath the LORD chosen to carry the ark of God, and to minister unto him for ever.

3 And David [d]gathered all Israel together to Jerusalem, to bring up the ark of the LORD unto his place, which he had prepared for it.

4 And David assembled the children of Aaron, and the Levites:

5 Of the sons of Kohath; Uriel the chief, and his [e]brethren a hundred and twenty:

6 Of the sons of Merari; Asaiah the chief, and his brethren two hundred and twenty:

7 Of the sons of Gershom; Joel the chief, and his brethren a hundred and thirty:

8 Of the sons of [f]Elizaphan; Shemaiah the chief, and his brethren two hundred:

9 Of the sons of [g]Hebron; Eliel the chief, and his brethren fourscore:

10 Of the sons of Uzziel; Amminadab the chief, and his brethren a hundred and twelve.

11 And David called for Zadok and Abiathar the priests, and for the Levites, for Uriel, Asaiah, and Joel, Shemaiah, and Eliel, and Amminadab,

12 And said unto them, Ye *are* the chief of the fathers of the Levites: sanctify yourselves, *both* ye and your brethren, that ye may bring up the ark of the LORD God of Israel unto *the place that* I have prepared for it.

13 For [h]because ye *did it* not at the first,

[i]the LORD our God made a breach upon us, for that we sought him not after the due order.

A. M. 2962
B. C. 1042
An. Exod. Isr.
449
Anno ante I.
Olymp. 266

14 So the priests and the Levites sanctified themselves to bring up the ark of the LORD God of Israel.

15 And the children of the Levites bare the ark of God upon their shoulders with the staves thereon, as [k]Moses commanded, according to the word of the LORD.

16 And David spake to the chief of the Levites to appoint their brethren *to be* the singers with instruments of music, psalteries and harps and cymbals, sounding, by lifting up the voice with joy.

17 So the Levites appointed [l]Heman the son of Joel; and of his brethren [m]Asaph the son of Berechiah; and of the sons of Merari their brethren, [n]Ethan the son of Kushaiah;

18 And with them their brethren of the second *degree,* Zechariah, Ben, and Jaaziel, Shemiramoth, and Jehiel, and Unni, Eliab, and Benaiah, and Maaseiah, and Mattithiah, and Elipheleh, and Mikneiah, and Obed-edom, and Jeiel, the porters.

19 So the singers, Heman, Asaph, and Ethan, *were appointed* to sound with cymbals of brass;

20 And Zechariah, and [o]Aziel, and Shemiramoth, and Jehiel, and Unni, and Eliab, and Maaseiah, and Benaiah, with psalteries [p]on Alamoth;

21 And Mattithiah, and Elipheleh, and Mikneiah, and Obed-edom, and Jeiel, and Azaziah, with harps [q]on the Sheminith to excel.

---

[a]Ch. xvi. 1——[b]Heb. It is *not to carry the ark of God, but for the Levites*——[c]Num. iv. 2, 15; Deut. x. 8; xxxi. 9 [d]1 Kings viii. 1; chapter xiii. 5——[e]Or, *kinsmen* [f]Exodus vi. 22——[g]Exod. vi. 18——[h]2 Samuel vi. 3;

chap. xiii. 7——[i]Chap. xiii. 10, 11——[k]Exod. xxv. 14; Num. iv. 15; vii. 9——[l]Ch. vi. 33——[m]Ch. vi. 39 [n]Ch. vi. 44——[o]Ver. 18, *Jaaziel*——[p]Psa. xlvi. title [q]Or, *on the eighth to oversee,* Psa. vi. title

---

NOTES ON CHAP. XV

Verse 1. *Made him houses*] One for himself, and one for the ark; in the latter was a tent, under which the ark was placed.

Verse 2. *None ought to carry the ark—but the Levites*] It was their business; and he should have thought of this sooner, and then the unfortunate breach on Uzza would have been prevented; see ver. 13.

Verse 15. *Upon their shoulders*] That is the staves which went through the rings rested on their shoulders, but the ark itself rested on the staves like a sedan on its poles.

As *Moses commanded*] See Num. iv. 5, 15.

Verse 17. *—Heman—Asaph—Ethan*] These were the *three* chief musicians in the time of David; see chap. vi. 31.

Verse 20. *With psalteries on Alamoth*] Some

suppose that the word signifies *virgins,* or *women singers,* the persons mentioned here being appointed to accompany them with psalteries, and preside over them.

The Vulgate says *arcana cantabant,* they sang *secret things* or *mysteries;* probably *prophetic hymns.*

Verse 21. *On the Sheminith*] According to the Targum, this signifies an instrument that sounded an octave, or, according to others, an instrument with *eight* strings. The Syriac and Arabic have it, instruments to sing with daily, at the *third, sixth,* and *ninth* hour; the Vulgate, an octave, *for a song of victory:* some think the *eighth* band of the musicians is intended, who had the *strongest* and most *sonorous* voices; and that it is in this sense that *shelomith* and *lenatstseach* should be understood.

A. M. 2962
B. C. 1042
An. Exod. Isr.
449
Anno ante I.
Olymp. 266

22 And Chenaniah, chief of the Levites, *was* for *song: he instructed about the song, because he *was* skilful.

23 And Berechiah and Elkanah *were* doorkeepers for the ark.

24 And Shebaniah, and Jehoshaphat, and Nethaneel, and Amasai, and Zechariah, and Benaiah, and Eliezer, the priests, *did blow with the trumpets before the ark of God: and Obed-edom and Jehiah *were* door-keepers for the ark.

25 So *David, and the elders of Israel, and the captains over thousands, went to bring up the ark of the covenant of the LORD out of the house of Obed-edom with joy.

26 And it came to pass, when God helped the Levites that bare the ark of the covenant of the LORD, that they offered seven bullocks and seven rams.

27 And David *was* clothed with a robe of fine linen, and all the Levites that bare the ark, and the singers, and Chenaniah the master of the *song with the singers: David also *had* upon him an ephod of linen.

28 *Thus all Israel brought up the ark of the covenant of the LORD with shouting, and with sound of the cornet, and with trumpets, and with cymbals, making a noise with psalteries and harps.

29 And it came to pass, *as the ark of the covenant of the LORD came to the city of David, that Michal the daughter of Saul looking out at a window saw King David dancing and playing: and she despised him in her heart.

A. M. 2962
B. C. 1042
An. Exod. Isr.
449
Anno ante I.
Olymp. 266

---

*Or, was *for the carriage; he instructed about the carriage* ——*Heb. *lifting up*——*Num. x. 8; Psa. lxxxi. 3

*2 Sam. vi. 12, 13, &c.; 1 Kings viii. 1——*Or, *carriage* ——*Chap. xiii. 8——*2 Sam. vi. 16

Verse 22. *Chenaniah—he instructed about the song*] This appears to have been the master singer; he gave the *key* and the *time*, for he presided במשא *bemassa*, in the *elevation*, probably meaning what is called *pitching the tune*, for *he was skilful* in music, and powerful in his voice, and well qualified to lead the band: he might have been *precentor*.

Verse 26. *God helped the Levites*] When they saw that God had made no breach among them, as he had in the case of Uzza, in gratitude for their preservation, and his acceptance of their labour, they sacrificed *seven bullocks and seven rams.*

Verse 27. *A robe of fine linen*] A robe made of בוץ *buts*, probably the tuft or beard of the

Pinna Magna, a species of muscle found everywhere on the shores of the Mediterranean, growing sometimes, as I have seen, to a foot and a half in length. I have seen a pair of gloves made of this very rich stuff; the colour is a deep dark yellow, something inclining to what is called the *lilac*. The *buts* or *byssus* was not heard of in Israel before the time of David: after that it is frequently mentioned.

Verse 29. *Michal—saw—David dancing—and she despised him*] See this whole business explained 2 Sam. vi. 20, &c., where David's conduct is vindicated, and the nature of Michal's disgrace and punishment hinted at, but all left to the reader's determination.

CHAPTER XVI

David brings the ark into its tent; and offers sacrifices, peace-offerings, and burnt-offerings, 1, 2; and gives portions to the people of Israel, 3. He appoints proper ministers and officers for the ark, 4–6. He delivers a solemn thanksgiving on the occasion, 7–36. How the different officers served at the ark, 37–42. The people return home, 43.

A. M. 2962
B. C. 1042
An. Exod. Isr.
449
Anno ante I.
Olymp. 266

SO *they brought the ark of God, and set it in the midst of the tent that David had pitched for it: and they offered burnt-sacrifices and peace-offerings before God.

2 And when David had made an end of offering the burnt-offerings and the peace-offerings, he blessed the people in the name of the LORD.

3 And he dealt to every one of Israel, both man and woman, to every one a loaf of bread,

A. M. 2962
B. C. 1042
An. Exod. Isr.
449
Anno ante I.
Olymp. 266

---

*2 Samuel   chap. vi. 17–19

NOTES ON CHAP. XVI

Verse 2. *He blessed the people*] "He blessed the people in the name of the WORD of the Lord."—*T.*

Verse 3. *To every one a loaf of bread*] A whole cake. *A good piece of flesh;* "the sixth part of an ox, and the sixth part of a hin of wine."—*T.* See 2 Sam. vi. 18-20; see *Jarchi* also.

A. M. 2962
B. C. 1042
An. Exod. Isr.
449
Anno ante I.
Olymp. 266

and a good piece of flesh, and a flagon *of wine.*

4 And he appointed *certain* of the Levites to minister before the ark of the LORD, and to ᵇrecord, and to thank and praise the LORD God of Israel:

5 Asaph the chief, and next to him Zechariah, Jeiel, and Shemiramoth, and Jehiel, and Mattithiah, and Eliab, and Benaiah, and Obed-edom: and Jeiel ᶜwith psalteries and with harps; but Asaph made a sound with cymbals;

6 Benaiah also and Jahaziel the priests with trumpets continually before the ark of the covenant of God.

7 Then on that day David delivered ᵈfirst *this psalm,* to thank the LORD, into the hand of Asaph and his brethren.

8 ᵉGive thanks unto the LORD, call upon his name, make known his deeds among the people.

9 Sing unto him, sing psalms unto him, talk ye of all his wondrous works.

10 Glory ye in his holy name: let the heart of them rejoice that seek the LORD.

11 Seek the LORD and his strength, seek his face continually.

12 Remember his marvellous works that he hath done, his wonders, and the judgments of his mouth;

13 O ye seed of Israel his servant, ye children of Jacob, his chosen ones.

14 He *is* the LORD our God; his judgments *are* in all the earth.

15 Be ye mindful always of his covenant; the word *which* he commanded to a thousand generations;

16 *Even of the* ᶠ*covenant* which he made with Abraham, and of his oath unto Isaac;

17 And hath confirmed the same to Jacob for a law, *and* to Israel *for* an everlasting covenant,

A. M. 2962
B. C. 1042
An. Exod. Isr.
449
Anno ante I.
Olymp. 266

18 Saying, Unto thee will I give the land of Canaan, ᵍthe lot of your inheritance;

19 When ye were but ʰfew, ⁱeven a few, and strangers in it.

20 And *when* they went from nation to nation, and from *one* kingdom to another people;

21 He suffered no man to do them wrong; yea, he ᵏreproved kings for their sakes,

22 *Saying,* ˡTouch not mine anointed, and do my prophets no harm.

23 ᵐSing unto the LORD, all the earth; show forth from day to day his salvation.

24 Declare his glory among the heathen; his marvellous works among all nations.

25 For great *is* the LORD, and greatly to be praised: he also *is* to be feared above all gods.

26 For all the gods ⁿof the people *are* idols: but the LORD made the heavens.

27 Glory and honour *are* in his presence; strength and gladness *are* in his place.

28 Give unto the LORD, ye kindreds of the people, give unto the LORD glory and strength.

29 Give unto the LORD the glory *due* unto his name: bring an offering, and come before him: worship the LORD in the beauty of holiness.

30 Fear before him, all the earth: the world also shall be stable, that it be not moved.

31 Let the heavens be glad, and let the earth rejoice: and let *men* say among the nations, The LORD reigneth.

32 Let the sea roar, and the fulness thereof:

ᵇPsa. xxxviii. and lxx. title——ᶜHeb. *with instruments of psalteries and harps*——ᵈSee 2 Sam. xxiii. 1 ᵉPsa. cv. 1–15——ᶠGen. xvii. 2; xxvi. 3; xxviii. 13; xxxv. 11

ᵍHeb. *the cord*——ʰHeb. *men of number*——ⁱGen. xxxiv. 30——ᵏGen. xii. 17; xx. 3; Exodus vii. 15–18 ˡPsalm cv. 15——ᵐPsalm xcvi. 1, &c.——ⁿLeviticus xix. 4

Verse 5. *Asaph*] See the preceding chapter, ver. 17, &c.

Verse 7. *David delivered first this psalm*] I believe the meaning of this place to be this: David made the psalm on the occasion above specified; and delivered it to Asaph, who was the musician, and to his brethren, to be sung by them in honour of what God had done in behalf of his people.

Verse 10. *That seek the Lord.*] "That seek the WORD of the Lord."—*T.*

Verse 12. *Remember his marvellous works*] The whole of the psalm refers to God's wondrous actions among the nations in behalf of Israel.

Verse 22. *Touch not mine anointed*] By this title the *patriarchs* are generally understood: they had a *regal* and *sacerdotal* power in the order of God. In the behalf of the patriarchs God had often especially interfered: in behalf of *Abraham,* Gen. xii. 17; and xx. 3; and of *Jacob,* Gen. xxxi. 24, and xxxiv. 26, and xxxv. 5. But the title may be applied to all the Jewish people, who *were* the *anointed,* as they were the *elect* and peculiar people of God. See on Heb. xi. 26.

Verse 31. *Let the heavens be glad*] "Let the supreme angels be glad, and the inhabitants of the earth rejoice."—*T.* In this place the Tar-

A. M. 2962
B. C. 1042
An. Exod. Isr.
449
Anno ante I.
Olymp. 266

let the fields rejoice, and all that *is* therein.

33 Then shall the trees of the wood sing out at the presence of the LORD, because he cometh to judge the earth.

34 °O give thanks unto the LORD; for *he is* good; for his mercy *endureth* for ever.

35 PAnd say ye, Save us, O God of our salvation, and gather us together, and deliver us from the heathen, that we may give thanks to thy holy name, *and* glory in thy praise.

36 ᑫBlessed *be* the LORD God of Israel for ever and ever. And all ʳthe people said, Amen, and praised the LORD.

37 So he left there before the ark of the covenant of the LORD Asaph and his brethren, to minister before the ark continually, as every day's work required:

38 And Obed-edom with their brethren, threescore and eight; Obed-edom also the son of Jeduthun, and Hosah, *to be* porters:

A. M. 2962
B. C. 1042
An. Exod. Isr.
449
Anno ante I.
Olymp. 266

39 And Zadok the priest, and his brethren the priests, ˢbefore the tabernacle of the LORD, ᵗin the high place that *was* at Gibeon,

40 To offer burnt-offerings unto the LORD upon the altar of the burnt-offering continually, ᵘmorning ᵛand evening, and *to do* according to all that is written in the law of the LORD, which he commanded Israel:

41 And with them Heman and Jeduthun, and the rest that were chosen, who were expressed by name, to give thanks to the LORD, ʷbecause his mercy *endureth* for ever;

42 And with them Heman and Jeduthun with trumpets and cymbals for those that should make a sound, and with musical instruments of God. And the sons of Jeduthun *were* ˣporters.

43 ʸAnd all the people departed every man to his house: and David returned to bless his house.

°Psalm cvi. 1; cvii. 1; cxviii. 1; cxxxvi. 1——ᵖPsa. cvi. 47, 48——ᑫ1 Kings viii. 15——ʳDeuteronomy xxvii. 15——ˢChapter xxi. 29; 2 Chronicles i. 3——ᵗ1 Kings iii. 4

ᵘExod. xxix. 38; Num. xxviii. 3——ᵛHeb. *in the morning, and in the evening*——ʷVer. 34; 2 Chron. v. 13; vii. 3; Ezra iii. 11; Jer. xxxiii. 11——ˣHeb. *for the gate* ʸ2 Sam. vi. 19, 20

---

gumist uses the Greek word αγγελοι, *angels*, in Hebrew letters thus, אנגלי *angeley*.

Verse 35. *Save us, O God of our salvation*] As he is the *saving* God, so we may pray to him to *save* us. To pray to God under the *attribute* the influence of which we need, serves to inspire much confidence. I am *weak; Almighty God, help* me! I am *ignorant; O* thou *Father of lights, teach* me! I am *lost; O merciful* God, *save* me; &c. See the notes on Psa. xcvi. and cv.

Verse 39. *Zadok the priest*] Both Zadok and Abiathar were high priests at this time: the former David established at *Gibeah*, or Gibeon, where the ark had been all the days of Saul; and the latter he established at Jerusalem, where the ark now was: so there were *two high priests*, and two distinct services; but there was only *one ark*. How long the service at Gibeon was continued we cannot tell; the principal functions were no doubt performed at Jerusalem.

Verse 42. *Musical instruments of God.*] *Ad canendum Deo*, "to sing to God."—*Vulgate.* Των ωδων του Θεου, "of the sons of God."—*Septuagint.* The *Syriac* is remarkable: "These were upright men who did not sing unto God with instruments of music, nor with drums, nor with listra, nor with straight nor crooked pipes, nor with cymbals; but they sang before the Lord Almighty with a joyous mouth, and with a pure and holy prayer, and with innocence and integrity." The *Arabic* is nearly the same. None of the *versions* understand the words שיר כלי

האלהים *keley shir haelohim* as implying *instruments of music of God*, but instruments employed in the song of God, or to praise God;

as also the *Targum. Query*, Did God ever ordain *instruments of music* to be used in his worship? Can they be used in *Christian assemblies* according to the spirit of Christianity? Has Jesus Christ, or his apostles, ever commanded or sanctioned the use of them? Were they ever used any where in the *apostolic Church?* Does the use of them at present, in Christian congregations, ever increase the spirit of devotion? Does it ever appear that *bands of musicians*, either in their *collective* or *individual* capacity, are *more spiritual*, or *as spiritual*, as the other parts of the Church of Christ? Is there less pride, self-will, stubbornness, insubordination, lightness, and frivolity, among such persons, than among the other professors of Christianity found in the same religious society? Is it ever remarked or known that musicians in the house of God have attained to any depth of piety, or superior soundness of understanding, in the things of God? Is it ever found that those Churches and Christian societies which have and use instruments of music in Divine worship are *more holy*. or *as holy*, as those societies which do not use them? And is it always found that the *ministers* which affect and recommend them to be used in the worship of Almighty God, are the most spiritual men, and the most spiritual and useful preachers? Can mere *sounds*, no matter how melodious, where no *word* nor *sentiment* is or can be uttered, be considered as giving praise to God? Is it possible that *pipes* or *strings* of any kind can give God praise? Can God be pleased with sounds which are emitted by no *sentient* being, and have in themselves *no meaning?* If these questions cannot be answered in the affirmative;

then, *query,* Is not the introduction of such instruments into the worship of God antichristian, and calculated to debase and ultimately ruin the spirit and influence of the Gospel of Jesus Christ? And should not all who wish well to the spread and establishment of pure and undefiled religion, lift up their hand, their influence, and their voice against them? The argument from their use in the *Jewish* service is futile in the extreme when applied to *Christianity.*

CHAPTER XVII

David consults Nathan about building a temple for God, 1, 2. God sends him an answer by Nathan, informing him that Solomon shall build the house, 3–14. David receives the Divine purpose with humility and joy, and gives God praise, 15–27.

A. M. 2962
B. C. 1042
An. Exod. Isr.
449
Anno ante I.
Olymp. 266

NOW ^ait came to pass, as David sat in his house, that David said to Nathan the prophet, Lo, I dwell in a house of cedars, but the ark of the covenant of the LORD *remaineth* under curtains.

2 Then Nathan said unto David, Do all that *is* in thine heart; for God *is* with thee.

3 And it came to pass the same night, that the word of God came to Nathan, saying,

4 Go and tell David my servant, Thus saith the LORD, Thou shalt not build me a house to dwell in:

5 For I have not dwelt in a house since the day that I brought up Israel unto this day; but ^bhave gone from tent to tent, and from *one* tabernacle *to another.*

6 Wheresoever I have walked with all Israel, spake I a word to any of the judges of Israel, whom I commanded to feed my people, saying, Why have ye not built me a house of cedars?

7 Now therefore thus shalt thou say unto my servant David, Thus saith the LORD of hosts, I took thee from the sheep-cote, *even* ^cfrom following the sheep, that thou shouldest be ruler over my people Israel:

8 And I have been with thee whithersoever thou hast walked, and have cut off all thine enemies from before thee, and have made thee a name like the name of the great men that *are* in the earth.

9 Also I will ordain a place for my people Israel, and will plant them, and they shall dwell in their place, and shall be moved no more; neither shall the children of wickedness waste them any more, as at the beginning,

A. M. 2962
B. C. 1042
An. Exod. Isr.
449
Anno ante I.
Olymp. 266

10 And since the time that I commanded judges *to be* over my people Israel. Moreover I will subdue all thine enemies. Furthermore I tell thee that the LORD will build thee a house.

11 And it shall come to pass, when thy days be expired that thou must go *to be* with thy fathers, that I will raise up thy seed after thee, which shall be of thy sons; and I will establish his kingdom.

12 He shall build me a house, and I will stablish his throne for ever.

13 ^dI will be his father, and he shall be my son: and I will not take my mercy away from him, as I took *it* from *him* that was before thee:

14 But ^eI will settle him in mine house and in my kingdom for ever: and his throne shall be established for evermore.

15 According to all these words, and according to all this vision, so did Nathan speak unto David.

16 ^fAnd David the king came and sat before the LORD, and said, Who *am* I, O LORD God, and what *is* mine house, that thou hast brought me hitherto?

---

^a2 Sam. vii. 1, &c.——^bHeb. *have been*——^cHeb. *from after*

^d2 Sam. vii. 14, 15——^eLuke i. 33——^f2 Sam. vii. 18

NOTES ON CHAP. XVII

Verse 1. *Now it came to pass*] See every thing recorded in this chapter amply detailed in the notes on 2 Sam. vii. 1, &c.

Verse 5. *But have gone from tent to tent*] "I have transferred my tabernacle from Gilgal to Nob, from Nob to Shiloh, and from Shiloh to Gibeon."—*Targum* and *Jarchi.*

Verse 9. *Neither shall the children of wickedness*] They shall no more be brought into servitude as they were in the time they sojourned in Egypt. This is what is here referred to.

Verse 12. *I will establish his throne for ever.*] David was a type of Christ; and concerning him the prophecy is literally true. See Isa. ix. 7, where there is evidently the same reference.

Verse 13. *I will not take my mercy away from him*] I will not cut off his family *from the throne,* as I did that of his predecessor Saul.

Verse 16. *And what is mine house, that thou*

A. M. 2962
B. C. 1042
An. Exod. Isr.
449
Anno ante I.
Olymp. 266

17 And *yet* this was a small thing in thine eyes, O God; for thou hast *also* spoken of thy servant's house for a great while to come, and hast regarded me according to the estate of a man of high degree, O LORD God.

18 What can David *speak* more to thee for the honour of thy servant? for thou knowest thy servant.

19 O LORD, for thy servant's sake, and according to thine own heart, hast thou done all this greatness, in making known all *these* [g]great things.

20 O LORD, *there is* none like thee, neither *is there any* God beside thee, according to all that we have heard with our ears.

21 And what one nation in the earth *is* like thy people Israel, whom God went to redeem *to be* his own people, to make thee a name of greatness and terribleness, by driving out nations from before thy people, whom thou hast redeemed out of Egypt?

22 For thy people Israel didst thou make thine own people for ever; and thou, LORD, becamest their God.

A. M. 2962
B. C. 1042
An. Exod. Isr.
449
Anno ante I.
Olymp. 266

23 Therefore now, LORD, let the thing that thou hast spoken concerning thy servant, and concerning his house, be established for ever, and do as thou hast said.

24 Let it even be established, that thy name may be magnified for ever, saying, The LORD of hosts *is* the God of Israel, *even* a God to Israel: and *let* the house of David thy servant *be* established before thee.

25 For thou, O my God, [h]hast told thy servant that thou wilt build him a house: therefore thy servant hath found *in his heart* to pray before thee.

26 And now, LORD, thou art God, and hast promised this goodness unto thy servant:

27 Now therefore [i]let it please thee to bless the house of thy servant, that it may be before thee for ever: for thou blessest, O LORD, and *it shall be* blessed for ever.

---

[g]Heb. *greatness*——[h]Heb. *hast revealed the ear*

of thy servant——[i]Or, *it hath pleased thee*

---

hast brought me hitherto?] I am not of any regal family, and have no natural right to the throne.

Verse 25. *Hath found* in his heart *to pray*] The Targum expresses a full sense: "Therefore thy servant hath found an opening of mouth, that he might pray before Thee."

Verse 27. *For thou blessest, O Lord*] "Thou

beginnest to bless the house of thy servant, therefore it shall be blessed for ever."—*T.*

THE reader is requested to refer to 2 Sam. vii., and the notes there for many particulars that belong to the parallel places here, and which it would answer no good purpose to repeat in this place.

CHAPTER XVIII

David smites the Philistines, and takes Gath, 1. *Reduces the Moabites,* 2. *Vanquishes Hadarezer, king of Zobah,* 3, 4. *Overcomes the Syrians of Damascus, and takes several of their cities,* 5–8. *Tou, king of Hamath, congratulates him on his victory, and sends him vessels of silver, gold, and brass,* 9, 10. *Those and the different spoils he had taken from the conquered nations, he dedicates to God,* 11. *Abishai defeats the Edomites,* 12, 13. *David reigns over all Israel,* 14. *His officers,* 15–17.

A. M. 2964
B. C. 1040
An. Exod. Isr.
451
Anno ante I.
Olymp. 264

NOW after this [a]it came to pass, that David smote the Philistines, and subdued them, and took Gath and her towns out of the hands of the Philistines.

2 And he smote Moab; and the Moabites became David's servants, *and* brought gifts.

3 And David smote [b]Hadarezer king of Zobah unto Hamath, as he went to stablish his dominion by the river Euphrates.

A. M. 2964
B. C. 1040
An. Exod. Isr.
451
Anno ante I.
Olymp. 264

4 And David took from him a thousand chariots, and [c]seven thousand horsemen, and twenty thousand footmen: David also houghed

---

[a]2 Sam. viii. 1, &c.——[b]Or, *Hadadezer,* 2 Sam. viii. 3

[c]2 Sam. viii. 4, *seven hundred*

NOTES ON CHAP. XVIII

Verse 1. *David—took Gath and her towns*] See the comparison between this chapter

and 2 Sam. viii. 1, &c., in the notes on the latter.

Verse 2. *Brought gifts*] Were laid under tribute.

A. M. 2964
B. C. 1040
An. Exod. Isr.
451
Anno ante I.
Olymp. 264
all the chariot *horses,* but reserved of them a hundred chariots.

5 And when the Syrians of dDamascus came to help Hadarezer king of Zobah, David slew of the Syrians two and twenty thousand men.

6 Then David put *garrisons* in Syriadamascus; and the Syrians became David's servants, *and* brought gifts. Thus the LORD preserved David whithersoever he went.

7 And David took the shields of gold that were on the servants of Hadarezer, and brought them to Jerusalem.

8 Likewise from eTibhath, and from Chun, cities of Hadarezer, brought David very much brass, wherewith fSolomon made the brazen sea, and the pillars, and the vessels of brass.

9 Now when gTou king of Hamath heard how David had smitten all the host of Hadarezer king of Zobah;

10 He sent hHadoram his son to King David, ito inquire of his welfare, and kto congratulate him because he had fought against Hadarezer, and smitten him; (for Hadarezer lhad war with Tou;) and *with him* all manner of vessels of gold, and silver, and brass.

11 Them also King David dedicated unto the LORD, with the silver and the gold that he brought from all *these* nations; A. M. 2964
B. C. 1040
An. Exod. Isr.
451
Anno ante I.
Olymp. 264 from Edom, and from Moab, and from the children of Ammon, and from the Philistines, and from Amalek.

12 Moreover mAbishai the son of Zeruiah slew of the Edomites in the valley of salt neighteen thousand.

13 oAnd he put garrisons in Edom; and all the Edomites became David's servants. Thus the LORD preserved David whithersoever he went.

14 So David reigned over all Israel, and executed judgment and justice among all his people.

15 And Joab the son of Zeruiah *was* over the host; and Jehoshaphat the son of Ahilud, precorder.

16 And Zadok the son of Ahitub, and qAbimelech the son of Abiathar *were* the priests; and rShavsha was scribe;

17 sAnd Benaiah the son of Jehoiada *was* over the Cherethites and the Pelethites; and the sons of David *were* chief tabout the king.

---

dHeb. *Darmesek*——eCalled in the book of Samuel *Betah and Berothai*——f1 Kings vii. 15, 23; 2 Chron. iv. 12, 15, 16——gOr, *Toi,* 2 Sam. viii. 9——hOr, *Joram,* 2 Sam. viii. 10——iOr, *to salute*——kHeb. *to bless* lHeb. *was the man of wars*

mHeb. *Abshai*——n2 Sam. vii. 13——o2 Sam. vii. 14, &c.——pOr, *remembrancer*——qCalled *Ahimelech,* 2 Sam. viii. 17——rCalled *Seraiah,* 2 Sam. viii. 17; and Shisha, 1 Kings iv. 3——s2 Sam. viii. 18——tHeb. *at the hand of the king*

Verse 9. *Tou king of Hamath*] Called *Toi* in 2 Sam. viii. 9.

Verse 12. *Abishai—slew of the Edomites*] This victory is attributed to *David,* 2 Sam. viii. 13. He sent Abishai against them, and he defeated them: this is with great propriety attributed to David as commander-in-chief; *qui facit per alterum, facit per se.*

Verse 15. *Joab—was over the host*] General-in-chief.

Jehoshaphat—recorder.] The king's remembrancer, or historiographer royal.

Verse 16. *Zadok—and Abimelech—priests*]

Both *high priests;* one at *Gibeon,* and the other at *Jerusalem,* as we have seen chap. xvi. 39.

Shavsha was scribe] Called *Seraiah,* 2 Sam. viii. 17.

Verse 17. *Cherethites and the Pelethites*] See the note on 2 Sam. viii. 18.

The *Targum* says, "Benaiah was over the great Sanhedrin and the small Sanhedrin, and consulted Urim and Thummim. And at his command the archers and slingers went to battle."

The sons of David] These were the highest in authority.

CHAPTER XIX

David sends a congratulatory message to Hanun, king of Ammon, 1, 2. *He treats the messengers with great incivility,* 3, 4. *David is exasperated, but condoles with the degraded messengers,* 5. *The Ammonites prepare for war, and hire* thirty-two thousand *chariots, and besiege Medeba,* 6, 7. *David sends Joab to attack them; he defeats the Syrians and Ammonites,* 8–15. *The discomfited Syrians recruit their army, and invade David's territories beyond Jordan; he attacks them, kills Shophach their general,* seven thousand *charioteers, and* forty thousand *of their infantry,* 16–18. *The Syrians abandon the Ammonites and make a separate peace with David,* 19.

A. M. 2967
B. C. 1037
An. Exod. Isr.
454
Anno ante I.
Olymp. 261

NOW [a]it came to pass after this, that Nahash the king of the children of Ammon died, and his son reigned in his stead.

2 And David said, I will show kindness unto Hanun the son of Nahash, because his father showed kindness to me. And David sent messengers to comfort him concerning his father. So the servants of David came into the land of the children of Ammon to Hanun, to comfort him.

3 But the princes of the children of Ammon said to Hanun, [b]Thinkest thou that David doth honour thy father, that he hath sent comforters unto thee? are not his servants come unto thee for to search, and to overthrow, and to spy out the land?

4 Wherefore Hanun took David's servants, and shaved them, and cut off their garments in the midst hard by their buttocks, and sent them away.

5 Then there went *certain,* and told David how the men were served. And he sent to meet them: for the men were greatly ashamed. And the king said, Tarry at Jericho until your beards be grown, and *then* return.

6 And when the children of Ammon saw that they had made themselves [c]odious to David, Hanun and the children of Ammon sent a thousand talents of silver to hire them chariots and horsemen out of Mesopotamia, and out of Syria-maachah, [d]and out of Zobah.

7 So they hired thirty and two thousand chariots, and the king of Maachah and his people; who came and pitched before Medeba. And the children of Ammon gathered themselves together from their cities, and came to battle.

8 And when David heard *of it,* he sent Joab, and all the host of the mighty men.

9 And the children of Ammon came out, and put the battle in array before the gate of the city: and the kings that were come *were* by themselves in the field.

A. M. 2967
B. C. 1037
An. Exod. Isr.
454
Anno ante I.
Olymp. 261

10 Now when Joab saw that [e]the battle was set against him before and behind, he chose out of all the [f]choice of Israel, and put *them* in array against the Syrians.

11 And the rest of the people he delivered unto the hand of [g]Abishai his brother, and they set *themselves* in array against the children of Ammon.

12 And he said, If the Syrians be too strong for me, then thou shalt help me: but if the children of Ammon be too strong for thee, then I will help thee.

13 Be of good courage, and let us behave ourselves valiantly for our people, and for the cities of our God: and let the LORD do *that which is* good in his sight.

14 So Joab and the people that *were* with him drew nigh before the Syrians unto the battle; and they fled before him.

15 And when the children of Ammon saw that the Syrians were fled, they likewise fled before Abishai his brother, and entered into the city. Then Joab came to Jerusalem.

16 And when the Syrians saw that they were put to the worse before Israel, they sent messengers, and drew forth the Syrians that *were* beyond the [h]river: and [i]Shophach the captain of the host of Hadarezer *went* before them.

A. M. 2968
B. C. 1036
An. Exod. Isr.
455
Anno ante I.
Olymp. 260

17 And it was told David; and he gathered all Israel, and passed over Jordan, and came upon them, and set *the battle* in array against them. So when David had put the battle in array against the Syrians, they fought with him.

18 But the Syrians fled before Israel; and

---

[a]2 Sam. x. 1, &c.——[b]Heb. *In thine eyes doth David,*&c. [c]Heb. *to stink*——[d]Ch. xviii. 5, 9——[e]Heb. *the face of* *the battle was*——[f]Or, *young men*——[g]Heb. *Abshai* [h]That is, *Euphrates*——[i]Or, *Shobach,* 2 Sam. x. 16

NOTES ON CHAP. XIX

Verse 1. *Now it came to pass*] See the same history, 2 Sam. x. 1, &c., and the notes there.

Verse 4. *And cut off their garments in the midst*] *Usque ad eorum pudenda.* So the *Targum, Jarchi,* and others; leaving exposed what nature and decency require to be concealed. See on 2 Sam. x. 4.

Verse 6. *Chariots and horsemen out of Mesopotamia*] These are not mentioned in the parallel place in *Samuel;* probably they did not

arrive till the Ammonites and their other allies were defeated by the Israelites in the first battle.

Verse 7. *Thirty and two thousand*] The whole number mentioned in Samuel is, *Syrians,* of Beth-rehob, and of Zoba, *twenty thousand;* of King Maacah, *one thousand;* of Ish-tob, *twelve thousand;* in all *thirty-three thousand.* Of chariots or cavalry there is no mention. These could not have been the whole army.

Verse 13. *Be of good courage*] See the note on 2 Sam. x. 12.

A. M. 2968
B. C. 1036
An. Exod. Isr.
455
Anno ante I.
Olymp. 260

David slew of the Syrians seven thousand *men which fought in* chariots, and forty thousand footmen, and killed Shophach the captain of the host.

19 And when the servants of Hadarezer saw

that they were put to the worse before Israel, they made peace with David, and became his servants: neither would the Syrians help the children of Ammon any more.

A. M. 2968
B. C. 1036
An. Exod. Isr.
455
Anno ante I.
Olymp. 260

Verse 18. *Forty thousand footmen*] See this number accounted for in the note on 2 Sam. x. 18.

Verse 19. *They made peace with David, and*

became his servants] See on 2 Sam. x. 19, and the concluding note in that place; and see for *omissions* in Chronicles, the preface to these books.

CHAPTER XX

Joab smites the city of Rabbah; and David puts the crown of its king upon his own head, and treats the people of the city with great rigour, 1–3. First battle with the Philistines, 4. Second battle with the Philistines, 5. Third battle with the Philistines, 6, 7. In these battles three giants are slain, 8.

A. M. 2969
B. C. 1035
An. Exod. Isr.
456
Anno ante I.
Olymp. 259

AND [a]it came to pass, that [b]after the year was expired, at the time that kings go out *to battle,* Joab led forth the power of the army, and wasted the country of the children of Ammon, and came and besieged Rabbah. But David tarried at Jerusalem. And [c]Joab smote Rabbah, and destroyed it.

2 And David [d]took the crown of their king from off his head, and found it [e]to weigh a talent of gold; and *there were* precious stones in it; and it was set upon David's head: and he brought also exceeding much spoil out of the city.

3 And he brought out the people that *were* in it, and cut *them* with saws, and with harrows of iron, and with axes. Even so dealt David with all the cities of the children of Ammon. And David and all the people returned to Jerusalem.

4 And it came to pass after this, [f]that there [g]arose [h]war at [i]Gezer with the Philistines, at which time [k]Sibbechai the Hushathite slew [l]Sippai, *that was* of the children of [m]the giant: and they were subdued.

A. M. 2969
B. C. 1035
An. Exod. Isr.
456
Anno ante I.
Olymp. 259

5 And there was war again with the Philistines: and Elhanan the son of [n]Jair slew Lahmi the brother of Goliath the Gittite, whose spear-staff *was* like a weaver's beam.

6 And yet again [o]there was war at Gath, where was [p]a man of *great* stature, whose fingers and toes *were* four and twenty, six *on each hand,* and six *on each foot:* and he also was [q]the son of the giant.

7 But when he [r]defied Israel, Jonathan, the son of [s]Shimea, David's brother, slew him.

8 These were born unto the giant in Gath; and they fell by the hand of David, and by the hand of his servants.

[a]2 Sam. xi. 1——[b]Heb. *at the return of the year*——[c]2 Sam. xii. 26——[d]2 Sam. xii. 30, 31——[e]Heb. *the weight of*——[f]2 Sam. xxi. 18——[g]Or, *continued*——[h]Heb. *stood*——[i]Or, *Gob*——[k]Ch. xi. 29——[l]Or, *Saph,* 2 Sam. xxi. 18

[m]Or, *Rapha*——[n]Called also, *Jaare-oregim,* 2 Sam. xxi. 19——[o]2 Sam. xxi. 20——[p]Heb. *a man of measure*——[q]Heb. *born to the giant,* or, *Rapha*——[r]Or, *reproached*——[s]Called *Shammah,* 1 Sam. xvi. 9

NOTES ON CHAP. XX

Verse 1. *After the year was expired, at the time that kings go out* to battle] About the *spring* of the year; see the note on 2 Sam. xi. 1.

After this verse the parallel place in Samuel relates the whole story of David and Bath-sheba, and the murder of Uriah, which the compiler of these books passes over as he designedly does almost every thing prejudicial to the character of David. All he states is, *but David tarried at Jerusalem;* and, while he thus tarried, and Joab conducted the war against the Ammonites, the awful transactions above referred to took place.

Verse 2. *David took the crown of their king —off his head*] See 2 Sam. xii. 30.

Precious stones in it] The Targum says,

"And there was set in it a precious stone, worth a talent of gold; this was that magnetic stone that supported the woven gold in the air." What does he mean?

Verse 3. *He brought out the people*] See this transaction particularly explained in the notes on the parallel places, 2 Sam. xii. 30, 31.

Verse 5. *Elhanan the son of Jair*] See the note on 2 Sam. xxi. 19. The *Targum* says, "David, the son of Jesse, a pious man, who rose at midnight to sing praises to God, slew Lachmi, the brother of Goliath, the same day on which he slew Goliath the Gittite, whose spear-staff was like a weaver's beam."

Verse 6. *Fingers and toes were four and twenty*] See the note on 2 Sam. xxi. 20.

Verse 8. *These were born unto the giant in*

Gath] "These were born לְהָרָפָא *leharapha, to that Rapha in Gath,* or *to Arapha."* So the *Vulgate, Septuagint,* and *Chaldee.*

THE compiler of these books passes by also the incest of Amnon with his sister Tamar, and the rebellion of Absalom, and the awful consequences of all these. These should have pre-

ceded the fourth verse. These facts could not be unknown to him, for they were notorious to all; but he saw that they were already amply detailed in books which were accredited among the people, and the relations were such as no friend to piety and humanity could delight to repeat. On these grounds the reader will give him credit for the *omission.* See on ver. 1.

CHAPTER XXI

David is tempted by Satan to take the numbers of the people of Israel and Judah, 1, 2. Joab remonstrates, but the king is determined, and Joab pleads in vain, 3, 4. He returns, and delivers in the number to the king, but reckons not Levi and Benjamin, 5. The Lord is displeased, and sends Gad to offer David his choice of three great national calamities; famine, war, or pestilence, 6–12. David submits himself to God, and a pestilence is sent, which destroys seventy thousand, 13, 14. *At David's intercession the destroying angel is restrained at the threshing-floor of Ornan, 15–17. He buys the piece of ground, builds an altar to the Lord and offers sacrifices, and the plague is stayed, 18–30.*

A. M. 2987
B. C. 1017
An. Exod. Isr. 474
Anno ante I. Olymp. 241

AND [a]Satan stood up against Israel, and provoked David to number Israel.

2 And David said to Joab and to the rulers of the people, Go, number Israel, from Beer-sheba even to Dan; [b]and bring the number of them to me, that I may know *it.*

3 And Joab answered, The LORD make his people a hundred times so many more as they *be:* but, my lord the king, *are* they not all my lord's servants? why then doth my lord require this thing? why will he be a cause of trespass to Israel?

4 Nevertheless the king's word prevailed against Joab. Wherefore Joab departed, and went throughout all Israel, and came to Jerusalem.

5 And Joab gave the sum of the number of the people unto David. And all *they of* Israel were a thousand thousand and a hundred thousand men that drew sword: and Judah *was* four hundred threescore and ten thousand men that drew sword.

6 [c]But Levi and Benjamin counted he not among them: for the king's word was abominable to Joab.

A. M. 2987
B. C. 1017
An. Exod. Isr. 474
Anno ante I. Olymp. 241

7 [d]And God was displeased with this thing; therefore he smote Israel.

8 And David said unto God, [e]I have sinned greatly, because I have done this thing: [f]but now, I beseech thee, do away the iniquity of thy servant; for I have done very foolishly.

9 And the LORD spake unto Gad, David's [g]seer, saying,

10 Go and tell David, saying, Thus saith the LORD, I [h]offer thee three *things:* choose thee one of them, that I may do *it* unto thee.

11 So Gad came to David, and said unto him, Thus saith the LORD, [i]Choose thee

12 [k]Either three years' famine; or three months to be destroyed before thy foes, while that the sword of thine enemies overtaketh *thee;* or else three days the sword of the LORD, even the pestilence in the land, and the angel of the LORD destroying throughout all the coasts of Israel. Now therefore advise thy-

---

[a]2 Samuel xxiv. 1, &c.——[b]Chapter xxvii. 23 [c]Chapter xxvii. 24——[d]Hebrew, *And it was evil in the eyes of the LORD concerning this thing*

[e]2 Sam. xxiv. 10——[f]2 Sam. xii. 13——[g]See 1 Sam. ix. 9——[h]Heb. *stretch out*——[i]Heb. *Take to thee*——[k]2 Sam. xxiv. 13

NOTES ON CHAP. XXI

Verse 1. *And Satan stood up against Israel*] See the notes on the parallel place, 2 Sam. xxiv. 1, &c.

Verse 5. *All they of Israel were a thousand thousand—Judah was four hundred threescore and ten thousand*] In the parallel place, 2 Sam. xxiv. 9, the men of Israel are reckoned *eight hundred thousand,* and the men of Judah *five hundred thousand:* see the note there.

Verse 6. *Levi and Benjamin counted he not*] The rabbins give the following reason for this: Joab, seeing that this would bring down de-

struction upon the people, purposed to save two tribes. Should David ask, Why have you not numbered the Levites? Joab purposed to say, Because the Levites are not reckoned among the children of Israel. Should he ask, Why have you not numbered Benjamin? he would answer, Benjamin has been already sufficiently punished, on account of the treatment of the woman at Gibeah: if, therefore, this tribe were to be again punished, who would remain?

Verse 12. *Three days—the pestilence in the land*] In 2 Sam. xxiv. 13, *seven years* of *famine* are mentioned: see the note there.

A. M. 2987
B. C. 1017
An. Exod. Isr.
474
Anno ante I.
Olymp. 241

self what word I shall bring again to him that sent me.

13 And David said unto Gad, I am in a great strait: let me fall now into the hand of the LORD; for very [l]great *are* his mercies: but let me not fall into the hand of man.

14 So the LORD sent pestilence upon Israel: and there fell of Israel seventy thousand men.

15 And God sent an [m]angel unto Jerusalem to destroy it; and as he was destroying, the LORD beheld, and [n]he repented him of the evil, and said to the angel that destroyed, It is enough, stay now thine hand. And the angel of the LORD stood by the threshing-floor of [o]Ornan the Jebusite.

16 And David lifted up his eyes, and [p]saw the angel of the LORD stand between the earth and the heaven, having a drawn sword in his hand stretched out over Jerusalem. Then David and the elders of *Israel, who were* clothed in sackcloth, fell upon their faces.

17 And David said unto God, *Is it* not I *that* commanded the people to be numbered? even I it is that have sinned and done evil indeed; but *as for* these sheep, what have they done? let thine hand, I pray thee, O LORD my God, be on me, and on my father's house; but not

on thy people, that they should be plagued.

A. M. 2987
B. C. 1017
An. Exod. Isr.
474
Anno ante I.
Olymp. 241

18 Then the [q]angel of the LORD commanded Gad to say to David, that David should go up, and set up an altar unto the LORD in the threshing-floor of Ornan the Jebusite.

19 And David went up at the saying of Gad, which he spake in the name of the LORD.

20 [r]And Ornan turned back, and saw the angel; and his four sons with him hid themselves. Now Ornan was threshing wheat.

21 And as David came to Ornan, Ornan looked and saw David, and went out of the threshing-floor, and bowed himself to David with *his* face to the ground.

22 Then David said to Ornan, [s]Grant me the place of *this* threshing-floor, that I may build an altar therein unto the LORD: thou shalt grant it me for the full price: that the plague may be stayed from the people.

23 And Ornan said unto David, Take *it* to thee, and let my lord the king do *that which is* good in his eyes: lo, I give *thee* the oxen also for burnt-offerings, and the threshing instruments for wood, and the wheat for the meat offering; I give it all.

24 And King David said to Ornan, Nay; but

---

[l]Or, *many*——[m]2 Sam. xxiv. 16——[n]See Gen. vi. 6
[o]Or, *Araunah;* 2 Sam. xxiv. 18——[p]2 Chron. iii. 1
[q]2 Chron. iii. 1

[r]Or, *When Ornan turned back and saw the angel, then he and his four sons with him hid themselves*
[s]Heb. *Give*

Verse 13. *David said—I am in a great strait*] The Targum reasons thus: "And David said to Gad, If I choose *famine,* the Israelites may say, The granaries of David are full of corn; neither doth he care should the people of Israel die with hunger. And if I choose *war,* and fly before an enemy, the Israelites may say, David is a strong and warlike man, and he cares not though the people of Israel should fall by the sword. I am brought into a great strait; I will deliver myself now into the HAND *of the* WORD *of the* LORD, בְּיַד מֵימְרָא דַיָי *beyad meymera dayai,* for his mercies are many; but into the hands of the children of men I will not deliver myself."

Verse 15. *And God sent an angel*] Thus the Targum: "And the WORD *of the* LORD sent the angel of death against Jerusalem to destroy it; and he beheld the ashes of the binding of Isaac at the foot of the altar, and he remembered his covenant with Abraham, which he made in the Mount of Worship; and the house of the upper sanctuary, where are the souls of the righteous, and the image of Jacob fixed on the throne of glory; and he turned *in his* WORD from the evil which he designed to do unto them; and he said to the destroying angel, Cease; take Abishai their chief from among them, and cease from smiting the rest of the people. And the angel

which was sent from the presence of the Lord stood at the threshing-floor of Araunah the Jebusite."

Verse 20. *Ornan turned back, and saw the angel*] The *Septuagint* say, And Orna turned, και ειδε τον βασιλεα, and saw the KING. The *Syriac* and *Arabic* say, David saw the angel; and do not mention Ornan in this place. *Houbigant* translates the same reading הַמֶּלֶךְ *hammalech, the king,* for הַמַּלְאָךְ *hammalach, the angel,* and vindicates his version from the parallel place, 2 Sam. xxiv. 20, where it is said, he *saw David:* but there is no word of his seeing the angel. But the seeing David is mentioned in ver. 21; though Houbigant supposes that the 20th verse refers to his seeing the king *while he was at a distance;* the 21st, to his seeing him *when he came into the threshing-floor.* In the first instance he and his sons were *afraid* when they saw the king coming, and this caused them to hide themselves; but when he came into the threshing-floor, they were obliged to appear before him. One of *Kennicott's* MSS. has הַמֶּלֶךְ *the king,* instead of הַמַּלְאָךְ *the angel.* Some learned men contend for the former reading.

Verse 24. *For the full price*] That is, *six hundred* shekels *full* weight of *pure* gold.

A. M. 2987
B. C. 1017
An. Exod. Isr.
474
Anno ante I.
Olymp. 241

I will verily buy it for the full price: for I will not take *that* which *is* thine for the LORD, nor offer burnt-offerings without cost.

25 So ᵗDavid gave to Ornan for the place six hundred shekels of gold by weight.

26 And David built there an altar unto the LORD, and offered burnt-offerings and peace-offerings, and called upon the LORD; and ᵘhe answered him from heaven by fire upon the altar of burnt-offering.

27 And the LORD commanded the angel;

and he put up his sword again into the sheath thereof.

A. M. 2987
B. C. 1017
An. Exod. Isr.
474
Anno ante I.
Olymp. 241

28 At that time, when David saw that the LORD had answered him in the threshing-floor of Ornan the Jebusite, then he sacrificed there.

29 ᵛFor the tabernacle of the LORD, which Moses made in the wilderness, and the altar of the burnt-offering, *were* at that season in the high place at ᵂGibeon.

30 But David could not go before it to inquire of God: for he was afraid because of the sword of the angel of the LORD.

ᵗ2 Sam. xxiv. 24——ᵘLev. ix. 24; 2 Chron. iii. 1; vii. 1

ᵛCh. xvi. 39——ᵂ1 Kings iii. 4; ch. xvi. 39; 2 Chron. i. 3

Verse 26. *He answered him—by fire*] In answer to David's prayers, God, to show that he had accepted him, and was now pacified towards him and the people, sent fire from heaven and consumed the offerings.

Verse 30. *Because of the sword of the angel*] This is given as a reason why David built an altar in the threshing-floor of Ornan: he was afraid to go to Gibeon, *because of the sword of the destroying angel*, or he was afraid of *delaying* the offerings so long as his going thither would require, lest the destroying angel should

in the mean while exterminate the people; therefore he hastily built an altar in that place, and on it made the requisite offerings; and by the fire from heaven God showed that he had accepted his act and his devotion. Such interventions as these must necessarily maintain in the minds of the people a full persuasion of the truth and Divine origin of their religion.

For a more circumstantial account of these transactions, see the notes on 2 Sam. xxiv. 1, &c., in which several difficulties of the text are removed.

CHAPTER XXII

David makes great preparations for building a temple to the Lord, 1–5; gives the necessary directions to Solomon concerning it, 6–16; and exhorts the princes of Israel to assist in the undertaking, 17–19.

A. M. 2987
B. C. 1017
An. Exod. Isr.
474
Anno ante I.
Olymp. 241

THEN David said, ªThis *is* the house of the LORD God, and this *is* the altar of the burnt-offering for Israel.

2 And David commanded to gather together ᵇthe strangers that *were* in the land of Israel; and he set masons to hew wrought stones to build the house of God.

3 And David prepared iron in abundance

for the nails for the doors of the gates, and for the joinings; and brass in abundance ᶜwithout weight;

A. M. 2987
B. C. 1017
An. Exod. Isr.
474
Anno ante I.
Olymp. 241

4 Also cedar trees in abundance: for the ᵈZidonians and they of Tyre brought much cedar wood to David.

5 And David said, ᵉSolomon my son *is* young and tender, and the house *that is* to be builded

---

ªDeut. xii. 5; 2 Sam. xxiv. 18; chap. xxi. 18, 19, 26, 28; 2 Chron. iii. 1

ᵇ1 Kings ix. 21——ᶜVer. 14; 1 Kings vii. 47——ᵈ1 Kings v. 6——ᵉChap. xxix. 1

NOTES ON CHAP. XXII

Verse 1. *David said, This is the house of the Lord*] Till a temple is built for his name, this place shall be considered the temple of God; and on this altar, and not on that at Gibeon, shall the burnt-offerings of Israel be made. David probably thought that this was the *place* on which God designed that his house should be built; and perhaps it was this that induced him to buy, not only the threshing-floor, but probably some adjacent ground also, as *Calmet* supposes, that there might be sufficient room for such a building.

Verse 2. *The strangers that were in the land*] Those who had become *proselytes* to the Jewish

religion, at least so far as to renounce idolatry, and keep what were called the seven Noahic precepts. These were to be employed in the more servile and difficult parts of the work: see on 1 Kings ix. 21. For the account of building the temple, see 1 Kings v.-ix., and the notes there.

Verse 3. *Iron—for the nails, &c.*] Iron for bolts, bars, hinges, &c., &c.

Verse 5. *Solomon—is young and tender*] He is as yet without complete knowledge and due experience; and it is necessary that I should make as much preparation for the work as I possibly can; especially as the house is to be exceedingly magnificent.

A. M. 2987
B. C. 1017
An. Exod. Isr.
474
Anno ante I.
Olymp. 241

for the LORD *must be* exceeding magnifical, of fame and of glory throughout all countries: I will *therefore* now make preparation for it. So David prepared abundantly before his death.

6 Then he called for Solomon his son, and charged him to build a house for the LORD God of Israel.

7 And David said to Solomon, My son, as for me, [f]it was in my mind to build a house [g]unto the name of the LORD my God:

8 But the word of the LORD came to me, saying, [h]Thou hast shed blood abundantly, and hast made great wars: thou shalt not build a house unto my name, because thou hast shed much blood upon the earth in my sight.

9 [i]Behold, a son shall be born to thee, who shall be a man of rest; and I will give him [k]rest from all his enemies round about: for his name shall be [l]Solomon, and I will give peace and quietness unto Israel in his days.

10 [m]He shall build a house for my name; and [n]he shall be my son, and I *will be* his father;

and I will establish the throne of his kingdom over Israel for ever.

A. M. 2987
B. C. 1017
An. Exod. Isr.
474
Anno ante I.
Olymp. 241

11 Now, my son, [o]the LORD be with thee; and prosper thou, and build the house of the LORD thy God, as he hath said of thee.

12 Only the LORD [p]give thee wisdom and understanding, and give thee charge concerning Israel, that thou mayest keep the law of the LORD thy God.

13 [q]Then shalt thou prosper, if thou takest heed to fulfil the statutes and judgments which the LORD charged Moses with concerning Israel: [r]be strong, and of good courage; dread not, nor be dismayed.

14 Now, behold, [s]in my trouble I have prepared for the house of the LORD a hundred thousand talents of gold, and a thousand thousand talents of silver; and of brass and iron [t]without weight; for it is in abundance: timber also and stone have I prepared, and thou mayest add thereto.

15 Moreover *there·are* workmen with thee in abundance, hewers and [u]workers of stone and

---

[f]2 Sam. vii. 2; 1 Kings viii. 17; ch. xvii. 1; xxviii. 2
[g]Deut. xii. 5, 11——[h]1 Kings v. 3; ch. xxviii. 3——[i]Ch.
xxviii. 5——[k]1 Kings iv. 25; v. 4—— [l]That is, *peaceable*
[m]2 Sam. vii. 13; 1 Kings v. 5; ch. xvii. 12, 13; xxviii. 6

[n]Heb. i. 5——[o]Ver. 16——[p]1 Kings iii. 9, 12; Psa.
lxxii. 1——[q]Josh. i. 7, 8; ch. xxviii. 7——[r]Deut. xxxi. 7,
8; Josh. i. 6, 7, 9; ch. xxviii. 20——[s]Or, *in my poverty*
[t]As verse 3——[u]That is, *masons and carpenters*

Verse 8. *Thou hast shed blood abundantly*]
Heathens, Jews, and Christians, have all agreed that *soldiers* of any kind should have nothing to do with Divine offices. Shedding of human blood but ill comports with the benevolence of God or the spirit of the Gospel.

Æneas, overpowered by his enemies, while fighting for his parents, his family, and his country, finding farther resistance hopeless, endeavours to carry off his aged father, his wife, young son, and his *household gods;* but as he was just come from slaughter, he would not even *handle* these objects of superstition, but confided them to his father, whom he took on his shoulders, and carried out of the burning of Troy.

Tu, genitor, cape sacra *manu*, patriosque penates:
Me bello *tanto digressum, et* cæde recenti,
Attrectare nefas; *donec me flumine vivo*
Abluero.   ÆN. ii., ver. 717.

"Our *country gods*, our *relics*, and the bands,
Hold you, my father, in your guiltless hands:
In me 'tis *impious holy things to bear*,
Red as I am with *slaughter, new from war;*
Till, in some living stream, I cleanse the guilt
Of dire debate, and blood in battle spilt."
           DRYDEN.

See the note at the end of 2 Sam. chap. vii.

Verse 9. *His name shall be Solomon*] שלמה
Shelomoh, from שלם *shalam*, he was *peaceable;* and therefore, says the Lord, alluding to the

name, *I will give* PEACE, שלום SHALOM, *in his days.*

Verse 14. *In my trouble I have prepared*]
Notwithstanding all the wars in which I have been engaged, all the treacheries with which I have been surrounded, all the domestic troubles with which I have been overwhelmed, I never lost sight of this great object, the building of a house for God, that his worship might be established in the land. I have curtailed my expenses, and have lived in comparative poverty that I might save all I possibly could for this building.

A hundred thousand talents of gold] A talent of gold weighed three thousand shekels, and was worth five thousand and seventy-five pounds, fifteen shillings, and seven pence halfpenny. One hundred thousand such talents would therefore amount to five hundred and seven millions, five hundred and seventy-eight thousand, one hundred and twenty-five pounds sterling. These sums are variously computed by several writers.

A thousand thousand talents of silver] A talent of silver weighed three thousand shekels, and was worth three hundred and fifty-three pounds, eleven shillings, and ten pence. A thousand thousand, or a million, of such talents would amount to the immense sum of three hundred and fifty-three millions, five hundred and ninety-one thousand, six hundred and sixty-six pounds, thirteen shillings, and four pence, sterling; both sums amounting to eight hundred and sixty-one millions, one hundred

A. M. 2987
B. C. 1017
An. Exod. Isr.
474
Anno ante I.
Olymp. 241

timber, and all manner of cunning men for every manner of work.

16 Of the gold, the silver, and the brass, and the iron, *there is* no number. Arise, *therefore,* and be doing, and ᵛthe LORD be with thee.

17 David also commanded all the princes of Israel to help Solomon his son, *saying,*

18 *Is* not the LORD your God with you? ʷand hath he *not* given you rest on every side?

for he hath given the inhabitants of the land into mine hand; and the land is subdued before the LORD, and before his people.

19 Now ˣset your heart and your soul to seek the LORD your God; arise therefore and build ye the sanctuary of the LORD God, to ʸbring the ark of the covenant of the LORD, and the holy vessels of God, into the house that is to be built ᶻto the name of the LORD.

A. M. 2987
B. C. 1017
An. Exod. Isr.
474
Anno ante I.
Olymp. 241

ᵛVer. 11——ʷDeut. xii. 10; Josh. xxii. 4; 2 Sam. vii. 1; chap. xxiii. 25

ˣ2 Chron. xx. 3——ʸ1 Kings viii. 6, 21; 2 Chron. v. 7; vi. 11——ᶻVer. 7; 1 Kings v. 3

---

and sixty-nine thousand, seven hundred and ninety-one pounds, thirteen shillings, and four pence.

Thou mayest add thereto.] Save as I have saved, out of the revenues of the state, and thou mayest also add something for the erection and splendour of this house. This was a gentle though pointed hint, which was not lost on Solomon.

Verse 18. *Is not the Lord your God with you?*] "Is not the WORD of the Lord your God your assistant?"—*T.*

Hath he not given you rest on every side?] David at this time was not only king of Judea,

but had also subdued most of the surrounding nations.

Thus Solomon came to the Jewish throne with every possible advantage. Had he made a proper use of his state and of his talents, he would have been the greatest as well as the wisest of sovereigns. But alas! how soon did this pure gold become dim! He began with an unlawful matrimonial connection; this led him to a commerce that was positively forbidden by the law of God: he then multiplied his matrimonial connections with heathen women; they turned his heart away from God, and the once wise and holy Solomon died a fool and an idolater.

CHAPTER XXIII

David makes Solomon king, 1. Numbers the Levites, and appoints them their work, 2–5. The sons of Levi, Gershom, Kohath, Merari, and their descendants, 6–12. The sons of Amram, and their descendants, 13. The sons of Moses, and their descendants, 14–24. David appoints the Levites to wait on the priests for the service of the sanctuary, 25–32.

A. M. 2989
B. C. 1015
An. Exod. Isr.
476
Anno ante I.
Olymp. 239

SO when David was old and full of days, he made ᵃSolomon his son king over Israel.

2 And he gathered together all the princes of Israel, with the priests and the Levites.

3 Now the Levites were numbered from the age of ᵇthirty years and upward: and their number by their polls, man by man, was thirty and eight thousand.

4 Of which, twenty and four thousand *were*

ᶜto set forward the work of the house of the LORD; and six thousand *were* ᵈofficers and judges.

5 Moreover four thousand *were* porters; and four thousand praised the LORD with the instruments ᵉwhich I made, *said David,* to praise *therewith.*

6 And ᶠDavid divided them into ᵍcourses among the sons of Levi, *namely,* Gershon, Kohath, and Merari.

A. M. 2989
B. C. 1015
An. Exod. Isr.
476
Anno ante I.
Olymp. 239

ᵃ1 Kings i. 33–39; chapter xxviii. 5——ᵇNum. iv. 3. 47——ᶜOr, *to oversee*——ᵈDeut. xvi. 18; chap. xxvi. 29; 2 Chron. xix. 8

ᵉSee 2 Chron. xxix. 25, 26; Amos vi. 5——ᶠExod. vi. 16; Num. xxvi. 57; chap. vi. 1, &c.; 2 Chron. viii. 14; xxix. 25——ᵍHeb. *divisions*

NOTES ON CHAP. XXIII

Verse 1. *David was old and full of days*] On the phrase *full of days,* see the note on Gen. xxv. 8.

Verse 3. *Thirty years and upward*] The enumeration of the Levites made in the desert, Num. iv. 3, was from *thirty* years upwards to *fifty* years. In this place, the latter limit is

not mentioned, probably because the service was not so laborious now; for the ark being fixed, they had no longer any heavy burdens to carry, and therefore even an old man might continue to serve the tabernacle. David made another ordinance afterwards; see on ver. 24 and 27.

Verse 5. *Four thousand praised the Lord*] David made this distribution according to his own judgment, and from the dictates of his

A. M. 2989
B. C. 1015
An. Exod. Isr.
476
Anno ante I.
Olymp. 239

7 Of the [b]Gershonites were, [i]Laadan, and Shimei.

8 The sons of Laadan; the chief was Jehiel, and Zetham, and Joel, three.

9 The sons of Shimei; Shelomith, and Haziel, and Haran, three. These were the chief of the fathers of Laadan.

10 And the sons of Shimei were, Jahath, [k]Zina, and Jeush, and Beriah. These four were the sons of Shimei.

11 And Jahath was the chief, and Zizah the second: but Jeush and Beriah [l]had not many sons; therefore they were in one reckoning, according to their father's house.

12 [m]The sons of Kohath; Amram, Izhar, Hebron, and Uzziel, four.

13 The sons of [n]Amram; Aaron and Moses: and [o]Aaron was separated, that he should sanctify the most holy things, he and his sons for ever, [p]to burn incense before the LORD, [q]to minister unto him, and [r]to bless in his name for ever.

14 Now concerning Moses, the man of God, [s]his sons were named of the tribe of Levi.

15 [t]The sons of Moses were, Gershom, and Eliezer.

16 Of the sons of Gershom, [u]Shebuel [v]was the chief.

17 And the sons of Eliezer were, [w]Rehabiah [x]the chief. And Eliezer had none other

sons; but the sons of Rehabiah [y]were very many.

18 Of the sons of Izhar; [z]Shelomith the chief.

19 [a]Of the sons of Hebron; Jeriah the first, Amariah the second, Jehaziel the third, and Jekameam the fourth.

20 Of the sons of Uzziel; Micah the first, and Jesiah the second.

21 [b]The sons of Merari; Mahli, and Mushi. The sons of Mahli; Eleazar, and [c]Kish.

22 And Eleazar died, and [d]had no sons, but daughters: and their [e]brethren the sons of Kish [f]took them.

23 [g]The sons of Mushi; Mahli, and Eder, and Jeremoth, three.

24 These were the sons of [h]Levi after the house of their fathers; even the chief of the fathers, as they were counted by number of names by their polls, that did the work for the service of the house of the LORD, from the age of [i]twenty years and upward.

25 For David said, The LORD God of Israel [k]hath given rest unto his people, [l]that they may dwell in Jerusalem for ever:

26 And also unto the Levites; they shall no more [m]carry the tabernacle, nor any vessels of it for the service thereof.

27 For by the last words of David the Levites were [n]numbered from twenty years old and above:

A. M. 2989
B. C. 1015
An. Exod. Isr.
476
Anno ante I.
Olymp. 239

---

[b]Ch. xxvi. 21——[i]Or, Libni, ch. vi. 17——[k]Or, Zizah, ver. 11——[l]Heb. did not multiply sons——[m]Exod. vi. 18 [n]Exod. vi. 20——[o]Exod. xxviii. 1; Heb. v. 4——[p]Exod. xxx. 7; Num. xvi. 40; 1 Sam. ii. 28——[q]Deut. xxi. 5 [r]Num. vi. 23——[s]See chap. xxvi. 23, 24, 25——[t]Exod. ii. 22; xviii. 3, 4——[u]Chap. xxvi. 24——[v]Shubael, chap. xxiv. 20——[w]Chap. xxvi. 25

[x]Or, the first——[y]Hebrew, were highly multiplied [z]Shelomoth, ch. xxiv. 22——[a]Ch. xxiv. 23——[b]Ch. xxiv. 26——[c]Ch. xxiv. 29——[d]Ch. xxiv. 28——[e]Or, kinsmen [f]See Num. xxxvi. 6, 8——[g]Ch. xxiv. 30——[h]Num. x. 17, 21——[i]Ver. 27; see Num. i. 3; iv. 3; viii. 24; Ezra iii. 8——[k]Ch. xxii. 18——[l]Or, and he dwelleth in Jerusalem, &c.——[m]Num. iv. 5, &c.——[n]Heb. numbers

---

piety; but it does not appear that he had any positive Divine authority for such arrangements. As to the instruments of music which he made they are condemned elsewhere; see Amos vi. 5, to which this verse is allowed to be the parallel.

Verse 11. Therefore they were in one reckoning] The family of Shimei, being small, was united with that of Laadan, that the two families might do that work which otherwise belonged to one, but which would have been too much for either of these separately.

Verse 13. To bless in his name] To bless the people by invoking the name of the Lord.

Verse 14. Moses the man of God] "Moses the prophet of God."—T.

Verse 16. To this verse the Targum adds, "The same Jonathan, who became a false prophet, repented in his old age; and David made him his chief treasurer."

Verse 17. But the sons of Rehabiah were

very many.] The Targum says, "On account of the merits of Moses, the posterity of Rehabiah were multiplied to more than sixty myriads."

Verse 22. Their brethren the sons of Kish took them.] This was according to the law made Num. xxvii. 1, &c., and xxxvi. 5-9, in favour of the daughters of Zelophehad, that women who were heiresses should marry in the family of the tribe of their father, and that their estates should not be alienated from them.

Verse 24. Twenty years and upward.] It appears that this was a different ordinance from that mentioned ver. 3. At first he appointed the Levites to serve from thirty years and upward; now from twenty years. These were David's last orders; see ver. 27. They should begin at an earlier age, and continue later.

This was not a very painful task; the ark being now fixed, and the Levites very numerous, there could be no drudgery.

A. M. 2989
B. C. 1015
An. Exod. Isr.
476
Anno ante I.
Olymp. 239

28 Because °their office *was* to wait on the sons of Aaron for the service of the house of the LORD, in the courts, and in the chambers, and in the purifying of all holy things, and the work of the service of the house of God;

29 Both for ᴾthe shew-bread, and for qthe fine flour for meat-offering, and for ʳthe unleavened cakes, and for ˢ*that which is baked in* the ᵗpan, and for that which is fried, and for all manner of ᵘmeasure and size;

30 And to stand every morning to thank and

praise the LORD, and likewise at even;

31 And to offer all burnt-sacrifices unto the LORD ᵛin the Sabbaths, in the new moons, and on the ʷset feasts, by number, according to the order commanded unto them, continually before the LORD:

32 And that they should ˣkeep the charge of the tabernacle of the congregation, and the charge of the holy *place,* and ʸthe charge of the sons of Aaron their brethren, in the service of the house of the LORD.

A. M. 2989
B. C. 1015
An. Exod. Isr.
476
Anno ante I.
Olymp. 239

°Heb. *Their station* was *at the hand of the sons of Aaron,* Neh. xi. 24——ᴾExod. xxv. 30——qLev. vi. 20; chap. ix. 29, &c.——ʳLev. ii. 4

ˢLev. ii. 5, 7——ᵗOr, *flat plate*——ᵘLev. xix. 35 ᵛNum. x. 10; Psalm lxxxi. 3——ʷLev. xxiii. 4——ˣNum. i. 53——ʸNum. iii. 6–9

Verse 28. *Purifying of all holy things*] Keeping all the vessels and utensils belonging to the sacred service clean and neat.

Verse 29. *Both for the shew-bread*] It was the *priests'* office to place this bread before the Lord, and it was their privilege to feed on the old loaves when they were replaced by the *new.* Some of the rabbins think that the priests sowed, reaped, ground, kneaded, and baked the grain of which the *shew-bread* was made. This appears to be a conceit. Jerome, in his comment on Mal. i. 6, mentions it in these words: "Panes propositionis quos, juxta traditiones Hebraicas, ipsi serere, ipsi demetere, ipsi molere, ipsi coquere debatis."

For all manner of measure and size] The

standards of all *weights* and *measures* were kept at the sanctuary, and by those there deposited all the *weights* and *measures* of the land were to be tried. See the note on Exod. xxx. 13.

Verse 30. *To stand every morning*] At the offering of the morning and evening sacrifice, they sounded their musical instruments, and sang praises to God.

Verse 32. *The charge of the sons of Aaron*] It was the priests' business to kill, flay, and dress, as well as to *offer,* the victims; but being *few,* they were obliged to employ the Levites to flay those animals. The Levites were, properly speaking, servants to the priests, and were employed about the more servile part of Divine worship.

CHAPTER XXIV

David divides the families of Eleazar and Ithamar, by lot, into twenty-four *courses, 1–19. How the rest of the sons of Levi were disposed of, 20–31.*

A. M. 2989
B. C. 1015
An. Exod. Isr.
476
Anno ante I.
Olymp. 239

NOW *these are* the divisions of the sons of Aaron. ªThe sons of Aaron; Nadab, and Abihu, Eleazar, and Ithamar.

2 But ᵇNadab and Abihu died before their father, and had no children: therefore Eleazar and Ithamar executed the priest's office.

3 And David distributed them, both Zadok and the sons of Eleazar, and Ahimelech of the sons of Ithamar, according to their offices in their service.

4 And there were more chief men found of the sons of Eleazar than of the sons of Ithamar; and *thus* were they divided. Among the sons of Eleazar *there were* sixteen chief men of the house of *their* fathers, and eight among the sons of Ithamar, according to the house of their fathers.

A. M. 2989
B. C. 1015
An. Exod. Isr.
476
Anno ante I.
Olymp. 239

5 Thus were they divided by lot, one sort with another; for the governors of the sanctuary, and governors *of the house* of God, were of the

---

ªLev. x. 1, 6; Num. xxvi. 60

ᵇNum. iii. 4; xxvi. 61

NOTES ON CHAP. XXIV

Verse 2. *Nadab and Abihu died before their father*] That is, during his lifetime.

Eleazar and Ithamar executed the priest's office.] These two served the office during the life of their father Aaron; after his death Eleazar succeeded in the high priesthood. And

under Eli the high priest, the family of Ithamar re-entered into that office.

Verse 3. *And Ahimelech*] Ahimelech is put here for *Abiathar,* who was high priest in the days of David. Abiathar had also the name of Ahimelech, as well as his father. See *Calmet.*

Verse 5. *They divided by lot*] This prevent-

A. M. 2989
B. C. 1015
An. Exod. Isr.
476
Anno ante I.
Olymp. 239

sons of Eleazar, and of the sons of Ithamar.

6 And Shemaiah the son of Nethaneel the scribe, *one* of the Levites, wrote them before the king, and the princes, and Zadok the priest, and Ahimelech the son of Abiathar, and *before* the chief of the fathers of the priests and Levites: one ᶜprincipal household being taken for Eleazar, and *one* taken for Ithamar.

7 Now the first lot came forth to Jehoiarib, the second to Jedaiah,

8 The third to Harim, the fourth to Seorim,

9 The fifth to Malchijah, the sixth to Mijamin,

10 The seventh to Hakkoz, the eighth to ᵈAbijah,

11 The ninth to Jeshuah, the tenth to Shecaniah,

12 The eleventh to Eliashib, the twelfth to Jakim,

13 The thirteenth to Huppah, the fourteenth to Jeshebeab,

14 The fifteenth to Bilgah, the sixteenth to Immer,

15 The seventeenth to Hezir, the eighteenth to Aphses,

16 The nineteenth to Pethahiah, the twentieth to Jehezekel,

17 The one and twentieth to Jachin, the two and twentieth to Gamul,

18 The three and twentieth to Delaiah, the four and twentieth to Maaziah.

19 These *were* the orderings of them in their service ᵉto come into the house of the

LORD, according to their manner, under Aaron their father, as the LORD God of Israel had commanded him.

A. M. 2989
B. C. 1015
An. Exod. Isr.
476
Anno ante I.
Olymp. 239

20 And the rest of the sons of Levi *were these:* Of the sons of Amram; ᶠShubael: of the sons of Shubael; Jehdeiah.

21 Concerning ᵍRehabiah: of the sons of Rehabiah, the first *was* Isshiah.

22 Of the Izharites; ʰShelomoth: of the sons of Shelomoth; Jahath.

23 And the sons *of* ¹*Hebron;* Jeriah *the first,* Amariah the second, Jahaziel the third, Jekameam the fourth.

24 *Of* the sons of Uzziel; Michah: of the sons of Michah; Shamir.

25 The brother of Michah *was* Isshiah: of the sons of Isshiah; Zechariah.

26 ᵏThe sons of Merari *were* Mahli and Mushi: the sons of Jaaziah; Beno.

27 The sons of Merari by Jaaziah; Beno, and Shoham, and Zaccur, and Ibri.

28 Of Mahli *came* Eleazar, ˡwho had no sons.

29 Concerning Kish: the son of Kish *was* Jerahmeel.

30 ᵐThe sons also of Mushi; Mahli, and Eder, and Jerimoth. These *were* the sons of the Levites after the house of their fathers.

31 These likewise cast lots over against their brethren the sons of Aaron in the presence of David the king, and Zadok, and Ahimelech, and the chief of the fathers of the priests and Levites, even the principal fathers over against their younger brethren.

ᶜHeb. *house of the father*——ᵈNeh. xii. 4, 17; Luke i. 5——ᵉChapter ix. 25——ᶠChapter xxiii. 16, *Shebuel* ᵍChapter xxiii. 17

ʰChap. xxiii. 18, *Shelomith*——¹Chap. xxiii. 19; xxvi. 31——ᵏExod. vi. 19; chap. xxiii. 21——ˡChap. xxiii. 22 ᵐChap. xxiii. 23

---

ed jealousies: for, as all the families were equally noble, they had equal right to all ecclesiastical and civil distinctions.

Verse 6. *And Shemaiah*] "Moses the great scribe, who is called Shemaiah, the son of Nethaneel, of the tribe of Levi, wrote them down."—*T.*

One principal household—for Eleazar] The family of Eleazar was the most illustrious of the sacerdotal families, because Eleazar was the *first-born* of Aaron, Ithamar's family was the *second* in order and dignity; therefore one of the principal families of Eleazar was *first* taken, and then one of Ithamar's, and thus alternately till the whole was finished.

Verse 19. *Under Aaron their father*] That is, they followed the order and plans laid down by Aaron during his lifetime.

Verse 26. *The sons of Merari*] It is remarkable that not a word is here spoken of the family of *Gershom.*

Verse 31. *These likewise cast lots*] The Levites were divided into *twenty-four* orders; and these were appointed by lot to serve under the *twenty-four* orders of the priests: the first order of Levites under the first order of priests, and so on. The meaning is not very clear: "both elder and younger," says Bishop Patrick, "had their places by lot, not by seniority of houses. They who were of greater dignity drew lots against those who were of less; and were to take their courses according to the lot they drew." This may have been the case; but we are very little interested in the subject.

CHAPTER XXV

The number and offices of the singers and players on musical instruments; and their division by lot into twenty-four courses, 1–31.

A. M. 2989
B. C. 1015
An. Exod. Isr.
476
Anno ante I.
Olymp. 239

MOREOVER David and the captains of the host separated to the service of the sons of ªAsaph, and of Heman, and of Jeduthun, who should prophesy with harps, with psalteries, and with cymbals: and the number of the workmen according to their service was:

2 Of the sons of Asaph; Zaccur, and Joseph, and Nethaniah, and ᵇAsarelah, the sons of Asaph under the hands of Asaph, which prophesied ᶜaccording to the order of the king.

3 Of Jeduthun: the sons of Jeduthun; Gedaliah, and ᵈZeri, and Jeshaiah, Hashabiah, and Mattithiah, ᵉsix, under the hands of their father Jeduthun, who prophesied with a harp, to give thanks and to praise the Lord.

4 Of Heman: the sons of Heman; Bukkiah, Mattaniah, ᶠUzziel, ᵍShebuel, and Jerimoth, Hananiah, Hanani, Eliathah, Giddalti, and Romamti-ezer, Joshbekashah, Mallothi, Hothir, *and* Mahazioth:

5 All these *were* the sons of Heman, the king's seer in the ʰwords of God, to lift up the horn. And God gave to Heman fourteen sons and three daughters.

6 All these *were* under the hands of their father for song *in* the house of the Lord, with cymbals, psalteries, and harps, for the

service of the house of God, ⁱaccording ᵏto the king's order to Asaph, Jeduthun, and Heman.

A. M. 2989
B. C. 1015
An. Exod. Isr.
476
Anno ante I.
Olymp. 239

7 So the number of them, with their brethren that were instructed in the songs of the Lord, *even* all that were cunning, was two hundred fourscore and eight.

8 And they cast lots, ward against *ward*, as well the small as the great, ˡthe teacher as the scholar.

9 Now the first lot came forth for Asaph to Joseph: the second to Gedaliah, who with his brethren and sons *were* twelve:

10 The third to ᵐZaccur, he, his sons, and his brethren, *were* twelve:

11 The fourth to Izri, *he,* his sons, and his brethren, *were* twelve:

12 The fifth to Nethaniah, *he,* his sons, and his brethren, *were* twelve:

13 The sixth to Bukkiah, *he,* his sons, and his brethren, *were* twelve:

14 The seventh to Jesharelah, *he,* his sons, and his brethren, *were* twelve:

15 The eighth to Jeshaiah, *he,* his sons, and his brethren, *were* twelve:

16 The ninth to Mattaniah, *he,* his sons, and his brethren, *were* twelve:

17 The tenth to Shimei, *he,* his sons, and his brethren, *were* twelve:

ªCh. vi. 33, 39, 44——ᵇOtherwise called *Jesharelah,* ver. 14——ᶜHeb. *by the hands of the king;* so ver. 6 ᵈOr, *Izri,* ver. 11——ᵉWith Shimei, mentioned ver. 17

ᶠOr, *Azareel,* ver. 18——ᵍOr, *Shubael,* ver. 20——ʰOr, *matters*——ⁱVer. 2——ᵏHeb. *by the hands of the king* ˡ2 Chron. xxiii. 13——ᵐVer. 2

NOTES ON CHAP. XXV

Verse 1. *David and the captains of the host*] The chiefs of those who formed the several orders: not *military* captains.

Should prophesy] Should accompany their musical instruments with prayer and singing.

Verse 2. *Which prophesied*] Sung hymns and prayed. But the *Targum* understands this of prophesying in the proper sense of the term; and therefore says, "Who prophesied by the Holy Spirit." *Jarchi* is of the same opinion; and quotes the case of Elisha, 2 Kings iii. 15: *While the minstrel played, the hand of the Lord* [i. e., the spirit of prophecy] *was upon him.*

Verse 3. *The sons of Jeduthun—six*] That is, *six* with their *father;* otherwise, there are but *five.* Hence it is said, *they were under the hands of their father Jeduthun, who prophesied with a harp, &c.*

Verse 5. *To lift up the horn*] "The horn of

prophecy," says *Jarchi;* "to sound with the trumpet in the words of prophecy before the Lord."—*T.*

Three daughters.] These also were employed among the singers.

Verse 7. *Two hundred fourscore and eight.*] That is, twelve classes of *twenty-four* Levites each; for *two hundred and eighty-eight* divided by *twelve* quotes *twenty-four.*

Verse 9. *For Asaph to Joseph*] His first-born.

The second to Gedaliah] The first-born of Jeduthun.

Verse 10. *The third to Zaccur*] The first-born of Asaph.

Verse 11. *The fourth to Izri*] The second son of Jeduthun.

Verse 12. *The fifth to Nethaniah*] The third son of Asaph. Thus we find the lot did not run in any particular kind of order.

Verse 14. *Jesharelah*] Supposed to be the same with Uzziel, son of Heman.

A. M. 2989
B. C. 1015
An. Exod. Isr.
476
Anno ante I.
Olymp. 239

18 The eleventh to Azareel, *he,* his sons, and his brethren, *were* twelve:

19 The twelfth to Hashabiah, *he,* his sons, and his brethren, *were* twelve:

20 The thirteenth to Shubael, *he,* his sons, and his brethren, *were* twelve:

21 The fourteenth to Mattithiah, *he,* his sons, and his brethren, *were* twelve:

22 The fifteenth to Jeremoth, *he,* his sons, and his brethren, *were* twelve:

23 The sixteenth to Hananiah, *he,* his sons, and his brethren, *were* twelve:

24 The seventeenth to Joshbekashah, *he,* his sons, and his brethren, *were* twelve:

25 The eighteenth to Hanani, *he,* his

sons, and his brethren, *were* twelve:

26 The nineteenth to Mallothi, *he,* his sons, and his brethren, *were* twelve:

27 The twentieth to Eliathah, *he,* his sons, and his brethren, *were* twelve:

28 The one and twentieth to Hothir, *he,* his sons, and his brethren, *were* twelve:

29 The two and twentieth to Giddalti, *he,* his sons, and his brethren, *were* twelve:

30 The three and twentieth to Mahazioth, *he,* his sons, and his brethren, *were* twelve:

31 The four and twentieth to ⁿRomamti-ezer, *he,* his sons, and his brethren, *were* twelve.

A. M. 2989
B. C. 1015
An. Exod. Isr.
476
Anno ante I.
Olymp. 239

ⁿ1 Chronicles,   chap. xxv. 4

Verse 31. *Romamti-ezer*] Both these names belong to the same person. He is mentioned also ver. 4.

With this immense parade of noise and show, (David's own invention,) Christianity has nothing to do.

CHAPTER XXVI

The divisions of the porters, 1–12. The gates assigned to them, 13–19. Those who were over the treasures, 20–28. Different officers, 29–32.

A. M. 2989
B. C. 1015
An. Exod. Isr.
476
Anno ante I.
Olymp. 239

CONCERNING the divisions of the porters: Of the Korhites *was* ªMeshelemiah the son of Kore, of the sons of ᵇAsaph.

2 And the sons of Meshelemiah *were,* Zechariah the first-born, Jediael the second, Zebadiah the third, Jathniel the fourth,

3 Elam the fifth, Jehohanan the sixth, Elioenai the seventh.

4 Moreover the sons of Obed-edom *were,* Shemaiah the first-born, Jehozabad the second, Joah the third, and Sacar the fourth, and Nethaneel the fifth,

5 Ammiel the sixth, Issachar the seventh, Peulthai the eighth: for God blessed ᶜhim.

6 Also unto Shemaiah his son were sons born, that ruled throughout the house of their father: for they *were* mighty men of valour.

A. M. 2989
B. C. 1015
An. Exod. Isr.
476
Anno ante I.
Olymp. 239

7 The sons of Shemaiah; Othni, and Rephael, and Obed, Elzabad, whose brethren *were* strong men, Elihu, and Semachiah.

8 All these of the sons of Obed-edom: they and their sons and their brethren, able men for strength for the service, *were* three-score and two of Obed-edom.

9 And Meshelemiah had sons and brethren, strong men, eighteen.

10 Also ᵈHosah, of the children of Merari,

ªOr, *Shelemiah,* ver. 14——ᵇOr,*Ebiasaph,* chap. vi. 37; ix. 19

ᶜThat is, Obed-edom, as chap. xiii. 14——ᵈChap. xvi. 38

NOTES ON CHAP. XXVI

Verse 1. *The divisions of the porters*] There were four classes of these, each of which belonged to one of the four gates of the temple, which opened to the four cardinal points of heaven. The *eastern* gate fell to Shelemiah; the *northern,* to Zechariah, ver. 14; the *southern,* to Obed-edom, ver. 15; the *western,* to Shuppim and Hosah, ver. 16. These several persons were *captains* of these porter-bands or door-keepers at the different gates. There were

probably *a thousand men* under each of these captains; as we find, from chap. xxiii. 5, that there were *four thousand* in all.

Verse 5. *For God blessed him.*] "That is, Obed-edom; because of the ark of the Lord which was in his house; and to him was given the honour that he should see his children and grand-children, even fourscore and two, masters of the Levites."—*T.* In ver. 8, we have only *sixty-two* mentioned.

Verse 6. *They* were *mighty men of valour.*] They were not only porters or door-keepers in

<table>
<tr><td>A. M. 2989
B. C. 1015
An. Exod. Isr.
476
Anno ante I.
Olymp. 239</td><td>had sons; Simri the chief, (for *though* he was not the first-born, yet his father made him the chief;)</td></tr>
</table>

11 Hilkiah the second, Tebaliah the third, Zechariah the fourth: all the sons and brethren of Hosah *were* thirteen.

12 Among these *were* the divisions of the porters, *even* among the chief men, *having* wards one against another, to minister in the house of the LORD.

13 And they cast lots, ^eas well the small as the great, according to the house of their fathers, for every gate.

14 And the lot eastward fell to ^fShelemiah. Then for Zechariah his son, a wise counsellor, they cast lots; and his lot came out northward.

15 To Obed-edom southward; and to his sons the house of ^gAsuppim.

16 To Shuppim and Hosah *the lot came forth* westward, with the gate Shallecheth, by the causeway of the going ^hup, ward against ward.

17 Eastward *were* six Levites, northward four a day, southward four a day, and toward Asuppim two *and* two.

18 At Parbar westward, four at the causeway, *and* two at Parbar.

19 These *are* the divisions of the porters

<table>
<tr><td></td><td>among the sons of Kore, and among the sons of Merari.</td><td>A. M. 2989
B. C. 1015
An. Exod. Isr.
476
Anno ante I.
Olymp. 239</td></tr>
</table>

20 And of the Levites, Ahijah *was* ⁱover the treasures of the house of God, and over the treasures of the ^kdedicated things.

21 *As concerning* the sons of ^lLaadan; the sons of the Gershonite Laadan, chief fathers, *even* of Laadan the Gershonite, *were* ^mJehieli.

22 The sons of Jehieli; Zetham, and Joel his brother, *which were* over the treasures of the house of the LORD.

23 Of the Amramites, *and* the Izharites, the Hebronites, *and* the Uzzielites:

24 And ⁿShebuel the son of Gershom, the son of Moses, *was* ruler of the treasures.

25 And his brethren by Eliezer; Rehabiah his son, and Jeshaiah his son, and Joram his son, and Zichri his son, and ^oShelomith his son.

26 Which Shelomith and his brethren *were* over all the treasures of the dedicated things, which David the king, and the chief fathers, the captains over thousands and hundreds, and the captains of the host, had dedicated.

27 ^pOut of the spoils won in battles did they dedicate to maintain the house of the LORD.

28 And all that Samuel ^qthe seer, and Saul the son of Kish, and Abner the son of Ner,

---

^eOr, *as well for the small as for the great*——^fCalled *Meshelemiah,* ver. 1——^gHeb. *gatherings*——^hSee 1 Kings x. 5; 2 Chron. ix. 4——ⁱChap. xxviii. 12; Mal. iii. 10

^kHeb. *holy things*——^lOr, *Libni,* ch. vi. 17——^mOr, *Jehiel,* ch. xxiii. 8; xxix. 8——ⁿCh. xxiii. 16——^oChap. xxiii. 18——^pHeb. *Out of the battles and spoils*——^q1 Sam. ix. 9

---

the ordinary sense of the word, but they were a military guard for the gates: and perhaps in this sense alone we are to understand their office.

Verse 12. The rest of this chapter, with the whole of the xxviiith, is wanting both in the *Syriac* and *Arabic*.

Verse 13. *They cast lots—for every gate.*] None of these captains or their companies were permitted to choose which gate they would guard, but each took his appointment by *lot*.

Verse 15. *The house of Asuppim.*] The house of the *collections;* the place where either the supplies of the porters, or the offerings made for the use of the priests and Levites, were laid up.

Verse 16. *The gate Shallecheth*] The gate of the *projections:* probably that through which all the offal of the temple was carried out.

Verse 17. *Eastward* were six Levites] It is supposed that there were more guards set at this *eastern gate,* because it was more frequented than the others. At each of the other gates were only *four;* at this, *six.*

Verse 20. *The treasures of the house of God*] Where the money was kept, which was to be expended in oblations for the temple.—*Jarchi.*

Verse 24. *Shebuel the son of Gershom*] "Shebuel, that is, Jonathan, the son of Gershom, the son of Moses, *who returned to God* [שבואל *shebuel.*] And David, seeing him expert in money matters, constituted him chief treasurer."—*T.*

Verse 27. *The spoils won in battles did they dedicate*] It seems these were intended for its *repairs*. This custom prevailed amongst almost all the people of the earth. All who acknowledged any supreme Being, believed that victory could only come through him; and therefore thought it quite rational to give him a share of the spoils. Proofs of this exist in all ancient histories: thus *Virgil:*—

Irruimus ferro, et divos, ipsumque vocamus
In partem prædamque Jovem.

ÆN. iii., ver. 222.

"With weapons we the welcome prey invade:
Then call the gods for partners of our feast,
And Jove himself, the chief invited guest."

DRYDEN.

On this passage *Servius* observes: Ipsum vocamus. *Ipsum regem deorum, cui de præda debetur aliquid: nam Romanis moris fuit, ut*

<table>
<tr><td>

A. M. 2989
B. C. 1015
An. Exod. Isr.
476
Anno ante I.
Olymp. 239

and Joab the son of Zeruiah, had dedicated; *and* whosoever had dedicated *any thing, it was* under the hand of Shelomith, and of his brethren.

29 Of the Izharites, Chenaniah and his sons *were* for the outward business over Israel, for ^rofficers and judges.

30 *And* of the Hebronites, Hashabiah and his brethren, men of valour, a thousand and seven hundred, *were* ^sofficers among them of Israel on this side Jordan westward in all the business of the LORD, and in the service of the king.

</td><td>

31 Among the Hebronites *was* ^tJerijah the chief, *even* among the Hebronites, according to the generations of his fathers. In the fortieth year of the reign of David they were sought for, and there were found among them mighty men of valour, ^uat Jazer of Gilead.

32 And his brethren, men of valour, *were* two thousand and seven hundred chief fathers, whom king David made rulers over the Reubenites, the Gadites, and the half tribe of Manasseh, for every matter pertaining to God, and ^vaffairs ^wof the king.

A. M. 2989
B. C. 1015
An. Exod. Isr.
476
Anno ante I.
Olymp. 239

</td></tr>
</table>

---

^rChapter xxiii. 4——^sHebrew, *over the charge*——^tChapter xxiii. 19

^uSee Joshua xxi. 39——^vHeb. *thing*——^w2 Chronicles xix. 11

---

bella gessuri de parte prædæ aliquid numinibus pollicerentur: adeo ut Romæ fuerit unum templum JOVIS PRÆDATORIS: *non quod prædæ præest, sed quod* ei ex præda aliquid debeatur. "Jupiter himself, the king of the gods, to whom a *portion* of the *prey* was due: for it was a custom among the Romans, when entering on a war, to promise some *part of the prey* to their *deities*. And there was a temple at Rome dedicated to JUPITER PRÆDATOR, not because he *presided* over the *prey*, but because a *part* of the *prey* was *due* to him."

Verse 29. *Outward business*] Work done without the city; cutting of timber, hewing stones, ploughing the fields belonging to the sanctuary.—*Jarchi.*

Verse 30. *In all the business of the Lord*] Every thing that concerned *ecclesiastical* matters.

In the service of the king.] Every thing that concerned *civil* affairs: see also ver. 32.

Thus courts of *ecclesiastical* and *civil* judicature were established in the land; and due care taken to preserve and insure the peace of the Church, and the safety of the state; without which the public welfare could neither be secured nor promoted. Whatever affects religion in any country, must affect the state or government of that country: true religion alone can dispose men to civil obedience. Therefore, it is the interest of every state to protect and encourage religion. It would certainly be ruinous to true religion, to make the state dependent on the Church; nor should the Church be dependent on the state. Let them mutually support each other; and let the state rule by the *laws*, and the Church live by the *Bible*.

CHAPTER XXVII

An account of the twelve *captains who were over the monthly course of* twenty-four thousand *men; each captain serving* one *month in turn,* 1. *The names of the* twelve, *and the months in which they served,* 2–15. *The names of the rulers of the* twelve *tribes,* 16–22. *The reasons why the whole number of Israel and Judah had not been taken,* 23, 24. *The persons who were over the king's property, treasures, fields, flocks, &c.,* 25–31. *His officers of state,* 32–34.

<table>
<tr><td>

A. M. 2989
B. C. 1015
An. Exod. Isr.
476
Anno ante I
Olymp. 239

NOW the children of Israel after their number, *to wit,* the chief fathers and captains of thousands and hundreds, and their officers that served the king in any mat-

</td><td>

ter of the courses, which came in and went out month by month throughout all the months of the year, of every course *were* twenty and four thousand.

A. M. 2989
B. C. 1015
An. Exod. Isr.
476
Anno ante I.
Olymp. 239

</td></tr>
</table>

NOTES ON CHAP. XXVII

Verse 1. *The chief fathers and captains of thousands*] The patriarchs, chief generals, or generals of brigade. This enumeration is widely different from the preceding. In *that,* we have the orders and courses of the *priests* and the *Levites* in their *ecclesiastical* ministrations; in *this,* we have the account of the order of the *civil* service, that which related simply to the *political state* of the king and the kingdom. Twenty-four persons, chosen out of David's

worthies, each of whom had a second, were placed over *twenty-four thousand* men, who all served a month in turn at a time; and this was the whole of their service during the year, after which they attended to their own affairs. Thus the king had always on foot a regular force of *twenty-four thousand,* who served without expense to him or the state, and were not oppressed by the service, which took up only a *twelfth* part of their time; and by this plan he could at any time, when the exigency of the state required it, bring into the field *twelve*

A. M. 2989
B. C. 1015
An. Exod. Isr.
476
Anno ante I.
Olymp. 239

2 Over the first course for the first month *was* [a]Jashobeam the son of Zabdiel: and in his course *were* twenty and four thousand.

3 Of the children of Perez *was* the chief of all the captains of the host for the first month.

4 And over the course of the second month *was* [b]Dodai an Ahohite, and of his course *was* Mikloth also the ruler: in his course likewise *were* twenty and four thousand.

5 The third captain of the host for the third month *was* Benaiah the son of Jehoiada, a [c]chief priest: and in his course *were* twenty and four thousand.

6 This *is that* Benaiah, *who was* [d]mighty among the thirty, and above the thirty: and in his course *was* Ammizabad his son.

7 The fourth *captain* for the fourth month *was* [e]Asahel the brother of Joab, and Zebadiah his son after him: and in his course *were* twenty and four thousand.

8 The fifth *captain* for the fifth month *was* Shamhuth the Izrahite: and in his course *were* twenty and four thousand.

9 The sixth *captain* for the sixth month *was* [f]Ira the son of Ikkesh the Tekoite: and in his course *were* twenty and four thousand.

10 The seventh *captain* for the seventh month *was* [g]Helez the Pelonite, of the children of Ephraim: and in his course *were* twenty and four thousand.

A. M. 2989
B. C. 1015
An. Exod. Isr.
476
Anno ante I.
Olymp. 239

11 The eighth *captain* for the eighth month *was* [h]Sibbecai the Hushathite, of the Zarhites: and in his course *were* twenty and four thousand.

12 The ninth *captain* for the ninth month *was* [i]Abiezer the Anetothite, of the Benjamites: and in his course *were* twenty and four *thousand.*

13 The tenth *captain* for the tenth month *was* [k]Maharai the Netophathite, of the Zarhites: and in his course *were* twenty and four thousand.

14 The eleventh *captain* for the eleventh month *was* [l]Benaiah the Pirathonite, of the children of Ephraim: and in his course *were* twenty and four thousand.

15 The twelfth *captain* for the twelfth month *was* [m]Heldai the Netophathite, of Othniel: and in his course *were* twenty and four thousand.

16 Furthermore over the tribes of Israel: the ruler of the Reubenites *was* Eliezer the son of Zichri: of the Simeonites, Shephatiah the son of Maachah:

17 Of the Levites, [n]Hashabiah the son of Kemuel: of the Aaronites, Zadok:

18 Of Judah, [o]Elihu, *one* of the brethren of David: of Issachar, Omri the son of Michael:

19 Of Zebulun, Ishmaiah the son of Obadiah: of Naphtali, Jerimoth the son of Azriel:

---

[a]2 Sam. xxiii. 8; chap. xi. 11——[b]Or, *Dodo*, 2 Sam. xxiii. 9——[c]Or, *principal officer*, 1 Kings iv. 5——[d]2 Sam. xxiii. 20, 22, 23; chap. xi. 22, &c.——[e]2 Sam. xxiii. 24; chap. xi. 26

[f]Chap. xi. 28——[g]Chap. xi. 27——[h]2 Sam. xxi. 18; chap. xi. 29——[i]Chap. xi. 28——[k]2 Sam. xxiii. 28; chap. xi. 30——[l]Chap. xi. 31——[m]Or, *Heled*, chap. xi. 30——[n]Chap. xxvi. 30——[o]1 Sam. xvi. 6, *Eliab*

---

times *twenty-four thousand*, or *two hundred and eighty-eight thousand* fighting men, independently of the *twelve thousand* officers, which made in the whole an effective force of *three hundred thousand* soldiers; and all these men were prepared, disciplined, and ready at a call, without the smallest expense to the state or the king. These were, properly speaking, the *militia* of the Israelitish kingdom. See *Calmet.*

Verse 2. *First course for the first month*] Instead of mentioning *first, second, third, &c., month*, the *Targum* names them thus: *First month, Nisan; second, Aiyar; third, Sivan; fourth, Tammuz; fifth, Ab; sixth, Elul; seventh, Tishri; eighth, Marchesvan; ninth, Cisleu; tenth, Tebeth; eleventh, Shebat; twelfth, Adar.* No mention is made of a *veadar* or intercalary month.

Verse 5. *Benaiah the son of Jehoiada, a chief priest*] Why should not this clause be read as it is in the Hebrew? "Benaiah, the son of Jehoiada the priest, a captain; and in his course," &c. Or, as the *Targum* has it, "The third

captain of the host for the month Sivan was Benaiah, the son of Jehoiada the priest, who was constituted a chief." He is distinguished from Benaiah, the Pirathonite, who was over the *eleventh month.* Some think that the original word הכהן *haccohen*, which generally signifies *priest*, should be translated here a *principal officer;* so the *margin* has it. But, in the Old Testament, כהן *cohen* signifies both *prince* and *priest;* and translating it by the former removes the difficulty from this place, for we well know that Benaiah never was a *priest.*

Verse 7. *Asahel the brother of Joab*] This verse proves that the division and arrangement mentioned above were made *before* David was acknowledged king in Hebron; for Asahel, the brother of Joab, who was fourth captain, was slain by *Abner*, while Ishbosheth reigned over Israel at Mahanaim, 2 Sam. ii. 19-23.

Verse 16. *Over the tribes of Israel*] In this enumeration there is no mention of the tribes of Asher and Gad. Probably the account of these has been lost from this register. These rulers

A. M. 2989
B. C. 1015
An. Exod. Isr.
476
Anno ante I.
Olymp. 239

20 Of the children of Ephraim, Hoshea the son of Azaziah: of the half tribe of Manasseh, Joel the son of Pedaiah:

21 Of the half *tribe* of Manasseh in Gilead, Iddo the son of Zechariah: of Benjamin, Jaasiel the son of Abner:

22 Of Dan, Azareel the son of Jeroham. These *were* the princes of the tribes of Israel.

23 But David took not the number of them from twenty years old and under: because Pthe LORD had said he would increase Israel like to the stars of the heavens.

A. M. 2987
B. C. 1017
An. Exod. Isr.
474
Anno ante I.
Olymp. 241

24 Joab the son of Zeruiah began to number, but he finished not, because qthere fell wrath for it against Israel; neither rwas the number put in the account of the chronicles of king David.

A. M. 2989
B. C. 1015
An. Exod. Isr.
476
Anno ante I.
Olymp. 239

25 And over the king's treasures *was* Azmaveth the son of Adiel: and over the storehouses in the fields, in the cities, and in the villages, and in the castles, *was* Jehonathan the son of Uzziah:

26 And over them that did the work of the field for tillage of the ground *was* Ezri the son of Chelub:

27 And over the vineyards *was* Shimei the Ramathite: sover the increase of the vineyards for the wine cellars *was* Zabdi the Shiphmite:

A. M. 2989
B. C. 1015
An. Exod. Isr.
476
Anno ante I.
Olymp. 239

28 And over the olive-trees and the sycamore-trees that *were* in the low plains *was* Baal-hanan the Gederite: and over the cellars of oil *was* Joash:

29 And over the herds that fed in Sharon *was* Shitrai the Sharonite: and over the herds *that were* in the valleys *was* Shaphat the son of Adlai:

30 Over the camels also *was* Obil the Ishmaelite: and over the asses *was* Jehdeiah the Meronothite:

31 And over the flocks *was* Jaziz the Hagerite. All these *were* the rulers of the substance which *was* king David's.

32 Also Jonathan David's uncle was a counsellor, a wise man, and a tscribe: and Jehiel the uson of Hachmoni *was* with the king's sons.

33 And vAhithophel *was* the king's counsellor; and wHushai the Archite *was* the king's companion:

34 And after Ahithophel *was* Jehoiada the son of Benaiah, and xAbiathar: and the general of the king's army *was* yJoab.

PGen. xv. 5——q2 Sam. xxiv. 15; ch. xxi. 7——rHeb. *ascended*——sHeb. *over that which* was *of the vineyards*

tOr, *secretary*——uOr, *Hachmonite*——v2 Sam. xv. 12 w2 Sam. xv. 37; xvi. 16——x1 Kings i. 7——yCh. xi. 6

---

appear to have been all honorary men, without pay, like the lords lieutenants of our counties.

Verse 24. *Neither was the number put in the account*] Joab did not return the whole number; probably the plague began before he had finished: or, he did not choose to give it in, as he had entered on this work with extreme reluctance; and he did not choose to tell the king how numerous they were.

Verses 25-31. *Over the king's treasures*] We see from these verses in what the *personal property* of David consisted:—1. Treasures, gold, silver, &c. 2. Goods and grain in castles, cities, villages, and in the fields. 3. Vineyards and their produce. 4. Olive-trees and their produce. 5. Neat cattle, in different districts. 6. Camels and asses: they had no horses. 7. Flocks, sheep, goats, &c.

Verse 34. *And after Ahithophel*] The Tar-

gum is curious: "When they went to war, they asked counsel of Ahithophel; and, after the counsel of Ahithophel, they inquired by Urim and Thummim of Jehoiada, the son of Benaiah, prince of the Sanhedrin, and chief of the priesthood; and from Abiathar, the high priest. And after they had inquired by Urim and Thummim, they went out to battle, well armed with bows and slings; and Joab, the general of the king's troops, led them on." It is worthy of remark, that Obil, an Ishmaelite or Arab, was put over the camels, which is a creature of Arabia; and that Jaziz, a Hagarene, (the Hagarenes were shepherds by profession,) was put over the flocks: nothing went by favour; each was appointed to the office for which he was best qualified; and thus men of worth were encouraged, and the public service effectually promoted.

CHAPTER XXVIII

David assembles the princes of Israel, and informs them that the temple was to be built by Solomon; to whom God had given the most gracious promises, 1-7. He exhorts them and him to be obedient to God, that they might continue to prosper, 8-10. He gives Solomon a pattern of the work, 11, 12; directs him concerning the courses of the priests and Levites, 13; gives also gold, by weight, for the different utensils of the temple, as God had directed him, 14-19; encourages Solomon to undertake the work, 20, 21.

A. M. 2989
B. C. 1015
An. Exod. Isr.
476
Anno ante I.
Olymp. 239

AND David assembled all the princes of Israel, [a]the princes of the tribes, and [b]the captains of the companies that ministered to the king by course, and the captains over the thousands, and captains over the hundreds, and [c]the stewards over all the substance and [d]possession of the king, [e]and of his sons, with the [f]officers, and with [g]the mighty men, and with all the valiant men, unto Jerusalem.

2 Then David the king stood up upon his feet, and said, Hear me, my brethren, and my people: *As for me,* [h]I *had* in mine heart to build a house of rest for the ark of the covenant of the Lord, and for [i]the footstool of our God, and had made ready for the building:

3 But God said unto me, [k]Thou shalt not build a house for my name, because thou *hast been* a man of war, and hast shed [l]blood.

4 Howbeit the Lord God of Israel [m]chose me before all the house of my father to be king over Israel for ever: for he hath chosen [n]Judah *to be* the ruler; and of the house of Judah, [o]the house of my father; and [p]among the sons of my father he liked me to make *me* king over all Israel:

5 [q]And of all my sons, (for the Lord hath given me many sons,) [r]he hath chosen Solomon my son to sit upon the throne of the kingdom of the Lord over Israel.

A. M. 2989
B. C. 1015
An. Exod. Isr.
476
Anno ante I.
Olymp. 239

6 And he said unto me, [s]Solomon thy son, he shall build my house and my courts: for I have chosen him *to be* my son, and I will be his father.

7 Moreover I will establish his kingdom for ever, [t]if he be [u]constant to do my commandments and my judgments, as at this day.

8 Now therefore in the sight of all Israel, the congregation of the Lord, and in the audience of our God, keep and seek for all the commandments of the Lord your God: that ye may possess this good land, and leave *it* for an inheritance for your children after you for ever.

9 And thou, Solomon my son, [v]know thou the God of thy father, and serve him [w]with a perfect heart and with a willing mind: for [x]the Lord searcheth all hearts, and understandeth all the imaginations of the thoughts: [y]if thou seek him, he will be found of thee; but if thou forsake him, he will cast thee off for ever.

10 Take heed now; [z]for the Lord hath chosen thee to build a house for the sanctuary; be strong, and do *it.*

11 Then David gave to Solomon his son [a]the pattern of the porch, and of the houses thereof, and of the treasuries thereof, and of

---

[a]Ch. xxvii. 16——[b]Ch. xxvii. 1, 2——[c]Ch. xxvii. 25 [d]Or, *cattle*——[e]Or, *and his sons*——[f]Or, *eunuchs* [g]Ch. xi. 10——[h]2 Sam. vii. 2; Psa. cxxxii. 3, 4, 5 [i]Psa. xcix. 5; cxxxii. 7——[k]2 Sam. vii. 5, 13; 1 Kings v. 3; ch. xvii. 4; xxii. 8——[l]Heb. *bloods*——[m]1 Sam. xvi. 7-13——[n]Gen. xlix. 8; ch. v. 2; Psa. lx. 7; lxxviii. 68 [o]1 Sam. xxvi. 1——[p]1 Sam. xvi. 12, 13

[q]Chap. iii. 1, &c.; xxiii. 1——[r]Ch. xxii. 9——[s]2 Sam. vii. 13, 14; ch. xxii. 9, 10; 2 Chron. i. 9——[t]Ch. xxii. 13 [u]Heb. *strong*——[v]Jer. ix. 24; Hos. iv. 1; John xvii. 3 [w]2 Kings xx. 3; Psa. ci. 2——[x]1 Sam. xvi. 7; 1 Kings viii. 39; ch. xxix. 17; Psa. vii. 9; cxxxix. 2; Prov. xvii. 3; Jer. xi. 20; xvii. 10; xx. 12; Rev. ii. 23——[y]2 Chron. xv. 2——[z]Ver. 6——[a]See Exod. xxv. 40; ver. 19

NOTES ON CHAP. XXVIII

Verse 1. *David assembled*] This refers to the persons whose names and offices we have seen in the preceding chapter.

Verse 2. *David—stood up upon his feet*] He was now very old, and chiefly confined to his bed, (see 1 Kings i. 47;) and while he was addressing his son Solomon, he continued on the bed; but when all the principal nobles of his kingdom came before him he received strength to arise and address them, standing on his feet.

Verse 3. *Thou shalt not build a house*] See 2 Sam. vii. 5, 13, and the observations at the end of that chapter.

Verse 4. *Over Israel for ever*] The government should have no end, provided they continued to walk according to the commandments of God; see ver. 7. The government, as referring to Christ, is, and will be, *without end.*

Verse 8. *In the audience of our God*] "Before the Word of the Lord."—*T.*

Verse 10. *The Lord hath chosen thee*] "The Word of the Lord hath chosen thee."—*T.*

Verse 11. *David gave to Solomon—the pattern*] He gave him an ichnograph of the building, with elevations, sections, and specifications of every part; and all this he received by inspiration from God himself, (see ver. 12 and 19,) just as Moses had received the plan of the tabernacle.

The treasuries thereof] נגזכיו *ganzaccaiv.* The word נגזך *ganzach* is not Hebrew, but is supposed to be *Persian,* the same word being found in Ezra iii. 19. In this tongue we have the word 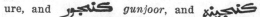 *ganj,* a granary, a hidden treasure, and كنجور *gunjoor,* and كنجينه *gunjineh,* a treasure, treasury, or barn. *Parkhurst* supposes that it is compounded of גנז *ganaz,* to treasure up, and זך *zach,* pure; *a treasury for the most precious things.*

A. M. 2989
B. C. 1015
An. Exod. Isr.
476
Anno ante I.
Olymp. 239
the upper chamber thereof, and of the inner parlours thereof, and of the place of the mercy-seat,

12 And the pattern [b]of all that he had by the Spirit, of the courts of the house of the LORD, and of all the chambers round about, [c]of the treasuries of the house of God, and of the treasuries of the dedicated things:

13 Also for the courses of the priests and the Levites, and for all the work of the service of the house of the LORD, and for all the vessels of service in the house of the LORD.

14 *He gave* of gold by weight for *things* of gold, for all instruments of all manner of service; *silver also* for all instruments of silver by weight, for all instruments of every kind of service:

15 Even the weight for the candlesticks of gold, and for their lamps of gold, by weight for every candlestick, and for the lamps thereof: and for the candlesticks of silver by weight, *both* for the candlestick, and *also* for the lamps thereof, according to the use of every candlestick.

16 And by weight *he gave* gold for the tables of shew-bread, for every table; and *likewise* silver for the tables of silver:

17 Also pure gold for the flesh-hooks, and the bowls, and the cups: and for the golden basons *he gave gold* by weight for every bason; and *likewise silver* by weight for every bason of silver:

A. M. 2989
B. C. 1015
An. Exod. Isr
476
Anno ante I.
Olymp. 239

18 And for the altar of incense refined gold by weight; and gold for the pattern of the chariot of the [d]cherubims, that spread out *their wings,* and covered the ark of the covenant of the LORD.

19 All *this, said David,* [e]the LORD made me understand in writing by *his* hand upon me, *even* all the works of this pattern.

20 And David said to Solomon his son, [f]Be strong and of good courage, and do *it:* fear not, nor be dismayed: for the LORD God, *even* my God, *will be* with thee; [g]he will not fail thee, nor forsake thee, until thou hast finished all the work for the service of the house of the LORD.

21 And, behold, [h]the courses of the priests and the Levites, *even they shall be with thee* for all the service of the house of God: and *there shall be* with thee for all manner of workmanship [i]every willing skilful man, for any manner of service: also the princes and all the people *will be* wholly at thy commandment.

---

[b]Heb, *of all that was with him*——[c]Chap. xxvi. 20
[d]Exod. xxv. 18–22; 1 Sam. iv. 4; 1 Kings vi. 23, &c.
[e]See Exod. xxv. 40; ver. 11, 12

[f]Deut. xxxi. 7, 8; Josh. i. 6, 7, 9; chap. xxii. 13
[g]Josh. i. 5——[h]Chap. xxiv., xxv., xxvi.——[i]Exod. xxxv. 25, 26; xxxvi. 1, 2

Verse 12. *All that he had by the Spirit*] "By the Spirit of prophecy that was with him."—*T.*

Verse 14. *Of gold by weight*] The quantity of gold which was to be put in *each article.*

Verse 15. *For the candlesticks*] There was but *one* chandelier in the tabernacle; there were *ten* in the temple. See 1 Kings vii. 49.

Verse 18. *The chariot of the cherubims*] "And the figure of the chariot, like to the figure of the propitiatory, where are the figures of the golden cherubim, extending their wings and covering the ark of the covenant of the Lord."—*T.*

Verse 19. *Understand in writing*] In some vision of ecstasy he had seen a regularly sketched out plan, which had made so deep an impression on his mind that he could readily describe it to his son.

"That the architecture of the temple," says Dr. Delaney, "was of Divine origin, I, for my part, am fully satisfied from this passage, and am confirmed in this opinion by finding from *Vilalpandus* that the Roman, at least the Greek, architecture is derived from this, as from its fountain; and in my humble opinion even an infidel may easily believe these to be of Divine original, inasmuch as they are, at least the latter is, found perfect in the earliest models; nor hath the utmost reach of human wisdom, invention, and industry, been ever able to improve it, or alter it but to disadvantage, through the course of so many ages."

Verse 20. *The Lord God—my God,* will be *with thee*] "The Word of the Lord my God will be thy assistant."—*T.*

Verse 21. *Behold, the courses of the priests*] The priests and the Levites, the cunning artificers, and the princes of the people, will be at thy command. Thus David, having assigned him his work, and described the manner in which it was to be done, shows him who were to be his assistants in it, and encourages him in the great undertaking.

Here we find piety, good sense, prudence, zeal for the public welfare and God's glory, the strongest attachments to the worship of Jehovah, and concern for the ordinances of religion, all united; and Solomon has his danger, his duty, and his interest placed before him in the truest and most impressive light by his pious and sensible father.

CHAPTER XXIX

David enumerates the gifts which he designed for the building of the temple; and exhorts the princes and people to make their offerings, 1–5. They offer willingly, and to a great amount, 6–9. David's thanksgiving and prayer to God on the occasion, 10–19. The princes and people praise God, offer sacrifices and feasts before him, make Solomon king, and do him homage, 20–24. The Lord magnifies Solomon, 25. Concluding account of David's reign, character, and death, 26–30.

A. M. 2989
B. C. 1015
An. Exod. Isr.
476
Anno ante
I. Olymp. 239

FURTHERMORE David the king said unto all the congregation, Solomon my son, whom God alone hath chosen, *is yet* ᵃyoung and tender, and the work *is* great: for the palace *is* not for man, but for the LORD God.

2 Now I have prepared with all my might for the house of my God the gold for *things to be made* of gold, and the silver for *things* of silver, and the brass for *things* of brass, the iron for *things* of iron, and wood for *things* of wood: ᵇonyx stones, and *stones* to be set, glistering stones, and of divers colours, and all manner of precious stones, and marble stones in abundance.

3 Moreover, because I have set my affection to the house of my God, I have of mine own proper good, of gold and silver, *which* I have given to the house of my God, over and above all that I have prepared for the holy house,

4 *Even* three thousand talents of gold, of the gold of ᶜOphir, and seven thousand talents of refined silver, to overlay the walls of the houses *withal*:

5 The gold for *things* of gold, and the silver for *things* of silver, and for all manner of work *to be made* by the hands of artificers. And who *then* is willing ᵈto consecrate his service this day unto the LORD?

A. M. 2989
B. C. 1015
An. Exod. Isr.
476
Anno ante
I. Olymp. 239

6 Then ᵉthe chief of the fathers and princes of the tribes of Israel, and the captains of thousands and of hundreds, with ᶠthe rulers of the king's work, offered willingly,

7 And gave for the service of the house of God of gold five thousand talents, and ten thousand drams, and of silver ten thousand talents, and of brass eighteen thousand talents, and one hundred thousand talents of iron.

8 And they with whom *precious* stones were found gave *them* to the treasure of the house of the LORD, by the hand of ᵍJehiel the Gershonite.

9 Then the people rejoiced, for that they offered willingly, because with perfect heart they ʰoffered willingly to the LORD: and David the king also rejoiced with great joy.

10 Wherefore David blessed the LORD before all the congregation: and David said,

---

ᵃ1 Kings iii. 7; chap. xxii. 5; Prov. iv. 3——ᵇSee Isa. liv. 11, 12; Rev. xxi. 18, &c.——ᶜ1 Kings ix. 28

ᵈHeb. *to fill his hand*——ᵉChap. xxvii. 1——ᶠChap. xxvii. 25, &c.——ᵍChap. xxvi. 21——ʰ2 Cor. ix. 7

NOTES ON CHAP. XXIX

Verse 1. *The palace is not for man*] "The palace is not prepared for the name of a son of man, but for the name of the Word of the Lord God."—*T*.

Verse 2. *And marble stones*] אבני שיש *abney shayish*, which the Vulgate translates *marmor Parium, Parian marble. Paros* was one of the Cyclade islands, and produced the *whitest* and *finest* marble, that of which most of the finest works of antiquity have been made. That the word *shaish* means *marble* is probable from the Chaldee, which has אבני מרמורייה *abney marmoraiyah, marble stones.* Josephus says that the temple was built of large blocks of white marble, beautifully polished, so as to produce a most splendid appearance.—Jos., *De Bell. Jud.*, lib. v., c. 5, s. 2.

Verse 5. *To consecrate his service*] למלאות ידו *lemalloth yado, to fill his hand;* to bring an offering to the Lord.

Verse 7. *Of gold five thousand talents*] These, at *five thousand and seventy-five pounds, fifteen shillings, and seven pence halfpenny* each,

amount to *twenty-five millions, three hundred and seventy-eight thousand nine hundred and six pounds, five shillings,* sterling. If, with Dr. Prideaux, we estimate the golden talent at upwards of *seven thousand pounds* sterling, the value of these *five thousand talents* will be much more considerable. See the notes on Exod. xxv. 39; Matt. xviii. 24; and the calculations at the end of the notes on 2 Chron. ix.

Ten thousand drams] Probably golden *darics*, worth each about *twenty shillings*, amounting to *ten thousand pounds.*

Of silver ten thousand talents] These, at *three hundred and fifty-three pounds, eleven shillings, and ten-pence halfpenny,* each, amount to *three millions five hundred and thirty-five thousand, nine hundred and thirty-seven pounds, ten shillings,* sterling.

Brass eighteen thousand talents] Each *six hundred and fifty-seven thousand talents,* amount to *one thousand and twenty-six tons, eleven hundred weight, and one quarter.*

One hundred thousand talents of iron] Each *six hundred and fifty-seven thousand grains,* amount to *five thousand seven hundred and three tons, two hundred weight, and a half.*

A. M. 2989
B. C. 1015
An. Exod. Isr. 476
Anno ante I. Olymp. 239

Blessed *be* thou, LORD God of Israel our father, for ever and ever.
11 [i]Thine, O LORD, *is* the greatness, and the power, and the glory, and the victory, and the majesty: for all *that is* in the heaven and in the earth *is thine;* thine *is* the kingdom, O LORD, and thou art exalted as head above all.
12 [k]Both riches and honour *come* of thee, and thou reignest over all; and in thine hand *is* power and might; and in thine hand *it is* to make great, and to give strength unto all.
13 Now therefore, our God, we thank thee, and praise thy glorious name.
14 But who *am* I, and what *is* my people, that we should be [l]able to offer so willingly after this sort? for all things *come* of thee, and [m]of thine own have we given thee.
15 For [n]we *are* strangers before thee, and sojourners, as *were* all our fathers: [o]our days on the earth *are* as a shadow, and *there is* none [p]abiding.
16 O LORD our God, all this store that we have prepared to build thee a house for thine holy name *cometh* of thine hand, and *is* all thine own.
17 I know also, my God, that thou [q]triest the heart, and [r]hast pleasure in uprightness. As for me, in the uprightness of mine heart I have willingly offered all these things: and now have I seen with joy thy people, which are [s]present here, to offer willingly unto thee.
18 O LORD God of Abraham, Isaac, and of Israel, our fathers, keep this for ever in the imagination of the thoughts of the heart of thy people, and [t]prepare their heart unto thee:
19 And [u]give unto Solomon my son a perfect heart, to keep thy commandments, thy testimonies, and thy statutes, and to do all *these things,* and to build the palace, *for* the which [v]I have made provision.
20 And David said to all the congregation, Now bless the LORD your God. And all the congregation blessed the LORD God of their fathers, and bowed down their heads, and worshipped the LORD, and the king.
21 And they sacrificed sacrifices unto the LORD, and offered burnt-offerings unto the

A. M. 2989
B. C. 1015
An. Exod. Isr. 476
Anno ante I. Olymp. 239

[i]Matthew vi. 13; 1 Timothy i. 17; Revelation v. 13 — [k]Romans xi. 36 — [l]Heb. *retain* or *obtain strength* — [m]Heb. *of thine hand* — [n]Chapter xxxix. 12; Hebrews xi. 13; 1 Peter ii. 11 — [o]Job xiv. 2; Psalm xc. 9; cii. 11; cxliv. 4 — [p]Heb. *expectation* — [q]1 Samuel xvi. 7; chap. xxviii. 9 — [r]Prov. xi. 20 — [s]Or, *found* — [t]Or, *stablish,* Psalm x. 17 — [u]Psalm lxxii. 1 — [v]Ver. 2; chap. xxii. 14

Verse 11. *Thine, O Lord,* is *the greatness*] This verse is thus paraphrased by the *Targum:* "*Thine, O Lord, is the magnificence;* for thou hast created the world by thy *great power,* and by thy *might* hast led our fathers out of Egypt, and with great signs hast caused them to pass through the Red Sea. Thou hast appeared *gloriously* on Mount Sinai, with troops of angels, in giving law to thy people. Thou hast *gained the victory* over Amalek; over Sihon and Og, kings of Canaan. By the splendour of thy majesty thou hast caused the sun to stand still on Gibeon, and the moon in the valley of Ajalon, until thy people, the house of Israel, were avenged of their enemies. All things that are in *heaven and earth* are the work of thy hands, and thou *rulest* over and *sustainest* whatsoever is in the heavens and in the earth. Thine, O Lord, is the *kingdom* in the firmament; and thou art *exalted* above the heavenly angels, and over all who are constituted *rulers* upon earth."

Verse 14. *Of thine own have we given thee.*] "For from thy presence all good comes, and of the blessings of thy hands have we given thee." —*Targum.*

Verse 15. *For we* are *strangers*] We have here neither *right* nor *property.*

And sojourners] Lodging as it were for a *night,* in the mansion of another.

As were all our fathers] These were, as we are, supported by thy bounty, and tenants at will to thee.

Our days on the earth are *as a shadow*] They are continually *declining, fading,* and *passing away.* This is the place of our sojourning, and here we have no *substantial,* permanent residence.

There is *none abiding.*] However we may wish to settle and remain in this state of things, it is impossible, because every earthly form is passing swiftly away, all is in a state of revolution and decay, and there is no abiding, מקוה *mikveh,* no *expectation,* that we shall be exempt from those changes and chances to which our fathers were subjected. "As the shadow of a bird flying in the air [אויר *avir*] of heaven, such are our days upon the earth; nor is there any *hope* to any son of man that he shall live for ever."—*Targum.*

Verse 18. *Keep this for ever*] All the good dispositions which myself and my people have, came from thee; continue to support and strengthen them by the same grace by which they have been inspired!

Verse 19. *Give unto Solomon—a perfect heart*] This he did, but Solomon abused his mercies.

Verse 20. *Worshipped the Lord, and the king.*] They did reverence to God as the *supreme Ruler,* and to the king as his *deputy.*

Verse 21. *With their drink-offerings*] The *Targum* says *a thousand drink-offerings,* making these *libations* equal in number to the other offerings.

And sacrifices] These were *peace-offerings,*

A. M. 2989
B. C. 1015
An. Exod. Isr. 476
Anno ante
I. Olymp. 239

LORD, on the morrow after that day, *even* a thousand bullocks, a thousand rams, *and* a thousand lambs, with their drink-offerings, and sacrifices in abundance for all Israel:

22 And did eat and drink before the LORD on that day with great gladness. And they made Solomon the son of David king the second time, and ʷanointed *him* unto the LORD *to be* the chief governor, and Zadok *to be* priest.

23 Then Solomon sat on the throne of the LORD as king instead of David his father, and prospered: and all Israel obeyed him.

24 And all the princes, and the mighty men, and all the sons likewise of King David, ˣsubmitted ʸthemselves unto Solomon the king.

25 And the LORD magnified Solomon exceedingly in the sight of all Israel, and ᶻbestowed upon him *such* royal majesty as had not

been on any king before him in Israel.

A. M. 2989
B. C. 1015
An. Exod. Isr. 476
Anno ante
I. Olymp. 239

26 Thus David the son of Jesse reigned over all Israel.

27 ᵃAnd the time that he reigned over Israel *was* forty years; ᵇseven years reigned he in Hebron, and thirty and three *years* reigned he in Jerusalem.

28 And he ᶜdied in a good old age, ᵈfull of days, riches, and honour: and Solomon his son reigned in his stead.

29 Now the acts of David the king, first and last, behold they *are* written in the ᵉbook ᶠof Samuel the seer, and in the book of Nathan the prophet, and in the book of Gad the seer,

30 With all his reign and his might, ᵍand the times that went over him, and over Israel, and over all the kingdoms of the countries.

ʷ1 Kings i. 35, 39——ˣEccles. viii. 2——ʸHeb. *gave the hand under Solomon.* See Gen. xxiv. 2; xlvii 29; 2 Chron. xxx. 8; Ezek. xvii. 18——ᶻ1 Kings iii. 13;

2 Chron. i. 12; Eccles. ii. 9——ᵃ2 Sam. v. 4; 1 Kings ii. 11——ᵇ2 Sam. v. 5——ᶜGen. xxv. 8——ᵈChap. xxiii. 1 ᵉOr, *history*——ᶠHeb. *words*——ᵍDan. ii. 21

---

offered for the people, and on the flesh of which they feasted.

Verse 22. *They made Solomon—king the second time*] The *first* time of his being anointed and proclaimed king was when his brother Adonijah affected the throne; and Zadok, Nathan, and Benaiah anointed and proclaimed him in a hurry, and without pomp. See 1 Kings i. 39. Now that all is quiet, and David his father dead, (for he was probably so at the time of the second anointing,) they anointed and proclaimed him afresh, with due ceremonies, sacrifices, &c.

To be *the chief governor*] To be the vicegerent or deputy of Jehovah; for God never gave up his right of king in Israel; those called kings were only his lieutenants: hence it is said, ver. 23, "that Solomon sat on *the throne of the Lord* as king instead of David his father."

Verse 24. *Submitted themselves*] נתנו יד תחת שלמה *nathenu yad tachath Shelomoh.* "They gave the hand under Solomon;" they *swore fealty* to him. We have already seen that *putting the hand under the thigh (super sectionem circumcisionis)* was the *form* of taking an oath. See the note on Gen. xxiv. 9.

Verse 28. *And he died*] David, at his death, had every thing that his heart could wish. 1. A *good old age;* having lived as long as living could be desirable, and having in the main enjoyed good health. 2. *Full of days;* having lived till he saw every thing that he lived for either accomplished or in a state of forwardness. 3. *Full of riches;* witness the immense sums left for the temple. 4. *Full of honour;* having gained more renown than any crowned head ever did, either before his time or since—laurels that are fresh to the present hour.

Verse 29. *The acts of David—first and last*] Those which concerned him in *private life,* as well as those which grew out of his *regal* government. All these were written by *three* emi-

nent men, personally acquainted with him through the principal part of his life; these were *Samuel* and *Gad* the seers, and *Nathan* the prophet. These writings are all lost, except the particulars interspersed in the books of *Samuel, Kings,* and *Chronicles,* none of which are the records mentioned here.

Verse 30. *The times that went over him*] The transactions of his reign, and the occurrences and vicissitudes in his own kingdom, as well as those which were *over all the kingdoms of the countries,* i. e., in the surrounding nations, in most of which David had a share during his forty years' reign. Relative to the *character* of David, see a few remarks in the note on 1 Kings ii. 10; and see more at the end of the *Psalms.*

Dr. Delaney gives a just view of his character in a few words: "To sum up all, David was a true believer, a zealous adorer of God, teacher of his law and worship, and inspirer of his praise. A glorious example, a perpetual and inexhaustible fountain of true piety. A consummate and unequalled hero; a skilful and fortunate captain; a steady patriot; a wise ruler; a faithful, generous, and magnanimous friend; and, what is yet rarer, a no less generous and magnanimous enemy. A true penitent a divine musician, a sublime poet, and an inspired prophet. By birth, a *peasant;* by merit, a *prince;* in youth, a *hero;* in manhood, a *monarch;* and in age, a *saint.*" The matter of Uriah and Bath-sheba is his great but only *blot!* There he sinned deeply; and no man ever suffered more in his body, soul, and domestic affairs, than he did in consequence. His penitence was as deep and as extraordinary as his crime; and nothing could surpass both but that eternal mercy that took away the guilt, assuaged the sorrow, and restored this most humbled transgressor to character, holiness, and happiness. Let the God of David be exalted for ever!

THE SECOND BOOK

OF

THE CHRONICLES

Chronological Notes relative to this Book

Year from the Creation, according to the English Bible, 2989.—Year before the Incarnation, 1015.—Year before the first Olympiad, 239.—Year before the building of Rome, according to Varro, 262.—Year of the Julian period, 3699.—Year of the Dionysian period, 507.—Cycle of the Sun, 3.—Cycle of the Moon, 13.—Year of Acastus, the second perpetual archon of the Athenians, 31.—Pyritiades was king over the Assyrians about this time, according to Scaliger and others. He was the *thirty-seventh* monarch, including Belus, according to Africanus; and the *thirty-third* according to Eusebius.—Year of Alba Sylvius, the sixth king of the Latins, 15.—Year of Solomon, king of the Hebrews, 1.

CHAPTER I

Solomon, and the chiefs of the congregation, go to Gibeon, where was the tabernacle of the Lord, and the brazen altar; and there he offers a thousand sacrifices, 1–6. The Lord appears to him in a dream, and gives him permission to ask any gift, 7. He asks wisdom, 8–10, which is granted; and riches, wealth, and honour besides, 11, 12. His kingdom is established, 13. His chariots, horsemen, and horses, 14. His abundant riches, 15. He brings horses, linen yarn, and chariots, at a fixed price, out of Egypt, 16, 17.

A. M. 2989
B. C. 1015
An. Exod. Isr.
476
Anno ante
I. Olymp. 239

AND [a]Solomon the son of David was strengthened in his kingdom, and [b]the LORD his God *was* with him, and [c]magnified him exceedingly.

2 Then Solomon spake unto all Israel, to [d]the captains of thousands and of hundreds, and to the judges, and to every governor of all Israel, the chief of the fathers.

3 So Solomon, and all the congregation with him, went to the high place that *was* at [e]Gibeon; for there was the tabernacle of the congregation of God, which Moses the servant of the LORD had made in the wilderness.

4 [f]But the ark of God had David brought up from Kirjath-jearim to *the place which* David had prepared for it: for he had pitched a tent for it at Jerusalem.

A. M. 2989
B. C. 1015
An. Exod. Isr.
476
Anno ante
I. Olymp. 239

5 Moreover [g]the brazen altar, that [h]Bezaleel the son of Uri, the son of Hur, had made, [i]he put before the tabernacle of the LORD: and Solomon and the congregation sought unto it.

6 And Solomon went up thither to the brazen altar before the LORD, which *was* at the tabernacle of the congregation, and [k]offered a thousand burnt-offerings upon it.

7 [l]In that night did God appear unto Solomon, and said unto him, Ask what I shall give thee.

---

[a]1 Kings ii. 46——[b]Gen. xxxix. 2——[c]1 Chron. xxix. 25——[d]1 Chron. xxvii. 1——[e]1 Kings iii. 4; 1 Chron. xvi. 39; xxi. 29

[f]1 Sam. vi. 2, 17; 1 Chron. xv. 1——[g]Exodus xxvii. 1, 2; xxxviii. 1, 2——[h]Exod. xxxi. 2——[i]Or, was *there* [k]1 Kings iii. 4——[l]1 Kings iii. 5, 6

NOTES ON CHAP. I

Verse 1. And Solomon the son of David] The very beginning of this book shows that it is a *continuation* of the preceding, and should not be thus formally separated from it. See the *preface* to the first book.

The Lord his God was with him] "The WORD of the Lord was his support."—*Targum.*

Verse 2. Then Solomon spake] This is sup-

posed to have taken place in the *second* year of his reign.

Verse 4. But the ark] The tabernacle and the brazen altar remained still at Gibeon; but David had brought away the ark out of the tabernacle, and placed it in a tent at Jerusalem; 2 Sam. vi. 2, 17.

Verse 5. Sought unto it.] Went to seek the Lord there.

Verse 7. In that night] The night follow-

A. M. 2989
B. C. 1015
An. Exod. Isr.
476
Anno ante
I. Olymp. 239

8 And Solomon said unto God, Thou hast showed great mercy unto David my father, and hast made me [m]to reign in his stead.

9 Now, O LORD God, let thy promise unto David my father be established: [n]for thou hast made me king over a people [o]like the dust of the earth in multitude.

10 [p]Give me now wisdom and knowledge, that I may [q]go out and come in before this people: for who can judge this thy people, *that is so* great?

11 [r]And God said to Solomon, Because this was in thine heart, and thou hast not asked riches, wealth, or honour, nor the life of thine enemies, neither yet hast asked long life; but hast asked wisdom and knowledge for thyself, that thou mayest judge my people, over whom I have made thee king:

12 Wisdom and knowledge *is* granted unto thee; and I will give thee riches, and wealth, and honour, such as [s]none of the kings have had that *have* been before thee, neither shall there any after thee have the like.

13 Then Solomon came *from his journey* to the high place that *was* at Gibeon to Jerusalem, from before the tabernacle of the congregation, and reigned over Israel.

A. M. 2989
B. C. 1015
An. Exod. Isr.
476
Anno ante
I. Olymp. 239

14 [t]And Solomon gathered chariots and horsemen: and he had a thousand and four hundred chariots, and twelve thousand horsemen, which he placed in the chariot cities, and with the king at Jerusalem.

15 [u]And the king [v]made silver and gold at Jerusalem *as plenteous* as stones, and cedar trees made he as the sycamore trees that *are* in the vale for abundance.

16 [w]And [x]Solomon had horses brought out of Egypt, and linen yarn: the king's merchants received the linen yarn at a price.

17 And they fetched up, and brought forth out of Egypt a chariot for six hundred *shekels* of silver, and a horse for a hundred and fifty: and so brought they out *horses* for all the kings of the Hittites, and for the kings of Syria, [y]by their means.

---

[m]1 Chron. xxviii. 5——[n]1 Kings iii. 7, 8——[o]Heb. *much as the dust of the earth*——[p]1 Kings iii. 9——[q]Num. xxvii. 17; Deut. xxxi. 2——[r]1 Kings iii. 11, 12, 13 [s]1 Chron. xxix. 25; chap. ix. 22; Eccles. ii. 9

[t]1 Kings iv. 26; x. 26, &c.; ch. ix. 25——[u]1 Kings x. 27; ch. ix. 27; Job xxii. 24——[v]Heb. *gave*——[w]1 Kings x. 28, 29; chap. ix. 28——[x]Heb. *the going forth of the horses which* was *Solomon's*——[y]Heb. *by their hand*

---

ing the sacrifice. On Solomon's *choice*, see the notes on 1 Kings iii. 5-15.

Verse 9. *Let thy promise*] דברך *debarcha, thy word;* פתגמך *pithgamach*, Targum. It is very remarkable that when either God or man is represented as having spoken a *word* then the noun פתגם *pithgam* is used by the *Targumist;* but when *word* is used personally, then he employs the noun מימרא *meymera*, which appears to answer to the Λογος of St. John, ch. i. 1, &c.

Verse 14. *He had a thousand and four hundred chariots*] For these numbers, see the notes on 1 Kings iv. 26.

Verse 15. *Made silver and gold*] See on 1 Kings x. 27, 28.

Verse 16. *Linen yarn*] See the note on 1 Kings x. 28, where this subject is particularly examined.

Verse 17. *A horse for a hundred and fifty*] Suppose we take the shekel at the utmost value at which it has been rated, *three shillings;* then the price of a horse was about *twenty-two pounds ten shillings.*

ON Solomon's multiplying horses, *Bishop Warburton* has made some judicious remarks:—

"Moses had expressly prohibited the multiplying of *horses*, Deut. xvii. 16, by which the future king was forbidden to establish a body of cavalry, because this could not be effected without sending into Egypt, with which people God had forbidden any communication, as this would be dangerous to religion. When Solomon had violated *this law*, and multiplied horses to excess, 1 Kings iv. 26, it was soon attended with those fatal consequences that the law foretold: for this wisest of kings having likewise, in violation of *another* law, married Pharaoh's daughter, (the early fruits of this commerce,) and then, by a repetition of the same crime, but a transgression of *another* law, having espoused more strange women, 1 Kings xi. 1; they first, in defiance of a *fourth* law, persuaded him to build them idol temples for *their use*, and afterwards, against a *fifth* law, brought him to erect other temples for his *own.* Now the original of all this mischief was the forbidden traffic with Egypt for *horses;* for thither were the agents of Solomon sent to mount his cavalry. Nay, this great king even turned factor for the neighbouring monarchs, ver. 17, and this opprobrious commerce was kept up by his successors and attended with the same pernicious consequences. Isaiah denounces the mischiefs of this traffic; and foretells that one of the good effects of leaving it would be the forsaking of their idolatries, Isa. xxxi. 1, 4, 6, 7."—See *Divine Legation*, vol. iii., p. 289 and *Dr. Dodd's* Notes.

CHAPTER II

Solomon determines to build a temple, 1. The number of his workmen, 2. Sends to Huram for artificers and materials, 3–10. Huram sends him a favourable answer, and makes an agreement with him concerning the labour to be done, and the wages to be paid to his men, 11–16. The number of strangers in the land, and how employed, 17, 18.

A. M. 2989
B. C. 1015
An. Exod. Isr.
476
Anno ante
I. Olymp. 239

AND Solomon [a]determined to build a house for the name of the LORD, and a house for his kingdom.

2 And [b]Solomon told out threescore and ten thousand men to bear burdens, and fourscore thousand to hew in the mountain, and three thousand and six hundred to oversee them.

3 And Solomon sent to [c]Huram the king of Tyre, saying, [d]As thou didst deal with David my father, and didst send him cedars to build him a house to dwell therein, *even so deal with me.*

4 Behold, [e]I build a house to the name of the LORD my God, to dedicate *it* to him, *and* [f]to burn before him [g]sweet incense, and for [h]the continual shew-bread, and for [i]the burnt-offerings morning and evening, on the Sabbaths, and on the new moons, and on the solemn feasts of the LORD our God. This *is an ordinance* for ever to Israel.

5 And the house which I build *is* great: for [k]great *is* our God above all gods.

6 [l]But who [m]is able to build him a house, seeing the heaven and heaven of heavens cannot contain him? who *am* I then, that I should build him a house, save only to burn sacrifice before him?

7 Send me now therefore a man cunning to work in gold, and in silver, and in brass, and in iron, and in purple, and crimson, and blue, and that can skill [n]to grave with the cunning men that *are* with me in Judah and in Jerusalem, [o]whom David my father did provide.

A. M. 2989
B. C. 1015
An. Exod. Isr.
476
Anno ante
I. Olymp. 239

8 [p]Send me also cedar trees, fir trees, and [q]algum trees, out of Lebanon: for I know that thy servants can skill to cut timber in Lebanon; and, behold, my servants *shall be* with thy servants,

9 Even to prepare me timber in abundance: for the house which I am about to build *shall be* [r]wonderful great.

10 [s]And, behold, I will give to thy servants, the hewers that cut timber, twenty thousand measures of beaten wheat, and twenty thousand measures of barley, and twenty thousand baths of wine, and twenty thousand baths of oil.

11 Then Huram the king of Tyre answered in writing, which he sent to Solomon, [t]Because the LORD hath loved his people, he hath made thee king over them.

12 Huram said moreover, [u]Blessed *be* the LORD God of Israel, [v]that made heaven and earth, who hath given to David the king a wise son, [w]endued with prudence and understanding, that might build a house for the LORD, and a house for his kingdom.

---

[a]1 Kings v. 5——[b]1 Kings v. 15; ver. 18——[c]Or, *Hiram,* 1 Kings v. 1——[d]1 Chron. xiv. 1——[e]Ver. 1 [f]Exod. xxx. 7——[g]Heb. *incense of spices*——[h]Exod. xxv. 30; Lev. xxiv. 8——[i]Num. xxviii. 3, 9, 11——[k]Psa. cxxxv. 5——[l]1 Kings viii. 27; ch. vi. 18; Isa. lxvi. 1 [m]Heb. *hath retained* or *obtained strength*

[n]Heb. *to grave gravings*——[o]1 Chron. xxii. 15——[p]1 Kings v. 6——[q]Or, *almuggim,* 1 Kings x. 11——[r]Heb. *great and wonderful*——[s]1 Kings v. 11——[t]1 Kings x. 9; ch. ix. 8——[u]1 Kings v. 7——[v]Gen. i. and ii; Psa. xxxiii. 6; cii. 25; cxxiv. 8; cxxxvi. 5, 6; Acts iv. 24; xiv. 15; Rev. x. 6——[w]Heb. *knowing prudence and understanding*

NOTES ON CHAP. II

Verse 1. *A house for the name of the Lord*] A temple for the worship of Jehovah.

A house for his kingdom.] A royal palace for his own use as king of Israel.

Verse 3. *Solomon sent to Huram*] This man's name is written חירם *Chiram* in Kings; and in Chronicles, חורם *Churam:* there is properly no difference, only a ו *yod* and a ו *vau* interchanged. See on 1 Kings v. 2.

Verse 6. *Seeing the heaven and heaven of heavens*] "For the lower heavens, the middle heavens, and the upper heavens cannot contain him, seeing he sustains all things by the arm of his power. Heaven is the throne of ʰis glory, the earth his footstool; the deep, and the whole world, are sustained by the spirit of his WORD, [ברוח מימריה *beruach meymereih.*] Who am I, then, that I should build him a house?"—*Targum.*

Save only to burn sacrifice] It is not under the hope that the house shall be able to contain him, but merely for the purpose of burning incense to him, and offering him sacrifice, that I have erected it.

Verse 7. *Send me—a man cunning to work*] A person of great ingenuity, who is capable of planning and directing, and who may be over the other artists.

Verse 11. *Answered in writing*] Though correspondence among persons of distinction was, in these early times, carried on by confidential messengers, yet we find that epistolary

A. M. 2989
B. C. 1015
An. Exod. Isr.
476
Anno ante
I. Olymp. 239

13 And now I have sent a cunning man, endued with understanding, of Huram my father's,

14 [x]The son of a woman of the daughters of Dan, and his father *was* a man of Tyre, skilful to work in gold, and in silver, in brass, in iron, in stone, and in timber, in purple, in blue, and in fine linen, and in crimson; also to grave any manner of graving, and to find out every device which shall be put to him, with thy cunning men, and with the cunning men of my lord David thy father.

15 Now therefore the wheat, and the barley, the oil, and the wine, which [y]my lord hath spoken of, let him send unto his servants:

16 [z]And we will cut wood out of Lebanon,

[a]as much as thou shalt need: and we will bring it to thee in floats by sea to [b]Joppa; and thou shalt carry it up to Jerusalem.

A. M. 2989
B. C. 1015
An. Exod. Isr.
476
Anno ante
I. Olymp. 239

17 [c]And Solomon numbered all [d]the strangers that *were* in the land of Israel after the numbering wherewith [e]David his father had numbered them; and they were found a hundred and fifty thousand and three thousand and six hundred.

18 And he sent [f]threescore and ten thousand of them *to be* bearers of burdens, and fourscore thousand *to be* hewers in the mountain, and three thousand and six hundred overseers to set the people a work.

---

[x]1 Kings vii. 13, 14——[y]Verse 10——[z]1 Kings v. 8, 9
[a]Heb. *according to all thy need*——[b]Heb. *Japho.* Josh. xix. 46; Acts ix. 36

[c]As ver. 2; 1 Kings v. 13, 15, 16; xix. 20, 21; chap. viii. 7, 8——[d]Heb. *the men the strangers*——[e]1 Chron. xxii. 2
[f]As it is ver. 2

---

correspondence did exist, and that kings could *write* and *read* in what were called by the proud and insolent *Greeks* and *Romans* barbarous nations. Nearly *two thousand* years after this we find a king on the British throne who could not sign his own name. About the year of our Lord 700, Withred, king of Kent, thus concludes a charter to secure the liberties of the Church: *Ego Wythredus rex Cantiæ hæc omnia suprascripta et confirmavi, atque, a me dictata propria manu signum sanctæ crucis pro*

ignorantia literarum expressi; "All the above dictated by myself, I have confirmed; and because I cannot write, I have with my own hand expressed this by putting the sign of the holy cross +."—See *Wilkins' Concilia.*

Verse 13. *I have sent a cunning man*] His name appears to have been *Hiram,* or *Hiram Abi:* see the notes on 1 Kings vii. 13, 14.

Verse 16. *In floats by sea to Joppa*] See the note on 1 Kings v. 9, and on the parallel places, for other matters contained in this chapter.

CHAPTER III

Solomon begins to build the temple in the fourth year of his reign on Mount Moriah, 1, 2. Its dimensions, ornaments, and pillars, 3–17.

A. M. 2993
B. C. 1011
An. Exod. Isr.
480
Anno ante
I. Olymp. 235

THEN [a]Solomon began to build the house of the LORD at [b]Jerusalem in Mount Moriah, [c]where *the LORD* appeared unto David his father, in the place that David had prepared in the threshing-floor of [d]Ornan [e]the Jebusite.

2 And he began to build in the second *day*

of the second month, in the fourth year of his reign.

A.M.2993-3000
B.C.1011-1004
Anno ante
I. Ol. 235–228

3 Now these *are the things* [f]wherein Solomon was [g]instructed for the building of the house of God. The length by cubits after the first measure *was* threescore cubits, and the breadth twenty cubits.

---

[a]1 Kings vi. 1, &c.——[b]Gen. xxii. 2, 14——[c]Or, *which was seen of David his father*

[d]1 Chron. xxi. 18; xii. 1——[e]Or, *Araunah,* 2 Sam. xxiv. 18——[f]1 Kings vi. 2——[g]Heb. *founded*

NOTES ON CHAP. III

Verse 1. *In Mount Moriah*] Supposed to be the same place where Abraham was about to offer his son Isaac; so the Targum: "Solomon began to build the house of the sanctuary of the Lord at Jerusalem, in the place where Abraham had prayed and worshipped in the name of the Lord. This is the place of the earth where all generations shall worship the Lord. Here Abraham was about to offer his son Isaac for a burnt-offering; but he was snatched away by the WORD of the Lord, and a ram placed in his stead. Here Jacob prayed when he fled from the face of Esau his brother; and

here the angel of the Lord appeared to David, at which time David built an altar unto the Lord in the threshing-floor which he bought from Araunah the Jebusite."

Verse 3. *The length—after the first measure was* threescore *cubits*] It is supposed that the *first measure* means the cubit used in the time of *Moses,* contradistinguished from that used in *Babylon,* and which the Israelites used after their return from captivity; and, as the books of Chronicles were written after the captivity, it was necessary for the writer to make this remark, lest it should be thought that the measurement was by the Babylonish cubit, which was a *palm,* or *one-sixth* shorter than the cubit

A.M.2993-3000
B.C.1011-1004
Anno ante
I. Ol. 235-228

4 And the [h]porch that *was* in the front *of the house,* the length *of it was* according to the breadth of the house, twenty cubits, and the height *was* a hundred and twenty: and he overlaid it within with pure gold.

5 And [i]the greater house he ceiled with fir tree, which he overlaid with fine gold, and set thereon palm trees and chains.

6 And he [k]garnished the house with precious stones for beauty: and the gold *was* gold of Parvaim.

7 He overlaid also the house, the beams, the posts, and the walls thereof, and the doors thereof, with gold; and graved cherubims on the walls.

8 And he made the most holy house, the length whereof *was* according to the breadth of the house, twenty cubits, and the breadth thereof twenty cubits: and he overlaid it with fine gold, *amounting* to six hundred talents.

9 And the weight of the nails *was* fifty shekels of gold. And he overlaid the upper chambers with gold.

10 [l]And in the most holy house he made two cherubims [m]of image work, and overlaid them with gold.

11 And the wings of the cherubims *were*

twenty cubits long: one wing *of the one cherub was* five cubits, reaching to the wall of the house: and the other wing *was likewise* five cubits, reaching to the wing of the other cherub.

A.M.2993-3000
B.C.1011-1004
Anno ante
I. Ol. 235-228

12 And *one* wing of the other cherub *was* five cubits, reaching to the wall of the house: and the other wing *was* five cubits *also,* joining to the wing of the other cherub.

13 The wings of these cherubims spread themselves forth twenty cubits: and they stood on their feet, and their faces *were* [n]inward.

14 And he made the [o]veil *of* blue, and purple, and crimson, and fine linen, and [p]wrought cherubims thereon.

15 Also he made before the house [q]two pillars of thirty and five cubits [r]high, and the chapiter that *was* on the top of each of them *was* five cubits.

16 And he made chains, *as* in the oracle, and put *them* on the heads of the pillars; and made [s]a hundred pomegranates, and put *them* on the chains.

17 And he [t]reared up the pillars before the temple, one on the right hand, and the other on the left; and called the name of that on the right hand [u]Jachin, and the name of that on the left [v]Boaz.

---

[h]1 Kings vi. 3——[i]1 Kings vi. 17——[k]Heb. *covered*
[l]1 Kings vi. 17——[m]Or, (as some think) *of moveable work*——[n]Or, *toward the house*——[o]Exodus xxvi. 31; Matt. xxvii. 51; Hebrews ix. 3——[p]Hebrew, *caused*

to ascend——[q]1 Kings vii. 15-21; Jeremiah lii. 21 [r]Hebrew, *long*——[s]1 Kings vii. 20——[t]1 Kings vii. 21——[u]That is, *he shall establish*——[v]That is, *in it is strength*

---

of Moses. See the same distinction observed by Ezekiel, chap. xl. 5; xliii. 13.

Verse 4. *The height was a hundred and twenty*] Some think this should be *twenty* only; but if the same building is spoken of as in 1 Kings vi. 2, the height was only *thirty cubits. Twenty* is the reading of the *Syriac,* the *Arabic,* and the *Septuagint* in the *Codex Alexandrinus.* The MSS. give us no help. There is probably a mistake here, which, from the similarity of the letters, might easily occur. The words, as they now stand in the Hebrew text, are מאה ואשרים *meah veesrim,* one hundred and twenty. But probably the letters in מאה *meah,* a hundred, are transposed for אמה *ammah,* a cubit; if, therefore, the א *aleph* be placed after the מ *mem,* then the word will be מאה *meah.* one hundred; if *before* it the word will be אמה *ammah.* a cubit; therefore אמה עשרים *ammah esrim* will be *twenty cubits;* and thus the *Syriac, Arabic,* and *Septuagint* appear to have read. This will bring it within the proportion of the other measures, but *a hundred and twenty* seems too great a height.

Verse 6. *Gold of Parvaim.*] We know not what this place was; some think it is the same as *Sepharvaim,* a place in *Armenia* or *Media,* conquered by the king of Assyria, 2 Kings xvii. 24, &c. Others, that it is *Taprobane,* now the

island of *Ceylon,* which *Bochart* derives from *taph,* signifying the border, and *Parvan,* i. e., the coast of *Parvan.* The rabbins say that it was gold of a *blood-red* colour, and had its name from פרים *parim, heifers,* being like to *bullocks' blood.*

The *Vulgate* translates the passage thus: *Stravit quoque pavimentum templi pretiosissimo marmore, decore multo; porro aurum erat probatissimum;* "And he made the pavement of the temple of the most precious marble; and moreover the gold was of the best quality," &c.

Verse 9. *The weight of the nails* was *fifty shekels*] Bolts must be here intended, as it would be preposterous to suppose *nails* of nearly *two pounds'* weight.

The upper chambers] Probably the *ceiling* is meant.

Verse 17. *He reared up the pillars*] "The name of that on the right hand was *Jachin,* because the kingdom of the house of David was *established;* and the name of the left was *Boaz,* from the name of *Boaz* the patriarch of the family of Judah, from whom all the kings of the house of Judah have descended."—*Targum.* See on 1 Kings vii. 21; and see the parallel places for other matters contained in this chapter.

CHAPTER IV

The brazen altar, 1. Molten sea, and its supporters, 2–5. The ten lavers, 6. Ten golden candlesticks, 7. Ten tables, the hundred golden basons, and the priests' court, 8–10. The works which Huram performed, 11–17. Solomon finishes the temple, and its utensils, 18–22.

A. M. 2993–3000
B. C. 1011–1004
Anno ante
I. Ol. 235–228

MOREOVER he made ^aan altar of brass, twenty cubits the length thereof, and twenty cubits the breadth thereof, and ten cubits the height thereof.

2 ^bAlso he made a molten sea of ten cubits ^cfrom brim to brim, round in compass, and five cubits the height thereof; and a line of thirty cubits did compass it round about.

3 ^dAnd under it *was* the similitude of oxen, which did compass it round about: ten in a cubit, compassing the sea round about. Two rows of oxen *were* cast, when it was cast.

4 It stood upon twelve oxen, three looking toward the north, and three looking toward the west, and three looking toward the south, and three looking toward the east: and the sea *was*

set above upon them, and all their hinder parts *were* inward.

A. M. 2993–3000
B. C. 1011–1004
Anno ante
I. Ol. 235–228

5 And the thickness of it *was* a hand-breadth, and the brim of it like the work of the brim of a cup, ^ewith flowers of lilies; *and* it received and held ^fthree thousand baths.

6 He made also ^gten lavers, and put five on the right hand, and five on the left, to wash in them: ^hsuch things as they offered for the burnt-offering they washed in them; but the sea *was* for the priests to wash in.

7 ⁱAnd he made ten candlesticks of gold ^kaccording to their form, and set *them* in the temple, five on the right hand, and five on the left.

8 ^lHe made also ten tables, and placed *them* in the temple, five on the right side, and five

---

^aExod. xxvii. 1, 2; 2 Kings xvi. 14; Ezek. xliii. 13, 16
^b1 Kings vii. 23——^cHeb. *from his brim to his brim*
^d1 Kings vii. 24, 25, 26——^eOr, *like a lily-flower*

^fSee 1 Kings vii. 26——^g1 Kings vii. 38——^hHeb. *the work of burnt-offering*——ⁱ1 Kings vii. 49——^kExod. xxv. 31, 40; 1 Chron. xxviii. 12, 19——^l1 Kings vii. 48

NOTES ON CHAP. IV

Verse 3. *Under it was the similitude of oxen*] In 1 Kings vii. 24, instead of *oxen*, בקרים *bekarim*, we have *knops*, פקעים *pekaim;* and this last is supposed by able critics to be the reading which ought to be received here. What we call *knops* may signify *grapes, mushrooms, apples,* or some such ornaments placed round about under the turned over lip or brim of this caldron. It is possible that בקרים *bekarim*, *oxen*, may be a corruption of פקעים *pekaim, grapes*, as the פ *pe* might be mistaken for a ב *beth*, to which in ancient MSS. it has often a great resemblance, the dot under the top being often faint and indistinct; and the ע *ain*, on the same account, might be mistaken for a ר *resh.* Thus *grapes* might be turned into *oxen.* *Houbigant* contends that the words in both places are right; but that בקר *bakar* does not signify *ox* here, but a large kind of *grape,* according to its meaning in Arabic: and thus both places will agree. But I do not find that بقر *bakar,* or بقرة *bakarat,* has any such meaning in Arabic. He was probably misled by the following, in the Arabic Lexicon, *Camus,* inserted under بقر *bakara,* both by *Giggeius* and *Golius,* عين البقر *aino albikri, ox-eye,* which is interpreted *Genus uvæ nigræ ac prægrandis, incredibilis dulcedinis. In Palæstina autem pro prunis absolute usurpatur.* "A species of black grape, very large, and of incredible sweetness. It is used in Palestine for *prune* or *plum.*" What is called the *Damascene plum* is doubtless meant; but בקרים *bekarim*, in the text, can never have this

meaning, unless indeed we found it associated with עין *ayin, eye,* and then עיני בקרים *eyney bekarim* might, according to the Arabic, be translated *plums, grapes, sloes,* or such like, especially those of the largest kind, which in *size* resemble the *eye of an ox.* But the criticism of this great man is not solid. The likeliest method of reconciling the two places is supposing a change in the letters, as specified above. The reader will at once see that what are called the *oxen,* ver. 3, said to be round about the brim, are widely different from those ver. 4, by which this molten sea was supported.

Verse 5. *It—held three thousand baths.*] In 1 Kings vii. 26, it is said to hold only *two thousand baths.* As this book was written afte^r the Babylonish captivity, it is very possible that reference is here made to the Babylonish *bath,* which might have been *less* than the Jewish. We have already seen that the *cubit* of Moses, or of the ancient Hebrews, was *longer* than the Babylonish by *one palm;* see on chap. iii. ver. 3. It might be the same with the measures of capacity; so that *two thousand* of the *ancient* Jewish baths might have been equal to *three thousand* of those used *after the captivity.* The *Targum* cuts the knot by saying, "It received *three thousand* baths of dry measure, and held *two thousand* of liquid measure."

Verse 6. *He made also ten lavers*] The lavers served to wash the different parts of the victims in; and the molten sea was for the use of the priests. In this they bathed, or drew water from it for their personal purification.

Verse 8. *A hundred basons of gold*] These were doubtless a sort of *pateræ,* or sacrificial spoons, with which they made *libations.*

VOL. II   640

A. M. 2993–3000
B. C. 1011–1004
Anno ante
I. Ol. 235–228

on the left. And he made a hundred ᵐbasons of gold.

9 Furthermore ⁿhe made the court of the priests, and the great court, and doors for the court, and overlaid the doors of them with brass.

10 And ᵒhe set the sea on the right side of the east end, over against the south.

11 And ᵖHuram made the pots, and the shovels, and the ᑫbasons. And Huram ʳfinished the work that he was to make for King Solomon for the house of God ;

12 *To wit,* the two pillars, and ˢthe pommels, and the chapiters *which were* on the top of the two pillars, and the two wreaths to cover the two pommels of the chapiters which *were* on the pillars ;

13 And ᵗfour hundred pomegranates on the two wreaths ; two rows of pomegranates on each wreath, to cover the two pommels of the chapiters which *were* ᵘupon the pillars.

14 He made also ᵛbases, and ʷlavers made he upon the bases ;

15 One sea, and twelve oxen under it.

A. M. 2993–3000
B. C. 1011–1004
Anno ante
I. Ol. 235–228

16 The pots also, and the shovels, and the flesh-hooks, and all their instruments, did ˣHuram his father make to King Solomon for the house of the Lᴏʀᴅ of ʸbright brass.

17 ᶻIn the plain of Jordan did the king cast them, in the ᵃclay ground between Succoth and Zeredathah.

18 ᵇThus Solomon made all these vessels in great abundance : for the weight of the brass could not be found out.

19 And ᶜSolomon made all the vessels that *were for* the house of God, the golden altar also, and the tables whereon ᵈthe shew-bread *was set ;*

20 Moreover the candlesticks with their lamps, that they should burn ᵉafter the manner before the oracle, of pure gold ;

21 And ᶠthe flowers, and the lamps, and the tongs, *made he of* gold, *and* that ᵍperfect gold ;

22 And the snuffers, and the ʰbasons, and the spoons, and the censers, *of* pure gold : and the entry of the house, the inner doors thereof for the most holy *place,* and the doors of the house of the temple, *were of* gold.

ᵐOr, *bowls*——ⁿ1 Kings vi. 36——ᵒ1 Kings vii. 39
ᵖSee 1 Kings vii. 40——ᑫOr, *bowls*——ʳHeb. *finished to make*——ˢ1 Kings vii. 41——ᵗSee 1 Kings vii. 20
ᵘHeb. *upon the face*——ᵛ1 Kings vii. 27, 43——ʷOr, *caldrons*——ˣ1 Kings vii. 14, 45

ʸHeb. *made bright, or scoured*——ᶻ1 Kings vii. 46
ᵃHeb. *thickness of the ground*——ᵇ1 Kings vii. 47——ᶜ1 Kings vii. 48, 49, 50——ᵈExod. xxv. 30——ᵉExod. xxvii. 20, 21——ᶠExod. xxv. 31, &c.——ᵍHeb. *perfections of gold*——ʰOr, *bowls*

Verse 9. *He made the court of the priests*] This was the *inner* court.

And the great court] This was the *outer* court, or place for the assembling of the people.

Verse 16. *Huram his father*] אב *ab, father,* is often used in Hebrew to signify a *master, inventor, chief operator,* and is very probably used here in the former sense by the Chaldee: *All these Chiram his master made for King Solomon;* or *Chiram Abi,* or rather *Hiram,* made for the king.

Verse 17. *In the clay ground*] See on 1 Kings vii. 46. Some suppose that he did not actually cast those instruments at those places, but that he brought the *clay* from that quarter, as being the most proper for making moulds to cast in.

Verse 21. *And the flowers, and the lamps*] Probably each branch of the chandelier was made like *a plant in flower,* and the opening of

the flower was either the *lamp,* or served to support it.

Verse 22. *The doors—were of gold.*] That is, were overlaid with *golden plates,* the thickness of which we do not know.

Tʜᴀᴛ every thing in the tabernacle and temple was *typical* or *representative* of some excellence of the Gospel dispensation may be readily credited, without going into all the detail produced by the pious author of *Solomon's Temple Spiritualized.* We can see the general reference and the principles of the great design, though we may not be able to make a particular application of the *knops,* the *flowers,* the *pomegranates,* the *tongs,* and the *snuffers,* to some Gospel doctrines: such spiritualizing is in most cases weak, silly, religious trifling; being ill calculated to produce respect for Divine revelation.

CHAPTER V

Solomon having finished the temple, brings in the things which his father had consecrated, 1. He assembles the elders and chiefs of Israel and the Levites, in order to bring up the ark from the city of David, 2, 3. They bring it and its vessels; and having offered innumerable sacrifices, place it in the temple, under the wings of the cherubim, 4–10. The Levites, singers, and trumpeters praise God; and his glory descends and fills the house, so that the priests cannot stand to minister, 11–14.

A. M. 3000
B. C. 1004
Anno ante
I. Olymp. 228
Ante Urbem
Conditam 251

THUS ^a all the work that Solomon made for the house of the LORD was finished: and Solomon brought in *all* the things that David his father had dedicated; and the silver, and the gold, and all the instruments, put he among the treasures of the house of God.

2 ^b Then Solomon assembled the elders of Israel, and all the heads of the tribes, the chief of the fathers of the children of Israel, unto Jerusalem, to bring up the ark of the covenant of the LORD ^c out of the city of David, which *is* Zion.

3 ^d Wherefore all the men of Israel assembled themselves unto the king ^e in the feast which *was* in the seventh month.

4 And all the elders of Israel came; and the Levites took up the ark.

5 And they brought up the ark, and the tabernacle of the congregation, and all the holy vessels that *were* in the tabernacle, these did the priests *and* the Levites bring up.

6 Also King Solomon, and all the congregation of Israel that were assembled unto him before the ark, sacrificed sheep and oxen, which could not be told nor numbered for multitude.

7 And the priests brought in the ark of the covenant of the LORD unto his place, to the oracle of the house, into the most holy *place,* *even* under the wings of the cherubims:

8 For the cherubims spread forth *their* wings over the place of the ark, and the cherubims covered the ark and the staves thereof above.

9 And they drew out the staves *of the ark,* that the ends of the staves were seen from the ark before the oracle; but they were not seen without. And ^f there it is unto this day.

A. M. 3000
B. C. 1004
Anno ante
I. Olymp. 228
Ante Urbem
Conditam 251

10 *There was* nothing in the ark save the two tables which Moses ^g put *therein* at Horeb, ^h when the LORD made *a covenant* with the children of Israel, when they came out of Egypt.

11 And it came to pass, when the priests were come out of the holy *place:* (for all the priests *that were* ^i present were sanctified *and* did not *then* wait by course:

12 ^k Also the Levites *which were* the singers, all of them of Asaph, of Heman, of Jeduthun, with their sons and their brethren, *being* arrayed in white linen, having cymbals and psalteries and harps, stood at the east end of the altar, ^l and with them a hundred and twenty priests sounding with trumpets:)

13 It came even to pass, as the trumpeters and singers *were* as one, to make one sound to be heard in praising and thanking the LORD; and when they lifted up *their* voice with the trumpets and cymbals and instruments of music, and praised the LORD, *saying,* ^m For *he is* good; for his mercy *endureth* for ever: that *then* the house was filled with a cloud, *even* the house of the LORD;

14 So that the priests could not stand to minister by reason of the cloud; ^n for the glory of the LORD had filled the house of God.

---

^a 1 Kings vii. 51——^b 1 Kings viii. 1, &c.——^c 2 Sam. vi. 12——^d 1 Kings viii. 2——^e See chap. vii. 8, 9, 10 ^f Or, *they are here,* as 1 Kings viii. 8——^g Deut. x. 2, 5; chap. vi. 11

^h Or, *where*——^i Hebrew, *found*——^k 1 Chronicles xxv. 1——^l 1 Chronicles xv. 24——^m Psalm cxxxvi. see 1 Chronicles xvi. 34, 41——^n Exodus xl. 35; chapter vii. 2

NOTES ON CHAP. V

Verse 1. *Brought in* all *the things*] See the note on 1 Kings vii. 51.

Verse 3. *The feast*] "That is, the feast of tabernacles, which was held in the seventh month."—*Targum.* See 1 Kings viii. 2.

Verse 9. *They drew out the staves*] As the ark was no longer to be carried about, these were unnecessary.

Verse 10. There was *nothing in the ark save*] The Chaldee paraphrases thus: "There was nothing put in the ark but the two tables which Moses placed there, after the first had been broken on account of the calf which they made in Horeb, and the two other tables had been confirmed which were written with writing expressed in the TEN WORDS."

Verse 11. *When the priests were come out*]

After having carried the ark into the holy of holies, before the sacred service had commenced.

Verse 12. *A hundred and twenty priests*] Cymbals, psalteries, and harps, of any kind, in union with *a hundred and twenty trumpets* or *horns,* could not produce much *harmony;* as to *melody,* that must have been impossible, as the *noise* was too great.

Verse 13. *For he is good*] This was either the whole of the song, or the *burden* of each verse. The Hebrew is very short:—

כי טוב כי לעולם חסדו

Ki tob, ki leolam chasdo.

For he is *good; for his mercy is endless.*

Verse 14. *The priests could not stand*] What a proof of the being of God, and of the Divine presence! What must those holy men have felt at this time!

CHAPTER VI

Solomon's prayer at the dedication of the temple, 1–42.

A. M. 3000
B. C. 1004
Anno ante
I. Olymp. 228
Ante Urbem
Conditam 251

THEN ªsaid Solomon, The LORD hath said that he would dwell in the ᵇthick darkness.

2 But I have built a house of habitation for thee, and a place for thy dwelling for ever.

3 And the king turned his face, and blessed the whole congregation of Israel: and all the congregation of Israel stood.

4 And he said, Blessed *be* the LORD God of Israel, who hath with his hands fulfilled *that* which he spake with his mouth to my father David, saying,

5 Since the day that I brought forth my people out of the land of Egypt I chose no city among all the tribes of Israel to build a house in, that my name might be there; neither chose I any man to be a ruler over my people Israel:

6 ᶜBut I have chosen Jerusalem that my name might be there; and ᵈhave chosen David to be over my people Israel.

7 Now ᵉit was in the heart of David my father to build a house for the name of the LORD God of Israel.

8 But the LORD said to David my father, Forasmuch as it was in thine heart to build a house for my name, thou didst well in that it was in thine heart:

9 Notwithstanding thou shalt not build the house; but thy son which shall come forth out of thy loins, he shall build the house for my name.

10 The LORD therefore hath performed his word that he hath spoken: for I am risen up in the room of David my father, and am set on the throne of Israel, as the LORD promised,

and have built the house for the name of the LORD God of Israel.

A. M. 3000
B. C. 1004
Anno ante
I. Olymp. 228
Ante Urbem
Conditam 251

11 And in it have I put the ark, ᶠwherein *is* the covenant of the LORD, that he made with the children of Israel.

12 ᵍAnd he stood before the altar of the LORD in the presence of all the congregation of Israel, and spread forth his hands:

13 For Solomon had made a brazen scaffold, of five cubits ʰlong, and five cubits broad, and three cubits high, and had set it in the midst of the court: and upon it he stood, and kneeled down upon his knees before all the congregation of Israel, and spread forth his hands toward heaven.

14 And said, O LORD God of Israel, ⁱ*there is* no God like thee in the heaven, nor in the earth; which keepest covenant, and *showest* mercy unto thy servants, that walk before thee will all their hearts:

15 ᵏThou which hast kept with thy servant David my father that which thou hast promised him; and spakest with thy mouth, and hast fulfilled *it* with thine hand, as *it is* this day.

16 Now therefore, O LORD God of Israel, keep with thy servant David my father that which thou hast promised him, saying, ¹There ᵐshall not fail thee a man in my sight to sit upon the throne of Israel; ⁿyet so that thy children take heed to their way to walk in my law, as thou hast walked before me.

17 Now then, O LORD God of Israel, let thy word be verified, which thou hast spoken unto thy servant David.

18 But will God in very deed dwell with men

ª1 Kings viii. 12, &c.——ᵇLeviticus xvi. 2——ᶜChap. xii. 13——ᵈ1 Chron. xxviii. 4——ᵉ2 Samuel vii. 2; 1 Chronicles xvii. 1; xxviii. 2——ᶠChapter v. 10 ᵍ1 Kings viii. 22——ʰHebrew, *the length thereof,* &c.

ⁱExodus xv. 11; Deuteronomy iv. 39; vii. 9——ᵏ1 Chron. xxii. 9——¹2 Sam. vii. 12, 16; 1 Kings ii. 4; vi. 12; chap. vii. 18——ᵐ*There shall not a man be cut off*——ⁿPsa. cxxxii. 12

NOTES ON CHAP. VI

Verse 1. *The Lord hath said that he would dwell*] Solomon, seeing the cloud descend and fill the house, immediately took for granted that the Lord had accepted the place, and was now present. What occurred now was precisely the same with what took place when Moses reared the tabernacle in the wilderness; see Exod. xl. 34, 35: *A cloud covered the tent— and the glory of the Lord filled the tabernacle. And Moses was not able to enter into the tent —because the glory of the Lord filled the tabernacle.*

The *Chaldee* paraphrases thus: "Then said Solomon, It has pleased God to place his majesty in the city of Jerusalem, in the house of the sanctuary which I have built to the name of his WORD, and he hath placed a dark cloud before him."

Verse 10. *For the name of the Lord*] "For the name of the WORD of the Lord God of Israel."—*Targum.*

Verse 14. *That walk before thee with all their hearts*] "With all the will of their souls, and with all the affection of their hearts."— *Targum.*

Verse 18. *But will God in very deed dwell*

A. M. 3000
B. C. 1004
Anno ante
I. Olymp. 228
Ante Urbem
Conditam 251

on the earth? [o]behold, heaven and the heaven of heavens cannot contain thee; how much less this house which I have built!

19 Have respect therefore to the prayer of thy servant, and to his supplication, O LORD my God, to hearken unto the cry and the prayer which thy servant prayeth before thee:

20 That thine eyes may be open upon this house day and night, upon the place whereof thou hast said that thou wouldest put thy name there; to hearken unto the prayer which thy servant prayeth [p]toward this place.

21 Hearken therefore unto the supplications of thy servant, and of thy people Israel, which they shall [q]make toward this place: hear thou from thy dwelling-place, *even* from heaven; and when thou hearest, forgive.

22 If a man sin against his neighbour, [r]and an oath be laid upon him to make him swear, and the oath come before thine altar in this house;

23 Then hear thou from heaven, and do, and judge thy servants, by requiting the wicked, by recompensing his way upon his own head; and by justifying the righteous, by giving him according to his righteousness.

24 And if thy people Israel [s]be put to the worse before the enemy, because they have sinned against thee; and shall return and confess thy name, and pray and make supplication before thee [t]in this house;

25 Then hear thou from the heavens, and forgive the sin of thy people Israel, and bring them again unto the land which thou gavest to them and to their fathers.

26 When the [u]heaven is shut up, and there is no rain, because they have sinned against thee; *yet* if they pray toward this place, and confess thy name, and turn from their sin, when thou dost afflict them;

27 Then hear thou from heaven, and forgive the sin of thy servants, and of thy people Israel, when thou hast taught them the good way, wherein they should walk; and send rain upon thy land, which thou hast given unto thy people for an inheritance.

A. M. 3000
B. C. 1004
Anno ante
I. Olymp. 228
Ante Urbem
Conditam 251

28 If there [v]be dearth in the land, if there be pestilence, if there be blasting, or mildew, locusts, or caterpillars; if their enemies besiege them [w]in the cities of their land; whatsoever sore or whatsoever sickness *there be:*

29 *Then* what prayer *or* what supplication soever shall be made of any man, or of all thy people Israel, when every one shall know his own sore and his own grief, and shall spread forth his hands [x]in this house:

30 Then hear thou from heaven thy dwelling-place, and forgive, and render unto every man according unto all his ways, whose heart thou knowest; (for thou only [y]knowest the hearts of the children of men;)

31 That they may fear thee, to walk in thy ways, [z]so long as they live [a]in the land which thou gavest unto our fathers.

32 Moreover concerning the stranger, [b]which is not of thy people Israel, but is come from a far country for thy great name's sake, and thy mighty hand, and thy stretched-out arm; if they come and pray in this house;

33 Then hear thou from the heavens, *even* from thy dwelling-place, and do according to all that the stranger calleth to thee for; that all people of the earth may know thy name, and fear thee, as *doth* thy people Israel, and may know that [c]this house which I have built is called by thy name.

34 If thy people go out to war against their enemies by the way that thou shalt send them, and they pray unto thee toward this city which thou hast chosen, and the house which I have built for thy name:

35 Then hear thou from the heavens their prayer and their supplication, and maintain their [d]cause.

---

[o]Chap. ii. 6; Isa. lxvi. 1; Acts vii. 49——[p]Or, *in this place*——[q]Heb. *pray*——[r]Heb. *and he require an oath of him*——[s]Or, *be smitten*——[t]Or, *toward*——[u]1 Kings xvii. 1——[v]Ch. xx. 9——[w]Heb. *in the land of their gates*——[x]Or, *toward this house*——[y]1 Chron. xxviii. 9——[z]Heb. *all the days which*——[a]Heb. *upon the face of the land*——[b]John xii. 20; Acts viii. 27——[c]Heb. *thy name is called upon this house*——[d]Or, *right*

---

with men] "But who could have imagined, who could have thought it credible, that God should place his majesty among men dwelling upon earth? Behold, the highest heavens, the middle heavens, and the lowest heavens, cannot bear the glory of thy majesty, (for thou art the God who sustainest all the heavens, and the earth, and the deep, and all that is in them,) nor can this house which I have built contain Thee."—*Targum.*

Verse 22. *If a man sin against his neighbour*] For the SEVEN *cases* put here by Solo-

A. M. 3000
B. C. 1004
Anno ante
I. Olymp. 228
Ante Urbem
Conditam 251

36 If they sin against thee, (for *there is* [e]no man which sinneth not,) and thou be angry with them, and deliver them over before *their* enemies, and [f]they carry them away captives unto a land far off or near;

37 Yet *if* they [g]bethink themselves in the land whither they are carried captive, and turn and pray unto thee in the land of their captivity, saying, We have sinned, we have done amiss, and have dealt wickedly;

38 If they return to thee with all their heart and with all their soul in the land of their captivity, whither they have carried them captives, and pray toward their land, which thou gavest unto their fathers, and *toward* the city which thou hast chosen, and toward the house which I have built for thy name:

39 Then hear thou from the heavens, *even* from thy dwelling-place, their prayer and their supplications, and maintain their [h]cause, and forgive thy people which have sinned against thee.

40 Now, my God, let, I beseech thee, thine eyes be open, and *let* thine ears *be* attent [i]unto the prayer *that is made* in this place.

41 Now [k]therefore arise, O LORD God, into thy [l]resting-place, thou, and the ark of thy strength: let thy priests, O LORD God, be clothed with salvation, and let thy saints [m]rejoice in goodness.

42 O LORD God, turn not away the face of thine anointed: [n]remember the mercies of David thy servant.

A. M. 3000
B. C. 1004
Anno ante
I. Olymp. 228
Ante Urbem
Conditam 251

---

[e]Prov. xx. 9; Eccles. vii. 20; James iii. 2; 1 John i. 8
[f]Heb. *they that take them captives carry them away*
[g]Heb. *bring back to their heart*

[h]Or, *right*——[i]Hebrew, *to the prayer of this place*
[k]Psalm cxxxii. 8, 9, 10, 16——[l]1 Chron. xxviii. 2
[m]Neh. ix. 25——[n]Psa. cxxxii. 1; Isa. lv. 3

---

mon in his prayer, see the notes on 1 Kings viii. 31-46.

Verse 36. *For* there is *no man which sinneth not*] See this case largely considered in the note on 1 Kings viii. 46.

Verse 37. If *they bethink themselves*] "If thy fear should return into their hearts."—*Targum.*

The whole of this prayer is amply considered in the parallel place, 1 Kings viii., where see the notes.

Verse 41. *Let thy saints rejoice in good-*

ness.] "In the abundance of the tithes and other goods which shall be given to the Levites, as their reward for keeping the ark, and singing before it."—*Jarchi.*

Verse 42. *Turn not away the face of thine anointed*] "At least do me good; and if not for *my* sake, do it for *thy own sake.*"—*Jarchi.*

These two last verses are not in the parallel place in 1 Kings viii. There are other differences between the two places in this prayer, but they are not of much consequence.

CHAPTER VII

Solomon having ended his prayer, the fire of the Lord comes down from heaven and consumes the offerings, 1. The people and the priests see this, and glorify God, and offer sacrifices, 2–4. Solomon offers twenty-two thousand oxen, and one hundred and twenty thousand sheep; and the priests and Levites attend in their offices, 5, 6. He keeps the feast seven days, and the dedication of the altar seven days, and dismisses the people, 7–11. The Lord appears unto him by night, and assures him that he has heard his prayer, 12–16; promises him and his posterity a perpetual government, if they be obedient, 17, 18; but utter destruction should they disobey, and become idolaters, 19–22.

A. M. 3000
B. C. 1004
Anno ante
I. Olymp. 228
Ante Urbem
Conditam 251

NOW [a]when Solomon had made an end of praying, the [b]fire came down from heaven, and consumed the burnt-offering and the sacrifices; and [c]the glory of the LORD filled the house.

2 [d]And the priests could not enter into the house of the LORD, because the glory of the LORD had filled the LORD's house.

3 And when all the children of Israel saw how the fire came down, and the glory of the LORD upon the house, they bowed themselves with their faces to the ground upon the pavement, and worshipped and praised the LORD, [e]*saying,* For *he is* good; [f]for his mercy *endureth* for ever.

4 [g]Then the king and all the people

A. M. 3000
B. C. 1004
Anno ante
I. Olymp. 228
Ante Urbem
Conditam 251

---

[a]1 Kings viii. 54——[b]Leviticus ix. 24; Judg. vi. 21; 1 Kings xviii. 38; 1 Chron. xxi. 26——[c]1 Kings viii. 10, 11; Chapter v. 13, 14; Ezekiel x. 3, 4——[d]Chapter

v. 14——[e]Chapter v. 13; Psalm cxxxvi. 1——[f]1 Chronicles xvi. 41; Chapter xx. 21——[g]1 Kings viii. 62, 63

NOTES ON CHAP. VII

Verse 1. *The fire came down*] The *cloud* had come down before, now the *fire* consumes

the *sacrifice*, showing that both the *house* and the *sacrifices* were accepted by the Lord.

Verse 4. *The king and all the people offered sacrifices*] They presented the victims to the

A. M. 3000
B. C. 1004
Anno ante
I. Olymp. 228
Ante Urbem
Conditam 251

offered sacrifices before the LORD.

5 And King Solomon offered a sacrifice of twenty and two thousand oxen, and a hundred and twenty thousand sheep; so the king and all the people dedicated the house of God.

6 ʰAnd the priests waited on their offices: the Levites also with instruments of music of the LORD, which David the king had made to praise the LORD, because his mercy *endureth* for ever, when David praised ʲby their ministry; and ᵏthe priests sounded trumpets before them, and all Israel stood.

7 Moreover ˡSolomon hallowed the middle of the court that *was* before the house of the LORD: for there he offered burnt-offerings, and the fat of the peace-offerings, because the brazen altar which Solomon had made was not able to receive the burnt-offerings, and the meat-offerings, and the fat.

8 ᵐAlso at the same time Solomon kept the feast seven days, and all Israel with him, a very great congregation, from the entering in of Hamath unto ⁿthe river of Egypt.

9 And in the eighth day they made a ᵒsolemn assembly: for they kept the dedication of the altar seven days, and the feast seven days.

10 And ᵖon the three and twentieth day of the seventh month he sent the people away into their tents, glad and merry in heart for the goodness that the LORD had showed unto

David, and to Solomon, and to Israel his people.

A. M. 3000
B. C. 1004
Anno ante
I. Olymp. 228
Ante Urbem
Conditam 251

11 Thus �q Solomon finished the house of the LORD, and the king's house: and all that came into Solomon's heart to make in the house of the LORD, and in his own house, he prosperously effected.

12 And the LORD appeared to Solomon by night, and said unto him, I have heard thy prayer, ʳand have chosen this place to myself for a house of sacrifice.

13 ˢIf I shut up heaven that there be no rain, or if I command the locusts to devour the land, or if I send pestilence among my people;

14 If my people, ᵗwhich are called by my name, shall ᵘhumble themselves, and pray, and seek my face, and turn from their wicked ways; ᵛthen will I hear from heaven, and will forgive their sin, and will heal their land.

15 Now ʷmine eyes shall be open, and mine ears attent ˣunto the prayer *that is made* in this place.

16 For now have ʸI chosen and sanctified this house, that my name may be there for ever: and mine eyes and mine heart shall be there perpetually.

17 ᶻAnd as for thee, if thou wilt walk before me, as David thy father walked, and do according to all that I have commanded thee, and shalt observe my statutes and my judgments;

ʰ1 Chron. xv. 16——ʲHeb. *by their hand*——ᵏChap. v. 12——ˡ1 Kings viii. 64——ᵐ1 Kings viii. 65 ⁿJosh. xiii. 3——ᵒHeb. *a restraint*——ᵖ1 Kings viii. 66 q1 Kings ix. 1, &c.——ʳDeut. xii. 5

ˢChap. vi. 26, 28——ᵗHeb. *upon whom my name is called*——ᵘJames iv. 10——ᵛChap. vi. 27, 30——ʷCh. vi. 40——ˣHeb. *to the prayer of this place*——ʸ1 Kings ix. 3; chap. vi. 6——ᶻ1 Kings ix. 4, &c.

---

priests, and they and the Levites slew them, and sprinkled the blood: or perhaps the people themselves slew them; and, having caught the blood, collected the fat, &c., presented them to the priests to be offered as the law required.

Verse 5. *Twenty and two thousand oxen, &c.*] The amount of all the victims that had been offered during the *seven* days of the feast of *tabernacles*, and the *seven* days of the feast of the *dedication*.

Verse 8. *The entering in of Hamath*] "From the entrance of Antioch to the Nile of Egypt." —*Targum*.

Verse 10. *On the three and twentieth day*] This was the *ninth* day of the dedication of the temple; but in 1 Kings viii. 66 it is called the *eighth* day. "The meaning is this," says *Jarchi:* "he gave them liberty to return on the *eighth* day, and many of them did then return: and he dismissed the remainder on the *ninth*, what is called here the *twenty-third*, reckoning

the *fourteen* days for the duration of the *two feasts;* in all, *twenty-three*."

The *Targum* paraphrases this verse thus: "The people departed with a glad heart, for all the good which God had done to David his servant, on whose account the doors of the sanctuary were open and for Solomon his son, because God had heard his prayer, and the majesty of the Lord had rested on the house of the sanctuary and for Israel, his people, because God had favourably accepted their oblations, and the heavenly fire had descended, and, burning on the altar, had devoured their sacrifices."

Verse 12. *The Lord appeared to Solomon*] This was a *second* manifestation; see 1 Kings ix. 2-9, and the notes there. The *Targum* says, "The WORD of the Lord appeared to Solomon."

Verse 13. *Or if I send pestilence*] "The angel of death."—*Targum*.

Verse 15. *Now mine eyes shall be open*] It

A. M. 3000
B. C. 1004
Anno ante
I. Olymp. 228
Ante Urbem
Conditam 251

18 Then will I stablish the throne of thy kingdom, according as I have covenanted with David thy father, saying, [a]There [b]shall not fail thee a man *to be* ruler in Israel.

19 [c]But if ye turn away, and forsake my statutes and my commandments, which I have set before you, and shall go and serve other gods, and worship them;

20 Then will I pluck them up by the roots out of my land which I have given them; and this house, which I have sanctified for my name, will I cast out of my sight, and

will make it *to be* a proverb and a by-word among all nations.

21 And this house, which is high, shall be an astonishment to every one that passeth by it; so that he shall say, [d]Why hath the LORD done thus unto this land, and unto this house?

22 And it shall be answered, Because they forsook the LORD God of their fathers, which brought them forth out of the land of Egypt, and laid hold on other gods, and worshipped them, and served them: therefore hath he brought all this evil upon them.

A. M. 3000
B. C. 1004
Anno ante
I. Olymp. 228
Ante Urbem
Conditam 251

---

[a]Chapter vi. 16——[b]Hebrew, *There shall not be cut off to thee*

[c]Lev. xxvii. 14, 33; Deut. xxviii. 15, 36, 37——[d]Deut. xxix. 24; Jer. xxii. 8, 9

---

shall be pleasing to me in the *sight* of *my* WORD, that I should incline mine ear," &c. —*Targum.*

Verse 18. *There shall not fail thee a man*] This *promise* was not fulfilled, because the *condition* was not fulfilled; they forsook God, and he cut *them* off, and the *throne* also.

Verse 20. *Then will I pluck them up by the roots*] How completely has this been fulfilled! not only all the *branches* of the Jewish political tree have been cut off, but the very *roots* have been plucked up; so that the day of the Lord's anger has left them neither *root* nor *branch*.

Verse 21. *Shall be an astonishment*] The *manner* in which these disobedient people have

been destroyed is truly *astonishing:* no nation was ever so highly favoured, and none ever so severely and signally punished.

Verse 22. *Because they forsook the Lord*] While they cleaved to God, the most powerful enemy could make no impression on them; but when they forsook him, then the weakest and most inconsiderable of their foes harassed, oppressed, and reduced them to bondage and misery. It was by no personal prowess, genuine heroism, or supereminent military tactics, that the Jews were enabled to resist and overcome their enemies; it was by the Divine power alone; for, destitute of this, they were even worse than other men.

CHAPTER VIII

Solomon's buildings, conquests, and officers, 1–10. He brings Pharaoh's daughter to his new-built palace, 11. His various sacrifices, and arrangement of the priests, Levites, and porters, 12–16. He sends a fleet to Ophir, 17, 18.

A. M. 3013
B. C. 991
Anno ante
I. Olymp. 215
Ante Urbem
Conditam 238

AND [a]it came to pass at the end of twenty years, wherein Solomon had built the house of the LORD, and his own house,

2 That the cities which Huram had restored to Solomon, Solomon built them, and caused the children of Israel to dwell there.

3 And Solomon went to Hamath-zobah, and prevailed against it.

4 [b]And he built Tadmor in the wilderness,

and all the store cities, which he built in Hamath.

5 Also he built Beth-horon the upper, and Beth-horon the nether, fenced cities, with walls, gates, and bars;

6 And Baalath, and all the store cities that Solomon had, and all the chariot cities, and the cities of the horsemen, and [c]all that Solomon desired to build in Jerusalem, and in Lebanon, and throughout all the land of his dominion.

A. M. 3013
B. C. 991
Anno ante
I. Olymp. 215
Ante Urbem
Conditam 238

---

[a]1 Kings ix. 10, &c.——[b]1 Kings ix. 17, &c.

[c]Heb. *all the desire of Solomon which he desired to build*

NOTES ON CHAP. VIII

Verse 1. *At the end of twenty years*] He employed *seven* years and a *half* in building the temple, and *twelve* and a *half*, or *thirteen*, in building his own house.—Compare this with 1 Kings vii. 1.

Verse 2. *The cities which Huram had restored*] See the note on 1 Kings ix. 11.

Verse 3. *Hamath-zobah*] "Emessa, on the river Orontes."—*Calmet.*

Verse 4. *Tadmor*] *Palmyra.* See the note on 1 Kings ix. 18, for an account of this superb city.

Verse 6. *All the store cities*] See the note on 1 Kings ix. 19.

A. M. 3013
B. C. 991
Anno ante
I. Olymp. 215
Ante Urbem
Conditam 238

7 ^d*As for* all the people *that were* left of the Hittites, and the Amorites, and the Perizzites, and the Hivites, and the Jebusites, which *were* not of Israel,

8 *But* of their children, who were left after them in the land, whom the children of Israel consumed not, them did Solomon make to pay tribute until this day.

9 But of the children of Israel did Solomon make no servants for his work; but they *were* men of war, and chief of his captains, and captains of his chariots, and horsemen.

10 And these *were* the chief of King Solomon's officers, *even* ^etwo hundred and fifty, that bare rule over the people.

11 And Solomon ^fbrought up the daughter of Pharaoh out of the city of David unto the house that he had built for her: for he said, My wife shall not dwell in the house of David king of Israel, because *the places are* ^gholy, whereunto the ark of the LORD hath come.

12 Then Solomon offered burnt-offerings unto the LORD on the altar of the LORD, which he had built before the porch,

13 Even after a certain rate ^hevery day, offering according to the commandment of Moses, on the Sabbaths, and on the new moons, and on the solemn feasts, ⁱthree times in the year, *even* in the feast of unleavened bread, and in the feast of weeks, and in the feast of tabernacles.

A. M. 3013
B. C. 991
Anno ante
I. Olymp. 215
Ante Urbem
Conditam 238

14 And he appointed, according to the order of David his father, the ^kcourses of the priests to their service, and ^lthe Levites to their charges, to praise and minister before the priests, as the duty of every day required: the ^mporters also by their courses at every gate: for ⁿso had David the man of God commanded.

15 And they departed not from the commandment of the king unto the priests and Levites concerning any matter, or concerning the treasures.

16 Now all the work of Solomon was prepared unto the day of the foundation of the house of the LORD, and until it was finished. *So* the house of the LORD was perfected.

17 Then went Solomon to ^oEzion-geber, and to ^pEloth, at the sea-side in the land of Edom.

18 ^qAnd Huram sent him, by the hands of his servants, ships, and servants that had knowledge of the sea; and they went with the servants of Solomon to Ophir, and took thence four hundred and fifty talents of gold, and brought *them* to King Solomon.

---

^d1 Kings ix. 20, &c.——^eSee 1 Kings ix. 23——^f1 Kings iii. 1; vii. 8; ix. 24——^gHeb. *holiness*——^hExod. xxix. 38; Num. xxviii. 3, 9, 11, 26; xxix. 1, &c.——ⁱExod. xxiii. 14; Deut. xvi. 16——^k1 Chron. xxiv. 1

^l1 Chron. xxv. 1——^m1 Chron. ix. 17; xxvi. 1 ⁿHeb. *so* was *the commandment of David the man of God* ^o1 Kings ix. 26——^pOr, *Elath*, Deut. ii. 8; 2 Kings xiv. 22——^q1 Kings ix. 27; chap. ix. 10, 13

Verse 9. *But of the children of Israel*] See the note on 1 Kings ix. 21.

Verse 11. *The daughter of Pharaoh*] "And Bithiah, the daughter of Pharaoh, Solomon brought up from the city of David to the palace which he had built for her."—*T.*

Because the places are *holy*] Is not this a proof that he considered his wife to be a *heathen*, and not proper to dwell in a place which had been sanctified? Solomon had not yet departed from the true God.

Verse 13. *Three times in the year*] These were the *three* great annual feasts.

Verse 15. *The commandment of the king*] The institutions of David.

Verse 17. *Then went Solomon to Ezion-geber*] See the notes on 1 Kings ix. 26-28, for conjectures concerning *Ezion-geber* and *Ophir.*

Verse 18. *Knowledge of the sea*] Skilful sailors. Solomon probably bore the expenses, and his friend, the Tyrian king, furnished him with expert sailors; for the Jews, at no period of their history, had any skill in maritime affairs, their navigation being confined to the lakes of their own country, from which they could never acquire any nautical skill. The Tyrians, on the contrary, lived on and in the sea.

CHAPTER IX

The queen of Sheba visits Solomon, and is sumptuously entertained by him, 1–12. His great riches, 13, 14 He makes targets and shields of beaten gold, and a magnificent ivory throne, and various utensils of gold, 15–20. His navigation to Tarshish, and the commodities brought thence, 21. His magnificence and political connections, 22–28. The writers of his life, 29. He reigns forty years, and is succeeded by his son Rehoboam, 30, 31.

A. M. 3014
B. C. 990
Anno ante
I. Olymp. 214
Ante Urbem
Conditam 237

AND [a]when the queen of Sheba heard of the fame of Solomon, she came to prove Solomon with hard questions at Jerusalem, with a very great company, and camels that bare spices, and gold in abundance, and precious stones: and when she was come to Solomon, she communed with him of all that was in her heart.

2 And Solomon told her all her questions: and there was nothing hid from Solomon which he told her not.

3 And when the queen of Sheba had seen the wisdom of Solomon, and the house that he had built,

4 And the meat of his table, and the sitting of his servants, and the attendance of his ministers, and their apparel; his [b]cupbearers also, and their apparel; and his ascent by which he went up into the house of the LORD; there was no more spirit in her.

5 And she said to the king, *It was* a true [c]report which I heard in mine own land of thine [d]acts, and of thy wisdom:

6 Howbeit I believed not their words, until I came, and mine eyes had seen *it:* and, behold, the one half of the greatness of thy wisdom was not told me: *for* thou exceedest the fame that I heard.

7 Happy *are* thy men, and happy *are* these thy servants, which stand continually before thee, and hear thy wisdom.

8 Blessed be the LORD thy God, which delighted in thee to set thee on his throne *to be* king for the LORD thy God: because thy God loved Israel, to establish them for ever, therefore made he thee king over them, to do judgment and justice.

9 And she gave the king a hundred and twenty talents of gold, and of spices great abundance, and precious stones: neither was there any such spice as the queen of Sheba gave King Solomon.

A. M. 3014
B. C. 990
Anno ante
I. Olymp. 214
Ante Urbem
Conditam 237

10 And the servants also of Huram, and the servants of Solomon, [e]which brought gold from Ophir, brought [f]algum trees and precious stones.

11 And the king made *of* the algum trees [g]terraces [h]to the house of the LORD, and to the king's palace, and harps and psalteries for singers; and there were none such seen before in the land of Judah.

12 And King Solomon gave to the queen of Sheba all her desire, whatsoever she asked, beside *that* which she had brought unto the king. So she turned, and went away to her own land, she and her servants.

A.M.2989-3029
B. C. 1015-975
Anno ante
I. Ol. 239-199

13 Now the weight of gold that came to Solomon in one year was six hundred and threescore and six talents of gold;

14 Beside *that which* chapmen and merchants brought. And all the kings of Arabia and [i]governors of the country brought gold and silver to Solomon.

15 And King Solomon made two hundred targets *of* beaten gold: six hundred *shekels* of beaten gold went to one target.

16 And three hundred shields *made he of* beaten gold: three hundred *shekels* of gold went to one shield. And the king put them in the house of the forest of Lebanon.

17 Moreover the king made a great throne of ivory, and overlaid it with pure gold.

18 And *there were* six steps to the throne, with a footstool of gold, *which were* fastened to the throne, and [k]stays on each side of the

---

[a]1 Kings x. 1, &c.; Matt. xii. 42; Luke xi. 31——[b]Or, *butlers*——[c]Heb. *word*——[d]Or, *sayings*

[e]Ch. viii. 18——[f]1 Kings x. 11, *almug trees*——[g]Or, *stays* [h]Heb. *highways*——[i]Or, *captains*——[k]Heb. *hands*

NOTES ON CHAP. IX

Verse 1. *The queen of Sheba*] See all the particulars of this royal visit distinctly marked and explained in the notes on 1 Kings x. 1-10. The *Targum* calls her *queen of Zemargad.*

Verse 12. *Beside* that *which she had brought unto the king*] In 1 Kings x. 13 it is stated that Solomon gave her all she asked, *besides that which he gave her of his royal bounty.* It is not at all likely that he gave her back the *presents* which she brought to *him*, and which he had accepted. She had, no doubt, asked for several things which were *peculiar* to the land of Judea, and would be curiosities in her own kingdom; and besides these, he gave her other valuable presents.

Verse 14. *The kings of Arabia*] "The kings of Sistevantha."—*Targum.*

Verse 15. *And King Solomon made two hundred targets of beaten gold*] For a more correct valuation of these targets and shields than that in 1 Kings x. 17, see at the end of the chapter.

Verse 17. *Made a great throne of ivory*] For a very curious description of the *throne of Solomon*, see at the end of the chapter.

A.M.2989-3029
B.C. 1015-975
Anno ante
I. Ol. 239-199 sitting place, and two lions standing by the stays:

19 And twelve lions stood there on the one side and on the other upon the six steps. There was not the like made in any kingdom.

20 And all the drinking vessels of King Solomon *were of* gold, and all the vessels of the house of the forest of Lebanon *were of* [^l]pure gold: [^m]none *were of* silver; it was *not* any thing accounted of in the days of Solomon.

21 For the king's ships went to Tarshish with the servants of Huram: every three years once came the ships of Tarshish bringing gold, and silver, [^n]ivory, and apes, and peacocks.

22 And King Solomon passed all the kings of the earth in riches and wisdom.

23 And all the kings of the earth sought the presence of Solomon, to hear his wisdom, that God had put in his heart.

24 And they brought every man his present, vessels of silver, and vessels of gold, and raiment, harness, and spices, horses, and mules, a rate year by year.

25 And Solomon [^o]had four A.M.2989-3029
B. C. 1015-975
Anno ante
I. Ol. 239-199 thousand stalls for horses and chariots, and twelve thousand horsemen; whom he bestowed in the chariot cities, and with the king at Jerusalem.

26 [^p]And he reigned over all the kings [^q]from the [^r]river even unto the land of the Philistines, and to the border of Egypt.

27 [^s]And the king [^t]made silver in Jerusalem as stones, and cedar trees made he as the sycamore trees that *are* in the low plains in abundance.

28 [^u]And they brought unto Solomon horses out of Egypt, and out of all lands.

29 [^v]Now the rest of the acts of Solomon, first and last, *are* they not written in the [^w]book of Nathan the prophet, and in the prophecy of [^x]Ahijah the Shilonite, and in the visions of [^y]Iddo the seer against Jeroboam the son of Nebat?

30 [^z]And Solomon reigned in Jerusalem over all Israel forty years.

31 And Solomon slept with his fathers, and he was buried in the city of David his father: and Rehoboam his son reigned in his stead.

A. M. 3029
B. C. 975
Anno ante
I. Olymp. 199
Ante Urbem
Conditam 222

[^l]Heb. *shut up*——[^m]Or, there was *no silver* in them [^n]Or, *elephants' teeth*——[^o]1 Kings iv. 26; x. 26; chap. i. 14——[^p]1 Kings iv. 21——[^q]Gen. xv. 18; Psa. lxxii. 8 [^r]That is, *Euphrates*

[^s]1 Kings x. 27; chap. i. 15——[^t]Heb. *gave*——[^u]1 Kings x. 28; chap. i. 16——[^v]1 Kings xi. 41——[^w]Heb. *words*——[^x]1 Kings xi. 29——[^y]Chap. xii. 25; xiii. 22 [^z]1 Kings xi. 42, 43

Verse 21. *The king's ships went to Tarshish*] "Went to *Africa*."—*Targum.*

Verse 25. *Four thousand stalls for horses*] See the note on 1 Kings iv. 26, where the *different numbers* in these two books are considered. The *Targum*, instead of *four thousand*, has ארבע מאה *arba meah*, *four hundred*.

Verse 29. *Nathan the prophet*] These books are all lost. See the account of Solomon, his character, and a review of his works, at the end of 1 Kings xi.

I. By the kindness of a learned friend, who has made this kind of subjects his particular study, I am able to give a more correct view of the value of the talent of gold and the talent of silver than that which I have quoted 1 Kings x. 17, from Mr. Reynold's *State of the Greatest King.*

1. To find the equivalent in British standard to an ounce troy of pure gold, valued at *eighty* shillings, and to a talent of the same which weighs *one thousand eight hundred* ounces troy.

The ounce contains *four hundred and eighty* grains, and the guinea weighs *one hundred and twenty-nine* grains, or *five pennyweights and nine* grains.

(1) As 129 grains : 21 shillings :: 480, the number of grains in an ounce : 78.1395348*s*. or

3*l*. 18*s*. 1*d*. 2.69767*q.*; the equivalent in our silver coin to *one ounce* of standard gold.

(2) As 78.1395348 shillings, the value of an ounce of *standard* gold, : 80 shillings, the value of an ounce troy of *pure* gold, :: 80 shillings : 81.9047619 shillings, the equivalent in *British standard* to *one ounce* of pure gold.

Instead of the preceding, the following proportions may be used:—

(1) As 21.5 shillings : 21 shillings :: 80 shillings : 78.1395348 shillings. This multiplied by 1800, the number of troy ounces in a Hebrew talent, gives 140651.16264*s*. or 7032*l*. 11*s*. 1*d*. 3.8*q.*, the equivalent to one talent of *standard* gold.

(2) As 21 standard : 21.5 pure :: 80 pure : 81.9047619 standard. This multiplied by 1800 gives 147428.57142*s*. or 7371*l*. 8*s*. 6*d*. 3.4*q.*, the equivalent to one talent of *pure* gold.

2. To find the equivalent in British standard to a talent of pure silver, which is valued at *four hundred and fifty pounds* sterling, or *five shillings* the ounce troy.

The pound troy is 240 pennyweights; and our silver coin has 18 pennyweights of alloy in the pound. From 240 pennyweights take 18, and there will remain 222 pennyweights, the pure silver in the pound.

Now as 240 pennyweights : 222 pennyweights :: 20 pennyweights, the weight of a crown piece, : 18½ pennyweights, the weight of the pure silver in the crown.

Then, as 18.5 pennyweights : 5 shillings :: 36000, the number of dwts. in a talent, : 9729.729729729729 shillings, or £486 9s. 8¾d., the equivalent in our coin to a talent of pure silver.

Example 1. To find the equivalent in British standard to the *one hundred and twenty* talents of gold which the queen of Sheba gave to King Solomon, 2 Chron. ix. 9.

147428.57142s. equivalent to one talent of pure gold,
120 number of talents [as found above.

17691428.5704 = £884,571 8s. 6¾d., the equivalent to 120 talents.

Example 2. To find the equivalent in British standard to Solomon's *two hundred* targets of beaten gold, each *six hundred* shekels; and to his *three hundred* shields, each *three hundred* shekels, 2 Chron. ix. 15, 16.

A talent is *three thousand* shekels; therefore *six hundred* shekels are *one-fifth*, and *three hundred* are *one-tenth* of a talent.

5)147428.57142s. equivalent to one talent.

29485.71428   equivalent to one target.
200 the number of targets.

2|0)589714|2.856

£294,857 2s. 10¼d. equivalent to 200 targets.
One-tenth of a talent is 14742.857142 = one shield.
300 number of shlds.

2|0)442285|7.1426

£221,142 17s. 1½d. = 300 shlds.

Example 3. To find the equivalent in British standard to the weight of gold which came to Solomon in one year, independently of what the chapmen and merchants brought him.

147428.57142s. = one talent.
666   number of talents.

88457142852
88457142852
88457142852

2|0)9818742|8.56572

£4,909,371 8s. 6¾d. equivalent to 666 talents.

Example 4. To find the equivalent in British standard, and to the *hundred thousand* talents of gold, and to the *million* of talents of silver, which were prepared by David for the temple, 1 Chron. xxii. 14.

THE GOLD

147428.57142s. = one talent.
100000 number of talents.

2|0)1474285714|2

£737,142,857 2s. the equivalent.

Or, *seven hundred and thirty-seven millions, one hundred and forty-two thousand, eight hundred and fifty-seven pounds, two shillings* sterling, for the gold.

THE SILVER

9729.729729729s. = one talent.
1000000 number of talents.

2|0)972972972|9.729

£486,486,486 9s. 8½d. the equivalent.

Or, *four hundred and eighty-six millions, four hundred and eighty-six thousand, four hundred and eighty-six pounds, nine shillings, and eightpence halfpenny* sterling, for the *silver*.

II. I have referred, in the note on ver. 17, to a curious account of Solomon's throne, taken from a Persian MS. entitled بيت المقدس *beet al mukuddus, the Holy House,* or *Jerusalem.* It has already been remarked, in the account of Solomon at the end of chap. xi. of 1 Kings, article 12, that among the oriental writers Solomon is considered, not only as the wisest of all men, but as having supreme command over *demons* and *genii* of all kinds; and that he knew the language of beasts and birds, &c.; and therefore the reader need not be surprised if he find, in the following account, Solomon employing preternatural agency in the construction of this celebrated *throne.*

"This famous throne was the work of the *Deev Sukhur;* it was called *Koukab al Jinna.* The beauty of this throne has never been sufficiently described; the following are the particulars:—

"The *sides* of it were pure gold; the *feet,* of emeralds and pearls, intermixed with other pearls, each of which was as large as the egg of an ostrich.

"The *throne* had SEVEN *steps;* on each side were delineated *orchards* full of trees, the branches of which were composed of precious stones, representing ripe and unripe fruits.

"On the tops of the trees were to be seen *fowls* of the most beautiful plumage; particularly the *peacock,* the *etaub,* and the *kurgus;* all these birds were artificially hollowed within, so as occasionally to utter a thousand melodious notes, such as the ears of mortals had never before heard.

"On the FIRST *step* were delineated *vine-branches,* having bunches of *grapes,* composed of various sorts of precious stones; fashioned in such a manner as to represent the different colours of *purple, violet, green,* and *red,* so as to exhibit the appearance of *real fruit.*

"On the SECOND *step,* on each side of the *throne,* were *two lions,* of massive gold, of terrible aspect, and as large as life.

"The property of this throne was such, that when the prophet Solomon placed his foot upon the FIRST *step,* all the *birds* spread their wings, and made a fluttering noise in the air.

"On his touching the SECOND *step,* the two *lions* expanded their claws.

"On his reaching the THIRD *step,* the whole assembly of *deevs, peris,* and *men,* repeated the praises of the Deity.

"When he arrived at the FOURTH *step,* voices were heard addressing him in the following manner: *Son of David be grateful for the blessings which the Almighty has bestowed upon thee.*

"The same was repeated on his reaching the FIFTH *step.*

"On his touching the SIXTH *step,* all the *children* sang praises.

"On his arrival at the SEVENTH *step,* the whole *throne,* with all the *birds* and other *animals,* became in motion, and ceased not till he had placed himself in the royal seat; and then the *birds, lions,* and other *animals,* by secret springs, discharged a shower of the *most precious musk* upon the prophet; after which two of the *kurguses,* descending placed a *golden crown* upon his head.

"Before the *throne* was a *column of burnished gold;* on the top of which was placed a *golden dove,* which had in its beak a *roll* bound in silver. In this *roll* were written the *Psalms* of the prophet *David;* and the *dove* having presented the *roll* to King Solomon, he read a portion of it to the children of Israel.

"It is farther related that, on the approach of *wicked* persons to this throne for judgment, the *lions* were wont to set up a terrible roaring, and to lash their tails about with violence; the *birds* also began to erect their feathers; and the whole *assembly* of *deeves* and *genii* uttered such loud cries, that for fear of them no person would dare to be guilty of falsehood, but instantly confess his crimes.

"Such was the *throne* of Solomon, the son of David."

Supposing even this splendid description to be *literally* true, there is nothing here that could not have been performed by *ingenuity* and *art;* nothing that needed the aid of *supernatural* influence.

In another MS., on which I cannot now lay my hand, the whole value of this throne, and its ornaments, is computed in *lacs* of *rupees!* The above description is founded in the main on the account given here, chap. ix. 17-19. The SIX *steps,* and the *footstool* of the sacred writer, make the SEVEN *steps,* in the above description. The *twelve* lions are not *distinguished* by the Mohammedan writer. Other matters are added from *tradition.*

This profusion of gold and precious stones was not beyond the reach of Solomon, when we consider the many millions left by his father; no less a sum than *one thousand two hundred and twenty-three millions, six hundred and twenty-nine thousand, three hundred and forty-three pounds, eleven shillings, and eight pence halfpenny,* besides what Solomon himself furnished.

CHAPTER X

The people apply to Rehoboam to ease them of their burdens, 1–4. Rejecting the advice of the aged counsellors, and following that of the young men, he gives them an ungracious answer, 5–14. The people are discouraged, and ten tribes revolt, 15–17. They stone Hadoram, who went to collect the tribute; and Rehoboam but barely escapes, 18, 19.

A. M. 3029
B. C. 975
Anno ante
I. Olymp. 199
Ante Urbem
Conditam 222

A ND ^aRehoboam went to Shechem: for to Shechem were all Israel come to make him king.

2 And it came to pass, when Jeroboam the son of Nebat, who *was* in Egypt, ^bwhither he had fled from the presence of Solomon the king, heard *it,* that Jeroboam returned out of Egypt.

3 And they sent and called him. So Jeroboam and all Israel came and spake to Rehoboam, saying,

4 Thy father made our yoke grievous: now therefore ease thou somewhat the grievous servitude of thy father, and his heavy yoke that he put upon us, and we will serve thee.

5 And he said unto them, Come again unto me after three days. And the people departed.

6 And King Rehoboam took counsel with the old men that had stood before Solomon his father while he yet lived, saying, What counsel give ye *me* to return answer to this people?

7 And they spake unto him, saying, If thou be kind to this people, and please them, and speak good words to them, they will be thy servants for ever.

8 But he forsook the counsel which the old men gave him, and took counsel with the young men that were brought up with him, that stood before him.

A. M. 3029
B. C. 975
Anno ante
I. Olymp. 199
Ante Urbem
Conditam 222

9 And he said unto them, What advice give ye that we may return answer to this people, which have spoken to me, saying, Ease somewhat the yoke that thy father did put upon us?

10 And the young men that were brought up with him spake unto him, saying, Thus shalt thou answer the people that spake unto thee, saying, Thy father made our yoke heavy, but make thou *it* somewhat lighter for us; thus shalt thou say unto them, My little *finger* shall be thicker than my father's loins.

11 For whereas my father ^cput a heavy yoke upon you, I will put more to your yoke; my father chastised you with whips, but I *will chastise you* with scorpions.

12 So Jeroboam and all the people came to Rehoboam on the third day, as the king bade, saying, Come again to me on the third day.

13 And the king answered them roughly; and King Rehoboam forsook the counsel of the old men,

---

^a1 Kings xii. 1, &c.——^b1 Kings xi. 40

^cHeb. *laded*

NOTES ON CHAP. X
Verse 1. *Rehoboam went to Shechem*] This chapter is almost word for word the same as

1 Kings xii., to the notes on which the reader is referred.
Verse 10. *My little finger shall be thicker*]

A. M. 3029
B. C. 975
Anno ante
I. Olymp. 199
Ante Urbem
Conditam 222

14 And answered them after the advice of the young men, saying, My father made your yoke heavy, but I will add thereto: my father chastised you with whips, but I *will chastise you* with scorpions.

15 So the king hearkened not unto the people: ᵈfor the cause was of God, that the LORD might perform his word, which he spake by the ᵉhand of Ahijah the Shilonite to Jeroboam the son of Nebat.

16 And when all Israel *saw* that the king would not hearken unto them, the people answered the king, saying, What portion have we in David? and *we have* none inheritance

in the son of Jesse: every man to your tents, O Israel: *and* now, David, see to thine own house. So all Israel went to their tents.

17 But *as for* the children of Israel that dwelt in the cities of Judah, Rehoboam reigned over them.

18 Then King Rehoboam sent Hadoram that *was* over the tribute; and the children of Israel stoned him with stones, that he died. But King Rehoboam ᶠmade speed to get him up to *his* chariot, to flee to Jerusalem.

19 ᵍAnd Israel rebelled against the house of David unto this day.

A. M. 3029
B. C. 975
Anno ante
I. Olymp. 199
Ante Urbem
Conditam 222

ᵈ1 Sam. ii. 25; 1 Kings xii. 15, 24——ᵉ1 Kings xi. 29

ᶠHeb. *strengthened himself*——ᵍ1 Kings xii. 19

"My weakness shall be stronger than the might of my father."—*Targum.*

Verse 15. *For the cause was of God*] "For there was an occasion Divinely given."—*Targum.*

Verse 16. *To your tents, O Israel*] "To your cities, O Israel."—*Targum.*

Now, David, see to thine own house.] "Now, David, rule over the men of thy own house." —*Targum.*

Verse 18. *Stoned him*] When he endeavoured to collect the tribute which Solomon had imposed on them.—*Jarchi.*

Verse 19. *Israel rebelled*] A few soft words, and the removal of a part of the oppressive taxes, (for they said, *Ease thou* SOMEWHAT *the grievous servitude,*) would have secured this people to the state, and prevented the shedding of a sea of human blood, which was the consequence of the separation of this kingdom. Rehoboam was a fool; and through his folly he

lost his kingdom. He is not the only example on record: the *Stuarts* lost the realm of England much in the same way; and, by a different mode of treatment, the House of Brunswick continues to fill the British throne. May the *thread* of its fortune, *woven* by the hand of God, never be undone! and may the *current* of its *power glide on* to the latest posterity!

Talia secla, suis dixerunt, currite, fusis Concordes stabili fatorum numine Parcæ.
VIRG. Ecl. iv., ver. 46.

"God's firm decree, by which this *web* was *spun,* Shall ever bless the *clue,* and bid it *smoothly* run."

Labitur, et labetur in omne volubilis Ævum.
HORAT. Epist., l. i., c. 2, v. 43.

"Still glides the river, and shall ever glide."
Amen! Amen!

CHAPTER XI

Rehoboam raises an army, purposing to reduce the ten tribes; but is prevented by Shemaiah the prophet, 1–4. He builds several cities of defence, and fortifies others, 5–12. The priests and Levites being turned out by Jeroboam, come to Rehoboam, 13, 14. Jeroboam's gross idolatry, 15. The pious of the land join with Judah, and strengthen the kingdom of Rehoboam, 16, 17. His wives, concubines, and numerous issue, 18–21. He places his own sons for governors in the different provinces, 22, 23.

A. M. 3029
B. C. 975
Anno ante
I. Olymp. 199
Ante Urbem
Conditam 222

AND ᵃwhen Rehoboam was come to Jerusalem, he gathered of the house of Judah and Benjamin a hundred and fourscore thousand chosen *men,* which were warriors, to fight against Israel, that he might bring the kingdom again to Rehoboam.

2 But the word of the LORD came ᵇto Shemaiah the man of God, saying,

3 Speak unto Rehoboam the son of Solomon, king of Judah, and to all Israel in Judah and Benjamin, saying,

4 Thus saith the LORD, Ye shall not go up, nor fight against your brethren: return every man to his house: for this thing is done of me. And they obeyed the words of the LORD, and returned from going against Jeroboam.

A. M. 3029
B. C. 975
Anno ante
I. Olymp. 199
Ante Urbem
Conditam 222

ᵃ1 Kings xii. 21, &c.

ᵇChap. xii. 15

NOTES ON CHAP. XI

Verse 1. *Gathered of the house of Judah*] See this account 1 Kings xii. 21-24, and the notes there.

Verse 5. *And built cities for defence in Judah.*]

He was obliged to strengthen his frontiers against the encroachments of the men of Israel; and Jeroboam did the same thing on his part, to prevent the inroads of Judah. See 1 Kings xii. 25.

A.M.3029-3032
B. C. 975–972
Anno ante
I. Ol. 199-196
5 And Rehoboam dwelt in Jerusalem, and built cities for defence in Judah.

6 He built even Beth-lehem, and Etam, and Tekoa,

7 And Beth-zur, and Shoco, and Adullam,

8 And Gath, and Mareshah, and Ziph,

9 And Adoraim, and Lachish, and Azekah,

10 And Zorah, and Aijalon, and Hebron, which *are* in Judah and in Benjamin, fenced cities.

11 And he fortified the strong holds, and put captains in them, and store of victual, and of oil and wine.

12 And in every several city *he put* shields and spears, and made them exceeding strong, having Judah and Benjamin on his side.

A. M. 3030
B. C. 974
Anno ante
I. Olymp. 198
Ante Urbem
Conditam 221
13 And the priests and the Levites that *were* in all Israel ^cresorted to him out of all their coasts.

14 For the Levites left ^dtheir suburbs and their possession, and came to Judah and Jerusalem: for ^eJeroboam and his sons had cast them off from executing the priest's office unto the LORD:

15 ^fAnd he ordained him priests for the high places, and for ^gthe devils, and for ^hthe calves which he had made.

16 ⁱAnd after them out of all the tribes of Israel such as set their hearts to seek the LORD God of Israel came to Jerusalem, to sacrifice unto the LORD God of their fathers.
A.M.3029-3032
B. C. 975–972
Anno ante
I. Ol. 199–196

17 So they ^kstrengthened the kingdom of Judah, and made Rehoboam the son of Solomon strong, three years: for three years they walked in the way of David and Solomon.

18 And Rehoboam took him Mahalath the daughter of Jerimoth the son of David to wife, *and* Abihail the daughter of Eliab the son of Jesse;
A.M.3029-3046
B. C. 975–958
Anno ante
I. Ol. 199–182

19 Which bare him children; Jeush, and Shamariah, and Zaham.

20 And after her he took ^lMaachah the daughter of Absalom; which bare him Abijah, and Attai, and Ziza, and Shelomith.

21 And Rehoboam loved Maachah the daughter of Absalom above all his wives and his concubines: (for he took eighteen wives, and threescore concubines; and begat twenty and eight sons, and threescore daughters.)

22 And Rehoboam ^mmade Abijah the son of Maachah the chief, *to be* ruler among his brethren: for *he thought* to make him king.

23 And he dealt wisely, and dispersed of all his children throughout all the countries of Judah and Benjamin, unto every fenced city: and he gave them victual in abundance. And he desired ⁿmany wives.

---

^cHeb. *presented themselves to him*——^dNum. xxxv. 2
^eChap. xiii. 9——^f1 Kings xii. 31; xiii. 33; xiv. 9; Hos.
xiii. 2——^gLev. xvii. 7; 1 Cor. x. 20——^h1 Kings xii. 28

ⁱSee ch. xv. 9; xxx. 11, 18——^kCh. xii. 1——^l1 Kings xv.
2; she is called Michaiah the daughter of Uriel, ch. xiii. 2
^mSee Deut. xxi. 15, 16, 17——ⁿHeb. *a multitude of wives*

Verse 11. *Store of victual*] In these places he laid up stores of provisions, not only to enable *them* to endure a siege; but also that they might be able, from their situation, to supply desolate places.

Verse 14. *The Levites left their suburbs*] They and the priests were expelled from their offices by Jeroboam, lest they should turn the hearts of the people to the true God, and then they would revolt to Judah, 1 Kings xii. 26; and therefore he established a new worship, and made new gods.

Verse 15. *And he ordained him priests—for the devils*] שעירים seirim, the *hairy ones;* probably *goats:* for as the *golden calves,* or *oxen,* were in imitation of the Egyptian ox-god, *Apis;* so they no doubt paid Divine honours to the *goat,* which we know was an object of religious veneration in Egypt.

Verse 16. *Such as set their hearts to seek the Lord*] All the truly pious joined him out of every tribe; and the whole tribe of *Levi,* being deprived of their functions, joined him also. Thus he had *Judah, Benjamin,* and *Levi,* and probably a part of *Simeon;* for he had

Etam, which was in that tribe, and the truly religious out of all the other tribes, for they could not bear Jeroboam's idolatry.

Verse 17. *For three years they walked in the way of David*] During this time he prospered; but for *fourteen* years after this he and the people were unfaithful to the Lord, except at such intervals as the hand of God's judgments was upon them.

Verse 18. *Took him Mahalath*] By marrying thus in the family of David, he strengthened his right to the Jewish throne.

Verse 20. *Maachah the daughter of Absalom*] See the note on 1 Kings xv. 10. She is called *Michaiah, the daughter of Uriel,* chap. xiii. 2. For this the *Targum* gives the following reason: "Abijah reigned *three* years in Jerusalem; and his mother's name was Michaiah, daughter of Uriel of Gibeatha. She is the same as Michah, the daughter of Absalom; but, because she was an upright woman, her name was changed into the more excellent name Michaiah, and her father's name into that of Uriel of Gibeatha, that the name of Absalom might not be remembered."

Verse 21. *Eighteen wives, and threescore con-*

cubines] Bad enough, but not so abandoned as his father. Of these marriages and concubinage the issue was *twenty-eight* sons and *sixty* daughters; *eighty-eight* children in the whole, to the education of the whole of whom he could pay but little attention. Numerous families are often neglected; and children by *different women*, must be yet in a worse state.

Verse 22. *Made Abijah—the chief*] Abijah certainly was not the *first-born* of Rehoboam; but as he loved Maachah more than any of his wives, so he preferred her son, probably through his mother's influence. In Deut. xxi. 16, this sort of preference is forbidden; but Rehoboam had a sort of precedent in the preference shown by David to Solomon.

Verse 23. *He dealt wisely*] It was true policy to disperse his own sons through the different provinces who were not likely to form any league with Jeroboam against their father.

He desired many wives.] He was much addicted to women; yet we do not find that he formed any heathenish alliances of this nature. And as no particulars are given, we do not know how far he indulged himself in this propensity. He probably strengthened his political connections by these means.

CHAPTER XII

Rehoboam and his subjects, forsaking the Lord, are delivered into the hands of Shishak, king of Egypt, 1-4. Shemaiah the prophet remonstrates with them, and they humble themselves, and Jerusalem is not destroyed; but Shishak takes away all the treasures, and the golden shields, instead of which Rehoboam makes shields of brass, 5-12. He reigns badly seventeen years, dies, and is succeeded by his son Abijah, 13-16.

A. M. 3032
B. C. 972
Anno ante
I. Olymp. 196
Ante Urbem
Conditam 219

AND ᵃit came to pass, when Rehoboam had established the kingdom, and had strengthened himself, ᵇhe forsook the law of the LORD, and all Israel with him.

A. M. 3034
B. C. 970
Anno ante
I. Olymp. 194
Ante Urbem
Conditam 217

2 ᶜAnd it came to pass, *that* in the fifth year of King Rehoboam, Shishak king of Egypt came up against Jerusalem, because they had transgressed against the LORD,

3 With twelve hundred chariots, and threescore thousand horsemen: and the people *were* without number that came with him out of Egypt; ᵈthe Lubims, the Sukkiims, and the Ethiopians.

4 And he took the fenced cities which *pertained* to Judah, and came to Jerusalem.

5 Then came ᵉShemaiah the prophet to Rehoboam, and *to* the princes of Judah, that were gathered together to Jerusalem because of Shishak, and said unto them, Thus saith the LORD, ᶠYe have forsaken me, and therefore have I also left you in the hand of Shishak.

A. M. 3034
B. C. 970
Anno ante
I. Olymp. 194
Ante Urbem
Conditam 217

6 Whereupon the princes of Israel and the king ᵍhumbled themselves; and they said, ʰThe LORD *is* righteous.

7 And when the LORD saw that they humbled themselves, ⁱthe word of the LORD came to Shemaiah, saying, They have humbled themselves; *therefore* I will not destroy them, but I will grant them ᵏsome deliverance; and my wrath shall not be poured out upon Jerusalem by the hand of Shishak.

ᵃChap. xi. 17——ᵇ1 Kings xiv. 22, 23, 24——ᶜ1 Kings xiv. 24, 25——ᵈChap. xvi. 8——ᵉChap. xi. 2

ᶠChap. xv. 2——ᵍJames iv. 10——ʰExod. ix. 27——ⁱ1 Kings xxi. 28, 29——ᵏOr, *a little while*

NOTES ON CHAP. XII

Verse 1. *He forsook the law of the Lord*] This was after the *three* years mentioned chap. xi. 17.

Verse 2. *Shishak king of Egypt*] Concerning this man, and the motive which led him to attack the Jews, see the note on 1 Kings xiv. 31.

Transgressed against the Lord] "Against the WORD of the Lord."—*Targum.*

Verse 3. *The Lubims*] Supposed to be a people of *Libya*, adjoining to Egypt; sometimes called *Phut* in Scripture, as the people are called *Lehabim* and *Ludim.*

The Sukkiims] The *Troglodytes*, a people of Egypt on the coast of the Red Sea. They were called *Troglodytes*, Τρωγλοδύται, οἱ εἰς τας τρωγλας οἰκουντες, "because they dwelt in caves."— *Hesych.* This agrees with what *Pliny* says of them, *Troglodytæ specus excavant, hæc illis*

domus; "The Troglodytes dig themselves caves; and these serve them for houses." This is not very different from the import of the original name סכיים *Sukkiyim,* from סכה *sachah,* to *cover* or *overspread;* (hence סוך *such,* a *tabernacle;*) the people who were *covered* (emphatically) *under the earth.* The Septuagint translate by the word Τρωγλοδύται, *Troglodytes.*

The Ethiopians.] כושים *Cushim.* Various people were called by this name, particularly a people bordering on the northern coast of the Red Sea; but *these* are supposed to have come from a country of that name on the south of Egypt.

Verse 6. *Whereupon the princes of Israel and the king humbled themselves*] This is not mentioned in the parallel place, 1 Kings xiv.: this was the sole reason why Jerusalem was not at this time *totally* destroyed, and the house of David entirely cut off; for they were totally

A. M. 3034
B. C. 970
Anno ante
I. Olymp. 194
Ante Urbem
Conditam 217

8 Nevertheless [1]they shall be his servants; that they may know [m]my service, and the service of the kingdoms of the countries.

9 [n]So Shishak king of Egypt came up against Jerusalem, and took away the treasures of the house of the LORD, and the treasures of the king's house; he took all: he carried away also the shields of gold which Solomon had [o]made.

10 Instead of which King Rehoboam made shields of brass, and committed *them* [p]to the hands of the chief of the guard, that kept the entrance of the king's house.

11 And when the king entered into the house of the LORD, the guard came and fetched them, and brought them again into the guard chamber.

12 And when he humbled himself, the wrath of the LORD turned from him, that he would not destroy *him* altogether: [q]and also in Judah things went well.

13 So King Rehoboam strengthened himself in Jerusalem, and reigned: for [r]Rehoboam *was* one and forty years old when he began *to* reign, and he reigned seventeen years in Jerusalem, [s]the city which the LORD had chosen out of all the tribes of Israel, to put his name there. And his mother's name *was* Naamah an Ammonitess.

A.M.3029-3046
B. C. 975-958
Anno ante
I. Ol. 199-182

14 And he did evil, because he [t]prepared not his heart to seek the LORD.

15 Now the acts of Rehoboam, first and last, *are* they not written in the [u]book of Shemaiah the prophet, [v]and of Iddo the seer concerning genealogies? [w]And *there were* wars between Rehoboam and Jeroboam continually.

16 And Rehoboam slept with his fathers, and was buried in the city of David: and [x]Abijah his son reigned in his stead.

A. M. 3046
B. C. 958
Anno ante
I. Olymp. 182
Ante Urbem
Conditam 205

---

[l]See Isaiah xxvi. 13——[m]Deut. xxviii. 47, 48——[n]1 Kings xiv. 25, 26——[o]1 Kings x. 16, 17; chapter ix. 15, 16——[p]2 Samuel viii. 18——[q]Or, *and yet in Judah there were good things;* see Genesis xviii. 24; and

1 Kings xiv. 13; chapter xix. 3——[r]1 Kings xiv. 21 [s]Chapter vi. 6——[t]Or, *fixed*——[u]Hebrew, *words* [v]Chapter ix. 29; xiii. 22——[w]1 Kings xiv. 30——[x]1 Kings xiv. 31, *Abijam*

---

incapable of defending themselves against this innumerable host.

Verse 8. *They shall be his servants*] They shall be preserved, and serve their enemies, that they may see the difference between the service of God and that of man. While they were pious, they found the service of the Lord to be *perfect freedom;* when they forsook the Lord, they found the fruit to be *perfect bondage.* A sinful life is both expensive and painful.

Verse 9. *Took away the treasures*] Such a booty as never had before, nor has since, come into the hand of man.

The shields of gold] These shields were the mark of the king's body-guard: it was in imitation of this Eastern magnificence that Alexander constituted his *Argyraspides,* adorned with the spoils taken from Darius. See Quintus Curtius, lib. viii., c. 5, et alibi.

Verse 13. *Was one and forty years old*] Houbigant thinks he was but *sixteen* years old when he began to reign; and brings many and forcible arguments to prove that the number *forty-one* must be a mistake. That he was *young*

when he came to the throne, is evident from his consulting *the young men that were brought up with him,* chap. x. 8, 10. They were *young men* then; and if *he* was *brought up with them,* he must have been *young then* also. Besides, Abijah, in his speech to Jeroboam, chap. xiii. 7, says that at the time Rehoboam came to the throne he was tender-hearted, and therefore could not withstand the children of Belial raised up against him by Jeroboam: but surely at that time no man could be reputed *young* and *tender-hearted*—quite devoid of experience, who was above *forty* years of age. Besides, if this reading were allowed, it would prove that he was born *before* his father Solomon began to reign, for Solomon reigned only *forty* years, and Rehoboam immediately succeeded him.

Verse 15. *Concerning genealogies*] "In the book of the genealogy of the family of David." —*Targum.*

Verse 16. *Abijah his son*] Concerning the many varieties in this king's name, see the note on 1 Kings xiv. 31.

CHAPTER XIII

Abijah begins to reign over Judah, and has war with Jeroboam, 1–3. His speech from Mount Zemaraim to Jeroboam, before the commencement of hostilities, 4–12. While thus engaged, Jeroboam despatches some troops, which come on the rear of Abijah's army, 13. Perceiving this, they cry unto the Lord, and the Israelites are defeated with the loss of five hundred thousand men, 14–18. Abijah retakes several cities from Jeroboam, who is smitten by the Lord, and dies, 19, 20. Abijah's marriages and issue, 21, 22.

A.M.3046-3049
B. C. 958–955
Anno ante
I. Ol. 182–179

NOW [a]in the eighteenth year of King Jeroboam began Abijah to reign over Judah.

2 He reigned three years in Jerusalem. His mother's name also *was* [b]Michaiah the

daughter of Uriel of Gibeah. And there was war between Abijah and Jeroboam.

3 And Abijah [c]set the battle in array with an army of valiant men of war,

A. M. 3047
B. C. 957
Anno ante
I. Olymp. 181
Ante Urbem
Conditam 204

---

[a]1 Kings xv. 1, &c.——[b]See chap. xi. 20

[c]Heb. *bound together*

NOTES ON CHAP. XIII

Verse 2. *His mother's name—was Michaiah*] See on chap. xi. 20.

Verse 3. *Abijah set the battle in array*] The *numbers* in this verse and in the seventeenth seem almost incredible. Abijah's army consisted of *four hundred thousand* effective men; that of Jeroboam consisted of *eight hundred thousand;* and the *slain* of Jeroboam's army were *five hundred thousand.* Now it is very possible that there is a *cipher* too much in all these numbers, and that they should stand thus: *Abijah's* army, *forty thousand; Jeroboam's, eighty thousand;* the *slain, fifty thousand.* Calmet, who defends the common reading, allows that the *Venice* edition of the Vulgate, in 1478; another, in 1489; that of *Nuremberg,* in 1521; that of *Basil,* by *Froben,* in 1538; that of *Robert Stevens,* in 1546; and many others, have the *smaller numbers.* Dr. *Kennicott* says: "On a particular collation of the *Vulgate* version, it appears that the number of chosen men here *slain,* which Pope *Clement's* edition in 1592 determines to be *five hundred thousand,* the edition of Pope *Sixtus,* printed two years before, determined to be only *fifty thousand;* and the two preceding numbers, in the edition of *Sixtus,* are *forty thousand* and *eighty thousand.* As to different *printed editions,* out of *fifty-two* from the year 1462 to 1592, *thirty-one* contain the *less* number. And out of *fifty-one* MSS. *twenty-three* in the *Bodleian* library, *four* in that of *Dean Aldrich,* and *two* in that of *Exeter College,* contain the *less* number, or else are corrupted irregularly, varying only one or two numbers."

This examination was made by Dr. *Kennicott* before he had finished his collation of Hebrew MSS., and before *De Rossi* had published his *Variæ Lectiones Veteris Testamenti;* but from these works we find little help, as far as the *Hebrew* MSS. are concerned. One Hebrew MS., instead of ארבע מאות אלף *arba meoth eleph, four hundred thousand,* reads ארבע עשר אלף *arba eser eleph, fourteen thousand.*

In all *printed* copies of the *Hebrew,* the numbers are as in the common text, *four hundred thousand, eight hundred thousand,* and *five hundred thousand.*

The *versions* are as follow:—The *Targum,* or *Chaldee,* the same in each place as the Hebrew.

The *Syriac* in ver. 3 has *four hundred thousand young men* for the army of Abijah, and *eight hundred thousand stout youth* for that of Jeroboam. For the *slain* Israelites, in ver. 17, it has ܚܡܫܡܐܐ *five hundred thousand,* falsely translated in the Latin text *quinque milia, five thousand,* both in the *Paris* and *London* Polyglots: another proof among many that little dependence is to be placed on the *Latin translation* of this version in either of the above Polyglots.

The *Arabic* is the same in all these cases with the *Syriac,* from which it has been translated.

The *Septuagint,* both as it is published in all the Polyglots, and as far as I have seen in MSS., is the same with the *Hebrew text.* So also is *Josephus.*

The *Vulgate* or *Latin* version is that alone that exhibits any important variations; we have had considerable proof of this in the above-mentioned collations of *Calmet* and *Kennicott.* I shall beg liberty to add others from my own collection.

In the *Editio Princeps* of the Latin Bible, though without *date* or *place,* yet evidently printed long before that of *Fust,* in 1462, the places stand thus: Verse 3. *Cumque inisset certamen, et haberet bellicosissimos viros, et electorum* QUADRAGINTA milia: *Iheroboam construxit e contra aciem* OCTOGINTA *milia virorum;* "With him Abia entered into battle; and he had of the most warlike and choice men *forty thousand;* and Jeroboam raised an army against him of *eighty thousand men.*"

And in ver. 17: *Et corruerunt vulnerati ex Israel,* QUINQUAGINTA *milia virorum fortium;* "And there fell down wounded *fifty thousand* stout men of Israel."

In the *Glossa Ordinaria,* by *Strabo Fuldensis,* we have *forty thousand* and *eighty thousand* in the two first instances, and *five hundred thousand* in the last.—*Bib. Sacr.* vol. ii., *Antv.* 1634.

In *six* ancient MSS. of my own, marked A, B, C, D, E, F, the text stands thus:—

A.—*Cumque inisset Abia certamen, et haberet bellicosissimos viros, et electorum* XL. MIL. *Jeroboam instruxit contra aciem* LXXX. MIL.

And in ver. 17: *Et corruerunt vulnerati ex Israel* L. MIL. *virorum fortium.* Here we have *forty thousand* for the army of *Abijah,* and *eighty thousand* for that of *Jeroboam,* and FIFTY *thousand* for the *slain* of the latter.

B.—QUADRAGINTA *milia,* OCTOGINTA *milia,* FORTY *thousand.* EIGHTY *thousand.*
QUINQUAGINTA *milia,* FIFTY *thousand.*

The numbers being here expressed in *words* at full length, there can be no suspicion of mistake.

C.—CCCC *milia,* DCCC *milibus,* D *milia,* 400 *thousand.* 800 *thousand.* 500 *thousand.*

This is the same as the Hebrew text, and very distinctly expressed.

D.—*xl.* m.   *lxxx.* m.   *l. v.* m. 40,000.   80,000.   50 and 5000.

This, in the two first numbers, is the same as the others above; but the last is confused, and appears to stand for *fifty thousand* and *five thousand.* A later hand has corrected the two first numbers in this MS., placing *over* the first four cccc, thus: *xl.,* thus changing *forty* into *four hundred;* and over the second thus, dccc *lxxx.,* thus changing *eighty* into *eight hundred.* Over the latter number, which is evidently a *mistake* of the scribe, there is no correction.

E.—*xl.* m.   OCTOGINTA m.   *l.* m. 40,000.   EIGHTY *thousand.* 50,000.

A. M. 3047
B. C. 957
Anno ante
I. Olymp. 181
Ante Urbem
Conditam 204

even four hundred thousand chosen men: Jeroboam also set the battle in array against him with eight hundred thousand chosen men, *being* mighty men of valour.

4 And Abijah stood up upon Mount ^dZemaraim, which *is* in Mount Ephraim, and said, Hear me, thou Jeroboam, and all Israel;

5 Ought ye not to know that the LORD God of Israel ^egave the kingdom over Israel to David for ever, *even* to him and to his sons ^fby a covenant of salt?

6 Yet Jeroboam the son of Nebat, the servant of Solomon the son of David, is risen up, and hath ^grebelled against his lord.

7 And there are gathered unto him ^hvain men, the children of Belial, and have strengthened themselves against Rehoboam the son of Solomon, when Rehoboam was young and tender-hearted, and could not withstand them.

8 And now ye think to withstand the kingdom of the LORD in the hand of the sons of David; and ye *be* a great multitude, and *there are* with you golden calves, which Jeroboam ⁱmade you for gods.

9 ^jHave ye not cast out the priests of the LORD, the sons of Aaron, and the Levites, and have made you priests after the manner of the nations of *other* lands? ^lso that whoso-

ever cometh ^mto consecrate himself with a young bullock and seven rams, *the same* may be a priest of *them that are* no gods.

10 But as for us, the LORD *is* our God, and we have not forsaken him; and the priests, which minister unto the LORD, *are* the sons of Aaron, and the Levites *wait* upon *their* business:

11 ⁿAnd they burn unto the LORD every morning and every evening burnt-sacrifices and sweet incense: the ^oshew-bread also *set they in order* upon the pure table; and the candlestick of gold with the lamps thereof, ^pto burn every evening: for we keep the charge of the LORD our God; but ye have forsaken him.

12 And, behold, God himself *is* with us for *our* captain, ^qand his priests with sounding trumpets to cry alarm against you. O children of Israel, ^rfight ye not against the LORD God of your fathers; for ye shall not prosper.

13 But Jeroboam caused an ambushment to come about behind them: so they were before Judah, and the ambushment *was* behind them.

14 And when Judah looked back, behold, the battle *was* before and behind: and they cried unto the LORD, and the priests sounded with the trumpets.

15 Then the men of Judah gave a shout:

A. M. 3047
B. C. 957
Anno ante
I. Olymp. 181
Ante Urbem
Conditam 204

---

^dJoshua xviii. 22——^e2 Samuel vii. 12, 13, 16 ^fNumbers xviii. 19——^g1 Kings xi. 26; xii. 20 ^hJudges ix. 4——ⁱ1 Kings xii. 28; xiv. 9; Hosea viii. 6——^kChapter xi. 14, 15——^lExodus xxix. 35

^mHebrew, *to fill his hand;* see Exodus xxix. 1; Leviticus viii, 2——ⁿChapter ii. 4——^oLev. xxiv. 6——^pExod. xxvii. 20, 21; Leviticus xxiv. 2, 3——^qNumbers x. 8 ^rActs v. 39

F.—cccc. m.	dccc. m.	d. m.
400,000.	800,000.	500,000.

This also is the same as the Hebrew.

The reader has now the whole evidence which I have been able to collect before him, and may choose; the *smaller* numbers appear to be the most correct. Corruptions in the numbers in these historical books we have often had cause to *suspect*, and to complain of.

Verse 4. *Stood up upon Mount Zemaraim*] "Which was a mount of the tribe of the house of Ephraim."—*Targum. Jarchi* thinks that Abijah went to the confines of the tribe of Ephraim to attack Jeroboam. It could not be *Shomeron*, the mount on which *Samaria* was built in the days of Omri king of Israel, 1 Kings xvi. 24.

Verse 5. *By a covenant of salt?*] For ever. "For as the waters of the sea never grow *sweet*, neither shall the dominion depart from the house of David."—*Targum.* See my note on Num. xviii. 19.

Verse 7. *When Rehoboam was young and tender-hearted*] Therefore he could not be *forty-one* when he came to the throne; see the note on ver. 3. *Children of Belial* here signifies

men of the most abandoned principles and characters; or men without consideration, education, or *brains*.

Verse 9. *A young bullock and seven rams*] He who could provide these for his own consecration was received into the order of this spurious and wicked priesthood. Some think he who could give to Jeroboam a young bullock and seven rams, was thereby received into the priesthood; this being the price for which the priesthood was conferred. The former is most likely.

Verse 10. *The Lord is our God*] We have not abandoned the Lord; and we still serve him according to his own law.

Verse 12. *God himself is with us*] Ye have *golden calves;* we have *the living and omnipotent Jehovah.*

With—trumpets to cry alarm against you.] This was appalling: When the priests sound their trumpets, it will be a proof that the vengeance of the Lord shall speedily descend upon you.

Verse 13. *But Jeroboam caused an ambushment*] While Abijah was thus employed in re-

| A. M. 3047 |
| B. C. 957 |
| Anno ante |
| I. Olymp. 181 |
| Ante Urbem |
| Conditam 204 |

and as the men of Judah shouted, it came to pass, that God ˢsmote Jeroboam and all Israel before Abijah and Judah.

16 And the children of Israel fled before Judah: and God delivered them into their hand.

17 And Abijah and his people slew them with a great slaughter: so there fell down slain of Israel five hundred thousand chosen men.

18 Thus the children of Israel were brought under at that time; and the children of Judah prevailed, ᵗbecause they relied upon the LORD God of their fathers.

19 And Abijah pursued after Jeroboam, and took cities from him, Beth-el with the towns thereof, and Jeshanah with the towns thereof, and ᵘEphraim with the towns thereof.

20 Neither did Jeroboam recover strength again in the days of Abijah: and the LORD ᵛstruck him, and ʷhe died.

21 But Abijah waxed mighty, and married fourteen wives, and begat twenty and two sons, and sixteen daughters.

| A. M. 3047 |
| B. C. 957 |
| Anno ante |
| I. Olymp. 181 |
| Ante Urbem |
| Conditam 204 |

| A.M. 3047-3049 |
| B. C. 957-955 |
| Anno ante |
| I. Ol. 181-179 |

22 And the rest of the acts of Abijah, and his ways, and his sayings, *are* written in the ˣstory of the prophet ʸIddo.

| A.M. 3046-3049 |
| B. C. 958-955 |
| Anno ante |
| I. Ol. 182-179 |

ˢChap. xiv. 12——ᵗ1 Chron. v. 20; Psalm xxii. 5 ᵘJosh. xv. 9

ᵛ1 Sam. xxv. 38——ʷ1 Kings xiv. 20——ˣOr, *commentary*——ʸChap. xii. 15

---

proving them, Jeroboam divided his army privately, and sent a part to take Abijah in the rear; and this must have proved fatal to the Jews, had not the Lord interposed.

Verse 17. *Slain—five hundred thousand chosen men.*] Query, *fifty thousand?* This was a great slaughter: see the note on ver. 3, where all these numbers are supposed to be overcharged.

Verse 18. *Judah prevailed, because*] "They depended on the WORD of the God of their fathers."—*T.*

Verse 19. *Beth-el*] "Beth-lehem."—*Targum.*

Jeshanah] We know not where these towns lay.

Verse 20. *The Lord struck him, and he died.*] Who died? *Abijah* or *Jeroboam?* Some think it was *Jeroboam;* some, that it was *Abijah.* Both *rabbins* and *Christians* are divided on this point; nor is it yet settled. The prevailing opinion is that *Jeroboam* is meant, who was struck *then* with that disease of which he died about *two years after;* for he did not die till two years after Abijah: see 1 Kings xiv. 20; xv. 9. It seems as if *Jeroboam* was meant, not *Abijah.*

Verse 21. *Married fourteen wives*] Probably he made alliances with the neighbouring powers, by taking their daughters to him for *wives.*

Verse 22. *Written in the story*] מדרש *bemidrash,* "in the commentary;" this, as far as I recollect, is the first place where a *midrash* or *commentary* is mentioned. The *margin* is right.

His ways, and his sayings] The *commentary* of the prophet Iddo is lost. What his *sayings* were we cannot tell; but from the specimen in this chapter, he appears to have been a very able speaker, and one who knew well how to make the best use of his argument.

CHAPTER XIV

Asa succeeds his father Abijah, reigns piously, and has peace for ten years, 1. He makes a great reformation in Judah, and builds cities of defence, 2–7. His military strength, 8. He is attacked by Zerah the Ethiopian, with an immense army; Asa cries to the Lord, attacks the Ethiopians, and gives them a total overthrow, 9–12. He takes several of their cities, their cattle, &c., and returns to Jerusalem, laden with spoils, 13–15.

| A. M. 3049 |
| B. C. 955 |
| Anno ante |
| I. Olymp. 179 |
| Ante Urbem |
| Conditam 202 |

SO Abijah slept with his fathers, and they buried him in the city of David: and ªAsa his son reigned in his stead. In his days the land was quiet ten years.

2 And Asa did *that which was* good and right in the eyes of the LORD his God:

3 For he took away the altars of the strange *gods,* and ᵇthe high places, and ᶜbrake down the ᵈimages, ᶜand cut down the groves:

| A.M.3063-3073 |
| B. C. 941-931 |
| Anno ante |
| I. Ol. 165-155 |
| A. M. 3063 |
| B. C. 941 |
| Anno ante |
| I. Olymp. 165 |
| Ante Urbem |
| Conditam 188 |

ª1 Kings xv. 8, &c.——ᵇSee 1 Kings xv. 14; chap. xv. 17

ᶜExod. xxxiv. 13——ᵈHeb. *statues*——ᶜ1 Kings xi. 7

NOTES ON CHAP. XIV

Verse 1. *The land was quiet ten years.*] Calmet thinks these years should be counted from the *fifth* to the *fifteenth* of Asa's reign.

Verse 2. *Did that which was good*] He attended to what the law required relative to the worship of God. He was no idolater, though, morally speaking, he was not exempt from faults, 1 Kings xv. 14. He suppressed idolatry universally, and encouraged the people to worship the true God: see verses 3, 4, 5.

<table>
<tr><td>A. M. 3063
B. C. 941
Anno ante
I. Olymp. 165
Ante Urbem
Conditam 188</td><td>

4 And commanded Judah to seek the LORD God of their fathers, and to do the law and the commandment.</td></tr>
</table>

5 Also he took away out of all the cities of Judah the high places and the [f]images: and the kingdom was quiet before him.

A.M.3063-3073
B. C. 931
Anno ante
I. Ol. 165-155

6 And he built fenced cities in Judah: for the land had rest, and he had no war in those years; because the LORD had given him rest.

7 Therefore he said unto Judah, Let us build these cities, and make about *them* walls, and towers, gates, and bars, *while* the land *is* yet before us; because we have sought the LORD our God, we have sought *him,* and he hath given us rest on every side. So they built and prospered.

8 And Asa had an army *of men* that bare targets and spears, out of Judah three hundred thousand; and out of Benjamin, that bare shields and drew bows, two hundred and fourscore thousand: all these *were* mighty men of valour.

A. M. 3063
B. C. 941
Anno ante
I. Olymp. 165
Ante Urbem
Conditam 188

9 [g]And there came out against them Zerah the Ethiopian with a host of a thousand thousand, and three hundred

chariots; and came unto [h]Mareshah.

A. M. 3063
B. C. 941
Anno ante
I. Olymp. 165
Ante Urbem
Conditam 188

10 Then Asa went out against him, and they set the battle in array in the valley of Zephathah at Mareshah.

11 And Asa [i]cried unto the LORD his God, and said, LORD, *it is* [k]nothing with thee to help, whether with many, or with them that have no power: help us, O LORD our God; for we rest on thee, and [l]in thy name we go against this multitude. O LORD, thou *art* our God; let not [m]man prevail against thee.

12 So the LORD [n]smote the Ethiopians before Asa, and before Judah; and the Ethiopians fled.

13 And Asa and the people that *were* with him pursued them unto [o]Gerar: and the Ethiopians were overthrown, that they could not recover themselves; for they were [p]destroyed before the LORD, and before his host; and they carried away very much spoil.

14 And they smote all the cities round about Gerar; for [q]the fear of the LORD came upon them: and they spoiled all the cities; for there was exceeding much spoil in them.

15 They smote also the tents of cattle, and carried away sheep and camels in abundance, and returned to Jerusalem.

---

[f]Heb. *sun images*——[g]Chap. xvi. 8——[h]Josh. xv. 44
[i]Exodus xiv. 10; chap. xiii. 14; Psalm xxii. 5——[k]1 Samuel xiv. 6

[l]1 Sam. xvii. 45; Prov. xviii. 10——[m]Or, *mortal man* [n]Chap. xiii. 15——[o]Gen. x. 19; xx. 1——[p]Heb. *broken* [q]Gen. xxxv. 5; chap. xvii. 10

Verse 6. *Fenced cities*] To preserve his territories from invasion, and strengthen the frontiers of his kingdom, see ver. 7.

Verse 8. *Targets and spears*] Probably targets with the *dagger in the centre,* and javelins for distant fight.

Bare shields and drew bows] They were not only archers, but had shield and sword for close fight.

Verse 9. *Zerah the Ethiopian*] Probably of that *Ethiopia* which lay on the south of Egypt, near to *Libya,* and therefore the *Libyans* are joined with them, chap. xvi. 8.

A thousand thousand] If this people had come from any great distance, they could not have had forage for such an immense army.

Verse 11. *Whether with many*] The same sentiment as that uttered by Jonathan, 1 Sam. xiv. 6, when he attacked the garrison of the Philistines.

O Lord our God—we rest on thee] "Help us, O Lord our God; because we depend on thy WORD, and in the name of thy WORD we come against this great host."—*Targum.*

Verse 14. *There was—much spoil in them.*] These cities being on the rear of this vast army, they had laid up much forage in them; and to get this the Jews overthrew the whole.

Verse 15. *Tents of cattle*] Those which had carried the baggage of the great army, and which they had left in such places as abounded with pasture. Perhaps sheepfolds, enclosures for camels, mules, &c., may also be intended. The discomfiture was great, because God fought for the people; and the spoil was immense, because the multitude was prodigious, indeed almost incredible, *a million* of men in one place is almost too much for the mind to conceive, but there may be some mistake in the numerals: it is evident from the whole account that the number was vast and the spoil great.

CHAPTER XV

Azariah's prophecy concerning Israel, and his exhortation to Asa, 1–7. Asa completes the reformation which he had begun, his kingdom is greatly strengthened, and all the people make a solemn covenant with the Lord, 8–15. His treatment of his mother Maachah, 16. He brings into the house of God the things that his father had dedicated, 17, 18. And he has no war till the thirty-fifth year of his reign, 19.

A. M. 3063
B. C. 941
Anno ante
I. Olymp. 165
Ante Urbem
Conditam 188

AND ^athe Spirit of God came upon Azariah the son of Oded:

2 And he went out to ^bmeet Asa, and said unto him, Hear ye me, Asa, and all Judah and Benjamin; ^cThe LORD *is* with you, while ye be with him; and ^dif ye seek him, he will be found of you; but ^eif ye forsake him, he will forsake you.

3 Now ^ffor a long season Israel *hath been* without the true God, and without ^ga teaching priest, and without law.

4 But ^hwhen they in their trouble did turn unto the LORD God of Israel, and sought him, he was found of them.

5 And ⁱin those times *there was* no peace to him that went out, nor to him that came in, but great vexations *were* upon all the inhabitants of the countries.

6 ^kAnd nation was ^ldestroyed of nation,

and city of city: for God did vex them with all adversity.

A. M. 3063
B. C. 941
Anno ante
I. Olymp. 165
Ante Urbem
Conditam 188

7 Be ye strong therefore, and let not your hands be weak: for your works shall be rewarded.

8 And when Asa heard these words, and the prophecy of Oded the prophet, he took courage, and put away the ^mabominable idols out of all the land of Judah and Benjamin, and out of the cities ⁿwhich he had taken from Mount Ephraim, and renewed the altar of the LORD, that *was* before the porch of the LORD.

9 And he gathered all Judah and Benjamin, and ^othe strangers with them out of Ephraim and Manasseh, and out of Simeon: for they fell to him out of Israel in abundance, when they saw that the LORD his God *was* with him.

10 So they gathered themselves together at

---

^aNum. xxiv. 2; Judges iii. 10; chap. xx. 14; xxiv. 20   ^bHeb. *before Asa* —— ^cJames iv. 8 —— ^dVer. 4, 15; 1 Chron. xxviii. 9; chap. xxxiii. 12, 13; Jer. xxix. 13; Matt. vii. 7

^eChap. xxiv. 20 —— ^fHos. iii. 4 —— ^gLev. x. 11   ^hDeut. iv. 29 —— ⁱJudg. v. 6 —— ^kMatt. xxiv. 7   ^lHeb. *beaten in pieces* —— ^mHeb. *abominations* —— ⁿCh. xiii. 19 —— ^oChap. xi. 16

NOTES ON CHAP. XV

Verse 1. *Azariah the son of Oded*] We know nothing of this prophet but what is related of him here.

Verse 2. *The Lord is with you, while ye be with him*] This is the settled and eternal purpose of God; to them who seek him he will ever be found propitious, and them alone will he abandon who forsake him. In this verse the unconditional perseverance of the saints has no place: a doctrine which was first the ruin of the human race, *Ye shall not die;* and ever since the fall, has been the plague and disgrace of the Church of Christ. The *Targum* is curious: "Hearken to me, Asa, and all Judah and Benjamin: The WORD of the Lord shall be your helper, while ye walk in *his* ways. If ye seek doctrine from *his presence*, he will be found of you in times of trouble; but if you cast away *his fear*, he will abandon you."

Verse 3. *Now for a long season Israel*] "Israel hath followed Jeroboam, and they have not worshipped the true God. They have burnt incense to their golden calves; their priestlings [כומריא] *cumeraiya*, their *black, sooty sacrificers*] have burnt perfumes with a strange worship, and have not exercised themselves in the law." —*Targum*. These priests could not *teach*, because they had not *learnt;* and as they had abandoned the *law* of the Lord, consequently they had no proper matter for instruction.

There is a great diversity of opinions concerning the meaning of this text. Some consider it a prophecy relative to the future state of this people, and the final destruction of the Jews as to their political existence: others consider it as referring to the state of the people under the reigns of Rehoboam and Abijah, which were happily changed under that of Asa; and this appears to me to be the most natural sense of the words.

Verse 5. *But great vexations*] Does not our Lord allude to this and the following verse in Matt. xxiv. 6, 7, 9, 13?

Verse 8. *Renewed the altar*] Dedicated it *afresh*, or perhaps *enlarged* it, that more sacrifices might be offered on it than ever before; for it cannot be supposed that this altar had no victims offered on it till the *fifteenth* year of the reign of Asa, who had previously been so zealous in restoring the Divine worship.

Verse 9. *And the strangers*] Many out of the different tribes, particularly out of *Simeon, Ephraim,* and *Manasseh,* having reflected that the Divine blessing was promised to the house of David, and finding the government of Jeroboam founded in idolatry, would naturally, through a spirit of piety, leave their own country, and go where they might enjoy the worship of the true God.

Verse 10. *The third month*] At the feast of *pentecost* which was held on the *third* month.

A. M. 3063
B. C. 941
Anno ante
I. Olymp. 165
Ante Urbem
Conditam 188

Jerusalem in the third month, in the fifteenth year of the reign of Asa.

11 [p]And they offered unto the LORD [q]the same time, of [r]the spoil *which* they had brought, seven hundred oxen and seven thousand sheep.

12 And they [s]entered into a covenant to seek the LORD God of their fathers with all their heart and with all their soul;

13 [t]That whosoever would not seek the LORD God of Israel [u]should be put to death, whether small or great, whether man or woman.

14 And they sware unto the LORD with a loud voice, and with shouting, and with trumpets, and with cornets.

15 And all Judah rejoiced at the oath: for they had sworn with all their heart, and [v]sought him with their whole desire; and he was found of them: and the LORD gave them rest round about.

A. M. 3063
B. C. 941
Anno ante
I. Olymp. 165
Ante Urbem
Conditam 188

16 And also *concerning* [w]Maachah the [x]mother of Asa the king, he removed her from *being* queen, because she had made an [y]idol in a grove: and Asa cut down her idol, and stamped *it*, and burnt *it* at the brook Kidron.

17 But [z]the high places were not taken away out of Israel: nevertheless the heart of Asa was perfect all his days.

18 And he brought into the house of God the things that his father had dedicated, and that he himself had dedicated, silver, and gold, and vessels.

19 And there was no *more* war unto the five and thirtieth year of the reign of Asa.

A.M.3063-3073
B. C. 941-931
Anno ante
I. Ol. 165-155

[p]Chap. xiv. 15——[q]Heb. *in that day*——[r]Chap. xiv. 13——[s]2 Kings xxiii. 3; chap. xxxiv. 31; Neh. x. 29
[t]Exodus xxii. 20

[u]Deut. xiii. 5, 9, 15——[v]Ver. 2——[w]1 Kings xv. 13
[x]That is, *grandmother*, 1 Kings xv. 2, 10——[y]Heb. *horror*——[z]Chap. xiv. 3, 5; 1 Kings xv. 14, &c.

Verse 11. ***The spoil*** **which** ***they had brought***] **The spoil which they had taken from Zerah and his auxiliaries, chap. xiv. 14, 15.**

Verse 12. ***They entered into a covenant***] **The covenant consisted of** ***two*** **parts: 1. We will seek the God of our fathers with all our heart, and with all our soul. 2. Whosoever, great or small, man or woman, will not worship the true God, and serve him alone, shall be put to death. Thus no toleration was given to idolatry, so that it must be rooted out: and that this covenant might be properly** ***binding***, **they confirmed it with an** ***oath;*** **and God accepted them and their services.**

Verse 16. Concerning ***Maachah***] **See the matter fully explained in the note on 1 Kings xv. 13.**

The Jews imagine that Maachah repented, and her name became changed into ***Michaiah, daughter of Uriel of Gibeah;*** **and that this was done that there might be no mention of her former name, lest it should be a reproach to her: but we have already seen another gloss on this name. See on chap. xi. 20.**

Verse 17. ***The high places were not taken away***] **He had totally suppressed or destroyed the** ***idolatry;*** **but some of the** ***places, buildings,*** **or** ***altars***, **he permitted to remain.**

Verse 18. ***The things that his father had dedicated***] **As it was a custom to dedicate a** ***part of the spoils taken from an enemy*** **to the service and honour of God, it is natural to suppose that Abijah, having so signally overthrown Jeroboam, (chap. xiii. 15-19,) had dedicated a part of the spoils to the Lord; but they had not been brought into the temple till this time.**

Silver, and gold, and vessels.] **The word** כלים ***kelim***, **which we translate** ***vessels***, **signifies** ***instruments, utensils, ornaments***, **&c.**

Verse 19. ***The five and thirtieth year of the reign of Asa***] **Archbishop Usher thinks that this should be counted from the** ***separation*** **of the kingdom, and that this fell on the** ***fifteenth*** **year of Asa's reign. To settle in every respect these chronologies is a most difficult undertaking; and the difficulty does not belong to the** ***sacred books*** **alone,** ***all*** **other chronological tables of** ***all*** **the nations in the world, are in the same predicament. With those of our own history I have often been puzzled, even while I had access to all the archives of the nation. Probably we should read here** ***the five and twentieth year***. **See the margin, and the note on 1 Kings xv. 16.**

CHAPTER XVI

Baasha, king of Israel, begins to build Ramah, to prevent his subjects from having any intercourse with the Jews, 1. Asa hires Ben-hadad, king of Syria, against him; and obliges him to leave off building Ramah, 2–5. Asa and his men carry the stones and timbers of Ramah away, and build therewith Geba and Mizpah, 6. Asa is reproved by Hanani, the seer, for his union with the king of Syria: he is offended with the seer, and puts him in prison, 7–10. Of his acts, 11. He is diseased in his feet, and seeks to physicians and not to God, and dies, 12, 13. His sumptuous funeral, 14.

<table>
<tr><td>A. M. 3074
B. C. 930
Anno ante
I. Olymp. 154
Ante Urbem
Conditam 177</td></tr>
</table>

IN the [a]six and thirtieth year of the reign of Asa [b]Baasha king of Israel came up against Judah, and built Ramah, [c]to the intent that he might let none go out or come in to Asa king of Judah.

2 Then Asa brought out silver and gold out of the treasures of the house of the LORD and of the king's house, and sent to Ben-hadad, king of Syria, that dwelt at [d]Damascus, saying,

3 *There is* a league between me and thee, as *there was* between my father and thy father : behold, I have sent thee silver and gold : go, break thy league with Baasha king of Israel, that he may depart from me.

4 And Ben-hadad hearkened unto King Asa, and sent the captains of [e]his armies against the cities of Israel ; and they smote Ijon, and Dan, and Abel-maim, and all the store cities of Naphtali.

5 And it came to pass, when Baasha heard *it,* that he left off building of Ramah, and let his work cease.

6 Then Asa the king took all Judah ; and they carried away the stones of Ramah, and the timber thereof, wherewith Baasha was building ; and he built therewith Geba and Mizpah.

7 And at that time [f]Hanani the seer came to Asa king of Judah, and said unto him, [g]Because thou hast relied on the king of Syria, and not relied on the LORD thy God, therefore is the host of the king of Syria escaped out of thine hand.

<table>
<tr><td>A. M. 3074
B. C. 930
Anno ante
I. Olymp. 154
Ante Urbem
Conditam 177</td></tr>
</table>

8 Were not [h]the Ethiopians and [i]the Lubims [k]a huge host, with very many chariots and horsemen ? yet, because thou didst rely on the LORD, he delivered them into thine hand.

9 [l]For the eyes of the LORD run to and fro throughout the whole earth, [m]to show himself strong in the behalf of *them* whose heart *is* perfect toward him. Herein [n]thou hast done foolishly : therefore from henceforth [o]thou shalt have wars.

10 Then Asa was wroth with the seer, and [p]put him in a prison house ; for *he was* in a rage with him because of this *thing.* And Asa [q]oppressed *some* of the people the same time.

11 [r]And, behold, the acts of Asa, first and last, lo, they *are* written in the book of the kings of Judah and Israel.

<table>
<tr><td>A.M.3049-3090
B. C. 955-914
Anno ante
I. Ol. 179-138</td></tr>
</table>

12 And Asa in the thirty and ninth year of his reign was diseased in his feet, until his disease *was* exceeding *great :* yet in his disease he [s]sought not to the LORD, but to the physicians.

<table>
<tr><td>A. M. 3088
B. C. 916
Anno ante
I. Olymp. 140
Ante Urbem
Conditam 163</td></tr>
</table>

---

[a]From the rending of the ten tribes from Judah, over which Asa was now king——[b]1 Kings xv. 17, &c. [c]Chap. xv. 9——[d]Heb. *Darmesek*——[e]Heb. *which* were *his*——[f]1 Kings xvi. 1 ; ch. xix. 2——[g]Isa. xxxi. 1 ; Jer. xvii. 5——[h]Chap. xiv. 9——[i]Chap. xii. 3

[k]Heb. *in abundance*——[l]Job xxxiv. 21 ; Prov. v. 21 ; xv. 3 ; Jer. xvi. 17 ; xxxii. 19 ; Zech. iv. 10——[m]Or, *strongly to hold with* them, &c.——[n]1 Sam. xiii. 13——[o]1 Kings xv. 32——[p]Chap. xviii. 26 ; Jer. xx. 2 ; Matt. xiv. 3 [q]Heb. *crushed*——[r]1 Kings xv. 23——[s]Jer. xvii. 5

NOTES ON CHAP. XVI

Verse 1. *The six and thirtieth year*] After the division of the kingdoms of Israel and Judah ; according to *Usher.* This opinion is followed in our *margin ;* see the note on 1 Kings xv. 16, where this subject is farther considered.

Concerning Baasha's building of Ramah, see the note on 1 Kings xv. 17.

Verse 3. There is *a league*] Let there be a treaty, offensive and defensive, between me and thee : see on 1 Kings xv. 22.

Verse 6. *Took all Judah*] See on 1 Kings xv. 22.

Verse 7. *Escaped out of thine hand.*] It is difficult to know what is here intended. Perhaps the Divine providence had intended to give Asa a grand victory over the *Syrians,* who had always been the inveterate enemies of the Jews ; but by this unnecessary and very improper alliance between Asa and Ben-hadad, this purpose of the Divine providence was prevented, and thus *the Syrians escaped out of his hands.*

Verse 9. *Therefore—thou shalt have wars.*] And so he had with Israel during the rest of his reign, 1 Kings xv. 32.

Verse 10. Asa *was wroth with the seer*] Instead of humbling himself, and deprecating the displeasure of the Lord, he persecuted his messenger : and having thus laid his impious hands upon the prophet, he appears to have got his heart hardened through the deceitfulness of sin ; and then he began to *oppress the people,* either by unjust imprisonments, or excessive taxations.

Verse 12. *Diseased in his feet*] He had a strong and long fit of the *gout ;* this is most likely.

He sought not to the Lord] "He did not seek discipline from the face of the Lord, but from the physicians."—*Targum.*

Are we not taught by this to make prayer and supplication to the Lord in our afflictions, with the expectation that *he* will heal us when he finds us duly humbled, i. e., when the *end* is answered for which he sends the affliction ?

A. M. 3090
B. C. 914
Anno ante
I. Olymp. 138
Ante Urbem
Conditam 161

13 [t]And Asa slept with his fathers, and died in the one and fortieth year of his reign.

14 And they buried him in his own sepulchres, which he had [u]made for himself in the city of David, and laid him in the bed which was filled [v]with sweet odours and divers kinds *of spices* prepared by the apothecaries' art: and they made [w]a very great burning for him.

A. M. 3090
B. C. 914
Anno ante
I. Olymp. 138
Ante Urbem
Conditam 161

---

[t]1 Kings xv. 24——[u]Heb. *digged*——[v]Gen. l. 2; Mark xvi. 1; John xix. 39, 40——[w]Chap. xxi. 19; Jer. xxxiv. 5

Verse 14. *And laid him in the bed*] It is very likely that the body of Asa was *burnt;* that the *bed* spoken of here was a *funeral pyre,* on which much *spices* and *odoriferous woods* had been placed; and then they set fire to the whole and consumed the body with the aromatics. Some think the body was not burned, but the *aromatics* only, in honour of the king.

How the ancients treated the bodies of the ilustrious dead we learn from *Virgil,* in the funeral rites paid to *Misenus.*

Nec minus interea *Misenum* in littore Teucri
Flebant, et cineri ingrato suprema ferebant.
Principio pinguem tædis et robore secto
Ingentem struxere pyram: cui frondibus atris
Intexunt latera, et ferales ante cupressas
Constituunt, decorantque super fulgentibus
    armis, &c.   *Æn.* vi. 214.

"Meanwhile the Trojan troops, with weeping eyes,
To dead *Misenus* pay their obsequies.
First from the ground a *lofty pile* they rear
Of *pitch trees, oaks,* and *pines,* and *unctuous fir.*
The fabric's front with *cypress twigs* they strew,
And stick the sides with boughs of *baleful yew.*
The topmost part his *glittering arms* adorn:
Warm waters, then, in brazen caldrons borne
Are *poured to wash his body joint* by *joint,*
And *fragrant oils* the stiffen'd limbs anoint.

With *groans* and *cries Misenus* they deplore:
Then on a *bier,* with *purple* cover'd o'er,
The breathless body thus bewail'd they lay,
And *fire the pile* (their faces turn'd away.)
Such reverend rites their fathers used to pay.
Pure *oil* and *incense* on the *fire* they throw,
And *fat* of *victims* which their friends bestow.
These gifts the greedy flames to dust devour,
Then on the living coals *red wine* they *pour:*
And last the *relics* by themselves dispose,
Which in a *brazen urn* the priests enclose.
Old Corineus compass'd thrice the crew,
And dipp'd an *olive branch* in holy dew;
Which *thrice he sprinkled* round, and thrice aloud
Invoked the dead, and then dismiss'd the crowd."   DRYDEN.

All these rites are of *Asiatic* extraction. *Virgil* borrows almost every circumstance from *Homer;* (see *Iliad,* xxiii., ver. 164, &c.;) and we well know that Homer ever describes Asiatic manners. Sometimes, especially in war, several captives were sacrificed to the manes of the departed hero. So, in the place above, the *mean-souled, ferocious demon,* ACHILLES, is represented sacrificing *twelve Trojan captives* to the ghost of his friend Patroclus. *Urns containing the ashes* and *half-calcined bones* of the dead occur frequently in *barrows* or *tumuli* in this country; most of them, no doubt, the work of the *Romans.* But all ancient nations, in funeral matters, have nearly the same rites.

CHAPTER XVII

Jehoshaphat succeeds his father Asa, and reigns piously, and is particularly blessed, 1–6. He establishes an itinerant ministry, for the instruction of the people, through all the cities of Judah, which produces the most beneficial effects, 7–10. The Philistines and Arabians bring him gifts, 11. His greatness, 12, 13. The commanders of his troops, 14–19.

A. M. 3090
B. C. 914
Anno ante
I. Olymp. 138
Ante Urbem
Conditam 161

AND [a]Jehoshaphat his son reigned in his stead, and strengthened himself against Israel.

2 And he placed forces in all the fenced cities of Judah, and set garrisons in the land of Judah, and in the cities of Ephraim, [b]which Asa his father had taken.

3 And the LORD was with Jehoshaphat, because he walked in the first ways of [c]his father David, and sought not unto Baalim;

A. M. 3090
B. C. 914
Anno ante
I. Olymp. 138
Ante Urbem
Conditam 161

---

[a]1 Kings xv. 24——[b]Chap. xv. 8   [c]Or, *of his father and of David*

NOTES ON CHAP. XVII

Verse 1. *Jehoshaphat—and strengthened himself against Israel*] The kingdoms of Israel and Judah were rivals from the beginning; sometimes one, sometimes the other, prevailed. Asa and Baasha were nearly matched; but, after Baasha's death, Israel was greatly weakened by civil contentions, and Jehoshaphat got the ascendancy. See 1 Kings xvi. 16-23.

Verse 2. *The cities of Ephraim*] This conquest from the kingdom of Israel is referred to, chap. xv. 8; but when it was made we do not know.

Verse 3. *The Lord was with Jehoshaphat*]

A. M. 3090
B. C. 914
Anno ante
I. Olymp. 138
Ante Urbem
Conditam 161

4 But sought to the *LORD* God of his father, and walked in his commandments, and not after ^dthe doings of Israel.

A. M. 3091
B. C. 913
Anno ante
I. Olymp. 137
Ante Urbem
Conditam 160

5 Therefore the LORD stablished the kingdom in his hand; and all Judah ^ebrought ^fto Jehoshaphat presents; ^gand he had riches and honour in abundance.

6 And his heart ^hwas lifted up in the ways of the LORD: moreover ⁱhe took away the high places and groves out of Judah.

A. M. 3092
B. C. 912
Anno ante
I. Olymp. 136
Ante Urbem
Conditam 159

7 Also in the third year of his reign he sent to his princes, *even* to Ben-hail, and to Obadiah, and to Zechariah, and to Nethaneel, and to Michaiah, ^kto teach in the cities of Judah.

8 And with them *he sent* Levites, *even* Shemaiah, and Nethaniah, and Zebadiah, and Asahel, and Shemiramoth, and Jehonathan, and Adonijah, and Tobijah, and Tob-adonijah,

Levites; and with them Elishama and Jehoram, priests.

A. M. 3092
B. C. 912
Anno ante
I. Olymp. 136
Ante Urbem
Conditam 159

9 ^lAnd they taught in Judah, and *had* the book of the law of the LORD with them, and went about throughout all the cities of Judah, and taught the people.

10 And ^mthe fear of the LORD ⁿfell upon all the kingdoms of the lands that *were* round about Judah, so that they made no war against Jehoshaphat.

11 Also *some* of the Philistines ^obrought Jehoshaphat presents, and tribute silver; and the Arabians brought him flocks, seven thousand and seven hundred rams, and seven thousand and seven hundred he-goats.

A.M.3092-3115
B. C. 912–889
Anno ante
I. Ol. 136–113

12 And Jehoshaphat waxed great exceedingly; and he built in Judah ^pcastles and cities of store.

13 And he had much business in the cities of Judah: and the men of war, mighty men of valour, *were* in Jerusalem.

---

^d1 Kings xii. 28——^e1 Sam. x. 27; 1 Kings x. 25 ^fHeb. *gave*——^g1 Kings x. 27; chap. xviii. 1——^hThat is, *was encouraged*

ⁱ1 Kings xxii. 43; ch. xv. 17; xix. 3; xx. 33——^kChap. xv. 3——^lCh. xxxv. 3; Neh. viii. 7——^mGen. xxxv. 5 ⁿHeb. *was*——^o2 Sam. viii. 2——^pOr, *palaces*

"The WORD of the Lord was Jehoshaphat's Helper."—*Targum.*

Verses 7-9. *To teach in the cities of Judah.*] "To teach the *fear of the Lord* in the cities of Judah."—*Targum.*

In these verses we find a remarkable account of an *itinerant ministry* established by Jehoshaphat; and in this work he employed *three* classes of men: 1. The *princes.* 2. The *Levites.* 3. The *priests.* We may presume that the *princes* instructed the people in the nature of the *civil law* and *constitution* of the *kingdom;* the *Levites* instructed them in every thing that appertained to the *temple service,* and *ritual law;* and the *priests* instructed them in the *nature* and *design* of the *religion* they professed. Thus the nation became thoroughly instructed in their duty to *God,* to the *king,* and to *each other.* They became, therefore, as *one man;* and against a people thus united, on such *principles,* no enemy could be successful.

Verse 9. Had *the book of the law of the Lord with them*] This was their *text book:* it was the *book of God;* they taught it *as such,* and as *such* the people received it. Its laws were *God's laws,* and the people *felt* their *obligation,* and their *consciences* were *bound.* Thus they were obedient to the laws of the land, on the principle of *religion.* In this they were encouraged and confirmed by the *example* of all, both in *Church* and *state.* The *princes* were not only *pious,* but were teachers of piety; the *Levites* showed them the worth and excellence of their ritual institutions; and the *priests* showed them the moral use they were to make of the whole: and thus the people became obedient to God as well as to the king, and kept all the civil ordinances, not merely for the sake

of a good king, but for the sake of a good and gracious God. By these means the nation enjoyed peace and prosperity; and all insurrections, seditions, and popular commotions, were prevented. The surrounding nations, perceiving this, saw that there was no hope of subduing such a people, so *they made no war with Jehoshaphat,* ver. 10. And they took care not to provoke such a people to fall on them; therefore, it is said, *The fear of the Lord fell on all the kingdoms and lands that were round about Judah.* Such an itinerant ministry established in these kingdoms for upwards of *fourscore years,* teaching the pure, unadulterated doctrines of the Gospel, with the propriety and necessity of obedience to the laws, has been the principal means, in the hand of God, of preserving these lands from those convulsions and revolutions that have ruined and nearly dissolved the European continent. The *itinerant ministry,* to which this refers, is that which was established in these lands by the late truly reverend, highly learned and cultivated, deeply pious and loyal JOHN WESLEY, A. M., formerly a fellow of Lincoln College, Oxford, whose followers are known by the name of METHODISTS; a people who are an honour to their country, and a blessing to the government under which they live.

Verse 11. *The Philistines brought—presents*] They and the *Arabians* purchased peace with the king of Judah by paying an annual *tribute.* The *Philistines* brought *silver,* and no doubt *different kinds of merchandise.* The *Arabs,* whose riches consisted in *cattle,* brought him *flocks* in great abundance, principally *rams* and *he-goats.*

Verse 13. *He had much business in the cities*]

A.M.3092-3115
B. C. 912-889
Anno ante
I. Ol. 136–113
14 And these *are* the numbers of them according to the house of their fathers: Of Judah, the captains of thousands; Adnah, the chief, and with him mighty men of valour three hundred thousand.

15 And qnext to him *was* Jehohanan the captain, and with him two hundred and fourscore thousand.

16 And next him *was* Amasiah the son of Zichri, rwho willingly offered himself unto the LORD; and with him two hundred

thousand mighty men of valour.

A.M.3092-3115
B. C. 912-889
Anno ante
I. Ol. 136–113

17 And of Benjamin; Eliada a mighty man of valour, and with him armed men with bow and shield two hundred thousand.

18 And next him *was* Jehozabad, and with him a hundred and fourscore thousand ready prepared for the war.

19 These waited on the king, beside sthose whom the king put in the fenced cities throughout all Judah.

---

qHeb. *at his hand*

rJudg. v. 2, 9——sVer. 2

He kept the people constantly employed; they had wages for their work; and by their labours the empire was both enriched and strengthened.

Verse 14. *Adnah, the chief*] He was *generalissimo* of all this host. These are the numbers of the *five battalions:* under *Adnah,* three hundred thousand; *Jehohanan,* two hundred and eighty thousand; *Amasiah,* two hundred thousand; *Eliada,* two hundred thousand; *Jehozabad,* one hundred and eighty thousand; in all, one million one hundred and sixty thousand.

Verse 19. *These waited on the king*] They were disposable forces, always at the king's command; and were independent of those by which the cities of Judah were *garrisoned.*

THERE is not a sovereign in Europe or in the world but might read this chapter with ad-

vantage. 1. It shows most forcibly that true religion is the basis of the state, and that, wherever it prospers, there the state prospers. 2. It shows also that it is the wisdom of kings to encourage religion with all their power and influence; for if the hearts of the subjects be not bound and influenced by true religion, vain is the application of laws, fines, imprisonments, or corporal punishment of any kind. 3. A religious nation is ever a great nation; it is loved by its friends, it is dreaded by its enemies. 4. It is ever a peaceable and united nation: the blessings of religion, and a wholesome and paternal government, are so fully felt and prized, that all find it their interest to preserve and defend them. Harmony, peace, piety, and strength, are the stability of such times. May Britain know and value them!

CHAPTER XVIII

Jehoshaphat joins affinity with Ahab, king of Israel, 1, 2; who invites him to assist him in the war against the Syrians, to which Jehoshaphat agrees, 3. They consult the prophets concerning the success of the war; and all, except Micaiah, promise Ahab victory, 4–17. Micaiah relates his vision concerning the lying spirit in the mouth of Ahab's prophets, 18–22. Zedekiah, a false prophet, opposes Micaiah; and Micaiah is put in prison, 23–27. Both the kings go against the Syrians; the confederate armies are defeated, and the king of Israel slain, 28–31.

A. M. 3107
B. C. 897
Anno ante
I. Olymp. 121
Ante Urbem
Conditam 144
NOW Jehoshaphat ahad riches and honour in abundance, and bjoined affinity with Ahab. 2 cAnd dafter *certain* years he went down to Ahab to Samaria. And Ahab killed sheep and oxen for him in abundance, and for the people, that *he had* with him, and persuaded him to go up *with him* to Ramoth-gilead.

3 And Ahab king of Israel said unto Jehoshaphat king of Judah, Wilt thou go with me to Ramoth-gilead? And he answered him, I *am* as thou *art,* and my people as thy people; and *we will be* with thee in the war.

A. M. 3107
B. C. 897
Anno ante
I. Olymp. 121
Ante Urbem
Conditam 144

4 And Jehoshaphat said unto the king of Israel, eInquire, I pray thee, at the word of the LORD to day.

---

aChap. xvii. 5——b2 Kings viii. 18——c1 Kings xxii. 2, &c.

dHeb. *at the end of years*——e1 Sam. xxiii. 2, 4, 9; 2 Samuel ii. 1

NOTES ON CHAP. XVIII
Verse 1. *Jehoshaphat had riches and honour*] The preceding chapter gives ample proof of this.
Joined affinity with Ahab.] Took his daughter *Athalia* to be wife to his son *Joram.*

Verse 3. *To Ramoth-gilead*] This place belonged to the Israelites, and was now held by the king of Syria.

The whole of this chapter is circumstantially explained in the note on 1 Kings xxii.

A. M. 3107
B. C. 897
Anno ante
I. Olymp. 121
Ante Urbem
Conditam 144

5 Therefore the king of Israel gathered together of prophets four hundred men, and said unto them, Shall we go to Ramoth-gilead to battle, or shall I forbear? And they said, Go up; for God will deliver *it* into the king's hand.

6 But Jehoshaphat said, *Is there* not here a prophet of the LORD [f]besides, that we might inquire of him?

7 And the king of Israel said unto Jehoshaphat, *There is* yet one man, by whom we may inquire of the LORD: but I hate him; for he never prophesied good unto me, but always evil: the same *is* Micaiah, the son of Imla. And Jehoshaphat said, Let not the king say so.

8 And the king of Israel called for one *of his* [g]officers, and said, [h]Fetch quickly Micaiah the son of Imla.

9 And the king of Israel and Jehoshaphat king of Judah sat either of them on his throne, clothed in *their* robes, and they sat in a [i]void place at the entering in of the gate of Samaria, and all the prophets prophesied before them.

10 And Zedekiah the son of Chenaanah had made him horns of iron, and said, Thus saith the LORD, With these thou shalt push Syria until [k]they be consumed.

11 And all the prophets prophesied so, saying, Go up to Ramoth-gilead, and prosper: for the LORD shall deliver *it* into the hand of the king.

12 And the messenger that went to call Micaiah spake to him, saying, Behold, the words of the prophets *declare* good to the king [l]with one assent; let thy word therefore, I pray thee, be like one of theirs, and speak thou good.

13 And Micaiah said, *As* the LORD liveth, [m]even what my God saith, that will I speak.

14 And when he was come to the king, the king said unto him, Micaiah, shall we go to Ramoth-gilead to battle, or shall I forbear? And he said, Go ye up, and prosper, and they shall be delivered into your hand.

A. M. 3107
B. C. 897
Anno ante
I. Olymp. 121
Ante Urbem
Conditam 144

15 And the king said to him, How many times shall I adjure thee that thou say nothing but the truth to me in the name of the LORD?

16 Then he said, I did see all Israel scattered upon the mountains, as sheep that have no shepherd: and the LORD said, These have no master; let them return *therefore* every man to his house in peace.

17 And the king of Israel said to Jehoshaphat, Did I not tell thee *that* he would not prophesy good unto me, [n]but evil?

18 Again he said, Therefore hear the word of the LORD: I saw the LORD sitting upon his throne, and all the host of heaven standing on his right hand and *on* his left.

19 And the LORD said, Who shall entice Ahab king of Israel, that he may go up and fall at Ramoth-gilead? And one spake, saying after this manner, and another saying after that manner.

20 Then there came out a [o]spirit, and stood before the LORD, and said, I will entice him. And the LORD said unto him, Wherewith?

21 And he said, I will go out, and be a lying spirit in the mouth of all his prophets. And *the LORD* said, Thou shalt entice *him*, and thou shalt also prevail: go out, and do *even* so.

22 Now therefore, behold, [p]the LORD hath put a lying spirit in the mouth of these thy prophets, and the LORD hath spoken evil against thee.

23 Then Zedekiah the son of Chenaanah came near, and [q]smote Micaiah upon the cheek, and said, Which way went the Spirit of the LORD from me to speak unto thee?

24 And Micaiah said, Behold, thou shalt see

[f]Heb. *yet*, or *more*——[g]Or, *eunuchs*——[h]Heb. *Hasten*——[i]Or, *floor*——[k]Heb. thou *consume them*——[l]Heb. *with one mouth*——[m]Num. xxii. 18, 20, 35; xxiii. 12, 26; xxiv. 13; 1 Kings xxii. 14——[n]Or, *but for evil*——[o]Job i. 6——[p]Job xii. 16; Isa. xix. 14; Ezek. xiv. 9——[q]Jer. xx. 2; Mark xiv. 65; Acts xxiii. 2

Verse 9. *The king of Israel and Jehoshaphat*] "Ahab consulted false prophets; but Jehoshaphat sought instruction from the presence of the Lord, and prayed at the entering in of Samaria; and before these all the false prophets prophesied lies."—*Targum.*

Verse 20. *Then there came out a spirit*] The *Targum* gives a strange gloss here: "Then the spirit of Naboth of Jezreel came out from the abode of the righteous, and stood before the Lord, and said, I will deceive him. And the Lord said, By what means? To which he answered, I will be a spirit of false prophecy in the mouth of his prophets. And the Lord said,

A. M. 3107
B. C. 897
Anno ante
I. Olymp. 121
Ante Urbem
Conditam 144

on that day when thou shalt go ʳinto ˢan inner chamber to hide thyself.

25 Then the king of Israel said, Take ye Micaiah, and carry him back to Amon the governor of the city, and to Joash the king's son;

26 And say, Thus saith the king, ᵗPut this *fellow* in the prison, and feed him with bread of affliction, and with water of affliction, until I return in peace.

27 And Micaiah said, If thou certainly return in peace, *then* hath not the LORD spoken by me. And he said, Hearken, all ye people.

28 So the king of Israel and Jehoshaphat the king of Judah went up to Ramoth-gilead.

29 And the king of Israel said unto Jehoshaphat, I will disguise myself, and will go to the battle: but put thou on thy robes. So the king of Israel disguised himself; and they went to the battle.

30 Now the king of Syria had commanded the captains of the chariots that *were* with

him, saying, Fight ye not with small or great, save only with the king of Israel.

A. M. 3107
B. C. 897
Anno ante
I. Olymp. 121
Ante Urbem
Conditam 144

31 And it came to pass, when the captains of the chariots saw Jehoshaphat, that they said, It *is* the king of Israel. Therefore they compassed about him to fight: but Jehoshaphat cried out, and the LORD helped him; and God moved them *to depart* from him.

32 For it came to pass, that, when the captains of the chariots perceived that it was not the king of Israel, they turned back again ᵘfrom pursuing him.

33 And a *certain* man drew a bow ᵛat a venture, and smote the king of Israel ʷbetween the joints of the harness: therefore he said to his chariot man, Turn thine hand, that thou mayest carry me out of the host; for I am ˣwounded.

34 And the battle increased that day: howbeit the king of Israel stayed *himself* up in *his* chariot against the Syrians until the even: and about the time of the sun going down he died.

ʳOr, *from chamber to chamber*——ˢHeb. *a chamber in a chamber*——ᵗChap. xvi. 10——ᵘHeb. *from after him*

ᵛHeb. *in his simplicity*——ʷHeb. *between the joints and between the breast-plate*——ˣHeb. *made sick*

Thou mayest then. But although the power of deceiving them is given unto thee, nevertheless it will not be lawful for thee to sit among the righteous; for whosoever shall speak falsely cannot have a mansion among the righteous. Therefore go forth from me, and do as thou hast said."—*Targum.*

Verse 29. *I will disguise myself*] See the note on 1 Kings xxii. 30.

Verse 31. *But Jehoshaphat cried out*] "Jehoshaphat cried, and the WORD of the Lord brought him assistance."—*Targum.*

Verse 33. *A certain man drew a bow*] The *Targum* tells us *who* it was. "Now, Naaman, the captain of the host of the great king of Syria, drew a bow against him, (that the prophecy of Elijah the Tishbite, and of Micaiah the son of Imla, might be fulfilled,) and smote the king of Israel between the heart and the caul of the liver, through the place where the coat of mail is joined." See the note on 2 Kings v. 1 for this tradition.

Verse 34. *Stayed* himself *up—against the Syrians*] There was a great deal of true personal courage and patriotism in this last act of the king of Israel: he well knew that if his

troops found that he was mortally wounded, they would immediately give way, and the battle would not only be lost, but the slaughter would be great in the pursuit; therefore he stayed himself up till the evening, when the termination of the day must necessarily bring the battle to a close: and when this was done, the Israelites found that their king was slain, and so they left the field of battle to their foes. Thus Israel had a great loss, and the *Syrians had got a great deliverance.* Had it not been for this accident, the Syrians had probably been defeated. See on 1 Kings xxii. 36.

IN the notes referred to above, the *quibbling* predictions of false prophets and *lying oracles* are mentioned, and several instances given; and the whole account of the *lying spirit* going forth from the Lord to deceive Ahab, particularly considered. See especially the notes as above on verses 19, 23, 24.

The reader should never forget a truth so very frequently occurring in the Bible, that God is repeatedly represented as *doing* what, in the course of his providence, he only *permits* to be done.

CHAPTER XIX

Jehoshaphat, on his return from Ramoth-gilead, is met by the prophet Jehu, and reproved, 1–3. He makes a farther reformation in the land, establishing courts of justice, and giving solemn and pertinent directions to the judges, Levites, &c., to do judgment and justice among the people. in the fear of God, 4–11.

A. M. 3108
B. C. 896
Anno ante
I. Olymp. 120
Ante Urbem
Conditam 143

A ND Jehoshaphat the king of Judah returned to his house in peace to Jerusalem.

2 And Jehu the son of Hanani [a]the seer went out to meet him, and said to King Jehoshaphat, Shouldest thou help the ungodly, and [b]love them that hate the LORD? therefore *is* [c]wrath upon thee from before the LORD.

3 Nevertheless there are [d]good things found in thee, in that thou hast taken away the groves out of the land, and hast [e]prepared thine heart to seek God.

4 And Jehoshaphat dwelt at Jerusalem: and [f]he went out again through the people from Beer-sheba to Mount Ephraim, and brought them back unto the LORD God of their fathers.

5 And he set judges in the land throughout all the fenced cities of Judah, city by city,

6 And said to the judges, Take heed what ye do: for [g]ye judge not for man, but for the LORD, [h]who *is* with you [i]in the judgment.

7 Wherefore now let the fear of the LORD be upon you; take heed and do *it:* for [k]*there is* no iniquity with the LORD our God, nor

[l]respect of persons, nor taking of gifts.

8 Moreover in Jerusalem did Jehoshaphat [m]set of the Levites, and *of* the priests, and of the chief of the fathers of Israel, for the judgment of the LORD, and for controversies, when they returned to Jerusalem.

9 And he charged them, saying, Thus shall ye do [n]in the fear of the LORD, faithfully, and with a perfect heart.

10 [o]And what cause soever shall come to you of your brethren that dwell in their cities, between blood and blood, between law and commandment, statutes and judgments, ye shall even warn them that they trespass not against the LORD, and *so* [p]wrath come upon [q]you, and upon your brethren: this do, and ye shall not trespass.

11 And, behold, Amariah the chief priest *is* over you [r]in all matters of the LORD; and Zebadiah the son of Ishmael, the ruler of the house of Judah, for all the king's matters: also the Levites *shall be* officers before you. [s]Deal courageously, and the LORD shall be [t]with the good.

A. M. 3108
B. C. 896
Anno ante
I. Olymp. 120
Ante Urbem
Conditam 143

---

[a]1 Sam. ix. 9——[b]Psa. cxxxix. 21——[c]Chap. xxxii. 25 [d]Chap. xvii. 4, 6; see chap. xii. 12——[e]Chap. xxx. 19; Ezra vii. 10——[f]Hebrew, *he returned and went out* [g]Deut. i. 17——[h]Psa. xxxii. 1; Eccles. v. 8——[i]Heb. *in the matter of judgment*——[k]Deut. xxxii. 4; Rom. ix. 14

[l]Deut. x. 17; Job xxxiv. 19; Acts x. 34; Rom. ii. 11; Gal. ii. 6; Eph. vi. 9; Col. iii. 25; 1 Pet. i. 17——[m]Deut. xvi. 18; ch. xvii. 8——[n]2 Sam. xxiii. 3——[o]Deut. xvii. 8, &c.——[p]Num. xvi. 46——[q]Ezek. iii. 18——[r]1 Chron. xxvi. 30——[s]*Take courage and do*——[t]Chap. xv. 2

NOTES ON CHAP. XIX

Verse 1. *Returned to his house in peace*] That is, in *safety*, notwithstanding he had been exposed to a danger so imminent, from which only the especial mercy of God could have saved him.

Verse 2. *Jehu the son of Hanani*] We have met with this prophet before; see the note on 1 Kings xvi. 7.

Therefore is *wrath upon thee*] That is, Thou *deservest* to be punished. And who can doubt this, who knows that he did *help* the *ungodly*, and did *love them* that *hated Jehovah?* And is not the wrath of God upon all those alliances which his people form with the *ungodly*, whether they be *social*, *matrimonial*, *commercial*, or *political?*

Verse 4. *From Beer-sheba to Mount Ephraim*] Before the separation of the ten tribes, in speaking of the extent of the land it was said, *From Dan to Beer-sheba;* but since that event, the kingdom of Judah was bounded on the *south* by Beer-sheba, and on the *north* by the mountains of Ephraim. This shows that Jehoshaphat had gone through all his territories to examine every thing himself, to see that judgment and justice were properly administered among the people.

Verse 6. *Take heed what ye do*] A very solemn and very necessary caution; judges should feel themselves in the place of God, and

judge as those who know they shall be judged for their judgments.

Verse 8. *And for controversies, when they returned to Jerusalem.*] Who were they that returned to Jerusalem? Some suppose that it means *Jehoshaphat and his courtiers*, who returned to Jerusalem after the expedition mentioned ver. 4: but if this were so, or if the text spoke of any person *returning to Jerusalem*, would not לירושלם *lirushalem*, TO *Jerusalem*, and not the simple word ירושלם *Yerushalem*, without the preposition, be used?

Learned men have supposed, with great plausibility, that the word וישבו *vaiyashubu*, "and they returned," should be written יושבי *yoshebey*, "the *inhabitants*," and that the words should be read, And *for the controversies of the inhabitants of Jerusalem*. That this was the original reading is very probable from its vestiges in the *Vulgate*, *habitatoribus ejus*, "its INHABITANTS;" and in the *Septuagint* it is found *totidem verbis*, Και κρινειν τους κατοικουντας εν Ἰερουσαλημ, And *to judge the inhabitants of Jerusalem.*

There is a clause in chap. xxxiv. 9 where we have a similar mistake in our version: *And they returned to Jerusalem*, וישבו ירושלם; where the false *keri*, or *marginal* note, directs it, in opposition to common sense and ALL the *versions*, to be read וישבו *and they returned*, which our translation has unhappily followed.

Verse 10. *Between blood and blood*] Cases

of man-slaughter or accidental murder, or cases of *consanguinity*, the settlement of inheritance, family claims, &c.

Between law and commandment] Whatsoever concerns the *moral precepts, rites,* and *ceremonies,* of the law, or whatsoever belongs to *civil* affairs.

Verse 11. *Behold, Amariah*] Here was a twofold jurisdiction, *ecclesiastical* and *civil:* in the *ecclesiastical court,* Amariah the high-priest was *supreme judge;* in the *civil court,* Zebadiah

was supreme. To assist both the *Levites* were a sort of *counsellors.*

WITHOUT good and wholesome *laws,* no nation can be prosperous: and vain are the best laws if they be not *judiciously* and *conscientiously* administered. The things of GOD and the things of the KING should never be confounded in the administration of justice. Amariah the priest, and Zebadiah the ruler, should ever have their distinct places of jurisdiction.

CHAPTER XX

The Moabites, Ammonites, and Edomites, invade Judah, 1, 2. Jehoshaphat proclaims a fast, and gathers the people together to seek the Lord, 3, 4. His prayer to God, 5–12. Jahaziel predicts the downfall of their enemies, 14–17. The king, the Levites, and the people take courage; praise and magnify God; and go forth to meet their enemies, 18–21. The enemies are confounded, and destroy each other, 22–24. The men of Judah take the spoil, praise the Lord, and return with joy to Jerusalem, 25–28. The fear of the Lord falls upon all their enemies round about; and the land has rest, 29, 30. Transactions and character of Jehoshaphat, 31–34. He joins with Ahaziah, king of Israel, in building a fleet of ships to go to Tarshish, but they are wrecked at Ezion-geber, 35–37.

A. M. 3108
B. C. 896
Anno ante
I. Olymp. 120
Ante Urbem
Conditam 143

IT came to pass after this also, *that* the children of Moab, and the children of Ammon, and with them *other* beside the Ammonites, came against Jehoshaphat to battle.

2 Then there came some that told Jehoshaphat, saying, There cometh a great multitude against thee from beyond the sea on this side Syria; and, behold, they *be* [a]in Hazazontamar, which *is* [b]En-gedi.

3 And Jehoshaphat feared, and set [c]himself

to [d]seek the LORD, and proclaimed a fast throughout all Judah.

A. M. 3108
B. C. 896
Anno ante
I. Olymp. 120
Ante Urbem
Conditam 143

4 And Judah gathered themselves together, to ask *help* of the LORD: even out of all the cities of Judah they came to seek the LORD.

5 And Jehoshaphat stood in the congregation of Judah and Jerusalem, in the house of the LORD, before the new court,

6 And said, O LORD God of our fathers, *art* not thou [e]God in heaven? and [f]rulest *not*

---

[a]Gen. xiv. 7——[b]Josh. xv. 62——[c]Heb. *his face*
[d]Chap. xix. 3

[e]Ezra viii. 21; Jer. xxxvi. 9; Jonah iii. 5——[f]Deut. iv. 39
Josh. ii. 11; 1 Kings viii. 23; Matt. vi. 9

NOTES ON CHAP. XX

Verse 1. *Children of Ammon, and with them* other *beside the Ammonites*] Here there must be a mistake; surely the *Ammonites* are the same as the *children of Ammon.* Our translators have falsified the text by inserting the words "other *beside*," which have nothing properly to represent them in the Hebrew. Literally translated, the words are: "And it happened after this, the children of Moab, and the children of Ammon, and with them of the Ammonites:" and thus the *Vulgate.* The *Syriac,* which the *Arabic* follows, has felt the difficulty, and translated, *Came together with warlike men to fight,* &c. The *Septuagint* have given it another turn: Καὶ μετ' αὐτων εκ των Μιναιων, *And with them people of the Minaites;* which were a people of Arabia Felix near the Red Sea. The *Targum* has עמהון מן אדומאי *Ve-immehon min Edomaey,* "And with them some of the Edomites." This is very likely to be the true reading, as we find from ver. 10, 22, 23, that they procured men from Mount *Seir;* and these were the *Idumeans* or *Edomites.* We should, in my opinion, read the text thus: *The children of Moab, and the children of Ammon, and with them some of the Edomites.*

Verse 2. *On this side Syria*] Instead of מארם *mearam, from Syria,* I would read with

one of *Kennicott's* MSS. (89) מאדם *meedom, from Edom,* which alteration brings it to truth, and does not require the change of *half a letter,* as it consists in the almost imperceptible difference between ר *resh* and ד *daleth.* We do not read of any *Syrians* in this invasion, but we know there were *Edomites,* or *inhabitants of Mount Seir.*

Hazazon-tamar] "In the wood of palm trees, that is, in Engedi."—*Targum.* This is the meaning of the word, and it is probable that they lay hid here.

Verse 3. *Jehoshaphat feared*] He found that he could not possibly stand against such a numerous army, and therefore could not expect to be delivered except by the strong arm of God. To get this assistance, it was necessary to *seek* it; and to get such *extraordinary* help, they should seek it in an *extraordinary way;* hence he proclaimed a *universal fast,* and all the people came up to Jerusalem to seek the Lord.

Verse 5. *Jehoshaphat stood*] What an instructive sight was this! The king who proclaimed the fast was foremost to observe it, and was on this occasion the priest of the people; offering in the congregation, without *form* or any *premeditation,* one of the most sensible, pious, correct, and as to its composition one of the most elegant prayers ever offered under the Old Testament dispensation.

A. M. 3108
B. C. 896
Anno ante
I. Olymp. 120
Ante Urbem
Conditam 143

thou over all the kingdoms of the heathen? and ^gin thine hand *is there not* power and might, so that none is able to withstand thee?

7 *Art* not thou ^hour God, ⁱ*who* ^kdidst drive out the inhabitants of this land before thy people Israel, and gavest it to the seed of Abraham ^lthy friend for ever?

8 And they dwelt therein, and have built thee a sanctuary therein for thy name, saying,

9 ^mIf, *when* evil cometh upon us, *as* the sword, judgment, or pestilence, or famine, we stand before this house, and in thy presence, (for thy ⁿname *is* in this house,) and cry unto thee in our affliction, then ^othou wilt hear and help.

10 And now, behold, the children of Ammon and Moab and Mount Seir, whom thou ^pwouldest not let Israel invade, when they came out of the land of Egypt, but ^qthey turned from them, and destroyed them not;

11 Behold, *I say, how* they reward us, ^rto come to cast us out of thy possession, which thou hast given us to inherit.

12 O our God, wilt thou not ^sjudge them? for we have no might against this great company that cometh against us; neither know we what to do: but ^tour eyes *are* upon thee.

13 And all Judah stood before the LORD, with their little ones, their wives, and their children.

14 Then upon Jahaziel the son of Zechariah, the son of Benaiah, the son of Jeiel, the son of Mattaniah, a Levite of the sons of Asaph, ^ucame the Spirit of the LORD in the midst of the congregation;

15 And he said, Hearken ye, all Judah, and ye inhabitants of Jerusalem, and thou king Jehoshaphat, Thus saith the LORD unto you, ^vBe not afraid nor dismayed by reason of this great multitude; for the battle *is* not yours, but God's.

A. M. 3108
B. C. 896
Anno ante
I. Olymp. 120
Ante Urbem
Conditam 143

16 To-morrow go ye down against them: behold, they come up by the ^wcliff of Ziz; and ye shall find them at the end of the ^xbrook, before the wilderness of Jeruel.

17 ^yYe shall not *need* to fight in this *battle:* set yourselves, stand ye *still,* and see the salvation of the LORD with you, O Judah and Jerusalem: fear not, nor be dismayed; tomorrow go out against them: ^zfor the LORD *will be* with you.

18 And Jehoshaphat ^abowed his head with *his* face to the ground: and all Judah and the inhabitants of Jerusalem fell before the LORD, worshipping the LORD.

19 And the Levites, of the children of the Kohathites, and of the children of the Korhites, stood up to praise the LORD God of Israel with a loud voice on high.

20 And they rose early in the morning, and went forth into the wilderness of Tekoa: and as they went forth, Jehoshaphat stood and said, Hear me, O Judah, and ye inhabitants of Jerusalem; ^bBelieve in the LORD your God, so shall ye be established; believe his prophets, so shall ye prosper.

21 And when he had consulted with the people, he appointed singers unto the LORD, ^cand ^dthat should praise the beauty of holiness, as they went out before the army, and

---

^gPsa. xlvii. 2, 8; Dan. iv. 17, 25, 32——^h1 Chron. xxix; 12; Psa. lxii. 11; Matt. vi. 13——ⁱGen. xvii. 7; Exod. vi. 7——^kHeb. *thou*——^lPsa. xliv. 2——^mIsa. xli. 8. James ii. 23——ⁿ1 Kings viii. 33, 37; chap. vi. 28, 29, 30 ^oChap. vi. 20——^pDeut. ii. 4, 9, 19——^qNum. xx. 21 ^rPsa. lxxxiii. 12——^s1 Sam. iii. 13

^tPsa. xxv. 15; cxxi. 1, 2; cxxiii. 1, 2; cxli. 8——^uNum. xi. 25, 26; xxiv. 2; ch. xv. 1; xxiv. 20——^vExod. xiv. 13, 14; Deut. i. 29, 30; xxxi. 6, 8; ch. xxxii. 7——^wHeb. *ascent*——^xOr, *valley*——^yExod. xiv. 13, 14——^zNum. xiv. 9; chap. xv. 2; xxxii. 8——^aExod. iv. 31——^bIsa. vii. 9——^c1 Chron. xvi. 29——^dHeb. *praisers*

Verse 7. *Art not thou our God*] "Hast not thou, by thy WORD, driven out."—*Targum.*

Verse 8. *Therein for thy name*] "For the name of thy WORD."—*Targum.*

Verse 9. *For thy name is in this house*] "Thy *Majesty* is in this house." Several of Kennicott's and De Rossi's MSS., with the *Vulgate, Syriac,* and *Arabic,* add נקרא *nikra,* "is invoked;" *Thy name is invoked in this house* —here thou dwellest, and here thou art worshipped.

Verse 11. *They reward us*] Six of Kennicott's and De Rossi's MSS. add רעה, *evil:* "Behold, they reward us EVIL." This is also the reading of the *Targum.*

Verse 12. *Wilt thou not judge them*] That is, Thou wilt inflict deserved punishment upon them.

Verse 15. *For the battle is not yours, but God's.*] God will not employ *you* in the discomfiture of this great host; he himself will take the matter in hand, deliver you, and destroy them.

Verse 17. *For the Lord will be with you.*] "The WORD of the Lord shall be your Helper." —*Targum.*

Verse 20. *Believe in the Lord your God*] "Believe in the WORD of the Lord your God, and believe in his law, and believe in his prophets; and ye shall prosper." Here the WORD and the

A. M. 3108
B. C. 896
Anno ante
I. Olymp. 120
Ante Urbem
Conditam 143

to say, [e]Praise the LORD; [f]for his mercy *endureth* for ever.

22 [g]And when they began [h]to sing and to praise, [i]the LORD set ambushments against the children of Ammon, Moab, and Mount Seir, which were come against Judah; and [k]they were smitten.

23 For the children of Ammon and Moab stood up against the inhabitants of Mount Seir, utterly to slay and destroy *them*: and when they had made an end of the inhabitants of Seir, every one helped [l]to destroy another.

24 And when Judah came toward the watchtower in the wilderness, they looked unto the multitude, and, behold, they *were* dead bodies fallen to the earth, and [m]none escaped.

25 And when Jehoshaphat and his people came to take away the spoil of them, they found among them in abundance both riches with the dead bodies, and precious jewels, which they stripped off for themselves, more than they could carry away: and they were three days in gathering of the spoil, it was so much.

26 And on the fourth day they assembled themselves in the valley of [n]Berachah; for there they blessed the LORD: therefore the name of the same place was called, The valley of Berachah, unto this day.

27 Then they returned, every man of Judah and Jerusalem, and Jehoshaphat in the [o]forefront of them, to go again to Jerusalem with joy; for the LORD had [p]made them to rejoice over their enemies.

28 And they came to Jerusalem with psalteries and harps and trumpets unto the house of the LORD.

29 And [q]the fear of God was on all the kingdoms of *those* countries, when they had heard that the LORD fought against the enemies of Israel.

30 So the realm of Jehoshaphat was quiet: for his [r]God gave him rest round about.

A.M.3090-3115
B. C. 914-889
Anno ante
I. Ol. 138-113

31 [s]And Jehoshaphat reigned over Judah: *he was* thirty and five years old when he began to reign, and he reigned twenty and five years in Jerusalem. And his mother's name *was* Azubah the daughter of Shilhi.

32 And he walked in the way of Asa his father, and departed not from it, doing *that which was* right in the sight of the LORD.

33 Howbeit [t]the high places were not taken away: for as yet the people had not [u]prepared their hearts unto the God of their fathers.

---

[e]1 Chron. xvi. 34; Psa. cxxxvi. 1——[f]1 Chron. xvi. 41; chap. v. 13; vii. 3, 6——[g]Heb. *And in the time that they,* &c.——[h]Hebrew, *in singing and praise* [i]Judges vii. 22; 1 Samuel xiv. 20——[k]Or, *they smote one another*

[l]Heb. *for the destruction*——[m]Heb. there was *not an escaping*——[n]That is, *blessing*——[o]Heb. *head* [p]Neh. xii. 43——[q]Chap. xvii. 10——[r]Chap. xv. 15; Job xxxiv. 29——[s]1 Kings xxii. 41, &c.——[t]See chap. xvii. 6——[u]Chap. xii. 14; xix. 3

---

revelation are most pointedly distinguished; the *Word* being used *personally*.

Verse 22. *The Lord set ambushments*] "The WORD of the Lord placed snares among the children of Ammon and Moab; and the inhabitants of the mountain of Gibla, who came to fight with Judah; and they were broken to pieces:" so the *Targum*.

Houbigant translates the place thus: "The Lord set against the children of Ammon and Moab ambushments of those who came from Mount Seir against Judah; and the children of Ammon and Moab were smitten: but they afterwards rose up against the inhabitants of Mount Seir, and utterly destroyed them; who being destroyed, they rose up one against another, and mutually destroyed each other." This is probably the meaning of these verses. *Calmet's* version is not very different.

Verse 25. *Both riches with the dead bodies*] For פגרים *pegarim*, dead bodies, בגדים *begadim*, *garments*, is the reading of *eight* MSS. in the collections of *Kennicott* and *De Rossi*, and in several ancient editions. None of the versions have *dead bodies* except the *Chaldee*. The words might be easily mistaken for each other, as the פ *pe*, if a little faint in the under dot might easily pass for a ב *beth*; and we know that the ר *resh* and ד *daleth*, are frequently interchanged and mistaken for each other, both in *Hebrew* and *Syriac*. I believe *garments* to be the true reading; and as to the clause *which they stripped off for themselves*, it should be understood thus: *Which they seized for themselves*, &c.

Verse 26. *Assembled themselves in the valley of Berachah*] "The valley of Benediction;" and so in the latter clause.—*Targum*.

Verse 27. *Jehoshaphat in the forefront of them*] He was their *leader* in all these spiritual, holy, fatiguing, and self-denying exercises. What a noble and persuasive pattern!

Verse 29. *The Lord fought*] "The WORD of the Lord made war against the enemies of Israel."—*Targum*.

Verse 33. *The high places were not taken away*] The idolatry, as we have seen, was universally suppressed; but some of the places where that worship had been performed were not destroyed. Some of them still remained:

A.M.3090-3115
B.C. 914-889
Anno ante
I. Ol. 138-113

34 Now the rest of the acts of Jehoshaphat, first and last, behold, they *are* written in the ᵛbook of Jehu the son of Hanani, ʷwho ˣ*is* mentioned in the book of the kings of Israel.

A. M. 3108
B. C. 896
Anno ante
I. Olymp. 120
Ante Urbem
Conditam 143

35 And after this ʸdid Jehoshaphat king of Judah join himself with Ahaziah king of Israel, who did very wickedly:

36 ᶻAnd he joined himself with him to make ships to go to Tarshish: and they made the ships in Ezion-geber.

A. M. 3108
B. C. 896
Anno ante
I. Olymp. 120
Ante Urbem
Conditam 143

37 Then Eliezer the son of Dodavah of Mareshah prophesied against Jehoshaphat, saying, Because thou hast joined thyself with Ahaziah, the LORD hath broken thy works. ᵃAnd the ships were broken, that they were not able to go ᵇto Tarshish.

ᵛHeb. *words*——ʷ1 Kings xvii. 1, 7——ˣHeb. *was made to ascend*——ʸ1 Kings xxii. 48, 49

ᵃAt first Jehoshaphat was unwilling, 1 Kings xxii. 49 ——ᵃ1 Kings xxii. 48——ᵇChap. ix. 21

---

and these, to such a fickle people, became the means of idolatry in reigns less propitious to truth and religion.

Verse 34. *In the book of Jehu*] This is totally lost, though it is evident that it was in being when the books of Chronicles were written.

Verse 36. *To go to Tarshish*] "In the great sea."—*Targum.* By which expression they always meant the *Mediterranean Sea.*

Verse 37. *The Lord hath broken, &c.*] "The WORD of the Lord hath broken."—*Targum.* Concerning *Tarshish, Ezion-geber,* and *Ophir,* and the voyage thither, see the notes on 1 Kings x. 22, and at the end of that chapter, and on chap. ix. 26-28. The Tarshish here is called by the Chaldee *Torsos in the great sea,* some place in the Mediterranean. On this subject the reader has, no doubt, already seen a great variety of opinions.

CHAPTER XXI

Jehoram succeeds his father Jehoshaphat; and commences his reign with the murder of his brethren, and of several of the princes of Israel, 1–5. He walks in the way of Ahab, whose bad daughter, Athaliah, he had married, 6. God remembers his covenant with David, and does not destroy the nation, 7. The Edomites revolt, 8–10. Jehoram restores the high places in the mountains of Judah, and greatly corrupts the morals of the people, 11. A letter comes to him from Elijah, 12–15. The Philistines and Arabians come up against him, pillage his house, and take away his wives, with all his sons except Jehoahaz, 16, 17. He is smitten with an incurable disease in his bowels; of which, in two years, he dies miserably, after a profligate reign of eight years, 18–20.

A. M. 3115
B. C. 889
Anno ante
I. Olymp. 113
Ante Urbem
Conditam 136

NOW ᵃJehoshaphat slept with his fathers, and was buried with his fathers in the city of David. And Jehoram his son ᵇreigned in his stead.

2 And he had brethren the sons of Jehoshaphat, Azariah, and Jehiel, and Zechariah, and Azariah, and Michael, and Shephatiah: all these *were* the sons of Jehoshaphat king of Israel.

3 And their father gave them great gifts of silver, and of gold, and of precious things, with fenced cities in Judah: but the kingdom gave he to ᶜJehoram; because he *was* the first-born.

A. M. 3115
B. C. 889
Anno ante
I. Olymp. 113
Ante Urbem
Conditam 136

4 Now when Jehoram was risen up to the kingdom of his father, he strengthened himself, and slew all his brethren with the sword, and *divers* also of the princes of Israel.

ᵃ1 Kings xxii. 50——ᵇAlone——ᶜJehoram made partner of the kingdom with his father, 2 Kings viii. 16

NOTES ON CHAP. XXI

Verse 2. *And he had brethren—the sons of Jehoshaphat, king of Israel.*] Jehoshaphat certainly was not king of *Israel,* but king of *Judah.* ישראל *Yisrael* must be a corruption in the text, for יהודה *Yehudah;* which is the reading of the *Syriac, Arabic, Septuagint,* and *Vulgate:* the *Chaldee,* only, agrees with the Hebrew text. And the reading of the *versions* is supported by *thirty-eight* of *Kennicott's* and *De Rossi's* MSS. The word *Judah* should therefore be restored to the text.

Verse 3. *The kingdom gave he to Jehoram*] He made him co-partner with himself in the kingdom about *three* years before his death; so that he reigned only *five* years after the death of his father Jehoshaphat. See the notes on 2 Kings viii. 16, &c.; and on the same, chap. i. 17, where an attempt is made to settle this disturbed chronology.

Verse 4. *Slew all his brethren*] What a truly diabolic thing is the *lust of power!* it destroys all the charities of life, and renders those who are under its influence the truest resemblants of the arch fiend. That he might sit the more secure upon his throne, this execrable man imbrues his hands in the blood of his own brothers! There are more instances of this species of cruelty among bad Asiatic kings than among any other class of men. The history of every country abounds in proofs; even that of our own is not the least barren.

A.M.3112-3119
B. C. 892–885
Anno ante
I. Ol. 116–109

5. ᵈJehoram *was* thirty and two years old when he began to reign, and he reigned eight years in Jerusalem.

6 And he walked in the way of the kings of Israel, like as did the house of Ahab: for he had the daughter of ᵉAhab to wife: and he wrought *that which was* evil in the eyes of the LORD.

7 Howbeit the LORD would not destroy the house of David, because of the covenant that he had made with David, and as he promised to give a ᶠlight to him and to his ᵍsons for ever.

A. M. 3115
B. C. 889
Anno ante
I. Olymp. 113
Ante Urbem
Conditam 136

8 ʰIn his days the Edomites revolted from under the ⁱdominion of Judah, and made themselves a king.

9 Then Jehoram went forth with his princes, and all his chariots with him: and he rose up by night, and smote the Edomites which compassed him in, and the captains of the chariots.

10 So the Edomites revolted from under the hand of Judah unto this day. The same time *also* did Libnah revolt from under his hand;

because he had forsaken the LORD God of his fathers.

A. M. 3115
B. C. 889
Anno ante
I. Olymp. 113
Ante Urbem
Conditam 136

11 Moreover he made high places in the mountains of Judah, and caused the inhabitants of Jerusalem to ᵏcommit fornication, and compelled Judah *thereto.*

12 And there came a ˡwriting to him from Elijah the prophet, saying, Thus saith the LORD God of David thy father, Because thou hast not walked in the ways of Jehoshaphat thy father, nor in the ways of Asa king of Judah,

A. M. 3116
B. C. 888
Anno ante
I. Olymp. 112
Ante Urbem
Conditam 135

13 But hast walked in the way of the kings of Israel, and hast ᵐmade Judah and the inhabitants of Jerusalem to ⁿgo a whoring, like to the ᵒwhoredoms of the house of Ahab, and also hast ᵖslain thy brethren of thy father's house, *which were* better than thyself:

14 Behold, with �q a great plague will the LORD smite thy people, and thy children, and thy wives, and all thy goods:

15 And thou *shalt have* great sickness by ʳdisease of thy bowels, until thy bowels fall out by reason of the sickness day by day.

ᵈIn consort, 2 Kings viii. 17, &c.——ᵉChap. xxii. 2
ᶠHeb. *lamp* or *candle*——ᵍ2 Sam. vii. 12, 13; 1 Kings xi. 36; 2 Kings viii. 19; Psa. cxxxii. 11, &c.——ʰ2 Kings viii. 20, &c.——ⁱHeb. *hand*——ᵏLev. xvii. 7; xx. 5; ver. 13

ˡWhich was writ before his assumption, 2 Kings ii. 1
ᵐVer. 11——ⁿExod. xxxiv. 15; Deut. xxxi. 16——ᵒ1 Kings xvi. 31–33; 2 Kings ix. 22——ᵖVer. 4——qHeb. *a great stroke*——ʳVer. 18, 19

Verse 6. *He had the daughter of Ahab to wife*] This was *Athaliah*, daughter of Ahab and Jezebel, who was famous for her impieties and cruelty, as was her most profligate mother. It is likely that she was the principal cause of Jehoram's cruelty and profaneness.

Verse 7. *To give a light to him*] To give him a *descendant*.

Verse 8. *In his days the Edomites revolted*] See on 2 Kings viii. 21.

Verse 11. *To commit fornication*] That is, to *serve idols*. The Israelites were considered as joined to Jehovah as a *woman* is joined to her *husband*: when *she* associates with *other men*, this is *adultery*; when *they* served *other gods*, this was called by the same name, it was *adultery* against Jehovah. This is frequently the only meaning of the terms *adultery* and *fornication* in the Scriptures.

Verse 12. *There came a writing to him from Elijah the prophet*] From 2 Kings ii. 11, it is evident that Elijah had been translated in the reign of Jehoshaphat, the father of Jehoram. How then could he send a letter to the son? Some say he sent it from heaven by an angel; others, that by the spirit of prophecy he foresaw this defection of Jehoram, and left the letter with Elisha, to be sent to him when this defection should take place; others say that Elijah is put here for *Elisha;* and others, that *this Elijah* was not the *same* that was trans-

lated, but another prophet of the same name. There are others who think that, as Elijah was still in the *body*, for he did not *die*, but was *translated*, he sent this letter from that secret place in which he was hidden by the Almighty. All the *versions* have *Elijah*, and all the MSS. the same reading. Dr. *Kennicott* contends that *Elisha* was the writer; for *Elijah* had been taken up to heaven *thirteen* years before the time of this writing. Our *margin* says, the letter *was written before his assumption*, and refers to 2 Kings ii. 1.

These are all *conjectures;* and I could add *another* to their number, but still we should be where we were. I should adopt the conjecture relative to *Elisha*, were not every *Hebrew* MS., and *all the Oriental versions*, against it; to which may be added, that the author of this book does not once mention *Elisha* in any part of his work. It is certainly a possible case that this *writing* might have been a *prediction* of Jehoram's impiety and miserable death, delivered in the time of the prophet, and which was now laid before this wicked king for the first time: and by it the prophet, though not among mortals, still continued to speak. I can see no solid reason against this opinion.

Verse 14. *Will the Lord smite*] "The WORD of the Lord will send a great mortality."—*Targum.*

Verse 15. *Until thy bowels fall out*] This

A. M. 3117
B. C. 887
Anno ante
I. Olymp. 111
Ante Urbem
Conditam 134

16 Moreover the LORD ᵃstirred up against Jehoram the spirit of the Philistines, and of the Arabians, that *were* near the Ethiopians.

17 And they came up into Judah, and brake into it, and ᵗcarried away all the substance that was found in the king's house, and ᵘhis sons also, and his wives; so that there was never a son left him, save ᵛJehoahaz, the youngest of his sons.

A.M.3117-3119
B. C. 887-885
Anno ante
I. Ol. 111-109

18 ᵂAnd after all this the LORD smote him ˣin his bowels with an incurable disease.

19 And it came to pass, that in process of time, after the end of two years, his bowels fell out by reason of his sickness: so he died of sore diseases. And his people made no burning for him, like ʸthe burning of his fathers.

A.M.3117-3119
B. C. 887-885
Anno ante
I. Ol. 111-109

20 Thirty and two years old was he when he began to reign, and he reigned in Jerusalem eight years, and departed ᶻwithout being desired. Howbeit they buried him in the city of David, but not in the sepulchres of the kings.

A.M.3112-3119
B. C. 892-885
Anno ante
I. Ol. 116-109

A. M. 3119
B. C. 885
Anno ante
I. Olymp. 109
Ante Urbem
Conditam 132

ᵃ1 Kings xi. 14, 23——ᵗHeb. *carried captive; see* chap. xxii. 1——ᵘChap. xxiv. 7——ᵛOr, *Ahaziah,* chap. xxii. 1; or *Azariah,* chap. xxii. 6

ᵂHis son, *Ahaziah Prorex,* 2 Kings ix. 29, soon after ˣVer. 15——ʸChapter xvi. 14——ᶻHebrew, *without desire;* Jeremiah xxii. 18

---

must have been occasioned by a violent inflammation: by the same death perished *Antiochus Epiphanes,* and *Herod Agrippa.*

Verse 16. *The Philistines, and—the Arabians*] We have no other account of this war. Though it was a predatory war, yet it appears to have been completely ruinous and destructive. What a general curse fell upon this bad king; in his *body, soul, substance, family,* and *government!*

Verse 17. *Save Jehoahaz the youngest*] This person had at least *three* names, *Jehoahaz, Ahaziah,* (chap. xxii. 1,) and *Azariah,* (ver. 6.)

Verse 18. *The Lord smote him*] "And after all these things the WORD of the Lord smote his bowels," &c.—*Targum.*

Verse 19. *After the end of two years, his bowels fell out*] The *Targum* seems to inti-

mate that he had a constipation and inflammation in his bowels; and that at last his bowels gushed out.

No burning] "His people made no burning of aromatic woods for him, as they had done for his forefathers."—*Targum.* See on chap. xvi. 14.

Verse 20. *Departed without being desired.*] He was hated while he lived, and neglected when he died; visibly cursed of God, and necessarily execrated by the people whom he had lived only to corrupt and oppress. No *annalist* is mentioned as having taken the pains to write any account of his vile life. This summary mention of him consigns him to the execration of posterity, and holds in the view of every prudent governor, the rock on which he split and wrecked the state.

CHAPTER XXII

Ahaziah begins to reign; and reigns wickedly under the counsels of his bad mother, 1–4. He is slain by Jehu, who destroys all the house of Ahab, 5–9. Athaliah destroys all the seed royal of Judah, except Joash, who is hidden by his nurse in the temple six years, 10–12.

A. M. 3119
B. C. 885
Anno ante
I. Olymp. 109
Ante Urbem
Conditam 132

AND the inhabitants of Jerusalem made ᵃAhaziah his youngest son king in his stead: for the band of men that came with the Arabians to the camp had slain all

the ᵇeldest. So Ahaziah the son of Jehoram king of Judah reigned.

2 ᶜForty and two years old *was* Ahaziah when he began to reign, and he reigned one year in Jerusalem. His mother's

A.M.3119-3120
B. C. 885-884
Anno ante
I. Ol. 109-108

ᵃ2 Kings viii. 24, &c.; see chap. xxi. 17; ver. 6

ᵇChap. xxi. 17——ᶜSee 2 Kings viii. 26

NOTES ON CHAP. XXII

Verse 1. *Made Ahaziah his youngest son king*] All the others had been slain by the Arabians, &c.; see the preceding chapter, ver. 17.

Verse 2. *Forty and two years old was Ahaziah*] See the note on 2 Kings viii. 26. Ahaziah might have been *twenty-two* years old, according to 2 Kings viii. 26, but he could not have been *forty-two,* as stated here, without being *two years older than his own father!* See the note there. The *Syriac* and *Arabic* have

twenty-two, and the *Septuagint,* in some copies, *twenty.* And it is very probable that the Hebrew text read so originally; for when *numbers* were expressed by *single letters,* it was easy to mistake מ *mem,* FORTY, for כ *caph,* TWENTY. And if this book was written by a scribe who used the *ancient Hebrew letters,* now called the *Samaritan,* the mistake was still more easy and probable, as the difference between ⳨ *caph* and ⵉ *mem* is very small, and can in many instances be discerned only by an accustomed eye.

A.M.3119-3120
B. C. 885-884
Anno ante
I. Ol. 109-108

name also *was* ^dAthaliah, the daughter of Omri.

3 He also walked in the ways of the house of Ahab: for his mother was his counsellor to do wickedly.

4 Wherefore he did evil in the sight of the LORD like the house of Ahab: for they were his counsellors after the death of his father to his destruction.

A. M. 3120
B. C. 884
Anno ante
I. Olymp. 108
Ante Urbem
Conditam 131

5 He walked also after their counsel, and ^ewent with Jehoram the son of Ahab king of Israel to war against Hazael king of Syria at Ramoth-gilead: and the Syrians smote Joram.

6 ^fAnd he returned to be healed in Jezreel, because of the wounds ^gwhich were given him at Ramah, when he fought with Hazael king of Syria. And ^hAzariah the son of Jehoram king of Judah went down to see Jehoram the son of Ahab at Jezreel, because he was sick.

7 And the ⁱdestruction of Ahaziah ^kwas of God by coming to Joram: for when **he was** come, he ^lwent out with Jehoram against Jehu the son of Nimshi, ^mwhom the LORD had anointed to cut off the house of Ahab.

8 And it came to pass, that when Jehu was

ⁿexecuting judgment upon the house of Ahab, and ^ofound the princes of Judah, and the sons of the brethren of Ahaziah, that ministered to Ahaziah, he slew them.

A. M. 3120
B. C. 884
Anno ante
I. Olymp. 108
Ante Urbem
Conditam 131

9 ^pAnd he sought Ahaziah: and they caught him, (for he was hid in Samaria,) and brought him to Jehu: and when they had slain him, they buried him: Because, said they, he *is* the son of Jehoshaphat, who ^qsought the LORD with all his heart. So the house of Ahaziah had no power to keep still the kingdom.

10 ^rBut when Athaliah the mother of Ahaziah saw that her son was dead, she arose and destroyed all the seed royal of the house of Judah.

11 But ^sJehoshabeath, the daughter of the king, took Joash the son of Ahaziah, and stole him from among the king's sons that were slain, and put him and his nurse in a bedchamber. So Jehoshabeath, the daughter of King Jehoram, the wife of Jehoiada the priest, (for she was the sister of Ahaziah,) hid him from Athaliah, so that she slew him not.

12 And he was with them hid in the house of God six years: and Athaliah reigned over the land.

A.M.3120-3126
B. C. 884-878
Anno ante
I. Ol. 108-102

---

^dCh. xxi. 6—^e2 Kings viii. 28, &c.—^f2 Kings ix. 15
^gHeb. *wherewith they wounded him*——^hOtherwise called
Ahaziah, ver. 1; and *Jehoahaz*, chap. xxi. 17——ⁱHeb.
treading down——^kJudg. xiv. 4; 1 Kings xii. 15; chap. x. 15

^l2 Kings ix. 21——^m2 Kings ix. 6, 7——ⁿ2 Kings x.
10, 11——^o2 Kings x. 13, 14——^p2 Kings ix. 27, at
Megiddo in the kingdom of *Samaria*——^qChap. xvii. 4
^r2 Kings xi. 1, &c.——^s2 Kings xi. 2, *Jehosheba*

The reading in 2 Kings is *right*, and any attempt to reconcile this in *Chronicles* with *that* is equally futile and absurd. *Both* readings cannot be *true; is* that therefore likely to be genuine that makes the *son two years older* than the *father* who begat him? *Apage hæ nugæ!*

Verse 3. *His mother was his counsellor*] Athaliah, the wicked daughter of a wicked parent, and the wicked spouse of an unprincipled king.

Verse 5. *Went with Jehoram*] See on 2 Kings viii. 28.

Verse 9. *He sought Ahaziah*] See a different account 2 Kings ix. 27, and the note there, where the accounts are reconciled.

Verse 10. *All the seed royal of the house of Judah*] Nothing but the miraculous interven-

tion of the Divine providence could have saved the line of David at this time, and preserved the prophecy relative to the Messiah. The whole truth of that prophecy, and the salvation of the world, appeared to be now suspended on the brittle thread of the life of an *infant* of a year old, (see chap. xxiv. 1,) to destroy whom was the interest of the reigning power! But God can save by few as well as by many. He had purposed, and vain were the counter-exertions of earth and hell.

Verse 12. *Hid in the house of God*] "In the house of the sanctuary of God."—*Targum.* Or, as he says on ver. 11, בקודש קודשיא *bekudash kudeshaiya*, "in the holy of holies." To this place Athaliah had no access, therefore Joash lay concealed, he and his affectionate aunt-nurse.—See on 2 Kings xi. 1.

CHAPTER XXIII

Jehoiada the priest, after having taken counsel with the captains, Levites, &c., proclaims Joash, and anoints him king, 1–11. Athaliah, endeavouring to prevent it, is slain, 12–15. He makes the people enter into a covenant, that they would serve the Lord, 16. The people break down the temple of Baal, and slay Mattan his priest, 17. Jehoiada makes several alterations, and remodels the kingdom, 18–21.

A. M. 3126
B. C. 878
Anno ante
I. Olymp. 102
Ante Urbem
Conditam 125

A ND ᵃin the seventh year Jehoiada strengthened him-
self, and took the captains of
hundreds, Azariah the son of
Jeroham, and Ishmael the son of Jehohanan,
and Azariah the son of Obed, and Maaseiah
the son of Adaiah, and Elishaphat the son of
Zichri, into covenant with him.

2 And they went about in Judah, and gathered the Levites out of all the cities of Judah,
and the chief of the fathers of Israel, and
they came to Jerusalem.

3 And all the congregation made a covenant
with the king in the house of God. And he
said unto them, Behold, the king's son shall
reign, as the LORD hath ᵇsaid of the sons of
David.

4 This *is* the thing that ye shall do; A
third part of you ᶜentering on the Sabbath,
of the priests and of the Levites, *shall be* porters of the ᵈdoors;

5 And a third part *shall be* at the king's
house; and a third part at the gate of the
foundation: and all the people *shall be* in the
courts of the house of the LORD.

6 But let none come into the house of the
LORD save the priests, and ᵉthey that minister
of the Levites; they shall go in, for they *are*
holy: but all the people shall keep the watch
of the LORD.

7 And the Levites shall compass the king
round about, every man with his weapons in
his hand; and whosoever *else* cometh into the
house, he shall be put to death: but be ye
with the king when he cometh in, and when
he goeth out.

8 So the Levites and all Judah did according to all things that Jehoiada the priest had
commanded, and took every man his men
that were to come in on the Sabbath, with
them that were to go *out* on the Sabbath: for

Jehoiada the priest dismissed
not ᶠthe courses.

A. M. 3126
B. C. 878
Anno ante
I. Olymp. 102
Ante Urbem
Conditam 125

9 Moreover Jehoiada the priest
delivered to the captains of hundreds spears, and bucklers, and shields, that
had been King David's, which *were* in the
house of God.

10 And he set all the people, every man
having his weapon in his hand, from the right
ᵍside of the ʰtemple to the left side of the
temple, along by the altar and the temple, by
the king round about.

11 Then they brought out the king's son,
and put upon him the crown, and ⁱ*gave him*
the testimony, and made him king. And
Jehoiada and his sons anointed him, and
said, ᵏGod save the king.

12 Now when Athaliah heard the noise of
the people running and praising the king, she
came to the people into the house of the LORD:

13 And she looked, and, behold, the king
stood at his pillar at the entering in, and the
princes and the trumpets by the king: and
all the people of the land rejoiced, and sounded with trumpets, also the singers with instruments of music, and ˡsuch as taught to
sing praise. Then Athaliah rent her clothes,
and said, ᵐTreason, Treason.

14 Then Jehoiada the priest brought out
the captains of hundreds that were set over
the hosts, and said unto them, Have her forth
of the ranges: and whoso followeth her, let
him be slain with the sword. For the priest
said, Slay her not in the house of the LORD.

15 So they laid hands on her; and when she
was come to the entering ⁿof the horse-gate
by the king's house, they slew her there.

16 And Jehoiada made a covenant between
him, and between all the people, and between
the king, that they should be the LORD's people.

17 Then all the people went to the house of

ᵃ2 Kings xi. 4, &c.——ᵇ2 Sam. vii. 12; 1 Kings ii. 4;
ix. 5; chap. vi. 16; vii. 18; xxi. 7——ᶜ1 Chron. ix. 25
ᵈHebrew, *thresholds*——ᵉ1 Chron. xxiii. 28, 29

ⁱSee 1 Chron. xxiv. and xxv——ᵍHeb. *shoulder*——ʰHeb.
house——ⁱDeut. xvii. 18——ᵏHeb. *Let the king live*——ˡ1
Chron. xxv. 8——ᵐHebrew, *Conspiracy*——ⁿNeh. iii. 28

NOTES ON CHAP. XXIII

Verse 1. *And in the seventh year*] See on
2 Kings xi. 4, &c.

Verse 9. *Spears and bucklers*] See on 2 Kings
xi. 10.

Verse 11. *God save the king.*] *May the king
live!* See on 2 Kings xi. 12.

Verse 14. *And whoso followeth her, let him
be slain with the sword.*] He who takes her

part, or endeavours to prevent the present
revolution, let him be immediately slain.

Verse 15. *Of the horse-gate*] See on 2 Kings
xi. 16.

Verse 16. *Made a covenant between him*]
The high priest was, on this occasion, the representative of GOD; whom both the people and the
king must have had in view, through the medium of his priest.

Verse 17. *Mattan the priest*] The *Targum*

A. M. 3126 B. C. 878 Anno ante I. Olymp. 102 Ante Urbem Conditam 125

Baal, and brake it down, and brake his altars and his images in pieces, and [o]slew Mattan the priest of Baal before the altars.

18 Also Jehoiada appointed the offices of the house of the LORD by the hand of the priests the Levites, whom David had [p]distributed in the house of the LORD, to offer the burnt-offerings of the LORD, as *it is* written in the [q]law of Moses, with rejoicing and with singing, *as it was ordained* [r]by David.

19 And he set the [s]porters at the gates of the house of the LORD, that none *which was* unclean in any thing should enter in.

A. M. 3126 B. C. 878 Anno ante I. Olymp. 102 Ante Urbem Conditam 125

20 [t]And he took the captains of hundreds, and the nobles, and the governors of the people, and all the people of the land, and brought down the king from the house of the LORD; and they came through the high gate into the king's house, and set the king upon the throne of the kingdom.

21 And all the people of the land rejoiced; and the city was quiet, after that they had slain Athaliah with the sword.

[o]Deut. xiii. 9——[p]1 Chron. xxiii. 6, 30, 31; xxiv. 1 [q]Num. xxviii. 2

[r]Heb. *by the hands of David;* 1 Chron. xxv. 2, 6——[s]1 Chron. xxvi. 1, &c.——[t]2 Kings xi. 19

will not prostitute the term *priest*, but calls him כומרא *cumera, priestling.*

Verse 21. *The city was quiet*] There was no attempt at a counter-revolution. Concerning the coronation of Joash, there is a curious circumstance mentioned by the *Targumist* on ver. 11; it is as follows:—

"And they brought forth the son of the king, and put on him the royal crown which David took from the head of the king of the children of Ammon. In it was inserted the precious attracting stone, in which was engraven and expressed the great and honourable NAME [יהוה] which David had placed there by the Holy Spirit: and it was of the weight of a talent of gold; it was therefore a testimony to the house of David that no king who was not of the seed of David should be able to put it on his head, nor be able to bear its weight. When, therefore, the people saw it placed on the head of Joash, and that he was able to bear this crown, they believed him to be of the seed of David, and immediately constituted him king. Therefore Jehoiada and his sons anointed him, and said, May the king be prosperous in his kingdom!"

The Jews say that this was the crown of the king of the Ammonites; and that it was always worn afterwards by the kings of the house of Judah. See *Jarchi* on this place.

CHAPTER XXIV

Joash begins to reign when seven years old, and reigns well all the days of Jehoiada the priest, 1–3. *He purposes to repair the temple of God; and makes a proclamation that the people should bring in the money prescribed by Moses,* 4–9. *They all contribute liberally; and the different artificers soon perfect the work,* 10–13. *The rest of the money is employed to form utensils for the temple,* 14. *Jehoiada dies,* 15, 16. *And the people after his death become idolaters,* 17, 18. *Prophets are sent unto them,* 19. *And among the rest Zechariah the son of Jehoiada, who testifies against them; and they stone him to death,* 20–22. *The Syrians come against Jerusalem, and spoil it,* 23, 24. *Joash is murdered by his own servants,* 25, 26. *His acts,* 27.

A.M.3126-3165 B. C. 878-839 Anno ante I. Ol. 102-63

JOASH [a]*was* seven years old when he began to reign, and he reigned forty years in Jerusalem. His mother's name also *was* Zibiah of Beer-sheba.

A.M.3126-3162 B. C. 878-842 Anno ante I. Ol. 102-66

2 And Joash [b]did *that which was* right in the sight of the LORD all the days of Jehoiada the priest.

A.M.3126-3162 B. C. 878-842 Anno ante I. Ol. 102-66

3 And Jehoiada took for him two wives; and he begat sons and daughters.

A. M. 3148 B. C. 856 Anno ante I. Olymp. 80 Ante Urbem Conditam 103

4 And it came to pass after this, *that* Joash was minded [c]to repair the house of the LORD.

5 And he gathered together the priests and the Levites, and said to them, Go out unto the cities of Judah, and [d]gather of

[a]2 Kings xi. 21; xii. 1, &c.——[b]See chap. xxvi. 5

[c]Heb. *to renew*——[d]2 Kings xii. 4

NOTES ON CHAP. XXIV

Verse 1. *Joash* was *seven years old*] As he was hidden *six* years in the temple, and was but *seven* when he came to the throne, he could have been but *one year* old when he was secreted by his aunt; see on chap. xxii. 10.

Verse 4. *To repair the house of the Lord.*] During the reigns of Joram and Athaliah, the temple of God had been pillaged to enrich that

A. M. 3148
B. C. 856
Anno ante
I. Olymp. 80
Ante Urbem
Conditam 103

all Israel money to repair the house of your God from year to year, and see that ye hasten the matter. Howbeit the Levites hastened *it* not.

6 ^eAnd the king called for Jehoiada the chief, and said unto him, Why hast thou not required of the Levites to bring in out of Judah and out of Jerusalem the collection, *according to the commandment* of ^fMoses the servant of the LORD, and of the congregation of Israel, for the ^gtabernacle of witness?

7 For ^hthe sons of Athaliah, that wicked woman, had broken up the house of God; and also all the ⁱdedicated things of the house of the LORD did they bestow upon Baalim.

8 And at the king's commandment ^kthey made a chest, and set it without at the gate of the house of the LORD.

9 And they made ^la proclamation through Judah and Jerusalem, to bring in to the LORD ^mthe collection *that* Moses the servant of God *laid* upon Israel in the wilderness.

10 And all the princes and all the people rejoiced, and brought in, and cast into the chest, until they had made an end.

11 Now it came to pass, that at what time the chest was brought unto the king's office by the hand of the Levites, and ⁿwhen they saw that *there was* much money, the king's scribe and the high priest's officer came and emptied the chest, and took it, and carried it to his place again. Thus they did day by day, and gathered money in abundance.

12 And the king and Jehoiada gave it to

such as did the work of the service of the house of the LORD, and hired masons and carpenters to repair the house of the LORD, and also such as wrought iron and brass to mend the house of the LORD.

A. M. 3148
B. C. 856
Anno ante
I. Olymp. 80
Ante Urbem
Conditam 103

13 So the workmen wrought, and ^othe work was perfected by them, and they set the house of God in his state, and strengthened it.

14 And when they had finished *it,* they brought the rest of the money before the king and Jehoiada, ^pwhereof were made vessels for the house of the LORD, *even* vessels to minister, and ^qto offer *withal,* and spoons, and vessels of gold and silver. And they offered burnt-offerings in the house of the LORD continually all the days of Jehoiada.

A. M. 3162
B. C. 842
Anno ante
I. Olymp. 66
Ante Urbem
Conditam 89

15 But Jehoiada waxed old, and was full of days when he died; a hundred and thirty years old *was he* when he died.

16 And they buried him in the city of David among the kings, because he had done good in Israel, both toward God, and toward his house.

17 Now after the death of Jehoiada came the princes of Judah, and made obeisance to the king. Then the king hearkened unto them.

A.M. 3162-3165
B. C. 842-839
Anno ante
I. Olymp. 66-68

18 And they left the house of the LORD God of their fathers, and served ^rgroves and idols: and ^swrath came upon Judah and Jerusalem for this their trespass.

19 Yet he ^tsent prophets to them, to bring them again unto the LORD; and they testified against them: but they would not give ear.

---

e2 Kings xii. 7——f Exodus xxx. 12, 13, 14, 16
g Num. i. 50; Acts vii. 44——h Chap. xxi. 17——i 2
Kings xii. 4——k 2 Kings xii. 9——l Hebrew, *a voice*
m Verse 16——n 2 Kings xii. 10

o Heb. *the healing went up upon the work*——p See 2
Kings xii. 13——q Or, *pestils*——r 1 Kings xiv. 23
s Judg. v. 8; ch. xix. 2; xxviii. 13; xxix. 8; xxxii. 25
t Chap. xxxvi. 15; Jer. vii. 25, 26; xxv. 4

---

of Baal, and the whole structure permitted to fall into decay; see ver. 7.

Verse 5. *Gather of all Israel money*] As the temple was the property of the whole nation, and the services performed in it were for the salvation of the people at large, it was right that each should come forward on an occasion of this kind, and lend a helping hand. This is the first instance of such a *general collection* for building or repairing a house of God.

From year to year] It must have been in a state of great dilapidation, when it required such annual exertions to bring it into a thorough state of repair.

Verse 6. *The collection—of Moses*] This was the poll-tax, fixed by Moses, of half a shekel, which was levied on every man from twenty years old and upward; and which was con-

sidered as a *ransom for their souls, that there might be no plague among them.* See Exod. xxx. 12-14.

Verse 8. *They made a chest*] See the notes on the parallel places, 2 Kings xii. 4, &c.

Verse 16. *They buried him—among the kings*] He had, in fact, been *king* in Judah; for Joash, who appears to have been a weak man, was always under his tutelage. Jehoiada governed the state in the name of the king; and his being buried among the kings is a proof of the high estimation in which he was held among the people.

Verse 17. *The princes of Judah—made obeisance to the king*] I believe the *Targum* has given the true sense of this verse: "After the death of Jehoiada, the great men of Judah came and adored King Joash, and seduced him;

A. M. 3164
B. C. 840
Anno ante
I. Olymp. 64
Ante Urbem
Conditam 87

20 And [u]the Spirit of God [v]came upon Zechariah the son of Jehoiada the priest, which stood above the people, and said unto them, Thus saith God, [w]Why transgress ye the commandments of the Lord, that ye cannot prosper? [x]Because ye have forsaken the Lord, he hath also forsaken you.

21 And they conspired against him, and [y]stoned him with stones at the commandment of the king in the court of the house of the Lord.

22 Thus Joash the king remembered not the kindness which Jehoiada his father had done to him, but slew his son. And when he died, he said, The Lord look upon *it*, and require *it*.

A. M. 3165
B. C. 839
Anno ante
I. Olymp. 63
Ante Urbem
Conditam 86

23 And it came to pass [z]at the end of the year, *that* [a]the host of Syria came up against him : and they came to Judah and Jerusalem, and destroyed all the princes of the people from among the people, and sent all the spoil of them unto the king of [b]Damascus.

24 For the army of the Syrians [c]came with a small company of men, and the Lord [d]delivered a very great host into their hand, because they had forsaken the Lord God of their fathers. So they [e]executed judgment against Joash.

A. M. 3165
B. C. 839
Anno ante
I. Olymp. 63
Ante Urbem
Conditam 86

25 And when they were departed from him, (for they left him in great diseases,) [f]his own servants conspired against him for the blood of the [g]sons of Jehoiada the priest, and slew him on his bed, and he died : and they buried him in the city of David, but they buried him not in the sepulchres of the kings.

26 And these are they that conspired against him ; [h]Zabad the son of Shimeath an Ammonitess, and Jehozabad the son of [i]Shimrith a Moabitess.

27 Now *concerning* his sons, and the greatness of [k]the burdens *laid* upon him, and the [l]repairing of the house of God, behold, they *are* written in the [m]story of the book of the kings. [n]And Amaziah his son reigned in his stead.

---

[u]Chapter xv. 1; xx. 14——[v]Hebrew, *clothed*, as Judges vi. 34——[w]Numbers xiv. 41——[x]Chapter xv. 2 [y]Matthew xxiii. 35; Acts vii. 58, 59——[z]Hebrew, *in the revolution of the year*——[a]2 Kings xii. 17——[b]Heb. *Darmesek*——[c]Leviticus xxvi. 8; Deuteronomy xxxii.

30; Isaiah xxx. 17——[d]Leviticus xxvi. 25; Deut. xxviii. 25——[e]Chap. xxii. 8; Isa. x. 5——[f]2 Kings xii. 20 [g]Verse 21——[h]Or, *Jozachar*, 2 Kings xii. 21——[i]Or, *Shomer*——[k]2 Kings xii. 18——[l]Heb. *founding*——[m]Or, *commentary*——[n]2 Kings xii. 21

---

and then the king received from them their idols."

Verse 20. *And the Spirit of God came upon Zechariah*] "When he saw the transgression of the king and of the people, burning incense to an idol in the house of the sanctuary of the Lord, on the day of expiation; and preventing the priests of the Lord from offering the burnt-offerings, sacrifices, daily oblations, and services, as written in the book of the law of Moses; he stood above the people, and said."—*Targum.*

Verse 21. *Stoned him—at the commandment of the king*] What a most wretched and contemptible man was this, who could imbrue his hands in the blood of a prophet of God, and the son of the man who had saved him from being murdered, and raised him to the throne! Alas, alas! Can even *kings* forget benefits? But when a man falls from God, the devil enters into him; and then he is capable of every species of cruelty.

Verse 22. *The Lord look upon* it, *and require* it.] And so he did; for, at the end of that year, the Syrians came against Judah, destroyed all the princes of the people, sent their spoils to Damascus; and Joash, the murderer of the prophet, the son of his benefactor, was himself murdered by his own servants. Here was a most signal display of the Divine retribution.

On the subject of the death of this prophet the reader is requested to refer to the note on Matt. xxiii. 34, 35.

Verse 26. *These are they that conspired*

against him] The two persons here mentioned were certainly not *Jews;* the *mother* of one was an *Ammonitess*, and the *mother* of the other was a *Moabitess.* Who their *fathers* were we know not; they were probably *foreigners* and *aliens.* Some suppose that these persons were of the *king's chamber*, and therefore could have the easiest access to him. It has been, and is still, the *folly* of kings to have foreigners for their valets and most confidential servants, and they have often been the causes of murders and treacheries of different kinds. *Foreigners* should be banished from the person of the sovereign by strong and efficient laws: even in this country they have often been the cause of much political wo.

Verse 27. *The greatness of the burdens* laid *upon him*] Meaning, probably, the heavy tribute laid upon him by the Syrians; though some think the vast sums amassed for the repairs of the temple are here intended.

Written in the story] מדרש *midrash*, the commentary, of the book of Kings. We have met with this before; but these works are all lost, except the extracts found in Kings, Chronicles, and Ezra. These *abridgments* were the cause of the neglect, and finally of the destruction, of the originals. This has been often the case in works of great consequence. *Trogus Pompeius* wrote a general history of the world, which he brought down to the reign of Augustus, in *forty-four* volumes. Justin abridged them into *one* volume, and the original is lost.

CHAPTER XXV

Amaziah succeeds his father Joash, and begins his reign well, 1, 2. He slays his father's murderers, but spares their children, 3, 4. He reviews and remodels the army, 5; and hires a hundred thousand soldiers out of Israel, whom, on the expostulation of a prophet, he sends home again, without bringing them into active service; at which they are greatly offended, 6-10. He attacks the Syrians, kills ten thousand, and takes ten thousand prisoners, whom he precipitates from the top of a rock, so that they are dashed to pieces, 11, 12. The Israelitish soldiers, sent back, ravage several of the cities of Judah, 13. Amaziah becomes an idolater, 14. Is reproved by a prophet, whom he threatens, and obliges to desist, 15, 16. He challenges Joash, king of Israel, 17; who reproves him by a parable, 18, 19. Not desisting, the armies meet, the Jews are overthrown, and Amaziah taken prisoner by Joash, who ravages the temple, and takes away all the treasures of the king, 20-24. The reign of Amaziah: a conspiracy is formed against him; he flees to Lachish, whither he is pursued and slain; is brought to Jerusalem, and buried with his fathers, 25-28.

A.M.3165-3194
B. C. 839-810
Anno ante
I. Olymp. 63-34

AMAZIAH ^a*was* twenty and five years old *when* he began to reign, and he reigned twenty and nine years in Jerusalem. And his mother's name *was* Jehoaddan of Jerusalem.

2 And he did *that which was* right in the sight of the LORD, ^bbut not with a perfect heart.

A. M. 3166
B. C. 838
Anno ante
I. Olymp. 62
Ante Urbem
Conditam 85

3 ^cNow it came to pass, when the kingdom was ^destablished to him, that he slew his servants that had killed the king his father.

4 But he slew not their children, but *did* as *it is* written in the law in the book of Moses, where the LORD commanded, saying, ^eThe fathers shall not die for the children, neither shall the children die for the fathers, but every man shall die for his own sin.

5 Moreover Amaziah gathered Judah together, and made them captains over thousands, and captains over hundreds, according to the houses of *their* fathers, throughout all Judah and Benjamin: and he numbered them ^ffrom twenty years old and above, and found them three hundred thousand choice *men, able* to go forth to war, that could handle spear and shield.

6 He hired also a hundred thousand mighty men of valour out of Israel for a hundred talents of silver.

7 But there came a man of God to him,

saying, O king, let not the army of Israel go with thee; for the LORD *is* not with Israel, *to wit,* with all the children of Ephraim.

A. M. 3166
B. C. 838
Anno ante
I. Olymp. 62
Ante Urbem
Conditam 85

8 But if thou wilt go, do *it,* be strong for the battle: God shall make thee fall before the enemy: for God hath ^gpower to help, and to cast down.

9 And Amaziah said to the man of God, But what shall we do for the hundred talents which I have given to the ^harmy of Israel? And the man of God answered, ⁱThe LORD is able to give thee much more than this.

10 Then Amaziah separated them, *to wit,* the army that was come to him out of Ephraim, to go ^khome again: wherefore their anger was greatly kindled against Judah, and they returned home in ^lgreat anger.

11 And Amaziah strengthened himself, and led forth his people, and went to ^mthe valley of salt, and smote of the children of Seir ten thousand.

A. M. 3177
B. C. 827
Anno ante
I. Olymp. 51
Ante Urbem
Conditam 74

12 And *other* ten thousand *left* alive did the children of Judah carry away captive, and brought unto the top of the rock, and cast them down from the top of the rock, that they all were broken in pieces.

13 But ⁿthe soldiers of the army which Amaziah sent back, that they should not go with him to battle, fell upon the cities of

---

^a2 Kings xiv. 1, &c.——^bSee 2 Kings xiv. 4; ver. 14——^c2 Kings xiv. 5, &c.——^dHeb. *confirmed upon him*——^eDeut. xxiv. 16; 2 Kings xiv. 6; Jer. xxxi. 30; Ezek. xviii. 20

^fNum. i. 3——^gChap. xx. 6——^hHeb. *band*——ⁱProv. x. 22——^kHeb. *to their place*——^lHeb. *in heat of anger* ^m2 Kings xiv. 7——ⁿHeb. *the sons of the band*

NOTES ON CHAP. XXV

Verse 2. *He did* that which was *right*] He began his reign well, but soon became an idolater, ver. 14, 15.

Verse 5. *Gathered Judah together*] He purposed to avenge himself of the Syrians, but wished to know his military strength before he came to a rupture.

Verse 7. *The* Lord is not with Israel] "The WORD of the Lord is not the helper of the Is-

raelites, nor of the kingdom of the tribe of Ephraim."—*Targum.*

Verse 9. *The* Lord is able to give thee much more than this.] Better lose the *money* than keep the *men,* for they will be a curse unto thee.

Verse 10. *They returned home in great anger*] They thought they were insulted, and began to meditate revenge. See the notes on 2 Kings xiv. 1-20, where almost every circumstance in this chapter is examined and explained.

A. M. 3177
B. C. 827
Anno ante
I. Olymp. 51
Ante Urbem
Conditam 74

Judah, from Samaria even unto Beth-horon, and smote three thousand of them, and took much spoil.

14 Now it came to pass, after that Amaziah was come from the slaughter of the Edomites, that [o]he brought the gods of the children of Seir, and set them up *to be* [p]his gods, and bowed down himself before them, and burned incense unto them.

15 Wherefore the anger of the LORD was kindled against Amaziah, and he sent unto him a prophet, which said unto him, Why hast thou sought after [q]the gods of the people, which [r]could not deliver their own people out of thine hand?

16 And it came to pass, as he talked with him, that *the king* said unto him, Art thou made of the king's counsel? forbear; why shouldest thou be smitten? Then the prophet forbare, and said, I know that God hath [s]determined [t]to destroy thee, because thou hast done this, and hast not hearkened unto my counsel.

A. M. 3178
B. C. 826
Anno ante
I. Olymp. 50
Ante Urbem
Conditam 73

17 Then [u]Amaziah king of Judah took advice, and sent to Joash, the son of Jehoahaz, the son of Jehu, king of Israel, saying, Come, let us see one another in the face.

18 And Joash king of Israel sent to Amaziah king of Judah, saying, The [v]thistle that *was* in Lebanon sent to the cedar that *was* in Lebanon, saying, Give thy daughter to my son to wife: and there passed by [w]a wild beast that *was* in Lebanon, and trode down the thistle.

19 Thou sayest, Lo, thou hast smitten the Edomites; and thine heart lifteth thee up to boast: abide now at home; why shouldest thou meddle to *thine* hurt, that thou shouldest fall, *even* thou, and Judah with thee?

A. M. 3178
B. C. 826
Anno ante
I. Olymp. 50
Ante Urbem
Conditam 73

20 But Amaziah would not hear; for [x]it *came* of God, that he might deliver them into the hand *of their enemies,* because they [y]sought after the gods of Edom.

21 So Joash the king of Israel went up; and they saw one another in the face, *both* he and Amaziah king of Judah, at Beth-shemesh, which *belongeth* to Judah.

22 And Judah was [z]put to the worse before Israel, and they fled every man to his tent.

23 And Joash the king of Israel took Amaziah king of Judah, the son of Joash, the son of [a]Jehoahaz, at Beth-shemesh, and brought him to Jerusalem, and brake down the wall of Jerusalem from the gate of Ephraim to [b]the corner gate, four hundred cubits.

24 And *he took* all the gold and the silver, and all the vessels that were found in the house of God with Obed-edom, and the treasures of the king's house, the hostages also, and returned to Samaria.

A.M.3179-3194
B. C. 825-810
Anno ante
I. Olymp. 49-34

25 [c]And Amaziah the son of Joash king of Judah lived after the death of Joash son of Jehoahaz king of Israel fifteen years.

A.M.3165-3194
B. C. 839-810
Anno ante
I. Olymp. 63-34

26 Now the rest of the acts of Amaziah, first and last, behold, *are* they not written in the book of the kings of Judah and Israel?

A. M. 3194
B. C. 810
Anno ante
I. Olymp. 34
Ante Urbem
Conditam 57

27 Now after the time that Amaziah did turn away [d]from following the LORD they [e]made a conspiracy against him in Jerusalem; and he fled to Lachish: but they sent to Lachish after him, and slew him there.

28 And they brought him upon horses, and buried him with his fathers in the city of [f]Judah.

[o]See ch. xxviii. 23——[p]Exod. xx. 3, 5——[q]Psa. xcvi. 5——[r]Ver. 11——[s]Heb. *counselled*——[t]1 Sam. ii. 25——[u]2 Kings xiv. 8, 9, &c.——[v]Or, *furze bush,* or *thorn*——[w]Heb. *a beast of the field*——[x]1 Kings xii. 15; ch. xxii. 7

[y]Ver. 14——[z]Heb. *smitten*——[a]See ch. xxi. 17; xxii. 1, 6——[b]Heb. *the gate of it that looketh*——[c]2 Kings xiv. 17——[d]Heb. *from after*——[e]*Conspired a conspiracy*——[f]That is, *the city of David,* as it is 2 Kings xiv. 20

Verse 14. *The gods of the children of Seir*] "The idols of the children of Gebal."—*Targum.*

Verse 16. *Art thou made of the king's counsel?*] How darest *thou* give advice to, or reprove, a king?

Verse 18. *The thistle that* was *in Lebanon*] See the explanation of this 2 Kings xiv. 9. After reciting this fable, the *Targum* adds, "Thus hast thou done in the time thou didst send unto me, and didst lead up from the house of Israel *a hundred thousand* strong warriors for *a hundred* talents of silver; and after they were sent, thou didst not permit them to go with thee to war, but didst send them back, greatly enraged, so that they spread themselves over the country; and having cut off *three thousand,* they brought back much spoil."

Verse 24. *In the house of God with Obed-edom*] From 1 Chron. xxvi. 15 we learn that to Obed-edom and his descendants was allotted the keeping of the house of *Asuppim* or *collections* for the Divine treasury.

And—the hostages] See on 2 Kings xiv. 14.

Verse 26. *The rest of the acts of Amaziah,*

first and last] Says the *Targum;* "The *first,* when he walked in the fear of the Lord; the *last,* when he departed from the right way before the Lord; are they not written," &c.

Verse 27. *Made a conspiracy*] He no doubt became very unpopular after having lost the battle with the Israelites; the consequence of which was the dismantling of Jerusalem, and the seizure of the royal treasures, with several

other evils. It is likely that the last *fifteen* years of his reign were greatly embittered: so that, finding the royal city to be no place of *safety,* he endeavoured to secure himself at Lachish; but all in vain, for thither his murderers pursued him; and he who forsook the Lord was forsaken by every friend, perished in his gainsaying, and came to an untimely end.

CHAPTER XXVI

Uzziah, the son of Amaziah, succeeds; and begins his reign piously and prosperously, which continued during the life of Zechariah the prophet, 1–5. He fights successfully against the Philistines, and takes and dismantles some of their chief cities, 6; prevails over the Arabians and Mehunims, 7; and brings the Ammonites under tribute, 8. He fortifies Jerusalem, and builds towers in different parts of the country, and delights in husbandry, 9, 10. An account of his military strength, warlike instruments, and machines, 11–15. He is elated with his prosperity, invades the priest's office, and is smitten with the leprosy, 16–20. He is obliged to abdicate the regal office, and dwell apart from the people, his son Jotham acting as regent, 21. His death and burial, 22, 23.

A. M. 3194 B. C. 810 Anno ante I. Olymp. 34 Ante Urbem Conditam 57 THEN all the people of Judah took ªUzziah,ᵇ who *was* sixteen years old, and made him king in the room of his father Amaziah.

2 He built Eloth, and restored it to Judah, after that the king slept with his fathers.

A.M.3194-3246 B. C. 810-758 Ante Urbem Conditam 57-5 3 Sixteen years old *was* Uzziah when he began to reign, and he reigned fifty and two years in Jerusalem. His mother's name also *was* Jecoliah of Jerusalem.

A.M.3194-3239 B. C. 810-765 Ante Urbem Conditam 57-12 4 And he did *that which was* right in the sight of the LORD according to all that his father Amaziah did.

5 And ᶜhe sought God in the days of Zechariah, who ᵈhad understanding ᵉin the visions of God: and as long as he sought the LORD, God made him to prosper.

6 And he went forth and ᶠwarred against the Philistines, and brake down the wall of Gath, and the wall of Jabneh, and the wall of Ashdod, and built cities ᵍabout Ashdod, and among the Philistines. **A.M.3194-3239 B. C. 810-765 Ante Urbem Conditam 57-12**

7 And God helped him against ʰthe Philistines, and against the Arabians that dwelt in Gur-baal, and the Mehunims.

8 And the Ammonites ⁱgave gifts to Uzziah: and his name ᵏspread abroad *even* to the entering in of Egypt; for he strengthened *himself* exceedingly.

9 Moreover Uzziah built towers in Jerusalem at the ˡcorner gate, and at the valley gate, and at the turning *of the wall,* and ᵐfortified them.

10 Also he built towers in the desert, and ⁿdigged many wells: for he had much cattle, both in the low country, and in the plains:

ª2 Kings xiv. 21, 22; xv. 1, &c.——ᵇOr, *Azariah* ᶜSee chapter xxiv. 2——ᵈGenesis xli. 15; Daniel i. 17; ii. 19; x. 1——ᵉHebrew, *in the seeing of God*——ᶠIsaiah. xiv. 29——ᵍOr, *in the country of Ashdod*——ʰChapter xxi. 16——ⁱ2 Sam. viii. 2; chapter xvii. 11——ᵏHebrew, *went*——ˡ2 Kings xiv. 13; Nehemiah iii. 13, 19, 32; Zech. xiv. 10——ᵐOr, *repaired*——ⁿOr, *cut out many cisterns*

NOTES ON CHAP. XXVI

Verse 1. *The people of Judah took Uzziah*] They all agreed to place this son on his father's throne.

Verse 2. *He built Eloth*] See the notes on 2 Kings xiv. 21. This king is called by several different names; see the note on 2 Kings xv. 1.

Verse 5. *In the days of Zechariah*] Who this was we know not, but by the character that is given of him here. He was wise *in the visions of God*—in giving the true interpretation of Divine prophecies. He was probably the tutor of Uzziah.

Verse 7. *And God helped him*] "And the WORD of the Lord helped him against the Philis-

tines, and against the Arabians who lived in Gerar, and the plains of Meun."—*Targum.* These are supposed to be the Arabs which are called the *Meuneons,* or *Munites,* or *Meonites.*

Verse 8. *The Ammonites gave gifts*] **Paid** an annual *tribute.*

Verse 10. *Built towers in the desert*] For the defence of his flocks, and his shepherds and husbandmen.

And in Carmel] Calmet remarks that there were *two* Carmels in Judea: one in the tribe of Judah, where Nabal lived; and the other on the coast of the Mediterranean Sea, near to Kishon; and both fertile in vines.

He loved husbandry.] This is a perfection in a king: on husbandry every state depends. Let

A.M.3194-3239
B. C. 810-765
Ante Urbem
Conditam 57-12

husbandmen *also,* and vinedressers in the mountains, and in [o]Carmel: for he loved [p]husbandry.

11 Moreover Uzziah had a host of fighting men that went out to war by bands, according to the number of their account by the hand of Jeiel the scribe and Maaseiah the ruler, under the hand of Hananiah, *one* of the king's captains.

12 The whole number of the chief of the fathers of the mighty men of valour *were* two thousand and six hundred.

13 And under their hand *was* [q]an army, three hundred thousand and seven thousand and five hundred, that made war with mighty power, to help the king against the enemy.

14 And Uzziah prepared for them throughout all the host shields, and spears, and helmets, and habergeons, and bows, and [r]slings *to cast* stones.

15 And he made in Jerusalem engines, invented by cunning men, to be on the towers and upon the bulwarks, to shoot arrows and great stones withal. And his name [s]spread far abroad; for he was marvellously helped, till he was strong.

16 But [t]when he was strong, his heart was [u]lifted up to *his* destruction: for he transgressed against the LORD his God, and [v]went into the temple of the LORD to burn incense upon the altar of incense.

A. M. 3239
B. C. 765
Olymp. III. 4
Ante Urbem
Conditam 12

17 And [w]Azariah the priest went in after him, and with him fourscore priests of the LORD, *that were* valiant men.

18 And they withstood Uzziah the king, and said unto him, *It* [x]*appertaineth* not unto thee, Uzziah, to burn incense unto the LORD, but to the [y]priests the sons of Aaron, that are consecrated to burn incense: go out of the sanctuary; for thou hast trespassed; neither *shall it be* for thine honour from the LORD God.

19 Then Uzziah was wroth, and *had* a censer in his hand to burn incense: and while he was wroth with the priests, [z]the leprosy even rose up in his forehead before the priests in the house of the LORD, from beside the incense altar.

20 And Azariah the chief priest, and all the priests, looked upon him, and, behold, he *was* leprous in his forehead, and they thrust him out from thence; yea, himself [a]hasted also to go out, because the LORD had smitten him.

21 [b]And Uzziah the king was a leper unto

[o]Or, *fruitful fields*——[p]Hebrew, *ground*——[q]Hebrew, *the power of an army*——[r]Hebrew, *stones of slings* [s]Heb. *went forth*——[t]Deut. xxxii. 15——[u]Deut. viii. 14; chap. xxv. 19

[v]So 2 Kings xvi. 12, 13——[w]1 Chronicles xvi. 10 [x]Num. xvi. 40; xviii. 7——[y]Exod. xxx. 7, 8——[z]Num. xii. 10; 2 Kings v. 27——[a]As Esther vi. 12——[b]2 Kings xv. 5

their trade or commerce be what they may, there can be no true national prosperity if agriculture do not prosper; for the king himself is served by the field. When, therefore, the king of a country encourages agriculture, an emulation is excited among his subjects; the science is cultivated; and the earth yields its proper increase; then, should trade and commerce fail, the people cannot be reduced to wretchedness, because there is plenty of bread.

Verse 14. *Shields, and spears*] He prepared a vast number of military weapons, that he might have them in readiness to put into the hands of his subjects on any exigency.

Verse 15. *Engines—to shoot arrows and great stones*] The *Targum* says, "He made in Jerusalem ingenious instruments, and little hollow towers, to stand upon the towers and upon the bastions, for the shooting of arrows, and projecting of great stones."

This is the very first intimation on record of any warlike engines for the *attack* or *defence* of besieged places; and this account is long prior to any thing of the kind among either the Greeks or Romans. Previously to such inventions, the besieged could only be *starved out,* and hence sieges were very *long* and *tedious.* Shalmaneser consumed *three* years before such an inconsiderable place as Samaria, 2 Kings xvii. 5, 6; Sardanapalus maintained himself in Nineveh for *seven* years, because the besiegers had no engines proper for the attack and destruction of walls, &c.; and it is well known that Troy sustained a siege of *ten* years, the Greeks not possessing any machine of the kind here referred to. The *Jews* alone were the inventors of such engines; and the invention took place in the reign of Uzziah, about *eight hundred* years before the Christian era. It is no wonder that, in consequence of this, *his name spread far abroad,* and struck terror into his enemies.

Verse 16. *He transgressed against the Lord*] "He sinned against the WORD of the Lord his God."—*T.*

Went into the temple to burn incense] Thus assuming to himself the priest's office. See this whole transaction explained in the notes on 2 Kings xv. 5.

Verse 20. *Because the Lord had smitten him.*] "Because the WORD of the Lord had brought the plague upon him."—*T.*

Verse 21. *And dwelt in a several house*] He was *separated,* because of the infectious nature of his disorder, from all society, domestic, civil, and religious.

A.M.3239-3246
B. C. 765-758
Ante Urbem
Conditam 12-5
the day of his death, and dwelt in a ^cseveral ^dhouse, *being* a leper; for he was cut off from the house of the LORD: and Jotham his son *was* over the king's house, judging the people of the land.

22 Now the rest of the acts of Uzziah, first

and last, did ^eIsaiah the prophet, the son of Amoz, write.

23 ^fSo Uzziah slept with his fathers, and they buried him with his fathers in the field of the burial which *belonged* to the kings; for they said, ^gHe *is* a leper: and Jotham his son reigned in his stead.

A. M. 3246
B. C. 758
Olymp. V. 3
Ante Urbem
Conditam 5

^cLev. xiii. 46; Num. v. 2——^dHeb. *free*

^eIsa. i. 1——^f2 Kings xv. 7; Isa. vi. 1——^gVer. 21

Jotham—was over the king's house] He became *regent* of the land; his father being no longer able to perform the functions of the regal office.

Verse 22. *The rest of the acts of Uzziah, first and last, did Isaiah the prophet—write.*] This work, however, is *totally lost;* for we have not any history of this king in the writings of

Isaiah. He is barely mentioned, Isa. i. 1, and vi. 1.

Verse 23. *They buried him—in the field of the burial*] As he was a *leper*, he was not permitted to be buried in the common burial-place of the kings; as it was supposed that even a place of sepulture must be defiled by the body of one who had died of this most afflictive and dangerous malady.

CHAPTER XXVII

Jotham succeeds his father Uzziah, and reigns well, 1, 2. His buildings, 3, 4. His successful wars, 5, 6. General account of his acts, reign, and death, 7-9.

A.M.3246-3262
B. C. 758-742
Olymp. V. 3
—IX. 3
JOTHAM ^awas twenty and five years old when he began to reign, and he reigned sixteen years in Jerusalem. His mother's name also *was* Jerushah, the daughter of Zadok.

2 And he did *that which was* right in the sight of the LORD, according to all that his father Uzziah did: howbeit he entered not into the temple of the LORD. And ^bthe people did yet corruptly.

3 He built the high gate of the house of the LORD, and on the wall of ^cOphel he built much.

4 Moreover he built cities in the mountains of Judah, and in the forests he built castles and towers.

5 He fought also with the king of the Ammonites, and prevailed against them. And the

children of Ammon gave him the same year a hundred talents of silver, and ten thousand measures of wheat, and ten thousand of barley. ^dSo much did the children of Ammon pay unto him, both the second year, and the third.

A.M.3246-3262
B. C. 758-742
Olymp. V. 3
—IX. 3

6 So Jotham became mighty, because he ^eprepared his ways before the LORD his God.

7 Now the rest of the acts of Jotham, and all his wars, and his ways, lo, they *are* written in the book of the kings of Israel and Judah.

8 He was five and twenty years old when he began to reign, and reigned sixteen years in Jerusalem.

9 ^fAnd Jotham slept with his fathers, and they buried him in the city of David: and Ahaz his son reigned in his stead.

A. M. 3262
B. C. 742
Olymp. IX. 3
Anno Urbis
Conditæ 12

^a2 Kings xv. 32, &c.——^b2 Kings xv. 35——^cOr, *the tower*, chap. xxxiii. 14; Neh. iii. 26

^dHeb. *This*——^eOr, *established*——^f2 Kings xv. 38

NOTES ON CHAP. XXVII

Verse 2. *He entered not into the temple*] He copied his father's conduct as far as it was constitutional; and avoided his transgression. See the preceding chapter.

Verse 3. *On the wall of Ophel*] The wall, says the *Targum*, of the *interior palace*. Ophel was some part of the wall of Jerusalem, that was most pregnable, and therefore Jotham fortified it in a particular manner.

Verse 4. *Castles and towers.*] These he built for the protection of the country people against marauders.

Verse 5. *He fought also with—the Am-*

monites] We find here that he brought them under a heavy tribute for *three* years; but whether this was the *effect* of his prevailing against them, is not so evident. Some think that they paid this tribute for three years, and then revolted; that, in consequence, he attacked them, and their utter subjection was the result.

Verse 7. *The rest of the acts of Jotham, and all his wars, and his ways*] It was in his days, according to 2 Kings xv. 37, that *Rezin* king of Syria, and *Pekah* king of Israel, *began to cut Judah short.* See the notes on 2 Kings xv. 36, 37.

Written in the book of the kings, &c.] There is not so much found in the books of *Kings* which we have now, as in this place of the *Chronicles.* In both places we have *abridged* accounts only: the larger histories have long been lost. The reign of Jotham was properly

the last *politically* prosperous reign among the Jews. *Hezekiah* and *Josiah* did much to preserve the Divine worship; but Judah continued to be cut short, till at last it was wholly ruined.

CHAPTER XXVIII

Ahaz succeeds his father Jotham, and reigns wickedly for sixteen years, 1. *He restores idolatry in its grossest forms,* 2–4; *and is delivered into the hands of the kings of Israel and Syria,* 5. *Pekah slays one hundred and twenty thousand Jews in one day, and carries away captive two hundred thousand of the people, whom, at the instance of Oded the prophet, they restore to liberty, and send home, clothed and fed,* 6–15. *Ahaz sends to the king of Assyria for help against the Edomites, Philistines, &c., from whom he receives no effectual succour,* 16–21. *He sins yet more, spoils and shuts up the temple of God, and propagates idolatry throughout the land,* 22–25. *A reference to his acts, his death, and burial,* 26, 27.

A.M.3246-3262
B. C. 758-742
Olymp. V. 3
—IX. 3

AHAZ [a]*was* twenty years old when he began to reign, and he reigned sixteen years in Jerusalem: but he did not *that which was* right in the sight of the LORD, like David his father:

2 For he walked in the ways of the kings of Israel, and made also [b]molten images for [c]Baalim.

3 Moreover he [d]burnt incense in [e]the valley of the son of Hinnom, and burnt [f]his children in the fire, after the abominations of the heathen whom the LORD had cast out before the children of Israel.

4 He sacrificed also and burnt incense in the high places, and on the hills, and under every green tree.

5 Wherefore [g]the LORD his God delivered

him into the hand of the king of Syria; and they [h]smote him, and carried away a great multitude of them captives, and brought *them* to [i]Damascus. And he was also delivered into the hand of the king of Israel, who smote him with a great slaughter.

A. M. 3263
B. C. 741
Olymp. IX. 4
Anno Urbis
Conditæ 13

6 For [k]Pekah the son of Remaliah slew in Judah a hundred and twenty thousand in one day, *which were* all [l]valiant men; because they had forsaken the LORD God of their fathers.

7 And Zichri, a mighty man of Ephraim, slew Maaseiah the king's son, and Azrikam the governor of the house, and Elkanah *that was* [m]next to the king.

8 And the children of Israel carried away captive of their [n]brethren two hundred thou-

---

[a]2 Kings xvi. 2——[b]Exod. xxxiv. 17; Lev. xix. 4
[c]Judg. ii. 11——[d]Or, *offered sacrifice*——[e]2 Kings xxiii.
10——[f]Lev. xviii. 21; 2 Kings xvi. 3; ch. xxxiii. 6

[g]Isa. vii. 1——[h]2 Kings xvi. 5, 6——[i]Heb. *Darmesek*
[k]2 Kings xv. 27——[l]Heb. *sons of valour*——[m]Heb. *the second to the king*——[n]Chap. xi. 4

NOTES ON CHAP. XXVIII

Verse 1. *Ahaz was twenty years old*] For the difficulties in this chronology, see the notes on 2 Kings xvi. 1.

Verse 3. *Burnt his children in the fire*] There is a most remarkable addition here in the *Chaldee,* which I shall give at length: "Ahaz burnt his children in the fire; but the WORD of the Lord snatched Hezekiah from among them; for it was manifest before the Lord that the *three* righteous men, *Hananiah, Mishael,* and *Azariah,* were to proceed from him; who should deliver up their bodies that they might be cast into a burning fiery furnace, on account of the great and glorious NAME, (יהוה,) and from which they should escape. *First,* Abram escaped from the furnace of fire among the Chaldeans, into which he had been cast by Nimrod, because he would not worship their idols. *Secondly, Tamar* escaped burning in the house of judgment of

Judah, who had said, Bring her out, that she may be burnt. *Thirdly, Hezekiah* the son of Ahaz escaped from the burning, when Ahaz his father cast him into the valley of the son of Hinnom, on the altars of Tophet. *Fourthly, Hananiah, Mishael,* and *Azariah,* escaped from the burning fiery furnace of Nebuchadnezzar king of Babylon. *Fifthly, Joshua,* the son of Josedek the high priest, escaped, when the impious Nebuchadnezzar had cast him into a burning fiery furnace, with Achaab the son of Kolia, and Zedekiah the son of Maaseiah, the false prophet. *They* were consumed by fire; but Joshua the son of Josedek escaped because of his righteousness."

Verse 5. *Delivered him into the hand of the king of Syria*] For the better understanding of these passages, the reader is requested to refer to what has been advanced in the notes on the sixteenth chapter of 2 Kings, ver. 5, &c.

Verse 6. *A hundred and twenty thousand*]

A. M. 3263 B. C. 741 Olymp. IX. 4 Anno Urbis Conditæ 13 sand, women, sons, and daughters, and took also away much spoil from them, and brought the spoil to Samaria.

9 But a prophet of the LORD was there, whose name *was* Oded: and he went out before the host that came to Samaria, and said unto them, Behold, [o]because the LORD God of your fathers was wroth with Judah, he hath delivered them into your hand, and ye have slain them in a rage *that* [p]reacheth up unto heaven.

10 And now ye purpose to keep under the children of Judah and Jerusalem for [q]bondmen and bond-women unto you: *but are there* not with you, even with you, sins against the LORD your God?

11 Now hear me therefore, and deliver the captives again, which ye have taken captive of your brethren: [r]for the fierce wrath of the LORD *is* upon you.

12 Then certain of the heads of the children of Ephraim, Azariah the son of Johanan, Berechiah the son of Meshillemoth, and Jehizkiah the son of Shallum, and Amasa the son of Hadlai, stood up against them that came from the war,

13 And said unto them, Ye shall not bring in the captives hither: for whereas we have offended against the LORD *already*, ye intend to add *more* to our sins and to our trespass: for our trespass is great, and *there is* fierce wrath against Israel.

14 So the armed men left the captives and the spoil before the princes and all the congregation. A. M. 3263 B. C. 741 Olymp. IX. 4 Anno Urbis Conditæ 13

15 And the men [s]which were expressed by name rose up, and took the captives, and with the spoil clothed all that were naked among them, and arrayed them, and shod them, and [t]gave them to eat and to drink, and anointed them, and carried all the feeble of them upon asses, and brought them to Jericho, [u]the city of palm trees, to their brethren: then they returned to Samaria.

16 [v]At that time did King Ahaz send unto the kings of Assyria to help him.

17 For again the Edomites had come and smitten Judah, and carried away [w]captives.

18 [x]The Philistines also had invaded the cities of the low country, and of the south of Judah, and had taken Beth-shemesh, and Ajalon, and Gederoth, and Shocho with the villages thereof, and Timnah with the villages thereof, Gimzo also and the villages thereof: and they dwelt there.

19 For the LORD brought Judah low because of Ahaz king of [y]Israel; for he [z]made Judah naked, and transgressed sore against the LORD.

20 And [a]Tilgath-pilneser king of Assyria came unto him, and distressed him, but strengthened him not. A. M. 3264 B. C. 740 Olymp. X. 1 Ante Urbem Conditæ 14

21 For Ahaz took away a portion *out* of

---

[o]Psa. lxix. 26; Isa. x. 5; xlvii. 6; Ezek. xxv. 12, 15; xxvi. 2; Obad. x. &c.; Zech. i. 15——[p]Ezra ix. 6; Rev. xviii. 5——[q]Leviticus xxv. 39, 42, 43, 46——[r]James ii. 13——[s]Ver. 12

[t]2 Kings vi. 22; Prov. xxv. 21, 22; Luke vi. 27; Rom. xii. 20——[u]Deut. xxxiv. 3; Judg. i. 16——[v]2 Kings xvi. 7——[w]Heb. *a captivity*——[x]Ezek. xvi. 27, 57——[y]Ch. xxi. 2——[z]Exod. xxxii. 35——[a]2 Kings xv. 29; xvi. 7, 8, 9

It is very probable that there is a mistake in this number. It is hardly possible that *a hundred and twenty thousand* men could have been slain in one day; yet all the *versions* and *MSS.* agree in this number. The whole people seem to have been given up into the hands of their enemies.

Verse 9. *But a prophet of the Lord—whose name* was *Oded*] To this beautiful speech nothing can be added by the best comment; it is simple, humane, pious, and overwhelmingly convincing: no wonder it produced the effect mentioned here. That there was much of humanity in the heads of the children of *Ephraim* who joined with the prophet on this occasion, the *fifteenth* verse sufficiently proves. They did not barely dismiss these most unfortunate captives, but they took that very spoil which their victorious army had brought away; and they clothed, fed, shod, and anointed, these distressed people, set the feeblest of them upon asses, and escorted them safely to Jericho. We can scarcely find a parallel to this in the universal history of the wars which savage man has carried on against his fellows, from the foundation of the world.

Verse 16. *The kings of Assyria to help him.*] Instead of מלכי *malchey;* KINGS; the *Vulgate, Syriac, Arabic,* and *Chaldee,* one MS., and the parallel place, 2 Kings xvi. 7, have מלך *melek,* KING, in the *singular* number. This king was *Tiglath-pileser,* as we learn from the second book of Kings.

Verse 21. *But he helped him not.*] He did him no ultimate service. See the note on 2 Kings xvi. 9.

After ver. 15, the 23d, 24th, and 25th verses are introduced before the 16th, in the *Syriac* and *Arabic;* and the 22d verse is wholly wanting in both, though some of the expressions may be found in the twenty-first verse.

A. M. 3264
B. C. 740
Olymp. X. 1
Anno Urbis
Conditæ 14
the house of the LORD, and *out* of the house of the king, and of the princes, and gave *it* unto the king of Assyria: but he helped him not.

22 And in the time of his distress did he trespass yet more against the LORD: this *is* that King Ah'az.

23 For bhe sacrificed unto the gods of cDamascus, which smote him: and he said, Because the gods of the kings of Syria help them, *therefore* will I sacrifice to them, that dthey may help me. But they were the ruin of him, and of all Israel.

24 And Ahaz gathered together the vessels of the house of God, and cut in pieces the vessels of the house of God, cand shut up the

doors of the house of the LORD, and he made him altars in every corner of Jerusalem. A. M. 3264
B. C. 740
Olymp. X. 1
Anno Urbis
Conditæ 14

25 And in every several city of Judah he made high places fto burn incense unto other gods, and provoked to anger the LORD God of his fathers.

26 gNow the rest of his acts and of all his ways, first and last, behold, they *are* written in the book of the kings of Judah and Israel. A.M.3262-3278
B. C. 742-726
Olymp. IX. 3
—XIII. 3

27 And Ahaz slept with his fathers, and they buried him in the city, *even* in Jerusalem: but they brought him not into the sepulchres of the kings of Israel: and Hezekiah his son reigned in his stead. A. M. 3278
B. C. 726
Olymp. XIII. 3
Anno Urbis
Conditæ 28

---

bSee chap. xxv. 14——cHeb. *Darmesek*——dJer. xliv. 17, 18

eSee chap. xxix. 3, 7——fOr, *to offer*——g2 Kings xvi. 19, 20

Verse 23. *He sacrificed unto the gods of Damascus, which smote him*] "This passage," says *Mr. Hallet*, "greatly surprised me; for the sacred historian himself is here represented as saying, *The gods of Damascus had smitten Ahaz*. But it is impossible to suppose that an *inspired* author could say this; for the Scripture everywhere represents the heathen *idols* as *nothing* and *vanity*, and as incapable of *doing either good* or *hurt*. All difficulty is avoided if we follow the *old Hebrew copies*, from which the *Greek translation* was made, Και ειπεν ὁ βασιλευς Αχαζ, εκζητησω τους Θεους Δαμασκου τους τυπτοντας με, *And King Ahaz said*, I WILL SEEK TO THE GODS OF DAMASCUS WHICH HAVE SMITTEN ME; and then it follows, both in Hebrew and Greek, *He said moreover, Because the gods of the king of Syria help them; therefore will I sacrifice to them, that they may*

help me. Both the *Syriac* and *Arabic* give it a similar turn; and say that *Ahaz sacrificed to the gods of Damascus, and said, Ye are my gods and my lords; you will I worship, and to you will I sacrifice.*"

Verse 24. *Shut up the doors*] He caused the Divine worship to be totally suspended; and they continued shut till the beginning of the reign of Hezekiah, one of whose first acts was to reopen them, and thus to restore the Divine worship, chap. xxix. 3.

Verse 27. *The kings of Israel*] It is a common thing for the writer of this book to put *Israel* for *Judah*. He still considers them as *one people*, because proceeding from one stock. The *versions* and *MSS*. have the same reading with the Hebrew; the matter is of little importance, and with this interpretation none can mistake.

CHAPTER XXIX

Hezekiah's good reign, 1, 2. He opens and repairs the doors of the temple, 3. He assembles and exhorts the priests and Levites, and proposes to renew the covenant with the Lord, 4–11. They all sanctify themselves and cleanse the temple, 12–17. They inform the king of their progress, 18, 19. He collects the rulers of the people: and they offer abundance of sin-offerings, and burnt-offerings, and worship the Lord, 20–30. Every part of the Divine service is arranged, and Hezekiah and all the people rejoice, 31–36.

A.M.3278-3306
B. C. 726-698
Ol. XIII. 3
—XX. 3
HEZEKIAH abegan to reign *when he was* five and twenty yearsold,andhe reigned nineand twenty years in Jerusalem. And his mother's name *was* Abijah, the daughter bof Zechariah.

2 And he did *that which was* right in the sight of the LORD, according to all that David his father had done.

3 He in the first year of his reign,in the first month, copened the doors of the house of the LORD, and repaired them. A. M. 3278
B. C. 726
Olymp. XIII. 3
Anno Urbis
Conditæ 28

4 And he brought in the priests and the Levites, and gathered them together into the east street,

5 And said unto them, Hear me, ye Le-

---

a2 Kings xviii. 1——bChap. xxvi. 5

cSee chap. xxviii. 24; ver. 7

NOTES ON CHAP. XXIX

Verse 2. *He did that which was right*] See the note on 2 Kings xviii. 3.

Verse 8. *He hath delivered them to trouble, to astonishment*] He probably refers here chieflv to that dreadful defeat by the Israelites

A. M. 3278
B. C. 726
Olymp. XIII. 3
Anno Urbis
Conditæ 28

vites, [d]sanctify now yourselves, and sanctify the house of the LORD God of your fathers, and carry forth the filthiness out of the holy *place*.

6 For our fathers have trespassed, and done *that which was* evil in the eyes of the LORD our God, and have forsaken him, and have [e]turned away their faces from the habitation of the LORD, and [f]turned *their* backs.

7 [g]Also they have shut up the doors of the porch, and put out the lamps, and have not burned incense nor offered burnt-offerings in the holy *place* unto the God of Israel.

8 Wherefore the [h]wrath of the LORD was upon Judah and Jerusalem, and he hath delivered them to [i]trouble, to astonishment, and to [k]hissing, as ye see with your eyes.

9 For, lo, [l]our fathers have fallen by the sword, and our sons and our daughters and our wives *are* in captivity for this.

10 Now *it is* in mine heart to make [m]a covenant with the LORD God of Israel, that his fierce wrath may turn away from us.

11 My sons, [n]be not now negligent: for the LORD hath [o]chosen you to stand before him, to serve him, and that ye should minister unto him, and [p]burn incense.

12 Then the Levites arose, Mahath the son of Amasai, and Joel the son of Azariah, of the sons of the Kohathites: and of the sons of Merari, Kish the son of Abdi, and Azariah the son of Jehalelel: and of the Gershonites; Joah the son of Zimmah, and Eden the son of Joah:

13 And of the sons of Elizaphan; Shimri,

and Jeiel: and of the sons of Asaph; Zechariah, and Mattaniah:

A. M. 3278
B. C. 726
Olymp. XIII. 3
Anno Urbis
Conditæ 28

14 And of the sons of Heman; Jehiel, and Shimei: and of the sons of Jeduthun; Shemaiah, and Uzziel.

15 And they gathered their brethren, and [q]sanctified themselves, and came, according to the commandment of the king, [r]by the words of the LORD, [s]to cleanse the house of the LORD.

16 And the priests went into the inner part of the house of the LORD, to cleanse *it,* and brought out all the uncleanness that they found in the temple of the LORD into the court of the house of the LORD. And the Levites took *it,* to carry *it* out abroad into the brook Kidron.

17 Now they began on the first *day* of the first month to sanctify, and on the eighth day of the month came they to the porch of the LORD; so they sanctified the house of the LORD in eight days; and in the sixteenth day of the first month they made an end.

18 Then they went in to Hezekiah the king and said, We have cleansed all the house of the LORD, and the altar of burnt-offering, with all the vessels thereof, and the shewbread table with all the vessels thereof.

19 Moreover all the vessels, which King Ahaz in his reign did [t]cast away in his transgression, have we prepared and sanctified, and, behold, they *are* before the altar of the LORD.

20 Then Hezekiah the king rose early, and gathered the rulers of the city, and went up to the house of the LORD.

[d]1 Chron. xv. 12; chap. xxxv. 6——[e]Jer. ii. 27; Ezek. viii. 16——[f]Heb. *given the neck*——[g]Chap. xxviii. 24——[h]Chap. xxiv. 18——[i]Heb. *commotion,* Deut. xxviii. 25——[k]1 Kings ix. 8; Jeremiah xviii. 16; xix. 8; xxv. 9, 18; xxix. 18

[l]Chap. xxviii. 5, 6, 8, 17——[m]Chap. xv. 12——[n]Or, *be not now deceived*——[o]Num. iii. 6; viii. 14; xviii. 2, 6 [p]Or, *offer sacrifice*——[q]Ver. 5——[r]Or, *in the business of the LORD,* chap. xxx. 12——[s]1 Chron. xxiii. 28 [t]Chap. xxviii. 24

in which *a hundred and twenty thousand* were slain, and *two hundred thousand* taken prisoners; see the preceding chapter, ver. 6, 8.

Verse 10. *To make a covenant*] To renew the covenant under which the whole people were constantly considered, and of which circumcision was the sign; and the *spirit* of which was, *I will be your God: Ye shall be my people.*

Verse 16. *And the priests went*] The priests and Levites cleansed first the courts both of the *priests* and of the *people.* On this labour they spent eight days. Then they cleansed the *interior* of the temple; but as the Levites had no right to enter the temple, the priests carried

all the dirt and rubbish to the *porch,* whence they were collected by the Levites, carried away, and cast into the brook Kidron; in this work eight days more were occupied, and thus the temple was purified in *sixteen days.*

Verse 17. *On the first* day] "They began on the first day of the first month Nisan."—*Targum.*

Verse 19. *All the vessels, which King Ahaz*] The *Targum* says, "All the vessels which King Ahaz had polluted and rendered abominable by strange idols, when he reigned in his transgression against the WORD of the Lord, we have collected and hidden; and others have we pre-

A. M. 3278
B. C. 726
Olymp. XIII. 3
Anno Urbis
Conditæ 28

21 And they brought seven bullocks, and seven rams, and seven lambs, and seven he-goats, for a ᵘsin-offering for the kingdom, and for the sanctuary, and for Judah. And he commanded the priests the sons of Aaron to offer *them* on the altar of the LORD.

22 So they killed the bullocks, and the priests received the blood, and ᵛsprinkled *it* on the altar: likewise, when they had killed the rams, they sprinkled the blood upon the altar: they killed also the lambs, and they sprinkled the blood upon the altar.

23 And they brought ʷforth the he-goats *for* the sin-offering before the king and the congregation; and they laid their ˣhands upon them;

24 And the priests killed them, and they made reconciliation with their blood upon the altar, ʸto make an atonement for all Israel: for the king commanded *that* the burnt-offering and the sin-offering *should be made* for all Israel.

25 ᶻAnd he set the Levites in the house of

the LORD with cymbals, with psalteries, and with harps, ᵃaccording to the commandment of David, and of ᵇGad the king's seer, and Nathan the prophet: ᶜfor *so was* the commandment ᵈof the LORD ᵉby his prophets.

26 And the Levites stood with the instruments ᶠof David, and the priests with ᵍthe trumpets.

27 And Hezekiah commanded to offer the burnt-offering upon the altar. And ʰwhen the burnt-offering began, ⁱthe song of the LORD began *also* with the trumpets, and with the ᵏinstruments *ordained* by David king of Israel.

28 And all the congregation worshipped, and the ˡsingers sang, and the trumpeters sounded: *and* all *this continued* until the burnt-offering was finished.

29 And when they had made an end of offering, ᵐthe king and all that were ⁿpresent with him bowed themselves, and worshipped.

30 Moreover Hezekiah the king and the princes commanded the Levites to sing praise

A. M. 3278
B. C. 726
Olymp. XIII. 3
Anno Urbis
Conditæ 28

ᵘLeviticus iv. 3, 14——ᵛLeviticus viii. 14, 15, 19, 24; Heb. ix. 21——ʷHeb. *near*——ˣLev. iv. 15, 24 ʸLev. xiv. 20——ᶻ1 Chron. xvi. 4; xxv. 6——ᵃ1 Chron. xxiii. 5; xxv. 1; chap. viii. 14——ᵇ2 Sam. xxiv. 11——ᶜChap. xxx. 12——ᵈHeb. *by the hand of* the LORD——ᵉHebrew, *by the hand of*——ᶠ1 Chron. xxiii. 5; Amos vi. 5——ᵍNum. x. 8, 10; 1 Chron. xv. 24; xvi. 6——ʰHeb. *in the time*——ⁱChap. xxiii. 18 ᵏHeb. *hands of instruments*——ˡHeb. *song*——ᵐChap. xx. 18——ⁿHeb. *found*

---

pared to replace them; and they are now before the Lord."

Verse 21. *They brought seven bullocks, &c.*] This was more than the law required; see Lev. iv. 13, &c. It ordered *one calf* or *ox* for the sins of the *people*, and *one he-goat* for the sins of the *prince;* but Hezekiah here offers many more. And the reason appears sufficiently evident: the law speaks only of *sins of ignorance;* but here were sins of every kind and every die—idolatry, apostasy from the Divine worship, profanation of the temple, &c., &c. The sin-offerings, we are informed, were offered, *first* for *the* KINGDOM—for the transgressions of the *king* and his family; *secondly,* for the SANCTUARY, which had been defiled and polluted, and for the *priests* who had been profane, negligent, and unholy; and, *finally,* for JUDAH—for the whole mass of the people, who had been led away into every kind of abomination by the above examples.

Verse 23. *They laid their hands upon them*] That is, they confessed their sin; and as they had by their transgression *forfeited their lives,* they now offer these animals to die as vicarious offerings, their life being taken for the life of their owners.

Verse 25. *With cymbals, with psalteries*] Moses had not appointed any musical instruments to be used in the divine worship; there was nothing of the kind under the first tabernacle. The *trumpets* or *horns* then used were not for song nor for praise, but as we use *bells,*

i. e., to give notice to the congregation of what they were called to perform, &c. But David did certainly introduce many *instruments* of music into God's worship, for which we have already seen he was solemnly reproved by the prophet Amos, chap. vi. 1-6. Here, however, the author of this book states he had the commandment of the prophet Nathan, and Gad the king's seer; and this is stated to have been *the commandment of the Lord by his prophets:* but the *Syriac* and *Arabic* give this a different turn—"Hezekiah appointed the Levites in the house of the Lord, with instruments of music, and the sound of harps, and with the HYMNS of DAVID, and the HYMNS of GAD, the king's prophet, and of NATHAN, the king's prophet: for David *sang the praises of the Lord his God, as from the mouth of the prophets.*" It was by the hand or *commandment* of the *Lord* and his *prophets* that the *Levites should praise* the *Lord;* for so the Hebrew text may be understood: and it was by the *order of David* that so many instruments of music should be introduced into the Divine service. But were it even evident, which it is not, either from this or any other place in the sacred writings, that instruments of music were prescribed by Divine authority *under the law,* could this be adduced with any semblance of reason, that they ought to be used in *Christian worship?* No: the whole spirit, soul, and genius of the Christian religion are against this: and those who know the Church of God best, and what *con-*

A. M. 3278
B. C. 726
Olymp. XIII. 3
Anno Urbis
Conditæ 28

unto the LORD with the words of David, and of Asaph the seer. And they sang praises with gladness, and they bowed their heads and worshipped.

31 Then Hezekiah answered and said, Now ye have °consecrated yourselves unto the LORD, come near and bring sacrifices and Pthank-offerings into the house of the LORD. And the congregation brought in sacrifices and thank-offerings; and as many as were of a free heart, burnt-offerings.

32 And the number of the burnt-offerings, which the congregation brought, was threescore and ten bullocks, a hundred rams, *and* two hundred lambs: all these *were* for a burnt-offering to the LORD.

33 And the consecrated things *were* six

hundred oxen and three thousand sheep.

A. M. 3278
B. C. 726
Olymp. XIII. 3
Anno Urbis
Conditæ 28

34 But the priests were too few, so that they could not flay all the burnt-offerings: wherefore ᵠtheir brethren the Levites ʳdid help them, till the work was ended, and until the *other* priests had sanctified themselves: ˢfor the Levites *were* more ᵗupright in heart to sanctify themselves than the priests.

35 And also the burnt-offerings *were* in abundance, with ᵘthe fat of the peace-offerings, and ᵛthe drink-offerings for *every* burnt-offering. So the service of the house of the LORD was set in order.

36 And Hezekiah rejoiced, and all the people, that God had prepared the people; for the thing was *done* suddenly.

°Or, *filled your hand*, chap. xiii. 9——PLev. vii. 12 ᵠChap. xxxv. 11

ʳHeb. *strengthened them*——ˢChap. xxx. 3——ᵗPsalm vii. 10——ᵘLev. iii. 16——ᵛNum. xv. 5, 7, 10

---

stitutes its *genuine spiritual state*, know that these things have been introduced as a substitute for the *life* and *power* of religion; and that where they prevail most, there is least of the *power* of Christianity. Away with such portentous baubles from the worship of that infinite Spirit who requires his followers to worship him *in spirit and in truth*, for to no such worship are those instruments friendly. See the texts in the margin; also the use of trumpets in the sanctuary, Num. x. 2, &c., and the notes there.

Verse 34. *They could not flay all the burnt-offerings*] Peace-offerings, and such like, the Levites might flay and dress; but the whole burnt-offerings, that is, those which were *entirely consumed* on the altar, could be touched only by the priests, unless in a case of necessity, such as is mentioned here.

The Levites were *more upright in heart*] The *priests* seem to have been very backward in this good work; the *Levites* were more ready to help forward this glorious reformation. Why the former should have been so backward is not easy to tell; but it appears to have been the fact. Indeed, it often happens that the

higher orders of the priesthood are less concerned for the prosperity of true religion than the lower. Why is this? They are generally too busy about *worldly things*, or too much satisfied with *secular emoluments*. A rich priesthood is not favourable either to the *spread* or *depth* of religion. Earthly gratifications are often put in the place of Divine influences: it is almost a miracle to see a very rich man deeply interested in behalf either of his own soul, or the souls of others.

Verse 36. *And Hezekiah rejoiced*] Both he and the people rejoiced that God had prepared their hearts to bring about so great a reformation in so short a time; *for*, it is added, *the thing was done suddenly*. The king's example and influence were here, under God, the grand spring of all those mighty and effectual movements. What amazing power and influence has God lodged with *kings!* They can sway a whole empire nearly as they please; and when they declare themselves in behalf of religion, they have the *people* uniformly on their side. *Kings*, on this very ground, are no indifferent beings; they must be either a great curse or a great blessing to the people whom they govern.

CHAPTER XXX

Hezekiah invites all Israel and Judah, and writes letters to Ephraim and Manasseh to come up to Jerusalem, and hold a passover to the Lord, 1–4. The posts go out with the king's proclamation from Dan to Beer-sheba, and pass from city to city through the coasts of Ephraim, Manasseh, and Zebulun, but are generally mocked in Israel, 5–10. Yet several of Asher, Manasseh, and Zebulun, humble themselves, and come to Jerusalem, 11. But in Judah they are all of one heart, 12, 13. They take away the idolatrous altars, kill the passover, sprinkle the blood, and, as circumstances will permit, sanctify the people, 14, 15. Many having eaten of the passover, who were not purified according to the law, Hezekiah prays for them; and the Lord accepts his prayer, and heals them, 16–20. Hezekiah exhorts them; and they hold the feast seven additional days, fourteen in all, and the people greatly rejoice, 21–26. The priests and the Levites bless the people, and God accepts their prayers and thanksgivings, 27.

A. M. 3278
B. C. 726
Olymp. XIII. 3
Anno Urbis
Conditæ 28

AND Hezekiah sent to all Israel and Judah, and wrote letters also to Ephraim and Manasseh, that they should come to the house of the LORD at Jerusalem, to keep the passover unto the LORD God of Israel.

2 For the king had taken counsel, and his princes, and all the congregation in Jerusalem, to keep the passover in the second [a]month.

3 For they could not keep it [b]at that time, [c]because the priests had not sanctified themselves sufficiently, neither had the people gathered themselves together to Jerusalem.

4 And the thing [d]pleased the king and all the congregation.

5 So they established a decree to make proclamation throughout all Israel, from Beer-sheba even to Dan, that they should come to keep the passover unto the LORD God of Israel at Jerusalem: for they had not done *it* for a long *time in such sort* as it was written.

6 So the posts went with the letters [e]from the king and his princes throughout all Israel and Judah, and according to the commandment of the king, saying, Ye children of Israel, [f]turn again unto the LORD God of Abraham, Isaac, and Israel, and he will return to the remnant of you, that are escaped out of the hand of [g]the kings of Assyria.

7 And be not ye [h]like your fathers, and like your brethren, which trespassed against the LORD God of their fathers, *who* therefore [i]gave them up to desolation, as ye see.

8 Now [k]be ye not [l]stiff-necked, as your fathers *were, but* [m]yield yourselves unto the LORD, and enter into his sanctuary, which he hath sanctified for ever: and serve the LORD your God, [n]that the fierceness of his wrath may turn away from you.

9 For if ye turn again unto the LORD, your brethren and your children *shall find* [o]compassion before them that lead them captive, so that they shall come again into this land: for the LORD your God *is* [p]gracious and merciful, and will not turn away *his* face from you, if ye [q]return unto him.

10 So the posts passed from city to city through the country of Ephraim and Manasseh even unto Zebulun: but [r]they laughed them to scorn, and mocked them.

11 Nevertheless [s]divers of Asher and Manasseh and of Zebulun humbled themselves, and came to Jerusalem.

12 Also in Judah [t]the hand of God was to give them one heart to do the commandment of the king and of the princes, [u]by the word of the LORD.

13 And there assembled at Jerusalem much people to keep the feast of unleavened bread in the second month, a very great congregation.

14 And they arose, and took away the [v]altars that *were* in Jerusalem, and all the altars for incense took they away, and cast *them* into the brook Kidron.

15 Then they killed the passover on the

A. M. 3278
B. C. 726
Olymp. XIII. 3
Anno Urbis
Conditæ 28

---

[a]Num. ix. 10, 11——[b]Exod. xii. 6, 18——[c]Chap. xxix. 34——[d]Heb. *was right in the eyes of the king* [e]Heb. *from the hand*——[f]Jer. iv. 1; Joel ii. 13——[g]2 Kings xv. 19, 29——[h]Ezek. xx. 18——[i]Chap. xxix. 8 [k]Heb. *harden not your necks*

[l]Deut. x. 16——[m]Heb. *give the hand;* see 1 Chron. xxix. 24; Ezra x. 19——[n]Chap. xxix. 10——[o]Psa. cvi. 46——[p]Exod. xxxiv. 6——[q]Isa. lv. 7——[r]Chap. xxxvi. 16——[s]So chap. xi. 16; ver. 18, 21——[t]Phil. ii. 13 [u]Chap. xxix. 25——[v]Chap. xxviii. 24

NOTES ON CHAP. XXX

Verse 1. *Hezekiah sent to all Israel*] It is not easy to find out how this was permitted by the king of Israel; but it is generally allowed that *Hoshea,* who then reigned over Israel, was one of their best kings. And as the Jews allow that at this time both the golden calves had been carried away by the Assyrians,—that at Dan by Tiglath-pileser, and that at Bethel by Shalmaneser,—the people who chose to worship Jehovah at Jerusalem were freely permitted to do it, and Hezekiah had encouragement to make the proclamation in question.

Verse 2. *In the second month.*] In *Ijar,* as they could not celebrate it in *Nisan,* the *fourteenth* of which month was the proper time. But as they could not complete the purgation of the temple, till the *sixteenth* of that month, therefore they were obliged to hold it now, or else adjourn it till the next year, which would

have been fatal to that spirit of reformation which had now taken place. The *law* itself had given permission to those who were at a distance, and could not attend to the *fourteenth* of the first month, and to those who were accidentally defiled, and ought not to attend, to celebrate the passover on the *fourteenth* of the second month; see Num. ix. 10, 11. Hezekiah therefore, and his counsellors, thought that they might extend that to the *people at large,* because of the delay necessarily occasioned by the cleansing of the temple, which was granted to *individuals* in such cases as the above, and the result showed that they had not mistaken the mind of the Lord upon the subject.

Verse 6. *So the posts went*] רצים *ratsim,* the *runners* or *couriers;* persons who were usually employed to carry messages; men who were *light of foot,* and *confidential.*

A. M. 3278
B. C. 726
Olymp. XIII. 3
Anno Urbis
Conditæ 28

fourteenth *day* of the second month: and the priests and the Levites were ^washamed, and sanctified themselves, and brought in the burnt-offerings into the house of the LORD.

16 And they stood in ^xtheir place after their manner, according to the law of Moses the man of God: the priests sprinkled the blood, *which they received* at the hand of the Levites.

17 For *there were* many in the congregation that were not sanctified; ^ytherefore the Levites had the charge of the killing of the passovers for every one *that was* not clean, to sanctify *them* unto the LORD.

18 For a multitude of the people, *even* ^zmany of Ephraim, and Manasseh, Issachar, and Zebulun, had not cleansed themselves, ^ayet did they eat the passover otherwise than it was written. But Hezekiah prayed for them, saying, The good LORD pardon every one

19 That ^bprepareth his heart to seek God, the LORD God of his fathers, though *he be* not *cleansed* according to the purification of the sanctuary.

20 And the LORD hearkened to Hezekiah, and healed the people.

21 And the children of Israel that were ^cpresent at Jerusalem kept ^dthe feast of unleavened bread seven days with great gladness; and the Levites and the priests praised the LORD day by day, *singing* with ^eloud instruments unto the LORD.

A. M. 3278
B. C. 726
Olymp. XIII. 3
Anno Urbis
Conditæ 28

22 And Hezekiah spake ^fcomfortably unto all the Levites ^gthat taught the good knowledge of the LORD; and they did eat throughout the feast seven days, offering peace-offerings, and ^hmaking confession to the LORD God of their fathers.

23 And the whole assembly took counsel to keep ⁱother seven days: and they kept *other* seven days with gladness.

24 For Hezekiah king of Judah ^kdid ^lgive to the congregation a thousand bullocks and seven thousand sheep; and the princes gave to the congregation a thousand bullocks and ten thousand sheep: and a great number of priests ^msanctified themselves.

25 And all the congregation of Judah, with the priests and the Levites, and all the congregation ⁿthat came out of Israel, and the strangers that came out of the land of Israel, and that dwelt in Judah, rejoiced.

26 So there was great joy in Jerusalem: for since the time of Solomon the son of David king of Israel *there was* not the like in Jerusalem.

27 Then the priests the Levites arose and ^oblessed the people: and their voice was heard, and their prayer came *up* to ^phis holy dwelling-place, *even* unto heaven.

---

^wChap. xxix. 34——^xHeb. *their standing*——^yChap. xxix. 34——^zVer. 11——^aExod. xii. 43, &c.——^bChap. xix. 3——^cHeb. *found*——^dExod. xii. 15; xiii. 6 ^eHeb. *instruments of strength*——^fHeb. *to the heart of all,* &c.; Isa. xl. 2

^gChap. xvii. 9; xxxv. 3; Deut. xxxiii. 10——^hEzra x. 11——ⁱSee 1 Kings viii. 65——^kHeb. *lifted up,* or *offered*——^lChap. xxxv. 7, 8——^mChap. xxix. 34 ⁿVer. 11, 18——^oNum. vi. 23——^pHeb. *the habitation of his holiness,* Psa. lxviii. 5

Verse 9. *And will not turn away* his *face from you*] Well expressed by the *Targum:* "For the Lord your God is gracious and merciful, and will not cause his majesty to ascend up from among you, if ye will return to his fear." The *shechinah,* of which the Targumist speaks, is the *dwelling* of the Divine Presence among men, and the *visible symbol* of that presence.

Verse 18. *A multitude of the people—had not cleansed themselves*] As there were men from Ephraim, Manasseh, Issachar, and Zebulun, they were excusable, because they came from countries that had been wholly devoted to idolatry.

The good Lord pardon every one] "The Lord, who is good, have mercy on this people who err."—*T.*

Verse 22. *Spake comfortably unto all the Levites*] On such occasions the priests and Levites had great fatigue, and suffered many privations; and therefore had need of that *encouragement* which this prudent and pious king gave. It is a fine and expressive character given of these men, "They taught the good knowledge of God to the people." This is the great work, or should be so, of every Christian minister. They should convey that knowledge of God to the people by which they may be *saved;* tnat is, *the good knowledge of the Lord.*

Verse 25. *The strangers that come out of the land of Israel*] That is, the *proselytes* of the covenant who had embraced Judaism, and had submitted to the rite of *circumcision;* for none others could be permitted to eat of the passover.

Verse 26. *Since the time of Solomon*—there was *not the like in Jerusalem.*] For from that time the ten tribes had been separated from the true worship of God, and now many of them for the first time, especially from Asher, Issachar, Ephraim, Manasseh, and Zebulun, joined to celebrate the passover.

Verse 27. *And their voice was heard*] God accepted the fruits of that pious disposition which himself had infused.

And their prayer came up] As the smoke of their sacrifices ascended to the clouds, so did their prayers, supplications, and thanksgivings, ascend to the heavens. The *Targum* says: "Their prayer came up to the dwelling-place of his holy *shechinah*, which is in heaven." Israel now appeared to be in a fair way of regaining what they had lost; but alas, how soon were all these bright prospects beclouded for ever!

It is not for the want of holy resolutions and heavenly influences that men are not saved, but through their own unsteadiness; they do not persevere, they forget the necessity of

continuing in prayer, and thus the Holy Spirit is grieved, departs from them, and leaves them to their own darkness and hardness of heart. When we consider the heavenly influences which many receive who draw back to perdition, and the good fruits which for a time they bore, it is blasphemy to say they had no genuine or saving grace; they had it, they showed it, they trifled with it, sinned against it, continued in their rebellions, and *therefore* are lost.

CHAPTER XXXI

The people destroy all traces of idolatry throughout Judah, Benjamin, Ephraim, and Manasseh, 1. Hezekiah reforms the state of religion in general; and the tithes are brought in from all quarters, and proper officers set over them, 2–13. They bring in also the freewill-offerings, and regulate the priests and Levites, and their families, according to their genealogies, 14–19. Hezekiah does every thing in sincerity and truth, and is prosperous, 20, 21.

A. M. 3278
B. C. 726
Olymp. XIII. 3
Anno Urbis
Conditæ 28

NOW when all this was finished, all Israel that were ªpresent went out to the cities of Judah, and ᵇbrake the ᶜimages in pieces, and cut down the groves, and threw down the high places and the altars out of all Judah and Benjamin, in Ephraim also and Manasseh, ᵈuntil they had utterly destroyed them all. Then all the children of Israel returned every man to his possession, into their own cities.

2 And Hezekiah appointed ᵉthe courses of the priests and the Levites after their courses, every man according to his service, the priests and Levites ᶠfor burnt-offerings and for peace-offerings, to minister, and to give thanks, and to praise in the gates of the tents of the LORD.

3 *He appointed* also the king's portion of his substance for the burnt-offerings, *to wit,* for the morning and evening burnt-offerings, and the burnt-offerings for the Sabbaths, and for the new moons, and for the set feasts, as *it is* written in the ᵍlaw of the LORD.

4 Moreover he commanded the people that

dwelt in Jerusalem to give the ʰportion of the priests and the Levites, that they might be encouraged in ⁱthe law of the LORD.

A. M. 3278
B. C. 726
Olymp. XIII. 3
Anno Urbis
Conditæ 28

5 And as soon as the commandment ᵏcame abroad, the children of Israel brought in abundance ˡthe first-fruits of corn, wine, and oil, and ᵐhoney, and of all the increase of the field; and the tithe of all *things* brought they in abundantly.

6 And *concerning* the children of Israel and Judah, that dwelt in the cities of Judah, they also brought in the tithe of oxen and sheep, and the ⁿtithe of holy things which were consecrated unto the LORD their God, and laid *them* ᵒby heaps.

7 In the third month they began to lay the foundation of the heaps, and finished *them* in the seventh month.

8 And when Hezekiah and the princes came and saw the heaps, they blessed the LORD, and his people Israel.

9 Then Hezekiah questioned with the priests and the Levites concerning the heaps.

ªHeb. *found*——ᵇ2 Kings xviii. 4——ᶜHeb. *statues,* chap. xxx. 14——ᵈHeb. *until to make an end*——ᵉ1 Chron. xxiii. 6; xxiv. 1——ᶠ1 Chron. xxiii. 30, 31 ᵍNum. xxviii., xxix

ʰNum. xviii. 8, &c.; Neh. xiii. 10——ⁱMal. ii. 7 ᵏHeb. *brake forth*——ˡExod. xxii. 29; Neh. xiii. 12 ᵐOr, *dates*——ⁿLev. xxvii. 30; Deut. xiv. 28——ᵒHeb. *heaps, heaps*

NOTES ON CHAP. XXXI

Verse 1. *Brake the images in pieces*] This species of reformation was not only carried on through *Judah,* but they carried it into *Israel;* whether through a transport of religious zeal, or whether with the *consent* of Hoshea the Israelitish king, we cannot tell.

Verse 2. *In the gates of the tents of the Lord.*] That is, in the temple; for this was the house, tabernacle, tent, and camp, of the Most High.

Verse 3. *The king's portion of his substance*

for the burnt-offerings] It is conjectured that the Jewish kings, at least from the time of David, furnished the morning and evening sacrifice daily at their own expense, and several others also.

Verse 5. *Brought—the first-fruits*] These were principally for the maintenance of the priests and Levites; they brought tithes of all the produce of the field, whether commanded or not, as we see in the instance of *honey,* which was not to be offered to the Lord, Lev. ii. 11, yet it appears it might be offered to the priests as *first-fruits,* or in the way of *tithes.*

A. M. 3278
B. C. 726
Olymp. XIII. 3
Anno Urbis
Conditæ 28

10 And Azariah the chief priest of the house of Zadok answered him, and said, ᵖSince *the people* began to bring the offerings into the house of the LORD, we have had enough to eat, and have left plenty: for the LORD hath blessed his people; and that which is left *is* this great store.

11 Then Hezekiah commanded to prepare �q̇chambers in the house of the LORD; and they prepared *them,*

12 And brought in the offerings and the tithes and the dedicated *things* faithfully: ʳover which Cononiah the Levite *was* ruler, and Shimei his brother *was* the next.

13 And Jehiel, and Azaziah, and Nahath, and Asahel, and Jerimoth, and Jozabad, and Eliel, and Ismachiah, and Mahath, and Benaiah, *were* overseers ˢunder the hand of Cononiah and Shimei his brother, at the commandment of Hezekiah the king, and Azariah the ruler of the house of God.

14 And Kore the son of Imnah the Levite, the porter toward the east, *was* over the freewill-offerings of God to distribute the oblations of the LORD, and the most holy things.

15 And ᵗnext him *were* Eden, and Miniamin, and Jeshua, and Shemaiah, Amariah, and Shecaniah, in the ᵘcities of the priests, in *their* ᵛset office, to give to their brethren by courses, as well to the great as to the small:

A. M. 3278
B. C. 726
Olymp. XIII. 3
Anno Urbis
Conditæ 28

16 Beside their genealogy of males, from three years old and upward, *even* unto every one that entereth into the house of the LORD, his daily portion for their service in their charges according to their courses;

17 Both to the genealogy of the priests by the house of their fathers, and the Levites ʷfrom twenty years old and upward, in their charges by their courses;

18 And to the genealogy of all their little ones, their wives, and their sons, and their daughters, through all the congregation: for in their ˣset office they sanctified themselves in holiness:

19 Also of the sons of Aaron the priests, *which were* in ʸthe fields of the suburbs of their cities, in every several city, the men that were ᶻexpressed by name, to give portions to all the males among the priests, and to all that were reckoned by genealogies among the Levites.

20 And thus did Hezekiah throughout all Judah, and ᵃwrought *that which was* good and right and truth, before the LORD his God.

21 And in every work that he began in the service of the house of God, and in the law, and in the commandments, to seek his God, he did *it* with all his heart, and prospered.

ᵖMal. iii. 10——qOr, *store-houses*——ʳNeh. xiii. 13
ˢHeb. *at the hand*——ᵗHeb. *at his hand*——ᵘJosh. xxi. 9
ᵛOr, *trust,* 1 Chron. ix. 22

ʷ1 Chron. xxiii. 24, 27——ˣOr, *trust*——ʸLev. xxv. 34; Numbers xxxv. 2——ᶻVerses 12, 13, 14, 15——ᵃ2 Kings xx. 3

Verse 7. *In the third month*] "The month *Sivan;* the *seventh, Tisri.*"—*Targum.*

The heaps] The vast *collections of grain* which they had from the tithes over and above their own consumption; see ver. 10.

Verse 11. *To prepare chambers*] To make granaries to lay up this superabundance.

Verse 12. *Shimei—was the next.*] He was assistant to Cononiah.

Verse 15. *And Miniamin*] Instead of מנימן, *Miniamin,* בנימן, *Benjamin,* is the reading of three of Kennicott's and De Rossi's MSS.; and this is the reading of the *Vulgate, Syriac, Septuagint,* and *Arabic.*

Verse 17. *From twenty years old*] Moses had ordered that the Levites should not begin their labour till they were *thirty* years of age; but David changed this order, and obliged them to begin at *twenty.*

Verse 20. *Wrought—good and right and truth*] Here is the proper character of a worthy king: he is GOOD, and he does *good;* he is UPRIGHT, and he acts *justly* and maintains *justice;* he is *truly* RELIGIOUS, and he lives according to that *truth* which he receives as a revelation from God.

Verse 21. *He did* it *with all his heart*] In every respect he was a thoroughly excellent man, saw his duty to God and to his people, and performed it with becoming zeal and diligence. May God ever send such *kings* to the nations of the world; and may the *people* who are blessed with such be duly obedient to them, and thankful to the God who sends them!

CHAPTER XXXII

Sennacherib invades Judea, 1. Hezekiah takes proper measures for the defence of his kingdom, 2–6. His exhortation, 7, 8. Sennacherib sends a blasphemous message to Hezekiah, and to the people, 9–15. His servants rail against God; and he and they blaspheme most grievously, 16–19. Hezekiah and the prophet Isaiah cry to God; he answers, and the Assyrians are destroyed, and Sennacherib is slain by his own sons, 20, 21. The Lord is magnified, 22, 23. Hezekiah's sickness and recovery, 24. His ingratitude, 25. His humiliation, 26. His riches, 27–30. His error relative to the Babylonish ambassadors, 31. His acts and death, 32, 33.

A. M. 3291
B. C. 713
Olymp. XVI. 4
Anno Urbis
Conditæ 41

A FTER ᵃthese things, and the establishment thereof, Sennacherib king of Assyria came, and entered into Judah, and encamped against the fenced cities, and thought ᵇto win them for himself.

2 And when Hezekiah saw that Sennacherib was come, and that ᶜhe was purposed to fight against Jerusalem,

3 He took counsel with his princes and his mighty men to stop the waters of the fountains which *were* without the city: and they did help him.

4 So there was gathered much people together, who stopped all the fountains, and the brook that ᵈran through the midst of the land, saying, Why should the kings of Assyria come, and find much water?

5 Also ᵉhe strengthened himself, and ᶠbuilt up all the wall that was broken, and raised *it* up to the towers, and another wall without, and repaired ᵍMillo *in* the city of David, and made ʰdarts and shields in abundance.

A. M. 3291
B. C. 713
Olymp. XVI. 4
Anno Urbis
Conditæ 41

6 And he set captains of war over the people,and gathered them together to him in the street of the gate of the city, and ⁱspake comfortably to them, saying,

7 ᵏBe strong and courageous, ˡbe not afraid nor dismayed for the king of Assyria, nor for all the multitude that *is* with him: for ᵐ*there be* more with us than with him:

8 With him *is* an ⁿarm of flesh; but ᵒwith us *is* the LORD our God to help us, and to fight our battles. And the people ᵖrested themselves upon the words of Hezekiah king of Judah.

A. M. 3294
B. C. 710
Olymp.XVII.3
Anno Urbis
Conditæ 44

9 �q After this did Sennacherib king of Assyria send his servants to Jerusalem, (but he *himself laid siege* against Lachish, and all his ʳpower with him,) unto Hezekiah king of Judah, and unto all Judah that *were* at Jerusalem, saying,

10 ˢThus saith Sennacherib king of Assyria,

ᵃ2 Kings xviii. 13, &c.; Isaiah xxxvi. 1, &c.——ᵇHeb. *to break them up*——ᶜHebrew, *his face was to war* ᵈHebrew, *overflowed*——ᵉIsaiah xxii. 9, 10——ᶠChap. xxv. 23——ᵍ2 Samuel v. 9; 1 Kings ix. 24——ʰOr, *swords* or *weapons*——ⁱHebrew, *spake to their heart,*

chap. xxx. 22; Isa. xl. 2——ᵏDeut. xxxi. 6——ˡChap. xx. 15——ᵐ2 Kings vi. 16——ⁿJeremiah xvii. 5; 1 John iv. 4——ᵒChap. xiii. 12; Romans viii. 31 ᵖHeb. *leaned*——q2 Kings xviii. 17——ʳHeb. *dominion* ˢ2 Kings xviii. 19

NOTES ON CHAP. XXXII

Verse 1. *After these things*] God did not permit this pious prince to be *disturbed* till he had completed the reformation which he had begun.

Verse 2. *When Hezekiah saw*] This was in the *fourteenth* year of the reign of Hezekiah; and at first the Jewish king *bought* him off at the great price of *three hundred talents of silver,* and *thirty talents of gold;* and even emptied his own treasures, and spoiled the house of the Lord, to gratify the oppressive avarice of the Assyrian king. See the whole account, 2 Kings xviii. 13, &c.

Verse 4. *Stopped all the fountains*] This was prudently done, for without water how could an immense army subsist in an *arid country?* No doubt the Assyrian army suffered much through this, as a Christian army did *eighteen hundred years* after this. When the crusaders came, in A. D. 1099, to besiege Jerusalem, the people of the city stopped up the wells, so that the Christian army was reduced to the greatest necessities and distress.

Verse 5. *Raised it up to the towers*] He built the wall up to the height of the towers, or, having built the wall, he raised towers on it.

Verse 6. *Set captains of war over the people —in the street of the gate of the city*] That is, the *open places* at the gate of the city, whither the people came for judgment, &c.

Verse 7. There be *more with us than with him*] We have more power than they have. (These words he quotes from the prophet Elisha, 2 Kings vi. 16.) This was soon proved to be true by the slaughter made by the angel of the Lord in the Assyrian camp.

Verse 9. *After this did Sennacherib*] Having received the silver and gold mentioned above, he withdrew his army, but shortly after he sent Rab-shakeh with a blasphemous message. This is the fact mentioned here.

Verse 10. *Thus saith Sennacherib*] See all these circumstances largely explained 2 Kings xviii. 17-36.

Verse 17. *Wrote also letters*] See 2 Kings xix. 9, 14.

Verse 21. *The Lord sent an angel*] See 2 Kings xix. 35, and the note there.

House of his god] Nisroch.

They that came forth of his own bowels] His sons Adrammelech and Sharezer.

Verse 23. *Many brought gifts unto the Lord*]

A. M. 3294
B. C. 710
Olymp. XVII. 3
Anno Urbis
Conditæ 44

Whereon do ye trust, that ye abide [t]in the siege in Jerusalem?

11 Doth not Hezekiah persuade you to give over yourselves to die by famine and by thirst, saying, [u]The LORD our God shall deliver us out of the hand of the king of Assyria?

12 [v]Hath not the same Hezekiah taken away his high places and his altars, and commanded Judah and Jerusalem, saying, Ye shall worship before one altar, and burn incense upon it?

13 Know ye not what I and my fathers have done unto all the people of *other* lands? [w]were the gods of the nations of those lands any ways able to deliver their lands out of mine hand?

14 Who *was there* among all the gods of those nations that my fathers utterly destroyed, that could deliver his people out of mine hand, that your God should be able to deliver you out of mine hand?

15 Now therefore [x]let not Hezekiah deceive you, nor persuade you on this manner, neither yet believe him: for no god of any nation or kingdom was able to deliver his people out of mine hand, and out of the hand of my fathers: how much less shall your God deliver you out of mine hand?

16 And his servants spake yet *more* against the LORD God, and against his servant Hezekiah.

17 [y]He wrote also letters to rail on the LORD God of Israel, and to speak against him, saying, [z]As the gods of the nations of *other* lands have not delivered their people out of mine hand, so shall not the God of Hezekiah deliver his people out of mine hand.

18 [a]Then they cried with a loud voice in the Jews' speech unto the people of Jerusalem [b]that *were* on the wall to affright them, and to trouble them; that they might take the city.

A. M. 3294
B. C. 710
Olymp. XVII. 3
Anno Urbis
Conditæ 44

19 And they spake against the God of Jerusalem, as against the gods of the people of the earth, *which were* [c]the work of the hands of man.

20 [d]And for this *cause* Hezekiah the king, and [e]the prophet Isaiah the son of Amoz, prayed and cried to heaven.

21 [f]And the LORD sent an angel, which cut off all the mighty men of valour, and the leaders and captains in the camp of the king of Assyria. So he returned with shame of face to his own land. And when he was come into the house of his god, they that came forth of his own bowels [g]slew him there with the sword.

22 Thus the LORD saved Hezekiah and the inhabitants of Jerusalem from the hand of Sennacherib the king of Assyria, and from the hand of all *other,* and guided them on every side.

23 And many brought gifts unto the LORD to Jerusalem, and [h]presents [i]to Hezekiah king of Judah: so that he was [k]magnified in the sight of all nations from thenceforth.

A. M. 3291
B. C. 713
Olymp. XVI. 4
Anno Urbis
Conditæ 41

24 [l]In those days Hezekiah was sick to the death, and prayed unto the LORD: and he spake unto him, and he [m]gave him a sign.

25 But Hezekiah [n]rendered not again according to the benefit *done* unto him; for [o]his heart was lifted up: [p]therefore there was wrath upon him, and upon Judah and Jerusalem.

26 [q]Notwithstanding Hezekiah humbled himself for [r]the pride of his heart, *both* he and the inhabitants of Jerusalem, so that the wrath of the LORD came not upon them [s]in the days of Hezekiah.

27 And Hezekiah had exceeding much

---

[t]Or, *in the strong hold*——[u]2 Kings xviii. 30——[v]2 Kings xviii. 22——[w]2 Kings xviii. 33, 34, 35——[x]2 Kings xviii. 29——[y]2 Kings xix. 9——[z]2 Kings xix. 12 [a]2 Kings xviii. 28——[b]2 Kings xviii. 26, 27, 28——[c]2 Kings xix. 18——[d]2 Kings xix. 15——[e]2 Kings xix. 2, 4——[f]2 Kings xix. 35, &c.

[g]Heb. *made him fall*——[h]Heb. *precious things* [i]Chap. xvii. 5——[k]Chap. i. 1——[l]2 Kings xx. 1; Isa. xxxviii. 1——[m]Or, *wrought a miracle for him*——[n]Psa. cxvi. 12——[o]Chap. xxvi. 16; Hab. ii. 4——[p]Chap. xxiv. 18——[q]Jer. xxvi. 18, 19——[r]Heb. *the lifting up* [s]2 Kings xx. 19

They plainly saw that Jehovah was the protector of the land.

And presents to Hezekiah] They saw that God was his *friend*, and would undertake for him; and they did not wish to have such a man for their *enemy*.

Verse 24. *Hezekiah was sick*] See 2 Kings xx. 1, &c., and the notes there.

Verse 25. *Hezekiah rendered not again*] He got into a vain confidence, took pleasure in his riches, and vainly showed them to the messengers of the king of Babylon. See on 2 Kings xx. 12, &c.

Verse 26. *Humbled himself*] Awoke from his sleep, was sorry for his sin, deprecated the wrath of God, and the Divine displeasure was turned away from him.

Verse 27. *Pleasant jewels*] כלי חמדה *keley chemdah*, desirable *vessels* or *utensils.*

A.M.3278-3306
B. C. 726-698
Olymp. XIII. 3
—XX. 3
riches and honour: and he made himself treasuries for silver, and for gold, and for precious stones, and for spices, and for shields, and for all manner of [t]pleasant jewels;

28 Storehouses also for the increase of corn, and wine, and oil; and stalls for all manner of beasts, and cotes for flocks.

29 Moreover he provided him cities, and possessions of flocks and herds in abundance: for [u]God had given him substance very much.

30 [v]This same Hezekiah also stopped the upper watercourse of Gihon, and brought it straight down to the west side of the city of David. And Hezekiah prospered in all his works.

31 Howbeit in *the business of* the [w]ambas-sadors of the princes of Babylon, who [x]sent unto him to inquire of the wonder that was *done* in the land, God left him, to [y]try him, that he might know all *that was* in his heart.

A. M. 3292
B. C. 712
Olymp. XVII. 1
Anno Urbis
Conditæ 42

32 Now the rest of the acts of Hezekiah, and his [z]goodness, behold, they *are* written in [a]the vision of Isaiah the prophet, the son of Amoz, *and* in the [b]book of the kings of Judah and Israel.

A.M.3278-3306
B. C. 726-698
Olymp. XIII. 3
—XX. 3

33 [c]And Hezekiah slept with his fathers, and they buried him in the [d]chiefest of the sepulchres of the sons of David: and all Judah and the inhabitants of Jerusalem did him [e]honour at his death. And Manasseh his son reigned in his stead.

A. M. 3306
B. C. 698
Olymp. XX. 3
Anno Urbis
Conditæ 56

---

[t]Heb. *instruments of desire*——[u]2 Chron. xxix. 12 [v]Isa. xxii. 9, 11——[w]Heb. *interpreters*——[x]2 Kings xx. 12; Isa. xxxix. 1——[y]Deut. viii. 2

[z]Heb. *kindnesses*——[a]Isa. xxxvi., xxxvii., xxxviii., xxxix——[b]2 Kings xviii., xix., xx——[c]2 Kings xx. 21 [d]Or, *highest*——[e]Prov. x. 7

Verse 30. *The upper watercourse*] He made canals to bring the waters of Gihon from the west side of Jerusalem to the west side of the city of David.

Verse 31. *Of the ambassadors*] See 2 Kings xx. 13, and the observations at the end of that chapter.

Verse 32. *The vision of Isaiah*] See this prophet, chap. xxxvi. to xxxix.

Verse 33. *Chiefest of the sepulchres*] This respect they paid to *him* who, since David, had been the best of all their kings.

I shall subjoin a few things from the *Targum* on this chapter.

Ver. 1. "After these things which Hezekiah did, and their establishment, the Lord appointed by his Word to bring Sennacherib, king of Assyria, and his army, into the land of Israel, that he might destroy the Assyrians in the land of the house of Judah, and smite their troops on the mountains of Jerusalem, and deliver all their spoils into the hands of Hezekiah and his people: wherefore Sennacherib came with immense armies, which could not be numbered; and having pitched his camps in the land of the tribe of Judah, besieged their fortified cities with his armies, hoping to overthrow them."

Verse 8. *Hezekiah said*—"His help is the strength of the flesh; but our auxiliary is the Word of the Lord."

Ver. 16. "His (Sennacherib's) servants spoke blasphemy against the Word of the Lord God."

Ver. 18. *In the Jews' speech*—"In the language of the holy house."

Ver. 21. "And the Word of the Lord sent Michael, and the angel Gabriel, and destroyed them on the night of the passover with a destructive fire; and burnt up their breath within their bodies, and consumed every soldier, cap-tain, and prince, in the army of the king of Assyria; and he returned with shame of face into his own land."

The destruction of God's enemies, and the support and salvation of the faithful, is in every instance in this *Targum* attributed to the Word of the Lord, *personally* understood. See the note on chap. xxxiv. 27.

Ver. 24. "In those days was Hezekiah sick, near to death; but he prayed before the Lord, who spoke to him by his Word to preserve him, and to add to his life *fifteen* years."

Ver. 31. "The king of Babylon sent, that they might inquire concerning the miracle that had been done in the land; that they might see the two tables of stone which were in the ark of the covenant of the Lord which Moses had placed there with the two tables which he had broken on account of the sin of the calf which they made in Horeb. The Word of the Lord permitted him to show them these; neither did he suffer for it; that he might try him, and see what was in his heart."

Thus God speaks after the manner of men: he either brings, or permits them to be brought, into such circumstances as shall cause them to show their prevailing propensities; and then warns them against the evils to which they are inclined, after having shown them that they are capable of those evils. To know ourselves, and our own character, is of the utmost importance to our religious growth and perfection. He who does not know where his weakness lies, is not likely to know where his strength lies. Many, by not being fully acquainted with their own character, have been unwatchful and unguarded, and so become an easy prey to their enemies. *Know thyself* is a lesson which no man can learn but from the Spirit of God.

CHAPTER XXXIII

Manasseh reigns fifty-five years, and restores idolatry, pollutes the temple, and practises all kinds of abomina-
tions, 1–9. He and the people are warned in vain, 10. He is delivered into the hands of the Assyrians,
bound with fetters, and carried to Babylon, 11. He humbles himself, and is restored, 12, 13. He destroys
idolatry, and restores the worship of God, 14–16. The people keep the high places, but sacrifice to the Lord
on them, 17. His acts, prayer, and death, 18–20. His son Amon succeeds him; and after a wicked idola-
trous reign of two years, is slain by his own servants in his own house, 21–24. The people rise up, and slay
his murderers, and make Josiah his son king in his stead, 25.

A.M.3306-3361
B. C. 698–643
Olymp. XX. 3
—XXXIV. 2

M ANASSEH [a]*was* twelve years old when he began to reign, and he reigned fifty

A.M.3306-3327
B. C. 698–677
Olymp. XX. 3
—XXV. 4

and five years in Jerusalem:

2 But did *that which was* evil in the sight of the LORD, like unto the [b]abominations of the heathen, whom the LORD had cast out before the children of Israel.

3 For [c]he built again the high places which Hezekiah his father had [d]broken down, and he reared up altars for Baalim, and [e]made groves, and worshipped [f]all the host of heaven, and served them.

4 Also he built altars in the house of the LORD, whereof the LORD had said, [g]In Jerusalem shall my name be for ever.

5 And he built altars for all the host of heaven [h]in the two courts of the house of the LORD.

6 [i]And he caused his children to pass through the fire in the valley of the son of Hinnom: [k]also he observed times, and used enchantments, and used witchcraft, and [l]dealt with a familiar spirit, and with wizards: he wrought much evil in the sight of the LORD, to provoke him to anger.

7 And [m]he set a carved image, the idol which he had made, in the house of God, of which God had said to David and to Solomon his son,

A.M.3306-3327
B. C. 698–677
Olymp. XX. 3
—XXV. 4

In [n]this house, and in Jerusalem, which I have chosen before all the tribes of Israel, will I put my name for ever:

8 [o]Neither will I any more remove the foot of Israel from out of the land which I have appointed for your fathers; so that they will take heed to do all that I have commanded them, according to the whole law and the statutes and the ordinances by the hand of Moses.

9 So Manasseh made Judah and the inhabitants of Jerusalem to err, *and* to do worse than the heathen, whom the LORD had destroyed before the children of Israel.

10 And the LORD spake to Manasseh, and to his people: but they would not hearken.

11 [p]Wherefore the LORD brought upon them the captains of the host [q]of the king of

A. M. 3327
B. C. 677
Olymp. XXV. 4
Anno Urbis
Conditæ 77

Assyria, which took Manasseh among the thorns, and [r]bound him with [s]fetters, and carried him to Babylon.

12 And when he was in affliction, he besought the LORD his God, and [t]humbled himself greatly before the God of his fathers,

---

[a]2 Kings xxi. 1, &c.——[b]Deut. xviii. 9; 2 Chron.
xxviii. 3——[c]Heb. *he returned and built*——[d]2 Kings
xviii. 4; ch. xxx. 14; xxxi. 1; xxxii. 12——[e]Deut. xvi. 21
[f]Deut. xvii. 3——[g]Deut. xii. 11; 1 Kings viii. 29; ix. 3;
ch. vi. 6; vii. 16——[h]Ch. iv. 9——[i]Lev. xviii. 21; Deut.

xviii. 10; 2 Kings xxiii. 10; ch. xxviii. 3; Ezek. xxiii. 37,
39——[k]Deut. xviii. 10, 11——[l]2 Kings xxi. 6——[m]2
Kings xxi. 7——[n]Psa. cxxxii. 14——[o]2 Sam. vii. 10
[p]Deut. xxviii. 36; Job xxxvi. 8——[q]Heb. *which were the*
king's——[r]Psa. cvii. 10, 11——[s]Or, *chains*——[t]1 Pet. v. 6

NOTES ON CHAP. XXXIII

Verse 1. *Manasseh was twelve years old*]
We do not find that he had any godly director;
his *youth* was therefore the more easily seduced.
But surely he had a *pious education;* how then
could the principles of it be so soon eradicated?

Verse 3. *Altars for Baalim*] The SUN and MOON.
And made groves, אשרות *Asheroth,* Astarte,
VENUS; *the host of heaven,* all the PLANETS and
STARS. These were the general objects of his
devotion.

Verse 5. *He built altars*] See the principal
facts in this chapter explained in the notes on
2 Kings xxi. 1-17.

Verse 7. *A carved image*] "He set up an
image, the likeness of himself, in the house of
the sanctuary." The *Targumist* supposes he
wished to procure himself Divine honours.

Verse 12. *And when he was in affliction*]
Here is a very large addition in the Chaldee:
"For the Chaldeans made a brazen mule, pierced
full of small holes, and put him within it, and
kindled fires all around it; and when he was in
this misery, he sought help of all the idols
which he had made, but obtained none, for they
were of no use. He therefore repented, and
prayed before the Lord his God, and was greatly
humbled in the sight of the Lord God of his
fathers."

A. M. 3327
B. C. 677
Olymp. XXV. 4
Anno Urbis
Conditæ 77

13 And prayed unto him: and he was [u]entreated of him, and heard his supplication, and brought him again to Jerusalem unto his kingdom. Then Manasseh [v]knew that the LORD he *was* God.

A.M. 3327-3361
B. C. 677–643
Olymp. XXV. 4
—XXXIV. 2

14 Now after this he built a wall without the city of David, on the west side of [w]Gihon, in the valley, even to the entering in at the fish-gate, and compassed [x]about [y]Ophel, and raised it up a very great height, and put captains of war in all the fenced cities of Judah.

15 And he took away the [z]strange gods, and the idol out of the house of the LORD, and all the altars that he had built in the mount of the house of the LORD, and in Jerusalem, and cast *them* out of the city.

16 And he repaired the altar of the LORD, and sacrificed thereon peace-offerings and [a]thank-offerings, and commanded Judah to serve the LORD God of Israel.

17 [b]Nevertheless the people did sacrifice still in the high places, *yet* unto the LORD their God only.

A.M. 3306-3361
B. C. 698–643
Olymp. XX. 3
—XXXIV. 2

18 Now the rest of the acts of Manasseh, and his prayer unto his God, and the words of [c]the seers that spake to him in the name of the LORD God of Israel, behold, they *are written*

in the book of the kings of Israel.

A.M. 3306-3361
B. C. 698–643
Olymp. XX. 3
—XXXIV. 2

19 His prayer also, and *how* God was entreated of him, and all his sins, and his trespass, and the places wherein he built high places, and set up groves, and graven images, before he was humbled: behold, they *are* written among the sayings of [d]the seers.

20 [e]So Manasseh slept with his fathers, and they buried him in his own house: and Amon his son reigned in his stead.

A. M. 3361
B. C. 643
An. Olymp.
XXXIV. 2
Anno Urbis
Conditæ 111

21 [f]Amon *was* two and twenty years old when he began to reign, and reigned two years in Jerusalem.

A.M. 3361-3363
B. C. 643–641
An. Olymp.
XXXIV. 2–4

22 But he did *that which was* evil in the sight of the LORD, as did Manasseh his father: for Amon sacrificed unto all the carved images which Manasseh his father had made, and served them;

23 And humbled not himself before the LORD [g]as Manasseh his father had humbled himself; but Amon [h]trespassed more and more.

24 [i]And his servants conspired against him, and slew him in his own house.

A. M. 3363
B. C. 641
Ol. XXXIV. 4
Anno Urbis
Conditæ 113

25 But the people of the land slew all them that had conspired against King Amon; and the people of the land made Josiah his son king in his stead.

---

[u]1 Chron. v. 20; Ezra viii. 23——[v]Psa. ix. 16; Dan. iv. 25——[w]1 Kings i. 33——[x]Chap. xxxii. 3——[y]Or, *the tower*——[z]Ver. 3, 5, 7——[a]Lev. vii. 12

[b]Chap. xxxii. 12——[c]1 Sam. ix. 9——[d]Or, *Hosai* [e]2 Kings xxi. 18——[f]2 Kings xxi. 19, &c.——[g]Ver. 12 [h]Heb. *multiplied trespass*——[i]2 Kings xxi. 23, 24

Verse 13. *And prayed unto him*] "While he was thus praying, all the presiding angels went away to the gates of prayer in heaven; and shut all the gates of prayer, and all the windows and apertures in heaven, lest that his prayer should be heard. Immediately the compassions of the Creator of the world were moved, whose right hand is stretched out to receive sinners, who are converted to his fear, and break their hearts' concupiscence by repentance. He made therefore a window and opening in heaven, under the throne of his glory; and having heard his prayer, he favourably received his supplication. And when his WORD had shaken the earth, the mule was burst and he escaped. Then the Spirit went out from between the wings of the cherubim; by which, being inspired through the decree of the WORD of the Lord, he returned to his kingdom in Jerusalem. And then Manasseh knew that it was the Lord God who had done these miracles and signs; and he *turned* to the Lord with his whole heart, left all his idols, and never served them more." This long addition gives the Jewish account of those particulars which the sacred writer has passed by:

it is curious, though in some sort trifling. The *gates of prayer* may be considered childish; but in most of those things the ancient rabbins purposely hid deep and important meanings.

Verse 14. *He built a wall*] This was probably a weak place that he fortified; or a part of the wall which the Assyrians had broken down, which he now rebuilt.

Verse 15. *He took away the strange gods*] He appears to have done every thing in his power to destroy the idolatry which he had set up, and to restore the pure worship of the true God. His repentance brought forth fruits meet for repentance. How *long* he was in captivity, and *when* or by *whom* he was delivered, we know not. The fact of his restoration is asserted; and we believe it on Divine testimony.

Verse 17. *The people did sacrifice*] "Nevertheless the people did sacrifice on the high places, but only to the name of the WORD of the Lord their God."—*Targum.*

Verse 18. *The words of the seers that spake to him*] "Which were spoken to him in the name of the WORD of the Lord God of Israel."—*Targum.*

Verse 19. *His prayer also*] What is called

the *Prayer of Manasseh, king of Judah, when he was holden captive in Babylon*, being found among our apocryphal books, I have inserted it at the end of the chapter, without either asserting or thinking that it is the identical prayer which this penitent king used when a captive in Babylon. But, as I have observed in another place, there are many good sentiments in it; and some sinners may find it a proper echo of the distresses of their hearts; I therefore insert it.

Written among the sayings of the seers.] "They are written in the words of Chozai."— *Targum.* So says the *Vulgate.* The *Syriac* has *Hunan the prophet;* and the *Arabic* has *Saphan the prophet.*

Verse 21. *Amon—reigned two years*] See on 2 Kings xxi. 19.

Verse 22. *Sacrificed unto all the carved images*] How astonishing is this! with his father's example before his eyes, he copies his father's *vices*, but not his *repentance*.

Verse 23. *Trespassed more and more.*] He appears to have exceeded his father, and would take no warning.

Verse 24. *His servants conspired against him*] On what account we cannot tell.

Verse 25. *The people of the land slew all them*] His murder was not a *popular* act, for the people slew the regicides. They were as prone to idolatry as their king was. We may rest satisfied that idolatry was accompanied with great *licentiousness* and sensual gratifications else it never, as a mere religious system, could have had any sway in the world.

FOR an explanation of the term *groves*, ver. 3, see the observations at the end of 2 Kings xxi.

I have referred to the *prayer* attributed to *Manasseh*, and found in what is called the *Apocrypha*, just before the first book of *Maccabees*. It was anciently used as a form of confession in the Christian Church, and is still as such received by the Greek Church. It is as follows:—

"O Lord, Almighty God of our fathers, Abraham, Isaac, and Jacob, and of their righteous seed; who hast made heaven and earth, with all the ornament thereof; who hast bound the sea by the word of thy commandment; who hast shut up the deep, and sealed it by thy terrible and glorious name; whom all men fear, and tremble before thy power; for the majesty of thy glory cannot be borne, and thine angry threatening towards sinners is insupportable; but thy merciful promise is unmeasurable and unsearchable; for thou art the most high Lord, of great compassion, long-suffering, very merciful, and repentest of the evils of men. Thou, O Lord, according to thy great goodness, hast promised repentance and forgiveness to them that have sinned against thee; and of thine infinite mercies hast appointed repentance unto sinners, that they may be saved. Thou, therefore, O Lord, that art the God of the just, has not appointed repentance to the just, as to Abraham, and Isaac, and Jacob, which have not sinned against thee; but thou hast appointed repentance unto me that am a sinner: for I have sinned above the number of the sands of the sea. My transgressions, O Lord, are multiplied; my transgressions are multiplied; and I am not worthy to behold and see the height of heaven for the multitude of mine iniquities. I am bowed down with many iron bands, that I cannot lift up mine head, neither have any release; for I have provoked thy wrath, and done evil before thee. I did not thy will, neither kept I thy commandments. I have set up abominations, and have multiplied offences. Now therefore I bow the knee of mine heart, beseeching thee of grace. I have sinned, O Lord, I have sinned, and I acknowledge mine iniquities: wherefore I humbly beseech thee, forgive me, O Lord, forgive me, and destroy me not in mine iniquities. Be not angry with me for ever, by reserving evil for me; neither condemn me into the lower parts of the earth. For thou art the God, the God of them that repent; and in me thou wilt show all thy goodness: for thou wilt save me, that am unworthy, according to thy great mercy. Therefore I will praise thee for ever all the days of my life: for all the powers of the heavens do praise thee, and thine is the glory for ever and ever.—*Amen.*

The above translation, which is that in our common Bibles, might be mended; but the piece is scarcely worth the pains.

CHAPTER XXXIV

Josiah reigns thirty-one *years; destroys idolatry in Judah, as also in Manasseh, Ephraim, Simeon, and even to Naphtali,* 1–7. *He begins to repair the temple, and collects money for the purpose, and employs workmen,* 8–13. *Hilkiah the priest finds the book of the law in the temple, which is read by Shaphan before the king,* 14–19. *He is greatly troubled, and consults Huldah the prophetess,* 20–22. *Her exhortation, and message to the king,* 23–28. *He causes it to be read to the elders of Judah, and they make a covenant with God,* 29, 32. *Josiah reforms every abomination, and the people serve God all his days,* 33.

A.M.3363-3394
B. C. 641-610
Ol. XXXIV. 4
—XLII. 3

JOSIAH [a]*was* eight years old when he began to reign, and he reigned in Jerusalem one and thirty years.

2 And he did *that which was* right in the sight of the LORD, and walked in the ways of David his father, and declined *neither* to

A.M.3363-3394
B. C. 641-610
Ol. XXXIV. 4
—XLII. 3

[a]2 Kings xxii. 1, &c.

NOTES ON CHAP. XXXIV

Verse 2. *He declined* neither *to the right hand, nor to the left.*] He never swerved from God and truth; he never omitted what he knew to be his duty to God and his kingdom; he carried on his reformation with a steady hand; *timidity* did not prevent him from going *far enough;* and *zeal* did not lead him beyond *due*

A. M. 3370
B. C. 634
An. Olymp.
XXXVI. 3
Anno Urbis
Conditæ 120

the right hand, nor to the left.

3 For in the eighth year of his reign, while he was yet young,

A. M. 3374
B. C. 630
An. Olymp.
XXXVII. 3
Anno Urbis
Conditæ 124

he began to [b]seek after the God of David his father: and in the twelfth year he began to [c]purge Judah and Jerusalem [d]from the high places, and the groves, and the carved images, and the molten images.

A.M.3374–3380
B. C. 630–624
Ol. XXXVII. 3
—XXXIX. 1

4 [e]And they brake down the altars of Baalim in his presence; and the [f]images, that *were* on high above them, he cut down; and the groves, and the carved images, and the molten images, he brake in pieces, and made dust *of them,* [g]and strowed *it* upon the [h]graves of them that had sacrificed unto them.

5 And he [i]burnt the bones of the priests upon their altars, and cleansed Judah and Jerusalem.

6 And *so did he* in the cities of Manasseh, and Ephraim, and Simeon, even unto Naphtali, with their [k]mattocks round about.

7 And when he had broken down the altars and the groves, and had [l]beaten the graven images [m]into powder, and cut down all the idols throughout all the land of Israel, he returned to Jerusalem.

8 Now [n]in the eighteenth year of his reign, when he had purged the land, and the house, he sent Shaphan the son of Azaliah, and Maaseiah the governor of the city, and Joah, the son of Joahaz the recorder, to repair the house of the LORD his God.

A. M. 3380
B. C. 624
An. Olymp.
XXXIX. 1
Anno Urbis
Conditæ 130

9 And when they came to Hilkiah the high priest, they delivered [o]the money that was brought into the house of God, which the Levites that kept the doors had gathered of the hand of Manasseh and Ephraim, and of all the remnant of Israel, and of all Judah and Benjamin; and they returned to Jerusalem.

10 And they put *it* in the hand of the workmen that had the oversight of the house of the LORD, and they gave it to the workmen that wrought in the house of the LORD, to repair and amend the house:

11 Even to the artificers and builders gave they *it,* to buy hewn stone, and timber for couplings, and [p]to floor the houses which the kings of Judah had destroyed.

12 And the men did the work faithfully: and the overseers of them *were* Jahath and Obadiah, the Levites, of the sons of Merari; and Zechariah and Meshullam, of the sons of the Kohathites, to set *it* forward; and *other*

---

[b]Chap. xv. 2——[c]1 Kings xiii. 2——[d]Chap. xxxiii. 17, 22——[e]Lev. xxvi. 30; 2 Kings xxiii. 4——[f]Or, *sun images*——[g]2 Kings xxiii. 4——[h]Heb. *face of the graves*

[i]1 Kings xiii. 2——[k]Or, *mauls*——[l]Deut. ix. 21 [m]Heb. *to make powder*——[n]2 Kings xxii. 3——[o]See 2 Kings xii. 4, &c.——[p]Or, *to rafter*

---

bounds. He walked in the *golden mean,* and his *moderation* was known unto all men. He went neither to the right nor to the left, he looked *inward,* looked *forward,* and looked *upward.* Reader, let the conduct of this pious youth be thy exemplar through life.

Verse 4. *The altars of Baalim*] How often have these been broken down, and how soon set up again! We see that the religion of a land is as the religion of its king. If the *king* were *idolatrous,* up went the altars, on them were placed the statues, and the smoke of incense ascended in ceaseless clouds to the honour of that which is *vanity,* and *nothing in the world;* on the other hand, when the king was *truly religious,* down went the idolatrous altars, broken in pieces were the images, and the sacrificial smoke ascended only to the true God: in all these cases the *people* were as one man with the *king.*

Verse 5. *He burnt the bones of the priests*] כומריא *kumeraiya,* the *kemarim,* says the *Targum.* See this word explained, 2 Kings xxiii. 5.

Verse 6. *The cities of Manasseh*] Even those who were under the government of the Israel-itish king permitted their idols and places of idolatry to be hewn down and destroyed: after

the truth was declared and acknowledged, the *spade* and the *axe* were employed to complete the reformation.

Verse 9. *And they returned to Jerusalem.*] Instead of וישבו *vaiyashubu,* "they returned," we should read ישבי *yoshebey,* "the inhabitants;" a reading which is supported by many *MSS.,* printed *editions,* and all the *versions,* as well as by *necessity* and *common sense.* See the note on chap. xix. 8, where a similar mistake is rectified.

Verse 12. *All that could skill of instruments of music*] Did the musicians play on their several instruments to encourage and enliven the workmen? Is not this a probable case from their mention here? If this were really the case, *instrumental music* was never better applied in any thing that refers to the worship of God. It is fabled of *Orpheus,* a most celebrated musician, that such was the enchanting *harmony* of his *lyre,* that he *built the city of Thebes* by it: the *stones* and *timbers danced* to his *melody;* and by the power of his *harmony* rose up, and *took* their respective *places* in the different parts of the wall that was to defend the city! This is *fable;* but as all fable is a representation of *truth,* where is the *truth* and *fact*

A. M. 3380
B. C. 624
An. Olymp.
XXXIX. 1
Anno Urbis
Conditæ 130

of the Levites, all that could skill of instruments of music.

13 Also *they were* over the bearers of burdens, and *were* overseers of all that wrought the work in any manner of service: �q and of the Levites *there were* scribes, and officers, and porters.

14 And when they brought out the money that was brought into the house of the LORD, Hilkiah the priest ʳfound a book of the law of the LORD *given* by ˢMoses.

15 And Hilkiah answered and said to Shaphan the scribe, I have found the book of the law in the house of the LORD. And Hilkiah delivered the book to Shaphan.

16 And Shaphan carried the book to the king, and brought the king word back again, saying, All that was committed ᵗto thy servants, they do *it*.

17 And they have ᵘgathered together the money that was found in the house of the

A. M. 3380
B. C. 624
An. Olymp.
XXXIX. 1
Anno Urbis
Conditæ 130

LORD, and have delivered it into the hand of the overseers, and to the hand of the workmen.

18 Then Shaphan the scribe told the king, saying, Hilkiah the priest hath given me a book. And Shaphan read ᵛit before the king.

19 And it came to pass, when the king had heard the words of the law, that he rent his clothes.

20 And the king commanded Hilkiah, and Ahikam the son of Shaphan, and ʷAbdon the son of Micah, and Shaphan the scribe, and Asaiah a servant of the king's, saying,

21 Go, inquire of the LORD for me, and for them that are left in Israel and in Judah, concerning the words of the book that is found: for great *is* the wrath of the LORD that is poured out upon us, because our fathers have not kept the word of the LORD, to do after all that is written in this book.

ᵠ1 Chron. xxiii. 4, 5——ʳ2 Kings xxii. 8, &c.——ˢHeb. *by the hand of*——ᵗHeb. *to the hand of*

ᵘHeb. *poured out* or *melted*——ᵛHeb. *in it*——ʷOr, *Achbor,* 2 Kings xxii. 12

---

to which this refers? How long has this question lain unanswered! But have we not the answer now? It is known in general, that the cities of *Herculaneum* and *Pompeii* were overwhelmed by an eruption of Mount *Vesuvius,* about the *seventy-ninth* year of the Christian era. It is also known that, in sinking for wells, the workmen of the king of Naples lighted on houses, &c., of those overwhelmed cities; that *excavations* have been carried on, and are now in the act of being carried on, which are bringing daily to view various *utensils, pictures,* and *books,* which have escaped the influence of the burning lava; and that some of those *parchment volumes* have been unrolled, and *fac similes* of them *engraved* and published; and that our late *Prince Regent,* afterwards George IV., king of Great Britain, expended considerable sums of money annually in searching for, unrolling, and deciphering those *rolls.* This I record to his *great credit* as the lover of science and literature. Now, among the books that have been unrolled and published, is a *Greek Treatise* on *Music,* by *Philodemus;* and here we have the *truth* represented which lay hidden under the *fables of Orpheus* and *Amphion.* This latter was a *skilful harper,* who was frequently employed by the Theban *workmen* to play to them while engaged in their labour, and for which they *rewarded him out of the proceeds of that labor.* So *powerful* and *pleasing* was his *music,* that they went lightly and comfortably through their work; and *time* and *labour* passed on without *tedium* or *fatigue;* and the *walls and towers were speedily raised.* This, by a metaphor, was attributed to the *dulcet sounds* of his *harp;* and *poetry* seized on and embellished it, and *mythology* incorporated it with her fabulous system. Orpheus is the same. By his skill in music he drew stones and trees after

him, i. e., he presided over and encouraged the workmen by his skill in music. Yet how simple and natural is the representation given by this ancient Greek writer of such matters! See *Philodemus, Col.* viii. and ix. *Orpheus,* and *Amphion,* by their music, moved the workmen to diligence and activity, and lessened and alleviated their toil. May we not suppose, then, that skilful musicians among the *Levites* did exercise their art among the *workmen* who were employed in the *repairs* of the house of the Lord? May I be allowed a gentle transition? Is it not the *power* and *harmony* of the *grace* of *Jesus Christ* in the *Gospel,* that convert, change, and purify the souls of men, and prepare them for and place them in that part of the house of God, the New Jerusalem? A most beautiful and chaste allusion to this *fact* and *fable* is made by an eminent poet, while praying for his own success as a *Christian* minister, who uses all his skill as a *poet* and *musician* for the glory of God:—

> Thy own musician, Lord, inspire,
> And may my consecrated lyre
>   Repeat the psalmist's part!
> His Son and thine reveal in me,
> And fill with sacred melody
>   The *fibres* of my heart.
> So shall I *charm* the *listening throng,*
> And *draw* the LIVING STONES along
>   By Jesus' *tuneful* name.
> The *living stones* shall *dance,* shall *rise,*
> And FORM a CITY in the *skies,*
>   The *New Jerusalem.*
>   CHARLES WESLEY.

Verse 14. *Found a book of the law*] See **on** 2 Kings xxii. 8.

A. M. 3380
B. C. 624
An. Olymp.
XXXIX. 1
Anno Urbis
Conditæ 130

22 And Hilkiah, and *they* that the king *had appointed,* went to Huldah the prophetess, the wife of Shallum the son of [x]Tikvath, the son of [y]Hasrah, keeper of the [z]wardrobe; (now she dwelt in Jerusalem [a]in the college;) and they spake to her to that *effect.*

23 And she answered them, Thus saith the LORD God of Israel, Tell ye the man that sent you to me,

24 Thus saith the LORD, Behold, I will bring evil upon this place, and upon the inhabitants thereof, *even* all the curses that are written in the book which they have read before the king of Judah:

25 Because they have forsaken me, and have burned incense unto other gods, that they might provoke me to anger with all the works of their hands; therefore my wrath shall be poured out upon this place, and shall not be quenched.

26 And as for the king of Judah, who sent you to inquire of the LORD, so shall ye say unto him, Thus saith the LORD God of Israel *concerning* the words which thou hast heard;

27 Because thine heart was tender, and thou didst humble thyself before God, when thou heardest his words against this place, and against the inhabitants thereof, and humbledst thyself before me, and didst rend thy clothes, and weep before me; I have even heard *thee* also, saith the LORD.

28 Behold, I will gather thee to thy fathers,

A. M. 3380
B. C. 624
An. Olymp.
XXXI. 1
Anno Urbis
Conditæ 130

and thou shalt be gathered to thy grave in peace; neither shall thine eyes see all the evil that I will bring upon this place, and upon the inhabitants of the same. So they brought the king word again.

29 [b]Then the king sent and gathered together all the elders of Judah and Jerusalem.

30 And the king went up into the house of the LORD, and all the men of Judah, and the inhabitants of Jerusalem, and the priests, and the Levites, and all the people [c]great and small: and he read in their ears all the words of the book of the covenant that was found in the house of the LORD.

31 And the king stood in his [d]place, and made a covenant before the LORD, to walk after the LORD, and to keep his commandments, and his testimonies, and his statutes, with all his heart, and with all his soul, to perform the words of the covenant which are written in this book.

32 And he caused all that were [e]present in Jerusalem and Benjamin to stand *to it.* And the inhabitants of Jerusalem did according to the covenant of God, the God of their fathers.

33 And Josiah took away all the [f]abominations out of all the countries that *pertained* to the children of Israel, and made all that were present in Israel to serve, *even* to serve the LORD their God. [g]*And* all his days they departed not [h]from following the LORD, the God of their fathers.

---

[x]2 Kings xxii. 14——[y]Or, *Harhas*——[z]Heb. *garments*
[a]Or, *in the school,* or *in the second part*——[b]2 Kings xxiii. 1, &c.

[c]Heb. *from great even to small*——[d]2 Kings xi. 14; xxiii. 3; chap. vi. 13——[e]Heb. *found*——[f]1 Kings xi. 5
[g]Jer. iii. 10——[h]Heb. *from after*

Verse 22. *Huldah the prophetess*] See on 2 Kings xxii. 14.

Verse 27. *Because thine heart was tender*] "Because thy heart was melted, and thou hast humbled thyself in the sight of the WORD of the Lord, דיי מימרא *meymera daya,* when thou didst hear his *words,* פתגמי ית *yath pithgamoi,* against this place," &c. Here the *Targum* most evidently distinguishes between מימרא *meymera,* the PERSONAL WORD, and פתגם *pithgam,* a *word spoken* or *expressed.*

Verse 28. *Gathered to thy grave in peace*] See particularly the note on 2 Kings xxii. 20.

Verse 30. *The king went*] See on 2 Kings xxiii. 1.

Verse 31. *Made a covenant*] See on 2 Kings xxiii. 3. And see the notes on that and the preceding chapter, for the circumstances detailed here.

Verse 32. *To stand to it.*] It is likely that he caused them all to *arise* when he read the terms of the covenant, and thus testify their approbation of the covenant itself, and their resolution to observe it faithfully and perseveringly.

CHAPTER XXXV

Josiah celebrates a passover, 1; regulates the courses of the priests; assigns them, the Levites, and the people, their portions; and completes the greatest passover ever celebrated since the days of Solomon, 2–19. Pharaoh Necho passes with his army through Judea, 20. Josiah meets and fights with him at Megiddo, and is mortally wounded, 21–23. He is carried to Jerusalem, where he dies, 24. Jeremiah laments for him, 25. Of his acts and deeds, and where recorded, 26, 27.

A. M. 3380
B. C. 624
An. Olymp.
XXXIX. 1
Anno Urbis
Conditæ 130

MOREOVER [a]Josiah kept a passover unto the LORD in Jerusalem: and they killed the passover on the [b]fourteenth *day* of the first month.

2 And he set the priests in their [c]charges, and [d]encouraged them to the service of the house of the LORD,

3 And said unto the Levites [e]that taught all Israel, which were holy unto the LORD, [f]Put the holy ark [g]in the house which Solomon the son of David king of Israel did build; [h]*it shall* not *be* a burden upon *your* shoulders: serve now the LORD your God, and his people Israel,

4 And prepare *yourselves* by the [i]houses of your fathers, after your courses, according to the [k]writing of David king of Israel, and according to the [l]writing of Solomon his son.

5 And [m]stand in the holy *place* according to the divisions of [n]the families of the fathers of your brethren [o]the people, and *after* the division of the families of the Levites.

6 So kill the passover, and [p]sanctify yourselves, and prepare your brethren, that *they* may do according to the word of the LORD by the hand of Moses.

7 And Josiah [q]gave [r]to the people of the flock, lambs and kids, all for the passover-offerings, for all that were present, to the number of thirty thousand, and three thousand bullocks: these *were* of the king's substance.

8 And his princes [s]gave willingly unto the people, to the priests, and to the Levites: Hilkiah and Zechariah and Jehiel, rulers of the house of God, gave unto the priests for the passover-offerings two thousand and six hundred *small cattle,* and three hundred oxen.

9 Conaniah also, and Shemaiah, and Nethaneel, his brethren, and Hashabiah, and Jeiel,

A. M. 3380
B. C. 624
An. Olymp.
XXXIX. 1
Anno Urbis
Conditæ 130

and Jozabad, chief of the Levites, [t]gave unto the Levites for passover-offerings five thousand *small cattle,* and five hundred oxen.

10 So the service was prepared, and the priests [u]stood in their place, and the Levites in their courses, according to the king's commandment.

11 And they killed the passover, and the priests [v]sprinkled *the blood* from their hands and the Levites [w]flayed *them.*

12 And they removed the burnt-offerings, that they might give according to the divisions of the families of the people, to offer unto the LORD, as *it is* written [x]in the book of Moses. And so *did they* with the oxen.

13 And they [y]roasted the passover with fire according to the ordinance: but the *other* holy *offerings* [z]sod they in pots, and in caldrons, and in pans, and [a]divided *them* speedily among all the people.

14 And afterward they made ready for themselves, and for the priests: because the priests the sons of Aaron *were busied* in offering of burnt-offerings and the fat until night; therefore the Levites prepared for themselves, and for the priests the sons of Aaron.

15 And the singers, the sons of Asaph, *were* in their [b]place, according to the [c]commandment of David, and Asaph, and Heman, and Jeduthun the king's seer; and the porters [d]*waited* at every gate; they might not depart from their service; for their brethren the Levites prepared for them.

16 So all the service of the LORD was prepared the same day, to keep the passover, and to offer burnt-offerings upon the altar of the LORD, according to the commandment of King Josiah.

---

[a]2 Kings xxiii. 21, 22; 1 Esd. i. 1, &c.——[b]Exod. xii. 6; Ezra vi. 19——[c]Ch. xxiii. 18; Ezra vi. 18——[d]Ch. xxix. 5, 11——[e]Deut. xxxiii. 10; ch. xxx. 22; Mal. ii. 7 [f]See ch. xxxiv. 14——[g]Ch. v. 7——[h]1 Chron. xxiii. 26 [i]1 Chron. ix. 10——[k]1 Chron. xxiii., xxiv., xxv., xxvi [l]Chap. viii. 14——[m]Psa. cxxxiv. 1——[n]Heb. *the house of the fathers*——[o]Heb. *the sons of the people*

[p]Chap. xxix. 5, 15; xxx. 3, 15; Ezra vi. 20——[q]Heb. *offered*——[r]Chap. xxx. 24——[s]Heb. *offered*——[t]Heb. *offered*——[u]Ezra vi. 18——[v]Chap. xxix. 22——[w]See chap. xxix. 34——[x]Lev. iii. 3——[y]Exod. xii. 8, 9; Deut. xvi. 7——[z]1 Samuel ii. 13, 14, 15——[a]Hebrew, *made them run*——[b]Hebrew, *station*——[c]1 Chronicles xxv. 1, &c.——[d]1 Chronicles ix. 17, 18; xxvi. 14, &c.

NOTES ON CHAP. XXXV

Verse 3. *Put the holy ark in the house*] It is likely that the priests had secured this when they found that the idolatrous kings were determined to destroy every thing that might lead the people to the worship of the true God. And now, as all appears to be well established, the ark is ordered to be put into its *own place.*

For an ample account of this passover and the reformation that was then made, see on 2 Kings xxiii. 1, &c., and the places marked in the margin.

Verse 11. *They killed the passover*] The people themselves might slay their own paschal lambs, and then present the *blood* to the *priests,* that they might *sprinkle* it before the altar;

A. M. 3380
B. C. 624
An. Olymp.
XXXIX. 1
Anno Urbis
Conditæ 130

17 And the children of Israel that were ᵉpresent kept the passover at that time, and the feast of ᶠunleavened bread seven days.

18 And ᵍthere was no passover like to that kept in Israel from the days of Samuel the prophet; neither did all the kings of Israel keep such a passover as Josiah kept, and the priests, and the Levites, and all Judah and Israel that were present, and the inhabitants of Jerusalem.

19 In the eighteenth year of the reign of Josiah was this passover kept.

A. M. 3394
B. C. 610
An. Olymp.
XLII. 3
Anno Urbis
Conditæ 144

20 ʰAfter all this, when Josiah had prepared the ⁱtemple, Necho king of Egypt came up to fight against Charchemish by Euphrates: and Josiah went out against him.

21 But he sent ambassadors to him, saying, What have I to do with thee, thou king of Judah? *I come* not against thee this day, but against ᵏthe house wherewith I have war: for God commanded me to make haste: forbear thee from *meddling with* God, who *is* with me, that he destroy thee not.

22 Nevertheless Josiah would not turn his face from him, but ¹disguised himself, that he might fight with him, and hearkened not unto the words of Necho ᵐfrom the mouth of God, and came to fight in the valley of Megiddo.

A. M. 3394
B. C. 610
An. Olymp.
XLII. 3
Anno Urbis
Conditæ 144

23 And the archers shot at King Josiah; and the king said to his servants, Have me away; for I am sore ⁿwounded.

24 ᵒHis servants therefore took him out of that chariot, and put him in the second chariot that he had; and they brought him to Jerusalem, and he died, and was buried ᵖin *one* of the sepulchres of his fathers. And �q all Judah and Jerusalem mourned for Josiah.

25 And Jeremiah ʳlamented for Josiah: and ˢall the singing men and the singing women spake of Josiah in their lamentations to this day, ᵗand made them an ordinance in Israel: and, behold, they *are* written in the lamentations.

26 Now the rest of the acts of Josiah, and his ᵘgoodness, according to *that which was* written in the law of the LORD,

27 And his deeds, first and last, behold, they *are* written in the book of the kings of Israel and Judah.

ᵉHeb. *found*——ᶠExod. xii. 15; xiii. 6; chap. xxx. 32
ᵍ2 Kings xxiii. 22, 23——ʰ2 Kings xxiii. 29; Jer. xlvi. 2;
1 Esd. i. 25——ⁱHeb. *house*——ᵏHeb. *the house of my war*——ˡSo 1 Kings xxii. 34——ᵐ1 Esd. i. 28

ⁿHeb. *made sick;* 1 Kings xxii. 34——ᵒ2 Kings xxiii.
30——ᵖOr, *among the sepulchres*——qZech. xii. 11
ʳLam. iv. 20——ˢSee Matt. ix. 23——ᵗJer. xxii. 20
ᵘHeb. *kindnesses*

---

and the *Levites* flayed them, and made them ready for dressing.

Verse 18. *There was no passover like to that*] "That which distinguished this passover from all the former was," says Calmet, "the great liberality of Josiah, who distributed to his people a greater number of victims than either David or Solomon had done."

Verse 20. *Necho king of Egypt*] *Pharaoh the lame,* says the *Targum.*

Verse 21. *God commanded me to make haste*] The *Targum* gives a curious turn to this and the following verse: "My idol commanded me to make haste; refrain therefore from me and my idol which is with me, that he betray thee not. When he heard him mention his idol, he would not go back; and he hearkened not unto the words of Necho, which he spake concerning his idol." Here is the rabbinical *excuse* for the conduct of Josiah.

Verse 24. *The second chariot*] Perhaps this means no more than that they took Josiah out of his own chariot and put him into another, either for *secrecy,* or because his own had been *disabled.* The chariot into which he was put might have been that of the *officer* or *aid-de-camp* who attended his master to the war. See the note on 2 Kings xxii. 20.

Verse 25. *Behold, they* are *written in the lamentations.*] The Hebrews had *poetical com-*

positions for all great and important events, *military* songs, songs of *triumph, epithalamia* or *marriage odes, funeral elegies,* &c. Several of these are preserved in different parts of the historical books of Scripture; and these were generally made by *prophets* or *inspired* men. That composed on the tragical end of this good king by Jeremiah is *now* lost. The *Targum* says, "Jeremiah bewailed Josiah with a great lamentation; and all the chiefs and matrons sing these lamentations concerning Josiah to the present day, and it was a statute in Israel annually to bewail Josiah. Behold, these are written in the book of Lamentations, which Baruch wrote down from the mouth of Jeremiah."

Verse 27. *And his deeds, first and last*] "The former things which he did in his childhood, and the latter things which he did in his youth; and all the judgments which he pronounced from his *eighth* year, when he came to the kingdom, to his *eighteenth,* when he was grown up, and began to repair the sanctuary of the LORD; and all that he brought of his substance to the hand of judgment, purging both the house of Israel and Judah from all uncleanness; behold, they are written in the book of the Kings of the house of Israel, and of the house of Judah."— *Targum.* These general histories are lost; but in the books of *Kings* and *Chronicles* we have the leading facts.

CHAPTER XXXVI

Jehoahaz made king on the death of his father Josiah, and reigns only three months, 1, 2.   He is dethroned by the king of Egypt, and Jehoiakim his brother made king in his stead, who reigns wickedly eleven years, and is dethroned and led captive to Babylon by Nebuchadnezzar, 3–8.   Jehoiachin is made king in his stead, and reigns wickedly three months and ten days, and is also led captive to Babylon, 9, 10.   Zedekiah begins to reign, and reigns wickedly eleven years, 11, 12.   He rebels against Nebuchadnezzar, and he and his people cast all the fear of God behind their backs; the wrath of God comes upon them to the uttermost; their temple is destroyed; and the whole nation is subjugated, and led into captivity, 13–21.   Cyrus, king of Persia, makes a proclamation to rebuild the temple of the Lord, 22, 23.

A. M. 3394
B. C. 610
An. Olymp.
XLII. 3
Anno Urbis
Conditæ 144

THEN [a]the people of the land took Jehoahaz the son of Josiah, and made him king in his father's stead in Jerusalem.

2 Jehoahaz *was* twenty and three years old when he began to reign, and he reigned three months in Jerusalem.

3 And the king of Egypt [b]put him down at Jerusalem, [c]and [d]condemned the land in a hundred talents of silver and a talent of gold.

4 And the king of Egypt made Eliakim his brother king over Judah and Jerusalem, and turned his name to Jehoiakim. And Necho took Jehoahaz his brother, and carried him to Egypt.

A.M.3394–3405
B. C. 610–599
An. Olymp.
XLII. 3
—XLV. 2

5 [e]Jehoiakim *was* twenty and five years old when he began to reign, and he reigned eleven years in Jerusalem: and he did *that which was* evil in the sight of the Lord his God.

A. M. 3397
B. C. 607
An. Olymp.
XLIII 2
Anno Urbis
Conditæ 147

6 [f]Against him came up Nebuchadnezzar king of Babylon, and bound him in [g]fetters to [h]carry him to Babylon.

A. M. 3398
B. C. 606
An. Olymp.
XLIII. 3
Anno Urbis
Conditæ 148

7 [i]Nebuchadnezzar also carried off the vessels of the house of the Lord to Babylon, and put them in his temple at Babylon.

8 Now the rest of the acts of Jehoiakim, and his abominations, which he did, and that which was found in him, behold, they *are* written in the book of the kings of Israel and Judah: and [k]Jehoiachin his son reigned in his stead.

A.M.3394–3405
B. C. 610–599
An. Olymp.
XLII. 3
—XLV. 2

9 [l]Jehoiachin *was* eight years old when he began to reign, and he reigned three months and ten days in Jerusalem; and he did *that which was* evil in the sight of the Lord.

A. M. 3405
B. C. 599
An. Olymp.
XLV. 2
Anno Urbis
Conditæ 155

10 And [m]when the year was expired, [n]King Nebuchadnezzar sent, and brought him to Babylon, [o]with the [p]goodly vessels of the house of the Lord, and made [q]Zedekiah [r]his brother king over Judah and Jerusalem.

11 [s]Zedekiah *was* one and twenty years old when he began to reign, and reigned eleven years in Jerusalem.

A.M.3405–3416
B. C. 599–588
An. Olymp.
XLV. 2
—XLVIII. 1

12 And he did *that which was* evil in the sight of the Lord his God, *and* humbled not himself before Jeremiah the prophet *speaking* from the mouth of the Lord.

13 And [t]he also rebelled against King Nebuchadnezzar, who had made him swear by God: but he [u]stiffened his neck, and hard-

---

[a]2 Kings xxiii. 30, &c.; 1 Esd. i. 34, &c.——[b]Heb. *removed him*——[c]1 Esd. i. 36——[d]Hebrew, *mulcted* [e]2 Kings xxiii. 36, 37——[f]2 Kings xxiv. 1——[g]Or, *chains:* foretold, Hab. i. 6——[h]See 2 Kings xxiv. 6; Jeremiah xxii. 18, 19; xxxvi. 30——[i]2 Kings xxiv. 13; Daniel i. 1, 2; v. 2——[k]Or, *Jeconiah,* 1 Chronicles

iii. 16; Or, *Coniah,* Jer. xxii. 24——[l]2 Kings xxiv. 8 [m]Heb. *at the return of the year*——[n]2 Kings xxiv. 10–17 [o]Dan. i. 1, 2; v. 2——[p]Heb. *vessels of desire*——[q]Or, *Mattaniah his father's brother,* 2 Kings xxiv. 17——[r]Jer. xxxvii. 1——[s]2 Kings xxiv. 18; Jer. lii. 1, &c.——[t]Jer. lii. 3; Ezek. xvii. 15, 18——[u]2 Kings xvii. 14

NOTES ON CHAP. XXXVI

Verse 1. *Took Jehoahaz*] It seems that after Necho had discomfited Josiah, he proceeded immediately against *Charchemish,* and in the interim, Josiah dying of his wounds, the people made his son king.

Verse 3. *The king of Egypt put him down*] He now considered Judah to be *conquered,* and *tributary* to him and because the people had set up Jehoahaz without his consent, he dethroned him, and put his brother in his place, perhaps for no other reason but to show his supremacy. For other particulars, see the notes on 2 Kings xxiii. 31-35.

Verse 6. *Came up Nebuchadnezzar*] See the

notes on 2 Kings xxiv. 1. Archbishop *Usher* believes that Jehoiakim remained *three* years after this tributary to the Chaldeans, and that it is from this period that the *seventy years'* captivity, predicted by Jeremiah, is to be reckoned.

Verse 9. *Jehoiachin was eight*] See on 2 Kings xxiv.

Verse 10. *Made Zedekiah—king*] His name was at first *Mattaniah,* but the king of Babylon changed it to *Zedekiah.* See 2 Kings xxiv. 17, and the notes there.

Verse 12. *Did that which was evil*] Was there ever such a set of weak, infatuated men as the Jewish kings in general? They had the

A.M.3405-3416 B. C. 599-588 An. Olymp. XLV. 2 —XLVIII. 1

ened his heart from turning unto the LORD God of Israel.

14 Moreover all the chief of the priests, and the people, transgressed very much after all the abominations of the heathen; and polluted the house of the LORD, which he had hallowed in Jerusalem.

15 [v]And the LORD God of their fathers sent to them [w]by his messengers, rising up [x]betimes, and sending; because he had compassion on his people, and on his dwelling-place:

16 [y]But they mocked the messengers of God, and [z]despised his words, and [a]misused his prophets, until the [b]wrath of the LORD arose against his people, till *there was* no [c]remedy.

A.M.3414-3416 B. C. 590-588 An. Olymp. XLVII. 3 —XLVIII. 1

17 [d]Therefore he brought upon them the king of the Chaldees, who [e]slew their young men with the sword in the house of their sanctuary, and had no compassion upon young man or maiden, old man, or him that stooped for age: he gave *them* all into his hand.

A. M. 3416 B. C. 588 An. Olymp. XLVIII. 1 Anno Urbis Conditæ 166

18 [f]And all the vessels of the house of God, great and small, and the treasures of the house of the LORD, and the treasures of the king, and of his princes; all *these* he brought to Babylon.

19 [g]And they burnt the house of God, and brake down the wall of Jerusalem, and burnt all the palaces thereof with fire, and destroyed all the goodly vessels thereof.

A. M. 3416 B. C. 588 An. Olymp. XLVIII. 1 Anno Urbis Conditæ 166

A.M.3416-3468 B. C. 588-536 An. Olymp. XLVIII. 1 —LXI. 1

20 And [h]them [i]that had escaped from the sword carried he away to Babylon; [k]where they were servants to him and his sons until the reign of the kingdom of Persia:

A.M.3398-3468 B. C. 606-536 An. Olymp. XLIII. 3 —LXI. 1

21 To fulfil the word of the LORD by the mouth of [l]Jeremiah, until the land [m]had enjoyed her Sabbaths; *for* as long as she lay desolate [n]she kept Sabbath, to fulfil three score and ten years.

A. M. 3468 B. C. 536 An. Olymp. LXI. 1 Anno Urbis Conditæ 218

22 [o]Now in the first year of Cyrus king of Persia, that the word of the LORD *spoken* by the mouth of [p]Jeremiah might be accomplished, the LORD stirred up the spirit of [q]Cyrus king of Persia, that he made a proclamation throughout all his kingdom, and *put it* also in writing, saying,

23 [r]Thus saith Cyrus king of Persia, All the kingdoms of the earth hath the LORD God of heaven given me; and he hath charged me to build him a house in Jerusalem, which *is* in Judah. Who *is there* among you of all his people? The LORD his God *be* with him, and let him go up.

[v]Jer. xxv. 3, 4; xxxv. 15; xliv. 4——[w]Heb. *by the hand of his messengers*——[x]That is, *continually and carefully* [y]Jer. v. 12, 13——[z]Prov. i. 25, 30——[a]Jer. xxxii. 3; xxxviii. 6; Matt. xxiii. 34——[b]Psa. lxxiv. 1; lxxix. 5 [c]Heb. *healing*——[d]Deut. xxviii. 49; 2 Kings xxv. 1, &c.; Ezra ix. 7——[e]Psa. lxxiv. 20; lxxix. 2, 3——[f]2 Kings xxv. 13, &c.

[g]2 Kings xxv. 9; Psa. lxxiv. 6, 7; lxxix. 1, 7——[h]Heb. *the remainder from the sword*——[i]2 Kings xxv. 11 [k]Jer. xxvii. 7——[l]Jeremiah xxv. 9, 11, 12; xxvi. 6, 7; xxix. 10——[m]Leviticus xxvi. 34, 35, 43; Daniel ix. 2 [n]Leviticus xxv. 4, 5——[o]Ezra i. 1——[p]Jeremiah xxv. 12, 13; xxix. 10; xxxiii. 10, 11, 14——[q]Isa. xliv. 28 [r]Ezra i. 2, 3

fullest evidence that they were only *deputies* to God Almighty, and that they could not expect to retain the throne any longer than they were faithful to their Lord; and yet with all this conviction they lived wickedly, and endeavoured to establish *idolatry* in the place of the worship of their Maker! After bearing with them long, the Divine mercy gave them up, as their case was utterly hopeless. *They sinned till there was* no *remedy.*

Verse 19. *They burnt the house of God*] Here was an end to the *temple;* the most superb and costly edifice ever erected by man.

Brake down the wall of Jerusalem] So it ceased to be a *fortified* city.

Burnt all the palaces] So it was no longer a *dwelling-place* for *kings* or *great* men.

Destroyed all the goodly vessels] Beat up all the silver and gold into masses, keeping only a few of the finest in their own shape. See ver. 18.

Verse 21. *To fulfil the word of the Lord*] See Jer. xxv. 9, 12, xxvi. 6, 7, xxix. 12. For the miserable death of Zedekiah, see 2 Kings xxv. 4, &c.

Verse 22. *Now in the first year of Cyrus*] This and the following verse are supposed to have been written by *mistake* from the *book of Ezra,* which begins in the same way. The book of the *Chronicles,* properly speaking, does close with the *twenty-first verse,* as then the Babylonish captivity *commences:* and these *two verses* speak of the transactions of a period *seventy years after.* This was in the first year of the reign of Cyrus over the *empire of the East* which is reckoned to be A. M. 3468. But he was king of *Persia* from the year 3444 or 3445. See *Calmet* and *Usher.*

Verse 23. *The Lord his God* be *with him*] "Let the WORD of the Lord be his helper, and let him go up."—*Targum.* See the notes on the beginning of Ezra.

THUS ends the history of a people the most fickle, the most ungrateful, and perhaps on the whole the most sinful, that ever existed on the face of the earth. But what a display does all this give of the power, justice, mercy, and long-suffering of the Lord! There was no people like this people, and no God like their God.

MASORETIC NOTES

The *sum* of the *verses* in both books of Chronicles is 1656. *Middle* verse, 1 Chron. xxvii. 25. Its Masoretic sections, *twenty-five*.

Having made particular remarks on every thing which I judged of importance in these and the preceding historical books, and in the course of this work having often found the want of a chronological list of the kings of Israel and Judah, in the consecutive order of their reigns; for the reader's information I have brought all the facts into a synopsis or general view, so that he may see at once the contemporary reigns in those two kingdoms, as well as the leading facts by which their reigns were distinguished. In this table will be seen, at one view, the year of the world; the year before Christ; the year before and after the First Olympiad; the year before and from the building of Rome; and under them the Jewish history, from its first kings till the time in which its regal state was entirely abolished, and both kingdoms led into captivity, never more to arise to any political consequence till they acknowledge the Lion of the tribe of Judah, and take Jesus the Christ, the son and only legitimate heir of David, for their Saviour and their Lord. I hope that the table which is here subjoined will be found, in every point of view, both interesting and instructive.

A. CLARKE.

Millbrook, December 7, 1819.

Finished correcting the two books of Chronicles, March 28th, 1828.—A. CLARKE.

A CHRONOLOGICAL LIST OF THE KINGS OF ISRAEL AND JUDAH

IN THE CONSECUTIVE ORDER OF THEIR REIGNS

*From their commencement to the destruction of the former by the Assyrians; and of the
latter by the Babylonians*

REGAL STATE OF JUDEA BEFORE THE DIVISION

SAUL reigned 40 years.—DAVID reigned 40 years.—SOLOMON reigned 40 years

ISRAEL AND JUDAH AFTER THE DIVISION OF THE TWELVE TRIBES

Year of the world	Year before Christ	Year before the first Olymp.	Year before the building of Rome		KINGDOM OF ISRAEL		KINGDOM OF JUDAH With the contemporary events of the Heathen nations
3029	975	199	222	1	JEROBOAM. Reigned 22 years.	1	REHOBOAM. Reigned 17 years. For-
3030	974	198	221	2	The disobedient prophet slain by a lion.	2	saking the counsel of the old men, ten
3031	973	197	220	3		3	tribes revolt from under his government;
3032	972	196	219	4	Jehoiadah the priest born about this time.	4	and are formed into a distinct kingdom.
3033	971	195	218	5	He lived in eight Jewish reigns, viz.,	5	Shishak king of Egypt (thought by Sir
3034	970	194	217	6	those of Rehoboam, Abijah, Asa, Jehosh-	6	Isaac Newton to have been the same
3035	969	193	216	7	aphat, Jehoram, Ahaziah, Athaliah, and	7	with the famous Sesostris) invades Ju-
3036	968	192	215	8	Joash.	8	dea and takes away the shields of gold
3037	967	191	214	9		9	out of the temple.
3038	966	190	213	10		10	
3039	965	189	212	11		11	
3040	964	188	211	12	Capys Sylvius succeeds Capetus in the	12	
3041	963	187	210	13	kingdom of Alba, and reigned 28 years.	13	
3042	962	186	209	14	The commencement of this reign hap-	14	
3043	961	185	208	15	pened (according to Dionysius of Hali-	15	
3044	960	184	207	16	carnassus) in the 221st year from the	16	
3045	959	183	206	17	destruction of Troy.	17	
3046	958	182	205	18			
3047	957	181	204	19		1	ABIJAH or ABIJAM. Reigned 3 years.
3048	956	180	203	20	Death of Abijah, the son of Jeroboam.	2	The king of Judah obtains a great victory
3049	955	179	202	21		3	over Jeroboam, and takes Beth-el, &c.
3050	954	178	201	22	1 NADAB. Reigned 2 years.	1	ASA. Reigned 41 years.
3051	953	177	200	2	1 BAASHA. Reigned 24 years.	2	
3052	952	176	199	2	About this time flourished the prophets	3	
3053	951	175	198	3	Jehu, Hanani, and Azariah. Baasha be-	4	Phorbas succeeds Thersippus as perpetual
3054	950	174	197	4	gins his reign by extirpating the whole	5	archon of the Athenians, and rules 31
3055	949	173	196	5	house of Jeroboam. The *dynasty of Jero-*	6	years.
3056	948	172	195	6	*boam* lasted not quite 24 years, and is	7	Birth of Jehoshaphat, who was afterwards
3057	947	171	194	7	followed by that of Baasha, which con-	8	king of Judah.
3058	946	170	193	8	tinues till the death of Elah, a period of	9	
3059	945	169	192	9	not quite 26 years.	10	
3060	944	168	191	10		11	
3061	943	167	190	11		12	
3062	942	166	189	12		13	
3063	941	165	188	13		14	
3064	940	164	187	14		15	Zerah, with an immense host of Ethiopi-
3065	939	163	186	15		16	ans and Lubims, invades Judea. Asa
3066	938	162	185	16		17	overcomes him in the valley of Zepha-
3067	937	161	184	17		18	thah at Mareshah, abolishes idolatry
3068	936	160	183	18	Calpetus Sylvius succeeds Capys in the	19	out of Judea, and enjoys a peace for *ten*
3069	935	159	182	19	kingdom of Alba, in the 249th year from	20	years. The number of men in Zerah's
3070	934	158	181	20	the destruction of Troy. He is named,	21	army is stated to have amounted to *a*
3071	933	157	180	21	by Eusebius, Carpetus Sylvius.	22	*million*, 2 Chron. xiv. 9.
3072	932	156	179	22		23	
3073	931	155	178	23	[7 days.	24	
3074	930	154	177	24	1 ELAH. Reigned 2 years. ZIMRI reigned	25	
3075	929	153	176	2	1 OMRI and TIBNI reign together about	26	Baasha comes up against Judah, and be-
3076	928	152	175	2	five years. Commencement of the *third*	27	gins to build Ramah, but is diverted from
3077	927	151	174	3	*dynasty* by the accession of Omri to the	28	his purpose by the policy of Asa. This
3078	926	150	173	4	throne.	29	is stated in 2 Chron. xvi. 1, to have
3079	925	149	172	5	TIBNI dying, OMRI reigns alone about	30	been in the 36th year of Asa; but there
3080	924	148	171	6	7 years.	31	is most manifestly a corruption in the
3081	923	147	170	7	Tiberinus Sylvius succeeds his father Cal-	32	sacred text; see on 1 Kings xv. 16.
3082	922	146	169	8	petus in the kingdom of Alba, and reigned	33	
3083	921	145	168	9	8 years. The river Tiber was so named	34	
3084	920	144	167	10	from this king.	35	Megacles succeeds Phorbas in the perpet-
3085	919	143	166	11		36	ual archonship of the Athenians, and
						37	rules 30 years.

Chronological account of the kings of Israel and Judah

Year of the world	Year before Christ	Year before the first Olymp.	Year before the building of Rome		KINGDOM OF ISRAEL With the contemporary		KINGDOM OF JUDAH events of Heathen nations
3086	918	142	165	12	1 AHAB. Reigned 22 years. In this	38	
3087	917	141	164	2	reign Jericho was rebuilt by Hiel, the	39	Asa begins to be diseased in his feet, and
3088	916	140	163	3	Beth-elite.	40	dies in the 41st year of his reign.
3089	915	139	162	4	About this time Agrippa Sylvius succeeds	41	
3090	914	138	161	5	Tiberinus Sylvius in the kingdom of	1	JEHOSHAPHAT. Reigned 25 years.
3091	913	137	160	6	Alba, and reigned 40 years.	2	
3092	912	136	159	7		3	The king of Judah sends Levites with the
3093	911	135	158	8		4	princes throughout his realm to instruct
3094	910	134	157	9	Commencement of the three years and six	5	the people in the law of the Lord.
3095	909	133	156	10	months' drought foretold by Elijah.	6	
3096	908	132	155	11		7	
3097	907	131	154	12	The widow's son raised to life.	8	Polydectus (of the family of the Proclidæ)
3098	906	130	153	13	The prophets of Baal slain by Elijah, at	9	succeeds Eunomus in the throne of
3099	905	129	152	14	the brook Kishon. Termination of the	10	Lacedæmon, and reigned 9 years.
3100	904	128	151	15	long drought. Great fall of rain in the	11	
3101	903	127	150	16	land of Israel.	12	
3102	902	126	149	17		13	
3103	901	125	148	18	The Syrians defeated by Ahab.	14	
3104	900	124	147	19	The Syrians again defeated by Ahab.	15	
3105	899	123	146	20	Naboth stoned to death.	16	[Spartans.
3106	898	122	145	21		17	Lycurgus begins his reign over the
3107	897	121	144	22	1 AHAZIAH. Reigned two years.	18	Jehoshaphat joins Ahab against the Syri-
3108	896	120	143	2	1 JORAM or JEHORAM. Reigned 12	19	ans. Ahab is slain at the siege of Ra-
3109	895	119	142	2	years. Assumption of Elijah in the first	20	moth-gilead, agreeably to the prophecy
3110	894	118	141	3	year of this reign. Elisha succeeds him	21	of Micaiah, and the dogs lick up his
3111	893	117	140	4	in the prophetic office.	22	blood, 1 Kings xxii. 2-38.
3112	892	116	139	5		23	1 JEHORAM associated with his father
3113	891	115	138	6	Diognetus succeeds Megacles in the per-	24	2 in the government, and reigns 8 years.
3114	890	114	137	7	petual archonship of the Athenians, and	25	3
3115	889	113	136	8	rules 28 years.	4	JEHORAM. Reigned 5 years alone.
3116	888	112	135	9		5	
3117	887	111	134	10		6	
3118	886	110	133	11		7	
3119	885	109	132	12		8	1 AHAZIAH. Reigned 1 year.
3120	884	108	131	1	JEHU. Reigned 28 years. End of the	1	ATHALIAH usurps the throne, and re-
3121	883	107	130	2	dynasty of Omri, after it had rules over	2	tains it six years.
3122	882	106	129	3	Israel 46 years. Jehu began his reign	3	
3123	881	105	128	4	by slaying all the posterity of Ahab, and	4	
3124	880	104	127	5	destroying the worshippers of Baal.	5	
3125	879	103	126	6	About this time Lycurgus, 42 years of	6	
3126	878	102	125	7	age, establishes his laws at Lacedæmon;	1	JOASH. Reigned 40 years. He main-
3127	877	101	124	8	and, together with Iphitus and Cleos-	2	tains the purity of the Jewish worship
3128	876	100	123	9	thenes, restores the Olympic games at	3	during the life of Jehoiada, the high
3129	875	99	122	10	Elis, about 108 years before the era	4	priest. In the fourth year of this reign
3130	874	98	121	11	usually called the first Olympiad. Awful	5	Alladius Sylvius succeeds Agrippa in
3131	873	97	120	12	death of Jezebel, the wife of Ahab.	6	the kingdom of Alba, and reigns 19
3132	872	96	119	13		7	years. This monarch is called Romu-
3133	871	95	118	14		8	lus Sylvius.
3134	870	94	117	15		9	
3135	869	93	116	16	Phidon, king of Argos, is supposed to have	10	
3136	868	92	115	17	invented scales and measures and coined	11	
3137	867	91	114	18	silver at Ægina. Carthage built by Dido.	12	
3138	866	90	113	19		13	
3139	865	89	112	20		14	
3140	864	88	111	21	[chonship of the Athenians.	15	
3141	863	87	110	22	Phereclus succeeds to the perpetual ar-	16	Birth of Amaziah, who was afterwards
3142	862	86	109	23	The Ninevites repent at the preaching of	17	king of Judah.
3143	861	85	108	24	Jonah the prophet. There are a few	18	
3144	860	84	107	25	years of uncertainty in the date of this	19	
3145	859	83	106	26	event. We here follow the margin of	20	
3146	858	82	105	27	our English Bibles.	21	
3147	857	81	104	28		22	
3148	856	80	103	1	JEHOAHAZ. Reigned 17 years. About the	23	Joash issues a mandate that the breaches
3149	855	79	102	2	commencement of this reign Aventinus	24	of the temple be repaired, and gives the
3150	854	78	101	3	Sylvius is supposed to have succeeded	25	charge thereof to Jehoiada the high
3151	853	77	100	4	Alladius Sylvius in the kingdom of Alba.	26	priest.
3152	852	76	99	5	He reigned 37 years, according to Diony-	27	
3153	851	75	98	6	sius of Halicarnassus, and was succeeded	28	
3154	850	74	97	7	by Procas Sylvius, who reigned 23 years.	29	

Year of the world	Year before Christ	Year before the first Olymp.	Year before the building of Rome	KINGDOM OF ISRAEL		KINGDOM OF JUDAH	
						With the contemporary events of Heathen nations	
				JEHOAHAZ.		JOASH.	
3155	849	73	96	8		30	
3156	848	72	95	9		31	
3157	847	71	94	10		32	
3158	846	70	93	11		33	
3159	845	69	92	12		34	
3160	844	68	91	13 Ariphron succeeds Phereclus in the per-		35	
3161	843	67	90	14 petual archonship of the Athenians.		36	
3162	842	66	89	15		37 Jehoiada, the high priest, dies at the age	
3163	841	65	88	16 1 JEHOASH reigns in consort with his		38 of 130.	
3164	840	64	87	17 2 father.		39 Zechariah, the priest, stoned to death.	
3165	839	63	86	3 Jehoash reigns alone. Hazael, king of		40 1 AMAZIAH. Reigned 29 years. Soon	
3166	838	62	85	4 Syria, dies about this time, and is suc-		2 after the commencement of his reign	
3167	837	61	84	5 ceeded by his son Ben-hadad. Elisha		3 he slew all his servants who had killed	
3168	836	60	83	6 dies in the second year of Ben-hadad,		4 his father.	
3169	835	59	82	7 king of Syria, after having been invested		5	
3170	834	58	81	8 with the prophetic office nearly 60		6	
3171	833	57	80	9 years.		7	
3172	832	56	79	10		8	
3173	831	55	78	11		9	
3174	830	54	77	12		10	
3175	829	53	76	13		11	
3176	828	52	75	14		12	
3177	827	51	74	15		13 Ten thousand of the children of Seir slain	
3178	826	50	73	16		14 by Amaziah in the Valley of Salt; and	
3179	825	49	72	1 JEROBOAM II. Reigned 41 years.		15 ten thousand precipitated from the top	
3180	824	48	71	2 Thespieus succeeds Ariphron in the gov-		16 of a rock, and dashed to pieces. Ama-	
3181	823	47	70	3 ernment of Athens.		17 ziah, proud of his victory over the	
3182	822	46	69	4		18 Edomites, provokes the Israelitish king	
3183	821	45	68	5		19 to battle. The following year Jehoash	
3184	820	44	67	6 The fall of the Assyrian empire by the		20 overcomes him, takes him prisoner,	
3185	819	43	66	7 death of Sardanapalus is supposed to		21 breaks down four hundred cubits of the	
3186	818	42	65	8 have taken place about this time. Ar-		22 wall of Jerusalem, and having spoiled	
3187	817	41	64	9 baces founds the empire of the Medes		23 the temple and the king's house of a	
3188	816	40	63	10 upon the ruins of the Assyrian empire.		24 vast treasure, returns to Samaria.	
3189	815	39	62	11		25	
3190	814	38	61	12 Caranus founds the kingdom of Macedon,		26	
3191	813	37	60	13 and reigns 28 years. This kingdom con-		27	
3192	812	36	59	14 tinued to the battle of Pydna, a period		28	
3193	811	35	58	15 of 646 years.		29	
3194	810	34	57	16		1 UZZIAH. Reigned 52 years. He is vic-	
3195	809	33	56	17 Charilaus, the successor of Lycurgus, dy-		2 torious over the Philistines, Arabians,	
3196	808	32	55	18 ing after a reign of 64 years, Nican-		3 and Mehunims. His standing army	
3197	807	31	54	19 der succeeds him in the kingdom of		4 consisted of 307,500 men. In this	
3198	806	30	53	20 Lacedæmon, and reigns 39 years.		5 reign lived the prophets Amos and	
3199	805	29	52	21		6 Hosea.	
3200	804	28	51	22		7	
3201	803	27	50	23		8	
3202	802	26	49	24		9	
3203	801	25	48	25		10	
3204	800	24	47	26		11	
3205	799	23	46	27		12	
3206	798	22	45	28		13 [government of the Athenians.	
3207	797	21	44	29 Ardysus begins his reign over Lydia, and		14 Agamestor succeeds Thespieus in the	
3208	796	20	43	30 rules 36 years.		15 Amulius Sylvius and Numitor succeed	
3209	795	19	42	31		16 Procas in the kingdom of Alba, the	
3210	794	18	41	32		17 former of whom reigned 44 years.	
3211	793	17	40	33		18 Numitor reigned alone two years, and	
3212	792	16	39	34 Sosarmus is supposed to have succeeded		19 was their last king. He died about	
3213	791	15	38	35 Arbaces in the government of the Medes		20 751 B. C.	
3214	790	14	37	36 about this time: but the chronology		21	
3215	789	13	36	37 of this event is very uncertain.		22	
3216	788	12	35	38 He is succeeded 30 years after by Me-		23	
3217	787	11	34	39 didus.		24	
3218	786	10	33	40 The triremes first invented by the Corin-		25 Cœnus, the second king of Macedon, be-	
3219	785	9	32	41 thians.		26 gins his reign.	
3220	784	8	31			27	
3221	783	7	30	After Jeroboam's death an interregnum of		28 Birth of Jotham, who was afterwards	
3222	782	6	29	11 years and a half is supposed to		29 king of Judah.	

Year of the world	Year before Christ	Year before the first Olymp.	Year before the building of Rome	Kingdom of the Romans	KINGDOM OF ISRAEL	KINGDOM OF JUDAH — With the contemporary events of Heathen nations
					JEROBOAM II.	**UZZIAH.**
3223	781	5	28		have taken place; for Zachariah,	30
3224	780	4	27		the son of Jeroboam, did not	31
3225	779	3	26		commence his reign till the 38th	32 The monarchial government
3226	778	2	25		year of Azariah, or Uzziah, king	33 abolished at Corinth, and the
3227	777	1	24		of Judah. See 2 Kings xv. 8.	34 Prytanes elected. Two years
		Era of the Olympiads.				
3228	776	I. 1	23		The *fourth dynasty* of Israelitish	35 after, Æschylus succeeds Aga-
3229	775	2	22		monarchs, viz., that of Jehu, is	36 mestor in the perpetual archon-
3230	774	3	21		terminated by the death of Za-	37 ship of the Athenians.
3231	773	4	20		chariah, B. C. 773.	38 Thurimas succeeds to the throne
3232	772	II. 1	19		ZACHARIAH. Reigned 6 m'ths.	39 of Macedon, and reigns 45
3233	771	2	18		1 SHALLUM. Reigned 1 month.	40 years.
3234	770	3	17		2 MENAHEM. Reigned 10 years.	41 Theopompus succeeds Nicander
3235	769	4	16		3 Here begins the *sixth dynasty* of	42 in the kingdom of Lacedæmon,
3236	768	III. 1	15		4 Israelitish kings, that of Shallum	43 and reigns 47 years.
3237	767	2	14		5 subsisting only a single month.	44
3238	766	3	13		6	45
3239	765	4	12		7	46 Uzziah, attempting to burn in-
3240	764	IV. 1	11		8	47 cense upon the altar of incense
3241	763	2	10		9	48 in the temple, is smitten with
3242	762	3	9		10	49 the leprosy.
3243	761	4	8		1 PEKAHIAH. Reigned 2 years.	50 Alyattes succeeds to the Lydian
3244	760	V. 1	7		2	51 throne.
3245	759	2	6		1 PEKAH. Reigned 20 years.	52 Isaiah begins to prophesy.
3246	758	3	5		2 Here begins the *seventh Israeli-*	1 JOTHAM. Reigned 16 years.
3247	757	4	4		3 *tish dynasty*, that of Menahem	2 This king overcomes the Am-
3248	756	VI. 1	3		4 having subsisted twelve years.	3 monites, whom he compels to
3249	755	2	2		5	4 pay tribute.
3250	754	3	1		6	5 Alcmæon, the last perpetual ar-
			A.U.C.			
3251	753	4	1	1	7 Rome built on the 20th of April	6 chon, begins his administration,
3252	752	VII. 1	2	2	8 of this year according to Varro.	7 and rules two years; after whom
3253	751	2	3	3	9	8 decennial archons are appointed,
3254	750	3	4	4	10 The rape of the Sabines.	9 Charops being first.
3255	749	4	5	5	11	10 Birth of Hezekiah, who succeeded
3256	748	VIII. 1	6	6	12	11 his father Ahaz in the kingdom
3257	747	2	7	7	13 Meles succeeds Alyattes in the	12 of Judah.
3258	746	3	8	8	14 Lydian throne.	13 Commencement of the era of
3259	745	4	9	9	15	14 Nabonassar, king of Babylon.
3260	744	IX. 1	10	10	16	15
3261	743	2	11	11	17 The first Messenian war begins;	16
3262	742	3	12	12	18 and continues 19 years, to the	1 AHAZ. Reigned 16 years. In the
3263	741	4	13	13	19 taking of Ithome.	2 first year of this reign Æsimedes
3264	740	X. 1	14	14	20 Pekah slain in the 4th year of Ahaz	3 succeeds Charops in the decen-
3265	739	2	15	15	by Hoshea, the son of Elah.	4 nial archonship of the Athenians.
3266	738	3	16	16	An anarchy is supposed to have	5 Æsimedes is succeeded by Clidi-
3267	737	4	17	17	succeeded for some years, as	6 cus, and ten years after Clidicus
3268	736	XI. 1	18	18	Hoshea is said not to have com-	7 is succeeded by Hippomenes.
3269	735	2	19	19	menced his reign before the 12th	8 Candaules succeeds Meles in the
3270	734	3	20	20	year of Ahaz, 2 Kings xvii. 1.	9 Lydian throne; who 17 years
3271	733	4	21	21	The beginning of Hoshea's reign	10 after is succeeded by Gyges.
3272	732	XII. 1	22	22	is placed two years later, that	11 Syracuse built by a Corinthian
3273	731	2	23	23	his 9th year may synchronize	12 colony.
3274	730	3	24	24	with Hezekiah's 6th.	13
3275	729	4	25	25	1 HOSHEA. Reigned 9 years.	14 Perdiccas succeeds to the throne
3276	728	XIII. 1	26	26	2 Here begins the *eighth* and *last*	15 of Macedon, and reigns 51 years.
3277	727	2	27	27	3 *dynasty* of Israelitish kings.	16
3278	726	3	28	28	4	1 HEZEKIAH. Reigned 29 years.
3279	725	4	29	29	5	2
3280	724	XIV. 1	30	30	6 Samaria besieged by Shalmane-	3 Zeuxidamus succeeds Theopom-
3281	723	2	31	31	7 ser king of Assyria. End of	4 pus in the throne of Lacedæmon,
3282	722	3	32	32	8 the first Messenian war.	5 and reigns 33 years.
3283	721	4	33	33	9	6 In the sixth year of Hezekiah
3284	720	XV. 1	34	34	7 **HEZEKIAH.**	(which was the 9th year of Ho-
3285	719	2	35	35	8 maneser, king of Assyria, took Samaria, carried the Israelites into	shea, the son of Elah) Shal-
3286	718	3	36	36	9 captivity, and so put an END TO THE KINGDOM OF ISRAEL,	
3287	717	4	37	37	10 254 years after the revolt of the ten tribes from Rehoboam.	

Romulus (Kingdom of the Romans).

Year of the world	Year before Christ	Era of the Olympiads	Year from the building of Rome	Kingdom of the Romans		KINGDOM OF JUDAH With the contemporary events of Heathen nations
3288	716	XVI. 1	38		11	HEZEKIAH.
3289	715	2	39	1	12	[the Medes, and rules 13 years.
3290	714	3	40	2	13	About this time Cerdiccas succeeds Medidus in the government of
3291	713	4	41	3	14	Sennacherib, king of Assyria, comes up against Judah, and takes
3292	712	XVII. 1	42	4	15	several of its fenced cities; but is pacified by a tribute. Hezekiah,
3293	711	2	43	5	16	falling sick, is miraculously restored to health.
3294	710	3	44	6	17	Sennacherib again invading Judea, the whole of the Assyrian army,
3295	709	4	45	7	18	consisting of 185,000 men, is destroyed in one night by an angel
3296	708	XVIII. 1	46	8	19	of the Lord. Birth of Manasseh, who succeeded Hezekiah in the
3297	707	2	47	9	20	kingdom of Judah.
3298	706	3	48	10	21	
3299	705	4	49	11	22	
3300	704	XIX. 1	50	12	23	[rentum by the Parthenians.
3301	703	2	51	13	24	Corcyra built by the Corinthians, four years after the building of Ta-
3302	702	3	52	14	25	Leocrates, the successor of Hippomenes, dying, Apsandras succeeds
3303	701	4	53	15	26	him in the Athenian government.
3304	700	XX. 1	54	16	27	Deioces, governor of the Medes, assumes the title of king, and reigns
3305	699	2	55	17	28	53 years. Ecbatana was built in this reign, according to Herodotus.
3306	698	3	56	18	29	1 MANASSEH. Reigned 55 years. This is the longest reign in the
3307	697	4	57	19	2	Jewish annals.
3308	696	XXI. 1	58	20	3	
3309	695	2	59	21	4	
3310	694	3	60	22	5	
3311	693	4	61	23	6	
3312	692	XXII. 1	62	24	7	Eryxias, the last perpetual archon of the Athenians, begins his ad-
3313	691	2	63	25	8	ministration.
3314	690	3	64	26	9	Anaxidamus succeeds his father Zeuxidamus in the throne of Lace-
3315	689	4	65	27	10	dæmon, and reigned 39 years. He was of the race of the Proclidæ.
3316	688	XXIII. 1	66	28	11	
3317	687	2	67	29	12	
3318	686	3	68	30	13	
3319	685	4	69	31	14	The second Messenian war begins; and continues 14 years to the
3320	684	XXIV. 1	70	32	15	taking of Ira, after a siege of 11 years.
3321	683	2	71	33	16	The government of Athens intrusted to annual archons, Creon being
3322	682	3	72	34	17	the first.
3323	681	4	73	35	18	
3324	680	XXV. 1	74	36	19	Ardysus II. succeeds Gyges in the Lydian throne, and reigns 49 years.
3325	679	2	75	37	20	
3326	678	3	76	38	21	Argæus, king of Macedon, begins his reign.
3327	677	4	77	39	22	Manasseh, on account of his impiety, is carried into captivity by the
3328	676	XXVI. 1	78	40	23	Assyrians, but upon his repentance, God restores him to his liberty
3329	675	2	79	41	24	and kingdom.
3330	674	3	80	42	25	End of the second Messenian war, which confirmed the Messenians
3331	673	4	81	43	26	under the power of the Lacedæmonians. The Messenians attempted
3332	672	XXVII. 1	82	1	27	a third time to free themselves from the power of Lacedæmon,
3333	671	2	83	2	28	B. C. 465: but it was not till 370 B. C. that the descendants of the
3334	670	3	84	3	29	Messenians finally returned into the Peloponnesus, after a long ban-
3335	669	4	85	4	30	ishment of upwards of 300 years.
3336	668	XXVIII. 1	86	5	31	
3337	667	2	87	6	32	Battle of the Horatii and Curiatii. Death of Metius Suffetius, the
3338	666	3	88	7	33	Alban dictator.
3339	665	4	89	8	34	Alba destroyed, and the inhabitants carried to Rome. Birth of Amon,
3340	664	XXIX. 1	90	9	35	son of Manasseh, king of Judah.
3341	663	2	91	10	36	
3342	662	3	92	11	37	
3343	661	4	93	12	38	
3344	660	XXX. 1	94	13	39	
3345	659	2	95	14	40	Cypselus usurps the government of Corinth, and keeps it for 30 years.
3346	658	3	96	15	41	The following year Byzantium is said to have been built by a
3347	657	4	97	16	42	colony of Argives, or Athenians. Paterculus says it was founded
3348	656	XXXI. 1	98	17	43	by the Milesians; Justin, that it was founded by the Lacedæmonians;
3349	655	2	99	18	44	and Ammianus, that it was founded by the Athenians. Byzantium
3350	654	3	100	19	45	is the same with what was afterwards called Constantinople.
3351	653	4	101	20	46	
3352	652	XXXII. 1	102	21	47	Birth of Pittacus, one of the seven wise men of Greece.
3353	651	2	103	22	48	Archidamus succeeds to the throne of Lacedæmon, and reigns 46
3354	650	3	104	23	49	years.
3355	649	4	105	24	50	Birth of Josiah, who was afterwards king of Judah.
3356	648	XXXIII. 1	106	25	51	

Vertical labels in the Kingdom of the Romans column: *Numa Pompilius*, *Tullus Hostilius*.

Year of the world	Year before Christ	Era of the Olympiads	Year from the building of Rome	Kingdom of the Romans		KINGDOM OF JUDAH With the contemporary events of Heathen nations
						MANASSEH.
3357	647	XXXIII. 2	107	26	52	Phraortes succeeds Deioces in the kingdom of Media. This monarch
3358	646	3	108	27	53	is supposed to be the same with the Arphaxad mentioned in Judith.
3359	645	4	109	28	54	
3360	644	XXXIV. 1	110	29	55	
3361	643	3	111	30	1	AMON. Reigned 2 years.
3362	642	3	112	31	2	[time.
3363	641	4	113	32	1	JOSIAH. Reigned 31 years. Birth of Thales happened about this
3364	640	XXXV. 1	114	1	2	Philip succeeds Argeus in the throne of Macedon, and reigns thirty-
3365	639	2	115	2	3	eight years.
3366	638	3	116	3	4	The celebrated Solon was born about this time. He died B. C. 558,
3367	637	4	117	4	5	at the age of 80.
3368	636	XXXVI. 1	118	5	6	
3369	635	2	119	6	7	
3370	634	3	120	7	8	Josiah (only 16 years of age) begins to manifest great zeal towards
3371	633	4	121	8	9	the pure worship of Jehovah.
3372	632	XXXVII. 1	122	9	10	
3373	631	2	123	10	11	Sadyattes succeeds Ardysus II. in the Lydian throne.
3374	630	3	124	11	12	Josiah commences a thorough reformation in the religion of Judea,
3375	629	4	125	12	13	which is completed in his eighteenth year. Cyrene built by Battus.
3376	628	XXXVIII. 1	126	13	14	
3377	627	2	127	14	15	
3378	626	3	128	15	16	[and Persia, and reigns 40 years.
3379	625	4	129	16	17	Cyaxares, or Cyaraxes, succeeds Phraortes in the kingdom of Media
3380	624	XXXIX. 1	130	17	18	Josiah repairs the temple, destroys the vessels of Baal and Asherah,
3381	623	2	131	18	19	puts down the idolatrous priests, breaks down the houses of the So-
3382	622	3	132	19	20	domites and the high places, defiles Topheth, takes away the horses
3383	621	4	133	20	21	of the sun, destroys Jeroboam's altar, and celebrates a great passover.
3384	620	XL. 1	134	21	22	
3385	619	2	135	22	23	Alyattes II. of the family of the Mermnadæ, and father of the cele-
3386	618	3	136	23	24	brated Crœsus, succeeds to the Lydian throne, and reigns 57 years.
3387	617	4	137	24	25	This king drove the Cimmerians from Asia, and made war against
3388	616	XLI. 1	138	1	26	the Medes. An eclipse of the sun terminated a battle between him
3389	615	2	139	2	27	and Cyaxares. He died when engaged in a war against Miletus.
3390	614	3	140	3	28	
3391	613	4	141	4	29	
3392	612	XLII. 1	142	5	30	
3393	611	2	143	6	31	
3394	610	3	144	7	1	JEHOAHAZ. Reigned 3 months.
3395	609	4	145	8	2	JEHOIAKIM. Reigned 11 years.
3396	608	XLIII. 1	146	9	3	[reign over Babylon.
3397	607	2	147	10	4	Jeremiah foretells the 70 years' captivity. Nebuchadnezzar begins his
3398	606	3	148	11	5	Nineveh taken and destroyed by Cyaxares and his allies.
3399	605	4	149	12	6	Agasicles succeeds to the throne of Lacedæmon, and reigns 41 years.
3400	604	XLIV. 1	150	13	7	The Phœnicians sailed around Africa by order of Necho. The age
3401	603	2	151	14	8	of Arion, Pittacus, Alcæus, &c.
3402	602	3	152	15	9	Æropas succeeds to the throne of Macedon, and reigns 20 years.
3403	601	4	153	16	10	
3404	600	XLV. 1	154	17	11	Birth of Sappho, the celebrated poetess, happened about this time.
3405	599	2	155	18	1	JEHOIACHIN. Reigned 3 months and 10 days.
3406	598	3	156	19	1	ZEDEKIAH. Reigned 11 years. He was the last Jewish king, and
3407	597	4	157	20	2	commenced his reign in the 8th year of Nebuchadnezzar.
3408	596	XLVI. 1	158	21	3	The Scythians are expelled from Asia Minor by Cyaxares, king of
3409	595	2	159	22	4	Media and Persia.
3410	594	3	160	23	5	
3411	593	4	161	24	6	About this time Zedekiah rebelled against Nebuchadnezzar, king of
3412	592	XLVII. 1	162	25	7	Babylon.
3413	591	2	163	26	8	The Pythian games first established at Delphi.
3414	590	3	164	27	9	Jerusalem besieged by Nebuchadnezzar; and two years after (viz.,
3415	589	4	165	28	10	in the 19th year of Nebuchadnezzar, Jer. lii. 12,) the city is taken,
3416	588	XLVIII. 1	166	29	11	the temple burnt, and the people carried away into captivity.

Thus ends THE KINGDOM OF JUDAH, after it had stood from
the death of Solomon 387 years, and from the captivity of the ten
tribes 133 years. About this time flourished Chilo, Anacharsis,
Thales, Epimenides, Solon, the prophets Ezekiel and Daniel, Æsop,
Stesichorus, &c. Nebuchadnezzar lived after the destruction of the
temple 24 years.

A. CLARKE.—*March 28th*, 1828.

INTRODUCTION TO THE BOOK

OF

EZRA

A T the conclusion of 2 Kings, and also of the preceding book, 2 Chronicles, we have seen
the state of misery and desolation to which the kingdoms of Israel and Judah were
reduced through their unparalleled ingratitude to God, and their innumerable backslidings
and rebellions. These at last issued in their captivity; the inhabitants of the former country being carried away by the Assyrians, and those of the latter by the Chaldeans. The
former never recovered their ancient territories, and were so disposed of by their enemies
that they either became amalgamated with the heathen nations, so as to be utterly undis-
tinguishable, or they were transported to some foreign and recluse place of settlement,
that the place of their existence, though repeatedly guessed at, has for more than *two thousand years* been totally unknown.

In mercy to the less polluted inhabitants of the kingdom of Judah, though delivered up
into the hands of their enemies, God had promised by his prophet, that at the expiration of
seventy years they should be enlarged, and restored to their own country. This prediction
was most literally fulfilled; and the books of *Ezra, Esther,* and *Nehemiah,* inform us *how*
the Divine goodness accomplished this most gracious design, and the *movers* and *agents* he
employed on the occasion. The writer of the following book was undoubtedly the chief
agent under God; and his history, as found in the most authentic writings of the Jews, is
too nearly connected with this book, and too important in every point of view, to be passed
by. No man has written on this subject with such perspicuity as Dean *Prideaux;* and from
his invaluable work, *The Connected History of the Old and New Testaments,* I shall freely
borrow whatever may be best calculated to throw light upon the ensuing history.

"In the beginning of the year 458 before the Christian era, Ezra obtained of King Artaxerxes and his seven counsellors a very ample commission for his return to Jerusalem, with
all of his nation that were willing to accompany him thither; giving him full authority there
to restore and settle the state, and reform the Church of the Jews, and to regulate and
govern both according to their own laws. This extraordinary favour, not being likely to
have been obtained but by some more than ordinary means, appears to have been granted
by King Artaxerxes to the solicitations of Esther, who, though not at that time advanced
to the dignity of his queen, was yet the best beloved of his concubines.

"Ezra was of the descendants of *Seraiah,* the high priest who was slain by Nebuchadnezzar when he burnt the temple and city of *Jerusalem.*

"As Ezra was a very holy, so also was he a very learned man, and especially skilled
excellently in the knowledge of the Holy Scriptures; and therefore he is said to have been
a very ready scribe in the law of God, for which he was so eminent that Artaxerxes takes
particular notice of it in his commission. He began his journey from Babylon on the first
day of the first month, called *Nisan,* which might fall about the middle of our March; and
having halted at the river of Ahava till the rest of his company was come up to him, he
there, in a solemn fast, recommended himself and all that were with him to the Divine
protection; and then, on the *twelfth* day, set forward for Jerusalem, they all having spent

four months in their journey from Babylon thither. On his arrival he delivered up to the temple the offerings which had been made to it by the king and his nobles, and the rest of the people of Israel that stayed behind; which amounted to *a hundred talents* of gold, with *twenty* basons of gold of the value of *a thousand* darics, and *six hundred* and *fifty* talents of silver, with vessels of silver of the weight of *a hundred* talents more: and then, having communicated his commission to the king's lieutenants and governors throughout all Syria and Palestine, he betook himself to the executing of the contents of it, whereby he was fully empowered to settle both the Church and the state of the Jews, according to the law of Moses; and to appoint magistrates and judges to punish all such as should be refractory; and that, not only by imprisonment and confiscation of goods, but also with banishment and death, according as their crimes should be found to deserve. And all this power *Ezra* was invested with, and continued faithfully to execute, for the space of *thirteen* years, till *Nehemiah* arrived with a new commission from the Persian court for the same work. *Ezra*, having found in the *second* year of his government (Ezra ix. and x.) that many of the people had taken strange wives, contrary to the law, and that several of the priests and Levites, as well as the chief men of Judah and Benjamin, had transgressed herein, after he had in fasting and prayer deprecated God's wrath for it, caused proclamation to be made for all the people of Israel that had returned from the captivity to gather themselves together at Jerusalem, under the penalty of excommunication, and forfeiture of all their goods. And when they were met, he made them sensible of their sins, and engaged them in promise and covenant before God, to depart from it by putting away their strange wives, and all such as were born of them, that the seed of Israel might not be polluted with such an undue commixture; and thereon commissioners were appointed to inquire into this matter, and cause every man to do according to the law.

"And they sat down the *first* day of the *tenth* month to examine into this matter, and made an end by the *first* day of the *first* month; so that in *three* months' time, that is, in the *tenth*, *eleventh*, and *twelfth* months of the Jewish year, a thorough reformation was made of this transgression: which *three* months answer to *January, February,* and *March* of our year.

"About this time (Esther ii. 21) Bigthan and Jeush, two eunuchs of the palace, entered into a conspiracy against the life of King Artaxerxes. Most likely they were of those who had attended Queen Vashti; and being now out of their offices by the degrading of their mistress, and the advancing of another in her place, took such a disgust at this as to resolve to revenge themselves on the king for it; of which Mordecai, having got the knowledge, made discovery to Queen Esther, and she in Mordecai's name to the king; whereon inquiry being made into the matter, and the whole treason laid open and discovered, the two traitors were both crucified for it, and the history of the whole matter was entered on the public registers and annals of the kingdom.

"Ezra continued in the government of Judea till the end of the year 446; and by virtue of the commission he had from the king, and the powers granted him thereby, he reformed the whole state of the Jewish Church, according to the law of Moses, in which he was excellently learned, and settled it upon that bottom upon which it afterwards stood till the time of our Saviour. The two chief things which he had to do, were to restore the observance of the Jewish law according to the ancient approved usages which had been in practice before the captivity, under the directions of the prophets; and to collect together and set forth a correct edition of the Holy Scriptures; in the performance of both which, the Jews inform us he had the assistance of what they call the Great Synagogue, which they tell us was a convention consisting of *one hundred and twenty* men, who lived all at the same time under the presidency of Ezra, and assisted him in both of these two works; and among these they name Daniel and his three friends, Shadrach, Meshach, and Abed-nego.

"But the whole conduct of the work, and the glory of accomplishing it, is by the Jews chiefly attributed to him under whose presidency they tell us it was done; and therefore they look upon him as another Moses: for the law, they say, was given by Moses; but it was reviewed and restored by Ezra, after it had in a manner been extinguished and lost in the Babylonish captivity. And therefore they reckon him as the second founder of it: and it is a common opinion among them that he was Malachi the prophet; that he was called Ezra as his proper name, and Malachi, which signifies an angel or messenger, from his office, because he was sent as the angel and messenger of God to restore again the Jewish religion, and establish it in the same manner as it was before the captivity on the foundation of the law and the prophets. And indeed, by virtue of that ample commission which he had from King Artaxerxes, he had an opportunity of doing more herein than any other of his nation; and he executed all the powers thereof to the utmost he was able, for the resettling both of the ecclesiastical and political state of the Jews in the best posture they were then capable of: and from hence his name is in so high esteem and veneration among the Jews, that it is a common saying among their writers, 'that if the law had not been given by Moses, Ezra was worthy, by whom it should have been given.' As to the ancient and approved usages of the Jewish Church which had been in practice before the captivity, they had by Joshua and Zerubbabel, with the chief elders, then contemporaries, and by others that after succeeded them, been gathering together from their first return to Jerusalem, as they could be recovered from the memories of the ancients of their nation who had either seen them practised themselves before the captivity, or who had been informed concerning them by their parents or others who had lived before them.

"All these, and whatsoever else was pretended to be of the same nature, Ezra brought under review, and, after due examination, allowed such of them as were to be allowed, and settled them by his approbation and authority: they gave birth to what the Jews now call their oral law; for they own a twofold law—the *first*, the written law, which is recorded in the Holy Scriptures; and the *second*, the oral law, which they have only by the tradition of their elders. And both these, they say, were given them by Moses from Mount Sinai, of which the former only was committed to writing, and the other delivered down to them from generation to generation by the tradition of the elders; and therefore holding them both to be of the same authority, as having both of them the same Divine original, they think themselves to be bound as much by the latter as the former, or rather much more; for the written law is, they say, in many places, obscure, scanty, and defective, and could be no perfect rule to them without the oral law, which, containing according to them a full, complete, and perfect interpretation of all that is included in the other, supplies all the defects and solves all the difficulties of it; and therefore they observe the written law no otherwise than according as it is explained and expounded by their oral law. And hence it is a common saying among them, 'that the covenant was made with them, not upon the written law, but upon the oral law;' and therefore they do in a manner lay aside the former to make room for the latter, and resolve their whole RELIGION into their traditions, in the same manner as the Romanists do theirs, having no farther regard to the written word of God than as it agrees with their traditionary explications of it, but always preferring them thereto, though in many particulars they are quite contradictory to it, which is a corruption that had grown to a great height among them even in our Saviour's time; for he charges them with it, and tells them *that they make the word of God of none effect through their traditions;* Mark vii. 13. But they have done it much more since, professing a greater regard to the latter than the former; and hence it is that we find it so often said in their writings, 'that the words of the scribes are lovely above the words of the law; that the words of the law are weighty and light, but the words of the scribes are all weighty; that the words of the elders are weightier than the words of the prophets;' where, by the words of the scribes and the words of the elders, they mean their traditions, delivered to them by their scribes and elders. And in other places, 'that the written text is only as water; but the *Mishnah* and *Talmud*, in which are contained the traditions, are as wine and hippocras.' And again, 'that the written law is only as salt, but the *Mishnah* and *Talmud* as pepper and sweet spices.' And in many other sayings, very common among them, do they express the very high veneration which they bear towards the oral or traditionary law, and the little regard which they have to the written word of God in comparison of it, making nothing of the latter but as expounded by the former; as if the written word were no more than the dead letter, and the traditionary law alone the soul that gives it the whole life and essence.

"And this being what they hold of their traditions, which they call their oral law, the account which they give of its original is as follows: they tell us that 'at the same time when God gave unto Moses the law in Mount Sinai, he gave unto him also the interpretation of it, commanding him to put the former into writing, but to deliver the other only by word of mouth, to be preserved in the memories of men, and to be transmitted down by them from generation to generation by tradition only; and from hence the former is called the written, and the other the oral, law.' And to this day all the determinations and dictates of the latter are termed by the Jews 'Constitutions of Moses from Mount Sinai,' because they do as firmly believe that he received them all from God in his *forty days'* converse with him in that mount, as that he then received the written text itself. That on his return from this converse he brought both of these laws with him, and delivered them unto the people of Israel in this manner: As soon as he was returned to his tent, he called Aaron thither unto him, and first delivered unto him the text, which was to be the written law, and after that the interpretation of it, which was the oral law, in the same order as he received both from God in the mount. Then Aaron arising and seating himself at the right hand of Moses, Eleazar and Ithamar his sons went next in, and both these being taught laws at the feet of the prophet in the same manner as Aaron had been, they also arose and seated themselves, the one on the left hand of Moses, the other on the right hand of Aaron; and then the *seventy* elders who constituted the Sanhedrin, or great senate of the nation, went in, and being taught by Moses both these laws in the same manner, they also seated themselves in the tent; and then entered all such of the people as were desirous of knowing the law of God, and were taught in the same manner. After this, Moses withdrawing, Aaron repeated the whole of the law as he had heard it from him, and also withdrew; and then Eleazar and Ithamar repeated the same, and on their withdrawing, the seventy elders made the same repetition to the people then present; so that each of them having heard both these laws repeated to them four times, they all had it thereby fixed in their memories; and that then they dispersed themselves among the whole congregation, and communicated to all the people of Israel what had been thus delivered to them by the prophet of God. That they did put the text into writing, but the interpretation of it they delivered down only by word of mouth to the succeeding generations; that the written text contained the *six hundred and thirteen precepts* into which they divide the law and the unwritten interpretations, all the manners, ways, and circumstances, that were to be observed in the keeping of them; that after this, towards the end of the *fortieth* year from their coming up out of the land of Egypt, in the beginning of the *eleventh* month, (which fell about the beginning of our June,) Moses, calling all the people of Israel together, acquainted them of the approaching time of his death, and therefore ordered that if any of them had forgot aught of what he had delivered to them, they should repair to him, and he would repeat to them what had slipped their memories, and farther explain to them every difficulty and doubt which might arise in their minds concerning what he had taught them of the law of their God; and that hereon they applying to him, all the remaining term of his life, that is, from the said beginning of the *eleventh* month till the *sixth* day of the *twelfth* month, was employed in instructing them in the text, which they call the written law, and in the interpretation of it, which they call the oral law; and that on the said *sixth* day having delivered unto them *thirteen* copies of the written law, all copied out with his own hand, from the beginning of Genesis to the end of Deuteronomy, one to each of the twelve tribes, to be kept by them throughout their generations, and the *thirteenth* to the Levites, to be laid up by them in the tabernacle before the Lord, and having moreover repeated the oral law to Joshua his successor, he went on the *seventh* day into Mount *Nebo*, and there died; that after his death Joshua delivered the same oral law to the elders who after succeeded him, and they delivered it to the prophets, and the prophets transmitted it down to each other till it came to *Jeremiah*, who delivered it to *Baruch*, and *Baruch* to Ezra, by whom it was delivered to the men of the great synagogue, the last of whom was *Simon the Just;* that by him it was delivered to Antigonus of Socho, and by him to Jose the son of Jochanan, and by him to Jose the son of Joeser, and by him to Nathan the Arbelite and Joshua the son of Berachiah, and by them to Judah the son of Jabhai, and, Simeon the son of Shatah, and by them to Shemaiah and Abitulion, and by them to Hillel and by Hillel to Simeon his son, who is supposed to have been the same who took our Saviour into his arms when he was brought to the temple to be there presented to the Lord at the time of his mother's purification; and by Simeon it was delivered to Gamaliel his son, the same at whose feet Paul was brought up, and by him to Simeon his son, by him to Gamaliel his son, and by him to Simeon his son, and by him to Rabbah Judah Hakkadosh his son, who wrote it into the book called the Mishnah. But all this is mere fiction spun out of the fertile invention of the Talmudists, without the least foundation either in Scripture or in any authentic history for it. But since all this has made a part of the Jewish creed, they do as firmly believe their traditions thus to have come from God in the manner I have related, as they do the written word itself; and have now, as it were, wholly resolved their religion into these traditions. There is no understanding what their religion at present is without it, and it is for this reason I have here inserted it.

"But the truth is this: After the death of *Simon the Just* there arose a sort of men whom they call *The Jarmain*, or the Mishnical doctors, who made it their business to study and descant upon those traditions which had been received and allowed by Ezra and the men of the great synagogue, and to draw inferences and consequences from them, all of which they ingrafted into the body of these ancient traditions, as if they had been as authentic as the others; which example being followed by those who after succeeded them in this profession, they continually added their own imaginations to what they had received from those who went before them, whereby the traditions, becoming as a snow-ball, the farther they rolled down from one generation to another the more they gathered, and the greater the bulk of them grew. And thus it went on till the middle of the second century after Christ, when *Antoninus Pius* governed the Roman empire, by which time they found it necessary to put all these traditions into writing; for they were then grown to so great a number, and enlarged to so huge a heap, as to exceed the possibility of being any longer preserved in the memory of men. And besides, in the second destruction which their country had undergone from the Romans a little before, in the reign of Adrian the preceding emperor, most of their learned men having been cut off, and the chiefest of their schools broken up and dissolved, and vast numbers of their people dissipated, and driven out of their land, the usual method of preserving their traditions had then in a great measure failed; and therefore, there being danger that under these disadvantages they might be all forgotten and lost, for the preservation of them it was resolved that they should be all collected together, and put into a book; and *Rabbi Judah*, the son of Simeon, who from the reputed sanctity of his life was called *Hakkadosh*, that is, The Holy, and was then rector of the school which they had at Tiberias in Galilee, and president of the Sanhedrin that there sat, undertook the work, and compiled it in *six* books, each consisting of several tracts, which altogether made up the number of *sixty-three;* in which, under their proper heads, he methodically digested all that had hitherto been delivered to them, of their law and their religion, by the tradition of their ancestors. And this is the book called *The Mishnah*, which book was forthwith received by the Jews with great veneration throughout all their dispersions, and has ever since been held in high estimation among them; for their opinion of it is, that all the particulars therein contained were dictated by God himself to Moses from Mount Sinai, as well as the written word itself, and consequently must be of the same Divine authority with it, and ought to be as sacredly observed. And therefore, as soon as it was published, it became the subject of the studies of all their learned men; and the chiefest of them, both in Judea and Babylonia, employed themselves to make comments on it; and these, with the *Mishnah*, make up both their *Talmuds;* that is, the Jerusalem Talmud and the Babylonish Talmud. These comments they call the *Gemara*, i. e., The Complement, because by them the Mishnah is fully explained, and the whole traditionary doctrines of their law and their religion completed. For the *Mishnah* is the *text*, and the *Gemara* the *comment;* and both together is what they call the *Talmud*. That made by the Jews of Judea is called the Jerusalem Talmud, that by the Jews of Babylonia is called the Babylonish Talmud. The former was completed about the year of our Lord 300, and is published in *one* large folio; the latter was published about *two hundred* years after, in the *beginning of the sixth century*, and has had several editions since the invention of printing. The last, published at Amsterdam, is in *twelve* folios; and in these two Talmuds, the law and the prophets being in a manner quite justled out of them, is contained the whole of the Jewish religion that is now professed among them; but the Babylonish Talmud is that which they chiefly follow; for the other, that is, the Jerusalem Talmud, being obscure, and hard to be understood, is not now much regarded by them. But this and the Mishnah, being the most ancient books which they have, except the *Chaldee* Paraphrases of *Onkelos* and *Jonathan*, and both written in the language and style of the Jews of Judea; our countryman, Dr. Lightfoot, has made very good use of them in explaining several places of the New Testament by parallel phrases and sayings out of them. For the one being composed about the *one hundred and fiftieth* year of our Lord, and the other about the *three hundredth*, the idioms, proverbial sayings, and phraseologies, used in our Saviour's time, might very well be preserved in them. But the other Talmud being written in the language and style of Babylonia, and not compiled till about the *five hundredth* year of our Lord, or, as some will have it, much later, this cannot so well serve for this purpose. However, it is now the Alcoran of the Jews, into which they have resolved all their faith, and all their religion, although framed almost with the same imposture as that of Mohammed, out of the doctrines falsely pretended to be brought from heaven. And in this book all that now pretend to any learning among them place their studies; and no one can be a master in their schools, or a teacher in their synagogues, who is not well instructed and versed herein; that is, not only in the text, which is the Mishnah, but also in the comment thereon, which is the Gemara; and this comment they so highly esteem beyond the other, that the name of Gemara is wholly engrossed by it; the Gemara of the Babylonish Talmud being that only which they now usually understand by that word; for this with the Mishnah, to which it is added, they think truly completes and makes up the whole of their religion, as fully and perfectly containing all the doctrines, rules, and rites thereof; and therefore it is, in their opinion, the most deserving of that name, which signifies what *completes, fills up*, or *perfects;* for this is the meaning of the word in the Hebrew language.

"They who professed this sort of learning, that is, taught and propagated this traditionary doctrine among them, have been distinguished by several different titles and appellations, according to the different ages in which they lived. From the time of the men of the great synagogue to the publishing of the Mishnah, they were called *Jarmain;* and they are the *Mishnical* doctors, out of whose doctrines and traditions the *Mishnah* was composed. And from the time of the publishing of the Mishnah to the publishing of the Babylonish Talmud, they were called *Amoraim;* and they are the *Gemarical* doctors, out of whose doctrines and traditions the *Gemara* was composed. And for about a *hundred* years after the publishing of the Talmud, they were called *Seburaim*, and after that *Georim*. And these were the several classes in which their learned men have been ranked, according to the several ages in which they lived. But for these later times, the general name of *Rabbi* is that only whereby their learned men are called, there being no other title whereby they have been distinguished for nearly *seven hundred* years past.

"For about the year 1040 all their schools in Mesopotamia, where only they enjoyed these high titles, being destroyed, and all their learned men thence expelled and driven out by the Mohammedan princes, who governed in those parts; they have since that, with the greatest number of their people, flocked into the western parts, especially into Spain, France, and England; and from that time all these pompous titles which they affected in the East being dropped, they have retained none other for their learned men from that time but that of *Rabbi;* excepting only that those of them who minister in their synagogues are called *Chacams,* i. e., wise men.

"But the great work of Ezra was, his collecting together and setting forth a correct edition of the Holy Scriptures, which he laboured much in, and went a great way in the perfecting of it. Of this both Christians and Jews gave him the honour; and many of the ancient fathers attribute more to him in this particular than the Jews themselves; for they hold that all the Scriptures were lost and destroyed in the Babylonish captivity, and that Ezra restored them all again by Divine revelation. Thus says *Irenæus* and thus say *Tertullian,* Clemens Alexandrinus, Basil, and others. But they had no other foundation for it than that fabulous relation which we have of it in the fourteenth chapter of the second Apocryphal book of Esdras, a book too absurd for the Romanists themselves to receive into their canon.

"Indeed, in the time of Josiah, through the impiety of the *two* preceding reigns of Manasseh and Amon, the book of the law was so destroyed and lost. The copy of it which *Hilkiah* is said to have found, and the grief which *Josiah* expressed at the hearing of it read, do plainly show that neither of them had ever seen it before.

"And if the king and the high priest, who were both men of eminent piety, were without this part of the Holy Scripture, it can scarcely be thought that any one else then had it. But so religious a prince as King Josiah could not leave this long unremedied. By his orders copies were written out from this original; and search being made for all the other parts of Holy Scripture, both in the colleges of the sons of the prophets, and all other places where they could be found, care was taken for transcripts to be made out of these also; and thenceforth copies of the whole became multiplied among the people; all those who were desirous of knowing the laws of their God, either writing them out themselves, or procuring others to do it for them; so that within a few years after the holy city and temple were destroyed, and the authentic copy of the law, which was laid up before the Lord, was burnt and consumed with them, yet by this time many copies, both of the law and the prophets, and all the other sacred writings, were got into private hands, who carried them with them into captivity.

"That Daniel had a copy of the Holy Scriptures with him in Babylon is certain, for he quotes the law, and also makes mention of the prophecies of the prophet Jeremiah, which he could not do had he never seen them. And in the sixth chapter of Ezra it is said, that on the finishing of the temple, in the *sixth* year of Darius, the priests and the Levites were settled in their respective functions, according as it is written in the law of Moses. But how could they do this according to the written law, if they had not copies of the law then among them? And this was nearly *sixty* years before Ezra came to Jerusalem.

"And farther, in Nehemiah, chap. viii., the people called for the law of Moses, to have it read to them, which the Lord had commanded Israel, which plainly shows that the book was then well known to have been extant, and not to need such a miraculous expedient as that of the Divine revelation for its restoration; all that Ezra did in this manner was to get together as many copies of the sacred writings as he could, and out of them all to set forth a correct edition; in the performance of which he took care of the following particulars: *First*, He corrected all the errors that had crept into these copies, through the negligence or mistakes of transcribers; for, by comparing them one with the other, he found out the true reading, and set all at rights. Whether the *keri cethib*, or various readings, that are in our present Hebrew Bibles were of these corrections, I dare not say. The generality of the Jewish writers tell us that they were; and others among them hold them as much more ancient, referring them, with absurdity enough, as far back as the times of the first writers of the books in which they are found, as if they themselves had designedly made these various readings for the sake of some mysteries comprised under them. It is most probable that they had their original from the mistakes of the transcribers after the time of Ezra, and the observations and corrections of the *Masorites* made thereon. If any of them were of those ancient various readings which had been observed by Ezra himself in the comparing of those copies he collated on this occasion, and were by him annexed in the margin as corrections of those errors which he found in the text, it is certain those could not be of that number which are now in those sacred books that were written by himself, or taken into the canon after his time; for there are *keri cethib* in them as well as in the other books of the Hebrew Scriptures. *Secondly*, He collected together all the books of which the Holy Scriptures did then consist, and disposed them in their proper order; and settled the canon of Scripture for his time. These books he divided into three parts: 1. The Law. 2. The Prophets. 3. The *Cethubim*, or *Hagiographa;* i. e., the Holy Writings: which division our Saviour himself takes notice of, Luke xxiv. 44, where he says: 'These are the words which I spake unto you, while I was yet with you, that all things might be fulfilled which are written in the law, and in the prophets, and in the Psalms, concerning me.' For there, by the Psalms, he means the whole third part called the Hagiographa; for, that part beginning with the Psalms, the whole was for that reason then commonly called by that name; as usually with the Jews, the particular books are named from the words with which they begin. Thus with them Genesis is called *Bereshith*, Exodus *Shemoth*, Leviticus *Vaijikra*, &c., because they begin with these Hebrew words.

"And Josephus makes mention of this same division; for he says, in his first book against Apion, 'We have only two and twenty books which are to be believed as of Divine authority, of which five are the books of Moses. From the death of Moses to the reign of Artaxerxes, the son of Xerxes, king of Persia, the prophets, who were the successors of Moses, have written in thirteen books. The remaining four books contain hymns to God, and documents of life for the use of men:' in which division, according to him, the law contains *Genesis, Exodus, Leviticus, Numbers, Deuteronomy.* The writings of the prophets, *Joshua, Judges*, with *Ruth, Samuel, Kings, Isaiah, Jeremiah,* with his *Lamentations, Ezekiel, Daniel*, the twelve minor prophets, *Job, Ezra, Nehemiah, Esther;* and the *Hagiographa*, i. e., the *Psalms, Proverbs, Ecclesiastes*, and *Song of Solomon*, which altogether make *two and twenty books.* This division was made for the sake of reducing the books to the number of their alphabet, in which were *twenty-two* letters. But at present they reckon these books to be *twenty-four*, and dispose of them in this order: *First*, the Law, which contains *Genesis, Exodus, Leviticus, Numbers*, and *Deuteronomy. Secondly*, the Writings of the Prophets, which they divide into the former prophets and the latter prophets: the books of the former prophets are, *Joshua, Judges, Samuel*, and *Kings;* the books of the latter prophets, *Isaiah, Jeremiah*, and *Ezekiel;* the twelve minor prophets; the *Hagiographa*, which are the *Psalms, Proverbs, Job*, the *Song of Solomon*, which they call the Song of Songs, *Ruth*, the *Lamentations, Ecclesiastes, Esther, Daniel, Ezra*, and the *Chronicles.* Under the name of *Ezra* they comprehend the book of *Nehemiah;* for the *Hebrews*, and also the *Greeks*, anciently reckoned *Ezra* and *Nehemiah* but as one book. But this order has not been always observed among the Jews; neither is it so now in all places, for there has been great variety as to this, and that not only among the Jews, but also among the Christians, as well as the Greeks and Latins: but no variation herein is of any moment, for in what order soever the books are placed, they are still the word of God; and no change as to this can make any change as to that Divine authority which is stamped upon them. But all these books were not received into the canon in *Ezra's* time, for Malachi it is supposed lived after him; and in *Nehemiah* mention is made of Jaddua as high priest, and of *Darius Codomannus* as king of Persia; who were at least *a hundred years* after his time. And in chap. iii. of the first book of Chronicles the genealogy of the sons of Zerubbabel is carried down for so many generations as must necessarily make it reach to the time of Alexander the Great; and therefore the book could not be put into the canon till after his time.

"It is most likely that the two books of *Chronicles, Ezra, Nehemiah,* and *Esther,* as well as *Malachi,* were afterwards added in the time of *Simon the Just,* and that it was not till then that the Jewish canon of the Holy Scriptures was fully completed: and indeed these last books seem very much to want the exactness and skill of *Ezra* in their publication, they falling far short of the correctness which is in the other parts of the Jewish Scriptures. The five books of the law are divided into *fifty-four* sections. This division many of the Jews hold to be one of the constitutions of Moses from *Mount Sinai;* but others, with more likelihood of truth, attribute it to *Ezra.* It was made for the use of their synagogues, and the better instructing of the people there in the law of God; for every Sabbath day one of these sections was read in their synagogues; and this, we are assured in the *Acts of the Apostles,* was done among them *of old time,* which may well be interpreted from the time of *Ezra.* They ended the last section with the last words of *Deuteronomy* on the Sabbath of the feast of tabernacles, and then recommenced with the first section from the beginning of *Genesis* the next Sabbath after; and so went on round in this circle every year. The number of the sections was *fifty-four;* because in their intercalated years (a month being added) there were *fifty-four* Sabbaths. [See complete tables of these in all their variations at the end of this comment on the book of Deuteronomy.]

"On other years they reduced them to the number of the Sabbaths which were in those years by joining two short ones several times into one; for they held themselves obliged to have the whole law thus read over to them in their synagogues every year. Until the time of the persecution of *Antiochus Epiphanes* they read only the law; but, being then forbid to read it any more, in the room of the *fifty-four* sections of the law, they substituted *fifty-four* sections out of the prophets, the reading of which they ever after continued. So that when the reading of the law was again restored by the Maccabees, the section which was read every Sabbath out of the law served for their first lesson, and the section out of the prophets for the second lesson; and so it was practised in the time of the apostles. And therefore, when *Paul* entered into the synagogue at *Antioch,* in *Pisidia,* it is said that 'he stood up to preach after the reading of the law and the prophets;' that is, after the reading of the first lesson out of he law, and the second lesson out of the prophets. And in that very sermon which he then preached, he tells them, 'That the prophets were read at *Jerusalem* every Sabbath day,' *that is,* in those lessons which were taken out of the prophets.

"These sections were divided into verses, which the Jews call *pesukim;* they were marked out in the Hebrew Bibles by two great points at the end of them, called from hence *sophpasuk,* i. e., *the end of the verse.* If Ezra himself was not the author of this division, (as most say,) it was not long after him that it was introduced, for certainly it is very ancient. It is most likely that it was introduced for the sake of the *Targumist* or *Chaldee* interpreters; for after the Hebrew language had ceased to be the mother tongue of the Jews, and the Chaldee grew up into use among them instead of it, (as was the case after their return from the Babylonish captivity,) their usage was that, in the public reading of the law to the people, it was read to them, first in the original Hebrew, and after that rendered by an interpreter into the Chaldee language, that so all might fully understand the same; and this was done period by period; and therefore, that these periods might be the better distinguished, and the reader more certainly know how much to read at every interval, and the interpreter know how much to interpret at every interval, there was a necessity that some marks should be invented for their direction herein. The rule given in the ancient books is, that in the law the reader was to read one verse, and then the interpreter was to render the same into Chaldee; but that in the prophets the reader was to read three verses together, and then the interpreter was to render the same three verses into Chaldee, in the same manner; which manifestly proves that the division of the Scriptures into verses must be as ancient as the way of interpreting them into the Chaldee language in their synagogues, which was from the very time that the synagogues were erected, and the Scriptures publicly read in them, after the Babylonish captivity. This was at first done only in the law; for till the time of the Maccabees, the law only was read in their synagogues: but afterwards, in imitation of this, the same was also done in the prophets, and in the *Hagiographa* especially. After that the prophets also began to be publicly read among them, as well as the law; and from hence the division of the Holy Scriptures into verses, it is most likely, was first made; but without any numerical figures annexed to them.

"The manner whereby they are now distinguished in their common Hebrew Bibles is by the two great points called *soph-pasuk* above mentioned; but whether this is the ancient way is by some made a question. The objection against it is this: If the distinction of verses was introduced for the sake of the Chaldee interpreters in their synagogues, and must therefore be held as ancient as that way of interpreting the Scriptures in them, it must then have place in their sacred synagogical books; for none others were used, either by their readers or their interpreters, in their public assemblies. But it has been anciently held as a rule among them, that any points or accents written into these sacred books pollute and profane them; and therefore, no copy of either the law or the prophets now used in their synagogues has any points or accents written in it. To this I answer, Whatever be the practice of the modern Jews, this is no rule to let us know what was the ancient practice among them, since in many particulars they have varied from the ancient usages, as they now do from each other, according to the different parts of the world in which they dwell. For mention is made of them in the *Mishnah;* and that the reason for this division was for the direction of the readers, and the Chaldee interpreters, is also there implied; and therefore, supposing a division for this use, it must necessarily follow, that there must have been some marks to set it out; otherwise it would not have answered the end intended.

"It is most likely that anciently the writing of those books was in long lines, from one side of the parchment to the other, and that the verses in them were distinguished in the same manner as the *stichi* afterwards were in the Greek Bibles; for the manner of their writing those *stichi* was, to allow a line to every *stichus*, and then to end the writing where they ended the *stichus*, leaving the rest of the line void, in the same manner as a line is left at a break: but this was losing too much of the parchment, and making the book too bulky; for the avoiding of both these inconveniences, the way afterwards was, to put a point at the end of every *stichus*, and so continue the writing without leaving any part of the line void as before. And in the same manner I conceive the *pesukim*, or verses of the Hebrew Bibles, were anciently written. At first they allowed a line to every verse, and a line drawn from one end of the parchment to the other, of the length as above mentioned, was sufficient to contain any verse that is now in the Hebrew Bible; but many verses falling short of this length, they found the same inconveniences that the Greeks after did in the first way of writing their *stichi;* and therefore came to the same remedy, that is, they did put the *two* points above mentioned (which they call *soph-pasuk*) at the place where the former verse ended, and continued the writing of the next verse in the same line, without leaving any void space at all in the line. And so their manner has continued ever since, excepting only that between their sections, as well the smaller as the larger, there is some void space left, to make the distinction between them; and I am the more inclined to think this to be the truth of the matter; that is, that anciently the verses of the Hebrew Bible were so many lines, because among the ancients of other nations, about the same time, the lines in the writings of prose authors, as well as the poets, were termed verses; and hence it is that we are told that *Zoroaster's* works contain *two millions* of verses, and *Aristotle's, four hundred and forty-five thousand two hundred and seventy;* though neither of them wrote any thing but in prose; and so also we find the writings of *Tully,* of *Origen,* of *Lactantius,* and others, who were all prose writers, reckoned by the number of verses, which could be no other than so many lines. And why then might not the Bible verses anciently have been of the same nature also? I mean when written in long lines as aforesaid. But the long lines often occasioning, that in reading to the end of one verse, they lost the beginning of the next, and so often did read wrong, either by skipping a line, or beginning the same again; for the avoiding of this they came to the way of writing in columns and in short lines, as above mentioned. But all this I mean of their sacred synagogical books. In their common Bibles they are not tied up to such rules, but write and print them so as they may serve for their instruction and convenience in common use.

"But the division of the Holy Scriptures into chapters, as we now have them, is of a much later date. The Psalms, indeed, were always divided as at present; for St. Paul, in his sermon at Antioch, in Pisidia, quotes the second Psalm: but as to the rest of the Holy Scriptures, the division of them into such chapters as we find at present is a matter of which the ancients knew nothing. Some attribute it to *Stephen Langton,* who was *archbishop* of *Canterbury* in the reigns of King *John* and King *Henry III.* his son. But the true author of this invention was *Hugo de Sancto Claro,* who being from a *Dominican* monk advanced to the dignity of a cardinal, and the first of that order that was so, is commonly called *Hugo Cardinalis.*

"The *third* thing that Ezra did about the Holy Scriptures in his edition of them was:— he added in several places, throughout the books of this edition, what appeared necessary for the illustrating, correcting, or completing of them, wherein he was assisted by the same Spirit by which they were at first written. Of this sort we may reckon the last chapter of Deuteronomy, which, giving an account of the death and burial of Moses, and of the succession of Joshua after him, could not be written by Moses himself, who undoubtedly was the penman of all the rest of that book. It seems most probable that it was added by Ezra at this time: and such also we may reckon the several interpolations which occur in many places of the Holy Scriptures. For that there are such interpolations is undeniable, there being many passages through the whole sacred writers which create difficulties which can never be solved without the allowing of them: as for instance, Gen. xii. 6, it is remarked on *Abraham's* coming into the land of *Canaan,* that the 'Canaanites were then in the land;' which is not likely to have been said till after the time of *Moses,* when the *Canaanites,* being extirpated by *Joshua,* were then no longer in the land: and Gen. xxii. 14, we read, 'As it is said to this day, In the Mount of the Lord it shall be seen.' But Mount *Moriah,* which is the mount there spoken of, was not called the Mount of the Lord till the temple was built on it many hundred years after; and this being here spoken of as a proverbial saying that obtained among the Israelites in after ages, the whole style of the text manifestly points at a time after *Moses,* when they were in the possession of the land in which this mountain stood; and, therefore, both these particulars prove the words cited to have been an interpolation. Gen. xxxvi. 3, it is written, 'And these are the kings that reigned in the land of Edom, before there reigned any king over the land of Israel,' which could not have been said till after there had been a king in *Israel;* and therefore they cannot be *Moses's* words, but must have been interpolated afterwards. Exod. xvi. 35, the words of the text are, 'And the children of Israel did eat manna forty years, till they came to a land inhabited. They did eat manna till they came into the borders of the land of Canaan.' But *Moses* was dead before the manna ceased; and, therefore, these cannot be his words, but must have been inserted afterwards. Deut. ii. 12, it is said, 'The Horims also dwelt in Seir beforetime, but the children of Esau succeeded them when they had destroyed them from before them, and dwelt in their stead, as Israel did unto the land of his possession which the Lord gave unto them.' Which could not have been written by *Moses,* Israel having not till after his death entered into the land of his possession, which the Lord gave unto them. Deut. iii. 11, it is said, 'Only Og, king of Bashan, remained of the remnant of giants; behold, his bedstead was a bedstead of iron. Is it not in Rabbath of the children of Ammon?' The whole style and strain of which text, especially that of the last clause of it, plainly speaks it to have been written a long while after that king was slain; and therefore it could not have been written by *Moses,* who died within five months after. In the same chapter, verse 14, it is said, 'Jair the son of Manasseh took all the country of Argob unto the coasts of Geshuri and Maachathi; and called them after his own name, Bashan-havoth-jair, unto this day.' Where the phrase *unto this day* speaks a much greater distance of time after the fact related than those few months in which *Moses* survived after the conquest; and therefore what is there written must have been inserted by some other hand than that of *Moses,* and long after his death. And in the book of *Proverbs,* which was certainly King *Solomon's,* in the beginning of the *twenty-fifth* chapter, it is written, 'These *are* also proverbs of Solomon, which the men of Hezekiah king of Judah copied out.' Which must certainly have been added many ages after *Solomon;* for Hezekiah was the *twelfth* generation in descent from him.

"Many more instances of such interpolated passages might be given; for throughout the whole Scriptures they have been frequently cast in by way of parentheses; where they have appeared necessary for the explaining, connecting, or illustrating the text, or supplying what was wanting in it: but those already mentioned are sufficient to prove the thing. Of which interpolations undoubtedly Ezra was the author, in all the books which passed his examination; and *Simon the Just* in all the rest which were added afterwards; for they all seem to refer to those latter times.

"But these additions do not at all detract from the Divine authority of the whole, because they were all inserted by the direction of the same Holy Spirit which dictated all the rest. This, as to Ezra, is without dispute, he being himself one of the Divine persons of the Holy Scriptures: for he was most certainly the writer of that book in the Old Testament which bears his name; and he is, upon good grounds, supposed to be the author of two more, that is, of the two books of *Chronicles,* as perchance he was also of the book of *Esther.* And if the books written by him be of Divine authority, why may not every thing else be so which he has added to any of the rest, since there is reason for us to suppose that he was as much directed by the Holy Spirit of God in the one as in the other? The great importance of the work proves the thing, for as it was necessary for the Church of God that this work should be done; so also it was necessary for the work that the person called thereto should be thus assisted in the completing of it.

"*Fourthly,* He changed the names of several places that were grown obsolete, putting instead of them the new names by which they were at that time called, that the people might the better understand what was written. Thus, Gen. xiv. 14, *Abraham* is said to have pursued the kings who carried *Lot* away captive as far as *Dan,* whereas the name of that place was *Laish* till the *Danites,* long after the death of *Moses,* possessed themselves of it, and called it, *Dan after the name of their father;* and, therefore, it could not be called *Dan* in the original copy of *Moses,* but that name must have been put in afterwards instead of that of *Laish* on this review. And so in several places in *Genesis,* and also in *Numbers,* we find mention made of *Hebron,* whereas the name of that city was *Kiriath-arba,* till *Caleb,* having the possession of it after the division of the land, called it *Hebron* after the name of *Hebron,* one of his sons: and, therefore, that name could not be had in the text, till placed there long after the time of *Moses*, by way of exchange for that of *Kiriath-arba*, which it is not to be doubted was done at the time of this review.

"And many other like examples of this may be given; whereby it appears that the study of those who governed the Church of God at those times was to render the Scriptures as plain and intelligible to the people as they could; and not to hide and conceal any of it from them.

"*Fifthly*, He wrote out the whole in the *Chaldee* character: for that having now grown wholly into use among the people after the *Babylonish* captivity, he changed the old *Hebrew* character for it, which hath since that time been retained only by the *Samaritans*, among whom it is preserved even to this day. This was the old *Phœnician* character, from which the *Greeks* borrowed theirs; and the old *Ionian* alphabet bears some resemblance to it, as *Scaliger* shows in his notes upon *Eusebius's Chronicon*. In this *Moses* and the other prophets recorded the sacred oracles of God; and in this the finger of God himself wrote the ten commandments in the two tables of stone. *Eusebius*, in his *Chronicon*, tells us so, and *St. Jerome* doth the same; and so do also both the *Talmuds;* and the generality of learned men, as well among the Jews as Christians, hold this opinion.

"Whether *Ezra* on this review did add the vowel points, which are now in the *Hebrew* Bibles, is a hard question to be decided: it went without contradiction in the affirmative till *Elias Levita*, a *German Jew*, wrote against it about the beginning of the Reformation. *Buxtorf*, the father, endeavoured to refute his argument; but *Capellus*, a Protestant divine of the *French* Church, and professor of Hebrew in their university at *Saumur*, hath, in a very elaborate discourse, made a thorough reply to all that can be said on this head, and very strenuously asserted the contrary. *Buxtorf*, the son, in vindication of his father's opinion, has written an answer to it, but not with that satisfaction to the learned world as to hinder the generality of them from going into the other opinion.

"There is in the church of *St. Dominic*, in *Bononia*, a copy of the Hebrew Scriptures, kept with a great deal of care, which they pretend to be the original copy written by Ezra himself, and therefore it is there valued at so high a rate that great sums of money have been borrowed by the *Bononians* upon the pawn of it, and again repaid for its redemption. It is written in a very fair character upon a sort of leather, and made up in a roll, according to the ancient manner; but it having the vowel points annexed, and the writing being fresh and fair, without any decay, both these particulars prove the novelty of that copy.

"But though Ezra's government over all *Judah* and *Jerusalem* expired in this year, 446; yet his labour to serve the Church of God did not end here; for he still went on as a preacher of righteousness, and a skilful scribe in the law of God, to perfect the reformation which he had begun, both in preparing for the people correct editions of the Scriptures, and also in bringing all things in Church and state to be conformed to Scripture rules. And this he continued to do so long as he lived, and in this he was thoroughly assisted and supported by the next governor, who, coming to Jerusalem with the same intention, and the same zeal for promoting the honour of God, and the welfare of his people in Judah and Jerusalem, as Ezra did, struck in heartily with Ezra in the work, so that Ezra went on still to do the same things by the authority of the new governor, which he before did by his own; and, by their thus joining together in the same holy undertaking, and their mutually assisting each other, it exceedingly prospered in their hands, till at length, notwithstanding all opposition, both from within and without, it was brought to full perfection *forty-nine* years after it had been begun by Ezra. Whether Ezra lived so long is uncertain; but what he had not time to do was completed by the piety and zeal of his successor."

See the Introduction to the book of Nehemiah; and see Prideaux's Connections, vol. i., edit. 1725.

For all other matters relative to the text, see the notes as they occur.

THE

BOOK OF EZRA

Chronological Notes relative to this Book

Year from the Creation, according to Archbishop Usher, whose system of chronology is most generally received, 3468.—Year before the birth of Christ, 532.—Year before the vulgar era of Christ's nativity, 536. Year of the Julian Period, 4178.—Year since the flood of Noah, according to the English Bible, 1812.—Year of the Cali Yuga, or Indian era of the Deluge, 2566.—Year from the vocation of Abram, 1386.—Year from the destruction of Troy, 649. This we collect from three passages in Dionysius of Halicarnassus, (who flourished in the Augustan age,) which state that an interval of *four hundred and thirty-two years* elapsed from the destruction of Troy to the building of Rome.—Year from the foundation of Solomon's temple, 475.—Year since the division of Solomon's monarchy into the kingdoms of Israel and Judah, 439.—Year of the era of Iphitus, who re-established the Olympic games, *three hundred and thirty-eight* years after their institution by Hercules, or about *eight hundred and eighty-four* years before the commencement of the Christian era, 349.—Year since the conquest of Corœbus at Elis, usually styled the first Olympiad, (being the *twenty-eighth* Olympiad after their re-establishment by Iphitus,) 241.— First year of the sixty-first Olympiad.—Year of the Varronian or generally received era of the building of Rome, 218. This is upon the supposition that Rome was built in the last year of the sixth Olympiad. —Year from the building of Rome, according to Cato and the Fasti Consulares, 217. Dionysius of Halicarnassus follows this account; for he says that the metropolis of the Roman world was built in the first year of the sixth Olympiad, which was the first year of Charops, the first decennial archon of the Athenians.—Year from the building of Rome, according to Polybius, 216.—Year from the building of Rome, according to Fabius Pictor, who lived about *two hundred and twenty-five* years before the Christian era, 212.—Year of the Nabonassarean era, 212.—Year since the destruction of the kingdom of Israel by Shalmaneser, king of Assyria, 186.—Year from the destruction of Solomon's temple by Nebuchadnezzar, king of Babylon, 53.—Year of Servius Tullius, the sixth king of the Romans, and father-in-law of Tarquin the Proud, 43.—Year of Ariston, king of Lacedæmon, and of the family of the Proclidæ, or Eurypontidæ, 29.—Year of Anaxandrides, king of Lacedæmon, and of the family of the Eurysthenidæ, or Agidæ, 28. N. B. The kings of the Lacedæmonians of the families of the Proclidæ and the Eurysthenidæ sat on the throne together for several hundred years.—Year of Amyntas, the ninth king of the Macedonians, 12.—Year of the reign of Cyrus, computing from the year in which he dethroned his grandfather Astyages, the last king of Media, 24. But this was only his *first year*, if with the Holy Scriptures, as well as Xenophon in the eighth book of his Institutes, we compute the years of his reign from the time in which he was put in possession of the whole Eastern empire. See *Ezra* i. 1.—Year of the Babylonish captivity, 70. The years of this captivity are generally reckoned from 606 B. C., when Jehoiakim king of Judah was put in chains to be carried to Babylon; and are supposed to be terminated by the edict of Cyrus to rebuild the temple at Jerusalem. But others are of opinion that the *seventy years' captivity* are to be computed from the total destruction of the Jewish monarchy; and that they reach down to the second year of Darius king of Persia, at which time Zerubbabel and Joshua were encouraged by the prophets Haggai and Zechariah to proceed with the rebuilding of the temple.

CHAPTER I

The proclamation of Cyrus for the rebuilding of the temple, 1–4. The people provide for their return, 5, 6. Cyrus restores to Sheshbazzar the vessels taken by Nebuchadnezzar out of the temple of Solomon, 7–11.

A. M. 3468
B. C. 536
Olymp. LXI. 1
Anno Urbis
Conditæ 218

NOW in the first year of Cyrus king of Persia, that the word of the LORD ᵃby the mouth of Jeremiah might be fulfilled, the LORD stirred up the spirit of Cyrus king

of Persia, ᵇthat ᶜhe made a proclamation throughout all his kingdom, and *put it* also in writing, saying,

2 Thus saith Cyrus king of Persia, The

A. M. 3468
B. C. 536
Olymp. LXI. 1
Anno Urbis
Conditæ 218

ᵃ2 Chron. xxxvi. 22, 23; Jer. xxv. 12; xxix. 10

ᵇChap. v. 13, 14——ᶜHeb. *caused a voice to pass*

In the introduction to this book the reader will find the history of Ezra detailed at considerable length. It is only necessary to say

here that he is generally allowed among the Jews to have been of the sacerdotal family, and therefore he is called ὁ ἱερεύς, *the priest* by the

A. M. 3468
B. C. 536
Olymp. LXI. 1
Anno Urbis
Conditæ 218

LORD God of heaven hath given me all the kingdoms of the earth; and he hath ^dcharged me to build him a house at Jerusalem, which *is* in Judah.

3 Who *is there* among you of all his people? his God be with him, and let him go up to Jerusalem, which *is* in Judah, and build the house of the LORD God of Israel, (^ehe *is* the God,) which *is* in Jerusalem.

4 And whosoever remaineth in any place

where he sojourneth, let the men of his place ^fhelp him with silver, and with gold, and with goods, and with beasts, beside the freewill-offering for the house of God that *is* in Jerusalem:

A. M. 3468
B. C. 536
Olymp. LXI. 1
Anno Urbis
Conditæ 218

5 Then rose up the chief of the fathers of Judah and Benjamin, and the priests, and the Levites, with all *them* whose spirit ^gGod had raised, to go up to build the house of the LORD which *is* in Jerusalem.

---

^dIsa. xliv. 28; xlv. 1, 13——^eDan. vi. 26

^fHeb. *lift him up*——^gPhil. ii. 13

Septuagint. Among the rabbins he passes for a most extraordinary critic, Divinely authorized to collect and arrange the different portions of the sacred writings, and digest them into a system. How far all they say on this subject is true, we cannot tell; he was, beyond all controversy, a very eminent man; and in all that he did, acted under the immediate direction and inspiration of the Almighty.

This history contains the transactions of about *eighty-two* years; from the *first* year of Cyrus in Babylon, according to Archbishop Usher, A. M. 3468, to the *ninteenth* year of *Ardsheer Diraz Dest,* or *Artaxerxes Longimanus,* who sent Nehemiah to Jerusalem, about A. M. 3550. For all other particulars, see the *introduction.*

NOTES ON CHAP. I

Verse 1. *Now in the first year*] This is word for word with the *two* last verses of the preceding book; which stand *here* in their proper place and connection, but there are entirely destitute of chronological connection and reference.

Cyrus] This prince, so eminent in antiquity, is said to have been the son of *Cambyses* king of Persia, and *Mandane,* daughter of *Astyages* king of the Medes; and was born about *six hundred* years before Christ. Josephus accounts for his partiality to the Jews from this circumstance; that he was shown the places in Isaiah the prophet where he is mentioned by name, and his exploits and conquests foretold: see Isa. xliv. 28, and xlv. 1, &c. Finding himself thus distinguished by the God of the Jews, he was anxious to give him proofs of his gratitude in return; and so made the decree in favour of the Jews, restored their sacred vessels, gave them liberty to return to their own land, and encouraged them to rebuild the temple of Jehovah, &c.

It is very probable that when Cyrus took Babylon he found *Daniel* there, who had been long famed as one of the wisest ministers of state in all the East; and it is most likely that it was this person who pointed out to him the prophecy of Isaiah, and gave him those farther intimations relative to the Divine will which were revealed to himself. Of his death there are contradictory accounts. *Herodotus* says, that having turned his arms against the Massagetes, and killed the son of *Tomyris* their queen, the mother, impatient to avenge the death of her son, sent him a defiance; promised to glut him with blood; and, having attacked

him, pretended to be worsted and to fly; and thus she drew him and his army into an ambuscade, where he was routed and slain, and a considerable part of his army destroyed. The enraged queen having found his body, cut off his head, and threw it into a vessel full of human blood, with this most bitter sarcasm:—

Εν μεν, εμευ ζωσης τε και νικωσης ες μαχην, απωλεσας παιδα τον εμον, ελων δολῳ· σε δ' εγω, καταπερ ηπειλησα, αιματος κορεσω.—HEROD. *Clio,* c. 214.

"Although living and victorious, thou hast destroyed me in slaying my son, whom thou hast overcome by deceit; but, as I have threatened, I will now slake thy thirst with blood."

Cyrus, thy thirst was blood, now drink thy fill.

By—Jeremiah] This prophet, chap. xxv. 12, and xxix. 11, had foretold that the Babylonish captivity should last only *seventy* years: these were now ended; Cyrus had given the Jews permission and encouragement to return to Judea, and rebuild the temple of the Lord; and thus the prediction of Jeremiah was fulfilled.

Verse 2. *The Lord God of heaven*] It is not unworthy of remark, that in all the books written *prior* to the captivity, Jehovah is called *The Lord of Hosts;* but in all the books written *after* the captivity, as 2 Chronicles, Ezra, Nehemiah, and Daniel, he is styled *The God of Heaven.* The words however have the same meaning.

All the kingdoms of the earth. At this time the empire of the Medo-Persians was very extensive: according to ancient writers, Cyrus, at this time, reigned over the Medes, Persians, Hyrcanians, Armenians, Syrians, Assyrians, Arabians, Cappadocians, Phrygians, Lydians, Phœnicians, Babylonians, Bactrians, Indians, Saci, Cilicians, Paphlagonians, Moriandrians, and many others. His empire extended on the EAST, to the Red Sea; on the NORTH, to the Euxine Sea; on the WEST, to the island of Cyprus and Egypt; and on the SOUTH, to Ethiopia.

Verse 4. *Whosoever remaineth in any place*] Every one was at liberty to go, but none was obliged to go. Thus their attachment to God was tried; he whose heart was right with God, went; he who was comfortably settled in Babylon, might go if he chose. Those who did not go, were commanded to assist their brethren who went.

A. M. 3468
B. C 536
Olymp. LXI. 1
Anno Urbis
Conditæ 218

6 And all they that *were* about them [h]strengthened their hands with vessels of silver, with gold, with goods, and with beasts, and with precious things, beside all *that* was willingly offered.

7 [i]Also Cyrus the king brought forth the vessels of the house of the LORD, [k]which Nebuchadnezzar had brought forth out of Jerusalem, and had put them in the house of his gods;

8 Even those did Cyrus king of Persia bring forth by the hand of Mithredath the treasurer, and numbered them [l]unto Sheshbazzar, the prince of Judah.

A. M. 3468
B. C. 536
Olymp. LXI. 1
Anno Urbis
Conditæ 218

9 And this *is* the number of them: thirty chargers of gold, a thousand chargers of silver, nine and twenty knives,

10 Thirty basons of gold, silver basons of a second *sort* four hundred and ten, *and* other vessels a thousand.

11 All the vessels of gold and of silver *were* five thousand and four hundred. All *these* did Sheshbazzar bring up with *them of* [m]the captivity that were brought up from Babylon unto Jerusalem.

---

[h]That is, *helped them*——[i]Chap. v. 14; vi. 5——[k]2 Kings xxiv. 13; 2 Chron. xxxvi. 7

[l]See chapter v. 14——[m]Hebrew, *the transportation*

Verse 6. *Vessels of silver*] *Articles* of silver, gold, &c.

Verse 7. *The king brought forth the vessels*] See on verses 9-11.

Verse 8. *Sheshbazzar, the prince of Judah.*] This was probably the Chaldean name of him who was originally called Zerubbabel: the former signifies *joy in affliction;* the latter, *a stranger in Babylon.* The latter may be designed to refer to his *captive state;* the former, to the *prospect of release.* Some think this was quite a different person; a Persian or Chaldean, sent by Cyrus to superintend whatever officers or men Cyrus might have sent to assist the Jews on their return; and to procure them help in the Chaldean provinces, through which they might be obliged to travel.

Verse 11. *All the vessels*—were *five thousand and four hundred.*] This place is without doubt corrupted; here it is said the sum of all the vessels, of every quality and kind, was *five thousand four hundred;* but the enumeration of the articles, as given in verses 9 and 10, gives the sum of *two thousand four hundred and ninety-nine* only. But we can correct this account from 1 Esdras ii. 13, 14.

I shall set both accounts down, that they may be compared together.

EZRA, chap. i. 9-11.

Golden chargers	30
Silver chargers	1000
Knives	29

Golden basons	30
Silver ditto, second sort	410
Other vessels	1000
Said to be 5400 only	2499
Difference of the *first* account from *itself.*	2901

1 ESDRAS, chap. ii. 13, 14.

Golden cups	1000
Silver cups	1000
Silver censers	29
Golden vials	30
Silver vials	2410
Other vessels	1000
Total	5469

Difference of the *second* account from the *first* ... 69

According, therefore, to the sum total in *Ezra,* the sum total in *Esdras* is only 69 different. See the next chapter.

It may be said that the vessels did actually amount to 5400, and that the chief of them only were intended to be specified; and these happen to amount to 2499; but that it was not the design of Ezra to insert the whole; and that the *ninth* verse should be considered as stating, *And of* the chief *of them,* that is, the gold and silver articles, *this is the number.* But the expression in ver. 10, *other vessels,* sets this conjecture aside: the place is most manifestly corrupted.

CHAPTER II

An account of those who returned from Babylon, 1–35. The children of the priests who returned, 36–39. Of the Levites, 40. Of the singers, 41. Of the porters, 42. Of the Nethinim, and the children of Solomon's servants, 43–58. Others who could not find out their registers, 59–62. The number of the whole congregation, 63, 64. Of their servants, maids, and singers, 65. Their horses and mules, 66. Their camels and asses, 67. The offerings of the chief men when they came to Jerusalem, 68, 69. The priests, Levites, singers, porters, and Nethinim, betake themselves to their respective cities, 70.

A. M. 3468
B. C. 536
Olymp. LXI. 1
Anno Urbis
Conditæ 218

NOW [a]these *are* the children of the province that went up out of the captivity, of those which had been carried away, [b]whom Nebuchadnezzar the king of Babylon had carried away unto Babylon, and came again unto Jerusalem and Judah, every one unto his city;

2 Which came with Zerubbabel: Jeshua, Nehemiah, [c]Seraiah, [d]Reelaiah, Mordecai, Bilshan, [e]Mizpar, Bigvai, [f]Rehum, Baanah. The number of the men of the people of Israel:

3 The children of Parosh, two thousand a hundred seventy and two.

4 The children of Shephatiah, three hundred seventy and two.

5 The children of Arah, [g]seven hundred seventy and five.

6 The children of [h]Pahath-moab, of the children of Jeshua *and* Joab, two thousand eight hundred and twelve.

7 The children of Elam, a thousand two hundred fifty and four.

8 The children of Zattu, nine hundred forty and five.

9 The children of Zaccai, seven hundred and three score.

A. M. 3468
B. C. 536
Olymp. LXI. 1
Anno Urbis
Conditæ 218

10 The children of [i]Bani, six hundred forty and two.

11 The children of Bebai, six hundred twenty and three.

12 The children of Azgad, a thousand two hundred twenty and two.

13 The children of Adonikam, six hundred sixty and six.

14 The children of Bigvai, two thousand fifty and six.

15 The children of Adin, four hundred fifty and four.

16 The children of Ater of Hezekiah, ninety and eight.

17 The children of Bezai, three hundred twenty and three.

18 The children of [k]Jorah, a hundred and twelve.

19 The children of Hashum, two hundred twenty and three.

20 The children of [l]Gibbar, ninety and five.

21 The children of Beth-lehem, a hundred twenty and three.

---

[a]Neh. vii. 6, &c.; 1 Esd. v. 7, &c.——[b]2 Kings xxiv. 14, 15, 16; xxv. 11; 2 Chron. xxxvi. 20——[c]Or, *Azaraiah*, Neh. vii. 7——[d]Or, *Raamiah*——[e]Or, *Mispereth*

[i]Or, *Nehum*——[g]See Neh. vii. 10——[h]Neh. vii. 11 [i]Or, *Binnui*, Neh. vii. 15——[k]Or, *Hariph*, Neh. vii. 24 [l]Or, *Gibeon*, Neh. vii. 25

NOTES ON CHAP. II

Verse 1. *These* are *the children of the province*] That is, of *Judea;* once a *kingdom*, and a flourishing *nation;* now a *province*, subdued, tributary, and ruined! Behold the goodness and severity of God! Some think Babylon is meant by *the province;* and that *the children of the province* means those Jews who were born in Babylon. But the first is most likely to be the meaning, for thus we find Judea styled, chap. v. 8. Besides, the *province* is contradistinguished from *Babylon* even in this first verse, *The children of the province—that had been carried away unto Babylon.*

Verse 2. *Which came with Zerubbabel*] There are many difficulties in this table of names; but as we have no less than *three* copies of it, *that* contained here from ver. 1-67, a *second* in Neh. vii. 6-69, and a *third* in 1 Esdras v. 7-43, on a careful examination they will be found to correct each other. The *versions* also, and the *Variæ Lectiones* of *Kennicott* and *De Rossi*, do much toward harmonizing the names.

Though the sum total at the end of each of these enumerations is equal, namely 42,360, yet the particulars reckoned up make in Ezra only 29,818, and in Nehemiah 31,089. We find that Nehemiah mentions 1765 persons which are not in Ezra, and Ezra has 494 not mentioned by Nehemiah. Mr. *Alting* thinks that this circumstance, which appears to render all hope of reconciling them impossible, is precisely the very point by which they can be reconciled; for if we add Ezra's *surplus* to the *sum* in Nehemiah, and the *surplus* of Nehemiah to the *number* in Ezra, the numbers will be equal.

Thus:—The number in Ezra......... 29,818
Surplus in Nehemiah................. 1,765

Sum total.......... 31,583
The number in Nehemiah............. 31,089
The surplus in Ezra................. 494

Sum total.......... 31,583

If we subtract this sum 31,583 from 42,360, we shall have a deficiency of 10,777 from the numbers as summed up in the text; and these are not named here, either because their registers were not found, or they were not of *Judah* and *Benjamin*, the tribes particularly concerned, but of the other Israelitish tribes; see ver. 36.

Verse 3. *The children of Parosh*] Where the word *children* is found in this table, prefixed to the name of a *man*, it signifies the *descendants* of that person, as from this verse to ver. 21. Where it is found prefixed to a *place*, *town*, &c., it signifies the *inhabitants* of that place, as from ver. 21 to ver. 35.

Verse 21. *The children of Beth-lehem*] The inhabitants; see before.

A. M. 3468
B. C. 536
Olymp. LXI. 1
Anno Urbis
Conditæ 218

22 The men of Netophah, fifty and six.

23 The men of Anathoth, a hundred twenty and eight.

24 The children of [m]Azmaveth, forty and two.

25 The children of Kirjath-arim, Chephirah, and Beeroth, seven hundred and forty and three.

26 The children of Ramah and Gaba, six hundred twenty and one.

27 The men of Michmas, a hundred twenty and two.

28 The men of Beth-el and Ai, two hundred twenty and three.

29 The children of Nebo, fifty and two.

30 The children of Magbish, a hundred fifty and six.

31 The children of the other [n]Elam, a thousand two hundred fifty and four.

32 The children of Harim, three hundred and twenty.

33 The children of Lod, [o]Hadid, and Ono, seven hundred twenty and five.

34 The children of Jericho, three hundred forty and five.

35 The children of Senaah, three thousand and six hundred and thirty.

36 The priests: the children of [p]Jedaiah, of the house of Jeshua, nine hundred seventy and three.

37 The children of [q]Immer, a thousand fifty and two.

38 The children of [r]Pashur, a thousand two hundred forty and seven.

39 The children of [s]Harim, a thousand and seventeen.

40 The Levites: the children of Jeshua and Kadmiel, of the children of [t]Hodaviah, seventy and four.

41 The singers: the children of Asaph, a hundred twenty and eight.

42 The children of the porters: the children of Shallum, the children of Ater, the children of Talmon, the children of Akkub, the children of Hatita, the children of Shobai, *in* all a hundred thirty and nine.

A. M. 3468
B. C. 536
Olymp. LXI. 1
Anno Urbis
Conditæ 218

43 [u]The Nethinims: the children of Ziha, the children of Hasupha, the children of Tabbaoth,

44 The children of Keros, the children of [v]Siaha, the children of Padon,

45 The children of Lebanah, the children of Hagabah, the children of Akkub,

46 The children of Hagab, the children of [w]Shalmai, the children of Hanan,

47 The children of Giddel, the children of Gahar, the children of Reaiah,

48 The children of Rezin, the children of Nekoda, the children of Gazzam,

49 The children of Uzza, the children of Paseah, the children of Besai,

50 The children of Asnah, the children of Mehunim, the children of [x]Nephusim,

51 The children of Bakbuk, the children of Hakupha, the children of Harhur,

52 The children of [y]Bazluth, the children of Mehida, the children of Harsha,

53 The children of Barkos, the children of Sisera, the children of Thamah,

54 The children of Neziah, the children of Hatipha.

55 The children of [z]Solomon's servants: the children of Sotai, the children of Sophereth, the children of [a]Peruda,

56 The children of Jaalah, the children of Darkon, the children of Giddel,

57 The children of Shephatiah, the children of Hattil, the children of Pochereth of Zebaim, the children of [b]Ami.

58 All the [c]Nethinims, and the children of [d]Solomon's servants, *were* three hundred ninety and two.

59 And these *were* they which went up from Tel-melah, Tel-harsa, Cherub, [e]Addan, *and* Immer: but they could not show their father's house, and their [f]seed, whether they *were* of Israel:

---

[m]Or, *Beth-azmaveth*, Neh. vii. 28——[n]See verse 7——[o]Or, *Harid*, as it is in some copies——[p]1 Chron. xxiv. 7——[q]1 Chron. xxiv. 14——[r]1 Chron. ix. 12——[s]1 Chron. xxiv. 8——[t]Or, *Judah*, ch. iii. 9; called also *Hodevah*, Neh. vii. 43——[u]1 Chron. ix. 2——[v]Or, Sia——[w]Or, *Shamlai*

[x]Or, *Nephishesim*——[y]Or, *Bazlith*, Nehemiah vii. 54——[z]1 Kings ix. 21——[a]Or, *Perida*, Nehemiah vii. 57——[b]Or, *Amon*, Nehemiah vii. 59——[c]Joshua ix. 21, 27; 1 Chronicles ix. 2——[d]1 Kings ix. 21——[e]Or, *Addon*, Nehemiah vii. 61——[f]Or, *pedigree*

Verse 33. *The children of Lod, Hadid, and Ono*] These were cities in the tribe of Benjamin; see on 1 Chron. viii. 12.

Verse 36. *The priests*] The preceding list takes in the census of Judah and Benjamin.

Verse 55. *The children of Solomon's ser-*

A. M. 3468
B. C. 536
Olymp. LXI. 1
Anno Urbis
Conditæ 218

60 The children of Delaiah, the children of Tobiah, the children of Nekoda, six hundred fifty and two.

61 And of the children of the priests: the children of Habaiah, the children of Koz, the children of Barzillai; which took a wife of the daughters of ᵍBarzillai the Gileadite, and was called after their name:

62 These sought their register *among* those that were reckoned by genealogy, but they were not found: ʰtherefore ⁱwere they, as polluted, put from the priesthood.

63 And the ᵏTirshatha said unto them, that they ˡshould not eat of the most holy things, till there stood up a priest with ᵐUrim and with Thummim.

64 ⁿThe whole congregation together *was* forty and two thousand three hundred *and* threescore,

65 Beside their servants and their maids, of whom *there were* seven thousand three hundred thirty and seven: and *there were* among them two hundred singing men and singing women.

66 Their horses *were* seven hundred thirty and six; their mules, two hundred forty and five;

67 Their camels, four hundred thirty and five; *their* asses, six thousand seven hundred and twenty.

68 ᵒAnd *some* of the chief of the fathers, when they came to the house of the LORD which *is* at Jerusalem, offered freely for the house of God to set it up in his place:

69 They gave after their ability unto the ᵖtreasure of the work threescore and one thousand drams of gold, and five thousand pounds of silver, and one hundred priests' garments.

70 ᑫSo the priests, and the Levites, and *some* of the people, and the singers, and the porters, and the Nethinims, dwelt in their cities, and all Israel in their cities.

A. M. 3468
B. C. 536
Olymp. LXI. 1
Anno Urbis
Conditæ 218

ᵍ2 Sam. xvii. 27——ʰNum. iii. 10——ⁱHeb. *they were polluted from the priesthood*——ᵏOr, *governor;* see Neh. viii. 9——ˡLev. xxii. 2, 10, 15, 16

ᵐExod. xxviii. 30; Num. xxvii. 21——ⁿNeh. vii. 67 ᵒNeh. vii. 70——ᵖ1 Chron. xxvi. 20——ᑫChap. vi. 16, 17; Neh. vii. 73

---

vants] The *Nethinim*, and others appointed to do the meaner services of the holy house.

Verse 63. *The Tirshatha*] This is generally supposed to be Nehemiah, or the person who was the commandant; see Neh. viii. 9, and x. 1, for the word appears to be the name of an *office.* The *Vulgate* and *Septuagint* write it *Atershatha,* the *Syriac* and *Arabic* render it *the princes of Judah.* Some suppose the word to be *Persian,* but nothing like it of the same import occurs in that language at present. If, as *Castel* supposed, it signifies *austerity,* or that *fear* which is impressed by the authority of a governor, it may come from ترس *ters,* FEAR, or ترش *tersh,* ACID, the former from ترسيدن *tarsidan,* to FEAR or DREAD.

Should not eat of the most holy things] There was a high priest then, but no *Urim* and *Thummim,* these having been lost in the captivity.

Verse 66. *Their horses—seven hundred, &c.*] They went into captivity, stripped of every thing; they now return from it, abounding in the most substantial riches, viz., horses 736, or, according to Esdras, 7036; mules, 245; camels, 435; asses, 6720; besides gold, and silver, and rich stuffs. See below.

Verse 69. *Threescore and one thousand drams of gold*] דרכמונים *darkemonim,* drakmons or darics; a Persian coin, always of gold, and worth about 1*l.* 5*s.;* not less than £76,250 sterling in gold.

Five thousand pounds of silver] מנים *manim,* manehs or minas. As a *weight,* the *maneh* was 100 shekels; as a coin, 60 shekels in value, or about 9*l.;* 5000 of these manehs therefore will amount to £45,000, making in the whole a sum of about £120,000; and in this are not included the 100 *garments for priests.*

Thus we find that God, in the midst of judgment, remembered mercy, and gave them favour in the land of their captivity.

Verse 70. *Dwelt in their cities*] They all went to those cities which belonged originally to their respective families.

CHAPTER III

The altar of burnt-offerings is set up, 1–3. They keep the feast of tabernacles, 4–6. They make provision for rebuilding the temple; and lay its foundation in the second month of the second year, 7, 8. Ceremonies observed in laying the foundation, 9–11. Some weep aloud, and others shout for joy, 12–18.

A. M. 3468
B. C. 536
Olymp. LXI. 1
Anno Urbis
Conditæ 218

AND [a]when the seventh month was come, and the children of Israel *were* in the cities, the people gathered themselves together as one man to Jerusalem.

2 Then stood up [b]Jeshua the son of Jozadak, and his brethren the priests, and [c]Zerubbabel the son of [d]Shealtiel, and his brethren, and builded the altar of the God of Israel, to offer burnt-offerings thereon, as *it is* [e]written in the law of Moses the man of God.

3 And they set the altar upon his bases; for fear *was* upon them because of the people of those countries: and they offered burnt-offerings thereon unto the LORD, *even* [f]burnt-offerings morning and evening.

4 [g]They kept also the feast of tabernacles, [h]as *it is* written, and [i]*offered* the daily burnt-offerings by number, according to the custom, [k]as the duty of every day required;

5 And afterward *offered* the [l]continual burnt-offering, both of the new moons, and of all the set feasts of the LORD that were consecrated, and of every one that willingly offered a freewill-offering unto the LORD.

6 From the first day of the seventh month began they to offer burnt-offerings unto the LORD. But [m]the foundation of the temple of the LORD was not *yet* laid.

7 They gave money also unto the masons, and to the [n]carpenters; and [o]meat, and drink, and oil, unto them of Zidon, and to them of Tyre, to bring cedar trees from Lebanon to the sea of [p]Joppa, [q]according to the grant that they had of Cyrus king of Persia.

A. M. 3468
B. C. 536
Olymp. LXI. 1
Anno Urbis
Conditæ 218

8 Now in the second year of their coming unto the house of God at Jerusalem, in the second month, began Zerubbabel the son of Shealtiel, and Jeshua the son of Jozadak, and the remnant of their brethren the priests and the Levites, and all they that were come out of the captivity unto Jerusalem, [r]and appointed the Levites, from twenty years old and upward, to set forward the work of the house of the LORD.

A. M. 3469
B. C. 535
Olymp. LXI. 2
Anno Urbis
Conditæ 219

9 Then stood [s]Jeshua *with* his sons and his brethren, Kadmiel and his sons, the sons of [t]Judah, [u]together, to set forward the workmen in the house of God: the sons of Henadad, *with* their sons and their brethren the Levites.

10 And when the builders laid the foundation of the temple of the LORD, [v]they set the priests in their apparel with trumpets, and the Levites the sons of Asaph with cymbals, to praise the LORD, after the [w]ordinance of David king of Israel.

---

[a]1 Esd. v. 47, &c.——[b]Or, *Joshua*, Hag. i. 1; ii. 2; Zech. iii. 1——[c]Called *Zorobabel*, Matt. i. 12; Luke iii. 27——[d]Matthew i. 12; Luke iii. 27, called *Salathiel*——[e]Deuteronomy xii. 5——[f]Num. xxviii. 3, 4——[g]Neh. viii. 14, 17; Zechariah xiv. 16, 17——[h]Exodus xxiii. 16 [i]Numbers xxix. 12, &c.——[k]Hebrew, *the matter of the day in his day*——[l]Exod. xxix. 38; Numbers xxviii. 3,

11, 19, 26; xxix. 2, 8, 13——[m]Heb. *the temple of the LORD was not yet founded*——[n]Or, *workmen*——[o]1 Kings v. 6, 9; 2 Chron. ii. 10; Acts xii. 20——[p]2 Chron. ii. 16; Acts ix. 36——[q]Chap. vi. 3——[r]1 Chron. xxiii. 24, 27——[s]Chap. ii. 40——[t]Or, *Hodaviah*, chap. ii. 40——[u]Heb. *as one*——[v]1 Chron. xvi. 5, 6, 42——[w]1 Chron. vi. 31; xvi. 4; xxv. 1

NOTES ON CHAP. III

Verse 1. *When the seventh month was come*] The month *Tisri*, which answers to the latter part of our *September*, and beginning of *October*. It seems that the Israelites had left Babylon about the *spring* of the year; that on their arrival at Jerusalem they constructed themselves huts and sheds to lodge in among the ruins, in which they must have spent some months. After this they rebuilt the altar of burnt-offerings, and kept the feast of tabernacles, which happened about this time, and continued to offer sacrifices regularly, as if the temple were standing.

Verse 2. *Jeshua the son of Jozadak*] He was grandson of Seraiah the high priest, who was put to death by Nebuchadnezzar, 2 Kings xxv. 18, 21. This Jeshua or Joshua was the first high priest after the captivity.

Verse 3. *They set the altar upon his bases*] Rebuilt it on the *same spot* on which it had formerly stood. As it was necessary to keep up the Divine worship during the time they should

be employed in re-edifying the temple, they first reared this altar of burnt-offerings; and all this they did, "*though* fear was upon them," because of the unfriendly disposition of their surrounding neighbours.

Verse 4. *They kept also the feast of tabernacles, as* it is *written*] This began on the *fifteenth* day of the seventh month; but they had begun the regular offerings from the *first day* of this month, ver. 6. And these were religiously continued all the time they were building the temple.

Verse 7. *They gave money also*] They copied the conduct of Solomon while he was building his temple; see 1 Kings v. 11. He employed the Tyrians, gave them meat and drink, &c.; and this permission they now had from Cyrus.

Verse 8. *In the second year*] The previous time had been employed in clearing the ground, felling timber, hewing stones, and transporting them to the place, and making other necessary preparations for the commencement of the building.

Verse 10. *After the ordinance of David*] With

A. M. 3469
B. C. 535
Olymp. LXI. 2
Anno Urbis
Conditæ 219
11 ˣAnd they sang together by course in praising and giving thanks unto the LORD; ʸbecause *he is* good, ᶻfor his mercy *endureth* for ever toward Israel. And all the people shouted with a great shout, when they praised the LORD, because the foundation of the house of the LORD was laid.

12 ᵃBut many of the priests and Levites and chief of the fathers, *who were* ancient men

that had seen the first house, when the foundation of this house was laid before their eyes, wept with a loud voice; and many shouted aloud for joy:
A. M. 3469
B. C. 535
Olymp. LXI. 2
Anno Urbis
Conditæ 219

13 So that the people could not discern the noise of the shout of joy from the noise of the weeping of the people: for the people shouted with a loud shout, and the noise was heard afar off.

ˣExod. xv. 21; 2 Chron. vii. 3; Neh. xii. 24——ʸ1 Chron. xvi. 34; Psa. cxxxvi. 1

ᶻ1 Chronicles xvi. 41; Jeremiah xxxiii. 11——ᵃSee Hag. ii. 3

---

psalms which he composed, acting in the *manner* which he directed.

Verse 12. *Wept with a loud voice*] They saw that the glory had departed from Israel; in their circumstances it was impossible to build such a house as the first temple was; and had this been even possible, still it would have been greatly inferior, because it wanted the ark of the covenant, the heavenly fire, the mercy-seat, the heavenly manna, Aaron's rod that budded, the Divine shechinah, the spirit of prophecy, and most probably the Urim and Thummim.

Many shouted for joy] Finding they were now restored to their own land, and to the wor-

ship of their God in his own peculiar city: these, in general, had not seen the original temple; and therefore could not feel affected in that way which the elderly people did.

The sight must have been very affecting: a whole people, one part *crying* aloud with *sorrow;* the other shouting aloud for *joy;* and on the same occasion too, in which both sides felt an equal interest! The prophet *Haggai* comforted them on this occasion by assuring them that the glory of this latter house should exceed that of the former, because the Lord (Jesus Christ) was to come to this temple, and fill it with his glory. See *Haggai*, chap. ii. 1-9.

CHAPTER IV

The Samaritans endeavour to prevent the rebuilding of the temple, 1–5. They send letters to Artaxerxes, against the Jews, 6–9. A copy of the letter, 10–16. He commands the Jews to cease from building the temple, which they do; nor was any thing farther done in the work till the second year of Darius, 17–24.

A. M. 3469
B. C. 535
Olymp. LXI. 2
Anno Urbis
Conditæ 219
NOW when ᵃthe adversaries of Judah and Benjamin heard that ᵇthe children of the captivity builded the temple unto the LORD God of Israel;

2 Then they came to Zerubbabel, and to the chief of the fathers, and said unto them, Let us build with you: for we seek your God, as ye *do;* and we do sacrifice unto him ᶜsince the days of Esarhaddon king of Assur, which brought us up hither.

3 But Zerubbabel, and Jeshua, and the rest of the chief of the fathers of Israel, said unto

them, ᵈYe have nothing to do with us to build a house unto our God; but we ourselves together will build unto the LORD God of Israel, as ᵉKing Cyrus the king of Persia hath commanded us.
A. M. 3469
B. C. 535
Olymp. LXI. 2
Anno Urbis
Conditæ 219

4 Then ᶠthe people of the land weakened the hands of the people of Judah, and troubled them in building,
A.M.3470-3475
B. C. 534–529
An. Ol. LXI. 3
—LXII. 4

5 And hired counsellors against them, to frustrate their purpose, all the days of Cyrus king of Persia, even until the reign of Darius king of Persia.

ᵃSee verse 7, 8, 9——ᵇHebrew, *The sons of the transportation*

ᶜ2 Kings xvii. 24, 32, 33; xix. 37; verse 10——ᵈNeh. ii. 20——ᵉChap. i. 1, 2, 3——ᶠChap. iii. 3

NOTES ON CHAP. IV

Verse 1. *Now when the adversaries*] These were the Samaritans, and the different nations with which the kings of Assyria had peopled Israel, when they had carried the original inhabitants away into captivity, see ver. 9.

Verse 2. *Let us build with you*] We acknowledge the same God, are solicitous for his glory, and will gladly assist you in this work.

But that they came with no friendly intention, the context proves.

Verse 3. *Ye have nothing to do with us*] We cannot acknowledge you as worshippers of the true God, and cannot participate with you in anything that relates to his worship.

Verse 4. *Weakened the hands*] Discouraged and opposed them by every possible means.

Verse 5. *Hired counsellors*] They found

A. M. 3475
B. C. 529
Olymp.LXII.4
Anno Urbis
Conditæ 225

6 And in the reign of ^gAhasuerus, in the beginning of his reign, wrote they *unto him* an accusation against the inhabitants of Judah and Jerusalem.

A. M. 3482
B. C. 522
Olymp.LXIV.3
Anno Urbis
Conditæ 232

7 And in the days of Artaxerxes wrote ^hBishlam, Mithredath, Tabeel, and the rest of their ⁱcompanions, unto Artaxerxes king of Persia; and the writing of the letter *was* written in the Syrian tongue, and interpreted in the Syrian tongue.

8 Rehum the chancellor, and Shimshai the ^kscribe, wrote a letter against Jerusalem to Artaxerxes the king in this sort:

9 Then *wrote* Rehum the chancellor, and Shimshai the scribe, and the rest of their ^lcompanions; ^mthe Dinaites, the Apharsath-

chites, the Tarpelites, the Apharsites, the Archevites, the Babylonians, the Susanchites, the Dehavites, *and* the Elamites,

A. M. 3482
B. C. 522
Olymp.LXIV.3
Anno Urbis
Conditæ 232

10 ⁿAnd the rest of the nations whom the great and noble Asnapper brought over, and set in the cities of Samaria, and the rest *that are* on this side the river, ^oand ^pat such a time.

11 This *is* the copy of the letter that they sent unto him, *even* unto Artaxerxes the king: Thy servants the men on this side the river, and at such a time.

12 Be it known unto the king, that the Jews which came up from thee to us are come unto Jerusalem, building the rebellious and the bad city, and have ^qset up the walls *thereof,* and ^rjoined the foundations.

---

^gHeb. *Ahashverosh*——^hOr, *in peace*——ⁱHebrew, *societies*——^kOr, *secretary*——^lChald. *societies*——^m2 Kings xvii. 30, 31

ⁿVerse 1——^oSo verse 11, 17; chapter vii. 12 ^pChald. *Cheeneth*——^qOr. *finished*——^rChald. *sewed together*

---

means to corrupt some of the principal officers of the Persian court, so that the orders of Cyrus were not executed; or at least so slowly as to make them nearly ineffectual.

Until the reign of Darius] This was probably *Darius* the son of *Hystaspes.*

Verse 6. *In the reign of Ahasuerus*] This is the person who is called *Cambyses* by the Greeks. He reigned seven years and five months; and during the whole of that time the building of the temple was interrupted.

Verse 7. *In the days of Artaxerxes*] After the death of Cambyses, one of the *Magi* named *Oropœstus* by Trogus Pompeius, *Smerdis* by Herodotus, *Mardus* by Æschylus, and *Sphendatates* by Ctesias, usurped the empire, feigning himself to be *Smerdis,* the brother of Cambyses, who had been put to death. This is the person named Artaxerxes in the text: or, following the Hebrew, *Artachshasta.* It is generally believed, that from the time of Cyrus the great, *Xerxes* and Artaxerxes were names assumed by the Persian sovereigns, whatever their names had been before.

Written in the Syrian tongue] That is, the Syrian or Chaldean *character* was used; not the *Hebrew.*

Interpreted in the Syrian tongue.] That is, the *language,* as well as the *character,* was the *Syriac* or *Chaldaic.*

Verse 8. *Rehum the chancellor*] With this verse the *Chaldee* part of the chapter begins; and the same language continues to the end of verse 18 of chap. vi. These men wrote to Darius in their own language; and the king in the same dialect returns an answer, chap. v. This circumstance adds authenticity to what is written: so scrupulous was the inspired penman, that he not only gave the words which each spoke and wrote, but he gave them also in the very language in which they were conceived, and in the *character* peculiar to that language.

Verse 10. *The great and noble Asnapper*] Whether this was *Shalmaneser,* or *Esar-haddon,*

or some *other person,* learned men and chronologists are not agreed. The Syriac terms him *Asphid;* but of this person we know no more than we do of *Asnapper.* He might have been the military officer who was appointed to escort this people to Judea.

Verse 11. *And at such a time.*] The word וכענת *ucheeneth* has greatly perplexed all commentators and critics. The versions give us no light; and the Vulgate translates it *et dicunt salutem,* "and they wish prosperity." Some translate it *and so forth;* and our translators supposed that it referred to the *date,* which however is not specified, and might have been as easily entered as the words *and at such a time.*

In our first translation of the Bible, that by *Coverdale,* in 1535, the passage stands thus: "And other on this syde the water, and in Canaan."

In that by *Becke,* 1549, it is thus: "And other on this syde the water, and in Ceneeth:" and in the margin he enters "or *peace,*" "or *health.*"

In *Cardmarden's* Bible, printed at Rouen, 1566, it stands thus: "And other that are nowe on thys syde the water."

In that printed by *Barker,* 1615, we find the text thus: "AND OTHER *that are beyond the river, and Cheeneth;*" on which is the following marginal note: "To wit, Euphrates: and he meaneth in respect of Babel, that they dwelt beyond it." And the note on *Cheeneth* is, "Which were a certain people that envied the Jews." All this is merely *guessing,* in the midst of obscurity; most of these having considered the original word כענת *Ceeneth* as the name of a people; and in this they follow the Syriac, which uses the word *Acaneth.*

Calmet thinks we should read ובעת *ubaeth,* "and at this time;" as if they had said, "We wish thee to enjoy the *same* health and prosperity at all *future* times, which thou dost at *present.*" This is not remote from the meaning of the *Chaldee* original.

A. M. 3482
B. C. 522
Olymp.LXIV.3
Anno Urbis
Conditæ 232

13 Be it known now unto the king, that, if this city be builded, and the walls set up *again, then* will they not ⁵pay ᵗtoll, tribute, and custom, and *so* thou shalt endamage the ᵘrevenue of the kings.

14 Now because ᵛwe have maintenance from *the king's* palace, and it was not meet for us to see the king's dishonour, therefore have we sent and certified the king;

15 That search may be made in the book of the records of thy fathers: so shalt thou find in the book of the records, and know that this city *is* a rebellious city, and hurtful unto kings and provinces, and that they have ʷmoved sedition ˣwithin the same of old time: for which cause was this city destroyed.

16 We certify the king, that if this city be builded *again,* and the walls thereof set up, by this means thou shalt have no portion on this side the river.

17 *Then* sent the king an answer unto Rehum the chancellor, and *to* Shimshai the scribe, and *to* the rest of their ʸcompanions that dwell in Samaria, and *unto* the rest beyond the river, Peace, and at such a time.

18 The letter which ye sent unto us hath been plainly read before me.

A. M. 3482
B. C. 522
Olymp.LXIV.3
Anno Urbis
Conditæ 232

19 And ᶻI commanded, and search hath been made, and it is found that this city of old time hath ᵃmade insurrection against kings, and *that* rebellion and sedition have been made therein.

20 There have been mighty kings also over Jerusalem, which have ᵇruled over all *countries* ᶜbeyond the river; and toll, tribute, and custom, was paid unto them.

21 ᵈGive ye now commandment to cause these men to cease, and that this city be not builded, until *another* commandment shall be given from me.

22 Take heed now that ye fail not to do this: why should damage grow to the hurt of the kings?

23 Now when the copy of King Artaxerxes' letter *was* read before Rehum, and Shimshai the scribe, and their companions, they went up in haste to Jerusalem unto the Jews, and made them to cease ᵉby force and power.

A.M.3482-3484
B. C. 522-520
An. Olymp.
LXIV. 3
—LXV. 1

24 Then ceased the work of the house of God which *is* at Jerusalem. So it ceased unto the ᶠsecond year of the reign of Darius king of Persia.

ᵃChald. *give*——ᵗChapter vii. 24——ᵘOr, *strength*
ᵛChald. *we are salted with the salt of the palace*
ʷChald. *made*——ˣChald. *in the midst thereof*
ʸChald. *societies*——ᶻChald. *by me a decree is set*

ᵃChald. *lifted up itself*——ᵇ1 Kings iv. 21; Psalm lxxii. 8——ᶜGen. xv. 18; Josh. i. 4——ᵈChald. *Make a decree*——ᵉChald. *by arm and power*——ᶠHag. i. 1; Zech. i. 1

Verse 13. *Toll, tribute, and custom*] The first term is supposed to imply the *capitation tax;* the second, an *excise on commodities* and *merchandise;* the third, a sort of *land tax.* Others suppose the first means a *property tax;* the second, a *poll tax;* and the third, what was paid on *imports* and *exports.* In a word, if you permit these people to rebuild and fortify their city, they will soon set you at naught, and pay you no kind of tribute.

Verse 14. *Now because we have maintenance from* the king's *palace*] More literally: *Now because at all times we are salted with the salt of the palace;* i. e., We live on the king's bounty, and must be faithful to our benefactor. Salt was used as the emblem of an incorruptible covenant; and those who ate bread and salt together were considered as having entered into a very solemn covenant. These hypocrites intimated that they felt their conscience bound by the league between them and the king; and therefore could not conscientiously see any thing going on that was likely to turn to the king's damage. They were probably also persons in the *pay* of the Persian king.

Verse 15. *The book of the records of thy fathers*] That is, the records of the *Chaldeans,* to whom the Persians succeeded.

Verse 17. *Peace, and at such a time*] The word וּכְעֶנֶת *ucheeth* is like that which we have already considered on ver. 10, and probably has the same meaning.

Verse 19. *Hath made insurrection against kings*] How true is the proverb, "It is an easy thing to find a staff to beat a dog!" The struggles of the Israelites to preserve or regain their independency, which they had from God, are termed insurrection, rebellion, and sedition: because at last they fell under the power of their oppressors. Had they been successful in these struggles, such offensive words had never been used. In 1688 the people of England struggled to throw off an oppressive government, that was changing the times and the seasons, and overthrowing the religion of the country, and setting up in its place the spurious offspring of popery and arbitrary government. They were successful; and it is called the Revolution: had they failed it would have been called rebellion; and the parties principally concerned would have been put to death.

Verse 20. *Beyond the river*] That is, the Euphrates. Both David and Solomon carried their conquests beyond this river. See 2 Sam. viii. 3, &c., and 1 Kings iv. 21, where it is said, *Solomon reigned over all kingdoms from the river* (Euphrates) *unto the land of the Philistines; and unto the borders of Egypt.*

Verse 21. *Until* another *commandment shall be given from me.*] The rebuilding was only provisionally suspended. The decree was, Let it cease for the present; nor let it proceed at any time without an order express from me.

Verse 23. *Made them to cease by force and power.*] Commanded them on pain of the king's displeasure not to proceed, obliging all to remit their labours, and probably bringing an armed force to prevent them from going forward.

Verse 24. *So it ceased unto the second year of—Darius*] They had begun in the first year of Cyrus, B. C. 536, to go up to Jerusalem, and they were obliged to desist from the building, B. C. 522; and thus they continued till the second year of Darius, B. C. 519. See the chronology in the margin and the following chapter.

CHAPTER V

Haggai and Zechariah the prophets encourage Zerubbabel and Jeshua to proceed with the building of the temple, 1, 2. Tatnai, the governor of the provinces on this side the Euphrates, and his companions, inquire by what authority they do this, 3–5. They write to Darius; a copy of the letter, 6–16. They request to know how they are to proceed, 17.

A. M. 3484
B. C. 520
Olymp. LXV. 1
Anno Urbis
Conditæ 234

THEN [a]the prophets, [b]Haggai the prophet, and [c]Zechariah the son of Iddo, prophesied unto the Jews that *were* in Judah and Jerusalem in the name of the God of Israel, *even* unto them.

2 Then rose up [d]Zerubbabel the son of Shealtiel, and Jeshua the son of Jozadak, and began to build the house of God which *is* at Jerusalem: and with them *were* the prophets of God helping them.

3 At the same time came to them [e]Tatnai, governor on this side the river, and Shethar-boznai, and their companions, and said thus unto them, [f]Who hath commanded you to build this house, and to make up this wall?

4 [g]Then said we unto them after this manner, What are the names of the men [h]that make this building?

5 But [i]the eye of their God was upon the elders of the Jews, that they could not cause them to cease, till the matter came to Darius: and then they returned [k]answer by letter concerning this *matter.*

A. M. 3484
B. C. 520
Olymp. LXV. 1
Anno Urbis
Conditæ 234

6 The copy of the letter that Tatnai, governor on this side the river, and Shethar-boznai, [l]and his companions the Apharsachites, which *were* on this side the river, sent unto Darius the king:

A. M. 3485
B. C. 519
Olymp. LXV. 2
Anno Urbis
Conditæ 235

7 They sent a letter unto him, [m]wherein was written thus; Unto Darius the king, all peace.

8 Be it known unto the king, that we went into the province of Judea, to the house of the great God, which is builded with [n]great stones, and timber is laid in the walls, and this work

---

[a]1 Esd. vi. 1, &c.——[b]Hag. i. 1——[c]Zech. i. 1
[d]Chapter iii. 2——[e]Verse 6; chap. vi. 6——[f]Verse 9
[g]Ver. 10——[h]Chald. *that build this building?*

[i]See chap. vii. 6, 28; Psa. xxxiii. 18——[k]Chap. vi. 6
[l]Chapter iv. 9——[m]Chald. *in the midst whereof*
[n]Chald. *stones of rolling*

NOTES ON CHAP. V

Verse 1. *Haggai—and Zechariah*] These are the same whose writings we have among the twelve minor prophets.

The son of Iddo] That is, the *grandson* of Iddo; for Zechariah was *the son of Barachiah, the son of Iddo.* See his prophecy, chap. i. ver. 1.

Verse 2. *Then rose up Zerubbabel*] Here we find *three classes* of men joining in the sacred work: *Zerubbabel* the *civil* governor; *Jeshua* the *high priest* or *ecclesiastical* governor; and *Haggai* and *Zechariah* the *prophets.* How glorious it is when we see the *civil government* joining with the *sacerdotal* and *prophetic* for the establishment and extension of true religion!

Verse 3. *Tatnai, governor*] He was governor of the provinces which belonged to the Persian empire on their side of the Euphrates, comprehending *Syria, Arabia Deserta, Phœnicia,* and *Samaria.* He seems to have been a mild and judicious man; and to have acted with great prudence and caution, and without any kind of *prejudice.* The manner in which he represented this to the king is a full proof of this disposition.

Verse 4. *What are the names*] It is most evident that this is the *answer* of the *Jews* to the inquiry of Tatnai, ver. 3, and the verse should be read thus: *Then said we unto them after this manner:* THESE *are the names of the men who make this building.*

Verse 5. *The eye of their God was upon the elders*] The *watchful care* of God was upon the elders. They were assured of his *favour;* and they found his especial *providence* working in their behalf.

Verse 8. *With great stones*] They are making a very *strong* and a very *costly* building.

A. M. 3485
B. C. 519
Olymp. LXV. 2
Anno Urbis
Conditæ 235

goeth fast on, and prospereth in their hands.

9 Then asked we those elders, *and* said unto them thus, °Who commanded you to build this house, and to make up these walls?

10 We asked their names also, to certify thee, that we might write the names of the men that *were* the chief of them.

11 And thus they returned us answer, saying, We are the servants of the God of heaven and earth, and build the house that was builded these many years ago, which a great king of Israel builded Pand set up.

A. M. 3468
B. C. 536
Olymp. LXI. 1
Anno Urbis
Conditæ 218

12 But qafter that our fathers had provoked the God of heaven unto wrath, he gave them into the hand of rNebuchadnezzar the king of Babylon, the Chaldean, who destroyed this house, and carried the people away into Babylon.

13 But in the first year of sCyrus the king of Babylon, *the same* King Cyrus made a decree to build this house of God.

14 And tthe vessels also of gold and silver

of the house of God, which
Nebuchadnezzar took out of the
temple that *was* in Jerusalem,
and brought them into the
temple of Babylon, those did Cyrus the king
take out of the temple of Babylon, and they
were delivered unto *one*, uwhose name *was*
Sheshbazzar, whom he had made vgovernor;

A. M. 3468
B. C. 536
Olymp. LXI. 1
Anno Urbis
Conditæ 218

15 And said unto him, Take these vessels, go, carry them into the temple that is in Jerusalem, and let the house of God be builded in his place.

16 Then came the same Sheshbazzar, *and* wlaid the foundation of the house of God which *is* in Jerusalem: and since that time even until now hath it been in building, and xyet it is not finished.

A.M.3468-3485
B. C. 536-519
Olymp. LXI. 1
—LXV. 2

17 Now therefore, if *it seem* good to the king, ylet there be search made in the king's treasure house, which *is* there at Babylon, whether it be *so*, that a decree was made of Cyrus the king to build this house of God at Jerusalem, and let the king send his pleasure to us concerning this matter.

A. M. 3485
B. C. 519
Olymp. LXV. 2
Anno Urbis
Conditæ 235

°Ver. 3, 4——P1 Kings vi. 1——q2 Chron. xxxvi. 16, 17
r2 Kings xxiv. 2; xxv. 8, 9, 11——sChap. i. 1

tCh. i. 7, 8; vi. 5——uHag. i. 14; ii. 2, 21——vOr, *deputy*
wChap. iii. 8, 10——xChap. vi. 15——yChap. vi. 1, 2

Verse 11. *We are the servants of the God of heaven*] How simple, plain, and ingenuous is this confession! They were the servants of the God of heaven. How came they then into bondage! Why, they *provoked the God of heaven* —*repeatedly sinned* against him, and then he gave them into the hands of their enemies.

Verse 16. *Sheshbazzar*] Probably the military officer that conducted the people from Babylon, and had the oversight of the work; but some think that Ezra is meant.

Verse 17. *The—treasure house*] גִּנְזַיָּא *ginzaiya*. This is a Persian word, گنجی *gunji*, a *treasury*.

There is a great deal of good sense and candour in this letter. Nothing of passion or prejudice appears in it. They laid before the king a fair statement, without any attempt to prejudice his mind; and gave him those directions which were most likely to lead him to the truth, and to form a correct judgment on a business which, however it issued, must be of considerable importance to the state. God was in all this business; he was now giving an additional proof of his continued regard for a disobedient people, whom, though he had punished in his *justice*, he had spared in his *mercy*.

CHAPTER VI

Darius orders search to be made for the edict of Cyrus, 1. It is found at Achmetha, 2. A transcript of this edict, 3–5. Darius confirms it, 6–12. Tatnai encourages the Jews to proceed; and they finish the temple in the sixth year of Darius, 13–15. They dedicate the temple, 16–18; keep the passover, 19–21, and the feast of unleavened bread, 22.

A. M. 3485
B. C. 519
Olymp. LXV. 2
Anno Urbis
Conditæ 235

THEN Darius the king made a decree, [a]and search was made in the house of the [b]rolls, where the treasures [c]were laid up in Babylon.

2 And there was found at [d]Achmetha, in the palace that *is* in the province of the Medes, a roll, and therein *was* a record thus written:

3 In the first year of Cyrus the king, *the same* Cyrus the king made a decree *concerning* the house of God at Jerusalem, Let the house be builded, the place where they offered sacrifices, and let the foundations thereof be strongly laid; the height thereof threescore cubits, *and* the breadth thereof threescore cubits;

4 [e]*With* three rows of great stones, and a row of new timber: and let the expenses be given out of the king's house:

5 And also let [f]the golden and silver vessels of the house of God, which Nebuchadnezzar took forth out of the temple which *is* at Jerusalem, and brought unto Babylon, be restored, and [g]brought again unto the temple which *is* at Jerusalem, *every one* to his place, and place *them* in the house of God.

6 [h]Now *therefore,* Tatnai, governor beyond the river, Shethar-boznai, and [i]your companions the Apharsachites, which *are* beyond the river, be ye far from thence:

7 Let the work of this house of God alone; let the governor of the Jews and the elders of the Jews build this house of God in his place.

A. M. 3485
B. C. 519
Olymp. LXV. 2
Anno Urbis
Conditæ 235

8 Moreover [k]I make a decree what ye shall do to the elders of these Jews for the building of this house of God: that of the king's goods, *even* of the tribute beyond the river, forthwith expenses be given unto these men, that they be not [l]hindered.

9 And that which they have need of, both young bullocks, and rams, and lambs, for the burnt-offerings of the God of heaven, wheat, salt, wine, and oil, according to the appointment of the priests which *are* at Jerusalem, let it be given them day by day without fail:

10 [m]That they may offer sacrifices [n]of sweet savours unto the God of heaven, and [o]pray for the life of the king, and of his sons.

11 Also I have made a decree, that whosoever shall alter this word, let timber be pulled down from his house, and being set up, [p]let him be hanged thereon; [q]and let his house be made a dunghill for this.

12 And the God that hath caused his [r]name to dwell there, destroy all kings and people that shall put to their hand to alter *and* to

---

[a]Chap. v. 17; 1 Esd. vi. 23——[b]Chald. *books*
[c]Chald. *made to descend*——[d]Or, *Ecbatana;* or, *in a coffer*——[e]1 Kings vi. 36——[f]Chap. i. 7, 8; v. 14
[g]Chald. *go*——[h]Chap. v. 3——[i]Chald. *their societies*

[k]Chald. *by me a decree is made*——[l]Chald. *made to cease*——[m]Chap. vii. 23; Jer. xxix. 7——[n]Chald. *of rest*
[o]1 Tim. ii. 1, 2——[p]Chald. *let him be destroyed*——[q]Dan. ii. 5; iii. 29——[r]1 Kings ix. 3

NOTES ON CHAP. VI

Verse 1. *In the house of the rolls*] בית ספריא *beith siphraiya,* the *house of the books,* the *king's library.* This is the first time we hear of a library.

Verse 2. *At Achmetha*] Ecbatana in India, whither it is probable all the records of Cyrus had been carried. This was a sort of summer residence for the kings of Persia.

Verse 3. *The height thereof threescore cubits*] This was much larger than the temple of Solomon. This was *sixty cubits high,* and *sixty cubits broad;* whereas Solomon's was only *twenty cubits* broad, and *thirty cubits* high.

Verse 4. *Three rows of great stones, and a row of new timber*] We have noticed this kind of building before, three courses of stones, and then a course of strong balk; and this continued to the square of the building.

And let the expenses be given] Cyrus had ordered *wood* to be cut at Libanus, and conveyed to Joppa at his expense; but it does not appear that he furnished the other expenses of the building, for we have already seen that the Jews contributed for the defraying of all others.

But it appears that he provided at his own expense the *sacrifices* and *offerings* for the temple. See ver. 9.

Verse 6. *Be ye far from thence*] Do not interrupt the Jews in their building; but, on the contrary, further them all in your power.

Verse 10. *And pray for the life of the king, and of his sons.*] Even heathens believed that offerings made in their behalf to the God of the Jews would be available. And this principle has had considerable influence in certain states, where there was even a form of religion established by the law, to induce them to tolerate other forms, that the state might have the benefit of their prayers.

Verse 11. *Let timber be pulled down*] Whether this refers to the punishment of hanging and gibbeting, of whipping at a post, or of empaling, is not quite clear. In China they tie culprits to posts; and the executioner cuts them open while alive, takes out their bowels, &c. Empaling, thrusting a sharp stake through the body till it comes out at the side of the neck, or hanging, seems to be intended here.

Let his house be made a dunghill] Let it be reduced to ruins, and never more used, except for the most sordid and unclean purposes.

A. M. 3185
B. C. 519
Olymp. LXV. 2
Anno Urbis
Conditæ 235

destroy this house of God which *is* at Jerusalem. I Darius have made a decree; let it be done with speed.

13 Then Tatnai, governor on this side the river, Shethar-boznai, and their companions, according to that which Darius the king had sent, so they did speedily.

14 [s]And the elders of the Jews builded, and they prospered through the prophesying of Haggai the prophet and Zechariah the son of Iddo. And they builded, and finished *it,* according to the commandment of the God of Israel, and according to the [t]commandment of [u]Cyrus, and [v]Darius, and [w]Artaxerxes king of Persia.

A. M. 3489
B. C. 515
Ol. LXVI. 2
Anno Urbis
Conditæ 239

15 And this house was finished on the third day of the month Adar, which was in the sixth year of the reign of Darius the king.

16 And the children of Israel, the priests, and the Levites and the rest of [x]the children of the captivity, kept [y]the dedication of this house of God with joy,

17 And [z]offered at the dedication of this house of God a hundred bullocks, two hun-

dred rams, four hundred lambs; and for a sin-offering for all Israel, twelve he-goats, according to the number of the tribes of Israel.

A. M. 3489
B. C. 515
Olymp. LXVI. 2
Anno Urbis
Conditæ 239

18 And they set the priests in their [a]divisions, and the Levites in their [b]courses, for the service of God, which *is* at Jerusalem; [c]as [d]it is written in the book of Moses.

19 And the children of the captivity kept the passover [e]upon the fourteenth *day* of the first month.

20 For the priests and the Levites were [f]purified together, all of them *were* pure, and [g]killed the passover for all the children of the captivity, and for their brethren the priests, and for themselves.

21 And the children of Israel which were come again out of captivity, and all such as had separated themselves unto them from the [h]filthiness of the heathen of the land, to seek the LORD God of Israel, did eat,

22 And kept the [i]feast of unleavened bread seven days with joy: for the LORD had made them joyful, and [k]turned the heart [l]of the king of Assyria unto them, to strengthen their hands in the work of the house of God, the God of Israel.

---

[s]Chap. v. 1, 2——[t]Chald. *decree*——[u]Chap. i. 1; v. 13; ver. 3——[v]Ch. iv. 24——[w]Ch. vii. 1——[x]Chald. *the sons of the transportation*——[y]1 Kings viii. 63; 2 Chron. vii. 5——[z]Ch. viii. 35——[a]1 Chron. xxiv. 1 [b]1 Chron. xxiii. 6——[c]Chald. *according to the writing*

[d]Num. iii. 6; viii. 9——[e]Exodus. xii. 6——[f]2 Chron. xxx. 15——[g]2 Chron. xxxv. 11——[h]Chap. ix. 11 [i]Exod. xii. 15; xiii. 6; 2 Chron. xxx. 21; xxxv. 17 [k]Proverbs xxi. 1——[l]2 Kings xxiii. 29; 2 Chron. xxxiii. 11; chapter i. 1; verse 6, &c.

Verse 14. *According to the commandment of the God of Israel*] He first gave the order, and stirred up the hearts of the following Persian kings to second that order.

Of Cyrus] This sovereign gave his orders for the rebuilding of the temple about A. M. 3468.

And Darius] Darius Hystaspes confirmed the above orders, A. M. 3485.

And Artaxerxes] Artaxerxes Longimanus sent Ezra to Judea with new privileges, A. M. 3547. With the permission of the same king, Nehemiah came to Judea in 3550. The writer recapitulates the different sovereigns who favoured the Jews after the Babylonish captivity. See *Calmet.*

Verse 15. *This house was finished*] The sixth year of Darius mentioned here was about A. M. 3489, twenty years after the foundation had been laid by Zerubbabel, under the reign of Cyrus.

Verse 17. *Twelve he-goats*] This was a sin-offering for every tribe.

Verse 18. *And they set the priests*] With this verse the Chaldee or Aramitic part of this chapter ends.

Verse 20. *The Levites were purified together*] They were all ready at one time to observe the proper rites and ceremonies, and had no need of having a second passover, which was appointed

by the law for those who had been accidentally defiled, or were at a distance from the tabernacle. See 2 Chron. xxx. 3.

Verse 21. *And all such as had separated themselves*] These were the *proselytes* who had embraced the Jewish religion by having mingled with the Jews in their captivity. This proves that there the poor captives had so acted according to the principles of their religion, that the heathens saw it, and walked in the light of the Lord with them. A good example is very persuasive; and particularly so when founded on pure principles.

Verse 22. *Turned the heart of the king of Assyria*] I am of Calmet's mind, that *king of Assyria* is here put for *king of Persia.* Cyrus and his successors possessed all the rights and estates of the ancient kings of Assyria, and therefore the same monarch may be styled king of Assyria as well as king of Persia.

DARIUS had a very high character, as a wise, just, and merciful prince. To strengthen his title to the crown, he married two of the daughters of *Cyrus;* and, no doubt, to show his affection to this family, he the more cheerfully confirmed the edict which Cyrus had made in favour of the Jews.

CHAPTER VII

In the seventh year of Artaxerxes, king of Persia, Ezra goes up to Jerusalem; and with him certain of the priests, Levites, porters, and Nethinim: his character, 1–10. The letter and decree of Artaxerxes in behalf of the Jews, 11–26. Ezra's thanksgiving to God for these mercies, 27, 28.

A. M. 3547
B. C. 457
Ol. LXXX. 4
Coss. Rom.
Q. Minucio
et C. Horatio

NOW [a]after these things, in the reign of [b]Artaxerxes king of Persia, Ezra [c]the son of Seraiah, the son of Azariah, the son of Hilkiah,

2 The son of Shallum, the son of Zadok, the son of Ahitub,

3 The son of Amariah, the son of Azariah, the son of Meraioth,

4 The son of Zerahiah, the son of Uzzi, the son of Bukki,

5 The son of Abishua, the son of Phinehas, the son of Eleazar, the son of Aaron the chief priest:

6 This Ezra went up from Babylon; and he *was* a [d]ready scribe in the law of Moses, which the LORD God of Israel had given: and the king granted him all his request, [e]according to the hand of the LORD his God upon him.

7 [f]And there went up *some* of the children of Israel, and of the priests, and [g]the Levites,

and the singers, and the porters, and [h]the Nethinims, unto Jerusalem, in the seventh year of Artaxerxes the king.

A. M. 3547
B. C. 457
Ol. LXXX. 4
Coss. Rom.
Q. Minucio
et C. Horatio

8 And he came to Jerusalem in the fifth month, which *was* in the seventh year of the king.

9 For upon the first *day* of the first month [i]began he to go up from Babylon, and on the first *day* of the fifth month came he to Jerusalem, [k]according to the good hand of his God upon him.

10 For Ezra had prepared his heart to [l]seek the law of the LORD, and to do *it,* and to [m]teach in Israel statutes and judgments.

11 Now this *is* the copy of the letter that the King Artaxerxes gave unto Ezra the priest, the scribe, *even* a scribe of the words of the commandments of the LORD, and of his statutes to Israel.

12 Artaxerxes, [n]king of kings, [o]unto Ezra the priest, a scribe of the law of the God of

---

[a]1 Esd. viii. 1, &c.——[b]Neh. ii. 1——[c]1 Chron. vi. 14
[d]Ver. 11, 12, 21——[e]Ver. 9; ch. viii. 22, 31——[f]Ch. viii.
1——[g]See chap. viii. 15, &c.——[h]Chap. ii. 43; viii. 20
[i]Heb. was *the foundation of the going up*

[k]Ver. 6; Neh. ii. 8, 18——[l]Psa. cxix. 45——[m]Ver. 6,
25; Deut. xxxiii. 10; Neh. viii. 1–8; Mal. ii. 7——[n]Ezek.
xxvi. 7; Dan. ii. 37——[o]Or, *To Ezra the priest, a perfect scribe of the law of the God of heaven,* peace, &c.

NOTES ON CHAP. VII

Verse 1. In the reign of Artaxerxes] This was Artaxerxes Longimanus, the seventh of whose reign chronologers place A. M. 3547, *sixty-eight* years after Cyrus had sent back Zerubbabel.—*Calmet.* See the *introduction.*

Son of Seraiah] Either this could not have been Seraiah the *high priest,* who had been put to death by Nebuchadnezzar *one hundred and twenty-one years* before this time, or the term *son* here must signify only his *descendants,* or *one of his descendants.* Were it otherwise, Ezra must now be at least *one hundred and twenty-two* years of age, supposing him to have been born in the year of his father's death; if, indeed, Seraiah the high priest was his father; but this is evidently impossible. In this place there are only *sixteen* generations reckoned between Ezra and Aaron, but in 1 Chron. vi. 3, 4, &c., there are not less than *twenty-two.* We must therefore supply the deficient generations from the above place, between Amariah son of Meraioth, 1 Chron. vi. 7, and Azariah the son of Johanan, ver. 10. There are other discrepancies relative to genealogies in these *historical* books which it would be useless to investigate. On these differences much has been already said in different parts of this comment.

Verse 6. A ready scribe] סופר מהיר *sopher machir* does not merely signify a *speedy writer*

or an *excellent penman,* but one who was eminently skilful in expounding the *law.* In this sense the word γραμματευς, *scribe,* is repeatedly used in the New Testament, and we find that both in the Old and New Testament it had the same signification. The *Syriac* gives the sense of the word by translating ܣܦܪ ܚܟܝܡܐ *sophro chocimo, a wise scribe,* or *expounder.*

Verse 8. He came to Jerusalem in the fifth month] From the following verse we learn that Ezra and his company set off from Babylon on the first day of the first month, and thus we find they were upwards of *four months* on their journey. They could not travel fast, as they were a great company, composed in part of the *aged* and *infirm,* besides multitudes of *women* and *children.* They appear also to have taken a circuitous route. See on chap. viii.

Verse 10. Ezra had prepared his heart] Here is a fine character of a minister of God: *He prepares,* הכין *hechin,* he fixes, purposes, and determines, לבבו *lebabo, with his heart*—with all his powers and affections, to *seek the law of God,* and *to do it* himself, that he may be properly qualified to *teach* its *statutes* and *judgments* to Israel.

Verse 12. Artaxerxes, king of kings] This letter, from the beginning of this verse to the end of ver. 26, is in the *Aramitic* or *Chaldee* language.

A. M. 3547
B. C. 457
Ol. LXXX. 4
Coss. Rom.
Q. Minucio
et C. Horatio

heaven, perfect *peace*, ᵖand at such a time.

13 I make a decree, that all they of the people of Israel, and *of* his priests and Levites, in my realm, which are minded of their own free-will to go up to Jerusalem, go with thee.

14 Forasmuch as thou art sent ᵠof the king, and of his ʳseven counsellors, to inquire concerning Judah and Jerusalem, according to the law of thy God which *is* in thine hand;

15 And to carry the silver and gold, which the king and his counsellors have freely offered unto the God of Israel, ˢwhose habitation *is* in Jerusalem;

16 ᵗAnd all the silver and gold that thou canst find in all the province of Babylon, with the freewill-offering of the people, and of the priests, ᵘoffering willingly for the house of their God which *is* in Jerusalem:

17 That thou mayest buy speedily with this money bullocks, rams, lambs, with their ᵛmeat-offerings and their drink-offerings, and ʷoffer them upon the altar of the house of your God which *is* in Jerusalem.

18 And whatsoever shall seem good to thee, and to thy brethren, to do with the rest of the silver and the gold, that do after the will of your God.

19 The vessels also that are given thee for the service of the house of thy God, *those* deliver thou before the God of Jerusalem.

20 And whatsoever more shall be needful for the house of thy God, which thou shalt have occasion to bestow, bestow it out of the king's treasure-house.

21 And I, *even* I, Artaxerxes the king, do make a decree to all the treasurers which *are* beyond the river, that whatsoever Ezra the priest, the scribe of the law of the God of heaven, shall require of you, it be done speedily,

22 Unto a hundred talents of silver, and to a hundred ˣmeasures of wheat, and to a hundred baths of wine, and to a hundred baths of oil, and salt without prescribing *how much*.

23 ʸWhatsoever is commanded by the God of heaven, let it be diligently done for the house of the God of heaven: for why should there be wrath against the realm of the king and his sons?

24 Also we certify you, that, touching any of the priests and Levites, singers, porters, Nethinims, or ministers of this house of God, it shall not be lawful to impose toll, tribute, or custom, upon them.

25 And thou, Ezra, after the wisdom of thy God, that *is* in thine hand, ᶻset magistrates and judges, which may judge all the people that *are* beyond the river, all such as know the laws of thy God; and ᵃteach ye them that know *them* not.

26 And whosoever will not do the law of thy God, and the law of the king, let judgment

A. M. 3547
B. C. 457
Ol. LXXX. 4
Coss. Rom.
Q. Minucio
et C. Horatio

ᵖChap. iv. 10——ᵠChald. *from before the king*
ʳEsth. i. 14——ˢ2 Chron. vi. 2; Psa. cxxxv. 21——ᵗCh. viii. 25——ᵘ1 Chron. xxix. 6, 9——ᵛNum. xv. 4–13

ʷDeut. xii. 5, 11——ˣChald. *cors*——ʸHeb. *Whatsoever* is *of the decree*——ᶻExod. xviii. 21, 22; Deut. xvi. 18
ᵃVer. 10; 2 Chron. xvii. 7; Mal. ii. 7; Matt. xxiii. 2, 3

This title of the king would, in Persian, run thus: اردشير شاهنشاه *Ardsheer shahinshah*, or پادشاه *padshah*, "Ardsheer, king of kings;" "*great* or *supreme king*, or *emperor*."

Verse 13. *Their own free-will*] None shall be *forced* either to *go* or to *stay*. He who loves his God will avail himself of this favourable opportunity.

Verse 14. *His seven counsellors*] It is very likely that the privy counsel of the king consisted of *seven* persons simply. The *names* of these seven counsellors or chamberlains may be found in the book of Esther, chap. i. 10.

Verse 16. *And all the silver and gold*] The king and his counsellors had already made a present to the house of the God of Israel; and Ezra is now empowered to receive any contribution which any of the inhabitants of the province of Babylon may think proper to give.

Verse 18. *After the will of your God*] He gave them the fullest liberty to order every

thing according to their own institutions, binding them to no form or mode of worship.

Verse 22. *A hundred talents of silver*] The talent of silver was 450*l*.

A hundred measures of wheat] A hundred *cors*; each *cor* was a little more than *seventy-five gallons, one quart*, and *a pint*, wine measure.

A hundred baths of wine] Each *bath* was seven gallons and *five pints*.

Verse 23. *Why should there be wrath*] As he believed he was appointed by the Almighty to do this work, he therefore wished to do it heartily, knowing that if he did not, God would be displeased, and that the kingdom would be cut off from *him* or his *posterity*.

Verse 24. *It shall not be lawful to impose toll*] As these persons had no private revenues, it would have been unreasonable to have laid them under *taxation*.

Verse 26. *Whether* it be *unto death*] These include almost *every* species of punishment which should be inflicted on culprits in any

A. M. 3547
B. C. 457
Ol. LXXX. 4
Coss. Rom.
Q. Minucio
et C. Horatio

be executed speedily upon him, whether *it be* unto death, or [b]to banishment, or to confiscation of goods, or to imprisonment.

27 [c]Blessed *be* the LORD God of our fathers, [d]which hath put *such a thing* as this in the king's heart, to beautify the house of the LORD which *is* in Jerusalem:

---

[b]Chald. *to rooting out*——[c]1 Chron. xxix. 10
[d]Chap. vi. 22

---

civilized state. With this verse the *Chaldee* part of this chapter ends.

Verse 28. *And I was strengthened*] In what the king decreed he saw the hand of God; he therefore gave *him* the praise, and took courage. There is a most amiable spirit of piety in these reflections. Ezra simply states the case; shows what the king had determined, and tells what he said; and then points out the grand

28 And [e]hath extended mercy unto me before the king, and his counsellors, and before all the king's mighty princes. And I was strengthened as [f]the hand of the LORD my God *was* upon me, and I gathered together out of Israel chief men to go up with me.

A. M. 3547
B. C. 457
Ol. LXXX. 4
Coss. Rom.
Q. Minucio
et C. Horatio

---

[e]Chap. ix. 9——[f]See chap. v. 5; ver. 6, 9; chap. viii. 18

---

agent in the whole business—it was the Lord God of his fathers. Thus God had put it into the king's heart to beautify the house of Jehovah; and, as that house was built for the salvation of the souls of men, he gives God praise for putting it into the king's heart to repair it: he who loves God and man will rejoice in the establishment of the Divine worship, because this is the readiest way to promote the best interests of man.

CHAPTER VIII

The genealogy of the chief persons who went with Ezra from Babylon, 1–14. He gathers them together at Ahava; and finding among them no Levites, he sends confidential persons to the river of Ahava, who return with many Levites and Nethinim, 15–20. He proclaims a fast at Ahava for Divine protection on their journey, 21–23. He delivers to the care of the priests, &c., the silver, gold, and sacred vessels, that they might carry them to Jerusalem, and deliver them to the high priest, 24–30. They depart from Ahava, and come to Jerusalem, 31, 32. The vessels are weighed and the weight registered, 33, 34. They offer burnt-offerings to God, 35; deliver the king's commissions to his lieutenants, by whom they are furthered in their work, 36.

A. M. 3547
B. C. 457
Ol. LXXX. 4
Coss. Rom.
Q. Minucio
et C. Horatio

THESE [a]*are* now the chief of their fathers, and *this is* the genealogy of them that went up with me from Babylon, in the reign of Artaxerxes the king.

2 Of the sons of Phinehas; Gershom: of the sons of Ithamar; Daniel: of the sons of David; [b]Hattush.

3 Of the sons of Shechaniah, of the sons of [c]Pharosh; Zechariah: and with him were reckoned by genealogy of the males a hundred and fifty.

4 Of the sons of Pahath-moab; Elihoenai the son of Zerahiah, and with him two hundred males.

5 Of the sons of Shechaniah; the son of Jahaziel, and with him three hundred males.

6 Of the sons also of Adin; Ebed the son

of Jonathan, and with him fifty males.

7 And of the sons of Elam; Jeshaiah the son of Athaliah, and with him seventy males.

8 And of the sons of Shephatiah; Zebadiah the son of Michael, and with him fourscore males.

9 Of the sons of Joab; Obadiah the son of Jehiel, and with him two hundred and eighteen males.

10 And of the sons of Shelomith; the son of Josiphiah, and with him a hundred and threescore males.

11 And of the sons of Bebai; Zechariah the son of Bebai, and with him twenty and eight males.

12 And of the sons of Azgad; Johanan [d]the

A. M. 3547
B. C. 457
Ol. LXXX. 4
Coss. Rom.
Q. Minucio
et C. Horatio

---

[a]1 Esd. viii. 28——[b]1 Chron. iii. 22

[c]Chap. ii. 3——[d]Or, *the youngest son*

NOTES ON CHAP. VIII

Verse 2. *Gershom*] One of the descendants of Phinehas, son of Eliazar.

Verse 3. *Of the sons of Shechaniah*] There

were three of this name; the second is mentioned ver. 5, and the third chap. x. 2. They were all different persons, as may be seen from their fathers' houses.

A. M. 3547
B. C. 457
Ol. LXXX. 4
Coss. Rom.
Q. Minucio
et C. Horatio

son of Hakkatan, and with him a hundred and ten males.

13 And of the last sons of Adonikam, whose names *are* these, Eliphelet, Jeiel, and Shemaiah, and with them threescore males.

14 Of the sons also of Bigvai; Uthai, and [e]Zabbud, and with them seventy males.

15 And I gathered them together to the river that runneth to Ahava; and there [f]abode we in tents three days: and I viewed the people, and the priests, and found there none of the [g]sons of Levi.

16 Then sent I for Eliezer, for Ariel, for Shemaiah, and for Elnathan, and for Jarib, and for Elnathan, and for Nathan, and for Zechariah, and for Meshullam, chief men; also for Joiarib, and for Elnathan, men of understanding.

17 And I sent them with commandment unto Iddo the chief at the place Casiphia, and [h]I told them what they should say unto Iddo, *and* to his brethren the Nethinims, at the place Casiphia, that they should bring unto us ministers for the house of our God.

18 And by the good hand of our God upon us they [i]brought us a man of understanding, of the sons of Mahli, the son of Levi, the son of Israel; and Sherebiah, with his sons and his brethren, eighteen;

19 And Hashabiah, and with him Jeshaiah of the sons of Merari, his brethren and their sons, twenty;

A. M. 3547
B. C. 457
Ol. LXXX. 4
Coss. Rom.
Q. Minucio
et C. Horatio

20 [k]Also of the Nethinims, whom David and the princes had appointed for the service of the Levites, two hundred and twenty Nethinims: all of them were expressed by name.

21 Then I [l]proclaimed a fast there, at the river of Ahava, that we might [m]afflict ourselves before our God, to seek of him a [n]right way for us, and for our little ones, and for all our substance.

22 For [o]I was ashamed to require of the king a band of soldiers and horsemen to help us against the enemy in the way: because we had spoken unto the king, saying, [p]The hand of our God *is* upon all them for [q]good that seek him; but his power and his wrath *is* [r]against all them that [s]forsake him.

23 So we fasted and besought our God for this: and he was [t]entreated of us.

24 Then I separated twelve of the chief of the priests, Sherebiah, Hashabiah, and ten of their brethren with them.

25 And weighed unto them [u]the silver, and the gold, and the vessels, *even* the offering of the house of our God, which the king, and his counsellors, and his lords, and all Israel *there* present, had offered:

[e]Or, *Zaccur*, as some read——[f]Or, *pitched*——[g]See ch. vii. 7——[h]*I put words in their mouth;* see 2 Sam. xiv. 3, 19——[i]Neh. viii. 7; ix. 4, 5——[k]See ch. ii. 43——[l]2 Chron. xx. 3——[m]Lev. xvi. 29; xxiii. 29; Isa. lviii. 3, 5 [n]Psa. v. 8

[o]So 1 Cor. ix. 15——[p]Chap. vii. 6, 9, 28——[q]Psa. xxxiii. 18, 19; xxxiv. 15, 22; Romans viii. 28——[r]Psalm xxxiv. 16——[s]2 Chronicles xv. 2——[t]1 Chronicles v. 20; 2 Chronicles xxxiii. 13; Isaiah xix. 22——[u]Chapter vii. 15, 16

Verse 15. *The river that runneth to Ahava*] Ahava was a *river* itself, which is supposed to be the same that is called *Diava* or *Adiava*, in the province of *Adiabene;* and perhaps the place whence the people of *Ava* came who were brought by the king of Assyria to Palestine, 2 Kings xvii. 24.

None of the sons of Levi.] None that were *simply Levites.* He found *priests,* and they were *sons of Levi;* but no *Levites* that were not *priests.*

Verse 17. *At the place Casiphia*] The most judicious commentators are agreed that by *Casiphia,* the *Caspian mountains,* between Media and Hyrcania, are intended; where, probably, the *Nethinim* were employed in working silver mines: כסף *keseph,* from which the word comes, signifies *silver.*

Verse 22. *I was ashamed to require—a band*] He had represented God, the object of his worship, as supremely powerful, and as having the strongest affection for his true followers: he could not, therefore, consistently with his declarations, ask a band of soldiers from the king to protect them on the way, when they were going expressly to rebuild the temple of Jehovah, and restore his worship. He therefore found it necessary to seek the Lord by *fasting* and *prayer,* that they might have from *Him* those succours without which they might become a prey to their enemies; and then the religion which they professed would be considered by the heathen as false and vain. Thus we see that this good man had more anxiety for the glory of God than for his own personal safety.

Verse 26. *Silver vessels a hundred talents*] That is, The *weight* of all the silver vessels amounted to one hundred talents; not that there were one hundred vessels of silver, *each a talent in weight.*

Reckoning in round sums, 650 *talents* of silver at £450 the talent, amount to £292,500 sterling. *Silver vessels,* 100 talents, amount to £45,000; *gold,* 100 talents, at £7,000 per talent, amount to £700,000 independently of the 20 *basons of gold,* amounting to 1000 *drachms.* Now the *golden drachm* or *daric* was worth about 1*l.* 2*s.*, therefore these basons were worth

A. M. 3547
B. C. 457
Ol. LXXX. 4
Coss. Rom.
Q. Minucio
et C. Horatio

26 I even weighed unto their hand six hundred and fifty talents of silver, and silver vessels a hundred talents, *and* of gold a hundred talents;

27 Also twenty basons of gold, of a thousand drams; and two vessels of ᵛfine copper ʷprecious as gold.

28 And I said unto them, Ye *are* ˣholy unto the LORD; the vessels *are* ʸholy also; and the silver and the gold *are* a freewill-offering unto the LORD God of your fathers.

29 Watch ye, and keep *them,* until ye weigh *them* before the chief of the priests and the Levites, and chief of the fathers of Israel, at Jerusalem, in the chambers of the house of the LORD.

30 So took the priests and the Levites the weight of the silver, and the gold, and the vessels, to bring *them* to Jerusalem unto the house of our God.

31 Then we departed from the river of Ahava on the twelfth *day* of the first month, to go unto Jerusalem: and ᶻthe hand of our God was upon us, and he delivered us from the hand of the enemy, and of such as lay in wait by the way.

32 And we ᵃcame to Jerusalem, and abode there three days.

A. M. 3547
B. C. 457
Ol. LXXX. 4
Coss. Rom.
Q. Minucio
et C. Horatio

33 Now on the fourth day was the silver and the gold and the vessels ᵇweighed in the house of our God by the hand of Meremoth the son of Uriah the priest; and with him *was* Eleazar the son of Phinehas; and with them *was* Jozabad the son of Jeshua, and Noadiah the son of Binnui, Levites;

34 By number *and* by weight of every one: and all the weight was written at that time.

35 *Also* the children of those that had been carried away, which were come out of the captivity, ᶜoffered burnt-offerings unto the God of Israel, twelve bullocks for all Israel, ninety and six rams, seventy and seven lambs, twelve he-goats *for* a sin-offering: all *this was* a burnt-offering unto the LORD.

36 And they delivered the king's ᵈcommissions unto the king's lieutenants, and to the governors on this side the river: and they furthered the people, and the house of God.

ᵛHeb. *yellow* or *shining brass*——ʷHeb. *desirable*
ˣLev. xxi. 6, 7, 8; Deut. xxxiii. 8——ʸLev. xxii. 2, 3;

Num. iv. 4, 15, 19, 20——ᶻCh. vii. 6, 9, 28——ᵃNeh. ii. 11——ᵇVer. 26, 30——ᶜSo ch. vi. 17——ᵈCh. vii. 21

£1100; the whole amounting to £1,038,600 sterling. But these different weights and coins are variously computed; some making the silver talent only £353 11s. 10½d., and the talent of gold £5057 15s. 1½d., calculations which I have elsewhere introduced.

Two vessels of fine copper, precious as gold] What these were we cannot tell. The Syriac translates **ܠܩܐ ܩܘܪܝܢܬܘܐ ܢܚܫܐ** *nechoso corinthio toba,* to be vessels of the *best Corinthian brass;* so called from the brass found after the burning of Corinth by *Lucius Mummius,* which was brass, copper, gold, and silver, all melted together, as is generally supposed. But it was probably some *factitious* metal made there, that took the polish and assumed the brightness of *gold,* and because of its *hardness* was more durable. There is still a certain factitious metal of this kind, made among the Asiatics. I have seen this metal often made; it is as bright and fine as gold, takes a most exquisite polish, and will scarcely tarnish. I have kept this exposed to every variation of the air, even among old iron, brass, copper, &c., for *twenty* years together, without being scarcely at all *oxidized.* It requires much art in the making, but the constituent materials are of small value. Vessels of this metal, because of their lustre and durability for ornamental and domestic uses, are in many respects more valuable than gold itself. The only difficulty is to get at first the *true colour,* which depends on the *degree of heat,* and the time employed in *fusion;* but there are, however, proper rules to ascertain them. This metal is widely different from the *or molu* of France and England, is less expensive, and much more valuable.

Verse 35. *Twelve bullocks for all Israel*] Though of *tribes* there were only *Judah* and *Benjamin,* yet they offered a bullock for *every* tribe, as if present. There can be little doubt that there were individuals there from all the twelve tribes, possibly some families of each; but no complete tribe but those mentioned above.

Verse 36. *The king's lieutenants*] אֲחַשְׁדַּרְפְּנֵי *achashdarpeney:* this is generally understood to mean *lieutenant* or *deputy,* and is probably of *Persian* origin, though here greatly corrupted. The *Vulgate* renders it *regis satrapis,* to the *satraps* of the king, which is the Persian سَتْرَب *satrab.* A *viceroy* in Persian is صوبه دار *soubah-dar; viceroys,* صوبه داران *soubahdaran.* دارافرين *darafreen* signifies a person in whom one has *confidence;* and اچی *achi* is an epithet of a *vizir.* These two words conjoined will make nearly that of the text. But I do not give any of these etymologies with confidence. Other words might be proposed as candidates, but where there is so little certainty, conjecture is useless. Were it necessary a dissertation might be written on the *Persian words,* and *Persian forms of speech,* in *this* and the *two following books;* but probably after my toil few of my readers would thank me for my pains.

CHAPTER IX

The princes inform Ezra that many of the people now settled in the land had married heathen wives; and several of the rulers were principal offenders in this thing, 1, 2. He is greatly afflicted, 3, 4. His prayer to God on this account, 5–15.

A. M. 3547
B. C. 457
Ol. LXXX. 4
Coss. Rom.
Q. Minucio
et C. Horatio

NOW [a]when these things were done, the princes came to me, saying, The people of Israel, and the priests, and the Levites, have not [b]separated themselves from the people of the lands, [c]*doing* according to their abominations, *even* of the Canaanites, the Hittites, the Perizzites, the Jebusites, the Ammonites, the Moabites, the Egyptians, and the Amorites.

2 For they have [d]taken of their daughters for themselves, and for their sons: so that the [e]holy seed have [f]mingled themselves with the people of *those* lands: yea, the hand of the princes and rulers hath been chief in this trespass.

3 And when I heard this thing, [g]I rent my garment and my mantle, and plucked off the hair of my head and of my beard, and sat down [h]astonied.

4 Then were assembled unto me every one that [i]trembled at the words of the God of Israel, because of the transgression of those that had been carried away; and I sat astonied until the [k]evening sacrifice.

5 And at the evening sacrifice I arose up from my [l]heaviness; and having rent my garment and my mantle, I fell upon my knees, and [m]spread out my hands unto the LORD my God,

6 And said, O my God, I am [n]ashamed and blush to lift up my face to thee, my God: for [o]our iniquities are increased over *our* head, and our [p]trespass is [q]grown up unto the heavens.

7 Since the days of our fathers *have* [r]we *been* in a great trespass unto this day; and for our iniquities [s]have we, our kings, *and* our priests, been delivered into the hand of the kings of the lands, to the sword, to captivity, and to a spoil, and to [t]confusion of face, as *it is* this day.

A. M. 3547
B. C. 457
Ol. LXXX. 4
Coss. Rom.
Q. Minucio
et C. Horatio

---

[a]1 Esd. viii. 68, &c.——[b]Chap. vi. 21; Neh. ix. 2 [c]Deut. vii. 30, 31——[d]Exod. xxxiv. 16; Deut. vii. 3; Neh. xiii. 23——[e]Exod. xix. 6; xxii. 31; Deut. vii. 6; xiv. 2——[f]2 Cor. xi. 14——[g]Job i. 20——[h]Psa. cxliii. 4——[i]Chap. x. 3; Isa. lxvi. 2

[k]Exodus xxix. 39——[l]Or, *affliction*——[m]Exodus ix. 29, 33——[n]Dan. ix. 7, 8——[o]Psa. xxxviii. 4——[p]Or, *guiltiness*——[q]2 Chron. xxviii. 9; Rev. xviii. 5——[r]Psa. cvi. 6; Dan. ix. 5, 6, 8——[s]Deut. xxviii. 36, 64; Neh. ix. 30——[t]Daniel ix. 7, 8

NOTES ON CHAP. IX

Verse 1. *The people of Israel*] These were they who had returned at first with Zerubbabel, and were settled in the land of Judea, and whom Ezra found on his arrival to be little better than the Canaanitish nations from whom God had commanded them ever to keep separate.

Verse 2. *Hath been chief in this trespass.*] They who are the *first* men have been the most *capital* offenders; so VIRGIL, *Æn.* ix. 783:—

Unus homo, vestris, o cives, undique septus
Aggeribus, tantas strages impune per urbem
Ediderit? Juvenum *primos* tot miserit orco?

"Shall one, and he enclosed within your walls,
One rash imprisoned warrior, vanquish all?
Calm you look on, and see the furious foe
Plunge crowds of *heroes* to the shades below!"
　　　　　　　　　　　　　　PITT.

The *first* of the *Trojan youth* were the *chief*, the most *illustrious;* so we say the *first* men of the kingdom for the *nobles*, &c.

Verse 3. *I rent my garment and my mantle*] The *outer* and *inner* garment, in sign of great grief. This significant act is frequently mentioned in the sacred writings, and was common among all ancient nations.

Plucked off the hair] *Shaving* the head and beard were signs of excessive grief; much more so the *plucking off the hair*, which must pro-duce exquisite pain. All this testified his abhorrence, not merely of the act of having taken strange wives, but their having also joined them in their *idolatrous* abominations.

Verse 4. *Those that had been carried away*] Those that had returned long before with Zerubbabel; see ver. 1.

Until the evening sacrifice.] The *morning* sacrifice was the *first* of all the offerings of the day, the *evening* sacrifice the *last*. As the latter was offered *between the two evenings*, i. e., between *sunset* and the *end of twilight*, so the former was offered between *break of day* and *sunrise.* Ezra *sat astonied*—confounded in his mind, distressed in his soul, and scarcely knowing what to do. He probably had withdrawn himself into some sequestered place, or into some secret part of the temple, spending the time in meditation and reflection.

Verse 5. *Fell upon my knees*] In token of the deepest *humility. Spread out my hands*, as if to *lay hold* on the mercy of God. We have already had occasion to explain these significant acts.

Verse 6. *I am ashamed and blush*] God had been so often provoked, and had so often pardoned them, and they had continued to transgress, that he was ashamed to go back again to the throne of grace to ask for mercy in their behalf. This is the genuine feeling of every reawakened *backslider.*

A. M. 3547
B. C. 457
Ol. LXXX. 4
Coss. Rom.
Q. Minucio
et C. Horatio

8 And now for a [u]little space grace hath been *show*ed from the LORD our God, to leave us a remnant to escape, and to give us [v]a nail in his holy place, that our God may [w]lighten our eyes, and give us a little reviving in our bondage.

9 [x]For we *were* bondmen; [y]yet our God hath not forsaken us in our bondage, but [z]hath extended mercy unto us in the sight of the kings of Persia, to give us a reviving, to set up the house of our God, and [a]to repair the desolations thereof, and to give us [b]a wall in Judah and in Jerusalem.

10 And now, O our God, what shall we say after this? for we have forsaken thy commandments,

11 Which thou hast commanded [c]by thy servants the prophets, saying, The land, unto which ye go to possess it, is an unclean land with the [d]filthiness of the people of the lands, with their abominations, which have filled it [e]from one end to another with their uncleanness.

A. M. 3547
B. C. 457
Ol. LXXX. 4
Coss. Rom.
Q. Minucio
et C. Horatio

12 Now therefore [f]give not your daughters unto their sons, neither take their daughters unto your sons, [g]nor seek their peace or their wealth for ever: that ye may be strong, and eat the good of the land, and [h]leave *it* for an inheritance to your children for ever.

13 And after all that is come upon us for our evil deeds, and for our great trespass, seeing that thou our God [i]hast [k]punished us less than our iniquities *deserve*, and hast given us *such* deliverance as this;

14 Should we [l]again break thy commandments, and [m]join in affinity with the people of these abominations? wouldest not thou be [n]angry with us till thou hadst consumed us, so that *there should be* no remnant nor escaping?

15 O LORD God of Israel, [o]thou *art* righteous: for we remain yet escaped, as *it is* this day: behold, we *are* [p]before thee, [q]in our trespasses: for we cannot [r]stand before thee because of this.

---

[u]Hebrew, *moment*——[v]Or, *a pin; that is, a constant and sure abode.* So Isaiah xxii. 23——[w]Psalm xiii. 3; xxxiv. 5——[x]Neh. ix. 36——[y]Psalm cxxxvi. 23——[z]Ch. vii. 28——[a]Hebrew, *to set up*——[b]Isaiah v. 2——[c]Heb. *by the hand of thy servants*——[d]Chap. vi. 21——[e]Heb. *from mouth to mouth:* as 2 Kings xxi. 16——[f]Exodus xxiii. 32; xxxiv. 16; Deut. vii. 3——[g]Deut. xxiii. 6 [h]Proverbs xiii. 22; xx. 7——[i]Psa. ciii. 10——[k]Hebrew, *hast withheld beneath our iniquities*——[l]John v. 14; 2 Peter ii. 20, 21——[m]Verse 2; Nehemiah xiii. 23, 27 [n]Deut. ix. 8——[o]Neh. ix. 33; Dan. ix. 14——[p]Rom. iii. 19——[q]1 Cor. xv. 17——[r]Psa. cxxx. 3

Verse 8. *And now for a little space*] This interval in which they were returning from servitude to their own land.

Grace hath been showed] God has disposed the hearts of the Persian kings to publish edicts in our *favour.*

To leave us a remnant to escape] The ten tribes are gone irrecoverably into captivity; a great part even of Judah and Benjamin had continued beyond the Euphrates: so that Ezra might well say, there was but a *remnant* which had *escaped.*

A nail in his holy place] Even so much ground as to fix our *tent-poles* in.

May lighten our eyes] To give us a thorough knowledge of ourselves and of our highest interest, and to enable us to re-establish his worship, is the reason why God has brought us back to this place.

A little reviving] We were *perishing,* and our hopes were almost *dead;* and, because of our sins, we were *sentenced to death:* but God in his great mercy has given us a *new trial;* and he begins with little, to see if we will make a wise and faithful use of it.

Verse 10. *What shall we say after this?*] Even in the midst of these beginnings of respite and mercy we have begun to provoke thee anew!

Verse 11. *Have filled it from one end to another*] The abominations have been like a sweeping mighty torrent, that has increased till it filled the whole land, and carried every thing before it.

Verse 13. *Hast punished us less than our iniquities*] Great, numerous, and oppressive as our calamities have been, yet merely as temporal punishments, they have been much less than our provocations have deserved.

Verse 15. *Thou* art *righteous*] Thou art *merciful;* this is one of the many meanings of the word צדק *tsedek;* and to this meaning St. Paul refers, when he says, God *declares his righteousness for the remission of sins that are past,* Rom. iii. 25. See the note there.

We remain yet escaped] Because of this *righteousness* or *mercy.*

In our trespasses] We have no righteousness; we are *clothed* and *covered* with our trespasses.

We cannot stand before thee because of this.] The parallel place, as noted in the margin, is Psa. cxxx. 3: *If thou, Lord, shouldest mark iniquities, O Lord, who shall stand?* Every man must stand before the judgment-seat of Christ: but who shall stand there with joy? No man against whom the Lord marks iniquities. There is a reference here to the temple service: the priests and Levites stood and ministered before the Lord, but they were not permitted to do so unless pure from all legal pollution; so no man shall stand before the judgment-seat of Christ who is not washed and made white in the blood of the Lamb. Reader, how dost thou expect to stand there?

CHAPTER X

The people are greatly afflicted by Ezra's prayer, 1. Shechaniah proposes that all who have taken strange wives should put them away, and the children they had by them; and make a covenant to serve God, 2–4. Ezra is encouraged; and makes a proclamation to collect the people, to find who had transgressed, 5–8. They come together on the twentieth day of the ninth month, 9. Ezra exhorts them to put away their strange wives, 10. The people agree to it, and require time, 11–14. This being granted, the business is completed by the first of the first month, 15–17. Some of the priests had taken strange wives; their names, and the names of all who were in the same trespass, 18–44.

A. M. 3547
B. C. 457
Ol. LXXX. 4
Coss. Rom.
Q. Minucio
et C. Horatio

NOW [a]when Ezra had prayed, and when he had confessed, weeping and casting himself down [b]before the house of God, there assembled unto him out of Israel a very great congregation of men and women and children: for the people [c]wept very sore.

2 And Shechaniah the son of Jehiel, *one of* the sons of Elam, answered and said unto Ezra, We have [d]trespassed against our God, and have taken strange wives of the people of the land: yet now there is hope in Israel concerning this thing.

3 Now therefore let us make a [e]covenant with our God [f]to put away all the wives, and such as are born of them, according to the counsel of my lord, and of those that [g]tremble at [h]the commandment of our God; and let it be done according to the law.

4 Arise; for *this* matter *belongeth* unto thee: we also *will be* with thee: [i]be of good courage, and do *it*.

5 Then arose Ezra, and made the chief priests, the Levites, and all Israel, [k]to swear that they should do according to this word. And they sware.

A. M. 3547
B. C. 457
Ol. LXXX. 4
Coss. Rom.
Q. Minucio
et C. Horatio

6 [l]Then Ezra rose up from before the house of God, and went into the chamber of Johanan the son of Eliashib: and *when* he came thither, he [m]did eat no bread, nor drink water: for he mourned because of the transgression of them that had been carried away.

7 And they made proclamation throughout Judah and Jerusalem unto all the children of the captivity, that they should gather themselves together unto Jerusalem;

8 And that whosoever would not come within three days, according to the counsel of the princes and the elders, all his substance should be [n]forfeited, and himself separated from the congregation of those that had been carried away.

9 Then all the men of Judah and Benjamin gathered themselves together unto Jerusalem

---

[a]1 Esd. viii. 91, &c.; Dan. ix. 20——[b]2 Chron. xx 9. •Heb. *wept a great weeping*——[d]Neh. xiii. 27——[e]2 Chron. xxxiv. 31——[f]Heb. *to bring forth*

[g]Chap. ix. 4——[h]Deut. vii. 2, 3——[i]1 Chron. xxviii. 10——[k]Neh. v. 12——[l]1 Esd. ix. 1, &c.——[m]Deut. ix. 18——[n]Heb. *devoted*

NOTES ON CHAP. X

Verse 1. *The people wept very sore.*] They were deeply affected at the thought of God's displeasure, which they justly feared was about to light upon them, because of their transgressions.

Verse 2. *Shechaniah the son of Jehiel*] He speaks here in the name of the *people*, not acknowledging *himself* culpable, for he is not in the following list. It is in the same form of speech with that in James, iii. 9. *With the tongue curse we men.* He seems to have been a *chief man* among the people; and Ezra, at present, stood in need of his influence and support.

Yet now there is hope in Israel] מקוה *mikveh*, expectation, of pardon; for the people were convinced of the evil, and were *deeply penitent:* hence it is said, ver. 1, that *they wept sore.*

Verse 3. *Let us make a covenant*] נכרת ברית *nichrath berith, let us cut* or *divide the covenant sacrifice.* See the notes on Gen. xv. 10.

Verse 4. *Arise; for* this *matter* belongeth unto thee] By the decree of Artaxerxes, he was authorized to do everything that the law of God required: see chap. vii. 23-28. And all officers were commanded to be aiding and assisting; hence Shechaniah says, *We are with you.*

Verse 5. *And they sware.*] The thing was evidently contrary to the law of God; and now he bound them by an *oath* to rectify the abuse.

Verse 6. *Johanan the son of Eliashib*] Eliashib was high priest, and was succeeded in that office by his son Joiada, Neh. xii. 10. Probably *Johanan* here is the same as *Jonathan* in Nehemiah, who was the son of *Joiada*, and grandson of *Eliashib.* Some suppose that *Johanan* and *Joiada* were two names for the same person.

Verse 8. *All his substance should be forfeited*] To *the use of the temple.* So the *Septuagint* understood the place: Αναθεματισθησεται πασα ἡ ὑπαρξις αυτου, "All his substance shall be devoted to a holy use."

Himself separated] *Excommunicated* from the Church of God, and *exiled* from Israel.

Verse 9. *Ninth month*] Answering to a part of our *December.*

Trembling because of—the great rain.] Απο του χειμωνος, *Because of the winter,* Septuagint; it

A. M. 3547
B. C. 457
Ol. LXXX. 4
Coss. Rom.
Q. Minucio
et C. Horatio

within three days. It *was* the
ninth month, and the twentieth
day of the month; and [o]all the
people sat in the street of the
house of God, trembling because of *this* matter, and for [p]the great rain.
10 And Ezra the priest stood up, and said
unto them, Ye have transgressed, and [q]have
taken strange wives, to increase the trespass
of Israel.
11 Now therefore [r]make confession unto the
LORD God of your fathers, and do his pleasure:
and [s]separate yourselves from the people of
the land, and from the strange wives.
12 Then all the congregation answered and
said with a loud voice, As thou hast said, so
must we do.
13 But the people *are* many, and *it is* a
time of much rain, and we are not able to
stand without, neither *is this* a work of one
day or two: for [t]we are many that have transgressed in this thing.
14 Let now our rulers of all the congregation stand, and let all them which have taken
strange wives in our cities come at appointed
times, and with them the elders of every city,
and the judges thereof, until [u]the fierce wrath
of our God [v]for this matter be turned from us.
15 Only Jonathan the son of Asahel and
Jahaziah the son of Tikvah [w]were employed
about this *matter:* and Meshullam and Shabbethai the Levite helped them.
16 And the children of the captivity did so.
And Ezra the priest, *with* certain chief of the
fathers, after the house of their fathers, and
all of them by *their* names,
were separated, and sat down in
the first day of the tenth month
to examine the matter.

A. M. 3547
B. C. 457
Ol. LXXX. 4
Coss. Rom.
Q. Minucio
et C. Horatio

17 And they made an end with all the men
that had taken strange wives by the first day
of the first month.
18 And among the sons of the
priests there were found that
had taken strange wives: *namely,*
of the sons of Jeshua the son of
Jozadak, and his brethren; Maaseiah, and
Eliezer, and Jarib, and Gedaliah.

A. M. 3548
B. C. 456
Ol. LXXXI.
1 Coss. Rom.
M. Valerio
et. Sp. Virginio

19 And they [x]gave their hands that they would
put away their wives; and *being* [y]guilty, *they
offered* a ram of the flock for their trespass.
20 And of the sons of Immer; Hanani, and
Zebadiah.
21 And of the sons of Harim; Maaseiah, and
Elijah, and Shemaiah, and Jehiel, and Uzziah.
22 And of the sons of Pashur; Elioenai,
Maaseiah, Ishmael, Nethaneel, Jozabad, and
Elasah.
23 Also of the Levites; Jozabad, and Shimei,
and Kelaiah, (the same *is* Kelita,) Pethahiah, Judah, and Eliezer.
24 Of the singers also; Eliashib: and of
the porters; Shallum, and Telem, and Uri.
25 Moreover of Israel: of the sons of Parosh; Ramiah, and Jeziah, and Malchiah,
and Miamin, and Eleazar, and Malchijah,
and Benaiah.
26 And of the sons of Elam; Mattaniah,
Zechariah, and Jehiel, and Abdi, and Jeremoth, and Eliah.

---

[o]See 1 Sam. xii. 18——[p]Heb. *the showers*——[q]Heb. *have caused to dwell,* or *have brought back*——[r]Josh. vii. 19; Prov. xxviii. 13——[s]Ver. 3——[t]Or, *we have greatly offended in this thing*

[u]2 Chronicles xxx. 8——[v]Or, *till this matter be despatched*——[w]Hebrew, *stood*——[x]2 Kings x. 15; 1 Chronicles xxix. 24; 2 Chronicles xxx. 8——[y]Leviticus vi. 4, 6

---

was now *December*, the coldest and most rainy part of the year in Palestine.

Verse 11. *Make confession*] Acknowledge your sins before God, with deep compunction of heart, and the fullest resolution to forsake them.

Verse 12. *As thou hast said, so must we do.*] They all resolved to do what Ezra then commanded; they did put away their wives, even those by whom they had children; ver. 44: this was a great hardship on the *women* and *children.* Though by the Jewish laws such marriages were *null* and *void,* yet as the *women* they had taken did not know these laws, their case was deplorable. However, we may take it for granted that each of them received a portion according to the circumstances of their husbands, and that they and their children were not turned away desolate, but had such a provision as their necessities required. *Humanity* must have dictated this, and no law of God is contrary to humanity. After all, there is some room to doubt whether they did put them *finally* away, for several years after Nehemiah found Jews that had married wives of *Ashdod, Ammon,* and *Moab;* Neh. xiii. 23. And if these were not the same women, we find that the same offence was continued.

Verse 17. *The first day of the first month*] So they were *three whole months* in examining into this affair, and making those *separations* which the law required.

Verse 19. *They gave their hands*] They bound themselves in the most solemn manner to do as the rest of the delinquents had done; and they made an acknowledgment of their

A. M. 3548
B. C. 456
Ol. LXXX. 1
Coss. Rom.
M. Valerio
et. Sp. Virginio

27 And of the sons of Zattu; Elioenai, Eliashib, Mattaniah, and Jeremoth, and Zabad, and Aziza.

28 Of the sons also of Bebai; Jehohanan, Hananiah, Zabbai, *and* Athlai.

29 And of the sons of Bani; Meshullam, Malluch, and Adaiah, Jashub, and Sheal, and Ramoth.

30 And of the sons of Pahath-moab; Adna, and Chelal, Benaiah, Maaseiah, Mattaniah, Bezaleel, and Binnui, and Manasseh.

31 And *of* the sons of Harim; Eliezer, Ishijah, Malchiah, Shemaiah, Shimeon,

32 Benjamin, Malluch, *and* Shemariah.

33 Of the sons of Hashum; Mattenai, Mat-

tathah, Zabad, Eliphelet, Jeremai, Manasseh, *and* Shimei.

34 Of the sons of Bani; Maadai, Amram, and Uel,

35 Benaiah, Bedeiah, Chelluh,

36 Vaniah, Meremoth, Eliashib,

37 Mattaniah, Mattenai, and Jaasau,

38 And Bani, and Binnui, Shimei,

39 And Shelemiah, and Nathan, and Adaiah,

40 ²Machnadebai, Shashai, Sharai,

41 Azareel, and Shelemiah, Shemariah,

42 Shallum, Amariah, *and* Joseph.

43 Of the sons of Nebo: Jeiel, Mattithiah, Zabad, Zebina, Jadau, and Joel, Benaiah.

44 All these had taken strange wives: and *some* of them had wives by whom they had children.

A. M. 3548
B. C. 456
Ol. LXXX. 1
Coss. Rom.
M. Valerio
et Sp. Virginio

---

²Or, *Mabnadebai,* according to some copies

---

iniquity to God by offering each a *ram* for a trespass-offering.

Verse 25. *Moreover of Israel*] That is, as *Calmet* observes, *simple Israelites*, to distinguish them from the *priests, Levites,* and *singers, mentioned* in verses 18, 23, and 24.

Verse 44. Some *of them had wives by whom they had children.*] This observation was probably intended to show that only a *few* of them had children; but it shows also how rigorously the law was put in execution.

According to a passage in *Justin Martyr's* dialogue with *Trypho,* a Jew, Ezra offered a paschal lamb on this occasion, and addressed the people thus: "And Ezra said to the people, This passover is our Saviour and our Refuge; and if ye will be persuaded of it, and let it enter into your hearts, that we are to humble ourselves to him in a sign, and afterwards shall

believe in him, this place shall not be destroyed for ever, saith the Lord of Hosts: but if ye will not believe in him, nor hearken to his preaching, ye shall be a laughing-stock to the Gentiles."—*Dial. cum Tryphone,* sec. 72.

This passage, *Justin* says, the Jews, through their enmity to Christ, blotted out of the book of Ezra. He charges them with cancelling several other places through the same spirit of enmity and opposition.

In the *Hebrew text* this and the following book make but one, though sometimes Nehemiah is distinguished as the *second book of Esdras.* In the Masoretic enumeration of sections, &c., both books are conjoined. This may be seen at the end of *Nehemiah.* I can add nothing of importance to the character of Ezra, which has already been given so much in detail in the *introduction* to this book.

Corrected, March, 1828.—A. CLARKE.

INTRODUCTION TO THE BOOK

OF

NEHEMIAH

IN the introduction to the book of Ezra, we have already seen those wonderful interferences of Divine Providence in which Nehemiah bore so large a share. Dr. Prideaux,
with his usual perspicuity, has interwoven the whole of the transactions of the mission of
Nehemiah with that part of the Persian history with which they are connected; which I
shall give, as in the preceding book, in his own words. He connects this book, as it ought
to be, with the book of *Ezra*. See before.

"He who succeeded Ezra in the government of Judah and Jerusalem was Nehemiah, a
very religious and most excellent man; one that was nothing behind his predecessor, saving
his learning and great knowledge in the law of God. He came to Jerusalem in the *twentieth*
year of *Artaxerxes Longimanus*, about *four hundred and forty-five* years before *Christ;* and
by a commission from him, superseded that of Ezra, and succeeded him in the government
of Judah and Jerusalem. He had in that commission, by an express clause therein inserted,
full authority to repair the walls, and set up the gates of Jerusalem; and to fortify it again in
that manner as it was before it was dismantled and destroyed by the Babylonians. He was
a Jew, whose ancestors had formerly been citizens of Jerusalem; for there, he says, was
the place of his fathers' sepulchres: but as to the tribe or family which he was of, no more
is said but only that his father's name was *Hachaliah*, who seems to have been of those
Jews who, having gotten good settlements in the land of their captivity, chose rather to
abide in them than return into their own country, when leave was granted for it. It is
most likely that Hachaliah was an inhabitant of the city of Shushan, and that it was his
dwelling there that gave his son an opportunity of gaining an advancement in the king's
palace; for he was one of the cup-bearers of King Artaxerxes, which was a place of great
honour and advantage in the Persian court, because of the privilege it gave him of being
daily in the king's presence, and the opportunity which he had thereby of gaining his
favour for the obtaining of any petition which he should make to him; and that, especially,
since the times of his attendance always were when the king was making his heart merry
with the wine which he served up to him; for this is the best opportunity with all men for
the obtaining any boon that shall be desired of them, because they are always then in the
best humour for complying: it was at such a time that he asked the government of Judea,
and obtained it. And by the like advantages of his place, no doubt it was that he gained
those immense riches which enabled him for so many years, out of his own private purse
only, to live in his government with that splendour and expense as will be hereafter related,
without burdening the people at all for it; and no doubt it was by the favour of Queen
Esther, as being of the same nation and people with her, that he abtained so honourable
and advantageous a preferment in that court. However, neither the honour nor advantage
of this place, nor the long settlement of his family out of his country, could make him forget
his love for it, or lay aside that zeal which he had fo the religion of his forefathers, who had
formerly dwelt in it. For though he had been born and bred in a strange land, yet he had a
great love for Sion, and a heart thoroughly set for the advancing the prosperity of it, and
was in all things a very religious observer of the law of his God; and therefore, when some

came from Jerusalem, and told him of the ill state of that city, how the walls of it were still in many places broken down, and the gates of it in the same demolished state as when burnt with fire by the Babylonians, and that, by reason thereof, the remnant of the captivity that dwelt there lay open, not only to the incursions and insults of their enemies, but also to the reproach and contempt of their neighbours as a mean and despicable people, and that they were in both these respects in great grief and affliction of heart; the good man, being suitably moved with this representation, applied himself in fasting and prayer unto the Lord his God, and earnestly supplicated him for his people Israel, and the place which he had chosen for his worship among them. And having thus implored he Divine mercy against this evil, he resolved next to make his application to the king for the redressing of it, trusting in God for the inclining of his heart thereto; and therefore, when his turn came next to wait in his office, the king, observing his countenance to be sad, which at other times used not to be so, and asking the cause thereof, he took this opportunity to lay before him the distressed state of his country; and, owning this to be the cause of great grief to him, prayed the king to send him there to remedy it. And by the favour of Queen Esther he had his petition granted unto him; for it being particularly marked in the sacred text that the queen was sitting with the king when *Nehemiah* obtained this grant, sufficiently indicates that her favour was assisting to him herein;* and accordingly a royal decree was issued out for the rebuilding of the walls and gates of Jerusalem; and Nehemiah was sent thither with it, as governor of the province of Judea, to put it into execution; and to do him the more honour, the king sent a guard of horse with him, under the command of some of the captains of his army, to conduct him safely to his government. And he wrote letters to all the governors on this side the river Euphrates, to further him in the work on which he was sent; and also gave his orders to Asaph, the keeper of the forests in those parts, to allow him as much timber out of them as should be needed for the finishing of it. However, the Ammonites, the Moabites, and the Samaritans, and other neighbouring nations round, did all they could to hinder him from proceeding therein; and to this they were excited, not only by the ancient and bitter enmity which those people bore to the whole Jewish nation, because of the different manners and different religions they professed; but most especially at this time because of their lands; for during the time that the Jews were in captivity, these nations, having seized their lands, were forced to restore them on their return; for which reason they did all they could to oppose their settlement, hoping that, if they could be kept low, they might find an opportunity, some time or other, of resuming the prey they had lost. But Nehemiah was not at all discouraged at this; for having, on his arrival at Jerusalem, made known to the people the commission with which he was sent, he took a view of the ruins of the old walls, and immediately set about the repairing of them, dividing the people into several companies, and assigning to each of them the quarter where they were to work, but reserving to himself the superintendence and direction of the whole, in which he laboured so effectually that all was finished by the end of the month *Elul,* within the compass of *thirty-two* days, notwithstanding all manner of opposition that was made against him, both from within and without; for within several false prophets, and other treacherous persons, endeavoured to create obstructions; and from without Sanballat the Horonite, Tobias the Ammonite, Geshem the Arabian, and several others, gave him all the disturbance they were able, not only by underhand dealings, and treacherous tricks and contrivances, but also by open force; so that while part of the people laboured in carrying on the building, the other part stood to their arms, to defend themselves against those who had any designs upon them. And all had their arms at hand, even while they worked, to be ready at a signal given to draw together at any part where the enemy should be discovered to be coming upon them: and by this means they secured themselves against the attempts and designs of their enemies till the work was brought to a conclusion. And

*See my note on this passage.—A. C.

when they had thus far finished the walls and set up the gates, a public dedication of them was celebrated with great solemnity by the priests and Levites, and all the people. The burden which the people underwent in the carrying on of this work, and the incessant labour which they were forced to undergo to bring it to so speedy a conclusion being very great, and such as made them faint and groan under it; to revive their drooping spirits, and make them the more easy and ready to proceed in that which was farther to be done, care was taken to relieve them from a much greater burden, the oppression of usurers, which they at that time lay under, and had much greater reason to complain of; for the rich, taking advantage of the necessities of the poor, had exacted heavy usury of them, making them pay the *centesimal* for all moneys lent them; that is, one *per cent.* for every month, which amounted to twelve *per cent.* for the whole year: so that they were forced to mortgage their lands, and sell some of their children into servitude, to have wherewith to buy bread for the support of themselves and families; which being a manifest breach of the law of God, given by Moses, (for that forbids all the race of Israel to take usury of any of their brethren,) Nehemiah, on his hearing of this, resolved forthwith to remove so great an iniquity; in order whereto he called a general assembly of all the people, where, having set forth unto them the nature of the offence, how great a breach it was of the Divine law, and how heavy an oppression upon their brethren, and how much it might provoke the wrath of God against them, he caused it to be enacted by the general suffrage of that whole assembly, that all should return to their brethren whatsoever had been exacted of them upon usury, and also release all the lands, vineyards, oliveyards, and houses, which had been taken of them upon mortgage on this account.

"And thus Nehemiah, having executed the main of the end for which he obtained the favour of the king to be sent to Jerusalem, appointed Hanani and Hananiah to be governors of the city, and returned again unto him into Persia; for a time had been set him for his return again to court, when he first obtained to be sent from thence on this commission; which, as expressed in the text, plainly imports a short time, and not that of *twelve* years, after which he again went unto the king, as some interpret it. And his having appointed governors of the city as soon as the walls were built evidently implies that he then went from thence, and was absent for some time; for, had he still continued at Jerusalem, he would not have needed any deputies to govern the place. And farthermore, the building of the walls of Jerusalem being all for which he prayed his first commission; when this was performed, he seems to have needed a new authority before he could go on to other proceedings, which were necessary for the well settling of the affairs of that country. But on his return to the king, and having given him an account how all things stood in that province, and what farther was needful to be done for the well regulating of it, he soon obtained to be sent back again to take care thereof: and the shortness of his absence seems to have been the cause why there is no mention of it in the text, though the particulars I have mentioned seem sufficiently to imply it.

"Nehemiah, being returned from the Persian court with a new commission, in the *twenty-first* year of Artaxerxes, [B. C. 444,] forthwith set himself to carry on the reformation of the Church, and the state of the Jews, which Ezra had begun; and took along with him the advice and direction of that learned and holy scribe in all that he attempted in this work.

"The first thing that he did was to provide for the security of the city, which he had now fortified, by settling rules for the opening and shutting of the gates, and keeping watch and ward on the towers and walls: but finding Jerusalem to be but thinly inhabited, and that to make this burden more easy there needed more inhabitants to bear their share with them in it, he projected the thorough repeopling of the place: in order to which he prevailed first with the rulers and great men of the nation to agree to build them houses there, and dwell in them; and then others following their example, offered themselves voluntarily to do the same; and of the rest of the people every tenth man was taken by lot, and obliged to come to Jerusalem, and there build them houses, and settle themselves and their families in them. And when the city was fortified, and all that had their dwellings in it were there well secured by walls and gates against the insults of their enemies, and the incursions of thieves and robbers, who before molested them, all willingly complied; by which means the houses, as well as the walls and gates, being again rebuilt, and fully replenished with inhabitants, it soon after this received its ancient lustre, and became again a city of great note in those parts.

"Nehemiah, finding it necessary to have the genealogies of the people well investigated and clearly stated, next examined into that matter; and this he did, not only for the sake of their civil rights, that all knowing of what tribe and family they were, they might be directed where to take their possessions; but more especially for the sake of the sanctuary, that none might be admitted to officiate, even as Levites, who were not of the tribe of Levi; or as priests, that were not of the family of Aaron. And therefore, for the true settling of this matter, search was made for the old registers; and, having among them found a register of the genealogies of those who came up at first from Babylon with Zerubbabel and Jeshua, he settled this matter according to it; adding such also as came up, and expunging others whose families were extinct. And this caused the difference that is between the accounts we have of these genealogies in Ezra and Nehemiah: for in the *second* chapter of Ezra we have the old register made by Zerubbabel; and in the *seventh* of Nehemiah, from the *sixth* verse to the end of the chapter, a copy of it as settled by Nehemiah with the alterations I have mentioned. Ezra, having completed his edition of the law of God, and written it out fairly and clearly in the Chaldean character, this year, on the feast of trumpets, publicly read it to the people of Jerusalem. This feast was celebrated on the *first* of *Tisri*, the *seventh* month of the Jews' ecclesiastical year, and the *first* of their civil year. Their coming out of Egypt having been in the month *Nisan*, from that time the beginning of the year, in all ecclesiastical matters, was reckoned among them from the beginning of that month, which happened about the time of the vernal equinox; but in all civil matters, such as contracts and bargains, they still continued to go by the old form, and began their year from the *first* of *Tisri* which happened about the time of the autumnal equinox, as all other nations of the East then did; and all instruments and writings relating to contracts and bargains, or other civil matters, were dated according to this year, and all their jubilees and Sabbatical years began with it; and, therefore, reckoning it their new-year's-day, they celebrated it with a festival; and this festival being solemnized by the sounding of trumpets, from the morning of that day to the end of it, to proclaim and give notice to all of the beginning of the new year, it was from thence called the feast of trumpets. To celebrate this feast, the people assembled from all parts of Jerusalem; and understanding that Ezra had finished his revisal of the law, and written out a fair copy of it, they called upon him to have it read to them; when a scaffold or large pulpit was erected in the largest street of the city, where most of the people might stand to hear it. Ezra ascended into it, with thirteen other principal elders; and having placed six on his right hand, and seven on his left, he stood up in the midst of them; and having blessed the Lord, the great God, he began to read the law out of the Hebrew text; and while he read it in this language, *thirteen* other of the Levites, whom he instructed for this purpose, rendered it period by period into Chaldee, which was then the vulgar language of the people, giving them the meaning of every particular part; thus making them understand it: thus the holy scribe, with these assistants, continued from morning till noon, reading and explaining the law of God unto the people in such a manner as suited their low capacities. But it being a festival day, and the dining hour approaching, Nehemiah, Ezra, and the rest that had been assisting, dismissed them to dinner, to eat and drink, and rejoice before the Lord the remainder of the day, because it was thus consecrated to be kept holy unto Him: but the next morning they assembled again, in the same place; and Ezra and his assistants went on farther to read and to explain the law of God in the same manner as they had done the day before; and when they came to the *twenty-third* chapter of Leviticus, wherein is written the law of the feast of tabernacles, and had explained to them the obligation they were under to observe it, and that the *fifteenth* day of that month was the day appointed for the beginning of it, he excited an eager desire in all the people to fulfil the law of God in this particular; and proclamation was therefore made through all Judah, to give notice of the festival, and to warn them all to be present at Jerusalem on that day for the observing of it. Accordngly they went thither at the time prescribed; and, as they were instructed by the law of God, prepared booths, made of the branches of trees, and kept the festival in them, through the whole *seven* days of its continuance, in so solemn a manner as had not been observed before since the days of Joshua to this time. Ezra, taking the advantage of having the people assembled in so great a number, and so well disposed towards the law of God, went on with his assistants farther to read and explain in the same way as he had done on the two former days; and this he did from the first to the last day of the festival, till they had gone through the whole law; by which the people, perceiving in how many things they had transgressed the law of God through ignorance, (for till now the law of God had never been read since their return from Babylon,) expressed much trouble of heart, being much grieved for their sins, and exceedingly terrified with the fear of God's wrath for the punishment of them. Nehemiah and Ezra, finding them so well disposed, applied themselves to make the best improvement they could of it for the honour of God, and the interests of religion; and, therefore, proclaimed a fast to be held the day but one after the festival was ended, to which having called all the people while the sense of these things was fresh in their minds, excited them to make a solemn confession of their sins before God, and also to enter into a solemn vow and covenant with God to avoid them for the future. The observances which they chiefly obliged themselves to in this covenant were: *Firstly,* Not to make intermarriages with the Gentiles, either by giving their daughters to them, or by taking any of their daughters to themselves. *Secondly,* To observe the Sabbaths and Sabbatical years. *Thirdly,* To pay their annual tribute to the temple for the repairing of it, and finding all the necessaries for the carrying on of the public service in it. And *Fourthly,* To pay the tithes and first-fruits to the priests and Levites. And these particulars being thus named in this covenant shows us that they were the laws of God which they had been neglectful of since their return from the captivity. It being their ignorance which led them into these transgressions, and this ignorance having been occasioned by their not having heard the law of God read to them; to prevent this for the future, they had from this time the most learned of the Levites and scribes that were skilled in the law, to read it to them in every city; which no doubt was at first done by gathering the people together in the most wide street, where all might the better hear it; but the inconvenience of this being soon felt, especially in the winter and stormy seasons of the year, they erected houses or tabernacles to meet in, and these were the original synagogues among them. That they had no synagogues before the Babylonish captivity is plain, not only from the silence of the Scriptures of the Old Testament, but also from several passages in them, which evidently prove that there were none in those days; for it is a common saying, among the Jews, that where there is no book kept of the law, there can be no synagogue; for the chief service of the synagogue being the reading of the law to the people, where there was no law, there certainly could be no synagogue. Many texts of Scripture tell us that the book of the law was very rare through all Judah before the Babylonish captivity. When Jehoshaphat sent teachers through all Judah to instruct the people in the law of God, they carried the law with them; which they need not have done if there had been copies of the law in those cities where they went, which there would have been had there been synagogues in them, it being the same absurdity to suppose a synagogue without a book of the law, as to suppose a parish church without a copy of the Bible in it; and therefore as this proves the want of the law through all Judah, so it proves the want of synagogues in them also. And when Hilkiah found the law in the temple, neither he nor the king Josiah would have been surprised at it, had books of the law been common in those times. Their behaviour on that occasion sufficiently proves that they had never seen it before, which could not have been the case had there been any copies of it to be found among the people; and if there were no copies of the law at that time among them, there could then be most certainly no synagogues for them to resort to for the hearing of it read. From hence it plainly follows that there could be no synagogues among the Jews till after the Babylonish captivity; and it is most probable that Ezra's reading to them the law, and the necessity which they perceived there was of having it oftener read to them, was the occasion of their erecting them after their captivity in the manner I have related; and most learned men are of this opinion, and some of the Jews themselves say as much.

"Nehemiah, after having held the government of Judah *twelve* years, returned to the Persian court, either recalled thither by the king, or else going thither to solicit a new commission after the expiration of the former, [32 Artax. B. C. 433.] During all the time that he had been in the government he managed it with great justice, and supported the dignity of his office, through these whole *twelve* years, with a very expensive and hospitable magnificence; for there sat at his table every day *a hundred and fifty* of the Jews and rulers, besides strangers who came to Jerusalem from among the heathen nations round about them; for when occasion brought them thither, if they were of any quality, they were always invited to the governor's house, and there hospitably and splendidly entertained; so that there were provided for Nehemiah's table every day *one* ox, *six* choice sheep, and fowls and kine, with all other things in proportion, which must have been a great expense; yet all this he bore through the whole *twelve* years, out of his own private purse, without burdening the province at all for it, or taking any part of that allowance which before was raised by other governors to support them in their station; which argues his great generosity, as well as his great love and tenderness to the people of his nation, in thus easing them of this burden; and also his vast wealth, in being able to do so. The office which he had been in at court gave him the opportunity of amassing great riches, and he thought he could no better expend them than in the service of his country, and by doing all he could to promote its true interest in Church and state; and God prospered him in the work, according to the great zeal with which he laboured in it.

"Nehemiah, on his return to the Persian court, in the *thirty-seventh* year of Artaxerxes, [B. C. 428,] having tarried there about *five* years in the execution, as it may be supposed, of his former office, at length obtained permission from the king to be sent back to Jerusalem with a new commission. The generality of chronologers as well as commentators on this part of Scripture make his going back there to have been much sooner; but considering the many and great corruptions which he tells us in the *thirteenth* chapter the Jews had run into during his absence, it cannot be conceived how, in less than *five* years' time, they could have grown to such a height among them. He had been *twelve* years in reforming what was amiss among them, and Ezra had been *thirteen* years doing the same before him; and they had brought their reformation to such a state of stability, that a little time would not have been sufficient to have unhinged it. It is indeed expressed in our English version, that *Nehemiah* came back from the *Persian* court to Jerusalem, *after certain days;* but the Hebrew word ימים *yamin,* which is there rendered *days,* signifies also *years;* and is in a great many places of the Hebrew Scriptures so used. About this time lived *Malachi* the prophet: the greatest of the corruptions he charged the Jews with are the same as those they had run into in the time of Nehemiah's absence; and therefore it is most probable that in this time his prophecies were delivered. It is certain that the temple was all finished, and every thing restored in it, before this time, for there are passages in his prophecies which clearly suppose it; for he does not charge the Jews with not restoring the templ , but their neglect of what pertained to the true worship of God in it. But at what time after the restoration of the temple it was that he wrote his prophecies, is nowhere stated; and therefore we have only conjecture about it, and I know of no conjecture that can place it with more probability than in the time I have mentioned.

"Many things having gone wrong among the Jews during the absence of Nehemiah, as soon as he was again settled in the government, he applied himself with his accustomed zeal to correct them. That which he first took notice of was a great profanation which had been introduced into the temple for the sake of *Tobiah* the *Ammonite*. This man, though he had made two alliances with the Jews, (for *Johanan* his son had married the daughter of *Meshullam* the son of *Berechiah*, who was one of the chief managers in the rebuilding of the walls of Jerusalem, under the direction of the governor, who himself had married the daughter of *Shecaniah* the son of Arah, another great man among the Jews,) yet being an *Ammonite*, he bore a national hatred to all who were of the race of Israel; and therefore, envying their prosperity, did the utmost he could to obstruct Nehemiah in all that he did for the good of that people, and confederated with *Sanballat*, their greatest enemy, to carry on this purpose. However, by reason of the alliances I have mentioned, he had many correspondents among the Jews, who were favourers of him, and acted insidiously with Nehemiah on this account; but he, being aware of their devices, withstood and baffled them all, so long as he continued in Jerusalem. But when he went from thence to the Persian court, *Eliashib* the high priest was prevailed upon, being one in the confederacy and alliance with *Tobiah*, to allow and provide for him lodging within the temple itself. In order for which he removed *the meat-offerings, the frankincense, and the vessels, and the tithes of corn, the new wine, and the oil, which had been commanded to be given to the Levites, and the singers, and the porters, and the offerings of the priests*, out of the chambers where they used to be laid; and to make out of them one large apartment for the reception of this heathen stranger. It is doubted by some whether this *Eliashib* were Eliashib the *high priest*, or only another priest of that name; for he is named in the text, where this is related of him, by the title only of priest, and is there said to have the oversight of the chambers in the house of God; from whence it is argued that he was only chamberlain of the temple, and not the high priest, who was above such an office. But the oversight of the chambers of the house of God may import the whole government of the temple, which belonged to the high priest only; and it is not easily to be conceived how any one less than the absolute governor of the whole temple could make such an innovation in it. Besides, *Eliashib* the high priest has no character in Scripture with which such a procedure can be said to be inconsistent. By what is said in the book of Ezra, chap. x. 18, it appears that the pontifical family was in his time grown very corrupt; and there is no act of his mentioned, either in Ezra or Nehemiah, except only his assisting in the repairing of the wall of Jerusalem. Had he done any thing else worthy of memory in the reforming of what was amiss, either in Church or state, in the times of Ezra or Nehemiah, it may be presumed mention would have been made of it in the books written by them. The silence of him in both these books, as to any good act done by him, is a sufficient proof that there was none to be recorded; for the high priest being head of the Jewish Church, had he borne any part with those two good men, when they laboured so much to reform that Church, it is utterly impossible that it should have been passed over in their writings, where they give an account of what was done in that reformation. What *Jeshua* his grandfather did, in concurrence with Zerubbabel the governor, and Haggai and Zechariah the prophets, in the resettling of the Church and state of the Jews, after their return from the Babylonish captivity, is all recorded in Scripture; and had Eliashib done any such thing in concurrence with Ezra and Nehemiah, we may be certain it would have been recorded also.

"Putting all this together, it appears most likely that it was Eliashib the high priest who was the author of this great profanation of the house of God. What was done, however, the text tells us, Nehemiah immediately withstood, as soon as he returned to Jerusalem; for, overruling what the high priest had ordered to be done by the authority which he had as governor, he commanded all the household stuff of *Tobiah* to be cast out, and the chambers to be cleansed and restored to their former use.

"The reading of the law to the people having been settled by Nehemiah, so as to be constantly carried on at certain stated times ever since it was begun under his government by Ezra, (probably on every Sabbath day,) when in the course of their lessons they came to chap. xxiii. of Deuteronomy, where it is commanded that *a Moabite or an Ammonite should not come into the congregation of the Lord even to the tenth generation for ever;* Nehemiah, taking advantage of it, separated all the mixed multitude from the rest of the people, that thereby it might be known with whom a true Israelite might lawfully marry; for neither this law, nor any other of the like nature, is to be understood as excluding any, of whatever nation, from entering into the congregation as a proselyte, and becoming a member of their Church. Neither did the Jews so interpret it; for they freely received into their religion all who would embrace it, and on their conversion admitted them to all its rights and privileges, and treated them in all respects as true Israelites, excepting only in the case of marriage; and therefore this phrase in the text, *of not entering into the congregation even to the tenth generation,* must be understood to imply no more than a prohibition not to be married with them till then; and thus all the Jewish doctors expound it.

"Among other corruptions that grew up during the absence of Nehemiah, one especially to be noticed was, the neglect of not carrying on the daily service of the house of God in the manner it ought; for the tithes, which were to maintain the ministers of the temple in their offices and stations, either being embezzled by the high priest or other rulers under him, or else subtracted by the laity, and not paid at all; for want of them the Levites and singers were driven from the temple, every one to his own house, there to seek for a subsistence some other way. This abuse the governor, whose piety led him always to attend to the public worship, could not be long without taking notice of, and when he had thoroughly informed himself of the cause, he soon provided very effectually for its remedy; for he again made those dues to be brought into the temple treasuries, and forced every man faithfully and fully to pay them; thus a maintenance being again provided for those who attended the service of the house of God, all was there again restored to its pristine order. And he also took care that the Sabbath should be duly observed, and made many good orders for the preventing of the profanation of it, and caused them all to be put into effectual execution. But though all these things are mentioned in one chapter, they were not all done at one time; but this good man brought them about as opportunities best served for the success of effecting them. In the same year [B. C. 425] in which Nehemiah went again to his government of Judea, from the Persian court, i. e., in the *fourth* year of the *eighty-seventh* Olympiad, *Plato,* the famous Athenian philosopher, was born, who came the nearest to the truth in Divine matters of any of the heathens; for, having in his travels to the East, (whither he went for his improvement in knowledge,) conversed with the Jews, and got some insight into the writings of Moses, and their other sacred books, he learned many things from them which the other philosophers could not attain unto, and therefore he is said by *Numenius* to be none other than Moses speaking Greek; and many of the ancient fathers speak of him to the same purpose."

With this book the general historical books of the Old Testament end; and the succeeding accounts of the Jewish people must be sought partly in the Apocryphal books, and in Josephus; but nowhere with so much *perspicuity* as in the remaining volumes of the industrious and judicious author of The Connected History of the Old and New Testaments, from which the reader has already had such copious extracts.

THE BOOK

OF

NEHEMIAH

Chronological Notes relative to this Book

Year from the Creation, according to Archbishop Usher, whose system of chronology is the most generally received, 3558.—Year before the birth of Christ, 442.—Year before the vulgar era of Christ's nativity, 446.—Year of the Julian period, 4268.—Year since the flood of Noah, according to the English Bible, 1902.—Year of the Cali Yuga, or Indian era of the Deluge, 2656.—Year from the vocation of Abram, 1476.—Year from the destruction of Troy, 739.—This we collect from three passages in Dionysius of Halicarnassus, (who flourished in the Augustan age,) which state that an interval of *four hundred and thirty-two years* elapsed from the destruction of Troy to the building of Rome.—Year from the foundation of Solomon's temple, 565.—Year since the division of Solomon's monarchy into the kingdoms of Israel and Judah, 529.—Year of the era of Iphitus, king of Elis, who re-established the Olympic games, *three hundred and thirty-eight* years after their institution by Hercules, or about *eight hundred and eighty-four* years before the commencement of the Christian era, 439.—This epoch is famous in chronological history, as every thing previous to it seems involved in fabulous obscurity.—Year since Corœbus won the prize at Olympia, a town of Elis in Peloponnesus, (being the *twenty-eighth* Olympiad after their re-establishment by Iphitus,) 331.—Third year of the *eighty-third* Olympiad.—The epoch of the Olympiads commenced according to the accurate and learned computations of some of the moderns, exactly *seven hundred and seventy-six* years before the Christian era, in the year of the Julian period 3938, and *twenty-three* years before the building of Rome. N. B. The Olympic games were celebrated at the time of the full moon which immediately followed the day of the summer solstice; therefore the Olympiads were not of equal length, because the time of the full moon differs about *eleven* days every year; and for that reason the Olympiads sometimes began the next day after the solstice, and at other times four weeks after. —Year of the Varronian or generally received era of the building of Rome, 308. This computation was used by the Romans in the celebration of their secular games.—Year from the building of Rome, according to Cato and the Fasti Consulares, 307. Dionysius of Halicarnassus follows this account in his Roman Antiquities.—Year from the building of Rome, according to Polybius the historian, (a native of Megalopolis in Peloponnesus, and son of Lycortas,) 306.—Year from the building of Rome, according to Fabius Pictor, (the first Roman who wrote a history of his own country, from the age of Romulus to the year of Rome 536,) 302.—Year of the era of Nabonassar, a king of Babylon after the division of the Assyrian monarchy, 302.—Year since the destruction of the kingdom of Israel by Shalmaneser, the king of Assyria, 276.—Year from the destruction of Solomon's temple by Nebuchadnezzar, king of Babylon, 143.—Year since the publication of the famous edict of Cyrus, king of Persia, empowering the Jews to rebuild their temple, 90. The commencement of this epoch was synchronical with the termination of the *seventy years* during which the Jews were under the dominion of the Babylonians.—Year since the expulsion of the Tarquins from Rome, which put an end to the regal government of the Romans, 63. The consular government immediately followed the expulsion of the Tarquins.—Year before the celebrated Peloponnesian war, 16. This war began on the seventh of May, *four hundred and thirty-one* years before the Christian era; and continued *twenty-seven* years between the Athenians and the inhabitants of Peloponnesus, with their allies.—Year before the commencement of the era of the Seleucidæ, 134. This era was named after Seleucus, one of the captains of Alexander the Great, surnamed Nicator, or The Conqueror. The year in which he conquered Babylon (viz. 312 B. C.) is called the first year of this era.—Year before the formation of the famous Achæan league, 165.—Year before the commencement of the first Punic war, 182. The Arundelian marbles are said to have been composed in the first year of this war.—Year before the fall of the Macedonian empire, 278.—Year before the extinction of the reign of the Seleucidæ in Syria, on the conquest of that country by Pompey, 381.—Year before the commencement of the era of the Roman emperors, 415. The year in which the famous battle of Actium was fought is the first year of this era.—Year of Archidamus, king of Lacedæmon, and of the family of the Proclidæ or Eurypontidæ, 24.—Year of Plistoanax, king of Lacedæmon, and of the family of the Eurysthenidæ or Agidæ, 21. This king was general of the Lacedæmonian armies in the Peloponnesian war. N. B. The kings of the Lacedæmonians of the families of the Proclidæ and the Eurysthenidæ sat on the throne together for several hundred years; viz., from 1102 B. C. to about 200 B. C.—Year of Perdiccas II. the eleventh king of Macedon, 9.—Year of Artaxerxes, surnamed Macrochir (Μακροχειρ) or Longimanus because his arms were so long that when standing erect, his hands reached down to his knees, 20.—Roman Consuls, T. Quintius Capitolinus the fourth time, and Agrippa Furius. During this consulship the Æqui and Volsci came near to the gates of Rome, and were defeated.

Eminent men who were contemporary with Nehemiah; upon the supposition that his birth happened about 500 B. C., and his death about 420 B. C.

Acron, a physician of Agrigentum; flourished 459 B. C.—*Æschylus*, the tragic poet of Athens; born, 525 B. C., died 456 B. C., at the age of 69.—*Alcidamus* the philosopher; flourished 424 B. C.—*Anaxagoras*, a Clazomenian philosopher; born B. C. 500., died 428 B. C., at the age of 72.—*Aristarchus* the tragic poet of Tegea in Arcadia; flourished about 454 B. C.—*Aristides*, the Athenian; flourished about 480 B. C.—*Aristophanes*, the comic poet; said to have flourished about 434 B. C.—*L. Furius Camillus*, celebrated Roman; born 445 B. C., and died 365 B. C., aged 80, after he had been five times dictator, once censor, three times interrex, twice a military tribune, and obtained four triumphs.—*Charandas*, who gave laws to the people of Thurium; died 446 B. C.—*Charon*, a historian of Lampsacus; flourished about 479 B. C.—*L. Q. Cincinnatus*, a celebrated Roman; flourished about 460 B. C.—*Cossus*, a Roman who killed Volumnius, king of Veii, and obtained the Spolia Opima, A. U. C. 317, B. C. 437.—*Cratinus*, the comic writer; born 528 B. C., died 431 B. C., at the age of 97.—*Democritus*, the philosopher; born 470 B. C., died 361 B. C., at the advanced age of 109.—*Empedocles*, a philosopher, poet, and historian, of Agrigentum in Sicily; flourished about 444 B. C.—*Epicharmus*, a poet and Pythagorean philosopher of Sicily, who, according to Aristotle and Pliny, added the two letters χ and θ to the Greek alphabet; flourished 440 B. C., and died in the 90th year of his age.—*Euctemon*, the astronomer; flourished about 431 B. C.—*Eupolis*, a comic poet of Athens; flourished about 435 B. C.—*Euripides*, the tragic poet, born at Salamis the day on which the army of Xerxes was defeated by the Greeks; torn to pieces by dogs, 407 B. C., in the 73d year of his age.—*Georgias*, a celebrated sophist and orator; born 508 B. C., died 400 B. C., at the advanced age of 108.—*Hellanicus*, the Greek historian; born at Mitylene, 496 B. C., died 411 B. C., in the 85th year of his age.—*Herodicus*, a physician surnamed Gymnastic; flourished 443 B. C.—*Herodotus*, a celebrated historian of Halicarnassus; born 484 B. C., read his history to the council of Athens, and received public honours, in the 39th year of his age, 445 B. C.—*Hippocrates*, a celebrated physician of Cos; born 460 B. C., died 361 B. C., nearly 100 years of age.—*Isocrates*, the orator; born 437 B. C., died about 338 B. C., aged 99.—*Leocrates*, an Athenian general; flourished about 460 B. C.—*Lysias*, the orator; born 459 B. C., died 378 B. C.—*Melissus*, the Samian philosopher; flourished about 440 B. C.—*Meton*, the astrologer and mathematician; flourished about 432 B. C.—*Pericles*, the celebrated minister of Athens; born 499 B. C., died of the plague about 429 B. C.—*Phidias*, a celebrated statuary of Athens; died 432 B. C.—*Pindar*, a celebrated lyric poet of Thebes; born 521 B. C., died 435 B. C., at the age of 86.—*Plato*, the Greek poet, called the prince of the middle comedy; flourished about 454 B. C.—*Protagoras*, a Greek philosopher; died at a very advanced age, about 400 B. C.—*Socrates*, one of the most celebrated philosophers of all antiquity; born 470 B. C., died 400 B. C., aged 70.—*Sophocles*, a celebrated tragic poet of Athens, educated in the school of Æschylus; born 497 B. C., died 406 B. C., at the age of 91.—*Thucydides*, a celebrated Greek historian; born at Athens 471 B. C., died 391 B. C., in his 80th year.—*Xenophon*, the celebrated general, historian, and philosopher; born 449 B. C., died 359 B. C., aged 90.—*Zeuxis*, a celebrated painter; flourished about 468 B. C.

CHAPTER I

Account of Nehemiah, 1. His inquiry about the Jews that had returned from their captivity, and concerning the state of Jerusalem, of which he receives the most discouraging information, 2, 3. He is greatly affected; fasts and prays, 4. His prayer and confession to God, 5–11.

A. M. 3558
B. C. 446
A. U. C. 308
Coss Rom. T.
Q. Capitolino 4
et Agrip. Furio

THE words of ᵃNehemiah the son of Hachaliah. And it came to pass in the month Chisleu, in the twentieth year,

as I was in Shushan the palace,

2 That Hanani, one of my brethren, came, he and *certain*

A. M. 3558
B. C. 446
A. U. C. 308
Coss. Rom. T.
Q. Capitolino 4
et Agrip. Furio

ᵃNehemiah,

chap. x. 1

NOTES ON CHAP. I

Verse 1. *The words of Nehemiah*] That this book was compiled out of the *journal* or *memoranda* made by *Nehemiah* himself, there can be no doubt: but that he was not the *compiler* is evident from several passages in the work itself. As it is written consecutively as one book

with Ezra, many have supposed that this latter was the author: but whoever compares the style of each, in the Hebrew, will soon be convinced that this is not correct; the style is so very different, that they could not possibly be the work of the same person.

It is doubtful even whether the Nehemiah who is mentioned *Ezra* ii. 2, who came to Jeru-

A. M. 3558
B. C. 446
A. U. C. 308
Coss. Rom. T.
Q. Capitolino 4
et Agrip. Furio

men of Judah; and I asked them concerning the Jews that had escaped, which were left of the captivity, and concerning Jerusalem.

3 And they said unto me, The remnant that are left of the captivity there in the province *are* in great affliction and reproach: ᵇthe wall of Jerusalem also ᶜ*is* broken down, and the gates thereof are burned with fire.

4 And it came to pass, when I heard these words, that I sat down and wept, and mourned *certain* days, and fasted, and prayed before the God of heaven,

5 And said, I beseech thee, ᵈO Lᴏʀᴅ God of heaven, the great and terrible God, ᵉthat keepeth covenant and mercy for them that love him and observe his commandments:

6 Let thine ear now be attentive, and ᶠthine

A. M. 3558
B. C. 446
A. U. C. 308
Coss. Rom. T.
Q. Capitolino 4
et Agrip. Furio

eyes open, that thou mayest hear the prayer of thy servant, which I pray before thee now, day and night, for the children of Israel thy servants, and ᵍconfess the sins of the children of Israel, which we have sinned against thee: both I and my father's house have sinned.

7 ʰWe have dealt very corruptly against thee, and have ⁱnot kept the commandments, nor the statutes, nor the judgments, which thou commandedst thy servant Moses.

8 Remember, I beseech thee, the word that thou commandedst thy servant Moses, saying, ᵏ*If* ye transgress, I will scatter you abroad among the nations:

9 ˡBut *if* ye turn unto me, and keep my commandments, and do them; ᵐthough there were of you cast out unto the uttermost part of the heaven, *yet* will I gather them from

---

ᵇCh. ii. 17——ᶜ2 Kings xxv. 10——ᵈDan. ix. 4——ᵉExod. xx. 6——ᶠ1 Kings viii. 28, 29; 2 Chron. vi. 40; Dan. ix. 7, 18——ᵍDan. ix. 20——ʰPsa. cvi. 6; Dan. ix. 5

ⁱDeut. xxviii. 15——ᵏLev. xxvi. 33; Deut. iv. 25, 26, 27; xxviii. 64——ˡLev. xxvi. 39, &c.; Deut. iv. 29, 30, 31; xxx. 2——ᵐDeut. xxx. 4

---

salem with Zerubbabel, be the same with him who is the reputed author of this book. By the computation of the best chronologists, *Zerubbabel* came to Jerusalem in A. M. 3468; and Nehemiah, who is here mentioned, did not come before the *twentieth* year of the reign of Artaxerxes, which falls in with A. M. 3558, *ninety* years after: and as his account here is carried down to A. M. 3570, *nearly twenty* years later, he must at his death have been about *a hundred and thirty*, allowing him to have been only *twenty* years old at the time that Zerubbabel went up to Jerusalem. This is by no means likely, as this would make him the king's cupbearer when he was upwards of *a hundred years of age!* It seems, therefore, evident that the Nehemiah of Ezra cannot be the same with the reputed author of this book, and the cup-bearer of the Persian king.

Son of Hachaliah] Of what tribe or lineage he was, we cannot tell: this is all we know of his parentage. Some suppose he was a priest, and of the house of Aaron, on the authority of 2 Mac. i. 18, 21; but this is but slender evidence. It is likely he was of a very eminent family, if not of the blood royal of Judah, as only persons of eminence could be placed in the office which he sustained in the Persian court.

The month Chisleu] Answering to a part of our November and December.

Twentieth year] That is, of Artaxerxes, A. M. 3558, B. C. 446.

Shushan the palace] The ancient city of *Susa;* called in Persian شُوشْتَر *Shuster:* the winter residence of the Persian kings.

Verse 2. *I asked them concerning the Jews*] Josephus gives a probable account of this business: "Nehemiah, being somewhere out of Susa, seeing some strangers, and hearing them converse in the Hebrew tongue, he went near; and finding they were Jews from Jerusalem, he asked them how matters went with their breth-

ren in that city, and what was their state?" And the answer they gave him is, in substance, that recorded in the text; though with several aggravations in Josephus.—*Joseph.* Ant. lib. xi., c. 5.

Verse 3. *The wall of Jerusalem also is broken down*] This must refer to the walls, which had been *rebuilt* after the people returned from their captivity: for it could not refer to the walls which were broken down and levelled with the dust by *Nebuchadnezzar;* for to hear of this could be no *news* to Nehemiah.

Verse 4. *And mourned certain days*] From the month *Chisleu* to the month *Nisan;* about *four* months from the time he received the above information, till the time that Artaxerxes noticed his grief, chap. ii. 1. All this time he probably spent in supplication to God; waiting for a favourable opening in the Divine providence. Every *good* work is not to be undertaken hastily; prayer and watchfulness are necessary to its completion. Many good works have been ruined by making *haste.*

Verse 5. *Lord God of heaven*] What was, before the captivity, *Jehovah, God of hosts* or *armies.*

Great] Able to do mighty things. *Terrible* —able to inflict the heaviest judgments.

Verse 6. *Let thine ear*] Hear what we *say* and *confess. Thine eyes open—see* what we *suffer.*

Verse 7. *Have not kept thy commandments*] The moral precepts by which our lives should be regulated.

Statutes] What refers to the rites and ceremonies of thy religion.

Judgments] The precepts of justice relative to our conduct to each other.

Verse 8. *Thy servant Moses*] See the parallel places in the margin, and the notes there. Though in an enemy's country, and far from

A. M. 3558
B. C. 446
A. U. C. 308
Coss. Rom. T.
Q. Capitolino 4
et Agrip. Furio

thence, and will bring them unto the place that I have chosen to set my name there.

10 ⁿNow these *are* thy servants and thy people, whom thou hast redeemed by thy great power, and by thy strong hand.

11 O LORD, I beseech thee, °let now thine

ear be attentive to the prayer of thy servant, and to the prayer of thy servants, ᵖwho desire to fear thy name: and prosper, I pray thee, thy servant this day, and grant him mercy in the sight of this man. For I was the king's ᑫcup-bearer.

A. M. 3558
B. C. 446
A. U. C. 308
Coss. Rom. T.
Q. Capitolino 4
et Agrip. Furio

ⁿDeut. ix. 29; Dan. ix. 15——°Ver. 6

ᵖIsa. xxvi. 8; Heb. xiii. 18——ᑫChap. ii. 1

---

the ordinances of God, Nehemiah did not forget the law: he read his Bible well, and quotes correctly.

Verse 11. *Mercy in the sight of this man.*] Favour before the king, Ahasuerus. He seems then to have been giving him the cup.

For I was the king's cup-bearer.] The king's *butler*, (the Persians call him ساقي *saky*,)

which gave him the opportunity of being frequently with the king; and to be in such a place of trust, he must be in the king's confidence. No Eastern potentate would have a cup-bearer with whom he could not trust his life, *poison* being frequently administered in this way. This verse seems to have been a mental prayer, which Nehemiah now put up as he was delivering the cup into the king's hand.

CHAPTER II

Artaxerxes, observing the sorrow of Nehemiah, inquires into the cause, 1, 2. *Nehemiah shows him the cause, and requests permission to go and rebuild the walls of Jerusalem,* 3–6. *The king grants it, and gives him letters to the governors beyond the river,* 7, 8. *He sets out on his journey,* 9. *Sanballat and Tobiah are grieved to find he had got such a commission,* 10. *He comes to Jerusalem; and, without informing any person of his business, examines by night the state of the city,* 11–16. *He informs the priests, nobles, and rulers, of his design and commission,* 17, 18. *The design is turned into contempt by Sanballat, Tobiah, and Geshem,* 19. *Nehemiah gives them a suitable answer,* 20.

A. M. 3559
B. C. 445
A. U. C. 309
Coss. Rom.
M. Genucio et
C. Curtio

AND it came to pass in the month Nisan, in the twentieth year of ᵃArtaxerxes the king, *that* wine *was* before him: and ᵇI took up the wine, and gave *it* unto the king. Now I had not been *beforetime* sad in his presence.

2 Wherefore the king said unto me, Why *is* thy countenance sad, seeing thou *art* not sick? this *is* nothing *else* but °sorrow of heart. Then I was very sore afraid,

3 And said unto the king, ᵈLet the king live

for ever: why should not my countenance be sad, when °the city, the place of my fathers' sepulchres, *lieth* waste, and the gates thereof are consumed with fire?

A. M. 3559
B. C. 445
A. U. C. 309
Coss. Rom.
M. Genucio et
C. Curtio

4 Then the king said unto me, For what dost thou make request? So I prayed to the God of heaven.

5 And I said unto the king, If it please the king, and if thy servant have found favour in thy sight, that thou wouldest send me unto Judah, unto the city of my fa-

---

ᵃEzra vii. 1——ᵇChap. i. 11——°Prov. xv. 13

ᵈ1 Kings i. 31; Dan. ii. 4; v. 10; vi. 6, 21——°Chap. i. 3

NOTES ON CHAP. II

Verse 1. *Month Nisan*] Answering to a part of our *March* and *April*.

I took up the wine] It is supposed that the kings of Persia had a different cup-bearer for each quarter of the year, and that it had just now come to Nehemiah's turn.

Verse 2. *Then I was very sore afraid.*] Probably the king spoke as if he had some suspicion that Nehemiah harboured some bad design, and that his face indicated some conceived treachery or remorse.

Verse 3. *Let the king live for ever*] Far from wishing ill to my master, I wish him on the contrary to live and prosper for ever.

ÆLIAN, *Hist. Var.* lib. i. c. 32, uses the same form of speech in reference to Artaxerxes Mnemon, one of the Persian kings, Βασιλεν Αρταξερξη, δι' αιωνος βασιλευοις, "O King Artaxerxes, may you reign for ever," when speaking of the custom of presenting them annually with an offering of earth and water; as if they had said, *May you reign for ever over these!*

Verse 4. *So I prayed to the God of heaven.*] Before he dared to prefer his request to the king, he made his prayer to God, that his suit might be acceptable: and this he does by mental prayer. To the spirit of prayer every place is a *praying place.*

Verse 5. *The city of my fathers' sepulchres*] The tombs of the dead were sacred among the

A. M. 3559
B. C. 445
A. U. C. 309
Coss. Rom.
M. Genucio et
C. Curtio thers' sepulchres, that I may build it.

6 And the king said unto me, (the ᶠqueen also sitting by him,) For how long shall thy journey be? and when wilt thou return? So it pleased the king to send me; and I set him ᵍa time.

7 Moreover I said unto the king, If it please the king, let letters be given me to the governors beyond the river, that they may convey me over till I come into Judah;

8 And a letter unto Asaph the keeper of the king's forest, that he may give me timber to make beams for the gates of the palace which *appertained* ʰto the house, and for the wall of the city, and for the house that I shall enter into. And the king granted me, ⁱaccording to the good hand of my God upon me.

9 Then I came to the governors beyond the river, and gave them the king's letters. Now

A. M. 3559
B. C. 445
A. U. C. 309
Coss. Rom.
M. Genucio et
C. Curtio the king had sent captains of the army and horsemen with me.

10 When Sanballat the Horonite, and Tobiah the servant, the Ammonite, heard *of it,* it grieved them exceedingly that there was come a man to seek the welfare of the children of Israel.

11 So I ᵏcame to Jerusalem, and was there three days.

12 And I arose in the night, I and some few men with me; neither told I *any* man what my God had put in my heart to do at Jerusalem: neither *was there any* beast with me, save the beast that I rode upon.

13 And I went out by night ˡby the gate of the valley, even before the dragon well, and to the dung port, and viewed the walls of Jerusalem, which were ᵐbroken down, and the gates thereof were consumed with fire.

ᶠHeb. *wife*——ᵍChap. v. 14; xiii. 6——ʰChap. iii. 7
ⁱEzra v. 5; vii. 6, 9, 28; ver. 18

ᵏEzra viii. 32——ˡ2 Chron. xxvi. 9; chap. iii. 13
ᵐChap. i. 3; ver. 17

ancients, and nothing could appear to them more detestable than disturbing the ashes or remains of the dead. Nehemiah knew that in mentioning this circumstance he should strongly interest the feelings of the Persian king.

Verse 6. *The queen also sitting by him*] Who probably forwarded his suit. This was not Esther, as Dean Prideaux supposes, nor perhaps the same Artaxerxes who had taken her to be queen; nor does שֵׁגָל *shegal* signify *queen,* but rather harlot or concubine, she who was chief favourite. The Septuagint translate it παλλακη, *harlot;* and properly too. See the introduction.

I set him a time.] How long this time was we are not told; it is by no means likely that it was long, probably no more than *six months* or a *year;* after which he either returned, or had his leave of absence *lengthened;* for in the same year we find he was made governor of the Jews, in which office he continued twelve years, viz., from the twentieth to the thirty-second year of Artaxerxes, chap. v. 14. He then returned to Susa; and after staying a short time, had leave to return to rectify some abuses that Tobiah the Ammonite had introduced into the temple, chap. xiii. 6, 7, and several others of which the people themselves were guilty. After having performed this service, it is likely he returned to the Persian king, and died in his office of cup-bearer; but of this *latter* circumstance we have no mention in the text.

Verse 8. *Asaph the keeper of the king's forest*] הַפַּרְדֵּס *hapardes* of the *paradise* of the king. This I believe is originally a *Persian* word; it frequently occurs in Arabic, قردوس *ferdoos,* and in Greek, παραδεισος, and in both signifies a *pleasant garden, vineyard, pleasure garden,* and what we call a *paradise.*

Above the hall of audience, in the imperial palace at Dehli, the following Persian couplet is inscribed:—

اگر فردوسی بر روئ زمی است
همین است همین است همین است

"If there be a *paradise* on the face of the earth, this is it, this is it, this is it."

Thus we find that the word is applied to denote *splendid apartments,* as well as *fine gardens;* in a word, any place of pleasure and delight. The *king's forest* mentioned in the text might have been the same to *Artaxerxes,* as the *New Forest* was to *William the Conqueror,* or *Windsor Forest* to the late amiable sovereign of the British people, GEORGE the THIRD.

And the king granted me, &c.] This noble spirited man attributes every thing to God. He might have said, I had been long a faithful servant to the king; and he was disposed, in reward of my fidelity, to grant my request; but he would not say so: "He granted my request, because the good *hand of my God was upon me.*" God favoured me, and influenced the king's heart to do what I desired.

Verse 10. *Sanballat the Horonite*] Probably a native of Horonaim, a *Moabite* by birth, and at this time governor of the Samaritans under the king of Persia.

Tobiah the servant] He was an *Ammonite;* and here, under the Persian king, joint governor with Sanballat. Some suppose that the Sanballat here mentioned was the same who persuaded Alexander to build a temple on Mount Gerizim in favour of the Samaritans. Pelagius thinks there were two governors of this name.

Verse 13. *The dragon well*] Perhaps so called because of the representation of a dragon, out of whose mouth the stream issued that proceeded from the well.

Dung port] This was the gate on the eastern side of the city, through which the filth of the city was carried into the valley of Hinnom.

A. M. 3559
B. C. 445
A. U. C. 309
Coss. Rom.
M. Genucio et
C. Curtio

14 Then I went on to the gate of the ᵑfountain, and to the king's pool: but *there was* no place for the beast *that was* under me to pass.

15 Then went I up in the night by the ᵒbrook, and viewed the wall, and turned back, and entered by the gate of the valley, and *so* returned.

16 And the rulers knew not whither I went, or what I did; neither had I as yet told *it* to the Jews, nor to the priests, nor to the nobles, nor to the rulers, nor to the rest that did the work.

17 Then said I unto them, Ye see the distress that we *are* in, how Jerusalem *lieth* waste, and the gates thereof are burned with fire: come, and let us build up the wall of Jerusalem, that we be no more ᵖa reproach.

18 Then I told them of ᑫthe hand of my God which was good upon me; as also the king's words that he had spoken unto me. And they said, Let us rise up and build. So they ʳstrengthened their hands for *this* good *work*.

A. M. 3559
B. C. 445
A. U. C. 309
Coss. Rom.
M. Genucio et
C. Curtio

19 But when Sanballat the Horonite, and Tobiah the servant, the Ammonite, and Geshem the Arabian, heard *it,* they ˢlaughed us to scorn, and despised us, and said, What *is* this thing that ye do? ᵗwill ye rebel against the king?

20 Then answered I them, and said unto them, The God of heaven, he will prosper us; therefore we his servants will arise and build: ᵘbut ye have no portion, nor right, nor memorial, in Jerusalem.

ᵑCh. iii. 15——ᵒ2 Sam. xv. 23; Jer. xxxi. 40——ᵖCh. i. 3; Psa. xliv. 13; lxxix. 4; Jer. xxiv. 9; Ezek. v. 14, 15;

xxii. 4——ᑫVer. 8——ʳ2 Sam. ii. 7——ˢPsa. xliv. 13; lxxix. 4; lxxx. 6——ᵗChap. vi. 6——ᵘEzra iv. 3

Verse 14. *The gate of the fountain*] Of *Siloah.*
The king's pool] Probably the *aqueduct* made by Hezekiah, to bring the waters of Gihon to the city of David. See 2 Chron. xxxii. 30.

Verse 15. *By the brook*] *Kidron.*
By the gate of the valley] The valley through which the brook Kidron flowed. It was by this gate he went out; so he went all round the city, and entered by the same gate from which he had gone out.

Verse 16. *The rulers knew not whither I went*] He made no person privy to his design, that he might hide every thing as much as possible from their enemies till he had all things in readiness; lest they should take measures to defeat the work.

Verse 18. *Then I told them*] He opened to them his design and his commission.

Verse 19. *Geshem the Arabian*] Some chief of the Arabs contiguous to Samaria, who had joined with Sanballat and Tobiah to distress the Jews, and hinder their work.
Will ye rebel against the king?] This they said in order to raise jealousies in the king's mind, and induce him to recall his ordinance.

Verse 20. *Ye have no portion, nor right*] To be a citizen of Jerusalem was a high honour; and they would not permit those who did not belong to the tribes of Israel to dwell there. Zerubbabel gave the same answer to the Samaritans, Ezra iv. 3.

CHAPTER III

The names of those who rebuilt the walls of Jerusalem; and the part assigned to each person, 1–32.

A. M. 3559
B. C. 445
A. U. C. 309
Coss. Rom.
M. Genucio et
C. Curtio

THEN ᵃEliashib the high priest rose up with his brethren the priests, ᵇand they builded the sheep gate; they sanctified it, and set up the doors of it; ᶜeven unto the tower of Meah they sanctified it, unto the tower of ᵈHananeel.

2 And ᵉnext unto him builded ᶠthe men of Jericho. And next to them builded Zaccur the son of Imri.

A. M. 3559
B. C. 445
A. U. C. 309
Coss. Rom.
M. Genucio et
C. Curtio

3 ᵍBut the fish gate did the sons of Hassenaah build, who *also* laid the beams thereof, and ʰset up the doors thereof, the

---

ᵃChap. xii. 10——ᵇJohn v. 2——ᶜChapter xii. 39
ᵈJer. xxxi. 38; Zech. xiv. 10——ᵉHeb. *at his hand*

ᶠEzra ii. 34——ᵍ2 Chron. xxxiii. 14; chap. xii. 39; Zeph. i. 10——ʰSee chap. vi. 1; vii. 1

NOTES ON CHAP. III

Verse 1. *Eliashib the high priest*] It was right that the priests should be *first* in this holy work; and perhaps the *sheep gate* which is mentioned here is that by which the offerings or sacrifices were brought into the temple.
They sanctified it] As they began with the

sacred offering as soon as they got an altar built, it was proper that the gate by which these sacrifices entered should be consecrated for this purpose, i. e., set apart, so that it should be for this use only.

Verse 3. *The fish gate*] We really know scarcely any thing about these gates—what they were, why called by these names, or in

A. M. 3559
B. C. 445
A. U. C. 309
Coss. Rom.
M. Genucio et
C. Curtio
locks thereof, and the bars thereof.

4 And next unto them repaired Meremoth the son of Urijah, the son of Koz. And next unto them repaired Meshullam the son of Berechiah, the son of Meshezabeel. And next unto them repaired Zadok, the son of Baana.

5 And next unto them the Tekoites repaired; but their nobles put not their necks to ¹the work of their Lord.

6 Moreover ᵏthe old gate repaired Jehoiada the son of Paseah, and Meshullam the son of Besodeiah; they laid the beams thereof, and set up the doors thereof, and the locks thereof, and the bars thereof.

7 And next unto them repaired Melatiah the Gibeonite, and Jadon the Meronothite, the men of Gibeon, and of Mizpah, unto the ¹throne of the governor on this side the river.

8 Next unto him repaired Uzziel the son of Harhaiah of the goldsmiths. Next unto him also repaired Hananiah the son of *one of* the apothecaries, and they ᵐfortified Jerusalem unto the ⁿbroad wall.

9 And next unto them repaired Rephaiah the son of Hur, the ruler of the half part of Jerusalem.

10 And next unto them repaired Jedaiah the

son of Harumaph, even over against his house. And next unto him repaired Hattush the son of Hashabniah.

A. M. 3559
B. C. 445
A. U. C. 309
Coss. Rom.
M. Genucio et
C. Curtio

11 Malchijah the son of Harim, and Hashub the son of Pahath-moab, repaired the °other piece, ᵖand the tower of the furnaces.

12 And next unto him repaired Shallum the son of Halohesh, the ruler of the half part of Jerusalem, he and his daughters.

13 �q The valley gate repaired Hanun, and the inhabitants of Zanoah; they built it, and set up the doors thereof, the locks thereof, and the bars thereof, and a thousand cubits on the wall unto ʳthe dung gate.

14 But the dung gate repaired Malchiah the son of Rechab, the ruler of part of Beth-haccerem; he built it, and set up the doors thereof, the locks thereof, and the bars thereof.

15 But ˢthe gate of the fountain repaired Shallun the son of Col-hozeh, the ruler of part of Mizpah; he built it, and covered it, and set up the doors thereof, the locks thereof, and the bars thereof, and the wall of the pool of ᵗSiloah by the king's garden, and unto the stairs that go down from the city of David.

16 After him repaired Nehemiah the son of Azbuk, the ruler of the half part of Beth-zur, unto *the place* over against the sepulchres of

---

ⁱJudg. v. 23——ᵏChap. xii. 39——ˡChap. ii. 8——ᵐOr, *left Jerusalem unto the broad wall*——ⁿChap. xii. 28

°Heb. *second measure*——ᵖChap. xii. 38——qChap. ii. 13——ʳChap. ii. 13——ˢChap. ii. 14——ᵗJohn ix. 7

---

what part of the wall situated. All plans of Jerusalem, its temple, walls, and gates, are mere works of conjecture; and yet how *learnedly* have some men written on all these subjects!

Verse 7. *The throne of the governor*] His house, and the place where he dispensed justice and judgment. Previously to the days of Nehemiah, Jerusalem was governed by a deputy from the Persian king; (see chap. v. 15;) but after this time they were governed by governors and judges chosen from among themselves.

Verse 8. *Goldsmiths.*] From the remotest period of the history of the Jews they had artists in all elegant and ornamental trades; and it is also evident that goldsmiths, apothecaries, and merchants were formed into *companies* in the time of Nehemiah.

Apothecaries] Rather such as dealt in *drugs, aromatics, spices,* &c., for embalming, or for furnishing the temple with the incense consumed there.

Verse 9. *Ruler of the half part of Jerusalem.*] Probably the city was divided into *two parts;* one for Judah, and the other for Benjamin, each having its proper governor. Rephaiah mentioned here was *one* of these governors, and *Shallum,* mentioned ver. 12, was the *other.* There were other rulers or governors of particular country or village districts.

Verse 11. *Repaired the other piece*] That which was left by *Jedaiah* after he had repaired the wall opposite to his own house. Probably some of the principal people were obliged to repair those parts of the wall opposite to their own dwellings. Perhaps this was the case generally.

Verse 12. *The son of Halohesh*] Or, the son of the *Enchanter:* conjectured to be thus named from having the art to *charm* serpents.

The ruler of the half part] See on ver. 9.

Verse 13. *The inhabitants of Zanoah*] This was a town in the tribe of Judah. Josh. xv. 34.

Verse 14. *Beth-haccerem*] A village or town in the tribe of Benjamin.—See Jer. vi. 1.

Verse 15. *The pool of Siloah*] This is probably the same as that mentioned by the evangelists.

The stairs that go down from the city of David.] Jerusalem being built on very *uneven ground,* and some *hills* being taken within the walls; there was a necessity that there should be in different places *steps* by which they could ascend and descend: probably similar to what we see in the city of *Bristol.*

Verse 16. *The pool that was made*] Calmet supposes that this was the reservoir made by Hezekiah, when besieged by Sennacherib, 2 Chron. xxxii. 4.

A. M. 3559
B. C. 445
A. U. C. 309
Coss. Rom.
M. Genucio et
C. Curtio

David, and to the ᵘpool that was made, and unto the house of the mighty.

17 And after him repaired the Levites, Rehum the sun of Bani. Next unto him repaired Hashabiah, the ruler of the half part of Keilah, in his part.

18 After him repaired their brethren, Bavai the son of Henadad, the ruler of the half part of Keilah.

19 And next to him repaired Ezer the son of Jeshua, the ruler of Mizpah, another piece over against the going up to the armoury at the ᵛturning *of the wall.*

20 After him Baruch the son of ʷZabbai earnestly repaired the other piece, from the turning *of the wall* unto the door of the house of Eliashib the high priest.

21 After him repaired Meremoth the son of Urijah the son of Koz another piece, from the door of the house of Eliashib even to the end of the house of Eliashib.

22 And after him repaired the priests, the men of the plain.

23 After him repaired Benjamin and Hashub over against their house. After him repaired Azariah the son of Maaseiah the son of Ananiah by his house.

24 After him repaired Binnui the son of Henadad another piece, from the house of Azariah unto ˣthe turning *of the wall,* even unto the corner.

25 Palal the son of Uzai, over against the turning *of the wall,* and the tower which lieth out from the king's high house, that *was* by the ʸcourt of the prison. After him Pedaiah the son of Parosh.

A. M. 3559
B. C. 445
A. U. C. 309
Coss. Rom.
M. Genucio et
C. Curtio

26 Moreover ᶻthe Nethinims ᵃdwelt in ᵇOphel,ᶜ unto *the place* over against ᵈthe water gate toward the east, and the tower that lieth out.

27 After them the Tekoites repaired another piece, over against the great tower that lieth out, even unto the wall of Ophel.

28 From above the ᵉhorse gate repaired the priests, every one over against his house.

29 After them repaired Zadok the son of Immer over against his house. After him repaired also Shemaiah the son of Shechaniah, the keeper of the east gate.

30 After him repaired Hananiah the son of Shelemiah, and Hanun the sixth son of Zalaph, another piece. After him repaired Meshullam the son of Berechiah over against his chamber.

31 After him repaired Malchiah the goldsmith's son unto the place of the Nethinims, and of the merchants, over against the gate Miphkad, and to the ᶠgoing up of the corner.

32 And between the going up of the corner unto the sheep gate repaired the goldsmiths and the merchants.

ᵘ2 Kings xx. 20; Isa. xxii. 11——ᵛ2 Chronicles xxvi. 9——ʷOr, *Zaccai*——ˣVerse 19——ʸJeremiah xxxii. 2; xxxiii. 1; xxxvii. 21——ᶻEzra ii. 43; chap. xi. 21

ᵃOr, which *dwelt in Ophel, repaired unto*——ᵇ2 Chron. xxvii. 3——ᶜOr, *the tower*——ᵈChapter viii. 1, 3; xii. 37——ᵉ2 Kings xi. 16; 2 Chron. xxiii. 15; Jer. xxxi. 40——ᶠOr, *corner-chamber*

The house of the mighty.] Probably a place where a *band of soldiers* was kept, or the *city guard.*

Verse 19. *The going up to the armoury*] This was either a *tower* that defended the angle where the two walls met; or the *city arsenal,* where shields, spears, &c., were kept to arm the people in time of danger.

Verse 20. *Earnestly repaired*] He distinguished himself by his *zeal* and *activity.*

Verse 22. *The priests, the men of the plain.*] Some of the officers of the temple, particularly the *singers,* dwelt in the *plain* country round about Jerusalem, chap. xii. 28; and it is likely that several of the *priests* dwelt in the same place.

Verse 28. *The horse gate*] The place through which the *horses* passed in order to be watered; it was near the temple. Some rabbins suppose that in order to go to the temple, a person might go on horseback to the place here referred to, but then was obliged to alight, as a horse could pass no farther. Horses were never very plentiful in Jerusalem.

Verse 32. *The goldsmiths and the merchants.*] The word צֹרְפִים *hatstsorephim* may signify *smiths,* or persons who worked in *metals* of any kind; but it is generally understood to mean those who worked in *gold.* I have already observed, that the mention of *merchants* and *goldsmiths* shows that these persons were formed into *bodies corporate* in those ancient times. But these terms are differently rendered in the *versions.* The *Vulgate* is the same as ours, which probably our translators copied: *aurifices et negociatores.* The *Syriac* is, *goldsmiths* and *druggists.* The *Arabic, smelters of metal* and *porters.* The *Septuagint,* in some copies, particularly in the *Roman* edition, and in the *Complutensian, Antwerp,* and *Paris Polyglots,* have οἱ χαλκεις και οἱ μεταβολοι, *smiths* and *merchants;* but in other copies, particularly the *London Polyglot,* for μεταβολοι we find ῥωποπωλαι, *seller of shields.* And here the learned reader will find a double mistake in the *London Polyglot,* ῥοποπωλαι for ῥωποπωλαι, and in the Latin version *scruta* for *scuta,* neither of which conveys any sense.

CHAPTER IV

Sanballat and Tobiah mock the Jews, and endeavour to prevent the completing of the wall, 1–3. Nehemiah prays against them, and the people complete one half of the wall, 4–6. The Arabians, Ammonites, and Ashdodites, conspire together, and come to fight against the Jews, 7, 8. The Jews commend themselves to God, and determine to fight for their lives and liberties; on hearing of which their enemies are disheartened, 9–16. The Jews divide themselves into two bands; one half working, and the other standing ready armed to meet their enemies. Even the workmen are obliged to arm themselves, while employed in building, for fear of their enemies, 17, 18. Nehemiah uses all precautions to prevent a surprise; and all labour with great fervour in the work, 19–22.

A. M. 3559
B. C. 445
A. U. C. 309
Coss. Rom.
M. Genucio et
C. Curtio

BUT it came to pass, [a]that when Sanballat heard that we builded the wall, he was wroth, and took great indignation, and mocked the Jews.

2 And he spake before his brethren and the army of Samaria, and said, What do these feeble Jews? will they [b]fortify themselves? will they sacrifice? will they make an end in a day? will they revive the stones out of the heaps of the rubbish which are burned?

3 Now [c]Tobiah the Ammonite *was* by him, and he said, Even that which they build, if a fox go up, he shall even break down their stone wall.

4 [d]Hear, O our God: for we are [e]despised: and [f]turn their reproach upon their own head, and give them for a prey in the land of captivity:

5 And [g]cover not their iniquity, and let not their sin be blotted out from before thee: for they have provoked *thee* to anger before the builders.

A. M. 3559
B. C. 445
A. U. C. 309
Coss. Rom.
M. Genucio et
C. Curtio

6 So built we the wall; and all the wall was joined together unto the half thereof: for the people had a mind to work.

7 But it came to pass, [h]*that* when Sanballat, and Tobiah, and the Arabians, and the Ammonites, and the Ashdodites, heard that the walls of Jerusalem [i]were made up, *and* that the breaches began to be stopped, then they were very wroth,

8 And [k]conspired all of them together to come *and* to fight against Jerusalem, and [l]to hinder it.

9 Nevertheless [m]we made our prayer unto our God, and set a watch against them

---

[a]Chap. ii. 10, 19——[b]Heb. *leave to themselves*——[c]Ch. ii. 10, 19——[d]Psa. cxxiii. 3, 4——[e]Hebrew, *despite* [f]Psa. lxxix. 12; Prov. iii. 34

[g]Psa. lxix. 27, 28; cix. 14, 15; Jer. xviii. 23——[h]Ver. 1 [i]Heb. *ascended*——[k]Psa. lxxxiii. 3, 4, 5——[l]Heb. *to make an error to it*——[m]Psa. l. 15

NOTES ON CHAP. IV

Verse 2. *The army of Samaria*] As he was *governor,* he had the command of the army, and he wished to excite the soldiers to second his views against Nehemiah and his men.

What do these feeble Jews?] We may remark here, in general, that the enemies of God's work endeavour by all means to *discredit* and *destroy* it, and *those* who are employed in it. 1. They *despise* the *workmen: What do these feeble Jews?* 2. They endeavour to turn all into *ridicule: Will they fortify themselves?* 3. They have recourse to *lying: If a fox go up, he shall even break down their stone wall.* 4. They sometimes use *fair* but *deceitful speeches;* see chap. vi. 2, &c.

Verse 4. *Turn their reproach upon their own head*] A prayer of this kind, understood literally, is not lawful for any *Christian.* Jesus, our great master, has said, "Love your enemies; do good to them that hate you; and pray for them that despitefully use you." Such sayings as the above are excusable in the mouth of a Jew, under severe irritation. See the next verse.

Verse 5. *Let not their sin be blotted out*] These are the most terrible imprecations; but probably we should understand them as *declaratory,* for the same form of the verb, in the Hebrew, is used as *precative* and *imperative. Turn their reproach*—Their reproach shall be

turned. *Give them for a prey*—They *shall be* given for a prey. *Cover not their iniquity*—Their iniquity *shall not* be covered. *Let not their sin be blotted out*—Their sin *shall not* be blotted out. All who know the genius of the Hebrew language, know that the *future* tense is used to express all these senses. Besides, we may rest assured that Nehemiah's curses, or declaration of God's judgments, had respect only to their *bodies,* and to *their life:* not to their *souls* and the *world* to come. And then they amount to no more than this: *What a man soweth that he shall reap.*

Verse 6. *For the people had a mind to work.*] The original is very emphatic: ויהי לב לעם

לעשות *vayehi leb leam laasoth,* "For the people had a *heart* to work." Their *hearts* were engaged in it; and where the *heart* is engaged, the work of God goes on well. The whole of this 6th verse is omitted by the *Septuagint.*

Verse 7. *The walls of Jerusalem were made up*] That is, they were made up *to the half height of the wall;* for the preceding verse seems to intimate that the *whole wall* was thus far built; not *half of the wall* completed, but the *whole wall* built to half its height.

Verse 9. *We made our prayer unto our God, and set a watch*] The strongest confidence in the protection and favour of God does not preclude the use of *all* or any of the *means of self-*

A. M. 3559
B. C. 445
A. U. C. 309
Coss. Rom.
M. Genucio et
C. Curtio

day and night, because of them.

10 And Judah said, The strength of the bearers of burdens is decayed, and *there is* much rubbish; so that we are not able to build the wall.

11 And our adversaries said, They shall not know, neither see, till we come in the midst among them, and slay them, and cause the work to cease.

12 And it came to pass, that when the Jews which dwelt by them came, they said unto us ten times, ⁿFrom all places whence ye shall return unto us *they will be upon you.*

13 Therefore set I °in the lower places behind the wall, *and* on the higher places, I even set the people after their families with their swords, their spears, and their bows.

14 And I looked, and rose up, and said unto the nobles, and to the rulers, and to the rest of the people,ᵖBe not ye afraid of them: remember the LORD, *which is* �q great and terrible, and ʳfight for your brethren, your sons, and your daughters, your wives, and your houses.

15 And it came to pass, when our enemies heard that it was known unto us, ˢand God had brought their counsel to naught, that we returned all of us to the wall, every one unto his work.

16 And it came to pass from that time forth, *that* the half of my servants wrought in the work, and the other half of them held both the spears, the shields, and the bows, and the habergeons; and the rulers *were* behind all the house of Judah.

A. M. 3559
B. C. 445
A. U. C. 309
Coss. Rom.
M. Genucio et
C. Curtio

ⁿOr, *That from all places ye must return to us*——°Heb. *from the lower parts of the place,* &c.

ᵖNum. xiv. 9; Deut. i. 29——�q Deut. x. 17——ʳ2 Sam. x. 12——ˢJob v. 12

---

preservation and defence which his providence has put in our power. While God works in us to *will and to do,* we should proceed to *willing,* through the *power* he has given us to *will;* and we should proceed to *action,* through the *power* he has given us to *act.* We cannot *will,* but through God's *power;* we cannot *act,* but through God's *strength.* The *power,* and the *use* of it, are two distinct things. We may *have the power to will,* and *not will;* and we may have the *power* to *do,* and *not act:* therefore, says the apostle, seeing God has wrought in you these powers, see that YOU WORK OUT YOUR OWN *salvation, with fear and trembling.*

Verse 10. *The strength of the bearers of burdens is decayed*] They worked both *day* and *night,* scarcely ever putting off their clothes, except for the purpose of being *washed,* ver. 21, 23.

Much rubbish] The ruins they were obliged to clear away, before they could dig the foundation for a new wall: and in this labour they were nearly exhausted; see chap. v. 15.

Verse 12. *From all places whence ye shall return unto us*] This verse is extremely difficult. Our translators have supplied the words, *they will be upon you,* which have nothing correspondent in the Hebrew. The Septuagint have given a good sense, Αναβαινουσιν εκ παντων των τοπων εφ' ἡμας, *They come up from all places against us.* The sense appears to be this: the Jews which dwelt among the Samaritans, &c., came often to Nehemiah from all quarters,where they sojourned, and told him the *designs* of his enemies against him: therefore, he set people with their swords, spears, and bows, to defend the walls. It is probable that instead of תשובו *tashubu,* "ye shall *return,*" we should read חשבו *chashebu,* "they *designed* or *meditated.*" This word is very similar to the other, and makes the sense very clear. "The Jews who dwelt among them told us frequently, from all places, what they *designed* against us." For this reading *Houbigant, Michaelis* and *Dathé* contend.

But this various reading is not found in any MS., and is not countenanced by any of the versions. See ver. 15.

Verse 14. *Be not ye afraid of them*] Are they more terrible or stronger than God?

Fight for your brethren] Your own *countrymen,* who worship the same God, and are come from the same stock; *your sons,* whom they wish to slay or lead into captivity; *your daughters* and *wives,* whom they wish to deflower and defile; and *your houses,* which they wish to seize and occupy as their own. They had every thing at stake; and therefore they must fight *pro aris et focis,* for their *religion,* their *lives,* and their *property.* A people thus interested, who once take up the sword, can never be *conquered.*

There is an address made to the Greeks by their leader in Æschylus, Pers. ver. 402, similar to this, to excite them against the Persians:—

——Ω Παιδες 'Ελληνων, ιτε,
Ελευθεροῦτε πατριδ', ελευθεροῦτε δε
Παιδας, γυναικας, θεων τε πατρῳων ἑδη,
Θηκας τε προγονων· νυν ὑπερ παντων αγων.

"——Sons of the Greeks, go on!
Free now your country, and your children free;
Your wives, the temples of your fathers' gods,
And dear abodes of farthest ancestors:—
Now strike the blow for all!" J. B. B. C.

Verse 15. *Their counsel to naught*] The word *counsel* used here countenances the *emendation* in the 12th verse.

Verse 16. *Half—wrought in the work*] This is no unusual thing, even in the present day, in Palestine: people sowing their seed are often attended by an armed man, to prevent the Arabs from robbing them of their seed, which they will not fail to do if not protected.

Habergeons] In the Franco-Gallic, *hautbergon* signifies *a coat of mail;* but as in *Teutonic* **hals** signifies the neck, and **bergen,** to *cover* or *de-*

A. M. 3559
B. C. 445
A. U. C. 309
Coss. Rom.
M. Genucio et
C. Curtio

17 They which builded on the wall, and they that bare burdens, with those that laded, *every one* with one of his hands wrought in the work, and with the other *hand* held a weapon.

18 For the builders, every one had his sword girded [t]by his side, and *so* builded. And he that sounded the trumpet *was* by me.

19 And I said unto the nobles, and to the rulers, and to the rest of the people, The work *is* great and large, and we are separated upon the wall, one far from another.

20 In what place *therefore* ye hear the sound of the trumpet, resort ye thither unto

us: [u]our God shall fight for us.

A. M. 3559
B. C. 445
A. U. C. 309
Coss. Rom.
M. Genucio et
C. Curtio

21 So we laboured in the work: and half of them held the spears from the rising of the morning till the stars appeared.

22 Likewise at the same time said I unto the people, Let every one with his servant lodge within Jerusalem, that in the night they may be a guard to us, and labour on the day.

23 So neither I, nor my brethren, nor my servants, nor the men of the guard which followed me, none of us put off our clothes, [v]*saving that* every one put them off for washing.

---

[t]Heb. *on his loins*——[u]Exod. xiv. 14, 25; Deut. i. 30; iii. 22; xx. 4; Josh. xxiii. 10

[v]Or, *every one* went *with his weapon for water; see* Judges v. 11

---

fend; it may be considered rather as signifying a *breastplate,* or *armour for the breast.*

Verse 17. *With one of his hands wrought in the work, and with the other* hand *held a weapon.*] That is, he had his *arms* at hand, and was as fully prepared to *fight* as to *work.* So OVID, *Epist.* xi., *Canace Macario,* ver. 1:—

Si qua tamen cæcis errabunt scripta lituris,
Oblitus a dominæ cæde libellus erit:
Dextra tenet calamum; strictum tenet altera
   ferrum:
Et jacet in gremio charta soluta meo.

If streaming blood my fatal letter stain,
Imagine, ere you read, the writer slain.
One hand the sword, and one the pen employs,
And in my lap the ready paper lies. DRYDEN.

By this mode of speech Canace does not intimate to her brother Macarius, that she actually *held* the *sword* in one hand while she held the *pen* in the other, but that she had it *ready* to slay herself as soon as she had written the epistle.

Verse 20. *Ye hear the sound of the trumpet*] As the walls were very extensive, and the workmen consequently much scattered, their enemies might easily attack and destroy them successively, he therefore ordered them all to work as near to each other as they could; and himself, who was everywhere surveying the work, kept a trumpeter always with him, who was to sound when the enemy approached; and all were instantly to run to the place where they heard the sound.

Verse 22. *Let every one with his servant lodge within Jerusalem*] The country people were accustomed, after their day's labour, to return to their families; now being so formidably threatened, he obliged them all to sleep in Jerusalem, that they might be ready, in case of attack, to help their brethren. All this man's arrangements were wise and judicious.

Verse 23. *None of us put off our clothes,* saving that *every one put them off for washing.*] The Hebrew for all this is only אין אנחנו פשטים

בגדינו איש שלחו המים *ein anachnu poshetim begadeynu ish shilcho hammayim;* which *Montanus* translates, *Non nos exuentes vestes nostras, vir missile suum aquas;* "We, not putting off our garments, a man his dart to the waters." Of this latter clause what sense can be made? Let us hear what the ancient *versions* say.

The *Vulgate, Unusquisque tantum nudabatur ad baptismum,* "Every one stripped himself for the bath."

The *Septuagint* omit the latter part of this clause, *And there was none of us who put off his garments.*

The *Syriac,* "None of us put off his clothes for a month each in his turn."

The *Arabic,* "Nor did we put off our clothes, but with our arms, at the end of a month."

There is a remarkable reading in one of *De Rossi's* MSS. אין אנחנו פשטים בגדינו משלחה על המים, *We did not lay aside our garments, but in order to send them to the washing.* This is most likely the sense of the place.

It is curious to see how our old versions translate the place.

Coverdale: We put neuer of our clothes, so much as to wash ourselues.—1535.

Becke: We put neuer of our clothes, so muche as to washe ourselues.—1549.

Cardmarden: We put neuer of oure clothes no more than the other dyd theyr harnesse, saue onely bycause of the water.—1566.

This shows how all interpreters have been puzzled with this vexatious clause.

THE reading from De Rossi's MS., given above, is the most likely to be the true one, because it gives a good sense, which cannot be found in the Hebrew text as it now stands. The general meaning is sufficiently evident: they worked nearly day and night, only had their hours by turns for repose; this did not permit them time sufficient to undress themselves in order to take regular sleep, therefore they only put off their clothes when they were obliged to get them washed.

CHAPTER V

The people complain that they are oppressed and enthralled by their richer brethren, 1–3. Nehemiah calls them to account; upbraids them for their cruelty; and obliges them to swear that they will forgive the debts, restore the mortgaged estates, and free their servants, 4–13. Nehemiah's generosity and liberality, 14–17. The daily provision for his table, 18, 19.

A. M. 3559
B. C. 445
A. U. C. 309
Coss. Rom.
M. Genucio et
C. Curtio

AND there was a great [a]cry of the people and of their wives against their [b]brethren the Jews.

2 For there were that said, We, our sons, and our daughters, *are* many: therefore we take up corn *for them,* that we may eat, and live.

3 *Some* also there were that said, We have mortgaged our lands, vineyards, and houses, that we might buy corn, because of the dearth.

4 There were also that said, We have borrowed money for the king's tribute, *and that* upon our lands and vineyards.

5 Yet now [c]our flesh *is* as the flesh of our brethren, our children as their children: and, lo, we [d]bring into bondage our sons and our daughters to be servants, and *some* of our daughters are brought unto bondage *already:* neither *is it* in our power *to redeem them;* for other men have our lands and vineyards.

6 And I was very angry when I heard their cry and these words.

A. M. 3559
B. C. 445
A. U. C. 309
Coss. Rom.
M. Genucio et
C. Curtio

7 Then [e]I consulted with myself, and I rebuked the nobles, and the rulers, and said unto them, [f]Ye exact usury, every one of his brother. And I set a great assembly against them.

8 And I said unto them, We after our ability have [g]redeemed our brethren the Jews, which were sold unto the heathen; and will ye even sell your brethren? or shall they be sold unto us? Then held they their peace, and found nothing *to answer.*

9 Also I said, It *is* not good that ye do: ought ye not to walk [h]in the fear of our God [i]because of the reproach of the heathen our enemies?

10 I likewise, *and* my brethren, and my servants, might exact of them money and corn: I pray you, let us leave off this usury.

---

[a]Isa. v. 7——[b]Lev. xxv. 35, 36, 37; Deut. xv. 7
[c]Isa. lviii. 7——[d]Exod. xxi. 7; Lev. xxv. 39——[e]Heb. *my heart consulted in me*

[f]Exod. xxii. 25; Lev. xxv. 36; Ezek. xxii. 12——[g]Lev. xxv. 48——[h]Lev. xxv. 36——[i]2 Sam. xii. 14; Rom. ii. 24; 1 Pet. ii. 12

NOTES ON CHAP. V

Verse 2. *We, our sons, and our daughters,* are *many*] Our families are larger than we can provide for; we are obliged to go in debt; and our richer brethren take advantage of our necessitous situation, and oppress us. The details which are given in the next verse are sufficiently plain.

Verse 3. *Because of the dearth.*] About the time of Zerubbabel, God had sent a judicial dearth upon the land, as we learn from *Haggai,* chap. i. 9, &c., for the people it seems were more intent on building houses for themselves than on rebuilding the house of the Lord: "Ye looked for much, and, lo, it is come to little; because of mine house that is waste; and ye run, every man unto his own house. Therefore the heaven over you is stayed from dew, and the earth is stayed from her fruit. And I called for a drought upon the land, and upon the mountains, and upon the corn, and upon the new wine, and upon the oil, and upon that which the ground brought forth; and upon men, and upon cattle, and upon all the labour of the hands." This dearth might have been continued, or its effects still felt; but it is more likely that there was a *new* dearth owing to the great number of people, for whose support the land that had been brought into cultivation was not sufficient.

Verse 4. *We have borrowed money*] This

should be read, *We have borrowed money for the king's tribute on our lands and vineyards.* They had a tax to pay to the Persian king in token of their subjection to him, and though it is not likely it was heavy, yet they were not able to pay it.

Verse 5. *We bring into bondage our sons*] The law permitted parents to sell their children in times of extreme necessity, Exod. xxi. 7.

Verse 7. *Ye exact usury*] This was expressly contrary to the law of God; and was doubly cruel at this time, when they were just returning out of the land of their captivity, and were suffering from the effects of a *dearth.* Some think that it was about the time of a Sabbatical year, when their land must have lain at rest without cultivation, and during which they were expressly commanded not to exact any debt, Deut. xv. 2.

I set a great assembly against them.] Brought all these delinquents before the rulers of the people.

Verse 9. *Ought ye not to walk in the fear of our God*] If ye wish to *accredit* that religion ye profess which comes from the God of *justice* and *mercy;* should you not, in the sight of the heathen, abstain from *injustice* and *cruelty?* Can they credit your profession, when they see such practices? The inconsistent conduct of some professors of religion does much harm in the Church of God.

A. M. 3559
B. C. 445
A. U. C. 309
Coss. Rom.
M. Genucio et
C. Curtio

11 Restore, I pray you, to them, even this day, their lands, their vineyards, their olive-yards, and their houses, also the hundredth *part* of the money, and of the corn, the wine, and the oil, that ye exact of them.

12 Then said they, We will restore *them,* and will require nothing of them; so will we do as thou sayest. Then I called the priests, ^kand took an oath of them, that they should do according to this promise.

13 Also ^lI shook my lap, and said, So God shake out every man from his house, and from his labour, that performeth not this promise, even thus be he shaken out, and ^memptied. And all the congregation said, Amen, and praised the LORD. ^nAnd the people did according to this promise.

14 Moreover from the time that I was appointed to be their governor in the land of Judah, from the twentieth year, ^oeven unto the two and thirtieth year of Artaxerxes the king, *that is,* twelve years, I and my brethren have not ^peaten the bread of the governor.

A. M. 3559
B. C. 445
A. U. C. 309
Coss. Rom.
M. Genucio et
C. Curtio

15 But the former governors that *had been* before me were chargeable unto the people, and had taken of them bread and wine, beside forty shekels of silver; yea, even their servants bare rule over the people: but ^qso did not I, because of the ^rfear of God.

16 Yea, also I continued in the work of this wall, neither bought we any land: and all my servants *were* gathered thither unto the work.

17 Moreover *there were* ^sat my table a hundred and fifty of the Jews and rulers, besides those that came unto us from among the heathen that *are* about us.

18 Now *that* ^twhich was prepared *for me* daily *was* one ox *and* six choice sheep; also fowls were prepared for me, and once in ten days store of all sorts of wine: yet for all this ^urequired not I the bread of the governor, because the bondage was heavy upon this people.

19 ^vThink upon me, my God, for good, *according* to all that I have done for this people.

---

^kEzra x. 5; Jer. xxxiv. 8, 9——^lMatt. x. 14; Acts xiii. 51; xviii. 6——^mHeb. *empty* or *void*——^n2 Kings xxiii. 3 ^oChap. xiii. 6

^p1 Cor. ix. 4, 15——^q2 Cor. xi. 9; xii. 13——^rVerse 9 ^s2 Sam. ix. 7; 1 Kings xviii. 19——^t1 Kings iv. 22 ^uVer. 14, 15——^vChap. xiii. 22

Verse 11. *Also the hundredth* part *of the money*] *Houbigant* contends, 1. That the word מאת *meath,* which *we* and the *Vulgate* translate one *hundredth* part, never means so anywhere; and 2. That it would have answered no end to have remitted to people so distressed merely the *one hundredth part* of the money which had been taken from them by usury. He understands מאת *meath* as signifying the same as מן את *min eth,* contracted into מאת *meeth,* a preposition and demonstrative particle joined together, *also a part* FROM THE *money.* Neither the *Syriac, Septuagint,* nor *Arabic* acknowledges this *hundredth part.* Some think that the *hundredth* part is that which they obliged the poor debtors to pay each month, which would amount to what we would call *twelve per cent.* interest for the money lent, or the debt contracted. See the *introduction.*

Verse 13. *Also I shook my lap*] This was a significant action frequent among the Hebrews; and something of the same nature was practised among other nations. "When the Roman ambassadors entered the senate of Carthage, they had their toga gathered up in their bosom. They said, We carry here *peace* and *war;* you may have *which* you will. The senate answered, You may give *which* you please. They then *shook their toga,* and said, We bring you war. To which all the senate answered, We cheerfully accept it." See *Livy.* lib. xxi., cap. 18; and see *Calmet.*

Verse 14. *I and my brethren have not eaten the bread of the governor.*] From what is related here, and in the following verse, we find

that the table of the governor was always supplied by the people with *bread* and *wine;* and, besides, they had *forty shekels* per diem for their other expenses. The people were also greatly oppressed by the *servants* and *officers* of the governor; but, during the *twelve years* that Nehemiah had been with them, he took not this salary, and ate none of their bread. Nor were his servants permitted to take or exact any thing from them. Having such an example, it was scandalous for their chiefs, priests, and nobles, thus to oppress an afflicted and distressed people.

Verse 16. *Neither bought we any land*] Neither he nor his officers took any advantage of the necessities of the people, to buy their lands, &c. He even made his own servants to work at the wall.

Verse 17. *A hundred and fifty of the Jews*] He kept *open house,* entertained *all comers;* besides having *one hundred and fifty* Jews who had their food constantly at his table, and at his expense. To be able to bear all these expenses, no doubt Nehemiah had saved money while he was cup-bearer to the Persian king in *Susa.*

Verse 18. *One ox* and *six choice sheep*] This was food sufficient for more than *two hundred* men.

Once in ten days store of all sorts of wine] It is supposed that every *tenth* day they drank wine; at all other times they drank *water;* unless we suppose the meaning of the phrase to be, that his servants laid *in a stock* of wine every ten days. Though the Asiatics drank sparingly of wine, yet it is not very likely that, in a case such as that above, *wine* was tasted only *thrice* in each month.

Bishop *Pococke* mentions the manner in which the *bey* of *Tunis* lived. He had daily *twelve sheep,* with *fish, fowls, soups, oranges, eggs, onions, boiled rice,* &c., &c., His *nobles* dined with him; after they had done, the *servants* sat down; and, when they had finished, the *poor* took what was left. Here is no mention of a *fat ox;* but there were *six sheep* at the bey's table *more* than were at the table of Nehemiah: so the *twelve sheep* were equal to *six sheep* and *one ox.* Probably the mode of living between these *two* was nearly alike.

Verse 19. *Think upon me, my God, for good*] Nehemiah wishes for no reward from *man;* and he only asks *mercy* at the hand of his God for

what his *providence* enabled him to do; and which, according to the good hand of his God upon him, he had done *faithfully.* He does not offer his *good deeds* to God in extenuation *of* his *sins,* or as a *compensation* for the *heaven* he expected. Nothing of the kind: he simply says, what any good man might say, My God, *as I* have done good to them, *so* do good to me; or as the poet has sung:—

> "Teach me to feel another's wo,
> To hide the fault I see:
> The mercy I to others show,
> That mercy show to me!"   POPE.

This is according to the precept of Christ: "Forgive, and ye shall be forgiven; give, and it shall be given unto you."

CHAPTER VI

Sanballat, Tobiah, and Geshem, insidiously desire a conference with Nehemiah, which he refuses, 1–4. They then charge him with the design of rebelling, and causing himself to be made king, 5–7; which he denies, and prays to God for support, 8, 9. A false prophet is hired by Tobiah and Sanballat, to put him in fear; he discovers the imposture, and defeats their design, 10–13. He prays to God against them, 14. The wall is finished in fifty-two days, 15. He discovers a secret and treasonable correspondence between Tobiah and some of the Jewish nobles, 16–19.

A. M. 3559
B. C. 445
A. U. C. 309
Coss. Rom.
M. Genucio et
C. Curtio

NOW it came to pass, [a]when Sanballat, and Tobiah, and [b]Geshem the Arabian, and the rest of our enemies, heard that I had builded the wall, and *that* there was no breach left therein; ([c]though at that time I had not set up the doors upon the gates;)

2 That Sanballat and Geshem [d]sent unto me, saying, Come, let us meet together in *some one of* the villages in the plain of [e]Ono. But they [f]thought to do me mischief.

3 And I sent messengers unto them, saying, I *am* doing a great work, so that I cannot

come down: why should the work cease, whilst I leave it and come down to you?

A. M. 3559
B. C. 445
A. U. C. 309
Coss. Rom.
M. Genucio et
C. Curtio

4 Yet they sent unto me four times after this sort; and I answered them after the same manner.

5 Then sent Sanballat his servant unto me in like manner the fifth time with an open letter in his hand;

6 Wherein *was* written, It is reported among the heathen, and [g]Gashmu saith *it,* [h]*that* thou and the Jews think to rebel: for which cause thou buildest the wall, that thou mayest be

---

[a]Chapter ii. 10, 19; iv. 1, 7——[b]Or, *Gashmu,* verse 6
[c]Chap. iii. 1, 3——[d]Prov. xxvi. 24, 25

[e]1 Chron. viii. 12; chap. xi. 35——[f]Psa. xxxvii. 12, 32
[g]Or, *Geshem,* ver. 1——[h]Chap. ii. 19

NOTES ON CHAP. VI

Verse 2. *Come, let us meet together in—the plain of Ono.*] They wished to get him out of Jerusalem from among his friends, that they might either carry him off, or murder him. *Ono* is supposed to have been in the tribe of Benjamin, near Jordan.

Verse 3. *I am doing a great work*] Though he knew their design, he does not think it prudent to mention it. Had he done so, they would probably have gone to extremities, finding that they were discovered; and perhaps in a formidable body attacked Jerusalem, when ill provided to sustain such a shock. They wished to effect their purpose rather by *treachery* than by open *violence.* I know not any language which a man who is employed on important labours can use more suitably, as an answer to the thou-

sand invitations and provocations he may have to remit his work, enter into useless or trivial conferences, or notice weak, wicked, and malicious attacks on his work and his motives: "I am doing a great work, so I cannot *stoop* to your nonsense, or notice your malevolence. Why should the work cease, while I leave it, and *come down* to such as *you?*"

Verse 5. *With an open letter in his hand*] This was an insult to a person of Nehemiah's quality: as letters sent to chiefs and governors in the East are always carefully folded up, and put in costly silken bags, and these carefully sealed. The circumstance is thus marked to show the contempt he (Sanballat) had for him.

Verse 6. *And Gashmu saith it*] You are accused of crimes against the state, and *Geshem,* the Arabian, is your accuser.

A. M. 3559
B. C. 445
A. U. C. 309
Coss. Rom.
M. Genucio et
C. Curtio

their king, according to these words.

7 And thou hast also appointed prophets to preach of thee at Jerusalem, saying, *There is* a king in Judah: and now shall it be reported to the king according to these words. Come now therefore, and let us take counsel together.

8 Then I sent unto him, saying, There are no such things done as thou sayest, but thou feignest them out of thine own heart.

9 For they all made us afraid, saying, Their hands shall be weakened from the work, that it be not done. Now therefore, *O God,* strengthen my hands.

10 Afterward I came unto the house of Shemaiah the son of Delaiah the son of Mehetabeel, who *was* shut up; and he said, Let us meet together in the house of God, within the temple, and let us shut the doors of the temple; for they will come to slay thee; yea, in the night will they come to slay thee.

11 And I said, Should such a man as I flee? and who *is there,* that, *being as I am,* would go into the temple to save his life? I will not go in.

12 And, lo, I perceived that God had not sent him; but that [i]he pronounced this prophecy against me: for Tobiah and Sanballat had hired him.

13 Therefore *was* he hired, that I should be afraid, and do so, and sin, and *that* they might have *matter* for an evil report, that they might reproach me.

14 [k]My God, think thou upon Tobiah and Sanballat according to these their works, and on the [l]prophetess Noadiah, and the rest of the prophets, that would have put me in fear.

15 So the wall was finished in the twenty and fifth *day* of *the month* Elul, in fifty and two days.

16 And it came to pass, that [m]when all our enemies heard *thereof,* and all the heathen

A. M. 3559
B. C. 445
A. U. C. 309
Coss. Rom.
M. Genucio et
C. Curtio

---

[i]Ezek. xiii. 22——[k]Chap. xiii. 29——[l]Ezek.
xiii. 17——[m]Chap. ii. 10; iv. 1, 7; vi. 1

Verse 7. *Thou hast also appointed prophets*] Persons who pretend to be commissioned to preach to the people, and say, *Nehemiah reigneth!*

Come now therefore, and let us take counsel] Come and justify yourself before me. This was a trick to get Nehemiah into his power.

Verse 8. *There are no such things done*] You well know that what you say is false: I shall not, therefore, trouble myself about a false charge.

Verse 10. *Who was shut up*] Lived in a sequestered, solitary state; pretending to sanctity, and to close intercourse with God.

Let us meet together in the house of God] The meaning is, "Shut yourself up in the temple; appear to have taken sanctuary there, for in it alone can you find safety." This he said to discourage and disgrace him, and to ruin the people; for, had Nehemiah taken his advice, the people would have been without a *leader,* their enemies would have come upon them at once, and they would have been an easy prey. Besides, had Nehemiah done this, he would have been shut up in the temple, his government would have been declared at an end, and Sanballat would have assumed the reins.

Verse 11. *Should such a man as I flee?*] Shall I, who am governor of the people, appointed both by God and the king, shall I betray my trust, and leave the flock without a shepherd? Shall I be a traitor, and abandon the office to which I am appointed?—No! Who, in my situation, with such responsibility, and such prospects, would go into the temple to save his life? *I* will not: I will stand at my post, and be ready to receive my enemies whensoever they come; so let Sanballat, Tobiah, and Geshem look to themselves.

Verse 14. *And on the prophetess Noadiah*] Whether this was a *prophet* or *prophetess,* we cannot tell; the *Hebrew* text only makes her a *prophetess;* all the *versions* have *Noadiah the prophet,* except the *Arabic* which has بودادع *Younadaa the prophet.* I think the ה *he* at the end of נביאה *nebiah* is a *mistake,* and that we should read *Noadiah the prophet.*

Verse 15. *The twenty and fifth—of—Elul*] This Jewish month answers to a part of our *August* and *September.*

Fifty and two days.] I see no difficulty in supposing that several thousand workmen, each of whom was working *as for God,* should be able to complete this wall in *fifty-two* days. There is little doubt that several parts of the old wall were entire; in many places the foundations still remained; there were all the *materials* of the old wall still at hand; and though they had to clear and carry away much rubbish, yet they do not appear to have had any stones to quarry. The work mentioned here was little when compared to what *Cæsar* did in Gaul and other places; and to what *Titus* did at Jerusalem, who built a wall round Jerusalem of *five thousand* paces in three days, besides, *thirteen towers* of *ten stadia* in circuit. And *Quintus Curtius* and *Arrian* inform us that Alexander the Great built the walls of Alexandria, on the Tanais, which were nearly *eight miles* in compass, in the space of between *twenty* and *thirty days.* Nehemiah therefore had time sufficient in *fifty-two* days to repair and restore the walls of Jerusalem. See *Calmet* on this place.

Verse 16. *This work was wrought of our God.*] This is an additional reason why we should not wonder at the *shortness* of the time in which so great a work was done, for God

A. M. 3559
B. C. 445
A. U. C. 309
Coss. Rom.
M. Genucio et
C. Curtio

that *were* about us saw *these things,* they were much cast down in their own eyes: for [n]they perceived that this work was wrought of our God.

17 Moreover in those days the nobles of Judah [o]sent many letters unto Tobiah, and *the letters* of Tobiah came unto them.

18 For *there were* many in Judah sworn

unto him, because he *was* the son-in-law of Shechaniah the son of Arah; and his son Johanan had taken the daughter of Meshullam the son of Berechiah.

19 Also they reported his good deeds before me, and uttered my [p]words to him. *And* Tobiah sent letters to put me in fear.

A. M. 3559
B. C. 445
A. U. C. 309
Coss. Rom.
M. Genucio et
C. Curtio

---

[n]Psa. cxxvi. 2——[o]Heb. *multiplied their*

letters passing to Tobiah——[p]Or, *matters*

---

helped them by an especial providence; and this was so very observable, that their *carnal* enemies could discover it.

Verse 17. *The nobles of Judah sent many letters*] The circumstances marked in this and the following verses show still more clearly the difficulties which Nehemiah had to encounter; he had enemies *without* and false friends *within*. A treacherous correspondence was carried on between the nobles of Judah and the Ammonites; and had almost any other man been at the head of the Jewish affairs, Jerusalem had never been re-established.

Verse 18. *He was the son-in-law of Shechaniah*] Previously to the coming of Nehemiah, the Jews seemed to be fast intermixing with the heathen, by *intermarriages* with *Ashdodites, Ammonites,* and *Moabites;* see chap. xiii. 23. Ezra had many evils of this kind to redress, (Ezra ix. 3, &c.,) chiefly among the common people, though there were both chiefs and priests in that trespass. But here we find the heathen and Jewish nobles interlinked; and the latter were so far imbued with the spirit of idolatry, that they forgot God, his service, their brethren, and their own souls.

CHAPTER VII

Nehemiah makes use of proper precautions in guarding the city gates, 1–4. He proposes to reckon the people according to their genealogies; and finds a register of those who came out of Babylon, with Zerubbabel, 5–7. A transcript of the register, 8–60. Account of those who came from other provinces; and of priests who, because they could not show their register, were put away from the priesthood as polluted, 61–65. The sum total of the congregation: of their men-servants and maid-servants; singing men and women; horses, mules, camels, and asses, 66–69. The sums given by different persons for the work, 70–72. All betake themselves to their several cities, 73.

A. M. 3559
B. C. 445
A. U. C. 309
Coss. Rom.
M. Genucio et
C. Curtio

NOW it came to pass, when the wall was built, and I had [a]set up the doors, and the porters and the singers and the Levites were appointed,

2 That I gave my brother Hanani, and Hananiah the ruler [b]of the palace, charge over Jerusalem: for he *was* a faithful man, and [c]feared God above many.

3 And I said unto them, Let not the gates of Jerusalem be opened until the sun be hot; and while they stand by, let them shut the doors, and bar *them:* and appoint watches of the inhabitants of Jerusalem, every one in his watch, and every one *to be* over against his house.

4 Now the city *was* [d]large and great; but

A. M. 3559
B. C. 445
A. U. C. 309
Coss. Rom.
M. Genucio et
C. Curtio

---

[a]Chap. vi. 1——[b]Chap. ii. 8——[c]Exod. xviii. 21

[d]Heb. *broad in spaces*

NOTES ON CHAP. VII

Verse 2. *My brother Hanani*] This was the person who gave Nehemiah the account of the desolate state of the Jews, chap. i. 2. He is now made ruler of Jerusalem, probably because Nehemiah was about to return to the Persian court. And he found this man to be one in whom he could trust: 1. Because *he was a faithful man*—one who had a proper *belief* in God, his government, and his protection; and being devoted to the interests of his people, would be *faithful* in the discharge of his office. 2. Because he *feared God above many*—was the most religious person in the congregation; would govern according to the laws; would take care of the interests of *pure religion;* would

not oppress, take bribes, nor abuse his authority; but act in all things as one who had the *fear of God* continually before his eyes. These are the proper qualifications of a governor.

Verse 3. *Until the sun be hot*] The meaning of this is, the gates were not to be *opened* before *sunrise*, and always *shut* at *sunset*. This is the custom to the present day in many of the cities of the East. If a traveller arrives *after sunset*, he finds the gates shut; and on no consideration will they open them till the next morning, so that those who come late are obliged to lodge in the plain, or *under the walls*.

Every one—over against his house.] Each was obliged to guard that part of the wall that was opposite to his own dwelling.

A. M. 3559
B. C. 445
A. U. C. 309
Coss. Rom.
M. Genucio et
C. Curtio

the people *were* few therein, and the houses *were* not builded.

5 And my God put into mine heart to gather together the nobles, and the rulers, and the people, that they might be reckoned by genealogy. And I found a register of the genealogy of them which came up at the first, and found written therein,

A. M. 3468
B. C. 536
Olymp. LXI. 1
Anno Urbis
Conditæ 218

6 [e]These *are* the children of the province, that went up out of the captivity, of those that had been carried away, whom Nebuchadnezzar the king of Babylon had carried away, and came again to Jerusalem and to Judah, every one unto his city;

7 Who came with Zerubbabel, Jeshua, Nehemiah, [f]Azariah, Raamiah, Nahamani, Mordecai, Bilshan, Mispereth, Bigvai, Nehum, Baanah. The number, *I say,* of the men of the people of Israel *was this;*

8 The children of Parosh, two thousand a hundred seventy and two.

9 The children of Shephatiah, three hundred seventy and two.

10 The children of Arah, six hundred fifty and two.

11 The children of Pahath-moab, of the children of Jeshua and Joab, two thousand and eight hundred *and* eighteen.

12 The children of Elam, a thousand two hundred fifty and four.

13 The children of Zattu, eight hundred forty and five.

14 The children of Zaccai, seven hundred and threescore.

15 The children of [g]Binnui, six hundred forty and eight.

A. M. 3468
B. C. 536
Olymp. LXI. 1
Anno Urbis
Conditæ 218

16 The children of Bebai, six hundred twenty and eight.

17 The children of Azgad, two thousand three hundred twenty and two.

18 The children of Adonikam, six hundred threescore and seven.

19 The children of Bigvai, two thousand threescore and seven.

20 The children of Adin, six hundred fifty and five.

21 The children of Ater of Hezekiah, ninety and eight.

22 The children of Hashum, three hundred twenty and eight.

23 The children of Bezai, three hundred twenty and four.

24 The children of [h]Hariph, a hundred and twelve.

25 The children of [i]Gibeon, ninety and five.

26 The men of Beth-lehem and Netophah, a hundred fourscore and eight.

27 The men of Anathoth, a hundred twenty and eight.

28 The men of [k]Beth-Azmaveth, forty and two.

29 The men of [l]Kirjath-jearim, Chephirah, and Beeroth, seven hundred forty and three.

30 The men of Ramah and Gaba, six hundred and twenty and one.

31 The men of Michmas, a hundred and twenty and two.

32 The men of Beth-el and Ai, a hundred twenty and three.

---

[e]Ezra ii. 1, &c.——[f]Or, *Seraiah;* see Ezra ii. 2——[g]Or, *Bani*

[h]Or, *Jora*——[i]Or, *Gibbar*——[k]Or, *Azmaveth*——[l]Or, *Kirjath-arim*

Verse 4. *The houses* were *not builded.*] The city was not yet rebuilt, only a row of houses in the inside of the wall all round.

Verse 5. *God put into mine heart*] With this good man every *good thing* was of GOD. If he *purposed* any good, it was because *God put it into his heart;* if he *did* any good, it was because *the good hand of his God was upon him;* if he *expected* any good, it was because he earnestly *prayed God to remember him for good.* Thus, in all his ways he acknowledged God, and God directed all his steps.

Verse 7. *Who came with Zerubbabel*] The register which he found was that of the persons only who came long before Zerubbabel, Ezra, and Joshua the son of Josedek, which register could not answer in every respect to the state

of the people then. Several persons and families were no doubt dead, and others had arrived since. Nehemiah probably altered it only in such parts, leaving the body of it as it was before; and this will account for the difference between it and the register that is found in *Ezra*, chap. ii.

Verse 8. *The children of Parosh*] As this chapter is almost entirely the *same* with the second chapter of the book of Ezra, it is not necessary to add any thing to what is said there; and to that chapter, and the accompanying notes, the reader is requested to refer.

Verse 19. *The children of Bigvai, two thousand threescore and seven*] Some MSS. read *two thousand and sixty-six,* as in Ezra ii. 14.

A. M. 3468
B. C. 536
Olymp. LXI. 1
Anno Urbis
Conditæ 218
33 The men of the other Nebo, fifty and two.

34 The children of the other [m]Elam, a thousand two hundred fifty and four.

35 The children of Harim three hundred and twenty.

36 The children of Jericho, three hundred forty and five.

37 The children of Lod, Hadid, and Ono, seven hundred twenty and one.

38 The children of Senaah, three thousand nine hundred and thirty.

39 The priests: the children of [n]Jedaiah, of the house of Jeshua, nine hundred seventy and three.

40 The children of [o]Immer, a thousand fifty and two.

41 The children of [p]Pashur, a thousand two hundred forty and seven.

42 The children of [q]Harim, a thousand and seventeen.

43 The Levites: the children of Jeshua, of Kadmiel, *and* of the children of [r]Hodevah, seventy and four.

44 The singers: the children of Asaph, a hundred forty and eight.

45 The porters: the children of Shallum, the children of Ater, the children of Talmon, the children of Akkub, the children of Hatita, the children of Shobai, a hundred thirty and eight.

46 The Nethinims: the children of Ziha, the children of Rashupha, the children of Tabbaoth,

47 The children of Keros, the children of [s]Sia, the children of Padon,

48 The children of Lebana, the children of Hagaba, the children of [t]Shalmai,

49 The children of Hanan, the children of Giddel, the children of Gahar,

50 The children of Reaiah, the children of Rezin, the children of Nekoda,

51 The children of Gazzam, the children of Uzza, the children of Phaseah,

52 The children of Besai, the children of Meunim, the children of [u]Nephishesim,

A. M. 3468
B. C. 536
Olymp. LXI. 1
Anno Urbis
Conditæ 218

53 The children of Bakbuk, the children of Hakupha, the children of Harhur,

54 The children of [v]Bazlith, the children of Mehida, the children of Harsha,

55 The children of Barkos, the children of Sisera, the children of Tamah,

56 The children of Neziah, the children of Hatipha.

57 The children of Solomon's servants: the children of Sotai, the children of Sophereth, the children of [w]Perida,

58 The children of Jaala, the children of Darkon, the children of Giddel,

59 The children of Shephatiah, the children of Hattil, the children of Pochereth of Zebaim, the children of [x]Amon.

60 All the Nethinims, and the children of Solomon's servants, *were* three hundred ninety and two.

61 [y]And these *were* they which went up *also* from Tel-melah, Tel-haresha, Cherub, [z]Addon, and Immer: but they could not show their father's house, nor their [a]seed, whether they *were* of Israel.

62 The children of Delaiah, the children of Tobiah, the children of Nekoda, six hundred forty and two.

63 And of the priests: the children of Habaiah, the children of Koz, the children of Barzillai, which took *one* of the daughters of Barzillai the Gileadite to wife, and was called after their name.

64 These sought their register *among* those that were reckoned by genealogy, but it was not found: therefore were they, as polluted, put from the priesthood.

65 And [b]the Tirshatha said unto them, that they should not eat of the most holy things, till there stood *up* a priest with Urim and Thummim.

66 The whole congregation together *was*

---

[m]See ver. 12——[n]1 Chron. xxiv. 7——[o]1 Chron. xxiv. 14
[p]See 1 Chron. ix. 12; xxiv. 9——[q]1 Chron. xxiv. 8——[r]Or, *Hodaviah*, Ezra ii. 40; or *Judah*, Ezra iii. 9——[s]Or, *Siaha*

[t]Or, *Shamlai*——[u]Or, *Nephusim*——[v]Or, *Bazluth*——[w]Or, *Peruda*——[x]Or, *Ami*——[y]Ezra ii. 59——[z]Or, *Addan*
[a]Or, *pedigree*——[b]Or, *the governor*, chap. viii. 9

Verse 33. *The men of the other Nebo*] The word *other* is not in the parallel place, Ezra ii. 29, and is wanting in many of *Kennicott's* and *De Rossi's* MSS. This *Nebo* is supposed to be the same as *Nob* or *Nobah*, in the tribe of Benjamin.

Verse 34. *The other Elam*] To distinguish him from the Elam mentioned ver. 12.

Verse 54. *The children of Mehida*] Many of *Kennicott's* and *De Rossi's* MSS., have *Mehira*.

A. M. 3468
B. C. 536
Olymp. LXI. 1
Anno Urbis
Conditæ 218
forty and two thousand three hundred and threescore,

67 Besides their man-servants and their maid-servants, of whom *there were* seven thousand three hundred thirty and seven: and they had two hundred forty and five singing men and singing women.

68 Their horses, seven hundred thirty and six: their mules, two hundred forty and five:

69 *Their* camels, four hundred thirty and five: six thousand seven hundred and twenty asses.

70 And ᶜsome of the chief of the fathers gave unto the work. ᵈThe Tirshatha gave to the treasure a thousand drams of gold, fifty

basons, five hundred and thirty priests' garments.

71 And *some* of the chief of the fathers gave to the treasure of the work ᵉtwenty thousand drams of gold, and two thousand and two hundred pounds of silver.

72 And *that* which the rest of the people gave *was* twenty thousand drams of gold, and two thousand pounds of silver, and threescore and seven priests' garments.

73 So the priests, and the Levites, and the porters, and the singers, and *some* of the people, and the Nethinims, and all Israel, dwelt in their cities; ᶠand when the seventh month came, the children of Israel *were* in their cities.

A. M. 3468
B. C. 536
Olymp. LXI. 1
Anno Urbis
Conditæ 218

ᵉHeb. *part*——ᵈChap. viii. 9

ᵉSo Ezra ii. 69——ᶠEzra iii. 1

Verse 68. *Their horses, &c.*] The whole of this verse is wanting in *fifty* of *Kennicott's* MSS., and in *twenty-nine* of those of *De Rossi*, in the edition of *Rab. Chayim*, 1525, in the *Roman Edit.* of the *Septuagint;* also in the *Syriac* and in the *Arabic*. It should however be observed, that the *Arabic* omits the *whole list*, having nothing of the chapter but the first five verses. The whole is found in the parallel place, Ezra ii. 66. *Calmet's* note on this passage is incorrect.

Verse 69. *Their camels, four hundred thirty and five*] After this verse St. Jerome has inserted the following words in the *Vulgate:*—

Hucusque refertur quid in commentario scriptum fuerit; exin Nehemiæ historia texitur.

"Thus far do the words extend which were written in the register; what follows belongs to the history of Nehemiah."

But this *addition* is not found either in the *Hebrew* or any of the ancient *versions*. It is wanting also in the *Complutum* and *Paris Polyglots*, but is in the *Editio Prima* of the *Vulgate*.

Verse 70. *The Tirshatha gave*] The *Septuagint*, particularly the copy in the *Codex Alex-*

andrinus, intimates that this sum was given *to the Tirshatha*, or Nehemiah: Και τῳ Αθερσαθᾳ εδωκαν εις θησαυρον, *And to the Athersatha they gave for the treasure, &c.*

For the meaning of the word *Tirshatha*, see on Ezra ii. 63.

Verse 71. *Two thousand and two hundred pounds*] The *Septuagint* has *two thousand* ᴛʜʀᴇᴇ *hundred minæ of silver.*

Verse 73. *All Israel, dwelt in their cities*] It was in reference to this particularly that the public registers were examined; for by them they found the different *families*, and consequently the cities, villages, &c., which belonged to them, according to the *ancient division* of the lands. It seems that the examination of the registers occupied about a *month;* for as soon as the walls were finished, which was in the *sixth* month, (*Elul*,) chap. vi. 15, Nehemiah instituted the examination mentioned in this chapter, ver. 5; and by the *concluding* verse we find that the different families had got into their paternal cities in the *seventh month*, Tisri, answering to a part of our *September* and *October*. Thus the register determined every thing: there was no room for complaint, and none to accuse the governor of partiality.

CHAPTER VIII

Ezra, Nehemiah, and the Levites, read and interpret the laws to the people, 1–7. The manner in which they do this important work, 8. The effect produced on the people's minds by hearing it, 9. The people are exhorted to be glad, and are told that the joy of the Lord is their strength, 10–12. On the second day they assemble, and find that they should keep the feast of tabernacles; which they accordingly religiously solemnize for seven days; and Ezra reads to them from the book of the law, 13–18.

A. M. 3559
B. C. 445
A. U. C. 309
Coss. Rom.
M. Genucio et
C. Curtio

AND all [a]the people gathered themselves together as one man into the street that *was* [b]before the water gate: and they spake unto Ezra the [c]scribe to bring the book of the law of Moses, which the LORD had commanded to Israel.

2 And Ezra the priest brought [d]the law before the congregation both of men and women, and all [e]that could hear with understanding, [f]upon the first day of the seventh month.

3 And he read therein before the street that *was* before the water gate [g]from the morning until mid-day, before the men and the women, and those that could understand; and the ears of all the people *were attentive* unto the book of the law.

4 And Ezra the scribe stood upon a [h]pulpit of wood, which they had made for the purpose; and beside him stood Mattithiah, and Shema, and Anaiah, and Urijah, and Hilkiah, and Maaseiah, on his right hand; and on his left hand, Pedaiah, and Mishael, and Malchiah, and Hashum, and Hashbadana, Zechariah, *and* Meshullam.

5 And Ezra opened the book in the [i]sight

A. M. 3559
B. C. 445
A. U. C. 309
Coss. Rom.
M. Genucio et
C. Curtio

of all the people; (for he was above all the people;) and when he opened it, all the people [k]stood up:

6 And Ezra blessed the LORD, the great God. And all the people [l]answered, Amen, Amen, with [m]lifting up their hands: and they [n]bowed their heads, and worshipped the LORD with *their* faces to the ground.

7 Also Jeshua, and Bani, and Sherebiah, Jamin, Akkub, Shabbethai, Hodijah, Maaseiah, Kelita, Azariah, Jozabad, Hanan, Pelaiah, and the Levites, [o]caused the people to understand the law: and the people *stood* in their place.

8 So they read in the book in the law of God distinctly, and gave the sense, and caused *them* to understand the reading.

9 [q]And Nehemiah, which *is* [q]the Tirshatha, and Ezra the priest the scribe, [r]and the Levites that taught the people, said unto all the people, [s]This day *is* holy unto the LORD your God; [t]mourn not, nor weep. For all the people wept, when they heard the words of the law.

10 Then he said unto them, Go your way, eat the fat, and drink the sweet, [u]and send portions unto them for whom nothing is pre-

---

[a]Ezra iii. 1; 1 Esd. ix. 38, &c.——[b]Chapter iii. 26 [c]Ezra vii. 6——[d]Deuteronomy xxxi. 11, 12——[e]Hebrew, *that understood in hearing*——[f]Leviticus xxiii. 24——[g]Hebrew, *from the light*——[h]Hebrew, *tower of wood*——[i]Hebrew, *eyes*——[k]Judges iii. 20——[l]1 Cor. xiv. 16——[m]Lam. iii. 41; 1 Tim. ii. 8

[n]Exod. iv. 31; xii. 27; 2 Chron. xx. 18——[o]Lev. x. 11; Deut. xxxiii. 10; 2 Chron. xvii. 7, 8, 9; Mal. ii. 7 [p]Ezra ii. 63; chap. vii. 65; x. 1——[q]Or, *the governor* [r]2 Chron. xxxv. 3; ver. 8——[s]Lev. xxiii. 24; Num. xxix. 1——[t]Deut. xvi. 14, 15; Eccles. iii. 4——[u]Esth. ix. 19, 22; Rev. xi. 10

NOTES ON CHAP. VIII

Verse 1. *The street that* was *before the water gate*] The gate which led from the temple to the brook *Kidron*.

Verse 2. *All that could hear with understanding*] Infants, idiots, and *children* not likely to receive instruction, were not permitted to attend this meeting; nor should any such, in any place, be ever brought to the house of God, if it can be avoided: yet, rather than a poor mother should be deprived of the ordinances of God, let her come with her child in her arms; and although it be inconvenient to the congregation, and to some ministers, to hear a child cry, it is cruel to exclude the mother on this account, who, having no person to take care of her child while absent, must bring it with her, or be totally deprived of the ordinances of the Christian Church.

Upon the first day of the seventh month.] This was the *first* day of what was called the *civil year;* and on it was the *feast of trumpets,* the year being ushered in by the sound of these instruments.

Verse 4. *Stood upon a pulpit of wood*] מגדל *migdal,* a *tower,* a *platform,* raised up for the purpose, to elevate him sufficiently for the people both to see and hear him; for it is said, ver.

5, that *he was above all the people.* This is the first intimation we have of a *pulpit,* or *structure* of this kind. But we must not suppose that it was any thing similar to those *tubs* or *barrels* ridiculously set up in churches and chapels, in which a preacher is nearly as much confined, during the time of his preaching, as if he was in the *stocks.*

Verse 5. *All the people stood up*] This was out of respect to the sacred word: in imitation of this, when the *gospel* for the day is read in our churches, all the people stand up.

Verse 6. *Ezra blessed the Lord*] In imitation of this, we say, when the gospel for the day is commenced, *Glory be to God for his holy Gospel!* and conclude this thanksgiving with, *Amen.*

Verse 8. *So they read in the book*] For an explanation of this verse, see the observations at the end of the chapter.

Verse 9. *Nehemiah, which* is *the Tirshatha*] This puts it out of doubt that, when the *Tirshatha* is mentioned, *Nehemiah* himself is intended, *Tirshatha* being the name of his *office.*

Mourn not, nor weep.] This is a holy day to God: a day appointed for *general rejoicing* in Him who has turned our captivity, restored to us his law, and again established among us his ordinances.

Verse 10. *Eat the fat, and drink the sweet*]

A. M. 3559
B. C. 445
A. U. C. 309
Coss. Rom.
M. Genucio et
C. Curtio

pared: for *this* day *is* holy unto our LORD: neither be ye sorry; for the joy of the LORD is your strength.

11 So the Levites stilled all the people, saying, Hold your peace, for the day *is* holy; neither be ye grieved.

12 And all the people went their way to eat, and to drink, and to ᵛsend portions, and to make great mirth, because they had ʷunderstood the words that were declared unto them.

13 And on the second day were gathered together the chief of the fathers of all the people, the priests, and the Levites, unto Ezra the scribe, even ˣto understand the words of the law.

14 And they found written in the law which the LORD had commanded ʸby Moses, that the children of Israel should dwell in ᶻbooths in the feast of the seventh month:

15 And ᵃthat they should publish and proclaim in all their cities, and ᵇin Jerusalem,

saying, Go forth unto the mount, and ᶜfetch olive branches, and pine branches, and myrtle branches, and palm branches, and branches of thick trees, to make booths, as *it is* written.

A. M. 3559
B. C. 445
A. U. C. 309
Coss. Rom.
M. Genucio et
C. Curtio

16 So the people went forth, and brought *them,* and made themselves booths, every one upon ᵈthe roof of his house, and in their courts, and in the courts of the house of God, and in the street of the ᵉwater gate, ᶠand in the street of the gate of Ephraim.

17 And all the congregation of them that were come again out of the captivity made booths, and sat under the booths: for since the days of Joshua the son of Nun unto that day had not the children of Israel done so. And there was very ᵍgreat gladness.

18 Also ʰday by day, from the first day unto the last day, he read in the book of the law of God. And they kept the feast seven days; and on the eighth day *was* ⁱa solemn assembly, ᵏaccording unto the manner.

ᵛVer. 10——ʷVer. 7, 8——ˣOr, *that they might instruct in the words of the law*——ʸHeb. *by the hand of* ᶻLev. xxiii. 34, 42; Deut. xvi. 13——ᵃLev. xxiii. 4 ᵇDeut. xvi. 16

ᶜLev. xxiii. 40——ᵈDeut. xxii. 8——ᵉChap. xii. 37 ᶠ2 Kings xiv. 13; chap. xii. 39——ᵍ2 Chron. xxx. 21 ʰDeut. xxxi. 10, &c.——ⁱHeb. *a restraint*——ᵏLev. xxiii. 36; Num. xxix. 35

Eat and drink the best that you have; and while ye are feeding yourselves in the fear of the Lord, remember those *who cannot feast;* and send *portions* to them, that the joy and the thanksgiving may be general. Let the poor have reason to rejoice as well as you.

For the joy of the Lord is your strength.] This is no gluttonous and drunken festival that *enervates* the body, and *enfeebles* the mind: from your religious feast your bodies will acquire *strength* and your minds power and fervour, so that you shall be able to DO HIS will, and to do it *cheerfully.* Religious joy. properly tempered with continual dependence on the help of God, meekness of mind, and self-diffidence, is a powerful means of strengthening the soul. In such a state every duty is practicable, and every duty delightful. In such a frame of mind no man ever fell, and in such a state of mind the general health of the body is much improved; a cheerful heart is not only a continual feast, but also a continual medicine.

Verse 14. *In the feast of the seventh month*] That is, the *feast of tabernacles,* which was held in commemoration of the sojourning of their fathers in the wilderness after they had been delivered from the Egyptian bondage. Now, having been delivered from the Babylonish captivity, and the proper time of the year occurring, it was their especial duty to keep the same feast.

Verse 15. *Fetch olive branches*] For every thing concerning this feast of tabernacles, see the notes on Lev. xxiii., and the other places *there* referred to.

Verse 16. *Upon the roof of his house*] It need scarcely be repeated, that the houses in the East

are generally built with *flat roofs.* On these they reposed; on these they took the air in the heats of summer; and on these they oftentimes slept.

Verse 17. *Since the days of Joshua*] No feast of tabernacles since Joshua's time had been so heartily and so piously celebrated. The story of the *sacred fire* now discovered, which had been hidden by the order of Jeremiah in a dry well, and now, some of the mud from the bottom being brought upon the altar, was kindled afresh by the rays of the sun, which suddenly broke out, though before covered with clouds, &c., is worthy of no credit. Those who wish to see the detail may consult 2 Mac. i. 18-36.

ON the subject in verse 8, I beg leave to make a few observations:—*So they read in the book in the law of God distinctly, and gave the sense, and caused them to understand the reading.* The Israelites, having been lately brought out of the Babylonish captivity, in which they had continued *seventy years,* according to the prediction of Jeremiah, chap. xxv. 11, were not only extremely corrupt, but it appears that they had in general lost the knowledge of the ancient Hebrew to such a degree, that when the book of the law was read, they did not understand it: but certain Levites *stood by, and gave the sense,* i. e., translated into the Chaldee dialect. This was not only the origin of the Chaldee *Targums,* or translation of the law and prophets into that tongue but was also, in all probability, the origin of *preaching from a text;* for it appears that the people were not only ignorant of their ancient language, but also of the rites and ceremonies of their religion, having been so long in Babylon, where they were not permitted to observe them. This being the case, not only the *language* must be *interpreted*, but the meaning of the *rites* and *ceremonies* must also be explained; for we find from ver. 13, &c., of this chapter, that they had even forgotten the *feast of tabernacles*, and every thing relative to that ceremony.

As we nowhere find that what is called *preaching on* or expounding a text was ever in use before that period, we are probably beholden to the Babylonish captivity for producing, in the hand of Divine Providence, a custom the most excellent and beneficial ever introduced among men.

What the nature of *preaching* or *expounding* the word of God was, at this early period of its institution, we learn from the above cited text.

I. *They read in the book of the law of God.*— The *words* of God, the doctrines of *Divine revelation*, are the proper *matter* of preaching; for they contain the wisdom of the Most High, and teach man the things which belong to his peace and happiness.

II. They read *distinctly*—מפרש *mephorash*, from פרש *parash*, to expand; they analyzed, dilated, and expounded it at large, showing the import and genuine meaning of every word.

III. They *gave the sense*—ושום שכל *vesom sechel*, they *put weight to it;* showed its value and utility, and how intimately concerned they were in all that was revealed: thus applying verbal criticism, and general exposition to their true and most important purposes.

IV. They *caused them to understand the reading*—ויבינו במקרא *vaiyabinu bammikra:* and they *understood*—had a *mental taste* and *perception* of the things which were in *the reading*, i. e., in the *letter* and *spirit* of the text. Thus *they knew* the Divine *will*, and *approved the things that were more excellent, being* (thus) *instructed out of the law*, Rom. ii. 18.

This was the ancient method of expounding the word of God among the Jews; and this mode is still more necessary for us:—

1. Because the sacred writings, as they came from God, are shut up in languages no longer vernacular; and no *translation* ever did or ever can reach the force of the *original* words, though perhaps our own in general, comes nearest to this of all versions, whether ancient or modern.

2. Ninety-nine out of a hundred know nothing of these languages; and consequently cannot, of themselves, reap all the requisite benefit from reading the Scriptures.

3. Sacred things are illustrated in the Bible by a reference to *arts* and *sciences*, of which the mass of the people are as ignorant as they are of the original tongues.

4. *Provincial customs* and *fashions* are mentioned in these writings, which must be understood, or the force and meaning of many texts cannot be comprehended.

5. There is a *depth* in the word of God which cannot be fathomed except either by Divine inspiration, or by deep study and research, for which the majority of the people have no time.

6. The people in general trust to the piety, learning and abilities of their ministers, and maintain them as persons capable of instructing them in all the deep things of God; and believing them to be *holy men*, they are confident they will not take their *tithes*, their *food*, and *their raiment*, under a pretence of doing a work for which they have not the ordinary qualifications. Where there is not such preaching as this, the people "sit in darkness, and in the valley of the shadow of death;" sinners are not converted unto God; neither are believers "built up on their most holy faith."

Reader—Art thou a *Christian minister?* Dost thou *feed the flock of God?* Let thy *conduct*, thy *conscience*, and the *fruits* of thy *ministry* answer for thee.

CHAPTER IX

On the twenty-fourth *day of the* seventh *month, the people hold a solemn fast unto the Lord, and confess their sins,* 1–3. *The Levites give a general account of God's kindness and forbearance to them and to their fathers; and acknowledge God's mercies and judgments,* 4–37. *They make a covenant with the Lord,* 38.

A. M. 3559
B. C. 445
A. U. C. 309
Coss. Rom.
M. Genucio et
C. Curtio

NOW in the twenty and fourth day of [a]this month the children of Israel were assembled with fasting, and with sackclothes, [b]and earth upon them.

2 And [c]the seed of Israel separated themselves from all [d]strangers, and stood and confessed their sins, and the iniquities of their fathers.

A. M. 3559
B. C. 445
A. U. C. 309
Coss. Rom.
M. Genucio et
C. Curtio

---

[a]Chap. viii. 2——[b]Josh. vii. 6; 1 Sam. iv. 12; 2 Sam. i. 2; Job ii. 12

[c]Ezra x. 11; chapter xiii. 3, 30——[d]Hebrew, *strange children*

NOTES ON CHAP. IX

Verse 1. *Now in the twenty and fourth day*] The *feast of trumpets* was on the *first* day of this month; on the *fourteenth* began the *feast of tabernacles*, which, lasting *seven days*, finished on the *twenty-second;* on the *twenty-third* they *separated* themselves from their *illegitimate wives* and *children;* and, on the *twenty-fourth*, they held a solemn *day of fasting* and *confession* of sin, and reading the law, which they closed by renewing their covenants.

Verse 2. *The seed of Israel separated themselves*] A reformation of this kind was begun by Ezra, x. 3; but it appears that either more were found out who had taken strange wives, or else those who had separated from them had taken them again.

And stood and confessed their sins, and the iniquities of their fathers.] They acknowledged that they had been sinners against God throughout all their generations; that their fathers had sinned and were punished; and that they, with this example before their eyes, had copied their fathers' offences.

A. M. 3559
B. C. 445
A. U. C. 309
Coss. Rom.
M. Genucio
C. Curtio

3 And they stood up in their place, and [e]read in the book of the law of the LORD their God *one* fourth part of the day; and *another* fourth part they confessed, and worshipped the LORD their God.

4 Then stood up upon the [f]stairs, of the Levites, Jeshua, and Bani, Kadmiel, Shebaniah, Bunni, Sherebiah, Bani, *and* Chenani, and cried with a loud voice unto the LORD their God.

5 Then the Levites, Jeshua, and Kadmiel, Bani, Hashabniah, Sherebiah, Hodijah, Shebaniah, *and* Pethahiah, said, Stand up *and* bless the LORD your God for ever and ever: and blessed be [g]thy glorious name, which is exalted above all blessing and praise.

6 [h]Thou, *even* thou, *art* LORD alone; [i]thou hast made heaven, [k]the heaven of heavens, with [l]all their hosts, the earth, and all *things* that *are* therein, the seas, and all that *is* therein, and thou [m]preservest them all; and the host of heaven worshippeth thee.

7 Thou *art* the LORD the God, who didst choose [n]Abram, and broughtest him forth out of Ur of the Chaldees, and gavest him the name of [o]Abraham;

8 And foundest his heart [p]faithful before

thee, and madest a [q]covenant with him to give the land of the Canaanites, the Hittites, the Amorites, and the Perizzites, and the Jebusites, and the Girgashites, to give *it, I say,* to his seed, and [r]hast performed thy words; for thou *art* righteous:

A. M. 3559
B. C. 445
A. U. C. 309
Coss. Rom.
M. Genucio et
C. Curtio

9 [s]And didst see the affliction of our fathers in Egypt, and [t]heardest their cry by the Red Sea;

10 And [u]showedst signs and wonders upon Pharaoh, and on all his servants, and on all the people of his land: for thou knewest that they [v]dealt proudly against them. So didst thou [w]get thee a name, as *it is* this day.

11 [x]And thou didst divide the sea before them, so that they went through the midst of the sea on the dry land; and their persecutors thou threwest into the deeps, [y]as a stone into the mighty waters.

12 Moreover thou [z]leddest them in the day by a cloudy pillar; and in the night by a pillar of fire, to give them light in the way wherein they should go.

13 [a]Thou camest down also upon Mount Sinai, and spakest with them from heaven, and gavest them [b]right judgments, and [c]true laws, good statutes and commandments:

14 And madest known unto them thy [d]holy

---

[e]Ch. viii. 7, 8——[f]Or, *scaffold*——[g]1 Chron. xxix. 13
[h]2 Kings xix. 15, 19; Psa. lxxxvi. 10; Isa. xxxvii. 16, 20
[i]Gen. ii. 1; Exod. xx. 11; Rev. xiv. 7——[k]Deut. x. 14;
1 Kings viii. 27——[l]Gen. i. 1——[m]Psa. xxxvi. 6
[n]Gen. xi. 31; xii. 1——[o]Gen. xvii. 5——[p]Gen. xv. 6
[q]Gen. xii. 7; xv. 18; xvii. 7, 8——[r]Josh. xxiii. 14
[s]Exod. ii. 25; iii. 7

[t]Exod. xiv. 10——[u]Exod. vii., viii., ix., x., xii., xiv.
[v]Exod. xviii. 11——[w]Exod. ix. 16; Isa. lxiii. 12, 14;
Jer. xxxii. 20; Dan. ix. 15——[x]Exod. xiv. 21, 22, 27,
28; Psa. lxxviii. 13——[y]Exod. xv. 5, 10——[z]Exod.
xiii. 21——[a]Exodus xix. 20; xx. 1——[b]Psalm xix. 8, 9;
Romans vii. 12——[c]Hebrew, *laws of truth*——[d]Gen.
ii. 3; Exod. xx. 8, 11

Verse 3. One *fourth part of the day*] As they did no manner of work on this day of fasting and humiliation, so they spent the whole of it in religious duties. They began, says *Calmet,* on the *first* hour, and continued these exercises to the *third* hour; from the *third* they recommenced, and continued till the *sixth* hour; from the *sixth* to the *ninth;* and from the *ninth,* to the *twelfth* or *last* hour. 1. They heard the law read, standing; 2. They prostrated themselves, and confessed their sins; 3. They arose to praise God for having spared and dealt thus mercifully with them.

Verse 5. *Stand up* and *bless the Lord your God*] It is the shameless custom of many congregations of people to sit still while they profess to bless and praise God, by singing the *Psalms of David* or *hymns* made on the plan of the Gospel! I ask such persons, Did they ever feel the *spirit of devotion* while thus employed? If they do, it must be owned that, by the prevalence of habit, they have counteracted the influence of an attitude most friendly to such acts of devotion.

Verse 6. *Thou preservest them all*] ואתה מחיה את כלם *vettah mechaiyeh eth cullam,* and thou *givest life* to them all; *and the host of the heavens,* לך משתחוים *lecha mishtachavim, prostrate themselves unto thee.* How near is this to the opinion of *Kepler,* that all the heavenly host are *instinct* with *life,* and navigate the great expanse on pinions adjusted to their situation in their respective orbits! But to *preserve in life,* or in *being,* is a very good meaning in the original, which does not necessarily imply *vitality.* We say a *tree* is *alive* when *flourishing,* a *plant* is *dead* when it *withers,* &c.

Verse 7. *Who didst choose Abram*] See the notes on the passages referred to in the margin.
The name of Abraham] For the explanation of this name, see the notes on Gen. xvii. 5.

Verse 12. *By a cloudy pillar*] See the notes on the parallel passages, both here and in the other verses.

Verse 14. *Madest known unto them thy holy Sabbath*] They appear to have forgotten this

A. M. 3559
B. C. 445
A. U. C. 309
Coss. Rom.
M. Genucio et
C. Curtio

Sabbath, and commandedst them precepts, statutes, and laws, by the hand of Moses thy servant:

15 And ^egavest them bread from heaven for their hunger, and ^fbroughtest forth water for them out of the rock for their thirst, and promisedst them that they should ^ggo in to possess the land ^hwhich thou hadst sworn to give them.

16 ⁱBut they and our fathers dealt proudly, and ^khardened their necks, and hearkened not to thy commandments,

17 And refused to obey, ^lneither were mindful of thy wonders that thou didst among them; but hardened their necks, and in their rebellion appointed ^ma captain to return to their bondage: but thou *art* ⁿa God ready to pardon, ^ogracious and merciful, slow to anger, and of great kindness, and forsookest them not.

18 Yea, ^pwhen they had made them a molten calf, and said, This *is* thy God that brought thee up out of Egypt, and had wrought great provocations;

19 Yet thou in thy ^qmanifold mercies forsookest them not in the wilderness; the ^rpillar of the cloud departed not from them by day, to lead them in the way; neither the pillar of

fire by night, to show them light, and the way wherein they should go.

A. M. 3559
B. C. 445
A. U. C. 309
Coss. Rom.
M. Genucio et
C. Curtio

20 Thou gavest also thy ^sgood Spirit to instruct them, and withheldest not thy ^tmanna from their mouth, and gavest them ^uwater for their thirst.

21 Yea, ^vforty years didst thou sustain them in the wilderness, *so that* they lacked nothing; their ^wclothes waxed not old, and their feet swelled not.

22 Moreover thou gavest them kingdoms and nations, and didst divide them into corners: so they possessed the land of ^xSihon, and the land of the king of Heshbon, and the land of Og king of Bashan.

23 ^yTheir children also multipliedst thou as the stars of heaven, and broughtest them into the land, concerning which thou hadst promised to their fathers, that they should go in to possess *it*.

24 So ^zthe children went in and possessed the land, and ^athou subduedst before them the inhabitants of the land, the Canaanites, and gavest them into their hands, with their kings, and the people of the land, that they might do with them ^bas they would.

---

^eExodus xvi. 14, 15; John vi. 31——^fExodus xvii. 6; Numbers xx. 9, &c.——^gDeuteronomy i. 8——^hHeb. *which thou hadst lift up thine hand to give them;* Numbers xiv. 30——ⁱVerse 29; Psalm cvi. 6——^kDeut. xxxi. 27; 2 Kings xvii. 14; 2 Chronicles xxx. 8; Jeremiah xix. 15 ——^lPsa. lxxviii. 11, 42, 43——^mNum. xiv. 4——ⁿHeb. *a God of pardons*——^oExod. xxxiv. 6; Num. xiv. 18;

Psalm lxxxvi. 5, 15; Joel ii. 13——^pExodus xxxii. 4 ^qVer. 27; Psa. cvi. 45——^rExod. xiii. 21, 22; Num. xiv. 14; 1 Cor. x. 1——^sNum. xi. 17; Isa. lxiii. 11 ^tExod. xvi. 15; Josh. v. 12——^uExod. xvii. 6——^vDeut. ii. 7——^wDeut. viii. 4; xxix. 5——^xNum. xxi. 21, &c. ^yGen. xxii. 17——^zJosh. i. 2, &c.——^aPsa. xliv. 2, 3 ^bHeb. *according to their will*

---

first of all the commandments of God, during their sojourning in Egypt.

Verse 17. *And in their rebellion appointed a captain*] This clause, read according to its order in the Hebrew text, is thus: *And appointed a captain to return to their bondage in their rebellion.* But it is probable that במרים *bemiryam, in their rebellion,* is a mistake for במצרים *bemitsrayim, in Egypt.* This is the reading of *seven* of *Kennicott's* and *De Rossi's* MSS., the *Neapolitan* edition of the *Hagiographa,* and the *Septuagint.* It is also the reading in Num. xiv. 4. The clause should undoubtedly be read, *They appointed a captain to return to their bondage in* EGYPT.

Verse 19. *The pillar of the cloud departed not from them*] מעליהם *mealeyhem,* "from over them." I have already had occasion to observe that this miraculous cloud, the symbol of the Divine presence, assumed *three* different positions while accompanying the Israelitish camp: 1. As a cloud in the form of a *pillar,* it went before them when they journey, to point out their way in the wilderness. 2. As a pillar of *fire,* it continued with them during the *night,* to give them light, and be a rallying point for the whole camp in the night season. 3. As an *ex-*

tended cloud, it *hovered over them* in their encampments, to refresh them with its dews, and to keep them from the ardours of the sun.

Verse 21. *Their clothes waxed not old*] See the note on Deut. viii. 4.

Verse 22. *The land of Og king of Bashan.*] It is most evident that *Sihon* was *king of Heshbon.* How then can it be said that they possessed *the land of Sihon, and the land of the king of Heshbon?* The words *the land of the king of Heshbon* are wanting in two of *De Rossi's* MSS. In another MS. the words *and the land of* are wanting; so that the clause is read, *They possessed the land of Sihon, king of Heshbon.* The *Septuagint* has the same reading; the *Arabic* nearly the same, viz., *the land of Sihon, the land of the king of Heshbon.* The *Syriac* has, *They possessed the land of Sihon, the land of the* KINGS *of Heshbon.* The reading of the text is undoubtedly wrong; that supported by the MSS. and by the *Septuagint* is most likely to be the true one. Those of the *Arabic* and *Syriac* contain at least no *contradictory* sense. The *and* in the *Hebrew* and *our version,* distinguishes *two lands* and *two kings;* the *land* of *Sihon* and the *land* of the *king of Heshbon:* when it is most certain that only *one land* and

A. M. 3559
B. C. 445
A. U. C. 309
Coss. Rom.
M. Genucio et
C. Curtio

25 And they took strong cities, and °a fat land, and possessed ᵈhouses full of all goods, ᵉwells digged, vineyards, and olive-yards, and ᶠfruit trees in abundance: so they did eat, and were filled, and ᵍbecame fat, and delighted themselves in thy great ʰgoodness.

26 Nevertheless they ⁱwere disobedient, and rebelled against thee, and ᵏcast thy law behind their backs, and slew thy ˡprophets which testified against them to turn them to thee, and they wrought great provocations.

27 ᵐTherefore thou deliveredst them into the hand of their enemies, who vexed them: and in the time of their trouble, when they cried unto thee, thou ⁿheardest *them* from heaven; and according to thy manifold mercies °thou gavest them saviours, who saved them out of the hand of their enemies.

28 But after they had rest, ᵖthey ᑫdid evil again before thee: therefore leftest thou them in the hand of their enemies, so that they had the dominion over them: yet when they returned, and cried unto thee, thou heardest *them* from heaven; and ʳmany times didst thou deliver them according to thy mercies;

29 And testifiedst against them, that thou mightest bring them again unto thy law: yet they ˢdealt proudly, and hearkened not unto thy commandments, but sinned against thy judgments, (ᵗwhich if a man do, he shall live in them;) and ᵘwithdrew the shoulder, and hardened their neck, and would not hear.

A. M. 3559
B. C. 445
A. U. C. 309
Coss. Rom.
M. Genucio et
C. Curtio

30 Yet many years didst thou ᵛforbear them, and testifiedst ʷagainst them by thy Spirit ˣin ʸthy prophets: yet would they not give ear: ᶻtherefore gavest thou them into the hand of the people of the lands.

31 Nevertheless for thy great mercies' sake ᵃthou didst not utterly consume them, nor forsake them; for thou *art* ᵇa gracious and merciful God.

32 Now therefore, our God, the great, the ᶜmighty, and the terrible God, who keepest covenant and mercy, let not all the ᵈtrouble seem little before thee, ᵉthat hath come upon us, on our kings, on our princes, and on our priests, and on our prophets, and on our fathers, and on all thy people, ᶠsince the time of the kings of Assyria unto this day.

33 Howbeit ᵍthou *art* just in all that is brought upon us; for thou hast done right, but ʰwe have done wickedly:

34 Neither have our kings, our princes, our priests, nor our fathers, kept thy law, nor

---

ᶜVer. 35; Num. xiii. 27; Deut. viii. 7, 8; Ezek. xx. 6
ᵈDeut. vi. 11——ᵉOr, *cisterns*——ᶠHeb. *tree of food*
ᵍDeut. xxxii. 15——ʰHos. iii. 5——ⁱJudg. ii. 11, 12;
Ezek. xx. 21——ᵏ1 Kings xiv. 9; Psa. l. 17——ˡ1 Kings
xviii. 4; xix. 10; 2 Chron. xxiv. 20, 21; Matt. xxiii. 37;
Acts vii. 52——ᵐJudg. ii. 14; iii. 8, &c.; Psa. cvi. 41, 42
ⁿPsa. cvi. 44——°Judg. ii. 18; iii. 9——ᵖHeb. *they returned to do evil*——ᑫSo Judg. iii. 11, 12, 30; iv. 1; v. 31;
vi. 1——ʳPsalm cvi. 43——ˢVer. 16

ᵗLev. xviii. 5; Ezek. xx. 11; Rom. x. 5; Gal. iii. 12
ᵘHeb. *they gave a withdrawing shoulder*, Zech. vii. 11
ᵛHeb. *protract over them*——ʷ2 Kings xvii. 13; 2 Chron.
xxxvi. 15; Jer. vii. 25; xxv. 4——ˣHeb. *in the hand of thy
prophets*——ʸSee Acts vii. 51; 1 Pet. i. 11; 2 Pet. i. 21
ᶻIsa. v. 5; xlii. 24——ᵃJer. iv. 27; v. 10, 18——ᵇVer. 17
ᶜExodus xxxiv. 6, 7; chap. i. 5——ᵈHeb. *weariness*
ᵉHeb. *that hath found us*——ᶠ2 Kings xvii. 3——ᵍDan.
ix. 14; Psa. cxix. 137——ʰPsa. cvi. 6; Dan. ix. 5, 6, 8

---

one *king* can be meant: but the ꝰ *vau* may be translated here as it often is, *even*: EVEN *the land of the king of Heshbon.*

Verse 25. *Became fat, and delighted them-selves*] They became effeminate, fell under the power of *luxury*, got totally corrupted in their manners, sinned against all the mercies of God, and then were destroyed by his judgments. We have an old nervous saying, "*War* begets *pov-erty*, *poverty* begets *peace*, *peace* begets *afflu-ence*, *affluence* begets *luxury* and *corruption* of *manners*; and hence *civil broils*, *foreign wars*, and *desolations.*" A sensible Roman historian has said the same: "*Imperium facile iis artibus retinetur, quibus initio* partum *est: verum ubi pro* LABORE, DESIDIA; *pro* continentia *et æqui-tate,* LIBIDO *atque* SUPERBIA *invasere: fortuna simul cum moribus* IMMUTATUR."

Verse 27. *Thou gavest them saviours*] The whole book of Judges is a history of God's mercies, and their rebellions.

Verse 30. *Many years didst thou forbear*] It is supposed that Nehemiah refers here princi-pally to the *ten tribes.* And many years did

God bear with *them;* not less than *two hundred and fifty-four* years from their separation from the house of *David*, till their captivity and utter dispersion under *Shalmaneser;* during the whole of which time God invariably warned them by his prophets; or, as it is here said, *by thy Spirit in thy prophets*, which gives us the true notion of *Divine inspiration.* God's Spirit was given to the prophets; and they testified to the people, *according* as they were *taught* and *influenced* by *this Spirit.*

Verse 32. *On our kings, on our princes*] I be-lieve Nehemiah in this place mentions the whole of *civil society* in its *officers* as they stand re-lated to each other in *dignity:*—1. KINGS, as supreme. 2. PRINCES. 3. PRIESTS. 4. PROPHETS. 5. The FATHERS, heads or chiefs of tribes and families. 6. The COMMON PEOPLE. Those who disturb this natural order (for it subsists even in *Britain*) are enemies to the peace of the *whole*, whatever they may pretend to the con-trary.

Verse 34. *Neither have our kings*] In this verse he acknowledges that the *kings, princes,*

A. M. 3559
B. C. 445
A. U. C. 309
Coss. Rom.
M. Genucio et
C. Curtio

hearkened unto thy command-ments and thy testimonies, wherewith thou didst testify against them.

35 For they have [l]not served thee in their kingdom, and in [k]thy great goodness that thou gavest them, and in the large and [l]fat land which thou gavest before them, neither turned they from their wicked works.

36 Behold, [m]we *are* servants this day, and *for* the land that thou gavest unto our fathers

---

[l]Deuteronomy xxviii. 47——[k]Ver. 25——[l]Verse 25 [m]Deut. xxviii. 48; Ezra ix. 9; Bar. iii. 8——[n]Deut. xxviii. 33, 51——[o]Deut. xxviii. 48

---

priests, and *fathers*, had broken the law: but the *prophets* are left out; for *they* continued faithful to God, testifying by his Spirit against the crimes of all; and this even at the risk of their lives.

Verse 35. *For they have not served thee in their kingdom*] Instead of במלכותם *bemalcu-tham*, "in THEIR kingdom," במלכותך *bemalcuthe-cha*, in THY kingdom," is the reading of two of *Kennicott's* MSS.; as also of the *Septuagint*, *Syriac*, and *Arabic*. This is most likely to be the true reading.

Verse 36. *Behold, we* are *servants*] They had no king of their own: and were under the government of the kings of Persia, to whom they paid a regular *tribute*.

Verse 37. *It yieldeth much increase unto the kings*] Good and fruitful as the land is, yet it profits *us little*; as the chief profits on all things go to the kings of Persia.

Over our bodies] Exacting *personal* and *feudal services* from us, and from our *cattle*; and this not by any *fixed rate*, or *rule*, of so much rent, so much labour, or boons; but *at their pleasure*; so that we can neither call our *persons*, our *time*, our *land*, nor our *cattle*, our own: therefore *we are in great distress*. Miserable are the people that live under such a government. Think of this, ye *Britons!* think of your liberties and rights. Compare them with any other nation under heaven, and see what a *balance* is in *your favour*. Almost all the nations of the earth acknowledge Britons the most happy of all men. May I not say,

---

to eat the fruit thereof and the good thereof, behold, we *are* servants in it:

37 And [n]it yieldeth much increase unto the kings whom thou hast set over us because of our sins: also they have [o]dominion over our bodies, and over our cattle, at their pleasure, and we *are* in great distress.

38 And because of all this we [p]make a sure *covenant,* and write *it;* and our princes, Levites, *and* priests, [q]seal [r]*unto it.*

A. M. 3559
B. C. 445
A. U. C. 309
Coss. Rom.
M. Genucio et
C. Curtio

---

[p]2 Kings xxiii. 3; 2 Chron. xxix. 10; xxxiv. 31; chap. x. 29; Ezra x. 3——[q]Heb. are *at the sealing,* or *sealed* [r]Chapter x. 1

O fortunatos nimium, sua si bona norint!

"How exceedingly happy would you be, could you but consider your many advantages!"

Verse 38. *Our princes, Levites,* and *priests, seal* unto it.] Persuaded that we have brought all the miseries upon ourselves by our transgressions, *feeling much* and *fearing more*, we make a covenant with thee to devote ourselves to thy service; to do with us as thou pleasest. From this *sealing* we learn that at this time the government of the Jews was a mixed *aristocracy;* composed of the *nobles* for the *civil* department, and the *priests* and *Levites* for the *ecclesiastical*.

THIS was not mixing the *Church* with the *state*, or the *state* with the *Church:* both were separate, yet both mutually supported each other. The *state* never attempted to model the Church according to its own mind; because the Church had been founded and regulated by God, and neither its *creed* nor its *ordinances* could be *changed*. The *Church* did not meddle with the *state*, to give it *new laws, new ordinances*, or *new officers*. Therefore the one could not be jealous of the other. Where this state of things prevails, every public blessing may be expected. In every *state* God says to the *governors* and the *governed:* "Render to Cæsar the things which are Cæsar's, and to GOD the things which are God's."

CHAPTER X

The names of those who sealed the covenant, 1-27. *All solemnly promise not to have affinity with the people of the land,* 28-30; *to observe the Sabbaths,* 31; *to provide for the sanctuary according to the law,* 32-36; *and to pay the regular tithes for the support of the priests, Levites, and other officers of the temple,* 37-39.

A. M. 3559
B. C. 445
A. U. C. 309
Coss. Rom.
M. Genucio et
C. Curtio

N OW ªthose that sealed *were,* ᵇNehemiah, ᶜthe Tirshatha, ᵈthe son of Hachaliah, and Zidkijah,

2 ᵉSeraiah, Azariah, Jeremiah,

3 Pashur, Amariah, Malchijah,

4 Hattush, Shebaniah, Malluch,

5 Harim, Meremoth, Obadiah,

6 Daniel, Ginnethon, Baruch,

7 Meshullam, Abijah, Mijamin,

8 Maaziah, Bilgai, Shemaiah: these *were* the priests.

9 And the Levites: both Jeshua the son of Azaniah, Binnui of the sons of Henadad, Kadmiel;

10 And their brethren, Shebaniah, Hodijah, Kelita, Pelaiah, Hanan,

11 Micha, Rehob, Hashabiah,

12 Zaccur, Sherebiah, Shebaniah,

13 Hodijah, Bani, Beninu.

14 The chief of the people: ᶠParosh, Pahath-moab, Elam, Zatthu, Bani,

15 Bunni, Azgad, Bebai,

16 Adonijah, Bigvai, Adin,

17 Ater, Hizkijah, Azzur,

18 Hodijah, Hashum, Bezai,

19 Hariph, Anathoth, Nebai,

20 Magpiash, Meshullam, Hezir,

21 Meshezabeel, Zadok, Jaddua,

22 Pelatiah, Hanan, Anaiah,

23 Hoshea, Hananiah, Hashub,

24 Hallohesh, Pileha, Shobek,

25 Rehum, Hashabnah, Maaseiah,

A. M. 3559
B. C. 445
A. U. C. 309
Coss. Rom.
M. Genucio et
C. Curtio

26 And Ahijah, Hanan, Anan,

27 Malluch, Harim, Baanah.

28 ᵍAnd the rest of the people, the priests, the Levites, the porters, the singers, the Nethinims, ʰand all they that had separated themselves from the people of the lands unto the law of God, their wives, their sons, and their daughters, every one having knowledge, and having understanding;

29 They clave to their brethren, their nobles, ⁱand entered into a curse, and into an oath, ᵏto walk in God's law, which was given ˡby Moses the servant of God, and to observe and do all the commandments of the LORD our Lord, and his judgments and his statutes;

30 And that we would not give ᵐour daughters unto the people of the land, nor take their daughters for our sons:

31 ⁿAnd *if* the people of the land bring ware or any victuals on the Sabbath day to sell, *that* we would not buy it of them on the Sabbath, or on the holy day: and *that* we would leave the ᵒseventh year, and the ᵖexaction of �q every debt.

32 Also we made ordinances for us, to charge ourselves yearly with the third part of a shekel for the service of the house of our God;

33 For ʳthe shew-bread, and for the ˢcontinual meat-offering, and for the continual burnt-offering, of the Sabbaths, of the new

---

ªHebrew, *at the sealings;* chapter ix. 38——ᵇChapter viii. 9——ᶜOr, *the governor*——ᵈChapter i. 1——ᵉSee chapter xii. 1–21——ᶠSee Ezra ii. 3, &c.; chapter vii. 8, &c.——ᵍEzra ii. 36-43——ʰEzra ix. 1; x. 11, 12, 19; chapter xiii. 3——ⁱDeut. xxix. 12, 14; chapter v. 12, 13; Psa. cxix. 106——ᵏ2 Kings xxiii. 3; 2 Chron.

xxxiv. 31——ˡHebrew, *by the hand of*——ᵐExodus xxxiv. 16; Deut. vii. 3; Ezra ix. 12, 14——ⁿExod. xx. 10; Lev. xxiii. 3; Deut. v. 12; chap. xiii. 15, &c.——ᵒExod. xxiii. 10, 11; Lev. xxv. 4——ᵖDeut. xv. 1, 2; chap. v. 12 ᵍHeb. *every band*——ʳLev. xxiv. 5, &c.; 2 Chron. ii. 4 ˢSee Num. xxviii., xxix.

NOTES ON CHAP. X

Verse 1. *Now those that sealed*] Four classes here seal. *Nehemiah first,* as their governor. And after him, *secondlly,* The *priests,* ver. 2-8. *Thirdly,* The *Levites,* ver. 9-13. *Fourthly,* The *chiefs of the people,* ver. 14-27.

It is strange that, among all these, we hear nothing of *Ezra,* nor of the high priest *Eliashib.* Nor are any of the *prophets* mentioned, though there must have been some of them at Jerusalem at this time.

The whole of this chapter, the two first verses excepted, is wanting in the *Arabic;* the word *Pashur* of the third verse is retained; and the rest of the chapter is summed up in these words, *and the rest of their assembly.*

Verse 28. *And the rest of the people*] All had, in one or other of the classes which sealed, their *representatives;* and by *their* sealing they considered themselves bound.

Verse 29. *They clave to their brethren*] Though they did not *sign* this instrument, yet they bound themselves under a *solemn oath* that they would fulfil the conditions of the covenant, and walk according to the law of Moses.

Verse 30. *Not give our daughters*] Make no affinity with the people of the land.

Verse 31. *Bring ware*] We will most solemnly keep the Sabbath. *Leave the seventh year*— We will let the land have its Sabbath, and rest every seventh year. See on Exod. xxiii. 10, 11.

Verse 32. *Charge ourselves yearly with the third part of a shekel*] According to the law, every one above *twenty* years of age was to give *half a shekel* to the sanctuary, which was called a *ransom for their souls.* See Exod. xxx. 11-16. But why is *one third* of a shekel now promised instead of the *half shekel,* which the law required? To this question no better answer can be given than this: the general *poverty* of the

A. M. 3559
B. C. 445
A. U. C. 309
Coss. Rom.
M. Genucio et
C. Curtio

moons, for the set feasts, and for the holy *things,* and for the sin-offerings to make an atone-ment for Israel, and *for* all the work of the house of our God.

34 And we cast the lots among the priests, the Levites, and the people, [t]for the wood-offering, to bring *it* into the house of our God, after the houses of our fathers, at times appointed year by year, to burn upon the altar of the LORD our God, [u]as *it is* written in the law:

35 And [v]to bring the first-fruits of our ground, and the first-fruits of all fruit of all trees, year by year, unto the house of the LORD:

36 Also the first-born of our sons, and of our cattle, as *it is* written [w]in the law, and the firstlings of our herds and of our flocks, to bring to the house of our God, unto the priests that minister in the house of our God:

37 [x]And *that* we should bring the first-fruits of our dough, and our offerings, and the fruit of all manner of trees, of wine, and of oil, unto the priests, to the chambers of the house of our God; and [y]the tithes of our ground unto the Levites, that the same Levites might have the tithes in all the cities of our tillage.

A. M. 3559
B. C. 445
A. U. C. 309
Coss. Rom.
M. Genucio et
C. Curtio

38 And the priest the son of Aaron shall be with the Levites, [z]when the Levites take tithes: and the Levites shall bring up the tithe of the tithes unto the house of our God, to [a]the chambers, into the treasure-house.

39 For the children of Israel and the children of Levi [b]shall bring the offering of the corn, of the new wine, and of the oil, unto the chambers, where *are* the vessels of the sanctuary, and the priests that minister, and the porters, and the singers: [c]and we will not forsake the house of our God.

---

[t]Chapter xiii. 31; Isaiah xl. 16——[u]Leviticus vi. 12
[v]Exod. xxiii. 19; xxxiv. 26; Lev. xix. 23; Numbers xviii. 12; Deuteronomy xxvi. 2——[w]Exodus xiii. 2, 12, 13; Leviticus xxvii. 26, 27; Numbers xviii. 15, 16

[x]Lev. xxiii. 17; Num. xv. 19; xviii. 12, &c.; Deut. xviii. 4; xxvi. 2——[y]Lev. xvii. 30; Num. xviii. 21, &c.
[z]Num. xviii. 26——[a]1 Chron. ix. 26; 2 Chron. xxxi. 11
[b]Deut. xii. 6, 11; 2 Chron. xxxi. 12; chap. xiii. 12
[c]Chap. xiii. 10, 11

---

people, occasioned by their wars, overthrows, heavy tributes, &c., in the land of their captivity: and now on their return, having little property, it was impossible for them to give more; and we know, from the terms of the law in this case, that the *poor* and the *rich* were obliged to give *alike,* because it was a *ransom for their souls;* and the souls of the *poor* and the *rich* were of *like value,* and stood equally in need of *redemption;* for all were *equally fallen,* and *all* had come equally short of the *glory of God.*

Though only a *third part* of a shekel was given at this time, and probably for the reason above assigned, yet when the people got into a state of greater prosperity, the *half* shekel was resumed: for it is clear that this sum was paid in the time of our Lord, though not to the *temple,* but to the *Roman government.* Hence when those who collected this as a *tribute* came to our Lord, it was for the δίδραχμα, *didrachma,* which was *half a shekel:* and the coin with which our Lord paid for himself and *Peter* was a *stater,* which contained exactly *two half shekels.* See Matt. xvii. 24-27.

Verse 34. *Cast the lots—for the wood-offering*] There does not appear to have been any *wood-offering* under the law. It was the business of the *Nethinim* to procure this; and hence they were called *hewers of wood* and *drawers of water* to the congregation. But it is very likely that after the captivity few Nethinim were found; for as such, who were the descendants of the Gibeonites, were considered only as *slaves* among the Israelites, they would doubtless find it *as much,* if not *more,* their *interest* to abide in the land of their captivity, than to

return with their former masters. As there was not enough of such persons to provide wood for the fires of the temple, the people now cast lots, not *who* should furnish the wood, but what class or district should furnish it at a particular time of the year, so that there might be a constant supply. One district furnished it for one whole year, or for the *first* month or year; another, for the second month or year; and so on. Now the lot was to determine which district should bring the supply on the first month or year; which on the second; and so on. When the wood was brought, it was delivered to the *Levites:* they cut, prepared, and stacked it; and when wanted, delivered it to the *priests,* whose business it was to lay it upon the altar. Perhaps this providing of the wood was done only *once a year* by one district, the next year by another district, and so on: and this bringing the wood to the temple at last became a great day; and was constituted into a *feast,* called by Josephus Ξυλοφορία, *the carrying of the wood.*—See *De Bell. Jud.* lib. ii., cap. xvii., sec. 6, p. 194. This feast is not mentioned in the sacred writings: then there was no need for such an institution, as the Nethinim were sufficiently numerous.

Verse 36. *Also the first-born*] See this law, and the reasons of it, Exod. xiii. 1-13. As by this law the Lord had a right to all the first-born, instead of these he was pleased to take the *tribe of Levi* for the whole; and thus the Levites served at the tabernacle and temple, instead of the *first-born* of all the tribes.

Verse 38. *Tithe of the tithes*] The tithes of all the produce of the fields were brought to the Levites; out of these a *tenth* part was given to the priests. This is what is called the *tithe of the tithes.* The law for this is found, Num. xviii. 26.

Verse 39. *We will not forsake the house of our God.*] Here was a glorious resolution; and had they been faithful to it, they had been a great and good people to the present day. But what is implied in, *We will not forsake the house of our God?* I answer:—

I. The Church of God is the house of God; there he has his constant *dwelling*-place.

II. True believers are his *family* in this house; and this family consists of, 1. *Fathers* and *mothers;* 2. *Young persons;* 3. *Little children;* And 4. *Servants.*

III. The ministers of the word of God are the officers and overseers of this house and family.

IV. The worship of God is the grand employment of this family.

V. The ordinances of God are the food of the members of this family; or the means of their spiritual support.

VI. Those who do not *forsake* the house of their God are those, 1. Who continue in the faith; 2. Who grow in grace; 3. Who labour in the vineyard; 4. Who bring forth fruit; 5. Who conscientiously attend all the ordinances; and 6. Who take care that the offerings of the house of God shall be duly made, providing for those who labour in the word and doctrine.

READER, 1. Art thou *of* this house? 2. Art thou *in* this house? 3. To what part *of* the family dost thou belong? 4. Art thou still an infant *in* this house? 5. Dost thou attend the ordinances *of* this house? 6. Hast thou *forsaken* this house? These questions are of great importance; answer them as in the sight of God.

CHAPTER XI

Lots are cast that a tenth of the people may constantly dwell at Jerusalem, and the other nine parts in the other cities and villages, 1. Some willingly offer themselves to dwell in Jerusalem, and the people bless them, 2. An enumeration of the families that dwell in Jerusalem, of Judah, and Benjamin, 3–9; of those of the priests, 10–12; of the chiefs of the fathers, 13; of the mighty men, 14; of the Levites, 15–18; of the porters, 19; of the residue of Israel and the officers, 20–24. The villages at which they dwell, 25–35. Certain divisions of the Levites were in Judah and Benjamin, 36.

A. M. 3559
B. C. 445
A. U. C. 309
Coss. Rom.
M. Genucio et
C. Curtio

AND the rulers of the people dwelt at Jerusalem: the rest of the people also cast lots, to bring one of ten to dwell in Jerusalem ªthe holy city, and nine parts *to* dwell in *other* cities.

2 And the people blessed all the men that ᵇwillingly offered themselves to dwell at Jerusalem.

3 ᶜNow these *are* the chief of the province that dwelt in Jerusalem: but in the cities of Judah dwelt every one in his possession in their cities, *to wit,* Israel, the priests, and the Levites, and ᵈthe Nethinims, and ᵉthe children of Solomon's servants.

4 And ᶠat Jerusalem dwelt *certain* of the children of Judah, and of the children of Benjamin. Of the children of Judah; Athaiah the

son of Uzziah, the son of Zechariah, the son of Amariah, the son of Shephatiah, the son of Mahalaleel, of the children of ᵍPerez;

5 And Maaseiah the son of Baruch, the son of Col-hozeh, the son of Hazaiah, the son of Adaiah, the son of Joiarib, the son of Zechariah, the son of Shiloni.

6 All the sons of Perez that dwelt at Jerusalem *were* four hundred threescore and eight valiant men.

7 And these *are* the sons of Benjamin; Sallu the son of Meshullam, the son of Joed, the son of Pedaiah, the son of Kolaiah, the son of Maaseiah, the son of Ithiel, the son of Jesaiah.

8 And after him Gabbai, Sallai, nine hundred twenty and eight.

9 And Joel the son of Zichri *was* their over-

A. M. 3559
B. C. 445
A. U. C. 309
Coss. Rom.
M. Genucio et
C. Curtio

ªVer. 18; Matt. iv. 5; xxvii. 53——ᵇJudg. v. 9——ᶜ1 Chron. ix. 2, 3

ᵈEzra ii. 43——ᵉEzra ii. 55——ᶠ1 Chron. ix. 3, &c. ᵍGen. xxxviii. 29, *Pharez*

NOTES ON CHAP. XI

Verse 1. *To bring one of ten*] Jerusalem certainly had many inhabitants at this time; but not sufficient to preserve the city, which was now encompassed with a wall, and the rebuilding of which was going on fast. Nehemiah therefore obliged *one tenth* of the *country people* to come and dwell in it, that the population might be sufficient for the preservation and defence of the city. *Ten* were set apart, and the lot cast among them to see *which one* of the ten should take up his residence in the city.

Verse 2. *All the men that willingly offered*] Some *volunteered* their services, which was

considered a sacrifice to patriotism at that time, as Jerusalem afforded very few advantages, and was a place of considerable danger; hence the *people spoke well of them,* and no doubt prayed for God's blessing upon them.

Verse 3. *Now these* are *the chief*] A good deal of difference will be found between the *enumeration* here and that in 1 Chron. ix. 2, &c. *There,* those only who came with Zerubbabel appear to be numbered; *here,* those, and the persons who came with Ezra and Nehemiah, enter into the account.

Verse 9. *And Joel—was their overseer*] Joel was chief or magistrate over those, and Judah was his *second* or *deputy.* Perhaps each had

A. M. 3559
B. C. 445
A. U. C. 309
Coss. Rom.
M. Genucio et
C. Curtio

seer: and Judah the son of Senuah *was* second over the city.

10 [h]Of the priests: Jedaiah the son of Joiarib, Jachin.

11 Seraiah the son of Hilkiah, the son of Meshullam, the son of Zadok, the son of Meraioth, the son of Ahitub, *was* the ruler of the house of God.

12 And their brethren that did the work of the house *were* eight hundred twenty and two: and Adaiah the son of Jeroham, the son of Pelaliah, the son of Amzi, the son of Zechariah, the son of Pashur, the son of Malchiah,

13 And his brethren, chief of the fathers, two hundred forty and two: and Amashai the son of Azareel, the son of Ahasai, the son of Meshillemoth, the son of Immer,

14 And their brethren, mighty men of valour, a hundred twenty and eight: and their overseer *was* Zabdiel, [i]the son of *one of* the great men.

15 Also of the Levites: Shemaiah the son of Hashub, the son of Azrikam, the son of Hashabiah, the son of Bunni;

16 And Shabbethai and Jozabad, of the chief of the Levites, [k]*had* the oversight of [l]the outward business of the house of God.

17 And Mattaniah the son of Micha, the son of Zabdi, the son of Asaph, *was* the principal to begin the thanksgiving in prayer: and Bakbukiah the second among his brethren, and Abda the son of Shammua, the son of Galal, the son of Jeduthun.

18 All the Levites in [m]the holy city *were* two hundred fourscore and four.

19 Moreover the porters, Akkub, Talmon, and their brethren that kept [n]the gates, *were* a hundred seventy and two.

20 And the residue of Israel, of the priests, *and* the Levites, *were* in all the cities of Judah, every one in his inheritance.

21 [o]But the Nethinims dwelt in [p]Ophel: and Ziha and Gispa *were* over the Nethinims.

22 The overseer also of the Levites at Jerusalem *was* Uzzi the son of Bani, the son of Hashabiah, the son of Mattaniah, the son of Micha. Of the sons of Asaph, the singers *were* over the business of the house of God.

23 For [q]*it was* the king's commandment concerning them, that [r]a certain portion should be for the singers, due for every day.

24 And Pethahiah the son of Meshezabeel, of the children of [s]Zerah the son of Judah, *was* [t]at the king's hand in all matters concerning the people.

25 And for the villages, with their fields, *some* of the children of Judah dwelt at [u]Kirjath-arba, and *in* the villages thereof, and at Dibon, and *in* the villages thereof, and at Jekabzeel, and *in* the villages thereof,

26 And at Jeshua, and at Moladah, and at Beth-phelet,

27 And at Hazar-shual, and at Beer-sheba, and *in* the villages thereof,

A. M. 3559
B. C. 445
A. U. C. 309
Coss. Rom.
M. Genucio et
C. Curtio

---

[h]1 Chron. ix. 10, &c.——[i]Or, *the son of Haggedolim*
[k]Heb. were *over*——[l]1 Chron. xxvi. 29——[m]Ver. 1
[n]Heb. *at the gates*——[o]See chap. iii. 26

[p]Or, *the tower*——[q]See Ezra vi. 8, 9; vii. 20, &c.
[r]Or, *to a sure ordinance*——[s]Gen. xxxviii. 30, *Zarah*
[t]1 Chron. xviii. 16; xxiii. 28——[u]Josh. xiv. 15

---

a *different* office, but that of Joel was the *chief*.

Verse 11. *Ruler of the house of God.*] He had the command over all *secular* matters, as the high priest had over those which were *spiritual*.

Verse 14. *Mighty men of valour*] Noted for strength of body, and military courage.

Verse 16. *And Shabbethai*] This verse, with verses 20, 21, 28, 29, 32, 33, 34, and 35, are all wanting in the *Septuagint* and the whole chapter is wanting in the *Arabic*, the translator not being concerned in Jewish *genealogies*.

The outward business] Calmet supposes that he provided the victuals for the priests, victims for the sacrifices, the sacerdotal vestments, the sacred vessels, and other necessaries for the service of the temple.

Verse 17. *The principal to begin the thanksgiving*] The *precentor, pitcher of the tune,* or *master-singer*.

Verse 22. *The overseer also of the Levites*]

פקיד *pekid*, the *visitant*, the *inspector;* translated επισκοπος, *bishop*, both by the *Septuagint* and *Vulgate*.

Verse 23. *It was the king's commandment*] By the *king* some understand *David*, and others *Artaxerxes*. It is most probable that it was the latter; who wished that a provision should be made for these, a part of whose office was to offer up *prayers* also, as well as *praises*. For we know that *Darius* made an ample provision for the priests, *that they might offer sacrifices of sweet savour unto the God of heaven; and pray for the life of the king and of his sons,* Ezra vi. 10. Some have thought that they had been Jewish singers employed in the service of the Persian king, to whom he had given a salary, and to whom he wished still to continue the same.

Verse 24. *Pethahiah—was at the king's hand*] He was the governor appointed by the Persian king over the Jewish nation in those matters in

A. M. 3559
B. C. 445
A. U. C. 309
Coss. Rom.
M. Genucio et
C. Curtio

28 And at Ziklag, and at Me-konah, and in the villages there-of,

29 And at En-rimmon, and at Zareah, and at Jarmuth,

30 Zanoah, Adullam, and in their villages, at Lachish, and the fields thereof, at Azekah, and in the villages thereof. And they dwelt from Beer-sheba unto the valley of Hin-nom.

---

^vOr, *of Geba*

---

which the civil government interfered with Jewish concerns. He no doubt fixed, levied, and received the tribute.

Verse 26. *And at Jeshua*] This city is no-where else mentioned.

Verse 28. *Mekonah*] This city is also un-known.

Verse 31. *Geba*] Probably the same as *Gibeah of Saul.*

Verse 32. *Ananiah*] No city of this name is known.

Verse 23. *Hadid*] This place is also unknown.

Neballat] Also unknown.

Verse 35. *Lod, and Ono*] These towns were built by the sons of Elpaal, 1 Chron. viii. 12.

The valley of craftsmen.] See 1 Chron. iv. 14.

31 The children also of Ben-jamin ^vfrom Geba *dwelt* ^wat Michmash, and Aija, and Beth-el, and *in* their villages,

32 *And* at Anathoth, Nob, Ananiah,

33 Hazor, Ramah, Gittaim,

34 Hadid, Zeboim, Neballat,

35 Lod, and Ono, ^xthe valley of craftsmen.

36 And of the Levites *were* divisions *in* Judah, *and* in Benjamin.

A. M. 3559
B. C. 445
A. U. C. 309
Coss. Rom.
M. Genucio et
C. Curtio

---

^wOr, *to Michmash*——^x1 Chron. iv. 14

Probably this latter town was built in this *valley.*

Verse 36. *And of the Levites* were *divisions*] The Levites had their dwellings in the divisions of Judah and Benjamin. This is probably the meaning: the *Syriac* says, *They had the half of Judah and Benjamin;* which is not likely.

THAT the people whose hearts were now turned towards the Lord, would make the best provision for the support of God's work, and all those engaged in it, we may naturally suppose; but this could not be very great, as the com-plete service was not yet established, and the Levites themselves were few in number.

CHAPTER XII

Account of the priests and Levites that came up with Zerubbabel, 1–7. Of the Levites, 8–21. The Levites in the days of Eliashib, 22–26. Of the dedication of the wall, and its ceremonies, 27–43. Different officers appointed, 44–47.

A. M. 3468
B. C. 536
Olymp. LXI. 1
Anno Urbis
Conditæ 218

NOW these *are* the ^apriests and the Levites that went up with Zerubbabel the son of Shealtiel, and Jeshua: ^bSeraiah, Jeremiah, Ezra,

2 Amariah, ^cMalluch, Hattush,

3 ^dShechaniah, ^eRehum, ^fMeremoth,

4 Iddo, ^gGinnetho, ^hAbijah,

5 ⁱMiamin, ^kMaadiah, Bilgah,

6 Shemaiah, and Joiarib, Jedaiah,

7 ^lSallu, Amok, Hilkiah, Je-daiah. These *were* the chief of the priests and of their brethren in the days of ^mJeshua.

8 Moreover the Levites: Jeshua, Binnui, Kadmiel, Sherebiah, Judah, *and* Mattaniah, ⁿwhich *was* over ^othe thanksgiving, he and his brethren.

9 Also Bakbukiah and Unni, their brethren, *were* over against them in the watches.

A. M. 3468
B. C. 536
Olymp. LXI. 1
Anno Urbis
Conditæ 218

---

^aEzra ii. 1, 2——^bSee chapter x. 2–8——^cOr, *Melicu*, verse 14——^dOr, *Shebaniah*, verse 14——^eOr, *Harim*, verse 15——^fOr, *Meraioth*, verse 15——^gOr, *Ginnethon*, verse 16

^hLuke i. 5——ⁱOr, *Miniamin*, verse 17——^kOr, *Moadiah*, verse 17——^lOr, *Sallai*, verse 20——^mEzra iii. 2; Hag. i. 1; Zech. iii. 1——ⁿChap. xi. 17——^oThat is, *the psalms of thanksgiving*

NOTES ON CHAP. XII

Verse 1. *Now these* are *the priests*] Not the *whole*, but the *chief* of them, as we are in-formed, ver. 7, 22, 23, and 24.

The *Septuagint* omit ver. 3, except the word *Shechaniah;* as also verses 4, 5, 6, 9, 37, 38, 39, 40, and 41. The *Arabic* omits the first *twenty-six* verses, and ver. 29. Mention is made of *Ezra* in this verse; and he is generally allowed to be that *Ezra* whose book the reader has already passed over, and who came to Jeru-salem in the time of Cyrus, with Zerubbabel. If this were the same, he must have been at

this time upward of *a hundred* years of age: and this case is not improbable, as an especial providence might preserve such a very useful man beyond the ordinary age of men. See what has been said on the case of Nehemiah, chap. i. 1.

Verse 7. *The chief of the priests*] They were *twenty-four* orders or courses in number, all subordinate to each other; as established by David, 1 Chron. xxiv. 18. And these orders or courses were continued till the destruction of Jerusalem by the Romans—See *Calmet.*

Verse 8. *Over the thanksgiving*] The *princi-pal singers:* see on chap. **xi. 17.**

A. M. 3468
B. C. 536
Olymp. LXI. 1
Anno Urbis
Conditæ 218

10 And Jeshua begat Joiakim, Joiakim also begat Eliashib, and Eliashib begat Joiada,

11 And Joiada begat Jonathan, and Jonathan begat Jaddua.

12 And in the days of Joiakim were priests, the chief of the fathers: of Seraiah, Meraiah; of Jeremiah, Hananiah;

13 Of Ezra, Meshullam; of Amariah, Jehohanan;

14 Of Melicu, Jonathan; of Shebaniah, Joseph;

15 Of Harim, Adna; of Meraioth, Helkai;

16 Of Iddo, Zechariah; of Ginnethon, Meshullam;

17 Of Abijah, Zichri; of Miniamin; of Moadiah, Piltai;

18 Of Bilgah, Shammua; of Shemaiah, Jehonathan;

19 And of Joiarib, Mattenai; of Jedaiah, Uzzi;

20 Of Sallai, Kallai; of Amok, Eber;

21 Of Hilkiah, Hashabiah; of Jedaiah, Nethaneel.

22 The Levites in the days of Eliashib,

Joiada, and Johanan, and Jaddua, *were* recorded chief of the fathers: also the priests, to the reign of Darius the Persian.

A. M. 3468
B. C. 536
Olymp. LXI. 1
Anno Urbis
Conditæ 218

23 The sons of Levi, the chief of the fathers, *were* written in the book of the Pchronicles, even until the days of Johanan the son of Eliashib.

24 And the chief of the Levites: Hashabiah, Sherebiah, and Jeshua the son of Kadmiel, with their brethren over against them, to praise *and* to give thanks, qaccording to the commandment of David the man of God, rward over against ward.

25 Mattaniah, and Bakbukiah, Obadiah, Meshullam, Talmon, Akkub, *were* porters keeping the ward at the sthresholds of the gates.

26 These *were* in the days of Joiakim the son of Jeshua, the son of Jozadak, and in the days of Nehemiah tthe governor, and of Ezra the priest, uthe scribe.

27 And at vthe dedication of the wall of Jerusalem they sought the Levites out of all their places, to bring them to

A. M. 3559
B. C. 445
A. U. C. 309
Coss. Rom.
M. Genucio et
C. Curtio

---

p1 Chron. ix. 14, &c.——q1 Chron. xxiii., xxv., xxvi
rEzra iii. 11——sOr *treasuries, or assemblies*

tChap. viii. 9——uEzra vii. 6, 11——vDeut. xx. 5; Psalm xxx. title

---

Verse 22. *Jaddua*] This was probably the high priest who went in his pontifical robes, accompanied by his brethren, to meet Alexander the Great, when he was advancing towards Jerusalem, with the purpose to destroy it, after having conquered Tyre and Gaza. Alexander was so struck with the appearance of the priest, that he forbore all hostilities against Jerusalem, prostrated himself before Jaddua, worshipped the Lord at the temple, and granted many privileges to the Jews. See *Josephus*, Ant. lib. xi., c. 8, and Prideaux's Connections, lib. 7, p. 695.

To the reign of Darius the Persian.] *Calmet* maintains that this must have been *Darius Codomanus*, who was defeated by Alexander the Great: but Archbishop *Usher* understands it of *Darius Nothus*, in whose reign he thinks Jaddua was born, who was high priest under *Darius Codomanus*.

Verse 23. *The book of the chronicles*] This is not the book of *Chronicles* which we have now, no such list being found in it; but some other book or register, which is lost.

Verse 25. *The thresholds of the gates.*] Some understand this of a sort of *porticoes* at the gates, and are puzzled about it, because they find no mention of porticoes elsewhere: but why may we not suppose these to resemble our *watch-boxes* or some temporary moveable shelters for those who took care of the gates? That there must have been some such conveniences, common sense dictates.

Verse 27. *At the dedication of the wall*] They

sent for the Levites from all quarters, that this dedication might be as solemn and majestic as possible; and it is likely that this was done as soon as convenient after the walls were finished. The dedication seems to have consisted in processions of the most eminent persons around the walls, and thanksgivings to God, who had enabled them to bring the work to so happy a conclusion: and no doubt to all this were added a particular *consecration* of the city to God, and the most earnest *invocation* that he would take it under his guardian care, and defend it and its inhabitants against all their enemies.

The ancients consecrated their cities to the gods, and the very *walls* were considered as sacred. *Ovid* gives us an account of the ceremonies used in laying the foundations of the *walls of the city of Rome*, by *Romulus*. After having consulted together who should give name to the city, and have the direction of the wall by which it was necessary to surround it, they agreed to let the case be decided by the flight of birds. One brother went to the top of the Mons Palatinus, the other to that of Mount Aventine. Romulus saw twelve birds, Remus saw but six; the former, therefore, according to agreement, took the command. The poet thus describes the ceremonies used on the occasion:—

Apta dies legitur, qua mœnia signet aratro;
 Sacra Palis suberant: inde movetur opus.
Fossa fit ad solidum: fruges jaciuntur in ima.
 Et de vicino terra petita solo.

A. M. 3559
B. C. 445
A. U. C. 309
Coss. Rom.
M. Genucio et
C. Curtio

Jerusalem, to keep the dedication with gladness, ᵂboth with thanksgivings, and with singing, *with* cymbals, psalteries, and with harps.

28 And the sons of the singers gathered themselves together, both out of the plain country round about Jerusalem, and from the villages of Netophathi;

29 Also from the house of Gilgal, and out of the fields of Geba and Azmaveth: for the singers had builded them villages round about Jerusalem.

30 And the priests and the Levites purified themselves, and purified the people, and the gates, and the walls.

31 Then I brought up the princes of Judah upon the wall, and appointed two great *companies of them that gave* thanks, *whereof* ˣ*one* went on the right hand upon the wall ʸtoward the dung gate:

32 And after them went Hoshaiah, and half of the princes of Judah,

33 And Azariah, Ezra, and Meshullam,

A. M. 3559
B. C. 445
A. U. C. 309
Coss. Rom.
M. Genucio et
C. Curtio

34 Judah, and Benjamin, and Shemaiah, and Jeremiah,

35 And *certain* of the priests' sons ᶻwith trumpets: *namely,* Zechariah the son of Jonathan, the son of Shemaiah, the son of Mattaniah, the son of Michaiah, the son of Zaccur, the son of Asaph:

36 And his brethren, Shemaiah, and Azarael, Milalai, Gilalai, Maai, Nethaneel, and Judah, Hanani, with ᵃthe musical instruments of David the man of God, and Ezra the scribe before them.

37 ᵇAnd at the fountain gate, which was over against them, they went up by ᶜthe stairs of the city of David, at the going up of the wall, above the house of David, even unto ᵈthe water gate eastward.

38 ᵉAnd the other *company of them that gave* thanks went over against *them,* and I after them, and the half of the people upon ᶠthe wall, from beyond ᵍthe tower of the

---

ᵂ1 Chronicles xxv. 6; 2 Chronicles v. 13; vii. 6 ——ˣSee verse 38——ʸChapter ii. 13; iii. 13——ᶻNumbers x. 2, 8——ᵃ1 Chronicles xxiii. 5——ᵇChapter ii. 14; iii. 15——ᶜChapter iii. 15——ᵈChapter iii. 26; viii. 1, 3, 16——ᵉSee verse 31——ᶠChapter iii. 11 ᵍChapter iii. 8

Fossa repletur humo, plenæque imponitur ara;
  Et novus accenso finditur igne focus.
Inde, premens stivam, designat mœnia sulco;
  Alba jugum niveo cum bove vacca tulit.
Vox fuit hæc regis; Condenti Jupiter urbem,
  Et genitor Mavors, Vestaque mater ades:
Quosque pium est adhibere deos, advertite
  cuncti:
Auspicibus vobis hoc mihi surgat opus.
Longa sit huic ætas, dominæque potentia terræ:
  Sitque sub hac oriens occiduusque dies!
Ille precabatur.　　OVID, Fast. lib. iv., ver. 819.

"A proper day is chosen in which he may mark out the walls with the plough: the festival of Pales was at hand when the work was begun. A ditch is dug down to the solid clay, into which they cast the fruits of the season; and bring earth from the neighbouring ground, with which they fill up the trench; and on it build an altar, by whose flames the newly made hearth is cleft asunder. Then Romulus, seizing the plough, which a white heifer yoked with a snowy bull drew along, marked out the walls with a furrow. And thus spoke the king: 'O Jupiter, and Father Mars, with Matron Vesta, prosper me in founding this city! And all ye gods, approach, whomsoever it is right to invoke! Under your auspices may the work arise; may it endure for countless ages, and be the mistress of the world; and may the East and the West be under its control!' Thus he prayed."

The above is a literal version, and the account is not a little curious.

Verse 29. *From the house of Gilgal, and out of the fields of Geba and Azmaveth*] Or, from Beth-Gilgal; a village erected in the place where the Israelites encamped after they had, under the direction of Joshua, passed over Jordan.

Verse 30. *The priests and the Levites purified themselves*] This consisted in washings, abstinence from wine, and other matters, which, on all other occasions, were lawful. And as to the purifying of the *gates* and the *walls,* nothing was requisite but to remove all filth from the former, and all rubbish that might have been laid against the latter.

Verse 31. *Then I brought up the princes*] Perhaps this verse should be read thus: "Then I caused the princes of Judah to go up on the wall, and appointed two great choirs, [to sing praises,] and *two* processions, one on the right hand, &c.

The following seems to have been the order of the procession: he divided the *priests,* the *Levites,* the *magistrates,* and the *people* into *two companies;* each company to go round one half of the wall. They began at the *dung gate,* one party going to the *right* and the other to the *left,* till they met at the *great space opposite to the temple,* where they all offered many sacrifices to God, and rejoiced with exceeding great joy; shouting so that the noise was heard a great way off.

Verse 38. *The broad wall*] What part this was, we know not: it might have been a place designed for a *public promenade,* or a *parade* for assembling the troops or guard of the temple.

A. M. 3559
B. C. 445
A. U. C. 309
Coss. Rom.
M. Genucio et
C. Curtio

furnaces even unto [h]the broad wall;

39 [i]And from above the gate of Ephraim, and above [k]the old gate, and above [l]the fish gate, [m]and the tower of Hananeel, and the tower of Meah, even unto [n]the sheep gate: and they stood still in [o]the prison gate.

40 So stood the two *companies of them that gave* thanks in the house of God, and I, and the half of the rulers with me:

41 And the priests: Eliakim, Maaseiah, Miniamin, Michaiah, Elioenai, Zechariah, *and* Hananiah, with trumpets;

42 And Maaseiah, and Shemaiah, and Eleazar, and Uzzi, and Jehohanan, and Malchijah, and Elam, and Ezer. And the singers [p]sang loud, with Jezrahiah *their* overseer.

43 Also that day they offered great sacrifices, and rejoiced: for God had made them rejoice with great joy: the wives also and the children rejoiced: so that the joy of Jerusalem was heard even afar off.

A. M. 3559
B. C. 445
A. U. C. 309
Coss. Rom.
M. Genucio et
C. Curtio

44 [q]And at that time were some appointed over the chambers for the treasures, for the offerings, for the first-fruits, and for the tithes, to gather into them out of the fields of the cities the portions [r]of the law for the priests and Levites: for Judah rejoiced for the priests and for the Levites [s]that waited.

45 And both the singers and the porters kept the ward of their God, and the ward of the purification, [t]according to the commandment of David, *and* of Solomon his son.

46 For in the days of David [u]and Asaph of old *there were* chief of the singers, and songs of praise and thanksgiving unto God.

47 And all Israel in the days of Zerubbabel, and in the days of Nehemiah, gave the portions of the singers and the porters, every day his portion: [v]and they [w]sanctified *holy things* unto the Levites; [x]and the Levites sanctified *them* unto the children of Aaron.

---

[h]2 Kings xiv. 13; ch. viii. 16——[i]Ch. iii. 6——[k]Ch. iii. 3——[l]Ch. iii. 1——[m]Ch. iii. 32——[n]Jer. xxxii. 2 [o]Heb. *made their voice to be heard*——[p]2 Chron. xiii. 11, 12; ch. xiii. 5, 12, 13——[q]That is, *appointed by the law*

[r]Heb. *for the joy of Judah*——[s]Heb. *that stood*——[t]1 Chron. xxv., xxvi——[u]1 Chron. xxv. 1, &c.; 2 Chron. xxix. 30——[v]Numbers xviii. 21, 24——[w]That is, *set apart*——[x]Numbers xviii. 26

Verse 47. *All Israel—gave the portions of the singers*] The *singers* and the *porters* were supported by the *people at large;* and each of these had their portions served out to them *daily.*

And they sanctified—unto the Levites] The things which were provided for *sacred uses* were delivered by the *people* to the *Levites,* and the Levites presented them to the *priests.*

The children of Aaron.] This may refer principally to the *tithes* which the people brought to the *Levites;* the *tithe* or *tenth* of which the Levites gave to the priests. The presenting these *tithes* is termed *sanctifying them;* that is, *dedicating* them to those sacred or ecclesiastical uses for which they were designed: this is a very general meaning of the word *sanctify* in Scripture.

CHAPTER XIII

The law is read, which commands that the Ammonite and Moabite should be separated from the congregation, on which they separate all the mixed multitude, 1–3. Eliashib the high priest having not only joined opinion with Sanballat, but being also allied to Tobiah the Ammonite, and having given him some of the chambers in the court of the house of God, 4, 5; Nehemiah casts out the goods of Tobiah, and purifies the chambers, 6–9. He rectifies several evils; and the people bring the tithes of all things to the treasuries, 10–12. He appoints treasurers, 13, 14; finds that the Sabbaths had been greatly profaned by buying and selling, and rectifies this abuse, 15–22; finds Jews that had married strange wives; against whom he testifies, and expels one of the priests who had married the daughter of Sanballat the Horonite, 23–29. He cleanses them from all strangers, makes a final regulation, and prays for God's mercy to himself, 30, 31.

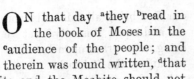

A. M. 3559
B. C. 445
A. U. C. 309
Coss. Rom.
M. Genucio et
C. Curtio

ON that day [a]they [b]read in the book of Moses in the [c]audience of the people; and therein was found written, [d]that the Ammonite and the Moabite should not come into the congregation of God for ever;

2 Because they met not the children of Israel with bread and with water, but [e]hired Balaam against them, that he should curse them: [f]howbeit our God turned the curse into a blessing.

3 Now it came to pass, when they had heard the law, [g]that they separated from Israel all the mixed multitude.

4 And before this, Eliashib the priest, [h]having the oversight of the chamber of the house of our God, *was* allied unto Tobiah:

5 And he had prepared for him a great chamber, [i]where aforetime they laid the meat-offerings, the frankincense, and the vessels, and the tithes of the corn, the new wine, and the oil, [k]which [l]was commanded *to be given* to the Levites, and the singers, and the porters; and the offerings of the priests.

6 But in all this *time* was not I at Jerusalem: [m]for in the two and thirtieth year of Artaxerxes king of Babylon came I unto the king, and [n]after certain days [o]obtained I leave of the king:

A. M. 3570
B. C. 434
A. U. C. 320
Coss. Rom.
C. Julio 2. et
L. Virginio 2

7 And I came to Jerusalem, and understood of the evil that Eliashib did for Tobiah, in [p]preparing him a chamber in the courts of the house of God.

8 And it grieved me sore: therefore I cast forth all the household stuff of Tobiah out of the chamber.

9 Then I commanded, and they [q]cleansed the chambers: and thither brought I again the vessels of the house of God, with the meat-offering and the frankincense.

10 And I perceived that the portions of the Levites had [r]not been given *them:* for the Levites and the singers, that did the work, were fled every one to [s]his field.

11 Then [t]contended I with the rulers, and said, [u]Why is the house of God forsaken? And I gathered them together, and set them in their [v]place.

---

[a]Deut. xxxi. 11, 12; 2 Kings xxiii. 2; chapter viii. 3, 8; ix. 3; Isaiah xxxiv. 16——[b]Hebrew, *there was read*——[c]Hebrew, *ears*——[d]Deuteronomy xxiii. 3, 4——[e]Num. xxii. 5; Josh. xxiv. 9, 10——[f]Numbers xxiii. 11; xxiv. 10; Deut. xxiii. 5——[g]Chap. ix. 2; x. 28——[h]Heb. *being set over,* chap. xii. 44

[i]Chap. xii. 44——[k]Heb. *the commandment of the Levites*——[l]Num. xviii. 21, 24——[m]Chap. v. 14 [n]Heb. *at the end of days*——[o]Or, *I earnestly requested* [p]Ver. 1, 5——[q]2 Chron. xxix. 5, 15, 16, 18——[r]Mal. iii. 8——[s]Num. xxxv. 2——[t]Ver. 17, 25; Prov. xxviii. 4 [u]Chap. x. 39——[v]Heb. *standing*

NOTES ON CHAP. XIII

Verse 1. *On that day*] I am quite of *Calmet's* mind that the transaction detailed in this chapter did not immediately succeed the dedication of the walls of Jerusalem. It is most likely that, when this dedication was ended, Nehemiah returned to Babylon, as himself particularly marks, ver. 6, for he did return in the *thirty-second* year of Artaxerxes; and then, after certain days, supposed to be about the term of *one* year, he got leave to return to Jerusalem to see how matters were conducted: and there he found the evils which he mentions in this chapter, and which he redressed in the manner himself describes. See the *introduction* to this book.

Should not come into the congregation] That is, Ye shall not form any kind of *matrimonial alliance* with them. This, and this alone, is the meaning of the *law*.

Verse 3. *They separated from Israel all the mixed multitude.*] They excluded all strange women, and all persons, young and old, who had been born of these illegal connections.

Verse 4. *Eliashib the priest*] *Perhaps* this was a different person from Eliashib the high priest; but there is no indubitable evidence that he was not the same. If he was high priest, he was very unfaithful to the high charge which he had received; and a reproach to the priesthood. He had married his grandson to Sanballat's daughter: this produced a connection with Tobiah, the fast friend of Sanballat; in whose favour he polluted the house of God, giving him one of the chambers for his ordinary residence, which were appointed for the reception of the tithes, oblations, &c., that came to the house of God.

Verse 6. *Was not I at Jerusalem*] Nehemiah came to Jerusalem in the *twentieth* year of Artaxerxes, and remained there till the *thirty-second* year, *twelve* years: then returned to Babylon, and staid one year; got leave to revisit his brethren; and found matters as stated in this chapter.

Verse 8. *I cast forth all the household stuff of Tobiah*] He acted as Jesus Christ did when he found the courts of the Lord's house profaned: He *overthrew the tables of the money-changers, and the seats of those who sold doves.*

Verse 10. *The portions of the Levites had not been given*] Hence we find they were obliged to abandon the sacred service, and betake themselves to cultivate the land for their support. This was the fault of the *rulers*, who *permitted* all these abuses.

Verse 11. *Why is the house of God forsaken?*] They had all solemnly promised, chap. x. 39, that *they would never forsake the house of their God;* but, alas, how soon is this forgotten! Nehemiah used their own words here by way of reproof.

A. M. 3570
B. C. 434
A. U. C. 320
Coss. Rom.
C. Julio 2. et
L. Virginio 2

12 [w]Then brought all Judah the tithe of the corn and the new wine and the oil unto the [x]treasuries.

13 [y]And I made treasurers over the treasuries, Shelemiah the priest, and Zadok the scribe, and of the Levites, Pedaiah: and [z]next to them *was* Hanan the son of Zaccur, the son of Mattaniah: for they were counted [a]faithful, and their [b]office *was* to distribute unto their brethren.

14 [c]Remember me, O my God, concerning this, and wipe not out my [d]good deeds that I have done for the house of my God, and for the [e]offices thereof.

15 In those days saw I in Judah *some* treading wine-presses [f]on the Sabbath, and bringing in sheaves, and lading asses; and also wine, grapes, and figs, and all *manner of* burdens, [g]which they brought into Jerusalem on the Sabbath day: and I testified *against them* in the day wherein they sold victuals.

16 There dwelt men of Tyre also therein, which brought fish and all manner of ware, and sold on the Sabbath unto the children of Judah, and in Jerusalem.

17 [h]Then I contended with the nobles of Judah, and said unto them, What evil thing *is* this that ye do, and profane the Sabbath day?

18 [i]Did not your fathers thus, and did not our God bring all this evil upon us, and upon this city? yet ye bring more wrath upon Israel by profaning the Sabbath.

A. M. 3570
B. C. 434
A. U. C. 320
Coss. Rom.
C. Julio 2. et
L. Virginio 2

19 And it came to pass, that when the gates of Jerusalem [k]began to be dark before the Sabbath, I commanded that the gates should be shut, and charged that they should not be opened till after the Sabbath: [l]and *some* of my servants set I at the gates, *that* there should no burden be brought in on the Sabbath day.

20 So the merchants and sellers of all kind of ware lodged without Jerusalem once or twice.

21 Then I testified against them, and said unto them, Why lodge ye [m]about the wall? if ye do *so* again, I will lay hands on you. From that time forth came they no *more* on the Sabbath.

22 And I commanded the Levites, that [n]they should cleanse themselves, and *that* they should come *and* keep the gates, to sanctify the Sabbath day. [o]Remember me, O my God, *concerning* this also, and spare me according to the [p]greatness of thy mercy.

23 In those days also saw I Jews *that* [q]had [r]married wives of Ashdod, of Ammon, *and* of Moab:

24 And their children spake half in the

[w]Chap. x. 38, 39; xii. 44——[x]Or, *store-houses*——[y]Ch. xii. 44; 2 Chron. xxxi. 12——[z]Heb. *at their hand* [a]Chap. vii. 2; 1 Cor. iv. 2——[b]Heb. it was *upon them* [c]Verse 22, 31; chap. v. 19——[d]Heb. *kindnesses*——[e]Or, *observations*——[f]Exod. xx. 10

[g]Jer. xvii. 21, 22; chap. x. 31——[h]Verse 11——[i]Jer. xvii. 21, 22, 23——[k]Lev. xxiii. 32——[l]Jer. xvii. 21, 22 [m]Heb. *before the wall?*——[n]Chap. xii. 30——[o]Verses 14, 31——[p]Or, *multitude*——[q]Heb. *had made to dwell* with them——[r]Ezra ix. 2

Verse 13. *They were counted faithful*] They were reported to me as persons in whom I could confide; they had been steady in God's ways and work, while others had been careless and relaxed.

Verse 14. *Wipe not out my good deeds*] If thou wert strict to mark what is done amiss, even my *good deeds* must be *wiped out;* but, Lord, remember me in thy mercy, and let my upright conduct be acceptable to thee!

Verse 15. *Treading wine-presses*] The Sabbath appears to have been totally disregarded.

Verse 17. I contended with the nobles] These evils took place through their negligence; and this I proved before them.

Verse 19. *When the gates—began to be dark*] After sunset on Friday evening he caused the gates to be shut, and kept them shut all the Sabbath; and, as he could not trust the ordinary officers, he set some of *his own servants* to watch the gates, that no person might enter for the purpose of traffic.

Verse 20. *So the merchants—lodged without Jerusalem*] They exposed their wares for sale on the outside of the walls.

Verse 21. *I will lay hands on you*] I will *imprison* every man of you. This had the desired effect; *they came no more.*

Verse 22. *Spare me according to the greatness of thy mercy.*] By some Nehemiah has been thought to deal with God too much on the principle of *merit.* That he wished God to *remember him for good,* is sufficiently evident; and who does not wish the same? But that he expected *heaven because of his good deeds,* does not appear. Indeed, the concluding clause of this verse proves the *contrary,* and shows that he expected nothing from God but through *the greatness of his mercy.* Shame on those who, with this evidence before them, brand this good man with the epithet of *workmonger!* a man who, in inward holiness, outward usefulness, and genuine love to God and man, was worth ten score of such *self-called* believers.

Verse 24. *Half in the speech of Ashdod*] There were children in the same family by *Jewish* and *Philistine mothers.* As the Jewish mother would always speak to *her* children in *Hebrew* or *Chaldee,* so *they* learnt to speak these languages; and as the *Ashdod mother*

A. M. 3570
B. C. 434
A. U. C. 320
Coss. Rom.
C. Julio 2. et
L. Virginio 2 speech of Ashdod, and ˢcould not speak in the Jews' language, but according to the language ᵗof each people.

25 And I ᵘcontended with them, and ᵛcursed them, and smote certain of them, and plucked off their hair, and made them ʷswear by God, *saying,* Ye shall not give your daughters unto their sons, nor take their daughters unto your sons, or for yourselves.

26 ˣDid not Solomon king of Israel sin by these things? yet ʸamong many nations was there no king like him, ᶻwho was beloved of his God, and God made him king over all Israel: ªnevertheless even him did outlandish women cause to sin.

27 Shall we then hearken unto you to do all this great evil, to ᵇtransgress against our God in marrying strange wives?

28 And *one* of the sons ᶜof Joiada, the son of Eliashib the high priest, *was* son-in-law to Sanballat the Horonite: therefore I chased him from me.

29 ᵈRemember them, O my God, ᵉbecause they have defiled the priesthood, and ᶠthe covenant of the priesthood, and of the Levites.

30 ᵍThus cleansed I them from all strangers, and ʰappointed the wards of the priests and the Levites, every one in his business;

31 And for ⁱthe wood-offering, at times appointed, and for the first-fruits. ᵏRemember me, O my God, for good.

A. M. 3570
B. C. 434
A. U. C. 320
Coss. Rom.
C. Julio 2. et
L. Virginio 2

ˢHeb. *they discerned not to speak*——ᵗHeb. *of people and people*——ᵘVer. 11; Prov. xxviii. 4——ᵛOr, *reviled them*——ʷEzra x. 5; chap. x. 29, 30——ˣ1 Kings xi. 1, &c.——ʸ1 Kings iii. 13; 2 Chron. i. 12

ᶻ2 Sam. xii. 24——ª1 Kings xi. 4, &c.——ᵇEzra x. 2 ᶜChap. xii. 10, 22——ᵈChap. vi. 14——ᵉHeb. *for the defilings*——ᶠMal. ii. 4, 11, 12——ᵍChap. x. 30——ʰCh. xii. 1, &c.——ⁱChap. x. 34——ᵏVer. 14, 22

---

would always speak to *her* children in the *Ashdod language,* so *they* learnt *that* tongue. Thus there were, in the same family, children who could not understand each other; *half,* or one *part,* speaking *one language,* and the *other* part *another.* Children of different wives did not ordinarily *mingle together;* and the wives had separate apartments. This is a better explanation than that which intimates that the *same child* spoke a *jargon,* half *Ashdod* and *half Hebrew.*

Verse 25. *I contended with them*] Proved the fact against these iniquitous fathers, in a legal assembly.

And cursed them] Denounced the judgments of God and the sentence of the law upon them.

Smote certain of them] Had them punished by *whipping.*

And plucked off their hair] Had them *shaven,* as a mark of the greatest ignominy.

And made them swear by God, saying, Ye shall not give] Caused them to bind themselves by an oath, that they would make no intermarriages with those who were not of the seed of Israel.

Verse 26. *Did not Solomon*] Have you not had an awful example before you? What a heavy curse did Solomon's conduct bring upon himself and upon the people, for a conduct such as *yours?*

Verse 27. *Shall we then hearken unto you*] If God spared not *Solomon,* who was so much beloved of Him, shall we spare *you,* who by your conduct are bringing down God's judgments upon Israel?

Verse 28. One *of the sons of Joiada*] This was *Manasseh,* brother of *Jaddua,* son of *Joiada,* and grandson of *Eliashib* the high priest.

I chased him from me.] Struck him off the list of the priests, and deemed him utterly unworthy of all connection and intercourse with truly religious people.

Verse 29. *Because they have defiled the priesthood*] God, therefore, will *remember* their iniq-

uities against them, and punish them for their transgressions. These words of Nehemiah are to be understood *declaratively.*

Verse 31. *For the wood-offering*] This was a most necessary regulation: without it the temple service could not have gone forward; and therefore Nehemiah mentions this as one of the most important services he had rendered to his nation. See chap. x. 34.

Remember me, O my God, for good.] This has precisely the same meaning with, *O my God, have mercy upon me!* and thus alone it should be understood.

Of Nehemiah the Jews speak as one of the greatest men of their nation. His concern for his country, manifested by such unequivocal marks, entitles him to the character of the first *patriot* that ever lived. In the course of the Divine providence, he was a captive in Babylon; but there his excellences were so apparent, that he was chosen by the Persian king to fill an office the most respectable and the most *confidential* in the whole court. Here he lived in ease and affluence; he lacked no manner of thing that was good; and here he might have *continued* to live, in the same affluence and in the same confidence: but he could enjoy neither, so long as his people were distressed, the sepulchres of his fathers trodden under foot, the altars of his God overturned, and his worship either totally neglected or corrupted. He sought the peace of Jerusalem; he prayed to God for it; and was willing to sacrifice wealth, ease, and safety, and even life itself, if he might be the instrument of restoring the desolations of Israel. And God, who saw the desire of his heart, and knew the excellences with which he had endowed him, granted his request, and gave him the high honour of restoring the desolated city of his ancestors, and the pure worship of their God. On this account he has been considered by several as an expressive *type* of Jesus Christ, and many parallels have been shown in their lives and conduct.

I have already, in several notes, vindicated him from all mercenary and interested views, as well as from all false notions of *religion*, grounded on *human merit*. For disinterestedness, philanthropy, patriotism, prudence, courage, zeal, humanity, and every virtue that constitutes a great mind, and proves a soul in deep communion with God, Nehemiah will ever stand conspicuous among the greatest men of the Jewish nation, and an *exemplar* worthy to be copied by the first patriots in every nation under heaven.

It has already been observed that, in the Jewish canon, Ezra and Nehemiah make but one book; and that both have been attributed, but without reason, to the same author: hence the *Syriac* version ends with this colophon— The end of the book of Ezra, the scribe, in which are contained *two thousand three hundred and sixty-one* verses.

MASORETIC NOTES.—Ezra and Nehemiah contain *six hundred and eighty-eight* verses. *Middle verse* is Neh. iii. 32. *Sections, ten.*

INTRODUCTION TO THE BOOK
OF
ESTHER

THE son and successor of the famous Persian king Xerxes was *Artaxerxes*, surnamed *Longimanus*, or, in Persian, اردشير ديراز دست *Ardsheer Diraz dest, the long-handed Ardshur*. This prince, on coming to the throne, had powerful opponents and competitors in the children of *Artabanus*, uncle to Xerxes, and in his own brother *Hystaspes*. The former, and their adherents, he overthrew in a bloody battle; and in the following year obtained a complete victory over his brother, and totally subdued the *Bactrians*, who had espoused his cause: and thus rendered himself the undisputed possessor of the Persian empire. About his *third* year, which was 462 before Christ, the history of *Esther* begins, which, in its connection with the Persian history, is thus ably introduced by Dr. *Prideaux:*—

"After Artaxerxes had obtained these successes, and thereby firmly settled himself in the peaceable possession of the whole Persian empire, (*Esther* i.,) he appointed a solemn rejoicing on this account: and caused it to be celebrated in the city of Shushan, or Susa, in feastings and shows, for the term of a *hundred and eighty days;* on the conclusion of which he gave a great feast for all the princes and people that were then in Shushan, for *seven* days; and Vashti, the queen, at the same time, made a like feast in her apartment for the women. On the *seventh* day, the king's heart being merry with wine, he commanded the *seven* chamberlains to bring Queen Vashti before him, with the crown royal on her head, that he might show to the princes and people her beauty. But for her thus to show herself in such an assembly being contrary to the usage of the Persians, and appearing to her, as indeed it was, very indecent, and much unbecoming the modesty of a lady, as well as the dignity of her station, she refused to comply, and would not come; whereon the king, being very much incensed, called his *seven* counsellors to take advice with them about it, who, fearing this might be a bad example through the whole empire, in encouraging women to contemn and disobey their husbands, advised that the king should put Vashti away for ever from him, and give her royal state to another, that should be better than her; and by his royal edict, give command throughout the whole empire that all wives should pay honour and obedience to their husbands, and that every man should rule absolutely in his own house. Which advice pleasing the king, he commanded it accordingly to be put in execution; and Vashti never more after that came again into the king's presence: for the decree whereby she was removed from him was registered among the laws of the Medes and Persians, and therefore it could never again be altered. After this, orders were given out through the whole empire for the gathering together at the palace at Shushan all the fair virgins in every province, that out of them one might be chosen whom the king should best like to be made queen in her place. At the time when this collection of virgins was made, (Esther ii.,) there lived in Shushan a certain Jew named Mordecai, who was of the descendants of those who had been carried captive to Babylon with Jeconiah king of Judah, and, by his attendance at the king's gate, seems to have been one of the porters of the royal palace. He, having no children, did bring up Hadassah, his uncle's daughter, and adopted her as his own. This young woman, being very beautiful and fair, was made choice of among other virgins on this occasion; and was carried to the king's palace, and there committed to the care of

Hege, the king's chamberlain, who was appointed to have the custody of these virgins; whom she pleased so well by her good carriage, that he showed her favour before all the other virgins under his care; and therefore he assigned her the best apartment of the house, and provided her first with those things that were requisite for her purification: for the custom was, that every virgin thus taken into the palace for the king's use was to go through a course of purification, by sweet oils and perfumes, for a whole year; and therefore Hadassah, having been, by the favour of the chamberlain, of the earliest provided with these things, was one of the first that was prepared and made ready for the king's bed, and therefore was one of the soonest that was called to it. The term, therefore, of her purification being accomplished, her turn came to go in unto the king; who was so much pleased with her that he often called her by name, which he used not to do but to those only of his women whom he was much delighted with. Esther growing still farther in the king's favour, and gaining his affections beyond all the rest of the women, (Esther ii.,) he advanced her to higher honour; and on the *tenth* day of the *tenth* month, which falls about the end of our year, did put the royal diadem upon her head, and declared her queen in the place of Vashti; and in consequence thereof, made a solemn feast for his princes and servants, which was called Esther's feast; and, in honour of her, at the same time made a release of taxes to the provinces, and gave donatives and presents to all that attended him, according to the grandeur and dignity of his royal estate. *Haman*, an *Amalekite*, of the posterity of *Agag*, who was king of *Amalek*, in the time of *Saul*, growing to be the chief favourite of King *Artaxerxes*, all the king's servants were commanded to pay reverence unto him, and bow before him; and all of them obeyed the king's order but *Mordecai* the *Jew*, who, sitting in the king's gate, according to his office, paid not any reverence to *Haman* at such times as he passed by into the palace, neither bowed he at all to him; at which, being told, he was exceedingly displeased: but scorning to lay hands on one man only, and being informed that he was a *Jew*, he resolved, in revenge of this affront, to destroy, not only him, but also his whole nation with him; and to this act he was not a little excited by the ancient enmity which was between them and the people of whom he was descended; and therefore, for the accomplishing of this design, on the *first day* of the *first month*, that is, in the month *Nisan*, he called together his diviners, to find out what day would be the most fortunate for the putting this plan into execution: and they having, according to the manner of divination then in use among those Eastern people, cast lots first upon each month, did thereby determine for the *thirteenth* day of the twelfth month following, called *Adar*, as the day which they judged would be the most lucky for the accomplishing of what he purposed: whereon he forthwith went in unto the king; and having insinuated to him that there was a certain people dispersed all over his empire who did not keep the king's laws, but followed laws of their own, diverse from the laws of all other people, to the disturbance of the good order of his kingdom, and the breach of that uniformity whereby it ought to be governed; and that, therefore, it was not for the king's profit that they should any longer be suffered; he proposed, and gave counsel that they should be all destroyed and extirpated out of the whole empire of *Persia;* and urged it as that which was necessary for the establishing of the peace and good order of his government: to which having gained the king's consent, and an order that on the *thirteenth* day of *Adar* following, according as was determined by the divination of the lots, it should be put in execution, he called the king's scribes together to write the decree; and it being drawn as he proposed, on the *thirteenth* day of the same month of *Nisan* copies thereof were written out, and sent into all the provinces of the empire, commanding the king's lieutenants, governors, and all other his officers in every one of them, to destroy, kill, and cause to perish, all *Jews*, both young and old, little children and women, in one day, even on the *thirteenth* day of *Adar* following; and to take the spoil of them for a prey: which day was full *eleven* months after the date of the decree. The lot which seems to have pointed out that day appears to have been directed by the special providence of God, that so long a space intervening, there might be time enough to take such measures as should be proper to prevent the mischief intended. It is hard to find a reason for *Mordecai's* refusing to pay his respect to *Haman*, which may be sufficient to excuse him for thus exposing himself and all his nation to that destruction which it had like to have drawn upon them. That which is commonly said is, that it was the same adoration which was made to the king of *Persia;* and that, consisting in the bowing of the knee, and the prostration of the whole body to the ground, it was avoided by *Mordecai*, upon a notion which he had of its being idolatrous: but this being the common compliment paid to the kings of *Persia*, by all that were admitted into their presence, it was no doubt paid to this very king by *Ezra* and *Nehemiah*, when they had access to him, and after also by *Mordecai* himself; for otherwise he could not have obtained that admission into his presence, and that advancement in his palace, which was afterwards there granted unto him; and if it were not idolatrous to pay this adoration to the king, neither was it idolatrous to pay it to *Haman*. The Greeks would not pay this respect to the kings of *Persia* out of pride; and excepting *Themistocles*, and two or three others, none of them could ever be brought to it. I will not say that this was the case with *Mordecai* in respect to *Haman:* it seems most probable that it was from a cause that was personal in *Haman* only. Perhaps it was because *Haman*, being of the race of the *Amalekites*, he looked upon him as under the curse which God had denounced against that nation; and therefore thought himself obliged not to give that honour to him. And if all the rest of the Jews thought the same, this might seem reason enough to him to extend his wrath against the whole nation, and to meditate the destruction of them all in revenge. But whatever was the cause that induced *Mordecai* to refuse the payment of this respect to the king's favourite, this provoked that favourite to procure the decree above mentioned, for the utter extirpation of the whole *Jewish* nation in revenge for it. When *Mordecai* heard of this decree, he made great lamentation, as did also all the *Jews* of *Shushan* with him; and therefore, putting on sackcloth, he sat in this mournful garb without the king's gate, (for he would not be allowed to enter within it in that dress,) which being told *Esther*, she sent to him to know what the matter was. Whereon *Mordecai* acquainted her with the whole state of the case; and sent her a copy of the decree, that she might fully see the mischief that was intended her people; to absolutely destroy them, and root them out from the face of the earth: and therefore commanded her forthwith to go in unto the king and make supplication for them. At first she excused herself, because of the law, whereby it was ordained that whosoever, whether man or woman, should come in unto the king in the inner court who was not called for, should be put to death, excepting such only to whom the king should hold out the golden sceptre in his hand that he might live; and she was afraid of hazarding her life in this cause. Whereon *Mordecai*, sending to her, again told her, that the decree extended universally to all of her nation, without any exception, and that, if it came to execution, she must not expect to escape more than any other of her people; that Providence seemed to have advanced her on purpose for this work; but if she refused to act her part in it, then deliverance should come some other way, and she and her father's house should perish; for he was fully persuaded that God would not suffer his people to be thus totally destroyed.

"Whereon Esther, resolving to put her life on the hazard for the safety of her people, desired *Mordecai* that he and all the *Jews* then in *Shushan* should fast three days for her, and offer up prayer and humble supplication that God would prosper her in the undertaking: which being accordingly done, on the third day *Esther* put on her royal apparel and went in unto the king, while he was sitting upon his throne in the inner part of his palace. And as soon as he saw her standing in the court, he showed favour unto her, and held out his golden sceptre; and *Esther*, going near and touching the top of it, had thereby her life secured unto her: and when the king asked her what her petition was, at first she only desired that he and *Haman* would come to a banquet which she had prepared for him.

"And when *Haman* was called, and the king and he were at the banquet, he asked her again of her petition, promising it should be granted her to the half of his kingdom: but then she desired only that the king and *Haman* should come again to the like banquet on the next day, intimating that she would then make known her request unto him. Her intention in claiming thus to entertain the king twice at her banquet before she made known her petition unto him was, that thereby she might the more endear herself unto him, and dispose him the better to grant the request which she had to make unto him.

"*Haman*, being proud of the honour of being thus admitted alone with the king to the queen's banquet, went home to his house much puffed up: but on his return thither, seeing *Mordecai* sitting at the gate of the palace, and still refusing to bow unto him; this moved his indignation to such a degree, that on his coming to his house, and calling his friends about him to relate to them the great honour that was done to him by the king and queen, and the high advancement which he had obtained in the kingdom, he could not forbear complaining of the disrespect and affront that was offered him by *Mordecai*. Whereon they advised him to cause a gallows to be built of *fifty* cubits in height, and next morning to ask the king to have *Mordecai* hanged thereon: and accordingly he ordered the gallows immediately to be made; and went early the next morning to the palace, for the obtaining of the grant from the king to have *Mordecai* hanged on it. But that morning the king awaking sooner than ordinary, and not being able to compose himself again to sleep, he called for the book of the records and chronicles of the kingdom, and caused them to be read unto him; wherein finding an account of the conspiracy of *Bigthan* and *Teresh*, and that it was discovered by *Mordecai* the *Jew*, the king inquired what honour had been done to him for the same. And being told that nothing had been done for him, he inquired who was in the court; and being told that *Haman* was standing there, he ordered him to be called in, and asked of him what should be done to the man whom the king delighted to honour: whereon *Haman*, thinking this honour was intended for himself, gave advice that the royal apparel should be brought which the king used to wear, and the horse which he kept for his own riding, and the crown which used to be set upon his head; and that this apparel and horse should be delivered into the hands of one of the king's most noble princes, that he might array therewith the man whom the king delighted to honour, and bring him on horseback through the whole city, and proclaim before him, 'Thus shall it be done to the man whom the king delighteth to honour.' Whereon the king commanded him forthwith to take the apparel and horse, and do this to *Mordecai* the *Jew*, who sat in the king's gate, in reward for his discovery of the treason of the two eunuchs: all which *Haman* having been forced to do in obedience to the king's command, he returned with great sorrow to his house, lamenting the disappointment and great mortification he had met with in being thus forced to pay such signal honour to his enemy, whom he had intended to have hanged on the gallows which he had provided for him. And on his relating this to his friends, they all told him, that if this *Mordecai* were of the seed of the *Jews*, this bad omen foreboded that he should not prevail against them, but should surely fall before him. While they were thus talking, one of the queen's chamberlains came to *Haman's* house to hasten him to the banquet: and seeing the gallows which had been set up the night before, fully informed himself of the intent for which it was prepared. On the king's and Haman's sitting down to the banquet, the king asked again of *Esther* what was her petition, with like promise that it should be granted to her to the half of his kingdom: whereon she humbly prayed the king that her life might be given her on her petition, and her people at her request; for that a design was laid for the destruction of her and all her kindred and nation. At which the king asking, with much anger, who it was that durst do this thing, she told him that *Haman* then present was the author of the wicked plot; and laid the whole of it open to the king. Whereon the king rose up with much wrath from the banquet, and walked out into the garden adjoining; which *Haman* perceiving, he fell down before the queen upon the bed on which she was sitting, to supplicate for his life; in which posture the king having found him upon his return, spoke out in great passion, What, will he force the queen before me in the house? At which words the servants present immediately covered his face, as was then the usage to condemned persons; and the chamberlain, who had that day called *Haman* to the banquet, acquainting the king with the gallows he saw in his house there prepared for *Mordecai*, who had saved the king's life in detecting the treason of the two eunuchs, the king ordered that he should be forthwith hanged thereon, which was accordingly done; and all his house, goods, and riches, were given to *Queen Esther;* and she appointed *Mordecai* to be her steward to manage the same. On the same day the queen made the king acquainted with the relation which *Mordecai* had unto her; whereon the king took him into his favour, and advanced him to great power, riches, and dignity in the empire; and made him the keeper of his signet, in the same manner as *Haman* had been be ore. But still the decree for the destruction of the *Jews* remaining in its full force, the queen petitioned the king a second time to put away this mischief from them; but, according to the laws of the *Medes* and *Persians*, nothing being to be reversed which had been decreed and written in the king's name, and sealed with the king's seal, and the decree procured by *Haman* against the *Jews* having been thus written and sealed, it could not be recalled. All therefore that the king could do, in compliance with her request, was, to give the *Jews*, by a new decree, such a power to defend themselves against such as should assault them, as might render the former decree ineffectual: and for that end he bid *Esther* and *Mordecai* draw such a decree in words as strong as could be devised, that so the former might be hindered from being executed, though it could not be annulled. And therefore the king's scribes being again called on the *twenty-third* day of the *third* month, a new decree was drawn just *two* months and *ten* days after the former; wherein the king granted to the *Jews*, which were in every city of the *Persian* empire, full license to gather themselves together and stand for their lives; and to destroy, slay, and cause to perish, all the power of the people and province that should assault them, with their little ones and women, and to take the spoil of them for a prey. And this decree being written in the king's hand, and sealed with his seal, copies thereof were drawn out, and especial messengers were despatched with them into all the provinces of the empire.

"The *thirteenth* day of *Adar* drawing near, when the decree obtained by *Haman* for the destruction of the *Jews* was to be put into execution, their adversaries everywhere prepared to act against them, according to the contents of it: and the *Jews*, on the other hand, by virtue of the second decree which was obtained in their favour, by *Esther* and *Mordecai*, gathered themselves together in every city where they dwelt, throughout all the provinces of King *Artaxerxes*, to provide for their safety: so that on the said *thirteenth* of *Adar*, through the means of these two different and discordant decrees, a war was commenced between the *Jews* and their enemies throughout the whole *Persian* empire. But the rulers of the provinces, and the lieutenants, the deputies, and the other officers of the king, knowing with what power *Esther* and *Mordecai* were then invested, through fear of them so favoured the *Jews*, that they prevailed everywhere against those that rose against them; and on that day, throughout the whole empire, slew of their enemies *seven thousand five hundred* persons; and in the city of *Shushan*, on that day and the next, *eight hundred* more; among whom were the ten sons of *Haman*, whom by a special order from the king they caused all to be hanged; perhaps upon the same gallows on which *Haman*, their father, had been hanged before. These transactions took place in the *hirteenth* year of *Artaxerxes*, about *four hundred and fifty-two* years before Christ." *The reader is requested to refer to the notes on all these passages.*

"The Jews, being delivered thus from this dangerous design which threatened them with nothing less than total extirpation, made great rejoicings for it on the two days following, that is, on the *fourteenth* and *fifteenth* days of the said month *Adar:* and by the order of *Esther* and *Mordecai* these two days, with the *thirteenth* that preceded them, were set apart, and consecrated to be annually observed for ever after in commemoration thereof; the *thirteenth* as a fast, because of the destruction on that day intended to have been brought upon them, and the other *two* as a feast because of their deliverance from it; and both this fast and feast they constantly observe every year on those days, even to this time. The fast they call the fast of *Esther;* and the feast, the feast of *Purim*, from the Persian word *Purim*, which signifies lots; because it was by the casting of lots that *Haman* did set out this time for their destruction. This feast is the *Bacchanals* of the *Jews*, which they celebrate with all manner of rejoicing, mirth, and jollity; and therein indulge themselves in all manner of luxurious excesses, especially in drinking wine, even to drunkenness; which they think part of the duty of the solemnity, because it was by means of the wine banquet, they say, that *Esther* made the king's heart merry, and brought him into that good humour which inclined him to grant the request which she made unto him for their deliverance; and therefore they think they ought to make their hearts merry also, when they celebrate the commemoration of it. During this festival the book of *Esther* is solemnly read in all their synagogues from the beginning to the end; at which they are all to be present, men, women, children, and servants, because all these had their part in this deliverance which *Esther* obtained for them. And as often as the name of *Haman* occurs in the reading of this book, the usage is for them all to clap with their hands, and stamp with their feet, and cry out: *Let his memory perish.*

"This is the last feast of the year among them, for the next that follows is the *Passover,* which always falls in the middle of the month, which begins the *Jewish* year."

THE BOOK

OF

ESTHER

_____

Chronological Notes relative to this Book

Year from the Creation, according to Archbishop Usher, 3540.—Year before the birth of Christ, 460.—
Year before the vulgar era of Christ's nativity, 464.—Year of the Julian Period, 4250.—Year since the
flood of Noah, 1904.—Year of the Cali Yuga, or Indian era of the Deluge, 2638.—Year from the vocation of Abram, 1458.—Year from the destruction of Troy, 721.—Year from the foundation of Solomon's
temple, 547.—Year since the division of Solomon's monarchy into the kingdoms of Israel and Judah,
511.—Year of the era of Iphitus, 421.—Year since Corœbus won the prize at the Olympic games, 313.
—First year of the _seventy-ninth_ Olympiad.—Year of the Varronian era of the building of Rome, 290.—
Year from the building of Rome, according to Cato and the Fasti Consulares, 289.—Year from the building of Rome according to Polybius the historian, 288.—Year from the building of Rome, according to
Fabius Pictor, 284.—Year of the era of Nabonassar, 284.—Year since the commencement of the first
Messenian war, 280.—Year since the destruction of the kingdom of Israel by Shalmaneser, the king of
Assyria, 258.—Year since the commencement of the second Messenian war, 222.—Year from the destruction of Solomon's temple by Nebuchadnezzar, king of Babylon, 125.—Year since the publication
of the famous edict of Cyrus, king of Persia, empowering the Jews to rebuild their temple, 72.—Year since
the conquest of Egypt by Cambyses, 62.—Year since the abolition of the tyranny of the Pisistratidæ
at Athens, 43.—Year since the expulsion of the Tarquins from Rome, which put an end to the regal
government of the Romans, 44.—Year since the famous battle of Marathon, 26.—Year after the commencement of the _third_ Messenian war, 2.—Year before the commencement of the _first_ sacred war concerning the temple at Delphi, 17.—Year before the commencement of the celebrated Peloponnesian
war, 34.—Year before the celebrated retreat of the _ten thousand_ Greeks, and the expulsion of the _thirty_
tyrants from Athens by Thrasybulus, 65.—Year before the commencement of the era of the Seleucidæ,
152.—Year before the formation of the famous Achæan league, 183.—Year before the commencement
of the first Punic war, 200.—Year before the fall of the Macedonian empire, 296.—Year before the destruction of Carthage by Scipio, and of Corinth by Mummius, 317.—Year before the commencement
of the Jugurthine war, which continued _five_ years, 354.—Year before the commencement of the Social
war, which continued for _five_ years, and was finished by Sylla, 374.—Year before the commencement
of the Mithridatic war, which continued for _twenty-six_ years, 376.—Year before the commencement
of the Servile war, under Spartacus, 392.—Year before the extinction of the reign of the Seleucidæ in
Syria, on the conquest of that country by Pompey, 399.—Year before the era of the Roman emperors,
433.—Year of Archidamus, king of Lacedæmon, and of the family of the Proclidæ, or Eurypontidæ, 6.
—Year of Plistoanax, king of Lacedæmon, and of the family of the Eurysthenidæ, or Agidæ, 3.—Year
of Alexander, the _tenth_ king of Macedon, 34.—Year of Artaxerxes Longimanus, king of Persia, 1.—
Roman Consuls, Aulus Postumius, and Sp. Furius.

_____

CHAPTER I

Ahasuerus makes royal feasts for his nobles and people, 1–9. Vashti is sent for by the king, but refuses to come,
10–12. Vashti is disgraced; and a law made for the subjection of women, 13–22.

A. M. 3540
B. C. 464
A. U. C. 290
Coss. Rom.
A. Postumio et
Sp. Furio

NOW it came to pass in the
days of ᵃAhasuerus, (this
_is_ Ahasuerus which reigned
ᵇfrom India even unto Ethiopia,
ᶜover a hundred and seven and
twenty provinces:)

2 _That_ in those days, when the
king Ahasuerus ᵈsat on the

A. M. 3540
B. C. 464
A. U. C. 290
Coss. Rom.
A. Postumio et
Sp. Furio

_____

ᵃEzra iv. 6; Dan. ix. 1——ᵇChap. viii. 9

ᶜDan. vi. 1; 1 Esd. iii. 2——ᵈ1 Kings i. 46

_____

The whole history of this book in its _con-_
nected order, with the occurrences in the
Persian empire at that time, will be found in

the _introduction;_ to which the reader is referred.

Concerning the _author_ of this book there are

A. M. 3542
B. C. 462
A. U. C. 292
Coss. Rom.
Tricipitino et
T. V. Gemino

throne of his kingdom, which *was* in ^eShushan the palace,

3 In the third year of his reign, he ^fmade a feast unto all his princes and his servants: the power of Persia

and Media, the nobles and princes of the provinces *being* before him:

4 When he showed the riches of his glorious kingdom and the honour of his

A. M. 3542
B. C. 462
A. U. C. 292
Coss. Rom.
Tricipitino et
T. V. Gemino

---

^eNeh. i. 1

^fGen. xl. 20; chap. ii. 18; Mark vi. 21

---

several opinions: some attribute the work to *Ezra;* some to one *Joachim,* a high priest; others, to the *men of the Great Synagogue;* and others to *Mordecai.* This latter is the most likely opinion: nor is that to be disregarded which gives to *Mordecai* for co-partner *Ezra* himself; though it is likely that the conclusion, from chap. ix. 23 to the end of the book, was inserted by another hand, and at a later time. Though some Christians have hesitated to receive the book of Esther into the sacred canon; yet it has always been received by the Jews, not only as perfectly *authentic,* but also as one of the most excellent of their sacred books. They call it מגילה *megillah,* THE VOLUME, by way of eminence; and hold it in the highest estimation. That it records the history of a real fact, the observation of the feast of *Purim,* to the present day, is a sufficient evidence. Indeed, this is one of the strongest evidences that any fact can have, viz., that, to commemorate it, a certain rite, procession, feast, or the like, should have been instituted at the time, which, without intermission, has been continued annually through every generation of *that people,* and in whatsoever place they or parties of them may have sojourned, to the present day. This is the fact concerning the feast of *Purim* here mentioned; which the Jews, in all places of their dispersion, have uninterruptedly celebrated, and do still continue to celebrate, from the time of their deliverance from the massacre intended by Haman to the present time. *Copies* of this book, widely differing from each other, exist in *Hebrew, Chaldee, Syriac, Greek,* and *Latin.* All these differ much from the *Hebrew* text, particularly the *Greek* and the *Chaldee:* the former has many additional paragraphs; and the latter, as it exists in the *London Polyglot,* contains five times more than the *Hebrew* text. To notice all the various readings, additions, and paraphrases, in the above copies, would require a volume of no inconsiderable magnitude. The reader who is curious may consult the above *Polyglot.* This book does not appear to be extant in *Arabic,* or in any other of the Oriental languages, besides the *Hebrew* and *Syriac.*

The question may naturally arise, What was the original of this book? or, In what language was it written? Though learned men in general decide in favour of a *Hebrew* original, yet there are many reasons which might be urged in favour of the *Persian.* Several of the proper names are evidently of a *Persian* origin; and no doubt all the others are so; but they are so transformed by passing through the *Hebrew,* that they are no longer discernible. The *Hebrew* has even retained some of the Persian words, having done little else than alter the character, e. g., *Esther, Mehuman, Mishak, Melzar, Vashti, Shushan, Pur, Darius, Paradise,* &c., several of which will be noted in their proper places. The *Targum* in the *London Polyglot* is widely different from that in the *Complutum,*

Antwerp, and *Paris* editions. The principal additions in the *Greek* are carefully marked in the *London Polyglot,* but are too long and too numerous to be inserted here. It is a singular circumstance that the *name of God* does not once occur in the whole of this book as it stands in Hebrew.

NOTES ON CHAP. I

Verse 1. *Now it came to pass*] The *Ahasuerus* of the *Romans,* the *Artaxerxes* of the *Greeks,* and *Ardsheer* of the *Persians,* are the same. Some think that this *Ahasuerus* was *Darius,* the son of *Hystaspes;* but *Prideaux* and others maintain that he was *Artaxerxes Longimanus.*

Reigned from India even unto Ethiopia] This is nearly the same account that is given by Xenophon. How great and glorious the kingdom of Cyrus was beyond all the kingdoms of Asia, was evident from this: Ὡρισθη μεν πρως εῳ τῃ Ερυθρᾳ θαλαττῃ· προσ αρκτον δε τῳ Ευξεινῳ ποντῳ· προς ἑσπεραν δε Κυπρῳ και Αιγυπτῳ· προς μεσημβριαν δε Αιθιοπιᾳ. "It was bounded on the east by the Red Sea; on the north by the Euxine Sea; on the west by Cyprus and Egypt; and on the south by Ethiopia."—CYROP. lib. viii., p. 241, edit. *Steph.* 1581.

Verse 2. *Sat on the throne of his kingdom*] Having subdued all his enemies, and brought universal peace to his empire. See the commencement of the *introduction.*

Shushan the palace] The ancient city of Susa, now called شُستر *Shuster* by the Persians. This, with Ecbatana and Babylon, was a residence of the Persian kings. The word הבירה *habbirah,* which we render *the palace,* should be rendered *the city,* εν Σουσοις τῃ πολει, as in the *Septuagint.*

Verse 4. *The riches of his glorious kingdom*] Luxury was the characteristic of the Eastern monarchs, and particularly of the *Persians.* In their feasts, which were superb and of long continuance, they made a general exhibition of their wealth, grandeur, &c., and received the highest encomiums from their poets and flatterers. Their ostentation on such occasions passed into a proverb: hence *Horace*—

Persicos *odi, puer,* apparatus:
Displicent nexæ philyra coronæ;
Mitte sectari, rosa quo locorum
Sera moretur.

I tell thee, boy, that I detest
The grandeur of a *Persian feast;*
Nor for me the linden's rind
Shall the flowery chaplet bind.
   Then search not where the curious rose
Beyond his season loitering grows.
                     FRANCIS.

A. M. 3542
B. C. 462
A. U. C. 292
Coss. Rom.
Tricipitino et
T. V. Gemino

excellent majesty many days, *even* a hundred and fourscore days.

5 And when these days were expired, the king made a feast unto all the people that were ᵍpresent in Shushan the palace, both unto great and small, seven days, in the court of the garden of the king's palace;

6 *Where were* white, green, and ʰblue *hangings,* fastened with cords of fine linen and purple to silver rings and pillars of marble: ⁱthe beds *were of* gold and silver, upon a pavement ᵏof red, and blue, and white, and black marble.

7 And they gave *them* drink in vessels of gold, (the vessels being diverse one from another,) and ˡroyal wine in abundance, ᵐaccording to the state of the king.

8 And the drinking *was* according to the law; none did compel: for so the king had appointed to all the officers of his house, that they should do according to every man's pleasure.

9 Also Vashti the queen made a feast for the women *in* the royal house which *belonged* to King Ahasuerus.

10 On the seventh day, when ⁿthe heart

A. M. 3542
B. C. 462
A. U. C. 292
Coss. Rom.
Tricipitino et
T. V. Gemino

—ᵍHebrew, *found*——ʰOr, *violet*——ⁱSee chapter vii. 8; Ezekiel xxiii. 41; Amos ii. 8; vi. 4——ᵏOr, *of porphyry, and marble, and alabaster, and stone of*

blue colour——ˡHeb. *wine of the kingdom*——ᵐHeb. *according to the hand of the king*——ⁿ2 Samuel xiii. 28

Verse 5. *A feast unto all the people*] The first was a feast for the *nobles* in general; this, for the *people* of the city at large.

In the court of the garden] As the company was very numerous that was to be received, no apartments in the palace could be capable of containing them; therefore the *court of the garden* was chosen.

Verse 6. *White, green, and blue* hangings] It was customary, on such occasions, not only to hang the place about with elegant curtains of the above colours, as Dr. Shaw and others have remarked, but also to have a *canopy* of rich stuffs suspended on cords from side to side of the place in which they feasted. And such courts were ordinarily paved with *different coloured marbles*, or with *tiles* painted, as above specified. And this was the origin of the *Musive* or *Mosaic work*, well known among the Asiatics, and borrowed from them by the *Greeks* and the *Romans*.

The *beds of gold and silver* mentioned here were the couches covered with gold and silver cloth, on which the guests reclined.

Verse 7. *Vessels being diverse*] They had different services of *plate*.

Verse 8. *None did compel: for so the king had appointed*] Every person drank what he pleased; he was not obliged to take more than he had reason to think would do him good.

Among the Greeks, each guest was obliged to *keep the round*, or leave the company: hence the proverb H πιθι, η απιθι; *Drink* or *begone*. To this *Horace* refers, but gives more license:—

Pasco libatis dapibus; prout cuique libido est,
Siccat inæquales calices conviva, solutus
Legibus insanis: seu quis capit acria fortis
Pocula; seu modicis humescit ætius.
      Horat. *Sat.* lib. ii., s. vi., ver. 67.

There, every guest may drink and fill
As *much* or *little* as *he will;*
Exempted from the *Bedlam rules*
Of roaring prodigals and fools,
Whether, in merry mood or whim,
He *fills his goblet to the brim;*
Or, *better pleased to let it pass,*
Is cheerful with a *moderate glass.*
                Francis.

At the Roman feasts there was a person chosen by the cast of *dice*, who was the *Arbiter bibendi*, and prescribed rules to the company, which all were obliged to observe. References to this custom may be seen in the same poet. Odar. lib. i., *Od.* iv., ver. 18:—

   Non regna vini sortiere talis.

And in lib. ii., *Od.* vii., ver. 25:—

  —— Quem Venus arbitrum
  Dicet bibendi?

Mr. *Herbert*, in his excellent poem, *The Church Porch*, has five verses on this vile custom and its rule:—

Drink not the *third glass*, which thou canst not *tame*
When once it is within thee, but before
Mayst rule it as thou list; and pour the shame,
Which it would pour on thee, upon the floor.
It is most just to throw that on the ground,
Which would throw me there if I *keep the round.*
He that is drunken may his mother kill,
Big with his sister; he hath lost the reins;
Is outlaw'd by himself. All kinds of ill
Did with his liquor slide into his veins.
The *drunkard* forfeits *man;* and doth divest
All worldly right, save what he hath by *beast.*

Nothing too severe can be said on this destructive practice.

Verse 9. *Also Vashti the queen*] دشتي

Vashti is a mere *Persian* word; and signifies a *beautiful* or *excellent woman*.

Made a feast for the women] The king, having subdued all his enemies, left no competitor for the kingdom; and being thus quietly and firmly seated on the throne, made this a time of *general* festivity. As the *women* of the East never mingle with the men in public, Vashti made a feast for the Persian ladies by themselves; and while the men were *in the court of the garden*, the women were *in the royal house*.

Verse 10. *He commanded Mehuman*] All these are doubtless *Persian* names; but so disguised by passing through a Hebrew medium,

A. M. 3542
B. C. 462
A. U. C. 292
Coss. Rom.
Tricipitino et
T. V. Gemino

of the king was merry with wine, he commanded Mehuman, Biztha, [o]Harbona, Bigtha, and Abagtha, Zethar, and Carcas, the seven [p]chamberlains that served in the presence of Ahasuerus the king,

11 To bring Vashti the queen before the king with the crown royal, to show the people and the princes her beauty: for she *was* [q]fair to look on.

12 But the queen Vashti refused to come at the king's commandment [r]by *his* chamberlains: therefore was the king very wroth, and his anger burned in him.

13 Then the king said to the [s]wise men, [t]which knew the times, (for so *was* the king's manner toward all that knew law and judgment:

14 And the next unto him *was* Carshena, Shethar, Admatha, Tarshish, Meres, Marsena, *and* Memucan, the [u]seven princes of Persia and Media, [v]which saw the king's face, *and* which sat the first in the kingdom;)

A. M. 3542
B. C. 462
A. U. C. 292
Coss. Rom.
Tricipitino et
T. V. Gemino

15 [w]What shall we do unto the queen Vashti according to law, because she hath not performed the commandment of the king Ahasuerus by the chamberlains?

16 And Memucan answered before the king and the princes, Vashti the queen hath not done wrong to the king only, but also to all the princes, and to all the people that are in all the provinces of the king Ahasuerus.

17 For *this* deed of the queen shall come abroad unto all women, so that they shall [x]despise their husbands in their eyes, when it shall be reported, The king Ahasuerus commanded Vashti the queen to be brought in before him, but she came not.

18 *Likewise* shall the ladies of Persia and Media say this day unto all the king's princes, which have heard of the deed of the queen. Thus *shall there arise* too much contempt and wrath.

19 [y]If it please the king, let there go a royal

---

[o]Chap. vii. 9——[p]Or, *eunuchs*——[q]Heb. *good of countenance*——[r]Heb. *which* was *by the hand of* his *eunuchs*——[s]Jer. x. 7; Dan. ii. 12; Matt. ii. 1

[t]1 Chron. xii. 32——[u]Ezra vii. 14——[v]2 Kings xxv. 19——[w]Heb. *What to do*——[x]Eph. v. 33——[y]Heb. *If it be good with the king*

---

that some of them can scarcely be known. مهمان *Mehuman* signifies a *stranger* or *guest.* We shall find other names and words in this book, the Persian etymology of which may be easily traced.

Verse 11. *To bring Vashti the queen*] The Targum adds *naked.*

For she was *fair to look on.*] Hence she had her name وشتي *Vashti,* which signifies *beautiful.* See verse 9.

Verse 12. *Vashti refused to come*] And much should she be commended for it. What woman, possessing even a common share of *prudence* and *modesty,* could consent to expose herself to the view of such a group of drunken Bacchanalians? Her *courage* was equal to her modesty: she would resist the royal mandate, rather than violate the rules of *chaste decorum.* Her *contempt* of *worldly grandeur,* when brought in competition with what every modest woman holds dear and sacred, is worthy of observation. She well knew that this act of disobedience would cost her her *crown,* if not her *life* also: but she was regardless of both, as she conceived her virtue and honour were at stake.

Her *humility* was greatly evidenced in this refusal. She was *beautiful;* and might have shown herself to great advantage, and have had a fine opportunity of gratifying her vanity, if she had any: but *she refused to come.*

Hail, noble woman! be thou a pattern to all thy sex on every similar occasion! Surely, every thing considered, we have few women like Vashti; for some of the highest of the land will dress and deck themselves with the utmost splendour, even to the *selvedge* of their fortunes, to exhibit themselves at balls, plays, galas, operas, and public assemblies of all kinds, (nearly half naked,) that they may be seen and admired of men, and even, to the endless reproach and broad suspicion of their honour and chastity, figure away in *masquerades!* Vashti must be considered at the top of her sex:—

Rara avis in terris, nigroque simillima cygno.

A *black swan* is not half so *rare* a bird.

Verse 13. *To the wise men*] Probably the *lawyers.*

Verse 14. *And the next unto him—the seven princes*] Probably, the privy counsellors of the king. *Which saw the king's face*—were at all times admitted to the royal presence.

Verse 16. *Vashti—hath not done wrong to the king only*] This reasoning or arguing was inconsequent and false. Vashti had not *generally* disobeyed the king, therefore she could be no *precedent* for the *general* conduct of the Persian women. She disobeyed only in *one particular;* and this, to serve a purpose, Memucan draws into a *general consequence;* and the rest came to the conclusion which he drew, being either too drunk to be able to discern *right* from *wrong,* or too intent on reducing the women to a state of vassalage, to neglect the present favourable opportunity.

Verse 18. *The ladies of Persia*] שרות *saroth,* the *princesses;* but the meaning is very well expressed by our term *ladies.*

Verse 19. *That it be not altered*] Let it be inserted among the *permanent laws,* and made a part of the *constitution* of the empire. Per-

A. M. 3542
B. C. 462
A. U. C. 292
Coss. Rom.
Tricipitino et
T. V. Gemino

commandment [z]from him, and let it be written among the laws of the Persians and the Medes, [a]that it be not altered, That Vashti come no more before King Ahasuerus; and let the king give her royal estate [b]unto another that is better than she.

20 And when the king's decree which he shall make shall be published throughout all his empire, (for it is great,) all the wives shall [c]give to their husbands honour, both to great and small.

21 And the saying [d]pleased the king and the princes; and the king did according to the word of Memucan;

22 For he sent letters into all the king's provinces, [e]into every province according to the writing thereof, and to every people after their language, that every man should [f]bear rule in his own house, and [g]that *it* should be published according to the language of every people.

A. M. 3542
B. C. 462
A. U. C. 292
Coss. Rom.
Tricipitino et
T. V. Gemino

---

[z]Heb. *from before him*——[a]Heb. *that it pass not away*, chap. viii. 8; Dan. vi. 8, 12, 15——[b]Heb. *unto her companion*——[c]Eph. v. 33; Col. iii. 18; 1 Pet. iii. 1

[d]Heb. *was good in the eyes of the king*——[e]Ch. viii. 9 [f]Eph. v. 22, 23, 24; 1 Tim. ii. 12——[g]Heb. *that one should publish it according to the language of his people*

---

haps the Persians affected such a degree of *wisdom* in the construction of their laws, that they *never could be amended*, and should never be *repeated*. And this we may understand to be the ground of the saying, *The laws of the Medes and Persians, that change not*.

Verse 22. *That every man should bear rule in his own house*] Both God's law and common sense taught this from the foundation of the world. And is it possible that this did not obtain in the Persian empire, previously to this edict? The *twentieth* verse has another clause, *That all wives shall give to their husbands honour, both to great and small*. This also was universally understood. This law did nothing.

I suppose the parade of enactment was only made to deprive honest Vashti of her crown. The Targum adds, "That each woman should speak the language of her husband." If she were even a *foreigner*, she should be obliged to learn and speak the language of the king. Perhaps there might be some common sense in this, as it would oblige the foreigner to devote much time to study and improvement; and, consequently, to make her a better woman, and a better wife. But there is no proof that this was a part of the decree. But there are so many additions to this book in the principal versions, that we know not what might have made a part of it originally.

CHAPTER II

The counsellors advise that a selection of virgins should be made throughout the empire, out of whom the king should choose one to be queen in place of Vashti, 1-4. Account of Mordecai and his cousin Esther, 5-7. She is chosen among the young women, and is placed under the care of Hegai, the king's chamberlain, to go through a year's purification, 8-11. The manner in which these young women were introduced to the king, and how those were disposed of who were not called again to the king's bed, 12-14. Esther pleases the king, and is set above all the women; and he makes her queen in the place of Vashti, and does her great honour, 15-20. Mordecai, sitting at the king's gate, discovers a conspiracy formed against the king's life by two of his chamberlains; he informs the king, the matter is investigated, they are found guilty and hanged, and the transaction is recorded, 21-23.

A. M. 3543
B. C. 461
A. U. C. 293
Coss. Rom.
P. Volumnio et
S. Sulpicio

AFTER these things, when the wrath of King Ahasuerus was appeased, he remembered Vashti, and what she had done, and [a]what was decreed against her.

2 Then said the king's servants that ministered unto him, Let there be fair young virgins sought for the king:

3 And let the king appoint officers in all the provinces of his kingdom, that they may gather together all the fair young virgins unto Shushan the palace, to the house of the women, [b]unto the custody of [c]Hege the king's chamberlain, keeper of the women; and let their things for purification be given *them*:

A. M. 3543
B. C. 461
A. U. C. 293
Coss. Rom.
P. Volumnio et
S. Sulpicio

---

[a]Chap. i. 19, 20——[b]Heb. *unto the hand*

[c]Or, *Hegai*, ver. 8

NOTES ON CHAP. II

Verse 2. *Let there be fair young virgins sought for the king*] This was the usual way in which the *harem* or *seraglio* was furnished: the finest women in the land, whether of high or low birth, were sought out, and brought to the *harem*. They all became the king's concubines:

but *one* was raised, as *chief wife* or *sultana*, to the throne; and her issue was specially entitled to inherit.

Verse 3. *Hege the king's chamberlain*] הגא סריס המלך *Hege seris hammelech*, "Hege, the king's *eunuch*;" so the Septuagint, Vulgate, Targum, and Syriac. In the Eastern countries

A. M. 3543
B. C. 461
A. U. C. 293
Coss. Rom.
P. Volumnio et
S. Sulpicio

4 And let the maiden which pleaseth the king be queen instead of Vashti. And the thing pleased the king; and he did so.

5 *Now* in Shushan the palace there was a certain Jew, whose name *was* Mordecai, the son of Jair, the son of Shimei, the son of Kish, a Benjamite;

6 [d]Who had been carried away from Jerusalem with the captivity which had been carried away with [e]Jeconiah king of Judah, whom Nebuchadnezzar the king of Babylon had carried away.

7 And he [f]brought up Hadassah, that *is,* Esther, [g]his uncle's daughter: for she had neither father nor mother, and the maid *was* [h]fair and beautiful; whom Mordecai, when her father and mother were dead, took for his own daughter.

8 So it came to pass, when the king's commandment and his decree was heard, and when many maidens were [i]gathered together unto Shushan the palace, to the custody of Hegai,

that Esther was brought also unto the king's house to the custody of Hegai, keeper of the women.

A. M. 3543
B. C. 461
A. U. C. 293
Coss. Rom.
P. Volumnio et
S. Sulpicio

9 And the maiden pleased him, and she obtained kindness of him; and he speedily gave her her [k]things for purification, with [l]such things as belonged to her, and seven maidens *which were* meet to be given her out of the king's house: and [m]he preferred her and her maids unto the best *place* of the house of the women.

10 [n]Esther had not showed her people nor her kindred: for Mordecai had charged her that she should not show *it.*

11 And Mordecai walked every day before the court of the women's house, [o]to know how Esther did, and what should become of her.

12 Now when every maid's turn was come to go in to King Ahasuerus, after that she had been twelve months, according

A. M. 3546
B. C. 458
A. U. C. 296
Coss. Rom.
L. Minucio et
C. Nautio 2

---

[d]2 Kings xxiv. 14, 15; 2 Chron. xxxvi. 10, 20; Jer. xxiv. 1——[e]Or, *Jehoiachin,* 2 Kings xxiv. 6——[f]Heb. *nourished,* Eph. vi. 4——[g]Ver. 15

[h]Heb. *fair of form, and good of countenance*——[i]Ver. 3 [k]Ver. 3, 12——[l]Heb. *her portions*——[m]Heb. *he changed her*——[n]Ver. 20——[o]Heb. *to know the peace*

---

the women are intrusted to the care of the *eunuchs* only.

Let their things for purification be given them] תמרקיהן *tamrukeyhen,* their *cosmetics.* What these were we are told in ver. 12; *oil of myrrh,* and *sweet odours.* The myrrh was employed for *six* months, and the odours for *six* months more, after which the person was brought to the king. This space was sufficient to show whether the young woman had been *chaste;* whether she were with *child* or not, that the king might not be imposed on, and be obliged to father a spurious offspring, which might have been the case had not this precaution been used.

Instead of the *oil of myrrh,* the Targum says it was the oil of unripe olives, which caused the hair to fall off, and rendered the skin delicate.

Verse 5. *Whose name* was *Mordecai*] The Targum says, "He was the son of Jair, the son of Shimea, the son of Gera, the son of Kish." And "this was the same Shimea that cursed David; and whom David forbade Joab to slay because he saw, in the spirit of prophecy, that he was to be the predecessor of *Esther* and *Mordecai;* but when he became *old,* and incapable of having children, David ordered Solomon to put him to death."

Verse 7. *He brought up Hadassah*] הדסה *hadassah* signifies a *myrtle* in Chaldee: this was probably her first or *Babylonish name.* When she came to the *Persian* court, she was called *Esther,* استر *aster,* or ستاره *sitara,* which signifies a *star* in Persian: the name is undoubtedly Persian. Esther was the daughter of Abihail, the uncle of Mordecai, and there-

fore must have been Mordecai's cousin, though the Vulgate and Josephus make her Mordecai's *niece:* but it is safest here to follow the Hebrew.

Verse 9. *The maiden pleased him*] He conceived a partiality for her above the rest, probably because of the propriety of his deportment, and her engaging though unassuming manners.

Seven maidens] These were to attend her to the *bath,* to anoint and adorn her, and be her servants in general.

Verse 10. *Esther had not showed her people*] This might have prejudiced her with the king; for it was certainly no credit at the Persian court to be a *Jew;* and we shall find from the sequel that those who were in the Persian dominions were far from being *reputable,* or in a *safe state.* Besides, had her lineage been known, envy might have prevented her from ever having access to the king.

Verse 12. *Six months with oil of myrrh*] See on ver. 3. The reason of this purification seems not to be apprehended by any writer I have seen. The most beautiful of all the young virgins of all the provinces of Babylon were to be selected; and these were taken out of all *classes* of the people, indiscriminately; consequently there must have been many who were brought up in low life. Now we know that those who feed on coarse strong food, which is not easily digested, have generally a copious perspiration, which is strongly odorous; and in many, though in every respect amiable, and even beautiful, this odour is far from being pleasant. Pure, wholesome, easily digested, and nourishing aliment, with the frequent use of the *hot bath,* continued for twelve months, the body fre-

A. M. 3546
B. C. 458
A. U. C. 296
Coss. Rom.
L. Minucio et
C. Nautio 2
to the manner of the women, (for so were the days of their purification accomplished, *to wit,* six months with oil of myrrh, and six months with sweet odours, and with *other* things for the purifying of the women;)

13 Then thus came *every* maiden unto the king; whatsoever she desired was given her to go with her out of the house of the women unto the king's house.

14 In the evening she went, and on the morrow she returned into the second house of the women, to the custody of Shaashgaz, the king's chamberlain, which kept the concubines: she came in unto the king no more, except the king delighted in her, and that she were called by name.

15 Now when the turn of Esther, ᵖthe daughter of Abihail the uncle of Mordecai, who had taken her for his daughter, was come to go in unto the king, she required nothing but what Hegai the king's chamberlain, the keeper of the women, appointed. And Esther obtained favour in the sight of all them that looked upon her.

16 So Esther was taken unto King Aha-suerus into his house royal in the tenth month, which *is* the month Tebeth, in the seventh year of his reign.

A. M. 3546
B. C. 458
A. U. C. 296
Coss. Rom.
L. Minucio et
C. Nautio 2

17 And the king loved Esther above all the women, and she obtained grace and ᑫfavour ʳin his sight more than all the virgins; so that he set the royal crown upon her head, and made her queen instead of Vashti.

18 Then the king ˢmade a great feast unto all his princes and his servants, *even* Esther's feast; and he made a ᵗrelease

A. M. 3547
B. C. 457
A. U. C. 297
Coss. Rom.
Q. Minucio et
C. Horatio
to the provinces, and gave gifts, according to the state of the king.

19 And when the virgins were gathered together the second time, then Mordecai sat ᵘin the king's gate.

20 ᵛEsther had not *yet* showed her kindred nor her people; as Mordecai had charged her: for Esther did the commandment of Mordecai, like as when she was brought up with him.

21 ʷIn those days, while Mordecai sat in the king's gate, two of the king's chamberlains, ˣBigthan and Teresh, of those which kept ʸthe door, were wroth, and sought to

---

ᵖVer. 7——ᑫOr, *kindness*——ʳHeb. *before him*——ˢCh. i. 3——ᵗHeb. *rest*——ᵘVer. 21; chap. iii. 2

ᵛVer. 10——ʷSee chap. xii. 1——ˣOr, *Bigthana,* chap. vi. 2——ʸHeb. *the threshold*

---

quently rubbed with *olive oil,* will in almost every case remove all that is disagreeable of this kind. This treatment will give a healthy action to all the subcutaneous vessels, and in every respect promote health and comfort.

Verse 13. *Whatsoever she desired*] When any of the young women were called to go to the king, it appears that it was an ordinance that whatever kind of *dress stuff, colour, jewels,* &c., they thought best to set off their persons, and render them more engaging, should be given them.

Verse 14. *She returned into the second house*] This was the place where the king's *concubines* were kept. They went out no more, and were never given in marriage to any man, and saw the king's face no more unless specially called.

Custody of Shaashgaz] This is probably another *Persian* name; شيشخونج *sheshkhunj, beardless,* a proper epithet of a *eunuch;* or سستگنج *sestgunj, weak loins,* for the same reason. Names of this kind at once show the reason of their imposition, by describing the *state* of the person.

Verse 15. *She required nothing*] She left this entirely to her friend Hege, who seems to have been intent on her success. She therefore left her decorations to his judgment alone, and went in that dress and in those ornaments which *he* deemed most suitable.

Verse 16. *The tenth month—Tebeth*] Answering to part of our *December* and *January.*

Verse 17. *Set the royal crown upon her head*] Made her what is now called in the East the SULTANA, the *queen.* She was the mistress of all the rest of the wives, all of whom were obliged to pay her the most profound respect.

Verse 18. *Made a release to the provinces*] Remitted some kind of *tribute* or *impost,* in honour of Esther, at her coronation, as our kings generally do when they are crowned, ordering a discharge from prison of many who are confined for minor offences. As it was the custom of the Persian kings to give their queens something like what is called with us the *aurum reginæ,* "queen gold," which was a tenth of all fines, &c., above what was given to the king; (for they gave them such a city to buy them *clothes,* another for their *hair,* a third for their *necklaces,* a fourth for their *pearls,* &c.;) it is probable that, on this occasion, Esther so wishing, he relieved those cities and provinces which had before paid this *queen gold* from all these expenses; and this would tend greatly to make the queen *popular.*

Verse 21. *Mordecai sat in the king's gate*] Mordecai might have been one of the *officers* of the king, as the *gate* was the place where such usually attended to await the king's call. It is not likely that he was the *porter;* had he been only such, *Haman* could have removed him at once.

A. M. 3547
B. C. 457
A. U. C. 297
Coss. Rom.
Q. Minucio et
C. Horatio

lay hand on the king Ahasuerus.

22 And the thing was known to Mordecai, [z]who told *it* unto Esther the queen; and Esther certified the king *thereof* in Mordecai's name.

[a]Chap. vi. 2

Two of the king's chamberlains] Eunuchs. *Why* they conspired against the life of the king, we are not informed. The *Targum* says that they found out that Esther had intended to use her influence with the king to get them removed from their office, and Mordecai put in their place; therefore they determined to poison Esther, and slay the king in his bedchamber. It is very likely that they were creatures of Haman, who probably affected the kingdom, and perhaps were employed by him to remove the king, and so make his way open to the throne.

Verse 22. *Was known to Mordecai*] Josephus says that a Jew, named *Barnabasus*, overheard the plot, told it to Mordecai, Mordecai to Esther, and Esther to the king, in Mordecai's name; and *he* was registered as the discoverer.

Verse 23. *It was found out*] It was proved against them, in consequence of which they were *hanged*. Perhaps the words ויתלו על עץ *vaiyittalu al ets, they were hung upon wood* or *a tree*, may refer to their being *impaled*. A

23 And when inquisition was made of the matter, it was found out; therefore they were both hanged on a tree: and it was written in [a]the book of the chronicles before the king.

A. M. 3547
B. C. 457
A. U. C. 297
Coss. Rom.
Q. Minucio et
C. Horatio

[a]Chap. vi. 1

pointed stake is set upright in the ground, and the culprit is taken, placed on the sharp point, and then pulled down by his legs till the stake that went in at the fundament passes up through the body and comes out by the side of the neck. A most dreadful species of punishment, in which *revenge* and *cruelty* may glut the utmost of their malice. The culprit lives a considerable time in excruciating agonies.

It has been observed that the *name of God* does not once occur in this book. This is true of the *Hebrew* text, and all *translations* from it; but in the *Septuagint* we find the following words, in ver. 20, after, *Esther had not showed her kindred:* Οὗτως γαρ ενετειλατο αυτη Μαρδοχαιος, φοβεισθαι τον Θεον, και ποιειν τα προσταγματα αυτου, καθως ην μετ' αυτου; "For so Mordecai had charged her to fear God, and to keep his commandments, as she did when with him." This, as far as the *Septuagint* is concerned, takes away the strange reproach from this book. It must be owned that it was not because there were not many fair opportunities that the sacred name has not been introduced.

CHAPTER III

Ahasuerus exalts Haman the Agagite, and commands all his officers to do him reverence, which Mordecai refuses, 1–3. Haman, informed of Mordecai's refusal, plots his destruction, and that of the Jews, 4–6. Lots are cast to find out the proper time, 7. Haman accuses the Jews to Ahasuerus, counsels him to destroy them, and offers ten thousand talents of silver for the damage which the revenue might sustain by their destruction, 8, 9. The king refuses the money, but gives Haman full authority to destroy them, 10, 11. Letters are written to this effect, and sent to the king's lieutenants throughout the empire, and the thirteenth day of the month Adar is appointed for the massacre, 12–15.

A. M. 3551
B. C. 453
A. U. C. 301
Coss. Rom.
P. Curiatio et
S. Quintilio

AFTER these things did King Ahasuerus promote [a]Haman the son of Hammedatha the [b]Agagite, and advanced him, and set his seat above all the princes that *were* with him.

[a]See chap. xvi. 10, 11——[b]Num. xxiv. 7; 1 Sam. xv. 8

NOTES ON CHAP. III

Verse 1. *Haman—the Agagite*] Perhaps he was some descendant of that *Agag*, king of the *Amalekites*, spared by Saul, but destroyed by Samuel; and on this ground might have an antipathy to the Jews.

Set his seat above all the princes] Made him his *prime minister*, and put all the officers of state under his direction.

Verse 2. *The king's servants, that were in the king's gate*] By *servants* here, certainly a

2 And all the king's servants, that *were* [c]in the king's gate, bowed, and reverenced Haman: for the king had so commanded concerning him. But Mordecai [d]bowed not, nor did *him* reverence.

A. M. 3551
B. C. 453
A. U. C. 301
Coss. Rom.
P. Curiatio et
S. Quintilio

[c]Chap. ii. 19——[d]Ver. 5; Psa. xv. 4; chap. xiii. 12

higher class of *officers* are intended than *porters;* and Mordecai was one of those officers, and came to the gate with the others who were usually there in attendance to receive the commands of the king.

Mordecai bowed not] לא יכרע *lo yichra.* "He did not bow down;" *nor did him reverence,* ולא ישתחוה *velo yishtachaveh,* "nor did he prostrate himself." I think it most evident, from these two words, that it was not *civil reverence* merely that Haman expected and *Mordecai re-*

A. M. 3551
B. C. 453
A. U. C. 301
Coss. Rom.
P. Curiatio et
S. Quintilio

3 Then the king's servants, which *were* in the king's gate, said unto Mordecai, Why transgressest thou the [e]king's commandment?

4 Now it came to pass, when they spake daily unto him, and he hearkened not unto them, that they told Haman, to see whether Mordecai's matters would stand: for he had told them that he *was* a Jew.

5 And when Haman saw that Mordecai [f]bowed not, nor did him reverence, then was Haman [g]full of wrath.

A. M. 3551
B. C. 453
A. U. C. 301
Coss. Rom.
P. Curiatio et
S. Quintilio

6 And he thought scorn to lay hands on Mordecai alone; for they had showed him the people of Mordecai: wherefore Haman [h]sought to destroy all the Jews that *were* throughout the whole kingdom of Ahasuerus, *even* the people of Mordecai.

7 In the first month, that *is,* the month Nisan, in the twelfth year of King Ahasuerus, [i]they cast Pur, that *is,* the lot, before Haman from day to day, and from month to month, *to* the twelfth *month,* that *is,* the month Adar.

8 And Haman said unto King Ahasuerus,

---

[e]Ver. 2——[f]Ver. 2; chap. v. 9——[g]Dan. iii. 19

[h]Psa. lxxxiii. 4——[i]Chap. ix. 24

---

fused; this sort of respect is found in the word כרע *cara,* to *bow.* This sort of reverence Mordecai could not refuse without being guilty of the most inexcusable *obstinacy,* nor did any part of the Jewish law forbid it. But Haman expected, what the Persian kings frequently received, a species of *Divine adoration;* and this is implied in the word שחה *shachah,* which signifies that kind of *prostration* which implies the *highest degree of reverence that can be paid to God or man,* lying down flat on the earth, with the hands and feet extended, and the mouth in the dust.

The *Targum,* says that Haman set up a *statue* for himself, to which every one was obliged to bow, and to adore Haman himself. The Jews all think that Mordecai refused this prostration because it implied *idolatrous adoration.* Hence, in the Apocryphal additions to this book, Mordecai is represented praying thus: "Thou knowest that if I have not adored Haman, it was not through pride, nor contempt, nor secret desire of glory; for I felt disposed to kiss the footsteps of his feet (gladly) for the salvation of Israel: but I feared to give to a man that honour which I know belongs only to my God."

Verse 7. *The first month*] That is, of the *civil* year of the Jews.

The month Nisan] Answering to a part of our *March* and *April.*

The twelfth year of King Ahasuerus] According to the chronology in our Bibles, about *five hundred and ten years* before Christ.

They cast Pur, that is, *the lot*] This appears to be the Hebrew corruption of the pure Persian word پاری *pari,* which signifies any thing that *happens fortuitously.* There is an addition here in the Greek text that was probably in the *original,* and which makes this place very plain. I shall set down the whole verse, and give the Greek in a parenthesis, that it may be read consecutively with what is in the Hebrew: "In the first month, that is, the month Nisan, in the twelfth year of King Ahasuerus, they cast Pur, that is, the lot, before Haman, from day to day, and from month to month." (ὥστε ἀπολέσαι ἐν μιᾷ ἡμερᾳ το γενος Μαρδοχαιου, και επεσεν ὁ κληρος εις την τεσσερακαιδεκατην του μηνος ὁς εστιν Αδαρ, "that they might destroy in one day the people of Mordecai; and the lot fell on the *fourteenth* day of the month Adar.")

We see plainly intimated by the Hebrew text

that they *cast lots,* or used a *species of divination,* to find *which* of the *twelve months* would be the most *favourable* for the execution of Haman's design; and, having found the desired *month,* then they *cast lots,* or used *divination,* to find out which *day* of the said month would be the *lucky day* for the accomplishment of the enterprise. But the *Hebrew* text does not tell us the result of this *divination;* we are left to guess it out; but the *Greek* supplies this deficiency, and makes all clear. From it we find that, when they cast for the *month,* the month *Adar* was taken; and when they cast for the *day,* the *fourteenth* (Heb. *thirteenth*) of that month was taken.

Some have questioned whether *Pur* may not have signified also some *game of chance,* which they played before or with Haman, from day to day, to divert him from his melancholy, till the lucky time came in which he was to have the gratification of slaying all the people who were objects of his enmity; or they cast lots, or played, who should get the property of such and such opulent families. *Holinshed,* one of our ancient historians, informs us that, previously to the battle of *Agincourt,* the English army, under Henry V., were so thinned and weakened by disease, and the French army so numerous, that "Frenchmen, in the mean while, as though they had been sure of victory, made great triumphe, for the captaines had determined before how to *divide the spoil;* and the souldiers, the night before, had *plaied the Englishmen at dice.*" To this the chorus of *Shakspeare* alludes:—

"Proud of their numbers, and secure of soul,
The confident and over-lusty French
Do the low-rated English play at dice.
————The poor condemned English,
Like sacrifices by their watchful fires,
Sit patiently, and inly ruminate
The morning's danger; and their gestures sad,
Investing lank-lean cheeks, and war-worn coats,
Presenteth them unto the gazing moon
So many horrid ghosts. Hen. V.

Monstrelet, who is an impartial writer, does not mention this.

Did *Haman* and his flatterers intend to divide the spoils of the designed-to-be-massacred Jews in some such manner as this?

Verse 8. *Their laws* are *diverse from all peo-*

A. M. 3551 B. C. 453 A. U. C. 301 Coss. Rom. P. Curiatio et S. Quintilio

There is a certain people scattered abroad and dispersed
among the people in all the provinces of thy kingdom; and
[k]their laws *are* diverse from all people; neither
keep they the king's laws: therefore it *is* not
[l]for the king's profit to suffer them.
9 If it please the king, let it be written
[m]that they may be destroyed: and I will

[k]Ezra iv. 13; Acts xvi. 20——[l]Heb. *meet* or *equal*——[m]Heb. *to destroy them*

[n]pay ten thousand talents of silver
to the hands of those that have
the charge of the business, to
bring *it* into the king's treasuries.
10 And the king [o]took [p]his ring from his
hand, and gave it unto Haman the son of
Hammedatha the Agagite, the Jews' [q]enemy.
11 And the king said unto Haman, The silver
is given to thee, the people also, to do with

A. M. 3551 B. C. 453 A. U. C. 301 Coss. Rom. P. Curiatio et S. Quintilio

[n]Heb. *weigh*——[o]Gen. xli. 42——[p]Chap. vii. 2, 8——[q]Or, *oppressor*, chap. vii. 6

ple] Such they certainly were; for they worshipped the *true* God according to *his own laws;* and this was not done by any other people then on the face of the earth.

Verse 9. *Let it be written that they may be destroyed*] Let it be *enacted* that they may all be put to death. By this he would throw all the odium off himself, and put it on the king and his counsellors; for he wished the thing to pass into a law, in which *he* could have but a small share of the blame.

I will pay ten thousand talents of silver] He had said before that *it was not for the king's profit to suffer them;* but here he is obliged to acknowledge that there will be a *loss* to the revenue, but that loss he is willing to make up out of his own property.

Ten thousand *talents of silver* is an immense sum indeed; which, counted by the *Babylonish* talent, amounts to *two millions one hundred and nineteen thousand pounds sterling;* but, reckoned by the *Jewish* talent, it makes more than double that sum.

Those who cavil at the Scriptures would doubtless call this *one* of the many absurdities which, they say, are so plenteously found in them, supposing it almost impossible for an individual to possess so much wealth. But though they do not believe the Bible, they do not scruple to credit *Herodotus*, who, lib. vii., says that when *Xerxes* went into Greece, *Pythius* the Lydian had *two thousand* talents of silver, and *four millions* of gold darics, which sums united make near *five millions and a half sterling.*

Plutarch tells us, in his life of *Crassus*, that after this Roman general had dedicated the tenth of all he had to Hercules, he entertained the Roman people at *ten thousand* tables, and distributed to every citizen as much corn as was sufficient for *three* months; and after all these expenses, he had *seven thousand one hundred* Roman talents remaining, which is more than a million and a half of English money.

In those days silver and gold were more plentiful than at present, as we may see in the yearly revenue of Solomon, who had of gold from *Ophir*, at one voyage, *four hundred and fifty* talents, which make *three millions two hundred and forty thousand* pounds sterling; and his annual income was *six hundred and sixty-six* talents of silver, which make *four millions seven hundred and ninety-five thousand two hundred* pounds English money.

In addition to the above I cannot help subjoining the following particulars:—

Crassus, who was mentioned before, had a landed estate valued at one million six hundred and sixty-six thousand six hundred and sixty-six pounds thirteen shillings and four pence.

C. Cœcilius Ridorus, after having lost much in the civil war, left by will effects amounting to one million forty-seven thousand one hundred and sixty pounds.

Lentullus, the augur, is said to have possessed no less than three millions three hundred and thirty-three thousand three hundred and thirty-three pounds six shillings and eight pence.

Apicius was worth more than nine hundred and sixteen thousand six hundred and seventy-one pounds thirteen shillings and four pence; who, after having spent in his kitchen eight hundred and thirty-three thousand three hundred and thirty-three pounds six shillings and eight pence, and finding that he had no more left than eighty-three thousand three hundred and thirty-three pounds six shillings and eight pence, considered it so little for his support, that he judged it best to put an end to his life by poison!

The superfluous furniture of *M. Scaurus*, which was burnt at *Tusculum*, was valued at no less than eight hundred and thirty-three thousand three hundred and thirty-two pounds thirteen shillings and four pence.

Anthony owed, at the *ides of March*, the sum of three hundred and thirty-three thousand three hundred and thirty-three pounds six shillings and six pence, which he paid before the *calends of April.*

None of these men were in trade, to account for the circulation of such immense sums through their hands. See DICKSON'S *Husband. of the Anc.*

Verse 10. *The king took his ring*] In this ring was no doubt included his *privy seal*, and he gave this to Haman, that when he had formed such a *decree* as he thought fit, he might seal it with this *ring*, which would give it its due force and influence among the rulers of the provinces. The *privy seal* of many of our sovereigns appears to have been inserted in their *rings;* and the seals of Eastern potentates were worn in rings upon their fingers. One such seal, once the property of the late *Tippoo Sultan*, lies before me; the inscription is deeply cut in *silver*, which is set in a *massy carriage of gold.* This, as fitted to the finger, he probably kept always on his hand, to be ready to seal despatches, &c., or it might be carried by a confidential officer for the same purpose, as it seems to refer to one of the *chief cutcheries*, or *military officers.*

A. M. 3551
B. C. 453
A. U. C. 301
Coss. Rom.
P. Curiatio et
S. Quintilio
them as it seemeth good to thee.

12 [r]Then were the king's [s]scribes called on the thirteenth day of the first month, and there was written according to all that Haman had commanded unto the king's lieutenants, and to the governors that *were* over every province, and to the rulers of every people of every province, [t]according to the writing thereof, and *to* every people after their language; [u]in the name of King Ahasuerus was it written, and sealed with the king's ring.

13 And the letters were [v]sent by posts into all the king's provinces, to destroy, to kill, and

to cause to perish, all Jews, both young and old, little children and women, [w]in one day, *even* upon [x]the thirteenth *day* of the twelfth month, which *is* the month Adar, and [y]*to take* the spoil of them for a prey.

A. M. 3551
B. C. 453
A. U. C. 301
Coss. Rom.
P. Curiatio et
S. Quintilio

14 [z]The copy of the writing for a commandment to be given in every province was published unto all people, that they should be ready against that day.

15 The posts went out, being hastened by the king's commandment, and the decree was given in Shushan the palace. And the king and Haman sat down to drink; but [a]the city Shushan was perplexed.

---

[r]Chap. viii. 9——[s]Or, *secretaries*——[t]Chap. i. 22; viii. 9
[u]1 Kings xxi. 8; chap. viii. 8, 10——[v]Chap. viii. 10

[w]Ch. viii. 12, &c.——[x]2 Mac. xv. 36——[y]Ch. viii. 11
[z]Chap. viii. 13, 14——[a]See chap. viii. 15; Prov. xxix. 2

Verse 12. *Unto the king's lieutenants*] אחשדרפני *achashdarpeney.* This is in all probability another *Persian* word, for there is nothing like it in the *Hebrew* language, nor can it be fairly deduced from any *roots* in that tongue. The *Vulgate* translates *ad omnes satrapas regis,* to all the *satraps* of the king. It is very likely that this is the true sense of the word, and that the אחשדרפני *achsadrapani,* as it may be pronounced, is the Chaldee or Hebrew corruption of the *Persian word* ستربا *satraban,* the plural of سترب *satrab,* a Persian peer, though the word is now nearly obsolete in the Persian language; for since the conquest of Persia by Mohammedanism, the names of officers are materially changed, as something of *Islamism* is generally connected with the titles of officers both civil and military, as well as religious.

Verse 13. *To destroy, to kill, and to cause to perish*] To put the whole of them to death in *any manner,* or by *every way* and *means.*

Take *the spoil of them for a prey.*] Thus, whoever killed a Jew had his property for his trouble! And thus the hand of every man was armed against this miserable people. Both in the *Greek* version and in the *Latin* the copy of this order is introduced at length, expressing "the king's desire to have all his dominions in quiet and prosperity; but that he is informed that this cannot be expected, while a certain detestable people are disseminated through all his provinces, who not only are not subject to the laws, but endeavour to change them; and that nothing less than their utter *extermination* will secure the peace and prosperity of the empire; and therefore he orders that they be all destroyed, both male and female, young and old," &c.

Verse 15. *The posts*] Literally, the *couriers,* the *hircarrahs,* those who carried the public despatches; a species of public functionaries, who have been in use in all nations of the world from the remotest antiquity.

The decree was given at Shushan] It was *dated* from the royal Susa, where the king then was.

The city Shushan was perplexed.] They saw that in a short time, by this wicked measure, the whole city would be thrown into confusion; for, although the *Jews* were the only objects of this decree, yet, as it armed the *populace* against them, even the Persians could not hope to escape without being spoiled, when a desperate mob had begun to taste of human blood, and enrich themselves with the property of the murdered. Besides, many Persian families had, no doubt, become united by intermarriages with Jewish families, and in such a massacre they would necessarily share the same fate with the Jews. A more impolitic, disgraceful, and cruel measure was never formed by any government; and one would suppose that the king who ordered it must have been an idiot, and the counsellors who advised it must have been madmen. But a despotic government is ever capable of extravagance and cruelty; for as it is the bane of popular freedom and happiness, so is it the disgrace of political wisdom and of all civil institutions. Despotism and tyranny in the state are the most direct curses which insulted justice can well inflict upon a sinful nation.

CHAPTER IV

On hearing the king's decree to exterminate the Jews, Mordecai mourns, and clothes himself in sackcloth, 1, 2. The Jews are filled with consternation, 3. Esther, perceiving Mordecai in distress at the palace gate, sends her servant Hatach to inquire the reason, 4–6. Hatach returns with the information, and also the express desire of Mordecai that she should go instantly to the king, and make supplication in behalf of her people, 7–9. Esther excuses herself on the ground that she had not been called by the king for thirty days past; and that the law was such that any one approaching his presence, without express invitation, should be put to death, unless the king should, in peculiar clemency, stretch out to such persons the golden sceptre, 10–12.

Mordecai returns an answer, insisting on her compliance, 13, 14. She then orders Mordecai to gather all the Jews of Shushan, and fast for her success three days, night and day; and resolves to make the attempt, though at the risk of her life, 15–17.

A. M. 3551
B. C. 453
A. U. C. 301
Coss. Rom.
P. Curiatio et
S. Quintilio

WHEN Mordecai perceived all that was done, Mordecai [a]rent his clothes, and put on sackcloth [b]with ashes, and went out into the midst of the city, and [c]cried with a loud and a bitter cry;

2 And came even before the king's gate: for none *might* enter into the king's gate clothed with sackcloth.

3 And in every province, whithersoever the king's commandment and his decree came, *there was* great mourning among the Jews, and fasting, and weeping, and wailing; and [d]many lay in sackcloth and ashes.

4 So Esther's maids and her [e]chamberlains came and told *it* her. Then was the queen exceedingly grieved; and she sent raiment to clothe Mordecai, and to take away his sackcloth from him: but he received *it* not.

5 Then called Esther for Hatach, *one* of the king's chamberlains, [f]whom he had appointed to attend upon her, and gave him a commandment to Mordecai, to know what it *was,* and why it *was.*

6 So Hatach went forth to Mordecai unto the street of the city, which *was* before the king's gate.

7 And Mordecai told him of all that had happened unto him, and of [g]the sum of the money that Haman had promised to pay to the king's treasuries for the Jews, to destroy them.

A. M. 3551
B. C. 453
A. U. C. 301
Coss. Rom.
P. Curiatio et
S. Quintilio

8 Also he gave him [h]the copy of the writing of the decree that was given at Shushan to destroy them, to show *it* unto Esther, and to declare *it* unto her, and to charge her that she should go in unto the king, to make supplication unto him, and to make request before him for her people.

9 And Hatach came and told Esther the words of Mordecai.

10 Again Esther spake unto Hatach, and gave him commandment unto Mordecai;

11 All the king's servants, and the people of the king's provinces, do know that whosoever, whether man or woman, shall come unto the king into [i]the inner court, who is not called, [k]*there is* one law of his to put *him* to death, except such [l]to whom the king shall hold out the golden sceptre, that he may live: but I have not been called to come in unto the king these thirty days.

12 And they told to Mordecai Esther's words.

---

[a]2 Sam. ii. 11——[b]Josh. vii. 6; Ezek. xxvii. 30 [c]Gen. xxvii. 34——[d]Heb. *sackcloth and ashes were laid under many;* Isa. lviii. 5; Dan. ix. 3

[e]Heb. *eunuchs*——[f]Heb. *whom he had set before her* [g]Chap. iii. 9——[h]Chap. iii. 14, 15——[i]Chap. v. 1 [k]Dan. ii. 9——[l]Chap. v. 2; viii. 4

NOTES ON CHAP. IV

Verse 1. *Mordecai rent his clothes*] He gave every demonstration of the most poignant and oppressive grief. Nor did he hide this from the city; and the Greek says that he uttered these words aloud: Αιρεται εθνος μηδεν ηδικηκος, *A people are going to be destroyed, who have done no evil!*

Verse 2. *Before the king's gate*] He could not enter into the gate, of the place where the officers waited, because he was in the habit of a mourner; for this would have been contrary to law.

Verse 3. *Fasting, and weeping, and wailing*] How astonishing, that in all this there is not the slightest intimation given *of praying to God!*

Verse 4. *Sent raiment*] She supposed that he must have been spoiled of his raiment by some means; and therefore sent him clothing.

Verse 5. *Then called Esther for Hatach*] This eunuch the king had appointed to wait upon her, partly, as is still the case in the East, to *serve her,* and partly, to *observe her conduct;*

for no despot is ever exempt from a twofold torture, *jealousy* and *suspicion.*

Verse 8. *That she should go in unto the king*] The Greek adds, "Remember the time of your low estate, and in what manner you have been nourished, and carried in my arms; and that Haman, who is next to the king, has got a decree for our destruction. Pray, therefore, to the Lord, and plead with the king, that we may be delivered from death." But there is not a word of this either in the *Hebrew, Syriac,* or *Vulgate.*

Verse 11. *Into the inner court*] We have already seen that the Persian sovereigns affected the highest degree of *majesty,* even to the *assuming of Divine honours.* No man nor woman dared to appear *unveiled* before them, without hazarding their lives; into the inner chamber of the *harem* no person ever entered but the king, and the woman he had chosen to call thither. None even of his courtiers or ministers dared to appear there; nor the most beloved of his concubines, except led thither by himself, or ordered to come to him. Here was Esther's difficulty; and that difficulty was **now**

A. M. 3551
B. C. 453
A. U. C. 301
Coss. Rom.
P. Curiatio et
S. Quintilio

13 Then Mordecai command-
ed to answer Esther, Think not
with thyself that thou shalt escape in the king's house, more
than all the Jews.

14 For if thou altogether holdest thy peace
at this time, *then* shall there ᵐenlargement
and deliverance arise to the Jews from another place; but thou and thy father's house
shall be destroyed: and who knoweth whether
thou art come to the kingdom for *such* a time
as this?

15 Then Esther bade *them*
return Mordecai *this answer:*

16 Go, gather together all the
Jews that are ⁿpresent in Shu-
shan, and fast ye for me, and neither eat nor
drink °three days, night or day: I also and
my maidens will fast likewise; and so will I
go in unto the king, which *is* not according to
the law: ᵖand if I perish, I perish.

17 So Mordecai �q went his way, and did according to all that Esther had commanded
him.

A. M. 3551
B. C. 453
A. U. C. 301
Cross. Rom.
P. Curiatio et
S. Quintilio

ᵐHeb. *respiration;* Job ix. 18——ⁿHeb. *found*

°See chap. v. 1——ᵖSee Gen. xliii. 14——q Heb. *passed*

---

increased by the circumstance of her not having
been sent for to the king's bed for *thirty* days.
In the last verse of the preceding chapter we
find that the *king and Haman sat down to
drink.* It is very likely that this wicked man
had endeavoured to draw the king's attention
from the queen, that his affection might be
lessened, as he must have known something of
the relationship between her and Mordecai;
and consequently viewed her as a person who,
in all probability, might stand much in the way
of the accomplishment of his designs. I cannot
but think that *he* had been the cause why
Esther had not seen the king for *thirty* days.

Verse 13. *Think not—that thou shalt escape*]
This confirms the suspicion that Haman knew
something of the relationship between Mordecai
and Esther; and therefore he gives her to understand that, although in the *king's palace,*
she should no more *escape than the Jews.*

Verse 14. Then *shall there enlargement and
deliverance arise*] He had a confidence that
deliverance would come by some means; and he
thought that *Esther* would be the most likely;
and that, if she did not use the influence which
her providential station gave her, she would be
highly culpable.

And who knoweth whether thou art come]
As if he had said, "Is it likely that Divine
providence would have so distinguished thee,
and raised thee from a state of abject obscurity,
merely for *thy own sake?* Must it not have
been on some *public account?* Did not *he* see
what was coming? and has he not put thee in
the place where thou mayest counteract one of
the most ruinous purposes ever formed?" Is
there a human being who has not some particular station by an especial providence, at some
particular time, in which he can be of some
essential service to his neighbour, in averting
evil or procuring good, if he be but faithful to
the *grace* and *opportunity* afforded by this station? Who dares give a negative to these questions? We lose much, both in reference to
ourselves and *others,* by not adverting to our
providental situation and *circumstances.* While
on this subject, I will give the reader two important sayings, from two eminent men, both
keen observers of human nature, and deeply
attentive in all such cases to the operations of
Divine providence:—

"To every thing there is a season; and a time
to every purpose under heaven. Therefore
withhold not good from them to whom it is
due, when it is in the power of thy hand to
do it."　　Solomon.

There is a *tide* in the affairs of men,
Which, taken at the *flood,* leads on to *fortune;*
Omitted, all the *voyage* of their life
Is *bound* in *shallows,* and in *miseries.*
　　　　　　　　Shakespeare.

Has there not been a case, *within time of
memory,* when evil was designed against a whole
people, through the Hamans who had poisoned
the ears of well-intentioned men; in which *one
poor man,* in consequence of a situation into
which he was brought by an astonishing providence, used the influence which his situation
gave him; and, by the mercy of his God, turned
the whole evil aside? By the association of
ideas the following passage will present itself
to the reader's memory, who may have any
acquaintance with the circumstance:—
"There was a little city, and few men within
it; and there came a great king against it, and
besieged it, and built great bulwarks against it.
Now there was found in it a poor wise man,
and he by his wisdom delivered the city; *yet
no man remembered that same poor man!*"
"Then *said, I, Ah, Lord God! They say of
me,* Doth he not speak parables?" Rem acu
tetigi.

Verse 16. *Fast ye for me, and neither eat nor
drink three days*] What a strange thing, that
still we hear nothing of *prayer,* nor of *God!*
What is the ground on which we can account
for this total silence? I know it not. She could
not suppose there was any *charm* in fasting,
sackcloth garments, and lying on the ground.
If these were not done to turn away the displeasure of God, which seemed now to have
unchained their enemies against them, what
were they done for?

If I perish, I perish.] If I lose my life in
this attempt to save my people, I shall lose it
cheerfully. I see it is my duty to make the attempt; and, come what will, I am resolved to
do it. She must, however, have depended much
on the efficacy of the humiliations she prescribed.

CHAPTER V

Esther presents herself before the king, and finds favour in his sight, 1, 2. He asks what her request is, and promises to grant it, 3. She invites him and Haman to a banquet, which they accept, 4, 5. He then desires to know her request; and she promises to make it known on the morrow, if they will again come to her banquet, 6–8. Haman, though overjoyed at the manner in which he was received by the queen, is indignant at the indifference with which he is treated by Mordecai, 9. He goes home, and complains of this conduct to his friends, and his wife Zeresh, 10–13. They counsel him to make a gallows of fifty cubits high, and to request the king that Mordecai may be hanged on it, which they take for granted the king will not refuse; and the gallows is made accordingly, 14.

A. M. 3551
B. C. 453
A. U. C. 301
Coss. Rom.
P. Curiatio et
S. Quintilio

NOW it came to pass [a]on the third day, that Esther put on *her* royal *apparel,* and stood in [b]the inner court of the king's house, over against the king's house: and the king sat upon his royal throne in the royal house, over against the gate of the house.

2 And it was so, when the king saw Esther the queen standing in the court, *that* [c]she obtained favour in his sight: and [d]the king held out to Esther the golden sceptre that *was* in his hand. So Esther drew near, and touched the top of the sceptre.

3 Then said the king unto her, What wilt thou, Queen Esther? and what *is* thy request? [e]it shall be even given thee to the half of the kingdom.

4 And Esther answered, If *it seem* good unto the king, let the king and Haman come this day unto the banquet that I have prepared for him.

5 Then the king said, Cause Haman to make haste, that he may do as Esther hath said. So the king and Haman came to the banquet that Esther had prepared.

A. M. 3551
B. C. 453
A. U. C. 301
Coss. Rom.
P. Curiatio et
S. Quintilio

6 [f]And the king said unto Esther at the banquet of wine, [g]What *is* thy petition? and it shall be granted thee: and what *is* thy request? even to the half of the kingdom it shall be performed.

7 Then answered Esther, and said, My petition and my request *is;*

8 If I have found favour in the sight of the king, and if it please the king to grant my petition, and [h]to perform my request, let the king and Haman come to the banquet that I shall prepare for them, and I will do to-morrow as the king hath said.

9 Then went Haman forth that day joyful and with a glad heart: but when Haman saw Mordecai in the king's gate, [i]that he stood not up, nor moved for him, he was full of indignation against Mordecai.

10 Nevertheless Haman [k]refrained himself: and when he came home, he sent and [l]called for his friends, and Zeresh his wife.

---

[a]See chapter iv. 16——[b]See chapter iv. 11; chapter vi. 4——[c]See Esther xv. 7, 8; Proverbs xxi. 1 [d]Chapter iv. 11; viii. 4——[e]So Mark vi. 23——[f]Chapter vii. 2——[g]Chapter ix. 12——[h]Hebrew, *to do* [i]Chapter iii. 5——[k]So 2 Samuel xiii. 22——[l]Heb. *caused to come*

NOTES ON CHAP. V

Verse 1. *On the third day*] Most probably the third day of the *fast* which she has prescribed to Mordecai and the Jews.

Verse 2. *She obtained favour in his sight*] The *Septuagint* represents "the king as being at first greatly enraged when he saw Esther, because she had dared to appear before him unveiled; and she, perceiving this, was so terrified that she fainted away; on which the king, touched with tenderness, sprung from his throne, took her up in his arms, laid the golden sceptre on her neck, and spoke to her in the most endearing manner." This is more circumstantial than the Hebrew, but is not *contrary* to it.

The golden sceptre that was in his hand.] That the kings of Persia did wear a *golden sceptre,* we have the following proof in *Xenophon:* Ὁτι ου τοδε το χρυσουν σκηπτρον το την βασιλειαν διασωξον εστιν, αλλ' οι πιστοι φιλοι σκηπτρον βασιλευσιν αληθεστατον και ασφαλεστατον. See Cyrop., lib. viii., p. 139, edit. *Steph.* 1581. *It is not,* said Cyrus to his son Cambyses, *the* GOLDEN SCEPTRE *that saves the kingdom; faithful friends are the truest and safest sceptre of the empire.*

Verse 4. *Let the king and Haman come this day unto the banquet*] It was necessary to invite Haman to prevent his suspicion, and that he might not take any hasty step which might have prevented the execution of the great design.

Verse 6. *The banquet of wine*] At that part of the banquet when the *wine* was introduced.

Verse 8. *I will do to-morrow*] She saw she was gaining on the king's affections; but she was not yet sufficiently confident; and therefore wished another interview, that she might ingratiate herself more fully in the king's favour, and thus secure the success of her design. But Providence disposed of things thus, to give time for the important event mentioned in the succeeding chapter.

Verse 9. *That he stood not up, nor moved for him*] This was certainly carrying his integrity or inflexibility to the highest pitch. But still we are left to conjecture that some rever-

A. M. 3551
B. C. 453
A. U. C. 301
Coss. Rom.
P. Curiatio et
S. Quintilio

11 And Haman told them of the glory of his riches, and [m]the multitude of his children, and all *the things* wherein the king had promoted him, and how he had [n]advanced him above the princes and servants of the king.

12 Haman said moreover, Yea, Esther the queen did let no man come in with the king unto the banquet that she had prepared but myself, and to-morrow am I invited unto her also with the king.

---

[m]Chap. ix. 7, &c.——[n]Chap. iii. 1——[o]Heb. *tree*

---

ence was required, which Mordecai could not conscientiously pay.

Verse 11. *The multitude of his children*] The Asiatic sovereigns delight in the number of their children; and this is one cause why they take so many wives and concubines.

Verse 13. *Yet all this availeth me nothing*] Pride will ever render its possessor unhappy. He has such a high opinion of his own worth, that he conceives himself defrauded by every one who does not pay him all the respect and homage which he conceives to be his due.

The soul was made for God, and nothing but God can fill it and make it happy. *Angels* could not be happy in *glory*, when they had cast off their allegiance to their Maker. As soon as his heart had departed from God, *Adam* would needs go to the forbidden fruit, to satisfy a desire which was only an indication of his having been unfaithful to his God. *Solomon*, in all his glory, possessing every thing heart could wish, found all to be *vanity* and *vexation of spirit;* because his soul had not God for its portion. *Ahab*, on the throne of Israel, takes to his bed, and refuses to eat bread, not merely because he cannot get the *vineyard of Naboth*, but because he had not God in his heart, who could alone satisfy its desires. *Haman*, on the

13 Yet all this availeth me nothing, so long as I see Mordecai the Jew sitting at the king's gate.

A. M. 3551
B. C. 453
A. U. C. 301
Coss. Rom.
P. Curiatio et
S. Quintilio

14 Then said Zeresh his wife and all his friends unto him, Let a [o]gallows [p]be made of fifty cubits high, and to-morrow [q]speak thou unto the king that Mordecai may be hanged thereon: then go thou in merrily with the king unto the banquet. And the thing pleased Haman; and he caused [r]the gallows to be made.

---

[p]Chap. vii. 9——[q]Chap. vi. 4——[r]Chap. vii. 10

---

same ground, though the prime favourite of the king, is wretched because he cannot have a *bow* from that man whom his heart even despised. O, how distressing are the inquietudes of vanity And how wretched is the man who has not the God of Jacob for his help, and in whose heart Christ dwells not by faith!

Verse 14. *Let a gallows be made of fifty cubits high*] The word עֵץ *ets*, which we translate *gallows*, signifies simply *wood*, a *tree*, or *pole;* and this was to be *seventy-five* feet high, that he might suffer the greater ignominy, and be a more public spectacle. I believe *impaling* is here also meant. See the note, chap. ii. 23.

IN former times the Jews were accustomed to burn Haman in effigy; and with him a *wooden cross*, which they pretended to be in memory of that which he had erected for the suspension of Mordecai; but which was, in fact, to deride the *Christian religion*. The emperors, *Justinian* and *Theodosius*, abolished it by their edicts; and the practice has ceased from that time, though the principle from which it sprang still exists, with the same virulence against Christianity and its glorious Author.

CHAPTER VI

That night the king, not being able to sleep, orders the chronicles of the kingdom to be read to him; and finds there the record concerning the discovery of the treason of the two eunuchs, made by Mordecai, 1, 2. He inquires whether Mordecai had been rewarded, and was answered in the negative, 3. At this time Haman arrives, in order to request the king's permission to hang Mordecai; and being suddenly asked what should be done to the man whom the king delighted to honour, supposing that himself must be meant, presented the ceremonial, 4–9. The king orders him to give Mordecai those honours; which he performs, to his extreme mortification, 10, 11. He informs his wife Zeresh of these transactions, who predicts his downfall, 12–13. He is hurried by the eunuchs to the queen's banquet, 14.

A. M. 3551
B. C. 453
A. U. C. 301
Coss. Rom.
P. Curiatio et
S. Quintilio

ON that night [a]could not the king sleep, and he commanded to bring [b]the book of records of the chronicles; and

---

[a]Heb. *the king's sleep fled away*——[b]Chap. iii. 23

NOTES ON CHAP. VI

Verse 1. *On that night could not the king sleep*] The *Targum* says the king had a dream,

they were read before the king.

A. M. 3551
B. C. 453
A. U. C. 301
Coss. Rom.
P. Curiatio et
S. Quintilio

2 And it was found written, that Mordecai had told of [c]Big-

---

[c]Or, *Bigthan*, chap. ii. 21

---

which was as follows:—"And the king saw one in the similitude of a man, who spoke these words to him: Haman desireth to slay thee, and to make himself king in thy stead. Behold, he

A. M. 3551
B. C. 453
A. U. C. 301
Coss. Rom.
P. Curiatio et
S. Quintilio
thana and Teresh, two of the king's chamberlains, the keepers of the ᵈdoors, who sought to lay hand on the king Ahasuerus.

3 And the king said, What honour and dignity hath been done to Mordecai for this? Then said the king's servants that ministered unto him, There is nothing done for him.

4 And the king said, Who *is* in the court? Now Haman was come into ᵉthe outward court of the king's house, ᶠto speak unto the king to hang Mordecai on the gallows that he had prepared for him.

5 And the king's servants said unto him, Behold, Haman standeth in the court. And the king said, Let him come in.

6 So Haman came in. And the king said unto him, What shall be done unto the man ᵍwhom the king delighteth to honour? Now Haman thought in his heart, To whom would the king delight to do honour more than to myself?

7 And Haman answered the king, For the man ʰwhom the king delighteth to honour,

8 ⁱLet the royal apparel be brought ᵏwhich the king *useth* to wear, and ˡthe horse that the king rideth upon, and the crown royal which is set upon his head:

9 And let this apparel and horse be delivered to the hand of one of the king's most noble princes, that they may array the man

A. M. 3551
B. C. 453
A. U. C. 301
Coss. Rom.
P. Curiatio et
S. Quintilio

ᵈHeb. *threshold*——ᵉChapter v. 1——ᶠChapter v. 14　　ˢHeb. *in whose honour the king delighteth*——ʰHeb. *in whose honour the king delighteth*

ⁱHebrew, *Let them bring the royal apparel*——ᵏHebrew, *wherewith the king clothed* himself——ˡ1 Kings i. 33

---

will come unto thee early in the morning, to ask from thee the man who rescued thee from death, that he may slay him: but say thou unto Haman, What shall be done for the man whose honour the king studieth? And thou wilt find that he will ask nothing less from thee than the royal vestments, the regal crown, and the horse on which the king is wont to ride."

The records of the chronicles] It may be well asked, Why should the king, in such a perturbed state of mind, wish such a dry detail, as *chronicles* afford, to be read to him? But the truth is, as chronicles were composed among the *Persians*, he could not have brought before him any work more instructive, and more entertaining; because they were all written in verse, and were generally the work of the most eminent poets in the empire. They are written in this way to the present time; and the famous epic poem of the finest Persian poet, *Ferdusi*, the *Homer* of India, is nothing else than a collection of chronicles brought down from the creation to the reign of Mohammed Ghezny, in the beginning of the *tenth* century. After *thirty* years' labour, he finished this poem, which contained *one hundred and twenty thousand* lines, and presented it to the Sultan Mahmoud, who had promised to give him a *dinar* (*eight shillings and sixpence*) for every line. The poem was finished A. D. 984; and was formed out of compositions of a similar nature made by *former poets*. This chronological poem is written in all the harmony, strength, and elegance of the most beautiful and harmonious language in the universe; and what adds greatly to its worth is, that it has few *Arabic* words, with which the beautiful Persian tongue was loaded, and in my opinion *corrupted*, after the conquest of the major part of Asia by the Mohammedans. The pedants of Hindoostan, whether they *speak* or *write*, in *prose* or in *verse*, affect this commixture of Arabic words; which, though they subjugate them to Persian rules, are producing a ruggedness in a language, which in *Ferdusi*, flows deep and strong, like a river of oil over every kind of channel. Such, I suppose, was the *chronicle* that was read to

Ahasuerus, when his distractions prevented his sleep, and his troubled mind required that soothing repose which the gentle though powerful hand of poetry is alone, in such circumstances, capable of affording. Even our *rough* English ancestors had their *poetic chronicles;* and, among many, the *chronicle of Robert of Gloucester* is proof in point. I need not add, that all that is real in *Ossian* is of the same complexion.

Verse 3. *What honour and dignity hath been done to Mordecai*] It is certain he found nothing in the record; and had any thing been done, that was the most likely place to find it.

Verse 4. *Who is in the court?*] This accords with the *dream* mentioned by the Targum; and given above.

Now Haman was come] This must have been very *early* in the morning. Haman's pride and revenge were both on the tenters to be gratified.

Verse 6. *The king said unto him*] He did not give him time to make his request; and put a question to him which, at the first view, promised him all that his heart could wish.

Verse 8. *Let the royal apparel be brought*] *Pride* and *folly* ever go hand in hand. What he asked would have been in any ordinary case against his own life: but he wished to reach the pinnacle of honour: never reflecting that the higher he rose, the more terrible would be his fall. The *royal apparel* was never worn but by the king: even when the king had lain them aside, it was death to put them on. The *Targum* has *purple robes*.

And the horse—and the crown royal] Interpreters are greatly divided whether what is called here *the crown royal* be not rather an *ornament* worn on the *head of the horse*, than what may be called the *royal crown*. The original may be understood both ways; and our version seems to favour the former opinion; but I think it more likely that the royal crown is meant; for why mention the ordinary trappings of the royal steed?

Verse 9. *One of the king's most noble princes*] Alas, poor Haman! Never was the fable of the

A. M. 3551 B. C. 453 A. U. C. 301 Coss. Rom. P. Curiatio et S. Quintilio

withal whom the king delighteth
to honour, and [m]bring him on
horseback through the street of
the city, [n]and proclaim before
him, Thus shall it be done to the man whom
the king delighteth to honour.
10 Then the king said to Haman, Make
haste, *and* take the apparel and the horse, as
thou hast said, and do even so to Mordecai
the Jew, that sitteth at the king's gate: [o]let
nothing fail of all that thou hast spoken.
11 Then took Haman the apparel and the
horse, and arrayed Mordecai, and brought him
on horseback through the street of the city, and
proclaimed before him, Thus shall it be done
unto the man whom the king delighteth to
honour.
12 And Mordecai came again
to the king's gate. But Haman
[p]hasted to his house
mourning, [q]and having his head
covered.
13 And Haman told Zeresh his wife and
all his friends every *thing* that had befallen
him. Then said his wise men and Zeresh
his wife unto him, If Mordecai *be*
of the seed of the Jews, before whom thou
hast begun to fall, thou shalt not prevail
against him, but shalt surely fall before
him.
14 And while they *were* yet talking with
him, came the king's chamberlains, and hasted
to bring Haman unto [r]the banquet that Esther
had prepared.

[m]Heb. *caused him to ride*——[n]Gen. xli. 43——[o]Heb. *suffer not a whit to fall*

[p]2 Chron. xxvi. 20——[q]2 Sam. xv. 30; Jer. xiv. 3, 4——[r]Chap. v. 8

dog and shadow more literally fulfilled. Thou didst gape at the *shadow*, and didst lose the *substance*.

Verse 10. *Make haste*, and *take the apparel—and do even so to Mordecai*] O mortifying reverse of human fortune! How could Haman bear this? The *Targumist might* speak according to *nature* when he said that "Haman besought the king to kill him rather than degrade him so." How astonishing is the conduct of Divine providence in all this business! From it we plainly see that there is neither counsel nor wisdom against the Lord; and that he who digs a pit for his neighbour, is sure to fall into it himself.

Verse 12. *Mordecai came again to the king's gate*] He resumed his former humble state; while Haman, ashamed to look up, *covered his face*, and ran home to hide himself in his own house. *Covering the head and face* was a sign of *shame* and *confusion*, as well as of *grief*, among most people of the earth.

Verse 13. *But shalt surely fall before him.*] The *Septuagint* adds, οτι ὁ Θεος ὁ ζων μετ' αυτου, *for the living God is with him.* But this is a sentiment that could scarcely be expected to proceed from the mouth of *heathens*, such as these were.

Verse 14. *Hasted to bring Haman*] There was a dreadful banquet before him, of which he knew nothing: and he could have little appetite to enjoy that which he knew was prepared at the palace of Esther.

ONE grand design of this history is, to show that he who lays a snare for the life of his neighbour, is most likely to fall into it himself: for, in the course of the Divine providence, men generally meet with those evils in life which they have been the means of inflicting on others: and this is exactly agreeable to the saying of our Lord: "With what measure ye mete, it shall be measured to you withal."

CHAPTER VII

The king at the banquet urges Esther to prefer her petition, with the positive assurance that it shall be granted, 1, 2. *She petitions for her own life, and the life of her people, who were sold to be destroyed,* 3, 4. *The king inquires the author of this project, and Haman is accused by the queen,* 5, 6. *The king is enraged: Haman supplicates for his life; but the king orders him to be hanged on the gallows he had prepared for Mordecai,* 7–10.

A. M. 3551 B. C. 453 A. U. C. 301 Coss. Rom. P. Curiatio et S. Quintilio

SO the king and Haman came
[a]to banquet with Esther
the queen.
2 And the king said again unto
Esther on the second day [b]at the banquet of
wine, What *is* thy petition,
Queen Esther? and it shall be
granted thee: and what *is* thy
request? and it shall be performed,
even to the half of the kingdom.

[a]Heb. *to drink*

[b]Chap. v. 6

NOTES ON CHAP. VII

Verse 2. *At the banquet of wine*] *Postquam vino incaluerat*, after he had been heated with wine, says the *Vulgate*. In such a state the king was more likely to come into the measures of the queen.

Verse 3. *Let my life be given me*] This was

A. M. 3551
B. C. 453
A. U. C. 301
Coss. Rom.
P. Curiatio et
S. Quintilio

3 Then Esther the queen answered and said, If I have found favour in thy sight, O king, and if it please the king, let my life be given me at my petition, and my people at my request:

4 For we are [c]sold, I and my people, [d]to be destroyed, to be slain, and to perish. But if we had been sold for bondmen and bondwomen, I had held my tongue, although the enemy could not countervail the king's damage.

5 Then the king Ahasuerus answered and said unto Esther the queen, Who is he, and where is he, [e]that durst presume in his heart to do so?

6 And Esther said, [f]The adversary and enemy *is* this wicked Haman. Then Haman was afraid [g]before the king and the queen.

7 And the king arising from the banquet of wine in his wrath *went* into the palace garden:

and Haman stood up to make request for his life to Esther the queen; for he saw that there was evil determined against him by the king.

A. M. 3551
B. C. 453
A. U. C. 301
Coss. Rom.
P. Curiatio et
S. Quintilio

8 Then the king returned out of the palace garden into the place of the banquet of wine; and Haman was fallen upon [h]the bed whereon Esther *was*. Then said the king, Will he force the queen also [i]before me in the house? As the word went out of the king's mouth, they [k]covered Haman's face.

9 And [l]Harbonah, one of the chamberlains, said before the king, Behold also, [m]the [n]gallows fifty cubits high, which Haman had made for Mordecai, who had spoken good for the king, standeth in the house of Haman. Then the king said, Hang him thereon.

10 So [o]they hanged Haman on the gallows that he had prepared for Mordecai. Then was the king's wrath pacified.

---

[c]Chapter iii. 9; iv. 7——[d]Hebrew, *that they should destroy, and kill, and cause to perish*——[e]Hebrew, *whose heart hath filled him*——[f]Hebrew, *The man adversary*

[g]Or, *at the presence of*——[h]Chap. i. 6——[i]Heb. *with me*——[k]Job ix. 24——[l]Chap. i. 10——[m]Chap. v. 14; Psa. vii. 16; Prov. xi. 5, 6——[n]Heb. *tree*——[o]Dan. vi. 24; Psa. xxxvii. 35, 36

---

very artfully, as well as very honestly, managed; and was highly calculated to work on the feelings of the king. What! is the life of the queen, whom I most tenderly love, in any kind of danger?

Verse 4. *To be destroyed, to be slain*] She here repeats the words which Haman put into the *decree.* See chap. iii. 13.

Could not countervail the king's damage.] Even the *ten thousand* talents of silver could not be considered as a compensation to the state for the loss of a whole nation of people *throughout all their generations.*

Verse 5. *Who is he, and where is he*] There is a wonderful abruptness and confusion in the original words, highly expressive of the state of mind in which the king then was: מי הוא זה

ואי זה הוא אשר מלאו לבו לעשות כן *mi hu zeh veey zeh hu asher melao libbo laasoth ken.* "Who? He? This one? And where? This one? He? Who hath filled his heart to do thus?" He was at once struck with the horrible nature of a conspiracy so cruel and diabolic.

Verse 7. *Haman stood up*] He rose from the table to make request for his life, as soon as the king had gone out; and then he fell on his knees before the queen, she still sitting upon her couch.

Verse 8. *Will he force the queen*] On the king's return he found him at the queen's knees; and, professing to think that he intended to do violence to her honour, used the above expressions; though he must have known that, in such circumstances, the thought of perpetrating an act of this kind could not possibly exist.

They covered Haman's face.] This was a sign of his being devoted to death: for the attendants saw that the king was determined on his destruction. When a criminal was condemned by a Roman judge, he was delivered into the hands of the serjeant with these words: *I, lictor; caput obnubito, arbori infelici suspendito.* "Go, serjeant; cover his head, and hang him on the accursed tree."

Verse 9. *Behold also, the gallows*] As if he had said, Besides all he has determined to do to the Jews, he has erected a very high gallows, on which he had determined, this very day, to hang Mordecai, who has saved the king's life.

Hang him thereon.] Let him be instantly impaled on the same post. "Harm watch, harm catch," says the proverb. *Perillus* was the first person burnt alive in the brazen bull which he had made for the punishment of *others;* hence the poet said:—

—— *Nec lex est justior ulla,*
Quam necis artifices arte perire sua.

"Nor can there be a juster law than that the artificers of death should perish by their own invention."

CHAPTER VIII

Ahasuerus invests Mordecai with the offices and dignities possessed by Haman, 1, 2. Esther begs that the decree of destruction gone out against the Jews may be reversed, 3–6. He informs her that the acts that had once passed the king's seal cannot be reversed; but he instructs her and Mordecai to write other letters in his name, and seal them with his seal, and send them to all the provinces in the empire, giving the Jews full liberty to defend themselves; which is accordingly done; and the letters are sent off with the utmost speed to all the provinces: in consequence, the Jews prepare for their own defence, 8–14. Mordecai appears publicly in the dress of his high office, 15. The Jews rejoice in every place; and many of the people become Jews, because the fear of the Jews had fallen upon them, 16, 17.

A. M. 3551
B. C. 453
A. U. C. 301
Coss. Rom.
P. Curiatio et
S. Quintilio

ON that day did the king Ahasuerus give the house of Haman the Jews' enemy unto Esther the queen. And Mordecai came before the king; for Esther had told ᵃwhat he *was* unto her.

2 And the king took off ᵇhis ring which he had taken from Haman, and gave it unto Mordecai. And Esther set Mordecai over the house of Haman.

3 And Esther spake yet again before the king and fell down at his feet, ᶜand besought him with tears to put away the mischief of Haman the Agagite, and his device that he had devised against the Jews.

4 Then ᵈthe king held out the golden sceptre towards Esther. So Esther arose, and stood before the king,

5 And said, If it please the king, and if I have found favour in his sight, and the thing *seem* right before the king, and I *be* pleasing in his eyes, let it be written to reverse ᵉthe letters devised by Haman the son of Hammedatha the Agagite, ᶠwhich he wrote to destroy the Jews which *are* in all the king's provinces;

6 For how can I ᵍendure to see ʰthe evil that shall come unto my people? or how can I endure to see the destruction of my kindred?

A. M. 3551
B. C. 453
A. U. C. 301
Coss. Rom.
P. Curiatio et
S. Quintilio

7 Then the king Ahasuerus said unto Esther the queen and to Mordecai the Jew, Behold, ⁱI have given Esther the house of Haman, and him they have hanged upon the gallows, because he laid his hand upon the Jews.

8 Write ye also for the Jews, as it liketh you, in the king's name, and seal *it* with the king's ring: for the writing which is written in the king's name, and sealed with the king's ring, ᵏmay no man reverse.

9 ˡThen were the king's scribes called at that time in the third month, that *is*, the month Sivan, on the three and twentieth *day* thereof; and it was written according to all that Mordecai commanded unto the Jews, and to the lieutenants, and the deputies and rulers of the provinces which *are* ᵐfrom India unto Ethiopia, a hundred twenty and seven provinces, unto every province ⁿaccording to the writing thereof, and unto every people after their lan-

---

ᵃChap. ii. 7——ᵇChap. iii. 10——ᶜHeb. *and she wept and besought him*——ᵈCh. iv. 11; v. 2——ᵉHeb. *the device*——ᶠOr, *who wrote*——ᵍHeb. *be able that I may see*

ʰChap. vii. 4; Neh. ii. 3——ⁱVer. 1; Prov. xiii. 22 ᵏSee chap. i. 19; Dan. vi. 8, 12, 15——ˡChap. iii. 12 ᵐChapter i. 1——ⁿChap. i. 22; iii. 12

NOTES ON CHAP. VIII

Verse 1. *The king—give the house of Haman*] As Haman was found guilty of treasonable practices against the peace and prosperity of the king and his empire, his life was forfeited, and his goods confiscated. And as Mordecai had been the means of preserving the king's life, and was the principal object of Haman's malice, it was but just to confer his property upon him, as well as his dignity and office, as Mordecai was found deserving of the former, and fit to discharge the duties of the latter.

Verse 2. *The king took off his ring*] In the *ring* was the *seal* of the king. *Giving the ring* to Mordecai was tantamount to giving him the *seal of the kingdom*, and constituting him the same as *lord chancellor* among us.

Verse 6. *To see the destruction of my kin-*

dred?] She had now informed the king that she was cousin to Mordecai, and consequently a *Jewess;* and though her own life and that of Mordecai were no longer in danger, Haman being dead, yet the decree that had gone forth was in full force against the *Jews;* and if not repealed, their destruction would be inevitable.

Verse 8. *May no man reverse.*] Whatever had passed the royal signet could never be revoked; no *succeeding* edict could destroy or repeal a *preceding* one: but one of a similar nature to the *Jews* against the *Persians*, as that to the *Persians* was against the *Jews*, might be enacted; and thus the Jews be enabled *legitimately* to defend themselves; and, consequently, placed on an equal footing with their enemies.

Verse 9. *The month Sivan*] This answers to a part of our *May* and *June*.

A. M. 3551
B. C. 453
A. U. C. 301
Coss. Rom.
P. Curiatio et
S. Quintilio

guage, and to the Jews according to their writing, and according to their language.

10 °And he wrote in the king Ahasuerus' name, and sealed *it* with the king's ring, and sent letters by posts on horseback, *and* riders on mules, camels, *and* young dromedaries.

11 Wherein the king granted the Jews which *were* in every city to gather themselves together, and to stand for their life, to destroy, to slay, and to cause to perish, all the power of the people and province that would assault them, *both* little ones and women, and Pto take the spoil of them for a prey,

12 qUpon one day in all the provinces of King Ahasuerus, *namely,* upon the thirteenth *day* of the twelfth month, which *is* the month Adar.

13 rThe copy of the writing for a commandment to be given in every province *was*

spublished unto all people, and that the Jews should be ready against that day to avenge themselves on their enemies.

A. M. 3551
B. C. 453
A. U. C. 301
Coss. Rom.
P. Curiatio et
S. Quintilio

14 *So* the posts that rode upon mules *and* camels went out, being hastened and pressed on by the king's commandment. And the decree was given at Shushan the palace.

15 And Mordecai went out from the presence of the king in royal apparel of tblue and white, and with a great crown of gold, and with a garment of fine linen and purple: and uthe city of Shushan rejoiced and was glad.

16 The Jews had vlight, and gladness, and joy, and honour.

17 And in every province, and in every city, whithersoever the king's commandment and his decree came, the Jews had joy and gladness, a feast wand a good day. And many of the people of the land xbecame Jews; for ythe fear of the Jews fell upon them.

---

o1 Kings xxi. 8; ch. iii. 12, 13——PSee ch. ix. 10, 15, 16
qCh. iii. 13, &c.; ix. 1——rCh. iii. 14, 15——sHeb. *revealed*——tOr, *violet*——uSee ch. iii. 15; Prov. xxix. 2

vPsa. xcvii. 11——w1 Sam. xxv. 8; chap. ix. 19, 22
xPsa. xviii. 43——yGen. xxxv. 5; Exod. xv. 16; Deut. ii. 25; xi. 25; chap. ix. 2

Verse 10. *On mules, camels, and young dromedaries*] What these beasts were is difficult to say. The word רכש *rechesh*, which we translate *mules*, signifies a *swift chariot horse.*

The strange word אחשתרנים *achashteranim* is probably a *Persian* word, but perhaps incurably corrupted. The most likely derivation is that of *Bochart,* from the *Persian* اخش *akhash,* huge, large, rough, and استر *aster,* a *mule;* large mules.

The words בני הרמכים *beney harammachim, the sons of mares,* which we translate *dromedaries,* are supposed to signify *mules,* produced between the *he ass* and the *mare,* to distinguish them from those produced between the *stallion* and the *ass.* But there is really so much confusion about these matters, and so little consent among learned men as to the signification of these words, and even the true knowledge of them is of such little importance, that we may well rest contented with such names as our modern translations have given us. They were, no doubt, the *swiftest* and *hardiest* beasts that the *city* or *country* could produce.

Verse 11. *To destroy, to slay, and to cause to perish*] The same words as in Haman's decree: therefore the Jews had as much authority to slay their enemies, as their enemies had to slay them.

Little ones and women] This was the ordinary custom, to destroy the whole family of those convicted of great crimes; and whether this was right or wrong, it was the custom of the people, and according to the laws. Besides, as this edict was to give the Jews the same power against their enemies as they had by the former decree against them, and the women and children were there included; consequently they must be included here,

Verse 14. *The decree was given at Shushan*] The contrary effect which it was to produce considered, this decree was in every respect like the former. See chap. iii.

Verse 15. *Blue and white*] Probably stripe interchanged with stripe; or *blue* faced and bordered with *white* fur.

A great crown of gold] A large *turban,* ornamented with gold, jewels, &c.

Fine linen and purple] See on Gen. xli. 42. The בוץ *buts,* here mentioned, is most probably the same with the *byssus* of the ancients; supposed to be the beautiful *tuft* or *beard,* growing out of the side of the *pinna longa,* a very large species of *muscle,* found on the coasts of the Mediterranean Sea, of which there are a pair of gloves in the British Museum. This *byssus* I have described elsewhere.

Shushan—was glad.] Haman was too *proud* to be *popular;* few lamented his fall.

Verse 17. *Many—became Jews; for—fear*] These were a species of *converts* not likely to bring much honour to true religion: but the sacred historian states the simple fact. They did profess Judaism for fear of the Jews, whether they continued steady in that faith or not.

It is only the Gospel which will not admit of coercion for the propagation and establishment of its doctrines. It is a spiritual system, and can be propagated only by spiritual influence. As it proclaims holiness of heart and life, which nothing but the Spirit of God can produce, so it is the Spirit of God alone that can persuade the understanding and change the heart. If the kingdom of Christ were of this *world,* then would his servants *fight.* But it is not from hence.

CHAPTER IX

On the thirteenth of the month Adar the Jews destroy their enemies, and the governors of the provinces assist them, 1–5. They slay five hundred in Shushan, and kill the ten sons of Haman, but take no spoil, 6–10. The king is informed of the slaughter in Shushan, 11. He desires to know what Esther requests farther; who begs that the Jews may be permitted to act on the following day as they had done on the preceding, and that Haman's sons may be hanged upon the gallows; which is granted; and they slay three hundred more in Shushan, and in the other provinces seventy-five thousand, 12–16. A recapitulation of what was done; and of the appointment of the feast of Purim to be observed through all their generations every year, 17–28. Esther writes to confirm this appointment, 29–32.

A. M. 3552
B. C. 452
A. U. C. 302
Coss. Rom.
C. Menenio et
P. Capitolino

NOW [a]in the twelfth month, that *is,* the month Adar, on the thirteenth day of the same, [b]when the king's commandment and his decree drew near to be put in execution, in the day that the enemies of the Jews hoped to have power over them, (though it was turned to the contrary, that the Jews [c]had rule over them that hated them;)

2 The Jews [d]gathered themselves together in their cities throughout all the provinces of the king Ahasuerus, to lay hands on such as [e]sought their hurt: and no man could withstand them; for [f]the fear of them fell upon all people.

3 And all the rulers of the provinces, and the lieutenants, and the deputies, and [g]officers of the king, helped the Jews; because the fear of Mordecai fell upon them.

4 For Mordecai *was* great in the king's house, and his fame went out throughout all the provinces: for this man Mordecai [h]waxed greater and greater.

5 Thus the Jews smote all their enemies with the stroke of the sword, and slaughter,

and destruction, and did [i]what they would unto those that hated them.

A. M. 3552
B. C. 452
A. U. C. 302
Coss. Rom.
C. Menenio et
P. Capitolino

6 And in Shushan the palace the Jews slew and destroyed five hundred men.

7 And Parshandatha, and Dalphon, and Aspatha,

8 And Poratha, and Adalia, and Aridatha,

9 And Parmashta, and Arisai, and Aridai, and Vajezatha,

10 [k]The ten sons of Haman the son of Hammedatha, the enemy of the Jews, slew they; [l]but on the spoil laid they not their hand.

11 On that day the number of those that were slain in Shushan the palace [m]was brought before the king.

12 And the king said unto Esther the queen, The Jews have slain and destroyed five hundred men in Shushan the palace, and the ten sons of Haman; what have they done in the rest of the king's provinces? now [n]what *is* thy petition? and it shall be granted thee: or what *is* thy request farther? and it shall be done.

13 Then said Esther, If it please the king, let it be granted to the Jews which *are* in

---

[a]Chap. viii. 12——[b]Chapter iii. 13——[c]2 Samuel xxii 41——[d]Chap. viii. 11; ver. 16——[e]Psa. lxxi. 13, 24 [f]Chap. viii. 17——[g]Heb. *those which did the business that* belonged *to the king*

[h]2 Sam. iii. 1; 1 Chron. xi. 9; Prov. iv. 18——[i]Heb. *according to their will*——[k]Chap. v. 11; Job xviii. 19; xxvii. 13, 14, 15; Psa. xxi. 10——[l]See chap. viii. 11 [m]Heb. *came*——[n]Chap. v. 6; vii. 2

NOTES ON CHAP. IX

Verse 1. Now in the twelfth month] What a number of providences, and none of them apparently of an extraordinary nature, concurred to preserve a people so signally, and to all human appearance so inevitably, doomed to destruction! None are ever too low for God to lift up, or too high for God to cast down. Must not these heathens have observed that the uncontrollable hand of an Almighty Being had worked in behalf of the Jews? And must not this have had a powerful tendency to discredit the idolatry of the country?

Verse 3. And all the rulers of the provinces] Mordecai being raised to the highest confidence of the king, and to have authority over the whole realm, these officers assisted the Jews, no doubt, with the troops under their command, to overthrow those who availed themselves of

the former decree to molest the Jews. For it does not appear that the Jews slew any person who did not rise up to destroy them. See ver. 5.

Verse 6. And in Shushan] It is strange that in this city, where the king's mind must have been so well known, there should be found *five hundred* persons to rise up in hostility against those whom they knew the king befriended!

Verse 10. The ten sons of Haman] Their names are given above. And it is remarked here, and in ver. 16, where the account is given of the number slain in the provinces, that the Jews *laid no hands on the spoil.* They stood for their lives, and gave full proof that they sought their own personal safety, and not the *property* of their enemies, though the decree in their favour gave them authority to take the property of all those who were their adversaries, chap. viii. 11.

Verse 13. Let Haman's ten sons be hanged]

A. M. 3552 B. C. 452 A. U. C. 302 Coss. Rom. C. Menenio et P. Capitolino

Shushan to do to-morrow also [o]according unto this day's decree, and [p]let Haman's ten sons [q]be hanged upon the gallows.

14 And the king commanded it so to be done: and the decree was given at Shushan; and they hanged Haman's ten sons.

15 For the Jews that *were* in Shushan [r]gathered themselves together on the fourteenth day also of the month Adar, and slew three hundred men at Shushan; [s]but on the prey they laid not their hand.

16 But the other Jews that *were* in the king's provinces [t]gathered themselves together, and stood for their lives, and had rest from their enemies, and slew of their foes seventy and five thousand, [u]but they laid not their hands on the prey,

17 On the thirteenth day of the month Adar; and on the fourteenth day [v]of the same rested they, and made it a day of feasting and gladness.

18 But the Jews that *were* at Shushan assembled together [w]on the thirteenth *day* thereof, and on the fourteenth thereof; and on the fifteenth *day* of the same they rested, and made it a day of feasting and gladness.

19 Therefore the Jews of the villages, that dwelt in the unwalled towns, made the fourteenth day of the month Adar [x]*a day of* gladness and feasting, [y]and a good day, and of [z]sending portions one to another.

A. M. 3552 B. C. 452 A. U. C. 302 Coss. Rom. C. Menenio et P. Capitolino

20 And Mordecai wrote these things, and sent letters unto all the Jews that *were* in all the provinces of the king Ahasuerus, *both* nigh and far,

21 To stablish *this* among them, that they should keep [a]the fourteenth day of the month Adar, and the fifteenth day of the same, yearly.

22 As the days wherein the Jews rested from their enemies, and the month which was [b]turned unto them from sorrow to joy, and from mourning into a good day: that they should make them days of feasting and joy, and of [c]sending portions one to another, and gifts to the poor.

23 And the Jews undertook to do as they had begun, and as Mordecai had written unto them;

24 Because Haman the son of Hammedatha, the Agagite, the enemy of all the Jews, [d]had devised against the Jews to destroy them, and had cast Pur, that *is,* the lot, to [e]consume them, and to destroy them;

25 But [f]when [g]*Esther* came before the king, he commanded by letters that his wicked device, which he devised against the Jews, should [h]return upon his own head, and that he and his sons should be hanged on the gallows.

---

[o]Chap. viii. 11——[p]Hebrew, *let men hang*——[q]2 Sam. xxi. 6, 9——[r]Verse 2; chapter viii. 11——[s]Verse 10——[t]Verse 2; chapter viii. 11——[u]See chapter vii. 11 [v]Hebrew, *in it*——[w]Verse 11, 15——[x]Deuteronomy xvi. 11, 14——[y]Chap. viii. 17

[z]Ver. 22; Neh. viii. 10, 12——[a]See 2 Mac. xv. 36 [b]Psa. xxx. 11——[c]Ver. 19; Neh. viii. 11——[d]Chap. iii. 6, 7——[e]Heb. *crush*——[f]Heb. *when she came* [g]Ver. 13, 14; chap. vii. 5, &c.; viii. 3, &c.——[h]Chap. vii. 10; Psa. vii. 16

They had been slain the preceding day, and now she requests that they may be exposed on posts or gibbets, as a terror to those who sought the destruction of the Jews.

Verse 15. *And slew three hundred men*] Esther had probably been informed by Mordecai that there were still many enemies of the Jews who sought their destruction, who had escaped the preceding day; and, therefore, begs that this *second* day be added to the former permission. This being accordingly granted, they found *three hundred* more, in all *eight hundred.* And thus Susa was purged of all their enemies.

Verse 18. *The Jews—assembled—on the thirteenth—and on the fourteenth*] These *two* days they were employed in slaying their enemies; and they rested on the *fifteenth.*

Verse 19. *The Jews of the villages*] They joined that to the preceding day, and made it a day of festivity, and *of sending portions to each other;* that is, the *rich* sent portions of the sacrifices slain on this occasion to the *poor,* that they also might be enabled to make the day a day of festivity; that as the *sorrow* was *general,* so also might the *joy* be.

It is worthy of remark that the ancient *Itala* or *Ante-hieronymian* version of this book omits the whole of these *nineteen* verses. Query, Were they originally in this book?

Verse 20. *Mordecai wrote these things*] It has been supposed that thus far that part of the book of Esther, which was written by *Mordecai* extends: what follows, to the end, was probably added either by *Ezra,* or the *men of the Great Synagogue;* though what is said here may refer only to the letters sent by Mordecai to the Jews of the provinces. From this to the end of the chapter is nothing else than a recapitulation of the chief heads of the preceding history, and an account of the appointment of an annual feast, called *the feast of Purim,* in commemoration of their providential deliverance from the malice of Haman.

Verse 23. *The Jews undertook to do as they had begun*] They had already kept the *fifteenth* day, and some of them in the country the *fourteenth* also, as a day of rejoicing: Mordecai wrote to them to bind themselves and their successors, and all their proselytes, to celebrate this as an *annual* feast throughout all their generations; and this they *undertook to do.* And it has been observed among them, in all

26 Wherefore they called these days Purim after the name of [1]Pur. Therefore for all the words of [k]this letter, and *of that* which they had seen concerning this matter, and which had come unto them,

27 The Jews ordained, and took upon them, and upon their seed, and upon all such as [l]joined themselves unto them, so as it should not [m]fail, that they would keep these two days according to their writing, and according to their *appointed* time every year;

28 And *that* these days *should be* remembered and kept throughout every generation, every family, every province, and every city; and *that* these days of Purim should not [n]fail from among the Jews, nor the memorial of them [o]perish from their seed.

29 Then Esther the queen, [p]the daughter of Abihail, and Mordecai the Jew, wrote with [q]all authority, to confirm this [r]second letter of Purim.

30 And he sent the letters unto all the Jews, to [s]the hundred twenty and seven provinces of the kingdom of Ahasuerus, *with* words of peace and truth.

31 To confirm these days of Purim in their times *appointed,* according as Mordecai the Jew and Esther the queen had enjoined them, and as they had decreed [t]for themselves and for their seed, the matters of [u]the fastings and their cry.

32 And the decree of Esther confirmed these matters of Purim; and it was written in the book.

A. M. 3552
B. C. 452
A. U. C. 302
Coss. Rom.
C. Menenio et
P. Capitolino

---

[i]That is, *lot*——[k]Ver. 20——[l]Chap. viii. 17; Isa. lvi. 3, 6; Zeph. ii. 11——[m]Heb. *pass*——[n]Heb. *pass* [o]Hebrew, *be ended*

[p]Chap. ii. 15——[q]Heb. *all strength*——[r]See chap viii. 10; ver. 20——[s]Chap. i. 1——[t]Heb. *for their souls* [u]Chap. iv. 3, 16

---

places of their dispersion, from that day to the present time, without any interruption.

Verse 26. *They called these days Purim*] That is from פור *pari, the lot;* because, as we have seen, Haman cast lots to find what month, and what day of the month, would be the most favourable for the accomplishment of his bloody designs against the Jews. See on chap. iii. 7.

And of that which they had seen] The *first letter* to which this *second* refers, must be that sent by Mordecai himself. See ver. 20.

Verse 29. *Esther—wrote with all authority*] Esther and Mordecai had the king's license so to do: and their own authority was great and extensive.

Verse 31. *As they had decreed for themselves and for their seed*] There is no mention of their receiving the approbation of any *high priest*, nor of any authority beyond that of Mor-

decai and Esther; the king could not join in such a business, as he had nothing to do with the Jewish religion, that not being the religion of the country.

Verse 32. *The decree of Esther confirmed these matters*] It was received by the Jews universally with all respect, and they bound themselves to abide by it.

The *Vulgate* gives a strange turn to this verse: *Et omnia quæ libri hujus, qui vocatur Esther, historia continentur;* "And all things which are contained in the history of this book, which is called Esther."

The *Targum* says, *And by the word of Esther all these things relative to Purim were confirmed;* and the *roll was transcribed in this book.* The *Syriac* is the same as the *Hebrew,* and the *Septuagint* in this place not very different.

CHAPTER X

Ahasuerus lays a tribute on his dominions, 1. *Mordecai's advancement under him,* 2. *His character,* 3.

A. M. 3552
B. C. 453
A. U. C. 302
Coss. Rom.
C. Menenio et
P. Capitolino

AND the king Ahasuerus laid a tribute upon the land, and upon [a]the isles of the sea.

2 And all the acts of his power and of his might, and the declaration of the greatness of Mordecai, [b]whereunto the king [c]advanced him, *are* they not written in the book of the chronicles of the kings of Media and Persia?

3 For Mordecai the Jew *was* [d]next unto King Ahasuerus, and great among the Jews, and accepted of the multitude of his brethren, [e]seeking the wealth of his people, and speaking peace to all his seed.

A. M. 3552
B. C. 452
A. U. C. 302
Coss. Rom.
C. Menenio et
P. Capitolino

---

[a]Genesis x. 5; Psalm lxxii. 10; Isa. xxiv. 15——[b]Chap. viii. 15; ix. 4

[c]Heb. *made him great*——[d]Gen. xli. 40; 2 Chron. xxviii. 7——[e]Neh. ii. 10; Psa. cxxii. 8, 9

NOTES ON CHAP. X

Verse 1. *Laid a tribute upon the land*] On

the *one hundred and twenty-seven* provinces of which we have already heard.

Probably the isles of the Ægean sea, which were conquered by *Darius Hystaspes.* *Calmet* supposes that this *Hystaspes* is the *Ahasuerus* of Esther.

Verse 2. *The book of the chronicles—of Media and Persia?*] The Persians have ever been remarkable for keeping exact chronicles of all public events. Their *Tareekhs,* which are compositions of this kind, are still very numerous, and indeed very important.

Verse 3. Was *next unto King Ahasuerus*] He was his prime minister; and, under him, was the governor of the whole empire.

The *Targum* is extravagant in its encomiums upon Mordecai: "All the kings of the earth feared and trembled before him: he was as resplendent as the evening star among the stars; and was as bright as Aurora beaming forth in the morning; and he was chief of the kings."

Seeking the wealth of his people] Studying to promote the Jewish interest to the utmost of his power.

Speaking peace to all his seed.] Endeavouring to settle their prosperity upon such a basis, that it might be *for ever permanent.* Here the *Hebrew* text ends; but in the ancient *Vulgate,* and in the *Greek, ten* verses are added to this chapter, and *six whole chapters* besides, so that the number of chapters in *Esther* amounts to *sixteen.* A translation of these may be found in the Apocrypha, bound up with the sacred text, in most of our larger English Bibles. On any part of this work it is not my province to add any comment.

THIS is the last of the historical books of the Old Testament, for from this time to the birth of Christ they had no *inspired writers;* and the interval of their history must be sought among the apocryphal writers and other historians who have written on Jewish affairs. The most complete *supplement* to this history will be found in that *most excellent work* of Dean *Prideaux,* entitled *The Old and New Testaments connected, in the History of the Jews and Neighbouring Nations, from the Declension of the Kingdoms of Israel and Judah to the time of* CHRIST, 4 vols. 8vo. 1725. The editions prior to this date are not so complete.

We have already seen what the *Feast of* PURIM means, and why it was instituted; if the reader is desirous of farther information on this subject, he may find it in the works of *Buxtorf, Leusden, Stehlin,* and *Calmet's* Dictionary, article *Pur.*

MASORETIC NOTES ON THE BOOK OF ESTHER

Number of verses, 167. Middle verse, chap. v. ver. 7. Sections, 5.

The following excellent remarks on the history of the Jews from the Babylonish captivity, I borrow from Dr. *John Taylor's* Scheme of *Scripture Divinity,* and make no doubt I shall have the thanks of every reader whose thanks are *worth having.*

"After the Babylonish captivity, the Jews no more lapsed into idolatry, but remained steady in the acknowledgment and worship of the one living and true God. Even then they fell into new ways of perverting religion, and the wise and holy intentions of the Divine law: 1. By laying all the stress on the *external* and *less momentous* parts of it, while they neglected the *weighty* and *substantial,* true holiness of heart and life. Mankind are too easily drawn into this error; while they retain a sense of religion,

they are too apt to listen to any methods by which it may be reduced to a consistency with the *gratification* of *their passions, pride,* and *avarice.* Thus, by placing religion in *mere profession,* or in the zealous observance of *rites* and *ceremonies,* instead of *real piety, truth, purity,* and *goodness,* they learn to be *religious* without *virtue.* 2. By speculating and commenting upon the Divine commands and institutions till their force is quite enervated, and they are refined into a sense that will commodiously allow a slight regard instead of sincere obedience. 3. By confirming and establishing the two former methods of corrupting religion by tradition, and the authority of learned rabbins, pretending that there was a system of religious rules delivered by *word of mouth* from Moses explanatory of the written law, known only to those rabbins, to whose judgment and decision, therefore, all the people were to submit.

"This in time (the space of *two hundred and nineteen* years) became the general state of religion among the Jews, after they had discarded idolatry: and this spirit prevailed among them for some ages (*two hundred and ninety* years) before the coming of Messiah; but, however, it did not interfere with the main system of Providence, or the introducing the knowledge of God among the nations, as they still continued steadfast in the worship of the true God, without danger of deviating from it.

"Thus the Jews were prepared by the preceding dispensation for the reception of the Messiah, and the just notions of religion which he was sent to inculcate; insomuch that their guilt must be highly aggravated if they rejected him and his instructions. It could not be for want of capacity, but of integrity, and must be assigned to *wilful* blindness and obduracy. Out of regard to temporal power, grandeur, and enjoyments, they loved darkness rather than light.

"For many ages the Jews had been well known in the *Eastern empire,* among the *Assyrians, Chaldeans, Medes,* and *Persians;* but till the time of Alexander the Great they had no communication with the *Grecians.*

"About the year before Christ 332 Alexander built Alexandria in Egypt; and to people his new city, removed thither many of the *Jews,* allowing them the use of their own laws and religion, and the same liberties with the *Macedonians* themselves. The Macedonians, who spake the Greek language, and other Greeks, were the principal inhabitants of Alexandria; from them the Jews learnt to speak Greek, which was the common language of the city, and which soon became the native language of the Jews that lived there, who on that account were called *Hellenists,* or *Greek Jews,* mentioned Acts vi. 1, 9; xi. 20. These Greek Jews had synagogues in Alexandria, and for their benefit the *Five Books of Moses,* which alone at first were publicly read, were translated into Greek, (by whom is uncertain,) and were read in their synagogues every Sabbath day; and in the time of *Antiochus Epiphanes,* about 168 years before Christ, the *prophets* were also translated into Greek for the use of the Alexandrian Jews.

"This translation contributed much to the spreading the knowledge of true religion among the nations in the western parts of the world.

"For the Jews, their synagogues and worship were, after Alexander's death, dispersed almost everywhere among the nations. *Ptolemy*, one of Alexander's successors, having reduced Jerusalem and all Judea about 320 years before Christ, carried *one hundred thousand* Jews into Egypt, and there raised considerable numbers of them to places of trust and power, and several of them he placed in *Cyrene* and *Libya*. *Seleucus*, another of Alexander's successors, about 300 years before Christ, built Antioch in Cilicia, and many other cities, in all *thirty-five*, and some of the capital cities in the Greater and Lesser Asia, in all which he planted the Jews, giving them equal privileges and immunities with the Greeks and Macedonians, especially at Antioch in Syria, where they settled in great numbers, and became almost as considerable a part of that city as they were at Alexandria. On that memorable day of Pentecost (Acts ii. 5, 9, 11, 12) were assembled in Jerusalem, *Jews, devout men, out of every nation under heaven*, namely, Parthians, Medes, and Persians, of the province of Elymais, inhabitants of Mesopotamia, Judea, Cappadocia, Pontus, Asia, Phrygia, Pamphylia, Egypt, Cyrene in Libya, and Rome, Cretes, and Arabs, who were all either Jews natural, or *devout men*, i. e., *proselytes* to the Jewish religion. And in every city of the Roman empire where Paul preached, he found a body of his countrymen the Jews, except in *Athens*, which was at that time, I suppose, a town of no considerable trade, which shows that the Jews and their synagogues, at the time of our Lord's appearance, were providentially scattered over all the Roman empire, and had in every place introduced, more or less, among the nations the knowledge and worship of God; and so had prepared great numbers for the reception of the Gospel.

"About the time that Alexander built Alexandria in Egypt, the use of the *papyrus* for writing was found out in that country. This invention was so favourable to literature, that *Ptolemy Soter* was thereby enabled to erect a *museum* or *library*, which, by his son and successor, *Philadelphus*, who died *two hundred and forty-seven years* before Christ, was augmented to *seven hundred thousand* volumes. Part of this library happened to be burnt when *Julius Cæsar* laid siege to Alexandria; but after that loss it was again much augmented, and soon grew up to be larger, and of more eminent note, than the former; till at length it was burnt and finally destroyed by the Saracens, in the year of our Lord 642. This plainly proves how much the invention of turning the *papyrus* into *paper* contributed to the increase of *books*, and the advancement of learning, for some ages before the coming of our Lord. Add to all this, that the world, after many changes and revolutions, was, by God's all-ruling wisdom, thrown into that form of civil affairs which best suited with the great intended alteration. The many petty states and tyrannies, whose passions and bigotry might have run counter to the schemes of Providence, were all swallowed up in one great power, the ROMAN, to which all appeals lay; the seat of which, *Rome*, lay at a great distance from *Jerusalem*, the spring from which the Gospel was to rise and flow to all nations; and therefore as no material obstruction to the Gospel could come but from *one quarter*, none could *suddenly* arise from thence, but only in *process*

of time, when the Gospel was sufficiently opened and established, as it did not in the least interfere with the *Roman polity* and *government*.

"The Gospel was first published in a time of *general peace* and *transquillity throughout the whole world*, which gave the preachers of it an opportunity of passing freely from one country to another, and the minds of men the advantage of attending calmly to it.

"Many savage nations were civilized by the Romans, and became acquainted with the arts and virtues of their conquerors. Thus the darkest countries had their thoughts awakened, and were growing to a capacity of receiving, at the stated time, the knowledge of true religion; so that all things and circumstances conspired now with the views of heaven, and made this apparently *the fulness of time*, (Gal. iv. 4,) or the *fittest juncture* for God to reveal himself to the Gentiles, and to put an end to idolatry throughout the earth. Now the minds of men were generally ripe for a purer and brighter dispensation; and the circumstances of the world were such as favoured the progress of it."—P. 368.

Hated and despised as the *Jews* were among the proud *Romans*, and the still more proud and supercilious *Greeks*, their sojourning among them, and their *Greek version* of the *Scriptures*, commonly called the *Septuagint*, were the means of furnishing them with truer notions, and a more distinct knowledge of *vice* and *virtue*, than they ever had before. And on examination we shall find that, from the time of Alexander's conquest of Judea, a little more than *three hundred* years before our Lord, both Greeks and Romans became more correct in their theological opinions; and the sect of *eclectic philosophers*, whose aim was to *select* from *all preceding sects* what was most consistent with reason and truth, were not a little indebted to the progress which the light of God, dispensed by means of the *Septuagint*, had made in the heathen world. And let it be remembered, that for *Jews*, who were settled in Grecian countries, this version was made, and by those *Jews* it was carried through all the places of their dispersion.

To this *version* Christianity, under God, owes much. To this version we are indebted for such a knowledge of the *Hebrew* originals of the Old Testament, as we could never have had without it, the pure Hebrew having ceased to be vernacular after the Babylonish captivity; and Jesus Christ and his apostles have stamped an infinite value upon it by the general use they have made of it in the New Testament; perhaps never once quoting, *directly*, the Hebrew text, or using any *other version* than *some copy* of the *Septuagint*. By this version, though prophecy had ceased from the times of Ezra, Daniel, and Malachi, yet the law and the prophets were *continued down to the time of Christ;* and this was the grand medium by which this conveyance was made. And why is this version neglected? I hesitate not to assert that no man can ever gain a thorough knowledge of the *phraseology* of the *New Testament writers*, who is unacquainted with this version, or has not profited by such writers as derived their knowledge from it.

A. CLARKE.

Millbrook, February 3, 1820.

Finished the correction of this volume, Oct. 16, 1828.—A. CLARKE.

VOL. II   829